W9-AQO-711

FROM BEOWULF TO THOMAS HARDY

VOLUME I

g

Ret chere made our ost to vs euerychon
And to soupere sette he vs anon
He serued vs wyth vytayll at the beste
Strong was the wyne & wel drynke vs lyste
A semely man our oste was wyth alle
Forto be a marchal in a lordes halle
A large man he was wyth eyen stepe
A feyrer burgeys is ther non in chepe
Bold of hys speche and wel was y taught
And of manhood lacked he right nought
Eke therto was he right a mery man
And aftir soupper to pleyen he began
And spak of myrthe among other thynges
Whan that we hadde made our rekenynges
He sayd thus now lordynges treuly
Ye be to me right welcome hertly
For by my trowthe yf I shal not lye
I saw not thys yeer so mery a companye

A page from Caxton's edition of Chaucer's *Canterbury Tales,* Westminster, 1484. This page shows the pilgrims around a table at the Tabard Inn, Southwark, the evening before starting on their pilgrimage. Below the woodcut are lines 749–766 of the "Prologue" (page 169). Caxton was the earliest English printer, and through his press helped to usher in the modern age. (Cou sy of the Pierpont Morgan Library.)

FROM BEOWULF TO THOMAS HARDY

NEW EDITION WITH PERIOD INTRODUCTIONS

ROBERT SHAFER
Professor of Literature and Fellow
of the Graduate School
University of Cincinnati

VOLUME I

DOUBLEDAY, DORAN & COMPANY, INC.

NEW YORK CITY

★

PRINTED IN THE U. S. A.
FIRST PRINTING OF NEW EDITION

Preface

In preparing the present new edition of *From Beowulf to Thomas Hardy* I have reconsidered the question of texts to be presented, much as if I were now compiling the work for the first time. The Revised Edition of 1931 included a number of writers not represented in the original edition. Expansion of this kind is tempting, and is always being suggested; nevertheless, it cannot continue without either increasing the size of the work beyond manageable proportions or causing me to abandon my first intention. I wished in 1924 to provide an acceptable book which would make possible a well-rounded survey of English literature without sacrifice of concentration. I then wrote, in the Preface to the first edition:

"These volumes are designed primarily for the introductory course in the general history of English literature given in many colleges and universities. The plan they follow is based on the conviction, gained from my own experience and that of many other teachers, that anthologies and collections of extracts are more useful to those who know literature than to those who are just learning to know it. It is of little permanent use for the learner to read a few pages of fragments from the work of an important writer; it may even do him harm rather than good. These volumes represent an effort to consult the learner's actual needs; and to this end not only have writers of minor importance, and works which can profitably be studied only by the mature student, been excluded, but the writers who are represented are, I hope, adequately represented."

The aim thus expressed still seems to me decidedly the most important one of such a textbook as *From Beowulf to Thomas Hardy*. Hence in the present edition I have not only refrained from increasing the number of writers included, but have actually reduced the number below the total in the Revised Edition of 1931; although eight writers or sections now first appear in the work and a great deal of new matter, including three additional plays, the passages from Bede and Pepys, letters by Gray, Cowper, Lamb, and FitzGerald, and some important poems—in particular the long narrative poem which in 1911 made Mr. John Masefield internationally famous. Even so, every teacher will miss some cherished writer or some favorite poem; I do myself, and regret, as much as anyone else, that we cannot have everything all of us would like. I hope, however, the book does now contain all that is needed for a solid foundation in the historical study of English literature.

To this end, moreover, I have for the first time divided the contents into sections, and have written a commentary on the several periods, including a final chapter on English literature of the present day. I cannot claim that these chapters constitute a "history of English literature," much less a "complete" one. I have never, indeed, been able to decide just what would constitute a "history of literature." Most books ostensibly falling in this category are not "histories" as the word is used in the field of social institutions. My own aim has been simply to provide a running commentary, designed to give students an adequate background for intelligent study of the texts, and thus to make it unnecessary to use, in connection with this new edition, any supplementary handbook. I should be inclined to call the chapters, taken by themselves, a "Preface to English Literature." I have made a strenuous effort to coördinate the commentary and the short introductions to the writers included, and hope the two kinds of introductory matter usefully complement each other throughout. Some small amount of repetition has seemed unavoidable, but this may serve the purpose of stressing matters that need to be firmly grasped. For the sake of precision in that skeleton of hard fact which is indispensable in historical study, I have added to this edition also a Chronological Outline. It may not be amiss to state here that I have, with the most recent writers on the period, accepted the corrected date for the death of Alfred which appears to be finally established; and that I have also, in both commentary and Outline, given the actual dates of publication of certain books, when known, even though the years given differ from those on the title pages of the books in question.

As in the Revised Edition, editorial omissions are indicated by asterisks (*) and, in one or two cases, by footnotes. One short passage omitted by Skeat in his translation of *Piers Plowman,* which has been used in the present edition, has not been supplied in a note, because it was thought best not to give possible occasion for scandal. For the same reason a single sentence has, with reluctance, been omitted from Dekker's *Shoemakers' Holiday.*

In the work of revision and change I have been assisted by Dr. Rudolf B. Gottfried. Dr. Gottfried is responsible for the completely revised glossary at the end of Volume I, for the modernized version of *The Second Shepherds' Play* here presented, for introductions to texts, such as this play and *The Shoemakers' Holiday,* now first included, for the Chronological Outline (in the main), and for many new footnotes. Besides acknowledging Dr. Gottfried's assistance, I must give hearty thanks to Dr. Siegmund A. E. Betz for some useful suggestions and for help with proofs. I wish also to thank Mr. Brett and Mr. Morehouse of The Macmillan Company for the unusual measures they kindly took to enable me to reprint Mr. Masefield's *Everlasting Mercy,* and to thank Mr. Masefield himself for his part in this matter. I wish further to express grateful appreciation to The Pierpont Morgan Library, The New York Public Library, and The Metropolitan Museum of Art for the use of their facilities and the generous help extended by their staffs in securing the illustrations included.

Other debts inevitably, in a work of this kind, are many, and important, and I am sorry that I cannot acknowledge them severally. It is not possible; and I must be content with a general expression of gratitude to the critics and scholars from whom I have learned.

R. S.

1 June, 1939.

Contents

I. EARLIEST TIMES: THE ANGLO-SAXONS, 449-1066

II. THE LATER MIDDLE AGES, 1066-1485

III. THE RENAISSANCE AND THE PROTESTANT REVOLT, 1485-1660

IV. THE RESTORATION AND THE EIGHTEENTH CENTURY, 1660–1784

Illustrations

FROM BEOWULF TO THOMAS HARDY

VOLUME I

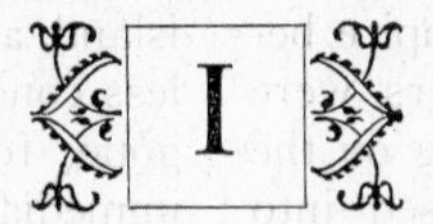

Earliest Times: The Anglo-Saxons, 449–1066

BRITAIN first appears on the page of history with Julius Caesar's expedition across the Channel from the European mainland in 55 B. C. Before this the largest of the British Isles had, indeed, been vaguely known to Mediterranean peoples; because Mediterranean traders for centuries had been bringing tin, gold, and pearls from the island. But only after Caesar's attempt at conquest was intercourse with civilized Europe maintained continuously enough and on such a level as to enable modern scholars to construct an authentic history, meager to be sure in the earliest periods, yet extending without a real break to the present.

When Caesar landed on the southern coast, Britain was inhabited by a mixed collection of people. Those whom he encountered were Celts, closely related to the Gallic tribes then living in northern Europe; and perhaps the chief reason for his invasion was the fact that the continental Celts were being aided in their resistance against Rome by men and ships from Britain. The Celts in Britain had come from the Continent probably in the period from 600 to about 400 B. C., and had gradually driven back their predecessors from the southern and eastern parts of the island. These predecessors had themselves at some time driven back still earlier settlers. For some thousands of years, and until after the Norman Conquest in 1066, southeastern Britain was the ultimate goal of all successive waves of migratory peoples who moved out from the interior to the coast of northern Europe—the coast line now held by France, Belgium, Holland, Germany, Denmark, Sweden, and Norway. At times these peoples were hard-pressed from behind; along much of the coast line, life was difficult and cheerless; and always Britain offered irresistible temptation to raiders and settlers. True, both foreigners and natives have long complained over the fogs and the heavy rainfall of the British Isles; but in return the land has been blessed with thick forests full of game, many rivers full of fish, rich pasturage, and fertile open fields. The climate of southern Britain, too, is remarkably free from extremes of cold or heat. And besides all these advantages there was, through many hundred years, the inducement of famous mines. The people, consequently, whom the Celts drove back were the mixed descendants of many earlier invaders, some of them of the dark-haired blue-eyed type, called "Iberian," still to be seen today in Ireland.

The Roman Conquest was yet another invasion, but it was not in the full sense a settlement, and it interrupted the normal or natural movement of peoples for more than three centuries after its effective beginning under the Emperor Claudius in A. D. 43. Moreover, it had but small lasting result. For the time being it transformed the southern part of Britain, with substantially constructed Roman towns, and the solid straight roads which the Romans built wherever they went; and it greatly encouraged agriculture.

But Britain was too far from the center of the Empire for that complete education and assimilation of a conquered people which was effected, for example, through a large part of France. And when the Empire began to crumble, and Roman soldiers were withdrawn from Britain for fighting on the Continent, the Celts quickly relapsed into something like their pre-Roman political condition. Before the Conquest the country had been divided up into small "kingdoms," the Celtic "kings" being really not much better than tribal chiefs, whose principal occupation was warfare against their neighbors.

The Coming of the Anglo-Saxons

This relapse was the more disastrous because a new wave of migration was advancing westward, and had been felt along the eastern and southern coasts of Britain, in the form of piratical raids, for a generation or more before the final withdrawal of the Roman legions. The people now moving outward from the European coast line were those whom we call the Anglo-Saxons. Several closely related Germanic tribes had taken possession, by about 200, of the neck of land whose northern part is modern Denmark. They were loosely organized under chiefs or "kings" as a military aristocracy, with a following of poor folk, some of them slaves, who engaged in rudimentary agriculture, fishing, and a few handicrafts. The fighting men disdained manual labor, and looked to their chiefs to find them means for a riotous existence. In battle they were determined and fierce; but they were also gluttonous at the table, unmeasured in their drinking, and the victims of dark melancholy when time hung heavy on their hands. They were multiplying rapidly, and soon were thickly settled along the coast; whereupon they readily took to the sea, in continued search for plunder.

The traditional date of the Germanic or Anglo-Saxon Conquest of Britain is A. D. 449; but actually this, like earlier movements of the same kind, was not an organized attack. It was rather a gradual infiltration, which had begun in a small way before the end of the fourth century and which continued for rather more than a hundred and fifty years. The object at first was simple robbery. The robbers, however, were quick to perceive the attractions of the island, and quick also to perceive its defenseless condition, once the Roman soldiers had gone; for the Celts, as was said above, had immediately resumed their ancient practice of fighting amongst themselves. And not only were they unable to unite against the Germanic invaders, but some of them made the fatal mistake of inviting the aid of these fierce warriors against their native rivals. The invaders, of course, were concerned only for themselves, and the invitation merely gave them a better opportunity than they could have expected to achieve their own lordship and settlement of the island. Gradually they dispossessed the Celts of all the land except, roughly, that comprised in modern Scotland, Wales, and Cornwall.

According to old tradition, the invaders belonged to three tribal groups—the Angles, the Saxons, and the Jutes. The Angles, or English, eventually gave their name to the greater part of the island, and to its inhabitants, and to the language which has spread over a large part of the modern world, wherever Englishmen have established themselves as settlers and rulers. There has been question in recent years as to how far the Angles and Saxons can really be distinguished from each other, and even more question as to exactly who the Jutes were. The truth seems to be that leaders, when recruiting bands of warriors, were indifferent to tribal affiliations; but that, nevertheless, the east coast of Britain, from the Firth of Forth or a little below to the River Stour, was predominantly settled by Angles, and from the Stour to the mouth of the Thames by Saxons, and south of the Thames by Jutes. The Jutes also settled in the Isle of Wight, and on the British coast opposite, though the rest of the south coast, except for modern Devon and Cornwall, was settled by Saxons.

The Language of the Anglo-Saxons

All of the invaders, however, spoke a common language. There were dialectal differences between the tribal groups, but these were, in the period of the Conquest, so slight that members of one group had no difficulty in understanding members of another. The language was a variety of what we now call Low German. Its appearance and its sound are very strange to us, as the late West-Saxon version of the first thirteen verses of the first chapter of the Gospel According to St. John will show:

On frymthe waes Word, and thaet Word waes mid Gode, and God waes thaet Word. Thaet waes on fruman mid Gode. Ealle thing waeron geworhte thurh hyne; and nan thing naes geworht butan him. Thaet waes lif the on him geworht waes; and thaet lif waes manna leoht. And thaet leoht lyht on thystrum; and thystro thaet ne genamon.

Mann waes fram Gode asend, thaes nama waes Johannes. Thes com to gewitnesse, thaet he gewitnesse cythde be tham leohte, thaet ealle menn thurh hyne gelyfdon. Naes he leoht, ac thaet he gewitnesse forth baere be tham leohte.

Soth leoht waes thaet onlyht aelcne cumendne man on thisne middaneard. He waes on middanearde, and middaneard waes geworht thurh hine, and middaneard hine ne underfengon. Sothlice swa hwylce swa hyne underfengon, he sealde him anweald thaet hi waeron Godes bearn, tham the gelyfath on his naman: tha ne synt acennede of blodum, ne of flaesces willan, ne of weres willan, ac hig synt of Gode acennede.

For comparison, the same verses from the Authorized Version of 1611 are subjoined:

In the beginning was the Word, and the Word was with God, and the Word was God. The same was in the beginning with God. All things were made by Him; and without Him was not anything made that was made. In Him was life; and the life was the light of men. And the light shineth in darkness; and the darkness comprehended it not.

There was a man sent from God, whose name was John. The same came for a witness, to bear witness of the Light, that all men through him might believe. He was not that Light, but was sent to bear witness of that Light.

That was the true Light, which lighteth every man that cometh into the world. He was in the world, and the world was made by Him, and the world knew Him not. He came unto His own, and His own received Him not. But as many as received Him, to them gave He power to become the sons of God, even to them that believe on His name: which were born, not of blood, nor of the will of the flesh, nor of the will of man, but of God.

If one patiently studies these two versions together, preferably with some help in pronouncing the earlier version aloud, one is likely to be surprised. The Anglo-Saxon speech remains, indeed, strange; but there is much more of similarity between the two versions than could at first sight have been supposed. And the fact is that while time and certain influences which we will later discuss have brought about many changes, and the German of the Angles and Saxons and Jutes has been remarkably transformed and enriched, still, this Anglo-Saxon language is the foundation and framework upon which our own modern English has been built. And for this reason many scholars prefer to call it, not Anglo-Saxon, but Old English.

The term "Old English," moreover, does have the advantage that it helps to emphasize the real continuity of English life and speech from the fifth century to the present. After the Anglo-Saxon Conquest there were to be, as we shall see, severe shocks and changes; and both the people and their language had a long rough road to travel before they could come to maturity and greatness; but the road *was continuous,* and on this account the study of English literature must begin, for full and proper understanding, with the earliest surviving remnants of the literature of the Anglo-Saxons, even though these remnants are written in what seems like—and is to us now—a foreign language.

Conversion to Christianity

By the end of the sixth century the Anglo-Saxons had firmly established themselves throughout the eastern and southern parts of Britain and had achieved a semblance of order, at least within large areas acknowledging the sovereignty of four or five kings. Nobody knows to what extent they absorbed the Celtic population. Some mingling of racial strains there probably was from the beginning, and it has of course continued since; but it appears altogether likely that most of the Celts not killed where they were found, were pushed back to the West, into Cornwall and Wales, and some of them up into Scotland. Many went across to Ireland, and others to the northwest corner of France (Brittany). In this retreat the Celts carried with them such culture as they had made their own during the centuries of Roman rule. Roman Britain had become Christianized along with the rest of the Empire, and in its clergy possessed a group of men who knew Latin and kept alive some rudiments of classical learning. Thus both Christianity and Latin passed into Ireland; and for several centuries some monastic centers of learning flourished there, while Christianity was embraced with extraordinary zeal—a zeal which presently caused Irish missionaries to go forth to the coast of Scotland and into northern England, and also to remote parts of continental Europe.

The Anglo-Saxons had, more or less, brought their own ancient religion with them. We do not know a great deal about it, except that it was weakened by passage across the sea, which suggests that part of its strength lay in its association with sacred places. On the Continent these tribes had worshiped an earth-goddess, Nerthus, to whom they occasionally offered a sacrifice of slaves, but neither this cult nor any practice of human sacrifice appears to have been carried over to Britain. Certain comparatively new gods did cross the sea, but though they gave us names we still use, they never attained so important a place in the esteem of the English as they did amongst the Scandinavians. Thus there was the god of war and warriors, Woden (Wednesday); the thunder-god, Thunor or Thor (Thursday); the Northern Venus, Frig (Friday); a minor war-god, Tiw (Tuesday); and, for a last example, a dawn-goddess, Eostra (Easter). Supreme above all gods and spirits was Wyrd (Fate), and Wyrd did long remain a real force in the minds and imaginations of the English. Below these deities, and closer than any of them save perhaps Wyrd to the hearts and daily lives of the mass of the people, were a confused rout of elves, mysterious monsters, dragons, and spirits of the wheat field, of the sunlight, of the rain, and the like. As a man lived and worked he supposed himself watched constantly by these powers, which were ready to plague him if he neglected the acts traditionally prescribed to please them or to frighten them off. Hence many sacrifices were necessary, such as the cakes offered to Sol in February or the cattle slaughtered in November; and magical charms had to be used, such as those to ward off rheumatism, or to help the field if crops were poor, or to bring back strayed cattle.

Some of these old beliefs or practices were long a-dying; nevertheless, the paganism of the Anglo-Saxons, taking it as a whole, was in a state of decline by the end of the sixth century, and the people, by and large, were ready for the change in their belief which was about to take place. In 597 Augustine and forty Benedictine monks landed on the southeastern coast of England to preach the gospel of Christ. They had been sent from Rome by Pope Gregory the Great. Gregory is reputed to have exclaimed years before, on seeing some fair-haired English boys in the slave-market at Rome, that they were "not Angles, but Angels," and to have resolved on the spot to carry Christianity to the land whence the boys came. The story may be true; at any rate Gregory long cherished the design of converting the English, made an effort at one time to go to England himself, and finally succeeded in sending Augustine and his band of monks, fearful though the monks were of "a barbarous, fierce, and unbelieving nation, to whose very language they were strangers." But those monks were pleasantly surprised. King Ethelbert of Kent—who had a Christian wife from the Continent—received them courteously, gave them an old Roman church in Canterbury, and promptly accepted baptism at their hands. He refused to allow his subjects to be forced into Christianity, but they soon followed their king's example, and within a year some 10,000 had been converted. The mission had many problems to solve, but from the beginning it was extraordinarily successful; and as testimony to its success Augustine—who should not be confused with the earlier famous theologian of the same name, who had died in 430—

was consecrated the first Archbishop of Canterbury.

Probably the most important reason for the rapid conversion of the English has already been mentioned—the failure of Germanic paganism in its new island surroundings to develop or even to hold its own. The ancient beliefs had become shadowy, had begun to seem childish, and offered little to an awakening reason. The English had indeed been "barbarous" and "fierce" as a necessity of the life they had lived until they were fairly settled in England; but amongst them were thoughtful men who, as soon as quieter circumstances permitted, began to ask themselves questions about the meaning of life, to which their own traditions afforded no satisfying answer. Such men had within them all the capacities requisite to what may be called a civilized maturity, and needed only the right stimulus and guidance in order to be quickly transformed. And what they needed, Christianity gave. The Christian interpretation of life won its way with them because it seemed obviously better than any they had hitherto known—better in itself and better in its fruits. For Augustine and some who came with him and after him seemed to embody and live what they preached. Augustine and his immediate successors were men of evident holiness, strong character, and remarkable practical intelligence. Moreover, they brought not only a system of worship and a rule of life, but all that still survived within the Roman Church of classical civilization. The very name of Rome was still powerful to impress barbarian peoples even while they were striking fatal blows at the old Empire. And the Roman Church, rising as the Empire fell—a new center of faith, hope, and courage—gathered up, conserved, and used all that could be saved from the wreckage. It was, of course, a shrunken heritage; still, it meant that along with Christianity, as the barbarians were converted, came some part of Greco-Roman philosophy, some classical literature, an elementary but firm educational discipline, and Roman standards of administration.

Hence to the English the acceptance of Christianity, both from the Irish in the north and from the Roman missionaries in the south, opened the door to civilization. From the early part of the seventh century, the Anglo-Saxon kings had at hand Roman ecclesiastics who were much better educated than they or any members of their courts, and who exerted a many-sided influence. Some were practical statesmen, who introduced improvements in law and administration. Further, in building up a unified organization of the Church, the priests promoted the ideal of unity amongst the English kingdoms. But above all they brought in education, and Latin, now the universal language of the Church and of educated men as it had been of the Empire in the past. Hence Latin remained the indispensable first step in education. One of Augustine's immediate successors at Canterbury knew Greek also, with the result that both classical languages were taught for a while at some English schools.

The English grasped eagerly at the opportunities thus placed before them, thereby showing from the very beginnings of their history a characteristic which through the centuries has been of primary importance in their development. The background of English intellectual, literary, artistic history is a series of external or foreign influences, so that the superficial student may be tempted to wonder if English literature is not a derivative phenomenon, a series of more or less distinguished imitations or adaptations. Yet the English character is unmistakable, and its impress is stamped no less firmly upon English literature than upon English political or social institutions. And the truth is that the English have been endlessly receptive, but have never been overpowered by foreign influences; rather, they have discovered themselves through them, and in doing so have made the foreign things their own and have built upon them.

The Venerable Bede

One of their earliest writers insisted that the English lost nothing by their conversion except what was "trivial or vain," and we may believe the venerable Bede in this, as we may also see in him much that was gained.

Bede was born in Northumbria, the northeastern part of England, only three-quarters of a century after the coming of Augustine to Kent. From the age of seven he spent his entire life within the monastery of Wearmouth-Jarrow, and amidst the observances of monastic rule found his constant delight in the pursuit of learning and in teaching and writing. There were competent teachers at hand, and Bede learned some Greek as well as Latin. There was also a library, well enough stocked to enable Bede to become acquainted with the whole range of knowledge still surviving from the classical world. By standards of the present day, or of any time from the fourteenth century to the present, Bede's learning was almost absurdly meager; nevertheless, it was sufficient to sharpen and develop his intelligence, and to make him a cultivated urbane man. This is plain from his *Ecclesiastical History of the English Nation,* for which he took the greatest pains to collect authentic information and, generally, did all that was humanly possible to make it what we should call a scholarly work. But, further, we can also see from the *Ecclesiastical History* that Bede had a composed assurance, an inward strength, which he could not have attained had he not really discovered himself through the tradition which entered into him. He was not the less an Englishman for the development he underwent; yet he was not a barbarian with a superficial veneer of Christian belief and traditional culture; he was really civilized, and if we could encounter him today we would find that he could meet us, across all the centuries, on equal terms. We could understand him, and he, with little effort, could understand us. In other words, Bede can meet us on equal terms so far as his capacities and the quality of his intelligence are concerned; and there is, moreover, a real continuity of intellectual background making, as it were, a bridge between Bede and ourselves.

Caedmon

All of Bede's books—about thirty-six in number—were written in Latin. Bede's Latin is remarkable for its simplicity and directness, in significant contrast to the absurdly embellished style which was fashionable in the seventh century; but though Bede's Latin is a mark of his genuine cultivation and good sense, it is still Latin, not English, so that his books are not properly a part of English literature. We owe to Bede, however, the name, and much more than the mere name, of the earliest English poet within the field of history. This was Caedmon, an unlearned lay-brother of the monastery at Whitby, who turned into English verse parts of the Bible which were translated for him, and who added to these Biblical narratives exhortations to virtue and the love of God, because he was a devout and humble believer in the new religion.

Early in the seventeenth century a manuscript was discovered containing four Old English poems, *Genesis, Exodus, Daniel,* and *Christ and Satan.* Because these seemed to correspond with some of the verses described as Caedmon's in Bede's *Ecclesiastical History,* they were for a time supposed to be his. We know today that these poems must have been composed somewhat later than the time of Caedmon, whose period of poetic activity centered in the decade 660–670; and nothing by Caedmon has survived except a few lines translated by Bede into Latin. But we also know today that Caedmon stands at the beginning of a short era in which the northeastern part of England, the kingdom of Northumbria, was the scene of great activity in education, in literature, and in art. On this account the first third of the eighth century has been called the "golden age" of Anglo-Saxon England. In the field of education, achievement was so remarkable that the schools of Northumbria did more than any in continental Europe to preserve and hand on the remnant of culture which did survive throughout the so-called Dark Ages. And when towards the close of the eighth century, in the reign of Charlemagne, something like order began to be re-established in parts of Europe, teachers and Christian missionaries from Northumbria assumed positions of leadership in the slow task of civilizing the barbarians who had overrun the Continent. When Charlemagne, for example, required a capable teacher and administrator in his court, he sent to the English school at York for Alcuin; but Alcuin is only the most famous amongst many who went out from Northumbria to carry learning back to Europe.

The Earliest English Poetry

At home, the impulse given by Christianity and education brought into being the earliest English literature and, at the same time, the earliest vernacular literature of any modern European country. A piece of literature is something written; and the Anglo-Saxons did not write until they were taught the use of the Roman alphabet. Perhaps as early as the second century of the Christian era they began to use an alphabet adapted from Greek and Roman characters, chiefly for carving inscriptions in stone. These letters were called runes, along with certain other characters or marks having a magic significance. Writing, however, did not develop as a native art from runes, but came in with Christianity and formal education. What was then written, from the late seventh century on, we of course can know only from that which has survived. Hence any general account of our earliest English literature must be based in part upon inference, because it is certain that only fragments from that time have been preserved. The Northumbrian kingdom was not long-lived. When it perished, from weakness and from external attack, it is altogether likely that manuscripts were destroyed at the same time that monasteries and royal residences were despoiled and burnt. Such Old English manuscripts as we now have, indeed, are copies made much later in the south of England. And there is no means of telling how much was copied, or how many manuscripts moldered away or were otherwise lost in succeeding centuries from sheer neglect, or were finally destroyed along with the monasteries that housed them, during the reign of Henry VIII, in the first half of the sixteenth century.

Nevertheless, within limits, we can speak with some assurance about our earliest English literature. The Angles and Saxons certainly possessed, from a time preceding their settlement in England, a traditional poetry, remembered and handed down by word of mouth, and therefore subject to gradual change. It was probably of two kinds, popular and aristocratic. The popular kind consisted of charms for many occasions, and of short narratives sung to simple tunes—poems similar to those of a much later time which we know as popular ballads. Somewhere between the two kinds fell poems in which the worldly wisdom or meditative life of these peoples was summed up or reflected—gnomic verse it is called. The aristocratic poetry consisted of short narratives connected specially with the warriors and their exploits, and was customarily chanted at feasts by minstrels. Such chanting in the halls of "kings" or chiefs was common enough to enable men with talent for composition and recitation to make this their profession.

It cannot be said with certainty that any of this pre-literary, pre-Christian poetry has been preserved unaltered. All of the Old English poetry we possess was written in its present form by Christians; and practically all of it is at least touched by Christianity—most of it, indeed, pervasively colored by Christian belief, and much of it directly intended, as we have seen Caedmon's was, to serve a religious purpose. But this does not mean that the older poetry which had been transmitted by word of mouth has completely perished. The Anglo-Saxons, as far as we know, were never subjected to enforced conversion. Moreover, Bede tells us how Gregory the Great wisely instructed the first missionaries to make the transition from paganism to Christianity as easy as possible. The missionaries were not to attempt to destroy the pagan past, to enforce a complete break and new beginning, but were rather to adapt old customs and beliefs to Christian uses, and to alter old standards and ideals in the light of Christianity. The aim, in other words, was to present Christianity as a natural growth, out of the native past into something better—and not in so doing to destroy the past, but to reinterpret it. Of course men differed in their reactions to novel demands quite as they differ today, and some, in their zeal for the new belief, became intolerant and destructive; but others were as temperate and wise as Bede; and still others—doubtless a very great number—remained practically unchanged in outlook and habit.

This is what we see reflected in the literature which has been preserved. The ancient charms, for example, to cure the rheumatism and the like, were not suppressed; they were simply altered as little as might be to give them a Christian appearance. And though at first, naturally enough, the energy generated by the conversion seems to have been turned exclusively to the writing of sacred poetry, still, even in this the Angles remained significantly true to themselves and their own past. Three of the early poems which have been mentioned above, *Genesis, Daniel,* and *Exodus,* were probably composed about 700—the third perhaps a little later than the first two. These pieces are in part loose poetical translations, or paraphrases, of books of the Old Testament. They are written in a verse form which was evidently traditional, and well developed, and which exercised a dominating influence upon style. The artistic medium, that is to say, was an inheritance unaltered from the pagan past; and it remained to the end of the Old English period practically the one verse form which the Anglo-Saxons were able to use. Furthermore, what the composers of these early poems really did was to seize upon passages which bore some resemblance to the kinds of subjects they were already familiar with, in their own native and pagan poetry, and which could be treated in the same traditional style, while they ignored the rest. The result was a thorough transformation of familiar Biblical stories and scenes.

In *Exodus,* for instance, the poet has confined himself for his matter chiefly to passages in the thirteenth, fourteenth, and fifteenth chapters. His imagination was aroused by the stir and movement of the Jewish flight from Egypt and the pursuit of the Egyptians, and by the dry path miraculously made for the Jews through the Red Sea; and to the poet's eye, Jews and Egyptians became armies of northern warriors, equipped like the fighting men he knew, with their habits, their outlook, their eye on treasure to be won and banquet halls to be wrested from foes, over them ravens wheeling, and nearby gray wolves ready to devour the slain. Moses became a "lord of men," a "bold folk-captain"—evidently the kind of war leader the poet knew—and he was surrounded by "earls." Doubtless something of the strangeness of this transformation arises from the limitations of language, but not all of it. The poet was fired by this moment in Jewish history, and proceeded vigorously to draw out a large battle picture in which all the figures were men of his own race and time. There was, to be sure, really no battle, and this difficulty appears to have bewildered the poet, though he made the best of such bloody destruction as did occur. Underlying the whole, moreover, and giving a species of unity to a rather confused poem, was a deeply felt Christian purpose. The poem was to glorify God, the righteous King, who rewarded His faithful followers and destroyed those who rebelled, or strove against Him. This *was* a Christian purpose, but in this and other sacred poems one can see how devotion to God was really felt by the Anglo-Saxons, as an extension of that loyalty to king or chief which was a primary article in their pagan ethical code.

Beowulf

Even more striking proof of the fact that Christianity brought about no sharp break with the past is afforded by *Beowulf,* which was written probably about 740, perhaps in the kingdom of Mercia, to the west and south of Northumbria, though more probably within Northumbria, where *Exodus* and the other poems already mentioned were written. At any rate the author of *Beowulf* knew *Genesis* and *Exodus* and *Daniel* and was influenced by them. He had also received a classical education, and appears to have been inspired in some parts of *Beowulf* by Virgil's *Aeneid*—perhaps also, as some think, by Homer's *Odyssey.* He was of course a Christian and, because of his education, we may safely assume he was an ecclesiastic, and one whose time was spent in or near a royal household. We can be sure that the poet was in some way closely connected with royalty because of the intimate acquaintance with the manners and customs of "courtly" circles displayed in *Beowulf,* and also because the author was steeped in the heroic lore of his people. Moreover, he loved the past reflected in that lore, and loved the aristocratic standards of conduct and bearing which it exemplified, and really took in from Christianity what could be fitted into his own native framework of convictions and loyalties. This does not mean that the poet's religion was perfunctory. The Christian interpretation of the story is all-pervasive and has been made an organic part of the poem; yet at the same time it is nowhere obtruded, and, what is more, we feel certain that the author has not distorted his matter, or even his reading of character and events, in order to square his tale with the new religion.

The point is worth dwelling on, because it so capitally illustrates what has already been said of the English in their whole history—that again and again they have been awakened, developed, inspired by external influences, but have not been overpowered by them. Again and again, indeed, they seem to have become only more truly and deeply themselves under the impact of the foreign thing, really conquering it and adapting it to their own uses, instead of being weakened or deflected by it. And exactly so the author of *Beowulf* was inspired by classical example to fashion an epic from traditional tales of heroism then current amongst the Northern peoples, and was enabled by Christianity to see a meaning in his hero's exploits which answered to Beowulf's nobility of character, while yet he remained faithful to his native or Germanic substance, atmosphere, and standards, and produced a thoroughly English poem. The ancient matter of the poem, to put it baldly, consists of a couple of fairy tales, which in the course of time had been placed inside an authentic historical framework. No poet could have made a single well-constructed poem out of two stories having no connection except in the person of the hero, and no poet could have brought either of the stories in *Beowulf* up to the level of the Homeric epics or of the *Aeneid.* Nevertheless, the author did fashion from his material a large poem in the heroic manner; and his Christianity did enable him to see Beowulf's conflicts, with Grendel and Grendel's mother and with the dragon, as symbols of the opposition in this world between good and evil—and it is this Christian interpretation of the legendary matter which dignifies alike the monsters and their opponent, and gives us the really heroic thing along with the heroic manner.

Beowulf possesses enduring human and literary interest. It is almost the only composition surviving from the Old English period—except the two spirited short battle pieces, *Brunanburh* and *Maldon,* written in the tenth century—for which such interest can be claimed. And though all literature from a remote period is valuable and interesting to historians, *Beowulf* rises above other Old English poetry in this respect too. For it is an unrivaled source of information about the early life and standards of the Germanic peoples at the stage of development reached when the invasion of Britain took place. "Germanic peoples," one says, because the poem has nothing whatever to do with England or with the ancestors of the warriors who invaded England. The scene of the poem is not only far from England, but far from the continental home of the Angles; and the first thing, accordingly, which the poem teaches us is the futility of trying to distinguish too precisely the Angles and Saxons and other Germanic tribes in the fifth and sixth centuries and even later. This was hinted above when the invasion was first spoken of; and there is no doubt that though there were tribal groups, movement to one group from another was easy for warriors, and common, and that linguistic differences were then so slight as to make no difficulty. This helps us to understand what we must take in as a fact: that it was enough for the English to see in Beowulf a typical Germanic hero engaged in characteristic activity, and that as such they could accept him as a symbol of their own heroic past or as an embodied ideal.

This is important, but it is more important to understand the kind of life depicted in *Beowulf*. It is aristocratic. The common people do not appear. We are in the presence of royalty, and of those who make up the royal circle or court. These, whatever they may be in addition, are first of all warriors. They are bound to loyal service; and lasting disgrace—in effect, banishment from aristocratic society—is the portion of any man who betrays or deserts his leader, no matter how hopeless the cause. If the leader and his band are trapped, it is the warrior's duty to stand his ground and die, if need be, in defense of his lord. In the poem, when Hygelac was surrounded and overpowered, Beowulf did escape with honor, but only after his lord had been slain, and only after he himself had slain Daeghrefn and so avenged Hygelac's death. The warriors, then, are governed by an uncompromising code of honor, in which loyalty until death is the first article. Obligation, however, is not one-sided. The king or leader is expected to support his warriors splendidly, in accordance with the standards of the time, to reward them generously, and to treat them with kindness. The great king is strong and brave, a terror to his foes, but to his retainers the mildest of men. For entrance into this aristocratic society, birth and family connections are important, but the prime requisite is personal bravery, and this is true not only for members of the royal circle but even for one becoming a king. Once entered into the fellowship, the warrior is above all productive labor. That is for slaves and menials. When not fighting and gathering spoil, the warrior is idle, and eats and drinks to excess, and listens to tales of brave adventure to keep his spirits up. He needs what help of this kind he can get, because he leads an extremely dangerous life; and even when amongst friends in his own lord's banqueting hall he is beset by fears of unknown malign forces of the darkness and, generally, of the incalculable world outside his snug, though smoky, haven. Such a society as this, we can see, was torn between two compelling necessities. The warrior had to be a terror to his foes, but, no less, he had to be devotedly loyal to his fellows. In other words, he had to cultivate in himself both a ruthless brutality and a fine humanity. That the problem could not always be solved is clear from *Beowulf* as it is from other early heroic poetry. Undoubtedly there was grievous reason for continually reminding warriors that the true hero was mild and courteous. Still, one is struck in *Beowulf* by the evidence of success. The love of splendor seen in courtly circles and the elaborate politeness encouraged are signs of a developing sense of human dignity.

We know there were other heroic tales stored in the minds of contemporaries of the poet who wrote *Beowulf,* but we cannot know whether or not any of them were fashioned into epics. The few fragments of other heroic poetry which survive are in too imperfect a condition to enable anyone to feel sure what they were parts of. We do have, however, two short poems, *Widsith* and *Deor,* in which the professional chanter speaks in his own person. From them one can learn a little of the life lived by these singers, and something of the range of the tales they told. Both poems contain some reflective passages, and are thus allied with such reflective pieces as *The Wanderer* and *The Seafarer.* From the scanty amount of such verse extant one would judge that the characteristic note of the more personal poetry of the time was one of somber gloom resolving itself into a bleak fatalism.

Cynewulf

Besides Caedmon we have the name of only one Old English poet. That one is Cynewulf, and of him, beyond his name, we know nothing except the little that can safely be inferred from his poems. We gather that he came of a noble family and in his youth was care-free and, as he later felt, sinful. As a man he was converted to Christianity and devoted himself henceforth to religion. This and the evidence he gives of education show that he must have entered a monastery. He wrote in the early years of the ninth century, when Northumbria's short period of greatness was drawing to a close and when the Anglian kingdom of the midlands, Mercia, was enjoying a short period of splendor. He may equally well have been a Northumbrian or a Mercian. His poems arose from his religious devotion, and just possibly from some desire to emulate, for the glory of God, the author of *Beowulf*. At any rate several of his poems show that he knew *Beowulf* and learned something from it. We happen to know his name, and to know at the same time that four poems were written by him, because into the fabric of each of these he wove runic characters which, when separated out, form his name, and so constitute a kind of signature. The poems so signed are entitled *Juliana, Christ, Elene,* and *Fates of the Apostles.* Of these, however, the second is regarded at present as a collection of three separate poems, of which only one, *The Ascension,* contains Cynewulf's runic signature.

Even with the deduction of *The Advent* and *Judgment Day,* which hitherto have been taken for the first and third parts of *Christ,* Cynewulf is left with some 2600 lines of verse to his credit. In the past a number of other poems have been assigned to him, without reason, and some against reason. Cynewulf has been called, too, a "great" poet, though in reality it is almost impossible to detect any important differences between his poems and the other later religious poetry which has been preserved. This is sufficiently proved by the fact that most of it has at one time or another been attributed to Cynewulf. The truth is that Cynewulf became something of a "hero" to a past generation of scholars simply because they had his name. The truth is also that Anglo-Saxon Christian culture was beginning to decline in the early years of the ninth century when Cynewulf wrote, and that neither his signed poems nor any other extant poetry of this period deserves to be called "great." None of it possesses much interest or importance except to the historian or the student of linguistic science, and nearly all of it shows weakness or decline of one kind or another.

All of these poems, Cynewulf's as well as the rest, are translations or paraphrases from Latin originals. *Juliana* and *Elene* and two others which formerly were ascribed to Cynewulf, *Andreas* and *Guthlac,* are saints' lives retold in verse. *Elene* and *Andreas* are the most readable of the four, the latter being indeed a rather exciting tale of marvelous adventure, over which the author has spread the atmosphere of heroic poetry, learned from his study of *Beowulf.* Other poems which may deserve mention are: *Judith,* a paraphrase of the story in the Apocrypha of Judith's slaying of the Assyrian leader Holofernes; *The Phoenix,* an expansion of a poem written in the fourth century by Lactantius; and *The Dream of the Rood,* apparently an expansion of a Latin hymn. The last may be considered something of an exception to the general depreciation of these poems expressed above. It has elements of real beauty and is vigorously conceived. The "dream" is a vision of the True Cross (Rood) which rises before the poet, adorned with gold and jewels and radiating light; as he sees it with awe its appearance changes and it is bathed in blood; then it speaks, telling its history, and how it is honored amongst men, and how those who hope to dwell with God must seek His Kingdom through it. Such a fanciful personification did not seem unnatural in the ninth century; more interesting, however, is the fact that it was presented through a dream. The dream, or vision, was a favorite medieval device, and we shall meet with other dream-poems before the close of the Middle Ages in England.

Limitations of Old English Poetry

Amongst the extant remnants of Old English poetry are a group of some ninety-five short pieces, all of which are riddles. Like most of the other poetry, they are based on Latin originals; and they are mentioned here not because of their merits, which are slight, but because they can help us to understand the poetic taste of the Anglo-Saxons, and also to understand one reason why Old English poetry failed to develop beyond the point reached in *Beowulf.* It is known that the Anglo-Saxons were fond of the riddles, and this suggests that they were fond of hearing someone talk in a roundabout enigmatic way, flinging out hints for them to puzzle their heads over, instead of coming forth with a simple downright statement. The suggestion is wearisomely confirmed by all of their poetry. A riddling fashion of utterance was the most prominent characteristic, evidently, of the traditional poetic style which their earliest writers perforce took up and used—and as far as we can tell both writers and those for whom they wrote were perfectly inured to it and wanted nothing else. It was unfortunate. It encouraged in the Old English poets the habit of talking all around what they intended to say, sometimes ingeniously to be sure, but always in many words and cloudily. And no one appeared, after the author of *Beowulf* had done the best that could be done with the traditional poetic medium, who had the desire and ability to break away in some new direction from the chains of custom. One of the latest of the Old English poems is a portion, as it stands in the manuscript, of the early *Genesis* mentioned above. It has attracted attention because its theme is the theme of Milton's *Paradise Lost,* and because there is just enough similarity of treatment to suggest doubtfully that Milton may have known *Genesis B,* as it is called; but, despite passages of some grandeur, the piece as a whole shows that Old English poetry was at a standstill. It is wordy, repetitious, rambling, really weak and nerveless.

The conclusion is unescapable that Old English poetry as a whole looks, not forward, but—as we see the poet himself looking in *Beowulf*—backward to a dying past. In that fine and interesting poem Old English poetry came to an early climax, and then declined. Many conditions have to be fulfilled for a developing art to flourish; and, if we are to feel surprise in contemplating Old English poetry, we should be surprised, not at its limitations, but at its even moderate success. The Christian culture of Northumbria was built on slender foundations in an untoward time. All of the Anglo-Saxon kingdoms were unstable, weak within and constantly threatened with violence from without; and settled orderly existence was rarely possible, and never possible for very long in one place. Able and intelligent men have always been few, and when the times are desperate such men are always drawn off into merely defensive activity. We can learn a good deal from the fact that soon after the establishment of Christianity in Northumbria some families began to turn their estates into sham monasteries, partly to escape the burdens and dangers of military service, partly to protect themselves and their property under the name of the new religion. The creative energy generated by religion-and-learning was a small flame which burned bravely, but soon began to flicker amidst wind and storms.

The Vikings

And in the ninth century the flame was snuffed out in Northumbria by new invaders. Fortunately, sparks had been carried to Mercia, to be cherished there and passed on later to the south of England, so that the work which had begun so well in the north was never lost. But Northumbria itself was despoiled and ruined in the early stages of a new migration—this time of Vikings, from the coast of Norway and from the Danish peninsula. The Vikings were closely related to the Angles and Saxons in language and race. At the beginning of the ninth century they were somewhat more advanced towards civilization, particularly in handicrafts, than the Angles and Saxons had been in the fifth century; but they were pagan barbarians, and to the inhabitants of Britain they seemed to be monsters of cruelty and savagery. So the Angles and Saxons had seemed to the Romanized and Christian Celts in the fifth and sixth centuries. The course of the Viking migration was, too, strikingly similar to that of the Anglo-Saxon migration. The Vikings, however, once they had begun to move, did not confine their expeditions to the British Isles, but in the north reached out as far as Iceland, Greenland, and America; and to the south ravaged the coast and the river-towns of France and Spain, and sailed the length of the Mediterranean Sea, where they almost met other Vikings from Sweden who had gone eastward into the heart of what is now Russia and had sailed down the

Dnieper to make themselves a nuisance in the Black Sea and at Constantinople. The reasons for this sudden tremendous outburst of Germanic energy, beyond the difficulties of supporting life along the Scandinavian coast, are not clear; but a sufficient spur to its continuance for a time was the discovery that piracy was extremely profitable. The Vikings in fact made a business of it, and systematically combined trade with intimidation and massacre. And though they were bold and took great risks, still, they were on the whole a shrewd hard-headed lot, by no means engaged in adventure for adventure's sake. They discovered that the British Isles and Europe, lacking sea-power, were defenseless against them, and promptly made the most of the discovery. Wherever defenses were developed, they did not linger to waste their time and lives, but simply pushed on to find new defenseless victims.

In their invasion of the British Isles the Norsemen, or Vikings from Norway, chiefly sailed around the northern end of Scotland and down the west coast into the Irish Sea, where the Isle of Man became their headquarters for attacks on Ireland and England. The Danes, or Vikings from Denmark, at the same time chiefly attacked the east coast of England from the Tyne to the Thames, with occasional expeditions along the south coast. And just as the Angles and Saxons had begun coming to England for plunder, but had ended by settling there, the Vikings were soon settling thickly in Northumbria and in the east Midlands, besides forming isolated smaller settlements on the west coast and in Ireland.

At this point, however, important differences between the two Germanic invasions become apparent. The Vikings did not kill or drive out the Angles in anything like the way in which the Anglo-Saxons had killed or driven out the Celts. Being traders as well as conquering settlers, the Vikings tended to gather in towns from which they could dominate and—to use a modern word—exploit the Anglian farmers. The consequence was that the Vikings very gradually were absorbed into the Anglian population, altering it certainly, but in time accepting its religion and language and finally becoming indistinguishable in the new amalgam. Moreover, the Vikings were not destined to overrun and conquer all England; for in the south a great leader appeared in Wessex who successfully opposed them, kept them within bounds, and at the same time contrived to reform the government of his kingdom and to revive there the cause of Christianity and education.

Alfred the Great

The leader was Alfred, justly called Alfred the Great, who reigned over Wessex from 871 until his death in 899. Throughout his life he was troubled by physical difficulties, first temptations of sex and then a succession of ailments, painful but not disabling. The first of his conquests was a conquest of himself; and with it or from it he developed a willingness extraordinary in his age to subordinate his individual interest to that of his family and his people. In addition, he had a keen trustworthy sense of reality. He could see through appearances; he could size up men and situations; and his deepest concern was not just to save his land from spoliation, but to civilize his people and to place Christianity upon a renewed strong foundation. For Alfred was imbued with piety; as a youngster he had spent some time on the Continent and had traveled as far as Rome, where he had learned enough to recognize that his West Saxons were falling into half-heathen barbarism, partly because of the demoralizing uncertainties of the time, partly because the early zeal of the English for learning had dwindled away. It is with this, the educational and religious side of Alfred's achievement, that we are concerned, because out of it arose the earliest English prose literature. But Alfred's greatness, we ought to remember, lies in his many-sidedness. In addition to his work as educator and religious reformer, he was a capable and successful warrior, he created the first English navy, he revised and codified the law, he rebuilt and improved the structure of government, and he transformed the old Germanic social relationships into the beginnings of English feudalism. We know, too, that Alfred was a devoted sportsman; and that he loved to hear the English poems recited, perhaps *Beowulf* amongst them.

Central in Alfred's mind was the conviction that wisdom could not fail, and that the English were degenerating because they had forsaken its pursuit. Hence he surrounded himself with learned men, chiefly from abroad, perhaps one or two from Mercia, since there were none at all in Wessex. He believed there was no member of the clergy south of the Thames, and very few anywhere in England at the beginning of his reign, who could translate even the simplest Latin. He set up a school as a part of his household, after the fashion of Charlemagne, and forced his officials as well as their children to learn all they could, he himself struggling to learn Latin after he was forty years old. But in addition he determined to place learning upon a more secure foundation by translating a few most needful books into English. He could not overnight bring Latin to all his clergy, but he could put into their own tongue some of the fruits of learning, so that they should not remain blind shepherds. This determination seems so obviously the sensible one in the circumstances that we are in danger of failing to recognize its revolutionary character. It had not occurred to Bede, or to any Englishman before Alfred. The poetical paraphrases we have discussed above, and even the translation of one of the gospels which Bede vainly hoped to complete before his death, were something quite different; if the former were useful, they were, speaking generally, useful only to excite a mood of devotion, and Bede's projected translation would seem to have been intended for the same purpose.

Alfred's translations were co-operative works. It is reasonably certain that he was mainly responsible for some, and equally certain that those around him were responsible for others, but all were at any rate made under his direction. Thus the *Dialogues* of Gregory the Great were translated by Bishop Werferth, but Gregory's *Pastoral Care*—a book about the duties of the clergy—was at least partly translated by Alfred himself. Other translations were: Bede's *Ecclesiastical History,* the *History of the World* by Orosius, *The Consolation of Philosophy* by Boethius, and the *Soliloquies* of St. Augustine of Hippo. In addition, it seems likely that the *Anglo-Saxon Chronicle* was compiled under Alfred's direction, so that with the *History* of Orosius and the *Chronicle* together the English might have a continuous view of history from the beginning to their own time. Five distinct versions of the *Chronicle* are extant, but it is supposed that the differences between them crept in gradually after the first copies had been deposited in various monasteries by Alfred. One of these was continued by the monks of Peterborough to the middle of the twelfth century. Finally it may be mentioned that we owe to Alfred such eighth-century and ninth-century poetry as we have, because it all survives only in West-Saxon versions made under his influence towards the close of his reign or in the following century.

The Alfredian translations possess interest of two kinds. Several of them are really free adaptations, with some passages omitted and others inserted; and these shed light on Alfred's widely ranging curiosity and on his thinking. We perceive, for instance, Alfred's special interest in his own part of the world when he inserts in his version of Orosius descriptions of all the regions in which Germanic dialects were spoken, and also the narratives of two sailors, given him by the sailors themselves, of their voyages in the Baltic Sea and all along the Norwegian coast by North Cape and thence into the White Sea. Again, to take a quite different example, Alfred speaks to his readers from his inmost self in this passage from his version of St. Augustine's *Soliloquies:* "I would know whether after the parting of the body and the soul I shall ever know more than I now know of all that which I have long wished to know; for I cannot find anything better in man than that he know, and nothing worse than that he be ignorant."

But besides their personal interest these translations possess a considerable linguistic and stylistic interest. One finds immediately upon looking into them that English speech in the ninth century was developing in the direction of our own speech of today. Many of Alfred's sentences are in structure almost exactly like the sentences we would ourselves form to say the same things; and his words too are often our words, underneath their superficially strange appearance. Even when these versions closely reflect the style of their Latin originals, moreover, they are only exhibiting an influence which was to remain important in forming the English prose style of later times. It can therefore be said with substantial truth that in Alfred's prose we have the beginnings of English literature. There were to be many changes in the language, there was to be much experimentation in style, in later centuries; but all of this is really a continuing development out of Alfred's beginnings.

Old English prose, then, looks forward, though Old English poetry looks back. What we know suggests strongly that, even had the Danes not overrun Northumbria and Mercia in the ninth century, there would have been no more poetry written in that period, or none worth having. And it is significant that when Alfred rescued Wessex from decline, there followed no poetical revival. The two battle poems of the tenth century, *Brunanburh* and *Maldon,* stand, as far as we know, alone; and in style, in their whole character, they are curious belated echoes of a past then remote and not to be recalled. In general, it is true, Alfred's efforts did not quickly or strikingly bear fruit. Yet his successors in the tenth century did become kings of all England; and despite ever-recurring wars, the struggle to keep learning alive was not abandoned; and at least two churchmen appeared, Aelfric in the latter half of the tenth century and early part of the eleventh, and Wulfstan in the first quarter of the eleventh century, who in their homilies, or sermons, show that much progress had been made since Alfred's time in developing the possibilities of literary prose.

The Last Anglo-Saxon King

But the times continued to be troubled and uncertain. Evidently there could be no secure or considerable advance towards civilization so long as disorder and violence continued. And disorder and violence were still normal in the tenth century and in the eleventh, with no leader appearing who was able to place government on a stable foundation. Danish raids were renewed towards the end of the tenth century, and were so successful that presently the southern part of England was paying heavy tribute to Sweyn Forkbeard, King of Denmark, for the sake of precarious peace. Then in 1016 Sweyn's son, Canute, forcibly seized the English crown. He was a wise and beneficent ruler; and as king also of Denmark, the conqueror of Norway, and lord of the Hebrides, he held what may be called a North-Sea empire which, under capable successors, might have wonderfully altered subsequent European history. But this "empire" was a house of cards which fell apart with the death of the man who erected it, and England was soon again the victim of forces of disruption. The country turned to Edward, known as the Confessor, son of the last Saxon king before Canute. Edward had been living in exile in Normandy, and had been in effect remade by the influences of French piety and French feudal civilization, so that he did what he could to alter Canute's Northern orientation of the island and to bring in Norman-French influences. Thus he prepared the way for the last invasion of England, and the momentous changes which followed and which brought England once and for all within the circle of Latin civilization.

BEOWULF[1]

There is only one extant manuscript of *Beowulf*. It is bound with some other Old English texts in a volume belonging to the collection of Sir Robert Cotton (1571–1631), which is now in the British Museum. This manuscript was written by two scribes about A. D. 1000. The poem was probably composed in the first half of the eighth century. Of its author nothing is directly known, though the internal evidence of the poem enables us to picture him to ourselves "as a man connected in some way with an Anglian court, a royal chaplain or abbot of noble birth or, it may be, a monk friend of his, who possessed an actual knowledge of court life and addressed himself to an aristocratic, in fact a royal audience. A man well versed in Germanic and Scandinavian heroic lore, familiar with secular Anglo-Saxon poems of the type exemplified by *Widsith, Finnsburg, Deor,* and *Waldere,* and a student of Biblical poems of the Caedmonian cycle, a man of notable taste and culture and informed with a spirit of broad-minded Christianity" (Fr. Klaeber, *Beowulf,* p. cxxii). The poem consists of two parts, joined to each other only by the person of the hero. The first part has three divisions: Beowulf's fight with Grendel, his fight with Grendel's mother, and his return to his own land. In the second part is narrated his struggle, after the passage of many years, with a dragon. The events of the poem take place entirely in Denmark and southern Sweden, and England is nowhere mentioned in it. It is considered practically certain that the stories of the conflict with the Grendel race and of the slaying of the dragon are of direct Scandinavian origin. The Anglian author, however, fuses with these many other elements from other sources—notably the pervasive Christian coloring, which deeply affects the character of the poem. But notwithstanding the latter, *Beowulf* gives us a faithful picture of many phases of ancient Germanic life, moral as well as material, and particularly of Germanic military ideals. Practically the only direct historical data of the poem are the several allusions to the raid of Hygelac which took place between A. D. 512 and 520. It has been conjectured that a person named Beowulf actually accompanied Hygelac on this raid and so distinguished himself by exceptional bravery that he gradually became a center of heroic legend. Whether this be so or not, the Beowulf of the poem is obviously an idealized, heroic figure, not an historical character.

The original poem, although it makes no use of rime, is written in a meter very similar to that of the translation here printed. Each verse contains four accented syllables together with a freely varying number of unaccented ones, and each verse contains a marked pause between the second and third accented syllables. The accented syllables are, with the exceptions presently to be noted, distinguished by alliteration—that is, they begin with the same sound. They occur at the beginning of a word, save that prefixes are disregarded. Like consonant sounds alliterate with each other, whether they are indicated by the same letter or not; thus *card* and *kitchen* alliterate with each other, as also *noon* and *knight,* and be*deck* and in*dict*. Any vowel sound alliterates with any other vowel sound. The fourth accented syllable never alliterates with the third in Old English verse of the best period; but the third always alliterates with the first or second, and in the majority of cases with both. Occasionally the fourth accented syllable alliterates with the second, and more rarely with the first, when either of these is not in alliteration with the third.

The first eleven lines of *Beowulf* are subjoined in their original form:

Hwæt, we Gar-Dena in geardagum,
þeodcyninga þrym gefrunon,
hu þa æþelingas ellen fremedon!
Oft Scyld Scefing sceaþena þreatum,
monegum mægþum meodo-setla ofteah,
egsode eorl[as], syððan ærest wearð
feasceaft funden; he þæs frofre gebad,
weox under wolcnum, weorðmyndum þah,
oðþæt him æghwylc þara ymbsittendra
ofer hron-rade hyran scolde,
gomban gyldan; þæt wæs god cyning!

[1]From *Beowulf, A New Verse Translation,* by William Ellery Leonard. Copyright 1923 by the Century Co. Used by permission of the translator and of D. Appleton-Century Company, Publishers.

A good edition of the original text, together with an excellent summary of the scholarship which has grown up around the poem, is *Beowulf and the Fight at Finnsburg,* ed. Franz Klaeber (Boston, 1922). The historical and literary background is discussed more fully by Raymond W. Chambers, *Beowulf; an Introduction to the Study of the Poem, with a Discussion of the Stories of Offa and Finn* (Cambridge, 1921), and by William W. Lawrence, *Beowulf and Epic Tradition* (Cambridge, U. S. A., 1928). For a standard work on the whole period see Francis B. Gummere, *Germanic Origins: A Study in Primitive Culture* (New York, 1892).

THE OPENING

What ho! We've heard the glory of Spear-Danes, clansmen-kings,
Their deeds of olden story,— how fought the aethelings![2]
Often Scyld Scefing reft his foemen all,
Reft the tribes at wassail of bench and mead in hall.
Smote the jarls[2] with terror; gat good recompense 5
For that he came a foundling, a child with no defense:
He waxed beneath the welkin, grew in honors great,
Till each and every people, of those around who sate
Off beyond the whale-road,[3] to him was underling,
To him must tender toll-fee. That was a goodly King! 10

Unto him thereafter, was an heir y-born,
Within his gates a youngling, whom God that folk forlorn
For recompense was sending. He marked the grievous wrong,
How they of old had suffered, without a prince so long.
And so the Wonder-Wielder, the Lord of Life, fulfilled 15
For them world's weal and honor, through him, the heir of Scyld.
For famous was this Beowulf,[4] and far and wide there came
O'er the lands of Scandia the vaunting of his name.
So shall youth achieve it, with good works before,
With bold gifts and largesse, from his father's store, 20
That in old age after, when the wars may come,
Willing comrades, liegemen loyal, may stand by at home.
Praiseful deed will bring good speed in what clan soe'er.

Then did Scyld betake him, when his hour was there,
The stout and staunch betook himself to his Lord's good care. 25
Then away they bore him to the sea-tides,—did,
They, his loving clansmen, as himself had bid,
Whilst he wielded speech-craft, he, the Scyldings' friend,
Prince so long who ruled them, dear to the end.
There in haven stood she, her prow a rounded ring, 30
Icy and out-bound, barge of the Aetheling.
Laid they then the dear Chief, Bracelet-Breaker of old,
Mighty King, by the mast there, within the good ship's hold.
And full many a treasure, many a shining thing,
They fetched from ways afar off, for his journeying. 35
Never heard I tell of keel more fairly dight
With the warrior-weapons and the weeds of fight,

---

[2]Noblemen. [3]The sea.
[4]Not the hero of the poem, who is a Geat, but an earlier, Danish king of the same name.

With the blades and byrnies.[5] On his bosom lay
Treasure to fare with him far o'er floods away.
Methinks not less a lading of lordly gifts they gave
Than those who sent him whilom a lone babe o'er the wave. 40
O'er his head they set, too, golden banner steep,
Let the billows bear him, gave him to the deep.
Theirs were souls of sorrow, theirs were hearts to weep.
And no man can say sooth,— none in halls of state, 45
None of battle-bold ones,— who took up that freight.

I

Ruled Beowulf, the Scylding, in burg[1] for many a year,
Famed among the people, a folk-king dear
(His father was ta'en elsewhere, that chief from home was ta'en[2]),
Until for him there woke a son, the high Halfdane.
And Halfdane, named the Aged and the Fierce-in-fray, 5
O'er the gracious Scyldings held, all his life, the sway.
And, lo, for him four children (to count them as they be)
Awoke unto the world's light: warrior-leaders three,
Heorogar, and Hrothgar, and Halga, named the good;
And daughter, queen (says story) in Sweden o'er the flood. 10

Now was there given to Hrothgar such valor in the van,
Such honor in the onset, that all his kin-of-clan
Eagerly obeyed him, till waxed around his throne
Host of comrade-tribesmen, warrior-youths well-grown.
It came into his mood then to bid his serfs up-raise 15
A hall-chamber, a mead-house, a mightier far for praise
Than sons of men e'er heard of, and then within the hall
Unto young and unto old to deal his treasures all,
Such as God had lent him, except men's lives and lands.
To many tribes (I 've heard too) he gave his wide commands 20
Around this earth to deck it, this folkstead, with their hands.
Nor was it long thereafter, men saw its finished frame,
The greatest of hall-houses: Heorot[3] was the name
That he whose word was mighty had fashioned for the same.
He failed not of his vaunting, he dealt the rings thereby, 25
The treasure at carousal. Heorot towered high,
With stag-horn on each gable . . waiting its fiery fate,
The burning after battle; nor far the day when hate,
After old feuds, should waken, once more betwixt the twain—
Betwixt the daughter's father and him her wedded thane.[4] 30
But now that bold Hobgoblin, who dwelt in fenways dark,
Ill bore the sullen grievance that he each day must hark
To revel loud at banquet. The noise of harp was there,
In hall clear song of singer. He spake who knew full fair

---

[5]Coats of mail.

[1]Stronghold. [2]An allusion to the death and sea-departure of Scyld Scefing just described.

[3]The word means stag (hart). The hall was so named because of decorations in the gables resembling the antlers of a deer.

[4]References to the eventual burning of Heorot and to the feud between Hrothgar and his son-in-law, Ingeld.

To tell mankind's beginning, how God Almighty wrought 35
The earth, that shining lea-land, which waters fold about;
Quoth how God set, triumphant, the sun and the moon
As lights to lighten landsfolk; how he adornéd soon
With leaf and limb the fold[5] all; and eke created birth
For every kind that moveth on ocean, air, or earth. 40

So lived the troop of tribesmen, in revel, wise and well,
Till One began to do misdeed— this selfsame Fiend of hell.
And that grim Hobgoblin was Grendel named by men,
Great Stalker of the marches, who held the moor and fen;
Housed with the brood of giants this joyless Wight the while, 45
After Lord Creator had doomed his damned exile.
(Upon Cain's kin the Eternal avengéd Abel's blood.
Cain gat no mirth from murder; God banished him from good,
Afar from man, for sin's sake. Thence woke the monster-brood,
Ettins,[6] elves, and ogres, and giants, too, that warred 50
So long with God, who paid them at last their fit reward.)

II

Then fared he forth, did Grendel, to seek at dead of night
The high house, how the Ring-Danes, after their beer, were dight.
The aethelings he found there, aslumber after mirth;
Naught they knew of sorrow, naught of human dearth.
The Creature of damnation, the grim, the greedy One, 5
The fierce One in his fury, was ready there anon;
And, where they rested, reft he thirty, thane by thane,
And thence went faring homeward, of his plunder fain,
With his fill of slaughter, to seek his lairs again.

In the dawning, at the daybreak, arose of men the wail, 10
A mickle morning-uproar, after their yester-ale,
When Grendel's strength in battle to sons of men was plain.
Blitheless sate the high Prince, the Aetheling so good;
That strong Heart stricken sate, o'er lost thanes abrood,
What time the court set eyes on the curséd Monster's trail,— 15
Too strong that strife for Danefolk, too long the bane and bale.

Eftsoons, but one night after, was he at work once more,
With more of loathly slaughter, nor mourned a whit therefore,
A whit for feud and foul deed— in sin was he so bound!
Then might ye mark full many who somewhat further found 20
Resting-places elsewhere,— in outer bowers[1] their bed,
When, by so clear a token, to them was soothly said
The hate of this new Hall-Thane.[2] More far, more tight, all such
Did keep themselves thereafter who 'scaped that devil's clutch!
So ruled he and so ravaged, in wrong the one 'gainst all, 25
Till idle stood and empty that excelling hall.
Mickle long the while was: twelve winters' tide
Hrothgar dreed[3] disaster, woes with never end,

---

[5]Earth. [6]Giants.
[1]Smaller buildings near the hall. [2]Grendel. [3]Suffered.

Sorrows unbounded, he, the Scyldings' Friend.
And the mournful tidings to courts and kingdoms wide 30
In gleemen's ballads traveled, how Grendel's hate defied
Hrothgar forever, how for many a year
Grendel waged his warfare, strife of ceaseless fear;
Would not, by a peace-pact, set the Danemen free,
Would not with the Aethelings e'er compound for fee. 35
And still less might any of the Wise-men wot,
'Gainst those paws of pillage, help for Hrothgar's lot.
The grisly Wretch kept reaving youth and age of breath;
He lurked, he lured them darkly, that skulking Shade of Death;
Made, through nights eternal, misty moors his home; 40
Though beyond man's ken the haunts, where Hell's wizards roam.
Such a tale of terrors, such heap of hard despite
Wrought this Foe of mankind, Stalker lone by night.
Heorot Hall, the gold-bright, was his dusky den.
(Yet not his the power— God forbade him then!— 45
E'er to greet the gift-stool, e'er to come anear
Throne itself of Hrothgar,[4] nor partake its cheer.)
And so soul of Hrothgar, Scylding good and great,
Long was wracked and broken. And chiefs together sate
Oft at rede,[5] devising, what to do were best, 50
For such stout-hearted clansmen, against such awful guest.

Whiles at their idol-temples they vowed their offerings fair,
And conjured the Soul-Destroyer, for help in folk-despair.
Such was their devil-practice, and hope of these heathen men,
'Twas Hell in their hearts they remembered; and God was not in their ken. 55
The Doomsman of Deeds, they wist not; wist not the Lord of Love;
Nor worshiped the Wielder-of-Wonders, the Helm of the Heavens above.
Woe to the soul that perversely shall fling to the fiery pit,
Never to ween of comfort, never to change a whit;
Weal to the soul that after the day of his death is come 60
May seek the Lord and crave there in arms of the Father a home.

III

And so the son of Halfdane was carked by cares which bide,
Nor might the brave and wise One the sorrow turn aside:
Too big the strife for Danefolk, too long the bale and bane,
This hugest of night-horrors, that on his people came.
Far in his home, that good man,[1] among the Geatish breeds, 5
Hyglac's thane and nephew, got word of Grendel's deeds.
Of all mankind the strongest in might and main was he,
In the days of this our life here, high-born and free.
Bade make ready for him a rider-of-the-sea;[2]
Quoth, he'd seek this War-King, o'er the swan-road,[3] he!— 10
Seek this noble Chieftain, "for that 't is men he needs."
The canny carls[4] did chide him (though he to them was dear)

[4]Like a good retainer, who comes up to receive gifts from the king on his throne.
[5]In consultation.
[1]Beowulf, the hero of the poem. [2]Ship. [3]The sea. [4]Men.

Little for his faring; nay, rather spake him cheer,
Him the battle-brave One, and looked for omens clear.
The Good One of the Geatfolk now picked his comrades keen: 15
When he sought his timbered vessel, he was one of bold fifteen;
And well he kenned the coast-marks, wise in sailor-craft.

The boat ere long they launchéd, under the bluffs abaft;
The ready warriors clambered over the wave-tossed side;
Against the sands the breakers were writhing with the tide; 20
On the breast of the bark the heroes bore their bright array,
Their battle-gear so gorgeous. They pushed the bark away,
Away on its eager voyage. The well-braced floater flew,
The foamy-necked, the bird-like, before the winds that blew,
Over the waves of the waters— till, after the risen sun 25
Of the next day, the curved prow her course so well had run
That these faring-men the land saw, the cliffs aglow o'er the deep,
Broad sea promontories, high hills steep.
Ocean now was o'er-wandered, now was their voyaging o'er.
Thence clomb the Weder-clansmen[5] speedily up on the shore; 30
Anchored well their sea-wood, whilst their armor clanked,
Their mailéd sarks[6] of battle; God Almighty thanked
Because for them the sea-paths had not been made too hard.

Then from the wall the Watchman, the Scylding set to guard
The water-cliffs, espied them over the gangway bear 35
Their glittering shields of linden, their ready fighting-gear.
His wits were seized with wonder, what men were these indeed!
Down to the strand he gat him, riding on a steed;
Henchman, he, of Hrothgar,— mightily did shake
With his hands his spear-shaft, and in parley spake: 40
"What are ye, ye mail-clad, what armor-bearing braves,
Who lead a keel so high-prowed hither o'er the waves,
O'er the ocean causeway? I 've been out-post long,
Long I 've held the sea-watch, lest a pirate throng
In their fleet might sometime do our Daneland wrong. 45
Here have strangers never made them more at home;
Yet to you no word-of-leave from my kin hath come,
No consent from braves here. Never did I view
O'er earth a mightier jarlman, than is one of you,—
That Hero in his harness: yon Man in weapons dight, 50
He is no mere retainer, if tells his face aright,
His peerless port and presence! But know I must your kin,
Your home, before from hence ye (as if some spies ye bin)
Farther fare on Daneland. Ye boatmen of the brine,
Ye far-off dwellers, hear now this simple thought of mine: 55
'T were best forthwith ye tell me whence your comings be!"

IV

Him answered then the eldest, the war-band Leader, he,
His chest of words unlocking: "Of Geatish kin are we,
And Hyglac's hearth-fellows. Wide was my father's fame;

[5] The Geats. [6] Shirts of mail.

The high-born Warrior-Chieftain, and Ecgtheow his name.
He tarried many winters before he fared away 5
From his courts, an old man; and wide o'er earth today
Him the wise remember. In faithful mood we come
Seeking the son of Halfdane, thy Folk-King at home.
Be to us good of guidance. To Danemen's monarch bold,
We have a mickle errand,— which must not lurk untold: 10
Thou wottest if it be so, as we have heard for sooth,
That 'mongst ye Danes some dusky Scather without ruth,
Some Doer in the dark night, is dealing spite uncouth,
Dastard shame and carnage. I can in generous mood
Teach a rede to Hrothgar, how he, the sage and good, 15
This Fiend may overmaster,— if e'er to be it is
That toil and teen shall alter, help come to him and his,
And seething cares grow cooler; or else forevermore
He tholeth[1] days of sorrow, dearth so sad and sore,
Whilst there upon its high-place the best of halls shall bide." 20

The Watchman, doughty servitor, from his steed replied:
"Behooveth the keen shieldman, he who thinketh well,
'Twixt words and works the tokens cunningly to tell.
I hear this band is friendly unto the great Scylding:
Bear forth your weeds and weapons; I 'll guide you to my King, 25
And bid my faithful kin-thanes 'gainst aught of foes to guard
Your boat upon the beach here, this floater newly-tarred,
Till once more, o'er the sea-streams, the curved-neck timber bear
To Weder-mark the dear men,— those to whomsoe'er
It shall be granted safely to bide the coming fray." 30

They gat them, then, to fare forth; at rest the floater lay,
On hawser fast at anchor, broad-breasted ship ashore.
O'er cheek-guards shone the golden body of the boar[2]—
Flashing, fire-hardened, keeping a life-guard o'er
The battle-eager Hero. Together on they sped, 35
Until they saw the gold-bright high hall timberéd.
Under the wide heavens, where'er men dwell, was that
The fairest of all houses wherein King Hrothgar sat;
The light whereof went streaming out o'er many lands.
Then showed their Guide that gleaming burg of battle-bands; 40
Bade their march be forward, thither where he show'th;
Reined around his palfrey, words thereafter quoth:
"Time for me to fare back; in his mercy may
The Almighty Father keep ye safe alway
On your voyage and venture. I will to the coast, 45
There to hold my sea-watch 'gainst a hostile host."

V

The street was laid with bright stones; the road led on the band;
The battle-byrnies shimmered, the hard, the linked-by-hand;
The iron-rings, the gleaming, amid their armor sang,

---

[1]Endures. [2]Images of boars on Beowulf's helmet.

Whilst thither, in dread war-gear, to hall they marched alang;
The ocean-weary warriors set down their bucklers wide, 5
Their shields, so hard and hardy, against that House's side;
They stacked points up, these seamen, their ash-wood, gray-tipped spears;
And bent to bench, as clankéd their byrnies, battle-gears—
An iron-troop well-weaponed! Then proud a Dane[1] forthwith
Did of these men-at-arms there enquire the kin and kith: 10
"Ye bear these plated bucklers hither from what realms;
These piléd shafts of onset, gray sarks, and visored helms?
The Henchman and the Herald of Hrothgar, lo, am I!
Never so many strangers I 've seen of mood more high.
I ween that 't is for prowess, and not for exile far, 15
That 't is indeed for glory, that ye have sought Hrothgár."

The valor-famed, the proud Prince of Weders, made reply,
As, hardy under helmet, he spake his words thereby:
"We 're Hyglac's board-fellows, Beowulf my name.
I would to son of Halfdane my errand here proclaim, 20
To the great King, thy Master, if he but thinketh meet
To grant to us that we may one so goodly greet."

Wulfgar made a speech then (Prince of the Wendels, he,
For soul of war and wisdom renowned exceedingly):
"Fain will I ask the Danes' Friend, the Lord of all Scyldings, 25
As to the boon thou beggest,— will ask the Breaker-of-Rings,
My ever-glorious Sovran, touching this thy quest,
And quickly fetch such answer as he, the good, deems best."

In haste he hied him thither where King Hrothgar sate,
The old man, the hoary, with his jarls in state. 30
He strode, the valor-faméd, until he stood before
The shoulders of his dear King— O he knew courtly lore!
Wulfgar made a speech then to his chief, Hrothgár:
"Hither have there ferried, coming from afar
O'er the ocean stretches, Geatfolk to our hall; 35
Him who is their eldest Beowulf they call.
These men-at-arms the boon beg that they, my Chief, of thee
May ask and hear a word now: O gracious Hrothgar, be
Not niggard of replyings! They in their warrior-dress
Of jarlman's fairest favor are worthy, as I guess,— 40
And he who led them hither is doughty prince indeed."

VI

Hrothgar made his speech then, Helm of the Scylding-Breed:
"I knew him as a child once; Ecgtheow his father old,
To whom, at home, Geat Hrethel, his only daughter gave;
And now is Ecgtheow's offspring hither come, the bold,
And seeketh now the faithful friend across the wave. 5
Of yore those seamen told me, who bore to Geatmen's land
Thither in thanks my royal gifts, that he in grip-of-hand,
He, the keen-at-contest, had the clinch of thirty thanes.

[1]Wulfgar.

Him holy God in mercy sent, methinks, to us West-Danes
Against the greed of Grendel. This goodly youth unto, 10
I trust to proffer treasure for this his derring-do.
Be speedy, bid them enter to see our banded thanes,
Say eke to them in right words they 're welcome guests to Danes."

Then went to doorway Wulfgar, and spake he from within:
"My high Lord, King of East-Danes,[1] bids say he knows your kin; 15
And that ye are to him all, from o'er the ocean crests,
Ye hardy-hearted seamen, hither welcome guests.
Now may ye under visors wend in warrior-gear
To see our Hrothgar, leaving your battle-bucklers here,
Your ash-woods, shafts-of-slaughter, to bide the parley's close." 20

Uprose the mighty Geat then; ringed around him, rose
His valiant throng of thanemen. Some remained without,
Guarding their martial trappings, as bade their chieftain stout.
They hied them in together, where the Herald led,
Under roof of Heorot. The Hero strode ahead, 25
The stout One under helmet, till at the hearth he stood.

Beowulf made his speech then (shone his corslet good,
A cunning net-work woven by olden wit of smith):
"Hail and health, O Hrothgar! Of Hyglac's kin and kith
Am I, who 've gained in young days glories not a few. 30
Afar this thing of Grendel on my home-turf I knew.
Sea-farers say it standeth, this excelling hall,
Idle and empty unto each and all,
When under heaven's hollows the evening-light is hid.
So my best of henchmen, my canny carls, they did 35
Teach me, Sovran Hrothgar, that I should seek thee out,
For that so well they wotted this strength of mine how stout.
Themselves had they seen me from sore straits come alive,
Blood-flecked from foemen, where I 'd bounden five,
Killed the kin of ettins, out upon the main 40
By night had smote the nicors,[2] suffered stress and pain,
Avenged their hate of Geatmen— (they hoped to harry us!)—
And crunched and crushed those grim ones. And now with Grendel thus,
With the Grisly, this Giant, alone I 'd hold debate.
So now, O Prince of Bright-Danes, thou Shelter-of-the-Great, 45
Of thee one boon I 'm begging: O Scyldings' Bulwark-Bar,
Deny not, noble Folk-Friend, now I have come so far,
That I alone with mine here, who still would share my lot,
This throng of hardy thanemen, may purge thee Heorot.
Eke have I learned this Terror, in wanton mood and vain, 50
Recketh not of weapons. Therefore will I disdain
(Thus Hyglac's heart, my Master's, may it rejoice through me)
To bear or sword or broad shield, that yellow disk, to strife.
With grip I 'll grasp this Grendel, and we 'll contend for life,
A loather 'gainst a loather. The one whom death shall hale, 55

---

[1]East-Danes, South-Danes, and North-Danes are the same people as the West-Danes mentioned just above.

[2]Sea monsters.

Let him believe the Lord's doom. He will, if he prevail,
Methinketh, in that war-hall, eat unfearingly
The Geatfolk, as so often the Danishmen did he.
No need for thee to hide, then, this head of mine or veil;[3]
He 'll have me, sprent with gore, if 't is I whom Death shall hale; 60
He 'll bear his bloody quarry, he 'll think to taste his prey;
He 'll eat—this lonely Stalker— unmournfully away;
He 'll track with me his fen-lair: the need will ne'er be thine
In death to have the care of the body which was mine.
Send Hygelac this war-coat, which wardeth now my breast 65
(Of all men's battle-byrnies the brightest and the best)—
If that Hild[4] should hale me— Hrethel left in trust,
And smith Weland[5] worked it. Wyrd[6] goeth as she must."

VII

Hrothgar made his speech then, Helm of Scylding-Breeds:
"Us hast thou sought, friend Beowulf, because of ancient deeds,
Because too of thy kindness. Thy father, when by hand
Heatholaf he slew there in the Wylfings' land,
The worst of feuds awakened. Then might his Weder-kin, 5
For fear of Wylfings' harryings, take not Ecgtheow in.
Thence he sought the South-Danes, over the sea-surging,
Us, the Glory-Scyldings, what time I first was King
Of Danefolk and in youth held this kingdom jeweled,
This treasure-burg of heroes. For Heorogar was dead, 10
Yes, he, my elder brother, bairn of Halfdane high,
Was not among the living— a better man than I!
Thereafter I compounded the feud for a fee:
I sent unto the Wylfings, over the ridge of the sea,
Goodly gifts and olden, and oaths he sware to me. 15

"Sorrow for soul of me 'tis to tell to any one
What shame to me, what dread spite, in Heorot Grendel's done
With his thoughts of hatred; is my folk-on-floor,
My warrior throng of house-carls, almost no more.
Them hath Wyrd away swept into Grendel's greed. 20
Yet can God that Scather mad turn from his deed!
Full oft across their ale-cups my men-at-arms would pledge,
When beer had roused their bosoms, to bide with fierce sword-edge,
Within these walls of wassail, Grendel's coming-on.
But then would be this mead-house, when the day would dawn, 25
This lordly chamber, gore-stained at the morning-tide;
Boards of all its benches with blood be-spattered wide,
With battle-blood this hall here. I had of trusty men,
Of dear and doughty, fewer— since death had taken them.
Sit thee now to banquet, the cords of speech untie, 30
Tell us of thy victor-vaunt, as whets thy soul thereby."

---

[3]The reference is either to interment or to the custom of covering the head of the deceased with a cloth.

[4]A personification of battle. [5]The Germanic Vulcan. [6]Destiny.

Then for Geatish tribesmen, close together all,
Was a bench made ready in the wassail-hall.
There the stout-in-spirit went to take their seat,
Proud of this their prowess. A henchman did as meet, 35
Mindful he to bear round the figured ale-tankárd,
And pour to each the clear mead. Whiles would sing a bard,
Clear of voice in Heorot. Reveled there the thanes—
A host of happy heroes, Wederfolk and Danes.

VIII

Unferth made his speech then, at Hrothgar's feet who sate;
Let loose that bairn of Ecglaf his secret grudge of hate.
Beowulf's quest, bold seaman, to him was mickle spite,
Because he might not own it that any other wight
Ever in this Middle-Yard more deeds of bravery 5
Had done beneath the heavens than himself had he:
"Art thou, then, that Beowulf, who strove with Breca, thou,
Who on the deep contested in swimming hard enow!—
When in your pride ye twain did attempt the waters wide,
And risked in rash vain-glory your lives upon the tide? 10
Nor might not any man then, whether lief or loath,
From fearful voyage dissuade ye, from breasting seaward both;
There ye stretched your arms out ocean streams among,
Measured ye the mere's[1] path, drew with your hands along,
Bounded over the billows. Flood was asurge with foam, 15
With the waves of winter. Ye on the water's home,
Seven nights ye swinkéd.[2] He outstripped in stroke!
Had the more of might, he! Him, when morrow broke,
Surf up-cast by Heathoreams. He sought his home therewith,
He, beloved of clansmen; sought dear Bronding-kith, 20
And his own fair stronghold, where he had a folk,
Had a town and treasures. All his vaunt 'gainst thee
Did the son of Beanstan[3] fulfill faithfully!
So I ween for thee now worser outcome there
(Though in battle-onset, though in grim warfare, 25
E'er wert thou so doughty!), if thou durst abide,
For coming-close of Grendel, one night-long tide."

Beowulf made his speech then, the son of Ecgtheow he:
"Aplenty hast thou prated, beer-drunken as thou be,
Friend Unferth, about Breca,— his feat hast told at length. 30
But truth I hold it, mine was a mightier ocean-strength,
A bigger toil in the billows, than any other man's.
We twain, when still but younglings, had talked and pledged our plans
To risk (we were but boys then) our lives far out to sea.
We did as we had vowed to! Our naked swords had we, 35
Our hardy swords, in hands there, on breasting seaward both,
To fend us from the whale-fish. He could no whit from me
Float o'er the sea-flood swifter— and I from him was loath.
Thus were we twain together five nights upon the wave,

[1]Ocean's. [2]Toiled. [3]Breca.

Till surge and weltering waters us both asunder drave; 40
The coldest of all weathers, dark night and northern blast,
Blew battle-grim against us; fierce were the floods we passed;
Roused was the wrath of mere-fish; but there against the foe
My mail-coat, hard and hand-linked, helped me even so!
My braided sark-of-battle lay about my breast, 45
My corslet gold-adornéd. Me bottom-ward did wrest
A spotted Devil-Scather— fast held the Grim his grip!
But unto me was given to pierce with swordsmanship,
Aye, with the blade-of-battle, the Monster of the brine.
The mighty Mere-Beast foundered through this hand of mine! 50

IX

"Thus the loathly lurkers pressed me sore and oft.
I served them with my dear sword in ways not soft.
For those foul devisers the hope of fill was o'er—
To eat me, to sit round a feast on ocean's floor!
But upon the morrow, wounded by the glaive, 5
They were lying up along the leavings of the wave,
Put to sleep by sword there— ne'er to thwart again
Sailor-folk in ferrying the fords of the main.
From the east a light rose— God's beacon bright;
The rolling seas subsided, so that see I might 10
Headlands and windy walls. Wyrd will often save
A jarl who is no fey[1] man, if he be but brave.
And so to me 'twas granted that with sword I slew
Nine there of the Nicors. Nay, I never knew
Under the vault of the heavens by night a fight more fierce, 15
Nor on the streams of the ocean a man put to it worse.
Way-weary, yet I 'scapéd the clutch of monsters fell;
And the sea up-cast me, flood-tide and swell,
On the land of Finn-men. Never about thee
Such straits of strife, such terrors of sword-blades heard I tell; 20
Ne'er yet at war-play Breca, nor neither one of ye,
Did deed so bold with bloody brands— nor boast thereof I will—
Though thou forsooth thy brothers, thy kin-of-heart, didst kill!
(Whence curse of hell awaits thee, though good thy wit may be.)
I say to thee in sooth now, thou of Ecglaf son, 25
That Grendel ne'er so many gruesome things had done,
The Grisly ne'er such havoc in Heorot to thy King,
If thought of thine, if soul of thine, were grim as thy telling.
But he hath found he needeth fear or feud or stroke
Little from thy people, the Victor-Scylding folk! 30
He taketh the forced pledges, unsparingly he rends,
He hath his lust of slaughter, he puts to sleep, he sends,—
He recketh not of any contest with the Dane.
But speedily 'tis mine now to show him might and main,
The warrior-work of Geatmen! Let him go who can 35
Blithe to mead tomorrow— when o'er bairns[2] of man

[1]Fated to die. [2]Children.

Shineth from the southward, on other day begun,
Once more that light-of-morning, the sky-girt sun."

Then the Prince of Bright-Danes, the Treasure-Breaker, he,
The old-haired and war-famed, had his time of glee. 40
Now in help he trusted; from Beowulf he caught,
He, his people's Shepherd, the firm-resolvéd thought.
Then was there heroes' laughter; and rang the shout and song,
And merry speech was bandied; and then stepped forth along
Wealhtheow, Queen of Hrothgar, mindful of manners all, 45
And gold-bedight she greeted the guest-men in the hall.
And then the high-born Lady erst gave the cup in hand
To him who was the Warder of East-Danes' fatherland;
And him she bade be blithesome at the bout-of-beer,
Him beloved of clansmen. He took with goodly cheer 50
The banquet and the beaker, the King of victory-fame.
Then round the hall to each and all she stepped, the Helmings' Dame,[3]
And gave to young and older the goblet rich-beseen,
Till came the happy moment when in hall the Queen,
Crown-bedight and high-souled, the cup to Beowulf bore. 55
She greeted the Geats' lord; God she thanked therefore,
Wise in her word-craft, that her wish had thriven
That she could trust some jarlman for help 'gainst horrors given.
He took the cup from Wealhtheow, a warsman fierce-to-smite;
And then he offered answer, eager for the fight. 60

Beowulf made his speech then, bairn of Ecgtheow, he:
"When with my troop of tribesmen, I mounted on the sea,
And sate me in my sailor-boat, I had this thought in me:
Either to work for all time thy people's will at last,
Or to fall afighting in grip of Grendel fast. 65
Firm am I to do my jarlman's deed withal,
Or to dree my end-of-days in this mead-hall."

Those words well pleased that woman,— the Geatman's battle-vows;
And gold-bedight she went, then, to sit beside her spouse,
Folk-Queen high-born. And once again there be 70
Brave words spoken, and hall-men in glee,
And uproar of victor-folk— until the King anon
Would seek his evening resting-place, Halfdane's Son.
He knew that battle waited the fiend on that high floor,
After they the sun-light could see no more, 75
After the dun night was over all about,
And the shapes of shadow should come aprowling out,
Wan beneath the welkin. Together rose the clan;
Then Hrothgar greeted Beowulf, man wishing luck to man,
Gave him of that wine-house the power and sway, and swore: 80
"Never have I trusted to any man before,—
Not since I could heave up hand and shield of me,—
This brave house of Danemen, until now to thee.
Have now and hold it— this excelling hall!
Remember thy glory,— make known thy might to all! 85

[3]She was apparently one of the Helmings by birth.

Watch against the Wrathful! Each wish of thine I 'll do,
If with thy life thou see'st this deed of daring through."

X

Then did Hrothgar hie him, the Scyldings' Bulwark-Bar,
Forth from the mead-hall with his band-of-war;
Wished that Warrior-Chieftain Wealhtheow for to seek,
His Queen for his bed-mate. The King-of-Glory there
Over against Grendel (so men had heard him speak) 5
Had set a chamber-warder; whose special task was care
Of him, the Danemen's Monarch, in keeping ogre-guard.
Truly, the Geatish Leader trusted well the Lord,
And his own proud mettle. His mail he then undid,
From his head his helmet, gave his figured sword 10
(That goodliest of iron-things) to his man and bid
Watch and ward his war-gear.
Then his boast he said,
Beowulf, the brave Geat, ere he clomb to bed:
"Not poorer in battle-prowess, do I reckon me,
In the works of warfare, than is Grendel, he! 15
So not with sword I purpose to spill his life tonight,
To put to sleep the Monster, though indeed I might.
Those goodly arts he knows not whereby to cut at me,
To hew against my buckler, though so bold he be
In the works of combat. But this eventide 20
To both of us behooveth leave the blade aside,
If he durst to seek out a lack-weapon fray,
And holy Lord, the wise God, thereafter either way
Let him decree the glory as him-thinketh best."

And then the Keen-in-contest laid him down to rest; 25
And in the pillow sank, then, that Jarlman's cheek and head;
And many a brisk one round him bent to his hall-bed—
Many an ocean-warrior. Not any of the band
Thought 't would e'er be his to seek from here his fatherland,
The dear folk, or free-burg, that fostered him and bore; 30
But they had heard that ere now more than many a man
Slaughter-death had taken off of the Danish clan.
But unto them the Lord gave the webs[1] of weal-in-war,
Gave unto the Weders aid and comfort so
That, through the strength of One, they all o'ercame their foe,— 35
Through his might of selfhood. 'T is known that God, the Giver,
Hath wielded over mankind forever and forever.

Striding through the wan night, the Shadow-Stalker stepped;
The holders of that hornéd house, the shooting-men, they slept—
All, save only one there. 'T was known to men that he, 40
That ghostly Scather, might not, against the Lord's decree,
Draw them down to Darkness. Watching the foe to smite,
In wrath the Geatman bided the issue of the fight.

---

[1]Destiny.

XI

And now from out the moorland, under the misty slopes,
Came astalking Grendel— God's anger on his hopes.
That Scather foul was minded to snare of human kin
Some one, or sundry, that high hall within.
Under the welkin strode he, until full well he spied 5
The wine-house, the gold-hall, with fret-work glittering wide.
Nor was that the first time Hrothgar's home he sought.
Yet never in his life-days, late or early, aught
Like this harsh welcome found he from thanemen in the hall.
He came afooting onward to the house withal, 10
This warring One that ever had been from bliss out-cast;
Forthwith the door sprang open, with forgéd-bolts though fast,
When with his paws he pressed it; yea, then, on bale-work bent,
Swoln as he was with fury, that house's mouth he rent.
Anon the Fiend was treading the shining floor in there; 15
On he moved in anger; from eyes of him did glare,
Unto fire likest, a light unfair.
He saw within the chamber many a man asleep,—
Kinsman band together, of clanfolk a heap;
Laughed his mood, was minded that Hobgoblin grim, 20
Ere the dawn to sunder each his life from limb,
Now that fill-of-feeding he weened awaited him!
But Wyrd it was that would not longer grant him might
To seize on more of mankind after that same night.

Was watching he, the stalwart Kin of Hygelac, 25
How with grip the Grisly would go at his attack.
He had no thought, this Goblin, that business to put off;
But pounced upon a sleeping man,[1] starting quick enough!
Unthwartedly he slit him, bit his bone-box,[2] drunk
From his veins the blood of him, gulped him chunk by chunk, 30
Till soon, then, he had there this un-living Geat
Altogether eaten down, even to hands and feet.
Then stepped he forth and nearer, and pawed by bed to nim[3]
The hardy-headed Hero, reaching toward him
With his claws be-deviled: with thoughts that boded harm, 35
Beowulf received him, propped upon an arm.
But soon he found, did Grendel,— this Herdsman-over-crimes,—
That never in this Middle-World, this earth of many climes,
He'd met a mightier hand-grip in any man than here.
Afeared in mood and spirit, small help he gat from fear! 40
Was bent on making-off, ho!— out to the dark would flee,
Would seek the din of devils! Not now in Heorot he
Fared as in the old-days!— And then the Bold-in-pride,
Hyglac's Thane, remembered his speech of eventide.
Up he stood and grasped him so tight the fingers[4] cracked. 45
The Ettin started outward— the Jarl upon him packed.
The monstrous One was minded, whereso'er he may,

---

[1]Handscio. [2]Skeleton. [3]Seize. [4]Grendel's.

To fling himself but farther, and from thence away
To flee to boggy dingles; his fingers' power he wist
Was in the grip of Grim One. That was a sorry quest 50
Whereon the Scather Grendel to Heorot Hall had pressed.
The lordly room resounded; and all the Danes did quail,
Those warrior jarls of walled-town, lest reft for aye of ale.
Wroth were the ramping twain there, those warders of the house;
The chamber rang with uproar; mickle wonder 'twas 55
How the wine-hall held out 'gainst shock of fighters there,
How adown did fall not that earthly dwelling fair.
But inside and outside it was too firmly wrought,
With the bands of iron, forged by cunning thought.
I 've heard that many a mead-bench, with gold gilded o'er, 60
There where tugged the foemen, started from the floor.
So had weened the wise ones of the Scyldings erst
That never any man by force might asunder burst
That brave house and bone-bright, nor by craft might split—
Save that bosoming fire in flame should swallow it. 65

Up there rose a shriek then, strange enough o'night;
On each and every North-Dane seized a grisly fright,
On each who from the wall there heard that "well-a-way"—
Heard this God-Forsaker chant his gruesome lay,
His song of loss-in-battle, heard bewail his wound 70
This Grendel, Hell's Bondsman. For held him tightly bound
That man who was of all men between the seas confessed,
In the days of this our life here, in strength the mightiest.

XII

The jarls' Defender would not, forsooth with a will,
Let him loose aliving— him who came to kill,
Deeming not his life-days of use to any folk.
More than once did jarlman of Beowulf try a stroke
With his father's falchion, fain the life to ward 5
Of the faméd Chieftain, their great Lord.
They wist not, these warsmen, these hardy-headed few,
The while they fell asmiting and thought the while to hew
On this side, on that side, seeking soul to kill,
That best of earthly iron blades, nor never battle-bill, 10
This accurséd Scather could hurt or harm:
For over victor-weapons he had cast a charm,
Over every sword-edge. Yet his passing-o'er,
In the days of his life here, was to be full sore;
And this alien Elf-Thing was to fare afar 15
To the under-places where the devils are.
For he had found, had Grendel,— this Striver against God,—
Who in such merry mood of old so oft on man had trod,
That his bulk-of-body would not help him moe,[1]
Now Hygelac's stout Kinsman held his fore-paw so! 20
Was each unto the other alive a loathly thing.

---

[1]More.

A body-sore he gat there, this wretched Ogreling:
There showed upon his shoulder a cureless wound anon;
His sinews sprang asunder; from socket burst the bone.
To Beowulf was given the glory of the fray; 25
And Grendel was to flee hence, sick-to-death, away,—
Off under fen-slopes, off to dens of gloom.
He wist, O well he wist it, his end-of-life had come,
His full tale of days now.— The wish of Danemen all,
After that gory set-to, had come to pass withal. 30

He had now y-cleanséd, he who came from far,
The Wise-head and Stout-Heart, the House of high Hrothgár,
Had freed it now from fury. His night-work made him glad,
His deed of might and glory. The Geatmen's Leader had
Now before the East-Danes fulfilled his vaunting there,— 35
Aye, all ills amended and the carking care,
Which they had dreed aforetime, and by stress and strain
Long been doomed to suffer— more than little pain.
Of this there was a token, clear enough in proof,
When the Victor-Fighter under the gabled roof 40
Hung on high the fore-paw, the arm and shoulder grim—
And there ye had together all Grendel's clutching-limb!

XIII

Then there was at morning —so I 've heard the tale—
Round about the gift-hall many a man-of-mail.
Thither fared the folk-chiefs, near and far asunder,
All along the wide-ways, for to view the wonder,—
The traces of the loathed Thing. Seemed his passing-out 5
Not a grievous sorrow to any thereabout,
Any who were viewing now the craven's trail—
How he, weary-hearted, beaten in the bout,
Death-doomed and routed, off away from here
Made for very life his tracks to the Nicors' mere. 10
Yonder were the waters weltering with blood;
Mingled all with hot gore, surged the gruesome flood;
With battle-spatter rolled the deep, where the death-doomed then
Laid forlorn his body down, his heathen soul, in fen—
There did Hell receive him!

Home on horse anew 15
Rode the old companions, many a younger too,
Back from merry journey, bold men back from mere,
Warriors on the white steeds. Then was sounded clear
Beowulf's deed of daring: all said it o'er and o'er,
That south or north none other, from shore to farthest shore, 20
Betwixt the seas none other, beneath the sky's domain,
Was better man to bear shield or worthier to reign.
(Nor they by this belied not their Friend in anything,
Hrothgar, their gracious Lord— but that was goodly King!)

Whiles these doughty warsmen let leap their fallow bays,[1] 25
Let run a race where fairest seemed the country-ways;
Whiles a thane of Hrothgar,— a man of boasts was he,
Stored with olden sagas, and deft at balladry,—
Found one good word for other and bound them soothfully;
So too this scop[2] made mention right well of Beowulf's quest, 30
And had good speed at speaking his phrases artfullest,
Linking words together.
He told an unknown story—
All he 'd heard of Sigemund, of his deeds of glory:
The warring of the Waelsing,[3] his wanderings so wide,
The feuds and the betrayals, whereof no men beside 35
Wist aught but only Fitela—[4] when he to him would tell,
The uncle to the nephew, somewhat of what befell;
For ever stood they comrades in need against the foe,
And countless of the ettin-kin they had with sword laid low.
After his death, for Sigemund upsprang a fame not least 40
When he, that hardy warsman, had quelled that Serpent-Beast,
That Guardian of the gold-hoard. Under the hoary stone
Dared he, the son of aetheling, that bold deed alone—
For Fitela was with him not. Yet luck to him was given,
That this wondrous dragon so by sword was riven 45
That the lordly steel with point the cavern wall did pierce.
The drake[5] he died a slaughter-death. And Sigemund, the fierce,
Had gained by prowess power to use at will the hoard;
A sea-boat he loaded; the rings he bare aboard;
He bare to the ship's bosom, this man whom Waels begot, 50
That gold-gleaming treasure.— But Dragon melted hot!
Chief was he of outlaws, through tribes anear and far,
For the deeds of daring, this warriors' Bulwark-Bar
(And so erewhile he prospered)— yes, chief since waned away
The battle-strength of Heremod, his force and fame in fray. 55
For Heremod was lured forth, when mid the Jutes was he,
Into the power of foemen, and sent off[6] speedily.
Too long the waves of sorrow had lamed this man of strife;
To jarls, to all the aethelings, he 'd been a care for life.
And often in the old days, the wanderings of their chief 60
Had been to his sage vassals a weary thing of grief,—
To many a one who 'd trusted he 'd be a help from harm,
Prosper as a king's bairn, achieve his father's arm,
And folk and hoard and stronghold guard from hostile band—
This kingdom of the heroes, the Scyldings' fatherland. 65
Therein the Kin of Hygelac[7] a fairer virtue showed
To all, to friends, to all mankind— than crime-curst Heremod.

So homeward, oft aracing, these warriors old and young
With swift horses followed the fallow paths along.
Now was the sun-of-morning urged higher up the skies; 70
Went many a bold retainer to see the wondrous prize

---

[1]The "white steeds" of a few lines earlier. [2]Bard. [3]Sigemund, the son of Waels.
[4]Nephew of Sigemund. [5]Dragon. [6]Murdered. [7]Beowulf, nephew of Hygelac.

At the high hall Heorot. The King himself no less,
The Warder of the ring-hoard, famed for worthiness,
From out the wedding-bowers strode in royal sheen,
Girt by many clansmen; and, lo, with him the Queen 75
With troop of maidens measured the mead-path to the scene.

XIV

Hrothgar made a speech then; he walked unto the hall;
Stood upon the fore-steps; looked at roof so tall,
So garnishéd with gold-work; at Grendel's paw looked he:
"Thanks to the All-Wielder at once for what I see!
From Grendel have I suffered such gruesome plight and plunder: 5
But ever God he worketh wonder upon wonder—
He is the King-of-Glory! It was but now that I
Weened no boot for sorrows for me until I die,
When stood this best of houses battle-sprent with gore,
A sorrow spread so widely for every councilor 10
Who weened they might not ever save from Fiends-of-murk,
From ogres and from demons, this great folk-work.
Now hath a thane by Lord's might a deed put through
That we for all our cunning erewhile could never do.
Well can she say, that woman (if yet she be on earth) 15
Who gave, among the tribes of men, to such an offspring birth,
That olden God was kindly to her in child-bearíng.
Now Beowulf, best of battlers, to my heart's fostering
For mine own son I 'll take thee. Guard it well from now,
This our new-born kinship! Never lack shalt thou 20
For aught of world's desires whereover I have power.
Full oft did I for less deed of old a largesse shower,
Rewards from out my treasure, upon a punier swain,
A slacker one at slaughter. By thine own might and main
Thou hast thyself achievéd that thy name shall live 25
Forever unto ages. May the All-Wielder give
Reward of good unto thee, as ever he hath done."

Beowulf made a speech then, who was of Ecgtheow son:
"We wrought that work of warfare, that fight, with goodly will;
Boldly we dared the might of that mystic Thing-of-ill. 30
O I would the rather that thou his very self
Hadst seen in his trappings, that weary, wavering Elf!
Swift I thought to pin him with my clutches firm
Down upon a bed of death, that he in vain should squirm,
Dying under hand-grip— unless his body fled. 35
That flight I could not hinder— God willed him free instead.
To him, this Life-Destroyer, I clave not well enough—
He was too strong at foot-work, this Fiend in making-off!
To save his life, however, he left his fingers back,
His arm and his shoulder, as witness of his track! 40
Yet by this the creature not any comfort wins;
None the longer lives he, harried by his sins.
But him his sore hath bounden fast by bonds of bale,

In a gripe of anguish. There abide he shall,
Outlawed by evil, the day of doom so grim, 45
Waiting how the shining Judge wills to sentence him!"

Then Unferth, son of Ecglaf, he was less noisy wight,
In brag of works of battle, when, thanks to this man's might,
The aethelings were gazing that high roof along
At paw and foeman's fingers— and foreward there they hung, 50
Each of the claws in place there, unto steel most like—
That heathen creature's hand-spur, that warrior's eery spike.
The gazers vowed no brave man's good old blade soever
Might touch him, might the Monster's bloody fight-paw sever.

XV

Then quick the hest was given. Within was Heorot then
By many hands bedeckéd. Of women and of men
Aye, full many were there who did make ready all
That wine-house and guest-room. Gleamed on every wall
Woven hangings, gold-gay— of wondrous sights so much, 5
For each and every mortal of those who gaze at such.
It had been greatly battered, that building brave and bright,
Though all within-ward bounden by bands of iron tight;
And the door-hinges rended; the roof alone held out
Sound all-together, when Grendel turned about, 10
That Ogre in his fleeing, outlawed by deeds of ill,
And of his life in wanhope.[1] Ah, let each try who will,
It is not over-easy to flee away from death!
But each of bairns of mankind, each who beareth breath,
Each who dwelleth on the ground, shall seek, as fate shall force, 15
The place made ready for him, where his body-corse
Shall sleep upon its resting-bed, when the feasting's done.

'Twas time and tide when hall-ward hied Halfdane's son;
The King himself, this Hrothgar, would in the revel share.
Ne'er heard I tell of tribesmen themselves who better bare 20
Around their treasure-giver, in a goodlier press.
They bent them to the benches, owners of success!
Merrily they feasted; took again, again,
Cheerily the mead-cup. And kinsmen still withal
Were both of those stout-hearted ones in that high hall— 25
Hrothgar and Hrothulf.[2] Within was Heorot then
Filled alone with friends all— never in those times
Had the folk of Scyldings wrought the traitor-crimes.

Then the bairn of Halfdane, to Beowulf he gave
A banneret of gold-work, broidered on a stave, 30
A helmet and a byrnie, as meed of victory.
And a glorious jeweled sword many there did see
Borne unto the Hero. Standing forth on floor,
Beowulf received the cup; that warrior-band before,
He needed not to suffer shame for these gifts of price. 35

---

[1]Despair. [2]Hrothgar's nephew.

I have not known many to give in friendlier wise
To others on the ale-bench golden treasures four!
Across the crown of the helmet, a ridge outside there rose,
Of wires interwoven, to guard the head from blows,
Lest the files'-remainders,[3] the battle-hardened glaive, 40
Too fiercely might scathe it, what time the brave
Behind his shield should hie him forth against his foes.
Bade then the jarlmen's Bulwark[4] bring adown the hall
Horses eight, with golden plate upon the cheeks of all.
On one a saddle rested with jewel-work replete, 45
Shining with deft devices— that was the battle-seat
Of Hrothgar, the high King, when Halfdane's son would fare
Forth unto the sword-play; and in the vanward ne'er
Failed his famous valor, while round him fell the slain!
And then the Lord of Ingwines[5] to Beowulf gave the twain, 50
The horses and the weapons, as his to have and hold—
Bade him well enjoy them! Hrothgar, the bold,
The Hoard-Guard of heroes, so manfully paid back,
With horses and with treasures, Beowulf's attack,
That none who 'll speak the truth aright can blame for any lack. 55

XVI

Then, too, the Lord of jarlmen at mead-bench bestowed
On each who had with Beowulf taken the ocean-road
Some treasure, some heirloom, and bade with gold requite
The death of him whom Grendel had foully slain that night—
As more of them he fain had slain, except that God, the good, 5
And the man's own courage, for them that wyrd withstood.
The Judge then ruled all races even as he doth yet—
So best is alway insight, and forethought of wit.
How much of lief and loathly shall fall to each man's life
Who long makes earth his dwelling here in these days of strife! 10

Now was there chant and music, together linked as one,
Before the Army-Chieftain, Halfdane's Son.
The merry harp was fingered, the lay was lilted free,
As Hrothgar's bard by mead-bench sang in hall his glee.

THE WOE OF HILDEBURH[1]

"The Hero of the Halfdanes, Hnaef of Scylding-folk, 15
In the Frisian struggle fell by fatal stroke
At the hands of sons of Finn when they in terror woke.

---

[3]Sword. [4]Hrothgar. [5]Danes.

[1]As with the story of Sigemund and Heremod above, the poet assumes that his readers know the tale of Finn and his feud, and so merely gives a summary of the following events: Finn, a Frisian chieftain, who nevertheless has a "castle" outside the Frisian border, marries Hildeburh, a Danish princess; and her brother, Hnaef, with many other Danes, pays Finn a visit. Relations between the two peoples have been strained before. Something starts the old feud anew; and the visitors are attacked in their quarters. Hnaef is killed; so is a son of Hildeburh. Many fall on both sides. Peace is patched up; a stately funeral is held; and the surviving visitors become in a way vassals or liegemen of Finn, going back with him to Frisia. So matters rest

Little cause had Hildeburh to praise the Jutemen's[2] troth:
Blameless bereaved was she of her dear ones both—
Her bairn and her brother, at the linden-play.[3] 20
Wounded by the lances, to doom dropped they.
That was a grieving Princess, and she, the daughter of Hoc,
Had good cause to mourn her fate when the morning broke,
And under the skies she set her eyes on murder-bale of kin,—
There, O where in all the world her greatest joys had been. 25

"The fray took off the thanes of Finn, all but only few;
He might not in the parley-place[4] 'gainst Hengest battle do,
Nor save by fight from Prince's Wight[5] the remnants of his crew.
And so did they, the Frisians, a truce with Danemen call:
They 'd yield another floor to them, a high-seat and hall, 30
And Danes with bairns of Jutemen should each rule half of all;
And Finn, the son of Folcwald, should, with gifts of pay,
Do the Danemen honor each and every day;
Should, with his ring-giving, favor Hengest's men,—
With costly boon of fretted gold, as much as Hengest then 35
In beer-hall should cheer all the folk of Frisian kin.
Then did they swear a peace-pact, unalterable for both;
Finn did unto Hengest vow, without all strife, on oath:
That, with his Witan's[6] counsel, he 'd use Hnaef's remnant right;
That no man there, by word or work, should break the pact they plight, 40
Nor Frisians e'er should speak thereof, by any evil sleight,
Though Danes, bereft of ruler, in their need now were
Followers of the man that slew Hnaef, their Ring-Giver;
And if then any Frisian should by foemen's taunt
Of old hate and slaughter to the Danemen vaunt, 45
Straight should it be settled then by the edge of sword.

"The oath was sworn, the costly gold uplifted from the hoard,
The best of braves of War-Danes, Hnaef, on the pile lay stark;
Upon that pyre was plain to sight the gore-bespattered sark,
His swine all golden,—[7] the boar-crest iron-strong,— 50
And aethelings, by wounds dead,— for they had fallen, a throng.
And Hildeburh behested that at Hnaef's own pyre
The bairn of her own body be given unto the fire,
His bone and brawn be burned there and laid upon the pile,
By the uncle's shoulder. The lady wept the while; 55
Bemoaning in dirges. Her warrior-son they raise.
There wound unto the welkin a huge bale's blaze,[8]
And crackled at the grave-mound. Heads did melt asunder;
Gashes burst and blood sprang from death-wounds under.
Flame, of spirits greediest, did all of those devour, 60
Of either folk, whom war had ta'en. Gone was their flower.

a while. Hengest is now leader of the Danes; but he is set upon revenge for his former lord, Hnaef. Probably he is killed in feud; but his clansmen, Guthlaf and Oslaf, gather at their home a force of sturdy Danes, come back to Frisia, storm Finn's stronghold, kill him, and carry back their kinswoman Hildeburh.

[2]The names *Jutemen* and *Frisians* are here used interchangeably, although the two peoples were actually distinct.

[3]Battle. [4]Field of battle. [5]Hengest, thane of Hnaef. [6]Council of wise men.

[7]The gilded image of a boar on his helmet. [8]Funeral fire.

XVII

"Then wended the warriors, bereft of friends, away;
Back unto their dwellings in Frisland wended they,
To homes of theirs and high-burg. But Hengest made his inn,
Still through winter grim and wan, peacefully with Finn.
His thoughts were of his home-land, although he might not drive 5
Over the sea his ringed prow. Waves with wind did strive;
With storm rolled the ocean; with ice-fetters fast
Winter locked the billows,— till there came at last
Another year to homes of men, as still it doth today—
The glory-gleaming weather that keeps its times alway. 10

"Then was gone the winter and fair was earth's breast;
Forth did fare the rover,— from Finn's courts, the guest;
But he was thinking rather of wreaking wrath for wrong,
Than of ocean-voyage: how he might be strong
To bring to pass a battle-parle, in the which he would 15
O not all unmindful be of the Jutemen's brood!
Thus did he refuse not what is world's behest,[1]
When the son of Hunlaf had laid upon his breast
The blade hight[2] Battle-Flame, of all bills[3] the best—
Whose edges to the Jutemen were known too well. 20
Likewise to the fierce-heart Finn in turn befell
The sword-bale bitter at his very home,
When Guthlaf and Oslaf o'er the sea did roam,
Bemoaning the sorrow, the onslaught so grim,
And for a deal of trouble blaming only him,— 25
Nor might they in their bold hearts restrain their restive mood.
Then the hall was reddened with the foemen's blood;
And King Finn was slaughtered, 'mid his body-corps,
And the queen was taken. The Scylding bowmen bore
All the wealth in household of the king of earth— 30
Whatsoe'er at Finn's home they could find of worth,
Of gems and wrought jewels— to their ships away.
On sea-voyage to the Danefolk the royal wife they bore;
Led her back to kinsmen."

Sung was now the lay,
The harp-chant of gleeman. Mirth arose once more, 35
Loud rang the bench-joy. Cup-bearers did pour
Wine from jars-of-wonder. Forth came Wealtheow there,
Walking under golden crown, to where the friendly pair,
The nephew and the uncle,[4] sate: then was their kinship still at one,
Each unto the other true: And Spokesman Unferth, Ecglaf's son, 40
Sate at the feet of Scyldings' King. Both trusted still his spirit bold,
That he was man of courage keen; though he unto his kin of old
Were not at sword-play merciful.

And then the Dame of Scyldings spake:
"Breaker-of-Rings and Free-Lord mine, now this beaker take;

[1]The duty required by the common opinion of the world. [2]Called. [3]Swords.
[4]Hrothulf and Hrothgar.

Be thou blithe of spirit, thou Gold-Friend in hall; 45
Bespeak the Geats in happy words, such as behooves withal;
Be gladsome to the Geatmen, and not forgetful be
Of good gifts anear or far which now thou havest free.
'Twas told me, this warrior thou 'dst take for son to thee.
This bright ring-chamber, this Heorot, is restored; 50
Use, while still thou mayest, thy times for fair reward;
And leave unto thy kinsmen the folk and the state,
When 'tis thine to fare forth, to greet eternal fate.
I know my gladsome Hrothulf— that 'tis his will to be
Gracious to these boys of ours, if earlier thou than he, 55
O thou Friend of Scyldings, leavest the world behind.
I ween, with goodness he 'll requite the offspring of us two,
If he all that remembers that you and I did do
For him when erst a youngling, with gifts and honors kind."

Thereat to bench she turned her where her lads were then, 60
Hrethric and Hrothmund, with bairns of fighting men—
The youth all together. There sate the doughty Thane,
Beowulf, the Geatman, between the brothers twain.

XVIII

To him she bare the goblet, and friendly words spake she,
And armlets twain of twisted gold she proffered graciously,
And rings and a war-coat, and best of collars too
That ever on earth I heard of.

Nay, I never knew
Under heaven a hero's treasure goodly more 5
Since Hama to his bright burg the Brisings' necklace bore,
With clasp and costly setting. (He fled the wily mood
Of Eormenric, that angry King, and chose eternal good.)
This was the very collar that Hygelac had on,
The Geatman, scion of Swerting, his last of raids upon, 10
When he beneath his banner was fending booty won,
And spoils of war was warding. Wyrd took him at a stroke,
When in his pride he trouble sought and feud with Frisian folk.
Yea, he, the mighty Chieftain, these precious stones had ta'en,
These fair adornments, with him across the bowl-of-the-main; 15
And now that he had fallen beneath his shield at last,
His corpse, his mail and collar, unto the Frankmen passed.
The weaker host was reaving the spoils of warriors dead
After this battle-hewing; and this slaughter-stead
The Geatish men were holding.

The hall rang out in glee; 20
Wealhtheow made a speech then; before the band spake she:
"Have joy of this collar, with weal, belovéd Youth!
This war-coat use, my Beowulf— a royal gift in sooth—
Thrive thou well and show thee ever strong and free,
And unto these my boys here kind in counsels be: 25
For that will I be mindful of recompense to thee!
Thou hast done so doughtily that for many a year

Men shall do thee honor both from far and near,
As widely as the sea-waves wash each windy wall;
As long as ever thou livest to thee may good befall! 30
I wish thee well with treasures! Unto this my boy
In deeds of thine be helpful, guarding him his joy!
Here is each jarl to other true and mild of mood,
Faithful to his Overlord; all the thanes are good,
The folk at one and ready, the reveling fighters free. 35
Do thou as I bid thee."

Unto her seat went she.

Here was the best of feastings; here drank of wine the bold;
They wist not Wyrd was walking, this grim Fate of old,
Forth for many a jarl there. When the eve had come
And Hrothgar had hied him unto his own home— 40
Unto his rest, the Chieftain— then did guard the floor
A goodly count of jarlmen as oft they did before.
The bench-boards they bare off; and through the hall did strew
The beddings and the bolsters. And of that boisterous crew
Was one to rest who laid him— ne'er to wake anew. 45
At heads they set their bucklers their war-wood bright.
On bench above each aetheling there was plain to sight
The steep battle-helmets, the byrnies of rings,
The spear-shafts sturdy. For these aethelings
Were wont to be full often ready for the fray 50
At home or on a harrying,— be whichever it may,—
Even on such of seasons as when befell some stroke
Against their Lord and Master. That was a doughty folk!

XIX

Sank they to sleep then; was one who purchased sore
His rest there of evening— as oft had chanced before,
Ever since this Grendel made Gold-Hall his home,
And wrought there at wrong deeds till his end did come—
His death after sinnings. And now 'twas seen by men, 5
And far and wide reported, that an Avenger then
Yet survived the Monster,— that all the time Another
Survived this battle-sorrow: Grendel's own Mother,
The She-Thing, the Witch-Wife, her pang was mourning near,
She who needs must make her home in grisly mere, 10
In the cold sea-currents— after the times when Cain
An only brother, his father's son, with the sword had slain.
Outlaw, marked for murder, he fled the joys of folk,
Haunted the wildernesses. So from him awoke
The breed of fated goblins; of these was Grendel kin, 15
That Horror, that Outcast— who Heorot Hall within
Had found that watchful Human, awaiting the fight.
There the Ogre gripped him, but of his strength of might
Beowulf was mindful— to him God's precious gift—
And trusted the Almighty for grace and cheer and shift.[1] 20

[1] Help.

Thereby he overcame the Foe; this Troll[2] of Hell he strook,
Who slunk off acringing, of his joys forsook,
For to see his death-place— this Foe of mankind.

And now his greedy, gloomy Mother was of mind
To go on quest of sorrow, to wreak the death of her son. 25
She came then to Heorot, where around the floor
The Ring-Danes were sleeping. Then came to jarls anon
Return of olden evils, when athrough the door
Burst the Mother of Grendel! But this was a terror less,
Less by as much as less is a woman's war-prowéss, 30
The battling might of maidens, than a man in fighting dress
(Whenever his falchion, banded, anvil-beat by the sledge,
His sword with blood bestainéd, cleaves with its doughty edge
Down through the foeman's boar-crest, over the helmet's crown).
Then in the hall of Hrothgar, many a blade was drawn, 35
Swords from over the benches; many a buckler tall
Was lifted tight in the hand there! Never a man in hall
Thought of his helm or corslet— on whom that fear did fall.
Hers was a sudden hasting— hers was a turning about
To save her life in the open, knowing herself found out. 40
But speedily the Ogress had seizéd tightly then
One of the Danish house-carls,[3] as off she fled to fen;
Hrothgar's dearest Hero in vassal's rank was he,
A mighty shield-warrior, between the sea and sea,
A fighter of a sure renown whom in his rest killed she. 45
And Beowulf was absent,— for to the Geatman bold
Another lodge allotted was after the gifts of gold.
Uproar was in Heorot. Away with her she bore
The famous paw of Grendel, dripping with its gore.
Sorrow was renewéd within their homes once more. 50
'Twas an exchange right grievous, where either side must pay
With the lives of loved ones.
Then that Warsman gray,
Old King Hrothgar, had a heart of pain,
Knowing this Prince was lifeless, dead this dearest Thane.
Speedily to bower was Beowulf fetched away, 55
The victory-blesséd Hero. And just at dawn of day
He wended with his jarlmen, this champion Aetheling,
Himself with his comrades, to where abode the King,
Waiting if All-Wielder might ever will to show
To him a turn-for-better after the spell of woe. 60
Strode along the floor, then, this Man, the brave-in-brawl,
With his hand-companions, whilst sounded planks in hall,
To greet with words the Wise One, and ask the Ingwines' Sire
If he had slept a quiet night after his desire.

XX

Hrothgar made a speech then, Helm of the Scylding-Brood:
"Nay, ask not after joyance! Sorrow is renewed

[2]Ogre. [3]Aescher.

Unto the folk of Daneland. Dead is now another—
Aescher, of Yrmenlaf who was the elder brother,
My councilor, my wise-man, and comrade at my right 5
Whenever our heads we warded amidst of the fight,
As clashed the foot-foemen, and rang the boar-crest—
A jarl should be like Aescher, an aetheling the best.
Him hath the hand in Heorot of roving Death-Sprite slain,
And I wot not whither its backward-ways 't has ta'en, 10
In its prey exulting, of its feasting fain.
She hath the feud avengéd whereby on yester-night
Thou slewest so grimly Grendel by gripping him so tight—
Because he rent and ravaged too long my folk in strife.
He fell at last in battle, paying with his life; 15
And now hath come another Scather lorn and lewd,
Who would avenge her offspring— and farther bears the feud:
So that indeed it seemeth unto many a thane,
Who weepeth for his Ring-Giver, a hard heart-bane;
Low lies the hand that wrought ye your every wish so well. 20

"I 've heard my land-dwellers, my folk's householders, tell
They 'd seen a pair of such ones, alien Sprites obscure,
Mickle Border-Stalkers, haunting the moor.
And of these the One was— as far as guess they might—
The likeness of a woman; the other wretched Wight 25
Trod his tracks of exile in a man's own mien,
Save that he was bigger than man hath ever been—
Whom the landfolk naméd Grendel of yore.
Knew they not the father— whether theretofore
Ever he'd begotten any troll-kin more. 30

"Their haunts are secret places, the wolf-slopes dim,
The headlands windy, the fen-ways grim,
Where the mountain waterfall downward away
Floweth under crag-head, under mists of spray.
And the mere it standeth off some mile or more: 35
Over it there hangeth a forest frosted hoar;
A wood, fast-rooted, the water over-hoods;
Each night is seen a wonder weird— a fire on the floods!
There lives no man so wise on earth whoso its bottom sounds:
Though the heath-ranger, harried by the hounds, 40
The hart, strong of antlers, hunted far in flight,
May seek this woodsy thicket, he 'll rather yield his sprite,
His life upon the brink there, than plunge for safety in.
A spot uncanny is it; whence wan to welkin spin
Welter of foam and waters, when the winds begin 45
Astirring the foul weather— till the air is murk,
And the heaven weepeth.

"Again we wait thy work,
Thine and thine only! That land not yet thou know'st,
The fearsome spot whereunder thou 'lt find that damnéd Ghost—
Seek it, if thou darest! For this fight to thee 50
I 'll give, as even erst I did, twisted gold in fee,
Aye, mine olden treasure, if back thou com'st to me."

XXI

Beowulf made a speech then,   son of Ecgtheow, he:
"Sorrow not, thou Sage One,—   for each it better be
That his friend he wreaketh   than bemourn him late.
Our end of life in world here   we must all await;
Let who is able win him   glory ere his death;   5
In after-years for warrior dead   that chiefly profiteth.
Arise thou Kingdom's Warden!   Speedily let us hie
Of this Kin of Grendel   the trail for to spy.
This to thee I promise: She 'll refuge in no rest—
Neither in earth's bosom   nor in hill-forést,   10
Nor in sea-bottom,   wheresoe'er she go!
For this day have patience   in thine every woe,
As I ween thou wilt have."
                    Upleapt the Graybeard now;
Thanked the Lord Almighty   for what this man did vow.
Then Hrothgar's horse was bridled,   his steed with braided mane;   15
Stately rode the royal Sage;   and afoot his train
Of shield-bearers was stepping.   Wide was there to see
Her tracks across the wood-ways,   her trail along the lea,
Whither fared she forward   over the murky moor,
And with her bare the dead man,   the best of kin-thanes sure   20
Of all who once with Hrothgar   warded well the home.
Then the Son of aethelings   now did over-roam
The narrow-passes,   the steep cliff-stone,
The close defiles and   the paths unknown,
The beetling cragheads,   the Nicors' den.   25
All ahead he[1] hastened with   a few wise men
For to view the region,   till a sudden he
Found the joyless forest,   found the mountain tree,
Leaning o'er the hoar cliff.   Under the wood,
Blood-stained and troubled,   there the waters stood.   30
Unto the friends of Scyldings,   unto every Dane,
It was a thing of sorrow,   a burden of heart's pain,
Aye, to many a clansman   a grief it was and dread,
When, upon the sea-cliff,   they met with Aescher's head!

The flood with blood was boiling,   yes, with the hot gore;   35
The folk saw down upon it;   the horn was singing o'er
Its battle-blast of onset.   The band all sate;
They watched along the water   the sea-worms[2] great,
Monsters of the dragon-breed,   trying there the sea,
And on the foreland ledges   Nicors lying free   40
(Who 're wont at early morning   their grievous quest to take
Out upon the sail-road[3])—   and wild-beast and snake.
Bitter and puffed with anger,   they hastened away—
They had heard that clangor,   the war-horn's lay.
One did the Geatish Leader   with arrow-bow from shore   45
Berob of life forever   and of the waves' uproar.

---

[1]Probably Hrothgar.   [2]Sea-serpents.   [3]Sea.

The warrior-shaft, the hardy, unto his heart went home—
He whom death had taken swam more sluggish on the foam!
Speedily on the billows with barbed boar-spears
They pressed him so sorely, they harried him so fierce, 50
And dragged him up the ledges, this wave-tossing Ranger.
The marveling warriors looked upon the grim and grisly Stranger.

Girded himself, did Beowulf, with his jarlman's weeds;
Naught for his life he mournéd. His coat of mail must needs,
Bright with deft devices, be trying the sea-quest— 55
This hand-woven byrnie big, that girt his bony-chest,
So never a grip-in-battle might do his bosom scath,
Nor life be hurt by vengeful grasp of this Thing-of-Wrath.
The head of him was guarded by the helmet white
That soon must seek the sounding surge and stir the deeps below: 60
With lordly bands 'twas bounden, with treasure-work 'twas dight,
As the weapon-smith had wrought it in days of long ago,
And wondrously had decked it and set with shapes of boar,
That brand nor blade of battle might bite it nevermore.

Nor was that the smallest of helps to mighty deed 65
Which Spokesman of Hrothgar[4] had loaned him in his need:
A good sword hafted, and Hrunting its name,
Of all old heirlooms the first it was in fame.
The edge of it was iron, etched with twig and spray,
Hardened by the battle-blood; ne'er did it betray 70
Any man that clasped it with hand amid the fray,—
Any man that dared to go on war-paths away,
To folk-stead[5] of foemen. Nor this the first time now
That Hrunting-sword of Unferth in mighty works should dow.[6]
In sooth the bairn of Ecglaf, great though his prowess be, 75
Remembered not his speech of late when drunk with wine was he,—
Now as he lent his weapon to a stouter swordsman here.
Himself he durst not hazard his own life in the mere,
Nor dree a warrior's duty. And thus he lost the fame,
The glory of a doughty deed. For the Other 'twas not so, 80
When he himself had girded for battle with the Foe.

XXII

Beowulf made his speech then, bairn of Ecgtheow, he:
"Bethink thee now, thou mighty son of Halfdane's name,
Gold-Friend of house-cards, Sovran wise and free,
Bethink thee, now I'm girt for quest, what we twain spake before:
If for thy need, O Hrothgar, my life I should give o'er, 5
That thou to me wouldst ever be, when I'm no longer here,
Still in the place of a father; every trusty fere,[1]
Each of these my kin-thanes, do thou as guardian tend,
If once the battle take me; and likewise, O my Friend,
These treasures that thou gavest me unto my Master send. 10

---

[4]Unferth. [5]Battle-place. [6]Prosper.
[1]Comrade.

Then Hyglac, son of Hrethel, may ken from all this gold,
Aye, see, when he beholdeth these giftings rich and old,
That I indeed had found me a Treasure-Giver bright,
And had my joy in him and his so long as still I might.
And let thou, too, thy Unferth, that far-famed soul, 15
Have the olden heirloom, the sword[2] with wavy scroll,
Hard of edge and jeweled. In Hrunting will I trust
To work my doom of glory— or I die the death I must."

After these his words the Geat, Beowulf, in pride
Hastened in his valor. No answer would he bide. 20
The billows took the Battle-Man. 'Twas a while of the day
Ere he arrived the sea-floor where the Monster lay.
And soon this grim and greedy She-Thing ravin-fierce,
That held the stretches of the floods a hundred half-years,
Found that there some one of men from up above had sought 25
The dwelling-place of eldritch-wights.[3] Against him then she caught,
With grisly claws she gripped him. His warrior-body sound
Thereby no whit she scathéd. His mail did shield him round
So that reach she might not, with loathly fingers stark,
Athrough his army-corslet, his linkéd battle-sark. 30
Then as she to the bottom came, this She-Wolf of the sea,
She bore unto her own home the Chieftain-of-the-Rings,
In such a wise he might not, albeit so wroth was he,
Ever wield his weapons. And many monstrous Things
Mauled him in the maelstrom, many a sea-beast tried, 35
With its battling tushes, to burst his sark aside,
And swarmed upon their Troubler. Then was the Jarl aware
That he was in some hall of hate— he knew not what or where—
In which not any water could scathe him at all,
Nor floods in onrush touch him because of rooféd hall; 40
And he saw a light of fire, a brightly flashing flare.
And Beowulf had a look then upon this deep-sea Troll,
This mighty Mere-Woman. Then up with sword and soul
He made a sudden onset, nor hand delayed the stroke,
And on her head the ringéd blade its greedy war-song woke. 45
But, lo, the Stranger found then his flasher-in-the-fray[4]
Would bite not, would scathe not the life it sought today,
For Hrunting's edge was failing the Chief in his distress,
Though often in the old days it had endured the press,
And cloven many a helmet, and war-coat of the fey; 50
This was the first of all times that low its glory lay.
Again had he but one thought,— nor courage did he lack,—
Still mindful of valor, this Kin of Hygelac!
In wrath the Champion hurléd the fretted[5] blade away,
Bound on hilt with ring-work, till there on earth it lay, 55
That stout sword and steel-edged; and on main strength relied,
The might of his old hand-grip. So must a man of pride,
Whenever he bethinks him to win in battle-strife
Praises everlasting, nor careth for his life.
The Chieftain of the Geatfolk,— who mourned not at the feud,— 60

---

[2]Beowulf's own sword. [3]Weird beings. [4]His sword, Hrunting. [5]Eaten.

Graspéd by her mane of hair Grendel's Mother lewd.
This hardy son of battle,— so did his anger swell,—
Flung the deadly She-Wolf till to ground she fell.
Speedily thereafter, with her grip so grim,
She gave him goodly payment and laid her hold on him. 65
And then with heart aweary, this Fighter fierce and lone
Stumbled in his footing, that there he tumbled prone.
Then on the Stranger in her hall The Mother squatted down,
And forth she drew her dagger, broad of blade and brown.
She would wreak her bairn now, her only child this day; 70
But on the Geatman's shoulders the woven breast-mail lay,
And that withstood the inthrust of point and edge at last.
For then the son of Ecgtheow to under-earth had passed,
Had not his battle-byrnie, his war-mesh stout and broad,
To him its help y-given, and had not holy God, 75
The Ruler, he, of Heaven, justly swayed the fight—
The wise Lord with his award— when Beowulf stood upright.

XXIII

For saw he 'mongst the war-gear one victorious bill,
An old sword of ettins, with edges doughty still,
The pick and choice of weapons, a warsman's prize indeed;
But more than any other man might bear in battle-need—
Good and brave to look on, the giants' handicraft. 5
The Bold One of the Scyldings he seized its belted haft;
And, battle-grim and savage, the ringéd blade he drew;
And, of his life all hopeless, in fury smote so true
That it gripped her sorely unto the neck, oho!
And brake in twain its bone-rings. The sword was keen to go 10
Athrough her doomèd body. She crumpled in the murk.
The old sword was bloody. The Hero liked his work.

And the gleam out-blazéd, within there stood a light,
As from heaven shineth the sky's Candle[1] bright.
He looked about the dwelling, he turned him to the wall, 15
He heaved by hilt the weapon, this hardiest sword of all;
Wroth and with but *one* thought, the Thane of Hygelac—
With its edge not useless for such a man's attack!—
Speedily was of a will to pay that Grendel back
For his many onslaughts made on folk West-Dane, 20
Mickle more than one time, when asleep he'd slain
Hrothgar's hearth-fellows, and slumbering eat with jaws
Fifteen of Danish folk and fifteen borne in claws
Outward, his ghastly prey. For Beowulf, the dread,
Paid him his award for that, where he beheld on bed 25
Grendel, the battle-weary, lying lorn of life,
Ev'n by scathe he'd gotten in Heorot at the strife.
The corse did spring asunder; it dreed a blow, though dead,
Oho, a swinging war-stroke,— and off was carved the head!

---

[1]Sun.

The wise earls that with Hrothgar sate peering at the flood
Soon saw the surges swirling, the sea all stained with blood. 30
The white-haired ones together about the brave Man speak:
Saying they ween the Aetheling no more will come to seek,
In the pride of victory, their glorious Overlord,
Since him it seemed to many the Sea-Wolf had devoured. 35
Then came the day's ninth hour; the Scyldings left the ness;[2]
The Gold-Friend of clansman, Hrothgar, hied him home;
Only the Geatish strangers sate in their distress,
Sick at heart with longing, and stared upon the foam.
They wished but never weened to see their dear Lord's self again. 40

Then the sword, the war-bill, 'gan wondrously to wane
In icicles of battle, by goblin-gore accurst:
Likest to ice it melted, when God, the Father, first
The bands of frost doth loosen, unfettering stream and pool,—
He 's Lord of times and seasons, and very sooth his rule! 45
The Chieftain of the Weder-Geats, he took not from the lair
Not any goods of treasure (though saw he many there),
Except the head of Grendel and hilt so bravely dight:
The fretted blade had burnt away, the sword had melted quite—
So hot had been the blood of her, so poison-fierce withal 50
Had been this eldritch Ogress that died there in the hall.
But he who in the combat did bide the demon-slaughter
Soon was at his swimming, up-diving through the water.

Cleansed were surge and stretches wide, where the grim Mere-Wife
Had left this fleeting world of ours and her days of life. 55
The sea-farer's Safe-guard, this Stout-Heart of toil,
Came striking out to landward, fain of his sea-spoil,
Fain of his booty-burden. Went to meet him then
His staunch troop of tribesmen, thanked the God of men,
Rejoiced in him their Leader to see him sound again. 60
Helm and mail of Hero they loosened with a will;
The waters under welkin, the bloody pool, was still;
Forth they fared in foot-prints, these happy aethelings;
The earth-way, the known road, they measured, bold as kings.
They bare the head from sea-cliff, a load for each, though stout, 65
And four upon the spear-pole scarce lifted it about
Onward to the Gold-Hall, till into hall bedene[3]
They came, these brave-in-battle, these Geatmen, the fourteen.
Their Chieftain in a mighty mood amid them trod the mead,
Till he, as first of clansmen, this Man so keen of deed, 70
Hero, battle-hardy, with glory honored,
Came to greet his Hrothgar. And now is Grendel's head
Borne by hair where warriors drink,— to jarls and Lady there
A gruesome vision wondrous. The Danes upon it stare.

XXIV

Beowulf made his speech then, son of Ecgtheow, he:
"Lo, thou Son of Halfdane, with joy we 've brought to thee,

[2]Promontory. [3]Straightway.

As token of glory, this spoil thou here dost see,
O Sovran of the Scyldings. I barely 'scaped with life;
Unsoftly did I risk the work in under-water strife; 5
Straight had the battle ended, had God not been my shield,
For Hrunting in the combat I might in no wise wield,
Though doughty be that weapon. But he, mankind's Defender,
Gave me upon the wall to see, hanging in its splendor,
A huge sword of old times. (Oft and oft withal 10
The Father guides the friendless.) I drew that sword from wall,
Then slew I at the onset, when my chance was good,
The Wardens of that under-house. But so sprang the blood,
The hottest gore of slaughter, that the fretted blade,
The battle-bill, was burnt all. From my foes I made, 15
Bearing thence the hilt away. I wreaked the crimes of hell,
The death-fall of Danishmen, as was fit and well.
I promise thee in Heorot a sleep care-free,
With band of thy retainers, each who follows thee,
Of the older, of the younger; and ever from that quarter, 20
O Sovran of the Scyldings, release from dread of slaughter
For these here, thy jarlmen, as erst 'twas thine to dree."

Then was that hilt, the golden, the giants' work of yore,
Giv'n to hand of the old King, the Battle-Leader hoar;
After the fall of devils, to Hrothgar's keep it fell— 25
This work of wonder-smithmen; yea, when this Heart-of-Hell,
God's Foeman, murder-guilty, this world of ours gave o'er
(And eke this Grendel's Mother), it passed into the power
Of him, the best of World-Kings of all between the seas
Who e'er on Scandia's island dealt men their golden fees. 30

Hrothgar made his speech then; on hilt he cast his eyes,
Relic of the olden time, whereon was writ the rise
Of that far-off warfare, when o'erwhelmed the flood
And the ocean's outpour once the giants' brood:
They bore themselves too boldly, a folk estranged from God; 35
For this the Lord made end-award by whelming under wave.
So on the golden sword-guard, in many a runic stave,[1]
Was marked aright and set and said for whom was wrought of yore
That best of steel with twinéd hilt, and etched with dragons o'er.

Then spake wise Son of Halfdane— and still were all the throng: 40
"Lo, one, like me, who 's warded a kingdom long and long,
And for his folk still worketh the right and the sooth,
One who remembers all of old, may say this thing indeed:
That here 's a very jarlman born of better breed.
Thy fame shall be uplifted, my belovéd youth, 45
Among all peoples, Beowulf, over the wide ways;
And thou shalt hold thy prowess with wisdom all thy days;
My troth to thee will I fulfill, e'en as we spake before.
Thou 'lt be unto thy people an aid forevermore,
A help unto the heroes.

---

[1]Letter in the runic or secret alphabet of the Germanic peoples.

"Not so was Heremod 50
Unto Ecgwela's children, the Scylding-folk, the good.
Nor waxed he to their pleasure, but unto every Dane
Was he the dire undoing and the deadly bane.
In wrath of heart he slew those who drank with him and ate
And stood beside his shoulders, till he, the King so great, 55
Lonely passed from cheer of men. Yet God advancéd him
And raised in power, in joys of strength, above all human kin.
His hoard of thoughts in bosom, however, bloodier grew;
He gave no rings to Danefolk, as kings are wont to do.
Lorn of joy he bided; the work of strife he dreed, 60
The long feud of his people.
"Learn from this thy rede;[2]
Know what is manly virtue. As one in winters gray,
For thee I 've told this story. A wonder 'tis to say
How mighty God on men bestows, in his forethought free,
Wisdom, lands, and earlship. All things ruleth he: 65
Whiles letteth he the heart-thought of men of noble birth
In lustihead go faring, giveth joy of earth,
Giveth in his native land a walled burg to keep,
Granteth stretches of the world, realms so wide of sweep,
That he himself the ends thereof may ween not in his thought. 70
Dwelleth he in fatness; him thwarteth never aught
Of either eld or sickness; nor any evil care
Beclouds in murk his spirit; nor feuding anywhere,
With sword and hatred, threatens. Unto his will and lot
All the world is wending. The worse he knoweth not. . . . 75

XXV

"Till wakes and waxeth in him pride, a mickle deal;
Whilst the Watchman[1] sleepeth, the Warden of souls' weal—
Aye, very fast that sleeping, and bound with busy woe,
The Slayer[2] very nigh him who shoots from grievous bow.
Then is he in his bosom, under helmet hit 5
By a bitter arrow— he knoweth not a whit
How he now may shield him from wonder-spells of wrong
Of the curséd Demon. What he held so long
He thinketh now too little. Greedy, grim, and bold,
He never gives with goodly boast the rings of plated gold; 10
Forgetteth he and spurneth the fate that comes to all,
Because the King-of-Glory him gave such good of old.
But in the end it happens his fleeting frame doth fall,—
Death-marked it sinketh. Another now succeeds,
Who gladly deals that jarl's old wealth and spurneth ugly deeds. 15

"Best of men, dear Beowulf, keep from bale and feud;
Choose for thyself the better part, the everlasting good.

---

[2]Advice.

[1]The conscience. [2]The Devil.

Spurn, renownéd Fighter, over-much of pride;
Now shall thy fame in valor a little while abide:
Soon shall be hereafter, that sickness or the glaive 20
Part thee from thy prowess— or the whelming wave,
Or the fang of fire, or the flight of spears,
Or the grip of falchion, or the aging years;
Or else thine eyes' brightness shall fail and darkened be,
And death anon, O Warrior-Son, shall over-master thee. 25

"Half a hundred winters, under the welkin, lo,
I held my sway o'er Ring-Danes, and warded them in war
With ash-stock[3] and steel-edge, 'gainst clans anear and far,
So well that I did count me 'neath all the skies no foe.
Behold! a change there came to me then in my father's home— 30
Grief instead of good times, when Grendel did become,
He, the olden Enemy, invader of my floor;
Ever for his raidings mickle care I bore.
Thanks to God eternal, that I did bide in life
Long enough with eyes to see, after olden strife, 35
That head from sword so gory. Go, now, to thy seat;
Enjoy the merry feasting, thou, honored by thy feat.
Many a gift between us twain there'll be upon the morrow."

Went to seek his seat then the Geat so free of sorrow,
As the Wise One bade him. And now, as erst, again 40
The feast was dight so fairly for valor-famous men,
The sitters in that hall-house. . . . The helmet of the night
Darkened dusky o'er the band. Arose each warrior-wight;
The hoary agéd Scylding was fain to seek his bed;
The Geat did list him[4] passing well to lay to rest his head, 45
He, the famous Shieldman. And soon the Thane-in-hall—
Who tended with meet courtesy the Hero's needments all
(Ev'n as these ocean-farers were worthy of the best)—
Led forth the Hero come from far, weary from his quest.
So rested he, the Great-Heart. That House it towered high, 50
Broad-roofed, gold-bright. Within it slept the guest,
Until the black raven with his blithesome cry
Boded the Joy-of-Heaven.[5] Onward came the Bright,
The Shine that follows shadow. Hastened every wight;
Aethelings were eager back to folk to fare; 55
The Big-Heart would take ship far away from there.
Bade he then, this Brave One, Unferth Hrunting bear,
Bade him take his sword again, the iron blade so lief;
Thanked him for the loan thereof; quoth, he counted it
A friend-in-war, a good and great; belied he not a whit 60
The edge of Unferth's falchion. That was a gallant chief!
And when the braves were forward, ready in their gear,
Then stepped he forth, the Hero, he to Danes so dear,
To where was there the Other high on kingly seat,
And then this battling Aetheling did his Hrothgar greet. 65

---

[3]Spear. [4]Was pleased. [5]The sun.

XXVI

Beowulf made his speech then, son of Ecgtheow, he:
"Lo, we far-comers, we farers on the sea,
Have a will to say now we 'd seek our Hygelac.
Thou hast been a goodly host; in nothing did we lack.
O Lord of men, if ever I may this earth upon 5
Earn me of thy heart's love more than yet I 've done,
By aught of work-of-battle, I 'll ready be anon.
If across the long seas, ever I should hear
That the dwellers round about burden thee with fear,
As the haters of thy realm have done of yester-year, 10
I 'll bring to thee a thousand thanes, braves for help to thee.
I wot me of my Hygelac, though so young he be,
This Sovran of us Geatmen, this Herdsman of our ledes,[1]
That he will well uphold me both by words and deeds,
That I may do thee honor, and to thy succor bear 15
Ashen spear and aid of might, if need of men be there.
If, too, thy Hrethric, bairn of kingly birth,
Betakes him to the Geatish court, he 'll find of friends no dearth:
'T is good to see a far countree, for one who trusts his worth."

Hrothgar made his speech then, answering him anon: 20
"The wise God these sayings sent into thy soul, my son.
Ne'er heard I more sagely so young a man take part;
Strong in might, and sound in thought, and wise in words thou art.
Most likely do I count it, if haply spear take him,
The offspring of Hrethel,[2] in battle bloody-grim,— 25
If illness, aye, or iron, take him to whom ye vow,
This Herdsman of your people,— and if alive art thou,
That then the Sea-Geats cannot make seemlier choice for King,
For Hoard-Ward of heroes, than thou, my Aetheling,
If then thou 'rt not unwilling thy kindred's realm to hold. 30
Me liketh thy brave spirit, belovéd Friend and bold,
The longer the better. Beowulf, 'twas thine
To bring to pass between us, between thy folk and mine,
The Geat-clan, the Spear-Danes, that common peace shall be,
And strife shall rest, the ugly feuds, which both erewhile did dree; 35
That there shall be, as long as I rule this Kingdom wide,
Treasures in common, and greetings either side,
Gifts the one to other over the gannet's bath;[3]
And that the ringéd ship shall bring over the ocean path
Offering and love-token. I wot our peoples hold, 40
Knit as one, to friend and foe, all blameless as of old."

Thereto the Son of Halfdane, whom "Shield of jarls" they call,
To Beowulf presented treasures twelve in hall.
And bade him with these giftings his own, his dear domain
To seek in weal and safety, and quickly come again. 45
And then the Lord of Scyldings, the King of birth so high,
Kissed the best of aethelings and clasped his neck thereby;

[1]Folk. [2]Hygelac. [3]Ocean.

The tears they were afalling from him, the old man hoar;—
Two likelihoods[4] he thought of— but one of them the more:
That never thereafter might they each other scan, 50
Proud men in parley. So lief was him this man
That now his breast's upheaving seemed too much to bear;
Bound within his bosom a secret longing there
After the man belovéd burned into his blood.

But Beowulf thence away the grass-plain trod, 55
War-man, gold-proud, fain of treasure-fee.
There at anchor riding, a goer-on-the-sea[5]
Was its master biding. And marching to the main,
The Geatmen spoke of Hrothgar's boon again and yet again.
That was a King all spotless . . . till from his joys of strength 60
Eld, that scathes so many men, took him too at length.

XXVII

So came the press of henchmen, these bold ones, to the bark;
Each bare his ringéd harness, the linkéd battle-sark.
The Land Guard, as erst, spied the jarls again on quest;
But not with any words of harm, from the headland's crest,
Greeted he the strangers. Toward he rode with hail; 5
Welcomed, as the scathers[1] fared to ship in shining mail.
Then on the sand was laden the boat of bulwarks wide,—
The ringéd craft was laden with armor side by side,
With horses and with treasures. The mast aloft it soared
Over Hrothgar's olden piléd treasure-hoard. 10
Beowulf gave the Boat Guard a gold-bound sword;
And ever thereafter upon the mead-bench he
Was worthier for that heirloom that gift from o 'er the sea.

The craft it clave deep water; from Daneland far it passed,
Upon the mast a sea-cloth, a sail by rope made fast; 15
Groaned and creaked the sea-wood;[2] the wind it never drave
From off its billowy course there that bounder-on-the-wave;
Foamy-necked it floated over the billows free,
Over the streams of ocean, that goer-on-the-sea—
Until the cliffs of Geatland the sailors sighted plain, 20
The old familiar nesses. The keel upsprang amain,
Speeded by the wildwinds, and rested on the land.

The Haven Guard was straightway helping at the strand,
He who long already, eager by the mere,
Had been awatching far-off for the men so dear. 25
He bound that boat of bosom broad with anchor-cordage fast,
Lest this their merry vessel the waves away should cast;
Then Beowulf bade bear out the wealth of aethelings,
The plated gold and trappings.
Not far from here it is
To seek the son of Hrethel, Giver-of-the-Rings, 30

---

[4]That they might or that they might not see each other again. [5]Ship.
[1]Warriors. [2]Ship.

Where at home he dwelleth, himself with comrades his,—
Hyglac near the sea-wall. That house was very fair;
Its lord a King renownéd, the halls were lofty there;
And Hygd,[3] of Haereth daughter, was young, but well-beseen,
Albeit so few her winters within the burg as queen— 35
Aye, none the less no chary, no niggard lady she
Unto the Geats with giftings, but one with treasures free.

Hygd, the goodly Folk-Queen, showed not the mood of Thryth,
Nor Thryth's misdeeds of terror. Was none of kin and kith
So brave, he durst adventure with eyes to face her[4] eyes 40
(Except her husband only). For well would he[5] surmise
Bonds of death would ready be, a hand-twisted cord;
And hard upon his seizure she'd summon her the sword,
For scrolléd blade to settle it, and thus his death reveal.
'Tis not a queenly custom, for woman so to deal, 45
E'en though she be so fair of face, aye, such a man to kill
(She who 's called "Peace-Weaver"[6]), in fury for no ill.
But Hemming's kinsman[7] verily did end her ruthless pride,
And men amid their ale-drinking often said beside
That less she wrought of folk-bale, and less all mercy scorned, 50
So soon as she was given, she, the gold-adorned,
Unto the youthful Fighter, the high-born and good,
When at her father's bidding she voyaged o'er the flood,
Unto the hall of Offa; where after on the throne
All her life she loved her lot, with a fair renown; 55
And fostered a deep fondness toward this Prince of thanes—
The best, as some have told me, in all the wide domains,
Of all the race of mankind, that dwell the seas between;
And therefore this Offa, this Man spear-keen,
Widely was honored for wars and gifts of hand; 60
With wisdom he ruléd his own home-land.
And unto him was born, then Eomaer, a son—
Grandson of Garmund, of Hemming's kinsman one,
A mighty man in battle, a help to every band.

XXVIII

'Gan then the Hardy One, himself along the sand,
To tread upon the sea-plains, the stretches of the strand,
With his feres, the trusty. The world's Candle shone,
The Spangle risen southward. They strode along alone;
Sturdily they marchéd, to where they heard that now 5
Hygelac, the Shield of jarls, slayer of Ongentheow,[1]
Within the burg was dealing ring upon ring,—
Hygelac, the good, he, the young War-King.
The coming-back of Beowulf to him was quickly told,
How thither to the King's house this Shield of battlers bold, 10

---

[3]Hygelac's queen. [4]Thryth's. [5]He who faced her eyes. [6]"Lady." [7]Offa.

[1]The slayer was really Hygelac's retainer, but a retainer's deed was customarily attributed to his chief.

And of the buckler-bearers, was coming on his way
Alive unto the court there, safe from battle-play.

Anon, as then the Sovran bade, the hall within was dight
For these guests, these way-farers. And he who fought the fight
Sate him by the King's self, kin his kin beside, 15
After he had greeted in courtesy and pride
His Liege-Lord, the gracious. With mead-draughts for all,
Hygd, of Haereth daughter, went round about the hall.
She lovéd these the people; she bare for the carouse
The stoup[2] to hands of Geatmen. In high hall-house 20
Hygelac in fair wise questionings addressed
To Beowulf, his house-carl; with longing burst his breast
To hear how well his Sea-Geats had thriven on their quest.

"Dear Beowulf, what luck, then, upon this voyage, for thee,
After thou bethoughtest, over the salt-sea, 25
To seek afar the battle, and strife at Heorot?
For Hrothgar, the great King, hast bettered now or not
That woe so widely told of? For this I seethed in breast
With care and surging sorrow. Me liked not such a quest
For man so much belovéd. And long I begged of thee 30
That thou that eldritch Ogre would let forever be,
And let themselves the South-Danes settle as they may
The warfare with Grendel. To God my thanks I say
That I can look upon thee sound again today."

Beowulf made his speech then, bairn of Ecgtheow, he; 35
"O that is no wise hidden from men, where'er they be,
That our famous meeting, Hygelac, my lord,—
How on that very field there I and Grendel warred
Where he so oft and often had wrought the sorrow-stroke
And miseries forever on Victor-Scylding folk. 40
All that so well I vengéd that none of Grendel's kin,
None on earth that longest lives begirt by sin,
Of this breed, the loathsome, will care to boast withal
Of the din there in the dawning.
"But unto the ring-hall[3]
First did I betake me Hrothgar to greet; 45
Soon when he, the mighty Child of Halfdane,
Knew the thought within me, he yielded me a seat
There beside his own son. Thane rejoiced with thane;
I never saw in all my life, under the heavens all,
More merriment at mead among sitters in a hall. 50
Whiles the Queen, the high-born, whom "Peace-Bringer" they call,
Passed, as she cheered the younger braves, around through all the hall,
And gave to many a warrior rings of wreathéd gold,
Ere yet she went unto her seat. And whiles unto the old,
To every jarl, the ale-stoup did Hrothgar's daughter bear— 55
She whom I heard the sitters within the hall-house there,
As she the bosséd beaker gave, Freawaru name.

[2]Cup. [3]Heorot, where Hrothgar distributed rings as gifts.

"Betrothed is Freawaru, the young, the golden dame,
To the glad son of Froda.[4] For Hrothgar did devise,
He, the Kingdom's Shepherd, a rede he counted wise:
Even through her, this Lady, to set old feuds at rest,
And end a deal of slaughter. But seldom 't is at best,
After a prince's death-fall, that spears are laid aside,
More than for a little while— however fair the bride.
And Ingeld may not like it, nor any of his thanes,
When there shall pace adown his hall a courtier of the Danes,
Leading in this Lady past many a Heathobard,
And shining with the heirloom, the fretted sword and hard—
The Heathobards' treasure, what time they wielded stroke,
Until they lost at linden-play their lives and fellow-folk.
And then shall some old spearsman, who marks the precious thing,
Grimly o'er the ale-cup speak remembering
The tribesmen pierced and fallen, and 'gin in grief of breast
To stir some stripling's bosom, his fighting soul to test,
To wake in him the war-hate. And this the word he saith:

" 'Canst thou not, my comrade, ken the sword of death,
Which to the fray thy father bore upon his final quest
Under his casque-of-battle,— this blade of iron dear,—
Where the Danemen slew him, and Scyldings bold-with-spear
Held the field of slaughter, victors over all,
When Withergild lay lifeless after our heroes' fall!
Lo, now some upstart youngling from out these men-of-bane,
Proud of these his trappings, paces down the hall,
Vaunteth of that murder, and doth that jewel[5] bear
The which by right, my comrade, thou alone shouldst wear.'

"So urgeth he and eggeth again and yet again
With words sore and bitter; till good time succeeds
When the Lady's serving Thane for his father's deeds,
After the bite of battle-bill, sleepeth and bleeds,
With his life a forfeit. The venger fleeth thence;
And living he escapeth, for well the land he kens.
The sworn oaths of jarlmen are broken on each side;
And welleth feud in Ingeld, and all his love of bride,
In surgings of his sorrows, waxeth cooler now.
Therefore I count the Heathobards' peace pact and vow
Guileful to Danishmen, their friendship not fast.

"But once again of Grendel I must speak at last,
That thou, O Treasure-Giver, may know the end aright
Of the hand-fray of the heroes. When heaven's Jewel bright
Had glided from the fields of earth, came that angry Sprite,
The grisly Evening-Goblin, for to seek us out,
Where we the hall were warding, Geatmen stout.
And then was unto Handscio the warfare come amain,
Bale to him, the fey man. 'Twas he that first was slain,
He, the girded Fighter. Our kindred's mighty Thane

[4]Ingeld, the Heathobard. [5]Sword.

Died in the mouth of Grendel. Grendel swallowed him,
The body of that dear man, head and trunk and limb.
Yet not for this the sooner would he quit withal,
He, the Slayer bloody-toothed, the gold-decked hall,
Still mindful of murders, still empty-handed, he! 110
But, terrible in prowess, did he try for me,—
Gripped with ready fore-paw! On him a pouch there hung;
Wide it was and wondrous, with cunning cordage strung,
And all y-wrought with artful thought, of very dragon's skin,
By the craft of devil. And me he'd thrust therein, 115
Me, a man unsinning, and many another too—
This savage Prince-of-Evil. But so he might not do,
When I myself in anger stood there upright.
Too long it is to tell ye how I did requite
This Scather of the people for each deed of ill; 120
I did thy people honor, my Lord, by strength and skill.
Away the Goblin scurried. 'Twas but a little space
He still had joy of living. But leaving there his trace,
His right paw in Heorot, thence forlorn in fear,
Sick at heart, he fell into the bottom of the mere. 125

"Hrothgar me rewarded for that onset bold
Well with many a treasure, yea, with plates of gold,
When had come the morning and we sat at ale.
There was glee and singing. Hrothgar hoar and hale,
Man of much adventure, of far times told. 130
Whiles he touched the joy-wood, the harp of man's delight,
He, the Brave-in-battle; whiles would he recite
A lay of sooth and sadness; whiles was he telling
Some legendary wonder, he, the great-heart King.
Or whiles, again, that old Man, the Warrior strook by time, 135
Began to mourn his lost youth, the prowess of his prime.
His bosom welled within him, when he, in years so grey,
Remembered so many things. Thus we the live-long day
Partook there of desire, until o'er sons of men
Another night was coming. Soon thereafter then 140
Was faring forth in sorrow, greedy to repay,
She, the Mother of Grendel. Death had ta'en her son,—
Death and Geatmen's war-hate. The eldritch Hag anon
Had her bairn avengéd, killed a man with might:
From Aescher, old councilor, the life took flight. 145
Nor could they, the Danefolk, when the morning came,
Burn their perished comrade with the brands of flame,
Nor lade upon the bale-fire the dear Man there:
His corse beneath the mountain-streams in devil-arms she bare.
O that was unto Hrothgar the sorrowfullest stroke 150
Of all that long beset him, this Chieftain of a folk.

"Then the grieving Sovran begged me by thy life
To do a deed of earlship amid the billows' strife,
To venture there my being and win me renown.
He vowed to me a meed for that. This Warden under mere, 155

I found, this Grim and Grisly, this Wave-Thing widely known.
Hand to hand the twain of us a while fought here.
With gore up-welled the waters; off I carved the head
Of this Grendel's Mother with a falchion dread,
In under-water hall of hers. With life I got away, 160
Though sorely and barely— as yet I was not fey.
Then did the Shield of jarlmen, give, as erst he'd done,
To me full many a treasure, Halfdane's Son.

XXXI[1]

"Thus he kept, this Folk-King, the customs of yore.
In naught was I the loser of reward therefor.
Of meed for my prowess,— nay, he gave me treasure,
He, the Kin of Halfdane, to do with at my pleasure.
Now I will to bring them, King of men, to thee, 5
To thee to proffer gladly. From now what comes to me
Of good is all thy favor; grievous is my lack
Of any closer kinsmen, save thee, O Hygelac."

Then he bade to bear in a banner with a boar,[2]
And a towering war-helm, and a byrnie hoar, 10
And a sword of splendor; and spake with accents grave:
"To me this battle-garment Hrothgar gave,
The wise son of Halfdane, and added then his hest
That first I should relate thee the tale of its bequest.
He quoth the Prince of Scyldings, Heorogar, the King, 15
A long while had owned it, this breast-garmenting;
But yet he would not give it to son of his so lief,
Heoroward, the daring. Enjoy it all, my chief."
I heard how as four horses, alike in swiftness all,
Apple-fallow horses, followed next in hall. 20
The gift of these and treasures before his King he set;
So alway should a kinsman do nor weave a wily net,
Nor plot with hidden cunning a near companion's slaughter.
To Hygelac, the hardy, the nephew was full leal,
And each was ever wistful of the other's weal. 25
I heard how as the necklace that she, the Prince's daughter,
Wealhtheow, had given him, on Hygd he did bestow,
A curious wonder-jewel; with palfreys three also,
Slender, bright-of-saddle. After the bequest
The Lady wore the necklace shining on her breast. 30

So he bore him boldly, bairn of Ecgtheow, he,
A man renowned for battles, for deeds of bravery;
He lived in right and honor; nor slew by foaming bowl
His comrades of the hearth-fire, nor ruthless was of soul.
With utmost might of mankind did he, the Battle-grim, 35
Guard the gift of strength that God had granted him.
Scorned he 'd been a long while; the bairns of Geatish race
Good had not accounted him; nor would the Weders' King

[1]Sections XXIX and XXX are not indicated in the original manuscript.
[2]With a boar pictured on it.

Make him on the mead-bench worthy much of grace—
Slack the strong men weened him, a sluggard aetheling: 40
But turn of fortune came to him, as one with honors blest,
For every shame he 'd suffered. The King gave his behest,
He, the jarlmen's Bulwark, then to fetch to hall
The heirloom of Hrethel,[3] with gold y-garnished all.
Never among the Geatmen was aught in shape of blade 45
Ever a prize more goodly. On Beowulf's lap he laid,
And gave him seven thousand,[4] a hall and high-seat.
Both possessed in common hereditary land,
A home, an olden birth-right, in country of the Geat,
Though th' Other's realm was broader, since his a King's command. 50

It came to pass in after-days, when Hygelac lay dead
After the battle-clashings, and battle-swords had sped
Heardred, his offspring, under the sheltering shield,
(What time the hardy foeman, the Scylfings,[5] fierce in field,
Had sought him in the vanguard, and laid him low with grame,[6] 55
Nephew of Hereric[7]), that Beowulf became
Ruler of the broad realms. Fifty winters told,[8]
He reigned till now an agéd King, a Folk-Ward old.
'Twas then that in the dark nights, a Thing began to lord—
A Dragon on a hollow heath, who watched there a hoard, 60
A steep stone-barrow. A path thereunder lay,
By sons of men unguessed of. There within did stray
Some nameless man or other, who with hand did nim
From out the heathen Hoard, whilst slept the Dragon grim,
A goblet, a golden one, nor gave it back to him, 65
Albeit was thus defrauded its Keeper thievishly. . .
Then the folk in burgs around found how wroth was he!

XXXII

But not of own accord there, not of his own will,
Brake he the Serpent's Hoard there, who did the Drake such ill;
But he, a slave of some one of human fellowship,
Seeking forlorn for cover, fled his master's whip,
And into the cave he entered, a man by guilt oppressed. 5
Anon he gazed with terror, he, the stranger guest;
Yet, even amid the horror, he, the wretched wight,
Espied the jeweled goblet. Was plain, besides, to sight
Many a treasure olden in that house-of-earth,
Precious heirlooms golden of kinsmen of high birth, 10
Which some jarl or other, in the days of yore,
Taking thought, had hidden there forevermore.
All his kin aforetime death away had taken,
And he alone of warrior-host lingering there forsaken,
A watcher, friends bewailing, weened like theirs his doom,— 15
That soon he too must leave each glad heirloom.

[3]A sword. [4]Probably seven thousand hides of land, each hide consisting of 120 acres.
[5]The Swedes. [6]Sorrow. [7]Probably the brother of Hygd, Hygelac's queen.
[8]Not perhaps to be taken literally but as meaning "a long time."

Ready to hand a barrow new lay by ness and moor,
Hard-by the sea-waves, secret and secure.
The Warden-of-Rings did thither the jarl-treasure bear,
Of plated gold a goodly deal, worth the hiding there. 20

Quoth he then in few words: "Earth, now hold,
Now that warriors can not, the jarlmen's gold—
Lo, from thee did brave men get it all of old.
Battle-death hath taken, body-bale hath slain
Every sturdy fighter, each folk-thane, 25
Of all who saw the joy in hall— ne'er to see again.
None have I who 'll wield the sword, none who 'll burnish fair
The golden-plated tankard, the drink-stoup rare:
All the valiant noblemen are gone . . . else . . . where.
From helmet hard, with gold dight, the platings shall depart; 30
The burnishers are sleeping who should prepare with art
The casques for every onset. E'en so the army-coat,
That braved amid the battle bite of steel on throat
Over the clashing bucklers, shall crumble with its bearer;
Yea, the ringéd byrnie, shall with its warrior-wearer 35
Fare afar no longer on the hero's frame.
Never joy of harp now, the glee-wood's game;
Never now the good hawk swingeth through the hall;
Never now the swift horse beateth court or stall;
Of my kith hath battle-death sent . . . forth . . . all." 40

Thus, with soul of sorrow, alone he mourned the rest;
By day and night he wandered, blitheless of breast,
Till waves of death o'erwhelmed him. His Hoard of dead delight
That old Dusk-Scather, who flieth in the night,
Enfolded in fire, found all open there,— 45
That naked Poison-Dragon, who, burning through the air,
Seeketh out the barrows. Him the folk on fold
Dreadeth very sorely. He needs must seek, I 'm told,
For hoards within the earth and guard the heathen gold,
A Worm of many winters— no good thereby gets he! 50
So this Plague-of-people for winters hundreds three,
This Drake so huge and mighty, held within the ground
His own hoard-cavern, until the man who found
Roused his wrath in bosom. The golden tankard then
He bare unto his Master; and begged for peace again 55
Of him, his angry Owner. Thus plundered was the den,
The hoard of booty lessened. The wretch received his boon.
His lord now first did look upon the olden work of men;
And when the Worm awoke, there was a new woe soon.
Along the stone he snuffed there, this Stark-Heart dread, 60
And found the foeman's footprints, who with secret tread
Had stepped there too forward near his Dragon-head.
(Thus may a man not fey yet survive, where'er he trod,
Woe and ways of exile who owns the grace of God.)
Greedily the Hoard-Ward sought along the ground 65
To find the man who gave his heart asleep so sore a wound;
Hot and fierce, he circled the barrow all around;

But in that barren moorland not any man he found.
Yet war was in his marrow, on battle-work his thought,—
Whiles darted into barrow, the precious flagon sought. 70
Soon he found that some man had searchéd out his gold,
His treasure-trove so lordly. Though restive he and bold,
The Hoard-Ward bided until the evening came;
Awrath the barrow's Keeper would requite with flame
The dear drink-flagon. . . . Now the day was fled, 75
To the joy of Dragon. Blazing now he sped,
Folded in fire, forth from the wall.[1]
That was a beginning horrible for all;
And folk within that Kingdom soon thereafter kenned
In fate of their Ring-Giver thereof the awful end. 80

XXXIII

Then began the Stranger One forth his gleeds[1] to spew,
And burn the bright homesteads; the glare ablazing flew,
Frightful to landsfolk. Nothing living there
Would he leave, this loathly One, Flier-in-the-air.
The warfare of the great Worm wide about was clear, 5
The rancor of this Ravager, afar and anear,—
How this fell Destroyer the folk of Geatish kin
Hated and hounded. He shot to Hoard within,
To his hidden King's-hall, ere the morning came.
The dwellers in the land he'd lapped about with flame, 10
With brand and with bale-fire. He trusted in his mound,
His wall and his warfare. His trust in vain he found.

Then was unto Beowulf the horror made known,
Speedily and soothly, that the home his own,
The goodliest of dwellings, the Geat's gift-throne, 15
In fiery surge had melted. That to this good King
Was a grief in bosom, the worst of sorrowing.
The Wise One he weenéd that he the Wielder might
Bitterly have angered, breaking olden right
Of the Lord eternal. Welled his bosom sore 20
With thoughts of black foreboding, as ne'er his wont before.
From beyond the water-land,[2] the Fire-Drake with gleeds
Now had laid in ashes the fastness of the ledes,
The stronghold of Geatmen. The Warrior-King for this,
The Sovran of the Weders, planned how vengeance should be his. 25
He, the clansmen's Bulwark, Lord of jarlmen, he,
Bade them work a wondrous shield, all of iron firm—
For well he wist that linden, wood of forest tree,
Could help him not against the flames of that great Worm.
He needs must now be meeting, this King of passing worth, 30
His end of days, the fleeting, and his life on earth—
And the Dragon with him, though long he held the Hoard.

---

[1]The wall of his cave.

[1]Flames. [2]Sea-board.

Yet there he scorned, did Beowulf, the Geats' Ring-Lord,
To follow the Far-Flier with troops of spear and sword.
He dreaded not the contest, despised the Dragon's war, 35
His vigor and his valor; because so oft before,
He'd passed so many perils, clashes in the van,
Hazarded so many straits, since as victor-man,
He'd cleansed the hall of Hrothgar, and at the grapple erst
Battling crushed the Grendel-kin— that breed accurst. 40

Nor least of fights was that fight where Hygelac was slain,
When the King of Geatmen, upon the Frisian plain,
The Lord-Friend of clansmen, amid the battle-raid,
The offspring of Hrethel, beaten down by blade,
Perished by the sword-drink.[3] Beowulf made shift, 45
'Scaping by a power his own, his goodly swimming-gift.
He had upon his arms then, though alone was he,
Thirty coats of armor, as he plunged to sea.
O never the Hetwaras boasted of that field
Who onward and before them bore the linden-shield, 50
For few escaped the War-Wolf to see again their home.
Then the son of Ecgtheow o'erswam the tracts of foam,
A hapless man and lonely, unto his folk again.
There Hygd to him did offer the riches and the reign,
The rings and the King's seat. Her bairn[4] she did not trow 55
Fit to fend the Fatherland from a foreign foe,
Now Hygelac had fallen. Yet not for this could they,
The stricken, move the Aetheling in purpose any way
To be the Lord of Heardred and hold the kingdom's sway.
However, he[5] upheld him[6] among the folk with lore, 60
With kindnesses of honor, until, a lad no more,
Heardred wielded Weder-Geats. Him o'er sea there sought
The outlaws, sons of Ohthere. These had set at naught
The Helmet of the Scylfings, the best of all sea-kings
Who ever there in Sweden dealt the treasure-rings— 65
Onela, the high prince. Heardred's end was that!
For sheltering the rebels a mortal wound he gat
By swinges of the sword-blade. And Bairn of Ongentheow[7]
Departed for to seek his home, at Heardred's overthrow,
Leaving unto Beowulf the seat of ring-giving 70
And lordship over Geatmen— that was a goodly King!

XXXIV

In after-days did Beowulf bethink him to requite
The downfall of Heardred; and that wretched Wight,
Eadgils, he befriended; Ohthere's son did he
Aid with a folk-band across the broad sea,
With warriors and weapons; and Eadgils then was bold 5
To slay the King in payment for paths of exile cold.
So the son of Ecgtheow had 'scapéd every harm

[3]By the wound from which the sword drank his blood. [4]Heardred. [5]Beowulf.
[6]Heardred. [7]Onela.

Of strife and stern encounter, by works of sturdy arm,
Until the day 'twas his at last to battle with the Worm.

He went with his eleven, wroth exceedingly, 10
He, the King of Geatmen, the Fire-Drake to see.
He 'd heard for why had risen this feud, this deadly hap;
The treasure-cup its finder's hand had given into his lap;
And he whose luckless finding that warfare all began
Was, amid that company, the thirteenth man. 15
A captive, a craven, 'twas his in cringing sorrow
Thence to lead the way along unto the moor and barrow;
Against his will he footed until the mound he found,
The one and only earth-hall, the cavern under ground,
Near the ocean billows, near the surges' sound. 20
Within 'twas full of jewels, of wire-work in gold;
And the frightful Watcher did the treasure hold,
Ready for the battle, the Old One in his lair—
'Twas no easy bargain for men to enter there!

Upon the ness he sat him, the King in battles bred; 25
Gold-Friend of Geatmen, while farewell he said
To all his hearth-fellows. His thoughts were sad and grim,
Wavering and deathward; and all too nigh to him
Wyrd was there awaiting to greet that agéd Heart,
Aye, to seek his soul's hoard, to sunder apart 30
The life from the body. Not long it was before
The spirit of the Aetheling was wound in flesh no more.

Beowulf made his speech then, son of Ecgtheow, he:
"From many a battle onset in youth I 'scapéd free,
From many a while of warfare— I mind me of them all. 35
I was seven winters, when from father's hall
That Prince-of-people took me, that Giver-of-the-Ring.
He held me, he had me, Hrethel, he, the King;
Fee and food he gave me, of kinship mindful, he;
Never was I loathlier to him in grace and gree,[1] 40
While a bairn in burg I lived, than his sons, the three,
Herebeald and Haethcyn, or my Hygelac.

"For Herebeald, the eldest, by unmeet attack,
By the deed of Kinsman, was strewn the death-bed,
When Haethcyn with arrow, from horn-bow sped, 45
Smote his own Herebeald, his Liege-Lord, dead;
He missed of his mark there, and shot his Kinsman's heart,
A brother the other, with a bloody dart.
That was a fight all fee-less,[2] of sin a fearful thing,
A horror unto Hrethel, and yet the Aetheling,[3] 50
Forever unavengéd, must from life depart.
It were a sight too awful for agéd man to bide,
To see his boy, his young boy, upon the gallows ride.

---

[1]Degree.

[2]The slaying could not be made good by money-payment to the kin of the slain since both the slayer and the slain were sons of one father. [3]Herebeald.

Then his lay he moaneth, his sorrow-song he speaks,
When his son is hanging, a joy for ravens' beaks; 55
And he may help him no wise, this old man[4] forlorn.
And he is reminded, each and every morn,
Of his bairn gone elsewhere. Nor doth the father care
To see within his burg-hall now another heir,
Since the one in death-pangs had suffered evil so. 60
Upon his son's own bower, he looketh, worn with woe—
The wine-hall a waste now, where the winds sweep,
Bereft now of revel. The rider is asleep,
The warrior in his under-grave; there is with harp no glee,
And in the courts no wassail, as there used to be. 65

XXXV

"To bed then he goeth; chanteth a sorrow-song,
The lone one for the lost one. Seemeth all too wide
His fields and his homestead. . . . So it did betide
The Helmet of the Weders;[1] his welling heart must long
Ever after Herebeald, but yet the bloody wrong 5
He might not venge on Haethcyn, by whom the brother died.
Nor even might he hound him, the warrior he begot,
By loathly deed of hatred, albeit he loved him not.
And so then for the sorrow he suffered from these blows,
The mirth of men he gave up and God's light chose. 10
He left unto his offspring (as doth a man of pelf)
His land and his folk-burgs, when death had ta'en himself.

"Then rose there crime and conteck[2] the Swedes and Geats between,
Over the wide water,— a conflict close and keen,
A war-hate of the hardy, after Hrethel died, 15
And the sons of Ongentheow were forward in their pride,
And would not hold the peace-pact with folk beyond the sea.
But raided oft round Hreosnabeorh in forays fierce and free.
That strife my friends and kinsmen repaid, as all men know,
That unholy warring; albeit another, though, 20
Bought with life the victory, a price not low—
To Haethcyn, Lord of Geatmen, was that fighting fell.
But upon the morrow, as I heard tell,
One brother the other[3] avenged right well
With sword upon the murderer, when Eofor met the King, 25
And war-helm of Ongentheow was split in plate and ring,
And battle-wan he dropped adown, this old Scylfing.
O Eofor's hand that smote him had not forgot, I trow,
The former feuds aplenty, nor withheld the blow!

"My master[4] I repaid in war with my sword so bright, 30
For treasures he had given me, as fully as I might.

---

[4]Not Hrethel but some father whose son has been hanged.

[1]Hrethel. [2]Strife.

[3]Hygelac, through his retainer Eofor, avenged his brother Haethcyn. [4]Hygelac.

With land had he endowed me, with stead[5] and joy of home;
He had no need to seek him from Danes across the foam,
From Gifths or realm of Sweden, a worser warrior-wight,
And buy the same with wages. Always I the man 35
To fight before the foremost, alone before the van;
And so forever shall I fight long as this sword shall last
That hath so often served me in years now past,
Ere since before the warriors 'twas mine to slay with hand
Daeghrefn, Champion of the Frankish band. 40
The spoils of slaughtered Hygelac it was not his to bring,
Not his, those deckings of the breast, unto the Frisian King;
But in the fight he crumpled, he, banner-bearer too,
This Aetheling of prowess; nor was 't the sword that slew,
But my battling arm-grip his bone-house broke, 45
And stopped his heart's surgings. And now by falchion's stroke,
By hand and by hard blade, I 'll battle for the Hoard."

Beowulf made his speech then; spake a vaunting word,
Even for the last time: "Lo, I dared my fill
Of battles in my youth, I. Now this day I will, 50
The folk's old Warden, dare another still,
And do a deed of glory, if this Pest-of-all
Forth will come to seek me from his earth-hall."

Then each man he greeted, the helmet-bearers grim,
Even for the final time, his fellows dear to him: 55
"No sword would I bear me, no weapon to this Snake,
If I only wist how to get upon the Drake
The boasted grip of arm that I once on Grendel got.
But yonder I do fear me battle-fire hot,
Reek of breath and poison. And so I have on me 60
Shield-board and byrnie. No foot-breadth I 'll flee
From the barrow's Keeper. Us twain it shall befall,
Even as Wyrd allotteth, fighting at the wall—
Wyrd who is the master ever of us all.
My mood is bold and I forbear my boast against this Flyer. 65
Bide ye by the barrow, in your war-attire,
Ye heroes in your harness, awaiting which of twain
Shall better bear the onset and the battle-pain.
This quest is not for you now, but mine alone the meed
To match a might with Monster and do a jarlman's deed. 70
I 'll win this gold with prowess, or war shall take me hence—
The death-bale take the fighting man, your dear Prince."

Upstood beside his buckler this Man-at-arms so stark,
Hardy under helmet. He bore his battle-sark
Down beneath the stone-cliff. He trusted at the test 75
The strength of one man only— not that a craven's quest!
Then he who 'd passed in hardihood unscathed so many blows,
So many battle-rushes where clashed afoot the foes,
Espied by the wall there a stone-arch stout,

[5]Homestead.

Whence a stream was breaking from the barrow out. 80
The billows of that burn[6] there were hot with fierce fire;
Nor that under-passage, to the Hoard nigher,
Might he any while endure, for the Dragon's flare.
From his breast he let then a word forth fare,
He, the Prince of Weder-Geats, swelling in his ire. 85
The Stark-Heart stormèd. His battle-clear tone
Went aringing inward under the hoar stone.
Dragon-hate was rousèd; the Hoard-Ward knew
'Twas indeed the voice of man. Now between the two
Was no time for peace-pact!
First from out the gloom 90
Burst the breath of Monster, hot battle-fume.
The hollow earth resounded. Against the grisly Guest
Beowulf in barrow swung his shield to chest;
Then Ring-Bow[7] in heart was ready for the test.
But the goodly War-King had drawn his sword[8] for blow, 95
An old-time heirloom, with edge not slow.
Each with thoughts of murder felt terror of his foe.
Stern of mood, the Chieftain stood against his buckler high.
The Worm now arched its back amain. The Mailed One waited nigh.
With body bowed[9] it burned and glode,[10] hastening to its fate; 100
But shield did fend in life and limb the King so good and great
A briefer while than wish of him did thereby await:
For there 'twas his to struggle the first time and day
In such a wise as Wyrd denies victory in the fray.
He had his hand uplifted, he, the Geatish Lord; 105
Hard smote the grisly Foeman with the ancient sword;
But, lo, its edge did crumble, brown upon the bone,
And bit there too slackly for need of Hero lone,
In the press of sore distress. The barrow's Keeper then
After that battle-swingeing was mad of mood again; 110
He scattered fires of slaughter; and wide sprang the flame.
The Gold-Friend of Geatmen bragged no victory-fame.
His war-bill weakened, naked in the feud,
As it ever ought not, an iron passing good.
That was no easy faring back o'er cavern's ground 115
For the Kin of Ecgtheow, the far-renowned.
'Twas his against his will now to make his home elsewhere,
To leave the life that 's loaned us, as every man must fare.
Anon the infuriate Foemen again together drew;
Heartened himself the Hoard-Ward, and belched his breath anew; 120
And he who once had wielded over a folk as Sire
Was laboring now in sore straits, folded round with fire.
Nor stood about him staunchly his own fighting crew,
The bairns of the aethelings; but to the woods they flew,
And there they saved their bodies. On one of them this wrought 125
Cark and care of spirit: there is never aught
Can alter loyal kinship for man of noble thought.

---

[6]Brook. [7]The Dragon with back arched like a bow. [8]Naegling. [9]Curved like a bow.
[10]Glided.

XXXVI

Hight was that one Wiglaf, the son of Weohstan,
And Lord of the Scylfings, belovéd Shield-man,
Aelfhere's kinsman. His Liege-Lord he saw
Under his casque of battle front that flaming maw.
Then he recalled the giftings from him his Lord and Head,— 5
The lands of the Waegmundings, the rich homestead,
And each of all the folk-rights his father used to wield.
No longer might he hold back; his fingers clasped the shield,
The wood of yellow linden; his olden sword he drew.

This sword was Eanmund's relic, as all men knew, 10
Whom in the fray by falchion-edge Weohstan slew—
Eanmund, son of Ohthere, the exile forlorn.
And Weohstan to Eanmund's Kin, Onela, had borne
The brown-bright helmet, the byrnie of the rings,
The old sword of ettins,— Eanmund's battle-things, 15
The war-gear furbished of a brother's son;
But these did Onela return to Weohstan anon,
Nor spake of feud for slaughter Weohstan had done.
These trappings Weohstan retained for many years his own,
The bill and the byrnie, until his boy had grown 20
Strong for deeds of jarlman like his father's feats.
He gave them to Wiglaf, now among the Geats,
War-weeds unnumbered, as he fared from life,
Old upon his forth-way.

And now in battle-strife
'Twas Wiglaf's for the first time to serve beside his Lord. 25
Nor did his spirit soften, nor did his father's sword
Weaken in the war-fare— as soon he found, the Drake,
When once they 'd met together! Wiglaf he spake;
Said to comrades sagely, as sorrow sore he dreed:
"The time I well remember, as we took the mead, 30
How we vowed in beer-hall to him who gave us rings,
Vowed unto our Overlord, that we, his aethelings,
Would requite for war-gear, for hard sword and helm,
If need like this should haply ever overwhelm.
For this it was he chose us, us for this his quest, 35
Of his own will, and deemed us worth the glorious test.
And gave to me these treasures, because he counted us
Good spear-wielders, helmets valorous,
Albeit our Lord was minded, as Fender of his folk,
Himself alone to compass for us the victor-stroke, 40
Since he of men hath compassed most of glory-fray,
Most of deeds of daring. Now is come the day
Our Master needs the prowess of war-men good.
Let us hasten to him, to help his hardihood,
Whilst the heat is round him, the grim horror-fire. 45
Of me, at least, God wotteth it is my dear desire
That flame embrace this body mine with his who gave me gold.
Methinketh it unseemly our bucklers home to bring

Before we fell the foe and save the Weders' King.
Well I wot it suits not with all his deeds of old 50
That he, alone of Geatland's tried men and bold,
Should suffer this sorrow and sink in battle down.
Sword, helm, byrnie, shield, between us shall be one."

Then strode he through the slaughter-reek with casque upon his head,
To be the standby of his Lord. A few words he said: 55
"Beowulf, belovéd, hold here, hold,
Even as in young days sworest thou of old
Ne'er to let thy glory fall, so long as life should be.
'Tis thine, O steadfast Aetheling, famed in bravery,
To guard thee now with all thy prow.[1] I will succor thee." 60

At the words the Worm came a second time in ire,
Shining in the surging flame, Stranger fierce and dire,
To seek his Foes, the loathéd men. Was burnt in waves of fire
His buckler to the very boss. Nor yet his byrnie might
Serve to shelter Wiglaf, the young Spear-Wight. 65
So dodged the Youth right speedily his Kingsman's shield behind,
Now his own was all consumed by the fury-wind.
Then again the War-King his glory called to mind,
And smote he then by main-strength with his battle-glaive,
That, under impulse of his hate, to the head it drave. 70
But Naegling was shivered: failed him in the fray,
This the sword of Beowulf, etched and old and gray.
To him it was not given that any edge of brand
Him could help at battle; so strong his arm and hand,
As I have heard the story, that every blade so'er 75
He overtaxed in swinging it, when he to battle bare
A weapon wondrous hardy. 'Twould stead him not a whit.

Then was the People-Scather, a third time too,
This bold Fire-Dragon, mindful to do;
He rushed upon the Hero, where his chance was fit, 80
Hot and battle-ugly. All the neck he bit
With his bitter fang-teeth. To death the Geat was hurt,
Bloodied o'er with his own gore, in welling wave and spurt.

XXXVII

Then at the need of Beowulf, as I heard tell,
The Jarlman upstanding proved his prowess well,
His craft and his keenness, as his indeed by birth.
He made not for the Monster's head; but in his will and worth,
His hand was all but burnt away, the while he helped his Kin, 5
As pierce he did the flamy Drake from under, up and in,—
This Hero in his harness. Deep the sword it ran,
Gleaming and gold-dight. And the fire began
To slacken thereafter. The King himself once more
Girt his wits together. His war-knife he drew, 10

[1] Prowess.

Biting and battle-sharp, which on his sark he wore.
The Weder down the middle then slit the Worm in two.
So they felled the Dragon, the fiery head and wings.
The dauntless twain the Pest had slain, Kinsman-Aethelings.
Each warrior it behooveth like Wiglaf to be, 15
Each thane at need of liege-lord.
But for the King was this
The last of victor-hours by any deed of his,
The last of work in world here. The wound he had to dree
From the Snake of under-earth began to burn and swell;
And soon he found a poison balefully did well 20
Deep in breast within him. Walked the King along,
Till by the wall he sate him, thinking, on the mold;
He looked upon the giants' works,— the earth-house old
With arches there-under on posts stone-strong.
Then with hands his Wiglaf, retainer without peer, 25
Laved him with water, his Overlord dear,
Laved the bleeding Hero, battle-worn and drear,
And loosened him his helmet.
Beowulf replied,
Spake, in spite of deadly wound pitifully wide;
Well he weened his time was come, his earth-joys passed, 30
His tale[1] of days all taken, and death anearing fast:
"Now would I give over, now unto my son,
To offspring, my war-weeds, if me were granted one—
An heir from my body, to wear them when I died.
I have ruled this people fifty winters' tide; 35
Nor is there any folk-king of all who dwell around
That durst me touch with sword of his, or me with terrors hound.
I bided in my homeland my appointed while;
Well mine own I warded; nor practiced feud and wile;
Nor sware, I guess, not many broken oaths of guile. 40
Of all of this my joy I have, though ill of wounds within,
Since me the God of men may not charge with murdered kin,
When life my body leaveth. . . . Go, now, quick,
To look upon the Hoard there under the hoar stone,
Wiglaf, belovéd, . . . now the Worm is prone, 45
And sleepeth, reft of treasure-trove, from the sword so sick.
Wiglaf, hasten now, that I may once behold
These riches of the foretime, these master-stores of gold. . . .
Yea, that once with gladness I may look upon
The bright and cunning jewels. For softlier anon, 50
After that golden seeing, I 'll leave behind, I know,
My life and the lordship I held from long ago."

XXXVIII

Then the son of Weohstan, as I heard tell,
Swiftly stirred to wish and word of him whose wound was fell,
Of him the battle-sick Man; and under barrow's roof

[1]Reckoning.

Took himself and ring-mesh, his woven sark of proof.
And then that dauntless Thane-man saw with victor-pride, 5
On passing where his Chieftain sate, store of gems inside:
Saw the gold glisten on the ground then,
Wonders on the wall there, and the Dragon's den,
Flier old by twilight, of standing jars a sight,
Vessels of the men of yore, with none to burnish bright, 10
Bereft of their adornments. Many a helmet old
There was lying rusty, and arm-rings of gold,
Artfully twisted. (Riches so rare,
Such booty in a barrow, may easily ensnare
Any one of mankind, Hide it whosoe'er.) 15
And also saw he hanging over Hoard on high
A banner all golden, wefted cunningly,
Of handiwork a wonder. And from it streamed a light,
Whereby the cavern's bottom well perceive he might,
And well o'er-count the prizes. But saw not there within 20
Any sign of Serpent— sword had taken him.

Then, as I heard the story, did one Man alone
Reave the Hoard from olden mound, the giants' work of stone;
With beakers and with platters, as his choice would seek,
He laded his bosom. He took the banner eke, 25
Brightest of beacons. The old King's bill—
O its edge was iron!— a while ago did kill
Him who had defended so long the treasure-found,
And spread o' midnights terror-flames, billowing fiercely round,
Hot before the Hoard there, until he died of wound. 30
Hastened now the Herald, eager to go back,
Spurred by splendor-booty. Him a doubt did rack
Whether he, the high-souled, would meet alive once more
The Sovran of the Weders, weakened now so sore,
There upon the moor-stead where him he 'd left before. 35

Then Wiglaf with the treasures found his King and Friend,
His glorious Chief, ableeding, near his life's end.
Again he plashed with water; until the point of word
Pierced athrough the breast-hoard[1] of Beowulf, the old,
And spake he in his grieving, with gaze upon the gold: 40
"For this splendor-booty be thanks unto the Lord,
Unto the King-of-Glory, for what I here behold,
To God, the everlasting, in that 'tis mine to give
Such gifts unto my people, while an hour I live.
Now have I bartered for the hoard of gold 45
The end of this my old life. Look ye well, my fere,
To my people's needs now. I 'm no longer here.
Bid the battle-bold men build a mound to me,
Shining, after death-pyre, on foreland by the sea;
Out upon Whale's Ness, it shall lift on high, 50
Reminder to my people of the man was I,
That ever thereafter sailor-folk will hail

[1]The thoughts and feelings in the breast.

'Beowulf's Barrow' when home from far they sail,
O'er the misty ocean, past the Ness-of-Whale."

From his neck he doffed then, he, the Sturdy-Souled, 55
And gave to his Retainer, a collar of gold;
Gave the young Spearman his helmet gold-bedight,
His ring and his byrnie; bade him use them right:
"Thou art only remnant of our common line,
The Kin of the Waegmundings, Wiglaf mine. 60
Wyrd has swept before ye all my stock and stem,
The jarlmen in their glory. I must after them."
The last of words was that for which that agéd Heart had breath,
Ere he chose the bale-fire, the hot waves of death.
And so from breast of Beowulf the soul took flight 65
To seek the just award of souls soothfast in the right.

XXXIX

Then it went O sorely with the young Friend,
When he saw his dearest at his life's end,
Faring so pitiful— his King upon the ground.
But lay the Slayer likewise, wasted with a wound,
Of his life bereavéd, Earth-Drake vile— 5
No longer crook-bow worm could lord o'er the treasure-pile,
Since the edge of iron, forged by hammer's play,
Blade so hard and battle-scarred, had ta'en him far away.
Thus the Wide-Flier, from his wound so still,
Sprawled upon the mold there, nigh his hoard-hill. 10
Nevermore o' midnights would he disport in air,
Or, proud of his prizes, show his shadow there.
But he to earth had fallen, by the work of hands
Of a Battle-Leader. Forsooth, in all the lands
But few, however hardy and dauntless of deed, 15
Have thriven when they bravéd the breath of Poison-Breed,
Or when they laid their hands on a drake's ring-hall,
If once they found the Warden watching by the wall,
Crouching at the barrow— few, as I recall.
This deal of lordly goods was bought by Beowulf's own death; 20
And each from out this fleeting life yielded up his breath.

Ere long the battle-laggards, the troth-breaking men,
The woodland abandoned, together the ten,
That durst not there awhile ago put their spears in play
For Beowulf, their Liege-Lord, in his mickle needs; 25
But each one bore his buckler and his battle-weeds,
Shambling and shame-faced, to where the Old One lay.
And they looked on Wiglaf. He o'erwearied kneeled
At his Master's shoulder, he, so brave with shield;
Would waken him with water. But help was none thereby, 30
And the Youth he might not, though yearned he so to try,
Hold on earth the life of him whom God had willed should die.
God, the mighty Deemster,[1] wielded his will

[1] Judge.

Then o'er deeds of human kind as he doeth still.
There was in the young Thane an answer grim withal, 35
Nor hard of understanding, to those cowards all.

Wiglaf made a speech then, son of Weohstan,
Gazing broken-hearted at each hated man:
"Lo, whoso will speak sooth, can say one thing:
That, when he gave ye good gear, he, your Lord and King, 40
Gave the battle-harness ye are standing in,
He threw away those war-weeds, unto shame and sin,
When the fight befell him— and oft enough withal
Bestowed he at the ale-bench on sitters in the hall,
This King unto his clansmen, helm and byrnie-gear, 45
The finest he could find for ye, from afar or near.
In sooth had he, your Folk-King, little cause to vaunt
Of comrades in this conquest! But God was kind to grant,
The Wielder over victories, that with knife, alone,
When he had need of valor, he laid the Monster prone. 50
Little could I offer of aid at the fight,
Yet I helped my Kinsman beyond my might.
When I struck the deadly Foeman with my sword,
Thereby was he the weaker and the slower poured
The fire from the wits of him. Of helpers, small the sum 55
That thronged around the Chieftain when his hour had come.
How shall fail forever for your Kin abhorred
The getting of the gold-rings, the gifting of the sword,
All the mirth of land of birth. Every man shall roam,
Beggared of his freehold, from his burg and home, 60
When aethelings from far away shall hear your deed of blame,
This your flight, ye cowards. For one of jarlman's name,
Death itself is better than a life of shame."

XL

Then Wiglaf bade a Herald the war-work to declare
Yonder at the fastness o'er the sea-cliff there,
Where the band of shieldmen had sat in brooding pain
All the long morning, between doubts twain:
The end of their belovéd, or . . . his coming-home again. 5
Of these new tidings the Rider to the ness
Was silent touching little; nay, in soothfastness
He told out the story in ears of all the band:
"Now is he, Joy-Giver of the Weder-land,
The Sovran of the Geatmen, on the couch-of-death,— 10
He woneth[1] on the slaughter-bed, from Dragon's tooth and breath.
Is lying there beside him the Queller of the Good,
Sick with thrusts of dagger; for with the sword he could
Work no wound soever, upon the Monster's hide.
Wiglaf is sitting, Beowulf beside, 15
Weohstan's youngling, the quick beside the dead.
Holdeth he with heart's woe a watch at his head,
O'er loved Lord and loathed Drake.

---

[1]Dwells.

"Now our folk may wait
Anew a while of warfare when our Prince's fate
Unto Franks and Frisians shall be widely told. 20
Started with this quarrel grievously of old,
When Hygelac to Frisian land afaring came with fleet.
And him the Hetwaras did in battle beat,
And valiantly achievéd by their over-might
That he, the byrnie-breasted, bowed and fell in fight— 25
To give unto his chivalry no more the treasures bright.
And ever thereafter could our Geatish clan
Count on little kindness from the Merovingian.

"Nor do I wait from Swedefolk aught but fray and feud—
For widely couth the story is how Ongentheow, the good, 30
Slaughtered Haethcyn, Hrethel's son, off at Ravenswood.

"In wanton over-weening, in earlier times before,
We Geatish folk had ravaged the Scylfings great in war;
Anon Ohthere's father, the ancient Ongentheow,
Old and full of fury, gave a counter-blow, 35
Killed the Viking Haethcyn, and freed his captive wife,—
The venerable lady, berobbed of gold in strife,
She who 'd born him Onela and Ohthere of yore,—
And followed then the foemen, until, forlorn and sore,
They hid themselves in Ravensholt, their Leader being dead. 40
Ongentheow beset then, with a host outspread,
This remnant of the carnage with wounds o'erwearied.
The live-long night he menaced with woe the wretched herd:
With sword-edge in the morning he 'd mow them, was his word,
Or hang them on the gallows-tree, a sport for every bird. 45
But comfort to the downcast came with dawn of day,
When heard they horn of Hygelac and trumpet boom away,
As fared he on the track of them with his war-array.

XLI

"The bloody swath of Swedes and Geats, the fighters' slaughter-storm,
Was seen afar, how either folk waked alike the harm.
So he went, did Ongentheow, with his arméd men,
This Agéd, sorely sorrowful, to seek his fastness then;
Yes, Ongentheow turned round to go up to his burg again. 5
He 'd learned about the hardihood of Geatman Hygelac,
The war-craft of the Proud One; he dared no counter-strife,
He knew not his the ablesse these sea-men to attack,
Or 'gainst these sailor-foes to fend hoard and bairns and wife.
And so unto his earth-wall the Old One bent him back,— 10
The Geatfolk chased the Swedefolk and flags of Hygelac
O'er their fended refuge forward forged along,
After his Victor-Hrethlings[1] did to the ramparts throng.

"But in that battle Ongentheow, the King with locks of gray,
By the edges of the swords was brought at last to bay; 15

[1]Geats.

And forced to dree the sole doom that Eofor's wrath did will:
Wulf, the son of Wonred, had strook the King with bill,
Even so that under blow sprang from veins the blood,
Out beneath his hair then. But fearlessly he stood,
And paid anon with better one for the slaughter-wound, 20
As he, the King, the old Scylfíng, had turned on him around.
And the swift Wonreding[2] no counter-buffet gave
Before the Jarl, that ancient carl, his head and helmet clave.
So Wulf, the son of Wonred, must bow, with gore bewet;
He tottered to the greensward, but fey was he not yet; 25
And well be waxed thereafter, albeit the wound was grave.
'T was then the hardy Eofor, thane of Hygelac,
E'en where Wulf, his brother, lay, over shield did hack
The giant helm of Ongentheow, with his broad glaive,
His old sword of ettins. The King he bowed in strife; 30
The Shepherd of his people was smitten to the life.
And then were there many the brother's wounds to bind,
And him to lift with speedy shift, when 'twas theirs to find
Themselves the masters of the field. And in the meanwhile now
One warrior reaved the other— Eofor Ongentheow. 35
He took the iron byrnie, helm and hilted sword,
And bare the Hoar One's harness to Hygelac, his Lord.
He received the war-spoils, and fairly pledged the Youth
A boon before the people— and kept his pledge in sooth.
For the Lord of Geatmen, son of Hrethel's name, 40
Rewarded for that onset, when as home he came,
Eofor and Wulf both, with treasure manifold;
To each of them he yielded, in measure of gold,
Of land and interlinkéd rings a hundred thousand told.
And no man in this Middle-Yard[3] had cause that boon to blame, 45
Seeing the two with strokes of swords had wrought such deeds of fame.
And as a pledge of favor, to Eofor for bride
He gave his only daughter, of his home the pride.

"This is the feud and hating, the deadly strife of men,
Wherewith, as I 'm awaiting, the Swedes will seek us then, 50
They, the battling Scylfings, for their heroes slain,
As they shall learn the loss of him our Overlord,
Him who once had guarded our Kingdom and the hoard,
And furthered the folk-weal, and done a jarlman's deed.

"Now is best that thither we hasten with speed 55
To look upon our people's Sire, and Beowulf to bring
Onward to the funeral pyre, who gave us ring by ring.
Nor shall a portion only melt with the man so bold,
But there is a hoard of treasures, and there is countless gold,
Purchased forsooth at a grim price,— circlet and sword and pelf, 60
Bought us now at the latest with life of the King himself.
These shall the fire devour, these shall the flame enfold;
Never a jarl shall bear him a token dear of the King,
No beautiful girl shall wear gem on neck in a noble ring;

[2]Wulf. [3]The earth.

But each, of the gold bereavéd, each in a mood of pain, 65
Shall wander the lands of strangers, over and over again,
Now that the Army-Leader hath lowered his laughter here,
His mirth and the joy of his revel. For this shall many a spear,
Iron-cold in the morning, be lifted up in the arm,
Clasped in the clansman's fingers; and never the harper's charm 70
Shall waken these of our warriors. Nay, but the raven wan,
Fluttering over the fallen, shall utter his croak anon,
Telling unto the eagle how he at his feasting sped,
The while with the wolf together he tore away on the dead."

Thus it was the Warsman the loathly tidings said; 75
Little was he lying in words or doom ahead.
Together rose the band then, with tears of sorrow-stress,
Blitheless they betook them under Eagles' Ness,
To gaze upon the wonder. They found o'er sandy shore
Him who gave the rings to them in the times before 80
Lifeless on his bed of rest. His ending-day had been
Unto him, the dauntless, the Prince of Weder-kin,
Unto him, the Warrior-King, a death of wondrous dying.
But erst had they espied there a stranger creature lying—
The Serpent him beside there, loathed for flame and flying. 85
That Drake, the grim and grisly, was scorched by fire about;
Fifty foot he measured long, all stretched out.
Aloft he'd had his joy of air in night-times past,
And down again had gone to den. In death now fast,
He would use his earthly lair nevermore at last. 90
The jars and the goblets were standing by him here,
And platters here were lying, and good swords dear,
Rusted and eaten through, even as of old
They'd houséd in earth's bosom a thousand winters told.
This heritage had magic might: this by-gone mortals' gold 95
Had been by spells encircled, that none of human kind
Could ever touch that treasure-hall, save him whom God designed
(The Sooth-King of victories, Helper, he, of men),
Whomsoe'er he deeméd fit to open hoard and den.

XLII

Then 'twas plain to seeing his[1] quest had fared not well
Who under wall had plundered wealth, within, against the spell.
Erst had the Keeper slaughtered someone[2] of a few,
And so the feud avengéd with horrible to-do.
A wonder 'tis the manner a man may meet his end, 5
Even a famous jarlman, when with kin and friend,
'Tis his within the mead-house no longer now to dwell.
And thus with Beowulf it was: when he that Keeper sought
And that close encounter, he himself knew naught
Of what should cause his parting from the world away; 10
For the mighty chieftains who there the treasure hid
Had spake a curse upon it till earth's doomsday—
That whosoever robbed the floor should be a man forbid,

[1]Beowulf's. [2]Beowulf.

Pent in demon-places, in hell-bonds fast,
A sinner racked by plague-spots. Yet Beowulf, he cast 15
His glances more on Heaven's grace than gold unto the last.

Wiglaf made a speech then, son of Weohstan:
"Many a jarl must often, for will of one man,
Suffer a great bitterness— even now as we.
Nor might we rede[3] our lief Lord, Shepherd of the free, 20
Not to greet that Gold-Guard, but to let him lie
Yonder where he long was and dwell his cavern by,
Ever unto world's end. But Beowulf, not he!—
Held he to his high fate. The Hoard is ours to see,
Albeit grimly gotten. Too strong the destiny 25
That thither lured our Folk-King. I was in the hall,
And of that chambered treasure had my look at all;
When by chance I 'd found there, none too pleasantly,
A pathway in and under that earth-wall.
With hands I seized me swiftly, from the treasure-store, 30
A burthen big and mickle; and hither out I bore
Back unto my own King. Quick as yet was he,
Wise, with wits about him, and spake he full and free,
The Agéd in his anguish, and sent farewells to ye,
And bade ye that ye build him, for deeds of him, your Friend, 35
A barrow, a high one, yonder on land's end,
Memorial, mickle barrow, where his pyre shall be—
For worthiest warrior was he, wide across the earth,
Whilst still he wielded burg-wealth, of all of human birth.
Let us hasten yonder to seek and see anew 40
Under wall the wonder— the heap I 'll show to you;
Where of rings and broad gold anear enough ye 'll view.
Be the bier ready, ordered anon,
By our coming back here; we will bear him on,
Our own Lord, our dear man, to where for long and late 45
In the Wielder's shelter he 'll abide his fate."

Then the Boy of Weohstan, Hero battle-stout,
Bade order many warriors of homesteads round about
Thither to fetch the bale-wood[4] from far for him, the Great,
Him, the people's Ruler: "Now shall fire devour, 50
As wax the murky flames now, the fighters' Man-of-power,
Him who oft abided of old the iron-shower,
When the storm of arrows, speeded by the strings,
Shot above the shield-wall swift on feathered wings,
And shaft fulfilled its duty and drave the barb to goal. 55

Of sooth, the son of Weohstan, Wiglaf, wise of soul,
Chose from out the followers thane-men of the King's,
The seven best together, and under roof of hate
Went he with the warriors, himself as one of eight,
And one who walked ahead there bare a torch in hand. 60
Nor was there any drawing-lots among that eager band
For who that Hoard should pillage, when they saw in hall

[3]Advise. [4]Wood for the funeral pyre.

It resting, reft of Keeper and lost, it lying all.
And little were they mourning, as out they carried fast
The treasure-trove, the priceless. The Dragon, eke, they cast, 65
The Worm, over the wall-cliff,— let the wave take,
Let the flood embosom the Hoard-Ward Drake.
The aethelings they piled a wain with twisted gold beyond a guess,
And bare the hoary Hero on, up Whale's Ness.

XLIII

Then for him the Geats made the pyre, firm on earth,
And hung it with helmets, with byrnies a-sheen,
And with battle-bucklers, as his prayer had been.
And they laid amid it the Prince of wondrous worth,
Laid their Lord belovéd, weeping in their dearth. 5
And upon the hill-top the warriors awoke
The mightiest of bale-fires. Rose the wood-smoke,
Swart above the blazing. And the roar of flame
Blended was with wailing, as still the winds became,
Till, hot unto his heart, it broke the Geat's bone-frame. 10
Unglad of mood, in grief they mourned their great Chief dead.
And his Wife,[1] with hair bound, her song of sorrow said,
Over and over: how 'twas hers to dread
Days of harm and hardship, warriors' fall and grame,
The terror of the raider, captivity and shame. 15

The sky the reek had swallowed. The Weders raised thereby
A mound upon the headland, that was broad and high,
Seen afar from ocean by sailors on their ways,
And built the battle-bold One a beacon in ten days.
Around the brands and ashes a wall they ran and wrought, 20
The worthiest contriving of men of wisest thought.
And in the barrow set they ring and gem and plate,
And all the splendor-booty out of hoard of late
Forth their hands had taken, urged by heads of hate.
They gave the wealth of jarlmen to earth for to hold, 25
Now where yet it liveth, in the mold, the gold,
As useless unto mortals as it was of old.

Then around the mound rode, with cry and call,
Bairns of the aethelings, twelve of all,
To mourn for their Master, their sorrow to sing, 30
Framing a word-chant, speaking of the King:
They vaunted his earlship, they honored doughtily
His wonder-works of glory. Let it ever be,
That heart of man shall cherish and word of man shall praise
The Master-Friend, when in the end his spirit goes its ways. 35
So the Geatish clansmen bemoanéd their dearth,
The passing-forth of Beowulf, these comrades of his hearth,
Calling him a World-King, the mildest under crown,
And to his kin the kindest, and keenest for renown.

[1]Nothing has been said of Beowulf's wife before this. It has been conjectured that he may have married Hygd.

THE VENERABLE BEDE

672?–735

Bede, or Baeda, as his name is written in Latin, was born near Jarrow in Northumbria about A. D. 672. Two years later a monastery was founded at Wearmouth in the same neighborhood by a certain Benedict Biscop, a learned churchman; here Bede was placed by his family at the age of seven. Soon after 681 Benedict established another house, also under his guidance, at Jarrow; and to this the boy seems to have been immediately transferred. At Jarrow Bede passed the whole of his maturity, probably leaving the monastery for short periods only, and never, as far as it is known, departing from England. He must have given early evidence of his abilities, for he became a deacon at the age of nineteen although canon law forbade that any man should do so before he became twenty-five; Bede, however, was ordained a priest only after he had reached the canonical age of thirty. He was employed by the monastery, not as an administrator, but as a teacher and a scholar. Benedict had brought a fair number of manuscripts from the Continent, and books could be borrowed from other monastic libraries in England. With the materials available, scanty as they may seem today, Bede composed scientific treatises on orthography, metrics, and chronology; but the majority of his works deal with theological subjects. He wrote the lives of several Northumbrian abbots; a martyrology, or calendar of the martyrs; and, what he undoubtedly regarded as his chief title to fame, a commentary on several books of the Bible. But from the modern point of view his masterpiece is the *Ecclesiastical History of the English Nation,* which he completed in 731. He died four years later, on 25 May, 735, engaged even to his last moments, if we may believe a contemporary account, in scholarly writing. At the time of his death he was about sixty-three; he has been called "the Venerable," not because he attained a great age, but as a tribute to his sanctity.

The *Ecclesiastical History* is modeled to some extent on the work of Eusebius which bears the same title, and on the *History of the Franks* by Gregory of Tours. In his opening chapters Bede epitomizes the affairs of England from Caesar's first invasion to the mission of Augustine in 597; he devotes the body of his work to the conversion of the English and the vicissitudes of their church between 597 and 731. His account is on the whole well ordered and well informed; it reveals a scholarly grasp of his material and a regard for accuracy which are unique among the histories written in that period; but it likewise enjoys the advantage of Bede's pure and lucid style as well as of his narrative skill. The immediate popularity of the *Ecclesiastical History* is indicated in a curious way: after the disappearance of Roman authority from western Europe it was customary for each kingdom to number years from the beginning of the reign of each of its kings; where, as in England, several small kingdoms existed side by side, this expedient was complex and awkward; although the modern system of dating the years uniformly from the incarnation of Christ had been invented about two centuries before Bede's time, the *Ecclesiastical History* was the first important work to adopt the improvement; and as soon as the *Ecclesiastical History* had adopted it, the modern system of dating became common throughout western Europe.

The standard edition of the original Latin is the *Venerabilis Baedae Historiam Ecclesiasticam Gentis Anglorum,* ed. Charles Plummer (Oxford, 1896); the so-called "Alfredian" translation is printed as *The Old English Version of Bede's Ecclesiastical History of the English People,* ed. Thomas Miller for the Early English Text Society (London, 1890–1898). *Bede, his Life, Times, and Writings,* ed. A. Hamilton Thompson (Oxford, 1935), is a convenient summary, by several experts, of all that is known about Bede and his background. The history of the Old English period is presented, largely through translations of original sources, by Raymond W. Chambers, *England before the Norman Conquest* (London, 1926).

THE ECCLESIASTICAL HISTORY OF THE ENGLISH NATION[1]

The Coming of Augustine

BOOK I

CHAPTER XXIII

How Pope Gregory Sent Augustine, with Other Monks, to Preach to the English Nation, and Encouraged Them by a Letter of Exhortation Not to Cease from Their Labor.

IN the year of our Lord 582, Mauritius, the fifty-fourth from Augustus, ascended the throne[2] and reigned twenty-one years. In the tenth year of his reign Gregory,[3] a man renowned for learning and behavior, was promoted to the apostolical see of Rome and presided over it thirteen years, six months, and ten days. He, being moved by divine inspiration, in the fourteenth year of the same emperor, and about the one hundred and fiftieth after the coming of the English into Britain, sent the servant of God, Augustine, and with him several other monks who feared the Lord, to preach the word of God to the English nation. They having, in obedience to the pope's commands, undertaken that work, were, on their journey, seized with a sluggish fear and began to think of returning home rather than proceed to a barbarous, fierce, and unbelieving nation, to whose very language they were strangers; and this they unanimously agreed was the safer course. In short, they sent back Augustine, who had been appointed to be consecrated bishop in case they were received by the English, that he might, by humble entreaty, obtain of the holy Gregory that they should not be compelled to undertake so dangerous, toilsome, and uncertain a journey. The pope, in reply, sent them a hortatory epistle, persuading them to proceed in the work of the divine word and rely on the assistance of the Almighty. The purport of which letter was as follows:—

5 "*Gregory, the servant of the servants of God, to the servants of our Lord.* Forasmuch as it had been better not to begin a good work than to think of desisting from that which has been begun, it behooves you, 10 my beloved sons, with the greatest zeal to fulfill the good work which, by the help of our Lord, you have undertaken. Let not, therefore, the toil of the journey, nor the tongues of evil-speaking men, deter you; 15 but with all possible earnestness and zeal perform that which, by God's direction, you have undertaken; being assured that much labor is followed by the greater glory of an eternal reward. When Augustine, your 20 chief, returns, whom we also constitute your abbot, humbly obey him in all things; knowing that whatsoever you shall do by his direction, will, in all respects, be available to your souls. Almighty God protect you with his 25 grace and grant that I may, in the heavenly country, see the fruits of your labor; inasmuch as, though I cannot labor with you, I shall partake in the joy of the reward, because I am willing to labor. God keep 30 you in safety, my most beloved sons. Dated the twenty-third of July in the fourteenth year of the reign of our pious and most august lord, Mauritius Tiberius, the thirteenth year after the consulship of our said 35 lord, the fourteenth indiction." [4]

CHAPTER XXV

How Augustine, Coming into Britain, First Preached in the Isle of Thanet to King Ethelbert and, Having Obtained License, Entered the Kingdom of Kent in Order to Preach Therein.

AUGUSTINE, thus strengthened by the con- 45 firmation of the blessed father, Gregory,

[1]From the translation of John Stevens (1723), revised by John A. Giles (1840); the passages included here have again been revised after a comparison with the Latin text.

[2]As emperor of the Western Roman Empire.

[3]Gregory I (later called the Great), who actually became pope in 590.

[4]In 596, the fourteenth year of the fifteen-year cycle (indiction), which began with the year in which Mauritius came to the throne.

returned to the work of the word of God with the servants of Christ, and arrived in Britain. The powerful Ethelbert was at that time king of Kent; he had extended his dominions as far as the great river Humber, by which the southern English are divided from the northern. On the east coast of Kent is the large Isle of Thanet containing, according to the English way of reckoning, six hundred families,[5] divided from the other land by the river Wantsum,[6] which is about three furlongs over and fordable only in two places, for both ends of it run into the sea. In this island landed the servant of our Lord, Augustine, and his companions, being, as is reported, nearly forty men. They had, by order of the blessed Pope Gregory, taken interpreters of the nation of the Franks and, sending to Ethelbert, signified that they were come from Rome and brought a joyful message, which most undoubtedly assured to all that took advantage of it everlasting joys in heaven and a kingdom that would never end, with the living and true God. The king, having heard this, ordered them to stay in that island where they had landed, and that they should be furnished with all necessaries, till he should consider what to do with them. For he had before heard of the Christian religion, having a Christian wife of the royal family of the Franks, called Bertha;[7] whom he had received from her parents upon condition that she should be permitted to practice her religion with the Bishop Luidhard, who was sent with her to preserve her faith. Some days after, the king came into the island and, sitting in the open air, ordered Augustine and his companions to be brought there into his presence. For he had taken precaution that they should not come to him in any house, lest, according to an ancient superstition, if they practiced any magical arts, they might by surprise impose upon him and so get the better of him. But they came furnished with divine, not with magic[8] virtue, bearing a silver cross for their banner, and the image of our Lord and Savior painted on a board; and singing the litanies, they offered up their prayers to the Lord for the eternal salvation both of themselves and of those to whom and for whose sake they were come. When they had sat down, pursuant to the king's commands, and preached to him and his attendants there present the word of life, the king answered thus:—"Your words and promises are very fair, but as they are new to us and of uncertain import, I cannot approve of them so far as to forsake those things which I have so long followed with the whole English nation. But because you are come from far into my kingdom and, as I conceive, are desirous to impart to us those things which you believe to be true and most beneficial, we will not molest you, but give you favorable entertainment and take care to supply you with your necessary sustenance; nor do we forbid you to preach and gain as many as you can to belief in your religion." Accordingly he permitted them to reside in the city of Canterbury, which was the metropolis of all his dominions, and, pursuant to his promise, besides allowing them sustenance, did not refuse them liberty to preach. It is reported that, as they drew near to the city after their manner, with the holy cross and the image of our sovereign Lord and King, Jesus Christ, they, in concert, sung this litany: "We beseech Thee, O Lord, in all Thy mercy, that Thy anger and wrath be turned away from this city and from Thy holy house, because we have sinned.[9] Hallelujah."

CHAPTER XXVI

How St. Augustine in Kent Followed the Doctrine and Manner of Living of the Primitive Church, and Settled His Episcopal See in the Royal City.

As soon as they entered the dwelling-place assigned them, they began to imitate the course of life practiced in the primitive Church; applying themselves to frequent prayer, watching, and fasting; preaching the word of life to as many as they could; despising all worldly things as not belonging

[5]Containing land enough to support six hundred families.

[6]Branch of the Stour.

[7]Daughter of Charibert, king of Paris.

[8]Diabolic.

[9]Daniel, 9:16.

to them; receiving only their necessary food from those they taught; living themselves in all respects conformably to what they prescribed to others, and being always disposed to suffer any adversity and even to die for that truth which they preached. In short, several believed and were baptized, admiring the simplicity of their innocent life and the sweetness of their heavenly doctrine. There was on the east side of the city a church dedicated to the honor of St. Martin, built whilst the Romans were still in the island, wherein the queen, who, as has been said before, was a Christian, used to pray. In this they first began to meet, to sing, to pray, to say mass, to preach, and to baptize, until the king, being converted to the faith, allowed them greater freedom to preach and build or repair churches in all places.

When he among the rest, gladdened by the unspotted life of these holy men and their delightful promises, which, by many miracles, they proved to be most certain, believed and was baptized, greater numbers began daily to flock together to hear the word and, forsaking their heathen rites, to associate themselves, by believing, to the unity of the Church of Christ. Their faith and conversion the king so far encouraged as that he compelled none to embrace Christianity, but only showed closer affection to the believers, as to his fellow-citizens in the heavenly kingdom. For he had learned from the instructors and authors of his salvation that the service of Christ ought to be voluntary, not by compulsion. Nor was it long before he gave his teachers a residence suitable to their degree[10] in his metropolis of Canterbury, with such possessions of different kinds as were necessary for their subsistence.

CHAPTER XXIX

How the Same Pope Sent Augustine the Pall,[11] an Epistle, and more Ministers of the Word.

MOREOVER, the same Pope Gregory, hearing from Bishop Augustine that he had a great harvest and but few laborers, sent to him, together with his aforesaid messengers,[12] more fellow laborers and ministers of the word, of whom the first and principal were Mellitus, Justus, Paulinus, and Rufinianus, and by them all things in general that were necessary for the worship and service of the church, *viz.*, sacred vessels and vestments for the altars, also ornaments for the churches and vestments for the priests and clerks, as likewise relics of the holy apostles and martyrs, besides many books. He also sent a letter wherein he signified that he had transmitted the pall to him, and at the same time directed how he should constitute bishops in Britain.

* * *

CHAPTER XXX

A Copy of the Letter Which Pope Gregory Sent to the Abbot Mellitus, Then Going into Britain.

THE aforesaid messengers[13] being departed, the holy father, Gregory, sent after them a letter worthy to be preserved in memory, wherein he plainly shows what care he took of the salvation of our nation. The letter was as follows:—

"*To his most beloved son, the Abbot Mellitus, Gregory, the servant of the servants of God.* We have been much concerned, since the departure of our congregation that is with you, because we have received no account of the success of your journey. When, therefore, Almighty God shall bring you to the most reverend Bishop Augustine, our brother, tell him what I have, upon mature deliberation on the affair of the English, determined upon, *viz.*, that the temples of the idols in that nation ought not to be destroyed; but let the idols that are in them be destroyed; let holy water be made and sprinkled in the said temples; let altars be erected and relics placed. For if those temples are well built, it is requisite that they be converted from the worship of devils to

[10]His own palace.

[11]Cloak, bestowed as mark of ecclesiastical honor.

[12]Lawrence and Peter, whom Augustine had sent to Rome with the report of his success (chapter xxvii).

[13]Lawrence, Peter, Mellitus, Justus, Paulinus, and Rufinianus.

the service of the true God; that the nation, seeing that their said temples are not destroyed, may remove error from their hearts and, knowing and adoring the true God, may the more familiarly resort to the places to which they have been accustomed. And because they have been used to slaughter many oxen in the sacrifices to devils, some solemnity must be exchanged for them on this account, as that on the day of the dedication, or the nativities of the holy martyrs whose relics are there deposited, they may build themselves huts of the boughs of trees about those churches which have been turned to that use from temples, and celebrate the solemnity with religious feasting, and no more offer beasts to the Devil but kill cattle to the praise of God in their eating, and return thanks to the Giver of all things for their abundance; to the end that, whilst some gratifications are outwardly permitted them, they may the more easily consent to the inward consolations of the grace of God. For there is no doubt that it is impossible to efface everything at once from their obdurate minds; because he who endeavors to ascend to the highest place, rises by degrees or steps, and not by leaps. Thus the Lord made Himself known to the people of Israel in Egypt; and yet He allowed them the use of the sacrifices which they were wont to offer to the Devil, in His own worship; so as to command them in His sacrifice to kill beasts, to the end that, changing their hearts, they might lay aside one part of the sacrifice, whilst they retained another; that whilst they offered the same beasts which they were wont to offer, they should offer them to the true God and not to idols; and thus they would no longer be the same sacrifices. This it behooves your affection to communicate to our aforesaid brother, that he, being there present, may consider how he is to order all things. God preserve you in safety, most beloved son.

"Given the eighteenth of July, in the nineteenth year of the reign of our lord, the most pious emperor, Mauritius Tiberius, the eighteenth year after the consulship of our said lord, the fourth indiction." [14]

[14]The fourth year in the second indiction of Mauritius.

BOOK II

CHAPTER I

On the Death of the Blessed Pope Gregory.

At this time, that is, in the year of our Lord 605,[15] the blessed Pope Gregory, after having most gloriously governed the Roman apostolic see thirteen years, six months, and ten days, died and was translated to the eternal see of the heavenly kingdom. Of him, in regard that he by his zeal converted our nation, the English, from the power of Satan to the faith of Christ, it behooves us to discourse more at large in our Ecclesiastical History, for we may and ought rightly to call him our apostle; because, as soon as he bore the pontifical power over all the world and was placed over the churches already reduced to the faith of truth, he made our nation, till then given up to idols, the Church of Christ, so that we may be allowed thus to attribute to him the character of an apostle; for though he is not an apostle to others, yet he is so to us; for we are the seal of his apostleship in our Lord.

* * *

To his works of piety and righteousness this also may be added, that he saved our nation, by the preachers he sent hither, from the teeth of the old enemy, and made it partaker of eternal liberty; in whose faith and salvation rejoicing and worthily commending the same, he in his exposition on holy Job says, "Behold, the tongue of Britain, which only knew a barbarous gnashing, has long since begun to resound the Hebrew Hallelujah! Behold, the once swelling ocean now serves prostrate at the feet of the saints; and its barbarous motions, which earthly princes could not subdue with the sword, are now, through the fear of God, bound by the mouths of priests with words only; and he that when an infidel stood not in awe of fighting troops, now a believer, fears the tongues of the humble! For by reason that the virtue of the divine knowledge is infused into it by precepts, heavenly words, and conspicuous miracles, it is curbed

[15]According to a corrected computation, 604.

by the dread of the same divinity, so as to fear to act wickedly, and bends all its desires to arrive at eternal glory." In which words holy Gregory declares this also, that St. Augustine and his companions brought the English to the knowledge of truth, not only by the preaching of words, but also by showing of heavenly signs.

* * *

Nor is the account of St. Gregory which has been handed down to us by the tradition of our ancestors to be passed by in silence in relation to his motives for taking such interest in the salvation of our nation. It is reported that some merchants, having just arrived at Rome on a certain day, exposed many things for sale in the market-place, and abundance of people resorted thither to buy: Gregory himself went with the rest, and, among other things, some boys were set to sale, their bodies white, their countenances beautiful, and their hair very fine. Having viewed them, he asked, as is said, from what country or nation they were brought? and was told, from the island of Britain, whose inhabitants were of such personal appearance. He again inquired whether those islanders were Christians or still involved in the errors of paganism? and was informed that they were pagans. Then fetching a deep sigh from the bottom of his heart, "Alas! what pity," said he, "that the author of darkness is possessed of men of such fair countenances; and that being remarkable for such graceful aspects, they should have minds void of inward grace." He therefore again asked what was the name of that nation? and was answered that they were called Angles. "Right," said he, "for they have an angelic face, and it becomes such to be co-heirs with the angels in heaven. What is the name," proceeded he, "of the province from which they are brought?" It was replied that the natives of that province were called Deiri.[16] "Truly are they *De ira*," said he, "withdrawn from wrath and called to the mercy of Christ. How is the king of that province called?" They told him his name was Aella; and he, alluding to the name, said, "Hallelujah, the praise of God, the Creator, must be sung in those parts."

Then repairing to the bishop of the Roman apostolical see[17] (for he was not himself then made pope), he entreated him to send some ministers of the word into Britain to the nation of the English, by whom it might be converted to Christ; declaring himself ready to undertake that work, by the assistance of God, if the apostolic pope should think fit to have it so done. Which not being then able to perform, because, though the pope was willing to grant his request, yet the citizens of Rome could not be brought to consent that he should depart so far from the city; as soon as he was himself made pope, he perfected the long-desired work, sending other preachers but himself by his prayers and exhortations assisting the preaching, that it might be successful. This account, as we have received it from the ancients, we have thought fit to insert in our Ecclesiastical History.

[16]Inhabitants of Deifyr, the district south of the Tees or the Tyne.

[17]Pope Benedict I.

The Conversion of Edwin

BOOK II

CHAPTER IX

Of the Reign of King Edwin, and How Paulinus, Coming to Preach the Gospel to Him, First Instructed His Daughter and Others in the Mysteries of the Christian Faith.

At this time[1] the nation of the Northumbrians, that is, the nation of the English that live on the north side of the river Humber, with their king, Edwin, received the faith through the preaching of Paulinus, above mentioned.[2] This Edwin, as an omen of his receiving the faith and of his share in the heavenly kingdom, received an increase of that which he enjoyed on earth, for he reduced under his dominion all the borders of Britain that were provinces either of the

[1]About 625.

[2]Cf. Book I, chapter xxix.

aforesaid nation,[3] or of the Britons, a thing which none of the English had ever done before; and he in like manner subjected to the English the Mevanian Islands, as has been said above.[4] The first whereof, which 5 is to the southward, is the largest in extent and most fruitful, containing nine hundred and sixty families according to the English computation; the other, above three hundred.

The occasion of this nation's embracing 10 the faith was that their aforesaid king was allied to the kings of Kent, having taken to wife Ethelberga, otherwise called Tata, daughter to King Ethelbert. He, having by his wooers asked her in marriage of her 15 brother Eadbald, who then reigned in Kent, was answered, "That it was not lawful to marry a Christian virgin to a pagan husband, lest the faith and the mysteries of the heavenly King should be profaned by her 20 cohabiting with a king that was altogether a stranger to the worship of the true God." This answer being brought to Edwin by his messengers, he promised in no manner to act in opposition to the Christian faith 25 which the virgin professed; but would give leave to her and all that went with her, men or women, priests or ministers, to follow their faith and worship after the custom of the Christians. Nor did he deny but that he 30 would embrace the same religion, if, being examined by wise persons, it should be found more holy and more worthy of God.

Hereupon the virgin was promised and sent to Edwin, and pursuant to what had 35 been agreed on, Paulinus, a man beloved of God, was ordained bishop, to go with her and by daily exhortations and celebrating the heavenly mysteries to confirm her and her company, lest they should be corrupted by 40 the company of the pagans. Paulinus was ordained bishop by the Archbishop Justus on the twenty-first of July in the year of our Lord 625, and so he came to King Edwin with the aforesaid virgin as a companion of 45 their union in the flesh. But his mind was wholly bent upon reducing the nation to which he was sent to the knowledge of truth; according to the words of the apostle, "To espouse her to one husband, that he might present her as a chaste virgin to Christ."[5] Being come into that province, he labored much, not only to retain those 5 that went with him, by the help of God, that they should not revolt from the faith, but, if he could, to convert some of the pagans to a state of grace by his preaching. But, as the apostle says, though he labored long 10 in the word, "The god of this world blinded the minds of them that believed not, lest the light of the glorious Gospel of Christ should shine unto them."[6]

The next year there came into the province 15 a certain assassin, called Eumer, sent by the king of the West-Saxons, whose name was Cuichelm, in hope at once to deprive King Edwin of his kingdom and his life. He had a two-edged short sword, dipped in poison 20 to the end that if the wound were not sufficient to kill the king, it might be aided by the venom. He came to the king on the first day of Easter at the river Derwent, where then stood the regal city, and being admitted 25 as if to deliver a message from his master, whilst he was in an artful manner delivering his pretended embassy, he started on a sudden and, drawing the sword from under his garment, assaulted the king; which Lilla, the 30 king's beloved minister, observing, having no buckler at hand to secure the king from death, interposed his own body to receive the stroke; but the wretch struck so home that he wounded the king through the slain 35 knight's body. Being then attacked on all sides with swords, he in that confusion also slew another soldier, whose name was Forthhere, with the same unlucky weapon.

On that same holy night of Easter Sunday 40 the queen had brought forth to the king a daughter, called Eanfled. The king, in the presence of Bishop Paulinus, gave thanks to his gods for the birth of his daughter; and the bishop, on the other hand, returned 45 thanks to Christ and endeavored to persuade the king that by his prayers to Him he had obtained that the queen should bring forth the child in safety and without much pain. The king, delighted with his words, prom- 50 ised that in case Christ would grant him life

[3] The Angles.

[4] Book II, chapter v. The Mevanian Islands are Anglesey and Man.

[5] II Corinthians, 11:2.

[6] II Corinthians, 11:4.

and victory over the king by whom the assassin who had wounded him had been sent, he would cast off his idols and serve Him; and as a pledge that he would perform his promise, he delivered up that same daughter to Paulinus, to be consecrated to Christ. She was the first baptized of the nation of the Northumbrians, on Whitsunday, with eleven others of her family. At that time, the king, being recovered of the wound which he had received, marched with his army against the nation of the West-Saxons; and having begun the war, either slew or subdued all those that he had been informed had conspired to murder him. Returning thus victorious unto his own country, he would not immediately and unadvisedly embrace the mysteries of the Christian faith, though he no longer worshiped idols ever since he made the promise that he would serve Christ; but thought fit first at leisure to be instructed by the venerable Paulinus in the knowledge of faith, and to confer with such as he knew to be the wisest of his prime men, to advise what they thought was fittest to be done in that case. And being a man of extraordinary sagacity, he often sat alone by himself a long time, silent as to his tongue but deliberating much in his heart how he should proceed, and which religion he should adhere to.

CHAPTER XII

How King Edwin Was Persuaded to Believe by a Vision Which He Had Seen When He Was in Exile.

But a heavenly vision, which the Divine Mercy was pleased once to reveal to this king when he was in banishment at the court of Redwald, king of the Angles, was of no little use in urging him to embrace and understand the doctrines of salvation. Paulinus, therefore, perceiving that it was a very difficult task to incline the king's lofty mind to the humility of the way of salvation and to embrace the mystery of the cross of life, and at the same time using both exhortation with men and prayer to God, for his and his subjects' salvation; at length, as we may suppose, it was shown him in spirit what and of what nature was the vision from heaven that had been formerly revealed to the king. Nor did he lose any time, but immediately admonished the king to perform the vow which he made when he received the oracle, promising to put the same in execution, if he were delivered from the trouble he was at that time under and should be advanced to the throne.

The vision was this. When Ethelfrid, his predecessor, was persecuting him, he for many years wandered in a private manner through several places and kingdoms, and at last came to Redwald, beseeching him to protect his life against the snares of his powerful persecutor. Redwald willingly admitted him and promised to perform what he requested. But when Ethelfrid understood that he had appeared in that province, and that he and his companions were hospitably entertained by Redwald, he sent messengers to offer that king a great sum of money to murder him, but without effect. He sent a second and a third time, bidding more and more money each time and threatening to make war on him if he refused. Redwald, either terrified by his threats or gained by his gifts, complied with his request and promised either to kill Edwin or to deliver him up to the ambassadors. This being observed by a trusty friend of his,[7] he went into his chamber where he[8] was going to bed, for it was the first hour of the night; and calling him out, discovered what the king had promised to do with him, adding, "If, therefore, you think fit, I will this very hour conduct you out of this province, and lead you to a place where neither Redwald nor Ethelfrid shall ever find you." He answered, "I thank you for your good will, yet I cannot do what you propose, or be guilty of breaking the compact I have made with so great a king, when he has done me no harm, nor offered me any injury; but, on the contrary, if I must die, let it rather be by his hand than by that of any meaner person. For whither shall I now fly, who have for so many years been a vagabond through all the provinces of Britain, to escape the hands of my enemies?" His

[7]Edwin's. [8]Edwin.

friend being gone, Edwin remained alone without, and sitting with a heavy heart before the palace, began to be overwhelmed with many thoughts, not knowing what to do or which way to turn himself.

When he had remained a long time in silence, brooding over his misfortunes in silent anguish of mind and pent-up misery, he, on a sudden, in the dead of night, saw approaching a person whose face and habit were equally strange, at which unknown and unexpected sight he was not a little frightened. The stranger, coming close up, saluted him and asked him, "Why he sat there alone and melancholy on a stone, keeping watch at that time when all others were taking their rest and were fast asleep?" Edwin, in his turn, asked, "What it was to him, whether he spent the night within doors or abroad?" The stranger, in reply, said, "Do not think that I am ignorant of the cause of your grief, your watching, and sitting alone without. For I know who you are, and why you grieve, and the evils which you fear will fall upon you. But tell me what reward you will give the man, if such there be, that shall deliver you out of this anguish and persuade Redwald neither to do you any harm himself nor to deliver you up to be murdered by your enemies." Edwin replied, "That he would give that person all that he was able for so singular a favor." The other further added, "What if I also assure you that you shall overcome your enemies, and surpass in power, not only all your own progenitors, but even all that have reigned before you over the English nation?" Edwin, encouraged by these questions, did not hesitate to promise that he would make a suitable return to him who should so highly oblige him. Then spoke the other for the third time, "But if he who foretells so much good as is to befall you can also give you better and more profitable advice for your life and salvation than any of your progenitors or kindred ever heard of, do you consent to submit to him and to follow his wholesome counsel?" Edwin did not hesitate to promise that he would in all things follow the directions of that man who should deliver him from so many and so great calamities and raise him to a throne.

Having received this answer, the person that talked to him laid his right hand on his head, saying, "When this sign shall be given you, remember this present discourse that has passed between us, and do not delay the performance of what you now promise." Having uttered these words, he is said to have immediately vanished, that the king might understand it was not a man, but a spirit, that had appeared to him.

Whilst the royal youth still sat there alone, glad of the comfort he had received, but preoccupied and seriously considering who he was, or whence he came, that had so talked to him, his above-mentioned friend came to him, and saluting him with a pleasant countenance, "Rise," said he, "go in and compose your mind and limbs to sleep without care or fear; for the king's resolution is altered, and he designs to do you no harm, but rather to perform the promise which he made you; for when he had privately acquainted the queen with his intention of doing what I told you before, she dissuaded him from it, declaring it was unworthy of so great a king to sell his good friend in such distress for gold and to sacrifice his honor, which is more valuable than all other ornaments, for the love of money." In short, the king did as he was advised and not only refused to deliver up the banished man to his enemy's messengers, but assisted him to recover his kingdom. For as soon as the ambassadors were returned home, he raised a mighty army to make war on Ethelfrid; who, meeting him with much inferior forces (for Redwald had not given him time to gather and unite all his power), was slain on the borders of the kingdom of Mercia,[9] on the east side of the river that is called Idle.[10] In this battle Redwald's son, called Regnhere, was killed; and thus Edwin, pursuant to the oracle he had received, not only escaped the danger from the king his enemy but, by his death, succeeded him in the throne.

King Edwin, therefore, delaying to receive the word of God at the preaching of Paulinus and using for some time, as has been said,

[9]The kingdom which embraced the central portion of what is now England.

[10]A tributary of the Trent.

to sit alone at suitable hours and seriously to ponder with himself what he was to do and what religion he was to follow, the man of God came to him, laid his right hand on his head, and asked, "Whether he knew that sign?" The king, in a trembling condition, was ready to fall down at his feet, but he raised him up and in a familiar manner said to him, "Behold, by the help of God you have escaped the hands of the enemies whom you feared. Behold, you have of his gift obtained the kingdom which you desired. Take heed not to delay the third part, that which you promised to perform; embrace the faith and keep the precepts of Him who, delivering you from temporal adversity, has raised you to the honor of a temporal kingdom; and if, from this time forward, you shall be obedient to His will, which through me He signifies to you, He will not only deliver you from the everlasting torments of the wicked, but also make you partaker with Him of His eternal kingdom in heaven."

CHAPTER XIII

What Counsel the Same Edwin Held with His Chief Men about Embracing the Faith of Christ, and How the High Priest Profaned His Own Altars.

THE king, hearing these words, answered that he was both willing and bound to receive the faith which he taught; but that he would confer about it with his principal friends and counselors, to the end that if they also were of his opinion, they might all together be cleansed in Christ, the Fountain of Life. Paulinus consenting, the king did as he said; for, holding a council with the wise men, he asked of every one in particular what he thought of this hitherto unknown doctrine and the new divine worship that was preached? To which the chief of his own priests, Coifi, immediately answered, "O king, consider what this is which is now preached to us; for I verily declare to you that the religion which we have hitherto professed has, as far as I can certainly learn, no virtue nor advantage in it. For none of your people has applied himself more diligently to the worship of our gods than I; and yet there are many who receive greater favors from you, and are more preferred than I, and are more prosperous in all they seek to do and to get. Now if the gods were good for anything, they would rather forward me, who have been more careful to serve them. It remains, therefore, that if upon examination you find those new doctrines which are now preached to us better and more efficacious, we immediately receive them without any delay."

Another of the king's chief men, approving of his prudent words and exhortations, presently added: "The present life of man on earth, O king, seems to me, in comparison of that time which is unknown to us, like to the swift flight of a sparrow through the room wherein you sit at supper in winter with your commanders and ministers, a good fire burning in the midst whilst the storms of rain and snow rage everywhere abroad; the sparrow, I say, flying in at one door and immediately out at another, whilst he is within is safe from the wintry storm; but after a short space of fair weather, lasting only a moment, he immediately vanishes out of your sight into the dark winter from which he had emerged. So this life of man appears for a short space, but of what went before or what is to follow we are utterly ignorant. If, therefore, this new doctrine contains something more certain, it seems justly to deserve to be followed." The other elders and king's counselors, by divine inspiration, spoke to the same effect.

But Coifi added that he wished more attentively to hear Paulinus discourse concerning the God whom he preached; which he having by the king's command performed, Coifi, hearing his words, cried out, "I have long since been sensible that there was nothing in that which we worshiped; because the more diligently I sought after truth in that worship, the less I found it. But now I freely confess that such truth evidently appears in this preaching as can confer on us the gifts of life, of salvation, and of eternal happiness. For which reason I advise, O king, that we instantly curse and set fire to those temples and altars which we have consecrated without reaping any benefit from them." In short, the king publicly gave his license to Paulinus to preach the Gospel and, renouncing idolatry, declared that he received the faith of Christ; and when he inquired of the aforesaid priest of his sacrifices who should first profane the altars and temples of their idols with the enclosures that were about them, he answered, "I; for who as an example to all others can now more properly than myself, through the wisdom which has been given me by the true God, destroy those things which I worshipped through my folly?" Then immediately, in contempt of his vain superstitions, he desired the king to furnish him with arms and a stallion, on which he might mount and set out to destroy the idols; for it was not lawful before for the high priest either to carry arms or to ride on any but a mare. Having, therefore, girt a sword about him, with a spear in his hand he mounted the king's stallion and proceeded to the idols. The multitude, beholding it, concluded he was distracted; but he lost no time, for as soon as he drew near the temple he profaned the same, casting into it the spear which he held; and rejoicing in the knowledge of the worship of the true God, he commanded his companions to destroy the temple, with all its enclosures, by fire. This place where the idols once were is still shown not far from York, to the eastward beyond the river Derwent, and is now called Godmundingham, where the high priest, by the inspiration of the true God, profaned and destroyed the altars which he had himself consecrated.

CHAPTER XIV

How King Edwin and His Nation Became Christians, and Where Paulinus Baptized Them.

KING EDWIN, therefore, with all the nobility of his nation and a large number of the common sort, received the faith and the washing of regeneration, in the eleventh year of his reign, which is the year of the incarnation of our Lord 627, and about one hundred and eighty after the coming of the English into Britain. He was baptized at York on the holy day of Easter, being the twelfth of April, in the church of St. Peter the Apostle which he himself had there hastily built of timber whilst he was catechizing and instructing in order to receive baptism. In that city also he appointed the see of the bishopric of his instructor and bishop, Paulinus. But as soon as he was baptized, he took care, by the direction of the same Paulinus, to build in the same place a larger and nobler church of stone, in the midst whereof that same oratory which he had first erected should be enclosed. Having therefore laid the foundation, he began to build the church square, encompassing the former oratory. But before the wall was raised to the proper height, the wicked assassination of the king left that work to be finished by Oswald his successor. Paulinus for the space of six years from that time, that is, till the end of the reign of that king, by his consent and favor, preached the word of God in that country, and all that were preordained to eternal life believed and were baptized; among whom were Osfrid and Eadfrid, King Edwin's sons, who were both born to him whilst he was in banishment, of Quenberga, the daughter of Cearl, king of the Mercians.

* * *

Caedmon

BOOK IV

CHAPTER XXIV

That There Was in the Same Monastery[1] a Brother on Whom the Gift of Writing Verses Was Bestowed by Heaven.

THERE was in this abbess's monastery a certain brother particularly remarkable for the grace of God, who was wont to make pious and religious verses, so that whatever was interpreted to him out of Scripture, he soon after put the same into poetical expressions of much sweetness and humility, in English, which was his native language. By his verses the minds of many were often

[1]The monastery of the Abbess Hilda at Whitby on the east coast of what is now Yorkshire; Bede, who supplies all that is known about Caedmon, apparently dates the discovery of the poet not long before the death of Hilda in 680.

excited to despise the world and to desire the heavenly life. Others after him attempted, in the English nation, to compose religious poems, but none could ever compare with him, for he did not learn the art 5 of poetry from men or through human help, but received it as a gift freely bestowed by God; for which reason he never could compose any trivial or vain poem, but only those which relate to religion suited his religious 10 tongue; for having lived in a secular habit until he was well advanced in years, he had never learned anything of versifying; for which reason being sometimes at entertainments, when it was agreed for the sake of 15 mirth that all present should sing in their turns, when he saw the harp come towards him, he rose up from the middle of the feast and returned home.

Having done so at a certain time and gone 20 out of the house where the entertainment was, to the stable where he had to take care of the horses that night, he there composed himself to rest at the proper time; a person appeared to him in his sleep and, saluting 25 him by his name, said, "Caedmon, sing some song to me." He answered, "I cannot sing; for that was the reason why I left the entertainment and retired to this place because I could not sing." The other who talked to 30 him replied, "However, you have to sing to me."—"What should I sing?" rejoined he. "Sing the beginning of created beings," said the other. Hereupon he presently began to sing to the praise of God, the Creator, verses 35 which he had never heard, the purport whereof was thus:—"We are now to praise the Maker of the heavenly kingdom, the power of the Creator and His counsel, the deeds of the Father of glory. How He, 40 being the eternal God, became the Author of all miracles, who first, as almighty Preserver of the human race, created heaven for the sons of men as the roof of the house, and next the earth." This is the sense, but not 45 the words in order as he sang them in his sleep; for verses, though never so well composed, cannot be literally translated word by word out of one language into another without losing much of their beauty and lofti- 50 ness. Awaking from his sleep, he remembered all that he had sung in his dream, and to these words soon added many more, in the same measure and worthy of the Deity.

In the morning he came to the steward, his superior, and, having acquainted him with the gift he had received, was conducted to the abbess, by whom he was ordered, in the presence of many learned men, to tell his dream and repeat the verses, that they might all give their judgment what and whence was the thing which he reported. They all concluded that heavenly grace had been conferred on him by our Lord. They expounded to him a passage in Holy Writ, either historical or doctrinal, ordering him, if he could, to put the same into verse. Having undertaken it, he went away and, returning the next morning, gave it to them composed in most excellent verse; whereupon the abbess, embracing the grace of God in the man, instructed him to quit the secular habit and take upon him the monastic vow; which being accordingly done, she associated him to the rest of the brethren in her monastery and ordered that he should be taught the whole series of sacred history. Thus Caedmon, keeping in mind all he could hear and learn and, as it were chewing the cud, converted the same into most harmonious verse; and sweetly repeating the same, made his masters in their turn his hearers. He sang the creation of the world, the origin of man, and all the history of Genesis; the departure of the children of Israel out of Egypt and their entering into the land of promise, with many other histories from Holy Writ; the incarnation, passion, resurrection of our Lord, and his ascension into heaven; the coming of the Holy Ghost and the preaching of the apostles. He also made many verses on the terror of future judgment, the horror of the pains of hell, and the delights of heaven, as well as many more about the divine benefits and judgments, by all of which he endeavored to turn away men from the love of vice and to excite in them the love of, and application to, good actions; for he was a very religious man, humbly submissive to regular discipline but full of zeal against those who behaved themselves otherwise; for which reason he ended his life happily.

For when the time of his departure drew near, he labored for the space of fourteen days under a bodily infirmity which seemed to prepare the way, yet so moderate that he could talk and walk the whole time. In his neighborhood was the house to which those that were sick and like shortly to die were wont to be carried. He desired the person that attended him, in the evening, as the night came on in which he was to depart this life, to make ready a place there for him to take his rest. This person, wondering why he should desire it, because there was as yet no sign of his dying soon, did what he had ordered. They accordingly went there; and, conversing pleasantly in a joyful manner with the rest that were in the house before, when it was past midnight, Caedmon asked them whether they had the Eucharist there? They answered, "What need of the Eucharist? for you are not likely to die, since you talk so merrily with us, as if you were in perfect health."—"However," said he again, "bring me the Eucharist." Having received the same into his hand, he asked whether they were all in charity with him and without any enmity or rancor? They answered that they were all in perfect charity and free from anger; and in their turn asked him whether he was in the same mind towards them? He immediately answered, "I am in charity, my children, with all the servants of God." Then strengthening himself with the heavenly viaticum,[2] he prepared for the entrance into another life and asked how near the time was when the brothers were to be awakened to sing the nocturnal praises of our Lord? They answered, "It is not far off." Then he said, "Well, let us wait that hour"; and signing himself with the sign of the cross, he laid his head on the pillow and, falling into a little slumber, ended his life so in silence.

Thus it came to pass that, as he had served God with a simple and pure mind and undisturbed devotion, so he now departed to His presence, leaving the world by a quiet death; and that tongue which had composed so many salutary words in praise of the Creator uttered its last words in His praise whilst he was in the act of signing himself with the cross and recommending himself into His hands; and by what has been here said, he seems to have had foreknowledge of his death.

[2]The Eucharist.

OLD ENGLISH POETRY

THE WANDERER[1]

This poem is preserved in the Exeter Book, a manuscript volume left with other books to his church by Leofric (first bishop of Exeter, died A. D. 1071). The volume is still in the cathedral library at Exeter. The author of the poem is unknown, as well as the date of its composition, though it has been conjectured that this elegiac lyric was written probably in the first quarter of the eighth century. "Over the body of the poem lie the shadows of fatalism, and a profound sense of the instability of the earth and its joys" (J. Duncan Spaeth, *Old English Poetry*, p. 247). This theme is a characteristic one in Old English literature.

The text of the original may be found in *An Anglo-Saxon Book of Verse and Prose*, ed. W. J. Sedgefield (Manchester, 1928), pp. 28–31. For a discussion of this and related Old English poems see Bernhard Ten Brink, *Early English Literature (to Wiclif)*, trans. Horace M. Kennedy (New York, 1883), pp. 59–67; and also Charles W. Kennedy, *Old English Elegies* (Princeton, 1936).

"Still the lone one and desolate waits for his Maker's ruth—
God's good mercy, albeit so long it tarry, in sooth.
Careworn and sad of heart, on the watery ways must he
Plow with the hand-grasped oar—how long?—the rime-cold sea,
Tread thy paths of exile, O Fate, who art cruelty." 5
Thus did a wanderer speak, being heart-full of woe, and all
Thoughts of the cruel slayings, and pleasant comrades' fall:
"Morn by morn I, alone, am fain to utter my woe;
Now is there none of the living to whom I dare to show
Plainly the thought of my heart; in very sooth I know 10
Excellent is it in man that his breast he straightly bind,
Shut fast his thinkings in silence, whatever he have in his mind.
The man that is weary in heart, he never can fate withstand;
The man that grieves in his spirit, he finds not the helper's hand.
Therefore the glory-grasper full heavy of soul may be. 15
So, far from my fatherland, and mine own good kinsmen free,
I must bind my heart in fetters, for long, ah! long ago,
The earth's cold darkness covered my giver of gold brought low;
And I, sore stricken and humbled, and winter-saddened, went
Far over the frost-bound waves to seek for the dear content 20
Of the hall of the giver of rings; but far nor near could I find
Who felt the love of the mead-hall, or who with comforts kind
Would comfort me, the friendless. 'T is he alone will know,
Who knows, being desolate too, how evil a fere[2] is woe;
For him the path of the exile, and not the twisted gold; 25
For him the frost in his bosom, and not earth-riches old.
"O, well he remembers the hall-men, the treasure bestowed in the hall;
The feast that his gold-giver made him, the joy at its height, at its fall;
He knows who must be forlorn for his dear lord's counsels gone,
Where sleep and sorrow together are binding the lonely one; 30
When himthinks he clasps and kisses his leader of men, and lays
His hands and head on his knee, as when, in the good yore-days,

[1]The translation is by Emily H. Hickey. It is reprinted here with the permission of the editors and publishers from *Select Translations from Old English Poetry*, edited by A. S. Cook and C. B. Tinker, and published by Ginn and Company.

[2]Comrade.

He sat on the throne of his might, in the strength that wins and saves.
But the friendless man awakes, and he sees the yellow waves,
And the sea-birds dip to the sea, and broaden their wings to the gale, 35
And he sees the dreary rime, and the snow commingled with hail.
O, then are the wounds of his heart the sorer much for this,
The brief for the loved and lost made new by the dream of old bliss.
His kinsmen's memory comes to him as he lies asleep,
And he greets it with joy, with joy, and the heart in his breast doth leap; 40
But out of his ken the shapes of his warrior-comrades swim
To the land whence seafarers bring no dear old saws for him;
Then fresh grows sorrow and new to him whose bitter part
Is to send o'er the frost-bound waves full often his weary heart.
For this do I look around this world, and cannot see 45
Wherefore or why my heart should not grow dark in me.
When I think of the lives of the leaders, the clansmen mighty in mood;
When I think how sudden and swift they yielded the place where they stood.
So droops this mid-earth and falls, and never a man is found
Wise ere a many winters have girt his life around. 50
Full patient the sage must be, and he that would counsel teach—
Not over-hot in his heart, nor over-swift in his speech;
Nor faint of soul nor secure, nor fain for the fight nor afraid;
Nor ready to boast before he know himself well arrayed.
The proud-souled man must bide when he utters his vaunt, until 55
He know of the thoughts of the heart, and whitherward turn they will.
The prudent must understand how terror and awe shall be,
When the glory and weal of the world lie waste, as now men see
On our mid-earth, many a where, the wind-swept walls arise,
And the ruined dwellings and void, and the rime that on them lies. 60
The wine-halls crumble, bereft of joy the warriors lie,
The flower of the doughty fallen, the proud ones fair to the eye.
War took off some in death, and one did a strong bird bear
Over the deep; and one—his bones did the gray wolf share;
And one was hid in a cave by a comrade sorrowful-faced. 65
O, thus the Shaper of men hath laid the earth all waste,
Till the works of the city-dwellers, the works of the giants of earth,
Stood empty and lorn of the burst of the mighty revelers' mirth.
"Who wisely hath mused on this wall-stead,[3] and ponders this dark life well,
In his heart he hath often bethought him of slayings many and fell, 70
And these be the words he taketh, the thoughts of his heart to tell:
'Where is the horse and the rider? Where is the giver of gold?
Where be the seats at the banquet? Where be the hall-joys of old?
Alas for the burnished cup, for the byrnied[4] chief to-day!
Alas for the strength of the prince! for the time hath passed away— 75
Is hid 'neath the shadow of night, as it never had been at all.
Behind the dear and doughty there standeth now a wall,
A wall that is wondrous high, and with wondrous snake-work wrought.
The strength of the spears hath fordone the earls and hath made them naught,
The weapons greedy of slaughter, and she, the mighty Wyrd;[5] 80
And the tempests beat on the rocks, and the storm-wind that maketh afeard—
The terrible storm that fetters the earth, the winter-bale,
When the shadow of night falls wan, and wild is the rush of the hail,
The cruel rush from the north, which maketh men to quail.
Hardship-full is the earth, o'erturned when the stark Wyrds say: 85
Here is the passing of riches, here friends are passing away;
And men and kinsfolk pass, and nothing and none may stay;
And all this earth-stead here shall be empty and void one day.'"

[3]Wall-place, earth. [4]Mail-coated. [5]Fate.

THE SEAFARER[1]

This poem is, like *The Wanderer*, preserved in the Exeter Book. Its author and date of composition are unknown, though it was written probably in the eighth century. The first part has been thought by some scholars to be a dialogue between an old mariner who knows the sea from bitter experience and a young man eager to become a sailor. This is only conjecture, though it is plain that two opposed moods are realized by the poet and expressed. It has also been supposed that the second part is by a different and later hand, but this too is only conjecture.

The text of the original may be found in *An Anglo-Saxon Book of Verse and Prose*, ed. W. J. Sedgefield (Manchester, 1928), pp. 32–4. For a discussion of this and related Old English poems see Bernhard Ten Brink, *Early English Literature (to Wiclif)*, trans. Horace M. Kennedy (New York, 1883), pp. 59–67; and also Charles W. Kennedy, *Old English Elegies* (Princeton, 1936).

PART I

I can sing of myself a true song, of my voyages telling,
How oft through laborious days, through the wearisome hours
I have suffered; have borne tribulations; explored in my ship,
Mid the terrible rolling of waves, habitations of sorrow.
Benumbed by the cold, oft the comfortless night-watch hath held me 5
At the prow of my craft as it tossed about under the cliffs.
My feet were imprisoned with frost, were fettered with ice-chains,
Yet hotly were wailing the querulous sighs round my heart;
And hunger within me, sea-wearied, made havoc of courage.
This he, whose lot happily chances on land, doth not know; 10
Nor how I on the ice-cold sea passed the winter in exile,
In wretchedness, robbed of my kinsmen, with icicles hung.
The hail flew in showers about me; and there I heard only
The roar of the sea, ice-cold waves, and the song of the swan;
For pastime the gannets' cry served me; the kittiwakes' chatter 15
For laughter of men; and for mead-drink the call of the sea-mews.
When storms on the rocky cliffs beat, then the terns, icy-feathered,
Made answer; full oft the sea-eagle forebodingly screamed,
The eagle with pinions wave-wet. There none of my kinsmen
Might gladden my desolate soul; of this little he knows 20
Who possesses the pleasures of life, who has felt in the city
Some hardship, some trifling adversity, proud and wine-flushed.
How weary I oft had to tarry upon the seaway!
The shadows of night became darker, it snowed from the north;
The world was enchained by the frost; hail fell upon earth; 25
'Twas the coldest of grain. Yet the thoughts of my heart now are throbbing
To test the high streams, the salt waves in tumultuous play.
Desire in my heart ever urges my spirit to wander,
To seek out the home of the stranger in lands afar off.
There is no one that dwells upon earth, so exalted in mind, 30
So large in his bounty, nor yet of such vigorous youth,
Nor so daring in deeds, nor to whom his liege lord is so kind,
But that he has always a longing, a seafaring passion
For what the Lord God shall bestow, be it honor or death.
No heart for the harp has he, nor for acceptance of treasure, 35
No pleasure has he in a wife, no delight in the world,
Nor in aught save the roll of the billows; but always a longing,
A yearning uneasiness, hastens him on to the sea.
The woodlands are captured by blossoms, the hamlets grow fair,

[1]The translation is by LaMotte Iddings. It is reprinted here with the permission of the editors and publishers from *Select Translations from Old English Poetry*, edited by A. S. Cook and C. B. Tinker, and published by Ginn and Company.

Broad meadows are beautiful, earth again bursts into life, 40
And all stir the heart of the wanderer eager to journey,
So he meditates going afar on the pathway of tides.
The cuckoo, moreover, gives warning with sorrowful note,
Summer's harbinger sings, and forebodes to the heart bitter sorrow.
The nobleman comprehends not, the luxurious man, 45
What some must endure, who travel the farthest in exile.
Now my spirit uneasily turns in the heart's narrow chamber,
Now wanders forth over the tide, o'er the home of the whale,
To the ends of the earth—and comes back to me. Eager and greedy,
The lone wanderer screams, and resistlessly drives my soul onward, 50
Over the whale-path, over the tracts of the sea.

PART II

The delights of the Lord are far dearer to me than this dead,
Fleeting life upon earth, for I cannot believe that earth's riches
For ever endure. Each one of three things, ere its time comes,
Is always uncertain: violence, age, and disease
Wrench the soul away, doomed to depart. This is praise from the living, 5
From those who speak afterwards, this the best fame after death—
That ere he departed he labored, and wrought daring deeds
'Gainst the malice of fiends, and the devil; so men shall extol him,
His praise among angels shall live, ever, world without end,
His the blessing of life everlasting, and joy mid the hosts. 10
The days have departed, all pomps of earth's kingdom have vanished;
There now are no kings, no emperors now, no gold-givers
As of yore, when they wrought in their midst the most glorious deeds,
And lived in the lordliest power. This glory has fallen,
Delights have all vanished away; the weak ones remain, 15
And these govern the world, obtaining their pleasure with effort.
Power has declined, earth's glory grows aged and sear,
Like every man now in the world; old age overtakes him,
His countenance loses its color, gray-haired he laments;
He has seen his old friends, sons of princes, consigned to the earth. 20
This garment of flesh has no power, when the spirit escapes,
To drink in the sweet nor to taste of the bitter; it then
Has no power to stretch forth the hands or to think with the mind.
Though the grave should be covered with gold by the nearest of kin,
Be buried along with the dead in masses of treasure, 25
Still that will not go with them. Gold can no substitute be
For the fear of the Lord, to the soul which is laden with sin,
Which aforetime, so long as it lived, kept that treasure concealed.
Great is the fear of the Lord; the earth trembles before it;
He established the unmovable earth, the world and the heavens. 30
Foolish is he who stands not in awe of the Lord—
Unexpectedly death comes upon him; but happy is he
Who lives humble in mind, to him cometh honor from heaven;
God doth establish the soul that believes in His might.
One should check a strong will, and should govern it firmly, 35
Be true unto men, and be clean in his manner of life. . . .
Fate, God the Creator, is stronger than any man's will.
Come, let us reflect where our home is, consider the way
By which we go thither; then let us each strive to press forward
To joy everlasting, where life has its source in God's love, 40
Where is heavenly hope. Then to Him who is holy be thanks,
Because He hath honored us; thanks to the Ruler of Heaven,
The Lord everlasting, throughout all the ages! Amen.

THE BATTLE OF BRUNANBURH[1]

This poem is preserved in four of the six extant manuscripts of the *Anglo-Saxon Chronicle*—in the Parker MS. in the library of Corpus Christi College, Cambridge, and in three Cotton MSS. in the British Museum. Its author is unknown, but the date under which it is entered in the *Chronicle* is A. D. 937. The poem describes an historical event. Tennyson, whose translation is printed here, prefixed to it the following note: "Constantinus, King of the Scots, after having sworn allegiance to Aethelstan, allied himself with the Danes of Ireland under Anlaf, and invading England, was defeated by Aethelstan and his brother Edmund with great slaughter at Brunanburh in the year 937." Aethelstan reigned over the West Saxons and Mercians from A. D. 925 to 940, and extended his influence throughout England. The site of Brunanburh is unknown. The most likely conjecture hitherto advanced is apparently that it is Bramber, near Preston in Lancashire.

The text of the original may be found in *An Anglo-Saxon Book of Verse and Prose,* ed. W. J. Sedgefield (Manchester, 1928), pp. 68–70. For a discussion and a literal translation of the poem see Bernhard Ten Brink, *Early English Literature (to Wiclif)*, trans. Horace M. Kennedy (New York, 1883), pp. 90–92.

I

Athelstan King,
Lord among Earls,
Bracelet-bestower and
Baron of Barons,
He with his brother, 5
Edmund Atheling,
Gaining a lifelong
Glory in battle,
Slew with the sword-edge
There by Brunanburh, 10
Brake the shield-wall,
Hewed the linden-wood,
Hacked the battle-shield,
Sons of Edward with hammered brands.

II

Theirs was a greatness 15
Got from their grandsires—
Theirs that so often in
Strife with their enemies
Struck for their hoards and their hearths and their homes.

III

Bowed the spoiler, 20
Bent the Scotsman,
Fell the ship-crews
Doomed to the death.
All the field with blood of the fighters
Flowed, from when first the great 25
Sun-star of morning-tide,
Lamp of the Lord God
Lord everlasting,
Glode over earth till the glorious creature
Sank to his setting. 30

IV

There lay many a man
Marred by the javelin,
Men of the Northland
Shot over shield.
There was the Scotsman 35
Weary of war.

V

We the West-Saxons,
Long as the daylight
Lasted, in companies
Troubled the track of the host that we hated; 40
Grimly with swords that were sharp from the grindstone,
Fiercely we hacked at the fliers before us.

VI

Mighty the Mercian,
Hard was his hand-play,
Sparing not any of 45
Those that with Anlaf,
Warriors over the
Weltering waters
Borne in the bark's-bosom,
Drew to this island— 50
Doomed to the death.

VII

Five young kings put asleep by the sword-stroke,
Seven strong Earls of the army of Anlaf
Fell on the war-field, numberless numbers,
Shipmen and Scotsmen. 55

[1]This translation is by Alfred Tennyson. Tennyson stated that he more or less availed himself of his son's prose translation of the poem published in the *Contemporary Review,* November, 1876.

VIII

Then the Norse leader—
Dire was his need of it,
Few were his following—
Fled to his war-ship;
Fleeted his vessel to sea with the king in it, 60
Saving his life on the fallow flood.

IX

Also the crafty one,
Constantinus,
Crept to his North again,
Hoar-headed hero! 65

X

Slender warrant had
He to be proud of
The welcome of war-knives—
He that was reft of his
Folk and his friends that had 70
Fallen in conflict,
Leaving his son too
Lost in the carnage,
Mangled to morsels,
A youngster in war! 75

XI

Slender reason had
He to be glad of
The clash of the war-glaive—
Traitor and trickster
And spurner of treaties— 80
He nor had Anlaf
With armies so broken
A reason for bragging
That they had the better
In perils of battle 85
On places of slaughter—
The struggle of standards,
The rush of the javelins,
The crash of the charges,
The wielding of weapons— 90
The play that they played with
The children of Edward.[2]

XII

Then with their nailed prows
Parted the Norsemen, a
Blood-reddened relic of 95
Javelins over
The jarring breaker, the deep-sea billow,
Shaping their way toward Dyflen[3] again,
Shamed in their souls.

XIII

Also the brethren, 100
King and Atheling,
Each in his glory,
Went to his own in his own West-Saxonland,
Glad of the war.

XIV

Many a carcase they left to be carrion, 105
Many a livid one, many a sallow-skin—
Left for the white-tailed eagle to tear it, and
Left for the horny-nibbed raven to rend it,
and
Gave to the garbaging war-hawk to gorge it,
and
That gray beast, the wolf of the weald.[4] 110

XV

Never had huger
Slaughter of heroes
Slain by the sword-edge—
Such as old writers
Have writ of in histories— 115
Hapt in this isle, since
Up from the East hither
Saxon and Angle from
Over the broad billow
Broke into Britain with 120
Haughty war-workers who
Harried the Welshman, when
Earls that were lured by the
Hunger of glory gat
Hold of the land. 125

[2]Athelstan and Edmund.

[3]Dublin. [4]Moorland.

The Later Middle Ages, 1066–1485

In 1066 Edward the Confessor died childless. Religion had been his central interest, and as a ruler he had not shown the strength which the times demanded. The actual government of the kingdom had fallen into the hands of a few powerful noblemen, and principally into the hands of Godwin, Earl of Wessex, and his sons. Edward, in fact, had obtained the throne chiefly through Godwin's influence, had married Godwin's daughter, and then had been unsuccessful in attempting to repel the domination of the family. Godwin had died in 1053, and his son Harold, of whom Edward was not fond, had succeeded to the earldom of Wessex and had become, in almost everything but name, the real ruler of England. On his deathbed Edward named Harold his successor; and the choice was afterwards confirmed by the Witan—the king's council composed of government officials, bishops, and noblemen.

Harold, however, knew that he would not be able to keep the throne without a struggle. William, Duke of Normandy across the Channel, had long been preparing to seize the English sovereignty upon Edward's death, and he now asserted his claims, gathered an army, secured the Pope's blessing upon the undertaking, and landed on the south coast of England towards the end of September, 1066. William's claims were based in part on kinship. Edward's mother was Emma, daughter of Richard, Duke of Normandy, from whom William was descended. But William also had secured from Edward in 1051 a promise—or so at any rate he now said—that he would be named Edward's successor; and in 1064 he had forced Harold to promise support for his claims when the time should come. Harold had no intention of keeping this forced promise, and Edward's promise, if really given, was not fulfilled. At bottom, William's position was that of a bold yet shrewd adventurer: he was determined to obtain England, and ready to risk everything upon armed invasion, but he also wanted to secure every advantage he could by giving a respectable appearance to the expedition.

The outcome made it appear that William had fate, whether or not he had justice and divine approval, on his side. Harold's sovereignty was also challenged by the King of Norway, who landed in the north of England, and drew Harold thither to meet him. Harold defeated the Norse army near York, but then had to hasten immediately south to encounter William. And in the battle which followed, at Hastings in October, Harold was killed, and his army routed. From that moment William's success was not in doubt, and he was soon accepted by the English, and crowned King in Westminster Abbey on Christmas Day. During the next five years William had some fighting to do in the north to complete his conquest, but he stamped out several attempts at rebellion, and made it clear that he had come to stay and that all England was to be firmly united under his rule.

Feudalism

William was indeed an extraordinary man, and the measures he took to consolidate his position were ingenious and effective. His fellow adventurers expected rewards, and he of course needed their continued aid. Hence he gave them land which had been owned by the English who fought against him, but he so divided up the land that none of the new owners had a large amount in any one place. Thus when he gave his more important followers several small estates, or manors, in different parts of the country, instead of a large estate all in one place, he scattered their strength, and made it as important to them as it was to him that the country should have a strong central government, able everywhere to enforce obedience and orderly conduct. Moreover, he made no outright gifts, but rather grants of land to be held subject to conditions. In this he introduced the principles of feudal tenure as they had grown up on the Continent. These principles were not wholly unfamiliar to the English, but feudalism had not developed in England before the Norman Conquest as it had in continental Europe, and particularly in France.

Under feudalism a king was, in theory, the sole absolute owner of all the land over which he exercised sovereignty. He merely granted the use of his land to his peers, or noblemen, in return for their oaths of fealty, or acknowledgment of loyalty and service due him; and the king could, in theory, take their estates from his noblemen, or vassals, if they violated their oaths. The service exacted was both military and administrative. The great noblemen held large estates, and administered them, in part, by dividing them into portions and granting the use of these portions to lesser men who swore fealty and promised services; and these in turn divided their estates and granted the use of small holdings, in return for loyalty and services, to still lesser men, until the end was reached with the peasants who actually tilled the soil. Social organization under feudalism may be likened to a pyramid. The broad base was composed of peasants. Some of these were bound to the soil; they had some rights to balance their services, and so were not slaves; but they could not leave the estates to which they were attached. They were called serfs; in England they gradually won their freedom before the close of the Middle Ages. The next and considerably smaller tier of the pyramid was composed of the smallest landholders—and so up it went with the king at the top. It is only essential for us to grasp the fact that this was a graded order, with an assigned place and prescribed duties for every man, so that no one was independent, though everyone received a certain measure of protection, or security, as compensation for what he gave up. This meant that the several ranks were bound together by ties of personal loyalty, extending through the whole social structure, besides being bound by the contractual arrangements which governed the use of land. It also meant, however, that society was divided sharply into classes, and that every man's station in life was determined pretty largely by the social rank and material circumstances of his parents.

Feudalism and the Church

The organization of the Catholic Church was also hierarchical, and had points of marked similarity to the feudal structure, with, however, the important difference that position within the Church could not be passed on by inheritance. But the medieval Church was a vast world in itself, based, materially, on a great accumulation of property. Lay rulers could not, or would not, allow the land acquired by the Church to pass completely beyond their control. Further, as bishops and abbots came to have at their command great wealth and power, these positions were sought by ambitious men who had no keen interest in religion but did have a strong desire for luxury or for important political or social position. Theoretically Church and State were two worlds, existing side by side; but practically they interpenetrated, and actually they were often in conflict. In general, in England, William and his successors managed to force abbots of monasteries and some bishops into the system of feudal tenure; so that these lords ecclesiastical became, in respect of their lands, subject to the king, bound by oaths of loyalty and obligated to military service, which they could perform by deputy. The king, however, could not rest content with this; in so far as abbots and bishops became important officers of state, he inevitably sought to control their appointment for purposes important to him as the lay ruler, not for the purposes of religion. Sometimes the king wished to reward a favorite or a follower for distinguished service; or again he wished to place an able man in a great position for the service of the State; and always he wished to maintain or increase his own power. The clergy, on their side, equally could not ignore the State, because it was only at the expense of the State that they could maintain or increase the power of the Church.

Life in the Middle Ages can only be understood in terms of these two institutions, feudalism and the Roman Catholic Church; uneasy bedfellows, both born of the effort to achieve order and security in the period of virtual anarchy which followed the breakup of the ancient Roman Empire and the resettlement of Europe by hordes of Germanic barbarians. This, of course, is said of the Church considered only, for the moment, as a form of social organization.

Norman Culture and Shrewdness

William and his followers were themselves, by descent, Vikings. While some Danes in the ninth century had been harrying and conquering the eastern part of England, others had gone to the north coast of France, and by the beginning of the tenth century had taken possession of the territory later called Normandy. In 911 this territory was formally granted by the king of the West Franks to Rollo, the Danish leader in possession at the time, as a feudal fief. Accordingly, Rollo became the first Duke of Normandy, acknowledging Charles the Simple of France as his feudal overlord; and William, in the middle of the eleventh century, was Rollo's direct descendant. In the interval, however, these Danes had shown an astonishing power of assimilation, and had besides become mixed, by intermarriage, with the Franks amongst whom they had settled. They had promptly accepted Christianity, and the French language, and French usages and manners. By 1066 they had become in effect Frenchmen—and this at a time when France was the center of the new social order and the new civilization which were now rapidly taking form after some centuries of chaos. Yet in becoming Frenchmen they had lost nothing of their native energy, shrewdness, and strength, and were still capable of acting like unscrupulous bullies when there was a purpose to be served by it.

William therefore brought to England not merely an army capable of holding his new kingdom by force, but also a rising civilization and culture, and well trained and educated administrators for both Church and State, who were able rapidly to alter the social organization, the intellectual outlook, and the manners of the English. Numerically, the Normans were a small group in comparison with the English, but they soon held throughout the kingdom all the positions of power and influence, from which they dominated the life of the island. And their hold was the more secure because of William's shrewdness in profiting by what he had seen, in France, of the dangers of feudalism. The prime danger was that a great noble might become, in effect, an independent ruler within his own estate, able to defy his king with impunity. It was William's greatest achievement that, in the way mentioned above and in other ways, he contrived to avoid this danger. He contrived to *use* feudalism in England, giving his new foreign aristocracy power and responsibility, yet keeping his central government so strong that, even under less competent successors, a useful working balance was maintained between king and nobles, and the unity of the realm was not seriously endangered for centuries.

Continuity of English Civilization

Undoubtedly the success of the Norman Conquest was facilitated by the fact that it did not at any point really break the continuity of civilization in England. The English were already Christian and Catholic; feudalism had been on the way, developing naturally under the stress of the same need that had brought it into being on the Continent; and Norman-French influence had begun to be felt strongly under Edward the Confessor. These things we need to remember, because the changes that were effected by the Norman invasion were so impressive that students have at times been led to think of this last foreign conquest of England as a sharp break and a new beginning.

For example, the English language seems, as we look back, practically to disappear in the years following the Conquest. Throughout the Middle Ages in Europe Latin was the universal language of the Church and of the learned. And the Normans brought in their own French for secular purposes, and imposed it upon the Englishmen who had to deal with them. The immediate result was that French became the language of all kinds of officials, of the law courts, even of the English stewards and other employees or servants of the Norman nobility. Moreover, in the eleventh century a new vernacular literature was beginning to appear in France which excited admiration everywhere, and led the way for the modern literatures of Germany and Italy as well as England; but in England it seemed for a while to have no effect, obviously because French was now the language in England of the aristocracy for whom the new literature was written. Indeed some of this new French literature was written in England; and it appears altogether probable that any enlightened and observant Englishman, a century after the Conquest, must have thought it the destiny of his country to become part and parcel of a great French domain extending from the Pyrenees to the northernmost tip of Scotland. He would have thought so because Henry II, the first of the Angevin or Plantagenet kings who were the rulers of England from 1154 until 1399, was not only king of England but also acknowledged overlord of Scotland, of South Wales, and of the eastern part of Ireland, and held as feudal fiefs from the king of France Normandy, Brittany, Maine, Anjou, Poitou, Aquitaine, and Gascony. On the one hand the king of France seemed powerless and insignificant, with Henry II his vassal only in name; and on the other hand French civilization and the French language seemed dominant in England.

Yet the appearance was deceptive. The "empire" of Henry II was an insubstantial structure, like the "empire" of Canute before the Norman Conquest; and both alike serve to show how many false starts had to be made, how many radical shifts in alignment were necessary, before the destinies of the modern European peoples became plain and enough stability could be achieved to render possible the growth of a new culture and of the modern European literatures. The "empire" of Canute, however, had been really ephemeral; whereas the problem of the relations between England and France continued unsolved during almost the whole of the period we are now concerned with. And it may almost be said that it was never quite the same problem from one decade to another. Politically the French possessions were never a real advantage to England; and as time went on it should have become clear, as it is now to us, that a real union between England and the French duchies was impossible. But, ironically enough, in the latest period of the long struggle, the French ambitions of the English kings actually fostered the emerging national consciousness and national pride of the English. This latest period is comprised in the so-called Hundred Years' War which began in 1338 and ended in 1453; and its progress was marked by three celebrated victories of the English—in the battles of Crécy, 1346, of Poitiers ten years later, and of Agincourt in 1415. Each of these victories was won primarily by English yeomen, using the English long bow against greatly superior numbers of mounted knights, who were drawn from the nobility of France. These great victories, consequently, were felt to be triumphs of the whole English people, in a sense that was not possible when fighting was confined, as in France, to the nobility and mercenaries. Each of these battles, too, was a blow at the feudal system on its important military side, because each showed that soldiers drawn from the mass of the common, or basely born, people could defeat the hitherto invincible noblemen.

Nevertheless, these famous victories were politically barren. At the end of the Hundred Years' War the French possessions of the English kings were so reduced as to be negligible, and it had become finally clear that England and France were to face each other across the Channel as independent countries, very different in temper, in political organization, and in language and literature. The next struggle in which the English were involved was an internal one, between the houses of Lancaster and York, both descended from Edward III, for the sovereignty of England. This period of conflict, known as the Wars of the Roses because a white rose was the emblem of the house of York and a red rose came to be regarded as emblematic of the opposing side, was precipitated by the ignominious close of the Hundred Years' War under the weak leadership of Henry VI, last of the Lancastrian kings. The Wars of the Roses ended in 1485, when Henry Tudor, not a Lancastrian but heir to the Lancastrian claims, defeated Richard III, the last of the three Yorkish kings, at the battle of Bosworth Field.

Though by the end of the Middle Ages, then, England and France were separate, each with a distinct national consciousness, this outcome was in doubt through most of the period under discussion. In this whole period, moreover, French and Latin influences were of decisive importance in remaking the English language and in the fashioning of a new English literature. The changes thus wrought were so great as to be almost revolutionary; yet they do not mark a break between Old and Modern English language or literature. The period is one of transition, but of transition through which threads of historical continuity firmly bind Old English to Modern. The term given to the period, to designate both the language and the literature, is Middle English, which properly emphasizes the fact of continuity persisting amidst great change.

The Middle English Language

We must notice first what happened to the language. We have already seen how French became the official speech of England immediately after the Conquest, and not only the public speech of officials but also the daily speech of the new aristocracy. William, in all the changes he introduced, showed a wise concern for English usage, and did no more than he considered necessary, to break the continuity of English life and custom. In the matter of language, however, he was helpless, if not heedless. It was something that would have to take care of itself—and it did. For English remained continuously the speech of the common people; and the Normans, though they held all the important positions in State and Church, remained so greatly in the minority that it was not long, as such things go, until they began to be absorbed into the English majority. This meant that in the end it was, not the English, but the descendants of the Normans who had to become first bilingual, and then gradually to give up the use of their own tongue. Barely three centuries after the Conquest, Edward III, in 1362, opened Parliament by a speech in English; and in the same year he sought to stop the use of French in the law courts. It was also about the middle of this century that English began to be taught in schools. And for a considerable time before this it had been true that the French spoken in England had become a provincial, if not an artificial dialect.

In the contest of tongues English had decisively won. In the years before the Norman Conquest there had been distinct signs that the West Saxon dialect was being accepted everywhere as the standard form of the language. But under Danish and then under Norman influence, when English persisted chiefly as a spoken language, and amongst people closely bound to their own localities, dialectal differences re-asserted themselves, and indeed increased, with the consequence that in the fourteenth century there were a number of very different kinds of English being used. The kinds fall into groups—Southern, Midland, and Northern

—all alike very different from Old English, but also very different from one another. Still, it can be said of all forms of Middle English that during the three centuries following the Norman Conquest two causes had been at work to produce change. One was the tendency to abandon inflectional endings; the language was turning into what is called an analytic, or mostly uninflected, tongue. This species of change had indeed begun before the Norman Conquest, but conditions after the Conquest greatly accelerated it, so that by the latter half of the fourteenth century only a remnant of inflection was still in use. The other most noticeable change which took place was the importation into English of a host of French and Latin words. Several hundred Latin words had come into Old English in the last centuries before the Conquest, but these made only a slight addition to the resources of the language in comparison with the great number which were imported from both Latin and French in the years between 1100 and 1500. About thirty-four hundred words from French alone had entered Middle English before 1400. Very considerable changes in pronunciation were also taking place in these centuries; and in the East Midlands (London and the surrounding country) pronunciation was much closer to French than it is now.

Altogether it is not surprising that some students formerly thought of English as practically a new language made up principally from French and Latin in the thirteenth and fourteenth centuries. But they judged hastily, and were wrong, as a single instance may show. In Chaucer's "Prologue" to his *Canterbury Tales* the French and Latin words number only thirteen *per cent.* of the whole. Doubtless in some other poems by Chaucer the foreign element is larger, but in general it is true that the words in commonest use, in the fourteenth century and still today, have come down from Old English, and that the foreign words, howsoever numerous then and since, have been genuinely drawn into the language and completely assimilated. In this the English ran true to form, showing a remarkable power to draw in the foreign thing and make it their own, until it no longer was foreign. And in the present instance their language remained at the center essentially unchanged and firm, so that real continuity was maintained. Some notion of what happened can be gained from the example used by Sir Walter Scott in *Ivanhoe,* where the jester is made to remark that living animals, under the care of English serfs, kept their native names—"ox," "sheep," "calf," "swine," "deer"—while the flesh of those animals when used for food, eaten by Norman nobles, came to be called by French names—"beef," "mutton," "veal," pork," "bacon," "venison." So also the words "master," "servant," "butler," "buttery," "bottle," "dinner," "supper," "banquet" are derived from the French. One could go on almost indefinitely giving familiar English words relating to law, government, property, trades, warfare, and the like, which had come in from French by the fourteenth century, but our conclusion would remain the same—that Middle English was English, and did take all these words into itself instead of being swallowed up by French and Latin.

Before leaving the subject of language, however, it should be said that the form of Middle English which was destined to survive and become the foundation of standard Modern English was the dialect spoken in and around London—the so-called East Midland dialect. This is the form of Middle English used by Chaucer, the greatest poet of the period and the most finished artist, and it is our good fortune, and in a sense his, that he did happen to be a Londoner and to use this dialect. For it has survived as the foundation of Modern English not because Chaucer used it, but because of the unique importance of London in the life and developing civilization of England.

The Continuity of English Literature: Influence of the Church

When we turn from language to literature there is more reason for wondering whether any real continuity between the pre-Conquest time and the later Middle Ages was maintained. Yet here too the answer must be in the affirmative. English did not at any time sink to the point of becoming merely a peasants' speech. We do not know as much about the use of English during the first two hundred years after the Conquest as we should like to. Indeed, throughout the whole period from 1066 to 1485 the evidence which has been preserved is fragmentary. We hear, for example, of a William Lichfield, rector of a parish in London and famous as a preacher, who, when he died in 1448, left over three thousand sermons all fully written out in English, besides many notes; yet nothing of what Lichfield wrote has survived except possibly one brief tract. Nevertheless, despite all that may have perished, we can see pretty clearly what happened.

We have already noticed that in the time of Alfred the Great a workmanlike English prose was formed which served very well the purposes of history and of education, chiefly religious instruction. We have also noticed that the *Anglo-Saxon Chronicle* was continued in one monastery, in Old English, for almost a century after the Conquest. But by the middle of the twelfth century Latin had come into use again, just as it had been used in the time of Bede, for all purposes of learning, including the writing of history. Even this, however, did not mean that English was being crowded out from every literary field. For there still remained the field of religious instruction, in which English steadily continued to be indispensable.

The Catholic Church of the Middle Ages, as it became wealthy and powerful, was perforce drawn into worldly affairs, after the fashion already mentioned in this chapter, and it sometimes seemed to contemporaries —as it does still today to some scholars— that the Church had become a worldly and corrupt institution. But the Church in its vastness was many-sided. As it touched and influenced medieval life at every point, so also it was touched and influenced by its surroundings, and it is not always possible to say from which side one or another development originated. After all, when an institution draws into itself something like one third of the population to occupy what may be called official positions, and when the whole population is comprised in the membership, the institution and society are scarcely distinguishable, and the officials must form really a cross section of the population, exhibiting all the varieties of character and interest and intelligence that humanity itself exhibits. And this is just what took place in the Catholic Church of the Middle Ages. Moreover, though we know that human beings were not in any significant way really different then from what they now are—not less intelligent, not less worldly, not less given to cheating and lying and hypocrisy, not less diverse—still, there is truth in the characterization of the Middle Ages as the ages of faith. There was throughout Europe, as the work of conversion was completed and the great medieval Church rose to its majestic height of power, a common framework of belief really shared by all, giving society a homogeneity more intimate than that conferred by the ancient Roman Empire, and a sense of unity which we almost totally lack today. Some, of course, were indifferent to that framework of belief, and some understood it frivolously, but all shared it; and those who took it seriously and with understanding were fired, through generation after generation, with a remarkable zeal. From this sprang nearly all the famous monuments of medieval civilization in literature and art and thought which are still the admiration of the modern world; from this sprang also a constantly renewed determination to go back in singleness of purpose to the original principles of Christianity, and to propagate them.

So it came about that the Catholic Church in England never lacked conscientious teachers who, like their brethren on the Continent, used every means which ingenuity could suggest to bring Christianity home to the mass of the people. And one vital means was instruction in English. It has been said of Aelfric, who died about 1020, that in his sermons, or homilies, he used the English prose he had inherited from Alfred and his contemporaries with an ease and simple directness "that would have been approved by Dryden." In the years following the Conquest Aelfric's sermons continued to be used, and also the English translation of the first seven books of the Old Testament which had been made under his supervision. This we know from copies made after the Conquest; and in the same way we learn that new discourses were being composed in English, upon the model furnished by Aelfric, during the twelfth century. This stream of good prose, confined by the Normans to the one service of popular religious instruction, was a slender trickle, which at the close of the twelfth century appeared to be dwindling away to nothing. There is indeed ground for thinking that about this time French had so far gained upon English that it seemed probable it was to become the language of all who dwelt in England. Yet just at the beginning of the thirteenth century some ecclesiastic wrote in English a set of directions for three young women who wished to lead a devout life in retirement and who had appealed to him for guidance—the *Ancren Riwle* it is called, or *Rule of Anchoresses* (nuns)—which is one of the masterpieces of English medieval literature. And the *Ancren Riwle* does not stand alone. It is one of half a dozen surviving prose pieces—three of them lives of women saints—all written about 1200, apparently in the West Midlands, for nuns. All are written with a competence and finish which would have been impossible had their authors not been in touch with a still-living tradition of good English prose; and they served to give this tradition a new lease on life.

Hence we owe it to the unlearned and especially, in the thirteenth and fourteenth centuries, to the needs of devout women, that the continuity of English prose was maintained. This is a fact of prime importance; and to importance is added a lively interest when we encounter on our way such a book as the *Ancren Riwle*. In content the *Riwle* consists mostly of traditional precepts for the outward and inward ordering of the cloistered life, supported after the medieval fashion by many passages quoted from the Bible and the Church Fathers. The author has no notion of aiming at originality; on the contrary, like most medieval writers on most subjects, he aims faithfully to hand on ancient truth, supported by ancient unquestionable authority. The power and the fascination of the *Riwle* arise from its author's complete mastery of his theme and his medium, and from his vividness and geniality. His substance is traditional; his way of speaking is his own, and there is life in every picture he draws. He is observant and thoughtful, and however often the things he says may have been said before, he makes them seem fresh and new because he has taken them up into himself and made them freshly his own in giving them new expression.

This fine quality in the *Ancren Riwle* was immediately felt. The book became a classic, was rewritten for general use, and for three centuries was one of the most widely read books in England. Indeed, in the course of time the *Riwle* was translated into French, and then into Latin; but of more concern to us is its long-continued popularity in its original English form. This enabled the *Riwle* to become a principal means of giving the great English religious writers of the fourteenth century a living, developed, flexible medium to work in. We do not know the names of some of these writers, but the most important of those whose names are known are Richard Rolle of Hampole, Walter Hilton, Juliana of Norwich, and Margery Kempe. The two latter lived on into the fifteenth century, but both are connected in spirit with the whole group of fourteenth-century writers who gave England in this period a great prose literature of Christian piety and mystical contemplation. Rolle, who died in 1349, wrote in both Latin and English; one of the more important of his treatises in English is *The Form of Living*. In this and other pieces he showed himself a master of a vivid, direct style which, underneath its reminiscences of Old English and its disguise of strange spellings, is surprisingly close to Modern English in structure. Walter Hilton was Rolle's later contemporary and lived until 1396. He was much influenced by Rolle, but was scarcely inferior to him in ability, and his writings appear to have been almost as popular as Rolle's. Both Rolle's writings and Hilton's still exist in very many more manuscript copies than can be found for the writings of Chaucer. And Hilton's continuing popularity is attested by the numerous editions of his *Scale of Perfection* and *Treatise of Mixed Life* which appeared after printing was introduced into England. Wynkyn de Worde printed both treatises about 1494, and they were reprinted in 1507, 1519, 1525, and 1533. There were also separate editions of the latter treatise in 1517 and 1531.

These mystical writings of the fourteenth century have been neglected by students of English literature, for reasons which are easy to understand, but impossible to defend. John Wiclif was a contemporary of Hilton, and a voluminous writer, at first in Latin, and then in English; and Wiclif also translated part of the Bible into English, and directed the translation of the rest. Wiclif was a man of learning, of great intellectual power, and of singular independence. He attacked worldliness and corruption in the Catholic Church, and was fired by opposition—very much as Martin Luther was, over a century later—to go further and further until he defiantly stigmatized the papacy as a personification of the spirit of Antichrist, denied the Catholic doctrine of transubstantiation, and encouraged all men to read the Bible and interpret it for themselves. Wiclif thus made himself a herald of the Protestant Reformation. In the light of subsequent events Protestant England looked back to him as a courageous leader, and remembered his controversial writings; whereas after the English Reformation in the sixteenth century Rolle and Hilton and the other mystical or devotional writers of the fourteenth century were almost completely forgotten.

As a consequence, one still hears Wiclif spoken of as "the father of English prose." Chaucer, to be sure, has never been forgotten, and Chaucer wrote prose, as well as verse, at about the same time as Wiclif. But it has rightly been felt that Chaucer's prose is undistinguished when not tiresomely pedestrian, and that Wiclif's is at least distinguished by vigor. Yet anyone who actually compares Wiclif and Hilton cannot fail to be struck at once by Hilton's superiority; and the explanation is not difficult to come by. The reader of Wiclif soon perceives that the great controversialist was hampered, when he turned to English late in life, by his earlier habit of writing in Latin, by his fund of Latin learning, and by his unfamiliarity with the living tradition of devotional English prose out of which Rolle and Hilton issued. The truth then is that Wiclif's prose really marks a retrogression; though it may be fair enough to say that Wiclif does stand at the head of a movement of more or less awkward experimentation which extended on through the fifteenth and sixteenth centuries and into the seventeenth, when writers were learning to use prose for many purposes other than devotional, and when at the same time they were being cut off from the tradition within which Rolle and Hilton worked.

The Fourteenth Century: Maturity and Independence

Discussion of Rolle and Hilton and Wiclif, and mention of Chaucer, has brought us into the great century of English medieval literature. We may say that by the early years of the fourteenth century the education of medieval man in England was complete. The problem of language was far from settled, but it became at any rate unmistakably clear as the century advanced that English was to be the spoken and literary tongue of Englishmen, even though it was not entirely clear until much later that English, and not Latin, was also to be the language of the learned and of works of learning. The problem of style too, in both prose and verse, was far from settled. But though experimentation was continuing, a great deal had been accomplished, and enough to make possible a literature in no need of indulgence from readers on the score of form or artistry. Above all, men themselves had become mature. Oxford had become a center of higher learning before the end of the twelfth century, and Cambridge early in the thirteenth, so that the English no longer were dependent on Paris and other continental universities for the sharpening of their wits. It is not easy to say just how important medieval university training was in the development of literature; but certainly by the fourteenth century Englishmen's wits were sharpened, and they were thoroughly at home in the fields of medieval learning and thought and story, could move about at their ease, and could handle traditional themes and forms with sure mastery—mastery and independence.

Often we associate independence with rebelliousness, because rebellion against the established order of things is an obvious sign of independence. In the fourteenth century the spirit of rebellion was active, as we have already seen in the case of Wiclif; and it was not confined to religion, but spread out into the whole field of social organization. The famous Peasants' Rising took place in 1381, and shows—in some ways even more impressively than the career of Wiclif or the remarkable, widespread literary activity of the time—the flood of energy which burst loose and animated the English people in the fourteenth century. England had suffered an especially severe visitation of the plague in 1348 and 1349, during which so many had died that a very serious shortage of labor had developed. The result was that wages rose and serfs began loudly to demand their freedom. They were already winning freedom gradually, which in part explains the situation. But now suddenly they began to demand freedom as a right. This was something new, and in it we catch our first glimpse of that sturdy self-respecting independence of spirit which in time came to be regarded as the peculiar characteristic of all Englishmen. "Freedom as a right" was revolutionary, and needed the most respectable and powerful sanction that could be found. It was immediately discovered that this had all along been the teaching of Christianity, which the Church had culpably neglected.

John Ball, a poor priest, was the chief instigator of the Rising, and for some twenty years before 1381 had been going about the countryside attacking both Church and State. We have a vivid report of his activities from Froissart, the French chronicler.

> Ball was accustomed [Froissart says] every Sunday after Mass, as the people were coming out of the church, to preach to them in the market-place and assemble a crowd around him, to whom he would say, "My good friends, things cannot go well in England, nor ever will until everything shall be in common; when there shall be neither vassal nor lord and all distinctions leveled, when the lords shall be no more masters than ourselves. How ill have they used us? And for what reason do they thus hold us in bondage? Are we not all descended from the same parents, Adam and Eve? And what can they show or what reasons give, why they should be more masters than ourselves?—except perhaps in making us labor and work for them to spend. They are clothed in velvets and rich stuffs, ornamented with ermine and other furs, while we are forced to wear poor cloth. They have handsome seats and manors, when we must brave the wind and rain in our labors in the field; but it is from our labor they have wherewith to support their pomp. We are called slaves, and if we do not perform our services we are beaten."

This incendiary appeal to what we now call class-hatred went further than the peasants themselves did when they finally rebelled in 1381; nevertheless, there is every reason to believe that a dissolving equalitarian doctrine was widely held. The popular cry was expressed in a couplet which was on everybody's lips:

> When Adam delved and Evé span,
> Who was then the gentleman?

And the noblemen, who based all their claims on birth and inheritance, not on their usefulness to society, had really nothing to answer to the question.

Still, though rebellion is unmistakable proof of independence, it is no necessary sign of it. Indeed, it generally defeats itself. The peasants in 1381 gained nothing by their rising, but on the contrary slowed up the economic change which was gradually giving them their freedom. Moreover, when we try to look at the fourteenth century as a whole, what we really see is a quite general awakening of the critical or questioning spirit, just as much awake and active in the author of *Piers Plowman* and in Chaucer as in Wiclif and John Ball. Yet neither Langland nor Chaucer was a rebel. Langland was passionately indignant over the corruption and abuses which he saw around him—but he was equally indignant at the friars and poor priests who were preaching communism as a quick and simple remedy:

They preach men of Plato and prove it by Seneca,
That all things under Heaven ought to be in common;
And yet he lieth, as I live, that to the unlearned so preacheth.

And Chaucer was not blind to any of the abuses or discontents of the time; his moral judgments are sound, even severe. Nevertheless, he was content to accept all he saw as part of a lively and varied picture which it would be no more sensible to attempt to change than it would be to wish for the moon—a picture which, too, was inexhaustibly interesting and amusing just as it was.

The New Verse

But when we turn from the prose literature we have been discussing to Chaucer's verse, we do instantly see that a literary revolution has occurred, whoever was responsible for it. Chaucer writes verse in accordance with the principles which, by and large, have governed English versification from his day to ours—and does it with a finished skill which has never been excelled. Briefly, Chaucer uses rime, and his lines have a regular number of syllables with the accents evenly distributed. Much of his verse is of the form that later was called the heroic couplet—lines normally of ten syllables and five accents each, riming in couplets. Some of his earlier verse is in the same form with a shorter line, of four feet—eight syllables with four accents—a form used often by Chaucer's predecessors on both sides of the Channel. The number of syllables may be, in the first of these forms, as few as nine or as many as eleven, or in the second as few as seven or as many as nine, the point of strict regularity being the number of accented or stressed syllables. Chaucer also uses a number of stanzaic forms, most often a stanza consisting of seven verses of five accents each, riming *a b a b b c c*, the so-called rime royal, which he introduced into English.

Now all of this marks a complete break with the Old English system of versification. It is something new, something radically different. But Chaucer did not invent it; he found it, and had the good sense to use it, and the talent to use it with perfect ease and sureness. The new versification came from France, and in a sense it was not new, even in England, by the time Chaucer began to write. Quite early in the Middle Ages, Catholic writers of hymns in Latin began to use rimes, and to desert ancient classical rhythms, based on quantity, for rhythms based on accent or stress, in which the length of syllables and, within rather narrow limits, the number also were secondary. These Latin hymns, many of them strikingly beautiful and exquisite in their artistry, served as examples in the matter of form when poets in the south of France, towards the beginning of the twelfth century, began to write secular lyrics in the vernacular. And this French poetry—or Provençal poetry, as it is usually called to distinguish it from northern French—served in turn as example and inspiration for all Europe.

We can easily see in a general way, even though the details are obscure and difficult, how the new versification became domesticated in England. As early as the beginning of the thirteenth century some English writers were trying to imitate in their own tongue the form of the Latin hymns. And the reason was that they were translating the hymns into English, and wanted their English versions to fit the music. There is no doubt that the requirements of music continued to exert pressure. One of the earliest Middle English secular lyrics, composed probably about 1225, is the famous "Cuckoo Song":

Sumer is icumen in,
Lhude sing cuccu!
Groweth sed and bloweth med
And springth the wude nu.
Sing cuccu!

Awe bleteth after lomb,
Lhouth after calve cu,
Bulluc sterteth, bucke verteth.
Murie sing cuccu!
Cuccu, cuccu,
Wel singes thu cuccu.
Ne swik thu naver nu!
Sing cuccu nu, Sing cuccu!
Sing cuccu, Sing cuccu nu!

This is not a translation, but it is a part song, written to be sung to music composed for a Latin hymn—and music which at the time was novel, indeed sophisticated. By far the greater portion of the surviving lyric poetry of the thirteenth and fourteenth centuries is religious, devotional, or moral in its content, and it is all in the new versification.

The Old Alliterative Verse

At the same time the Old English alliterative verse form was not forgotten. There is very little evidence to show how it was transmitted through the twelfth and thirteenth centuries, but in the second half of the fourteenth it was used by the author of *Piers Plowman,* and also by the poet from the northwestern part of England who wrote *Sir Gawain and the Green Knight* and, probably, *The Pearl, Purity,* and *Patience.* Others besides these two great poets used it in the fourteenth century, and it continued to be used occasionally in the next century, and even in the sixteenth. It was, however, a dying form. *Piers Plowman* is the last poem of any importance in strict alliterative verse, and it is in effect a demonstration that the old traditional form would no longer do. For one thing, though the rules are followed carefully enough, the result is very different from that obtained in Old English. And here we see another influence making for the new versification, in addition to the Latin hymns and the requirements of music. The linguistic changes which have already been discussed were great enough to make the language really a new kind of medium, with a new movement of its own, lighter and quicker than that of Old English. The rhythm of *Piers Plowman,* to the sensitive ear, is neither one thing nor the other; it falls between two stools, and seems merely awkward and slovenly. We continue to value *Piers Plowman,* not because its author was a great artist, but because he had deep feeling and keen insight and vivid imagination, and so contrived, despite grave artistic faults, to give us a picture of his age which still lives and breathes—and a picture, moreover, which is complementary to Chaucer's, so that anyone who hopes to understand the latter half of the fourteenth century must always study both writers.

What we see in *Sir Gawain* and *The Pearl* and in other poetry of the fourteenth century is more what we might expect—experimental work in which an attempt was being made to combine the traditional alliteration with the new verse forms. In these transitional pieces, however, the actual effect was mostly achieved by virtue of what was new—new and French; for the French influence on both form and content had by then become unmistakable and strong. From this poetry to Chaucer it is only a step or two; nevertheless, there was no gradual development out of the old alliterative verse into the new measures. The two systems are genuinely different, and the attempts made in the fourteenth century to effect a compromise between them led to nothing.

The Ballads

The popular poetry of the time shows how radical the change really was. Since the alliterative verse form did die slowly, it might have been expected to live on in poetry written for the unlearned mass of the people. But apparently nothing of the sort happened. Of course we do not know what has perished; still, a few ballads have survived which must have been originally composed in the thirteenth century or the fourteenth, and their verse form is clearly derived from the Latin hymns. Indeed it can be said in general of the popular English verse of the Middle Ages that it was passed down to the common people from the learned and aristocratic writers of the time. It was more or less transformed in its passage, and once the first impulses had been given, some independence in development took place. But the first impulses did come from Church and Court, and a firm grasp on this fact can help us to understand how completely true it is that English literature has issued out of an assimilation of foreign influences, even though it has remained unmistakably and thoroughly English. The popular ballads are justly admired by modern readers for their directness and freshness and simplicity, their apparent lack of sophistication united with a certain rude intensity. In many of the ballads, too, one finds a perception of the tragic quality of life which is elsewhere lacking in medieval literature—a perception suggesting that the composers were looking directly at realities of experience, undistracted by literary conventions. If, finally, we remember that these poems really were popular in appeal, we may fairly conclude that their character is indigenous. The ballads, in other words, actually are what they seem to be, and yet their points of origin are learned and foreign. And this is true not only of their form, but, in a number of cases, also of their themes—both showing the French influence.

Provençal Love Poetry and French Romances

The new French poetry which transformed the literature not only of England, but of Europe, was novel, and dazzling, in content as well as in versification. The new poetry of the south of France, of Provence, was chiefly lyrical, and its theme was love—the love of man for woman. The new poetry of northern France was chiefly narrative, and its theme was adventure, under the guise of far-off history. The first thing to strike us is that both kinds of poetry were secular, not religious. The Catholic Church had sought to encompass and dominate the whole life of man; the newly developing civilization of the Middle Ages was to be centered in the love of God; all of men's earthly activities were to be evaluated in terms of the spirit in which they were carried out. This was the theory, and a vast deal of practical wisdom went into its application. Amongst other things, a widespread if rather childish love for tales of strange adventure was not neglected. If we are tempted to smile upon being told that this love was satisfied by lives of saints, that is only because we are ignorant of the marvelous doings with which many of the saints were credited. Still, in the end, lives of saints did not satisfy; and the whole program of trying to give man's present existence, interests, and acts a religious coloring began to crack. As a new civilization developed, with the aid of the Church, upon the ruins of the Roman Empire, men's active interests in their own immediate affairs in this world developed too—and developed at the expense of interest in a promised life beyond death. The change in outlook was slow, and by no means always conscious or deliberate or consistent. Gradually it gained force and self-consciousness, but today it is not yet completed, and there is no reason to suppose it ever will be.

We at present are concerned only with the fact that tacit rebellion against the all-embracing claims of medieval Christianity showed itself distinctly in the Provençal and French poetry of the twelfth and thirteenth centuries. The new narrative poems composed in northern France were called romances, simply because *romance* was the term used to denote the language in which the poems were written. It was not until later that all of the European tongues derived from Latin were called *romance* languages. And meanwhile the word "romance" was acquiring a new and distinct literary meaning, derived from the special character of the French narratives. They were, in the beginning, merely tales of remote and strange adventure. Remoteness was necessary, because it helped belief. Medieval people are thought of as credulous, but they were quite as sharp-witted as we are, and often as skeptical or cynical as any sophisticated person of the present day, in the fields where they did have knowledge gained by experience or direct observation.

The difference between them and ourselves is that their knowledge of the external world was very limited, and that they all had an overwhelming sense of inferiority to the great men of ancient times, so that they tended to accept without question whatever they found in old books. Medieval people never lost consciousness of the fact that they were living upon the ruins of a great civilization, and the more civilized they themselves became, the more highly did they value whatever they could rescue, and understand, from the mighty past. Thus they were at one with the Church in giving a high authority to tradition. When they read in an ancient book that something or other was true of a remote place, they felt they had good reason for believing it, even though nothing at all like it was true within the limited field of their own experience. The world was large in those days, and might very well be full of wonders.

An instance or two may help us a great deal to understand this state of mind. We all know that there are no snakes in Ireland. About 1250 Bartholomaeus Anglicus (Bartholomew the Englishman) wrote a book in Latin which became famous all over Europe and was translated into English, French, and Spanish, and was much used, even as late as the end of the sixteenth century. It is entitled *De Proprietatibus Rerum,* and was written to explain allusions to the world of nature found in the Bible. As Bartholomew worked on it, it became in fact a kind of encyclopedia of natural knowledge—an account of the properties of things in general. And Bartholomew had learned what we know—that there are no snakes in Ireland; but he had also learned much more than this, which seemed to him equally reasonable and credible, and which he set down in good faith. He says:

> In Ireland is no serpent, no frogs, nor venomous spider; but all the land is so contrary to venomous beasts that if the earth of that land be brought into another land, and sprinkled on the ground, it slayeth serpents and toads. Also venomous beasts flee Irish wool, skins, and hides. And if serpents or toads be brought into Ireland by shipping, they die anon.

Bartholomew does not say where he learned this, but he used all the ancient authorities he could lay his hands on, and usually mentions them, as he does in his interesting account of the eagle:

> Augustine saith, and Pliny also, that in age the eagle hath darkness and dimness in eyes, and heaviness in wings. And against this disadvantage she is taught by nature to seek a well of springing water, and then she flieth up into the air as far as she may, till she be full hot by heat of the air, and by the labor of flight, and so then by heat the pores are opened and the feathers chafed, and she falleth suddenly into the well, and there the feathers are changed, and the dimness of her eyes is wiped away and purged, and she taketh again her might and strength.

The French romances, then, were written for people who were not childishly credulous, but who nevertheless could believe very strange things on the authority of tradition. The matter of these tales came from old books which purported to be histories, and the characters were historical figures out of the mighty past. Three spacious fields of history, or of presumed history, had the strongest appeal: Stories were told of Charlemagne and his peers, of King Arthur of Britain and his Knights of the Round Table, and of "Rome the Great." This last field really included all of classical antiquity, and within it fell tales of Alexander the Great, of Thebes, and of Troy. The fact that these stories were supposed to have a basis in history gave them a considerable part of their value. Hence as the demand grew for more tales, writers did not go out into new fields, but multiplied incidents and characters related to what was already familiar. So cycles grew up, and particularly in the case of King Arthur an immense body of legend accumulated which formed in a rough way a detailed account of Arthur's whole life and of the lives and adventures of all his knights. The story of Sir Gawain, exquisitely retold in English by a northern poet late in the fourteenth century, gained incalculably in interest because, though it was an episode complete in itself, it was told about one of Arthur's knights and had its beginning and its end at Arthur's court.

So far, these romances, though obviously secular, not sacred, in their theme and intent, may not appear to bear out the assertion that they represent a movement of rebellion, or of emancipation, from medieval Christianity. But though the matter—the characters and events—of these tales was historical, or supposedly historical, and remote; the dress, the manners, customs, social relationships, the whole atmosphere and life were contemporary. Under the guise of "history" the poets drew idealized pictures of the feudal society around them, and put into graphic form the code of conduct and the scale of values which governed that society. We have seen earlier in this chapter how feudalism, though it was an organization built on close personal loyalties, drew a sharp line between classes, and threw its whole weight behind the strict determination of status by heredity. If you were born a peasant, you were basely born and had a base nature, and basely must you live. It was not admitted that you could have good personal qualities; the mere circumstance of your inherited status answered every question about you, and determined your position in life—unless, indeed, you escaped into the Church, which was always possible, but often far from easy. You could not then be noble, in any sense of the word, unless your parentage was noble; but if your parentage was noble, you were presumed because of that fact to have the qualities of nobility, in the widest sense of the word. You were expected to be a person worthy of your birth, to live up to your birth. You had blue blood, you were a superior being, and the outward marks of your superiority were loyalty, bravery, courtesy, generosity, and gallantry to women. Except for the last, these were virtues agreeable to the spirit of Christianity, and indeed the Church played an important part in helping to civilize feudal brigands and bullies by inculcating the principle that *noblesse oblige;* and as feudalism flowered into chivalry in the eleventh and twelfth centuries the Church tried to make knighthood a consecration to piety as well as to the moral code of the gentleman. But in the long run nothing could obscure the fact that secular standards of conduct, to some extent inherited from pagan Germanic ancestors, were developing independently of Christianity, and not only that, but in opposition to the spirit and letter of Christian belief.

For it was of the essence of the medieval knightly system which we call chivalry that the standards of the gentleman were based on birth and breeding—not on grace or on any religious foundation, but on noble blood and what is due to noble blood. No acquirement, bestowed, or gained by good works, could be a substitute. (At the beginning of the seventeenth century James I said to his old nurse: "I'll mak' your son a *baronet* gin ye like, Luckie, but the de'il himself couldna' mak' him a gentleman.") Furthermore, as the most important achievement of the lyric poets of Provence in the twelfth century, there was developed, in fundamental opposition to Christianity, what can only be called a rival religion, which became an integral part of the chivalric code. This was the worship of gentle-born women—or what we still call romantic love, though in modern times the medieval assumption that such love was possible only for the gentle-born has practically been discarded. It was a new thing; there had been nothing like it in the ancient world, or amongst the pagan Germanic tribes. No one has been able to explain exactly how or why it appeared. Briefly, it demanded that a gentlewoman be regarded as the incarnation of a spirit as worthy of worship as the true God—there is no other way to express it—and that she receive abject and wholehearted devotion from her knightly lover. He was to submit himself humbly to her every wish; whatever he did, whatever warlike exploits he performed, whatever adventures he undertook—all were to be looked upon as services in honor of his lady. In sum, the knight owed his lady the kind of loyalty he owed his feudal lord. And there was the further correspondence with the feudal system that a lady was expected to reward devotion, and was considered unworthy if she did not meet love with love. Since, moreover, love must be entirely free if it really is love, it was for the medieval knight and his lady a thing wholly apart from marriage. Normally the medieval knight devoted himself to another man's wife, as Launcelot devoted himself to Guinevere, the wife of King Arthur. It has been said that medieval courtly love can be expressed in the words Humility, Courtesy, Worship, Adultery. Howsoever abject the knight might be, he was not content with worship from afar, and complete union with his beloved was his object.

Romantic love was not only opposed to Christianity because it was lawless love, but, perhaps even more, because it was earthly love—such devotion paid to a creature as could properly be paid only to the Creator. However it began, it took fast hold upon medieval courtly society; and when priests condemned it, the poets retaliated by centering all knightly virtues more and more in love as a noble and ennobling passion which alone could kindle honor, courtesy, true loyalty, and the rest. The audacity of Aucassin, in the thirteenth-century romance entitled *Aucassin and Nicolette,* is famous, and typical of the spirit which was aroused by opposition. Aucassin is told by the captain who had bought Nicolette as a slave-girl that if he had succeeded in making her his mistress, his soul would certainly be destined to lie in Hell. To this Aucassin replies:

In Paradise what have I to win? Therein I seek not to enter, but only to have Nicolette, my sweet lady that I love so well. For into Paradise go none but such folk as I shall tell thee now: Thither go these same old priests, and halt old men and maimed, who all day and night cower continually before the altars, and in the crypts; and such folk as wear old amices and old clouted frocks, and naked folk and shoeless, and covered with sores, perishing of hunger and thirst, and of cold, and of little ease. These be they that go into Paradise, with them have I naught to make. But into Hell would I fain go; for into Hell fare the goodly clerks, and goodly knights that fall in tourneys and great wars, and stout men at arms, and all men noble. With these would I gladly go. And thither pass the sweet ladies and courteous that have two lovers, or three, and their lords also thereto. Thither goes the gold, and the silver, and cloth of vair, and cloth of gris, and harpers, and poets, and the prince of this world. With these I would gladly go, let me but have with me Nicolette, my sweetest lady.

Allegory and Romance

The French romances which began as tales of knightly adventure under the guise of history were rapidly transformed by this new discovery of the Provençal poets into love stories. And whereas the persons in these tales had been at first only pegs on which to hang the action, in which interest was centered, characters began, with the growth of sentiment, to be individualized, and action tended to be subordinated to inward conflicts of feeling. For the representation of such conflicts the medieval poet inevitably turned to allegory. The allegorical method was not invented in the Middle Ages, as we might imagine from what is sometimes said of it. The early Christians inherited it from late classical literature; and in truth, as we perceive the moment we stop to ask what it really is, allegory must go back well-nigh to the beginnings of human effort to express thought. For, in essence, allegory is simply the representation of something immaterial by a visible or picturable embodiment. The more apt or appropriate the embodiment seems to be, the more effective the allegory; but, in general, allegory is simply an emblematic way of speaking. Nevertheless, there is reason for associating allegory particularly with the Middle Ages, because it was then an all-pervasive mode of thought and art. Christian preachers were confirmed in the habit of interpreting everything in the Bible as possessing an emblematic significance lying behind its literal meaning; and this habit had been extended to the whole visible world and the course of human history. It was indeed a magnificent conception—the world of nature itself regarded as an allegory devised by the Creator—but we cannot help feeling that medieval writers ran it into the ground. The odd behavior of the eagle, for example, as recorded by Bartholomew in a passage quoted earlier in this chapter, was interpreted as follows:

Man is like the eagle—old in his hidden sins, before he becomes a Christian. And thus he renews himself when he goes to church. Before he was able to bethink him of his sins his eyes were dim. At church, forsaking Satan and every sinful deed, he betaketh himself to Jesus Christ, for He shall be his reward. He believes in our Lord Christ, and learns the priest's teachings, and from his eyes departs the mist while he tarries there. His hope is all turned to God, and he learns of His love—that is the sun certainly—and thus he regains his sight. Naked he falls into the font-vessel, and comes out all new.

This is sad stuff, but all the more convincing as evidence of the extent to which the habit of seeing things emblematically was ingrained. Hence it was natural—really, as was said above, inevitable—that when the medieval poet wished to represent something invisible he should personify it. The classical example of this, and the source of much that followed it in English as well as French poetry, is *The Romance of the Rose,* written in the thirteenth century by Guillaume de Lorris, and continued, in a satirical spirit, by Jean de Meung. The narrator falls asleep and in his dream finds himself by a walled garden which Idleness invites him to enter. The garden is the world of courtly society, and in its midst is a rose plot hedged about, which represents a young girl. The efforts of the poet to pluck a rose are obstructed by Shame, Danger, and the like personages, and aided by Pity, Innocence, and Fair Welcome. The plan may seem coldly artificial when reduced to a bare skeleton, but the poet was really engaged in representing the conflict of feelings within the mind and heart of the young girl, and anyone who reads the poem with close attention is altogether likely to conclude that the poet's method is strikingly successful.

Progress of Romance in England

The whole development of romance here sketched can be illustrated from English poems of the late thirteenth and the fourteenth centuries, modeled upon or, often, freely translated from French romances. Thus the English *Guy of Warwick* and *Sir Bevis of Hampton* illustrate the first stage, in which martial adventure was the main thing. A reader of *Sir Bevis* has calculated that this hero, aside from slaughter which he effected with others in set battles, killed more than six hundred and fifty human beings with his own hand before he settled down into tranquil domestic life. Professor Hearnshaw continues: Sir Bevis "lived as dangerously as even a Nietzsche or a Mussolini could desire; but of any good that he did, or ideal that inspired him, or end that he achieved, there is not a suggestion. Psychologically he is no more interesting than a modern machine-gun."

Yet from such an unpromising beginning there did develop the romance in which, while strange and thrilling adventure was still prominent, the representation of knights and ladies as embodiments of the courtly ideal became a chief object. The fourteenth-century *Sir Launfal* attributed to Thomas Chester is a good example of an early stage in this transition; for in this tale politeness and good breeding are shown through a course of action which is irresponsibly conceived, without any regard for serious characterization. But in *Sir Gawain and the Green Knight* we have a fine instance of the same kind of tale in which the interest in characterization has become strong, and the ability to satisfy it mature.

And then finally in *The Pearl* and in *Piers Plowman* and in Chaucer's *House of Fame* we have English examples of the dream which furnishes the setting for an allegory in which the poet emblematically sets forth his theme. Only the last of these deals with earthly love, but of course the dream-setting and the allegorical method could, once they had become established, be used for the handling of any theme. In the greatest of English medieval love romances, Chaucer's *Troilus and Criseyde,* the allegorical method is cast aside, though the center of interest is where the French allegorical romance had finally placed it—in characterization and in inward conflicts of feeling. In this beautifully and subtly wrought tale we see Chaucer, as we see him again, though in a different way, in the *Canterbury Tales,* stepping outside of the enchanted realm of romance, into the more familiar field of direct observation and realistic treatment. He saw the unreality of the high-flown heroes of romance and their ladies, and parodied chivalrous adventure and courtly love in *Sir Thopas.* The Nun's Priest says humorously that his tale of Chanticleer is just as true, he can promise his fellow-pilgrims, as is the book of *Lancelot du Lac* which women hold in high esteem; and the Squire, when he comes to tell of his knight at the court of Cambuscan, says he spoke so politely

> That Gawain, with his olde curteisye,
> Though he were come ageyn out of Fairye,
> Ne coude him nat amende with a word.

The Squire also feels that no man but Launcelot could have been adequate to describe the courteous love-making at Cambuscan's court—and Launcelot is dead.

Reaction Against Romance

This kind of thing, we say, shows that Chaucer is "modern." And indeed Chaucer

The Green Knight appears at the Court of King Arthur

"For he held up the head in his hand, and turned the face towards them that sat on the high daïs, and it lifted up the eyelids and looked upon them and spake as ye shall hear. 'Look, Gawain, that thou art ready to go as thou hast promised, and seek loyally till thou find me, even as thou hast sworn in this hall in the hearing of these knights. Come thou, I charge thee, to the Green Chapel; such a stroke as thou hast dealt thou hast deserved, and it shall be promptly paid thee on New Year's morn. Many men know me as the Knight of the Green Chapel, and if thou askest, thou shall not fail to find me. Therefore it behooves thee to come, or to yield thee as recreant.'" (See page 123.)

The two illustrations on this page are copies of the original pictures in the manuscript of *Sir Gawain and the Green Knight* in the British Museum.

Sir Gawain meets the Green Knight at the Green Chapel

"Then the Green Knight drew off from him and leaned on his ax, setting the shaft on the ground, and looked on Gawain as he stood all armed and faced him fearlessly—at heart it pleased him well. Then he spake merrily in a loud voice, and said to the knight, 'Bold sir, be not so fierce; no man here hath done thee wrong, nor will do, save by covenant, as we made at Arthur's court.'" (See page 140.)

¶The Tale of The Nonnys preest

¶ And here begynnyth his tale

A Poure wydow som dele y stept in age
Was somtyme dwellyng in a cotage
Beside a groue stondyng in a dale
This wydow of which I telle you my tale
Syn that day that she was last a wyf
In pacience ledde a ful sympyl lyf
For lytil was her catel and her rent
By husbondry of suche as god her sent
She fonde her self and eke her doughtryn two
Thre large sowys had she and nomo
Thre kyne & eek a sheep that hight malle
Wel soty was her bour and eek her halle
In whyche she eet many a slender meel
Of poynaunt sawce ne knewe she neuer a deel
Ne deynte morsel passyd thorough her throte

E iij

The illustrations on this page and the facing page are from the first illustrated edition of Chaucer's *The Canterbury Tales*. (Courtesy of The Pierpont Morgan Library.)

¶ The tale of the Pardoner

For though my self be a ful vicious man
A moralle tale yet I you telle can
Whiche I am wont for to preche and also wynne
Now holde your pees my tale I wol begynne

¶ Here endyth the prologue
Of the Pardoner

¶ And begynneth the Tale

IN flaundris sumtyme was a companye
Of yonge folke that haunteden folye
As ryot hazard Stewys and tauarnys
Where as wyth harpes lutes and gyternes
They daunce and pleye at the dyce both day & nyght
And etyn also & drynkyn aboue her myght
Thorow whiche they doon the deuyl sacrifise

This illustrated edition of *The Canterbury Tales* was printed by William Caxton at his press in Westminster in 1484. (Courtesy of The Pierpont Morgan Library.)

¶ Capitulum primum

It was a kyng that hyghte Melyodas/and he
was lord and kynge of the countre of Lyonas
And this Melyodas was a lykely knyght as
ony was that tyme lyuynge/And by fortune
he wedded kynge Markys syster of Cornewaille / And she
was called Elyzabeth that was callyd bothe good and fair
And at that tyme kynge Arthur regned / and he was hole
kynge of Englond / walys and Scotland & of many other
royammes how be it there were many kynges that were lordes
of many countreyes/but alle they held their landes of kyng
Arthur/for in walys were two kynges/and in the north we
re many kynges / And in Cornewail and in the west were
two kynges/ ¶ Also in Irland were two or thre kynges
and al were vnder the obeissaunce of kyng Arthur/So was
the kynge of Fraunce and the kyng of Bretayn and all the
lordshippes vnto Rome/So whan this kyng Melyodas hadde
ben with his wyf/within a whyle she waxid grete with child
and she was a ful meke lady/and wel she loued her lord/&
he her ageyne/soo there was grete ioye betwixe them / Thenne
ther was a lady in that countrey that had loued kynge Melyodas longe/And by no meane she neuer coude gete his loue
therfore she lete ordeyne vpon a day as kynge Melyodas rode
on huntynge/for he was a grete chacer / and there by an en-
chauntement she made hym chace an herte by hym self alone/til
that he came to an old Castel/ and there anone he was taken
prysoner by the lady that hym loued/Whanne Elyzabeth kyng
Melyodas myst her lord/and she was nygh oute of her wytte
and also as grete with child as she was she took a gentylwo
man with her/and ranne in to the forest to seke her lord /
And whanne she was ferre in the forest she myghte no ferther
for she bygan to trauaille fast of her child/And she had ma
ny grymly throwes/her gentylwoman halp her alle that she
myghte/And soo by myracle of oure lady of heuen she was
delyuerd with grete paynes/But she had taken suche cold for
the defaute of helpe that depe draughtes of deth toke her / that
nedes she must dye and departe oute of this world/ther was

¶ Here begynneth a treatyse how ẏ hye
fader of heuen sendeth dethe to so-
mon euery creature to come and
gyue a counte of theyr lyues in
this worlde/and is in maner
of a morall playe.

Above is a page from Sir Thomas Malory's *Le Morte D'Arthur,* printed by William Caxton in 1485. (Courtesy of The Pierpont Morgan Library.) At the right is a page from the edition of *Everyman* printed about 1530 by John Skot, another early English printer.

is just as "modern" as we are "medieval." For he was by no means alone in perceiving that the proper home of the heroes and ladies of the age of chivalry was in fairyland. Many before him, and some of them in England, had revolted against the violation of common sense, or common observation, of which the writers of conventional romance were guilty. In particular, the romantic idealization of woman provoked satirical retort, often savage in its intensity of denunciation—the general opinion being that actually women were incapable of constancy or truth, and were sensual, impulsive, and inherently trivial in nature. But of wider scope in their anti-romantic character were the numerous beast stories, similar to the Nun's Priest's tale of Chanticleer, which exhibit a humorous but determined worldly wisdom—shrewd, selfish, practical, close to reality as medieval people knew it in their own experience.

Similar in effect were the *fabliaux*—usually coarse, always comic, often dealing with people from the middle or lower classes—and more destructive of the fragile spell of romance than direct satire. *Fabliau* means in this connection simply "tale" or "story"; but the kind of story to which this name has been attached is the medieval form of what today would be called the "dirty" or "smutty" story. Members of the clergy running after women were favorite objects of rudely humorous attack in these stories, as were, also, inconstant women themselves, and foolish husbands. Practically the only English examples of the *fabliau* which have survived are to be found in the *Canterbury Tales*. It is considered certain that *fabliaux* circulated in England, but in days when comparatively few could read, and when books existed only in expensive manuscript copies, much was passed about by word of mouth, to perish at last without trace.

Miracle Plays

Fortunately, however, another species of popular literature has survived in a considerable number of examples, to prove that in the fourteenth century the English were fond of broad realistic comedy. This species is the vernacular miracle play. In the wreck of ancient civilization drama had disappeared from view more completely than other kinds of literature, and in the Middle Ages it had a new birth, followed by an independent development up to the time of the Renaissance. The new birth occurred at the church altar, as early as the ninth century, though in England not before the end of the tenth century. It came as one consequence of the varied and pertinacious efforts of clerics to impress the gospel story upon those who could not read. A certain dramatic element is inherent in the ceremonial of the mass itself; and in the ninth and tenth centuries the Divine Office for Easter, and then that for Christmas, began to be elaborated in order to render more vivid the sacred events which they commemorated. The Divine Office is a service distinct from the mass, and was early divided into eight "hours"—Matins, Lauds, Prime, Terce, Sext, None, Vespers, and Compline—distributed throughout the day. At Easter during Matins there was a representation of the three Marys at the Sepulcher, and at Christmas during the Divine Office a representation of the Shepherds seeking the Manger and also of the Magi prostrating themselves before the infant Christ. These representations were accompanied by tropes, which were brief dialogues sung, not spoken, in Latin. Once begun, these innovations proved so popular that they gradually underwent expansion; and by the end of the twelfth century fairly well-developed dramatic scenes were being presented, with the dialogue spoken—no longer sung—and spoken in French.

As the thirteenth century opened, sacred dramatizations were outgrowing the churches. First they were banished to the church porch, and then in time they were banished wholly from the church precincts, while some of the clergy endeavored vainly to abolish them altogether. The miracles, as they were now called, had become too popular—too popular in the sense that they were being enjoyed, not for the light they cast on sacred story, but for their own dramatic qualities; and also in the sense that they were being transformed into grotesque and hilarious pieces of buffoonery. The first impulse in this latter direction had probably also been given from within the Church, in the extraordinary license long permitted the clergy in minor orders and the choir-boys, in many great churches, at the Feast of Fools and on other occasions.

In 1264 the Feast of Corpus Christi was instituted, though it was not officially established until 1311. Before the latter date, however, it began to be celebrated, on the Thursday after Trinity Sunday, in part by a processional service in which the guilds, or merchants' associations, marched with great banners. Coming in the early summer, it was a convenient time for open-air activities. And the guilds took over the miracle plays which were being banished from the churches and which the populace would not let die, and began to perform them on Corpus Christi Day. Just when the miracles came completely under secular control, or when they began to be written and spoken in English, or when they came to be grouped in series, we do not know, except that it was during the fourteenth century. But we do know that by this time the miracles had grown until they formed series, or cycles, of scenes representing in order the whole course of sacred history. We still have the cycles performed at York, Wakefield (though an attempt has recently been made to show that many of these plays really belong to some town in Lancashire), and Chester, and the so-called Coventry Cycle, mistakenly attributed to the town of Coventry in the seventeenth century. These cycles were under the control of the municipalities where they were performed, and plays were assigned to different guilds. At York the Armorers had the responsibility of staging the Expulsion from Paradise, the Shipwrights the Building of Noah's Ark, the Fishermen and Mariners the Flood, the Goldsmiths the Adoration of the Magi, the Bakers the Last Supper, and so on. The York Cycle was comprised in fifty-four scenes, of which forty-eight are extant. The Chester Cycle was comprised in twenty-five scenes. Because of the procession above mentioned, the cycles usually were played processionally. For each scene there was a raised platform on wheels, with space underneath the platform to which the actors retired in the intervals between their appearances, and in which also stage properties were kept. At various points in the streets were stations at which each movable stage stopped in turn, while the scene for which it was designed was enacted. As the cycles grew, more time was required for their presentation, and the annual performances could not be confined to Corpus Christi Day. At Chester three days were needed, during which the town was crowded, and there was a joyful holiday spirit much in evidence.

The composers were of course for the most part restricted by their source, the Bible; but in certain scenes they were allowed considerable freedom. Throughout they consulted popular taste, and where there was opportunity they introduced clowning and comedy. In general it cannot be said that the writers of the miracles advanced very far towards drama in the full sense, but they did give satisfaction to a strong and widespread taste for dramatic representation, which in the fifteenth century expanded into a demand for performances in which purely secular themes were treated dramatically and in which there was more scope for comedy. These were called interludes—the word meaning, most probably, a play carried on between two or more performers. The interludes were usually quite short, and were enacted by strolling companies of players. Looking back, we can see them as one essential connecting link between the miracle plays and the fully developed English drama of the late sixteenth century; but in the fifteenth century they were considered a troublesome innovation by those who performed the miracles, and there were conflicts between the amateur actors of the guilds and the emerging class of professional actors.

Morality Plays

Another service performed by the writers of the miracles was the sanction their practice gave to the mixture of the comic with the serious. And they did, in some of their scenes, make an advance towards the study and representation of individual character. But as the interest in character developed, the same thing happened that had happened in the case of the romances. At the end of the fourteenth century and in the fifteenth, writers turned to allegory in order to represent dramatically, by personifications, inward conflicts of feeling or motive. The subject most often treated in this fashion was the universal one—the conflict between the vices and the virtues for the soul of man. Hence comes the name applied to these pieces—morality plays. There are some thirty of them extant, dating from the fifteenth and early sixteenth centuries. By far the best is the famous play entitled *Everyman*. The moralities suffered from a number of limitations which made the type inevitably a temporary or transitional one, but in the fifteenth century they marked an important advance towards fully developed drama. The essence of the dramatic is a situation—a conflict between two sides—and this is exactly what was achieved in the moralities. But beyond this, English drama did not go within our present period.

Fifteenth Century Decadence

In the field of poetry the fifteenth century achieved nothing of great importance. Chaucer died at the end of the fourteenth century, and his well-bred and talented contemporary, John Gower, a few years later. The two together overawed their successors. Some, especially in Scotland, were by no means insignificant or without talent. Nevertheless, taking them as a whole, they were mere imitators; and some of them quite failed to perceive how far Chaucer had gone beyond conventional medieval practice. The names of these weak brethren are mentioned by conscientious historians—Thomas Occleve and John Lydgate, both of whom died about 1450; and, amongst Scottish Chaucerians, King James I (1394–1436), Robert Henryson (1425–1500), William Dunbar (who lived until about 1520), Gawin Douglas (died about 1522), and Sir David Lyndsay (1490–1555). Dunbar and Douglas carry us well beyond our period; and Lyndsay, though he too was a poetical son of Chaucer, was not even born before the close of our period.

The internal condition of England during the fifteenth century was very unsettled. The medieval social organization was breaking up, and no one saw what was to come next, nor was there a strong central government able to preserve even an outward semblance of order. Political and social unrest certainly were not favorable to literature, but these factors alone cannot account for the stagnation into which England fell in the fifteenth century. Probably the best explanation is simply this: the framework of belief and aspiration which had sufficed for the Middle Ages had lost its compelling force under disillusioning experience, and nothing was yet in sight to take its place.

How drab, confined, and materialized people had become can be seen from the long series of *The Paston Letters* written to one another in this century by members of a Norfolk family who were almost wholly concerned with the preservation and increase of their property during troubled times. And those who were not wholly absorbed, like the Pastons, with their own day-to-day practical affairs, could only look back with longing to the good old days, or amuse themselves with accounts of the marvelous things to be observed in distant lands. Thus the *Voiage and Travaile of Sir John Maundeville* was put into English early in the century, and long had a great vogue. "Maundeville" was supposed to have been a fourteenth-century Englishman, but was really an invented character upon whom the supposed travels were fathered by the actual author, who lived in Liége, gathered his material from earlier travel narratives, and wrote his book in French. "Sir John" entertained his readers with many decidedly curious observations. He would not have believed these things himself, he says, had he not actually seen them. In Ethiopia, for example, he saw men with only a single foot who could travel extraordinarily fast by hopping, "and the foot is so large that it shades all the body from the sun, when they lie down to rest." Elsewhere he saw dog-headed men; and he saw ant-hills of gold dust; and diamonds the size of hazel-nuts which fed on the dew of heaven, and grew together, male and female, and brought forth small diamonds.

Sir Thomas Malory

There was, however, one superlative achievement which issued in this century from discontent with present realities and longing for the departed grandeur of the age of chivalry. This was the *Morte d'Arthur,* written by Sir Thomas Malory, and printed by Caxton in 1485. Malory used a great many French romances, adapting and condensing them, and loosely binding them together. In effect he gives a view of Arthur's whole imagined career, interrupted by accounts of the adventures of the Knights of the Round Table—one of these being the long search for the Holy Grail. It has been said that in parts of his book Malory only half understood the material he was using, and certainly the *Morte d'Arthur* is at times mystifying, incoherent, fragmentary, and inconsistent. Nevertheless, one would not have it different. It does possess unity of style and atmosphere, and both, one feels, are exactly right. The prose of Malory is almost childlike, the right kind for a fairy story; and the atmosphere is that of an enchanted world, so different from the real one that a reader is perplexed to find creatures of flesh and blood with very human passions moving about in it. All in all, Malory caught better than any other English writer the unreality, the noble and moving aspiration, the beauty, the brutality, the aristocratic courtliness, and the vague conventionalized scenery of medieval romance, and in so doing caught a great part of what is most distinctive in the Middle Ages, and bequeathed it to following generations.

Caxton

It was said above that the *Morte d'Arthur* was printed by Caxton in 1485. William Caxton deserves a place in any account of English literature, because he introduced printing into England. He learned the art on the Continent, and then set up a press at Westminster in 1475. He printed over seventy different books, of which the *Morte d'Arthur* was the fifty-second. Many of his books were translations, and he himself translated some twenty of the works he printed; for he was a translator and editor as well as a printer. Not only do his prefaces and epilogues possess great personal interest, but they have a place in the development of prose. Caxton admired the clarity and ease of French prose, and himself attained both qualities in some of his own writing, though he also had notions about the "improving" of English which were not fortunate. His printing press brings us to the threshold of the modern age, but Caxton himself, like so many of his contemporaries, looked back towards the Middle Ages. It has been remarked that his collection of printed books bears a close resemblance to the library formed by the Paston family, containing "the same mixture of poetry, chivalrous romances, moral allegories, and books of devotion." The fact is that Caxton was first of all a practical tradesman, and anxiously consulted existing popular taste. His immediate successors were men much like him, though perhaps without his abundant energy and geniality. The net result was that in England the modern age was ushered in by a flood of books recalling and in a sense renewing the atmosphere and spirit of medievalism.

SIR GAWAIN AND THE GREEN KNIGHT[1]

This poem is preserved in a manuscript of the Cotton collection in the British Museum. The manuscript dates from the end of the fourteenth century or early in the fifteenth, but *Sir Gawain and the Green Knight* was probably composed about 1370. Of the author nothing is known save what can be gathered from this work—or from this work and from the *Pearl, Purity,* and *Patience* (three other poems found in the same manuscript), if, as most scholars think on the basis of internal evidence, all four are by the same author. In either case we can say that he was probably a native of Lancashire, as he uses the West Midland dialect; he was also a highly educated and cultivated gentleman, familiar with the best society of his day. "He had a keen eye, a vivid imagination, and a love for external phenomena, that gave him a power for description unequaled in Middle English literature. He was a lover of details; but he handled the details with a constructive power and a picturesqueness that create vivid impressions or realistic scenes. His observation of dress, of color, of position, of relative location, of deportment, enabled him at the opening of the piece to make of a conventional situation an intense, rich, dramatic scene with a splendid background. . . . He caught, and makes us feel, the very spirit of nature in varied moods, spring, summer, autumn—but especially nature in her wilder aspects, the biting winter, the icy rain, the dreary forest, the rugged rocks, the snow-covered country, and the cold hills lost in mist" (J. E. Wells, *Manual of the Writings in Middle English,* pp. 56–57). It should be added that this author had, too, real feeling for the higher spirit of chivalry and an uncommon fineness of nature. It is believed that he drew the materials for his story from a Norman-French romance now lost—which, in turn, was based on Celtic legend—but that his delicate treatment of the materials is all his own. *Sir Gawain and the Green Knight* is by general consent the best of the English romances. It is also interesting for the picture it gives of the earlier Gawain; for in the beginning he was without peer for courage and courtesy among the knights of the Round Table. It was only later that he came to be depreciated for the sake of others, and it is unfortunate that both Malory and Tennyson have contributed to make him best known as an "empty-headed, empty-hearted worldling."

For the Middle English text see *Sir Gawain and the Green Knight,* ed. with Introduction, full notes, and glossary by J. R. R. Tolkien and E. V. Gordon (Oxford, corrected edition 1930). The original manuscript has been reproduced in *Pearl, Cleanness, Patience and Sir Gawain,* ed. Israel Gollancz, the Early English Text Society (Oxford, 1923). Jessie L. Weston supplies commentary and background in *The Legend of Sir Gawain; Studies upon its Original Scope and Significance* (London, 1897); more recent is *A Study of Gawain and the Green Knight,* by G. L. Kittredge (Cambridge, U. S. A., 1916). Miss Weston has given complete translations, in the original meters, of *Sir Gawain* and the three other poems attributed to the same poet in a volume entitled *Romance, Vision, and Satire* (Boston, 1912).

I

AFTER the siege and the assault of Troy, when that burg was destroyed and burnt to ashes, and the traitor tried for his treason, 5 the noble Aeneas and his kin sailed forth to become princes and patrons of well-nigh all the Western Isles. Thus Romulus built Rome (and gave to the city his own name, which it bears even to this day); and Ticius turned him to Tuscany; and Langobard raised him up dwellings in Lombardy; and Felix Brutus sailed far over the French flood, and founded the kingdom of Britain,

[1]This translation is by Miss Jessie L. Weston. It forms the first volume in the series of "Arthurian Romances unrepresented in Malory's *Morte d' Arthur*" published by David Nutt.

wherein have been war and waste and wonder, and bliss and bale, ofttimes since.

And in that kingdom of Britain have been wrought more gallant deeds than in any other; but of all British kings Arthur was the most valiant, as I have heard tell; therefore will I set forth a wondrous adventure that fell out in his time. And if ye will listen to me, but for a little while, I will tell it even as it stands in story stiff and strong, fixed in the letter, as it hath long been known in the land.

King Arthur lay at Camelot upon a Christmas-tide, with many a gallant lord and lovely lady, and all the noble brotherhood of the Round Table. There they held rich revels with gay talk and jest; one while they would ride forth to joust and tourney, and again back to the court to make carols;[2] for there was the feast holden fifteen days with all the mirth that men could devise, song and glee, glorious to hear, in the daytime, and dancing at night. Halls and chambers were crowded with noble guests, the bravest of knights and the loveliest of ladies, and Arthur himself was the comeliest king that ever held a court. For all this fair folk were in their youth, the fairest and most fortunate under heaven, and the king himself of such fame that it were hard now to name so valiant a hero.

Now the New Year had but newly come in, and on that day a double portion was served on the high table to all the noble guests, and thither came the king with all his knights, when the service in the chapel had been sung to an end. And they greeted each other for the New Year, and gave rich gifts, the one to the other (and they that received them were not wroth, that may ye well believe!), and the maidens laughed and made mirth till it was time to get them to meat. Then they washed and sat them down to the feasting in fitting rank and order, and Guinevere the queen, gaily clad, sat on the high daïs. Silken was her seat, with a fair canopy over her head, of rich tapestries of Tars, embroidered, and studded with costly gems; fair she was to look upon, with her shining gray eyes, a fairer woman might no man boast himself of having seen.

But Arthur would not eat till all were served, so full of joy and gladness was he, even as a child; he liked not either to lie long, or to sit long at meat, so worked upon him his young blood and his wild brain. And another custom he had also, that came of his nobility, that he would never eat upon an high day till he had been advised of some knightly deed, or some strange and marvelous tale, of his ancestors, or of arms, or of other ventures. Or till some stranger knight should seek of him leave to joust with one of the Round Table, that they might set their lives in jeopardy, one against another, as fortune might favor them. Such was the king's custom when he sat in hall at each high feast with his noble knights; therefore on that New Year tide, he abode, fair of face, on the throne, and made much mirth withal.

Thus the king sat before the high tables, and spake of many things; and there good Sir Gawain was seated by Guinevere the queen, and on her other side sat Agravain, *à la dure main;*[3] both were the king's sister's sons and full gallant knights. And at the end of the table was Bishop Bawdewyn, and Ywain, King Urien's son, sat at the other side alone. These were worthily served on the daïs, and at the lower tables sat many valiant knights. Then they bare the first course with the blast of trumpets and waving of banners, with the sound of drums and pipes, of song and lute, that many a heart was uplifted at the melody. Many were the dainties, and rare the meats; so great was the plenty they might scarce find room on the board to set on the dishes. Each helped himself as he liked best, and to each two were twelve dishes, with great plenty of beer and wine.

Now I will say no more of the service, but that ye may know there was no lack, for there drew near a venture that the folk might well have left their labor to gaze upon. As the sound of the music ceased, and the first course had been fitly served, there came in at the hall door one terrible to behold, of stature greater than any on earth; from neck to loin so strong and thickly made, and with limbs so long and so great that he seemed even as a

[2]Dances accompanied by song.

[3]Of the hard hand.

giant. And yet he was but a man, only the mightiest that might mount a steed; broad of chest and shoulders and slender of waist, and all his features of like fashion; but men marveled much at his color, for he rode even as a knight, yet was green all over.

For he was clad all in green, with a straight coat, and a mantle above; all decked and lined with fur was the cloth and the hood that was thrown back from his locks and lay on his shoulders. Hose had he of the same green, and spurs of bright gold with silken fastenings richly worked; and all his vesture was verily green. Around his waist and his saddle were bands with fair stones set upon silken work, 't were too long to tell of all the trifles that were embroidered thereon—birds and insects in gay gauds of green and gold. All the trappings of his steed were of metal of like enamel, even the stirrups that he stood in stained of the same, and stirrups and saddle-bow alike gleamed and shone with green stones. Even the steed on which he rode was of the same hue, a green horse, great and strong, and hard to hold, with broidered bridle, meet for the rider.

The knight was thus gaily dressed in green, his hair falling around his shoulders; on his breast hung a beard, as thick and green as a bush, and the beard and the hair of his head were clipped all round above his elbows. The lower part of his sleeves was fastened with clasps in the same wise as a king's mantle. The horse's mane was crisp and plaited with many a knot folded in with gold thread about the fair green, here a twist of the hair, here another of gold. The tail was twined in like manner, and both were bound about with a band of bright green set with many a precious stone; then they were tied aloft in a cunning knot, whereon rang many bells of burnished gold. Such a steed might no other ride, nor had such ever been looked upon in that hall ere that time; and all who saw that knight spake and said that a man might scarce abide his stroke.

The knight bore no helm nor hauberk, neither gorget nor breast-plate, neither shaft nor buckler to smite nor to shield, but in one hand he had a holly-bough, that is greenest when the groves are bare, and in his other an ax, huge and uncomely, a cruel weapon in fashion, if one would picture it. The head was an ell-yard long, the metal all of green steel and gold, the blade burnished bright, with a broad edge, as well shapen to shear as a sharp razor. The steel was set into a strong staff, all bound round with iron, even to the end, and engraved with green in cunning work. A lace was twined about it, that looped at the head, and all adown the handle it was clasped with tassels on buttons of bright green richly broidered.

The knight rideth through the entrance of the hall, driving straight to the high daïs, and greeted no man, but looked ever upwards; and the first words he spake were, "Where is the ruler of this folk? I would gladly look upon that hero, and have speech with him." He cast his eyes on the knights, and mustered[4] them up and down, striving ever to see who of them was of most renown.

Then was there great gazing to behold that chief, for each man marveled what it might mean that a knight and his steed should have even such a hue as the green grass; and that seemed even greener than green enamel on bright gold. All looked on him as he stood, and drew near unto him, wondering greatly what he might be; for many marvels had they seen, but none such as this, and phantasm and faërie did the folk deem it. Therefore were the gallant knights slow to answer, and gazed astounded, and sat stone still in a deep silence through that goodly hall, as if a slumber were fallen upon them. I deem it was not all for doubt, but some for courtesy that they might give ear unto his errand.

Then Arthur beheld this adventurer before his high daïs, and knightly he greeted him, for fearful was he never. "Sir," he said, "thou art welcome to this place—lord of this hall am I, and men call me Arthur. Light thee down, and tarry awhile, and what thy will is, that shall we learn after."

"Nay," quoth the stranger, "so help me He that sitteth on high, 't was not mine errand to tarry any while in this dwelling; but the praise of this thy folk and thy city is lifted up on high, and thy warriors are holden for the best and most valiant of those who ride mail-clad to the fight. The wisest and the

[4]Surveyed.

worthiest of this world are they, and well proven in all knightly sports. And here, as I have heard tell, is fairest courtesy; therefore have I come hither as at this time. Ye may be sure by the branch that I bear here that I come in peace, seeking no strife. For had I willed to journey in warlike guise I have at home both hauberk and helm, shield and shining spear, and other weapons to mine hand, but since I seek no war, my raiment is that of peace. But if thou be as bold as all men tell, thou wilt freely grant me the boon I ask."

And Arthur answered, "Sir Knight, if thou cravest battle here thou shalt not fail for lack of a foe."

And the knight answered, "Nay, I ask no fight; in faith here on the benches are but beardless children; were I clad in armor on my steed there is no man here might match me. Therefore I ask in this court but a Christmas jest, for that it is Yule-tide and New Year, and there are here many fain for sport. If any one in this hall holds himself so hardy, so bold both of blood and brain, as to dare strike me one stroke for another, I will give him as a gift this ax, which is heavy enough, in sooth, to handle as he may list, and I will abide the first blow, unarmed as I sit. If any knight be so bold as to prove my words, let him come swiftly to me here, and take this weapon; I quit claim to it, he may keep it as his own, and I will abide his stroke, firm on the floor. Then shalt thou give me the right to deal him another, the respite of a year and a day shall he have. Now haste, and let see whether any here dare say aught."

Now if the knights had been astounded at the first, yet stiller were they all, high and low, when they had heard his words. The knight on his steed straightened himself in the saddle, and rolled his eyes fiercely round the hall; red they gleamed under his green and bushy brows. He frowned and twisted his beard, waiting to see who should rise, and when none answered he cried aloud in mockery, "What, is this Arthur's hall, and these the knights whose renown hath run through many realms? Where are now your pride and your conquests, your wrath, and anger, and mighty words? Now are the praise and the renown of the Round Table overthrown by one man's speech, since all keep silence for dread ere ever they have seen a blow!"

With that he laughed so loudly that the blood rushed to the king's fair face for very shame; he waxed wroth, as did all his knights, and sprang to his feet, and drew near to the stranger and said, "Now by heaven, foolish is thy asking, and thy folly shall find its fitting answer. I know no man aghast at thy great words. Give me here thine ax and I shall grant thee the boon thou hast asked." Lightly he sprang to him and caught at his hand, and the knight, fierce of aspect, lighted down from his charger.

Then Arthur took the ax and gripped the haft, and swung it round, ready to strike. And the knight stood before him, taller by the head than any in the hall; he stood, and stroked his beard, and drew down his coat, no more dismayed for the king's threats than if one had brought him a drink of wine.

Then Gawain, who sat by the queen, leaned forward to the king and spake, "I beseech ye, my lord, let this venture be mine. Would ye but bid me rise from this seat, and stand by your side, so that my liege lady thought it not ill, then would I come to your counsel before this goodly court. For I think it not seemly when such challenges be made in your hall that ye yourself should undertake it, while there are many bold knights who sit beside ye; none are there, methinks, of readier will under heaven, or more valiant in open field. I am the weakest, I wot, and the feeblest of wit, and it will be the less loss of my life if ye seek sooth. For save that ye are mine uncle, naught is there in me to praise, no virtue is there in my body save your blood, and since this challenge is such folly that it beseems ye not to take it, and I have asked it from ye first, let it fall to me, and if I bear myself ungallantly, then let all this court blame me."

Then they all spake with one voice that the king should leave this venture and grant it to Gawain.

Then Arthur commanded the knight to rise, and he rose up quickly and knelt down before the king, and caught hold of the weapon; and the king loosed his hold of it, and lifted up his hand, and gave him his blessing, and bade him be strong both of heart and hand. "Keep thee well, nephew," quoth Arthur, "that thou give him but the one blow, and if thou redest[5] him rightly I trow thou shalt well abide the stroke he may give thee after."

Gawain stepped to the stranger, ax in hand, and he, never fearing, awaited his coming. Then the Green Knight spake to Sir Gawain, "Make we our covenant ere we go further. First, I ask thee, knight, what is thy name? Tell my truly, that I may know thee."

"In faith," quoth the good knight, "Gawain am I, who give thee this buffet, let what may come of it; and at this time twelvemonth will I take another at thine hand with whatsoever weapon thou wilt, and none other."

Then the other answered again, "Sir Gawain, so may I thrive as I am fain to take this buffet at thine hand," and he quoth further, "Sir Gawain, it liketh me well that I shall take at thy fist that which I have asked here, and thou hast readily and truly rehearsed all the covenant that I asked of the king, save that thou shalt swear me, by thy troth, to seek me thyself wherever thou hopest that I may be found, and win thee such reward as thou dealest me to-day, before this folk."

"Where shall I seek thee?" quoth Gawain. "Where is thy place? By him that made me, I wot never where thou dwellest, nor know I thee, knight, thy court, nor thy name. But teach me truly all that pertaineth thereto, and tell me thy name, and I shall use all my wit to win my way thither, and that I swear thee for sooth, and by my sure troth."

"That is enough in the New Year, it needs no more," quoth the Green Knight to the gallant Gawain, "if I tell thee truly when I have taken the blow, and thou hast smitten me; then will I teach thee of my house and home, and mine own name, then mayest thou ask thy road and keep covenant. And if I waste no words then farest thou the better, for thou canst dwell in thy land, and seek no further. But take now thy toll, and let see how thou strikest."

"Gladly will I," quoth Gawain, handling his ax.

Then the Green Knight swiftly made him ready; he bowed down his head, and laid his long locks on the crown that his bare neck might be seen. Gawain gripped his ax and raised it on high; the left foot he set forward on the floor, and let the blow fall lightly on the bare neck. The sharp edge of the blade sundered the bones, smote through the neck, and clave it in two, so that the edge of the steel bit on the ground, and the fair head fell to the earth that many struck it with their feet as it rolled forth. The blood spurted forth, and glistened on the green raiment, but the knight neither faltered nor fell; he started forward with out-stretched hand, and caught the head, and lifted it up; then he turned to his steed, and took hold of the bridle, set his foot in the stirrup, and mounted. His head he held by the hair, in his hand. Then he seated himself in his saddle as if naught ailed him, and he were not headless. He turned his steed about, the grim corpse bleeding freely the while, and they who looked upon him doubted them much for the covenant.

For he held up the head in his hand, and turned the face towards them that sat on the high daïs, and it lifted up the eyelids and looked upon them and spake as ye shall hear. "Look, Gawain, that thou art ready to go as thou hast promised, and seek loyally till thou find me, even as thou hast sworn in this hall in the hearing of these knights. Come thou, I charge thee, to the Green Chapel; such a stroke as thou hast dealt thou hast deserved, and it shall be promptly paid thee on New Year's morn. Many men know me as the Knight of the Green Chapel, and if thou askest, thou shalt not fail to find me. Therefore it behooves thee to come, or to yield thee as recreant."

With that he turned his bridle, and galloped out at the hall door, his head in his hands, so that the sparks flew from beneath his horse's hoofs. Whither he went none knew, no more than they wist whence he had come; and the king and Gawain they gazed and laughed, for in sooth this had proved a greater marvel than any they had known aforetime.

Though Arthur the king was astonished at his heart, yet he let no sign of it be seen,

---

[5]Handlest.

but spake in courteous wise to the fair queen: "Dear lady, be not dismayed, such craft is well suited to Christmas-tide when we seek jesting, laughter, and song, and fair carols of knights and ladies. But now I may well get me to meat, for I have seen a marvel I may not forget." Then he looked on Sir Gawain, and said gaily, "Now, fair nephew, hang up thine ax, since it has hewn enough," and they hung it on the dossal[6] above the daïs, where all men might look on it for a marvel, and by its true token tell of the wonder. Then the twain sat them down together, the king and the good knight, and men served them with a double portion, as was the share of the noblest, with all manner of meat and of minstrelsy. And they spent that day in gladness, but Sir Gawain must well bethink him of the heavy venture to which he had set his hand.

II

This beginning of adventures had Arthur at the New Year; for he yearned to hear gallant tales, though his words were few when he sat at the feast. But now had they stern work on hand. Gawain was glad to begin the jest in the hall, but ye need have no marvel if the end be heavy. For though a man be merry in mind when he has well drunk, yet a year runs full swiftly, and the beginning but rarely matches the end.

For Yule was now over-past, and the year after, each season in its turn following the other. For after Christmas comes crabbed Lent, that will have fish for flesh and simpler cheer. But then the weather of the world chides with winter; the cold withdraws itself, the clouds uplift, and the rain falls in warm showers on the fair plains. Then the flowers come forth, meadows and grove are clad in green, the birds make ready to build, and sing sweetly for solace of the soft summer that follows thereafter. The blossoms bud and blow in the hedgerows rich and rank, and noble notes enough are heard in the fair woods.

After the season of summer, with the soft winds, when zephyr breathes lightly on seeds and herbs, joyous indeed is the growth that waxes thereout when the dew drips from the leaves beneath the blissful glance of the bright sun. But then comes harvest and hardens the grain, warning it to wax ripe ere the winter. The drought drives the dust on high, flying over the face of the land; the angry wind of the welkin wrestles with the sun; the leaves fall from the trees and light upon the ground, and all brown are the groves that but now were green, and ripe is the fruit that once was flower. So the year passes into many yesterdays, and winter comes again, as it needs no sage to tell us.

When the Michaelmas moon was come in with warnings of winter, Sir Gawain bethought him full oft of his perilous journey. Yet till All Hallows Day he lingered with Arthur, and on that day they made a great feast for the hero's sake, with much revel and richness of the Round Table. Courteous knights and comely ladies, all were in sorrow for the love of that knight, and though they spake no word of it, many were joyless for his sake.

And after meat, sadly Sir Gawain turned to his uncle, and spake of his journey, and said, "Liege lord of my life, leave from you I crave. Ye know well how the matter stands without more words; to-morrow am I bound to set forth in search of the Green Knight." Then came together all the noblest knights, Ywain and Erec, and many another. Sir Dodinel le Sauvage, the Duke of Clarence, Launcelot and Lionel, and Lucan the Good, Sir Bors and Bedivere, valiant knights both, and many another hero, with Sir Mador de la Porte, and they all drew near, heavy at heart, to take counsel with Sir Gawain. Much sorrow and weeping was there in the hall to think that so worthy a knight as Gawain should wend his way to seek a deadly blow, and should no more wield his sword in fight. But the knight made ever good cheer, and said, "Nay, wherefore should I shrink? What may a man do but prove his fate?"

He dwelt there all that day, and on the morn he arose and asked betimes for his armor; and they brought it unto him on this wise: first, a rich carpet was stretched on the floor (and brightly did the gold gear glitter upon it), then the knight stepped upon it, and handled the steel; clad he was in a

[6]Tapestry.

doublet of silk, with a close hood, lined fairly throughout. Then they set the steel shoes upon his feet, and wrapped his legs with greaves, with polished knee-caps, fastened with knots of gold. Then they cased his thighs in cuisses closed with thongs, and brought him the byrnie[1] of bright steel rings sewn upon a fair stuff. Well burnished braces they set on each arm with good elbow-pieces, and gloves of mail, and all the goodly gear that should shield him in his need. And they cast over all a rich surcoat, and set the golden spurs on his heels, and girt him with a trusty sword fastened with a silken bawdrick. When he was thus clad his harness was costly, for the least loop or latchet gleamed with gold. So armed as he was he hearkened Mass and made his offering at the high altar. Then he came to the king, and the knights of his court, and courteously took leave of lords and ladies, and they kissed him, and commended him to Christ.

With that was Gringalet ready, girt with a saddle that gleamed gaily with many golden fringes, enriched and decked anew for the venture. The bridle was all barred about with bright gold buttons, and all the covertures and trappings of the steed, the crupper and the rich skirts, accorded with the saddle; spread fair with the rich red gold that glittered and gleamed in the rays of the sun.

Then the knight called for his helmet, which was well lined throughout, and set it high on his head, and hasped it behind. He wore a light kerchief over the ventail, that was broidered and studded with fair gems on a broad silken ribbon, with birds of gay color, and many a turtle[2] and true-lover's knot interlaced thickly, even as many a maiden had wrought diligently for seven winters long. But the circlet which crowned his helmet was yet more precious, being adorned with a device in diamonds. Then they brought him his shield, which was of bright red, with the pentangle painted thereon in gleaming gold. And why that noble prince bare the pentangle I am minded to tell you, though my tale tarry thereby. It is a sign that Solomon set ere-while, as betokening truth; for it is a figure with five points and each line overlaps the other, and nowhere hath it beginning or end, so that in English it is called "the endless knot." And therefore was it well suiting to this knight and to his arms, since Gawain was faithful in five and five-fold, for pure was he as gold, void of all villainy and endowed with all virtues. Therefore he bare the pentangle on shield and surcoat as truest of heroes and gentlest of knights.

For first he was faultless in his five senses; and his five fingers never failed him; and all his trust upon earth was in the five wounds that Christ bare on the cross, as the Creed tells. And wherever this knight found himself in stress of battle he deemed well that he drew his strength from the five joys which the Queen of Heaven had of her Child. And for this cause did he bear an image of Our Lady on the one half of his shield, that whenever he looked upon it he might not lack for aid. And the fifth five that the hero used were frankness and fellowship above all, purity and courtesy that never failed him, and compassion that surpasses all; and in these five virtues was that hero wrapped and clothed. And all these, fivefold, were linked one in the other, so that they had no end, and were fixed on five points that never failed, neither at any side were they joined or sundered, nor could ye find beginning or end. And therefore on his shield was the knot shapen, red-gold upon red, which is the pure pentangle. Now was Sir Gawain ready, and he took his lance in hand, and bade them all farewell, he deemed it had been for ever.

Then he smote the steed with his spurs, and sprang on his way, so that sparks flew from the stones after him. All that saw him were grieved at heart, and said one to the other, "By Christ, 't is great pity that one of such noble life should be lost! I' faith, 't were not easy to find his equal upon earth. The king had done better to have wrought more warily. Yonder knight should have been made a duke; a gallant leader of men is he, and such a fate had beseemed him better than to be hewn in pieces at the will of an elfish man, for mere pride. Who ever knew a king to take such counsel as to risk his knights on a Christmas jest?" Many

[1]Coat of mail. [2]Turtle-dove.

were the tears that flowed from their eyes when that goodly knight rode from the hall. He made no delaying, but went his way swiftly, and rode many a wild road, as I heard say in the book.

So rode Sir Gawain through the realm of Logres,[3] on an errand that he held for no jest. Often he lay companionless at night, and must lack the fare that he liked. No comrade had he save his steed, and none save God with whom to take counsel. At length he drew nigh to North Wales, and left the isles of Anglesey on his left hand, crossing over the fords by the foreland over at Holyhead, till he came into the wilderness of Wirral,[4] where but few dwell who love God and man of true heart. And ever he asked, as he fared, of all whom he met, if they had heard any tidings of a Green Knight in the country thereabout, or of a Green Chapel? And all answered him, "Nay," never in their lives had they seen any man of such a hue. And the knight wended his way by many a strange road and many a rugged path, and the fashion of his countenance changed full often ere he saw the Green Chapel.

Many a cliff did he climb in that unknown land, where afar from his friends he rode as a stranger. Never did he come to a stream or a ford but he found a foe before him, and that one so marvelous, so foul and fell, that it behooved him to fight. So many wonders did that knight behold, that it were too long to tell the tenth part of them. Sometimes he fought with dragons and wolves; sometimes with wild men that dwelt in the rocks; another while with bulls, and bears, and wild boars, or with giants of the high moorland that drew near to him. Had he not been a doughty knight, enduring, and of well-proved valor, and a servant of God, doubtless he had been slain, for he was oft in danger of death. Yet he cared not so much for the strife; what he deemed worse was when the cold clear water was shed from the clouds, and froze ere it fell on the fallow ground. More nights than enough he slept in his harness on the bare rocks, near slain with the sleet, while the stream leapt bubbling from the crest of the hills, and hung in hard icicles over his head.

Thus in peril and pain, and many a hardship, the knight rode alone till Christmas Eve, and in that tide he made his prayer to the Blessed Virgin that she would guide his steps and lead him to some dwelling. On that morning he rode by a hill, and came into a thick forest, wild and drear; on each side were high hills, and thick woods below them of great hoar oaks, a hundred together, of hazel and hawthorn with their trailing boughs intertwined, and rough ragged moss spreading everywhere. On the bare twigs the birds chirped piteously, for pain of the cold. The knight upon Gringalet rode lonely beneath them, through marsh and mire, much troubled at heart lest he should fail to see the service of the Lord, who on that self-same night was born of a maiden for the cure of our grief; and therefore he said, sighing, "I beseech thee, Lord, and Mary thy gentle Mother, for some shelter where I may hear Mass, and thy matins at morn. This I ask meekly, and thereto I pray my Paternoster, Ave, and Credo." Thus he rode praying, and lamenting his misdeeds, and he crossed himself, and said, "May the Cross of Christ speed me."

Now that knight had crossed himself but thrice ere he was aware in the wood of a dwelling within a moat, above a lawn, on a mound surrounded by many mighty trees that stood round the moat. 'Twas the fairest castle that ever a knight owned; built in a meadow with a park all about it, and a spiked palisade, closely driven, that enclosed the trees for more than two miles. The knight was ware of the hold from the side, as it shone through the oaks. Then he lifted off his helmet, and thanked Christ and Saint Julian that they had courteously granted his prayer, and hearkened to his cry. "Now," quoth the knight, "I beseech ye, grant me fair hostel." Then he pricked Gringalet with his golden spurs, and rode gaily towards the great gate, and came swiftly to the bridge end.

The bridge was drawn up and the gates close shut; the walls were strong and thick, so that they might fear no tempest. The knight on his charger abode on the bank of

[3]England. [4]In Cheshire.

the deep double ditch that surrounded the castle. The walls were set deep in the water, and rose aloft to a wondrous height; they were of hard hewn stone up to the corbels, which were adorned beneath the battlements with fair carvings, and turrets set in between with many a loophole; a better barbican Sir Gawain had never looked upon. And within he beheld the high hall, with its tower and many windows with carven cornices, and chalk-white chimneys on the turreted roofs that shone fair in the sun. And everywhere, thickly scattered on the castle battlements, were pinnacles, so many that it seemed as if it were all wrought out of paper, so white was it.

The knight on his steed deemed it fair enough, if he might come to be sheltered within it to lodge there while that the holy-day lasted. He called aloud, and soon there came a porter of kindly countenance, who stood on the wall and greeted this knight and asked his errand.

"Good sir," quoth Gawain, "wilt thou go mine errand to the high lord of the castle, and crave for me lodging?"

"Yea, by Saint Peter," quoth the porter. "In sooth I trow that ye be welcome to dwell here so long as it may like ye."

Then he went, and came again swiftly, and many folk with him to receive the knight. They let down the great drawbridge, and came forth and knelt on their knees on the cold earth to give him worthy welcome. They held wide open the great gates, and courteously he bade them rise, and rode over the bridge. Then men came to him and held his stirrup while he dismounted, and took and stabled his steed. There came down knights and squires to bring the guest with joy to the hall. When he raised his helmet there were many to take it from his hand, fain to serve him, and they took from him sword and shield.

Sir Gawain gave good greeting to the noble and the mighty men who came to do him honor. Clad in his shining armor they led him to the hall, where a great fire burned brightly on the floor; and the lord of the household came forth from his chamber to meet the hero fitly. He spake to the knight, and said: "Ye are welcome to do here as it likes ye. All that is here is your own to have at your will and disposal."

"Gramercy!" quoth Gawain, "may Christ requite ye."

As friends that were fain each embraced the other; and Gawain looked on the knight who greeted him so kindly, and thought 't was a bold warrior that owned that burg.

Of mighty stature he was, and of high age; broad and flowing was his beard, and of a bright hue. He was stalwart of limb, and strong in his stride, his face fiery red, and his speech free: in sooth he seemed one well fitted to be a leader of valiant men.

Then the lord led Sir Gawain to a chamber, and commanded folk to wait upon him, and at his bidding there came men enough who brought the guest to a fair bower. The bedding was noble, with curtains of pure silk wrought with gold, and wondrous coverings of fair cloth all embroidered. The curtains ran on ropes with rings of red gold, and the walls were hung with carpets of Orient, and the same spread on the floor. There with mirthful speeches they took from the guest his byrnie and all his shining armor, and brought him rich robes of the choicest in its stead. They were long and flowing, and became him well, and when he was clad in them all who looked on the hero thought that surely God had never made a fairer knight: he seemed as if he might be a prince without peer in the field where men strive in battle.

Then before the hearth-place, whereon the fire burned, they made ready a chair for Gawain, hung about with cloth and fair cushions; and there they cast around him a mantle of brown samite, richly embroidered and furred within with costly skins of ermine, with a hood of the same, and he seated himself in that rich seat, and warmed himself at the fire, and was cheered at heart. And while he sat thus, the serving men set up a table on trestles, and covered it with a fair white cloth, and set thereon salt-cellar, and napkin, and silver spoons; and the knight washed at his will, and set him down to meat.

The folk served him courteously with many dishes seasoned of the best, a double portion. All kinds of fish were there, some baked in bread, some broiled on the embers, some sodden,[5] some stewed and savored with spices, with all sorts of cunning devices to his taste. And often he called it a feast, when they spake gaily to him all together, and said, "Now take ye this penance, and it shall be for your amendment." Much mirth thereof did Sir Gawain make.

Then they questioned that prince courteously of whence he came; and he told them that he was of the court of Arthur, who is the rich royal king of the Round Table, and that it was Gawain himself who was within their walls, and would keep Christmas with them, as the chance had fallen out. And when the lord of the castle heard those tidings he laughed aloud for gladness, and all men in that keep were joyful that they should be in the company of him to whom belonged all fame, and valor, and courtesy, and whose honor was praised above that of all men on earth. Each said softly to his fellow, "Now shall we see courteous bearing, and the manner of speech befitting courts. What charm lieth in gentle speech shall we learn without asking, since here we have welcomed the fine father of courtesy. God has surely shown us His grace since He sends us such a guest as Gawain! When men shall sit and sing, blithe for Christ's birth, this knight shall bring us to the knowledge of fair manners, and it may be that hearing him we may learn the cunning speech of love."

By the time the knight had risen from dinner it was near nightfall. Then chaplains took their way to the chapel, and rang loudly, even as they should, for the solemn evensong of the high feast. Thither went the lord, and the lady also, and entered with her maidens into a comely closet, and thither also went Gawain. Then the lord took him by the sleeve and led him to a seat, and called him by his name, and told him he was of all men in the world the most welcome. And Sir Gawain thanked him truly, and each kissed the other, and they sat gravely together throughout the service.

Then was the lady fain to look upon that knight; and she came forth from her closet with many fair maidens. The fairest of ladies was she in face, and figure, and coloring, fairer even than Guinevere, so the knight thought. She came through the chancel to greet the hero; another lady held her by the left hand, older than she, and seemingly of high estate, with many nobles about her. But unlike to look upon were those ladies, for if the younger were fair, the elder was yellow. Rich red were the cheeks of the one, rough and wrinkled those of the other; the kerchiefs of the one were broidered with many glistening pearls, her throat and neck bare, and whiter than the snow that lies on the hills; the neck of the other was swathed in a gorget, with a white wimple over her black chin. Her forehead was wrapped in silk with many folds, worked with knots, so that naught of her was seen save her black brows, her eyes, her nose, and her lips, and those were bleared, and ill to look upon. A worshipful lady in sooth one might call her! In figure was she short and broad, and thickly made—far fairer to behold was she whom she led by the hand.

When Gawain beheld that fair lady, who looked at him graciously, with leave of the lord he went towards them, and, bowing low, he greeted the elder, but the younger and fairer he took lightly in his arms, and kissed her courteously, and greeted her in knightly wise. Then she hailed him as friend, and he quickly prayed to be counted as her servant, if she so willed. Then they took him between them, and talking, led him to the chamber, to the hearth, and bade them bring spices, and they brought them in plenty with the good wine that was wont to be drunk at such seasons. Then the lord sprang to his feet and bade them make merry, and took off his hood, and hung it on a spear, and bade him win the worship thereof who should make most mirth that Christmas-tide. "And I shall try, by my faith, to fool it with the best, by the help of my friends, ere I lose my raiment." Thus with gay words the lord made trial to gladden Gawain with jests that night, till it was time to bid them light the tapers, and Sir Gawain took leave of them and gat him to rest.

In the morn when all men call to mind how Christ our Lord was born on earth to die for us, there is joy, for his sake, in all dwellings

[5]Boiled.

of the world; and so was there here on that day. For high feast was held, with many dainties and cunningly cooked messes. On the daïs sat gallant men, clad in their best. The ancient dame sat on the high seat with the lord of the castle beside her. Gawain and the fair lady sat together, even in the midst of the board when the feast was served; and so throughout all the hall each sat in his degree, and was served in order. There was meat, there was mirth, there was much joy, so that to tell thereof would take me too long, though peradventure I might strive to declare it. But Gawain and that fair lady had much joy of each other's company through her sweet words and courteous converse. And there was music made before each prince, trumpets and drums, and merry pipings; each man hearkened his minstrel, and they too hearkened theirs.

So they held high feast that day and the next, and the third day thereafter, and the joy on Saint John's Day was fair to hearken, for 't was the last of the feast and the guests would depart in the gray of the morning. Therefore they awoke early, and drank wine, and danced fair carols, and at last, when it was late, each man took his leave to wend early on his way. Gawain would bid his host farewell, but the lord took him by the hand, and led him to his own chamber beside the hearth, and there he thanked him for the favor he had shown him in honoring his dwelling at that high season, and gladdening his castle with his fair countenance. "I wis, sir, that while I live I shall be held the worthier that Gawain has been my guest at God's own feast."

"Gramercy, sir," quoth Gawain, "in good faith, all the honor is yours, may the High King give it you, and I am but at your will to work your behest, inasmuch as I am beholden to you in great and small by rights."

Then the lord did his best to persuade the knight to tarry with him, but Gawain answered that he might in no wise do so. Then the host asked him courteously what stern behest had driven him at the holy season from the king's court, to fare all alone, ere yet the feast was ended?

"Forsooth," quoth the knight, "ye say but the truth: 't is a high quest and a pressing that hath brought me afield, for I am summoned myself to a certain place, and I know not whither in the world I may wend to find it; so help me Christ, I would give all the kingdom of Logres an I might find it by New Year's morn. Therefore, sir, I make request of you that ye tell me truly if ye ever heard word of the Green Chapel, where it may be found, and the Green Knight that keeps it. For I am pledged by solemn compact sworn between us to meet that knight at the New Year if so I were on life; and of that same New Year it wants but little—I' faith, I would look on that hero more joyfully than on any other fair sight! Therefore, by your will, it behooves me to leave you, for I have but barely three days, and I would as fain fall dead as fail of mine errand."

Then the lord quoth, laughing, "Now must ye needs stay, for I will show you your goal, the Green Chapel, ere your term be at an end, have ye no fear! But ye can take your ease, friend, in your bed, till the fourth day, and go forth on the first of the year and come to that place at mid-morn to do as ye will. Dwell here till New Year's Day, and then rise and set forth, and ye shall be set in the way; 't is not two miles hence."

Then was Gawain glad, and he laughed gaily. "Now I thank you for this above all else. Now my quest is achieved I will dwell here at your will, and otherwise do as ye shall ask."

Then the lord took him, and set him beside him, and bade the ladies be fetched for their greater pleasure, tho' between themselves they had solace. The lord, for gladness, made merry jest, even as one who wist not what to do for joy; and he cried aloud to the knight, "Ye have promised to do the thing I bid ye: will ye hold to this behest, here, at once?"

"Yea, forsooth," said that true knight, "while I abide in your burg I am bound by your behest."

"Ye have traveled from far," said the host, "and since then ye have waked with me, ye are not well refreshed by rest and sleep, as I know. Ye shall therefore abide in your chamber, and lie at your ease tomorrow at Mass-tide, and go to meat when ye will with my wife, who shall sit with you, and comfort you with her company till I return; and I shall rise early and go forth to the chase." And Gawain agreed to all this courteously.

"Sir knight," quoth the host, "we will make a covenant. Whatsoever I win in the wood shall be yours, and whatever may fall to your share, that shall ye exchange for it. Let us swear, friend, to make this exchange, however our hap may be, for worse or for better."

"I grant ye your will," quoth Gawain the good; "if ye list so to do, it liketh me well."

"Bring hither the wine-cup, the bargain is made," so said the lord of that castle. They laughed each one, and drank of the wine, and made merry, these lords and ladies, as it pleased them. Then with gay talk and merry jest they rose, and stood, and spoke softly, and kissed courteously, and took leave of each other. With burning torches, and many a serving-man, was each led to his couch; yet ere they gat them to bed the old lord oft repeated their covenant, for he knew well how to make sport.

III

Full early, ere daylight, the folk rose up; the guests who would depart called their grooms, and they made them ready, and saddled the steeds, tightened up the girths, and trussed up their mails.[1] The knights, all arrayed for riding, leapt up lightly, and took their bridles, and each rode his way as pleased him best.

The lord of the land was not the last. Ready for the chase, with many of his men, he ate a sop hastily when he had heard Mass, and then with blast of the bugle fared forth to the field. He and his nobles were to horse ere daylight glimmered upon the earth.

Then the huntsmen coupled their hounds, unclosed the kennel door, and called them out. They blew three blasts gaily on the bugles, the hounds bayed fiercely, and they that would go a-hunting checked and chastised them. A hundred hunters there were of the best, so I have heard tell. Then the trackers gat them to the trysting-place and uncoupled the hounds, and the forest rang again with their gay blasts.

At the first sound of the hunt the game quaked for fear, and fled, trembling, along the vale. They betook them to the heights, but the liers in wait turned them back with loud cries; the harts they let pass them, and the stags with their spreading antlers, for the lord had forbidden that they should be slain, but the hinds and the does they turned back, and drave down into the valleys. Then might ye see much shooting of arrows. As the deer fled under the boughs a broad whistling shaft smote and wounded each sorely, so that, wounded and bleeding, they fell dying on the banks. The hounds followed swiftly on their tracks, and hunters, blowing the horn, sped after them with ringing shouts as if the cliffs burst asunder. What game escaped those that shot was run down at the outer ring. Thus were they driven on the hills, and harassed at the waters, so well did the men know their work, and the greyhounds were so great and swift that they ran them down as fast as the hunters could slay them. Thus the lord passed the day in mirth and joyfulness, even to nightfall.

So the lord roamed the woods, and Gawain, that good knight, lay ever a-bed, curtained about, under the costly coverlet, while the daylight gleamed on the walls. And as he lay half slumbering, he heard a little sound at the door, and he raised his head, and caught back a corner of the curtain, and waited to see what it might be. It was the lovely lady, the lord's wife; she shut the door softly behind her, and turned towards the bed; and Gawain was shamed, laid him down softly and made as if he slept. And she came lightly to the bedside, within the curtain, and sat herself down beside him, to wait till he wakened. The knight lay there awhile, and marveled within himself what her coming might betoken; and he said to himself, "'T were more seemly if I asked her what hath brought her hither." Then he made feint to waken, and turned towards her, and opened his eyes as one astonished, and crossed himself; and she looked on him laughing, with her cheeks red and white, lovely to behold, and small smiling lips.

[1] Bags.

"Good morrow, Sir Gawain," said that fair lady; "ye are but a careless sleeper, since one can enter thus. Now are ye taken unawares, and lest ye escape me I shall bind you in your bed; of that be ye assured!" Laughing, she spake these words.

"Good morrow, fair lady," quoth Gawain blithely. "I will do your will, as it likes me well. For I yield me readily, and pray your grace, and that is best, by my faith, since I needs must do so." Thus he jested again, laughing. "But an ye would, fair lady, grant me this grace that ye pray your prisoner to rise. I would get me from bed, and array me better, then could I talk with ye in more comfort."

"Nay, forsooth, fair sir," quoth the lady, "ye shall not rise, I will rede[2] ye better. I shall keep ye here, since ye can do no other, and talk with my knight whom I have captured. For I know well that ye are Sir Gawain, whom all the world worships, wheresoever ye may ride. Your honor and your courtesy are praised by lords and ladies, by all who live. Now ye are here and we are alone, my lord and his men are afield; the serving men in their beds, and my maidens also, and the door shut upon us. And since in this hour I have him that all men love I shall use my time well with speech, while it lasts. Ye are welcome to my company, for it behooves me in sooth to be your servant."

"In good faith," quoth Gawain, "I think me that I am not him of whom ye speak, for unworthy am I of such service as ye here proffer. In sooth, I were glad if I might set myself by word or service to your pleasure; a pure joy would it be to me!"

"In good faith, Sir Gawain," quoth the gay lady, "the praise and the prowess that pleases all ladies I lack them not, nor hold them light; yet are there ladies enough who would liever now have the knight in their hold, as I have ye here, to dally with your courteous words, to bring them comfort and to ease their cares, than much of the treasure and the gold that are theirs. And now, through the grace of Him who upholds the heavens, I have wholly in my power that which they all desire!"

Thus the lady, fair to look upon, made him great cheer, and Sir Gawain, with modest words, answered her again: "Madam," he quoth, "may Mary requite ye, for in good faith I have found in ye a noble frankness. Much courtesy have other folk shown me, but the honor they have done me is naught to the worship of yourself, who knoweth but good."

"By Mary," quoth the lady, "I think otherwise; for were I worth all the women alive, and had I the wealth of the world in my hand, and might choose me a lord to my liking, then, for all that I have seen in ye, Sir Knight, of beauty and courtesy and blithe semblance, and for all that I have hearkened and hold for true, there should be no knight on earth to be chosen before ye."

"Well, I wot," quoth Sir Gawain, "that ye have chosen a better; but I am proud that ye should so prize me, and as your servant do I hold ye my sovereign, and your knight am I, and may Christ reward ye."

So they talked of many matters till mid-morn was past, and ever the lady made as though she loved him, and the knight turned her speech aside. For though she were the brightest of maidens, yet had he forborne to show her love for the danger that awaited him, and the blow that must be given without delay.

Then the lady prayed her leave from him, and he granted it readily. And she gave him good-day, with laughing glance, but he must needs marvel at her words:

"Now He that speeds fair speech reward ye this disport; but that ye be Gawain my mind misdoubts me greatly."

"Wherefore?" quoth the knight quickly, fearing lest he had lacked in some courtesy.

And the lady spake: "So true a knight as Gawain is holden, and one so perfect in courtesy, would never have tarried so long with a lady but he would of his courtesy have craved a kiss at parting."

Then quoth Gawain, "I wot I will do even as it may please ye, and kiss at your commandment, as a true knight should who forbears to ask for fear of displeasure."

At that she came near and bent down and kissed the knight, and each commended the other to Christ, and she went forth from the chamber softly.

[2]Manage.

Then Sir Gawain rose and called his chamberlain and chose his garments, and when he was ready he gat him forth to Mass, and then went to meat, and made merry all day till the rising of the moon, and never had a knight fairer lodging than had he with those two noble ladies, the elder and the younger.

And ever the lord of the land chased the hinds through holt and heath till eventide, and then with much blowing of bugles and baying of hounds they bore the game homeward; and by the time daylight was done all the folk had returned to that fair castle. And when the lord and Sir Gawain met together, then were they both well pleased. The lord commanded them all to assemble in the great hall, and the ladies to descend with their maidens, and there, before them all, he bade the men fetch in the spoil of the day's hunting, and he called unto Gawain, and counted the tale of the beasts, and showed them unto him, and said, "What think ye of this game, Sir Knight? Have I deserved of ye thanks for my woodcraft?"

"Yea, I wis," quoth the other, "here is the fairest spoil I have seen this seven year in the winter season."

"And all this do I give ye, Gawain," quoth the host, "for by accord of covenant ye may claim it as your own."

"That in sooth," quoth the other, "I grant you that same; and I have fairly won this within walls, and with as good will do I yield it to you." With that he clasped his hands round the lord's neck and kissed him as courteously as he might. "Take ye here my spoils, no more have I won; ye should have it freely, though it were greater than this."

"'T is good," said the host, "gramercy thereof. Yet were I fain to know where ye won this same favor, and if it were by your own wit?"

"Nay," answered Gawain, "that was not in the bond. Ask me no more: ye have taken what was yours by right, be content with that."

They laughed and jested together, and sat them down to supper, where they were served with many dainties; and after supper they sat by the hearth, and wine was served out to them; and oft in their jesting they promised to observe on the morrow the same covenant that they had made before, and whatever chance might betide, to exchange their spoil, be it much or little, when they met at night. Thus they renewed their bargain before the whole court, and then the night-drink was served, and each courteously took leave of the other and gat him to bed.

By the time the cock had crowed thrice the lord of the castle had left his bed; Mass was sung and meat fitly served. The folk were forth to the wood ere the day broke; with hound and horn they rode over the plain, and uncoupled their dogs among the thorns. Soon they struck on the scent, and the hunt cheered on the hounds who were first to seize it, urging them with shouts. The others hastened to the cry, forty at once, and there rose such a clamor from the pack that the rocks rang again. The huntsmen spurred them on with shouting and blasts of the horn; and the hounds drew together to a thicket betwixt the water and a high crag in the cliff beneath the hillside. There where the rough rock fell ruggedly they, the huntsmen, fared to the finding, and cast about round the hill and the thicket behind them. The knights wist well what beast was within, and would drive him forth with the bloodhounds. And as they beat the bushes, suddenly over the beaters there rushed forth a wondrous great and fierce boar; long since had he left the herd to roam by himself. Grunting, he cast many to the ground, and fled forth at his best speed, without more mischief. The men hallooed loudly and cried, "Hay! Hay!" and blew the horns to urge on the hounds, and rode swiftly after the boar. Many a time did he turn to bay and tare the hounds, and they yelped, and howled shrilly. Then the men made ready their arrows and shot at him, but the points were turned on his thick hide, and the barbs would not bite upon him, for the shafts shivered in pieces, and the head but leapt again wherever it hit.

But when the boar felt the stroke of the arrows he waxed mad with rage, and turned on the hunters and tare many, so that, affrightened, they fled before him. But the lord on a swift steed pursued him, blowing his bugle; as a gallant knight he rode through the woodland, chasing the boar till the sun grew low.

So did the hunters this day, while Sir Gawain lay in his bed lapped in rich gear; and the lady forgat not to salute him, for early was she at his side, to cheer his mood.

She came to the bedside and looked on the knight, and Gawain gave her fit greeting, and she greeted him again with ready words, and sat her by his side and laughed, and with a sweet look she spoke to him:

"Sir, if ye be Gawain, I think it a wonder that ye be so stern and cold, and care not for the courtesies of friendship, but if one teach ye to know them ye cast the lesson out of your mind. Ye have soon forgotten what I taught ye yesterday, by all the truest tokens that I knew!"

"What is that?" quoth the knight. "I trow I know not. If it be sooth that ye say, then is the blame mine own."

"But I taught ye of kissing," quoth the fair lady. "Wherever a fair countenance is shown him, it behooves a courteous knight quickly to claim a kiss."

"Nay, my dear," said Sir Gawain, "cease that speech; that durst I not do lest I were denied, for if I were forbidden I wot I were wrong did I further entreat."

"I' faith," quoth the lady merrily, "ye may not be forbid, ye are strong enough to constrain by strength an ye will, were any so discourteous as to give ye denial."

"Yea, by heaven," said Gawain, "ye speak well; but threats profit little in the land where I dwell, and so with a gift that is given not of good will! I am at your commandment to kiss when ye like, to take or to leave as ye list."

Then the lady bent her down and kissed him courteously.

And as they spake together she said, "I would learn somewhat from ye, an ye would not be wroth, for young ye are and fair, and so courteous and knightly as ye are known to be, the head of all chivalry, and versed in all wisdom of love and war—'t is ever told of true knights how they adventured their lives for their true love, and endured hardships for her favors, and avenged her with valor, and eased her sorrows, and brought joy to her bower; and ye are the fairest knight of your time, and your fame and your honor are everywhere, yet I have sat by ye here twice, and never a word have I heard of love! Ye who are so courteous and skilled in such love ought surely to teach one so young and unskilled some little craft of true love! Why are ye so unlearned who art otherwise so famous? Or is it that ye deemed me unworthy to hearken to your teaching? For shame, Sir Knight! I come hither alone and sit at your side to learn of ye some skill; teach me of your wit, while my lord is from home."

"In good faith," quoth Gawain, "great is my joy and my profit that so fair a lady as ye are should deign to come hither, and trouble ye with so poor a man, and make sport with your knight with kindly countenance; it pleaseth me much. But that I, in my turn, should take it upon me to tell of love and such like matters to ye who know more by half, or a hundred fold, of such craft than I do, or ever shall in all my lifetime, by my troth 't were folly indeed! I will work your will to the best of my might as I am bounden, and evermore will I be your servant, so help me Christ!"

Then often with guile she questioned that knight that she might win him to woo her, but he defended himself so fairly that none might in any wise blame him, and naught but bliss and harmless jesting was there between them. They laughed and talked together till at last she kissed him, and craved her leave of him, and went her way.

Then the knight rose and went forth to Mass, and afterward dinner was served and he sat and spake with the ladies all day. But the lord of the castle rode ever over the land chasing the wild boar, that fled through the thickets, slaying the best of his hounds and breaking their backs in sunder; till at last he was so weary he might run no longer, but made for a hole in a mound by a rock. He got the mound at his back and faced the hounds, whetting his white tusks and foaming at the mouth. The huntsmen stood aloof, fearing to draw nigh him; so many of them had been already wounded that they were loath to be torn with his tusks, so fierce he was and mad with rage. At length the lord himself came up, and saw the beast at bay, and the men standing aloof. Then quickly he sprang to the ground and drew out a bright blade, and waded through the stream to the boar.

When the beast was aware of the knight with weapon in hand, he set up his bristles and snorted loudly, and many feared for their lord lest he should be slain. Then the boar leapt upon the knight so that beast and man were one atop of the other in the water; but the boar had the worst of it, for the man had marked, even as he sprang, and set the point of his brand to the beast's chest, and drove it up to the hilt, so that the heart was split in twain, and the boar fell snarling, and was swept down by the water to where a hundred hounds seized on him, and the men drew him to shore for the dogs to slay.

Then was there loud blowing of horns and baying of hounds; the huntsmen smote off the boar's head, and hung the carcass by the four feet to a stout pole, and so went on their way homewards. The head they bore before the lord himself, who had slain the beast at the ford by force of his strong hand.

It seemed him o'er long ere he saw Sir Gawain in the hall, and he called, and the guest came to take that which fell to his share. And when he saw Gawain the lord laughed aloud, and bade them call the ladies and the household together, and he showed them the game, and told them the tale, how they hunted the wild boar through the woods, and of his length and breadth and height; and Sir Gawain commended his deeds and praised him for his valor, well proven, for so mighty a beast had he never seen before.

Then they handled the huge head, and the lord said aloud, "Now, Gawain, this game is your own by sure covenant, as ye right well know."

"'T is sooth," quoth the knight, "and as truly will I give ye all I have gained." He took the host round the neck, and kissed him courteously twice. "Now are we quits," he said, "this eventide, of all the covenants that we made since I came hither."

And the lord answered, "By Saint Giles, ye are the best I know; ye will be rich in a short space if ye drive such bargains!"

Then they set up the tables on trestles, and covered them with fair cloths, and lit waxen tapers on the walls. The knights sat and were served in the hall, and much game and glee was there round the hearth, with many songs, both at supper and after; song of Christmas, and new carols, with all the mirth one may think of. And ever that lovely lady sat by the knight, and with still stolen looks made such feint of pleasing him, that Gawain marveled much, and was wroth with himself, but he could not for his courtesy return her fair glances, but dealt with her cunningly, however she might strive to wrest the thing.

When they had tarried in the hall so long as it seemed them good, they turned to the inner chamber and the wide hearth-place, and there they drank wine, and the host proffered to renew the covenant for New Year's Eve; but the knight craved leave to depart on the morrow, for it was nigh to the term when he must fulfill his pledge. But the lord would withhold him from so doing, and prayed him to tarry, and said:

"As I am a true knight I swear my troth that ye shall come to the Green Chapel to achieve your task on New Year's morn, long before prime.[3] Therefore abide ye in your bed, and I will hunt in this wood, and hold ye to the covenant to exchange with me against all the spoil I may bring hither. For twice have I tried ye, and found ye true, and the morrow shall be the third time and the best. Make we merry now while we may, and think on joy, for misfortune may take a man whensoever it wills."

Then Gawain granted his request, and they brought them drink, and they gat them with lights to bed.

Sir Gawain lay and slept softly, but the lord, who was keen on woodcraft, was afoot early. After Mass he and his men ate a morsel, and he asked for his steed; all the knights who should ride with him were already mounted before the hall gates.

'T was a fair frosty morning, for the sun rose red in ruddy vapor, and the welkin was clear of clouds. The hunters scattered them by a forest side, and the rocks rang again with the blast of their horns. Some came on the scent of a fox, and a hound gave

[3]Probably nine o'clock.

tongue; the huntsmen shouted, and the pack followed in a crowd on the trail. The fox ran before them, and when they saw him they pursued him with noise and much shouting, and he wound and turned through many a thick grove, often cowering and hearkening in a hedge. At last by a little ditch he leapt out of a spinney, stole away slily by a copse path, and so out of the wood and away from the hounds. But he went, ere he wist, to a chosen tryst, and three started forth on him at once, so he must needs double back, and betake him to the wood again.

Then was it joyful to hearken to the hounds; when all the pack had met together and had sight of their game they made as loud a din as if all the lofty cliffs had fallen clattering together. The huntsmen shouted and threatened, and followed close upon him so that he might scarce escape, but Reynard was wily, and he turned and doubled upon them and led the lord and his men over the hills, now on the slopes, now in the vales, while the knight at home slept through the cold morning beneath his costly curtains.

But the fair lady of the castle rose betimes, and clad herself in a rich mantle that reached even to the ground, left her throat and her fair neck bare, and was bordered and lined with costly furs. On her head she wore no golden circlet, but a network of precious stones, that gleamed and shone through her tresses in clusters of twenty together. Thus she came into the chamber, closed the door after her, and set open a window, and called to him gaily, "Sir Knight, how may ye sleep? The morning is so fair."

Sir Gawain was deep in slumber, and in his dream he vexed him much for the destiny that should befall him on the morrow, when he should meet the knight of the Green Chapel, and abide his blow; but when the lady spake he heard her, and came to himself, and roused from his dream and answered swiftly. The lady came laughing, and kissed him courteously, and he welcomed her fittingly with a cheerful countenance. He saw her so glorious and gaily dressed, so faultless of features and complexion, that it warmed his heart to look upon her.

They spake to each other smiling, and all was bliss and good cheer between them. They exchanged fair words, and much happiness was therein, yet was there a gulf between them, and she might win no more of her knight, for that gallant prince watched well his words—he would neither take her love, nor frankly refuse it. He cared for his courtesy, lest he be deemed churlish, and yet more for his honor lest he be traitor to his host. "God forbid," quoth he to himself, "that it should so befall." Thus with courteous words did he set aside all the special speeches that came from her lips.

Then spake the lady to the knight, "Ye deserve blame if ye hold not that lady who sits beside ye above all else in the world, if ye have not already a love whom ye hold dearer, and like better, and have sworn such firm faith to that lady that ye care not to loose it—and that am I now fain to believe. And now I pray ye straitly that ye tell me that in truth, and hide it not."

And the knight answered, "By Saint John" (and he smiled as he spake) "no such love have I, nor do I think to have yet awhile."

"That is the worst word I may hear," quoth the lady, "but in sooth I have mine answer; kiss me now courteously, and I will go hence; I can but mourn as a maiden that loves much."

Sighing, she stooped down and kissed him, and then she rose up and spake as she stood, "Now, dear, at our parting do me this grace, give me some gift, if it were but thy glove, that I may bethink me of my knight, and lessen my mourning."

"Now, I wis," quoth the knight, "I would that I had here the most precious thing that I possess on earth that I might leave ye as love-token, great or small, for ye have deserved forsooth more reward than I might give ye. But it is not to your honor to have at this time a glove for reward as gift from Gawain, and I am here on a strange errand, and have no man with me, nor mails with goodly things—that mislikes me much, lady, at this time; but each man must fare as he is taken, if for sorrow and ill."

"Nay, knight highly honored," quoth that lovesome lady, "though I have naught of yours, yet shall ye have somewhat of mine."

With that she reached him a ring of red gold with a sparkling stone therein, that shone even as the sun (wit ye well, it was worth many marks); but the knight refused it, and spake readily.

"I will take no gift, lady, at this time. I have none to give, and none will I take."

She prayed him to take it, but he refused her prayer, and sware in sooth that he would not have it.

The lady was sorely vexed, and said, "If ye refuse my ring as too costly, that ye will not be so highly beholden to me, I will give you my girdle as a lesser gift." With that she loosened a lace that was fastened at her side, knit upon her kirtle under her mantle. It was wrought of green silk, and gold, only braided by the fingers, and that she offered to the knight, and besought him though it were of little worth that he would take it, and he said nay, he would touch neither gold nor gear ere God give him grace to achieve the adventure for which he had come hither. "And therefore, I pray ye, displease ye not, and ask me no longer, for I may not grant it. I am dearly beholden to ye for the favor ye have shown me, and ever, in heat and cold, will I be your true servant."

"Now," said the lady, "ye refuse this silk, for it is simple in itself, and so it seems, indeed; lo, it is small to look upon and less in cost, but whoso knew the virtue that is knit therein he would, peradventure, value it more highly. For whatever knight is girded with this green lace, while he bears it knotted about him there is no man under heaven can overcome him, for he may not be slain for any magic on earth."

Then Gawain bethought him, and it came into his heart that this were a jewel for the jeopardy that awaited him when he came to the Green Chapel to seek the return blow—could he so order it that he should escape unslain, 't were a craft worth trying. Then he bare with her chiding, and let her say her say, and she pressed the girdle on him and prayed him to take it, and he granted her prayer, and she gave it him with good will, and besought him for her sake never to reveal it but to hide it loyally from her lord, and the knight agreed that never should any man know it, save they two alone. He thanked her often and heartily, and she kissed him for the third time.

Then she took her leave of him, and when she was gone Sir Gawain rose, and clad him in rich attire, and took the girdle, and knotted it round him, and hid it beneath his robes. Then he took his way to the chapel, and sought out a priest privily and prayed him to teach him better how his soul might be saved when he should go hence; and there he shrived him, and showed his misdeeds, both great and small, and besought mercy and craved absolution; and the priest assoiled[4] him, and set him as clean as if doomsday had been on the morrow. And afterwards Sir Gawain made him merry with the ladies, with carols, and all kinds of joy, as never he did but that one day, even to nightfall; and all the men marveled at him, and said that never since he came thither had he been so merry.

Meanwhile the lord of the castle was abroad chasing the fox; awhile he lost him, and as he rode through a spinney he heard the hounds near at hand, and Reynard came creeping through a thick grove, with all the pack at his heels. Then the lord drew out his shining brand, and cast it at the beast, and the fox swerved aside for the sharp edge, and would have doubled back, but a hound was on him ere he might turn, and right before the horse's feet they all fell on him, and worried him fiercely, snarling the while.

Then the lord leapt from his saddle, and caught the fox from the jaws, and held it aloft over his head, and hallooed loudly, and many brave hounds bayed as they beheld it; and the hunters hied them thither, blowing their horns; all that bare bugles blew them at once, and all the others shouted. 'T was the merriest meeting that ever men heard, the clamor that was raised at the death of the fox. They rewarded the hounds, stroking them and rubbing their heads, and took Reynard and stripped him of his coat; then blowing their horns, they turned them homewards, for it was nigh nightfall.

The lord was gladsome at his return, and found a bright fire on the hearth, and the knight beside it, the good Sir Gawain, who

[4] Absolved.

was in joyous mood for the pleasure he had had with the ladies. He wore a robe of blue, that reached even to the ground, and a surcoat richly furred, that became him well. A hood like to the surcoat fell on his shoulders, and all alike were done about with fur. He met the host in the midst of the floor, and jesting, he greeted him, and said, "Now shall I be first to fulfill our covenant which we made together when there was no lack of wine." Then he embraced the knight, and kissed him thrice, as solemnly as he might.

"Of a sooth," quoth the other, "ye have good luck in the matter of this covenant, if ye made a good exchange!"

"Yet, it matters naught of the exchange," quoth Gawain, "since what I owe is swiftly paid."

"Marry," said the other, "mine is behind, for I have hunted all this day, and naught have I got but this foul fox-skin, and that is but poor payment for three such kisses as ye have here given me."

"Enough," quoth Sir Gawain, "I thank ye, by the Rood."

Then the lord told them of his hunting, and how the fox had been slain.

With mirth and minstrelsy, and dainties at their will, they made them as merry as a folk well might till 't was time for them to sever, for at last they must needs betake them to their beds. Then the knight took his leave of the lord, and thanked him fairly.

"For the fair sojourn that I have had here at this high feast may the High King give ye honor. I give ye myself, as one of your servants, if ye so like; for I must needs, as you know, go hence with the morn, and ye will give me, as ye promised, a guide to show me the way to the Green Chapel, an God will suffer me on New Year's Day to deal the doom of my weird." [5]

"By my faith," quoth the host, "all that ever I promised, that shall I keep with good will." Then he gave him a servant to set him in the way, and lead him by the downs, that he should have no need to ford the stream, and should fare by the shortest road through the groves; and Gawain thanked the lord for the honor done him. Then he would take leave of the ladies, and courteously he kissed them, and spake, praying them to receive his thanks, and they made like reply; then with many sighs they commended him to Christ, and he departed courteously from that fold. Each man that he met he thanked him for his service and his solace, and the pains he had been at to do his will; and each found it as hard to part from the knight as if he had ever dwelt with him.

Then they led him with torches to his chamber, and brought him to his bed to rest. That he slept soundly I may not say, for the morrow gave him much to think on. Let him rest awhile, for he was near that which he sought, and if ye will but listen to me I will tell ye how it fared with him thereafter.

IV

Now the New Year drew nigh, and the night passed, and the day chased the darkness, as is God's will; but wild weather wakened therewith. The clouds cast the cold to the earth, with enough of the north to slay them that lacked clothing. The snow drave smartly, and the whistling wind blew from the heights, and made great drifts in the valleys. The knight, lying in his bed, listened, for though his eyes were shut, he might sleep but little, and hearkened every cock that crew.

He arose ere the day broke, by the light of a lamp that burned in his chamber, and called to his chamberlain, bidding him bring his armor and saddle his steed. The other gat him up, and fetched his garments, and robed Sir Gawain.

First he clad him in his clothes to keep off the cold, and then in his harness, which was well and fairly kept. Both hauberk and plates were well burnished, the rings of the rich byrnie freed from rust, and all as fresh as at first, so that the knight was fain to thank them. Then he did on each piece, and bade them bring his steed, while he put the fairest raiment on himself; his coat with its fair cognizance, adorned with precious stones upon velvet, with broidered seams, and all furred within with costly skins. And he left not the lace, the lady's gift, that Gawain for-

[5] To take the judgment of my fate.

got not, for his own good. When he had girded on his sword he wrapped the gift twice about him, swathed around his waist. The girdle of green silk set gaily and well upon the royal red cloth, rich to behold, but the knight ware it not for pride of the pendants, polished though they were with fair gold that gleamed brightly on the ends, but to save himself from sword and knife, when it behooved him to abide his hurt without question. With that the hero went forth, and thanked that kindly folk full often.

Then was Gringalet ready, that was great and strong, and had been well cared for and tended in every wise; in fair condition was that proud steed, and fit for a journey. Then Gawain went to him, and looked on his coat, and said by his sooth, "There is a folk in this place that thinketh on honor; much joy may they have, and the lord who maintains them, and may all good betide that lovely lady all her life long. Since they for charity cherish a guest, and hold honor in their hands, may He who holds the heaven on high requite them, and also ye all. And if I might live anywhile on earth, I would give ye full reward, readily, if so I might." Then he set foot in the stirrup and bestrode his steed, and his squire gave him his shield, which he laid on his shoulder. Then he smote Gringalet with his golden spurs, and the steed pranced on the stones and would stand no longer.

By that his man was mounted, who bare his spear and lance, and Gawain quoth, "I commend this castle to Christ, may He give it ever good fortune." Then the drawbridge was let down, and the broad gates unbarred and opened on both sides; the knight crossed himself, and passed through the gateway, and praised the porter, who knelt before the prince, and gave him good-day, and commended him to God. Thus the knight went on his way, with the one man who should guide him to that dread place where he should receive rueful payment.

The two went by hedges where the boughs were bare, and climbed the cliffs where the cold clings. Naught fell from the heavens, but 't was ill beneath them; mist brooded over the moor and hung on the mountains; each hill had a cap, a great cloak, of mist. The streams foamed and bubbled between their banks, dashing sparkling on the shores where they shelved downwards. Rugged and dangerous was the way through the woods, till it was time for the sun-rising. Then were they on a high hill; the snow lay white beside them, and the man who rode with Gawain drew rein by his master.

"Sir," he said, "I have brought ye hither, and now ye are not far from the place that ye have sought so specially. But I will tell ye for sooth, since I know ye well, and ye are such a knight as I well love, would ye follow my counsel ye would fare the better. The place whither ye go is accounted full perilous, for he who liveth in that waste is the worst on earth, for he is strong and fierce; and loveth to deal mighty blows; taller he is than any man on earth, and greater of frame than any four in Arthur's court, or in any other. And this is his custom at the Green Chapel; there may no man pass by that place, however proud his arms, but he does him to death by force of his hand, for he is a discourteous knight, and shows no mercy. Be he churl or chaplain who rides by that chapel, monk or mass-priest, or any man else, he thinks it as pleasant to slay them as to pass alive himself. Therefore, I tell ye, as sooth as ye sit in saddle, if ye come there, and that knight know it, ye shall be slain, though ye had twenty lives; trow me that truly! He has dwelt here full long and seen many a combat; ye may not defend ye against his blows. Therefore, good Sir Gawain, let the man be, and get ye away some other road; for God's sake seek ye another land, and there may Christ speed ye! And I will hie me home again, and I promise ye further that I will swear by God and the saints, or any other oath ye please, that I will keep counsel faithfully, and never let any wit the tale that ye fled for fear of any man."

"Gramercy," quoth Gawain, but ill-pleased. "Good fortune be his who wishes me good, and that thou wouldst keep faith with me I will believe; but didst thou keep it never so truly, an I passed here and fled for fear as thou sayest, then were I a coward knight, and might not be held guiltless. So I will to the chapel let chance what may, and talk with that man, even as I may list, whether for weal or for woe as fate may have it. Fierce though he may be in fight, yet God knoweth well how to save His servants."

"Well," quoth the other, "now that ye have said so much that ye will take your own harm on yourself, and ye be pleased to lose your life, I will neither let[1] nor keep ye. Have here your helm and the spear in your hand, and ride down this same road beside the rock till ye come to the bottom of the valley, and there look a little to the left hand, and ye shall see in that vale the chapel, and the grim man who keeps it. Now fare ye well, noble Gawain; for all the gold on earth I would not go with ye nor bear ye fellowship one step further." With that the man turned his bridle into the wood, smote the horse with his spurs as hard as he could, and galloped off, leaving the knight alone.

Quoth Gawain, "I will neither greet[2] nor moan, but commend myself to God, and yield me to His will."

Then the knight spurred Gringalet, and rode adown the path close in by a bank beside a grove. So he rode through the rough thicket, right into the dale, and there he halted, for it seemed him wild enough. No sign of a chapel could he see, but high and burnt banks on either side and rough rugged crags with great stones above. An ill-looking place he thought it.

Then he drew in his horse and looked round to seek the chapel, but he saw none and thought it strange. Then he saw as it were a mound on a level space of land by a bank beside the stream where it ran swiftly; the water bubbled within as if boiling. The knight turned his steed to the mound, and lighted down and tied the rein to the branch of a linden; and he turned to the mound and walked around it, questioning with himself what it might be. It had a hole at the end and at either side, and was overgrown with clumps of grass, and it was hollow within as an old cave or the crevice of a crag; he knew not what it might be.

"Ah," quoth Gawain, "can this be the Green Chapel? Here might the devil say his matins at midnight! Now I wis there is wizardry here. 'T is an ugly oratory, all overgrown with grass, and 't would well beseem that fellow in green to say his devotions on devil's wise. Now feel I in five wits, 't is the foul fiend himself who hath set me this tryst, to destroy me here! This is a chapel of mischance: ill-luck betide it, 't is the cursedest kirk that ever I came in!"

Helmet on head and lance in hand, he came up to the rough dwelling, when he heard over the high hill beyond the brook, as it were in a bank, a wondrous fierce noise, that rang in the cliff as if it would cleave asunder. 'Twas as if one ground a scythe on a grindstone; it whirred and whetted like water on a mill-wheel and rushed and rang, terrible to hear.

"By God," quoth Gawain, "I trow that gear is preparing for the knight who will meet me here. Alas! naught may help me, yet should my life be forfeit, I fear not a jot!" With that he called aloud. "Who waiteth in this place to give me tryst? Now is Gawain come hither: if any man will aught of him let him hasten hither now or never."

"Stay," quoth one on the bank above his head, "and ye shall speedily have that which I promised ye." Yet for a while the noise of whetting went on ere he appeared, and then he came forth from a cave in the crag with a fell weapon, a Danish ax newly dight, wherewith to deal the blow. An evil head it had, four feet large, no less, sharply ground, and bound to the handle by the lace that gleamed brightly. And the knight himself was all green as before, face and foot, locks and beard, but now he was afoot. When he came to the water he would not wade it, but sprang over with the pole of his ax, and strode boldly over the bent[3] that was white with snow.

Sir Gawain went to meet him, but he made no low bow. The other said, "Now, fair sir, one may trust thee to keep tryst. Thou art welcome, Gawain, to my place. Thou hast timed thy coming as befits a true man. Thou knowest the covenant set between us: at this time twelve months agone thou didst take that which fell to thee, and

[1]Hinder. [2]Weep.

[3]Field.

I at this New Year will readily requite thee. We are in this valley, verily alone; here are no knights to sever us, do what we will. Have off thy helm from thine head, and have here thy pay; make me no more talking than I did then when thou didst strike off my head with one blow."

"Nay," quoth Gawain, "by God that gave me life, I shall make no moan whatever befall me, but make thou ready for the blow and I shall stand still and say never a word to thee, do as thou wilt."

With that he bent his head and showed his neck all bare, and made as if he had no fear, for he would not be thought a-dread.

Then the Green Knight made him ready and grasped his grim weapon to smite Gawain. With all his force he bore it aloft with a mighty feint of slaying him: had it fallen as straight as he aimed he who was ever doughty of deed had been slain by the blow. But Gawain swerved aside as the ax came gliding down to slay him as he stood, and shrank a little with the shoulders, for the sharp iron. The other heaved up the blade and rebuked the prince with many proud words:

"Thou art not Gawain," he said, "who is held so valiant, that never feared he man by hill or vale, but thou shrinkest for fear ere thou feelest hurt. Such cowardice did I never hear of Gawain! Neither did *I* flinch from thy blow, or make strife in King Arthur's hall. My head fell to my feet, and yet I fled not; but thou didst wax faint of heart ere any harm befell. Wherefore must I be deemed the braver knight."

Quoth Gawain, "I shrank once, but so will I no more; though an my head fall on the stones I cannot replace it. But haste, Sir Knight, by thy faith, and bring me to the point, deal me my destiny, and do it out of hand, for I will stand thee a stroke and move no more till thine ax have hit me—my troth on it."

"Have at thee, then," quoth the other, and heaved aloft the ax with fierce mien, as if he were mad. He struck at him fiercely but wounded him not, withholding his hand ere it might strike him.

Gawain abode the stroke, and flinched in no limb, but stood still as a stone or the stump of a tree that is fast rooted in the rocky ground with a hundred roots.

Then spake gaily the man in green, "So now thou hast thine heart whole it behooves me to smite. Hold aside thy hood that Arthur gave thee, and keep thy neck thus bent lest it cover it again."

Then Gawain said angrily, "Why talk on thus? Thou dost threaten too long. I hope thy heart misgives thee."

"For sooth," quoth the other, "so fiercely thou speakest I will no longer let thine errand wait its reward." Then he braced himself to strike, frowning with lips and brow, 't was no marvel that it pleased but ill him who hoped for no rescue. He lifted the ax lightly and let it fall with the edge of the blade on the bare neck. Though he struck swiftly, it hurt him no more than on the one side where it severed the skin. The sharp blade cut into the flesh so that the blood ran over his shoulder to the ground. And when the knight saw the blood staining the snow, he sprang forth, swift-foot, more than a spear's length, seized his helmet and set it on his head, cast his shield over his shoulder, drew out his bright sword, and spake boldly (never since he was born was he half so blithe), "Stop, Sir Knight, bid me no more blows; I have stood a stroke here without flinching, and if thou give me another, I shall requite thee, and give thee as good again. By the covenant made betwixt us in Arthur's hall but one blow falls to me here. Halt, therefore."

Then the Green Knight drew off from him and leaned on his ax, setting the shaft on the ground, and looked on Gawain as he stood all armed and faced him fearlessly—at heart it pleased him well. Then he spake merrily in a loud voice, and said to the knight, "Bold sir, be not so fierce; no man here hath done thee wrong, nor will do, save by covenant, as we made at Arthur's court. I promised thee a blow and thou hast it—hold thyself well paid! I release thee of all other claims. If I had been so minded I might perchance have given thee a rougher buffet. First I menaced thee with a feigned one, and hurt thee not for the covenant that we made in the first night, and which thou didst hold truly. All the gain didst thou give me as a true man should. The other feint I proffered thee for the morrow: my fair wife kissed thee, and thou didst give me her kisses—for both those days I gave thee two blows without scathe—true man, true return. But the third time thou didst fail, and therefore hadst thou that blow. For 't is *my* weed thou wearest, that same woven girdle, my own wife wrought it, that do I wot for sooth. Now know I well thy kisses, and thy conversation, and the wooing of my wife, for 't was mine own doing. I sent her to try thee, and in sooth I think thou art the most faultless knight that ever trod earth. As a pearl among white peas is of more worth than they, so is Gawain, i' faith, by other knights. But thou didst lack a little, Sir Knight, and wast wanting in loyalty, yet that was for no evil work, nor for wooing neither, but because thou lovedst thy life—therefore I blame thee the less."

Then the other stood a great while, still sorely angered and vexed within himself; all the blood flew to his face, and he shrank for shame as the Green Knight spake; and the first words he said were, "Cursed be ye, cowardice and covetousness, for in ye is the destruction of virtue." Then he loosed the girdle, and gave it to the knight. "Lo, take there the falsity, may foul befall it! For fear of thy blow cowardice bade me make friends with covetousness and forsake the customs of largess and loyalty, which befit all knights. Now am I faulty and false and have been afeared: from treachery and untruth come sorrow and care. I avow to thee, Sir Knight, that I have ill done; do then thy will. I shall be more wary hereafter."

Then the other laughed and said gaily, "I wot I am whole of the hurt I had, and thou hast made such free confession of thy misdeeds, and hast so borne the penance of mine ax edge, that I hold thee absolved from that sin, and purged as clean as if thou hadst never sinned since thou wast born. And this girdle that is wrought with gold and green, like my raiment, do I give thee, Sir Gawain, that thou mayest think upon this chance when thou goest forth among princes of renown, and keep this for a token of the adventure of the Green Chapel, as it chanced between chivalrous knights. And thou shalt come again with me to my dwelling and pass the rest of this feast in gladness." Then the lord laid hold of him, and said, "I wot we shall soon make peace with my wife, who was thy bitter enemy."

"Nay, forsooth," said Sir Gawain, and seized his helmet and took it off swiftly, and thanked the knight: "I have fared ill, may bliss betide thee, and may He who rules all things reward thee swiftly. Commend me to that courteous lady, thy fair wife, and to the other my honored ladies, who have beguiled their knight with skilful craft. But 't is no marvel if one be made a fool and brought to sorrow by women's wiles, for so was Adam beguiled by one, and Solomon by many, and Samson all too soon, for Delilah dealt him his doom; and David thereafter was wedded with Bathsheba, which brought him much sorrow—if one might love a woman and believe her not, 't were great gain! And since all they were beguiled by women, methinks 't is the less blame to me that I was misled! But as for thy girdle, that will I take with good will, not for gain of the gold, nor for samite, nor silk, nor the costly pendants, neither for weal nor for worship, but in sign of my frailty. I shall look upon it when I ride in renown and remind myself of the fault and faintness of the flesh; and so when pride uplifts me for prowess of arms, the sight of this lace shall humble my heart. But one thing would I pray, if it displease thee not: since thou art lord of yonder land wherein I have dwelt, tell me what thy rightful name may be, and I will ask no more."

"That will I truly," quoth the other. "Bernlak de Hautdesert am I called in this land. Morgain le Fay dwelleth in mine house, and through knowledge of clerkly craft hath she taken many. For long time was she the mistress of Merlin, who knew well all you knights of the court. Morgain the goddess is she called therefore, and there is none so haughty but she can bring him low. She sent me in this guise to yon fair hall to test the truth of the renown that is spread abroad of the valor of the Round Table. She taught me this marvel to betray your wits, to vex Guinevere and fright her to death by the man who spake with his head in his hand at the high table. That is she who is at home, that ancient lady; she is even thine aunt, Arthur's half-sister, the daughter of the Duchess of Tintagel, who afterward married King Uther. Therefore I bid thee, knight, come to thine aunt, and make merry in thine house; my folk love thee, and I wish thee as well as any man on earth, by my faith, for thy true dealing."

But Sir Gawain said nay, he would in no wise do so; so they embraced and kissed, and commended each other to the Prince of Paradise, and parted right there, on the cold ground. Gawain on his steed rode swiftly to the king's hall, and the Green Knight got him whithersoever he would.

Sir Gawain, who had thus won grace of his life, rode through wild ways on Gringalet; oft he lodged in a house, and oft without, and many adventures did he have and came off victor full often, as at this time I cannot relate in tale. The hurt that he had in his neck was healed, he bare the shining girdle as a baldric bound by his side, and made fast with a knot 'neath his left arm, in token that he was taken in a fault—and thus he came in safety again to the court.

Then joy awakened in that dwelling when the king knew that the good Sir Gawain was come, for he deemed it gain. King Arthur kissed the knight, and the queen also, and many valiant knights sought to embrace him. They asked him how he had fared, and he told them all that had chanced to him—the adventure of the chapel, the fashion of the knight, the love of the lady—at last of the lace. He showed them the wound in the neck which he won for his disloyalty at the hand of the knight; the blood flew to his face for shame as he told the tale.

"Lo, lady," he quoth, and handled the lace, "this is the bond of the blame that I bear in my neck, this is the harm and the loss I have suffered, the cowardice and covetousness in which I was caught, the token of my covenant in which I was taken. And I must needs wear it so long as I live, for none may hide his harm, but undone it may not be, for if it hath clung to thee once, it may never be severed."

Then the king comforted the knight, and the court laughed loudly at the tale, and all made accord that the lords and the ladies who belonged to the Round Table, each hero among them, should wear bound about him a baldric of bright green for the sake of Sir Gawain. And to this was agreed all the honor of the Round Table, and he who ware it was honored the more thereafter, as it is testified in the book of romance. That in Arthur's days this adventure befell, the book of Brutus bears witness. For since that bold knight came hither first, and the siege and the assault were ceased at Troy, I wis

Many a venture herebefore
Hath fallen such as this:
May He that bare the crown of thorn
Bring us unto His bliss.

Amen.

WILLIAM LANGLAND(?)

The Vision of William concerning Piers the Plowman has been traditionally attributed to one William Langland, to whom Skeat assigned, for convenience' sake, the conjectural dates *c.* 1332–*c.* 1400. On the basis of the author's supposed references to himself within the poem a biography has also been made up. His name, however, has been disputed, and likewise the identification with him of the "Will" of the poem; as a matter of fact nothing is certainly known about the authorship of the work. *Piers Plowman* exists in three versions, known as the A-, B-, and C-texts. The A-text was written in 1362 or shortly thereafter. It is 2567 lines in length. The B-text was written probably in 1376 or 1377; for this the A-text was taken as a basis, was thoroughly made over, and was considerably enlarged, the number of lines in this text being 7242. The C-text was written probably some time between 1393 and 1399; it is a revision of the B-text with many comparatively small changes, and contains 7357 lines. Until a generation ago these versions were accepted as the work of one writer. In 1906, however, Professor J. M. Manly asserted that the A-text was the work of three writers, and that the B- and C-texts were by two different authors, each other than the writers of the A-text. Proof of these assertions has not yet appeared, and the published work of other scholars since 1906 has on the whole gone to show that their proof would be more difficult than may have been at first supposed. Consequently, although the question of single or multiple authorship remains an open one and can perhaps never be settled, it seems justifiable to retain, at least provisionally, the traditional name William Langland.

Piers Plowman was in its own age and in the fifteenth century one of the most popular and valued pieces of literature in the English language, as is evinced by the fact that no less than forty-seven manuscripts of it are still extant. This popularity was deserved. The poem is, after *The Canterbury Tales* of Chaucer, "the greatest piece of Middle English literature; it is one of the greatest of the medieval vision poems, and, as a vision poem, in many respects second only to the *Divine Comedy;* it is one of the foremost of the writings in English in which allegory is used" (J. E. Wells, *Manual of the Writings in Middle English,* p. 264). Moreover, to any student of the fourteenth century the poem is a necessary complement to the work of Chaucer, picturing as it does the life of the lower classes, and reflecting as it does the convictions and aspirations of simple-hearted men of deep feeling. *Piers Plowman* has little of conscious art, its language is rough and broken, and it is written in the old alliterative meter, but its author felt intensely, saw deeply, and dealt greatly with the great issues of life.

The A-, B-, and C-texts are reproduced in parallel columns in *The Vision of William concerning Piers the Plowman,* ed. Walter W. Skeat (Oxford, 1886). Greta Hort's *Piers Plowman and Contemporary Religious Thought* (London, n. d.) is a valuable study of a side of the poem which is too often neglected at the present time. For the medieval background see also D. Chadwick, *Social Life in the Days of Piers Plowman* (Cambridge, 1922), and *Life in the Middle Ages,* ed. and trans. George G. Coulton (Cambridge, 1928–1930). *The Vision of Piers Plowman* is the title of a recent complete translation into modern English by Henry W. Wells, with Introduction by Nevill Coghill (London and New York, 1935).

THE VISION OF PIERS THE PLOWMAN[1]

PROLOGUE

THE FIELD FULL OF FOLK

In a summer season, when soft was the sun,
I enshrouded me well in a shepherd's garb,
And robed as a hermit, unholy of works,
Went wide through the world, all wonders to hear.
And on a May morning, on Malvern Hills,[2] 5

[1]From the translation of W. W. Skeat in "The Medieval Library."

[2]In Worcestershire.

Strange fancies befell me, and fairy-like dreams.
I was weary of wand'ring, and went to repose
On a broad green bank, by a burn-side;
As I lay there and leaned and looked on the waters,
I slumbered and slept, they sounded so merry. 10

Came moving before me a marvelous vision;
I was lost in a wild waste; but *where,* I discerned not.
I beheld in the east, on high, near the sun,
A tower on a hill-top, with turrets well wrought;
A deep dale beneath, and a dungeon therein, 15
With deep ditches and dark, and dreadful to see.
A fair field, full of folk, I found there between,[3]
Of all manner of men, the mean and the rich,
All working or wand'ring, as the world requires.

Some plowed with the plow; their play was but seldom; 20
Some sowing, some earning, with sweat of their brows,
The gain which the great ones in gluttony waste.

In pride of apparel some passed on their way,
And in costliest clothing were quaintly disguised.
In prayer and in penance some placed their delight, 25
And all for our Lord's love lived strictly and hard,
In hope to have after their heavenly meed;
These hermits and anchorites held to their cells,
Not caring to roam through the country around
For doles of sweet dainties, their flesh to delight. 30

Some chose to be chapmen, to chaffer for gain;
As it seems to our sight, such surely succeed.
And some, to make merry, as minstrels are wont,
Getting gold with their glee, yet guiltless, I trust.

As for jugglers and jesters, all Judas's children, 35
That feign silly fancies, appareled as fools,
Having wit, if they willed it, to work as they ought—
I pass o'er what Paul would have preached of these sinners;[4]
For the speaker of evil is Satan's own son.

Next beggars and beadsmen were bustling about, 40
Their bags and their bellies with bread were well crammed.
By falsehood they fed them, and fought o'er their ale,
As greedy as gluttons they go to their beds,
And rise up as ribalds, these robberlike knaves;
Sleep and vile sloth pursue them forever. 45

Next, pilgrims and palmers would plight them together
To seek out Saint James[5] and saints known in Rome;
They went on their way with many wise tales,
And had leave to tell lies all their lifetime after.
Some saw I that said they had sought out the saints; 50
In each tale that they told their tongue fashioned lies
Much sooner than sooth, as it seemed by their speech.

Of hermits a huge heap, with hooks to their staves,
To Walsingham[6] went; and their wenches went after;
Great lubbers and long, that to labor were loath; 55
They clothed them in cloaks, to be known from all others
And arrayed them as hermits, more ease to enjoy.

I found there some friars of all the four orders,[7]
Who preached to the people for personal profit;

[3]The world, midway between heaven and hell.

[4]"If any would not work, neither should he eat" (II Thessalonians, 3:10).

[5]The shrine of St. James at Compostella in Spain.

[6]The shrine of our Lady at Walsingham in Norfolk.

[7]Carmelites, Augustinians, Dominicans, and Minorites or Franciscans.

As it seemed to them good, put a gloss on the gospel, 60
And explained it at pleasure; they coveted copes.
Many of these masters may wear what they will;
Their money and merchandise meet well together;
Since Charity was chapman, and chief to shrive lords,
What sights we have seen in a few short years! 65
Unless they and the Church keep closer together,
The most mischief e'er made will be mounting up fast.

There preached, too, a pardoner, a priest, as he seemed,
Who brought forth a bull, with the bishop's seals,
And said he himself might absolve them all 70
Of falsehood in fasting, or vows they had broken.
The laymen believed him, and liked well his words,
Came up and came kneeling, to kiss the said bull;
He blessed them right bravely, and blinded their eyes,
And won with his roll both their rings and their brooches. 75
Thus they give up their gold for such gluttons to spend,
And lose to loose livers their lawful gains.
If the bishop were wiser, or worth both his ears,
His seal ne'er were sent, to deceive so the people.
Small blame of the bishop such boys will express; 80
For the parish-priest and pardoner part all the silver
That the poor of the parish would otherwise share.

The parsons and parish-priests complained to the bishop
That their parishes were poor since the pestilence-year,[8]
Asking license and leave in London to dwell, 85
To sing there for simony; for silver is sweet.

Bishops and bachelors, both masters and doctors,
Having cures[9] under Christ, and crowned with the tonsure
To show they should hear their parishioners' shrift,
Preaching and praying, and feeding the poor, 90
Are lodged now in London, in Lent-time and ever.
Some serve there the king, and count out his silver,
In chancery and exchequer make claims of his dues
From wards and from ward-motes,[10] his waifs and his strays.
And some serve as servants both ladies and lords, 95
Are as stewards enstalled, or as judges take seat.
Their masses and matins and many of their prayers
Are done undevoutly. I dread, at the last,
Lest Christ, at the Judgment, will curse not a few.
I pondered on the power that Peter had to keep— 100
"To bind and to unbind"—as the Book tells us.[11]
How he left it, with love, as our Lord him bade,
In trust of four virtues—the best of all virtues—
As "cardinal" known, or "the closing of gates,"
Where Christ's in His kingdom, to close and to shut, 105
Or to open to good men the glory of heaven.[12]
But for cardinals at court, who have caught up the name,
And presume on their power a pope to appoint,
To have Peter's own power—impugn it I dare not;
To learning and love that election belongeth; 110
I might, but I must not, say more of that court.

Then came there a king, with knights in a troop;
The might of the commons had made him to reign;

[8]Probably 1348–9, the year of the Great Pestilence.

[9]Spiritual duties. [10]Ward-meetings.

[11]Matthew, 16:19.

[12]Prudence, Temperance, Fortitude, and Justice are called the four "cardinal," or all-important, virtues. The poet puns on the derivation of "cardinal" from *cardo,* the Latin word for a door-hinge, and connects this idea with that of St. Peter's keys.

And then came Kind-Wit,[13] and clerks he appointed
To counsel the king, and the commons to save. 115
The king and his knights, and the clergy also
Decreed that the commons must toil for their bread.

The commons contrived for the craftsmen their trades,
And for profit o' the people set plowmen to work,
To till and to travail, as true life requires; 120
While the king and the commons, with Kind-Wit as third,
Made laws for protecting all loyal men's goods.

Then looked up a lunatic, a lean man withal,
Knelt down to the king, and full clerk-like spake:—
"Christ keep thee, sir king! and thy kingdom eke, 125
So to reign in thy land that thy lieges may love thee,
And thy righteous rule be rewarded in heaven!"

Then, high in the air, an angel from heaven
Spake loudly in Latin, that laymen might fail
To object or to judge, or justly to doubt, 130
But suffer and serve:—and thus said the angel—
"Know, prince, that thy power soon passes forever;
Thy kingdom is Christ's, and in keeping His laws
Thou 'rt just; but let justice be joined to discretion!
Array naked justice in raiment of mercy; 135
Sow wisely such grain as thou gladly wouldst reap.
Who deals in bare justice, bare justice be dealt him;
To him who has mercy shall mercy be meted."

A riotous rich one, who rambled in talk,
To the angel on high made answer in anger:— 140
"Since *rex* is derived, sure, from *rego*, I rule,
Kings rule by the laws, or they rule but in name."

Then cried out the commons, exclaiming in Latin,
To the king and his knights (let him construe, who will)—
Precepta regis sunt nobis vincula legis: 145
"Commandments of kings are the canons of law."

Then forth ran a rout of great rats, all at once,
Where met them small mice, yea, more than a thousand;
All came to a council for their common profit.[14]
For a cat of the court would come, when he liked, 150
And chase them and clutch them, and catch them at will,
Play with them perilously, and push them about:—
"For dread of the danger, look round us we dare not;
If we grudge him his game, he will grieve us the more,
Tease us or toss us, or take in his claws, 155
That we loathe our own lives, ere he lets us go free.
If by wit or by wile we his will might withstand,
We might lord it aloft, and might live at our ease."

Then a rat of renown, very ready of tongue,
Said, for a sovereign help to themselves, 160
"Some cits have I seen, in the city of London,
Wear chains on their necks of the choicest gold,
Or collars of crafty work; uncoupled they go
Both in warren and waste, as their will inclines,
And elsewhere at odd times, as I hear tell. 165
If they bore each a bell, by its ringing, me thinketh,
One might wit where they were, and away soon run!

[13] Common Sense; or perhaps the natural intelligence enlightened by revelation.

[14] "This fable refers to events following the Good Parliament (1376). The King, Edward III, is the cat. The rats are certain nobles, desiring to depose the king (to 'bell the cat'), but lacking the power and courage to put their plan into effect. The poet sympathizes with the desire of the nobles to bring pressure on the rulers, but refuses to go so far as to favor the deposition of the aged king and the establishment of a regency" (Henry W. Wells).

Right so," quoth the rat, "doth reason suggest
To buy a bell of brass or of bright silver,
To be bound on a collar, for our common profit, 170
On the cat's neck to hang; then each hearer can tell
If he rambles or rests him, or runs out to play!
When mild is his mood, we can move as we list
And appear in his presence, when playful and pleased,
Or, when angry, beware; and away will we run!" 175

All the rout of great rats to his reasons assented,
But when bought was the bell, and well bound on the collar,
Not a rat in the rout, for the realm of all France,
Durst bind the said bell about the cat's neck,
Nor hang it beside him, all England to win! 180
They owned they were cowards, and their counsel weak;
So their labor was lost, and all their long study.

Then a mouse of mind, who had merit, methought,
Strode forth sternly, and stood before them all,
And to the rout of rats rehearsèd these words: 185
"Though we killed the old cat, yet another would come
To catch all our kin, though we crept under benches.
I counsel the commons to let the cat be;
Be we never so bold as to show him the bell.
For I heard my sire say, some seven years since, 190
'Where the cat is a kitten, the court is a sad one';
So witnesseth Scripture, who willeth may read it,
Woe to thee, land, when thy king is a child![15]
For no one could rest him, for rats in the night!
While the cat catches rabbits, he covets us less, 195
But is fed as with venison; defame we him never!
Better a little loss than a livelong sorrow,
By loss of a loathed one to live in disorder!
For many men's malt we mice would destroy,
And ye, rout of rats, would rend men's clothes, 200
If the cat of the court could not catch you at will!
Ye rats, if unruled, could not rule o'er yourselves.
I see," quoth the mouse, "such a mischief might follow,
Neither kitten nor cat, by my counsel, shall suffer;
Nor care I for collars that have cost me nothing; 205
Had they cost me a crown, I would keep it unknown,
And suffer our rulers to rove where they like,
Uncoupled, or coupled, to catch what they can.
I warn well each wise man to ward well his own."
What this vision may mean, ye men that are merry, 210
Discern ye! I dare not discern it myself!

I saw then a hundred, in hoods all of silk,
All serjeants, it seemed, that served at the bar,
Pleading their causes for pence or for pounds,
But for love of our Lord their lips moved never! 215
Sooner measure the mist upon Malvern Hills
Than see a mouth mumble ere money be shown!

Barons and burgesses, and bondmen also
I saw in this assembly, as soon ye shall hear;
Bakers and brewers, and butchers full many, 220
Websters of woollen, and weavers of linen,
Tailors and tinkers, and tollers[16] in markets,
Masons and miners, and many other crafts.
Of laborers of all kinds there leapt forth some,
Such as dikers and delvers; ill done was their work; 225
They drawled through the day, singing, *"Dieu vous save, dame Emme!"*[17]

Cooks and kitchen-lads cried—"Hot pies, hot!"—
"Good geese and good bacon!"—"Good dinners! come, dine!"

[15]Ecclesiastes, 10:16.

[16]Takers of toll.

[17]God save you, Lady Emma! (Evidently the refrain of some popular song.)

Taverners touted—"A taste here, for nothing!"
"White wine of Alsace!"—"Red Gascony wine!" 230
"Here's Rhine wine!" "Rochelle wine, your roast to digest!"
All this saw I sleeping, and seven times more.

PASSUS V[1]

THE SEVEN DEADLY SINS

The king and his knights to the kirk went
To hear matins of the day, and the mass after.
Then I waked from my sleep, and was woful withal
That I had not slept sounder, and seen much more.
Scarce fared I a furlong, ere faintness o'ercame me, 5
Nor further could foot it, for default of repose.
Sat I softly adown, and said my belief,[2]
And babbled o'er my beads; which brought me asleep.

Then saw I much more than I marked hitherto;
The field full of folk I saw, as before, 10
Where Reason was ready to preach to the realm;
With a cross, 'fore the king, he commenced his teaching.

He proved that the pestilences were purely for sin,
And the south-west wind, on Saturday at even,[3]
Was plainly for our pride, and for no point else. 15
Pear-trees and plum-trees were puffed to the earth
For example to sinners, to serve God better.
Beeches and broad oaks were blown to the ground,
Turning upward their tails, as a token of dread
That deadly sin, at Doomsday, would condemn us all. 20

I might, of this matter, be muttering long;
But I say what I saw—so God be my help!—
How plainly Sir Reason 'gan preach to the people.

He bade Waster to work at what he knew best,
To win what he wasted, with wise employ. 25
Maid Parnel he prayed fine apparel to leave,
And keep it in chests, as a chattel at need.
Tom Stow then he taught to take two staves,
And fight for his Phyllis, when ducked for a scold!

He warned also Wat that his wife was to blame, 30
For her head[4] cost a half-mark, his hood not a groat.
He bade also Bat cut a bough or e'en twain,
And beat Betty therewith, unless she would work.
He charged also chapmen to chasten their children,
Not spoil them, though wealthy, the while they were young, 35
Nor please them too fondly, in pestilence-time.
"My sire to me said once, and so did my dame,
'The liefer[5] the child, the more lore it behooveth';
And Solomon likewise, in Sapience, wrote,
He that spareth his rod hateth his son.[6] 40
The sense of this saying, if some one would know,
Is, 'who spareth the birch-sprig, his children he spoileth.'"

And next he prayed prelates and priests together,
"What ye preach to the people, first prove on yourselves,
And do so in deed; it will draw you to good; 45
If ye live by your lore, we believe you the better."

[1] Canto V. The sections which follow the Prologue describe a series of dreams which come to the poet while he is resting on Malvern Hills: Holy Church instructs him in Truth and Love, and warns him against Falsehood and Flattery; he sees arrangements made for the marriage of Falsehood to Lady Meed (Reward or Bribery); when the legality of the union is called in question, Lady Meed is brought before the king at Westminster; and in the end her plea is overcome by the arguments of Reason. At the opening of Passus V the poet awakes for a moment from his dream of the trial at Westminster.

[2] Creed.

[3] The violent tempest on Saturday, 15 January, 1362.

[4] Head-covering.

[5] Dearer.

[6] Proverbs, 13:24.

Religion he counseled his rule to observe,
"Lest the king and his council your commons[7] impair,
And be stewards of your steads, till ye're better established."

Then he counseled the king the commons to love, 50
"'Tis thy treasure 'gainst treason, an antidote true."

Then prayed he the pope to have pity on the Church;
Ere he granted a grace, first to govern himself.
"Ye that laws have to keep, first covet the truth
More than gold or great gifts, if God ye would please. 55
The traitor to truth has been told in the Gospel
That neither God knows him, nor saints in the skies:
Verily I say unto you, I know you not.[8]
Ye that seek[9] to Saint James, and the saints in Rome,
Seek rather Saint Truth, who can save you all; 60
Who with Father and Son:[10]—fair hap them befall
Who assent to my sermon!"—And thus said Sir Reason.

With that ran Repentance, rehearsing the text,
And making Will[11] weep many watery tears.

The Confession of Pride

Maid Parnel Proud-heart fell prone on the earth, 65
Lying long ere she looked up, and "Lord, mercy!" cried.
She vowed then a vow to the Father in heaven,
Her smock to unsow, and a hair-shirt to wear,
To enfeeble her flesh, that so fierce was to sin:—
"Shall no high heart upheave me; I'll hold myself low, 70
And suffer men slight me—and so did I never!

[7]Provisions. [8]Matthew, 15:12. [9]Resort.

[10]An abbreviated formula for ending sermons.

[11]Probably the poet himself and not a personification of the will.

I pray for more meekness, and mercy beseech
For all I have hitherto hated in heart."

The Confession of Lechery

Then said Lecher, "Alas!"—to our Lady he cried
To have mercy, for misdeeds, 'twixt God and his soul, 75
And said that on Saturdays, seven years after,
He would drink with the duck, and would dine only once!

The Confession of Envy

Next Envy, with heavy heart, asked to have shrift;
As a sorrowful sinner his sins he confessed.
He was pale as a stone, in a palsy he seemed, 80
And clothed in a coarse suit I scarce can describe,
In a short coat and kirtle,[12] a knife by his side.
Of a friar's frock were the two fore-sleeves;
Like a leek that has lain too long in the sun
He looked, with his lean cheeks, lowering on all. 85
With wrath swelled his body, he bit both his lips,
Fast clenching his fists; to avenge him he thought
With works or with words, still awaiting his time.
He uttered his tales with an adder's tongue;
Chiding and challenging chose he as food; 90
To backbite and blacken, and bear false witness
Was his care and his courtesy, whereso he came.

"I'd be shriven," quoth this shrew, "if for shame I might dare;
My gladness is greater, when Gib fares amiss,
Than in winning a wey[13] of your fine Essex cheese! 95

"I've a neighbor full nigh, I annoy him full oft,
And belie him to lords, till he loses his pelf;
His friends are made foes through my false report;
His gains and his good luck oft grieve me full sore.

[12]Under-jacket. [13]Weight of 336 pounds.

'Twixt household and household such hatred I raise 100
That both lives and limbs have been lost by my means.
When I meet him at market whom most I detest,
I heartily hail him in haste, as a friend;
He's more doughty than I, so I dare do naught else;
Had I mast'ry and might, God knows my desire! 105

"When I come to the kirk, and should kneel to the cross,
And pray for the people, as teacheth the priest,
For pilgrims and palmers, and people at large,
Then I cry on my knees, 'may Christ give him sorrow
Who bore off my bowl, or my broken plate!' 110
Away from the altar then turn I mine eyes,
And note how Elaine hath a new-made gown;
I wish it were mine, with the rest of the web.

"I laugh when men lose, for that my heart liketh;
I weep when they win, and bewail the time; 115
I doom the ill-doer, myself doing worse;
With him that upbraids me I'm angry forever.
I would that each wight were my servant and slave;
Who hath what I have not, him hate I full sore.
Thus loveless I live, like a low-bred cur, 120
That my body nigh bursts for bitterest gall.

"I oft cannot eat, as a man ought to do,
For envy and ill-will are hard to digest.
Can no sugar nor sweet thing assuage my swelling,
Nor medicinal drug drive it out of my heart, 125
Nor yet shrift nor shame, save my maw be scraped?"

"Yes; readily," said Repentance, "this rule is the best—
Sorrow for sins is salvation of souls."

"I am sorry," quoth that sinner, "I am seldom aught else;
This makes me so meager—I miss my revenge! 130
I have been among burgesses, dwelling in London,
Getting brokers to backbite and blame men's ware.

"If my neighbor could sell, while I sold not, right soon
Would I lower and lie, and lay on him blame.
I'll amend, if I may, by th' Almighty's help!" 135

The Confession of Wrath

Now Wrath awaketh, with two white eyes;
He sniveled with his nose, with a neck low bent.

"I am Wrath," quoth he; "I once was a friar,
And the convent-gardener, to graft young shoots.
On limiters and lectors such lies I engrafted,[14] 140
They bore leaves of low-speech, great lords for to please,
And then blossomed abroad, to hear shrifts in bowers,[15]
Till there fell this fruit—that folk would far rather
Show shrifts unto them than be shriven by priests.

"Now that priests have perceived how friars claim part, 145
These prebend'ries preach, and deprave the friars.
Then friars find fault, as the folk bear witness,
And preach to the people in places around;
I, Wrath, with them rove, and teach them to rail.
Thus clerks of the Church one another contemn 150
Till both are but beggars, and live by their begging,
Or else all are rich, and go riding about.
I, Wrath, never rest, but rove evermore,
And follow these false ones; for such is my grace.

"My aunt is a nun, and an abbess to boot;
She sooner would swoon than once suffer a pain. 156

[14] I taught such lies to those sent out by their convents to beg within certain limits, and to church-readers.

[15] Ladies' chambers.

I was cook in her kitchen, the convent I served
For many a month; and with monks have I stayed;
Made pottage for the prioress, and other poor dames.
Their broth was to backbite—'Dame Joan is a bastard'— 160
'Dame Clarice, a knight's girl, a cuckold's her sire'—
'Dame Parnel's a priest's wench, a prioress never;
She childed in cherry-time, the chapter all know it.'

"Their worts[16] I commingled with wicked words,
Till 'liar!' and 'liar!' leapt forth from their lips, 165
And each hit the other just under the cheek;
They had dealt many deaths, had daggers been near!

"Saint Gregory, pope,[17] had a good foreknowledge,
And granted no prioress power to shrive;
For surely, with women, no secret is safe! 170

"To remain among monks I mostly refuse;
Too keen are some brothers my counsels to spy,
Such as prior, sub-prior, and *pater*[18] the abbot.
If I tell any tales, they take me to task,
And make me fast Fridays on bread and on water. 175
I am chidden in chapter-house, like to a child,
And beaten on bare flesh, rebuked and abused.
With such men to linger small liking is mine;
Salt fish is their diet, and feeblest of ale.
If wine, once a while, in my way comes at eve, 180
I defame them, with foul mouth, some five days after.
All sins I had seen any brother consent to
I discussed in the cloister; the convent soon knew them."

"Repent," quoth Repentance; "rehearse nevermore
Such facts as thou findest by favor or right; 185
Nor drink over deeply, nor delicate drafts,
Lest rashly thy will unto wrath should incline.
Be sober," he said; and absolved him thereafter,
Bade him weep with good will, and his wickedness mend.

The Confession of Avarice

Next Coveting came; whom I scarce can describe; 190
So hungry and hollow Sir Harvey appeared.
He had beetling brows, coarse bulging lips,
And two bleary eyes, like a blind old hag;
Like a leathern purse were his loose-hung cheeks,
Lower than his chin low-drooping with age. 195
His beard, like a boor's, was beslobbered with bacon;
A hood on his head, and a lousy old hat;
In a tawny tabard, some twelve years old,
All tattered and torn, with lice for its tenants;—
By nature a louse is a lively leaper, 200
Or it could not have crawled on that threadbare cloth.

"I've been covetous," quoth that caitiff, "I confess it here;
For some time I served old Sim at-the-Stile,
And was plighted his 'prentice, his profit to serve.
First learnt I, in lying, a lesson or twain; 205
Wickedly to weigh was my first lesson;
To Weyhill[19] and Winchester I went to the fair
With all manner of wares, as my master bade;
If Guile had not given some grace to my ware,
It had still been unsold, were it seven years since! 210

"Then I drew me to drapers, my duties to learn,
To stretch out the stuff, till it looked the longer.
One lesson I learnt as to long striped cloths;
To pierce them with a needle, and piece them together,
Put them in a press, and press them thereunder 215
Till ten yards or twelve were turned to thirteen!

[16] Vegetables. [17] Gregory IX, d. 1241.
[18] Father.

[19] In Hampshire.

"My wife was a weaver, and woollen cloth made;
She spoke to the spinners to spin it well out;
But the pound that she paid by surpassed by a quarter
The standard of weight that the steelyard[20] gave! 220
I barley-malt bought her, she brewed it to sell,
Thick ale and thin ale she thoroughly mingled
For laborers and low folk; this lay by itself.
The best ale in bower or bed-room we kept;
He that tasted thereof was contented to buy it, 225
A groat for a gallon; he gave never less;
Yet it came forth in cups;[21] such craft would she use.
Rose the Retailer she rightly was named;
The trade of a huckster is hers, as at first.
I swear now, so thrive I! that sin will I leave, 230
Nor chaffer so falsely, nor false measures use,
But wend unto Walsingham, and with me my wife,
And pray Bromholm-rood[22] to reprieve me from sin."

"Hast never repented, nor made restitution?"
"Yes; once was I housed with a host of chapmen; 235
I rose while they rested, and rifled their bags."

"That was no restitution, but a robber's deed;
For which thou more highly hast claim to be hanged
Than for all the misdeeds thou hast hitherto done."

"I thought theft restitution; for read could I never; 240
Such French as I know is of further Norfolk."

"Was usury ever a usage of thine?"
"Nay, soothly!" he answered, "except in my youth.
I learnt among Lombards and Jews this lesson,
To weigh the king's pence, and the heavy ones pare, 245
And lend them (to lose them) for love of the pledge;
So I worded the deed, if the day should be broken.
More manors are mine through arrears than mercy.

"I have lent things to lords, and to ladies also,
And then been their broker, and bought them myself. 250
Exchanges and loans are the chaffer I deal with.
When I lend, of each noble[23] a portion they lose;
And with letters of Lombards bear money to Rome,
Here take it by tally, there tell it as less."

"Hast lent aught to lords, for love of their aid?" 255
"I have lent oft to lords, that ne'er loved me thereafter,
And made of a knight both a mercer and draper[24]
Who paid, as apprentice, not one pair of gloves!"

"Hast thou pity on poor men, persuaded to borrow?"
"Such pity on poor men, as a pedlar on cats; 260
Could he catch them, he'd kill them; he covets their skins."

"Dost deal out to neighbors thy drink and thy meat?"
"I'm as courteous," he cried, "as a cur in a kitchen;
Such a name, among neighbors, is noted as mine!"

"Now God never grant thee, unless thou repent, 265
His grace, on this ground, thy goods to bestow,
Nor thine heirs have, after thee, aught of thy gains,
Nor executors spend well the silver thou leavest!
What was wrongfully won will be wickedly spent.
Were I friar of a house, where faith is and love, 270

[20]Scales. [21]To prevent accurate measurement.
[22]The Cross of Bromholm, in Norfolk.

[23]A gold coin.
[24]Since he had to take part of the loan in goods.

Thy coin should not clothe us, nor our kirk amend,
Nor a penny of thine should our pittance improve
For the best book we have, though bright gold were the leaves,
If I knew for a sooth thou wert such as thou sayest,
Or could witness, by watching, thy works and thy ways. 275
Seek a man's feasts, and you serve him as slave;
Live on thy loaf, and thy life then is free!
Thou'rt a creature unkind, whom I cannot assoil
Till thou make restitution, and reckon with all.
Till Reason enroll, i' th' register of heaven, 280
Thou hast made full amends, I may not absolve thee:—
The sin is not remitted, till the stolen thing be restored.
All that gain by thy goods, so God have my troth!
At the high day of doom, must help thee restore.
Who sees not this sooth, let him seek in the Psalter, 285
In *Miserere-mei,*[25] that I mean the truth:—
Behold, thou desirest truth in the inward parts.[26]
No workman i' th' world shall thrive on thy winnings;
Cum sancto eris sanctus; expound that in English:—
With the holy thou shalt be holy."[27] 290

Then lost he all hope, and himself would have hanged,
Had not quickly Repentance the wretch reassured—
"Keep mercy in mind, and with mouth implore it;
God's mercy is more than His mightiest works:—
His mercy is over all his works.[28] 295
All the wickedness i' th' world that men work or devise
Is no more, to God's mercy, than sparks in the main:—
All iniquity, compared with God's mercy, is as a spark in the midst of the sea.
Keep mercy in mind, and thy merchandise leave;
Thou hast no better way to win thee a loaf 300
Than by aid of thy tongue or thy two good hands.
The gain thou hast gotten began with deceit,
And while buying therewith, thou wast borrowing ever!

"If thou wit not whereby or to whom to restore,
Bear it to the bishop; beseech him, of grace, 305
To bestow it himself as is best for thy soul.
He shall answer for thee, at the awful doom,
For thee and for many that man shall account—
As his lore was in Lent (believe this is true)—
How the Lord's grace he lent you, to lead you from sin." 310

The Confession of Gluttony

Now beginneth Sir Glutton to go to his shrift;
His course is to kirkward, as culprit to pray.
But Betty the brewster just bade him "Good-morrow,"
And asked him therewith as to whither he went.

"To holy church haste I, to hear me a mass, 315
And straight to be shriven, and sin nevermore."
"Good ale have I, gossip; Sir Glutton, assay it!"
"But hast thou hot spices at hand, in thy bag?"
"I have pepper and peony-seed, and a pound of garlic,
And a farthingworth of fennel-seed, for fasting-days." 320

Then Glutton goes in, and with him great oaths.
Cicely the shoe-seller sat on the bench,
The warrener[29] Wat, and his wife also,
Timothy the tinker, with two of his lads,
The hackney-man Hick, the needle-man Hugh, 325
Clarice of Cock-lane,[30] the clerk of the church,

[25]Have mercy on me. [26]Psalms, 51:6.
[27]Psalms, 18:25. [28]Psalms, 145:9.

[29]Game-keeper.
[30]A section of London inhabited by women of ill repute.

Davy the ditcher, and a dozen others;
Sir Piers the priest, and Parnel of Flanders,
A fiddler, a ratcatcher, a Cheapside raker,[31]
A rider,[32] a rope-seller, dish-selling Rose, 330
Godfrey of Garlickhithe, Griffin of Wales;
And a heap of upholsterers, early assembled,
Gave Glutton, with glad cheer, a treat of good ale.

Then Clement, the cobbler, cast off his cloak,
Which he offered to any, by way of exchange; 335
Hick the hackney-man hitched off his hood,
And bade Bat the butcher to be on his side.
Then chapmen were chosen the choice to appraise;
He that hath but the hood shall have more for amends.

Two rose up in haste, and reasoned together, 340
Appraising these pen'orths apart by themselves.
They could not, in conscience, accord together
Till Robin the roper arose from his place,
And was ordered, as umpire, to end the dispute,
And tell the true value between them at last. 345

So Hickey the ostler laid hold of the cloak,
In covenant that Clement should fill up his cup,
And have Hick's hood, the ostler's, and hold him content;
Who soonest repented must after arise,
And grant to Sir Glutton a gallon of ale. 350

There was laughing and lowering, and "let go the cup!"[33]
They sat so till evensong, and sung now and then,
Till Glutton had gulped down a gallon and a gill.[34]

* * *

He neither could step, nor without a staff stand;
Then began he to go like a gleeman's dog,[35] 355
Sometimes aside, and sometimes arear,
Like one that lays lines, young larks to ensnare.

As he drew to the door, then dim grew his eyes,
He was tripped by the threshold and thrown to the earth.
Clement the cobbler him caught by the middle, 360
To lift him aloft, and him laid on his knees;
But Glutton, that great churl, was grievous to lift,
And coughed up a caudle in Clement's lap;
So hungry no hound is in Hertfordshire lane
As would lap up the leavings, unlovely of scent. 365

With all woe in the world his wife and his wench
Bore him home to his bed, and brought him therein.
And after this surfeit he slept, in his sloth,
All Saturday and Sunday, till sunset had come.
Then woke he in wonder, and wiped both his eyes; 370
The word he first uttered was—"Where is the bowl?"
His wife sadly warned him, how wicked his ways,
And Repentance full rightly rebuked him of sin:—
"Both in words and in works thou hast wrought much evil,
Now shrive thee with shame, and show me thy sins." 375

"I, Glutton," he granted, "am guilty indeed;
I have trespassed with tongue, I can tell not how oft,
Have sworn 'by God's soul,' and 'so help me the saints,'
Where never was need, nine hundred of times.
I'd a surfeit at supper, and sometimes at noon, 380
Till I, Glutton, it gulped up, ere gone was a mile,
And spilt what should spared be, and spent on the hungry.
Too delicately, on fast-days, I drank and ate both,
And sat sometimes so long that I slept while I ate.

[31] Scavenger. [32] Groom. [33] Pass the cup round.
[34] Skeat here omits five lines in which some of the first consequences of Glutton's drinking are graphically described.
[35] A dog who led a blind minstrel.

To hear tales, in taverns, to drink more, I dined, 385
And feasted ere noon, when the fasting-days came."
"This showing of shrift shall be to thy merit."

Then Glutton 'gan groan; great mourning he made
For the loathsome life he had lived such a while;
And vowed he would fast:—"For hunger or thirst 390
Shall no fish on the Friday be found in my maw
Till Abstinence, my aunt, hath accorded me leave;
And yet have I hitherto hated her ever!"

The Confession of Sloth

Then came Sloth all beslobbered, with two slimy eyes;
"I must sit," quoth this sinner, "or else shall I doze; 395
I stand not, nor stoop, nor kneel without stool.
Were I brought to my bed, save for bitterest need,
Should no ringing arouse me, ere ripe time for dinner."
Benedictite he began, and smote on his breast;
He grumbled, and stretched him, and grunted at last. 400

"Awake!" quoth Repentance, "make ready for shrift."

"This day should I die, no duties for me!
Paternoster I know not, as priests intone it,
But rhymes of Robin Hood, or Randolph of Chester;[36]
Of our Lady or Lord, not the least ever made! 405
Forty vows have I made, and forgot them the morrow;
I performed never penance as the priest appointed;
Right sorry for my sins as yet was I never.
If I bid any beads,[37] but it be in my wrath,
What I tell with my tongue is two miles from my heart. 410
Each day am I occupied, holidays and others,
With idle tales at ale-house, and sometimes in churches;
God's pain and His passion I ponder on seldom.

"I visit no feeble men, or fettered men in jails;
I'd sooner hear ribaldry, or summer-games[38] of cobblers, 415
Or lying tales to laugh at, and belie my neighbors,
Than all that e'er Mark wrote, John, Matthew, or Luke.
All vigils and fastdays I simply let slide,
And lie abed in Lent, in a lazy sleep,
Till past matins and mass; then I move to the friars; 420
To come to the mass-end, for me, is enough.
I seldom am shriven, save sickness impel me,
Not twice in two years; when I shrive me by guess!
I've been parson and priest past thirty long years,
Yet I sing not, nor *sol-fa*,[39] nor Saints' Lives read; 425
I can find in a field or a furlong[40] a hare
Better than in *beatus-vir* or in *beati-omnes*.[41]
Construe a clause, or full clearly expound it.
I can hold well lovedays,[42] or hear a reeve's reckoning,
But in canon-law and decretals can read not a line. 430

"If I buy aught and pledge it—but it be on the tally—
I forget it right soon; and, when settlement's sought,
Six times or seven I forswear it with oaths;
Thus true men I trouble ten hundred of times.

"My servingmen's salary is sometimes behind; 435
Rueful is the reckoning, to read the accounts;
With wrath and ill-will all my workmen I pay.

"If a service is shown me, or succor at need,
I requite it unkindly; I cannot conceive it;
For I have, and have had, the ways of a hawk, 440
Being lured, not by love, but by meat in the hand.

[36] Earl of Chester, 1181–1231 or 1232.

[37] Say any prayers.

[38] Probably May games. [39] Sing by notes.

[40] Furrow. [41] In Psalms, 1 or 128.

[42] Days for the arbitration of disputes.

"The favors my fellows once fondly accorded,
I, Sloth, have forgotten them sixty times since;
In speech, or in sparing speech, spoilt many times
Both flesh-meat and fishes, and many such victuals: 445
Both bread and eke ale, milk, butter, and cheese,
Would I waste in my service, till none would they serve.

"I ran wild in youth, still refusing to learn,
And since, for my sloth, as a beggar subsisted.
How barren, alas! was the life of my youth!" 450

"Dost repent?" quoth Repentance; and straightway he swooned;
Vigilate, the watchful, drew water from his eyes
Which he flung in his face, and with firmness of speech
Said, "Beware of Despair, that will work thee but woe;
'I am sorry for my sins,' thus say to thyself, 455
And beat on thy breast, and beseech God's grace;
No guilt is so great but His goodness is more."

Then sat Sloth up, made the sign of the cross,
And vowed, before God, for his foul neglect:—
"Each Sunday, for seven years, except I am sick, 460
Will I draw me, ere day, to the dear-loved church,
To hear matins and mass, like a monk devout.
No ale after meat shall hold me thence
Till I've evensong heard; so help me the Rood!
Of wealth will I strip me, and strive to restore 465
What I wickedly won by my cunning wits.
Though I lack good living, no labor I'll spare
Till each have his own, ere I hence depart;
And with help of the remnant, by the rood of Chester,
Will I seek Saint Truth, ere I see far Rome!" 470

Robert the robber was fain to restore;
But wealth had he none, wherefore sorely he wept.
The sorrowing sinner thus said to himself:—
"Christ, that on Calvary didst die on the cross,
When Dismas my brother besought Thee for grace, 475
And had mercy on the man who 'Remember me' said,[43]
Have ruth on the robber that naught can restore,
Nor ween to win wealth with skill of my own.
Mitigation I pray for; Thy mercy is great,
Nor condemn me at Doomsday for deeds I did ill." 480

What befell of this felon I failed to discern;
With both his eyes water, I wot well, he wept,
And acknowledged moreover his crimes unto Christ
Till Penitence, his pike-staff, was polished anew,
To leap with, o'er land, while his life should endure.[44] 485

* * *

Then Repentance had ruth, and advised them to kneel:—
"For sinners I pray to our Savior for grace
To amend our misdeeds, and show mercy to all.
Now, God! that in goodness the great world didst make,
Of naught madest all, and man most like Thyself, 490
And didst suffer him to sin, which was sickness to all,
Yet all for the best, as the book[45] hath expressed:—
Oh happy fault! Oh necessary sin of Adam!
Thy Son, through that sin, was sent to this earth,
Made man of a maid, mankind for to save; 495
Like Thyself and Thy Son we sinners were made;
Let us make man in our image, after our likeness.[46]

---

[43] Luke, 23:42.

[44] Skeat here omits a line which may be translated: "For he had lain with Latro (Robbery), Lucifer's aunt."

[45] The Sarum Missal. [46] Genesis, 1:26.

He that dwelleth in love, dwelleth in God, and God in him.[47]
And since, in Thy Son, in our suit didst die
On Good Friday, for man's sake, at full time of day; 500
Nor Thyself, nor Thy Son, didst feel sorrow in death,
In our suit[48] was the sorrow; Thy Son led it captive:—
He led captivity captive.[49]

"The sun then, for sorrow, lost sight for a time;
At midday, when's most light, the mealtime of saints, 505
Thou fed'st, with Thy fresh blood, our forefathers in darkness;—
The people that walked in darkness have seen a great light.[50]
By the light that then leapt out was Lucifer blinded;
It blew all Thy blessèd to Paradise' bliss.

"The third day thereafter saw Thee in our suit; 510
Frail Mary beheld Thee ere Mary Thy mother;
To solace all sinners Thou sufferedst thus:—
I am not come to call the righteous, but sinners to repentance.[51]
All that Mark ever made, John, Matthew, and Luke—
Thy doughtiest deeds—were done in our armor:— 515
The word was made flesh, and dwelt among us.[52]
By so much, me seemeth, more surely may we
Both pray and beseech, if it be Thy will,
Our Father and Brother, Thy mercy be shown us;
Have ruth on these ribalds, repenting them sorely 520
They wrought Thee to wrath, in word, thought, or deed."

Then Hope seized a horn, *Thou-shalt-quicken-us-again,*[53]
And blew it with *blessed-is-he-whose-sin-is-forgiven,*[54]
Till saints high in heaven all sang in accord:—

O Lord, Thou preservest man and beast; how excellent is Thy loving-kindness.[55] 525

A thousand of men then came thronging together,
Crying upward to Christ and His kindly mother
That grace might go with them, to seek Saint Truth.

No wight was so wise that the way there he knew;
They blundered, like beasts, over banks and o'er hills, 530
A long while, till late, when a lithe one they met,
Appareled as a pagan, in pilgrim's guise.
He bare him a staff, with a broad strip bound,
That round it was twined like a woodbine's twist;
A bowl and a bag he bare by his side; 535
A hundred of vials[56] were set on his hat,
Signs from Sinai, Gallician[57] shells;
With crosses on his cloak, and the keys of Rome,
And the vernicle[58] before, for that men should discern
And see by his signs what shrines he had sought. 540

Then fain would this folk know from whence he had come?
"From Sinai," he said, "and the Sepulcher Holy,
Bethlehem and Babylon, I've been in them both,
Armenia, Alexandria, and other like places.
Ye may see by the signs that here sit on my hat 545
I have walkèd full widely, in wet and in dry,
And sought out good saints, for the health of my soul."
"Know'st thou a saint men entitle Saint Truth?
Canst thou walk in the way now, to where He resides?"

---

[47] I John, 4:16. [48] Flesh. [49] Psalms, 68:18.
[50] Isaiah, 9:2. [51] Matthew, 9:13. [52] John 1:14.
[53] Psalms, 71:20. [54] Psalms, 32:1.

[55] Psalms, 36:6.
[56] Signifying that he had visited the shrine of St. Thomas at Canterbury.
[57] From the shrine of St. James at Compostella in Galicia, Spain.
[58] Copy of St. Veronica's handkerchief, impressed with the image of Christ. It signified that he had made a pilgrimage to Rome.

"Nay," said the good man, "so God be my guide, 550
I saw never palmer with pikestaff or scrip
That asked for Him ever, ere now in this place!"

"By Peter!" quoth a plowman,[59] and put forth his head,
"I know him as closely as clerk doth his books!
Through Conscience and Kind-Wit I ken where He dwelleth; 555
They safely ensured me to serve Him forever,
Both to sow and to set, while my strength shall endure.
I have faithfully followed Him fifty long years,
Both sown Him His seed, and His cattle preserved;
Within and without have I watched o'er His profit. 560
I dike and I delve, and do that He biddeth;
Sometimes I sow, and sometimes I thrash;
I am tailor or tinker, as Truth doth appoint;
I weave or I wind, doing what so He biddeth.

"Though I say it myself, my service He values; 565
I have meed in good measure, and sometimes have more;
None prompter to pay can a poor man find,
He withholds none his hire; he hath it at even.
He's lowly as a lamb, and loving in speech;
And would ye now wit well, where that He dwelleth, 570
Full well can I wend on my way to His place."

"Yea, Piers!" quoth the pilgrims, and proffered him hire
To teach them the true way to Truth's own abode.

"By my soul's health," quoth Piers, and was fain for to swear,
"Not a farthing I finger, for Saint Thomas's shrine! 575
Truth would love me the less for a long time after.
But would ye now wend there, the way there is this
That I set now before you; I say you the sooth.—
Commence it through Meekness, ye men and ye women,
Till ye come unto Conscience; let Christ know the truth 580
How ye love well our Lord as the liefest of things,
And your neighbor the next, and in no wise requite him
Otherwise than thou wouldst he should do to thyself.
Bend forth by a brook named Be-courtly-of-speech,
Till ye find there a ford, called Honor-your-fathers:— 585
Honor thy father and thy mother:[60]
Wade through that water, and wash you well there;
Ye shall leap then the lightlier, your lifetime after!
Then see shall ye Swear-not-except-ye-have-need-
And-name-not-in-vain-the-great-name-of-the Lord. 590

"Next come near a croft, but ne'er come ye therein;
That croft is called Covet-not-men's-cattle-or-wives-
And-none-of-their-servants-that-might-them-annoy;
So break ye no boughs there, save boughs of your own.
Two stocks there are standing, but stay ye not there, 595
Named Steal-not and Slay-not, but slip by them both,
Leave them on the left hand, and look not upon them;
And Hold-well-thy-holiday-holy-till-even.
Next bend past a barrow, Bear-no-false-witness,
'Tis fenced in with florins and other like fees; 600
Then pluck thou no plant there, for peril of thy soul.
Then see shall ye Say-Sooth-as-sooth-is-indeed-
And-otherwise-never-at-no-one's-request.
Next come to a court, as clear as the sun,
Its moat is of Mercy, the manor around, 605
The walls are of Wit, to guard against Will,
Embattled with Christendom, Christians to save,
Buttressed with Believe-so-or-savéd-be-never.

[59]Piers the plowman. This is his first appearance in the poem.

[60]Exodus, 20:12.

The house is all covered, both chambers and
halls,
Not with lead, but with Love, and Low-
speech-of-brethren; 610
The bridge is of Pray-well-the-better-to-
speed;
Each pillar, of Penance or Prayers-to-the-
Saints,
And of Almsdeeds, the hooks whereon hung
are the gates.

"Grace is the gate-ward, a good man forsooth;
His man is Amend-you, full many men know
him. 615
Tell him this token, which Truth will approve,
'I performed all the penance the priest did
enjoin,
And am sorry for my sins, and so shall be
ever
When thoughts of them throng me, yea,
though I were pope!
Pray Amend-you full meekly his Master to
ask 620
To throw wide the wicket the woman once
shut
When Adam and Eve ate their apples un-
roasted:—
*Through Eve was it closed to all, and through
the Virgin Mary was it opened again.*
For His is the key, though the king should
slumber.
If Grace shall once grant thee to go through
the gate, 625
Thou shalt see, in thyself, Truth sit in thine
heart,
In a chain of Charity, a child as thou wert,
To suffer but say naught, gainst will of thy
sire.
Beware then of Wrath-thee, most wicked of
all,
He hath envy of Him that should sit in thine
heart, 630
And putteth forth Pride and the Praise-of-
thyself;
Thy boasting of benefits maketh thee blind,
Till out thou art driven, and the door shut
fast,
And closed with a key, to keep thee outside
A hundred years, haply, ere ever thou
enter. 635
Thus thou losest His love, by uplifting
thyself,
Ne'er, haply, to enter, save only by grace.

"There are seven sweet sisters that serve
Truth forever,
Porters of posterns assigned to that place.
Abstinence is one, and Humility next, 640
Charity and Chastity, chief of His maidens,
Patience and Peace, many people they help;
And Largesse, the lady that lets many in;
From the pinfold of hell she hath helped out
a thousand.
He that kinship can claim with these sisters
seven 645
Is wondrously welcome, and well is receivèd.
And except ye're akin to some one of the
seven
'Tis full hard, by my head, for any of you all
To go through the gate there, save grace
may be yours."

"By Christ!" quoth a cutpurse, "no kin
have I there!" 650
"Nor I," quoth an ape-ward, "for aught that
I know."
"Wist I," quoth a wafer-man,[61] "such were
the truth,
No further I'd foot it, by friars' advice!"

"Yes!" quoth Piers Plowman (their profit
he sought),
"Mercy's a maid there, hath might over
all, 655
Akin to all sinners, as her Son is also;
By help of these two (there is hope in none
other)
Grace shalt thou get there, by going betimes."

"By Saint Paul," quoth a pardoner, "perhaps I'm unknown there;
Where's my brief-box, my bull, and my
bishop's letters?" 660

A common wench cried—"Thy companion
I'll be,
And say I'm thy sister; but see! they are
gone!"

[61] Confectioner, whose occupation frequently allowed him to serve as a go-between.

GEOFFREY CHAUCER

c. 1340–1400

Chaucer was born in London, the son of a wine-merchant who was in some way connected with the court of Edward III. He is the earliest English writer about whose life and works we have reasonably full knowledge. Though our knowledge of his life is confined almost exclusively to its external course, still, what we do know is definite and dependable. The reason is that Chaucer from an early age was connected with the English court or government, so that the outlines of his public career can be traced from documentary evidence. We first hear of him as attached to the household of the wife of Prince Lionel, the third son of Edward III, in 1357. The only known evidence concerning the date of Chaucer's birth is contained in testimony he gave in a suit in 1386, when he stated that he was forty years or more of age and had borne arms for twenty-seven years. This statement agrees with the record of his service with the English army in France in 1359 (when he was taken prisoner by the French), and suggests 1340 as a probable date for his birth. In the absence of knowledge this generally accepted date is open to question, and an attempt has been made to show, from what has been learned of the ages at which youths took arms, that Chaucer may have been born as late as 1345. This seems improbable, though perhaps he was born in 1342 or 1343. He may have studied law at some time between 1360 and 1367; in the latter year he was granted a pension for his services as valet in the king's household. Probably about this time Chaucer married Philippa, a lady who is thought to have been a sister-in-law of John of Gaunt. In 1372–1373 he was sent on a diplomatic mission to Italy. In 1374 he was given a post in the customs. In 1377 he was in Flanders and France on diplomatic service, and in 1378 went again to Italy. In 1382 he was given an additional post in the customs and three years later was allowed to exercise his office through a deputy. In 1386 he sat as a member of Parliament for Kent; in the same year he was for some reason deprived of his offices in the customs. Later he again held public offices, being appointed clerk of the king's works at Westminster in 1389 and holding the same office at Windsor in 1390, while he received a pension which was increased in 1394 and again in 1399; but despite this help Chaucer seems to have been in some financial difficulty from the time of his reverses in 1386 until shortly before his death. He died in 1400 and was buried in Westminster Abbey.

Chaucer's literary career has been divided into three periods: the French and Latin period (to 1373), the Italian period (1373–1385), and the English period (1385–1400). This division is convenient and is roughly in accordance with the facts. It should be kept in mind, however, that it is only approximate and that the so-called periods are not mutually exclusive. As a young man Chaucer made himself familiar with what was closest to hand—the Latin literature that was known to everyone of any education, and French poetry of his own time or shortly before. His acquaintance with the work of Dante, Petrarch, and Boccaccio probably dates from his first Italian journey in 1373. All that he learned from these varied sources was of use to him throughout his life, and what is meant in terming his last fifteen years an "English" period is that his apprenticeship was definitely over, and that he then wrote with a free command of his material which enabled him, more clearly than before, to exhibit himself in his work. In his first period Chaucer translated at least parts of the French *Romance of the Rose,* an allegorical poem of the thirteenth century, and wrote the *Book of the Duchess,* which shows the influence of French allegorical love poetry. In his second period he began, but did not finish, *The House of Fame,* he wrote *The Parliament of Fowls,* he translated Boethius' *Consolation of Philosophy,* and he wrote *Troilus and Criseyde,* a long and highly finished narrative poem based upon, and in part translated from, Boccaccio's *Filostrato.* In his third period he wrote *The Legend of Good Women* and *The Canterbury Tales,* leaving both unfinished.

Chaucer won for himself immediately a foremost place in literature, and his works exerted a dominating influence upon later poets in the fifteenth and sixteenth centuries. In the middle of the sixteenth century it was said that fine courtiers would "talk nothing but Chaucer," and it is possible that this vogue of archaic speech helped, towards the close of the century, to strengthen Spenser's allegiance to him. Though Spenser could not appreciate Chaucer's skill, because of linguistic changes, the elder poet was a deft craftsman, and his verse is remarkable for its smoothness, ease, grace, and variety. He was not a man of deep seriousness, and this has cost him a place among the greatest poets; but he was a keen observer of the appearances of things and of the external traits of human character, which, with his mastery of a precise and finished style, enabled him to tell a story supremely well. His poetry might show us, even if we knew nothing of his public career, that he was a successful man of the world. He took men and things as he found them and was content to describe, as he so well could, and not to judge. He had, to be sure, his standards, and they were not low, but neither were they deeply felt. His nature was catholic and he viewed the human scene with whimsical detachment;—with a constant enjoyment, too, which he still communicates to all his readers.

The edition of Chaucer which is most useful to the scholar is still *The Complete Works,* ed. Walter W. Skeat (Oxford, 1894–1897); but a much more compact and up-to-date edition has recently appeared, *The Complete Works of Geoffrey Chaucer,* ed. F. N. Robinson, the "Cambridge Poets" (Boston, 1933).

Information about the poet and his work is found in Robert D. French's *Chaucer Handbook* (New York, 1927). In *Some New Light on Chaucer* (New York, 1926) John M. Manly attempts to relate several of the Canterbury Pilgrims to real persons of the fourteenth century. The best literary interpretations are George L. Kittredge, *Chaucer and his Poetry* (Cambridge, U. S. A., 1915); John L. Lowes, *Geoffrey Chaucer and the Development of his Genius* (Boston, 1934); and Robert K. Root, *The Poetry of Chaucer; a Guide to its Study and Appreciation,* revised edition (Boston, 1922). For the contemporary background see George G. Coulton, *Chaucer and his England* (London, 1908), and Jules J. Jusserand, *English Wayfaring Life in the Middle Ages,* trans. L. Toulmin Smith, revised edition (London, 1921).

THE CANTERBURY TALES

The Prologue[1]

Whan that Aprille with his shoures sote
The droghte of Marche hath perced to the rote,
And bathed every veyne in swich licour,
Of which vertu engendred is the flour;
Whan Zephirus eek with his swete breeth 5
Inspired hath in every holt and heeth
The tendre croppes, and the yonge sonne
Hath in the Ram[2] his halfe cours y-ronne,
And smale fowles maken melodye,
That slepen al the night with open yë, 10
(So priketh hem nature in hir corages):
Than longen folk to goon on pilgrimages
(And palmers for to seken straunge strondes)
To ferne halwes, couthe in sondry londes;
And specially, from every shires ende 15
Of Engelond, to Caunterbury they wende,
The holy blisful martir[3] for to seke,
That hem hath holpen, whan that they were seke.
Bifel that, in that seson on a day,[4]
In Southwerk at the Tabard as I lay 20
Redy to wenden on my pilgrimage
To Caunterbury with ful devout corage,
At night was come in-to that hostelrye
Wel nyne and twenty in a companye,
Of sondry folk, by aventure y-falle 25
In felawshipe, and pilgrims were they alle,
That toward Caunterbury wolden ryde;
The chambres and the stables weren wyde,
And wel we weren esed atte beste.
And shortly, whan the sonne was to reste, 30
So hadde I spoken with hem everichon,
That I was of hir felawshipe anon,
And made forward erly for to ryse,
To take our wey, ther as I yow devyse.
But natheles, whyl I have tyme and space,
Er that I ferther in this tale pace, 36

[1]The *Prologue,* besides describing the pilgrims, outlines Chaucer's general design. This calls for about 120 stories, two told by each pilgrim on the way to Canterbury, and two on the way back. Chaucer seems later to have modified this plan, reducing the number of tales by one-half. But even so he left the work far from completed. We have only 24 tales, several of them unfinished.

[2]Sign of the zodiac, Aries.

[3]Thomas à Becket.

[4]The day was 16 April, and the year may be supposed to be 1387 (Skeat).

Me thinketh it acordaunt to resoun,
To telle yow al the condicioun
Of ech of hem, so as it semed me,
And whiche they weren, and of what degree;
And eek in what array that they were inne: 41
And at a knight than wol I first biginne.

A KNIGHT ther was, and that a worthy man,
That fro the tyme that he first bigan
To ryden out, he loved chivalrye, 45
Trouthe and honour, fredom and curteisye.
Ful worthy was he in his lordes werre,
And therto hadde he riden (no man ferre)
As wel in Cristendom as hethenesse,
And ever honoured for his worthinesse. 50

At Alisaundre he was, whan it was wonne;
Ful ofte tyme he hadde the bord bigonne
Aboven alle naciouns in Pruce.
In Lettow hadde he reysed and in Ruce,
No Cristen man so ofte of his degree. 55
In Gernade at the sege eek hadde he be
Of Algezir, and riden in Belmarye.
At Lyeys was he, and at Satalye,
Whan they were wonne; and in the Grete See
At many a noble aryve hadde he be. 60
At mortal batailles hadde he been fiftene,
And foughten for our feith at Tramissene
In listes thryes, and ay slayn his fo.
This ilke worthy knight had been also
Somtyme with the lord of Palatye, 65
Ageyn another hethen in Turkye:
And evermore he hadde a sovereyn prys.
And though that he were worthy, he was wys,
And of his port as meke as is a mayde.
He never yet no vileinye ne sayde 70
In al his lyf, un-to no maner wight.
He was a verray parfit gentil knight.
But for to tellen yow of his array,
His hors were gode, but he was nat gay.
Of fustian he wered a gipoun 75
Al bismotered with his habergeoun;
For he was late y-come from his viage,
And wente for to doon his pilgrimage.

With him ther was his sone, a yong SQUYER,
A lovyere, and a lusty bacheler, 80
With lokkes crulle, as they were leyd in presse.
Of twenty yeer of age he was, I gesse.
Of his stature he was of evene lengthe,
And wonderly deliver, and greet of strengthe.
And he had been somtyme in chivachye, 85
In Flaundres, in Artoys, and Picardye,
And born him wel, as of so litel space,
In hope to stonden in his lady grace.
Embrouded was he, as it were a mede
Al ful of fresshe floures, whyte and rede. 90
Singinge he was, or floytinge, al the day;
He was as fresh as is the month of May.
Short was his goune, with sleves longe and wyde.
Wel coude he sitte on hors, and faire ryde.
He coude songes make and wel endyte, 95
Juste and eek daunce, and wel purtreye and wryte.
So hote he lovede, that by nightertale
He sleep namore than dooth a nightingale.
Curteys he was, lowly, and servisable,
And carf biforn his fader at the table. 100

A YEMAN hadde he, and servaunts namo
At that tyme, for him liste ryde so;
And he was clad in cote and hood of grene;
A sheef of pecok-arwes brighte and kene
Under his belt he bar ful thriftily; 105
(Wel coude he dresse his takel yemanly:
His arwes drouped noght with fetheres lowe),
And in his hand he bar a mighty bowe.
A not-heed hadde he, with a broun visage.
Of wode-craft wel coude he al the usage. 110
Upon his arm he bar a gay bracer,
And by his syde a swerd and a bokeler,
And on that other syde a gay daggere,
Harneised wel, and sharp as point of spere;
A Cristofre on his brest of silver shene. 115
An horn he bar, the bawdrik was of grene;
A forster was he, soothly, as I gesse.

Ther was also a Nonne, a PRIORESSE,
That of hir smyling was ful simple and coy;
Hir grettest ooth was but by sëynt Loy; 120
And she was cleped madame Eglentyne.
Ful wel she song the service divyne,
Entuned in hir nose ful semely;
And Frensh she spak ful faire and fetisly,
After the scole of Stratford atte Bowe,[5] 125
For Frensh of Paris was to hir unknowe.
At mete wel y'taught was she with-alle;
She leet no morsel from hir lippes falle,
Ne wette hir fingres in hir sauce depe.
Wel coude she carie a morsel, and wel kepe,
That no drope ne fille up-on hir brest 131
In curteisye was set ful muche hir lest.
Hir over lippe wyped she so clene,
That in hir coppe was no ferthing sene
Of grece, whan she dronken hadde hir draughte. 135
Ful semely after hir mete she raughte,
And sikerly she was of greet disport,
And ful plesaunt, and amiable of port,
And peyned hir to countrefete chere
Of court, and been estatlich of manere, 140

[5] A convent near London.

And to ben holden digne of reverence.
But, for to speken of hir conscience,
She was so charitable and so pitous,
She wolde wepe, if that she sawe a mous
Caught in a trappe, if it were deed or bledde.
Of smale houndes had she, that she fedde 146
With rosted flesh, or milk and wastel-breed.
But sore weep she if oon of hem were deed,
Or if men smoot it with a yerde smerte:
And al was conscience and tendre herte. 150
Ful semely hir wimpel pinched was;
Hir nose tretys; hir eyen greye as glas;
Hir mouth ful smal, and ther-to softe and
reed;
But sikerly she hadde a fair forheed;
It was almost a spanne brood, I trowe; 155
For, hardily, she was nat undergrowe.
Ful fetis was hir cloke, as I was war.
Of smal coral aboute hir arm she bar
A peire of bedes, gauded al with grene; 159
And ther-on heng a broche of gold ful shene,
On which ther was first write a crowned A,
And after, *Amor vincit Omnia*.[6]
Another NONNE with hir hadde she,
That was hir chapeleyne, and PREESTES
THREE. 164
A MONK ther was, a fair for the maistrye,
An out-rydere, that lovede venerye;
A manly man, to been an abbot able.
Ful many a deyntee hors hadde he in stable:
And, whan he rood, men mighte his brydel
here
Ginglen in a whistling wind as clere, 170
And eek as loude as dooth the chapel-belle
Ther as this lord was keper of the celle.
The reule of seint Maure or of seint Beneit,
By-cause that it was old and som-del streit,
This ilke monk leet olde thinges pace, 175
And held after the newe world the space.
He yaf nat of that text a pulled hen,
That seith, that hunters been nat holy men;
Ne that a monk, whan he is cloisterlees,
Is lykned til a fish that is waterlees; 180
This is to seyn, a monk out of his cloistre.
But thilke text held he nat worth an oistre;
And I seyde, his opinioun was good.
What sholde he studie, and make him-selven
wood,
Upon a book in cloistre alwey to poure, 185
Or swinken with his handes, and laboure,
As Austin bit? How shal the world be
served?
Lat Austin have his swink to him reserved.
Therfore he was a pricasour aright;

[6]Love conquers all things (Virgil, *Eclogues*, x, 69).

Grehoundes he hadde, as swifte as fowel in
flight; 190
Of priking and of hunting for the hare
Was al his lust, for no cost wolde he spare.
I seigh his sleves purfiled at the hond
With grys, and that the fyneste of a lond;
And, for to festne his hood under his chin, 195
He hadde of gold y-wroght a curious pin:
A love-knotte in the gretter ende ther was.
His heed was balled, that shoon as any glas,
And eek his face, as he had been anoint.
He was a lord ful fat and in good point; 200
His eyen stepe, and rollinge in his heed,
That stemed as a forneys of a leed;
His botes souple, his hors in greet estat.
Now certeinly he was a fair prelat;
He was nat pale as a for-pyned goost. 205
A fat swan loved he best of any roost.
His palfrey was as broun as is a berye.
A FRERE ther was, a wantown and a merye,
A limitour, a ful solempne man.
In alle the ordres foure[7] is noon that can 210
So muche of daliaunce and fair langage.
He hadde maad ful many a mariage
Of yonge wommen, at his owne cost.
Un-to his ordre he was a noble post.
Ful wel biloved and famulier was he 215
With frankeleyns over-al in his contree,
And eek with worthy wommen of the toun:
For he had power of confessioun,
As seyde him-self, more than a curat,
For of his ordre he was licentiat. 220
Ful swetely herde he confessioun,
And plesaunt was his absolucioun;
He was an esy man to yeve penaunce
Ther as he wiste to han a good pitaunce;
For unto a povre ordre for to yive 225
Is signe that a man is wel y-shrive.
For if he yaf, he dorste make avaunt,
He wiste that a man was repentaunt.
For many a man so hard is of his herte, 229
He may nat wepe al-thogh him sore smerte.
Therfore, in stede of weping and preyeres,
Men moot yeve silver to the povre freres.
His tipet was ay farsed ful of knyves
And pinnes, for to yeven faire wyves.
And certeinly he hadde a mery note; 235
Wel coude he singe and pleyen on a rote.
Of yeddinges he bar utterly the prys.
His nekke whyt was as the flour-de-lys;
Ther-to he strong was as a champioun.
He knew the tavernes wel in every toun, 240
And everich hostiler and tappestere
Bet than a lazar or a beggestere;
For un-to swich a worthy man as he

[7]Dominicans, Franciscans, Carmelites, and Augustinians.

Acorded nat, as by his facultee,
To have with seke lazars aqueyntaunce. 245
It is nat honest, it may nat avaunce
For to delen with no swich poraille,
But al with riche and sellers of vitaille.
And over-al, ther as profit sholde aryse,
Curteys he was, and lowly of servyse. 250
Ther nas no man no-wher so vertuous.
He was the beste beggere in his hous;
And yaf a certeyn ferme for the graunt;
Noon of his bretheren cam ther in his haunt;
For thogh a widwe hadde noght a sho, 255
So plesaunt was his *"In principio,"*[8]
Yet wolde he have a ferthing, er he wente.
His purchas was wel bettre than his rente.
And rage he coude, as it were right a whelpe.
In love-dayes ther coude he muchel helpe. 260
For there he was nat lyk a cloisterer,
With a thredbar cope, as is a povre scoler,
But he was lyk a maister or a pope.
Of double worsted was his semi-cope,
That rounded as a belle out of the presse. 265
Somwhat he lipsed, for his wantownesse,
To make his English swete up-on his tonge;
And in his harping, whan that he had songe,
His eyen twinkled in his heed aright,
As doon the sterres in the frosty night. 270
This worthy limitour was cleped Huberd.

A MARCHANT was ther with a forked berd,
In mottelee, and hye on horse he sat,
Up-on his heed a Flaundrish bever hat;
His botes clasped faire and fetisly. 275
His resons he spak ful solempnely,
Souninge alway th'encrees of his winning.
He wolde the see were kept for any thing
Bitwixe Middelburgh and Orewelle.[9]
Wel coude he in eschaunge sheeldes selle. 280
This worthy man ful wel his wit bisette;
Ther wiste no wight that he was in dette,
So estatly was he of his governaunce,
With his bargaynes, and with his chevisaunce.
For sothe he was a worthy man with-alle, 285
But sooth to seyn, I noot how men him calle.

A CLERK ther was of Oxenford also,
That un-to logik hadde longe y-go.
As lene was his hors as is a rake,
And he nas nat right fat, I undertake; 290
But loked holwe, and ther-to soberly.
Ful thredbar was his overest courtepy;
For he had geten him yet no benefyce,
Ne was so worldly for to have offyce.
For him was lever have at his beddes heed 295
Twenty bokes, clad in blak or reed,
Of Aristotle and his philosophye,
Than robes riche, or fithele, or gay sautrye.
But al be that he was a philosophre,
Yet hadde he but litel gold in cofre;[10] 300
But al that he mighte of his freendes hente,
On bokes and on lerninge he it spente,
And bisily gan for the soules preye
Of hem that yaf him wher-with to scoleye.
Of studie took he most cure and most hede. 305
Noght o word spak he more than was nede,
And that was seyd in forme and reverence,
And short and quik, and ful of hy sentence.
Souninge in moral vertu was his speche, 309
And gladly wolde he lerne, and gladly teche.

A SERGEANT OF THE LAWE, war and wys,
That often hadde been at the parvys,
Ther was also, ful riche of excellence.
Discreet he was, and of greet reverence:
He semed swich, his wordes weren so wyse. 315
Justyce he was ful often in assyse,
By patente, and by pleyn commissioun;
For his science, and for his heigh renoun
Of fees and robes hadde he many oon.
So greet a purchasour was no-wher noon. 320
Al was fee simple to him in effect,[11]
His purchasing mighte nat been infect.
No-wher so bisy a man as he ther nas,
And yet he semed bisier than he was.
In termes hadde he caas and domes alle, 325
That from the tyme of king William were falle.
Therto he coude endyte, and make a thing,
Ther coude no wight pinche at his wryting;
And every statut coude he pleyn by rote.
He rood but hoomly in a medlee cote 330
Girt with a ceint of silk, with barres smale;
Of his array telle I no lenger tale.

A FRANKELEYN was in his companye;
Whyt was his berd, as is the dayesye.
Of his complexioun he was sangwyn. 335
Wel loved he by the morwe a sop in wyn.
To liven in delyt was ever his wone,
For he was Epicurus owne sone,
That heeld opinioun, that pleyn delyt
Was verraily felicitee parfyt. 340
An housholdere, and that a greet, was he;
Seint Julian[12] he was in his contree.
His breed, his ale, was alwey after oon;

[8]In the beginning (opening words of the Gospel of St. John, a text much quoted by the friars).

[9]The former a port on an island off the coast of The Netherlands, the latter an English port at the mouth of the Orwell River. He wanted the sea-route between the two kept open at any expense.

[10]The reference is to the alchemists, who were also termed philosophers. It was commonly believed that they could turn base metals into gold.

[11]The meaning is that he could untie any entail, or restriction on land.

[12]The patron saint of hospitality.

A bettre envyned man was no-wher noon.
With-oute bake mete was never his hous, 345
Of fish and flesh, and that so plentevous,
It snewed in his hous of mete and drinke,
Of alle deyntees that men coude thinke.
After the sondry sesons of the yeer,
So chaunged he his mete and his soper. 350
Ful many a fat partrich hadde he in mewe,
And many a breem and many a luce in stewe.
Wo was his cook, but-if his sauce were
Poynaunt and sharp, and redy al his gere.
His table dormant in his halle alway 355
Stood redy covered al the longe day.
At sessiouns ther was he lord and sire;
Ful ofte tyme he was knight of the shire.
An anlas and a gipser al of silk
Heng at his girdel, whyt as morne milk. 360
A shirreve hadde he been, and a countour;
Was no-wher such a worthy vavasour.

An HABERDASSHER and a CARPENTER,
A WEBBE, a DYERE, and a TAPICER,
Were with us eek, clothed in o liveree, 365
Of a solempne and greet fraternitee.
Ful fresh and newe hir gere apyked was;
Hir knyves were y-chaped noght with bras,
But al with silver, wroght ful clene and weel,
Hir girdles and hir pouches every-deel. 370
Wel semed ech of hem a fair burgeys,
To sitten in a yeldhalle on a deys.
Everich, for the wisdom that he can,
Was shaply for to been an alderman.
For catel hadde they y-nogh and rente, 375
And eek hir wyves wolde it wel assente;
And elles certein were they to blame.
It is ful fair to been y-clept *"ma dame,"*
And goon to vigilyës al bifore,
And have a mantel royalliche y-bore. 380

A COOK they hadde with hem for the nones,
To boille the chiknes with the mary-bones,
And poudre-marchant tart, and galingale.
Wel coude he knowe a draughte of London ale.
He coude roste, and sethe, and broille, and frye, 385
Maken mortreux, and wel bake a pye.
But greet harm was it, as it thoughte me,
That on his shine a mormal hadde he;
For blankmanger, that made he with the beste.

A SHIPMAN was ther, woning fer by weste; 390
For aught I woot, he was of Dertemouthe.
He rood up-on a rouncy, as he couthe,
In a gowne of falding to the knee.
A daggere hanging on a laas hadde he
Aboute his nekke under his arm adoun. 395
The hote somer had maad his hewe al broun;
And, certeinly, he was a good felawe.
Ful many a draughte of wyn had he y-drawe
From Burdeux-ward, whyl that the chapman sleep.[13]
Of nyce conscience took he no keep. 400
If that he faught, and hadde the hyer hond,
By water he sente hem hoom to every lond.[14]
But of his craft to rekene wel his tydes,
His stremes and his daungers him bisydes, 404
His herberwe and his mone, his lodemenage,
Ther nas noon swich from Hulle to Cartage.
Hardy he was, and wys to undertake;
With many a tempest hadde his berd been shake.
He knew wel alle the havenes, as they were,
From Gootlond to the cape of Finistere, 410
And every cryke in Britayne and in Spayne;
His barge y-cleped was the Maudelayne.

With us ther was a DOCTOUR OF PHISYK,
In al this world ne was ther noon him lyk
To speke of phisik and of surgerye; 415
For he was grounded in astronomye.[15]
He kepte his pacient a ful greet del
In houres, by his magik naturel.
Wel coude he fortunen the ascendent
Of his images for his pacient. 420
He knew the cause of everich maladye,
Were it of hoot or cold, or moiste, or drye,
And where engendred, and of what humour;
He was a verrey parfit practisour.
The cause y-knowe, and of his harm the rote, 425
Anon he yaf the seke man his bote.
Ful redy hadde he his apothecaries,
To sende him drogges and his letuaries,
For ech of hem made other for to winne;
Hir frendschipe nas nat newe to beginne. 430
Wel knew he th'olde Esculapius,
And Deiscorides, and eek Rufus,
Old Ypocras, Haly, and Galien;
Serapion, Razis, and Avicen;
Averrois, Damascien, and Constantyn; 435
Bernard, and Gatesden, and Gilbertyn.[16]
Of his diete mesurable was he,
For it was of no superfluitee,
But of greet norissing and digestible.
His studie was but litel on the bible. 440
In sangwin and in pers he clad was al,
Lyned with taffata and with sendal;

[13] He had stolen wine from the casks he was carrying from Bordeaux.

[14] Threw them overboard.

[15] "Astronomye." This is really astrology. The physician knew well how to watch for a favorable astrological hour for the making of images to be used as charms in the treatment of his patient.

[16] All great medical authorities.

And yet he was but esy of dispence;
He kepte that he wan in pestilence.
For gold in phisik is a cordial, 445
Therfore he lovede gold in special.
A good WYF was ther of bisyde BATHE,
But she was som-del deef, and that was scathe.
Of clooth-making she hadde swiche an haunt,
She passed hem of Ypres and of Gaunt. 450
In al the parisshe wyf ne was ther noon
That to the'offring bifore hir sholde goon;
And if ther dide, certeyn, so wrooth was she,
That she was out of alle charitee.
Hir coverchiefs ful fyne were of ground; 455
I dorste swere they weyeden ten pound
That on a Sonday were upon hir heed.
Hir hosen weren of fyn scarlet reed,
Ful streite y-teyd, and shoos ful moiste and newe.
Bold was hir face, and fair, and reed of hewe. 460
She was a worthy womman al hir lyve,
Housbondes at chirche-dore she hadde fyve,
Withouten other companye in youthe;
But therof nedeth nat to speke as nouthe.
And thryes hadde she been at Jerusalem; 465
She hadde passed many a straunge streem;
At Rome she hadde been, and at Boloigne,
In Galice at seint Jame,[17] and at Coloigne.
She coude muche of wandring by the weye:
Gat-tothed was she, soothly for to seye. 470
Up-on an amblere esily she sat,
Y-wimpled wel, and on hir heed an hat
As brood as is a bokeler or a targe;
A foot-mantel aboute hir hipes large,
And on hir feet a paire of spores sharpe. 475
In felawschip wel coude she laughe and carpe.
Of remedyes of love she knew per-chaunce,
For she coude of that art the olde daunce.
A good man was ther of religioun,
And was a povre PERSOUN of a toun; 480
But riche he was of holy thoght and werk.
He was also a lerned man, a clerk,
That Cristes gospel trewely wolde preche;
His parisshens devoutly wolde he teche.
Benigne he was, and wonder diligent, 485
And in adversitee ful pacient;
And swich he was y-preved ofte sythes.
Ful looth were him to cursen for his tythes,
But rather wolde he yeven, out of doute,
Un-to his povre parisshens aboute 490
Of his offring, and eek of his substaunce.
He coude in litel thing han suffisaunce.
Wyd was his parisshe, and houses fer a-sonder,

[17]Compostella in Spain.

But he ne lafte nat, for reyn ne thonder,
In siknes nor in meschief, to visyte 495
The ferreste in his parisshe, muche and lyte,
Up-on his feet, and in his hand a staf.
This noble ensample to his sheep he yaf,
That first he wroghte, and afterward he taughte;
Out of the gospel he tho wordes caughte;[18] 500
And this figure he added eek ther-to,
That if gold ruste, what shal iren do?
For if a preest be foul, on whom we truste,
No wonder is a lewed man to ruste;
And shame it is, if a preest take keep, 505
A shiten shepherde and a clene sheep.
Wel oghte a preest ensample for to yive,
By his clennesse, how that his sheep shold live.
He sette nat his benefice to hyre,
And leet his sheep encombred in the myre, 510
And ran to London, un-to sëynt Poules,
To seken him a chaunterie for soules,[19]
Or with a bretherhed to been withholde;[20]
But dwelte at hoom, and kepte wel his folde,
So that the wolf ne made it nat miscarie; 515
He was a shepherde and no mercenarie.
And though he holy were, and vertuous,
He was to sinful man nat despitous,
Ne of his speche daungerous ne digne,
But in his teching discreet and benigne. 520
To drawen folk to heven by fairnesse
By good ensample, was his bisinesse:
But it were any persone obstinat,
What-so he were, of heigh or lowe estat, 524
Him wolde he snibben sharply for the nones.
A bettre preest, I trowe that nowher noon is.
He wayted after no pompe and reverence,
Ne maked him a spyced conscience,
But Cristes lore, and his apostles twelve, 529
He taughte, and first he folwed it him-selve.
With him ther was a PLOWMAN, was his brother,
That hadde y-lad of dong ful many a fother,
A trewe swinker and a good was he,
Livinge in pees and parfit charitee.
God loved he best with al his hole herte 535
At alle tymes, thogh him gamed or smerte,
And thanne his neighebour right as him-selve.
He wolde thresshe, and ther-to dyke and delve,
For Cristes sake, for every povre wight,
Withouten hyre, if it lay in his might. 540

[18]St. Matthew, 5:19.

[19]There were thirty-five chantries at St. Paul's, served by fifty-four priests who said masses for the dead.

[20]"Or to remain in retirement with some fraternity."

His tythes payed he ful faire and wel,
Bothe of his propre swink and his catel.
In a tabard he rood upon a mere.
Ther was also a Reve and a Millere,
A Somnour and a Pardoner also, 545
A Maunciple, and my-self; ther were namo.
The MILLER was a stout carl, for the nones,
Ful big he was of braun, and eek of bones;
That proved wel, for over-al ther he cam, 549
At wrastling he wolde have alwey the ram.[21]
He was short-sholdred, brood, a thikke knarre,
Ther nas no dore that he nolde heve of harre,
Or breke it, at a renning, with his heed.
His berd as any sowe or fox was reed,
And ther-to brood, as though it were a spade.
Up-on the cop right of his nose he hade 556
A werte, and ther-on stood a tuft of heres,
Reed as the bristles of a sowes eres;
His nose-thirles blake were and wyde.
A swerd and bokeler bar he by his syde; 560
His mouth as greet was as a greet forneys.
He was a janglere and a goliardeys,
And that was most of sinne and harlotryes.
Wel coude he stelen corn, and tollen thryes;
And yet he hadde a thombe of gold, pardee.
A whyt cote and a blew hood wered he. 566
A baggepype wel coude he blowe and sowne,
And ther-with-al he broghte us out of towne.
A gentil MAUNCIPLE was ther of a temple,
Of which achatours mighte take exemple 570
For to be wyse in bying of vitaille.
For whether that he payde, or took by taille,
Algate he wayted so in his achat,
That he was ay biforn and in good stat.
Now is nat that of God a ful fair grace, 575
That swich a lewed mannes wit shal pace
The wisdom of an heep of lerned men?
Of maistres hadde he mo than thryes ten,
That were of lawe expert and curious;
Of which ther were a doseyn in that hous 580
Worthy to been stiwardes of rente and lond
Of any lord that is in Engelond,
To make him live by his propre good,
In honour dettelees, but he were wood,
Or live as scarsly as him list desire; 585
And able for to helpen al a shire
In any cas that mighte falle or happe;
And yit this maunciple sette hir aller cappe.
The REVE was a sclendre colerik man,
His berd was shave as ny as ever he can. 590
His heer was by his eres round y-shorn.
His top was dokked lyk a preest biforn.
Ful longe were his legges, and ful lene,
Y-lyk a staf, ther was no calf y-sene.

[21]The prize.

Wel coude he kepe a gerner and a binne; 595
Ther was noon auditour coude on him winne.
Wel wiste he, by the droghte, and by the reyn,
The yelding of his seed, and of his greyn.
His lordes sheep, his neet, his dayerye,
His swyn, his hors, his stoor, and his pultrye,
Was hoolly in this reves governing, 601
And by his covenaunt yaf the rekening,
Sin that his lord was twenty yeer of age;
Ther coude no man bringe him in arrerage.[22]
Ther nas baillif, ne herde, ne other hyne, 605
That he ne knew his sleighte and his covyne;
They were adrad of him, as of the deeth.
His woning was ful fair up-on an heeth,
With grene treës shadwed was his place.
He coude bettre than his lord purchace. 610
Ful riche he was astored prively,
His lord wel coude he plesen subtilly,
To yeve and lene him of his owne good,
And have a thank, and yet a cote and hood.
In youthe he lerned hadde a good mister; 615
He was a wel good wrighte, a carpenter.
This reve sat up-on a ful good stot,
That was al pomely grey, and highte Scot.
A long surcote of pers up-on he hade,
And by his syde he bar a rusty blade, 620
Of Northfolk was this reve, of which I telle,
Bisyde a toun men clepen Baldeswelle.
Tukked he was, as is a frere, aboute,
And ever he rood the hindreste of our route.
A SOMNOUR was ther with us in that place,
That hadde a fyr-reed cherubinnes face, 626
For sawcefleem he was, with eyen narwe.
As hoot he was, and lecherous, as a sparwe;
With scalled browes blake, and piled berd;
Of his visage children were aferd. 630
Ther nas quik-silver, litarge, ne brimstoon,
Boras, ceruce, ne oille of tartre noon,
Ne oynement that wolde clense and byte,
That him mighte helpen of his whelkes whyte,
Nor of the knobbes sittinge on his chekes. 635
Wel loved he garleek, oynons, and eek lekes,
And for to drinken strong wyn, reed as blood.
Than wolde he speke, and crye as he were wood.
And whan that he wel dronken hadde the wyn,
Than wolde he speke no word but Latyn. 640
A fewe termes hadde he, two or three,
That he had lerned out of som decree;
No wonder is, he herde it al the day;
And eek ye knowen wel, how that a jay 644
Can clepen "Watte," as well as can the pope.

[22]Catch him in arrears.

But who-so coude in other thing him grope,
Thanne hadde he spent al his philosophye;
Ay *"Questio quid iuris"*[23] wolde he crye.
He was a gentil harlot and a kinde;
A bettre felawe sholde men noght finde. 650
He wolde suffre, for a quart of wyn,
A good felawe to have his concubyn
A twelf-month, and excuse him atte fulle:
Full prively a finch eek coude he pulle.
And if he fond o-wher a good felawe, 655
He wolde techen him to have non awe,
In swich cas, of the erchedeknes curs,
But-if a mannes soule were in his purs;
For in his purs he sholde y-punisshed be.
"Purs is the erchedeknes helle," seyde he. 660
But wel I woot he lyed right in dede;
Of cursing oghte ech gilty man him drede—
For curs wol slee, right as assoilling saveth—
And also war him of a *significavit*.[24]
In daunger hadde he at his owne gyse 665
The yonge girles of the diocyse,
And knew hir counseil, and was al hir reed.
A gerland hadde he set up-on his heed,
As greet as it were for an ale-stake;
A bokeler hadde he maad him of a cake. 670
With him ther rood a gentil PARDONER
Of Rouncival,[25] his freend and his compeer,
That streight was comen fro the court of Rome.
Ful loude he song, "Com hider, love, to me."
This somnour bar to him a stif burdoun, 675
Was never trompe of half so greet a soun.
This pardoner hadde heer as yelow as wex,
But smothe it heng, as dooth a strike of flex;
By ounces henge his lokkes that he hadde, 679
And ther-with he his shuldres overspradde;
But thinne it lay, by colpons oon and oon;
But hood, for jolitee, ne wered he noon,
For it was trussed up in his walet.
Him thoughte, he rood al of the newe jet;
Dischevele, save his cappe, he rood all bare. 685
Swiche glaringe eyen hadde he as an hare.
A vernicle hadde he sowed on his cappe.
His walet lay biforn him in his lappe,
Bret-ful of pardoun come from Rome al hoot.
A voys he hadde as smal as hath a goot. 690
No berd hadde he, ne never sholde have,
As smothe it was as it were late y-shave;
I trowe he were a gelding or a mare.
But of his craft, fro Berwik into Ware,
Ne was ther swich another pardoner. 695
For in his male he hadde a pilwe-beer,
Which that, he seyde, was our lady veyl:
He seyde, he hadde a gobet of the seyl
That sëynt Peter hadde, whan that he wente
Up-on the see, til Jesu Crist him hente. 700
He hadde a croys of latoun, ful of stones,
And in a glas he hadde pigges bones.
But with thise relikes, whan that he fond
A povre person dwelling up-on lond,
Up-on a day he gat him more moneye 705
Than that the person gat in monthes tweye.
And thus, with feyned flaterye and japes,
He made the person and the peple his apes.
But trewely to tellen, atte laste,
He was in chirche a noble ecclesiaste. 710
Wel coude he rede a lessoun or a storie,
But alderbest he song an offertorie;
For wel he wiste, whan that song was songe,
He moste preche, and wel affyle his tonge,
To winne silver, as he ful wel coude; 715
Therefore he song so meriely and loude.
Now have I told you shortly, in a clause,
Th'estat, th'array, the nombre, and eek the cause
Why that assembled was this companye
In Southwerk, at this gentil hostelrye, 720
That highte the Tabard, faste by the Belle.
But now is tyme to yow for to telle
How that we baren us that ilke night,
Whan we were in that hostelrye alight.
And after wol I telle of our viage, 725
And al the remenaunt of our pilgrimage.
But first I pray yow, of your curteisye,
That ye n'arette it nat my vileinye,
Thogh that I pleynly speke in this matere,
To telle yow hir wordes and hir chere; 730
Ne thogh I speke hir wordes properly.
For this ye knowen al-so wel as I,
Who-so shal telle a tale after a man,
He moot reherce, as ny as ever he can,
Everich a word, if it be in his charge, 735
Al speke he never so rudeliche and large;
Or elles he moot telle his tale untrewe,
Or feyne thing, or finde wordes newe.
He may nat spare, al-thogh he were his brother;
He moot as wel seye o word as another. 740
Crist spak him-self ful brode in holy writ,
And wel ye woot, no vileinye is it.
Eek Plato seith, who-so that can him rede,
The wordes mote be cosin to the dede.[26]
Also I prey yow to foryeve it me, 745
Al have I nat set folk in hir degree
Here in this tale, as that they sholde stonde;
My wit is short, ye may wel understonde.

---

[23] What is the law on this point?

[24] A writ of excommunication, which usually began with this word.

[25] An hospital near Charing Cross, London.

[26] Chaucer took this from Boethius, *De Consolatione*, bk. III, pr. 12. Cf. Plato, *Timaeus*, 29B.

Greet chere made our hoste us everichon,
And to the soper sette us anon; 750
And served us with vitaille at the beste.
Strong was the wyn, and wel to drinke us leste.
A semely man our hoste was with-alle
For to han been a marshal in an halle;
A large man he was with eyen stepe, 755
A fairer burgeys is ther noon in Chepe:[27]
Bold of his speche, and wys, and wel y-taught,
And of manhod him lakkede right naught.
Eek therto he was right a mery man,
And after soper pleyen he bigan, 760
And spak of mirthe amonges othere thinges,
Whan that we hadde maad our rekeninges;
And seyde thus: "Now, lordinges, trewely,
Ye been to me right welcome hertely:
For by my trouthe, if that I shal nat lye, 765
I ne saugh this yeer so mery a companye
At ones in this herberwe as is now.
Fayn wolde I doon yow mirthe, wiste I how.
And of a mirthe I am right now bithoght,
To doon yow ese, and it shal coste noght. 770
"Ye goon to Caunterbury; God yow spede,
The blisful martir quyte yow your mede.
And wel I woot, as ye goon by the weye,
Ye shapen yow to talen and to pleye;
For trewely, confort ne mirthe is noon 775
To ryde by the weye doumb as a stoon;
And therfore wol I maken yow disport,
As I seyde erst, and doon yow som confort.
And if yow lyketh alle, by oon assent,
Now for to stonden at my jugement, 780
And for to werken as I shal yow seye,
To-morwe, whan ye ryden by the weye,
Now, by my fader soule, that is deed,
But ye be merye, I wol yeve yow myn heed.
Hold up your hond, withouten more speche."
Our counseil was nat longe for to seche; 786
Us thoughte it was noght worth to make it wys,
And graunted him withouten more avys,
And bad him seye his verdit, as him leste.
"Lordinges," quod he, "now herkneth for the beste; 790
But tak it not, I prey yow, in desdeyn;
This is the poynt, to speken short and pleyn,
That ech of yow, to shorte with your weye,
In this viage, shal telle tales tweye,
To Caunterbury-ward, I mene it so, 795
And hom-ward he shal tellen othere two,
Of aventures that whylom han bifalle,
And which of yow that bereth him best of alle,
That is to seyn, that telleth in this cas
Tales of best sentence and most solas, 800
Shal have a soper at our aller cost
Here in this place, sitting by this post,
Whan that we come agayn fro Caunterbury.
And for to make yow the more mery,
I wol my-selven gladly with yow ryde, 805
Right at myn owne cost, and be your gyde.
And who-so wol my jugement withseye
Shal paye al that we spenden by the weye.
And if ye vouche-sauf that it be so,
Tel me anon, with-outen wordes mo, 810
And I wol erly shape me therfore."
This thing was graunted, and our othes swore
With ful glad herte, and preyden him also
That he wold vouche-sauf for to do so,
And that he wolde been our governour, 815
And of our tales juge and reportour,
And sette a soper at a certeyn prys;
And we wold reuled been at his devys,
In heigh and lowe; and thus, by oon assent,
We been acorded to his jugement. 820
And ther-up-on the wyn was fet anon;
We dronken, and to reste wente echon,
With-outen any lenger taryinge.
A-morwe, whan that day bigan to springe,
Up roos our host, and was our aller cok, 825
And gadrede us togidre, alle in a flok,
And forth we riden, a litel more than pas,
Un-to the watering of seint Thomas.[28]
And there our host bigan his hors areste,
And seyde, "Lordinges, herkneth, if yow leste. 830
Ye woot your forward, and I it yow recorde.
If even-song and morwe-song acorde,
Lat see now who shal telle the firste tale.
As ever mote I drinke wyn or ale,
Who-so be rebel to my jugement 835
Shal paye for al that by the weye is spent.
Now draweth cut, er that we ferrer twinne;
He which that hath the shortest shal biginne.
Sire knight," quod he, "my maister and my lord,
Now draweth cut, for that is myn acord. 840
Cometh neer," quod he, "my lady prioresse;
And ye, sir clerk, lat be your shamfastnesse,
Ne studieth noght; ley hond to, every man."
Anon to drawen every wight bigan,
And shortly for to tellen, as it was, 845
Were it by aventure, or sort, or cas,
The sothe is this, the cut fil to the knight,
Of which ful blythe and glad was every wight;
And telle he moste his tale, as was resoun,
By forward and by composicioun, 850
As ye han herd; what nedeth wordes mo?

[27]Cheapside.

[28]Two miles from Southwark.

And whan this gode man saugh it was so,
As he that wys was and obedient
To kepe his forward by his free assent,
He seyde: "Sin I shal beginne the game, 855
What, welcome be the cut, a Goddes name!
Now lat us ryde, and herkneth what I seye."
And with that word we riden forth our weye;
And he bigan with right a mery chere
His tale anon, and seyde in this manere.[29] 860

The Prioresses Prologue

"Wel seyd, by *corpus dominus*,"[1] quod our hoste,
"Now longe moot thou sayle by the coste,
Sir gentil maister, gentil marineer!
God yeve this monk a thousand last quad yeer!
A ha! felawes! beth ware of swiche a jape! 5
The monk putte in the mannes hood an ape,
And in his wyves eek, by seint Austin!
Draweth no monkes more un-to your in.
"But now passe over, and lat us seke aboute,
Who shal now telle first, of al this route, 10
Another tale"; and with that word he sayde,
As curteisly as it had been a mayde,
"My lady Prioresse, by your leve,
So that I wiste I sholde yow not greve,
I wolde demen that ye tellen sholde 15
A tale next, if so were that ye wolde.
Now wol ye vouche-sauf, my lady dere?"
"Gladly," quod she, and seyde as ye shal here.

The Prioresses Tale

Domine, dominus noster.[2]

O Lord our lord, thy name how merveillous
Is in this large worlde y-sprad—quod she:—
For noght only thy laude precious
Parfourned is by men of dignitee,
But by the mouth of children thy bountee 5
Parfourned is, for on the brest soukinge
Som tyme shewen they thyn heryinge.

Wherfor in laude, as I best can or may,
Of thee, and of the whyte lily flour
Which that thee bar, and is a mayde alway, 10
To telle a storie I wol do my labour;
Not that I may encresen hir honour;
For she hir-self is honour, and the rote
Of bountee, next hir sone, and soules bote.—

O moder mayde! o mayde moder free! 15
O bush unbrent, brenninge in Moyses sighte,
That ravisedest doun fro the deitee,
Thurgh thyn humblesse, the goost that in th'alighte,
Of whos vertu, whan he thyn herte lighte,
Conceived was the fadres sapience, 20
Help me to telle it in thy reverence!

Lady! thy bountee, thy magnificence,
Thy vertu, and thy grete humilitee
Ther may no tonge expresse in no science;
For som-tyme, lady, er men praye to thee, 25
Thou goost biforn of thy benignitee,
And getest us the light, thurgh thy preyere,
To gyden us un-to thy sone so dere.

My conning is so wayk, o blisful quene,
For to declare thy grete worthinesse, 30
That I ne may the weighte nat sustene,
But as a child of twelf monthe old, or lesse,
That can unnethes any word expresse,
Right so fare I, and therfor I yow preye,
Gydeth my song that I shal of yow seye. 35

Here Biginneth the Prioresses Tale[3]

Ther was in Asie, in a greet citee,
Amonges Cristen folk, a Jewerye,
Sustened by a lord of that contree
For foule usure and lucre of vilanye,
Hateful to Crist and to his companye; 40
And thurgh the strete men mighte ryde or wende,
For it was free, and open at either ende.

A litel scole of Cristen folk ther stood
Doun at the ferther ende, in which ther were
Children an heep, y-comen of Cristen blood, 45
That lerned in that scole yeer by yere
Swich maner doctrine as men used there,
This is to seyn, to singen and to rede,
As smale children doon in hir childhede.

Among thise children was a widwes sone, 50
A litel clergeon, seven yeer of age,
That day by day to scole was his wone,
And eek also, wher-as he saugh th'image
Of Cristes moder, hadde he in usage,

[29] Here follow the tales of the Knight, the Miller, the Reeve, and the Cook, the last unfinished. On the morning of the second day the Man of Law tells the first tale, then the Shipman tells one, and then the Host turns to the Prioress.

[1] By the body of our Lord.

[2] O Lord, our Lord.

[3] Chaucer probably based this tale on some Latin prose legend current in his day. The theme, the murder of a Christian child by Jews, was a popular one in the Middle Ages, and at least 29 versions of it are known.

As him was taught, to knele adoun and seye 55
His *Ave Marie,*[4] as he goth by the weye.

Thus hath this widwe hir litel sone y-taught
Our blisful lady, Cristes moder dere,
To worshipe ay, and he forgat it naught,
For sely child wol alday sone lere; 60
But ay, whan I remembre on this matere,
Seint Nicholas stant ever in my presence,
For he so yong to Crist did reverence.

This litel child, his litel book lerninge,
As he sat in the scole at his prymer, 65
He *Alma redemptoris*[5] herde singe,
As children lerned hir antiphoner;
And, as he dorste, he drough him ner and ner,
And herkned ay the wordes and the note,
Til he the firste vers coude al by rote. 70

Noght wiste he what this Latin was to seye,
For he so yong and tendre was of age;
But on a day his felaw gan he preye
T'expounden him this song in his langage,
Or telle him why this song was in usage; 75
This preyde he him to construe and declare
Ful ofte tyme upon his knowes bare.

His felaw, which that elder was than he,
Answerde him thus: "this song, I have herd seye,
Was maked of our blisful lady free, 80
Hir to salue, and eek hir for to preye
To been our help and socour whan we deye.
I can no more expounde in this matere;
I lerne song, I can but smal grammere."

"And is this song maked in reverence 85
Of Cristes moder?" seyde this innocent;
"Now certes, I wol do my diligence
To conne it al, er Cristemasse is went;
Though that I for my prymer shal be shent,
And shal be beten thryës in an houre, 90
I wol it conne, our lady for to honoure."

His felaw taughte him homward prively,
Fro day to day, til he coude it by rote,
And than he song it wel and boldely
Fro word to word, acording with the note; 95
Twyës a day it passed thurgh his throte,
To scoleward and homward whan he wente;
On Cristes moder set was his entente.

As I have seyd, thurgh-out the Jewerye
This litel child, as he cam to and fro, 100
Ful merily than wolde he singe, and crye
O Alma redemptoris ever-mo.
The swetnes hath his herte perced so
Of Cristes moder, that, to hir to preye,
He can nat stinte of singing by the weye. 105

Our firste fo, the serpent Sathanas,
That hath in Jewes herte his waspes nest,
Up swal, and seide, "O Hebraik peple, allas!
Is this to yow a thing that is honest,
That swich a boy shal walken as him lest 110
In your despyt, and singe of swich sentence,
Which is agayn your lawes reverence?"

Fro thennes forth the Jewes han conspyred
This innocent out of this world to chace;
An homicyde ther-to han they hyred, 115
That in an aley hadde a privee place;
And as the child gan for-by for to pace,
This cursed Jew him hente and heeld him faste,
And kitte his throte, and in a pit him caste.

I seye that in a wardrobe they him threwe 120
Wher-as these Jewes purgen hir entraille.
O cursed folk of Herodes al newe,
What may your yvel entente yow availle?
Mordre wol out, certein, it wol nat faille, 124
And namely ther th'onour of god shal sprede,
The blood out cryeth on your cursed dede.

"O martir, souded to virginitee,
Now maystou singen, folwing ever in oon
The whyte lamb celestial," quod she,
"Of which the grete evangelist, seint John, 130
In Pathmos wroot, which seith that they that goon
Biforn this lamb, and singe a song al newe,
That never, fleshly, wommen they ne knewe."

This povre widwe awaiteth al that night
After hir litel child, but he cam noght; 135
For which, as sone as it was dayes light,
With face pale of drede and bisy thoght,
She hath at scole and elles-wher him soght,
Til finally she gan so fer espye
That he last seyn was in the Jewerye. 140

With modres pitee in hir brest enclosed,
She gooth, as she were half out of hir minde,
To every place wher she hath supposed
By lyklihede hir litel child to finde;
And ever on Cristes moder meke and kinde 145
She cryde, and atte laste thus she wroghte,
Among the cursed Jewes she him soghte.

---

[4]Hail Mary (the first two words of a short prayer made up from St. Luke, 1:28 and 42).

[5]Gracious Mother of the Redeemer. There is more than one medieval hymn with this beginning.

She frayneth and she preyeth pitously
To every Jew that dwelte in thilke place,
To telle hir, if hir child wente oght for-by. 150
They seyde, "nay"; but Jesu, of his grace,
Yaf in hir thought, inwith a litel space,
That in that place after hir sone she cryde,
Wher he was casten in a pit bisyde.

O grete god, that parfournest thy laude 155
By mouth of innocents, lo heer thy might!
This gemme of chastitee, this emeraude,
And eek of martirdom the ruby bright,
Ther he with throte y-corven lay upright,
He *"Alma redemptoris"* gan to singe 160
So loude, that al the place gan to ringe.

The Cristen folk, that thurgh the strete wente,
In coomen, for to wondre up-on this thing,
And hastily they for the provost sente;
He cam anon with-outen tarying, 165
And herieth Crist that is of heven king,
And eek his moder, honour of mankinde,
And after that, the Jewes leet he binde.

This child with pitous lamentacioun
Up-taken was, singing his song alway; 170
And with honour of greet processioun
They carien him un-to the nexte abbay.
His moder swowning by the bere lay;
Unnethe might the peple that was there
This newe Rachel bringe fro his bere. 175

With torment and with shamful deth echon
This provost dooth thise Jewes for to sterve
That of this mordre wiste, and that anon;
He nolde no swich cursednesse observe.
Yvel shal have, that yvel wol deserve. 180
Therfor with wilde hors he dide hem drawe,[6]
And after that he heng hem by the lawe.

Up-on his bere ay lyth this innocent
Biforn the chief auter, whyl masse laste,
And after that, the abbot with his covent 185
Han sped hem for to burien him ful faste;
And whan they holy water on him caste,
Yet spak this child, whan spreynd was holy water,
And song—*"O Alma redemptoris mater!"*

This abbot, which that was an holy man 190
As monkes been, or elles oghten be,
This yonge child to conjure he bigan,
And seyde, "o dere child, I halse thee,
In vertu of the holy Trinitee,
Tel me what is thy cause for to singe, 195
Sith that thy throte is cut, to my seminge?"

"My throte is cut un-to my nekke-boon,"
Seyde this child, "and, as by wey of kinde,
I sholde have deyed, ye, longe tyme agoon,
But Jesu Crist, as ye in bokes finde, 200
Wil that his glorie laste and be in minde;
And, for the worship of his moder dere,
Yet may I singe *'O Alma'* loude and clere.

"This welle of mercy, Cristes moder swete,
I lovede alwey, as after my conninge; 205
And whan that I my lyf sholde forlete,
To me she cam, and bad me for to singe
This antem verraily in my deyinge,
As ye han herd, and, whan that I had songe,
Me thoughte, she leyde a greyn up-on my tonge. 210

"Wherfor I singe, and singe I moot certeyn
In honour of that blisful mayden free,
Til fro my tonge of-taken is the greyn;
And afterward thus seyde she to me,
'My litel child, now wol I fecche thee 215
Whan that the greyn is fro thy tonge y-take;
Be nat agast, I wol thee nat forsake.' "

This holy monk, this abbot, him mene I,
His tonge out-caughte, and took a-wey the greyn,
And he yaf up the goost ful softely. 220
And whan this abbot had this wonder seyn,
His salte teres trikled doun as reyn,
And gruf he fil al plat up-on the grounde,
And stille he lay as he had been y-bounde.

The covent eek lay on the pavement 225
Weping, and herien Cristes moder dere,
And after that they ryse, and forth ben went,
And toke awey this martir fro his bere,
And in a tombe of marbul-stones clere
Enclosen they his litel body swete; 230
Ther he is now, god leve us for to mete.

O yonge Hugh of Lincoln, slayn also
With cursed Jewes, as it is notable,
For it nis but a litel whyle ago;
Preye eek for us, we sinful folk unstable, 235
That, of his mercy, god so merciable
On us his grete mercy multiplye,
For reverence of his moder Marye. Amen.

[6] *Sc.* to the gallows.

The Prologue of the Nonne Prestes Tale[1]

"Ho!" quod the knight, "good sir, namore of this,
That ye han seyd is right y-nough, y-wis,
And mochel more; for litel hevinesse
Is right y-nough to mochel folk, I gesse.
I seye for me, it is a greet disese 5
Wher-as men han ben in greet welthe and ese,
To heren of hir sodeyn fal, allas!
And the contrarie is joie and greet solas,
As whan a man hath been in povre estaat,
And clymbeth up, and wexeth fortunat, 10
And ther abydeth in prosperitee,
Swich thing is gladsom, as it thinketh me,
And of swich thing were goodly for to telle."
"Ye," quod our hoste, "by seint Poules belle,
Ye seye right sooth; this monk, he clappeth loude, 15
He spak how 'fortune covered with a cloude'
I noot never what, and als of a 'Tragedie'
Right now ye herde, and parde! no remedie
It is for to biwaille, ne compleyne
That that is doon, and als it is a peyne, 20
As ye han seyd, to here of hevinesse.
Sir monk, na-more of this, so god yow blesse!
Your tale anoyeth al this companye;
Swich talking is nat worth a boterflye;
For ther-in is ther no desport ne game. 25
Wherfor, sir Monk, or dan Piers by your name,
I preye yow hertely, telle us somwhat elles,
For sikerly, nere clinking of your belles,
That on your brydel hange on every syde,
By heven king, that for us alle dyde, 30
I sholde er this han fallen doun for slepe,
Although the slough had never been so depe;
Than had your tale al be told in vayn.
For certeinly, as that thise clerkes seyn,
'Wher-as a man may have noon audience, 35
Noght helpeth it to tellen his sentence.'
And wel I woot the substance is in me,
If any thing shal wel reported be.
Sir, sey somwhat of hunting, I yow preye."
"Nay," quod this monk, "I have no lust to pleye; 40
Now let another telle, as I have told."
Than spak our host, with rude speche and bold,
And seyde un-to the Nonnes Preest anon,
"Com neer, thou preest, com hider, thou sir John,
Tel us swich thing as may our hertes glade, 45
Be blythe, though thou ryde up-on a jade.
What though thyn hors be bothe foule and lene,
If he wol serve thee, rekke nat a bene;
Look that thyn herte be mery evermo."
"Yis, sir," quod he, "yis, host, so mote I go, 50
But I be mery, y-wis, I wol be blamed."—
And right anon his tale he hath attamed,
And thus he seyde un-to us everichon,
This swete preest, this goodly man, sir John.

The Nonne Preestes Tale[2]

A povre widwe, somdel stape in age,
Was whylom dwelling in a narwe cotage,
Bisyde a grove, stonding in a dale.
This widwe, of which I telle yow my tale,
Sin thilke day that she was last a wyf, 5
In pacience ladde a ful simple lyf,
For litel was hir catel and hir rente;
By housbondrye, of such as God hir sente,
She fond hir-self, and eek hir doghtren two.
Three large sowes hadde she, and namo, 10
Three kyn, and eek a sheep that highte Malle.
Ful sooty was hir bour, and eek hir halle,
In which she eet ful many a sclendre meel.
Of poynaunt sauce hir neded never a deel.
No deyntee morsel passed thurgh hir throte;
Hir dyete was accordant to hir cote. 16
Repleccioun ne made hir never syk;
Attempree dyete was al hir phisyk,
And exercyse, and hertes suffisaunce.
The goute lette hir no-thing for to daunce, 20
N'apoplexye shente nat hir heed;
No wyn ne drank she, neither whyt ne reed;
Hir bord was served most with whyt and blak,
Milk and broun breed, in which she fond no lak,
Seynd bacoun, and somtyme an ey or tweye,
For she was as it were a maner deye. 26
A yerd she hadde, enclosed al aboute
With stikkes, and a drye dich with-oute,
In which she hadde a cok, hight Chauntecleer,
In al the land of crowing nas his peer. 30
His vois was merier than the mery orgon
On messe-dayes that in the chirche gon;

[1]After the Prioress's tale the Host asks Chaucer for a story. He begins *Sir Thopas,* a burlesque of the popular romances of the day, but is soon interrupted by the Host, who is bored. Thereupon Chaucer begins anew, and tells the edifying prose *Tale of Melibeus.* The Monk's tale which follows consists of a series of "tragedies," or sad stories, illustrating the instability of human good fortune; these prove to be too much for the patience of the Knight.

[2]The immediate source of this story is not known, but there were popular cycles dealing with Reynard the Fox.

Wel sikerer was his crowing in his logge,
Than is a clokke, or an abbey orlogge.
By nature knew he ech ascencioun 35
Of equinoxial in thilke toun;
For whan degrees fiftene were ascended,[3]
Thanne crew he, that it mighte nat ben amended.
His comb was redder than the fyn coral,
And batailed, as it were a castel-wal. 40
His bile was blak, and as the jeet it shoon;
Lyk asur were his legges, and his toon;
His nayles whytter than the lilie flour,
And lyk the burned gold was his colour.
This gentil cok hadde in his governaunce 45
Sevene hennes, for to doon al his plesaunce,
Whiche were his sustres and his paramours,
And wonder lyk to him, as of colours.
Of whiche the faireste hewed on hir throte
Was cleped faire damoysele Pertelote. 50
Curteys she was, discreet, and debonaire,
And compaignable, and bar hir-self so faire,
Sin thilke day that she was seven night old,
That trewely she hath the herte in hold
Of Chauntecleer loken in every lith; 55
He loved hir so, that wel was him therwith.
But such a joye was it to here hem singe,
Whan that the brighte sonne gan to springe,
In swete accord, "my lief is faren in londe."
For thilke tyme, as I have understonde, 60
Bestes and briddes coude speke and singe.
And so bifel, that in a daweninge,
As Chauntecleer among his wyves alle
Sat on his perche, that was in the halle,
And next him sat this faire Pertelote, 65
This Chauntecleer gan gronen in his throte,
As man that in his dreem is drecched sore.
And whan that Pertelote thus herde him rore,
She was agast, and seyde, "O herte dere,
What eyleth yow, to grone in this manere? 70
Ye been a verray sleper, fy for shame!"
And he answerde and seyde thus, "madame,
I pray yow, that ye take it nat a-grief:
By god, me mette I was in swich meschief
Right now, that yet myn herte is sore afright.
Now god," quod he, "my swevene recche aright, 76
And keep my body out of foul prisoun!
Me mette, how that I romed up and doun
Withinne our yerde, wher-as I saugh a beste,
Was lyk an hound, and wolde han maad areste 80
Upon my body, and wolde han had me deed.
His colour was bitwixe yelwe and reed;
And tipped was his tail, and bothe his eres,
With blak, unlyk the remenant of his heres;
His snowte smal, with glowinge eyen tweye.
Yet of his look for fere almost I deye; 86
This caused me my groning, doutelees."
"Avoy!" quod she, "fy on yow, hertelees!
Allas!" quod she, "for, by that god above,
Now han ye lost myn herte and al my love; 90
I can nat love a coward, by my feith.
For certes, what so any womman seith,
We alle desyren, if it mighte be,
To han housbondes hardy, wyse, and free,
And secree, and no nigard, ne no fool, 95
Ne him that is agast of every tool,
Ne noon avauntour, by that god above!
How dorste ye seyn for shame unto your love,
That any thing mighte make yow aferd?
Have ye no mannes herte, and han a berd? 100
Allas! and conne ye been agast of swevenis?
No-thing, god wot, but vanitee, in sweven is.
Swevenes engendren of replecciouns,
And ofte of fume, and of complecciouns, 104
Whan humours been to habundant in a wight.
Certes this dreem, which ye han met to-night,
Cometh of the grete superfluitee
Of youre rede *colera,* pardee,
Which causeth folk to dreden in here dremes
Of arwes, and of fyr with rede lemes, 110
Of grete bestes, that they wol hem byte,
Of contek, and of whelpes grete and lyte;
Right as the humour of malencolye
Causeth ful many a man, in sleep, to crye,
For fere of blake beres, or boles blake, 115
Or elles, blake develes wole hem take.
Of othere humours coude I telle also,
That werken many a man in sleep ful wo;
But I wol passe as lightly as I can. 119
"Lo Catoun,[4] which that was so wys a man,
Seyde he nat thus, ne do no fors of dremes?
Now, sire," quod she, "whan we flee fro the bemes,
For Goddes love, as tak som laxatyf;
Up peril of my soule, and of my lyf,
I counseille yow the beste, I wol nat lye, 125
That bothe of colere and of malencolye
Ye purge yow; and for ye shul nat tarie,
Though in this toun is noon apotecarie,
I shal my-self to herbes techen yow,
That shul ben for your hele, and for your prow; 130
And in our yerd tho herbes shal I finde,
The whiche han of hir propretee, by kinde,
To purgen yow binethe, and eek above.
Forget not this, for goddes owene love!
Ye been ful colerik of compleccioun. 135
Ware the sonne in his ascencioun
Ne fynde yow nat repleet of humours hote;
And if it do, I dar wel leye a grote,

[3]When an hour had passed.

[4]Dionysius Cato, a medieval writer.

That ye shul have a fevere terciane,
Or an agu, that may be youre bane. 140
A day or two ye shul have digestyves
Of wormes, er ye take your laxatyves,
Of lauriol, centaure, and fumetere,
Or elles of ellebor, that groweth there,
Of catapuce, or of gaytres beryis, 145
Of erbe yve, growing in our yerd, that mery
is;
Pekke hem up right as they growe, and ete
hem in.
Be mery, housbond, for your fader kin!
Dredeth no dreem; I can say yow namore."
"Madame," quod he, "*graunt mercy* of[5]
your lore. 150
But nathelees, as touching daun Catoun,
That hath of wisdom such a greet renoun,
Though that he bad no dremes for to drede,
By god, men may in olde bokes rede
Of many a man, more of auctoritee 155
Than ever Catoun was, so mote I thee,
That al the revers seyn of his sentence,
And han wel founden by experience,
That dremes ben significaciouns,
As wel of joye as tribulaciouns 160
That folk enduren in this lyf present.
Ther nedeth make of this noon argument;
The verray preve sheweth it in dede.
"Oon of the gretteste auctours that men
rede[6]
Seith, thus, that whylom two felawes wente
On pilgrimage, in a ful good entente; 166
And happed so, thay come into a toun,
Wher-as ther was swich congregacioun
Of peple, and eek so streit of herbergage,
That they ne founde as muche as o cotage 170
In which they bothe mighte y-logged be.
Wherfor thay mosten, of necessitee,
As for that night, departen compaignye;
And ech of hem goth to his hostelrye,
And took his logging as it wolde falle. 175
That oon of hem was logged in a stalle,
Fer in a yerd, with oxen of the plough;
That other man was logged wel y-nough,
As was his aventure, or his fortune,
That us governeth alle as in commune. 180
"And so bifel, that, longe er it were day,
This man mette in his bed, ther-as he lay,
How that his felawe gan up-on him calle,
And seyde, 'allas! for in an oxes stalle
This night I shal be mordred ther I lye. 185
Now help me, dere brother, er I dye;
In alle haste com to me,' he sayde.
This man out of his sleep for fere abrayde;
But whan that he was wakned of his sleep,
He turned him, and took of this no keep; 190

[5]Many thanks for. [6]Cicero in *De Divinatione*.

Him thoughte his dreem nas but a vanitee.
Thus twyës in his sleping dremed he.
And atte thridde tyme yet his felawe
Cam, as him thoughte, and seide, 'I am now
slawe;
Bihold my blody woundes, depe and wyde! 195
Arys up erly in the morwe-tyde,
And at the west gate of the toun,' quod he,
'A carte ful of dong ther shaltow see,
In which my body is hid ful prively;
Do thilke carte aresten boldely. 200
My gold caused my mordre, sooth to sayn';
And tolde him every poynt how he was slayn,
With a ful pitous face, pale of hewe.
And truste wel, his dreem he fond ful trewe;
For on the morwe, as sone as it was day, 205
To his felawes in he took the way;
And whan that he cam to this oxes stalle,
After his felawe he bigan to calle.
"The hostiler answered him anon,
And seyde, 'sire, your felawe is agon, 210
As sone as day he wente out of the toun.'
This man gan fallen in suspecioun,
Remembring on his dremes that he mette,
And forth he goth, no lenger wolde he lette,
Unto the west gate of the toun, and fond 215
A dong-carte, as it were to donge lond,
That was arrayed in the same wyse
As ye han herd the dede man devyse;
And with an hardy herte he gan to crye
Vengeaunce and justice of this felonye:— 220
'My felawe mordred is this same night,
And in this carte he lyth gapinge upright.
I crye out on the ministres,' quod he,
'That sholden kepe and reulen this citee;
Harrow! allas! her lyth my felawe slayn!' 225
What sholde I more un-to this tale sayn?
The peple out-sterte, and caste the cart to
grounde,
And in the middel of the dong they founde
The dede man, that mordred was al newe.
"O blisful god, that art so just and
trewe! 230
Lo, how that thou biwreyest mordre alway!
Mordre wol out, that see we day by day.
Mordre is so wlatsom and abhominable
To god, that is so just and resonable,
That he ne wol nat suffre it heled be; 235
Though it abyde a yeer, or two, or three,
Mordre wol out, this my conclusioun.[7]
And right anoon, ministres of that toun
Han hent the carter, and so sore him pyned,
And eek the hostiler so sore engyned, 240
That they biknewe hir wikkednesse anoon,
And were an-hanged by the nekke-boon.

[7]Cf. the Prioress's tale, l. 124.

"Here may men seen that dremes been to
drede,
And certes, in the same book I rede,
Right in the nexte chapitre after this 245
(I gabbe nat, so have I joye or blis),
Two men that wolde han passed over see,
For certeyn cause, in-to a fer contree,
If that the wind ne hadde been contrarie,
That made hem in a citee for to tarie, 250
That stood ful mery upon an haven-syde.
But on a day, agayn the even-tyde,
The wind gan chaunge, and blew right as hem
leste.
Jolif and glad they wente un-to hir reste,
And casten hem ful erly for to saille; 255
But to that oo man fil a greet mervaille.
That oon of hem, in sleping as he lay,
Him mette a wonder dreem, agayn the day;
Him thoughte a man stood by his beddes
syde,
And him comaunded, that he sholde abyde, 260
And seyde him thus, 'if thou to-morwe
wende,
Thou shalt be dreynt; my tale is at an ende.'
He wook, and tolde his felawe what he mette,
And preyde him his viage for to lette;
As for that day, he preyde him to abyde. 265
His felawe, that lay by his beddes syde,
Gan for to laughe, and scorned him ful faste.
'No dreem,' quod he, 'may so myn herte
agaste,
That I wol lette for to do my thinges.
I sette not a straw by thy dreminges, 270
For swevenes been but vanitees and japes.
Men dreme al-day of owles or of apes,
And eke of many a mase therwithal;
Men dreme of thing that never was ne shal.
But sith I see that thou wolt heer abyde, 275
And thus for-sleuthen wilfully thy tyde,
God wot it reweth me; and have good day.'
And thus he took his leve, and wente his way.
But er that he hadde halfe his cours y-seyled,
Noot I nat why, ne what mischaunce it eyled,
But casuelly the shippes botme rente, 281
And ship and man under the water wente
In sighte of othere shippes it byside,
That with hem seyled at the same tyde.
And therfor, faire Pertelote so dere, 285
By swiche ensamples olde maistow lere,
That no man sholde been to recchelees
Of dremes, for I sey thee, doutelees,
That many a dreem ful sore is for to drede.
"Lo, in the lyf of seint Kenelm, I rede, 290
That was Kenulphus sone, the noble king
Of Mercenrike, how Kenelm mette a thing;
A lyte er he was mordred, on a day,
His mordre in his avisioun he say.
His norice him expouned every del 295
His sweven, and bad him for to kepe him wel
For traisoun; but he nas but seven yeer old,
And therfore litel tale hath he told
Of any dreem, so holy was his herte.
By god, I hadde lever than my sherte 300
That ye had rad his legende, as have I.
Dame Pertelote, I sey yow trewely,
Macrobeus, that writ th'avisioun
In Affrike of the worthy Cipioun,
Affermeth dremes, and seith that they
been 305
Warning of thinges that men after seen.
"And forther-more, I pray yow loketh wel
In th'olde testament, of Daniel,
If he held dremes any vanitee.
Reed eek of Joseph, and ther shul ye see 310
Wher dremes ben somtyme (I sey nat alle)
Warning of thinges that shul after falle.
Loke of Egipt the king, daun Pharao,
His bakere and his boteler also,
Wher they ne felte noon effect in dremes. 315
Who-so wol seken actes of sondry remes,
May rede of dremes many a wonder thing.
"Lo Cresus, which that was of Lyde king,[8]
Mette he nat that he sat upon a tree,
Which signified he sholde anhanged be? 320
Lo heer Andromacha, Ectores wyf,
That day that Ector sholde lese his lyf,
She dremed on the same night biforn,
How that the lyf of Ector sholde be lorn,
If thilke day he wente in-to bataille; 325
She warned him, but it mighte nat availle;
He wente for to fighte nathelees,
But he was slayn anoon of Achilles.
But thilke tale is al to long to telle,
And eek it is ny day, I may nat dwelle. 330
Shortly I seye, as for conclusioun,
That I shal han of this avisioun
Adversitee; and I seye forther-more,
That I ne telle of laxatyves no store,
For they ben venimous, I woot it wel; 335
I hem defye, I love hem never a del.
"Now let us speke of mirthe, and stinte al
this;
Madame Pertelote, so have I blis,
Of o thing god hath sent me large grace;
For whan I see the beautee of your face, 340
Ye ben so scarlet-reed about your yën,
It maketh al my drede for to dyen;
For, also siker as *In principio,*
Mulier est hominis confusio;[9]
Madame, the sentence of this Latin is— 345

[8]The story of Croesus had been the last of the tragedies told by the Monk before the Knight interrupted him.

[9]In the beginning woman is man's undoing.

Womman is mannes joye and al his blis.
For whan I fele a-night your softe syde,
Al-be-it that I may nat on you ryde,
For that our perche is maad so narwe, alas!
I am so ful of joye and of solas 350
That I defye bothe sweven and dreem."
And with that word he fley doun fro the
beem,
For it was day, and eek his hennes alle;
And with a chuk he gan hem for to calle,
For he had founde a corn, lay in the yerd. 355
Royal he was, he was namore aferd;
He fethered Pertelote twenty tyme,
And trad as ofte, er that it was pryme.
He loketh as it were a grim leoun;
And on his toos he rometh up and doun, 360
Him deyned not to sette his foot to grounde.
He chukketh, whan he hath a corn y-founde,
And to him rennen thanne his wyves alle.
Thus royal, as a prince is in his halle,
Leve I this Chauntecleer in his pasture; 365
And after wol I telle his aventure.
Whan that the month in which the world
bigan,
That highte March, whan god first maked
man,
Was complet, and [y]-passed were also,
Sin March bigan, thritty dayes and two, 370
Bifel that Chauntecleer, in al his pryde,
His seven wyves walking by his syde,
Caste up his eyen to the brighte sonne,
That in the signe of Taurus hadde
y-ronne 374
Twenty degrees and oon, and somwhat more;
And knew by kynde, and by noon other lore,
That it was pryme, and crew with blisful
stevene.
"The sonne," he sayde, "is clomben up on
hevene
Fourty degrees and oon, and more, y-wis.
Madame Pertelote, my worldes blis, 380
Herkneth thise blisful briddes how they
singe,
And see the fresshe floures how they springe;
Ful is myn herte of revel and solas."
But sodeinly him fil a sorweful cas;
For ever the latter ende of joye is wo. 385
God woot that worldly joye is sone ago;
And if a rethor coude faire endyte,
He in a cronique saufly mighte it wryte,
As for a sovereyn notabilitee.
Now every wys man, lat him herkne me; 390
This storie is al-so trewe, I undertake,
As is the book of Launcelot de Lake,[10]
That wommen holde in ful gret reverence.
Now wol I torne agayn to my sentence.

[10]A prose romance.

A col-fox, ful of sly iniquitee, 395
That in the grove hadde woned yeres three,
By heigh imaginacioun forn-cast,
The same night thurgh-out the hegges brast
Into the yerd, ther Chauntecleer the faire
Was wont, and eek his wyves, to repaire; 400
And in a bed of wortes stille he lay,
Til it was passed undern of the day,
Wayting his tyme on Chauntecleer to falle,
As gladly doon thise homicydes alle,
That in awayt liggen to mordre men. 405
O false mordrer, lurking in thy den!
O newe Scariot, newe Genilon![11]
False dissimilour, O Greek Sinon,
That broghtest Troye al outrely to sorwe!
O Chauntecleer, acursed be that morwe, 410
That thou into that yerd flough fro the
bemes!
Thou were ful wel y-warned by thy dremes,
That thilke day was perilous to thee.
But what that god forwoot mot nedes be,
After the opinioun of certeyn clerkis. 415
Witnesse on him, that any perfit clerk is,
That in scole is gret altercacioun
In this matere, and greet disputisoun,
And hath ben of an hundred thousand men.
But I ne can not bulte it to the bren, 420
As can the holy doctour Augustyn,
Or Boëce, or the bishop Bradwardyn,
Whether that goddes worthy forwiting
Streyneth me nedely for to doon a thing
(Nedely clepe I simple necessitee); 425
Or elles, if free choys be graunted me
To do that same thing, or do it noght,
Though god forwoot it, er that it was wroght;
Or if his witing streyneth nevere a del
But by necessitee condicionel. 430
I wol not han to do of swich matere;
My tale is of a cok, as ye may here,
That took his counseil of his wyf, with sorwe,
To walken in the yerd upon that morwe
That he had met the dreem, that I yow tolde.
Wommennes counseils been ful ofte
colde; 436
Wommannes counseil broghte us first to wo,
And made Adam fro paradys to go,
Ther-as he was ful mery, and wel at ese.—
But for I noot, to whom it mighte displese,
If I counseil of wommen wolde blame, 441
Passe over, for I seyde it in my game.
Rede auctours, wher they trete of swich
matere,
And what thay seyn of wommen ye may
here.
Thise been the cokkes wordes, and nat myne;
I can noon harm of no womman divyne.— 446

[11]The betrayer of Roland.

Faire in the sond, to bathe hir merily,
Lyth Pertelote, and alle hir sustres by,
Agayn the sonne; and Chauntecleer so free
Song merier than the mermayde in the see; 450
For Phisiologus[12] seith sikerly,
How that they singen wel and merily.
And so bifel that, as he caste his yë,
Among the wortes, on a boterflye,
He was war of this fox that lay ful lowe. 455
No-thing ne liste him thanne for to crowe,
But cryde anon, "cok, cok," and up he sterte,
As man that was affrayed in his herte.
For naturelly a beest desyreth flee
Fro his contrarie, if he may it see, 460
Though he never erst had seyn it with his yë.
This Chauntecleer, whan he gan him espye,
He wolde han fled, but that the fox anon
Seyde, "Gentil sire, allas! wher wol ye gon?
Be ye affrayed of me that am your freend? 465
Now certes, I were worse than a feend,
If I to yow wolde harm or vileinye.
I am nat come your counseil for t'espye;
But trewely, the cause of my cominge
Was only for to herkne how that ye singe. 470
For trewely ye have as mery a stevene
As eny aungel hath, that is in hevene;
Therwith ye han in musik more felinge
Than hadde Boëce, or any that can singe.
My lord your fader (god his soule blesse!) 475
And eek your moder, of hir gentilesse,
Han in myn hous y-been, to my gret ese;
And certes, sire, ful fayn wolde I yow plese.
But for men speke of singing, I wol saye,
So mote I brouke wel myn eyen tweye, 480
Save yow, I herde never man so singe,
As dide your fader in the morweninge;
Certes, it was of herte, al that he song.
And for to make his voys the more strong,
He wolde so peyne him, that with bothe his yën 485
He moste winke, so loude he wolde cryen,
And stonden on his tiptoon ther-with-al,
And strecche forth his nekke long and smal.
And eek he was of swich discrecioun,
That ther nas no man in no regioun 490
That him in song or wisdom mighte passe.
I have wel rad in daun Burnel the Asse,[13]
Among his vers, how that ther was a cok,
For that a preestes sone yaf him a knok
Upon his leg, whyl he was yong and nyce, 495
He made him for to lese his benefyce.
But certeyn, ther nis no comparisoun
Bitwix the wisdom and discrecioun
Of youre fader, and of his subtiltee.
Now singeth, sire, for seinte Charitee, 500
Let see, conne ye your fader countrefete?"
This Chauntecleer his winges gan to bete,
As man that coude his tresoun nat espye,
So was he ravisshed with his flaterye.
Allas! ye lordes, many a fals flatour 505
Is in your courtes, and many a losengeour,
That plesen yow wel more, by my feith,
Than he that soothfastnesse unto yow seith.
Redeth Ecclesiaste of flaterye;[14]
Beth war, ye lordes, of hir trecherye. 510
This Chauntecleer stood hye up-on his toos,
Strecching his nekke, and heeld his eyen cloos,
And gan to crowe loude for the nones;
And daun Russel the fox sterte up at ones,
And by the gargat hente Chauntecleer, 515
And on his bak toward the wode him beer,
For yet ne was ther no man that him sewed.
O destinee, that mayst nat been eschewed!
Allas, that Chauntecleer fleigh fro the bemes!
Allas, his wyf ne roghte nat of dremes! 520
And on a Friday fil al this meschaunce.
O Venus, that art goddesse of plesaunce,
Sin that thy servant was this Chauntecleer,
And in thy service dide al his poweer,
More for delyt, than world to multiplye, 525
Why woldestow suffre him on thy day to dye?
O Gaufred,[15] dere mayster soverayn,
That, whan thy worthy king Richard was slayn
With shot, compleynedest his deth so sore,
Why ne hadde I now thy sentence and thy lore, 530
The Friday for to chyde, as diden ye?
(For on a Friday soothly slayn was he.)
Than wolde I shewe yow how that I coude pleyne
For Chauntecleres drede, and for his peyne.
Certes, swich cry ne lamentacioun 535
Was never of ladies maad, whan Ilioun
Was wonne, and Pirrus with his streite swerd,
Whan he hadde hent king Priam by the berd,
And slayn him (as saith us *Eneydos*),[16]
As maden alle the hennes in the clos, 540
Whan they had seyn of Chauntecleer the sighte.

[12] The Bestiary, a popular collection containing moralized descriptions of animals.

[13] A Latin poem by Nigellus Wireker entitled *Burnellus or the Mirror of Fools* (written towards the close of the twelfth century).

[14] Ecclesiasticus (in *Apocrypha*), 12:10, 11, 16.

[15] Geoffrey de Vinsauf, Anglo-Norman trouvère.

[16] *Aeneid*, II, 544.

But sovereynly dame Pertelote shrighte,
Ful louder than dide Hasdrubales wyf,
Whan that hir housbond hadde lost his lyf,
And that the Romayns hadde brend Cartage; 545
She was so ful of torment and of rage,
That wilfully into the fyr she sterte,
And brende hir-selven with a stedfast herte.
O woful hennes, right so cryden ye,
As, whan that Nero brende the citee 550
Of Rome, cryden senatoures wyves,
For that hir housbondes losten alle hir lyves;
Withouten gilt this Nero hath hem slayn.
Now wol I torne to my tale agayn:— 554
This sely widwe, and eek hir doghtres two,
Herden thise hennes crye and maken wo,
And out at dores sterten they anoon,
And syen the fox toward the grove goon,
And bar upon his bak the cok away; 559
And cryden, "Out! harrow! and weylaway!
Ha, ha, the fox!" and after him they ran,
And eek with staves many another man;
Ran Colle our dogge, and Talbot, and Gerland,
And Malkin, with a distaf in hir hand; 564
Ran cow and calf, and eek the verray hogges
So were they fered for berking of the dogges
And shouting of the men and wimmen eke,
They ronne so, hem thoughte hir herte breke.
They yelleden as feendes doon in helle; 569
The dokes cryden as men wolde hem quelle;
The gees for fere flowen over the trees;
Out of the hyve cam the swarm of bees;
So hidous was the noyse, a! *benedicite!*[17]
Certes, he Jakke Straw,[18] and his meynee,
Ne made never shoutes half so shrille, 575
Whan that they wolden any Fleming kille,
As thilke day was maad upon the fox.
Of bras thay broghten bemes, and of box,
Of horn, of boon, in whiche they blewe and pouped,
And therwithal thay shryked and they houped; 580
It semed as that heven sholde falle.
Now, gode men, I pray yow herkneth alle!
Lo, how fortune turneth sodeinly
The hope and pryde eek of hir enemy!
This cok, that lay upon the foxes bak, 585
In al his drede, un-to the fox he spak,
And seyde, "sire, if that I were as ye,
Yet sholde I seyn (as wis god helpe me),
Turneth agayn, ye proude cherles alle!
A verray pestilence up-on yow falle! 590

[17]Literally, "Blessings on you."

[18]Leader of an insurrection in 1381. Thomas Walsingham states that when he and his men killed Flemings they raised a "most horrible clamor."

Now am I come un-to this wodes syde,
Maugree your heed, the cok shal heer abyde;
I wol him ete in feith, and that anon."—
The fox answerde, "in feith, it shal be don,"—
And as he spak that word, al sodeinly 595
This cok brak from his mouth deliverly,
And heighe up-on a tree he fleigh anon.
And whan the fox saugh that he was y-gon,
"Allas!" quod he, "O Chauntecleer, allas!
I have to yow," quod he, "y-doon trespas, 600
In-as-muche as I maked yow aferd,
Whan I yow hente, and broghte out of the yerd;
But, sire, I dide it in no wikke entente;
Com doun, and I shal telle yow what I mente.
I shal seye sooth to yow, god help me so." 605
"Nay than," quod he, "I shrewe us bothe two,
And first I shrewe my-self, bothe blood and bones,
If thou bigyle me ofter than ones.
Thou shalt na-more, thurgh thy flaterye,
Do me to singe and winke with myn yë. 610
For he that winketh, whan he sholde see,
Al wilfully, god lat him never thee!"
"Nay," quod the fox, "but god yeve him meschaunce,
That is so undiscreet of governaunce,
That jangleth whan he sholde holde his pees."
Lo, swich it is for to be recchelees, 616
And necligent, and truste on flaterye.
But ye that holden this tale a folye,
As of a fox, or of a cok and hen,
Taketh the moralitee, good men. 620
For seint Paul seith, that al that writen is,
To our doctryne it is y-write, y-wis.[19]
Taketh the fruyt, and lat the chaf be stille.
Now, gode god, if that it be thy wille, 624
As seith my lord,[20] so make us alle good men;
And bringe us to his heighe blisse. Amen.

Words of the Host[1]

Our Hoste gan to swere as he were wood,
"Harrow!" quod he, "by nayles and by blood!

[19]II Timothy, 3:16.

[20]A note in one of the manuscripts explains this as referring to the Archbishop of Canterbury.

[1]Following the Nun's Priest's Tale there is an evident break, after which, in the now accepted arrangement of the tales, come the Physician's Tale (immediately preceding the above "words of the Host") and the Pardoner's Tale. The Physician's Tale, to which the Host refers, was one of afflicted innocence, the story of Appius and Virginia, in which the latter's father slays her as the only means of protecting her from shame at the hands of Appius.

This was a fals cherl and a fals justyse!
As shamful deeth as herte may devyse
Come to thise juges and hir advocats! 5
Algate this sely mayde is slayn, allas!
Allas! to dere boghte she beautee!
Wherfore I seye al day, as men may see,
That yiftes of fortune or of nature
Ben cause of deeth to many a creature. 10
Hir beautee was hir deeth, I dar wel sayn;
Allas! so pitously as she was slayn!
Of bothe yiftes that I speke of now
Men han ful ofte more harm than prow.
But trewely, myn owene mayster dere, 15
This is a pitous tale for to here.
But natheles, passe over, is no fors;
I prey to god, so save thy gentil cors,
And eek thyne urinals and thy jordanes,
Thyn Ypocras, and eek thy Galianes, 20
And every boist ful of thy letuarie;
God blesse hem, and our lady seinte Marie!
So mot I theen, thou art a propre man,
And lyk a prelat, by seint Ronyan![2] 24
Seyde I nat wel? I can nat speke in terme;
But wel I woot, thou doost my herte to erme,
That I almost have caught a cardiacle.
By corpus bones! but I have triacle,
Or elles a draught of moyste and corny ale,
Or but I here anon a mery tale, 30
Myn herte is lost for pitee of this mayde.
Thou bel amy, thou Pardoner," he seyde,
"Tell us som mirthe or japes right anon."
"It shall be doon," quod he, "by seint Ronyon!
But first," quod he, "heer at this ale-stake 35
I wol both drinke, and eten of a cake."
But right anon thise gentils gonne to crye,
"Nay! lat him telle us of no ribaudye;
Tel us som moral thing, that we may lere
Som wit, and thanne wol we gladly here." 40
"I graunte, y-wis," quod he, "but I mot thinke
Up-on som honest thing, whyl that I drinke."

The Prologue of the Pardoners Tale

Radix malorum est Cupiditas: Ad Thimotheum, sexto.[3]

"Lordings," quod he, "in chirches whan I preche,
I peyne me to han an hauteyn speche,
And ringe it out as round as gooth a belle,
For I can al by rote that I telle.
My theme is alwey oon, and ever was— 5
'*Radix malorum est Cupiditas.*'
"First I pronounce whennes that I come,
And than my bulles shewe I, alle and somme.
Our lige lordes seel on my patente,
That shewe I first, my body to warente, 10
That no man be so bold, ne preest ne clerk,
Me to destourbe of Cristes holy werk;
And after that than telle I forth my tales,
Bulles of popes and of cardinales,
Of patriarkes, and bishoppes I shewe; 15
And in Latyn I speke a wordes fewe,
To saffron with my predicacioun,
And for to stire men to devocioun.
Than shewe I forth my longe cristal stones,
Y-crammed ful of cloutes and of bones; 20
Reliks been they, as wenen they echoon.
Than have I in latoun a sholder-boon
Which that was of an holy Jewes shepe.
'Good men,' seye I, 'tak of my wordes kepe;
If that this boon be wasshe in any welle, 25
If cow, or calf, or sheep, or oxe swelle
That any worm hath ete, or worm y-stonge,
Tak water of that welle, and wash his tonge,
And it is hool anon; and forthermore,
Of pokkes and of scabbe, and every sore 30
Shal every sheep be hool, that of this welle
Drinketh a draughte; tak kepe eek what I telle.
If that the good-man, that the bestes oweth,
Wol every wike, er that the cok him croweth,
Fastinge, drinken of this welle a draughte, 35
As thilke holy Jewe our eldres taughte,
His bestes and his stoor shal multiplye.
And, sirs, also it heleth jalousye;
For, though a man be falle in jalous rage,
Let maken with this water his potage, 40
And never shal he more his wyf mistriste,
Though he the sooth of hir defaute wiste;
Al had she taken preestes two or three.
"Heer is a miteyn eek, that ye may see.
He that his hond wol putte in this miteyn, 45
He shal have multiplying of his greyn,
Whan he hath sowen, be it whete or otes,
So that he offre pens, or elles grotes.
" 'Good men and wommen, o thing warne I yow.
If any wight be in this chirche now, 50
That hath doon sinne horrible, that he
Dar nat, for shame, of it y-shriven be,
Or any womman, be she yong or old,
That hath y-maad hir housbond cokewold,
Swich folk shul have no power ne no grace 55
To offren to my reliks in this place.
And who-so findeth him out of swich blame,
He wol com up and offre in goddes name,
And I assoille him by the auctoritee
Which that by bulle y-graunted was to me.' 60

[2] St. Ronan, whose name will be familiar to readers of Scott. Little besides his name is known of him.

[3] Greed is the root of all evil (I Timothy, 6:10).

"By this gaude have I wonne, yeer by yeer,
An hundred mark sith I was Pardoner.
I stonde lyk a clerk in my pulpet,
And whan the lewed peple is doun y-set,
I preche, so as ye han herd bifore, 65
And telle an hundred false japes more.
Than peyne I me to strecche forth the nekke,
And est and west upon the peple I bekke,
As doth a dowve sitting on a berne.
Myn hondes and my tonge goon so yerne, 70
That it is joye to see my bisinesse.
Of avaryce and of swich cursednesse
Is al my preching, for to make hem free
To yeve her pens, and namely un-to me.
For my entente is nat but for to winne, 75
And no-thing for correccioun of sinne.
I rekke never, whan that they ben beried,
Though that her soules goon a-blakeberied!
For certes, many a predicacioun
Comth ofte tyme of yvel entencioun; 80
Som for plesaunce of folk and flaterye,
To been avaunced by ipocrisye,
And som for veyne glorie, and som for hate.
For, whan I dar non other weyes debate,
Than wol I stinge him with my tonge smerte
In preching, so that he shal nat asterte 86
To been defamed falsly, if that he
Hath trespased to my brethren or to me.
For, though I telle noght his propre name,
Men shal wel knowe that it is the same 90
By signes and by othere circumstances.
Thus quyte I folk that doon us displesances;
Thus spitte I out my venim under hewe
Of holynesse, to seme holy and trewe.
"But shortly myn entente I wol devyse; 95
I preche of no-thing but for coveityse.
Therfor my theme is yet, and ever was—
'*Radix malorum est cupiditas.*'
Thus can I preche agayn that same vyce
Which that I use, and that is avaryce. 100
But, though my-self be gilty in that sinne,
Yet can I maken other folk to twinne
From avaryce, and sore to repente.
But that is nat my principal entente.
I preche no-thing but for coveityse; 105
Of this matere it oughte y-nogh suffyse.
"Than telle I hem ensamples many oon
Of olde stories, longe tyme agoon:
For lewed peple loven tales olde; 109
Swich thinges can they wel reporte and holde.
What? trowe ye, the whyles I may preche,
And winne gold and silver for I teche,
That I wol live in povert wilfully?
Nay, nay, I thoghte it never trewely! 114
For I wol preche and begge in sondry londes;
I wol not do no labour with myn hondes,
Ne make baskettes, and live therby,
Because I wol nat beggen ydelly.
I wol non of the apostles counterfete; 119
I wol have money, wolle, chese, and whete,
Al were it yeven of the povrest page,
Or of the povrest widwe in a village,
Al sholde hir children sterve for famyne.
Nay! I wol drinke licour of the vyne,
And have a joly wenche in every toun. 125
But herkneth, lordings, in conclusioun;
Your lyking is that I shal telle a tale.
Now, have I dronke a draughte of corny ale,
By god, I hope I shal yow telle a thing
That shal, by resoun, been at your lyking. 130
For, though myself be a ful vicious man,
A moral tale yet I yow telle can,
Which I am wont to preche, for to winne.
Now holde your pees, my tale I wol be-
ginne."

The Pardoners Tale[4]

In Flaundres whylom was a companye
Of yonge folk, that haunteden folye,
As ryot, hasard, stewes, and tavernes,
Wher-as, with harpes, lutes, and gitermes,
They daunce and pleye at dees bothe day and
night, 5
And ete also and drinken over hir might,
Thurgh which they doon the devel sacrifyse
With-in that develes temple, in cursed wyse,
By superfluitee abhominable;
Hir othes been so grete and so dampnable, 10
That it is grisly for to here hem swere;
Our blissed lordes body they to-tere;
Hem thoughte Jewes rente him noght
y-nough;
And ech of hem at otheres sinne lough.
And right anon than comen tombesteres 15
Fetys and smale, and yonge fruytesteres,
Singers with harpes, baudes, wafereres,
Whiche been the verray develes officeres
To kindle and blowe the fyr of lecherye,
That is annexed un-to glotonye; 20
The holy writ tak I to my witnesse,
That luxurie is in wyn and dronkenesse.
Lo, how that dronken Loth, unkindely,
Lay by his doghtres two, unwitingly;
So dronke he was, he niste what he
wroghte. 25
Herodes (who-so wel the stories soghte),
Whan he of wyn was replet at his feste,

[4]This story is of Eastern origin, and its theme has been often used from early times to the present day—for example by Boccaccio, *Decameron*, 6th Day, 10th Tale (apparently not Chaucer's source, which is unknown) and by Kipling, *The King's Ankus*. The Pardoner's final comment makes the tale a sort of sermon or *exemplum* of avarice.

Right at his owene table he yaf his heste
To sleen the Baptist John ful giltelees.
 Senek seith eek a good word doutelees; 30
He seith, he can no difference finde
Bitwix a man that is out of his minde
And a man which that is dronkelewe,
But that woodnesse, y-fallen in a shrewe,
Persevereth lenger than doth dronkenesse. 35
O glotonye, ful of cursednesse,
O cause first of our confusioun,
O original of our dampnacioun,
Til Crist had boght us with his blood agayn!
Lo, how dere, shortly for to sayn, 40
Aboght was thilke cursed vileinye;
Corrupt was al this world for glotonye!
 Adam our fader, and his wyf also,
Fro Paradys to labour and to wo
Were driven for that vyce, it is no drede; 45
For whyl that Adam fasted, as I rede,
He was in Paradys; and whan that he
Eet of the fruyt defended on the tree,
Anon he was out-cast to wo and peyne.
O glotonye, on thee wel oghte us pleyne! 50
O, wiste a man how many maladyes
Folwen of excesse and of glotonyes,
He wolde been the more mesurable
Of his diete, sittinge at his table.
Allas! the shorte throte, the tendre mouth, 55
Maketh that, Est and West, and North and
 South,
In erthe, in eir, in water men to-swinke
To gete a glotoun deyntee mete and drinke!
Of this matere, o Paul, wel canstow trete,
"Mete un-to wombe, and wombe eek un-to
 mete, 60
Shal god destroyen bothe," as Paulus seith.[5]
Allas! a foul thing is it, by my feith,
To seye this word, and fouler is the dede,
Whan man so drinketh of the whyte and rede,
That of his throte he maketh his privee, 65
Thurgh thilke cursed superfluitee.
 The apostel weping seith ful pitously,
"Ther walken many of whiche yow told have
 I,
I seye it now weping with pitous voys,
[That] they been enemys of Cristes croys, 70
Of whiche the ende is deeth, wombe is her
 god."[6]
O wombe! O bely! O stinking cod,
Fulfild of donge and of corrupcioun!
At either ende of thee foul is the soun.
How greet labour and cost is thee to finde! 75
Thise cokes, how they stampe, and streyne,
 and grinde,
And turnen substaunce in-to accident,[7]
To fulfille al thy likerous talent!
Out of the harde bones knokke they
The mary, for they caste noght a-wey 80
That may go thurgh the golet softe and
 swote;
Of spicerye, of leef, and bark, and rote
Shal been his sauce y-maked by delyt,
To make him yet a newer appetyt.
But certes, he that haunteth swich delyces 85
Is deed, whyl that he liveth in tho vyces.
 A lecherous thing is wyn, and dronkenesse
Is ful of stryving and of wrecchednesse.
O dronke man, disfigured is thy face,
Sour is thy breeth, foul artow to embrace, 90
And thurgh thy dronke nose semeth the soun
As though thou seydest ay, "Sampsoun,
 Sampsoun";
And yet, god wot, Sampsoun drank never no
 wyn.
Thou fallest, as it were a stiked swyn;
Thy tonge is lost, and al thyn honest cure; 95
For dronkenesse is verray sepulture
Of mannes wit and his discrecioun.
In whom that drinke hath dominacioun,
He can no conseil kepe, it is no drede.
Now kepe yow fro the whyte and fro the
 rede, 100
And namely fro the whyte wyn of Lepe,[8]
That is to selle in Fish-strete or in Chepe.[9]
This wyn of Spayne crepeth subtilly
In othere wynes, growing faste by,[10]
Of which ther ryseth swich fumositee, 105
That whan a man hath dronken draughtes
 three,
And weneth that he be at hoom in Chepe,
He is in Spayne, right at the toune of Lepe,
Nat at the Rochel, ne at Burdeux toun;
And thanne wol he seye, "Sampsoun, Samp-
 soun." 110
But herkneth, lordings, o word, I yow preye,
That alle the sovereyn actes, dar I seye,
Of victories in th'olde testament,
Thurgh verray god, that is omnipotent,
Were doon in abstinence and in preyere; 115
Loketh the Bible, and ther ye may it lere.
 Loke, Attila, the grete conquerour,
Deyde in his sleep, with shame and dishonour,

---

[5]I Corinthians, 6:13. [6]Philippians, 3: 18–19.

[7]An allusion to disputes between the realists and the nominalists among medieval philosophers. The meaning is that cooks so changed the very nature of the things they prepared that those who ate them could not tell what they originally were.

[8]Near Cadiz. [9]Cheapside, London.

[10]The Pardoner says that the mixture must come from the closeness of the vineyards to each other, but means that it comes from the closeness of the casks in the vintners' cellars. The wines of La Rochelle and Bordeaux were milder than the Spanish wines.

Bledinge ay at his nose in dronkenesse;
A capitayn shoulde live in sobrenesse. 120
And over al this, avyseth yow right wel
What was comaunded un-to Lamuel—[11]
Nat Samuel, but Lamuel, seye I—
Redeth the Bible, and finde it expresly
Of wyn-yeving to hem that han justyse. 125
Na-more of this, for it may wel suffyse.
And now that I have spoke of glotonye,
Now wol I yow defenden hasardrye.
Hasard is verray moder of lesinges,
And of deceite, and cursed forsweringes, 130
Blaspheme of Crist; manslaughtre, and wast also
Of catel and of tyme; and forthermo,
It is repreve and contrarie of honour
For to ben holde a commune hasardour.
And ever the hyër he is of estaat, 135
The more is he holden desolaat.
If that a prince useth hasardrye,
In alle governaunce and policye
He is, as by commune opinioun,
Y-holde the lasse in reputacioun. 140
Stilbon,[12] that was a wys embassadour,
Was sent to Corinthe, in ful greet honour,
Fro Lacidomie, to make hir alliaunce.
And whan he cam, him happede, par chaunce,
That alle the grettest that were of that lond,
Pleyinge atte hasard he hem fond. 146
For which, as sone as it mighte be,
He stal him hoom agayn to his contree,
And seyde, "ther wol I nat lese my name;
N'I wol nat take on me so greet defame, 150
Yow for to allye un-to none hasardours.
Sendeth othere wyse embassadours;
For, by my trouthe, me were lever dye,
Than I yow sholde to hasardours allye.
For ye that been so glorious in honours 155
Shul nat allyen yow with hasardours
As by my wil, ne as by my tretee."
This wyse philosophre thus seyde he.
Loke eek that, to the king Demetrius
The king of Parthes, as the book seith us,[13] 160
Sente him a paire of dees of gold in scorn,
For he hadde used hasard ther-biforn;
For which he heeld his glorie or his renoun
At no value or reputacioun.
Lordes may finden other maner pley 165
Honeste y-nough to dryve the day awey.
Now wol I speke of othes false and grete
A word or two, as olde bokes trete.
Gret swering is a thing abhominable,

[11]Lemuel. Proverbs, 31: 1, 4, 5.

[12]Should be Chilon. The story is in John of Salisbury's *Policraticus,* bk. I, ch. 5.

[13]*Policraticus,* bk. I, ch. 5.

And false swering is yet more reprevable. 170
The heighe god forbad swering at al,
Witnesse on Mathew;[14] but in special
Of swering seith the holy Jeremye,[15]
"Thou shalt seye sooth thyn othes, and nat lye,
And swere in dome, and eek in rightwisnesse"; 175
But ydel swering is a cursednesse.
Bihold and see, that in the firste table
Of heighe goddes hestes honurable,
How that the seconde heste of him is this—
"Tak nat my name in ydel or amis."[16] 180
Lo, rather[17] he forbedeth swich swering
Than homicyde or many a cursed thing;
I seye that, as by ordre, thus it stondeth;
This knowen, that his hestes understondeth,
How that the second heste of god is that. 185
And forther over, I wol thee telle al plat,
That vengeance shal nat parten from his hous,
That of his othes is to outrageous.
"By goddes precious herte, and by his nayles,
And by the blode of Crist, that it is in Hayles,[18] 190
Seven is my chaunce, and thyn is cink and treye;
By goddes armes, if thou falsly pleye,
This dagger shal thurgh-out thyn herte go"—
This fruyt cometh of the bicched bones two,
Forswering, ire, falsnesse, homicyde. 195
Now, for the love of Crist that for us dyde,
Leveth your othes, bothe grete and smale;
But, sirs, now wol I telle forth my tale.

Thise ryotoures three, of whiche I telle,
Longe erst er pryme rong of any belle, 200
Were set hem in a taverne for to drinke;
And as they satte, they herde a belle clinke
Biforn a cors, was caried to his grave;
That oon of hem gan callen to his knave,
"Go bet," quod he, "and axe redily, 205
What cors is this that passeth heer forby;
And look that thou reporte his name wel."
"Sir," quod this boy, "it nedeth never-a-del.
It was me told, er ye can heer, two houres;

[14]St. Matthew, 5:34. [15]Jeremiah, 4:2.

[16]Formerly the first and second commandments were considered as one, the tenth being divided into two to make up the number; hence the Pardoner refers to the third commandment as the second. It is in the first table, i. e., the group teaching man's duty to God, those in the second table teaching his duty to his neighbor.

[17]Earlier in the list of commandments.

[18]The Abbey of Hailes, or Hales, in Gloucestershire.

He was, pardee, an old felawe of youres; 210
And sodeynly he was y-slayn to-night,
For-dronke, as he sat on his bench upright;
Ther cam a privee theef, men clepeth Deeth,
That in this contree al the peple sleeth, 214
And with his spere he smoot his herte a-two,
And wente his wey with-outen wordes mo.
He hath a thousand slayn this pestilence:
And, maister, er ye come in his presence,
Me thinketh that it were necessarie
For to be war of swich an adversarie: 220
Beth redy for to mete him evermore.
Thus taughte me my dame, I sey na-more."
"By seinte Marie," seyde this taverner,
"The child seith sooth, for he hath slayn this yeer,
Henne over a myle, with-in a greet village, 225
Both man and womman, child and hyne, and page.
I trowe his habitacioun be there;
To been avysed greet wisdom it were,
Er that he dide a man a dishonour."
"Ye, goddes armes," quod this ryotour, 230
"Is it swich peril with him for to mete?
I shal him seke by wey and eek by strete,
I make avow to goddes digne bones!
Herkneth, felawes, we three been al ones;
Lat ech of us holde up his hond til other, 235
And ech of us bicomen otheres brother,
And we wol sleen this false traytour Deeth;
He shal be slayn, which that so many sleeth,
By goddes dignitee, er it be night."
Togidres han thise three her trouthes plight, 240
To live and dyen ech of hem for other,
As though he were his owene y-boren brother.
And up they sterte al dronken, in this rage,
And forth they goon towardes that village,
Of which the taverner had spoke biforn, 245
And many a grisly ooth than han they sworn,
And Cristes blessed body they to-rente—
"Deeth shal be deed, if that they may him hente."
Whan they han goon nat fully half a myle,
Right as they wolde han troden over a style,
An old man and a povre with hem mette. 251
This olde man ful mekely hem grette,
And seyde thus, "now, lordes, god yow see!"
The proudest of thise ryotoures three
Answerde agayn, "what? carl, with sory grace, 255
Why artow al forwrapped save thy face?
Why livestow so longe in so greet age?"
This olde man gan loke in his visage,
And seyde thus, "for I ne can nat finde
A man, though that I walked in-to Inde, 260
Neither in citee nor in no village,
That wolde chaunge his youthe for myn age;
And therfore moot I han myn age stille,
As longe time as it is goddes wille.
"Ne deeth, allas! ne wol nat han my lyf; 265
Thus walke I, lyk a restelees caityf,
And on the ground, which is my modres gate,
I knokke with my staf, bothe erly and late,
And seye, 'leve moder, leet me in! 269
Lo, how I vanish, flesh, and blood, and skin!
Allas! whan shul my bones been at reste?
Moder, with yow wolde I chaunge my cheste,
That in my chambre longe tyme hath be,
Ye! for an heyre clout to wrappe me!'
But yet to me she wol nat do that grace, 275
For which ful pale and welked is my face.
"But, sirs, to yow it is no curteisye
To speken to an old man vileinye,
But he trespasse in worde, or elles in dede.
In holy writ ye may your-self wel rede, 280
'Agayns an old man, hoor upon his heed,
Ye sholde aryse';[19] wherfor I yeve yow reed,
Ne dooth un-to an old man noon harm now,
Na-more than ye wolde men dide to yow
In age, if that ye so longe abyde; 285
And god be with yow, wher ye go or ryde.
I moot go thider as I have to go."
"Nay, olde cherl, by god, thou shalt nat so,"
Seyde this other hasardour anon; 289
"Thou partest nat so lightly, by seint John!
Thou spak right now of thilke traitour Deeth,
That in this contree alle our frendes sleeth.
Have heer my trouthe, as thou art his aspye,
Tel wher he is, or thou shalt it abye,
By god, and by the holy sacrament! 295
For soothly thou art oon of his assent,
To sleen us yonge folk, thou false theef!"
"Now, sirs," quod he, "if that yow be so leef
To finde Deeth, turne up this croked wey,
For in that grove I lafte him, by my fey, 300
Under a tree, and ther he wol abyde;
Nat for your boost he wol him no-thing hyde.
See ye that ook? right ther ye shul him finde.
God save yow, that boghte agayn mankinde,
And yow amende!"—thus seyde this olde man. 305
And everich of thise ryotoures ran,
Til he cam to that tree, and ther they found
Of florins fyne of golde y-coyned rounde
Wel ny an eighte busshels, as hem thoughte.
No lenger thanne after Deeth they soughte,
But ech of hem so glad was of that sighte, 311
For that the florins been so faire and brighte,
That doun they sette hem by this precious hord.

---

[19] Leviticus, 19:32.

The worste of hem he spake the firste word.
"Brethren," quod he, "tak kepe what I seye; 315
My wit is greet, though that I bourde and pleye.
This tresor hath fortune un-to us yiven,
In mirthe and jolitee our lyf to liven,
And lightly as it comth, so wol we spende.
Ey! goddes precious dignitee! who wende 320
To-day, that we sholde han so fair a grace?
But mighte this gold be caried fro this place
Hoom to myn hous, or elles un-to youres—
For wel ye woot that al this gold is oures—
Than were we in heigh felicitee. 325
But trewely, by daye it may nat be;
Men wolde seyn that we were theves stronge,
And for our owene tresor doon us honge.
This tresor moste y-caried be by nighte
As wysly and as slyly as it mighte. 330
Wherfore I rede that cut among us alle
Be drawe, and lat see wher the cut wol falle;
And he that hath the cut with herte blythe
Shal renne to the toune, and that ful swythe,
And bringe us breed and wyn ful prively. 335
And two of us shul kepen subtilly
This tresor wel; and, if he wol nat tarie,
Whan it is night, we wol this tresor carie
By oon assent, wher-as us thinketh best." 339
That oon of hem the cut broughte in his fest,
And bad hem drawe, and loke wher it wol falle;
And it fil on the yongeste of hem alle;
And forth toward the toun he wente anon.
And al-so sone as that he was gon, 344
That oon of hem spak thus un-to that other,
"Thou knowest wel thou art my sworne brother,
Thy profit wol I telle thee anon.
Thou woost wel that our felawe is agon;
And heer is gold, and that ful greet plentee,
That shal departed been among us three. 350
But natheles, if I can shape it so
That it departed were among us two,
Hadde I nat doon a freendes torn to thee?"
That other answerde, "I noot how that may be; 354
He woot how that the gold is with us tweye,
What shal we doon, what shal we to him seye?"
"Shal it be conseil?" seyde the firste shrewe,
"And I shal tellen thee, in wordes fewe,
What we shal doon, and bringe it wel aboute."
"I graunte," quod that other, "out of doute, 360
That, by my trouthe, I wol thee nat biwreye."
"Now," quod the firste, "thou woost wel we be tweye,
And two of us shul strenger be than oon.
Look whan that he is set, and right anoon 364
Arys, as though thou woldest with him pleye;
And I shal ryve him thurgh the sydes tweye
Whyl that thou strogelest with him as in game,
And with thy dagger look thou do the same;
And than shal al this gold departed be,
My dere freend, bitwixen me and thee; 370
Than may we bothe our lustes al fulfille,
And pleye at dees right at our owene wille."
And thus acorded been thise shrewes tweye
To sleen the thridde, as ye han herd me seye.
This yongest, which that wente un-to the toun, 375
Ful ofte in herte he rolleth up and doun
The beautee of thise florins newe and brighte.
"O lord!" quod he, "if so were that I mighte
Have al this tresor to my-self allone,
Ther is no man that liveth under the trone 380
Of god, that sholde live so mery as I!"
And atte laste the feend, our enemy,
Putte in his thought that he shold poyson beye,
With which he mighte sleen his felawes tweye; 384
For-why the feend fond him in swich lyvinge,
That he had leve him to sorwe bringe,
For this was outrely his fulle entente
To sleen hem bothe, and never to repente.
And forth he gooth, no lenger wolde he tarie,
Into the toun, un-to a pothecarie, 390
And preyed him, that he him wolde selle
Som poyson, that he mighte his rattes quelle;
And eek ther was a polcat in his hawe,
That, as he seyde, his capouns hadde y-slawe,
And fayn he wolde wreke him, if he mighte, 395
On vermin, that destroyed him by nighte.
The pothecarie answerde, "and thou shalt have
A thing that, al-so god my soule save,
In al this world ther nis no creature,
That ete or dronke hath of this confiture 400
Noght but the mountance of a corn of whete,
That he ne shal his lyf anon forlete;
Ye, sterve he shal, and that in lasse whyle
Than thou wolt goon a paas nat but a myle;
This poyson is so strong and violent." 405
This cursed man hath in his hond y-hent
This poyson in a box, and sith he ran
In-to the nexte strete, un-to a man,
And borwed [of] him large botels three;
And in the two his poyson poured he; 410
The thridde he kepte clene for his drinke.

For al the night he shoop him for to swinke
In caryinge of the gold out of that place.
And whan this ryotour, with sory grace,
Had filled with wyn his grete botels three, 415
To his felawes agayn repaireth he.
What nedeth it to sermone of it more?
For right as they had cast his deeth bifore,
Right so they han him slayn, and that anon.
And whan that this was doon, thus spak that oon, 420
"Now lat us sitte and drinke, and make us merie,
And afterward we wol his body berie."
And with that word it happed him, par cas,
To take the botel ther the poyson was,
And drank, and yaf his felawe drinke also, 425
For which anon they storven bothe two.
But, certes, I suppose that Avicen[20]
Wroot never in no canon, ne in no fen,
Mo wonder signes of empoisoning 429
Than hadde thise wrecches two, er hir ending.
Thus ended been thise homicydes two,
And eek the false empoysoner also.

O cursed sinne, ful of cursednesse!
O traytours homicyde, o wikkednesse!
O glotonye, luxurie, and hasardrye! 435
Thou blasphemour of Crist with vileinye
And othes grete, of usage and of pryde!
Allas! mankinde, how may it bityde,
That to thy creatour which that thee wroghte,
And with his precious herte-blood thee boghte, 440
Thou art so fals and so unkinde, allas!
Now, goode men, god forgeve yow your trespas,
And ware yow fro the sinne of avaryce.
Myn holy pardoun may yow alle waryce,
So that ye offre nobles or sterlinges, 445
Or elles silver broches, spones, ringes.
Boweth your heed under this holy bulle!
Cometh up, ye wyves, offreth of your wolle!
Your name I entre heer in my rolle anon;
In-to the blisse of hevene shul ye gon; 450
I yow assoile, by myn heigh power,
Yow that wol offre, as clene and eek as cleer
As ye were born; and, lo, sirs, thus I preche.
And Jesu Crist, that is our soules leche,
So graunte yow his pardon to receyve; 455
For that is best; I wol yow nat deceyve.
But sirs, o word forgat I in my tale,
I have relikes and pardon in my male,
As faire as any man in Engelond,
Whiche were me yeven by the popes hond. 460
If any of yow wol, of devocioun,
Offren, and han myn absolucion,
Cometh forth anon, and kneleth heer adoun,
And mekely receyveth my pardoun:
Or elles, taketh pardon as ye wende, 465
Al newe and fresh, at every tounes ende,
So that ye offren alwey newe and newe
Nobles and pens, which that be gode and trewe.
It is an honour to everich that is heer,
That ye mowe have a suffisant pardoneer 470
T'assoille yow, in contree as ye ryde,
For aventures which that may bityde.
Peraventure ther may falle oon or two
Doun of his hors, and breke his nekke atwo.
Look which a seuretee is it to yow alle 475
That I am in your felaweship y-falle,
That may assoille yow, bothe more and lasse,
Whan that the soule shal fro the body passe.
I rede that our hoste heer shal biginne,
For he is most envoluped in sinne. 480
Com forth, sir hoste, and offre first anon,
And thou shalt kisse the reliks everichon,
Ye, for a grote! unbokel anon thy purs.
"Nay, nay," quod he, "than have I Cristes curs! 484
Lat be," quod he, "it shal nat be, so thee'ch!
Thou woldest make me kisse thyn old breech,
And swere it were a relik of a seint,
Thogh it were with thy fundement depeint!
But by the croys which that seint Eleyne fond,
I wolde I hadde thy coillons in myn hond 490
In stede of relikes or of seintuarie;
Lat cutte hem of, I wol thee helpe hem carie;
They shul be shryned in an hogges tord."
This pardoner answerde nat a word; 494
So wrooth he was, no word ne wolde he seye.
"Now," quod our host, "I wol no lenger pleye
With thee, ne with noon other angry man."
But right anon the worthy Knight bigan,
Whan that he saugh that al the peple lough,
"Na-more of this, for it is right y-nough; 500
Sir Pardoner, be glad and mery of chere;
And ye, sir host, that been to me so dere,
I prey yow that ye kisse the Pardoner.
And Pardoner, I prey thee, drawe thee neer,
And, as we diden, lat us laughe and pleye." 505
Anon they kiste, and riden forth hir weye.[21]

---

[20]Avicenna (A. D. 980–1037), celebrated Arabian physician and philosopher. As Chaucer (or the Pardoner) perhaps did not understand, "Canon" is the general title of Avicenna's treatise on medicine.

[21]The Pardoner's tale concludes what, in the present arrangement of *The Canterbury Tales*, is the third group. There follow six more groups, in which eleven stories are told.

CHAUCERS WORDES UNTO ADAM, HIS OWNE SCRIVEYN

Adam scriveyn, if ever it thee bifalle
Boece or Troilus to wryten newe,
Under thy lokkes thou most have the scalle,
But after my making thou wryte trewe.
So ofte a daye I mot thy werk renewe, 5
Hit to correcte and eek to rubbe and scrape;
And al is through thy negligence and rape.

TRUTH

Balade de Bon Conseyl

Flee fro the prees, and dwelle with soth-fastnesse,
Suffyce unto thy good, though hit be smal;
For hord hath hate, and climbing tikelnesse,
Prees hath envye, and wele blent overal;
Savour no more than thee bihove shal; 5
Werk wel thy-self, that other folk canst rede;
And trouthe shal delivere, hit is no drede.

Tempest thee noght al croked to redresse,
In trust of hir that turneth as a bal:[1]
Gret reste stant in litel besinesse; 10
And eek be war to sporne ageyn an al;
Stryve noght, as doth the crokke with the wal.
Daunte thy-self, that dauntest otheres dede;
And trouthe shal delivere, hit is no drede.

That thee is sent, receyve in buxumnesse, 15
The wrastling for this worlde axeth a fal.
Her nis non hoom, her nis but wildernesse:
Forth, pilgrim, forth! Forth, beste, out of thy stal!
Know thy contree, look up, thank God of al;
Holde the hye wey, and lat thy gost thee lede:
And trouthe shal delivere, hit is no drede. 21

ENVOY

Therfore, thou vache,[2] leve thyn old wrecch-ednesse
Unto the worlde; leve now to be thral;
Crye him mercy, that of his hy goodnesse
Made thee of noght, and in especial 25
Draw unto him, and pray in general
For thee, and eek for other, hevenlich mede;
And trouthe shal delivere, hit is no drede.

[1]Fortune.

[2]It is now known that this poem was addressed to one of Chaucer's friends, Sir Philip la Vache; "vache" (beast) is therefore used with double meaning.

LAK OF STEDFASTNESSE

Balade

Som tyme this world was so stedfast and stable,
That mannes word was obligacioun,
And now hit is so fals and deceivable,
That word and deed, as in conclusioun,
Ben no-thing lyk, for turned up so doun 5
Is al this world for mede and wilfulnesse,
That al is lost for lak of stedfastnesse.

What maketh this world to be so variable,
But lust that folk have in dissensioun?
Among us now a man is holde unable, 10
But-if he can, by som collusioun,
Don his neighbour wrong or oppressioun.
What causeth this, but wilful wrecchednesse,
That al is lost, for lak of stedfastnesse?

Trouthe is put doun, resoun is holden fable;
Vertu hath now no dominacioun, 16
Pitee exyled, no man is merciable.
Through covetyse is blent discrecioun;
The world hath mad a permutacioun
Fro right to wrong, fro trouthe to fikel-nesse, 20
That al is lost, for lak of stedfastnesse.

LENVOY TO KING RICHARD

O prince, desyre to be honourable,
Cherish thy folk and hate extorcioun!
Suffre no thing, that may be reprevable
To thyn estat, don in thy regioun. 25
Shew forth thy swerd of castigacioun,
Dred God, do law, love trouthe and worthi-nesse,
And wed thy folk agein to stedfastnesse.

THE COMPLEINT OF CHAUCER TO HIS EMPTY PURSE[3]

To you, my purse, and to non other wight
Compleyne I, for ye be my lady dere!
I am so sory, now that ye be light;
For certes, but ye make me hevy chere,
Me were as leef be leyd up-on my bere; 5
For whiche un-to your mercy thus I crye:
Beth hevy ageyn, or elles mot I dye!

[3]This is probably one of the last poems Chaucer wrote, inasmuch as the envoy, at least, cannot have been written before 30 September, 1399, when Parliament formally acknowledged Henry IV's right to the English throne. Chaucer's appeal, it may be added, was successful.

Now voucheth sauf this day, or hit be night,
That I of you the blisful soun may here,
Or see your colour lyk the sonne bright, 10
That of yelownesse hadde never pere.
Ye be my lyf, ye be myn hertes stere,
Quene of comfort and of good companye:
Beth hevy ageyn, or elles mot I dye!

Now purs, that be to me my lyves light, 15
And saveour, as doun in this worlde here,
Out of this toune help me through your might,
Sin that ye wole nat been my tresorere;
For I am shave as nye as any frere.
But yit I pray un-to your curtesye: 20
Beth hevy ageyn, or elles mot I dye!

LENVOY DE CHAUCER

O conquerour of Brutes Albioun!
Which that by lyne and free eleccioun
Ben verray king, this song to you I sende;
And ye, that mowen al our harm amende, 25
Have minde up-on my supplicacioun!

POPULAR BALLADS

A popular ballad is "a song that tells a story," and that has come out of the past through oral tradition. We do not know the authors of any true ballads; on the contrary, it has been contended that none was composed by an individual. Ballads, according to this theory, originated at a very early stage of culture when communities were still largely undifferentiated, when they acted spontaneously as groups, and when the individual had scarcely become conscious of himself. "Persons," in other words, had not yet appeared, although communities had, and the homogeneous members of these communities lived one collective life. So, it is thought, they danced and sang, and what they sang were ballads; yet no one had composed a ballad, but around some refrain, perhaps beginning in a mere inarticulate cry, here a member of the group and there a member of the group had thrown a line or two which simply "came" on the spur of the moment, with the ultimate result that a song telling a connected story sprang into existence. It was thus unpremeditated, spontaneous, the composition not of a person but of a community. All this, however, evidently relates to a stage of life about which we know very little and may accordingly theorize with considerable freedom. The account just given has been widely accepted, but it has, too, been acutely challenged on the ground that while we know little enough about primitive life, what we do know hardly bears out these claims for the possibilities of spontaneous collective action. Consequently it is urged that ballads, like other and later kinds of literature, must have had individual authors. But, while the question of origins remains unsettled, it is of course true that, as long as a poem is handed from one generation to another orally, it is subject to change and thus does become in a real sense the product as well as the possession of a community; and so much we can safely say of the English and Scottish popular ballads. As we have them, they show no obvious signs of individual authorship; they are objective, impersonal, unreflective, and in many cases evidently had a long period of life before they attained a fixed form through being written down. More than three hundred of them are extant. Of these only eleven come from manuscripts older than the seventeenth century, but the time when a ballad reached its final form through writing or printing is not significant of its real age. The oldest of the English and Scottish ballads may have had their origin in the thirteenth century, and others which are founded on historical events can be definitely assigned to the fourteenth and fifteenth centuries. Cultivated people took no serious interest in this field of poetry before the middle of the eighteenth century. It was then that Bishop Percy discovered a folio manuscript, written about 1650, which still remains the most important collection of ballads. He printed his famous *Reliques of Ancient English Poetry* in 1765. The book was at once a sign of growing interest in ballad-literature and a stimulant to further search for additional material. A little later Sir Walter Scott became a notable collector of ballads from the mouths of people in whose families they had been handed down orally.

Simplicity is the outstanding characteristic of the ballads. Their language is direct and unfigurative. Conventional epithets and standing phrases abound. A dramatic framework is frequently assumed. Stanzas consist generally either of a couplet of verses of four accents with alternating refrain, or of four lines riming *a b c b,* of which the first and third have four accents and the second and fourth three. The usual themes fall into a few broadly popular types—domestic tragedy, supernatural occurrences, the life of outlaws, riddles, historical events, and humorous incidents.

The English and Scottish Popular Ballads, ed. Francis J. Child (Boston, 1882–1898), contains all save a few ballads, which have been discovered since; this collection has been published in an abridged form, under the same title, ed. Helen C. Sargent and George L. Kittredge (Boston, 1904). *The Popular Ballad,* by F. B. Gummere (Boston, 1907), has long been a standard book on its subject, and is still useful as a critical study. The theory that the ballads were of communal origin, which was accepted by Gummere, is notably attacked by Louise Pound in *Poetic Origins and the Ballad* (New York, 1921). For a more inclusive commentary see Gordon H. Gerould, *The Ballad of Tradition* (Oxford, 1932).

RIDDLES WISELY EXPOUNDED

There was a lady of the North Country,
  Lay the bent to the bonny broom
And she had lovely daughters three.
  Fa la la la, fa la la la ra re.

There was a knight of noble worth 5
Which also livéd in the North.

The knight, of courage stout and brave,
A wife he did desire to have.

He knockéd at the ladie's gate
One evening when it was late. 10

The eldest sister let him in,
And pinned the door with a silver pin.

The second sister she made his bed,
And laid soft pillows under his head.

The youngest daughter that same night, 15
She went to bed to this young knight.

And in the morning, when it was day,
These words unto him she did say:

"Now you have had your will," quoth she,
"I pray, sir knight, will you marry me?" 20

The young brave knight to her replied,
"Thy suit, fair maid, shall not be denied.

"If thou canst answer me questions three,
This very day will I marry thee."

"Kind sir, in love, O then," quoth she, 25
"Tell me what your [three] questions be."

"O what is longer than the way,
Or what is deeper than the sea?

"Or what is louder than the horn,
Or what is sharper than a thorn? 30

"Or what is greener than the grass,
Or what is worse then a woman was?"

"O love is longer than the way,
And hell is deeper than the sea.

"And thunder is louder than the horn, 35
And hunger is sharper than a thorn.

"And poyson is greener than the grass,
And the Devil is worse than woman was."

When she these questions answered had,
The knight became exceeding glad. 40

And having [truly] tried her wit,
He much commended her for it.

And after, as it is verified,
He made of her his lovely bride.

So now, fair maidens all, adieu, 45
This song I dedicate to you.

I wish that you may constant prove
Unto the man that you do love.

THE DOUGLAS TRAGEDY

"Rise up, rise up, now Lord Douglas," she says,
  "And put on your armour so bright;
Let it never be said that a daughter of thine
  Was married to a lord under night.

"Rise up, rise up, my seven bold sons, 5
  And put on your armour so bright,
And take better care of your youngest sister,
  For your eldest's awa the last night."

He's mounted her on a milk-white steed,
  And himself on a dapple gray, 10
With a bugelet horn hung down his side;
  And lightly they rode away.

Lord William looked o'er his left shoulder,
  To see what he could see,
And there he spyed her seven brethren bold 15
  Come riding over the lea.

"Light down, light down, Lady Margret," he said,
  "And hold my steed in your hand,
Until that against your seven brethren bold,
  And your father, I mak' a stand." 20

O, there she stood, and bitter she stood,
  And never did shed one tear,
Until that she saw her seven brethren fa',
  And her father, who loved her so dear. 24

"O hold your hand, Lord William!" she said,
"For your strokes they are wondrous sair;
True lovers I can get many an ane,
But a father I can never get mair."

O she's ta'en out her handkerchief,
It was o' the holland sae fine, 30
And aye she dighted her father's wounds,
That were redder than the wine.

"O chuse, O chuse, Lady Margret," he said,
"O whether will ye gang or bide?"
"I'll gang, I'll gang, Lord William," she said,
"For ye've left me no other guide." 36

He's lifted her on a milk-white steed,
And himself on a dapple gray,
With a bugelet horn hung down by his side;
And slowly they baith rade away. 40

O they rade on, and on they rade,
And a' by the light of the moon,
Until they came to yon wan water,
And there they lighted doun.

They lighted doun to tak' a drink 45
Of the spring that ran sae clear,
And doun the stream ran his gude heart's blood,
And sair she gan to fear.

"Hold up, hold up, Lord William," she says,
"For I fear that you are slain."— 50
"'Tis naething but the shadow of my scarlet cloak,
That shines in the water sae plain."

O they rade on, and on they rade,
And a' by the light of the moon,
Until they cam' to his mother's ha' door, 55
And there they lighted doun.

"Get up, get up, lady mother," he says,
"Get up, and let me in!
Get up, get up, lady mother," he says,
"For this night my fair lady I've win. 60

"O mak my bed, lady mother," he says,
"O mak it braid and deep,
And lay Lady Margret close at my back,
And the sounder I will sleep."

Lord William was dead lang ere midnight, 65
Lady Margaret lang ere day,
And all true lovers that go thegither,
May they have mair luck than they!

Lord William was buried in St. Mary's kirk,
Lady Margret in Mary's quire; 70
Out o' the lady's grave grew a bonny red rose,
And out o' the knight's a brier.

And they twa met, and they twa plat,
And fain they wad be near;
And a' the warld might ken right weel 75
They were twa lovers dear.

But bye and rade the Black Douglas,
And wow but he was rough!
For he pulled up the bonny brier,
And flang 't in St. Mary's Lough. 80

ROBIN HOOD AND GUY OF GISBORNE[1]

When shawes beene sheene, and shradds full fayre,
And leeves both large and longe,
Itt is merry, walking in the fayre fforrest,
To heare the small birds songe.

The woodweele sang, and wold not cease, 5
Amongst the leaves a lyne:
And it is by two wight yeomen,
By deare God, that I meane.

. . . . .

"Me thought they did mee beate and binde,
And tooke my bow mee froe; 10
If I bee Robin a-live in this lande,
I 'le be wrocken on both them towe."

"Sweavens are swift, master," quoth John,
"As the wind that blowes ore a hill;
Ffor if itt be never soe lowde this night, 15
To-morrow it may be still."

"Buske yee, bowne yee, my merry men all,
Ffor John shall goe with mee;
For I 'le goe seeke yond wight yeomen
In greenwood where the bee." 20

---

[1]Tradition has it that Robin Hood was an historical character, an outlaw of the early fourteenth century. This is, to say the least, extremely improbable. As he is portrayed in the ballads, at any rate, he is a typical figure, an idealized outlaw, the champion of common folk against oppression. As such he was extremely popular, there being some 40 ballads about him. We know from a reference in the B-text of *Piers Plowman* that he was a familiar character at least as early as 1377.

A few verses are lost between stanzas 2 and 3, and the story itself has suffered some derangement. Robin dreams that two yeomen beat and bind him, and goes to seek them. One is Sir Guy, the other the sheriff of Nottingham; but we are not told how Robin knew that the sheriff was out against him, had attacked his camp, and had taken John prisoner.

They cast on their gowne of greene,
  A shooting gone are they,
Untill they came to the merry greenwood,
  Where they had gladdest bee;
There were the ware of [a] wight yeoman, 25
  His body leaned to a tree.

A sword and a dagger he wore by his side,
  Had beene many a mans bane,
And he was cladd in his capull-hyde,
  Topp, and tayle, and mayne. 30

"Stand you still, master," quoth Litle John,
  "Under this trusty tree,
And I will goe to yond wight yeoman,
  To know his meaning trulye."

"A, John, by me thou setts noe store, 35
  And that's a ffarley thinge;
How offt send I my men beffore,
  And tarry my-selfe behinde?

"It is noe cunning a knave to ken,
  And a man but heare him speake; 40
And itt were not for bursting of my bowe,
  John, I wold thy head breake."

But often words they breeden bale,
  That parted Robin and John;
John is gone to Barn[e]sdale, 45
  The gates he knowes eche one.

And when hee came to Barnesdale,
  Great heavinesse there hee hadd;
He ffound two of his fellowes
  Were slaine both in a slade, 50

And Scarlett a ffoote flyinge was,
  Over stockes and stone,
For the sheriffe with seven score men
  Fast after him is gone.

"Yett one shoote I 'le shoote," sayes Litle
  John, 55
  "With Crist his might and mayne;
I 'le make yond fellow that flyes soe fast
  To be both glad and ffaine."

John bent up a good veiwe bow,
  And ffetteled him to shoote; 60
The bow was made of a tender boughe,
  And fell downe to his foote.

"Woe worth thee, wicked wood," sayd Litle
  John,
  "That ere thou grew on a tree!
Ffor this day thou art my bale, 65
  My boote when thou shold bee!"

This shoote it was but looselye shott,
  The arrowe flew in vaine,
And it mett one of the sheriffes men;
  Good William a Trent was slaine. 70

It had beene better for William a Trent
  To hange upon a gallowe
Then for to lye in the greenwoode,
  There slaine with an arrowe.

And it is sayd, when men be mett, 75
  Six can doe more then three:
And they have tane Litle John,
  And bound him ffast to a tree.

"Thou shalt be drawen by dale and downe,"
  quoth the sheriffe,
  "And hanged hye on a hill": 80
"But thou may ffayle," quoth Litle John,
  "If itt be Christs owne will."

Let us leave talking of Litle John,
  For hee is bound fast to a tree,
And talke of Guy and Robin Hood, 85
  In the green woode where they bee.

How these two yeomen together they mett,
  Under the leaves of lyne,
To see what marchandise they made
  Even at that same time. 90

"Good morrow, good fellow," quoth Sir Guy;
  "Good morrow, good ffellow," quoth hee;
"Methinkes by this bow thou beares in thy
  hand,
  A good archer thou seems to bee."

"I am wilfull of my way," quoth Sir Guye, 95
  "And of my morning tyde":
"I 'le lead thee through the wood," quoth
  Robin,
  "Good ffellow, I 'le be thy guide."

"I seeke an outlaw," quoth Sir Guye;
  "Men call him Robin Hood; 100
I had rather meet with him upon a day
  Then forty pound of golde."

"If you tow mett, itt wold be seene whether
  were better
  Afore yee did part awaye;
Let us some other pastime find, 105
  Good ffellow, I thee pray.

"Let us some other masteryes make,
  And wee will walke in the woods even;
Wee may chance mee[t] with Robin Hoode
  Att some unsett steven." 110

They cutt them downe the summer shroggs
  Which grew both under a bryar,
And sett them three score rood in twinn,
  To shoote the prickes full neare.

"Leade on, good ffellow," sayd Sir Guye, 115
  "Lead on, I doe bidd thee":
"Nay, by my faith," quoth Robin Hood,
  "The leader thou shalt bee."

The first good shoot that Robin ledd
  Did not shoote an inch the pricke ffroe; 120
Guy was an archer good enoughe,
  But he cold neere shoote soe.

The second shoote Sir Guy shott,
  He shott within the garlande;
But Robin Hoode shott it better then hee, 125
  For he clove the good pricke-wande.

"Gods blessing on thy heart!" sayes Guye,
  "Goode ffellow, thy shooting is goode;
For an thy hart be as good as thy hands,
  Thou were better then Robin Hood. 130

"Tell me thy name, good ffellow," quoth Guy,
  "Under the leaves of lyne":
"Nay, by my faith," quoth good Robin,
  "Till thou have told me thine." 134

"I dwell by dale and downe," quoth Guye,
  "And I have done many a curst turne;
And he that calles me by my right name
  Calles me Guye of good Gysborne."

"My dwelling is in the wood, sayes Robin;
  "By thee I set right nought; 140
My name is Robin Hood of Barnesdale,
  A ffellow thou has long sought."

He that had neither beene a kithe nor kin
  Might have seene a full fayre sight,
To see how together these yeomen went, 145
  With blades both browne and bright.

To have seene how these yeomen together foug[ht],
  Two howers of a summers day;
Itt was neither Guy nor Robin Hood
  That ffettled them to flye away. 150

Robin was reacheles on a roote,
  And stumbled at that tyde,
And Guy was quicke and nimble withall,
  And hitt him ore the left side.

"Ah, deere Lady!" sayd Robin Hoode, 155
  "Thou art both mother and may!
I thinke it was never mans destinye
  To dye before his day."

Robin thought on Our Lady deere,
  And soone leapt up againe, 160
And thus he came with an awkwarde stroke;
  Good Sir Guy hee has slayne.

He tooke Sir Guys head by the hayre,
  And sticked itt on his bowes end:
"Thou hast beene traytor all thy liffe, 165
  Which thing must have an ende."

Robin pulled forth an Irish kniffe,
  And nicked Sir Guy in the fface,
That hee was never on a woman borne
  Cold tell who Sir Guye was. 170

Saies, Lye there, lye there, good Sir Guye,
  And with me be not wrothe;
If thou have had the worse strokes at my hand,
  Thou shalt have the better cloathe.

Robin did off his gowne of greene, 175
  Sir Guye hee did it throwe;
And hee put on that capull-hyde,
  That cladd him topp to toe.

"The bowe, the arrowes, and litle horne,
  And with me now I 'le beare; 180
Ffor now I will goe to Barn[e]sdale,
  To see how my men doe ffare."

Robin sett Guyes horne to his mouth,
  A lowd blast in it he did blow;
That beheard the sheriffe of Nottingham, 185
  As he leaned under a lowe.

"Hearken! hearken!" sayd the sheriffe,
  "I heard noe tydings but good;
For yonder I heare Sir Guyes horne blowe,
  For he hath slaine Robin Hoode. 190

"For yonder I heare Sir Guyes horne blow,
  Itt blowes soe well in tyde,
For yonder comes that wighty yeoman,
  Cladd in his capull-hyde.

"Come hither, thou good Sir Guy, 195
  Aske of mee what thou wilt have":
"I 'le none of thy gold," sayes Robin Hood,
  "Nor I 'le none of itt have.

"But now I have slaine the master," he sayd,
  "Let me goe strike the knave; 200
This is all the reward I aske,
  Nor noe other will I have."

"Thou art a madman," said the shiriffe,
"Thou sholdest have had a knights ffee;
Seeing thy asking [hath] beene soe badd, 205
Well granted it shall be."

But Litle John heard his master speake,
Well he knew that was his steven;
"Now shall I be loset," quoth Litle John,
"With Christs might in heaven." 210

But Robin hee hyed him towards Litle John,
Hee thought hee wold loose him belive;
The sheriffe and all his companye
Fast after him did drive. 214

"Stand abacke! stand abacke!" sayd Robin;
"Why draw you mee soe neere?
Itt was never the use in our countrye
One's shrift another shold heere."

But Robin pulled forth an Irysh kniffe,
And losed John hand and ffoote, 220
And gave him Sir Guyes bow in his hand,
And bade it be his boote.

But John tooke Guyes bow in his hand—
His arrowes were rawstye by the roote;
The sherriffe saw Litle John draw a bow 225
And ffettle him to shoote.

Towards his house in Nottingam
He ffled full fast away,
And soe did all his companye,
Not one behind did stay. 230

But he cold neither soe fast goe,
Nor away soe fast runn,
But Litle John, with an arrow broade,
Did cleave his heart in twinn.

ROBIN HOOD AND THE MONK[1]

In somer, when the shawes be sheyne,
And leves be large and long,
Hit is full mery in feyre foreste
To here the foulys song:

To se the dere draw in the dale, 5
And leve the hilles hee,
And shadow hem in the levés grene,
Under the grene-wode tre.

Hit befel on Whitsontide,
Erly in a May mornyng, 10
The son up feyre can shyne,
And the briddis mery can syng.

"This is a mery mornyng," said Litull John,
"Be hym that dyed on tre;
A more mery man then I am one 15
Lyves not in Cristianté.

"Pluk up thi hert, my dere mayster,"
Litull John can sey,
"And thynk hit is a full fayre tyme
In a mornyng of May." 20

"Ye, on thyng greves me," seid Robyn,
"And does my hert mych woo;
That I may not no solem day
To mas nor matyns goo.

"Hit is a fourtnet and more," seid he, 25
"Syn I my savyour see;
To day wil I to Notyngham," seid Robyn,
"With the myght of mylde Marye."

Than spake Moche, the mylner sun,
Ever more wel hym betyde! 30
"Take twelve of thi wyght yemen,
Well weppynd, be thi side.
Such on wolde thi selfe slon,
That twelve dar not abyde."

"Of all my mery men," seid Robyn, 35
"Be my feith I wil non have,
But Litull John shall beyre my bow,
Till that me list to drawe."

"Thou shall beyre thin own," seid Litull Jon,
"Maister, and I wyl beyre myne, 40
And we well shete a peny," seid Litull Jon,
"Under the grene-wode lyne."

"I will not shete a peny," seyd Robyn Hode,
"In feith, Litull John, with the,
But ever for on as thou shetis," seide Robyn,
"In feith I holde the thre." 46

Thus shet thei forth, these yemen too
Bothe at buske and brome,
Til Litull John wan of his maister
Five shillings to hose and shone. 50

A ferly strife fel them betwene,
As they went bi the wey;
Litull John seid he had won five shillings,
And Robyn Hode seid schortly nay.

[1]This is the oldest of the extant Robin Hood ballads. It comes from a manuscript of about 1450 which is now in the Cambridge University Library.

With that Robyn Hode lyed Litul Jon, 55
 And smote hym with his hande;
Litul Jon waxed wroth therwith,
 And pulled out his bright bronde.

"Were thou not my maister," seid Litull John,
 "Thou shuldis by hit ful sore; 60
Get the a man wher thou w[ilt],
 For thou getis me no more."

Then Robyn goes to Notyngham,
 Hym selfe mornyng allone,
And Litull John to mery Scherwode, 65
 The pathes he knew ilkone.

Whan Robyn came to Notyngham,
 Sertenly withouten layn,
He prayed to God and myld Mary
 To bryng hym out save agayn. 70

He gos in to Seynt Mary chirch,
 And kneled down before the rode;
Alle that ever were the church within
 Beheld wel Robyn Hode.

Beside hym stod a gret-hedid munke, 75
 I pray to God woo he be!
Fful sone he knew gode Robyn,
 As sone as he hym se.

Out at the durre he ran,
 Fful sone and anon; 80
Alle the gatis of Notyngham
 He made to be sparred everychon.

"Rise up," he seid, "thou prowde schereff,
 Buske the and make the bowne;
I have spyed the kynggis felon, 85
 Ffor sothe he is in this town.

"I have spyed the false felon,
 As he stondis at his masse;
Hit is long of the," seide the munke,
 "And ever he fro us passe. 90

"This traytur name is Robyn Hode,
 Under the grene-wode lynde;
He robbyt me onys of a hundred pound,
 Hit shalle never out of my mynde."

Up then rose this prowde shereff, 95
 And radly made hym gare;
Many was the moder son
 To the kyrk with hym can fare.

In at the durres thei throly thrast,
 With staves full gode wone; 100

"Alas, alas!" seid Robyn Hode,
 "Now mysse I Litull John."

But Robyn toke out a too-hond sworde,
 That hangit down be his kne;
Ther as the schereff and his men stode
 thyckust, 105
 The thurwarde wolde he.

Thryes thorowout them he ran then,
 For sothe as I yow sey,
And woundyt mony a moder son,
 And twelve he slew that day. 110

His sworde upon the schireff hed
 Sertanly he brake in too;
"The smyth that the made," seid Robyn,
 "I pray to God wyrke hym woo!

"Ffor now am I weppynlesse," said Robyn,
 "Alasse! agayn my wylle; 116
But if I may fle these traytors fro,
 I wot thei wil me kyll."

Robyn in to the churché ran,
 Throout hem everilkon, 120

. . . . .

Sum fel in swonyng as thei were dede,
 And lay stil as any stone;
Non of theym were in her mynde
 But only Litull Jon.

"Let be your rule," seid Litull Jon, 125
 "Ffor his luf that dyed on tre,
Ye that shulde be dugty men;
 Het is gret shame to se.

"Oure maister has been hard bystode
 And yet scapyd away; 130
Pluk up your hertis, and leve this mone,
 And harkyn what I shal say.

"He has servyd Oure Lady many a day,
 And yet wil, securly;
Therfor I trust in hir specialy 135
 No wyckud deth shal he dye.

"Therfor be glad," seid Litul John,
 "And let this mournyng be;
And I shal be the munkis gyde,
 With the myght of mylde Mary. 140

. . . .

"We will go but we too;
And I mete hym," seid Litul John,

. . . . .

"Loke that ye kepe wel owre tristil-tre,
  Under the levys smale,
And spare non of this venyson, 145
  That gose in thys vale."

Fforthe then went these yemen too,
  Litul John and Moche on fere,
And lokid on Moch emys hows,
  The hye way lay full nere. 150

Litul John stode at a wyndow in the
    mornyng,
  And lokid forth at a stage;
He was war wher the munke came ridyng,
  And with hym a litul page.

"Be my feith," seid Litul John to Moch, 155
  "I can the tel tithyngus gode;
I see wher the munke cumys rydyng,
  I know hym be his wyde hode."

They went in to the way, these yemen bothe,
  As curtes men and hende; 160
Thei spyrred tithyngus at the munke,
  As they hade bene his frende.

"Ffro whens come ye?" seid Litull Jon,
  "Tel us tithyngus, I yow pray,
Off a false owtlay, [callid Robyn Hode,] 165
  Was takyn yisterday.

"He robbyt me and my felowes bothe
  Of twenti marke in serten;
If that false owtlay be takyn,
  Ffor sothe we wolde be fayn." 170

"So did he me," seid the munke,
  "Of a hundred pound and more;
I layde furst hande hym apon,
  Ye may thonke me therfore."

"I pray God thanke you," seid Litull John,
  "And we will when we may; 176
We wil go with you, with your leve,
  And bryng yow on your way.

"Ffor Robyn Hode hase many a wilde felow,
  I tell you in certen; 180
If thei wist ye rode this way,
  In feith ye shulde be slayn."

As thei went talking by the way,
  The munke and Litull John,
John toke the munkis horse be the hede, 185
  Fful sone and anon.

Johne toke the munkis horse be the hed,
  Ffor sothe as I yow say;
So did Much the litull page,
  Ffor he shulde not scape away. 190

Be the golett of the hode
  John pulled the munke down;
John was nothyng of hym agast,
  He lete hym falle on his crown.

Litull John was so[re] agrevyd, 195
  And drew owt his swerde in hye;
This munke saw he shulde be ded,
  Lowd mercy can he crye.

"He was my maister," seid Litull John,
  "That thou hase browgt in bale; 200
Shalle thou never cum at our kyng,
  Ffor to telle hym tale."

John smote of the munkis hed,
  No longer wolde he dwell;
So did Moch the litull page, 205
  Ffor ferd lest he wolde tell.

Ther thei beryed hem bothe,
  In nouther mosse nor lyng,
And Litull John and Much infere
  Bare the letturs to oure kyng. 210

. . . . .

He knelid down upon his kne:
"God yow save, my lege lorde,
  Ihesus yow save and se!

"God yow save, my lege kyng!"
  To speke John was full bolde; 215
He gaf hym the letturs in his hond,
  The kyng did hit unfold.

The kyng red the letturs anon,
  And seid, "So mot I the,
Ther was never yoman in mery Inglond 220
  I longut so sore to se.

"Wher is the munke that these shuld have
    brougt?"
  Oure kyng can say:
"Be my trouth," seid Litull John,
  "He dyed after the way." 225

The kyng gaf Moch and Litul Jon
  Twenti pound in sertan,
And made theim yemen of the crown,
  And bade theim go agayn.

He gaf John the seel in hand, 230
  The sheref for to bere,
To bryng Robyn hym to,
  And no man do hym dere.

John toke his leve at oure kyng,
  The sothe as I yow say; 235
The next way to Notyngham
  To take, he gede the way.

Whan John came to Notyngham
  The gatis were sparred ychon;
John callid up the porter, 240
  He answerid sone anon.

"What is the cause," seid Litul Jon,
  "Thou sparris the gates so fast?"
"Because of Robyn Hode," seid [the] porter,
  "In depe prison is cast. 245

"John and Moch and Wyll Scathlok,
  Ffor sothe as I yow say,
Thei slew oure men upon our wallis,
  And sawten us every day."

Litull John spyrred after the schereff, 250
  And sone he hym fonde;
He oppyned the kyngus prive seell,
  And gaf hym in his honde.

Whan the scheref saw the kyngus seell,
  He did of his hode anon: 255
"Where is the munke that bare the letturs?"
  He seid to Litull John.

"He is so fayn of hym," seid Litul John,
  "Ffor sothe as I yow say,
He has made hym abot of Westmynster, 260
  A lorde of that abbay."

The scheref made John gode chere,
  And gaf hym wyne of the best;
At nygt thei went to her bedde,
  And every man to his rest. 265

When the scheref was on slepe,
  Dronken of wyne and ale,
Litul John and Moch for sothe
  Toke the way unto the jale.

Litul John callid up the jayler, 270
  And bade hym rise anon:
He seyd Robyn Hode had brokyn prison,
  And out of hit was gon.

The porter rose anon sertan,
  As sone as he herd John calle; 275
Litul John was redy with a swerd,
  And bare hym to the walle.

"Now wil I be porter," seid Litul John,
  "And take the keyes in honde":
He toke the way to Robyn Hode, 280
  And sone he hym unbonde.

He gaf hym a gode swerd in his hond,
  His hed [ther] with for to kepe,
And ther as the walle was lowyst
  Anon down can thei lepe. 285

Be that the cok began to crow,
  The day began to spryng;
The scheref fond the jaylier ded,
  The comyn bell made he ryng.

He made a crye thoroout al the tow[n], 290
  Wheder he be yoman or knave,
That cowthe bryng hym Robyn Hode,
  His warison he shuld have.

"Ffor I dar never," said the scheref,
  "Cum before oure kyng; 295
Ffor if I do, I wot serten
  Ffor sothe he wil me heng."

The scheref made to seke Notyngham,
  Bothe be strete and stye,
And Robyn was in mery Scherwode, 300
  As ligt as lef on lynde.

Then bespake gode Litull John,
  To Robyn Hode can he say,
I have done the a gode turne for an evyll,
  Quyte the whan thou may. 305

"I have done the a gode turne," seid Litull
    John,
  "Ffor sothe as I yow say;
I have brougt the under grene-wode lyne;
  Ffare wel, and have gode day."

"Nay, be my trouth," seid Robyn Hode, 310
  "So shall hit never be;
I make the maister," seid Robyn Hode,
  "Off alle my men and me."

"Nay, be my trouth," seid Litull John,
  "So shalle hit never be; 315
But lat me be a felow," seid Litull John,
  "No noder kepe I be."

Thus John gate Robyn Hod out of prison,
  Sertan withoutyn layn;
Whan his men saw hym hol and sounde, 320
  Ffor sothe they were full fayne.

They filled in wyne, and made hem glad,
  Under the levys smale,
And gete pastes of venyson,
  That gode was with ale. 325

Than worde came to oure kyng
  How Robyn Hode was gon,
And how the scheref of Notyngham
  Durst never loke hym upon.

Then bespake oure cumly kyng, 330
  In an angur hye:
"Litull John hase begyled the schereff,
  In faith so hase he me.

"Litul John has begyled us bothe,
  And that full wel I se; 335
Or ellis the schereff of Notyngham
  Hye hongut shulde he be.

"I made hem yemen of the crowne,
  And gaf hem fee with my hond;
I gaf hem grith," seid oure kyng, 340
  "Thorowout all mery Inglond.

"I gaf theym grith," then seid oure kyng;
  "I say, so mot I the,
Ffor sothe soch a yeman as he is on
  In all Inglond ar not thre. 345

"He is trew to his maister," seid our kyng;
  "I sey, be swete Seynt John,
He lovys better Robyn Hode
  Then he dose us ychon.

"Robyn Hode is ever bond to hym, 350
  Bothe in strete and stalle;
Speke no more of this mater," seid oure kyng,
  "But John has begyled us alle."

Thus endys the talkyng of the munke
  And Robyn Hode i-wysse; 355
God, that is ever a crowned kyng,
  Bryng us all to his blisse!

ROBIN HOOD'S DEATH

When Robin Hood and Little John,
  Down a down a down a down,
Went oer yon bank of broom,
  Said Robin Hood bold to Little John,
We have shot for many a pound. 5
  Hey, *etc.*

But I am not able to shoot one shot more,
  My broad arrows will not flee;
But I have a cousin lives down below,
  Please God, she will bleed me. 10

Now Robin he is to fair Kirkly gone,
  As fast as he can win;
But before he came there, as we do hear,
  He was taken very ill.

And when he came to fair Kirkly-hall, 15
  He knocked all at the ring,
But none was so ready as his cousin herself
  For to let bold Robin in.

"Will you please to sit down, cousin Robin," she said,
  "And drink some beer with me?" 20
"No, I will neither eat nor drink,
  Till I am blooded by thee."

"Well, I have a room, cousin Robin," she said,
  "Which you did never see,
And if you please to walk therein, 25
  You blooded by me shall be."

She took him by the lily-white hand,
  And led him to a private room,
And there she blooded bold Robin Hood,
  While one drop of blood would run down. 30

She blooded him in a vein of the arm,
  And locked him up in the room;
Then did he bleed all the live-long day,
  Until the next day at noon.

He then bethought him of a casement there, 35
  Thinking for to get down;
But was so weak he could not leap,
  He could not get him down.

He then bethought him of his buglehorn,
  Which hung low down to his knee; 40
He set his horn unto his mouth,
  And blew out weak blasts three.

Then Little John, when hearing him,
  As he sat under a tree,
"I fear my master is now near dead, 45
  He blows so wearily."

Then Little John to fair Kirkly is gone,
  As fast as he can dree;
But when he came to Kirkly-hall,
  He broke locks two or three: 50

Until he came bold Robin to see,
  Then he fell on his knee;
"A boon, a boon," cries Little John,
  "Master, I beg of thee."

"What is that boon," said Robin Hood, 55
  "Little John, [thou] begs of me?"
"It is to burn fair Kirkly-hall,
  And all their nunnery."

"Now nay, now nay," quoth Robin Hood,
  "That boon I'll not grant thee; 60
I never hurt woman in all my life,
  Nor men in woman's company.

"I never hurt fair maid in all my time,
  Nor at mine end shall it be;
But give me my bent bow in my hand, 65
  And a broad arrow I'll let flee
And where this arrow is taken up,
  There shall my grave digged be.

"Lay me a green sod under my head,
  And another at my feet; 70
And lay my bent bow by my side,
  Which was my music sweet;
And make my grave of gravel and green,
  Which is most right and meet.

"Let me have length and breadth enough, 75
  With a green sod under my head;
That they may say, when I am dead,
  Here lies bold Robin Hood."

These words they readily granted him,
  Which did bold Robin please: 80
And there they buried bold Robin Hood,
  Within the fair Kirkleys.

THE HUNTING OF THE CHEVIOT[1]

The Persë owt off Northombarlonde,
  and avowe to God mayd he
That he wold hunte in the mowntayns
  off Chyviat within days thre,
In the magger of doughtë Dogles, 5
  and all that ever with him be.

The fattiste hartes in all Cheviat
  he sayd he wold kyll, and cary them away;
"Be my feth," sayd the dougheti Doglas
    agayn,
  "I wyll let that hontyng yf that I may." 10

[1]This is probably a later and confused account of the fight dealt with in the ballad called *The Battle of Otterburn.* The battle took place in 1388. Sir Philip Sidney's famous praise is generally referred to this ballad, though it would fit *Otterburn* almost as well: "Certainly I must confess my own barbarousness. I never heard the old song of Percy and Douglas that I found not my heart moved more than with a trumpet," *etc.* (*Defense of Poesie*). Addison criticized with high praise a younger and more corrupted version (*Chevy Chase*) of *The Hunting of the Cheviot,* in Nos. 70 and 74 of the *Spectator.*

The[n] the Persë owt off Banborowe cam,
  with him a myghtee meany,
With fifteen hondrith archares bold off blood
    and bone;
  the wear chosen owt of shyars thre.

This begane on a Monday at morn, 15
  in Cheviat the hillys so he;
The chylde may rue that ys un-born,
  it wos the mor pittë.

The dryvars thorowe the woodës went,
  for to reas the dear; 20
Bomen byckarte uppone the bent
  with ther browd aros cleare.

Then the wyld thorowe the woodës went,
  on every sydë shear;
Greahondes thorowe the grevis glent, 25
  for to kyll thear dear.

This begane in Chyviat the hyls abone,
  yerly on a Monnyn-day;
Be that it drewe to the oware off none,
  a hondrith fat hartës ded ther lay. 30

The blewe a mort uppone the bent,
  the semblyde on sydis shear;
To the quyrry then the Persë went,
  to se the bryttlynge off the deare.

He sayd, "It was the Duglas promys 35
  this day to met me hear;
But I wyste he wolde faylle, verament";
  a great oth the Persë swear.

At the laste a squyar off Northomberlonde
  lokyde at his hand full ny; 40
He was war a the doughetie Doglas com-
    mynge,
  with him a myghttë meany.

Both with spear, bylle, and brande,
  yt was a myghtti sight to se;
Hardyar men, both off hart nor hande, 45
  wear not in Cristiantë.

The wear twenti hondrith spear-men good,
  withoute any feale;
The wear borne along be the watter a Twyde,
  yth bowndës of Tividale. 50

"Leave of the brytlyng of the dear," he sayd,
  "and to your boÿs lock ye tayk good hede;
For never sithe ye wear on your mothars
    borne
  had ye never so mickle nede."

The dougheti Dogglas on a stede, 55
he rode alle his men beforne;
His armor glytteryde as dyd a glede;
a boldar barne was never born.

"Tell me whos men ye ar," he says,
"Or whos men that ye be: 60
Who gave youe leave to hunte in this Chyviat chays,
in the spyt of myn and of me."

The first mane that ever him an answear mayd,
yt was the good lord Persë:
"We wyll not tell the whoys men we ar," he says, 65
"nor whos men that we be;
But we wyll hounte hear in this chays,
in the spyt of thyne and of the.

"The fattiste hartës in all Chyviat
we have kyld, and cast to carry them away": 70
"Be my troth," sayd the doughetë Dogglas agay[n],
"therfor the ton of us shall de this day."

Then sayd the doughtë Doglas
unto the lord Persë:
"To kyll alle these giltles men, 75
alas, it wear great pittë!

"But, Persë, thowe art a lord of lande,
I am a yerle callyd within my contrë;
Let all our men uppone a parti stande,
and do the battell off the and of me." 80

"Nowe Cristes cors on his crowne," sayd the lorde Persë,
"who-so-ever ther-to says nay!
Be my troth, doughttë Doglas," he says,
"thou shalt never se that day.

"Nethar in Ynglonde, Skottlonde, nar France, 85
nor for no man of a woman born,
But, and fortune be my chance,
I dar met him, on man for on."

Then bespayke a squyar off Northombarlonde,
Richard Wytharyngton was his nam; 90
"It shall never be told in Sothe-Ynglonde," he says,
"To Kyng Herry the Fourth for sham.

"I wat youe byn great lordës twaw,
I am a poor squyar of lande;
I wylle never se my captayne fyght on a fylde, 95
and stande my selffe and loocke on,
But whylle I may my weppone welde,
I wylle not [fayle] both hart and hande."

That day, that day, that dredfull day!
The first fit here I fynde; 100
And youe wyll here any mor a the hountynge a the Chyviat,
yet ys ther mor behynde.

The Ynglyshe men hade ther bowys yebent,
ther hartes wer good yenoughe;
The first off arros that the shote off, 105
seven skore spear-men the sloughe.

Yet byddys the yerle Doglas uppon the bent,
a captayne good yenoughe,
And that was sene verament,
for he wrought hom both woo and wouche.

The Dogglas partyd his ost in thre, 111
lyk a cheffe cheften off pryde;
With suar spears off myghttë tre,
the cum in on every syde;

Thrughe our Ynglyshe archery 115
gave many a wounde fulle wyde;
Many a doughetë the garde to dy,
which ganyde them no pryde.

The Ynglyshe men let ther boÿs be,
and pulde owt brandes that wer brighte;
It was a hevy syght to se 121
bryght swordes on basnites lyght.

Thorowe ryche male and myneyeple,
many sterne the strocke done streght;
Many a freyke that was fulle fre, 125
ther undar foot dyd lyght.

At last the Duglas and the Persë met,
lyk to captayns of myght and of mayne;
The swapte togethar tylle the both swat,
with swordes that wear of fyn myllan. 130

Thes worthë freckys for to fyght,
ther-to the wear fulle fayne,
Tylle the bloode owte off thear basnetes sprente,
as ever dyd heal or ra[y]n.

"Yelde the, Persë," sayde the Doglas, 135
"and i feth I shalle the brynge
Wher thowe shalte have a yerls wagis
of Jamy our Skottish kynge.

"Thoue shalte have thy ransom fre,
  I hight the hear this thinge; 140
For the manfullyste man yet art thowe
  that ever I conqueryd in filde fighttynge."

"Nay," sayd the lord Persë,
  "I tolde it the beforne,
That I wolde never yeldyde be 145
  to no man of a woman born."

With that ther cam an arrowe hastely,
  forthe off a myghttë wane;
Hit hathe strekene the yerle Duglas
  in at the brest-bane. 150

Thorowe lyvar and longës bathe
  the sharpe arrowe ys gane,
That never after in all his lyffe-days
  he spayke mo wordës but ane:
That was, "Fyghte ye, my myrry men,
    whyllys ye may, 155
  for my lyff-days ben gan."

The Persë leanyde on his brande,
  and sawe the Duglas de;
He tooke the dede mane by the hande,
  and sayd, "Wo ys me for the! 160

"To have savyde thy lyffe, I wolde have
    partyde with
  my landes for years thre,
For a better man, of hart nare of hande,
  was nat in all the north contrë."

Off all that se a Skottishe knyght, 165
  was callyd Ser Hewe the Monggombyrry;
He sawe the Duglas to the deth was dyght,
  he spendyd a spear, a trusti tre.

He rod uppone a corsiare
  throughe a hondrith archery: 170
He never stynttyde, nar never blane,
  tylle he came to the good lord Persë.

He set uppone the lorde Persë
  a dynte that was full soare;
With a suar spear of a myghttë tre 175
  clean thorow the body he the Persë ber,

A the tothar syde that a man myght se
  a large cloth-yard and mare:
Towe bettar captayns wear nat in Cristiantë
  then that day slan wear ther. 180

An archar off Northomberlonde
  say slean was the lord Persë;
He bar a bende bowe in his hand,
  was made off trusti tre.

An arow that a cloth-yarde was lang 185
  to the harde stele halyde he;
A dynt that was both sad and soar
  he sat on Ser Hewe the Monggombyrry.

The dynt yt was both sad and sar
  that he of Monggomberry sete; 190
The swane-fethars that his arrowe bar
  with his hart-blood the wear wete.

Ther was never a freake wone foot wolde fle,
  but still in stour dyd stand,
Heawyng on yche othar, whylle the myghte
    dre, 195
  with many a balfull brande.

This battell begane in Chyviat
  an owar before the none,
And when even-songe bell was rang,
  the battell was nat half done. 200

The tocke . . . on ethar hande[2]
  be the lyght off the mone;
Many hade no strength for to stande,
  in Chyviat the hillys abon.

Of fifteen hondrith archars of Ynglonde 205
  went away but seventi and thre;
Of twenti hondrith spear-men of Skotlonde,
  but even five and fifti.

But all wear slayne Cheviat within;
  the hade no streng[th]e to stand on by; 210
The chylde may rue that ys unborne,
  it was the mor pittë.

Thear was slayne, withe the lord Persë,
  Ser Johan of Agerstone,
Ser Rogar, the hinde Hartly, 215
  Ser Wyllyam, the bolde Hearone.

Ser Jorg, the worthë Loumle,
  a knyghte of great renowen,
Ser Raff, the ryche Rugbe,
  with dyntes wear beaten dowene. 220

For Wetharryngton my harte was wo,
  that ever he slayne shulde be;
For when both his leggis wear hewyne in to,
  yet he knyled and fought on hys kny.

Ther was slayne, with the dougheti Duglas,
  Ser Hewe the Monggombyrry, 226
Ser Davy Lwdale, that worthë was,
  his sistars son was he.

---

[2]Words are missing in the manuscript. "Rest" has been suggested to fill the gap; and also "them off"—i. e., "they took themselves off."

Ser Charls a Murrë in that place,
that never a foot wolde fle; 230
Ser Hewe Maxwelle, a lorde he was,
with the Doglas dyd he dey.

So on the morrowe the mayde them byears
off birch and hasell so g[r]ay;
Many wedous, with wepyng tears, 235
cam to fache ther makys away.

Tivydale may carpe off care,
Northombarlond may mayk great mon,
For towe such captayns as slayne wear thear
on the March-parti shall never be non. 240

Word ys commen to Eddenburrowe,
to Jamy the Skottishe kynge,[3]
That dougheti Duglas, lyff-tenant of the Marches,
he lay slean Chyviot within.

His handdës dyd he weal and wryng, 245
he sayd, "Alas, and woe ys me!
Such an othar captayn Skotland within,"
he sayd, "ye-feth shuld never be."

Worde ys commyn to lovly Londone,
till the fourth Harry our kynge, 250
That lord Persë, leyff-tenante of the Marchis,
he lay slayne Chyviat within.

"God have merci on his solle," sayde Kyng Harry,
"good lord, yf thy will it be!
I have a hondrith captayns in Ynglonde," he sayd, 255
"as good as ever was he:
But, Persë, and I brook my lyffe,
thy deth well quyte shall be."

As our noble kynge mayd his avowe,
lyke a noble prince of renowen, 260
For the deth of the lord Persë
he dyde the battell of Hombylldown;

Wher syx and thrittë Skottishe knyghtes
on a day wear beaten down;
Glendale glytteryde on ther armor bryght, 265
over castille, towar, and town.

This was the hontynge off the Cheviat,
that tear begane this spurn;
Old men that knowen the grownde well yenoughe
call it the battell of Otterburn. 270

At Otterburn begane this spurne,
uppone a Monnynday;
Ther was the doughtë Doglas slean,
the Persë never went away.

Ther was never a tym on the Marche-partës
sen the Doglas and the Persë met, 276
But yt ys mervele and the rede blude ronne not,
as the reane doys in the stret.

Ihesue Crist our balys bete,
and to the blys us brynge! 280
Thus was the hountynge of the Chivyat:
God send us alle good endyng!

[3]James I of Scotland.

SIR PATRICK SPENS

The king sits in Dunfermlin town,
Sae merrily drinkin the wine:
"Whare will I get a mariner,
Will sail this ship o mine?"

Then up bespak a bonny boy, 5
Sat just at the king's knee:
"Sir Patrick Spence is the best seaman,
That eer set foot on sea."

The king has written a braid letter,
Seald it wi his ain hand; 10
He has sent word to Sir Patrick,
To come at his command.

"O wha is this, or wha is that,
Has tald the king o me?
For I was never a good seaman, 15
Nor ever intend to be."

They mounted sail on Munenday morn,
Wi a' the haste they may,
And they hae landed in Norraway,
Upon the Wednesday. 20

They hadna been a month, a month
In Norraway but three,
Till lads o Norraway began to say,
"Ye spend a' our white monie.

"Ye spend a' our good kingis goud, 25
But and our queenis fee":
"Ye lie, ye lie, ye liars loud,
Sae weel's I hear you lie.

"For I brought as much white money
As will gain my men and me; 30
I brought half a fou o good red goud
Out oer the sea with me.

"Be 't wind or weet, be 't snaw or sleet,
 Our ships maun sail the morn:"
"O ever alack! my master dear, 35
 I fear a deadly storm.

"I saw the new moon late yestreen,
 Wi the auld moon in her arm;
And if we gang to sea, master,
 I fear we'll suffer harm." 40

They hadna sailed a league on sea,
 A league but barely ane,
Till anchors brak, and tap-masts lap;
 There came a deadly storm.

"Whare will I get a bonny boy 45
 Will tak thir sails in hand,
That will gang up to the tap-mast,
 See an he ken dry land?"

Laith, laith were our good Scots lords
 To weet their leathern shoon; 50
But or the morn at fair day-light,
 Their hats were wat aboon.

Mony was the feather bed,
 That flottered on the faem,
And mony was the good Scots lord 55
 Gaed awa that neer cam hame,
And mony was the fatherless bairn
 That lay at hame greetin.

It's forty miles to Aberdeen,
 And fifty fathoms deep; 60
And there lyes a' our good Scots lords,
 Wi Sir Patrick at their feet.

The ladies crackt their fingers white,
 The maidens tore their hair,
A' for the sake o their true loves, 65
 For them they neer saw mair.

Lang, lang may our ladies stand,
 Wi their fans in their hand,
Ere they see Sir Patrick and his men
 Come sailing to the land. 70

THE THREE RAVENS

There were three ravens sat on a tree,
 Downe a downe, hay down, hay downe,
There were three ravens sat on a tree,
 With a downe,
There were three ravens sat on a tree, 5
They were as blacke as they might be.
 With a downe, derrie, derrie, derrie,
 downe, downe.

The one of them said to his mate,
"Where shall we our breakefast take?"

"Downe in yonder greene field, 10
There lies a knight slain under his shield.

"His hounds they lie downe at his feete,
So well they can their master keepe.

"His haukes they flie so eagerly,
There's no fowle dare him come nie." 15

Downe there comes a fallow doe,
As great with yong as she might goe.

She lift up his bloudy hed,
And kist his wounds that were so red.

She got him up upon her backe, 20
And carried him to earthen lake.

She buried him before the prime,
She was dead herselfe ere even-song time.

God send every gentleman, 24
Such haukes, such hounds, and such a leman.

EDWARD

"Why dois your brand sae drap wi bluid,
 Edward, Edward,
Why dois your brand sae drap wi bluid,
 And why sae sad gang yee O?"
"O I hae killed my hauke sae guid, 5
 Mither, mither,
O I hae killed my hauke sae guid,
 And I had nae mair bot hee O."

"Your haukis bluid was nevir sae reid,
 Edward, Edward, 10
Your haukis bluid was nevir sae reid,
 My deir son I tell thee O."
"O I hae killed my reid-roan steid,
 Mither, mither,
O I hae killed my reid-roan steid, 15
 That erst was sae fair and frie O."

"Your steid was auld, and ye hae gat mair,
 Edward, Edward,
Your steid was auld, and ye hae gat mair,
 Sum other dule ye drie O." 20
"O I hae killed my fadir deir,
 Mither, mither,
O I hae killed my fadir deir,
 Alas, and wae is mee O!"

"And whatten penance wul ye drie for that, 25
Edward, Edward?
And whatten penance will ye drie for that?
My deir son, now tell me O."
"Ile set my feit in yonder boat,
Mither, mither, 30
Ile set my feit in yonder boat,
And Ile fare ovir the sea O."

"And what wul ye doe wi your towirs and your ha,
Edward, Edward?
And what wul ye doe wi your towirs and your ha, 35
That were sae fair to see O?"
"Ile let thame stand tul they doun fa,
Mither, mither,
Ile let thame stand tul they doun fa,
For here nevir mair maun I bee O." 40

"And what wul ye leive to your bairns and your wife,
Edward, Edward?
And what wul ye leive to your bairns and your wife,
Whan ye gang ovir the sea O?"
"The warldis room, late them beg thrae life, 45
Mither, mither,
The warldis room, late them beg thrae life,
For thame nevir mair wul I see O."

"And what wul ye leive to your ain mither deir,
Edward, Edward? 50
And what wul ye leive to your ain mither deir?
My deir son, now tell me O."
"The curse of hell frae me sall ye beir,
Mither, mither,
The curse of hell frae me sall ye beir, 55
Sic counseils ye gave to me O."

BABYLON; OR, THE BONNIE BANKS O FORDIE

There were three ladies lived in a bower,
Eh vow bonnie
And they went out to pull a flower.
On the bonnie banks o Fordie.

They hadna pu'ed a flower but ane, 5
When up started to them a banisht man.

He's taen the first sister by her hand,
And he's turned her round and made her stand.

"It's whether will ye be a rank robber's wife,
Or will ye die by my wee pen-knife?" 10

"It's I'll not be a rank robber's wife,
But I'll rather die by your wee pen-knife."

He's killed this may, and he's laid her by,
For to bear the red rose company.

He's taken the second ane by the hand, 15
And he's turned her round and made her stand.

"It's whether will ye be a rank robber's wife,
Or will ye die by my wee pen-knife?"

"I'll not be a rank robber's wife,
But I'll rather die by your wee pen-knife." 20

He's killed this may, and he's laid her by,
For to bear the red rose company.

He's taken the youngest ane by the hand,
And he's turned her round and made her stand.

Says, "Will ye be a rank robber's wife, 25
Or will ye die by my wee pen-knife?"

"I'll not be a rank robber's wife,
Nor will I die by your wee pen-knife.

"For I hae a brother in this wood,
And gin ye kill me, it's he'll kill thee." 30

"What's thy brother's name? come tell to me."
"My brother's name is Baby Lon."

"O sister, sister, what have I done!
O have I done this ill to thee!

"O since I've done this evil deed, 35
Good sall never be seen o me."

He's taken out his wee pen-knife,
And he's twyned himsel o his ain sweet life.

THE TWA SISTERS

There was twa sisters in a bowr,
Edinburgh, Edinburgh,
There was twa sisters in a bowr,
Stirling for ay.
There was twa sisters in a bowr, 5
There came a knight to be their wooer;
Bonny Saint Johnston stands upon Tay.

He courted the eldest wi glove an ring,
But he lovd the youngest above a' thing.

He courted the eldest wi brotch an knife, 10
But lovd the youngest as his life.

The eldest she was vexéd sair,
An much envi'd her sister fair.

Into her bowr she could not rest,
Wi grief an spite she almos brast. 15

Upon a morning fair an clear,
She cried upon her sister dear:

"O sister, come to yon sea stran,
And see our father's ships come to lan."

She's taen her by the milk-white han, 20
And led her down to yon sea stran.

The younges[t] stood upon a stane,
The eldest came an threw her in.

She tooke her by the middle sma,
An dashd her bonny back to the jaw. 25

"O sister, sister, tak my han,
An Ise mack you heir to a' my lan.

"O sister, sister, tak my middle,
An yes get my goud and my gouden girdle.

"O sister, sister, save my life, 30
An I swear Ise never be nae man's wife."

"Foul fa the han that I should tacke,
It twin'd me an my wardles make.

"Your cherry cheeks an yallow hair
Gars me gae maiden for evermair." 35

Sometimes she sank, an sometimes she swam,
Till she came down yon bonny mill-dam.

O out it came the miller's son,
An saw the fair maid swimmin in.

"O father, father, draw your dam, 40
Here's either a mermaid or a swan."

The miller quickly drew the dam,
An there he found a drownd woman.

You coudna see her yallow hair
For gold and pearle that were so rare. 45

You coudna see her middle sma
For gouden girdle that was sae braw.

You coudna see her fingers white,
For gouden rings that was sae gryte.

An by there came a harper fine, 50
That harpéd to the king at dine.

When he did look that lady upon,
He sighd and made a heavy moan.

He's taen three locks o her yallow hair,
An wi them strung his harp sae fair. 55

The first tune he did play and sing,
Was, "Farewell to my father the king."

The nextin tune that he playd syne,
Was, "Farewell to my mother the queen."

The lasten tune that he playd then, 60
Was, "Wae to my sister, fair Ellen."

THE TWA BROTHERS

There were twa brethren in the north,
They went to school thegithar;
The one unto the other said,
Will you try a warsle afore?

They wrestled up, they wrestled down, 5
Till Sir John fell to the ground,
And there was a knife in Sir Willie's pouch,
Gied him a deadlie wound.

"Oh brither dear, take me on your back,
Carry me to yon burn clear, 10
And wash the blood from off my wound,
And it will bleed nae mair."

He took him up upon his back,
Carried him to yon burn clear,
And washd the blood from off his wound, 15
And aye it bled the mair.

"Oh brother dear, take me on your back,
Carry me to yon kirk-yard,
And dig a grave baith wide and deep,
And lay my body there." 20

He's taen him up upon his back,
Carried him to yon kirk-yard,
And dug a grave both deep and wide,
And laid his body there.

"But what will I say to my father dear, 25
Should he chance to say, Willie, whar's
John?"
"Oh say that he's to England gone,
To buy him a cask of wine."

"And what shall I say to my mother dear,
Should she chance to say, Willie, whar's John?" 30
"Oh say that he's to England gone,
To buy her a new silk gown."

"And what will I say to my sister dear,
Should she chance to say, Willie, whar's John?"
"Oh say that he's to England gone, 35
To buy her a wedding ring."

"What will I say to her you loe dear,
Should she cry, Why tarries my John?"
"Oh tell her I lie in fair Kirk-land,
And home will never come." 40

THE CRUEL BROTHER

There was three ladies playd at the ba,
With a hey ho and a lillie gay,
There came a knight and played oer them a'.
As the primrose spreads so sweetly.

The eldest was baith tall and fair, 5
But the youngest was beyond compare.

The midmost had a graceful mien,
But the youngest looked like beautie's queen.

The knight bowd low to a' the three,
But to the youngest he bent his knee. 10

The ladie turned her head aside,
The knight he woo'd her to be his bride.

The ladie blushd a rosy red,
And sayd, "Sir knight, I'm too young to wed."

"O ladie fair, give me your hand, 15
And I'll make you ladie of a' my land."

"Sir knight, ere ye my favor win,
You maun get consent frae a' my kin."

He's got consent frae her parents dear,
And likewise frae her sisters fair. 20

He's got consent frae her kin each one,
But forgot to spiek to her brother John.

Now, when the wedding day was come,
The knight would take his bonny bride home.

And many a lord and many a knight 25
Came to behold that ladie bright.

And there was nae man that did her see,
But wishd himself bridegroom to be.

Her father dear led her down the stair,
And her sisters twain they kissd her there. 30

Her mother dear led her thro the closs,
And her brother John set her on her horse.

She leand her oer the saddle-bow,
To give him a kiss ere she did go.

He has taen a knife, baith lang and sharp, 35
And stabbd that bonny bride to the heart.

She hadno ridden half thro the town,
Until her heart's blude staind her gown.

"Ride softly on," says the best young man,
"For I think our bonny bride looks pale and wan." 40

"O lead me gently up yon hill,
And I'll there sit down, and make my will."

"O what will you leave to your father dear?"
"The silver-shode steed that brought me here."

"What will you leave to your mother dear?"
"My velvet pall and my silken gear." 46

"What will you leave to your sister Anne?"
"My silken scarf and my gowden fan."

"What will you leave to your sister Grace?"
"My bloody cloaths to wash and dress." 50

"What will you leave to your brother John?"
"The gallows-tree to hang him on."

"What will you leave to your brother John's wife?"
"The wilderness to end her life."

This ladie fair in her grave was laid, 55
And many a mass was oer her said.

But it would have made your heart right sair,
To see the bridegroom rive his haire.

THE WIFE OF USHER'S WELL

There lived a wife at Usher's Well,
And a wealthy wife was she;
She had three stout and stalwart sons,
And sent them oer the sea.

They hadna been a week from her, 5
A week but barely ane,
Whan word came to the carline wife
That her three sons were gane.

They hadna been a week from her,
A week but barely three, 10
Whan word came to the carlin wife
That her sons she'd never see.

"I wish the wind may never cease,
Nor fashes in the flood,
Till my three sons come hame to me, 15
In earthly flesh and blood."

It fell about the Martinmass,
When nights are lang and mirk,
The carlin wife's three sons came hame,
And their hats were o the birk. 20

It neither grew in syke nor ditch,
Nor yet in only sheugh;
But at the gates o Paradise,
That birk grew fair eneugh.

. . . . .

"Blow up the fire, my maidens, 25
Bring water from the well;
For a' my house shall feast this night,
Since my three sons are well."

And she has made to them a bed,
She's made it large and wide, 30
And she's taen her mantle her about,
Sat down at the bed-side.

. . . . .

Up then crew the red, red cock,
And up and crew the gray;
The eldest to the youngest said, 35
" 'Tis time we were away."

The cock he hadna crawd but once,
And clappd his wings at a',
When the youngest to the eldest said,
"Brother, we must awa." 40

"The cock doth craw, the day doth daw,
The channerin worm doth chide;
Gin we be mist out o our place,
A sair pain we maun bide.

"Fare ye weel, my mother dear! 45
Fareweel to barn and byre!
And fare ye weel, the bonny lass
That kindles my mother's fire!"

KEMP OWYNE[1]

Her mother died when she was young,
Which gave her cause to make great moan;
Her father married the warst woman
That ever lived in Christendom.

She servéd her with foot and hand, 5
In every thing that she could dee,
Till once, in an unlucky time,
She threw her in ower Craigy's sea.

Says, "Lie you there, dove Isabel,
And all my sorrows lie with thee; 10
Till Kemp Owyne come ower the sea,
And borrow you with kisses three,
Let all the warld do what they will,
Oh borrowed shall you never be!"

Her breath grew strang, her hair grew lang, 15
And twisted thrice about the tree,
And all the people, far and near,
Thought that a savage beast was she.

These news did come to Kemp Owyne,
Where he lived, far beyond the sea; 20
He hasted him to Craigy's sea,
And on the savage beast lookd he.

Her breath was strang, her hair was lang,
And twisted was about the tree,
And with a swing she came about: 25
"Come to Craigy's sea, and kiss with me.

"Here is a royal belt," she cried,
"That I have found in the green sea;
And while your body it is on,
Drawn shall your blood never be; 30
But if you touch me, tail or fin,
I vow my belt your death shall be."

He steppéd in, gave her a kiss,
The royal belt he brought him wi;
Her breath was strang, her hair was lang, 35
And twisted twice about the tree,
And with a swing she came about:
"Come to Craigy's sea, and kiss with me.

"Here is a royal ring," she said,
"That I have found in the green sea; 40
And while your finger it is on,
Drawn shall your blood never be;
But if you touch me, tail or fin,
I swear my ring your death shall be."

[1]Owyne is Owain or Ywain, one of King Arthur's knights. Disenchantment by a kiss is common in romance, but none is known in which Ywain has this adventure.

He steppéd in, gave her a kiss, 45
  The royal ring he brought him wi;
Her breath was strang, her hair was lang,
  And twisted ance about the tree,
And with a swing she came about:
  "Come to Craigy's sea, and kiss with me. 50

"Here is a royal brand," she said,
  "That I have found in the green sea;
And while your body it is on,
  Drawn shall your blood never be;
But if you touch me, tail or fin, 55
  I swear my brand your death shall be."

He steppéd in, gave her a kiss,
  The royal brand he brought him wi;
Her breath was sweet, her hair grew short,
  And twisted nane about the tree, 60
And smilingly she came about,
  As fair a woman as fair could be.

THOMAS RYMER[1]

True Thomas lay oer yond grassy bank,
  And he beheld a ladie gay,
A ladie that was brisk and bold,
  Come riding oer the fernie brae.

Her skirt was of the grass-green silk, 5
  Her mantel of the velvet fine,
At ilka tett of her horse's mane
  Hung fifty silver bells and nine.

True Thomas he took off his hat,
  And bowed him low down till his knee: 10
"All hail, thou mighty Queen of Heaven!
  For your peer on earth I never did see."

"O no, O no, True Thomas," she says,
  "That name does not belong to me;
I am but the queen of fair Elfland, 15
  And I'm come here for to visit thee.

. . . . .

"But ye maun go wi me now, Thomas,
  True Thomas, ye maun go wi me,
For ye maun serve me seven years,
  Thro weel or wae as may chance to be." 20

[1]This story is told in fuller detail in the poem called *Thomas of Erceldoune,* a fifteenth-century romance and probably the source of the ballad. Thomas of Erceldoune is an historical character; he lived in southern Scotland in the thirteenth century.

She turned about her milk-white steed,
  And took True Thomas up behind,
And aye wheneer her bridle rang,
  The steed flew swifter than the wind.

For forty days and forty nights 25
  He wade thro red blude to the knee,
And he saw neither sun nor moon,
  But heard the roaring of the sea.

O they rade on, and further on,
  Until they came to a garden green: 30
"Light down, light down, ye ladie free,
  Some of that fruit let me pull to thee."

"O no, O no, True Thomas," she says,
  "That fruit maun not be touched by thee,
For a' the plagues that are in hell 35
  Light on the fruit of this countrie.

"But I have a loaf here in my lap,
  Likewise a bottle of claret wine,
And now ere we go farther on,
  We'll rest a while, and ye may dine." 40

When he had eaten and drunk his fill,
  "Lay down your head upon my knee,"
The lady sayd, "ere we climb yon hill,
  And I will show you fairlies three.

"O see not ye yon narrow road, 45
  So thick beset wi thorns and briers?
That is the path of righteousness,
  Tho after it but few enquires.

"And see not ye that braid braid road,
  That lies across yon lillie leven? 50
That is the path of wickedness,
  Tho some call it the road to heaven.

"And see not ye that bonny road,
  Which winds about the fernie brae?
That is the road to fair Elfland, 55
  Whe[re] you and I this night maun gae.

"But Thomas, ye maun hold your tongue,
  Whatever you may hear or see,
For gin ae word you should chance to speak,
  You will neer get back to your ain countrie." 60

He has gotten a coat of the even cloth,
  And a pair of shoes of velvet green,
And till seven years were past and gone
  True Thomas on earth was never seen.

SIR HUGH, OR, THE JEW'S DAUGHTER[1]

Four and twenty bonny boys
Were playing at the ba,
And by it came him sweet Sir Hugh,
And he playd oer them a'.

He kicked the ba with his right foot, 5
And catchd it wi his knee,
And throuch-and-thro the Jew's window
He gard the bonny ba flee.

He's doen him to the Jew's castell,
And walkd it round about; 10
And there he saw the Jew's daughter,
At the window looking out.

"Throw down the ba, ye Jew's daughter,
Throw down the ba to me!"
"Never a bit," says the Jew's daughter, 15
"Till up to me come ye."

"How will I come up? How can I come up?
How can I come to thee?
For as ye did to my auld father,
The same ye'll do to me." 20

She's gane till her father's garden,
And pu'd an apple red and green;
'T was a' to wyle him sweet Sir Hugh,
And to entice him in.

She's led him in through ae dark door, 25
And sae has she thro nine;
She's laid him on a dressing-table,
And stickit him like a swine.

And first came out the thick, thick blood,
And syne came out the thin, 30
And syne came out the bonny heart's blood;
There was nae mair within.

She's rowd him in a cake o lead,
Bade him lie still and sleep;
She's thrown him in Our Lady's draw-well, 35
Was fifty fathom deep.

When bells were rung, and mass was sung,
And a' the bairns came hame,
When every lady gat hame her son,
The Lady Maisry gat nane. 40

She's taen her mantle her about,
Her coffer by the hand,
And she's gane out to seek her son,
And wanderd oer the land.

She's doen her to the Jew's castell, 45
Where a' were fast asleep:
"Gin ye be there, my sweet Sir Hugh,
I pray you to me speak."

She's doen her to the Jew's garden,
Thought he had been gathering fruit: 50
"Gin ye be there, my sweet Sir Hugh,
I pray you to me speak."

She neard Our Lady's deep draw-well,
Was fifty fathom deep:
"Whareer ye be, my sweet Sir Hugh, 55
I pray you to me speak."

"Gae hame, gae hame, my mither dear,
Prepare my winding sheet,
And at the back o merry Lincoln
The morn I will you meet." 60

Now Lady Maisry is gane hame,
Made him a winding sheet,
And at the back o merry Lincoln
The dead corpse did her meet.

And a' the bells o merry Lincoln 65
Without men's hands were rung,
And a' the books o merry Lincoln
Were read without man's tongue,
And neer was such a burial
Sin Adam's days begun. 70

THE DAEMON LOVER

"O where have you been, my long, long love,
This long seven years and mair?"
"O I'm come to seek my former vows
Ye granted me before."

"O hold your tongue of your former vows, 5
For they will breed sad strife;
O hold your tongue of your former vows,
For I am become a wife."

He turned him right and round about,
And the tear blinded his ee: 10
"I wad never hae trodden on Irish ground,
If it had not been for thee.

[1]This is based on an alleged murder which took place in 1255. The popularity of such stories in the Middle Ages has been mentioned in the note to Chaucer's Prioress's tale, which has the same theme. As has been said, these stories are as credible as the miracles asserted to have been worked by the relics of the young saints.

"I might hae had a king's daughter,
Far, far beyond the sea;
I might have had a king's daughter, 15
Had it not been for love o thee."

"If ye might have had a king's daughter,
Yer sel ye had to blame;
Ye might have taken the king's daughter,
For ye kend that I was nane. 20

"If I was to leave my husband dear,
And my two babes also,
O what have you to take me to,
If with you I should go?"

"I hae seven ships upon the sea— 25
The eighth brought me to land—
With four-and-twenty bold mariners,
And music on every hand."

She has taken up her two little babes,
Kissd them baith cheek and chin: 30
"O fair ye weel, my ain two babes,
For I'll never see you again."

She set her foot upon the ship,
No mariners could she behold;
But the sails were o the taffetie, 35
And the masts o the beaten gold.

She had not sailed a league, a league,
A league but barely three,
When dismal grew his countenance,
And drumlie grew his ee. 40

They had not saild a league, a league,
A league but barely three,
Until she espied his cloven foot,
And she wept right bitterlie.

"O hold your tongue of your weeping," says he, 45
"Of your weeping now let me be;
I will shew you how the lilies grow
On the banks of Italy."

"O what hills are yon, yon pleasant hills,
That the sun shines sweetly on?" 50
"O yon are the hills of heaven," he said,
"Where you will never win."

"O whaten a mountain is yon," she said,
"All so dreary wi frost and snow?"
"O yon is the mountain of hell," he cried, 55
"Where you and I will go."

He strack the tap-mast wi his hand,
The fore-mast wi his knee,
And he brake that gallant ship in twain,
And sank her in the sea. 60

GET UP AND BAR THE DOOR

It fell about the Martinmas time,
And a gay time it was then,
When our goodwife got puddings to make,
And she's boild them in the pan.

The wind sae cauld blew south and north, 5
And blew into the floor;
Quoth our goodman to our goodwife,
"Gae out and bar the door."

"My hand is in my hussyfskap,
Goodman, as ye may see; 10
An it should nae be barrd this hundred year,
It's no be barrd for me."

They made a paction tween them twa,
They made it firm and sure,
That the first word whaeer shoud speak, 15
Shoud rise and bar the door.

Then by there came two gentlemen,
At twelve o clock at night,
And they could neither see house nor hall,
Nor coal nor candle-light. 20

"Now whether is this a rich man's house,
Or whether is it a poor?"
But neer a word wad ane o them speak,
For barring of the door.

And first they ate the white puddings, 25
And then they ate the black;
Tho muckle thought the goodwife to hersel,
Yet neer a word she spake.

Then said the one unto the other,
"Here, man, tak ye my knife; 30
Do ye tak aff the auld man's beard,
And I'll kiss the goodwife."

"But there's nae water in the house,
And what shall we do than?"
"What ails ye at the pudding-broo, 35
That boils into the pan?"

O up then started our good man,
An angry man was he:
"Will ye kiss my wife before my een,
And scad me wi pudding-bree?" 40

Then up and started our goodwife,
Gied three skips on the floor:
"Goodman, you've spoken the foremost word,
Get up and bar the door."

THE SECOND SHEPHERDS' PLAY[1]

The Second Shepherds' Play belongs to a group of miracles known as *The Towneley Plays,* so called because the manuscript containing them was long preserved at Towneley Hall in Lancashire. Although the manuscript can be dated about 1450, the plays themselves were probably composed during the second half of the fourteenth and the early years of the fifteenth century. It has generally been assumed, on the basis of tradition and internal evidence, that the whole cycle is that which is known to have been performed at Wakefield in Yorkshire; but recent investigations suggest that a majority of the plays may have been originally compiled for presentation at some place in Lancashire, near Towneley Hall. In any case, it is clear that eight complete miracles, out of the thirty-two which compose the cycle, form a well-defined group and are the work of one poet, the Wakefield Master, as he has come to be known. An unsuccessful attempt has been made to identify him with a certain Gilbert Pilkington, a fourteenth-century ecclesiastic of Wakefield; the plays themselves, however, tell all that is as yet known about their author. He employs a characteristic stanza, consisting of nine lines which are of various lengths and which rime *a a a a b c c c b*. Through this medium, awkward though it be for the purposes of drama, he recreates the Bible stories in his own vigorous and highly realistic manner. "This unnamed playwright makes out of life something full of trouble and racy with fun; a field for cutting satire and playful humor, for colossal irreverence and the touching faith of child-like men. He sees its multitudinous diversities and yet by the skill of his crude but certain art weaves out of its many strands a consistent picture" (Frank W. Cady, *University of California Chronicle,* XXIX, 272).

The Second Shepherds' Play is easily the most effective of the eight miracles by the Wakefield Master; nor is this hard to understand. Unlike the others, it is a second and more mature treatment of a subject which he had already handled. In *The First Shepherds' Play* of the Towneley group he had already told the Nativity story in a form similar to that which appears in other cycles: the three shepherds greet one another, converse, dine, fall asleep, are awakened by the angel, imitate his song, and proceed to Bethlehem, where they give their presents to the Christ Child. These traditional incidents are included in the second as well as the first of the Towneley shepherd plays; but in returning to familiar material the Wakefield Master has also improved on himself by adding, probably from English folklore, the episode of Mak and the stolen sheep. And the Mak episode, with its dramatic skill, its nice delineation of character, and the brilliant juxtaposition of its profane theme with the sacred parallel of the Nativity, is what ensures *The Second Shepherds' Play* a pre-eminence in any discussion of the early English drama.

The best edition of the complete *Towneley Plays* is that published by the Early English Text Society, ed. George England and Alfred W. Pollard (London, 1897); *The Second Shepherds' Play* has been published with other miracles on the same subject in *English Nativity Plays,* ed. Samuel B. Hemingway (New York, 1909). For a minute and comprehensive survey of the early drama see Edmund K. Chambers, *The Medieval Stage* (Oxford, 1903). A briefer treatment is to be found in *English Miracle Plays and Moralities,* by E. H. Moore (1907).

CHARACTERS

FIRST SHEPHERD	GILL, *Mak's wife*
SECOND SHEPHERD	THE VIRGIN MARY
THIRD SHEPHERD	THE CHRIST CHILD
MAK	AN ANGEL

[1]Modernized by Rudolf Gottfried.

FIRST SHEPHERD. Lord, but these weathers are cold! And I am ill-wrapped,
Almost frozen, behold, so long have I napped;
My legs crack and fold; my fingers are chapped;

It is not as I would, for I am all lapped
In sorrow. 5
In storms and tempest,
Now in east, now in west,
Woe to him has no rest
Midday or morrow.

But we simple sheephands that walk on the moor, 10
In faith, we are husbands[2] out of the door!
No wonder, as it stands, if we be poor;
For the tilth of our lands fallow lies as the floor.
You ken,
We are so lamed, 15
O'er-taxed and maimed,
We are made hand-tamed
By these gentry men.

Thus they rob us of rest—Our Lady them harry!
Those who are lord-possessed, they cause the plow tarry. 20
That, men say, is for the best; we find it contrary.
Thus are husbandmen pressed in point to miscarry
While alive.
Thus hold they us under;
Thus they bring us in blunder; 25
It were great wonder
If e'er should we thrive.

There shall come a swain, a peacock for show;
He must borrow my wain, my plow also;
Then am I full fain to grant ere he go. 30
Thus live we in pain, anger, and woe,
By night and by day.
He must have, if he sigh
For what I lose thereby;
It were better to die 35
Than once say him nay.

For if he get a painted sleeve or a brooch now-a-days,
Woe to who would him grieve or him once gainsays!
Dares no man him reprove however he brays;
And yet may no man believe one word that he says, 40
One letter.
He can find sustenance,
With boast and bragrance;
And all is through maintenance
By men that are greater. 45

It does me good, as I walk thus on my own,
Of this world for to talk in manner of moan.
To my sheep will I stalk and hearken anon;
There abide on a balk,[3] or sit on a stone
Full soon. 50
For I trow, pardie,
True men if they be,
We get more company
Ere it be noon.

SECOND SHEPHERD. Bless me! Lord bless us! What may this all mean? 55
Why fares the world thus? Oft have we not seen!
Lord, this wind is malicious, and the weather full keen;
And the frosts are so vicious my eyes water e'en;
No lie.
Now in dry, now in wet, 60
Now in snow, now in sleet,
When shoes freeze to my feet,
Small ease then have I.

But as far as I ken, ere yet as I go,
We poor married men do suffer much woe; 65
We have sorrow now and then, oft it falls so.
Good Capel, our hen, both to and fro
She cackles;
But begin she to chuck,
To grumble or cluck, 70
Woe be to our cock,
For he's in the shackles.

These men that are wed have not all their will.
When they're badly bestead, they sigh very still.
God knows, they are led full hard and full ill; 75
In bedroom or bed they say not their fill.
By now
My part have I found,
Can my lesson expound:
Woe to him that is bound, 80
For he must all allow.

But now late in our lives—a marvel to me,
That I think my heart rives such wonders to see,

[2]Husbandmen.

[3]A ridge between furrows.

What our destiny drives, that so it should be!—
Some men have two wives, and some men have three 85
In store.
Some are sad that have any!
But so far as I ken, he
Too is sad that has many,
For he feels it sore. 90

But, young men a-wooing, as God saved you and bought,
Beware well of wedding, and think in your thought:
"Had I wist" is a thing which serves you for naught.
Much silent mourning has wedding home brought,
Cause to misgive 95
With many a sharp shower;
For ye may catch in an hour
What shall savor full sour
As long as ye live.

For, if I read e'er epistle,[4] I have one for my dear 100
As sharp as a thistle, as rough as a briar;
She is browed like a bristle, with a sour-faced cheer;
Had she once wet her whistle, she could sing full clear
Her Pater Noster.
She is as great as a whale; 105
She has a gallon of gall;
By Him that died for us all,
I would I had run till I lost her!

FIRST SHEPHERD. God! as ever I saw!
Full deafly you stand.
SECOND SHEPHERD. Yea, the devil in thy maw! So behindhand 110
Saw thou anywhere Daw?
FIRST SHEPHERD. Yea, from a pasture-land
His horn heard I draw near, for he comes at hand
Over there.
Stand still.
SECOND SHEPHERD. Why?
FIRST SHEPHERD. For he comes, hope I. 115
SECOND SHEPHERD. He will tell us both a lie
Unless we beware.

THIRD SHEPHERD. Christ's cross me speed, and St. Nicholas!
Thereof have I need; it is worse than it was.
Whoso knows it, take heed and let the world pass; 120
Uncertain at need and brittle as glass,
It slides.
This world fared never so,
With marvels that grow,
Now in weal, now in woe; 125
For nothing abides.

Were never since Noah's flood such floods seen,
Winds and rains ne'er so rude, and storms ne'er so keen!
Some have stammered, some stood in doubt, as I ween.
Now God turn all to good! I say as I mean; 130
For ponder
How these floods will drown
All in field and town,
How they bear all down;
And that is a wonder. 135

We that walk in the nights our cattle to keep,
We see sudden sights when other men sleep.
Yet methinks my heart lights; I see rascals peep.
Ye are two tall wights! I will lead my sheep
To and fro. 140
No more discontent;
As I walk on this bent,[5]
I may quickly repent
If I stub my toe.

Ah, sir, God you save! and you, master mine! 145
A drink do I crave and somewhat to dine.
FIRST SHEPHERD. Christ's curse, my knave, thou ill servant mine!
SECOND SHEPHERD. What! the boy would rave? Think not to dine
Before we have done.
Ill luck on thy pate! 150
Though the rogue came late,
Yet is he in state
For his meal,—had he one.

THIRD SHEPHERD. Such servants as I, that sweat, toil, and stink,
Eat our bread very dry; and that makes me think. 155
We are oft wet and weary when master-men wink;[6]

[4]Apostolical epistle in the New Testament.

[5]Field. [6]Sleep.

Yet comes not full early either dinner or drink.
But straight
Both our dame and our sire,
When we have run in the mire, 160
Take a nip from our hire
And pay us full late.

But hear my oath, master: for the table you lay,
I shall do thereafter,—work as you pay;
I a little shall do, sir, and between times shall play; 165
For on stomach my supper did never yet weigh
Afield.
Why argue should I?
With my staff can I fly;
Men say, "Dealings sly 170
Poorly yield."

FIRST SHEPHERD. Thou wert an ill lad to ride a-wooing
With a master that had but little for spending.
SECOND SHEPHERD. Peace, boy, I bad! No more of this babbling,
Or I shall make thee afraid, by the heavens' great King, 175
With thy gauds.[7]
Where are our sheep, boy, for scorn?
THIRD SHEPHERD. Sir, this same day at morn
I them left in the corn
When the bells rang for lauds.[8] 180

They have pasture good; they cannot go wrong.
FIRST SHEPHERD. That is right. By the rood, these nights are too long!
Ere we parted I would that one gave us a song.
SECOND SHEPHERD. So I thought as I stood, to make mirth us among.
THIRD SHEPHERD. I grant. 185
FIRST SHEPHERD. I the tenor will try.
SECOND SHEPHERD. And I the treble so high.
THIRD SHEPHERD. Then the mid-part am I.
Let's hear how ye chant.

(MAK *enters with a cloak covering his ordinary dress.*)

MAK. Now, Lord, by Thy names seven, who mad'st both moon and sun, 190
From Thy will am I riven by things whose names I shun.
My wits are oft hard-driven; luck have I none.
Now would God I were in heaven, where weeps no little one,
In quiet still.
FIRST SHEPHERD. Who is't that pipes so poor? 195
MAK. If ye wist what I endure!
FIRST SHEPHERD. Lo, a man that walks on the moor
And has not all his will.
SECOND SHEPHERD. Mak, where hast thou gone? Tell us tiding.
THIRD SHEPHERD. Is he come? Let every one take heed for his thing. 200

(*He takes the cloak from him.*)

MAK. What! Ich[9] be a yeoman, Ich tell you, of the king;
The self-same, a henchman sent by a great lording
So rich.
Fie on you! Go hence!
Out of my presence! 205
Ich must have reverence,
And you ask who be Ich!

FIRST SHEPHERD. Why mak'st thou this feint? Mak, thou dost wrong.
SECOND SHEPHERD. List thou, Mak, play the saint? For that well may'st thou long.
THIRD SHEPHERD. The rogue can false paint! Him the devil should have hung. 210
MAK. Ich shall make complaint, and have your withers all wrung
At a word.
And tell e'en how ye doth.
FIRST SHEPHERD. But, Mak, is that truth?
Now take out that southern tooth, 215
And put in a turd!

SECOND SHEPHERD. Mak, the devil take thee! A stroke would I lend thee.
THIRD SHEPHERD. Mak, know'st thou not me? By God, I could shend thee.
MAK. God save you all three! Methought I had kenned ye.
Ye are a fair company.
FIRST SHEPHERD. Can memory mend thee? 220

[7] Tricks.

[8] The first canonical service of the day, held just before dawn.

[9] To deceive the shepherds, Mak adopts the southern pronunciation of the first person singular pronoun. Allusion is made to it in line 215.

SECOND SHEPHERD. A fine sham!
Thus late as thou goes,
What will men suppose?
Thou art thought one who knows
About stealing a lamb. 225

MAK. That I am true as steel all men surely wot!
But a sickness I feel that keeps me full hot;
My belly turns from a meal; in good state it is not.
THIRD SHEPHERD. Seldom lies the de'il really dead on the spot.
MAK. Full sore 230
Am I therefore and ill
If I stand stone-still;
I've not eaten my fill
This month and more.

FIRST SHEPHERD. How fares thy wife? By my hood, how does she do? 235
MAK. Lies lolling, by the rood, near the fire unto.
And a house full of brood! She drinks quite well too.
Ill speed other good that, besides these few,
She will do!
Eats she as fast as a rat; 240
And each year it comes pat,
She brings forth a brat,—
And some years it's two.

But had I more than would glut, and were richer by much,
I were eaten out of hut and also of hutch. 245
Yet is she a foul slut, if you come close to touch;
Worse wife, in what is known of all such,
Than any.
Now will ye see what I proffer?
To give all in my coffer 250
And tomorrow it offer
For her funeral penny.

SECOND SHEPHERD. I wot so tired a lad is none in this shire.
I would sleep, though I had less for my hire.
THIRD SHEPHERD. I am cold and unclad, and would fain have a fire. 255
FIRST SHEPHERD. I am weary and sad with running the mire.
Watch ye.

SECOND SHEPHERD. Nay, I'll lie down nearby,
For I must sleep now, no lie.
THIRD SHEPHERD. As good a man's son was I 260
As each of you be.

But, Mak, come hither. Between us thou shalt lie firmer.
MAK. Then might I be a screen, if ye would murmur.[10]

. . .

Me indeed,
Top to toe, end to end, 265
"Into thy hands I commend,"[11]
Pontius Pilate, my friend.
Christ's cross me speed!

(*While the* SHEPHERDS *sleep, he arises and says:*)

Now were time for a man that lacks what he'd hold
To privily plan, then stalk to a fold, 270
Nimbly do what he can, and be not too bold;
What as bargain began might cost dear, if 'twere told,
At the ending.
Better do now than tell;
But he needs good counsel 275
That fain would fare well
And has little for spending.

Draw about you a circle as round as a moon;
Till I have done what I will, until it be noon,
Here lie ye stone-still, until I have done;
And aloud I will of good words a rune 281
Recite:
Over your heads my hand I lift.
Out go your eyes! Blind be your sight!—
But yet I must make better shift 285
If it be right.

Lord, how hard they do sleep! that may ye all hear.
Never did I tend sheep; now begins my career.
Though fear make the flock leap, yet shall I steal near.
How! It hither does creep! Now mends our good cheer 290
From sorrow.

---

[10]At this point there appear to be some lines omitted in the original.

[11]A parody of Luke, 23:46.

A fat sheep, I dare say!
A good fleece I waylay!
When I can I'll repay,
But this will I borrow. 295

How, Gill, art thou in? Get us some light.
MAK'S WIFE. Who makes such a din this time of the night?
I am settled to spin; there's no hope that I might
By rising now win a penny. Loud curses light
On such lobs! 300
A housewife's not seated
But to rise she's entreated!
Here is no work completed
For such little jobs.

MAK. Good wife, ope the door. Seest thou not what I cart? 305
WIFE. Thyself draw the latch, I implore.
Ah, come in, my sweetheart!
MAK. Yea, thou cared not how sore long standing might be on my part.
WIFE. By the bare neck much more art thou like for to smart.
MAK. Away!
I am worthy my meat; 310
In a pinch can I get
More than they who toil and sweat
All the long day.

Thus it fell to my lot; I had; Gill, such grace!
WIFE. It were a foul blot to be hanged for disgrace. 315
MAK. Oft as hard a swat, Gill, have I dared to outface.
WIFE. But so long goes the pot to the water, always
At last
Comes it home broken.
MAK. Well know I the token; 320
Let it never be spoken,
But come and help fast.

I would he were slain; I list well to eat.
This year have I not been more fain of good sheep's meat.
WIFE. Come they ere he be slain and hear the sheep bleat,— 325
MAK. Then might I be ta'en! That were not very sweet.
The door
Go fasten.
WIFE. Yes. Mak,
For if they come at thy back,—
MAK. Then might I get from the pack 330
The devil and more!

WIFE. A good trick have I spied, since thou hast none of thy own.
Here shall we hide him till they be gone;
In my cradle he'll bide; let me alone,
And I'll lie him beside in childbed, and groan. 335
MAK. Well thought!
And I shall say that this night
Thy boy child saw the light.
WIFE. Now that day was bright
When forth was I brought: 340

This is a clever device and a subtle cast![12]
Always a woman's advice gives help at the last!
I care never who spies. Back again go thou fast.
MAK. Unless I come ere they rise, it will blow a cold blast.
I'll go sleep. 345
Still sleeps all this crew;
Privily stalk I thereto,
As though I never knew
Who bore off their sheep.

FIRST SHEPHERD. *Resurrex a mortruis!*[13]
Take hold of my hand. 350
Iudas carnas dominus! I may not well stand.
My foot sleeps, by Jesus; and a drink would be grand.
Methought sleep did seize us full near to England.
SECOND SHEPHERD. Ah me!
Lord, how sleep does one heal! 355
As fresh as an eel,
As light I now feel
As a leaf on a tree.

THIRD SHEPHERD. Blessings be herein!
So my body doth quake;
My heart is out of my skin; it throbs as if it would break. 360
Who makes all this din? Black grow my brows and they ache.
I'll find the doer of sin. Hark, fellows, awake!
We were four:
Saw ye aught of Mak now?
FIRST SHEPHERD. We were up ere thou. 365

[12]Trick.

[13]The italicized words in this and the following line are Scriptural tags in a corrupt Latin.

SECOND SHEPHERD. Man, I give God a vow,
Mak stayed here to snore.

THIRD SHEPHERD. Methought he was lapped in a wolf's skin.
FIRST SHEPHERD. So have many been wrapped ere now—namely, within.
THIRD SHEPHERD. When we had long napped, methought with a gin[14] 370
A fat sheep he trapped; but he made no din.
SECOND SHEPHERD. Be still!
Dreams like thine are mad and delude;
Mere fancy it is, by the rood.
FIRST SHEPHERD. Now God turn all to good, 375
If so be his will.

SECOND SHEPHERD. Rise, Mak! For shame! thou liest right long.
MAK. Now Christ's holy name be us among!
What is this, by St. James? I may not move along!
I trow I be the same. Oh, my neck, wry and wrong 380
Has it lain.
Many thanks! Since yestereven,
Now by St. Stephen,
With a dream's sour leaven
My poor heart was slain. 385

I thought Gill gan to croak and travail full sad,
Well-nigh at first cock, of another young lad
For to fill out our flock. Then I never am glad;
I have more tow on my rock[15] than ever I had.
Oh, my head! 390
A house full of young fat!
The devil knock their skulls flat!
Woe to him has much brat,
And withal little bread!

I must go home, by your leave, if Gill is as I thought. 395
I pray you, search my sleeve that I steal naught;
I am loth you to grieve or take from you aught.

THIRD SHEPHERD. Go forth; ill luck to thee cleave! Now would I we sought
This morn
That we had all our store. 400
FIRST SHEPHERD. But I'll go before;
Let us meet—
SECOND SHEPHERD. Where?
THIRD SHEPHERD. Afore
The old crooked thorn.

MAK. Undo this door! Who is there?
How long shall I stand?
WIFE. Whose voice splits my ear? In the old moon[16] go stand! 405
MAK. Ah, Gill, what cheer? It is I, Mak, your husband.
WIFE. Then may we see here how the devil has planned:
Sir Guile,
Lo, thou com'st with a croak
As though a rope made thee choke. 410
I may not sit at my yoke
The scantiest while.

MAK. Will ye hear how she fakes with her fuss and her pose?
Naught but pleasure she takes and scratches her toes.
WIFE. Why, who walks, and who wakes?
Who comes, and who goes? 415
Who brews, and who bakes? Who makes me thus hose?
Besides
It is sad to behold,
Now in hot, now in cold,
How woeful the household 420
That no woman guides.

But what end hast thou made with the shepherds, Mak?
MAK. The last word that they said, when I turned my back,
Was they'd look that no raid had been made on their pack.
I hope they be not well paid when they their sheep lack, 425
Pardie.
But howso the game goes,
My guilt must they suppose,
And loudly expose,
And cry out upon me. 430

But perform thou thy plight.

---

[14]Device.
[15]Distaff.

[16]The wane of the moon was considered an unlucky period.

WIFE. I agree to it still;
I shall swaddle him right, as though for the chill.
If it needed more sleight, yet had I the skill.
I'll lie down forthright. Come wrap me.
MAK. I will.
WIFE. Behind! 435
Come Coll and his whelp,
They will nip us and yelp.
MAK. But I may cry out, "Help, help!"
The sheep if they find.

WIFE. Hearken aye till they call, for they will come anon. 440
Go and make ready all, and sing thou alone;
Lullaby shalt thou bawl, while my part is to groan
And cry out by the wall on Mary and John,
Stricken sore.
Sing lullaby fast 445
When thou hear'st them at last;
And but I play a false cast,
Trust me no more!

THIRD SHEPHERD. Ah, Coll, good morn! Why sleepest thou not?
FIRST SHEPHERD. Alas, that e'er was I born! we have a foul blot. 450
A fat sheep has been torn from us.
THIRD SHEPHERD. Lord, say it not!
SECOND SHEPHERD. Who could show us that scorn? That were a foul spot.
FIRST SHEPHERD. Some shrew.[17]
With my dogs did I wake
All Horbury brake, 455
And for fifteen lambs o'ertake
But one little ewe.

THIRD SHEPHERD. Now trust me if ye will: by St. Thomas of Kent
Either Mak or Gill did this theft invent.
FIRST SHEPHERD. Peace, man! Be still!
I saw when he went. 460
Thou slander'st him ill. Thou ought'st to repent
With speed.
SECOND SHEPHERD. Now as ever I thrive,
Though my death here arrive,
I say that of any alive 465
Mak did that same deed.

THIRD SHEPHERD. Straight to his farmstead let us run on our feet.

[17]Rogue.

Shall I never eat bread the truth till I weet.
FIRST SHEPHERD. Nor I drink in my head with him till I meet.
SECOND SHEPHERD. I will rest in no bed until I him greet, 470
My brother.
One thing will I plight:
Till I see him in sight
Shall I ne'er sleep one night
Where I slept another. 475

THIRD SHEPHERD. Will ye hear how they croak? Our sire would croon.
FIRST SHEPHERD. Heard I never voice crack so clear out of tune!
Call on him.
SECOND SHEPHERD. Mak! undo your door soon.
MAK. Who is that who spoke as if it were noon,
Loud and aloft? 480
Who is that, I say?
THIRD SHEPHERD. Good fellows, were it day—
MAK. As far as ye may,
I beg you, speak soft

O'er a sick woman's head that is at ill ease; 485
I had rather be dead than her torments increase.
WIFE. Go elsewhere, I said. I may not well wheeze:
Each step that ye tread does my breathing displease
And impair.
FIRST SHEPHERD. Tell us, Mak, if you may, 490
How fare you, I say?
MAK. Are ye in this quarter today?
Now how do ye fare?

Ye have run in the mire, and are wet as my spit.
I shall make you a fire if ye care for to sit. 495
A nurse would I hire: know ye one who is fit?
Well quit is my hire: my dream—this is it,
In season.
I have babes, as ye knew,
Many more than a few; 500
But we must drink as we brew,
And that is but reason.

I would ye dined ere ye wend. Methinks that ye sweat.

SECOND SHEPHERD. Nay, our mood would not mend if we drank or we eat.
MAK. Why, does aught ail my friend?
THIRD SHEPHERD. Yea, our sheep that we get 505
Have been stollen unkenned. Our loss is hard met.
MAK. Sirs, now drink!
Had I also been there,
Sore had some paid their fare.
FIRST SHEPHERD. Marry, some men trow that you were; 510
And that gives us to think.

SECOND SHEPHERD. Mak, one well trows that thou it should be.
THIRD SHEPHERD. Either thou or thy spouse, so say we.
MAK. Now if ye smell a mouse on Gill or on me,
Come and rip up our house, and then may ye see 515
Who's afraid.
If any sheep stole I somehow,
Either bullock or cow
(For Gill has not risen now
Since her head was here laid), 520

As I true am like steel, to God here I pray
That this be the first meal I shall eat on this day.[18]
FIRST SHEPHERD. Mak, as I hope for my weal, consider, I say:
He learned early to steal that could not say nay.
WIFE. I faint! 525
Out, thieves, from my dwelling!
Ye come to rob with your yelling.
MAK. Her grief hear ye not swelling?
Your hearts should melt at her plaint.

WIFE. From my babe, thieves, for scorn!
Draw not near to explore! 530
MAK. Wist ye what she had borne, your hearts would be sore.
Ye do wrong, I you warn, that ye thus come before
One whom her labors have torn. But I say no more!
WIFE. Oh, my middle!
I pray God so mild, 535
If you e'er I beguiled,
That I eat this child
That lies in this cradle.

MAK. Peace, woman, by God's pain! and cry not so!
Thou dost harm to thy brain, and fill'st me with woe. 540
SECOND SHEPHERD. I trow our sheep be slain. What find ye two though?
THIRD SHEPHERD. All work we in vain; as well may we go.
But I swear
I can find no flesh,
Hard or nesh,[19] 545
Salt or fresh,
But two plates that are bare.

Living cattle but this,[20] rough or mild,
Here is none which, iwis, as our sheep smells so wild.
WIFE. No, so God give me bliss and joy of my child! 550
FIRST SHEPHERD. We've proceeded amiss; I hold us beguiled.
SECOND SHEPHERD. So have we done.
Sir, Our Lady him save:
Is it a boy that Gill gave?
MAK. Any lord might well crave 555
This child for his son.

When he wakens he grips, it is joy to espy.
THIRD SHEPHERD. Good luck to his hips and happiness high!
But who were his gossips,[21] so ready and nigh?
MAK. Blessed be their lips!
FIRST SHEPHERD. Hark now, a lie! 560
MAK. So God give them thanks:
Perkin and Gibbon Waller,[22] I say,
And gentle John Horn,—in his way
He made all the horseplay
With his great shanks. 565

SECOND SHEPHERD. Mak, friends will we be, for we are at one.
MAK. We! for my part I shall see when amends have begun.
Farewell, all three! I'd be glad were ye gone!
THIRD SHEPHERD. Fair words may there be, but love is there none
This year. 570
FIRST SHEPHERD. Gave ye the child anything?

[18]Here Mak probably points to the cradle.

[19]Soft.

[20]He probably points to the cradle.

[21]Sponsors at baptism.

[22]The names of two of the shepherds in the "First Shepherds' Play" of the same cycle.

SECOND SHEPHERD. I trow, not one farthing.

THIRD SHEPHERD. Back again will I fling;
Abide for me here.[23]

Thy child, Mak, I'd see; receive it not ill nor in spite. 575

MAK. Nay, me thou didst disbelieve, and thou dost me great slight.

THIRD SHEPHERD. The child will not grieve, that day-star so bright.
Mak, by thy leave, let me give thy sweet mite
But six pence.

MAK. Nay, get away! He sleeps. 580

THIRD SHEPHERD. Methinks that he peeps.

MAK. When he wakens he weeps.
I pray thee, go hence.

THIRD SHEPHERD. Give me leave him to kiss, and lift up the clout.
What the devil is this? he has a long snout! 585

FIRST SHEPHERD. He is shapen amiss.
Why wait longer about?

SECOND SHEPHERD. From ill-spun woof, iwis, aye comes foul out.
Ay, so!
He is like to our sheep!

THIRD SHEPHERD. How, Gib? may I peep? 590

FIRST SHEPHERD. I trow, nature will creep
Where it may not go!

SECOND SHEPHERD. This was a shrewd gaud and a subtle cast!
It was a high fraud!

THIRD SHEPHERD. Yea, sirs, I'm aghast.
Let's burn her, this bawd, and bind her fast. 595
A false scold, by God, will hang at the last!
So shalt thou.
Will ye see how they swaddled
His four feet, and remodeled?
In cradle ne'er saw I coddled 600
A horned lad ere now!

MAK. Peace bid I! What! Let be your fanfare!
It was I him begot, and yonder woman him bare.

FIRST SHEPHERD. What name has the tot?
"Mak"? Lo, God, Mak's heir!

SECOND SHEPHERD. With the rascal joke not. Now God give him care, 605
I say.

WIFE. As pretty a child is he
As sits on a woman's knee;
A dillydown darling, pardie,
To make a man gay. 610

THIRD SHEPHERD. I know him by the earmark; that is a good token.

MAK. I tell you, sirs, hark! his nose was born broken;
A scholar since made the remark he is by magic forspoken.

FIRST SHEPHERD. This is work false and dark. Would I had a good oaken
Staff! 615

WIFE. He was changed by an elf;
I saw it myself.
When the clock had struck twelve
He became a moon-calf.

SECOND SHEPHERD. Ye two, it is plain, are endowed with one vice. 620

THIRD SHEPHERD. Since their theft they maintain, let death be the price.

MAK. If I trespass again, off with my head in a trice!
At your will I remain.

FIRST SHEPHERD. Sirs, take my advice:
For this cheat
We will neither curse nor accuse, 625
Neither fight nor abuse,
But suddenness use,
And him toss in a sheet.[24]

Lord, but I'm sore! I shall burst at the wrist.
In faith, I can do no more; I shall therefore desist. 630

SECOND SHEPHERD. As a sheep of seven score pounds he weighed in my fist.
Anywhere for to snore methinks that I list.

THIRD SHEPHERD. Now I pray,
Lie down on this green.

FIRST SHEPHERD. On these thieves my thoughts lean. 635

THIRD SHEPHERD. Why not be serene?
Come do as I say!

(An ANGEL *sings "Glory to God in the highest"; then let him say:)*

ANGEL. Arise, ye who kindly tend sheep! for now is He born

---

[23]The third shepherd goes to Mak's dwelling, while the other two follow more slowly.

[24]Here Mak must be tossed by the shepherds.

That shall from the fiend rend what Adam
had lorn;
The devil to shend this night is he born; 640
God is made your friend even now on this
morn.
He doth ordain
That ye to Bethlehem go,
Where lies a babe high-born, though
In a poor manger low 645
Between cattle twain.

FIRST SHEPHERD. This voice had a spell
like none I e'er heard.
It is a marvel to tell, thus to be stirred.
SECOND SHEPHERD. About God's Son now
fell from heaven his word.
Methought the whole dell his lightening
did gird 650
In a streak.
THIRD SHEPHERD. Of a child did I hear
In Bethlehem, near.
FIRST SHEPHERD. Yon star makes it clear;
Let us thither him seek. 655

SECOND SHEPHERD. Say, what was his song?
Heard ye not how he sang it,
Three breves to a long?[25]
THIRD SHEPHERD. Yea, he did twang it;
Was no crotchet[26] wrong; none might
better clang it.
FIRST SHEPHERD. For to sing us among,
right as he rang it,
I know how. 660
SECOND SHEPHERD. Let us hear how you
croon.
Can you bark at the moon?
THIRD SHEPHERD. Hold your tongue, loon!
FIRST SHEPHERD. Sing after me now.

SECOND SHEPHERD. He to Bethlehem bad
that we move right along; 665
Some fear have I had that we tarry too
long.
THIRD SHEPHERD. Be merry, not sad; of
mirth is our song;
Eternity glad to us shall belong
For reward.
FIRST SHEPHERD. Then hie we in humor
mild, 670
Though wet and weary and wild,
To that mother and child.
Ill we that loss could afford.

SECOND SHEPHERD. We find by the prophecy—let be your din!—
Of David, Isaiah, and nigh more than my
mind holds within, 675
They prophecied by learning high that in
a virgin
Should He light and lie, to slacken our sin
And to slake it,
Our nature, from woe.
For Isaiah said so: 680
"A virgin, lo,
Shall conceive"[27] a child that is
naked.

THIRD SHEPHERD. Full glad may we be,
and await that day
That dear one to see that all powers will
sway.
Lord, well were me, for now and for
aye, 685
Might I kneel on my knee some word for
to say
To that child.
But the angel bewrayed
In a crib was he laid;
He was poorly arrayed, 690
Both meek and mild.

FIRST SHEPHERD. Patriarchs that have been
and prophets outworn,
They desired to have seen this child that
is born.
They are gone full clean, and that have
they lorn.
We shall see him, I ween, ere it be
morn, 695
For a token.
When I see him and feel,
I shall know in my zeal
It is true as steel
What the prophets have spoken: 700

That he to ones so bare as we would
appear;
Them first find and declare by his messenger dear.
SECOND SHEPHERD. Go we now; let us
fare. The place is nigh here.
THIRD SHEPHERD. I am ready and ware;
let's together draw near
To that boy. 705
Lord, if Thy will it be,—
We are untaught all three,—
Grant for our comfort that we
Have in some kind this joy.

FIRST SHEPHERD. Hail, comely and clean!
Hail, thou young child! 710

[25]Breves were short musical notes, three of which were equivalent to a long note.

[26]A note one eighth as long as a breve.

[27]Isaiah, 7:14.

Hail, Maker! born hast thou been from a maiden so mild!
Thou hast cursed, as I ween, the devil so wild;
The false beguiler is seen where now goes he beguiled.
How merry's!
Lo, laughs he, my sweeting! 715
Most happy this meeting,
My promise completing!
Have a bob of these cherries!

SECOND SHEPHERD. Hail, sovereign Savior, for thou hast us sought!
Hail, noble scion and flower, that all things hast wrought! 720
Hail, thou full of favor, that mad'st all of nought!
Hail! I kneel and I cower. A bird have I brought
To my child.
Hail, thou wee little mite!
Of our creed thou the height! 725
May thy cup me requite,
Thou day-star so mild!

THIRD SHEPHERD. Hail, darling dear, delight of our creed!
I pray thee be near when I have the need.
Hail! Sweet is thy cheer! My heart nigh would bleed 730
To see thee sit here in so poor a weed,[28]
With no pennies.
Hail! thy fist stretch forth small.
Thee I bring but a ball:
Have it and play withal, 735
And use it for tennis.

MARY. The Father of heavenly light, God omnipotent,
That set all things aright, his Son has he sent.
He named me; his Sprite had begot ere he went;
And e'en through his might I conceived as he meant; 740
Now he is born.
May he keep you from woe!
I shall pray him do so.
Tell it forth as ye go,
And remember this morn. 745

FIRST SHEPHERD. Farewell, lady, to thee, so fair to behold
With thy child on thy knee.
SECOND SHEPHERD. But he lies very cold,
Lord, well is me! Now we must go, behold.
THIRD SHEPHERD. Forsooth, new though it be, it seems it was told
Full oft. 750
FIRST SHEPHERD. What grace have we found!
SECOND SHEPHERD. Come forth; now are we sound!
THIRD SHEPHERD. To sing are we bound:
Sing aloud and aloft!

Here ends the pageant of the shepherds.

[28] Garment.

EVERYMAN

The authorship of *Everyman* is not known. The play made its appearance some time during the fifteenth century. Its text is preserved in four early editions, none of which is dated, though all must have appeared between 1493 and 1537—dates which mark the limits of the period during which the two printers of the editions, Pynson and Skot, did their work. It is considered probable by some scholars that *Everyman* is a translation of a Dutch play, *Elckerlijk* (ascribed to Dorlandus), which was in print before the earliest edition of *Everyman.* This, however, is by no means certain, as *Everyman* may be really the earlier of the two, or both may go back to some common source now unknown. The importance of this unsettled question, moreover, may easily be exaggerated, inasmuch as *Everyman* as it now stands is a thoroughly English play, with none of the earmarks of a mere translation, and has its inherent right to the place it has won in English literature.

The English moralities, of which *Everyman* is an outstanding example, were in the beginning vehicles of religious and moral instruction; later the type was made the instrument of religious controversy and was also used in exhibiting the value of learning. The chief theme of the earlier moralities was the life of man conceived as a conflict between good and evil, a conflict which begins with birth and ends only with death. In its entirety this is a practically endless subject, and writers tended to narrow its scope, with a proportionate gain in simplicity of structure, in directness, and in power. Thus some moralities exhibit a crucial conflict between two groups, virtues and vices, for possession of the soul of man. Another plan was to picture the coming of death, and this is done in *Everyman.* The play shows the measure of dramatic quality and power which the morality was capable of attaining when it was at its best.

A good text of *Everyman* may be found in *Chief Pre-Shakespearean Dramas,* ed. Joseph Q. Adams (Boston, 1924), pp. 288–303. For a discussion of the play and its background see C. F. Tucker Brooke, *The Tudor Drama; a History of English National Drama to the Retirement of Shakespeare* (Boston, 1911).

CHARACTERS

EVERYMAN	STRENGTH
GOD: ADONAI	DISCRETION
DEATH	FIVE-WITS
MESSENGER	BEAUTY
FELLOWSHIP	KNOWLEDGE
COUSIN	CONFESSION
KINDRED	ANGEL
GOODS	DOCTOR
GOOD-DEEDS	

Here beginneth a treatis how the High Father of Heaven sendeth death to summon every creature to come and give account of their lives in this world and is in manner of a moral play.

MESSENGER. I pray you all give your audience,
And hear this matter with reverence,
By figure a moral play—
The *Summoning of Everyman* called it is,
That of our lives and ending shows 5
How transitory we be all day.
This matter is wondrous precious,
But the intent of it is more gracious,
And sweet to bear away.
The story saith,—Man, in the beginning, 10
Look well, and take good heed to the ending,
Be you never so gay!
Ye think sin in the beginning full sweet,
Which in the end causeth thy soul to weep,
When the body lieth in clay. 15
Here shall you see how *Fellowship* and *Jollity,*
Both *Strength, Pleasure,* and *Beauty,*
Will fade from thee as flower in May.
For ye shall hear how our Heaven King
Calleth *Everyman* to a general reckoning: 20

Give audience, and hear what he doth say.
God. I perceive here in my majesty,
How that all creatures be to me unkind,
Living without dread in worldly prosperity:
Of ghostly sight[1] the people be so blind, 25
Drowned in sin, they know me not for their God;
In worldly riches is all their mind,
They fear not my rightwiseness, the sharp rod;
My law that I showed, when I for them died,
They forget clean, and shedding of my blood red; 30
I hanged between two, it cannot be denied;
To get them life I suffered to be dead;
I healed their feet, with thorns hurt was my head:
I could do no more than I did truly,
And now I see the people do clean forsake me. 35
They use the seven deadly sins damnable;
As pride, covetise, wrath, and lechery,
Now in the world be made commendable;
And thus they leave of angels the heavenly company; 39
Everyman liveth so after his own pleasure,
And yet of their life they be nothing sure:
I see the more that I them forbear
The worse they be from year to year;
All that liveth appaireth[2] fast,
Therefore I will in all the haste 45
Have a reckoning of Everyman's person;
For and I leave the people thus alone
In their life and wicked tempests,
Verily they will become much worse than beasts;
For now one would by envy another up eat; 50
Charity they all do clean forget.
I hoped well that Everyman
In my glory should make his mansion,
And thereto I had them all elect;
But now I see, like traitors deject, 55
They thank me not for the pleasure that I to them meant,
Nor yet for their being that I them have lent;
I proffered the people great multitude of mercy,
And few there be that asketh it heartily;
They be so cumbered with worldly riches, 60
That needs on them I must do justice,
On Everyman living without fear.
Where art thou, *Death,* thou mighty messenger?
Death. Almighty God, I am here at your will,
Your commandment to fulfil. 65
God. Go thou to *Everyman,*
And show him in my name
A pilgrimage he must on him take,
Which he in no wise may escape;
And that he bring with him a sure reckoning 70
Without delay or any tarrying.
Death. Lord, I will in the world go run over all,
And cruelly outsearch both great and small;
Every man will I beset that liveth beastly
Out of God's laws, and dreadeth not folly:
He that loveth riches I will strike with my dart, 76
His sight to blind, and from heaven to depart,
Except that alms be his good friend,
In hell for to dwell, world without end.
Lo, yonder I see *Everyman* walking; 80
Full little he thinketh on my coming;
His mind is on fleshly lusts and his treasure,
And great pain it shall cause him to endure
Before the Lord Heaven King.
Everyman, stand still; whither art thou going 85
Thus gaily? Hast thou thy Maker forget?
Everyman. Why askst thou?
Wouldest thou wete?[3]
Death. Yea, sir, I will show you;
In great haste I am sent to thee 90
From God out of his majesty.
Everyman. What, sent to me?
Death. Yea, certainly.
Though thou have forgot him here,
He thinketh on thee in the heavenly sphere, 95
As, or we depart, thou shalt know.
Everyman. What desireth God of me?
Death. That shall I show thee;
A reckoning he will needs have
Without any longer respite. 100
Everyman. To give a reckoning longer leisure I crave;
This blind matter troubleth my wit.
Death. On thee thou must take a long journey:

[1] Spiritual insight.
[2] Is impaired.
[3] Know.

Therefore thy book of count with thee
thou bring;
For turn again thou cannot by no way, 105
And look thou be sure of thy reckoning:
For before God thou shalt answer, and
show
Thy many bad deeds and good but a few;
How thou hast spent thy life, and in what
wise,
Before the chief lord of paradise. 110
Have ado that we were in that way,
For, wete thou well, thou shalt make none
attournay.[4]

EVERYMAN. Full unready I am such reckoning to give.
I know thee not: what messenger art thou?

DEATH. I am *Death,* that no man dreadeth.[5]
For every man I rest[6] and no man spareth;
For it is God's commandment 117
That all to me should be obedient.

EVERYMAN. O *Death,* thou comest when I
had thee least in mind;
In thy power it lieth me to save, 120
Yet of my good will I give thee, if ye will
be kind,
Yea, a thousand pound shalt thou have,
And defer this matter till another day.

DEATH. *Everyman,* it may not be by no
way;
I set not by gold, silver, nor riches, 125
Nor by pope, emperor, king, duke, nor
princes.
For and I would receive gifts great,
All the world I might get;
But my custom is clean contrary.
I give thee no respite: come hence, and not
tarry. 130

EVERYMAN. Alas, shall I have no longer
respite?
I may say *Death* giveth no warning:
To think on thee, it maketh my heart sick,
For all unready is my book of reckoning.
But twelve year and I might have abiding, 135
My counting book I would make so clear,
That my reckoning I should not need to
fear.
Wherefore, *Death,* I pray thee, for God's
mercy,
Spare me till I be provided of remedy.

DEATH. Thee availeth not to cry, weep, and
pray: 140
But haste thee lightly that you were gone
the journey,
And prove thy friends if thou can.
For, wete thou well, the tide abideth no
man,
And in the world each living creature
For *Adam's* sin must die of nature. 145

EVERYMAN. *Death,* if I should this pilgrimage take,
And my reckoning surely make,
Show me, for saint *charity,*
Should I not come again shortly?

DEATH. No, *Everyman;* and thou be once
there, 150
Thou mayst never more come here,
Trust me verily.

EVERYMAN. O gracious God, in the high
seat celestial,
Have mercy on me in this most need;
Shall I have no company from this vale
terrestrial 155
Of mine acquaintance that way me to lead?

DEATH. Yea, if any be so hardy,
That would go with thee and bear thee
company.
Hie thee that you were gone to God's
magnificence, 159
Thy reckoning to give before his presence.
What, weenest thou thy life is given thee,
And thy worldly goods also?

EVERYMAN. I had wend so, verily.

DEATH. Nay, nay; it was but lent thee;
For as soon as thou art go, 165
Another awhile shall have it, and then go
therefro
Even as thou hast done.
Everyman, thou art mad; thou hast thy
wits five,
And here on earth will not amend thy life,
For suddenly I do come. 170

EVERYMAN. O wretched caitiff, whither
shall I flee,
That I might scape this endless sorrow!
Now, gentle *Death,* spare me till tomorrow,
That I may amend me
With good advisement. 175

DEATH. Nay, thereto I will not consent,
Nor no man will I respite,
But to the heart suddenly I shall smite
Without any advisement.
And now out of thy sight I will me hie; 180
See thou make thee ready shortly,
For thou mayst say this is the day
That no man living may scape away.

EVERYMAN. Alas, I may well weep with
sighs deep;
Now have I no manner of company 185

[4] Mediator.
[5] That respecteth no man.
[6] Arrest.

To help me in my journey, and me to keep;
And also my writing is full unready.
How shall I do now for to excuse me?
I would to God I had never be gete![7]
To my soul a full great profit it had be; 190
For now I fear pains huge and great.
The time passeth; Lord, help that all wrought;
For though I mourn it availeth nought.
The day passeth, and is almost a-go;
I wot not well what for to do. 195
To whom were I best my complaint to make?
What, and I to *Fellowship* thereof spake,
And showed him of this sudden chance?
For in him is all mine affiance;
We have in the world so many a day 200
Be on good friends in sport and play.
I see him yonder, certainly;
I trust that he will bear me company;
Therefore to him will I speak to ease my sorrow.
Well met, good *Fellowship,* and good morrow! 205

FELLOWSHIP *speaketh. Everyman,* good morrow by this day.
Sir, why lookest thou so piteously?
If any thing be amiss, I pray thee, me say,
That I may help to remedy.

EVERYMAN. Yea, good *Fellowship,* yea, 210
I am in great jeopardy.

FELLOWSHIP. My true friend, show to me your mind;
I will not forsake thee, unto my life's end,
In the way of good company.

EVERYMAN. That was well spoken, and lovingly. 215

FELLOWSHIP. Sir, I must needs know your heaviness;
I have pity to see you in any distress;
If any have you wronged ye shall revenged be,
Though I on the ground be slain for thee,—
Though that I know before that I should die. 220

EVERYMAN. Verily, *Fellowship,* gramercy.

FELLOWSHIP. Tush! by thy thanks I set not a straw.
Show me your grief, and say no more.

EVERYMAN. If I my heart should to you break,
And then you to turn your mind from me,
And would not me comfort, when you hear me speak, 226
Then should I ten times sorrier be.

FELLOWSHIP. Sir, I say as I will do in deed.

EVERYMAN. Then be you a good friend at need:
I have found you true here before. 230

FELLOWSHIP. And so ye shall evermore;
For, in faith, and thou go to Hell,
I will not forsake thee by the way!

EVERYMAN. Ye speak like a good friend; I believe you well;
I shall deserve it, and I may. 235

FELLOWSHIP. I speak of no deserving, by this day.
For he that will say and nothing do
Is not worthy with good company to go;
Therefore show me the grief of your mind,
As to your friend most loving and kind. 240

EVERYMAN. I shall show you how it is;
Commanded I am to go a journey,
A long way, hard and dangerous,
And give a strait count without delay
Before the high judge Adonai.[8] 245
Wherefore I pray you, bear me company,
As ye have promised, in this journey.

FELLOWSHIP. That is matter indeed! Promise is duty,
But, and I should take such a voyage on me,
I know it well, it should be to my pain: 250
Also it make me afeard, certain.
But let us take counsel here as well as we can,
For your words would fear a strong man.

EVERYMAN. Why, ye said, If I had need,
Ye would me never forsake, quick nor dead, 255
Though it were to hell truly.

FELLOWSHIP. So I said, certainly,
But such pleasures be set aside, thee sooth to say:
And also, if we took such a journey,
When should we come again? 260

EVERYMAN. Nay, never again till the day of doom.

FELLOWSHIP. In faith, then will not I come there!
Who hath you these tidings brought?

EVERYMAN. Indeed, *Death* was with me here.

FELLOWSHIP. Now, by God that all hath bought,[9] 265
If *Death* were the messenger,
For no man that is living to-day
I will not go that loath journey—
Not for the father that begat me!

EVERYMAN. Ye promised other wise, pardie.

FELLOWSHIP. I wot well I say so truly; 271

[7]Been born.

[8]God. [9]Redeemed.

And yet if thou wilt eat, and drink, and make good cheer,
Or haunt to women, the lusty company,
I would not forsake you, while the day is clear,
Trust me verily! 275
EVERYMAN. Yea, thereto ye would be ready;
To go to mirth, solace, and play,
Your mind will sooner apply
Than to bear me company in my long journey.
FELLOWSHIP. Now, in good faith, I will not that way. 280
But and thou wilt murder, or any man kill,
In that I will help thee with a good will!
EVERYMAN. O that is a simple advice indeed!
Gentle *fellow,* help me in my necessity;
We have loved long, and now I need, 285
And now, gentle *Fellowship,* remember me.
FELLOWSHIP. Whether ye have loved me or no,
By Saint John, I will not with thee go.
EVERYMAN. Yet I pray thee, take the labor, and do so much for me
To bring me forward, for saint charity, 290
And comfort me till I come without the town.
FELLOWSHIP. Nay, and thou would give me a new gown,
I will not a foot with thee go;
But and you had tarried I would not have left thee so.
And as now, God speed thee in thy journey, 295
For from thee I will depart as fast as I may.
EVERYMAN. Whither away, *Fellowship?* will you forsake me?
FELLOWSHIP. Yea, by my fay, to God I betake[10] thee.
EVERYMAN. Farewell, good *Fellowship;* for this my heart is sore;
Adieu for ever, I shall see thee no more. 300
FELLOWSHIP. In faith, *Everyman,* farewell now at the end;
For you I will remember that parting is mourning.
EVERYMAN. Alack! shall we thus depart indeed?
Our Lady, help, without any more comfort,
Lo, *Fellowship* forsaketh me in my most need: 305
For help in this world whither shall I resort?
Fellowship herebefore with me would merry make;
And now little sorrow for me doth he take.
It is said, in prosperity men friends may find,
Which in adversity be full unkind. 310
Now whither for succor shall I flee,
Since that *Fellowship* hath forsaken me?
To my kinsmen I will truly,
Praying them to help me in my necessity;
I believe that they will do so, 315
For kind will creep where it may not go.
I will go say,[11] for yonder I see them go.
Where be ye now, my friends and kinsmen?
KINDRED. Here be we now at your commandment.
Cousin, I pray you show us your intent 320
In any wise, and not spare.
COUSIN. Yea, *Everyman,* and to us declare
If ye be disposed to go any whither,
For wete you well, we will live and die together.
KINDRED. In wealth and woe we will with you hold, 325
For over his kin a man may be bold.
EVERYMAN. Gramercy, my friends and kinsmen kind.
Now shall I show you the grief of my mind:
I was commanded by a messenger,
That is an high king's chief officer; 330
He bade me go a pilgrimage to my pain,
And I know well I shall never come again;
Also I must give a reckoning straight,
For I have a great enemy, that hath me in wait,
Which intendeth me for to hinder. 335
KINDRED. What account is that which ye must render?
That would I know.
EVERYMAN. Of all my works I must show
How I have lived and my days spent;
Also of ill deeds, that I have used 340
In my time, since life was me lent;
And of all virtues that I have refused.
Therefore I pray you go thither with me,
To help to make mine account, for saint *charity.*
COUSIN. What, to go thither? Is that the matter? 345
Nay, *Everyman,* I had liefer fast bread and water
All this five year and more.
EVERYMAN. Alas, that ever I was bore![12]

[10]Commit.

[11]Put it to the trial. [12]Born.

For now shall I never be merry
If that you forsake me. 350
KINDRED. Ah, sir; what, ye be a merry man!
Take good heart to you, and make no moan.
But one thing I warn you, by Saint Anne,
As for me, ye shall go alone.
EVERYMAN. My *Cousin,* will you not with me go? 355
COUSIN. No, by Our Lady; I have the cramp in my toe.
Trust not to me, for, so God me speed,
I will deceive you in your most need.
KINDRED. It availeth not us to tice. 359
Ye shall have my maid with all my heart;
She loveth to go to feasts, there to be nice,
And to dance, and abroad to start:
I will give her leave to help you in that journey,
If that you and she may agree.
EVERYMAN. Now show me the very effect of your mind. 365
Will you go with me, or abide behind?
KINDRED. Abide behind? yea, that I will and I may!
Therefore farewell until another day.
EVERYMAN. How should I be merry or glad?
For fair promises to me make, 370
But when I have most need, they me forsake.
I am deceived; that maketh me sad.
COUSIN. Cousin *Everyman,* farewell now,
For verily I will not go with you;
Also of mine own an unready reckoning 375
I have to account; therefore I make tarrying.
Now, God keep thee, for now I go.
EVERYMAN. Ah, *Jesus,* is all come hereto?
Lo, fair words maketh fools feign; 379
They promise and nothing will do certain.
My kinsmen promised me faithfully
For to abide with me steadfastly,
And now fast away do they flee:
Even so *Fellowship* promised me.
What friend were best me of to provide? 385
I lose my time here longer to abide.
Yet in my mind a thing there is;—
All my life I have loved riches;
If that my good now help me might,
He would make my heart full light. 390
I will speak to him in this distress.—
Where art thou, my *Goods* and riches?
GOODS. Who calleth me? *Everyman?* what haste thou hast.
I lie here in corners, trussed and piled so high,
And in chests I am locked so fast, 395
Also sacked in bags, thou mayst see with thine eye,
I cannot stir; in packs low I lie.
What would ye have, lightly me say.
EVERYMAN. Come hither, *Good,* in all the haste thou may,
For of counsel I must desire thee. 400
GOODS. Sir, and ye in the world have trouble or adversity,
That can I help you to remedy shortly.
EVERYMAN. It is another disease[13] that grieveth me;
In this world it is not, I tell thee so.
I am sent for another way to go, 405
To give a straight account general
Before the highest *Jupiter* of all;
And all my life I have had joy and pleasure in thee.
Therefore I pray thee go with me,
For, peradventure, thou mayst before God Almighty 410
My reckoning help to clean and purify;
For it is said ever among,
That money maketh all right that is wrong.
GOODS. Nay, *Everyman,* I sing another song,
I follow no man in such voyages; 415
For and I went with thee
Thou shouldst fare much the worse for me;
For because on me thou did set thy mind,
Thy reckoning I have made blotted and blind, 419
That thine account thou cannot make truly;
And that hast thou for the love of me.
EVERYMAN. That would grieve me full sore,
When I should come to that fearful answer.
Up, let us go thither together.
GOODS. Nay, not so, I am too brittle, I may not endure; 425
I will follow no man one foot, be ye sure.
EVERYMAN. Alas, I have thee loved, and had great pleasure
All my life-days on good and treasure.
GOODS. That is to thy damnation without leasing,[14]
For my love is contrary to the love everlasting. 430
But if thou had me loved moderately during,
As, to the poor give part of me,
Then shouldst thou not in this dolor be,
Nor in this great sorrow and care.
EVERYMAN. Lo, now was I deceived or I was ware, 435
And all I may wyte[15] my spending of time.

[13]Trouble. [14]Lying. [15]Blame.

GOODS. What, weenest thou that I am thine?
EVERYMAN. I had wend so.
GOODS. Nay, *Everyman,* I say no;
As for a while I was lent thee, 440
A season thou hast had me in prosperity;
My condition is man's soul to kill;
If I save one, a thousand I do spill;
Weenest thou that I will follow thee?
Nay, from this world, not verily. 445
EVERYMAN. I had wend otherwise.
GOODS. Therefore to thy soul *Good* is a thief;
For when thou art dead, this is my guise
Another to deceive in the same wise
As I have done thee, and all to his soul's reprief. 450
EVERYMAN. O false *Good,* cursed thou be!
Thou traitor to God, that hast deceived me,
And caught me in thy snare.
GOODS. Marry, thou brought thyself in care,
Whereof I am glad, 455
I must needs laugh, I cannot be sad.
EVERYMAN. Ah, *Good,* thou hast had long my hearty love;
I gave thee that which should be the Lord's above.
But wilt thou not go with me in deed?
I pray thee truth to say. 460
GOODS. No, so God me speed,
Therefore farewell, and have good day.
EVERYMAN. Oh, to whom shall I make my moan
For to go with me in that heavy journey?
First *Fellowship* said he would with me gone; 465
His words were very pleasant and gay,
But afterward he left me alone.
Then spake I to my kinsmen all in despair,
And also they gave me words fair;
They lacked no fair speaking; 470
But all forsake me in the ending.
Then went I to my *Goods* that I loved best,
In hope to have comfort, but there had I least!
For my *Goods* sharply did me tell
That he bringeth many into hell. 475
Then of myself I was ashamed,
And so I am worthy to be blamed;
Thus may I well myself hate.
Of whom shall I now counsel take?
I think that I shall never speed 480
Till that I go to my *Good-Deed,*
But alas, she is so weak,
That she can neither go nor speak;
Yet will I venture on her now.—
My *Good-Deeds,* where be you? 485
GOOD-DEEDS. Here I lie cold in the ground;
Thy sins hath me sore bound,
That I cannot stir.
EVERYMAN. O, *Good-Deeds,* I stand in fear;
I must you pray of counsel, 490
For help now should come right well.
GOOD-DEEDS. *Everyman,* I have understanding
That ye be summoned account to make
Before *Messias,* of Jerusalem King;
And you do by me[16] that journey with you will I take. 495
EVERYMAN. Therefore I come to you, my moan to make;
I pray you, that ye will go with me.
GOOD-DEEDS. I would full fain, but I cannot stand verily.
EVERYMAN. Why, is there anything on you fall?
GOOD-DEEDS. Yea, sir, I may thank you of all; 500
If ye had perfectly cheered me,
Your book of account now full ready had be.
Look, the books of your works and deeds eke;
Oh, see how they lie under the feet,
To your soul's heaviness. 505
EVERYMAN. Our Lord *Jesus,* help me!
For one letter here I cannot see.
GOOD-DEEDS. There is a blind reckoning in time of distress!
EVERYMAN. *Good-Deeds,* I pray you, help me in this need,
Or else I am for ever damned indeed; 510
Therefore help me to make reckoning
Before the redeemer of all things,
That king is, and was, and ever shall.
GOOD-DEEDS. *Everyman,* I am sorry of your fall,
And fain would I help you, and I were able. 515
EVERYMAN. *Good-Deeds,* your counsel I pray you give me.
GOOD-DEEDS. That shall I do verily;
Though that on my feet I may not go.
I have a sister, that shall with you also,
Called *Knowledge,* which shall with you abide, 520
To help you to make that dreadful reckoning.
KNOWLEDGE. *Everyman,* I will go with thee, and be thy guide,
In thy most need to go by thy side.
EVERYMAN. In good condition I am now in every thing,

---

[16]If you take my counsel.

And am wholly content with this good thing; 525
Thanked be God my Creator.
GOOD-DEEDS. And when he hath brought thee there,
Where thou shalt heal thee of thy smart,
Then go you with your reckoning and your *Good-Deeds* together
For to make you joyful at heart 530
Before the blessed Trinity.
EVERYMAN. My *Good-Deeds,* gramercy;
I am well content, certainly,
With your words sweet. 534
KNOWLEDGE. Now go we together lovingly,
To *Confession,* that cleansing river.
EVERYMAN. For joy I weep; I would we were there;
But, I pray you, give me cognition
Where dwelleth that holy man, *Confession.*
KNOWLEDGE. In the house of salvation: 540
We shall find him in that place.
That shall us comfort by God's grace.
Lo, this is *Confession;* kneel down and ask mercy,
For he is in good conceit[17] with God Almighty.
EVERYMAN. O glorious fountain that all uncleanness doth clarify, 545
Wash from me the spots of vices unclean,
That on me no sin may be seen;
I come with *Knowledge* for my redemption,
Repent with hearty and full contrition; 549
For I am commanded a pilgrimage to take,
And great accounts before God to make.
Now, I pray you, *Shrift,* mother of salvation,
Help my good deeds for my piteous exclamation.
CONFESSION. I know your sorrow well, *Everyman;*
Because with *Knowledge* ye come to me, 555
I will you comfort as well as I can,
And a precious jewel I will give thee,
Called penance, wise voider of adversity;
Therewith shall your body chastised be,
With abstinence and perseverance in God's service: 560
Here shall you receive that scourge of me
Which is penance strong, that ye must endure,
To remember thy Savior was scourged for thee
With sharp scourges, and suffered it patiently;
So must thou, or thou scape that painful pilgrimage; 565
Knowledge, keep him in this voyage,
And by that time *Good-Deeds* will be with thee.
But in any wise, be sure of mercy,
For your time draweth fast, and ye will saved be;
Ask God mercy, and He will grant truly. 570
When with the scourge of penance man doth him bind,
The oil of forgiveness then shall he find.
EVERYMAN. Thanked be God for his gracious work!
For now I will my penance begin;
This hath rejoiced and lighted my heart, 575
Though the knots be painful and hard within.
KNOWLEDGE. *Everyman,* look your penance that ye fulfil,
What pain that ever it to you be,
And *Knowledge* shall give you counsel at will, 579
How your accounts ye shall make clearly.
EVERYMAN. O eternal God, O heavenly figure,
O way of rightwiseness, O goodly vision,
Which descended down in a virgin pure
Because he would *Everyman* redeem,
Which *Adam* forfeited by his disobedience; 585
O blessed Godhead, elect and high-divine,
Forgive my grievous offense;
Here I cry thee mercy in this presence.
O ghostly treasure, O ransomer and redeemer
Of all the world, hope and conductor, 590
Mirror of joy, and founder of mercy,
Which illumineth heaven and earth thereby,
Hear my clamorous complaint, though it late be;
Receive my prayers; unworthy in this heavy life
Though I be, a sinner most abominable, 595
Yet let my name be written in *Moses'* table;
O *Mary,* pray to the Maker of all thing,
Me for to help at my ending,
And save me from the power of my enemy,
For *Death* assaileth me strongly; 600
And, Lady, that I may by means of thy prayer
Of your Son's glory to be partaker,
By the means of his passion I it crave,
I beseech you, help my soul to save.—

[17]Esteem.

Knowledge, give me the scourge of penance; 605
My flesh therewith shall give a quittance:
I will now begin, if God give me grace.

KNOWLEDGE. *Everyman,* God give you time and space:
Thus I bequeath you in the hands of our Savior, 609
Thus may you make your reckoning sure.

EVERYMAN. In the name of the Holy Trinity,
My body sore punished shall be:
Take this body for the sin of the flesh;
Also thou delightest to go gay and fresh,
And in the way of damnation thou did me bring; 615
Therefore suffer now strokes and punishing.
Now of penance I will wade the water clear
To save me from purgatory, that sharp fire.

GOOD-DEEDS. I thank God, now I can walk and go; 619
And am delivered of my sickness and woe.
Therefore with *Everyman* I will go, and not spare;
His good works I will help him to declare.

KNOWLEDGE. Now, *Everyman,* be merry and glad;
Your *Good-Deeds* cometh now; ye may not be sad;
Now is your *Good-Deeds* whole and sound, 625
Going upright upon the ground.

EVERYMAN. My heart is light, and shall be evermore;
Now will I smite faster than I did before.

GOOD-DEEDS. *Everyman,* pilgrim, my special friend,
Blessed be thou without end; 630
For thee is prepared the eternal glory.
Ye have me made whole and sound,
Therefore I will bide by thee in every stound.[18]

EVERYMAN. Welcome, my *Good-Deeds;* now I hear thy voice,
I weep for very sweetness of love. 635

KNOWLEDGE. Be no more sad, but ever rejoice;
God seeth thy living in his throne above;
Put on this garment to thy behove,
Which is wet with your tears,
Or else before God you may it miss, 640
When you to your journey's end come shall.

EVERYMAN. Gentle *Knowledge,* what do you it call?

KNOWLEDGE. It is a garment of sorrow:
From pain it will you borrow;
Contrition it is, 645
That getteth forgiveness;
It pleaseth God passing well.

GOOD-DEEDS. *Everyman,* will you wear it for your heal?

EVERYMAN. Now blessed be *Jesu, Mary's* Son!
For now have I on true contrition. 650
And let us go now without tarrying;
Good-Deeds, have we clear our reckoning?

GOOD-DEEDS. Yea, indeed I have it here.

EVERYMAN. Then I trust we need not fear;
Now, friends, let us not part in twain. 655

KNOWLEDGE. Nay, *Everyman,* that will we not, certain.

GOOD-DEEDS. Yet must thou lead with thee
Three persons of great might.

EVERYMAN. Who should they be?

GOOD-DEEDS. *Discretion* and *Strength* they hight,[19] 660
And thy *Beauty* may not abide behind.

KNOWLEDGE. Also ye must call to mind
Your *Five-Wits* as for your counselors.

GOOD-DEEDS. You must have them ready at all hours.

EVERYMAN. How shall I get them hither? 665

KNOWLEDGE. You must call them all together,
And they will hear you incontinent.

EVERYMAN. My friends, come hither and be present,
Discretion, Strength, my *Five-Wits,* and *Beauty.* 669

BEAUTY. Here at your will we be all ready.
What will ye that we should do?

GOOD-DEEDS. That ye would with *Everyman* go,
And help him in his pilgrimage,
Advise you, will ye with him or not in that voyage?

STRENGTH. We will bring him all thither, 675
To his help and comfort, ye may believe me.

DISCRETION. So will we go with him all together.

EVERYMAN. Almighty God, loved thou be,
I give thee laud that I have hither brought
Strength, Discretion, Beauty, and *Five-Wits;* lack I nought; 680
And my *Good-Deeds,* with *Knowledge* clear,
All be in my company at my will here;
I desire no more to my business.

[18]Season.

[19]Are called.

STRENGTH. And I, *Strength,* will by you stand in distress,
Though thou would in battle fight on the ground. 685
FIVE-WITS. And though it were through the world round,
We will not depart for sweet nor sour.
BEAUTY. No more will I unto death's hour,
Whatsoever thereof befall.
DISCRETION. *Everyman,* advise you first of all; 690
Go with a good advisement and deliberation;
We all give you virtuous monition
That all shall be well.
EVERYMAN. My friends, hearken what I will tell:
I pray God reward you in his heavenly sphere. 695
Now hearken, all that be here,
For I will make my testament
Here before you all present.
In alms half my good I will give with my hands twain
In the way of charity, with good intent, 700
And the other half still shall remain
In quiet to be returned there it ought to be.
This I do in despite of the fiend of hell
To go quite out of his peril
Ever after and this day. 705
KNOWLEDGE. *Everyman,* hearken what I say;
Go to priesthood, I you advise,
And receive of him in any wise
The holy sacrament and ointment together;
Then shortly see ye turn again hither; 710
We will all abide you here.
FIVE-WITS. Yea, *Everyman,* hie you that ye ready were;
There is no emperor, king, duke, nor baron,
That of God hath commission, 714
As hath the least priest in the world being;
For of the blessed sacraments pure and benign,
He beareth the keys and thereof hath the cure
For man's redemption, it is ever sure;
Which God for our soul's medicine
Gave us out of his heart with great pine; 720
Here in this transitory life, for thee and me
The blessed sacraments seven there be,
Baptism, confirmation, with priesthood good,
And the sacrament of God's precious flesh and blood,
Marriage, the holy extreme unction, and penance; 725
These seven be good to have in remembrance,
Gracious sacraments of high divinity.
EVERYMAN. Fain would I receive that holy body,
And meekly to my ghostly[20] father I will go.
FIVE-WITS. *Everyman,* that is the best that ye can do: 730
God will you to salvation bring,
For priesthood exceedeth all other thing;
To us Holy Scripture they do teach,
And converteth man from sin heaven to reach;
God hath to them more power given 735
Than to any angel that is in heaven;
With five words he may consecrate
God's body in flesh and blood to make,
And handleth his maker between his hands;
The priest bindeth and unbindeth all bands, 740
Both in earth and in heaven;
Thou ministers all the sacraments seven;
Though we kissed thy feet thou were worthy;
Thou art surgeon that cureth sin deadly:
No remedy we find under God 745
But all only priesthood.
Everyman, God gave priests that dignity,
And setteth them in his stead among us to be;
Thus be they above angels in degree.
KNOWLEDGE. If priests be good it is so surely; 750
But when Jesus hanged on the cross with great smart
There he gave, out of his blessed heart,
The same sacrament in great torment:
He sold them not to us, that Lord Omnipotent.
Therefore Saint Peter the apostle doth say
That Jesu's curse hath all they 756
Which God their Savior do buy or sell,
Or they for any money do take or tell.
Sinful priests giveth the sinners example bad;
Their children sitteth by other men's fires, I have heard; 760
And some haunteth women's company,
With unclean life, as lusts of lechery:
These be with sin made blind.

[20]Spiritual.

FIVE-WITS. I trust to God no such may we find;
Therefore let us priesthood honor, 765
And follow their doctrine for our souls' succor;
We be their sheep, and they shepherds be
By whom we all be kept in surety.
Peace, for yonder I see *Everyman* come,
Which hath made true satisfaction. 770
GOOD-DEEDS. Methinketh it is he indeed.
EVERYMAN. Now Jesu be our alder speed.[21]
I have received the sacrament for my redemption,
And then mine extreme unction:
Blessed be all they that counseled me to take it! 775
And now, friends, let us go without longer respite;
I thank God that ye have tarried so long.
Now set each of you on this rod your hand,
And shortly follow me:
I go before, there I would be; God be our guide. 780
STRENGTH. *Everyman,* we will not from you go
Till ye have gone this voyage long.
DISCRETION. I, *Discretion,* will bide by you also.
KNOWLEDGE. And though this pilgrimage be never so strong,
I will never part you fro: 785
Everyman, I will be as sure by thee
As ever I did by Judas Maccabee.
EVERYMAN. Alas, I am so faint I may not stand,
My limbs under me do fold;
Friends, let us not turn again to this land,
Not for all the world's gold. 791
For into this cave must I creep
And turn to the earth and there to sleep.
BEAUTY. What, into this grave? alas!
EVERYMAN. Yea, there shall you consume more and less. 795
BEAUTY. And what, should I smother here?
EVERYMAN. Yea, by my faith, and never more appear.
In this world live no more we shall,
But in heaven before the highest Lord of all.
BEAUTY. I cross out all this; adieu by Saint *John;* 800
I take my tap in my lap and am gone.[22]

[21]Jesu help us all.

[22]A proverbial expression used to describe a hasty departure. In the beginning it was used literally of a woman taking her tap—a quantity of flax for spinning—and distaff in her lap or apron, in going to or from a friend's house.

EVERYMAN. What, *Beauty,* whither will ye?
BEAUTY. Peace, I am deaf; I look not behind me,
Not and thou would give me all the gold in thy chest.
EVERYMAN. Alas, whereto may I trust? 805
Beauty goeth fast away hie;
She promised with me to live and die.
STRENGTH. *Everyman,* I will thee also forsake and deny;
Thy game liketh me not at all.
EVERYMAN. Why, then ye will forsake me all. 810
Sweet *Strength,* tarry a little space.
STRENGTH. Nay, sir, by the rood of grace
I will hie me from thee fast,
Though thou weep till thy heart brast.[23]
EVERYMAN. Ye would ever bide by me, ye said. 815
STRENGTH. Yea, I have you far enough conveyed;
Ye be old enough, I understand,
Your pilgrimage to take on hand;
I repent me that I hither came.
EVERYMAN. *Strength,* you to displease I am to blame; 820
Will you break promise that is debt?
STRENGTH. In faith, I care not;
Thou art but a fool to complain,
You spend your speech and waste your brain;
Go thrust thee into the ground. 825
EVERYMAN. I had wend surer I should you have found.
He that trusteth in his *Strength*
She him deceiveth at the length.
Both *Strength* and *Beauty* forsaketh me,
Yet they promised me fair and lovingly. 830
DISCRETION. *Everyman,* I will after *Strength* be gone,
As for me I will leave you alone.
EVERYMAN. Why, *Discretion,* will ye forsake me?
DISCRETION. Yea, in faith, I will go from thee,
For when *Strength* goeth before 835
I follow after evermore.
EVERYMAN. Yet, I pray thee, for the love of the Trinity,
Look in my grave once piteously.
DISCRETION. Nay, so nigh will I not come.
Farewell, every one! 840
EVERYMAN. O all thing faileth, save God alone;

[23]Burst.

Beauty, Strength, and *Discretion;*
For when *Death* bloweth his blast,
They all run from me full fast.
FIVE-WITS. *Everyman,* my leave now of thee I take; 845
I will follow the other, for here I thee forsake.
EVERYMAN. Alas! then may I wail and weep,
For I took you for my best friend.
FIVE-WITS. I will no longer thee keep;
Now farewell, and there an end. 850
EVERYMAN. O Jesu, help, all hath forsaken me!
GOOD-DEEDS. Nay, *Everyman,* I will bide with thee,
I will not forsake thee indeed;
Thou shalt find me a good friend at need.
EVERYMAN. Gramercy, *Good-Deeds;* now may I true friends see; 855
They have forsaken me every one;
I loved them better than my *Good-Deeds* alone.
Knowledge, will ye forsake me also?
KNOWLEDGE. Yea, *Everyman,* when ye to death do go:
But not yet for no manner of danger. 860
EVERYMAN. Gramercy, *Knowledge,* with all my heart.
KNOWLEDGE. Nay, yet I will not from hence depart,
Till I see where ye shall be come.
EVERYMAN. Methinketh, alas, that I must be gone,
To make my reckoning and my debts pay,
For I see my time is nigh spent away. 866
Take example, all ye that this do hear or see,
How they that I loved best do forsake me,
Except my *Good-Deeds* that bideth truly.
GOOD-DEEDS. All earthly things is but vanity: 870
Beauty, Strength, and *Discretion* do man forsake,
Foolish friends and kinsmen, that fair spake,
All fleeth save *Good-Deeds,* and that am I.
EVERYMAN. Have mercy on me, God most mighty;
And stand by me, thou Mother and Maid, holy *Mary.* 875
GOOD-DEEDS. Fear not, I will speak for thee.
EVERYMAN. Here I cry God mercy.
GOOD-DEEDS. Short our end, and minish our pain;
Let us go and never come again.
EVERYMAN. Into thy hands, Lord, my soul I commend; 880
Receive it, Lord, that it be not lost;
As thou me boughtest, so me defend,
And save me from the fiend's boast,
That I may appear with that blessed host
That shall be saved at the day of doom. 885
In manus tuas—of might's most
For ever—*commendo spiritum meum.*[24]
KNOWLEDGE. Now hath he suffered that we all shall endure;
The *Good-Deeds* shall make all sure.
Now hath he made ending; 890
Methinketh that I hear angels sing
And make great joy and melody,
Where *Everyman's* soul received shall be.
ANGEL. Come, excellent elect spouse to Jesu:
Hereabove thou shalt go 895
Because of thy singular virtue:
Now the soul is taken the body fro;
Thy reckoning is crystal-clear.
Now shalt thou into the heavenly sphere,
Unto the which all ye shall come 900
That liveth well before the day of doom.
DOCTOR. This moral men may have in mind;
Ye hearers, take it of worth, old and young,
And forsake pride, for he deceiveth you in the end,
And remember *Beauty, Five-Wits, Strength,* and *Discretion,* 905
They all at the last do *Everyman* forsake,
Save his *Good-Deeds,* there doth he take.
But beware, and they be small
Before God, he hath no help at all.
None excuse may be there for *Everyman;* 910
Alas, how shall he do then?
For after death amends may no man make,
For then mercy and pity do him forsake.
If his reckoning be not clear when he do come,
God will say—*ite, maledicti, in ignem aeternum.*[25] 915
And he that hath his account whole and sound,
High in heaven he shall be crowned;
Unto which place God bring us all thither
That we may live body and soul together.
Thereto help the Trinity, 920
Amen, say ye, for saint *charity.*

[24] To thy hands I commend my soul.
[25] Hence, accursed one, into eternal fire.

SIR THOMAS MALORY

c. 1400–1471

Very little is known about the life of Malory. The year generally given as that of his birth is approximate only. He lived at Newbold Revell, in Warwickshire. He served in the French wars with Richard Beauchamp, Earl of Warwick, a renowned representative of the chivalric ideal. Malory was also conspicuous on the Lancastrian side in the Wars of the Roses, and for this reason he was imprisoned towards the close of his life. In 1445, he was a member of Parliament for Warwickshire. He was "a gentleman of an ancient house, and a soldier"—a man whose career, as far as we know anything about it, seems eminently appropriate to the compiler of the *Morte d'Arthur.* This book Malory finished in 1469 or 1470, and it was first printed in 1485, by William Caxton (*c.* 1421–1491), the earliest English printer.

Caxton tells us in the Preface printed below that Malory took the *Morte d'Arthur* "out of certain books of French, and reduced it into English." Malory, in fact, used some English material; but he translated the greater part of his work from a number of French romances, whose volume is said to be about ten times as great as that of the *Morte d'Arthur* itself. These romances told no connected story; on the contrary, they were frequently inconsistent with each other, and this, together with their number, probably accounts sufficiently for the incongruities in Malory's book. He seems to have chosen the stories that pleased him best, with the general design of giving an account of Arthur's life from birth to death. This is done only in the loosest fashion, but it is a mark of originality on Malory's part, inasmuch as Arthur is thus given an importance which he does not have in the old romances.

The definitive text is *Le Morte Darthur,* ed. H. Oskar Sommer (London, 1889–1891); this also contains an essay on Malory's prose style by Andrew Lang. Sir Edmund K. Chambers has given a brief but well-considered interpretation in *Sir Thomas Malory,* a pamphlet published by the English Association (London, 1922). For a full discussion of Malory's life and sources see Eugène Vinaver, *Malory* (Oxford, 1929).

LE MORTE D'ARTHUR

CAXTON'S PREFACE

After that I had accomplished and finished divers histories, as well of contemplation as of other historical and worldly acts of great 5 conquerors and princes, and also certain books of ensamples and doctrine, many noble and divers gentlemen of this realm of England came and demanded me, many and ofttimes, wherefore that I have not do made[1] and im- 10 printed the noble history of the Sangreal, and of the most renowned Christian king, first and chief of the three best Christian and worthy, King Arthur, which ought most to be remembered among us English men to- 15 fore all other Christian kings. For it is notoriously known through the universal world that there be nine worthy and the best that ever were. That is, to wit, three paynims, three Jews, and three Christian men. As for the paynims they were tofore the Incarnation of Christ, which were named, the first Hector of Troy, of whom the history is come both in ballad and in prose; the second Alexander the Great; and the third Julius Caesar, Emperor of Rome, of whom the histories be well-known and had. And as for the three Jews which also were tofore the Incarnation of our Lord, of whom the first was Duke Joshua which brought the children of Israel into the land of behest; the second David, King of Jerusalem; and the third Judas Maccabaeus. of these three the

[1] Had made.

Bible rehearseth all their noble histories and acts. And sith the said Incarnation have been three noble Christian men stalled[2] and admitted through the universal world into the number of the nine best and worthy, of whom was first the noble Arthur, whose noble acts I purpose to write in this present book here following. The second was Charlemagne or Charles the Great, of whom the history is had in many places both in French and English; and the third and last was Godfrey of Bouillon, of whose acts and life I made a book unto the excellent prince and king of noble memory, King Edward the Fourth. The said noble gentlemen instantly required me to imprint the history of the said noble king and conqueror, King Arthur, and of his knights, with the history of the Sangreal, and of the death and ending of the said Arthur; affirming that I ought rather to imprint his acts and noble feats, than of Godfrey of Bouillon, or any of the other eight, considering that he was a man born within this realm, and king and emperor of the same; and that there be in French divers and many noble volumes of his acts, and also of his knights. To whom I answered, that divers men hold opinion that there was no such Arthur, and that all such books as be made of him be but feigned and fables, by cause that some chronicles make of him no mention nor remember him no thing, nor of his knights. Whereto they answered and one in special said, that in him that should say or think that there was never such a king called Arthur, might well be credited great folly and blindness; for he said that there were many evidences of the contrary: first ye may see his sepulture in the Monastery of Glastonbury. And also in Polichronicon,[3] in the fifth book the sixth chapter, and in the seventh book the twenty-third chapter, where his body was buried and after found and translated into the said monastery. Ye shall see also in the history of Bochas,[4] in his book *De Casu Principum,* part of his noble acts, and also of his fall. Also Galfridus[5] in his British book recounteth his life; and in divers places of England many remembrances be yet of him and shall remain perpetually, and also of his knights. First in the Abbey of Westminster, at Saint Edward's shrine, remaineth the print of his seal in red wax closed in beryl, in which is written *Patricius Arthurus, Britannie, Gallie, Germanie, Dacie, Imperator.*[6] Item in the castle of Dover ye may see Gawaine's skull and Craddock's mantle: at Winchester the Round Table: at other places Launcelot's sword and many other things. Then all these things considered, there can no man reasonably gainsay but there was a king of this land named Arthur. For in all places, Christian and heathen, he is reputed and taken for one of the nine worthy, and the first of the three Christian men. And also he is more spoken of beyond the sea, more books made of his noble acts than there be in England, as well in Dutch, Italian, Spanish, and Greek, as in French. And yet of record remain in witness of him in Wales, in the town of Camelot,[7] the great stones and marvelous works of iron, lying under the ground, and royal vaults, which divers now living hath seen. Wherefore it is a marvel why he is no more renowned in his own country, save only it accordeth to the Word of God, which saith that no man is accept for a prophet in his own country. Then all these things foresaid alleged, I could not well deny but that there was such a noble king named Arthur, and reputed one of the nine worthy, and first and chief of the Christian men; and many noble volumes be made of him and of his noble knights in French, which I have seen and read beyond the sea, which be not had in our maternal tongue, but in Welsh be many and also in French, and some in English, but no where nigh all. Wherefore, such as have late been drawn out briefly into English I have after the simple conning that God hath sent to me, under the favor and correction of all noble lords and

[2]Installed.

[3]A history of the world, written in Latin by Ranulph Higden (died *c.* 1364).

[4]Boccaccio. The book (*On the Fall of Princes*) tells of the misfortunes of illustrious men.

[5]Geoffrey of Monmouth, whose *History of the Kings of Britain* (written in Latin, probably about 1140) contains much fabulous matter.

[6]Noble Arthur, Emperor of Britain, Gaul, Germany, and Dacia.

[7]A legendary town, where Arthur held his court.

gentlemen, emprised[8] to imprint a book of the noble histories of the said King Arthur, and of certain of his knights, after a copy unto me delivered, which copy Sir Thomas Malory did take out of certain books of French, and reduced it into English. And I, according to my copy, have done set it in imprint, to the intent that noble men may see and learn the noble acts of chivalry, the gentle and virtuous deeds that some knights used in those days, by which they came to honor; and how they that were vicious were punished and oft put to shame and rebuke; humbly beseeching all noble lords and ladies, with all other estates, of what estate or degree they be of, that shall see and read in this said book and work, that they take the good and honest acts in their remembrance, and to follow the same. Wherein they shall find many joyous and pleasant histories, and noble and renowned acts of humanity, gentleness, and chivalries. For herein may be seen noble chivalry, courtesy, humanity, friendliness, hardiness, love, friendship, cowardice, murder, hate, virtue, and sin. Do after the good and leave the evil, and it shall bring you to good fame and renown. And for to pass the time this book shall be pleasant to read in; but for to give faith and believe that all is true that is contained herein, ye be at your liberty; but all is written for our doctrine, and for to beware that we fall not to vice nor sin; but to exercise and follow virtue; by which we may come and attain to good fame and renown in this life, and after this short and transitory life, to come unto everlasting bliss in heaven, the which He grant us that reigneth in heaven, the blessed Trinity. Amen.

Then to proceed forth in this said book, which I direct unto all noble princes, lords and ladies, gentlemen or gentlewomen, that desire to read or hear read of the noble and joyous history of the great conqueror and excellent king, King Arthur, sometime king of this noble realm, then called Britain. I, William Caxton, simple person, present this book following, which I have emprised to imprint; and treateth of the noble acts, feats of arms of chivalry, prowess, hardiness, humanity, love, courtesy and very gentleness, with many wonderful histories and adventures. And for to understand briefly the content of this volume, I have divided it into twenty-one books, and every book chaptered as hereafter shall by God's grace follow. The first book shall treat how Uther Pendragon gat the noble conqueror King Arthur, and containeth twenty-eight chapters. The second book treateth of Balin the noble knight, and containeth nineteen chapters. The third book treateth of the marriage of King Arthur to Queen Guenever, with other matters, and containeth fifteen chapters. The fourth book, how Merlin was assotted,[9] and of war made to King Arthur, and containeth twenty-nine chapters. The fifth book treateth of the conquest of Lucius the emperor, and containeth twelve chapters. The sixth book treateth of Sir Launcelot and Sir Lionel, and marvelous adventures, and containeth eighteen chapters. The seventh book treateth of a noble knight called Sir Gareth, and named by Sir Kay, Beaumains, and containeth thirty-six chapters. The eighth book treateth of the birth of Sir Tristram the noble knight, and of his acts, and containeth forty-one chapters. The ninth book treateth of a knight named by Sir Kay, La Cote Male Taile, and also of Sir Tristram, and containeth forty-four chapters. The tenth book treateth of Sir Tristram and other marvelous adventures, and containeth eighty-eight chapters. The eleventh book treateth of Sir Launcelot and Sir Galahad, and containeth fourteen chapters. The twelfth book treateth of Sir Launcelot and his madness, and containeth fourteen chapters. The thirteenth book treateth how Galahad came first to King Arthur's court, and the quest now the Sangreal was begun, and containeth twenty chapters. The fourteenth book treateth of the quest of the Sangreal, and containeth ten chapters. The fifteenth book treateth of Sir Launcelot, and containeth six chapters. The sixteenth book treateth of Sir Bors and Sir Lionel his brother, and containeth seventeen chapters. The seventeenth book treateth of the Sangreal, and containeth twenty-three chapters. The eighteenth book treateth of Sir Launcelot and the queen, and

[8]Undertaken.

[9]Besotted.

containeth twenty-five chapters. The nineteenth book treateth of Queen Guenever and Launcelot, and containeth thirteen chapters. The twentieth book treateth of the piteous death of Arthur, and containeth twenty-two chapters. The twenty-first book treateth of his last departing, and how Sir Launcelot came to revenge his death, and containeth thirteen chapters. The sum is twenty-one books, which contain the sum of five hundred and seven chapters, as more plainly shall follow hereafter.

BOOK XXI

CHAPTER I

How Sir Mordred Presumed and Took on Him to Be King of England, and Would Have Married the Queen, His Uncle's Wife

As Sir Mordred was ruler of all England, he did do make[1] letters as though that they came from beyond the sea, and the letters specified that King Arthur was slain in battle with Sir Launcelot. Wherefore Sir Mordred made a parliament, and called the lords together, and there he made them to choose him king; and so was he crowned at Canterbury, and held a feast there fifteen days; and afterward he drew him unto Winchester, and there he took the Queen Guenever, and said plainly that he would wed her which was his uncle's wife and his father's wife. And so he made ready for the feast, and a day prefixed that they should be wedded; wherefore Queen Guenever was passing heavy. But she durst not discover her heart, but spake fair, and agreed to Sir Mordred's will. Then she desired of Sir Mordred for to go to London, to buy all manner of things that longed unto the wedding. And by cause of her fair speech Sir Mordred trusted her well enough, and gave her leave to go. And so when she came to London she took the Tower of London, and suddenly in all haste possible she stuffed it with all manner of victual, and well garnished it with men, and so kept it. Then when Sir Mordred wist[2] and understood how he was beguiled, he was passing wroth out of measure. And a short tale for to make, he went and laid a mighty siege about the Tower of London, and made many great assaults thereat, and threw many great engines unto them, and shot great guns. But all might not prevail[3] Sir Mordred, for Queen Guenever would never for fair speech nor for foul, would never trust to come in his hands again. Then came the Bishop of Canterbury, the which was a noble clerk and an holy man, and thus he said to Sir Mordred: Sir, what will ye do? will ye first displease God and sithen[4] shame yourself and all knighthood? Is not King Arthur your uncle, no farther but your mother's brother, and on her himself King Arthur begat you upon his own sister, therefore how may you wed your father's wife? Sir, said the noble clerk, leave this opinion or I shall curse you with book and bell and candle. Do thou thy worst, said Sir Mordred, wit thou well I shall defy thee. Sir, said the Bishop, and wit you well I shall not fear me to do that me ought to do. Also where ye noise where my lord Arthur is slain, and that is not so, and therefore ye will make a foul work in this land. Peace, thou false priest, said Sir Mordred, for an thou chafe me any more I shall make strike off thy head. So the Bishop departed and did the cursing in the most orgulist[5] wise that might be done, and then Sir Mordred sought the Bishop of Canterbury, for to have slain him. Then the Bishop fled, and took part of his goods with him, and went nigh unto Glastonbury; and there he was as priest hermit in a chapel, and lived in poverty and in holy prayers, for well he understood that mischievous war was at hand. Then Sir Mordred sought on Queen Guenever by letters and sondes,[6] and by fair means and foul means, for to have her to come out of the Tower of London; but all this availed not, for she answered him shortly, openly and privily, that she had lever slay herself than to be married with him. Then came word to Sir Mordred that King Arthur had araised the siege for Sir Launcelot, and he was coming homeward with a great host, to be avenged upon Sir Mordred; wherefore Sir Mordred made write[7] writs to

[1]Have made. [2]Heard.

[3]Avail. [4]Afterwards. [5]Insolent.
[6]Messages. [7]Had written.

all the barony of this land, and much people drew to him. For then was the common voice among them that with Arthur was none other life but war and strife, and with Sir Mordred was great joy and bliss. Thus was Sir Arthur depraved,[8] and evil said of. And many there were that King Arthur had made up of nought, and given them lands, might not then say him a good word. Lo ye, all Englishmen, see ye not what a mischief here was! for he that was the most king and knight of the world, and most loved the fellowship of noble knights, and by him they were all upholden, now might not these Englishmen hold them content with him. Lo thus was the old custom and usage of this land; and also men say that we of this land have not yet lost nor forgotten that custom and usage. Alas, this is a great default of us Englishmen, for there may no thing please us no term. And so fared the people at that time, they were better pleased with Sir Mordred than they were with King Arthur; and much people drew unto Sir Mordred, and said they would abide with him for better and for worse. And so Sir Mordred drew with a great host to Dover, for there he heard say that Sir Arthur would arrive, and so he thought to beat his own father from his lands; and the most part of all England held with Sir Mordred, the people were so newfangle.[9]

CHAPTER II

How after that King Arthur Had Tidings, He Returned and Came to Dover, where Sir Mordred Met Him to Let[10] His Landing; and of the Death of Sir Gawaine

AND so as Sir Mordred was at Dover with his host, there came King Arthur with a great navy of ships, and galleys, and carracks. And there was Sir Mordred ready awaiting upon his landing, to let[10] his own father to land upon the land that he was king over. Then there was launching of great boats and small, and full of noble men of arms; and there was much slaughter of gentle knights, and many a full bold baron was laid full low, on both parties. But King Arthur was so courageous that there might no manner of knights let him to land, and his knights fiercely followed him; and so they landed maugre[11] Sir Mordred and all his power, and put Sir Mordred aback, that he fled and all his people. So when this battle was done, King Arthur let bury his people that were dead. And then was noble Sir Gawaine found in a great boat, lying more than half dead. When Sir Arthur wist that Sir Gawaine was laid so low, he went unto him; and there the king made sorrow out of measure, and took Sir Gawaine in his arms, and thrice he there swooned. And then when he awaked, he said: Alas, Sir Gawaine, my sister's son, here now thou liest, the man in the world that I loved most; and now is my joy gone, for now, my nephew, Sir Gawaine, I will discover me unto your person: in Sir Launcelot and you I most had my joy, and mine affiance,[12] and now have I lost my joy of you both; wherefore all mine earthly joy is gone from me. Mine uncle, King Arthur, said Sir Gawaine, wit you well my death day is come, and all is through mine own hastiness and willfulness; for I am smitten upon the old wound the which Sir Launcelot gave me, on the which I feel well I must die; and had Sir Launcelot been with you as he was, this unhappy war had never begun; and of all this am I causer, for Sir Launcelot and his blood, through their prowess, held all your cankered enemies in subjection and danger. And now, said Sir Gawaine, ye shall miss Sir Launcelot. But alas, I would not accord with him, and therefore, said Sir Gawaine, I pray you, fair uncle, that I may have paper, pen, and ink, that I may write to Sir Launcelot a cedle[13] with mine own hands. And then when paper and ink was brought, then Gawaine was set up weakly by King Arthur, for he was shriven a little tofore; and then he wrote thus, as the French book maketh mention: Unto Sir Launcelot, flower of all noble knights that ever I heard of or saw by my days, I, Sir Gawaine, King Lot's son of Orkney, sister's son unto the noble King Arthur, send thee greeting, and let thee have knowledge that the tenth day of May I was smitten upon the old wound that thou gavest

[8]Slandered. [9]New-fashioned. [10]Prevent. [11]Despite. [12]Trust. [13]Note.

me afore the city of Benwick,[14] and through the same wound that thou gavest me I am come to my death day. And I will that all the world wit, that I, Sir Gawaine, knight of the Table Round, sought my death, and not through thy deserving, but it was mine own seeking; wherefore I beseech thee, Sir Launcelot, to return again unto this realm, and see my tomb, and pray some prayer more or less for my soul. And this same day that I wrote this cedle, I was hurt to the death in the same wound, the which I had of thy hand, Sir Launcelot; for of a more nobler man might I not be slain. Also, Sir Launcelot, for all the love that ever was betwixt us, make no tarrying, but come over the sea in all haste, that thou mayst with thy noble knights rescue that noble king that made thee knight, that is my lord Arthur; for he is full straitly bestad[15] with a false traitor, that is my half-brother, Sir Mordred; and he hath let crown him king, and would have wedded my lady Queen Guenever, and so had he done had she not put herself in the Tower of London. And so the tenth day of May last past, my lord Arthur and we all landed upon them at Dover; and there we put that false traitor, Sir Mordred, to flight, and there it misfortuned me to be stricken upon thy stroke. And at the date of this letter was written, but two hours and a half afore my death, written with mine own hand, and so subscribed with part of my heart's blood. And I require thee, most famous knight of the world, that thou wilt see my tomb. And then Sir Gawaine wept, and King Arthur wept; and then they swooned both. And when they awaked both, the king made Sir Gawaine to receive his Savior. And then Sir Gawaine prayed the king for to send for Sir Launcelot, and to cherish him above all other knights. And so at the hour of noon Sir Gawaine yielded up the spirit; and then the king let inter him in a chapel within Dover Castle; and there yet all men may see the skull of him, and the same wound is seen that Sir Launcelot gave him in battle. Then was it told the king that Sir Mordred had pyghte a new field[16] upon Barham Down.

[14]Launcelot had, in fact, wounded him twice on the head (Book XX, Chaps. xxi, xxii).

[15]Hard pressed. [16]Taken up a new position.

And upon the morn the king rode thither to him, and there was a great battle betwixt them, and much people was slain on both parties; but at the last Sir Arthur's party stood best, and Sir Mordred and his party fled into Canterbury.

CHAPTER III

How after, Sir Gawaine's Ghost Appeared to King Arthur, and Warned Him that He Should Not Fight That Day

And then the king let search all the towns for his knights that were slain, and interred them; and salved them with soft salves that so sore were wounded. Then much people drew unto King Arthur. And then they said that Sir Mordred warred upon King Arthur with wrong. And then King Arthur drew him with his host down by the seaside westward toward Salisbury; and there was a day assigned betwixt King Arthur and Sir Mordred, that they should meet upon a down beside Salisbury, and not far from the seaside; and this day was assigned on a Monday after Trinity Sunday, whereof King Arthur was passing glad, that he might be avenged upon Sir Mordred. Then Sir Mordred araised much people about London, for they of Kent, Southsex, and Surrey, Estsex, and of Southfolk, and of Northfolk, held the most part with Sir Mordred; and many a full noble knight drew unto Sir Mordred and to the king: but they that loved Sir Launcelot drew unto Sir Mordred. So upon Trinity Sunday at night, King Arthur dreamed a wonderful dream, and that was this: that him seemed he sat upon a chaflet[17] in a chair, and the chair was fast to a wheel, and thereupon sat King Arthur in the richest cloth of gold that might be made; and the king thought there was under him, far from him, an hideous deep black water, and therein were all manner of serpents, and worms, and wild beasts foul and horrible; and suddenly the king thought the wheel turned up so down, and he fell among the serpents, and every beast took him by a limb; and then the king cried as he lay in his bed and slept: Help. And then knights, squires, and yeomen

[17]Platform.

awaked the king; and then he was so amazed that he wist not where he was; and then he fell on slumbering again, not sleeping nor thoroughly waking. So the king seemed verily that there came Sir Gawaine unto him with 5 a number of fair ladies with him. And when King Arthur saw him, then he said: Welcome, my sister's son; I weened thou hadst been dead, and now I see thee on live, much am I beholding unto almighty Jesu. 10 O fair nephew and my sister's son, what be these ladies that hither be come with you? Sir, said Sir Gawaine, all these be ladies for whom I have foughten when I was man living, and all these are those that I did battle 15 for in righteous quarrel; and God hath given them that grace at their great prayer, by cause I did battle for them, that they should bring me hither unto you: thus much hath God given me leave, for to warn you of your 20 death; for an ye fight as tomorn with Sir Mordred, as ye both have assigned, doubt ye not ye must be slain, and the most part of your people on both parties. And for the great grace and goodness that almighty Jesu 25 hath unto you, and for pity of you, and many more other good men there shall be slain, God hath sent me to you of His special grace, to give you warning that in no wise ye do battle as tomorn, but that ye take a treaty 30 for a month day; and proffer you largely,[18] so as tomorn to be put in a delay. For within a month shall come Sir Launcelot with all his noble knights, and rescue you worshipfully, and slay Sir Mordred, and all 35 that ever will hold with him. Then Sir Gawaine and all the ladies vanished. And anon the king called upon his knights, squires, and yeomen, and charged them wightly[19] to fetch his noble lords and wise bishops unto him. 40 And when they were come, the king told them his avision, what Sir Gawaine had told him, and warned him that if he fought on the morn he should be slain. Then the king commanded Sir Lucan the Butler, and his 45 brother, Sir Bedivere, with two bishops with them, and charged them in any wise, an they might, Take a treaty for a month day with Sir Mordred, and spare not, proffer him lands and goods as much as ye think 50 best. So then they departed, and came to Sir Mordred, where he had a grim host of an hundred thousand men. And there they entreated Sir Mordred long time; and at the last Sir Mordred was agreed for to have Cornwall and Kent, by Arthur's days: after, all England, after the days of King Arthur.

CHAPTER IV

How by Misadventure of an Adder the Battle Began, where Mordred Was Slain, and Arthur Hurt to the Death

THEN were they condescended that King Arthur and Sir Mordred should meet betwixt both their hosts, and every each of them should bring fourteen persons; and they came with this word unto Arthur. Then said he: I am glad that this is done: and so he went into the field. And when Arthur should depart, he warned all his host that an they see any sword drawn: Look ye come on fiercely, and slay that traitor, Sir Mordred, for I in no wise trust him. In likewise Sir Mordred warned his host that: An ye see any sword drawn, look that ye come on fiercely, and so slay all that ever before you standeth; for in no wise I will not trust for this treaty, for I know well my father will be avenged on me. And so they met as their appointment was, and so they were agreed and accorded thoroughly; and wine was fetched, and they drank. Right soon came an adder out of a little heath bush, and it stung a knight on the foot. And when the knight felt him stung, he looked down and saw the adder, and then he drew his sword to slay the adder, and thought of none other harm. And when the host on both parties saw that sword drawn, then they blew beamous,[20] trumpets, and horns, and shouted grimly. And so both hosts dressed them together. And King Arthur took his horse, and said: Alas, this unhappy day! and so rode to his party. And Sir Mordred in likewise. And never was there seen a more dolefuller battle in no Christian land; for there was but rushing and riding, foining[21] and striking, and many a grim word was there spoken either to other, and many a deadly stroke. But ever King

[18]Make generous proposals. [19]Quickly.

[20]Horns. [21]Thrusting.

Arthur rode throughout the battle of Sir Mordred many times, and did full nobly as a noble king should, and at all times he fainted never; and Sir Mordred that day put him in devoir,[22] and in great peril. And thus they fought all the long day, and never stinted till the noble knights were laid to the cold earth; and ever they fought still till it was near night, and by that time was there an hundred thousand laid dead upon the down. Then was Arthur wood[23] wroth out of measure, when he saw his people so slain from him. Then the king looked about him, and then was he ware, of all his host and of all his good knights, were left no more on live but two knights; that one was Sir Lucan the Butler, and his brother Sir Bedivere, and they were full sore wounded. Jesu mercy, said the king, where are all my noble knights become? Alas that ever I should see this doleful day, for now, said Arthur, I am come to mine end. But would to God that I wist where were that traitor Sir Mordred, that hath caused all this mischief. Then was King Arthur ware where Sir Mordred leaned upon his sword among a great heap of dead men. Now give me my spear, said Arthur unto Sir Lucan, for yonder I have espied the traitor that all this woe hath wrought. Sir, let him be, said Sir Lucan, for he is unhappy; and if ye pass this unhappy day ye shall be right well revenged upon him. Good lord, remember ye of your night's dream, and what the spirit of Sir Gawaine told you this night, yet God of his great goodness hath preserved you hitherto. Therefore for God's sake, my lord, leave off by this, for blessed be God ye have won the field, for here we be three on live, and with Sir Mordred is none on live; and if ye leave off now this wicked day of destiny is past. Tide me death, betide me life, saith the king, now I see him yonder alone he shall never escape mine hands, for at a better avail shall I never have him. God speed you well, said Sir Bedivere. Then the king gat his spear in both his hands, and ran toward Sir Mordred, crying: Traitor, now is thy death day come. And when Sir Mordred heard Sir Arthur, he ran until him with his sword drawn in his hand. And there King Arthur smote Sir Mordred under the shield, with a foin of his spear, throughout the body, more than a fathom. And when Sir Mordred felt that he had his death wound he thrust himself with the might that he had up to the bur[24] of King Arthur's spear. And right so he smote his father Arthur, with his sword holden in both his hands, on the side of the head, that the sword pierced the helmet and the brain pan, and therewithal Sir Mordred fell stark dead to the earth; and the noble Arthur fell in a swoon to the earth, and there he swooned ofttimes. And Sir Lucan the Butler and Sir Bedivere ofttimes heaved him up. And so weakly they led him betwixt them both, to a little chapel not far from the seaside. And when the king was there he thought him well eased. Then heard they people cry in the field. Now go thou, Sir Lucan, said the king, and do me to wit what betokens that noise in the field. So Sir Lucan departed, for he was grievously wounded in many places. And so as he yede,[25] he saw and hearkened by the moonlight, how that pillers[26] and robbers were come into the field, to pill and to rob many a full noble knight of brooches, and beads, of many a good ring, and of many a rich jewel; and who that were not dead all out, there they slew them for their harness and their riches. When Sir Lucan understood this work, he came to the king as soon as he might, and told him all what he had heard and seen. Therefore by my rede,[27] said Sir Lucan, it is best that we bring you to some town. I would it were so, said the king.

CHAPTER V

How King Arthur Commanded to Cast His Sword Excalibur into the Water, and How He Was Delivered to Ladies in a Barge

BUT I may not stand, mine head works so. Ah Sir Launcelot, said King Arthur, this day have I sore missed thee; alas, that ever I was against thee, for now have I my death, whereof Sir Gawaine me warned in my dream. Then Sir Lucan took up the king the one

[22]Duty. [23]Mad.

[24]Ring to prevent the hand from slipping.
[25]Went. [26]Pillagers. [27]Counsel.

part, and Sir Bedivere the other part, and in the lifting the king swooned; and Sir Lucan fell in a swoon with the lift, that the part of his guts fell out of his body, and therewith the noble knight's heart brast.[28] And when the king awoke, he beheld Sir Lucan, how he lay foaming at the mouth, and part of his guts lay at his feet. Alas, said the king, this is to me a full heavy sight, to see this noble duke so die for my sake, for he would have holpen me, that had more need of help than I. Alas, he would not complain him, his heart was so set to help me: now Jesu have mercy upon his soul! Then Sir Bedivere wept for the death of his brother. Leave this mourning and weeping, said the king, for all this will not avail me, for wit thou well an I might live myself, the death of Sir Lucan would grieve me evermore; but my time hieth fast, said the king. Therefore, said Arthur unto Sir Bedivere, take thou Excalibur, my good sword, and go with it to yonder water side, and when thou comest there I charge thee throw my sword in that water, and come again and tell me what thou there seest. My lord, said Bedivere, your commandment shall be done, and lightly[29] bring you word again. So Sir Bedivere departed, and by the way he beheld that noble sword, that the pommel and the haft was all of precious stones; and then he said to himself: If I throw this rich sword in the water, thereof shall never come good, but harm and loss. And then Sir Bedivere hid Excalibur under a tree. And so, as soon as he might, he came again unto the king, and said he had been at the water, and had thrown the sword in the water. What saw thou there? said the king. Sir, he said, I saw nothing but waves and winds. That is untruly said of thee, said the king, therefore go thou lightly again, and do my commandment; as thou art to me lief and dear, spare not, but throw it in. Then Sir Bedivere returned again, and took the sword in his hand; and then him thought sin and shame to throw away that noble sword, and so eft[30] he hid the sword, and returned again, and told to the king that he had been at the water, and done his commandment. What saw thou there? said the king. Sir, he said, I saw nothing but the

[28]Burst. [29]Swiftly. [30]Again.

waters wappe[31] and waves wanne.[32] Ah, traitor untrue, said King Arthur, now hast thou betrayed me twice. Who would have weened that, thou that hast been to me so lief and dear? and thou art named a noble knight, and would betray me for the richness of the sword. But now go again lightly, for thy long tarrying putteth me in great jeopardy of my life, for I have taken cold. And but if thou do now as I bid thee, if ever I may see thee, I shall slay thee with mine own hands; for thou wouldst for my rich sword see me dead. Then Sir Bedivere departed, and went to the sword, and lightly took it up, and went to the water side; and there he bound the girdle about the hilts, and then he threw the sword as far into the water as he might; and there came an arm and an hand above the water and met it, and caught it, and so shook it thrice and brandished, and then vanished away the hand with the sword in the water. So Sir Bedivere came again to the king, and told him what he saw. Alas, said the king, help me hence, for I dread me I have tarried over long. Then Sir Bedivere took the king upon his back, and so went with him to that water side. And when they were at the water side, even fast by the bank hoved a little barge with many fair ladies in it, and among them all was a queen, and all they had black hoods, and all they wept and shrieked when they saw King Arthur. Now put me into the barge, said the king. And so he did softly; and there received him three queens with great mourning; and so they set them down, and in one of their laps King Arthur laid his head. And then that queen said: Ah, dear brother, why have ye tarried so long from me? alas, this wound on your head hath caught over-much cold. And so then they rowed from the land, and Sir Bedivere beheld all those ladies go from him. Then Sir Bedivere cried: Ah, my lord Arthur, what shall become of me, now ye go from me and leave me here alone among mine enemies? Comfort thyself, said the king, and do as well as thou mayest, for in me is no trust for to trust in; for I will into the vale of Avilion[33] to heal me of my grievous wound: and if thou hear never more of me,

[31]Ripple. [32]Grow dark.
[33]Avalon, home of spirits of the departed.

pray for my soul. But ever the queens and ladies wept and shrieked, that it was pity to hear. And as soon as Sir Bedivere had lost the sight of the barge, he wept and wailed, and so took the forest; and so he went all that night, and in the morning he was ware betwixt two holts[34] hoar, of a chapel and an hermitage.

CHAPTER VI

How Sir Bedivere Found Him on the Morrow Dead in an Hermitage, and How He Abode There with the Hermit

THEN was Sir Bedivere glad, and thither he went; and when he came into the chapel, he saw where lay an hermit groveling on all four, there fast by a tomb was new graven.[35] When the hermit saw Sir Bedivere he knew him well, for he was but little tofore Bishop of Canterbury, that Sir Mordred flemed.[36] Sir, said Bedivere, what man is there interred that ye pray so fast for? Fair son, said the hermit, I wot not verily, but by deeming. But this night, at midnight, here came a number of ladies, and brought hither a dead corpse, and prayed me to bury him; and here they offered an hundred tapers, and they gave me an hundred besants.[37] Alas, said Sir Bedivere, that was my lord King Arthur, that here lieth buried in this chapel. Then Sir Bedivere swooned; and when he awoke he prayed the hermit he might abide with him still there, to live with fasting and prayers. For from hence will I never go, said Sir Bedivere, by my will, but all the days of my life here to pray for my lord Arthur. Ye are welcome to me, said the hermit, for I know ye better than ye ween that I do. Ye are the bold Bedivere, and the full noble duke, Sir Lucan the Butler, was your brother. Then Sir Bedivere told the hermit all as ye have heard tofore. So there bode Sir Bedivere with the hermit that was tofore Bishop of Canterbury, and there Sir Bedivere put upon him poor clothes, and served the hermit full lowly in fasting and in prayers. Thus of Arthur I find never more written in books that be authorized nor more of the very certainty of his death heard I never read, but thus was he led away in a ship wherein were three queens; that one was King Arthur's sister, Queen Morgan le Fay; the other was the Queen of Northgalis; the third was the Queen of the Waste Lands. Also there was Nimue, the chief lady of the lake, that had wedded Pelleas the good knight; and this lady had done much for King Arthur, for she would never suffer Sir Pelleas to be in no place where he should be in danger of his life; and so he lived to the uttermost of his days with her in great rest. More of the death of King Arthur could I never find, but that ladies brought him to his burials; and such one was buried there, that the hermit bare witness that sometime was Bishop of Canterbury, but yet the hermit knew not in certain that he was verily the body of King Arthur: for this tale Sir Bedivere, knight of the Table Round, made it to be written.

CHAPTER VII

Of the Opinion of Some Men of the Death of King Arthur; and How Queen Guenever Made Her a Nun in Almesbury

YET some men say in many parts of England that King Arthur is not dead, but had by the will of our Lord Jesu into another place; and men say that he shall come again, and he shall win the holy cross. I will not say it shall be so, but rather I will say, here in this world he changed his life. But many men say that there is written upon his tomb this verse: *Hic jacet Arthurus Rex, quondam Rexque futurus.*[38] Thus leave I here Sir Bedivere with the hermit, that dwelled that time in a chapel beside Glastonbury, and there was his hermitage. And so they lived in their prayers, and fastings, and great abstinence. And when Queen Guenever understood that King Arthur was slain, and all the noble knights, Sir Mordred and all the remnant, then the queen stole away, and five ladies with her, and so she went to

[34]Wooded hills. Later (Chap. x) they are spoken of as cliffs.

[35]Dug. [36]Put to flight.

[37]Coin first made at Byzantium (Constantinople).

[38]Here lies King Arthur, King formerly and so to be in the future.

Almesbury; and there she let make herself a nun, and ware white clothes and black, and great penance she took, as ever did sinful lady in this land, and never creature could make her merry; but lived in fasting, prayers, and alms-deeds, that all manner of people marveled how virtuously she was changed. Now leave we Queen Guenever in Almesbury, a nun in white clothes and black, and there she was abbess and ruler as reason would; and turn we from her, and speak we of Sir Launcelot du Lake.

CHAPTER VIII

How when Sir Launcelot Heard of the Death of King Arthur, and of Sir Gawaine, and Other Matters, He Came into England

AND when he heard in his country that Sir Mordred was crowned king in England, and made war against King Arthur, his own father, and would let him to land in his own land; also it was told Sir Launcelot how that Sir Mordred had laid siege about the Tower of London, by cause the queen would not wed him; then was Sir Launcelot wroth out of measure, and said to his kinsmen: Alas, that double traitor Sir Mordred, now me repenteth that ever he escaped my hands, for much shame hath he done unto my lord Arthur; for all I feel by the doleful letter that my lord Sir Gawaine sent me, on whose soul Jesu have mercy, that my lord Arthur is full hard bestad. Alas, said Sir Launcelot, that ever I should live to hear that most noble king that made me knight thus to be overset with his subject in his own realm. And this doleful letter that my lord, Sir Gawaine, hath sent me afore his death, praying me to see his tomb, wit you well his doleful words shall never go from mine heart, for he was a full noble knight as ever was born; and in an unhappy hour was I born that ever I should have that unhap to slay first Sir Gawaine, Sir Gaheris the good knight, and mine own friend Sir Gareth, that full noble knight. Alas, I may say I am unhappy, said Sir Launcelot, that ever I should do thus unhappily, and, alas, yet might I never have hap to slay that traitor, Sir Mordred. Leave your complaints, said Sir Bors, and first revenge you of the death of Sir Gawaine; and it will be well done that ye see Sir Gawaine's tomb, and secondly that ye revenge my lord Arthur, and my lady, Queen Guenever. I thank you, said Sir Launcelot, for ever ye will my worship. Then they made them ready in all the haste that might be, with ships and galleys, with Sir Launcelot and his host to pass into England. And so he passed over the sea till he came to Dover, and there he landed with seven kings, and the number was hideous to behold. Then Sir Launcelot spered[39] of men of Dover where was King Arthur become. Then the people told him how that he was slain, and Sir Mordred and an hundred thousand died on a day; and how Sir Mordred gave King Arthur there the first battle at his landing, and there was good Sir Gawaine slain; and on the morn Sir Mordred fought with the king upon Barham Down, and there the king put Sir Mordred to the worse. Alas, said Sir Launcelot, this is the heaviest tidings that ever came to me. Now, fair sirs, said Sir Launcelot, show me the tomb of Sir Gawaine. And then certain people of the town brought him into the Castle of Dover, and showed him the tomb. Then Sir Launcelot kneeled down and wept, and prayed heartily for his soul. And that night he made a dole, and all they that would come had as much flesh, fish, wine and ale, and every man and woman had twelve pence, come who would. Thus with his own hand dealt he this money, in a mourning gown; and ever he wept, and prayed them to pray for the soul of Sir Gawaine. And on the morn all the priests and clerks that might be gotten in the country were there, and sang mass of *requiem*;[40] and there offered first Sir Launcelot, and he offered an hundred pound; and then the seven kings offered forty pound apiece; and also there was a thousand knights, and each of them offered a pound; and the offering dured from morn till night, and Sir Launcelot lay two nights on his tomb in prayers and weeping. Then on the third day Sir Launcelot called the kings, dukes, earls, barons, and knights, and said thus: My fair lords, I thank you all of your coming into this country with me, but we

[39] Asked. [40] Mass for the dead.

came too late, and that shall repent me while I live, but against death may no man rebel. But sithen[41] it is so, said Sir Launcelot, I will myself ride and seek my lady, Queen Guenever, for as I hear say she hath had great pain and much disease; and I heard say that she is fled into the west. Therefore ye all shall abide me here, and but if I come again within fifteen days, then take your ships and your fellowship, and depart into your country, for I will do as I say to you.

CHAPTER IX

How Sir Launcelot Departed to Seek the Queen Guenever, and How He Found Her at Almesbury

THEN came Sir Bors de Ganis, and said: My lord Sir Launcelot, what think ye for to do, now to ride in this realm? wit ye well ye shall find few friends. Be as be may, said Sir Launcelot, keep you still here, for I will forth on my journey, and no man nor child shall go with me. So it was no boot to strive, but he departed and rode westerly, and there he sought a seven or eight days; and at the last he came to a nunnery, and then was Queen Guenever ware of Sir Launcelot as he walked in the cloister. And when she saw him there she swooned thrice, that all the ladies and gentlewomen had work enough to hold the queen up. So when she might speak, she called ladies and gentlewomen to her, and said: Ye marvel, fair ladies, why I make this fare. Truly, she said, it is for the sight of yonder knight that yonder standeth; wherefore I pray you all call him to me. When Sir Launcelot was brought to her, then she said to all the ladies: Through this man and me hath all this war been wrought, and the death of the most noblest knights of the world; for through our love that we have loved together is my most noble lord slain. Therefore, Sir Launcelot, wit thou well I am set in such a plight to get my soul heal; and yet I trust through God's grace that after my death to have a sight of the blessed face of Christ, and at domesday to sit on His right side, for as sinful as ever I was are saints in heaven. Therefore, Sir Launcelot, I require thee and beseech thee heartily, for all the love that ever was betwixt us, that thou never see me more in the visage; and I command thee, on God's behalf, that thou forsake my company, and to thy kingdom thou turn again, and keep well thy realm from war and wrake;[42] for as well as I have loved thee, mine heart will not serve me to see thee, for through thee and me is the flower of kings and knights destroyed; therefore, Sir Launcelot, go to thy realm, and there take thee a wife, and live with her with joy and bliss; and I pray thee heartily, pray for me to our Lord that I may amend my misliving. Now, sweet madam, said Sir Launcelot, would ye that I should now return again unto my country, and there to wed a lady? Nay, madam, wit you well that shall I never do, for I shall never be so false to you of that I have promised; but the same destiny that ye have taken you to, I will take me unto, for to please Jesu, and ever for you I cast me specially to pray. If thou wilt do so, said the queen, hold thy promise, but I may never believe but that thou wilt turn to the world again. Well, madam, said he, ye say as pleaseth you, yet wist you me never false of my promise, and God defend but I should forsake the world as ye have done. For in the quest of the Sangreal I had forsaken the vanities of the world had not your lord been. And if I had done so at that time, with my heart, will, and thought, I had passed all the knights that were in the Sangreal except Sir Galahad, my son. And therefore, lady, sithen ye have taken you to perfection, I must needs take me to perfection, of right. For I take record of God, in you I have had mine earthly joy; and if I had found you now so disposed, I had cast to have you into mine own realm.

CHAPTER X

How Sir Launcelot Came to the Hermitage where the Archbishop of Canterbury Was, and How He Took the Habit on Him

BUT sithen I find you thus disposed, I ensure you faithfully, I will ever take me to penance, and pray while my life lasteth, if I

[41] Since.

[42] Ruin.

may find any hermit, either gray or white, that will receive me. Wherefore, madam, I pray you kiss me and never no more. Nay, said the queen, that shall I never do, but abstain you from such works: and they departed. But there was never so hard an hearted man but he would have wept to see the dolor that they made; for there was lamentation as they had been stung with spears; and many times they swooned, and the ladies bare the queen to her chamber. And Sir Launcelot awoke and went and took his horse, and rode all that day and all night in a forest, weeping. And at the last he was ware of an hermitage and a chapel stood betwixt two cliffs; and then he heard a little bell ring to mass, and thither he rode and alit, and tied his horse to the gate, and heard mass. And he that sang mass was the Bishop of Canterbury. Both the Bishop and Sir Bedivere knew Sir Launcelot, and they spake together after mass. But when Sir Bedivere had told his tale all whole, Sir Launcelot's heart almost brast for sorrow, and Sir Launcelot threw his arms abroad, and said: Alas, who may trust this world. And then he kneeled down on his knee, and prayed the Bishop to shrive him and assoil[43] him. And then he besought the Bishop that he might be his brother. Then the Bishop said: I will gladly; and there he put an habit upon Sir Launcelot, and there he served God day and night with prayers and fastings. Thus the great host abode at Dover. And then Sir Lionel took fifteen lords with him, and rode to London to seek Sir Launcelot; and there Sir Lionel was slain and many of his lords. Then Sir Bors de Ganis made the great host for to go home again; and Sir Bors, Sir Ector de Maris, Sir Blamore, Sir Bleoberis, with more other of Sir Launcelot's kin, took on them to ride all England over-thwart[44] and endlong, to seek Sir Launcelot. So Sir Bors by fortune rode so long till he came to the same chapel where Sir Launcelot was; and so Sir Bors heard a little bell knell, that rang to mass; and there he alit and heard mass. And when mass was done, the Bishop, Sir Launcelot, and Sir Bedivere came to Sir Bors. And when Sir Bors saw Sir Launcelot in that manner clothing, then he prayed the Bishop that he might be in the same suit. And so there was an habit put upon him, and there he lived in prayers and fasting. And within half a year, there was come Sir Galihud, Sir Galihodin, Sir Blamore, Sir Bleoberis, Sir Villiars, Sir Clarras, and Sir Gahalantine. So all these seven noble knights there abode still. And when they saw Sir Launcelot had taken him to such perfection, they had no list to depart, but took such an habit as he had. Thus they endured in great penance six year; and then Sir Launcelot took the habit of priesthood of the Bishop, and a twelvemonth he sang mass. And there was none of these other knights but they read in books, and holp for to sing mass, and rang bells, and did bodily all manner of service. And so their horses went where they would, for they took no regard of no worldly riches. For when they saw Sir Launcelot endure such penance, in prayers and fastings, they took no force[45] what pain they endured, for to see the noblest knight of the world take such abstinence that he waxed full lean. And thus upon a night, there came a vision to Sir Launcelot, and charged him, in remission of his sins, to haste him unto Almesbury: And by then thou come there, thou shalt find Queen Guenever dead. And therefore take thy fellows with thee, and purvey them of an horse bier, and fetch thou the corpse of her, and bury her by her husband, the noble King Arthur. So this avision came to Sir Launcelot thrice in one night.

CHAPTER XI

How Sir Launcelot Went with His Seven Fellows to Almesbury, and Found There Queen Guenever Dead, Whom They Brought to Glastonbury

THEN Sir Launcelot rose up or[46] day, and told the hermit. It were well done, said the hermit, that ye made you ready, and that you disobey not the avision. Then Sir Launcelot took his seven fellows with him, and on foot they yede[47] from Glastonbury to Almesbury, the which is little more than thirty mile. And thither they came within

[43] Absolve. [44] Across.

[45] Account. [46] Before. [47] Went.

two days, for they were weak and feeble to go. And when Sir Launcelot was come to Almesbury within the nunnery, Queen Guenever died but half an hour afore. And the ladies told Sir Launcelot that Queen Guenever told them all or she passed, that Sir Launcelot had been priest near a twelvemonth, And hither he cometh as fast as he may to fetch my corpse; and beside my lord, King Arthur, he shall bury me. Wherefore the queen said in hearing of them all: I beseech Almighty God that I may never have power to see Sir Launcelot with my worldly eyen; and thus, said all the ladies, was ever her prayer these two days, till she was dead. Then Sir Launcelot saw her visage, but he wept not greatly, but sighed. And so he did all the observance of the service himself, both the dirge at night, and on the morn he sang mass. And there was ordained an horse bier; and so with an hundred torches ever burning about the corpse of the queen, and ever Sir Launcelot with his seven fellows went about the horse bier, singing and reading many an holy orison, and frankincense upon the corpse incensed. Thus Sir Launcelot and his seven fellows went on foot from Almesbury unto Glastonbury. And when they were come to the chapel and the hermitage, there she had a dirge, with great devotion. And on the morn the hermit that sometime was Bishop of Canterbury sang the mass of *requiem* with great devotion. And Sir Launcelot was the first that offered, and then also his seven fellows. And then she was wrapped in cered cloth of Raines,[48] from the top to the toe, in thirtyfold; and after she was put in a web[49] of lead, and then in a coffin of marble. And when she was put in the earth Sir Launcelot swooned, and lay long still, while the hermit came and awaked him, and said: Ye be to blame, for ye displease God with such manner of sorrow making. Truly, said Sir Launcelot, I trust I do not displease God, for He knoweth mine intent. For my sorrow was not, nor is not, for any rejoicing of sin, but my sorrow may never have end. For when I remember of her beauty, and of her noblesse that was both with her king and with her, so when I saw his corpse and her corpse so lie together, truly mine heart would not serve to sustain my careful[50] body. Also when I remember me how by my default, mine orgulity[51] and my pride, that they were both laid full low, that were peerless that ever was living of Christian people, wit you well, said Sir Launcelot, this remembered, of their kindness and mine unkindness, sank so to mine heart, that I might not sustain myself. So the French book maketh mention.

CHAPTER XII

How Sir Launcelot Began to Sicken, and After Died, Whose Body Was Borne to Joyous Gard for to Be Buried

THEN Sir Launcelot never after ate but little meat, ne drank, till he was dead. For then he sickened more and more, and dried, and dwined[52] away. For the Bishop nor none of his fellows might not make him to eat, and little he drank, that he was waxen by a cubit[53] shorter than he was, that the people could not know him. For evermore, day and night, he prayed, but sometime he slumbered a broken sleep; ever he was lying groveling on the tomb of King Arthur and Queen Guenever. And there was no comfort that the Bishop, nor Sir Bors, nor none of his fellows could make him, it availed not. So within six weeks after, Sir Launcelot fell sick, and lay in his bed; and then he sent for the Bishop that there was hermit, and all his true fellows. Then Sir Launcelot said with dreary steven:[54] Sir Bishop, I pray you give to me all my rites that longeth to a Christian man. It shall not need you, said the hermit and all his fellows, it is but heaviness of your blood, ye shall be well mended by the grace of God tomorn. My fair lords, said Sir Launcelot, wit you well my careful body will into the earth, I have warning more than now I will say; therefore give me my rites. So when he was houseled and enelid,[55] and had all that a Christian man ought to have, he prayed the Bishop that his fellows might bear his body to Joyous Gard. Some men

[48]Waxed cloth from Rennes, in Brittany.
[49]Thin sheet.
[50]Distressed. [51]Arrogance. [52]Dwindled.
[53]About eighteen inches. [54]Voice.
[55]Given the Holy Sacrament and anointed.

say it was Alnwick, and some men say it was Bamborough. Howbeit, said Sir Launcelot, me repenteth sore, but I made mine avow sometime, that in Joyous Gard I would be buried. And by cause of breaking of mine avow, I pray you all, lead me thither. Then there was weeping and wringing of hands among his fellows. So at a season of the night they all went to their beds, for they all lay in one chamber. And so after midnight, against day, the Bishop that was hermit, as he lay in his bed asleep, he fell upon a great laughter. And therewithal the fellowship awoke, and came to the Bishop, and asked him what he ailed. Ah Jesu mercy, said the Bishop, why did ye awake me? I was never in all my life so merry and so well at ease. Wherefore? said Sir Bors. Truly, said the Bishop, here was Sir Launcelot with me with more angels than ever I saw men in one day. And I saw the angels heave up Sir Launcelot unto heaven, and the gates of heaven opened against him. It is but dretching of swevens,[56] said Sir Bors, for I doubt not Sir Launcelot aileth nothing but good. It may well be, said the Bishop; go ye to his bed, and then shall ye prove the sooth. So when Sir Bors and his fellows came to his bed they found him stark dead, and he lay as he had smiled, and the sweetest savor about him that ever they felt. Then was there weeping and wringing of hands, and the greatest dole they made that ever made men. And on the morn the Bishop did his mass of *requiem;* and after, the Bishop and all the nine knights put Sir Launcelot in the same horse bier that Queen Guenever was laid in tofore that she was buried. And so the Bishop and they all together went with the body of Sir Launcelot daily, till they came to Joyous Gard; and ever they had an hundred torches burning about him. And so within fifteen days they came to Joyous Gard. And there they laid his corpse in the body of the quire, and sang and read many psalters and prayers over him and about him. And ever his visage was laid open and naked, that all folks might behold him. For such was the custom in those days, that all men of worship should so lie with open visage till that they were buried. And right thus as they were at their service, there came Sir Ector de Maris, that had seven years sought all England, Scotland, and Wales, seeking his brother, Sir Launcelot.

[56]The troubling of dreams.

CHAPTER XIII

How Sir Ector Found Sir Launcelot His Brother Dead, and How Constantine Reigned Next after Arthur; and of the End of This Book

AND when Sir Ector heard such noise and light in the quire of Joyous Gard, he alit and put his horse from him, and came into the quire, and there he saw men sing and weep. And all they knew Sir Ector, but he knew not them. Then went Sir Bors unto Sir Ector, and told him how there lay his brother, Sir Launcelot, dead; and then Sir Ector threw his shield, sword, and helm from him. And when he beheld Sir Launcelot's visage, he fell down in a swoon. And when he waked it were hard any tongue to tell the doleful complaints that he made for his brother. Ah Launcelot, he said, thou were head of all Christian knights, and now I dare say, said Sir Ector, thou Sir Launcelot, there thou liest, that thou were never matched of earthly knight's hand. And thou were the courteoust knight that ever bare shield. And thou were the truest friend to thy lover that ever bestrad horse. And thou were the truest lover of a sinful man that ever loved woman. And thou were the kindest man that ever struck with sword. And thou were the goodliest person that ever came among press of knights. And thou were the meekest man and the gentlest that ever ate in hall among ladies. And thou were the sternest knight to thy mortal foe that ever put spear in the rest. Then there was weeping and dolor out of measure. Thus they kept Sir Launcelot's corpse on loft fifteen days, and then they buried it with great devotion. And then at leisure they went all with the Bishop of Canterbury to his hermitage, and there they were together more than a month. Then Sir Constantine, that was Sir Cador's son of Cornwall, was chosen king of England. And he was a full noble knight, and worshipfully he ruled this realm.

And then this King Constantine sent for the Bishop of Canterbury, for he heard say where he was. And so he was restored unto his Bishopric, and left that hermitage. And Sir Bedivere was there ever still hermit to his life's end. Then Sir Bors de Ganis, Sir Ector de Maris, Sir Gahalantine, Sir Galihud, Sir Galihodin, Sir Blamore, Sir Bleoberis, Sir Villiars le Valiant, Sir Clarrus of Clermont, all these knights drew them to their countries. Howbeit King Constantine would have had them with him, but they would not abide in this realm. And there they all lived in their countries as holy men. And some English books make mention that they went never out of England after the death of Sir Launcelot, but that was but favor of makers.[57] For the French book maketh mention, and is authorized, that Sir Bors, Sir Ector, Sir Blamore, and Sir Bleoberis went into the Holy Land thereas Jesu Christ was quick and dead, and anon as they had stablished their lands. For the book saith, so Sir Launcelot commanded them for to do, or ever he passed out of this world. And these four knights did many battles upon the miscreants[58] or Turks. And there they died upon a Good Friday for God's sake.

Here is the end of the book of King Arthur, and of his noble knights of the Round Table, that when they were whole together there was ever an hundred and forty. And here is the end of the death of Arthur. I pray you all, gentlemen and gentlewomen that readeth this book of Arthur and his knights, from the beginning to the ending, pray for me while I am on live, that God send me good deliverance, and when I am dead, I pray you all pray for my soul. For this book was ended the ninth year of the reign of King Edward the Fourth, by Sir Thomas Maleore, knight, as Jesu help him for his great might, as he is the servant of Jesu both day and night.

Thus endeth this noble and joyous book entitled Le Morte Darthur. Notwithstanding it treateth of the birth, life, and acts of the said King Arthur, of his noble knights of the Round Table, their marvelous enquests and adventures, the achieving of the Sangreal, and in the end the dolorous death and departing out of this world of them all. Which book was reduced into English by Sir Thomas Malory, knight, as afore is said, and by me divided into twenty-one books, chaptered and imprinted, and finished in the abbey Westminster the last day of July the year of our Lord MCCCCLXXXV.

Caxton me fieri fecit.[59]

[57] The fiction of poets. [58] Misbelievers.

[59] Caxton caused me to be made.

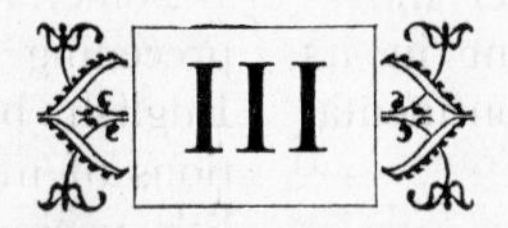

The Renaissance and the Protestant Revolt, 1485–1660

RENAISSANCE is a word of French origin which means literally "rebirth." It is used by all historians to denote the period following the Middle Ages—the period when the modern world took form. This was a period of extraordinary and far-reaching change. Some of the changes which occurred were deliberate and conscious; others were impersonal and unconscious—changes in conditions under which men lived and worked, not brought about deliberately by any person or group of persons. The meaning and influence of the latter were slow in becoming apparent. Yet the two kinds of change went together, and worked to the same end. And men of that time, participating in the movement, felt that what was taking place was a rebirth of civilization after a long night, or perhaps nightmare, of barbarism. They knew all along, as we have seen, that the Mediterranean world, and in fact all Europe, had enjoyed a remarkable civilization before the coming of Christianity. They knew that early in the Christian era this civilization had been shattered, seemingly by the barbarian invasions. They now began to feel that through the intervening centuries until their own time men had been sunk in shameful ignorance, had remained blind to the good possibilities of earthly life, and so had not only continued in a state of barbarism but had gradually declined into a state of corruption. At length, however, men's eyes were being opened; men were becoming conscious of what they had neglected and lost, were reaching out to recover it, and civilization was being reborn.

This conscious effort at recovery had its beginnings in Italy in the fourteenth century, and spread out from Italy over Europe. We, of course, are concerned with England, and in England with the effect of the Renaissance on literature; but we have already seen in earlier periods that we cannot understand what happened or what was written in England without constant reference to continental Europe, and here again it is necessary first to look beyond England. We have to realize that the Renaissance was a lengthy period of complex change, European in its extent, and that it did not effectively touch England or English literature until late in its course. As a conscious effort at recovery it traveled slowly northward, and only began to be felt in England towards the close of the fifteenth century. By that time, moreover, the Renaissance had attained its full complexity, and had produced abundant fruit in Italy, and some in France. In addition, it must always be remembered that any external influence is conditioned in its working by the character of the people who feel it and by their circumstances. And the English, we have noticed, have shown through the centuries a perhaps unique power to absorb foreign influences without being overmastered by them, converting the foreign things into instruments of their own growth after their own fashion. Hence we should not be surprised to find that though the English Renaissance is part and parcel of a larger movement, it is also markedly different in its character and results from its continental sources.

The Age of Discovery

If now we ask what were the great impersonal causes of change which were altering the medieval conditions of life, and giving men a new outlook and new hopes, we find standing in front of all others three late medieval inventions or discoveries: the mariner's compass, gunpowder, and the art of printing with movable types. The Chinese have been credited with making these discoveries long before they were made in Europe—wrongly, it appears, in the case of the compass. But in any event there is no doubt that the compass and gunpowder and the art of printing were independently discovered in Europe late in the Middle Ages, though Europe does owe to the Chinese the art of making paper, without which printing could not have become a means for the multiplication of cheap books. The Arabians learned how to make paper from some Chinese captives in the eighth century, and the art spread rapidly throughout Mohammedan dominions, and was brought by the Moors into Spain in the middle of the twelfth century, whence it spread into France, and then Italy, and later into Germany and England. Printing itself, however, was much the latest of these discoveries, and can only be regarded as antedating the Renaissance because that movement, as has been said, traveled somewhat slowly northward. Printing is generally supposed to have begun about 1440 in the German city of Mainz, and its discovery is ascribed to Johann Gutenberg. Gunpowder was apparently discovered in the thirteenth century by the Englishman, Friar Roger Bacon; and in Italy, France, and England it was being used to discharge projectiles from cannon as early as the first half of the fourteenth century. No one attempts to say who discovered the mariner's compass; but the earliest known description of the instrument occurs in a manuscript written in 1269, and it had come into general use by the early part of the fifteenth century.

Something has already been said in the preceding chapter of the importance of English bowmen in changing the conditions of medieval warfare. What the English yeomen with their deadly long bows began, firearms rapidly completed; and the social importance, or usefulness, of the feudal nobility of Europe tended to disappear as rapidly as it became apparent that a common man with a gun could defeat the best armed and mounted knight without one. The whole character of warfare suffered a revolution, and besides the social consequences just mentioned within Europe, the possession of firearms gave European powers a military advantage which enabled them to dominate the rest of the world. At the same time, thanks to the mariner's compass, the rest of the world was being discovered and opened up for commerce and colonization. Commerce was the stimulus which brought the mariner's compass into use, and sent a host of adventurous and bold explorers out upon the sea. The Crusades exercised so slight an influence on medieval English literature that it was not necessary even to allude to them in the last chapter. Now, however, we must notice that though the efforts of European Christendom between 1096 and 1272 to recover the Holy Land from the Mohammedans failed, except temporarily, of their purpose, still, the Crusades had a lasting and important effect in opening the eyes of Europeans to oriental luxuries and thus creating a demand which resulted in permanent commercial relations between Europe and the East. We think, quite rightly, of a subsistence economy as being characteristic of medieval times; but the self-sufficient community, producing and consuming its own goods, persisted only so long as men saw no opportunity for further economic development. This economy broke down everywhere as rapidly as opportunities for interregional commerce were perceived; and it is scarcely too much to say that the gradual collapse of the feudal social system in the face of growing commercial opportunity during the later Middle Ages was the one great underlying cause of the Renaissance.

Commerce between Europe and the East was carried on principally through Venice, and was so profitable that it aroused the envy of other states and caused them to try to open up a sea route to the Indies and China which could compete with the overland route controlled by the Venetians. The sensational climax, as it now appears to us, was the discovery of America in 1492 by Christopher Columbus; but this was only one episode, and at the time a disappointing one, in a long-continued effort to reach Asia by sea. Success was achieved five years later by the Portuguese when Vasco da Gama, sailing south along the coast of Africa, rounded the Cape of Good Hope, and then proceeded up through the Indian Ocean to Calicut. And in the same year England entered the race by sending John Cabot, a Venetian citizen who had settled in Bristol, on a westward voyage. He reached Labrador or Newfoundland, and went back thinking he had found the coast of China. It did not take long for the Spaniards, for whom Columbus had made his several voyages, to learn that though their explorer had not succeeded in his aim, he had led them to a country rich in gold and silver, and of vast extent, whose very existence had been unguessed.

No words can be adequate to describe, no effort of the imagination can be sufficient to grasp, the full effect of these exploits upon the life of Europe. They forced a revolution in thought which was at once exhilarating and bewildering. The world was proved to be larger, more various, richer in yet unknown possibilities of all kinds—including of course the acquisition of wealth—than had been dreamed; and human capacities were proved to be equal to the challenge. Life here and now was a better thing than Christian teachers had admitted—life was action, which could lead to earthly power and earthly happiness, proving the worth of positive human effort directed to the control of natural forces for the satisfaction of desire. There came, then, an indefinite enlargement of the sense of personality, a conviction of the worth of present earthly life considered simply in and for itself, without necessary reference to a life of the soul after death, and a new self-confidence. This was a growth of individualism, and individualism was further promoted by the development of commerce which had stimulated exploration. Commerce gave scope for personal initiative, ambition, and even heroism; it was the open door out of the medieval world of inherited status; and the wealth which was its end, when achieved, gave opportunity for the expression of individuality.

Rediscovery of the Ancient World

The economic development which awakened individualism, and the prosperity which enabled men to seek the refinements of life, came earliest in Italy. And accordingly it was first in Italy that men began, more than a century before the spectacular successes of the explorers, to look back to classical civilization with a new sense of what had been lost throughout the Middle Ages. We should be prepared to think of this backward look as inevitable. We have to keep remembering that medieval people were never without consciousness of the greatness of Rome, and also that they used such fragments saved from the wreck of classical culture as they could appropriate. Zealous Christians argued in vain for a complete divorce between the pagans and themselves. Other Christians no less zealous, and wiser—such for example as St. Augustine—argued for the appropriation from classical antiquity of all that might serve the cause of sound learning. And in general, whatever seemed to be the attitude of the Church, medieval people took over from the ancient world what they could, and used it according to their lights. We noticed in the last chapter that allegory and allegorical interpretation, for instance, which are generally regarded as distinctively medieval, were inherited from classical literature. The whole question is really one of cultural development. In the thousand years before the fourteenth century the barbarians who had overrun Europe had become humanized, had built up with considerable help from antiquity a distinctive culture of their own which had rather quickly reached its limits, and were now at length ready, and anxious, to learn more from antiquity.

Influence of Petrarch

The great and justly celebrated pioneer in this attempt was Francis Petrarch, who was born near Florence in 1304 and died in 1374. Somebody has called him the first man who felt contempt for the Middle Ages. "Contempt" is perhaps too strong a word, but it is unqualifiedly true that Petrarch felt a boundless and lifelong enthusiasm for classical culture, born of the conviction that the great writers of antiquity were more completely developed human beings, were wiser, and were far more accomplished artists than any the Middle Ages could show. He took the utmost pains to ferret out neglected manuscripts, studied them with loving minuteness, and managed to gain a comprehensive close knowledge of classical Latin literature. He learned enough to realize that a knowledge of Greek literature would be more important and rewarding to him than his Latin studies; but he could only have learned Greek with the help of some Byzantine scholar, and the opportunity never came. This was by no means the only limitation he suffered; his appreciation of Virgil was vitiated by the notion that the *Aeneid* was an allegory, and he remained in many other ways a man of the Middle Ages. But what is remarkable and significant is the extent of his success in leading the way out of the Middle Ages. He communicated his enthusiasm wherever he went; and his aim was not merely the study of classical literature, but study for the sake of revival, study for the sake of emulation, study to the end that men might again become fully and maturely human, and might again write great poetry. He himself ardently desired fame, and won it abundantly in his own lifetime as well as in after ages to this day. And he remains endlessly interesting because of his own clear consciousness of the opposition between the Christian and the classical, or pagan, views of life. Of course the classical Greco-Roman civilization was not a tight little society whose members from one generation to another all thought and felt and wrote alike; hence it is nonsense to speak of "the Greek view of life" as if there were only one. Nevertheless, while Christians early and late have found elements of close kinship, almost of identity, between themselves and some classical philosophers and poets, there does remain not only a difference, but an undeniable opposition between Christian and pagan—and Petrarch knew it, felt it within himself, and wrestled with it unsuccessfully through a great part of his life.

Indeed, it is this inner contradiction, and the self-consciousness at once heightened and troubled which issued from it, that earns for Petrarch the title of "the first modern man." He blamed himself for the earthly passion which inspired his famous series of sonnets to Laura—sonnets in which he developed and refined the medieval discovery of romantic love, and so handed it on as a source of lyric inspiration to a host of Renaissance poets in Italy, France, and England. But even after he had repentantly detached himself from idealized yet earthly love, he could not give up his desire for fame, though he recognized this as being, from a strict Christian point of view, equally a vanity—a worthless bauble in comparison with the eternal life of the soul. This was the way in which the opposition presented itself to him. We may put it more generally by saying that to the Greeks and Romans human life was significant and full of solid worth in and for itself, whereas to the Christian it was only a means to an end beyond itself. The Greeks and Romans had studied to obtain the most from life, in the sense of developing, refining, and exercising all human capacities to the fullest extent; they had held determinedly to a belief in the dignity and greatness of human nature, and in the possibility of a sufficing happiness in this life, regardless of any life to come. This confidence had persisted even after they had recognized the tragic issues of life; for they had succeeded in showing that the full grandeur of human nature scarcely appears until man is confronted by defeat, when he yet in a true sense can remain superior, through sheer heroic integrity, to death itself. The ancients had vindicated their faith nobly in the sculpture, in the architecture, and above all in the literature they had created and bequeathed to posterity. No one could become acquainted with their heroic poetry and not long to emulate them, in action and in artistic creation. No one could become acquainted with them and fail to see that medieval Christianity had been blind to possibilities in life and in human nature which make an irresistible appeal to what is best in ourselves; and equally no one could fail to see that medieval people, and institutions—the Church itself—had been corrupted by slavery to dogmas which gave no adequate encouragement or outlet to our temporal activities while we are temporal beings.

This is the kind of thinking we can see expressed or implied in Petrarch's writings; and yet, beside it we see something very different. For Petrarch went back to the "ancients" within Christianity as well as to those who lived before Christ, and, in the writings of St. Augustine most especially, he was confronted by the unescapable logic of the otherworldly faith which he devoutly accepted. If it *is true* that the soul of man is to live on eternally after death, in perfect happiness in Heaven or in complete torment in Hell; and if it *is true* that every man deserves eternal punishment, but that some by God's grace may escape it, yet assuredly none will be snatched from the fire who does not consecrate himself to righteousness and worship;—why, then, it behooves man to cut himself loose just as far as is humanly possible from every earthly attachment, to live here as a stranger on pilgrimage, and to realize that every appeal of this world, no matter of what kind, is an evil deception which will ensnare him if he yield, and distract him, perhaps fatally, from his goal.

Petrarch saw no way of reconciling these two views of life, yet he could not let go of either; consequently he remained a troubled and divided spirit, trying somehow to make the best of both worlds. Not least for this reason, the more one studies him the more enlightening does he seem as the prototype of modern humanity. Through him we see better than through any others after him how the Renaissance, as a movement in art and literature, was integrally joined to the heroic work of the explorers, who also in their way were opening up the modern world and shattering some medieval conceptions. We see, too, how inevitably the Renaissance was, in its artistic and literary phases, a revival of classical studies. And, finally, in Petrarch's divided allegiance—which forced him to keep trying to make independent judgments—we see not only the birth of individualism and of the modern critical intelligence, but also the beginning of a progressive disintegration which has led, from his time to ours, continually away from the unity of thought and feeling achieved in Europe in the twelfth and thirteenth centuries.

Study of Greek

By the end of the fourteenth century there were one or two Byzantine scholars in Italy teaching Greek; and after the Turks captured Constantinople in the middle of the fifteenth century a good many Greek scholars fled to Italy, bringing Greek manuscripts. From this time, the new study of classical antiquity meant everywhere the study of Greek as well as Latin; and most of those throughout Europe and England who followed Petrarch's lead recognized, as he had, that the study of Greek was of the first importance, because Latin literature and thought and taste were all derived from what the ancient Greeks had done. Nevertheless, throughout the Renaissance, Latin was studied much more than Greek, just as it has been, on the whole, throughout modern times, always for the same reason: Latin was a great deal closer, and Greek required more time, and far more strenuous application, for anything like mastery. To medieval people, of course, Latin was already a familiar language, and what was required was not so much linguistic study as new eyes. A few writers of the twelfth and thirteenth centuries had become acquainted with most of the Latin literature that deeply influenced Petrarch without, however, seeing that they had entered into a very different world from their own, and that the whole spirit, and the standards and achievements, of classical civilization offered a disturbing challenge to medieval Christian culture. This Petrarch did perceive clearly, and it is exactly this that makes his career a turning-point in history.

Humanism

Those who followed Petrarch as students of Greek and Latin were called humanists —that is, the exponents of *humanism.* This new word was found for the new kind of study, which very quickly spread over Italy in the fifteenth century, and forced its way into university teaching. Renaissance humanism has often been defined as simply the study of the ancient Greek and Roman poets, philosophers, and historians. The definition is correct enough but incomplete, because the word "humanism" denotes the object of this study, which is the important thing to grasp. Petrarch and the scholars who succeeded him aimed to bring in and foster the study of "humanity" as a subject no less worthy of attention than the "divinity" or theology which in the Middle Ages held the supreme place in the field of higher learning. And they were all convinced, as has been said in discussing Petrarch, that the best material for studying mature and cultivated humanity was to be found in Greek and Roman literature. What the ancients had done had been accomplished without benefit of divine revelation; their civilization was "human" in that sense. In addition, the ancients had sedulously developed their humanity, instead of fearing it, repressing it, and trying to escape from it, as it was felt the Middle Ages had. And finally it seemed self-evident from classical literature and art that the cultivation of humanity was as well worth attention and effort as the study of divinity.

Obviously this was a serious conclusion which set up a serious purpose as the aim of humanism. There are several obstacles in the way of our understanding clearly what was taking place. We are always tending to think too well of ourselves and others, and we do not readily recognize how frivolous and stupid, or at any rate wrong-headed, very many people have been in every generation. Many disciples of the humanists promptly took the superficial view that the conflict between humanism and Christianity was one between "body" and "soul," and accordingly they celebrated the rights and rewards of present bodily life (adducing classical precedent), tried to discredit Christian morality by asserting that it was founded on dogma and prejudice rather than on reason, and ended by encouraging the spread of a sophisticated sensuality which often descended into sheer animalism.

Machiavellianism

Many considerations of different kinds united during the Renaissance to suggest that Christianity was a congeries of superstitions rather than a divine revelation, and the suggestion was eagerly and undiscriminatingly accepted by men impatient of restraint. A spread of animalism was only one result; another was the spread of what came to be called Machiavellianism. Niccolò Machiavelli, a Florentine statesman of the late fifteenth and early sixteenth centuries, was a patriot who longed to see Italy united under one sovereign and who possessed an acute mind and had a genius for seeing events and people as they really were. When he was forced into retirement, he wrote a short treatise on the art of government, entitled *The Prince,* which became famous, and then notorious. For the notion quickly gained currency that Machiavelli was a kind of monster who justified and advised every crime known to man in the pursuit of power. Innumerable references in English Renaissance literature show that to call a man a Machiavellian came to be regarded as a short way of saying that he was a hardened and unscrupulous villain who would stop at nothing to gain his end. This was a gross perversion of what *The Prince* actually contains, but it had this basis, that Machiavelli did give unabashed expression to the doctrine that "the end justifies the means." The end Machiavelli had in view was the welfare of the whole Italian people; but all around him were men who, "emancipated" as he was from the trammels of Christian morality, seemed ready without hesitation to commit any crime for *their own personal ends*—a

To the left above is St. Thomas More. (Courtesy of the Frick Collection.) To the right above is Erasmus, the great Dutch scholar. (Courtesy of the New York Public Library.) To the left below is Henry VIII (collection of Earl Spencer, Althorp); and to the right below is John Colet (courtesy of the New York Public Library). These portraits were made by Henry VIII's court painter, Hans Holbein the Younger (1497–1543).

Above is an engraving of London made in 1616 by Claes Jan Visscher. London at this time had a population of about 100,000, and extended some four miles from east to west along the Thames ("Thamesis Fluvius" in the engraving). On the south side of the River ("South Warke" in the engraving, towards the bottom) may be seen at the right some taverns, clustered about the Bridge Gate, on the top of which are traitors' heads, stuck on poles. Extending beyond the Gate across the River is old London Bridge, covered with buildings. At the extreme left on the south side may be seen the Bear Garden, and the Globe Theater built in 1598. On the north side of the Thames, at the extreme left, rises old St. Paul's, destroyed, with much of the City around it, in the Great Fire of 1666 (see Pepys's description, pages 680–685). The north side of the River was lined with palaces of the nobility. (Courtesy of the Folger Shakespeare Library.)

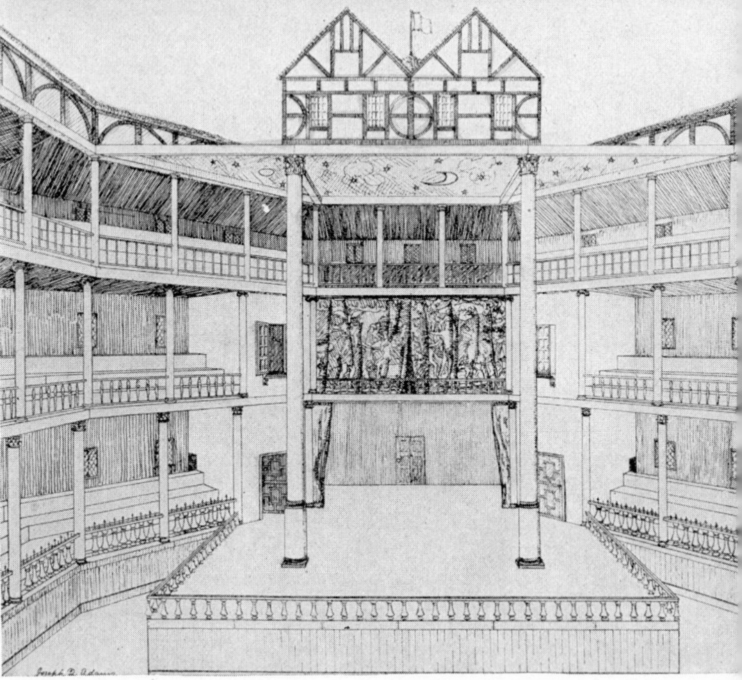

Above is a reconstruction of the interior of the Globe Theater, from John Quincy A *A Life of William Shakespeare* (used by permission of Mr. Adams). The stage proje into the unroofed center of the theater, though there is a roof (with painted stars and c moon on the ceiling) extending over part of it. Only the small backstage area could be at need, by curtains. Above this section of the stage is a balcony. To the right are the ti and facing page of the first collected edition of Shakespeare's plays, commonly referred to First Folio. On the facing page are Ben Jonson's verses on the portrait. The portr engraved by Martin Droeshout, and is one of only two likenesses of Shakespeare which h claim to authenticity (the other being the bust in Stratford Church by Gerard John Janssen, of Southwark). (Courtesy of the Pierpont Morgan Library.)

To the Reader.

This Figure, that thou here seest put,
It was for gentle Shakespeare cut;
Wherein the Grauer had a strife
with Nature, to out-doo the life:
O, could he but haue drawne his wit
As well in brasse, as he hath hit
His face; the Print would then surpasse
All, that vvas euer vvrit in brasse.
But, since he cannot, Reader, looke
Not on his Picture, but his Booke.

B. I.

Mr. WILLIAM SHAKESPEARES COMEDIES, HISTORIES, & TRAGEDIES.

Published according to the True Originall Copies.

LONDON
Printed by Isaac Iaggard, and Ed. Blount. 1623.

To the left above is Sir Thomas Wyatt, and to the right above, Henry Howard, Earl of Surrey—the two most important poets of the first half of the sixteenth century represented in *Tottel's Miscellany* (1557). Both portraits are reproduced from Bartolozzi's engravings after Hans Holbein's contemporary drawings. To the left below is George Herbert, a poet of the "metaphysical school," as represented in Izaak Walton's *Life of Herbert,* 1670. To the right below is an engraved portrait of Sir Philip Sidney, whose *Astrophel and Stella* contains some of the best sonnets of the Elizabethan era. (These portraits are reproduced by courtesy of the New York Public Library.)

very different thing, of course, yet not different enough to keep people from calling unscrupulous villainy Machiavellianism.

Neo-Latin Literature

The "Machiavellian," as well as the sensualist, adduced classical precedent for his unmoral creed, and, in general, classical precedent became a criterion: Whatever was "classical" was excellent; whatever was not "classical" was barbarous or, as everybody later began to say, "Gothic." "Gothic" remained until the nineteenth century a term of opprobrium, signifying what was thought to be rude, uncouth, irregular, or uncivilized in art, literature, or manners. So high did enthusiasm for the "classical" mount that precise or slavish imitation, rather than emulation, became the ideal of many humanists; and to write prose exactly as Cicero wrote it, or poetry exactly as Virgil or Horace wrote it, and in Cicero's or Virgil's Latin, was the aim now cherished. Nor did imitation stop here. Pagan customs, observances, worship were revived. Every kind of effort to turn back the clock was made. In England late in the sixteenth century at Cambridge University Gabriel Harvey tried to induce English poets, Spenser amongst them, if they would not write in Latin, at least to write English verse in imitation of classical quantitative measures.

The saying that history never repeats itself is truer than some popular sayings, and all attempts to turn the clock back, to return to good old days and customs, are predestined to failure. As any change gathers momentum, there are always people who will try to push it to impossible extremes, and who make themselves, if not the movement, ridiculous, and do a good deal of mischief. So it was during the Renaissance. The artificial and frigid Latin prose and verse of the Renaissance is a buried monument to human wrong-headedness. It fell barren and lifeless from its creators' hands and was promptly buried in a few libraries where it has since lain undisturbed. Nevertheless, these slavish imitators, and the sensualists and Machiavellians, still attract undue attention to themselves and obstruct our view of the real nature and service of humanism. At its center, we must recall, humanism was a re-assertion, parallel with the heroic exploits we have noticed as one side of the Renaissance, of confidence in the worth and dignity of human nature, and an effort to restore the balance between this world and the next which it was thought the Middle Ages had lost. Humanism resorted to classical studies because classical civilization seemed to offer the best available guidance for exploring the higher possibilities of earthly life and for cultivating and refining crude human nature.

Humanistic Educational and Literary Standards

From the study of classical civilization came the humanistic ideal of life as itself an art. This ideal received unsurpassed expression in the famous book entitled *The Courtier,* by Baldassare Castiglione; and of education as a discipline calculated for the symmetrical and harmonious development of all human abilities. The professional soldier or theologian, musician or logician, actor or lawyer, to the extent that his development was one-sided for the sake of a limited expertness, was believed to be dehumanized; and only the well-rounded man, whose training developed equally his body, emotions, and mind, who possessed varied accomplishments but was not too expert in any of them, who had varied knowledge but was not a narrow specialist in any field—only the man who was thus balanced, cultivated, and accomplished could be called fully human. To set up such a standard was to bring disinterested reason to bear on all exclusive claims—those of the Church or of any other institution or profession—and to establish independent criticism.

In art and literature it seemed reasonable to ask for the same balance, symmetry, restraint, and smoothness that were required for acceptable practice of the art of living. Whatever was whimsical or merely fanciful, extreme, impulsive, disordered, or vague was therefore condemnable. It was generally acknowledged that poets are born, not made, and that the best poetry attains a happiness of effect which no rules of composition can teach; but it was confidently believed that the poet, no matter how great his genius, must be disciplined and formed, taught to avoid faults, to observe decorum, and to subdue native wildness to reason. "Decorum" in this connection meant simply fitness or appropriateness in the delineation of character. A prince must act and talk like a prince, a merchant like a merchant, and so on, else the effect would be merely grotesque, and truth would be sacrificed to sensationalism. To the objection that in actual life one could find unprincely princes, the answer was that the poet should not be concerned with the representation of the eccentric or exceptional, but of the broadly typical human being. Poetry should not be the mirror of particular fact, but of generalized truth rendered vivid and concrete by embodiment in the life and speech of appropriately formed characters. In actual life we find much confusion—men and women whose natures are mixed and contradictory, men whose capacities are only half-realized, people whose lives are twisted or snuffed out by sheer unmeaning accident, hypocrites and liars and backbiters apparently prospering at the expense of the righteous, and so on. It was held to be the office of the poet to draw meaning out of this confusion, and to represent life, not photographically as it is, but as it might be and should be, and so to achieve a higher truth, by bringing out clearly and unmistakably what in particular cases is only more or less hinted at in actual life. Thus the poet himself must be an informed and critical observer, capable in selection and rejection, with a view to making his picture more real than actual life, and more significant and impressive. Thus too the poet accepts a fearful responsibility, because he must see more clearly and deeply than ordinary men, and rise equal to the demands of his theme, and so become a leader and teacher of mankind.

This, briefly, was the critical standard for imaginative literature set up by humanism. It had behind it, of course, the authority of classical precedent; but it derived weight rather from its seriousness and from the claim, more and more emphasized as time went on, that it was based, not on tradition, but on reason. And though the study of classical literature was regarded as indispensable for the guidance and development of the poet, the forms and style of classical poetry were not held to be sacrosanct, except by a few fanatics, who were not taken very seriously by their contemporaries. Ben Jonson expressed the general view when he said the ancients were to be looked to as guides, not commanders. And, in general, modern poets were encouraged to emulate rather than merely imitate classical writers. It became a patriotic ambition to try to do for one's own time and people what the most celebrated ancient writers had done for theirs. The humanists were, it is true, strong for discipline, and they erected high hurdles over which modern poets were to leap, but the effect of their doctrine was not repressive; it was extraordinarily stimulating.

Medieval Survivals in the Renaissance

Today, when we look back on the Renaissance, we cannot see it as did those who took part in it. In our study of the later Middle Ages we noticed that an unmistakable assertion of the claims of secular earthly life occurred in France as early as the twelfth century, and received literary expression in the romances of chivalry and in the poetry of romantic love (see page 110). Life in this world, developing along its own line, independently of the Church, and even in opposition to the Church, was not an innovation which had to await the Renaissance. The decisive step in that direction had already been taken, and the Renaissance is nowadays correctly seen as a further step, not so revolutionary as its own leaders supposed. Furthermore, both in literature and in thought much that is regarded as characteristically medieval persisted through the Renaissance. We can see this almost everywhere in English literature of the end of the sixteenth century, and it appears to be a logical consequence of the fact already mentioned (see page 118), that the first half-century of printing in England flooded the country with books renewing the atmosphere and spirit of medievalism. The truth is that even the greatest changes are slower and less complete than we like to imagine, and the generations of men are bound to one another by invisible ties not easily severed. In retrospect we can always see this, though even in retrospect we cannot always see how or why it has been so. What we do see, in Spenser, in Marlowe, in Shakespeare, is, not a sharp break or repudiation, but continuity with the later Middle Ages. Spenser in writing his *Faerie Queene* consciously looked back to Chaucer, to the romances of chivalry, and to the moralities, and felt that there he was on firm ground. His imagination could work freely and surely with what was familiar and ingrained; it could not suddenly leap into fields entirely new. So, too, Marlowe's *Doctor Faustus* is in form really a morality play; and Shakespeare's plays have intimate bonds of connection with the whole native medieval development of dramatic art, out of which they seem to issue almost as a natural growth and culmination. Or, again, if we look not to authors, but to streams of influence, we see the medieval conception of courtesy, the medieval discovery of romantic love, and medieval symbolism or allegory carried on into and through the Renaissance —until finally we may begin to think the Renaissance a fiction.

Mingling of Old and New: Marlowe's "Doctor Faustus"

To think the Renaissance a fiction would be a grave mistake—fortunately a mistake no unprejudiced student will be tempted to make. For the evidence that along with the old there is also something in this literature which is distinctly new and transforming is spread everywhere, and cannot be escaped. When we first look at *Doctor Faustus* we see personified virtues and vices contesting for man's soul, and we see Marlowe apparently unable to escape what had been a cardinal difficulty in the moralities—the reduction of the hero to a passive role, while the real struggle which gives the specifically dramatic interest goes on about him. But then, before we are through, at our first quick reading, we cannot help seeing also that the old symbolic framework has been put to a new kind of use. Despite his passive role, Faustus begins to have for us a personal interest. The colorless "Mankind" or "Everyman" of the old moralities has become an individual with positive qualities, with a boundless curiosity, a soaring desire for knowledge and power and full experience of life, and daring self-confidence. Faustus, in a word, is still a type, but he is the typical new man of the Renaissance, determined to see and learn and experience all things for himself, at whatever cost. The cost, in accordance with traditional belief, is high, and the end is agony, but at least Faustus has been himself.

There can be no doubt of the meaning of this. Marlowe has a new theme, which shadows forth, imperfectly but unmistakably, a whole new realm of thought and aspiration. Entrance into this realm of worldliness places man in mortal conflict with medieval otherworldliness, as Marlowe seems to recognize. Nevertheless, the impulse towards fullness of earthly life is irresistible, and Marlowe himself is intoxicated by the new prospect, and gives it grand expression in verse which itself is a revelation of new power in the language. Hence in studying the English Renaissance we have constantly to remember that though the new literature of the sixteenth century had vital connections with the native medieval past, and to a certain extent was a growth out of that past, still, it was also really new—permeated with the Renaissance spirit of worldliness and also with influences from the Renaissance literature of Italy and from ancient classical literature. The result was a peculiarly English amalgam, the foreign thing once more completely assimilated and naturalized, not all at once, but gradually working its way in without violent disturbance, and producing its effect as a leavening influence rather than an overmastering one. At the same time, however, we must also remember that whether they were altogether right or not, Englishmen of the later sixteenth century *felt* they were living in a new world of thought and aspiration, *felt* a deep opposition between themselves and the Middle Ages, and *felt* they were pioneers in literature and in life.

Conflict between Old and New: Roger Ascham

Naturally this feeling, howsoever general, was a varying quantity from one person to another. But we may profitably look, before we go further, at an extreme example of it. Roger Ascham was one of the earlier English humanists; and he took the study of literature seriously. Here is his judgment of Sir Thomas Malory's great redaction of the medieval Arthurian romances:

> In our forefathers' time, when Papistry as a standing pool covered and overflowed all England, few books were read in our tongue, saving certain books of chivalry, as they said, for pastime and pleasure, which, as some say, were made in monasteries by idle monks or wanton canons: as one for example, *Morte d'Arthur,* the whole pleasure of which book standeth in two special points, in open manslaughter and bold bawdry. In which book those be counted the noblest knights that do kill most men without any quarrel, and commit foulest adulteries by subtlest shifts: as Sir Launcelot, with the wife of King Arthur his master; Sir Tristram, with the wife of King Mark his uncle; Sir Lamorak, with the wife of King Lot that was his own aunt. This is good stuff for wise men to laugh at, or honest men to take pleasure at. Yet I know when God's Bible was banished the Court, and *Morte d'Arthur* received into the Prince's chamber.

Whatever may be thought of this opinion, there is no mistaking the fact that Ascham felt himself to be living in a different world from the one reflected in the romances of chivalry. The Middle Ages cast no glamorous spell over him, and he only wished he could convince others of the truth, as he saw it—that medievalism was synonymous with barbarity, immorality, and superstition. Ascham was not, however, a narrow-minded moralist. He was said by a contemporary to have died a poor man, despite important public employments, because of his addiction to gambling with dice and to cock-fighting—and he himself confessed his interest in the latter. He had a deep faith in the power of sound education to re-form human nature; and he conceived of education broadly, as a symmetrical development of body, emotions, and intellect, with a view to maturity of the whole person, or of character. The study of literature was centrally important in this scheme as a means to learn the realities of life; and Ascham judged that ancient classical literature, especially Greek, was invaluable for this purpose, and that medieval literature was by comparison worse than childish.

Linguistic Change

Ascham, with his solid learning and his informed critical intelligence, was prophetic, in the middle of the sixteenth century, rather than typical. Yet most men of the time shared for one reason or another his sense of a gulf dividing the Middle Ages from their own new age. Some of these reasons were peculiar to England. One is simply that the English language was still changing rapidly throughout the fifteenth century and in the early part of the sixteenth. Language, the experts assure us, is always changing, but there are periods when it changes very little and very slowly. Printing, Shakespeare, and the English Bible have combined to standardize and fix modern English, not stopping growth, but holding down fundamental change to a minimum from the end of the sixteenth century to our time. But within less than a hundred years after Chaucer's death no one knew how Chaucer's Middle English had been pronounced. From the latter part of the fifteenth century until fairly late in the nineteenth it was supposed that Chaucer's versification was an awkward, irregular compromise—unpleasing, rough, outlandish, but doubtless the best poor Chaucer could achieve in an ignorant barbarous age when, as he himself had complained in *Troilus and Criseyde,* the language was in a state of chaos. Hence nearly all that Chaucer had done with consummate skill to make the new regular versification native to the English tongue was quickly lost, and had to be done over again in the sixteenth century. The principal, but by no means the only, change in pronunciation was the dropping of the final "e" so frequent in Chaucer. It disappeared first from the spoken language, and then, more slowly, from the written and printed language. Throughout the fifteenth century, too, and into the sixteenth, differences in pronunciation and vocabulary were so great from one locality to another, as they had been in Chaucer's day, that Englishmen traveling through England often had real difficulty in making themselves understood. Hence there was abundant reason for men to feel at the beginning of the sixteenth century that the English language was still a barbarous unformed tongue, in need of discipline and enrichment before it could stand up as a worthy rival to French. "Discipline" seems to be the right word for one part of what was felt, because Caxton in the last years of the fifteenth century complained that speech was subject to such rapid and capricious changes that one of his translations was outmoded in its language before he could complete it and print it.

Amidst all this change and confusion, there was a center of fixity in English religious prose as it had been taken up and developed in the fourteenth century by Rolle and Hilton and others, whose works—especially Hilton's—continued to be read. And there is convincing reason for believing that this prose was the foundation of St. Thomas More's easy, unaffected, yet eloquent English in the first quarter of the sixteenth century. Certainly St. Thomas More could say anything he wanted, without difficulty and in surprisingly "modern" English. But both More and his teachers were cut off from the main stream of English life by the break between England and the Roman Catholic Church which caused the martyrdom of More in 1535. Thereafter, Hilton promptly disappears from view; and More's own English writings were soon neglected and forgotten, with the consequence that the long tradition which culminated in More was of practically no service at a time when it might have saved a great deal of trouble and misguided experimentation.

Language itself, then, gives us an important reason why men felt, in the fields of both prose and verse, that they were sharply separated from the Middle Ages, and that they were pioneers confronted with the task of shaping and refining a rude tongue so that it might become a fit and sufficient medium for the literary uses of cultivated people. The other important reasons for this same feeling of separation cannot be disentangled from one another for discussion. They can be summarized at the outset, however, as the accession of the new Tudor dynasty, the entrance of humanism into England, and the Protestant Reformation. To understand these changes we have to look at them in their interrelations; but we must remember as we proceed that we are trying to see why Englishmen in the sixteenth century began to feel that they were living in a new world.

The Tudors

When Henry Tudor won the English crown by defeating and slaying Richard III at the battle of Bosworth Field in 1485, a very long period of consolidation, of growing national feeling, and of political uncertainty and dissension was ended. The greater part of the old feudal nobility was gone. Many members of noble houses were killed in the Wars of the Roses, and other families had become extinct from natural causes. The new king, known as Henry VII, had therefore an unusual opportunity to build up a strong administration. Relatively free from the jealous claims and demands of powerful families, he could choose aides for their merits, and could count on the undivided loyalty of men whose fortunes depended solely on his favor. The nation, moreover, wanted a strong central government, able to keep order and to give security which would encourage private enterprise. During the later Middle Ages considerable progress had been made in England in the direction of a limited monarchy and parliamentary government, with disappointing results. The country had become a battle-ground for hostile factions, and a reign of lawlessness had set in. This produced an overwhelming reaction of sentiment in favor of public order and private security. Henry VII was steady, capable, and strong. Himself a "new man," founder of a new dynasty, he gave England the new deal her people wanted. He and his successors in the next century were practically absolute sovereigns, and would have been execrated as tyrants had they not given the English people as a whole exactly what they needed and welcomed. As it was, they received grateful support from a people who enjoyed under them peace, great and constantly increasing prosperity, and rising national prestige, which reached a magnificent climax in the defeat of the Spanish Armada in the latter half of the long reign of Elizabeth, the last of the Tudor sovereigns.

The reign of the Tudor dynasty was a fortunate and successful period of absolutism because of the conditions at the outset just mentioned, and because of the astuteness of the Tudor sovereigns in holding popular support, or, to put it in another way, the astuteness of the Tudor sovereigns in carrying out only such designs as the people of England really approved, or could be got to approve. This was the way in which Henry VII limited himself, and what his son Henry VIII on the whole unquestionably did, and what Henry VIII's daughter Elizabeth brilliantly did under very difficult conditions. Between Henry VIII's death in 1547 and the accession of Elizabeth there was a period of eleven years during which Tudor popularity was severely tested, and shown to be closely connected with Tudor astuteness. In the first half of this period the government was carried on under a regency because Henry VIII's son, Edward VI, was only nine years old when be became king; and factional troubles immediately proved that England still needed a strong ruler. In the second half of the period Henry's daughter Mary reigned, and showed that she possessed Tudor strength or imperiousness without that regard for popular opinion, and ability to foresee it, which her father and her half-sister Elizabeth both had. Her reign was short, but she died embittered by failure and unmourned by her subjects.

Erasmus, More, and Others

Duke Humphrey of Gloucester, who died in 1447, appears to have been the first man in England to exhibit an active interest in Renaissance humanism. He studied classical Latin literature, learned to read the new Italian literature, and emulated Petrarch in collecting manuscripts. These he bequeathed to Oxford, and so became the founder of what is now the great Bodleian Library, the oldest part of which was built to house his collection. What he did as a "noble patron," however, would scarcely have been important had he not been followed by some younger men of tenacious purpose who were eager not only to partake of the new classical learning but to implant it in England and transmit it. The most notable of these were Thomas Linacre and William Grocyn, who learned Greek in Italy, and returned to establish the teaching of Greek at Oxford about 1490; and John Colet, who also traveled and studied in Italy, and came back to become Dean of St. Paul's in London, and the founder, in 1504, of St. Paul's School. This was the first secondary school in England to adopt, under Colet's direction, the classical curriculum in which all teaching was based on Latin, and study was centered in Greek and Latin literature and history—a curriculum which was soon adopted by other secondary schools all over England, and held its place as the basis of English higher education until towards the close of the nineteenth century, when "modern subjects" began to displace it.

With these founders of humanism in England must be mentioned another, the famous Dutch scholar Erasmus, who was brought over from Paris by a pupil, Lord Mountjoy, at the end of the fifteenth century, was influenced especially by Colet to become a serious student of Greek, and made himself in the course of several long visits a co-founder of Greek learning in England. From 1511 to 1514 he taught Greek at Cambridge University. The closest and most congenial friend Erasmus made in England was St. Thomas More, who learned some Greek under Linacre and

Grocyn at Oxford and became thoroughly imbued with the humanistic spirit then and later when he was establishing himself as a lawyer in London.

St. Thomas More is one of the two most vivid and significant figures who stand out boldly from the rather dim background of the very early sixteenth century in England. He was a man of the middle class, with a strict father. He later thought his father's strictness had helped to give him backbone. At the age of twelve, after being grounded in Latin and in the practice of debating at a London school, he was placed in the household of John Morton, then Archbishop of Canterbury and Lord Chancellor, and afterwards a cardinal. This arrangement was in accordance with medieval usage, which in the sixteenth century was to give way before the advantages of education in such schools as the one which Colet founded. Morton lived, as befitted his station, in princely fashion; and to be a page in attendance upon him was, for a perceptive boy, an education in manners and in the ways of the world. There was plenty of good and solid discussion to be heard too, in Latin and in English, from which much could be learned. More saw also, and took part in, the dramatic entertainments which by this time had become usual in the houses of great men. It is even possible that he witnessed a performance of the earliest wholly secular play written in the English tongue—a play entitled *Fulgens and Lucrece,* by Henry Medwall, the Archbishop's chaplain. In any event More certainly learned, in the two years he spent in Morton's household, that piety and firm religious convictions were not necessarily inconsistent with rough humor, informal manners, and worldly shrewdness. In later life More showed himself capable of courtly deportment when it was needed, and of courtly flattery also, but he had none of that elaborate and refined courtesy which, whether or not it was often attained, was everywhere regarded in the later Middle Ages as an indispensable mark of the gentleman. More was, in this and in other ways, as far removed from the medieval world as his younger contemporary, Roger Ascham.

When More was fourteen—about the average age of students entering the universities in those days—he was sent to Oxford. After two years at Oxford he proceeded to the Inns of Court in London for his legal training. In following years More underwent a prolonged inward struggle. He felt strongly inclined to withdraw from the world and become a monk; at the same time he felt unable to endure the pains of celibacy. While he vacillated, he continued to work hard at Greek, with Linacre and Grocyn who had left Oxford for London, and continued also to carry on his study of the law. In the end he decided upon marriage and life in the world, and about the same time he opened his public career by entering Parliament. Thereafter for a quarter of a century he almost continuously held one public office after another, in the City of London and at Court, finally becoming Lord Chancellor, and then, unable to follow his sovereign against the Pope, dying under the ax in 1535.

Religious Reform

More, Grocyn, Colet, and Erasmus were all formed and developed by their classical studies, and were the earliest notable representatives of what may be called Northern Humanism. The effect everywhere of the new classical learning was to awaken the independent critical intelligence, and to give form and direction to that revolt against medieval Catholicism which, as we have seen, had long, in one fashion or another, and more or less waywardly, been gathering strength. In the south, in Italy, the revolt took the form of an attempted return to paganism. There are always exceptions to a general statement in the field of history; but on the whole, in Italy, Christian belief and Christian morals were tacitly or openly rejected, though the Church continued to flourish as an important temporal institution. It was part of the social framework. Not only did it everywhere control, as we saw in the last chapter, a vast amount of property; it entered actively into all phases of life; and gradually it had built up a body of formal usages, or habitual practices, which seemed more important than belief, and really tended to take the place of belief. In addition, in Italy the Pope was a temporal sovereign, exercising full rule over part of the peninsula, besides being the spiritual sovereign of all European Christendom. Practically to abandon Christian belief and yet retain the Church's temporalities—its property, its administrative activities, its political connections, its worldly dignities—involved grave dishonesty, and promoted the decadence and corruption which helped to cause revolt.

This, however, was the easiest path; and in Italy its worst fruits were the Machiavellianism and the "pagan" animalism, in both life and literature, which have been discussed earlier in this chapter. In England, and in northern Europe generally, these fruits of the Renaissance excited a kind of horrified fascination. Everything Italian seemed devilish in the extreme. Pernicious as Roger Ascham thought Malory's *Morte d'Arthur* to be, it seemed to him innocent in comparison with Italian literature and vice. The earliest English humanists were serious men, to whom religion was the basis of the good life. This does not mean that they were narrow and sadly solemn. St. Thomas More had high spirits, wit, abundant geniality, and eager interest in all that the new classical learning could contribute to cultivated life. To all appearances he was an urbane man of the world—yet next to his skin he wore the hair shirt of the medieval penitent, with no feeling of incongruity between his outward life and his religious faith. To men like St. Thomas More, therefore, it was natural that the critical temper awakened by the new learning should suggest, not abandonment of Christianity for pre-Christian culture, but rather a reformation of the clergy and of Christian institutions. John Colet, More's senior by twelve years, led the way in lectures he gave at Oxford on the epistles of St. Paul. Colet said in effect that medieval interpreters of the Bible had found a means of making the Bible appear to say anything they might want it to, in the famous fourfold method of exposition which had been developed. It was taught that every passage in the Bible had four meanings: anagogical, tropological, allegorical, and literal. Of these the literal meaning came to be regarded as the least important. Colet boldly asserted that St. Paul's epistles were first of all historical documents, to be examined as real letters written by one man to other men, and that their literal meaning was all-important. Hence he proceeded in his lectures to examine them critically, in an attempt to recover their literal meaning.

So obviously sensible and right does Colet's approach now seem that it may be hard to realize its revolutionary character. Yet such treatment of any part of the Bible *was* revolutionary, and shows as clearly as anything we have discussed the really sharp line of cleavage between the medieval spirit and the modern critical spirit. It seems probable too that Colet's influence determined Erasmus to prepare and publish the original Greek text of the New Testament, with a commentary and a new translation into Latin, as an indispensable step in the critical return to the sources of Christian belief and practice. Erasmus's commentary contained many sharp thrusts at clerical abuses, though his most widely effective thrusts at the clergy of the time had earlier appeared in his *Praise of Folly,* a satirical attack on all the wickedness and foolishness of the age.

Social Reform: More's "Utopia"

More's contribution to the cause of enlightenment and reform was a small book written in Latin, amidst his public employments, and entitled *Utopia,* which is Greek for "Nowhere." The fact that Latin was used may suggest that when Renaissance Latin literature was spoken of earlier in this chapter as being artificial and frigid, More's *Utopia* and perhaps other works were forgotten. There is, however, an important distinction to be remembered. Latin in the sixteenth century, and indeed in the seventeenth, was still the natural language of learned men writing learned works addressed to an international audience. Some learned men also doubted the stability of the new national tongues. For one of these reasons or the other, such seventeenth-century Englishmen as Francis Bacon, Milton, Thomas Hobbes, and Isaac Newton, to mention no more, composed some of their works in Latin. The writings earlier referred to were works of literary art. The *Utopia* has been accepted as a classic of modern literature, partly because it has been misunderstood; but, as we shall see, it was not written primarily as a work of art.

More's book is a picture, inspired by Plato's *Republic* and *Laws,* of an imaginary commonwealth, supposed to have been found by one of the adventurous mariners of the early sixteenth century in the New World beyond the Atlantic. It is not a picture of an "ideal" commonwealth; it is, exactly like Plato's *Republic,* an imaginative study constructed for a special, definite purpose. More's humanistic training encouraged the free play of reason, and his aim was to describe the kind of commonwealth which could be imagined as issuing logically from the use of reason in conjunction with the human virtues—wisdom, fortitude, temperance, and justice. Reason was common to all men, whether Christian or not, and through reason these virtues could be achieved by non-Christians as well as Christians. This More learned both from Plato and from medieval Christian philosophy. Christianity had added to these rational or cardinal virtues, as they were called, three more peculiar to itself, not discoverable by reason but divinely revealed—faith, hope, and charity or love. More's description of Utopia is preceded by a picture of Christian England and Christian Europe as he saw them, impoverished by expenditures for armament, distracted by perpetual warfare, governed by faithless and corrupt statesmen, while real social welfare was neglected, farmers were cruelly turned adrift so that capitalists might obtain their land for sheep pasture, and general unemployment was causing waves of crime which no ruthless exercise of "justice" could repress. And More's object was simply to emphasize the shameful contrast between his two pictures. The Christians, he says, with not only reason but revelation to guide them, and having within their reach the three Christian virtues besides the four rational virtues, have sunk into a morass of wretchedness and iniquity, whereas the non-Christian Utopians, with only reason and the rational virtues, have achieved a justly ordered society and a happy existence. From their merely rational viewpoint More's Utopians condemn ascetic practices; and they are perfectly logical in regarding such practices as "mad"—that is, non-rational. For those who remember the hair shirt he wore next his skin, this is enough to prove that More had no intention of picturing his own "ideal" in his description of Utopia.

Henry VIII and the New Courtly Poetry

The *Utopia* was completed and published in 1516, only thirty-one years after the publication of Malory's *Morte d'Arthur.* In 1509 Henry VII had died and Henry VIII had ascended the throne. It was said above that More is one of the two most vivid and significant figures in the England of the early sixteenth century. Henry VIII is the other. Henry VII's great achievement as king has been described; but Henry VII excited no enthusiastic feeling, and helped not at all to advance the cause of the new learning. His strikingly handsome young son, however, awakened unbounded admiration and seemed to personify all the virtues, including a love for learning. His accession seemed unmistakably to mark a new and happy era. What was felt about him can hardly be understood unless we turn to the actual words of a contemporary. The Lord Mountjoy who had been a pupil of Erasmus, and who had first brought him to England, now summoned him back, from Rome, in this letter written a few weeks after Henry VIII had become king:

> I have no fear, my Erasmus, but when you heard that our prince, now Henry VIII, whom we may well call our Octavius, had succeeded to his father's throne, all your melancholy left you at once. For what may you not promise yourself from a prince, with whose extraordinary and almost divine character you are well acquainted, and to whom you are not only known but intimate, having received from him (as few others have) a letter traced with his own fingers? But when you know what

a hero he now shows himself, how wisely he behaves, what a lover he is of justice and goodness, what affection he bears to the learned, I will venture to swear that you will need no wings to make you fly to behold this new and auspicious star. Oh, my Erasmus, if you could see how all the world here is rejoicing in the possession of so great a prince, how his life is all their desire, you could not contain your tears for joy. The heavens laugh, the earth exults, all things are full of milk, of honey, and of nectar! Avarice is expelled the country. Liberality scatters wealth with bounteous hand. Our King does not desire gold or gems or precious metals, but virtue, glory, immortality. I will give you an example. The other day he wished he was more learned. I said, that is not what we expect of your Grace, but that you will foster and encourage learned men. Yea surely, said he, for indeed without them we should scarcely exist at all. What more splendid saying could fall from the lips of a prince? . . . Make up your mind that the last day of your wretchedness has dawned. You will come to a Prince, who will say, Accept our wealth and be our greatest sage.

This is rhetorical, but there is ample reason to believe that it expresses the genuine feelings and expectations of Henry's subjects. Probably no one could have satisfied such golden anticipations; certainly Henry did not; yet to the end he commanded a more complete loyalty from the mass of his people than we today find it quite easy to understand. And for a while things went very well. Modern English poetry was born at Henry's court, during the early years of his reign, before his life was darkened by struggle; and this alone is enough to prove that the court promptly became a center of Renaissance influences.

Poetry, which had been sinking steadily through the fifteenth century, continued in the early years of the sixteenth to be imitative, dull, and lifeless—and metrically, owing to the changes in the language which have been discussed, almost formless. We can see a good deal from even a few lines out of *The Example of Virtue* by Stephen Hawes:

Sapience bade me marvel nothing
  For she would show me the signification
Why he so sat, by short reckoning,
  According to a moralization.

Hawes was so misguided as to admire Lydgate and accept him as his master. He praised Chaucer because Lydgate had praised him, but learned nothing from him. *The Example of Virtue* is, like several anonymous pieces of about the same time, an allegory in a dream-setting, in conformity with one of the most popular of medieval conventions. The chief poem written by Hawes is an allegory called *The Pastime of Pleasure,* published in 1506, two years after *The Example of Virtue.* The only thing of importance for us to remember about Hawes, and his master Lydgate too, is that they were popular, and remained popular longer than they should have. Hawes's *Pastime of Pleasure* was reprinted in 1517, in 1554, and *twice* in 1555.

But alongside of Hawes there were some stirrings of new life in poetry. John Skelton was a tutor of Henry VIII and a person of lively temper, who at least made departures from outworn convention, even though it cannot be said that he led the way forward. He was no artist. He was something of a humanist but derived no artistic lessons from his classical studies. In its formal qualities his verse remains mostly as rough and irregular as that of Lydgate or Hawes, and he used current frames—the framework of the morality play, for example, in his *Magnificence,* though the *theme* of this play is new, and humanistic, as it is a study of the virtues to be desired in a prince or ruler and of the way in which the prince may achieve his appropriate excellence despite temptation. Similarly Skelton's *Bowge at Court* is in form an allegory in a dream-setting, but the old form is used for a new purpose, a satirical attack on the vices which flourish at a royal court; and in his representation Skelton shows that he is a keen observer. In many of his poems he went back to the short lines, with three or only two stressed syllables, used in some medieval Latin verse, and made this form so much his own that it has come to be known by his name. In its effect it is rather breathless, and thus is characteristic of the man. He threw himself into things pell-mell, and scrambled out the best way he could. At times he seems to be only a coarse buffoon, but at any rate he dares boldly to be himself—instead of something fine which he was not—and he does have energy and serious things to say.

Though my rime be ragged,
Tattered and jagged,
Rudely rain-beaten,
Rusty and moth-eaten;
If ye take well therewith
It hath in it some pith.

Skelton is interesting chiefly as a sign that as Henry VIII entered manhood there was new life stirring around him outside of the new learning, which itself was not an end, but a means. And though Mountjoy wrote to Erasmus as if the young Henry was wrapped up in the cause of learning, it soon became apparent that the King was in love rather with "glory" and pleasure. Henry VII had accumulated a large treasure, and his son now spent it, not in support of such scholars as Erasmus, who came to England only to have his hopes disappointed, but in gorgeous pageantry, in gay entertainments, and in continental warfare designed to make him stand out as a splendid monarch exerting a decisive influence in European affairs.

Yet the new régime was by no means only an outward show of Renaissance magnificence. Henry did have some real interest in the new learning, and, moreover, was fond of music, which at this time meant chiefly song. He is said himself to have been a creditable composer, and he encouraged song-writing at his court. The importance of this can hardly be exaggerated. Music had been popular in England through the later Middle Ages, and now again it was to exercise a beneficent influence when the secret of writing smooth verse in English had to be rediscovered. Henry's encouragement made this cultivated pastime fashionable, and led directly to the great age of English music in the reigns of Elizabeth and James. This is the great age also of English lyric poetry, when poets were writing directly for music, were often skilled musicians themselves, were sometimes composers of the music for their own poems, and in any event had the inspiration of working with a group of composers well-nigh as fine as any the modern world has seen. It is considered certain that many of the songs written during Henry's reign have not been preserved. They were written by gentlemen, who thought it beneath their position to vie with professional poets by publication—an attitude shared later by Sir Philip Sidney and others, which did not become ridiculous until well into the eighteenth century. Consequently these noblemen and courtiers wrote for their own amusement and read one another's works in manuscript. There was, too, a feeling when the printing-press was young that lyric poems were inconsiderable trifles. What we do know of the new kinds of poems written in the first half of the sixteenth century we owe almost entirely to the enterprise of one Richard Tottel who, ten years after the death of Henry VIII, gathered together 271 poems and printed them under the title *Songs and Sonnets,* with a preface in which he said, "That to have well written in verse, yea and in small parcels, deserveth great praise, the works of divers, Latins, Italians, and other, do prove."

Two Courtly Poets: Wyatt and Surrey

Tottel's Miscellany, as it is called, stands at the threshold of the poetry of the English Renaissance, and owes its fame to this position. Most of the pieces it contains are historically interesting as a record of the struggling efforts which had to be made in rediscovering the art of writing English verse, but have no other value. The most notable poems in the first edition—the book proved so popular that nine editions appeared in the next thirty years—are in two groups which make up just over half of the pieces printed. One group contains ninety-six poems by Sir Thomas Wyatt, and the other, forty by Henry Howard, Earl of Surrey. Wyatt had been to Italy and, whatever else he learned there, had encountered Petrarch's famous sonnets. He introduced into England the lyric of courtly love and the Petrarchian or Italian sonnet-form. This was the most popular verse-form of the Renaissance, in Italy, in France, and later in England. As written in Italy it contained fourteen iambic pentameter lines, divided into two stanzas, an octave (first eight lines) and a sestet (the remaining six lines), usually riming *a b b a a b b a c d e c d e*. This form was too difficult for Wyatt, as his efforts show, and Surrey made a change, in the sonnets he wrote, which was accepted later by Shakespeare and others. Hence the altered form is often called the Shakespearian sonnet. Surrey's innovation turned the form into three four-line stanzas followed by a couplet, riming *a b a b c d c d e f e f g g*. Both Wyatt's sonnets and Surrey's are in many cases simply translations from Petrarch; and many of the sonnets written in the second half of the century also are translations or adaptations from Italian or French originals, though occasionally it seems a pity that this has been discovered. More than two thousand Elizabethan sonnets found their way into print, and a majority may be stigmatized as "rank imitations" without causing the lover of poetry to feel any concern or regret. But others are moving and beautiful English poems, which are not the less genuine for having analogues or origins or for being written in conformity with a prevailing style and prevailing ideas. The truth is that though we owe thanks to originators and pioneers—as we certainly owe gratitude to Wyatt and Surrey—still, we do not get masterpieces from them, but from their successors who enter into a heritage of experimentation and thought and happen to possess the genius to make the fullest and happiest use of what they find ready to hand.

We see other important beginnings in *Tottel's Miscellany* which show that Renaissance impulses at this time were really striking home in England. There are Horatian odes, and epigrams from Martial, and satires and reflective lyrics in the classical manner. We also owe to Surrey a translation of two books of Virgil's *Aeneid,* published by Tottel though not in the *Miscellany,* in which he used blank verse—iambic pentameter lines without rime—and so earned the commendation of classical scholars, like Ascham, who thought rime a piece of Gothic barbarism. It is fortunate that the views on this subject of Ascham and others did not prevail, but no less fortunate that Surrey was so influenced by classical literature as to invent an English substitute for Virgil's dactylic hexameter. For, a few years later, Surrey's invention was taken up and used by Thomas Sackville (later Earl of Dorset) and Thomas Norton in *Gorboduc,* the earliest English classical tragedy, and so was passed on to Marlowe, who finally showed its possibilities and made it the verse of Elizabethan drama, above all of Shakespearian drama; thence it passed to Milton to become the verse of *Paradise Lost* and *Paradise Regained;* and since then it has been the verse most commonly used in England for long poems, whether dramatic, reflective, or narrative.

When all is said, however, none of the verse written by Surrey or by other courtly poets of the first half of the sixteenth century has much value beyond its historical importance, with the exception of certain songs, chiefly by Wyatt. In the best of his songs Wyatt has a sure control over metrical form without sacrifice of spontaneity, and he raises poetry "in small parcels" to a position of dignity and strength which it has held almost continuously from his day to ours. And though they do have dignity, there is nothing heavy or over-formal in these songs; on the contrary, they are simple, and full of a light grace which reminds us that, although Wyatt was a man of some learning, he was also an accomplished and highly cultivated courtier.

The Protestant Reformation

But behind the exquisite song, the gayety and splendor of Henry's court, storms were brewing, which were to burst forth in violence in the 1530's and were to continue for many a year, plaguing and dividing the English people, even to the point of civil war in the next century. The first open sign of grievous division appeared, not in England, but in the Saxon town of Wittenberg, not far from Berlin, in 1517, when the Augustinian monk Martin Luther nailed his celebrated ninety-five theses to the door of the Schlosskirche. This proved to be the first decisive step leading quickly to the Protestant Reformation. Luther's defiance of the Pope almost immediately found sympathizers in England. Wiclif in the fourteenth century, as we have seen, had led a formidable English movement of rebellion against the worldly power of the Church and the authority of the Pope; but the Lollards, as his followers were called, had been hunted down and persecuted, and the movement so far suppressed that it had little or no influence upon Englishmen of the sixteenth century. Many manuscripts of the Wiclifite translations of the Bible had been put in circulation, but these it had been necessary to keep in hiding, for the most part, and by the end of the fifteenth century they were practically unknown.

The movement for reform of the Catholic Church, therefore, which we have noticed as springing up amongst the earliest English humanists towards the end of the fifteenth century, was a new thing. It was born, as has been said, of the critical attitude awakened by the new Renaissance learning. It was distinct not only from the earlier Lollard movement, but also from mere outcry against the ignorance, self-seeking, and worldliness of the clergy. Protest against the gross failings of the clergy was one of the traditional subjects of medieval literature, often satirically handled. Such protests are to be found in the writings of Hawes and of Skelton, and, as is proved by his subsequent abuse of Luther, Skelton at any rate had no inclination to revolt from the Church. The new species of attack undertaken by the humanists went much deeper, but they also had no wish to take part in a revolt. Indeed it is practically certain that no one in England *began* reforming efforts with any notion of separating from Rome. But a few young men, principally at Cambridge University, were so deeply convinced of the necessity of radical reform that they did promptly welcome Luther's leadership; and amongst them was William Tyndale, who was a graduate of Oxford but had afterwards gone to Cambridge.

Tyndale and the English Bible

Tyndale remains personally somewhat obscure to us despite all efforts of biographers, but there is no doubt that he was a man of genius and of heroic determination. He became convinced that it was an immediate necessity, for the renovation of Christianity amongst his countrymen, to translate the Bible into English. When it appeared that he could not safely undertake the task in England, he went to Germany, lived for some months in Wittenberg near Luther, and began there his work on the New Testament. He was a competent Greek scholar, and used the new edition of the Greek text which had been published by Erasmus. He had also the aid afforded by Erasmus's new Latin translation, and by Luther's German translation. It is thought that he must have known of the Lollard English versions, but certainly he made no use of them. He began to print his version at Cologne in 1525, but was forced to flee when only a small part had been done. He then established himself in Worms and began the printing anew. The first printed New Testament in English was completed at Worms in 1526, and immediately began to circulate in England.

St. Thomas More had by this time ranged himself on the side of Christian unity, as something even more important than reform, and he now made the grave accusation that Tyndale had willfully mistranslated the New Testament to serve heretical ends. The accusation has been repeated in our own day. It is true that Tyndale had become, to all intents and purposes, what we should now call a Lutheran; it is also true that in half a dozen cases, though even then not consistently, he avoided words associated with Catholic doctrine and used other English equivalents of the Greek; but he was not guilty of willful mistranslation, and he produced a version which is almost miraculously good. He had an extraordinary command of idiomatic English; he aimed to convey the meaning of the gospel in a form which the simplest reader might grasp; and he had a spirit which responded nobly to the height and dignity, nobly to every demand, of his text. He went on at once to learn Hebrew in order to translate the Old Testament directly from the language in which it had been written, and published his version of the Pentateuch—the first five books attributed to Moses—in 1530. He completed other books of the Old Testament, but was not allowed to finish his task. Branded as an arch-heretic, he had to live in hiding. In the late spring of 1535 he was betrayed by a fellow-Englishman, and in the following year was condemned as a heretic, degraded from the priesthood, and turned over to the officers of the Emperor Charles V for execution. In a village near Antwerp he was tied to a stake, strangled, and his body burned.

The Reformation in England

Meanwhile in England Henry VIII had been having his own troubles, of a very different kind, with the Papacy. Henry had married his deceased brother's wife, Catherine of Aragon, but their children had died in infancy with the one exception of a daughter. Though there was no English law which would bar this daughter, Mary, from the throne, to which in fact she did succeed in 1553, still, Henry was most extremely anxious for a male heir; and by the time it was evident he would get none from Catherine he also had become passionately attached to Anne Boleyn, a relative of the great Howard family. It is useless to speculate upon the turnings of Henry's mind, but there is reason to believe he was sincere in thinking that his marriage with Catherine had been cursed. Ecclesiastical law forbade marriage with a deceased brother's wife, and papal dispensation had been obtained for Henry and Catherine; nevertheless, Henry now decided that this dispensation had been irregular, and applied to the Pope for annulment of the marriage. Henry had himself written and published an attack on Luther, and in 1521 had been rewarded by the Pope with the title "Defender of the Faith." Henry and everybody else knew that the request for annulment was nothing extraordinary, and that normally it would have been granted, and all the more readily to one who had come forward in support of orthodoxy when serious rebellion was spreading like fire in northern Europe. Yet the Pope hesitated. His reason was purely political. Catherine was the aunt of Charles V, King of Spain and Emperor, and the most powerful sovereign on the Continent. The Pope did not dare to offend Charles, and hence placed one obstacle after another in the way of Henry's petition.

The consequence was the English Reformation. So mixed are the causes, very often, of great events. Henry in effect appealed to English national feeling against foreign dictatorship over internal affairs of the Kingdom. He carried his subjects with him because there was acute dissatisfaction of long standing over the amount of property held by the Church and over the amount of money annually drawn out of England for the support of Italian prelates and the policies of the Papacy; but he also carried many Englishmen with him who were convinced of the necessity of religious reformation, and who were willing to seize any opportunity for separation from Rome. In 1533 Thomas Cranmer, one of Tyndale's former associates at Cambridge, and now just made Archbishop of Canterbury, annulled Henry's marriage on the findings of an English court. Before this, Henry had forced the clergy to acknowledge him as supreme head of the Church in England "as far as the law of Christ allows," and had then married Anne Boleyn, in January, 1533. Cranmer's pronouncement several months later validated this marriage in England, but not, of course, in the eyes of Roman Catholics. Hence Anne's daughter Elizabeth, later Queen, who was born in September, was regarded by Catholics as an illegitimate child. It was because, still devoted to Christian unity, he refused to acknowledge Henry as head of the English Church, after Parliament's Act of Supremacy in 1534, that St. Thomas More was beheaded (1535).

About this time a great change began to take place in Henry, which accounts for the conception of him most people entertain today. His appearance altered sadly—he may have been afflicted with the disease called elephantiasis—and his personal qualities no less. He showed himself fickle, heartlessly selfish, callous, materialized, and, indeed, altogether a disagreeable and sinister figure. It is not to our purpose to discuss further Henry's marital adventures—he had six wives in all—but something must still be said of the progress of "reformation" in his reign. Henry did not at any time desire the slightest change in Catholic doctrine, worship, or clerical organization. But he had spent the treasure amassed by his father and did need money. For this reason in the years from 1536 to 1539 he proceeded to dissolve the English monasteries and to confiscate their vast estates. Also, after he had been excommunicated and "deposed" by the Pope, he was forced to make concessions to Protestant demands, the most important being his authorization in 1539 of the use of an English Bible in the churches. The Bible used was one which incorporated Tyndale's translation as far as that martyred scholar had been able to carry it. In addition, some steps were taken in the last years of Henry's reign towards the change from Latin to English in the Church services, though the first English *Book of Common Prayer* was not printed until 1548, the year after Henry's death. This was largely the work of Cranmer, who, although he did not possess Tyndale's heroism, did have nothing less than genius, of the same quality as Tyndale's, in his command of an English style at once simple and elevated, and very perfectly suited to the liturgical offices.

As nearly as so difficult a question can be answered, English feeling after Henry's death was tending to favor a position midway between Catholic claims and Protestant wishes. The reformers carried things too far in the Protestant direction during the brief reign of Edward VI, but the reversal to Catholicism under Mary also provoked strong opposition, so that there was general rejoicing when Elizabeth succeeded to the throne in 1558. Elizabeth, in so far as she was religious at all, was Catholic in her sympathies; but the circumstances of her birth, hardly less than the demands of prudent policy, compelled her to espouse Protestantism. She aimed to effect a characteristically English compromise, and during her long and brilliant reign she did succeed in holding an even course between extremists on both sides. The question at issue, however, was not one that could be settled so easily, and the great queen accomplished no more than a postponement of conflict.

The Elizabethan Voyagers

Meanwhile, Elizabeth did give England nearly a half-century of relative quiet and peace at just the time when, as it turned out, the opportunity could be used to the greatest conceivable advantage. In the first half of the sixteenth century England took practically no part in the work of exploration at which we have already glanced. It appeared that both the glory and the prizes were to go to Spain and Portugal. But in the second half of the century English sailors, with Elizabeth's encouragement, began to make up for lost time. Active efforts to find a northern route to China and India were resumed, following the attempts made by John Cabot and his son Sebastian in the 1490's, and simultaneously Englishmen began to rob the Spaniards of their American gold and silver, by capturing Spanish treasure-ships and by raids on Spanish coastal settlements in South America. Strictly speaking this was piracy, but Elizabeth favored it as a method of undeclared warfare against a great and dangerous Catholic power; and to the English populace the sailors who brought home Spanish treasure were national heroes. The greatest of them all was Sir Francis Drake. He personifies the daring, expanding, conquering Elizabethan spirit in action as perfectly as Marlowe personifies it in the world of imagination. And Drake did what all of the sailors and explorers dreamed of doing, but what none of the others so wonderfully achieved: When he returned from his three years' voyage around the world in the *Golden Hind* he paid the shareholders in the venture a profit of 4700 per cent. The best known of the explorers, next to Drake, are Sir Martin Frobisher, Sir John Hawkins, and Sir Humphrey Gilbert; and the best known of the "gentlemen promoters" who stood behind them is Gilbert's half-brother, Sir Walter Ralegh.

No one could have foreseen at the time that by the shift from the Mediterranean, immemorial center of European civilization, to the Atlantic as the all-important ocean highway, England was removed from the position of a remote border-state to the most advantageous place at the table of world commerce which was being spread. No one could have foreseen that England, despite her late start, was to benefit far more than any other nation from the work of all the explorers and discoverers. No one could have foreseen that the Elizabethan voyagers were laying the foundations of the vast British Empire of the nineteenth century. Yet what contemporaries did see was enough to arouse their enthusiasm and wonder, to give them a sense of the surprisingness of life and the world, and of expanding opportunity for themselves, and to make them glow with exuberance and self-confidence. All that they felt received full confirmation when, in the summer of 1588, the Spanish Armada of Philip II, which was expected to destroy the rising British sea power and prepare the way for an invasion by a Spanish army, was decisively defeated and largely destroyed. English supremacy on the sea has been more than once challenged since 1588, but has never been overthrown. Contemporary feeling was reflected pervasively in the literature written in the half-century from 1575 to 1625, but most directly in a folio volume published the year after the repulse of the Armada, under the title, *The Principal Navigations, Voyages, and Discoveries of the English Nation.* This has been called "the prose epic" of modern England, and the collection of the heroic narratives it contains was the life's work of Richard Hakluyt, who continued to amass more material for an enlarged edition in three volumes which appeared in 1598–1600.

The Elizabethan Translators

Hakluyt's great collection gives us the background of action against which Elizabethan life and letters took form. But the sea captains were not the only explorers who were at work. The task of opening up the riches of classical literature, and also of the newer literatures of Italy and France, was carried on steadily in England throughout the sixteenth century, but gained a new momentum in the reign of Elizabeth. The age is notable not least for its wealth of translations, which often were very unscholarly but nearly always were vivid and lively, so that some of them have held a place in English literature in preference to later more exact renderings. One of the most famous of the Tudor translations belongs rather to the medieval tradition than to the Renaissance, but still deserves mention here, both because it has won an enduring place in English literature and because it was influential in giving some renewed life to the chivalric ideal in the later sixteenth century. This was the version of *The Chronicles of Froissart* made by Lord Berners and published in 1523–1525.

Nearly all of the earlier translations from Greek were made from Italian or French versions, and it was not until the very end of the century that men like George Chapman and Philemon Holland began translating directly from Greek. William Tyndale's New Testament was the most important exception to this rule. Nevertheless, though the versions were made mostly by Greekless men, Aristotle's *Ethics* was put into English in 1547, the *History* of Thucydides in 1550, Epictetus's *Manual* in 1567, the *Ethiopian History* of Heliodorus (a late Greek romance) in about 1569, and Plutarch's *Lives of the Noble Grecians and Romans* in 1579. The last was the work of Sir Thomas North, and stands out above other translations both because of the use made of it by Shakespeare and because, like Berners's *Froissart,* it has won an important place of its own in English literature. Translations from Isocrates, Demosthenes, Herodotus, Galen, Homer, Euripides, Theocritus, Longus, and Achilles Tatius also appeared before the end of the century. George Chapman began to publish his famous translation of Homer's *Iliad* in 1598, and completed it in 1611. He completed his translation of the *Odyssey* in 1615.

Translation from Latin did not offer the difficulties in the sixteenth century that were encountered in making English versions of Greek classics, because every man who was educated at all had some Latin, and most could read it with ease. For this reason also there was not so much need of translation from Latin; yet in fact during the Tudor period practically all of the most important classical Latin prose was translated, beginning indeed before 1485 with several of Cicero's treatises. A play by Terence was translated as early as about 1520; part of Livy in the 1540's; Virgil in the 1550's; Ovid and Horace and most of the tragedies of Seneca in the 1560's. Ovid had been found a congenial poet in the later Middle Ages, and throughout the Tudor period he continued to be the most widely read and best liked of the classical poets. Arthur Golding's translation of Ovid's *Metamorphoses,* which was used by Shakespeare, was completed in 1567. The classical writer who exerted the strongest influence on the Elizabethan mind was Seneca, whose philosophical treatises expounded Stoic morality; and from Seneca's plays, too, the Elizabethans derived their conception of classical tragedy.

The age was no less interested in the Renaissance literature of Italy and France, and also Spain, than in ancient classical literature. We have already noticed this in speaking of the sonnet, and everywhere in Elizabethan verse scholars find evidence that the continental Renaissance poets were being studied and used. Spenser, for example, in his *Faerie Queene* made extensive use of Ariosto's *Orlando Furioso* and of Tasso's *Jerusalem Delivered.* And in the next century Milton—and others besides—made considerable use of the French Protestant Du Bartas's *Divine Weeks and Works.* The Italian epics of Ariosto and Tasso were both translated into English in the 1590's; and Du Bartas was translated by Joshua Sylvester a few years later.

But popular interest was most strongly attracted by the short stories in prose which had become fashionable in Italy early in the Renaissance—a species of literature which has indeed been popular in almost every age throughout the world. The Middle Ages had had, as we have noticed, their own popular form of the short story, in verse, in the *fabliau.* Boccaccio's *Decameron,* written in the middle of the fourteenth century, set the Renaissance fashion for short tales in prose—called, in Italian, *novelle.* The first English collection of such tales, translated from Italian and other languages, was compiled by William Painter, under the title, *The Palace of Pleasure.* It was published in 1566, and was followed by a second volume in 1567, and an enlarged edition of the first volume in 1569. In all, *The Palace of Pleasure* contains one hundred tales, thirty-two of them taken from such classical authors as Herodotus, Plutarch, Livy, Tacitus, and Aulus Gellius. Sixteen are from Boccaccio, twenty-six from Bandello, sixteen from the *Heptameron* of Margaret of Navarre, and the remaining ten from several Italian and Spanish writers. The story of Shakespeare's *Romeo and Juliet* is in *The Palace of Pleasure,* and also the source of his *All's Well that Ends Well;* and from a later collection of translated *novelle* Shakespeare took the plot of his *Measure for Measure.*

This account is far from giving a complete picture of the wealth of foreign literature made English in the Tudor period. The work of translation continued, moreover, very actively in the seventeenth century. John Florio's translation of the *Essays* of Montaigne appeared in 1603, and Thomas Shelton's version of Cervantes' *Don Quixote* in 1612—both notable achievements, though Florio has been overpraised. No praise, however, can be too high for the Authorized, or King James, Version of the Bible which appeared in 1611. This was the culmination of nearly a century's work by various men, beginning with Tyndale's New Testament. It owes more to Tyndale than to anyone else—perhaps more to Tyndale than to all others combined—and we must therefore think of Tyndale as chiefly responsible for the most influential book in English that has ever been published from the beginning to the present.

The Elizabethan Antiquaries and Chroniclers

Our glance at the Elizabethan voyagers and the Elizabethan translators does not quite cover the work of exploration which was carried on in the latter half of the sixteenth century, and which forms the rich and varied background of Elizabethan literature. The pride of nationality had been growing in England, as we have noticed, in the later Middle Ages; it greatly increased in the sixteenth century, and especially in the reign of Elizabeth. It then showed itself in a heightened interest in English antiquity and history. The greatest of the antiquaries of the time was William Camden. He had an able predecessor in Matthew Parker, whom Elizabeth made Archbishop of Canterbury in 1559. Parker, with the aid of John Stow, edited and first printed the works of the chief medieval English chroniclers. Stow also wrote an invaluable description of Elizabethan London, published in 1598, and had earlier compiled his own history of England from its supposed beginnings with the coming of the Trojan Brutus to the year 1580, when the book was published. But the greatest achievement in the realm of history in this period was the composite work known as *Holinshed's Chronicle,* the first edition of which appeared, in two folio volumes, in 1578. This contains a celebrated *Description of England* by William Harrison, and other descriptive or historical sections by several writers. It goes under the name of Raphael Holinshed because he more or less supervised the whole and himself wrote the most important part, the *History of England*. Holinshed freely used the work of previous chroniclers, and his compilation became in some sense a classic. It is the principal source not only for Shakespeare's historical plays but for other Elizabethan plays dealing with England's past.

We can now see the first part of Elizabeth's reign for what it was: a time when the accustomed framework of life and thought and imagination, the medieval scheme of things, had fallen apart; and when men with youthful energy and confidence were busily exploring new worlds—a new physical world, the whole field, new to them, of classical literature and culture, the brave new field of continental literature inspired by the Italian Renaissance, and finally their own national history seen with new eyes and a growing pride.

"The Mirror for Magistrates"

The student looking at literature alone does not find much to reward him in the first twenty years after Elizabeth's accession. The one really fine piece of verse these years have to show was composed about 1560. This is the *Induction,* or preface, written by Thomas Sackville (who has already been mentioned as part-author of *Gorboduc)* for a projected series of narratives—so William Baldwin, the editor, says—to be included in an enlarged edition of *The Mirror for Magistrates.* The *Mirror* is a collection of narratives following an established medieval convention. When dramatic art disappeared from Europe with the coming of the so-called Dark Ages (see page 115), and then had a new and independent beginning, the words "tragedy" and "comedy" survived, but were used in a new way peculiar to the Middle Ages. A "comedy" was a story with a happy ending, and this explains why Dante could call his great poem *The Divine Comedy.* Similarly, "tragedy" was used to denote a narrative with an unhappy ending. The stories told by Chaucer's Monk in *The Canterbury Tales* are "tragedies" in this medieval sense of the word, and they are simply brief narratives exhibiting the way in which Fortune or Fate has brought great persons from high estate to low. Boccaccio wrote, in Latin, a famous series of "tragedies" of this kind entitled *De Casibus Virorum Illustrium,* and the English poet Lydgate's *Fall of Princes* is a paraphrase of Boccaccio's series. *The Mirror for Magistrates* was originally planned as a continuation of Lydgate's poem, which should deal with "such as Fortune had dallied with" in England, and "might be as a mirror for all men as well noble as others, to show the slippery deceits of the wavering lady and the due reward of all kind of vices." Owing to some difficulties, however, the *Mirror* appeared, in 1559, not as an appendix to *The Fall of Princes* but as a separate work. It was exceedingly popular for half a century, though as poetry it is almost worthless except for Sackville's *Induction* in the second edition, published in 1563.

The *Mirror* as a whole shows the persistence, despite all changes taking place, of the medieval kind of thing; Sackville's *Induction* shows the new thing entering in. It is a thoroughly humanistic poem; but there is nothing to compare it with until we reach Spenser's *Faerie Queene,* which began to appear in 1590. In the twenty years from

1560 to 1580 there was a certain amount of literary activity. Verse "in small parcels" continued to be written, and the popularity of *Tottel's Miscellany* suggested the publication of additional miscellanies. In the quite varied works of George Gascoigne one can see how the new influences from classical studies and from the Italian Renaissance were being assimilated. Gascoigne and his contemporaries, however, were only able to do what may be called apprentice work. Importance has been conferred upon it by the literature which followed.

Drama

This is true, on the whole, in the field of drama—into which Gascoigne entered—as well as in the field of non-dramatic poetry. There was throughout the sixteenth century a constantly increasing interest in dramatic performances, and the pieces written, or used, to satisfy this interest have been much studied, not because of their intrinsic merits, for the most part, but because we can see in the changes occurring and in the different kinds of plays the development which brought the drama in England to the point where Shakespeare and his contemporaries took it up. Drama, as the word has been understood from Shakespeare's time to the present, is the representation, through speech and act, by persons on a stage, of a conflict of some kind. As a play opens, we are confronted by a situation which has in it possibilities of trouble; and the situation more or less rapidly develops to the point of conflict—conflict between two persons, or groups of persons, or conflict really within one person, but externalized sufficiently to make possible its representation. The point of actual conflict is the climax of the play, and this is followed by the outcome or resolution of the conflict, which concludes the play. In accordance with the medieval use of the two words, a play in which the conflict was happily resolved was in the Elizabethan age and for long afterwards called a comedy, although it might not be at all what we would call a comic piece; and a play in which the conflict was resolved unhappily was called a tragedy—the tragic event *par excellence* being the death of the hero after he has enlisted our sympathies.

Hence a play in the full sense of the word must have a plot, a story or, as it used to be called, a fable, whose essential element is a conflict and its resolution. We have seen (page 117) that the moralities, despite all their limitations, met this requirement. It was fundamental, and the problem of the sixteenth century was how to transcend the morality's limitations. Of course writers of the time did not see it in this simplified way, and what we actually find is a disorderly advance on several fronts, with the gains finally consolidated by the genius of Shakespeare. The early moralities, as was said in the last chapter, had only one theme—the conflict between virtues and vices for the soul of man. At the beginning of the sixteenth century the method or framework of the morality was used for other themes: interests aroused by humanism were allegorically treated; later, towards the middle of the century, religious controversy. At the same time, writers of interludes were getting away from allegory and exploring the possibilities of realistic presentation of human characters, with comic scenes depending for their effect upon character rather than upon mere clowning. There was also during the sixteenth century an independent development along a different line, whose beginnings are obscure. This was the dramatized presentation of an heroic story from legend or history, out of which grew the chronicle-plays.

Classical Drama in England

The fatal trouble with the chronicle-plays was that they lacked plot; and it is true of all the native efforts that they were structurally very deficient, and that they showed very little understanding of the relation between character and the genuinely dramatic conflict. On the side of structure essential help now came from the new knowledge of classical literature. The Latin comedies of Terence and Plautus and the tragedies of Seneca were not only being read; at schools and the universities they were being acted by the students, and new plays were being written in Latin for school performance which were modeled on Terence, Plautus, and Seneca. Presently the next step was taken, and plays modeled upon Latin tragedy and comedy were written in English for performance before learned audiences. The Inns of Court in London, which were, and still are, the law schools of England, were also at this time centers of humanistic learning and culture. Queen Elizabeth, moreover, who had been taught by Roger Ascham, was one of the most accomplished of the classically learned ladies of the sixteenth century, and her court was the dominating center of culture in England. Hence learned audiences were to be found in the third quarter of the sixteenth century not only at the universities and at schools, but also at the court of Elizabeth and in the London law schools. *Gorboduc* has already been mentioned as the earliest English tragedy modeled on Seneca; Sackville and Norton, its authors, were members of the Inner Temple, one of the law schools; and the play was performed before Queen Elizabeth in January, 1562. The earliest English plays modeled on Latin comedy were *Gammer Gurton's Needle,* written by a Cambridge man, and performed at Christ's College, Cambridge; and *Ralph Roister Doister,* written by Nicholas Udall, who was Headmaster at Eton and later at Westminster.

These plays and other similar ones which followed them were "academic" in the sense that they grew out of no native tradition, but were the foreign or exotic products of the new classical learning, and were enjoyed only by those who shared that learning. They were not publicly performed for popular audiences. Public demand for dramatic spectacle was eager, but was being satisfied in the 1560's and 1570's by beggarly professional actors who wandered about performing, mostly in the courtyards of inns, chronicle-plays and interludes with a liberal admixture of clowning and ribaldry. If a genuine English drama was to appear, somehow a union would have to be effected between these two kinds. The popular writers of crude formless dramatic spectacles would have to learn the lessons the Latin dramatists could teach them about orderly structure and plot, and many refinements of technique; or the "academic" writers would have to learn how to use what they knew about structure and technique in some way which would give popular audiences what they already wanted and enjoyed, but would give it to them in a genuinely dramatic form, recognizable as an improvement over the pieces they had been seeing.

The Great Elizabethan Writers and the New Learning

We can now see the first twenty years of Elizabeth's reign as a period, in the field of literature, of continuing experiment with apparently small result. It was a time of exploration in many fields, all of which could contribute something to a new literature, if only the writers should appear who could take full advantage of the opportunity. And suddenly at the end of the 1570's and in the 1580's they did appear, not merely one or two, but a whole group, who felt keenly the bewildering variety of influences and changes we have been reviewing, who had confidence, energy, and genius, and who rapidly proceeded to make the end of the sixteenth century the great age of English literature. Almost without exception these new writers were university men. Oxford and Cambridge were still trying to hold on to the medieval scholastic discipline, which had come to be centered in logic; but, as we have seen, they had both felt the influence of humanism, had long since admitted the teaching of Greek, and were now in fact, even if still unofficially, important homes or the new learning. The most notable of the men who came thence to create a new literature were Sir Philip Sidney, Edmund Spenser, Sir Walter Ralegh, John Lyly, Christopher Marlowe, Robert Greene, George Peele, Thomas Lodge, Thomas Nashe, and Francis Bacon. Perhaps Thomas Kyd should be included, even in a short list; he did not go to either Oxford or Cambridge, but did receive a classical education at the Merchant Taylors' School in London.

The least learned of them all, as it happened, was Shakespeare, not only the greatest poet and dramatist of the age, but the greatest poet in the whole range of English and of modern European literature. Shakespeare's formal education was obtained at the grammar school in Stratford, where he was born, and it was early concluded. Traditionally he is said to have had "small Latin and less Greek." Somehow or other it is often implied, even by people who would not be so foolish as to say it outright, that Shakespeare's slender education is a commentary on the usefulness of learning. It may therefore be well to say at once that his extraordinary endowments by no means took the place of education, and that he had to pick up as best he could outside of school and university a great deal that his more fortunate contemporaries learned with the help of teachers. No amount of innate genius, not even Shakespeare's, can ever enable anyone to create a work of art without materials, which must be acquired in one way if not in another. The truth about Shakespeare consequently is, not that he rose to a supreme height of literary achievement without education, but that he was better able to educate himself, sufficiently for his purposes, than most men; and that he came from his country town to London at just the time when enough had been done by others to enable him, with his keen eye and receptive mind, to enter into a heritage which we may think was almost providentially prepared for him. This in fact is one of the secrets of his achievement—that he did not build from the ground up, but took what others had done—as Robert Greene bitterly complained, accusing him of being an upstart crow beautified with other men's feathers—and immeasurably improved it.

Spenser's "Shepherd's Calendar"

But, as was just implied, Shakespeare entered into a literary career several years later than most of those above mentioned; and before anything more is said of his achievement we should glance at what was done in the first years of this great period. By general consent, the publication of Edmund Spenser's *Shepherd's Calendar* in 1579 was the beginning. The book created a stir; it was recognized promptly as something new and promising, by a talented poet. Thus its historical importance is very great, but, save for a few passages, it is scarcely readable today. Nor is this surprising. The poems are too consciously and purely experimental; they are in fact something like school-exercises, and have the same kind of importance as such exercises, strictly dependent upon what they lead to. The book consists of twelve eclogues, modeled on French and Italian pastoral writers of the Renaissance, who in turn had modeled their poems on the pastoral eclogues of Virgil and Theocritus. Spenser was not the first to bring the pastoral eclogue into English; this had been done near the beginning of the sixteenth century by Alexander Barclay, whose model had been the Italian Renaissance writer, Mantuan; but Spenser seemed to contemporaries a pioneer, and his eclogues were rightly recognized as the herald of a new day, because of the attempt he made in them to effect a fusion between humanism and native tradition.

He was thoroughly indoctrinated with Renaissance humanism, and fired with the wish to create a new English poetry which might satisfy humanistic criteria. He shared the contempt felt by his classically educated Cambridge friends for the "rakehelly rout of ragged rimers"—such as all the writers of *The Mirror for Magistrates* except Sackville—who were still feebly echoing the feeble Lydgate. Yet at the same time he had a firm conviction that a new and better English poetry could not be made simply by imitating the foreigners or by trying to carry them bodily into English. All the translators and adapters might be performing an indispensable task of education; nevertheless, they were not creating a new English literature. He would boldly leap over the intervening years and go back to the undefiled source of the English poetic tradition in Chaucer; he would found his language and poetic style and verse, as far as he could, directly on Chaucer; he would also look to English scenery for his pastoral setting, and make his shepherds English in their customs and beliefs as well as in their names (Hobbinol, Piers, Willie); and thus he would create a poetry truly English in substance and form, but infused with the spirit of classical pastoral, handled freely as Virgil himself had handled it, and also Mantuan and Marot in Renaissance Italy and France.

This was the central aim, and it is worth pausing over because here we see Spenser engaged in the characteristic English task of assimilating a new foreign influence, and using it, while maintaining real continuity of native tradition. Spenser's practice in *The Shepherd's Calendar* was not, as was intimated above, so successful as his intention was sound. The work was a young man's experiment, carried through with spirit, and launched with a flourish, in the form of an elaborate commentary written by a friend. The whole enterprise might easily have looked ridiculous. But Spenser's talent did save it from that, and he was encouraged, fortunately, to continue what he had begun. His work culminated in *The Faerie Queene,* which has placed him securely amongst the five or six greatest English poets.

"The Faerie Queene"

Now *The Faerie Queene* is to be contemplated first of all as a continuance of the kind of effort made in *The Shepherd's Calendar*. It is Spenser's English embodiment of the aims of Renaissance humanism. In it he meant to accomplish for England what Homer had done for Greece, and Virgil for Rome—as these classical achievements were understood, of course, in the Renaissance. He meant, then, to write an heroic poem which should teach by example, not precept, the art of right living, with a due value set upon all the good and enjoyable possibilities of present life, and a due emphasis upon the life to come, maintaining a rational balance between this world and the next. His characters were to be, not men and women as they are, but living embodiments of ideal types or qualities—men and women as they ought to be, or as they ought not to be. Here, it is true, the necessities of his allegorical method seem to interfere with this aim, since the Red Cross Knight, for example, is said to represent only holiness—only one of the qualities entering into the "ideal" man—but, as Spenser handles the matter, this difficulty is more apparent than real. The Red Cross Knight is in fact much more than a personified quality, and becomes an ideal type. Everything, moreover, was to be harmonized with this central purpose; for instance, the landscapes of *The Faerie Queene* were to be appropriate scenes for such actors as Spenser would create, and not only subordinated to the action but as far removed from crude verisimilitude as the characters themselves. Further, the style was to be worthy of the height and seriousness of the theme. As it is fit that the crown of an emperor should be elaborately and curiously carved and encrusted with jewels, the fineness and richness of the work symbolizing the ruler's supreme authority, so the heroic poem should have a stately movement, a formal elaborated style, and magnitude.

All of this Spenser accomplishes, yet nothing could be more striking than the differences the reader instantly perceives between *The Faerie Queene* and the *Iliad* or the *Odyssey*. In the first lines of Spenser's poem we encounter an armed knight riding on a plain, and we know that we shall travel with him into the realm of medieval chivalry. But we must remember that humanism at its best, in the field of literature, aimed to emulate the classical poets, not servilely to imitate them. Spenser set out to write, not an *Iliad* or an *Aeneid* in English, but an English heroic poem—a poem, in other words, rooted in the native English past, using everything medieval and familiar that could be used. In this we see how *The Faerie Queene* is a continuance of the kind of effort Spenser made in *The Shepherd's Calendar*. First he went back to Chaucer; now he also went back to Malory's *Morte d'Arthur*. Undoubtedly he was influenced in this by the Italian poet Ariosto, who had made a Renaissance poem out of matter from the romances; but he was guided also by a sound instinct. Granted that Roger Ascham was right about the *Morte d'Arthur,* it still was not necessary to make a disastrous sacrifice of so much of England's imaginative past. A great part of the old familiar matter could be taken up and reinterpreted, made new by a new spirit and aim, yet not too new.

A good deal has been made of the fact that Spenser was not a classical scholar; that he and other Elizabethan poets and playwrights took matter, and ideas, from classical literature at second or third hand, and hence made mistakes in using what they took. But such discoveries should not confuse us, and indeed ought not to surprise us. The recapture of the ancient world was a slow and arduous undertaking, and could be itself a life's work or more than a life's work. The English Renaissance had its scholars from the beginning, as we have seen; we may be grateful that it also had its poets who were able to catch the new spirit, the new outlook, and *something* from the riches of the ancient world which they could use to great effect, while still saving time, amidst busy active lives, to write their poems. None of Spenser's poetry is "classical," though much deriving ultimately from the ancient literatures is gathered into it. Spenser's poetry is English, and has its roots in the English past. Not only does it look back to Chaucer and Malory—*The Faerie Queene* is a series of medieval allegories, and the allegory of the first book is identical with the theme of the earlier morality plays. Nevertheless, the poem is inconceivable except as the production of a writer of the Renaissance. And although Spenser's direct classical learning was meager, he was widely read in the French and Italian literature of the Renaissance. He was not a "classical" poet, but he was unequivocally and completely a Renaissance poet, carrying out the aims of Renaissance humanism. *The Faerie Queene* indeed can best be understood as an English poet's re-creation, in his own way, of such a work as Castiglione's *Book of the Courtier*.

One of the most significant things about *The Faerie Queene* is the way in which Spenser has sought to bring together in it the whole range of matter, thought, and feeling which the age presented to him. The poem is medieval, yet Protestant; Christian and pagan; ethical, yet sensuous in the extreme; idyllic, but also heroic. If proof were needed, this would suffice to prove how completely the poem is the product of Renaissance influences. Spenser was certainly no less aware than Petrarch had been of contradictions between things which still irresistibly appealed to him. Since they did irresistibly appeal, he somehow got everything into his poem; and while we read it we feel that all is subdued and harmonized to his slow and stately music, in which, after all, he has said a great part of what he has to say to us; but when the spell of that music is broken, and we look for intellectual, or even emotional, harmony, we are disappointed. Spenser is "modern" as Petrarch is; both are divided and enigmatic souls, unable to reconcile flesh and spirit, unable to cleave to either, and so trying to make the best of both worlds.

Sir Philip Sidney

Spenser's *Shepherd's Calendar* had been dedicated to Sir Philip Sidney; and though Sidney wrote nothing which can place him beside the author of *The Faerie Queene*, anyone who would understand the English Renaissance must know Sidney as well as Spenser. There are interesting points of contact between the two. Sidney was the paragon of the age, the living embodiment of the hero as Spenser conceived that ideal type. He was a thorough aristocrat, early famous for his courtesy and taste, and the best example England could show of humanistic education, rhetorical and literary, and of the symmetrically developed man of many accomplishments. His *Defense of Poesy* is almost the earliest set piece of literary criticism in the language and is an eloquent, even distinguished presentation of Renaissance literary theory. Spenser accepted for himself substantially what Sidney says in the *Defense*. For Sidney, however, as an independent gentleman, the writing of poetry—indeed all writing—was only an avocation. A gentleman should be able to write a copy of verses, on occasion, as he should be able to play a musical instrument, or take his part in a song, or acquit himself well on the tennis court or in a fencing bout. And Sidney did write, but published nothing, which was also, as was said earlier in this chapter, the gentlemanly thing. His writings found their way into print only after his early death. His series of sonnets, *Astrophel and Stella,* contains some of the best sonnets written in the Elizabethan era—better than any Spenser wrote, better than any except some of Shakespeare's. Sidney also wrote a very long prose romance, the *Arcadia,* which contains some charming lyrics. As a connected story it is almost as complete a failure as *The Faerie Queene,* though fortunately neither of these works depends for its interest upon a neat or practicable plan. The interest of Sidney's romance lies partly in the extent to which it is a prose counterpart of *The Faerie Queene.* The *Arcadia* is an heroic tale in a pastoral setting, whose characters are much occupied with love and with everything that can be said about love.

The Themes of Elizabethan Literature

Spenser and Sidney between them in all their writings supplement and confirm each other. From either we can learn the three chief subjects of English literature at the end of the sixteenth century: courtly love, heroism, and pastoralism. These are aristocratic subjects, and sophisticated subjects; they are the fruit of learning—Renaissance learning rather than classical learning. Elizabethan literature is a learned and courtly literature, and the popular literature of the time follows, on the whole, the lead of the aristocrats, just as it had in the Middle Ages. Heroism, as should be clear from what has already been said in this chapter, was a subject which the Renaissance owed directly to humanism—to the effort of the humanists to give this life its due. Courtly love in the Renaissance, when Plato came to be studied but was ill understood, was perversely connected with the doctrine of love expounded by Plato in the *Symposium,* and turned, in some hands, into what we still call "Platonic love." This, which really had nothing to do with Plato, was a pretense that the lover cared only for the spiritual (divine) qualities of the beloved, and sought only a spiritual, not a bodily, union. Pastoral poetry in its origin, in the latest period of Greek literature, had been a sophisticated townsman's dream of life in the country, far from the complexities and corruptions of the city, where men and women were simple—almost to the point of being child-like—direct, honest, and (except in love) trustworthy. This dream of simple kindly people leading an easy life, in company with their sheep, in unspoiled natural surroundings, which were conceived as "ideally" as the shepherds and shepherdesses themselves, fascinated the Elizabethans—as indeed it was to fascinate others, until almost our own time—and was transmuted by them into a picture of the fabled golden age, to which they could in imagination withdraw, far from all the uncertainties and hardships and malignancies of their actual experience.

John Lyly and "Fine Writing"

Spenser and Sidney also illustrate, in different ways, the Elizabethan exuberance which led, in literature, to unrestrained flights of "fine writing," just as it also led, with rapidly growing wealth, to unrestrained gorgeousness of costume amongst courtiers and all who aspired to enter "high life." But the prime example of this characteristic of Elizabethan literature was given to the world, as early as 1578, by John Lyly in a book called *Euphues, the Anatomy of Wit,* which excited so much interest that Lyly wrote a sequel, and Lodge, Greene, and others wrote popular imitations. Lodge's *Rosalind,* which Shakespeare in effect dramatized in *As You Like It,* had for its subtitle "Euphues' Golden Legacy." Lyly's book is really a humanistic treatise on the art of living. The story is a framework for chapters on education, friendship, manners, morals, religion, and clothes, all intended for gentle folk. But it was the literary style, not the subject-matter, which at once attracted eager attention. Lyly's guiding principles were not new; they were to be found in textbooks on rhetoric. But these rhetorical devices had not previously been used to create an English prose so formal, so highly elaborated, so rich in decorative qualities as Lyly's; and the effects he achieved were vastly admired by a generation in love with words and with all the wonderful things to be done with them.

Exuberance leads to wild extremes. The Elizabethans were guilty of every wild excess, and for a time liked them all. Euphuism was one of them—but so obvious an extreme that a reaction quickly set in. By the time Shakespeare was fairly in the way of writing plays, Euphuism had become a proper subject for parody and satire. Certain other extremes had a less transitory vogue, but, as we shall see, they also provoked reactions.

The First Theater

English love of clowning and buffoonery; Elizabethan love of gaudy display, elaborate pageantry, and high-flown rhetoric; spreading humanistic passion for the heroic and for earthly glory;—these not altogether harmonious interests came, as the reign of Elizabeth continued, to find their fullest satisfaction in the theater. And in Elizabethan drama one can perhaps most instructively see youthful exuberance leading to extremes which provoked strong reactions. We have noticed how widespread love for dramatization steadily grew through the sixteenth century, and have seen the various steps towards drama, in the full sense of the word, which were being taken. Now we must see what these preparatory gropings led to.

In 1576 a carpenter who had turned professional actor, one James Burbage, became convinced that it would be profitable to erect a building in London exclusively for dramatic performances. He was not permitted to do so within the precincts of the City, but had to build his theater in the suburbs where already there were facilities for other popular amusements—rings for bull-baiting and bear-baiting, pits for cockfighting, butts for archery, and playing fields for football. Burbage's notion of a theater was derived partly from a bear-baiting ring, partly from courtyards of inns where, as was said earlier in this chapter, traveling players had for some time been giving their performances. The building was circular, with tiers of galleries running towards the stage from either side of the entrance, and with the center open to the sky. The stage was a platform projecting from the side opposite the entrance into the unroofed center, so that the audience surrounded three sides of the stage. There was no front curtain. There was also no painted scenery, and not very much in the way of theatrical properties. But these deficiencies were compensated as fully as possible by expensive and gaudy costumes and much impressive display.

The New Plays of the 1580's

Burbage's instinct for business was excellent. His theater more than paid its way, and soon had rivals. Much study has been devoted to these first theaters and their organization, and to the history of stage-production, none of which is more than a side issue to the student of literature. What is important for us to realize is that a company of traveling players could go a long way with a few pieces to perform, because when its repertory was exhausted the company could move on to another place. But with the erection of theaters in the London suburbs the situation changed. A varied fare became vitally necessary to insure profitable attendance. Hence from 1576 there was an active market for plays, and a man with the right talent who was desperate for money could earn a living by writing—a miserable and precarious living, to be sure, but the possibility was enough to attract certain very needy and dissolute young men from the universities who could find nothing else to do for their bread and wine. These young men had learned a great deal from the Senecan tragedies and the comedies of Plautus and Terence, and they had some Renaissance learning, besides talent and plenty of exuberance. They had to meet a commercial demand, and were restricted by it; but they succeeded, not all at once yet quickly, in effecting a fusion of classical structure and motifs with native liveliness and freedom which was something new and unique. Elizabethan drama could not have come into being without this fusion—or at any rate did not. The foreign elements were as essential as the native, but not more essential.

"Classical" and "Romantic"

The result was a drama so far from "classical"—especially as "classical" requirements had been rationalized and stiffened by Renaissance critics—that it has been called, like the greater part of Elizabethan literature, and for the same reason, "romantic." Critics and historians cannot dispense with these two troublesome words, but no one should suppose that all literature can be divided into two portions, one "classical," the other "romantic," and that consequently if a piece of literature is not "classical" it must be "romantic." It would be just about as sensible, and useful, to divide all men into two classes, one drunk, one sober. Confusion enough is caused by attaching quite various and even unrelated meanings to "classical" and "romantic"; but a worse mischief encouraged by this dual classification is a spirit of partisanship which has too long infected writers on modern literature. Before we judge, we should at least try to understand what we are judging. It may therefore be suggested as a wise rule for any student that he should try to discover just what a writer or lecturer really means whenever he uses "classical" or "romantic," and that he should substitute that meaning wherever possible. If it appears, to take the latter word alone, that by "romantic" somebody really means "flamboyant," or "unrestrained," or "thrilling," or "sentimental," or—as is often the case with Elizabethan drama—simply "non-classical in form," the definite right word or phrase should be fixed in one's mind in place of the unnecessary vague word.

We have seen that *The Faerie Queene* is "romantic" in the sense that it is composed largely of matter derived from chivalric romance, but we have also seen that this matter is used for a controlling humanistic purpose. Similarly a great many Elizabethan plays are more or less "romantic" in some sense and at the same time more or less "classical" in some sense. What is most useful at present for us to understand is chiefly that Elizabethan drama is a fusion, a genuine fusion of elements often held to be disparate. The fusion was effected under the stress of practical needs by a small group of writers who did have some classical learning. These writers did feel contempt for the formless dramatizations of the time, and they wished to free the theater, as Marlowe, the greatest of them, proclaimed,

> From jigging veins of riming mother wits,
> And such conceits as clownage keeps in pay.

They had, however, no notion of working towards anything except dramatic effectiveness according to their lights, and within the limits imposed by what their audiences found interesting and exciting.

William Shakespeare

When Shakespeare came to London, in the late 1580's, the groundwork had been completed, as was said above. He found a thriving business into which, somehow, he entered; and by combining in his own career the offices of actor, playwright, manager, and owner he contrived to make a good thing out of it; and towards the close of his life he was able to retire to Stratford as a gentleman and modest property-holder. As far as we can see, Elizabethan drama would have run exactly the same course had Shakespeare never written anything, and it would also have become the dominant literary form in the half-century from 1590 to 1640 had he not written a play. He was not a pioneer or innovator. The themes of his plays are, almost wholly, those which have been named as the themes of Elizabethan literature in general—courtly or romantic love, pastoralism, and the heroic character. In his early dramas he shows the same exuberance, and the same delight in rich effects and in sheer play with words, that we have seen in his contemporaries. Shakespeare, in short, accepted what he found, grew into it as any apprentice might unquestioningly learn a craft, and finally used the dramatic medium with the mastery of supreme genius. This is the difference between Shakespeare and his fellow-dramatists; he did what they were doing, but did it better. A student should not read too many Elizabethan plays—they are not worth the time and effort in comparison with much else in English literature—but the reading of a few will show him the truth and meaning of this distinction more impressively than any number of critical superlatives bestowed on "Avonian Willy, bard Divine," as he was called by a great actor (but not great poet) of the eighteenth century.

Nevertheless, we cannot say that Shakespeare is "better" without at least briefly suggesting what this means. The bard is far from "divine"; he is often careless, even slovenly, sometimes bombastic, sometimes barbaric; but he triumphs over all faults in the matchless expressiveness of his poetic vein. We hear of Marlowe's "mighty line," wonderfully expressive of the pomp of earthly grandeur. Marlowe is famous for it. But Shakespeare could be equally expressive of the whole range of human moods, the whole range of human character, the whole range of human perceptions. The English vocabulary had more than doubled itself during the sixteenth century, and Shakespeare had all of it under command—the word and phrase so perfect for whatever he needed to say that we are brought to a pause, and can only call it a species of magic. No one, perhaps, ever thought so constantly through images as Shakespeare; and by his wealth of imagery, so apt for his meaning and intention that his pictures have entered into the mind of the race, he seems not so much to *say* this or that as to express it directly after the fashion of the painter or the musician. And he was a subtle and effortless musician who with a touch of his bow could summon the one perfectly right tone for every utterance of every character.

Shakespeare, we know, wrote rapidly, sometimes too rapidly; but, in compensation, there is nothing labored, painfully forced out, in his plays. The man himself seems enigmatic to many, in a very different way from such a one as Petrarch: he seems completely impersonal—an unexpressive mask looking down impartially on his vast concourse of extraordinarily varied characters. But this is another reason for his "betterness." He had the dramatic imagination in its greatest purity and intensity. He became possessed by a plot, by a character, by one character after another, and was himself merely the recording instrument. In this sense Shakespeare *is* impersonal: his eye is on the object, his heart is in it, for the moment he *is,* in effect, "the object." He is not engaged in self-expression; with complete objectiveness he is engaged in dramatic expression.

No one has ever equaled Shakespeare in this, and he was so perfectly equipped with catholic sympathies, right feeling, and sound perception that he succeeded in making his characters life-like to the point of giving them a kind of existence outside of and beyond his plays. In this he had no notion of what was later to be called "realism." He adopted the practices of fellow-dramatists in simplifying, heightening, underlining for dramatic effectiveness; and for this purpose he did not hesitate to make his characters act at times in most improbable ways. Granted his conditions, or postulates, as he lays out his scheme, all follows with perfect logic—but the postulates are sometimes wild. Shakespeare does not materially differ from his contemporaries in this; he differs from them rather in making us accept his postulates without any feeling that they are wild. And he succeeds better than any magician in creating his illusions because of the amount and kind of human truth which conceals the wires and pulleys by which his puppets are directed. The Elizabethan audience wanted to be thrilled, shocked, staggered by a tragic performance. Dramatists gave the audience what it wanted by boldly making their characters larger and livelier than people are in real life, and by using every device to make situations more clear-cut and striking than they are in real life. There is an instructive analogy in the heroic figures of one of the world's greatest painters and sculptors, Michelangelo. The danger in the procedure followed alike by

Elizabethan dramatists and by Michelangelo is that it may easily degenerate into mere revolting sensationalism. Shakespeare's contemporaries and successors fell into this trap, and too often evoke only a morbid horror, worked up for its own sake. Shakespeare avoided the danger, not because his methods were different, but through his unexcelled skill and truth in characterization and his sense of the kind of character really demanded by this or that tragic situation.

We do not always realize as clearly as we should that a fully developed tragic art requires a certain maturity of thought. The tragic writer wrestles with a problem—in Milton's famous words, he seeks to "justify the ways of God to men." Expressing this more generally, we may say that the tragic writer seeks to show that justice is not really violated, though it seems to be. The Middle Ages could have no tragic art because medieval people were not aware of the problem. God's ways seemed clear to them; no matter what the appearances, human beings were really fallen and corrupt creatures who deserved whatever punishment they received, here or hereafter. Through medieval literature there also moves somewhat uncertainly the conception of Fate—a bequest of paganism—as an inscrutable power controlling all men and things, so that really we are helpless puppets. The ancient Greek dramatists had struggled to moralize Fate, and had in this manner achieved tragic meaning, picturing the hero as accountable to moral law, even when his only fault was ignorance. But in the Middle Ages Fate was thought of as capricious, or, at the other extreme, was sometimes merged with Christian Providence. And in either case there could be no development of tragic art, because justice was not seen as a tragic problem. This development had to await the coming of humanism—the coming, that is to say, of a conviction that our present earthly human nature contains elements of real goodness and greatness rising to heroic proportions, so that calamity befalling the heroic man demands explanation. The humanistic challenge to historic Christianity might be answered in a Christian way, but humanism brought it out that here was a problem requiring an answer. The difference at this point between Shakespeare and his fellows was that they tended to shirk the problem, if they saw it, conceiving the hero as simply bigger than the ordinary man, impressive as a giant would be amongst pigmies, and for this reason the more awe-inspiring in his fall; whereas Shakespeare made his heroes impressive by their nobility of nature. At the same time, the nobility embodied in these heroes is peculiarly personal and individual—imagine, as readers have been asked a thousand times to imagine, Othello in Hamlet's place or Hamlet in Othello's. Hence the Shakespearian heroes do not have a broadly representative character. Modern individualism and humanism came in together, as we saw at the beginning of this chapter, and both are reflected in Hamlet and Othello and Lear and the rest.

What is Shakespeare's solution of the tragic question he so clearly raises? Up to a point the answer is obvious: Shakespeare's heroes, for all their nobility or grandeur of nature, have fatal flaws of character, which explain and in a sense justify the calamities by which they are overwhelmed. But here we stop in perplexity—and perhaps one reason why Shakespeare continues to hold his supreme place with us is that here too the modern world stops in perplexity. "What a piece of work is a man! how noble in reason! how infinite in faculty! in form and moving how express and admirable! in action how like an angel! in apprehension how like a god! the beauty of the world! the paragon of animals!"—and yet "this quintessence of dust" is born to suffer, born to encounter the one trial he is least able to face, born to calamity, born to die and, for all we know, to be swallowed up for ever by the earth. Why should it be so? Shakespeare does not know. Is there a law of justice by which all is swayed? or a covenant of grace? Shakespeare does not know. Quite possibly we are all mere creatures of illusion, as truly as the feigned characters of the stage:

> Tomorrow, and tomorrow, and tomorrow,
> Creeps in this petty pace from day to day
> To the last syllable of recorded time,
> And all our yesterdays have lighted fools

The way to dusty death. Out, out, brief candle!
Life's but a walking shadow, a poor player
That struts and frets his hour upon the stage
And then is heard no more: it is a tale
Told by an idiot, full of sound and fury
Signifying nothing.

In his latest plays Shakespeare exhibits an untroubled serenity. It is worth notice that these are romances, in the sense that they are unearthly fantasies. Of Prospero in *The Tempest* an English critic has said that he "is the supreme manifestation in poetry of the full-grown wisdom of humanism"; yet Prospero has nothing different to say from Macbeth, except in the manner:

Our revels now are ended. These our actors,
As I foretold you, were all spirits, and
Are melted into air, into thin air:
And, like the baseless fabric of this vision,
The cloud-capp'd towers, the gorgeous palaces,
The solemn temples, the great globe itself,
Yea, all which it inherit, shall dissolve
And like this insubstantial pageant faded
Leave not a wrack behind. We are such stuff
As dreams are made on, and our little life
Is rounded with a sleep.

Later Plays and the Comedy of Manners

Plays continued to be written in very large numbers from the time of Shakespeare's retirement until the London theaters were closed by the Puritans in 1642. Some of the later plays are "remarkable," rather than great; and in general the drama suffered a sharp decline into unabashed sensationalism. There was one kind of play, however, of which Shakespeare wrote no example, which began to appear towards the end of the 1590's, which flourished especially in the early years of the seventeenth century, but which continued to be written later with no decline of power or zest. This, moreover, is the one type of Elizabethan play which has real and influential connections with later English drama of the Restoration and eighteenth century. It may be described as the comedy, often but not always satirical, of London life and manners. It is thought to have grown out of the popularity, with Londoners, of scenes having to do with London in the chronicle-plays. Thomas Dekker's *Shoemakers' Holiday* is one of the earliest, pleasantest, and most successful of the comedies of this type.

Ben Jonson

Another dramatist who wrote comedies with a London setting was the redoubtable Ben Jonson; but his comedies were satirical, and the satire was directed against follies not confined to any one time or place. In these plays, in other words, Jonson aimed consciously and directly at the criticism of life for "the correction of manners." His conception of comedy as something which could be "throughout pleasant and ridiculous" and yet should stick close to real life and serve a useful purpose he had derived from his study of classical literature. Elizabethan literature had been pervasively influenced by the *outlook* of humanism, and a great deal of matter derived ultimately from classical sources had been taken up by Elizabethan writers and used—as Plutarch's *Lives* were used by Shakespeare in his Roman plays; but classical urbanity, moderation, purity of style, and firmness of design were still quite foreign to England, along with much else that could be learned from the ancient literatures, including this conception of the proper function of comedy.

Jonson had been apprenticed to his stepfather's trade of bricklaying, but had come under the influence of William Camden, the great antiquarian, who was also a classical scholar and Headmaster of Westminster School. With Camden's help Jonson had acquired a wide and close knowledge of Greek and Latin literature, which enabled him to take a critical view of Elizabethan drama and poetry. He reacted strongly against Elizabethan exuberance, extravagance, facility, and fancifulness, and tried by his own example to show the way to a more controlled and mature literary art. He undertook this missionary work at an opportune time. "Youth's a stuff will not endure," and by 1600 Elizabethan high spirits were evidently beginning to fail. Moreover, though Jonson had some faults commonly found in the self-made man or the conscious pioneer—he was both arrogant and truculent—he had good sense and genuine talent. It was he, we may recall, who uttered the sound dictum that classical writers should be accepted as guides, not commanders; and he had no notion of leading to an imitation classical literature, but aimed at something very different, assimilation of the foreign thing and growth through it.

Jonson wrote not only satirical comedies, but tragedies, Horatian satires, epigrams, odes, and elegies. He was also the great master of that courtly and elaborate form of entertainment called the masque, in which spoken dialogue, song, and dancing were mingled, and which flourished especially during the reign of Elizabeth's successor, James I. The masques were performed not only with expensive costume, but with magnificent scenery and other stage devices, mostly designed by Inigo Jones, a great architect; and it is from these performances that the painted scenes of the modern stage are descended. Jonson was one of the earliest all-round professional men of letters in England. His whole life was centered in the cause of literature, and he achieved amongst contemporaries a position of acknowledged leadership comparable to that later attained successively by Dryden, Pope, and Samuel Johnson. He did not, it is true, exert an immediate influence on the drama, which proceeded, by and large, on the downward course already mentioned. He did, however, form amongst the lyric poets of the first half of the seventeenth century a definite school of followers who learned his classical lessons and wrote the most urbane, finely controlled, and exquisitely designed lyrics in the language. Amongst this "tribe of Ben" were Randolph, Carew, Lovelace, Suckling, Waller, and—the best of them—Robert Herrick.

John Donne

Jonson was not the only one who reacted critically against Elizabethan literature at the end of the sixteenth century, or who attracted a following amongst Jacobean and Caroline writers. The poetry of the first half of the seventeenth century can be roughly classified as of three kinds—a sign that culture as well as society was now fast losing homogeneity. There were a number of poetic followers of Spenser, the brothers Giles and Phineas Fletcher, George Wither, and William Browne of Tavistock being the most notable. But the Spenserians did not have the positive qualities of mind or feeling that would have been requisite to infuse their school with new life. The other two schools had far more vitality—the school of Jonson and the school of John Donne.

Donne reacted against the "sugared sweetness" of Elizabethan love poetry, against what had come to be the conventional praise of ladies as models of constancy, purity, and all other virtues, and as surpassingly beautiful. Like Jonson, he wanted to lead a return from Arcadia and other dream-lands, and bring literature down to earth and reality. But his method was very different from Jonson's—was indeed more simply and purely a *reaction,* of the kind noticeable in some of Shakespeare's sonnets. Since he found Elizabethan love-poems diffuse, obvious, cloyingly sweet, false in their "idealistic" pictures of womankind, and equally false in the pretense that love was purely spiritual, he would write poems about love in a completely opposed style, and picture women as they really were, and love as a fever of the body. Hence his poems tend to be crabbed, compressed, recondite, sometimes bitter, sometimes cynical, realistic in the modern sense, and paradoxical. Donne had in him as a young man a good deal of that impudent desire to shock conventional people which was to reappear in English literature in the 1890's. But he had also a kind of dark intensity of feeling, and a wretched sense that love was really at one and the same time both a devil and a saint; hence his poems express an inward struggle and strange uneasiness which is occasionally painful but always arresting.

What particularly struck contemporaries, however, was Donne's new literary style, the most remarkable feature of which was the conceit. The word is the equivalent of the Italian *concetto,* and signifies an ingenious, unexpected comparison or turn of thought. *Unexpected* is the emphatic word in this definition. The conceit was not invented by Donne, nor was he the first to bring it into English literature. Lyly's *Euphues* is full of conceits of a kind. Donne, however, used the conceit more seriously than his predecessors, in the sense that with him it was not an ornament or a plaything, but became an integral part of his effort to fuse style and meaning; and what he sought to express was an unsatisfied questioning spirit, the mind aroused so to problems, which it could not finally solve and could not let go, that acuteness, learning, every aid must be summoned. This appearance in his verse of the intellect stretched and taxed, together with some comparisons Donne drew from his knowledge of medieval philosophy, probably encouraged Dryden in the 1690's to say that Donne "affected the metaphysics." Nearly a century later Dr. Johnson in his account of Cowley in *The Lives of the English Poets* spoke of Donne as the father of "a race of writers that may be termed the metaphysical poets";—and since then the name has stuck to Donne and his successors, to the perplexity of many, including Wordsworth. It appears, from Johnson's use of the word elsewhere in a sense characteristic of the eighteenth century, and also from what he says of these poets in his life of Cowley, that all he meant by "metaphysical" was "unnatural," "unreal," or "fantastic."

When he was forty-three, Donne became a priest of the Anglican Church, and six years later was made Dean of St. Paul's Cathedral in London. He continued to write poetry, with not much change in style, but an appropriate change in subject. This later verse is religious and devotional. And it was this that influenced George Herbert in the style of his devotional poetry. Herbert in turn exerted an influence on Henry Vaughan; and these three, together with the Roman Catholic poet, Richard Crashaw, are by far the best of the "metaphysical" poets. Hence, somewhat oddly, Donne's strained and crabbed style became the vehicle of the only really fine religious poetry that modern English literature can show.

How uncertain Dr. Johnson was over connections and influences may be inferred from the fact that he couples Donne and Ben Jonson as joint founders of the "metaphysical" style. Yet he had some excuse. Jonson and Donne alike, as we have seen, rebelled against what they regarded as the empty prettiness of the Elizabethans and the falsehood of romantic or courtly love; and both brought the critical intellect into poetry, to give it more solidity and reality. Moreover, Carew, Lovelace, and Suckling, because of their use of conceits and because Suckling makes fun of "Platonic" love, have often been counted amongst the "metaphysicals," while Vaughan in his most characteristic vein seems only tenuously related to them. The truth is that classifications in literary history can be only approximate. Jonson formed a more distinct "school" than Donne, but each was at the head of a movement that would have taken place, somehow, without the example of either. Jonson represents an inevitable further stage of the impact of the ancient literatures on the modern mind; Donne represents more simply, as was said, a *reaction,* and his peculiar style, impressive as it was in his hands and George Herbert's, easily and quickly degenerated into a tasteless, and sometimes cheap, straining after merely rhetorical effects. In Cowley's hands, in the middle of the century, it became palpably "false wit," and died.

Francis Bacon

We have noticed how the first fruits of humanism in England were a sharpening of the critical sense—the awakening of the spirit of independent, fresh inquiry, which turned men away from tradition and back to sources. This is the key to the age. The new impulse was slow and fitful in its development. There were distractions and pauses. If at times we seem to have lost sight of this spirit of inquiry in our review of this greatest, richest, most significant period of English letters, that is part of a true picture of the age. At the end of the sixteenth century the impulse acquired a new force. It reappeared not only in poetry and drama, but in religion, and also extended itself to philosophy. There it found voice in Francis Bacon. There are many parallels, not only curious but significant, between Bacon and certain of his fellow-countrymen from the end of the fifteenth century to the end of the sixteenth. This is not the place to go far into them, but it should be understood that Bacon had predecessors, such as John Colet, who saw how medieval philosophy had degenerated into profitless and puerile disputation about words, and had lost all contact with reality; that Bacon was like his contemporaries Jonson and Donne in wanting to get back to reality; and that finally he was like many Elizabethans who felt themselves to be in a new world wholly distinct from the discredited medieval world, but who in fact were less changed than they supposed.

It is well to remember this, because it is important to see that Bacon was limited like others by the conditions of the age, and inspired also by the same impulse that others felt. What is distinctive in him is that he came into the field of philosophic thought with the mind and something of the experience of the practical statesman—the politician engaged in managing men for their own good. He was a searcher after truth, but he tended to value truth largely for its practical uses. He wished to put aside the whole method of medieval philosophy, and begin the search for truth anew; he wished no less to concentrate the search upon physical reality within reach of man's powers of first-hand, immediate observation. It is quite possible that Machiavelli's realistic discussion of the art of managing men and of the uses of power had not a little to do with the vision Bacon formed, of men learning how to manage Nature so as to use the physical resources of the earth to further their own purposes. At any rate, this was Bacon's vision—the improvement of man's earthly estate through the increase of exact knowledge of the physical world.

The question was just how to go about this new search for real, as against merely pretended, knowledge. Bacon had a clear conception of the distinction between the two, as well as the definitely conceived aim just set forth; he spent most of his leisure in fiddling with the all-important question of method. He has been disparaged by some undiscriminating critics because he did not reach a fruitful solution of this problem On the Continent Kepler and Galileo were his contemporaries; in England William Harvey, the famous discoverer of the circulation of the blood, was his younger contemporary. These were actual founders of modern scientific inquiry, and Bacon was either ignorant of their work or indifferent to it. Instead of learning from them, he sat alone, sketching out large plans, making many beginnings, surveying the existing state of knowledge, and eloquently pleading for recognition of the importance and possibilities of systematic scientific research. Nevertheless, though he failed to elaborate a useful scientific method, and though his works are a mass of fragments, of great beginnings left incomplete, and of notes, he did succeed in expressing more eloquently and impressively than anyone else the inestimable value of scientific inquiry, in words which seem prophetic of the revolution in our ways of life and in our thinking which science has progressively brought about since the seventeenth century. And in so acting as the missionary of modern science he made a deeper impression on his own age than has always been realized. Sir Thomas Browne was a delightful, if not—scientifically considered—fruitful, follower of Bacon; and the founders and early members of the Royal Society were all influenced by him. He did, in short, a very great deal to turn men's minds towards science and keep them working energetically and hopefully, until at the end of the century the new kind of inquiry gained irresistible prestige and momentum from the discoveries of Sir Isaac Newton.

Prose of the First Half of the Seventeenth Century

It is in keeping with the altered temper of the seventeenth century that we find, practically speaking, no professedly imaginative work in prose. The imagination is actively at work in prose writers of the time, and the first half of this century is notable for prose composed with fine literary art. But the *ends* writers set before them are not literary. Outside of Bacon, we have Robert Burton, whose extraordinary *Anatomy of Melancholy* is, in intention, a medical treatise; and Sir Thomas Browne, whose works are antiquarian, or speculative, or ethical; and Izaak Walton, who wrote biographical sketches of his friends or of men he admired, and a treatise on fishing. If we look beyond these we encounter the succession of divines of the Anglican Church, whose treatises and sermons during the first half of the century are indeed one of the glories of English literature too much neglected—but, still, they are writings composed to serve a cause not literary.

Religious Writings and Controversy

The works of the divines fall into two classes: they are either, like the eloquent sermons of Donne and of Lancelot Andrewes, primarily devotional; or they are treatises in defense of Anglican Protestantism, some directed against Rome, and some against Calvinists and other kinds of Protestants who felt that the Church of England was not sufficiently reformed to be genuinely Protestant. The significant feature of these treatises, from Richard Hooker's *Of Ecclesiastical Polity* to Jeremy Taylor's *Liberty of Prophesying,* is that their writers place their reliance on human reason as the final authority man can appeal to, even in questions of religion.

The average person today will say that literature is one thing, and religion another, and of course he is quite right; yet we have seen that thus far from the beginning the course of literature in England has been intimately bound up with Christianity, and we shall see as we go on that this close relationship continued to the end of the nineteenth century. Not only is it true that much religious prose and some religious poetry has become an integral part of English literature. Not only is it true that the Authorized Version of the English Bible has been the most influential of all books in the language—and influential upon English writers to the point that it is impossible to study English literature intelligently without a knowledge of the Bible. It is also true that Christianity in England has so continuously affected, in one way or another, the outlook of writers and the character of their writing, that anyone studying English literature without constant reference to the history of Christianity in England is in very much the same position as a deaf man at a concert.

It is therefore necessary that we stop to ask how it was that English divines began, with Richard Hooker at the end of the sixteenth century, to rely on human reason as the final court of appeal in matters of religious belief. This was something new, and was an unforeseen consequence of the Reformation. It is also something startling, because Christianity is a religion founded on divine revelation, so that this revelation itself, or, in other words, the direct Word of God, should be, for those who receive and accept it, the final and supreme authority. The difficulty was that the alleged revelation took place a long time ago, so that if a question did arise about it, direct verification —after the manner in which we can at any time verify a scientific "law"—was impossible. The revelation was recorded in the Bible, but how could anyone be sure that this record was authentic? The answer of the Roman Catholic Church was that the Church had been founded by one of Christ's Apostles, entrusted with that duty by Christ Himself, and had passed on from one generation to another without a break this direct Apostolic testimony to the authenticity of the revelation recorded in the Bible. But the Protestant Reformers had challenged the Roman Catholic Church's authority as thus based on tradition, asserting that the tradition in the Church's hands had been corrupted. They had gone on to make the dreadful accusation that the Pope was Antichrist (because only if this were true could their rebellion be justified), and had then proclaimed the Bible itself the sole authority for Christian belief.

This was the thing that got the Reformers into inextricable difficulties, though there was nothing else they could do if they were determined to separate themselves from the historic Church. The question about the authenticity of the Bible as the inspired Word of God was immediately raised. It came up plainly in controversial exchanges between

St. Thomas More and William Tyndale. When More asked how we can know what the Divine Word is unless there is an infallible custodian (the Church) to inform us, Tyndale could only reply:

> Who taught the eagles to spy out their prey? Even so the children of God spy out their Father; and Christ's elect spy out their Lord, and trace out the paths of His feet and follow. . . . Hereby ye see that it is a plain and an evident conclusion, as bright as the sun's shining, that the truth of God's word dependeth not of the truth of the congregation. And therefore, when thou art asked, why thou believest that thou shalt be saved through Christ, and of such like principles of our faith; answer, Thou wottest and feelest that it is true. And when he asketh, how thou knowest that it is true; answer, Because it is written in thine heart. And if he ask who wrote it; answer, The Spirit of God. And if he ask how thou camest first by it; tell him whether by reading in books, or hearing it preached, as by an outward instrument, but that inwardly thou wast taught by the Spirit of God. And if he ask, whether thou believest it not because it is written in books, or because the priests so preach; answer, No, not now, but only because it is written in thine heart, and because the Spirit of God so preacheth and so testifieth unto thy soul.

Tyndale's confidence in the sufficiency of this answer was absolute, but it is hardly doubtful that it would have been severely shaken had he lived longer. What he says is, in plain words, that every individual's own private inner conviction of the truth is to be that person's final authority. There was not only the question of the Bible's authenticity; there was also the question how the Bible was to be understood when you read it, or had it read to you; and, as Tyndale saw, it was no more possible to answer such questions directly from the Bible than it would be to fly to the moon. Yet, rejecting the Church, the only course open to him was to invite every man to regard himself individually as divinely commissioned to interpret the Word of God as he pleased. This was to bring in sheer anarchy, as subversive of the State and of ordered social life as it was of any commonly held religious faith. And in fact anarchy became a real danger. Differing Protestant sects multiplied rapidly, each claiming to be the custodian of the one and indivisible truth vouchsafed to its leader by his inner conviction, and many claiming on this basis an authority above that of the State.

The individualism to which the Reformers were committed in spite of themselves, and the unlimited fanaticism thus encouraged did not become apparent in England at once. The Reformation in England and the Renaissance were not two separate movements which happened to take place at the same time. As we have seen, in England the Reformation and the Renaissance were really united into one complex movement of change, and this for some years obscured their fundamental disharmony, and helped to make possible the compromise which Elizabeth maintained, through a Church which claimed to be Catholic though Reformed. The convinced Protestants under Elizabeth felt strongly that the English Church still savored in its ritual and organization of "popery," and wanted thoroughly to purify it of the taint. Hence arose the term, contemptuously applied, of "Puritanism," which happened to stick, so that we have it yet. Spenser and Lyly were Puritans, which is enough to prove that Protestantism in their time had not yet become fanatical and opposed to secular, or "worldly," cultivation. But it was headed that way, as a logical result both of the doctrine of private inspiration and of the aim of Protestants to effect a return to the pure sources of Christian belief. The Renaissance as a return to the sources of secular culture, as we have seen, was a movement back to classical pre-Christian civilization. The Reformation as a return to the sources of Christianity was a movement back to the early Christian writers and thus inevitably to a revival of the otherworldly attitude of historic Christianity.

We can now see why divines of the Church of England began to appeal to reason. They were in search of something which should be the same in all men, assent to the authority of which would head off the dangers of fanaticism and anarchy inherent in the doctrine of private inspiration. Hooker and his immediate successors said substantially what Roman Catholic theologians had long said: Reason is a faculty implanted in man whereby he can become possessed of absolute truth; revelation therefore cannot contradict reason, and does not (so it was held), though it goes beyond what reason of itself can discover; and since reason *is* an organ of universal truth, it must be the same in all men. Hence a conviction peculiar to one, or to a group or sect, no matter how firmly held, must be suspect. So far we encounter nothing really new; but the Anglican divines were pushed further, because, like all other Protestants, they had to deny the authority of tradition. Hence they had to acknowledge reason as the final arbiter in all questions about the Bible, and this had far-reaching consequences. When two interpretations of a given text, for instance, seemed equally reasonable, there was nothing to do but declare that the text contained no message necessary for salvation. And this opened the way for endless sniping at the Bible.

Nevertheless, the attempt to justify separation from Rome and yet hold Englishmen together in one Christian Church founded on reason might have succeeded, at least for a time, had it had a fair chance. But it did not. James Stuart, Elizabeth's successor, was a foolish king who held that he ruled by Divine Right, and who had none of Elizabeth's power to see what Englishmen would willingly endure. There were other forces besides Protestantism making for the development of individualism in the sixteenth century, as we have seen, and particularly the growth of industrial and commercial activity. These forces by the beginning of the seventeenth century were producing men of very independent temper, jealous of their rights, and ready to make a determined stand against tyranny. James was blind to this new condition and obstinate in asserting claims to absolute arbitrary power. Hence, inevitably, he succeeded in alarming many of his subjects and so encouraged the spirit of rebellion against both Church and State. His son, Charles I, added fuel to the flame, and did so especially by handing the administration of the Church to Archbishop Laud, who was suspected—wrongly but not unnaturally—of wanting to lead the English Church back to Rome.

The consequence, during the years from 1603 to about 1640, was that the growth of fanatical Protestant beliefs in England was accelerated, that Puritan grievances became combined with political grievances, and that finally open rebellion against Church and State broke out, and civil war followed. The Puritans found an able military commander in Oliver Cromwell, and through his ability won the war. They then were guilty of the cardinal blunder, to say no more, of beheading Charles I, in 1649, and so of making a royal martyr of him. But this was only the beginning of their troubles. They had fought against despotism. Immediately upon their victory, one faction, the Presbyterians, wanted to erect a new despotism after the example set by Calvin at Geneva. Cromwell himself, and many of the Puritans, were Independents, as they were called, or belonged to one of numerous non-Presbyterian Protestant groups. They were determined not to hand themselves over to a new ecclesiastical tyranny. But agreement upon any course proved impossible. Protestant fanaticism and Protestant anarchy had descended upon England, and there was union only in repression of "worldliness." Against his own desire Cromwell was forced to govern England by a military despotism, and by the time he died, in 1658, it seemed evident to most Englishmen that they had merely jumped out of the frying pan into the fire.

John Milton

The last representative of the English Renaissance was John Milton, who grew up amidst the thickening clouds and the increasing discords that led to the Civil War. As a young man he seemed wholly unconscious of the actual state of the country. He *was* conscious of his own ability, and determined to prepare himself for the writing of an heroic poem—the great crowning literary achievement which was the dream and the ambition of poets wherever Renaissance humanism penetrated. When the Civil War came, however, he had no hesitation in allying himself with the Puritan cause, put aside his poetical ambition, and spent some ten years as official propagandist and as a member of Cromwell's government. During all that time he nursed his early intention, and after his years of public service, when old and blind, returned to it, to write *Paradise Lost,* and then *Paradise Regained* and *Samson Agonistes.* He acknowledged Spenser as his master, and this should be remembered and pondered, because what strikes most readers is the great difference between the two. Yet there is no doubt that Milton did feel himself to be really indebted to Spenser; and the fact, accepted even if it cannot readily be understood, may help us to place Milton justly. He is often regarded as a lonely figure, out of relation to the highway of literary development. He was, of course, monumentally self-dependent; but he only appears isolated in his final triumphant literary activity because by the middle of the century he was the last man still trying to unite in himself discordant elements which Spenser had, as we have seen, not so much united as simply accepted. Milton, then, was the product of Renaissance culture, and of a wonderfully complete assimilation of classical art, and of Protestant individualism. For better, for worse, what he did represents what could be done with this combination, by a man possessed of genius and an iron determination proof against every difficulty.

JOHN LYLY

1554?–1606

Of Lyly's life not much is known. He was born in either 1553 or 1554. In the spring of 1569 he entered Magdalen College, Oxford, taking his bachelor's degree in 1573 and his master's degree in 1575. In the following year he was perhaps at Cambridge; he became a master of arts of that university in 1579. In 1578 he published the book for which he is still most widely known, *Euphues, the Anatomy of Wit,* the immediate success of which led to the publication of a second part, *Euphues and his England,* in 1580. Lyly's comedies, which he produced in the years that followed, are chiefly important for the part they played in helping to affect the transition from medieval to Elizabethan drama; the best known of them are *Endimion, Sapho and Phao, Campaspe,* and *Gallathea.* As these titles serve to indicate, he drew his subject-matter from pastoral tradition or classical myth; though this, in many of his plays, he used to veil political or social allegory bearing on current events. In 1588 Lyly obtained a minor post in the Revels Office which he held until 1604. He made repeated attempts to gain the Mastership of the Revels, but failed to do so and was apparently embittered by his failure. He sat in Parliament four times between 1589 and 1601.

To the modern reader the style of *Euphues* seems frigid, as indeed it is, and one concedes that its interest is chiefly historical. Yet the book will hardly be read except because of its style. It is a tale, and it has been called "the earliest English novel," but this unduly stretches the meaning of "novel," for the story is slight and of secondary importance, serving really as a framework to hold together a collection of letters and moral discussions. Moreover, the content of the book as a whole is primarily a means to an end. That is to say, it was meant as a vehicle for a certain kind of style, Euphuism, as it is called, which has three chief characteristics: (1) Balanced sentences are the rule, with frequent use of antithesis and alliteration. Euphues is described, for example, as having more wit than wealth, yet more wealth than wisdom. (2) Every fact is referred to some ancient authority, usually classical. (3) Besides the profusion of classical references, Lyly's pages are filled with allusions to natural history, mostly fabulous. Shakespeare's Falstaff knew that a lion will not harm a true prince; and Lyly gathered and used an extraordinary amount of this kind of lore. Lyly's prose, in short, is extremely mannered and artificial. We do not need Seneca's authority for the statement that "too much bending breaketh the bow"; and this absurd example will show why Euphuism soon became a proper subject for jokes. But Euphuism is misunderstood if it is thought of as a mere affectation in speech. The truth is that Lyly was a literary pioneer. We owe it to him probably more than to any other one man that prose came to be regarded equally with verse as an artistic medium. If his style now seems merely quaint and curious, it should be remembered that Lyly was one who showed the way, and that our better standards have been made possible by the fact that later writers were able to take advantage of his successes as well as of his failures.

The best edition of *Euphues: The Anatomy of Wit; Euphues & his England* is that edited by Morris W. Croll and Harry Clemons (New York, 1916). *The Complete Works of John Lyly,* ed. R. Warwick Bond (Oxford, 1902), supplies a voluminous scholarly apparatus. For a discussion of the whole development of which *Euphues* is a part see George P. Krapp, *The Rise of English Literary Prose* (New York, 1915).

EUPHUES, THE ANATOMY OF WIT

Very pleasant for all Gentlemen to read, and most necessary to remember: wherein are contained the delights that Wit followeth in his youth by the pleasantness of Love, and the happiness he reapeth in age by the perfectness of Wisdom.

A COOLING CARD[1] FOR PHILAUTUS AND ALL FOND LOVERS[2]

MUSING with myself, being idle, how I might be well employed, friend Philautus, I could find nothing either more fit to continue our friendship, or of greater force to dissolve our folly, than to write a remedy for that which many judge past cure; for love, Philautus, with the which I have been so tormented that I have lost my time, thou so troubled that thou hast forgot reason, both so mangled with repulse, inveigled by deceit, and almost murdered by disdain, that I can neither remember our miseries without grief, nor redress our mishaps without groans. How wantonly, yea, and how willingly have we abused our golden time and misspent our gotten treasure! How curious were we to please our lady, how careless to displease our Lord! How devout in serving our goddess, how desperate in forgetting our God! Ah, my Philautus, if the wasting of our money might not dehort us, yet the wounding of our minds should deter us; if reason might nothing persuade us to wisdom, yet shame should provoke us to wit. If Lucilla[3] read this trifle, she will straight proclaim Euphues for a traitor, and, seeing me turn my tippet,[4] will either shut me out for a wrangler, or cast me off for a wiredrawer;[5] either convince me of malice in bewraying their sleights, or condemn me of mischief in arming young men against fleeting minions. And what then? Though Curio be as hot as a toast, yet Euphues is as cold as a clock;[6] though he be a cock of the game, yet Euphues is content to be craven and cry creek;[7] though Curio be old huddle, and twang "*ipse,* he,"[8] yet Euphues had rather shrink in the wetting than waste in the wearing. I know Curio to be steel to the back, standard-bearer in Venus's camp, sworn to the crew, true to the crown, knight marshal to Cupid, and heir apparent to his kingdom. But by that time that he hath eaten but one bushel of salt with[9] Lucilla, he shall taste ten quarters[10] of sorrow in his love; then shall he find for every pint of honey a gallon of gall, for every dram of pleasure an ounce of pain, for every inch of mirth an ell of moan. And yet, Philautus, if there be any man in despair to obtain his purpose, or so obstinate in his opinion that, having lost his freedom by folly, would also lose his life for love, let him repair hither, and he shall reap such profit as will either quench his flames or assuage his fury; either cause him to renounce his lady as most pernicious, or redeem his liberty as most precious. Come, therefore, to me, all ye lovers that have been deceived by fancy, the glass of pestilence, or deluded by women, the gate to perdition; be as earnest to seek a medicine as you were eager to run into a mischief; the earth bringeth forth as well endive to delight the people as hemlock to endanger the patient; as well the rose to distill as the nettle to sting; as well the bee to give honey as the spider to yield poison.

If my lewd life, gentlemen, have given you offense, let my good counsel make amends; if by my folly any be allured to lust, let them by my repentance be drawn to continency. Achilles's spear could as well heal as hurt;

[1] Guide; sailor's compass.

[2] A "pamphlet" written by Euphues to "bridle the overlashing affections" of his friend Philautus, "yet generally to be applied to all lovers."

[3] Lucilla was betrothed to Philautus, but, when she saw Euphues, fell in love with him, he returning her love. This broke the friendship of Euphues and Philautus; but a little later Lucilla fell in love anew with one Curio and married him, whereupon Euphues and Philautus renewed their friendship.

[4] Proverbial expression meaning to change sides.

[5] An over-precise person.

[6] As free from passion as a machine.

[7] Confess himself beaten.

[8] Though Curio be embraced as her loved one and sing "I am the man."

[9] Seen a great deal of.

[10] There are eight bushels to the quarter.

the Scorpion, though he sting, yet he stints the pain; though the herb Nerius poison the sheep, yet is it a remedy to man against poison; though I have infected some by example, yet I hope I shall comfort many by repentance. Whatsoever I speak to men, the same also I speak to women; I mean not to run with the hare and hold with the hound, to carry fire in the one hand and water in the other; neither to flatter men as altogether faultless, neither to fall out with women as altogether guilty; for, as I am not minded to pick a thank with the one, so am I not determined to pick a quarrel with the other; if women be not perverse, they shall reap profit by remedy of pleasure. If Phyllis were now to take counsel, she would not be so foolish to hang herself, neither Dido so fond to die for Aeneas, neither Pasiphaë so monstrous to love a bull, nor Phedra so unnatural to be enamored of her son.

This is, therefore, to admonish all young imps and novices in love not to blow the coals of fancy with desire, but to quench them with disdain. When love tickleth thee, decline it, lest it stifle thee; rather fast than surfeit; rather starve than strive to exceed. Though the beginning of love bring delight, the end bringeth destruction. For, as the first draught of wine doth comfort the stomach, the second inflame the liver, the third fume into the head, so the first sip of love is pleasant, the second perilous, the third pestilent. If thou perceive thyself to be enticed with their wanton glances or allured with their wicked guiles, either enchanted with their beauty or enamored with their bravery, enter with thyself into this meditation: What shall I gain if I obtain my purpose? nay, rather, what shall I lose in winning my pleasure? If my lady yield to be my lover, is it not likely she will be another's leman? and if she be a modest matron, my labor is lost. This, therefore, remaineth, that either I must pine in cares or perish with curses.

If she be chaste, then is she coy; if light, then is she impudent; if a grave matron, who can woo her? if a lewd minion, who would wed her? if one of the Vestal Virgins, they have vowed virginity; if one of Venus's court, they have vowed dishonesty. If I love one that is fair, it will kindle jealousy; if one that is foul, it will convert me into frenzy. If fertile to bear children, my care is increased; if barren, my curse is augmented; if honest, I shall fear her death; if immodest, I shall be weary of her life.

To what end, then, shall I live in love, seeing always it is life more to be feared than death? for all my time wasted in sighs and worn in sobs, for all my treasure spent on jewels and spilled in jollity, what recompense shall I reap besides repentance? What other reward shall I have than reproach? What other solace than endless shame? But haply thou wilt say, "If I refuse their courtesy I shall be accounted a mecock,[11] a milksop, taunted and retaunted with check and checkmate, flouted and reflouted with intolerable glee."

Alas, fond fool, art thou so pinned to their sleeves that thou regardest more their babble than thine own bliss, more their frumps than thine own welfare? Wilt thou resemble the kind spaniel,[12] which, the more he is beaten the fonder he is, or the foolish eyas,[13] which will never away? Dost thou not know that women deem none valiant unless he be too venturous?—that they account one a dastard if he be not desperate, a pinch-penny if he be not prodigal; if silent, a sot, if full of words, a fool? Perversely do they always think of their lovers and talk of them scornfully, judging all to be clowns[14] which be no courtiers, and all to be pinglers[15] that be not coursers.

Seeing therefore the very blossom of love is sour, the bud cannot be sweet. In time prevent danger, lest untimely thou run into a thousand perils. Search the wound while it is green; too late cometh the salve when the sore festereth, and the medicine bringeth double care when the malady is past cure.

Beware of delays. What less than the grain of mustard seed?—in time, almost what thing is greater than the stalk thereof? The slender twig groweth to a stately tree, and that which with the hand might easily have been pulled up will hardly with the ax be hewn down. The least spark, if it be not

[11] A tame-spirited man. [12] True-bred spaniel.
[13] Nestling or unfledged bird. [14] Peasants.
[15] Loiterers.

quenched, will burst into a flame; the least moth in time eateth the thickest cloth; and I have read that, in a short space, there was a town in Spain undermined with conies, in Thessaly with moles, with frogs in France, in Africa with flies. If these silly worms in tract of time overthrow so stately towns, how much more will love, which creepeth secretly into the mind (as the rust doth into the iron and is not perceived), consume the body, yea, and confound the soul. Defer not from hour to day, from day to month, from month to year, and always remain in misery.

He that to-day is not willing will to-morrow be more willful. But, alas, it is no less common than lamentable to behold the tottering estate of lovers, who think by delays to prevent dangers, with oil to quench fire, with smoke to clear the eyesight. They flatter themselves with a feinting farewell, deferring ever until to-morrow, when as their morrow doth always increase their sorrow. Let neither their amiable countenances, neither their painted protestations, neither their deceitful promises, allure thee to delays. Think this with thyself, that the sweet songs of Calypso were subtle snares to entice Ulysses; that the crab then catcheth the oyster when the sun shineth; that hyena, when she speaketh like a man, deviseth most mischief; that women when they be most pleasant pretend most treachery.

Follow Alexander, which, hearing the commendation and singular comeliness of the wife of Darius, so courageously withstood the assaults of fancy that he would not so much as take a view of her beauty. Imitate Cyrus, a king endued with such continency that he loathed to look on the heavenly hue of Panthea; and, when Araspus told him that she excelled all mortal wights in amiable show, "By so much the more," said Cyrus, "I ought to abstain from her sight; for if I follow thy counsel in going to her, it may be I shall desire to continue with her, and by my light affection neglect my serious affairs." Learn of Romulus to refrain from wine, be it never so delicate; of Agesilaus to despise costly apparel, be it never so curious; of Diogenes to detest women, be they never so comely. He that toucheth pitch shall be defiled; the sore eye infecteth the sound; the society with women breedeth security in the soul, and maketh all the senses senseless. Moreover, take this counsel as an article of thy creed, which I mean to follow as the chief argument of my faith, that idleness is the only nurse and nourisher of sensual appetite, the sole maintenance of youthful affection, the first shaft that Cupid shooteth into the hot liver of a heedless lover. I would to God I were not able to find this for a truth by mine own trial, and I would the example of others' idleness had caused me rather to avoid that fault than experience of mine own folly. How dissolute have I been in striving against good counsel, how resolute in standing in mine own conceit, how forward to wickedness, how wanton with too much cockering,[16] how wayward in hearing correction! Neither was I much unlike these abbey lubbers in my life (though far unlike them in belief) which labored till they were cold, ate till they sweat, and lay in bed till their bones ached. Hereof cometh it, gentlemen, that love creepeth into the mind of privy craft, and keepeth this hold by main courage.

The man being idle, the mind is apt to all uncleanness; the mind being void of exercise, the man is void of honesty. Doth not the rust fret[17] the hardest iron if it be not used? Doth not the moth eat the finest garment if it be not worn? Doth not moss grow on the smoothest stone if it be not stirred? Doth not impiety infect the wisest wit if it be given to idleness? Is not the standing water sooner frozen than the running stream? Is not he that sitteth more subject to sleep than he that walketh? Doth not common experience make this common unto us, that the fattest ground bringeth forth nothing but weeds if it be not well tilled, that the sharpest wit inclineth only to wickedness if it be not exercised? Is it not true which Seneca reporteth, that as too much bending breaketh the bow, so too much remission spoileth the mind? Besides this, immoderate sleep, immodest play, unsatiable swilling of wine doth so weaken the senses and bewitch the soul that, before we feel the motion of love, we are resolved into lust. Eschew idleness, my Philautus, so shalt thou easily unbend the

[16]Coddling. [17]Eat.

bow and quench the brands of Cupid. Love gives place to labor; labor, and thou shalt never love. Cupid is a crafty child, following those at an inch[18] that study pleasure, and flying those swiftly that take pains. Bend thy mind to the law, whereby thou mayest have understanding of old and ancient customs; defend thy clients; enrich thy coffers; and carry credit in thy country. If law seem loathsome unto thee, search the secrets of physic, whereby thou mayest know the hidden natures of herbs; whereby thou mayest gather profit to thy purse and pleasure to thy mind. What can be more exquisite in human affairs than for every fever, be it never so hot, for every palsy, be it never so cold, for every infection, be it never so strange, to give a remedy? The old verse standeth as yet in his old virtue: That Galen giveth goods, Justinian honors. If thou be so nice that thou canst no way brook the practice of physic, or so unwise that thou wilt not beat thy brains about the institutes of the law, confer all thy study, all thy time, all thy treasure to the attaining of the sacred and sincere knowledge of divinity; by this mayest thou bridle thine incontinency, rein thine affections, restrain thy lust. Here shalt thou behold, as it were in a glass, that all the glory of man is as the grass; that all things under heaven are but vain; that our life is but a shadow, a warfare, a pilgrimage, a vapor, a bubble, a blast; of such shortness that David saith it is but a span long; of such sharpness that Job noteth it replenished with all miseries; of such uncertainty that we are no sooner born but we are subject to death; the one foot no sooner on the ground but the other ready to slip into the grave. Here shalt thou find ease for thy burden of sin, comfort for the conscience pined with vanity, mercy for thine offenses by the martyrdom of thy sweet Savior. By this thou shalt be able to instruct those that be weak, to confute those that be obstinate, to confound those that be erroneous, to confirm the faithful, to comfort the desperate, to cut off the presumptuous, to save thine own soul by thy sure faith, and edify the hearts of many by thy sound doctrine. If this seem too strait a diet for thy straining disease,[19] or too holy a profession for so hollow a person, then employ thyself to martial feats, to jousts, to tourneys, yea, to all torments, rather than to loiter in love and spend thy life in the laps of ladies; what more monstrous can there be than to see a young man abuse those gifts to his own shame which God hath given him for his own preferment? What greater infamy than to confer the sharp wit to the making of lewd sonnets, to the idolatrous worshiping of their ladies, to the vain delights of fancy, to all kind of vice, as it were against kind and course of nature? Is it not folly to show wit to women, which are neither able nor willing to receive fruit thereof? Dost thou not know that the tree Silvacenda beareth no fruit in Pharos?[20] That the Persian trees in Rhodes do only wax green but never bring forth apple?[21]

That amomus and nardus will only grow in India, balsamum only in Syria; that in Rhodes no eagle will build her nest, no owl live in Crete, no wit spring in the will of women? Mortify, therefore, thy affections, and force not nature against nature to strive in vain. Go into the country, look to thy grounds, yoke thine oxen, follow thy plow, graft thy trees, behold thy cattle, and devise with thyself how the increase of them may increase thy profit. In autumn pull thine apples, in summer ply thy harvest, in the spring trim thy gardens, in the winter, thy woods, and thus, beginning to delight to be a good husband,[22] thou shalt begin to detest to be in love with an idle housewife; when profit shall begin to fill thy purse with gold, then pleasure shall have no force to defile thy mind with love. For honest recreation after thy toil, use hunting or hawking; either rouse the deer, or unperch the pheasant; so shalt thou root out the remembrance of thy former love, and repent thee of thy foolish lust. And, although thy sweetheart bind thee by oath always to hold a candle at her shrine, and to offer thy devotion to thine own de-

[18]Close behind.

[19]Craving for freedom.

[20]The island near Alexandria on which Ptolemy I built a lighthouse.

[21]Lyly has in mind Pliny's statement (*Natural History*, xvi, 58) that in general trees do not bear except where they are indigenous.

[22]Husbandman.

struction, yet go, run, fly into the country; neither water thou thy plants, in that thou departest from thy pigsny,[23] neither stand in a mammering[24] whether it be best to depart or not; but how much the more thou art unwilling to go, by so much the more hasten thy steps, neither feign for thyself any sleeveless excuse whereby thou mayest tarry. Neither let rain nor thunder, neither lightning nor tempest, stay thy journey; and reckon not with thyself how many miles thou hast gone—that showeth weariness; but how many thou hast to go—that proveth manliness. But foolish and frantic lovers will deem my precepts hard, and esteem my persuasions haggard;[25] I must of force confess that it is a corrosive to the stomach of a lover, but a comfort to a godly liver to run through a thousand pikes[26] to escape ten thousand perils. Sour potions bring sound health; sharp purgations make short diseases; and the medicine, the more bitter it is, the more better it is in working. To heal the body we try physic, search cunning, prove sorcery, venture through fire and water, leaving nothing unsought that may be gotten for money, be it never so much or procured by any means, be they never so unlawful. How much more ought we to hazard all things for the safeguard of mind, and quiet of conscience! And, certes, easier will the remedy be when the reason is espied; do you not know the nature of women, which is grounded only upon extremities?

Do they think any man to delight in them unless he dote on them? Any to be zealous except they be jealous? Any to be fervent in case he be not furious? If he be cleanly, then term they him proud; if mean in apparel, a sloven; if tall, a longis; if short, a dwarf; if bold, blunt; if shamefaced, a coward; insomuch as they have neither mean in their frumps, nor measure in their folly. But at the first the ox wieldeth not the yoke, nor the colt the snaffle, nor the lover good counsel; yet time causeth the one to bend his neck, the other to open his mouth, and should enforce the third to yield his right to reason. Lay before thine eyes the slights and deceits of thy lady, her snatching in jest and keeping in earnest, her perjury, her impiety, the countenance she showeth to thee of course,[27] the love she beareth to others of zeal, her open malice, her dissembled mischief.

O, I would in repeating their vices thou couldst be as eloquent as in remembering them thou oughtst to be penitent! Be she never so comely, call her counterfeit; be she never so straight, think her crooked. And wrest all parts of her body to the worst, be she never so worthy. If she be well set, then call her a boss; if slender, a hazel twig; if nutbrown, as black as a coal; if well colored, a painted wall; if she be pleasant, then is she a wanton; if sullen, a clown; if honest, then is she coy; if impudent, a harlot.

Search every vein and sinew of their disposition; if she have no sight in descant,[28] desire her to chant it; if no cunning to dance, request her to trip it; if no skill in music, proffer her the lute; if an ill gait, then walk with her; if rude in speech, talk with her; if she be jag-toothed, tell her some merry jest to make her laugh; if pink-eyed, some doleful history to cause her weep: in the one her grinning will show her deformed; in the other her whining, like a pig half roasted.

It is a world to see how commonly we are blinded with the collusions of women, and more enticed by their ornaments being artificial than their proportion being natural. I loathe almost to think on their ointments and apothecary drugs, the sleeking of their faces, and all their slibber[29] sauces which bring queasiness to the stomach and disquiet to the mind.

Take from them their periwigs, their paintings, their jewels, their rolls, their bolsterings, and thou shalt soon perceive that a woman is the least part of herself. When they be once robbed of their robes, then will they appear so odious, so ugly, so monstrous, that thou wilt rather think them serpents than saints; and so like hags that thou wilt fear rather to be enchanted than enamored. Look in their closets, and there shalt thou find an apothecary's shop of sweet confections, a surgeon's box of sundry salves, a pedlar's pack of new fangles. Besides all

[23]Thy loved one. [24]Hesitation.

[25]Wild? A haggard is a wild hawk. [26]Rocks.

[27]Outwardly.

[28]No knowledge of musical harmony.

[29]Dirty.

this, their shadows,[30] their spots,[31] their lawns, their lyfkies,[32] their ruffs, their rings, show them rather cardinals' courtesans than modest matrons, and more carnally affected than moved in conscience. If every one of these things severally be not of force to move thee, yet all of them jointly shall mortify thee.

Moreover, to make thee the more stronger to strive against these sirens, and more subtle to deceive these tame serpents, my counsel is that thou have more strings to thy bow than one; it is safe riding at two anchors; a fire divided in twain burneth slower; a fountain running into many rivers is of less force; the mind enamored on two women is less affected with desire and less infected with despair: one love expelleth another, and the remembrance of the latter quencheth the concupiscence of the first.

Yet, if thou be so weak, being bewitched with their wiles that thou hast neither will to eschew nor wit to avoid their company, if thou be either so wicked that thou wilt not, or so wedded that thou canst not abstain from their glances, yet at the least dissemble thy grief. If thou be as hot as the mount Etna, feign thyself as cold as the hill Caucasus; carry two faces in one hood; cover thy flaming fancy with feigned ashes; show thyself sound when thou art rotten; let thy hue be merry when thy heart is melancholy; bear a pleasant countenance with a pined[33] conscience, a painted sheath with a leaden dagger.[34] Thus, dissembling thy grief, thou mayest recure thy disease. Love creepeth in by stealth, and by stealth slideth away.

If she break promise with thee in the night, or absent herself in the day, seem thou careless, and then will she be careful; if thou languish, then will she be lavish of her honor, yea, and of the other strange beast, her honesty. Stand thou on thy pantofles,[35] and she will veil bonnet. Lie thou aloof, and she will seize on the lure; if thou pass by her door and be called back, either seem deaf and not to hear, or desperate, and not to care.

Fly the places, the parlors, the portals wherein thou hast been conversant with thy lady; yea, Philautus, shun the street where Lucilla doth dwell, lest the sight of her window renew the sum of thy sorrow.

Yet, although I would have thee precise in keeping these precepts, yet would I have thee to avoid solitariness—that breeds melancholy; melancholy, madness; madness, mischief and utter desolation. Have ever some faithful fere[36] with whom thou mayest communicate thy counsels: some Pylades to encourage Orestes, some Damon to release Pythias, some Scipio to recure[37] Laelius. Phyllis in wandering the woods hanged herself; Asiarchus, forsaking company, spoiled himself with his own bodkin;[38] Biarus, a Roman, more wise than fortunate, being alone, destroyed himself with a potsherd. Beware solitariness. But, although I would have thee use company for thy recreation, yet would I have thee always to leave the company of those that accompany thy lady; yea, if she have any jewel of thine in her custody, rather lose it than go for it, lest in seeking to recover a trifle thou renew thine old trouble. Be not curious to curl thy hair, nor careful to be neat in thine apparel; be not prodigal of thy gold nor precise in thy going; be not like the Englishman, which preferreth every strange fashion before the use of his country; be thou dissolute,[39] lest thy lady think thee foolish in framing thyself to every fashion for her sake. Believe not their oaths and solemn protestations, their exorcisms and conjurations, their tears which they have at commandment, their alluring looks, their treading on the toe, their unsavory toys.

Let every one loathe his lady and be ashamed to be her servant. It is riches and ease that nourisheth affection; it is play, wine, and wantonness that feedeth a lover as fat as a fool; refrain from all such meats as shall provoke thine appetite to lust, and all such means as may allure thy mind to folly. Take clear water for strong wine, brown bread for fine manchet,[40] beef and brewis[41] for quails and partridge; for ease,

[30]Borders attached to bonnets to shield complexion.

[31]Patches. [32]Bodices. [33]Tortured.

[34]A proverbial expression for false appearances.

[35]A proverbial expression for pride.

[36]Comrade. [37]Recover. [38]Small dagger.

[39]Disheveled. [40]The finest white bread.

[41]Broth obtained from boiling salted beef.

labor; for pleasure, pain; for surfeiting, hunger; for sleep, watching; for the fellowship of ladies, the company of philosophers. If thou say to me, "Physician, heal thyself," I answer that I am meetly well purged of that disease; and yet was I never more willing to cure myself than to comfort my friend. And, seeing the cause that made in me so cold a devotion should make in thee also as frozen a desire, I hope thou wilt be as ready to provide a salve as thou wast hasty in seeking a sore. And yet, Philautus, I would not that all women should take pepper in the nose,[42] in that I have disclosed the legerdemains of a few, for well I know none will wince unless she be galled, neither any be offended unless she be guilty. Therefore I earnestly desire thee that thou show this cooling card to none except thou show also this my defense to them all. For, although I weigh nothing the ill will of light housewives, yet would I be loath to lose the good will of honest matrons. Thus, being ready to go to Athens, and ready there to entertain thee whensoever thou shalt repair thither, I bid thee farewell, and fly women.

Thine ever,

EUPHUES.

[42] Take offense.

CHRISTOPHER MARLOWE

1564–1593

Marlowe was born at Canterbury in February, 1564. His father belonged to the shoemakers' and tanners' guild of the town. In 1579 the boy entered the King's School at Canterbury, and two years later passed thence to Corpus Christi College, Cambridge. He was graduated B. A. in 1584, M. A. in 1587. While at the King's School he had held a scholarship, and during his Cambridge years he held another—one created in 1575 by the will of Archbishop Matthew Parker. After 1584 his periods of residence at the University were much broken, and in the spring of 1587 his absence apparently gave opportunity for the spread of damaging rumors concerning him, which threatened to prevent his receiving his higher degree. He seems to have been in reality engaged in some secret governmental service on the Continent, and he obtained his degree as a consequence of the intervention of the Privy Council. His retention of his scholarship for six years implied the intention of taking orders in the Anglican Church; it has been inferred that his failure to do so was the result of "the growth of his speculative views" (F. S. Boas, *Marlowe and his Circle)*. At all events, he went from Cambridge to London, and at once began writing for the theaters, chiefly for the Lord Admiral's Company. On 18 September, 1589, he engaged in a duel with a certain William Bradley, whom a friend of Marlowe's, joining the fight, proceeded to slay; Marlowe, after being imprisoned and then released on bond, was finally cleared of the charge of murder. Three years later, at the petition of two constables, he was bound over to keep the peace. In May, 1593, he was summoned before the Privy Council, but before the month was out he lay murdered in a Deptford tavern. He had gone thither on 30 May with three companions, Ingram Frizer, Nicholas Skeres, and Robert Poley. The four had spent most of the day in the tavern of Eleanor Bull, and in the evening Frizer and Marlowe had begun to quarrel over the payment of the reckoning. Marlowe, in sudden anger, had seized Frizer's dagger and inflicted two wounds on his head; whereupon the latter, struggling with Marlowe, had managed to get back his dagger and had given Marlowe a mortal wound over his right eye, causing instant death. This is the account returned by the coroner's jury of sixteen men (an account discovered in the Public Record Office, London, in 1925, by Professor J. Leslie Hotson), and there is no good reason to doubt its substantial accuracy. Frizer was soon pardoned on the ground that he had acted in self-defense, and he survived—a churchwarden during his last twenty-two years—until August, 1627.

Immediately after his death Marlowe was charged with atheism by an informer, Richard Baines, and by his one-time friend Thomas Kyd, author of *The Spanish Tragedy.* Later, others joined in the accusation, and it seems evident that wild utterances of the poet's gave a more than plausible basis for it, though what was meant was not atheism in the present sense of the word. Marlowe was associated more or less closely with a small group of men who were interested in the new birth of science which was one phase of the Renaissance, and interested in religious problems turned up by the revolt of philosophy and science against scholasticism; and there can be no doubt that he held opinions definitely heterodox in character. But there is no proof that he embraced an antitheistic philosophy. The extant evidence suggests simply that he was encouraged by the new skepticism to indulge in ribald speech concerning the miraculous element in Christianity.

Marlowe's *Tamburlaine,* Part I, was performed in 1587, *Doctor Faustus* at some time between 1588 and 1592, and *The Jew of Malta* in 1589. In these three plays and in *Tamburlaine,* Part II, and *Edward II* he wrote such poetry as England had not before known. To a lofty and intense imagination he united a command of language and a skill in versification which put him easily above the other dramatists who preceded Shakespeare. He wrote his plays in blank verse, and with such mastery that he established it as the verse of Elizabethan tragedy. And in the pictures he drew, in *Tamburlaine* of the craving for universal political power, in *Doctor Faustus* of the craving for unlimited power got through knowledge, and in *The Jew of Malta* of the craving for boundless wealth, he exhibited an important—if not indeed the central—aspect of the Renaissance, with its sudden accession of unbounded confidence in human capacity and its corresponding expansion of desires. In so doing he seems, it is true, to be curiously remote from the ways and life of his time—but this is a mere deceptive appearance. "The Elizabethan world is never photographed or portrayed in his works; but its ideas and aspirations find nowhere a truer revelation; none of his contemporaries reflect its spirit, its desires and efforts better than he. A simple instance of such transmutation comes to mind. To us, looking back over 300 years, one of the most significant series of events in that age is the vast enterprise which inspired and organized the voyages of discovery. . . . The wonders and highly-colored fantasies reported by the voyagers appealed to the credulity of poets and public alike; Shakespeare clothes with concrete forms the marvels of the Bermudas. But if we turn back to the year 1593 when much of this was already current, Marlowe has little to tell us of the wonders and marvels, of dog-headed men and the sun coming up like thunder out of the far East. . . . Yet this is not the whole truth." For "deep in Marlowe's mind lay certain memories, the impressions left by those Westward voyages." Witness the dying words of Mortimer in *Edward II:*

> Weep not for Mortimer
> That scorns the world, and as a traveler
> Goes to discover countries yet unknown.

"The lives and deaths of the voyagers had made no emotional—far less any sentimental—appeal to him. But they had remained an image of eternal forth-faring." And in fact "Marlowe is, of all Elizabethans, the truest explorer. His career is a long voyage of discovery; his America is always just beyond the horizon. He endeavors, blindly and passionately at first, later with more sureness and clarity, to map new territory; new thought, and truths ascertained by thought; new dreams, visions and ecstasies created by the imagination" (U. M. Ellis-Fermor, *Marlowe).*

The Works and Life of Christopher Marlowe, ed. R. H. Case (London, 1930–1933), is the best edition; it contains a concise life of Marlowe, by C. F. Tucker Brooke, in vol. I, and *Faustus,* ed. Frederick S. Boas, in vol. V. The fullest and most recent, but not the most scholarly, biography is that by John Bakeless, *Christopher Marlowe; the Man in his Time* (New York, 1937). For the dramatic background see Edmund K. Chambers, *The Elizabethan Stage* (Oxford, 1923); for the intellectual background, Hardin Craig, *The Enchanted Glass; the Elizabethan Mind in Literature* (New York, 1936).

THE TRAGICAL HISTORY OF DOCTOR FAUSTUS[1]

DRAMATIS PERSONAE

THE POPE.
CARDINAL OF LORRAIN.
THE EMPEROR OF GERMANY.
DUKE OF VANHOLT.
FAUSTUS.
VALDES *and* CORNELIUS, *friends to Faustus.*
WAGNER, *servant to Faustus.*
CLOWN.
ROBIN.
RALPH.
VINTNER.
HORSE-COURSER.
A KNIGHT.
AN OLD MAN.
SCHOLARS, FRIARS, *and* ATTENDANTS.
DUCHESS OF VANHOLT.
LUCIFER.
BELZEBUB.
MEPHISTOPHILIS.
GOOD ANGEL.
EVIL ANGEL.
THE SEVEN DEADLY SINS.
DEVILS.
SPIRITS *in the shapes of Alexander the Great, of his Paramour, and of Helen.*
CHORUS.

[1]The earliest edition of *Doctor Faustus* extant is the quarto of 1604, on which the present reprint is based. In 1616 and in 1663 appeared versions which differ widely from the text of 1604, but the generally accepted opinion is that the earliest version of the play is the one nearest to what Marlowe wrote. The German *Faustbuch,* as it is usually called, in which the legend of Faustus first appeared in print, was published at Frankfurt in 1587. It instantly attained wide popularity, and from it Marlowe drew the

Enter CHORUS.

CHORUS. Not marching now in fields of Thrasymene,
Where Mars did mate[2] the Carthaginians;
Nor sporting in the dalliance of love,
In courts of kings where state is overturned; 4
Nor in the pomp of proud audacious deeds,
Intends our Muse to vaunt her heavenly verse:
Only this, gentlemen,—we must perform
The form of Faustus' fortunes, good or bad:
To patient judgments we appeal our plaud,
And speak for Faustus in his infancy. 10
Now is he born, his parents base of stock,
In Germany, within a town called Rhodes:[3]
Of riper years, to Wertenberg he went,
Whereas his kinsmen chiefly brought him up.
So soon he profits in divinity, 15
The fruitful plot of scholarism graced,[4]
That shortly he was graced[5] with doctor's name,
Excelling all whose sweet delight disputes
In heavenly matters of theology;
Till swol'n with cunning,[6] of a self-conceit, 20
His waxen wings did mount above his reach,
And, melting, heavens conspired his overthrow;[7]
For, falling to a devilish exercise,
And glutted now with learning's golden gifts,
He surfeits upon cursèd necromancy; 25
Nothing so sweet as magic is to him,
Which he prefers before his chiefest bliss:
And this the man that in his study sits.
[*Exit.*

FAUSTUS *discovered in his study.*

FAUST. Settle thy studies, Faustus, and begin
To sound the depth of that thou wilt profess:[8] 30
Having commenced, be a divine in show,
Yet level[9] at the end of every art,
And live and die in Aristotle's works.
Sweet Analytics,[10] 'tis thou hast ravished me!
Bene disserere est finis logices.[11] 35
Is to dispute well logic's chiefest end?
Affords this art no greater miracle?
Then read no more; thou hast attained the end:
A greater subject fitteth Faustus' wit:
Bid 'ὸν καὶ μὴ 'ὸν[12] farewell; Galen come, 40
Seeing, *Ubi desinit philosophus, ibi incipit medicus:*[13]
Be a physician, Faustus; heap up gold,
And be eternized for some wondrous cure:
Summum bonum medicinae sanitas,[14]
The end of physic is our body's health. 45
Why, Faustus, hast thou not attained that end?
Is not thy common talk sound aphorisms?
Are not thy bills[15] hung up as monuments,
Whereby whole cities have escaped the plague,
And thousand desperate maladies been eased? 50
Yet art thou still but Faustus, and a man.
Wouldst thou make men to live eternally,
Or, being dead, raise them to life again,
Then this profession were to be esteemed.
Physic, farewell! Where is Justinian? 55
[*Reads.*
Si una eademque res legatur duobus, alter rem, alter valorem rei, etc.[16]
A pretty case of paltry legacies! [*Reads.*
Exhaereditare filium non potest pater, nisi, etc.[17]
Such is the subject of the institute,
And universal body of the law: 60
His[18] study fits a mercenary drudge,
Who aims at nothing but external trash;
Too servile and illiberal for me.
When all is done, divinity is best:
Jerome's Bible,[19] Faustus, view it well. 65
[*Reads.*

---

material for his play. There is difficulty in the question whether he used the German book or had access to a manuscript translation (the English translation was apparently not printed before 1590 at the earliest); the latter supposition, however, is the more probable one.

[2]Pit himself against.

[3]Roda, not far from Jena. [4]I. e., gracing.

[5]Took his degree. [6]Knowledge.

[7]Like Icarus who flew too near the sun.

[8]Teach.

[9]Aim. [10]Logic.

[11]To argue well is the end of logic.

[12]Being and not being (an Aristotelian phrase).

[13]Where the philosopher leaves off the physician begins.

[14]Translated in the following line. Other passages in Latin translated in the text are left without note.

[15]Pronouncements.

[16]If one and the same thing is willed to two persons, one receives the thing, the other the value of the thing, etc.

[17]A father cannot disinherit his son, unless, etc.

[18]Its. [19]The Vulgate.

Stipendium peccati mors est. Ha! *Stipendium, etc.*
The reward of sin is death: that's hard.
[*Reads.*
Si peccasse negamus, fallimur, et nulla est in nobis veritas;
If we say that we have no sin, we deceive ourselves, and there's no truth in us. Why, then, belike we must sin, and so consequently die: 72
Ay, we must die an everlasting death.
What doctrine call you this, *Che sera, sera,*
What will be, shall be? Divinity, adieu!
These metaphysics of magicians, 76
And necromantic books are heavenly;
Lines, circles, scenes, letters, and characters;
Ay, these are those that Faustus most desires.
O, what a world of profit and delight, 80
Of power, of honor, of omnipotence,
Is promised to the studious artisan!
All things that move between the quiet poles
Shall be at my command: emperors and kings
Are but obeyed in their several provinces,
Nor can they raise the wind, or rend the clouds; 86
But his dominion that exceeds in this,
Stretcheth as far as doth the mind of man;
A sound magician is a mighty god:
Here, Faustus, try thy brains to gain a deity. 90

Enter WAGNER.

Wagner, commend me to my dearest friends,
The German Valdes and Cornelius;
Request them earnestly to visit me.

WAG. I will, sir. [*Exit.*

FAUST. Their conference will be a greater help to me 95
Than all my labors, plod I ne'er so fast.

Enter GOOD ANGEL *and* EVIL ANGEL.

G. ANG. O Faustus, lay thy damnéd book aside,
And gaze not on it, lest it tempt thy soul,
And heap God's heavy wrath upon thy head!
Read, read the Scriptures:—that is blasphemy. 100

E. ANG. Go forward, Faustus, in that famous art
Wherein all Nature's treas'ry is contained:
Be thou on earth as Jove is in the sky,
Lord and commander of these elements.
[*Exeunt* ANGELS.

FAUST. How am I glutted with conceit[20] of this! 105
Shall I make spirits fetch me what I please,
Resolve me of all ambiguities,
Perform what desperate enterprise I will?
I'll have them fly to India for gold,
Ransack the ocean for orient pearl, 110
And search all corners of the new-found world
For pleasant fruits and princely delicates;
I'll have them read me strange philosophy,
And tell the secrets of all foreign kings;
I'll have them wall all Germany with brass,
And make swift Rhine circle fair Wertenberg; 116
I'll have them fill the public schools with silk,
Wherewith the students shall be bravely clad;
I'll levy soldiers with the coin they bring,
And chase the Prince of Parma from our land;[21] 120
And reign sole king of all our provinces;
Yea, stranger engines for the brunt of war,
Than was the fiery keel at Antwerp's bridge,
I'll make my servile spirits to invent.

Enter VALDES *and* CORNELIUS.

Come, German Valdes and Cornelius, 125
And make me blest with your sage conference.
Valdes, sweet Valdes, and Cornelius,
Know that your words have won me at the last
To practice magic and concealéd arts:
Yet not your words only, but mine own fantasy, 130
That will receive no object; for my head
But ruminates on necromantic skill.
Philosophy is odious and obscure;
Both law and physic are for petty wits;
Divinity is basest of the three, 135
Unpleasant, harsh, contemptible, and vile:
'Tis magic, magic, that hath ravished me.
Then, gentle friends, aid me in this attempt;
And I, that have with concise syllogisms
Graveled the pastors of the German Church, 140
And made the flowering pride of Wertenberg

[20] Thought. [21] The Netherlands.

Swarm to my problems, as the infernal spirits
On sweet Musaeus when he came to hell,
Will be as cunning as Agrippa was,
Whose shadow made all Europe honor him. 145
VALD. Faustus, these books, thy wit, and our experience,
Shall make all nations to canonize us.
As Indian Moors[22] obey their Spanish lords,
So shall the subjects of every element
Be always serviceable to us three; 150
Like lions shall they guard us when we please;
Like Almain rutters[23] with their horsemen's staves.
Or Lapland giants, trotting by our sides;
Sometimes like women, or unwedded maids,
Shadowing more beauty in their airy brows
Than have the white breasts of the queen of love: 156
From Venice shall they drag huge argosies,
And from America the golden fleece
That yearly stuffs old Philip's treasury;
If learnéd Faustus will be resolute. 160
FAUST. Valdes, as resolute am I in this
As thou to live: therefore object it not.
CORN. The miracles that magic will perform
Will make thee vow to study nothing else.
He that is grounded in astrology, 165
Enriched with tongues, well seen[24] in minerals,
Hath all the principles magic doth require:
Then doubt not, Faustus, but to be renowned,
And more frequented for this mystery
Than heretofore the Delphian oracle. 170
The spirits tell me they can dry the sea,
And fetch the treasure of all foreign wrecks,
Ay, all the wealth that our forefathers hid
Within the massy entrails of the earth:
Then tell me, Faustus, what shall we three want? 175
FAUST. Nothing, Cornelius. Oh, this cheers my soul!
Come, show me some demonstrations magical,
That I may conjure in some lusty grove,
And have these joys in full possession.
VALD. Then haste thee to some solitary grove, 180
And bear wise Bacon's[25] and Albertus' works,
The Hebrew Psalter, and New Testament;
And whatsoever else is requisite
We will inform thee ere our conference cease.
CORN. Valdes, first let him know the words of art; 185
And then, all other ceremonies learned,
Faustus may try his cunning by himself.
VALD. First I'll instruct thee in the rudiments,
And then wilt thou be perfecter than I.
FAUST. Then come and dine with me, and, after meat, 190
We'll canvass every quiddity[26] thereof;
For, ere I sleep, I'll try what I can do:
This night I'll conjure, though I die therefore.
[*Exeunt.*

Enter two SCHOLARS.

FIRST SCHOL. I wonder what's become of Faustus, that was wont to make our schools ring with *sic probo*.[27] 196

SEC. SCHOL. That shall we know, for see, here comes his boy.

Enter WAGNER.

FIRST SCHOL. How now, sirrah! where's thy master? 200
WAG. God in heaven knows.
SEC. SCHOL. Why, dost not thou know?
WAG. Yes, I know; but that follows not.
FIRST SCHOL. Go to, sirrah! leave your jesting, and tell us where he is. 205
WAG. That follows not necessary by force of argument, that you, being licentiates, should stand upon; therefore acknowledge your error, and be attentive.
SEC. SCHOL. Why, didst thou not say thou knewest? 211
WAG. Have you any witness on't?
FIRST SCHOL. Yes, sirrah, I heard you.
WAG. Ask my fellow if I be a thief.
SEC. SCHOL. Well, you will not tell us? 215
WAG. Yes, sir, I will tell you; yet, if you were not dunces, you would never ask me such a question, for is not he *corpus naturale?*[28] and is not that *mobile?*[29] then wherefore should you ask me such a question? But that I am by nature phlegmatic, slow to wrath, and prone to

[22]American Indians. [23]Troopers.
[24]Versed.
[25]Roger Bacon's. [26]Subtlety.
[27]Thus I demonstrate.
[28]Natural body. [29]Movable.

lechery (to love, I would say), it were not for you to come within forty foot of the place of execution, although I do not doubt to see you both hanged the next sessions. Thus having triumphed over you, I will set my countenance like a precisian,[30] and begin to speak thus:—Truly, my dear brethren, my master is within at dinner, with Valdes and Cornelius, as this wine, if it could speak, it would inform your worships: and so, the Lord bless you, preserve you, and keep you, my dear brethren, my dear brethren! [*Exit.* 236

FIRST SCHOL. Nay, then, I fear he is fallen into that damned art for which they two are infamous through the world.

SEC. SCHOL. Were he a stranger, and not allied to me, yet should I grieve for him. But, come, let us go and inform the Rector, and see if he by his grave counsel can reclaim him. 244

FIRST SCHOL. Oh, but I fear me nothing can reclaim him!

SEC. SCHOL. Yet let us try what we can do. [*Exeunt.*

Enter FAUSTUS *to conjure.*

FAUST. Now that the gloomy shadow of the earth,
Longing to view Orion's drizzling look,
Leaps from th' antarctic world unto the sky,
And dims the welkin with her pitchy breath, 250
Faustus, begin thine incantations,
And try if devils will obey thy hest,
Seeing thou hast prayed and sacrificed to them.
Within this circle is Jehovah's name, 254
Forward and backward anagrammatized,
Th' abbreviated names of holy saints,
Figures of every adjunct to[31] the heavens,
And characters of signs and erring stars,[32]
By which the spirits are enforced to rise:
Then fear not, Faustus, but be resolute, 260
And try the uttermost magic can perform.—
Sint mihi dei Acherontis propitii! Valeat numen triplex Jehovae! Ignei, aërii, aquatici spiritus, salvete! Orientis princeps Belzebub, inferni ardentis monarcha, et Demogorgon, propitiamus vos, ut appareat et surgat Mephistophilis; quid tu moraris? Per Jehovam, Gehennam, et consecratam aquam quam nunc spargo, signumque crucis quod nunc facio, et per vota nostra, ipse nunc surgat nobis dicatus Mephistophilis![33] 272

Enter MEPHISTOPHILIS.

I charge thee to return, and change thy shape;
Thou art too ugly to attend on me:
Go, and return an old Franciscan friar; 275
That holy shape becomes a devil best.
[*Exit* MEPHISTOPHILIS.
I see there's virtue in my heavenly words:
Who would not be proficient in this art?
How pliant is this Mephistophilis,
Full of obedience and humility! 280
Such is the force of magic and my spells:
Now, Faustus, thou art conjurer laureate,
That canst command great Mephistophilis:
Quin regis Mephistophilis fratris imagine.[34]

Re-enter MEPHISTOPHILIS *like a Franciscan friar.*

MEPH. Now, Faustus, what wouldst thou have me do? 285

FAUST. I charge thee wait upon me whilst I live,
To do whatever Faustus shall command,
Be it to make the moon drop from her sphere,
Or the ocean to overwhelm the world.

MEPH. I am a servant to great Lucifer, 290
And may not follow thee without his leave:
No more than he commands must we perform.

FAUST. Did not he charge thee to appear to me?

MEPH. No, I came now hither of mine own accord.

FAUST. Did not my conjuring speeches raise thee? speak. 295

MEPH. That was the cause, but yet *per accidens,*[35]
For, when we hear one rack the name of God,

[30] I. e., a puritan. [31] Every star belonging to.

[32] Planets.

[33] Gods of Acheron, grant me your aid! The triple deity of Jehovah assist me! Spirits of fire, air, water, all hail! Belzebub, Prince of the East, ruler of the fiery realms, and Demogorgon, I supplicate you, that Mephistophilis may rise and appear; why do you delay? By Jehovah, Gehenna, and the holy water I now sprinkle, and the sign of the cross I now make, and by my prayer, may Mephistopholis now called by me arise!

[34] Verily you have power in the image of your brother Mephistophilis.

[35] By accident.

Abjure the Scriptures and his Saviour Christ,
We fly, in hope to get his glorious soul;
Nor will we come, unless he use such means 300
Whereby he is in danger to be damned.
Therefore the shortest cut for conjuring
Is stoutly to abjure the Trinity,
And pray devoutly to the prince of hell.

FAUST. So Faustus hath 305
Already done; and holds this principle,
There is no chief but only Belzebub;
To whom Faustus doth dedicate himself.
This word "damnation" terrifies not him,
For he confounds hell in Elysium: 310
His ghost be with the old philosophers!
But, leaving these vain trifles of men's souls,
Tell me what is that Lucifer, thy lord?

MEPH. Arch-regent and commander of all spirits.

FAUST. Was not that Lucifer an angel once?

MEPH. Yes, Faustus, and most dearly loved of God. 316

FAUST. How comes it, then, that he is prince of devils?

MEPH. Oh, by aspiring pride and insolence;
For which God threw him from the face of heaven.

FAUST. And what are you that live with Lucifer? 320

MEPH. Unhappy spirits that fell with Lucifer,
Conspired against our God with Lucifer,
And are for ever damned with Lucifer.

FAUST. Where are you damned?

MEPH. In hell. 325

FAUST. How comes it, then, that thou art out of hell?

MEPH. Why, this is hell, nor am I out of it.
Think'st thou that I, who saw the face of God,
And tasted the eternal joys of heaven,
Am not tormented with ten thousand hells,
In being deprived of everlasting bliss? 331
O, Faustus, leave these frivolous demands,
Which strike a terror to my fainting soul!

FAUST. What, is great Mephistophilis so passionate[36]
For being deprivéd of the joys of heaven?
Learn thou of Faustus manly fortitude, 336
And scorn these joys thou never shalt possess.
Go bear these tidings to great Lucifer:
Seeing Faustus hath incurred eternal death
By desperate thoughts against Jove's deity,
Say, he surrenders up to him his soul, 341
So he will spare him four-and-twenty years,
Letting him live in all voluptuousness;
Having thee ever to attend on me,
To give me whatsoever I shall ask, 345
To tell me whatsoever I demand,
To slay mine enemies, and aid my friends,
And always be obedient to my will.
Go and return to mighty Lucifer,
And meet me in my study at midnight, 350
And then resolve me of thy master's mind.

MEPH. I will, Faustus. [*Exit.*

FAUST. Had I as many souls as there be stars,
I'd give them all for Mephistophilis. 354
By him I'll be great emperor of the world,
And make a bridge through the moving air,
To pass the ocean with a band of men;
I'll join the hills that bind the Afric shore,
And make that country continent to Spain,
And both contributory to my crown: 360
The Emperor shall not live but by my leave,
Nor any potentate of Germany.
Now that I have obtained what I desired,
I'll live in speculation[37] of this art,
Till Mephistophilis return again. [*Exit.* 365

Enter WAGNER *and* CLOWN.

WAG. Sirrah boy, come hither.

CLOWN. How, boy! swowns, boy! I hope you have seen many boys with such pickadevaunts[38] as I have: boy, quotha! 369

WAG. Tell me, sirrah, hast thou any comings in?

CLOWN. Ay, and goings out too; you may see else. 373

WAG. Alas, poor slave! see how poverty jesteth in his nakedness! the villain is bare and out of service, and so hungry that I know he would give his soul to the devil for a shoulder of mutton, though it were blood-raw. 379

CLOWN. How! my soul to the devil for a shoulder of mutton, though 'twere blood-raw! not so, good friend: by'r lady, I had need have it well roasted, and good sauce to it, if I pay so dear. 384

WAG. Well, wilt thou serve me, and I'll make thee go like *Qui mihi discipulus?*[39]

CLOWN. How, in verse? 387

---

[36]Saddened.

[37]Study. [38]Beards trimmed to a sharp point.
[39]Who will be my pupil?

WAG. No, sirrah; in beaten silk and staves-acre.[40]

CLOWN. How, how, knaves-acre![41] ay, I thought that was all the land his father left him. Do you hear? I would be sorry to rob you of your living. 393

WAG. Sirrah, I say in staves-acre.

CLOWN. Oho, oho, staves-acre! why then, belike, if I were your man I should be full of vermin. 397

WAG. So thou shalt, whether thou beest with me or no. But, sirrah, leave your jesting, and bind yourself presently unto me for seven years, or I'll turn all the lice about thee into familiars, and they shall tear thee in pieces. 403

CLOWN. Do you hear, sir? you may save that labor; they are too familiar with me already: swowns, they are as bold with my flesh as if they had paid for their meat and drink. 408

WAG. Well, do you hear, sirrah? hold, take these guilders. [*Gives money.*

CLOWN. Gridirons! what be they?

WAG. Why, French crowns. 412

CLOWN. Mass, but for the name of French crowns, a man were as good have as many English counters. And what should I do with these? 416

WAG. Why, now, sirrah, thou art at an hour's warning, whensoever and wheresoever the devil shall fetch thee.

CLOWN. No, no; here, take your gridirons again.

WAG. Truly, I'll none of them. 422

CLOWN. Truly, but you shall.

WAG. Bear witness I gave them him.

CLOWN. Bear witness I give them you again.

WAG. Well, I will cause two devils presently to fetch thee away—Baliol and Belcher!

CLOWN. Let your Baliol and your Belcher come here, and I'll knock them, they were never so knocked since they were devils: say I should kill one of them, what would folks say? "Do ye see yonder tall fellow in the round slop?[42] he has killed the devil." So I should be called Kill-devil all the parish over. 435

Enter two DEVILS; *and the* CLOWN *runs up and down crying.*

WAG. Baliol and Belcher,—spirits, away! [*Exeunt* DEVILS.

[40]Species of larkspur, used for destroying vermin.
[41]Name given to Poultney Street, London.
[42]Wide knickerbockers.

CLOWN. What, are they gone? a vengeance on them! they have vile long nails. There was a he-devil and a she-devil: I'll tell you how you shall know them; all he-devils has horns, and all she-devils has clifts and cloven feet. 442

WAG. Well, sirrah, follow me.

CLOWN. But, do you hear? if I should serve you, would you teach me to raise up Banios and Belcheos?

WAG. I will teach thee to turn thyself to anything, to a dog, or a cat, or a mouse, or a rat, or anything. 449

CLOWN. How! a Christian fellow to a dog or a cat, a mouse or a rat! no, no, sir; if you turn me into anything, let it be in the likeness of a little pretty frisking flea, that I may be here and there and everywhere: Oh, I'll tickle the pretty wenches' plackets! I'll be amongst them, i'faith.

WAG. Well, sirrah, come. 457

CLOWN. But, do you hear, Wagner?

WAG. How!—Baliol and Belcher!

CLOWN. O Lord! I pray, sir, let Baliol and Belcher go sleep. 461

WAG. Villain, call me Master Wagner, and let thy left eye be diametarily[43] fixed upon my right heel, with *quasi vestigias nostras insistere*.[44] [*Exit.*

CLOWN. God forgive me, he speaks Dutch fustian. Well, I'll follow him; I'll serve him, that's flat. [*Exit.* 468

FAUSTUS *discovered in his study.*

FAUST. Now, Faustus, must
Thou needs be damned, and canst thou not be saved:
What boots it, then, to think of God or heaven? 471
Away with such vain fancies, and despair;
Despair in God, and trust in Belzebub:
Now go not backward; no, Faustus, be resolute:
Why waver'st thou? Oh, something soundeth in mine ears, 475
"Abjure this magic, turn to God again!"
Ay, and Faustus will turn to God again.
To God? he loves thee not;
The god thou serv'st is thine own appetite,
Wherein is fixed the love of Belzebub: 480
To him I'll build an altar and a church,
And offer lukewarm blood of new-born babes.

[43]Diametrically.
[44]As if to follow in my footsteps.

Enter GOOD ANGEL *and* EVIL ANGEL.

G. ANG. Sweet Faustus, leave that execrable art.

FAUST. Contrition, prayer, repentance—what of them?

G. ANG. Oh, they are means to bring thee unto heaven! 485

E. ANG. Rather illusions, fruits of lunacy,
That make men foolish that do trust them most.

G. ANG. Sweet Faustus, think of heaven and heavenly things.

E. ANG. No, Faustus; think of honor and of wealth. [*Exeunt* ANGELS.

FAUST. Of wealth! 490
Why, the signiory of Emden shall be mine.
When Mephistophilis shall stand by me,
What god can hurt thee, Faustus? thou art safe:
Cast no more doubts.—Come, Mephistophilis,
And bring glad tidings from great Lucifer;—
Is't not midnight?—come, Mephistophilis,
Veni, veni, Mephistophile![45]

Enter MEPHISTOPHILIS.

Now tell me what says Lucifer, thy lord?

MEPH. That I shall wait on Faustus whilst he lives,
So he will buy my service with his soul. 500

FAUST. Already Faustus hath hazarded that for thee.

MEPH. But, Faustus, thou must bequeath it solemnly,
And write a deed of gift with thine own blood;
For that security craves great Lucifer.
If thou deny it, I will back to hell. 505

FAUST. Stay, Mephistophilis, and tell me, what good will my soul do thy lord?

MEPH. Enlarge his kingdom.

FAUST. Is that the reason why he tempts us thus?

MEPH. *Solamen miseris socios habuisse doloris.*[46] 510

FAUST. Why, have you any pain that tortures others?

MEPH. As great as have the human souls of men.
But, tell me, Faustus, shall I have thy soul?
And I will be thy slave, and wait on thee,
And give thee more than thou hast wit to ask. 515

[45]Come, come, Mephistophilis!

[46]Misery loves company.

FAUST. Ay, Mephistophilis, I give it thee.

MEPH. Then, Faustus, stab thine arm courageously,
And bind thy soul, that at some certain day
Great Lucifer may claim it as his own;
And then be thou as great as Lucifer. 520

FAUST. [*Stabbing his arm*] Lo, Mephistophilis, for love of thee,
I cut mine arm, and with my proper blood
Assure my soul to be great Lucifer's,
Chief lord and regent of perpetual night!
View here the blood that trickles from mine arm, 525
And let it be propitious for my wish.

MEPH. But, Faustus, thou must
Write it in manner of a deed of gift.

FAUST. Ay, so I will [*Writes*]. But, Mephistophilis, 529
My blood congeals, and I can write no more.

MEPH. I'll fetch thee fire to dissolve it straight. [*Exit.*

FAUST. What might the staying of my blood portend?
Is it unwilling I should write this bill?
Why streams it not, that I may write afresh?
Faustus gives to thee his soul: ah, there it stayed! 535
Why shouldst thou not? is not thy soul thine own?
Then write again, *Faustus gives to thee his soul.*

Re-enter MEPHISTOPHILIS *with a chafer of coals.*

MEPH. Here's fire; come, Faustus, set it on.

FAUST. So, now the blood begins to clear again;
Now will I make an end immediately. 540 [*Writes.*

MEPH. O, what will not I do t' obtain his soul! [*Aside.*

FAUST. *Consummatum est;*[47] this bill is ended,
And Faustus hath bequeathed his soul to Lucifer.
But what is this inscription on mine arm?
Homo, fuge;[48] whither should I fly? 545
If unto God, he'll throw me down to hell.
My senses are deceived; here's nothing writ:—
I see it plain; here in this place is writ,
Homo, fuge: yet shall not Faustus fly.

MEPH. I'll fetch him somewhat to delight his mind. [*Aside, and then exit.* 550

[47]It is finished. [48]O man, flee!

Re-enter MEPHISTOPHILIS *with* DEVILS, *who give crowns and rich apparel to* FAUSTUS, *dance, and then depart.*

FAUST. Speak, Mephistophilis, what means this show?
MEPH. Nothing, Faustus, but to delight thy mind withal,
And to show thee what magic can perform.
FAUST. But may I raise up spirits when I please?
MEPH. Ay, Faustus, and do greater things than these. 555
FAUST. Then there's enough for a thousand souls.
Here, Mephistophilis, receive this scroll,
A deed of gift of body and of soul:
But yet conditionally that thou perform
All articles prescribed between us both. 560
MEPH. Faustus, I swear by hell and Lucifer
To effect all promises between us made!
FAUST. Then hear me read them. [*Reads.*] *On these conditions following. First, that Faustus may be a spirit in form and substance. Secondly, that Mephistophilis shall be his servant, and at his command. Thirdly, that Mephistophilis shall do for him, and bring him whatsoever he desires. Fourthly, that he shall be in his chamber or house invisible. Lastly, that he shall appear to the said John Faustus, at all times, in what form or shape soever he please. I, John Faustus, of Wertenberg, Doctor, by these presents, do give both body and soul to Lucifer, prince of the East, and his minister Mephistophilis; and furthermore grant unto them that, twenty-four years being expired, the articles above-written inviolate, full power to fetch or carry the said John Faustus, body and soul, flesh, blood, or goods, into their habitation wheresoever. By me, John Faustus.* 583
MEPH. Speak, Faustus, do you deliver this as your deed?
FAUST. Ay, take it, and the devil give thee good on't!
MEPH. Now, Faustus, ask what thou wilt.
FAUST. First will I question with thee about hell.
Tell me, where is the place that men call hell?
MEPH. Under the heavens.
FAUST. Ay, but whereabout? 590
MEPH. Within the bowels of these elements,
Where we are tortured and remain for ever:
Hell hath no limits, nor is circumscribed
In one self place; for where we are is hell,
And where hell is, there must we ever be:
And, to conclude, when all the world dissolves, 596
And every creature shall be purified,
All places shall be hell that are not heaven.
FAUST. Come, I think hell's a fable.
MEPH. Ay, think so still, till experience change thy mind. 600
FAUST. Why, think'st thou, then, that Faustus shall be damned?
MEPH. Ay, of necessity, for here's the scroll
Wherein thou hast given thy soul to Lucifer.
FAUST. Ay, and body too: but what of that?
Think'st thou that Faustus is so fond[49] to imagine 605
That, after this life, there is any pain?
Tush, these are trifles and mere old wives' tales.
MEPH. But, Faustus, I am an instance to prove the contrary,
For I am damnéd, and am now in hell.
FAUST. How! now in hell! 610
Nay, an this be hell, I'll willingly be damned here:
What! walking, disputing, etc.
But, leaving off this, let me have a wife,
The fairest maid in Germany;
For I am wanton and lascivious, 615
And cannot live without a wife.
MEPH. How! a wife!
I prithee, Faustus, talk not of a wife.
FAUST. Nay, sweet Mephistophilis, fetch me one, for I will have one. 620
MEPH. Well, thou wilt have one? Sit there till I come: I'll fetch thee a wife in the devil's name. [*Exit.*

Re-enter MEPHISTOPHILIS *with a* DEVIL *dressed like a woman, with fireworks.*

MEPH. Tell me, Faustus, how dost thou like thy wife?
FAUST. A plague on her for a hot whore! 625
MEPH. Tut, Faustus,
Marriage is but a ceremonial toy;
If thou lovest me, think no more of it.
I'll cull thee out the fairest courtesans, 629
And bring them every morning to thy bed:
She whom thine eye shall like, thy heart shall have,
Be she as chaste as was Penelope,
As wise as Saba,[50] or as beautiful

[49]Foolish. [50]Queen of Sheba.

As was bright Lucifer before his fall. 634
Hold, take this book, peruse it thoroughly:
[*Gives book.*
The iterating of these lines brings gold;
The framing of this circle on the ground
Brings whirlwinds, tempests, thunder, and lightning;
Pronounce this thrice devoutly to thyself,
And men in armor shall appear to thee, 640
Ready to execute what thou desir'st.

FAUST. Thanks, Mephistophilis: yet fain would I have a book wherein I might behold all spells and incantations, that I might raise up spirits when I please.

MEPH. Here they are in this book. 646
[*Turns to them.*

FAUST. Now would I have a book where I might see all characters and planets of the heavens, that I might know their motions and dispositions. 650

MEPH. Here they are too. [*Turns to them.*

FAUST. Nay, let me have one book more,—and then I have done,—wherein I might see all plants, herbs, and trees that grow upon the earth. 655

MEPH. Here they be.

FAUST. Oh, thou art deceived.

MEPH. Tut, I warrant thee.
[*Turns to them. Exeunt.*

Enter FAUSTUS *in his study, and* MEPHISTOPHILIS.

FAUST. When I behold the heavens, then I repent,
And curse thee, wicked Mephistophilis, 660
Because thou hast deprived me of those joys.

MEPH. Why, Faustus,
Thinkest thou heaven is such a glorious thing?
I tell thee, 'tis not half so fair as thou,
Or any man that breathes on earth. 665

FAUST. How prov'st thou that?

MEPH. 'Twas made for man, therefore is man more excellent.

FAUST. If it were made for man, 'twas made for me:
I will renounce this magic and repent.

Enter GOOD ANGEL *and* EVIL ANGEL.

G. ANG. Faustus, repent; yet God will pity thee. 670

E. ANG. Thou art a spirit; God cannot pity thee.

FAUST. Who buzzeth in mine ears I am a spirit?
Be I a devil, yet God may pity me;
Ay, God will pity me, if I repent. 674

E. ANG. Ay, but Faustus never shall repent.
[*Exeunt* ANGELS.

FAUST. My heart's so hardened, I cannot repent:
Scarce can I name salvation, faith, or heaven,
But fearful echoes thunder in mine ears,
"Faustus, thou art damned!" Then swords, and knives,
Poison, guns, halters, and envenomed steel
Are laid before me to dispatch myself; 681
And long ere this I should have slain myself,
Had not sweet pleasure conquered deep despair.
Have not I made blind Homer sing to me
Of Alexander's love and Oenon's death?
And hath not he that built the walls of Thebes 686
With ravishing sound of his melodious harp,
Made music with my Mephistophilis?
Why should I die, then, or basely despair!
I am resolved; Faustus shall ne'er repent.—
Come, Mephistophilis, let us dispute again,
And argue of divine astrology. 692
Tell me, are there many heavens above the moon?
Are all celestial bodies but one globe,
As is the substance of this centric earth?

MEPH. As are the elements, such are the spheres, 696
Mutually folded in each other's orb,
And, Faustus,
All jointly move upon one axletree,
Whose terminus is termed the world's wide pole; 700
Nor are the names of Saturn, Mars, or Jupiter
Feigned, but are erring stars.

FAUST. But, tell me, have they all one motion, both *situ et tempore?*[51] 704

MEPH. All jointly move from east to west in twenty-four hours upon the poles of the world; but differ in their motion upon the poles of the zodiac.

FAUST. Tush,
These slender trifles Wagner can decide:
Hath Mephistophilis no greater skill? 711
Who knows not the double motion of the planets?
The first is finished in a natural day; 713
The second thus; as Saturn in thirty years;

[51]In direction and time.

Jupiter in twelve; Mars in four; the Sun, Venus, and Mercury in a year; the Moon in twenty-eight days. Tush, these are freshmen's suppositions. But, tell me, hath every sphere a dominion or *intelligentia?* 720

MEPH. Ay.

FAUST. How many heavens or spheres are there?

MEPH. Nine; the seven planets, the firmament, and the empyreal heaven. 725

FAUST. Well, resolve me in this question: why have we not conjunctions, oppositions, aspects, eclipses, all at one time, but in some years we have more, in some less?

MEPH. *Per inaequalem motum respectu totius.*[52]

FAUST. Well, I am answered. Tell me, who made the world? 732

MEPH. I will not.

FAUST. Sweet Mephistophilis, tell me.

MEPH. Move me not, for I will not tell thee.

FAUST. Villain, have I not bound thee to tell me anything? 737

MEPH. Ay, that is not against our kingdom; but this is.
Think thou on hell, Faustus, for thou art damned.

FAUST. Think, Faustus, upon God that made the world. 740

MEPH. Remember this. [*Exit.*

FAUST. Ay, go, accursèd spirit, to ugly hell!
'Tis thou hast damned distressèd Faustus' soul.
Is't not too late?

Re-enter GOOD ANGEL *and* EVIL ANGEL.

E. ANG. Too late. 745

G. ANG. Never too late, if Faustus can repent.

E. ANG. If thou repent, devils shall tear thee in pieces.

G. ANG. Repent, and they shall never raze thy skin. [*Exeunt* ANGELS.

FAUST. Ah, Christ, my Savior,
Seek to save distressèd Faustus' soul! 750

Enter LUCIFER, BELZEBUB, *and* MEPHISTOPHILIS.

LUC. Christ cannot save thy soul, for he is just:
There's none but I have interest in the same.

[52]On account of their unequal motion in relation to the whole.

FAUST. Oh, who art thou that look'st so terrible?

LUC. I am Lucifer,
And this is my companion-prince in hell. 755

FAUST. O Faustus, they are come to fetch away thy soul!

LUC. We come to tell thee thou dost injure us;
Thou talk'st of Christ, contrary to thy promise:
Thou shouldst not think of God: think of the devil,
And of his dam too. 760

FAUST. Nor will I henceforth: pardon me in this,
And Faustus vows never to look to heaven,
Never to name God, or to pray to him,
To burn his Scriptures, slay his ministers,
And make my spirits pull his churches down. 765

LUC. Do so, and we will highly gratify thee. Faustus, we are come from hell to show thee some pastime: sit down, and thou shalt see all the Seven Deadly Sins appear in their proper shapes. 770

FAUST. That sight will be as pleasing unto me
As Paradise was to Adam the first day
Of his creation.

LUC. Talk not of Paradise nor creation; but mark this show: talk of the devil, and nothing else.—Come away! 776

Enter the SEVEN DEADLY SINS.

Now, Faustus, examine them of their several names and dispositions.

FAUST. What art thou, the first? 779

PRIDE. I am Pride. I disdain to have any parents. I am like to Ovid's flea; I can creep into every corner of a wench; sometimes, like a periwig, I sit upon her brow; or, like a fan of feathers, I kiss her lips; indeed, I do—what do I not? But, fie, what a scent is here! I'll not speak another word, except the ground were perfumed, and covered with cloth of arras.

FAUST. What art thou, the second? 790

COVET. I am Covetousness, begotten of an old churl, in an old leathern bag: and, might I have my wish, I would desire that this house and all the people in it were turned to gold, that I might lock you up in my good chest: O my sweet gold!

FAUST. What art thou, the third? 798

WRATH. I am Wrath. I had neither father

nor mother: I leaped out of a lion's mouth when I was scarce half an hour old; and ever since I have run up and down the world with this case[53] of rapiers, wounding myself when I had nobody to fight withal. I was born in hell; and look to it, for some of you shall be my father.[54]

FAUST. What art thou, the fourth? 808

ENVY. I am Envy, begotten of a chimney-sweeper and an oyster-wife. I cannot read, and therefore wish all books were burned. I am lean with seeing others eat. O that there would come a famine through all the world, that all might die, and I live alone! then thou shouldst see how fat I would be. But must thou sit, and I stand? come down, with a vengeance!

FAUST. Away, envious rascal!—What art thou, the fifth? 820

GLUT. Who I, sir? I am Gluttony. My parents are all dead, and the devil a penny they have left me, but a bare pension, and that is thirty meals a day, and ten bevers,[55]—a small trifle to suffice nature. Oh, I come of a royal parentage! my grandfather was a Gammon of Bacon, my grandmother a Hogshead of Claret-wine; my godfathers were these, Peter Pickle-herring and Martin Martlemas-beef; O but my godmother, she was a jolly gentlewoman, and well-beloved in every good town and city; her name was Mistress Margery March-beer. Now, Faustus, thou hast heard all my progeny;[56] wilt thou bid me to supper? 837

FAUST. No, I'll see thee hanged: thou wilt eat up all my victuals.

GLUT. Then the devil choke thee!

FAUST. Choke thyself, glutton!—What art thou, the sixth? 841

SLOTH. I am Sloth. I was begotten on a sunny bank, where I have lain ever since; and you have done me great injury to bring me from thence: let me be carried thither again by Gluttony and Lechery. I'll not speak another word for a king's ransom.

FAUST. What are you, Mistress Minx, the seventh and last? 850

LECHERY. Who I, sir? I am one that loves an inch of raw mutton better than an ell of fried stock-fish; and the first letter of my name begins with L.

LUC. Away, to hell, to hell! 855

[*Exeunt the* SINS.

Now, Faustus, how dost thou like this?

FAUST. Oh, this feeds my soul!

LUC. Tut, Faustus, in hell is all manner of delight.

FAUST. O might I see hell, and return again,
How happy were I then! 861

LUC. Thou shalt; I will send for thee at midnight.
In meantime take this book; peruse it thoroughly,
And thou shalt turn thyself into what shape thou wilt.

FAUST. Great thanks, mighty Lucifer! 865
This will I keep as chary as my life.

LUC. Farewell, Faustus, and think on the devil.

FAUST. Farewell, great Lucifer.

[*Exeunt* LUCIFER *and* BELZEBUB.

Come, Mephistophilis. [*Exeunt.* 870

Enter CHORUS.

CHOR. Learnéd Faustus,
To know the secrets of astronomy
Graven in the book of Jove's high firmament,
Did mount himself to scale Olympus' top,
Being seated in a chariot burning bright,
Drawn by the strength of yoky dragons' necks. 876
He now is gone to prove cosmography,
And, as I guess, will first arrive in Rome,
To see the Pope and manner of his court,
And take some part of holy Peter's feast,
That to this day is highly solemnized. 881

[*Exit.*

Enter FAUSTUS *and* MEPHISTOPHILIS.

FAUST. Having now, my good Mephistophilis,
Passed with delight the stately town of Trier,[57]
Environed round with airy mountain-tops,
With walls of flint, and deep-entrenchéd lakes, 885
Not to be won by any conquering prince;
From Paris next, coasting the realm of France,
We saw the river Maine fall into Rhine,
Whose banks are set with groves of fruitful vines;

[53] Pair.

[54] I. e., one of the devils must be my father.

[55] Refreshments between breakfast and dinner.

[56] Lineage.

[57] Trèves.

Then up to Naples, rich Campania, 890
Whose buildings fair and gorgeous to the eye,
The streets straight forth, and paved with finest brick,
Quarter the town in four equivalents:
There saw we learnéd Maro's[58] golden tomb,
The way he cut, an English mile in length,
Thorough a rock of stone, in one night's space; 896
From thence to Venice, Padua, and the rest,
In one of which a sumptuous temple stands,
That threats the stars with her aspiring top. 899
Thus hitherto hath Faustus spent his time:
But tell me now what resting-place is this?
Hast thou, as erst I did command,
Conducted me within the walls of Rome?

MEPH. Faustus, I have; and, because we will not be unprovided, I have taken up[59] his Holiness' privy-chamber for our use. 906

FAUST. I hope his Holiness will bid us welcome.

MEPH. Tut, 'tis no matter, man; we'll be bold with his good cheer.
And now, my Faustus, that thou mayst perceive 910
What Rome containeth to delight thee with,
Know that this city stands upon seven hills
That underprop the groundwork of the same:
Just through the midst runs flowing Tiber's stream
With winding banks that cut it in two parts; 915
Over the which four stately bridges lean,
That make safe passage to each part of Rome:
Upon the bridge called Ponte Angelo
Erected is a castle passing strong,
Within whose walls such store of ordnance are, 920
And double cannons framed of carvéd brass,
As match the days within one complete year;
Besides the gates, and high pyramidés,[60]
Which Julius Caesar brought from Africa.

FAUST. Now, by the kingdoms of infernal rule, 925
Of Styx, of Acheron, and the fiery lake
Of ever-burning Phlegethon, I swear
That I do long to see the monuments
And situation of bright-splendent Rome:
Come, therefore, let's away. 930

MEPH. Nay, Faustus, stay: I know you'd fain see the Pope
And take some part of holy Peter's feast,
Where thou shalt see a troop of bald-pate friars,
Whose *summum bonum*[61] is in belly-cheer.

FAUST. Well, I'm content to compass then some sport, 935
And by their folly make us merriment.
Then charm me, that I
May be invisible, to do what I please,
Unseen of any whilst I stay in Rome.
[MEPHISTOPHILIS *charms him.*

MEPH. So, Faustus; now 940
Do what thou wilt, thou shalt not be discerned.

Sound a Sennet.[62] *Enter the* POPE *and the* CARDINAL OF LORRAIN *to the banquet, with* FRIARS *attending.*

POPE. My lord of Lorrain, will't please you draw near?

FAUST. Fall to, and the devil choke you, an you spare! 945

POPE. How now! who's that which spake?—Friars, look about.

FIRST FRIAR. Here's nobody, if it like your Holiness.

POPE. My lord, here is a dainty dish was sent me from the Bishop of Milan. 951

FAUST. I thank you, sir. [*Snatches the dish.*

POPE. How now! who's that which snatched the meat from me? will no man look?—My lord, this dish was sent me from the Cardinal of Florence. 956

FAUST. You say true; I'll ha't.
[*Snatches the dish.*

POPE. What, again!—My lord, I'll drink to your grace.

FAUST. I'll pledge your grace. 960
[*Snatches the cup.*

C. OF LOR. My lord, it may be some ghost newly crept out of purgatory, come to beg a pardon of your Holiness.

POPE. It may be so.—Friars, prepare a dirge to lay the fury of this ghost.—Once again, my lord, fall to. 966
[*The* POPE *crosses himself.*

FAUST. What, are you crossing of yourself?

---

[58]Virgil's, who in the Middle Ages was thought to have been a magician.

[59]Engaged. [60]Obelisks.

[61]Highest good.

[62]Set of notes on trumpet or cornet.

Well, use that trick no more, I would advise you.

[*The* POPE *crosses himself again.*

Well, there's the second time. Aware[63] the third;
I give you fair warning. 970

[*The* POPE *crosses himself again, and* FAUSTUS *hits him a box on the ear; and they all run away.*

Come on, Mephistophilis; what shall we do?

MEPH. Nay, I know not: we shall be cursed with bell, book, and candle.

FAUST. How! bell, book, and candle,—candle, book, and bell,—
Forward and backward, to curse Faustus to hell! 975
Anon you shall hear a hog grunt, a calf bleat, and an ass bray,
Because it is Saint Peter's holiday.

Re-enter all the FRIARS *to sing the Dirge.*

FIRST FRIAR. Come, brethren, let's about our business with good devotion. 979

They sing:

Cursed be he that stole away his Holiness' meat from the table!
maledicat Dominus![64]
Cursed be he that struck his Holiness a blow on the face!
maledicat Dominus!
Cursed be he that took Friar Sandelo a blow on the pate!
maledicat Dominus! 985
Cursed be he that disturbeth our holy dirge!
maledicat Dominus!
Cursed be he that took away his Holiness' wine!
maledicat Dominus! Et omnes Sancti![65]
Amen! 990

[MEPHISTOPHILIS *and* FAUSTUS *beat the* FRIARS, *and fling fireworks among them; and so exeunt.*

Enter CHORUS.

CHOR. When Faustus had with pleasure ta'en the view
Of rarest things, and royal courts of kings,
He stayed his course, and so returnéd home;
Where such as bear his absence but with grief,
I mean his friends and near'st companions, 995
Did gratulate his safety with kind words,
And in their conference of what befell,
Touching his journey through the world and air,
They put forth questions of astrology,
Which Faustus answered with such learnéd skill 1000
As they admired and wondered at his wit.
Now is his fame spread forth in every land:
Amongst the rest the Emperor is one,
Carolus the Fifth, at whose palace now
Faustus is feasted 'mongst his noblemen.
What there he did, in trial of his art, 1006
I leave untold; your eyes shall see performed. [*Exit.*

Enter ROBIN *the Ostler, with a book in his hand.*

ROBIN. Oh, this is admirable! here I ha' stolen one of Doctor Faustus' conjuring books, and, i'faith, I mean to search some circles for my own use. Now will I make all the maidens in our parish dance at my pleasure, stark naked before me; and so by that means I shall see more than e'er I felt or saw yet. 1015

Enter RALPH, *calling* ROBIN.

RALPH. Robin, prithee, come away; there's a gentleman tarries to have his horse, and he would have his things rubbed and made clean: he keeps such a chafing with my mistress about it; and she has set me to look thee out; prithee, come away. 1022

ROBIN. Keep out, keep out, or else you are blown up, you are dismembered, Ralph: keep out, for I am about a roaring piece of work. 1026

RALPH. Come, what doest thou with that same book? thou canst not read?

ROBIN. Yes, my master and mistress shall find that I can read, he for his forehead, she for her private study; she's born to bear with me, or else my art fails. 1032

RALPH. Why, Robin, what book is that?

ROBIN. What book! why, the most intolerable book for conjuring that e'er was invented by any brimstone devil.

RALPH. Canst thou conjure with it? 1037

ROBIN. I can do all these things easily with it: first, I can make thee drunk with

---

[63]Beware. [64]May the Lord curse him.
[65]And all the saints.

ippocras[66] at any tavern in Europe for nothing; that's one of my conjuring works. 1042

RALPH. Our Master Parson says that's nothing.

ROBIN. True, Ralph: and more, Ralph, if thou hast any mind to Nan Spit, our kitchen-maid, then turn her and wind her to thy own use, as often as thou wilt, and at midnight. 1049

RALPH. O brave Robin! shall I have Nan Spit, and to mine own use? On that condition I'll feed thy devil with horse-bread as long as he lives, of free cost. 1053

ROBIN. No more, sweet Ralph: let's go and make clean our boots, which lie foul upon our hands, and then to our conjuring in the devil's name. [*Exeunt.* 1057

Enter ROBIN *and* RALPH *with a silver goblet.*

ROBIN. Come, Ralph: did not I tell thee, we were for ever made by this Doctor Faustus' book? *ecce, signum!*[67] here's a simple purchase[68] for horse-keepers: our horses shall eat no hay as long as this lasts. 1062

RALPH. But, Robin, here comes the vintner.

ROBIN. Hush! I'll gull him supernaturally.

Enter VINTNER.

Drawer, I hope all is paid; God be with you!—Come, Ralph. 1066

VINT. Soft, sir; a word with you. I must yet have a goblet paid from you, ere you go.

ROBIN. I a goblet, Ralph, I a goblet!—I scorn you; and you are but a, etc.[69] I a goblet! search me. 1072

VINT. I mean so, sir, with your favor.
[*Searches* ROBIN.

ROBIN. How say you now?

VINT. I must say somewhat to your fellow.—You, sir! 1076

RALPH. Me, sir! me, sir! search your fill. [VINTNER *searches him.*] Now, sir, you may be ashamed to burden honest men with a matter of truth. 1080

VINT. Well, th' one of you hath this goblet about you.

ROBIN. You lie, drawer; 'tis afore me [*Aside*]. Sirrah you, I'll teach you to impeach honest men;—stand by;—I'll scour you for a goblet;—stand aside you had best, I charge you in the name of Belzebub.—Look to the goblet, Ralph [*Aside to* RALPH]. 1089

VINT. What mean you, sirrah?

ROBIN. I'll tell you what I mean. [*Reads from a book*] *Sanctobulorum Periphrasticon*—nay, I'll tickle you, vintner.—Look to the goblet, Ralph [*Aside to* RALPH]. [*Reads*] *Polypragmos Belseborams framanto pacostiphos tostu, Mephistophilis, etc.*

Enter MEPHISTOPHILIS, *sets squibs at their backs, and then exit. They run about.*

VINT. *O, nomine Domini!*[70] what meanest thou, Robin? thou hast no goblet. 1099

RALPH. *Peccatum peccatorum!*[71] — Here's thy goblet, good vintner.
[*Gives the goblet to* VINTNER, *who exit.*

ROBIN. *Misericordia pro nobis!*[72] what shall I do? Good devil, forgive me now, and I'll never rob thy library more.

Re-enter MEPHISTOPHILIS.

MEPH. Monarch of hell, under whose black survey 1105
Great potentates do kneel with awful fear,
Upon whose altars thousand souls do lie,
How am I vexéd with these villains' charms?
From Constantinople am I hither come,
Only for pleasure of these damnéd slaves.

ROBIN. How, from Constantinople! you have had a great journey: will you take sixpence in your purse to pay for your supper and be gone? 1114

MEPH. Well, villains, for your presumption, I transform thee into an ape, and thee into a dog; and so be gone! [*Exit.*

ROBIN. How, into an ape! that's brave: I'll have fine sport with the boys; I'll get nuts and apples enow. 1120

RALPH. And I must be a dog.

ROBIN. I'faith, thy head will never be out of the pottage-pot.
[*Exeunt.*

Enter EMPEROR, FAUSTUS, *and a* KNIGHT, *with* ATTENDANTS.

EMP. Master Doctor Faustus, I have heard strange report of thy knowledge in the black art, how that none in my empire

---

[66] Wine sweetened and spiced.

[67] Behold, the proof! [68] A clear gain.

[69] The actor was expected to speak the abuse extemporaneously.

[70] In the name of the Lord.

[71] Sin of sins. [72] Mercy upon us.

nor in the whole world can compare with thee for the rare effects of magic: they say thou hast a familiar spirit, by whom thou canst accomplish what thou list. This, therefore, is my request, that thou let me see some proof of thy skill, that mine eyes may be witnesses to confirm what mine ears have heard reported: and here I swear to thee, by the honor of mine imperial crown, that, whatever thou doest, thou shalt be no ways prejudiced or endamaged. 1138

KNIGHT. I'faith, he looks much like a conjurer. [*Aside.*

FAUST. My gracious sovereign, though I must confess myself far inferior to the report men have published, and nothing answerable to the honor of your imperial majesty, yet, for that love and duty binds me thereunto, I am content to do whatsoever your majesty shall command me. 1148

EMP. Then, Doctor Faustus, mark what I shall say.
As I was sometime solitary set
Within my closet, sundry thoughts arose
About the honor of mine ancestors,
How they had won by prowess such exploits,
Got such riches, subdued so many kingdoms, 1154
As we that do succeed, or they that shall
Hereafter possess our throne, shall
(I fear me) ne'er attain to that degree
Of high renown and great authority:
Amongst which kings is Alexander the Great,
Chief spectacle of the world's pre-eminence, 1160
The bright shining of whose glorious acts
Lightens the world with his reflecting beams,
As when I hear but motion[73] made of him,
It grieves my soul I never saw the man:
If, therefore, thou, by cunning of thine art,
Canst raise this man from hollow vaults below, 1166
Where lies entombed this famous conqueror,
And bring with him his beauteous paramour,
Both in their right shapes, gesture, and attire
They used to wear during their time of life,
Thou shalt both satisfy my just desire 1171
And give me cause to praise thee whilst I live.

FAUST. My gracious lord, I am ready to accomplish your request, so far forth as by art and power of my spirit I am able to perform. 1176

KNIGHT. I'faith, that's just nothing at all. [*Aside.*

FAUST. But, if it like your grace, it is not in my ability to present before your eyes the true substantial bodies of those two deceased princes, which long since are consumed to dust. 1182

KNIGHT. Ay, marry, Master Doctor, now there's a sign of grace in you, when you will confess the truth. [*Aside.*

FAUST. But such spirits as can lively resemble Alexander and his paramour shall appear before your grace, in that manner that they best lived in, in their most flourishing estate; which I doubt not shall sufficiently content your imperial majesty. 1192

EMP. Go to, Master Doctor; let me see them presently.

KNIGHT. Do you hear, Master Doctor? you bring Alexander and his paramour before the Emperor!

FAUST. How then, sir?

KNIGHT. I'faith, that's as true as Diana turned me to a stag. 1200

FAUST. No, sir; but, when Actaeon died, he left the horns for you.—Mephistophilis, be gone. [*Exit* MEPHISTOPHILIS.

KNIGHT. Nay, an you go to conjuring, I'll be gone. [*Exit.*

FAUST. I'll meet with you anon for interrupting me so.—Here they are, my gracious lord. 1208

Re-enter MEPHISTOPHILIS *with* SPIRITS *in the shapes of* ALEXANDER *and his* PARAMOUR.

EMP. Master Doctor, I heard this lady, while she lived, had a wart or mole in her neck: how shall I know whether it be so or no? 1212

FAUST. Your highness may boldly go and see.

EMP. Sure, these are no spirits, but the true substantial bodies of those two deceased princes. [*Exeunt* SPIRITS.

FAUST. Wilt please your highness now to send for the knight that was so pleasant with me here of late? 1219

EMP. One of you call him forth. [*Exit* ATTENDANT.

[73] Mention.

Re-enter the KNIGHT *with a pair of horns on his head.*

How now, sir knight! why, I had thought thou hadst been a bachelor, but now I see thou hast a wife, that not only gives thee horns, but makes thee wear them. Feel on thy head. 1225

KNIGHT. Thou damnéd wretch and execrable dog,
Bred in the concave of some monstrous rock,
How dar'st thou thus abuse a gentleman?
Villain, I say, undo what thou hast done!

FAUST. Oh, not so fast, sir! there's no haste: but, good, are you remembered how you crossed me in my conference with the Emperor? I think I have met[74] with you for it. 1234

EMP. Good Master Doctor, at my entreaty release him: he hath done penance sufficient.

FAUST. My gracious lord, not so much for the injury he offered me here in your presence, as to delight you with some mirth, hath Faustus worthily requited this injurious knight; which being all I desire, I am content to release him of his horns:—and, sir knight, hereafter speak well of scholars.—Mephistophilis, transform him straight. [MEPHISTOPHILIS *removes the horns.*]—Now, my good lord, having done my duty, I humbly take my leave.

EMP. Farewell, Master Doctor; yet, ere you go, 1250
Expect from me a bounteous reward.
[*Exeunt* EMPEROR, KNIGHT, *and* ATTENDANTS.

FAUST. Now, Mephistophilis, the restless course
That time doth run with calm and silent foot,
Shortening my days and thread of vital life,
Calls for the payment of my latest years:
Therefore, sweet Mephistophilis, let us 1256
Make haste to Wertenberg.

MEPH. What, will you go on horse-back or on foot?

FAUST. Nay, till I am past this fair and pleasant green, I'll walk on foot. 1260

Enter a HORSE-COURSER.[75]

HORSE-C. I have been all this day seeking one Master Fustian: mass, see where he is!—God save you, Master Doctor!

[74]I am even. [75]Horse dealer.

FAUST. What, horse-courser! you are well met. 1265

HORSE-C. Do you hear, sir? I have brought you forty dollars for your horse.

FAUST. I cannot sell him so: if thou likest him for fifty, take him. 1269

HORSE-C. Alas, sir, I have no more!—I pray you, speak for me.

MEPH. I pray you, let him have him: he is an honest fellow, and he has a great charge, neither wife nor child. 1274

FAUST. Well, come, give me your money [HORSE-COURSER *gives* FAUSTUS *the money*]: my boy will deliver him to you. But I must tell you one thing before you have him; ride him not into the water, at any hand. 1280

HORSE-C. Why, sir, will he not drink of all waters?

FAUST. O, yes, he will drink of all waters; but ride him not into the water; ride him over hedge or ditch, or where thou wilt, but not into the water. 1286

HORSE-C. Well, sir.—Now am I made man forever: I'll not leave my horse for forty: if he had but the quality of hey-ding-ding, hey-ding-ding, I'd make a brave living on him: he has a buttock as slick as an eel [*Aside*].—Well, God b'wi'ye, sir: your boy will deliver him me: but, hark you, sir; if my horse be sick or ill at ease, if I bring his water to you, you'll tell me what it is? 1296

FAUST. Away, you villain! what, dost think I am a horse-doctor?
[*Exit* HORSE-COURSER.
What art thou, Faustus, but a man condemned to die?
Thy fatal time doth draw to final end; 1300
Despair doth drive distrust unto my thoughts:
Confound these passions with a quiet sleep:
Tush, Christ did call the thief upon the Cross; 1303
Then rest thee, Faustus, quiet in conceit.
[*Sleeps in his chair.*

Re-enter HORSE-COURSER, *all wet, crying.*

HORSE-C. Alas, alas! Doctor Fustian, quotha? mass, Doctor Lopus[76] was never such a doctor: has given me a purgation, has purged me of forty dollars; I

[76]Roderigo Lopez, private physician to Queen Elizabeth, hanged in 1594 for conspiring to poison her.

shall never see them more. But yet, like an ass as I was, I would not be ruled by him, for he bade me I should ride him into no water; now I, thinking my horse had had some rare quality that he would not have had me known of, I, like a venturous youth, rid him into the deep pond at the town's end. I was no sooner in the middle of the pond, but my horse vanished away, and I sat upon a bottle[77] of hay, never so near drowning in my life. But I'll seek out my doctor, and have my forty dollars again, or I'll make it the dearest horse!—Oh, yonder is his snipper-snapper. Do you hear? you hey-pass,[78] where's your master? 1324

MEPH. Why, sir, what would you? you cannot speak with him.

HORSE-C. But I will speak with him.

MEPH. Why, he's fast asleep: come some other time. 1329

HORSE-C. I'll speak with him now, or I'll break his glass-windows about his ears.

MEPH. I tell thee, he has not slept this eight nights.

HORSE-C. An he have not slept this eight weeks, I'll speak with him. 1335

MEPH. See, where he is, fast asleep.

HORSE-C. Ay, this is he.—God save you, Master Doctor, Master Doctor, Master Doctor Fustian! forty dollars, forty dollars for a bottle of hay! 1340

MEPH. Why, thou seest he hears thee not.

HORSE-C. So-ho, ho! so-ho, ho! [*Hollows in his ear.*] No, will you not wake? I'll make you wake ere I go. [*Pulls* FAUSTUS *by the leg, and pulls it away.*] Alas, I am undone! what shall I do? 1346

FAUST. Oh, my leg, my leg!—Help, Mephistophilis! call the officers.—My leg, my leg!

MEPH. Come, villain, to the constable.

HORSE-C. O Lord, sir, let me go, and I'll give you forty dollars more! 1351

MEPH. Where be they?

HORSE-C. I have none about me: come to my ostry,[79] and I'll give them you.

MEPH. Be gone quickly. 1355

[HORSE-COURSER *runs away.*

FAUST. What, is he gone? farewell he! Faustus has his leg again, and the horse-courser, I take it, a bottle of hay for his labor: well, this trick shall cost him forty dollars more. 1360

Enter WAGNER.

How now, Wagner! what's the news with thee?

WAG. Sir, the Duke of Vanholt doth earnestly entreat your company.

FAUST. The Duke of Vanholt! an honorable gentleman, to whom I must be no niggard of my cunning.—Come, Mephistophilis, let's away to him. [*Exeunt.* 1368

Enter the DUKE OF VANHOLT, *the* DUCHESS, *and* FAUSTUS.

DUKE. Believe me, Master Doctor, this merriment hath much pleased me.

FAUST. My gracious lord, I am glad it contents you so well.—But it may be, madam, you take no delight in this. I have heard that great-bellied women do long for some dainties or other: what is it, madam? tell me, and you shall have it. 1377

DUCHESS. Thanks, good Master Doctor: and, for I see your courteous intent to pleasure me, I will not hide from you the thing my heart desires; and, were it now summer, as it is January and the dead time of the winter, I would desire no better meat than a dish of ripe grapes. 1384

FAUST. Alas, madam, that's nothing!—Mephistophilis, be gone. [*Exit* MEPHISTOPHILIS.] Were it a greater thing than this, so it would content you, you should have it. 1389

Re-enter MEPHISTOPHILIS *with grapes.*

Here they be, madam: wilt please you taste on them?

DUKE. Believe me, Master Doctor, this makes me wonder above the rest, that being in the dead time of winter and in the month of January, how you should come by these grapes. 1396

FAUST. If it like your grace, the year is divided into two circles over the whole world, that, when it is here winter with us, in the contrary circle it is summer with them, as in India, Saba, and farther countries in the east; and by means of a swift spirit that I have, I had them brought hither, as you see.—How do you like them, madam? be they good?

DUCHESS. Believe me, Master Doctor, they be the best grapes that e'er I tasted in my life before. 1408

FAUST. I am glad they content you so, madam.

---

[77] Bundle. [78] Juggler. [79] Inn.

DUKE. Come, madam, let us in, where you must well reward this learned man for the great kindness he hath showed to you.

DUCHESS. And so I will, my lord; and, whilst I live, rest beholding for this courtesy.

FAUST. I humbly thank your grace. 1416

DUKE. Come, Master Doctor, follow us, and receive your reward. [*Exeunt.*

Enter WAGNER.

WAG. I think my master means to die shortly,
For he hath given to me all his goods: 1420
And yet, methinks, if that death were near,
He would not banquet, and carouse, and swill
Amongst the students, as even now he doth,
Who are at supper with such belly-cheer
As Wagner ne'er beheld in all his life. 1425
See, where they come! belike the feast is ended. [*Exit.*

Enter FAUSTUS *with two or three* SCHOLARS *and* MEPHISTOPHILIS.

FIRST SCHOL. Master Doctor Faustus, since our conference about fair ladies, which was the beautifulest in all the world, we have determined with ourselves that Helen of Greece was the admirablest lady that ever lived: therefore, Master Doctor, if you will do us that favor, as to let us see that peerless dame of Greece, whom all the world admires for majesty, we should think ourselves much beholding unto you. 1437

FAUST. Gentlemen,
For that I know your friendship is unfeigned,
And Faustus' custom is not to deny 1440
The just requests of those that wish him well
You shall behold that peerless dame of Greece,
No otherways for pomp and majesty
Than when Sir Paris crossed the seas with her,
And brought the spoils to rich Dardania.
Be silent then, for danger is in words. 1446

Music sounds, and HELEN passeth over the *stage.*

SEC. SCHOL. Too simple is my wit to tell her praise,
Whom all the world admires for majesty.

THIRD SCHOL. No marvel though the angry Greeks pursued
With ten years' war the rape of such a queen, 1450
Whose heavenly beauty passeth all compare.

FIRST SCHOL. Since we have seen the pride of Nature's works,
And only paragon of excellence,
Let us depart; and for this glorious deed
Happy and blest be Faustus evermore! 1455

FAUST. Gentlemen, farewell: the same I wish to you. [*Exeunt* SCHOLARS.

Enter an OLD MAN.

OLD MAN. Ah, Doctor Faustus, that I might prevail
To guide thy steps unto the way of life,
By which sweet path thou mayst attain the goal
That shall conduct thee to celestial rest!
Break heart, drop blood, and mingle it with tears, 1461
Tears falling from repentant heaviness
Of thy most vile and loathsome filthiness,
The stench whereof corrupts the inward soul
With such flagitious crimes of heinous sin
As no commiseration may expel, 1466
But mercy, Faustus, of thy Savior sweet,
Whose blood alone must wash away thy guilt.

FAUST. Where art thou, Faustus? wretch, what hast thou done?
Damned art thou, Faustus, damned; despair and die! 1470
Hell calls for right, and with a roaring voice
Says, "Faustus, come; thine hour is almost come";
And Faustus now will come to do thee right.
[MEPHISTOPHILIS *gives him a dagger.*

OLD MAN. Ah, stay, good Faustus, stay thy desperate steps!
I see an angel hovers o'er thy head, 1475
And, with a vial full of precious grace,
Offers to pour the same into thy soul:
Then call for mercy, and avoid despair.

FAUST. Ah, my sweet friend, I feel 1479
Thy words to comfort my distresséd soul!
Leave me a while to ponder on my sins.

OLD MAN. I go, sweet Faustus; but with heavy cheer,
Fearing the ruin of thy hopeless soul.
[*Exit.*

FAUST. Accurséd Faustus, where is mercy now?
I do repent, and yet I do despair: 1485
Hell strives with grace for conquest in my breast:
What shall I do to shun the snares of death?

MEPH. Thou traitor, Faustus, I arrest thy soul
For disobedience to my sovereign lord: 1489
Revolt, or I'll in piece-meal tear thy flesh.

FAUST. Sweet Mephistophilis, entreat thy lord
To pardon my unjust presumption,
And with my blood again I will confirm
My former vow I made to Lucifer.

MEPH. Do it, then, quickly, with unfeignéd heart, 1495
Lest greater danger do attend thy drift.

FAUST. Torment, sweet friend, that base and crooked age,[80]
That durst dissuade me from thy Lucifer,
With greatest torments that our hell affords.

MEPH. His faith is great; I cannot touch his soul; 1500
But what I may afflict his body with
I will attempt, which is but little worth.

FAUST. One thing, good servant, let me crave of thee,
To glut the longing of my heart's desire,—
That I might have unto my paramour 1505
That heavenly Helen which I saw of late,
Whose sweet embracings may extinguish clean
Those thoughts that do dissuade me from my vow,
And keep mine oath I made to Lucifer.

MEPH. Faustus, this, or what else thou shalt desire, 1510
Shall be performed in twinkling of an eye.

Re-enter HELEN.

FAUST. Was this the face that launched a thousand ships,
And burnt the topless towers of Ilium?—
Sweet Helen, make me immortal with a kiss.— [*Kisses her.*
Her lips suck forth my soul: see, where it flies! 1515
Come, Helen, come, give me my soul again.
Here will I dwell, for heaven is in these lips,
And all is dross that is not Helena.
I will be Paris, and for love of thee,
Instead of Troy, shall Wertenberg be sacked; 1520
And I will combat with weak Menelaus,
And wear thy colors on my pluméd crest;
Yes, I will wound Achilles in the heel,
And then return to Helen for a kiss.
Oh, thou art fairer than the evening air 1525
Clad in the beauty of a thousand stars;
Brighter art thou than flaming Jupiter
When he appeared to hapless Semele;
More lovely than the monarch of the sky
In wanton Arethusa's azured arms; 1530
And none but thou shalt be my paramour!
[*Exeunt.*

Enter the OLD MAN.

OLD MAN. Accurséd Faustus, miserable man,
That from thy soul exclud'st the grace of heaven,
And fly'st the throne of his tribunal-seat!

Enter DEVILS.

Satan begins to sift me with his pride: 1535
As in this furnace God shall try my faith,
My faith, vile hell, shall triumph over thee.
Ambitious fiends, see how the heavens smile
At your repulse, and laugh your state to scorn!
Hence, hell! for hence I fly unto my God.
[*Exeunt—on one side,* DEVILS; *on the other,* OLD MAN.

Enter FAUSTUS, *with* SCHOLARS.

FAUST. Ah, gentlemen! 1541

FIRST SCHOL. What ails Faustus?

FAUST. Ah, my sweet chamber-fellow, had I lived with thee, then had I lived still! but now I die eternally. Look, comes he not? comes he not? 1546

SEC. SCHOL. What means Faustus?

THIRD SCHOL. Belike he is grown into some sickness by being over-solitary.

FIRST SCHOL. If it be so, we'll have physicians to cure him.—'Tis but a surfeit; never fear, man. 1552

FAUST. A surfeit of deadly sin, that hath damned both body and soul.

SEC. SCHOL. Yet, Faustus, look up to heaven; remember God's mercies are infinite. 1556

FAUST. But Faustus' offense can ne'er be pardoned: the serpent that tempted Eve may be saved, but not Faustus. Ah, gentlemen, hear me with patience, and tremble not at my speeches! Though

[80] The Old Man.

my heart pants and quivers to remember that I have been a student here these thirty years, O would I had never seen Wertenberg, never read book! and what wonders I have done, all Germany can witness, yea, all the world; for which Faustus hath lost both Germany and the world, yea, heaven itself, heaven, the seat of God, the throne of the blessed, the kingdom of joy; and must remain in hell for ever, hell, ah, hell, for ever! Sweet friends, what shall become of Faustus, being in hell for ever? 1574

THIRD SCHOL. Yet, Faustus, call on God.

FAUST. On God, whom Faustus hath abjured! on God, whom Faustus hath blasphemed! Ah, my God, I would weep! but the devil draws in my tears. Gush forth blood, instead of tears! yea, life and soul! Oh, he stays my tongue! I would lift up my hands; but see, they hold them, they hold them! 1583

ALL. Who, Faustus?

FAUST. Lucifer and Mephistophilis. Ah, gentlemen, I gave them my soul for my cunning!

ALL. God forbid! 1588

FAUST. God forbade it, indeed; but Faustus hath done it: for vain pleasure of twenty-four years hath Faustus lost eternal joy and felicity. I writ them a bill with mine own blood: the date is expired; the time will come, and he will fetch me. 1594

FIRST SCHOL. Why did not Faustus tell us of this before, that divines might have prayed for thee?

FAUST. Oft have I thought to have done so; but the devil threatened to tear me in pieces, if I named God, to fetch both body and soul, if I once gave ear to divinity: and now 'tis too late. Gentlemen, away, lest you perish with me. 1603

SEC. SCHOL. Oh, what shall we do to save Faustus?

FAUST. Talk not of me, but save yourselves, and depart.

THIRD SCHOL. God will strengthen me; I will stay with Faustus. 1609

FIRST SCHOL. Tempt not God, sweet friend; but let us into the next room, and there pray for him.

FAUST. Ay, pray for me, pray for me; and what noise soever ye hear, come not unto me, for nothing can rescue me. 1615

SEC. SCHOL. Pray thou, and we will pray that God may have mercy upon thee.

FAUST. Gentlemen, farewell: if I live till morning, I'll visit you; if not, Faustus is gone to hell. 1620

ALL. Faustus, farewell.

[*Exeunt* SCHOLARS.—*The clock strikes eleven.*

FAUST. Ah, Faustus,
Now hast thou but one bare hour to live,
And then thou must be damned perpetually!
Stand still, you ever-moving spheres of heaven, 1625
That time may cease, and midnight never come;
Fair Nature's eye, rise, rise again, and make
Perpetual day; or let this hour be but
A year, a month, a week, a natural day,
That Faustus may repent and save his soul! 1630
O lente, lente currite, noctis equi![81]
The stars move still, time runs, the clock will strike,
The devil will come, and Faustus must be damned.
Oh, I'll leap up to my God!—Who pulls me down?—
See, see, where Christ's blood streams in the firmament! 1635
One drop would save my soul, half a drop: ah, my Christ!—
Ah, rend not my heart for naming of my Christ!
Yet will I call on Him: O spare me, Lucifer!—
Where is it now? 'tis gone: and see, where God
Stretcheth out His arm and bends His ireful brows! 1640
Mountains and hills, come, come, and fall on me,
And hide me from the heavy wrath of God!
No, no!
Then will I headlong run into the earth:
Earth, gape! O no, it will not harbor me!
You stars that reigned at my nativity, 1646
Whose influence hath allotted death and hell,
Now draw up Faustus, like a foggy mist,
Into the entrails of yon laboring clouds,
That, when you vomit forth into the air, 1650
My limbs may issue from your smoky mouths,

[81] Run slowly, slowly, horses of night (Ovid, *Amores*, i, 13).

So that my soul may but ascend to heaven!
[*The clock strikes the half-hour.*
Ah, half the hour is past! 'twill all be past anon.
O God, 1654
If Thou wilt not have mercy on my soul,
Yet for Christ's sake, whose blood hath ransomed me,
Impose some end to my incessant pain;
Let Faustus live in hell a thousand years,
A hundred thousand, and at last be saved;
Oh, no end is limited to damnéd souls! 1660
Why wert thou not a creature wanting soul?
Or why is this immortal that thou hast?
Ah, Pythagoras' metempsychosis, were that true,
This soul should fly from me, and I be changed
Unto some brutish beast! All beasts are happy, 1665
For, when they die,
Their souls are soon dissolved in elements;
But mine must live still to be plagued in hell.
Curst be the parents that engendered me!
No, Faustus, curse thyself; curse Lucifer
That hath deprived thee of the joys of heaven. 1671
[*The clock strikes twelve.*
Oh, it strikes, it strikes! Now, body, turn to air,
Or Lucifer will bear thee quick to hell!
[*Thunder and lightning.*
O soul, be changed into little water-drops,
And fall into the ocean—ne'er be found!
My God, my God, look not so fierce on me!

Enter DEVILS.

Adders and serpents, let me breathe a while! 1677
Ugly hell, gape not! come not, Lucifer!
I'll burn my books!—Ah, Mephistophilis!
[*Exeunt* DEVILS *with* FAUSTUS.

Enter CHORUS.

CHOR. Cut is the branch that might have grown full straight, 1680
And burnéd is Apollo's laurel-bough,
That sometime grew within this learnéd man.
Faustus is gone: regard his hellish fall,
Whose fiendful fortune may exhort the wise,
Only to wonder at unlawful things, 1685
Whose deepness doth entice such forward wits
To practice more than heavenly power permits. [*Exit.*

SIR PHILIP SIDNEY

1554–1586

Sidney came of a distinguished family and was born at Penshurst on 30 November, 1554. King Philip of Spain, then in England, was one of his godfathers (whence the boy's name). In 1564 he entered Shrewsbury School. Fulke Greville, later the first Baron Brooke, of Warwick Castle, and Sidney's constant and admiring friend, entered the same school on the same day. Many years after the death of his friend, Greville, in dedicating his own works to Sidney's memory, wrote: Of his youth "I will report no other wonder but this, that though I lived with him, and knew him from a child, yet I never knew him other than a man; with such staidness of mind, lovely and familiar gravity, as carried grace and reverence above greater years. His talk ever of knowledge, and his very play tending to enrich his mind, so as even his teachers found something in him to observe and learn, above that which they had usually read or taught." From Shrewsbury Sidney proceeded to Christ Church, Oxford, in 1567 or 1568, where he found in the University—if we are to believe a contemporary writer—some 1700 fit companions, all "distinguished for their modesty, taciturnity, obedience, and devotion to their studies." Notwithstanding, it seems highly probable that he left Oxford to study, for at least a short time, at Cambridge. In May, 1572, he went to the Continent, traveling first to Paris, where he witnessed the massacre of St. Bartholomew, and thence to Frankfort, where he spent about nine months with the humanist and diplomatist Hubert Languet. He went next (with Languet) to Vienna, penetrated Hungary, and then spent some months in Italy, returning to stay through a winter in Vienna, and then to journey on through the Low Countries to England in May, 1575. In July he was at Kenilworth when the Earl of Leicester received Queen Elizabeth there; and later in the summer, it is said, he first saw Stella (Penelope Devereux, daughter of the Earl of Essex), then aged about thirteen. Sidney's sonnets, *Astrophel and Stella,* were mostly written by 1581 (first published 1591, 1598). In 1577 he was sent as an ambassador to the Continent. In 1580 he was virtually banished from Elizabeth's court because of his protest against her project of marriage with Francis, Duke of Anjou (also known as Alençon); and at this time Sidney seems to have written the later and longer version of his pastoral romance, the *Arcadia* (published 1590, 1593). In the following year he sat in Parliament, and in 1583 Elizabeth knighted him. In the same year he married Frances, daughter of Sir Francis Walsingham, who bore him a daughter in 1585.

In 1579 one Stephen Gosson published an attack upon stage-plays and upon "poets and pipers and such peevish cattle," entitled *The School of Abuse*. This he dedicated to Sidney without having obtained leave to do so, and was —as Edmund Spenser wrote—"for his labor scorned, if at least it be in the goodness of that nature to scorn." It is frequently said, though with little reason, that Sidney wrote his *Defense of Poesy* in reply to Gosson. He does, of course, unmistakably refer to Gosson's pamphlet, but also to other recent attacks; and, in any case, the *Defense* is far more than a reply to ignorant zealots who thought they were serving the causes of religion and decency in attacking drama and poetry. The *Defense* was probably begun in 1580, and finished in 1583 or 1584 (first published in 1595). It remains to this day one of the fairest monuments of English literary criticism. "In its mingling of gravity and gayety, of colloquialism and dignified, elevated speech, it is a true reflection of Sidney's character. His mind plays easily over the field which he is treating, and the enthusiasm of his personality fuses the seemingly incongruous elements. More than history or philosophy or any of the sciences, he maintains, poetry tends to elevate the whole man. Its delightful teach ing leads us to virtuous action, the rational object of all learning. Sidney's love of beauty includes the beauty of a well-ordered life; all other beauty reaches but to dust. It is because, like Arnold, he believes that as time passes our race will find a surer and surer stay in poetry that he urges its claims in such unqualified terms. . . . His criticisms of contemporary literature missed the mark in some instances, but his book endures because in essence it is profoundly true, and because it is a true reflex of the author's versatile, high-minded, gracious personality." (M. W. Wallace, *Life of Sidney,* p. 240.)

During the winter of 1584–1585 Sidney sat again in Parliament, and in the latter year he was appointed Governor of Flushing, assuming the office on 21 November. He thus went to play his part in the unwilling assistance which Elizabeth gave to the Dutch against Spain. Ten months later occurred the battle at Zutphen in which Sidney received a mortal wound. Instantly weakened, he was forced to retire, though still able to ride his horse. "In which sad progress," wrote Fulke Greville, "passing along by the rest of the army, where his uncle the general was, and being thirsty with excess of bleeding, he called for drink which was presently brought him; but as he was putting the bottle to his mouth, he saw a poor soldier carried along, who had eaten his last at the same feast, ghastly casting up his eyes at the bottle. Which Sir Philip perceiving, took it from his head before he drank, and delivered it to the poor man with these words, 'Thy necessity is yet greater than mine.' And when he had pledged this poor soldier, he was presently carried to Arnheim." There he awaited death twenty-six days, until the end came on 17 October. Amidst universal mourning his body was conveyed to London and given a magnificent burial in old St. Paul's Cathedral. To contemporaries Sidney was the ideal embodiment of the virtues of the Renaissance gentleman and courtier; and this he has remained in the eyes of posterity.

The Complete Works of Sir Philip Sidney, ed. Albert Feuillerat (Cambridge, 1912–1926), contains the *Defense of Poesy* in vol. III; a good, fully annotated edition of the *Defense* alone is that edited by Albert S. Cook (Boston, 1890). The most scholarly biography is still Malcolm W. Wallace's *Life of Sir Philip Sidney* (Cambridge, 1915); a sound, if more popular, account is Mona Wilson's *Sir Philip Sidney* (New York, 1932). Joel E. Spingarn summarizes the background of the *Defense* in his *History of Literary Criticism in the Renaissance* (New York, 1899).

THE DEFENSE OF POESY[1]

(1595)

WHEN the right virtuous Edward Wotton[2] and I were at the Emperor's[3] court together, we gave ourselves to learn horsemanship of John Pietro Pugliano, one that with great commendation had the place of an esquire in 5 his stable; and he, according to the fertileness of the Italian wit, did not only afford us the demonstration of his practice, but sought to enrich our minds with the contemplations therein which he thought most precious. 10 But with none I remember mine ears were at any time more loaden than when—either angered with slow payment, or moved with our learner-like admiration—he exercised his speech in the praise of his faculty. He said 15 soldiers were the noblest estate of mankind, and horsemen the noblest of soldiers. He said they were the masters of war and ornaments of peace, speedy goers and strong abiders, triumphers both in camps and courts. Nay, to so unbelieved a point he proceeded, as that no earthly thing bred such wonder to a prince as to be a good horseman; skill of government was but a *pedanteria*[4] in comparison. Then would he add certain praises, by telling what a peerless beast the horse was, the only serviceable courtier without flattery, the beast of most beauty, faithfulness, courage, and such more, that if I had not been a piece of a logician before I came to him, I think he would have persuaded me to have wished myself a horse. But thus much at least with his no few words he drave into me, that self-love is better than any gilding to make that seem gorgeous wherein ourselves be parties.

20 Wherein if Pugliano's strong affection and weak arguments will not satisfy you, I will give you a nearer example of myself, who, I

[1]In preparation of the text, A. S. Cook's modernization, based on both of the editions of 1595, was found useful.

[2]Later first Baron Wotton, half-brother to Sir Henry Wotton; lived 1548–1626. One of the pallbearers at Sidney's funeral.

[3]Maximilian II (1527–1576).

[4]Species of pedantry.

know not by what mischance, in these my not old years and idlest times, having slipped into the title of a poet, am provoked to say something unto you in the defense of that my unelected vocation, which if I handle with more good will than good reasons, bear with me, since the scholar is to be pardoned that followeth the steps of his master. And yet I must say that, as I have just cause to make a pitiful defense of poor poetry, which from almost the highest estimation of learning is fallen to be the laughing-stock of children, so have I need to bring some more available proofs, since the former is by no man barred of his deserved credit, the silly[5] latter hath had even the names of philosophers used to the defacing of it, with great danger of civil war among the Muses.

And first, truly, to all them that, professing learning, inveigh against poetry, may justly be objected that they go very near to ungratefulness, to seek to deface that which, in the noblest nations and languages that are known, hath been the first light-giver to ignorance, and first nurse, whose milk by little and little enabled them to feed afterwards of tougher knowledges. And will they now play the hedgehog, that, being received into the den, drave out his host? Or rather the vipers, that with their birth kill their parents? Let learned Greece in any of her manifold sciences be able to show me one book before Musaeus, Homer, and Hesiod, all three nothing else but poets. Nay, let any history be brought that can say any writers were there before them, if they were not men of the same skill, as Orpheus, Linus, and some other are named, who, having been the first of that country that made pens deliverers of their knowledge to their posterity, may justly challenge to be called their fathers in learning. For not only in time they had this priority—although in itself antiquity be venerable—but went before them as causes, to draw with their charming sweetness the wild untamed wits to an admiration of knowledge. So as Amphion was said to move stones with his poetry to build Thebes, and Orpheus to be listened to by beasts,—indeed stony and beastly people. So among the Romans were Livius Andronicus and Ennius; so in the Italian language the first that made it aspire to be a treasure-house of science were the poets Dante, Boccaccio, and Petrarch; so in our English were Gower and Chaucer, after whom, encouraged and delighted with their excellent foregoing, others have followed to beautify our mother-tongue, as well in the same kind as in other arts.

This did so notably show itself, that the philosophers of Greece durst not a long time appear to the world but under the masks of poets. So Thales, Empedocles, and Parmenides sang their natural philosophy in verses; so did Pythagoras and Phocylides their moral counsels; so did Tyrtaeus in war matters, and Solon in matters of policy; or rather they, being poets, did exercise their delightful vein in those points of highest knowledge which before them lay hidden to the world. For that wise Solon was directly a poet it is manifest, having written in verse the notable fable of the Atlantic Island which was continued by Plato. And truly even Plato whosoever well considereth shall find that in the body of his work though the inside and strength were philosophy, the skin as it were and beauty depended most of poetry. For all standeth upon dialogues; wherein he feigneth many honest burgesses of Athens to speak of such matters that, if they had been set on the rack, they would never have confessed them; besides his poetical describing the circumstances of their meetings, as the well-ordering of a banquet, the delicacy of a walk,[6] with interlacing mere tales, as Gyges' Ring[7] and others, which who knoweth not to be flowers of poetry did never walk into Apollo's garden.

And even historiographers, although their lips sound of things done, and verity be written in their foreheads, have been glad to borrow both fashion and perchance weight of the poets. So Herodotus entitled his history by the name of the nine Muses; and both he and all the rest that followed him either stole or usurped of poetry their passionate describing of passions, the many particularities of battles which no man could affirm, or, if that be denied me, long orations put in the mouths

[5]Poor.

[6]*Symposium; Phaedrus.*

[7]*Republic,* II, 359–360.

of great kings and captains, which it is certain they never pronounced.

So that truly neither philosopher nor historiographer could at the first have entered into the gates of popular judgments, if they had not taken a great passport of poetry, which in all nations at this day, where learning flourisheth not, is plain to be seen; in all which they have some feeling of poetry. In Turkey, besides their lawgiving divines, they have no other writers but poets. In our neighbor country Ireland, where truly learning goeth very bare, yet are their poets held in a devout reverence. Even among the most barbarous and simple Indians, where no writing is, yet have they their poets, who make and sing songs (which they call *areytos*[8]), both of their ancestors' deeds and praises of their gods,—a sufficient probability that, if ever learning come among them, it must be by having their hard dull wits softened and sharpened with the sweet delights of poetry; for until they find a pleasure in the exercise of the mind, great promises of much knowledge will little persuade them that know not the fruits of knowledge. In Wales, the true remnant of the ancient Britons, as there are good authorities to show the long time they had poets which they called bards, so through all the conquests of Romans, Saxons, Danes, and Normans, some of whom did seek to ruin all memory of learning from among them, yet do their poets even to this day last; so as it is not more notable in soon beginning than in long continuing.

But since the authors of most of our sciences were the Romans, and before them the Greeks, let us a little stand upon their authorities, but even[9] so far as to see what names they have given unto this now scorned skill. Among the Romans a poet was called *vates,* which is as much as a diviner, foreseer, or prophet, as by his conjoined words, *vaticinium* and *vaticinari,* is manifest; so heavenly a title did that excellent people bestow upon this heart-ravishing knowledge. And so far were they carried into the admiration thereof, that they thought in the chanceable hitting upon any such verses great foretokens of their following fortunes were placed; whereupon grew the word of *Sortes Virgilianae,* when by sudden opening Virgil's book they lighted upon some verse of his making. Whereof the *Histories of the Emperors' Lives*[10] are full: as of Albinus, the governor of our island, who in his childhood met with this verse,

Arma amens capio, nec sat rationis in armis,[11]

and in his age performed it. Although it were a very vain and godless superstition, as also it was to think that spirits were commanded by such verses—whereupon this word charms, derived of *carmina,* cometh—so yet serveth it to show the great reverence those wits were held in, and altogether not[12] without ground, since both the oracles of Delphos[13] and Sibylla's prophecies were wholly delivered in verses; for that same exquisite observing of number and measure in words, and that high-flying liberty of conceit[14] proper to the poet, did seem to have some divine force in it.

And may not I presume a little further to show the reasonableness of this word *vates,* and say that the holy David's Psalms are a divine poem? If I do, I shall not do it without the testimony of great learned men, both ancient and modern. But even the name of Psalms will speak for me, which, being interpreted, is nothing but Songs; then, that it is fully written in meter, as all learned Hebricians agree, although the rules be not yet fully found; lastly and principally, his handling his prophecy, which is merely poetical. For what else is the awaking his musical instruments, the often and free changing of persons, his notable prosopopoeias,[15] when he maketh you, as it were, see God coming in His majesty, his telling of the beasts' joyfulness and hills' leaping, but a heavenly poesy, wherein almost he showeth himself a passionate lover of that unspeakable and everlasting beauty to be seen by the eyes of the mind, only cleared by faith? But truly

[8]The native word was picked up by the Spaniards in the West Indies.

[9]Merely.

[10]The *Augustan Histories.*

[11]To arms I rush in frenzy,—not that good cause is shown for arms (*Aeneid,* II, 314).

[12]Not altogether. [13]Delphi.

[14]Imaginative invention. [15]Personifications.

now having named him, I fear I seem to profane that holy name, applying it to poetry, which is among us thrown down to so ridiculous an estimation. But they that with quiet judgments will look a little deeper into it shall find the end and working of it such as, being rightly applied, deserveth not to be scourged out of the Church of God.

But now let us see how the Greeks named it and how they deemed of it. The Greeks called him ποιητήν, which name hath, as the most excellent, gone through other languages. It cometh of this word ποιεῖν, which is "to make"; wherein I know not whether by luck or wisdom we Englishmen have met with the Greeks in calling him a maker.[16] Which name how high and incomparable a title it is, I had rather were known by marking the scope of other sciences than by any partial allegation. There is no art delivered unto mankind that hath not the works of nature for his principal object, without which they could not consist, and on which they so depend as they become actors and players, as it were, of what nature will have set forth. So doth the astronomer look upon the stars and, by that he seeth, set down what order nature hath taken therein. So do the geometrician and arithmetician in their divers sorts of quantities. So doth the musician in times tell you which by nature agree, which not. The natural philosopher thereon hath his name, and the moral philosopher standeth upon the natural virtues, vices, and passions of man; and "follow nature," saith he, "therein, and thou shalt not err." The lawyer saith what men have determined, the historian what men have done. The grammarian speaketh only of the rules of speech, and the rhetorician and logician, considering what in nature will soonest prove and persuade, thereon give artificial rules, which still are compassed within the circle of a question, according to the proposed matter. The physician weigheth the nature of man's body, and the nature of things helpful or hurtful unto it. And the metaphysic, though it be in the second and abstract notions, and therefore be counted supernatural, yet doth he, indeed, build upon the depth of nature.

[16]The word was used to signify a poet particularly in Scotland and by the Scottish Chaucerians.

Only the poet, disdaining to be tied to any such subjection, lifted up with the vigor of his own invention, doth grow, in effect, into another nature, in making things either better than nature bringeth forth, or, quite anew, forms such as never were in nature, as the heroes, demi-gods, cyclops, chimeras, furies, and such like; so as he goeth hand in hand with nature, not enclosed within the narrow warrant of her gifts, but freely ranging within the zodiac of his own wit. Nature never set forth the earth in so rich tapestry as divers poets have done; neither with pleasant rivers, fruitful trees, sweet-smelling flowers, nor whatsoever else may make the too-much-loved earth more lovely; her world is brazen, the poets only deliver a golden.

But let those things alone, and go to man—for whom as the other things are, so it seemeth in him her uttermost cunning is employed—and know whether she have brought forth so true a lover as Theagenes,[17] so constant a friend as Pylades; so valiant a man as Orlando;[18] so right a prince as Xenophon's Cyrus; so excellent a man every way as Virgil's Aeneas? Neither let this be jestingly conceived, because the works of the one be essential, the other in imitation or fiction; for any understanding knoweth the skill of each artificer standeth in that idea, or fore-conceit of the work, and not in the work itself. And that the poet hath that idea is manifest, by delivering them forth in such excellency as he hath imagined them. Which delivering forth, also, is not wholly imaginative, as we are wont to say by[19] them that build castles in the air; but so far substantially it worketh, not only to make a Cyrus, which had been but a particular excellency, as nature might have done, but to bestow a Cyrus upon the world to make many Cyruses, if they will learn aright why and how that maker made him. Neither let it be deemed too saucy a comparison to balance the highest point of man's wit with the efficacy of nature; but rather give right honor to the Heavenly Maker of that maker, who, having made man to His own likeness, set him beyond and over all the works of that

[17]In the romance, *Ethiopic History*, by Heliodorus.

[18]Hero of Ariosto's *Orlando Furioso*. [19]Of.

second nature. Which in nothing he showeth so much as in poetry, when with the force of a divine breath he bringeth things forth far surpassing her doings, with no small argument to the incredulous of that first accursed fall of Adam,—since our erected wit maketh us know what perfection is, and yet our infected will keepeth us from reaching unto it. But these arguments will by few be understood, and by fewer granted; thus much I hope will be given me, that the Greeks with some probability of reason gave him the name above all names of learning.

Now let us go to a more ordinary opening of him, that the truth may be the more palpable; and so, I hope, though we get not so unmatched a praise as the etymology of his names will grant, yet his very description, which no man will deny, shall not justly be barred from a principal commendation.

Poesy, therefore, is an art of imitation, for so Aristotle termeth it in his word *μίμησις*, that is to say, a representing, counterfeiting, or figuring forth; to speak metaphorically, a speaking picture, with this end,—to teach and delight.

Of this have been three general kinds. The chief, both in antiquity and excellency, were they that did imitate the inconceivable excellencies of God. Such were David in his Psalms; Solomon in his Song of Songs, in his Ecclesiastes and Proverbs; Moses and Deborah in their Hymns; and the writer of Job; which, beside other, the learned Emanuel Tremellius[20] and Franciscus Junius[21] do entitle the poetical part of the Scripture. Against these none will speak that hath the Holy Ghost in due holy reverence. In this kind, though in a full wrong divinity, were Orpheus, Amphion, Homer in his *Hymns,* and many other, both Greeks and Romans. And this poesy must be used by whosoever will follow St. James's counsel in singing psalms when they are merry;[22] and I know is used with the fruit of comfort by some, when, in sorrowful pangs of their death-bringing sins, they find the consolation of the never-leaving goodness.

The second kind is of them that deal with matters philosophical: either moral, as Tyrtaeus, Phocylides, and Cato;[23] or natural, as Lucretius and Virgil's *Georgics;* or astronomical, as Manilius and Pontanus;[24] or historical, as Lucan; which who mislike, the fault is in their judgment quite out of taste, and not in the sweet food of sweetly uttered knowledge.

But because this second sort is wrapped within the fold of the proposed subject, and takes not the free course of his own invention, whether they properly be poets or no let grammarians dispute, and go to the third, indeed right poets, of whom chiefly this question ariseth. Betwixt whom and these second is such a kind of difference as betwixt the meaner sort of painters, who counterfeit only such faces as are set before them, and the more excellent, who having no law but wit, bestow that in colors upon you which is fittest for the eye to see,—as the constant though lamenting look of Lucretia,[25] when she punished in herself another's fault; wherein he painteth not Lucretia, whom he never saw, but painteth the outward beauty of such a virtue. For these third be they which most properly do imitate to teach and delight; and to imitate borrow nothing of what is, hath been, or shall be; but range, only reined with learned discretion, into the divine consideration of what may be and should be. These be they that, as the first and most noble sort may justly be termed *vates,* so these are waited on in the excellentest languages and best understandings with the foredescribed name of poets. For these, indeed, do merely make to imitate, and imitate both to delight and teach, and delight to move men to take that goodness in hand, which without delight they would fly as from a stranger; and teach to make them know that goodness whereunto they are moved:—

[20]Biblical scholar (1510–1580). A Jew of Ferrara, he was converted to Catholic Christianity, later became a Protestant, and lived for a time at Oxford.

[21]French Protestant (1545–1602); taught theology at Neustadt, Heidelberg, and Leyden.

[22]See James, 5:13.

[23]A certain Dionysius Cato who lived, perhaps, in the third century A. D. His moral distichs were widely popular in the Middle Age, and were still used in Elizabethan schools.

[24]Italian scholar of the Renaissance (1426–1503). Sidney refers to his *Urania,* an astronomical poem in five books.

[25]See Livy, i, 58.

which being the noblest scope to which ever any learning was directed, yet want there not idle tongues to bark at them.

These be subdivided into sundry more special denominations. The most notable be the heroic, lyric, tragic, comic, satiric, iambic, elegiac, pastoral, and certain others, some of these being termed according to the matter they deal with, some by the sort of verse they liked best to write in,—for indeed the greatest part of poets have appareled their poetical inventions in that numberous kind of writing which is called verse. Indeed but appareled, verse being but an ornament and no cause to poetry, since there have been many most excellent poets that never versified, and now swarm many versifiers that need never answer to the name of poets. For Xenophon, who did imitate so excellently as to give us *effigiem justi imperii*—the portraiture of a just empire under the name of Cyrus (as Cicero saith of him)—made therein an absolute heroical poem; so did Heliodorus in his sugared[26] invention of that picture of love in Theagenes and Chariclea;[27] and yet both these wrote in prose. Which I speak to show that it is not riming and versing that maketh a poet—no more than a long gown maketh an advocate, who, though he pleaded in armor, should be an advocate and no soldier—but it is that feigning notable images of virtues, vices, or what else, with that delightful teaching, which must be the right describing note to know a poet by. Although indeed the senate of poets hath chosen verse as their fittest raiment, meaning, as in matter they passed all in all, so in manner to go beyond them; not speaking, table-talk fashion, or like men in a dream, words as they chanceably fall from the mouth, but peizing[28] each syllable of each word by just proportion, according to the dignity of the subject.

Now therefore it shall not be amiss, first to weigh this latter sort of poetry by his works, and then by his parts; and if in neither of these anatomies he be condemnable, I hope we shall obtain a more favorable sentence. This purifying of wit, this enriching of memory, enabling of judgment, and enlarging of conceit, which commonly we call learning, under what name soever it come forth or to what immediate end soever it be directed, the final end is to lead and draw us to as high a perfection as our degenerate souls, made worse by their clay lodgings, can be capable of. This, according to the inclination of man, bred many-formed impressions. For some that thought this felicity principally to be gotten by knowledge, and no knowledge to be so high or heavenly as acquaintance with the stars, gave themselves to astronomy; others, persuading themselves to be demigods if they knew the causes of things, became natural and supernatural philosophers. Some an admirable delight drew to music, and some the certainty of demonstration to the mathematics; but all, one and other, having this scope:—to know, and by knowledge to lift up the mind from the dungeon of the body to the enjoying his own divine essence. But when by the balance of experience it was found that the astronomer, looking to the stars, might fall into a ditch, that the inquiring philosopher might be blind in himself, and the mathematician might draw forth a straight line with a crooked heart; then lo! did proof, the over-ruler of opinions, make manifest, that all these are but serving sciences, which, as they have each a private end in themselves, so yet are they all directed to the highest end of the mistress-knowledge, by the Greeks called ἀρχιτεκτονική,[29] which stands, as I think, in the knowledge of a man's self, in the ethic and politic consideration, with the end of well-doing, and not of well-knowing only:—even as the saddler's next end is to make a good saddle, but his further end to serve a nobler faculty, which is horsemanship; so the horseman's to soldiery; and the soldier not only to have the skill, but to perform the practice of a soldier. So that the ending end of all earthly learning being virtuous action, those skills that most serve to bring forth that have a most just title to be princes over all the rest; wherein, if we can show, the poet is worthy to have it before any other competitors.

Among whom as principal challengers step

[26] Charming.

[27] The *Ethiopic History,* referred to above.

[28] Poising, weighing.

[29] Fulke Greville calls this the "architectonical art."

forth the moral philosophers; whom, me thinketh, I see coming towards me with a sullen gravity, as though they could not abide vice by daylight; rudely clothed, for to witness outwardly their contempt of outward things; with books in their hands against glory, whereto they set their names; sophistically speaking against subtility; and angry with any man in whom they see the foul fault of anger. These men, casting largess as they go of definitions, divisions, and distinctions, with a scornful interrogative do soberly ask whether it be possible to find any path so ready to lead a man to virtue, as that which teacheth what virtue is, and teacheth it not only by delivering forth his very being, his causes and effects, but also by making known his enemy, vice, which must be destroyed, and his cumbersome servant, passion, which must be mastered; by showing the generalities that contain it, and the specialities that are derived from it; lastly, by plain setting down how it extendeth itself out of the limits of a man's own little world, to the government of families, and maintaining of public societies?

The historian scarcely giveth leisure to the moralist to say so much, but that he, loaden with old mouse-eaten records, authorizing himself for the most part upon other histories, whose greatest authorities are built upon the notable foundation of hearsay; having much ado to accord differing writers, and to pick truth out of partiality; better acquainted with a thousand years ago than with the present age, and yet better knowing how this world goeth than how his own wit runneth; curious for antiquities and inquisitive of novelties, a wonder to young folks and a tyrant in table-talk; denieth, in a great chafe, that any man for teaching of virtue and virtuous actions is comparable to him. "I am *testis temporum, lux veritatis, vita memoriae, magistra vitae, nuntia vetustatis.*[30] The philosopher," saith he, "teacheth a disputative virtue, but I do an active. His virtue is excellent in the dangerless Academy of Plato, but mine showeth forth her honorable face in the battles of Marathon, Pharsalia, Poitiers, and Agincourt. He teacheth virtue by certain abstract considerations, but I only bid you follow the footing of them that have gone before you. Old-aged experience goeth beyond the fine-witted philosopher; but I give the experience of many ages. Lastly, if he make the song-book, I put the learner's hand to the lute; and if he be the guide, I am the light." Then would he allege you innumerable examples, confirming story by story, how much the wisest senators and princes have been directed by the credit of history, as Brutus, Alphonsus of Aragon[31]—and who not, if need be? At length the long line of their disputation maketh a point[32] in this,—that the one giveth the precept, and the other the example.

Now whom shall we find, since the question standeth for the highest form in the school of learning, to be moderator? Truly, as me seemeth, the poet; and if not a moderator, even the man that ought to carry the title from them both, and much more from all other serving sciences. Therefore compare we the poet with the historian and with the moral philosopher; and if he go beyond them both, no other human skill can match him. For as for the divine, with all reverence it is ever to be excepted, not only for having his scope as far beyond any of these as eternity exceedeth a moment, but even for passing each of these in themselves. And for the lawyer, though *Jus* be the daughter of Justice, and Justice the chief of virtues, yet because he seeketh to make men good rather *formidine poenae* than *virtutis amore,*[33] or, to say righter, doth not endeavor to make men good, but that their evil hurt not others, having no care, so he be a good citizen, how bad a man he be; therefore, as our wickedness maketh him necessary, and necessity maketh him honorable, so is he not in the deepest truth to stand in rank with these, who all endeavor to take naughtiness away, and plant goodness even in the secretest cabinet of our souls. And these four are all

[30]History, the evidence of time, the light of truth, the life of memory, the directress of life, the herald of antiquity (Cicero, *De Oratore,* II, ix, 36).

[31]Alphonso V of Aragon and I of Sicily (1416-1458).

[32]Cometh to an end.

[33]Rather from the fear of punishment than from the love of virtue (Horace, *Epistles,* I, xvi, 52-53).

that any way deal in that consideration of men's manners, which being the supreme knowledge, they that best breed it deserve the best commendation.

The philosopher therefore and the historian are they which would win the goal, the one by precept, the other by example; but both not having both, do both halt. For the philosopher, setting down with thorny arguments the bare rule, is so hard of utterance and so misty to be conceived that one that hath no other guide but him shall wade in him till he be old, before he shall find sufficient cause to be honest. For his knowledge standeth so upon the abstract and general that happy is that man who may understand him, and more happy that can apply what he doth understand. On the other side, the historian, wanting the precept, is so tied, not to what should be but to what is, to the particular truth of things and not to the general reason of things, that his example draweth no necessary consequence, and therefore a less fruitful doctrine.

Now doth the peerless poet perform both; for whatsoever the philosopher saith should be done, he giveth a perfect picture of it in some one by whom he presupposeth it was done, so as he coupleth the general notion with the particular example. A perfect picture, I say; for he yieldeth to the powers of the mind an image of that whereof the philosopher bestoweth but a wordish description, which doth neither strike, pierce, nor possess the sight of the soul so much as that other doth. For as, in outward things, to a man that had never seen an elephant or a rhinoceros, who should tell him most exquisitely all their shapes, color, bigness, and particular marks; or of a gorgeous palace, an architector,[34] with declaring the full beauties, might well make the hearer able to repeat, as it were by rote, all he had heard, yet should never satisfy his inward conceit with being witness to itself of a true lively[35] knowledge; but the same man, as soon as he might see those beasts well painted, or that house well in model, should straightways grow, without need of any description, to a judicial comprehending of them: so no doubt the philosopher, with his learned definitions, be it of virtues or vices, matters of public policy or private government, replenisheth the memory with many infallible grounds of wisdom, which notwithstanding lie dark before the imaginative and judging power, if they be not illuminated or figured forth by the speaking picture of poesy.

Tully[36] taketh much pains, and many times not without poetical helps, to make us know the force love of our country hath in us. Let us but hear old Anchises speaking in the midst of Troy's flames,[37] or see Ulysses, in the fullness of all Calypso's delights, bewail his absence from barren and beggarly Ithaca.[38] Anger, the Stoics said, was a short madness.[39] Let but Sophocles bring you Ajax on a stage, killing and whipping sheep and oxen, thinking them the army of Greeks, with their chieftains Agamemnon and Menelaus, and tell me if you have not a more familiar insight into anger, than finding in the schoolmen his genus and difference.[40] See whether wisdom and temperance in Ulysses and Diomedes, valor in Achilles, friendship in Nisus and Euryalus,[41] even to an ignorant man carry not an apparent shining. And, contrarily, the remorse of conscience in Oedipus; the soon-repenting pride of Agamemnon;[42] the self-devouring cruelty in his father Atreus;[43] the violence of ambition in the two Theban brothers;[44] the sour sweetness of revenge in Medea;[45] and, to fall lower, the Terentian Gnatho[46] and our Chaucer's Pandar[47] so expressed that we now use their names to signify their trades; and finally, all virtues, vices, and passions so in their own natural states laid to the view, that we seem not to hear of them, but clearly to see through them.

But even in the most excellent determination of goodness, what philosopher's counsel can so readily direct a prince, as the feigned

[34]Architect. [35]Living.

[36]M. Tullius Cicero. [37]*Aeneid,* II, 634–650.

[38]*Odyssey,* V, 149–158.

[39]Horace, *Epistles,* I, ii, 62; Seneca, *De Ira,* I, 1.

[40]In Sophocles's *Ajax.*

[41]*Aeneid,* IX, 176–182, 433–445.

[42]In Aeschylus's *Agamemnon.*

[43]*Ibid.,* ll. 1555–1580.

[44]Eteocles and Polynices, in Aeschylus's *Seven against Thebes.*

[45]In Euripides' *Medea.* [46]In Terence's *Eunuch.*

[47]In Chaucer's *Troilus and Cressida.*

Cyrus in Xenophon? Or a virtuous man in all fortunes, as Aeneas in Virgil? Or a whole commonwealth, as the way of Sir Thomas More's *Utopia?* I say the way, because where Sir Thomas More erred, it was the fault of the man, and not of the poet; for that way of patterning a commonwealth was most absolute, though he, perchance, hath not so absolutely performed it. For the question is, whether the feigned image of poesy, or the regular instruction of philosophy, hath the more force in teaching. Wherein if the philosophers have more rightly showed themselves philosophers than the poets have attained to the high top of their profession,—as in truth,

> *Mediocribus esse poetis*
> *Non Dii, non homines, non concessere columnae,*—[48]

it is, I say again, not the fault of the art, but that by few men that art can be accomplished.

Certainly, even our Savior Christ could as well have given the moral commonplaces of uncharitableness and humbleness as the divine narration of Dives and Lazarus; or of disobedience and mercy, as that heavenly discourse of the lost child and the gracious father; but that his through-searching wisdom knew the estate of Dives burning in hell, and of Lazarus in Abraham's bosom, would more constantly, as it were, inhabit both the memory and judgment. Truly, for myself, meseems I see before mine eyes the lost child's disdainful prodigality, turned to envy a swine's dinner; which by the learned divines are thought not historical acts, but instructing parables.

For conclusion, I say the philosopher teacheth, but he teacheth obscurely, so as the learned only can understand him; that is to say, he teacheth them that are already taught. But the poet is the food for the tenderest stomachs; the poet is indeed the right popular philosopher. Whereof Aesop's tales give good proof; whose pretty allegories, stealing under the formal[49] tales of beasts, make many, more beastly than beasts, begin to hear the sound of virtue from those dumb speakers.

But now may it be alleged that if this imagining of matters be so fit for the imagination, then must the historian needs surpass, who bringeth you images of true matters, such as indeed were done, and not such as fantastically or falsely may be suggested to have been done. Truly, Aristotle himself, in his *Discourse of Poesy,* plainly determineth this question, saying that poetry is φιλοσοφώτερον and σπουδαιό ερ) , that is to say, it is more philosophical and more studiously serious than history. His reason is, because poesy dealeth with καθόλου, that is to say with the universal consideration, and the history with καφ' ἕκαστον, the particular. "Now," saith he, "the universal weighs what is fit to be said or done, either in likelihood or necessity—which the poesy considereth in his imposed names; and the particular only marketh whether Alcibiades did, or suffered, this or that": thus far Aristotle. Which reason of his, as all his, is most full of reason.

For, indeed, if the question were whether it were better to have a particular act truly or falsely set down, there is no doubt which is to be chosen, no more than whether you had rather have Vespasian's picture right as he was, or, at the painter's pleasure, nothing resembling. But if the question be for your own use and learning, whether it be better to have it set down as it should be or as it was, then certainly is more doctrinable[50] the feigned Cyrus in Xenophon than the true Cyrus in Justin;[51] and the feigned Aeneas in Virgil than the right Aeneas in Dares Phrygius;[52] as to a lady that desired to fashion her countenance to the best grace, a painter should more benefit her to portrait a most sweet face, writing Canidia upon it, than to paint Canidia as

---

[48]Mediocrity in poets is condemned by gods and men, and by booksellers too (Horace, *De Arte Poetica,* 372–373).

[49]Circumstantial.

[50]Instructive.

[51]Second century A. D. His history is an abridgment of an older one. His account of Cyrus (I, 4–8) probably comes ultimately from Herodotus.

[52]"An apocryphal history of the Trojan war passed current in the Middle Age under this name, and was regarded as the authentic account of an eyewitness and participant" (Cook). Sidney followed contemporaries in still assuming it to be authentic.

she was, who, Horace sweareth, was foul and ill-favored.[53]

If the poet do his part aright, he will show you in Tantalus, Atreus, and such like, nothing that is not to be shunned; in Cyrus, Aeneas, Ulysses, each thing to be followed. Where[54] the historian, bound to tell things as things were, cannot be liberal—without he will be poetical—of a perfect pattern; but, as in Alexander, or Scipio himself, show doings, some to be liked, some to be misliked; and then how will you discern what to follow but by your own discretion, which you had without reading Quintus Curtius? And whereas a man may say, though in universal consideration of doctrine the poet prevaileth, yet that the history, in his saying such a thing was done, doth warrant a man more in that he shall follow,—the answer is manifest: that if he stand upon that *was,* as if he should argue, because it rained yesterday therefore it should rain to-day, then indeed it hath some advantage to a gross conceit. But if he know an example only informs a conjectured likelihood, and so go by reason, the poet doth so far exceed him as he is to frame his example to that which is most reasonable, be it in warlike, politic, or private matters; where the historian in his bare *was* hath many times that which we call fortune to overrule the best wisdom. Many times he must tell events whereof he can yield no cause; or if he do, it must be poetically.

For, that a feigned example hath as much force to teach as a true example—for as for to move, it is clear, since the feigned may be tuned to the highest key of passion—let us take one example wherein a poet and a historian do concur. Herodotus and Justin do both testify that Zopyrus, king Darius's faithful servant, seeing his master long resisted by the rebellious Babylonians, feigned himself in extreme disgrace of his king; for verifying of which he caused his own nose and ears to be cut off, and so flying to the Babylonians, was received, and for his known valor so far credited, that he did find means to deliver them over to Darius. Much-like matter doth Livy record of Tarquinius and his son. Xenophon excellently feigneth such another stratagem, performed by Abradatas in Cyrus's behalf. Now would I fain know, if occasion be presented unto you to serve your prince by such an honest dissimulation, why do you not as well learn it of Xenophon's fiction as of the other's verity? and, truly, so much the better, as you shall save your nose by the bargain; for Abradatas did not counterfeit so far.

So, then, the best of the historian is subject to the poet; for whatsoever action or faction, whatsoever counsel, policy, or war-stratagem the historian is bound to recite, that may the poet, if he list, with his imitation make his own, beautifying it both for further teaching and more delighting, as it pleaseth him; having all, from Dante's Heaven to his Hell, under the authority of his pen. Which if I be asked what poets have done? so as I might well name some, yet say I, and say again, I speak of the art, and not of the artificer.

Now, to that which commonly is attributed to the praise of history, in respect of the notable learning is gotten by marking the success, as though therein a man should see virtue exalted and vice punished,—truly that commendation is peculiar to poetry and far off from history. For, indeed, poetry ever setteth virtue so out in her best colors, making Fortune her well-waiting handmaid, that one must needs be enamored of her. Well may you see Ulysses in a storm and in other hard plights; but they are but exercises of patience and magnanimity, to make them shine the more in the near following prosperity. And, of the contrary part, if evil men come to the stage, they ever go out—as the tragedy writer answered to one that misliked the show of such persons—so manacled as they little animate folks to follow them. But the historian, being captived to the truth of a foolish world, is many times a terror from well-doing, and an encouragement to unbridled wickedness. For see we not valiant Miltiades[55] rot in his fetters? The just Phocion[56] and the accomplished Socrates put to death like traitors? The cruel Severus[57] live prosperously? The

[53]See his *Epodes,* V, and *Satires,* I, viii.

[54]Whereas.

[55]The victor at Marathon. (Cf. Cicero, *Republic,* I, iii, 5.)

[56]See Plutarch's life of him.

[57]Septimius Severus (A. D. 193–211).

excellent Severus[58] miserably murdered? Sylla and Marius dying in their beds? Pompey and Cicero slain then, when they would have thought exile a happiness? See we not virtuous Cato[59] driven to kill himself, and rebel Caesar so advanced that his name yet, after sixteen hundred years, lasteth in the highest honor? And mark but even Caesar's own words of the forenamed Sylla—who in that only did honestly, to put down his dishonest tyranny—*literas nescivit:*[60] as if want of learning caused him to do well. He meant it not by poetry, which, not content with earthly plagues, deviseth new punishments in hell for tyrants; nor yet by philosophy, which teacheth *occidendos esse;*[61] but, no doubt, by skill in history, for that indeed can afford you Cypselus, Periander,[62] Phalaris,[63] Dionysius,[64] and I know not how many more of the same kennel, that speed well enough in their abominable injustice or usurpation.

I conclude, therefore, that he excelleth history, not only in furnishing the mind with knowledge, but in setting it forward to that which deserveth to be called and accounted good; which setting forward, and moving to well-doing, indeed setteth the laurel crown upon the poet as victorious, not only of the historian, but over the philosopher, howsoever in teaching it may be questionable. For suppose it be granted—that which I suppose with great reason may be denied—that the philosopher, in respect of his methodical proceeding, teach more perfectly than the poet, yet do I think that no man is so much φιλοφιλόσοφος[65] as to compare the philosopher in moving with the poet. And that moving is of a higher degree than teaching, it may by this appear, that it is well nigh both the cause and the effect of teaching; for who will be taught, if he be not moved with desire to be taught? And what so much good doth that teaching bring forth—I speak still of moral doctrine—as that it moveth one to do that which it doth teach? For, as Aristotle saith, it is not γνῶσις but πρᾶξις[66] must be the fruit; and how πρᾶξις cannot be, without being moved to practice, it is no hard matter to consider. The philosopher showeth you the way; he informeth you of the particularities, as well of the tediousness of the way, as of the pleasant lodging you shall have when your journey is ended, as of the many by-turnings that may divert you from your way; but this is to no man but to him that will read him, and read him with attentive, studious painfulness; which constant desire whosoever hath in him, hath already passed half the hardness of the way, and therefore is beholding to the philosopher but for the other half. Nay, truly, learned men have learnedly thought that where once reason hath so much overmastered passion as that the mind hath a free desire to do well, the inward light each mind hath in itself is as good as a philosopher's book; since in nature we know it is well to do well, and what is well and what is evil, although not in the words of art which philosophers bestow upon us; for out of natural conceit the philosophers drew it. But to be moved to do that which we know, or to be moved with desire to know, *hoc opus, hic labor est.*[67]

Now therein of all sciences—I speak still of human and according to the human conceit—is our poet the monarch. For he doth not only show the way, but giveth so sweet a prospect into the way as will entice any man to enter into it. Nay, he doth, as if your journey should lie through a fair vineyard, at the very first give you a cluster of grapes, that full of that taste you may long to pass further. He beginneth not with obscure definitions, which must blur the margent with interpretations, and load the memory with doubtfulness. But he cometh to you with words set in delightful proportion, either accompanied with, or prepared for, the well-enchanting skill of music; and with a tale, forsooth, he cometh unto you, with a tale which holdeth children from play and old

[58]Alexander Severus (A. D. 222–235).

[59]Cato of Utica.

[60]Was an ignorant fellow.

[61]That they are to be slain.

[62]Concerning both see Herodotus, V, 92.

[63]Tyrant of Agrigentum. (Cf. Cicero, *De Officiis,* II, vii, 26.)

[64]Tyrant of Syracuse. (Cf. Cicero, *Tusc. Disp.,* V, 20.)

[65]A friend to the philosopher.

[66]Not knowledge but practice.

[67]This is the task, this is the struggle (*Aeneid,* VI, 129).

men from the chimney-corner, and, pretending no more, doth intend the winning of the mind from wickedness to virtue; even as the child is often brought to take most wholesome things by hiding them in such other as have a pleasant taste,—which, if one should begin to tell them the nature of the aloes or rhubarb they should receive, would sooner take their physic at their ears than at their mouth. So is it in men, most of which are childish in the best things, till they be cradled in their graves,—glad they will be to hear the tales of Hercules, Achilles, Cyrus, Aeneas; and, hearing them, must needs hear the right description of wisdom, valor, and justice; which, if they had been barely, that is to say philosophically, set out, they would swear they be brought to school again.

That imitation whereof poetry is hath the most conveniency to nature of all other; insomuch that, as Aristotle saith, those things which in themselves are horrible, as cruel battles, unnatural monsters, are made in poetical imitation delightful. Truly, I have known men that even with reading *Amadis de Gaule,* which, God knoweth, wanteth much of a perfect poesy, have found their hearts moved to the exercise of courtesy, liberality, and especially courage. Who readeth Aeneas carrying old Anchises on his back, that wisheth not it were his fortune to perform so excellent an act? Whom do not those words of Turnus move, the tale of Turnus having planted his image in the imagination:

Fugientem haec terra videbit?
Usque adeone mori miserum est?[68]

Where the philosophers, as they scorn to delight, so must they be content little to move—saving wrangling whether virtue be the chief or the only good, whether the contemplative or the active life do excel—which Plato and Boethius well knew, and therefore made Mistress Philosophy very often borrow the masking raiment of Poesy. For even those hard-hearted evil men who think virtue a school-name, and know no other good but *indulgere genio,*[69] and therefore despise the austere admonitions of the philosopher, and feel not the inward reason they stand upon, yet will be content to be delighted, which is all the good-fellow poet seemeth to promise; and so steal to see the form of goodness—which seen, they cannot but love—ere themselves be aware, as if they took a medicine of cherries.

Infinite proofs of the strange effects of this poetical invention might be alleged; only two shall serve, which are so often remembered as I think all men know them. The one of Menenius Agrippa,[70] who, when the whole people of Rome had resolutely divided themselves from the senate, with apparent show of utter ruin, though he were, for that time, an excellent orator, came not among them upon trust either of figurative speeches or cunning insinuations, and much less with far-fet[71] maxims of philosophy, which, especially if they were Platonic, they must have learned geometry before they could well have conceived; but, forsooth, he behaves himself like a homely and familiar poet. He telleth them a tale, that there was a time when all the parts of the body made a mutinous conspiracy against the belly, which they thought devoured the fruits of each other's labor; they concluded they would let so unprofitable a spender starve. In the end, to be short—for the tale is notorious, and as notorious that it was a tale—with punishing the belly they plagued themselves. This, applied by him, wrought such effect in the people as I never read that ever words brought forth but then so sudden and so good an alteration; for upon reasonable conditions a perfect reconcilement ensued.

The other is of Nathan the prophet,[72] who, when the holy David had so far forsaken God as to confirm adultery with murder, when he was to do the tenderest office of a friend, in laying his own shame before his eyes,—sent by God to call again so chosen a servant, how doth he it but by telling of a man whose beloved lamb was ungratefully taken from his bosom? The application

[68] Shall this land see Turnus a fugitive? Is it so passing hard to die? (*Aeneid,* XII, 645–646.)

[69] To give their genius free play (Persius, *Satires,* V, 151).

[70] See Livy, II, 32.

[71] Far-fetched.

[72] See II Samuel, 12.

most divinely true, but the discourse itself feigned; which made David (I speak of the second and instrumental cause) as in a glass to see his own filthiness, as that heavenly Psalm of Mercy well testifieth.

By these, therefore, examples and reasons, I think it may be manifest that the poet with that same hand of delight doth draw the mind more effectually than any other art doth. And so a conclusion not unfitly ensueth: that as virtue is the most excellent resting-place for all worldly learning to make his end of, so poetry, being the most familiar to teach it, and most princely to move towards it, in the most excellent work is the most excellent workman.

But I am content not only to decipher him by his works—although works in commendation or dispraise must ever hold a high authority—but more narrowly will examine his parts; so that, as in a man, though all together may carry a presence full of majesty and beauty, perchance in some one defectious piece we may find a blemish.

Now in his parts, kinds, or species, as you list to term them, it is to be noted that some poesies have coupled together two or three kinds,—as tragical and comical, whereupon is risen the tragi-comical; some, in the like manner, have mingled prose and verse, as Sannazaro[73] and Boethius;[74] some have mingled matters heroical and pastoral; but that cometh all to one in this question, for, if severed they be good, the conjunction cannot be hurtful. Therefore, perchance forgetting some, and leaving some as needless to be remembered, it shall not be amiss in a word to cite the special kinds, to see what faults may be found in the right use of them.

Is it then the pastoral poem which is misliked?—for perchance where the hedge is lowest they will soonest leap over. Is the poor pipe disdained, which sometimes out of Meliboeus' mouth can show the misery of people under hard lords and ravening soldiers, and again, by Tityrus, what blessedness is derived to them that lie lowest from the goodness of them that sit highest? sometimes, under the pretty tales of wolves and sheep, can include the whole considerations of wrongdoing and patience; sometimes show that contention for trifles can get but a trifling victory; where perchance a man may see that even Alexander and Darius, when they strave who should be cock of this world's dunghill, the benefit they got was that the after-livers may say:

Haec memini et victum frustra contendere Thyrsim;
Ex illo Corydon, Corydon est tempore nobis.[75]

Or is it the lamenting elegiac, which in a kind heart would move rather pity than blame; who bewaileth, with the great philosopher Heraclitus, the weakness of mankind and the wretchedness of the world; who surely is to be praised, either for compassionate accompanying just causes of lamentation, or for rightly painting out how weak be the passions of woefulness?

Is it the bitter but wholesome iambic, who rubs the galled mind, in making shame the trumpet of villainy with bold and open crying out against naughtiness?

Or the satiric? who

Omne vafer vitium ridenti tangit amico;[76]

who sportingly never leaveth till he make a man laugh at folly, and at length ashamed to laugh at himself, which he cannot avoid without avoiding the folly; who, while *circum praecordia ludit,*[77] giveth us to feel how many headaches a passionate life bringeth us to,—how, when all is done,

Est Ulubris, animus si nos non deficit aequus.[78]

No, perchance it is the comic; whom naughty play-makers and stage-keepers have justly made odious. To the argument of abuse I will answer after. Only thus much now is to be said, that the comedy is an imitation of the common errors of our life,

[73]Neapolitan scholar and poet (1458–1530). Sidney refers to his *Arcadia*.

[74]In his *Consolation of Philosophy*.

[75]These verses I remember, and how the vanquished Thyrsis vainly strove; from that day it has been with us Corydon, none but Corydon (Virgil, *Eclogues*, VII, 69–70).

[76]Cunningly probes every fault while making his friend laugh (Persius, *Sat.*, I, 116).

[77]He plays about the heart-strings (*Ibid.*, 117).

[78]Even Ulubrae may be a happy place of abode, if we preserve a balanced mind. (The line cannot be translated without expanding it. Horace, *Epistles*, I, xi, 30.)

which he representeth in the most ridiculous and scornful sort that may be, so as it is impossible that any beholder can be content to be such a one. Now, as in geometry the oblique must be known as well as the right, and in arithmetic the odd as well as the even; so in the actions of our life who seeth not the filthiness of evil wanteth a great foil to perceive the beauty of virtue. This doth the comedy handle so, in our private and domestical matters, as with hearing it we get, as it were, an experience what is to be looked for of a niggardly Demea, of a crafty Davus, of a flattering Gnatho, of a vain-glorious Thraso;[79] and not only to know what effects are to be expected, but to know who be such, by the signifying badge given them by the comedian. And little reason hath any man to say that men learn evil by seeing it so set out; since, as I said before, there is no man living but by the force truth hath in nature, no sooner seeth these men play their parts but wisheth them *in pistrinum,*[80] although perchance the sack of his own faults lie so behind his back that he seeth not himself to dance the same measure,—whereto yet nothing can more open his eyes than to find his own actions contemptibly set forth.

So that the right use of comedy will, I think, by nobody be blamed, and much less of the high and excellent tragedy that openeth the greatest wounds, and showeth forth the ulcers that are covered with tissue; that maketh kings fear to be tyrants, and tyrants manifest their tyrannical humors; that with stirring the effects of admiration and commiseration teacheth the uncertainty of this world, and upon how weak foundations gilden roofs are builded; that maketh us know:

Qui sceptra saevus duro imperio regit,
Timet timentes, metus in auctorem redit.[81]

But how much it can move, Plutarch yieldeth a notable testimony of the abominable tyrant Alexander Pheraeus;[82] from whose eyes a tragedy, well made and represented, drew abundance of tears, who without all pity had murdered infinite numbers, and some of his own blood; so as he that was not ashamed to make matters for tragedies, yet could not resist the sweet violence of a tragedy. And if it wrought no further good in him, it was that he, in despite of himself, withdrew himself from hearkening to that which might mollify his hardened heart. But it is not the tragedy they do mislike, for it were too absurd to cast out so excellent a representation of whatsoever is most worthy to be learned.

Is it the lyric that most displeaseth, who with his tuned lyre and well-accorded voice, giveth praise, the reward of virtue, to virtuous acts; who giveth moral precepts and natural problems; who sometimes raiseth up his voice to the height of the heavens, in singing the lauds of the immortal God? Certainly I must confess mine own barbarousness; I never heard the old song of Percy and Douglas that I found not my heart moved more than with a trumpet; and yet it is sung but by some blind crowder,[83] with no rougher voice than rude style; which being so evil appareled in the dust and cobwebs of that uncivil age, what would it work, trimmed in the gorgeous eloquence of Pindar? In Hungary I have seen it the manner at all feasts, and other such meetings, to have songs of their ancestors' valor, which that right soldier-like nation think the chiefest kindlers of brave courage. The incomparable Lacedaemonians did not only carry that kind of music ever with them to the field, but even at home as such songs were made, so were they all content to be singers of them; when the lusty men were to tell what they did, the old men what they had done, and the young men what they would do. And where a man may say that Pindar many times praiseth highly victories of small moment, matters rather of sport than virtue; as it may be answered it was the fault of the poet, and not of the poetry, so indeed the chief fault was in the time and custom of the Greeks, who set those toys at so high a price that Philip of Macedon reckoned a horse-race won at Olympus[84] among his three fearful felicities. But as

[79] All characters in the plays of Terence.

[80] In the mill (the place of punishment, as one learns from Plautus and Terence, for troublesome slaves).

[81] The savage tyrant who governs his peoples harshly fears those who fear him, and thus fear recoils upon the author of fear (Seneca, *Oedipus,* 705–706).

[82] In his *Life of Pelopidas,* 29.

[83] Fiddler.

[84] I. e., Olympia.

the unimitable Pindar often did, so is that kind most capable and most fit to awake the thoughts from the sleep of idleness, to embrace honorable enterprises.

There rests the heroical, whose very name, I think, should daunt all backbiters. For by what conceit can a tongue be directed to speak evil of that which draweth with it no less champions than Achilles, Cyrus, Aeneas, Turnus, Tydeus,[85] Rinaldo?[86] who doth not only teach and move to a truth, but teacheth and moveth to the most high and excellent truth; who maketh magnanimity and justice shine through all misty fearfulness and foggy desires; who, if the saying of Plato and Tully be true, that who could see virtue would be wonderfully ravished with the love of her beauty, this man setteth her out to make her more lovely, in her holiday apparel, to the eye of any that will deign not to disdain until they understand. But if anything be already said in the defense of sweet poetry, all concurreth to the maintaining the heroical, which is not only a kind, but the best and most accomplished kind of poetry. For, as the image of each action stirreth and instructeth the mind, so the lofty image of such worthies most inflameth the mind with desire to be worthy, and informs with counsel how to be worthy. Only let Aeneas be worn in the tablet of your memory, how he governeth himself in the ruin of his country; in the preserving his old father, and carrying away his religious ceremonies; in obeying the god's commandment to leave Dido, though not only all passionate kindness, but even the human consideration of virtuous gratefulness, would have craved other of him; how in storms, how in sports, how in war, how in peace, how a fugitive, how victorious, how besieged, how besieging, how to strangers, how to allies, how to enemies, how to his own; lastly, how in his inward self, and how in his outward government; and I think, in a mind most prejudiced with a prejudicating humor, he will be found in excellency fruitful,—yea, even as Horace saith, *melius Chrysippo et Crantore*.[87] But truly I imagine it falleth out with these poet-whippers as with some good women who often are sick, but in faith they cannot tell where. So the name of poetry is odious to them, but neither his cause nor effects, neither the sum that contains him nor the particularities descending from him, give any fast handle to their carping dispraise.

Since, then, poetry is of all human learnings the most ancient and of most fatherly antiquity, as from whence other learnings have taken their beginnings; since it is so universal that no learned nation doth despise it, nor barbarous nation is without it; since both Roman and Greek gave divine names unto it, the one of "prophesying," the other of "making," and that indeed that name of "making" is fit for him, considering that whereas other arts retain themselves within their subject, and receive, as it were, their being from it, the poet only bringeth his own stuff, and doth not learn a conceit out of a matter, but maketh matter for a conceit; since neither his description nor his end containeth any evil, the thing described cannot be evil; since his effects be so good as to teach goodness, and delight the learners of it; since therein—namely in moral doctrine, the chief of all knowledges—he doth not only far pass the historian, but for instructing is well nigh comparable to the philosopher, and for moving leaveth him behind him; since the Holy Scripture, wherein there is no uncleanness, hath whole parts in it poetical, and that even our Savior Christ vouchsafed to use the flowers of it; since all his kinds are not only in their united forms, but in their several dissections fully commendable; I think, and think I think rightly, the laurel crown appointed for triumphant captains doth worthily, of all other learnings, honor the poet's triumph.

But because we have ears as well as tongues, and that the lightest reasons that may be will seem to weigh greatly if nothing be put in the counter-balance, let us hear, and, as well as we can, ponder, what objections be made against this art, which may be worthy either of yielding or answering.

First, truly, I note not only in these μισομούσοι, poet-haters, but in all that kind of people who seek a praise by dispraising others, that they do prodigally spend a great

[85] See *Iliad*, IV.

[86] See Tasso's *Jerusalem Delivered.*

[87] Better than Chrysippus and Crantor (*Epistles*, I, ii, 4).

many wandering words in quips and scoffs, carping and taunting at each thing which, by stirring the spleen, may stay the brain from a through-beholding the worthiness of the subject. Those kind of objections, as they are full of a very idle easiness—since there is nothing of so sacred a majesty but that an itching tongue may rub itself upon it—so deserve they no other answer, but, instead of laughing at the jest, to laugh at the jester. We know a playing wit can praise the discretion of an ass, the comfortableness of being in debt, and the jolly commodity of being sick of the plague. So of the contrary side, if we will turn Ovid's verse,

Ut lateat virtus proximitate mali,[88]

"that good lie hid in nearness of the evil," Agrippa[89] will be as merry in showing the vanity of science as Erasmus[90] was in commending of folly; neither shall any man or matter escape some touch of these smiling railers. But for Erasmus and Agrippa, they had another foundation than the superficial part would promise. Marry, these other pleasant fault-finders, who will correct the verb before they understand the noun, and confute others' knowledge before they confirm their own, I would have them only remember that scoffing cometh not of wisdom; so as the best title in true English they get with their merriments is to be called good fools,—for so have our grave forefathers ever termed that humorous kind of jesters.

But that which giveth greatest scope to their scorning humor is riming and versing. It is already said, and as I think truly said, it is not riming and versing that maketh poesy. One may be a poet without versing, and a versifier without poetry. But yet presuppose it were inseparable—as indeed it seemeth Scaliger[91] judgeth—truly it were an inseparable commendation. For if *oratio* next to *ratio*, speech next to reason, be the greatest gift bestowed upon mortality, that cannot be praiseless which doth most polish that blessing of speech; which considereth each word, not only as a man may say by his forcible quality, but by his best-measured quantity; carrying even in themselves a harmony,—without, perchance, number, measure, order, proportion be in our time grown odious.

But lay aside the just praise it hath by being the only fit speech for music—music, I say, the most divine striker of the senses—thus much is undoubtedly true, that if reading be foolish without remembering, memory being the only treasurer of knowledge, those words which are fittest for memory are likewise most convenient for knowledge. Now that verse far exceedeth prose in the knitting up of the memory, the reason is manifest; the words, besides their delight, which hath a great affinity to memory, being so set, as one cannot be lost but the whole work fails; which, accusing itself, calleth the remembrance back to itself, and so most strongly confirmeth it. Besides, one word so, as it were, begetting another, as, be it in rime or measured verse, by the former a man shall have a near guess to the follower. Lastly, even they that have taught the art of memory have showed nothing so apt for it as a certain room divided into many places, well and throughly known; now that hath the verse in effect perfectly, every word having his natural seat, which seat must needs make the word remembered. But what needeth more in a thing so known to all men? Who is it that ever was a scholar that doth not carry away some verses of Virgil, Horace, or Cato, which in his youth he learned, and even to his old age serve him for hourly lessons? as:

Percontatorem fugito, nam garrulus idem est.
Dum sibi quisque placet, credula turba sumus.[92]

But the fitness it hath for memory is notably proved by all delivery of arts, wherein, for the most part, from grammar to logic, mathematic, physic, and the rest, the rules chiefly necessary to be borne away are compiled in

[88] *Art of Love,* II, 662.

[89] Henry Cornelius Agrippa (1486–1535), German scholar, whose treatise *On the Vanity of Arts and Sciences* (written in Latin) was published in 1527.

[90] His *Praise of Folly* was written in 1509.

[91] Julius Caesar Scaliger (1484–1558), Italian humanist. His *Poetics,* one of the important sources of Sidney's *Defense,* was published in 1561.

[92] Avoid a curious man; he is sure to be a gossip (Horace, *Epistles,* I, xviii, 69). And: While each one is satisfying himself, we are ever a credulous set (Ovid, *Rem. Love,* 686).

verses. So that verse being in itself sweet and orderly, and being best for memory, the only handle of knowledge, it must be in jest that any man can speak against it.

Now then go we to the most important imputations laid to the poor poets; for aught I can yet learn they are these:

First, that there being many other more fruitful knowledges, a man might better spend his time in them than in this.

Secondly, that it is the mother of lies.

Thirdly, that it is the nurse of abuse, infecting us with many pestilent desires, with a siren's sweetness drawing the mind to the serpent's tail of sinful fancies,—and herein especially comedies give the largest field to ear,[93] as Chaucer saith; how, both in other nations and in ours, before poets did soften us, we were full of courage, given to martial exercises, the pillars of manlike liberty, and not lulled asleep in shady idleness with poets' pastimes.

And, lastly and chiefly, they cry out with an open mouth, as if they had overshot Robin Hood, that Plato banished them out of his Commonwealth. Truly this is much, if there be much truth in it.

First, to the first, that a man might better spend his time is a reason indeed; but it doth, as they say, but *petere principium*.[94] For if it be, as I affirm, that no learning is so good as that which teacheth and moveth to virtue, and that none can both teach and move thereto so much as poesy, then is the conclusion manifest that ink and paper cannot be to a more profitable purpose employed. And certainly, though a man should grant their first assumption, it should follow, me thinks, very unwillingly, that good is not good because better is better. But I still and utterly deny that there is sprung out of earth a more fruitful knowledge.

To the second, therefore, that they should be the principal liars, I answer paradoxically, but truly, I think truly, that of all writers under the sun the poet is the least liar; and though he would, as a poet can scarcely be a liar. The astronomer, with his cousin the geometrician, can hardly escape when they take upon them to measure the height of the stars. How often, think you, do the physicians lie, when they aver things good for sicknesses, which afterwards send Charon a great number of souls drowned in a potion before they come to his ferry? And no less of the rest which take upon them to affirm. Now for the poet, he nothing affirmeth, and therefore never lieth. For, as I take it, to lie is to affirm that to be true which is false; so as the other artists, and especially the historian, affirming many things, can, in the cloudy knowledge of mankind, hardly escape from many lies. But the poet, as I said before, never affirmeth. The poet never maketh any circles about your imagination, to conjure you to believe for true what he writeth. He citeth not authorities of other histories, but even for his entry calleth the sweet Muses to inspire into him a good invention; in troth, not laboring to tell you what is or is not, but what should or should not be. And therefore though he recount things not true, yet because he telleth them not for true he lieth not; without we will say that Nathan lied in his speech, before alleged, to David; which, as a wicked man durst scarce say, so think I none so simple would say that Aesop lied in the tales of his beasts; for who thinketh that Aesop wrote it for actually true, were well worthy to have his name chronicled among the beasts he writeth of. What child is there that, coming to a play, and seeing Thebes written in great letters upon an old door, doth believe that it is Thebes? If then a man can arrive at that child's-age, to know that the poet's persons and doings are but pictures what should be, and not stories what have been, they will never give the lie to things not affirmatively but allegorically and figuratively written. And therefore, as in history looking for truth, they may go away full-fraught with falsehood, so in poesy looking but for fiction, they shall use the narration but as an imaginative ground-plot of a profitable invention. But hereto is replied that the poets give names to men they write of, which argueth a conceit of an actual truth, and so, not being true, proveth a falsehood. And doth the lawyer lie then, when, under the names of John of the Stile, and John of the Nokes, he putteth his case?[95] But that is

[93]To plow. [94]Beg the question.

[95]Analogous to our "John Doe" legal actions.

easily answered: their naming of men is but to make their picture the more lively, and not to build any history. Painting men, they cannot leave men nameless. We see we cannot play at chess but that we must give names to our chess-men; and yet, me thinks, he were a very partial champion of truth that would say we lied for giving a piece of wood the reverend title of a bishop. The poet nameth Cyrus and Aeneas no other way than to show what men of their fames, fortunes, and estates should do.

Their third is, how much it abuseth men's wit, training it to wanton sinfulness and lustful love. For indeed that is the principal, if not the only, abuse I can hear alleged. They say the comedies rather teach than reprehend amorous conceits. They say the lyric is larded with passionate sonnets, the elegiac weeps the want of his mistress, and that even to the heroical Cupid hath ambitiously climbed. Alas! Love, I would thou couldst as well defend thyself as thou canst offend others! I would those on whom thou dost attend could either put thee away, or yield good reason why they keep thee! But grant love of beauty to be a beastly fault, although it be very hard, since only man, and no beast, hath that gift to discern beauty; grant that lovely name of Love to deserve all hateful reproaches, although even some of my masters the philosophers spent a good deal of their lamp-oil in setting forth the excellency of it; grant, I say, whatsoever they will have granted,—that not only love, but lust, but vanity, but, if they list, scurrility, possesseth many leaves of the poets' books; yet think I when this is granted, they will find their sentence may with good manners put the last words foremost, and not say that poetry abuseth man's wit, but that man's wit abuseth poetry. For I will not deny but that man's wit may make poesy, which should be εἰκαστική, which some learned have defined, figuring forth good things, to be φανταστική, which doth contrariwise infect the fancy with unworthy objects;[96] as the painter that should give to the eye either some excellent perspective, or some fine picture fit for building or fortification, or containing in it some notable example, as Abraham sacrificing his son Isaac, Judith killing Holofernes, David fighting with Goliath, may leave those, and please an ill-pleased eye with wanton shows of better-hidden matters. But what! shall the abuse of a thing make the right use odious? Nay, truly, though I yield that poesy may not only be abused, but that being abused, by the reason of his sweet charming force, it can do more hurt than any other army of words, yet shall it be so far from concluding that the abuse should give reproach to the abused, that contrariwise it is a good reason that whatsoever, being abused, doth most harm, being rightly used—and upon the right use each thing receiveth his title—doth most good. Do we not see the skill of physic, the best rampire[97] to our often-assaulted bodies, being abused, teach poison, the most violent destroyer? Doth not knowledge of law, whose end is to even and right all things, being abused, grow the crooked fosterer of horrible injuries? Doth not, to go in the highest, God's word abused breed heresy, and His name abused become blasphemy? Truly a needle cannot do much hurt, and as truly—with leave of ladies be it spoken—it cannot do much good. With a sword thou mayst kill thy father, and with a sword thou mayst defend thy prince and country. So that, as in their calling poets the fathers of lies they say nothing, so in this their argument of abuse they prove the commendation.

They allege herewith that before poets began to be in price our nation hath set their hearts' delight upon action, and not upon imagination; rather doing things worthy to be written, than writing things fit to be done. What that before-time was, I think scarcely Sphinx can tell; since no memory is so ancient that hath the precedence of poetry. And certain it is that, in our plainest homeliness, yet never was the Albion nation without poetry. Marry, this argument, though it be leveled against poetry, yet is it indeed a chain-shot[98] against all learning,—or bookishness, as they commonly term it. Of such mind were certain Goths, of whom it is

[96]This distinction is derived from Plato's *Sophist*, 235–236.

[97]Rampart, defense.

[98]Two cannon-balls connected by a chain to do more extensive damage.

written that having in the spoil of a famous city taken a fair library, one hangman—belike fit to execute the fruits of their wits—who had murdered a great number of bodies, would have set fire in it. "No," said another very gravely, "take heed what you do; for while they are busy about these toys, we shall with more leisure conquer their countries." This, indeed, is the ordinary doctrine of ignorance, and many words sometimes I have heard spent in it; but because this reason is generally against all learning, as well as poetry, or rather all learning but poetry; because it were too large a digression to handle, or at least too superfluous, since it is manifest that all government of action is to be gotten by knowledge, and knowledge best by gathering many knowledges, which is reading; I only, with Horace, to him that is of that opinion

Jubeo stultum esse libenter;[99]

for as for poetry itself, it is the freest from this objection, for poetry is the companion of the camps. I dare undertake Orlando Furioso or honest King Arthur will never displease a soldier; but the quiddity of *ens,* and *prima materia,*[100] will hardly agree with a corselet. And therefore, as I said in the beginning, even Turks and Tartars are delighted with poets. Homer, a Greek, flourished before Greece flourished; and if to a slight conjecture a conjecture may be opposed, truly it may seem that as by him their learned men took almost their first light of knowledge, so their active men received their first motions of courage. Only Alexander's example may serve, who by Plutarch is accounted of such virtue that Fortune was not his guide but his footstool; whose acts speak for him, though Plutarch did not; indeed the phoenix of warlike princes. This Alexander left his schoolmaster, living Aristotle, behind him, but took dead Homer with him. He put the philosopher Callisthenes to death, for his seeming philosophical, indeed mutinous, stubbornness; but the chief thing he was ever heard to wish for was that Homer had been alive. He well found he received more bravery of mind by the pattern of Achilles than by hearing the definition of fortitude. And therefore if Cato misliked Fulvius for carrying Ennius with him to the field, it may be answered that if Cato misliked it, the noble Fulvius liked it, or else he had not done it. For it was not the excellent Cato Uticensis, whose authority I would much more have reverenced; but it was the former,[101] in truth a bitter punisher of faults, but else a man that had never sacrificed to the Graces. He misliked and cried out upon all Greek learning; and yet, being fourscore years old, began to learn it, belike fearing that Pluto understood not Latin. Indeed, the Roman laws allowed no person to be carried to the wars but he that was in the soldiers' roll. And therefore though Cato misliked his unmustered person, he misliked not his work. And if he had, Scipio Nasica,[102] judged by common consent the best Roman, loved him. Both the other Scipio brothers, who had by their virtues no less surnames than of Asia and Afric, so loved him that they caused his body to be buried in their sepulcher. So as Cato's authority being but against his person, and that answered with so far greater than himself, is herein of no validity.

But now, indeed, my burthen is great, that Plato's name is laid upon me, whom, I must confess, of all philosophers I have ever esteemed most worthy of reverence; and with great reason, since of all philosophers he is the most poetical; yet if he will defile the fountain out of which his flowing streams have proceeded, let us boldly examine with what reasons he did it.

First, truly, a man might maliciously object that Plato, being a philosopher, was a natural enemy of poets. For, indeed, after the philosophers had picked out of the sweet mysteries of poetry the right discerning true points of knowledge, they forthwith, putting it in method, and making a school-art of

[99]Cheerfully bid him to be a fool. (This is Sidney's meaning. The words are altered from Horace, *Satires,* I, i, 63.)

[100]Metaphysical terms.

[101]I. e., Cato the Censor. Cato of Utica was his great-grandson.

[102]See Livy, XXIX, 14.

that which the poets did only teach by a divine delightfulness, beginning to spurn at their guides, like ungrateful prentices were not content to set up shops for themselves, but sought by all means to discredit their masters; which by the force of delight being barred them, the less they could overthrow them the more they hated them. For, indeed, they found for Homer seven cities strave who should have him for their citizen; where many cities banished philosophers, as not fit members to live among them. For only repeating certain of Euripides' verses, many Athenians had their lives saved of the Syracusans, where the Athenians themselves thought many philosophers unworthy to live. Certain poets, as Simonides and Pindar, had so prevailed with Hiero the First that of a tyrant they made him a just king; where Plato could do so little with Dionysius that he himself of a philosopher was made a slave. But who should do thus, I confess, should requite the objections made against poets with like cavilations against philosophers; as likewise one should do that should bid one read *Phaedrus* or *Symposium* in Plato, or the *Discourse of Love* in Plutarch, and see whether any poet do authorize abominable filthiness, as they do.

Again, a man might ask out of what commonwealth Plato doth banish them. In sooth, thence where he himself alloweth community of women.[103] So as belike this banishment grew not for effeminate wantonness, since little should poetical sonnets be hurtful when a man might have what woman he listed. But I honor philosophical instructions, and bless the wits which bred them, so as they be not abused, which is likewise stretched to poetry. Saint Paul himself, who yet, for the credit of poets, allegeth twice two poets, and one of them by the name of a prophet,[104] setteth a watchword upon philosophy,[105]—indeed upon the abuse. So doth Plato upon the abuse, not upon poetry. Plato found fault that the poets of his time filled the world with wrong opinions of the gods, making light tales of that unspotted essence, and therefore would not have the youth depraved with such opinions. Herein may much be said; let this suffice: the poets did not induce such opinions, but did imitate those opinions already induced. For all the Greek stories can well testify that the very religion of that time stood upon many and many-fashioned gods; not taught so by the poets, but followed according to their nature of imitation. Who list may read in Plutarch the discourses of Isis and Osiris, of the cause why oracles ceased, of the Divine Providence, and see whether the theology of that nation stood not upon such dreams,—which the poets indeed superstitiously observed; and truly, since they had not the light of Christ, did much better in it than the philosophers, who, shaking off superstition, brought in atheism.

Plato therefore, whose authority I had much rather justly construe than unjustly resist, meant not in general of poets, in those words of which Julius Scaliger saith, *Qua authoritate barbari quidam atque hispidi abuti velint ad poetas e republica exigendos;*[106] but only meant to drive out those wrong opinions of the Deity, whereof now, without further law, Christianity hath taken away all the hurtful belief, perchance, as he thought, nourished by the then esteemed poets. And a man need go no further than to Plato himself to know his meaning; who, in his dialogue called *Ion,* giveth high and rightly divine commendation unto poetry. So as Plato, banishing the abuse, not the thing, not banishing it, but giving due honor unto it, shall be our patron and not our adversary. For, indeed, I had much rather, since truly I may do it, show their mistaking of Plato, under whose lion's skin they would make an ass-like braying against poesy, than go about to overthrow his authority; whom, the wiser a man is, the more just cause he shall find to have in admiration; especially since he attributeth unto poesy more than myself do, namely to be a very inspiring of

[103] This statement and that which follows are very misleading.

[104] In Acts, 17:28 (Aratus, Cleanthes); Titus, 1:12 (Epimenides); I Corinthians, 15:33 (Menander). St. Paul does not name these poets, but quotes from them. The passage in Acts is found in both Aratus and Cleanthes.

[105] See Colossians, 2:8.

[106] Which authority [Plato's] certain rude and barbarous persons desire to abuse, in order to banish poets out of the commonwealth (*Poetics,* i, 2).

a divine force, far above man's wit, as in the forenamed dialogue is apparent.

Of the other side, who would show the honors have been by the best sort of judgments granted them, a whole sea of examples would present themselves: Alexanders, Caesars, Scipios, all favorers of poets; Laelius, called the Roman Socrates, himself a poet, so as part of *Heautontimoroumenos* in Terence was supposed to be made by him. And even the Greek Socrates, whom Apollo confirmed to be the only wise man, is said to have spent part of his old time in putting Aesop's *Fables* into verses; and therefore full evil should it become his scholar, Plato, to put such words in his master's mouth against poets. But what needs more? Aristotle writes the *Art of Poesy;* and why, if it should not be written? Plutarch teacheth the use to be gathered of them; and how, if they should not be read? And who reads Plutarch's either history or philosophy shall find he trimmeth both their garments with guards of poesy. But I list not to defend poesy with the help of his underling historiography. Let it suffice that it is a fit soil for praise to dwell upon; and what dispraise may set upon it, is either easily overcome, or transformed into just commendation.

So that since the excellencies of it may be so easily and so justly confirmed, and the low-creeping objections so soon trodden down: it not being an art of lies, but of true doctrine; not of effeminateness, but of notable stirring of courage; not of abusing man's wit, but of strengthening man's wit; not banished, but honored by Plato; let us rather plant more laurels for to engarland our poets' heads—which honor of being laureate, as besides them only triumphant captains were, is a sufficient authority to show the price they ought to be held in—than suffer the ill-savored breath of such wrong speakers once to blow upon the clear springs of poesy.

But since I have run so long a career in this matter, me thinks, before I give my pen a full stop, it shall be but a little more lost time to inquire why England, the mother of excellent minds, should be grown so hard a stepmother to poets; who certainly in wit ought to pass all others, since all only proceedeth from their wit, being indeed makers of themselves, not takers of others. How can I but exclaim,

Musa, mihi causas memora, quo numine laeso?[107]

Sweet poesy! that hath anciently had kings, emperors, senators, great captains, such as, besides a thousand others, David, Adrian,[108] Sophocles, Germanicus,[109] not only to favor poets, but to be poets; and of our nearer times can present for her patrons a Robert, King of Sicily;[110] the great King Francis of France;[111] King James of Scotland;[112] such cardinals as Bembus and Bibbiena;[113] such famous preachers and teachers as Beza and Melancthon;[114] so learned philosophers as Fracastorius[115] and Scaliger; so great orators as Pontanus and Muretus;[116] so piercing wits as George Buchanan;[117] so grave counselors as—besides many, but before all—that Hospital of France,[118] than whom, I think, that realm never brought forth a more accomplished judgment, more firmly builded upon virtue; I say these, with numbers of others, not only to read others' poesies but to poetize for others' reading. That poesy, thus embraced in all other places, should only find in our time a hard welcome in England, I think the very earth lamenteth it, and therefore decketh our soil with fewer laurels than it was accustomed. For heretofore poets have in England also flourished; and, which is to be noted, even in those times when the trumpet of Mars did sound loudest. And now that an over-faint quietness should seem to strew the house for poets, they are almost in as good reputation as the mountebanks at Venice. Truly even that, as of the

---

[107]O Muse, relate to me the causes, tell me in what had her will been offended? (*Aeneid*, I, 12.)

[108]Hadrian, Roman emperor (A. D. 76–138).

[109]Nephew and adopted son of the emperor Tiberius (15 B. C.–A. D. 19).

[110]Robert II of Anjou (1275–1343).

[111]Francis I (1494–1547).

[112]Probably James I (1394–1437).

[113]Bembus (1470–1547); Bibbiena (1470–1520).

[114]Beza (1519–1605); Melancthon (1497–1560).

[115]Lived 1483–1553, chiefly at Verona.

[116]French humanist (1526–1585).

[117]Scottish humanist (1506–1582).

[118]Michel de l'Hôpital (1504–1573), Chancellor of France.

one side it giveth great praise to poesy, which, like Venus—but to better purpose—hath rather be troubled in the net with Mars than enjoy the homely quiet of Vulcan; so serves it for a piece of a reason why they are less grateful to idle England, which now can scarce endure the pain of a pen. Upon this necessarily followeth that base men with servile wits undertake it, who think it enough if they can be rewarded of the printer. And so as Epaminondas is said with the honor of his virtue to have made an office, by his exercising it, which before was contemptible, to become highly respected; so these men, no more but setting their names to it, by their own disgracefulness disgrace the most graceful poesy. For now, as if all the Muses were got with child to bring forth bastard poets, without any commission they do post over the banks of Helicon, till they make their readers more weary than post-horses; while, in the mean time, they,

Queis meliore luto finxit praecordia Titan,[119]

are better content to suppress the outflowings of their wit than by publishing them to be accounted knights of the same order.

But I that, before ever I durst aspire unto the dignity, am admitted into the company of the paper-blurrers, do find the very true cause of our wanting estimation is want of desert, taking upon us to be poets in despite of Pallas. Now wherein we want desert were a thankworthy labor to express; but if I knew, I should have mended myself. But as I never desired the title, so have I neglected the means to come by it; only, overmastered by some thoughts, I yielded an inky tribute unto them. Marry, they that delight in poesy itself should seek to know what they do and how they do; and especially look themselves in an unflattering glass of reason, if they be inclinable unto it. For poesy must not be drawn by the ears, it must be gently led, or rather it must lead; which was partly the cause that made the ancient learned affirm it was a divine gift, and no human skill, since all other knowledges lie ready for any that hath strength of wit; a poet no industry can make if his own genius be not carried into it. And therefore is it an old proverb: *Orator fit, poeta nascitur.*[120] Yet confess I always that, as the fertilest ground must be manured, so must the highest-flying wit have a Daedalus to guide him. That Daedalus, they say, both in this and in other, hath three wings to bear itself up into the air of due commendation: that is, art, imitation, and exercise. But these, neither artificial rules nor imitative patterns, we much cumber ourselves withal. Exercise indeed we do, but that very fore-backwardly, for where we should exercise to know, we exercise as having known; and so is our brain delivered of much matter which never was begotten by knowledge. For there being two principal parts, matter to be expressed by words and words to express the matter, in neither we use art or imitation rightly. Our matter is *quodlibet*[121] indeed, though wrongly performing Ovid's verse,

Quicquid conabar dicere, versus erat,[122]

never marshaling it into any assured rank, that almost the readers cannot tell where to find themselves.

Chaucer, undoubtedly, did excellently in his *Troilus and Cressida;* of whom, truly, I know not whether to marvel more, either that he in that misty time could see so clearly, or that we in this clear age walk so stumblingly after him. Yet had he great wants, fit to be forgiven in so reverend antiquity. I account the *Mirror of Magistrates*[123] meetly furnished of beautiful parts; and in the Earl of Surrey's lyrics many things tasting of a noble birth, and worthy of a noble mind. The *Shepherd's Calendar*[124] hath much poetry in his eclogues indeed worthy the reading, if I be not deceived. That same framing of his style to an old rustic language I dare not allow, since neither Theocritus in Greek, Virgil in Latin, nor Sannazaro in Italian did affect it. Besides these, I do not remember to have seen but

[119]Whose hearts the Titan [Prometheus] has molded out of better clay (altered from Juvenal, *Satires,* XIV, 34–35).

[120]The orator is made, the poet is born.

[121]Indifferent.

[122]Whatever I tried to express turned out to be poetry (quoted inexactly from *Tristia,* IV, x, 26).

[123]First published in 1559.

[124]By Edmund Spenser. It was dedicated to Sidney.

few (to speak boldly) printed that have poetical sinews in them. For proof whereof, let but most of the verses be put in prose, and then ask the meaning, and it will be found that one verse did but beget another, without ordering at the first what should be at the last; which becomes a confused mass of words, with a tinkling sound of rime, barely accompanied with reason.

Our tragedies and comedies not without cause cried out against, observing rules neither of honest civility nor of skilful poetry, excepting *Gorboduc*[125] (again I say of those that I have seen); which notwithstanding as it is full of stately speeches and well-sounding phrases, climbing to the height of Seneca's style, and as full of notable morality, which it doth most delightfully teach, and so obtain the very end of poesy; yet in truth it is very defectious in the circumstances, which grieveth me, because it might not remain as an exact model of all tragedies. For it is faulty both in place and time, the two necessary companions of all corporal actions. For where the stage should always represent but one place, and the uttermost time presupposed in it should be, both by Aristotle's precept and common reason, but one day; there is both many days and many places inartificially imagined.

But if it be so in *Gorboduc,* how much more in all the rest? where you shall have Asia of the one side, and Afric of the other, and so many other under-kingdoms that the player, when he cometh in, must ever begin with telling where he is, or else the tale will not be conceived. Now ye shall have three ladies walk to gather flowers, and then we must believe the stage to be a garden. By and by we hear news of shipwreck in the same place, and then we are to blame if we accept it not for a rock. Upon the back of that comes out a hideous monster with fire and smoke, and then the miserable beholders are bound to take it for a cave. While in the mean time two armies fly in, represented with four swords and bucklers, and then what hard heart will not receive it for a pitched field?

[125]By Thomas Sackville, Lord Buckhurst (1536–1608) and Thomas Norton (1532–1584). First published in 1565.

Now of time they are much more liberal. For ordinary it is that two young princes[126] fall in love; after many traverses she is got with child, delivered of a fair boy; he is lost, groweth a man, falleth in love, and is ready to get another child,—and all this in two hours' space; which how absurd it is in sense even sense may imagine, and art hath taught, and all ancient examples justified, and at this day the ordinary players in Italy will not err in. Yet will some bring in an example of *Eunuchus*[127] in Terence, that containeth matter of two days, yet far short of twenty years. True it is, and so was it to be played in two days, and so fitted to the time it set forth. And though Plautus have in one place done amiss, let us hit with him, and not miss with him. But they will say, How then shall we set forth a story which containeth both many places and many times? And do they not know that a tragedy is tied to the laws of poesy, and not of history; not bound to follow the story, but having liberty either to feign a quite new matter, or to frame the history to the most tragical conveniency? Again, many things may be told which cannot be showed,—if they know the difference betwixt reporting and representing. As for example, I may speak, though I am here, of Peru, and in speech digress from that to the description of Calicut;[128] but in action I cannot represent it without Pacolet's horse.[129] And so was the manner the ancients took, by some *nuntius*[130] to recount things done in former time or other place.

Lastly, if they will represent a history, they must not, as Horace saith, begin *ab ovo,*[131] but they must come to the principal point of that one action which they will represent. By example this will be best expressed. I have a story of young Polydorus,[132] delivered for safety's sake, with

[126]Title applied to both sexes.

[127]A slip. Sidney meant to refer to the *Heautontimoroumenos* of Terence.

[128]In India.

[129]In the romance of *Valentine and Orson.*

[130]Messenger.

[131]From the very beginning (*Satires,* I, iii, 6; also *De Arte Poetica,* 147).

[132]Euripides, *Hecuba.*

great riches, by his father Priamus to Polymnestor, King of Thrace, in the Trojan war time. He, after some years, hearing the overthrow of Priamus, for to make the treasure his own murdereth the child; the body of the child is taken up by Hecuba; she, the same day, findeth a sleight to be revenged most cruelly of the tyrant. Where now would one of our tragedy-writers begin, but with the delivery of the child? Then should he sail over into Thrace, and so spend I know not how many years, and travel numbers of places. But where doth Euripides? Even with the finding of the body, leaving the rest to be told by the spirit of Polydorus. This needs no further to be enlarged; the dullest wit may conceive it.

But, besides these gross absurdities, how all their plays be neither right tragedies nor right comedies, mingling kings and clowns, not because the matter so carrieth it, but thrust in the clown by head and shoulders to play a part in majestical matters, with neither decency nor discretion; so as neither the admiration and commiseration, nor the right sportfulness, is by their mongrel tragi-comedy obtained. I know Apuleius did somewhat so,[133] but that is a thing recounted with space of time, not represented in one moment; and I know the ancients have one or two examples of tragi-comedies, as Plautus hath *Amphytrio*. But, if we mark them well, we shall find that they never, or very daintily, match hornpipes and funerals. So falleth it out that, having indeed no right comedy in that comical part of our tragedy, we have nothing but scurrility, unworthy of any chaste ears, or some extreme show of doltishness, indeed fit to lift up a loud laughter, and nothing else; where the whole tract of a comedy should be full of delight, as the tragedy should be still maintained in a well-raised admiration.

But our comedians think there is no delight without laughter, which is very wrong; for though laughter may come with delight, yet cometh it not of delight, as though delight should be the cause of laughter; but well may one thing breed both together. Nay, rather in themselves they have, as it were, a kind of contrariety. For delight we scarcely do, but in things that have a conveniency to ourselves, or to the general nature; laughter almost ever cometh of things most disproportioned to ourselves and nature. Delight hath a joy in it either permanent or present; laughter hath only a scornful tickling. For example, we are ravished with delight to see a fair woman, and yet are far from being moved to laughter. We laugh at deformed creatures, wherein certainly we cannot delight. We delight in good chances; we laugh at mischances. We delight to hear the happiness of our friends and country, at which he were worthy to be laughed at that would laugh. We shall, contrarily, laugh sometimes to find a matter quite mistaken and go down the hill against the bias, in the mouth of some such men, as for the respect of them one shall be heartily sorry he cannot choose but laugh, and so is rather pained than delighted with laughter. Yet deny I not but that they may go well together. For as in Alexander's picture well set out we delight without laughter, and in twenty mad antics we laugh without delight; so in Hercules, painted, with his great beard and furious countenance, in woman's attire, spinning at Omphale's commandment, it breedeth both delight and laughter; for the representing of so strange a power in love, procureth delight, and the scornfulness of the action stirreth laughter.

But I speak to this purpose, that all the end of the comical part be not upon such scornful matters as stir laughter only, but mixed with it that delightful teaching which is the end of poesy. And the great fault, even in that point of laughter, and forbidden plainly by Aristotle, is that they stir laughter in sinful things, which are rather execrable than ridiculous; or in miserable, which are rather to be pitied than scorned. For what is it to make folks gape at a wretched beggar or a beggarly clown, or, against law of hospitality, to jest at strangers because they speak not English so well as we do? what do we learn? since it is certain:

> *Nil habet infelix paupertas durius in se*
> *Quam quod ridiculos homines facit.*[134]

[133] In his *Metamorphoses.*

[134] Poverty, bitter though it be, has no sharper pang than this, that it makes men ridiculous (Juvenal, *Satires,* III, 152–153).

But rather a busy loving courtier; a heartless threatening Thraso; a self-wise-seeming schoolmaster; a wry-transformed traveler: these if we saw walk in stage-names, which we play naturally, therein were delightful laughter and teaching delightfulness,—as in the other, the tragedies of Buchanan do justly bring forth a divine admiration.

But I have lavished out too many words of this play-matter. I do it, because as they are excelling parts of poesy, so is there none so much used in England, and none can be more pitifully abused; which, like an unmannerly daughter, showing a bad education, causeth her mother Poesy's honesty to be called in question.

Other sorts of poetry almost have we none, but that lyrical kind of songs and sonnets, which, Lord if He gave us so good minds, how well it might be employed, and with how heavenly fruits both private and public, in singing the praises of the immortal beauty, the immortal goodness of that God who giveth us hands to write, and wits to conceive!—of which we might well want words, but never matter; of which we could turn our eyes to nothing, but we should ever have new-budding occasions.

But truly, many of such writings as come under the banner of unresistible love, if I were a mistress, would never persuade me they were in love; so coldly they apply fiery speeches, as men that had rather read lovers' writings, and so caught up certain swelling phrases—which hang together like a man which once told me the wind was at northwest and by south, because he would be sure to name winds enough—than that in truth they feel those passions, which easily, as I think, may be bewrayed by that same forcibleness, or *energia* (as the Greeks call it) of the writer. But let this be a sufficient, though short note, that we miss the right use of the material point of poesy.

Now for the outside of it, which is words, or (as I may term it) diction, it is even well worse, so is that honey-flowing matron eloquence appareled, or rather disguised, in a courtesan-like painted affectation: one time with so far-fet words, that many seem monsters—but must seem strangers—to any poor Englishman; another time with coursing of a letter, as if they were bound to follow the method of a dictionary; another time with figures and flowers extremely winter-starved.

But I would this fault were only peculiar to versifiers, and had not as large possession among prose-printers, and, which is to be marveled, among many scholars, and, which is to be pitied, among some preachers. Truly I could wish—if at least I might be so bold to wish in a thing beyond the reach of my capacity—the diligent imitators of Tully and Demosthenes (most worthy to be imitated) did not so much keep Nizolian[135] paper-books of their figures and phrases, as by attentive translation, as it were devour them whole, and make them wholly theirs. For now they cast sugar and spice upon every dish that is served to the table; like those Indians, not content to wear ear-rings at the fit and natural place of the ears, but they will thrust jewels through their nose and lips, because they will be sure to be fine. Tully, when he was to drive out Catiline as it were with a thunderbolt of eloquence, often used that figure of repetition, as *Vivit. Vivit? Immo vero etiam in senatum venit,*[136] *etc.* Indeed, inflamed with a well-grounded rage, he would have his words, as it were, double out of his mouth; and so do that artificially which we see men in choler do naturally. And we, having noted the grace of those words, hale them in sometime to a familiar epistle, when it were too much choler to be choleric. How well store of *similiter*[137] cadences doth sound with the gravity of the pulpit, I would but invoke Demosthenes' soul to tell, who with a rare daintiness useth them. Truly they have made me think of the sophister that with too much subtility would prove two eggs three, and though he might be counted a sophister, had none for his labor. So these men bringing in such a kind of eloquence, well may they obtain an opinion of a seeming fineness, but persuade few,—which should be the end of their fineness.

Now for similitudes in certain printed

---

[135]The Italian Marius Nizolius (1498–1566) compiled a Ciceronian lexicon.

[136]He lives. He lives? Yes, he comes even into the senate (Cicero, *Catiline,* I, 2).

[137]Similar.

discourses, I think all herbarists, all stories of beasts, fowls, and fishes are rifled up, that they may come in multitudes to wait upon any of our conceits, which certainly is as absurd a surfeit to the ears as is possible. For the force of a similitude not being to prove any thing to a contrary disputer, but only to explain to a willing hearer; when that is done, the rest is a most tedious prattling, rather overswaying the memory from the purpose whereto they were applied, than any whit informing the judgment, already either satisfied or by similitudes not to be satisfied.

For my part, I do not doubt, when Antonius and Crassus, the great forefathers of Cicero in eloquence, the one (as Cicero testifieth of them) pretended not to know art, the other not to set by it, because with a plain sensibleness they might win credit of popular ears, which credit is the nearest step to persuasion, which persuasion is the chief mark of oratory,—I do not doubt, I say, but that they used these knacks very sparingly; which who doth generally use any man may see doth dance to his own music, and so be noted by the audience more careful to speak curiously than truly. Undoubtedly (at least to my opinion undoubtedly) I have found in divers small-learned courtiers a more sound style than in some professors of learning; of which I can guess no other cause, but that the courtier following that which by practice he findeth fittest to nature, therein, though he know it not, doth according to art, though not by art; where the other, using art to show art and not to hide art—as in these cases he should do—flieth from nature, and indeed abuseth art.

But what! me thinks I deserve to be pounded for straying from poetry to oratory. But both have such an affinity in the wordish consideration that I think this digression will make my meaning receive the fuller understanding:—which is not to take upon me to teach poets how they should do, but only, finding myself sick among the rest, to show some one or two spots of the common infection grown among the most part of writers; that, acknowledging ourselves somewhat awry, we may bend to the right use both of matter and manner: whereto our language giveth us great occasion, being, indeed, capable of any excellent exercising of it.

I know some will say it is a mingled language. And why not so much the better, taking the best of both the other? Another will say it wanteth grammar. Nay, truly, it hath that praise that it wanteth not grammar. For grammar it might have, but it needs it not; being so easy in itself, and so void of those cumbersome differences of cases, genders, moods, and tenses, which, I think, was a piece of the Tower of Babylon's curse, that a man should be put to school to learn his mother-tongue. But for the uttering sweetly and properly the conceits of the mind, which is the end of speech, that hath it equally with any other tongue in the world; and is particularly happy in compositions of two or three words together, near the Greek, far beyond the Latin,—which is one of the greatest beauties can be in a language.

Now of versifying there are two sorts, the one ancient, the other modern. The ancient marked the quantity of each syllable, and according to that framed his verse; the modern observing only number, with some regard of the accent, the chief life of it standeth in that like sounding of the words which we call rime. Whether of these be the more excellent would bear many speeches; the ancient no doubt more fit for music, both words and tune observing quantity; and more fit lively to express divers passions, by the low or lofty sound of the well-weighed syllable. The latter likewise with his rime striketh a certain music to the ear; and, in fine, since it doth delight, though by another way, it obtaineth the same purpose; there being in either, sweetness, and wanting in neither, majesty. Truly the English, before any other vulgar language I know, is fit for both sorts. For, for the ancient, the Italian is so full of vowels that it must ever be cumbered with elisions; the Dutch so, of the other side, with consonants, that they cannot yield the sweet sliding fit for a verse. The French in his whole language hath not one word that hath his accent in the last syllable saving two, called antepenultima, and little more hath the

Spanish; and therefore very gracelessly may they use dactyls. The English is subject to none of these defects. Now for rime, though we do not observe quantity, yet we observe the accent very precisely, which other languages either cannot do, or will not do so absolutely. That caesura, or breathing-place in the midst of the verse, neither Italian nor Spanish have; the French and we never almost fail of.

Lastly, even the very rime itself the Italian cannot put in the last syllable, by the French named the masculine rime, but still in the next to the last, which the French call the female, or the next before that, which the Italians term *sdrucciola.* The example of the former is *buono:suono;* of the *sdrucciola* is *femina:semina.* The French, of the other side, hath both the male, as *bon: son,* and the female, as *plaise:taise;* but the *sdrucciola* he hath not. Where the English hath all three, as *due:true, father:rather, motion:potion;* with much more which might be said, but that already I find the triflingness of this discourse is much too much enlarged.

So that since the ever praiseworthy poesy is full of virtue-breeding delightfulness, and void of no gift that ought to be in the noble name of learning; since the blames laid against it are either false or feeble; since the cause why it is not esteemed in England is the fault of poet-apes, not poets; since, lastly, our tongue is most fit to honor poesy, and to be honored by poesy; I conjure you all that have had the evil luck to read this ink-wasting toy of mine, even in the name of the Nine Muses, no more to scorn the sacred mysteries of poesy; no more to laugh at the name of poets, as though they were next inheritors to fools; no more to jest at the reverend title of "a rimer"; but to believe, with Aristotle, that they were the ancient treasurers of the Grecians' divinity; to believe, with Bembus, that they were first bringers-in of all civility; to believe, with Scaliger, that no philosopher's precepts can sooner make you an honest man than the reading of Virgil; to believe, with Clauserus, the translator of Cornutus, that it pleased the Heavenly Deity by Hesiod and Homer, under the veil of fables, to give us all knowledge, logic, rhetoric, philosophy natural and moral, and *quid non?*[138] to believe, with me, that there are many mysteries contained in poetry which of purpose were written darkly, lest by profane wits it should be abused; to believe, with Landino,[139] that they are so beloved of the gods that whatsoever they write proceeds of a divine fury; lastly, to believe themselves, when they tell you they will make you immortal by their verses.

Thus doing, your name shall flourish in the printers' shops. Thus doing, you shall be of kin to many a poetical preface. Thus doing, you shall be most fair, most rich, most wise, most all; you shall dwell upon superlatives. Thus doing, though you be *libertino patre natus,*[140] you shall suddenly grow *Herculea proles,*[141]

Si quid mea carmina possunt.[142]

Thus doing, your soul shall be placed with Dante's Beatrice or Virgil's Anchises.

But if—fie of such a but!—you be born so near the dull-making cataract of Nilus, that you cannot hear the planet-like music of poetry; if you have so earth-creeping a mind that it cannot lift itself up to look to the sky of poetry, or rather, by a certain rustical disdain, will become such a mome[143] as to be a Momus of poetry; then, though I will not wish unto you the ass's ears of Midas, nor to be driven by a poet's verses, as Bubonax[144] was, to hang himself; nor to be rimed to death, as is said to be done in Ireland; yet thus much curse I must send you in the behalf of all poets:—that while you live you live in love, and never get favor for lacking skill of a sonnet; and when you die, your memory die from the earth for want of an epitaph.

[138] What not?

[139] Florentine humanist (1424–1504).

[140] The son of a freedman (Horace, *Satires,* I, vi, 6).

[141] Herculean offspring.

[142] If my song can aught avail (*Aeneid,* IX, 446).

[143] Fool.

[144] "Sidney is referring to the tale of *Hippomax,* . . . of whom one story was that he satirized the statuary *Bupalus* so bitterly that he hanged himself. By some confusion . . . he has combined the two names" (Shuckburgh).

EDMUND SPENSER

1552?–1599

The year of Spenser's birth is known only by inference from a sonnet which he wrote in 1593. His father was a man in humble circumstances and followed the trade of cloth-making in London. Spenser was sent to the Merchant Tailors' School, then newly founded under the direction of Richard Mulcaster, one of the most distinguished teachers of the time. Thence he proceeded in 1569 to Pembroke Hall, Cambridge, where he was a sizar, or undergraduate, some of whose expenses were paid in return for certain menial services. He took his B. A. in 1573 and his M. A. in 1576. At Cambridge Spenser formed a lasting friendship with Gabriel Harvey, a Fellow of Pembroke and later one of the notable figures of the University; there too, of course, he came under strong Puritan influences which also were lasting in their effects. When he left Cambridge Spenser may have gone for a time among his kinsmen in the north of England. In 1578 he was a secretary in the household of John Young, Bishop of Rochester. A year later he was back in London, in the household of Robert Dudley, Earl of Leicester, where he came to know and admire Leicester's nephew, Sir Philip Sidney. On 27 October, 1579, he married his first wife, Machabyas Childe. In 1579, too, Spenser published *The Shepherd's Calendar,* a series of twelve eclogues, in which he clearly announced himself as a significant new force in English poetry. But poetry, of course, brought in no money, and Spenser was perforce at this time seeking public office. In 1580 he was successful in a manner which, it has generally been thought, was little to his taste. He went to Ireland as secretary to Lord Grey of Wilton, then Lord Deputy of Ireland. And in Ireland Spenser stayed, save for two lengthy visits to London, until within a month of his death. In 1589 he came to London with Sir Walter Ralegh, who had been in Ireland, to publish the first three books of *The Faerie Queene* in 1590; and five years later he again returned to England to oversee the publication (in 1596) of a new edition of *The Faerie Queene,* containing three additional books, and, in separate volumes, of his *Four Hymns* and *Prothalamion.* In publishing *The Faerie Queene* Spenser sought something more than the pension which Elizabeth gave him. It is probable, however, that Spenser's disappointment has been exaggerated. His eyes were open to the corruption which surrounded life at Court, and at the same time his career in Ireland was at once honorable and moderately successful. He filled several minor offices there, and in 1589 was granted an estate of some 3000 acres in the County of Cork. He found congenial friends in Ireland, and there he met and married his second wife, Elizabeth Boyle (1594). Certainly also his virtual retirement from the larger world was conducive to that sober, meditative life which was most natural to him and which found a lofty expression in *The Faerie Queene* and in such shorter poems as the *Four Hymns.* And to this, one thinks, Spenser himself can hardly have been blind, however much at times he may have yearned for a life which would have made his achievement as a poet immeasurably more difficult, if not impossible. In 1598 there occurred an insurrection in Ireland in the course of which Spenser's castle of Kilcolman was pillaged and burned, he and his family escaping to Cork. In December he was sent thence to London with dispatches, and there he fell ill, and died on 13 January, 1599. He was buried in Westminster Abbey. According to tradition he died not only broken-hearted over the loss of a child in the burning of Kilcolman, but also in the direst poverty, unable to buy necessary food. Contemporaries, among them Ben Jonson and Camden, gave countenance to the story, and it may well be that Spenser was suffering a lack of ready money.

Spenser is, as has been well said, "among the very greatest of our poets, but the significance of his poetry in the history of our literature is even greater than its intrinsic value. He re-created English prosody, giving back to our verse the fluidity and the grace that it had lost since the days of Chaucer, and extending the range of its achievement; he created English poetic diction, lifting it from anarchy and stiffness, daring greatly, but triumphing whether in the simple or the ornate, widening its scope, but at the same time never failing to give it ease and flexibility, so that language became to him a willing servant, and could voice the subtlest shades of mood or fancy. By means of this rich and varied style, fully expressive of his high seriousness, his spirituality, his inexhaustible sense of beauty, he has exercised a spell that has been potent for three centuries, and none has called so many poets to their vocation" (E. de Selincourt, Introduction to Spenser's *Poetical Works,* pp. xxxix-xl).

The Works of Edmund Spenser, ed. Edwin Greenlaw, Charles G. Osgood, Frederick M. Padelford, and Ray Heffner (Baltimore, 1932–1938), is a variorum edition, the object of which is to summarize Spenser scholarship, as well as to present the best text of his work; this edition has been completed only through the first six volumes, containing the whole of *The Faerie Queene. Spenser's Minor Poems,* ed. Ernest de Selincourt (Oxford, 1910), offers a good text of the remainder.

A compact volume of commentary is H. S. V. Jones's *Spenser Handbook* (New York, 1930). B. E. C. Davis, *Edmund Spenser, a Critical Study* (Cambridge, 1933) is valuable on the interpretative rather than on the biographical side. Outstanding studies are Emile Legouis, *Edmund Spenser* (New York, 1926), and William L. Renwick, *Edmund Spenser; an Essay on Renaissance Poetry* (London, 1925).

THE FAERIE QUEENE

A LETTER OF THE AUTHOR'S,

Expounding His Whole Intention in the Course of This Worke: Which, for that It Giveth Great Light to the Reader, for the Better Understanding Is Hereunto Annexed.

To the Right Noble and Valorous Sir Walter Ralegh, Knight; Lord Wardein of the Stanneryes, and Her Majesties Liefetenaunt of the County of Cornewayll.

Sir, knowing how doubtfully all allegories may be construed, and this booke of mine, which I have entituled the *Faery Queene,* being a continued allegory, or darke conceit, I have thought good, as well for avoyding of gealous opinions and misconstructions, as also for your better light in reading thereof (being so by you commanded), to discover unto you the general intention and meaning, which in the whole course thereof I have fashioned, without expressing of any particular purposes, or by-accidents therein occasioned. The generall end therefore of all the booke is to fashion a gentleman or noble person in vertuous and gentle discipline: which for that I conceived shoulde be most plausible and pleasing, being coloured with an historicall fiction, the which the most part of men delight to read, rather for variety of matter than for profite of the ensample, I chose the historye of King Arthure, as most fitte for the excellency of his person, being made famous by many men's former workes, and also furthest from the daunger of envy, and suspition of present time. In which I have followed all the antique poets historicall: first Homere, who in the persons of Agamemnon and Ulysses hath ensampled a good governour and a vertuous man, the one in his Ilias, the other in his Odysseis; then Virgil, whose like intention was to doe in the person of Aeneas; after him Ariosto comprised them both in his Orlando: and lately Tasso dissevered them againe, and formed both parts in two persons, namely that part which they in philosophy call ethice, or vertues of a private man, coloured in his Rinaldo; the other named politice in his Godfredo. By ensample of which excellente poets, I labour to pourtraict in Arthure, before he was king, the image of a brave knight, perfected in the twelve private morall vertues, as Aristotle hath devised; the which is the purpose of these first twelve bookes:[1] which if I finde to be well accepted, I may be perhaps encoraged to frame the other part

[1] Of these Spenser completed only six, and a fragment probably designed for the seventh.

of pollliticke vertues in his person, after that hee came to be king.

To some, I know, this methode will seeme displeasaunt, which had rather have good discipline delivered plainly in way of precepts, or sermoned at large, as they use, than thus clowdily enwrapped in allegoricall devices. But such, me seeme, should be satisfide with the use of these dayes, seeing all things accounted by their showes, and nothing esteemed of, that is not delightfull and pleasing to commune sence.[2] For this cause is Xenophon preferred before Plato, for that the one, in the exquisite depth of his judgement, formed a commune welth, such as it should be; but the other in the person of Cyrus, and the Persians, fashioned a governement, such as might best be: so much more profitable and gratious is doctrine by ensample, than by rule. So have I laboured to doe in the person of Arthure: whome I conceive, after his long education by Timon, to whom he was by Merlin delivered to be brought up, so soone as he was borne of the Lady Igrayne, to have seene in a dream or vision the Faery Queen, with whose excellent beauty ravished, he awaking resolved to seeke her out; and so being by Merlin armed, and by Timon throughly instructed, he went to seeke her forth in Faerye Land. In that Faery Queene I meane glory in my generall intention, but in my particular I conceive the most excellent and glorious person of our soveraine the Queene, and her kingdome in Faery Land. And yet, in some places els, I doe otherwise shadow her. For considering she beareth two persons, the one of a most royall queene or empresse, the other of a most vertuous and beautifull lady, this latter part in some places I doe expresse in Belphoebe, fashioning her name according to your owne excellent conceipt of Cynthia (Phoebe and Cynthia being both names of Diana). So in the person of Prince Arthure I sette forth magnificence in particular, which vertue, for that (according to Aristotle and the rest) it is the perfection of all the rest, and conteineth in it them all, therefore in the whole course I mention the deedes of Arthure applyable to that vertue which I write of in

[2] I. e., the senses, in opposition to the reason.

that booke. But of the xii. other vertues, I make xii. other knights the patrones, for the more variety of the history: of which these three bookes contayn three.[3] The first of the Knight of the Redcrosse, in whome I expresse Holynes: The seconde of Sir Guyon, in whome I sette forth Temperaunce: The third of Britomartis, a lady knight, in whome I picture Chastity. But, because the beginning of the whole worke seemeth abrupte, and as depending upon other antecedents, it needs that ye know the occasion of these three knights severall adventures. For the methode of a poet historical is not such as of an historiographer. For an historiographer discourseth of affayres orderly as they were donne, accounting as well the times as the actions; but a poet thrusteth into the middest, even where it most concerneth him, and there recoursing to the thinges forepaste, and divining of thinges to come, maketh a pleasing analysis of all.

The beginning therefore of my history, if it were to be told by an historiographer, should be the twelfth booke, which is the last; where I devise that the Faery Queene kept her annuall feaste xii. dayes; upon which xii. severall dayes, the occasions of the xii. severall adventures happed, which, being undertaken by xii. severall knights, are in these xii. books severally handled and discoursed. The first was this. In the beginning of the feast, there presented himselfe a tall clownishe younge man, who, falling before the Queene of Faries, desired a boone (as the manner then was) which during that feast she might not refuse: which was that hee might have the atchievement of any adventure, which during that feaste should happen: that being graunted, he rested him on the floore, unfitte through his rusticity for a better place. Soone after entred a faire ladye in mourning weedes, riding on a white asse, with a dwarfe behind her leading a warlike steed, that bore the armes of a knight, and his speare in the dwarfes hand. Shee, falling before the Queene of Faeries, complayned that her father and mother, an ancient king and

[3] This letter was first published in the edition of 1590, which contained only the first three books.

queene, had bene by an huge dragon many years shut up in a brasen castle, who thence suffred them not to yssew; and therefore besought the Faery Queene to assygne her some one of her knights to take on him that exployt. Presently that clownish person, upstarting, desired that adventure: whereat the Queene much wondering, and the lady much gaine-saying, yet he earnestly importuned his desire. In the end the lady told him, that unlesse that armour which she brought, would serve him (that is, the armour of a Christian man specified by Saint Paul, v. Ephes.[4]), that he could not succeed in that enterprise: which being forthwith put upon him with dewe furnitures thereunto, he seemed the goodliest man in al that company, and was well liked of the lady. And eftesoones taking on him knighthood, and mounting on that straunge courser, he went forth with her on that adventure: where beginneth the first booke, *viz.*,

A gentle knight was pricking on the playne, *etc.*

The second day there came in a palmer, bearing an infant with bloody hands, whose parents he complained to have bene slayn by an enchaunteresse called Acrasia; and therefore craved of the Faery Queene, to appoint him some knight to performe that adventure; which being assigned to Sir Guyon, he presently went forth with that same palmer: which is the beginning of the second booke and the whole subject thereof. The third day there came in a groome, who complained before the Faery Queene, that a vile enchaunter, called Busirane, had in hand a most faire lady, called Amoretta, whom he kept in most grievous torment, because she would not yield him the pleasure of her body. Whereupon Sir Scudamour, the lover of that lady, presently tooke on him that adventure. But being unable to performe it by reason of the hard enchauntments, after long sorrow, in the end met with Britomartis, who succoured him, and reskewed his love.

But by occasion hereof many other adventures are intermedled, but rather as accidents then intendments: as the love of Britomart, the overthrow of Marinell, the misery of Florimell, the vertuousness of Belphoebe, the lasciviousnes of Hellenora, and many the like.

Thus much, Sir, I have briefly overronne, to direct your understanding to the welhead of the history, that from thence gathering the whole intention of the conceit ye may, as in a handfull, gripe al the discourse, which otherwise may happily seeme tedious and confused. So, humbly craving the continuance of your honourable favour towards me, and th'eternall establishment of your happines, I humbly take leave.

23 January, 1589.

Yours most humbly affectionate,

Ed. Spenser.

[4] A mistake for "vi. Ephes."

THE FIRST BOOKE OF THE FAERIE QUEENE

Contayning

The Legende of the Knight of the Red Crosse, or of Holinesse

1

Lo I the man, whose Muse whilome did maske,
As time her taught, in lowly Shepheards weeds,[1]
Am now enforst a far unfitter taske,
For trumpets sterne to chaunge mine Oaten reeds,
And sing of Knights and Ladies gentle deeds; 5
Whose prayses having slept in silence long,
Me, all too meane, the sacred Muse areeds
To blazon broad emongst her learnéd throng:
Fierce warres and faithfull loves shall moralize my song.

2

Helpe then, O holy Virgin chiefe of nine,[2] 10
Thy weaker Novice to performe thy will,
Lay forth out of thine everlasting scryne
The antique rolles, which there lye hidden still,

[1] In *The Shepherd's Calendar* (1579).

[2] Calliope, muse of heroic poetry; though according to some, Spenser means Clio, the muse of history.

Of Faerie knights and fairest *Tanaquill*,[3]
Whom that most noble Briton Prince[4] so long
Sought through the world, and suffered so much ill, 16
That I must rue his undeservéd wrong:
O helpe thou my weake wit, and sharpen my dull tong.

3

And thou most dreaded impe of highest *Jove*,
Faire *Venus* sonne, that with thy cruell dart 20
At that good knight so cunningly didst rove,
That glorious fire it kindled in his hart,
Lay now thy deadly Heben bow apart,
And with thy mother milde come to mine ayde:
Come both, and with you bring triumphant *Mart*, 25
In loves and gentle jollities arrayd,
After his murdrous spoiles and bloudy rage allayd.

4

And with them eke, O Goddesse heavenly bright,[5]
Mirrour of grace and Majestie divine,
Great Lady of the greatest Isle, whose light 30
Like *Phoebus* lampe throughout the world doth shine,
Shed thy faire beames into my feeble eyne,
And raise my thoughts too humble and too vile,
To thinke of that true glorious type of thine,
The argument of mine afflicted stile: 35
The which to heare, vouchsafe, O dearest dred a-while.

CANTO I

The Patron of true Holinesse,
Foule Errour doth defeate:
Hypocrisie him to entrape,
Doth to his home entreate.

1

A gentle knight was pricking on the plaine,
Y-cladd in mightie armes and silver shielde,
Wherein old dints of deepe wounds did remaine,
The cruell markes of many' a bloudy fielde;
Yet armes till that time did he never wield: 5
His angry steede did chide his foming bitt,
As much disdayning to the curbe to yield:
Full jolly knight he seemd, and faire did sitt,
As one for knightly giusts and fierce encounters fitt.

2

But on his brest a bloudie Crosse he bore, 10
The deare remembrance of his dying Lord,
For whose sweete sake that glorious badge he wore,
And dead as living ever him ador'd:
Upon his shield the like was also scor'd,
For soveraine hope, which in his helpe he had: 15
Right faithfull true he was in deede and word,
But of his cheere did seeme too solemne sad;
Yet nothing did he dread, but ever was ydrad.

3

Upon a great adventure he was bond,
That greatest *Gloriana*[6] to him gave, 20
That greatest Glorious Queene of *Faerie* lond,
To winne him worship, and her grace to have,
Which of all earthly things he most did crave;
And ever as he rode, his hart did earne
To prove his puissance in battell brave 25
Upon his foe, and his new force to learne;
Upon his foe, a Dragon horrible and stearne.[7]

4

A lovely Ladie[8] rode him faire beside,
Upon a lowly Asse more white then snow,
Yet she much whiter, but the same did hide 30
Under a vele, that wimpled was full low,
And over all a blacke stole she did throw,
As one that inly mournd: so was she sad,
And heavie sat upon her palfrey slow;
Seeméd in heart some hidden care she had, 35
And by her in a line a milke white lambe she lad.

5

So pure and innocent, as that same lambe,
She was in life and every vertuous lore,
And by descent from Royall lynage came
Of ancient Kings and Queenes, that had of yore 40
Their scepters stretcht from East to Westerne shore,
And all the world in their subjection held;
Till that infernall feend with foule uprore
Forwasted all their land, and them expeld:
Whom to avenge, she had this Knight from far compeld. 45

[3]A British princess, representing Queen Elizabeth.
[4]Prince Arthur. [5]Queen Elizabeth.

[6]Queen Elizabeth. [7]The dragon typifies sin.
[8]Una, who typifies truth.

6

Behind her farre away a Dwarfe[9] did lag,
That lasie seemd in being ever last,
Or wearied with bearing of her bag
Of needments at his backe. Thus as they past, 49
The day with cloudes was suddeine overcast,
And angry *Jove* an hideous storme of raine
Did poure into his Lemans lap so fast,
That every wight to shrowd it did constrain,
And this fair couple eke to shroud themselves were fain.

7

Enforst to seeke some covert nigh at hand, 55
A shadie grove not far away they spide,
That promist ayde the tempest to withstand:
Whose loftie trees yclad with sommers pride,
Did spred so broad, that heavens light did hide,
Not perceable with power of any starre: 60
And all within were pathes and alleies wide,
With footing worne, and leading inward farre:
Faire harbour that them seemes; so in they entred arre.

8

And foorth they passe, with pleasure forward led,
Joying to heare the birdes sweete harmony, 65
Which therein shrouded from the tempest dred,
Seemd in their song to scorne the cruell sky.
Much can they prayse the trees so straight and hy,
The sayling Pine, the Cedar proud and tall,
The vine-prop Elme, the Poplar never dry,[10] 70
The builder Oake, sole king of forrests all,
The Aspine good for staves, the Cypresse funerall.[11]

9

The Laurell, meed of mightie Conquerours
And Poets sage, the Firre that weepeth still,[12]
The Willow worne of forlorne Paramours, 75
The Eugh obedient to the benders will,
The Birch for shaftes, the Sallow for the mill,
The Mirrhe sweete bleeding in the bitter wound,[13]
The warlike Beech,[14] the Ash for nothing ill,
The fruitful Olive, and the Platane round, 80
The carver Holme, the Maple seeldom inward sound.

10

Led with delight, they thus beguile the way,
Untill the blustring storme is overblowne;
When weening to returne, whence they did stray,
They cannot finde that path, which first was showne, 85
But wander too and fro in wayes unknowne,
Furthest from end then, when they neerest weene,
That makes them doubt, their wits be not their owne:
So many pathes, so many turnings seene,
That which of them to take, in diverse doubt they been. 90

11

At last resolving forward still to fare,
Till that some end they finde or in or out,
That path they take, that beaten seemd most bare,
And like to lead the labyrinth about;
Which when by tract they hunted had throughout, 95
At length it brought them to a hollow cave,
Amid the thickest woods. The Champion stout
Eftsoones dismounted from his courser brave,
And to the Dwarfe awhile his needlesse spere he gave. 99

12

Be well aware, quoth then that Ladie milde,
Least suddaine mischiefe ye too rash provoke:
The danger hid, the place unknowne and wilde,
Breedes dreadfull doubts: Oft fire is without smoke,
And perill without show: therefore your stroke
Sir knight with-hold, till further triall made.
Ah Ladie (said he) shame were to revoke 106
The forward footing for an hidden shade:[15]
Vertue gives her selfe light, through darkenesse for to wade.

---

[9]Typifying prudence.
[10]Because it grows best in moist soil.
[11]Symbolic of death. [12]It exudes resin.
[13]Myrrh is fragrant though bitter.
[14]"There is a tradition that the war chariots of the ancients were made of beech" (Winstanley).
[15]It were a shame to turn back because of an imagined danger.

13

Yea but (quoth she) the perill of this
place 109
I better wot then you, though now too late,
To wish you backe returne with foule disgrace,
Yet wisedome warnes, whilest foot is in the
gate,
To stay the steppe, ere forcéd to retrate.
This is the wandring wood, this *Errours den,*
A monster vile, whom God and man does
hate: 115
Therefore I read beware. Fly fly (quoth
then
The fearefull Dwarfe:) this is no place for
living men.

14

But full of fire and greedy hardiment,
The youthfull knight could not for ought be
staide,
But forth unto the darksome hole he went, 120
And lookéd in: his glistring armor made
A little glooming light, much like a shade,
By which he saw the ugly monster plaine,
Halfe like a serpent horribly displaide,
But th'other halfe did womans shape retaine,
Most lothsom, filthie, foule, and full of vile
disdaine. 126

15

And as she lay upon the durtie ground,
Her huge long taile her den all overspred,
Yet was in knots and many boughtes upwound,
Pointed with mortall sting. Of her there
bred 130
A thousand yong ones, which she dayly fed,
Sucking upon her poisonous dugs, eachone
Of sundry shapes, yet all ill favoréd:
Soone as that uncouth light upon them shone,
Into her mouth they crept, and suddain all
were gone. 135

16

Their dam upstart, out of her den effraide,
And rushéd forth, hurling her hideous taile
About her curséd head, whose folds displaid
Were stretcht now forth at length without
entraile.
She lookt about, and seeing one in mayle 140
Arméd to point, sought backe to turne againe;
For light she hated as the deadly bale,
Ay wont in desert darknesse to remaine,
Where plaine none might her see, nor she see
any plaine.

17

Which when the valiant Elfe[16] perceiv'd, he
lept 145
As Lyon fierce upon the flying pray,
And with his trenchand blade her boldly kept
From turning backe, and forcéd her to stay:
Therewith enrag'd she loudly gan to bray,
And turning fierce, her speckled taile advaunst, 150
Threatning her angry sting, him to dismay:
Who nought aghast, his mightie hand enhaunst:
The stroke down from her head unto her
shoulder glaunst.

18

Much daunted with that dint, her sence was
dazd,
Yet kindling rage, her selfe she gathered
round, 155
And all attonce her beastly body raizd
With doubled forces high above the ground:
Tho wrapping up her wrethed sterne arownd,
Lept fierce upon his shield, and her huge
traine
All suddenly about his body wound, 160
That hand or foot to stirre he strove in vaine;
God helpe the man so wrapt in *Errours* endlesse traine.

19

His Lady sad to see his sore constraint,
Cride out, Now now Sir Knight, shew what
ye bee, 164
Add faith unto your force, and be not faint:
Strangle her, else she sure will strangle thee.
That when he heard, in great perplexitie,
His gall did grate for griefe and high disdaine,[17]
And knitting all his force got one hand free,
Wherewith he grypt her gorge with so great
paine, 170
That soone to loose her wicked bands did
her constraine.

20

Therewith she spewd out of her filthy maw
A floud of poyson horrible and blacke,
Full of great lumpes of flesh and gobbets
raw,
Which stunck so vildly, that it forst him
slacke 175

[16]The Knight is so called because he is a fairy knight.

[17]His anger was kindled by his pain and great disgust.

His grasping hold, and from her turne him
backe:
Her vomit full of bookes and papers was,[18]
With loathly frogs and toades, which eyes
did lacke,
And creeping sought way in the weedy gras:
Her filthy parbreake all the place defiléd has.

21

As when old father *Nilus* gins to swell 181
With timely pride above the *Aegyptian* vale,
His fattie waves do fertile slime outwell,
And overflow each plaine and lowly dale:
But when his later spring gins to avale, 185
Huge heapes of mudd he leaves, wherein
there breed
Ten thousand kindes of creatures, partly
male
And partly female of his fruitfull seed;
Such ugly monstrous shapes elswhere may
no man reed.

22

The same so sore annoyéd has the knight, 190
That welnigh chokéd with the deadly stinke,
His forces faile, ne can no longer fight.
Whose corage when the feend perceiv'd to
shrinke,
She pouréd forth out of her hellish sinke
Her fruitfull curséd spawne of serpents
small, 195
Deforméd monsters, fowle, and blacke as
inke,
Which swarming all about his legs did crall,
And him encombred sore, but could not hurt
at all.

23

As gentle Shepheard in sweete even-tide,
When ruddy *Phoebus* gins to welke in
west, 200
High on an hill, his flocke to vewen wide,
Markes which do byte their hasty supper
best;
A cloud of combrous gnattes do him molest,
All striving to infixe their feeble stings,
That from their noyance he no where can
rest, 205
But with his clownish hands their tender
wings
He brusheth oft, and oft doth mar their
murmurings.

24

Thus ill bestedd, and fearefull more of
shame,
Then of the certaine perill he stood in,
Halfe furious unto his foe he came, 210
Resolv'd in minde all suddenly to win,
Or soone to lose, before he once would lin;
And strooke at her with more then manly
force,
That from her body full of filthie sin
He raft her hatefull head without re-
morse; 215
A streame of cole black bloud forth gushéd
from her corse.

25

Her scattred brood, soone as their Parent
deare
They saw so rudely falling to the ground, 218
Groning full deadly, all with troublous feare,
Gathred themselves about her body round,
Weening their wonted entrance to have found
At her wide mouth: but being there with-
stood
They flockéd all about her bleeding wound,
And suckéd up their dying mothers blood,
Making her death their life, and eke her hurt
their good. 225

26

That detestable sight him much amazde,
To see th'unkindly Impes of heaven accurst,
Devoure their dam; on whom while so he
gazd,
Having all satisfide their bloudy thurst,
Their bellies swolne he saw with fulnesse
burst, 230
And bowels gushing forth: well worthy end
Of such as drunke her life, the which them
nurst;
Now needeth him no lenger labour spend,
His foes have slaine themselves, with whom
he should contend. 234

27

His Ladie seeing all, that chaunst, from farre
Approcht in hast to greet his victorie,
And said, Faire knight, borne under happy
starre,
Who see your vanquisht foes before you lye:
Well worthy be you of that Armorie,[19] 239
Wherein ye have great glory wonne this day,
And proov'd your strength on a strong eni-
mie,
Your first adventure: many such I pray,
And henceforth ever wish, that like succeed
it may.

[18]The allusion is to pamphlets written by Catholics against Protestantism.

[19]The armor of a Christian man.

28

Then mounted he upon his Steede againe,
And with the Lady backward sought to wend; 245
That path he kept, which beaten was most plaine.
Ne ever would to any by-way bend,
But still did follow one unto the end,
The which at last out of the wood them brought.
So forward on his way (with God to frend) 250
He passéd forth, and new adventure sought;
Long way he travelléd, before he heard of ought.

29

At length they chaunst to meet upon the way
An agéd Sire,[20] in long blacke weedes yclad,
His feete all bare, his beard all hoarie gray, 255
And by his belt his booke he hanging had;
Sober he seemde, and very sagely sad,
And to the ground his eyes were lowly bent,
Simple in shew, and voyde of malice bad,
And all the way he prayéd, as he went, 260
And often knockt his brest, as one that did repent.

30

He faire the knight saluted, louting low,
Who faire him quited, as that courteous was:
And after askéd him, if he did know
Of straunge adventures, which abroad did pas. 265
Ah my deare Sonne (quoth he) how should, alas,
Silly old man, that lives in hidden cell,
Bidding his beades all day for his trespas,
Tydings of warre and worldly trouble tell?
With holy father sits not with such things to mell. 270

31

But if of daunger which hereby doth dwell,
And homebred evill ye desire to heare,
Of a straunge man I can you tidings tell,
That wasteth all this countrey farre and neare.
Of such (said he) I chiefly do inquere, 275
And shall you well reward to shew the place,
In which that wicked wight his dayes doth weare
For to all knighthood it is foule disgrace,
That such a curséd creature lives so long a space. 279

[20] Archimago, a disguised enchanter, who typifies hypocrisy.

32

Far hence (quoth he) in wastfull wildernesse
His dwelling is, by which no living wight
May ever passe, but thorough great distresse.
Now (sayd the Lady) draweth toward night,
And well I wote, that of your later fight
Ye all forwearied be: for what so strong, 285
But wanting rest will also want of might?
The Sunne that measures heaven all day long,
At night doth baite his steedes the *Ocean* waves emong.

33

Then with the Sunne take Sir, your timely rest,
And with new day new worke at once begin:
Untroubled night they say gives counsell best. 291
Right well Sir knight ye have adviséd bin,
(Quoth then that aged man;) the way to win
Is wisely to advise: now day is spent;
Therefore with me ye may take up your In
For this same night. The knight was well content: 296
So with that godly father to his home they went.

34

A little lowly Hermitage it was,
Downe in a dale, hard by a forests side,
Far from resort of people, that did pas 300
In travell to and froe: a little wyde
There was an holy Chappell edifyde,
Wherein the Hermite dewly wont to say
His holy things each morne and eventyde:
Thereby a Christall streame did gently play,
Which from a sacred fountaine welléd forth alway. 306

35

Arrivéd there, the little house they fill,
Ne looke for entertainement, where none was:
Rest is their feast, and all things at their will;
The noblest mind the best contentment has. 310
With faire discourse the evening so they pas:
For that old man of pleasing wordes had store,
And well could file his tongue as smooth as glas;
He told of Saintes and Popes, and evermore
He strowd an *Ave-Mary* after and before. 315

36

The drouping Night thus creepeth on them
fast,
And the sad humour loading their eye liddes,
As messenger of *Morpheus* on them cast
Sweet slombring deaw, the which to sleepe
them biddes.
Unto their lodgings then his guestes he
riddes: 320
Where when all drownd in deadly sleepe he
findes,
He to his study goes, and there amiddes
His Magick bookes and artes of sundry
kindes,
He seekes out mighty charmes, to trouble
sleepy mindes. 324

37

Then choosing out few wordes most horrible,
(Let none them read) thereof did verses
frame,
With which and other spelles like terrible,
He bad awake blacke *Plutoes* griesly Dame,[21]
And curséd heaven, and spake reprochfull
shame
Of highest God, the Lord of life and
light; 330
A bold bad man, that dar'd to call by name
Great *Gorgon,* Prince of darknesse and dead
night,
At which *Cocytus* quakes, and *Styx* is put to
flight.[22]

38

And forth he cald out of deepe darknesse
dred
Legions of Sprights, the which like little
flyes 335
Fluttring about his ever damnéd hed,
A-waite whereto their service he applyes,
To aide his friends, or fray his enimies:
Of those he chose out two, the falsest twoo,
And fittest for to forge true-seeming lyes; 340
The one of them he gave a message too,
The other by him selfe staide other worke to
doo.

39

He making speedy way through spersèd ayre,
And through the world of waters wide and
deepe,
To *Morpheus* house doth hastily repaire. 345
Amid the bowels of the earth full steepe,
And low, where dawning day doth never
peepe,
His dwelling is; there *Tethys*[23] his wet bed
Doth ever wash, and *Cynthia*[24] still doth
steepe
In silver deaw his ever-drouping hed, 350
Whiles sad Night over him her mantle black
doth spred.

40

Whose double gates he findeth lockéd fast,
The one faire fram'd of burnisht Yvory,
The other all with silver overcast;
And wakefull dogges before them farre do
lye, 355
Watching to banish Care their enimy,
Who oft is wont to trouble gentle sleepe.
By them the Sprite doth passe in quietly,
And unto *Morpheus* comes, whom drownéd
deepe
In drowsie fit he findes: of nothing he takes
keepe. 360

41

And more, to lulle him in his slumber soft,
A trickling streame from high rocke tum-
bling downe
And ever-drizling raine upon the loft,
Mixt with a murmuring winde, much like
the sowne 364
Of swarming Bees, did cast him in a swowne:
No other noyse, nor peoples troublous cryes,
As still are wont t'annoy the walléd towne,
Might there be heard: but carelesse Quiet
lyes,
Wrapt in eternall silence farre from ene-
myes.

42

The messenger approching to him spake, 370
But his wast wordes returnd to him in vaine:
So sound he slept, that nought mought him
awake.
Then rudely he him thrust, and pusht with
paine,
Whereat he gan to stretch: but he againe
Shooke him so hard, that forcéd him to
speake. 375
As one then in a dreame, whose dryer
braine[25]
Is tost with troubled sights and fancies
weake,
He mumbled soft, but would not all his
silence breake.

---

[21]Proserpine. [22]Two rivers in Hades.

[23]The ocean. [24]The moon.

[25]It was once supposed that the brain, when too dry, gave rise to troubled dreams.

43

The Sprite then gan more boldly him to wake,
And threatned unto him the dreaded name 380
Of *Hecate*:[26] whereat he gan to quake,
And lifting up his lumpish head, with blame
Halfe angry askéd him, for what he came.
Hither (quoth he) me *Archimago* sent,
He that the stubborne Sprites can wisely tame, 385
He bids thee to him send for his intent
A fit false dreame, that can delude the sleepers sent.

44

The God obayde, and calling forth straight way
A diverse dreame out of his prison darke,
Delivered it to him, and downe did lay 390
His heavie head, devoide of carefull carke,
Whose sences all were straight benumbd and starke.
He backe returning by the Yvorie dore,
Remounted up as light as chearefull Larke,
And on his litle winges the dreame he bore 395
In hast unto his Lord, where he him left afore.

45

Who all this while with charmes and hidden artes,
Had made a Lady of that other Spright,
And fram'd of liquid ayre her tender partes
So lively, and so like in all mens sight, 400
That weaker sence it could have ravisht quight:
The maker selfe for all his wondrous witt,
Was nigh beguiléd with so goodly sight:
Her all in white he clad, and over it
Cast a blacke stole, most like to seeme for *Una* fit. 405

46

Now when that ydle dreame was to him brought,
Unto that Elfin knight he bad him fly,
Where he slept soundly void of evill thought,
And with false shewes abuse his fantasy,
In sort as he him schooléd privily: 410
And that new creature borne without her dew,[27]
Full of the makers guile, with usage sly
He taught to imitate that Lady trew,
Whose semblance she did carrie under feignéd hew.

[26] Goddess of Hades, the patroness of witches.
[27] Born unnaturally.

47

Thus well instructed, to their worke they hast, 415
And comming where the knight in slomber lay,
The one upon his hardy head him plast,
And made him dreame of loves and lustfull play,
That nigh his manly hart did melt away,
Bathéd in wanton blis and wicked joy: 420
Then seeméd him his Lady by him lay,
And to him playnd, how that false wingéd boy,[28]
Her chast hart had subdewd, to learne Dame pleasures toy.

48

And she her selfe of beautie soveraigne Queene,
Faire Venus seemde unto his bed to bring 425
Her, whom he waking evermore did weene,
To be the chastest flowre, that ay did spring
On earthly braunch, the daughter of a king,
Now a loose Leman to vile service bound:
And eke the *Graces* seeméd all to sing, 430
Hymen Iö Hymen,[29] dauncing all around,
Whilst freshest *Flora*[30] her with Yvie girlond crownd.

49

In this great passion of unwonted lust,
Or wonted feare of doing ought amis,
He started up, as seeming to mistrust 435
Some secret ill, or hidden foe of his:
Lo there before his face his Lady is,
Under blake stole hyding her bayted hooke,
And as halfe blushing offred him to kis,
With gentle blandishment and lovely looke, 440
Most like that virgin true, which for her knight him took.

50

All cleane dismayd to see so uncouth sight,
And halfe enragéd at her shamelesse guise,
He thought have slaine her in his fierce despight:
But hasty heat tempring with sufferance wise, 445
He stayde his hand, and gan himselfe advise
To prove his sense, and tempt her faignéd truth.
Wringing her hands in wemens pitteous wise,

[28] Cupid.
[29] Hymn to Hymen, god of marriage.
[30] Goddess of flowers.

Tho can she weepe, to stirre up gentle ruth,
Both for her noble bloud, and for her tender
youth. 450

51

And said, Ah Sir, my liege Lord and my love,
Shall I accuse the hidden cruell fate,
And mightie causes wrought in heaven above,
Or the blind God, that doth me thus amate,
For hopéd love to winne me certaine hate? 455
Yet thus perforce he bids me do, or die.
Die is my dew: yet rew my wretched state
You, whom my hard avenging destinie
Hath made judge of my life or death indif-
ferently.

52

Your owne deare sake forst me at first to
leave 460
My Fathers kingdome, There she stopt with
teares;
Her swollen hart her speach seemd to be-
reave,
And then againe begun, My weaker yeares
Captiv'd to fortune and frayle worldly feares,
Fly to your faith for succour and sure
ayde: 465
Let me not dye in languor and long teares.
Why Dame (quoth he) what hath ye thus
dismayd?
What frayes ye, that were wont to comfort
me affrayd?

53

Love of your selfe, she said, and deare constraint
Lets me not sleepe, but wast the wearie
night 470
In secret anguish and unpittied plaint,
Whiles you in carelesse sleepe are drownéd
quight.
Her doubtfull words made that redoubted
knight
Suspect her truth: yet since no'untruth he
knew,
Her fawning love with foule disdainefull
spight 475
He would not shend, but said, Deare dame I
rew,
That for my sake unknowne such griefe unto
you grew.

54

Assure your selfe, it fell not all to ground;
For all so deare as life is to my hart,
I deeme your love, and hold me to you
bound; 480
Ne let vaine feares procure your needlesse
smart,
Where cause is none, but to your rest depart.
Not all content, yet seemd she to appease
Her mournefull plaintes, beguiléd of her art,
And fed with words, that could not chuse but
please, 485
So slyding softly forth, she turnd as to her
ease.

55

Long after lay he musing at her mood,
Much griev'd to thinke that gentle Dame so
light,
For whose defence he was to shed his blood.
At last dull wearinesse of former fight 490
Having yrockt asleepe his irkesome spright,
That troublous dreame gan freshly tosse his
braine,
With bowres, and beds, and Ladies deare
delight:
But when he saw his labour all was vaine,
With that misforméd spright he backe re-
turnd againe. 495

CANTO II

The guilefull great Enchaunter parts
The Redcrosse Knight from Truth:
Into whose stead faire falshood steps,
And workes him wofull ruth.

1

By this the Northerne wagoner[1] had set
His sevenfold teme[2] behind the stedfast
starre,[3]
That was in Ocean waves yet never wet,
But firme is fixt, and sendeth light from farre
To all, that in the wide deepe wandring
arre: 5
And chearefull Chaunticlere with his note
shrill
Had warnéd once, that *Phoebus* fiery carre
In hast was climbing up the Easterne hill,
Full envious that night so long his roome did
fill.

2

When those accurséd messengers of hell, 10
That feigning dreame, and that faire-forgéd
Spright
Came to their wicked maister, and gan tell
Their bootelesse paines, and ill succeeding
night:

---

[1]Boötes. [2]Charles's Wain, or the Great Bear.
[3]The pole star.

Who all in rage to see his skilfull might
Deluded so, gan threaten hellish paine 15
And sad *Proserpines* wrath, them to affright.
But when he saw his threatning was but vaine,
He cast about, and searcht his balefull bookes againe.

3

Eftsoones he tooke that miscreated faire,
And that false other Spright, on whom he spred 20
A seeming body of the subtile aire,
Like a young Squire, in loves and lusty-hed
His wanton dayes that ever loosely led,
Without regard of armes and dreaded fight:
Those two he tooke, and in a secret bed, 25
Covered with darknesse and misdeeming night,
Them both together laid, to joy in vaine delight.

4

Forthwith he runnes with feignéd faithfull hast
Unto his guest, who after troublous sights
And dreames, gan now to take more sound repast, 30
Whom suddenly he wakes with fearefull frights,
As one aghast with feends or damnéd sprights,
And to him cals, Rise rise unhappy Swaine,
That here wex old in sleepe, whiles wicked wights
Have knit themselves in *Venus* shamefull chaine; 35
Come see, where your false Lady doth her honour staine.

5

All in amaze he suddenly up start
With sword in hand, and with the old man went;
Who soone him brought into a secret part,
Where that false couple were full closely ment 40
In wanton lust and lewd embracément:
Which when he saw, he burnt with gealous fire,
The eye of reason was with rage yblent,
And would have slaine them in his furious ire,
But hardly was restreinéd of that agéd sire. 45

6

Returning to his bed in torment great,
And bitter anguish of his guiltie sight,
He could not rest, but did his stout heart eat,
And wast his inward gall with deepe despight,
Yrkesome of life, and too long lingring night. 50
At last faire *Hesperus* in highest skie
Had spent his lampe,[4] and brought forth dawning light,
Then up he rose, and clad him hastily;
The Dwarfe him brought his steed: so both away do fly.

7

Now when the rosy-fingred Morning faire, 55
Weary of agéd *Tithones* saffron bed,
Had spred her purple robe through deawy aire,
And the high hils *Titan*[5] discoveréd,
The royall virgin shooke off drowsy-hed,
And rising forth out of her baser bowre, 60
Lookt for her knight, who far away was fled,
And for her Dwarfe, that wont to wait each houre;
Then gan she waile and weepe, to see that woefull stowre.

8

And after him she rode with so much speede
As her slow beast could make, but all in vaine; 65
For him so far had borne his light-foot steede,
Prickéd with wrath and fiery fierce disdaine,
That him to follow was but fruitlesse paine;
Yet she her weary limbes would never rest,
But every hill and dale, each wood and plaine 70
Did search, sore grievéd in her gentle brest,
He so ungently left her, whom she lovéd best.

9

But subtill *Archimago,* when his guests
He saw divided into double parts,
And *Una* wandring in woods and forrests, 75
Th'end of his drift, he praisd his divelish arts,
That had such might over true meaning harts;
Yet rests not so, but other meanes doth make,
How he may worke unto her further smarts:
For her he hated as the hissing snake, 80
And in her many troubles did most pleasure take.

---

[4]The morning star had yielded place to dawn.
[5]The sun.

10

He then devisde himselfe how to disguise;
For by his mightie science[6] he could take
As many formes and shapes in seeming wise,
As ever *Proteus*[7] to himselfe could make: 85
Sometime a fowle, sometime a fish in lake,
Now like a foxe, now like a dragon fell,
That of himselfe he oft for feare would
quake,
And oft would flie away. O who can tell
The hidden power of herbes, and might of
Magicke spell? 90

11

But now seemde best, the person to put on
Of that good knight, his late beguiléd guest:
In mighty armes he was yclad anon,
And silver shield: upon his coward brest
A bloudy crosse, and on his craven crest 95
A bounch of haires discolourd diversly:
Full jolly knight he seemde, and well ad-
drest,
And when he sate upon his courser free,
Saint George himself ye would have deeméd
him to be.

12

But he the knight, whose semblaunt he did
beare, 100
The true *Saint George* was wandred far
away,
Still flying from his thoughts and gealous
feare;
Will was his guide, and griefe led him astray.
At last him chaunst to meete upon the way
A faithlesse Sarazin[8] all arm'd to point, 105
In whose great shield was writ with letters
gay
Sans foy:[9] full large of limbe and every joint
He was, and caréd not for God or man a
point.

13

He had a faire companion of his way,
A goodly Lady[10] clad in scarlot red, 110
Purfled with gold and pearle of rich assay,
And like a *Persian* mitre[11] on her hed.

[6]His magic. [7]A sea-god.

[8]Used as a generic term for pagans.

[9]Faithless.

[10]Duessa, typifying falsehood, who calls herself Fidessa. She probably represents Mary, Queen of Scots—though it has also been suggested that she represents Mary Tudor—and the Roman Catholic Church.

[11]The papal crown is meant.

She wore, with crownes and owches gar-
nishéd,
The which her lavish lovers to her gave;
Her wanton palfrey all was overspred 115
With tinsell trappings, woven like a wave,
Whose bridle rung with golden bels and
bosses brave.

14

With faire disport and courting dalliaunce
She intertainde her lover all the way:
But when she saw the knight his speare ad-
vaunce, 120
She soone left off her mirth and wanton play,
And bad her knight addresse him to the fray:
His foe was nigh at hand. He, prickt with
pride
And hope to winne his Ladies heart that day,
Forth spurréd fast: adowne his coursers
side 125
The red bloud trickling staind the way, as he
did ride.

15

The knight of the *Redcrosse* when him he
spide,
Spurring so hote with rage dispiteous,
Gan fairely couch his speare, and towards
ride:
Soone meete they both, both fell and furious,
That daunted with their forces hideous, 131
Their steeds do stagger, and amazéd stand,
And eke themselves too rudely rigorous,
Astonied with the stroke of their owne hand,
Do backe rebut, and each to other yeeldeth
land. 135

16

As when two rams stird with ambitious pride,
Fight for the rule of the rich fleecéd flocke,
Their hornéd fronts so fierce on either side
Do meete, that with the terrour of the shocke
Astonied both, stand sencelesse as a blocke,
Forgetfull of the hanging victory: 141
So stood these twaine, unmovéd as a rocke,
Both staring fierce, and holding idely
The broken reliques of their former cru-
elty.[12]

17

The *Sarazin* sore daunted with the buffe 145
Snatcheth his sword, and fiercely to him flies;
Who well it wards, and quyteth cuff with
cuff:
Each others equall puissaunce envies,

[12]The broken shafts of their lances.

And through their iron sides with cruell spies
Does seeke to perce: repining courage yields
No foote to foe. The flashing fier flies 151
As from a forge out of their burning shields,
And streames of purple bloud new dies the verdant fields.

18

Curse on that Crosse (quoth then the *Sarazin*)
That keepes thy body from the bitter fit;[13] 155
Dead long ygoe I wote thou haddest bin,
Had not that charme from thee forwarnéd it:
But yet I warne thee now assuréd sitt,
And hide thy head. Therewith upon his crest
With rigour so outrageous he smitt, 160
That a large share it hewd out of the rest,
And glauncing downe his shield, from blame him fairely blest.

19

Who thereat wondrous wroth, the sleeping spark
Of native vertue gan eftsoones revive,
And at his haughtie helmet making mark, 165
So hugely stroke, that it the steele did rive,
And cleft his head. He tumbling downe alive,
With bloudy mouth his mother earth did kis,
Greeting his grave: his grudging ghost did strive
With the fraile flesh; at last it flitted is, 170
Whither the soules do fly of men, that live amis.

20

The Lady when she saw her champion fall,
Like the old ruines of a broken towre,
Staid not to waile his woefull funerall,
But from him fled away with all her powre; 175
Who after her as hastily gan scowre,
Bidding the Dwarfe with him to bring away
The *Sarazins* shield, signe of the conquer-oure.
Her soone he overtooke, and bad to stay,
For present cause was none of dread her to dismay. 180

21

She turning backe with ruefull countenaunce,
Cride, Mercy mercy Sir vouchsafe to show
On silly Dame, subject to hard mischaunce,
And to your mighty will. Her humblesse low

[13] Death.

In so ritch weedes and seeming glorious show, 185
Did much emmove his stout heroïcke heart,
And said, Deare dame, your suddein over-throw
Much rueth me; but now put feare apart,
And tell, both who ye be, and who that tooke your part. 189

22

Melting in teares, then gan she thus lament;
The wretched woman, whom unhappy howre
Hath now made thrall to your commande-ment,
Before that angry heavens list to lowre,
And fortune false betraide me to your powre,
Was (O what now availeth that I was!) 195
Borne the sole daughter of an Emperour,
He that the wide West under his rule has,
And high hath set his throne, where *Tiberis* doth pas.[14]

23

He in the first flowre of my freshest age,
Betrothéd me unto the onely haire 200
Of a most mighty king, most rich and sage;
Was never Prince so faithfull and so faire,
Was never Prince so meeke and debonaire;
But ere my hopéd day of spousall shone,
My dearest Lord fell from high honours staire, 205
Into the hands of his accurséd fone,
And cruelly was slaine, that shall I ever mone.

24

His blesséd body spoild of lively breath,
Was afterward, I know not how, convaid
And from me hid: of whose most innocent death 210
When tidings came to me unhappy maid,
O how great sorrow my sad soule assaid.
Then forth I went his woefull corse to find,
And many yeares throughout the world I straid,
A virgin widow; whose deepe wounded mind
With love, long time did languish as the striken hind. 216

25

At last it chauncéd this proud *Sarazin*,
To meete me wandring, who perforce me led
With him away, but yet could never win
The Fort, that Ladies hold in soveraigne dread. 220

[14] The Pope, at Rome, where the river Tiber passes.

There lies he now with foule dishonour dead,
Who whiles he liv'de, was calléd proud *Sans foy,*
The eldest of three brethren, all three bred
Of one bad sire, whose youngest is *Sans joy,*[15]
And twixt them both was borne the bloudy bold *Sans loy.*[16] 225

26

In this sad plight, friendlesse, unfortunate,
Now miserable I *Fidessa* dwell,
Craving of you in pitty of my state,
To do none ill, if please ye not do well.
He in great passion all this while did dwell, 230
More busying his quicke eyes, her face to view,
Then his dull eares, to heare what she did tell;
And said, faire Lady hart of flint would rew
The undeservéd woes and sorrowes, which ye shew.

27

Henceforth in safe assuraunce may ye rest, 235
Having both found a new friend you to aid,
And lost an old foe, that did you molest:
Better new friend then an old foe is said.
With chaunge of cheare the seeming simple maid 239
Let fall her eyen, as shamefast to the earth,
And yeelding soft, in that she nought gain-said,
So forth they rode, he feining seemely merth,
And she coy lookes: so dainty they say maketh derth.[17]

28

Long time they thus together traveiléd,
Till weary of their way, they came at last, 245
Where grew two goodly trees, that faire did spred
Their armes abroad, with gray mosse overcast,
And their greene leaves trembling with every blast, 248
Made a calme shadow far in compasse round:
The fearefull Shepheard often there aghast
Under them never sat, ne wont there sound
His mery oaten pipe, but shund th'unlucky ground.

[15]Joyless. [16]Lawless.

[17]The proverb, meaning that fastidiousness causes scarcity, by a play on words is made to mean that coyness causes desire.

29

But this good knight soone as he them can spie,
For the coole shade him thither hastly got:
For golden *Phoebus* now ymounted hie, 255
From fiery wheeles of his faire chariot
Hurléd his beame so scorching cruell hot,
That living creature mote it not abide;
And his new Lady it enduréd not. 259
There they alight, in hope themselves to hide
From the fierce heat, and rest their weary limbs a tide.

30

Faire seemely pleasaunce each to other makes,
With goodly purposes there as they sit:
And in his falséd fancy he her takes
To be the fairest wight, that livéd yit; 265
Which to expresse, he bends his gentle wit,
And thinking of those braunches greene to frame
A girlond for her dainty forehead fit,
He pluckt a bough: out of whose rift there came
Small drops of gory bloud, that trickled downe the same. 270

31

Therewith a piteous yelling voyce was heard,
Crying, O spare with guilty hands to teare
My tender sides in this rough rynd embard,
But fly, ah fly far hence away, for feare 274
Least to you hap, that happened to me heare,
And to this wretched Lady, my deare love,
O too deare love, love bought with death too deare.
Astond he stood, and up his haire did hove,
And with that suddein horror could no member move.

32

At last whenas the dreadfull passion 280
Was overpast, and manhood well awake,
Yet musing at the straunge occasion,
And doubting much his sence, he thus bespake;
What voyce of damnéd Ghost from *Limbo* lake,[18] 284
Or guilefull spright wandring in empty aire,
Both which fraile men do oftentimes mistake,
Sends to my doubtfull eares these speaches rare,
And ruefull plaints, me bidding guiltlesse bloud to spare?

[18]Hades.

33

Then groning deepe, Nor damnéd Ghost (quoth he),
Nor guilefull sprite to thee these wordes doth speake, 290
But once a man *Fradubio,*[19] now a tree,
Wretched man, wretched tree; whose nature weake,
A cruell witch her curséd will to wreake,
Hath thus transformd, and plast in open plaines,
Where *Boreas*[20] doth blow full bitter bleake, 295
And scorching Sunne does dry my secret vaines:
For though a tree I seeme, yet cold and heat me paines.

34

Say on *Fradubio* then, or man, or tree,
Quoth then the knight, by whose mischievous arts
Art thou misshapéd thus, as now I see? 300
He oft finds med'cine, who his griefe imparts;
But double griefs afflict concealing harts,
As raging flames who striveth to suppresse.
The author then (said he) of all my smarts,
Is one *Duessa* a false sorceresse, 305
That many errant knights hath brought to wretchednesse.

35

In prime of youthly yeares, when corage hot
The fire of love and joy of chevalree
First kindled in my brest, it was my lot
To love this gentle Lady, whom ye see, 310
Now not a Lady, but a seeming tree;
With whom as once I rode accompanyde,
Me chauncéd of a knight encountred bee,
That had a like faire Lady by his syde, 314
Like a faire Lady, but did fowle *Duessa* hyde.

36

Whose forgéd beauty he did take in hand,
All other Dames to have exceeded farre;
I in defence of mine did likewise stand,
Mine, that did then shine as the Morning starre:
So both to battell fierce arraungéd arre, 320
In which his harder fortune was to fall
Under my speare: such is the dye of warre:
His Lady left as a prise martiall,
Did yield her comely person, to be at my call.

[19]One of doubtful faith. [20]The north wind.

37

So doubly lov'd of Ladies unlike faire, 325
Th'one seeming such, the other such indeede,
One day in doubt I cast for to compare,
Whether in beauties glorie did exceede;
A Rosy girlond was the victors meede:
Both seemde to win, and both seemde won to bee, 330
So hard the discord was to be agreede.
Fraelissa[21] was as faire, as faire mote bee,
And ever false *Duessa* seemde as faire as shee.

38

The wicked witch now seeing all this while
The doubtfull ballaunce equally to sway, 335
What not by right, she cast to win by guile,
And by her hellish science raisd streightway
A foggy mist, that overcast the day,
And a dull blast, that breathing on her face,
Dimméd her former beauties shining ray, 340
And with foule ugly forme did her disgrace:
Then was she faire alone, when none was faire in place.

39

Then cride she out, Fye, fye, deforméd wight,
Whose borrowed beautie now appeareth plaine
To have before bewitchéd all mens sight; 345
O leave her soone, or let her soone be slaine.
Her loathly visage viewing with disdaine,
Eftsoones I thought her such, as she me told,
And would have kild her; but with faignéd paine,
The false witch did my wrathfull hand withhold; 350
So left her, where she now is turnd to treen mould.

40

Thenceforth I tooke *Duessa* for my Dame,
And in the witch unweeting joyd long time,
Ne ever wist, but that she was the same,
Till on a day (that day is every Prime, 355
When Witches wont do penance for their crime)
I chaunst to see her in her proper hew,
Bathing her selfe in origane and thyme:
A filthy foule old woman I did vew,
That ever to have toucht her, I did deadly rew. 360

[21]Typifies such faith as is possible to a doubter.

41

Her neather partes misshapen, monstruous,
Were hidd in water, that I could not see,
But they did seeme more foule and hideous,
Then womans shape man would beleeve to
bee.
Thenceforth from her most beastly companie
I gan refraine, in minde to slip away, 366
Soone as appeard safe opportunitie:
For danger great, if not assur'd decay
I saw before mine eyes, if I were knowne to
stray.

42

The divelish hag by chaunges of my cheare
Perceiv'd my thought, and drownd in sleepie
night, 371
With wicked herbes and ointments did be-
smeare
My bodie all, through charmes and mag-
icke might,
That all my senses were bereavéd quight:
Then brought she me into this desert waste,
And by my wretched lovers side me pight, 376
Where now enclosd in wooden wals full
faste,
Banisht from living wights, our wearie dayes
we waste.

43

But how long time, said then the Elfin
knight,
Are you in this misforméd house to dwell? 380
We may not chaunge (quoth he) this evil
plight,
Till we be bathéd in a living well;
That is the terme prescribéd by the spell.
O how, said he, mote I that well out find,
That may restore you to your wonted well?
Time and suffiséd fates to former kynd 386
Shall us restore, none else from hence may
us unbynd.

44

The false *Duessa,* now *Fidessa* hight,
Heard how in vaine *Fradubio* did lament,
And knew well all was true. But the good
knight 390
Full of sad feare and ghastly dreriment,
When all this speech the living tree had
spent,
The bleeding bough did thrust into the
ground,
That from the bloud he might be innocent,
And with fresh clay did close the wooden
wound: 395
Then turning to his Lady, dead with feare
her found.

45

Her seeming dead he found with feignéd
feare,
As all unweeting of that well she knew,
And paynd himselfe with busie care to reare
Her out of carelesse swowne. Her eylids
blew 400
And dimméd sight with pale and deadly hew
At last she up gan lift: with trembling
cheare
Her up he tooke, too simple and too trew,
And oft her kist. At length all passéd
feare,
He set her on her steede, and forward forth
did beare. 405

CANTO III

Forsaken Truth long seekes her love,
And makes the Lyon mylde,
Marres blind Devotions mart, and fals
In hand of leachour vylde.

1

Nought is there under heav'ns wide hollow-
nesse,
That moves more deare compassion of mind,
Then beautie brought t'unworthy wretched-
nesse
Through envies snares or fortunes freakes
unkind:
I, whether lately through her[1] brightnesse
blind, 5
Or through alleageance and fast fealtie,
Which I do owe unto all woman kind,
Feele my heart perst with so great agonie,
When such I see, that all for pittie I could
die.

2

And now it is empassionéd so deepe, 10
For fairest *Unaes* sake, of whom I sing,
That my fraile eyes these lines with teares
do steepe,
To thinke how she through guilefull handel-
ing,
Though true as touch, though daughter of a
king,
Though faire as ever living wight was
faire, 15
Though nor in word nor deede ill meriting,
Is from her knight divorcéd in despaire
And her due loves deriv'd to that vile witches
share.

[1]Beauty's.

3

Yet she most faithfull Ladie all this while
Forsaken, wofull, solitarie mayd 20
Farre from all peoples prease, as in exile,
In wildernesse and wastfull deserts strayd,
To seeke her knight; who subtilly betrayd
Through that late vision, which th'Enchaunter wrought,
Had her abandond. She of nought affrayd, 25
Through woods and wastnesse wide him daily sought;
Yet wishéd tydings none of him unto her brought.

4

One day nigh wearie of the yrkesome way,
From her unhastie beast she did alight,
And on the grasse her daintie limbes did lay 30
In secret shadow, farre from all mens sight:
From her faire head her fillet she undight,
And laid her stole aside. Her angels face
As the great eye of heaven shynéd bright,
And made a sunshine in the shadie place; 35
Did never mortall eye behold such heavenly grace.

5

It fortunéd out of the thickest wood
A ramping Lyon[2] rushéd suddainly,
Hunting full greedie after salvage blood;
Soone as the royall virgin he did spy, 40
With gaping mouth at her ran greedily,
To have attonce devour'd her tender corse:
But to the pray when as he drew more ny,
His bloudie rage asswagéd with remorse,
And with the sight amazd, forgat his furious forse. 45

6

In stead thereof he kist her wearie feet,
And lickt her lilly hands with fawning tong,
As he her wrongéd innocence did weet.
O how can beautie maister the most strong,
And simple truth subdue avenging wrong? 50
Whose yeelded pride and proud submission,
Still dreading death, when she had markéd long,
Her hart gan melt in great compassion,
And drizling teares did shed for pure affection.

[2] Probably typifying reason.

7

The Lyon Lord of every beast in field, 55
Quoth she, his princely puissance doth abate,
And mightie proud to humble weake does yield,
Forgetfull of the hungry rage, which late
Him prickt, in pittie of my sad estate:
But he my Lyon, and my noble Lord, 60
How does he find in cruell hart to hate
Her that him lov'd, and ever most adord,
As the God of my life? why hath he me abhord?

8

Redounding teares did choke th'end of her plaint,
Which softly ecchoed from the neighbour wood; 65
And sad to see her sorrowfull constraint
The kingly beast upon her gazing stood;
With pittie calmd, downe fell his angry mood.
At last in close hart shutting up her paine,
Arose the virgin borne of heavenly brood, 70
And to her snowy Palfrey got againe,
To seeke her strayéd Champion, if she might attaine.

9

The Lyon would not leave her desolate,
But with her went along, as a strong gard
Of her chast person, and a faithfull mate 75
Of her sad troubles and misfortunes hard:
Still when she slept, he kept both watch and ward,
And when she wakt, he waited diligent,
With humble service to her will prepard:
From her faire eyes he tooke commandement, 80
And ever by her lookes conceivéd her intent.

10

Long she thus traveiléd through deserts wyde,
By which she thought her wandring knight shold pas,
Yet never shew of living wight espyde; 84
Till that at length she found the troden gras,
In which the tract of peoples footing was,
Under the steepe foot of a mountaine hore;
The same she followes, till at last she has
A damzell[3] spyde slow footing her before,
That on her shoulders sad a pot of water bore. 90

[3] Abessa, representing superstition.

11

To whom approching she to her gan call,
To weet, if dwelling place were nigh at hand;
But the rude wench her answer'd nought at all,
She could not heare, nor speake, nor understand;
Till seeing by her side the Lyon stand, 95
With suddaine feare her pitcher downe she threw,
And fled away: for never in that land
Face of faire Ladie she before did vew,[4]
And that dread Lyons looke her cast in deadly hew.

12

Full fast she fled, ne ever lookt behynd, 100
As if her life upon the wager lay,
And home she came, whereas her mother blynd[5]
Sate in eternall night: nought could she say,
But suddaine catching hold, did her dismay
With quaking hands, and other signes of feare: 105
Who full of ghastly fright and cold affray,
Gan shut the dore. By this arrivéd there
Dame *Una,* wearie Dame, and entrance did requere.

13

Which when none yeelded, her unruly Page
With his rude clawes the wicket open rent, 110
And let her in; where of his cruell rage
Nigh dead with feare, and faint astonishment,
She found them both in darkesome corner pent;
Where that old woman day and night did pray
Upon her beades devoutly penitent; 115
Nine hundred *Pater nosters* every day,
And thrise nine hundred *Aves* she was wont to say.

14

And to augment her painefull pennance more,
Thrise every weeke in ashes she did sit,
And next her wrinkled skin rough sackcloth wore, 120
And thrise three times did fast from any bit:[6]
But now for feare her beads she did forget.
Whose needlesse dread for to remove away,
Faire *Una* framéd words and count'nance fit:
Which hardly doen, at length she gan them pray, 125
That in their cotage small, that night she rest her may.

15

The day is spent, and commeth drowsie night,
When every creature shrowded is in sleepe;
Sad *Una* downe her laies in wearie plight, 129
And at her feet the Lyon watch doth keepe:
In stead of rest, she does lament, and weepe
For the late losse of her deare lovéd knight,
And sighes, and grones, and evermore does steepe
Her tender brest in bitter teares all night,
All night she thinks too long, and often lookes for light. 135

16

Now when *Aldeboran*[7] was mounted hie
Above the shynie *Cassiopeias* chaire,[8]
And all in deadly sleepe did drownéd lie,
One[9] knockéd at the dore, and in would fare;
He knockéd fast, and often curst, and sware,
That readie entrance was not at his call: 141
For on his backe a heavy load he bare
Of nightly stelths and pillage severall,[10]
Which he had got abroad by purchase criminall.

17

He was to weet a stout and sturdie thiefe, 145
Wont to robbe Churches of their ornaments,
And poore mens boxes of their due reliefe,
Which given was to them for good intents;
The holy Saints of their rich vestiments 149
He did disrobe, when all men carelesse slept,
And spoild the Priests of their habiliments,
Whiles none the holy things in safety kept;
Then he by cunning sleights in at the window crept.

18

And all that he by right or wrong could find,
Unto this house he brought, and did bestow
Upon the daughter of this woman blind, 156
Abessa daughter of *Corceca* slow,

[4]Abessa has never beheld Truth, whose very appearance now terrifies her.
[5]Corceca, representing blind devotion.
[6]She fasted three whole days of each week.
[7]A star of the constellation of Taurus.
[8]The constellation called by this name.
[9]Kirkrapine, or Church-Robber.
[10]Thefts by night and pillage in various places.

With whom he whoredome used, that few
did know,
And fed her fat with feast of offerings,
And plentie, which in all the land did grow;
Ne sparéd he to give her gold and rings: 161
And now he to her brought part of his stolen
things.

19

Thus long the dore with rage and threats he
bet,
Yet of those fearefull women none durst
rize,
The Lyon frayéd them, him in to let: 165
He would no longer stay him to advize,
But open breakes the dore in furious wize,
And entring is; when that disdainfull beast
Encountring fierce, him suddaine doth sur-
prize, 169
And seizing cruell clawes on trembling brest,
Under his Lordly foot him proudly hath
suppresst.

20

Him booteth not resist, nor succour call,
His bleeding hart is in the vengers hand,
Who streight him rent in thousand peeces
small, 174
And quite dismembred hath: the thirstie land
Drunke up his life; his corse left on the
strand.
His fearefull friends weare out the wofull
night,
Ne dare to weepe, nor seeme to understand
The heavie hap, which on them is alight,
Affraid, least to themselves the like mishap-
pen might. 180

21

Now when broad day the world discoveréd
has,
Up *Una* rose, up rose the Lyon eke,
And on their former journey forward pas,
In wayes unknowne, her wandring knight to
seeke,
With paines farre passing that long wan-
dring *Greeke,*[11] 185
That for his love refuséd deitie;
Such were the labours of this Lady meeke,
Still seeking him, that from her still did flie,
Then furthest from her hope, when most she
weenéd nie.

22

Soone as she parted thence, the fearefull
twaine, 190
That blind old woman and her daughter deare
Came forth, and finding *Kirkrapine* there
slaine,
For anguish great they gan to rend their
heare,
And beat their brests, and naked flesh to
teare.
And when they both had wept and wayld
their fill, 195
Then forth they ranne like two amazéd
deare,
Halfe mad through malice, and revenging
will,
To follow her, that was the causer of their ill.

23

Whom overtaking, they gan loudly bray,
With hollow howling, and lamenting cry, 200
Shamefully at her rayling all the way,
And her accusing of dishonesty,
That was the flowre of faith and chastity;
And still amidst her rayling, she did pray,
That plagues, and mischiefs, and long misery
Might fall on her, and follow all the way, 206
And that in endlesse error she might ever
stray.

24

But when she saw her prayers nought pre-
vaile,
She backe returnéd with some labour lost;
And in the way as she did weepe and
waile, 210
A knight her met in mighty armes embost,
Yet knight was not for all his bragging bost,
But subtill *Archimag,* that *Una* sought
By traynes into new troubles to have tost:
Of that old woman tydings he besought, 215
If that of such a Ladie she could tellen ought.

25

Therewith she gan her passion to renew,
And cry, and curse, and raile, and rend her
heare,
Saying, that harlot she too lately knew, 219
That causd her shed so many a bitter teare,
And so forth told the story of her feare:
Much seeméd he to mone her haplesse
chaunce,
And after for that Ladie did inquere;
Which being taught, he forward gan ad-
vaunce
His faire enchaunted steed, and eke his
charméd launce. 225

---

[11] Ulysses.

26

Ere long he came, where *Una* traveild slow,
And that wilde Champion wayting her beside:
Whom seeing such, for dread he durst not show
Himselfe too nigh at hand, but turnéd wyde
Unto an hill; from whence when she him spyde, 230
By his like seeming shield, her knight by name
She weend it was, and towards him gan ryde:
Approching nigh, she wist it was the same,
And with faire fearefull humblesse towards him shee came.

27

And weeping said, Ah my long lackéd Lord,
Where have ye bene thus long out of my sight? 236
Much fearèd I to have bene quite abhord,
Or ought have done, that ye displeasen might,
That should as death unto my deare hart light:
For since mine eye your joyous sight did mis,
My chearefull day is turnd to chearelesse night, 241
And eke my night of death the shadow is;
But welcome now my light, and shining lampe of blis.

28

He thereto meeting said, My dearest Dame,
Farre be it from your thought, and fro my will, 245
To thinke that knighthood I so much should shame,
As you to leave, that have me lovéd still,
And chose in Faery court of meere goodwill,
Where noblest knights were to be found on earth: 249
The earth shall sooner leave her kindly skill
To bring forth fruit, and make eternall derth,
Then I leave you, my liefe, yborne of heavenly berth.

29

And sooth to say, why I left you so long,
Was for to seeke adventure in strange place,
Where *Archimago* said a felon strong 255
To many knights did daily worke disgrace;
But knight he now shall never more deface:
Good cause of mine excuse; that mote ye please
Well to accept, and evermore embrace
My faithfull service, that by land and seas 260
Have vowd you to defend, now then your plaint appease.

30

His lovely words her seemd due recompence
Of all her passéd paines: one loving howre
For many yeares of sorrow can dispence:
A dram of sweet is worth a pound of sowre: 265
She has forgot, how many a wofull stowre
For him she late endur'd; she speakes no more
Of past: true is, that true love hath no powre
To looken backe; his eyes be fixt before.
Before her stands her knight, for whom she toyld so sore. 270

31

Much like, as when the beaten marinere,
That long hath wandred in the *Ocean* wide,
Oft soust in swelling *Tethys*[12] saltish teare,
And long time having tand his tawney hide
With blustring breath of heaven, that none can bide, 275
And scorching flames of fierce *Orions* hound,[13]
Soone as the port from farre he has espide,
His chearefull whistle merrily doth sound,
And *Nereus*[14] crownes with cups; his mates him pledg around.

32

Such joy made *Una,* when her knight she found; 280
And eke th'enchaunter joyous seemd no lesse,
Then the glad marchant, that does vew from ground
His ship farre come from watrie wildernesse;
He hurles out vowes, and *Neptune* oft doth blesse:
So forth they past, and all the way they spent 285
Discoursing of her dreadfull late distresse,
In which he askt her, what the Lyon ment:
Who told her all that fell in journey as she went.[15]

---

[12]Sea-goddess, wife of Oceanus.

[13]Sirius, the dog star.

[14]The sea-god.

[15]I. e., who told all that befell her, etc. Possibly the line should be emended to read, "Who told all that her fell," etc.

33

They had not ridden farre, when they might see
One pricking towards them with hastie heat,
Full strongly armd, and on a courser free, 291
That through his fiercenesse foméd all with sweat,
And the sharpe yron did for anger eat,
When his hot ryder spurd his chaufféd side;
His looke was sterne, and seeméd still to threat 295
Cruell revenge, which he in hart did hyde,
And on his shield *Sans loy* in bloudie lines was dyde.

34

When nigh he drew unto this gentle payre
And saw the Red-crosse, which the knight did beare,
He burnt in fire, and gan eftsoones prepare 300
Himselfe to battell with his couchéd speare.
Loth was that other, and did faint through feare,
To taste th'untryéd dint of deadly steele;
But yet his Lady did so well him cheare,
That hope of new goodhap he gan to feele; 305
So bent his speare, and spurnd his horse with yron heele.

35

But that proud Paynim forward came so fierce,
And full of wrath, that with his sharp-head speare
Through vainely crosséd shield he quite did pierce,
And had his staggering steede not shrunke for feare, 310
Through shield and bodie eke he should him beare:
Yet so great was the puissance of his push,
That from his saddle quite he did him beare:
He tombling rudely downe to ground did rush,
And from his goréd wound a well of bloud did gush. 315

36

Dismounting lightly from his loftie steed,
He to him lept, in mind to reave his life,
And proudly said, Lo there the worthie meed
Of him, that slew *Sansfoy* with bloudie knife;
Henceforth his ghost freed from repining strife, 320
In peace may passen over *Lethe* lake,[16]
When morning altars purgd with enemies life,
The blacke infernall *Furies* doen aslake:
Life from *Sansfoy* thou tookst, *Sansloy* shall from thee take.

37

Therewith in haste his helmet gan unlace, 325
Till *Una* cride, O hold that heavie hand,
Deare Sir, what ever that thou be in place:
Enough is, that thy foe doth vanquisht stand
Now at thy mercy: Mercie not withstand:
For he is one the truest knight alive, 330
Though conquered now he lie on lowly land,
And whilest him fortune favourd, faire did thrive
In bloudie field: therefore of life him not deprive.

38

Her piteous words might not abate his rage,
But rudely rending up his helmet, would 335
Have slaine him straight: but when he sees his age,
And hoarie head of *Archimago* old,
His hastie hand he doth amazéd hold,
And halfe ashaméd, wondred at the sight:
For that old man well knew he, though untold, 340
In charmes and magicke to have wondrous might,
Ne ever wont in field, ne in round lists to fight.

39

And said, Why *Archimago,* lucklesse syre,
What doe I see? what hard mishap is this,
That hath thee hither brought to taste mine yre? 345
Or thine the fault, or mine the error is,
In stead of foe to wound my friend amis?
He answered nought, but in a traunce still lay,
And on those guilefull dazéd eyes of his
The cloud of death did sit. Which doen away, 350
He left him lying so, ne would no lenger stay.

[16]Lethe: river of forgetfulness in Hades. The lines mean that Sansfoy's soul had been kept from entering Hades because of his desire that he be revenged, and that now he may enter because the Furies, who demand vengeance for the slain, will be appeased by the death of the (supposed) Red Cross Knight.

40

But to the virgin comes, who all this while
Amaséd stands, her selfe so mockt to see
By him, who has the guerdon of his guile,
For so misfeigning her true knight to bee: 355
Yet is she now in more perplexitie,
Left in the hand of that same Paynim bold,
From whom her booteth not at all to flie;
Who by her cleanly garment catching hold,
Her from her Palfrey pluckt, her visage to behold. 360

41

But her fierce servant full of kingly awe
And high disdaine, when as his soveraine Dame
So rudely handled by her foe he sawe,
With gaping jawes full greedy at him came,
And ramping on his shield, did weene the same 365
Have reft away with his sharpe rending clawes:
But he was stout, and lust did now inflame
His corage more, that from his griping pawes
He hath his shield redeem'd, and foorth his swerd he drawes.

42

O then too weake and feeble was the forse 370
Of salvage beast, his puissance to withstand
For he was strong, and of so mightie corse,
As ever wielded speare in warlike hand,
And feates of armes did wisely understand.
Eftsoones he percéd through his chauféd chest 375
With thrilling point of deadly yron brand,
And launcht his Lordly hart: with death opprest
He roar'd aloud, whiles life forsooke his stubborne brest.

43

Who now is left to keepe the forlorne maid
From raging spoile of lawlesse victors will? 380
Her faithfull gard remov'd, her hope dismaid,
Her selfe a yeelded pray to save or spill.
He now Lord of the field, his pride to fill,
With foule reproches, and disdainfull spight
Her vildly entertaines, and will or nill, 385
Beares her away upon his courser light:
Her prayers nought prevaile, his rage is more of might.

44

And all the way, with great lamenting paine,
And piteous plaints she filleth his dull eares,
That stony hart could riven have in twaine,
And all the way she wets with flowing teares:
But he enrag'd with rancor, nothing heares.
Her servile beast yet would not leave her so, 393
But followes her farre off, ne ought he feares,
To be partaker of her wandring woe, 395
More mild in beastly kind, then that her beastly foe.

CANTO IV

To sinfull house of Pride, Duessa
guides the faithfull knight,
Where brothers death to wreak Sansjoy
doth chalenge him to fight.

1

Young knight, what ever that dost armes professe,
And through long labours huntest after fame,
Beware of fraud, beware of ficklenesse,
In choice, and change of thy deare lovéd Dame,
Least thou of her beleeve too lightly blame, 5
And rash misweening doe thy hart remove:
For unto knight there is no greater shame,
Then lightnesse and inconstancie in love;
That doth this *Redcrosse* knights ensample plainly prove.

2

Who after that he had faire *Una* lorne, 10
Through light misdeeming of her loialtie,
And false *Duessa* in her sted had borne,
Calléd *Fidess'*, and so supposed to bee;
Long with her traveild, till at last they see
A goodly building,[1] bravely garnishéd, 15
The house of mightie Prince it seemd to bee:
And towards it a broad high way that led,
All bare through peoples feet, which thither traveiléd.

3

Great troupes of people traveild thitherward
Both day and night, of each degree and place, 20
But few returnéd, having scapéd hard,
With balefull beggerie, or foule disgrace,

[1]The House of Pride.

Which ever after in most wretched case,
Like loathsome lazars, by the hedges lay.
Thither *Duessa* bad him bend his pace: 25
For she is wearie of the toilesome way,
And also nigh consuméd is the lingring day.

4

A stately Pallace built of squaréd bricke,
Which cunningly was without morter laid,
Whose wals were high, but nothing strong, nor thick, 30
And golden foile all over them displaid,
That purest skye with brightnesse they dismaid:
High lifted up were many loftie towres,
And goodly galleries farre over laid,
Full of faire windowes, and delightfull bowres; 35
And on the top a Diall told the timely howres.

5

It was a goodly heape for to behould,
And spake the praises of the workmans wit;
But full great pittie, that so faire a mould
Did on so weake foundation ever sit: 40
For on a sandie hill, that still did flit,
And fall away, it mounted was full hie,
That every breath of heaven shakéd it:
And all the hinder parts, that few could spie,
Were ruinous and old, but painted cunningly. 45

6

Arrivéd there they passéd in forth right,
For still to all the gates stood open wide,
Yet charge of them was to a Porter hight
Cald *Malvenu,*[2] who entrance none denide:
Thence to the hall, which was on every side 50
With rich array and costly arras dight:
Infinite sorts of people did abide
There waiting long, to win the wishéd sight
Of her, that was the Lady of that Pallace bright.

7

By them they passe, all gazing on them round, 55
And to the Presence mount; whose glorious vew
Their frayle amazéd senses did confound:
In living Princes court none ever knew
Such endlesse richesse, and so sumptuous shew;
Ne *Persia* selfe, the nourse of pompous pride 60
Like ever saw. And there a noble crew
Of Lordes and Ladies stood on every side,
Which with their presence faire, the place much beautifide.

8

High above all a cloth of State was spred,
And a rich throne, as bright as sunny day, 65
On which there sate most brave embellishéd
With royall robes and gorgeous array,
A mayden Queene, that shone as *Titans* ray,[3]
In glistring gold, and peerelesse pretious stone:
Yet her bright blazing beautie did assay 70
To dim the brightnesse of her glorious throne,
As envying her selfe, that too exceeding shone.

9

Exceeding shone, like *Phoebus* fairest childe,[4]
That did presume his fathers firie wayne,
And flaming mouthes of steedes unwonted wilde 75
Through highest heaven with weaker hand to rayne;
Proud of such glory and advancement vaine,
While flashing beames do daze his feeble eyen,
He leaves the welkin way most beaten plaine,
And rapt with whirling wheeles, inflames the skyen, 80
With fire not made to burne, but fairely for to shyne.

10

So proud she shynéd in her Princely state,
Looking to heaven, for earth she did disdayne;
And sitting high, for lowly she did hate: 84
Lo underneath her scornefull feete, was layne
A dreadfull Dragon with an hideous trayne,
And in her hand she held a mirrhour bright,
Wherein her face she often vewéd fayne,
And in her selfe-lov'd semblance tooke delight;
For she was wondrous faire, as any living wight. 90

11

Of griesly *Pluto* she the daughter was,
And sad *Proserpina* the Queene of hell;

[2]Ill-come.

[3]As the sun's rays. [4]Phaëthon, Apollo's son.

Yet did she thinke her pearelesse worth to pas
That parentage, with pride so did she swell,
And thundring *Jove*, that high in heaven doth dwell, 95
And wield the world, she claymèd for her syre,
Or if that any else did *Jove* excell:
For to the highest she did still aspyre,
Or if ought higher were then that, did it desyre.

12

And proud *Lucifera* men did her call, 100
That made her selfe a Queene, and crowned to be,
Yet rightfull kingdome she had none at all,
Ne heritage of native soveraintie,
But did usurpe with wrong and tyrannie
Upon the scepter, which she now did hold: 105
Ne ruld her Realmes with lawes, but pollicie,
And strong advizement of six wizards old,[5]
That with their counsels bad her kingdome did uphold.

13

Soone as the Elfin knight in presence came,
And false *Duessa* seeming Lady faire, 110
A gentle Husher, *Vanitie* by name
Made rowme, and passage for them did prepaire:
So goodly brought them to the lowest staire
Of her high throne, where they on humble knee
Making obeysaunce, did the cause declare, 115
Why they were come, her royall state to see,
To prove the wide report of her great Majestee.

14

With loftie eyes, halfe loth to looke so low,
She thankèd them in her disdainefull wise,
Ne other grace vouchsafèd them to show 120
Of Princesse worthy, scarse them bad arise.
Her Lordes and Ladies all this while devise
Themselves to setten forth to straungers sight:
Some frounce their curlèd haire in courtly guise,
Some prancke their ruffes, and others trimly dight 125
Their gay attire: each others greater pride does spight.

15

Goodly they all that knight do entertaine,
Right glad with him to have increast their crew:
But to *Duess'* each one himselfe did paine
All kindnesse and faire courtesie to shew; 130
For in that court whylome her well they knew:
Yet the stout Faerie mongst the middest crowd
Thought all their glorie vaine in knightly vew,
And that great Princesse too exceeding prowd,
That to strange knight no better countenance allowd. 135

16

Suddein upriseth from her stately place
The royall Dame, and for her coche doth call:
All hurtlen forth; and she with Princely pace,
As faire *Aurora* in her purple pall,
Out of the East the dawning day doth call: 140
So forth she comes: her brightnesse brode doth blaze;
The heapes of people thronging in the hall,
Do ride each other, upon her to gaze:
Her glorious glitterand light doth all mens eyes amaze.

17

So forth she comes, and to her coche does clyme, 145
Adornèd all with gold, and girlonds gay,
That seemd as fresh as *Flora* in her prime,
And strove to match, in royall rich array,
Great *Junoes* golden chaire, the which they say
The Gods stand gazing on, when she does ride 150
To *Joves* high house through heavens braspavèd way
Drawne of fair Pecocks, that excell in pride,
And full of *Argus* eyes[6] their tailes dispredden wide.

18

But this was drawne of six unequall beasts,
On which her six sage Counsellours did ryde, 155

[5]The rest of the Seven Deadly Sins, of which Pride (Lucifera) is the chief.

[6]Argus, who had a hundred eyes, perished in Juno's service. She placed his eyes in the tail of her peacock as a memorial to him.

Taught to obay their bestiall beheasts,
With like conditions to their kinds applyde:[7]
Of which the first, that all the rest did guyde,
Was sluggish *Idlenesse* the nourse of sin;
Upon a slouthfull Asse he chose to ryde, 160
Arayd in habit blacke, and amis thin,
Like to an holy Monck, the service to begin.

19

And in his hand his Portesse still he bare,
That much was worne, but therein little red,
For of devotion he had little care, 165
Still drownd in sleepe, and most of his dayes ded;
Scarse could he once uphold his heavie hed,
To looken, whether it were night or day:
May seeme the wayne was very evill led,
When such an one had guiding of the way, 170
That knew not, whether right he went, or else astray.

20

From worldly cares himselfe he did esloyne,
And greatly shunnéd manly exercise,
From every worke he chalengéd essoyne,
For contemplation sake: yet otherwise, 175
His life he led in lawlesse riotise;
By which he grew to grievous malady;
For in his lustlesse limbs through evill guise
A shaking fever raignd continually:
Such one was *Idlenesse,* first of this company. 180

21

And by his side rode loathsome *Gluttony,*
Deforméd creature, on a filthie swyne,
His belly was up-blowne with luxury,
And eke with fatnesse swollen were his eyne,
And like a Crane his necke was long and fyne, 185
With which he swallowd up excessive feast,
For want whereof poore people oft did pyne;
And all the way, most like a brutish beast,
He spuéd up his gorge, that all did him deteast.

22

In greene vine leaves he was right fitly clad;
For other clothes he could not weare for heat, 191
And on his head an yvie girland had,
From under which fast trickled downe the sweat:
Still as he rode, he somewhat still did eat,
And in his hand did beare a bouzing can, 195
Of which he supt so oft, that on his seat
His dronken corse he scarse upholden can,
In shape and life more like a monster, then a man.

23

Unfit he was for any worldly thing,
And eke unhable once to stirre or go, 200
Not meet to be of counsell to a king,
Whose mind in meat and drinke was drownéd so,
That from his friend he seldome knew his fo:
Full of diseases was his carcas blew,
And a dry dropsie[8] through his flesh did flow,
Which by misdiet daily greater grew: 206
Such one was *Gluttony,* the second of that crew.

24

And next to him rode lustfull *Lechery,*
Upon a bearded Goat, whose rugged haire,
And whally eyes (the signe of gelosy) 210
Was like the person selfe, whom he did beare:
Who rough, and blacke, and filthy did appeare,
Unseemely man to please faire Ladies eye;
Yet he of Ladies oft was lovéd deare,
When fairer faces were bid standen by: 215
O who does know the bent of womens fantasy?

25

In a greene gowne he clothéd was full faire,
Which underneath did hide his filthinesse,
And in his hand a burning hart he bare,
Full of vaine follies, and new fanglenesse: 220
For he was false, and fraught with ficklenesse,
And learnéd had to love with secret lookes,
And well could daunce, and sing with ruefulnesse,
And fortunes tell, and read in loving bookes,
And thousand other wayes, to bait his fleshly hookes. 225

26

Inconstant man, that lovéd all he saw,
And lusted after all, that he did love,
Ne would his looser life be tide to law,
But joyd weake wemens hearts to tempt, and prove

[7]The animals are of like nature with their riders.

[8]Perhaps Spenser means a dropsy causing thirst.

If from their loyall loves he might them move; 230
Which lewdnesse fild him with reprochfull paine
Of that fowle evill, which all men reprove,
That rots the marrow, and consumes the braine:
Such one was *Lecherie,* the third of all this traine.

27

And greedy *Avarice* by him did ride, 235
Upon a Camell loaden all with gold;
Two iron coffers hong on either side,
With precious mettall full, as they might hold,
And in his lap an heape of coine he told;
For of his wicked pelfe his God he made, 240
And unto hell him selfe for money sold;
Accurséd usurie was all his trade,
And right and wrong ylike in equall ballaunce waide.

28

His life was nigh unto deaths doore yplast,
And thred-bare cote, and cobled shoes he ware, 245
Ne scarse good morsell all his life did tast,
But both from backe and belly still did spare,
To fill his bags, and richesse to compare;
Yet chylde ne kinsman living had he none
To leave them to; but thorough daily care 250
To get, and nightly feare to lose his owne,
He led a wretched life unto him selfe unknowne.

29

Most wretched wight, whom nothing might suffise,
Whose greedy lust did lacke in greatest store,[9]
Whose need had end, but no end covetise, 255
Whose wealth was want, whose plenty made him pore,
Who had enough, yet wishéd ever more;
A vile disease, and eke in foote and hand
A grievous gout tormented him full sore,
That well he could not touch, nor go, nor stand: 260
Such was one *Avarice,* the fourth of this faire band.

30

And next to him malicious *Envie* rode,
Upon a ravenous wolfe, and still did chaw
Betweene his cankred teeth a venemous tode,
That all the poison ran about his chaw; 265
But inwardly he chawéd his owne maw
At neighbours wealth, that made him ever sad;
For death it was, when any good he saw,
And wept, that cause of weeping none he had,
But when he heard of harme, he wexéd wondrous glad. 270

31

All in a kirtle of discolourd say
He clothéd was, ypainted full of eyes;
And in his bosome secretly there lay
An hatefull Snake, the which his taile uptyes
In many folds, and mortall sting implyes. 275
Still as he rode, he gnasht his teeth, to see
Those heapes of gold with griple Covetyse,
And grudgéd at the great felicitie
Of proud *Lucifera,* and his owne companie.

32

He hated all good workes and vertuous deeds, 280
And him no lesse, that any like did use,[10]
And who with gracious bread the hungry feeds,
His almes for want of faith he doth accuse;
So every good to bad he doth abuse:
And eke the verse of famous Poets witt 285
He does backebite, and spightfull poison spues
From leprous mouth on all, that ever writt:
Such one vile *Envie* was, that fifte in row did sitt.

33

And him beside rides fierce revenging *Wrath,*
Upon a Lion, loth for to be led; 290
And in his hand a burning brond he hath,
The which he brandisheth about his hed;
His eyes did hurle forth sparkles fiery red,
And staréd sterne on all, that him beheld,
As ashes pale of hew and seeming ded; 295
And on his dagger still his hand he held,
Trembling through hasty rage, when choler in him sweld.

34

His ruffin raiment all was staind with blood,
Which he had spilt, and all to rags yrent,
Through unadvizéd rashnesse woxen wood;
For of his hands he had no governement, 301

[9]He was greedy, yet amidst wealth denied his desires.

[10]He hated not only good deeds but also any who performed them.

Ne car'd for bloud in his avengement:
But when the furious fit was overpast,
His cruell facts he often would repent;
Yet wilfull man he never would forecast, 305
How many mischieves should ensue his heed-
lesse hast.

35

Full many mischiefes follow cruell *Wrath:*
Abhorréd bloudshed, and tumultuous strife,
Unmanly murder, and unthrifty scath,
Bitter despight, with rancours rusty knife, 310
And fretting griefe the enemy of life;
All these, and many evils moe haunt ire,
The swelling Splene,[11] and Frenzy raging
rife,
The shaking Palsey, and Saint *Fraunces*
fire:[12]
Such one was *Wrath,* the last of this ungodly
tire. 315

36

And after all, upon the wagon beame
Rode *Satan,* with a smarting whip in hand,
With which he forward lasht the laesie teme,
So oft as *Slowth* still in the mire did stand.
Huge routs of people did about them
band, 320
Showting for joy, and still before their way
A foggy mist had covered all the land;
And underneath their feet, all scattered lay
Dead sculs and bones of men, whose life
had gone astray.

37

So forth they marchen in this goodly sort, 325
To take the solace of the open aire,
And in fresh flowring fields themselves to
sport;
Emongst the rest rode that false Lady faire,
The fowle *Duessa,* next unto the chaire
Of proud *Lucifera,* as one of the traine: 330
But that good knight would not so nigh
repaire,
Him selfe estraunging from their joyaunce
vaine,
Whose fellowship seemd far unfit for war-
like swaine.

38

So having solacéd themselves a space 334
With pleasaunce of the breathing fields yfed,
They backe returnéd to the Princely Place;
Whereas an errant knight in armes ycled,
And heathnish shield, wherein with letters
red
Was writ *Sans joy,* they new arrivéd find:
Enflam'd with fury and fiers hardy-hed, 340
He seemd in hart to harbour thoughts
unkind,
And nourish bloudy vengeaunce in his bitter
mind.

39

Who when the shaméd shield of slaine *Sans
foy*
He spide with that same Faery champions
page,
Bewraying him, that did of late destroy 345
His eldest brother, burning all with rage
He to him leapt, and that same envious gage
Of victors glory from him snatcht away:
But th'Elfin knight, which ought that warlike
wage, 349
Disdaind to loose the meed he wonne in fray,
And him rencountring fierce, reskewd the
noble pray.

40

Therewith they gan to hurtlen greedily,
Redoubted battaile ready to darrayne,
And clash their shields, and shake their
swords on hy,
That with their sturre they troubled all the
traine; 355
Till that great Queene upon eternall paine
Of high displeasure, that ensewen might,
Commaunded them their fury to refraine,
And if that either to that shield had right,
In equall lists they should the morrow next
it fight. 360

41

Ah dearest Dame (quoth then the Paynim
bold),
Pardon the errour of enragéd wight,
Whom great griefe made forget the raines
to hold
Of reasons rule, to see this recreant knight,
No knight, but treachour full of false
despight 365
And shamefull treason, who through guile
hath slayn
The prowest knight, that ever field did fight,
Even stout *Sans foy* (O who can then
refrayn?)
Whose shield he beares renverst, the more
to heape disdayn.

[11] The spleen was thought to be the seat of anger.
[12] Probably erysipelas.

42

And to augment the glorie of his guile, 370
His dearest love the faire *Fidessa* loe
Is there possesséd of the traytour vile,
Who reapes the harvest sowen by his foe,
Sowen in bloudy field, and bought with woe:
That brothers hand shall dearely well re-
quight 375
So be, O Queene, you equall favour showe.
Him litle answerd th'angry Elfin knight;
He never meant with words, but swords to
plead his right.

43

But threw his gauntlet as a sacred pledge,
His cause in combat the next day to try: 380
So been they parted both, with harts on
edge,[13]
To be aveng'd each on his enimy.
That night they pas in joy and jollity,
Feasting and courting both in bowre and
hall;
For Steward was excessive *Gluttonie,* 385
That of his plenty pouréd forth to all;
Which doen, the Chamberlain *Slowth* did to
rest them call.

44

Now whenas darkesome night had all dis-
playd
Her coleblacke curtein over brightest skye, 389
The warlike youthes on dayntie couches layd,
Did chace away sweet sleepe from sluggish
eye,
To muse on meanes of hopéd victory.
But whenas *Morpheus*[14] had with leaden
mace
Arrested all that courtly company,
Up-rose *Duessa* from her resting place, 395
And to the Paynims lodging comes with
silent pace.

45

Whom broad awake she finds, in troublous
fit,
Forecasting, how his foe he might annoy,
And him amoves with speaches seeming fit:
Ah deare *Sans joy,* next dearest to *Sans foy,*
Cause of my new griefe, cause of my new
joy, 401
Joyous, to see his ymage in mine eye,
And greev'd, to thinke how foe did him de-
stroy,
That was the flowre of grace and chevalrye;
Lo his *Fidessa* to thy secret faith I flye. 405

[13]In furious anger. [14]God of sleep.

46

With gentle wordes he can her fairely greet,
And bad say on the secret of her hart.
Then sighing soft, I learne that litle sweet
Oft tempred is (quoth she) with muchell
smart:
For since my brest was launcht with lovely
dart 410
Of deare *Sansfoy,* I never joyéd howre,
But in eternall woes my weaker hart
Have wasted, loving him with all my powre,
And for his sake have felt full many an
heavie stowre.

47

At last when perils all I weenéd past, 415
And hop'd to reape the crop of all my
care,
Into new woes unweeting I was cast,
By this false faytor, who unworthy ware
His worthy shield, whom he with guilefull
snare
Entrappéd slew, and brought to shamefull
grave. 420
Me silly maid away with him he bare,
And ever since hath kept in darksome cave,
For that I would not yeeld, that to *Sans-foy*
I gave.

48

But since faire Sunne hath sperst that
lowring clowd,
And to my loathéd life now shewes some
light, 425
Under your beames I will me safely shrowd,
From dreaded storme of his disdainfull
spight:
To you th'inheritance belongs by right
Of brothers prayse, to you eke longs his love.
Let not his love, let not his restlesse spright
Be unreveng'd, that calles to you above 431
From wandring *Stygian* shores,[15] where it
doth endlesse move.

49

Thereto said he, faire Dame be nought dis-
maid
For sorrowes past; their griefe is with them
gone:
Ne yet of present perill be affraid; 435
For needlesse feare did never vantage none,
And helplesse hap it booteth not to mone,
Dead is *Sans-foy,* his vitall paines are past,

[15]Shores of the Styx where ghosts wander till they are carried across that river.

Though greevéd ghost for vengeance deepe do grone; 439
He lives, that shall him pay his dewties last,
And guiltie Elfin bloud shall sacrifice in hast.

50

O but I feare the fickle freakes (quoth shee)
Of fortune false, and oddes of armes in field.
Why dame (quoth he) what oddes can ever bee,
Where both do fight alike, to win or yield? 445
Yea but (quoth she) he beares a charméd shield,
And eke enchaunted armes, that none can perce,
Ne none can wound the man, that does them wield.
Charmd or enchaunted (answerd he then ferce)
I no whit reck, ne you the like need to reherce. 450

51

But faire *Fidessa,* sithens fortunes guile,
Or enimies powre hath now captivéd you,
Returne from whence ye came, and rest a while
Till morrow next, that I the Elfe subdew,
And with *Sans-foyes* dead dowry you endew.
Ay me, that is a double death (she said) 456
With proud foes sight my sorrow to renew:
Where ever yet I be, my secret aid
Shall follow you, So passing forth she him obaid.

CANTO V

The faithfull knight in equall field
subdewes his faithlesse foe.
Whom false Duessa saves, and for
his cure to hell does goe.

1

The noble hart, that harbours vertuous thought,
And is with child of glorious great intent,
Can never rest, untill it forth have brought
Th'eternall brood of glorie excellent:
Such restlesse passion did all night torment 5
The flaming corage of that Faery knight,
Devizing, how that doughtie turnament
With greatest honour he atchieven might;
Still did he wake, and still did watch for dawning light.

2

At last the golden Orientall gate 10
Of greatest heaven gan to open faire,
And *Phoebus* fresh, as bridegrome to his mate,
Came dauncing forth, shaking his deawie haire:
And hurld his glistring beames through gloomy aire.
Which when the wakeful Elfe perceiv'd, streight way 15
He started up, and did him selfe prepaire,
In sun-bright armes, and battailous array:
For with that Pagan proud he combat will that day.

3

And forth he comes into the commune hall,
Where earely waite him many a gazing eye, 20
To weet what end to straunger knights may fall.
There many Minstrales maken melody,
To drive away the dull melancholy,
And many Bardes, that to the trembling chord
Can tune their timely voyces cunningly, 25
And many Chroniclers, that can record
Old loves, and warres for Ladies doen by many a Lord.

4

Soone after comes the cruell Sarazin,
In woven maile all arméd warily,
And sternly lookes at him, who not a pin 30
Does care for looke of living creatures eye.
They bring them wines of *Greece* and *Araby,*
And daintie spices fetcht from furthest *Ynd,*
To kindle heat of corage privily:
And in the wine a solemne oth they bynd 35
T'observe the sacred lawes of armes, that are assynd.

5

At last forth comes that far renowméd Queene,
With royall pomp and Princely majestie;
She is ybrought unto a paléd greene,
And placéd under stately canapee, 40
The warlike feates of both those knights to see.
On th'other side in all mens open vew
Duessa placéd is, and on a tree
Sans-foy his shield is hangd with bloudy hew:
Both those the lawrell girlonds to the victor dew.[1] 45

[1] I. e., both Duessa and the shield are to be the victor's rewards.

6

A shrilling trompet sownded from on hye,
And unto battaill bad them selves addresse:
Their shining shieldes about their wrestes they tye,
And burning blades about their heads do blesse,
The instruments of wrath and heavinesse: 50
With greedy force each other doth assayle,
And strike so fiercely, that they do impresse
Deepe dinted furrowes in the battred mayle;
The yron walles to ward their blowes are weake and fraile. 54

7

The Sarazin was stout, and wondrous strong,
And heapéd blowes like yron hammers great:
For after bloud and vengeance he did long.
The knight was fiers, and full of youthly heat:
And doubled strokes, like dreaded thunders threat:
For all for prayse and honour he did fight. 60
Both stricken strike, and beaten both do beat,
That from their shields forth flyeth firie light,
And helmets hewen deepe, shew marks of eithers might.

8

So th'one for wrong, the other strives for right:
As when a Gryfon seizéd of his pray, 65
A Dragon fiers encountreth in his flight,
Through widest ayre making his ydle way,
That would his rightfull ravine rend away:
With hideous horrour both together smight,
And souce so sore, that they the heavens affray: 70
The wise Southsayer seeing so sad sight,
Th'amazéd vulgar tels of warres and mortall fight.

9

So th'one for wrong, the other strives for right,
And each to deadly shame would drive his foe:
The cruell steele so greedily doth bight 75
In tender flesh, that streames of bloud down flow,
With which the armes, that earst so bright did show,
Into a pure vermillion now are dyde:
Great ruth in all the gazers harts did grow,
Seeing the goréd woundes to gape so wyde, 80
That victory they dare not wish to either side.

10

At last the Paynim chaunst to cast his eye,
His suddein eye, flaming with wrathfull fyre,
Upon his brothers shield, which hong thereby:
Therewith redoubled was his raging yre, 85
And said, Ah wretched sonne of wofull syre,
Doest thou sit wayling by black *Stygian* lake,
Whilest here thy shield is hangd for victors hyre,
And sluggish german doest thy forces slake,
To after-send his foe, that him may overtake? 90

11

Goe caytive Elfe, him quickly overtake,
And soone redeeme from his long wandring woe;
Goe guiltie ghost, to him my message make,
That I his shield have quit from dying foe.
Therewith upon his crest he stroke him so, 95
That twise he reeléd, readie twise to fall;
End of the doubtfull battell deeméd tho
The lookers on, and lowd to him gan call
The false *Duessa,* Thine the shield, and I, and all.

12

Soone as the Faerie heard his Ladie speake, 100
Out of his swowning dreame he gan awake,
And quickning faith, that earst was woxen weake,
The creeping deadly cold away did shake:
Tho mov'd with wrath, and shame, and Ladies sake,
Of all attonce he cast avengd to bee, 105
And with so'exceeding furie at him strake,
That forcéd him to stoupe upon his knee;
Had he not stoupéd so, he should have cloven bee.

13

And to him said, Goe now proud Miscreant,
Thy selfe thy message doe to german deare, 110
Alone he wandring thee too long doth want:
Goe say, his foe thy shield with his doth beare.
Therewith his heavie hand he high gan reare,
Him to have slaine; when loe a darkesome clowd
Upon him fell: he no where doth appeare, 115
But vanisht is. The Elfe him cals alowd,
But answer none receives: the darknes him does shrowd.

14

In haste *Duessa* from her place arose,
And to him running said, O prowest knight,
That ever Ladie to her love did chose, 120
Let now abate the terror of your might,
And quench the flame of furious despight,
And bloudie vengeance; lo th'infernall powres
Covering your foe with cloud of deadly night,
Have borne him hence to *Plutoes* balefull bowres. 125
The conquest yours, I yours, the shield, and glory yours.

15

Not all so satisfide, with greedie eye
He sought all round about his thirstie blade
To bath in bloud of faithlesse enemy;
Who all that while lay hid in secret shade: 130
He standes amazéd, how he thence should fade.
At last the trumpets, Triumph sound on hie,
And running Heralds humble homage made,
Greeting him goodly with new victorie,
And to him brought the shield, the cause of enmitie. 135

16

Wherewith he goeth to that soveraine Queene,
And falling her before on lowly knee,
To her makes present of his service seene:
Which she accepts, with thankes, and goodly gree,
Greatly advauncing his gay chevalree. 140
So marcheth home, and by her takes the knight,
Whom all the people follow with great glee,
Shouting, and clapping all their hands on hight,
That all the aire it fils, and flyes to heaven bright.

17

Home is he brought, and laid in sumptuous bed: 145
Where many skilfull leaches him abide,
To salve his hurts, that yet still freshly bled.
In wine and oyle they wash his woundés wide,
And softly can embalme on every side.
And all the while, most heavenly melody 150
About the bed sweet musicke did divide,
Him to beguile of griefe and agony:
And all the while *Duessa* wept full bitterly.

18

As when a wearie traveller that strayes
By muddy shore of broad seven-mouthéd *Nile,* 155
Unweeting of the perillous wandring wayes,
Doth meet a cruell craftie Crocodile,
Which in false griefe hyding his harmefull guile,
Doth weepe full sore, and sheddeth tender teares:
The foolish man, that pitties all this while 160
His mournefull plight, is swallowd up unwares,
Forgetfull of his owne, that mindes anothers cares.

19

So wept *Duessa* untill eventide,
That shyning lampes in *Joves* high house were light:
Then forth she rose, ne lenger would abide, 165
But comes unto the place, where th'Hethen knight
In slombring swownd nigh voyd of vitall spright,
Lay cover'd with inchaunted cloud all day:
Whom when she found, as she him left in plight,[2]
To wayle his woefull case she would not stay,
But to the easterne coast of heaven makes speedy way. 171

20

Where griesly *Night,* with visage deadly sad,
That *Phoebus* chearefull face durst never vew,
And in a foule blacke pitchie mantle clad,
She findes forth comming from her darkesome mew, 175
Where she all day did hide her hated hew.
Before the dore her yron charet stood,
Alreadie harnesséd for journey new;
And coleblacke steedes yborne of hellish brood,
That on their rustie bits did champ, as they were wood. 180

21

Who when she saw *Duessa* sunny bright,
Adornd with gold and jewels shining cleare,
She greatly grew amazéd at the sight,
And th'unacquainted light began to feare: 184

[2]She found him in the same condition as when she had left him.

For never did such brightnesse there appeare,
And would have backe retyréd to her cave,
Untill the witches speech she gan to heare,
Saying, Yet O thou dreaded Dame, I crave
Abide, till I have told the message, which I have. 189

22

She stayd, and foorth *Duessa* gan proceede,
O thou most auncient Grandmother of all,[3]
More old then *Jove,* whom thou at first didst breede,
Or that great house of Gods caelestiall,
Which wast begot in *Daemogorgons* hall, 194
And sawst the secrets of the world unmade,[4]
Why suffredst thou thy Nephewes deare to fall
With Elfin sword, most shamefully betrade?
Lo where the stout *Sansjoy* doth sleepe in deadly shade.

23

And him before, I saw with bitter eyes
The bold *Sansfoy* shrinke underneath his speare; 200
And now the pray of fowles in field he lyes,
Nor wayld of friends, nor laid on groning beare,
That whylome was to me too dearely deare.
O what of Gods then boots it to be borne,
If old *Aveugles*[5] sonnes so evill heare?[6] 205
Or who shall not great *Nightés* children scorne,
When two of three her Nephews are so fowle forlorne?

24

Up then, up dreary Dame, of darknesse Queene,
Go gather up the reliques of thy race,
Or else goe them avenge, and let be seene, 210
That dreaded *Night* in brightest day hath place,
And can the children of faire light deface.
Her feeling speeches some compassion moved
In hart, and chaunge in that great mothers face:
Yet pittie in her hart was never proved 215
Till then: for evermore she hated, never loved.

25

And said, Deare daughter rightly may I rew
The fall of famous children borne of mee,
And good successes, which their foes ensew:
But who can turne the streame of destinee, 220
Or breake the chayne of strong necessitee,
Which fast is tyde to *Joves* eternall seat?
The sonnes of Day he favoureth, I see,
And by my ruines thinkes to make them great:
To make one great by others losse, is bad excheat. 225

26

Yet shall they not escape so freely all;
For some shall pay the price of others guilt:
And he the man that made *Sansfoy* to fall,
Shall with his owne bloud price that he hath spilt. 229
But what art thou, that telst of Nephews kilt?
I that do seeme not I, *Duessa* am,
(Quoth she) how ever now in garments gilt,
And gorgeous gold arayd I to thee came;
Duessa I, the daughter of Deceipt and Shame. 234

27

Then bowing downe her agéd backe, she kist
The wicked witch, saying; In that faire face
The false resemblance of Deceipt, I wist
Did closely lurke; yet so true-seeming grace
It carried, that I scarse in darkesome place
Could it discerne, though I the mother bee 240
Of falshood, and root of *Duessaes* race.
O welcome child, whom I have longd to see,
And now have seene unwares. Lo now I go with thee.

28

Then to her yron wagon she betakes,
And with her beares the fowle welfavourd witch: 245
Through mirkesome aire her readie way she makes.
Her twyfold Teme, of which two blacke as pitch,
And two were browne, yet each to each unlich,
Did softly swim away, ne ever stampe,
Unlesse she chaunst their stubborne mouths to twitch; 250
Then foming tarre, their bridles they would champe,
And trampling the fine element,[7] would fiercely rampe.

[3]Night and Earth were daughters of Chaos and older than the Olympian gods.

[4]The secrets of Chaos, existing when the world was yet unmade.

[5]Spiritual Blindness.

[6]Are brought to such disgrace.

[7]The air.

29

So well they sped, that they be come at length
Unto the place, whereas the Paynim lay,
Devoid of outward sense,[8] and native strength, 255
Coverd with charméd cloud from vew of day,
And sight of men, since his late luckelesse fray.
His cruell wounds with cruddy bloud congealéd,
They binden up so wisely, as they may,
And handle softly, till they can be healéd: 260
So lay him in her charet, close in night concealéd.

30

And all the while she stood upon the ground,
The wakefull dogs did never cease to bay,
As giving warning of th'unwonted sound,
With which her yron wheeles did them affray, 265
And her darke griesly looke them much dismay;
The messenger of death, the ghastly Owle
With drearie shriekes did also her bewray;
And hungry Wolves continually did howle,
At her abhorréd face, so filthy and so fowle. 270

31

Thence turning backe in silence soft they stole,
And brought the heavie corse with easie pace
To yawning gulfe of deepe *Avernus* hole,
By that same hole an entrance darke and bace
With smoake and sulphure hiding all the place, 275
Descends to hell: there creature never past,
That backe returnéd without heavenly grace;
But dreadfull *Furies,* which their chaines have brast,
And damnéd sprights sent forth to make ill men aghast.

32

By that same way the direfull dames doe drive 280
Their mournefull charet, fild with rusty blood,
And downe to *Plutoes* house are come bilive:
Which passing through, on every side them stood

[8]Unconscious.

The trembling ghosts with sad amazéd mood, 284
Chattring their yron teeth, and staring wide
With stonie eyes; and all the hellish brood
Of feends infernall flockt on every side,
To gaze on earthly wight, that with the Night durst ride.

33

They pas the bitter waves of *Acheron,*[9]
Where many soules sit wailing woefully, 290
And come to fiery flood of *Phlegeton,*[9]
Whereas the damnéd ghosts in torments fry,
And with sharpe shrilling shriekes doe bootlesse cry,
Cursing high *Jove,* the which them thither sent. 294
The house of endlesse paine is built thereby,
In which ten thousand sorts of punishment
The curséd creatures doe eternally torment.

34

Before the threshold dreadfull *Cerberus*[10]
His three deforméd heads did lay along,
Curléd with thousand adders venemous, 300
And lilléd forth his bloudie flaming tong:
At them he gan to reare his bristles strong,
And felly gnarre, untill dayes enemy
Did him appease; then downe his taile he hong
And suffered them to passen quietly: 305
For she in hell and heaven had power equally.

35

There was *Ixion* turnéd on a wheele,
For daring tempt the Queene of heaven[11] to sin;
And *Sisyphus* an huge round stone did reele
Against an hill, ne might from labour lin; 310
There thirstie *Tantalus* hong by the chin;[12]
And *Tityus* fed a vulture on his maw;
Typhoeus joynts were stretchéd on a gin, 313
Theseus condemned to endlesse slouth by law,
And fifty sisters[13] water in leake vessels draw. 315

36

They all beholding worldly wights in place,
Leave off their worke, unmindfull of their smart,

[9]River of Hades.
[10]The dog who guarded Hades.
[11]Hera.
[12]Tantalus was punished with the sight of food and water which he could never reach.
[13]The Danaides, who slew their husbands.

To gaze on them; who forth by them doe
pace,
Till they be come unto the furthest part:
Where was a Cave ywrought by wondrous
art, 320
Deepe, darke, uneasie, dolefull, comfortlesse,
In which sad *Aesculapius* farre apart
Emprisond was in chaines remedilesse,
For that *Hippolytus* rent corse he did re-
dresse.

37

Hippolytus a jolly huntsman was, 325
That wont in charet chace the foming Bore;
He all his Peeres in beautie did surpas,
But Ladies love as losse of time forbore:
His wanton stepdame[14] lovéd him the more,
But when she saw her offred sweets re-
fused 330
Her love she turnd to hate, and him before
His father fierce of treason false accused,
And with her gealous termes his open eares
abused.

38

Who all in rage his Sea-god syre besought,
Some curséd vengeance on his sonne to cast:
From surging gulf two monsters straight
were brought, 336
With dread whereof his chasing steedes
aghast,
Both charet swift and huntsman overcast.
His goodly corps on ragged cliffs yrent,
Was quite dismembred, and his members
chast 340
Scattered on every mountaine, as he went,
That of *Hippolytus* was left no moniment.

39

His cruell stepdame seeing what was donne,
Her wicked dayes with wretched knife did
end, 344
In death avowing th'innocence of her sonne.
Which hearing, his rash Syre began to rend
His haire, and hastie tongue, that did offend:
Tho gathering up the relicks of his smart[15]
By *Dianes* meanes, who was *Hippolyts*
frend, 349
Them brought to *Aesculape,* that by his art
Did heale them all againe, and joynéd every
part.

40

Such wondrous science in mans wit to raine
When *Jove* avizd, that could the dead revive,
And fates expiréd could renew againe,
Of endlesse life he might him not deprive, 355
But unto hell did thrust him downe alive,
With flashing thunderbolt ywounded sore:
Where long remaining, he did alwaies strive
Himselfe with salves to health for to restore,
And slake the heavenly fire, that ragéd ever-
more. 360

41

There auncient Night arriving, did alight
From her nigh wearie waine, and in her
armes
To *Aesculapius* brought the wounded knight:
Whom having softly disarayd of armes,
Tho gan to him discover all his harmes, 365
Beseeching him with prayer, and with praise,
If either salves, or oyles, or herbes, or
charmes
A fordonne wight from dore of death mote
raise,
He would at her request prolong her nephews
daies.

42

Ah Dame (quoth he) thou temptest me in
vaine, 370
To dare the thing, which daily yet I rew,
And the old cause of my continued paine
With like attempt to like end to renew.
Is not enough, that thrust from heaven dew
Here endlesse penance for one fault I pay, 375
But that redoubled crime with vengeance new
Thou biddest me to eeke? Can Night defray
The wrath of thundring *Jove,* that rules both
night and day?

43

Not so (quoth she) but sith that heavens
king
From hope of heaven hath thee excluded
quight, 380
Why fearest thou, that canst not hope for
thing,
And fearest not, that more thee hurten
might,
Now in the powre of everlasting Night?
Goe to then, O thou farre renowméd sonne
Of great *Apollo,* shew thy famous might 385
In medicine, that else hath to thee wonne
Great paines, and greater praise, both never
to be donne.

[14]Phaedra.

[15]The fragments of Hippolytus's body.

44

Her words prevaild: And then the learnéd leach
His cunning hand gan to his wounds to lay,
And all things else, the which his art did teach: 390
Which having seene, from thence arose away
The mother of dread darknesse, and let stay
Aveugles sonne there in the leaches cure,
And backe returning tooke her wonted way,
To runne her timely race, whilst *Phoebus* pure 395
In westerne waves his wearie wagon did recure.

45

The false *Duessa* leaving noyous Night,
Returnd to stately pallace of dame Pride;
Where when she came, she found the Faery knight
Departed thence, albe his woundés wide 400
Not throughly heald, unreadie were to ride.
Good cause he had to hasten thence away;
For on a day his wary Dwarfe had spide,
Where in a dongeon deepe huge numbers lay
Of caytive wretched thrals, that wayléd night and day. 405

46

A ruefull sight, as could be seene with eie;
Of whom he learnéd had in secret wise
The hidden cause of their captivitie,
How mortgaging their lives to *Covetise,* 409
Through wastfull Pride, and wanton Riotise,
They were by law of that proud Tyrannesse
Provokt with *Wrath,* and *Envies* false surmise,
Condemnéd to that Dongeon mercilesse,
Where they should live in woe, and die in wretchednesse.

47

There was that great proud king of *Babylon,*[16] 415
That would compell all nations to adore,
And him as onely God to call upon,
Till through celestiall doome throwne out of dore,
Into an Oxe he was transform'd of yore: 419
There also was king *Croesus,* that enhaunst
His heart too high through his great riches store;
And proud *Antiochus,* the which advaunst
His curséd hand gainst God, and on his altars daunst.

[16]Nebuchadnezzar.

48

And then long time before, great *Nimrod* was,
That first the world with sword and fire warrayd; 425
And after him old *Ninus*[17] farre did pas
In princely pompe, of all the world obayd;
There also was that mightie Monarch[18] layd
Low under all, yet above all in pride, 429
That name of native syre did fowle upbrayd,
And would as *Ammons* sonne be magnifide,
Till scornd of God and man a shamefull death he dide.[19]

49

All these together in one heape were throwne,
Like carkases of beasts in butchers stall.
And in another corner wide were strowne 435
The antique ruines of the *Romaines* fall:
Great *Romulus* the Grandsyre of them all,
Proud *Tarquin,* and too lordly *Lentulus,*
Stout *Scipio,* and stubborne *Hanniball,*
Ambitious *Sylla,* and sterne *Marius,* 440
High *Caesar,* great *Pompey,* and fierce *Antonius.*[20]

50

Amongst these mighty men were wemen mixt,
Proud wemen, vaine, forgetfull of their yoke:[21]
The bold *Semiramis,*[22] whose sides transfixt
With sonnes owne blade, her fowle reproches spoke; 445
Faire *Sthenoboea,*[23] that her selfe did choke
With wilfull cord, for wanting of her will;
High minded *Cleopatra,* that with stroke
Of Aspés sting her selfe did stoutly kill:
And thousands moe the like, that did that dongeon fill. 450

51

Besides the endlesse routs of wretched thralles,
Which thither were assembled day by day,

[17]According to legend, the founder of Nineveh.

[18]Alexander the Great, who dishonored the name of his father Philip, in allowing himself to be called the son of Jupiter Ammon.

[19]It was believed that Alexander died of drunkenness.

[20]Mark Antony.

[21]Forgetful of the subordination proper to their sex.

[22]According to legend, the wife of Ninus.

[23]Slew herself because of love for Bellerophon.

From all the world after their wofull falles,
Through wicked pride, and wasted wealthes decay.
But most of all, which in that Dongeon lay 455
Fell from high Princes courts, or Ladies bowres,
Where they in idle pompe, or wanton play,
Consuméd had their goods, and thriftlesse howres,
And lastly throwne themselves into these heavy stowres.

52

Whose case when as the carefull Dwarfe had tould, 460
And made ensample of their mournefull sight
Unto his maister, he no lenger would
There dwell in perill of like painefull plight,
But early rose, and ere that dawning light
Discovered had the world to heaven wyde, 465
He by a privie Posterne tooke his flight,
That of no envious eyes he mote be spyde:
For doubtlesse death ensewd, if any him descryde.

53

Scarce could he footing find in that fowle way,
For many corses, like a great Lay-stall 470
Of murdred men which therein strowéd lay,
Without remorse, or decent funerall:
Which all through that great Princesse pride did fall
And came to shamefull end. And them beside
Forth ryding underneath the castell wall, 475
A donghill of dead carkases he spide,
The dreadfull spectacle of that sad house of *Pride*.

CANTO VI

From lawlesse lust by wondrous grace
fayre Una is releast:
Whom salvage nation does adore,
and learnes her wise beheast.

1

As when a ship, that flyes faire under saile,
An hidden rocke escapéd hath unwares,
That lay in waite her wrack for to bewaile,[1]
The Marriner yet halfe amazéd stares
At perill past, and yet in doubt ne dares 5
To joy at his foole-happie oversight:
So doubly is distrest twixt joy and cares
The dreadlesse courage of this Elfin knight,
Having escapt so sad ensamples in his sight.

2

Yet sad he was that his too hastie speed 10
The faire *Duess'* had forst him leave behind;
And yet more sad, that *Una* his deare dreed
Her truth had staind with treason so unkind;
Yet crime in her could never creature find,
But for his love, and for her owne selfe sake,
She wandred had from one to other *Ynd*,[2] 16
Him for to seeke, ne ever would forsake,
Till her unwares the fierce *Sansloy* did overtake.

3

Who after *Archimagoes* fowle defeat,
Led her away into a forrest wilde, 20
And turning wrathfull fire to lustfull heat,
With beastly sin thought her to have defilde,
And made the vassall of his pleasures vilde.
Yet first he cast by treatie, and by traynes, 24
Her to perswade, that stubborne fort to yilde:
For greater conquest of hard love he gaynes,
That workes it to his will, then he that it constraines.

4

With fawning wordes he courted her a while,
And looking lovely, and oft sighing sore,
Her constant hart did tempt with diverse guile: 30
But wordes, and lookes, and sighes she did abhore,
As rocke of Diamond stedfast evermore.
Yet for to feed his fyrie lustfull eye,
He snatcht the vele, that hong her face before;
Then gan her beautie shine, as brightest skye, 35
And burnt his beastly hart t'efforce her chastitye.

5

So when he saw his flatt'ring arts to fayle,
And subtile engines bat from batteree,
With greedy force he gan the fort assayle,
Whereof he weend possesséd soone to bee, 40
And win rich spoile of ransackt chastetee.
Ah heavens, that do this hideous act behold,
And heavenly virgin thus outragéd see,
How can ye vengeance just so long withhold,
And hurle not flashing flames upon that Paynim bold? 45

[1]To cause her wreck to be bewailed.

[2]From the East to the West Indies, figurative expression for a great distance.

6

The pitteous maiden carefull comfortlesse,
Does throw out thrilling shriekes, and shrieking cryes,
The last vaine helpe of womens great distresse,
And with loud plaints importuneth the skyes,
That molten starres do drop like weeping eyes; 50
And *Phoebus* flying so most shamefull sight,
His blushing face in foggy cloud implyes,
And hides for shame. What wit of mortall wight
Can now devise to quit a thrall from such a plight?

7

Eternall providence exceeding thought, 55
Where none appeares can make her selfe a way:
A wondrous way it for this Lady wrought,
From Lyons clawes to pluck the gripéd pray.
Her shrill outcryes and shriekes so loud did bray,
That all the woodes and forestes did resownd; 60
A troupe of *Faunes* and *Satyres*[3] far away
Within the wood were dauncing in a rownd,
Whiles old *Sylvanus*[4] slept in shady arber sownd.

8

Who when they heard that pitteous strainéd voice,
In hast forsooke their rurall meriment, 65
And ran towards the far rebownded noyce,
To weet, what wight so loudly did lament.
Unto the place they come incontinent:
Whom when the raging Sarazin espide,
A rude, misshapen, monstrous rablement, 70
Whose like he never saw, he durst not bide,
But got his ready steed, and fast away gan ride.

9

The wyld woodgods arrivéd in the place,
There find the virgin dolefull desolate,
With ruffled rayments, and faire blubbred face, 75
As her outrageous foe had left her late,
And trembling yet through feare of former hate;
All stand amazéd at so uncouth sight,
And gin to pittie her unhappie state;
All stand astonied at her beautie bright, 80
In their rude eyes unworthie of so wofull plight.

10

She more amaz'd, in double dread doth dwell;
And every tender part for feare does shake:
As when a greedie Wolfe through hunger fell
A seely Lambe farre from the flocke does take, 85
Of whom he meanes his bloudie feast to make,
A Lyon spyes fast running towards him,
The innocent pray in hast he does forsake,
Which quit from death yet quakes in every lim
With chaunge of feare, to see the Lyon looke so grim. 90

11

Such fearefull fit assaid her trembling hart,
Ne word to speake, ne joynt to move she had:
The salvage nation feele her secret smart,
And read her sorrow in her count'nance sad;
Their frowning forheads with rough hornes yclad, 95
And rusticke horror all aside doe lay,
And gently grenning, shew a semblance glad
To comfort her, and feare to put away,
Their backward bent knees teach her humbly to obay.[5] 99

12

The doubtfull Damzell dare not yet commit
Her single person to their barbarous truth,
But still twixt feare and hope amazd does sit,
Late learnd what harme to hastie trust ensu'th,
They in compassion of her tender youth,
And wonder of her beautie soveraine, 105
Are wonne with pitty and unwonted ruth,
And all prostrate upon the lowly plaine,
Do kisse her feete, and fawne on her with count'nance faine.

13

Their harts she ghesseth by their humble guise,
And yieldes her to extremitie of time;[6] 110
So from the ground she fearelesse doth arise,
And walketh forth without suspect of crime:

[3] The Latin and Greek wood-gods. Here, however, they represent unenlightened mankind, "common people."

[4] Roman woodland deity, here simply the chief figure among the fauns and satyrs.

[5] They teach their knees (backward-bent like those of a goat) to obey her humbly—i. e., they kneel or bow low to her.

[6] Accommodates herself to the extremity she is in.

They all as glad, as birdes of joyous Prime,
Thence lead her forth, about her dauncing
round, 114
Shouting, and singing all a shepheards ryme
And with greene braunches strowing all the
ground,
Do worship her, as Queene, with olive girlond
cround.

14

And all the way their merry pipes they sound,
That all the woods with doubled Eccho ring,
And with their hornéd feet do weare the
ground, 120
Leaping like wanton kids in pleasant Spring.
So towards old *Sylvanus* they her bring;
Who with the noyse awakéd, commeth out,
To weet the cause, his weake steps governing,
And agéd limbs on Cypresse stadle stout, 125
And with an yvie twyne his wast is girt about.

15

Far off he wonders, what them makes so
glad,
Or *Bacchus* merry fruit they did invent,
Or *Cybeles* franticke rites have made them
mad;
They drawing nigh, unto their God pre-
sent 130
That flowre of faith and beautie excellent.
The God himselfe vewing that mirrhour
rare,[7]
Stood long amazd, and burnt in his intent;
His owne faire *Dryope* now he thinkes not
faire,
And *Pholoe* fowle, when her to this he doth
compaire. 135

16

The woodborne people fall before her flat,
And worship her as Goddesse of the wood:
And old *Sylvanus* selfe bethinkes not, what
To thinke of wight so faire, but gazing stood,
In doubt to deeme her borne of earthly
brood; 140
Sometimes Dame *Venus* selfe he seemes to
see,
But *Venus* never had so sober mood;
Sometimes *Diana* he her takes to bee,
But misseth bow, and shaftes, and buskins to
her knee.

17

By vew of her he ginneth to revive 145
His ancient love, and dearest *Cyparisse*,
And calles to mind his pourtraiture alive,
How faire he was, and yet not faire to this,
And how he slew with glauncing dart amisse
A gentle Hynd, the which the lovely boy 150
Did love as life, above all worldly blisse;
For griefe whereof the lad n'ould after joy,
But pynd away in anguish and selfe-wild
annoy.

18

The wooddy Nymphes, faire *Hamadryades*[8]
Her to behold do thither runne apace, 155
And all the troupe of light-foot *Naiades*,[9]
Flocke all about to see her lovely face:
But when they vewéd have her heavenly
grace,
They envie her in their malitious mind,
And fly away for feare of fowle disgrace: 160
But all the *Satyres* scorne their woody kind,
And henceforth nothing faire, but her on
earth they find.

19

Glad of such lucke, the luckelesse lucky maid,
Did her content to please their feeble eyes,[10]
And long time with that salvage people
staid, 165
To gather breath in many miseries.
During which time her gentle wit she plyes,
To teach them truth, which worshipt her in
vaine,
And made her th'Image of Idolatryes;
But when their bootlesse zeale she did re-
straine 170
From her own worship, they her Asse would
worship fayn.

20

It fortunéd a noble warlike knight,[11]
By just occasion to that forrest came,
To seeke his kindred, and the lignage right,
From whence he tooke his well deservéd
name: 175
He had in armes abroad wonne muchell fame,
And fild far landes with glorie of his might,
Plaine, faithfull, true, and enimy of shame,
And ever lov'd to fight for Ladies right,
But in vaine glorious frayes he litle did de-
light. 180

[7]Una is a mirror in the sense that in her appearance she reflects the heavenly beauty.

[8]Spirits of the trees.

[9]Water-nymphs.

[10]Feeble to discern spiritual things. As immediately appears, they cannot distinguish between truth and its symbols.

[11]Sir Satyrane, who typifies natural morality, not enlightened by revealed truth.

21

A Satyres sonne yborne in forrest wyld,
By straunge adventure as it did betyde,
And there begotten of a Lady myld,
Faire *Thyamis* the daughter of *Labryde,*
That was in sacred bands of wedlocke tyde 185
To *Therion,* a loose unruly swayne;
Who had more joy to raunge the forrest wyde,
And chase the salvage beast with busie payne,
Then serve his Ladies love, and wast in pleasures vayne.

22

The forlorne mayd did with loves longing burne, 190
And could not lacke her lovers company,
But to the wood she goes, to serve her turne,
And seeke her spouse, that from her still does fly,
And followes other game and venery:
A Satyre chaunst her wandring for to find, 195
And kindling coles of lust in brutish eye,
The loyall links of wedlocke did unbind,
And made her person thrall unto his beastly kind.

23

So long in secret cabin there he held
Her captive to his sensuall desire, 200
Till that with timely fruit her belly sweld,
And bore a boy unto that salvage sire:
Then home he suffred her for to retire,
For ransome leaving him the late borne childe;
Whom till to ryper yeares he gan aspire, 205
He noursled up in life and manners wilde,
Emongst wild beasts and woods, from lawes of men exilde.

24

For all he taught the tender ymp, was but
To banish cowardize and bastard feare;
His trembling hand he would him force to put 210
Upon the Lyon and the rugged Beare,
And from the she Beares teats her whelps to teare;
And eke wyld roring Buls he would him make
To tame, and ryde their backes not made to beare;
And the Robuckes in flight to overtake, 215
That every beast for feare of him did fly and quake.

25

Thereby so fearelesse, and so fell he grew,
That his owne sire and maister of his guise
Did often tremble at his horrid vew, 219
And oft for dread of hurt would him advise,
The angry beasts not rashly to despise,
Not too much to provoke; for he would learne
The Lyon stoup to him in lowly wise,
(A lesson hard) and make the Libbard sterne
Leave roaring, when in rage he for revenge did earne. 225

26

And for to make his powre approvéd more,
Wyld beasts in yron yokes he would compell;
The spotted Panther, and the tuskéd Bore,
The Pardale swift, and the Tigre cruell; 229
The Antelope, and Wolfe both fierce and fell;
And them constraine in equall teme to draw.
Such joy he had, their stubborne harts to quell,
And sturdie courage tame with dreadfull aw,
That his beheast they fearéd, as a tyrans law.

27

His loving mother came upon a day 235
Unto the woods, to see her little sonne;
And chaunst unwares to meet him in the way,
After his sportes, and cruell pastime donne,
When after him a lyonesse did runne, 239
That roaring all with rage, did lowd requere
Her children deare, whom he away had wonne:
The Lyon whelpes she saw how he did beare,
And lull in rugged armes, withouten childish feare.

28

The fearefull Dame all quakéd at the sight,
And turning backe, gan fast to fly away, 245
Untill with love revokt from vaine affright
She hardly yet perswaded was to stay,
And then to him these womanish words gan say;
Ah *Satyrane,* my dearling, and my joy,
For love of me leave off this dreadfull play, 250
To dally thus with death, is no fit toy,
Go find some other play-fellowes, mine own sweet boy.

29

In these and like delights of bloudy game
He traynéd was, till ryper yeares he raught,

And there abode, whilst any beast of name 255
Walkt in that forest, whom he had not
taught
To feare his force: and then his courage
haught
Desird of forreine foemen to be knowne,
And far abroad for straunge adventures
sought: 259
In which his might was never overthrowne,
But through all Faery lond his famous worth
was blown.

30

Yet evermore it was his manner faire,
After long labours and adventures spent,
Unto those native woods for to repaire,
To see his sire and ofspring auncient. 265
And now he thither came for like intent;
Where he unwares the fairest *Una* found,
Straunge Lady, in so straunge habiliment,
Teaching the Satyres, which her sat around,
Trew sacred lore,[12] which from her sweet lips
did redound. 270

31

He wondred at her wisedome heavenly rare,
Whose like in womens wit he never knew;
And when her curteous deeds he did compare,
Gan her admire, and her sad sorrowes rew,
Blaming of Fortune, which such troubles
threw, 275
And joyd to make proofe of her crueltie
On gentle Dame, so hurtlesse, and so trew:
Thenceforth he kept her goodly company,
And learnd her discipline of faith and veritie.

32

But she all vowd unto the *Redcrosse* knight,
His wandring perill closely did lament, 281
Ne in this new acquaintaunce could delight,
But her deare heart with anguish did torment,
And all her wit in secret counsels spent,
How to escape. At last in privie wise 285
To *Satyrane* she shewéd her intent;
Who glad to gain such favour, gan devise,
How with that pensive Maid he best might
thence arise.

33

So on a day when Satyres all were gone,
To do their service to *Sylvanus* old, 290
The gentle virgin left behind alone
He led away with courage stout and bold.
Too late it was, to Satyres to be told,
Or ever hope recover her againe: 294
In vaine he seekes that having cannot hold.
So fast he carried her with carefull paine,
That they the woods are past, and come now
to the plaine.

34

The better part now of the lingring day,
They traveild had, when as they farre espide
A wearie wight forwandring by the way, 300
And towards him they gan in hast to ride,
To weet of newes, that did abroad betide,
Or tydings of her knight of the *Redcrosse*.
But he them spying, gan to turne aside,
For feare as seemd, or for some feignéd
losse; 305
More greedy they of newes, fast towards him
do crosse.

35

A silly man, in simple weedes forworne,
And soild with dust of the long driéd way;
His sandales were with toilesome travell
torne,
And face all tand with scorching sunny ray,
As he had traveild many a sommers day, 311
Through boyling sands of *Arabie* and *Ynde;*
And in his hand a *Jacobs* staffe, to stay
His wearie limbes upon: and eke behind,
His scrip did hang, in which his needments
he did bind. 315

36

The knight approching nigh, of him inquerd
Tydings of warre, and of adventures new;
But warres, nor new adventures none he
herd.
Then *Una* gan to aske, if ought he knew,
Or heard abroad of that her champion trew,
That in his armour bare a croslet red. 321
Aye me, Deare dame (quoth he) well may I
rew
To tell the sad sight, which mine eies have
red:
These eyes did see that knight both living
and eke ded.

37

That cruell word her tender hart so thrild, 325
That suddein cold did runne through every
vaine,
And stony horrour all her sences fild
With dying fit, that downe she fell for paine.

[12]The Gospel as interpreted by the Protestant reformers.

The knight her lightly rearéd up againe,
And comforted with curteous kind reliefe: 330
Then wonne from death, she bad him tellen plaine
The further processe of her hidden griefe;[13]
The lesser pangs can beare, who hath endur'd the chiefe.

38

Then gan the Pilgrim thus, I chaunst this day,
This fatall day, that shall I ever rew, 335
To see two knights in travell on my way
(A sory sight) arraung'd in battell new,
Both breathing vengeaunce, both of wrathfull hew;
My fearefull flesh did tremble at their strife,
To see their blades so greedily imbrew, 340
That drunke with bloud, yet thristed after life:
What more? the *Redcrosse* knight was slaine with Paynim knife.

39

Ah dearest Lord (quoth she) how might that bee,
And he the stoutest knight, that ever wonne?
Ah dearest dame (quoth he) how might I see 345
The thing, that might not be, and yet was donne?
Where is (said *Satyrane*) that Paynims sonne,
That him of life, and us of joy hath reft?
Not far away (quoth he) he hence doth wonne
Foreby a fountaine, where I late him left 350
Washing his bloudy wounds, that through the steele were cleft.

40

Therewith the knight thence marchéd forth in hast,
Whiles *Una* with huge heavinesse opprest,
Could not for sorrow follow him so fast;
And soone he came, as he the place had ghest, 355
Whereas that *Pagan* proud him selfe did rest,
In secret shadow by a fountaine side:
Even he it was, that earst would have supprest
Faire *Una:* whom when *Satyrane* espide,
With fowle reprochfull words he boldly him defide. 360

41

And said, Arise thou curséd Miscreaunt,
That hast with knightlesse guile and trecherous train
Faire knighthood fowly shamed, and doest vaunt
That good knight of the *Redcrosse* to have slain:
Arise, and with like treason now maintain 365
Thy guilty wrong, or else thee guilty yield.
The Sarazin this hearing, rose amain,
And catching up in hast his three square shield,
And shining helmet, soone him buckled to the field.

42

And drawing nigh him said, Ah misborne Elfe, 370
In evill houre thy foes thee hither sent,
Anothers wrongs to wreake upon thy selfe:
Yet ill thou blamest me, for having blent
My name with guile and traiterous intent;
That *Redcrosse* knight, perdie, I never slew,
But had he beene, where earst his armes were lent,[14] 376
Th'enchaunter vaine his errour should not rew:
But thou his errour shalt, I hope now proven trew.

43

Therewith they gan, both furious and fell,
To thunder blowes, and fiersly to assaile 380
Each other bent his enimy to quell,
That with their force they perst both plate and maile,
And made wide furrowes in their fleshes fraile,
That it would pitty any living eie.
Large floods of bloud adowne their sides did raile; 385
But floods of bloud could not them satisfie:
Both hungred after death: both chose to win, or die.

44

So long they fight, and fell revenge pursue,
That fainting each, themselves to breathen let,
And oft refreshéd, battell oft renue: 390
As when two Bores with rancling malice met,

[13] The details as yet unknown to her.

[14] Had he been wearing the armor which Archimago borrowed from him.

Their gory sides fresh bleeding fiercely fret,
Till breathlesse both them selves aside retire,
Where foming wrath, their cruell tuskes they whet,
And trample th'earth, the whiles they may respire; 395
Then backe to fight againe, new breathéd and entire.

45

So fiersly, when these knights had breathéd once,
They gan to fight returne, increasing more
Their puissant force, and cruell rage attonce,
With heapéd strokes more hugely, then before, 400
That with their drerie wounds and bloudy gore
They both deforméd, scarsely could be known.
By this sad *Una* fraught with anguish sore,
Led with their noise, which through the aire was thrown,
Arriv'd, where they in erth their fruitles bloud had sown. 405

46

Whom all so soone as that proud Sarazin
Espide, he gan revive the memory
Of his lewd lusts, and late attempted sin,
And left the doubtfull battell hastily,
To catch her, newly offred to his eie: 410
But *Satyrane* with strokes him turning, staid,
And sternely bad him other businesse plie,
Then hunt the steps of pure unspotted Maid:
Wherewith he all enrag'd, these bitter speaches said.

47

O foolish faeries sonne, what furie mad 415
Hath thee incenst, to hast thy dolefull fate?
Were it not better, I that Lady had,
Then that thou hadst repented it too late?
Most sencelesse man he, that himselfe doth hate,
To love another. Lo then for thine ayd 420
Here take thy lovers token on thy pate.
So they two fight; the whiles the royall Mayd
Fled farre away, of that proud Paynim sore afrayd.

48

But that false *Pilgrim,* which that leasing told,
Being in deed old *Archimage,* did stay 425
In secret shadow, all this to behold,
And much rejoycéd in their bloudy fray:
But when he saw the Damsell passe away
He left his stond, and her pursewd apace,
In hope to bring her to her last decay. 430
But for to tell her lamentable cace,
And eke this battels end, will need another place.[15]

CANTO VII

The Redcrosse knight is captive made
by Gyaunt proud opprest,
Prince Arthur meets with Una greatly
with those newes distrest.

1

What man so wise, what earthly wit so ware,
As to descry the crafty cunning traine,
By which deceipt doth maske in visour faire,
And cast her colours dyéd deepe in graine,
To seeme like Truth, whose shape she well can faine, 5
And fitting gestures to her purpose frame,
The guiltlesse man with guile to entertaine?
Great maistresse of her art was that false Dame,
The false *Duessa,* clokéd with *Fidessaes* name.

2

Who when returning from the drery *Night,* 10
She fownd not in that perilous house of *Pryde,*
Where she had left, the noble *Redcrosse* knight,
Her hopéd pray, she would no lenger bide,
But forth she went, to seeke him far and wide.
Ere long she fownd, whereas he wearie sate, 15
To rest him selfe, foreby a fountaine side,
Disarméd all of yron-coted Plate,
And by his side his steed the grassy forage ate.

3

He feedes upon the cooling shade, and bayes
His sweatie forehead in the breathing wind, 20
Which through the trembling leaves full gently playes
Wherein the cherefull birds of sundry kind
Do chaunt sweet musick, to delight his mind:
The Witch approching gan him fairely greet,
And with reproch of carelesnesse unkind 25

[15] But Spenser never told the outcome of this battle.

Upbrayd, for leaving her in place unmeet,
With fowle words tempring faire, soure gall with hony sweet.

4

Unkindnesse past, they gan of solace treat,
And bathe in pleasaunce of the joyous shade,
Which shielded them against the boyling heat, 30
And with greene boughes decking a gloomy glade,
About the fountaine like a girlond made;
Whose bubbling wave did ever freshly well,
Ne ever would through fervent sommer fade:
The sacred Nymph, which therein wont to dwell, 35
Was out of *Dianes* favour, as it then befell.

5

The cause was this: one day when *Phoebe*[1] fayre
With all her band was following the chace,
This Nymph, quite tyr'd with heat of scorching ayre,
Sat downe to rest in middest of the race: 40
The goddesse wroth gan fowly her disgrace,
And bad the waters, which from her did flow,
Be such as she her selfe was then in place.
Thence forth her waters waxéd dull and slow,
And all that drunke thereof, did faint and feeble grow. 45

6

Hereof this gentle knight unweeting was,
And lying downe upon the sandie graile,
Drunke of the streame, as cleare as cristall glas;
Eftsoones his manly forces gan to faile,
And mightie strong was turnd to feeble fraile. 50
His chaungéd powres at first them selves not felt,
Till crudled cold his corage gan assaile,
And chearefull bloud in faintnesse chill did melt,
Which like a fever fit through all his body swelt.

7

Yet goodly court he made still to his Dame, 55
Pourd out in loosnesse on the grassy grownd,
Both carelesse of his health, and of his fame:
Till at the last he heard a dreadful sownd,
Which through the wood loud bellowing, did rebownd, 59
That all the earth for terrour seemd to shake,
And trees did tremble. Th'Elfe therewith astownd,
Upstarted lightly from his looser make,
And his unready weapons gan in hand to take.

8

But ere he could his armour on him dight,
Or get his shield, his monstrous enimy 65
With sturdie steps came stalking in his sight,
An hideous Geant[2] horrible and hye,
That with his talnesse seemd to threat the skye,
The ground eke gronéd under him for dreed:
His living like saw never living eye, 70
Ne durst behold: his stature did exceed
The hight of three the tallest sonnes of mortall seed.

9

The greatest Earth his uncouth mother was,
And blustring *Aeolus* his boasted sire,
Who with his breath, which through the world doth pas, 75
Her hollow womb did secretly inspire,
And fild her hidden caves with stormie yre,
That she conceiv'd; and trebling the dew time,
In which the wombes of women do expire,
Brought forth this monstrous masse of earthly slime, 80
Puft up with emptie wind, and fild with sinfull crime.

10

So growen great through arrogant delight
Of th'high descent, whereof he was yborne,
And through presumption of his matchlesse might,
All other powres and knighthood he did scorne. 85
Such now he marcheth to this man forlorne,
And left to losse: his stalking steps are stayde
Upon a snaggy Oke, which he had torne
Out of his mothers bowelles, and it made
His mortall mace, wherewith his foemen he dismayde. 90

[1] Artemis.

[2] Orgoglio, typifying pride; not the pride of life typified by Lucifera, but the pride of a corrupt church immersed in temporal affairs—the Roman Catholic Church as Spenser saw it.

11

That when the knight he spide, he gan advance
With huge force and insupportable mayne,
And towardes him with dreadfull fury praunce;
Who haplesse, and eke hopelesse, all in vaine
Did to him pace, sad battaile to darrayne, 95
Disarmd, disgrast, and inwardly dismayde,
And eke so faint in every joynt and vaine,
Through that fraile fountaine, which him feeble made,
That scarsely could he weeld his bootlesse single blade.

12

The Geaunt strooke so maynly mercilesse, 100
That could have overthrowne a stony towre.
And were not heavenly grace, that him did blesse,
He had beene pouldred all, as thin as flowre:
But he was wary of that deadly stowre, 104
And lightly lept from underneath the blow:
Yet so exceeding was the villeins powre,
That with the wind it did him overthrow,
And all his sences stound, that still he lay full low.

13

As when that divelish yron Engin wrought
In deepest Hell, and framd by *Furies* skill, 110
With windy Nitre and quick Sulphur fraught
And ramd with bullet round, ordaind to kill,
Conceiveth fire, the heavens it doth fill
With thundring noyse, and all the ayre doth choke,
That none can breath, nor see, nor heare at will, 115
Through smouldry cloud of duskish stincking smoke,
That th'onely breath him daunts, who hath escapt the stroke.

14

So daunted when the Geaunt saw the knight,
His heavie hand he heavéd up on hye,
And him to dust thought to have battred quight, 120
Untill *Duessa* loud to him gan crye;
O great *Orgoglio,* greatest under skye,
O hold thy mortall hand for Ladies sake,
Hold for my sake, and do him not to dye,
But vanquisht thine eternall bondslave make,
And me thy worthy meed unto thy Leman take. 126

15

He hearkned, and did stay from further harmes,
To gayne so goodly guerdon, as she spake:
So willingly she came into his armes,
Who her as willingly to grace did take, 130
And was possesséd of his new found make,
Then up he tooke the slombred sencelesse corse,
And ere he could out of his swowne awake,
Him to his castle brought with hastie forse,
And in a Dongeon deepe him threw without remorse. 135

16

From that day forth *Duessa* was his deare,
And highly honourd in his haughtie eye,
He gave her gold and purple pall to weare,
And triple crowne set on her head full hye,
And her endowd with royall majestye: 140
Then for to make her dreaded more of men,
And peoples harts with awfull terrour tye,
A monstrous beast[3] ybred in filthy fen
He chose, which he had kept long time in darksome den.

17

Such one it was, as that renowméd Snake[4] 145
Which great *Alcides* in *Stremona* slew,
Long fostred in the filth of *Lerna* lake,
Whose many heads out budding ever new,
Did breed him endlesse labour to subdew: 149
But this same Monster much more ugly was;
For seven great heads out of his body grew,
And yron brest, and backe of scaly bras,
And all embrewd in bloud, his eyes did shine as glas.

18

His tayle was stretchéd out in wondrous length, 154
That to the house of heavenly gods it raught,
And with extorted powre, and borrow'd strength,
The ever-burning lamps from thence it brought,
And prowdly threw to ground, as things of nought;
And underneath his filthy feet did tread
The sacred things, and holy heasts foretaught. 160
Upon this dreadful Beast with sevenfold head
He set the false *Duessa,* for more aw and dread.

[3]Cf. Revelation, 17:3.
[4]The Lernean Hydra, slain by Hercules.

19

The wofull Dwarfe, which saw his maisters fall,
Whiles he had keeping of his grasing steed, 164
And valiant knight become a caytive thrall,
When all was past, tooke up his forlorne weed,
His mightie armour, missing most at need;
His silver shield, now idle maisterlesse;
His poynant speare, that many made to bleed,
The ruefull moniments of heavinesse, 170
And with them all departes, to tell his great distresse.

20

He had not travaild long, when on the way
He wofull Ladie, wofull *Una* met,
Fast flying from the Paynims greedy pray,
Whilest *Satyrane* him from pursuit did let: 175
Who when her eyes she on the Dwarfe had set,
And saw the signes, that deadly tydings spake,
She fell to ground for sorrowfull regret,
And lively breath her sad brest did forsake,
Yet might her pitteous hart be seene to pant and quake. 180

21

The messenger of so unhappie newes,
Would faine have dyde: dead was his hart within,
Yet outwardly some little comfort shewes:
At last recovering hart, he does begin
To rub her temples, and to chaufe her chin, 185
And every tender part does tosse and turne:
So hardly he the flitted life does win,
Unto her native prison to retourne:
Then gins her grievéd ghost thus to lament and mourne.

22

Ye dreary instruments of dolefull sight, 190
That doe this deadly spectacle behold,
Why do ye lenger feed on loathéd light,
Or liking find to gaze on earthly mould,
Sith cruell fates the carefull threeds unfould,
The which my life and love together tyde? 195
Now let the stony dart of senselesse cold
Perce to my hart, and pas through every side,
And let eternall night so sad sight fro me hide.

23

O lightsome day, the lampe of highest *Jove*,
First made by him, mens wandring wayes to guyde, 200
When darkenesse he in deepest dongeon drove,
Henceforth thy hated face for ever hyde,
And shut up heavens windowes shyning wyde:
For earthly sight can nought but sorrow breed,
And late repentance, which shall long abyde.
Mine eyes no more on vanitie shall feed, 206
But seeléd up with death, shall have their deadly meed.

24

Then downe againe she fell unto the ground;
But he her quickly rearéd up againe:
Thrise did she sinke adowne in deadly swownd, 210
And thrise he her reviv'd with busie paine:
At last when life recover'd had the raine,
And over-wrestled his strong enemie,
With foltring tong, and trembling every vaine,
Tell on (quoth she) the wofull Tragedie, 215
The which these reliques sad present unto mine eie.

25

Tempestuous fortune hath spent all her spight,
And thrilling sorrow throwne his utmost dart;
Thy sad tongue cannot tell more heavy plight, 219
Then that I feele, and harbour in mine hart:
Who hath endur'd the whole, can beare each part.
If death it be, it is not the first wound,
That launchéd hath my brest with bleeding smart.
Begin, and end the bitter balefull stound;
If lesse, then that I feare, more favour I have found. 225

26

Then gan the Dwarfe the whole discourse declare,
The subtill traines of *Archimago* old;
The wanton loves of false *Fidessa* faire,
Bought with the bloud of vanquisht Paynim bold:
The wretched payre transform'd to treen mould; 230

The house of Pride, and perils round about;
The combat, which he with *Sansjoy* did
hould;
The lucklesse conflict with the Gyant stout,
Wherein captiv'd, of life or death he stood
in doubt.[5]

27

She heard with patience all unto the end, 235
And strove to maister sorrowfull assay,
Which greater grew, the more she did con-
tend,
And almost rent her tender hart in tway;
And love fresh coles unto her fire did lay:
For greater love, the greater is the losse. 240
Was never Ladie lovéd dearer day,
Then she did love the knight of the *Red-
crosse;*[6]
For whose deare sake so many troubles her
did tosse.

28

At last when fervent sorrow slakéd was,
She up arose, resolving him to find 245
Alive or dead: and forward forth doth pas,
All as the Dwarfe the way to her assynd:
And evermore in constant carefull mind
She fed her wound with fresh renewéd bale;
Long tost with stormes, and bet with bitter
wind. 250
High over hils, and low adowne the dale,
She wandred many a wood, and measurd
many a vale.

29

At last she chauncéd by good hap to meet
A goodly knight,[7] faire marching by the way
Together with his Squire, arayéd meet: 255
His glitterand armour shinéd farre away,
Like glauncing light of *Phoebus* brightest
ray;
From top to toe no place appearéd bare,
That deadly dint of steele endanger may:
Athwart his brest a bauldrick brave he ware,
That shynd, like twinkling stars, with stons
most pretious rare. 261

30

And in the midst thereof one pretious stone
Of wondrous worth, and eke of wondrous
mights,
Shapt like a Ladies head, exceeding shone,
Like *Hesperus* emongst the lesser lights, 265
And strove for to amaze the weaker sights;
Thereby his mortall blade full comely hong
In yvory sheath, ycarv'd with curious slights;
Whose hilts were burnisht gold, and handle
strong
Of mother pearle, and buckled with a golden
tong. 270

31

His haughtie helmet, horrid all with gold,
Both glorious brightnesse, and great terrour
bred;
For all the crest a Dragon did enfold 273
With greedie pawes, and over all did spred
His golden wings: his dreadfull hideous hed
Close couchéd on the bever, seem'd to throw
From flaming mouth bright sparkles fierie
red,
That suddeine horror to faint harts did show;
And scaly tayle was stretcht adowne his
backe full low.

32

Upon the top of all his loftie crest, 280
A bunch of haires discolourd diversly,
With sprincled pearle, and gold full richly
drest,
Did shake, and seem'd to daunce for jollity,
Like to an Almond tree ymounted hye
On top of greene Selinis all alone, 285
With blossomes brave bedecked daintily;
Whose tender locks do tremble every one
At every little breath, that under heaven is
blowne.

33

His warlike shield all closely cover'd was,
Ne might of mortall eye be ever seene; 290
Not made of steele, nor of enduring bras,
Such earthly mettals soone consumed bene:
But all of Diamond perfect pure and cleene
It framéd was, one massie entire mould,
Hewen out of Adamant rocke with engines
keene, 295
That point of speare it never percen could,
Ne dint of direfull sword divide the sub-
stance would.

34

The same to wight he never wont disclose,
But when as monsters huge he would dismay,
Or daunt unequall armies of his foes, 300
Or when the flying heavens he would affray;

[5]Since the knight had been carried off a captive, the dwarf did not know whether he was still alive or dead.

[6]Lady never loved daylight more than she loved the Red Cross Knight.

[7]Prince Arthur, typifying that virtue which comprehends all the rest, magnanimity, and, in this book of the *Faerie Queene,* Heavenly Grace.

For so exceeding shone his glistring ray,
That *Phoebus* golden face it did attaint,[8]
As when a cloud his beames doth over-lay;
And silver *Cynthia* wexéd pale and faint, 305
As when her face is staynd with magicke arts constraint.[9]

35

No magicke arts hereof had any might,
Nor bloudie wordes of bold Enchaunters call,
But all that was not such, as seemd in sight,
Before that shield did fade, and suddeine fall: 310
And when him list the raskall routes appall,
Men into stones therewith he could transmew,
And stones to dust, and dust to nought at all;
And when him list the prouder lookes subdew,
He would them gazing blind, or turne to other hew. 315

36

Ne let it seeme, that credence this exceedes,
For he that made the same, was knowne right well
To have done much more admirable deedes.
It *Merlin* was, which whylome did excell 319
All living wightes in might of magicke spell:
Both shield, and sword, and armour all he wrought
For this young Prince, when first to armes he fell;
But when he dyde, the Faerie Queene it brought
To Faerie lond, where yet it may be seene, if sought.

37

A gentle youth, his dearely lovéd Squire 325
His speare of heben wood behind him bare,
Whose harmefull head, thrice heated in the fire,
Had riven many a brest with pikehead square;
A goodly person, and could menage faire,
His stubborne steed with curbéd canon bit, 330
Who under him did trample as the aire,
And chauft, that any on his backe should sit;
The yron rowels into frothy fome he bit.

38

When as this knight nigh to the Ladie drew,
With lovely court he gan her entertaine; 335
But when he heard her answeres loth, he knew
Some secret sorrow did her heart distraine:
Which to allay, and calme her storming paine,
Faire feeling words he wisely gan display,
And for her humour fitting purpose faine, 340
To tempt the cause it selfe for to bewray;
Wherewith emmov'd, these bleeding words she gan to say.

39

What worlds delight, or joy of living speach
Can heart, so plung'd in sea of sorrowes deepe, 344
And heapéd with so huge misfortunes, reach?
The carefull cold[10] beginneth for to creepe,
And in my heart his yron arrow steepe,
Soone as I think upon my bitter bale:
Such helplesse harmes yts better hidden keepe, 349
Then rip up griefe, where it may not availe,
My last left comfort is, my woes to weepe and waile.

40

Ah Ladie deare, quoth then the gentle knight,
Well may I weene, your griefe is wondrous great;
For wondrous great griefe groneth in my spright,
Whiles thus I heare you of your sorrowes treat. 355
But wofull Ladie let me you intrete,
For to unfold the anguish of your hart:
Mishaps are maistred by advice discrete,
And counsell mittigates the greatest smart;
Found never helpe, who never would his hurts impart. 360

41

O but (quoth she) great griefe will not be tould,
And can more easily be thought, then said.
Right so; (quoth he) but he, that never would,
Could never: will to might gives greatest aid.
But griefe (quoth she) does greater grow displaid, 365
If then it find not helpe, and breedes despaire.
Despaire breedes not (quoth he) where faith is staid.

[8]It was more brilliant than the sun. The light of truth outshines all others.

[9]It was believed that witches caused eclipses of the moon.

[10]The chill of grief.

No faith so fast (quoth she) but flesh does paire.
Flesh may empaire (quoth he) but reason can repaire.

42

His goodly reason, and well guided speach 370
So deepe did settle in her gratious thought,
That her perswaded to disclose the breach,
Which love and fortune in her heart had wrought,
And said; Faire Sir, I hope good hap hath brought
You to inquire the secrets of my griefe, 375
Or that your wisedome will direct my thought,
Or that your prowesse can me yield reliefe:
Then heare the storie sad, which I shall tell you briefe.

43

The forlorne Maiden, whom your eyes have seene
The laughing stocke of fortunes mockeries, 380
Am th'only daughter of a King and Queene,
Whose parents deare, whilest equall destinies
Did runne about,[11] and their felicities
The favourable heavens did not envy,
Did spread their rule through all the territories, 385
Which *Phison* and *Euphrates* floweth by,
And *Gehons*[12] golden waves doe wash continually.

44

Till that their cruell curséd enemy,
An huge great Dragon horrible in sight,
Bred in the loathly lakes of *Tartary*,[13] 390
With murdrous ravine, and devouring might
Their kingdome spoild, and countrey wasted quight:
Themselves, for feare into his jawes to fall,
He forst to castle strong to take their flight,
Where fast embard in mightie brasen wall,
He has them now foure yeres besiegd to make them thrall. 396

45

Full many knights adventurous and stout
Have enterprizd that Monster to subdew;
From every coast that heaven walks about,[14]
Have thither come the noble Martiall crew,
That famous hard atchievements still pursew, 401
Yet never any could that girlond win,
But all still shronke, and still he greater grew:
All they for want of faith, or guilt of sin,
The pitteous pray of his fierce crueltie have bin. 405

46

At last yledd with farre reported praise,
Which flying fame throughout the world had spred,
Of doughtie knights, whom Faery land did raise,
That noble order high of Maidenhed,
Forthwith to court of *Gloriane* I sped, 410
Of *Gloriane* great Queene of glory bright,
Whose kingdomes seat *Cleopolis*[15] is red,
There to obtaine some such redoubted knight,
That Parents deare from tyrants powre deliver might.

47

It was my chance (my chance was faire and good) 415
There for to find a fresh unprovéd knight,
Whose manly hands imbrew'd in guiltie blood
Had never bene, ne ever by his might
Had throwne to ground the unregarded right:
Yet of his prowesse proofe he since hath made 420
(I witnesse am) in many a cruell fight;
The groning ghosts of many one dismaide
Have felt the bitter dint of his avenging blade.

48

And ye the forlorne reliques of his powre,
His byting sword, and his devouring speare,
Which have enduréd many a dreadful stowre,
Can speake his prowesse, that did earst you beare, 427
And well could rule: now he hath left you heare,
To be the record of his ruefull losse,
And of my dolefull disaventurous deare: 430
O heavie record of the good *Redcrosse*,
Where have you left your Lord, that could so well you tosse?

[11] While the destinies moved equably.

[12] The three rivers of the Garden of Eden. Una's parents represent mankind, and were dispossessed of their territory by the dragon of sin.

[13] Tartarus, or hell.

[14] Spenser speaks in terms of the Ptolemaic astronomy, according to which the heavens revolve about the earth.

[15] The city of glory.

49

Well hopéd I, and faire beginnings had,
That he my captive langour should redeeme,
Till all unweeting, an Enchaunter bad 435
His sence abusd, and made him to misdeeme
My loyalty, not such as it did seeme;
That rather death desire, then such despight.
Be judge ye heavens, that all things right esteeme, 439
How I him lov'd, and love with all my might,
So thought I eke of him, and thinke I thought aright.

50

Thenceforth me desolate he quite forsooke,
To wander, where wilde fortune would me lead,
And other bywaies he himselfe betooke,
Where never foot of living wight did tread,
That brought not backe the balefull body dead; 446
In which him chauncéd false *Duessa* meete,
Mine onely foe, mine onely deadly dread,
Who with her witchcraft and misseeming sweete, 449
Inveigled him to follow her desires unmeete.

51

At last by subtill sleights she him betraid
Unto his foe, a Gyant huge and tall,
Who him disarméd, dissolute, dismaid,
Unwares surprised, and with mightie mall
The monster mercilesse him made to fall, 455
Whose fall did never foe before behold;
And now in darkesome dungeon, wretched thrall,
Remedilesse, for aie he doth him hold;
This is my cause of griefe, more great, then may be told.

52

Ere she had ended all, she gan to faint: 460
But he her comforted and faire bespake,
Certes, Madame, ye have great cause of plaint,
That stoutest heart, I weene, could cause to quake.
But be of cheare, and comfort to you take:
For till I have acquit your captive knight, 465
Assure your selfe, I will you not forsake.
His chearefull words reviv'd her chearelesse spright,
So forth they went, the Dwarfe them guiding ever right.

CANTO VIII

Faire virgin to redeeme her deare
brings Arthur to the fight:
Who slayes that Gyant, wounds the beast,
and strips Duessa quight.

1

Ay me, how many perils doe enfold
The righteous man, to make him daily fall?
Were not, that heavenly grace doth him uphold,
And stedfast truth acquite him out of all.
Her love is firme, her care continuall, 5
So oft as he through his owne foolish pride,
Or weaknesse is to sinfull bands made thrall:
Else should this *Redcrosse* knight in bands have dyde,
For whose deliverance she this Prince doth thither guide.

2

They sadly traveild thus, untill they came 10
Nigh to a castle builded strong and hie:
Then cryde the Dwarfe, lo yonder is the same,
In which my Lord my liege doth lucklesse lie,
Thrall to that Gyants hatefull tyrannie:
Therefore, deare Sir, your mightie powres assay. 15
The noble knight alighted by and by
From loftie steede, and bad the Ladie stay.
To see what end of fight should him befall that day.

3

So with the Squire, th'admirer of his might,
He marchéd forth towards that castle wall;
Whose gates he found fast shut, ne living wight 21
To ward the same, nor answere commers call.
Then tooke that Squire an horne of bugle small,
Which hong adowne his side in twisted gold,
And tassels gay. Wyde wonders over all 25
Of that same hornes great vertues weren told,
Which had approvéd bene in uses manifold.

4

Was never wight, that heard that shrilling sound,
But trembling feare did feele in every vaine;
Three miles it might be easie heard around,
And Ecchoes three answerd it selfe againe: 31
No false enchauntment, nor deceiptfull traine

Might once abide the terror of that blast,
But presently was voide and wholly vaine:
No gate so strong, no locke so firme and fast,
But with that percing noise flew open quite,
or brast. 36

5

The same before the Geants gate he blew,
That all the castle quakéd from the ground,
And every dore of freewill open flew. 39
The Gyant selfe dismaiéd with that sownd,
Where he with his *Duessa* dalliance fownd,
In hast came rushing forth from inner bowre,
With staring countenance sterne, as one
astownd,
And staggering steps, to weet, what suddein
stowre,
Had wrought that horror strange, and dar'd
his dreaded powre. 45

6

And after him the proud *Duessa* came,
High mounted on her manyheaded beast,
And every head with fyrie tongue did flame,
And every head was crownéd on his creast,
And bloudie mouthéd with late cruell feast. 50
That when the knight beheld, his mightie
shild
Upon his manly arme he soone addrest,
And at him fiercely flew, with courage fild,
And eger greedinesse through every mem-
ber thrild.

7

Therewith the Gyant buckled him to fight, 55
Inflam'd with scornefull wrath and high dis-
daine,
And lifting up his dreadfull club on hight,
All arm'd with ragged snubbes and knottie
graine,
Him thought at first encounter to have slaine.
But wise and warie was that noble Pere, 60
And lightly leaping from so monstrous maine,
Did faire avoide the violence him nere;
It booted nought, to thinke, such thunder-
bolts to beare.

8

Ne shame he thought to shunne so hideous
might:
The idle stroke, enforcing furious way, 65
Missing the marke of his misayméd sight
Did fall to ground, and with his heavie sway
So deepely dinted in the driven clay,
That three yardes deepe a furrow up did
throw:
The sad earth wounded with so sore assay, 70
Did grone full grievous underneath the blow,
And trembling with strange feare, did like an
earthquake show.

9

As when almightie *Jove* in wrathfull mood,
To wreake the guilt of mortall sins is bent,
Hurles forth his thundring dart with deadly
food, 75
Enrold in flames, and smouldring dreriment,
Through riven cloudes and molten firma-
ment;
The fierce threeforkéd engin making way,
Both loftie towres and highest trees hath
rent, 79
And all that might his angrie passage stay,
And shooting in the earth, casts up a mount
of clay.

10

His boystrous club, so buried in the ground,
He could not rearen up againe so light,
But that the knight him at avantage found,
And whiles he strove his combred clubbe to
quight 85
Out of the earth, with blade all burning
bright
He smote off his left arme, which like a
blocke
Did fall to ground, depriv'd of native might;
Large streames of bloud out of the trunckéd
stocke
Forth gushéd, like fresh water streame from
riven rocke. 90

11

Dismaiéd with so desperate deadly wound,
And eke impatient of unwonted paine,
He loudly brayd with beastly yelling sound,
That all the fields rebellowéd againe;
As great a noyse, as when in Cymbrian
plaine[1] 95
An heard of Bulles, whom kindly rage doth
sting,
Do for the milkie mothers want complaine,
And fill the fields with troublous bellowing,
The neighbour woods around with hollow
murmur ring. 99

12

That when his deare *Duessa* heard, and saw
The evill stownd, that daungerd her estate,
Unto his aide she hastily did draw
Her dreadfull beast, who swolne with bloud
of late

[1]Possibly the modern Crimea.

Came ramping forth with proud presumpteous gate,
And threatned all his heads like flaming brands. 105
But him the Squire made quickly to retrate,
Encountring fierce with single sword in hand,
And twixt him and his Lord did like a bulwarke stand.

13

The proud *Duessa* full of wrathfull spight,
And fierce disdaine, to be affronted so, 110
Enforst her purple beast with all her might
That stop out of the way to overthroe,
Scorning the let of so unequall foe:
But nathemore would that courageous swayne 114
To her yeeld passage, gainst his Lord to goe,
But with outrageous strokes did him restraine,
And with his bodie bard the way atwixt them twaine.

14

Then tooke the angrie witch her golden cup,[2]
Which still she bore, replete with magick artes;
Death and despeyre did many thereof sup, 120
And secret poyson through their inner parts,
Th'eternall bale of heavie wounded harts;
Which after charmes and some enchauntments said,
She lightly sprinkled on his weaker parts;
Therewith his sturdie courage soone was quayd, 125
And all his senses were with suddeine dread dismayd.

15

So downe he fell before the cruell beast,
Who on his necke his bloudie clawes did seize,
That life nigh crusht out of his panting brest:
No powre he had to stirre, nor will to rize. 130
That when the carefull knight gan well avise,
He lightly left the foe, with whom he fought,
And to the beast gan turne his enterprise:
For wondrous anguish in his hart it wrought,
To see his lovéd Squire into such thraldome brought. 135

16

And high advauncing his bloud-thirstie blade,
Stroke one of those deforméd heads so sore,
That of his puissance proud ensample made;
His monstrous scalpe downe to his teeth it tore, 139
And that misforméd shape mis-shapéd more:
A sea of bloud gusht from the gaping wound,
That her gay garments staynd with filthy gore,
And overflowéd all the field around;
That over shoes in bloud he waded on the ground.

17

Thereat he roaréd for exceeding paine, 145
That to have heard, great horror would have bred,
And scourging th'emptie ayre with his long traine,
Through great impatience of his grievéd hed
His gorgeous ryder from her loftie sted
Would have cast downe, and trod in durtie myre, 150
Had not the Gyant soone her succouréd;
Who all enrag'd with smart and franticke yre,
Came hurtling in full fierce, and forst the knight retyre.

18

The force, which wont in two to be disperst,
In one alone left hand he now unites, 155
Which is through rage more strong then both were erst;
With which his hideous club aloft he dites,
And at his foe with furious rigour smites,
That strongest Oake might seeme to overthrow:
The stroke upon his shield so heavie lites, 160
That to the ground it doubleth him full low:
What mortall wight could ever beare so monstrous blow?

19

And in his fall his shield, that covered was,
Did loose his vele by chaunce, and open flew:
The light whereof, that heavens light did pas, 165
Such blazing brightnesse through the aier threw,
That eye mote not the same endure to vew.
Which when the Gyaunt spyde with staring eye,
He downe let fall his arme, and soft withdrew
His weapon huge, that heavéd was on hye 170
For to have slaine the man, that on the ground did lye.

[2]Cf. Revelation, 17:4.

20

And eke the fruitfull-headed beast, amaz'd
At flashing beames of that sunshiny shield,
Became starke blind, and all his senses daz'd,
That downe he tumbled on the durtie field, 175
And seem'd himselfe as conqueréd to yield.
Whom when his maistresse proud perceiv'd to fall,
Whiles yet his feeble feet for faintnesse reeld,
Unto the Gyant loudly she gan call, 179
O helpe *Orgoglio,* helpe, or else we perish all.

21

At her so pitteous cry was much amoov'd
Her champion stout, and for to ayde his frend,
Againe his wonted angry weapon proov'd:
But all in vaine: for he has read his end
In that bright shield, and all their forces[3] spend 185
Themselves in vaine: for since that glauncing sight,
He hath no powre to hurt, nor to defend;
As where th'Almighties lightning brond does light,
It dimmes the dazéd eyen, and daunts the senses quight.

22

Whom when the Prince, to battell new addrest, 190
And threatning high his dreadfull stroke did see,
His sparkling blade about his head he blest,
And smote off quite his right leg by the knee,
That downe he tombled; as an agéd tree,
High growing on the top of rocky clift, 195
Whose hartstrings with keene steele nigh hewen be,
The mightie trunck halfe rent, with ragged rift
Doth roll adowne the rocks, and fall with fearefull drift.

23

Or as a Castle rearéd high and round,
By subtile engins and malitious slight 200
Is underminéd from the lowest ground,
And her foundation forst, and feebled quight,
At last downe falles, and with her heapéd hight
Her hastie ruine does more heavie make,
And yields it selfe unto the victours might;
Such was this Gyaunts fall, that seemd to shake 206
The stedfast globe of earth, as it for feare did quake.

24

The knight then lightly leaping to the pray,
With mortall steele him smot againe so sore,
That headlesse his unweldy bodie lay, 210
All wallowd in his owne fowle bloudy gore,
Which flowéd from his wounds in wondrous store,
But soone as breath out of his breast did pas,
That huge great body, which the Gyaunt bore,
Was vanisht quite, and of that monstrous mas 215
Was nothing left, but like an emptie bladder was.

25

Whose grievous fall, when false *Duessa* spide,
Her golden cup she cast unto the ground,
And crownéd mitre rudely threw aside;
Such percing griefe her stubborne hart did wound, 220
That she could not endure that dolefull stound,
But leaving all behind her, fled away:
The light-foot Squire her quickly turnd around,
And by hard meanes enforcing her to stay,
So brought unto his Lord, as his deservéd pray. 225

26

The royall Virgin, which beheld from farre,
In pensive plight, and sad perplexitie,
The whole atchievement of this doubtfull warre,
Came running fast to greet his victorie,
With sober gladnesse, and myld modestie, 230
And with sweet joyous cheare him thus bespake;
Faire braunch of noblesse, flowre of chevalrie,
That with your worth the world amazéd make,
How shall I quite the paines, ye suffer for my sake?

27

And you fresh bud of vertue springing fast,[4]
Whom these sad eyes saw nigh unto deaths dore, 236

[3]Referring to Duessa as well as Orgoglio?

[4]The Squire.

What hath poore Virgin for such perill past,
Wherewith you to reward? Accept therefore
My simple selfe, and service evermore;
And he that high does sit, and all things see
With equall eyes, their merites to restore, 241
Behold what ye this day have done for mee,
And what I cannot quite, requite with usuree.

28

But sith the heavens, and your faire handeling 244
Have made you maister of the field this day,
Your fortune maister eke with governing,
And well begun end all so well, I pray,
Ne let that wicked woman scape away;
For she it is, that did my Lord bethrall,
My dearest Lord, and deepe in dongeon lay,
Where he his better dayes hath wasted all. 251
O heare, how piteous he to you for ayd does call.

29

Forthwith he gave in charge unto his Squire,
That scarlot whore to keepen carefully;
Whiles he himselfe with greedie great desire
Into the Castle entred forcibly, 256
Where living creature none he did espye;
Then gan he lowdly through the house to call:
But no man car'd to answere to his crye.
There raignd a solemne silence over all, 260
Nor voice was heard, nor wight was seene in bowre or hall.

30

At last with creeping crooked pace forth came
An old old man, with beard as white as snow,
That on a staffe his feeble steps did frame,
And guide his wearie gate both too and fro: 265
For his eye sight him failéd long ygo,
And on his arme a bounch of keyes he bore,
The which unuséd rust did overgrow:
Those were the keyes of every inner dore,
But he could not them use, but kept them still in store. 270

31

But very uncouth sight was to behold,
How he did fashion his untoward pace,
For as he forward moov'd his footing old,
So backward still was turned his wrincled face,
Unlike to men, who ever as they trace, 275
Both feet and face one way are wont to lead.
This was the auncient keeper of that place,
And foster father of the Gyant dead;
His name *Ignaro*[5] did his nature right aread.

32

His reverend haires and holy gravitie 280
The knight much honord, as beseeméd well,
And gently askt, where all the people bee,
Which in that stately building wont to dwell.
Who answerd him full soft, he could not tell.
Againe he askt, where that same knight was layd, 285
Whom great *Orgoglio* with his puissaunce fell
Had made his caytive thrall; againe he sayde,
He could not tell: ne ever other answere made.

33

Then askéd he, which way he in might pas:
He could not tell, againe he answeréd. 290
Thereat the curteous knight displeaséd was,
And said, Old sire, it seemes thou hast not red
How ill it fits with that same silver hed
In vaine to mocke, or mockt in vaine to bee:
But if thou be, as thou art pourtrahéd 295
With natures pen, in ages grave degree,
Aread in graver wise, what I demaund of thee.

34

His answere likewise was, he could not tell.
Whose sencelesse speach, and doted ignorance
When as the noble Prince had markéd well,
He ghest his nature by his countenance, 301
And calmd his wrath with goodly temperance.
Then to him stepping, from his arme did reach
Those keyes, and made himselfe free enterance.
Each dore he opened without any breach; 305
There was no barre to stop, nor foe him to empeach.

35

There all within full rich arayd he found,
With royall arras and resplendent gold,
And did with store of every thing abound,
That greatest Princes presence might behold.

[5]Ignorance.

But all the floore (too filthy to be told) 311
With bloud of guiltlesse babes, and innocents trew,
Which there were slaine, as sheepe out of the fold,
Defiléd was, that dreadfull was to vew,
And sacred ashes over it was strowéd new. 315

36

And there beside of marble stone was built
An Altare, carv'd with cunning imagery,
On which true Christians bloud was often spilt,
And holy Martyrs often doen to dye,
With cruell malice and strong tyranny: 320
Whose blesséd sprites from underneath the stone
To God for vengeance cryde continually,
And with great griefe were often heard to grone,
That hardest heart would bleede, to heare their piteous mone.

37

Through every rowme he sought, and every bowr, 325
But no where could he find that wofull thrall:
At last he came unto an yron doore,
That fast was lockt, but key found not at all
Emongst that bounch, to open it withall;
But in the same a little grate was pight, 330
Through which he sent his voyce, and lowd did call
With all his powre, to weet, if living wight
Were houséd there within, whom he enlargen might.

38

Therewith an hollow, dreary, murmuring voyce
These piteous plaints and dolours did resound: 335
O who is that, which brings me happy choyce
Of death, that here lye dying every stound,
Yet live perforce in balefull darkenesse bound?
For now three Moones have changéd thrice their hew,
And have beene thrice hid underneath the ground, 340
Since I the heavens chearefull face did vew:
O welcome thou, that doest of death bring tydings trew.

39

Which when that Champion heard, with percing point
Of pitty deare his hart was thrilléd sore,
And trembling horrour ran through every joynt, 345
For ruth of gentle knight so fowle forlore:
Which shaking off, he rent that yron dore,
With furious force, and indignation fell;
Where entred in, his foot could find no flore,
But all a deepe descent, as darke as hell, 350
That breathéd ever forth a filthie banefull smell.

40

But neither darkenesse fowle, nor filthy bands,
Nor noyous smell his purpose could withhold,
(Entire affection hateth nicer hands)
But that with constant zeale, and courage bold, 355
After long paines and labours manifold,
He found the meanes that Prisoner up to reare;
Whose feeble thighes, unhable to uphold
His pinéd corse, him scarce to light could beare,
A ruefull spectacle of death and ghastly drere. 360

41

His sad dull eyes deepe sunck in hollow pits,
Could not endure th'unwonted sunne to view;
His bare thin cheekes for want of better bits,
And empty sides deceivéd of their dew,
Could make a stony hart his hap to rew; 365
His rawbone armes, whose mighty brawnéd bowrs
Were wont to rive steele plates, and helmets hew,
Were cleane consum'd, and all his vitall powres
Decayd, and all his flesh shronk up like withered flowres.

42

Whom when his Lady saw, to him she ran
With hasty joy: to see him made her glad, 371
And sad to view his visage pale and wan,
Who earst in flowres of freshest youth was clad.
Tho when her well of teares she wasted had,
She said, Ah dearest Lord, what evill starre
On you hath fround, and pourd his influence bad, 376

That of your selfe ye thus berobbéd arre,
And this misseeming hew your manly looks
doth marre?

43

But welcome now my Lord, in wele or woe,
Whose presence I have lackt too long a day;
And fie on Fortune mine avowéd foe, 381
Whose wrathfull wreakes them selves do
now alay.
And for these wrongs shall treble penaunce
pay
Of treble good; good growes of evils priefe.
The chearelesse man, whom sorrow did dis-
may, 385
Had no delight to treaten of his griefe;
His long enduréd famine needed more re-
liefe.

44

Faire Lady, then said that victorious knight,
The things, that grievous were to do, or
beare,
Them to renew, I wote, breeds no delight; 390
Best musicke breeds delight in loathing eare:
But th'onely good, that growes of passéd
feare,
Is to be wise, and ware of like agein.
This dayes ensample hath this lesson deare
Deepe written in my heart with yron pen, 395
That blisse may not abide in state of mor-
tall men.

45

Henceforth sir knight, take to you wonted
strength,
And maister these mishaps with patient
might;
Loe where your foe lyes stretcht in mon-
strous length,
And loe that wicked woman in your sight, 400
The roote of all your care, and wretched
plight,
Now in your powre, to let her live, or dye.
To do her dye (quoth *Una*) were despight,
And shame t'avenge so weake an enimy;
But spoile her of her scarlot robe, and let her
fly. 405

46

So as she bad, that witch they disaraid,
And robd of royall robes, and purple pall,
And ornaments that richly were displaid;
Ne sparéd they to strip her naked all.
Then when they had despoild her tire and
call, 410
Such as she was, their eyes might her be-
hold,
That her misshapéd parts did them appall,
A loathly, wrinckled hag, ill favoured, old,
Whose secret filth good manners biddeth not
be told.

47

Her craftie head was altogether bald, 415
And as in hate of honorable eld,
Was overgrowne with scurfe and filthy scald;
Her teeth out of her rotten gummes were
feld,
And her sowre breath abhominably smeld;
Her driéd dugs, like bladders lacking wind,
Hong downe, and filthy matter from them
weld; 421
Her wrizled skin as rough, as maple rind,
So scabby was, that would have loathd all
womankind.

48

Her neather parts, the shame of all her kind,
My chaster Muse for shame doth blush to
write; 425
But at her rompe she growing had behind
A foxes taile, with dong all fowly dight;
And eke her feete most monstrous were in
sight;
For one of them was like an Eagles claw,
With griping talaunts armd to greedy fight,
The other like a Beares uneven paw: 431
More ugly shape yet never living creature
saw.

49

Which when the knights beheld, amazd they
were,
And wondred at so fowle deforméd wight.
Such then (said *Una*) as she seemeth
here, 435
Such is the face of falshood, such the sight
Of fowle *Duessa,* when her borrowed light
Is laid away, and counterfesaunce knowne.
Thus when they had the witch disrobéd
quight,
And all her filthy feature open showne, 440
They let her goe at will, and wander wayes
unknowne.

50

She flying fast from heavens hated face,
And from the world that her discovered
wide,
Fled to the wastfull wildernesse apace,
From living eyes her open shame to hide, 445

And lurkt in rocks and caves long unespide.
But that faire crew of knights, and *Una* faire
Did in that castle afterwards abide,
To rest them selves, and weary powres repaire,
Where store they found of all, that dainty was and rare. 450

CANTO IX

His loves and lignage Arthur tells,
The knights knit friendly bands:
Sir Trevisan flies from Despayre,
Whom Redcrosse knight withstands.

1

O goodly golden chaine,[1] wherewith yfere
The vertues linkéd are in lovely wize:
And noble minds of yore allyéd were,
In brave poursuit of chevalrous emprize,
That none did others saféty despize, 5
Nor aid envy to him, in need that stands,
But friendly each did others prayse devize,
How to advaunce with favourable hands,
As this good Prince redeemd the *Redcrosse* knight from bands.

2

Who when their powres, empaird through labour long, 10
With dew repast they had recuréd well,
And that weake captive wight now wexéd strong,
Them list no lenger there at leasure dwell,
But forward fare, as their adventures fell,
But ere they parted, *Una* faire besought 15
That straunger knight his name and nation tell;
Least so great good, as he for her had wrought,
Should die unknown, and buried be in thankless thought.

3

Faire virgin (said the Prince) ye me require
A thing without the compas of my wit: 20
For both the lignage and the certain Sire,
From which I sprong, from me are hidden yit.
For all so soone as life did me admit
Into this world, and shewéd heavens light,
From mothers pap I taken was unfit: 25
And streight delivered to a Faery knight,
To be upbrought in gentle thewes and martiall might.

4

Unto old *Timon* he me brought bylive,
Old *Timon,* who in youthly yeares hath beene
In warlike feates th'expertest man alive, 30
And is the wisest now on earth I weene;
His dwelling is low in a valley greene,
Under the foot of *Rauran* mossy hore,
From whence the river *Dee* as silver cleene
His tombling billowes rolls with gentle rore:
There all my dayes he traind me up in vertuous lore. 36

5

Thither the great Magicien *Merlin* came,
As was his use, ofttimes to visit me:
For he had charge my discipline to frame,
And Tutours nouriture to oversee.[2] 40
Him oft and oft I askt in privitie,
Of what loines and what lignage I did spring:
Whose aunswere bad me still assuréd bee,
That I was sonne and heire unto a king,
As time in her just terme the truth to light should bring. 45

6

Well worthy impe, said then the Lady gent,
And Pupill fit for such a Tutours hand.
But what adventure, or what high intent
Hath brought you hither into Faery land,
Aread Prince *Arthur,* crowne of Martiall band? 50
Full hard it is (quoth he) to read aright
The course of heavenly cause, or understand
The secret meaning of th'eternall might,
That rules mens wayes, and rules the thoughts of living wight. 54

7

For whither he through fatal deepe foresight
Me hither sent, for cause to me unghest,
Or that fresh bleeding wound, which day and night
Whilome doth rancle in my riven brest,
With forcéd fury following his[3] behest, 59
Me hither brought by wayes yet never found,
You to have helpt I hold my selfe yet blest.
Ah curteous knight (quoth she) what secret wound
Could ever find, to grieve the gentlest hart on ground?

[1]The quality typified by Arthur, "magnificence," or magnanimity, in which all other virtues meet.

[2]And to supervise the training imposed by my tutor.

[3]Its.

8

Deare Dame (quoth he) you sleeping sparkes
awake,
Which troubled once, into huge flames will
grow, 65
Ne ever will their fervent fury slake,
Till living moysture into smoke do flow,
And wasted life do lye in ashes low.
Yet sithens silence lesseneth not my fire,
But told it flames, and hidden it does glow, 70
I will revele, what ye so much desire:
Ah Love, lay downe thy bow, the whiles I
may respire.

9

It was in freshest flowre of youthly yeares,
When courage first does creepe in manly
chest,
Then first the coale of kindly heat appeares
To kindle love in every living brest; 76
But me had warnd old *Timons* wise behest,
Those creeping flames by reason to subdew,
Before their rage grew to so great unrest,
As miserable lovers use to rew, 80
Which still wex old in woe, whiles woe still
wexeth new.

10

That idle name of love, and lovers life,
As losse of time, and vertues enimy
I ever scornd, and joyd to stirre up strife,
In middest of their mournfull Tragedy, 85
Ay wont to laugh, when them I heard to cry,
And blow the fire, which them to ashes brent:
Their God himselfe, griev'd at my libertie,
Shot many a dart at me with fiers intent,
But I them warded all with wary govern-
ment. 90

11

But all in vaine: no fort can be so strong,
Ne fleshly brest can armèd be so sound,
But will at last be wonne with battrie long,
Or unawares at disavantage found;
Nothing is sure, that growes on earthly
ground: 95
And who most trustes in arme of fleshly
might,
And boasts, in beauties chaine not to be
bound,
Doth soonest fall in disaventrous fight,
And yeeldes his caytive neck to victours most
despight.

12

Ensample make of him your haplesse joy,[4]
And of my selfe now mated, as ye see; 101
Whose prouder vaunt that proud avenging
boy
Did soone pluck downe, and curbd my lib-
ertie.
For on a day prickt forth with jollitie
Of looser life, and heat of hardiment, 105
Raunging the forest wide on courser free,
The fields, the floods, the heavens with one
consent
Did seeme to laugh on me, and favour mine
intent.

13

For-wearied with my sports, I did alight
From loftie steed, and downe to sleepe me
layd; 110
The verdant gras my couch did goodly
dight,
And pillow was my helmet faire displayd:
Whiles every sence the humour sweet em-
bayd,
And slombring soft my hart did steale away,
Me seemèd, by my side a royall Mayd 115
Her daintie limbes full softly down did lay:
So faire a creature yet saw never sunny day.

14

Most goodly glee and lovely blandishment
She to me made, and bad me love her deare,
For dearely sure her love was to me bent, 120
As when just time expired[5] should appeare.
But whether dreames delude, or true it were,
Was never hart so ravisht with delight,
Ne living man like words did ever heare,
As she to me delivered all that night; 125
And at her parting said, She Queene of
Faeries hight.

15

When I awoke, and found her place devoyd,
And nought but pressèd gras, where she had
lyen,
I sorrowed all so much, as earst I joyd,
And washèd all her place with watry eyen. 130
From that day forth I lov'd that face divine;
From that day forth I cast in carefull mind,
To seeke her out with labour, and long tyne,
And never vow to rest,[6] till her I find,
Nine monethes I seeke in vaine yet ni'll that
vow unbind. 135

[4] The Red Cross Knight.
[5] As in due course of time.
[6] And vow never to rest.

16

Thus as he spake, his visage wexéd pale,
And chaunge of hew great passion did
bewray;
Yet still he strove to cloke his inward bale,
And hide the smoke, that did his fire display,
Till gentle *Una* thus to him gan say; 140
O happy Queene of Faeries, that hast found
Mongst many, one that with his prowesse
may
Defend thine honour, and thy foes con-
found:
True Loves are often sown, but seldom grow
on ground.

17

Thine, O then, said the gentle *Redcrosse*
knight, 145
Next to that Ladies love, shalbe the place,
O fairest virgin, full of heavenly light,
Whose wondrous faith, exceeding earthly
race,
Was firmest fixt in mine extremest case.
And you, my Lord, the Patrone of my
life, 150
Of that great Queene may well gaine worthy
Grace:
For onely worthy you through prowes priefe
Yf living man mote worthy be, to be her
liefe.

18

So diversly discoursing of their loves,
The golden Sunne his glistring head gan
shew, 155
And sad remembraunce now the Prince
amoves,
With fresh desire his voyage to pursew:
Als *Una* earnd her traveill to renew.
Then those two knights, fast friendship for
to bynd,
And love establish each to other trew, 160
Gave goodly gifts, the signes of gratefull
mynd,
And eke the pledges firme, right hands to-
gether joynd.

19

Prince *Arthur* gave a boxe of Diamond sure,
Embowd with gold and gorgeous ornament,
Wherein were closd few drops of liquor
pure, 165
Of wondrous worth, and vertue excellent,
That any wound could heale incontinent:
Which to requite, the *Redcrosse* knight him
gave
A booke, wherein his Saveours testament
Was writ with golden letters rich and brave;
A worke of wondrous grace, and able soules
to save. 171

20

Thus beene they parted, *Arthur* on his way
To seeke his love, and th'other for to fight
With *Unaes* foe, that all her realme did pray.
But she now weighing the decayéd plight, 175
And shrunken synewes of her chosen knight,
Would not a while her forward course
pursew,
Ne bring him forth in face of dreadfull fight,
Till he recovered had his former hew:
For him to be yet weake and wearie well
she knew. 180

21

So as they traveild, lo they gan espy
An arméd knight towards them gallop fast,
That seeméd from some fearéd foe to fly,
Or other griesly thing, that him agast.
Still as he fled, his eye was backward cast, 185
As if his feare still followed him behind;
Als flew his steed, as he his bands had brast,
And with his wingéd heeles did tread the
wind,
As he had beene a fole of *Pegasus* his kind.[7]

22

Nigh as he drew, they might perceive his
head 190
To be unarmd, and curld uncombéd heares
Upstaring stiffe, dismayd with uncouth
dread;
Nor drop of bloud in all his face appeares
Nor life in limbe: and to increase his feares,
In fowle reproch of knighthoods faire de-
gree, 195
About his neck an hempen rope he weares,
That with his glistring armes does ill agree;[8]
But he of rope or armes has now no memoree.

23

The *Redcrosse* knight toward him crosséd
fast,
To weet, what mister wight was so dis-
mayd: 200
There him he finds all sencelesse and aghast,
That of him selfe he seemd to be afrayd;
Whom hardly he from flying forward stayd.
Till he these wordes to him deliver might;
Sir knight, aread who hath ye thus arayd, 205

[7]Of the race of Pegasus.

[8]Hanging was a punishment reserved for common criminals. A knight if executed would be beheaded.

And eke from whom make ye this hasty flight:
For never knight I saw in such misseeming plight.

24

He answerd nought at all, but adding new
Feare to his first amazment, staring wide
With stony eyes, and hartlesse hollow hew, 210
Astonisht stood, as one that had aspide
Infernall furies, with their chaines untide.
Him yet againe, and yet againe bespake
The gentle knight; who nought to him replide,
But trembling every joynt did inly quake, 215
And foltring tongue at last these words seemd forth to shake.

25

For Gods deare love, Sir knight, do me not stay;
For loe he comes, he comes fast after mee.
Eft looking backe would faine have runne away;
But he him forst to stay, and tellen free 220
The secret cause of his perplexitie:
Yet nathemore by his bold hartie speach,
Could his bloud-frosen hart emboldned bee,
But through his boldnesse rather feare did reach,
Yet forst, at last he made through silence suddein breach. 225

26

And am I now in safetie sure (quoth he)
From him, that would have forcéd me to dye?
And is the point of death now turnd fro mee,
That I may tell this haplesse history?
Feare nought (quoth he), no daunger now is nye. 230
Then shall I you recount a ruefull cace
(Said he), the which with this unlucky eye
I late beheld, and had not greater grace
Me reft from it, had bene partaker of the place.

27

I lately chaunst (Would I had never chaunst)
With a faire knight to keepen companee, 236
Sir *Terwin* hight, that well himselfe advaunst
In all affaires, and was both bold and free,
But not so happie as mote happie bee:
He lov'd, as was his lot, a Ladie gent, 240
That him againe lov'd in the least degree.[9]
For she was proud, and of too high intent,
And joyd to see her lover languish and lament.

28

From whom returning sad and comfortlesse,
As on the way together we did fare, 245
We met that villen (God from him me blesse)
That curséd wight, from whom I scapt whyleare,
A man of hell, that cals himselfe *Despaire:*
Who first us greets, and after faire areedes
Of tydings strange, and of adventures rare: 250
So creeping close, as Snake in hidden weedes,
Inquireth of our states, and of our knightly deedes.

29

Which when he knew, and felt our feeble harts
Embost with bale, and bitter byting griefe,
Which love had launchéd with his deadly darts, 255
With wounding words and termes of foule repriefe,
He pluckt from us all hope of due reliefe,
That earst us held in love of lingring life;
Then hopelesse hartlesse, gan the cunning thiefe
Perswade us die, to stint all further strife: 260
To me he lent this rope, to him a rustie knife.

30

With which sad instrument of hastie death,
That wofull lover, loathing lenger light,
A wide way made to let forth living breath.
But I more fearefull, or more luckie wight, 265
Dismayd with that deforméd dismall sight,
Fled fast away, halfe dead with dying feare:
Ne yet assur'd of life by you, Sir knight,
Whose like infirmitie like chaunce may beare:
But God you never let his charméd speeches heare. 270

31

How may a man (said he) with idle speach
Be wonne, to spoyle the Castle of his health?
I wote (quoth he) whom triall late did teach,
That like would not for all this worldés wealth:

[9]Not at all.

His subtill tongue, like dropping honny, mealt'th 275
Into the hart, and searcheth every vaine,
That ere one be aware, by secret stealth
His powre is reft, and weaknesse doth remaine.
O never Sir desire to try his guilefull traine.

32

Certes (said he) hence shall I never rest, 280
Till I that treachours art have heard and tride;
And you Sir knight, whose name mote I request,
Of grace do me unto his cabin guide.
I that hight *Trevisan* (quoth he) will ride
Against my liking backe, to doe you grace:
But nor for gold nor glee will I abide 286
By you, when ye arrive in that same place;
For lever had I die, then see his deadly face.

33

Ere long they come, where that same wicked wight
His dwelling has, low in an hollow cave, 290
Farre underneath a craggie clift ypight,
Darke, dolefull, drearie, like a greedie grave,
That still for carrion carcases doth crave:
On top whereof aye dwelt the ghastly Owle,
Shrieking his balefull note, which ever drave
Farre from that haunt all other chearefull fowle; 296
And all about it wandring ghostes did waile and howle.

34

And all about old stockes and stubs of trees,
Whereon nor fruit, nor leafe was ever seene,
Did hang upon the ragged rocky knees; 300
On which had many wretches hangéd beene,
Whose carcases were scattered on the greene,
And throwne about the cliffs. Arrivéd there,
That bare-head knight for dread and dolefull teene,
Would faine have fled, ne durst approchen neare, 305
But th'other forst him stay, and comforted in feare.

35

That darkesome cave they enter, where they find
That curséd man, low sitting on the ground,
Musing full sadly in his sullein mind;
His griesie lockes, long growén, and unbound, 310
Disordred hong about his shoulders round,
And hid his face; through which his hollow eyne
Lookt deadly dull, and staréd as astound;
His raw-bone cheekes through penurie and pine,
Were shronke into his jawes as he did never dine. 315

36

His garment nought but many ragged clouts,
With thornes together pind and patchéd was,
The which his naked sides he wrapt abouts;
And him beside there lay upon the gras
A drearie corse, whose life away did pas, 320
All wallowd in his owne yet luke-warme blood,
That from his wound yet welléd fresh alas;
In which a rustie knife fast fixéd stood,
And made an open passage for the gushing flood.

37

Which piteous spectacle, approving trew 325
The wofull tale that *Trevisan* had told,
When as the gentle *Redcrosse* knight did vew,
With firie zeale he burnt in courage bold,
Him to avenge, before his bloud were cold,
And to the villein said, Thou damnéd wight, 330
The author of this fact, we here behold,
What justice can but judge against the right,
With thine owne bloud to price his bloud, here shed in sight?

38

What franticke fit (quoth he) hath thus distraught
Thee, foolish man, so rash a doome to give? 335
What justice ever other judgement taught,
But he should die, who merites not to live?
None else to death this man despayring drive,
But his owne guiltie mind deserving death.
Is then unjust to each his due to give? 340
Or let him die, that loatheth living breath?
Or let him die at ease, that liveth here uneath?

39

Who travels by the wearie wandring way,
To come unto his wishéd home in haste,
And meetes a flood, that doth his passage stay, 345
Is not great grace to helpe him over past,

Or free his feet, that in the myre sticke fast?
Most envious man, that grieves at neighbours good,
And fond, that joyest in the woe thou hast,
Why wilt not let him passe, that long hath stood 350
Upon the banke, yet wilt thy selfe not passe the flood?

40

He there does now enjoy eternall rest
And happie ease, which thou doest want and crave,
And further from it daily wanderest:
What if some litle paine the passage have, 355
That makes fraile flesh to feare the bitter wave?
Is not short paine well borne, that brings long ease,
And layes the soule to sleepe in quiet grave?
Sleepe after toyle, port after stormie seas,
Ease after warre, death after life does greatly please. 360

41

The knight much wondred at his suddeine wit,
And said, The terme of life is limited,
Ne may a man prolong, nor shorten it;
The souldier may not move from watchfull sted,
Nor leave his stand, untill his Captaine bed.
Who life did limit by almightie doome, 366
(Quoth he) knowes best the termes establishéd;
And he, that points the Centonell his roome,
Doth license him depart at sound of morning droome.

42

Is not his deed, what ever thing is donne, 370
In heaven and earth? did not he all create
To die againe? all ends that was begonne.
Their times in his eternall booke of fate
Are written sure, and have their certaine date.
Who then can strive with strong necessitie, 375
That holds the world in his still chaunging state,
Or shunne the death ordaynd by destinie?
When houre of death is come, let none aske whence, nor why.

43

The lenger life, I wote the greater sin,
The greater sin, the greater punishment: 380
All those great battels, which thou boasts to win,
Through strife, and bloud-shed, and avengément,
Now praysd, hereafter deare thou shalt repent:
For life must life, and bloud must bloud repay.
Is not enough thy evill life forespent?[10] 385
For he, that once hath misséd the right way,
The further he doth goe, the further he doth stray.

44

Then do no further goe, no further stray,
But here lie downe, and to thy rest betake,
Th'ill to prevent, that life ensewen may. 390
For what hath life, that may it lovéd make,
And gives not rather cause it to forsake?
Feare, sicknesse, age, losse, labour, sorrow, strife,
Paine, hunger, cold, that makes the hart to quake;
And ever fickle fortune rageth rife, 395
All which, and thousands mo do make a loathsome life.

45

Thou wretched man, of death hast greatest need,
If in true ballance thou wilt weigh thy state:
For never knight, that daréd warlike deede,
More lucklesse disaventures did amate: 400
Witnesse the dongeon deepe, wherein of late
Thy life shut up, for death so oft did call;
And though good lucke prolongéd hath thy date,
Yet death then, would the like mishaps forestall,
Into the which hereafter thou maiest happen fall. 405

46

Why then doest thou, O man of sin, desire
To draw thy dayes forth to their last degree?
Is not the measure of thy sinfull hire
High heapéd up with huge iniquitie,
Against the day of wrath, to burden thee? 410
Is not enough, that to this Ladie milde
Thou falséd hast thy faith with perjurie,
And sold thy selfe to serve *Duessa* vilde,
With whom in all abuse thou hast thy selfe defilde?

[10] Is not enough of your life spent in evil-doing?

47

Is not he just, that all this doth behold 415
From highest heaven, and beares an equall
eye?
Shall he thy sins up in his knowledge fold,
And guiltie be of thine impietie?
Is not his law, Let every sinner die:
Die shall all flesh? what then must needs be
donne, 420
Is it not better to doe willinglie,
Then linger, till the glasse be all out ronne?
Death is the end of woes: die soone, O
faeries sonne.

48

The knight was much enmovéd with his
speach,
That as a swords point through his hart did
perse, 425
And in his conscience made a secret breach,
Well knowing true all, that he did reherse,
And to his fresh remembrance did reverse
The ugly vew of his deforméd crimes,
That all his manly powres it did disperse, 430
As he were charméd with inchaunted rimes,
That oftentimes he quakt, and fainted often-
times.

49

In which amazement, when the Miscreant
Perceivéd him to waver weake and fraile,
Whiles trembling horror did his conscience
dant, 435
And hellish anguish did his soule assaile,
To drive him to despaire, and quite to quaile,
He shew'd him painted in a table plaine,
The damnéd ghosts, that doe in torments
waile,
And thousand feends that doe them endlesse
paine 440
With fire and brimstone, which for ever shall
remaine.

50

The sight whereof so throughly him dismaid,
That nought but death before his eyes he
saw,
And ever burning wrath before him laid,
By righteous sentence of th'Almighties law:
Then gan the villein him to overcraw, 446
And brought unto him swords, ropes, poison,
fire,
And all that might him to perdition draw;
And bad him choose, what death he would
desire:
For death was due to him, that had provokt
Gods ire. 450

51

But when as none of them he saw him take,
He to him raught a dagger sharpe and keene,
And gave it him in hand: his hand did quake,
And tremble like a leafe of Aspin greene,
And troubled bloud through his pale face
was seene 455
To come, and goe with tydings from the hart,
As it a running messenger had beene.
At last resolv'd to worke his finall smart,
He lifted up his hand, that backe againe did
start.

52

Which when as *Una* saw, through every
vaine 460
The crudled cold ran to her well of life,
As in a swowne: but soone reliv'd againe;
Out of his hand she snatcht the curséd knife,
And threw it to the ground, enragéd rife,
And to him said, Fie, fie, faint harted
knight, 465
What meanest thou by this reprochfull
strife?
Is this the battell, which thou vauntst to fight
With that fire-mouthéd Dragon, horrible and
bright?

53

Come, come away, fraile, feeble, fleshly
wight,
Ne let vaine words bewitch thy manly
hart, 470
Ne divelish thoughts dismay thy constant
spright.
In heavenly mercies hast thou not a part?
Why shouldst thou then despeire, that chosen
art?
Where justice growes, there grows eke
greater grace,
The which doth quench the brond of hellish
smart, 475
And that accurst hand-writing doth deface.
Arise, Sir knight arise, and leave this curséd
place.

54

So up he rose, and thence amounted streight.
Which when the carle beheld, and saw his
guest
Would safe depart, for all his subtill
sleight, 480
He chose an halter from among the rest,
And with it hung himselfe, unbid unblest.
But death he could not worke himselfe
thereby;
For thousand times he so himselfe had drest,
Yet nathelesse it could not doe him die, 485
Till he should die his last, that is eternally.

CANTO X

Her faithfull knight faire Una brings
to house of Holinesse,
Where he is taught repentance, and
the way to heavenly blesse.

1

What man is he, that boasts of fleshly might,
And vaine assurance of mortality,
Which all so soone, as it doth come to fight,
Against spirituall foes, yeelds by and by,
Or from the field most cowardly doth fly? 5
Ne let the man ascribe it to his skill,
That thorough grace hath gainéd victory.
If any strength we have, it is to ill,
But all the good is Gods, both power and eke will.

2

By that, which lately hapned, *Una* saw, 10
That this her knight was feeble, and too faint;
And all his sinews woxen weake and raw,
Through long enprisonment, and hard constraint,
Which he enduréd in his late restraint,
That yet he was unfit for bloudie fight: 15
Therefore to cherish him with diets daint,
She cast to bring him, where he chearen might,
Till he recovered had his late decayéd plight.

3

There was an auntient house not farre away,
Renowmd throughout the world for sacred lore, 20
And pure unspotted life: so well they say
It governd was, and guided evermore,
Through wisedome of a matrone grave and hore;
Whose onely joy was to relieve the needes
Of wretched soules, and helpe the helpelesse pore: 25
All night she spent in bidding of her bedes,
And all the day in doing good and godly deedes.

4

Dame *Caelia*[1] men did her call, as thought
From heaven to come, or thither to arise,
The mother of three daughters, well upbrought 30
In goodly thewes, and godly exercise:
The eldest two most sober, chast, and wise,
Fidelia and *Speranza*[2] virgins were
Though spousd, yet wanting wedlocks solemnize;
But faire *Charissa*[3] to a lovely fere 35
Was linckéd, and by him had many pledges dere.

5

Arrivéd there, the dore they find fast lockt;
For it was warely watchéd night and day,
For feare of many foes: but when they knockt,
The Porter opened unto them streight way:
He was an agéd syre, all hory gray, 41
With lookes full lowly cast, and gate full slow,
Wont on a staffe his feeble steps to stay,
Hight *Humiltá*.[4] They passe in stouping low;
For streight and narrow was the way, which he did show. 45

6

Each goodly thing is hardest to begin,
But entred in a spacious court they see,
Both plaine, and pleasant to be walkéd in,
Where them does meete a francklin faire and free,
And entertaines with comely courteous glee, 50
His name was *Zele,* that him right well became,
For in his speeches and behaviour hee
Did labour lively to expresse the same,
And gladly did them guide, till to the Hall they came.

7

There fairely them receives a gentle Squire, 55
Of milde demeanure, and rare courtesie,
Right cleanly clad in comely sad attire;
In word and deede that shew'd great modestie,
And knew his good to all of each degree,[5]
Hight *Reverence*. He them with speeches meet 60
Does faire entreat; no courting nicetie,
But simple true, and eke unfainéd sweet,
As might become a Squire so great persons to greet.

8

And afterwards them to his Dame he leades,
That agéd Dame, the Ladie of the place: 65

[1] Knowledge of heavenly things.
[2] Faith and Hope.
[3] Charity.
[4] Humility.
[5] Knew how to bear himself towards men of every rank.

Who all this while was busie at her beades:
Which doen, she up arose with seemely grace,
And toward them full matronely did pace.
Where when that fairest *Una* she beheld,
Whom well she knew to spring from heavenly race, 70
Her hart with joy unwonted inly sweld,
As feeling wondrous comfort in her weaker eld.

9

And her embracing said, O happie earth,
Whereon thy innocent feet doe ever tread,
Most vertuous virgin borne of heavenly berth, 75
That to redeeme thy woefull parents head,
From tyrans rage, and ever-dying dread,
Hast wandred through the world now long a day;
Yet ceasest not thy wearie soles to lead,
What grace hath thee now hither brought this way? 80
Or doen thy feeble feet unweeting hither stray?

10

Strange thing it is an errant knight to see
Here in this place, or any other wight,
That hither turnes his steps. So few there bee,
That chose the narrow path, or seeke the right: 85
All keepe the broad high way, and take delight
With many rather for to go astray,
And be partakers of their evill-plight,
Then with a few to walke the rightest way;
O foolish men, why haste ye to your owne decay? 90

11

Thy selfe to see, and tyréd limbs to rest,
O matrone sage (quoth she) I hither came,
And this good knight his way with me addrest,
Led with thy prayses and broad-blazéd fame,
That up to heaven is blowne. The auncient Dame 95
Him goodly greeted in her modest guise,
And entertaynd them both, as best became,
With all the court'sies, that she could devise,
Ne wanted ought, to shew her bounteous or wise.

12

Thus as they gan of sundry things devise, 100
Loe two most goodly virgins came in place,
Ylinkéd arme in arme in lovely wise,
With countenance demure, and modest grace,
They numbred even steps and equall pace:
Of which the eldest, that *Fidelia* hight, 105
Like sunny beames threw from her Christall face,
That could have dazd the rash beholders sight,
And round about her head did shine like heavens light.

13

She was araiéd all in lilly white,
And in her right hand bore a cup of gold, 110
With wine and water fild up to the hight,
In which a Serpent did himselfe enfold,[6]
That horrour made to all, that did behold;
But she no whit did chaunge her constant mood:
And in her other hand she fast did hold 115
A booke,[7] that was both signd and seald with blood,
Wherein darke things were writ, hard to be understood.

14

Her younger sister, that *Speranza* hight,
Was clad in blew,[8] that her beseeméd well;
Not all so chearefull seeméd she of sight, 120
As was her sister; whether dread did dwell,
Or anguish in her hart, is hard to tell:
Upon her arme a silver anchor lay,[9]
Whereon she leanéd ever, as befell:
And ever up to heaven, as she did pray, 125
Her stedfast eyes were bent, ne swarvéd other way.

15

They seeing *Una,* towards her gan wend,
Who them encounters with like courtesie;
Many kind speeches they betwene them spend,
And greatly joy each other well to see: 130
Then to the knight with shamefast modestie
They turne themselves, at *Unaes* meeke request,
And him salute with well beseeming glee;
Who faire them quites, as him beseeméd best,
And goodly gan discourse of many a noble gest. 135

[6]The serpent, because it casts off its skin, has sometimes been taken as a type of immortality.

[7]The New Testament, signed and sealed with Christ's blood.

[8]The color of constancy.

[9]Another symbol of constancy.

16

Then *Una* thus: But she your sister deare,
The deare *Charissa* where is she become?
Or wants she health, or busie is elsewhere?
Ah no, said they, but forth she may not come:
For she of late is lightned of her wombe, 140
And hath encreast the world with one sonne more,
That her to see should be but troublesome.
Indeede (quoth she) that should be trouble sore,
But thankt be God, and her encrease so evermore.

17

Then said the agéd *Caelia,* Deare dame, 145
And you good Sir, I wote that of your toyle,
And labours long, through which ye hither came,
Ye both forwearied be: therefore a whyle
I read you rest, and to your bowres recoyle.
Then calléd she a Groome, that forth him led 150
Into a goodly lodge, and gan despoile
Of puissant armes, and laid in easie bed;
His name was meeke *Obedience* rightfully ared.

18

Now when their wearie limbes with kindly rest,
And bodies were refresht with due repast, 155
Faire *Una* gan *Fidelia* faire request,
To have her knight into her schoolehouse plaste,
That of her heavenly learning he might taste,
And heare the wisedome of her words divine.
She graunted, and that knight so much agraste, 160
That she him taught celestiall discipline,
And opened his dull eyes, that light mote in them shine.

19

And that her sacred Booke, with bloud ywrit,
That none could read, except she did them teach,
She unto him discloséd every whit, 165
And heavenly documents thereout did preach,
That weaker wit of man could never reach,
Of God, of grace, of justice, of free will,
That wonder was to heare her goodly speach:
For she was able, with her words to kill, 170
And raise againe to life the hart, that she did thrill.

20

And when she list poure out her larger spright,
She would commaund the hastie Sunne to stay,
Or backward turne his course from heavens hight;
Sometimes great hostes of men she could dismay; 175
Dry-shod to passe, she parts the flouds in tway;
And eke huge mountaines from their native seat
She would commaund, themselves to beare away,
And throw in raging sea with roaring threat.
Almightie God her gave such powre, and puissance great. 180

21

The faithfull knight, now grew in litle space,
By hearing her, and by her sisters lore,
To such perfection of all heavenly grace,
That wretched world he gan for to abhore,
And mortall life gan loath, as thing forlore, 185
Greev'd with remembrance of his wicked wayes,
And prickt with anguish of his sinnes so sore,
That he desirde to end his wretched dayes:
So much the dart of sinfull guilt the soule dismayes. 189

22

But wise *Speranza* gave him comfort sweet,
And taught him how to take assuréd hold
Upon her silver anchor, as was meet;
Else had his sinnes so great, and manifold
Made him forget all that *Fidelia* told.
In this distresséd doubtfull agonie, 195
When him his dearest *Una* did behold,
Disdeining life, desiring leave to die,
She found her selfe assayld with great perplexitie.

23

And came to *Caelia* to declare her smart,
Who well acquainted with that commune plight, 200
Which sinfull horror workes in wounded hart,
Her wisely comforted all that she might,
With goodly counsell and advisement right;
And streightway sent with carefull diligence,
To fetch a Leach, the which had great insight

In that disease of grievéd conscience, 206
And well could cure the same; His name was
Patience.

24

Who comming to that soule-diseaséd knight,
Could hardly him intreat, to tell his griefe:
Which knowne, and all that noyd his heavie
spright, 210
Well searcht, eftsoones he gan apply reliefe
Of salves and med'cines, which had passing
priefe,
And thereto added words of wondrous
might:
By which to ease he him recuréd briefe,
And much asswag'd the passion of his plight,
That he his paine endur'd, as seeming now
more light. 216

25

But yet the cause and root of all his ill,
Inward corruption, and infected sin,
Not purg'd nor heald, behind remainéd still,
And festring sore did rankle yet within, 220
Close creeping twixt the marrow and the skin.
Which to extirpe, he laid him privily
Downe in a darkesome lowly place farre in,
Whereas he meant his corrosives to apply,
And with streight diet tame his stubborne
malady. 225

26

In ashes and sackcloth he did array
His daintie corse, proud humors to abate,
And dieted with fasting every day,
The swelling of his wounds to mitigate,
And made him pray both earely and eke
late: 230
And ever as superfluous flesh did rot
Amendment readie still at hand did wayt,
To pluck it out with pincers firie whot,
That soone in him was left no one corrupted
jot.

27

And bitter *Penance* with an yron whip, 235
Was wont him once to disple every day:
And sharpe *Remorse* his hart did pricke and
nip,
That drops of bloud thence like a well did
play;
And sad *Repentance* uséd to embay,
His bodie in salt water smarting sore, 240
The filthy blots of sinne to wash away.
So in short space they did to health restore
The man that would not live, but earst lay
at deathes dore.

28

In which his torment often was so great,
That like a Lyon he would cry and rore, 245
And rend his flesh, and his owne synewes
eat.
His owne deare *Una* hearing evermore
His ruefull shriekes and gronings, often tore
Her guiltlesse garments, and her golden
heare,
For pitty of his paine and anguish sore; 250
Yet all with patience wisely she did beare;
For well she wist, his crime could else be
never cleare.

29

Whom thus recover'd by wise *Patience,*
And trew *Repentance* they to *Una* brought:
Who joyous of his curéd conscience, 255
Him dearely kist, and fairely eke besought
Himselfe to chearish, and consuming
thought
To put away out of his carefull brest.
By this *Charissa,* late in child-bed brought,
Was woxen strong, and left her fruitfull
nest: 260
To her faire *Una* brought this unacquainted
guest.

30

She was a woman in her freshest age,
Of wondrous beauty, and of bountie rare,
With goodly grace, and comely personage,
That was on earth not easie to compare; 265
Full of great love, but *Cupids* wanton snare
As hell she hated, chast in worke and will;
Her necke and breasts were ever open bare,
That ay thereof her babes might sucke their
fill;
The rest was all in yellow robes[10] arayéd
still. 270

31

A multitude of babes about her hong,
Playing their sports, that joyd her to behold,
Whom still she fed, whiles they were weake
and young,
But thrust them forth still, as they wexéd
old:
And on her head she wore a tyre of gold, 275
Adornd with gemmes and owches wondrous
faire,
Whose passing price uneath was to be told;
And by her side there sate a gentle paire
Of turtle doves, she sitting in an yvorie
chaire.

[10]Symbolic of maternity.

32

The knight and *Una* entring, faire her greet,
And bid her joy of that her happie brood; 281
Who them requites with court'sies seeming meet,
And entertaines with friendly chearefull mood.
Then *Una* her besought, to be so good,
As in her vertuous rules to schoole her knight, 285
Now after all his torment well withstood,
In that sad house of *Penaunce,* where his spright
Had past the paines of hell, and long enduring night.

33

She was right joyous of her just request,
And taking by the hand that Faeries sonne,
Gan him instruct in every good behest, 291
Of love, and righteousnesse, and well to donne,
And wrath, and hatred warély to shonne,
That drew on men Gods hatred, and his wrath,
And many soules in dolours had fordonne: 295
In which when him she well instructed hath,
From thence to heaven she teacheth him the ready path.

34

Wherein his weaker wandring steps to guide,
An auncient matrone she to her does call,
Whose sober lookes her wisedome well descride: 300
Her name was *Mercie,* well knowne over all,
To be both gratious, and eke liberall:
To whom the carefull charge of him she gave,
To lead aright, that he should never fall
In all his wayes through this wide worldés wave, 305
That Mercy in the end his righteous soule might save.

35

The godly Matrone by the hand him beares
Forth from her presence, by a narrow way,
Scattred with bushy thornes, and ragged breares,
Which still before him she remov'd away, 310
That nothing might his ready passage stay:
And ever when his feet encombred were,
Or gan to shrinke, or from the right to stray,
She held him fast, and firmely did upbeare,
As carefull Nourse her child from falling oft does reare. 315

36

Eftsoones unto an holy Hospitall,
That was fore by the way, she did him bring,
In which seven Bead-men that had vowéd all
Their life to service of high heavens king
Did spend their dayes in doing godly thing: 320
There gates to all were open evermore,
That by the wearie way were traveiling,
And one sate wayting ever them before,
To call in commers-by, that needy were and pore.

37

The first of them that eldest was, and best, 325
Of all the house had charge and governement,
As Guardian and Steward of the rest:
His office was to give entertainement
And lodging, unto all that came, and went:
Not unto such, as could him feast againe, 330
And double quite, for that he on them spent
But such, as want of harbour did constraine:
Those for Gods sake his dewty was to entertaine.

38

The second was as Almner of the place,
His office was, the hungry for to feed, 335
And thristy give to drinke, a worke of grace:
He feard not once him selfe to be in need,
Ne car'd to hoord for those, whom he did breede:
The grace of God he layd up still in store,
Which as a stocke he left unto his seede: 340
He had enough, what need him care for more?
And had he lesse, yet some he would give to the pore.

39

The third had of their wardrobe custodie,
In which were not rich tyres, nor garments gay,
The plumes of pride, and wings of vanitie, 345
But clothes meet to keepe keene could away,
And naked nature seemely to aray;
With which bare wretched wights he dayly clad,
The images of God in earthly clay;
And if that no spare cloths to give he had, 350
His owne coate he would cut, and it distribute glad.

40

The fourth appointed by his office was,
Poore prisoners to relieve with gratious ayd,
And captives to redeeme with price of bras,
From Turkes and Sarazins, which them had
stayd; 355
And though they faultie were, yet well he
wayd,
That God to us forgiveth every howre
Much more then that, why they in bands
were layd,
And he[11] that harrowd hell with heavie
stowre,
The faultie soules from thence brought to
his heavenly bowre. 360

41

The fift had charge sicke persons to attend,
And comfort those, in point of death which
lay;
For them most needeth comfort in the end,
When sin, and hell, and death do most dismay
The feeble soule departing hence away. 365
All is but lost, that living we bestow,
If not well ended at our dying day.
O man have mind of that last bitter throw;
For as the tree does fall, so lyes it ever low.

42

The sixt had charge of them now being dead,
In seemely sort their corses to engrave, 371
And deck with dainty flowres their bridall
bed,
That to their heavenly spouse both sweet and
brave
They might appeare, when he their soules
shall save.
The wondrous workemanship of Gods owne
mould, 375
Whose face he made, all beasts to feare, and
gave
All in his hand, even dead we honour should.
Ah dearest God me graunt, I dead be not
defould.

43

The seventh now after death and buriall
done,
Had charge the tender Orphans of the dead
And widowes ayd, least they should be
undone: 381
In face of judgement he their right would
plead,
Ne ought the powre of mighty men did dread
In their defence, nor would for gold or fee
Be wonne their rightfull causes downe to
tread: 385
And when they stood in most necessitee,
He did supply their want, and gave them ever
free.

44

There when the Elfin knight arrivéd was,
The first and chiefest of the seven, whose
care
Was guests to welcome, towardes him did
pas: 390
Where seeing *Mercie*, that his steps up bare,
And alwayes led, to her with reverence rare
He humbly louted in meeke lowlinesse,
And seemely welcome for her did prepare:
For of their order she was Patronesse, 395
Albe *Charissa* were their chiefest founder-
esse.

45

There she awhile him stayes, him selfe to
rest,
That to the rest more able he might bee:
During which time, in every good behest
And godly worke of Almes and charitee 400
She him instructed with great industree;
Shortly therein so perfect he became,
That from the first unto the last degree,
His mortall life he learnéd had to frame
In holy righteousnesse, without rebuke or
blame. 405

46

Thence forward by that painfull way they
pas,
Forth to an hill, that was both steepe and hy;
On top whereof a sacred chappell was,
And eke a litle Hermitage thereby,
Wherein an aged holy man did lye, 410
That day and night said his devotion,
Ne other worldly busines did apply;
His name was heavenly *Contemplation;*
Of God and goodnesse was his meditation.

47

Great grace that old man to him given had;
For God he often saw from heavens hight, 416
All were his earthly eyen both blunt and bad,
And through great age had lost their kindly
sight,
Yet wondrous quick and persant was his
spright,
As Eagles eye, that can behold the Sunne: 420
That hill they scale with all their powre and
might,

[11]Christ who, when he descended into hell, redeemed the souls of the patriarchs and of others.

That his frayle thighes nigh wearie and fordonne
Gan faile, but by her helpe the top at last he wonne.

48

There they do finde that godly agéd Sire,
With snowy lockes adowne his shoulders shed, 425
As hoarie frost with spangles doth attire
The mossy braunches of an Oke halfe ded.
Each bone might through his body well be red,
And every sinew seene through his long fast:
For nought he car'd his carcas long unfed; 430
His mind was full of spirituall repast,
And pyn'd his flesh, to keepe his body low and chast.

49

Who when these two approching he aspide,
At their first presence grew agrievéd sore,
That forst him lay his heavenly thoughts aside; 435
And had he not that Dame respected more,
Whom highly he did reverence and adore,
He would not once have movéd for the knight.
They him saluted standing far afore;
Who well them greeting, humbly did requight, 440
And askéd, to what end they clomb that tedious height.

50

What end (quoth she) should cause us take such paine,
But that same end, which every living wight
Should make his marke, high heaven to attaine?
Is not from hence the way, that leadeth right 445
To that most glorious house, that glistreth bright
With burning starres, and everliving fire,
Whereof the keyes are to thy hand behight
By wise *Fidelia?* she doth thee require,
To shew it to this knight, according his desire. 450

51

Thrise happy man, said then the father grave,
Whose staggering steps thy steady hand doth lead,
And shewes the way, his sinfull soule to save.
Who better can the way to heaven aread,
Then thou thy selfe, that was both borne and bred 455
In heavenly throne, where thousand Angels shine?
Thou doest the prayers of the righteous sead
Present before the majestie divine,
And his avenging wrath to clemencie incline.

52

Yet since thou bidst, thy pleasure shalbe donne. 460
Then come thou man of earth, and see the way,
That never yet was seene of Faeries sonne,
That never leads the traveiler astray,
But after labours long, and sad delay, 464
Brings them to joyous rest and endlesse blis.
But first thou must a season fast and pray,
Till from her bands the spright assoiléd is,
And have her strength recur'd from fraile infirmitis.

53

That done, he leads him to the highest Mount; 469
Such one, as that same mighty man of God,[12]
That bloud-red billowes like a walléd front
On either side disparted with his rod,
Till that his army dry-foot through them yod,
Dwelt fortie dayes upon; where writ in stone
With bloudy letters by the hand of God, 475
The bitter doome of death and balefull mone
He did receive, while flashing fire about him shone.

54

Or like that sacred hill,[13] whose head full hie,
Adornd with fruitfull Olives all arownd,
Is, as it were for endlesse memory 480
Of that deare Lord, who oft thereon was fownd,
For ever with a flowring girlond crownd:
Or like that pleasaunt Mount,[14] that is for ay
Through famous Poets verse each where renownd,
On which the thrise three learnéd Ladies[15] play 485
Their heavenly notes, and make full many a lovely lay.

55

From thence, far off he unto him did shew
A litle path, that was both steepe and long,

[12]Moses. [13]The Mount of Olives.
[14]Parnassus. [15]The nine muses.

Which to a goodly Citie led his vew;
Whose wals and towres were builded high
and strong 490
Of perle and precious stone, that earthly tong
Cannot describe, nor wit of man can tell;
Too high a ditty for my simple song;
The Citie of the great king hight it well,
Wherein eternall peace and happinesse doth
dwell. 495

56

As he thereon stood gazing, he might see
The blessèd Angels to and fro descend
From highest heaven, in gladsome companee,
And with great joy into that Citie wend, 499
As commonly as friend does with his frend.
Whereat he wondred much, and gan enquere,
What stately building durst so high extend
Her loftie towres unto the starry sphere,
And what unknowen nation there empeopled
were.

57

Faire knight (quoth he) *Hierusalem* that is,
The new *Hierusalem,* that God has built 506
For those to dwell in, that are chosen his,
His chosen people purg'd from sinfull guilt,
With pretious bloud, which cruelly was spilt
On cursèd tree, of that unspotted lam, 510
That for the sinnes of all the world was kilt:
Now are they Saints all in that Citie sam,
More deare unto their God, then younglings
to their dam.

58

Till now, said then the knight, I weenèd well,
That great *Cleopolis,* where I have beene, 515
In which that fairest *Faerie Queene* doth
dwell,
The fairest Citie was, that might be seene;
And that bright towre all built of christall
cleene,
Panthea, seemd the brightest thing, that was:
But now by proofe all otherwise I weene; 520
For this great Citie that does far surpas,
And this bright Angels towre quite dims that
towre of glas.

59

Most trew, then said the holy agèd man;
Yet is *Cleopolis* for earthly frame,
The fairest peece, that eye beholden can: 525
And well beseemes all knights of noble name,
That covet in th'immortall booke of fame
To be eternizèd, that same to haunt,
And doen their service to that soveraigne
Dame, 529
That glorie does to them for guerdon graunt:
For she is heavenly borne, and heaven may
justly vaunt.

60

And thou faire ymp, sprong out from Eng-
lish race,
How ever now accompted Elfins sonne,
Well worthy doest thy service for her grace,
To aide a virgin desolate foredonne. 535
But when thou famous victorie hast wonne,
And high emongst all knights hast hong thy
shield,
Thenceforth the suit of earthly conquest
shonne,
And wash thy hands from guilt of bloudy
field:
For bloud can nought but sin, and wars but
sorrowes yield. 540

61

Then seeke this path, that I to thee presage,
Which after all to heaven shall thee send;
Then peaceably thy painefull pilgrimage
To yonder same *Hierusalem* do bend,
Where is for thee ordaind a blessèd end: 545
For thou emongst those Saints, whom thou
doest see,
Shalt be a Saint, and thine owne nations
frend
And Patrone: thou Saint *George* shalt callèd
bee,
Saint *George* of mery England, the signe of
victoree.

62

Unworthy wretch (quoth he) of so great
grace, 550
How dare I thinke such glory to attaine?
These that have it attaind, were in like cace
(Quoth he) as wretched, and liv'd in like
paine.
But deeds of armes must I at last be faine,
And Ladies love to leave so dearely bought?
What need of armes, where peace doth ay
remaine, 556
(Said he) and battailes none are to be
fought?
As for loose loves are vaine, and vanish into
nought.

63

O let me not (quoth he) then turne againe
Backe to the world, whose joyes so fruitlesse
are; 560
But let me here for aye in peace remaine,
Or streight way on that last long voyage fare,

That nothing may my present hope empare.
That may not be (said he) ne maist thou yit
Forgo that royall maides bequeathéd care, 565
Who did her cause into thy hand commit,
Till from her curséd foe thou have her freely quit.

64

Then shall I soone, (quoth he) so God me grace,
Abet that virgins cause disconsolate,
And shortly backe returne unto this place, 570
To walke this way in Pilgrims poore estate.
But now aread, old father, why of late
Didst thou behight me borne of English blood,
Whom all a Faeries sonne doen nominate?
That word shall I (said he) avouchen good, 575
Sith to thee is unknowne the cradle of thy brood.

65

For well I wote, thou springst from ancient race
Of *Saxon* kings, that have with mightie hand
And many bloudie battailes fought in place
High reard their royall throne in *Britane* land, 580
And vanquisht them, unable to withstand:
From thence a Faerie thee unweeting reft,
There as thou slepst in tender swadling band,
And her base Elfin brood there for thee left.
Such men do Chaungelings call, so chaunged by Faeries theft. 585

66

Thence she thee brought into this Faerie lond,
And in an heapéd furrow did thee hyde,
Where thee a Ploughman all unweeting fond,
As he his toylesome teme that way did guyde,
And brought thee up in ploughmans state to byde, 590
Whereof *Georgos*[16] he thee gave to name;
Till prickt with courage, and thy forces pryde,
To Faery court thou cam'st to seeke for fame,
And prove thy puissaunt armes, as seemes thee best became.

67

O holy Sire (quoth he) how shall I quight 595
The many favours I with thee have found,
That hast my name and nation red aright,
And taught the way that does to heaven bound?
This said, adowne he lookéd to the ground,
To have returnd, but dazéd were his eyne, 600
Through passing brightnesse, which did quite confound
His feeble sence, and too exceeding shyne.
So darke are earthly things compard to things divine.

68

At last whenas himselfe he gan to find,
To *Una* back he cast him to retire; 605
Who him awaited still with pensive mind.
Great thankes and goodly meed to that good syre,
He thence departing gave for his paines hyre.
So came to *Una*, who him joyd to see,
And after little rest, gan him desire, 610
Of her adventure mindfull for to bee.
So leave they take of *Caelia*, and her daughters three.

[16]Greek γεωργός, meaning husbandman.

CANTO XI

The knight with that old Dragon fights
two dayes incessantly:
The third him overthrowes, and gayns
most glorious victory.

1

High time now gan it wex for *Una faire*,
To thinke of those her captive Parents deare,
And their forwasted kingdome to repaire:
Whereto whenas they now approchéd neare,
With hartie words her knight she gan to cheare, 5
And in her modest manner thus bespake;
Deare knight, as deare, as ever knight was deare,
That all these sorrowes suffer for my sake,
High heaven behold the tedious toyle, ye for me take.

2

Now are we come unto my native soyle, 10
And to the place, where all our perils dwell;
Here haunts that feend, and does his dayly spoyle,
Therefore henceforth be at your keeping well,[1]
And ever ready for your foeman fell.
The sparke of noble courage now awake, 15
And strive your excellent selfe to excell;

[1]Be carefully on your guard.

That shall ye evermore renowméd make,
Above all knights on earth, that batteill undertake.

3

And pointing forth, lo yonder is (said she)
The brasen towre in which my parents deare 20
For dread of that huge feend emprisond be,
Whom I from far see on the walls appeare,
Whose sight my feeble soule doth greatly cheare:
And on the top of all I do espye
The watchman wayting tydings glad to heare, 25
That O my parents might I happily
Unto you bring, to ease you of your misery.

4

With that they heard a roaring hideous sound,
That all the ayre with terrour filléd wide,
And seemd uneath to shake the stedfast ground. 30
Eftsoones that dreadfull Dragon they espide,
Where stretcht he lay upon the sunny side,
Of a great hill, himselfe like a great hill.
But all so soone, as he from far descride
Those glistring armes, that heaven with light did fill, 35
He rousd himselfe full blith, and hastned them untill.

5

Then bad the knight his Lady yede aloofe,
And to an hill her selfe withdraw aside,
From whence she might behold that battailles proof
And eke be safe from daunger far descryde: 40
She him obayd, and turnd a little wyde.
Now O thou sacred Muse,[2] most learnéd Dame,
Faire ympe of *Phoebus,* and his agéd bride,[3]
The Nourse of time, and everlasting fame,
That warlike hands ennoblest with immortall name; 45

6

O gently come into my feeble brest,
Come gently, but not with that mighty rage,
Wherewith the martiall troupes thou doest infest,
And harts of great Heroës doest enrage,
That nought their kindled courage may aswage, 50
Soone as thy dreadfull trompe begins to sownd;
The God of warre with his fiers equipage
Thou doest awake, sleepe never he so sownd,
And scaréd nations doest with horrour sterne astownd.

7

Faire Goddesse lay that furious fit aside, 55
Till I of warres and bloudy *Mars* do sing,
And Briton fields with Sarazin bloud bedyde,
Twixt that great faery Queene and Paynim king,[4]
That with their horrour heaven and earth did ring,
A worke of labour long, and endlesse prayse: 60
But now a while let downe that haughtie string,
And to my tunes thy second tenor rayse,
That I this man of God his godly armes may blaze.

8

By this the dreadfull Beast drew nigh to hand,
Halfe flying, and halfe footing in his hast, 65
That with his largenesse measuréd much land,
And made wide shadow under his huge wast;
As mountaine doth the valley overcast.
Approching nigh, he rearéd high afore
His body monstrous, horrible, and vast, 70
Which to increase his wondrous greatnesse more,
Was swolne with wrath, and poyson, and with bloudy gore.

9

And over, all with brasen scales was armd,
Like plated coate of steele, so couchéd neare,
That nought mote perce, ne might his corse be harmd 75
With dint of sword, nor push of pointed speare;
Which as an Eagle, seeing pray appeare,
His aery plumes doth rouze, full rudely dight,
So shakéd he, that horrour was to heare,
For as the clashing of an Armour bright, 80
Such noyse his rouzéd scales did send unto the knight.

[2] Calliope (but see note above, Introd. Stanzas, 2).

[3] The muses were the children of Apollo and Mnemosyne, or Memory.

[4] Spenser here refers to a later part of the *Faerie Queene,* which was never written.

10

His flaggy wings when forth he did display,
Were like two sayles, in which the hollow wynd
Is gathered full, and worketh speedy way:
And eke the pennes, that did his pineons bynd, 85
Were like mayne-yards, with flying canvas lynd,
With which whenas him list the ayre to beat,
And there by force unwonted passage find,
The cloudes before him fled for terrour great,
And all the heavens stood still amazéd with his threat. 90

11

His huge long tayle wound up in hundred foldes,
Does overspred his long bras-scaly backe,
Whose wreathéd boughts when ever he unfoldes,
And thicke entangled knots adown does slacke,
Bespotted as with shields of red and blacke, 95
It sweepeth all the land behind him farre,
And of three furlongs does but litle lacke;
And at the point two stings in-fixéd arre,
Both deadly sharpe, that sharpest steele exceeden farre.

12

But stings and sharpest steele did far exceed 100
The sharpnesse of his cruell rending clawes;
Dead was it sure, as sure as death in deed,
What ever thing does touch his ravenous pawes,
Or what within his reach he ever drawes. 104
But his most hideous head my toung to tell,
Does tremble: for his deepe devouring jawes
Wide gapéd, like the griesly mouth of hell,
Through which into his darke abisse all ravin fell.

13

And that more wondrous was, in either jaw
Three ranckes of yron teeth enraungéd were, 110
In which yet trickling bloud and gobbets raw
Of late devouréd bodies did appeare,
That sight thereof bred cold congealéd feare:
Which to increase, and all atonce to kill,
A cloud of smoothering smoke and sulphur seare 115
Out of his stinking gorge forth steeméd still,
That all the ayre about with smoke and stench did fill.

14

His blazing eyes, like two bright shining shields,
Did burne with wrath, and sparkled living fyre;
As two broad Beacons, set in open fields, 120
Send forth their flames farre off to every shyre,
And warning give, that enemies conspyre,
With fire and sword the region to invade;
So flam'd his eyne with rage and rancorous yre:
But farre within, as in a hollow glade, 125
Those glaring lampes were set, that made a dreadfull shade.

15

So dreadfully he towards him did pas,
Forelifting up aloft his speckled brest,
And often bounding on the bruséd gras,
As for great joyance of his newcome guest. 130
Eftsoones he gan advance his haughtie crest,
As chaufféd Bore his bristles doth upreare,
And shoke his scales to battell readie drest;
That made the *Redcrosse* knight nigh quake for feare,
As bidding bold defiance to his foeman neare.

16

The knight gan fairely couch his steadie speare, 136
And fiercely ran at him with rigorous might:
The pointed steele arriving rudely theare,
His harder hide would neither perce, nor bight,
But glauncing by forth passéd forward right; 140
Yet sore amovéd with so puissant push,
The wrathfull beast about him turnéd light,
And him so rudely passing by, did brush
With his long tayle, that horse and man to ground did rush.

17

Both horse and man up lightly rose againe, 145
And fresh encounter towards him addrest:
But th'idle stroke yet backe recoyld in vaine,
And found no place his deadly point to rest.
Exceeding rage enflam'd the furious beast,
To be avengéd of so great despight; 150
For never felt his imperceable brest
So wondrous force, from hand of living wight;
Yet had he prov'd the powre of many a puissant knight.

18

Then with his waving wings displayéd wyde,
Himselfe up high he lifted from the ground,
And with strong flight did forcibly divide 156
The yielding aire, which nigh too feeble found
Her flitting partes, and element unsound,
To beare so great a weight: he cutting way
With his broad sayles, about him soaréd round: 160
At last low stouping with unweldie sway,
Snatcht up both horse and man, to beare them quite away.

19

Long he them bore above the subject plaine,
So farre as Ewghen bow a shaft may send,
Till struggling strong did him at last constraine, 165
To let them downe before his flightés end:
As hagard hauke presuming to contend
With hardie fowle, above his hable might,
His wearie pounces all in vaine doth spend,
To trusse the pray too heavie for his flight; 170
Which comming downe to ground, does free it selfe by fight.

20

He so disseizéd of his gryping grosse,
The knight his thrillant speare againe assayd
In his bras-plated body to embosse,
And three mens strength unto the stroke he layd; 175
Wherewith the stiffe beame quakéd, as affrayd,
And glauncing from his scaly necke, did glyde
Close under his left wing, then broad displayd.
The percing steele there wrought a wound full wyde,
That with the uncouth smart the Monster lowdly cryde. 180

21

He cryde, as raging seas are wont to rore,
When wintry storme his wrathfull wreck does threat,
The rolling billowes beat the ragged shore,
As they the earth would shoulder from her seat,
And greedie gulfe does gape, as he would eat
His neighbour element in his revenge: 186
Then gin the blustring brethren boldly threat,
To move the world from off his stedfast henge,
And boystrous battell make, each other to avenge.

22

The steely head stucke fast still in his flesh, 190
Till with his cruell clawes he snatcht the wood,
And quite asunder broke. Forth flowéd fresh
A gushing river of blacke goarie blood,
That drownéd all the land, whereon he stood;
The streame thereof would drive a watermill.
Trebly augmented was his furious mood 196
With bitter sense of his deepe rooted ill,
That flames of fire he threw forth from his large nosethrill.

23

His hideous tayle then hurléd he about, 199
And therewith all enwrapt the nimble thyes
Of his froth-fomy steed, whose courage stout
Striving to loose the knot, that fast him tyes,
Himselfe in streighter bandes too rash implyes,
That to the ground he is perforce constraynd
To throw his rider: who can quickly ryse 205
From off the earth, with durty bloud distaynd,
For that reprochfull fall right fowly he disdaynd.

24

And fiercely tooke his trenchand blade in hand,
With which he stroke so furious and so fell,
That nothing seemd the puissance could withstand: 210
Upon his crest the hardned yron fell,
But his more hardned crest was armd so well,
That deeper dint therein it would not make;
Yet so extremely did the buffe him quell,
That from thenceforth he shund the like to take, 215
But when he saw them come, he did them still forsake.

25

The knight was wrath to see his stroke beguyld,
And smote againe with more outrageous might;
But backe againe the sparckling steele recoyld,
And left not any marke, where it did light; 220

As if in Adamant rocke it had bene pight.
The beast impatient of his smarting wound,
And of so fierce and forcible despight,
Thought with his wings to stye above the ground;
But his late wounded wing unserviceable found. 225

26

Then full of griefe and anguish vehement,
He lowdly brayd, that like was never heard,
And from his wide devouring oven sent
A flake of fire, that flashing in his beard,
Him all amazd, and almost made affeard: 230
The scorching flame sore swingéd all his face,
And through his armour all his bodie seard,
That he could not endure so cruell cace,
But thought his armes to leave, and helmet to unlace.

27

Now that great Champion of the antique world,[5] 235
Whom famous Poetes verse so much doth vaunt,
And hath for twelve huge labours high extold,
So many furies and sharpe fits did haunt,
When him the poysoned garment did enchaunt
With *Centaures* bloud, and bloudie verses charm'd, 240
As did this knight twelve thousand dolours daunt,
Whom fyrie steele now burnt, that earst him arm'd,
That erst him goodly arm'd, now most of all him harm'd.

28

Faint, wearie, sore, emboyléd, grievéd, brent
With heat, toyle, wounds, armes, smart, and inward fire 245
That never man such mischiefes did torment;
Death better were, death did he oft desire,
But death will never come, when needes require.
Whom so dismayd when that his foe beheld,
He cast to suffer him no more respire, 250
But gan his sturdie sterne about to weld,
And him so strongly stroke, that to the ground him feld.

29

It fortunéd (as faire it then befell) 253
Behind his backe unweeting, where he stood,

[5]Hercules.

Of auncient time there was a springing well,
From which fast trickled forth a silver flood,
Full of great vertues, and for med'cine good.
Whylome, before that curséd Dragon got
That happie land, and all with innocent blood
Defyld those sacred waves, it rightly hot 260
The well of life,[6] ne yet his vertues had forgot.

30

For unto life the dead it could restore,
And guilt of sinfull crimes cleane wash them quite away;
Those that with sicknesse were infected sore,
It could recure, and agéd long decay 265
Renew, as one were borne that very day.
Both *Silo*[7] this, and *Jordan*[8] did excell,
And th'English *Bath,* and eke the german *Spau,*
Ne can *Cephise,*[9] nor *Hebrus*[10] match this well:
Into the same the knight backe overthrowen, fell. 270

31

Now gan the golden *Phoebus* for to steepe
His fierie face in billowes of the west,
And his faint steedes watred in Ocean deepe,
Whiles from their journall labours they did rest,
When that infernall Monster, having kest 275
His wearie foe into that living well,
Can high advance his broad discoloured brest,
Above his wonted pitch, with countenance fell,
And clapt his yron wings, as victor he did dwell.

32

Which when his pensive Ladie saw from farre, 280
Great woe and sorrow did her soule assay,
As weening that the sad end of the warre,
And gan to highest God entirely pray,
That fearéd chance from her to turne away;
With folded hands and knees full lowly bent
All night she watcht, ne once adowne would lay 286

[6]Cf. Revelation, 22:1. The well represents divine grace.

[7]The pool of Siloam (St. John, 9:7).

[8]Naaman was healed in the Jordan (II Kings, 5:14).

[9]The river Cephisus, near Athens.

[10]A river in Thrace.

Her daintie limbs in her sad dreriment,
But praying still did wake, and waking did lament.

33

The morrow next gan early to appeare,
That Titan rose to runne his daily race; 290
But early ere the morrow next gan reare
Out of the sea faire *Titans* deawy face,
Up rose the gentle virgin from her place,
And lookéd all about, if she might spy
Her lovéd knight to move his manly pace: 295
For she had great doubt of his safety,
Since late she saw him fall before his enemy.

34

At last she saw, where he upstarted brave
Out of the well, wherein he drenchéd lay;
As Eagle fresh out of the Ocean wave, 300
Where he hath left his plumes all hoary gray,
And deckt himselfe with feathers youthly gay,[11]
Like Eyas hauke up mounts unto the skies,
His newly budded pineons to assay,
And marveiles at himselfe, still as he flies: 305
So new this new-borne knight to battell new did rise.

35

Whom when the damnéd feend so fresh did spy,
No wonder if he wondred at the sight,
And doubted, whether his late enemy
It were, or other new supplied knight. 310
He, now to prove his late renewéd might,
High brandishing his bright deaw-burning[12] blade,
Upon his crested scalpe so sore did smite,
That to the scull a yawning wound it made:
The deadly dint his dulléd senses all dismaid.

36

I wote not, whether the revenging steele 316
Were hardned with that holy water dew,
Wherein he fell, or sharper edge did feele,
Or his baptizéd hands now greater grew;
Or other secret vertue did ensew; 320
Else never could the force of fleshly arme,
Ne molten mettall[13] in his bloud embrew:
For till that stownd could never wight him harme,
By subtilty, nor slight, nor might, nor mighty charme.

[11] The tradition that the eagle could renew its youth is an old one (cf. Psalms, 103:5).

[12] Shining with the dew of the well.

[13] Metal that was ever melted.

37

The cruell wound enragéd him so sore, 325
That loud he yeldéd for exceeding paine;
As hundred ramping Lyons seem'd to rore,
Whom ravenous hunger did thereto constraine:
Then gan he tosse aloft his stretchéd traine,
And therewith scourge the buxome aire so sore, 330
That to his force to yeelden it was faine;
Ne ought his sturdie strokes might stand afore,
That high trees overthrew, and rocks in peeces tore.

38

The same advauncing high above his head,
With sharpe intended sting so rude him smot, 335
That to the earth him drove, as stricken dead,
Ne living wight would have him life behot:
The mortall sting his angry needle shot
Quite through his shield, and in his shoulder seasd,
Where fast it stucke, ne would there out be got: 340
The griefe thereof him wondrous sore diseasd,
Ne might his ranckling paine with patience be appeasd.

39

But yet more mindfull of his honour deare,
Then of the grievous smart, which him did wring, 344
From loathéd soile he can him lightly reare,
And strove to loose the farre infixéd sting:
Which when in vaine he tryde with struggeling,
Inflam'd with wrath, his raging blade he heft,
And stroke so strongly, that the knotty string
Of his huge taile he quite a sunder cleft, 350
Five joynts thereof he hewd, and but the stump him left.

40

Hart cannot thinke, what outrage, and what cryes,
With foule enfouldred smoake and flashing fire,
The hell-bred beast threw forth unto the skyes,
That all was coveréd with darknesse dire: 355

Then fraught with rancour, and engorgéd ire,
He cast at once him to avenge for all,
And gathering up himselfe out of the mire,
With his uneven wings did fiercely fall,
Upon his sunne-bright shield, and gript it fast withall. 360

41

Much was the man encombred with his hold,
In feare to lose his weapon in his paw,
Ne wist yet, how his talants to unfold;
Nor harder was from *Cerberus* greedie jaw
To plucke a bone, then from his cruell claw 365
To reave by strength the gripéd gage away:
Thrise he assayd it from his foot to draw,
And thrise in vaine to draw it did assay,
It booted nought to thinke, to robbe him of his pray.

42

Tho when he saw no power might prevaile, 370
His trustie sword he cald to his last aid,
Wherewith he fiercely did his foe assaile,
And double blowes about him stoutly laid,
That glauncing fire out of the yron plaid;
As sparckles from the Andvile used to fly, 375
When heavie hammers on the wedge are swaid;
Therewith at last he forst him to unty
One of his grasping feete, him to defend thereby.

43

The other foot, fast fixéd on his shield,
Whenas no strength, nor stroks mote him constraine 380
To loose, ne yet the warlike pledge to yield,
He smot thereat with all his might and maine,
That nought so wondrous puissance might sustaine;
Upon the joynt the lucky steele did light,
And made such way, that hewd it quite in twaine; 385
The paw yet misséd not his minisht might,
But hong still on the shield, as it at first was pight.

44

For griefe thereof, and divelish despight,
From his infernall fournace forth he threw
Huge flames, that dimméd all the heavens light, 390
Enrold in duskish smoke and brimstone blew;
As burning *Aetna* from his boyling stew
Doth belch out flames, and rockes in peeces broke,
And ragged ribs of mountaines molten new,
Enwrapt in coleblacke clouds and filthy smoke, 395
That all the land with stench, and heaven with horror choke.

45

The heate whereof, and harmefull pestilence
So sore him noyd, that forst him to retire
A little backward for his best defence,
To save his bodie from the scorching fire, 400
Which he from hellish entrailes did expire.
It chaunst (eternall God that chaunce did guide)
As he recoyléd backward, in the mire
His nigh forwearied feeble feet did slide,
And downe he fell, with dread of shame sore terrifide. 405

46

There grew a goodly tree him faire beside,
Loaden with fruit and apples rosie red,
As they in pure vermilion had beene dide,
Whereof great vertues over all were red:
For happie life to all, which thereon fed, 410
And life eke everlasting did befall:
Great God it planted in that blesséd sted
With his almightie hand, and did it call
The tree of life, the crime of our first fathers fall.[14]

47

In all the world like was not to be found, 415
Save in that soile, where all good things did grow,
And freely sprong out of the fruitfull ground,
As incorrupted Nature did them sow,
Till that dread Dragon all did overthrow.
Another like faire tree eke grew thereby, 420
Whereof who so did eat, eftsoones did know
Both good and ill:[15] O mornefull memory:
That tree through one mans fault hath doen us all to dy.

48

From that first tree forth flowd, as from a well,
A trickling streame of Balme,[16] most soveraine 425

[14]Cf. Genesis, 3:22–23.
[15]Cf. Genesis, 2:9.
[16]Suggested by Revelation, 22:2.

And daintie deare, which on the ground still fell,
And overflowéd all the fertill plaine,
As it had deawéd bene with timely raine:
Life and long health that gratious ointment gave,
And deadly woundes could heale and reare againe 430
The senselesse corse appointed for the grave.
Into that same he fell: which did from death him save.

49

For nigh thereto the ever damnéd beast
Durst not approch, for he was deadly made,
And all that life preservéd, did detest: 435
Yet he it oft adventur'd to invade.
By this the drouping day-light gan to fade,
And yeeld his roome to sad succeeding night,
Who with her sable mantle gan to shade
The face of earth, and wayes of living wight,
And high her burning torch[17] set up in heaven bright. 441

50

When gentle *Una* saw the second fall
Of her deare knight, who wearie of long fight,
And faint through losse of bloud, mov'd not at all,
But lay as in a dreame of deepe delight, 445
Besmeard with pretious Balme, whose vertuous might
Did heale his wounds, and scorching heat alay,
Againe she stricken was with sore affright,
And for his safetie gan devoutly pray;
And watch the noyous night, and wait for joyous day. 450

51

The joyous day gan early to appeare,
And faire *Aurora* from the deawy bed
Of aged *Tithone* gan herselfe to reare,
With rosie cheekes, for shame as blushing red;
Her golden lockes for haste were loosely shed 455
About her eares, when *Una* her did marke
Clymbe to her charet, all with flowers spred,
From heaven high to chase the chearelesse darke;
With merry note her loud salutes the mounting larke.

[17]The moon.

52

Then freshly up arose the doughtie knight, 460
All healéd of his hurts and woundés wide,
And did himselfe to battell readie dight;
Whose early foe awaiting him beside
To have devourd, so soone as day he spyde,
When now he saw himselfe so freshly reare, 465
As if late fight had nought him damnifyde,
He woxe dismayd, and gan his fate to feare;
Nathlesse with wonted rage he him advauncéd neare.

53

And in his first encounter, gaping wide,
He thought attonce him to have swallowd quight, 470
And rusht upon him with outrágious pride;
Who him r'encountring fierce, as hauke in flight,
Perforce rebutted backe. The weapon bright
Taking advantage of his open jaw,
Ran through his mouth with so importune might, 475
That deepe emperst his darksome hollow maw,
And back retyrd, his life bloud forth with all did draw.

54

So downe he fell, and forth his life did breath,
That vanisht into smoke and cloudés swift;
So downe he fell, that th'earth him underneath 480
Did grone, as feeble so great load to lift;
So downe he fell, as an huge rockie clift,
Whose false foundation waves have washt away,
With dreadfull poyse is from the mayneland rift,
And rolling downe, great *Neptune* doth dismay; 485
So downe he fell, and like an heapéd mountaine lay.

55

The knight himselfe even trembled at his fall,
So huge and horrible a masse it seem'd;
And his deare Ladie, that beheld it all,
Durst not approch for dread, which she misdeem'd, 490

But yet at last, when as the direfull feend
She saw not stirre, off-shaking vaine affright,
She nigher drew, and saw that joyous end:
Then God she praysd, and thankt her faithfull knight,
That had atchiev'd so great a conquest by his might. 495

CANTO XII

Faire Una to the Redcrosse knight
betrouthéd is with joy:
Though false Duessa it to barre
her false sleights doe imploy.

1

Behold I see the haven nigh at hand,
To which I meane my wearie course to bend;
Vere the maine shete, and beare up with the land,
The which afore is fairely to be kend,
And seemeth safe from stormes, that may offend; 5
There this faire virgin wearie of her way
Must landed be, now at her journeyes end:
There eke my feeble barke a while may stay,
Till merry wind and weather call her thence away.

2

Scarsely had *Phoebus* in the glooming East 10
Yet harnesséd his firie-footed teeme,
Ne reard above the earth his flaming creast,
When the last deadly smoke aloft did steeme,
That signe of last outbreathéd life did seeme,
Unto the watchman on the castle wall; 15
Who thereby dead that balefull Beast did deeme,
And to his Lord and Ladie lowd can call,
To tell, how he had seene the Dragons fatall fall.

3

Uprose with hastie joy, and feeble speed
That agéd Sire, the Lord of all that land, 20
And lookéd forth, to weet, if true indeede
Those tydings were, as he did understand,
Which whenas true by tryall he out fond,
He bad to open wyde his brazen gate,
Which long time had bene shut, and out of hond 25
Proclayméd joy and peace through all his state;
For dead now was their foe, which them forrayéd late.

4

Then gan triumphant Trompets sound on hie,
That sent to heaven the ecchoéd report
Of their new joy, and happie victorie 30
Gainst him, that had them long opprest with tort,
And fast imprisonéd in siegéd fort.
Then all the people, as in solemne feast,
To him assembled with one full consort,
Rejoycing at the fall of that great beast, 35
From whose eternall bondage now they were releast.

5

Forth came that auncient Lord and agéd Queene,
Arayd in antique robes downe to the ground,
And sad habiliments right well beseene;
A noble crew about them waited round 40
Of sage and sober Peres, all gravely gownd;
Whom farre before did march a goodly band
Of tall young men, all hable armes to sownd,
But now they laurell braunches bore in hand;
Glad signe of victorie and peace in all their land. 45

6

Unto that doughtie Conquerour they came,
And him before themselves prostrating low,
Their Lord and Patrone loud did him proclame,
And at his feet their laurell boughes did throw.
Soone after them all dauncing on a row 50
The comely virgins came, with girlands dight,
As fresh as flowres in medow greene do grow,
When morning deaw upon their leaves doth light:
And in their hands sweet Timbrels all upheld on hight.

7

And them before, the fry of children young 55
Their wanton sports and childish mirth did play,
And to the Maydens sounding tymbrels sung
In well attunéd notes, a joyous lay,
And made delightfull musicke all the way,
Untill they came, where that faire virgin stood; 60
As faire *Diana* in fresh sommers day,
Beholds her Nymphes, enraung'd in shadie wood,
Some wrestle, some do run, some bathe in christall flood.

8

So she beheld those maydens meriment
With chearefull vew; who when to her they came, 65
Themselves to ground with gratious humblesse bent,
And her ador'd by honorable name,
Lifting to heaven her everlasting fame:
Then on her head they set a girland greene,
And crownéd her twixt earnest and twixt game; 70
Who in her selfe-resemblance well beseene,[1]
Did seeme such, as she was, a goodly maiden Queene.

9

And after, all the raskall many ran,
Heapéd together in rude rablement,
To see the face of that victorious man: 75
Whom all admiréd, as from heaven sent,
And gazd upon with gaping wonderment.
But when they came, where that dead Dragon lay,
Stretcht on the ground in monstrous large extent,
The sight with idle feare did them dismay, 80
Ne durst approch him nigh, to touch, or once assay.

10

Some feard, and fled; some feard and well it faynd;
One that would wiser seeme, then all the rest,
Warnd him not touch, for yet perhaps remaynd
Some lingring life within his hollow brest, 85
Or in his wombe might lurke some hidden nest
Of many Dragonets, his fruitfull seed;
Another said, that in his eyes did rest
Yet sparckling fire, and bad thereof take heed;
Another said, he saw him move his eyes indeed. 90

11

One mother, when as her foolehardie chyld
Did come too neare, and with his talants play,
Halfe dead through feare, her litle babe revyld,
And to her gossips gan in counsell say;
How can I tell, but that his talants may 95
Yet scratch my sonne, or rend his tender hand?
So diversly themselves in vaine they fray;
Whiles some more bold, to measure him nigh stand,
To prove how many acres he did spread of land. 99

12

Thus flockéd all the folke him round about,
The whiles that hoarie king, with all his traine,
Being arrivéd, where that champion stout
After his foes defeasance did remaine,
Him goodly greetes, and faire does entertaine,
With princely gifts of yvorie and gold, 105
And thousand thankes him yeelds for all his paine.
Then when his daughter deare he does behold,
Her dearely doth imbrace, and kisseth manifold.

13

And after to his Pallace he them brings,
With shaumes, and trompets, and with Clarions sweet; 110
And all the way the joyous people sings,
And with their garments strowes the pavéd street:
Whence mounting up, they find purveyance meet
Of all, that royall Princes court became,
And all the floore was underneath their feet 115
Bespred with costly scarlot of great name,
On which they lowly sit, and fitting purpose frame.

14

What needs me tell their feast and goodly guize,
In which was nothing riotous nor vaine?
What needs of daintie dishes to devize, 120
Of comely services, or courtly trayne?
My narrow leaves cannot in them containe
The large discourse of royall Princes state.
Yet was their manner then but bare and plaine:
For th'antique world excesse and pride did hate; 125
Such proud luxurious pompe is swollen up but late.

---

[1] I. e., she now looked like her real self.

15

Then when with meates and drinkes of every
kinde
Their fervent appetites they quenchéd had,
That auncient Lord gan fit occasion finde,
Of straunge adventures, and of perils sad, 130
Which in his travell him befallen had,
For to demaund of his renowméd guest:
Who then with utt'rance grave, and count-
'nance sad,
From point to point, as is before exprest,
Discourst his voyage long, according his re-
quest. 135

16

Great pleasure mixt with pittifull regard,
That godly King and Queene did passionate,
Whiles they his pittifull adventures heard,
That oft they did lament his lucklesse state,
And often blame the too importune fate, 140
That heapd on him so many wrathfull
wreakes:
For never gentle knight, as he of late,
So tosséd was in fortunes cruell freakes;
And all the while salt teares bedeawd the
hearers cheaks.

17

Then said the royall Pere in sober wise; 145
Deare Sonne, great beene the evils, which ye
bore
From first to last in your late enterprise,
That I note, whether prayse, or pitty more:
For never living man, I weene, so sore
In sea of deadly daungers was distrest; 150
But since now safe ye seiséd have the shore,
And well arrivéd are (high God be blest),
Let us devize of ease and everlasting rest.

18

Ah dearest Lord, said then that doughty
knight,
Of ease or rest I may not yet devize; 155
For by the faith, which I to armes have
plight,
I bounden am streight after this emprize,
As that your daughter can ye well advize,
Backe to returne to that great Faerie Queene,
And her to serve six yeares in warlike
wize, 160
Gainst that proud Paynim king, that workes
her teene:
Therefore I ought crave pardon, till I there
have beene.

19

Unhappie falles that hard necessitie,
(Quoth he) the troubler of my happie peace,
And vowéd foe of my felicitie; 165
Ne I against the same can justly preace:
But since that band ye cannot now release,
Nor doen undo (for vowes may not be
vaine);
Soone as the terme of those six yeares shall
cease,
Ye then shall hither backe returne againe, 170
The marriage to accomplish vowd betwixt
you twain.

20

Which for my part I covet to performe,
In sort as through the world I did proclame,
That who so kild that monster most deforme,
And him in hardy battaile overcame, 175
Should have mine onely daughter to his
Dame,
And of my kingdome heire apparaunt bee:
Therefore since now to thee perteines the
same,
By dew desert of noble chevalree,
Both daughter and eke kingdome, lo I yield
to thee. 180

21

Then forth he calléd that his daughter faire,
The fairest *Un'* his onely daughter deare,
His onely daughter, and his onely heyre;
Who forth proceeding with sad sober cheare,
As bright as doth the morning starre ap-
peare 185
Out of the East, with flaming lockes bedight,
To tell that dawning day is drawing neare,
And to the world does bring long wishéd
light;
So faire and fresh that Lady shewd her selfe
in sight.

22

So faire and fresh, as freshest flowre in
May; 190
For she had layd her mournefull stole aside,
And widow-like sad wimple throwne away,
Wherewith her heavenly beautie she did
hide,
Whiles on her wearie journey she did ride;
And on her now a garment she did weare, 195
All lilly white, withoutten spot, or pride,
That seemd like silke and silver woven neare,
But neither silke nor silver therein did ap-
peare.

23

The blazing brightnesse of her beauties
beame,
And glorious light of her sunshyny face 200
To tell, were as to strive against the streame.
My ragged rimes are all too rude and bace,
Her heavenly lineaments for to enchace.
Ne wonder; for her owne deare lovéd
knight,
All were she dayly with himselfe in place, 205
Did wonder much at her celestiall sight:
Oft had he seene her faire, but never so faire
dight.

24

So fairely dight, when she in presence came,
She to her Sire made humble reverence,
And bowéd low, that her right well became,
And added grace unto her excellence: 211
Who with great wisedome, and grave elo-
quence
Thus gan to say. But eare he thus had said,
With flying speede, and seeming great pre-
tence,
Came running in, much like a man dismaid,
A Messenger with letters, which his message
said. 216

25

All in the open hall amazéd stood,
At suddeinnesse of that unwarie sight,
And wondred at his breathlesse hastie mood.
But he for nought would stay his passage
right, 220
Till fast before the king he did alight;
Where falling flat, great humblesse he did
make,
And kist the ground, whereon his foot was
pight;
Then to his hands that writ he did betake,
Which he disclosing, red thus, as the paper
spake. 225

26

To thee, most mighty king of *Eden* faire,
Her greeting sends in these sad lines addrest,
The wofull daughter, and forsaken heire
Of that great Emperour of all the West;[2]
And bids thee be advizéd for the best, 230
Ere thou thy daughter linck in holy band
Of wedlocke to that new unknowen guest:
For he already plighted his right hand
Unto another love, and to another land.

[2]The pope.

27

To me sad mayd, or rather widow sad, 235
He was affiauncéd long time before,
And sacred pledges he both gave, and had,
False erraunt knight, infamous, and for-
swore:
Witnesse the burning Altars, which he
swore,
And guiltie heavens of[3] his bold perjury, 240
Which though he hath polluted oft of yore,
Yet I to them for judgement just do fly,
And them conjure t'avenge this shamefull
injury.

28

Therefore since mine he is, or free or bond,
Or false or trew, or living or else dead, 245
Withhold, O soveraine Prince, your hasty
hond
From knitting league with him, I you aread;
Ne weene my right with strength adowne to
tread,
Through weakenesse of my widowhed, or
woe:
For truth is strong, her rightfull cause to
plead, 250
And shall find friends, if need requireth soe.
So bids thee well to fare, Thy neither friend,
nor foe, *Fidessa.*

29

When he these bitter byting words had red,
The tydings straunge did him abashéd make,
That still he sate long time astonishéd 255
As in great muse, ne word to creature spake.
At last his solemne silence thus he brake,
With doubtfull eyes fast fixéd on his guest;
Redoubted knight, that for mine onely sake
Thy life and honour late adventurest, 260
Let nought be hid from me, that ought to be
exprest.

30

What meane these bloudy vowes, and idle
threats,
Throwne out from womanish impatient
mind?
What heavens? what altars? what enragéd
heates
Here heapéd up with termes of love un-
kind, 265
My conscience cleare with guilty bands
would bind?
High God be witnesse, that I guiltlesse ame.
But if your selfe, Sir knight, ye faultie find,

[3]Heavens infected by.

Or wrappéd be in loves of former Dame,
With crime do not it cover, but disclose the same. 270

31

To whom the *Redcrosse* knight this answere sent,
My Lord, my King, be nought hereat dismayd,
Till well ye wote by grave intendiment,
What woman, and wherefore doth me upbrayd
With breach of love, and loyalty betrayd. 275
It was in my mishaps, as hitherward
I lately traveild, that unwares I strayd
Out of my way, through perils straunge and hard;
That day should faile me, ere I had them all declard.

32

There did I find, or rather I was found 280
Of this false woman, that *Fidessa* hight,
Fidessa hight the falsest Dame on ground,
Most false *Duessa,* royall richly dight,
That easie was t'invegle weaker sight:
Who by her wicked arts, and wylie skill, 285
Too false and strong for earthly skill or might,
Unwares me wrought unto her wicked will,
And to my foe betrayd, when least I fearéd ill.

33

Then steppéd forth the goodly royall Mayd,
And on the ground her selfe prostrating low, 290
With sober countenaunce thus to him sayd;
O pardon me, my soveraigne Lord, to show
The secret treasons, which of late I know
To have bene wroght by that false sorceresse.
She onely she it is, that earst did throw 295
This gentle knight into so great distresse,
That death him did awaite in dayly wretchednesse.

34

And now it seemes, that she subornéd hath
This craftie messenger with letters vaine,
To worke new woe and improvided scath, 300
By breaking of the band betwixt us twaine;
Wherein she uséd hath the practicke paine
Of this false footman, clokt with simplenesse,
Whom if ye please for to discover plaine,
Ye shall him *Archimago* find, I ghesse, 305
The falsest man alive; who tries shall find no lesse.

35

The king was greatly movéd at her speach,
And all with suddein indignation fraight,
Bad on that Messenger rude hands to reach.
Eftsoones the Gard, which on his state did wait, 310
Attacht that faitor false, and bound him strait:
Who seeming sorely chaufféd at his band,
As chainéd Beare, whom cruell dogs do bait,
With idle force did faine them to withstand,
And often semblaunce made to scape out of their hand. 315

36

But they him layd full low in dungeon deepe,
And bound him hand and foote with yron chains.
And with continuall watch did warely keepe;
Who then would thinke, that by his subtile trains
He could escape fowle death or deadly paines? 320
Thus when that Princes wrath was pacifide,
He gan renew the late forbidden banes,
And to the knight his daughter deare he tyde,
With sacred rites and vowes for ever to abyde.

37

His owne two hands the holy knots did knit, 325
That none but death for ever can devide;
His owne two hands, for such a turne most fit,
The housling fire did kindle and provide,
And holy water thereon sprinckled wide;
At which the bushy Teade a groome did light, 330
And sacred lampe in secret chamber hide,
Where it should not be quenchéd day nor night,
For feare of evill fates, but burnen ever bright.

38

Then gan they sprinckle all the posts with wine,
And made great feast to solemnize that day; 335
They all perfumde with frankencense divine,
And precious odours fetcht from far away,

That all the house did sweat with great aray:
And all the while sweete Musicke did apply
Her curious skill, the warbling notes to play,
To drive away the dull Melancholy; 341
The whiles one sung a song of love and jollity.

39

During the which there was an heavenly noise
Heard sound through all the Pallace pleasantly,
Like as it had bene many an Angels voice, 345
Singing before th'eternall majesty,
In their trinall triplicities[4] on hye;
Yet wist no creature, whence that heavenly sweet
Proceeded, yet each one felt secretly
Himselfe thereby reft of his sences meet, 350
And ravishéd with rare impression in his sprite.

40

Great joy was made that day of young and old,
And solemne feast proclaimd throughout the land,
That their exceeding merth may not be told:
Suffice it heare by signes to understand 355
The usuall joyes at knitting of loves band.

[4]It was believed that there were nine orders of angels, grouped in three ranks of three each.

Thrise happy man the knight himselfe did hold,
Possesséd of his Ladies hart and hand,
And ever, when his eye did her behold,
His heart did seeme to melt in pleasures manifold. 360

41

Her joyous presence and sweet company
In full content he there did long enjoy,
Ne wicked envie, ne vile gealosy
His deare delights were able to annoy:
Yet swimming in that sea of blisfull joy, 365
He nought forgot, how he whilome had sworne,
In case he could that monstrous beast destroy,
Unto his Farie Queene backe to returne:
The which he shortly did, and *Una* left to mourne.

42

Now strike your sailes ye jolly Mariners, 370
For we be come unto a quiet rode,
Where we must land some of our passengers,
And light this wearie vessell of her lode.
Here she a while may make her safe abode,
Till she repairéd have her tackles spent, 375
And wants supplide. And then againe abroad
On the long voyage whereto she is bent:
Well may she speede and fairely finish her intent.

EPITHALAMION[1]

Ye learnéd sisters,[2] which have oftentimes
Beene to me ayding, others to adorne,
Whom ye thought worthy of your gracefull rymes,
That even the greatest did not greatly scorne
To heare theyr names sung in your simple layes, 5
But joyéd in theyr prayse;
And when ye list your owne mishaps to mourne,
Which death, or love, or fortunes wreck[3] did rayse,
Your string could soone to sadder tenor turne,
And teach the woods and waters to lament 10
Your dolefull dreriment:
Now lay those sorrowfull complaints aside,
And having all your heads with girland crownd,
Helpe me mine owne loves prayses to resound;
Ne let the same of any be envide: 15
So Orpheus did for his owne bride:
So I unto my selfe alone will sing;
The woods shall to me answer, and my Eccho ring.

Early, before the worlds light-giving lampe
His golden beame upon the hils doth spred, 20
Having disperst the nights unchearefull dampe,
Doe ye awake, and, with fresh lustyhed
Go to the bowre of my belovéd love,
My truest turtle dove:
Bid her awake; for Hymen[4] is awake, 25

[1]Written, as Spenser tells in the poem, for his own marriage in 1594.

[2]The muses. [3]Violence.

[4]God of marriage.

And long since ready forth his maske to move,
With his bright Tead[5] that flames with many a flake,
And many a bachelor to waite on him,
In theyr fresh garments trim.
Bid her awake therefore, and soone her dight, 30
For lo! the wishéd day is come at last,
That shall, for al the paynes and sorrowes past,
Pay to her usury of long delight:
And whylest she doth her dight,
Doe ye to her of joy and solace sing, 35
That all the woods may answer, and your eccho ring.

Bring with you all the Nymphes that you can heare,
Both of the rivers and the forrests greene,
And of the sea that neighbours to her neare,[6]
Al with gay girlands goodly wel beseene.[7] 40
And let them also with them bring in hand
Another gay girland,
For my fayre love, of lillyes and of roses,
Bound truelove wize with a blew silke riband.
And let them make great store of bridale poses,
And let them eeke bring store of other flowers,
To deck the bridale bowers.
And let the ground whereas her foot shall tread,
For feare the stones her tender foot should wrong,
Be strewed with fragrant flowers all along, 50
And diapred[8] lyke the discolored mead.
Which done, doe at her chamber dore awayt,
For she will waken strayt;
The whiles doe ye this song unto her sing,
The woods shall to you answer, and your Eccho ring. 55

Ye nymphes of Mulla,[9] which with carefull heed
The silver scaly trouts doe tend full well,
And greedy pikes which use therein to feed,
(Those trouts and pikes all others doo excell)
And ye likewise which keepe the rushy lake,[10] 60

[5]Torch.

[6]The home of Elizabeth Boyle was on the Bay of Youghal.

[7]Well arrayed. [8]Variegated.

[9]The river Awbeg, south of Kilcolman.

[10]Kilcolman was beside a lake.

Where none doo fishes take,
Bynd up the locks the which hang scatterd light,
And in his waters, which your mirror make,
Behold your faces as the christall bright,
That when you come whereas my love doth lie, 65
No blemish she may spie.
And eke ye lightfoot mayds which keepe the deere
That on the hoary mountayne use to towre,[11]
And the wylde wolves, which seeke them to devoure,
With your steele darts doo chace from comming neer, 70
Be also present heere,
To helpe to decke her, and to help to sing,
That all the woods may answer, and your eccho ring.

Wake now, my love, awake! for it is time:
The Rosy Morne long since left Tithones bed, 75
All ready to her silver coche to clyme,
And Phoebus gins to shew his glorious hed.
Hark how the cheerefull birds do chaunt theyr laies,
And carroll of loves praise!
The merry Larke hir mattins sings aloft, 80
The thrush replyes, the Mavis[12] descant playes,
The Ouzell[13] shrills, the Ruddock[14] warbles soft,
So goodly all agree, with sweet consent,[15]
To this dayes merriment.
Ah! my deere love, why doe ye sleepe thus long, 85
When meeter were that ye should now awake,
T'awayt the comming of your joyous make,[16]
And hearken to the birds love-learnéd song,
The deawy leaves among?
For they of joy and pleasance to you sing, 90
That all the woods them answer, and theyr eccho ring.

My love is now awake out of her dreames,
And her fayre eyes, like stars that dimméd were
With darksome cloud, now shew theyr goodly beams
More bright then Hesperus[17] his head doth rere. 95

[11]Climb. [12]Song-thrush. [13]Blackbird.
[14]Robin. [15]Harmony. [16]Mate.
[17]The morning star.

Come now, ye damzels, daughters of delight,
Helpe quickly her to dight.
But first come ye, fayre houres, which were begot
In Joves sweet paradice, of Day and Night,
Which doe the seasons of the yeare allot, 100
And al that ever in this world is fayre
Do make and still repayre.
And ye three handmayds[18] of the Cyprian Queene,
The which doe still adorne her beauties pride,
Helpe to addorne my beautifullest bride: 105
And as ye her array, still throw betweene
Some graces to be seene:
And as ye use to Venus, to her sing,
The whiles the woods shal answer, and your eccho ring.

Now is my love all ready forth to come: 110
Let all the virgins therefore well awayt,
And ye fresh boyes, that tend upon her groome,
Prepare your selves, for he is comming strayt.
Set all your things in seemely good aray,
Fit for so joyfull day, 115
The joyfulst day that ever sunne did see.
Faire Sun, shew forth thy favourable ray,
And let thy lifull heat not fervent be,
For feare of burning her sunshyny face,
Her beauty to disgrace. 120
O fayrest Phoebus, father of the Muse,
If ever I did honour thee aright,
Or sing the thing that mote[19] thy mind delight,
Doe not thy servants simple boone refuse,
But let this day, let this one day be myne, 125
Let all the rest be thine.
Then I thy soverayne prayses loud wil sing,
That all the woods shal answer, and theyr eccho ring.

Harke how the Minstrels gin to shrill aloud
Their merry Musick that resounds from far, 130
The pipe, the tabor,[20] and the trembling Croud,[21]
That well agree withouten breach or jar.
But most of all the Damzels doe delite,
When they their tymbrels smyte,
And thereunto doe daunce and carrol sweet, 135
That all the sences they doe ravish quite,
The whyles the boyes run up and downe the street,
Crying aloud with strong confuséd noyce,
As if it were one voyce.
Hymen, Iö Hymen, Hymen,[22] they do shout, 140
That even to the heavens theyr shouting shrill
Doth reach, and all the firmament doth fill;
To which the people, standing all about,
As in approvance doe thereto applaud,
And loud advaunce her laud, 145
And evermore they Hymen, Hymen sing,
That al the woods them answer, and theyr eccho ring.

Loe! where she comes along with portly pace,
Lyke Phoebe, from her chamber of the East,
Arysing forth to run her mighty race, 150
Clad all in white, that seemes a virgin best.
So well it her beseemes, that ye would weene
Some angell she had beene.
Her long loose yellow locks lyke golden wyre,
Sprinckled with perle, and perling flowers atweene, 155
Doe lyke a golden mantle her attyre,
And being crownéd with a girland greene,
Seeme lyke some mayden Queene.
Her modest eyes, abashéd to behold
So many gazers as on her do stare, 160
Upon the lowly ground affixéd are;
Ne dare lift up her countenance too bold,
But blush to heare her prayses sung so loud,
So farre from being proud.
Nathlesse doe ye still loud her prayses sing,
That all the woods may answer, and your eccho ring. 166

Tell me, ye merchants daughters, did ye see
So fayre a creature in your towne before,
So sweet, so lovely, and so mild as she,
Adornd with beautyes grace and vertues store? 170
Her goodly eyes lyke Saphyres shining bright,
Her forehead yvory white,
Her cheekes lyke apples which the sun hath rudded,
Her lips lyke cherryes charming men to byte,

[18] The Graces. [19] Might.
[20] Drum. [21] Fiddle.

[22] Refrain of Roman nuptial song. Spenser in this poem follows in a general way the Latin tradition exemplified in Catullus LXI and LXII.

Her brest like to a bowle of creame uncrudded,[23] 175
Her paps lyke lyllies budded,
Her snowie necke lyke to a marble towre,
And all her body like a pallace fayre,
Ascending uppe, with many a stately stayre,
To honors seat and chastities sweet bowre. 180
Why stand ye still, ye virgins, in amaze,
Upon her so to gaze,
Whiles ye forget your former lay to sing,
To which the woods did answer, and your eccho ring.

But if ye saw that which no eyes can see, 185
The inward beauty of her lively spright,[24]
Garnisht with heavenly guifts of high degree,
Much more then would ye wonder at that sight,
And stand astonisht lyke to those which red[25]
Medusaes mazeful hed.[26] 190
There dwels sweet love and constant chastity,
Unspotted fayth, and comely womanhead,
Regard of honour, and mild modesty;
There vertue raynes as Queene in royal throne,
And giveth lawes alone, 195
The which the base affections doe obay,
And yeeld theyr services unto her will;
Ne thought of thing uncomely ever may
Thereto approch to tempt her mind to ill.
Had ye once seene these her celestial threasures, 200
And unrevealéd pleasures,
Then would ye wonder, and her prayses sing,
That al the woods should answer, and your echo ring.

Open the temple gates unto my love,
Open them wide that she may enter in, 205
And all the postes adorne as doth behove,
And all the pillours deck with girlands trim,
For to recyve this Saynt with honour dew,
That commeth in to you.
With trembling steps and humble reverence, 210
She commeth in before th' almighties vew:
Of her, ye virgins, learne obedience,
When so ye come into those holy places,
To humble your proud faces.
Bring her up to th' high altar, that she may 215
The sacred ceremonies there partake,
The which do endlesse matrimony make;
And let the roring Organs loudly play
The praises of the Lord in lively notes,
The whiles with hollow throates 220
The Choristers the joyous Antheme sing,
That al the woods may answere, and their eccho ring.

Behold, whiles she before the altar stands,
Hearing the holy priest that to her speakes,
And blesseth her with his two happy hands,
How the red roses flush up in her cheekes, 226
And the pure snow with goodly vermill stayne,
Like crimsin dyde in grayne:[27]
That even th' Angels, which continually
About the sacred Altare doe remaine, 230
Forget their service and about her fly,
Ofte peeping in her face, that seemes more fayre,
The more they on it stare.
But her sad[28] eyes, still fastened on the ground,
Are governéd with goodly modesty, 235
That suffers not one looke to glaunce awry,
Which may let in a little thought unsownd.
Why blush ye, love, to give to me your hand,
The pledge of all our band?[29]
Sing, ye sweet Angels, Alleluya sing, 240
That all the woods may answere, and your eccho ring.

Now al is done; bring home the bride againe,
Bring home the triumph of our victory,
Bring home with you the glory of her gaine,
With joyance bring her and with jollity. 245
Never had man more joyfull day then this,
Whom heaven would heape with blis.
Make feast therefore now all this live long day;
This day for ever to me holy is; 249
Poure out the wine without restraint or stay,
Poure not by cups, but by the belly full,
Poure out to all that wull,
And sprinkle all the postes and wals with wine,
That they may sweat, and drunken be withall.
Crowne ye God Bacchus with a coronall, 255
And Hymen also crowne with wreathes of vine;
And let the Graces daunce unto the rest,
For they can doo it best:
The whiles the maydens doe theyr carroll sing,
The which the woods shal answer, and theyr eccho ring. 260

[23]Uncurdled. [24]Spirit. [25]Saw.
[26]Medusa's hair was turned into serpents.

[27]In scarlet dye. [28]Sober. [29]Tie.

Ring ye the bels, ye yong men of the towne,
And leave your wonted labors for this day:
This day is holy; doe ye write it downe,
That ye for ever it remember may.
This day[30] the sunne is in his chiefest hight, 265
With Barnaby the bright,
From whence declining daily by degrees,
He somewhat loseth of his heat and light,
When once the Crab[31] behind his back he sees.
But for this time it ill ordainéd was, 270
To chose the longest day in all the yeare,
And shortest night, when longest fitter weare:
Yet never day so long, but late would passe.
Ring ye the bels, to make it weare away,
And bonefiers make all day, 275
And daunce about them, and about them sing:
That all thé woods may answer, and your eccho ring.

Ah! when will this long weary day have end,
And lende me leave to come unto my love?
How slowly do the houres theyr numbers spend! 280
How slowly does sad Time his feathers move!
Haste thee, O fayrest Planet,[32] to thy home
Within the Westerne fome:
Thy tyréd steedes long since have need of rest.
Long though it be, at last I see it gloome, 285
And the bright evening star with golden creast
Appeare out of the East.
Fayre childe of beauty, glorious lampe of love,
That all the host of heaven in rankes doost lead,
And guydest lovers through the nightés dread, 290
How chearefully thou lookest from above,
And seemst to laugh atweene thy twinkling light,
As joying in the sight
Of these glad many, which for joy doe sing,
That all the woods them answer, and their echo ring! 295

Now ceasse, ye damsels, your delights forepast;
Enough is it that all the day was youres:
Now day is doen, and night is nighing fast:
Now bring the Bryde into the brydall boures.
Now night is come, now soone her disaray, 300
And in her bed her lay;
Lay her in lillies and in violets,
And silken courteins over her display,
And odourd sheetes, and Arras[33] coverlets.
Behold how goodly my faire love does ly 305
In proud humility!
Like unto Maia, when as Jove her tooke
In Tempe, lying on the flowry gras,
Twixt sleepe and wake, after she weary was
With bathing in the Acidalian brooke. 310
Now it is night, ye damsels may be gon,
And leave my love alone,
And leave likewise your former lay to sing:
The woods no more shal answere, nor your echo ring.

Now welcome, night! thou night so long expected, 315
That long daies labour doest at last defray,
And all my cares, which cruell love collected,
Hast sumd in one, and cancelléd for aye:
Spread thy broad wing over my love and me,
That no man may us see, 320
And in thy sable mantle us enwrap,
From feare of perrill and foule horror free.
Let no false treason seeke us to entrap,
Nor any dread disquiet once annoy
The safety of our joy: 325
But let the night be calme and quietsome,
Without tempestuous storms or sad afray:
Lyke as when Jove with fayre Alcmena lay,
When he begot the great Tirynthian groome:[34]
Or lyke as when he with thy selfe did lie, 330
And begot Majesty.
And let the mayds and yongmen cease to sing:
Ne let the woods them answer, nor theyr eccho ring.

Let no lamenting cryes, nor dolefull teares,
Be heard all night within, nor yet without: 335
Ne let false whispers, breeding hidden feares,
Breake gentle sleepe with misconceivéd dout.
Let no deluding dreames, nor dreadful sights,
Make sudden sad affrights;
Ne let house-fyres, nor lightnings helplesse[35] harmes, 340
Ne let the Pouke,[36] nor other evill sprights,
Ne let mischivous witches with theyr charmes,

[30] St. Barnabas's day is 11 June. The old calendar being ten days out, it was also the longest day.
[31] One of the signs of the zodiac. [32] The sun.

[33] Coverlets from Arras. [34] Hercules.
[35] Irreparable. [36] Puck, Robin Goodfellow.

Ne let hob Goblins, names whose sence we
see not,
Fray us with things that be not.
Let not the shriech Oule, nor the Storke be
heard, 345
Nor the night Raven that still deadly yels,
Nor damnéd ghosts cald up with mighty
spels,
Nor griesly vultures make us once affeard:
Ne let th' unpleasant Quyre of Frogs still
croking
Make us to wish theyr choking. 350
Let none of these theyr drery accents sing;
Ne let the woods them answer, nor theyr
eccho ring.

But let stil Silence trew night watches keepe,
That sacred peace may in assurance rayne,
And tymely sleep, when it is tyme to sleepe,
May poure his limbs forth on your pleasant
playne, 356
The whiles an hundred little wingéd loves,
Like divers fethered doves,
Shall fly and flutter round about our bed,
And in the secret darke that none re-
proves, 360
Their prety stealthes shall worke, and snares
shal spread
To filch away sweet snatches of delight,
Conceald through covert night.
Ye sonnes of Venus, play your sports at will:
For greedy pleasure, careless of your
toyes, 365
Thinks more upon her paradise of joyes,
Then what ye do, albe it good or ill.
All night therefore attend your merry play,
For it will soone be day:
Now none doth hinder you, that say or sing,
Ne will the woods now answer, nor your
Eccho ring. 371

Who is the same which at my window
peepes?
Or whose is that faire face that shines so
bright?
Is it not Cinthia,[37] she that never sleepes,
But walkes about high heaven al the night?
O fayrest goddesse, do thou not envy[38] 376
My love with me to spy:
For thou likewise didst love, though now
unthought,
And for a fleece of woll, which privily
The Latmian shephard[39] once unto thee
brought,
His pleasures with thee wrought. 380
Therefore to us be favorable now;
And sith of wemens labours thou hast
charge,
And generation goodly dost enlarge,
Encline thy will t' effect our wishfull vow, 385
And the chast wombe informe with timely
seed,
That may our comfort breed:
Till which we cease our hopefull hap[40] to
sing,
Ne let the woods us answere, nor our Eccho
ring.

And thou, great Juno, which with awful
might 390
The lawes of wedlock still dost patronize,
And the religion of the faith first plight
With sacred rites hast taught to solemnize,
And eeke for comfort often calléd art
Of women in their smart, 395
Eternally bind thou this lovely band,
And all thy blessings unto us impart.
And thou, glad Genius, in whose gentle hand
The bridale bowre and geniall bed remaine,
Without blemish or staine, 400
And the sweet pleasures of theyr loves
delight
With secret ayde doest succour and supply,
Till they bring forth the fruitfull progeny,
Send us the timely fruit of this same night.
And thou, fayre Hebe,[41] and thou, Hymen
free, 405
Grant that it may so be.
Til which we cease your further prayse to
sing,
Ne any woods shal answer, nor your Eccho
ring.

And ye high heavens, the temple of the gods,
In which a thousand torches flaming bright
Doe burne, that to us wretched earthly
clods 411
In dreadful darknesse lend desiréd light,
And all ye powers which in the same re-
mayne,
More then we men can fayne,[42]
Poure out your blessing on us plentiously, 415
And happy influence upon us raine,
That we may raise a large posterity,
Which from the earth, which they may long
possesse

[37]The moon. [38]Begrudge. [39]Endymion.

[40]Fortune. [41]Cup-bearer to the gods.
[42]Imagine.

With lasting happinesse,
Up to your haughty pallaces may mount, 420
And for the guerdon[43] of theyr glorious merit,
May heavenly tabernacles there inherit,
Of blesséd Saints for to increase the count.
So let us rest, sweet love, in hope of this,
And cease till then our tymely joyes to sing:
The woods no more us answer, nor our eccho ring. 426

[43]Reward.

Song, made in lieu of many ornaments
With which my love should duly have bene dect,
Which cutting off through hasty accidents,[44]
Ye would not stay your dew time to expect,[45] 430
But promist both to recompens,
Be unto her a goodly ornament,
And for[46] short time an endlesse moniment.

[44]Accidents of haste.
[45]Await. [46]Rather than for.

THOMAS DEKKER

1570?–1641?

The biographical facts of which we can be certain in the case of Thomas Dekker are few, and they do not include the dates of either his birth or his death. It is generally assumed, however, that he was born about 1570. He himself called London "the mother of his life and the nurse of his being"; presumably he came of Dutch stock, spent his formative years among lower middle-class surroundings, and received a good grammar-school education. At the beginning of 1598 his name appears in the diary of Philip Henslowe, a theatrical manager, who notes the sums given to Dekker for writing certain plays, as well as a payment of forty shillings to free him from imprisonment for debt. Henslowe's record shows that during the next six years the young dramatist was paid for some twelve plays which were almost entirely his own work and for more than twenty in which he assisted or collaborated with other writers. *The Shoemakers' Holiday* was performed by the Lord Admiral's Players in 1599, and printed in the following year, without Dekker's name on the title page. In 1600 he also published *Old Fortunatus,* a romantic comedy; in 1602 *Satiromastix,* a strange mingling of historical tragedy with contemporary satire on Ben Jonson; and in 1604 the First Part of *The Honest Whore,* which, in spite of a division of interest between comic and tragic elements, is his most powerful play. In the years that followed, as if he had not been sufficiently versatile already, Dekker turned his hand largely to non-dramatic writing. Among his numerous prose pamphlets, two, both published in 1609, have reached a permanent fame: *The Gull's Hornbook,* a satire on the life of the London gallants, containing, in particular, a vivid account of their conduct during the performance of plays; and the *Four Birds of Noah's Ark,* a series of prayers whose simplicity and beauty are unique even in the devotional literature of that period. Dekker's realism and piety may well be reflections of his own misfortunes. He seems to have been in prison again between 1613 and 1616; thereafter his career grows more and more obscure. Of his death it is only known that it occurred in 1632 or later.

The plot of *The Shoemakers' Holiday* is derived from Thomas Deloney's *Gentle Craft* (1598), a group of stories concerning the shoemakers of London; to this plot is added information about the historical Simon Eyre, a great London merchant of the fifteenth century; but the characterization of Eyre as a humorous madcap, the bourgeois pretensions of his wife, and in general the robust gayety which is the predominant mood of the comedy were probably recreated by Dekker out of the unwritten traditions of the city. In unfolding his story he displays little conscious art: his style is frequently uneven or incongruous, the motivation of his characters unconvincing, the dramatic structure loose and inconsequential. And yet in the traditions of the London tradesmen and in his own knowledge of their life he discovered material of the greatest literary value. "With a . . . fore-feeling for the direction literature was to take in the distant future, he realized the artistic possibilities in the unsophisticated life of the humble, and he represented it upon the stage with more fidelity to fact, humor, grace, and sympathy than any other Elizabethan" (Mary L. Hunt, *Thomas Dekker, a Study* [New York, 1911], p. 201).

An excellent edition of *The Shoemakers' Holiday,* edited with a critical essay by Alexis F. Lange, appears in *Representative English Comedies,* ed. Charles M. Gayley (New York, 1903–1936), III, 1–103. For Dekker's life and development see the study by Mary L. Hunt noted above. Edmund K. Chambers, *The Elizabethan Stage* (Oxford, 1923), supplies the theatrical background; the social background may be found in Louis B. Wright, *Middle-Class Culture in Elizabethan England* (Chapel Hill, 1935).

THE SHOEMAKERS' HOLIDAY

or a Pleasant Comedy of the Gentle Craft

(1600)

To all good Fellows, Professors of the Gentle Craft,[1] *of what degree soever.*

KIND gentlemen and honest boon companions, I present you here with a merry conceited comedy called *The Shoemakers' Holiday,* acted by my Lord Admiral's Players this present Christmas before the Queen's Most Excellent Majesty, for the mirth and pleasant matter by her Highness graciously accepted, being indeed no way offensive. The argument of the play I will set down in this epistle: Sir Hugh Lacy, Earl of Lincoln, had a young gentleman of his own name, his near kinsman, that loved the lord mayor's daughter of London, to prevent and cross which love the earl caused his kinsman to be sent colonel of a company into France, who resigned his place to another gentleman his friend, and came disguised like a Dutch shoemaker to the house of Simon Eyre in Tower Street, who served the mayor and his household with shoes. The merriments that passed in Eyre's house, his coming to be mayor of London, Lacy's getting his love, and other accidents, with two merry three-men's songs—take all in good worth that is well intended, for nothing is purposed but mirth; mirth lengtheneth long life, which, with all other blessings, I heartily wish you. 28

Farewell.

The First Three-man's
Song

O the month of May, the merry month of May,
So frolic, so gay, and so green, so green, so green!
O and then did I unto my true love say:
"Sweet Peg, thou shalt be my summer's queen!

"Now the nightingale, the pretty nightingale, 5
The sweetest singer in all the forest's choir,
Entreats thee, sweet Peggy, to hear thy true love's tale;
Lo, yonder she sitteth, her breast against a brier.

"But Oh, I spy the cuckoo, the cuckoo, the cuckoo;
See where she sitteth: come away, my joy; 10
Come away, I prithee, I do not like the cuckoo
Should sing where my Peggy and I kiss and toy."

O the month of May, the merry month of May,
So frolic, so gay, and so green, so green, so green!
And then did I unto my true love say: 15
"Sweet Peg, thou shalt be my summer's queen!"

The Second Three-man's
Song

(This is to be sung at the latter end.)

Cold's the wind, and wet's the rain,
St. Hugh[2] be our good speed:
Ill is the weather that bringeth no gain,
Nor helps good hearts in need.

Trowl[3] the bowl, the jolly nut-brown bowl, 5
And here, kind mate, to thee:
Let's sing a dirge for St. Hugh's soul,
And down it merrily.

Down a down, hey down a down,
[*Close with the tenor boy.*
Hey derry derry, down a down! 10
Ho, well done; to me let come!
Ring compass,[4] gentle joy.

Trowl the bowl, the nut-brown bowl,
And here, kind, *&c. as often as there be men to drink.*

(At last when all have drunk, this verse:)

Cold's the wind, and wet's the rain, 15
St. Hugh be our good speed:
Ill is the weather that bringeth no gain,
Nor helps good hearts in need.

---

[1]Shoemaking.

[2]Patron saint of shoemakers.

[3]Pass round.

[4]Produce the full range of notes.

The Prologue as it was pronounced
before the Queen's
Majesty.

As wretches in a storm (expecting day),
With trembling hands and eyes cast up to
heaven,
Make prayers the anchor of their conquered
hopes,
So we, dear goddess, wonder of all eyes,
Your meanest vassals (through mistrust and
fear 5
To sink into the bottom of disgrace
By our imperfect pastimes) prostrate thus
On bended knees, our sails of hope do strike,
Dreading the bitter storms of your dislike.
Since then, unhappy men, our hap is such, 10
That to ourselves ourselves no help can
bring,
But needs must perish, if your saint-like
ears
(Locking the temple where all mercy sits)
Refuse the tribute of our begging tongues:
O grant, bright mirror of true chastity, 15
From those life-breathing stars, your sun-
like eyes,
One gracious smile: for your celestial breath
Must send us life, or sentence us to death.

DRAMATIS PERSONAE

THE KING
THE EARL OF CORNWALL
SIR HUGH LACY, *Earl of Lincoln*
ROWLAND LACY, *otherwise* HANS, } *his Nephews*
ASKEW, } *his Nephews*
SIR ROGER OTELEY, *Lord Mayor of London*
MASTER HAMMON, } *Citizens of London*
MASTER WARNER, } *Citizens of London*
MASTER SCOTT, } *Citizens of London*
SIMON EYRE, *the Shoemaker*
ROGER, *commonly called* HODGE, } *Eyre's Journeymen*
FIRK, } *Eyre's Journeymen*
RALPH, } *Eyre's Journeymen*
LOVELL, *a courtier*
DODGER, *Servant to the Earl of Lincoln*
A DUTCH SKIPPER
A BOY
ROSE, *Daughter of Sir Roger*
SYBIL, *her maid*
MARGERY, *Wife of Simon Eyre*
JANE, *Wife of Ralph*
Courtiers, Attendants, Officers, Soldiers, Hunters, Shoemakers, Apprentices, Servants

ACT I

SCENE I

Enter LORD MAYOR *and* LINCOLN.

LINCOLN. My lord mayor, you have sun-
dry times
Feasted myself and many courtiers more:
Seldom or never can we be so kind
To make requital of your courtesy.
But leaving this, I hear my cousin Lacy 5
Is much affected to your daughter Rose.

LORD MAYOR. True, my good lord, and
she loves him so well
That I mislike her boldness in the chase.

LINCOLN. Why, my lord mayor, think
you it then a shame,
To join a Lacy with an Oteley's name? 10

LORD MAYOR. Too mean is my poor girl
for his high birth;
Poor citizens must not with courtiers wed,
Who will in silks and gay apparel spend
More in one year than I am worth, by far:
Therefore your honor need not doubt[1] my
girl. 15

LINCOLN. Take heed, my lord, advise you
what you do!
A verier unthrift lives not in the world
Than is my cousin; for I'll tell you what:
'Tis now almost a year since he requested
To travel countries for experience; 20
I furnished him with coin, bills of exchange,
Letters of credit, men to wait on him,
Solicited my friends in Italy
Well to respect him: but to see the end:
Scant had he journeyed through half Ger-
many, 25
But all his coin was spent, his men cast off,
His bills embezzled,[2] and my jolly coz,
Asham'd to show his bankrupt presence here,
Became a shoemaker in Wittenberg,
A goodly science for a gentleman 30
Of such descent! Now judge the rest by
this:
Suppose your daughter have a thousand
pound,
He did consume me more in one half year;
And, make him heir to all the wealth you
have,
One twelvemonth's rioting will waste it all. 35
Then seek, my lord, some honest citizen
To wed your daughter to.

LORD MAYOR. I thank your lordship.—
[*Aside.*] Well, fox, I understand your
subtilty.—
As for your nephew, let your lordship's eye

[1]Fear. [2]Squandered.

But watch his actions, and you need not
fear, 40
For I have sent my daughter far enough.
And yet your cousin Rowland might do well,
Now he hath learned an occupation;
And yet I scorn to call him son-in-law.
LINCOLN. Ay, but I have a better trade
for him: 45
I thank his grace, he hath appointed him
Chief colonel of all those companies
Mustered in London and the shires about,
To serve his highness in those wars of
France.
See where he comes!—Lovell, what news
with you? 50

Enter LOVELL, LACY, *and* ASKEW.

LOVELL. My Lord of Lincoln, 'tis his
highness' will
That presently your cousin ship for France
With all his powers; he would not for a
million,
But they should land at Dieppe within four
days.
LINCOLN. Go certify his grace it shall be
done. 55
[*Exit* LOVELL.
Now, Cousin Lacy, in what forwardness
Are all your companies?
LACY. All well prepared.
The men of Hertfordshire lie at Mile-end;
Suffolk and Essex train in Tothill-fields;
The Londoners and those of Middlesex, 60
All gallantly prepared in Finsbury,
With frolic spirits long for their parting
hour.
LORD MAYOR. They have their imprest,[3]
coats, and furniture,
And, if it please your cousin Lacy come
To the Guildhall, he shall receive his pay; 65
And twenty pounds besides my brethren
Will freely give him, to approve our loves
We bear unto my lord your uncle here.
LACY. I thank your honor.
LINCOLN. Thanks, my good
lord mayor.
LORD MAYOR. At the Guildhall we will
expect your coming. [*Exit.*
LINCOLN. To approve your loves to me?
No subtilty! 71
Nephew, that twenty pound he doth bestow
For joy to rid you from his daughter Rose.
But, cousins both, now here are none but
friends,
I would not have you cast an amorous eye 75

[3]Advance pay.

Upon so mean a project as the love
Of a gay, wanton, painted citizen.
I know, this churl even in the height of scorn
Doth hate the mixture of his blood with thine.
I pray thee, do thou so! Remember, coz, 80
What honorable fortunes wait on thee:
Increase the king's love, which so brightly
shines
And gilds thy hopes. I have no heir but
thee,—
And yet not thee, if with a wayward spirit
Thou start from the true bias of[4] my love. 85
LACY. My lord, I will (for honor, not
desire
Of land or livings, or to be your heir)
So guide my actions in pursuit of France
As shall add glory to the Lacys' name.
LINCOLN. Coz, for those words here 's
thirty Portigues,[5] 90
And, nephew Askew, there 's a few for you.
Fair Honor in her loftiest eminence
Stays in France for you, till you fetch her
thence.
Then, nephews, clap swift wings on your
designs:
Begone, begone, make haste to the Guild-
hall; 95
There presently I'll meet you. Do not stay:
Where honor beckons, shame attends delay.
[*Exit.*
ASKEW. How gladly would your uncle
have you gone!
LACY. True, coz, but I'll o'erreach his
policies.
I have some serious business for three
days, 100
Which nothing but my presence can dispatch.
You, therefore, cousin, with the companies
Shall haste to Dover; there I'll meet with
you:
Or, if I stay past my prefixéd time,
Away for France; we'll meet in Nor-
mandy. 105
The twenty pounds my lord mayor gives
to me
You shall receive, and these ten Portigues,
Part of mine uncle's thirty. Gentle coz,
Have care to our great charge; I know your
wisdom
Hath tried itself in higher consequence. 110
ASKEW. Coz, all myself am yours: yet
have this care,
To lodge in London with all secrecy;
Our uncle Lincoln hath, besides his own,

[4]Course dictated by.
[5]Gold coins, each worth three or four pounds.

Many a jealous eye that in your face
Stares only to watch means for your disgrace. 115

LACY. Stay, cousin, who be these?

Enter SIMON EYRE, MARGERY *his wife,* HODGE, FIRK, JANE, *and* RALPH *with a piece.*[6]

EYRE. Leave whining, leave whining! Away with this whimpering, this puling, these blubbering tears, and these wet eyes! I'll get thy husband discharged, I warrant thee, sweet Jane; go to! 120

HODGE. Master, here be the captains.

EYRE. Peace, Hodge; husht, ye knave, husht!

FIRK. Here be the cavaliers and the colonels, master. 125

EYRE. Peace, Firk; peace, my fine Firk! Stand by with your pishery-pashery,[7] away! I am a man of the best presence; I'll speak to them, an they were Popes.—Gentlemen, captains, colonels, commanders! Brave men, brave leaders, may it please you to give me audience. I am Simon Eyre, the mad shoemaker of Tower Street; this wench with the mealy mouth that will never tire is my wife, I can tell you; here's Hodge, my man and my foreman; here's Firk, my fine firking[8] journeyman; and this is blubbered Jane. All we come to be suitors for this honest Ralph. Keep him at home, and as I am a true shoemaker and a gentleman of the gentle craft, buy spurs yourself, and I'll find ye boots these seven years. 142

MARGERY. Seven years, husband?

EYRE. Peace, midriff, peace! I know what I do. Peace!

FIRK. Truly, master cormorant, you shall do God good service to let Ralph and his wife stay together. She's a young new-married woman; if you take her husband away from her a night, you undo her; she may beg in the daytime; for he 's as good a workman at a prick and an awl, as any is in our trade. 153

JANE. Oh, let him stay, else I shall be undone.

FIRK. Ay, truly, she shall be laid at one side like a pair of old shoes else, and be occupied for no use.

LACY. Truly, my friends, it lies not in my power:

The Londoners are pressed, paid, and set forth 160

By the lord mayor; I cannot change a man.

HODGE. Why, then you were as good be a corporal as a colonel, if you cannot discharge one good fellow; and I tell you true, I think you do more than you can answer, to press a man within a year and a day of his marriage.

EYRE. Well said, melancholy Hodge; gramercy, my fine foreman. 169

MARGERY. Truly, gentlemen, it were ill done for such as you, to stand so stiffly against a poor young wife; considering her case, she is new-married, but let that pass: I pray, deal not roughly with her; her husband is a young man, and but newly entered, but let that pass.

EYRE. Away with your pishery-pashery, your pols and your edipols! Peace, midriff; silence, Cicely Bumtrinket![9] Let your head speak. 180

FIRK. Yea, and the horns too, master.

EYRE. Too soon, my fine Firk, too soon! Peace, scoundrels!—See you this man? Captains, you will not release him? Well, let him go; he's a proper shot; let him vanish! Peace, Jane; dry up thy tears; they'll make his powder dankish. Take him, brave men; Hector of Troy was an hackney to him, Hercules and Termagant[10] scoundrels; Prince Arthur's round table—by the Lord of Ludgate—ne'er fed such a tall,[11] such a dapper swordman; by the life of Pharaoh, a brave, resolute swordman! Peace, Jane! I say no more, mad knaves.

FIRK. See, see, Hodge, how my master raves in commendation of Ralph! 196

HODGE. Ralph, th'art a gull,[12] by this hand, an thou goest not.

ASKEW. I am glad, good Master Eyre, it is my hap
To meet so resolute a soldier.
Trust me, for your report and love to him,
A common slight regard shall not respect him.

LACY. Is thy name Ralph?

RALPH. Yes, sir.

LACY. Give me thy hand;
Thou shalt not want, as I am a gentleman.
Woman, be patient; God, no doubt, will send
Thy husband safe again; but he must go;
His country's quarrel says it shall be so.

---

[6]Piece of work. [7]Twiddle-twaddle.
[8]Frisking.

[9]Margery's maid. [10]Imaginary Saracen god.
[11]Brave. [12]Fool.

HODGE. Th'art a gull, by my stirrup, if thou dost not go. I will not have thee strike thy gimlet into these weak vessels; prick thine enemies, Ralph. 211

Enter DODGER

DODGER. My lord, your uncle on the Tower-hill
Stays with the lord mayor and the aldermen,
And doth request you with all speed you may
To hasten thither.
ASKEW. Cousin, let's go.
LACY. Dodger, run you before; tell them we come.—
[*Exit* DODGER.
This Dodger is mine uncle's parasite,
The arrant'st varlet that e'er breathed on earth;
He sets more discord in a noble house
By one day's broaching of his pickthank[13] tales 220
Than can be salved again in twenty years;
And he, I fear, shall go with us to France,
To pry into our actions.
ASKEW. Therefore, coz,
It shall behoove you to be circumspect.
LACY. Fear not, good cousin.—Ralph, hie to your colors.
RALPH. I must, because there's no remedy;
But, gentle master and my loving dame,
As you have always been a friend to me,
So in my absence think upon my wife. 229
JANE. Alas, my Ralph.
MARGERY. She cannot speak for weeping.

EYRE. Peace, you cracked groats, you mustard tokens;[14] disquiet not the brave soldier. Go thy ways, Ralph!

JANE. Ay, ay, you bid him go; what shall I do when he is gone?

FIRK. Why, be doing with me or my fellow Hodge; be not idle. 237

EYRE. Let me see thy hand, Jane. This fine hand, this white hand, these pretty fingers must spin, must card, must work; work, you bombast-cotton-candle-quean; work for your living, with a pox to you.—Hold thee, Ralph; here's five sixpences for thee; fight for the honor of the gentle craft, for the gentlemen shoemakers, the courageous cordwainers, the flower of St. Martin's, the mad knaves of Bedlam, Fleet Street, Tower Street, and Whitechapel; crack me the crowns of the French knaves, a pox on them, crack them; fight, by the Lord of Ludgate, fight, my fine boy! 251

FIRK. Here, Ralph, here's three twopences: two carry into France, the third shall wash our souls at parting, for sorrow is dry. For my sake, firk the *Basa mon cues*.[15]

HODGE. Ralph, I am heavy at parting, but here's a shilling for thee. God send thee to cram thy slops[16] with French crowns, and thy enemies' bellies with bullets. 260

RALPH. I thank you, master, and I thank you all.
Now, gentle wife, my loving lovely Jane,
Rich men, at parting, give their wives rich gifts,
Jewels and rings, to grace their lily hands.
Thou know'st our trade makes rings for women's heels:
Here take this pair of shoes, cut out by Hodge,
Stitched by my fellow Firk, seamed by myself,
Made up and pinked[17] with letters for thy name.
Wear them, my dear Jane, for thy husband's sake,
And every morning, when thou pull'st them on, 270
Remember me, and pray for my return.
Make much of them; for I have made them so
That I can know them from a thousand mo.

Sound drum. Enter LORD MAYOR, LINCOLN, LACY, ASKEW, DODGER, *and* Soldiers. *They pass over the stage;* RALPH *falls in amongst them;* FIRK *and the rest cry "Farewell," &c., and so exeunt.*

ACT II

SCENE I

Enter ROSE, *alone, making a garland.*

ROSE. Here sit thou down upon this flow'ry bank,
And make a garland for thy Lacy's head.
These pinks, these roses, and these violets,
These blushing gilliflowers, these marigolds,
The fair embroidery of his coronet, 5
Carry not half such beauty in their cheeks
As the sweet countenance of my Lacy doth.

[13]Told to curry favor.

[14]Yellow spots, denoting that a body was infected by the plague.

[15]Trounce the kiss-my-tails (the French).

[16]Trousers. [17]Perforated.

O my most unkind father! O my stars,
Why lowered you so at my nativity,
To make me love, yet live robbed of my love? 10
Here as a thief am I imprisoned
(For my dear Lacy's sake) within those walls
Which by my father's cost were builded up
For better purposes; here must I languish

Enter SYBIL.

For him that doth as much lament, I know, 15
Mine absence as for him I pine in woe.

SYBIL. Good morrow, young mistress; I am sure you make that garland for me, against I shall be Lady of the Harvest.

ROSE. Sybil, what news at London? 20

SYBIL. None but good; my lord mayor, your father, and master Philpot, your uncle, and Master Scot, your cousin, and Mistress Frigbottom by Doctors' Commons, do all, by my troth, send you most hearty commendations.

ROSE. Did Lacy send kind greetings to his love?

SYBIL. Oh, yes, out of cry.[1] By my troth, I scant knew him; here 'a wore a scarf, and here a scarf, here a bunch of feathers, and here precious stones and jewels and a pair of garters,—Oh, monstrous! like one of our yellow silk curtains at home here in Old Ford house, here in Master Bellymount's chamber. I stood at our door in Cornhill, looked at him, he at me indeed, spake to him, but he not to me, not a word: marry gup, thought I, with a wanion![2] He passed by me as proud—Marry foh! are you grown humorous,[3] thought I; and so shut the door, and in I came. 42

ROSE. O Sybil, how dost thou my Lacy wrong!
My Rowland is as gentle as a lamb;
No dove was ever half so mild as he.

SYBIL. Mild? yea, as a bushel of stamped crabs.[4] He looked upon me as sour as verjuice. Go thy ways, thought I; thou may'st be much in my gaskins,[5] but nothing in my nether-stocks.[6] This is your fault, mistress, to love him that loves not you; he thinks scorn to do as he's done to; but if I were as you, I'd cry: "Go by, Jeronimo, go by!"[7]

I'd set mine old debts against my new driblets, 55
And the hare's foot against the goose giblets;[8]
For if ever I sigh, when sleep I should take,
Pray God I may lose my maidenhead when I wake.

ROSE. Will my love leave me then, and go to France?

SYBIL. I know not that, but I am sure I see him stalk before the soldiers. By my troth, he is a proper man; but he is proper that proper doth. Let him go snick up,[9] young mistress. 65

ROSE. Get thee to London, and learn perfectly
Whether my Lacy go to France or no:
Do this, and I will give thee for thy pains
My cambric apron and my Romish gloves,
My purple stockings and a stomacher.
Say, wilt thou do this, Sybil, for my sake?

SYBIL. Will I, quoth a? At whose suit? By my troth, yes, I'll go. A cambric apron, gloves, a pair of purple stockings, and a stomacher! I'll sweat in purple, mistress, for you; I'll take anything that comes, a God's name. O rich! a cambric apron! Faith, then have at "up tails all."[10] I'll go jiggy-joggy to London, and be here in a trice, young mistress. [*Exit.*

ROSE. Do so, good Sybil. Meantime wretched I 81
Will sit and sigh for his lost company. [*Exit.*

SCENE II

Enter ROWLAND LACY *like a Dutch Shoemaker.*

LACY. How many shapes have gods and kings devised,
Thereby to compass their desired loves!
It is no shame for Rowland Lacy, then,
To clothe his cunning with the gentle craft,
That, thus disguised, I may unknown possess 5
The only happy presence of my Rose.
For her have I forsook my charge in France,
Incurred the king's displeasure, and stirred up
Rough hatred in mine uncle Lincoln's breast.
O love, how powerful art thou, that canst change 10
High birth to baseness, and a nobler mind
To the mean semblance of a shoemaker!

---

[1]Beyond measure. [2]Vengeance. [3]Capricious.
[4]Crushed crab apples.
[5]Breeches. [6]Stockings.
[7]A parody of words in Thomas Kyd's *Spanish Tragedy*.

[8]I'd balance accounts. [9]Go and be hanged.
[10]A popular tune.

But thus it must be, for her cruel father,
Hating the single union of our souls,
Hath secretly conveyed my Rose from London, 15
To bar me of her presence; but I trust
Fortune and this disguise will further me
Once more to view her beauty, gain her sight.
Here in Tower Street with Eyre the shoemaker
Mean I a while to work; I know the trade, 20
I learnt it when I was in Wittenberg.
Then cheer thy hoping spirits; be not dismayed;
Thou canst not want, do Fortune what she can;
The gentle craft is living for a man. [*Exit.*

SCENE III

Enter EYRE, *making himself ready.*

EYRE. Where be these boys, these girls, these drabs, these scoundrels? They wallow in the fat brewis[11] of my bounty and lick up the crumbs of my table, yet will not rise to see my walks cleansed. Come out, you powder-beef-queans! What, Nan! what, Madge Mumble-crust! Come out, you fat midriff-swag-belly-whores, and sweep me these kennels,[12] that the noisome stench offend not the nose of my neighbors. What, Firk, I say; what, Hodge! Open my shop-windows! What, Firk, I say! 12

Enter FIRK.

FIRK. O master, is't you that speak bandog and Bedlam[13] this morning? I was in a dream, and mused what madman was got into the street so early; have you drunk this morning that your throat is so clear?

EYRE. Ah, well said, Firk; well said, Firk. To work, my fine knave, to work! Wash thy face, and thou'lt be more blest.

FIRK. Let them wash my face that will eat it. Good master, send for a souse-wife,[14] if you'll have my face cleaner. 23

Enter HODGE.

EYRE. Away, sloven! avaunt, scoundrel!—Good-morrow, Hodge; good-morrow, my fine foreman.

HODGE. O master, good-morrow; y'are an early stirrer. Here's a fair morning.—Good-morrow, Firk, I could have slept this hour. Here's a brave day towards. 30

EYRE. Oh, haste to work, my fine foreman; haste to work.

FIRK. Master, I am dry as dust to hear my fellow Roger talk of fair weather; let us pray for good leather, and let clowns and ploughboys and those that work in the fields pray for brave days. We work in a dry shop; what care I if it rain?

Enter MARGERY.

EYRE. How now, Dame Margery, can you see to rise? Trip and go, call up the drabs your maids. 41

MARGERY. See to rise? I hope 'tis time enough; 'tis early enough for any woman to be seen abroad. I marvel how many wives in Tower Street are up so soon! Gods me, 'tis not noon;—here's a yawling!

EYRE. Peace, Margery, peace! Where's Cicely Bumtrinket, your maid? She has a privy fault; she farts in her sleep. Call the quean up; if my men want shoe-thread, I'll swinge her in[15] a stirrup. 51

FIRK. Yet, that's but a dry beating; here's still a sign of drought.

Enter LACY *singing.*

LACY. Der was een bore van Gelderland,
Frolick sie byen;
He was als dronck he cold nyet stand,
Upsolce sie byen.
Tap eens de canneken,
Drincke, schone mannekin.[16]

FIRK. Master, for my life, yonder's a brother of the gentle craft; if he bear not St. Hugh's bones,[17] I'll forfeit my bones; he's some uplandish[18] workman; hire him, good master, that I may learn some gibble-gabble; 'twill make us work the faster. 65

EYRE. Peace, Firk! A hard world! Let him pass, let him vanish; we have journeymen enow. Peace, my fine Firk!

MARGERY. Nay, nay, y'are best follow your man's counsel; you shall see what will come on't: we have not men enow, but we

[11]Broth. [12]Gutters.

[13]Like a watch dog and a lunatic.

[14]Woman who washed and pickled pigs' faces.

[15]With.

[16]There was a peasant from Gelderland,
Frolic they be;
He was so drunk he could not stand,
Tipsy they be.
Draw us a cannikin,
Drink, pretty mannikin.

[17]Shoemakers' tools. [18]Foreign.

must entertain every butter-box;[19] but let that pass.

HODGE. Dame, 'fore God, if my master follow your counsel, he'll consume little beef. He shall be glad of men, an he can catch them.

FIRK. Ay, that he shall. 78

HODGE. 'Fore God, a proper man and, I warrant, a fine workman. Master, farewell; dame, adieu; if such a man as he cannot find work, Hodge is not for you. [*Offer to go.*

EYRE. Stay, my fine Hodge.

FIRK. Faith, an your foreman go, dame, you must take a journey to seek a new journeyman; if Roger remove, Firk follows. If St. Hugh's bones shall not be set a-work, I may prick mine awl in the walls, and go play. Fare ye well, master; good-bye, dame. 89

EYRE. Tarry, my fine Hodge, my brisk foreman! Stay, Firk!—Peace, pudding-broth! By the Lord of Ludgate, I love my men as my life. Peace, you gallimaufry![20] —Hodge, if he want work, I'll hire him. One of you to him; stay,—he comes to us.

LACY. Goeden dach, meester, ende u vro oak.[21]

FIRK. Nails, if I should speak after him without drinking, I should choke. And you, friend Oake, are you of the gentle craft? 100

LACY. Yaw, yaw, ik bin den skomawker.[22]

FIRK. "Den skomaker," quoth a! And hark you, "skomaker," have you all your tools, a good rubbing-pin, a good stopper, a good dresser, your four sorts of awls, and your two balls of wax, your paring knife, your hand- and thumb-leathers, and good St. Hugh's bones to smooth up to your work?

LACY. Yaw, yaw; be niet vorveard. Ik hab all de dingen voour mack skoos groot and cleane.[23] 112

FIRK. Ha, ha! Good master, hire him; he'll make me laugh so that I shall work more in mirth than I can in earnest.

EYRE. Hear ye, friend, have ye any skill in the mystery of cordwainers?

LACY. Ik weet niet wat yow seg; ich verstaw you niet.[24] 119

FIRK. Why, thus, man: [*Makes gesture.*] "Ich verste u niet," quoth a!

LACY. Yaw, yaw, yaw; ick can dat wel doen.[25]

FIRK. "Yaw, yaw!" He speaks yawing like a jackdaw that gapes to be fed with cheese-curds. Oh, he'll give a villainous pull at a can of double-beer; but Hodge and I have the vantage, we must drink first, because we are the eldest journeymen.

EYRE. What is thy name? 130

LACY. Hans—Hans Meulter.

EYRE. Give me thy hand; th'art welcome.—Hodge, entertain him; Firk, bid him welcome; come, Hans. Run, wife, bid your maids, your trullibubs, make ready my fine men's breakfasts. To him, Hodge!

HODGE. Hans, th'art welcome; use thyself friendly, for we are good fellows; if not, thou shalt be fought with, wert thou bigger than a giant. 140

FIRK. Yea, and drunk with, wert thou Gargantua. My master keeps no cowards, I tell thee.—Ho, boy, bring him an heel-block;[26] here's a new journeyman.

Enter BOY.

LACY. Oh, ich wersto you; ich moet een halve dossen cans betaelen; here, boy, nempt dis skilling; tap eens freelicke.[27] [*Exit* BOY.

EYRE. Quick, snipper-snapper, away! Firk, scour thy throat; thou shalt wash it with Castilian liquor. 150

Enter BOY.

Come, my last of the fives, give me a can. Have to thee, Hans; here, Hodge; here Firk; drink, you mad Greeks, and work like true Trojans, and pray for Simon Eyre, the shoemaker.—Here, Hans, and th'art welcome.

FIRK. Lo, dame, you would have lost a good fellow that will teach us to laugh. This beer came hopping in well.

MARGERY. Simon, it is almost seven. 159

EYRE. Is't so, Dame Clapper-dudgeon,[28] is't seven a clock, and my men's breakfast not ready! Trip and go, you soused conger, away! Come, you mad Hyperboreans; follow me, Hodge; follow me, Hans; come after, my fine Firk; to work, to work a while, and then to breakfast! [*Exit.*

FIRK. Soft! Yaw, yaw, good Hans,

---

[19]Dutchman. [20]Hodge-podge.

[21]Good day, master, and you, mistress, too.

[22]Yes, yes, I am a shoemaker.

[23]Yes, yes; be not afraid. I have all the things for making shoes great and small.

[24]I know not what you say; I understand you not.

[25]Yes, yes, yes; I can do that well.

[26]Block for fixing a new heel on a shoe.

[27]Oh, I understand you; I must pay for half a dozen cans; here, boy, take this shilling; draw for us freely.

[28]Beggar.

though my master have no more wit but to call you afore me, I am not so foolish to go behind you, I being the elder journeyman. 170

[*Exeunt.*

SCENE IV

Holloaing within. Enter WARNER *and* HAMMON, *like Hunters.*

HAMMON. Cousin, beat every brake; the game's not far;
This way with wingèd feet he fled from death,
Whilst the pursuing hounds, scenting his steps,
Find out his highway to destruction.
Besides, the miller's boy told me even now, 5
He saw him take soil,[29] and he holloaed him,
Affirming him to have been so embossed[30]
That long he could not hold.

WARNER. If it be so,
'Tis best we trace these meadows by Old Ford.

A noise of Hunters within. Enter a BOY.

HAMMON. How now, boy! Where's the deer? speak, saw'st thou him? 11

BOY. Oh, yea; I saw him leap through a hedge, and then over a ditch, then at my lord mayor's pale. Over he skipped me, and in he went me, and "holla" the hunters cried, and "there, boy; there, boy!" But there he is, 'a mine honesty.

HAMMON. Boy, God amercy. Cousin, let's away;
I hope we shall find better sport today. 19

[*Exeunt.*

SCENE V

Hunting within. Enter ROSE *and* SYBIL.

ROSE. Why, Sybil, wilt thou prove a forester?

SYBIL. Upon some,[31] no; forester, go by; no, faith, mistress. The deer came running into the barn through the orchard and over the pale; I wot well, I looked as pale as a new cheese to see him. But whip, says goodman Pin-close, up with his flail, and our Nick with a prong; and down he fell, and they upon him, and I upon them. By my troth, we had such sport; and in the end we ended him; his throat we cut, flayed him, unhorned him, and my lord mayor shall eat of him anon, when he comes. 32

[*Horns sound within.*

[29]Take to water. [30]Driven to extremity.
[31]Indeed.

ROSE. Hark, hark, the hunters come; y'are best take heed,
They'll have a saying to you for this deed.

Enter HAMMON, WARNER, Huntsmen, *and* Boy.

HAMMON. God save you, fair ladies.

SYBIL. Ladies! O gross!

WARNER. Came not a buck this way?

ROSE. No, but two does.

HAMMON. And which way went they? Faith, we'll hunt at those.

SYBIL. At those? upon some, no: when, can you tell?

WARNER. Upon some, ay.

SYBIL. Good Lord!

WARNER. Wounds! Then farewell!

HAMMON. Boy, which way went he?

BOY. This way, sir, he ran.

HAMMON. This way he ran indeed, fair Mistress Rose; 41
Our game was lately in your orchard seen.

WARNER. Can you advise, which way he took his flight?

SYBIL. Follow your nose; his horns will guide you right.

WARNER. Th'art a mad wench.

SYBIL. O rich!

ROSE. Trust me, not I.
It is not like that the wild forest-deer
Would come so near to places of resort;
You are deceived; he fled some other way.

WARNER. Which way, my sugar-candy, can you show?

SYBIL. Come up, good honeysops, upon some, no. 50

ROSE. Why do you stay, and not pursue your game?

SYBIL. I'll hold my life, their hunting-nags be lame.

HAMMON. A deer more dear is found within this place.

ROSE. But not the deer, sir, which you had in chase.

HAMMON. I chased the deer, but this dear chaseth me.

ROSE. The strangest hunting that ever I see.
But where's your park?

[*She offers to go away.*

HAMMON. 'Tis here: Oh, stay!

ROSE. Impale me in't, and then I will not stray.

WARNER. They wrangle, wench; we are more kind than they.

SYBIL. What kind of hart is that dear heart you seek? 60

WARNER. A hart, dear heart.
SYBIL. Who ever saw the like?
ROSE. To lose your heart, is't possible you can?
HAMMON. My heart is lost.
ROSE. Alack, good gentleman!
HAMMON. This poor lost heart would I wish you might find.
ROSE. You, by such luck, might prove your hart a hind.
HAMMON. Why, Luck had horns, so have I heard some say.
ROSE. Now, God, an't be his will, send Luck into your way.

Enter the LORD MAYOR *and* Servants.

LORD MAYOR. What, Master Hammon! Welcome to Old Ford!
SYBIL. God's pittikins, hands off, sir! Here's my lord.
LORD MAYOR. I hear you had ill luck, and lost your game. 70
HAMMON. 'Tis true, my lord.
LORD MAYOR. I am sorry for the same.
What gentleman is this?
HAMMON. My brother-in-law.
LORD MAYOR. Y'are welcome both; sith Fortune offers you
Into my hands, you shall not part from hence
Until you have refreshed your wearied limbs.—
Go, Sybil, cover the board!—You shall be guest
To no good cheer, but even a hunter's feast.
HAMMON. I thank your lordship.—Cousin, on my life,
For our lost venison I shall find a wife.
[*Exeunt.*
LORD MAYOR. In, gentlemen; I'll not be absent long.— 80
This Hammon is a proper gentleman,
A citizen by birth, fairly allied;
How fit an husband were he for my girl!
Well, I will in, and do the best I can,
To match my daughter to this gentleman.
[*Exit.*

ACT III

SCENE I

Enter LACY, SKIPPER, HODGE, *and* FIRK.

SKIPPER. Ick sal yow wat seggen, Hans; dis skip, dat comen from Candy, is al wol, by Got's sacrament, van sugar, civet, almonds, cambrick, end alle dingen, towsand towsand ding. Nempt it, Hans, nempt it vor u meester. Daer be de bils van laden. Your meester, Simon Eyre, sal hae good copen. Wat seggen yow, Hans?[1]

FIRK. Wat seggen de reggen, de copen slopen—laugh, Hodge, laugh! 10

LACY. Mine liever broder, Firk, bringt Meester Eyre tot det signe un Swannekin; daer sal yow finde dis skipper end me. Wat seggen yow, broder Firk? Doot it, Hodge.[2] Come, skipper. [*Exeunt* LACY *and* SKIPPER.

FIRK. Bring him, quoth you? Here's no knavery, to bring my master to buy a ship worth the lading of two or three hundred thousand pounds. Alas, that's nothing; a trifle, a bauble, Hodge. 20

HODGE. The truth is, Firk, that the merchant owner of the ship dares not show his head, and therefore this skipper that deals for him, for the love he bears to Hans, offers my master Eyre a bargain in the commodities. He shall have a reasonable day of payment; he may sell the wares by that time, and be an huge gainer himself.

FIRK. Yea, but can my fellow Hans lend my master twenty porpentines as an earnest penny? 31

HODGE. Portigues, thou wouldst say; here they be, Firk; hark, they jingle in my pocket like St. Mary Overy's bells.

Enter EYRE *and* MARGERY.

FIRK. Mum, here comes my dame and my master. She'll scold, on my life, for loitering this Monday; but all's one, let them all say what they can, Monday's our holiday.

MARGERY. You sing, Sir Sauce, but I beshrew your heart;
I fear, for this your singing we shall smart.

FIRK. Smart for me, dame? why, dame, why? 41

HODGE. Master, I hope you'll not suffer my dame to take down your journeymen.

FIRK. If she take me down, I'll take her up; yea, and take her down too, a buttonhole lower.

EYRE. Peace, Firk; not I, Hodge; by

---

[1] I'll tell you what, Hans; this ship, that comes from Candy, is all full, by God's Sacrament, of sugar, civet, almonds, cambric, and all things, a thousand thousand things. Take it, Hans, take it for your master. There be the bills of lading. Your master, Simon Eyre, will have a good bargain. What say you, Hans?

[2] My dear brother, Firk, bring Master Eyre to the sign of the Swan; there shall you find this skipper and me. What say you, brother Firk? Do it, Hodge.

the life of Pharaoh, by the Lord of Ludgate, by this beard every hair whereof I value at a king's ransom, she shall not meddle with you.—Peace, you bombast-cotton-candle-quean; away, queen of clubs; quarrel not with me and my men, with me and my fine Firk; I'll firk you, if you do. 54

MARGERY. Yea, yea, man, you may use me as you please; but let that pass.

EYRE. Let it pass, let it vanish away; peace! Am I not Simon Eyre! Are not these my brave men, brave shoemakers, all gentlemen of the gentle craft? Prince am I none; yet am I nobly born, as being the sole son of a shoemaker. Away, rubbish! vanish, melt, melt like kitchen-stuff! 63

MARGERY. Yea, yea, 'tis well, I must be called rubbish, kitchen-stuff, for a sort[3] of knaves.

FIRK. Nay, dame, you shall not weep and wail in woe for me. Master, I'll stay no longer; here's a vennentory of my shop-tools. Adieu, master; Hodge, farewell. 70

HODGE. Nay, stay, Firk; thou shalt not go alone.

MARGERY. I pray, let them go; there be more maids than Mawkin, more men than Hodge, and more fools than Firk.

FIRK. Fools? Nails! if I tarry now, I would my guts might be turned to shoe-thread.

HODGE. And if I stay, I pray God I may be turned to a Turk, and set in Finsbury for boys to shoot at.—Come, Firk. 81

EYRE. Stay, my fine knaves, you arms of my trade, you pillars of my profession. What, shall a tittle-tattle's words make you forsake Simon Eyre?—Avaunt, kitchen-stuff! Rip, you brown-bread Tannikin![4] Out of my sight! Move me not! Have not I ta'en you from selling tripes in Eastcheap, and set you in my shop, and made you hail-fellow with Simon Eyre, the shoemaker? And now do you deal thus with my journey-men? Look, you powder-beef-quean, on the face of Hodge; here's a face for a lord! 93

FIRK. And here's a face for any lady in Christendom.

EYRE. Rip, you chitterling, avaunt! Boy, bid the tapster of the Boar's Head fill me a dozen cans of beer for my journeymen.

FIRK. A dozen cans? O brave! Hodge, now I'll stay. 100

EYRE. [*Aside to the* Boy.] An the knave fills any more than two, he pays for them. [*Exit Boy. Aloud.*] A dozen cans of beer for my journeymen. [*Re-enter* Boy.] Hear you, mad Mesopotamians! wash your livers with this liquor. Where be the odd ten? [*Aside.*] No more, Madge, no more.—Well said. Drink and to work!—What work dost thou, Hodge? what work? 109

HODGE. I am a-making a pair of shoes for my lord mayor's daughter, Mistress Rose.

FIRK. And I a pair of shoes for Sybil, my lord's maid. I deal with her.

EYRE. Sybil? Fie, defile not thy fine workmanly fingers with the feet of kitchen-stuff and basting-ladles. Ladies of the court, fine ladies, my lads, commit their feet to our apparelling; put gross work to Hans. Yark[5] and seam, yark and seam! 120

FIRK. For yarking and seaming let me alone, an I come to't.

HODGE. Well, master, all this is from the bias.[6] Do you remember the ship my fel-low Hans told you of? The skipper and he are both drinking at the Swan. Here be the Portigues to give earnest. If you go through with it, you cannot choose but be a lord at least. 129

FIRK. Nay, dame, if my master prove not a lord, and you a lady, hang me.

MARGERY. Yea, like enough, if you may loiter and tipple thus.

FIRK. Tipple, dame? No, we have been bargaining with Skellum Skanderbag:[7] can you Dutch spreaken for a ship of silk Cyprus, laden with sugar-candy?

Enter the Boy *with a velvet coat and an Alderman's gown.* EYRE *puts it on.*

EYRE. Peace, Firk; silence, Tittle-tattle! Hodge, I'll go through with it. Here's a seal-ring, and I have sent for a guarded[8] gown and a damask cassock. See where it comes; look here, Maggy; help me, Firk; apparel me, Hodge; silk and satin, you mad Philistines, silk and satin. 144

FIRK. Ha, ha, my master will be as proud as a dog in a doublet, all in beaten[9] damask and velvet.

EYRE. Softly, Firk, for rearing of the nap, and wearing threadbare my garments. How dost thou like me, Firk? How do I look, my fine Hodge? 151

HODGE. Why, now you look like yourself,

[3]Pack. [4]Name given to Dutchwomen.

[5]Stitch. [6]Beside the mark.

[7]Rogue Scanderbeg, the Albanian hero, John Castriot.

[8]With facings. [9]Embroidered.

master. I warrant you, there's few in the city but will give you the wall, and come upon you with the "right worshipful."

FIRK. Nails, my master looks like a threadbare cloak new turn'd and dress'd. Lord, Lord, to see what good raiment doth! Dame, dame, are you not enamoured? 159

EYRE. How say'st thou, Maggy, am I not brisk? Am I not fine?

MARGERY. Fine! By my troth, sweetheart, very fine! By my troth, I never liked thee so well in my life, sweetheart. But let that pass; I warrant, there be many women in the city have not such handsome husbands, but only for their apparel; but let that pass too. 168

Enter LACY *and* SKIPPER.

LACY. Godden day, mester. Dis be de skipper dat heb de skip van marchandice; de commodity ben good; nempt it, master, nempt it.[10]

EYRE. Godamercy, Hans; welcome, skipper. Where lies this ship of merchandise?

SKIPPER. De ship ben in revere; dor be van Sugar, cyvet, almonds, cambrick, and a towsand towsand tings; gotz sacrament, nempt it, mester, ye sal heb good copen.[11]

FIRK. To him, master! O sweet master! O sweet wares! Prunes, almonds, sugar-candy, carrot-roots, turnips! O brave fatting meat! Let not a man buy a nutmeg but yourself. 183

EYRE. Peace, Firk! Come, skipper, I'll go aboard with you.—Hans, have you made him drink?

SKIPPER. Yaw, yaw, ic heb veale gedrunck.[12] 188

EYRE. Come, Hans, follow me. Skipper, thou shalt have my countenance in the city. [*Exeunt.*

FIRK. "Yaw, heb veale gedrunck," quoth a! They may well be called butter-boxes when they drink fat veal and thick beer too! But come, dame, I hope you'll chide us no more.

MARGERY. No, faith, Firk; no, perdy, Hodge. I do feel honor creep upon me, and which is more, a certain rising in my flesh; but let that pass. 200

FIRK. Rising in your flesh do you feel, say you? Ay, you may be with child; but why should not my master feel a rising in his flesh, having a gown and a gold ring on? But you are such a shrew, you'll soon pull him down.

MARGERY. Ha, ha! prithee, peace! Thou mak'st my worship laugh; but let that pass. Come, I'll go in; Hodge, prithee, go before me; Firk, follow me. 210

FIRK. Firk doth follow: Hodge, pass out in state. [*Exeunt.*

SCENE II

Enter LINCOLN *and* DODGER.

LINCOLN. How now, good Dodger, what's the news in France?

DODGER. My lord, upon the eighteenth day of May
The French and English were prepared to fight;
Each side with eager fury gave the sign
Of a most hot encounter. Five long hours 5
Both armies fought together; at the length
The lot of victory fell on our sides.
Twelve thousand of the Frenchmen that day died,
Four thousand English, and no man of name
But Captain Hyam and young Ardington, 10
Two gallant gentlemen; I knew them well.

LINCOLN. But, Dodger, prithee tell me, in this fight
How did my cousin Lacy bear himself?

DODGER. My lord, your cousin Lacy was not there.

LINCOLN. Not there?

DODGER. No, my good lord.

LINCOLN. Sure, thou mistakest.
I saw him shipped, and a thousand eyes beside 16
Were witnesses of the farewells which he gave,
When I, with weeping eyes, bid him adieu.
Dodger, take heed.

DODGER. My lord, I am advised,
That what I spake is true: to prove it so, 20
His cousin Askew, that supplied his place,
Sent me for him from France, that secretly
He might convey himself thither.

LINCOLN. Is't even so?
Dares he so carelessly venture his life
Upon the indignation of a king? 25
Has he despised my love, and spurned those favors
Which I with prodigal hand poured on his head?

[10]Good day, master. This is the skipper that has the ship of merchandise; the commodity is good; take it, master, take it.

[11]The ship is in the river; there are sugar, civet, almonds, cambric, and a thousand thousand things; God's Sacrament, take it, master! you will have a good bargain.

[12]Yes, yes; I have drunk much.

He shall repent his rashness with his soul;
Since of my love he makes no estimate,
I'll make him wish he had not known my hate. 30
Thou hast no other news?

DODGER. None else, my lord.

LINCOLN. None worse I know thou hast.—Procure the king
To crown his giddy brows with ample honors,
Send him chief colonel, and all my hope
Thus to be dashed! But 'tis in vain to grieve; 35
One evil cannot a worse relieve.
Upon my life, I have found out his plot;
That old dog, Love, that fawned upon him so,
Love to that puling girl, his fair-cheeked Rose,
The lord mayor's daughter, hath distracted him; 40
And in the fire of that love's lunacy
Hath he burnt up himself, consumed his credit,
Lost the king's love, yea, and I fear, his life,
Only to get a wanton to his wife:
Dodger, it is so.

DODGER. I fear so, my good lord. 45

LINCOLN. It is so—nay, sure it cannot be!
I am at my wits' end. Dodger!

DODGER. Yea, my lord.

LINCOLN. Thou art acquainted with my nephew's haunts;
Spend this gold for thy pains; go seek him out;
Watch at my lord mayor's—there if he live, 50
Dodger, thou shalt be sure to meet with him.
Prithee, be diligent.—Lacy, thy name
Lived once in honor, now 'tis dead in shame.—
Be circumspect. [*Exit.*

DODGER. I warrant you, my lord. [*Exit.*

SCENE III

Enter LORD MAYOR *and* MASTER SCOTT.

LORD MAYOR. Good Master Scott, I have been bold with you,
To be a witness to a wedding-knot
Betwixt young Master Hammon and my daughter.
Oh, stand aside; see where the lovers come.

Enter HAMMON *and* ROSE.

ROSE. Can it be possible you love me so? 5
No, no, within those eyeballs I espy
Apparent likelihoods of flattery.
Pray now, let go my hand.

HAMMON. Sweet Mistress Rose,
Misconstrue not my words, nor misconceive
Of my affection, whose devoted soul 10
Swears that I love thee dearer than my heart.

ROSE. As dear as your own heart? I judge it right;
Men love their hearts best when th' are out of sight.

HAMMON. I love you, by this hand.

ROSE. Yet hands off now!
If flesh be frail, how weak and frail's your vow! 15

HAMMON. Then by my life I swear.

ROSE. Then do not brawl;
One quarrel loseth wife and life and all.
Is not your meaning thus?

HAMMON. In faith, you jest.

ROSE. Love loves to sport; therefore leave love, y'are best.

LORD MAYOR. What? square they, Master Scott?

SCOTT. Sir, never doubt, 20
Lovers are quickly in and quickly out.

HAMMON. Sweet Rose, be not so strange in fancying me.
Nay, never turn aside, shun not my sight:
I am not grown so fond, to fond my love
On any that shall quite it with disdain; 25
If you will love me, so—if not, farewell.

LORD MAYOR. Why, how now, lovers, are you both agreed?

HAMMON. Yes, faith, my lord.

LORD MAYOR. 'Tis well, give me your hand.
Give me yours, daughter.—How now, both pull back?
What means this, girl?

ROSE. I mean to live a maid. 30

HAMMON. [*Aside.*] But not to die one; pause, ere that be said.

LORD MAYOR. Will you still cross me, still be obstinate?

HAMMON. Nay, chide her not, my lord, for doing well;
If she can live an happy virgin's life,
'Tis far more blessèd than to be a wife. 35

ROSE. Say, sir, I cannot: I have made a vow,
Whoever be my husband, 'tis not you.

LORD MAYOR. Your tongue is quick; but, Master Hammon, know
I bade you welcome to another end.

HAMMON. What, would you have me pule and pine and pray, 40
With "lovely lady, mistress of my heart,

Pardon your servant," and the rhymer play,
Railing on "Cupid and his tyrant's dart";
Or shall I undertake some martial spoil,
Wearing your glove at tourney and at tilt, 45
And tell how many gallants I unhorsed—
Sweet, will this pleasure you?

ROSE. Yea, when wilt begin?
What, love-rhymes, man? Fie on that deadly sin!

LORD MAYOR. If you will have her, I'll make her agree.

HAMMON. Enforcéd love is worse than hate to me.— 50
[*Aside.*] There is a wench keeps shop in the Old Change;
To her will I; it is not wealth I seek;
I have enough, and will prefer her love
Before the world.—[*Aloud.*] My good lord mayor, adieu. 54
Old love for me, I have no luck with new. [*Exit.*

LORD MAYOR. Now, mammet,[13] you have well behaved yourself;
But you shall curse your coyness if I live.—
Who's within there? See you convey your mistress
Straight to th'Old Ford! I'll keep you straight enough;
Fore God, I would have sworn the puling girl 60
Had willingly accepted Hammon's love;
But banish him, my thoughts!—Go, minion, in! [*Exit* ROSE.
Now tell me, Master Scott, would you have thought
That Master Simon Eyre, the shoemaker,
Had been of wealth to buy such merchandise? 65

SCOTT. 'Twas well, my lord, your honor and myself
Grew partners with him; for your bills of lading
Show that Eyre's gains in one commodity
Rise at the least to full three thousand pound,
Besides like gain in other merchandise. 70

LORD MAYOR. Well, he shall spend some of his thousands now,
For I have sent for him to the Guildhall.

Enter EYRE.

See, where he comes.—Good morrow, Master Eyre.

EYRE. Poor Simon Eyre, my lord, your shoemaker.

LORD MAYOR. Well, well, it likes yourself to term you so. 75

Enter DODGER.

Now, Master Dodger, what's the news with you?

DODGER. I'd gladly speak in private to your honor.

LORD MAYOR. You shall, you shall.—Master Eyre and Master Scott,
I have some business with this gentleman;
I pray, let me entreat you to walk before 80
To the Guildhall; I'll follow presently.
Master Eyre, I hope ere noon to call you sheriff.

EYRE. I would not care, my lord, if you might call
Me King of Spain.—Come, Master Scott. [*Exeunt* EYRE *and* SCOTT.

LORD MAYOR. Now, Master Dodger, what's the news you bring? 85

DODGER. The Earl of Lincoln by me greets your lordship,
And earnestly requests you, if you can,
Inform him where his nephew Lacy keeps.

LORD MAYOR. Is not his nephew Lacy now in France?

DODGER. No, I assure your lordship, but disguised 90
Lurks here in London.

LORD MAYOR. London? is't even so?
It may be; but upon my faith and soul,
I know not where he lives, or whether he lives:
So tell my Lord of Lincoln.—Lurks in London?
Well, Master Dodger, you perhaps may start[14] him; 95
Be but the means to rid him into France,
I'll give you a dozen angels[15] for your pains,
So much I love his honor, hate his nephew.
And, prithee, so inform thy lord from me.

DODGER. I take my leave. [*Exit* DODGER.

LORD MAYOR. Farewell, good Master Dodger. 100
Lacy in London? I dare pawn my life
My daughter knows thereof, and for that cause
Denied young Master Hammon in his love.
Well, I am glad I sent her to Old Ford.
God's Lord, 'tis late; to Guildhall I must hie; 105
I know my brethren stay my company. [*Exit.*

[13]Puppet.

[14]Discover.

[15]Coins, each worth ten shillings.

SCENE IV

Enter FIRK, MARGERY, LACY, *and* HODGE.

MARGERY. Thou goest too fast for me, Roger. O Firk!

FIRK. Ay, forsooth.

MARGERY. I pray thee, run—do you hear? —run to Guildhall, and learn if my husband, Master Eyre, will take that worshipful vocation of Master Sheriff upon him. Hie thee, good Firk.

FIRK. Take it? Well, I go; an he should not take it, Firk swears to forswear him. Yes, forsooth, I go to Guildhall. 11

MARGERY. Nay, when? thou art too compendious and tedious.

FIRK. O rare, your excellence is full of eloquence. [*Aside.*] How like a new cartwheel my dame speaks, and she looks like an old musty ale-bottle going to scalding.

MARGERY. Nay, when? thou wilt make me melancholy. 19

FIRK. God forbid your worship should fall into that humor;—I run. [*Exit.*

MARGERY. Let me see now, Roger and Hans.

HODGE. Ay, forsooth, dame—mistress I should say, but the old term so sticks to the roof of my mouth, I can hardly lick it off.

MARGERY. Even what thou wilt, good Roger; dame is a fair name for any honest Christian; but let that pass. How dost thou, Hans? 30

LACY. Mee tanck you, vro.[16]

MARGERY. Well, Hans and Roger, you see God hath blest your master, and, perdy, if ever he comes to be Master Sheriff of London—as we are all mortal—you shall see, I will have some odd thing or other in a corner for you: I will not be your back-friend;[17] but let that pass. Hans, pray thee, tie my shoe.

LACY. Yaw, ic sal, vro.[18] 40

MARGERY. Roger, thou know'st the length of my foot; as it is none of the biggest, so I thank God, it is handsome enough; prithee, let me have a pair of shoes made, cork, good Roger, wooden heel too.

HODGE. You shall.

MARGERY. Art thou acquainted with never a farthingale-maker nor a French hoodmaker? I must enlarge my bum, ha, ha! How shall I look in a hood, I wonder! Perdy, oddly, I think. 51

[16]I thank you, mistress. [17]Faithless friend.

[18]Yes, I shall, mistress.

HODGE. [*Aside.*] As a cat out of a pillory. —Very well, I warrant you, mistress.

MARGERY. Indeed all flesh is grass; and, Roger, canst thou tell where I may buy a good hair?

HODGE. Yes, forsooth, at the poulterer's in Gracious Street.

MARGERY. Thou art an ungracious wag, perdy; I mean a false hair for my periwig.

HODGE. Why, mistress, the next time I cut my beard, you shall have the shavings of it; but they are all true hairs.

MARGERY. It is very hot; I must get me a fan or else a mask. 65

HODGE. [*Aside.*] So you had need, to hide your wicked face.

MARGERY. Fie upon it, how costly this world's calling is; perdy, but that it is one of the wonderful works of God, I would not deal with it. Is not Firk come yet? Hans, be not so sad; let it pass and vanish, as my husband's worship says.

LACY. Ick bin vrolicke; lot see yow soo.[19]

HODGE. Mistress, will you drink a pipe of tobacco?

MARGERY. Oh, fie upon it, Roger, perdy! These filthy tobacco-pipes are the most idle, slavering baubles that ever I felt. Out upon it! God bless us, men look not like men that use them. 81

Enter RALPH, *being lame.*

HODGE. What, fellow Ralph! Mistress, look here, Jane's husband! Why, how now, lame? Hans, make much of him; he's a brother of our trade, a good workman, and a tall soldier.

LACY. You be welcome, broder.

MARGERY. Perdy, I knew him not. How dost thou, good Ralph? I am glad to see thee well. 90

RALPH. I would God you saw me, dame, as well
As when I went from London into France.

MARGERY. Trust me, I am sorry, Ralph, to see thee impotent. Lord, how the wars have made him sunburnt! The left leg is not well; 'twas a fair gift of God the infirmity took not hold a little higher, considering thou camest from France; but let that pass.

RALPH. I am glad to see you well, and I rejoice 99
To hear that God hath blest my master so
Since my departure.

[19]I am merry; let's see you so.

MARGERY. Yea, truly, Ralph, I thank my Maker; but let that pass.

HODGE. And, sirrah Ralph, what news, what news in France?

RALPH. Tell me, good Roger, first, what news in England?
How does my Jane? When didst thou see my wife?
Where lives my poor heart? She'll be poor indeed,
Now I want limbs to get whereon to feed.

HODGE. Limbs? Hast thou not hands, man? Thou shalt never see a shoemaker want bread, though he have but three fingers on a hand. 112

RALPH. Yet all this while I hear not of my Jane.

MARGERY. O Ralph, your wife,—perdy, we know not what's become of her. She was here a while and, because she was married, grew more stately than became her; I checked her, and so forth; away she flung, never returned, nor said bye nor bah;[20] and, Ralph, you know, "ka me, ka thee."[21] And so, as I tell ye—— Roger, is not Firk come yet?

HODGE. No, forsooth.

MARGERY. And so, indeed, we heard not of her, but I hear she lives in London; but let that pass. If she had wanted, she might have opened her case to me or my husband, or to any of my men; I am sure there's not any of them, perdy, but would have done her good to his power. Hans, look if Firk be come. 132

LACY. Yaw, ik sal, vro.[22] [*Exit* LACY.

MARGERY. And so, as I said—but, Ralph, why dost thou weep? Thou knowest that naked we came out of our mother's womb, and naked we must return; and, therefore, thank God for all things.

HODGE. No, faith, Jane is a stranger here; but, Ralph, pull up a good heart; I know thou hast one. Thy wife, man, is in London; one told me, he saw her awhile ago very brave and neat; we'll ferret her out, an London hold her.

MARGERY. Alas, poor soul, he's overcome with sorrow; he does but as I do, weep for the loss of any good thing. But, Ralph, get thee in; call for some meat and drink; thou shalt find me worshipful towards thee. 149

[20]Gave a courteous or an insulting farewell.

[21]Scratch me, and I'll scratch thee.

[22]Yes, I shall, mistress.

RALPH. I thank you, dame; since I want limbs and lands,
I'll trust to God, my good friends, and to my hands. [*Exit.*

Enter LACY *and* FIRK *running.*

FIRK. Run, good Hans! O Hodge! O mistress!. Hodge, heave up thine ears; mistress, smug[23] up your looks; on with your best apparel; my master is chosen; my master is called, nay, condemned by the cry of the country to be sheriff of the city for this famous year now to come. And time now being, a great many men in black gowns were asked for their voices and their hands, and my master had all their fists about his ears presently, and they cried "Ay, ay, ay, ay,"—and so I came away—

Wherefore without all other grieve
I do salute you, Mistress Shrieve.

LACY. Yaw, my mester is de groot man, de shrieve.[24]

HODGE. Did not I tell you, mistress? Now I may boldly say: Good-morrow to your worship. 170

MARGERY. Good-morrow, good Roger. I thank you, my good people all.—Firk, hold up thy hand: here's a threepenny piece for thy tidings.

FIRK. 'Tis but three-half-pence, I think. Yes, 'tis three-pence; I smell the rose.[25]

HODGE. But, mistress, be ruled by me, and do not speak so pulingly.

FIRK. 'Tis her worship speaks so, and not she. No, faith, mistress, speak me in the old key: "To it, Firk," "there, good Firk," "ply your business, Hodge," "Hodge, with a full mouth," "I'll fill your bellies with good cheer, till they cry twang." 184

Enter SIMON EYRE, *wearing a gold chain.*

LACY. See, myn liever broder, heer compt my meester.[26]

MARGERY. Welcome home, Master Shrieve; I pray God continue you in health and wealth.

EYRE. See here, my Maggy, a chain, a gold chain for Simon Eyre. I shall make thee a lady; here's a French hood for thee; on with it, on with it! dress thy brows with this flap of a shoulder of mutton, to make thee look

[23]Smarten.

[24]Yes, my master is a great man, a sheriff.

[25]The rose appearing on certain coins at this time.

[26]See, my dear brother, here comes my master.

lovely. Where be my fine men? Roger, I'll make over my shop and tools to thee; Firk, thou shalt be the foreman; Hans, thou shalt have an hundred for twenty. Be as mad knaves as your master Sim Eyre hath been, and you shall live to be sheriffs of London.—How dost thou like me, Margery? Prince am I none, yet am I princely born. Firk, Hodge, and Hans!

ALL THREE. Ay, forsooth, what says your worship, Master Sheriff? 105

EYRE. Worship and honor, you Babylonian knaves, for the gentle craft. But I forgot myself; I am bidden by my lord mayor to dinner to Old Ford; he's gone before; I must after. Come, Madge, on with your trinkets! Now, my true Trojans, my fine Firk, my dapper Hodge, my honest Hans, some device, some odd crotchets, some morris, or such like, for the honor of the gentlemen shoemakers. Meet me at Old Ford; you know my mind. Come, Madge, away. Shut up the shop, knaves, and make holiday.
[*Exeunt.*

FIRK. O rare! O brave! Come, Hodge; follow me, Hans;
We'll be with them for a morris-dance. 119
[*Exeunt.*

SCENE V

Enter LORD MAYOR, ROSE, EYRE, MARGERY *in a French hood,* SYBIL, *and other* Servants.

LORD MAYOR. Trust me, you are as welcome to Old Ford
As I myself.

MARGERY. Truly, I thank your lordship.

LORD MAYOR. Would our bad cheer were worth the thanks you give.

EYRE. Good cheer, my lord mayor, fine cheer!
A fine house, fine walls, all fine and neat. 5

LORD MAYOR. Now, by my troth, I'll tell thee, Master Eyre,
It does me good, and all my brethren,
That such a madcap fellow as thyself
Is entered into our society.

MARGERY. Ay, but, my lord, he must learn now to put on gravity.

EYRE. Peace, Maggy; a fig for gravity! When I go to Guildhall in my scarlet gown, I'll look as demurely as a saint, and speak as gravely as a justice of peace; but now I am here at Old Ford, at my good lord mayor's house, let it go by, vanish; Maggy, I'll be merry; away with flip-flap, these fooleries, these gulleries. What, honey? Prince am I none, yet am I princely born. What says my lord mayor? 21

LORD MAYOR. Ha, ha, ha! I had rather than a thousand pound I had an heart but half so light as yours.

EYRE. Why, what should I do, my lord? A pound of care pays not a dram of debt. Hum, let's be merry whiles we are young; old age, sack, and sugar will steal upon us ere we be aware.[27] 29

LORD MAYOR. It's well done; Mistress Eyre, pray, give good counsel to my daughter.

MARGERY. I hope Mistress Rose will have the grace to take nothing that's bad.

LORD MAYOR. Pray God she do; for i' faith, Mistress Eyre,
I would bestow upon that peevish girl
A thousand marks more than I mean to give her
Upon condition she'd be ruled by me.
The ape still crosseth me. There came of late
A proper gentleman of fair revenues,
Whom gladly I would call son-in-law: 40
But my fine cockney would have none of him.—
You'll prove a coxcomb for it, ere you die:
A courtier, or no man must please your eye.

EYRE. Be ruled, sweet Rose: th'art ripe for a man. Marry not with a boy that has no more hair on his face than thou hast on thy cheeks. A courtier? wash, go by! stand not upon pishery-pashery: those silken fellows are but painted images, outsides, outsides, Rose; their inner linings are torn. No, my fine mouse, marry me with a gentleman grocer like my lord mayor, your father; a grocer is a sweet trade: plums, plums. Had I a son or daughter should marry out of the generation and blood of the shoemakers, he should pack; what, the gentle trade is a living for a man through Europe, through the world. 58

A noise within of a tabor and a pipe.

LORD MAYOR. What noise is this?

EYRE. O my lord mayor, a crew of good fellows that for love to your honor are come hither with a morris-dance. Come in, my Mesopotamians, cheerily.

---

[27]At this point some editors insert the "First Three-man's Song" which the present edition, like the early ones, places before the Prologue of the play.

Enter HODGE, LACY, RALPH, FIRK, *and other* Shoemakers, *in a morris; after a little dancing the* LORD MAYOR *speaks.*

LORD MAYOR. Master Eyre, are all these shoemakers?

EYRE. All cordwainers, my good lord mayor.

ROSE. [*Aside.*] How like my Lacy looks yond shoemaker!

LACY. [*Aside.*] Oh, that I durst but speak unto my love!

LORD MAYOR. Sybil, go fetch some wine to make these drink.
You are all welcome.

ALL. We thank your lordship.

[ROSE *takes a cup of wine and goes to* LACY.]

ROSE. For his sake whose fair shape thou represent'st, 70
Good friend, I drink to thee.

LACY. Ic bedancke, good frister.[28]

MARGERY. I see, Mistress Rose, you do not want judgment; you have drunk to the properest man I keep.

FIRK. Here be some have done their parts to be as proper as he.

LORD MAYOR. Well, urgent business calls me back to London:
Good fellows, first go in and taste our cheer,
And to make merry as you homeward go, 80
Spend these two angels in beer at Stratford-Bow.

EYRE. To these two, my mad lads, Sim Eyre adds another; then cheerily, Firk; tickle it, Hans, and all for the honor of shoemakers. [*All go dancing out.*

LORD MAYOR. Come, Master Eyre, let's have your company. [*Exeunt.*

ROSE. Sybil, what shall I do?

SYBIL. Why, what's the matter?

ROSE. That Hans the shoemaker is my love Lacy,
Disguised in that attire to find me out.
How should I find the means to speak with him? 90

SYBIL. What, mistress, never fear; I dare venture my maidenhead to nothing, and that's great odds, that Hans the Dutchman, when we come to London, shall not only see and speak with you, but in spite of all your father's policies[29] steal you away and marry you. Will not this please you?

ROSE. Do this, and ever be assured of my love. 99

SYBIL. Away, then, and follow your father to London, lest your absence cause him to suspect something:
To-morrow, if my counsel be obeyed,
I'll bind you prentice to the gentle trade. [*Exeunt.*

[28] I thank you, good maid. [29] Schemes.

ACT IV

SCENE I

Enter JANE *in a Seamster's shop, working, and* HAMMON, *muffled, at another door; he stands aloof.*

HAMMON. Yonder's the shop, and there my fair love sits.
She's fair and lovely, but she is not mine.
Oh, would she were! Thrice have I courted her,
Thrice hath my hand been moistened with her hand,
Whilst my poor famished eyes do feed on that 5
Which made them famish. I am unfortunate:
I still love one, yet nobody loves me.
I muse, in other men what women see
That I so want! Fine Mistress Rose was coy,
And this too curious![1] Oh, no, she is chaste, 10
And for she thinks me wanton, she denies
To cheer my cold heart with her sunny eyes.
How prettily she works, O pretty hand!
O happy work! It doth me good to stand
Unseen to see her. Thus I oft have stood 15
In frosty evenings, a light burning by her,
Enduring biting cold only to eye her.
One only look hath seemed as rich to me
As a king's crown; such is love's lunacy.
Muffled I'll pass along, and by that try 20
Whether she know me.

JANE. Sir, what is't you buy?
What is't you lack, sir, calico or lawn,
Fine cambric shirts or bands; what will you buy?

HAMMON. [*Aside.*] That which thou wilt not sell. Faith, yet I'll try:
How do you sell this handkerchief?

JANE. Good cheap. 25

HAMMON. And how these ruffs?

JANE. Cheap too.

HAMMON. And how this band?

JANE. Cheap too.

HAMMON. All cheap; how sell you then this hand?

JANE. My hands are not to be sold.

[1] Fastidious.

HAMMON. To be given then!
Nay, faith, I come to buy.
JANE. But none knows when.
HAMMON. Good sweet, leave work a little while; let's play. 30
JANE. I cannot live by keeping holiday.
HAMMON. I'll pay you for the time which shall be lost.
JANE. With me you shall not be at so much cost.
HAMMON. Look, how you wound this cloth, so you wound me.
JANE. It may be so.
HAMMON. 'Tis so.
JANE. What remedy? 35
HAMMON. Nay, faith, you are too coy.
JANE. Let go my hand.
HAMMON. I will do any task at your command;
I would let go this beauty, were I not
In mind to disobey you by a power
That controls kings: I love you!
JANE. So, now part. 40
HAMMON. With hands I may, but never with my heart.
In faith, I love you.
JANE. I believe you do.
HAMMON. Shall a true love in me breed hate in you?
JANE. I hate you not.
HAMMON. Then you must love?
JANE. I do.
What are you better now? I love not you. 45
HAMMON. All this, I hope, is but a woman's fray,
That means "Come to me," when she cries "Away!"
In earnest, mistress,—I do not jest—
A true chaste love hath entered in my breast.
I love you dearly, as I love my life, 50
I love you as a husband loves a wife;
That, and no other love, my love requires.
Thy wealth, I know, is little; my desires
Thirst not for gold. Sweet, beauteous Jane, what's mine
Shall, if thou make myself thine, all be thine. 55
Say, judge, what is thy sentence, life or death?
Mercy or cruelty lies in thy breath.
JANE. Good sir, I do believe you love me well;
For 'tis a silly conquest, silly pride
For one like you—I mean a gentleman— 60
To boast that by his love-tricks he hath brought
Such and such women to his amorous lure;
I think you do not so; yet many do,
And make it even a very trade to woo.
I would be coy, as many women be, 65
Feed you with sunshine smiles and wanton looks,
But I detest witchcraft; say that I
Do constantly believe you, constant have——
HAMMON. Why dost thou not believe me?
JANE. I believe you;
But yet, good sir, because I will not grieve you 70
With hopes to taste fruit which will never fall,
In simple truth this is the sum of all:
My husband lives; at least I hope he lives.
Pressed was he to these bitter wars in France;
Bitter they are to me by wanting him. 75
I have but one heart, and that heart's his due.
How can I then bestow the same on you?
Whilst he lives, his I live, be it ne'er so poor,
And rather be his wife than a king's whore.
HAMMON. Chaste and dear woman, I will not abuse thee, 80
Although it cost my life, if thou refuse me.
Thy husband, pressed for France, what was his name?
JANE. Ralph Damport.
HAMMON. Damport?—Here's a letter sent
From France to me, from a dear friend of mine,
A gentleman of place; here he doth write 85
Their names that have been slain in every fight.
JANE. I hope death's scroll contains not my love's name.
HAMMON. Cannot you read?
JANE. I can.
HAMMON. Peruse the same.
To my remembrance such a name I read
Amongst the rest. See here.
JANE. Ay me, he's dead! 90
He's dead! if this be true, my dear heart's slain!
HAMMON. Have patience, dear love.
JANE. Hence, hence!
HAMMON. Nay, sweet Jane,
Make not poor sorrow proud with these rich tears.
I mourn thy husband's death, because thou mourn'st.
JANE. That bill is forged; 'tis signed by forgery. 95
HAMMON. I'll bring thee letters sent besides to many,
Carrying the like report: Jane, 'tis too true.

Come, weep not: mourning, though it rise
from love,
Helps not the mournéd, yet hurts them that
mourn.

JANE. For God's sake, leave me. 99

HAMMON. Whither dost thou turn?
Forget the dead; love them that are alive.
His love is faded; try how mine will thrive.

JANE. 'Tis now no time for me to think on
love—

HAMMON. 'Tis now best time for you to
think on love,
Because your love lives not.

JANE. Though he be dead, 105
My love to him shall not be buriéd;
For God's sake, leave me to myself alone.

HAMMON. 'Twould kill my soul to leave
thee drowned in moan.
Answer me to my suit, and I am gone;
Say to me yea or no.

JANE. No.

HAMMON. Then farewell! 110
One farewell will not serve; I come again.
Come, dry these wet cheeks; tell me, faith,
sweet Jane,
Yea or no, once more.

JANE. Once more I say no;
Once more be gone, I pray; else will I go.

HAMMON. Nay, then I will grow rude; by
this white hand, 115
Until you change that cold "no," here I'll
stand
Till by your hard heart——

JANE. Nay, for God's love, peace!
My sorrows by your presence more increase.
Not that you thus are present, but all grief
Desires to be alone: therefore in brief 120
Thus much I say, and saying bid adieu:
If ever I wed man, it shall be you.

HAMMON. O blesséd voice! Dear Jane,
I'll urge no more,
Thy breath hath made me rich.

JANE. Death makes me poor.

[*Exeunt.*

SCENE II

Enter HODGE, *at his shop-board,* RALPH, FIRK, LACY, *and a* Boy *at work.*

ALL. Hey, down a down, down, derry.

HODGE. Well said, my hearts; ply your work today; we loitered yesterday; to it pell-mell, that we may live to be lord mayors, or aldermen at least.

FIRK. Hey, down a down, derry.

HODGE. Well said, i' faith! How say'st thou, Hans: doth not Firk tickle it?

LACY. Yaw, mester. 9

FIRK. Not so neither; my organ-pipe squeaks this morning for want of liquoring. Hey, down a down, derry!

LACY. Forward, Firk, tow best un jolly yongster. Hort, ay, mester; ic bid yo, cut me un pair vampres vor Mester Jeffre's boots.[2]

HODGE. Thou shalt, Hans.

FIRK. Master!

HODGE. How now, boy? 19

FIRK. Pray, now you are in the cutting vein, cut me out a pair of counterfeits,[3] or else my work will not pass current; hey, down a down!

HODGE. Tell me, sirs, are my cousin Mistress Priscilla's shoes done?

FIRK. Your cousin? No, master; one of your aunts,[4] hang her; let them alone.

RALPH. I am in hand with them; she gave charge that none but I should do them for her. 30

FIRK. Thou do for her? then 'twill be a lame doing, and that she loves not. Ralph, thou might'st have sent her to me, in faith; I would have yerk'd and firk'd your Priscilla. Hey, down a down, derry. This gear will not hold.

HODGE. How say'st thou, Firk: were we not merry at Old Ford?

FIRK. How, merry? why, our buttocks went jiggy-joggy like a quagmire. Well, Sir Roger Oatmeal, if I thought all meal of that nature, I would eat nothing but bagpuddings.

RALPH. Of all good fortunes my fellow Hans had the best.

FIRK. 'Tis true, because Mistress Rose drank to him.

HODGE. Well, well, work apace. They say, seven of the aldermen be dead or very sick. 50

FIRK. I care not; I'll be none.

RALPH. No, nor I; but then my Master Eyre will come quickly to be lord mayor.

Enter SYBIL.

FIRK. Whoop, yonder comes Sybil.

HODGE. Sybil, welcome, i' faith; and how dost thou, mad wench?

FIRK. Syb-whore, welcome to London.

SYBIL. Godamercy, sweet Firk; good lord,

---

[2]Forward, Firk, thou art a jolly youngster. Hark ye, master; I ask you to cut me a pair of vamps for Master Jeffrey's boots.

[3]Vamps. [4]Bawds.

Hodge, what a delicious shop you have got! You tickle it,[5] i' faith. 60

RALPH. Godamercy, Sybil, for our good cheer at Old Ford.

SYBIL. That you shall have, Ralph.

FIRK. Nay, by the mass, we had tickling cheer, Sybil; and how the plague dost thou and Mistress Rose and my lord mayor? I put the women in first.

SYBIL. Well, Godamercy; but God's me, I forget myself: where's Hans the Fleming?

FIRK. Hark, butter-box; now you must yelp out some spreken. 71

LACY. Wat begaie you? Vat vod you, Frister?[6]

SYBIL. Marry, you must come to my young mistress, to pull on her shoes you made last.

LACY. Vare ben your egle fro; vare ben your mistris?[7]

SYBIL. Marry, here at our London house in Cornhill.

FIRK. Will nobody serve her turn but Hans? 81

SYBIL. No, sir. Come, Hans, I stand upon needles.

HODGE. Why then, Sybil, take heed of pricking.

SYBIL. For that let me alone. I have a trick in my budget. Come, Hans.

LACY. Yaw, yaw, ic sall meete yo gane.[8]

[*Exit* LACY *and* SYBIL.

HODGE. Go, Hans, make haste again. Come, who lacks work? 90

FIRK. I, master, for I lack my breakfast; 'tis munching-time and past.

HODGE. Is't so? why, then leave work, Ralph. To breakfast! Boy, look to the tools. Come, Ralph; come, Firk. [*Exeunt.*

Enter a SERVING-MAN.

SERVING-MAN. Let me see now, the sign of the Last in Tower Street. Mass, yonder's the house. What, haw! Who's within? 99

Enter RALPH.

RALPH. Who calls there? What want you, sir?

SERVING-MAN. Marry, I would have a pair of shoes made for a gentlewoman against tomorrow morning. What, can you do them?

RALPH. Yes, sir, you shall have them. But what length's her foot?

SERVING-MAN. Why, you must make them in all parts like this shoe; but, at any hand,[9] fail not to do them, for the gentlewoman is to be married very early in the morning. 111

RALPH. How? by this shoe must it be made? by this? Are you sure, sir, by this?

SERVING-MAN. How, by this? Am I sure, by this? Art thou in thy wits? I tell thee, I must have a pair of shoes, dost thou mark me? a pair of shoes, two shoes, made by this very shoe, this same shoe, against tomorrow morning by four a clock. Dost understand me? Canst thou do't? 120

RALPH. Yes, sir, yes—ay, ay!—I can do't. By this shoe, you say? I should know this shoe. Yes, sir, yes, by this shoe, I can do't. Four a clock, well. Whither shall I bring them?

SERVING-MAN. To the sign of the Golden Ball in Watling Street; inquire for one Master Hammon, a gentleman, my master.

RALPH. Yea, sir; by this shoe, you say?

SERVING-MAN. I say, Master Hammon at the Golden Ball; he's the bridegroom, and those shoes are for his bride.

RALPH. They shall be done by this shoe; well, well, Master Hammon at the Golden Shoe—I would say, the Golden Ball; very well, very well. But I pray you, sir, where must Master Hammon be married?

SERVING-MAN. At St. Faith's Church, under Paul's. But what's that to thee? Prithee, dispatch those shoes, and so farewell. [*Exit.*

RALPH. By this shoe, said he. How am I amazed 142
At this strange accident! Upon my life,
This was the very shoe I gave my wife
When I was pressed for France; since when, alas!
I never could hear of her: it is the same,
And Hammon's bride no other but my Jane.

Enter FIRK.

FIRK. 'Snails, Ralph, thou hast lost thy part of three pots a countryman of mine gave me to breakfast. 150

RALPH. I care not; I have found a better thing.

FIRK. A thing? away! Is it a man's thing, or a woman's thing?

RALPH. Firk, dost thou know this shoe?

FIRK. No, by my troth; neither doth that

[5]Work briskly.

[6]What want you? What would you, maid?

[7]Where is your noble mistress; where is your mistress?

[8]Yes, yes, I will go with you.

[9]In any case.

know me! I have no acquaintance with it; 'tis a mere stranger to me.

RALPH. Why, then I do; this shoe, I durst be sworn,
Once covered the instep of my Jane. 160
This is her size, her breadth; thus trod my love;
These true-love knots I pricked; I hold[10] my life,
By this old shoe I shall find out my wife.

FIRK. Ha, ha! Old shoe, that wert new! How a murrain came this ague-fit of foolishness upon thee?

RALPH. Thus, Firk: even now here came a serving-man;
By this shoe would he have a new pair made
Against tomorrow morning for his mistress
That's to be married to a gentleman. 170
And why may not this be my sweet Jane?

FIRK. And why may'st not thou be my sweet ass? Ha, ha!

RALPH. Well, laugh and spare not! But the truth is this:
Against tomorrow morning I'll provide
A lusty crew of honest shoemakers
To watch the going of the bride to church.
If she prove Jane, I'll take her in despite
From Hammon and the devil, were he by.
If it be not my Jane, what remedy? 180
Hereof I am sure: I shall live till I die,
Although I never with a woman lie. [*Exit.*

FIRK. Thou lie with a woman, to build nothing but Cripple-gates! Well, God sends fools fortune, and it may be he may light upon his matrimony by such a device; for wedding and hanging goes by destiny. [*Exit.*

SCENE III

Enter LACY *and* ROSE, *arm in arm.*

LACY. How happy am I by embracing thee!
Oh, I did fear such cross mishaps did reign,
That I should never see my Rose again.

ROSE. Sweet Lacy, since fair opportunity
Offers herself to further our escape, 5
Let not too over-fond esteem of me
Hinder that happy hour. Invent the means,
And Rose will follow thee through all the world.

LACY. Oh, how I surfeit with excess of joy,
Made happy by thy rich perfection! 10
But since thou pay'st sweet interest to my hopes,

[10] Wager.

Redoubling love on love, let me once more
Like to a bold-faced debtor crave of thee
This night to steal abroad, and at Eyre's house,
Who now by death of certain aldermen 15
Is mayor of London, and my master once,
Meet thou thy Lacy, where in spite of change,
Your father's anger, and mine uncle's hate,
Our happy nuptials will we consummate. 19

Enter SYBIL.

SYBIL. O God, what will you do, mistress? Shift for yourself; your father is at hand! He's coming, he's coming! Master Lacy, hide yourself! In, my mistress! For God's sake, shift for yourselves!

LACY. Your father come, sweet Rose—what shall I do? 25
Where shall I hide me? How shall I escape?

ROSE. A man, and want wit in extremity!
Come, come, be Hans still; play the shoemaker;
Pull on my shoe.

Enter the LORD MAYOR.

LACY. Mass, and that's well remembered.

SYBIL. Here comes your father. 30

LACY. Forware, metresse, 'tis un good skow; it sal vel dute, or ye sal neit betallen.[11]

ROSE. O God, it pincheth me; what will you do?

LACY. [*Aside.*] Your father's presence pincheth, not the shoe.

LORD MAYOR. Well done; fit my daughter well, and she shall please thee well. 35

LACY. Yaw, yaw, ick weit dat well; forware, 'tis un good skoo; 'tis gimait van neits leither; se euer, mine here.[12]

Enter a PRENTICE.

LORD MAYOR. I do believe it.—What's the news with you?

PRENTICE. Please you, the Earl of Lincoln at the gate 40
Is newly lighted, and would speak with you.

LORD MAYOR. The Earl of Lincoln come to speak with me?
Well, well, I know his errand. Daughter Rose,

[11] Truly, mistress, it is a good shoe; it will fit well, or you shall not pay.

[12] Yes, yes, I know that well; truly, it is a good shoe; it is made of neat's leather; only look, sir.

Send hence your shoemaker; dispatch; have done!
Syb, make things handsome! Sir boy, follow me. [*Exit.*

LACY. Mine uncle come! Oh, what may this portend? 46
Sweet Rose, this of our love threatens an end.

ROSE. Be not dismayed at this; whate'er befall,
Rose is thine own. To witness I speak truth,
Where thou appoints the place, I'll meet with thee. 50
I will not fix a day to follow thee,
But presently steal hence. Do not reply:
Love which gave strength to bear my father's hate,
Shall now add wings to further our escape. [*Exeunt.*

SCENE IV

Enter LORD MAYOR *and* LINCOLN.

LORD MAYOR. Believe me, on my credit, I speak truth:
Since first your nephew Lacy went to France,
I have not seen him. It seemed strange to me,
When Dodger told me that he stayed behind,
Neglecting the high charge the king imposed. 5

LINCOLN. Trust me, Sir Roger Oteley, I did think
Your counsel had given head to this attempt,
Drawn to it by the love he bears your child.
Here I did hope to find him in your house;
But now I see mine error and confess 10
My judgment wronged you by conceiving so.

LORD MAYOR. Lodge in my house, say you? Trust me, my lord,
I love your nephew Lacy too too dearly,
So much to wrong his honor; and he hath done so,
That first gave him advice to stay from France. 15
To witness I speak truth, I let you know
How careful I have been to keep my daughter
Free from all conference or speech of him;
Not that I scorn your nephew, but in love
I bear your honor, lest your noble blood 20
Should by my mean worth be dishonored.

LINCOLN. [*Aside.*] How far the churl's tongue wanders from his heart!
—Well, well, Sir Roger Oteley, I believe you,
With more than many thanks for the kind love
So much you seem to bear me. But, my lord, 25
Let me request your help to seek my nephew,
Whom if I find, I'll straight embark for France.
So shall your Rose be free, my thoughts at rest,
And much care die which now lies in my breast.

Enter SYBIL.

SYBIL. O Lord! Help, for God's sake! my mistress! oh, my young mistress! 30

LORD MAYOR. Where is thy mistress? What's become of her?

SYBIL. She's gone; she's fled!

LORD MAYOR. Gone! Whither is she fled?

SYBIL. I know not, forsooth; she's fled out of doors with Hans the shoemaker; I saw them scud, scud, scud, apace, apace! 35

LORD MAYOR. Which way? What, John! Where be my men? Which way?

SYBIL. I know not, an it please your worship.

LORD MAYOR. Fled with a shoemaker? Can this be true?

SYBIL. O Lord, sir, as true as God's in Heaven. 40

LINCOLN. [*Aside.*] Her love turned shoemaker? I am glad of this.

LORD MAYOR. A Fleming butter-box, a shoemaker!
Will she forget her birth, requite my care
With such ingratitude? Scorned she young Hammon
To love a honnikin, a needy knave? 45
Well, let her fly; I'll not fly after her;
Let her starve, if she will; she's none of mine.

LINCOLN. Be not so cruel, sir.

Enter FIRK *with shoes.*

SYBIL. [*Aside.*] I am glad, she's 'scaped.

LORD MAYOR. I'll not account of her as of my child.
Was there no better object for her eyes 50
But a foul drunken lubber, swill-belly,
A shoemaker? That's brave!

FIRK. Yea, forsooth; 'tis a very brave shoe, and as fit as a pudding.

LORD MAYOR. How now, what knave is this? From whence comest thou?

FIRK. No knave, sir. I am Firk the shoemaker, lusty Roger's chief lusty journeyman, and I come hither to take up the pretty leg of sweet Mistress Rose; and thus hoping your worship is in as good health as I was at the making thereof, I bid you farewell, yours, Firk. 61

LORD MAYOR. Stay, stay, Sir Knave!

LINCOLN. Come hither, shoemaker!

FIRK. 'Tis happy the knave is put before the shoemaker, or else I would not have vouchsafed to come back to you. I am moved, for I stir. 66

LORD MAYOR. My lord, this villain calls us knaves by craft.

FIRK. Then 'tis by the gentle craft, and to call one knave gently is no harm. Sit your worship merry! [*Aside to* SYBIL.]—Syb, your young mistress—I'll so bob[13] them, now my Master Eyre is lord mayor of London.

LORD MAYOR. Tell me, sirrah, whose man are you? 74

FIRK. I am glad to see your worship so merry. I have no maw to this gear, no stomach as yet to a red petticoat.

[*Pointing to* SYBIL.

LINCOLN. He means not, sir, to woo you to his maid,
But only doth demand whose man you are. 79

FIRK. I sing now to the tune of Rogero. Roger, my fellow, is now my master.

LINCOLN. Sirrah, know'st thou one Hans, a shoemaker?

FIRK. Hans, shoemaker? Oh, yes; stay; yes. I have him. I tell you what, I speak it in secret: Mistress Rose and he are by this time—no, not so, but shortly are to come over one another with "Can you dance the shaking of the sheets?" It is that Hans—[*Aside.*] I'll so gull these diggers![14]

LORD MAYOR. Know'st thou, then, where he is? 90

FIRK. Yes, forsooth; yea, marry!

LINCOLN. Canst thou, in sadness?[15]

FIRK. No, forsooth; no marry!

LORD MAYOR. Tell me, good honest fellow, where he is, 94
And thou shalt see what I'll bestow of thee.

FIRK. Honest fellow? No, sir; not so, sir; my profession is the gentle craft; I care not for seeing; I love feeling; let me feel it here; *aurium tenus,* ten pieces of gold; *genuum tenus,* ten pieces of silver;[16] and then Firk is your man—[*Aside*] in a new pair of stretchers.[17] 102

LORD MAYOR. Here is an angel, part of thy reward,
Which I will give thee; tell me where he is.

FIRK. No point![18] Shall I betray my brother? no! Shall I prove Judas to Hans? no! Shall I cry treason to my corporation? no! I shall be firked and yerked then. But give me your angel; your angel shall tell you. 111

LINCOLN. Do so, good fellow; 'tis no hurt to thee.

FIRK. Send simpering Syb away.

LORD MAYOR. Huswife, get you in.

[*Exit* SYBIL.

FIRK. Pitchers have ears, and maids have wide mouths; but for Hauns-prauns, upon my word, tomorrow morning he and young Mistress Rose go to this gear: they shall be married together, by this rush, or else turn Firk to a firkin of butter to tan leather withal. 121

LORD MAYOR. But art thou sure of this?

FIRK. Am I sure that Paul's steeple is a handful higher than London Stone, or that the Pissing-Conduit leaks nothing but pure Mother Bunch? Am I sure I am lusty Firk? God's nails, do you think I am so base to gull you?

LINCOLN. Where are they married? Dost thou know the church? 129

FIRK. I never go to church, but I know the name of it; it is a swearing church—stay a while, 'tis—Ay, by the mass; no, no,—'tis—Ay, by my troth; no, nor that; 'tis—Ay, by my faith, that, that, 'tis, Ay, by my Faith's Church under Paul's Cross. There they shall be knit like a pair of stockings in matrimony; there they'll be inconie.[19]

LINCOLN. Upon my life, my nephew Lacy walks
In the disguise of this Dutch shoemaker.

FIRK. Yes, forsooth. 140

LINCOLN. Doth he not, honest fellow?

FIRK. No, forsooth; I think Hans is nobody but Hans, no spirit.

LORD MAYOR. My mind misgives me now; 'tis so, indeed.

LINCOLN. My cousin speaks the language, knows the trade.

LORD MAYOR. Let me request your company, my lord;
Your honorable presence may, no doubt,

---

[13]Fool. [14]Diggers for information.

[15]Knowest thou in earnest?

[16]Firk obviously mistranslates the Latin phrases, which mean "up to the ears" and "up to the knees."

[17]Lies. [18]Not at all. [19]A fine sight.

Refrain their headstrong rashness, when myself 148
Going alone perchance may be o'erborne.
Shall I request this favor?

LINCOLN. This, or what else.

FIRK. Then you must rise betimes, for they mean to fall to their "hey-pass and repass," "pindy-pandy, which hand will you have," very early.

LORD MAYOR. My care shall every way equal their haste.
This night accept your lodging in my house;
The earlier shall we stir, and at St. Faith's
Prevent this giddy hare-brained nuptial.
This traffic of hot love shall yield cold gains:
They ban[20] our loves, and we'll forbid their banns. [*Exit.*

LINCOLN. At St. Faith's Church, thou say'st? 161

FIRK. Yes, by my troth.

LINCOLN. Be secret, on thy life. [*Exit.*

FIRK. Yes, when I kiss your wife! Ha, ha, here's no craft in the gentle craft! I came hither of purpose with shoes to Sir Roger's worship, whilst Rose, his daughter, be cony-catched by Hans. Soft now; these two gulls will be at St. Faith's Church tomorrow morning to take Master Bridegroom and Mistress Bride napping; and they, in the meantime, shall chop up the matter at the Savoy. But the best sport is Sir Roger Oteley will find my fellow lame Ralph's wife going to marry a gentleman, and then he'll stop her instead of his daughter. Oh, brave! there will be fine tickling sport. Soft now; what have I to do? Oh, I know; now a mess of shoemakers meet at the Woolsack in Ivy Lane to cozen my gentleman of lame Ralph's wife, that's true. 182

Alack, alack!
Girls, hold out tack![21]
For now smocks for this jumbling
Shall go to wrack. [*Exit.*

ACT V

SCENE I

Enter EYRE, MARGERY, LACY, *and* ROSE.

EYRE. This is the morning, then, say, my bully, my honest Hans, is it not?

LACY. This is the morning that must make us two happy or miserable; therefore, if you——

EYRE. Away with these ifs and ans, Hans, and these *et ceteras!* By mine honor, Rowland Lacy, none but the king shall wrong thee. Come, fear nothing; am not I Sim Eyre? Is not Sim Eyre lord mayor of London? Fear nothing, Rose: let them all say what they can; dainty, come thou to me —laughest thou? 13

MARGERY. Good my lord, stand her friend in what thing you may.

EYRE. Why, my sweet Lady Madgy, think you Simon Eyre can forget his fine Dutch journeyman? No, vah! Fie, I scorn it; it shall never be cast in my teeth that I was unthankful. Lady Madgy, thou had'st never covered thy Saracen's head with this French flap, nor loaden thy bum with this farthingale ('tis trash, trumpery, vanity); Simon Eyre had never walked in a red petticoat nor wore a chain of gold, but for my fine journeyman's Portigues; and shall I leave him? No! Prince am I none, yet bear a princely mind.

LACY. My lord, 'tis time for us to part from hence. 30

EYRE. Lady Madgy, Lady Madgy, take two or three of my pie-crust-eaters, my buff-jerkin varlets, that do walk in black gowns at Simon Eyre's heels; take them, good Lady Madgy; trip and go, my brown queen of periwigs, with my delicate Rose and my jolly Rowland to the Savoy; see them linked, countenance the marriage; and when it is done, cling, cling together, you Hamborow turtle-doves. I'll bear you out; come to Simon Eyre; come, dwell with me, Hans, thou shalt eat minced-pies and marchpane. Rose, away, cricket; trip and go, my Lady Madgy, to the Savoy; Hans, wed, and to bed; kiss, and away! Go, vanish! 45

MARGERY. Farewell, my lord.

ROSE. Make haste, sweet love.

MARGERY. She'd fain the deed were done.

LACY. Come, my sweet Rose; faster than deer we'll run. [*They go out.*

EYRE. Go, vanish, vanish! Avaunt, I say! By the Lord of Ludgate, it's a mad life to be a lord mayor; it's a stirring life, a fine life, a velvet life, a careful life. Well, Simon Eyre, yet set a good face on it, in the honor of St. Hugh. Soft, the king this day comes to dine with me, to see my new buildings; his majesty is welcome; he shall have good cheer, delicate cheer, princely cheer. This day my fellow prentices of London come to dine with me too; they shall have fine cheer, gentlemanlike cheer. I promised the mad Cappadocians, when we

[20]Curse. [21]Hold your own.

all served at the Conduit[1] together, that if ever I came to be mayor of London, I would feast them all; and I'll do 't, I'll do 't, by the life of Pharaoh; by this beard, Sim Eyre will be no flincher. Besides, I have procured that upon every Shrove Tuesday, at the sound of the pancake bell, my fine dapper Assyrian lads shall clap up their shop windows, and away. This is the day, and this day they shall do 't, they shall do 't. 72

Boys, that day are you free, let masters care;
And prentices shall pray for Simon Eyre. [*Exit.*

SCENE II

Enter HODGE, FIRK, RALPH, *and five or six* SHOEMAKERS, *all with cudgels or such weapons.*

HODGE. Come, Ralph; stand to it, Firk. My masters, as we are the brave bloods of the shoemakers, heirs apparent to St. Hugh, and perpetual benefactors to all good fellows, thou shalt have no wrong; were Hammon a king of spades, he should not delve in thy close[2] without thy sufferance. But tell me, Ralph, art thou sure 'tis thy wife? 8

RALPH. Am I sure this is Firk? This morning, when I stroked on her shoes, I looked upon her, and she upon me, and sighed, asked me if ever I knew one Ralph. "Yes," said I. "For his sake," said she—tears standing in her eyes—"and for thou art somewhat like him, spend this piece of gold." I took it; my lame leg and my travel beyond sea made me unknown. All is one for that: I know she's mine. 18

FIRK. Did she give thee this gold? O glorious, glittering gold! She's thine own, 'tis thy wife, and she loves thee; for I'll stand to 't, there's no woman will give gold to any man, but she thinks better of him than she thinks of them she gives silver to. And for Hammon, neither Hammon nor hangman shall wrong thee in London. Is not our old master Eyre lord mayor? Speak, my hearts.

ALL. Yes, and Hammon shall know it to his cost. 30

Enter HAMMON, *his* MAN, JANE, *and others.*

HODGE. Peace, my bullies; yonder they come.

RALPH. Stand to 't, my hearts. Firk, let me speak first.

[1]Served as apprentices. [2]Enclosure; property.

HODGE. No, Ralph, let me.—Hammon, whither away so early?

HAMMON. Unmannerly, rude slave, what's that to thee?

FIRK. To him, sir? Yes, sir, and to me, and others. Good-morrow, Jane, how dost thou? Good Lord, how the world is changed with you! God be thanked! 41

HAMMON. Villains, hands off! How dare you touch my love?

ALL THE SHOEMAKERS. Villains? Down with them! Cry clubs[3] for prentices!

HODGE. Hold, my hearts! Touch her, Hammon? Yea, and more than that: we'll carry her away with us. My masters and gentlemen, never draw your bird-spits; shoemakers are steel to the back, men every inch of them, all spirit. 50

ALL OF HAMMON'S SIDE. Well, and what of all this?

HODGE. I'll show you.—Jane, dost thou know this man? 'Tis Ralph, I can tell thee; nay, 'tis he in faith, though he be lamed by the wars. Yet look not strange; run to him; fold him about the neck and kiss him.

JANE. Lives then my husband? O God, let me go,
Let me embrace my Ralph.

HAMMON. What means my Jane?

JANE. Nay, what meant you, to tell me he was slain? 61

HAMMON. Pardon me, dear love, for being misled. 'Twas rumored here in London, thou wert dead.

FIRK. Thou seest he lives. Lass, go, pack home with him. Now, Master Hammon, where's your mistress, your wife?

SERVING-MAN. 'Swounds, master, fight for her! Will you thus lose her?

SHOEMAKERS. Down with that creature! Clubs! Down with him! 71

HODGE. Hold, hold!

HAMMON. Hold, fool! Sirs, he shall do no wrong. Will my Jane leave me thus, and break her faith?

FIRK. Yea, sir! She must, sir! She shall, sir! What then? Mend it!

HODGE. Hark, fellow Ralph, follow my counsel: set the wench in the midst, and let her choose her man, and let her be his woman. 81

JANE. Whom should I choose? Whom should my thoughts affect
But him whom Heaven hath made to be my love?

[3]The cry for a public affray.

Thou art my husband, and these humble weeds
Make thee more beautiful than all his wealth.
Therefore I will but put off his attire,
Returning it into the owner's hand,
And after ever be thy constant wife.

HODGE. Not a rag, Jane! The law's on our side; he that sows in another man's ground, forfeits his harvest. Get thee home, Ralph; follow him, Jane; he shall not have so much as a busk-point[4] from thee. 93

FIRK. Stand to that, Ralph; the appurtenances are thine own. Hammon, look not at her!

SERVING-MAN. Oh, 'swounds, no!

FIRK. Blue coat, be quiet; we'll give you a new livery else; we'll make Shrove Tuesday St. George's Day for you. Look not, Hammon; leer not! I'll firk you! For thy head now,—one glance, one sheep's eye, anything, at her! Touch not a rag, lest I and my brethren beat you to clouts. 104

SERVING-MAN. Come, Master Hammon, there's no striving here.

HAMMON. Good fellows, hear me speak; and, honest Ralph,
Whom I have injured most by loving Jane,
Mark what I offer thee: here in fair gold
Is twenty pound; I'll give it for thy Jane;
If this content thee not, thou shalt have more.

HODGE. Sell not thy wife, Ralph: make her not a whore.

HAMMON. Say, wilt thou freely cease thy claim in her,
And let her be my wife?

ALL THE SHOEMAKERS. No, do not, Ralph.

RALPH. Sirrah Hammon, Hammon, dost thou think a shoemaker is so base to be a bawd to his own wife for commodity? Take thy gold; choke with it! Were I not lame, I would make thee eat thy words.

FIRK. A shoemaker sell his flesh and blood? Oh, indignity! 120

HODGE. Sirrah, take up your pelf, and be packing.

HAMMON. I will not touch one penny, but in lieu
Of that great wrong I offered thy Jane,
To Jane and thee I give that twenty pound.
Since I have failed of her, during my life,
I vow no woman else shall be my wife.
Farewell, good fellows of the gentle trade:
Your morning mirth my mourning day hath made. [*Exeunt.*

[4]A lace used to keep the stays in position.

FIRK. Touch the gold, creature, if you dare! Y'are best be trudging. Here, Jane, take thou it. Now let's home, my hearts. 131

HODGE. Stay! Who comes here? Jane, on again with thy mask!

Enter LINCOLN, LORD MAYOR, *and* Servants.

LINCOLN. Yonder's the lying varlet mocked us so.

LORD MAYOR. Come hither, sirrah!

FIRK. I, sir? I am sirrah? You mean me, do you not?

LINCOLN. Where is my nephew married?

FIRK. Is he married? God give him joy; I am glad of it. They have a fair day, and the sign is in a good planet, Mars in Venus.

LORD MAYOR. Villain, thou toldst me that my daughter Rose 143
This morning should be married at St. Faith's;
We have watched there these three hours at the least,
Yet see we no such thing.

FIRK. Truly, I am sorry for 't; a bride's a pretty thing.

HODGE. Come to the purpose. Yonder's the bride and bridegroom you look for, I hope. Though you be lords, you are not to bar by your authority men from women, are you? 153

LORD MAYOR. See, see, my daughter's masked.

LINCOLN. True, and my nephew,
To hide his guilt, counterfeits him lame.

FIRK. Yea, truly; God help the poor couple, they are lame and blind.

LORD MAYOR. I'll ease her blindness.

LINCOLN. I'll his lameness cure.

FIRK. [*Aside to the* Shoemakers.] Lie down, sirs, and laugh! My fellow Ralph is taken for Rowland Lacy, and Jane for Mistress Damask Rose. This is all my knavery. 163

LORD MAYOR. What, have I found you, minion?

LINCOLN. O base wretch!
Nay, hide thy face; the horror of thy guilt
Can hardly be washed off. Where are thy powers?
What battles have you made? O yes, I see,
Thou fought'st with Shame, and Shame hath conquered thee.
This lameness will not serve.

LORD MAYOR. Unmask yourself.

LINCOLN. Lead home your daughter. 170

LORD MAYOR. Take your nephew hence.

RALPH. Hence! 'Swounds, what mean

you? Are you mad? I hope you cannot enforce my wife from me. Where's Hammon?

LORD MAYOR. Your wife?

LINCOLN. What Hammon?

RALPH. Yea, my wife; and, therefore, the proudest of you that lays hands on her first, I'll lay my crutch 'cross his pate. 179

FIRK. To him, lame Ralph! Here's brave sport!

RALPH. Rose call you her? Why, her name is Jane. Look here else; do you know her now?—

LINCOLN. Is this your daughter?

LORD MAYOR. No, nor this your nephew.
My Lord of Lincoln, we are both abused
By this base, crafty varlet.

FIRK. Yea, forsooth, no varlet; forsooth, no base; forsooth, I am but mean; no crafty neither, but of the gentle craft. 191

LORD MAYOR. Where is my daughter Rose? Where is my child?

LINCOLN. Where is my nephew Lacy married?

FIRK. Why, here is good laced mutton,[5] as I promised you.

LINCOLN. Villain, I'll have thee punished for this wrong.

FIRK. Punish the journeyman villain, but not the journeyman shoemaker.

Enter DODGER.

DODGER. My lord, I come to bring unwelcome news. 199
Your nephew Lacy and your daughter Rose
Early this morning wedded at the Savoy,
None being present but the lady mayoress.
Besides, I learnt among the officers,
The lord mayor vows to stand in their defence
'Gainst any that shall seek to cross the match.

LINCOLN. Dares Eyre, the shoemaker, uphold the deed?

FIRK. Yes, sir, shoemakers dare stand in a woman's quarrel, I warrant you, as deep as another, and deeper too.

DODGER. Besides, his grace today dines with the mayor, 210
Who on his knees humbly intends to fall
And beg a pardon for your nephew's fault.

LINCOLN. But I'll prevent him! Come, Sir Roger Oteley;
The king will do us justice in this cause.
Howe'er their hands have made them man and wife,
I will disjoin the match, or lose my life.
[*Exeunt.*

[5] A woman.

FIRK. Adieu, Monsieur Dodger! Farewell, fools! Ha, ha!—Oh, if they had stayed, I would have so lambed[6] them with flouts! O heart, my codpiece-point is ready to fly in pieces every time I think upon Mistress Rose; but let that pass, as my lady mayoress says.

HODGE. This matter is answered. Come, Ralph, home with thy wife. Come, my fine shoemakers, let's to our master's, the new lord mayor, and there swagger this Shrove Tuesday. I'll promise you wine enough, for Madge keeps the cellar. 229

ALL. O rare! Madge is a good wench.

FIRK. And I'll promise you meat enough, for simpering Susan keeps the larder. I'll lead you to victuals, my brave soldiers; follow your captain. O brave! Hark, hark!
[*Bell rings.*

ALL. The pancake-bell rings, the pancake-bell! Trilill, my hearts!

FIRK. O brave! O sweet bell! O delicate pancakes! Open the doors, my hearts, and shut up the windows! keep in the house; let out the pancakes! Oh, rare, my hearts! Let's march together for the honor of St. Hugh to the great new hall in Gracious Street corner, which our master, the new lord mayor, hath built.

RALPH. O the crew of good fellows that will dine at my lord mayor's cost today!

HODGE. By the Lord, my lord mayor is a most brave man. How shall prentices be bound to pray for him and the honor of the gentlemen shoemakers! Let's feed and be fat with my lord's bounty. 251

FIRK. O musical bell, still! O Hodge! O my brethren! There's cheer for the heavens: venison pasties walk up and down piping hot, like sergeants; beef and brewis comes marching in dry-fats;[7] fritters and pancakes comes trowling in, in wheelbarrows; hens and oranges hopping in porters' baskets; collops and eggs in scuttles; and tarts and custards comes quavering in, in malt-shovels. 261

Enter more PRENTICES.

ALL. Whoop, look here, look here!

HODGE. How now, mad lads, whither away so fast?

1ST PRENTICE. Whither? Why, to the great new hall, know you not why? The lord mayor hath bidden all the prentices in London to breakfast this morning.

[6] Whipped. [7] Hogsheads.

ALL. O brave shoemaker! O brave lord of incomprehensible good fellowship! Whoo! Hark you! The pancake-bell rings. 271

[*Cast up caps.*

FIRK. Nay, more, my hearts! Every Shrove Tuesday is our year of jubilee; and when the pancake-bell rings, we are as free as my lord mayor; we may shut up our shops, and make holiday. I'll have it called St. Hugh's Holiday.

ALL. Agreed, agreed! St. Hugh's Holiday.

HODGE. And this shall continue forever.

ALL. O brave! Come, come, my hearts! Away, away! 280

FIRK. O eternal credit to us of the gentle craft! March fair, my hearts! O rare!

[*Exeunt.*

SCENE III

Enter KING *and his* Train *over the stage.*

KING. Is our lord mayor of London such a gallant?

NOBLEMAN. One of the merriest madcaps in your land.
Your grace will think, when you behold the man,
He's rather a wild ruffian than a mayor:
Yet thus much I'll ensure your majesty, 5
In all his actions that concern his state
He is as serious, provident, and wise,
As full of gravity amongst the grave,
As any mayor hath been these many years.

KING. I am with child[8] till I behold this huff-cap, 10
But all my doubt is, when we come in presence,
His madness will be dashed clean out of countenance.

NOBLEMAN. It may be so, my liege.

KING. Which to prevent
Let some one give him notice, 'tis our pleasure
That he put on his wonted merriment. 15
Set forward!

ALL. On afore! [*Exeunt.*

SCENE IV

Enter EYRE, HODGE, FIRK, RALPH, *and other* Shoemakers, *all with napkins on their shoulders.*

EYRE. Come, my fine Hodge, my jolly gentlemen shoemakers; soft, where be these cannibals, these varlets, my officers? Let them all walk and wait upon my brethren; for my meaning is that none but shoemakers, none but the livery of my company shall in their satin hoods wait upon the trencher of my sovereign.

FIRK. O my lord, it will be rare! 9

EYRE. No more, Firk; come, lively! Let your fellow prentices want no cheer; let wine be plentiful as beer, and beer as water. Hang these penny-pinching fathers, that cram wealth in innocent lambskins. Rip, knaves, avaunt! Look to my guests!

HODGE. My lord, we are at our wits' end for room; those hundred tables will not feast the fourth part of them. 18

EYRE. Then cover me those hundred tables again and again, till all my jolly prentices be feasted. Avoid,[9] Hodge! Run, Ralph! Frisk about, my nimble Firk! Carouse me fathom-healths to the honor of the shoemakers. Do they drink lively, Hodge? Do they tickle it, Firk?

FIRK. Tickle it? Some of them have taken their liquor standing so long that they can stand no longer; but for meat, they would eat it, an they had it. 29

EYRE. Want they meat? Where's this swag-belly, this greasy kitchenstuff cook? Call the varlet to me! Want meat? Firk, Hodge, lame Ralph, run, my tall men, beleaguer the shambles, beggar all Eastcheap, serve me whole oxen in chargers, and let sheep whine upon the tables like pigs for want of good fellows to eat them. Want meat? Vanish, Firk! Avaunt, Hodge! 38

HODGE. Your lordship mistakes my man, Firk; he means, their bellies want meat, not the boards; for they have drunk so much, they can eat nothing.[10]

Enter LACY, ROSE, *and* MARGERY.

MARGERY. Where is my lord?

EYRE. How now, Lady Madgy?

MARGERY. The king's most excellent majesty is new come; he sends me for thy honor; one of his most worshipful peers bade me tell thou must be merry, and so forth; but let that pass. 49

EYRE. Is my sovereign come? Vanish, my tall shoemakers, my nimble brethren; look to my guests, the prentices. Yet stay

[8] In suspense.

[9] Away.

[10] At this point some editors have inserted the "Second Three-man's Song," which the present edition, like the early ones, places before the Prologue of the play.

a little! How now, Hans? How looks my little Rose?

LACY. Let me request you to remember me.
I know your honor easily may obtain
Free pardon of the king for me and Rose,
And reconcile me to my uncle's grace. 58

EYRE. Have done, my good Hans, my honest journeyman; look cheerily! I'll fall upon both my knees, till they be as hard as horn, but I'll get thy pardon.

MARGERY. Good my lord, have a care what you speak to his grace.

EYRE. Away, you Islington whitepot![11] hence, you hopperarse! you barley-pudding full of maggots! you broil'd carbonado![12] avaunt, avaunt, avoid, Mephistophilis! Shall Sim Eyre learn to speak of you, Lady Madgy? Vanish, Mother Miniver-cap;[13] vanish, go, trip and go; meddle with your partlets[14] and your pishery-pashery, your flewes and your whirligigs; go, rub, out of mine alley! Sim Eyre knows how to speak to a Pope, to Sultan Soliman, to Tamburlaine, an he were here; and shall I melt, shall I droop before my sovereign? No! Come, my Lady Madgy! Follow me, Hans! About your business, my frolic freebooters! Firk, frisk about, and about, and about, for the honor of mad Simon Eyre, lord mayor of London. 82

FIRK. Hey, for the honor of the shoemakers. [*Exeunt.*

SCENE V

A long flourish or two. Enter KING, NOBLES, EYRE, MARGERY, LACY, ROSE. LACY *and* ROSE *kneel.*

KING. Well, Lacy, though the fact was very foul
Of your revolting from our kingly love
And your own duty, yet we pardon you.
Rise both, and, Mistress Lacy, thank my lord mayor
For your young bridegroom here. 5

EYRE. So, my dear liege, Sim Eyre and my brethren, the gentlemen shoemakers, shall set your sweet majesty's image cheek by jowl by St. Hugh for this honor you have done poor Simon Eyre. I beseech your grace, pardon my rude behavior; I am a handicraftsman, yet my heart is without craft; I would be sorry at my soul that my boldness should offend my king.

KING. Nay, I pray thee, good lord mayor, be even as merry 15
As if thou wert among thy shoemakers;
It does me good to see thee in this humor.

EYRE. Say'st thou me so, my sweet Diocesian? Then, humph! Prince am I none, yet am I princely born. By the Lord of Ludgate, my liege, I'll be as merry as a pie.[15]

KING. Tell me, in faith, mad Eyre, how old thou art. 22

EYRE. My liege, a very boy, a stripling, a younker; you see not a white hair on my head, not a grey in this beard. Every hair, I assure thy majesty, that sticks in this beard, Sim Eyre values at the King of Babylon's ransom; Tamar Cham's beard was a rubbing brush to't: yet I'll shave it off, and stuff tennis-balls with it, to please my bully king. 31

KING. But all this while I do not know your age.

EYRE. My liege, I am six and fifty year old, yet I can cry Humph! with a sound heart for the honor of St. Hugh. Mark this old wench, my king: I danced the shaking of the sheets with her six and thirty years ago, and yet I hope to get two or three young lord mayors ere I die. I am lusty still, Sim Eyre still. Care and cold lodging brings white hairs. My sweet Majesty, let care vanish; cast it upon thy nobles; it will make thee look always young like Apollo, and cry Humph! Prince am I none, yet am I princely born. 45

KING. Ha, ha! Say, Cornwall, didst thou ever see his like?

NOBLEMAN. Not I, my lord.

Enter LINCOLN *and* LORD MAYOR.

KING. Lincoln, what news with you?

LINCOLN. My gracious lord, have care unto yourself,
For there are traitors here.

ALL. Traitors! Where? Who?

EYRE. Traitors in my house? God forbid! Where be my officers? I'll spend my soul, ere my king feel harm. 52

KING. Where is the traitor, Lincoln?

LINCOLN. Here he stands.

KING. Cornwall, lay hold on Lacy!—Lincoln, speak;
What canst thou lay unto thy nephew's charge?

[11]Custard. [12]Steak.

[13]Fur cap (worn by the wives of the wealthier citizens).

[14]Collars or ruffs.

[15]Magpie.

LINCOLN. This, my dear liege: your Grace, to do me honor,
Heaped on the head of this degenerous boy
Desertless favors; you made choice of him
To be commander over powers in France.
But he——

KING. Good Lincoln, prithee pause a while! 60
Even in thine eyes I read what thou wouldst speak.
I know how Lacy did neglect our love,
Ran himself deeply, in the highest degree,
Into vile treason——

LINCOLN. Is he not a traitor?

KING. Lincoln, he was; now have we pardoned him.
'Twas not a base want of true valor's fire
That held him out of France, but love's desire.

LINCOLN. I will not bear his shame upon my back.

KING. Nor shalt thou, Lincoln; I forgive you both. 69

LINCOLN. Then, good my liege, forbid the boy to wed
One whose mean birth will much disgrace his bed.

KING. Are they not married?

LINCOLN. No, my liege.

BOTH. We are.

KING. Shall I divorce them then? Oh, be it far,
That any hand on earth should dare untie
The sacred knot, knit by God's majesty;
I would not for my crown disjoin their hands,
That are conjoin'd in holy nuptial bands.
How say'st thou, Lacy, wouldst thou lose thy Rose?

LACY. Not for all India's wealth, my sovereign.

KING. But Rose, I am sure, her Lacy would forgo. 80

ROSE. If Rose were asked that question, she'd say no.

KING. You hear them, Lincoln?

LINCOLN. Yea, my liege, I do.

KING. Yet canst thou find i'th' heart to part these two?
Who seeks, besides you, to divorce these lovers?

LORD MAYOR. I do, my gracious lord; I am her father.

KING. Sir Roger Oteley, our last mayor, I think?

NOBLEMAN. The same, my liege.

KING. Would you offend Love's laws?
Well, you shall have your wills. You sue to me
To prohibit the match. Soft, let me see—
You are both married, Lacy, art thou not? 90

LACY. I am, dread sovereign.

KING. Then, upon thy life,
I charge thee not to call this woman wife.

LORD MAYOR. I thank your grace.

ROSE. O my most gracious lord! [*Kneel.*

KING. Nay, Rose, never woo me; I tell you true,
Although as yet I am a bachelor,
Yet I believe I shall not marry you.

ROSE. Can you divide the body from the soul,
Yet make the body live?

KING. Yea, so profound?
I cannot, Rose, but you I must divide.
Fair maid, this bridegroom cannot be your bride. 100
Are you pleased, Lincoln? Oteley, are you pleased?

BOTH. Yes, my lord.

KING. Then must my heart be eased;
For, credit me, my conscience lives in pain,
Till these whom I divorced, be joined again.
Lacy, give me thy hand; Rose, lend me thine!
Be what you would be! Kiss now! So, that's fine.
At night, lovers, to bed!—Now, let me see,
Which of you all mislikes this harmony.

LORD MAYOR. Will you then take from me my child perforce?

KING. Why, tell me, Oteley: shines not Lacy's name 110
As bright in the world's eye as the gay beams
Of any citizen?

LINCOLN. Yea, but, my gracious lord,
I do mislike the match far more than he;
Her blood is too too base.

KING. Lincoln, no more.
Dost thou not know that love respects no blood,
Cares not for difference of birth or state?
The maid is young, well-born, fair, virtuous,
A worthy bride for any gentleman.
Besides, your nephew for her sake did stoop
To bare necessity, and, as I hear, 120
Forgetting honors and all courtly pleasures,
To gain her love became a shoemaker.
As for the honor which he lost in France,
Thus I redeem it: Lacy, kneel thee down!—
Arise, Sir Rowland Lacy! Tell me now,
Tell me in earnest, Oteley, canst thou chide,
Seeing thy Rose a lady and a bride?

LORD MAYOR. I am content with what your grace hath done.

LINCOLN. And I, my liege, since there's no remedy.

KING. Come on, then; all shake hands: I'll have you friends; 130
Where there is much love, all discord ends.
What says my mad lord mayor to all this love?

EYRE. O my liege, this honor you have done to my fine journeyman here, Rowland Lacy, and all these favors which you have shown to me this day in my poor house, will make Simon Eyre live longer by one dozen of warm summers more than he should.

KING. Nay, my mad lord mayor—that shall be thy name,—
If any grace of mine can length thy life, 140
One honor more I'll do thee: that new building,
Which at thy cost in Cornhill is erected,
Shall take a name from us; we'll have it called
The Leadenhall, because in digging it
You found the lead that covereth the same.

EYRE. I thank your majesty.

MARGERY. God bless your grace!

KING. Lincoln, a word with you!

Enter HODGE, FIRK, RALPH, *and more* SHOEMAKERS.

EYRE. How now, my mad knaves? Peace; speak softly; yonder is the king.

KING. With the old troop which there we keep in pay
We will incorporate a new supply. 150
Before one summer more pass o'er my head,
France shall repent England was injuréd.
What are all those?

LACY. All shoemakers, my liege,
Sometimes my fellows; in their companies
I lived as merry as an emperor.

KING. My mad lord mayor, are all these shoemakers?

EYRE. All shoemakers, my liege; all gentlemen of the gentle craft, true Trojans, courageous cordwainers; they all kneel to the shrine of holy St. Hugh. 160

ALL THE SHOEMAKERS. God save your majesty!

KING. Mad Simon, would they anything with us?

EYRE. Mum, mad knaves! Not a word! I'll do't; I warrant you.—They are all beggars, my liege; all for themselves, and I for them all, on both my knees do entreat that for the honor of poor Simon Eyre and the good of his brethren, these mad knaves, your grace would vouchsafe some privilege to my new Leadenhall, that it may be lawful for us to buy and sell leather there two days a week. 173

KING. Mad Sim, I grant your suit; you shall have patent
To hold two market-days in Leadenhall;
Mondays and Fridays, those shall be the times.
Will this content you?

ALL. Jesus bless your grace!

EYRE. In the name of these my poor brethren shoemakers, I most humbly thank your grace. But before I rise, seeing you are in the giving vein and we in the begging, grant Sim Eyre one boon more. 182

KING. What is it, my lord mayor?

EYRE. Vouchsafe to taste of a poor banquet that stands sweetly waiting for your sweet presence.

KING. I shall undo thee, Eyre, only with feasts;
Already have I been too troublesome;
Say, have I not? 189

EYRE. O my dear king, Sim Eyre was taken unawares upon a day of shroving, which I promised long ago to the prentices of London. For, an't please your highness, in time past,
I bare the water-tankard, and my coat
Sits not a whit the worse upon my back;
And then, upon a morning, some mad boys,—
It was Shrove Tuesday, even as 'tis now,— 198
gave me my breakfast; and I swore then by the stopple of my tankard, if ever I came to be lord mayor of London, I would feast all the prentices. This day, my liege, I did it, and the slaves had an hundred tables five times covered; they are gone home and vanished;
Yet add more honor to the gentle trade;
Taste of Eyre's banquet, Simon's happy made.

KING. Eyre, I will taste of thy banquet, and will say
I have not met more pleasure on a day. 209
Friends of the gentle craft, thanks to you all,
Thanks, my kind lady mayoress, for our cheer.—
Come, lords, a while let's revel it at home!
When all our sports and banquetings are done,
Wars must right wrongs which Frenchmen have begun. [*Exeunt.*

FRANCIS BACON

1561–1626

Francis Bacon was a younger son of Sir Nicholas Bacon, lord keeper of the great seal under Queen Elizabeth. His mother was the sister-in-law of Lord Burghley, long Elizabeth's trusted adviser, so that it may fairly be said that Bacon was born a member of the governing class of England; and as one destined for public service he was brought up. In 1573 he went to Trinity College, Cambridge, staying there until the end of 1575. In 1576 he entered Gray's Inn to study the law, leaving in 1577, however, for two years' residence in France in the household of the English ambassador. The death of his father in 1579 left him to shift largely for himself, and he turned immediately to the law. He was admitted an utter barrister in 1582. In 1584 he entered Parliament and thus actively began his long political career. He persistently sought advancement through the friendship of the great—through Lord Burghley, then through the Earl of Essex, and then through Sir Robert Cecil, Burghley's son—and he sought to deserve friendship by his statesmanlike advice. His abilities were striking and his advice was good; yet the opening he wanted to a great career was long denied him. He was knighted in 1603, at the accession of James; in 1607 he was made solicitor-general, in 1613 attorney-general, in 1616 privy councilor, in 1617 lord keeper of the great seal, and in 1618 lord chancellor. In the same year he was created Baron Verulam, and in 1621 Viscount St. Alban. Later in 1621, however, came his sudden and complete downfall. He was impeached on the charge of bribery, confessed his guilt, and was sentenced by the House of Lords to a fine of £40,000 and to imprisonment in the Tower during the king's pleasure, while he was disabled from sitting in Parliament and from coming within the verge, i. e., within twelve miles, of the Court. The fine was immediately converted into a trust fund for Bacon's use and his imprisonment lasted only a few days; within a year, too, he was allowed again to present himself at Court; but his exclusion from Parliament was not relaxed, and Bacon was politically a broken man. The remaining years of his life were devoted to study and writing. Born on 22 January, 1561, he died on 9 April, 1626.

Pope called Bacon "the wisest, brightest, meanest of mankind," and the line has stuck. Yet, while no one would for a moment contend that Bacon had either the elevation of character or the detachment of a saint, it is no less certain that he has suffered from grave misunderstanding. While not condoning his moral obtuseness, one should in justice remember that he simply suffered from the defects, as he enjoyed the advantages, of the clearly marked type of mind to which we owe the achievements of modern science. Morality is concerned with imperfectly realized ideals, it seeks to bend men to the commands of an invisible kingdom. Bacon, on the other hand, saw things and men as they are, and viewed his world as a field for the realization of human purposes.

In politics he undoubtedly wished to find a place for himself, and in this took, not a mean, but a common-sense view of his situation. No less clearly, however, he wanted to use his power when he obtained it for public ends, for furthering the greatness of his country and bettering the condition of its members. And for the achievement of his personal and public purposes he followed what, as things were in his day, was the only practicable method—the method of rising through favor of the great. If he was blind to the loss of dignity involved in seeking such favor, this was because his mind was centered on his end and because he judged means simply in relation to their probable efficacy. Again, in accepting gifts as a judge, Bacon merely followed the common custom of his day, and he was more scrupulous than other judges in that he appears not to have allowed the gifts to bias his judgments. If we may smile at the naïveté which blinded him to the enmities this was bound to arouse, still we cannot avoid agreement with his own statement. "I was," he said, "the justest judge that was in

England these fifty years, but it was the justest sentence in Parliament that was these two hundred years."

When he was a young man Bacon wrote, in a letter hinting his desire for preferment, "I have as vast contemplative ends as I have moderate civil ends; for I have taken all knowledge to be my province." This was the second of the two related purposes of his life. A child of the Renaissance both in the vastness of his outlook and in his confidence in human powers, he saw the importance of knowledge in life as he understood it. And as he sought in public life an opportunity for the application of knowledge to the betterment of the condition of his country and its inhabitants, so he sought also to map out the field of knowledge and to elaborate a right method for its discovery. The former he attempted to achieve in *The Advancement of Learning* (1605) and, more fully, in the amplified Latin version of that book published in 1623. His imperfect formulation of scientific method is contained in his *Novum Organum* (1620). His fragmentary *New Atlantis* is a literary picture of the advantages to man which he saw in the pursuit of science. His *History of Henry VII,* one of the fruits of his retirement after 1621, is a masterly historical work which also occupies a deservedly high place in literature. But to most readers Bacon will always be known chiefly through his *Essays,* those "dispersed meditations," "set down rather significantly than curiously," on which, in all probability, he never supposed that his fame would largely depend. Ten essays were published in 1597; in the second edition of 1612 they had grown to thirty-eight; and in the third edition of 1625 there were fifty-eight, while many of the earlier essays were amplified. They probably take their title from Montaigne's *Essais* (1580), though the two books have little in common save that both consist of dispersed notes on life set down by a man of the world. Bacon's *Essays* introduced a new form into English literature; and they represent the man as he was, shrewd, incisive, somewhat hard, and yet on occasion finely imaginative.

The Works of Francis Bacon, ed. James Spedding, Robert L. Ellis, Douglas D. Heath, revised edition (New York, 1869), contains the *Essays* in vol. XII; a more up-to-date edition is the volume *Essays, Advancement of Learning, New Atlantis, and Other Pieces,* ed. Richard F. Jones (Garden City, 1937). For a sympathetic study of Bacon as a man see James Spedding, *The Letters and Life of Francis Bacon, Including All his Occasional Works* (London, 1861–1874); Lytton Strachey's *Elizabeth and Essex, a Tragic History* (New York, 1928) gives an effective and damaging portrait of the younger Bacon. Two studies which deal with Bacon's intellectual importance are Basil Willey, *The Seventeenth Century Background; Studies in the Thought of the Age in Relation to Poetry and Religion* (London, 1934), and Richard F. Jones, *Ancients and Moderns, a Study in the Background of the Battle of the Books* (St. Louis, 1936).

ESSAYS OR COUNSELS CIVIL AND MORAL

1.—Of Truth

"WHAT is truth?" said jesting Pilate,[1] and would not stay for an answer. Certainly there be that delight in giddiness, and count it a bondage to fix a belief; affecting free-will in thinking, as well as in acting. And though the sects of philosophers of that kind be gone, yet there remain certain discoursing wits which are of the same veins, though there be not so much blood in them as was in those of the ancients. But it is not only the difficulty and labor which men take in finding out of truth, nor again that when it is found it imposeth upon men's thoughts, that doth bring lies in favor; but a natural though corrupt love of the lie itself. One of the later school of the Grecians examineth the matter, and is at a stand to think what should be in it that men should love lies; where neither they make for pleasure, as with poets; nor for advantage, as with the merchant; but for the lie's sake. But I cannot tell: this same truth is a naked and open day-light that doth not show the masques and mummeries and triumphs of the world half so stately and daintily as candle-lights. Truth may perhaps come to the price of a pearl, that showeth best by day; but it will not rise to the price of a diamond or carbuncle, that showeth best in varied lights. A mixture of a lie doth ever add pleasure. Doth any man doubt that if

[1] Cf. St. John, 18:38.

there were taken out of men's minds vain opinions, flattering hopes, false valuations, imaginations as one would, and the like, but it would leave the minds of a number of men poor shrunken things, full of melancholy and indisposition, and unpleasing to themselves? One of the fathers, in great severity, called poesy *vinum daemonum*,[2] because it filleth the imagination, and yet it is but with the shadow of a lie. But it is not the lie that passeth through the mind, but the lie that sinketh in and settleth in it, that doth the hurt, such as we spake of before. But howsoever these things are thus in men's depraved judgments and affections, yet truth, which only doth judge itself, teacheth that the inquiry of truth, which is the lovemaking or wooing of it, the knowledge of truth, which is the presence of it, and the belief of truth, which is the enjoying of it, is the sovereign good of human nature. The first creature of God, in the works of the days, was the light of the sense; the last was the light of reason; and his sabbath work, ever since, is the illumination of his Spirit. First he breathed light upon the face of the matter or chaos; then he breathed light into the face of man; and still he breatheth and inspireth light into the face of his chosen. The poet[3] that beautified the sect[4] that was otherwise inferior to the rest, saith yet excellently well: "It is a pleasure to stand upon the shore, and to see ships tossed upon the sea: a pleasure to stand in the window of a castle, and to see a battle and the adventures thereof below: but no pleasure is comparable to the standing upon the vantage ground of truth" (a hill not to be commanded, and where the air is always clear and serene), "and to see the errors, and wanderings, and mists, and tempests, in the vale below": so always that this prospect be with pity, and not with swelling or pride. Certainly, it is heaven upon earth to have a man's mind move in charity, rest in providence, and turn upon the poles of truth.

To pass from theological and philosophical truth to the truth of civil business: it will be acknowledged, even by those that practice it not, that clear and round[5] dealing is the honor of man's nature; and that mixture of falsehood is like alloy in coin of gold and silver, which may make the metal work the better, but it embaseth it. For these winding and crooked courses are the goings of the serpent; which goeth basely upon the belly, and not upon the feet. There is no vice that doth so cover a man with shame as to be found false and perfidious. And therefore Montaigne saith prettily, when he inquired the reason why the word of the lie should be such a disgrace and such an odious charge? saith he: "If it be well weighed, to say that a man lieth is as much to say as that he is brave towards God and a coward towards men."[6] For a lie faces God, and shrinks from man. Surely the wickedness of falsehood and breach of faith cannot possibly be so highly expressed, as in that it shall be the last peal to call the judgments of God upon the generations of men; it being foretold that when Christ cometh, "he shall not find faith upon the earth."[7]

5.—*Of Adversity*

It was an high speech of Seneca (after the manner of the Stoics), "That the good things which belong to prosperity are to be wished; but the good things that belong to adversity are to be admired." *Bona rerum secundarum optabilia, adversarum mirabilia.* Certainly, if miracles be the command over nature, they appear most in adversity. It is yet a higher speech of his than the other (much too high for a heathen), "It is true greatness to have in one the frailty of a man, and the security of a god." *Vere magnum, habere fragilitatem hominis, securitatem dei.*[1] This would have done better in poesy, where transcendences[2] are more allowed. And the poets indeed have been busy with it; for it is in effect the thing which is

[2]Wine of devils. A phrase of similar meaning is used by Augustine (*Confessions,* I, xvi, 26).

[3]Lucretius. Bacon paraphrases a passage at the beginning of Bk. II of Lucretius's poem *On the Nature of Things.*

[4]The Epicureans.

[5]Straightforward. [6]*Essays,* II, 18.

[7]St. Luke, 18:8.

[1]Both passages are inexactly quoted from Seneca's *Epistles.*

[2]Exaggerations.

figured in that strange fiction of the ancient poets, which seemeth not to be without mystery; nay, and to have some approach to the state of a Christian: that "Hercules, when he went to unbind Prometheus (by whom human nature is represented), sailed the length of the great ocean in an earthen pot or pitcher": lively describing Christian resolution, that saileth in the frail bark of the flesh through the waves of the world. But to speak in a mean.[3] The virtue of prosperity is temperance; the virtue of adversity is fortitude, which in morals is the more heroical virtue. Prosperity is the blessing of the Old Testament; adversity is the blessing of the New, which carrieth the greater benediction, and the clearer revelation of God's favor. Yet even in the Old Testament, if you listen to David's harp, you shall hear as many hearse-like airs as carols; and the pencil of the Holy Ghost hath labored more in describing the afflictions of Job than the felicities of Solomon. Prosperity is not without many fears and distastes; and adversity is not without comforts and hopes. We see in needleworks and embroideries, it is more pleasing to have a lively work upon a sad and solemn ground, than to have a dark and melancholy work upon a lightsome ground: judge therefore of the pleasure of the heart by the pleasure of the eye. Certainly virtue is like precious odors, most fragrant when they are incensed or crushed: for prosperity doth best discover vice; but adversity doth best discover virtue.

6.—*Of Simulation and Dissimulation*

Dissimulation is but a faint kind of policy or wisdom; for it asketh a strong wit and a strong heart to know when to tell truth, and to do it. Therefore it is the weaker sort of politics[1] that are the great dissemblers.

Tacitus saith: "Livia sorted well with the arts of her husband and dissimulation of her son";[2] attributing arts or policy to Augustus, and dissimulation to Tiberius. And again, when Mucianus encourageth Vespasian to take arms against Vitellius, he saith: "We rise not against the piercing judgment of Augustus, nor the extreme caution or closeness of Tiberius."[3] These properties, of arts or policy and dissimulation or closeness, are indeed habits and faculties several and to be distinguished. For if a man have that penetration of judgment as he can discern what things are to be laid open, and what to be secreted, and what to be showed at half lights, and to whom, and when (which indeed are arts of state and arts of life, as Tacitus well calleth them), to him a habit of dissimulation is a hindrance and a poorness. But if a man cannot obtain to that judgment, then it is left to him, generally, to be close, and a dissembler. For where a man cannot choose or vary in particulars, there it is good to take the safest and wariest way in general; like the going softly by one that cannot well see. Certainly the ablest men that ever were have had all an openness and frankness of dealing, and a name of certainty and veracity; but then they were like horses well managed; for they could tell passing well when to stop or turn; and at such times when they thought the case indeed required dissimulation, if then they used it, it came to pass that the former opinion spread abroad of their good faith and clearness of dealing made them almost invisible.

There be three degrees of this hiding and veiling of a man's self. The first, closeness, reservation, and secrecy; when a man leaveth himself without observation, or without hold to be taken, what he is. The second, dissimulation, in the negative; when a man lets fall signs and arguments, that he is not that he is. And the third, simulation, in the affirmative; when a man industriously and expressly feigns and pretends to be that he is not.

For the first of these, secrecy: it is indeed the virtue of a confessor; and assuredly the secret man heareth many confessions; for who will open himself to a blab or a babbler? But if a man be thought secret, it inviteth discovery; as the more close air sucketh in the more open: and as in confession the revealing is not for worldly use, but for the ease of a man's heart, so secret men come

[3]To speak temperately.

[1]Politicians. [2]*Annals,* V, 1.

[3]Tacitus, *Hist.*, II, 76.

to the knowledge of many things in that kind; while men rather discharge their minds than impart their minds. In few words, mysteries are due to secrecy. Besides (to say truth) nakedness is uncomely, as well in mind as body; and it addeth no small reverence to men's manners and actions, if they be not altogether open. As for talkers and futile persons, they are commonly vain and credulous withal. For he that talketh what he knoweth will also talk what he knoweth not. Therefore set it down *that an habit of secrecy is both politic and moral.* And in this part, it is good that a man's face give his tongue leave to speak. For the discovery of a man's self by the tracts[4] of his countenance is a great weakness and betraying; by how much it is many times more marked and believed than a man's words.

For the second, which is dissimulation: it followeth many times upon secrecy by a necessity; so that he that will be secret must be a dissembler in some degree. For men are too cunning to suffer a man to keep an indifferent[5] carriage between both, and to be secret, without swaying the balance on either side. They will so beset a man with questions, and draw him on, and pick it out of him that, without an absurd silence, he must show an inclination one way; or if he do not, they will gather as much by his silence as by his speech. As for equivocations, or oraculous speeches, they cannot hold out long. So that no man can be secret except he give himself a little scope of dissimulation; which is, as it were, but the skirts or train of secrecy.

But for the third degree, which is simulation and false profession: that I hold more culpable, and less politic; except it be in great and rare matters. And therefore a general custom of simulation (which is this last degree) is a vice, rising either of a natural falseness or fearfulness, or of a mind that hath some main faults, which because a man must needs disguise, it maketh him practice simulation in other things, lest his hand should be out of use.

The great advantages of simulation and dissimulation are three. First, to lay asleep opposition, and to surprise. For where a man's intentions are published, it is an alarm to call up all that are against them. The second is, to reserve to a man's self a fair retreat. For if a man engage himself by a manifest declaration, he must go through, or take a fall. The third is, the better to discover the mind of another. For to him that opens himself men will hardly show themselves adverse; but will (fair)[6] let him go on, and turn their freedom of speech to freedom of thought. And therefore it is a good shrewd proverb of the Spaniard, "Tell a lie and find a truth"; as if there were no way of discovery but by simulation. There be also three disadvantages to set it even. The first, that simulation and dissimulation commonly carry with them a show of fearfulness, which in any business doth spoil the feathers of round[7] flying up to the mark. The second, that it puzzleth and perplexeth the conceits[8] of many that perhaps would otherwise co-operate with him, and makes a man walk almost alone to his own ends. The third and greatest is, that it depriveth a man of one of the most principal instruments for action, which is trust and belief. The best composition and temperature[9] is to have openness in fame and opinion; secrecy in habit; dissimulation in seasonable use; and a power to feign, if there be no remedy.

7.—*Of Parents and Children*

THE joys of parents are secret, and so are their griefs and fears: they cannot utter the one, nor they will not utter[1] the other. Children sweeten labors, but they make misfortunes more bitter; they increase the cares of life, but they mitigate the remembrance of death. The perpetuity by generation is common to beasts; but memory, merit, and noble works are proper to men; and surely a man shall see the noblest works and foundations have proceeded from childless men, which have sought to express the images of their minds, where those of their bodies have failed; so the care of posterity is most in them that have no posterity. They that are the first raisers of their houses are most

[4]Features. [5]Impartial.

[6]Rather. [7]I. e., swiftly. [8]Thoughts.
[9]Temperament.
[1]Nor will they utter.

indulgent towards their children, beholding them as the continuance not only of their kind but of their work, and so both children and creatures.

The difference in affection of parents towards their several children is many times unequal, and sometimes unworthy, especially in the mother; as Solomon saith: "A wise son rejoiceth the father, but an ungracious son shames the mother."[2] A man shall see, where there is a house full of children, one or two of the eldest respected, and the youngest made wantons; but in the midst some that are as it were forgotten, who many times nevertheless prove the best. The illiberality of parents in allowance towards their children is an harmful error; makes them base; acquaints them with shifts;[3] makes them sort with mean company; and makes them surfeit more when they come to plenty: and therefore the proof is best when men keep their authority towards their children, but not their purse. Men have a foolish manner (both parents and schoolmasters and servants) in creating and breeding an emulation between brothers during childhood, which many times sorteth to discord when they are men, and disturbeth families. The Italians make little difference between children and nephews or near kinsfolks; but so they be of the lump, they care not though they pass not through their own body. And, to say truth, in nature it is much a like matter; insomuch that we see a nephew sometimes resembleth an uncle or a kinsman more than his own parents, as the blood happens. Let parents choose betimes the vocations and courses they mean their children should take, for then they are most flexible; and let them not too much apply themselves to the disposition of their children, as thinking they will take best to that which they have most mind to. It is true, that if the affection or aptness of the childen be extraordinary, then it is good not to cross it; but generally the precept is good, *Optimum elige, suave et facile illud faciet consuetudo.*[4] Younger brothers are commonly fortunate, but seldom or never where the elder are disinherited.

[2]Proverbs, 10:1. [3]Deceptions.

[4]Choose the best; habit will make it pleasant and easy. (Plutarch attributes this saying to Pythagoras.)

8.—*Of Marriage and Single Life*

He that hath wife and children hath given hostages to fortune; for they are impediments to great enterprises, either of virtue or mischief. Certainly, the best works, and of greatest merit for the public, have proceeded from the unmarried or childless men, which both in affection and means have married and endowed the public. Yet it were great reason that those that have children should have greatest care of future times; unto which they know they must transmit their dearest pledges. Some there are who though they lead a single life, yet their thoughts do end with themselves, and account future times impertinences. Nay, there are some other that account wife and children but as bills of charges. Nay more, there are some foolish rich covetous men that take a pride in having no children, because they may be thought so much the richer. For perhaps they have heard some talk: "Such an one is a great rich man," and another except to it: "Yea, but he hath a great charge of children"; as if it were an abatement to his riches. But the most ordinary cause of a single life is liberty; especially in certain self-pleasing and humorous[1] minds, which are so sensible of every restraint, as they will go near to think their girdles and garters to be bonds and shackles. Unmarried men are best friends, best masters, best servants, but not always best subjects; for they are light to run away; and almost all fugitives are of that condition. A single life doth well with churchmen; for charity will hardly water the ground where it must first fill a pool. It is indifferent for judges and magistrates; for if they be facile and corrupt, you shall have a servant five times worse than a wife. For soldiers, I find the generals commonly in their hortatives[2] put men in mind of their wives and children; and I think the despising of marriage amongst the Turks maketh the vulgar soldier more base. Certainly wife and children are a kind of discipline of

[1]Whimsical. [2]Exhortations.

humanity; and single men, though they be many times more charitable, because their means are less exhaust,[3] yet, on the other side, they are more cruel and hardhearted (good to make severe inquisitors), because their tenderness is not so oft called upon. Grave natures, led by custom, and therefore constant, are commonly loving husbands; as was said of Ulysses, *Vetulam suam praetulit immortalitati.*[4] Chaste women are often proud and froward, as presuming upon the merit of their chastity. It is one of the best bonds both of chastity and obedience in the wife, if she think her husband wise; which she will never do if she find him jealous. Wives are young men's mistresses; companions for middle age; and old men's nurses. So as a man may have a quarrel[5] to marry when he will. But yet he was reputed one of the wise men, that made answer to the question, when a man should marry? "A young man not yet, an elder man not at all."[6] It is often seen that bad husbands have very good wives; whether it be that it raiseth the price of their husband's kindness when it comes, or that the wives take a pride in their patience. But this never fails, if the bad husbands were of their own choosing, against their friends' consent; for then they will be sure to make good their own folly.

10.—Of Love

THE stage is more beholding to love than the life of man. For as to the stage, love is ever matter of comedies, and now and then of tragedies; but in life it doth much mischief, sometimes like a siren, sometimes like a fury. You may observe that amongst all the great and worthy persons (whereof the memory remaineth, either ancient or recent) there is not one that hath been transported to the mad degree of love; which shows that great spirits and great business do keep out this weak passion. You must except, nevertheless, Marcus Antonius,[1] the half partner of the empire of Rome, and Appius Claudius,[2] the decemvir and lawgiver: whereof the former was indeed a voluptuous man, and inordinate; but the latter was an austere and wise man: and therefore it seems (though rarely) that love can find entrance not only into an open heart, but also into a heart well fortified, if watch be not well kept. It is a poor saying of Epicurus, *Satis magnum alter alteri theatrum sumus:*[3] as if man, made for the contemplation of heaven and all noble objects, should do nothing but kneel before a little idol, and make himself subject, though not of the mouth (as beasts are), yet of the eye, which was given them for higher purposes. It is a strange thing to note the excess of this passion, and how it braves[4] the nature and value of things, by this, that the speaking in a perpetual hyperbole is comely in nothing but in love. Neither is it merely in the phrase; for whereas it hath been well said[5] that the arch-flatterer, with whom all the petty flatterers have intelligence, is a man's self, certainly the lover is more. For there was never proud man thought so absurdly well of himself as the lover doth of the person loved; and therefore it was well said: "That it is impossible to love and to be wise."[6] Neither doth this weakness appear to others only, and not to the party loved, but to the loved most of all, except the love be reciprocal. For it is a true rule, that love is ever rewarded either with the reciproque[7] or with an inward and secret contempt. By how much the more men ought to beware of this passion, which loseth not only other things, but itself. As for the other losses, the poet's relation doth well figure them: That he[8] that preferred Helena quitted the gifts of Juno and Pallas. For whosoever esteemeth too much of amorous affection quitteth both riches and wisdom. This passion hath his floods in the very times of weakness; which are great prosperity and great adversity (though this latter

[3]Exhausted.

[4]He preferred his aged wife to immortality (which had been offered him by Calypso).

[5]An excuse.

[6]The saying is ascribed by Plutarch to Thales, one of the "seven wise men" of Greece.

[1]Cleopatra's lover.

[2]The lover of Virginia.

[3]We are to one another an ample spectacle (quoted by Seneca, *Epistles*, I, vii, 11).

[4]Exaggerates. [5]By Plutarch.

[6]By Publius Syrus. [7]Returned affection.

[8]Paris.

hath been less observed): both which times kindle love, and make it more fervent, and therefore show it to be the child of folly. They do best who, if they cannot but admit love, yet make it keep quarter,[9] and sever it wholly from their serious affairs and actions of life; for if it check[10] once with business, it troubleth men's fortunes, and maketh men that they can no ways be true to their own ends. I know not how, but martial men are given to love: I think it is but as they are given to wine; for perils commonly ask to be paid in pleasures. There is in man's nature a secret inclination and motion towards love of others, which, if it be not spent upon some one or a few, doth naturally spread itself towards many, and maketh men become humane and charitable; as it is seen sometime in friars. Nuptial love maketh mankind; friendly love perfecteth it; but wanton love corrupteth and embaseth it.

11.—*Of Great Place*

MEN in great places are thrice servants: servants of the sovereign or state; servants of fame; and servants of business. So as they have no freedom, neither in their persons, nor in their actions, nor in their times. It is a strange desire, to seek power and to lose liberty; or to seek power over others and to lose power over a man's self. The rising unto place is laborious, and by pains men come to greater pains; and it is sometimes base, and by indignities men come to dignities. The standing is slippery; and the regress is either a downfall, or at least an eclipse, which is a melancholy thing. *Cum non sis qui fueris, non esse cur velis vivere.*[1] Nay, retire men cannot when they would; neither will they when it were reason; but are impatient of privateness, even in age and sickness, which require the shadow:[2] like old townsmen, that will be still sitting at their street door, though thereby they offer age to scorn. Certainly, great persons had need to borrow other men's opinions to think themselves happy; for if they judge by their own feeling, they cannot find it: but if they think with themselves what other men think of them, and that other men would fain be as they are, then they are happy as it were by report, when perhaps they find the contrary within. For they are the first that find their own griefs, though they be the last that find their own faults. Certainly, men in great fortunes are strangers to themselves, and while they are in the puzzle of business they have no time to tend their health, either of body or mind. *Illi mors gravis incubat, qui notus nimis omnibus, ignotus moritur sibi.*[3] In place there is license to do good and evil; whereof the latter is a curse: for in evil the best condition is not to will, the second not to can.[4] But power to do good is the true and lawful end of aspiring. For good thoughts (though God accept them) yet towards men are little better than good dreams, except they be put in act; and that cannot be without power and place, as the vantage and commanding ground. Merit and good works is the end of man's motion; and conscience[5] of the same is the accomplishment of man's rest. For if a man can be partaker of God's theater, he shall likewise be partaker of God's rest. *Et conversus Deus ut aspiceret opera quae fecerunt manus suae, vidit quod omnia essent bona nimis;*[6] and then the Sabbath. In the discharge of thy place, set before thee the best examples; for imitation is a globe[7] of precepts. And after a time set before thee thine own example; and examine thyself strictly, whether thou didst not best at first. Neglect not also the examples of those that have carried themselves ill in the same place; not to set off thyself by taxing their memory, but to direct thyself what to avoid. Reform, therefore, without bravery[8] or scandal of former times and persons; but yet set it down to thyself as

[9]Keep within bounds. [10]Interfere.

[1]When you are no longer what you were, there is no reason why you should wish to keep on living (Cicero).

[2]Retirement.

[3]Sad is the fate of him who ends his days all too well known to others, but a stranger to himself (Seneca, *Thyestes*).

[4]To know. [5]Consciousness.

[6]And God, turning back to look upon the works which his hands had made, saw that all were very good (Genesis, 1:31, quoted inexactly from the Vulgate).

[7]A complete or perfect body. [8]Boast.

well to create good precedents as to follow them. Reduce things to the first institution, and observe wherein and how they have degenerate; but yet ask counsel of both times; of the ancient time, what is best; and of the latter time, what is fittest. Seek to make thy course regular, that men may know beforehand what they may expect; but be not too positive and peremptory; and express thyself well when thou digressest from thy rule. Preserve the right of thy place, but stir not questions of jurisdiction: and rather assume thy right in silence and *de facto*[9] than voice it with claims and challenges. Preserve likewise the rights of inferior places; and think it more honor to direct in chief than to be busy in all. Embrace and invite helps and advices touching the execution of thy place; and do not drive away such as bring thee information as meddlers, but accept of them in good part. The vices of authority are chiefly four: delays, corruption, roughness, and facility.[10] For delays: give easy access; keep times appointed; go through with that which is in hand; and interlace not business but of necessity. For corruption: do not only bind thine own hands or thy servants' hands from taking, but bind the hands of suitors also from offering. For integrity used doth the one; but integrity professed, and with a manifest detestation of bribery, doth the other. And avoid not only the fault, but the suspicion. Whosoever is found variable, and changeth manifestly without manifest cause, giveth suspicion of corruption. Therefore always when thou changest thine opinion or course, profess it plainly and declare it, together with the reasons that move thee to change; and do not think to steal[11] it. A servant or a favorite, if he be inward,[12] and no other apparent cause of esteem, is commonly thought but a by-way to close corruption. For roughness, it is a needless cause of discontent: severity breedeth fear, but roughness breedeth hate. Even reproofs from authority ought to be grave, and not taunting. As for facility, it is worse than bribery. For bribes come but now and then; but if importunity or idle respects[13] lead a man, he shall never be without. As Solomon saith: "To respect persons is not good; for such a man will transgress for a piece of bread."[14] It is most true that was anciently spoken, "A place showeth the man": and it showeth some to the better, and some to the worse. *Omnium consensu capax imperii, nisi imperasset,*[15] saith Tacitus of Galba; but of Vespasian he saith, *Solus imperantium Vespasianus mutatus in melius:*[16] though the one was meant of sufficiency,[17] the other of manners and affection. It is an assured sign of a worthy and generous spirit, whom honor amends. For honor is, or should be, the place of virtue; and as in nature things move violently to their place, and calmly in their place; so virtue in ambition is violent, in authority settled and calm. All rising to great place is by a winding stair; and if there be factions, it is good to side a man's self whilst he is in the rising, and to balance himself when he is placed. Use the memory of thy predecessor fairly and tenderly; for if thou dost not, it is a debt will sure be paid when thou art gone. If thou have colleagues, respect them, and rather call them when they look not for it than exclude them when they have reason to look to be called. Be not too sensible or too remembering of thy place in conversation and private answers to suitors; but let it rather be said, "When he sits in place he is another man."

12.—Of Boldness

It is a trivial grammar-school text, but yet worthy a wise man's consideration. Question was asked of Demosthenes, "What was the chief part of an orator?" he answered "Action": what next? "Action": what next again? "Action." He said it that knew it best, and had by nature himself no advantage in that he commended. A strange thing, that that part of an orator which is but superficial, and rather the

[9]As a matter of fact. [10]Lack of firmness.
[11]Hide. [12]Intimate.

[13]Considerations. [14]Proverbs, 28:21.
[15]All men would have thought him competent to rule if they had not seen him as a ruler.
[16]Of all the emperors Vespasian alone changed for the better.
[17]Ability.

virtue of a player, should be placed so high above those other noble parts of invention, elocution, and the rest; nay, almost alone, as if it were all in all. But the reason is plain. There is in human nature generally more of the fool than of the wise; and therefore those faculties by which the foolish part of men's minds is taken are most potent. Wonderful like is the case of boldness in civil business: what first? "Boldness": what second and third? "Boldness." And yet boldness is a child of ignorance and baseness, far inferior to other parts. But nevertheless it doth fascinate and bind hand and foot those that are either shallow in judgment or weak in courage, which are the greatest part; yea, and prevaileth with wise men at weak times. Therefore we see it hath done wonders in popular[1] states, but with senates and princes less; and more ever upon the first entrance of bold persons into action than soon after; for boldness is an ill keeper of promise. Surely, as there are mountebanks for the natural body, so are there mountebanks for the politic body; men that undertake great cures, and perhaps have been lucky in two or three experiments, but want the grounds[2] of science, and therefore cannot hold out. Nay, you shall see a bold fellow many times do Mahomet's miracle. Mahomet made the people believe that he would call an hill to him, and from the top of it offer up his prayers for the observers of his law. The people assembled; Mahomet called the hill to come to him, again and again; and when the hill stood still, he was never a whit abashed, but said: "If the hill will not come to Mahomet, Mahomet will go to the hill." So these men, when they have promised great matters and failed most shamefully, yet (if they have the perfection of boldness) they will but slight it over, and make a turn, and no more ado. Certainly, to men of great judgment, bold persons are a sport to behold; nay, and to the vulgar also, boldness hath somewhat of the ridiculous. For if absurdity be the subject of laughter, doubt you not but great boldness is seldom without some absurdity. Especially it is a sport to see, when a bold fellow is out of countenance; for that puts his face into a

[1]Democratic. [2]Foundations.

most shrunken and wooden posture; as needs it must; for in bashfulness the spirits do a little go and come; but with bold men, upon like occasion, they stand at a stay; like a stale[3] at chess, where it is no mate, but yet the game cannot stir. But this last were fitter for a satire than for a serious observation. This is well to be weighed, that boldness is ever blind; for it seeth not dangers and inconveniences. Therefore it is ill in counsel, good in execution; so that the right use of bold persons is, that they never command in chief, but be seconds, and under the direction of others. For in counsel it is good to see dangers; and in execution not to see them, except they be very great.

16.—Of Atheism

I HAD rather believe all the fables in the Legend,[1] and the Talmud, and the Alcoran,[2] than that this universal frame is without a mind. And therefore God never wrought miracle to convince[3] atheism, because his ordinary works convince it. It is true, that a little philosophy[4] inclineth man's mind to atheism; but depth in philosophy bringeth men's minds about to religion: for while the mind of man looketh upon second causes scattered, it may sometimes rest in them, and go no further; but when it beholdeth the chain of them, confederate and linked together, it must needs fly to Providence and Deity. Nay, even that school which is most accused of atheism doth most demonstrate religion; that is, the school of Leucippus and Democritus and Epicurus. For it is a thousand times more credible that four mutable elements and one immutable fifth essence, duly and eternally placed, need no God than that an army of infinite small portions or seeds unplaced should have produced this order and beauty without a divine marshal. The Scripture saith: "The fool hath said in his heart there is no God":[5] it is not said,

[3]Stale-mate, where the king cannot move, save into check.

[1]The *Legenda Aurea,* a medieval collection of the lives of saints.

[2]Koran. [3]Confute.

[4]Natural philosophy, or science.

[5]Psalms, 14:1, and 53:1.

"The fool hath thought in his heart"; so as he rather saith it by rote to himself, as that he would have, than that he can thoroughly believe it, or be persuaded of it. For none deny there is a God but those for whom it maketh that there were no God. It appeareth in nothing more that atheism is rather in the lip than in the heart of man than by this: that atheists will ever be talking of that their opinion, as if they fainted in it within themselves, and would be glad to be strengthened by the consent of others: nay more, you shall have atheists strive to get disciples, as it fareth with other sects: and, which is most of all, you shall have of them that will suffer for atheism, and not recant; whereas, if they did truly think that there were no such thing as God, why should they trouble themselves? Epicurus is charged that he did but dissemble for his credit's sake, when he affirmed there were blessed natures, but such as enjoyed themselves without having respect to the government of the world. Wherein they say he did temporize, though in secret he thought there was no God. But certainly he is traduced; for his words are noble and divine: *Non deos vulgi negare profanum, sed vulgi opiniones diis applicare profanum.*[6] Plato could have said no more. And although he had the confidence to deny the administration, he had not the power to deny the nature. The Indians of the West have names for their particular gods, though they have no name for God: as if the heathens should have had the names *Jupiter, Apollo, Mars, etc.,* but not the word *Deus;* which shows that even those barbarous people have the notion, though they have not the latitude and extent of it. So that against atheists the very savages take part with the very subtlest philosophers. The contemplative atheist is rare: a Diagoras, a Bion, a Lucian perhaps, and some others; and yet they seem to be more than they are, for that all that impugn a received religion, or superstition, are, by the adverse part, branded with the name of atheists. But the great atheists indeed are hypocrites; which are ever handling holy things, but without feeling; so as they must needs be cauterized in the end. The causes of atheism are: divisions in religion, if they be many; for any one main division addeth zeal to both sides, but many divisions introduce atheism. Another is, scandal of priests; when it is come to that which S. Bernard saith: *Non est jam dicere, ut populus, sic sacerdos; quia nec sic populus, ut sacerdos.*[7] A third is, custom of profane scoffing in holy matters, which doth by little and little deface the reverence of religion. And lastly, learned times, specially with peace and prosperity; for troubles and adversities do more bow men's minds to religion. They that deny a God destroy man's nobility; for certainly man is of kin to the beasts by his body; and if he be not of kin to God by his spirit, he is a base and ignoble creature. It destroys likewise magnanimity, and the raising of human nature; for take an example of a dog, and mark what a generosity and courage he will put on when he finds himself maintained by a man, who to him is in stead of a god, or *melior natura;*[8] which courage is manifestly such as that creature, without that confidence of a better nature than his own, could never attain. So man, when he resteth and assureth himself upon divine protection and favor, gathereth a force and faith which human nature in itself could not obtain. Therefore, as atheism is in all respects hateful, so in this, that it depriveth human nature of the means to exalt itself above human frailty. As it is in particular persons, so it is in nations: never was there such a state for magnanimity as Rome: of this state hear what Cicero saith: *Quam volumus licet, patres conscripti, nos amemus, tamen nec numero Hispanos, nec robore Gallos, nec calliditate Poenos, nec artibus Graecos, nec denique hoc ipso hujus gentis et terrae domestico nativoque sensu Italos ipsos et Latinos; sed pietate, ac religione, atque hac una sapientia, quod Deorum immortalium numine omnia regi gubernarique perspeximus, omnes gentes nationesque superavimus.*[9]

---

[6]It is not impious to say that the gods of men do not exist; it is impious rather to apply to the gods the foolish notions of men (Diogenes Laertius).

[7]It can no longer be said, "As the people are so is the priest," because the people are not now like the priest (i. e., the priest is worse).

[8]Better nature.

[9]We may plume ourselves as we will, O senators, yet we have not conquered the Spaniards by force

23.—Of Wisdom for a Man's Self

An ant is a wise creature for itself, but it is a shrewd[1] thing in an orchard or garden. And certainly men that are great lovers of themselves waste the public. Divide with reason between self-love and society; and be so true to thyself as thou be not false to others, specially to thy king and country. It is a poor center of a man's actions, himself. It is right earth. For that only stands fast upon his own center; whereas all things that have affinity with the heavens move upon the center of another, which they benefit.[2] The referring of all to a man's self is more tolerable in a sovereign prince; because themselves are not only themselves, but their good and evil is at the peril of the public fortune. But it is a desperate evil in a servant to a prince, or a citizen in a republic. For whatsoever affairs pass such a man's hands, he crooketh them to his own ends; which must needs be often eccentric to[3] the ends of his master or state. Therefore let princes, or states, choose such servants as have not this mark; except they mean their service should be made but the accessory. That which maketh the effect more pernicious is that all proportion is lost. It were disproportion enough for the servant's good to be preferred before the master's; but yet it is a greater extreme, when a little good of the servant shall carry things against a great good of the master's. And yet that is the case of bad officers, treasurers, ambassadors, generals, and other false and corrupt servants; which set a bias upon their bowl,[4] of their own petty ends and envies, to the overthrow of their master's great and important affairs. And for the most part, the good such servants receive is after the model of their own fortune; but the hurt they sell for that good is after the model of their master's fortune. And certainly it is the nature of extreme self-lovers, as they will set an house on fire, and it were but to roast their eggs; and yet these men many times hold credit with their masters, because their study is but to please them and profit themselves; and for either respect[5] they will abandon the good of their affairs.

Wisdom for a man's self is, in many branches thereof, a depraved thing. It is the wisdom of rats, that will be sure to leave a house somewhat before it fall. It is the wisdom of the fox, that thrusts out the badger who digged and made room for him. It is the wisdom of crocodiles, that shed tears when they would devour. But that which is specially to be noted is that those which (as Cicero says of Pompey) are *sui amantes sine rivali*[6] are many times unfortunate. And whereas they have all their time sacrificed to themselves, they become in the end themselves sacrifices to the inconstancy of fortune, whose wings they thought by their self-wisdom to have pinioned.

27.—Of Friendship

It had been hard for him that spake it to have put more truth and untruth together in a few words than in that speech: "Whosoever is delighted in solitude is either a wild beast or a god."[1] For it is most true that a natural and secret hatred and aversation[2] towards society, in any man, hath somewhat of the savage beast; but it is most untrue that it should have any character at all of the divine nature; except it proceed, not out of a pleasure in solitude, but out of a love and desire to sequester a man's self for a higher conversation:[3] such as is found to have been falsely and feignedly in some of the heathen; as Epimenides the Candian, Numa the Roman, Empedocles the Sicilian, and Apollonius of Tyana; and truly and really in

of numbers, nor the Gauls by superior might, nor the Carthaginians by strategy, nor the Greeks by our culture, nor lastly the Italians and Latins by the power of internal organization which is peculiar to this people and this land; but it is because of our devotion and our piety and, above all, our realization that human events are ruled and guided by the power of the immortal gods that we have conquered all nations and all peoples.

[1]Mischievous.

[2]Bacon writes in terms of the Ptolemaic astronomy, which he accepted, and according to which the earth is the center of the universe.

[3]Different from.

[4]Place a weight in one side of their ball in bowling.

[5]Consideration.

[6]Lovers of themselves without a rival.

[1]Aristotle, in his *Politics*.

[2]Aversion. [3]Mode of life.

divers of the ancient hermits and holy fathers of the church. But little do men perceive what solitude is, and how far it extendeth. For a crowd is not company, and faces are but a gallery of pictures, and talk but a 5 tinkling cymbal, where there is no love. The Latin adage meeteth with it a little, *Magna civitas, magna solitudo,*[4] because in a great town friends are scattered, so that there is not that fellowship, for the most part, which 10 is in less neighborhoods. But we may go further and affirm most truly that it is a mere and miserable solitude to want true friends, without which the world is but a wilderness; and even in this sense also of 15 solitude, whosoever in the frame of his nature and affections is unfit for friendship, he taketh it of the beast, and not from humanity.

A principal fruit of friendship is the ease 20 and discharge of the fullness and swellings of the heart, which passions of all kinds do cause and induce. We know diseases of stoppings and suffocations are the most dangerous in the body; and it is not much other- 25 wise in the mind: you may take sarza[5] to open the liver, steel to open the spleen, flower of sulphur for the lungs, castoreum[6] for the brain; but no receipt openeth the heart but a true friend, to whom you may 30 impart griefs, joys, fears, hopes, suspicions, counsels, and whatsoever lieth upon the heart to oppress it, in a kind of civil shrift or confession.

It is a strange thing to observe how high 35 a rate great kings and monarchs do set upon this fruit of friendship whereof we speak: so great as they purchase it many times at the hazard of their own safety and greatness. For princes, in regard of the distance of their 40 fortune from that of their subjects and servants, cannot gather this fruit, except (to make themselves capable thereof) they raise some persons to be as it were companions and almost equals to themselves, which 45 many times sorteth to inconvenience. The modern languages give unto such persons the name of favorites, or *privadoes;* as if it were matter of grace, or conversation. But the Roman name attaineth the true use and 50 cause thereof, naming them *participes curarum,*[7] for it is that which tieth the knot. And we see plainly that this hath been done, not by weak and passionate princes only, but by the wisest and most politic that ever reigned; who have oftentimes joined to themselves some of their servants, whom both themselves have called friends, and allowed others likewise to call them in the same manner, using the word which is received between private men.

L. Sylla, when he commanded Rome, raised Pompey (after surnamed the Great) to that height that Pompey vaunted himself for Sylla's overmatch. For when he had carried the consulship for a friend of his, against the pursuit of Sylla, and that Sylla did a little resent thereat, and began to speak great, Pompey turned upon him again, and in effect bade him be quiet, "for that more men adored the sun rising than the sun setting."[8] With Julius Caesar, Decimus Brutus had obtained that interest as he set him down in his testament for heir in remainder after his nephew. And this was the man that had power with him to draw him forth to his death. For when Caesar would have discharged the senate, in regard of some ill presages, and specially a dream of Calpurnia, this man lifted him gently by the arm out of his chair telling him he hoped he would not dismiss the senate till his wife had dreamed a better dream.[9] And it seemeth his favor was so great as Antonius, in a letter which is recited *verbatim* in one of Cicero's *Philippics,* calleth him *venefica,* "witch"; as if he had enchanted Caesar. Augustus raised Agrippa (though of mean birth) to that height as, when he consulted with Maecenas about the marriage of his daughter Julia, Maecenas took the liberty to tell him, "that he must either marry his daughter to Agrippa, or take away his life; there was no third way, he had made him so great."[10] With Tiberius Caesar, Sejanus had ascended to that height, as they two were termed and reckoned as a pair of friends. Tiberius in a letter to him saith, *Haec pro amicitia nostra*

[4]A great city is a great solitude.

[5]Sarsaparilla. [6]A secretion of the beaver.

[7]Partners of their sorrows.

[8]Plutarch, *Life of Pompey.*

[9]Plutarch, *Life of Caesar.*

[10]Dion Cassius, LVI, 6.

non occultavi;[11] and the whole senate dedicated an altar to Friendship, as to a goddess, in respect of the great dearness of friendship between them two. The like or more was between Septimius Severus and Plautianus. For he forced his eldest son to marry the daughter of Plautianus, and would often maintain Plautianus in doing affronts to his son, and did write also in a letter to the senate by these words: "I love the man so well as I wish he may over-live me."[12] Now if these princes had been as a Trajan, or a Marcus Aurelius, a man might have thought that this had proceeded of an abundant goodness of nature; but being men so wise, for such strength and severity of mind, and so extreme lovers of themselves, as all these were, it proveth most plainly that they found their own felicity (though as great as ever happened to mortal men) but as an half piece, except they might have a friend to make it entire: and yet, which is more, they were princes that had wives, sons, nephews; and yet all these could not supply the comfort of friendship.

It is not to be forgotten, what Commineus[13] observeth of his first master, Duke Charles the Hardy; namely, that he would communicate his secrets with none; and least of all, those secrets which troubled him most. Whereupon he goeth on and saith that towards his latter time "that closeness did impair and a little perish his understanding." Surely Commineus might have made the same judgment also, if it had pleased him, of his second master, Lewis the Eleventh, whose closeness was indeed his tormentor. The parable of Pythagoras is dark, but true; *Cor ne edito,* "Eat not the heart." Certainly, if a man would give it a hard phrase, those that want friends to open themselves unto are cannibals of their own hearts. But one thing is most admirable (wherewith I will conclude this first fruit of friendship), which is, that this communicating of a man's self to his friend works two contrary effects; for it redoubleth joys, and cutteth griefs in halfs. For there is no man that imparteth his joys to his friend but he joyeth the more; and no man that imparteth his griefs to his friend but he grieveth the less. So that it is in truth of operation upon a man's mind, of like virtue as the alchemists use to attribute to their stone for man's body, that it worketh all contrary effects, but still to the good and benefit of nature. But yet, without praying in aid[14] of alchemists, there is a manifest image of this in the ordinary course of nature. For in bodies, union strengtheneth and cherisheth any natural action, and, on the other side, weakeneth and dulleth any violent impression; and even so is it of minds.

The second fruit of friendship is healthful and sovereign for the understanding, as the first is for the affections. For friendship maketh indeed a fair day in the affections, from storm and tempests; but it maketh daylight in the understanding, out of darkness and confusion of thoughts. Neither is this to be understood only of faithful counsel, which a man receiveth from his friend; but before you come to that, certain it is that whosoever hath his mind fraught with many thoughts, his wits and understanding do clarify and break up, in the communicating and discoursing with another: he tosseth his thoughts more easily; he marshaleth them more orderly; he seeth how they look when they are turned into words; finally, he waxeth wiser than himself, and that more by an hour's discourse than by a day's meditation. It was well said by Themistocles to the king of Persia, "that speech was like cloth of Arras, opened and put abroad; whereby the imagery doth appear in figure; whereas in thoughts they lie but as in packs."[15] Neither is this second fruit of friendship, in opening the understanding, restrained only to such friends as are able to give a man counsel (they indeed are best); but even without that, a man learneth of himself, and bringeth his own thoughts to light, and whetteth his wits as against a stone, which itself cuts not. In a word, a man were better relate himself to a statue or picture than to suffer his thoughts to pass in smother.

[11] Such is our friendship that even this I have not kept from you (Tacitus, *Annals,* IV, 40).

[12] Dion Cassius, LXXV, 15.

[13] Philippe de Comines, the French historian (*c.* 1445–1519).

[14] Calling in the aid.

[15] Plutarch, *Life of Themistocles.*

Add now, to make this second fruit of friendship complete, that other point, which lieth more open, and falleth within vulgar observation; which is faithful counsel from a friend. Heraclitus saith well in one of his enigmas: "Dry light is ever the best." And certain it is that the light that a man receiveth by counsel from another is drier and purer than that which cometh from his own understanding and judgment; which is ever infused and drenched in his affections and customs. So as there is as much difference between the counsel that a friend giveth, and that a man giveth himself, as there is between the counsel of a friend and of a flatterer. For there is no such flatterer as is a man's self; and there is no such remedy against flattery of a man's self as the liberty of a friend. Counsel is of two sorts; the one concerning manners, the other concerning business. For the first: the best preservative to keep the mind in health is the faithful admonition of a friend. The calling of a man's self to a strict account is a medicine, sometime, too piercing and corrosive. Reading good books of morality is a little flat and dead. Observing our faults in others is sometimes unproper for our case. But the best receipt (best, I say, to work, and best to take) is the admonition of a friend. It is a strange thing to behold what gross errors and extreme absurdities many (especially of the greater sort) do commit, for want of a friend to tell them of them, to the great damage both of their fame and fortune. For as S. James saith, they are as men, "that look sometimes into a glass, and presently forget their own shape and favor."[16] As for business, a man may think, if he will, that two eyes see no more than one; or that a gamester seeth always more than a looker-on; or that a man in anger is as wise as he that hath said over the four and twenty letters; or that a musket may be shot off as well upon the arm as upon a rest; and such other fond and high imaginations, to think himself all in all. But when all is done, the help of good counsel is that which setteth business straight. And if any man think that he will take counsel, but it shall be by pieces; asking counsel in one business of one man, and in another business of another man; it is well (that is to say, better perhaps than if he asked none at all); but he runneth two dangers. One, that he shall not be faithfully counseled; for it is a rare thing except it be from a perfect and entire friend to have counsel given, but such as shall be bowed and crooked to some ends which he hath that giveth it. The other, that he shall have counsel given, hurtful and unsafe (though with good meaning), and mixed partly of mischief and partly of remedy: even as if you would call a physician that is thought good for the cure of the disease you complain of, but is unacquainted with your body; and therefore may put you in way for a present cure, but overthroweth your health in some other kind; and so cure the disease and kill the patient. But a friend that is wholly acquainted with a man's estate will beware, by furthering any present business, how he dasheth upon other inconvenience. And therefore rest not upon scattered counsels; they will rather distract and mislead than settle and direct.

After these two noble fruits of friendship (peace in the affections, and support of the judgment) followeth the last fruit, which is like the pomegranate, full of many kernels; I mean aid and bearing a part in all actions and occasions. Here the best way to represent to life the manifold use of friendship is to cast and see how many things there are which a man cannot do himself; and then it will appear that it was a sparing speech of the ancients to say, "that a friend is another himself"; for that a friend is far more than himself. Men have their time, and die many times in desire of some things which they principally take to heart; the bestowing of a child, the finishing of a work, or the like. If a man have a true friend, he may rest almost secure that the care of those things will continue after him. So that a man hath as it were two lives in his desires. A man hath a body, and that body is confined to a place; but where friendship is, all offices of life are as it were granted to him and his deputy. For he may exercise them by his friend. How many things are there which a man cannot, with any face or comeliness, say or do himself! A man can scarce allege his

[16] St. James, 1:23–24.

own merits with modesty, much less extol them; a man cannot sometimes brook to supplicate or beg; and a number of the like. But all these things are graceful in a friend's mouth, which are blushing in a man's own. So again, a man's person hath many proper relations which he cannot put off. A man cannot speak to his son but as a father; to his wife but as a husband; to his enemy but upon terms: whereas a friend may speak as the case requires, and not as it sorteth with the person. But to enumerate these things were endless: I have given the rule, where a man cannot fitly play his own part: if he have not a friend, he may quit the stage.

42.—Of Youth and Age

A MAN that is young in years may be old in hours, if he have lost no time. But that happeneth rarely. Generally, youth is like the first cogitations, not so wise as the second. For there is a youth in thoughts as well as in ages. And yet the invention of young men is more lively than that of the old; and imaginations stream into their minds better, and, as it were, more divinely. Natures that have much heat, and great and violent desires and perturbations, are not ripe for action till they have passed the meridian of their years: as it was with Julius Caesar, and Septimius Severus. Of the latter of whom it is said, *Juventutem egit erroribus, imo furoribus, plenam.*[1] And yet he was the ablest emperor, almost, of all the list. But reposed natures may do well in youth. As it is seen in Augustus Caesar, Cosmus, Duke of Florence,[2] Gaston de Foix, and others. On the other side, heat and vivacity in age is an excellent composition for business. Young men are fitter to invent than to judge; fitter for execution than for counsel; and fitter for new projects than for settled business. For the experience of age, in things that fall within the compass of it, directeth them; but in new things, abuseth them. The errors of young men are the ruin of business; but the errors of aged men amount but to this, that more might have been done, or sooner. Young men, in the conduct and manage[3] of actions, embrace more than they can hold; stir more than they can quiet; fly to the end, without consideration of the means and degrees; pursue some few principles which they have chanced upon absurdly; care[4] not to innovate, which draws unknown inconveniences; use extreme remedies at first; and, that which doubleth all errors, will not acknowledge or retract them, like an unready horse that will neither stop nor turn. Men of age object too much, consult too long, adventure too little, repent too soon, and seldom drive business home to the full period, but content themselves with a mediocrity of success. Certainly, it is good to compound employments of both; for that will be good for the present, because the virtues of either age may correct the defects of both; and good for succession, that young men may be learners, while men in age are actors; and, lastly, good for extern[5] accidents, because authority followeth old men, and favor and popularity youth. But for the moral part, perhaps youth will have the pre-eminence, as age hath for the politic. A certain rabbin, upon the text, "Your young men shall see visions, and your old men shall dream dreams,"[6] inferreth that young men are admitted nearer to God than old, because vision is a clearer revelation than a dream. And certainly, the more a man drinketh of the world, the more it intoxicateth; and age doth profit rather in the powers of understanding than in the virtues of the will and affections. There be some have an over-early ripeness in their years, which fadeth betimes. These are, first, such as have brittle wits, the edge whereof is soon turned; such as was Hermogenes the rhetorician, whose books are exceeding subtle, who afterwards waxed stupid. A second sort is of those that have some natural dispositions which have better grace in youth than in age; such as is a fluent and luxuriant speech, which becomes youth well, but not age; so Tully saith of Hortensius, *Idem manebat, neque idem decebat.*[7] The

---

[1]He spent his youth in folly, nay, in madness (Spartianus).

[2]I. e., Cosimo de' Medici.

[3]Management. [4]Hesitate.

[5]External. [6]Joel, 2:28.

[7]He remained the same, but it was no longer becoming (Cicero).

third is of such as take too high a strain at the first, and are magnanimous more than tract of years can uphold. As was Scipio Africanus, of whom Livy saith in effect, *Ultima primis cedebant.*[8]

47.—*Of Negotiating*

It is generally better to deal by speech than by letter; and by the mediation of a third than by a man's self. Letters are good, when a man would draw an answer by letter back again; or when it may serve for a man's justification afterwards to produce his own letter; or where it may be danger to be interrupted, or heard by pieces. To deal in person is good, when a man's face breedeth regard, as commonly with inferiors; or in tender cases, where a man's eye upon the countenance of him with whom he speaketh may give him a direction how far to go; and generally, where a man will reserve to himself liberty either to disavow or to expound. In choice of instruments, it is better to choose men of a plainer sort, that are like to do that that is committed to them, and to report back again faithfully the success,[1] than those that are cunning to contrive out of other men's business somewhat to grace themselves, and will help the matter in report for satisfaction sake. Use also such persons as affect[2] the business wherein they are employed, for that quickeneth much; and such as are fit for the matter, as bold men for expostulation, fair-spoken men for persuasion, crafty men for inquiry and observation, froward and absurd men for business that doth not well bear out itself. Use also such as have been lucky and prevailed before in things wherein you have employed them; for that breeds confidence, and they will strive to maintain their prescription.[3] It is better to sound a person, with whom one deals, afar off, than to fall upon the point at first; except you mean to surprise him by some short question. It is better dealing with men in appetite[4] than with those that are where they would be. If a man deal with another upon conditions, the start or first performance is all, which a man cannot reasonably demand, except either the nature of the thing be such which must go before; or else a man can persuade the other party that he shall still need him in some other thing; or else that he be counted the honester man. All practice[5] is to discover, or to work. Men discover themselves in trust; in passion; at unawares; and of necessity, when they would have somewhat done and cannot find an apt pretext. If you would work[6] any man, you must either know his nature and fashions, and so lead him; or his ends, and so persuade him; or his weakness and disadvantages, and so awe him; or those that have interest in him, and so govern him. In dealing with cunning persons, we must ever consider their ends, to interpret their speeches; and it is good to say little to them, and that which they least look for. In all negotiations of difficulty, a man may not look to sow and reap at once; but must prepare business, and so ripen it by degrees.

50.—*Of Studies*

Studies serve for delight, for ornament, and for ability. Their chief use for delight is in privateness and retiring; for ornament, is in discourse; and for ability, is in the judgment and disposition of business. For expert men can execute, and perhaps judge of particulars, one by one; but the general counsels, and the plots and marshaling of affairs come best from those that are learned. To spend too much time in studies is sloth; to use them too much for ornament is affectation; to make judgment wholly by their rules is the humor of a scholar. They perfect nature, and are perfected by experience; for natural abilities are like natural plants, that need pruning by study; and studies themselves do give forth directions too much at large, except they be bounded in by experience. Crafty men contemn studies; simple men admire them; and wise men use them: for they teach not their own use; but that is a wisdom without them and above them, won by observation. Read not to contradict and confute; nor to believe and take for granted; nor to find talk and discourse; but to weigh

[8]His latter days fell short of the first.

[1]Result. [2]Are inclined to. [3]Reputation.

[4]Anxious to advance.

[5]Negotiation. [6]Manage.

and consider. Some books are to be tasted, others to be swallowed, and some few to be chewed and digested: that is, some books are to be read only in parts; others to be read, but not curiously;[1] and some few to be read wholly, and with diligence and attention. Some books also may be read by deputy, and extracts made of them by others; but that would be only in the less important arguments, and the meaner sort of books; else distilled books are like common distilled waters, flashy[2] things. Reading maketh a full man; conference a ready man; and writing an exact man. And therefore, if a man write little, he had need have a great memory; if he confer little, he had need have a present wit; and if he read little, he had need have much cunning, to seem to know that he doth not. Histories make men wise; poets witty; the mathematics subtle; natural philosophy deep; moral grave; logic and rhetoric able to contend. *Abeunt studia in mores.*[3] Nay, there is no stond[4] or impediment in the wit, but may be wrought out by fit studies, like as diseases of the body may have appropriate exercises. Bowling is good for the stone and reins;[5] shooting for the lungs and breast; gentle walking for the stomach; riding for the head; and the like. So if a man's wit be wandering, let him study the mathematics; for in demonstrations, if his wit be called away never so little, he must begin again: if his wit be not apt to distinguish or find differences, let him study the schoolmen; for they are *cymini sectores:*[6] if he be not apt to beat over matters, and to call one thing to prove and illustrate another, let him study the lawyers' cases: so every defect of the mind may have a special receipt.

56.—*Of Judicature*

JUDGES ought to remember that their office is *jus dicere,* and not *jus dare;* to interpret law, and not to make law, or give law. Else will it be like the authority claimed by the church of Rome; which, under pretext of exposition of Scripture, doth not stick[1] to add and alter, and to pronounce that which they do not find, and by show of antiquity to introduce novelty. Judges ought to be more learned than witty, more reverend than plausible, and more advised than confident. Above all things, integrity is their portion and proper virtue. "Cursed" (saith the law) "is he that removeth the land-mark.[2] The mislayer of a mere stone is to blame. But it is the unjust judge that is the capital remover of land-marks, when he defineth amiss of lands and property. One foul sentence doth more hurt than many foul examples. For these do but corrupt the stream; the other corrupteth the fountain. So saith Solomon: *Fons turbatus, et vena corrupta, est justus cadens in causa sua coram adversario.*[3] The office of judges may have reference unto the parties that sue; unto the advocates that plead; unto the clerks and ministers of justice underneath them; and to the sovereign or state above them.

First, for the causes or parties that sue. "There be" (saith the Scripture) "that turn judgment into wormwood";[4] and surely there be also that turn it into vinegar, for injustice maketh it bitter, and delays make it sour. The principal duty of a judge is to suppress force and fraud; whereof force is the more pernicious when it is open, and fraud when it is close and disguised. Add thereto contentious suits, which ought to be spewed out, as the surfeit of courts. A judge ought to prepare his way to a just sentence, as God useth to prepare his way, by raising valleys and taking down hills; so when there appeareth on either side an high hand, violent prosecution, cunning advantages taken, combination, power, great counsel, then is the virtue of a judge seen, to make inequality equal, that he may plant his judgment as upon an even ground. *Qui fortiter emungit, elicit sanguinem,*[5] and where the

[1]Not with great care. [2]Insipid.

[3]Studies develop into manners (Ovid, *Heroides,* XV, 83).

[4]Hindrance. [5]Kidneys.

[6]Splitters of cumin, i. e., hair-splitters.

[1]Hesitate. [2]Deuteronomy, 27:17.

[3]As a troubled fountain and corrupted spring, so is the righteous man that must give way before his opponent (Proverbs, 25:26).

[4]Amos, 5:7.

[5]Hard pressure draws blood (Proverbs, 30:33).

wine-press is hard wrought, it yields a harsh wine, that tastes of the grapestone. Judges must beware of hard constructions and strained inferences; for there is no worse torture than the torture of laws. Specially in case of laws penal, they ought to have care that that which was meant for terror be not turned into rigor; and that they bring not upon the people that shower whereof the Scripture speaketh, *Pluet super eos laqueos:*[6] for penal laws pressed are a *shower of snares* upon the people. Therefore let penal laws, if they have been sleepers of long, or if they be grown unfit for the present time, be by wise judges confined in the execution:

Judicis officium est, ut res, ita tempora rerum, etc.[7]

In causes of life and death, judges ought (as far as the law permitteth) in justice to remember mercy; and to cast a severe eye upon the example, but a merciful eye upon the person.

Secondly, for the advocates and counsel that plead. Patience and gravity of hearing is an essential part of justice; and an over-speaking judge is no well tuned cymbal. It is no grace to a judge first to find that which he might have heard in due time from the bar; or to show quickness of conceit in cutting off evidence or counsel too short; or to prevent information by questions, though pertinent. The parts of a judge in hearing are four: to direct the evidence; to moderate length, repetition, or impertinency of speech; to recapitulate, select, and collate the material points of that which hath been said; and to give the rule or sentence. Whatsoever is above these is too much; and proceedeth either of glory and willingness to speak or of impatience to hear, or of shortness of memory, or of want of a staid and equal attention. It is a strange thing to see that the boldness of advocates should prevail with judges; whereas they should imitate God, in whose seat they sit, who "represseth the presumptuous," and "giveth grace to the modest."[8] But it is more strange that judges should have noted favorites; which cannot but cause multiplication of fees, and suspicion of by-ways. There is due from the judge to the advocate some commendation and gracing, where causes are well handled and fair pleaded, especially towards the side which obtaineth not; for that upholds in the client the reputation of his counsel, and beats down in him the conceit[9] of his cause. There is likewise due to the public a civil reprehension of advocates, where there appeareth cunning counsel, gross neglect, slight information, indiscreet pressing, or an over-bold defense. And let not the counsel at the bar chop[10] with the judge, nor wind himself into the handling of the cause anew after the judge hath declared his sentence; but on the other side, let not the judge meet the cause half way, nor give occasion to the party to say his counsel or proofs were not heard.

Thirdly, for that that concerns clerks and ministers. The place of justice is an hallowed place; and therefore not only the bench, but the foot-pace[11] and precincts and purprise[12] thereof ought to be preserved without scandal and corruption. For certainly, "Grapes" (as the Scripture saith) "will not be gathered of thorns or thistles";[13] neither can justice yield her fruit with sweetness amongst the briars and brambles of catching and polling[14] clerks and ministers. The attendance of courts is subject to four bad instruments. First, certain persons that are sowers of suits; which make the court swell, and the country pine. The second sort is of those that engage courts in quarrels of jurisdiction, and are not truly *amici curiae*, but *parasiti curiae*,[15] in puffing a court up beyond her bounds, for their own scraps and advantage. The third sort is of those that may be accounted the left hands of courts; persons that are full of nimble and sinister tricks and shifts, whereby they pervert the plain and direct courses of courts,

[6] He will rain down snares upon them (Psalms, 11:6).

[7] The judge must consider the times as well as the circumstances of things (Ovid).

[8] St. James, 4:6. [9] Opinion. [10] Have words.

[11] Step on which the lawyer stands.

[12] Enclosure. [13] St. Matthew, 7:16.

[14] Plundering.

[15] Friends of the court, but parasites of the court.

and bring justice into oblique lines and labyrinths. And the fourth is the poller[16] and exacter of fees; which justifies the common resemblance of the courts of justice to the bush, whereunto while the sheep flies for defense in weather, he is sure to lose part of his fleece. On the other side, an ancient clerk, skillful in precedents, wary in proceeding, and understanding in the business of the court, is an excellent finger of a court, and doth many times point the way to the judge himself.

Fourthly, for that which may concern the sovereign and estate. Judges ought above all to remember the conclusion of the Roman Twelve Tables, *Salus populi suprema lex;*[17] and to know that laws, except they be in order to that end, are but things captious, and oracles not well inspired. Therefore it is an happy thing in a state when kings and states do often consult with judges; and again, when judges do often consult with the king and state: the one, when there is matter of law intervenient in business of state; the other, when there is some consideration of state intervenient in matter of law. For many times the things deduced to judgment may be *meum* and *tuum,*[18] when the reason and consequence thereof may trench to point of estate.[19] I call matter of estate not only the parts of sovereignty, but whatsoever introduceth any great alteration or dangerous precedent, or concerneth manifestly any great portion of people. And let no man weakly conceive that just laws and true policy have any antipathy; for they are like the spirits and sinews, that one moves with the other. Let judges also remember that Solomon's throne was supported by lions on both sides; let them be lions, but yet lions under the throne, being circumspect that they do not check or oppose any points of sovereignty. Let not judges also be so ignorant of their own right as to think there is not left to them, as a principal part of their office, a wise use and application of laws. For they may remember what the Apostle saith of a greater law than theirs: *Nos scimus quia lex bona est, modo quis ea utatur legitime.*[20]

[16]Plunderer.

[17]The people's safety is the supreme law (Cicero, *Of Laws,* III, 3).

[18]Mine and thine.

[19]May extend to concern the state.

[20]We know that the law is good if a man use it lawfully (I Timothy, 1:8).

57.—*Of Anger*

To SEEK to extinguish anger utterly is but a bravery[1] of the Stoics. We have better oracles: "Be angry, but sin not. Let not the sun go down upon your anger."[2] Anger must be limited and confined, both in race and in time. We will first speak how the natural inclination and habit *to be angry* may be attempered and calmed. Secondly, how the particular motions of anger may be repressed, or at least refrained from doing mischief. Thirdly, how to raise anger, or appease anger, in another.

For the first: there is no other way but to meditate and ruminate well upon the effects of anger, how it troubles man's life. And the best time to do this is to look back upon anger when the fit is thoroughly over. Seneca saith well, "that anger is like ruin, which breaks itself upon that it falls." The Scripture exhorteth us "to possess our souls in patience."[3] Whosoever is out of patience, is out of possession of his soul. Men must not turn bees;

——*animasque in vulnere ponunt.*[4]

Anger is certainly a kind of baseness; as it appears well in the weakness of those subjects in whom it reigns, children, women, old folks, sick folks. Only men must beware that they carry their anger rather with scorn than with fear, so that they may seem rather to be above the injury than below it; which is a thing easily done, if a man will give law to himself in it.

For the second point: the causes and motives of anger are chiefly three. First, to be too sensible of hurt; for no man is angry that feels not himself hurt, and therefore tender and delicate persons must needs be oft angry; they have so many things to trouble them which more robust natures have little sense of. The next is the apprehension

[1]Boast. [2]Ephesians, 4:26. [3]St. Luke, 21:19.

[4]And spend their lives in stinging (Virgil, *Georgics,* IV, 238).

and construction of the injury offered to be, in the circumstances thereof, full of contempt. For contempt is that which putteth an edge upon anger, as much or more than the hurt itself. And therefore, when men are ingenious in picking out circumstances of contempt, they do kindle their anger much. Lastly, opinion of the touch[5] of a man's reputation, doth multiply and sharpen anger. Wherein the remedy is, that a man should have, as Consalvo was wont to say, *telam honoris crassiorem.*[6] But in all refrainings of anger, it is the best remedy to win time; and to make a man's self believe, that the opportunity of his revenge is not yet come, but that he foresees a time for it; and so to still himself in the mean time, and reserve it.

To contain[7] anger from mischief, though it take hold of a man, there be two things whereof you must have special caution. The one, of extreme bitterness of words, especially if they be aculcate[8] and proper; for *communia maledicta*[9] are nothing so much; and again, that in anger a man reveal no secrets, for that makes him not fit for society. The other, that you do not peremptorily break off, in any business, in a fit of anger; but howsoever you show bitterness, do not act anything that is not revocable.

For raising and appeasing anger in another; it is done chiefly by choosing of times, when men are frowardest and worst disposed, to incense them. Again, by gathering (as was touched before) all that you can find out, to aggravate the contempt. And the two remedies are by the contraries. The former, to take good times, when first to relate to a man an angry business; for the first impression is much. And the other is to sever, as much as may be, the construction of the injury from the point of contempt, imputing it to misunderstanding, fear, passion, or what you will.

[5]Censure. [6]A stout web of honor. [7]Restrain.

[8]Stinging. [9]General abuses.

LYRIC POETRY OF THE SIXTEENTH AND EARLY SEVENTEENTH CENTURIES

English lyric poetry of the sixteenth century is a new beginning, and has its sources not in older native literature, but in Italy. Late in the century Spenser went back to Chaucer, and to some extent in language, even more in the modulation and melody of his verse, continued and developed a national tradition, which he in turn handed on to Milton. The evidence for this is to be found, however, chiefly in Spenser's longer poems, *The Shepherd's Calendar* and *The Faerie Queene,* while much earlier in the century the course which the Elizabethan lyric was to take had been pretty clearly marked out by members of the Renaissance court of Henry VIII. The two chief poets of this earlier period were Sir Thomas Wyatt and Henry Howard, Earl of Surrey. And that a new thing had come into English poetry was made unmistakable when many of the poems written by Wyatt and Surrey, together with others by Grimald and by "uncertain authors," were gathered together and printed in *Tottel's Miscellany* (1557), the first of a series of collections of lyrics by various writers which appeared during the latter half of the sixteenth century. Full mastery of the new kind of poetry and complete freedom of expression hardly came before 1580; but their coming, when it did occur, was sudden, and for some fifteen or twenty years there was a veritable outburst of lyric song, gay, easy, rich, and musical, as remarkable for its spontaneity as for its frequent intensity, and perhaps even more remarkable for the great numbers who not only felt the lyrical impulse but were able to express it in a smooth and charming form. The more notable of the miscellanies into which many, though by no means all, of the lyrics of the period were collected were *The Phoenix' Nest* (1593), *England's Helicon* (1600), and the Davisons' *Poetical Rhapsody* (1602).

Of the various forms which the lyric took only one can be specifically mentioned here—the sonnet. Petrarch had not only written some of his greatest poetry in sonnet-form but had connected his sonnets in a sequence, so that in effect they told the story of his moods and feelings, above all of the course of his love, and of other things as they related themselves to that central theme. The sonnet-sequence made its way to England along with the rest, and became popular in the decade from 1590 to 1600. The most notable of the sequences were Sir Philip Sidney's *Astrophel and Stella,* Samuel Daniel's *Delia,* Michael Drayton's *Idea,* Spenser's *Amoretti,* and Shakespeare's *Sonnets.*

On the whole, the Elizabethan burst of song was as brief as it was splendid. Spontaneous expression quickly develops into more deliberate art, and so it was with the lyric in the closing years of the sixteenth century. Its exuberance became distasteful, its sweetness cloying, and Ben Jonson, lifting the same chastening voice of good sense in the lyric as in the drama, set the example of restraint, of greater attention to form, and of practice enlightened by study of the best models of classical Greek and Roman poetry. At the same time John Donne reacted harshly and powerfully from the sweetness and the conventional themes of the Petrarchians in their love-poetry. Probably literary historians have tended to make too much of the personal influence of Jonson and Donne. Perhaps they were not so much actually leaders of new movements in poetry as the earliest men to feel strongly, each in his own way, a pronounced change in the whole intellectual and emotional life of England which gathered force in the early years of the seventeenth century. One way of putting it is that a period of expansive, youthful feeling was succeeded by a period of doubt mixed with disillusionment. Certainly something like this took place, and the change made itself felt throughout literature, not merely within the little field of the lyric; yet it still remains useful within that field to remember that Jonson and Donne were the prophets of the new age. It should also be remembered, however, that some continued, as in every generation, to live in the past and to express the influences which for them were still potent, the most notable instance of this being the so-called school of Spenserians who continued to echo their master until well into the troubled years of the middle of the seventeenth century.

Tottel's Miscellany has been thoroughly edited by Hyder E. Rollins (Cambridge, U. S. A., 1928); vol. II of this edition contains an abundance of scholarly material. *The Poems of Sir Thomas Wiat,* ed. A. K. Foxwell (London, 1913), and *The Poems of Henry Howard, Earl of Surrey,* ed. Frederick M. Padelford, revised edition (Seattle, 1928), may also be recommended. John M. Berdan's *Early Tudor Poetry, 1485–1547* (New York, 1920) contains much interesting commentary, but it must be used guardedly.

Norman Ault has edited a useful anthology of *Elizabethan Lyrics* (London, 1925); Sir Sidney Lee's *Elizabethan Sonnets* (London, 1904) supplies the text of several sequences and an introduction which emphasizes the continental background for the poems written in this form. The most important Elizabethan miscellany, *England's Helicon,* has been edited by A. H. Bullen (London, 1899). The editions of individual Elizabethan poets, as well as studies devoted to them, are numerous. For Lyly's poetry see his *Complete Works,* ed. R. Warwick Bond (Oxford, 1902). *The Complete Works of Sir Philip Sidney,* ed. Albert Feuillerat (Cambridge, 1912–1926), and Mona Wilson's *Sir Philip Sidney* (New York, 1932) supply all that is needed to begin a study of that poet. Ralph M. Sargent's *At the Court of Queen Elizabeth; the Life and Lyrics of Sir Edward Dyer* (London, 1935) contains Dyer's poems and all that is known about him. *The Poems of Sir Walter Ralegh* are gathered together in Agnes M. C. Latham's edition (London, 1929); the most recent biography, Edward Thompson's *Sir Walter Ralegh, Last of the Elizabethans* (New Haven, 1936), is a sympathetic, rather than a judicious, study. The poetry of George Peele may be found in his *Works,* ed. A. H. Bullen (London, 1888). The most complete edition of *The Plays and Poems of Robert Greene* is the work of J. Churton Collins (Oxford, 1905). Of *The Works of Michael Drayton,* ed. J. William Hebel (Oxford, 1931–1933), four volumes, containing the complete text, have already appeared. *The Shakespeare Songs* have been edited by C. F. Tucker Brooke, with an introduction by Walter De La Mare (New York, 1929); the same editor has presented *Shakespeare's Sonnets,* arranged in a new order and accompanied by an acute introduction (New York, 1936); for information on the life and background of Shakespeare see Edmund K. Chambers, *William Shakespeare* (Oxford, 1930), and C. F. Tucker Brooke, *Shakespeare of Stratford, a Handbook for Students* (New Haven, 1926); *Shakespeare's England; an Account of the Life & Manners of His Age* (Oxford, 1916) is an anthology of essays by experts, each dealing with a side of Elizabethan life which appears in Shakespeare's work. Thomas Campion's *Works* have been edited by Percival Vivian (Oxford, 1909). Ben Jonson's poems have been reprinted by the Shakespeare Head Press (Oxford); the new collected edition of his complete works, ed. C. H. Herford, Percy Simpson, and Evelyn Simpson (Oxford, 1925–1938), has only been completed through the volumes containing the biography and the plays; for a popular life see John Palmer, *Ben Jonson* (London, 1934).

Metaphysical Lyrics & Poems of the Seventeenth Century, ed. Sir Herbert J. C. Grierson (Oxford, 1921), is an excellent anthology with a valuable introduction. The definitive edition of *The Poems of John Donne* is edited by Sir Herbert J. C. Grierson (Oxford, 1912), but a more compact volume is the *Complete Poetry and Selected Prose,* ed. John Hayward (New York, 1930); *A Garland for John Donne, 1631–1931,* ed. Theodore Spencer (Cambridge, U. S. A., 1931), contains essays of tribute by T. S. Eliot, Evelyn Simpson, Mario Praz, John Hayward, Mary P. Ramsay, John Sparrow, George Williamson, Theodore Spencer; George Williamson gives an artistic evaluation of seventeenth-century poetry in *The Donne Tradition; a Study in English Poetry from Donne to the Death of Cowley* (Cambridge, U. S. A., 1930), while Helen C. White's *Metaphysical Poets; a Study in Religious Experience* (New York, 1936) treats Donne, Herbert, Crashaw, Vaughan, and Traherne primarily as mystics. The standard editions of the remaining poets in this section are as follows: *The Poetical Works of Robert Herrick,* ed. F. W. Moorman (Oxford, 1915); *The English Works of George Herbert,* ed. George H. Palmer (Boston, 1905); *The Poems of Edmund Waller,* ed. G. Thorn Drury (London, 1904); *The Works of Sir John Suckling in Prose and Verse,* ed. A. Hamilton Thompson (London, 1910); *The Poems of Richard Lovelace,* ed. C. H. Wilkinson (Oxford, 1930); *The Poems & Letters of Andrew Marvell,* ed. H. M. Margoliouth (Oxford, 1927); *The Works of Henry Vaughan,* ed. Leonard C. Martin (Oxford, 1914).

SIR THOMAS WYATT

(1503–1542)

THE LOVER FOR SHAME-FASTNESS HIDETH HIS DESIRE WITHIN HIS FAITHFUL HEART

The long love that in my thought doth harbor,
And in my heart doth keep his residence,
Into my face presseth with bold pretense,
And therein campeth spreading his banner.
She that me learns to love and suffer, 5
And wills that my trust and lust's negligence[1]
Be reined by reason, shame, and reverence,
With his hardiness takes displeasure.
Wherewithal[2] into the heart's forest he fleeth,
Leaving his enterprise with pain and cry, 10
And there him hideth, and not appeareth.
What may I do, when my master feareth?
But in the field with him to live and die?
For good is the life ending faithfully.

THE WAVERING LOVER WILLETH, AND DREADETH, TO MOVE HIS DESIRE

Such vain thought as wonted to mislead me
In desert hope, by well assuréd moan,
Makes me from company to live alone,
In following her whom reason bids me flee.
She flyeth as fast by gentle cruelty; 5
And after her my heart would fain be gone,
But armėd sighs my way do stop anon,
'Twixt hope and dread locking my liberty.
Yet as I guess, under disdainful brow
One beam of pity is in her cloudy look, 10
Which comforteth the mind, that erst for fear shook;
And therewithal bolded, I seek the way how
To utter the smart that I suffer within;
But such it is, I not[3] how to begin.

THE LOVER HAVING DREAMED ENJOYING OF HIS LOVE, COMPLAINETH THAT THE DREAM IS NOT EITHER LONGER OR TRUER

Unstable dream, according to the place,
Be steadfast once, or else at least be true.
By tasted sweetness make me not to rue
The sudden loss of thy false feignéd grace.
By good respect in such a dangerous case 5
Thou broughtst not her into this tossing mew,[4]
But madest my sprite[5] live, my care to renew.
My body in tempest her succor to embrace.
The body dead, the sprite had his desire;
Painless was th' one, the other in delight. 10
Why then, alas! did it not keep it right,
Returning to leap into the fire,
And where it was at wish, it could not remain?
Such mocks of dreams they turn to deadly pain!

DESCRIPTION OF THE CONTRARIOUS PASSIONS IN A LOVER

I find no peace, and all my war is done;
I fear and hope, I burn, and freeze like ice;
I fly above the wind, yet can I not arise;
And nought I have, and all the world I seize on,
That loseth nor locketh, holdeth me in prison, 5
And holdeth me not, yet can I scape no wise;
Nor letteth me live, nor die, at my devise,[6]
And yet of death it giveth me occasion.
Without eye I see; and without tongue I plain.[7]
I desire to perish, and yet I ask health; 10
I love another, and thus I hate myself;
I feed me in sorrow, and laugh in all my pain.
Likewise displeaseth me both death and life,
And my delight is causer of this strife.

THE LOVER COMPARETH HIS STATE TO A SHIP IN PERILOUS STORM TOSSED ON THE SEA

My galley chargéd with forgetfulness
Thorough sharp seas in winter nights doth pass,
'Tween rock and rock; and eke mine enemy, alas,
That is my lord, steereth with cruelness,
And every hour, a thought in readiness, 5
As though that death were light in such a case.
And endless wind doth tear the sail apace
Of forcéd sighs and trusty fearfulness.
A rain of tears, a cloud of dark disdain
Hath done the wearied cords great hinderance, 10
Wreathed with error, and eke with ignorance.
The stars be hid that led me to this pain;
Drownéd is reason that should me comfort,
And I remain despairing of the port.

---

[1]Careless confidence. [2]Whereupon.
[3]Know not. [4]Cage.

[5]Spirit. [6]Desire. [7]Lament.

A RENOUNCING OF LOVE

Farewell, Love, and all thy laws for ever!
Thy baited hooks shall tangle me no more:
Senec[8] and Plato call me from thy lore
To perfect wealth my wit for to endeavor.[9]
In blind error when I did persever, 5
Thy sharp repulse, that pricketh aye so sore,
Hath taught me to set in trifles no store;
And 'scape forth, since liberty is lever[10]
Therefore, farewell! go trouble younger hearts,
And in me claim no more authority. 10
With idle youth go use thy property,
And thereon spend thy many brittle darts;
For hitherto though I have lost my time,
Me list no longer rotten boughs to climb.

THE LOVER SENDETH SIGHS TO MOAN HIS SUIT

Go, burning sighs, unto the frozen heart
Go, break the ice which pity's painful dart
Might never pierce; and if mortal prayer
In heaven may be heard, at least I desire
That death or mercy be end of smart. 5
Take with thee pain, whereof I have my part,
And eke the flame from which I cannot start,
And leave me then in rest, I you require.
Go, burning sighs, fulfill that I desire,
I must go work, I see, by craft and art, 10
For truth and faith in her is laid apart:
Alas, I cannot therefore assail her
With pitiful complaint and scalding fire
That from my breast deceivably doth start.

THE LOVER COMPLAINETH THE UNKINDNESS OF HIS LOVE

My lute, awake, perform the last
Labor that thou and I shall waste,
And end that I have now begun.
And when this song is sung and past,
My lute, be still, for I have done. 5

As to be heard where ear is none,
As lead to grave[11] in marble stone,
My song may pierce her heart as soon.
Should we then sigh, or sing, or moan?
No, no, my lute, for I have done. 10

The rocks do not so cruelly
Repulse the waves continually
As she my suit and affection;
So that I am past remedy,
Whereby my lute and I have done. 15

Proud of the spoil that thou hast got
Of simple hearts through Lovës shot,
By whom unkind thou hast them won,
Think not he hath his bow forgot,
Although my lute and I have done. 20

Vengeance shall fall on thy disdain
That makest but game on earnest pain.
Think not alone under the sun
Unquit to cause thy lovers plain,[12]
Although my lute and I have done. 25

Perchance thee lie withered and old,
The winter nights that are so cold,
Plaining in vain unto the moon;
Thy wishes then dare not be told.
Care then who list, for I have done. 30

And then may chance thee to repent
The time that thou hast lost and spent
To cause thy lovers sigh and swoon;
Then shalt thou know beauty but lent,
And wish and want, as I have done. 35

Now cease, my lute; this is the last
Labor that thou and I shall waste,
And ended is that we begun.
Now is the song both sung and past;
My lute, be still, for I have done. 40

AN EARNEST SUIT TO HIS UNKIND MISTRESS NOT TO FORSAKE HIM

And wilt thou leave me thus?
Say nay, say nay, for shame!
To save thee from the blame
Of all my grief and grame.[13]
And wilt thou leave me thus? 5
Say nay! say nay!

And wilt thou leave me thus,
That hath loved thee so long
In wealth and woe among:
And is thy heart so strong 10
As for to leave me thus?
Say nay! say nay!

And wilt thou leave me thus,
That hath given thee my heart
Never for to depart, 15
Neither for pain nor smart:
And wilt thou leave me thus?
Say nay! say nay!

---

[8]Seneca. [9]Exert. [10]Preferable. [11]Engrave.

[12]To lament. [13]Sorrow.

And wilt thou leave me thus,
And have no more pity 20
Of him that loveth thee?
Alas, thy cruelty!
And wilt thou leave me thus?
Say nay! say nay!

THE LOVER BESEECHETH HIS MISTRESS NOT TO FORGET HIS STEADFAST FAITH AND TRUE INTENT

Forget not yet the tried intent
Of such a truth as I have meant;
My great travail so gladly spent,
Forget not yet!

Forget not yet when first began 5
The weary life ye know, since when
The suit, the service none tell can;
Forget not yet!

Forget not yet the great assays,
The cruel wrong, the scornful ways, 10
The painful patience in delays,
Forget not yet!

Forget not yet, forget not this,
How long ago hath been, and is,
The mind that never meant amiss— 15
Forget not yet!

Forget not then thine own approved,
The which so long hath thee so loved,
Whose steadfast faith yet never moved:
Forget not this! 20

OF THE MEAN AND SURE ESTATE[14]

Written to John Poins

My mother's maids, when they did sew and spin,
They sung sometime a song of the field mouse
That, for because her livelod[15] was but thin,
Would needs go seek her townish sister's house.
She thought herself enduréd too much pain; 5
The stormy blasts her cave so sore did souse
That when the furrows swimméd with the rain,
She must lie cold and wet in sorry plight;
And worse than that, bare meat there did remain
To comfort her when she her house had dight;[16] 10
Sometime a barley corn; sometime a bean,
For which she labored hard both day and night
In harvest time whilst she might go and glean;
And when her store was stroyéd[17] with the flood,
Then welaway! for she undone was clean. 15
Then was she fain to take, instead of food,
Sleep, if she might, her hunger to beguile.
"My sister," quoth she, "hath a living good,
And hence from me she dwelleth not a mile;
In cold and storm she lieth warm and dry 20
In bed of down; the dirt doth not defile
Her tender foot; she laboreth not as I.
Richly she feedeth, and at the rich man's cost,
And for her meat she needs not crave nor cry.
By sea, by land, of delicates the most 25
Her cater[18] seeks and spareth for no peril,
She feedeth on boiled bacon, meat, and roast,
And hath thereof neither charge nor travail;
And, when she list, the liquor of the grape
Doth glad her heart till that her belly swell."
And at this journey she maketh but a jape;[19] 31
So forth she goeth, trusting of all this wealth
With her sister her part so for to shape
That if she might keep herself in health,
To live a lady while her life doth last. 35
And to the door now is she come by stealth,
And with her foot anon she scrapeth full fast.
Th' other, for fear, durst not well scarce appear,
Of every noise so was the wretch aghast.
At last she askéd softly who was there, 40
And in her language as well as she could.
"Peep!" quoth the other sister, "I am here."
"Peace," quoth the town mouse, "why speakest thou so loud?"
And by the hand she took her fair and well.
"Welcome," quoth she, "my sister, by the Rood!" 45
She feasted her, that joy it was to tell
The fare they had; they drank the wine so clear,
And, as to purpose now and then it fell,
She cheeréd her with "How, sister, what cheer!"

[14]This poem is based upon Horace, *Satires* II, 6. It is not, of course, a lyric, but deserves inclusion here to indicate the range of Wyatt's experiments.
[15]Livelihood.
[16]Ordered. [17]Destroyed. [18]Caterer. [19]Jest.

Amid this joy befell a sorry chance, 50
That, welaway! the stranger bought full dear
The fare she had, for, as she looked askance,
Under a stool she spied two steaming[20] eyes
In a round head with sharp ears. In France
Was never mouse so feared, for, though unwise 55
Had not y-seen such a beast before,
Yet had nature taught her after her guise
To know her foe and dread him evermore.
The towny mouse fled, she knew whither to go;
Th'other had no shift, but wonders sore 60
Feared of her life. At home she wished her tho,[21]
And to the door, alas! as she did skip,
The heaven it would, lo! and eke her chance was so,
At the threshold her silly foot did trip;
And ere she might recover it again, 65
The traitor cat had caught her by the hip,
And made her there against her will remain,
That had forgot her poor surety and rest
For seeming wealth wherein she thought to reign.
Alas, my Poins, how men do seek the best 70
And find the worst by error as they stray!
And no marvel; when sight is so opprest,
And blinds the guide, anon out of the way
Goeth guide and all in seeking quiet life.
O wretched minds, there is no gold that may 75
Grant that you seek; no war, no peace, no strife.
No, no, although thy head were hooped with gold,
Sergeant with mace, halberd, sword, nor knife,
Cannot repulse the care that follow should.
Each kind of life hath with him his disease. 80
Live in delight even as thy lust would,
And thou shalt find, when lust doth most thee please,
It irketh straight, and by itself doth fade.
A small thing is it that may thy mind appease.
None of ye all there is that is so mad 85
To seek for grapes on brambles or on briars;
Nor none, I trow, that hath his wit so bad
To set his hay[22] for conies[23] over rivers,
Nor ye set not a drag-net for an hare;
And yet the thing that most is your desire 90
Ye do mis-seek with more travail and care.
Make plain thine heart, that it be not knotted
With hope or dread, and see thy will be bare
From all effects whom vice hath ever spotted.
Thyself content with that is thee assigned, 95
And use it well that is to thee allotted.
Then seek no more out[24] of thyself to find
The thing that thou hast sought so long before,
For thou shalt feel it sticking in thy mind.
Mad, if ye list to continue your sore, 100
Let present pass and gape on time to come,
And deep yourself in travail more and more.
Henceforth, my Poins, this shall be all and some,
These wretched fools shall have naught else of me;
But to the great God and to his high dome,[25]
None other pain pray I for them to be, 106
But, when the rage doth lead them from the right,
That, looking backward, virtue they may see,
Even as she is so goodly fair and bright,
And whilst they clasp their lusts in arms across, 110
Grant them, good Lord, as thou mayst of thy might,
To fret inward for losing such a loss.

[20]Gleaming. [21]Then. [22]Snare. [23]Rabbits.

[24]Outside. [25]Judgment.

HENRY HOWARD, EARL OF SURREY

(1517?–1547)

DESCRIPTION OF SPRING WHEREIN EACH THING RENEWS, SAVE ONLY THE LOVER

The soote[1] season that bud and bloom forth brings,
With green hath clad the hill and eke the vale;
The nightingale with feathers new she sings;
The turtle[2] to her make[3] hath told her tale:
Summer is come, for every spray now springs; 5
The hart hath hung his old head on the pale;
The buck in brake his winter coat he flings;
The fishes float with new repairéd scale;
The adder all her slough away she slings;
The swift swallow pursueth the flies smale; 10
The busy bee her honey now she mings.[4]
Winter is worn, that was the flowers' bale:
And thus I see among these pleasant things
Each care decays, and yet my sorrow springs!

[1]Sweet. [2]Turtle-dove. [3]Mate. [4]Mixes.

COMPLAINT OF A LOVER REBUKED

Love, that doth reign and live within my thought,
And build his seat within my captive breast,
Clad in the arms wherein with me he fought,
Oft in my face he doth his banner rest.
But she that taught me love and suffer pain, 5
My doubtful hope and eke my hot desire
With shamefast look to shadow and refrain,
Her smiling grace converteth straight to ire.
And coward Love then to the heart apace
Taketh his flight, where he doth lurk and plain 10
His purpose lost, and dare not show his face.
For my lord's guilt thus faultless bide I pain.
Yet from my lord shall not my foot remove;
Sweet is the death that taketh end by love.

VOW TO LOVE FAITHFULLY HOWSOEVER HE BE REWARDED

Set me whereas the sun doth parch the green,
Or where his beams may not dissolve the ice;
In temperate heat, where he is felt and seen;
In presence prest of people, mad or wise;
Set me in high, or yet in low degree; 5
In longest night, or in the longest day;
In clearest sky, or where clouds thickest be;
In lusty youth, or when my hairs are gray:
Set me in heaven, in earth, or else in hell;
In hill, or dale, or in the foaming flood; 10
Thrall, or at large, alive whereso I dwell;
Sick or in health, in evil fame or good;
Hers will I be, and only with this thought
Content myself, although my chance be naught.

COMPLAINT OF THE ABSENCE OF HER LOVER BEING UPON THE SEA

O happy dames! that may embrace
The fruit of your delight;
Help to bewail the woeful case,
And eke the heavy plight,
Of me, that wonted to rejoice 5
The fortune of my pleasant choice:
Good ladies, help to fill my mourning voice.

In ship freight[5] with rememberance
Of thoughts and pleasures past,
He sails that hath in governance 10
My life, while it will last;
With scalding sighs, for lack of gale,
Furthering his hope, that is his sail,
Toward me, the sweet port of his avail.[6]

Alas, how oft in dreams I see 15
Those eyes that were my food;
Which sometime so delighted me,
That yet they do me good;
Wherewith I wake with his return,
Whose absent flame did make me burn: 20
But when I find the lack, Lord, how I mourn!

When other lovers in arms across
Rejoice their chief delight,
Drownéd in tears to mourn my loss,
I stand the bitter night 25
In my window, where I may see
Before the winds how the clouds flee:
Lo, what a mariner love hath made me!

And in green waves when the salt flood
Doth rise by rage of wind, 30
A thousand fancies in that mood
Assail my restless mind.
Alas, now drencheth[7] my sweet foe,
That with the spoil of my heart did go,
And left me; but, alas, why did he so? 35

And when the seas wax calm again
To chase from me annoy,
My doubtful hope doth cause me pain;
So dread cuts off my joy.
Thus is my wealth mingled with woe, 40
And of each thought a doubt doth grow;
Now he comes! Will he come? Alas, no, no!

A PRAISE OF HIS LOVE WHEREIN HE REPROVETH THEM THAT COMPARE THEIR LADIES WITH HIS

Give place, ye lovers, here before
That spent your boasts and brags in vain;
My lady's beauty passeth more
The best of yours, I dare well sayn,[8]
Than doth the sun the candle light, 5
Or brightest day the darkest night.

And thereto hath a troth[9] as just
As had Penelope the fair;
For what she saith, ye may it trust
As it by writing sealéd were: 10
And virtues hath she many mo[10]
Than I with pen have skill to show.

I could rehearse, if that I would,
The whole effect of Nature's plaint,
When she had lost the perfect mold, 15
The like to whom she could not paint:

[5]Freighted. [6]Advantage.

[7]Drowneth. [8]Say. [9]Faithfulness. [10]More.

With wringing hands, how she did cry,
And what she said, I know it, I.

I know she swore with raging mind,
Her kingdom only set apart, 20
There was no loss by law of kind[11]
That could have gone so near her heart.
And this was chiefly all her pain:
She could not make the like again.

Sith[12] Nature thus gave her the praise, 25
To be the chiefest work she wrought;
In faith, methink, some better ways
On your behalf might well be sought
Than to compare, as ye have done,
To match the candle with the sun. 30

THE MEANS TO ATTAIN HAPPY LIFE[13]

Martial, the things that do attain
The happy life be these, I find:
The riches left, not got with pain;
The fruitful ground; the quiet mind;
The equal friend; no grudge, no strife; 5
No charge of rule, no governance;
Without disease, the healthful life;
The household of continuance;
The mean[14] diet, no delicate fare;
True wisdom joined with simpleness; 10
The night dischargéd of all care,
Where wine the wit may not oppress;
The faithful wife, without debate;
Such sleeps as may beguile the night:
Contented with thine own estate, 15
Ne wish for death, ne fear his might.

OF THE DEATH OF SIR T[HOMAS] W[YATT]

W. resteth here, that quick[15] could never rest;
Whose heavenly gifts, encreaséd by disdain,
And virtue sank the deeper in his breast;
Such profit he by envy could obtain.
A head where wisdom mysteries did frame; 5
Whose hammers beat still in that lively brain
As on a stithe[16] where that some work of fame
Was daily wrought to turn to Britain's gain.
A visage stern and mild, where both did grow,
Vice to condemn, in virtue to rejoice; 10
Amid great storms, whom grace assuréd so
To live upright and smile at fortune's choice.
A hand that taught what might be said in rime;
That reft[17] Chaucer the glory of his wit:
A mark, the which (unparfited,[18] for time) 15
Some may approach, but never none shall hit.
A tongue that served in foreign realms his king;
Whose courteous talk to virtue did enflame
Each noble heart; a worthy guide to bring
Our English youth by travail unto fame. 20
An eye whose judgment none affect[19] could blind,
Friends to allure, and foes to reconcile;
Whose piercing look did represent a mind
With virtue fraught, reposéd, void of guile.
A heart where dread was never so imprest 25
To hide the thought that might the truth advance;
In neither fortune lost, nor yet represt,
To swell in wealth, or yield unto mischance.
A valiant corse,[20] where force and beauty met;
Happy, alas, too happy, but for foes! 30
Lived, and ran the race that Nature set:
Of manhood's shape, where she the mold did lose.
But to the heavens that simple[21] soul is fled,
Which left with such as covet Christ to know
Witness of faith that never shall be dead, 35
Sent for our health, but not receivéd so.
Thus for our guilt, this jewel have we lost;
The earth his bones, the heavens possess his ghost!

[11]Nature. [12]Since.
[13]Translated from Martial's *Epigrams,* x, 47. The Latin poet is addressing a friend also named Martial.
[14]Moderate. [15]Alive. [16]Anvil.
[17]Took from. [18]Unperfected.
[19]No affections. [20]Body.
[21]I. e., incorruptible.

ANONYMOUS

A STUDENT AT HIS BOOK[1]

A student at his book, so placed
That wealth he might have won,
From book to wife did fleet in haste,
From wealth to woe did run.
Now, who hath played a feater cast,[2] 5
Since juggling first begun?
In knitting of himself so fast,
Himself he hath undone.

[1]One of the poems by "uncertain authors" in Tottel's *Miscellany* (1557).
[2]A neater trick.

BACK AND SIDE GO BARE[3]

CHORUS

Back and side go bare, go bare;
Both foot and hand go cold;
But, belly, God send thee good ale enough,
Whether it be new or old.

I cannot eat but little meat, 5
My stomach is not good;
But sure I think that I can drink
With him that wears a hood.
Though I go bare, take ye no care,
I am nothing a-cold; 10
I stuff my skin so full within
Of jolly good ale and old.

I love no roast but a nutbrown toast,
And a crab[4] laid in the fire;
A little bread shall do me stead,[5] 15
Much bread I not desire.
No frost nor snow, no wind, I trow,
Can hurt me if I would,
I am so wrapped and thoroughly lapped
Of jolly good ale and old. 20

And Tib, my wife, that as her life
Loveth well good ale to seek,
Full oft drinks she, till ye may see
The tears run down her cheek.
Then doth she trowl[6] to me the bowl, 25
Even as a maltworm should,
And saith, "Sweetheart, I have take my part
Of this jolly good ale and old."

Now let them drink till they nod and wink,
Even as good fellows should do; 30
They shall not miss to have the bliss
Good ale doth bring men to.
And all poor souls that have scoured bowls,
Or have them lustily trowled,
God save the lives of them and their wives, 35
Whether they be young or old.

JOHN LYLY

(1553–1606)

APELLES' SONG[1]

Cupid and my Campaspe played
At cards for kisses; Cupid paid.
He stakes his quiver, bow, and arrows,
His mother's doves and team of sparrows;
Loses them too; then down he throws 5
The coral of his lip, the rose
Growing on's cheek (but none knows how);
With these, the crystal of his brow,
And then the dimple of his chin;
All these did my Campaspe win. 10
At last he set[2] her both his eyes;
She won, and Cupid blind did rise.
O Love, has she done this to thee?
What shall, alas! become of me?

[3]From *Gammer Gurton's Needle* (written *c.* 1562).

[4]Apple. [5]Be sufficient. [6]Pass.

[1]This and the following song are both from *Campaspe* (1584). It is possible that the songs in Lyly's plays are by another hand.

[2]Wagered.

SPRING'S WELCOME

What bird so sings, yet so does wail?
O 'tis the ravished nightingale.
"Jug, jug, jug, jug, tereu," she cries,
And still her woes at midnight rise.
Brave prick-song! who is 't now we hear? 5
None but the lark so shrill and clear;
Now at heaven's gates she claps her wings,
The morn not waking till she sings.
Hark, hark, with what a pretty throat
Poor robin redbreast tunes his note! 10
Hark how the jolly cuckoos sing,
"Cuckoo," to welcome in the spring!
"Cuckoo," to welcome in the spring!

SIR PHILIP SIDNEY

(1554–1586)

ASTROPHEL AND STELLA

I

Loving in truth, and fain in verse my love to show,
That she, dear she, might take some pleasure of my pain,—
Pleasure might cause her read, reading might make her know,
Knowledge might pity win, and pity grace obtain,—
I sought fit words to paint the blackest face of woe, 5
Studying inventions fine, her wits to entertain,
Oft turning others' leaves, to see if thence would flow
Some fresh and fruitful showers upon my sunburnt brain.

But words came halting forth, wanting Invention's stay;
Invention, Nature's child, fled step-dame Study's blows; 10
And others' feet still seemed but strangers' in my way.
Thus, great with child to speak, and helpless in my throes,
Biting my truant pen, beating myself for spite;
"Fool," said my Muse to me, "look in thy heart, and write."

15

You that do search for every purling spring
Which from the ribs of old Parnassus[1] flows,
And every flower, not sweet perhaps, which grows
Near thereabouts, into your poesy wring;
You that do dictionary's method bring 5
Into your rimes, running in rattling rows;
You that poor Petrarch's long deceaséd woes
With new-born sighs and denizened[2] wit do sing;
You take wrong ways; those far-fet[3] helps be such
As do bewray a want of inward touch.[4] 10
And sure, at length stolen goods do come to light:
But if, both for your love and skill, your name
You seek to nurse at fullest breasts of Fame,
Stella behold, and then begin to indite.

31

With how sad steps, O Moon, thou climb'st the skies!
How silently, and with how wan a face!
What, may it be that even in heavenly place
That busy archer his sharp arrows tries!
Sure, if that long-with-love-acquainted eyes 5
Can judge of love, thou feel'st a lover's case;
I read it in thy looks; thy languished grace,
To me, that feel the like, thy state descries,
Then, even of fellowship, O Moon, tell me,
Is constant love deemed there but want of wit? 10
Are beauties there as proud as here they be?
Do they above love to be lovèd, and yet
Those lovers scorn whom that love doth possess?
Do they call virtue there ungratefulness?[5]

[1]Abode of Apollo and the Muses.
[2]Adopted, i. e., borrowed. [3]Far-fetched.
[4]Emotion. [5]Call ungratefulness a virtue.

39

Come, Sleep! O Sleep, the certain knot of peace,
The baiting-place of wit, the balm of woe,
The poor man's wealth, the prisoner's release,
Th' indifferent judge between the high and low;
With shield of proof shield me from out the press 5
Of those fierce darts Despair at me doth throw:
O make in me those civil wars to cease;
I will good tribute pay, if thou do so.
Take thou of me smooth pillows, sweetest bed,
A chamber deaf of noise and blind of light, 10
A rosy garland and a weary head:
And if these things, as being thine by right,
Move not thy heavy grace, thou shalt in me,
Livelier than elsewhere, Stella's image see.

41

Having this day my horse, my hand, my lance
Guided so well that I obtained the prize,
Both by the judgment of the English eyes
And of some sent from that sweet enemy, France;
Horsemen my skill in horsemanship advance,[6] 5
Town folks my strength; a daintier judge applies
His praise to sleight which from good use doth rise;
Some lucky wits impute it but to chance;
Others, because of both sides I do take
My blood from them who did excel in this, 10
Think Nature me a man-at-arms did make.
How far they shot awry! the true cause is,
Stella looked on, and from her heavenly face
Sent forth the beams which made so fair my race.

64

No more! My Dear, no more these counsels try!
O give my passions leave to run their race!
Let Fortune lay on me her worst disgrace!
Let folk o'ercharged with brain against me cry!
Let clouds bedim my face, break in mine eye! 5
Let me no steps but of lost labor trace!

[6]Praise.

Let all the earth in scorn recount my case;
But do not will me from my love to fly!
I do not envy Aristotle's wit;
Nor do aspire to Caesar's bleeding fame; 10
Nor ought do care, though some above me sit;
Nor hope, nor wish another course to frame:
But that which once may win thy cruel heart.
Thou art my wit, and thou my virtue art.

95

Leave me, O Love, which reachest but to dust,
And thou, my mind, aspire to higher things!
Grow rich in that which never taketh rust:
Whatever fades, but fading pleasure brings. 4
Draw in thy beams, and humble all thy might
To that sweet yoke where lasting freedoms be;
Which breaks the clouds and open forth the light
That doth both shine and give us sight to see.
O take fast hold! let that light be thy guide
In this small course which birth draws out to death, 10
And think how evil becometh him to slide
Who seeketh Heaven, and comes of heavenly breath.
Then farewell, world! thy uttermost I see:
Eternal Love, maintain thy life in me!

Eleventh Song

"Who is it that this dark night
Underneath my window plaineth?"
It is one who from thy sight
Being, ah! exiled, disdaineth
Every other vulgar light. 5

"Why, alas! and are you he?
Be not yet those fancies changed?"
Dear, when you find change in me,
Though from me you be estranged,
Let my change to ruin be. 10

"Well, in absence this will die;
Leave to see, and leave to wonder."
Absence sure will help, if I
Can learn how myself to sunder
From what in my heart doth lie. 15

"But time will these thoughts remove;
Time doth work what no man knoweth."
Time doth as the subject prove;
With time still the affection groweth
In the faithful turtle-dove. 20

"What if we new beauties see?
Will not they stir new affection?"
I will think they pictures be,
(Image-like, of saint's perfection)
Poorly counterfeiting thee. 25

"But your reason's purest light
Bids you leave such minds to nourish."
Dear, do reason no such spite;
Never doth thy beauty flourish
More than in my reason's sight. 30

"But the wrongs Love bears will make
Love at length leave undertaking."
No, the more fools it do shake,
In the ground of so firm making,
Deeper still they drive the stake. 35

"Peace, I think that some give ear!
Come no more, lest I get anger!"
Bliss, I will my bliss forbear;
Fearing, sweet, you to endanger;
But my soul shall harbor there. 40

"Well, be gone! be gone, I say,
Lest that Argus' eyes[7] perceive you!"
O unjust is Fortune's sway,
Which can make me thus to leave you;
And from louts to run away. 45

MY TRUE-LOVE HATH MY HEART

My true-love hath my heart and I have his,
By just exchange one for the other given:
I hold his dear, and mine he cannot miss;
There never was a better bargain driven: 4
My true-love hath my heart, and I have his.

His heart in me keeps him and me in one.
My heart in him his thoughts and senses guides:
He loves my heart, for once it was his own;
I cherish his because in me it bides: 9
My true-love hath my heart, and I have his.

MY SHEEP ARE THOUGHTS[8]

My sheep are thoughts, which I both guide and serve;
Their pasture is fair hills of fruitless love;
On barren sweets they feed, and feeding sterve.[9]
I wail their lot, but will not other prove;

---

[7]Argus had one hundred eyes.
[8]From Sidney's *Arcadia*. [9]Starve.

My sheep-hook is wan hope, which all upholds; 5
My weeds,[10] desire, cut out in endless folds;
What wool my sheep shall bear, whilst thus they live,
In you it is, you must the judgment give.

SIR EDWARD DYER

(1550?–1607)

MY MIND TO ME A KINGDOM IS

My mind to me a kingdom is;
Such present joys therein I find
That it excels all other bliss
That earth affords or grows by kind:[1] 4
Though much I want which most would have,
Yet still my mind forbids to crave.

No princely pomp, no wealthy store,
No force to win the victory,
No wily wit to salve a sore,
No shape to feed a loving eye, 10
To none of these I yield as thrall:
For why? My mind doth serve for all.

I see how plenty surfeits oft,
And hasty climbers soon do fall;
I see that those which are aloft 15
Mishap doth threaten most of all;
They get with toil, they keep with fear:
Such cares my mind could never bear.

Content to live, this is my stay;
I seek no more than may suffice; 20
I press to bear no haughty sway;
Look, what I lack my mind supplies:
Lo, thus I triumph like a king,
Content with that my mind doth bring.

Some have too much, yet still do crave; 25
I little have, and seek no more.
They are but poor, though much they have,
And I am rich with little store:
They poor, I rich; they beg, I give;
They lack, I leave; they pine, I live. 30

I laugh not at another's loss;
I grudge not at another's pain;
No worldly waves my mind can toss;
My state at one doth still remain:
I fear no foe, I fawn no friend; 35
I loathe not life, nor dread my end.

Some weigh their pleasure by their lust,
Their wisdom by their rage of will;
Their treasure is their only trust;
A cloakéd craft their store of skill: 40
But all the pleasure that I find
Is to maintain a quiet mind.

My wealth is health and perfect ease;
My conscience clear my chief defense;
I neither seek by bribes to please, 45
Nor by deceit to breed offense:
Thus do I live; thus will I die;
Would all did so as well as I!

[10]Clothes.

[1]Nature.

SIR WALTER RALEGH

(1552?–1618)

HIS PILGRIMAGE

Give me my scallop-shell[1] of quiet,
My staff of faith to walk upon,
My scrip[2] of joy, immortal diet,
My bottle of salvation,
My gown of glory, hope's true gage,[3] 5
And thus I'll take my pilgrimage.

Blood must be my body's balmer;
No other balm will there be given;
Whilst my soul, like a quiet palmer,
Traveleth towards the land of heaven, 10
Over the silver mountains,
Where spring the nectar fountains.
There will I kiss
The bowl of bliss,
And drink mine everlasting fill 15
Upon every milken hill.
My soul will be a-dry before;
But, after, it will thirst no more.

Then by that happy blissful day
More peaceful pilgrims I shall see, 20
That have cast off their rags of clay,
And walk appareled fresh like me.
I'll take them first,
To quench their thirst
And taste of nectar suckets,[4] 25
At those clear wells
Where sweetness dwells,
Drawn up by saints in crystal buckets.

And when our bottles and all we
Are filled with immortality, 30

[1]One of the badges of a pilgrim.

[2]Wallet. [3]Pledge. [4]Sweetmeats.

Then the blesséd paths we'll travel,
Strowed with rubies thick as gravel;
Ceilings of diamonds, sapphire floors,
High walls of coral, and pearly bowers.

From thence to heaven's bribeless hall, 35
Where no corrupted voices brawl;
No conscience molten into gold;
No forged accuser bought or sold;
No cause deferred, no vain-spent journey;
For there Christ is the king's attorney, 40
Who pleads for all, without degrees,
And he hath angels[5] but no fees.

And when the grand twelve million jury
Of our sins, with direful fury,
Against our souls black verdicts give, 45
Christ pleads his death; and then we live.
Be Thou my speaker, taintless pleader!
Unblotted lawyer! true proceeder!
Thou giv'st salvation, even for alms,
Not with a bribéd lawyer's palms. 50

And this is mine eternal plea
To him that made heaven and earth and sea:
That, since my flesh must die so soon,
And want a head to dine next noon,
Just at the stroke, when my veins start and spread, 55
Set on my soul an everlasting head!

Then am I ready, like a palmer fit,
To tread those blest paths, which before I writ.

GEORGE PEELE

(1558?–1597?)

CUPID'S CURSE[1]

OENONE. Fair and fair, and twice so fair,
As fair as any may be;
The fairest shepherd on our green,
A love for any lady.
PARIS. Fair and fair, and twice so fair, 5
As fair as any may be;
Thy love is fair for thee alone,
And for no other lady.
OEN. My love is fair, my love is gay,
As fresh as been the flowers in May, 10
And of my love my roundelay,
My merry, merry roundelay,
Concludes with Cupid's curse,—
"They that do change old love for new, 14
Pray gods they change for worse!"
AMBO SIMUL.[2] They that do change, *etc.*
OEN. Fair and fair, *etc.*
PAR. Fair and fair, *etc.*
Thy love is fair, *etc.* 19
OEN. My love can pipe, my love can sing,
My love can many a pretty thing,
And of his lovely praises ring
My merry, merry roundelays,
Amen to Cupid's curse,—
"They that do change," *etc.* 25
PAR. They that do change, *etc.*
AMBO. Fair and fair, *etc.*

HARVESTMEN A-SINGING[3]

All ye that lovely lovers be,
Pray you for me:
Lo, here we come a-sowing, a-sowing,
And sow sweet fruits of love;
In your sweet hearts well may it prove! 5
Lo, here we come a-reaping, a-reaping,
To reap our harvest-fruit!
And thus we pass the year so long,
And never be we mute.

ROBERT GREENE

(1560?–1592)

SWEET ARE THE THOUGHTS THAT SAVOR OF CONTENT[1]

Sweet are the thoughts that savor of content;
The quiet mind is richer than a crown;
Sweet are the nights in careless slumber spent;
The poor estate scorns fortune's angry frown:
Such sweet content, such minds, such sleep, such bliss, 5
Beggars enjoy, when princes oft do miss.

The homely house that harbors quiet rest;
The cottage that affords no pride nor care;
The mean that 'grees with country music best;
The sweet consort of mirth and music's fare; 10
Obscuréd life sets down a type of bliss:
A mind content both crown and kingdom is.

---

[5]Used with double meaning; it was also the name of a coin.
[1]From the *Arraignment of Paris* (1584).
[2]Both together.
[3]From *The Old Wives' Tale* (*c.* 1590).
[1]From *The Farewell to Folly* (1591).

WEEP NOT, MY WANTON[2]

Weep not, my wanton; smile upon my knee;
When thou art old there's grief enough for thee.
Mother's wag, pretty boy,
Father's sorrow, father's joy;
When thy father first did see 5
Such a boy by him and me,
He was glad, I was woe;
Fortune changéd made him so;
When he left his pretty boy
Last his sorrow, first his joy. 10

Weep not, my wanton; smile upon my knee;
When thou art old there's grief enough for thee.
Streaming tears that never stint,
Like pearl-drops from a flint,
Fell by course from his eyes, 15
That one another's place supplies;
Thus he grieved in every part,
Tears of blood fell from his heart,
When he left his pretty boy,
Father's sorrow, father's joy. 20

Weep not, my wanton; smile upon my knee;
When thou art old there's grief enough for thee.
The wanton smiled, father wept;
Mother cried, baby leapt;
More he crowed, more we cried; 25
Nature could not sorrow hide:
He must go, he must kiss
Child and mother, baby bless,
For he left his pretty boy,
Father's sorrow, father's joy. 30
Weep not, my wanton; smile upon my knee;
When thou art old there's grief enough for thee.

[2]From *Menaphon* (1589). A wanton is a spoiled child.

MICHAEL DRAYTON
(1563–1631)

TO HIS COY LOVE

I pray thee, leave, love me no more;
Call home the heart you gave me!
I but in vain that saint adore
That can but will not save me.
These poor half-kisses kill me quite— 5
Was ever man thus servéd?
Amidst an ocean of delight
For pleasure to be stervéd?[1]
Show me no more those snowy breasts
With azure riverets branchéd, 10
Where, whilst mine eye with plenty feasts,
Yet is my thirst not stanchéd;
O Tantalus, thy pains ne'er tell!
By me thou art prevented:[2]
'Tis nothing to be plagued in hell, 15
But thus in heaven tormented!

Clip[3] me no more in those dear arms,
Nor thy life's cömfort call me,
O these are but too powerful charms,
And do but more enthral me! 20
But see how patient I am grown
In all this coil[4] about thee:
Come, nice thing, let my heart alone,
I cannot live without thee!

[1]Starved.

[2]Anticipated. [3]Embrace. [4]Disturbance.

IDEA

To the Reader of These Sonnets

Into these loves who but for passion looks,
At this first sight, here let him lay them by,
And seek elsewhere in turning other books
Which better may his labor satisfy.
No far-fetched sigh shall ever wound my breast; 5
Love from mine eye a tear shall never wring;
Nor in "Ah me's!" my whining sonnets drest!
A libertine! fantasticly I sing!
My verse is the true image of my mind,
Ever in motion, still desiring change; 10
And as thus, to variety inclined,
So in all humors sportively I range!
My Muse is rightly of the English strain,
That cannot long one fashion entertain.

61

Since there's no help, come, let us kiss and part!
Nay, I have done; you get no more of me!
And I am glad, yea, glad with all my heart
That thus so cleanly I myself can free.
Shake hands for ever! Cancel all our vows! 5
And when we meet at any time again,
Be it not seen in either of our brows
That we one jot of former love retain!
Now at the last gasp of Love's latest breath,
When, his pulse failing, Passion speechless lies; 10
When Faith is kneeling by his bed of death,
And Innocence is closing up his eyes—

Now, if thou wouldst, when all have given
him over,
From death to life thou might'st him yet
recover!

ODE XI

To the Virginian Voyage

You brave heroic minds,
Worthy your country's name,
That honor still pursue;
Go and subdue!
Whilst loitering hinds[5] 5
Lurk here at home with shame.

Britons, you stay too long;
Quickly aboard bestow you!
And with a merry gale
Swell your stretched sail, 10
With vows as strong
As the winds that blow you!

Your course securely steer,
West-and-by-south forth keep!
Rocks, lee-shores, nor shoals, 15
When Eolus[6] scowls,
You need not fear,
So absolute the deep.

And cheerfully at sea,
Success you still entice 20
To get the pearl and gold;
And ours to hold,
Virginia,
Earth's only Paradise;

Where Nature hath in store 25
Fowl, venison, and fish;
And the fruitful'st soil,—
Without your toil,
Three harvests more,
All greater than your wish. 30

And the ambitious vine
Crowns with his purple mass
The cedar reaching high
To kiss the sky,
The cypress, pine, 35
And useful sassafras.

To whom the Golden Age[7]
Still Nature's laws doth give:
Nor other cares attend,
But them to defend 40
From winter's rage,
That long there doth not live.

[5]Peasants. [6]God of winds.

[7]A fabled period of peace and plenty.

When as the luscious smell
Of that delicious land,
Above the seas that flows, 45
The clear wind throws,
Your hearts to swell,
Approaching the dear strand.

In kenning[8] of the shore
(Thanks to God first given!) 50
O you, the happiest men,
Be frolic then!
Let cannons roar,
Frightening the wide heaven!

And in regions far 55
Such heroes bring ye forth
As those from whom we came!
And plant our name
Under that star
Not known unto our North! 60

And as there plenty grows
The laurel everywhere,
Apollo's sacred tree,
You may it see
A poet's brows 65
To crown, that may sing there.

Thy Voyages attend,
Industrious Hakluyt![9]
Whose reading shall inflame
Men to seek fame, 70
And much commend
To after times thy wit.

ODE XII

To the Cambro-Britons and Their Harp His Ballad of Agincourt

Fair stood the wind for France,
When we our sails advance;
Nor now to prove our chance
Longer will tarry;
But putting to the main, 5
At Caux, the mouth of Seine,
With all his martial train
Landed King Harry.[10]

And taking many a fort,
Furnished in warlike sort, 10

[8]Recognition.

[9]Richard Hakluyt (1553–1616), compiler of a famous collection of narratives of Elizabethan voyages, first published in 1589.

[10]Henry V.

Marcheth towards Agincourt[11]
In happy hour;
Skirmishing day by day,
With those that stopped his way,
Where the French general lay 15
With all his power.

Which, in his height of pride,
King Henry to deride,
His ransom to provide
To the King sending; 20
Which he neglects the while,
As from a nation vile,
Yet, with an angry smile,
Their fall portending.

And turning to his men, 25
Quoth our brave Henry then:
"Though they to one be ten
Be not amazéd!
Yet have we well begun:
Battles so bravely won 30
Have ever to the sun
By Fame been raiséd!

"And for myself," quoth he,
"This my full rest shall be:
England ne'er mourn for me, 35
Nor more esteem me!
Victor I will remain
Or on this earth lie slain;
Never shall she sustain
Loss to redeem me! 40

"Poitiers and Crécy[12] tell,
When most their pride did swell,
Under our swords they fell.
No less our skill is
Than when our grandsire great, 45
Claiming the regal seat,
By many a warlike feat
Lopped the French lilies."

The Duke of York so dread
The eager vanward led; 50
With the main, Henry sped
Amongst his henchmen;
Exeter had the rear,
A braver man not there!
O Lord, how hot they were 55
On the false Frenchmen!

[11]The battle of Agincourt was fought on 25 October, 1415.

[12]Victories of the English in France during the Hundred Years' War. The battle of Crécy took place on 26 August, 1346; that of Poitiers on 19 September, 1356.

They now to fight are gone;
Armor on armor shone;
Drum now to drum did groan:
To hear was wonder; 60
That, with the cries they make,
The very earth did shake;
Trumpet to trumpet spake;
Thunder to thunder.

Well it thine age became, 65
O noble Erpingham,
Which didst the signal aim
To our hid forces!
When, from a meadow by,
Like a storm suddenly, 70
The English archery
Struck the French horses

With Spanish yew so strong;
Arrows a cloth-yard long,
That like to serpents stung, 75
Piercing the weather.
None from his fellow starts;
But, playing manly parts,
And like true English hearts,
Stuck close together. 80

When down their bows they threw,
And forth their bilboes[13] drew,
And on the French they flew:
Not one was tardy.
Arms were from shoulders sent, 85
Scalps to the teeth were rent,
Down the French peasants went:
Our men were hardy.

This while our noble King,
His broad sword brandishing, 90
Down the French host did ding,[14]
As to o'erwhelm it.
And many a deep wound lent;
His arms with blood besprent,
And many a cruel dent 95
Bruiséd his helmet.

Gloucester, that duke so good,
Next of the royal blood,
For famous England stood
With his brave brother. 100
Clarence, in steel so bright,
Though but a maiden knight,
Yet in that furious fight
Scarce such another!

[13]Swords. [14]Strike.

Warwick in blood did wade; 105
Oxford, the foe invade,
And cruel slaughter made,
Still as they ran up.
Suffolk his ax did ply;
Beaumont and Willoughby 110
Bare them right doughtily;
Ferrers and Fanhope.

Upon Saint Crispin's Day
Fought was this noble fray,
Which Fame did not delay 115
To England to carry.
O, when shall English men
With such acts fill a pen?
Or England breed again
Such a King Harry? 120

WILLIAM SHAKESPEARE

(1564–1616)

SONNETS

15

When I consider everything that grows
Holds in perfection but a little moment,
That this huge stage presenteth nought but shows
Whereon the stars in secret influence comment;
When I perceive that men as plants increase, 5
Cheeréd and checked e'en by the self-same sky,
Vaunt in their youthful sap, at height decrease,
And wear their brave state out of memory:
Then the conceit[1] of this inconstant stay
Sets you most rich in youth before my sight, 10
Where wasteful Time debateth[2] with decay,
To change your day of youth to sullied night;
And all in war with Time for love of you,
As he takes from you, I engraft you new.

18

Shall I compare thee to a summer's day?
Thou art more lovely and more temperate:
Rough winds do shake the darling buds of May,
And summer's lease hath all too short a date;

[1]Thought. [2]Contends.

Sometime too hot the eye of heaven shines, 5
And often is his gold complexion dimmed;
And every fair from fair sometime declines,
By chance or nature's changing course untrimmed:
But thy eternal summer shall not fade
Nor lose possession of that fair thou ow'st;[3] 10
Nor shall Death brag thou wand'rest in his shade,
When in eternal lines to time thou grow'st;[4]
So long as men can breathe or eyes can see,
So long lives this and this gives life to thee.

25

Let those who are in favor with their stars,
Of public honor and proud titles boast,
Whilst I, whom fortune of such triumph bars,
Unlooked for,[5] joy in that I honor most.
Great princes' favorites their fair leaves spread 5
But as the marigold at the sun's eye,
And in themselves their pride lies buriéd,
For at a frown they in their glory die.
The painful[6] warrior famouséd for worth,
After a thousand victories once foiled, 10
Is from the book of honor razéd forth,
And all the rest forgot for which he toiled.
Then happy I, that love and am beloved
Where I may not remove nor be removed.

29

When, in disgrace with Fortune and men's eyes,
I all alone beweep my outcast state,
And trouble deaf heaven with my bootless cries,
And look upon myself and curse my fate,
Wishing me like to one more rich in hope, 5
Featured like him, like him with friends possessed,
Desiring this man's art, and that man's scope,
With what I most enjoy contented least.
Yet in these thoughts myself almost despising,
Haply I think on thee; and then my state, 10
Like to the lark at break of day arising
From sullen earth, sings hymns at heaven's gate;

[3]Ownest.
[4]When you reach future times in my eternal lines.
[5]Unexpectedly. [6]Suffering pain.

For thy sweet love remembered such wealth brings
That then I scorn to change my state with kings.

30

When to the sessions of sweet silent thought
I summon up[7] remembrance of things past,
I sigh the lack of many a thing I sought,
And with old woes new wail my dear time's waste;
Then can I drown an eye, unused to flow, 5
For precious friends hid in death's dateless night,
And weep afresh love's long since canceled woe,
And moan th' expense[8] of many a vanished sight:
Then can I grieve at grievances foregone,
And heavily from woe to woe tell[9] o'er 10
The sad account of fore-bemoanéd moan,
Which I new pay as if not paid before.
But if the while I think on thee, dear friend,
All losses are restored and sorrows end.

31

Thy bosom is endearéd with all hearts
Which I by lacking have supposéd dead;
And there reigns love, and all love's loving parts,
And all those friends which I thought buriéd.
How many a holy and obsequious[10] tear 5
Hath dear religious love stol'n from mine eye
As interest of the dead, which now appear
But things removed that hidden in thee lie!
Thou art the grave where buried love doth live,
Hung with the trophies of my lovers gone, 10
Who all their parts of me to thee did give,
That due of many[11] now is thine alone.
Their images I loved I view in thee,
And thou, all they, hast all the all of me.

55

Not marble, nor the gilded monuments
Of princes, shall outlive this powerful rime;
But you shall shine more bright in these contents[12]
Than[13] unswept stone besmeared with sluttish time.

[7]Summon up as in a court of justice. [8]Cost.
[9]Count. [10]Funereal.
[11]So that what belonged to many.
[12]In these verses. [13]Than in.

When wasteful war shall statues overturn, 5
And broils root out the work of masonry,
Nor Mars his sword nor war's quick fire shall burn
The living record of your memory.
'Gainst death and all-oblivious enmity
Shall you pace forth; your praise shall still find room, 10
Even in the eyes of all posterity
That wear this world out to the ending doom.
So, till the judgment that[14] yourself arise,
You live in this, and dwell in lovers' eyes.

57

Being your slave, what should I do but tend
Upon the hours and times of your desire?
I have no precious time at all to spend,
Nor services to do, till you require.
Nor dare I chide the world-without-end hour 5
Whilst I, my sovereign, watch the clock for you,
Nor think the bitterness of absence sour
When you have bid your servant once adieu.
Nor dare I question with my jealous thought
Where you may be, or your affairs suppose, 10
But, like a sad slave, stay and think of nought
Save, where you are how happy you make those.
So true a fool is love that in your will,[15]
Though you do anything, he thinks no ill.

60

Like as the waves make towards the pebbled shore,
So do our minutes hasten to their end;
Each changing place with that which goes before,
In sequent toil all forwards do contend.
Nativity, once in the main of light,[16] 5
Crawls to maturity, wherewith being crowned,
Crooked[17] eclipses 'gainst his glory fight,
And Time that gave doth now his gift confound.
Time doth transfix the flourish[18] set on youth
And delves the parallels[19] in beauty's brow, 10

[14]When.
[15]The original text reads "Will," and perhaps a play was intended on Shakespeare's own first name.
[16]The sky. [17]Malignant.
[18]Doth remove the garland.
[19]Parallels are, literally, trenches parallel with a fortification which is besieged.

Feeds on the rarities of nature's truth,
And nothing stands but for his scythe to mow;
And yet to times in hope[20] my verse shall stand,
Praising thy worth, despite his cruel hand.

64

When I have seen by Time's fell hand defaced
The rich proud cost of outworn buried age;
When sometime[21] lofty towers I see down-razed
And brass eternal slave to mortal rage;
When I have seen the hungry ocean gain 5
Advantage on the kingdom of the shore,
And the firm soil win of the watery main,
Increasing store with loss and loss with store;
When I have seen such interchange of state,
Or state[22] itself confounded to decay: 10
Ruin hath taught me thus to ruminate,
That Time will come and take my love away.
This thought is as a death, which cannot choose
But weep to have that which it fears to lose.

71

No longer mourn for me when I am dead
Than you shall hear the surly sullen bell
Give warning to the world that I am fled
From this vile world, with vilest worms to dwell.
Nay, if you read this line, remember not 5
The hand that writ it; for I love you so
That I in your sweet thoughts would be forgot,
If thinking on me then should make you woe.
O, if, I say, you look upon this verse
When I perhaps compounded am with clay, 10
Do not so much as my poor name rehearse,
But let your love even with my life decay,
Lest the wise world should look into your moan
And mock you with me after I am gone.

73

That time of year thou mayst in me behold
When yellow leaves, or none, or few, do hang
Upon those boughs which shake against the cold,
Bare ruined choirs where late the sweet birds sang.

[20]Future times. [21]Once. [22]Greatness.

In me thou see'st the twilight of such day 5
As after sunset fadeth in the west,
Which by and by black night doth take away,
Death's second self, that seals up all in rest.
In me thou see'st the glowing of such fire
That on the ashes of his youth doth lie, 10
As the death-bed whereon it must expire,
Consumed with that which it was nourished by[23]
This thou perceiv'st, which makes thy love more strong,
To love that well which thou must leave ere long.

90

Then hate me when thou wilt; if ever, now;
Now, while the world is bent my deeds to cross,
Join with the spite of fortune, make me bow,
And do not drop in for an after-loss:
Ah, do not, when my heart hath 'scaped this sorrow, 5
Come in the rearward of a conquered woe;
Give not a windy night a rainy morrow,
To linger out a purposed overthrow.
If thou wilt leave me, do not leave me last,
When other petty griefs have done their spite, 10
But in the onset come; so shall I taste
At first the very worst of fortune's might,
And other strains[24] of woe, which now seem woe,
Compared with loss of thee will not seem so.

94

They that have power to hurt and will do none,
That do not do the thing they most do show,
Who, moving others, are themselves as stone,
Unmovéd, cold, and to temptation slow,
They rightly do inherit heaven's graces 5
And husband nature's riches from expense;
They are the lords and owners of their faces,
Others but stewards of their excellence.[25]
The summer's flower is to the summer sweet,
Though to itself it only live and die; 10
But if that flower with base infection meet,
The basest weed outbraves his dignity:

[23]Choked by the ashes of the wood by which it was nourished.

[24]Kinds.

[25]Beautiful persons who are commanded by their passions hold their beauty as stewards for the commanders, their passions, which are the real owners.

For sweetest things turn sourest by their deeds;
Lilies that fester smell far worse than weeds.

97

How like a winter hath my absence been
From thee, the pleasure of the fleeting year!
What freezings have I felt, what dark days seen!
What old December's bareness everywhere!
And yet this time removed[26] was summer's time, 5
The teeming autumn, big with rich increase,
Bearing the wanton burden of the prime,[27]
Like widowed wombs after their lords' decease.
Yet this abundant issue seemed to me
But hope of orphans[28] and unfathered fruit; 10
For summer and his pleasures wait on thee,
And, thou away, the very birds are mute;
Or, if they sing, 'tis with so dull a cheer
That leaves look pale, dreading the winter's near.

98

From you have I been absent in the spring,
When proud-pied[29] April, dressed in all his trim,
Hath put a spirit of youth in everything,
That heavy Saturn[30] laughed and leaped with him.
Yet nor the lays of birds nor the sweet smell 5
Of different flowers in[31] odor and in hue
Could make me any summer's story tell,[32]
Or from their proud lap pluck them where they grew;
Nor did I wonder at the lily's white,
Nor praise the deep vermilion in the rose; 10
They were but sweet, but figures of delight
Drawn after you, you pattern of all those.
Yet seemed it winter still, and, you away,
As with your shadow I with these did play.

106

When in the chronicle of wasted time
I see descriptions of the fairest wights,[33]
And beauty making beautiful old rime
In praise of ladies dead and lovely knights;
Then, in the blazon of sweet beauty's best, 5
Of hand, of foot, of lip, of eye, of brow,
I see their antique pen would have expressed
Even such a beauty as you master[34] now.
So all their praises are but prophecies
Of this our time, all you prefiguring; 10
And, for they looked but with divining eyes,
They had not skill enough your worth to sing:
For we, which now behold these present days,
Have eyes to wonder, but lack tongues to praise.

109

O, never say that I was false of heart,
Though absence seemed my flame to qualify.[35]
As easy might I from myself depart
As from my soul, which in thy breast doth lie.
That is my home of love; if I have ranged, 5
Like him that travels I return again,
Just to the time, not with the time exchanged,[36]
So that myself bring water for my stain.
Never believe, though in my nature reigned
All frailties that besiege all kinds of blood,[37] 10
That it could so preposterously be stained
To leave for nothing all thy sum of good;
For nothing this wide universe I call,
Save thou, my rose; in it thou art my all.

110

Alas, 'tis true I have gone here and there
And made myself a motley to the view,[38]
Gored[39] mine own thoughts, sold cheap what is most dear,
Made old offenses of affections new;
Most true it is that I have looked on truth 5
Askance and strangely: but, by all above,
These blenches[40] gave my heart another youth,
And worse essays proved thee my best of love.

---

[26]Time of my absence.

[27]The children of the wanton spring.

[28]Hope such as orphans bring.

[29]Gaily colored.

[30]Planet credited in astrology with producing a sluggish and gloomy temperament in those born under its influence.

[31]Flowers different in.

[32]Could make me tell a cheerful story; or, could put me in harmony with the season.

[33]People. [34]Have. [35]Moderate.

[36]Punctual, not altered by the time.

[37]Temperament. [38]A public jester.

[39]Injured. [40]Aberrations.

Now all is done, have what shall have no end:
Mine appetite I never more will grind[41] 10
On newer proof, to try an older friend,
A god in love, to whom I am confined.
Then give me welcome, next my heaven the best,
Even to thy pure and most most loving breast.

111

O, for my sake do you with Fortune chide,
The guilty goddess of[42] my harmful deeds,
That did not better for my life provide
Than public means which public manners breeds.
Thence comes it that my name receives a brand, 5
And almost thence my nature is subdued
To what it works in, like the dyer's hand.
Pity me, then, and wish I were renewed;
Whilst, like a willing patient, I will drink
Potions of eisel[43] 'gainst my strong infection; 10
No bitterness that I will bitter think,
Nor double penance, to correct correction.
Pity me then, dear friend, and I assure ye
Even that your pity is enough to cure me.

116

Let me not to the marriage of true minds
Admit impediments. Love is not love
Which alters when it alteration finds,
Or bends with the remover to remove.
O, no! it is an ever-fixéd mark 5
That looks on tempests and is never shaken;
It is the star to every wand'ring bark,
Whose worth's unknown, although his height be taken.
Love's not Time's fool,[44] though rosy lips and cheeks
Within his bending sickle's compass come; 10
Love alters not with his brief hours and weeks,
But bears it out even to the edge of doom.[45]
If this be error and upon me proved,
I never writ, nor no man ever loved.

129

Th' expense of spirit in a waste of shame
Is lust in action;[46] and till action, lust
Is perjured, murd'rous, bloody, full of blame,

[41]Whet. [42]Goddess guilty of. [43]Vinegar.
[44]The sport of time. [45]Doomsday.
[46]Lust in action is a shameful expenditure of energy.

Savage, extreme, rude, cruel, not to trust,
Enjoyed no sooner but despiséd straight, 5
Past reason hunted, and no sooner had,
Past reason hated, as a swallowed bait
On purpose laid to make the taker mad;
Mad in pursuit and in possession so;
Had, having, and in quest to have, extreme; 10
A bliss in proof,[47] and, proved, a very woe;
Before, a joy proposed; behind, a dream.
All this the world well knows; yet none knows well
To shun the heaven that leads men to this hell.

130

My mistress' eyes are nothing like the sun;
Coral is far more red than her lips' red;
If snow be white, why then her breasts are dun;
If hairs be wires, black wires grow on her head.
I have seen roses damasked, red and white, 5
But no such roses see I in her cheeks;
And in some perfumes is there more delight
Than in the breath that from my mistress reeks.
I love to hear her speak, yet well I know
That music hath a far more pleasing sound; 10
I grant I never saw a goddess go;[48]
My mistress, when she walks, treads on the ground:
And yet, by heaven, I think my love as rare
As any she belied with false compare.

146

Poor soul, the center of my sinful earth,[49]
Rebuke these rebel powers that thee array!
Why dost thou pine within and suffer dearth,
Painting thy outward walls so costly gay?
Why so large cost, having so short a lease, 5
Dost thou upon thy fading mansion spend?
Shall worms, inheritors of this excess,
Eat up thy charge?[50] Is this thy body's end?
Then, soul, live thou upon thy servant's loss,
And let that pine to aggravate[51] thy store; 10
Buy terms divine[52] in selling hours of dross;
Within be fed, without be rich no more;
So shalt thou feed on Death,[53] that feeds on men,
And Death once dead, there's no more dying then.

[47]In experience. [48]Walk. [49]My body.
[50]The body on which so much has been spent.
[51]Increase. [52]Eternity.
[53]Consume the mortal elements.

Songs from the Plays

WHEN DAISIES PIED[54]

When daisies pied and violets blue,
And lady-smocks all silver-white,
And cuckoo-buds of yellow hue
Do paint the meadows with delight,
The cuckoo then, on every tree, 5
Mocks married men; for thus sings he,
Cuckoo!
Cuckoo, cuckoo!—O word of fear,
Unpleasing to a married ear!

When shepherds pipe on oaten straws, 10
And merry larks are plowmen's clocks,
When turtles[55] tread, and rooks, and daws,
And maidens bleach their summer smocks,
The cuckoo then, on every tree,
Mocks married men; for thus sings he, 15
Cuckoo!
Cuckoo, cuckoo!—O word of fear,
Unpleasing to a married ear!

WHEN ICICLES HANG BY THE WALL

When icicles hang by the wall,
And Dick the shepherd blows his nail,
And Tom bears logs into the hall,
And milk comes frozen home in pail,
When blood is nipped and ways be foul, 5
Then nightly sings the staring owl,
"Tu-whit, tu-who!" a merry note,
While greasy Joan doth keel[56] the pot.

When all aloud the wind doth blow,
And coughing drowns the parson's saw,[57] 10
And birds sit brooding in the snow,
And Marian's nose looks red and raw,
When roasted crabs[58] hiss in the bowl,
Then nightly sings the staring owl,
"Tu-whit, tu-who!" a merry note, 15
While greasy Joan doth keel the pot.

WHO IS SYLVIA?[59]

Who is Sylvia? what is she,
That all our swains commend her?
Holy, fair, and wise is she;
The heaven such grace did lend her,
That she might admiréd be. 5

Is she kind as she is fair?
For beauty lives with kindness.
Love doth to her eyes repair
To help him of his blindness,
And, being helped, inhabits there. 10

Then to Sylvia let us sing,
That Sylvia is excelling;
She excels each mortal thing
Upon the dull earth dwelling:
To her let us garlands bring. 15

TELL ME, WHERE IS FANCY BRED[60]

Tell me, where is fancy bred,
Or in the heart, or in the head?
How begot, how nourished?
Reply, reply.
It is engendered in the eyes, 5
With gazing fed; and fancy dies
In the cradle where it lies:
Let us all ring fancy's knell;
I'll begin it,—Ding-dong, bell.
Ding, dong, bell. 10

UNDER THE GREENWOOD TREE[61]

Under the greenwood tree
Who loves to lie with me,
And turn his merry note
Unto the sweet bird's throat,
Come hither! come hither! come hither! 5
Here shall he see
No enemy
But winter and rough weather.

Who doth ambition shun
And loves to live i' the sun, 10
Seeking the food he eats
And pleased with what he gets,
Come hither! come hither! come hither!
Here shall he see
No enemy 15
But winter and rough weather.

BLOW, BLOW, THOU WINTER WIND

Blow, blow, thou winter wind!
Thou art not so unkind
As man's ingratitude;
Thy tooth is not so keen,
Because thou art not seen, 5
Although thy breath be rude.

---

[54]This and the following song are from *Love's Labor's Lost.*
[55]Turtle-doves. [56]Skim. [57]Discourse.
[58]Apples. [59]From *Two Gentlemen of Verona.*
[60]From *The Merchant of Venice.*
[61]This and the following song are from *As You Like It.*

Heigh ho! sing, heigh ho! unto the green holly:
Most friendship is feigning, most loving mere folly:
Then, heigh ho, the holly!
This life is most jolly. 10

Freeze, freeze, thou bitter sky!
That dost not bite so nigh
As benefits forgot;
Though thou the waters warp,[62]
Thy sting is not so sharp 15
As friend remembered not.

Heigh ho! sing, heigh ho! *etc.*

SIGH NO MORE[63]

Sigh no more, ladies, sigh no more!
Men were deceivers ever,
One foot in sea and one on shore,
To one thing constant never:
Then sigh not so, but let them go, 5
And be you blithe and bonny,
Converting all your sounds of woe
Into Hey nonny, nonny!

Sing no more ditties, sing no moe[64]
Of dumps so dull and heavy! 10
The fraud of men was ever so,
Since summer first was leafy:
Then sigh not so, but let them go,
And be you blithe and bonny,
Converting all your sounds of woe 15
Into Hey nonny, nonny!

O MISTRESS MINE[65]

O mistress mine, where are you roaming?
O stay and hear; your true love's coming,
That can sing both high and low:
Trip no further, pretty sweeting;
Journeys end in lovers meeting, 5
Every wise man's son doth know.

What is love? 't is not hereafter;
Present mirth hath present laughter;
What's to come is still unsure:
In delay there lies no plenty; 10
Then come kiss me, sweet and twenty;
Youth's a stuff will not endure.

[62]Cause to shrink.
[63]From *Much Ado about Nothing.*
[64]More. [65]From *Twelfth Night*

TAKE, O TAKE THOSE LIPS AWAY[66]

Take, O take those lips away,
That so sweetly were forsworn;
And those eyes, the break of day,
Lights that do mislead the morn:
But my kisses bring again, 5
Bring again;
Seals of love, but sealed in vain,
Sealed in vain!

COME, THOU MONARCH OF THE VINE[67]

Come, thou monarch of the vine,
Plumpy Bacchus with pink eyne![68]
In thy vats our cares be drowned,
With thy grapes our hairs be crowned!
Cup us, till the world go round, 5
Cup us, till the world go round!

HARK, HARK! THE LARK[69]

Hark, hark! the lark at heaven's gate sings,
And Phoebus 'gins arise,
His steeds to water at those springs
On chaliced flowers that lies;
And winking Mary-buds begin 5
To ope their golden eyes:
With everything that pretty is,
My lady sweet, arise!
Arise, arise!

FEAR NO MORE THE HEAT O' THE SUN

Fear no more the heat o' th' sun,
Nor the furious winter's rages;
Thou thy worldly task hast done;
Home art gone, and ta'en thy wages:
Golden lads and girls all must, 5
As chimney-sweepers, come to dust.

Fear no more the frown o' th' great;
Thou art past the tyrant's stroke;
Care no more to clothe and eat;
To thee the reed is as the oak: 10
The Scepter, Learning, Physic must
All follow this, and come to dust.

Fear no more the lightning-flash,
Nor th' all-dreaded thunder-stone;
Fear not slander, censure rash; 15
Thou hast finished joy and moan:

[66]From *Measure for Measure.*
[67]From *Antony and Cleopatra.* [68]Eyes.
[69]This and the following song are from *Cymbeline.*

All lovers young, all lovers must
Consign[70] to thee, and come to dust.

No exorciser harm thee!
Nor no witchcraft charm thee! 20
Ghost unlaid forbear thee!
Nothing ill come near thee!
Quiet consummation have;
And renownéd be thy grave!

FULL FATHOM FIVE THY FATHER LIES[71]

Full fathom five thy father lies:
Of his bones are coral made;
Those are pearls that were his eyes;
Nothing of him that doth fade
But doth suffer a sea-change 5
Into something rich and strange.
Sea-nymphs hourly ring his knell;
Ding-dong!
Hark! now I hear them,—Ding-dong, bell!

THOMAS CAMPION

(1567-1619)

FOLLOW THY FAIR SUN

Follow thy fair sun, unhappy shadow,
Though thou be black as night,
And she made all of light;
Yet follow thy fair sun, unhappy shadow.

Follow her whose light thy light depriveth, 5
Though here thou liest disgraced,
And she in heaven is placed;
Yet follow her whose light the world reviveth.

Follow those pure beams whose beauty burneth,
That so have scorchéd thee 10
As thou still black must be,
Till her kind beams thy black to brightness turneth.

Follow her while yet her glory shineth:
There comes a luckless night
That will dim all her light; 15
And this the black unhappy shade divineth.

Follow still, since so thy fates ordainéd;
The Sun must have his shade,
Till both at once do fade,
The Sun still proud, the shadow still disdainéd. 20

FOLLOW YOUR SAINT

Follow your saint, follow with accents sweet;
Haste you, sad notes; fall at her flying feet;
There, wrapt in cloud of sorrow, pity move,
And tell the ravisher of my soul I perish for her love:
But if she scorns my never-ceasing pain, 5
Then burst with sighing in her sight and ne'er return again.

All that I sung still to her praise did tend;
Still she was first; still she my songs did end.
Yet she my love and music both doth fly,
The music that her echo is and beauty's sympathy; 10
Then let my notes pursue her scornful flight:
It shall suffice that they were breathed and died for her delight.

THERE IS A GARDEN IN HER FACE

There is a garden in her face
Where roses and white lilies grow;
A heavenly paradise is that place,
Wherein all pleasant fruits do flow:
There cherries grow which none may buy 5
Till "Cherry-ripe" themselves do cry.

Those cherries fairly do enclose
Of orient pearl a double row,
Which when her lovely laughter shows,
They look like rosebuds filled with snow; 10
Yet them nor peer nor prince can buy
Till "Cherry-ripe" themselves do cry.

Her eyes like angels watch them still;
Her brows like bended bows do stand,
Threatening with piercing frowns to kill 15
All that attempt, with eye or hand,
Those sacred cherries to come nigh
Till "Cherry-ripe" themselves do cry.

WHEN THOU MUST HOME

When thou must home to shades of underground,
And there arrived, a new admiréd guest,
The beauteous spirits do engirt thee round,
White Iöpe, blithe Helen, and the rest,
To hear the stories of thy finished love 5
From that smooth tongue whose music hell can move;

[70] Agree. [71] From *The Tempest*.

Then wilt thou speak of banqueting delights,
Of masques and revels which sweet youth did make,
Of tourneys and great challenges of knights,
And all these triumphs for thy beauty's sake: 10
When thou hast told these honors done to thee,
Then tell, O tell, how thou didst murder me.

NOW WINTER NIGHTS ENLARGE

Now winter nights enlarge
The number of their hours;
And clouds their storms discharge
Upon the airy towers.
Let now the chimneys blaze, 5
And cups o'erflow with wine;
Let well-tuned words amaze
With harmony divine.
Now yellow waxen lights
Shall wait on honey love; 10
While youthful revels, masques, and courtly sights
Sleep's leaden spells remove.

This time doth well dispense
With lovers' long discourse;
Much speech hath some defense, 15
Though beauty no remorse.
All do not all things well:
Some measures comely tread,
Some knotted riddles tell,
Some poems smoothly read. 20
The summer hath his joys,
And winter his delights;
Though love and all his pleasures are but toys,
They shorten tedious nights.

ROSE-CHEEKED LAURA

Rose-cheeked Laura, come,
Sing thou smoothly with thy beauty's
Silent music, either other
Sweetly gracing.

Lovely forms do flow 5
From consent[1] divinely framéd;
Heav'n is music, and thy beauty's
Birth is heavenly.

These dull notes we sing
Discords need for helps to grace them; 10
Only beauty purely loving
Knows no discord,

But still moves delight,
Like clear springs renewed by flowing,
Ever perfect, ever in them- 15
selves eternal.

[1]Harmony.

NEVER LOVE

Never love, unless you can
Bear with all the faults of man:
Men sometimes will jealous be,
Though but little cause they see,
And hang the head, as discontent, 5
And speak what straight they will repent.

Men that but one saint adore
Make a show of love to more:
Beauty must be scorned in none,
Though but truly served in one: 10
For what is courtship but disguise?
True hearts may have dissembling eyes.

Men, when their affairs require,
Must awhile themselves retire;
Sometimes hunt, and sometimes hawk, 15
And not ever sit and talk.
If these and such like you can bear,
Then like, and love, and never fear.

BEAUTY IS BUT A PAINTED HELL

Beauty is but a painted hell:
Aye me, aye me,
She wounds them that admire it;
She kills them that desire it;
Give her pride but fuel, 5
No fire is more cruel.

Pity from ev'ry heart is fled:
Aye me, aye me,
Since false desire could borrow
Tears of dissembled sorrow, 10
Constant vows turn truthless,
Love cruel, Beauty ruthless.

Sorrow can laugh, and Fury sing:
Aye me, aye me,
My raving griefs discover 15
I lived too true a lover;
The first step to madness
Is the excess of sadness.

THE MAN OF LIFE UPRIGHT

The man of life upright,
Whose guiltless heart is free
From all dishonest deeds,
Or thought of vanity;

The man whose silent days 5
In harmless joys are spent,
Whom hopes cannot delude
Nor sorrow discontent;

That man needs neither towers
Nor armor for defense, 10
Nor secret vaults to fly
From thunder's violence.

He only can behold
With unaffrighted eyes
The horrors of the deep 15
And terrors of the skies.

Thus, scorning all the cares
That fate or fortune brings,
He makes the heav'n his book,
His wisdom heav'nly things, 20

Good thoughts his only friends,
His wealth a well-spent age,
The earth his sober inn
And quiet pilgrimage.

BEN JONSON

(1573?–1637)

HYMN TO DIANA

Queen and Huntress, chaste and fair,
Now the sun is laid to sleep,
Seated in thy silver chair
State in wonted manner keep:
Hesperus[1] entreats thy light, 5
Goddess excellently bright.

Earth, let not thy envious shade
Dare itself to interpose;
Cynthia's shining orb was made
Heaven to clear when day did close: 10
Bless us then with wishéd sight,
Goddess excellently bright.

Lay thy bow of pearl apart
And thy crystal-shining quiver;
Give unto the flying hart 15
Space to breathe, how short soever:
Thou that mak'st a day of night,
Goddess excellently bright.

[1]The evening star.

SONG: TO CELIA[2]

Come, my Celia, let us prove,
While we can, the sports of love.
Time will not be ours for ever;
He, at length, our good will sever;
Spend not then his gifts in vain. 5
Suns that set may rise again;
But if once we lose this light,
'T is with us perpetual night.
Why should we defer our joys?
Fame and rumor are but toys. 10
Cannot we delude the eyes
Of a few poor household spies?
Or his easier ears beguile,
Thus removéd by our wile?
'T is no sin love's fruits to steal; 15
But the sweet theft to reveal,
To be taken, to be seen,
These have crimes accounted been.

TO CELIA

Drink to me only with thine eyes,
And I will pledge with mine;
Or leave a kiss but in the cup,
And I'll not look for wine.
The thirst that from the soul doth rise 5
Doth ask a drink divine;
But might I of Jove's nectar sup,
I would not change for[3] thine.

I sent thee late a rosy wreath,
Not so much honoring thee 10
As giving it a hope that there
It could not withered be.
But thou thereon didst only breathe,
And sent'st it back to me;
Since when it grows, and smells, I swear, 15
Not of itself, but thee.

SONG: THAT WOMEN ARE BUT MEN'S SHADOWS

Follow a shadow, it still flies you;
Seem to fly it, it will pursue:
So court a mistress, she denies you;
Let her alone, she will court you.
Say are not women truly, then, 5
Styled but the shadows of us men?

At morn and even shades are longest;
At noon they are or short or none:
So men at weakest, they are strongest,
But grant us perfect, they're not known. 10
Say are not women truly, then,
Styled but the shadows of us men?

[2]An adaptation of Catullus (*Carmina*, v).
[3]From.

STILL TO BE NEAT

Still to be neat, still to be drest,
As you were going to a feast;
Still to be powdered, still perfumed;—
Lady, it is to be presumed,
Though art's hid causes are not found, 5
All is not sweet, all is not sound.

Give me a look, give me a face,
That makes simplicity a grace;
Robes loosely flowing, hair as free:
Such sweet neglect more taketh me 10
Than all th' adulteries of art;
They strike mine eyes, but not my heart.

HER TRIUMPH

See the chariot at hand here of Love,
Wherein my lady rideth!
Each that draws is a swan or a dove,
And well the car Love guideth.
As she goes, all hearts do duty 5
Unto her beauty;
And enamored, do wish, so they might
But enjoy such a sight,
That they still were to run by her side,
Through swords, through seas, whither she would ride. 10

Do but look on her eyes: they do light
All that Love's world compriseth!
Do but look on her hair: it is bright
As Love's star when it riseth!
Do but mark: her forehead's smoother 15
Than words that soothe her;
And from her arched brows, such a grace
Sheds itself through the face
As alone there triumphs to the life
All the gain, all the good, of the elements' strife. 20

Have you seen but a bright lily grow
Before rude hands have touched it?
Have you marked but the fall of the snow
Before the soil hath smutched[4] it?
Have you felt the wool of the beaver? 25
Or swan's down ever?
Or have smelt o' the bud of the briar?
Or the nard in the fire?
Or have tasted the bag of the bee!
O so white! O so soft! O so sweet is she! 30

[4]Dirtied.

AN ODE

High-spirited friend,
I send nor balms, nor corsives[5] to your wound;
Your faith hath found
A gentler and more agile hand to tend
The cure of that which is but corporal, 5
And doubtful days, which were named critical,
Have made their fairest flight,
And now are out of sight.
Yet doth some wholesome physic for the mind
Wrapt in this paper lie, 10
Which in the taking if you misapply,
You are unkind.

Your covetous hand,
Happy in that fair honor it hath gained,
Must now be reined. 15
True valor doth her own renown command
In one full action; nor have you now more
To do than be a husband of that store.
Think but how dear you bought
This same which you have caught; 20
Such thoughts will make you more in love with truth:
'Tis wisdom, and that high,
For men to use their fortune reverently,
Even in youth.

A SONG

O do not wanton with those eyes,
Lest I be sick with seeing;
Nor cast them down, but let them rise,
Lest shame destroy their being.

O be not angry with those fires, 5
For then their threats will kill me;
Nor look too kind on my desires,
For then my hopes will spill me.

O do not steep them in thy tears,
For so will sorrow slay me; 10
Nor spread them as distract with fears;
Mine own enough betray me.

A NYMPH'S PASSION

I love, and he loves me again,
Yet dare I not tell who;
For if the nymphs should know my swain,
I fear they'd love him too;

[5]A corrosive medicine.

Yet if he be not known, 5
The pleasure is as good as none,
For that's a narrow joy is but our own.

I'll tell, that if they be not glad,
They yet may envy me;
But then if I grow jealous mad, 10
And of them pitied be,
It were a plague 'bove scorn;
And yet it cannot be forborn,
Unless my heart would, as my thought, be torn.

He is, if they can find him, fair, 15
And fresh and fragrant too,
As summer's sky, or purgéd air,
And looks as lilies do
That are this morning blown;
Yet, yet I doubt he is not known, 20
And fear much more that more of him be shown.

But he hath eyes so round, and bright,
As make away my doubt,
Where Love may all his torches light
Though hate had put them out: 25
But then, t' increase my fears,
What nymph so'er his voice but hears
Will be my rival, though she have but ears.

I'll tell no more, and yet I love,
And he loves me; yet no 30
One unbecoming thought doth move
From either heart, I know;
But so exempt from blame,
As it would be to each a fame,
If love or fear would let me tell his name. 35

TO THE MEMORY OF MY BELOVED MASTER WILLIAM SHAKESPEARE

To draw no envy, Shakespeare, on thy name,
Am I thus ample to thy book and fame;
While I confess thy writings to be such
As neither man, nor muse, can praise too much.
'T is true, and all men's suffrage.[6] But these ways 5
Were not the paths I meant unto thy praise;
For silliest ignorance on these may light,
Which, when it sounds at best, but echoes right;
Or blind affection, which doth ne'er advance
The truth, but gropes, and urgeth all by chance; 10
Or crafty malice might pretend this praise,
And think to ruin, where it seemed to raise.
These are as some infamous bawd or whore

[6]Opinion.

Should praise a matron. What could hurt her more?
But thou art proof against them and, indeed, 15
Above the ill fortune of them, or the need.
I therefore will begin. Soul of the age!
The applause, delight, the wonder of our stage!
My Shakespeare, rise! I will not lodge thee by
Chaucer, or Spenser, or bid Beaumont lie 20
A little further, to make thee a room:
Thou art a monument without a tomb,
And art alive still while thy book doth live
And we have wits to read and praise to give.
That I not mix thee so, my brain excuses, 25
I mean with great, but disproportioned muses;
For if I thought my judgment were of years,
I should commit thee surely with thy peers,
And tell how far thou didst our Lyly outshine,
Or sporting Kyd, or Marlowe's mighty line. 30
And though thou hadst small Latin and less Greek,
From thence to honor thee I would not seek
For names; but call forth thundering Aeschylus,
Euripides, and Sophocles to us;
Pacuvius[7] Accius,[7] him of Cordova[8] dead, 35
To life again, to hear thy buskin[9] tread,
And shake a stage; or, when thy socks[10] were on,
Leave thee alone for the comparison
Of all that insolent Greece or haughty Rome
Sent forth, or since did from their ashes come. 40
Triumph, my Britain, thou hast one to show
To whom all scenes of Europe homage owe.
He was not of an age, but for all time!
And all the Muses still were in their prime
When, like Apollo, he came forth to warm 45
Our ears, or like a Mercury to charm!
Nature herself was proud of his designs
And joyed to wear the dressing of his lines!
Which were so richly spun, and woven so fit,
As, since, she will vouchsafe no other wit. 50
The merry Greek, tart Aristophanes,
Neat Terence, witty Plautus, now not please;
But antiquated and deserted lie,
As they were not of Nature's family.

[7]Roman tragic poet. [8]Seneca the tragic poet.

[9]The high boot worn in classical times by actors in tragedy.

[10]Light shoes worn in classical times by actors in comedy.

Yet must I not give Nature all; thy art, 55
My gentle Shakespeare, must enjoy a part.
For though the poet's matter Nature be,
His art doth give the fashion; and that he
Who casts to write a living line must sweat,
(Such as thine are) and strike the second heat 60
Upon the Muses' anvil; turn the same
(And himself with it) that he thinks to frame,
Or, for the laurel, he may gain a scorn;
For a good poet's made, as well as born.
And such wert thou! Look how the father's face 65
Lives in his issue; even so the race
Of Shakespeare's mind and manners brightly shines
In his well turnéd, and true filéd lines;
In each of which he seems to shake a lance,
As brandished at the eyes of ignorance. 70
Sweet Swan of Avon! what a sight it were
To see thee in our waters yet appear,
And make those flights upon the banks of Thames,
That so did take Eliza, and our James![11]
But stay; I see thee in the hemisphere 75
Advanced, and made a constellation there!
Shine forth, thou star of poets, and with rage
Or influence, chide or cheer the drooping stage,
Which, since thy flight from hence, hath mourned like night,
And despairs day, but for thy volume's light. 80

A PINDARIC ODE

To the Immortal Memory and Friendship of that Noble Pair, Sir Lucius Cary and Sir H. Morison[12]

I

THE STROPHE, OR TURN

Brave infant of Saguntum,[13] clear
Thy coming forth in that great year
When the prodigious Hannibal did crown
His rage with razing your immortal town.
Thou looking then about, 5
Ere thou were half got out,
Wise child, didst hastily return,
And mad'st thy mother's womb thine urn.
How summed[14] a circle didst thou leave mankind
Of deepest lore, could we the center find! 10

THE ANTISTROPHE, OR COUNTER-TURN

Did wiser nature draw thee back
From out the horror of that sack,
Where shame, faith, honor, and regard of right
Lay trampled on? the deeds of death and night
Urged, hurried forth, and hurled 15
Upon the affrighted world;
Fire, famine, and fell fury met,
And all on utmost ruin set:
As, could they but life's miseries foresee,
No doubt all infants would return like thee. 20

THE EPODE, OR STAND

For what is life, if measured by the space,
Not by the act?
Or maskéd man, if valued by his face
Above his fact?[15]
Here's one outlived his peers 25
And told forth fourscore years;
He vexéd time, and busied the whole state,
Troubled both foes and friends,
But ever to no ends:
What did this stirrer but die late? 30
How well at twenty had he fallen or stood![16]
For three of his four score he did no good.

II

THE STROPHE, OR TURN

He entered well by virtuous parts,
Got up, and thrived with honest arts,
He purchased friends, and fame, and honors then,
And had his noble name advanced with men;
But weary of that flight, 5
He stooped in all men's sight
To sordid flatteries, acts of strife,
And sunk in that dead sea of life,
So deep as he did then death's waters sup,
But that the cork of title buoyed him up. 10

[11] Queen Elizabeth and James I.

[12] Pindar was the greatest of Greek lyric poets. This poem is modeled upon his odes in its stanzaic structure, and to some extent in its style and tone. Sir Lucius Cary, Viscount Falkland, was himself a poet and the friend of men of letters, who visited him freely at his country house near Oxford. He married the sister of Sir Henry Morison. Morison died in 1629, shortly before Jonson's ode was written.

[13] A city in Spain captured by Hannibal after a painful siege (219 B. C.) The story told by Jonson is recorded by Pliny, *Natural History,* VII, iii.

[14] Complete. [15] Deed. [16] Stopped.

THE ANTISTROPHE, OR COUNTER-TURN

Alas! but Morison fell young!
He never fell,—thou fall'st, my tongue.
He stood a soldier to the last right end,
A perfect patriot and a noble friend;
But most, a virtuous son. 15
All offices were done
By him, so ample, full, and round,
In weight, in measure, number, sound,
As, though his age imperfect might appear,
His life was of humanity the sphere.[17] 20

THE EPODE, OR STAND

Go now, and tell[18] our days summed up with fears,
And make them years;
Produce thy mass of miseries on the stage,
To swell thine age;
Repeat of things a throng, 25
To show thou hast been long,
Not lived; for life doth her great actions spell
By what was done and wrought
In season, and so brought
To light: her measures are, how well 30
Each syllabe answered, and was formed how fair;
These make the lines of life, and that's her air!

III

THE STROPHE, OR TURN

It is not growing like a tree
In bulk, doth make men better be;
Or standing long an oak, three hundred year,
To fall a log at last, dry, bald, and sear:
A lily of a day 5
Is fairer far in May,
Although it fall and die that night;
It was the plant and flower of light.
In small proportions we just beauties see;
And in short measures life may perfect be. 10

THE ANTISTROPHE, OR COUNTER-TURN

Call, noble Lucius, then, for wine,
And let thy looks with gladness shine;
Accept this garland, plant it on thy head,
And think, nay know, thy Morison's now dead.
He leaped the present age, 15
Possest with holy rage,
To see that bright eternal day,
Of which we priests and poets say
Such truths as we expect for happy men;
And there he lives with memory and Ben 20

THE EPODE, OR STAND

Jonson, who sung this of him, ere he went
Himself to rest,
Or taste a part of that full joy he meant
To have exprest,
In this bright asterism;[19] 25
Where it were friendship's schism,
Were not his Lucius long with us to tarry,
To separate these twi-
Lights, the Dioscuri;[20]
And keep the one half from his Harry. 30
But fate doth so altérnate the design,
Whilst that in heaven, this light on earth must shine.

IV

THE STROPHE, OR TURN

And shine as you exalted are;
Two names of friendship, but one star:
Of hearts the union, and those not by chance
Made, or indenture, or leased out t' advance
The profits for a time. 5
No pleasures vain did chime
Of rimes, or riots, at your feasts,
Orgies of drink, or feigned protests;
But simple love of greatness and of good,
That knits brave minds and manners more than blood. 10

THE ANTISTROPHE, OR COUNTER-TURN

This made you first to know the why
You liked, then after to apply
That liking; and approach so one the t' other,
Till either grew a portion of the other;
Each styléd by his end, 15
The copy of his friend.
You lived to be the great sir-names
And titles by which all made claims
Unto the virtue: nothing perfect done,
But as a Cary or a Morison. 20

THE EPODE, OR STAND

And such a force the fair example had
As they that saw
The good and durst not practice it, were glad
That such a law

[17] I. e., included all that humanity may achieve.
[18] Count.
[19] Constellation.
[20] Castor and Pollux, children of Zeus.

Was left yet to mankind; 25
Where they might read and find
Friendship, indeed, was written not in words;
And with the heart, not pen,
Of two so early men,
Whose lines her rolls were, and records; 30
Who, ere the first down bloomèd on the chin,
Had sowed these fruits, and got the harvest in.

EPITAPH ON ELIZABETH, L. H.

Would'st thou hear what man can say
In a little? Reader, stay.

Underneath this stone doth lie
As much beauty as could die:
Which in life did harbor give 5
To more virtue than doth live.

If at all she had a fault,
Leave it buried in this vault.
One name was Elizabeth,
The other, let it sleep with death! 10
Fitter where it died to tell
Than that it lived at all. Farewell!

EPITAPH ON SALATHIEL PAVY

Weep with me, all you that read
This little story;
And know, for whom a tear you shed
Death's self is sorry.
'T was a child that so did thrive 5
In grace and feature
As heaven and nature seemed to strive
Which owned the creature.
Years he numbered scarce thirteen
When fates turned cruel; 10
Yet three filled zodiacs[21] had he been
The stage's jewel,
And did act, what now we moan,
Old men so duly
As, sooth, the Parcae[22] thought him one, 15
He played so truly.
So, by error, to his fate
They all consented;
But viewing him since, alas, too late!
They have repented; 20
And have sought, to give new birth,
In baths to steep him;
But being so much too good for earth,
Heaven vows to keep him.

[21]Full years. [22]The Fates.

JOHN DONNE

(1573–1631)

SONG

Go and catch a falling star,
Get with child a mandrake root,[1]
Tell me where all past years are,
Or who cleft the devil's foot;
Teach me to hear mermaids singing, 5
Or to keep off envy's stinging,
And find
What wind
Serves to advance an honest mind.

If thou be'st born to strange sights, 10
Things invisible to see,
Ride ten thousand days and nights
Till age snow white hairs on thee;
Thou, when thou return'st, wilt tell me
All strange wonders that befell thee, 15
And swear
No where
Lives a woman true and fair.

If thou find'st one, let me know;
Such a pilgrimage were sweet. 20
Yet do not; I would not go,
Though at next door we might meet.
Though she were true when you met her,
And last till you write your letter,
Yet she 25
Will be
False, ere I come, to two or three.

THE INDIFFERENT

I can love both fair and brown;
Her whom abundance melts, and her whom want betrays;
Her who loves loneness best, and her who[2] masks and plays;
Her whom the country formed, and whom the town;
Her who believes, and her who tries; 5
Her who still weeps with spongy eyes,
And her who is dry cork and never cries.
I can love her, and her, and you, and you;
I can love any, so she be not true.

Will no other vice content you? 10
Will it not serve your turn to do as did your mothers?

[1]This root has a shape somewhat like that of the human body.
[2]Who loves.

Or have you all old vices spent and now
would find out others?
Or doth a fear that men are true torment
you?
O we are not, be not you so;
Let me—and do you—twenty know; 15
Rob me, but bind me not, and let me go.
Must I, who came to travel thorough you,
Grow your fixed subject, because you are
true?

Venus heard me sigh this song;
And by love's sweetest part, variety, she
swore 20
She heard not this till now; it should be so
no more.
She went, examined, and returned ere long,
And said, "Alas! some two or three
Poor heretics in love there be, 24
Which think to stablish dangerous constancy.
But I have told them, 'Since you will be true,
You shall be true to them who're false to
you.'"

THE CANONIZATION

For God's sake hold your tongue, and let me
love,
Or chide my palsy or my gout;
My five gray hairs or ruin'd fortune flout;
With wealth your state, your mind with
arts improve;
Take you a course, get you a place, 5
Observe his Honor or his Grace;
Or the king's real, or his stamped face
Contemplate; what you will, approve,
So you will let me love.

Alas, alas, who's injur'd by my love? 10
What merchant's ships have my sighs
drown'd?
Who says my tears have overflow'd his
ground?
When did my colds a forward spring
remove?
When did the heats which my veins
fill
Add one more to the plaguy bill?[3] 15
Soldiers find wars, and lawyers find out still
Litigious men which quarrels move,
Though she and I do love.

Call us what you will, we are made such
by love;
Call her one, me another fly, 20
We're tapers too and at our own cost die;
And we in us find th'eagle and the dove.[4]
The phoenix riddle[5] hath more wit
By us: we two, being one, are it.
So to one neutral thing both sexes fit; 25
We die and rise the same and prove
Mysterious by this love.

We can die by it, if not live by love;
And if unfit for tombs and hearse
Our legend be, it will be fit for verse; 30
And if no piece of chronicle we prove,
We'll build in sonnets pretty rooms.
As well a well-wrought urn becomes
The greatest ashes, as half-acre tombs;
And by these hymns all shall approve 35
Us canonized for love,

And thus invoke us: "You whom reverend
love
Made one another's hermitage;
You to whom love was peace, that now is
rage;
Who did the whole world's soul contract,
and drove 40
Into the glasses of your eyes
(So made such mirrors and such spies
That they did all to you epitomize)
Countries, towns, courts: beg from above
A pattern of your love!" 45

LOVERS' INFINITENESS

If yet I have not all thy love,
Dear, I shall never have it all;
I cannot breathe one other sigh to move,
Nor can intreat one other tear to fall,
And all my treasure which should purchase
thee, 5
Sighs, tears, and oaths, and letters, I have
spent.
Yet no more can be due to me
Than at the bargain made was meant;
If then thy gift of love were partial,
That some to me, some should to others
fall, 10
Dear, I shall never have thee all.

Or if then thou gavest me all,
All was but all which thou hadst then;
But if in thy heart, since, there be or shall
New love created be by other men, 15

[3]The official record of the number of those who had died by the plague.

[4]The respective symbols of strength and purity.

[5]After living 500 or 1000 years the phoenix burned itself to ashes and was reborn from the fire.

Which have their stocks entire, and can in tears,
In sighs, in oaths, and letters outbid me,
This new love may beget new fears,
For this love was not vowed by thee;
And yet it was, thy gift being general; 20
The ground, thy heart, is mine, whatever shall
Grow there, dear; I should have it all.

Yet I would not have all yet;
He that hath all can have no more,
And since my love doth every day admit 25
New growth, thou shouldst have new rewards in store;
Thou canst not every day give me thy heart;
If thou canst give it, then thou never gavest it:
Love's riddles are that, though thy heart depart,
It stays at home, and thou with losing savest it: 30
But we will have a way more liberal
Than changing hearts, to join them; so we shall
Be one, and one another's all.

SONG

Sweetest love, I do not go
For weariness of thee,
Nor in hope the world can show
A fitter love for me;
But since that I 5
Must die at last, 'tis best
To use myself in jest
Thus by fain'd deaths to die.

Yesternight the sun went hence
And yet is here today; 10
He hath no desire nor sense,
Nor half so short a way.
Then fear not me,
But believe that I shall make
Speedier journeys, since I take 15
More wings and spurs than he.

O how feeble is man's power,
That if good fortune fall
Cannot add another hour,
Nor a lost hour recall! 20
But come bad chance,
And we join to't our strength,
And we teach it art and length[6]
Itself o'er us t'advance.

When thou sigh'st, thou sigh'st not wind, 25
But sigh'st my soul away;
When thou weep'st, unkindly kind,
My life's blood doth decay.
It cannot be
That thou lov'st me as thou say'st, 30
If in thine my life thou waste
That art the best of me.

Let not thy divining heart
Forethink me any ill;
Destiny may take thy part 35
And may thy fears fulfil.
But think that we
Are but turn'd aside to sleep;
They who one another keep
Alive, ne'er parted be. 40

THE DREAM

Dear love, for nothing less than thee
Would I have broke this happy dream;
It was a theme
For reason, much too strong for fantasy.
Therefore thou waked'st me wisely; yet 5
My dream thou brok'st not, but continued'st it.
Thou art so true that thoughts of thee suffice
To make dreams truths and fables histories;
Enter these arms, for since thou thought'st it best 9
Not to dream all my dream, let's act the rest.

As lightning, or a taper's light,
Thine eyes, and not thine noise, waked me;
Yet I thought thee—
For thou lov'st truth—an angel, at first sight;
But when I saw thou saw'st my heart, 15
And knew'st my thoughts beyond an angel's art,
When thou knew'st what I dreamt, when thou knew'st when
Excess of joy would wake me, and cam'st then,
I must confess it could not choose but be
Profane to think thee anything but thee. 20

Coming and staying showed thee thee,
But rising makes me doubt that now
Thou art not thou.
That love is weak where fear's as strong as he;
'T is not all spirit pure and brave 25
If mixture it of fear, shame, honor have.
Perchance as torches, which must ready be,
Men light and put out, so thou deal'st with me.

[6]Endurance.

Thou cam'st to kindle, go'st to come: then I
Will dream that hope again, but else would
  die.

THE ECSTASY

Where, like a pillow on a bed,
  A pregnant bank swelled up, to rest
The violet's reclining head,
  Sat we two, one another's best.
Our hands were firmly cemented 5
  With a fast balm, which thence did spring;
Our eye-beams twisted, and did thread
  Our eyes upon one double string;
So t' intergraft our hands as yet
  Was all the means to make us one, 10
And pictures in our eyes to get
  Was all our propagation.
As 'twixt two equal armies, fate
  Suspends uncertain victory,
Our souls (which to advance their state, 15
  Were gone out) hung 'twixt her and me.
And whil'st our souls negotiate there,
  We like sepulchral statues lay;
All day the same our postures were,
  And we said nothing all the day. 20
If any, so by love refined
  That he soul's language understood,
And by good love were grown all mind,
  Within convenient distance stood,
He (though he knew not which soul spake, 25
  Because both meant, both spake the same)
Might thence a new concoction take,
  And part far purer than he came.
This Ecstasy doth unperplex
  (We said) and tell us what we love; 30
We see by this it was not sex;
  We see we saw not what did move:[7]
But as all several souls contain
  Mixture of things, they know not what,
Love, these mixed souls, doth mix again, 35
  And makes both one, each this and that.
A single violet transplant,
  The strength, the color, and the size,
(All which before was poor, and scant)
  Redoubles still, and multiplies. 40
When love with one another so
  Interinanimates two souls,
That abler soul, which thence doth flow,
  Defects of loneliness controls.
We then, who are this new soul, know 45
  Of what we are composed, and made,
For th' atomies of which we grow,
  Are souls, whom no change can invade.
But O alas, so long, so far
  Our bodies why do we forbear? 50

[7]We see now that we did not before know the true source of our love.

They're ours, though they're not we; we are
  The intelligences, they the sphere.[8]
We owe them thanks, because they thus
  Did us to us at first convey,
Yielded their forces, sense, to us, 55
  Nor are dross to us, but allay.[9]
On man heaven's influence works not so
  But that it first imprints the air;
So soul into the soul may flow,
  Though it to body first repair. 60
As our blood labors to beget
  Spirits as like souls as it can,
Because such fingers need to knit
  That subtle knot which makes us man:
So must pure lovers' souls descend 65
  T' affections, and to faculties,
Which sense may reach and apprehend;
  Else a great prince in prison lies.
T' our bodies turn we then, that so
  Weak men on love revealed may look; 70
Love's mysteries in souls do grow,
  But yet the body is his book.
And if some lover, such as we,
  Have heard this dialogue of one,
Let him still mark us: he shall see 75
  Small change when we're to bodies gone.

THE FUNERAL

Whoever comes to shroud me, do not harm
  Nor question much
That subtle wreath of hair[10] about mine
  arm:
The mystery, the sign you must not touch,
  For 'tis my outward soul, 5
Viceroy to that which, unto heav'n being
  gone,[11]
  Will leave this to control
And keep these limbs, her provinces, from
  dissolution.

For if the sinewy thread my brain lets fall
  Through every part[12] 10
Can tie those parts, and make me one of all,
Those hairs which upward grew, and
  strength and art
  Have from a better brain,[13]
Can better do't; except she meant that I
  By this should know my pain, 15
As prisoners then are manacled when they're
  condemned to die.

[8]The astronomical spheres were supposed to be moved by spirits known as intelligences.

[9]Alloy.

[10]Bracelet of the lady's hair.

[11]Viceroy to the inward, true soul which has departed from the body.

[12]Probably the soul. [13]The lady's.

Whate'er she meant by 't, bury it with me;
For since I am
Love's martyr, it might breed idolatry
If into other hands these relics came; 20
As 'twas humility
To afford to it all that a soul can do,
So 'tis some bravery[14]
That, since you would have none of me, I bury some of you.

HOLY SONNET

Death, be not proud, though some have calléd thee
Mighty and dreadful, for thou art not so;
For those whom thou think'st thou dost overthrow
Die not, poor Death; nor yet canst thou kill me.
From rest and sleep, which but thy picture be, 5
Much pleasure; then from thee much more must flow;
And soonest our best men with thee do go—
Rest of their bones and souls' delivery!
Thou'rt slave to fate, chance, kings, and desperate men,
And dost with poison, war, and sickness dwell; 10
And poppy or charms can make us sleep as well
And better than thy stroke. Why swell'st thou then?
One short sleep past, we wake eternally,
And Death shall be no more: Death, thou shalt die!

A HYMN TO GOD THE FATHER

Wilt thou forgive that sin where I begun,
Which was my sin, though it were done before?[15]
Wilt thou forgive that sin through which I run,
And do run still, though still I do deplore?
When thou hast done, thou hast not done; 5
For I have more.

Wilt thou forgive that sin which I have won
Others to sin, and made my sins their door?
Wilt thou forgive that sin which I did shun
A year or two, but wallowed in a score? 10
When thou hast done, thou has not done;
For I have more.

I have a sin of fear, that when I've spun
My last thread, I shall perish on the shore;
But swear by thyself that at my death thy Son 15
Shall shine as he shines now and heretofore;
And having done that, thou hast done;
I fear no more.

[14]Bravado.

[15]Original sin, derived from Adam and Eve.

ROBERT HERRICK
(1591–1674)

THE ARGUMENT OF HIS BOOK

I sing of brooks, of blossoms, birds, and bowers,
Of April, May, of June and July-flowers;
I sing of May-poles, hock-carts, wassails, wakes,[1]
Of bridegrooms, brides, and of their bridal cakes;
I write of youth, of love, and have access 5
By these to sing of cleanly wantonness;
I sing of dews, of rains, and, piece by piece,
Of balm, of oil, of spice, and ambergris;
I sing of times trans-shifting, and I write
How roses first came red and lilies white; 10
I write of groves, of twilights, and I sing
The court of Mab, and of the Fairy King;
I write of hell; I sing (and ever shall)
Of heaven, and hope to have it after all.

UPON THE LOSS OF HIS MISTRESSES

I have lost, and lately, these
Many dainty mistresses:
Stately Julia, prime of all;
Sapho next, a principal;
Smooth Anthea, for a skin 5
White and heaven-like crystalline;
Sweet Electra; and the choice
Myrha, for the lute and voice.
Next Corinna, for her wit,
And the graceful use of it; 10
With Perilla: all are gone;
Only Herrick's left alone,
For to number sorrow by
Their departures hence, and die.

[1]A hock-cart is the last cart drawn from the field at harvest. Wassail is a drinking-bout. Wake is a merry-making or fair held on the anniversary of the dedication of a church.

CHERRY-RIPE

Cherry-ripe, ripe, ripe, I cry,
Full and fair ones; come and buy!
If so be you ask me where
They do grow, I answer, there
Where my Julia's lips do smile; 5
There's the land, or cherry-isle,
Whose plantations fully show
All the year where cherries grow.

DELIGHT IN DISORDER

A sweet disorder in the dress
Kindles in clothes a wantonness.
A lawn about the shoulders thrown
Into a fine distraction;
An erring lace, which here and there 5
Enthralls the crimson stomacher,[2]
A cuff neglectful, and thereby
Ribbons to flow confusedly;
A winning wave (deserving note)
In the tempestuous petticoat; 10
A careless shoe-string, in whose tie
I see a wild civility;—
Do more bewitch me than when art
Is too precise in every part.

CORINNA'S GOING A-MAYING

Get up, get up for shame; the blooming morn
Upon her wings presents the god unshorn.
See how Aurora throws her fair
Fresh-quilted colors through the air:
Get up, sweet slug-a-bed, and see 5
The dew bespangling herb and tree.
Each flower has wept and bowéd toward the east
Above an hour since: yet you not dressed;
Nay! not so much as out of bed?
When all the birds have matins said 10
And sung their thankful hymns, 'tis sin,
Nay, profanation, to keep in,
Whenas a thousand virgins on this day
Spring, sooner than the lark, to fetch in May.

Rise, and put on your foliage, and be seen 15
To come forth, like the spring-time, fresh and green,
And sweet as Flora.[3] Take no care
For jewels for your gown or hair:
Fear not; the leaves will strew
Gems in abundance upon you: 20
Besides, the childhood of the day has kept,
Against you come, some orient pearls unwept;
Come and receive them while the light
Hangs on the dew-locks of the night:
And Titan[4] on the eastern hill 25
Retires himself, or else stands still
Till you come forth. Wash, dress, be brief in praying:
Few beads[5] are best when once we go a-Maying.

Come, my Corinna, come; and coming mark
How each field turns a street, each street a park 30
Made green and trimmed with trees; see how
Devotion gives each house a bough
Or branch: each porch, each door ere this
An ark, a tabernacle is,
Made up of white-thorn, neatly interwove; 35
As if here were those cooler shades of love.
Can such delights be in the street
And open fields and we not see 't?
Come, we'll abroad; and let's obey
The proclamation made for May: 40
And sin no more, as we have done, by staying;
But, my Corinna, come, let's go a-Maying.

There's not a budding boy or girl this day
But is got up, and gone to bring in May.
A deal of youth, ere this, is come 45
Back, and with white-thorn laden home.
Some have dispatched their cakes and cream
Before that we have left to dream:
And some have wept, and wooed, and plighted troth,
And chose their priest, ere we can cast off sloth: 50
Many a green-gown[6] has been given;
Many a kiss, both odd and even;
Many a glance too has been sent
From out the eye, love's firmament;
Many a jest told of the keys betraying 55
This night, and locks picked, yet we're not a-Maying.

Come, let us go while we are in our prime;
And take the harmless folly of the time.
We shall grow old apace, and die
Before we know our liberty. 60
Our life is short, and our days run
As fast away as does the sun;
And, as a vapor or a drop of rain,
Once lost, can ne'er be found again,

---

[2]Front-piece of woman's dress.
[3]Goddess of flowers.
[4]The sun. [5]Prayers.
[6]Many a tumble on the grass.

So when or you or I are made 65
A fable, song, or fleeting shade,
All love, all liking, all delight
Lies drowned with us in endless night.
Then while time serves, and we are but decaying,
Come, my Corinna, come let's go a-Maying. 70

TO THE VIRGINS TO MAKE MUCH OF TIME

Gather ye rosebuds while ye may;
Old Time is still a-flying;
And this same flower that smiles to-day
To-morrow will be dying.

The glorious lamp of heaven, the sun, 5
The higher he's a-getting,
The sooner will his race be run,
And nearer he's to setting.

That age is best which is the first,
When youth and blood are warmer; 10
But being spent, the worse and worst
Times still succeed the former.

Then be not coy, but use your time,
And while ye may, go marry;
For, having lost but once your prime, 15
You may forever tarry.

TO MUSIC, TO BECALM HIS FEVER

Charm me asleep, and melt me so
With thy delicious numbers
That, being ravished, hence I go
Away in easy slumbers.
Ease my sick head, 5
And make my bed,
Thou power that canst sever
From me this ill;
And quickly still,
Though thou not kill, 10
My fever.

Thou sweetly canst convert the same
From a consuming fire
Into a gentle-licking flame,
And make it thus expire. 15
Then make me weep
My pains asleep,
And give me such reposes
That I, poor I,
May think, thereby, 20
I live and die
'Mongst roses.

Fall on me like a silent dew,
Or like those maiden showers,
Which, by the peep of day, do strew 25
A baptism o'er the flowers.
Melt, melt my pains
With thy soft strains,
That having ease me given,
With full delight 30
I leave this light,
And take my flight
For heaven.

TO ANTHEA, WHO MAY COMMAND HIM ANYTHING

Bid me to live, and I will live
Thy protestant[7] to be:
Or bid me love, and I will give
A loving heart to thee.

A heart as soft, a heart as kind, 5
A heart as sound and free
As in the whole world thou canst find,
That heart I'll give to thee.

Bid that heart stay, and it will stay,
To honor thy decree: 10
Or bid it languish quite away,
And 't shall do so for thee.

Bid me to weep, and I will weep,
While I have eyes to see:
And having none, yet I will keep 15
A heart to weep for thee.

Bid me despair, and I'll despair,
Under that cypress tree:
Or bid me die, and I will dare
E'en death, to die for thee. 20

Thou art my life, my love, my heart,
The very eyes of me,
And hast command of every part,
To live and die for thee.

UPON A CHILD THAT DIED

Here she lies, a pretty bud,
Lately made of flesh and blood:
Who as soon fell fast asleep,
As her little eyes did peep.
Give her strewings, but not stir 5
The earth that lightly covers her.

[7] Suitor.

TO DAFFODILS

Fair Daffodils, we weep to see
You haste away so soon;
As yet the early rising sun
Has not attained his noon.
Stay, stay, 5
Until the hasting day
Has run
But to the even-song;
And, having prayed together, we
Will go with you along. 10

We have short time to stay as you;
We have as short a spring;
As quick a growth to meet decay
As you, or anything.
We die 15
As your hours do, and dry
Away,
Like to the summer's rain;
Or as the pearls of morning's dew,
Ne'er to be found again. 20

TO DAISIES, NOT TO SHUT SO SOON

Shut not so soon; the dull-eyed night
Has not as yet begun
To make a seizure on the light,
Or to seal up the sun.

No marigolds yet closéd are, 5
No shadows great appear;
Nor doth the early shepherd's star
Shine like a spangle here.

Stay but till my Julia close
Her life-begetting eye; 10
And let the whole world then dispose
Itself to live or die.

TO ENJOY THE TIME

While fates permit us, let's be merry:
Pass all we must the fatal ferry;
And this our life too whirls away
With the rotation of the day.

HIS WINDING-SHEET

Come thou, who art the wine and wit
Of all I've writ;
The grace, the glory, and the best
Piece of the rest.
Thou art of what I did intend 5
The all and end;
And what was made, was made to meet
Thee, thee, my sheet.
Come then, and be to my chaste side
Both bed and bride. 10
We two as relics left will have
One rest, one grave;
And, hugging close, we will not fear
Lust ent'ring here,
Where all desires are dead, or cold 15
As is the mold,
And all affections are forgot,
Or trouble not.
Here, here the slaves and pris'ners be
From shackles free, 20
And weeping widows, long oppressed,
Do here find rest.
The wrongéd client ends his laws
Here, and his cause;
Here those long suits of chancery lie 25
Quiet, or die,
And all star-chamber bills[8] do cease,
Or hold their peace.
Here needs no court for our request,
Where all are best, 30
All wise, all equal, and all just,
Alike i' th' dust;
Nor need we here to fear the frown
Of court, or crown;
Where fortune bears no sway o'er things, 35
There all are kings.
In this securer place we'll keep,
As lulled asleep;
Or for a little time we'll lie,
As robes laid by, 40
To be another day re-worn,—
Turned, but not torn;
Or like old testaments engrossed,[9]
Locked up, not lost:
And for a while lie here concealed, 45
To be revealed
Next at that great Platonic year,[10]
And then meet here.

ART ABOVE NATURE. TO JULIA

When I behold a forest spread
With silken trees upon thy head,
And when I see that other dress
Of flowers set in comeliness;
When I behold another grace 5
In the ascent of curious lace,
Which like a pinnacle doth show
The top, and the top-gallant too;

---

[8]Bills handled by the court which originally sat in the Star Chamber at Westminster.

[9]Collected.

[10]The year in which everything will return to its original state.

Then, when I see thy tresses bound
Into an oval, square, or round, 10
And knit in knots far more than I
Can tell by tongue, or true-love tie;
Next, when those lawny films I see
Play with a wild civility,
And all those airy silks to flow, 15
Alluring me, and tempting so:
I must confess, mine eye and heart
Dotes less on nature than on art.

THE PRIMROSE

Ask me why I send you here
This sweet infanta of the year?
Ask me why I send to you
This primrose, thus bepearled with dew?
I will whisper to your ears, 5
The sweets of love are mixed with tears.
Ask me why this flower does show
So yellow-green, and sickly too?
Ask me why the stalk is weak
And bending, yet it doth not break? 10
I will answer, these discover
What fainting hopes are in a lover.

THE NIGHT-PIECE, TO JULIA

Her eyes the glow-worm lend thee;
The shooting stars attend thee;
And the elves also,
Whose little eyes glow
Like the sparks of fire, befriend thee. 5

No Will-o'-th'-Wisp mis-light thee,
Nor snake nor slow-worm bite thee;
But on, on thy way,
Not making a stay,
Since ghost there's none to affright thee. 10

Let not the dark thee cumber;
What though the moon does slumber?
The stars of the night
Will lend thee their light,
Like tapers clear without number. 15

Then, Julia, let me woo thee,
Thus, thus, to come unto me:
And when I shall meet
Thy silvery feet
My soul I'll pour into thee. 20

TO ELECTRA

I dare not ask a kiss;
I dare not beg a smile;
Lest having that or this,
I might grow proud the while.

No, no, the utmost share 5
Of my desire shall be
Only to kiss that air
That lately kissèd thee.

UPON JULIA'S CLOTHES

Whenas in silks my Julia goes,
Then, then methinks how sweetly flows
That liquefaction of her clothes.

Next, when I cast mine eyes and see
That brave vibration each way free, 5
O how that glittering taketh me!

AN ODE FOR BEN JONSON

Ah, Ben!
Say how or when
Shall we, thy guests,
Meet at those lyric feasts,
Made at the Sun, 5
The Dog, the Triple Tun;[11]
Where we such clusters had,
As made us nobly wild, not mad?
And yet each verse of thine
Out-did the meat, out-did the frolic wine. 10

My Ben!
Or come again,
Or send to us
Thy wit's great overplus;
But teach us yet 15
Wisely to husband it,
Lest we that talent spend;
And having once brought to an end
That precious stock, the store 19
Of such a wit the world should have no more.

COMFORT TO A YOUTH THAT HAD LOST HIS LOVE

What needs complaints,
When she a place
Has with the race
Of saints?
In endless mirth, 5
She thinks not on
What's said or done
In earth.
She sees no tears,
Or any tone 10
Of thy deep groan
She hears;

[11] Names of London taverns.

Nor does she mind,
Or think on't now,
That ever thou 15
Wast kind.
But changed above,
She likes not there,
As she did here,
Thy love, 20
Forbear therefore,
And lull asleep
Thy woes, and weep
No more.

HIS LITANY, TO THE HOLY SPIRIT

In the hour of my distress,
When temptations me oppress,
And when I my sins confess,
Sweet Spirit, comfort me!

When I lie within my bed, 5
Sick in heart, and sick in head,
And with doubts discomforted,
Sweet Spirit, comfort me!

When the house doth sigh and weep,
And the world is drowned in sleep, 10
Yet mine eyes the watch do keep,
Sweet Spirit, comfort me!

When the artless doctor sees
No one hope, but of his fees,
And his skill runs on the lees, 15
Sweet Spirit, comfort me!

When his potion and his pill
Has or none or little skill,
Meet for nothing but to kill,
Sweet Spirit, comfort me! 20

When the passing-bell doth toll,
And the furies in a shoal
Come to fright a parting soul,
Sweet Spirit, comfort me!

When the tapers now burn blue, 25
And the comforters are few,
And that number more than true,
Sweet Spirit, comfort me!

When the priest his last hath prayed,
And I nod to what is said, 30
'Cause my speech is now decayed,
Sweet Spirit, comfort me!

When, God knows, I'm tossed about,
Either with despair or doubt,
Yet before the glass be out, 35
Sweet Spirit, comfort me!

When the Tempter me pursu'th
With the sins of all my youth,
And half damns me with untruth,
Sweet Spirit, comfort me! 40

When the flames and hellish cries
Fright mine ears and fright mine eyes,
And all terrors me surprise,
Sweet Spirit, comfort me!

When the judgment is revealed, 45
And that opened which was sealed,
When to thee I have appealed,
Sweet Spirit, comfort me!

A THANKSGIVING TO GOD FOR HIS HOUSE

Lord, thou hast given me a cell
Wherein to dwell,
A little house, whose humble roof
Is weather-proof;
Under the spars[12] of which I lie 5
Both soft and dry;
Where thou my chamber for to ward
Hast set a guard
Of harmless thoughts, to watch and keep
Me while I sleep. 10
Low is my porch as is my fate,
Both void of state;
And yet the threshold of my door
Is worn by'th poor,
Who thither come and freely get 15
Good words or meat.
Like as my parlor, so my hall
And kitchen's small:
A little buttery and therein
A little bin, 20
Which keeps my little loaf of bread
Unchipt, unflead.
Some brittle sticks of thorn or briar
Make me a fire,
Close by whose living coal I sit 25
And glow like it.
Lord, I confess too, when I dine
The pulse[13] is thine,
And all those other bits that be
There plac'd by thee, 30
The worts,[14] the purslane, and the mess
Of water-cress,
Which of thy kindness thou hast sent;
And my content
Makes those and my belovéd beet 35
To be more sweet.

---

[12]Rafters.
[13]Edible seeds of plants that bear pods.
[14]Greens.

'Tis thou that crown'st my glittering hearth
With guiltless mirth,
And giv'st me wassail bowls to drink,
Spic'd to the brink. 40
Lord, 'tis thy plenty-dropping hand
That soils[15] my land,
And giv'st me for my bushel sown
Twice ten for one.
Thou mak'st my teeming hen to lay 45
Her egg each day,
Besides my healthful ewes to bear
Me twins each year;
The while the conduits of my kine
Run cream, for wine. 50
All these and better thou dost send
Me, to this end,
That I should render, for my part,
A thankful heart;
Which, fir'd with incense, I resign 55
As wholly thine.
But the acceptance, that must be,
My Christ, by thee.

A GRACE FOR A CHILD

Here, a little child, I stand,
Heaving up my either hand:
Cold as paddocks[16] though they be,
Here I lift them up to thee,
For a benison to fall 5
On our meat, and on us all. Amen.

GEORGE HERBERT

(1593–1633)

THE COLLAR

I struck the board, and cried, "No more; I will abroad!
What! shall I ever sigh and pine?
My lines[1] and life are free; free as the road,
Loose as the wind, as large as store.[2]
Shall I be still in suit? 5
Have I no harvest but a thorn
To let me blood, and not restore
What I have lost with cordial fruit?
Sure there was wine
Before my sighs did dry it; there was corn 10
Before my tears did drown it;
Is the year only lost to me?
Have I no bays to crown it,
No flowers, no garlands gay? all blasted,
All wasted? 15
Not so, my heart, but there is fruit,
And thou hast hands.
Recover all thy sigh-blown age
On double pleasures; leave thy cold dispute
Of what is fit and not; forsake thy cage, 20
Thy rope of sands
Which petty thoughts have made, and made to thee
Good cable, to enforce and draw,
And be thy law,
While thou didst wink[3] and wouldst not see. 25
Away! take heed;
I will abroad.
Call in thy death's head there, tie up thy fears;
He that forbears
To suit and serve his need 30
Deserves his load."
But as I raved, and grew more fierce and wild
At every word,
Methought I heard one calling, "Child";
And I replied, "My Lord." 35

DISCIPLINE

Throw away thy rod;
Throw away thy wrath:
O my God,
Take the gentle path.

For my heart's desire 5
Unto thine is bent:
I aspire
To a full consent.[4]

Not a word or look
I affect to own, 10
But by book,
And thy book alone.

Though I fail, I weep;
Though I halt in pace,
Yet I creep 15
To the throne of grace.

Then let wrath remove;
Love will do the deed:
For with love
Stony hearts will bleed. 20

Love is swift of foot;
Love's a man of war,
And can shoot,
And can hit from far.

---

[15] Manures. [16] Toads.

[1] Appointed lot. [2] An abundance.

[3] Blink, or perhaps sleep. [4] Harmony.

Who can scape his bow? 25
That which wrought on thee,
Brought thee low,
Needs must work on me.

Throw away thy rod;
Though man frailties hath, 30
Thou art God:
Throw away thy wrath.

THE PULLEY

When God at first made man,
Having a glass of blessing standing by,
"Let us," said he, "pour on him all we can:
Let the world's riches, which disperséd lie,
Contract into a span." 5

So Strength first made a way;
Then Beauty flowed; then Wisdom, Honor, Pleasure.
When almost all was out, God made a stay,
Perceiving that alone, of all his treasure,
Rest in the bottom lay. 10

"For if I should," said he,
"Bestow this jewel also on my creature,
He would adore my gifts instead of me,
And rest in Nature, not the God of Nature;
So both should losers be. 15

"Yet let him keep the rest,
But keep them with repining restlessness;
Let him be rich and weary, that at least,
If goodness lead him not, yet weariness
May toss him to my breast." 20

LOVE

Love bade me welcome; yet my soul drew back,
Guilty of dust and sin.
But quick-eyed Love, observing me grow slack
From my first entrance in,
Drew nearer to me, sweetly questioning, 5
If I lacked anything.

"A guest," I answered, "worthy to be here";
Love said, "You shall be he."
"I, the unkind, ungrateful? Ah, my dear,
I cannot look on thee!" 10
Love took my hand and smiling did reply,
"Who made the eyes but I?"

"Truth, Lord; but I have marred them: let my shame
Go where it doth deserve."
"And know you not," says Love, "who bore the blame?" 15
"My dear, then I will serve."
"You must sit down," says Love, "and taste my meat."
So I did sit and eat.

EDMUND WALLER
(1606–1687)

GO, LOVELY ROSE!

Go, lovely rose!
Tell her that wastes her time and me,
That now she knows,
When I resemble her to thee,
How sweet and fair she seems to be. 5

Tell her that's young,
And shuns to have her graces spied,
That hadst thou sprung
In deserts, where no men abide,
Thou must have uncommended died. 10

Small is the worth
Of beauty from the light retired;
Bid her come forth,
Suffer herself to be desired,
And not blush so to be admired. 15

Then die! that she
The common fate of all things rare
May read in thee;
How small a part of time they share
That are so wondrous sweet and fair! 20

SIR JOHN SUCKLING
(1609–1642)

A DOUBT OF MARTYRDOM

O for some honest lover's ghost,
Some kind unbodied post
Sent from the shades below!
I strangely long to know
Whether[1] the noble chaplets wear, 5
Those that their mistress' scorn did bear
Or those that were used kindly.

For whatso'er they tell us here
To make those sufferings dear,
'Twill there, I fear, be found 10
That to the being crowned

[1]Which.

T' have loved alone will not suffice,
Unless we also have been wise
And have our loves enjoyed.

What posture can we think him in 15
That, here unloved, again
Departs, and 's thither gone
Where each sits by his own?
Or how can that Elysium be
Where I my mistress still must see 20
Circled in other's arms?

For there the judges all are just,
And Sophonisba[2] must
Be his whom she held dear,
Not his who loved her here. 25
The sweet Philoclea,[3] since she died,
Lies by her Pirocles his side,
Not by Amphialus.

Some bays, perchance, or myrtle bough
For difference crowns the brow 30
Of those kind souls that were
The noble martyrs here;
And if that be the only odds
(As who can tell?) ye kinder gods,
Give me the woman here! 35

THE CONSTANT LOVER

Out upon it, I have loved
Three whole days together!
And am like to love three more,
If it prove fair weather.

Time shall molt away his wings 5
Ere he shall discover
In the whole wide world again
Such a constant lover.

But the spite on't is, no praise
Is due at all to me: 10
Love with me had made no stays,
Had it any been but she.

Had it any been but she,
And that very face,
There had been at least ere this 15
A dozen dozen in her place.

[2]A Carthaginian. She was betrothed to a Numidian prince but married another; later, however, she married the Numidian when he conquered her husband.

[3]Philoclea and the two following are characters in Sir Philip Sidney's *Arcadia*.

WHY SO PALE AND WAN?

Why so pale and wan, fond lover?
Prithee, why so pale?
Will, when looking well can't move her,
Looking ill prevail?
Prithee, why so pale? 5

Why so dull and mute, young sinner?
Prithee, why so mute?
Will, when speaking well can't win her,
Saying nothing do 't?
Prithee, why so mute? 10

Quit, quit for shame! This will not move;
This cannot take her.
If of herself she will not love,
Nothing can make her:
The devil take her! 15

RICHARD LOVELACE
(1618–1658)

TO ALTHEA, FROM PRISON

When Love with unconfinéd wings
Hovers within my gates,
And my divine Althea brings
To whisper at the grates;
When I lie tangled in her hair 5
And fettered to her eye,
The birds that wanton in the air
Know no such liberty.

When flowing cups ran swiftly round
With no allaying Thames, 10
Our careless heads with roses bound,
Our hearts with loyal flames;
When thirsty grief in wine we steep,
When healths and draughts go free,
Fishes that tipple in the deep 15
Know no such liberty.

When, like committed[1] linnets, I
With shriller throat will sing
The sweetness, mercy, majesty,
And glories of my king; 20
When I shall voice aloud how good
He is, how great should be,
Enlargéd winds, that curl the flood,
Know no such liberty.

Stone walls do not a prison make, 25
Nor iron bars a cage;
Minds innocent and quiet take
That for an hermitage;

[1]Confined.

If I have freedom in my love
And in my soul am free, 30
Angels alone, that soar above,
Enjoy such liberty.

ANDREW MARVELL

(1621-1678)

AN HORATIAN ODE UPON CROMWELL'S RETURN FROM IRELAND

The forward youth that would appear
Must now forsake his muses dear,
Nor in the shadows sing
His numbers languishing:

'Tis time to leave the books in dust, 5
And oil the unused armor's rust,
Removing from the wall
The corselet of the hall.

So restless Cromwell would not cease
In the inglorious arts of peace, 10
But through adventurous war
Urgéd his active star;

And, like the three-forked lightning, first
Breaking the clouds where it was nursed,
Did thorough his own side 15
His fiery way divide,[1]

For 'tis all one to courage high,
The emulous, or enemy,
And with such to enclose
Is more than to oppose. 20

Then burning through the air he went,
And palaces and temples rent;
And Caesar's[2] head at last
Did through his laurels[3] blast.

'Tis madness to resist or blame 25
The face of angry heaven's flame;
And if we would speak true,
Much to the man is due

Who from his private gardens, where
He lived reservéd and austere, 30
As if his highest plot
To plant the bergamot,[4]

Could by industrious valor climb
To ruin the great work of Time,
And cast the kingdoms old, 35
Into another mold,

Though Justice against Fate complain,
And plead the ancient rights in vain;
But those do hold or break,
As men are strong or weak. 40

Nature, that hateth emptiness,
Allows of penetration less,
And therefore must make room
Where greater spirits come.

What field of all the civil war 45
Where his were not the deepest scar?
And Hampton[5] shows what part
He had of wiser art;

Where, twining subtle fears with hope,
He wove a net of such a scope 50
That Charles himself might chase
To Caresbrooke's narrow case,

That thence the royal actor borne
The tragic scaffold might adorn,
While round the armèd bands 55
Did clap their bloody hands.

He[6] nothing common did, or mean,
Upon that memorable scene,
But with his keener eye
The ax's edge did try; 60

Nor called the gods with vulgar spite
To vindicate his helpless right,
But bowed his comely head
Down, as upon a bed.

This was that memorable hour 65
Which first assured the forcéd power;
So, when they did design
The capitol's first line,

A bleeding head, where they begun,
Did fright the architects to run;[7] 70
And yet in that the state
Foresaw its happy fate.

---

[1]The allusion is to differences which arose between the Puritan army and the Puritan parliament—differences which Cromwell forcibly resolved by bringing the army to London.

[2]Charles I's. [3]Spite of his crown.

[4]A variety of pear.

[5]Hampton Court. Marvell shared the belief of other contemporaries (as the following lines show) that Cromwell tacitly abetted Charles I's flight from Hampton Court to Carisbrooke Castle.

[6]Charles I.

[7]Pliny tells this story (*Natural History,* XXVIII, 4).

And now the Irish are ashamed
To see themselves in one year tamed;
So much one man can do, 75
That does both act and know.

They can affirm his praises best,
And have, though overcome, confessed
How good he is, how just,
And fit for highest trust; 80

Nor yet grown stiffer with command,
But still in the republic's hand,
How fit he is to sway
That can so well obey!

He to the Common's feet presents 85
A kingdom[8] for his first year's rents;
And, what he may, forbears
His fame, to make it theirs;

And has his sword and spoils ungirt,
To lay them at the public's skirt: 90
So when the falcon high
Falls heavy from the sky,

She, having killed, no more doth search,
But on the next green bough to perch;
Where, when he first does lure, 95
The falconer has her sure.

What may not then our isle presume,
While victory his crest does plume?
What may not others fear,
If thus he crowns each year? 100

As Caesar he, ere long, to Gaul,
To Italy a Hannibal,
And to all states not free
Shall climacteric be.[9]

The Pict[10] no shelter now shall find 105
Within his parti-colored[11] mind,
But, from this valor sad,[12]
Shrink underneath the plaid;

Happy if in the tufted brake
The English hunter him mistake, 110
Nor lay his hounds in[13] near
The Caledonian deer.

But thou, the war's and Fortune's son,
March undefatigably on;
And for the least effect, 115
Still keep the sword erect;

Besides the force it has to fright
The spirits of the shady night,
The same arts that did gain
A power must it maintain. 120

[8]Ireland. [9]Shall be a dangerous menace.
[10]The Scot. [11]I. e., fickle. [12]Resolute; sober.
[13]Put his hounds on the scent.

BERMUDAS[14]

Where the remote Bermudas ride,
In the ocean's bosom unespied,
From a small boat that rowed along
The listening winds received this song:

"What should we do but sing his praise 5
That led us through the watery maze,
Unto an isle so long unknown,
And yet far kinder than our own?
Where he the huge sea-monsters wracks,
That lift the deep upon their backs, 10
He lands us on a grassy stage,
Safe from the storms' and prelates' rage.
He gave us this eternal spring,
Which here enamels everything,
And sends the fowls to us in care, 15
On daily visits through the air;
He hangs in shades the orange bright,
Like golden lamps in a green night,
And does in the pomegranates close
Jewels more rich than Ormus[15] shows; 20
He makes the figs our mouths to meet,
And throws the melons at our feet,
But apples[16] plants of such a price
No tree could ever bear them twice;
With cedars chosen by his hand 25
From Lebanon he stores the land,
And makes the hollow seas, that roar,
Proclaim the ambergris on shore;
He cast (of which we rather boast)
The Gospel's pearl upon our coast, 30
And in these rocks for us did frame
A temple, where to sound his name.
Oh! let our voice his praise exalt,
Till it arrive at heaven's vault,
Which, thence (perhaps) rebounding, may 35
Echo beyond the Mexique Bay."

Thus sung they, in the English boat,
A holy and a cheerful note,
And all the way, to guide their chime,
With falling oars they kept the time. 40

[14]The Bermudas were settled early in the seventeenth century by Englishmen, who, like those who came to New England, sought to escape tyranny at home.
[15]An island in the Persian Gulf. [16]Pineapples.

TO HIS COY MISTRESS

Had we but world enough, and time,
This coyness, Lady, were no crime;
We would sit down and think which way
To walk and pass our long love's day.
Thou by the Indian Ganges' side 5
Shouldst rubies find; I by the tide
Of Humber would complain. I would
Love you ten years before the Flood,
And you should, if you please, refuse
Till the conversion of the Jews. 10
My vegetable love should grow
Vaster than empires, and more slow;
An hundred years should go to praise
Thine eyes and on thy forehead gaze;
Two hundred to adore each breast, 15
But thirty thousand to the rest;
An age at least to every part,
And the last age should show your heart.
For, Lady, you deserve this state,
Nor would I love at lower rate. 20
But at my back I always hear
Time's wingéd chariot hurrying near;
And yonder all before us lie
Deserts of vast eternity.
Thy beauty shall no more be found, 25
Nor, in thy marble vault, shall sound
My echoing song; then worms shall try
That long preserved virginity,
And your quaint honor turn to dust,
And into ashes all my lust: 30
The grave's a fine and private place,
But none, I think, do there embrace.
Now therefore, while the youthful hue
Sits on thy skin like morning dew,
And while thy willing soul transpires 35
At every pore with instant fires,
Now let us sport us while we may,
And now, like amorous birds of prey,
Rather at once our time devour 39
Than languish in his slow-chapt[17] power.
Let us roll all our strength and all
Our sweetness up into one ball,
And tear our pleasures with rough strife
Thorough the iron gates of life:
Thus, though we cannot make our sun 45
Stand still, yet we will make him run.

THE GARDEN

How vainly men themselves amaze
To win the palm, the oak, or bays,
And their uncessant labors see
Crown'd from some single herb or tree,
Whose short and narrow-vergéd shade 5
Does prudently their toils upbraid;
While all flowers and all trees do close
To weave the garlands of repose.

Fair Quiet, have I found thee here,
And Innocence, thy sister dear? 10
Mistaken long, I sought you then
In busy companies of men.
Your sacred plants, if here below,
Only among the plants will grow.
Society is all but[18] rude 15
To this delicious solitude.

No white nor red was ever seen
So am'rous as this lovely green.
Fond lovers, cruel as their flame,
Cut in these trees their mistress' name. 20
Little, alas, they know or heed
How far these beauties hers exceed!
Fair trees! wheres'e'er your barks I wound,
No name shall but your own be found.

When we have run our passion's heat, 25
Love hither makes his best retreat.
The gods that mortal beauty chase
Still in a tree did end their race.
Apollo hunted Daphne so,
Only that she might laurel grow. 30
And Pan did after Syrinx speed,
Not as a nymph, but for a reed.[19]

What wond'rous life is this I lead!
Ripe apples drop about my head;
The luscious clusters of the vine 35
Upon my mouth do crush their wine;
The nectarine and curious[20] peach
Into my hands themselves do reach;
Stumbling on melons as I pass,
Insnar'd with flowers, I fall on grass. 40

Meanwhile the mind, from pleasure less,
Withdraws into its happiness:
The mind, that ocean where each kind
Does straight its own resemblance find;
Yet it creates, transcending these, 45
Far other worlds and other seas,
Annihilating all that's made
To a green thought in a green shade.

Here at the fountain's sliding foot
Or at some fruit-tree's mossy root, 50
Casting the body's vest aside,
My soul into the boughs does glide.

[17]Slow-devouring (a chap is a jaw).

[18]Only.

[19]Daphne, fleeing from Apollo, and Syrinx, fleeing from Pan, were saved by being changed, respectively, into a laurel-tree and into a reed.

[20]Exquisite.

There like a bird it sits and sings,
Then whets and combs its silver wings;
And, till prepar'd for longer flight, 55
Waves in its plumes the various light.

Such was that happy garden-state,
While Man there walk'd without a mate:
After a place so pure and sweet
What other help could yet be meet? 60
But 'twas beyond a mortal's share
To wander solitary there:
Two paradises 'twere in one
To live in Paradise alone.

How well the skilful gardener drew 65
Of flowers and herbs this dial new,
Where from above the milder sun
Does through a fragrant zodiac run;
And, as it works, th'industrious bee
Computes its time as well as we. 70
How could such sweet and wholesome hours
Be reckon'd but with herbs and flowers!

HENRY VAUGHAN

(1622–1695)

THE WORLD[1]

I saw Eternity the other night,
Like a great ring of pure and endless[2] light,
All calm as it was bright;
And round beneath it, Time, in hours, days, years,
Driv'n by the spheres, 5
Like a vast shadow moved; in which the world
And all her train were hurled.
The doting lover in his quaintest strain
Did there complain;
Near him, his lute, his fancy, and his flights,
Wit's four delights, 11
With gloves, and knots,[3] the silly snares of pleasure,
Yet his dear treasure,
All scattered lay, while he his eyes did pour
Upon a flower. 15

The darksome statesman, hung with weights and woe,
Like a thick midnight-fog, moved there so slow,
He did not stay, nor go;
Condemning thoughts, like sad eclipses, scowl
Upon his soul, 20
And clouds of crying witnesses without
Pursued him with one shout.
Yet digged the mole, and lest his ways be found,
Worked under ground,
Where he did clutch his prey; but one did see
That policy:[4] 26
Churches and altars fed him; perjuries
Were gnats and flies;
It rained about him blood and tears, but he
Drank them as free.[5] 30

The fearful miser on a heap of rust
Sat pining all his life there, did scarce trust
His own hands with the dust,
Yet would not place one piece above,[6] but lives
In fear of thieves. 35
Thousands there were as frantic as himself,
And hugged each one his pelf;
The downright epicure placed heaven in sense,
And scorned pretense;
While others, slipt into a wide excess, 40
Said little less;
The weaker sort, slight, trivial wares enslave,
Who think them brave;
And poor, despiséd Truth sat counting by
Their victory. 45

Yet some, who all this while did weep and sing,
And sing and weep, soared up into the ring;
But most would use no wing.
O fools, said I, thus to prefer dark night
Before true light! 50
To live in grots and caves, and hate the day
Because it shows the way,
The way, which from this dead and dark abode
Leads up to God;
A way where you might tread the sun, and be 55
More bright than he!
But, as I did their madness so discuss,
One whispered thus,
"This ring the Bridegroom did for none provide
But for his bride." 60

---

[1]Vaughan printed I John, 2:16–17, at the end of this poem.
[2]Endless not only in time but also, being a ring, in space.
[3]Love-knots.
[4]Craft.
[5]As freely as if it had not rained blood and tears.
[6]In heaven.

THE RETREAT

Happy those early days, when I
Shined in my angel-infancy!
Before I understood this place
Appointed for my second race,
Or taught my soul to fancy aught 5
But a white, celestial thought;
When yet I had not walked above
A mile or two from my first love,
And looking back at that short space,
Could see a glimpse of his bright face; 10
When on some gilded cloud or flower
My gazing soul would dwell an hour,
And in those weaker glories spy
Some shadows of eternity;
Before I taught my tongue to wound 15
My conscience with a sinful sound,
Or had the black art to dispense,
A several sin to every sense,
But felt through all this fleshly dress
Bright shoots of everlastingness. 20
O, how I long to travel back,
And tread again that ancient track,
That I might once more reach that plain,
Where first I felt my glorious train;
From whence th' enlightened spirit sees 25
That shady city of palm trees.[7]
But ah! my soul with too much stay
Is drunk, and staggers in the way!
Some men a forward motion love,
But I by backward steps would move; 30
And when this dust falls to the urn,
In that state I came, return.

PEACE

My soul, there is a country
Far beyond the stars,
Where stands a wingéd sentry
All skilful in the wars.
There above noise and danger 5
Sweet peace sits crown'd with smiles,
And one born in a manger
Commands the beauteous files.
He is thy gracious friend,
And (O my soul, awake!) 10
Did in pure love descend
To die here for thy sake.
If thou canst get but thither,
There grows the flower of peace,
The rose that cannot wither, 15
Thy fortress, and thy ease.
Leave then thy foolish ranges;
For none can thee secure,
But one who never changes,
Thy God, thy life, thy cure. 20

[7] I. e., Jericho.

MAN

Weighing the steadfastness and state
Of some mean things which here below reside,
Where birds like watchful clocks the noiseless date
And intercourse of times divide,
Where bees at night get home and hive, and flowers 5
Early, as well as late,
Rise with the sun, and set in the same bowers;

I would (said I) my God would give
The staidness of these things to man! for these
To his divine appointments ever cleave, 10
And no new business breaks their peace;
The birds nor sow, nor reap, yet sup and dine;
The flowers without clothes live,
Yet Solomon was never dressed so fine.

Man hath still either toys, or care; 15
He hath no root, nor to one place is tied,
But ever restless and irregular
About this earth doth run and ride;
He knows he hath a home, but scarce knows where;
He says it is so far 20
That he hath quite forgot how to go there.

He knocks at all doors, strays and roams,
Nay hath not so much wit as some stones[8] have
Which in the darkest nights point to their homes,
By some hid sense their Maker gave; 25
Man is the shuttle, to whose winding quest
And passage through these looms
God ordered motion, but ordained no rest.

ASCENSION HYMN

They are all gone into the world of light!
And I alone sit ling'ring here;
Their very memory is fair and bright,
And my sad thoughts doth clear.

It glows and glitters in my cloudy breast 5
Like stars upon some gloomy grove,
Or those faint beams in which this hill is drest,
After the sun's remove.

[8] Loadstones.

I see them walking in an air of glory,
Whose light doth trample on my days: 10
My days, which are at best but dull and hoary,
Mere glimmering and decays.

O holy hope! and high humility,
High as the heavens above!
These are your walks, and you have showed them me 15
To kindle my cold love.

Dear, beauteous death! the jewel of the just,
Shining nowhere, but in the dark;
What mysteries do lie beyond thy dust;
Could man outlook that mark! 20

He that hath found some fledged bird's nest may know
At first sight, if the bird be flown;
But what fair well[9] or grove he sings in now,
That is to him unknown.

And yet, as angels in some brighter dreams
Call to the soul, when man doth sleep: 26
So some strange thoughts transcend our wonted themes,
And into glory peep.

If a star were confined into a tomb 29
Her captive flames must needs burn there;
But when the hand that locked her up gives room,
She'll shine through all the sphere.

O Father of eternal life, and all
Created glories under thee!
Resume[10] thy spirit from this world of thrall
Into true liberty. 36

Either disperse these mists, which blot and fill
My perspective still as they pass,
Or else remove me hence unto that hill,
Where I shall need no glass. 40

[9]Spring or fountain. [10]Take back to thyself.

THE WATERFALL

With what deep murmurs through time's silent stealth
Doth thy transparent, cool, and wat'ry wealth
Here flowing fall,
And chide, and call,
As if his liquid, loose retinue stayed 5
Ling'ring, and were of this steep place afraid;
The common pass
Where, clear as glass,
All must descend
Not to an end, 10
But, quickened by this deep and rocky grave,
Rise to a longer course more bright and brave.

Dear stream! dear bank, where often I
Have sat, and pleased my pensive eye:
Why, since each drop of thy quick store 15
Runs thither, whence it flowed before,
Should poor souls fear a shade or night,
Who came, sure, from a sea of light?
Or since those drops are all sent back
So sure to thee, that none doth lack, 20
Why should frail flesh doubt any more
That what God takes, he'll not restore?

O useful element and clear!
My sacred wash and cleanser here,
My first consigner unto those 25
Fountains of life, where the Lamb goes![11]
What sublime truths, and wholesome themes,
Lodge in thy mystical, deep streams!—
Such as dull man can never find
Unless that Spirit lead his mind, 30
Which first upon thy face did move,
And hatched all with his quick'ning love.
As this loud brook's incessant fall
In streaming rings restagnates all
Which reach by course the bank, and then
Are no more seen, just so pass men. 36
O my invisible estate,
My glorious liberty, still late!
Thou art the channel my soul seeks,
Not this with cataracts and creeks. 40

[11]I. e., in baptism.

SIR THOMAS BROWNE

1605–1682

Sir Thomas Browne was born on 19 October, 1605. His father was a London mercer. Browne was sent to Winchester School in 1616, and in 1623 he went thence to Broadgates Hall (now Pembroke College), Oxford. He took his B. A. in 1626, his M. A. in 1629, and little else is known about his Oxford years. In 1630 he began a period of travel and study on the Continent, going first to Montpellier, in the south of France, then famous for its medical school. He continued his medical studies at Padua, and then at Leyden, where it is thought he obtained a medical degree. In 1633 he returned to England and settled himself near Halifax. He was made doctor of medicine at Oxford in 1637. Soon after this he began to practice medicine at Norwich, where he remained until his death. He married, in 1641, Dorothy Mileham, "a lady of such symmetrical proportion to her worthy husband, both in the graces of her body and mind, that they seemed to come together by a kind of natural magnetism." About 1635 Browne had written, "at leisurable hours," for his "private exercise and satisfaction," his famous confession of faith, the *Religio Medici.* He apparently had no intention of publishing this, but allowed friends to read it in manuscript and to make copies of it; and thus, being admired, it came to be widely known (there are at least five manuscripts of the book extant, or were in the early nineteenth century). The result was that in 1642 an unauthorized edition was printed from one of these copies and so quickly sold out that a second edition was printed within a few months. This troubled Browne because the book was about so serious a subject as religion, and was now being much more widely read, and not only read but criticized, in a form very different from that in which it had actually been written. The copy which reached the press was, Browne wrote, "most depraved," as the result of successive transcriptions, and so in 1643 he published as a kind of duty the first authorized edition of the book. The general scandal of his profession, Browne said, might help to persuade the world that he had no religion at all, but it was not so. On the contrary he was disposed rather to wish, if for anything, for more curious tests of his faith than Christianity afforded. "Methinks," he says, "there be not impossibilities enough in religion for an active faith; the deepest mysteries ours contains have not only been illustrated, but maintained, by syllogism and the rule of reason. I love to lose myself in a mystery, to pursue my reason to an *O altitudo!* 'Tis my solitary recreation to pose my apprehension with those involved enigmas and riddles of the Trinity, with Incarnation, and Resurrection." In this Browne told the simple truth; a touch of mystery fired his mind and sent it soaring on its speculative way. Whatever was odd or strange was food for him, and he became one of the most curiously learned men of any age. At the same time his wide reading helped him to clothe his grave meditations in a style which for richness and dignity is not surpassed even by any other of the great prose-writers of his own century.

Browne was a royalist, but lived through the Civil War without, apparently, being much disturbed by outward events. In 1646 he published an eminently characteristic book, his *Pseudodoxia Epidemica or Enquiries into very many received Tenets and commonly presumed Truths, which examined prove but Vulgar and Common Errors.* Some years later certain urns were unearthed in Norfolk, which were exactly the sort of thing to set his mind in motion, and the result was that he wrote and, in 1658, published *Hydriotaphia;* in this essay the qualities of his mind and of his personality are finely exhibited. Two other works, *A Letter to a Friend* and *Christian Morals,* were not published until after his death. In 1671 Browne was knighted, in consequence of the singular modesty of the then mayor of Norwich. Charles II was visting Norwich and proposed to confer knighthood on the mayor, who declined it and begged that it be conferred instead on Browne, as the citizen of Norwich who most deserved the honor.

The Works of Sir Thomas Browne have been well edited by Geoffrey Keynes (London, 1928–1931). For an able essay on Browne, see Sir Leslie Stephen, *Hours in a Library,* Second Series (London, 1876). Browne's intellectual position has more recently been treated by Basil Willey in *The Seventeenth Century Background; Studies in the Thought of the Age in Relation to Poetry and Religion* (London, 1934).

HYDRIOTAPHIA, URN-BURIAL

CHAPTER V

Now since these dead bones[1] have already out-lasted the living one of Methuselah, and in a yard under ground, and thin walls of clay, out-worn all the strong and specious buildings above it, and quietly rested under the drums and tramplings of three conquests: what prince can promise such diuturnity[2] unto his relics, or might not gladly say,

Sic ego componi versus in ossa velim?[3]

Time, which antiquates antiquities, and hath an art to make dust of all things, hath yet spared these minor monuments.

In vain we hope to be known by open and visible conservatories,[4] when to be unknown was the means of their continuation, and obscurity their protection. If they died by violent hands, and were thrust into their urns, these bones become considerable, and some old philosophers would honor them, whose souls they conceived most pure, which were thus snatched from their bodies, and to retain a stronger propension unto them; whereas they weariedly left a languishing corpse, and with faint desires of re-union. If they fell by long and aged decay, yet wrapped up in the bundle of time, they fall into indistinction,[5] and make but one blot with infants. If we begin to die when we live, and long life be but a prolongation of death, our life is a sad composition; we live with death, and die not in a moment. How many pulses made up the life of Methuselah, were work for Archimedes: common counters sum up the life of Moses his man.[6] Our days become considerable, like petty sums, by minute accumulations; where numerous fractions make up but small round numbers; and our days of a span long, make not one little finger.

If the nearness of our last necessity brought a nearer conformity into it, there were a happiness in hoary hairs, and no calamity in half-senses. But the long habit of living indisposeth us for dying; when avarice makes us the sport of death, when even David grew politicly cruel and Solomon could hardly be said to be the wisest of men. But many are too early old, and before the date of age. Adversity stretcheth our days, misery makes Alcmena's nights,[7] and time hath no wings unto it. But the most tedious being is that which can unwish itself, content to be nothing, or never to have been, which was beyond the malcontent of Job, who cursed not the day of his life, but his nativity; content to have so far been, as to have a title to future being, although he had lived here but in an hidden state of life, and as it were an abortion.

What song the Syrens sang, or what name Achilles assumed when he hid himself among women, though puzzling questions,[8] are not beyond all conjecture. What time the persons of these ossuaries entered the famous nations of the dead, and slept with princes and counselors, might admit a wide solution. But who were the proprietaries of these bones, or what bodies these ashes made up,

[1]The bones in the urns found near Walsingham, in northern Norfolk, which caused Browne to write *Hydriotaphia.* The essay as a whole, of which the last chapter is here reprinted, is a general account of ancient burial customs. The funeral urns, which modern antiquaries regard as of Saxon origin, merely served to bring Browne's learning into play and to set his mind in motion.

[2]Lastingness.

[3]Thus I should wish to be buried when turned to bones (Tibullus, III, ii, 26).

[4]Repositories. [5]Obscurity.

[6]The allusion is to Psalms, 90:10, where the normal life of man is said to be 70 years.

[7]One night as long as three (Browne's note).

[8]Browne says in a note that these are two of the three questions which Tiberius put to grammarians.

were a question above antiquarism; not to be resolved by man, nor easily perhaps by spirits, except we consult the provincial guardians, or tutelary observators.[9] Had they made as good provision for their 5 names, as they have done for their relics, they had not so grossly erred in the art of perpetuation. But to subsist in bones, and be but pyramidally[10] extant, is a fallacy in duration. Vain ashes which in the oblivion 10 of names, persons, times, and sexes, have found unto themselves a fruitless continuation, and only arise unto late posterity, as emblems of mortal vanities, antidotes against pride, vain-glory, and madding vices. Pagan 15 vain-glories, which thought the world might last for ever, had encouragement for ambition; and, finding no Atropos[11] unto the immortality of their names, were never damped with the necessity of oblivion. Even old 20 ambitions had the advantage of ours, in the attempts of their vain-glories, who acting early, and before the probable meridian of time,[12] have by this time found great accomplishment of their designs, whereby the an- 25 cient heroes have already out-lasted their monuments and mechanical preservations. But in this latter scene of time, we cannot expect such mummies unto our memories, when ambition may fear the prophecy of 30 Elias, and Charles the Fifth can never hope to live within two Methuselahs of Hector.

And therefore, restless unquiet for the diuturnity of our memories unto present considerations seems a vanity almost out of 35 date, and superannuated piece of folly. We cannot hope to live so long in our names as some have done in their persons. One face of Janus holds no proportion unto the other. 'Tis too late to be ambitious. The 40 great mutations of the world are acted, or time may be too short for our designs. To extend our memories by monuments, whose death we daily pray for, and whose duration we cannot hope without injury to our ex- 45 pectations in the advent of the last day, were a contradiction to our beliefs. We whose generations are ordained in this setting part of time, are providentially taken off from such imaginations; and, being necessitated to eye the remaining particle of futurity, are naturally constituted unto thoughts of the next world, and cannot excusably decline the consideration of that duration which maketh pyramids pillars of snow, and all that's past a moment.

Circles and right lines limit and close all bodies, and the mortal right-lined circle[13] must conclude and shut up all. There is no antidote against the opium of time, which temporally considereth all things: our fathers find their graves in our short memories, and sadly tell us how we may be buried in our survivors. Gravestones tell truth scarce forty years. Generations pass while some trees stand, and old families last not three oaks. To be read by bare inscriptions like many in Gruter,[14] to hope for eternity by enigmatical epithets or first letters of our names, to be studied by antiquaries, who we were, and have new names given us like many of the mummies, are cold consolations unto the students of perpetuity, even by everlasting languages.

To be content that times to come should only know there was such a man, not caring whether they knew more of him, was a frigid ambition in Cardan;[15] disparaging his horoscopical inclination and judgment of himself. Who cares to subsist like Hippocrates' patients, or Achilles' horses in Homer, under naked nominations, without deserts and noble acts, which are the balsam[16] of our memories, the *entelechia*[17] and soul of our subsistences? To be nameless in worthy deeds exceeds an infamous history. The Canaanitish woman lives more happily without a name than Herodias with one. And who had not rather been the good thief than Pilate?

But the iniquity of oblivion blindly scattereth her poppy, and deals with the memory of men without distinction to merit of perpetuity. Who can but pity the founder of the pyramids? Herostratus lives that burned the temple of Diana; he is almost lost that

[9]Protecting spirits of the place.

[10]After the manner of a mummy.

[11]One of the Fates. She cut the thread of life.

[12]Noon of the world's life.

[13]The Greek letter θ, which stands for θάνατος, or death.

[14]A Dutch philologer.

[15]An Italian mathematician, physician, and philosopher.

[16]Preservative. [17]Entelechy, actual existence.

built it. Time hath spared the epitaph of Adrian's horse, confounded that of himself. In vain we compute our felicities by the advantage of our good names, since bad have equal durations, and Thersites is like to live as long as Agamemnon. Who knows whether the best of men be known, or whether there be not more remarkable persons forgot than any that stand remembered in the known account of time? Without the favor of the everlasting register, the first man had been as unknown as the last, and Methuselah's long life had been his only chronicle.

Oblivion is not to be hired. The greater part must be content to be as though they had not been, to be found in the register of God, not in the record of man. Twenty-seven names make up the first story,[18] and the recorded names ever since contain not one living century. The number of the dead long exceedeth all that shall live. The night of time far surpasseth the day, and who knows when was the equinox? Every hour adds unto that current arithmetic,[19] which scarce stands one moment. And since death must be the Lucina[20] of life, and even Pagans could doubt whether thus to live were to die; since our longest sun sets at right descensions, and makes but winter arches, and therefore it cannot be long before we lie down in darkness, and have our light in ashes; since the brother of death daily haunts us with dying mementos, and time, that grows old in itself, bids us hope no long duration;—diuturnity is a dream and folly of expectation.

Darkness and light divide the course of time, and oblivion shares with memory a great part even of our living beings; we slightly remember our felicities, and the smartest strokes of affliction leave but short smart upon us. Sense endureth no extremities, and sorrows destroy us or themselves. To weep into stones are fables. Afflictions induce callosities;[21] miseries are slippery, or fall like snow upon us, which notwithstanding is no unhappy stupidity. To be ignorant of evils to come, and forgetful of evils past, is a merciful provision in nature, whereby we digest the mixture of our few and evil days, and, our delivered senses not relapsing into cutting remembrances, our sorrows are not kept raw by the edge of repetitions. A great part of antiquity contented their hopes of subsistency with a transmigration of their souls,—a good way to continue their memories, while having the advantage of plural successions, they could not but act something remarkable in such variety of beings, and enjoying the fame of their passed selves, make accumulation of glory unto their last durations. Others, rather than be lost in the uncomfortable night of nothing, were content to recede into the common being, and make one particle of the public soul of all things, which was no more than to return into their unknown and divine original again. Egyptian ingenuity was more unsatisfied, contriving their bodies in sweet consistencies, to attend the return of their souls. But all was vanity, feeding the wind, and folly. The Egyptian mummies, which Cambyses or time hath spared, avarice now consumeth. Mummy is become merchandise,[22] Mizraim[23] cures wounds, and Pharaoh is sold for balsams.

In vain do individuals hope for immortality, or any patent from oblivion, in preservations below the moon; men have been deceived even in their flatteries above the sun, and studied conceits to perpetuate their names in heaven. The various cosmography of that part hath already varied the names of contrived constellations; Nimrod is lost in Orion, and Osyris in the Dog-star. While we look for incorruption in the heavens, we find they are but like the earth;—durable in their main bodies, alterable in their parts; whereof, beside comets and new stars, perspectives[24] begin to tell tales, and the spots that wander about the sun, with Phaëton's favor, would make clear conviction.

There is nothing strictly immortal but immortality. Whatever hath no beginning, may be confident of no end (all others have

[18]The time before the Flood.

[19]That running account—i. e., continuously moving time.

[20]Goddess of childbirth.

[21]Cause insensibility.

[22]The substance of mummies was in use as a medicine in Browne's day and before.

[23]Hebrew name of Egypt.

[24]Telescopes.

a dependent being and within the reach of destruction); which is the peculiar of that necessary Essence that cannot destroy itself; and the highest strain of omnipotency, to be so powerfully constituted as not to suffer even from the power of itself. But the sufficiency of Christian immortality frustrates all earthly glory, and the quality of either state after death makes a folly of posthumous memory. God who can only[25] destroy our souls, and had assured our resurrection, either of our bodies or names hath directly promised no duration. Wherein there is so much of chance, that the boldest expectants have found unhappy frustration; and to hold long subsistence, seems but a scape in oblivion.[26] But man is a noble animal, splendid in ashes, and pompous in the grave, solemnizing nativities and deaths with equal luster, nor omitting ceremonies of bravery in the infamy of his nature.

Life is a pure flame, and we live by an invisible sun within us. A small fire sufficeth for life; great flames seemed too little after death, while men vainly affected precious pyres, and to burn like Sardanapalus; but the wisdom of funeral laws found the folly of prodigal blazes, and reduced undoing fires unto the rule of sober obsequies, wherein few could be so mean as not to provide wood, pitch, a mourner, and an urn.

Five languages secured not the epitaph of Gordianus. The man of God lives longer without a tomb than any by one, invisibly interred by angels, and adjudged to obscurity, though not without some marks directing human discovery. Enoch and Elias, without either tomb or burial, in an anomalous state of being, are the great examples of perpetuity, in their long and living memory, in strict account being still on this side death, and having a late part yet to act upon this stage of earth. If in the decretory term of the world,[27] we shall not all die but be changed, according to received translation, the last day will make but few graves; at least quick resurrections will anticipate lasting sepultures. Some graves will be opened before they be quite closed, and Lazarus be no wonder. When many that feared to die shall groan that they can die but once, the dismal state is the second and living death, when life puts despair on the damned; when men shall wish the coverings of mountains, not of monuments, and annihilations shall be courted.

While some have studied monuments, others have studiously declined them, and some have been so vainly boisterous[28] that they durst not acknowledge their graves; wherein Alaricus seems most subtle, who had a river turned to hide his bones at the bottom. Even Sylla, that thought himself safe in his urn, could not prevent revenging tongues, and stones thrown at his monument. Happy are they whom privacy makes innocent, who deal so with men in this world that they are not afraid to meet them in the next; who, when they die, make no commotion among the dead, and are not touched with that poetical taunt of Isaiah.[29]

Pyramids, arches, obelisks, were but the irregularities of vain-glory, and wild enormities of ancient magnanimity. But the most magnanimous resolution rests in the Christian religion, which trampleth upon pride, and sits on the neck of ambition, humbly pursuing that infallible perpetuity unto which all others must diminish their diameters, and be poorly seen in angles of contingency.

Pious spirits who passed their days in raptures of futurity, made little more of this world than the world that was before it, while they lay obscure in the chaos of preordination, and night of their fore-beings. And if any have been so happy as truly to understand Christian annihilation, ecstasies, exolution, liquefaction, transformation, the kiss of the spouse, gustation of God, and ingression into the divine shadow,[30] they have already had an handsome anticipation of heaven; the glory of the world is surely over, and the earth in ashes unto them.

To subsist in lasting monuments, to live in their productions, to exist in their names and predicament of chimaeras,[31] was large

[25]I. e., who only can.

[26]But a chance of escaping oblivion.

[27]If at the day of judgment.

[28]Turbulent.

[29]Cf. Isaiah, 14:9, and following verses.

[30]These terms are descriptive of the experiences of mystics.

[31]Condition of unfounded conceptions.

satisfaction unto old expectations, and made one part of their Elysiums. But all this is nothing in the metaphysics of true belief. To live indeed, is to be again ourselves, which being not only an hope, but an evidence in noble believers, 'tis all one to lie in St. Innocents' church-yard, as in the sands of Egypt. Ready to be anything, in the ecstasy of being ever, and as content with six foot as the *moles* of Adrianus.[32]

—tabesne cadavera solvat,
An rogus, haud refert.[33]

[32]The monument of Hadrian, now known in its altered form as the castle of St. Angelo.

[33]It matters not whether our bodies rot in the grave or are consumed by the funeral pyre (Lucan, *Pharsalia*, vii, 809–810).

IZAAK WALTON

1593-1683

Walton was born at Stafford on 9 August, 1593. Of his youth and education nothing is known—and indeed little enough is known of the whole course of his long life. He obeyed a text which he more than once used: "Study to be quiet, and to do your own business" (I Thessalonians, 4:11). He was in London by 1611, and in 1618 was admitted a "free brother" of the Ironmongers' Company. He followed his trade in Fleet Street and in Chancery Lane for many years, though just when he abandoned active connection with it cannot be determined. He left his house in Chancery Lane in 1644, because it had become a dangerous neighborhood "for honest men"—that is, for Royalists. But he probably did not then leave London. He is said to have been living in Clerkenwell in 1650. Meanwhile on 27 December, 1626, he had married Rachel Floud of Canterbury. Their carved marriage-chest, for which Walton wrote an inscription, is now in the hall of Warwick Castle. Rachel Walton died in 1640, having borne her husband six children, all of whom died in infancy. In 1646 Walton married Anne Ken, a half-sister of Bishop Ken of Winchester, who bore him three children, of whom a daughter and a son survived him. Anne Walton died at Worcester in 1662. George Morley, then Bishop of Worcester, later Bishop of Winchester, had appointed Walton his steward, and much of his time during his later years was spent at Farnham Castle, the bishop's residence. During these years he also lived at times with his daughter, whose husband was Prebendary of Winchester, and in her home he died on 15 December, 1683. He was buried in a chapel of the Cathedral, in accordance with a request in his will: "I desire my burial may be near the place of my death; and free from any ostentation or charge, but privately."

Walton must have been from his youth interested in literature, and he must also have been, all his life, a reading man. He was besides, as everybody knows, a devoted fisherman. Guileless, simple, easy, charming, he had a genius for friendship, though—as his younger friend Charles Cotton said plainly—he was not everybody's friend: "My father Walton will be seen twice in no man's company he does not like, and likes none but such as he believes to be very honest men." Amongst these "very honest men" were Ben Jonson, Michael Drayton, John Hales of Eton, Henry King, Thomas Fuller, Sir Henry Wotton, and John Donne. And out of his friendships and "the contemplative man's recreation" issued Walton's unassuming and singularly perfect writings. When he began to write cannot be known; but his earliest publication was an elegy on Donne, printed in the first edition of Donne's *Poems* in 1633. Thereafter he collected material for a biography of Donne which their common friend Sir Henry Wotton intended to write. But Wotton died without having written it, and Walton then took up the task, and his *Life of Donne* was published with Donne's *LXXX Sermons,* 1640. Eleven years later the *Life of Wotton* was published in *Reliquiae Wottonianae,* and in 1653 appeared the first edition of *The Compleat Angler.* Walton modestly thought, "Most readers may receive so much pleasure or profit by it as may make it worthy the time of their perusal, if they be not very busy men." He disallowed "severe, sour-complexioned men" to be competent judges of his book, and these have in fact held their peace; for no dissenting voice has marred the chorus of grateful and affectionate praise which has followed the quiet angler and biographer down the years. The *Life of Hooker* was first published in 1665, the *Life of Herbert* in 1670, and the *Life of Bishop Sanderson* in 1678.

Walton's writings have been conveniently gathered together in one volume, *The Compleat Angler, The Lives of Donne, Wotton, Hooker, Herbert & Sanderson, with Love and Truth & Miscellaneous Writings,* ed. Geoffrey Keynes (London, 1929). For Walton's life and personality see S. Martin, *Izaak Walton and his Friends* (London, 1904).

PASSAGES FROM

THE LIFE OF DR. JOHN DONNE

Late Dean of St. Paul's Church, London

MASTER John Donne was born in London in the year 1573,[1] of good and virtuous parents; and, though his own learning and other multiplied merits may justly appear sufficient to dignify both himself and his posterity, yet the reader may be pleased to know that his father was masculinely and lineally descended from a very ancient family in Wales, where many of his name now live that deserve and have great reputation in that country.

By his mother he was descended of the family of the famous and learned Sir Thomas More,[2] sometime Lord Chancellor of England; as also from that worthy and laborious Judge Rastell[3] who left posterity the vast statutes of the law of this nation most exactly abridged.

He had his first breeding in his father's house, where a private tutor had the care of him until the tenth year of his age; and, in his eleventh year, was sent to the University of Oxford, having at that time a good command both of the French and Latin tongue. This and some other of his remarkable abilities made one then give this censure[4] of him: that this age had brought forth another Picus Mirandola,[5] of whom story says that he was rather born than made wise by study.

There he remained for some years in Hart Hall, having for the advancement of his studies tutors of several sciences to attend and instruct him, till time made him capable, and his learning expressed in public exercises declared him worthy to receive his first degree in the schools; which he forbore by advice from his friends, who being for their religion of the Romish persuasion, were conscionably averse to some parts of the oath that is always tendered at those times, and not to be refused by those that expect the titulary honor of their studies.

About the fourteenth year of his age he was transplanted from Oxford to Cambridge, where, that he might receive nourishment from both soils, he stayed till his seventeenth year; all which time he was a most laborious student, often changing his studies, but endeavoring to take no degree for the reasons formerly mentioned.

About the seventeenth year of his age he was removed to London, and then admitted into Lincoln's Inn, with an intent to study the law; where he gave great testimonies of his wit, his learning, and of his improvement in that profession, which never served him for other use than an ornament and self-satisfaction.

His father died before his admission into this society, and being a merchant, left him his portion in money (it was £3000). His mother and those to whose care he was committed were watchful to improve his knowledge, and to that end appointed him tutors both in the mathematicks and in all the other liberal sciences, to attend him. But with these arts they were advised to instil into him particular principles of the Romish Church; of which those tutors professed (though secretly) themselves to be members.

They had almost obliged him to their faith, having for their advantage, besides many opportunities, the example of his dear and pious parents, which was a most powerful persuasion, and did work much upon him, as he professeth in his Preface to his *Pseudo-Martyr,* a book of which the reader shall have some account in what follows.

He was now entered into the eighteenth

[1] It now seems more likely that he was born in 1571 or 1572.

[2] The great English humanist and statesman (1478–1535).

[3] William Rastell, nephew of Sir Thomas More, published his *Abridgement of the Statutes* in 1559.

[4] Judgment.

[5] Italian humanist (1463–1494).

year of his age, and at that time had betrothed himself to no religion that might give him any other denomination than a Christian. And reason and piety had both persuaded him that there could be no such sin as schism, if an adherence to some visible church were not necessary.

About the nineteenth year of his age he, being then unresolved what religion to adhere to, and considering how much it concerned his soul to choose the most orthodox, did therefore (though his youth and health promised him a long life), to rectify all scruples that might concern that, presently lay aside all study of the law and of all other sciences that might give him a denomination, and begun seriously to survey and consider the body of divinity, as it was then controverted betwixt the Reformed and the Roman Church. And as God's blessed Spirit did then awaken him to the search, and in that industry did never forsake him (they be his own words), so he calls the same Holy Spirit to witness this protestation: that in that disquisition and search he proceeded with humility and diffidence in himself, and by that which he took to be the safest way, namely, frequent prayers and an indifferent affection to both parties.[6] And indeed truth had too much light about her to be hid from so sharp an inquirer; and he had too much ingenuity not to acknowledge he had found her.

Being to undertake this search, he believed the Cardinal Bellarmine[7] to be the best defender of the Roman cause, and therefore betook himself to the examination of his reasons. The cause was weighty, and wilful delays had been inexcusable both towards God and his own conscience; he therefore proceeded in this search with all moderate[8] haste, and about the twentieth year of his age did shew the then Dean of Gloucester (whose name my memory hath now lost) all the cardinal's works marked with many weighty observations under his own hand; which works were bequeathed by him at his death as a legacy to a most dear friend.

About a year following he resolved to travel; and the Earl of Essex going first the Cales and after the Island Voyages,[9] the first *anno* 1596, the second 1597, he took the advantage of those opportunities, waited upon his lordship, and was an eye-witness of those happy and unhappy employments.

But he returned not back into England till he had staid some years first in Italy, and then in Spain, where he made many useful observations of those countries, their laws and manner of government, and returned perfect in their languages.

The time that he spent in Spain was at his first going into Italy designed for traveling to the Holy Land, and for viewing Jerusalem and the sepulcher of our Savior. But at his being in the furthest parts of Italy, the disappointment of company, or of a safe convoy, or the uncertainty of returns of money into those remote parts, denied him that happiness; which he did often occasionally mention with a deploration.

Not long after his return into England that exemplary pattern of gravity and wisdom, the Lord Ellesmere,[10] then Keeper of the Great Seal and Lord Chancellor of England, taking notice of his learning, languages, and other abilities, and much affecting his person and behavior, took him to be his chief secretary; supposing and intending it to be an introduction to some more weighty employment in the state, for which, his lordship did often protest, he thought him very fit.

Nor did his lordship, in this time of Master Donne's attendance upon him, account him to be so much his servant as to forget he was his friend; and to testify it did always use him with much courtesy, appointing him a place at his own table, to which he esteemed his company and discourse to be a great ornament.

He continued that employment for the space of five years, being daily useful and not mercenary to his friends. During which time he (I dare not say unhappily) fell into such a liking, as (with her approbation) increased into a love with a young gentlewoman that lived in that family, who was

[6] *Pseudo-Martyr,* Preface.

[7] A leading Catholic controversialist (1542–1621).

[8] Fairly good.

[9] The voyages to Cadiz and to the Azores.

[10] Sir Thomas Egerton, Lord Ellesmere (*c.* 1540–1617).

niece to the Lady Ellesmere, and daughter to Sir George More, then Chancellor of the Garter and Lieutenant of the Tower.[11]

Sir George had some intimation of it, and knowing prevention to be a great part of wisdom, did therefore remove her with much haste from that to his own house at Lothesley, in the county of Surrey; but too late, by reason of some faithful promises which were so interchangeably passed as never to be violated by either party.

These promises were only known to themselves, and the friends of both parties used much diligence and many arguments to kill or cool their affections to each other; but in vain, for love is a flattering mischief, that hath denied aged and wise men a foresight of those evils that too often prove to be the children of that blind father, a passion! that carries us to commit errors with as much ease as whirlwinds remove feathers, and begets in us an unwearied industry to the attainment of what we desire. And such an industry did, notwithstanding much watchfulness against it, bring them secretly together (I forbear to tell the manner how) and at last to a marriage too,[12] without the allowance of those friends whose approbation always was and ever will be necessary to make even a virtuous love become lawful.

And that the knowledge of their marriage might not fall like an unexpected tempest on those that were unwilling to have it so, and that preapprehensions might make it the less enormous when it was known, it was purposely whispered into the ears of many that it was so, yet by none that could affirm it. But to put a period to the jealousies of Sir George (doubt often begetting more restless thoughts than the certain knowledge of what we fear) the news was in favor to Mr. Donne, and with his allowance made known to Sir George by his honorable friend and neighbor, Henry, Earl of Northumberland. But it was to Sir George so immeasurably unwelcome, and so transported him, that, as though his passion of anger and inconsideration might exceed theirs of love and error, he presently engaged his sister, the Lady Ellesmere, to join with him to procure her lord to discharge Mr. Donne of the place he held under his lordship.—This request was followed with violence; and though Sir George were remembered that errors might be overpunished, and desired therefore to forbear till second considerations might clear some scruples, yet he became restless until his suit was granted, and the punishment executed. And though the Lord Chancellor did not at Mr. Donne's dismission give him such a commendation as the great Emperor Charles V, did of his secretary Eraso, when he presented him to his son and successor, Philip II, saying that in his Eraso he gave to him a greater gift then all his estate and all the kingdoms which he then resigned to him; yet the Lord Chancellor said he parted with a friend, and such a secretary as was fitter to serve a king then a subject.

Immediately after his dismission from his service he sent a sad letter to his wife, to acquaint her with it; and after the subscription of his name writ,

John Donne, Anne Donne, Vn-done;

and God knows it proved too true.

For this bitter physic of Mr. Donne's dismission was not strong enough to purge out all Sir George's choler; for he was not satisfied till Mr. Donne and his sometime compupil in Cambridge that married him, namely, Samuel Brooke (who was after doctor in divinity and Master of Trinity College) and his brother, Mr. Christopher Brooke, sometime Mr. Donne's chamber-fellow in Lincoln's Inn, who gave Mr. Donne his wife and witnessed the marriage, were all committed to three several prisons.

Mr. Donne was first enlarged, who neither gave rest to his body or brain, nor to any friend in whom he might hope to have an interest, until he had procured an enlargement for his two imprisoned friends.

He was now at liberty, but his days were still cloudy; and being past these troubles, others did still multiply upon him, for his wife was (to her extreme sorrow) detained from him. And though with Jacob he endured not an hard service for her,[13] yet he

[11] Born 1533; died 1632.

[12] In 1601.

[13] Allusion to Jacob's services under Laban before he won Rachel (Genesis, 29).

lost a good one, and was forced to make good his title, and to get possession of her by a long and restless suit in law; which proved troublesome and sadly chargeable to him, whose youth, and travel, and needless bounty, had brought his estate into a narrow compass.

It is observed, and most truly, that silence and submission are charming qualities, and work most upon passionate men; and it proved so with Sir George; for these and a general report of Mr. Donne's merits, together with his winning behavior (which, when it would intice, had a strange kind of elegant, irresistible art), these and time had so dispassionated Sir George that as the world had approved his daughter's choice, so he also could not but see a more then ordinary merit in his new son. And this at last melted him into so much remorse (for love and anger are so like agues as to have hot and cold fits; and love in parents, though it may be quenched, yet is easily rekindled, and expires not till death denies mankind a natural heat) that he labored his son's restoration to his place, using to that end both his own and his sister's power to her lord; but with no success, for his answer was that though he was unfeignedly sorry for what he had done, yet it was inconsistent with his place and credit to discharge and readmit servants at the request of passionate petitioners.

Sir George's endeavor for Mr. Donne's readmission was by all means to be kept secret (for men do more naturally reluct[14] for errors than submit to put on those blemishes that attend their visible acknowledgment). But, however, it was not long before Sir George appeared to be so far reconciled as to wish their happiness and not to deny them his paternal blessing, but yet refused to contribute any means that might conduce to their livelihood.

Mr. Donne's estate was the greatest part spent in many and chargeable travels, books and dear-bought experience; he, out of all employment that might yield a support for himself and wife, who had been curiously and plentifully educated; both their natures generous, and accustomed to confer, and not to receive courtesies: these and other considerations, but chiefly that his wife was to bear a part in his sufferings, surrounded him with many sad thoughts and some apparent apprehensions of want.

But his sorrows were lessened and his wants prevented[15] by the seasonable courtesy of their noble kinsman, Sir Francis Wolley of Pirford in Surrey,[16] who intreated them to a cohabitation with him, where they remained with much freedom to themselves and equal content to him for some years; and, as their charge encreased (she had yearly a child), so did his love and bounty.

It hath been observed by wise and considering men that wealth hath seldom been the portion, and never the mark to discover good people; but that Almighty God, who disposeth all things wisely, hath of his abundant goodness denied it (he only knows why) to many whose minds he hath enriched with the greater blessings of knowledge and virtue as the fairer testimonies of his love to mankind. And this was the present condition of this man of so excellent erudition and endowments, whose necessary and daily expenses were hardly reconcilable with his uncertain and narrow estate. Which I mention, for that at this time there was a most generous offer made him for the moderating of his worldly cares, the declaration of which shall be the next employment of my pen.

God hath been so good to his church as to afford it in every age some such men to serve at his altar as have been piously ambitious of doing good to mankind, a disposition that is so like to God himself that it owes it self only to him who takes a pleasure to behold it in his creatures. These times he did bless with many such, some of which still live to be patterns of apostolical charity, and of more than human patience. I have said this because I have occasion to mention one of them in my following discourse: namely, Dr. Morton,[17] the most laborious and learned Bishop of Durham, one that God hath blessed with perfect intellectuals and a cheerful heart at the age

[14]Hesitate.

[15]Forestalled.

[16]Anne Donne's first cousin (1583–1610).

[17]Thomas Morton (1564–1659), Dean of Gloucester 1607, Bishop of Durham 1632.

of 94 years (and is yet living), one that in his days of plenty had so large a heart as to use his large revenue to the encouragement of learning and virtue, and is now (be it spoken with sorrow) reduced to a narrow estate, which he embraces without repining; and still shows the beauty of his mind by so liberal a hand, as if this were an age in which tomorrow were to care for itself. I have taken a pleasure in giving the reader a short but true character of this good man, my friend, from whom I received this following relation:——He sent to Mr. Donne, and intreated to borrow an hour of his time for a conference the next day. After their meeting there was not many minutes passed before he spake to Mr. Donne to this purpose: "Mr. Donne, the occasion of sending for you is to propose to you what I have often revolved in my own thought since I last saw you; which nevertheless I will not declare but upon this condition, that you shall not return me a present answer, but forbear three days, and bestow some part of that time in fasting and prayer, and after a serious consideration of what I shall propose then return to me with your answer. Deny me not, Mr. Donne; for it is the effect of a true love which I would gladly pay as a debt due for yours to me."

This request being granted, the doctor exprest himself thus: "Mr. Donne, I know your education and abilities; I know your expectation of a state employment; and I know your fitness for it; and I know too the many delays and contingencies that attend court promises; and let me tell you that my love begot by our long friendship, and your merits, hath prompted me to such an inquisition after your present temporal estate as makes me no stranger to your necessities, which I know to be such as your generous spirit could not bear, if it were not supported with a pious patience. You know I have formerly persuaded you to waive your court hopes, and enter into holy orders; which I now again persuade you to embrace, with this reason added to my former request: The King hath yesterday made me Dean of Gloucester, and I am also possessed of a benefice the profits of which are equal to those of my deanery; I will think my deanery enough for my maintenance (who am and resolved to die a single man) and will quit my benefice and estate you in[18] it (which the patron is willing I shall do), if God shall incline your heart to embrace this motion. Remember, Mr. Donne, no man's education or parts make him too good for this employment, which is to be an ambassador for the God of glory, that God who by a vile death opened the gates of life to mankind. Make me no present answer; but remember your promise, and return to me the third day with your resolution."

At the hearing of this Mr. Donne's faint breath and perplexed countenance gave a visible testimony of an inward conflict; but he performed his promise and departed without returning an answer till the third day.[19]

* * *

At this time of Mr. Donne's and his wife's living in Sir Robert's house,[20] the Lord Hay was by King James sent upon a glorious embassy to the then French King, Henry IV, and Sir Robert put on a sudden resolution to accompany him to the French Court, and, to be present at his audience there. And Sir Robert put on as sudden a resolution to solicit Mr. Donne to be his companion in that journey; and this desire was suddenly made known to his wife, who was then with child and otherways under so dangerous a habit of body, as to her health, that she professed an unwillingness to allow him any absence from her, saying her divining soul boded her some ill in his absence; and therefore desired him not to leave her. This made Mr. Donne lay aside all thoughts of the journey, and really to resolve against it. But Sir Robert became restless in his persuasions for it; and Mr. Donne was so generous as to think he had sold his liberty when he received so many charitable kindnesses from him, and told his wife so; who did therefore with an unwilling willingness give a faint consent to the journey, which was proposed to be but for two months, for about that time they determined their return.

[18] Put you in possession of.

[19] Donne decided at this time that he could not enter into holy orders with an easy conscience.

[20] Sir Robert Drury's house, Drury Lane, London.

—Within a few days after this resolve the ambassador, Sir Robert, and Mr. Donne left London, and were the twelfth day got all safe to Paris.—Two days after their arrival there Mr. Donne was left alone in that room in which Sir Robert and he and some other friends had dined together. To this place Sir Robert returned within half an hour; and, as he left, so he found Mr. Donne alone, but in such an ecstasy and so altered as to his looks as amazed Sir Robert to behold him; insomuch that he earnestly desired Mr. Donne to declare what had befallen him in the short time of his absence? to which Mr. Donne was not able to make a present answer but, after a long and perplexed pause, did at last say, "I have seen a dreadful vision since I saw you; I have seen my dear wife pass twice by me through this room, with her hair hanging about her shoulders and a dead child in her arms; this I have seen since I saw you." To which Sir Robert replied, "Sure, sir, you have slept since I saw you; and this is the result of some melancholy dream, which I desire you to forget, for you are now awake." To which Mr. Donne's reply was: "I cannot be surer that I now live than that I have not slept since I saw you, and am as sure that at her second appearing she stopped, and looked me in the face, and vanished."——Rest and sleep had not altered Mr. Donne's opinion the next day; for he then affirmed this vision with a more deliberate and so confirmed a confidence that he inclined Sir Robert to a faint belief that the vision was true.——It is truly said that desire and doubt have no rest; and it proved so with Sir Robert, for he immediately sent a servant to Drury House with a charge to hasten back, and bring him word whether Mrs. Donne were alive? and if alive, in what condition she was as to her health?—The twelfth day the messenger returned with this account:—That he found and left Mrs. Donne very sad and sick in her bed; and that after a long and dangerous labor she had been delivered of a dead child. And, upon examination, the abortion proved to be the same day and about the very hour that Mr. Donne affirmed he saw her pass by him in his chamber.

* * *

I return from my account of the vision to tell the reader that both before Mr. Donne's going into France, at his being there, and after his return many of the nobility, and others that were powerful at Court were watchful and solicitous to the king for some secular employment for him. The king had formerly both known and put a value upon his company, and had also given him some hopes of a state employment; being always much pleased when Mr. Donne attended him, especially at his meals, where there were usually many deep discourses of general learning, and very often friendly disputes or debates of religion betwixt His Majesty and those divines whose places required their attendance on him at those times, particularly the Dean of the Chapel, who then was Bishop Montague (the publisher of the learned and eloquent works of His Majesty) and the most reverend Dr. Andrewes,[21] the late learned Bishop of Winchester, who then was the king's Almoner.

About this time there grew many disputes that concerned the oath of supremacy and allegiance, in which the king had appeared and engaged himself by his public writings now extant; and His Majesty, discoursing with Mr. Donne concerning many of the reasons which are usually urged against the taking of those oaths, apprehended such a validity and clearness in his stating the questions and his answers to them that His Majesty commanded him to bestow some time in drawing the arguments into a method, and then to write his answers to them, and, having done that, not to send but be his own messenger and bring them to him. To this he presently and diligently applied himself, and within six weeks brought them to him under his own handwriting, as they be now printed, the book bearing the name of *Pseudo-Martyr,* printed *anno* 1610.

When the king had read and considered that book, he persuaded Mr. Donne to enter into the ministry, to which at that time he was and appeared very unwilling, apprehending it (such was his mistaking modesty)

---

[21] Launcelot Andrewes (1555–1626), one of the translators of the King James Version of the Bible, and one of the outstanding sermon-writers of the period.

to be too weighty for his abilities; and though His Majesty had promised him a favor, and many persons of worth mediated with His Majesty for some secular employment for him (to which his education had apted him), and particularly the Earl of Somerset[22] when in his greatest height of favor, who being then at Theobalds[23] with the king, where one of the clerks of the council died that night, the Earl posted a messenger for Mr. Donne to come to him immediately, and at Mr. Donne's coming said, "Mr. Donne, to testify the reality of my affection and my purpose to prefer you, stay in this garden till I go up to the king, and bring you word that you are clerk of the council; doubt not my doing this, for I know the king loves you, and know the king will not deny me." But the king gave a positive denial to all requests and, having a discerning spirit, replied, "I know Mr. Donne is a learned man, has the abilities of a learned divine, and will prove a powerful preacher; and my desire is to prefer him that way, and in that way I will deny you nothing for him." After that time, as he professeth, "The king descended to a persuasion, almost to a solicitation of him, to enter into sacred orders";[24] which though he then denied not, yet he deferred it for almost three years. All which time he applied himself to an incessant study of textual divinity, and to the attainment of a greater perfection in the learned languages, Greek and Hebrew.

In the first and most blessed times of Christianity, when the clergy were looked upon with reverence and deserved it, when they overcame their opposers by high examples of virtue, by a blessed patience and long suffering, those only were then judged worthy the ministry whose quiet and meek spirits did make them look upon that sacred calling with an humble adoration and fear to undertake it; which indeed requires such great degrees of humility, and labor, and care, that none but such were then thought worthy of that celestial dignity. And such only were then sought out, and solicited to undertake it. This I have mentioned because forwardness and inconsideration could not in Mr. Donne, as in many others, be an argument of insufficiency or unfitness; for he had considered long, and had many strifes within himself concerning the strictness of life and competency of learning required in such as enter into sacred orders; and doubtless, considering his own demerits, did humbly ask God with St. Paul, "Lord, who is sufficient for these things?" and with meek Moses, "Lord, who am I?"[25] And sure, if he had consulted with flesh and blood, he had not for these reasons put his hand to that holy plow. But God, who is able to prevail, wrestled with him, as the angel did with Jacob, and marked him; marked him for his own; marked him with a blessing; a blessing of obedience to the motions of his blessed Spirit. And then, as he had formerly asked God with Moses, "Who am I?" so now being inspired with an apprehension of God's particular mercy to him, in the king's and other solicitations of him, he came to ask King David's thankful question, "Lord, who am I, that thou art so mindful of me?" so mindful of me as to lead me for more then forty years through this wilderness of the many temptations and various turnings of a dangerous life; so merciful to me as to move the learnedest of kings to descend to move me to serve at the altar! so merciful to me as at last to move my heart to embrace this holy motion. Thy motions I will and do embrace; and I now say with the blessed Virgin, "Be it with thy servant as seemeth best in thy sight";[26] and so, blessed Jesus, I do take the cup of salvation, and will call upon thy name, and will preach thy Gospel.

Such strifes as these St. Austin had when St. Ambrose endeavored his conversion to Christianity; with which he confesseth he acquainted his friend Alipius. Our learned author (a man fit to write after no mean copy) did the like; and declaring his intentions to his dear friend, Dr. King,[27] then Bishop of London, a man famous in his generation and no stranger to Mr. Donne's abilities (for he had been chaplain to the

[22]Robert Carr, royal favorite, disgraced in 1615 for having poisoned Sir Thomas Overbury.

[23]A royal palace near London.

[24]In *Devotions upon Emergent Occasions* (1624).

[25]Exodus, 3:11.

[26]St. Luke, 1:38.

[27]John King (*c.* 1559–1621).

This is the elaborately engraved title page of the 1616 folio edition of *The Works* of Ben Jonson. This is reproduced from a presentation copy, and at the bottom of the page can be seen Jonson's inscription and signature: "To his most worthy, & learned friend Mr. John Wilson. Ben: Jonsons guift & testimony of his love." (Courtesy of the Pierpont Morgan Library.)

Above are two engravings made to illustrate an edition of Izaak Walton's *Compleat Angler* published in London in 1750. The picture to the left was used as the frontispiece in this edition, and illustrates "the contemplative man's recreation." That to the right illustrates the meeting of Piscator and Venator with the Milkmaid and her daughter, when Piscator presents her with a chub and begs her and her daughter to sing the "choicely good" songs by Christopher Marlowe and Sir Walter Ralegh which he had heard them sing when he was last fishing in the same place (see pages 568–569). (Courtesy of the New York Public Library.)

To the left is the portrait of John Donne which appeared as the frontispiece to the edition of Walton's *Lives of Donne, Wotton, Hooker, and Herbert* published in London in 1670. Passages from Walton's *Life of Donne* appear on pages 554–563. (Courtesy of the New York Public Library.)

Lord Chancellor at the time of Mr. Donne's being his lordship's secretary), that reverend man did receive the news with much gladness; and, after some expressions of joy and a persuasion to be constant in his pious purpose, he proceeded with all convenient speed to ordain him first deacon, and then priest not long after.[28]

Now the English Church had gained a second St. Austin, for, I think, none was so like him before his conversion, none so like St. Ambrose after it; and if his youth had the infirmities of the one, his age had the excellencies of the other, the learning and holiness of both.

And now all his studies, which had been occasionally diffused, were all concentered in divinity. Now he had a new calling, new thoughts, and a new employment for his wit and eloquence. Now all his earthly affections were changed into divine love; and all the faculties of his own soul were engaged in the conversion of others: in preaching the glad tidings of remission to repenting sinners, and peace to each troubled soul. To these he applied himself with all care and diligence; and now such a change was wrought in him that he could say with David, "Oh, how amiable are thy tabernacles, O Lord, God of Hosts!" Now he declared openly that when he required a temporal, God gave him a spiritual blessing; and that he was now gladder to be a door-keeper in the house of God than he could be to enjoy the noblest of all temporal employments.

Presently after he entered into his holy profession, the king sent for him, and made him his chaplain in ordinary, and promised to take a particular care for his preferment.

And though his long familiarity with scholars and persons of greatest quality was such as might have given some men boldness enough to have preached to any eminent auditory; yet his modesty in this employment was such that he could not be persuaded to it, but went usually accompanied with some one friend to preach privately in some village not far from London: his first sermon being preached at Paddington. This he did, till His Majesty sent and appointed him a day to preach to him at Whitehall; and, though much were expected from him both by His Majesty and others, yet he was so happy (which few are) as to satisfy and exceed their expectations, preaching the word so as showed his own heart was possessed with those very thoughts and joys that he labored to distill into others: a preacher in earnest, weeping sometimes for his auditory, sometimes with them; always preaching to himself, like an angel from a cloud, but in none; carrying some, as St. Paul was, to heaven in holy raptures, and enticing others by a sacred art and courtship to amend their lives; here picturing a vice so as to make it ugly to those that practised it, and a virtue so as to make it be beloved even by those that loved it not; and all this with a most particular grace and an unexpressible addition of comeliness.

* * *

About a year after his return out of Germany,[29] Dr. Cary was made Bishop of Exeter, and by his removal the Deanery of St. Paul's being vacant, the king sent to Dr. Donne, and appointed him to attend him at dinner the next day. When His Majesty was sate down, before he had eat any meat he said after his pleasant manner, "Dr. Donne, I have invited you to dinner; and, though you sit not down with me, yet I will carve to you of a dish that I know you love well; for knowing you love London, I do therefore make you Dean of St. Paul's; and when I have dined, then do you take your beloved dish home to your study; say grace there to your self, and much good may it do you."

* * *

The latter part of his life may be said to be a continued study; for as he usually preached once a week, if not oftener, so after his sermon he never gave his eyes rest till he had chosen out a new text, and that night cast his sermon into a form and his text into divisions, and the next day betook himself to consult the Fathers, and so commit his meditations to his memory, which was excellent. But upon Saturday he usu-

[28] In 1615.

[29] In 1621. Donne had been sent thither to assist the Earl of Doncaster in a diplomatic mission.

ally gave himself and his mind a rest from the weary burthen of his week's meditations, and usually spent that day in visitation of friends or some other diversions of his thoughts; and would say that "he gave both his body and mind that refreshment that he might be enabled to do the work of the day following not faintly, but with courage and cheerfulness."

Nor was his age only so industrious, but in the most unsettled days of his youth his bed was not able to detain him beyond the hour of four in a morning; and it was no common business that drew him out of his chamber till past ten, all which time was employed in study, though he took great liberty after it. And if this seem strange, it may gain a belief by the visible fruits of his labors, some of which remain as testimonies of what is here written; for he left the resultance of 1400 authors, most of them abridged and analyzed with his own hand; he left also sixscore of his sermons, all written with his own hand; also an exact and laborious treatise concerning self-murther, called *Biathanatos,*[30] wherein all the laws violated by that act are diligently surveyed and judiciously censured: a treatise written in his younger days, which alone might declare him then not only perfect in the civil and canon law, but in many other such studies and arguments as enter not into the consideration of many that labor to be thought great clerks, and pretend to know all things.

Nor were these only found in his study; but all businesses that past of any public consequence, either in this or any of our neighbor nations, he abbreviated either in Latin or in the language of that nation, and kept them by him for useful memorials. So he did the copies of divers letters and cases of conscience that had concerned his friends, with his observations and solutions of them, and divers other businesses of importance, all particularly and methodically digested by himself.

* * *

Before that month[31] ended he was appointed to preach upon his old constant day, the first Friday in Lent; he had notice of it, and had in his sickness so prepared for that employment that as he had long thirsted for it, so he resolved his weakness should not hinder his journey; he came therefore to London some few days before his appointed day of preaching. At his coming thither many of his friends (who with sorrow saw his sickness had left him but so much flesh as did only cover his bones) doubted his strength to perform that task, and did therefore dissuade him from undertaking it, assuring him, however, it was like to shorten his life; but he passionately denied their requests, saying, he would not doubt that that God who in so many weaknesses had assisted him with an unexpected strength would now withdraw it in his last employment, professing an holy ambition to perform that sacred work. And when to the amazement of some beholders he appeared in the pulpit, many of them thought he presented himself not to preach mortification by a living voice, but mortality by a decayed body and a dying face. And doubtless many did secretly ask that question in Ezekiel: "Do these bones live?"[32] or can that soul organize that tongue to speak so long time as the sand in that glass will move towards its center, and measure out an hour of this dying man's unspent life? Doubtless it cannot; and yet, after some faint pauses in his zealous prayer, his strong desires enabled his weak body to discharge his memory of his preconceived meditations, which were of dying, the text being "To God, the Lord, belong the issues from death"; many that then saw his tears and heard his faint and hollow voice professing they thought the text prophetically chosen and that Dr. Donne had preached his own funeral sermon.[33]

Being full of joy that God had enabled him to perform this desired duty, he hastened to his house; out of which he never moved till like St. Stephen he was carried by devout men to his grave.

* * *

I must here look so far back as to tell the

[30] First published in 1644.

[31] January, 1631.

[32] Ezekiel, 37:3.

[33] This sermon was published in 1633 with the title "Death's Duel."

reader that at his first return out of Essex to preach his last sermon his old friend and physician, Dr. Fox, a man of great worth, came to him to consult his health; and that after a sight of him and some queries concerning his distempers he told him that by cordials and drinking milk twenty days together there was a probability of his restoration to health; but he passionately denied to drink it. Nevertheless, Dr. Fox, who loved him most entirely, wearied him with solicitations till he yielded to take it for ten days; at the end of which time he told Dr. Fox he had drunk it more to satisfy him than to recover his health; and that he would not drink it ten days longer upon the best moral assurance of having twenty years added to his life; for he loved it not, and was so far from fearing death, which to others is the king of terrors, that he longed for the day of his dissolution.

It is observed that a desire of glory or commendation is rooted in the very nature of man; and that those of the severest and most mortified lives, though they may become so humble as to banish self-flattery, and such weeds as naturally grow there, yet they have not been able to kill this desire of glory, but that, like our radical heat, it will both live and die with us. And many think it should do so; and we want not sacred examples to justify the desire of having our memory to out-live our lives. Which I mention because Dr. Donne, by the persuasion of Dr. Fox, easily yielded at this very time to have a monument made for him; but Dr. Fox undertook not to persuade him how or what monument it should be; that was left to Dr. Donne himself.

A monument being resolved upon, Dr. Donne sent for a carver to make for him in wood the figure of an urn, giving him directions for the compass and height of it, and to bring with it a board of the just height of his body. These being got, then without delay a choice painter was got to be in a readiness to draw his picture, which was taken as followeth: Several charcoal fires being first made in his large study, he brought with him into that place his winding-sheet in his hand, and, having put off all his clothes, had this sheet put on him and so tied with knots at his head and feet, and his hands so placed, as dead bodies are usually fitted to be shrouded and put into their coffin or grave. Upon this urn he thus stood with his eyes shut, and with so much of the sheet turned aside as might show his lean, pale, and death-like face, which was purposely turned toward the east, from whence he expected the second coming of his and our Savior Jesus. In this posture he was drawn at his just height; and when the picture was fully finished, he caused it to be set by his bed-side, where it continued and became his hourly object till his death, and was then given to his dearest friend and executor, Dr. Henry King, then chief Residenciary of St. Paul's, who caused him to be thus carved in one entire piece of white marble, as it now stands in that church.

* * *

I. W.

THE COMPLEAT ANGLER,
or
The Contemplative Man's Recreation

CHAP. I

A Conference betwixt an ANGLER, a FALCONER, *and a* HUNTER, *each commending his recreation*

PISCATOR
VENATOR
AUCEPS[1]

PISC. You are well overtaken, Gentlemen! A good morning to you both; I have stretched my legs up Tottenham-hill to overtake you, hoping your business may occasion you towards Ware[2] this fine, fresh May morning.

VENAT. Sir, I, for my part, shall almost answer your hopes, for my purpose is to drink my morning's draught at the Thatched House in Hodsden;[3] and I think not to rest

[1]Angler, Hunter, Falconer.

[2]A market town about twenty miles north of London.

[3]Place on the road from London to Ware.

till I come thither, where I have appointed a friend or two to meet me: but for this Gentleman that you see with me, I know not how far he intends his journey; he came so lately into my company, that I have scarce had time to ask him the question.

Auceps. Sir, I shall by your favor bear you company as far as Theobalds, and there leave you; for then I turn up to a friend's house, who mews[4] a Hawk for me, which I now long to see.

Venat. Sir, we are all so happy as to have a fine, fresh, cool morning; and I hope we shall each be the happier in the others' company. And, Gentlemen, that I may not lose yours, I shall either abate or amend my pace to enjoy it, knowing that (as the Italians say) Good company in a journey makes the way to seem the shorter.

Auceps. It may do so, Sir, with the help of good discourse, which, methinks, we may promise from you, that both look and speak so cheerfully: and for my part, I promise you, as an invitation to it, that I will be as free and openhearted as discretion will allow me to be with strangers.

Ven. And, Sir, I promise the like.

Pisc. I am right glad to hear your answers, and, in confidence you speak the truth, I shall put on a boldness to ask you, Sir, whether business or pleasure caused you to be so early up, and walk so fast, for this other Gentleman hath declared he is going to see a Hawk, that a friend mews for him.

Ven. Sir, mine is a mixture of both, a little business and more pleasure; for I intend this day to do all my business, and then bestow another day or two in hunting the Otter, which a friend, that I go to meet, tells me is much pleasanter than any other chase whatsoever: howsoever, I mean to try it; for to-morrow morning we shall meet a pack of Otter-dogs of noble Mr. Sadler's, upon Amwell hill, who will be there so early, that they intend to prevent[5] the sun-rising.

Pisc. Sir, my fortune has answered my desires, and my purpose is to bestow a day or two in helping to destroy some of those villainous vermin; for I hate them perfectly, because they love fish so well, or rather, because they destroy so much; indeed so much, that in my judgment all men that keep Otter-dogs ought to have pensions from the King, to encourage them to destroy the very breed of those base Otters, they do so much mischief.

Ven. But what say you to the Foxes of the Nation, would not you as willingly have them destroyed? for doubtless they do as much mischief as Otters do.

Pisc. Oh, Sir, if they do, it is not so much to me and my fraternity, as those base vermin the Otters do.

Auc. Why Sir, I pray, of what fraternity are you, that you are so angry with the poor Otters?

Pisc. I am, Sir, a Brother of the Angle, and therefore an enemy to the Otter: for you are to note, that we Anglers all love one another, and therefore do I hate the Otter both for my own and for their sakes who are of my brotherhood.

Ven. And I am a lover of Hounds; I have followed many a pack of dogs many a mile, and heard many merry men make sport and scoff at Anglers.

Auc. And I profess myself a Falconer, and have heard many grave, serious men pity them, 'tis such a heavy, contemptible, dull recreation.

Pisc. You know, Gentlemen, 'tis an easy thing to scoff at any Art or Recreation; a little wit mixed with ill nature, confidence, and malice, will do it; but though they often venture boldly, yet they are often caught, even in their own trap, according to that of Lucian, the father of the family of Scoffers.

Lucian, well skilled in scoffing, this hath writ,
Friend, that's your folly, which you think your
  wit:
This you vent oft, void both of wit and fear,
Meaning another, when yourself you jeer.

If to this you add what Solomon says of Scoffers, that they are abomination to mankind.[6] Let him that thinks fit be a Scoffer still; but I account them enemies to me, and to all that love virtue and Angling.

And for you that have heard many grave, serious men pity Anglers; let me tell you,

[4]Confines during moulting.

[5]Anticipate.

[6]Proverbs, 24:9.

Sir, there be many men that are by others taken to be serious, grave men, which we contemn and pity. Men that are taken to be grave, because Nature hath made them of a sour complexion, money-getting-men, men that spend all their time, first in getting, and next, in anxious care to keep it; men that are condemned to be rich, and then always busy or discontented: for these poor-rich-men, we Anglers pity them perfectly, and stand in no need to borrow their thoughts to think ourselves happy. No, no, Sir, we enjoy a contentedness above the reach of such dispositions, and as the learned and ingenuous Montaigne says, like himself, freely, "When my Cat and I entertain each other with mutual apish tricks (as playing with a garter) who knows but that I make my Cat more sport than she makes me? Shall I conclude her to be simple, that has her time to begin or refuse sportiveness as freely as I myself have? Nay, who knows but that it is a defect of my not understanding her language (for doubtless Cats talk and reason with one another) that we agree no better: and who knows but that she pities me for being no wiser, and laughs and censures my folly, for making sport for her, when we play together?"[7]

Thus freely speaks Montaigne concerning Cats, and I hope I may take as great a liberty to blame any man, and laugh at him too, let him be never so serious, that hath not heard what Anglers can say in the justification of their Art and Recreation; which I may again tell you is so full of pleasure, that we need not borrow their thoughts, to think ourselves happy.

VENAT. Sir, you have almost amazed me, for though I am no scoffer, yet I have, I pray let me speak it without offense, always looked upon Anglers as more patient and more simple men, than I fear I shall find you to be.

PISC. Sir, I hope you will not judge my earnestness to be impatience: and for my simplicity, if by that you mean a harmlessness, or that simplicity which was usually found in the primitive Christians, who were, as most Anglers are, quiet men, and followers of peace; men that were so simply-wise, as not to sell their consciences to buy riches, and with them vexation and a fear to die, if you mean such simple men as lived in those times when there were fewer Lawyers; when men might have had a Lordship safely conveyed to them in a piece of parchment no bigger than your hand (though several sheets will not do it safely in this wiser age); I say, Sir, if you take us Anglers to be such simple men as I have spoke of, then myself and those of my profession will be glad to be so understood: But if by simplicity you meant to express a general defect in those that profess and practice the excellent Art of Angling, I hope in time to disabuse you, and make the contrary appear so evidently, that if you will but have patience to hear me, I shall remove all the anticipations that discourse, or time, or prejudice, have possessed you with against that laudable and ancient art; for I know it is worthy the knowledge and practice of a wise man.

* * *

CHAP. IV[8]

Observations of the nature and breeding of the Trout; and how to fish for him. And the Milkmaid's Song.

PISC. The Trout is a fish highly valued both in this and foreign Nations: he may be justly said, (as the old Poet said of wine, and we English say of venison) to be a generous[9] fish: a fish that is so like the Buck that he also has his seasons; for it is observed, that he comes in and goes out of season with the Stag and Buck; Gesner[10] says, his name is of a German off-spring,[11] and says he is a fish that feeds clean and purely, in the swiftest streams, and on the hardest gravel; and that he may justly contend with all fresh-water-fish, as the Mullet may with all sea-fish, for precedency and daintiness of taste, and that being in right season, the most dainty palates have allowed precedency to him.

[7]*Essays,* "Apology for Raymond Sebond."

[8]Since Chapter I, a day has intervened during which Piscator has accompanied Venator in an otter hunt; and now on the third day Venator accompanies Piscator in his fishing.

[9]Of noble birth.

[10]Conrad Gesner (1516–1565), author of the *Historia Naturalis Animalium.*

[11]Origin.

And before I go farther in my Discourse, let me tell you, that you are to observe, that as there be some barren Does, that are good in summer, so there be some barren Trouts that are good in winter, but there are not many that are so; for usually they be in their perfection in the month of May, and decline with the Buck. Now you are to take notice, that in several Countries, as in Germany and in other parts, compared to ours, fish do differ much in their bigness, and shape, and other ways, and so do Trouts; it is well known that in the Lake Leman (the Lake of Geneva) there are Trouts taken of three cubits long, as is affirmed by Gesner, a writer of good credit; and Mercator[12] says, the Trouts that are taken in the Lake of Geneva, are a great part of the merchandise of that famous city. And you are further to know, that there be certain waters that breed Trouts remarkable both for their number and smallness. I know a little brook in Kent, that breeds them to a number incredible, and you may take them twenty or forty in an hour, but none greater than about the size of a Gudgeon. There are also in divers rivers, especially that relate to, or be near to the sea (as Winchester, or the Thames about Windsor) a little Trout called a Samlet or Skegger Trout (in both which places I have caught twenty or forty at a standing) that will bite as fast and as freely as Minnows; these be by some taken to be young Salmons, but in those waters they never grow to be bigger than a Herring.

There is also in Kent near to Canterbury, a Trout (called there a Fordidge Trout) a Trout (that bears the name of the town where it is usually caught) that is accounted the rarest of fish; many of them near the bigness of a Salmon, but known by their different color, and in their best season they cut very white; and none of these have been known to be caught with an Angle, unless it were one that was caught by Sir George Hastings (an excellent Angler, and now with God) and he hath told me, he thought that Trout bit not for hunger but wantonness; and it is the rather to be believed, because both he then, and many others before him, have been curious to search into their bellies, what the food was by which they lived; and have found out nothing by which they might satisfy their curiosity.

Concerning which you are to take notice, that it is reported by good authors, that there is a fish, that hath not any mouth, but lives by taking breath by the porings of her gills, and feeds and is nourished by no man knows what; and this may be believed of the Fordidge Trout, which (as it is said of the Stork, that he knows his season, so he) knows his times (I think almost his day) of coming into that river out of the sea, where he lives (and it is like, feeds) nine months of the year, and fasts three in the River of Fordidge. And you are to note, that the townsmen are very punctual in observing the very time of beginning to fish for them; and boast much that their river affords a Trout, that exceeds all others. And just so does Sussex boast of several fish; as namely, a Shelsey Cockle, a Chichester Lobster, an Arundel Mullet, and an Amerly Trout.

And now for some confirmation of the Fordidge Trout, you are to know that this Trout is thought to eat nothing in the fresh water; and it may be the better believed, because it is well known, that Swallows, which are not seen to fly in England for six months in the year, but about Michaelmas[13] leave us for a hotter climate; yet some of them that have been left behind their fellows, have been found (many thousands at a time) in hollow trees, where they have been observed to live and sleep out the whole winter without meat; and so Albertus[14] observes, that there is one kind of Frog that hath her mouth naturally shut up about the end of August, and that she lives so all the winter: and though it be strange to some, yet it is known to too many among us to be doubted.

And so much for these Fordidge trouts, which never afford an Angler sport, but either live their time of being in the fresh water, by their meat formerly gotten in the sea (not unlike the Swallow or Frog) or by

[12]Gerard Mercator (1512–1594). Flemish geographer.

[13]September 29.

[14]Albertus Magnus (d. 1280), whose observation Walton seems to have found in Edward Topsell's *Historie of Serpents* (1608).

the virtue of the fresh water only; or as the birds of Paradise, and the Chameleon are said to live by the sun and the air.

There is also in Northumberland a Trout called a Bull-trout, of a much greater length and bigness, than any in these Southern parts: and there are in many rivers that relate to the sea, Salmon-trouts, as much different from others, both in shape and in their spots, as we see sheep differ one from another in their shape and bigness, and in the fineness of their wool: and certainly, as some pastures do breed larger sheep, so do some rivers, by reason of the ground over which they run, breed larger Trouts.

Now the next thing that I will commend to your consideration is, that the Trout is of a more sudden growth than other fish: concerning which you are also to take notice, that he lives not so long as the Perch and divers other fishes do, as Sir Francis Bacon hath observed in his *History of Life and Death.*[15]

And next you are to take notice, that he is not like the Crocodile, which if he lives never so long, yet always thrives till his death: but 'tis not so with the Trout; for after he is come to his full growth, he declines in his body, but keeps his bigness or thrives only in his head till his death. And you are to know, that he will about (especially before) the time of his spawning, get almost miraculously through Weirs and Floodgates against the stream; even through such high and swift places as is almost incredible. Next, that the Trout usually spawns about October or November, but in some rivers a little sooner or later: which is the more observable, because most other fish spawn in the spring or summer, when the sun hath warmed both the earth and water, and made it fit for generation. And you are to note, that he continues many months out of season: for it may be observed of the Trout, that he is like the Buck or the Ox, that will not be fat in many months, though he go in the very same pastures that horses do, which will be fat in one month; and so you may observe, that most other fishes recover strength, and grow sooner fat, and in season than the Trout doth.

And next, you are to note, that till the sun gets to such a height as to warm the earth and the water, the Trout is sick and lean, and lousy, and unwholesome: for you shall in winter find him to have a big head, and then to be lank, and thin, and lean; at which time many of them have sticking on them Sugs, or Trout lice, which is a kind of a worm, in shape like a clove or pin with a big head, and sticks close to him and sucks his moisture; those, I think, the Trout breeds himself, and never thrives till he free himself from them, which is till warm weather comes; and then, as he grows stronger, he gets from the dead, still water, into the sharp streams, and the gravel, and there rubs off these worms or lice; and then, as he grows stronger, so he gets him into swifter and swifter streams, and there lies at the watch for any fly or Minnow, that comes near to him; and he especially loves the May-fly, which is bred of the Cod-worm, or Caddis; and these make the Trout bold and lusty, and he is usually fatter and better meat at the end of that month, than at any time of the year.

Now you are to know, that it is observed, that usually the best trouts are either red or yellow, though some (as the Fordidge Trout) be white and yet good; but that is not usual: and it is a note observable, that the female Trout hath usually a less head, and a deeper body than the male Trout; and is usually the better meat: and note that a hogback, and a little head to any fish, either Trout, Salmon, or other fish, is a sign that that fish is in season.

But yet you are to note, that as you see some Willows or palm-trees bud and blossom sooner than others do, so some Trouts be in rivers sooner in season; and as some Hollies or Oaks are longer before they cast their leaves, so are some Trouts, in some rivers, longer before they go out of season.

And you are to note, that there are several kinds of Trouts, though they all go under that general name; just as there be tame and wild Pigeons: and of tame, there be Cropers, Carriers, Runts, and too many to name, which all differ, and so do Trouts,

[15] A part of the *History Naturall and Experimental.*

in their bigness, shape, and color. The great Kentish Hens may be an instance, compared to other Hens; and doubtless there is a kind of small Trout, which will never thrive to be big, that breeds very many more than others do, that be of a larger size; which you may rather believe, if you consider, that the little Wren and Titmouse will have twenty young at a time, when usually the noble Hawk, or the Musical Throstle or Black-bird exceed not four or five.

And now I shall try my skill to catch a Trout, and at my next walking either this evening, or to-morrow morning, I will give you direction, how you yourself shall fish for him.

VENAT. Trust me, Master, I see now it is a harder matter to catch a Trout than a Chub: for I have put on patience, and followed you these two hours, and not seen a fish stir, neither at your Minnow nor your Worm.

PISC. Well, Scholar, you must endure worse luck sometime, or you will never make a good Angler. But what say you now? there is a Trout now, and a good one too, if I can but hold him, and two or three turns more will tire him: now you see he lies still, and the sleight is to land him: reach me that landing net. So, Sir, now he is mine own, what say you now? is not this worth all my labor and your patience?

VENAT. On my word, Master, this is a gallant Trout, what shall we do with him?

PISC. Marry, e'en eat him to supper: we'll go to my Hostess from whence we came; she told me, as I was going out of door, that my brother Peter, a good Angler and a cheerful companion, had sent word he would lodge there to-night, and bring a friend with him. My Hostess has two beds, and I know, you and I may have the best: we'll rejoice with my brother Peter and his friend, tell tales, or sing Ballads, or make a Catch,[16] or find some harmless sport to content us, and pass away a little time without offense to God or man.

VENAT. A match, good Master, let's go to that house for the linen looks white, and smells of lavender, and I long to lie in a pair of sheets that smell so: let's be going, good Master, for I am hungry again with fishing.

PISC. Nay, stay a little good Scholar, I caught my last Trout with a Worm, now I will put on a Minnow, and try a quarter of an hour about yonder trees for another, and so walk towards our lodging. Look you, Scholar, thereabout we shall have a bite presently, or not at all: have with you, Sir, on my word I have him! Oh, it is a great loggerheaded Chub; come, hang him upon that Willow-twig, and let's be going. But turn out of the way a little, good Scholar, towards yonder high hedge; we'll sit whilst this shower falls so gently upon the teeming earth, and gives yet a sweeter smell to the lovely flowers that adorn these verdant meadows.

Look! under that broad Beech-tree, I sate down, when I was last this way a-fishing, and the birds in the adjoining grove seemed to have a friendly contention with an echo, whose dead voice seemed to live in a hollow tree, near to the brow of that primrose-hill; there I sate viewing the silver streams glide silently towards their center, the tempestuous sea; yet, sometimes opposed by rugged roots, and pebble-stones, which broke their waves, and turned them into foam: and sometimes I beguiled time by viewing the harmless lambs, some leaping securely in the cool shade, whilst others sported themselves in the cheerful sun; and saw others craving comfort from the swollen udders of their bleating dams. As I thus sate, these and other sights had so fully possessed my soul with content, that I thought as the Poet has happily expressed it:

I was for that time lifted above earth;
And possessed joys not promised in my birth.

As I left this place, and entered into the next field, a second pleasure entertained me, 'twas a handsome Milkmaid that had cast away all care, and sung like a Nightingale: her voice was good, and the Ditty fitted for it; 'twas that smooth song, which was made by Kit. Marlowe, now at least fifty years ago:[17] and the Milkmaid's Mother sung an

[16] Song in which one singer catches up the words of another.

[17] Marlowe had already been dead sixty years. His song, which the milkmaid sings, was first published over his name in *England's Helicon* (1600). Ralegh's satiric reply, sung by the milkmaid's mother, likewise appeared in that collection.

answer to it, which was made by Sir Walter Ralegh in his younger days.

They were old-fashioned Poetry, but choicely good, I think much better than the strong[18] lines that are now in fashion in this critical age. Look yonder! on my word, yonder they both be a-milking again, I will give her the Chub, and persuade them to sing those two songs to us.

God speed you, good woman, I have been a-fishing, and am going to Bleak-Hall, to my bed, and having caught more fish than will sup myself and my friend, I will bestow this upon you and your Daughter; for I use to sell none.

MILK. Marry, God requite you, Sir, and we'll eat it cheerfully: and if you come this way a-fishing two months hence, a grace of God I'll give you a Sillybub[19] of new Verjuice in a new made Hay-cock, for it, and my Maudlin shall sing you one of her best Ballads, for she and I both love all Anglers, they be such honest, civil, quiet men; in the meantime will you drink a draught of Red-Cows milk, you shall have it freely.

PISC. No, I thank you, but I pray do us a courtesy that shall stand you and your daughter in nothing, and yet we will think ourselves still something in your debt: it is but to sing us a Song, that was sung by your daughter, when I last passed over this meadow, about eight or nine days since.

MILK. What Song was it, I pray? was it "Come, Shepherds, deck your herds," or "As at noon Dulcina rested," or "Phillida flouts me," or "Chevy Chase"?[20]

PISC. No, it is none of those: it is a Song that your daughter sung the first part, and you sung the answer to it.

MILK. Oh, I know it now, I learned the first part in my golden age, when I was about the age of my poor daughter; and the latter part, which indeed fits me best now, but two or three years ago, when the cares of the world began to take hold of me: but you shall, God willing, hear them both, and sung as well as we can, for we both love Anglers. Come, Maudlin, sing the first part to the Gentlemen, with a merry heart, and I'll sing the second, when you have done.

THE MILKMAID'S SONG

Come live with me, and be my Love,
And we will all the pleasures prove
That valleys, groves, or hills, or fields,
Or woods, and steepy mountain yields.

Where we will sit upon the Rocks,
And see the Shepherds feed our flocks,
By shallow *Rivers,* to whose falls,
Melodious birds sing *Madrigals.*

And I will make thee beds of *Roses,*
And then a thousand fragrant Posies,
A Cap of flower, and a Kirtle,[21]
Embroidered all with leaves of myrtle.

A Gown made of the finest Wool
Which from our pretty Lambs we pull;
Slippers lined choicely for the cold,
With buckles of the purest gold.

A Belt of Straw, and Ivy-buds,
With Coral Clasps and Amber studs:
And if these pleasures may thee move,
Come live with me and be my Love.

Thy silver dishes for thy meat,
As precious as the Gods do eat,
Shall on an Ivory Table be
Prepared each day for thee and me.

The Shepherds' Swains shall dance and sing
For thy delight each May-morning:
If these delights thy mind may move,
Then live with me, and be my Love.

VENAT. Trust me, Master, it is a choice Song, and sweetly sung by honest Maudlin. I now see it was not without cause, that our good Queen Elizabeth did so often wish herself a Milkmaid all the month of May, because they are not troubled with cares, but sing sweetly all the day, and sleep securely all the night: and without doubt, honest, innocent, pretty Maudlin does so. I'll bestow Sir Thomas Overbury's Milkmaid's wish upon her, That she may die in the Spring, and have good store of flowers stuck round about her winding sheet.[22]

[18]Pointed.
[19]Drink of cream, curdled with some acidic admixture and then sweetened.
[20]All popular songs, the last the most famous of the ballads of the Scotch border.
[21]Skirt or outer petticoat.
[22]From Overbury's *Characters* (1615). The sketch of "A Fair and Happy Milkmaid," here quoted, is now thought to be the work of the dramatist, John Webster.

THE MILKMAID'S MOTHER'S ANSWER

If all the world and Love were young,
And truth in every Shepherd's tongue,
These pretty pleasures might me move
To live with thee, and be thy Love.

But Time drives flocks from field to fold,
When Rivers rage, and rocks grow cold,
Then *Philomel* becometh dumb,
The Rest complains of care to come.

The flowers do fade, and wanton fields
To wayward Winter reckoning yields,
A honey tongue, a heart of gall,
Is fancy's spring, but sorrow's fall;

Thy gowns, thy shoes, thy beds of roses,
Thy cap, thy kirtle, and thy posies,
Soon break, soon wither, soon forgotten,
In folly ripe, in reason rotten.

Thy Belt of Straw, and Ivy-buds,
Thy Coral clasps, and Amber-studs,
All these in me no means can move
To come to thee, and be thy Love.

What should we talk of dainties then,
Of better meat than 's fit for men?
These are but vain: that's only good
Which God hath blest, and sent for food.

But could Youth last, and love still breed,
Had joys no date, nor age no need;
Then those delights my mind might move,
To live with thee, and be thy Love.

PISC. Well sung, good Woman, I thank you. I'll give you another dish of fish one of these days; and then beg another song of you. Come, Scholar, let Maudlin alone: do not you offer to spoil her voice. Look, yonder comes mine Hostess, to call us to supper. How now? is my brother Peter come?

HOSTESS. Yes, and a friend with him, they are both glad to hear that you are in these parts, and long to see you, and are hungry, and long to be at supper.

CHAP. VIII[23]

Observations of the Luce or Pike, with directions how to fish for him.

PISC. The mighty Luce or Pike is taken to be the Tyrant (as the Salmon is the King) of the fresh waters. 'Tis not to be doubted, but that they are bred, some by generation, and some not: as namely, of a Weed called 5 Pickerel-weed, unless learned Gesner be much mistaken; for he says, this weed and other glutinous matter, with the help of the sun's heat in some particular months, and some ponds apted for it by nature, do be-10 come Pikes. But doubtless divers Pikes are bred after this manner, or are brought into some ponds some other ways that is past man's finding out, of which we have daily testimonies.

15 Sir Francis Bacon, in his *History of Life and Death,* observes the Pike to be the longest lived of any fresh-water-fish, and yet he computes it to be not usually above forty years; and others think it to be not above 20 ten years; and yet Gesner mentions a Pike taken in Swedeland in the year 1449 with a ring about his neck, declaring he was put into the pond by Frederick the second, more than two hundred years before he was last 25 taken, as by the inscription of that ring (being Greek) was interpreted by the then Bishop of Worms. But of this no more, but that it is observed, that the old or very great Pikes have in them more of state than good-30 ness; the smaller or middle sized Pikes being by the most and choicest palates observed to be the best meat; and contrary, the Eel is observed to be the better for age and bigness.

All Pikes that live long prove chargeable 35 to their keepers, because their life is maintained by the death of so many other fish, even those of his own kind, which has made him by some writers to be called the Tyrant of the rivers, or the Fresh-water-wolf, by 40 reason of his bold, greedy, devouring disposition; which is so keen, as Gesner relates, a man going to a pond (where it seems a Pike had devoured all the fish) to water his Mule, had a Pike bite his Mule by the lips; to 45 which the Pike hung so fast, that the Mule drew him out of the water; and by that accident the owner of the Mule got the Pike. And the same Gesner observes, that a maid in Poland had a Pike bite her by the foot, 50 as she was washing clothes in a pond. And I have heard the like of a woman in Killingworth Pond not far from Coventry. But I

[23]Piscator continues his explanations to Venator on the day following that of the milkmaid's song.

have been assured by my friend Mr. Segrave, of whom I spake to you formerly,[24] that keeps tame Otters, that he hath known a Pike in extreme hunger fight with one of his Otters for a Carp that the Otter had caught and was then bringing out of the water. I have told you who relates these things, and tell you they are persons of credit; and shall conclude this observation, by telling you what a wise man has observed, It is a hard thing to persuade the belly, because it has no ears.

But if these relations be disbelieved, it is too evident to be doubted, that a Pike will devour a fish of his own kind, that shall be bigger than his belly or throat will receive, and swallow a part of him, and let the other part remain in his mouth till the swallowed part be digested, and then swallow that other part that was in his mouth, and so put it over by degrees; which is not unlike the Ox and some other beasts, taking their meat not out of their mouth into their belly, but first into some place betwixt, and then chaw it, or digest it after, which is called Chewing the Cud. And doubtless Pikes will bite when they are not hungry, but as some think in very anger, when a tempting bait comes near to them.

And it is observed, that the Pike will eat venomous things (as some kind of Frogs are) and yet live without being harmed by them: for, as some say, he has in him a natural Balsam or Antidote against all poison: and others, that he never eats the venomous Frog till he have first killed her, and then (as Ducks are observed to do to Frogs in spawning time, at which time some Frogs are observed to be venomous) so thoroughly washed her, by tumbling her up and down in the water, that he may devour her without danger. And Gesner affirms, that a Polonian Gentleman, did faithfully assure him, he had seen two young Geese at one time in the belly of a Pike. And doubtless a Pike in his height of hunger will bite at and devour a dog that swims in a pond, and there have been examples of it, or the like; for as I told you, The belly has no ears when hunger comes upon it.

The Pike is also observed to be a solitary, melancholy and a bold fish: melancholy, because he always swims or rests himself alone, and never swims in shoals or with company, as Roach and Dace, and most other fish do: and bold, because he fears not a shadow, or to see or be seen of anybody, as the Trout and Chub, and all other fish do.

And it is observed by Gesner, that the jaw-bones, and hearts, and galls of Pikes, are very medicinable for several diseases, or to stop blood, to abate fevers, to cure agues, to oppose or expel the infection of the plague, and to be many ways medicinable and useful for the good of Mankind; but he observes, that the biting of a Pike is venomous and hard to be cured.

And it is observed, that the Pike is a fish that breeds but once a year, and that other fish (as namely Loaches) do breed oftener: as we are certain tame Pigeons do almost every month, and yet the Hawk (a Bird of Prey, as the Pike is of Fish) breeds but once in twelve months: and you are to note, that his time of breeding or spawning is usually about the end of February, or somewhat later, in March, as the weather proves colder or warmer; and to note, that his manner of breeding is thus, a He and a She Pike will usually go together out of a river into some ditch or creek, and that there the Spawner casts her eggs, and the Milter[25] hovers over her all that time that she is casting her spawn, but touches her not.

I might say more of this, but it might be thought curiosity or worse, and shall therefore forbear it, and take up so much of your attention, as to tell you, that the best of Pikes are noted to be in rivers, next those in great ponds or meres, and the worst in small ponds.

But before I proceed further, I am to tell you that there is a great antipathy betwixt the Pike and some Frogs; and this may appear to the reader of Dubravius (a Bishop in Bohemia), who in his Book of Fish and Fish-ponds,[26] relates what, he says, he saw with his own eyes, and could not forbear to tell the reader. Which was:

As he and the Bishop Thurzo were walking by a large pond in Bohemia, they saw a Frog, when the Pike lay very sleepily and quiet by the shore side, leap upon his head,

[24]In Chapter II, not included here.

[25]Male fish.

[26]Janus Dubravius Scala, *De Piscinis, etc.* (1559).

and the Frog having expressed malice or anger by his swollen cheeks and staring eyes, did stretch out his legs and embrace the Pike's head, and presently reached them to his eyes, tearing with them and his teeth those tender parts; the Pike moved with anguish, moves up and down the water, and rubs himself against weeds, and whatever he thought might quit him of his enemy; but all in vain, for the Frog did continue to ride triumphantly, and to bite and torment the Pike, till his strength failed, and then he sunk with the Pike to the bottom of the water; then presently the Frog appeared again at the top, and croaked, and seemed to rejoice like a Conqueror, and then presently retired to his secret hole. The Bishop, that had beheld the battle, called his fisherman to fetch his nets, and by all means to get the Pike that they might declare what had happened: and the Pike was drawn forth, and both his eyes eaten out, at which when they began to wonder, the Fisherman wished them to forbear, and assured them he was certain that Pikes were often so served.

I told this (which is to be read in the sixth chapter of the book of Dubravius), unto a friend, who replied, It was as improbable as to have the mouse scratch out the cat's eyes. But he did not consider, that there be fishing Frogs (which the Dalmatians call the Water-Devil) of which I might tell you as wonderful a story, but I shall tell you, that 'tis not to be doubted, but that there be some Frogs so fearful of the Water-snake, that, when they swim in a place in which they fear to meet with him, they get a reed across into their mouths, which if they two meet by accident, secures the frog from the strength and malice of the Snake, and note, that the frog swims the fastest.

And let me tell you, that as there be Water and Land-frogs, so there be Land and Water-Snakes. Concerning which take this observation, that the Land-snake breeds, and hatches her eggs, which become young snakes, in some old dunghill, or a like hot place; but the Water-snake, which is not venomous (and as I have been assured by a great observer of such secrets) does breed her young alive, which she does not then forsake, but bides with them, and in case of danger will take them all into her mouth and swim away from any apprehended danger, and then let them out again when she thinks all danger to be past; these be accidents that we Anglers sometimes see and often talk of.

But whither am I going? I had almost lost myself by remembering the Discourse of Dubravius. I will therefore stop here, and tell you according to my promise how to catch this fish.

His feeding is usually of fish or frogs, and sometimes a weed of his own called Pickerel-weed. Of which I told you some think some Pikes are bred; for they have observed, that where none have been put into ponds, yet they have there found many: and that there has been plenty of that weed in those ponds, and that that weed both breeds and feeds them; but whether those Pikes so bred will ever breed by generation as the others do, I shall leave to the disquisitions of men of more curiosity and leisure than I profess myself to have; and shall proceed to tell you that you may fish for a Pike, either with a ledger or a walking-bait; and you are to note, that I call that a ledger-bait, which is fixed, or made to rest in one certain place when you shall be absent; and I call that a walking-bait, which you take with you, and have ever in motion. Concerning which two, I shall give you this direction; that your ledger-bait is best to be a living bait, whether it be a fish or a frog; and that you may make them live the longer, you may, or indeed you must, take this course.

First, for your live bait of fish, a Roach or Dace is (I think) best and most tempting, and a Perch is the longest-lived on a hook, and having cut off his fin on his back, which may be done without hurting him, you must take your knife (which cannot be too sharp), and betwixt the head and the fin on the back, cut or make an incision, or such a scar, as you may put the arming wire of your hook into it, with as little bruising or hurting the fish as art and diligence will enable you to do; and so carrying your arming wire along his back, unto, or near the tail of your fish, betwixt the skin and the body of it, draw out that wire or arming of your hook at another scar near to his tail: then tie him about it with thread, but no harder than of necessity you must to prevent hurting the fish; and the better to avoid hurting the fish, some have a kind of probe to open the way, for the more easy entrance and passage of your wire or arming: but as for these, time, and a little experience will teach you better than I can by words; therefore I will for the present say no more of this, but come next to give you some directions, how to bait your hook with a frog.

VEN. But, good Master, did you not say even now, that some Frogs were venomous, and is it not dangerous to touch them?

PISC. Yes, but I will give you some rules or cautions concerning them: and first, you are to note, that there are two kinds of Frogs; that is to say (if I may so express myself), a flesh, and a fish-frog. By flesh-frogs, I mean frogs that breed and live on the land; and of these there be several sorts also and colors, some being peckled,[27] some greenish, some blackish, or brown: the green Frog, which is a small one, is, by Topsell taken to be venomous; and so is the padock, or Frog-padock, which usually keeps or breeds on the land, and is very large and bony, and big, especially the She frog of that kind; yet these will sometimes come into the water, but it is not often: and the land frogs are some of them observed by him, to breed by laying eggs: and others to breed of the slime and dust of the earth, and that in winter they turn to slime again, and that the next summer that very slime returns to be a living creature; this is the opinion of Pliny: And Cardanus undertakes to give a reason for the raining of Frogs:[28] but if it were in my power, it should rain none but water-Frogs, for those I think are not venomous, especially the right water-Frog, which about February or March breeds in ditches by slime, and blackish eggs in that slime: about which time of breeding the He and She frogs are observed to use divers somersaults, and to croak and make a noise, which the land-frog, or Padock-frog, never does. Now of these water-frogs, if you intend to fish with a frog for a Pike, you are to choose the yellowest that you can get, for that the Pike ever likes best. And thus use your frog, that he may continue long alive:

Put your hook into his mouth, which you may easily do from the middle of April till August, and then the frog's mouth grows up, and he continues so for at least six months without eating, but is sustained, none but he whose name is Wonderful, knows how: I say, put your hook, I mean the arming wire, through his mouth, and out at his gills, and then with a fine needle and silk sew the upper part of his leg with only one stitch to the arming wire of your hook, or tie the frog's leg above the upper joint, to the armed wire; and in so doing, use him as though you loved him, that is, harm him as little as you may possibly, that he may live the longer.

And now, having given you this direction for the baiting your ledger-hook with a live fish or frog, my next must be to tell you, how your hook thus baited must or may be used: and it is thus. Having fastened your hook to a line, which if it be not fourteen yards long, should not be less than twelve; you are to fasten that line to any bough near to a hole where a Pike is, or is likely to lie, or to have a haunt, and then wind your line on any forked stick, all your line, except half a yard of it or rather more, and split that forked stick with such a nick or notch at one end of it, as may keep the line from any more of it raveling from about the stick, than so much of it as you intended; and choose your forked stick to be of that bigness as may keep the fish or frog from pulling the forked stick under the water till the Pike bites, and then the Pike having pulled the line forth of the cleft or nick of that stick in which it was gently fastened, will have line enough to go to his hold and pouch the bait: and if you would have this ledger-bait to keep at a fixed place, undisturbed by wind or other accidents which may drive it to the shore side (for you are to note, that it is likeliest to catch a Pike in the midst of the water), then hang a small plummet of lead, a stone, or piece of tile, or a turf in a string, and cast it into the water, with the forked stick, to hang upon the ground, to be a kind of anchor to keep the forked stick from moving out of your intended place till the Pike come. This I take to be a very

---

[27] Speckled.

[28] Jerome Cardan (1501–1576) in *De Subtilitate* (1551).

good way, to use so many ledger-baits as you intend to make trial of.

Or if you bait your hooks thus with live fish or frogs, and in a windy day, fasten them thus to a bough or bundle of straw, and by the help of that wind can get them to move cross a pond or mere, you are like to stand still on the shore and see sport, if there be any store of Pikes; or these live baits may make sport, being tied about the body or wings of a Goose or Duck, and she chased over a pond: and the like may be done with turning three or four live baits thus fastened to bladders, or boughs, or bottles of hay or flags,[29] to swim down a river, whilst you walk quietly alone on the shore, and are still in expectation of sport. The rest must be taught you by practice, for time will not allow me to say more of this kind of fishing with live baits.

And for your dead bait for a Pike, for that you may be taught by one day's going a-fishing with me, or any other body that fishes for him, for the baiting your hook with a dead Gudgeon or a Roach, and moving it up and down the water, is too easy a thing to take up any time to direct you to do it; and yet, because I cut you short in that, I will commute[30] for it, by telling you that that was told me for a secret; it is this:

Dissolve Gum of Ivy in Oil of Spike, and therewith anoint your dead bait for a Pike, and then cast it into a likely place, and when it has lain a short time at the bottom, draw it towards the top of the water and so up the stream, and it is more than likely that you have a Pike follow with more than common eagerness.

And some affirm, that any bait anointed with the marrow of the thigh-bone of an Heron is a great temptation to any fish.

These have not been tried by me, but told me by a friend of note, that pretended to do me a courtesy, but if this direction to catch a Pike thus, do you no good, yet I am certain this direction how to roast him when he is caught, is choicely good, for I have tried it, and it is somewhat the better for not being common; but with my direction you must take this caution, that your Pike must not be a small one, that is, it must be more than half a yard, and should be bigger.

First, open your Pike at the gills, and if need be, cut also a little slit towards the belly; out of these, take his guts, and keep his liver, which you are to shred very small with Thyme, Sweet-Marjoram, and a little Winter-savory; to these put some pickled Oysters, and some Anchovies, two or three, both these last whole (for the Anchovies will melt, and the Oysters should not); to these you must add also a pound of sweet butter, which you are to mix with the herbs that are shred, and let them all be well salted (if the Pike be more than a yard long, then you may put into these herbs more than a pound, or if he be less, then less Butter will suffice); these being thus mixed with a blade or two of Mace, must be put into the Pike's belly, and then his belly sewed up, as to keep all the Butter in his belly if it be possible, if not, then as much of it as you possibly can, but take not off the scales; then you are to thrust the spit through his mouth, out at his tail. And then with four or five or six split sticks, or very thin lathes, and a convenient quantity of Tape or Filleting, these lathes are to be tied round about the Pike's body from his head to his tail, and the Tape tied somewhat thick to prevent his breaking or falling off from the spit; let him be roasted very leisurely, and often basted with Claret wine, and Anchovies, and butter mixed together, and also with what moisture falls from him into the pan: when you have roasted him sufficiently you are to hold under him (when you unwind or cut the Tape that ties him), such a dish as you purpose to eat him out of; and let him fall into it with the sauce that is roasted in his belly, and by this means the Pike will be kept unbroken and complete: then, to the sauce which was within, and also in the pan, you are to add a fit quantity of the best Butter, and to squeeze the juice of three or four Oranges: lastly, you may either put into the Pike, with the Oysters, two cloves of Garlic, and take it whole out, when the Pike is cut off the spit, or, to give the sauce a hogo,[31] let the dish (into which you let the Pike fall) be rubbed with it: the using

[29] Bundles of hay or turf. [30] Compound.

[31] A strong flavor (*haut-goût*).

or not using of this Garlic is left to your discretion.

M. B.

This dish of meat is too good for any but Anglers or honest men; and I trust, you will prove both, and therefore I have trusted you with this secret.

Let me next tell you, that Gesner tells us there are no Pikes in Spain, and that the largest are in the Lake Thrasimene in Italy; and the next, if not equal to them, are the Pikes of England, and that in England, Lincolnshire boasteth to have the biggest. Just so doth Sussex boast of four sorts of fish; namely, an Arundel Mullet, a Chichester Lobster, a Shelsey Cockle, and an Amerly Trout.

But I will take up no more of your time with this relation, but proceed to give you some observations of the Carp, and how to angle for him.

JOHN MILTON

1608–1674

Milton was born in London on 9 December, 1608. His father was a scrivener or solicitor, and a convinced Puritan. There was indeed so much feeling behind his Puritanism as to have caused him to break with his family on this account, Milton's grandfather having been a Catholic recusant in the reign of Elizabeth. It should be remembered, however, that Puritanism had not yet become the narrow, ascetic, intolerant force that we generally associate with the name; and Milton, as a matter of fact, was brought up in an environment of cultivation in which music and poetry were ever-present realities. As a boy he attended St. Paul's School in London, and went thence to Christ's College, Cambridge, in 1625. There he remained for seven years, reading widely and deeply, laying the foundations of his immense learning, writing his first important poem, the ode *On the Morning of Christ's Nativity* (1629), and other shorter poems, and exhibiting already that spirit of independence which remained throughout his life a major characteristic. The immediate circumstances, it is true, of Milton's trouble with his college tutor are obscure; but it is at least a probable supposition that his independent spirit had something to do with his temporary banishment from Cambridge in 1626 and his transference to another tutor on his return. In 1632 Milton left Cambridge and went to Horton, in Buckinghamshire, where his father had retired from his London business. Here he spent six years, perhaps the happiest of his life, continuing his studies with the conscious purpose of preparing himself for some great poetical achievement. For Milton was a dedicated spirit; from an early time aware of his great powers, he proceeded deliberately to make himself fit for the execution of his high purpose, the creation of a noble monument in verse. Many years later he expressed what was his abiding conviction from youth to old age: "He who would not be frustrate of his hope to write well hereafter in laudable things ought himself to be a true poem . . . not presuming to sing high praises of heroic men or famous cities unless he have in himself the experience and practice of all that which is praiseworthy." During the years at Horton, too, Milton not only read himself into the spirit of great poetry in ages past, but also sent forth those trial barks which remain still among the loveliest of their kind in English verse. For at Horton he wrote *L'Allegro, Il Penseroso, Comus,* and *Lycidus,* as well as other of his so-called minor poems. In 1638 he left England to travel southward to Italy, where he spent some months in pleasant intercourse with learned and cultivated men in several Italian cities. He was planning to travel farther, to Greece and Palestine, when the news of Charles's first expedition against the Scots reached him and determined him to turn his steps homeward. He knew the political situation in England well enough to realize that this was probably the beginning of worse things, and he wrote afterwards, "I thought it base to be traveling for amusement abroad while my fellow citizens were fighting for liberty at home." On his way back he had the opportunity of meeting Galileo—then old, blind, and in partial confinement at the hand of the Inquisition—at Florence.

Milton reached England in August, 1639, and proceeded to become a schoolmaster. This result of his anxiety to share in his countrymen's fight for liberty has, certainly, the air of anticlimax, but his serious purpose was to fight in the way he best could, with his pen, and his teaching was punctuated by the writing of controversial pamphlets, some of which won him appointment in 1649 as Latin Secretary in the Puritan government. He never made himself, however, the instrument of a party. His guiding star was liberty, and he was ready to turn against the Puritans themselves when they seemed to him in danger of deserting that principle for which, as he thought, they fundamentally stood. In 1641 and 1642 he wrote five pamphlets against episcopacy, or government of the church by bishops, fighting therein for religious liberty. In 1643 he began a series of pamphlets in which he contended passionately for easy divorce. The immediate occasion of these was his own unhappy marriage in that year, but the battle he waged was entirely consistent with his previously formed conviction that liberty was essential to human well-being. In 1644 he wrote his tract on liberal education, designed to principle the mind in virtue, "the only genuine source of political and individual liberty"; and also his *Areopagitica,* an eloquent defense of freedom of speech, in the course of which he uttered his celebrated praise of Spenser, "our sage and serious poet." After three years of work as Latin Secretary, Milton's devotion to his duties in the service of the Commonwealth caused his blindness, though he did not allow this to stop either his official work or his controversial writing, any more than he allowed it to prevent the later accomplishment of his purpose of writing a great poem. That purpose he never relinquished through all the central years of his life when the cause of liberty and public duty claimed his energy, and before the Restoration in 1660 he had begun the writing of *Paradise Lost.* There is no reason for thinking that either the theme or his execution of it in the poem was influenced by the decay of the Commonwealth and Charles II's return, bitter blows to Milton though both were. The theme was chosen, after long hesitation, simply on the ground that it was the most heroic in its proportions of all possible subjects. Milton suffered surprisingly little annoyance from the new government, and lived his remaining years quietly enough, save for disturbances within his family, at work upon various tasks, but chiefly *Paradise Lost, Paradise Regained,* and *Samson Agonistes.* The first was finished by the summer of 1665 and was published in 1667; *Paradise Regained* and *Samson Agonistes* appeared in 1671. *Paradise Lost* in the first edition has ten books; in the year of his death Milton published a second edition in which two of the original ten books were divided, making the twelve in which the poem has ever since been printed.

The "Columbia" Edition of *The Works of John Milton,* ed. Frank A. Patterson and others (New York, 1931–1938), represents an effort to establish a final text of both the poetry and prose; the one-volume *Student's Milton,* edited by Frank A. Patterson (New York, 1934), presents the complete poetry and the greater part of the prose in a less elaborate form; editions of *Paradise Lost* and of *Paradise Regained, the Minor Poems, and Samson Agonistes* have been published with full annotations and critical introductions by Merritt Y. Hughes (Garden City, 1935 and 1937). James H. Hanford's *Milton Handbook* (New York, 1926) is a compact summary of scholarship on Milton. David Masson's *Life of John Milton: Narrated in Connexion with the Political, Ecclesiastical, and Literary History of his time* (London, 1877–1896) is a mine of information and a work still to be reckoned with; among more recent studies the most important are Denis Saurat, *Milton, Man and Thinker* (New York, 1925), and Eustace M. W. Tillyard, *Milton* (London, 1930). In *Cross Currents in English Literature of the XVIIth Century* (London, 1929) Sir Herbert J. C. Grierson discusses the opposition between humanism and Puritanism as it appears in Milton and his age.

ON TIME

Fly, envious Time, till thou run out thy race:
Call on the lazy leaden-stepping Hours,
Whose speed is but the heavy plummet's pace;[1]
And glut thyself with what thy womb devours,
Which is no more than what is false and vain, 5
And merely mortal dross;
So little is our loss,
So little is thy gain!
For, when as each thing bad thou hast entombed,
And, last of all, thy greedy self consumed, 10
Then long Eternity shall greet our bliss
With an individual kiss,
And Joy shall overtake us as a flood;
When everything that is sincerely good,
And perfectly divine, 15
With Truth, and Peace, and Love, shall ever shine
About the supreme throne
Of him, to whose happy-making sight alone
When once our heavenly-guided soul shall climb,
Then, all this earthly grossness quit, 20
Attired with stars we shall for ever sit,
Triumphing over Death, and Chance, and thee, O Time!

[1] I. e., the gradual descent of the weights in a clock.

AT A SOLEMN MUSIC

Blest pair of Sirens, pledges of Heaven's joy,
Sphere-born harmonious sisters, Voice and Verse,
Wed your divine sounds, and mixed power employ,
Dead things with inbreathed sense able to pierce;
And to our high-raised fantasy present 5
That undisturbéd song of pure consent,[2]
Aye sung before the sapphire-colored throne
To him that sits thereon,
With saintly shout and solemn jubilee;
Where the bright Seraphim in burning row 10
Their loud uplifted angel-trumpets blow,
And the Cherubic host in thousand quires,[3]
Touch their immortal harps of golden wires,
With those just Spirits that wear victorious palms,
Hymns devout and holy psalms 15
Singing everlastingly:
That we on Earth, with undiscording voice,
May rightly answer that melodious noise;
As once we did, till disproportioned sin
Jarred against nature's chime, and with harsh din 20
Broke the fair music that all creatures made
To their great Lord, whose love their motion swayed
In perfect diapason,[4] whilst they stood
In first obedience, and their state of good.
O, may we soon again renew that song, 25
And keep in tune with Heaven, till God ere long
To his celestial consort[5] us unite,
To live with him, and sing in endless morn of light!

ON SHAKESPEARE

What needs my Shakespeare for his honored bones
The labor of an age in piléd stones?
Or that his hallowed relics should be hid
Under a star-ypointing pyramid?
Dear son of memory, great heir of fame, 5
What need'st thou such weak witness of thy name?
Thou in our wonder and astonishment
Has built thyself a livelong monument.
For whilst, to the shame of slow-endeavoring art,
Thy easy numbers flow, and that each heart 10
Hath from the leaves of thy unvalued[6] book
Those Delphic[7] lines with deep impression took,
Then thou, our fancy of itself bereaving,
Dost make us marble with too much conceiving,
And so sepúlchered in such pomp dost lie 15
That kings for such a tomb would wish to die.

[2]Harmony. [3]Choirs.
[4]Combination of notes or parts in harmonious whole.
[5]Symphony.

[6]Invaluable. [7]Inspired.

L'ALLEGRO

Hence, loathéd Melancholy,
Of Cerberus and blackest Midnight born
In Stygian cave forlorn
'Mongst horrid shapes, and shrieks, and sights unholy!
Find out some uncouth[1] cell, 5
Where brooding Darkness spreads his jealous wings,
And the night-raven sings;
There, under ebon[2] shades and low-browed rocks,
As ragged as thy locks,
In dark Cimmerian desert[3] ever dwell. 10
But come, thou Goddess fair and free,
In heaven yclept[4] Euphrosyne,
And by men heart-easing Mirth;
Whom lovely Venus, at a birth,
With two sister Graces more, 15
To ivy-crownéd Bacchus bore:
Or whether (as some sager sing)
The frolic wind that breathes the spring,
Zephyr, with Aurora playing,
As he met her once a-Maying, 20
There, on beds of violets blue,
And fresh-blown roses washed in dew,
Filled her with thee, a daughter fair,
So buxom,[5] blithe, and debonair.
Haste thee, Nymph, and bring with thee 25
Jest, and youthful Jollity,
Quips and cranks[6] and wanton wiles,
Nods and becks and wreathéd smiles,
Such as hang on Hebe's cheek,
And love to live in dimple sleek; 30
Sport that wrinkled Care derides,
And Laughter holding both his sides.
Come, and trip it, as you go,
On the light fantastic toe;
And in thy right hand lead with thee 35
The mountain-nymph, sweet Liberty;
And, if I give thee honor due,

[1]Unknown, strange. [2]Black.
[3]A mythical land involved in perpetual mist and darkness (*Odyssey*, XI, 14).
[4]Called. [5]Lively.
[6]Humorous turns of speech.

Mirth, admit me of thy crew,
To live with her, and live with thee,
In unreprovéd[7] pleasures free; 40
To hear the lark begin his flight,
And, singing, startle the dull night,
From his watch-tower in the skies,
Till the dappled dawn doth rise;
Then to come, in spite of sorrow, 45
And at my window bid good-morrow,
Through the sweet-briar or the vine,
Or the twisted eglantine;
While the cock, with lively din,
Scatters the rear of darkness thin; 50
And to the stack, or the barn-door,
Stoutly struts his dames before:
Oft listening how the hounds and horn
Cheerly rouse the slumbering morn,
From the side of some hoar hill, 55
Through the high wood echoing shrill:
Sometime walking, not unseen,
By hedgerow elms, on hillocks green,
Right against the eastern gate
Where the great Sun begins his state, 60
Robed in flames and amber light,
The clouds in thousand liveries dight;[8]
While the plowman, near at hand,
Whistles o'er the furrowed land,
And the milkmaid singeth blithe, 65
And the mower whets his scythe,
And every shepherd tells his tale[9]
Under the hawthorn in the dale.
Straight mine eye hath caught new pleasures
Whilst the landscape round it measures: 70
Russet lawns, and fallows gray,
Where the nibbling flocks do stray,
Mountains on whose barren breast
The laboring clouds do often rest;
Meadows trim, with daisies pied; 75
Shallow brooks, and rivers wide;
Towers and battlements it sees
Bosomed high in tufted trees,
Where perhaps some beauty lies,
The cynosure[10] of neighboring eyes. 80
Hard by a cottage chimney smokes
From betwixt two agéd oaks,
Where Corydon and Thyrsis[11] met
Are at their savory dinner set
Of herbs and other country messes, 85
Which the neat-handed Phyllis dresses;
And then in haste her bower she leaves,
With Thestylis to bind the sheaves;
Or, if the earlier season lead,
To the tanned haycock in the mead. 90

[7]Innocent. [8]Adorned. [9]Counts his sheep.
[10]Center of attention.
[11]These and the two other names in following lines are conventional names drawn from pastoral poetry.

Sometimes, with secure[12] delight,
The upland hamlets will invite,
When the merry bells ring round,
And the jocund rebecks[13] sound
To many a youth and many a maid 95
Dancing in the checkered shade,
And young and old come forth to play
On a sunshine holiday,
Till the livelong daylight fail:
Then to a spicy nut-brown ale, 100
With stories told of many a feat,
How Faery Mab the junkets eat.
She was pinched and pulled, she said;
And he, by Friar's lantern[14] led,
Tells how the drudging goblin[15] sweat 105
To earn his cream-bowl duly set,
When in one night, ere glimpse of morn,
His shadowy flail hath threshed the corn
That ten day-laborers could not end;
Then lies him down, the lubber[16] fiend, 110
And, stretched out all the chimney's length,
Basks at the fire his hairy strength,
And crop-full out of doors he flings,
Ere the first cock his matin rings.
Thus done the tales, to bed they creep, 115
By whispering winds soon lulled asleep.
Towered cities please us then,
And the busy hum of men,
Where throngs of knights and barons bold,
In weeds[17] of peace, high triumphs hold, 120
With store of ladies, whose bright eyes
Rain influence, and judge the prize
Of wit or arms, while both contend
To win her grace whom all commend.
There let Hymen[18] oft appear 125
In saffron robe, with taper clear,
And pomp, and feast, and revelry,
With mask and antique pageantry;
Such sights as youthful poets dream
On summer eves by haunted stream. 130
Then to the well-trod stage anon,
If Jonson's learnéd sock[19] be on,
Or sweetest Shakespeare, Fancy's child,
Warble his native wood-notes wild.
And ever, against eating cares, 135
Lap me in soft Lydian airs,
Married to immortal verse,
Such as the meeting soul may pierce,
In notes with many a winding bout[20]
Of linkéd sweetness long drawn out 140
With wanton heed and giddy cunning,

[12]Carefree. [13]Fiddles.
[14]Will-o'-the-wisp. [15]Robin Goodfellow.
[16]Clumsy. [17]Garments. [18]God of marriage.
[19]The light shoe worn in classical times by actors in comedy.
[20]Turn.

The melting voice through mazes running,
Untwisting all the chains that tie
The hidden soul of harmony;
That Orpheus' self may heave his head 145
From golden slumber on a bed
Of heaped Elysian flowers, and hear
Such strains as would have won the ear
Of Pluto to have quite set free
His half-regained Eurydice. 150
These delights if thou canst give,
Mirth, with thee I mean to live.

IL PENSEROSO

Hence, vain deluding Joys,
The brood of Folly without father bred!
How little you bested,[1]
Or fill the fixéd mind with all your toys!
Dwell in some idle brain, 5
And fancies fond[2] with gaudy shapes possess,
As thick and numberless
As the gay motes that people the sunbeam,
Or likest hovering dreams,
The fickle pensioners of Morpheus' train. 10
But, hail! thou Goddess sage and holy!
Hail, divinest Melancholy!
Whose saintly visage is too bright
To hit the sense of human sight,
And therefore to our weaker view 15
O'erlaid with black, staid Wisdom's hue;
Black, but such as in esteem
Prince Memnon's sister might beseem,
Or that starred Ethiop queen[3] that strove
To set her beauty's praise above 20
The Sea-Nympths, and their powers offended.
Yet thou art higher far descended:
Thee bright-haired Vesta long of yore
To solitary Saturn bore;
His daughter she; in Saturn's reign 25
Such mixture was not held a stain.
Oft in glimmering bowers and glades
He met her, and in secret shades
Of woody Ida's inmost grove,
Whilst yet there was no fear of Jove. 30
Come, pensive Nun, devout and pure,
Sober, steadfast, and demure,
All in a robe of darkest grain,[4]
Flowing with majestic train,
And sable stole of cypress lawn[5] 35
Over thy decent shoulders drawn.
Come; but keep thy wonted state,

[1]Profit. [2]Foolish.
[3]Cassiopeia, who was placed among the stars.
[4]Color. [5]A light crape.

With even step, and musing gait,
And looks commercing with the skies,
Thy rapt soul sitting in thine eyes: 40
There, held in holy passion still,
Forget thyself to marble, till
With a sad leaden downward cast
Thou fix them on the earth as fast.
And join with thee calm Peace and Quiet, 45
Spare Fast, that oft with gods doth diet,
And hears the Muses in a ring
Aye round about Jove's altar sing;
And add to these retiréd Leisure,
That in trim gardens takes his pleasure; 50
But, first and chiefest, with thee bring
Him that yon soars on golden wing,
Guiding the fiery-wheeléd throne,
The Cherub Contemplation;
And the mute Silence hist along, 55
'Less Philomel[6] will deign a song,
In her sweetest saddest plight,
Smoothing the rugged brow of Night,
While Cynthia[7] checks her dragon yoke
Gently o'er the accustomed oak. 60
Sweet bird, that shunn'st the noise of folly,
Most musical, most melancholy!
Thee, chauntress, oft the woods among
I woo, to hear thy even-song;
And, missing thee, I walk unseen 65
On the dry smooth-shaven green
To behold the wandering moon,
Riding near her highest noon,
Like one that had been led astray
Through the heaven's wide pathless way, 70
And oft, as if her head she bowed,
Stooping through a fleecy cloud.
Oft, on a plat of rising ground,
I hear the far-off curfew sound,
Over some wide-watered shore, 75
Swinging slow with sullen roar;
Or, if the air will not permit,
Some still removéd place will fit,
Where glowing embers through the room
Teach light to counterfeit a gloom, 80
Far from all resort of mirth,
Save the cricket on the hearth,
Or the bellman's[8] drowsy charm
To bless the doors from nightly harm.
Or let my lamp, at midnight hour, 85
Be seen in some high lonely tower,
Where I may oft outwatch the Bear,[9]
With thrice great Hermes,[10] or unsphere[11]

[6]The nightingale. [7]The moon. [8]Watchman's.
[9]The Great Bear never sets in England, consequently he would have to sit up until dawn.
[10]Hermes Trismegistus, a fabled Egyptian ruler to whom were ascribed many books.
[11]Call his spirit from the sphere where it abides.

The spirit of Plato, to unfold
What worlds or what past regions hold 90
The immortal mind that hath forsook
Her mansion in this fleshly nook;
And of those demons that are found
In fire, air, flood, or underground,
Whose power hath a true consent[12] 95
With planet or with element.
Sometimes let gorgeous Tragedy
In sceptered pall come sweeping by,
Presenting Thebes, or Pelops' line,
Or the tale of Troy divine, 100
Or what (though rare) of later age
Ennobled hath the buskined[13] stage.
But, O sad Virgin! that thy power
Might raise Musaeus from his bower;
Or bid the soul of Orpheus sing 105
Such notes as, warbled to the string,
Drew iron tears down Pluto's cheek,
And made Hell grant what love did seek;
Or call up him[14] that left half-told
The story of Cambuscan bold, 110
Of Camball, and of Algarsife,
And who had Canace to wife,
That owned the virtuous ring and glass,
And of the wondrous horse of brass
On which the Tartar king did ride; 115
And if aught else great bards beside
In sage and solemn tunes have sung,
Of turneys, and of trophies hung,
Of forests, and enchantments drear,
Where more is meant than meets the ear.[15] 120
Thus, Night, oft see me in thy pale career,
Till civil-suited Morn appear,
Not tricked and frounced, as she was wont
With the Attic boy[16] to hunt,
But kerchiefed in a comely cloud, 125
While rocking winds are piping loud,
Or ushered with a shower still,
When the gust hath blown his fill,
Ending on the rustling leaves,
With minute-drops from off the eaves. 130
And, when the sun begins to fling
His flaring beams, me, Goddess, bring
To archéd walks of twilight groves,
And shadows brown, that Sylvan loves,
Of pine, or monumental oak, 135
Where the rude ax with heavéd stroke
Was never heard the nymphs to daunt,

[12]Sympathy.

[13]Tragic (the buskin was the heavy boot worn by tragic actors in classical times).

[14]Chaucer (the allusion is to the uncompleted Squire's Tale).

[15]The allusion is probably to Spenser.

[16]Cephalus, loved by Aurora.

Or fright them from their hallowed haunt.
There, in close covert, by some brook,
Where no profaner eye may look, 140
Hide me from day's garish eye,
While the bee with honeyed thigh,
That at her flowery work doth sing,
And the waters murmuring,
With such consort as they keep, 145
Entice the dewy-feathered Sleep.
And let some strange mysterious dream
Wave at his wings, in airy stream
Of lively portraiture displayed,
Softly on my eyelids laid; 150
And, as I wake, sweet music breathe
Above, about, or underneath,
Sent by some Spirit to mortals good,
Or the unseen Genius of the wood.
But let my due feet never fail 155
To walk the studious cloister's pale,[17]
And love the high embowéd roof,
With antique pillars massy-proof,
And storied windows richly dight,[18]
Casting a dim religious light. 160
There let the pealing organ blow,
To the full-voiced quire below,
In service high and anthems clear,
As may with sweetness, through mine ear,
Dissolve me into ecstasies, 165
And bring all Heaven before mine eyes.
And may at last my weary age
Find out the peaceful hermitage,
The hairy gown and mossy cell,
Where I may sit and rightly spell[19] 170
Of every star that heaven doth shew,
And every herb that sips the dew,
Till old experience do attain
To something like prophetic strain.
These pleasures, Melancholy, give; 175
And I with thee will choose to live.

LYCIDAS[1]

Yet once more, O ye laurels, and once more,
Ye myrtles brown, with ivy never sere,
I come to pluck your berries harsh and crude,
And with forced fingers rude

[17]Enclosure.

[18]Windows richly adorned with stories (from the Bible).

[19]Read.

[1]In this monody the author bewails a learned friend, unfortunately drowned in his passage from Chester on the Irish seas, 1637, and by occasion foretells the ruin of our corrupted clergy, then in their height (Milton's note). Milton's learned friend was Edward King of Christ's College, Cambridge.

Shatter your leaves before the mellowing year.[2] 5
Bitter constraint and sad occasion dear
Compels me to disturb your season due;
For Lycidas[3] is dead, dead ere his prime,
Young Lycidas, and hath not left his peer.
Who would not sing for Lycidas? he knew 10
Himself to sing, and build the lofty rime.
He must not float upon his watery bier
Unwept, and welter to the parching wind,
Without the meed of some melodious tear.
Begin, then, Sisters of the sacred well[4] 15
That from beneath the seat of Jove doth spring;
Begin, and somewhat loudly sweep the string.
Hence with denial vain and coy excuse:
So may some gentle Muse
With lucky words favor *my* destined urn, 20
And as he passes turn,
And bid fair peace be to my sable shroud!
For we were nursed upon the self-same hill,
Fed the same flock, by fountain, shade, and rill;
Together both, ere the high lawns appeared 25
Under the opening eyelids of the Morn,
We drove a-field, and both together heard
What time the gray-fly winds her sultry horn,
Battening[5] our flocks with the fresh dews of night,
Oft till the star that rose at evening bright[6] 30
Toward heaven's descent had sloped his westering wheel.
Meanwhile the rural ditties were not mute;
Tempered to the oaten flute,
Rough Satyrs danced, and Fauns with cloven heel
From the glad sound would not be absent long; 35
And old Damoetas[7] loved to hear our song.
But, oh! the heavy change, now thou art gone,
Now thou art gone and never must return!
Thee, Shepherd, thee the woods and desert caves,
With wild thyme and the gadding vine o'ergrown, 40
And all their echoes, mourn.
The willows, and the hazel copses green,
Shall now no more be seen
Fanning their joyous leaves to thy soft lays.
As killing as the canker to the rose, 45
Or taint-worm to the weanling herds that graze,
Or frost to flowers, that their gay wardrobe wear,
When first the white-thorn blows;
Such, Lycidas, thy loss to shepherd's ear.
Where were ye, Nymphs, when the remorseless deep 50
Closed o'er the head of your loved Lycidas?
For neither were ye playing on the steep
Where your old bards, the famous Druids, lie,
Nor on the shaggy top of Mona high,
Nor yet where Deva spreads her wizard stream.[8] 55
Ay me! I fondly[9] dream
"Had ye been there," . . . for what could that have done?
What could the Muse[10] herself that Orpheus bore,
The Muse herself, for her enchanting son,
Whom universal nature did lament, 60
When, by the rout that made the hideous roar,
His gory visage down the stream was sent,
Down the swift Hebrus to the Lesbian shore?
Alas! what boots[11] it with uncessant care
To tend the homely, slighted, shepherd's trade, 65
And strictly meditate the thankless Muse?
Were it not better done, as others use,
To sport with Amaryllis in the shade,
Or with the tangles of Neaera's hair?
Fame is the spur that the clear spirit doth raise 70
(That last infirmity of noble mind)
To scorn delights and live laborious days;
But the fair guerdon when we hope to find,
And think to burst out into sudden blaze,
Comes the blind Fury[12] with the abhorréd shears, 75

[2]I. e., Milton was forced to break his resolution not to write until his powers were fully matured.

[3]The name occurs in the seventh Idyll of Theocritus.

[4]Muses of the Pierian spring.

[5]Feeding. [6]Hesperus, which appears at evening.

[7]A conventional name drawn from pastoral poetry. Probably some fellow or the master of Christ's College is meant.

[8]Neither on the Welsh hills, nor on Anglesea (Mona), nor along the river Dee: all places near the scene of King's shipwreck.

[9]Foolishly.

[10]Calliope. Orpheus was torn to pieces by Thracian women, and his head was thrown into the river Hebrus.

[11]Avails.

[12]Atropos, a Fate. Perhaps Milton here calls her a Fury because of his anger.

And slits the thin-spun life. "But not the praise,"
Phoebus replied, and touched my trembling ears:
"Fame is no plant that grows on mortal soil,
Nor in the glistening foil[13]
Set off to the world, nor in broad rumor lies, 80
But lives and spreads aloft by those pure eyes
And perfect witness of all-judging Jove;
As he pronounces lastly on each deed,
Of so much fame in heaven expect thy meed."

O fountain Arethuse, and thou honored flood, 85
Smooth-sliding Mincius, crowned with vocal reeds,
That strain I heard was of a higher mood.
But now my oat[14] proceeds,
And listens to the Herald of the Sea,
That came in Neptune's plea. 90
He asked the waves, and asked the felon winds,
What hard mishap hath doomed this gentle swain?
And questioned every gust of rugged wings
That blows from off each beakéd promontory.
They knew not of his story; 95
And sage Hippotades[15] their answer brings,
That not a blast was from his dungeon strayed:
The air was calm, and on the level brine
Sleek Panope[16] with all her sisters played.
It was that fatal[17] and perfidious bark, 100
Built in the eclipse, and rigged with curses dark,
That sunk so low that sacred head of thine.

Next, Camus,[18] reverend sire, went footing slow,
His mantle hairy, and his bonnet sedge,
Inwrought with figures dim, and on the edge
Like to that sanguine flower inscribed with woe.[19] 106
"Ah! who hath reft," quoth he, "my dearest pledge?"[20]
Last came, and last did go,
The Pilot of the Galilean Lake;[21]
Two massy keys he bore of metals twain[22] 110
(The golden opes, the iron shuts amain[23]).
He shook his mitered locks, and stern bespake:—
"How well could I have spared for thee, young swain,
Enow of such as, for their bellies' sake,
Creep, and intrude, and climb into the fold! 115
Of other care they little reckoning make
Than how to scramble at the shearers' feast,
And shove away the worthy bidden guest.
Blind mouths! that scarce themselves know how to hold
A sheep-hook, or have learned aught else the least 120
That to the faithful herdman's art belongs!
What recks[24] it them? What need they? They are sped;[25]
And, when they list, their lean and flashy songs
Grate on their scrannel[26] pipes of wretched straw;
The hungry sheep look up, and are not fed, 125
But, swoln with wind and the rank mist they draw,
Rot inwardly, and foul contagion spread;
Besides what the grim wolf with privy paw
Daily devours apace, and nothing said.
But that two-handed engine[27] at the door 130
Stands ready to smite once, and smite no more."

Return, Alpheus;[28] the dread voice is past
That shrunk thy streams; return, Sicilian Muse,
And call the vales, and bid them hither cast
Their bells and flowerets of a thousand hues. 135
Ye valleys low, where the mild whispers use
Of shades, and wanton winds, and gushing brooks,
On whose fresh lap the swart star[29] sparely looks,
Throw hither all your quaint enameled eyes
That on the green turf suck the honeyed showers, 140
And purple all the ground with vernal flowers.

---

[13]Glittering setting of a gem. [14]Shepherd's pipe.
[15]Aeolus, god of winds.
[16]One of the Nereids. [17]Fated.
[18]The god of the Cam, the river at Cambridge.
[19]The hyacinth, whose leaves have certain markings, said by the ancients to be AI, AI (alas!), in mourning for Hyacinthus.
[20]Bereaved me of my dearest child.

[21]St. Peter. [22]Cf. St. Matthew, 16:19.
[23]With force. [24]Concerns.
[25]Provided for. [26]Thin.
[27]Perhaps the ax of St. Matthew, 3:10, and St. Luke, 3:9.
[28]River of Arcadia, whose spirit loved Arethusa.
[29]The dog-star, supposed to be injurious to plants.

Bring the rathe[30] primrose that forsaken dies,
The tufted crow-toe, and pale jessamine,
The white pink, and the pansy freaked[31] with jet,
The growing violet, 145
The musk rose, and the well-attired woodbine,
With cowslips wan that hang the pensive head,
And every flower that sad embroidery wears;
Bid amaranthus all his beauty shed,
And daffadillies fill their cups with tears, 150
To strew the laureate hearse where Lycid lies.
For so, to interpose a little ease,
Let our frail thoughts dally with false surmise,
Ay me! whilst thee the shores and sounding seas
Wash far away, where'er thy bones are hurled; 155
Whether beyond the stormy Hebrides,
Where thou perhaps under the whelming tide
Visit'st the bottom of the monstrous world;[32]
Or whether thou, to our moist vows denied,
Sleep'st by the fable of Bellerus old,[33] 160
Where the great Vision of the guarded mount[34]
Looks toward Namancos and Bayona's hold.[35]
Look homeward, Angel,[36] now, and melt with ruth:[37]
And, O ye dolphins, waft the hapless youth.
Weep no more, woeful shepherds, weep no more, 165
For Lycidas, your sorrow, is not dead,
Sunk though he be beneath the watery floor.
So sinks the day-star in the ocean bed,
And yet anon repairs his drooping head,
And tricks[38] his beams, and with new-spangled ore[39] 170
Flames in the forehead of the morning sky:
So Lycidas sunk low, but mounted high,
Through the dear might of him that walked the waves,
Where, other groves and other streams along,
With nectar pure his oozy locks he laves, 175
And hears the unexpressive[40] nuptial song,
In the blest kingdoms meek of joy and love.

[30]Early. [31]Sprinkled.
[32]World of monsters. [33]Land's End.
[34]St. Michael's Mount, near Land's End.
[35]In Spain, near Cape Finisterre.
[36]Either Lycidas or St. Michael. [37]Pity.
[38]Adorns. [39]Brightness. [40]Inexpressible.

There entertain him all the Saints above,
In solemn troops, and sweet societies,
That sing, and singing in their glory move, 180
And wipe the tears for ever from his eyes.
Now, Lycidas, the shepherds weep no more;
Henceforth thou art the Genius of the shore,
In thy large recompense, and shalt be good
To all that wander in that perilous flood. 185
Thus sang the uncouth swain to the oaks and rills,
While the still morn went out with sandals gray:
He touched the tender stops of various quills,[41] 188
With eager thought warbling his Doric lay:[42]
And now the sun had stretched out all the hills,
And now was dropped into the western bay.
At last he rose, and twitched his mantle blue:
To-morrow to fresh woods, and pastures new.

SONNETS[1]

VII

How soon hath Time, the subtle thief of youth,
Stolen on his wing my three-and-twentieth year!
My hasting days fly on with full career,
But my late spring no bud or blossom shew'th.
Perhaps my semblance might deceive the truth 5
That I to manhood am arrived so near;
And inward ripeness doth much less appear,
That some more timely-happy spirits endu'th.
Yet, be it less or more, or soon or slow,
It shall be still in strictest measure even 10
To that same lot, however mean or high,
Toward which Time leads me, and the will of Heaven;
All is, if I have grace to use it so,
As ever in my great Task-Master's eye.

VIII[2]

Captain or Colonel, or Knight in Arms,
Whose chance on these defenseless doors may seize,

[41]Reeds, i. e., pipes. [42]Pastoral poem.
[1]The Sonnets are numbered as in H. C. Beeching's edition.
[2]Written in the fall of 1642 when the army of Charles I was advancing on London.

If ever deed of honor did thee please,
Guard them, and him within protect from harms:
He can requite thee, for he knows the charms 5
That call fame on such gentle acts as these;
And he can spread thy name o'er lands and seas,
Whatever clime the sun's bright circle warms.
Lift not thy spear against the Muses' bower:
The great Emathian conqueror[3] bid spare 10
The house of Pindarus, when temple and tower
Went to the ground; and the repeated air
Of sad Electra's poet[4] had the power
To save the Athenian walls from ruin bare.

IX

Lady, that in the prime of earliest youth
Wisely hast shunned the broad way and the green,
And with those few art eminently seen
That labor up the hill of heavenly Truth,
The better part with Mary and with Ruth, 5
Chosen thou hast; and they that overween,
And at thy growing virtues fret their spleen,
No anger find in thee, but pity and ruth.
Thy care is fixed, and zealously attends
To fill thy odorous lamp with deeds of light, 10
And hope that reaps not shame.[5] Therefore be sure
Thou, when the Bridegroom with his feastful friends
Passes to bliss at the mid-hour of night,
Hast gained thy entrance, Virgin wise and pure.

XI

A book was writ of late called *Tetrachordon*,[6]
And woven close, both matter, form, and style;
The subject new: it walked the town a while,
Numbering good intellects; now seldom pored on.
Cries the stall-reader, "Bless us! what a word on 5
A title-page is this!"; and some in file
Stand spelling false, while one might walk to Mile-
End Green. Why, is it harder, sirs, than *Gordon*,
Colkitto, or *Macdonnel*, or *Galasp*?[7]
Those rugged names to our like mouths grow sleek, 10
That would have made Quintilian stare and gasp.
Thy age, like ours, O soul of Sir John Cheke,[8]
Hated not learning worse than toad or asp,
When thou taught'st Cambridge and King Edward Greek.

XII

On the Same

I did but prompt the age to quit their clogs
By the known rules of ancient liberty,
When straight a barbarous noise environs me
Of owls and cuckoos, asses, apes, and dogs;
As when those hinds that were transformed to frogs 5
Railed at Latona's twin-born progeny,[9]
Which after held the Sun and Moon in fee.
But this is got by casting pearl to hogs,
That bawl for freedom in their senseless mood,
And still revolt when Truth would set them free. 10
Licence they mean when they cry Liberty;
For who loves that must first be wise and good:
But from that mark how far they rove we see,
For all this waste of wealth and loss of blood.

XV

On the Late Massacre in Piedmont[10]

Avenge, O Lord, thy slaughtered saints, whose bones
Lie scattered on the Alpine mountains cold;

[3] Alexander the Great, when he sacked Thebes.

[4] Euripedes.

[5] See the parable of the wise and foolish virgins (St. Matthew, 25:6).

[6] One of Milton's pamphlets on divorce.

[7] Names of Scottish generals during the war of 1644–1645.

[8] English humanist of the mid-sixteenth century, first professor of Greek at Cambridge and tutor of Edward VI.

[9] Apollo and Diana.

[10] In 1655 the Duke of Savoy subjected the Protestants of Piedmont to bitter persecution, cruelly killing a number of them.

Even them who kept thy truth so pure of old,
When all our fathers worshiped stocks and stones,
Forget not: in thy book record their groans 5
Who were thy sheep, and in their ancient fold
Slain by the bloody Piemontese, that rolled
Mother with infant down the rocks. Their moans
The vales redoubled to the hills, and they
To heaven. Their martyred blood and ashes sow 10
O'er all th' Italian fields, where still doth sway
The triple Tyrant;[11] that from these may grow
A hundred fold, who, having learned thy way,
Early may fly the Babylonian woe.

XVI ✔

When I consider how my light is spent
Ere half my days in this dark world and wide,
And that one talent[12] which is death to hide
Lodged with me useless, though my soul more bent
To serve therewith my Maker, and present 5
My true account, lest He returning chide,
"Doth God exact day-labor, light denied?"
I fondly ask. But Patience, to prevent
That murmur, soon replies, "God doth not need
Either man's work or his own gifts. Who best 10
Bear his mild yoke, they serve him best. His state
Is kingly: thousands at his bidding speed,
And post o'er land and ocean without rest;
They also serve who only stand and wait."

XVII

Lawrence, of virtuous father virtuous son,
Now that the fields are dank, and ways are mire,
Where shall we sometimes meet, and by the fire
Help waste a sullen day, what may be won
From the hard season gaining? Time will run 5

[11] The pope. The Puritans identified Rome with Babylon (cf. Revelation, 17:5).

[12] See the parable of the servant with whom one talent (a sum of money) was left (St. Matthew, 25:26).

On smoother, till Favonius[13] reinspire
The frozen earth, and clothe in fresh attire
The lily and rose, that neither sowed nor spun.
What neat repast shall feast us, light and choice,
Of Attic taste, with wine, whence we may rise, 10
To hear the lute well touched, or artful voice
Warble immortal notes and Tuscan air?
He who of those delights can judge, and spare
To interpose them oft, is not unwise.

XVIII

Cyriack, whose grandsire[14] on the royal bench
Of British Themis,[15] with no mean applause,
Pronounced, and in his volumes taught, our laws,
Which others at their bar so often wrench,
To-day deep thoughts resolve with me to drench 5
In mirth that after no repenting draws;
Let Euclid rest, and Archimedes pause,
And what the Swede intend, and what the French.[16]
To measure life learn thou betimes, and know
Towards solid good what leads the nearest way; 10
For other things mild Heaven a time ordains,
And disapproves that care, though wise in show,
That with superfluous burden loads the day,
And, when God sends a cheerful hour, refrains.

XIX

Methought I saw my late espouséd saint[17]
Brought to me like Alcestis from the grave,
Whom Jove's great son[18] to her glad husband gave,

[13] The spring wind from the southwest.

[14] Sir Edward Coke. [15] Goddess of justice.

[16] Charles X of Sweden was at war with Poland and Russia, and Louis XIV was fighting the Spanish in the Netherlands.

[17] Catherine Woodcock, Milton's second wife, who died in childbirth in February, 1658.

[18] Hercules.

Rescued from Death by force, though pale
and faint.
Mine, as whom washed from spot of child-
bed taint 5
Purification in the Old Law[19] did save,
And such as yet once more I trust to have
Full sight of her in Heaven without re-
straint,
Came vested all in white, pure as her mind.
Her face was veiled; yet to my fancied
sight 10
Love, sweetness, goodness, in her person
shined
So clear as in no face with more delight.
But, oh! as to embrace me she inclined,
I waked, she fled, and day brought back my
night.

TO THE LORD GENERAL CROMWELL MAY, 1652

On the Proposals of Certain Ministers at the Committee for Propagation of the Gospel

Cromwell, our chief of men, who through a
cloud
Not of war only, but detractions rude,
Guided by faith and matchless fortitude,
To peace and truth thy glorious way hast
plowed,
And on the neck of crownéd Fortune proud 5
Hast reared God's trophies, and his work
pursued,
While Darwen stream, with blood of Scots
imbrued,
And Dunbar field, resounds thy praises
loud,
And Worcester's laureate wreath:[20] yet much
remains
To conquer still; Peace hath her vic-
tories 10
No less renowned than War: new foes
arise,
Threatening to bind our souls with secular
chains.[21]
Help us to save free conscience from the
paw
Of hireling wolves, whose Gospel is their
maw.

TO MR. CYRIACK SKINNER

Upon His Blindness

Cyriack, this three years' day these eyes,
though clear
To outward view, of blemish or of spot,
Bereft of light, their seeing have forgot;
Nor to their idle orbs doth sight appear
Of sun, or moon, or star, throughout the
year, 5
Or man, or woman. Yet I argue not
Against Heaven's hand or will, nor bate a
jot
Of heart or hope, but still bear up and
steer
Right onward. What supports me, dost
thou ask?
The conscience, friend, to have lost them
overplied 10
In Liberty's defense, my noble task,
Of which all Europe rings from side to side;
This thought might lead me through the
world's vain mask
Content, though blind, had I no better
guide.

PARADISE LOST

THE VERSE

THE measure is English heroic verse without rime, as that of Homer in Greek, and of Virgil in Latin; rime being no necessary adjunct or true ornament of poem or good verse, in longer works especially, but the invention of a barbarous age to set off wretched matter and lame meter; graced indeed since by the use of some famous modern poets, carried away by custom, but much to their own vexation, hindrance, and constraint to express many things otherwise, and for the most part worse, than else they would have expressed them. Not without cause therefore, some both Italian and Spanish poets of prime note have rejected rime both in longer and shorter works, as have long since our best English tragedies; as a thing of itself, to all judicious ears, trivial and of no true musical delight; which consists only in apt numbers, fit quantity of syllables, and the sense variously drawn out from one verse into another;

[19] Leviticus, 12.

[20] Three victories of Cromwell over the Scotch, respectively in 1648, 1650, and 1651.

[21] Government control. The proposals to which Milton objected were that Puritan ministers be supported by the state.

not in the jingling sound of like endings, a fault avoided by the learned ancients both in poetry and all good oratory. This neglect then of rime so little is to be taken for a defect, though it may seem so perhaps to vulgar readers, that it is rather to be esteemed an example set, the first in English, of ancient liberty recovered to heroic poem, from the troublesome and modern bondage of riming.

BOOK I

THE ARGUMENT

This First Book proposes, first in brief, the whole subject—Man's disobedience, and the loss thereupon of Paradise, wherein he was placed: then touches the prime cause of his fall—the Serpent, or rather Satan in the Serpent; who, revolting from God, and drawing to his side many legions of Angels, was, by the command of God, driven out of Heaven, with all his crew, into the great Deep. Which action passed over, the Poem hastens into the midst of things; presenting Satan, with his Angels, now fallen into Hell—described here not in the Center (for heaven and earth may be supposed as yet not made, certainly not yet accursed), but in a place of utter darkness, fitliest called Chaos. Here Satan, with his Angels lying on the burning lake, thunderstruck and astonished, after a certain space recovers, as from confusion; calls up him who, next in order of dignity, lay by him: they confer of their miserable fall. Satan awakens all his legions, who lay till then in the same manner confounded. They rise: their numbers; array of battle; their chief leaders named, according to the idols known afterwards in Canaan and the countries adjoining. To these Satan directs his speech; comforts them with hope yet of regaining Heaven; but tells them, lastly, of a new world and new kind of creature to be created, according to an ancient prophecy, or report, in Heaven—for that Angels were long before this visible creation was the opinion of many ancient Fathers. To find out the truth of this prophecy, and what to determine thereon, he refers to a full council. What his associates thence attempt. Pandemonium, the palace of Satan, rises, suddenly built out of the Deep: the infernal Peers there sit in council.

Of man's first disobedience, and the fruit
Of that forbidden tree whose mortal taste
Brought death into the World, and all our woe,
With loss of Eden, till one greater Man
Restore us, and regain the blissful seat, 5
Sing, Heavenly Muse, that, on the secret top
Of Oreb, or of Sinai, didst inspire
That shepherd[1] who first taught the chosen seed
In the beginning how the heavens and earth
Rose out of Chaos: or, if Sion hill 10
Delight thee more, and Siloa's brook that flowed
Fast[2] by the oracle of God,[3] I thence
Invoke thy aid to my adventrous song,
That with no middle flight intends to soar
Above the Aonian mount,[4] while it pursues 15
Things unattempted yet in prose or rime.
And chiefly thou, O Spirit, that does prefer
Before all temples the upright heart and pure,
Instruct me, for thou know'st; thou from the first
Wast present, and, with mighty wings outspread, 20
Dove-like sat'st brooding on the vast Abyss,
And mad'st it pregnant: what in me is dark
Illumine, what is low raise and support;
That, to the highth of this great argument,
I may assert[5] Eternal Providence, 25
And justify the ways of God to men.
Say first—for Heaven hides nothing from thy view,
Nor the deep tract of Hell—say first what cause
Moved our grand[6] Parents, in that happy state,
Favored of Heaven so highly, to fall off 30
From their Creator, and transgress his will
For[7] one restraint, lords of the World besides.
Who first seduced them to that foul revolt?
The infernal Serpent; he it was whose guile,
Stirred up with envy and revenge, deceived 35
The mother of mankind, what time his pride
Had cast him out from Heaven, with all his host
Of rebel Angels, by whose aid, aspiring
To set himself in glory above his peers,
He trusted to have equaled the Most High, 40
If he opposed, and, with ambitious aim
Against the throne and monarchy of God,
Raised impious war in Heaven and battle proud,
With vain attempt. Him the Almighty Power
Hurled headlong flaming from the ethereal sky, 45

[1]Moses. [2]Close. [3]The temple of Jerusalem. [4]Helicon, home of the muses. [5]Vindicate. [6]First. [7]Because of.

With hideous ruin and combustion, down
To bottomless perdition, there to dwell
In adamantine chains and penal fire,
Who durst defy the Omnipotent to arms.[8]
Nine times the space that measure day and night 50
To mortal men, he, with his horrid crew,
Lay vanquished, rolling in the fiery gulf,
Confounded, though immortal. But his doom
Reserved him to more wrath; for now the thought
Both of lost happiness and lasting pain 55
Torments him: round he throws his baleful eyes,
That witnessed huge affliction and dismay,
Mixed with obdurate pride and steadfast hate.
At once, as far as Angels ken, he views
The dismal situation waste and wild. 60
A dungeon horrible, on all sides round,
As one great furnace flamed; yet from those flames
No light; but rather darkness visible
Served only to discover sights of woe,
Regions of sorrow, doleful shades, where peace 65
And rest can never dwell, hope never comes
That comes to all, but torture without end
Still urges, and a fiery deluge, fed
With ever-burning sulphur unconsumed.
Such place Eternal Justice had prepared 70
For those rebellious; here their prison ordained
In utter darkness, and their portion set,
As far removed from God and light of Heaven
As from the center thrice to the utmost pole.
Oh how unlike the place from whence they fell! 75
There the companions of his fall, o'erwhelmed
With floods and whirlwinds of tempestuous fire,
He soon discerns; and, weltering by his side,
One next himself in power, and next in crime,
Long after known in Palestine, and named 80
BEËLZEBUB. To whom the Arch-Enemy,
And thence in Heaven called SATAN,[9] with bold words
Breaking the horrid silence, thus began:—
"If thou beest he—but Oh how fallen! how changed
From him!—who, in the happy realms of light, 85
Clothed with transcendent brightness, didst outshine
Myriads, though bright—if he whom mutual league,
United thoughts and counsels, equal hope
And hazard in the glorious enterprise,
Joined with me once, now misery hath joined
In equal ruin; into what pit thou seest 91
From what highth fallen: so much the stronger proved
He with his thunder: and till then who knew
The force of those dire arms? Yet not for those,
Nor what the potent Victor in his rage 95
Can else inflict, do I repent, or change,
Though changed in outward luster, that fixed mind,
And high disdain from sense of injured merit,
That with the Mightiest raised me to contend,
And to the fierce contention brought along 100
Innumerable force of Spirits armed,
That durst dislike his reign, and, me preferring,
His utmost power with adverse power opposed
In dubious battle on the plains of Heaven,
And shook his throne. What though the field be lost? 105
All is not lost—the unconquerable will,
And study of revenge, immortal hate,
And courage never to submit or yield;

[8]Milton's conception of the universe and of its relation to heaven and hell should be grasped at the outset. He follows the Ptolemaic system, according to which the earth is the center of the universe, about which the other bodies revolve. These (sun, moon, etc.) are supposed to be fastened in a series of hollow spheres, made of some transparent substance, which move around the earth as a common center. The hollow spheres were, in medieval and early modern times, supposed to be ten in number, the outermost being the *primum mobile,* or "first moved." Thus the starry universe has the form of a large globe, and it is suspended from the wall of heaven by a golden chain. Heaven is the region lying entirely outside the starry universe and immediately above it. Surrounding the universe and separated from heaven by a wall is chaos, the region of unformed, warring elements through which Satan and his host were hurled from heaven. At the bottom of this region of chaos is hell, the place of punishment prepared for Satan and his followers when they rebelled. Hell, then, is under the universe and is separated from it by a distance through chaos equal to the distance from the center of the earth to the *primum mobile* (see where Milton says the distance from heaven to hell is three times the radius of the universe).

[9]A Hebrew word meaning adversary.

And what is else not to be overcome?
That glory never shall his wrath or might 110
Extort from me. To bow and sue for grace
With suppliant knee, and deify his power
Who, from the terror of this arm, so late
Doubted[10] his empire—that were low indeed;
That were an ignominy and shame beneath
This downfall; since, by fate, the strength of Gods, 116
And this empyreal substance, cannot fail;
Since, through experience of this great event,
In arms not worse, in foresight much advanced,
We may with more successful hope resolve 120
To wage by force or guile eternal war,
Irreconcilable to our grand Foe,
Who now triumphs, and in the excess of joy
Sole reigning holds the tyranny of Heaven."
So spake the apostate Angel, though in pain, 125
Vaunting aloud, but racked with deep despair;
And him thus answered soon his bold compeer:—
"O Prince, O Chief of many thronéd Powers
That led the embattled Seraphim to war
Under thy conduct, and, in dreadful deeds 130
Fearless, endangered Heaven's perpetual King,
And put to proof his high supremacy,
Whether upheld by strength, or chance, or fate,
Too well I see and rue the dire event
That, with sad overthrow and foul defeat, 135
Hath lost us Heaven, and all this mighty host
In horrible destruction laid thus low,
As far as Gods and Heavenly Essences
Can perish: for the mind and spirit remains
Invincible, and vigor soon returns, 140
Though all our glory extinct, and happy state
Here swallowed up in endless misery.
But what if he our Conqueror (whom I now
Of force believe almighty, since no less
Than such could have o'erpowered such force as ours) 145
Have left us this our spirit and strength entire,
Strongly to suffer and support our pains,
That we may so suffice[11] his vengeful ire,
Or do him mightier service as his thralls
By right of war, whate'er his business be, 150
Here in the heart of Hell to work in fire,
Or do his errands in the gloomy Deep?
What can it then avail though yet we feel
Strength undiminished, or eternal being
To undergo eternal punishment?" 155
Whereto with speedy words the Arch-Fiend replied:—
"Fallen Cherub, to be weak is miserable,
Doing or suffering: but of this be sure—
To do ought good never will be our task,
But ever to do ill our sole delight, 160
As being the contrary to his high will
Whom we resist. If then his providence
Out of our evil seek to bring forth good,
Our labor must be to pervert that end,
And out of good still to find means of evil; 165
Which ofttimes may succeed so as perhaps
Shall grieve him, if I fail not,[12] and disturb
His inmost counsels from their destined aim.
But see! the angry Victor hath recalled
His ministers of vengeance and pursuit 170
Back to the gates of Heaven: the sulphurous hail,
Shot after us in storm, o'erblown hath laid
The fiery surge that from the precipice
Of Heaven received us falling; and the thunder,
Winged with red lightning and impetuous rage, 175
Perhaps hath spent his shafts, and ceases now
To bellow through the vast and boundless Deep.
Let us not slip the occasion, whether scorn
Or satiate fury yield it from our Foe.
Seest thou yon dreary plain, forlorn and wild, 180
The seat of desolation, void of light,
Save what the glimmering of these livid flames
Casts pale and dreadful? Thither let us tend
From off the tossing of these fiery waves;
There rest, if any rest can harbor there; 185
And, re-assembling our afflicted powers,
Consult how we may henceforth most offend
Our enemy, our own loss how repair,
How overcome this dire calamity,
What reinforcement we may gain from hope,
If not, what resolution from despair." 191
Thus Satan, talking to his nearest mate,
With head uplift above the wave, and eyes
That sparkling blazed; his other parts besides
Prone on the flood, extended long and large,
Lay floating many a rood, in bulk as huge 196

[10]Feared for. [11]Satisfy.

[12]If I mistake not.

As whom the fables name of monstrous size,
Titanian or Earth-born, that warred on
Jove,[13]
Briareos or Typhon, whom the den
By ancient Tarsus held, or that sea-beast 200
Leviathan, which God of all his works
Created hugest that swim the ocean-stream.
Him, haply slumbering on the Norway foam,
The pilot of some small night-foundered[14]
skiff,
Deeming some island, oft, as seamen tell, 205
With fixéd anchor in his scaly rind,
Moors by his side under the lee, while night
Invests the sea, and wishéd morn delays.
So stretched out huge in length the Arch-Fiend lay,
Chained on the burning lake; nor ever thence
Had risen, or heaved his head, but that the
will 211
And high permission of all-ruling Heaven
Left him at large to his own dark designs,
That with reiterated crimes he might
Heap on himself damnation, while he sought
Evil to others, and enraged might see 216
How all his malice served but to bring forth
Infinite goodness, grace, and mercy, shown
On Man by him seduced, but on himself
Treble confusion, wrath, and vengeance
poured. 220
Forthwith upright he rears from off the
pool
His mighty stature; on each hand the flames
Driven backward slope their pointing spires,
and, rolled
In billows, leave i'the midst a horrid vale.
Then with expanded wings he steers his
flight 225
Aloft, incumbent on the dusky air,
That felt unusual weight; till on dry land
He lights—if it were land that ever burned
With solid, as the lake with liquid fire,
And such appeared in hue as when the force
Of subterranean wind transports a hill 231
Torn from Pelorus, or the shattered side
Of thundering Aetna, whose combustible
And fueled entrails, thence conceiving fire,
Sublimed with mineral fury, aid the
winds, 235
And leave a singéd bottom all involved
With stench and smoke. Such resting found
the sole
Of unblest feet. Him followed his next
mate;
Both glorying to have scaped the Stygian
flood
As gods, and by their own recovered
strength, 240
Not by the sufferance of supernal power.
"Is this the region, this the soil, the clime,"
Said then the lost Archangel, "this the seat
That we must change for Heaven?—this
mournful gloom
For that celestial light? Be it so, since he 245
Who now is sovran can dispose and bid
What shall be right: farthest from him is
best,
Whom reason hath equaled, force hath made
supreme
Above his equals. Farewell, happy fields,
Where joy for ever dwells! Hail, horrors!
hail, 250
Infernal World! and thou, profoundest Hell,
Receive thy new possessor—one who brings
A mind not to be changed by place or time.
The mind is its own place, and in itself
Can make a Heaven of Hell, a Hell of
Heaven. 255
What matter where, if I be still the same,
And what I should be, all but less than[15] he
Whom thunder hath made greater? Here
at least
We shall be free; the Almighty hath not
built
Here for his envy, will not drive us hence: 260
Here we may reign secure; and, in my choice,
To reign is worth ambition, though in Hell:
Better to reign in Hell than serve in Heaven.
But wherefore let we then our faithful
friends,
The associates and co-partners of our
loss, 265
Lie thus astonished on the oblivious pool,[16]
And call them not to share with us their part
In this unhappy mansion, or once more
With rallied arms to try what may be yet
Regained in Heaven, or what more lost in
Hell?" 270
So Satan spake; and him Beëlzebub
Thus answered:—"Leader of those armies
bright
Which, but the Omnipotent, none could have
foiled!
If once they hear that voice, their liveliest
pledge
Of hope in fears and dangers—heard so
oft 275
In worst extremes, and on the perilous edge

[13]The Titans warred on Uranus, the Giants (earth-born) on Jove (Zeus). Briareos was a Titan, Typhon a Giant.

[14]Overtaken by night and so brought to a stand.

[15]I. e., only less than.

[16]Lie thus thunderstruck on the benumbing pool.

Of battle, when it raged, in all assaults
Their surest signal—they will soon resume
New courage and revive, though now they lie
Groveling and prostrate on yon lake of fire, 280
As we erewhile, astounded and amazed;
No wonder, fallen such a pernicious highth!"
He scarce had ceased when the superior Fiend
Was moving toward the shore; his ponderous shield,
Ethereal temper, massy, large, and round, 285
Behind him cast. The broad circumference
Hung on his shoulders like the moon, whose orb
Through optic glass[17] the Tuscan artist views
At evening, from the top of Fesolé,
Or in Valdarno, to descry new lands, 290
Rivers, or mountains, in her spotty globe.
His spear—to equal which the tallest pine
Hewn on Norwegian hills, to be the mast
Of some great ammiral,[18] were but a wand—
He walked with, to support uneasy steps 295
Over the burning marl, not like those steps
On Heaven's azure; and the torrid clime
Smote on him sore besides, vaulted with fire.
Nathless[19] he so endured, till on the beach
Of that inflaméd sea he stood, and called 300
His legions—Angel Forms, who lay entranced
Thick as autumnal leaves that strow the brooks
In Vallombrosa,[20] where the Etrurian shades
High over-arched embower; or scattered sedge
Afloat, when with fierce winds Orion armed
Hath vexed the Red-Sea coast, whose waves o'erthrew 306
Busiris and his Memphian chivalry,[21]
While with perfidious hatred they pursued
The sojourners of Goshen, who beheld
From the safe shore their floating carcases 310
And broken chariot-wheels. So thick bestrown,
Abject and lost, lay these, covering the flood,
Under amazement of their hideous change.
He called so loud that all the hollow deep
Of Hell resounded:—"Princes, Potentates, 315
Warriors, the Flower of Heaven—once yours; now lost,
If such astonishment as this can seize
Eternal Spirits! Or have ye chosen this place
After the toil of battle to repose
Your wearied virtue,[22] for the ease you find 320
To slumber here, as in the vales of Heaven?
Or in this abject posture have ye sworn
To adore the Conqueror, who now beholds
Cherub and Seraph rolling in the flood
With scattered arms and ensigns, till anon 325
His swift pursuers from Heaven-gates discern
The advantage, and, descending, tread us down
Thus drooping, or with linkéd thunderbolts
Transfix us to the bottom of this gulf?—
Awake, arise, or be for ever fallen!" 330
They heard, and were abashed, and up they sprung
Upon the wing, as when men wont to watch,
On duty sleeping found by whom they dread,
Rouse and bestir themselves ere well awake.
Nor did they not perceive[23] the evil plight 335
In which they were, or the fierce pains not feel;
Yet to their General's voice they soon obeyed
Innumerable. As when the potent rod
Of Amram's son,[24] in Egypt's evil day,
Waved round the coast, up-called a pitchy cloud 340
Of locusts, warping on the eastern wind,
That o'er the realm of impious Pharaoh hung
Like Night, and darkened all the land of Nile;
So numberless were those bad Angels seen 344
Hovering on wing under the cope of Hell,
'Twixt upper, nether, and surrounding fires;
Till, as a signal given, the uplifted spear
Of their great Sultan waving to direct 348
Their course, in even balance down they light
On the firm brimstone, and fill all the plain:
A multitude like which the populous North
Poured never from her frozen loins to pass
Rhene or the Danaw,[25] when her barbarous sons
Came like a deluge on the South, and spread
Beneath Gibraltar to the Libyan sands. 355
Forthwith, from every squadron and each band,

[17]The telescope, greatly improved by Galileo (the Tuscan artist). Fiesole is a hill just outside of Florence; Val d'Arno, the valley in which Florence lies.

[18]Chief vessel in a fleet. [19]Nevertheless.

[20]Eighteen miles from Florence.

[21]Busiris, Pharaoh; Memphian, Egyptian.

[22]Courage.

[23]Nor did they fail to perceive. [24]Aaron.

[25]Rhine or the Danube.

bove are illustrations for Books I and II of *aradise Lost,* made for the first illustrated edi-
on of Milton's epic, published in London in 88. These pictures are historically interesting, examples of the earliest attempt to make ilton's tremendous scenes visible to the eye. o artist could really succeed in this attempt, d something of the quality of Milton's achieve-
ent can be learned by comparison of these venteenth-century pictures with Milton's own ords. (Courtesy of the New York Public Library.)

o the right is reproduced the portrait of Milton twenty-one, which is preserved at Nuneham. his is the most attractive, and perhaps also the ost illuminating, of the extant contemporary ortraits of Milton. From other portraits made hen he was older one receives not much more an the impression of severity and determina-
on; but from this almost youthful likeness one n see that Milton's countenance did not belie e splendor of his genius. His clear, fresh eauty, indeed, caused his contemporaries at ambridge to nickname him "the lady of hrist's"; but this was not discriminating, be-
use masculine force is as evident in this por-
trait as beauty.

Fr. Baconi
DE VERULAMIO
SERMONES FIDELES,
ETHICI,
POLITICI,
ŒCONOMICI:
Sive
INTERIORA RERUM.
Accedit
FABER FORTUNÆ &c.

C.V. Dalen sculp.

LUG. BATAVORUM,
Apud Franciſcum Hackium. A°. 1641.

Bridget Hitchcock her Book

THE
FAERIE QVEEN:
THE
Shepheards Calendar:
Together
WITH THE OTHER
Works of England's Arch-Poët,
EDM. SPENSER:
¶ *Collected into one Volume, and carefully corrected.*
Printed by *H. L.* for *Mathew Lownes.*
Anno Dom. 1611.

The Tragicall Hiſtory of the Life and Death of Doctor FAVSTVS.

With new Additions.

Written by *Ch. Mar.*

Printed at London for *Iohn Wright*, and are to be ſold at his ſhop without Newgate. 1624.

The title page reproduced to the left above is that o edition, in Latin, of Bacon's *Essays* published at Ley Holland, in 1641. The interest of this pictorial title lies in the engraver's representation of Bacon discour learnedly to three men who listen with close atten (Courtesy of the New York Public Library.) The page directly above is that of the first collected editio the works of Edmund Spenser—a folio published in (Courtesy of the Pierpont Morgan Library.) The page of the 1624 edition of Marlowe's *Doctor Faustu* the left, is interesting because the woodcut illustrat scene from the play (see page 306). Faustus in academic robe, holding a wand in one hand and a boo magic in the other, says,

> "Within this circle is Jehovah's name,
> Forward and backward anagrammatized,
> Th' abbreviated names of holy saints,
> Figures of every adjunct to the heavens,
> And characters of signs and erring stars,
> By which the spirits are enforced to rise."

He then repeats the Latin incantation which ca Mephistopheles to appear through a trap door in the st The figure of Faustus is a likeness of Edward Al (1566–1626), the actor, who played the part at the For Theater. Alleyn, who became wealthy, was the fou of Dulwich College. (Reproduced from the copy in Bodleian Library, Oxford.)

The heads and leaders thither haste where stood
Their great Commander—godlike Shapes, and Forms
Excelling human; princely Dignities;
And Powers that erst[26] in Heaven sat on thrones, 360
Though of their names in Heavenly records now
Be no memorial, blotted out and razed
By their rebellion from the Books of Life.
Nor had they yet among the sons of Eve
Got them new names, till, wandering o'er the earth, 365
Through God's high sufferance for the trial of man,
By falsities and lies the greatest part
Of mankind they corrupted to forsake
God their Creator, and the invisible
Glory of him that made them, to transform
Oft to the image of a brute, adorned 371
With gay religions full of pomp and gold,
And devils to adore for deities:
Then were they known to men by various names,
And various idols through the Heathen World.
Say, Muse, their names then known, who first, who last, 376
Roused from the slumber on that fiery couch,
At their great Emperor's call, as next in worth
Came singly where he stood on the bare strand,
While the promiscuous crowd stood yet aloof. 380
The chief were those who, from the pit of Hell
Roaming to seek their prey on Earth, durst fix
Their seats, long after, next the seat of God,
Their altars by his altar, gods adored
Among the nations round, and durst abide
Jehovah thundering out of Sion, throned 386
Between the Cherubim; yea, often placed
Within his sanctuary itself their shrines,
Abominations; and with curséd things
His holy rites and solemn feasts profaned, 390
And with their darkness durst affront his light.
First, *Moloch,* horrid king, besmeared with blood
Of human sacrifice, and parents' tears;
Though, for the noise of drums and timbrels loud,
Their children's cries unheard that passed through fire 395
To his grim idol. Him the Ammonite
Worshiped in Rabba and her watery plain,
In Argob and in Basan, to the stream
Of utmost Arnon. Nor content with such
Audacious neighborhood, the wisest heart 400
Of Solomon he led by fraud to build
His temple right against the temple of God
On that opprobrious hill,[27] and made his grove
The pleasant valley of Hinnom, Tophet thence
And black Gehenna called, the type of Hell.
Next *Chemos,* the obscene dread of Moab's sons, 406
From Aroar to Nebo and the wild
Of southmost Abarim; in Hesebon
And Horonaim, Seon's realm, beyond
The flowery dale of Sibma clad with vines, 410
And Eleålé to the Asphaltic Pool:[28]
Peor his other name, when he enticed
Israel in Sittim on their march from Nile,
To do him wanton rites, which cost them woe.
Yet thence his lustful orgies he enlarged 415
Even to that hill of scandal, by the grove
Of Moloch homicide, lust hard by hate,
Till good Josiah drove them thence to Hell.
With these came they who, from the bordering flood
Of old Euphrates to the brook that parts 420
Egypt from Syrian ground, had general names
Of *Baälim* and *Ashtaroth*—those male,
These feminine. For spirits, when they please,
Can either sex assume, or both; so soft
And uncompounded is their essence pure, 425
Not tied or manacled with joint or limb,
Nor founded on the brittle strength of bones,
Like cumbrous flesh; but, in what shape they choose,
Dilated or condensed, bright or obscure,
Can execute their aery purposes, 430
And works of love or enmity fulfill.
For those the race of Israel oft forsook
Their Living Strength, and unfrequented left
His righteous altar, bowing lowly down 434
To bestial gods; for which their heads, as low
Bowed down in battle, sunk before the spear
Of despicable foes. With these in troop
Came *Astoreth,* whom the Phoenicians called

[26]Formerly.

[27]The Mount of Olives, later called the Mount of Offense.

[28]The Dead Sea.

Astarté, queen of heaven, with crescent horns;
To whose bright image nightly by the moon 440
Sidonian virgins paid their vows and songs;
In Sion also not unsung, where stood
Her temple on the offensive mountain, built
By that uxorious king[29] whose heart, though large,
Beguiled by fair idolatresses, fell 445
To idols foul. *Thammuz* came next behind,
Whose annual wound in Lebanon allured
The Syrian damsels to lament his fate
In amorous ditties all a summer's day, 449
While smooth Adonis[30] from his native rock
Ran purple to the sea, supposed with blood,
Of Thammuz yearly wounded: the love-tale
Infected Sion's daughters with like heat,
Whose wanton passions in the sacred porch
Ezekiel saw, when, by the vision led, 455
His eye surveyed the dark idolatries
Of alienated Judah. Next came one
Who mourned in earnest, when the captive ark
Maimed his brute image, head and hands lopped off,
In his own temple, on the grunsel[31] edge, 460
Where he fell flat and shamed his worshipers:
Dagon his name, sea-monster, upward man
And downward fish; yet had his temple high
Reared in Azotus, dreaded through the coast
Of Palestine, in Gath and Ascalon, 465
And Accaron and Gaza's frontier bounds.
Him followed *Rimmon,* whose delightful seat
Was fair Damascus, on the fertile banks
Of Abbana and Pharphar, lucid streams. 469
He also against the house of God was bold:
A leper[32] once he lost, and gained a king—
Ahaz, his sottish conqueror, whom he drew
God's altar to disparage and displace
For one of Syrian mode, whereon to burn
His odious offerings, and adore the gods 475
Whom he had vanquished. After these appeared
A crew who, under names of old renown—
Osiris, Isis, Orus, and their train—
With monstrous shapes and sorceries abused
Fanatic Egypt and her priests to seek 480
Their wandering gods disguised in brutish forms
Rather than human. Nor did Israel scape
The infection, when their borrowed gold[33] composed
The calf in Oreb; and the rebel king[34]
Doubled that sin in Bethel and in Dan, 485
Likening his Maker to the grazéd ox—
Jehovah, who, in one night, when he[35] passed
From Egypt marching, equaled[36] with one stroke
Both her first-born and all her bleating gods.
Belial came last; than whom a Spirit more lewd 490
Fell not from Heaven, or more gross to love
Vice for itself. To him no temple stood
Or altar smoked; yet who more oft than he
In temples and at altars, when the priest
Turns atheist, as did Eli's sons, who filled 495
With lust and violence the house of God?
In courts and palaces he also reigns,
And in luxurious cities, where the noise
Of riot ascends above their loftiest towers,
And injury and outrage; and, when night 500
Darkens the streets, then wander forth the sons
Of Belial, flown[37] with insolence and wine.
Witness the streets of Sodom, and that night
In Gibeah, when the hospitable door
Exposed a matron, to avoid worse rape. 505
These were the prime in order and in might:
The rest were long to tell; though far renowned
The Ionian gods—of Javan's issue held
Gods, yet confessed later than Heaven and Earth,
Their boasted parents;—*Titan,* Heaven's first-born, 510
With his enormous brood, and birthright seized
By younger *Saturn:* he from mightier Jove,
His own and Rhea's son, like measure found;
So *Jove* usurping reigned. These, first in Crete
And Ida known, thence on the snowy top 515
Of cold Olympus ruled the middle air,
Their highest heaven; or on the Delphian cliff,
Or in Dodona, and through all the bounds
Of Doric land; or who with Saturn old
Fled over Adria to the Hesperian fields, 520
And o'er the Celtic roamed the utmost Isles.
All these and more came flocking; but with looks

---

[29] Solomon.
[30] A river in Phoenicia whose waters are colored by the soil through which it flows.
[31] Threshold. [32] Naaman.

[33] "Borrowed" from the Egyptians. [34] Jeroboam.
[35] I. e., Israel. [36] Struck down. [37] Flushed.

Downcast and damp;[38] yet such wherein appeared
Obscure some glimpse of joy to have found their Chief
Not in despair, to have found themselves not lost 525
In loss itself; which on his countenance cast
Like doubtful hue. But he, his wonted pride
Soon recollecting,[39] with high words, that bore
Semblance of worth, not substance, gently raised
Their fainting courage, and dispelled their fears: 530
Then straight commands that, at the warlike sound
Of trumpets loud and clarions, be upreared
His mighty standard. That proud honor claimed
Azazel as his right, a Cherub tall:
Who forthwith from the glittering staff unfurled 535
The imperial ensign; which, full high advanced,
Shone like a meteor streaming to the wind,
With gems and golden luster rich emblazed,
Seraphic arms and trophies; all the while
Sonorous metal blowing martial sounds: 540
At which the universal host up-sent
A shout that tore Hell's concave, and beyond
Frighted the reign of Chaos and old Night.
All in a moment through the gloom were seen
Ten thousand banners rise into the air, 545
With orient[40] colors waving: with them rose
A forest huge of spears; and thronging helms
Appeared, and serried shields in thick array
Of depth immeasurable. Anon they move
In perfect phalanx to the Dorian mood[41] 550
Of flutes and soft recorders[42]—such as raised
To highth of noblest temper heroes old
Arming to battle, and instead of rage
Deliberate valor breathed, firm, and unmoved[43]
With dread of death to flight or foul retreat;
Nor wanting power to mitigate and swage[44]
With solemn touches troubled thoughts, and chase 557
Anguish and doubt and fear and sorrow and pain
From mortal or immortal minds. Thus they,
Breathing united force with fixéd thought, 560
Moved on in silence to soft pipes that charmed
Their painful steps o'er the burnt soil. And now
Advanced in view they stand—a horrid[45] front
Of dreadful length and dazzling arms, in guise
Of warriors old, with ordered spear and shield, 565
Awaiting what command their mighty Chief
Had to impose. He through the arméd files
Darts his experienced eye, and soon traverse[46]
The whole battalion views—their order due,
Their visages and stature as of gods; 570
Their number last he sums. And now his heart
Distends with pride, and, hardening in his strength,
Glories: for never, since created Man,[47]
Met such embodied force as, named with these,
Could merit more than that small infantry 575
Warred on by cranes[48]—though all the giant brood
Of Phlegra with the heroic race were joined
That fought at Thebes and Ilium, on each side
Mixed with auxiliar gods; and what resounds
In fable or romance of Uther's son[49] 580
Begirt with British and Armoric[50] knights;
And all who since, baptized or infidel,
Jousted in Aspramont, or Montalban,
Damasco, or Marocco, or Trebisond,
Or whom Biserta sent from Afric shore 585
When Charlemagne with all his peerage fell
By Fontarabbia. Thus far these beyond
Compare of mortal prowess, yet observed[51]
Their dread Commander. He, above the rest
In shape and gesture proudly eminent, 590
Stood like a tower. His form had yet not lost
All her original brightness, nor appeared
Less than Archangel ruined, and the excess
Of glory obscured: as when the sun new-risen
Looks through the horizontal misty air 595
Shorn of his beams, or from behind the moon,
In dim eclipse, disastrous twilight sheds
On half the nations, and with fear of change
Perplexes monarchs. Darkened so, yet shone
Above them all the Archangel: but his face 600
Deep scars of thunder had intrenched, and care
Sat on his faded cheek, but under brows
Of dauntless courage, and considerate[52] pride
Waiting revenge. Cruel his eye, but cast

---

[38]Depressed. [39]Regaining. [40]Bright.
[41]It was grave, or even stern, in character—suitable for soldiers.
[42]A kind of flute. [43]Immovable. [44]Assuage.

[45]Bristling. [46]Across. [47]Since man's creation.
[48]The Pygmies (*Iliad*, III, 5). [49]King Arthur.
[50]Breton. [51]Obeyed. [52]Thoughtful.

Signs of remorse and passion,[53] to behold 605
The fellows of his crime, the followers rather
(Far other once beheld in bliss), condemned
For ever now to have their lot in pain—
Millions of Spirits for his fault amerced[54] 609
Of Heaven, and from eternal splendors flung
For his revolt—yet faithful how they stood,
Their glory withered; as, when heaven's fire
Hath scathed[55] the forest oaks or mountain pines,
With singéd top their stately growth, though bare,
Stands on the blasted heath. He now prepared 615
To speak; whereat their doubled ranks they bend
From wing to wing, and half enclose him round
With all his peers: Attention held them mute.
Thrice he assayed, and thrice, in spite of scorn,
Tears, such as angels weep, burst forth: at last 620
Words interwove with sighs found out their way:—
"O myriads of immortal Spirits! O Powers
Matchless, but with the Almighty!—and that strife
Was not inglorious, though the event[56] was dire,
As this place testifies, and this dire change, 625
Hateful to utter. But what power of mind,
Foreseeing or presaging, from the depth
Of knowledge past or present, could have feared
How such united force of gods, how such 629
As stood like these, could ever know repulse?
For who can yet believe, though after loss,
That all these puissant legions, whose exile
Hath emptied Heaven, shall fail to re-ascend,
Self-raised, and re-possess their native seat?
For me, be witness all the host of Heaven, 635
If counsels different, or danger shunned
By me, have lost our hopes. But he who reigns
Monarch in Heaven till then as one secure
Sat on his throne, upheld by old repute,
Consent or custom, and his regal state 640
Put forth at full, but still his strength concealed—
Which tempted our attempt, and wrought our fall.

[53]Pity and strong emotion. [54]Punished by loss.
[55]Injured. [56]Result.

Henceforth his might we know, and know our own,
So as not either to provoke, or dread 644
New war provoked: our better part remains
To work in close design, by fraud or guile,
What force effected not; that he no less
At length from us may find, who overcomes
By force hath overcome but half his foe.
Space may produce new Worlds; whereof so rife 650
There went a fame in Heaven that he ere long
Intended to create, and therein plant
A generation whom his choice regard
Should favor equal to the Sons of Heaven.
Thither, if but to pry, shall be perhaps 655
Our first eruption—thither, or elsewhere;
For this infernal pit shall never hold
Celestial Spirits in bondage, nor the Abyss
Long under darkness cover. But these thoughts
Full counsel must mature. Peace is despaired; 660
For who can think submission? War, then, war
Open or understood,[57] must be resolved."
He spake; and, to confirm his words, outflew
Millions of flaming swords, drawn from the thighs
Of mighty Cherubim; the sudden blaze 665
Far round illumined Hell. Highly they raged
Against the Highest, and fierce with graspéd arms
Clashed on their sounding shields the din of war, 668
Hurling defiance toward the vault of Heaven.
There stood a hill not far, whose grisly top
Belched fire and rolling smoke; the rest entire
Shone with a glossy scurf—undoubted sign
That in his womb was hid metallic ore,
The work of sulphur.[58] Thither, winged with speed, 674
A numerous brigad hastened: as when bands
Of pioneers, with spade and pickax armed,
Forerun the royal camp, to trench a field,
Or cast a rampart. Mammon led them on—
Mammon, the least erected Spirit that fell
From Heaven; for even in Heaven his looks and thoughts 680
Were always downward bent, admiring more
The riches of Heaven's pavement, trodden gold,
Than aught divine or holy else enjoyed

[57]Not openly declared.
[58]Sulphur was formerly believed to be the formative element of metals.

In vision beatific. By him first
Men also, and by his suggestion taught, 685
Ransacked the center,[59] and with impious hands
Rifled the bowels of their mother earth
For treasures better hid. Soon had his crew
Opened into the hill a spacious wound,
And digged out ribs[60] of gold. Let none admire[61] 690
That riches grow in Hell; that soil may best
Deserve the precious bane. And here let those
Who boast in mortal things, and wondering tell
Of Babel, and the works of Memphian kings,[62]
Learn how their greatest monuments of fame
And strength, and art, are easily outdone 696
By Spirits reprobate, and in an hour
What in an age they, with incessant toil
And hands innumerable, scarce perform.
Nigh on the plain, in many cells prepared, 700
That underneath had veins of liquid fire
Sluiced from the lake, a second multitude
With wondrous art founded[63] the massy ore,
Severing each kind, and scummed the bullion-dross. 704
A third as soon had formed within the ground
A various mold, and from the boiling cells
By strange conveyance filled each hollow nook;
As in an organ, from one blast of wind,
To many a row of pipes the sound-board breathes.
Anon out of the earth a fabric huge 710
Rose like an exhalation, with the sound
Of dulcet symphonies and voices sweet—
Built like a temple, where pilasters round
Were set, and Doric pillars overlaid[64] 714
With golden architrave; nor did there want
Cornice or frieze, with bossy[65] sculptures graven;
The roof was fretted[66] gold. Not Babylon
Nor great Alcairo such magnificence
Equaled in all their glories, to enshrine
Belus or Serapis their gods, or seat 720
Their kings, when Egypt with Assyria strove
In wealth and luxury. The ascending pile
Stood fixed her stately highth; and straight the doors,
Opening their brazen folds, discover, wide
Within, her ample spaces o'er the smooth 725
And level pavement: from the archéd roof,
Pendent by subtle magic, many a row
Of starry lamps and blazing cressets, fed
With naphtha and asphaltus, yielded light
As from a sky. The hasty multitude 730
Admiring entered; and the work some praise,
And some the architect. His hand was known
In Heaven by many a towered structure high,
Where sceptered Angels held their residence,
And sat as Princes, whom the supreme King
Exalted to such power, and gave to rule, 736
Each in his hierarchy, the Orders bright.
Nor was his name unheard or unadored
In ancient Greece; and in Ausonian land[67]
Men called him Mulciber; and how he fell 740
From Heaven they fabled, thrown by angry Jove
Sheer o'er the crystal battlements: from morn
To noon he fell, from noon to dewy eve,
A summer's day, and with the setting sun
Dropped from the zenith, like a falling star,
On Lemnos, the Aegæan isle. Thus they relate, 746
Erring; for he with this rebellious rout
Fell long before; nor aught availed him now
To have built in Heaven high towers; nor did he scape
By all his engines,[68] but was headlong sent, 750
With his industrious crew, to build in Hell.
Meanwhile the wingéd heralds, by command
Of sovran power, with awful ceremony
And trumpet's sound, throughout the host proclaim
A solemn council forthwith to be held 755
At Pandemonium,[69] the high capital
Of Satan and his peers. Their summons called
From every band and squaréd regiment
By place or choice the worthiest: they anon
With hundreds and with thousands trooping came 760
Attended. All access was thronged; the gates
And porches wide, but chief the spacious hall
(Though like a covered field, where champions bold
Wont ride in armed, and at the soldan's[70] chair
Defied the best of paynim[71] chivalry 765
To mortal combat, or career with lance),
Thick swarmed, both on the ground and in the air,

[59]The earth. [60]Bars. [61]Wonder.
[62]The pyramids. [63]Melted. [64]Surmounted.
[65]Projecting.
[66]Checkered; or adorned with embossed designs.

[67]Italy. [68]Contrivances.
[69]Abode of all demons. [70]Sultan's. [71]Pagan.

Brushed with the hiss of rustling wings. As bees
In spring-time, when the Sun with Taurus[72] rides,
Pour forth their populous youth about the hive 770
In clusters; they among fresh dews and flowers
Fly to and fro, or on the smoothéd plank,
The suburb of their straw-built citadel,
New rubbed with balm, expatiate,[73] and confer[74]
Their state-affairs: so thick the aery crowd
Swarmed and were straitened; till, the signal given, 776
Behold a wonder! They but now who seemed
In bigness to surpass earth's giant sons,
Now less than smallest dwarfs, in narrow room
Throng numberless—like that pygmean race
Beyond the Indian mount; or faery elves, 781
Whose midnight revels, by a forest-side
Or fountain, some belated peasant sees,
Or dreams he sees, while overhead the Moon
Sits arbitress,[75] and nearer to the earth 785
Wheels her pale course: they, on their mirth and dance
Intent, with jocund music charm his ear;
At once with joy and fear his heart rebounds.
Thus incorporeal Spirits to smallest forms
Reduced their shapes immense, and were at large, 790
Though without number still, amidst the hall
Of that infernal court. But far within,
And in their own dimensions like themselves,
The great Seraphic Lords and Cherubim
In close recess[76] and secret conclave sat, 795
A thousand demi-gods on golden seats,
Frequent[77] and full. After short silence then,
And summons read, the great consult[78] began.

BOOK II

THE ARGUMENT

THE consultation begun, Satan debates whether another battle be to be hazarded for the recovery of Heaven: some advise it, others dissuade. A third proposal is preferred, mentioned before by Satan—to search the truth of that prophecy or tradition in Heaven concerning another world, and another kind of creature, equal, or not much inferior, to themselves, about this time to be created. Their doubt who shall be sent on this difficult search: Satan, their chief, undertakes alone the voyage; is honored and applauded. The council thus ended, the rest betake them several ways and to several employments, as their inclinations lead them, to entertain the time till Satan return. He passes on his journey to Hell-gates; finds them shut, and who sat there to guard them; by whom at length they are opened, and discover to him the great gulf between Hell and Heaven. With what difficulty he passes through, directed by Chaos, the Power of that place, to the sight of this new World which he sought.

High on a throne of royal state, which far
Outshone the wealth of Ormus[1] and of Ind,
Or where the gorgeous East with richest hand
Showers on her kings barbaric pearl and gold,
Satan exalted sat, by merit raised 5
To that bad eminence; and, from despair
Thus high uplifted beyond hope, aspires
Beyond thus high, insatiate to pursue
Vain war with Heaven; and, by success[2] untaught,
His proud imaginations thus displayed:— 10
"Powers and Dominions, Deities of Heaven!—
For, since no deep within her gulf can hold
Immortal vigor, though oppressed and fallen,
I give not Heaven for lost: from this descent
Celestial Virtues rising will appear 15
More glorious and more dread than from no fall,
And trust themselves to fear no second fate!—
Me though just right, and the fixed laws of Heaven,
Did first create your leader—next, free choice,
With what besides in council or in fight 20
Hath been achieved of merit—yet this loss,
Thus far at least recovered, hath much more
Established in a safe, unenvied throne,
Yielded with full consent. The happier state
In Heaven, which follows dignity, might draw 25
Envy from each inferior; but who here
Will envy whom the highest place exposes
Foremost to stand against the Thunderer's aim
Your bulwark, and condemns to greatest share

[72]Sign of the zodiac (the time is 19 April to 20 May).
[73]Walk abroad. [74]Discuss. [75]Witness.
[76]Retirement. [77]Numerous. [78]Consultation.

[1]An island in the Persian Gulf. [2]Experience.

Of endless pain? Where there is, then, no good 30
For which to strive, no strife can grow up there
From faction: for none sure will claim in Hell
Precedence; none whose portion is so small
Of present pain that with ambitious mind
Will covet more! With this advantage, then, 35
To union, and firm faith, and firm accord,
More than can be in Heaven, we now return
To claim our just inheritance of old,
Surer to prosper than prosperity
Could have assured us; and by what best way, 40
Whether of open war or covert guile,
We now debate. Who can advise may speak."

He ceased; and next him Moloch, sceptered king,
Stood up—the strongest and the fiercest Spirit
That fought in Heaven, now fiercer by despair. 45
His trust was with the Eternal to be deemed
Equal in strength, and rather than be less
Cared not to be at all; with that care lost
Went all his fear: of God, or Hell, or worse,
He recked[3] not, and these words thereafter spake:— 50

"My sentence is for open war. Of wiles,
More unexpert,[4] I boast not: them let those
Contrive who need, or when they need; not now.
For, while they sit contriving, shall the rest—
Millions that stand in arms, and longing wait 55
The signal to ascend—sit lingering here,
Heaven's fugitives, and for their dwelling-place
Accept this dark opprobrious den of shame,
The prison of his tyranny who reigns
By our delay? No! let us rather choose, 60
Armed with Hell-flames and fury, all at once
O'er Heaven's high towers to force resistless way,
Turning our tortures into horrid arms
Against the Torturer; when, to meet the noise
Of his almighty engine, he shall hear 65
Infernal thunder, and, for lightning, see
Black fire and horror shot with equal rage
Among his Angels, and his throne itself
Mixed with Tartarean[5] sulphur and strange fire,
His own invented torments. But perhaps 70
The way seems difficult, and steep to scale
With upright wing against a higher foe!
Let such bethink them, if the sleepy drench
Of that forgetful lake benumb not still,
That in our proper[6] motion we ascend 75
Up to our native seat; descent and fall
To us is adverse. Who but felt of late,
When the fierce foe hung on our broken rear
Insulting, and pursued us through the Deep,
With what compulsion and laborious flight 80
We sunk thus low? The ascent is easy, then;
The event[7] is feared! Should we again provoke
Our stronger, some worse way his wrath may find
To our destruction, if there be in Hell
Fear to be worse destroyed! What can be worse 85
Than to dwell here, driven out from bliss, condemned
In this abhorréd deep to utter woe!
Where pain of unextinguishable fire
Must exercise[8] us without hope of end
The vassals of his anger, when the scourge 90
Inexorably, and the torturing hour,
Calls us to penance? More destroyed than thus,
We should be quite abolished, and expire.
What fear we then? what doubt we to incense
His utmost ire? which, to the highth enraged, 95
Will either quite consume us, and reduce
To nothing this essential[9]—happier far
Than miserable to have eternal being!—
Or, if our substance be indeed divine,
And cannot cease to be, we are at worst 100
On this side nothing; and by proof we feel
Our power sufficient to disturb his Heaven
And with perpetual inroads to alarm,
Though inaccessible, his fatal throne:
Which, if not victory, is yet revenge." 105

He ended frowning, and his look denounced[10]
Desperate revenge, and battle dangerous
To less than gods. On the other side up rose
Belial, in act more graceful and humane.
A fairer person lost not Heaven; he seemed 110

---

[3]Cared. [4]Inexperienced.

[5]Infernal. [6]Natural.

[7]Its result. [8]Torment.

[9]Substance (adjective for substantive, as frequently with Milton).

[10]Indicated.

For dignity composed, and high exploit.
But all was false and hollow; though his tongue
Dropped manna, and could make the worse appear
The better reason, to perplex and dash
Maturest counsels: for his thoughts were low— 115
To vice industrious, but to nobler deeds
Timorous and slothful. Yet he pleased the ear,
And with persuasive accent thus began:—
"I should be much for open war, O Peers,
As not behind in hate, if what was urged 120
Main reason to persuade immediate war
Did not dissuade me most, and seem to cast
Ominous conjecture on the whole success;
When he who most excels in fact[11] of arms,
In what he counsels and in what excels 125
Mistrustful, grounds his courage on despair
And utter dissolution, as the scope
Of all his aim, after some dire revenge.
First, what revenge? The towers of Heaven are filled
With armèd watch, that render all access 130
Impregnable: oft on the bordering Deep
Encamp their legions, or with obscure wing
Scout far and wide into the realm of Night,
Scorning surprise. Or, could we break our way
By force, and at our heels all Hell should rise 135
With blackest insurrection to confound
Heaven's purest light, yet our great Enemy,
All incorruptible, would on his throne
Sit unpolluted, and the ethereal mold,[12]
Incapable of stain, would soon expel 140
Her mischief, and purge off the baser fire,
Victorious. Thus repulsed, our final hope
Is flat despair: we must exasperate
The Almighty Victor to spend all his rage;
And that must end us; that must be our cure— 145
To be no more. Sad cure! for who would lose,
Though full of pain, this intellectual being,
Those thoughts that wander through eternity,
To perish rather, swallowed up and lost
In the wide womb of uncreated Night, 150
Devoid of sense and motion? And who knows,
Let this be good, whether our angry Foe
Can give it, or will ever? How he can
Is doubtful; that he never will is sure.
Will he, so wise, let loose at once his ire, 155

[11]Deeds. [12]Substance.

Belike[13] through impotence or unaware,
To give his enemies their wish, and end
Them in his anger whom his anger saves
To punish endless? 'Wherefore cease we, then?'
Say they who counsel war; 'we are decreed, 160
Reserved, and destined to eternal woe;
Whatever doing, what can we suffer more,
What can we suffer worse?' Is this, then, worst—
Thus sitting, thus consulting, thus in arms?
What when we fled amain, pursued and strook 165
With Heaven's afflicting thunder, and besought
The Deep to shelter us? This Hell then seemed
A refuge from those wounds. Or when we lay
Chained on the burning lake? That sure was worse.
What if the breath that kindled those grim fires, 170
Awaked, should blow them into sevenfold rage
And plunge us in the flames; or from above
Should intermitted vengeance arm again
His red right hand to plague us? What if all
Her stores were opened, and this firmament 175
Of Hell should spout her cataracts of fire,
Impendent horrors, threatening hideous fall
One day upon our heads; while we perhaps,
Designing or exhorting glorious war
Caught in a fiery tempest, shall be hurled, 180
Each on his rock transfixed, the sport and prey
Of racking whirlwinds, or for ever sunk
Under yon boiling ocean, wrapped in chains,
There to converse with everlasting groans,
Unrespited, unpitied, unreprieved, 185
Ages of hopeless end? This would be worse.
War, therefore, open or concealed, alike
My voice dissuades; for what can force or guile
With him, or who deceive his mind, whose eye
Views all things at one view? He from Heaven's highth 190
All these our motions vain sees and derides,
Not more almighty to resist our might
Than wise to frustrate all our plots and wiles.
Shall we, then, live thus vile—the race of Heaven

[13]Probably.

Thus trampled, thus expelled, to suffer here 195
Chains and these torments? Better these than worse,
By my advice; since fate inevitable
Subdues us, and omnipotent decree,
The Victor's will. To suffer, as to do,
Our strength is equal; nor the law unjust 200
That so ordains. This was at first resolved,
If we were wise, against so great a foe
Contending, and so doubtful what might fall.
I laugh when those who at the spear are bold
And venturous, if that fail them, shrink, and fear 205
What yet they know must follow—to endure
Exile, or ignominy, or bonds, or pain,
The sentence of their conqueror. This is now
Our doom; which if we can sustain and bear,
Our Supreme Foe in time may much remit 210
His anger, and perhaps, thus far removed,
Not mind us not offending, satisfied
With what is punished; whence these raging fires
Will slacken, if his breath stir not their flames.
Our purer essence then will overcome 215
Their noxious vapor; or, inured, not feel;
Or, changed at length, and to the place conformed
In temper and in nature, will receive
Familiar the fierce heat; and, void of pain,
This horror will grow mild, this darkness light; 220
Besides what hope the never-ending flight
Of future days may bring, what chance, what change
Worth waiting—since our present lot appears
For happy though but ill, for ill not worst,[14]
If we procure not to ourselves more woe." 225
Thus Belial, with words clothed in reason's garb,
Counseled ignoble ease and peaceful sloth,
Not peace; and after him thus Mammon spake:—
"Either to disenthrone the King of Heaven
We war, if war be best, or to regain 230
Our own right lost. Him to unthrone we then
May hope, when everlasting Fate shall yield
To fickle Chance, and Chaos judge the strife.
The former, vain to hope, argues as vain
The latter; for what place can be for us 235
Within Heaven's bound, unless Heaven's Lord Supreme
We overpower? Suppose he should relent,
And publish grace to all, on promise made
Of new subjection; with what eyes could we
Stand in his presence humble, and receive 240
Strict laws imposed, to celebrate his throne
With warbled hymns, and to his Godhead sing
Forced Halleluiahs, while he lordly sits
Our envied sovran, and his altar breathes
Ambrosial odors and ambrosial flowers, 245
Our servile offerings? This must be our task
In Heaven, this our delight. How wearisome
Eternity so spent in worship paid
To whom we hate! Let us not then pursue,
By force impossible, by leave obtained 250
Unacceptable, though in Heaven, our state
Of splendid vassalage; but rather seek
Our own good from ourselves, and from our own
Live to ourselves, though in this vast recess,
Free and to none accountable, preferring 255
Hard liberty before the easy yoke
Of servile pomp. Our greatness will appear
Then most conspicuous when great things of small,
Useful of hurtful, prosperous of adverse,
We can create, and in what place soe'er 260
Thrive under evil, and work ease out of pain
Through labor and endurance. This deep world
Of darkness do we dread? How oft amidst
Thick clouds and dark doth Heaven's all-ruling Sire
Choose to reside, his glory unobscured, 265
And with the majesty of darkness round
Covers his throne, from whence deep thunders roar,
Mustering their rage, and Heaven resembles Hell!
As he our darkness, cannot we his light
Imitate when we please? This desert soil 270
Wants not her hidden luster, gems and gold;
Nor want we skill or art from whence to raise
Magnificence; and what can Heaven show more?
Our torments also may, in length of time,
Become our elements, these piercing fires 275
As soft as now severe, our temper changed
Into their temper; which must needs remove
The sensible[15] of pain. All things invite

[14]Since our present lot appears ill, indeed, compared with happiness, yet not so bad as it might be.

[15]Sense.

To peaceful counsels, and the settled state
Of order, how in safety best we may 280
Compose our present evils, with regard
Of what we are and where, dismissing quite
All thoughts of war. Ye have what I advise."

He scarce had finished, when such murmur filled
The assembly as when hollow rocks retain 285
The sound of blustering winds, which all night long
Had roused the sea, now with hoarse cadence lull
Seafaring men o'erwatched,[16] whose bark by chance,
Or pinnace, anchors in a craggy bay
After the tempest. Such applause was heard 290
As Mammon ended, and his sentence pleased,
Advising peace: for such another field[17]
They dreaded worse than Hell; so much the fear
Of thunder and the sword of Michaël
Wrought still within them; and no less desire 295
To found this nether empire, which might rise,
By policy and long process of time,
In emulation opposite to Heaven.
Which when Beëlzebub perceived—than whom,
Satan except, none higher sat—with grave 300
Aspect he rose, and in his rising seemed
A pillar of state. Deep on his front engraven
Deliberation sat, and public care;
And princely counsel in his face yet shone,
Majestic, though in ruin. Sage he stood, 305
With Atlantean shoulders,[18] fit to bear
The weight of mightiest monarchies; his look
Drew audience and attention still as night
Or summer's noontide air, while thus he spake:—

"Thrones and Imperial Powers, Offspring of Heaven, 310
Ethereal Virtues! or these titles now
Must we renounce, and, changing style, be called
Princes of Hell? for so the popular vote
Inclines—here to continue, and build up here
A growing empire; doubtless! while we dream, 315
And know not that the King of Heaven hath doomed
This place our dungeon—not our safe retreat
Beyond his potent arm, to live exempt
From Heaven's high jurisdiction, in new league
Banded against his throne, but to remain 320
In strictest bondage, though thus far removed,
Under the inevitable curb, reserved
His captive multitude. For He, be sure,
In highth or depth, still first and last will reign
Sole king, and of his kingdom lose no part 325
By our revolt, but over Hell extend
His empire, and with iron scepter rule
Us here, as with his golden those in Heaven.
What sit we then projecting peace and war?
War hath determined[19] us and foiled with loss 330
Irreparable; terms of peace yet none
Vouchsafed or sought; for what peace will be given
To us enslaved, but custody severe,
And stripes and arbitrary punishment
Inflicted? and what peace can we return, 335
But, to[20] our power, hostility and hate,
Untamed reluctance, and revenge, though slow,
Yet ever plotting how the Conqueror least
May reap his conquest, and may least rejoice
In doing what we most in suffering feel? 340
Nor will occasion want, nor shall we need
With dangerous expedition to invade
Heaven, whose high walls fear no assault or siege,
Or ambush from the Deep. What if we find
Some easier enterprise? There is a place 345
(If ancient and prophetic fame[21] in Heaven
Err not)—another World, the happy seat
Of some new race, called Man, about this time
To be created like to us, though less
In power and excellence, but favored more 350
Of him who rules above; so was his will
Pronounced among the gods, and by an oath
That shook Heaven's whole circumference confirmed.
Thither let us bend all our thoughts, to learn
What creatures there inhabit, of what mold
Or substance, how endued, and what their power. 356
And where their weakness: how attempted best
By force or subtlety. Though Heaven be shut,

[16]Wearied with watching. [17]Battle.
[18]Shoulders like those of Atlas, who supported the columns on which the heavens rest.

[19]Undone. [20]To the limit of. [21]Report.

And Heaven's high Arbitrator sit secure
In his own strength, this place may lie exposed, 360
The utmost border of his kingdom, left
To their defense who hold it: here, perhaps,
Some advantageous act may be achieved
By sudden onset—either with Hell-fire
To waste his whole creation, or possess 365
All as our own, and drive, as we are driven,
The puny habitants; or, if not drive,
Seduce them to our party, that their God
May prove their foe, and with repenting hand
Abolish his own works. This would surpass 370
Common revenge, and interrupt his joy
In our confusion, and our joy upraise
In his disturbance; when his darling sons,
Hurled headlong to partake with us, shall curse
Their frail original, and faded bliss— 375
Faded so soon! Advise[22] if this be worth
Attempting, or to sit in darkness here
Hatching vain empires." Thus Beëlzebub
Pleaded his devilish counsel—first devised 379
By Satan, and in part proposed: for whence,
But from the author of all ill, could spring
So deep a malice, to confound the race
Of mankind in one root, and Earth with Hell
To mingle and involve, done all to spite
The great Creator? But their spite still serves 385
His glory to augment. The bold design
Pleased highly those Infernal States,[23] and joy
Sparkled in all their eyes: with full assent
They vote: whereat his speech he thus renews:—
"Well have ye judged, well ended long debate, 390
Synod of Gods, and, like to what ye are,
Great things resolved, which from the lowest deep
Will once more lift us up, in spite of fate,
Nearer our ancient seat—perhaps in view
Of those bright confines, whence, with neighboring arms, 395
And opportune excursion, we may chance
Re-enter Heaven; or else in some mild zone
Dwell, not unvisited of Heaven's fair light,
Secure, and at the brightening orient beam
Purge off this gloom: the soft delicious air, 400
To heal the scar of these corrosive fires,

[22]Consider. [23]Councilors.

Shall breathe her balm. But, first, whom shall we send
In search of this new World? whom shall we find
Sufficient? who shall tempt[24] with wandering feet
The dark, unbottomed, infinite Abyss, 405
And through the palpable obscure[25] find out
His uncouth[26] way, or spread his aery flight,
Upborne with indefatigable wings
Over the vast Abrupt,[27] ere he arrive
The happy Isle? What strength, what art, can then 410
Suffice, or what evasion bear him safe,
Through the strict senteries and stations thick
Of angels watching round? Here he had need
All circumspection: and we now no less
Choice[28] in our suffrage; for on whom we send 415
The weight of all, and our last hope, relies."
This said, he sat; and expectation held
His look suspense,[29] awaiting who appeared
To second, or oppose, or undertake
The perilous attempt. But all sat mute, 420
Pondering the danger with deep thoughts; and each
In other's countenance read his own dismay,
Astonished. None among the choice and prime
Of those Heaven-warring champions could be found
So hardy as to proffer or accept, 425
Alone, the dreadful voyage; till, at last,
Satan, whom now transcendent glory raised
Above his fellows, with monarchal pride
Conscious of highest worth, unmoved thus spake:—
"O Progeny of Heaven! Empyreal Thrones! 430
With reason hath deep silence and demur[30]
Seized us, though undismayed. Long is the way
And hard, that out of Hell leads up to Light.
Our prison strong, this huge convex of fire,
Outrageous to devour, immures us round 435
Ninefold; and gates of burning adamant,
Barred over us, prohibit all egress.
These passed, if any pass, the void profound
Of unessential[31] Night receives him next,
Wide-gaping, and with utter loss of being 440

[24]Try. [25]Obscurity. [26]Unknown.
[27]The region of chaos. [28]Care.
[29]In suspense [30]Hesitancy. [31]Void of being.

Threatens him, plunged in that abortive[32] gulf.
If thence he scape, into whatever world,
Or unknown region, what remains[33] him less
Than unknown dangers, and as hard escape?
But I should ill become this throne, O Peers, 445
And this imperial sovranty, adorned
With splendor, armed with power, if aught proposed
And judged of public moment in the shape
Of difficulty or danger, could deter
Me from attempting. Wherefore do I assume 450
These royalties, and not refuse to reign,
Refusing to accept as great a share
Of hazard as of honor, due alike
To him who reigns, and so much to him due
Of hazard more as he above the rest 455
High honored sits? Go, therefore, mighty Powers,
Terror of Heaven, though fallen: intend[34] at home,
While here shall be our home, what best may ease
The present misery, and render Hell
More tolerable; if there be cure or charm 460
To respite, or deceive,[35] or slack the pain
Of this ill mansion: intermit no watch
Against a wakeful foe, while I abroad
Through all the coasts of dark destruction seek
Deliverance for us all. This enterprise 465
None shall partake with me." Thus saying, rose
The Monarch, and prevented all reply;
Prudent lest, from his resolution raised,[36]
Others among the chief might offer now,
Certain to be refused, what erst they feared,
And, so refused, might in opinion stand 471
His rivals, winning cheap the high repute
Which he through hazard huge must earn. But they
Dreaded not more the adventure than his voice
Forbidding; and at once with him they rose. 475
Their rising all at once was as the sound
Of thunder heard remote. Towards him they bend
With awful reverence prone, and as a God
Extol him equal to the Highest in Heaven.

[32]Dangerous. [33]Awaits.
[34]Consider. [35]Divert us from.
[36]Lest, encouraged by his bravery.

Nor failed they to express how much they praised 480
That for the general safety he despised
His own: for neither do the Spirits damned
Lose all their virtue; lest bad men should boast
Their specious deeds on earth, which glory excites,
Or close[37] ambition varnished o'er with zeal. 485
Thus they their doubtful consultations dark
Ended, rejoicing in their matchless Chief:
As, when from mountain-tops the dusky clouds
Ascending, while the North-wind sleeps, o'erspread
Heaven's cheerful face, the louring element 490
Scowls o'er the darkened landscape snow or shower,
If chance the radiant sun, with farewell sweet,
Extend his evening beam, the fields revive,
The birds their notes renew, and bleating herds
Attest their joy, that hill and valley rings. 495
O shame to men! Devil with devil damned
Firm concord holds; men only disagree
Of creatures rational, though under hope
Of heavenly grace, and, God proclaiming peace,
Yet live in hatred, enmity, and strife 500
Among themselves, and levy cruel wars
Wasting the earth, each other to destroy:
As if (which might induce us to accord)
Man had not hellish foes enow[38] besides,
That day and night for his destruction wait! 505
The Stygian council thus dissolved; and forth
In order came the grand Infernal Peers:
Midst came their mighty Paramount,[39] and seemed
Alone the antagonist of Heaven, nor less
Than Hell's dread Emperor, with pomp supreme, 510
And god-like imitated state: him round
A globe of fiery Seraphim enclosed
With bright emblazonry, and horrent[40] arms.
Then of their session ended they bid cry
With trumpet's regal sound the great result: 515
Toward the four winds four speedy Cherubim

[37]Secret. [38]Enough. [39]Chief. [40]Bristling.

Put to their mouths the sounding alchemy,[41]
By herald's voice explained;[42] the hollow Abyss
Heard far and wide, and all the host of Hell
With deafening shout returned them loud acclaim. 520
Thence more at ease their minds, and somewhat raised
By false presumptuous hope, the rangéd Powers
Disband; and, wandering, each his several way
Pursues, as inclination or sad choice
Leads him perplexed, where he may likeliest find 525
Truce to his restless thoughts, and entertain
The irksome hours, till his great Chief return.
Part on the plain, or in the air sublime,
Upon the wing or in swift race contend, 529
As at the Olympian games or Pythian fields;
Part curb their fiery steeds, or shun the goal
With rapid wheels, or fronted brigads form:
As when, to warn proud cities, war appears
Waged in the troubled sky, and armies rush
To battle in the clouds; before each van 535
Prick[43] forth the aery knights, and couch their spears,
Till thickest legions close; with feats of arms
From either end of heaven the welkin[44] burns.
Others, with vast Typhoean rage, more fell,
Rend up both rocks and hills, and ride the air 540
In whirlwind; Hell scarce holds the wild uproar:—
As when Alcides,[45] from Oechalia crowned
With conquest, felt the envenomed robe, and tore
Through pain up by the roots Thessalian pines,
And Lichas from the top of Oeta threw 545
Into the Euboic sea. Others, more mild,
Retreated in a silent valley, sing
With notes angelical to many a harp
Their own heroic deeds, and hapless fall
By doom of battle, and complain that Fate 550
Free Virtue should enthrall to Force or Chance.
Their song was partial; but the harmony
(What could it less when Spirits immortal sing?)
Suspended Hell, and took with ravishment
The thronging audience. In discourse more sweet 555
(For Eloquence the Soul, Song charms the Sense)
Others apart sat on a hill retired,
In thoughts more elevate, and reasoned high
Of Providence, Foreknowledge, Will, and Fate— 559
Fixed fate, free will, foreknowledge absolute,
And found no end, in wandering mazes lost.
Of good and evil much they argued then,
Of happiness and final misery,
Passion and apathy, and glory and shame:
Vain wisdom all, and false philosophy!— 565
Yet, with a pleasing sorcery, could charm
Pain for a while or anguish, and excite
Fallacious hope, or arm the obduréd breast
With stubborn patience as with triple steel.
Another part, in squadrons and gross[46] bands, 570
On bold adventure to discover wide
That dismal world, if any clime perhaps
Might yield them easier habitation, bend
Four ways their flying march, along the banks
Of four infernal rivers, that disgorge 575
Into the burning lake their baleful streams—
Abhorréd Styx, the flood of deadly hate;
Sad Acheron of sorrow, black and deep;
Cocytus, named of lamentation loud
Heard on the rueful stream; fierce Phlegeton, 580
Whose waves of torrent fire inflame with rage.
Far off from these, a slow and silent stream,
Lethe, the river of oblivion, rolls
Her watery labyrinth, whereof who drinks
Forthwith his former state and being forgets— 585
Forgets both joy and grief, pleasure and pain.
Beyond this flood a frozen continent
Lies dark and wild, beat with perpetual storms
Of whirlwind and dire hail, which on firm land
Thaws not, but gathers heap, and ruin seems 590
Of ancient pile; all else deep snow and ice,
A gulf profound as that Serbonian bog
Betwixt Damiata and Mount Casius old,[47]
Where armies whole have sunk: the parching air

---

[41]Trumpets.
[42]I. e., the herald states the meaning of the trumpet blasts.
[43]Ride. [44]Sky.
[45]Hercules. The robe is the poisoned shirt which his wife obtained from the centaur Nessus and sent to him by his servant Lichas.
[46]Large. [47]I. e., in Egypt.

Burns frore,[48] and cold performs the effect
of fire. 595
Thither, by harpy-footed Furies haled,
At certain revolutions all the damned
Are brought; and feel by turns the bitter
change
Of fierce extremes, extremes by change more
fierce,
From beds of raging fire to starve in ice 600
Their soft ethereal warmth, and there to pine
Immovable, infixed, and frozen round
Periods of time—thence hurried back to fire.
They ferry over this Lethean sound
Both to and fro, their sorrow to augment, 605
And wish and struggle, as they pass, to reach
The tempting stream, with one small drop to
lose
In sweet forgetfulness all pain and woe,
All in one moment, and so near the brink;
But Fate withstands, and, to oppose the at-
tempt, 610
Medusa with Gorgonian terror guards
The ford, and of itself the water flies
All taste of living wight,[49] as once it fled
The lip of Tantalus. Thus roving on
In confused march forlorn, the adventurous
bands, 615
With shuddering horror pale, and eyes aghast,
Viewed first[50] their lamentable lot, and found
No rest. Through many a dark and dreary
vale
They passed, and many a region dolorous,
O'er many a frozen, many a fiery Alp, 620
Rocks, caves, lakes, fens, bogs, dens, and
shades of death—
A universe of death, which God by curse
Created evil, for evil only good;
Where all life dies, death lives, and Nature
breeds,
Perverse, all monstrous, all prodigious
things, 625
Abominable, inutterable, and worse
Than fables yet have feigned or fear con-
ceived,
Gorgons, and Hydras, and Chimaeras dire.
Meanwhile the Adversary of God and
Man,
Satan, with thoughts inflamed of highest
design, 630
Puts on swift wings, and toward the gates of
Hell
Explores his solitary flight: sometimes
He scours the right hand coast, sometimes the
left;

[48]Frozen. [49]Living being.
[50]Viewed for the first time.

Now shaves with level wing the deep, then
soars
Up to the fiery concave towering high. 635
As when far off at sea a fleet descried
Hangs in the clouds, by equinoctial winds
Close sailing from Bengala, or the isles
Of Ternate and Tidore,[51] whence merchants
bring
Their spicy drugs; they on the trading
flood, 640
Through the wide Ethiopian to the Cape,[52]
Ply stemming nightly toward the pole:[53] so
seemed
Far off the flying Fiend. At last appear
Hell-bounds, high reaching to the horrid
roof,
And thrice threefold the gates; three folds
were brass, 645
Three iron, three of adamantine rock,
Impenetrable, impaled with circling fire,
Yet unconsumed. Before the gates there sat
On either side a formidable Shape,
The one seemed woman to the waist, and
fair, 650
But ended foul in many a scaly fold,
Voluminous and vast—a serpent armed
With mortal sting. About her middle round
A cry[54] of Hell-hounds never-ceasing barked
With wide Cerberean mouths full loud, and
rung 655
A hideous peal; yet, when they list, would
creep,
If aught disturbed their noise, into her womb,
And kennel there; yet there still barked and
howled
Within unseen. Far less abhorred[55] than
these
Vexed Scylla, bathing in the sea that parts 660
Calabria from the hoarse Trinacrian shore;[56]
Nor uglier follow the night-hag, when, called
In secret, riding through the air she comes,
Lured with the smell of infant blood, to dance
With Lapland witches,[57] while the laboring
moon 665
Eclipses at their charms. The other Shape—
If shape it might be called that shape had
none
Distinguishable in member, joint, or limb;

[51]Two of the Moluccas.
[52]Through the Indian Ocean to the Cape of Good Hope.
[53]The South Pole. [54]Pack.
[55]Less to be abhorred.
[56]The sea between Italy and Sicily.
[57]Lapland was believed to be a favorite home of witches.

Or substance might be called that shadow
seemed,
For each seemed either—black it stood as
Night, 670
Fierce as ten Furies, terrible as Hell,
And shook a dreadful dart: what seemed his
head
The likeness of a kingly crown had on.
Satan was now at hand, and from his seat
The monster moving onward came as fast 675
With horrid strides; Hell trembled as he
strode.
The undaunted Fiend what this might be
admired[58]—
Admired, not feared (God and his Son ex-
cept,
Created thing naught valued he nor
shunned),
And with disdainful look thus first be-
gan:— 680
"Whence and what art thou, execrable
Shape,
That dar'st, though grim and terrible, advance
Thy miscreated front athwart my way
To yonder gates? Through them I mean to
pass,
That be assured, without leave asked of
thee. 685
Retire; or taste thy folly, and learn by proof,
Hell-born, not to contend with Spirits of
Heaven."
To whom the Goblin,[59] full of wrath, re-
plied:—
"Art thou that Traitor-Angel, art thou he,
Who first broke peace in Heaven and faith,
till then 690
Unbroken, and in proud rebellious arms
Drew after him the third part of Heaven's
sons,
Conjured[60] against the Highest—for which
both thou
And they, outcast from God, are here con-
demned
To waste eternal days in woe and pain? 695
And reckon'st thou thyself with Spirits of
Heaven,
Hell-doomed, and breath'st defiance here and
scorn,
Where I reign king, and, to enrage thee more,
Thy kind and lord? Back to thy punishment,
False fugitive; and to thy speed add
wings, 700
Lest with a whip of scorpions I pursue
Thy lingering, or with one stroke of this dart
Strange horror seize thee, and pangs unfelt
before."
So spake the grisly Terror, and in shape,
So speaking and so threatening, grew ten-
fold 705
More dreadful and deform. On the other
side,
Incensed with indignation, Satan stood
Unterrified, and like a comet burned,
That fires the length of Ophiuchus[61] huge
In the arctic sky, and from his horrid hair 710
Shakes pestilence and war. Each at the head
Leveled his deadly aim; their fatal hands
No second stroke intend; and such a frown
Each cast at the other as when two black
clouds,
With heaven's artillery fraught, come rattling
on 715
Over the Caspian—then stand front to front
Hovering a space, till winds the signal blow
To join their dark encounter in mid-air.
So frowned the mighty combatants that Hell
Grew darker at their frown; so matched they
stood; 720
For never but once more was either like
To meet so great a foe.[62] And now great
deeds
Had been achieved, whereof all Hell had
rung,
Had not the snaky Sorceress, that sat
Fast by Hell-gate and kept the fatal key, 725
Risen, and with hideous outcry rushed be-
tween.
"O father, what intends thy hand," she
cried,
"Against thy only son? What fury, O son,
Possesses thee to bend that mortal dart
Against thy father's head? And know'st for
whom;[63] 730
For him who sits above, and laughs the while
At thee, ordained his drudge to execute
Whate'er his wrath, which he calls justice,
bids—
His wrath, which one day will destroy ye
both!"
She spake, and at her words the hellish
Pest 735
Forbore: then these to her Satan returned:—
"So strange thy outcry, and thy words so
strange
Thou interposest, that my sudden hand,
Prevented, spares to tell thee yet by deeds
What it intends, till first I know of thee 740

[58]Wondered. [59]I. e., demon, or fiend.
[60]Banded by oath.

[61]A large constellation.
[62]Christ (cf. I Corinthians, 25:26, and Hebrews, 2:14).
[63]I. e., and though thou knowest for whom.

What thing thou art, thus double-formed, and why,
In this infernal vale first met, thou call'st
Me father, and that phantasm call'st my son.
I know thee not, nor ever saw till now
Sight more detestable than him and thee." 745
To whom thus the Portress of Hell-gate replied:—
"Hast thou forgot me, then; and do I seem
Now in thine eye so foul?—once deemed so fair
In Heaven, when at the assembly, and in sight
Of all the Seraphim with thee combined 750
In bold conspiracy against Heaven's King,
All on a sudden miserable pain
Surprised thee, dim thine eyes and dizzy swum
In darkness, while thy head flames thick and fast
Threw forth, till on the left side opening wide, 755
Likest to thee in shape and countenance bright,
Then shining heavenly fair, a goddess armed,
Out of thy head I sprung. Amazement seized
All the host of Heaven; back they recoiled afraid
At first, and called me *Sin,* and for a sign 760
Portentous held me; but, familiar grown,
I pleased, and with attractive graces won
The most averse—thee chiefly, who, full oft
Thyself in me thy perfect image viewing,
Becam'st enamored; and such joy thou took'st 765
With me in secret that my womb conceived
A growing burden. Meanwhile war arose,
And fields were fought in Heaven: wherein remained
(For what could else?) to our Almighty Foe
Clear victory; to our part loss and rout 770
Through all the Empyrean. Down they fell,
Driven headlong from the pitch of Heaven, down
Into this Deep; and in the general fall
I also: at which time this powerful key
Into my hands was given, with charge to keep 775
These gates for ever shut, which none can pass
Without my opening. Pensive here I sat
Alone; but long I sat not, till my womb,
Pregnant by thee, and now excessive grown,
Prodigious motion felt and rueful throes. 780
At last this odious offspring whom thou seest,
Thine own begotten, breaking violent way,
Tore through my entrails, that, with fear and pain
Distorted, all my nether shape thus grew
Transformed: but he my inbred enemy 785
Forth issued, brandishing his fatal dart,
Made to destroy. I fled, and cried out *Death!*
Hell trembled at the hideous name, and sighed
From all her caves, and back resounded *Death!*
I fled; but he pursued (though more, it seems, 790
Inflamed with lust than rage), and, swifter far,
Me overtook, his mother, all dismayed,
And, in embraces forcible and foul
Engendering with me, of that rape begot
These yelling monsters, that with ceaseless cry 795
Surround me, as thou saw'st—hourly conceived
And hourly born, with sorrow infinite
To me; for, when they list, into the womb
That bred them they return, and howl, and gnaw 799
My bowels, their repast; then, bursting forth
Afresh, with conscious terrors vex me round,
That rest or intermission none I find.
Before mine eyes in opposition sits
Grim Death, my son and foe, who sets them on,
And me, his parent, would full soon devour 805
For want of other prey, but that he knows
His end with mine involved, and knows that I
Should prove a bitter morsel, and his bane,
Whenever that shall be: so Fate pronounced.
But thou, O father, I forewarn thee, shun 810
His deadly arrow; neither vainly hope
To be invulnerable in those bright arms,
Though tempered heavenly; for that mortal dint,[64]
Save he who reigns above, none can resist."
She finished; and the subtle Fiend his lore 815
Soon learned, now milder, and thus answered smooth:—
"Dear daughter—since thou claim'st me for thy sire,
And my fair son here show'st me, the dear pledge
Of dalliance had with thee in Heaven, and joys
Then sweet, now sad to mention, through dire change 820

---

[64]Blow.

Befallen us unforeseen, unthought-of—know,
I come no enemy, but to set free
From out this dark and dismal house of pain
Both him and thee, and all the Heavenly host
Of Spirits that, in our just pretenses[65] armed, 825
Fell with us from on high. From them I go
This uncouth[66] errand sole, and one for all
Myself expose, with lonely steps to tread
The unfounded[67] Deep, and through the void immense
To search, with wandering quest, a place foretold 830
Should be—and, by concurring signs, ere now
Created vast and round—a place of bliss
In the purlieus[68] of Heaven; and therein placed
A race of upstart creatures, to supply
Perhaps our vacant room, though more removed, 835
Lest Heaven, surcharged with potent multitude,
Might hap to move new broils. Be this, or aught
Than this more secret, now designed, I haste
To know; and, this once known, shall soon return,
And bring ye to the place where thou and Death 840
Shall dwell at ease, and up and down unseen
Wing silently the buxom[69] air, embalmed
With odors. There ye shall be fed and filled
Immeasurably; all things shall be your prey."
He ceased; for both seemed highly pleased, and Death 845
Grinned horrible a ghastly smile, to hear
His famine should be filled, and blessed his maw
Destined to that good hour. No less rejoiced
His mother bad, and thus bespake her sire:—
"The key of this infernal Pit, by due 850
And by command of Heaven's all-powerful king,
I keep, by him forbidden to unlock
These adamantine gates; against all force
Death ready stands to interpose his dart,
Fearless to be o'ermatched by living might. 855
But what owe I to his commands above,
Who hates me, and hath hither thrust me down
Into this gloom of Tartarus profound,
To sit in hateful office here confined,
Inhabitant of Heaven and heavenly born 860
Here in perpetual agony and pain,
With terrors and with clamors compassed round
Of mine own brood, that on my bowels feed?
Thou art my father, thou my author, thou
My being gav'st me; whom should I obey 865
But thee? whom follow? Thou wilt bring me soon
To that new world of light and bliss, among
The gods who live at ease, where I shall reign
At thy right hand voluptuous, as beseems
Thy daughter and thy darling, without end." 870
Thus saying, from her side the fatal key,
Sad instrument of all our woe, she took;
And, towards the gate rolling her bestial train,
Forthwith the huge portcullis[70] high up-drew,
Which, but herself, not all the Stygian Powers 875
Could once have moved; then in the key-hole turns
The intricate wards,[71] and every bolt and bar
Of massy iron or solid rock with ease
Unfastens. On a sudden open fly,
With impetuous recoil and jarring sound, 880
The infernal doors, and on their hinges grate
Harsh thunder, that the lowest bottom shook
Of Erebus. She opened; but to shut
Excelled her power: the gates wide open stood,
That with extended wings a bannered host, 885
Under spread ensigns marching, might pass through
With horse and chariots ranked in loose array;
So wide they stood, and like a furnace-mouth
Cast forth redounding[72] smoke and ruddy flame.
Before their eyes in sudden view appear 890
The secrets of the hoary Deep—a dark
Illimitable ocean, without bound,
Without dimension; where length, breadth, and highth,
And time, and place, are lost; where eldest Night
And Chaos, ancestors of Nature, hold 895
Eternal anarchy, amidst the noise
Of endless wars, and by confusion stand.

---

[65]Claims. [66]Unknown, strange.
[67]Without foundation. [68]Suburbs. [69]Yielding.

[70]Heavy grating sliding up and down in grooves placed at sides of gateway.
[71]Notches and projections in key and lock.
[72]Rolling in billows.

For Hot, Cold, Moist, and Dry,[73] four champions fierce,
Strive here for mastery, and to battle bring
Their embryon atoms: they around the flag 900
Of each his faction, in their several clans,
Light-armed or heavy, sharp, smooth, swift, or slow,
Swarm populous, unnumbered as the sands
Of Barca or Cyrene's[74] torrid soil,
Levied to side with warring winds, and poise 905
Their lighter wings. To whom these most adhere
He rules a moment: Chaos umpire sits,
And by decision more embroils the fray
By which he reigns: next him, high arbiter,
Chance governs all. Into this wild Abyss, 910
The womb of Nature, and perhaps her grave,
Of neither Sea, nor Shore, nor Air, nor Fire,[75]
But all these in their pregnant causes mixed
Confusedly, and which thus must ever fight,
Unless the Almighty Maker them ordain 915
His dark materials to create more worlds—
Into this wild Abyss the wary Fiend
Stood on the brink of Hell and looked a while,
Pondering his voyage; for no narrow frith[76]
He had to cross. Nor was his ear less pealed 920
With noises loud and ruinous (to compare
Great things with small) than when Bellona[77] storms
With all her battering engines, bent to raze
Some capital city; or less than if this frame
Of Heaven were falling, and these elements 925
In mutiny had from her axle torn
The steadfast Earth. At last his sail-broad vans[78]
He spread for flight, and, in the surging smoke
Uplifted, spurns the ground; thence many a league,
As in a cloudy chair, ascending rides 930
Audacious; but, that seat soon failing, meets
A vast vacuity. All unawares,
Fluttering his pennons vain, plumb-down he drops
Ten thousand fathom deep, and to this hour
Down had been falling, had not, by ill chance, 935
The strong rebuff of some tumultuous cloud,
Instinct with fire and niter, hurried him
As many miles aloft. That fury stayed—
Quenched in a boggy Syrtis,[79] neither sea,
Nor good dry land—nigh foundered, on he fares, 940
Treading the crude consistence, half on foot,
Half flying; behoves him now both oar and sail.
As when a gryphon through the wilderness
With wingéd course, o'er hill or moory dale,
Pursues the Arimaspian,[80] who by stealth 945
Had from his wakeful custody purloined
The guarded gold; so eagerly the Fiend
O'er bog or steep, through strait, rough, dense, or rare,
With head, hands, wings, or feet, pursues his way,
And swims, or sinks, or wades, or creeps, or flies. 950
At length a universal hubbub wild
Of stunning sounds, and voices all confused,
Borne through the hollow dark, assaults his ear
With loudest vehemence. Thither he plies
Undaunted, to meet there whatever Power 955
Or Spirit of the nethermost Abyss
Might in that noise reside, of whom to ask
Which way the nearest coast of darkness lies
Bordering on light; when straight behold the throne
Of *Chaos,* and his dark pavilion spread 960
Wide on the wasteful Deep! With him enthroned
Sat sable-vested *Night,* eldest of things,
The consort of his reign; and by them stood
Orcus and Ades, and the dreaded name 964
Of Demogorgon; Rumor next, and Chance,
And Tumult, and Confusion, all embroiled,
And Discord with a thousand various mouths.
To whom Satan, turning boldly, thus:—"Ye Powers
And Spirits of this nethermost Abyss,
Chaos and ancient Night, I come no spy 970
With purpose to explore or to disturb
The secrets of your realm; but, by constraint
Wandering this darksome desert, as my way
Lies through your spacious empire up to light,
Alone and without guide, half lost, I seek, 975

[73]The four humors of medieval medicine.
[74]Cities of northern Africa.
[75]The four elements of the older physical science.
[76]Arm of the sea. [77]Goddess of war. [78]Wings.

[79]The Syrtes were two quicksands off the north coast of Africa.

[80]The Arimaspians were a one-eyed people of Scythia who, according to ancient writers, were continually fighting the griffins for the sake of the gold guarded by the latter.

What readiest path leads where your gloomy bounds
Confine with Heaven; or, if some other place,
From your dominion won, the Ethereal King
Possesses lately, thither to arrive
I travel this profound. Direct my course: 980
Directed, no mean recompense it brings
To your behoof,[81] if I that region lost,
All usurpation thence expelled, reduce
To her original darkness and your sway
(Which is my present journey[82]), and once more 985
Erect the standard there of ancient Night.
Yours be the advantage all, mine the revenge!"
Thus Satan; and him thus the Anarch old,
With faltering speech and visage incomposed,
Answered:—"I know thee, stranger, who thou art— 990
That mighty leading Angel, who of late
Made head against Heaven's King, though overthrown.
I saw and heard; for such a numerous host
Fled not in silence through the frighted Deep,
With ruin upon ruin, rout on rout, 995
Confusion worse confounded; and Heaven-gates
Poured out by millions her victorious bands.
Pursuing. I upon my frontiers here
Keep residence; if all I can will serve
That little which is left so to defend, 1000
Encroached on still through our intestine broils
Weakening the scepter of old Night: first, Hell,
Your dungeon, stretching far and wide beneath,
Now lately Heaven and Earth, another world
Hung o'er my realm, linked in a golden chain
To that side Heaven from whence your legions fell! 1006
If that way be your walk, you have not far;
So much the nearer danger. Go, and speed;
Havoc, and spoil, and ruin, are my gain."
He ceased; and Satan stayed not to reply,
But, glad that now his sea should find a shore,
With fresh alacrity and force renewed 1012
Springs upward, like a pyramid of fire,
Into the wild expanse, and through the shock
Of fighting elements, on all sides round
Environed, wins his way; harder beset 1016

[81]Advantage. [82]Work.

And more endangered than when Argo[83] passed
Through Bosporus betwixt the justling rocks,[84]
Or when Ulysses on the larboard shunned
Charybdis, and by the other whirlpool steered. 1020
So he with difficulty and labor hard
Moved on. With difficulty and labor he;
But, he once passed, soon after, when Man fell,
Strange alteration! Sin and Death amain,[85]
Following his track (such was the will of Heaven) 1025
Paved after him a broad and beaten way
Over the dark Abyss, whose boiling gulf
Tamely endured a bridge of wondrous length,
From Hell continued, reaching the utmost Orb[86]
Of this frail World; by which the Spirits perverse 1030
With easy intercourse pass to and fro
To tempt or punish mortals, except whom
God and good Angels guard by special grace.
But now at last the sacred influence
Of light appears, and from the walls of Heaven 1035
Shoots far into the bosom of dim Night
A glimmering dawn. Here Nature first begins
Her farthest verge, and Chaos to retire,
As from her outmost works, a broken foe,
With tumult less and with less hostile din; 1040
That[87] Satan with less toil, and now with ease,
Wafts on the calmer wave by dubious light,
And, like a weather-beaten vessel, holds[88]
Gladly the port, though shrouds and tackle torn;
Or in the emptier waste, resembling air, 1045
Weighs his spread wings, at leisure to behold
Far off the empyreal Heaven, extended wide
In circuit, undetermined square or round,
With opal towers and battlements adorned
Of living sapphire, once his native seat, 1050
And, fast by, hanging in a golden chain,
This pendent World, in bigness as a star

[83]The boat in which Jason went to Colchis for the golden fleece.

[84]The Symplegades, at the entrance of the Black Sea.

[85]In great haste.

[86]The outermost of the concentric spheres surrounding the earth.

[87]So that. [88]Makes for.

Of smallest magnitude close by the moon.
Thither, full fraught with mischievous revenge,
Accursed, and in a curséd hour, he hies. 1055

BOOK III

THE ARGUMENT

GOD, sitting on his throne, sees Satan flying towards this World, then newly created; shows him to the Son, who sat at his right hand; foretells the success of Satan in perverting mankind; clears his own justice and wisdom from all imputation, having created Man free, and able enough to have withstood his Tempter; yet declares his purpose of grace towards him, in regard he fell not of his own malice, as did Satan, but by him seduced. The Son of God renders praises to his Father for the manifestation of his gracious purpose towards Man: but God again declares that grace cannot be extended towards Man without the satisfaction of divine justice; Man hath offended the majesty of God by aspiring to Godhead, and therefore, with all his progeny, devoted to death, must die, unless some one can be found sufficient to answer for his offence, and undergo his punishment. The Son of God freely offers himself a ransom for Man: the Father accepts him, ordains his incarnation, pronounces his exaltation above all Names in Heaven and Earth; commands all the Angels to adore him. They obey, and, hymning to their harps in full choir, celebrate the Father and the Son. Meanwhile Satan alights upon the bare convex of this World's outermost orb; where wandering he finds a place since called the Limbo of Vanity; what persons and things fly up thither: thence comes to the gate of Heaven, described ascending by stairs, and the waters above the firmament that flow about it. His passage thence to the orb of the Sun: he finds there Uriel, the regent of that orb, but first changes himself into the shape of a meaner Angel, and, pretending a zealous desire to behold the new Creation, and Man whom God had placed here, inquires of him the place of his habitation, and is directed: alights first on Mount Niphates.

BOOK IV

THE ARGUMENT

SATAN, now in prospect of Eden, and nigh the place where he must now attempt the bold enterprise which he undertook alone against God and Man, falls into many doubts with himself, and many passions—fear, envy, and despair; but at length confirms himself in evil; journeys on to Paradise, whose outward prospect and situation is described; overleaps the bounds; sits, in the shape of a cormorant, on the Tree of Life, as highest in the Garden, to look about him. The Garden described; Satan's first sight of Adam and Eve; his wonder at their excellent form and happy state, but with resolution to work their fall; overhears their discourse; thence gathers that the Tree of Knowledge was forbidden them to eat of under penalty of death, and thereon intends to found his temptation by seducing them to transgress; then leaves them a while, to know further of their state by some other means. Meanwhile Uriel, descending on a sunbeam, warns Gabriel, who had in charge the gate of Paradise, that some evil Spirit has escaped the Deep, and passed at noon by his Sphere, in the shape of a good Angel, down to Paradise, discovered after by his furious gestures in the mount. Gabriel promises to find him ere morning. Night coming on, Adam and Eve discourse of going to their rest; their bower described; the evening worship. Gabriel, drawing forth his bands of night-watch to walk the rounds of Paradise, appoints two strong Angels to Adam's bower, lest the evil Spirit should be there doing some harm to Adam or Eve sleeping; there they find him at the ear of Eve, tempting her in a dream, and bring him, though unwilling, to Gabriel; by whom questioned, he scornfully answers; prepares resistance; but, hindered by a sign from Heaven, flies out of Paradise.

BOOK V

THE ARGUMENT

MORNING approached, Eve relates to Adam her troublesome dream; he likes it not, yet comforts her. They come forth to their day labors: their Morning Hymn at the door of their Bower. God, to render Man inexcusable, sends Raphael to admonish him of his obedience, of his free estate, of his enemy near at hand;—who he is, and why his enemy, and whatever else may avail Adam to know. Raphael comes down to Paradise; his appearance described, his coming discerned by Adam afar off, sitting at the door of his Bower; he goes out to meet him, brings him to his lodge, entertains him with the choicest fruits of Paradise, got together by Eve; their discourse at table: Raphael performs his message, minds Adam of his state and of his enemy; relates at Adam's request who that enemy is, and how he came to be so, beginning from his first revolt in Heaven, and the occasion thereof; how he drew his Legions after him to the parts of the North, and there incited them to rebel with him, persuading all but only Abdiel, a Seraph, who in argument dissuades and opposes him, then forsakes him.

BOOK VI

THE ARGUMENT

RAPHAEL continues to relate how Michael and Gabriel were sent forth to battle against Satan and his Angels. The first fight described: Satan and his Powers retire under Night; he calls a council, invents devilish engines, which in the second day's fight put Michael and his Angels to some disorder; but they, at length pulling up mountains, overwhelmed both the force and machines of Satan. Yet the tumult not so ending, God on the third day sends Messiah, his Son, for whom he had reserved the glory of that victory: He, in the Power of his Father coming to the place, and causing all his Legions to stand still on either side, with his chariot and thunder driving into the midst of his enemies, pursues them, unable to resist, towards the wall of Heaven; which opening, they leap down with horror and confusion into the place of punishment prepared for them in the Deep. Messiah returns with triumph to his Father.

BOOK VII

THE ARGUMENT

RAPHAEL at the request of Adam relates how and wherefore this world was first created; that God, after the expelling of Satan and his Angels out of Heaven, declared his pleasure to create another World and other Creatures to dwell therein; sends his Son with glory and attendance of Angels to perform the work of Creation in six days: the Angels celebrate with hymns the performance thereof, and his reascension into Heaven.

BOOK VIII

THE ARGUMENT

ADAM inquires concerning celestial motions, is doubtfully answered, and exhorted to search rather things more worthy of knowledge. Adam assents, and, still desirous to detain Raphael, relates to him what he remembered since his own creation, his placing in Paradise, his talk with God concerning solitude and fit society, his first meeting and nuptials with Eve, his discourse with the Angel thereupon; who after admonitions repeated departs.

BOOK IX

THE ARGUMENT

SATAN, having compassed the Earth, with meditated guile returns as a mist by night into Paradise; enters into the Serpent sleeping. Adam and Eve in the morning go forth to their labors, which Eve proposes to divide in several places, each laboring apart: Adam consents not, alleging the danger lest that enemy of whom they were forewarned should attempt her found alone. Eve, loath to be thought not circumspect or firm enough, urges her going apart, the rather desirous to make trial of her strength; Adam at last yields. The Serpent finds her alone: his subtle approach, first gazing, then speaking, with much flattery extolling Eve above all other creatures. Eve, wondering to hear the Serpent speak, asks how he attained to human speech and such understanding not till now; the Serpent answers that by tasting of a certain tree in the Garden he attained both to speech and reason, till then void of both. Eve requires him to bring her to that tree, and finds it to be the Tree of Knowledge forbidden: the Serpent, now grown bolder with many wiles and arguments, induces her at length to eat. She, pleased with the taste, deliberates a while whether to impart thereof to Adam or not; at last brings him of the fruit; relates what persuaded her to eat thereof. Adam, at first amazed, but perceiving her lost, resolves, through vehemence of love, to perish with her, and, extenuating the trespass, eats also of the fruit. The effect thereof in them both; they seek to cover their nakedness; then fall to variance and accusation of one another.

BOOK X

THE ARGUMENT

MAN'S transgression known, the guardian Angels forsake Paradise, and return up to Heaven to approve their vigilance, and are approved; God declaring that the entrance of Satan could not be by them prevented. He sends his Son to judge the transgressors; who descends, and gives sentence accordingly; then, in pity, clothes them both, and reascends. Sin and Death, sitting till then at the gates of Hell, by wondrous sympathy feeling the success of Satan in this new world, and the sin of man there committed, resolve to sit no longer confined in Hell, but to follow Satan, their sire, up to the place of man: to make the way easier from Hell to this world to and fro, they pave a broad highway or bridge over Chaos, according to the track that Satan first made; then, preparing for earth, they meet him, proud of his success, returning to Hell; their mutual gratulation. Satan arrives at Pandemonium; in full assembly relates, with boasting, his success against man; instead of applause is entertained with a general hiss by all his audience, transformed, with himself also, suddenly into Serpents, according to his doom given in Paradise; then, deluded with a show of the Forbidden Tree springing up before them, they, greedily reaching to take of the fruit, chew dust and bitter ashes. The proceedings of Sin and Death: God foretells the final victory of his Son over them, and the renewing of all things; but, for the present, commands his Angels to make several alterations in the heavens and elements. Adam, more and more perceiving his fallen condition, heavily bewails, rejects the condolement of Eve; she persists, and at length appeases him: then, to evade the curse likely to fall on their offspring, proposes to Adam violent ways; which he approves not, but, conceiving better hope, puts her in mind of the late promise made them, that her seed should be revenged on the Serpent, and exhorts her, with him, to seek peace of the offended Deity by repentance and supplication.

BOOK XI

THE ARGUMENT

THE Son of God presents to his Father the prayers of our first Parents, now repenting, and intercedes for them. God accepts them, but declares that they must no longer abide in Paradise; sends Michael with a Band of Cherubim to dispossess them, but first to reveal to Adam future things: Michael's coming down. Adam shows to Eve certain ominous signs; he discerns Michael's approach; goes out to meet him: the Angel denounces[1] their departure. Eve's lamentation. Adam pleads, but submits: the Angel leads him up to a high hill; sets before him in vision what shall happen till the Flood.

BOOK XII

THE ARGUMENT

THE Angel Michael continues from the Flood to relate what shall succeed; then, in the mention of Abraham, comes by degrees to explain who that Seed of the Woman shall be, which was promised Adam and Eve in the Fall: his Incarnation, Death, Resurrection, the Ascension; the state of the Church till his second Coming. Adam, greatly satisfied and recomforted by these relations and promises, descends the hill with Michael; wakens Eve, who all this while had slept, but with gentle dreams composed to quietness of mind and submission. Michael in either hand leads them out of Paradise, the fiery Sword waving behind them, and the Cherubim taking their stations to guard the Place.

[1]Proclaims.

AREOPAGITICA[1]

A Speech for the Liberty of Unlicensed Printing

TO THE PARLIAMENT OF ENGLAND

This is true liberty, when free-born men,
Having to advise the public, may speak free;
Which he who can and will deserves high praise,
Who neither can nor will may hold his peace. 5
What can be juster in a state than this?

Euripides, *The Suppliants*

THEY who to states and governors of the Commonwealth direct their speech, High 10 Court of Parliament, or wanting such access in a private condition, write that which they foresee may advance the public good, I suppose them as at the beginning of no mean endeavor not a little altered[2] and moved inwardly in their minds, some with doubt of what will be the success, others with fear of what will be the censure;[3] some with hope, others with confidence of what they have to speak. And me perhaps each of these dispositions, as the subject was whereon I entered, may have at other times variously

[1]The title is borrowed from the Areopagitic Oration of Isocrates, addressed to the Areopagus, or Great Council of Athens, and like Milton's work intended to be read rather than heard.

[2]Disturbed. [3]Judgment.

affected; and likely might in these foremost expressions now also disclose which of them swayed most, but that the very attempt of this address thus made, and the thought of whom it hath recourse to, hath got the power within me to a passion far more welcome than incidental to a preface. Which though I stay not to confess ere any ask, I shall be blameless, if it be no other than the joy and gratulation which it brings to all who wish and promote their country's liberty; whereof this whole discourse proposed will be a certain testimony, if not a trophy.[4] For this is not the liberty which we can hope, that no grievance ever should arise in the Commonwealth; that let no man in this world expect; but when complaints are freely heard, deeply considered, and speedily reformed, then is the utmost bound of civil liberty attained that wise men look for. To which if I now manifest by the very sound of this which I shall utter that we are already in good part arrived, and yet from such a steep disadvantage of tyranny and superstition grounded into our principles as was beyond the manhood of a Roman recovery,[5] it will be attributed first, as is most due, to the strong assistance of God, our deliverer, next to your faithful guidance and undaunted wisdom, Lords and Commons of England. Neither is it in God's esteem the diminution of his glory when honorable things are spoken of good men and worthy magistrates; which if I now first should begin to do, after so fair a progress of your laudable deeds and such a long obligement upon the whole realm to your indefatigable virtues, I might be justly reckoned among the tardiest and the unwillingest of them that praise ye. Nevertheless there being three principal things without which all praising is but courtship[6] and flattery: first, when that only is praised which is solidly worth praise; next, when greatest likelihoods are brought that such things are truly and really in those persons to whom they are ascribed: the other, when he who praises, by showing that such his actual persuasion is of whom he writes, can demonstrate that he flatters not. The former two of these I have heretofore endeavored, rescuing the employment from him who went about to impair your merits with a trivial and malignant encomium;[7] the latter, as belonging chiefly to mine own acquittal, that whom I so extolled I did not flatter, hath been reserved opportunely to this occasion. For he who freely magnifies what hath been nobly done, and fears not to declare as freely what might be done better, gives ye the best covenant of his fidelity, and that his loyalest affection and his hope waits on your proceedings. His highest praising is not flattery, and his plainest advice is a kind of praising; for though I should affirm and hold by argument that it would fare better with truth, with learning, and the Commonwealth, if one of your published orders, which I should name, were called in, yet at the same time it could not but much redound to the luster of your mild and equal government whenas private persons are hereby animated to think ye better pleased with public advice than other statists have been delighted heretofore with public flattery. And men will then see what difference there is between the magnanimity of a triennial parliament, and that jealous haughtiness of prelates and cabin[8] counsellors that usurped of late, whenas they shall observe ye in the midst of your victories and successes more gently brooking written exceptions against a voted order than other courts, which had produced nothing worth memory but the weak ostentation of wealth, would have endured the least signified dislike at any sudden proclamation. If I should thus far presume upon the meek demeanor of your civil and gentle greatness, Lords and Commons, as what your published order hath directly said, that to gainsay, I might defend myself with ease, if any should accuse me of being new or insolent, did they but know how much better I find ye esteem it to imitate the old and elegant humanity of Greece than the barbaric pride of a Hunnish and Norwegian stateliness. And out of those ages to whose polite wisdom and letters we owe that we are not yet Goths and Jut-

[4]Even though unsuccessful.

[5]The recovery of Rome from her many disasters.

[6]Fawning of courtiers.

[7]Bishop Joseph Hall in his *Humble Remonstrance* to Parliament against the abolition of episcopacy, against which Milton wrote his *Apology for Smectymnuus.*

[8]Cabinet.

landers I could name him[9] who from his private house wrote that discourse to the Parliament of Athens that persuades them to change the form of democracy which was then established. Such honor was done in those days to men who professed the study of wisdom and eloquence, not only in their own country but in other lands, that cities and signories heard them gladly and with great respect, if they had aught in public to admonish the state. Thus did Dion Prusaeus, a stranger and a private orator, counsel the Rhodians against a former edict; and I abound with other like examples, which to set here would be superfluous. But if from the industry of a life wholly dedicated to studious labors, and those natural endowments haply not the worst for two and fifty degrees of northern latitude, so much must be derogated as to count me not equal to any of those who had this privilege, I would obtain to be thought not so inferior as yourselves are superior to the most of them who received their counsel; and how far you excel them, be assured, Lords and Commons, there can no greater testimony appear than when your prudent spirit acknowledges and obeys the voice of reason, from what quarter soever it be heard speaking, and renders ye as willing to repeal any act of your own setting forth as any set forth by your predecessors.

If ye be thus resolved, as it were injury to think ye were not, I know not what should withold me from presenting ye with a fit instance wherein to show both that love of truth which ye eminently profess, and that uprightness of your judgment which is not wont to be partial to yourselves, by judging over again that order[10] which ye have ordained to regulate printing: "that no book, pamphlet, or paper shall be henceforth printed unless the same be first approved and licensed by such, or at least one of such, as shall be thereto appointed." For that part which preserves justly every man's copy[11] to himself, or provides for the poor, I touch not, only wish they be not made pretences to abuse and persecute honest and painful[12] men who offend not in either of these particulars. But that other clause of licensing books, which we thought had died with his brother quadragesimal and matrimonial[13] when the prelates expired, I shall now attend with such a homily as shall lay before ye: first, the inventors of it to be those whom ye will be loath to own; next, what is to be thought in general of reading, whatever sort the books be, and that this Order avails nothing to the suppressing of scandalous, seditious, and libellous books, which were mainly intended to be suppressed; last, that it will be primely to the discouragement of all learning and the stop of truth, not only by disexercising and blunting our abilities in what we know already, but by hindering and cropping the discovery that might be yet further made both in religious and civil wisdom.

I deny not but that it is of greatest concernment in the Church and Commonwealth to have a vigilant eye how books demean themselves as well as men, and thereafter to confine, imprison, and do sharpest justice on them as malefactors. For books are not absolutely dead things, but do contain a potency of life in them to be as active as that soul was whose progeny they are; nay, they do preserve as in a vial the purest efficacy and extraction of that living intellect that bred them. I know they are as lively and as vigorously productive as those fabulous dragon's teeth,[14] and, being sown up and down, may chance to spring up armed men. And yet on the other hand, unless wariness be used, as good almost kill a man as kill a good book; who kills a man kills a reasonable creature, God's image; but he who destroys a good book kills reason itself, kills the image of God, as it were, in the eye. Many a man lives a burden to the earth; but a good book is the precious life-blood of a master-spirit, embalmed and treasured up on purpose to a life beyond life. 'Tis true, no age can restore a life, whereof perhaps there is no great loss; and revolutions of ages do not oft recover the loss of a rejected truth, for the want of which whole

---

[9] Isocrates. [10] Of June 14, 1643.

[11] Copyright. [12] Painstaking.

[13] Ecclesiastical licenses for eating forbidden foods in Lent and for marriage.

[14] Which, when sown, sprang up as armed men in the legends of both Jason and Cadmus.

nations fare the worse. We should be wary therefore what persecution we raise against the living labors of public men, how we spill that seasoned life of man preserved and stored up in books; since we see a kind of homicide may be thus committed, sometimes a martyrdom, and if it extend to the whole impression, a kind of massacre, whereof the execution ends not in the slaying of an elemental life, but strikes at that ethereal and fifth essence,[15] the breath of reason itself, slays an immortality rather than a life. But lest I should be condemned of introducing licence, while I oppose licensing, I refuse not the pains to be so much historical as will serve to show what hath been done by ancient and famous commonwealths against this disorder, till the very time that this project of licensing crept out of the Inquisition, was catched up by our prelates, and hath caught some of our presbyters.

In Athens, where books and wits were ever busier than in any other part of Greece, I find but only two sorts of writings which the magistrate cared to take notice of: those either blasphemous and atheistical, or libellous. Thus the books of Protagoras[16] were by the judges of Areopagus commanded to be burnt, and himself banished the territory for a discourse begun with his confessing not to know whether there were gods, or whether not. And against defaming it was decreed that none should be traduced by name, as was the manner of *Vetus Comoedia,*[17] whereby we may guess how they censured libelling. And this course was quick enough, as Cicero writes, to quell both the desperate wits of other atheists and the open way of defaming, as the event showed. Of other sects and opinions, though tending to voluptuousness and the denying of divine providence, they took no heed. Therefore we do not read that either Epicurus, or that libertine school of Cyrene, or what the Cynic impudence uttered,[18] was ever questioned by the laws. Neither is it recorded that the writings of those old comedians[19] were suppressed, though the acting of them were forbid; and that Plato commended the reading of Aristophanes, the loosest of them all, to his royal scholar, Dionysius, is commonly known, and may be excused, if holy Chrysostom,[20] as is reported, nightly studied so much the same author and had the art to cleanse a scurrilous vehemence into the style of a rousing sermon. That other leading city of Greece, Lacedaemon, considering that Lycurgus, their law-giver, was so addicted to elegant learning as to have been the first that brought out of Ionia the scattered works of Homer, and sent the poet Thales from Crete to prepare and mollify the Spartan surliness with his smooth songs and odes, the better to plant among them law and civility, it is to be wondered how museless and unbookish they were, minding nought but the feats of war. There needed no licensing of books among them, for they disliked all but their own Laconic apophthegms, and took a slight occasion to chase Archilochus out of their city, perhaps for composing in a higher strain than their own soldierly ballads and roundels could reach to; or if it were for his broad verses, they were not therein so cautious but they were as dissolute in their promiscuous conversing; whence Euripides affirms in *Andromache* that their women were all unchaste. Thus much may give us light after what sort books were prohibited among the Greeks. The Romans also, for many ages trained up only to a military roughness, resembling most the Lacedaemonian guise, knew of learning little but what their twelve tables and the Pontific College with their augurs and flamens[21] taught them in religion and law, so unacquainted with other learning that when Carneades and Critolaus, with the Stoic Diogenes coming ambassadors to Rome, took thereby occasion to give the city a taste of their philosophy, they were sus-

[15]Fifth or spiritual essence, as opposed to the four elements, the material essences.

[16]The first of the Greek Sophists (B. C. 480–*c.* 411).

[17]The early Greek comedy, of which Aristophanes was the chief representative.

[18]Epicurus (B. C. 342–270) believed that happiness was the highest good; the school of Cyrene in northern Africa gave the pre-eminence to pleasure; and the Cynic philosophers made a point of impudently flouting human pretensions.

[19]Writers of comedies.

[20]St. Chrysostom (A. D. 347–407), Bishop of Constantinople.

[21]Various orders of priests in pagan Rome.

pected for seducers by no less a man than Cato, the censor, who moved it in the Senate to dismiss them speedily and to banish all such Attic babblers out of Italy. But Scipio and others of the noblest senators withstood him and his old Sabine austerity; honored and admired the men; and the censor himself at last in his old age fell to the study of that whereof before he was so scrupulous. And yet at the same time Naevius and Plautus, the first Latin comedians, had filled the city with all the borrowed scenes of Menander and Philemon.[22] Then began to be considered there also what was to be done to libellous books and authors; for Naevius was quickly cast into prison for his unbridled pen, and released by the tribunes upon his recantation. We read also that libels were burnt, and the makers punished by Augustus. The like severity no doubt was used if aught were impiously written against their esteemed gods. Except in these two points, how the world went in books the magistrate kept no reckoning. And therefore Lucretius without impeachment versifies his Epicurism to Memmius, and had the honor to be set forth the second time by Cicero, so great a father of the Commonwealth, although himself disputes against that opinion in his own writings. Nor was the satirical sharpness or naked plainness of Lucilius, or Catullus, or Flaccus[23] by any order prohibited. And for matters of state, the story of Titus Livius, though it extolled that part which Pompey held, was not therefore suppressed by Octavius Caesar of the other faction. But that Naso[24] was by him banished in his old age for the wanton poems of his youth was but a mere covert[25] of state over some secret cause; and besides, the books were neither banished nor called in. From hence we shall meet with little else but tyranny in the Roman Empire, that we may not marvel if not so often bad as good books were silenced. I shall therefore deem to have been large enough in producing what among the ancients was punishable to write, save only which all other arguments were free to treat on.

By this time the emperors were become Christians, whose discipline in this point I do not find to have been more severe than what was formerly in practice. The books of those whom they took to be grand heretics were examined, refuted, and condemned in the general councils, and not till then were prohibited or burnt by authority of the emperor. As for the writings of heathen authors, unless they were plain invectives against Christianity, as those of Porphyrius and Proclus,[26] they met with no interdict that can be cited till about the year 400 in a Carthaginian council, wherein bishops themselves were forbid to read the books of gentiles,[27] but heresies they might read; while others long before them on the contrary scrupled more the books of heretics than of gentiles. And that the primitive councils and bishops were wont only to declare what books were not commendable, passing no further but leaving it to each one's conscience to read or to lay by, till after the year 800 is observed already by Padre Paolo, the great unmasker of the Trentine Council.[28] After which time the popes of Rome, engrossing what they pleased of political rule into their own hands, extended their dominion over men's eyes, as they had before over their judgments, burning and prohibiting to be read what they fancied not, yet sparing in their censures, and the books not many which they so dealt with; till Martin V[29] by his bull not only prohibited, but was the first that excommunicated the reading of heretical books; for about that time Wicliffe and Huss, growing terrible, were they who first drove the Papal Court to a stricter policy of prohibiting. Which course Leo X[30] and his successors followed, until the Council of Trent and the Spanish Inquisition, engendering together, brought forth, or perfected those catalogues and expurging indexes that rake through the entrails of many an old good author, with a violation worse than any could be offered to his tomb. Nor did they

[22] Two leading writers of "new," or later, Greek comedy.

[23] Horace. [24] Ovid. [25] Pretext.

[26] Neoplatonic philosophers of the fourth and fifth centuries A. D.

[27] Pagans.

[28] Fra Paolo Sarpi, a Venetian scholar of the late sixteenth century, whose best known work was a history of the Catholic Council of Trent.

[29] Pope, 1417–1431. [30] Pope, 1513–1521.

stay in matters heretical, but any subject that was not to their palate they either condemned in a prohibition, or had it straight into the new purgatory of an index. To fill up the measure of encroachment their last invention was to ordain that no book, pamphlet, or paper should be printed (as if St. Peter had bequeathed them the keys of the press also out of Paradise) unless it were approved and licensed under the hands of two or three glutton friars. For example:

"Let the Chancellor Cini be pleased to see if in this present work be contained aught that may withstand the printing.
Vincent Rabatta, Vicar of Florence."

"I have seen this present work, and find nothing athwart the Catholic faith and good manners: in witness whereof I have given, *etc.*
Niccolò Cini, Chancellor of Florence."

"Attending the precedent relation, it is allowed that this present work of Davanzati may be printed.
Vincent Rabatta, *etc.*"

"It may be printed, 15 July.
Friar Simon Mompei d'Amelia Chancellor of the holy office in Florence."[31]

Sure they have a conceit, if he of the bottomless pit had not long since broke prison, that this quadruple exorcism would bar him down. I fear their next design will be to get into their custody the licensing of that which they say Claudius intended, but went not through with.[32] Vouchsafe to see another of their forms, the Roman stamp:

"*Imprimatur,*[33] if it seem good to the reverend Master of the Holy Palace,
Belcastro, vicegerent."

"*Imprimatur.*
Friar Niccolò Rodolphi, Master of the Holy Palace."

Sometimes five *imprimaturs* are seen together dialogue-wise in the piazza of one title-page, complimenting and ducking each to other with their shaven reverences, whether the author, who stands by in perplexity at the foot of his epistle, shall to the press or to the sponge. These are the pretty responsories, these are the dear antiphonies that so bewitched of late our prelates and their chaplains with the goodly echo they made; and besotted us to the gay imitation of a lordly *imprimatur,* one from Lambeth House, another from the west end of Paul's,[34] so apishly Romanizing that the word of command still was set down in Latin, as if the learned, grammatical pen that wrote it would cast no ink without Latin, or perhaps, as they thought, because no vulgar tongue was worthy to express the pure conceit of an *imprimatur;* but rather, as I hope, for that our English, the language of men ever famous and foremost in the achievements of liberty, will not easily find servile letters enow to spell such a dictatory presumption English. And thus ye have the inventors and the original of book-licensing ripped up, and drawn as lineally as any pedigree. We have it not, that can be heard of, from any ancient state, or polity, or church, nor by any statute left us by our ancestors elder or later; nor from the modern custom of any reformed city or church abroad; but from the most Anti-Christian Council and the most tyrannous Inquisition that ever inquired. Till then books were ever as freely admitted into the world as any other birth; the issue of the brain was no more stifled than the issue of the womb; no envious Juno sate cross-legged[35] over the nativity of any man's intellectual offspring; but if it proved a monster, who denies but that it was justly burnt, or sunk into the sea. But that a book, in worse condition than a peccant soul, should be to stand before a jury ere it be born to the world, and undergo yet in darkness the judgment of Radamanth and his colleagues[36] ere it can pass the ferry backward into light, was never heard before till that mysterious iniquity, provoked and troubled at the first entrance of reformation, sought out new limboes and new hells wherein they might

[31] This example of licensing is taken from Bernardo Davanzati Bostichi's *Scisma d'Inghilterra,* published at Florence in 1638, probably during Milton's visit in that city.

[32] "*Quo veniam daret flatum crepitumque ventris in convivio emittendi. Sueton. in Claudio*" (Milton's note).

[33] Let it be printed.

[34] One from the London house of the Archbishop of Canterbury, another from the house of the Bishop of London.

[35] Juno put a curse.

[36] Radamanth and the other judges of Hades.

include our books also within the number of their damned. And this was the rare morsel so officiously snatched up, and so ill-favoredly imitated by our inquisiturient[37] bishops and the attendant Minorites[38] their chaplains. That ye like not now these most certain authors of this licensing order, and that all sinister intention was far distant from your thoughts when ye were importuned the passing it, all men who know the integrity of your actions, and how ye honor truth, will clear ye readily.

But some will say, "What though the inventors were bad? the thing for all that may be good." It may so; yet if that thing be no such deep invention, but obvious and easy for any man to light on, and yet best and wisest commonwealths through all ages and occasions have forborne to use it, and falsest seducers and oppressors of men were the first who took it up, and to no other purpose but to obstruct and hinder the first approach of reformation; I am of those who believe, it will be a harder alchemy than Lullius[39] ever knew to sublimate any good use out of such an invention. Yet this only is what I request to gain from this reason, that it may be held a dangerous and suspicious fruit, as certainly it deserves, for the tree that bore it, until I can dissect one by one the properties it has. But I have first to finish, as was propounded, what is to be thought in general of reading books, whatever sort they be, and whether be more the benefit or the harm that thence proceeds.

Not to insist upon the examples of Moses, Daniel, and Paul, who were skilful in all the learning of the Egyptians, Chaldeans, and Greeks, which could not probably be without reading their books of all sorts, in Paul especially, who thought it no defilement to insert into holy Scripture the sentences of three Greek poets, and one of them a tragedian,[40] the question was, notwithstanding, sometimes controverted among the primitive doctors, but with great odds on that side which affirmed it both lawful and profitable, as was then evidently perceived when Julian,[41] the Apostate and subtlest enemy to our faith, made a decree forbidding Christians the study of heathen learning; for, said he, they wound us with our own weapons, and with our own arts and sciences they overcome us. And indeed the Christians were put so to their shifts by this crafty means, and so much in danger to decline into all ignorance, that the two Appollinarii were fain, as a man may say, to coin all the seven liberal sciences[42] out of the Bible, reducing it into divers forms of orations, poems, dialogues, even to the calculating of a new Christian grammar. But, saith the historian Socrates,[43] the providence of God provided better than the industry of Appollinarius and his son, by taking away that illiterate law with the life of him who devised it. So great an injury they then held it to be deprived of Hellenic learning, and thought it a persecution more undermining and secretly decaying the Church than the open cruelty of Decius or Diocletian. And perhaps it was the same politic drift that the Devil whipped St. Jerome in a lenten dream for reading Cicero; or else it was a phantasm bred by the fever which had then seized him.[44] For had an angel been his discipliner, unless it were for dwelling too much upon Ciceronianisms, and had chastised the reading, not the vanity, it had been plainly partial; first, to correct him for grave Cicero and not for scurril Plautus, whom he confesses to have been reading not long before; next, to correct him only and let so many more ancient fathers wax old in those pleasant and florid studies without the lash of such a tutoring apparition, insomuch that Basil teaches how some good use may be made of *Margites,* a sportful poem, not now extant, writ by Homer; and why not then of *Morgante,*[45] an Italian romance much to the same purpose? But if it be agreed we shall be tried by visions,

[37]Desirous of being inquisitors.

[38]Franciscan friars.

[39]Raymond Lully (1234–1315), alchemist.

[40]Euripides, from whom Paul is supposed to have taken I Corinthians, 15:33.

[41]Roman emperor and leader of a movement to return to paganism (A. D. 331–363).

[42]Grammar, logic, rhetoric, arithmetic, music, geometry, and astronomy.

[43]Flourished in the fifth century A. D.

[44]St. Jerome (A. D. *c.* 345–420) in a letter to the nun Eustochium ascribes the dream to the Devil.

[45]The *Morgante Maggiore* of Luigi Pulci (1431–1487).

there is a vision recorded by Eusebius[46] far ancienter than this tale of Jerome to the nun Eustochium, and besides has nothing of a fever in it. Dionysius Alexandrinus was about the year 240 a person of great name in the Church for piety and learning, who had wont to avail himself much against heretics by being conversant in their books, until a certain presbyter laid it scrupulously to his conscience how he durst venture himself among those defiling volumes. The worthy man, loath to give offence, fell into a new debate with himself what was to be thought; when suddenly a vision sent from God (it is his own epistle that so avers it) confirmed him in these words: "Read any books whatever come to thy hands, for thou art sufficient both to judge aright, and to examine each matter." To this revelation he assented the sooner, as he confesses, because it was answerable to that of the Apostle to the Thessalonians: "Prove all things; hold fast that which is good." And he might have added another remarkable saying of the same author: "To the pure all things are pure," not only meats and drinks, but all kind of knowledge whether of good or evil; the knowledge cannot defile, nor consequently the books, if the will and conscience be not defiled. For books are as meats and viands are, some of good, some of evil substance; and yet God in that unapocryphal[47] vision said without exception, "Rise Peter, kill and eat," leaving the choice to each man's discretion. Wholesome meats to a vitiated stomach differ little or nothing from unwholesome; and best books to a naughty mind are not unappliable to occasions of evil. Bad meats will scarce breed good nourishment in the healthiest concoction; but herein the difference is of bad books that they to a discreet and judicious reader serve in many respects to discover, to confute, to forewarn, and to illustrate. Whereof what better witness can ye expect I should produce than one of your own now sitting in Parliament, the chief of learned men reputed in this land, Mr. Selden?[48] whose volume of natural and national laws proves, not only by great authorities brought together, but by exquisite reasons and theorems almost mathematically demonstrative, that all opinions, yea errors, known, read, and collated, are of main service and assistance toward the speedy attainment of what is truest. I conceive therefore that when God did enlarge the universal diet of man's body, saving ever the rules of temperance, he then also, as before, left arbitrary the dieting and repasting of our minds, as wherein every mature man might have to exercise his own leading capacity. How great a virtue is temperance, how much of moment through the whole life of man! yet God commits the managing so great a trust, without particular law or prescription, wholly to the demeanor[49] of every grown man. And therefore, when he himself tabled the Jews from heaven, that omer which was every man's daily portion of manna is computed to have been more than might have well sufficed the heartiest feeder thrice as many meals. For those actions which enter into a man rather than issue out of him, and therefore defile not, God uses not to captivate under a perpetual childhood of prescription, but trusts him with the gift of reason to be his own chooser; there were but little work left for preaching if law and compulsion should grow so fast upon those things which heretofore were governed only by exhortation. Solomon informs us that much reading is a weariness to the flesh, but neither he nor other inspired author tells us that such or such reading is unlawful; yet certainly had God thought good to limit us herein, it had been much more expedient to have told us what was unlawful than what was wearisome. As for the burning of those Ephesian books by St. Paul's converts, 'tis replied the books were magic: the Syriac so renders them. It was a private act, a voluntary act, and leaves us to a voluntary imitation; the men in remorse burnt those books which were their own; the magistrate by this example is not appointed; these men practised the books; another might perhaps have read them in some sort usefully. Good and evil we know in the field of this world grow up together almost inseparably; and

[46]Bishop of Caesarea at the beginning of the fourth century A. D.

[47]In the Bible (Acts, 10:9–16).

[48]John Selden (1584–1654), author of *De Jure Naturali et Gentium* (1640).

[49]Management.

the knowledge of good is so involved and interwoven with the knowledge of evil, and in so many cunning resemblances hardly to be discerned, that those confused seeds which were imposed on Psyche as an incessant labor to cull out and sort asunder were not more intermixed.[50] It was from out the rind of one apple tasted that the knowledge of good and evil as two twins cleaving together leaped forth into the world. And perhaps this is that doom which Adam fell into of knowing good and evil, that is to say, of knowing good by evil. As therefore the state of man now is, what wisdom can there be to choose, what continence to forbear without the knowledge of evil? He that can apprehend and consider vice with all her baits and seeming pleasures, and yet abstain, and yet distinguish, and yet prefer that which is truly better, he is the true wayfaring[51] Christian. I cannot praise a fugitive and cloistered virtue, unexercised and unbreathed, that never sallies out and sees her adversary, but slinks out of the race where that immortal garland is to be run for not without dust and heat. Assuredly we bring not innocence into the world; we bring impurity much rather; that which purifies us is trial, and trial is by what is contrary. That virtue therefore which is but a youngling in the contemplation of evil, and knows not the utmost that vice promises to her followers, and rejects it, is but a blank virtue, not a pure; her whiteness is but an excremental[52] whiteness. Which was the reason why our sage and serious poet Spenser, whom I dare be known to think a better teacher than Scotus or Aquinas,[53] describing true temperance under the person of Guyon,[54] brings him in with his palmer through the cave of Mammon and the bower of earthly bliss, that he might see and know, and yet abstain. Since therefore the knowledge and survey of vice is in this world so necessary to the constituting of human virtue, and the scanning of error to the confirmation of truth, how can we more safely and with less danger scout into the regions of sin and falsity than by reading all manner of tractates, and hearing all manner of reason? And this is the benefit which may be had of books promiscuously read. But of the harm that may result hence three kinds are usually reckoned. First is feared the infection that may spread; but then all human learning and controversy in religious points must remove out of the world, yea the Bible itself; for that ofttimes relates blasphemy not nicely, it describes the carnal sense of wicked men not unelegantly, it brings in holiest men passionately murmuring against providence through all the arguments of Epicurus; in other great disputes it answers dubiously and darkly to the common reader; and ask a Talmudist what ails the modesty of his marginal *keri,* that Moses and all the prophets cannot persuade him to pronounce the textual *chetiv.*[55] For these causes we all know the Bible itself put by the Papist into the first rank of prohibited books. The ancientest Fathers must be next removed, as Clement of Alexandria and that Eusebian book of evangelic preparation, transmitting our ears through a hoard of heathenish obscenities to receive the Gospel. Who finds not that Irenaeus, Epiphanius, Jerome, and others discover more heresies than they well confute, and that oft for heresy which is the truer opinion. Nor boots it to say for these and all the heathen writers of greatest infection, if it must be thought so, with whom is bound up the life of human learning, that they writ in an unknown tongue, so long as we are sure those languages are known as well to the worst of men, who are both most able and most diligent to instil the poison they suck, first into the courts of princes, acquainting them with the choicest delights and criticisms of sin; as perhaps did that Petronius whom Nero called his arbiter, the master of his revels, and that notorious ribald of Arezzo, dreaded and yet dear to the Italian courtiers.[56] I name not him for posterity's sake whom

[50]The story is told in *The Golden Ass* of Apuleius.

[51]In one copy of the *Areopagitica* Milton himself corrected "wayfaring" to "warfaring."

[52]External.

[53]Duns Scotus and St. Thomas Aquinas, the greatest medieval philosophers.

[54]Hero of the second book of the *Faerie Queene.*

[55]The original text of the *Talmud,* or great compilation of Jewish laws; the *keri* are marginal annotations.

[56]Petronius Arbiter, author of the *Satyricon,* and Pietro Aretino (1492-1557), the "Scourge of Princes."

Harry VIII named in merriment his Vicar of Hell.[57] By which compendious way all the contagion that foreign books can infuse will find a passage to the people far easier and shorter than an Indian voyage, though it could be sailed either by the north of Cataio[58] eastward, or of Canada westward, while our Spanish licensing gags the English press never so severely. But on the other side, that infection which is from books of controversy in religion is more doubtful and dangerous to the learned than to the ignorant; and yet those books must be permitted untouched by the licenser. It will be hard to instance where any ignorant man hath been ever seduced by papistical book in English, unless it were commended and expounded to him by some of that clergy: and indeed all such tractates, whether false or true, are as the prophecy of Isaiah was to the eunuch, not to be understood without a guide. But of our priests and doctors how many have been corrupted by studying the comments of Jesuits and Sorbonists,[59] and how fast they could transfuse that corruption into the people, our experience is both late and sad. It is not forgot since the acute and distinct[60] Arminius[61] was perverted merely by the perusing of a nameless discourse written at Delft, which at first he took in hand to confute. Seeing therefore that those books, and those in great abundance which are likeliest to taint both life and doctrine, cannot be suppressed without the fall of learning and of all ability in disputation, and that these books of either sort are most and soonest catching to the learned, from whom to the common people whatever is heretical or dissolute may quickly be conveyed, and that evil manners are as perfectly learnt without books a thousand other ways which cannot be stopped, and evil doctrine not with books can propagate, except a teacher guide, which he might also do without writing, and so beyond prohibiting, I am not able to unfold how this cautelous[62] enterprise of licensing can be exempted from the number of vain and impossible attempts. And he who were pleasantly disposed could not well avoid to liken it to the exploit of that gallant man who thought to pound up the crows by shutting his park gate. Besides another inconvenience: if learned men be the first receivers out of books and dispreaders both of vice and error, how shall the licensers themselves be confided in, unless we can confer upon them, or they assume to themselves above all others in the land, the grace of infallibility and uncorruptedness? And again, if it be true that a wise man like a good refiner can gather gold out of the drossiest volume, and that a fool will be a fool with the best book, yea or without book, there is no reason that we should deprive a wise man of any advantage to his wisdom, while we seek to restrain from a fool that which being restrained will be no hindrance to his folly. For if there should be so much exactness always used to keep that from him which is unfit for his reading, we should in the judgment of Aristotle not only, but of Solomon and of our Savior, not vouchsafe him good precepts, and by consequence not willingly admit him to good books, as being certain that a wise man will make better use of an idle pamphlet than a fool will do of sacred Scripture. 'Tis next alleged we must not expose ourselves to temptations without necessity, and next to that not employ our time in vain things. To both these objections one answer will serve, out of the grounds already laid, that to all men such books are not temptations nor vanities, but useful drugs and materials wherewith to temper and compose effective and strong medicines, which man's life cannot want.[63] The rest, as children and childish men, who have not the art to qualify and prepare these working minerals, well may be exhorted to forbear, but hindered forcibly they cannot be by all the licensing that Sainted Inquisition could ever yet contrive. Which is what I promised to deliver next: that this order of licensing conduces nothing to the end for which it was framed; and hath almost prevented[64] me by being clear already while thus much hath been explaining. See

[57]Perhaps the poet John Skelton. [58]Cathay.

[59]Scholars of the Sorbonne, the great theological school in Paris.

[60]Clear-headed.

[61]Dutch theologian, converted to an anti-Calvinistic position.

[62]Dangerous.

[63]Do without.

[64]Forestalled.

the ingenuity[65] of Truth, who, when she gets a free and willing hand, opens herself faster than the pace of method and discourse can overtake her. It was the task which I began with, to shew that no nation or well instituted state, if they valued books at all, did ever use this way of licensing; and it might be answered that this is a piece of prudence lately discovered. To which I return that, as it was a thing slight and obvious to think on, so if it had been difficult to find out, there wanted not among them long since who suggested such a course; which they not following, leave us a pattern of their judgment, that it was not the not knowing but the not approving which was the cause of their not using it. Plato, a man of high authority indeed, but least of all for his commonwealth, in the book of his laws, which no city ever yet received, fed his fancy with making many edicts to his airy burgomasters, which they who otherwise admire him wish had been rather buried and excused in the genial cups of an Academic night-sitting. By which laws he seems to tolerate no kind of learning but by unalterable decree, consisting most of practical traditions, to the attainment whereof a library of smaller bulk than his own dialogues would be abundant; and there also enacts that no poet should so much as read to any private man what he had written, until the judges and law-keepers had seen it and allowed it. But that Plato meant this law peculiarly to that commonwealth which he had imagined, and to no other, is evident. Why was he not else a law-giver to himself, but a transgressor and to be expelled by his own magistrates, both for the wanton epigrams and dialogues which he made, and his perpetual reading of Sophron Mimus[66] and Aristophanes, books of grossest infamy, and also for commending the latter of them, though he were the malicious libeller of his chief friends, to be read by the tyrant Dionysius, who had little need of such trash to spend his time on? but that he knew this licensing of poems had reference and dependence to many other provisoes there set down in his fancied republic, which in this world could have no place; and so neither he himself, nor any magistrate or city ever imitated that course, which taken apart from those other collateral injunctions must needs be vain and fruitless. For if they fell upon one kind of strictness, unless their care were equal to regulate all other things of like aptness to corrupt the mind, that single endeavor they knew would be but a fond labor, to shut and fortify one gate against corruption, and be necessitated to leave others round about wide open. If we think to regulate printing, thereby to rectify manners, we must regulate all recreations and pastimes, all that is delightful to man. No music must be heard, no song be set or sung but what is grave and Doric.[67] There must be licensing dancers that no gesture, motion, or deportment be taught our youth but what by their allowance shall be thought honest; for such Plato was provided of. It will ask more than the work of twenty licensers to examine all the lutes, the violins, and the guitars in every house; they must not be suffered to prattle as they do, but must be licensed what they may say. And who shall silence all the airs and madrigals that whisper softness in chambers? The windows also and the balconies must be thought on. There are shrewd[68] books with dangerous frontispieces set to sale; who shall prohibit them? shall twenty licensers? The villages also must have their visitors to inquire what lectures the bagpipe and the rebeck[69] reads even to the ballatry, and the gamut of every municipal fiddler, for these are the countryman's *Arcadias,* and his Montemayors.[70] Next, what more national corruption, for which England hears ill[71] abroad, than household gluttony? who shall be the rectors of our daily rioting? and what shall be done to inhibit the multitudes that frequent those houses where drunkenness is sold and harbored? Our garments also should be referred to the licensing of some more sober work-masters to see them cut into a less wanton garb. Who shall regulate all

[65]Ingenuousness.

[66]Writer of coarse farces (fifth century B. C.).

[67]Of a martial character. [68]Malicious.

[69]Fiddle.

[70]Pastoral entertainments like the *Arcadia* of Sir Philip Sidney or the *Diana* of the Portuguese poet, Jorge de Montemayor (*c.* 1520–1562).

[71]Is ill spoken of.

the mixed conversation of our youth, male and female together, as is the fashion of this country? who shall still appoint what shall be discoursed, what presumed, and no further? Lastly, who shall forbid and separate all idle resort, all evil company? These things will be, and must be; but how they shall be least hurtful, how least enticing, herein consists the grave and governing wisdom of a state. To sequester out of the world into Atlantic and Utopian polities,[72] which never can be drawn into use, will not mend our condition, but to ordain wisely as in this world of evil, in the midst whereof God hath placed us unavoidably. Nor is it Plato's licensing of books will do this, which necessarily pulls along with it so many other kinds of licensing as will make us all both ridiculous and weary, and yet frustrate; but those unwritten, or at least unconstraining laws of virtuous education, religious and civil nurture, which Plato there mentions as the bonds and ligaments of the commonwealth, the pillars and the sustainers of every written statute, these they be which will bear chief sway in such matters as these, when all licensing will be easily eluded. Impunity and remissness for certain are the bane of a commonwealth; but here the great art lies to discern in what the law is to bid restraint and punishment, and in what things persuasion only is to work. If every action which is good or evil in man at ripe years were to be under pittance,[73] and prescription, and compulsion, what were virtue but a name? what praise could be then due to well-doing? what gramercy to be sober, just, or continent? Many there be that complain of divine providence for suffering Adam to transgress: foolish tongues! When God gave him reason, he gave him freedom to choose, for reason is but choosing; he had been else a mere artificial Adam, such an Adam as he is in the motions.[74] We ourselves esteem not of that obedience, or love, or gift, which is of force; God therefore left him free, set before him a provoking object, ever almost in his eyes herein consisted his merit, herein the right of his reward, the praise of his abstinence. Wherefore did he create passions within us, pleasures round about us, but that these rightly tempered are the very ingredients of virtue? They are not skilful considerers of human things who imagine to remove sin by removing the matter of sin; for, besides that it is a huge heap increasing under the very act of diminishing, though some part of it may for a time be withdrawn from some persons, it cannot from all in such a universal thing as books are; and when this is done, yet the sin remains entire. Though ye take from a covetous man all his treasure, he has yet one jewel left; ye cannot bereave him of his covetousness. Banish all objects of lust; shut up all youth into the severest discipline that can be exercised in any hermitage; ye cannot make them chaste that came not thither so: such great care and wisdom is required to the right managing of this point. Suppose we could expel sin by this means; look how much we thus expel of sin, so much we expel of virtue, for the matter of them both is the same; remove that, and ye remove them both alike. This justifies the high providence of God, who though he commands us temperance, justice, continence, yet pours out before us even to a profuseness all desirable things, and gives us minds that can wander beyond all limit and satiety. Why should we then affect a rigor contrary to the manner of God and of nature, by abridging or scanting those means, which books freely permitted are, both to the trial of virtue and the exercise of truth? It would be better done to learn that the law must needs be frivolous which goes to restrain things, uncertainly and yet equally working to good and to evil. And were I the chooser, a dram of well-doing should be preferred before many times as much the forcible hindrance of evil-doing. For God sure esteems the growth and completing of one virtuous person more than the restraint of ten vicious. And albeit whatever thing we hear or see, sitting, walking, travelling, or conversing may be fitly called our book, and is of the same effect that writings are, yet, grant the things to be prohibited were only books, it appears that this order hitherto is far insufficient to the end which it intends.

[72] Ideal states like the New Atlantis of Bacon and the Utopia of More.

[73] A system of allowances.

[74] Puppet-shows.

Do we not see, not once or oftener but weekly, that continued court libel[75] against the Parliament and city printed, as the wet sheets can witness, and dispersed among us for all that licensing can do? yet this is the prime service, a man would think, wherein this order should give proof of itself. If it were executed, you'll say. But certain, if execution be remiss or blindfold now, and in this particular, what will it be hereafter, and in other books? If then the order shall not be vain and frustrate, behold a new labor, Lords and Commons; ye must repeal and proscribe all scandalous and unlicensed books already printed and divulged, after ye have drawn them up into a list that all may know which are condemned and which not, and ordain that no foreign books be delivered out of custody till they have been read over. This office will require the whole time of not a few overseers, and those no vulgar men. There be also books which are partly useful and excellent, partly culpable and pernicious; this work will ask as many more officials, to make expurgations and expunctions that the commonwealth of learning be not damnified.[76] In fine, when the multitude of books increase upon their hands, ye must be fain to catalogue all those printers who are found frequently offending, and forbid the importation of their whole suspected typography. In a word, that this your order may be exact and not deficient, ye must reform it perfectly according to the model of Trent and Seville,[77] which I know ye abhor to do. Yet though ye should condescend[78] to this, which God forbid, the order still would be but fruitless and defective to that end whereto ye meant it. If to prevent sects and schisms, who is so unread or so uncatechised in story[79] that hath not heard of many sects refusing books as a hindrance and preserving their doctrine unmixed for many ages, only by unwritten traditions. The Christian faith (for that was once a schism) is not unknown to have spread all over Asia ere any gospel or epistle was seen in writing. If the amendment of manners be aimed at, look into Italy and Spain, whether those places be one scruple the better, the honester, the wiser, the chaster, since all the inquisitional rigor that hath been executed upon books.

Another reason whereby to make it plain that this order will miss the end it seeks, consider by the quality which ought to be in every licenser. It cannot be denied but that he who is made judge to sit upon the birth or death of books, whether they may be wafted into this world or not, had need to be a man above the common measure, both studious, learned, and judicious; there may be else no mean mistakes in the censure of what is passable or not, which is also no mean injury. If he be of such worth as behoves him, there cannot be a more tedious and unpleasing journey-work,[80] a greater loss of time levied upon his head, than to be made the perpetual reader of unchosen books and pamphlets, oft-times huge volumes. There is no book that is acceptable unless at certain seasons; but to be enjoined the reading of that at all times, and in a hand scarce legible, whereof three pages would not down at any time in the fairest print, is an imposition which I cannot believe how he that values time and his own studies, or is but of a sensible[81] nostril, should be able to endure. In this one thing I crave leave of the present licensers to be pardoned for so thinking, who doubtless took this office up, looking on it through their obedience to the Parliament, whose command perhaps made all things seem easy and unlaborious to them; but that this short trial hath wearied them out already their own expressions and excuses to them who make so many journeys to solicit their license are testimony enough. Seeing therefore those who now possess the employment by all evident signs wish themselves well rid of it, and that no man of worth, none that is not a plain unthrift of his own hours, is ever likely to succeed them, except he mean to put himself to the salary of a press-corrector, we may easily foresee what kind of licensers we are to expect hereafter, either ignorant, imperious, and

[75]The weekly Royalist paper, the *Mercurius Aulicus*.

[76]Made to suffer injury.

[77]The Council of Trent and the Inquisition of Seville.

[78]Give consent to.

[79]History.

[80]Day-laborer's work.

[81]Sensitive.

remiss, or basely pecuniary. This is what I had to show wherein this order cannot conduce to that end whereof it bears the intention.

I lastly proceed from the no good it can do to the manifest hurt it causes in being, first, the greatest discouragement and affront that can be offered to learning and to learned men. It was the complaint and lamentation of prelates, upon every least breath of a motion to remove pluralities and distribute more equally church revenues, that then all learning would be forever dashed and discouraged. But as for that opinion, I never found cause to think that the tenth part of learning stood or fell with the clergy; nor could I ever but hold it for a sordid and unworthy speech of any churchman who had a competency left him. If therefore ye be loath to dishearten utterly and discontent, not the mercenary crew of false pretenders to learning, but the free and ingenuous sort of such as evidently were born to study, and love learning for itself, not for lucre or any other end but the service of God and of truth, and perhaps that lasting fame and perpetuity of praise which God and good men have consented shall be the reward of those whose published labors advance the good of mankind; then know that so far to distrust the judgment and the honesty of one who hath but a common repute in learning, and never yet offended, as not to count him fit to print his mind without a tutor and examiner, lest he should drop a schism or something of corruption, is the greatest displeasure and indignity to a free and knowing spirit that can be put upon him. What advantage is it to be a man over it is to be a boy at school, if we have only escaped the ferule to come under the fescue[87] of an *imprimatur?* if serious and elaborate writings, as if they were no more than the theme of a grammar-lad under his pedagogue, must not be uttered without the cursory eyes of a temporizing and extemporizing licenser. He who is not trusted with his own actions, his drift not being known to be evil, and standing to the hazard of law and penalty, has no great argument to think himself reputed in the commonwealth wherein he was born for other than a fool or a foreigner. When a man writes to the world, he summons up all his reason and deliberation to assist him; he searches, meditates, is industrious, and likely consults and confers with his judicious friends; after all which done he takes himself to be informed in what he writes as well as any that writ before him; if in this the most consummate act of his fidelity and ripeness, no years, no industry, no former proof of his abilities can bring him to that state of maturity as not to be still mistrusted and suspected, unless he carry all his considerate diligence, all his midnight watchings, and expense of Palladian[83] oil, to the hasty view of an unleisured licenser, perhaps much his younger, perhaps far his inferior in judgment, perhaps one who never knew the labor of book-writing, and if he be not repulsed, or slighted, must appear in print like a puny[84] with his guardian, and his censor's hand on the back of his title to be his bail and surety that he is no idiot or seducer, it cannot be but a dishonor and derogation to the author, to the book, to the privilege and dignity of learning. And what if the author shall be one so copious of fancy as to have many things well worth the adding come into his mind after licensing, while the book is yet under the press, which not seldom happens to the best and diligentest writers, and that perhaps a dozen times in one book. The printer dares not go beyond his licensed copy; so often then must the author trudge to his leave-giver that those his new insertions may be viewed; and many a jaunt will be made ere that licenser, for it must be the same man, can either be found, or found at leisure; meanwhile either the press must stand still, which is no small damage, or the author lose his accuratest thoughts, and send the book forth worse than he had made it, which to a diligent writer is the greatest melancholy and vexation that can befall. And how can a man teach with authority, which is the life of teaching, how can he be a doctor in his book as he ought to be, or else had better be silent, whenas all he teaches, all he delivers, is but under the tuition, under the correction of his patriarchal licenser to blot

[82]Escaped the rod to come under the pointer.

[83]Learned (concerning Pallas Athene).

[84]Minor.

or alter what precisely accords not with the hide-bound humor which he calls his judgment? When every acute reader upon the first sight of a pedantic license will be ready with these like words to ding[85] the book a quoit's distance from him, I hate a pupil teacher; I endure not an instructor that comes to me under the wardship of an overseeing fist. I know nothing of the licenser but that I have his own hand here for his arrogance; who shall warrant me his judgment? "The state, sir," replies the stationer, but has a quick return, "The state shall be my governors, but not my critics; they may be mistaken in the choice of a licenser as easily as this licenser may be mistaken in an author; this is some common stuff." And he might add from Sir Francis Bacon that such authorized books are but the language of the times.[86] For though a licenser should happen to be judicious more than ordinary, which will be a great jeopardy of the next succession,[87] yet his very office and his commission enjoins him to let pass nothing but what is vulgarly received already. Nay, which is more lamentable, if the work of any deceased author, though never so famous in his lifetime, and even to this day, come to their hands for license to be printed or reprinted, if there be found in his book one sentence of a venturous edge, uttered in the height of zeal, and who knows whether it might not be the dictate of a divine spirit, yet not suiting with every low decrepit humor of their own, though it were Knox himself, the reformer of a kingdom that spake it, they will not pardon him their dash; the sense of that great man shall to all posterity be lost for the fearfulness or the presumptuous rashness of a perfunctory licenser. And to what an author this violence hath been lately done, and in what book of greatest consequence to be faithfully published, I could now instance, but shall forbear till a more convenient season. Yet if these things be not resented seriously and timely by them who have the remedy in their power, but that such iron molds[88] as these shall have authority to gnaw out the choicest periods of exquisitest books and to commit such a treacherous fraud against the orphan remainders of worthiest men after death, the more sorrow will belong to that hapless race of men whose misfortune it is to have understanding. Henceforth let no man care to learn, or care to be more than worldly wise; for certainly in higher matters to be ignorant and slothful, to be a common steadfast dunce will be the only pleasant life, and only in request.

And as it is a particular disesteem of every knowing person alive, and most injurious to the written labors and monuments of the dead, so to me it seems an undervaluing and vilifying of the whole nation. I cannot set so light by all the invention, the art, the wit, the grave and solid judgment which is in England, as that it can be comprehended in any twenty capacities how good soever, much less that it should not pass except their superintendence be over it, except it be sifted and strained with their strainers, that it should be uncurrent without their manual stamp. Truth and understanding are not such wares as to be monopolized and traded in by tickets and statutes and standards. We must not think to make a staple commodity of all the knowledge in the land, to mark and license it like our broad-cloth and our woolpacks. What is it but a servitude like that imposed by the Philistines, not to be allowed the sharpening of our own axes and colters, but we must repair from all quarters to twenty licensing forges. Had any one written and divulged erroneous things and scandalous to honest life, misusing and forfeiting the esteem had of his reason among men, if after conviction this only censure were adjudged him, that he should never henceforth write but what were first examined by an appointed officer, whose hand should be annexed to pass his credit for him that now he might be safely read, it could not be apprehended less than a disgraceful punishment. Whence to include the whole nation, and those that never yet thus offended, under such a diffident and suspectful prohibition may plainly be under-

[85] Throw.

[86] See Bacon's *Advertisement Touching the Controversies in the Church of England.*

[87] Which will make it hard to find a worthy successor.

[88] Rusts.

stood what a disparagement it is. So much the more whenas debtors and delinquents may walk abroad without a keeper, but inoffensive books must not stir forth without a visible jailer in their title. Nor is it to the common people less than a reproach; for if we be so jealous over them as that we dare not trust them with an English pamphlet, what do we but censure them for a giddy, vicious, and ungrounded people, in such a sick and weak estate of faith and discretion as to be able to take nothing down but through the pipe[89] of a licenser? That this is care or love of them we cannot pretend, whenas in those Popish places where the laity are most hated and despised the same strictness is used over them. Wisdom we cannot call it, because it stops but one breach of license, nor that neither; whenas those corruptions which it seeks to prevent break in faster at other doors which cannot be shut.

And in conclusion it reflects to the disrepute of our ministers also, of whose labors we should hope better, and of the proficiency which their flock reaps by them, than that after all this light of the Gospel which is, and is to be, and all this continual preaching, they should be still frequented with such an unprincipled, unedified, and laic rabble as that the whiff of every new pamphlet should stagger them out of their catechism and Christian walking. This may have much reason to discourage the ministers when such a low conceit is had of all their exhortations and the benefiting of their hearers as that they are not thought fit to be turned loose to three sheets of paper without a licenser, that all the sermons, all the lectures preached, printed, vented in such numbers and such volumes as have now well-nigh made all other books unsalable, should not be armor enough against one single *enchiridion,*[90] without the castle St. Angelo[91] of an *imprimatur.*

And lest some should persuade ye, Lords and Commons, that these arguments of learned men's discouragement at this your order are mere flourishes and not real, I could recount what I have seen and heard in other countries, where this kind of inquisition tyrannizes; when I have sat among their learned men, for that honor I had, and been counted happy to be born in such a place of philosophic freedom as they supposed England was, while themselves did nothing but bemoan the servile condition into which learning amongst them was brought, that this was it which had damped the glory of Italian wits, that nothing had been there written now these many years but flattery and fustian. There it was that I found and visited the famous Galileo grown old,[92] a prisoner to the Inquisition for thinking in astronomy otherwise than the Franciscan and Dominican licensers thought. And though I knew that England then was groaning loudest under the prelatical yoke, nevertheless I took it as a pledge of future happiness that other nations were so persuaded of her liberty. Yet was it beyond my hope that those worthies were then breathing in her air who should be her leaders to such a deliverance as shall never be forgotten by any revolution of time that this world hath to finish. When that was once begun, it was as little in my fear that what words of complaint I heard among learned men of other parts uttered against the Inquisition, the same I should hear by as learned men at home uttered in time of Parliament against an order of licensing; and that so generally that when I had disclosed myself a companion of their discontent, I might say, if without envy, that he whom an honest quaestorship had endeared to the Sicilians,[93] was not more by them importuned against Verres than the favorable opinion which I had among many who honor ye, and are known and respected by ye, loaded me with entreaties and persuasions that I would not despair to lay together that which just reason should bring into my mind toward the removal of an undeserved thraldom upon learning. That this is not therefore the disburdening of a particular fancy, but the common grievance of all those who had prepared their minds and studies above the vulgar pitch to advance truth in others, and from others to entertain it, thus much may satisfy. And in their name I

[89]Tube used to feed patients.

[90]Handbook.

[91]Papal fortress in Rome.

[92]Near Florence in 1638, when Galileo was 74.

[93]Cicero.

shall for neither friend nor foe conceal what the general murmur is: that if it come to inquisitioning again and licensing, and that we are so timorous of ourselves and so suspicious of all men as to fear each book and the shaking of every leaf before we know what the contents are, if some who but of late were little better than silenced from preaching shall come now to silence us from reading except what they please, it cannot be guessed what is intended by some but a second tyranny over learning, and will soon put it out of controversy that bishops and presbyters are the same to us both name and thing. That those evils of prelaty which before from five or six and twenty sees were distributively charged upon the whole people will now light wholly upon learning is not obscure to us; whenas now the pastor of a small, unlearned parish on the sudden shall be exalted archbishop over a large diocese of books, and yet not remove but keep his other cure too, a mystical pluralist. He who but of late cried down the sole ordination of every novice bachelor of art, and denied sole jurisdiction over the simplest parishioner, shall now at home in his private chair assume both these over worthiest and excellentest books and ablest authors that write them. This is not, ye covenants and protestations that we have made, this is not to put down prelaty; this is but to chop an episcopacy; this is but to translate the palace metropolitan[94] from one kind of dominion into another; this is but an old canonical sleight of commuting our penance. To startle thus betimes at a mere unlicensed pamphlet will after a while be afraid of every conventicle, and a while after will make a conventicle of every Christian meeting. But I am certain that a state governed by the rules of justice and fortitude, or a church built and founded upon the rock of faith and true knowledge, cannot be so pusillanimous. While things are yet not constituted in religion that freedom of writing should be restrained by a discipline imitated from the prelates, and learned by them from the Inquisition, to shut us up all again into the breast of a licenser must needs give cause of doubt and discouragement to all learned and religious men. Who cannot but discern the fineness of this politic drift and who are the contrivers? that while bishops were to be baited[95] down, then all presses might be open; it was the people's birthright and privilege in time of Parliament; it was the breaking forth of light. But now the bishops abrogated and voided out of the Church, as if our reformation sought no more but to make room for others into their seats under another name, the episcopal arts begin to bud again; the cruise of truth must run no more oil; liberty of printing must be enthralled again under a prelatical commission of twenty, the privilege of the people nullified; and which is worse, the freedom of learning must groan again, and to her old fetters: all this the Parliament yet sitting, although their own late arguments and defences against the prelates might remember them that this obstructing violence meets for the most part with an event utterly opposite to the end which it drives at. Instead of suppressing sects and schisms, it raises them and invests them with a reputation. *"The punishing of wits enhances their authority,"* saith the Viscount St. Albans,[96] *"and a forbidden writing is thought to be a certain spark of truth that flies up in the faces of them who seek to tread it out."* This order therefore may prove a nursing mother to sects, but I shall easily show how it will be a step-dame to Truth, and first by disenabling us to the maintenance of what is known already.

Well knows he who uses to consider, that our faith and knowledge thrives by exercise, as well as our limbs and complexion. Truth is compared in Scripture to a streaming fountain; if her waters flow not in a perpetual progression, they sicken into a muddy pool of conformity and tradition. A man may be a heretic in the truth; and if he believe things only because his pastor says so, or the assembly so determines, without knowing other reason, though his belief be true, yet the very truth he holds becomes his heresy. There is not any burden that some would gladlier post off to another than the

[94] Lambeth Palace, standing for the Archbishopric of Canterbury.

[95] Hunted. [96] Francis Bacon.

charge and care of their religion. There be, who knows not that there be of Protestants and professors[97] who live and die in as arrant an implicit faith as any lay Papist of Loretto? A wealthy man addicted to his pleasure and to his profits finds religion to be a traffic so entangled and of so many piddling accounts that of all mysteries[98] he cannot skill to keep a stock going upon that trade. What should he do? fain he would have the name to be religious; fain he would bear up with his neighbors in that. What does he therefore but resolves to give over toiling and to find himself out some factor to whose care and credit he may commit the whole managing of his religious affairs? some divine of note and estimation that must be. To him he adheres, resigns the whole warehouse of his religion, with all the locks and keys, into his custody; and indeed makes the very person of that man his religion; esteems his associating with him a sufficient evidence and commendatory of his own piety; so that a man may say his religion is now no more within himself, but is become a dividual[99] movable and goes and comes near him according as that good man frequents the house. He entertains him, gives him gifts, feasts him, lodges him; his religion comes home at night, prays, is liberally supped, and sumptuously laid to sleep, rises, is saluted; and after the malmsey or some well-spiced brewage, and better breakfasted than he whose morning appetite would have gladly fed on green figs between Bethany and Jerusalem, his religion walks abroad at eight, and leaves his kind entertainer in the shop trading all day without his religion.

Another sort there be who when they hear that all things shall be ordered, all things regulated and settled, nothing written but what passes through the custom-house of certain publicans[100] that have the tonnaging and the poundaging of all free-spoken truth, will straight give themselves up into your hands, make 'em and cut 'em out what religion ye please. There be delights, there be recreations and jolly pastimes that will fetch the day about from sun to sun, and rock the tedious year as in a delightful dream. What need they torture their heads with that which others have taken so strictly and so unalterably into their own purveying? These are the fruits which a dull ease and cessation of our knowledge will bring forth among the people. How goodly and how to be wished were such an obedient unanimity as this? what a fine conformity would it starch us all into? doubtless a staunch and solid piece of framework, as any January could freeze together.

Nor much better will be the consequence even among the clergy themselves. It is no new thing, never heard of before, for a parochial minister, who has his reward and is at his Hercules' pillars[101] in a warm benefice, to be easily inclinable, if he have nothing else that may rouse up his studies, to finish his circuit in an English concordance and a topic folio, the gatherings and savings of a sober graduateship, a harmony and a catena,[102] treading the constant round of certain common doctrinal heads, attended with their uses, motives, marks, and means; out of which as out of an alphabet or sol-fa[103] by forming and transforming, joining and disjoining variously a little bookcraft, and two hours' meditation might furnish him unspeakably to the performance of more than a weekly charge of sermoning, not to reckon up the infinite helps of interliniaries, breviaries, synopses, and other loitering gear. But as for the multitude of sermons ready printed and piled up on every text that is not difficult, our London trading St. Thomas in his vestry, and add to boot St. Martin and St. Hugh, have not within their hallowed limits more vendible ware of all sorts ready made; so that penury he never need fear of pulpit provision, having where so plenteously to refresh his magazine. But if his rear and flanks be not impaled, if his back door be not secured by the rigid licenser, but that a bold book may now and then issue forth and give the assault to some of his old

[97]Those who make open profession of their religion, particularly Puritans.

[98]Trades. [99]Dividable.

[100]Tax-collectors.

[101]Has reached the height of his expectations.

[102]A synopsis of the four Gospels and a series of extracts from the Church Fathers.

[103]Musical gamut.

collections in their trenches, it will concern him then to keep waking, to stand in watch, to set good guards and sentinels about his received opinions, to walk the round and counter-round with his fellow-inspectors, fearing lest any of his flock be seduced, who also then would be better instructed, better exercised and disciplined. And God send that the fear of this diligence which must then be used do not make us affect the laziness of a licensing church.

For if we be sure we are in the right, and do not hold the truth guiltily, which becomes not if we ourselves condemn not our own weak and frivolous teaching, and the people for an untaught and irreligious gadding rout, what can be more fair than when a man judicious, learned, and of a conscience, for aught we know, as good as theirs that taught us what we know, shall not privily from house to house, which is more dangerous, but openly by writing publish to the world what his opinion is, what his reasons, and wherefore that which is now thought cannot be sound? Christ urged it as wherewith to justify himself that he preached in public; yet writing is more public than preaching, and more easy to refutation, if need be, there being so many whose business and profession merely it is, to be the champions of truth; which if they neglect, what can be imputed but their sloth or inability?

Thus much we are hindered and disinured[104] by this course of licensing toward the true knowledge of what we seem to know. For how much it hurts and hinders the licensers themselves in the calling of their ministry more than any secular employment, if they will discharge that office as they ought, so that of necessity they must neglect either the one duty or the other, I insist not, because it is a particular, but leave it to their own conscience how they will decide it there.

There is yet, behind of what I purposed to lay open, the incredible loss and detriment that this plot of licensing puts us to; more than if some enemy at sea should stop up all our havens and ports and creeks, it hinders and retards the importation of our richest merchandise, truth. Nay, it was first established and put in practice by Anti-Christian malice and mystery on set purpose to extinguish, if it were possible, the light of reformation and to settle falsehood, little differing from that policy wherewith the Turk upholds his Alcoran by the prohibition of printing. 'Tis not denied, but gladly confessed, we are to send our thanks and vows to heaven, louder than most of nations, for that great measure of truth which we enjoy, especially in those main points between us and the Pope, with his appurtenances, the prelates; but he who thinks we are to pitch our tent here, and have attained the utmost prospect of reformation that the mortal glass wherein we contemplate can show us till we come to beatific vision, that man by this very opinion declares that he is yet far short of truth.

Truth indeed came once into the world with her divine master, and was a perfect shape most glorious to look on; but when he ascended, and his apostles after him were laid asleep, then straight arose a wicked race of deceivers who, as that story goes of the Egyptian Typhon with his conspirators, how they dealt with the good Osiris, took the virgin Truth, hewed her lovely form into a thousand pieces, and scattered them to the four winds. From that time ever since the said friends of Truth, such as durst appear, imitating the careful[105] search that Isis made for the mangled body of Osiris, went up and down gathering up limb by limb still as they could find them. We have not yet found them all, Lords and Commons, nor ever shall do till her master's second coming; he shall bring together every joint and member, and shall mold them into an immortal feature of loveliness and perfection. Suffer not these licensing prohibitions to stand at every place of opportunity, forbidding and disturbing them that continue seeking, that continue to do our obsequies to the torn body of our martyred saint. We boast our light; but if we look not wisely on the sun itself, it smites us into darkness. Who can discern those planets that are oft combust,[106] and those stars of brightest magnitude that rise and set with the sun, until the opposite motion

[104] Made unaccustomed.

[105] Sorrowful.

[106] So near the sun as to be invisible.

of their orbs bring them to such a place in the firmament where they may be seen evening or morning? The light which we have gained was given us, not to be ever staring on, but by it to discover onward things more remote from our knowledge. It is not the unfrocking of a priest, the unmitering of a bishop, and the removing him from off the presbyterian shoulders that will make us a happy nation; no, if other things as great in the church and in the rule of life both economical[107] and political be not looked into and reformed, we have looked so long upon the blaze that Zuinglius and Calvin[108] hath beaconed up to us that we are stark blind. There be who perpetually complain of schisms and sects, and make it such a calamity that any man dissents from their maxims. 'Tis their own pride and ignorance which causes the disturbing, who neither will hear with meekness nor can convince, yet all must be suppressed which is not found in their syntagma.[109] They are the troublers; they are the dividers of unity, who neglect and permit not others to unite those dissevered pieces which are yet wanting to the body of Truth. To be still searching what we know not by what we know, still closing up truth to truth as we find it (for all her body is homogeneal[110] and proportional), this is the golden rule in theology as well as in arithmetic, and makes up the best harmony in a church, not the forced and outward union of cold, and neutral, and inwardly divided minds.

Lords and Commons of England, consider what nation it is whereof ye are and whereof ye are the governors: a nation not slow and dull, but of a quick, ingenious, and piercing spirit, acute to invent, subtle and sinewy to discourse, not beneath the reach of any point the highest that human capacity can soar to. Therefore the studies of learning in her deepest sciences have been so ancient and so eminent among us that writers of good antiquity and ablest judgment have been persuaded that even the school of Pythagoras and the Persian wisdom took beginning from the old philosophy of this island. And that wise and civil Roman, Julius Agricola, who governed once here for Caesar,[111] preferred the natural wits of Britain before the labored studies of the French. Nor is it for nothing that the grave and frugal Transylvanian sends out yearly from as far as the mountainous borders of Russia, and beyond the Hercynian wilderness,[112] not their youth, but their staid men to learn our language and our theologic arts. Yet that which is above all this, the favor and the love of heaven, we have great argument to think in a peculiar manner propitious and propending towards us. Why else was this nation chosen before any other, that out of her as out of Sion should be proclaimed and sounded forth the first tidings and trumpet of reformation to all Europe. And had it not been the obstinate perverseness of our prelates against the divine and admirable spirit of Wicliffe, to suppress him as a schismatic and innovator, perhaps neither the Bohemian Huss and Jerome, no, nor the name of Luther or of Calvin had been ever known; the glory of reforming all our neighbors had been completely ours. But now, as our obdurate clergy have with violence demeaned the matter, we are become hitherto the latest and the backwardest scholars, of whom God offered to have made us the teachers. Now once again by all concurrence of signs and by the general instinct of holy and devout men, as they daily and solemnly express their thoughts, God is decreeing to begin some new and great period in his Church, even to the reforming of reformation itself; what does he then but reveal himself to his servants and, as his manner is, first to his Englishmen? I say, as his manner is, first to us, though we mark not the method of his counsels and are unworthy. Behold now this vast city, a city of refuge, the mansion-house of liberty, encompassed and surrounded with his protection; the shop of war hath not there more anvils and hammers waking, to fashion out the plates and in-

[107]Concerning private management.

[108]Swiss and French reformers of the sixteenth century.

[109]Personal collections of beliefs.

[110]Homogeneous.

[111]For the emperors Vespasian, Titus, and Domitian.

[112]The forests of southern Germany.

struments of armed justice in defence of beleaguered truth, than there be pens and heads there, sitting by their studious lamps, musing, searching, revolving new notions and ideas wherewith to present, as with their homage and their fealty, the approaching reformation; others as fast reading, trying all things, assenting to the force of reason and convincement. What could a man require more from a nation so pliant and so prone to seek after knowledge? What wants there to such towardly[113] and pregnant soil but wise and faithful laborers, to make a knowing people, a nation of prophets, of sages, and of worthies? We reckon more than five months yet to harvest; there need not be five weeks; had we but eyes to lift up, the fields are white already. Where there is much desire to learn, there of necessity will be much arguing, much writing, many opinions; for opinion in good men is but knowledge in the making. Under these fantastic terrors of sect and schism we wrong the earnest and zealous thirst after knowledge and understanding which God hath stirred up in this city. What some lament of we rather should rejoice at, should rather praise this pious forwardness among men to reassume the ill-deputed care of their religion into their own hands again. A little generous prudence, a little forbearance of one another, and some grain of charity might win all these diligences to join and unite into one general and brotherly search after truth, could we but forego this prelatical tradition of crowding free consciences and Christian liberties into canons and precepts of men. I doubt not, if some great and worthy stranger should come among us, wise to discern the mold and temper of a people, and how to govern it, observing the high hopes and aims, the diligent alacrity of our extended thoughts and reasonings in the pursuance of truth and freedom, but that he would cry out as Pyrrhus[114] did, admiring the Roman docility and courage, "if such were my Epirots, I would not despair the greatest design that could be attempted to make a church or kingdom happy." Yet these are the men cried out against for schismatics and sectaries, as if, while the Temple of the Lord was building, some cutting, some squaring the marble, others hewing the cedars, there should be a sort of irrational men who could not consider there must be many schisms and many dissections made in the quarry and in the timber, ere the house of God can be built. And when every stone is laid artfully together, it cannot be united into a continuity, it can but be contiguous in this world; neither can every piece of the building be of one form; nay, rather the perfection consists in this, that out of many moderate varieties and brotherly dissimilitudes that are not vastly disproportional arises the goodly and the graceful symmetry that commends the whole pile and structure. Let us therefore be more considerate builders, more wise in spiritual architecture, when great reformation is expected. For now the time seems come wherein Moses, the great prophet, may sit in heaven rejoicing to see that memorable and glorious wish of his fulfilled, when not only our seventy elders but all the Lord's people are become prophets. No marvel then though some men, and some good men too perhaps, but young in goodness, as Joshua then was, envy them. They fret, and out of their own weakness are in agony lest these divisions and sub-divisions will undo us. The adversary again applauds and waits the hour: "When they have branched themselves out," saith he, "small enough into parties and partitions, then will be our time." Fool! he sees not the firm root out of which we all grow, though into branches; nor will beware until he see our small divided maniples cutting through at every angle of his ill-united and unwieldy brigade. And that we are to hope better of all these supposed sects and schisms, and that we shall not need that solicitude, honest perhaps though over-timorous, of them that vex in this behalf, but shall laugh in the end at those malicious applauders of our differences, I have these reasons to persuade me.

First, when a city shall be as it were besieged and blocked about, her navigable river infested, inroads and incursions round, defiance and battle oft rumored to be marching up even to her walls and suburb trenches, that then the people, or the greater part,

[113] Easily cultivated.

[114] King of Epirus (B. C. 318–272).

more than at other times wholly taken up with the study of highest and most important matters to be reformed, should be disputing, reasoning, reading, inventing, discoursing, even to a rarity and admiration, things not before discoursed or written of, argues first a singular good will, contentedness and confidence in your prudent foresight and safe government, Lords and Commons; and from thence derives itself to a gallant bravery and well-grounded contempt of their enemies, as if there were no small number of as great spirits among us as his was who when Rome was nigh besieged by Hannibal, being in the city, bought that piece of ground at no cheap rate whereon Hannibal himself encamped his own regiment. Next it is a lively and cheerful presage of our happy success and victory. For as in a body, when the blood is fresh, the spirits pure and vigorous, not only to vital but to rational faculties, and those in the acutest and the pertest[115] operations of wit and subtlety, it argues in what good plight and constitution the body is; so when the cheerfulness of the people is so sprightly up as that it has, not only wherewith to guard well its own freedom and safety, but to spare and to bestow upon the solidest and sublimest points of controversy and new invention, it betokens us not degenerated nor drooping to a fatal decay, but casting off the old and wrinkled skin of corruption to outlive these pangs and wax young again, entering the glorious ways of truth and prosperous virtue destined to become great and honorable in these latter ages. Methinks I see in my mind a noble and puissant nation rousing herself like a strong man after sleep, and shaking her invincible locks. Methinks I see her as an eagle mewing[116] her mighty youth and kindling her undazzled eyes at the full mid-day beam, purging and unscaling her long-abused sight at the fountain itself of heavenly radiance; while the whole noise of timorous and flocking birds, with those also that love the twilight, flutter about, amazed at what she means, and in their envious gabble would prognosticate a year of sects and schisms.

What should ye do then, should ye suppress all this flowery crop of knowledge and new light sprung up and yet springing daily in this city; should ye set an oligarchy of twenty engrossers[117] over it, to bring a famine upon our minds again, when we shall know nothing but what is measured to us by their bushel? Believe it, Lords and Commons, they who counsel ye to such a suppressing do as good as bid ye suppress yourselves; and I will soon show how. If it be desired to know the immediate cause of all this free writing and free speaking, there cannot be assigned a truer than your own mild, and free, and humane government; it is the liberty, Lords and Commons, which your own valorous and happy counsels have purchased us, liberty which is the nurse of all great wits; this is that which hath rarefied and enlightened our spirits like the influence of heaven; this is that which hath enfranchised, enlarged, and lifted up our apprehensions degrees above themselves. Ye cannot make us now less capable, less knowing, less eagerly pursuing of the truth, unless ye first make yourselves, that made us so, less the lovers, less the founders of our true liberty. We can grow ignorant again, brutish, formal, and slavish, as ye found us; but you then must first become that which ye cannot be, oppressive, arbitrary, and tyrannous, as they were from whom ye have freed us. That our hearts are now more capacious, our thoughts more erected to the search and expectation of greatest and exactest things is the issue of your own virtue propagated in us; ye cannot suppress that unless ye reinforce an abrogated and merciless law that fathers may dispatch at will their own children. And who shall then stick closest to ye and excite others? not he who takes up arms for coat and conduct[118] and his four nobles of Danegelt.[119] Although I dispraise not the defence of just immunities, yet love my peace better, if that[120] were all. Give me the liberty to know, to utter, and to argue

[115]Liveliest. [116]Renewing.

[117]Monopolizers.

[118]Takes up arms to resist taxation for clothing and transporting troops.

[119]Originally, a land-tax for protection against Danish raids; here, referring to the ship-money which Charles I had exacted, supposedly to afford naval protection.

[120]Immunity from taxation.

freely according to conscience, above all liberties.

What would be best advised then, if it be found so hurtful and so unequal to suppress opinions for the newness, or the unsuitableness to a customary acceptance, will not be my task to say; I only shall repeat what I have learned from one of your own honorable number, a right noble and pious lord, who, had he not sacrificed his life and fortunes to the Church and Commonwealth, we had not now missed and bewailed a worthy and undoubted patron of this argument. Ye know him I am sure; yet I for honor's sake, and may it be eternal to him, shall name him the Lord Brooke.[121] He, writing of episcopacy, and by the way treating of sects and schisms, left ye his vote, or rather now the last words of his dying charge, which I know will ever be of dear and honored regard with ye, so full of meekness and breathing charity that next to his last testament, who bequeathed love and peace to his disciples, I cannot call to mind where I have read or heard words more mild and peaceful. He there exhorts us to hear with patience and humility those, however they be miscalled, that desire to live purely, in such a use of God's ordinances as the best guidance of their conscience gives them, and to tolerate them, though in some disconformity to ourselves. The book itself will tell us more at large, being published to the world and dedicated to the Parliament by him who both for his life and for his death deserves that what advice he left be not laid by without perusal.

And now the time in special is by privilege to write and speak what may help to the further discussing of matters in agitation. The Temple of Janus with his two controversal faces might now not unsignificantly be set open. And though all the winds of doctrine were let loose to play upon the earth, so Truth be in the field, we do injuriously by licensing and prohibiting to misdoubt her strength. Let her and Falsehood grapple; who ever knew Truth put to the worse in a free and open encounter. Her confuting is the best and surest suppressing. He who hears what praying there is for light and clearer knowledge to be sent down among us would think of other matters to be constituted beyond the discipline of Geneva, framed and fabricked already to our hands. Yet when the new light which we beg for shines in upon us, there be who envy and oppose if it come not first in at their casements. What a collusion is this, whenas we are exhorted by the wise man[122] to use diligence, to seek for wisdom as for hidden treasures early and late, that another order shall enjoin us to know nothing but by statute. When a man hath been laboring the hardest labor in the deep mines of knowledge, hath furnished out his findings in all their equipage, drawn forth his reasons as it were a battle ranged, scattered and defeated all objections in his way, calls out his adversary into the plain, offers him the advantage of wind and sun, if he please, only that he may try the matter by dint of argument, for his opponents then to skulk, to lay ambushments, to keep a narrow bridge of licensing where the challenger should pass, though it be valor enough in soldiership, is but weakness and cowardice in the wars of Truth. For who knows not that Truth is strong next to the Almighty; she needs no policies, nor stratagems, nor licensings to make her victorious; those are the shifts and the defences that Error uses against her power; give her but room, and do not bind her when she sleeps, for then she speaks not true, as the old Proteus did, who spake oracles only when he was caught and bound, but then rather she turns herself into all shapes except her own, and perhaps tunes her voice according to the time, as Micaiah did before Ahab, until she be adjured into her own likeness. Yet is it not impossible that she may have more shapes than one. What else is all that rank of things indifferent wherein Truth may be on this side, or on the other, without being unlike herself. What but a vain shadow else is the abolition of those ordinances, that hand-writing nailed to the cross? what great purchase is this Christian liberty which Paul so often boasts of? His doctrine is that he who eats or eats not, regards a day, or regards it not, may do

[121] Robert Greville (1607–1643), author of *A Discourse on Episcopacy.*

[122] Christ (St. Matthew, 13:44).

either to the Lord. How many other things might be tolerated in peace and left to conscience, had we but charity, and were it not the chief stronghold of our hypocrisy to be ever judging one another. I fear yet this iron yoke of outward conformity hath left a slavish print upon our necks; the ghost of a linen decency[123] yet haunts us. We stumble and are impatient at the least dividing of one visible congregation from another, though it be not in fundamentals; and through our forwardness to suppress and our backwardness to recover any enthralled piece of truth out of the gripe[124] of custom we care not to keep truth separated from truth, which is the fiercest rent and disunion of all. We do not see that while we still affect by all means a rigid external formality, we may as soon fall again into a gross conforming stupidity, a stark and dead congealment of wood and hay and stubble forced and frozen together, which is more to the sudden degenerating of a church than many sub-dichotomies[125] of petty schisms. Not that I can think well of every light separation, or that all in a church is to be expected gold and silver and precious stones; it is not possible for man to sever the wheat from the tares, the good fish from the other fry; that must be the angel's ministry at the end of mortal things. Yet if all cannot be of one mind, as who looks they should be? this doubtless is more wholesome, more prudent, and more Christian that many be tolerated rather than all compelled. I mean not tolerated Popery and open superstition, which as it extirpates all religions and civil supremacies, so itself should be extirpate, provided first that all charitable and compassionate means be used to win and regain the weak and the misled; that also which is impious or evil absolutely either against faith or manners no law can possibly permit, that intends not to unlaw itself; but those neighboring differences, or rather indifferences, are what I speak of, whether in some point of doctrine or of discipline which though they may be many, yet need not interrupt the unity of spirit, if we could but find among us the bond of peace. In the meanwhile if any one would write and bring his helpful hand to the slow-moving reformation which we labor under, if truth have spoken to him before others, or but seemed at least to speak, who hath so bejesuited us that we should trouble that man with asking license to do so worthy a deed? and not consider this, that if it come to prohibiting, there is not aught more likely to be prohibited than truth itself; whose first appearance to our eyes, bleared and dimmed with prejudice and custom, is more unsightly and unplausible than many errors, even as the person is of many a great man slight and contemptible to see to. And what do they tell us vainly of new opinions, when this very opinion of theirs, that none must be heard but whom they like, is the worst and newest opinion of all others, and is the chief cause why sects and schisms do so much abound, and true knowledge is kept at distance from us, besides yet a greater danger which is in it? For when God shakes a kingdom with strong and healthful commotions to a general reforming, 'tis not untrue that many sectaries and false teachers are then busiest in seducing; but yet more true it is that God then raises to his own work men of rare abilities and more than common industry not only to look back and revise what hath been taught heretofore, but to gain further and go on some new enlightened steps in the discovery of truth. For such is the order of God's enlightening his Church, to dispense and deal out by degrees his beam, so as our earthly eyes may best sustain it. Neither is God appointed and confined where and out of what place these his chosen shall be first heard to speak; for he sees not as man sees, chooses not as man chooses, lest we should devote ourselves again to set places, and assemblies, and outward callings of men, planting our faith one while in the old convocation house, and another while in the chapel at Westminster;[126] when all the faith and religion that shall be there canonized is not sufficient without plain convincement and the charity of patient instruction to supple[127] the least

[123]The controversy over ecclesiastical vestments.

[124]Grip. [125]Minute divisions.

[126]One while in the place where the clergy of the Church of England assembled, and another in the place where the Presbyterian Church held its meetings when it became the state religion in 1643.

[127]Soften.

bruise of conscience, to edify the meanest Christian who desires to walk in the spirit and not in the letter of human trust, for all the number of voices that can be there made; no, though Harry VII himself there,[128] with all his liege tombs about him, should lend them voices from the dead to swell their number. And if the men be erroneous who appear to be the leading schismatics, what withholds us but our sloth, our self-will and distrust in the right cause, that we do not give them gentle meetings and gentle dismissions, that we debate not and examine the matter thoroughly with liberal and frequent audience, if not for their sakes, yet for our own? seeing no man who hath tasted learning but will confess the many ways of profiting by those who not contented with stale receipts are able to manage and set forth new positions to the world. And were they but as the dust and cinders of our feet, so long as in that notion they may yet serve to polish and brighten the armory of truth, even for that respect they were not utterly to be cast away. But if they be of those whom God hath fitted for the special use of these times with eminent and ample gifts, and those perhaps neither among the priests nor among the pharisees, and we in the haste of a precipitant zeal shall make no distinction but resolve to stop their mouths, because we fear they come with new and dangerous opinions, as we commonly forejudge them ere we understand them, no less than woe to us, while thinking thus to defend the Gospel, we are found the persecutors.

There have been not a few since the beginning of this Parliament, both of the presbytery and others, who by their unlicensed books to the contempt of an *imprimatur* first broke that triple ice clung about our hearts and taught the people to see day; I hope that none of those were the persuaders to renew upon us this bondage which they themselves have wrought so much good by contemning. But if neither the check that Moses gave to young Joshua, nor the countermand which our Savior gave to young John, who was so ready to prohibit those whom he thought unlicensed, be not enough to admonish our elders how unacceptable to God their testy mood of prohibiting is; if neither their own remembrance what evil hath abounded in the Church by this let[129] of licensing, and what good they themselves have begun by transgressing it, be not enough but that they will persuade and execute the most Dominican part of the Inquisition over us, and are already with one foot in the stirrup so active at suppressing; it would be no unequal distribution in the first place to suppress the suppressors themselves, whom the change of their condition hath puffed up more than their late experience of harder times hath made wise.

And as for regulating the press, let no man think to have the honor of advising ye better than yourselves have done in that order published next before this, that no book be printed unless the printer's and the author's name, or at least the printer's, be registered. Those which otherwise come forth, if they be found mischievous and libellous, the fire and the executioner will be the timeliest and the most effectual remedy that man's prevention can use. For this authentic Spanish policy of licensing books, if I have said aught, will prove the most unlicensed book itself within a short while; and was the immediate image of a Star-Chamber decree[130] to that purpose made in those very times when that court did the rest of those her pious works for which she is now fallen from the stars with Lucifer. Whereby ye may guess what kind of state prudence, what love of the people, what care of religion or good manners there was at the contriving, although with singular hypocrisy it pretended to bind books to their good behavior. And how it got the upper hand of your precedent order so well constituted before, if we may believe those men whose profession gives them cause to inquire most, it may be doubted there was in it the fraud of some old patentees and monopolizers in the trade of book-selling; who under pretence of the poor in their company not to be defrauded and the just retaining of each man his several copy, which God forbid should be gainsaid,

[128] Henry VII is buried in the chapel at Westminster.

[129] Hindrance.

[130] A decree by the royal court of the Star Chamber, abolished in 1641.

brought divers glossing colors to the House, which were indeed but colors and serving to no end except it be to exercise a superiority over their neighbors, men who do not therefore labor in an honest profession to which learning is indebted, that they should be made other men's vassals. Another end is thought was aimed at by some of them in procuring by petition this order, that having power in their hands, malignant books might the easier escape abroad, as the event shows. But of these sophisms and elenches[131] of merchandise I skill not. This I know, that errors in a good government and in a bad are equally almost incident; for what magistrate may not be misinformed, and much the sooner, if liberty of printing be reduced into the power of a few; but to redress willingly and speedily what hath been erred, and in highest authority to esteem a plain advertisement more than others have done a sumptuous bribe is a virtue (honored Lords and Commons) answerable to your highest actions, and whereof none can participate but greatest and wisest men.

[131] Fallacious arguments.

The Restoration and the Eighteenth Century, 1660–1784

Upon the death of Oliver Cromwell in 1658 it became rapidly clear that the Puritan Commonwealth was a failure. Oliver named his son Richard as his successor, but Richard had none of his father's overmastering force of character, and soon found himself helpless in the hands of the council of military officers through which Oliver had ruled the country. Richard summoned a Parliament to help him. Though Parliament and Army began to quarrel with each other, Richard himself was not helped. He was forced to abdicate within less than a year after he had become Protector. Oliver had risen to that position only because the Puritans could not agree amongst themselves once they had overturned the Stuart monarchy. It now became clear that Oliver's personal strength, or genius, had alone kept the so-called Commonwealth together for even a few years, and that there was no one capable of taking Oliver's place.

With the virtual collapse of government, the widespread discontent which had been aroused by the severity of "Godly" military rule became active and vocal. Royalists were ready with the only practical solution that presented itself—the recall of Charles I's son from across the water. When complete confusion threatened after Richard's abdication, one of Oliver Cromwell's generals, George Monk, who had been stationed in Scotland, came south with his army. Monk acted in accordance with the desire of the great majority in bringing about the restoration of royal government through the return, in 1660, of Charles II. Charles had been sent abroad for safety in 1645. He had come back to Scotland, where he was proclaimed king, after the Puritans had beheaded Charles I; but within a few months Cromwell had secured control of Scotland, and Charles II had been forced to return to France. An exile for virtually fifteen years, he had spent the greater part of that time in France, surrounded by a considerable number of loyal Englishmen. Life had not been easy for the royal exile, and he was very glad to come home. General Monk advised him to be liberal with pardons, and he accepted the advice. He was, indeed, more disposed to let bygones be bygones than was Parliament, which refused to sanction the religious toleration Charles advocated, and imposed severe penalties or disabilities on those who would not come within the re-established Church of England.

Charles II and His Influence

Charles II was not without characteristic Stuart ambitions and beliefs. He wanted like his father and grandfather, to become an absolute ruler, and he also wanted to bring the country back to Catholicism. He had, however, learned some lessons. Providence had at length given him a position of great affluence and of the highest dignity, and he was resolved to enjoy the gift to the utmost and not on any account to allow it to be snatched away. Hence, when opposition to one or another of his designs became stiff, he would abandon his plan rather than fight for it. During his last years the English grew suspicious of him, but even then did not know that he was accepting large sums of money from the king of France as an inducement to act against the interests of his own people. It was not until he was on his death-bed, in 1685, that he acknowledged himself a Roman Catholic. Doubtless Charles's readiness to throw over schemes when they provoked serious trouble was a consequence not only of his desire to hold the throne, for himself and for his family, but also of the licentious life he led. He was easygoing, and always ready to sacrifice business for pleasure.

The "merry monarch" was merriest when he was with one of his mistresses, and Charles's court is notorious for the open and gross immorality which flourished there. The court, moreover, was still the center of the nation's life as it had been in the reign of Elizabeth and in the reigns of the first two Stuarts. The moral standards, the manners, the tastes and interests, the dress, the household furniture, the whole order and setting of life brought in by the king exerted an influence stronger than we today can easily imagine, not only upon London but upon the nation at large. Charles himself might complain that a king forced to consult his parliament was a king only in name, but the name was majestic, as a ludicrous example may show. One Sunday in the Chapel Royal the preacher of the day stopped in his sermon to cry out to the sleeping Earl of Lauderdale, "My lord, my lord, you snore so loud you will wake the king!"

But Charles's overpowering influence made itself felt in a kind of worldliness which we would not be prepared to expect simply from hearing of the great number of his mistresses and of his ability to sleep through the "disease of sermons" which he could only thus escape. Charles had a genuine, persistent interest in chemistry, and maintained a laboratory in his palace; indeed, he had an active interest in the whole realm of science, and, considering his incapacity for study, a surprising fund of practical knowledge. He not only "understood navigation well," as Bishop Burnet has recorded, "but above all he knew the architecture of ships so perfectly that in that respect he was exact rather more than became a prince." In addition, Charles inherited his father's love of the painter's art. He tried to gather again the pictures Charles I had collected, which had been dispersed under the Commonwealth, and specially cherished the paintings of Raphael, Titian, and Holbein with which he surrounded himself. He was also a liberal patron of living artists, and kept some half a dozen of them busy. Music too he loved, and he drew to his court the best English and some of the best foreign masters of that art. From France he brought gilt mirrors and furniture and colorful clothes. Paris in the middle of the seventeenth century had become the brilliant center of all European culture, art, and polished elegance, and Charles introduced into England every new thing Paris could boast of, until the stream of refinements gathered a momentum of its own and no longer needed royal encouragement. To give one example, trifling enough in itself, in the summer of 1669 four thousand gilt mirrors were sent from Paris to supply the London trade.

Much more important than mirrors was good breeding. When Charles returned, he found England, on the whole, a country of boors, rough in their play, always jeering at anything strange, stiff and awkward in manner, and much inclined to be morose. The type is not wholly extinct today in backward corners of the island; but Charles set a very different standard, which had an immediate and permanent influence. His conception of a gentleman was, "to be easy himself and to make everybody else so." It can be expressed in ten words, but it would be difficult in as many pages to explain all that this new ideal meant and to outline its bearings upon English life and letters for the next hundred years and more. Without this change in manners, the flood of other French influences could have had but little effect; with it, everything hung together, and the total effect we can see fairly reflected in the new prose and poetry of the time.

Continuity of Renaissance Tradition

The contrast between Restoration literature and Elizabethan literature is so striking, and so significant, that there is some temptation to treat it dramatically. Merely to underline differences, however, is to lose the truth for a fancy picture. Hence before we turn to the new prose and poetry we must understand that there were elements of continuity in English artistic and intellectual life through the seventeenth century no less important than the changes we see. Charles II's scientific interests, for example, represented nothing new or foreign. From the early years of the century scientific investigation had been actively carried on in England; and when, in 1662, Charles gave a charter to the Royal Society, he was merely recognizing, and encouraging, a group of men who had been meeting regularly to discuss scientific problems and projects since 1645. Modes of thought which were to prevail in the new age similarly go back to Bacon, and to the rationalism which we have seen growing in the work of Anglican divines of the first half of the century.

The literature of the Restoration and the eighteenth century also has its roots in England, going back chiefly to Ben Jonson and the "sons of Ben," as his followers gratefully styled themselves. Restoration comedy does not owe a great deal directly to Jonson, but does owe much to several courtly dramatists of the second quarter of the century who themselves were of Jonson's school. This element of continuity can be seen most distinctly in some of the lyrical poetry of the Restoration period, but it is present everywhere, and is unmistakable once we begin to look closely for it. As the eighteenth century advances, moreover, we find poets looking back to Spenser and even more to Milton as their teachers and sources of inspiration. The consequences, with a few exceptions, were not happy, but at present what we are concerned with is simply the evidence, which is abundant, that men of the Restoration and the eighteenth century did not think of themselves as having broken with the Elizabethan or Renaissance tradition.

On the contrary, they thought of themselves as continuing this tradition and building upon it, or advancing from it. What is more, they were, within limits, quite right. This is the first thing concerning this new period that we must get clearly fixed in mind. We have seen that the revival of classical studies was, for literature, a central part of that very complex movement of change called the Renaissance. We have seen that this revival had a pervasive, yet on the whole superficial, influence upon late sixteenth-century literature. The revival at first took strongest hold, as we might expect, upon a few scholars, and then spread slowly outward. The consequence was that Elizabethan literature was rather humanistic than classical. It expressed primarily, in other words, the spirit of the age: the new confidence in human powers, the new conviction of the dignity and worth of earthly human nature, and the new desire to emulate the cultural achievements of the ancient pre-Christian world. These convictions and aspirations broadly distinguish the early manifestations of what we call "the modern spirit" from "the medieval spirit," and they were of the essence of Renaissance humanism. Elizabethan imaginative writers were not, by and large, deeply read in the ancient literatures; but they were emphatically men of the Renaissance. With Ben Jonson, however, literature began to be more genuinely classical in form and spirit. By this it is not meant that poets set about the creation of museum pieces. As they became more intimately and appreciatively acquainted with Virgil, with Martial, with the poets of the *Greek Anthology,* and, above all, with Horace, they became more critical, and better able to use what they were learning, in verse which was not less English for being smooth, carefully modulated, and urbane. When in the 1650's Sir John Denham, altering his *Cooper's Hill* (first published in 1642), apostrophized the Thames in lines which became famous, it was felt that a new height had been reached in the refinement of English verse.

O could I flow like thee, and make thy stream
My great example, as it is my theme!
Though deep, yet clear, though gentle, yet not dull,
Strong without rage, without o'erflowing full.

The Heroic Couplet

These couplets can tell us a great deal. To aim at clarity, ease, and steady control, without sacrifice of interest, strength, or depth, may be accepted as a classical standard, or, alternatively, as a fit standard for a cultivated society which has attained a high level of civilization. And in the new age Denham and his contemporary Edmund Waller were given most credit for showing the way to a kind of verse which could meet this standard. It was said that the "ideal" verse should combine Waller's "sweetness" with Denham's "strength." Actually the kind of thing aimed at was the "closed couplet," as it is called, in which a complete general statement is made with neatness and point:

Know then thyself, presume not God to scan;
The proper study of Mankind is Man.

For Forms of Government let fools contest;
Whate'er is best administered is best.

Worth makes the man, and want of it the fellow;
The rest is all but leather or prunella.

Men, some to Business, some to Pleasure take;
But every Woman is at heart a Rake.

Pope is the author of these familiar examples. He has no English rival in this field, and remains the undisputed brilliant master of our aphoristic verse. Dryden bridges the long distance between Denham and Pope. Dryden used the rimed couplet for many purposes, for narrative and heroic poetry, for heroic drama, for satire, for reasoned argument, and for many of the conversational prologues and epilogues which he wrote. He used it in these varied ways with unfailing energy, and did more than anyone else to fix it, for several generations, as the dominant form of English verse. Yet it was gaining ground so unmistakably in the earliest years of Dryden's career that Milton felt compelled to justify himself, somewhat acrimoniously, for his use of blank verse—or "English heroic verse without rime," as he called it—when he came to publish *Paradise Lost.* What the fortune of the couplet would have been without Dryden no one can say, but, as we can see from Milton's self-defense, it was coming to be regarded as the one form of verse suitable for heroic poetry; and for this reason it is often termed the "heroic couplet." In practice, however, as was just said, it was put to many uses; and Dryden himself rebelled against the restrictions it imposed upon heroic drama, and employed it most successfully for satire and argument.

Now the rimed couplet, as it was used by Dryden in such poems as *Absalom and Achitophel* and *Mac Flecknoe,* is so far different from any typical example of Elizabethan poetic art as to suggest that somehow a revolution in taste has occurred. But we can see, even from the brief account just given, that the change is sufficiently explicable without resort to any suggestion of so violent or sudden a break as the word revolution implies. The change in fact came about gradually, as a natural result of the classical influence set in motion by the Renaissance. That influence, when classical education had really taken hold in England, began, with Ben Jonson and his followers, to alter poetic style. By the time we come to the polished aphoristic verse of Pope a radical transformation has been effected; yet this is only the latest consequence of a true development or natural progression under Renaissance impulses from classical literature. The evidence suggests that had there been no civil strife, no Puritan Commonwealth, no Restoration, no influx of French influences, the same development would have taken place in England during the seventeenth century. This may remind us that far-reaching changes can, and often do, come about with no violation of historical continuity. If therefore we are to reach a genuine understanding of the Restoration and the eighteenth century, we must attempt—as we now are attempting—to distinguish those changes which were mainly caused by the continuous operation of Renaissance impulses from other changes which were really caused by the religious and political strife of the seventeenth century.

French Influence

It was at one time generally believed that the new characteristics of Restoration literature were largely the result of French influences brought in by Charles II and those loyal Englishmen who shared his years of exile. As has already been said, the French did exert a strong influence upon the English people, particularly upon the court and those at all close to the court, in the years following the Restoration; and this influence extended beyond gilt mirrors and the like to literature, and was certainly important in the field of literature. Nevertheless, we cannot really be sure that any important difference between Elizabethan literature and that of the Restoration can be ascribed to influences from France felt after 1660. The fact is that French influence in the later seventeenth century really worked, not to alter, but to reinforce the natural English progression from exuberant spontaneity to critical and orderly restraint, of which we have just seen an example in that development of poetic technique which brought in the reign of the heroic couplet. In addition, French influence began to be important a whole generation before 1660, and in this earlier period also reinforced Renaissance impulses which had already been felt in England.

Influence of d'Urfé's "Astrée"

The earlier period of French influence is centered in the 1630's, and was promoted by the interests of Charles I's French wife, Henrietta Maria. The medieval discovery of courtly love, as revitalized especially by Petrarch in his sonnets to Laura, had been, as we have seen, an important strain in Renaissance literature throughout Europe. In the early seventeenth century in France the related themes of courtly love and courtly honor had been taken up anew, and had found literary expression in the interminable prose romance, *Astrée*, written by Honoré d'Urfé—or written mostly by him, because he did not live to complete it, and the last part was composed by another hand. The book is really a kind of record of endless discussions, carried on in the most cultivated French society, as evidence of perfect refinement. The love in question was now miscalled by everybody "Platonic" love, or love so spiritualized that physical expression was entirely excluded, and it came to mean an irreproachable friendship between man and woman founded wholly on admiration felt for inner qualities. The theme of honor was similarly lifted above the plane of average human nature by requirements which only the most refined and spiritualized could meet, or indeed feel. Evidently this development hovered on the verge of the ridiculous, as contemporaries were prompt to perceive; but it had a side which gave it importance. The beings who exemplified the workings of "Platonic" love and courtly honor, because they were refined beyond the capacities of average human nature, could be conceived as living in the "heroic" way. The "heroic" character had to be in some fashion larger than life, or lifted above life as we ordinarily experience it. Hence d'Urfé's *Astrée* could be regarded as a fulfillment of the consuming ambition of Renaissance writers to produce, for their own time and country, something "heroic" in quality, something comparable in spirit and intent to what Homer and Virgil had done. *Astrée* was a modern epic in prose, or was at any rate so regarded.

And as such the book not only initiated a vogue, becoming the father of a family of seventeenth-century heroic romances popular in both France and England, but had a wide influence. It elaborated an "heroic" theme which had a genuine contemporary interest, and thus it seemed for a while to answer directly to the need of men who were trying, not to write correct imitations of classical masterpieces, but to create a modern literature, appealing to existing tastes and interests, in the light of classical example. *Astrée* and the other heroic romances thus became a major influence in the creation of the heroic drama of the Restoration, which was in fact simply a refashioning in dramatic form of the stuff of these romances. Nor did their influence stop here; for, both positively and negatively, they exerted a controlling effect upon Restoration comedy; and they also had a determining effect, by way of reaction, upon the novel of the eighteenth century.

Influence of the French Classical Critics

The most important new influence from France felt in the 1660's and 1670's, and later, came from the French classical critics, and above all from Boileau's treatise, in verse, on the art of poetry. The authority of the French critics stood very high in England, and their discourses encouraged thought about literary aims and methods, and helped to give precision to such thought. At the same time, the development of literary criticism in England was encouraged. This was salutary, but even more wholesome was the appearance—not wholly yet largely under French influence—of a new critical attitude. Dryden's many and delightful critical essays are written on the conversational level; they are not pronouncements from on high, but are genial discussions, such as cultivated gentlemen with a natural and intelligent concern for the arts might be expected to participate in. This is a change, like much else we find in the Restoration and eighteenth century, which is a perfectly appropriate fulfillment of Renaissance humanism; but it is not a change for which any English criticism before the Restoration prepares the way.

Critical Standards of the Restoration and the Eighteenth Century

There was, indeed, a surprising suddenness of change with the Restoration—a change fairly typified by the quite extraordinary difference between Dryden's prose and Milton's or Sir Thomas Browne's. Moreover, Restoration literature as a whole cannot be explained simply in terms of a natural development of Renaissance humanism. In fact, the more clearly we see that it was, *in part,* such a natural development, the more conscious do we become of characteristics of the period which *cannot* be so explained. In particular we find a pronounced discrepancy between what may be called the literary hopes and standards of the new age and its actual performance, which we must now try to account for. We may first recall that Renaissance humanism had been expansive and optimistic; it had taken a generous and kindly view of human nature; it had inspired confidence in human powers; it had placed a high valuation upon present earthly life as a field of significant action and of heroic effort, and as a field also wherein man's whole nature could achieve true satisfaction. Present life, in other words, was not, according to this view, a means to an end, as Christianity had taught, but was itself an adequate end, to a rightly ordered nature. Full humanity, however, was not something given, but something to be attained through guided all-round development. Hence the importance attached to education by the humanists, and their belief in the power of general or liberal education to civilize man. The best teachers, furthermore, were the best men; and the best men were those inspired ancient poets who had seen most fully and deeply into the constitution and possibilities of human nature and had succeeded in constructing vivid concrete imitations of life, not as it is, but as it might be and should be.

Here is the basis, evidently, of a theory of poetry—a theory, set forth briefly in the last chapter, according to which poetry was seen as the embodiment of all wisdom attainable by man. Thus we sometimes hear it said that Homer's *Iliad* was the Bible of the ancient Greeks; and certain Renaissance critics placed poetry, considered as the fountain of inspired earthly or human wisdom, alongside the Christian Bible, considered as the repository of a wisdom above nature, or divinely revealed wisdom. We must now observe that this theory continued to dominate thought about poetry, and indeed about the function of literature in general, until the end of the eighteenth century. One of the most interesting expressions of the theory was put, by Dr. Johnson in 1759, into the mouth of Imlac, the "sage," when he made Imlac tell the story of his life to

Rasselas, in the tale called *The History of Rasselas, Prince of Abyssinia.* The passage is somewhat long for quotation, yet it is worth giving in its entirety. Imlac says:

Wherever I went, I found that poetry was considered as the highest learning, and regarded with a veneration somewhat approaching to that which man would pay to the angelic nature. And yet it fills me with wonder that, in almost all countries, the most ancient poets are considered as the best: whether it be that every other kind of knowledge is an acquisition gradually attained, and poetry is a gift conferred at once; or that the first poetry of every nation surprised them as a novelty, and retained the credit by consent which it received by accident at first; or whether, as the province of poetry is to describe nature and passion, which are always the same, the first writers took possession of the most striking objects for description, and the most probable occurrences for fiction, and left nothing to those that followed them but transcription of the same events, and new combinations of the same images:—whatever be the reason, it is commonly observed that the early writers are in possession of nature, and their followers of art; that the first excel in strength and invention, and the latter in elegance and refinement.

I was desirous to add my name to this illustrious fraternity. I read all the poets of Persia and Arabia, and was able to repeat by memory the volumes that are suspended in the mosque of Mecca. But I soon found that no man was ever great by imitation. My desire of excellence impelled me to transfer my attention to nature and to life. Nature was to be my subject, and men to be my auditors: I could never describe what I had not seen; I could not hope to move those with delight or terror whose interests and opinions I did not understand.

Being now resolved to be a poet, I saw everything with a new purpose; my sphere of attention was suddenly magnified; no kind of knowledge was to be overlooked. I ranged mountains and deserts for images and resemblances, and pictured upon my mind every tree of the forest and flower of the valley. I observed with equal care the crags of the rock and the pinnacles of the palace. Sometimes I wandered along the mazes of the rivulet, and sometimes watched the changes of the summer clouds. To a poet nothing can be useless. Whatever is beautiful, and whatever is dreadful, must be familiar to his imagination: he must be conversant with all that is awfully vast or elegantly little. The plants of the garden, the animals of the wood, the minerals of the earth, and meteors of the sky, must all concur to store his mind with inexhaustible variety: for every idea is useful for the enforcement or decoration of moral or religious truth; and he who knows most will have most power of diversifying his scenes, and of gratifying his reader with remote allusions and unexpected instruction.

All the appearances of nature I was therefore careful to study; and every country which I have surveyed has contributed something to my poetical powers.

At this, Rasselas observed that surely Imlac must have left a great deal unnoticed, because he himself had found that there was really no end to the examination of the minute particulars of natural phenomena; upon every walk he took he beheld something which he had not before seen, or heeded. Imlac replied:

The business of a poet is to examine, not the individual, but the species; to remark general properties and large appearances. He does not number the streaks of the tulip, or describe the different shades in the verdure of the forest: he is to exhibit in his portraits of nature such prominent and striking features as recall the original to every mind; and must neglect the minuter discriminations which one may have remarked and another have neglected, for those characteristics which are alike obvious to vigilance and carelessness.

But the knowledge of nature is only half the task of a poet: he must be acquainted likewise with all the modes of life. His character requires that he estimate the happiness and misery of every condition, observe the power of all the passions in all their combinations, and trace the changes of the human mind as they are modified by various institutions and accidental influences of climate or custom, from the sprightliness of infancy to the despondence of decrepitude. He must divest himself of the prejudices of his age and country; he must consider right and wrong in their abstracted and invariable state; he must disregard present laws and opinions, and rise to general and transcendental truths, which will always be the same. He must therefore content himself with the slow progress of his name, contemn the applause of his own time, and commit his claims to the justice of posterity. He must write as the interpreter of nature, and the legislator of mankind, and consider himself as presiding over the thoughts and manners of future generations; as a being superior to time and place.

His labor is not yet at an end; he must know many languages and many sciences; and, that his style may be worthy of his thoughts, must, by incessant practice, familiarize to himself every delicacy of speech and grace of harmony.

Here Imlac was stopped by Rasselas, who exclaimed, "Thou hast convinced me that no human being can ever be a poet." The standard was lofty, yet not too exacting for a Spenser or a Milton, or indeed for a Shakespeare; and if no one met it successfully in the eighteenth century, one reason, too little considered, is that men of extraordinary genius are really rare. Literature is never completely independent of surrounding conditions, but a danger arising from the historical study of literature is that we may fall into the mistake of supposing that external conditions completely determine not only what is done, but what can be done, in a given period. The eighteenth century has been blamed as a time when the creative imagination was bound down, and indeed stifled, by the general acceptance of rigid and narrow rules, by a species of social control which not only was misguided, but was in itself pernicious. From this condemnation, some historians and critics have gone on to assert that the eighteenth century was a comparatively barren period in the annals of English literature. Such an assertion means no more than this: that in the time from 1660 to 1784 no writer of the highest poetic genius appeared; but the only reason we can be sure of is that such writers are rare. We do not certainly know that any external conditions under which civilized life is possible can obstruct the man of high poetic genius when he does appear. The whole subject is much more obscure than would be supposed from what is often written about it; yet at least it may be accepted as certain that no external conditions, short of such all-embracing absolutism as is spreading over Europe today, can either "produce" or "stifle" the greatest men, that great poets are not born in every generation, and that the greatest, when they do appear, show their genius through their transcendence of local and temporary conditions.

Masterpieces of the Restoration and the Eighteenth Century

No age can be called "barren" which has to its credit such acknowledged masterpieces in their several fields as the verse satires of Dryden and Pope, the comedies of Congreve, the prose satires of Swift, the narratives of Defoe, the mock-heroic poems of Pope, the essays of Addison and Steele and Goldsmith, the novels of Richardson and Fielding and Sterne, the prose of Chesterfield, the history of Gibbon, the oratory of Burke, and the *Life of Dr. Johnson* by Boswell. It is one of the glories of British literature that through the centuries men of the British Isles have written unsurpassed masterpieces in many different kinds of prose and verse, and we owe to the eighteenth century a great extension of the range of supreme performance. We ought then to study this period as we study other ages of British literature—not to belittle, to find fault, to emphasize limitations or deficiencies—but to learn disinterestedly what the distinctive character of the period was, and to discover what it has contributed to the permanent enrichment of English letters.

New Characteristics of Restoration Literature

Thus far we have seen that the change in the character of literature after 1660 was at least in part the consequence of a natural progression or development, that the roots of Restoration literature are to be found in England in the first half of the seventeenth century, that the standards of the new age were largely those of Renaissance humanism, and that French influence before and after the Restoration did not, on the whole, deflect English writers from their own course. In this there has been no intention of minimizing the change that did take place with the Restoration, and it was said above that some part of this change cannot be accounted for in terms of natural progression. We have now to inquire into the conditions which did alter the writing and, to a lesser extent, the critical standards of the new age.

In so doing we must remember that the Renaissance conception of poetry as a fountain of wisdom persisted straight through this period. This is why Dr. Johnson's *Rasselas,* written near the end of the period, could be quoted in illustration of it. Dr. Johnson spoke about poetry in *Rasselas* not for himself alone, but as the representative of a living and generally accepted tradition. From Imlac's words, however, we can see that the Renaissance conception has undergone, if not a serious modification, at least a significant change of emphasis. For, though Imlac alludes in passing to "inspiration" (when he says poetry may be "a gift conferred at once"), he does not place any confidence in it as a source of wisdom. His discourse as a whole shows clearly that the poetic teacher of mankind is, in his opinion, to gain wisdom, as well as skill in writing, from observation and study. This shift in emphasis is an important new thing, characteristic of the new age; and the change affected not only thought about poetry, but the practice of writers. It is therefore necessary for us to inquire why men came to distrust "inspiration" as a source of wisdom, and turned instead to systematic rational contemplation. But, as has been said above, we find in the Restoration and the eighteenth century not only a modification of traditional standards; we find also a discrepancy between accepted standards and actual performance. We find the persistence of a lofty ideal to be served by literary creation, while nevertheless the "creative" part of literary production is restricted to the mere decoration of scientific truth, or to its attractive or memorable expression. More than this, we find a licentious literature growing up in the years following the Restoration, and, alongside it, a literature of mockery. We shall discover that these contrasts are all related to the distrust of "inspiration" which arose after 1660, and that this distrust, or even hatred, was in turn the result of the ignominious failure of the Puritans under the Commonwealth. The new literature of the Restoration and the eighteenth century, we shall see, was the legacy of religious and political strife and disunion, gradually affected also by the growth of the rational scientific spirit, and finally undermined by a revolt against both immoralism and calculating rationalism.

England Still Divided after the Restoration

Though England as a whole welcomed the return of Charles II, the Puritans were by no means disposed to abandon their religious convictions, nor, as has already been said, were those who rode into power with Charles disposed to conciliate them. The result was that a large part of the population was forced into the position of an outcast element, living a submerged life of its own. This would have been bad enough, for both sides, had the country been divided into only two camps; but it was really divided into a considerable number of separated elements. The Puritans, as we have seen, under the guidance of "private inspiration," had split up into various sects, and in addition there were the Roman Catholics. The loss of homogeneity which had begun with the Reformation was thus perpetuated and the growth of provincial narrowness and exclusiveness encouraged. Everybody was the weaker for it, and everybody tended, of course, to be blind to his own deficiencies and keenly aware of the failings of those outside of his immediate circle. Inasmuch as the royal court remained, as has been said, the unchallenged center of cultivated life, writers gathered around it and wrote for the courtly circle; but this meant that Restoration literature was written not only for a small aristocratic public, but also for a public that no longer fairly represented the nation as the court had represented it in the sixteenth century. The fact that Charles and his closest associates had spent years in France made matters worse, because all the strange French elegance of the new régime was for some time an added bar separating the court from the country.

Anti-Puritan Attitude of the Court

Further, the opinion held at the court, certainly with some justification, was that Puritanism had degenerated into hypocrisy. We may be just as sure that this opinion did not represent the whole truth as that there was some truth in it—and enough truth to give courtiers the feeling that they were on solid ground in refusing to be hypocrites themselves. Thus there was an element of principle, even of serious conviction, underlying the bold outspoken worldliness and irreligion of the Restoration court. The anti-Puritan attitude was brilliantly and wittily expressed very soon after Charles's return, towards the end of 1662, by Samuel Butler in *Hudibras:*

When civil fury first grew high,
And men fell out, they knew not why,
When hard words, jealousies, and fears
Set folks together by the ears,
And made them fight, like mad or drunk,
For dame Religion as for punk;
Whose honesty they all durst swear for,
Though not a man of them knew wherefore:
When Gospel-Trumpeter, surrounded
With long-eared rout, to battle sounded,
And pulpit, drum ecclesiastick,
Was beat with fist, instead of a stick;
Then did Sir Knight abandon dwelling,
And out he rode a coloneling. . . .
 For his Religion, it was fit
To match his learning and his wit:
'Twas Presbyterian true blue,
For he was of that stubborn crew
Of errant saints, whom all men grant
To be the true church militant:
Such as do build their faith upon
The holy text of pike and gun;
Decide all controversies by
Infallible artillery;
And prove their doctrine orthodox
By apostolic blows and knocks;
Call fire, and sword, and desolation,
A *godly-thorough Reformation,*
Which always must be carried on,
And still be doing, never done:
As if religion were intended
For nothing else but to be mended.
A sect, whose chief devotion lies
In odd perverse antipathies;
In falling out with that or this,
And finding somewhat still amiss:
More peevish, cross, and splenetick
Than dog distract, or monkey sick:
That with more care keep holy-day
The wrong, than others the right way:
Compound for sins they are inclined to
By damning those they have no mind to;
Still so perverse and opposite,
As if they worshiped God for spite,
The self-same thing they will abhor
One way, and long another for.
Free-will they one way disavow,
Another, nothing else allow.
All piety consists therein
In them, in other men all sin.
Rather than fail, they will defy
That which they love most tenderly,
Quarrel with minced pies, and disparage
Their best and dearest friend, plum-porridge;
Fat pig and goose itself oppose,
And blaspheme custard through the nose.
Th' apostles of this fierce religion,
Like Mahomet's, were ass and widgeon,
To whom our knight, by fast instinct
Of wit and temper, was so linked
As if hypocrisy and nonsense
Had got th' advowson of his conscience.

Emergence of the Satiric Spirit

If now we recall that ideal picture of the poet, his training, his aim, his temper, which has been quoted in the words of Dr. Johnson's Imlac, and compare it with actual performance in these verses describing the religion of Sir Hudibras, we will be led a long way towards a right understanding of Restoration literature. Though *Rasselas* was written nearly a century later than *Hudibras,* we have already seen that Imlac gives voice to a traditional conception of poetry which was inherited alike by Butler and by Dr. Johnson. Butler, however, was one of the earliest to exhibit in literature the changed temper of the Restoration period; and readers of *Hudibras* are at once struck so forcibly by the poem's spirit of contemptuous hatred—mirrored in its rough and ready style, its witty forced rimes, and its mock-heroic scheme—that they are likely to see only a glaring contrast between Dr. Johnson's standards and Butler's performance. Significant contrast there is, and we must see in what it consists. Yet Butler and Dr. Johnson are in complete agreement on certain fundamental points, and in order to grasp the meaning of the contrast between them we must first observe that both Dr. Johnson's Imlac and Butler are *objective.* To both of them equally the aim of the writer is not self-expression or self-revelation, but discovery and expression of general truth, reached by observation of the world and men. Both feel definitely that the observer must try to distinguish between mere appearances, which may be deceptive and are at any rate ephemeral, and underlying reality. Both are anxious to get at and hold fast to what is objectively real and solid, and are therefore critical.

Imlac, however, is serene and dispassionate, though steadfastly devoted, and his aim is positive—the discovery of "general and transcendental truths which will always be the same." If it were not for Imlac's concern over problems of style, of presentation worthy of his thoughts and delightful to his audience, we would find his attitude and aim identical with the attitude and aim of the man of science; and even as an artist, we should observe, Imlac has no notion of depending upon his native unaided powers. He does not wish to be an imitator or to take anything at secondhand; nevertheless, he forms and develops himself by assiduous study of the best poets, and leaves as little as possible to happy chance or to merely personal genius. He works as a social being, subordinating and correcting individuality by constant reference to what is common or shared; and realizing that no one person in and by himself contributes greatly to the sum of human achievement.

Butler, on the contrary, is anything but dispassionate; and he seizes upon particular facts, deliberately distorts the matter he uses, and has a negative aim. He is impelled by an indignant sense of the vice and folly of mankind, and holds up the Puritans as a special example. His method is that of ridicule. Inspired by *Don Quixote,* in which Cervantes had made the outworn conventions and ideals of chivalry ridiculous by burlesquing them, Butler writes a burlesque poem in which he parodies the persons, aims, and activities of the Puritans. This is his way of getting underneath appearances to reality. He wants to convince us that beneath their sanctimonious disguises the Puritans were really a crackbrained, opinionated, stubbornly perverse lot, and hypocritical to boot. And though *Hudibras* is a burlesque in form, it is satirical in aim. Butler, in other words, is above all conscious of the divided state of the nation—is, we may say, obsessed by that cruel fact, and cannot get by it or outside of it to any positive universal truths. He is caught up in the strife of parties and forced to become a party man himself, who attacks the opposed faction by merciless derision. He may be compared to a ship's officer in a furious storm, who cannot pause calmly to observe, from this instance, anything generally true of storms or of human behavior, but must hastily attempt any measure to protect his ship and the lives of his crew. The analogy is instructive, yet not perfect; because Butler is not wholly reduced to partisanship or to immediate practical necessities. He is reduced, however, by the pressure of events, from any optimistic contemplation of what man might be or should be, to a disillusioned recognition of what men, alas, actually are, too often, too generally—a vicious compound of "hypocrisy and nonsense." And by the spectacle he is impelled to satire.

Satire and Irony Defined

Satire may be defined as a kind of writing, in verse or prose, in which vice, folly, and even individual human beings are held up to ridicule. Satirical verse is not the highest kind of poetry, as was fully understood by everybody in the seventeenth and eighteenth centuries, but we ought not to make the mistake of denying that it is poetry at all. It is indeed one of the offices of the historical study of literature to open our eyes to the fact that true poetry of widely differing kinds does exist, and to put us on our guard against parochial or narrowly exclusive definitions. It is incontestable that verse, as Butler, Dryden, Pope, and, in the next age, Byron used it, is far more effective for satirical purposes than prose in their hands would have been. As these masters employ it, verse-satire is not statement or argument, coldly intellectual, which merely happens to be given metrical form; it is a true and passionately imagined *embodiment* of a critical attitude, and hence is true poetry, whether of the kind we like best or not. The real difficulty felt by some readers of verse-satire is that it does not give scope for what they regard as *the* "poetical" passions; but this is merely a burden of prejudice from which education should relieve us. A further difficulty is that satire is a product of disillusion, and so usually appears late in any train of cultural development, after writers and their public have become sophisticated, and have begun to look with a skeptical eye upon human hopes and aims, and upon human character itself. Unless we have reached a like stage of development, we look at the human scene, and at ourselves, in a more kindly way, and we resent the cold water dashed by the satirist upon our generous confidence. Hence we tend to look on the satirist as an unpleasant fellow, a misanthrope; in short, we do all we can to close our ears to the kind of truth he tells. Matters are not helped when we observe the satirist's methods. He has no reverence, else he would not burlesque the highest kinds of literature, or institutions or conventions in which are enshrined lofty, even sacred, aspirations. He is sarcastic; and he is ironical.

Irony, in the hands of a master, can be the most effective of satirical methods. Nevertheless, there are readers who dislike it and complain against it. They take up a poem or an essay in good faith, and are gradually bewildered as they begin to suspect that the author cannot mean what he is saying. And of course this is just what the ironist aims at. He is not a dogmatist; he does not set himself up as a judge; he desires to force the reader into judging for himself, and perhaps even against himself, and to this end he follows a course of deliberate indirection. By appearing to accept it himself, he forces his reader to recognize some absurdity for what it really is. Hence irony can be defined as an assertion of the opposite of what one actually means. The ironist explodes some plausible fallacy or hidden vice by taking it at its apparent value and then drawing out the logical consequences. These are so patently absurd that we are forced to see that the fallacy is a fallacy and the vice really vicious. If we ourselves have been cherishing the fallacy, or shutting our eyes to the consequences of the vice, we do not enjoy the exposure of our mistake. Swift is the great master of solemn irony, who has been excelled by no one, ancient or modern; yet, while everybody acknowledges his power and extraordinary genius, he is not loved for his irony. Those who love him, do so for other reasons—because of his warmth and loyalty in friendship, because of his playful but deeply rooted and noble human sympathy, and because of the unique flight of his imagination in *Gulliver's Travels,* where he has succeeded in giving his mordant pictures of humanity an outer form perennially delightful to children, who do not suspect the underlying satire.

Satire and the Humanistic Tradition

The commonly held objections to satire, then, arise for the most part from immaturity and inexperience. And so far are naïve complaints against irony beside the point that one critic has justly said: In literature, "the history of irony is the history of good manners." Perhaps we ought to be most grateful to the satirists of the half-century and more after 1660 for their demonstration that it is possible to be serious, even profound, and devotedly on the side of the angels, without being solemn, labored, fanatical, or obscure. For though the work of satire is in a sense negative, since it makes clear the folly of the foolish and the like, we must remember that there are always positive standards to which the satirist is tacitly appealing, and which he is enforcing in a manner bound to command our assent. Positively, Butler, when he is ridiculing the Puritans, is advancing the cause of honesty and common sense and balance, and we are not allowed to remain in doubt about this. It may seem odd in Butler's case and in the case of most satirists to say that they are "on the side of the angels"; but at any rate they are on the side of reason and sweetness and light, and the positive ideal of the eighteenth-century satirists was a cultivated and developed humanity, intelligent enough to put first things first and tolerant enough to live together amicably. Butler was no more favorable to the licentiousness of Restoration society than he was to Puritan individualism, fanaticism, and hypocrisy; and he may have been right when he insisted that the scientists of the Royal Society were trifling their time away over gadgets which, however fascinating, could contribute nothing material to human welfare. At least his meaning was that those scientists were not putting first things first, and that an instrument, for example, enabling us to acquire knowledge of the moon's surface contributes little to the problem of forming an ordered society composed of well-balanced men and women. The truth is that Butler and Swift—who drew more from Butler all along the line than seems generally to be realized—were campaigning for sanity. And in this they were carrying on the program of Renaissance humanism.

Nevertheless, we have only to repeat the word—sanity—to realize that however admirable, and needed, the campaign was, and however brilliant its prosecution, the new aim represents a shrinkage of Renaissance optimism. We are helped to see how great the shrinkage was when we discover that satire had been duly revived under classical auspices by the Elizabethans, and extensively practiced. Even Butler's accusation that the Puritans were hypocrites was by no means new; it had been resoundingly made by Ben Jonson. But in the varied wealth of Elizabethan literature satire had remained a minor and almost alien element. It was not until after 1660 that classical satire had a congenial home in England; and it then for two generations assumed a foremost place not only because it was written with genius and was eagerly received but also because it had no effective competition. The times were such that satire could be written effectively; and no one with outstanding genius for higher forms of literature appeared within courtly or sophisticated circles.

"Enthusiasm" Displaced by Disillusioned Common Sense

The reasons for this change of temper, and this shrinkage, are to be found in the fact—partly explained in the last chapter—that Renaissance humanism was made up of really discordant elements, which in time were bound to come into open conflict, and did. The Renaissance, it was said in the last chapter, was first of all a movement of the awakened critical intelligence, sending men back to original sources, in the hope of discovering a better and firmer basis for civilization than that afforded by decadent tradition. In England, Renaissance and Reformation were in the beginning one movement, not two that happened to coincide in time. They were there the fruit of a common impulse and confidence; they followed a common aim of exploration and recovery; and for a while no disharmony between them was felt. But gradually it became clear, not only that Protestantism was and must be individualistic—the Renaissance was individualistic as well—but that Protestantism had no secure basis this side of the daemonic element in human nature which is, if not above reason, at least beyond reason and completely deaf to all mere reasoning. There is, of course, an obvious disharmony between paganism and asceticism, between extreme worldliness and extreme otherworldliness. Yet it is possible, if not to resolve this disharmony, at least to effect a fair working compromise between pagan humanity and Christian spirituality. Agreement may be precarious, but it has been achieved. Protestantism, however, ran promptly into the worst extremes of fanatical intolerance, under the guidance of the doctrine of "private inspiration" which has earlier been mentioned, and which is simply another name for absolute confidence in the individual's own inward, non-rational conviction that what he happens to believe is the whole truth and nothing but the truth. And this kind of Protestantism had had its innings in the years of the Puritan Commonwealth, and had fizzled out ignominiously.

We can hardly by any means bring ourselves to a full realization of the force of this impact upon contemporaries. It was utterly confounding. In the name of what was best and highest the horrors of civil war had been wantonly invoked; there had appeared the threat, and some part of the reality, of anarchic social dissolution, and by way of answer a brutally repressive tyranny. The conclusion was unescapable: the daemonic element in human nature was purely malevolent. To credit its behests, to follow it, was to walk blindly over a precipice.

Was the truly hellish force of "inspiration" only scotched by the return of Charles II, or was it really killed? If civilized life was to be a continuing possibility, it must at any cost be killed. Here we have the explanation of that eighteenth-century phenomenon which is at first astonishing to readers—the widespread hatred felt for what the men of that time called "enthusiasm." The enthusiastic person is one who is carried away, carried out of himself, by an inward conviction of the worth of something. This is a non-rational persuasion; it is a species of "possession" closing the ears of its victim to argument. The English came to fear it and hate it as a result of devastating experience, and along with it all "transcendental truths" not based firmly on objective evidence or on clear demonstration from self-evident premises. What they needed and longed for was plain unoriginal common sense.

Growth of the Scientific Spirit and Its Influence

At this point another element which had been an integral part of the Renaissance, and which had, with Francis Bacon, begun to take a separate line of its own in England, entered in to reinforce distrust of the inspired imagination. This was the growth of the scientific spirit. It was of the essence of this spirit to reject not only the authority of tradition but also man's alleged intuitive powers, and to rely exclusively upon methodical observation. What was wanted was knowledge; not a strong inward persuasion of knowledge, but verifiable knowledge, knowledge which could be experimentally tested and so, in a sense, proved. Such a demand limited the knowledge sought to that which the eye could see, or the hand touch—in short, to the field of phenomena apprehended through the five senses. It thus tended to transform and limit the conception of knowledge, though this was not clearly perceived at once, nor indeed until practically our own time. But it did immediately begin to rob poetry of serious justification. The Renaissance poet had set up to be, at his highest, an inspired teacher of mankind. His claim to inspiration had been challenged and derided by religious enthusiasts, who had in turn themselves discredited their own claim to inspiration. The outcome was a clean sweep. Serious men would henceforth know better than to look to poets, or to any literary folk, for the discovery of truth. Poets could still be useful in disseminating truth in pleasing form; and they could continue to make their delightful contributions, of a merely decorative or ornamental kind, to the rational enjoyment of leisure. The role, however, of a skillful popularizer or of what might be called a mental decorator was a sadly shrunken one for the inheritors of the proud Renaissance tradition. And it was no comfort that the claims of religion were undergoing an exactly similar deflation.

New Emphasis on Control over Natural World

The rise of science in the seventeenth century did indeed keep alive the optimistic and expansive temper of Renaissance humanism, but at the same time transformed it. The change is not easy to put into words without distortion, because, though it is startlingly great, it is only a change in emphasis. Perhaps it can be indicated fairly by saying that the early leaders of the Renaissance placed their faith in education, whereas the later men of science placed theirs in power over the world of nature. Both groups had in view the improvement of life. But the earlier group looked at the problem in terms of a change from barbarism, from brutality, from superstition, to a developed, re-formed, civilized humanity. Life itself, as was said in the last chapter, was regarded as an art to be learned. This conception persisted, in a somewhat weakened and debased form, throughout the eighteenth century. The famous letters of the Earl of Chesterfield to his son make use of an exquisitely polished and refined prose style to inculcate what was left of the old aim. But meanwhile under the influence of successful scientific research a quite different view of "improvement" was taking possession of men's minds. According to this view it was not the re-formation of man that was primarily needed for human welfare, but the improvement of his material circumstances. The emphasis was shifted from man to his material environment, just as rapidly as the progress of science enabled men to command and use nature, or material resources, for their own purposes. Thus the progress of civilization came to be thought of in terms of improved agriculture, improved transport, the multiplication of cheap articles of use, and the like; and human welfare began to be measured in terms of available power, or material wealth. The underlying assumption, which was to become clearer as the eighteenth century advanced, was that man was by nature a good and civilized being, and that the ills of life arose from an insufficient command, or an unequally distributed command, over the means to physical well-being and to enjoyment.

Rationalism and the Prescription to "Follow Nature"

This new view, like the doctrine of progress that developed along with it, had been foreshadowed from the beginning in the writings of Bacon. It was later called utilitarianism, and also, when sentimentalized, humanitarianism. It began to make itself felt as early as the end of the seventeenth century in a demand for education directed not so much to self-knowledge and self-development as to "practical subjects"—a demand which has been steadily growing ever since. The educational shift—for better, for worse, very slowly accomplished—illustrates clearly the nature of the change which was taking place. Considered broadly, it was a change from humanism to rationalism. And what this meant for literature can be seen as early as 1650, when Thomas Hobbes was writing derisively of the poets who pretended "to speak by inspiration, like a bagpipe." He went on to state summarily the genesis, as he saw it, of poetry: "Time and education begets experience; experience begets memory; memory begets judgment and fancy: Judgment begets the strength and structure, and Fancy begets the ornaments of a poem."

Here in a sentence we have the conception which the combined influences under discussion imposed upon the eighteenth-century man of letters. The "strength," not only of a poem indeed, but of any piece of serious literature, was to be supplied by reason; in other words, a writer was to express and inculcate the collective wisdom, the received truths or common sense, of mankind. He was to aim, not at originality, but at the perfect expression of what was received for universal truth, rationally or scientifically determined. This was what the eighteenth-century man of letters had in mind when he agreed that his cardinal rule was to "follow Nature." The "nature" he had in mind was the nature of the universe or of its many component parts as these can be discovered by scientific observation and rational deduction, and expressed in universal "laws," or what we call nowadays scientific laws. The nature of man was to be found, not in the peculiarities which distinguish one man from another, but in the traits common to all men, and especially in those distinguishing man from other animals. The nature of the scoundrel was to be found in what was really or universally scoundrelly in him; and so on. Further, it was accepted that the universe throughout is a rationally ordered structure—a view which had long been entertained alike by ancient philosophers and by Christian theologians, and which seemed to be magnificently confirmed in the 1680's by Sir Isaac Newton's discovery of the laws of motion. Newton was the one man of the very highest genius in England whose work falls wholly within the period from 1660 to 1784, and it is significant not only that he was a man of science, but that his discoveries seemed to confirm what was already being thought. Now order implies subordination, or arrangement of parts in a certain right way—as in a jig-saw puzzle—to form a whole. Thence a scale of values or order of importance can be derived. It was accepted that the most important object on earth was Man, who stood at the head of the animal creation, the needs of which in turn were served by the vegetable kingdom and, in general, by the inanimate parts of the earth. Hence to "follow Nature" discriminatingly, a writer should give his attention principally to man and to man's concerns, duly subordinating man's environment. More than this, amongst men a "natural" scale of values could be discovered. All men were, not rational, but, as Swift insisted, "capable of reason"—a very different thing. And only those who were rational were more human than animal. Thus, again, to "follow Nature" discriminatingly, a writer should give his principal attention, not just to "man," but to those men who were most completely humanized. At the beginning of the eighteenth century it was assumed that the most fully humanized men were cultivated and civilized men; but the assumption was early questioned, because of the manifold corruptions which seemed inseparable from life in cities and around courts, with the consequence that men began to look for "ideal humanity" in out-of-the-way places where simple people dwelt.

The Search for Universal Artistic Laws

Hobbes also laid it down, in the sentence quoted above, that "judgment" begets the "structure" of a work of literary art. There is a right way and a wrong way to fashion an automobile tire or to build a house. Fitness for the purpose is the standard. The right way may have to be discovered by trial and error, or may be discovered by the use of rational intelligence. The critics of the later Renaissance, moved by such considerations as these, set about the discovery of the universal or immutable laws of literary art. They were convinced that there were such laws, exactly as there were laws of motion awaiting discovery. The object was that to which Bacon had eloquently summoned the best efforts of man. In their sphere they wanted to substitute knowledge for stupid hit-or-miss methods, or for a blind following of tradition. The intention was not inherently absurd; it was prosecuted with some understanding, not perfect but certainly intelligent, of the limits of any "science" in the sphere of art; and some sound conclusions were reached. What we should specially notice, however, is that in proportion as the practice of literary art was reduced to law, or rule, the task of the writer was, exactly as in the case of the "strength" of his work, a problem of conformity, and not of origination.

The Dramatic Unities

The most famous of the "rules," and the one most frequently referred to with misunderstanding, is that of the three dramatic unities, of time, place, and action. Aristotle, the father of dramatic criticism, had insisted only on the unity of action. He had added that "tragedy endeavors, as far as possible, to confine itself to a single revolution of the sun, or but slightly to exceed this limit." About unity of place he had said nothing at all. Critics of the Renaissance, therefore, who insisted on the observance equally of all three unities, and who even went so far as to assert that the best tragedy should require no more time than that needed for actual representation on the stage, were departing from Aristotle. As we have seen, the Renaissance as a literary movement had at its center a return to the ancient writers as supreme masters of literary art, who were to be emulated, and who could not be emulated without close and even reverent study of what they had achieved. The allegiance given the ancients had not been, on the whole, blind, unreasoning, or slavish. Nevertheless, their authority stood high. Hence some critics disguised their departure from Aristotle by declaring, in effect, that he must have intended to insist equally on all three unities and would doubtless have made his intention clear had he been writing exhaustively; and that therefore they were only filling out the gaps in his treatment. Actually, they were inaugurating a movement towards a set of artistic standards based, not on tradition, but on reason, or common sense. The transition was a confused one, but the tendency is unmistakable, and was generally recognized by the latter part of the seventeenth century. The assumption underlying this particular departure from Aristotle was that the tragic dramatist ought to aim at strict verisimilitude; and the inference that all three unities must be carefully observed to attain such verisimilitude was sound. The trouble was with the assumption, not the inference. As Dr. Johnson said in his emphatic way: "It is false that any representation is mistaken for reality; that any dramatic fable, in its materiality, was ever credible, or for a single moment was ever credited."

Poetic Diction

One of the other rules of the time which should be mentioned here is that concerning diction. It was generally held that a writer should avoid technical terms, colloquialisms, words which had become "debased by vulgar mouths," words not fully domesticated (such as French phrases or turns of speech), and, in general, any words which might distract attention from what was being said because they seemed inappropriate in the context. As the standard is explained in many passages in Dr. Johnson's writings, and by other eighteenth-century critics, it is reasonable. It is a special development of the Renaissance doctrine of "decorum," which means, we may recall, "appropriateness." It led to a decided preference for general and often abstract expressions, instead of concrete words, and so opened the way to some absurdities, especially from mediocre or worse than mediocre writers. Erasmus Darwin at the end of the century, in his anxiety not to call a spade a spade, called it a

> Metallic Blade, wedded to ligneous Rod.

But it is not proper to judge a standard by the worst instances of its application one can find. James Thomson's *Seasons* has been castigated on the ground that "one might suppose the poem written for a wager, to prove that country life may be described, and nothing called by its name." Study of the *Seasons* shows, however, that very many of Thomson's periphrastic expressions really mirror with precision the poet's close and careful observation.

The one tendency of the standard which cannot be defended, and cannot be justified by examples from the best eighteenth-century writers, is brought out, unconsciously, by Dr. Johnson when he observes in *The Rambler:* "He that will not condescend to recommend himself by external embellishments, must submit to the fate of just sentiment meanly expressed, and be ridiculed and forgotten before he is understood." Hobbes had said that "Fancy" begets the "ornaments" of a work of literary art. The whole view of art under discussion did unfortunately encourage the restriction of what we should call the free imagination of the artist to mere ornament, or "external embellishments" simply stuck on. What disgusts us in rococo furniture or architecture is lack of organic unity; and it is the rococo quality of some eighteenth-century poetry, engendered by the sharp separation of reason and imagination, and the shrinkage of the latter into mere fancy to be called upon, almost as an afterthought, for a bit of extraneous ornament, that is responsible for much of the dislike felt for this period.

Restoration Drama

One extreme almost inevitably produces another. Men of the eighteenth century should be no more blamed for the opposition between reason and the imagination than the Puritans and the men of science who together forced it on them. And the Puritans' extreme of "enthusiasm" was not the only one they were guilty of. Their extremity of moral and cultural repression ushered in the cynical worldliness and immorality of the Restoration court and its zealous devotion to French elegance and polish. It was natural that a principal part of the effort to restore the worldliness which Puritanism had sought to banish should center in the stage. The glories of the English drama were to be revived, with much help from France. But nothing great in art can be made to order. Tragedies were written and the heroic drama ran its brief course, to demonstrate that demand could not create supply. The best tragedy that was composed in full obedience to so-called classical standards was Dryden's *All for Love.* It is a more than respectable achievement, all the more interesting because it is a rewriting of Shakespeare's *Antony and Cleopatra.* Dryden had unfailing energy, inexhaustible professional interest, and an active mind which, in a thoroughly congenial undertaking, became incisive. He shared, too, the Renaissance ambition to write in the heroic way, though practical

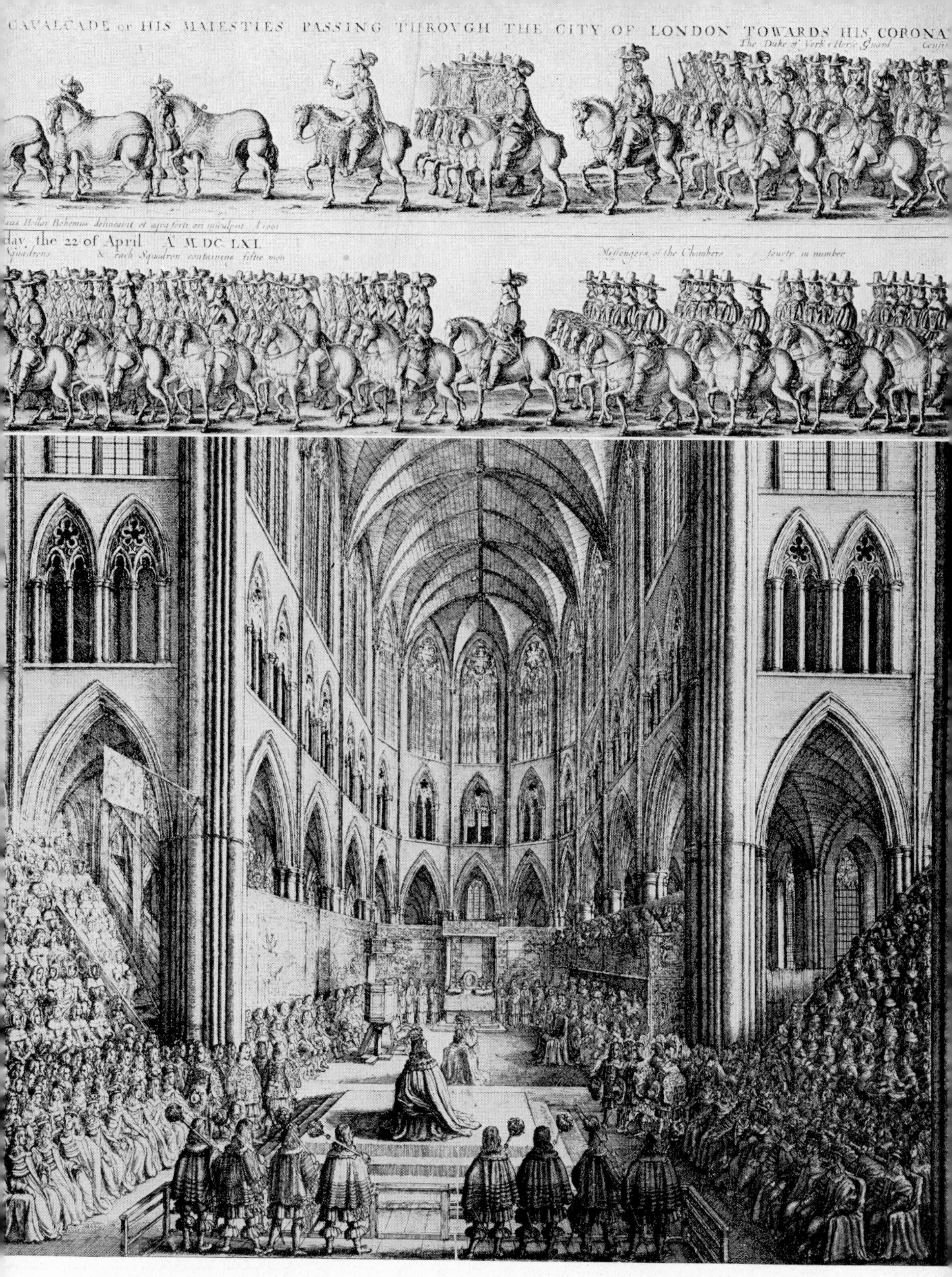

At the top of this page is shown part of Charles II's cavalcade, preceding his coronation. The procession passed through the City of London on 22 April, 1661, and the coronation took place on the following day in Westminster Abbey. The lower engraving shows the interior of the Abbey, with Charles in the center, in his royal robes, crowned, and seated on his throne. For Pepys's description of the ceremony, see pages 677–679, "Coronation Day." Both of these prints were engraved immediately after the coronation by Wenceslaus Hollar, who also engraved many interesting views of seventeenth-century London. (Courtesy of the Metropolitan Museum of Art.)

The upper picture is an aquatint by Pugin and Rowlandson (published in 1808) of the interior of Drury Lane Theater, showing John Philip Kemble as "Coriolanus." This aquatint pictures the theater as rebuilt by Sir Christopher Wren in 1674. Richard Steele was for several years manager of this famous theater; and here, later on, David Garrick, Mrs. Siddons, and Edmund Kean acted. (Courtesy of the Metropolitan Museum of Art.) The lower picture is a French print (preserved in the Bodleian Library, Oxford) of an early eighteenth-century coffee-house, such as those referred to by Steele in the first *Tatler* paper (see page 803).

exigencies forced him to try to satisfy that ambition through plays, for which there was a commercial demand. But neither Dryden nor the Restoration court had anything at all of the true heroic temper, and *All for Love,* like Dryden's other serious plays, has many false notes and no sublimity.

Restoration society found its true expression in comedy—the comedy of manners as it is called—and in this field some masterpieces of a kind were written, by Sir George Etherege, by William Wycherley, by William Congreve, and by Sir John Vanbrugh, to name only the four most notable of the comic playwrights of the time. The characteristics of this comedy are its wit and fashionable raillery, its moral cynicism descending at times to the grossest brutality and license of speech, with action to match, its almost exclusive concern with adulterous intrigue, and its restriction, for its field of representation, to aristocratic society. Congreve was the most distinguished of all the Restoration dramatists, and no English writer has excelled him in the portrayal of polished manners, or in his achievement of a prose flawless for its purpose, along with perfect unity of tone.

Nevertheless, even at its brilliant best in Congreve's *Way of the World,* Restoration comedy repels a great many readers. Doubtless some are repelled for much the same reason that prevents them from appreciating the satire in which this generation and the next achieved its fullest and most congenial expression—because they lack the maturity and experience needed in order to meet these writers on their own ground. But in the case of Restoration comedy there is an added reason. Charles Lamb, in his essay "On the Artificial Comedy of the Last Century" defended these plays against the moral strictures of his earnest contemporaries by pleading that they belong to

> . . . a world of themselves, almost as much as fairy-land. Take one of their characters, male or female (with few exceptions they are alike), and place it in a modern play, and my virtuous indignation shall rise against the profligate wretch as warmly as the Catos of the pit could desire; because in a modern play I am to judge of the right and the wrong. . . . But in its own world do we feel the creature is so very bad?—The Fainalls and the Mirabels, the Dorimants and the Lady Touchwoods, in their own sphere, do not offend my moral sense; in fact they do not appeal to it at all. . . . They break through no laws, or conscientious restraints. They know of none. They have got out of Christendom. . . . It is altogether a speculative scene of things, which has no reference whatever to the world that is.

In one sense Lamb was wrong. The Restoration comedies are examples of realistic art in that, as was implied above, they do faithfully reflect the spirit and activities of contemporary society. Yet Lamb was right also in a very important sense, in that both the society and the plays which mirror it were really dehumanized. The escape from morality was a descent, which no external elegances could disguise, into animalism where all true and genuine human feeling was lost. And it is at bottom the sense of this calamitous loss, however obscurely felt, which makes us conclude that Restoration society was hollow and decadent and that its comedy is empty and sterile and really worthless, no matter how brilliant in execution.

Modern Literature Increasingly Written for Small Groups

In pondering this we have to remember what has earlier been said about the divided condition of England, and how small a circle the society of the Restoration court was. The literature which we think of as characteristic of the period was written for this small public, not for the nation. And here we encounter a situation which has continued to the present day—the multiplication of special publics with barriers between them through which only a few writers succeed in bursting their way, and those without altering the condition itself. Owing to this condition, moreover, any attempt to give a complete picture of literary production in England from the seventeenth century to the present becomes extremely complicated—in fact so complicated that historians tend to content themselves with accounts of the most prominent developments and the most popular books, or else turn to the writing of monographs, treatments of the novel in isolation from other literature, or of lyric poetry considered by itself, or even of the sonnet separated off from other lyrics. Distortion—or sometimes downright falsification—results from following either course. In trying to avoid this, and yet give a solid foundation for historical understanding, we shall be forced to give our attention more and more to underlying conditions, and less to even brief discussion of individual writers. Dutiful historians, who cannot bring themselves to omit names which are found in all the handbooks, are reduced too often to the compilation of mere catalogues of names and dates. At whatever risk of omission, this course cannot be followed here.

Nevertheless, there *are* names which cannot on any account be omitted. Literature arises out of social and intellectual conditions, and, as has been said earlier, is never entirely independent of its immediate environment. Yet it is not produced by "conditions." It is written by individuals; and, further, the change from medieval to modern conditions, which it has been a part of our undertaking to follow, has been, as we have noticed, a change from a homogeneous, relatively undifferentiated society to one which increasingly is divided and subdivided into separate groups, and, at the same time, to one which, even within groups, is increasingly individualistic. Hence literature itself, as we approach our own time, becomes more and more personal, and is more and more concerned with persons. Always, moreover, early and late, the wind of inspiration bloweth where it listeth, in the last analysis unaccountably.

John Bunyan's Achievement of Universality

Hence it is not enough to point out that what we call "characteristic" Restoration literature arose from a relatively small circle, not fairly representative of the nation, and perhaps not so much really dominant as temporarily on the crest of a wave. Nor is it enough to point out that Puritanism, though defeated and submerged, still existed. For despite the most unfavorable conditions, not only did Milton go on triumphantly to complete *Paradise Lost* after the Restoration, but also to write *Paradise Regained* and *Samson Agonistes.* We think of Milton, quite properly, as was explained at the end of the last chapter, as really belonging to and surviving from an earlier time; but we ought to remember that he was not crushed or essentially changed by the Restoration. And after Milton there followed John Bunyan. With every disadvantage from surrounding conditions and also from personal circumstances, Bunyan somehow contrived to write several books which are classics of English literature, above all *The Pilgrim's Progress.* Some of Bunyan's writings, like certain memoirs of the period and the diaries or journals of such different men as Pepys, John Evelyn, and George Fox (the founder of the Society of Friends, or Quakers), show the increasingly personal character of literature; but in *The Pilgrim's Progress* Bunyan has gone, as it were, through personal feeling and experience to universality, and has produced a narrative which can give something of both pleasure and heightened understanding to every kind of reader, young or old, learned or unlearned, in any country in the world, of whatever faith or creed; and which, like the other books deserving to be called classics, gives its readers ever more upon their return to it than they had realized was there. Bunyan, in other words, really succeeded in striking through all limitations of time and place to "transcendental truths which will always be the same"—always and everywhere; and he succeeded in making what he had learned a true work of art by, not just saying it, but *embodying* it in the persons and lives of real men and women, in a story which has variety within unity, and which exhibits constructive ability comparable to Milton's and far above Spenser's. But though it must be emphasized that Bunyan did rise beyond sect, beyond seventeenth-century Puritanism, to a conception of life which is true to human experience everywhere, it is also true that he spoke for a very large number of his contemporaries who were not much longer to remain silent and apparently acquiescent before the frivolous and obscene spectacle of Restoration society.

The Revolution of 1688–1689 and Its Consequences

Charles II died in 1685, and was succeeded by his brother, James II, who was not only an avowed Roman Catholic but was determined, as was believed from his efforts, to restore England to the Catholic fold. This suggests that he was blind to conditions in the country as well as imperious, like most of the Stuarts. Nevertheless, he was a man of some ability, and had a strong following—many Englishmen believing firmly that sovereignty was inalienable for any cause—and he might have kept the throne if, in the summer of 1688, his second wife, herself a Roman Catholic, had not borne him a son. His first wife had been a Protestant, and by her he had had two daughters, Mary and Anne, who had lived (six other children had died in infancy) and had remained Protestants. Thus until the son (James Edward Stuart) was born, Mary was James's heir, and the future seemed secure for Protestantism. But with a Catholic Prince of Wales all was suddenly changed. A few years before Charles II's death, the country had become divided over the question of a Catholic successor, and the party names, Whig and Tory, had come into use—the former designating those, chiefly men of the middle class with a sprinkling of powerful country families, who were opposed to the accession of James II; and Tory designating those who were royal legitimists. The Tories were in a difficult position. They were not Roman Catholics—the number of Catholics in England at this time was quite small—and they supported inalienable sovereignty as Church of England men, opposed to Protestant individualism, or dissent from Anglicanism. The Whigs were so strengthened by the prospect of a Catholic successor to James II, that, at the end of 1688, they took the bold step of calling upon William of Orange, a Dutch prince who had married James's older daughter Mary, to rescue the country. When William landed in England, it immediately became clear that the country as a whole approved of this solution, and James II fled to France. A second revolution had taken place, with practically no fighting.

This revolution of 1688–1689 had consequences of the utmost importance. William and Mary became joint sovereigns in the latter year upon their acceptance of terms laid down by Parliament. Intermittently and uncertainly the English people had been moving for centuries in the direction of limiting kingly power. Now it was recognized that if Parliament could make a king it could unmake him; and henceforth the people of the realm through Parliament were in a genuine sense their own rulers. Of course a democratic government was not achieved overnight—the right to vote for members of Parliament was much restricted, and many boroughs were completely in the control of powerful families, or could be bought; the hereditary House of Lords had as much legislative power as the United States Senate; and the sovereign continued for some years to rule as well as reign—even though his rule was now definitely limited. Nevertheless, the center of control had shifted, and the fundamental step towards democracy had been made. In actual fact the country was ruled for the next eighty years—with the exception of four, early in the eighteenth century, when the Tories were in power—by a Whig oligarchy. Yet there was a widespread, and on the whole correct, feeling that a momentous alteration had been effected, and that Englishmen enjoyed a liberty which the oppressed peoples of continental Europe might envy. And those "oppressed peoples" took English liberty at its face value, and did envy "free-born Englishmen," and got into the way of thinking of England as the enlightened leader in the march of progress. Within a few years after the revolution, party government in the modern sense of the phrase was firmly established, as were freedom of the press and a wide measure of religious tolerance. Questions indeed which had been the cause of dissension and strife for nearly a century were now so satisfactorily settled that no new major political reform was felt to be necessary until well into the nineteenth century.

Queen Mary died childless in 1694, and William reigned alone until his death in 1702. He was succeeded by Mary's younger sister Anne. She had seventeen children, but all of them died in infancy save one, and he died at the age of eleven before Anne became queen. Hence at her death in 1714 there was some threat of trouble from James Edward Stuart, who had, in France, been proclaimed King of England upon the death of his father, James II, in 1701. Parliament, however, had settled succession to the throne upon a Protestant German prince—George, Elector of Hanover, who was a great-grandson of James I of England—and he took possession without difficulty. His descendants have reigned over England ever since, although during the Great War of 1914–1918 they changed their name to Windsor. The last of the Stuarts was a Cardinal of the Roman Catholic Church, who was impoverished by the French Revolution. George III thereupon gave him a liberal pension; and the cardinal in return, at his death in 1807, bequeathed to the House of Hanover the crown jewels which his grandfather, James II, had carried off in 1688.

It is pleasing to think of these final acts of friendliness, even though we may reflect that George III could well afford to be generous. He, and England, did lose the American colonies; but save for this one reverse the country steadily throughout the century grew in wealth and power, and George III was firmly established in what by his time was the greatest secular position the earth had to bestow. At the beginning of the century the Duke of Marlborough had brought high prestige to the country through his brilliant victories at Blenheim and elsewhere, and his success remained politically important for many years. But even more important was the combined expansion of commerce and empire which followed, and which continued throughout the eighteenth and nineteenth centuries. And satisfaction with this "progress," and with existing social, intellectual, cultural conditions was on the whole dominant—not unquestioned, not universal, but dominant—until about the time of the French Revolution. Hence arises the picture often painted of the eighteenth century as a happy time, with peace and prosperity at home, with Common Sense holding the reins—a time when there were "no troublesome people with philanthropic or political or religious nostrums, proposing to turn the world upside down and introduce an impromptu millennium"—a time of "rest and refreshment" when cultivation had reached a level leaving nothing more to be desired, and men could begin to look back with tolerance at all the ages of Gothic barbarism which had preceded their own enlightened era, and could even begin to find some amusement in poking about amongst Gothic ruins.

The "Virtuoso" and the "Man of Taste"

There is truth in this picture, enough truth to help us to understand why the "virtuoso" and the "man of taste" flourished in the eighteenth century, and why men of that time did tend to be complacent, as we feel, to our annoyance, that the Earl of Chesterfield and Horace Walpole and others were. The "virtuoso" was the man who had nothing more important to do than to indulge an idle miscellaneous curiosity. He was a "collector," the early representative of a type still very familiar. And, like his modern descendants, he might collect anything. There was the man who prided himself, if we are to believe contemporary report, on possession of a bottle containing water which "was formerly an icicle on the crags of Caucasus," and of "a snail that has crawled upon the Wall of China"; also the man who had acquired Pontius Pilate's wife's chambermaid's sister's hat. These are satirical exaggerations, because common sense was quick to perceive in the collector's activities an opportunity for effective ridicule. Common sense has since been rebuked, after the discovery that some eighteenth-century collections had scientific interest. But such scientific value was exceptional, and the impulse animating the majority of the collectors was really an idle one, and a symptom of what is too likely to happen in an age of "rest and refreshment." The "virtuoso," however, was sometimes also a "man of taste," and might collect paintings, or build and adorn a great house in the country, or spend a fortune in remodeling the landscape around his house in accordance with new standards of gardening which began to be fashionable at the very beginning of the eighteenth century. The "man of taste" was an idle man too, who, regarding all vital or troublesome questions as settled for the best, could indulge himself in the solution of nice problems of fit adornment.

We owe a good deal to both of these types. Modern historical research, archaeology, and natural history all have their foundation, in part, in the idle activities of the "virtuoso"; and the restrained splendors of Georgian architecture and interior decoration, the beautiful furniture of Chippendale, Hepplewhite, and others, the china of Wedgwood, and modern landscape gardening are the chief items in the legacy of the "man of taste." These are not small debts, and we ought not to forget them or discount them in forming our own conception and estimate of the eighteenth century. Nevertheless, the picture they suggest is something less than a half-truth concerning the age. How much it leaves out we begin to see as soon as we ask ourselves whether Swift, for example, was full of complacent optimism; and whether he gives us the impression that all vexing problems had been satisfactorily solved, and that he was free to amuse himself, and us, in a time of "rest and refreshment." Swift certainly had complacency, and did feel free to amuse himself and a select circle by the hoaxes he loved; yet even from his jokes we catch at times the aroma of brimstone, and we know that he was, through the greater part of his life, burning with indignant rage against all he saw around him of human folly and stupidity, pedantry, corruption, empty pride, and senseless conflict. No one worth listening to has ever contended that Swift was simply the victim of a morbid sensibility, or that he imagined the evils which aroused his indignation. Nor are Swift's the only writings of the time which show us that under the splendid decorative surface of the full eighteenth century there were turbulent cross-currents which were forcing thought in new directions and forcing men of letters into new paths.

The Birth of Journalism: Government by Organized Public Opinion

To understand this significant aspect of the time we have to remember that the Civil War of the second quarter of the seventeenth century had been an attempt to settle by force conflicts, both political and religious, of opinion and principles which could not be thus settled. It had been preceded by a flood of argument, and the resort to arms had only intensified and embittered this verbal warfare. In the hundreds of pamphlets and printed addresses of the 1640's and 1650's some have seen the birth of journalism in England; and certainly with the Restoration it seems to have been assumed that henceforth the dissemination of officially doctored news was one necessary governmental activity. The Revolution of 1688–1689 carried this development several steps further. It was quickly recognized that the shift in the center of government from king to parliament gave an increased importance to public opinion on legislative questions. The emergence with the Revolution of party government meant, indeed, that henceforth England was more and more to be ruled by organized public opinion. Hence it became a practical necessity for party leaders to try to sway public opinion, by employing writers skillful in argument, and ready to give versions of public affairs favorable to the party hiring them and unfavorable to the opposed party. At the same time other developments were making the control of public opinion through the printed word more feasible than it would have been in any earlier period. The reading public was growing in size quite rapidly; and the new readers were members of the middle class who were becoming prosperous through the enlargement of commerce. As they acquired property they grew in importance, and simultaneously the policies of Government became more important to them. Throughout the eighteenth century the transition from aristocratic government by the great landed interests to middle-class government by the trading and industrial interests was under way. The rising middle class was, on the whole, earnest, orderly, thrifty, ambitious, pious, and anxious for education and information.

The other major change at the beginning of the eighteenth century which gave journalism a much enlarged field was the phenomenal growth in London of coffee-houses and of clubs. The first coffee-house was opened in London at about the same time as the first French restaurant—both shortly after the Restoration. By 1700 or soon thereafter it has been estimated there were about three thousand coffee-houses and no French restaurant. The coffee-houses were places where men gathered with their friends to smoke, drink, read the latest pamphlets and the news of the day, and discuss whatever interested them. They were comfortable lounging places, where free and easy intercourse with congenial friends could be indulged at all times—and the more satisfactorily because women were wholly excluded. They were places of escape from uncomfortable lodgings, nagging wives, loneliness, troublesome business, or whatever men wanted to escape from. They became specialized, in that one house got to be known as a Whig gathering place, another as a Tory sanctuary, another as the resort of the men of letters, and so on. And public opinion on all kinds of questions—political, religious, literary, and the rest—came to be formed in the coffee-houses and to be spread abroad from them. In this the growing journalism of the time played a crucial part, as we have much evidence to show that the coffee-house politicians and critics depended upon the journalists for topics of discussion and also very often for the substance of their talk.

Daniel Defoe

The first writer of importance who was, in a sense, produced by these new conditions was Daniel Defoe, the author of *Robinson Crusoe*. He was one of the most rapid and prolific writers the world has ever seen, and we do not know today, and probably never will know, exactly how much he did write, because many of his pamphlets were published under various disguises and it is hard to track him down. The important thing for us to recognize in his work is that he was the journalist incarnate in everything he wrote. He wrote voluminously for party leaders who would pay him, disseminating news, propaganda, and argument; but he also saw that the new middle-class reading public would eagerly buy any exciting book that could plausibly be regarded as a source of useful or improving information. His most famous books, of enduring interest, were written to satisfy this new demand. *Robinson Crusoe* purports to be an historical narrative, and does have objective fact as its starting-point. But Defoe found it easier, quicker, and more effective for his purpose to leave fact behind once he had begun, and to rely on his imagination for the development of his narratives, though he was always very careful to preserve the air of a simple reporter of actual events, narrated just as they had taken place. Robinson Crusoe is the middle-class individualist *par excellence,* with every admirable quality the middle-class reader might envy, and would rejoice to see embodied in a man successfully making his own way against the most extraordinary obstacles. The English novel is one of the gifts of the rising middle class to literature, and we trace its ancestry from *The Pilgrim's Progress* through *Robinson Crusoe* to Samuel Richardson, who actually created it, by accident.

Before we discuss the novel, however, we must notice that the development of journalism, particularly in Defoe's hands, brought into being another new kind of literature in the opening years of the eighteenth century. It was Defoe's *Review*—a journal which combined brief news-reports with brief discussions of public questions—that suggested to Richard Steele the possibility of carrying popular easy discussion of an improving tendency outside of the field of politics into the broad realm of cultural standards—manners, social customs, morals, literary taste, the whole round of questions interesting to "the polite world" or the would-be polite world. This was the origin of the famous *Tatler,* which in turn became the father of a very numerous family, from *The Spectator* through Dr. Johnson's *Rambler* and *Idler* to Goldsmith's *Citizen of the World* and beyond.

"The Spectator": Joseph Addison

Steele was a very talented as well as a lovable man; yet the greatest of his services to letters was the opportunity he gave in the *Tatler* to his friend Joseph Addison. Addison found in the informal periodical essay exactly the right medium for the full exercise of his powers and the perfect development of his genius. And it was he, chiefly in *The Spectator,* who established the vogue of the periodical essay so firmly that almost every eighteenth-century man of letters had to try his hand at it. Addison discussed with exquisite urbanity and unfailing clarity every kind of problem; aimed with unqualified success to be understood by everybody, including frivolous and empty-headed ladies of fashion, and to make his discussions interesting to everybody; and hammered away tirelessly at his critical object—the creation of an enlightened, tolerant, well-balanced body of public opinion. Obviously Addison could not be at once expertly informed and deeply thoughtful over the whole range of the subjects he discussed in his easy and apparently confident way; hence it has become an indispensable mark of historical and critical competence to insist that he was superficial. To this objection he could have replied with telling force; and it must be said for him that at any rate he was read appreciatively by those whom he addressed—an important goal not invariably achieved by those who aim to instruct—and, further, that he was, like Swift, usually very much in the right as far as he did go. Those who complain that he dealt in commonplaces could learn by a little historical study that the Addisonian commonplace was not a commonplace when the "Spectator" began his work, and that, if it has since become a commonplace, this is due very largely to the success of the "Spectator" and his followers. Moreover, time has shown that, however it may be with Addison's supercilious critics, with the public at large it is true that the "Spectator's" lessons are still needed. A generation or more ago it appeared that society was in such secure possession of Addison's important "lessons" that the enduring portion of his work was comprised in his imaginative creations, and principally in Sir Roger de Coverley. Today, worthy Sir Roger is likely to seem a bit stuffy, whereas Addison's attacks upon factious intolerance, upon pedantry, upon false wit, and his steady good-humored advocacy of humanity, reasonableness, moderation, and common sense are, alas, as pertinent as ever they were in his own time.

Revolt Against Moral Insensibility

It is not so much to our immediate purpose, however, to sing Addison's praises as to understand the situation which he confronted both intelligently and effectively. The bitter antagonisms of the seventeenth century had not been extinguished by the beginning of the eighteenth. The cynical reaction against "enthusiasm" had been ostensibly a turning towards "reason," with the inevitable corollary that the two were regarded as sharply opposed to each other. Hence "reason" tended to become a species of unfeeling calculation for a man's own advantage. And since the reaction from "enthusiasm" was also a reaction from asceticism and otherworldliness, "advantage" practically meant immoral indulgence and material gain. A spirit of calculating and corrupt selfishness appeared to be spreading through society. Restoration comedy at its best was a representation of complete moral bankruptcy in those who had been the leaders and were still largely the governors of the nation—moral bankruptcy accompanied by every evidence of social cultivation and refinement and intellectual acuteness. The spectacle was regarded with horror by a large part of the nation. In the 1690's there was a concerted effort to combat the influences spreading out from aristocratic circles by the recruitment of societies for the reformation of manners. Men were beginning to say that reason had been betrayed by false friends; that the assimilation of reason to a species of mechanical calculation of self-interest was a travesty of a noble faculty, producing evils as great as had unchecked "enthusiasm"; that man was not by nature a mere self-regarding being, but also and at least equally a social being; and that rational benevolence was as integral a part of our natural endowment as rational self-regard. In 1698 Jeremy Collier published his famous *Short View of the Immorality and Profaneness of the English Stage,* which Dryden met by a frank confession of guilt, and other dramatists by some very lame defenses. Collier, it should be remembered, was not a Puritan, but a "high" Anglican clergyman. He was on the side of intelligence and cultivation, but clear-headed enough to see that moral insensibility masquerading under the reputable name of rational enlightenment was leading the nation towards disaster. Steele attempted in the early years of the eighteenth century to write comedies of manners coated over with moral sentiment, but only succeeded in showing that the existing dramatic tradition could not thus be humanized; and through the eighteenth century, though the stage itself flourished, thanks to a succession of great actors and actresses, with the celebrated David Garrick at their head, dramatic creation languished, because others did not succeed even as well as Steele in plausibly mixing immoral intrigue and moral sentiment.

Addison's Attempt to Reunite Society

The situation, then, which Addison confronted was this: On the one side was refinement, educated taste, and cultivation united with moral insensibility against which a large part of the nation was revolting with a violence which threatened a renewal of fanaticism. On the other side was the rising middle class, which tended to be narrowly moral and was not socially or aesthetically educated. At the same time society was torn by violent political differences between Whig and Tory. The complete disruption of civilized social existence seemed to be threatened. The middle class might be the backbone of the nation, but it was extremely desirable to get it organically connected with the head. Addison's task was one of reconciliation. If it could not be achieved by tinkering with a literary form which was really as bankrupt as the high society it mirrored, the effort might more hopefully be made by use of a new literary form which was just emerging out of changing social conditions. The form of essay suggested by Defoe, created by Steele, and perfected by Addison may be described as a genial lay sermon, addressed to people who did want to be improved and who found it refreshing to be amused at the same time. Addison provided amusement lavishly, as he still can; but his serious aim was the noble one of reconciling differences. He tried to reunite moral sensibility and cultivation. He wanted to bring together warring individualists into a real society. He hoped people of good will could come together on a platform of enlightened common sense.

Critical Scrutiny of "Reason"

As this may sufficiently indicate, Addison shared the common trust in reason, and had no wish to undermine it. On the social side the general problem left by the Renaissance was that of discovering an adequate substitute for tradition as a basis for ordered life. Reason was everywhere advanced as eminently satisfactory for the purpose. Developments of the seventeenth century which have been touched on in this and the preceding chapter showed clearly that "reason" was a word which meant different things to different men. Thus it became needful to subject reason itself to critical scrutiny—an endeavor which was taken up by John Locke, and carried on in turn by Bishop Berkeley and by David Hume. In quite different ways all three reached conclusions which were damaging to reason. Locke, to be sure, vindicated an enlightened common sense as sufficient for all practical purposes in the conduct of life; and this was good enough not only for Addison but for most men of the eighteenth century. But both Berkeley and Hume found it easy to prove too much, in opposed directions. Berkeley seemed to leave earth and earthly concerns altogether behind him in a high-flying idealism which was too paradoxical to win credence. Hume, on the other hand, dissolved reason in an all-embracing skepticism which, he acknowledged, seemed unreal the moment he stepped from his desk, though he saw no logical escape from it. He ended by simply turning his back on the abyss he had opened up, and threw himself, like his great contemporary, Edward Gibbon, into the writing of history.

Shaftesbury and Deism

After all, Addison, in his superficial way, had dealt more effectively with the social or moral problem of the time than the profound inquirers into the character and possibilities of rational knowledge were able to. Yet Addison did not get much further with the problem of rational moral sanctions than a tentative implication that moral behavior was a matter of good taste as well as of good sense. Such a view was elaborated and buttressed, without much system and none too clearly, by the third Earl of Shaftesbury, the grandson of Dryden's "Achitophel." Shaftesbury also was a rationalist, and praised tolerance and attacked fanaticism like his contemporaries, and even wrote a defense of satire as the most effective touchstone for exposing folly and vice. But he parted from Locke, who had directed his education, in his conception of reason. He erected the good taste which enables us to recognize beauty into a direct intuition of good and evil—the good being identical with the beautiful, evil with ugliness—which he declared to be something ultimate and absolute. Furthermore, the fellow-feeling or sympathy which causes us to be unhappy in the presence of suffering or misery he declared to be an evidence of our inborn or instinctive altruism. It is because of something integral in human nature itself that we instinctively feel satisfaction in the presence of others who are well and happy, and find our own well-being is best served when we are promoting the general welfare. Not every man so feels, to be sure, but he who does not is "unnatural" or inwardly deformed.

Here we see what Shaftesbury is driving at: Human nature, unless deformed or diseased from one cause or another, is good. Man is naturally good. According to historic Christianity, man had been created good, but as a consequence of the fall of our first parents human nature had been corrupted. Hence, on the Christian view, all men born of human parents, as long as the race may continue to live, are brought forth in sin and are in their own nature corrupt, or evil. There is not necessarily any difference over facts of observation between these views; Shaftesbury and Christian teachers see and acknowledge that moral deformity is widespread; but there is a profound difference between Shaftesbury and Christianity in the explanation of the fact and in the estimate of its significance. Shaftesbury's thought is developed in complete independence of Christianity, and goes back to ancient Stoicism and to Plato. Shaftesbury, moreover, is full of the optimism, and confidence in the worth of earthly human nature, which we have seen to be characteristic of Renaissance humanism. And his thinking brings him to this conclusion: Man is naturally good, here and now, and his goodness is to be seen in his altruistic feeling. Shaftesbury was led on to declare, on the principle that man is a microcosm—or has in himself in little all the qualities which the universe, the macrocosm, exhibits in the large—that the universe, considered as a whole, is perfect, partaking of the nature of its Creator, the all-perfect Deity. This is what Pope set out to expound in his *Essay on Man.* The famous last words of Epistle I of this *Essay,* "Whatever is, is right," mean that since the universe as a whole is perfect, the parts considered separately are imperfect, but still are such parts as are required to make up, together, a perfect whole. This gives Pope's saying a more plausible meaning than at first sight one would suppose it could have; nevertheless, it is true that the reality of evil in the world is denied. Evil fades away into a deceptive appearance, into mere deprivation, or deformity, and loses all positive character.

The kind of thought represented by Shaftesbury is called deistical. It developed from the acceptance of rationalism, and became, as we have just seen, completely independent of historic Christianity and in some respects contradictory of it. Shaftesbury and other deists considered it expedient to conform outwardly to the Church of England as by law established; but actually the whole current of philosophical thought and rational theology was carrying laymen and clergymen alike away from any real belief in Christianity as a divine revelation. This we shall have reason to recall as we proceed into the next age. At present we must barely notice that just as Bunyan's work shows a powerful current of truly religious and Christian conviction flowing under the surface in the Restoration era, so in the first half of the eighteenth century the work of William Law shows us the same thing continuing. Law is best known for a devotional book, *A Serious Call to a Devout and Holy Life,* published in 1729, which was eagerly and widely read. Dr. Johnson ascribed to this book his own religious awakening; and, in addition, John Wesley regarded it as a prime source of the Methodist revival of religion which shortly after began under Wesley's leadership and, in the mid-eighteenth century, swept the country.

It cannot be said of deism, however, as it could of Restoration comedy, that it represented only a small circle of emancipated spirits. Deism is one stage in the development of modern rationalistic philosophy, and the movement of which it is a part was to continue and gain strength with every year and was to remain non-Christian, or in some respects anti-Christian, just as we have seen it in Shaftesbury. In other words, all the efforts made in the first half of the eighteenth century to draw men together into a real society founded on reason or common sense were in the end unsuccessful. Something was accomplished, but not enough. The nation continued to be much divided, and the Wesleyan movement profoundly strengthened oppositions. John Wesley and his brother Charles had in the beginning no thought of founding a new church, and Charles in particular was bitterly opposed to separation from the Church of England; yet in the end separation was forced on the Methodists, and a further step away from the ideal of a united society was taken.

Cultivation of Sensibility

Shaftesbury's work was destined to have repercussions which would have astonished and disgusted him, had he lived to witness the dazzling apparition of Jean Jacques Rousseau later in the century and the outbreak of the French Revolution. As was said above, Shaftesbury was on the side of balanced good sense. And in his moral theory, though he tried to swing free of utilitarianism he did not in fact succeed. His ethical system at bottom is, as much as any other rationalist's, a calculation in terms of self-interest. Nevertheless, aside from his very great influence on the Continent, which was later to return in force, he did express, and perhaps reinforce, that movement of revulsion, which we have noticed as appearing even before the beginning of the century, against widespread and shameless moral insensibility. We have seen how Shaftesbury contended that moral feeling was *natural* to man, and how as a consequence the unfeeling or unsympathetic man was stigmatized as a deformed or diseased person. The reaction against brutal callousness more and more took form as a cultivation of the emotions. It began to be a sign of refinement, even of genuine humanity, to have feelings, or at least to be able to produce promptly some distinct sign of the emotion considered appropriate to this or that exigency. Tears, sighs, and groans began to be fashionable, and, in time, even fainting fits amongst members of the tender sex. The rising tide of sensibility produced, quite naturally, a rising interest in the inward workings of the sensitive heart, and, generally, in the springs of personality.

Samuel Richardson: "Pamela"

Perhaps no one guessed how absorbing this new interest could be until it was gratified in 1740 by the publication of Samuel Richardson's *Pamela, or Virtue Rewarded.* And Richardson himself was sufficiently isolated from the circles where philosophical or literary discussion flourished to make it certain that what he did was spontaneous. In other words, the interest he satisfied was one already diffused and "in the air," as people say. Richardson was a mousy little printer, precise, fussy, perfectly conventional, very religious, industrious, and prosperous. Eighteenth-century printers were sometimes editors also, and Richardson not only made indexes for some books he printed but wrote dedicatory letters capably. He had always been timid, and as a youth had found the company of some young women more congenial than that of rough boys of his own age. The young women on their side had found him full of sympathetic understanding, and had entrusted to him the delicate task of writing, better than they could themselves, love letters to young men. This was the character and extent of Richardson's literary experience when, at the age of fifty, he was asked by some booksellers to compile a volume of model letters for the use of maidservants, sailors, countrymen, and the like, who occasionally had to write but did not know how to go about it. Richardson accepted the task, and in due time completed the book, which was published under the following title, worth reproducing in full: *Letters Written to and for Particular Friends, On the Most Important Occasions, Directing not only the Requisite Style and Forms to be Observed in Writing Familiar Letters; But how to Think and Act* Justly *and* Prudently, *in the Common Concerns of Human Life* (1741). Richardson, in other words, was, like most of his contemporaries, a moralist, and he could not let this opportunity slip without doing his bit for the moral improvement of those who might use the book. *Pamela* happened to be written because Richardson became so interested in one group of model letters that he laid aside the booksellers' job in order to expand those dealing with a not uncommon problem confronting maidservants in great eighteenth-century houses—the attempts of young masters in those households to seduce them. Thus the first full-fledged English novel was produced, in what some would call a characteristically English fashion, by accident. In so far as it was the result of literary influence, the book expressed a reaction against the "vain," "empty," high-flying heroic romances of the seventeenth century. It brought fiction down to earth and reality, for the sake of moral betterment.

Pamela is a very pretty young maidservant, whose virtue is assailed by the wealthy young Mr. B——. The story is told in a series of letters: how Pamela repels Mr. B—— with abhorrence, how in time she falls in love with him despite his villainy, but keeps her head, and how thus she finally succeeds in making him marry her—the reward for her virtue. There is a good deal of action, but the interest is centered in character portrayal achieved through Pamela's own minute self-analysis and detailed record of all her feelings, their rise and fall, in every circumstance in which she is involved. In his two later, and longer, novels, *Clarissa Harlowe* and *The History of Sir Charles Grandison,* Richardson had the same aim and stuck to the same method, of telling the story through a series of letters written by the characters to one another. It is an awkward way of telling a story—some amusing calculations have been made of the time that must have been required for all the writing done by Richardson's most important characters—and not many of Richardson's successors have adopted it. Yet it does lend itself admirably to the purpose of building up gradually, through many small touches, a portrait of inward character, seen through all its minutest workings, until a reader feels that he knows one of Richardson's heroines far better than he can ever know anyone in actual life.

"Novel" and "Romance" Defined

Richardson came to regard himself as the originator of an entirely new species of writing, and he was substantially right. Moreover, he was phenomenally successful. He was the one man of the eighteenth century who wrote a book which instantly broke through all barriers and divisions and was devoured literally by everybody. How are we to define the novel, which Richardson created, and which from his day to ours has been the most popular kind of imaginative literature, taking up the central place which had been held by drama? The word "romance," used to denote a type of fiction, has kept the meaning which became attached to it in the beginning. It was first used, as we have seen, to designate narratives of strange adventure. In the early medieval romances the interest was centered in the action itself, and the characters were interesting only because of their exploits. As those for whom the romances were written became more mature, the center of interest, we may recall, shifted from action to delineation of character. Chaucer's *Troilus and Criseyde* has often been called a novel in verse because, though Chaucer used matter of romance, he made it merely the setting for a tale whose interest lies, not in the plot, but in the detailed subtle presentation of inward character, realistically conceived.

This gives us the key to the meaning of "novel." The modern novel has been a very elastic literary form, but in all its varieties of treatment it has, on the whole, preserved the qualities which Richardson gave it. The novel requires a certain amplitude of treatment; it must have a plot in order that the characters may be seen not only in action but in conflict which serves to reveal them; but the action is subordinated to the delineation of character, and perhaps, though not necessarily, of character developing through experience; and finally the novel is realistic, or is a transcript of real life in the real world of our own experience. As early as the end of the fifteenth century "romance" had come to be used as a synonym for "lie," obviously because, in their lack of regard for truth to life and experience, the writers of medieval romances had idly indulged in every kind of extravagance and inconsequence. The words "romance" and "romantic" have kept something of this meaning ever since. Pepys in his *Diary* speaks of some things which, he says, "are almost romantic, and yet true." And the fashionable "heroic" fictions of the seventeenth century, which have been discussed earlier in this chapter, are "romances" because, though the treatment in them is the realistic one of character analysis, the characters themselves are extravagantly conceived, and never lived anywhere save in the irresponsible imaginations of their creators. In the modern world the romance has persisted alongside the novel. The prose tales of G. A. Henty and of Robert Louis Stevenson are alike romances—though there is a world of difference in their quality—because in them the interest is centered in action, and not in character.

Sentimentalism: Laurence Sterne

Dr. Johnson said, "If you were to read Richardson for the story, your impatience would be so much fretted that you would hang yourself. But you must read him for the sentiment, and consider the story as only giving occasion to the sentiment." This was perfectly sound advice, but advice that most of Richardson's contemporary readers did not need. The novelist wonderfully gratified the rising tide of sensibility by drawing out the sentiment with loving exhaustiveness, until the emotions of readers were not only touched, but harrowed. And they loved it. Richardson was helping to produce a brood of sentimentalists; though it must be said, for his credit, that they would certainly have appeared without his help. Sentimentalism may be defined as the love and cultivation of emotion for its own sake. The sentimentalist seeks occasion for pity, for tears, because he *enjoys* being emotionally stirred; and when he has become thus deranged almost any occasion will suffice for his purpose. This is illustrated capitally in the work of Richardson's younger contemporary, Laurence Sterne, author of *Tristram Shandy* and *A Sentimental Journey through France and Italy*. Sterne is the incarnation of whimsicality, and, beyond all his monkey tricks and elaborate absurdities, at the same time a masterly delineator of character; but he is also a mawkish sentimentalist, who shows the worst lengths to which this trivial and in the end unmeaning emotionalism could go.

Henry Fielding: "Tom Jones"

What Henry Fielding would have thought of Sterne's sentimentalism, had he lived to read *Tristram Shandy* and the *Sentimental Journey,* would probably be unprintable, though certainly his judgment would have been tempered by a genial appreciation of Sterne's sophisticated artistry and disarming good nature. Fielding died in 1754, six years before *Tristram* began to appear. He had lived hard and worked incessantly, as playwright and essayist and poet, when Richardson's *Pamela* appeared. That book disgusted him, and caused him to write a parody in which he ruthlessly exposed what he took to be the real bearing and tendency of *Pamela,* and laughed at Richardson's pious pretension to the name of moralist. He entitled the book, *An Apology for the Life of Mrs. Shamela Andrews, in which the Many*

Notorious Falsehoods and Misrepresentations of a Book Called Pamela *are Exposed and Refuted; and All the Matchless Arts of that Young Politician Set in a True and Just Light.* But this witty and devastating skit did not exhaust Fielding's satirical impulse. He went on to mock at *Pamela* in a book giving the alleged history of her brother, Joseph Andrews, a virtuous young serving-man whose mistress tries to tempt him into misconduct. In *Joseph Andrews,* however, Fielding was carried far beyond his first intention, and produced a novel which could stand on its own feet by virtue of its portrayal of the lovable Parson Adams and its pictures of English country life. Having thus discovered his powers, Fielding went on to write *Tom Jones,* a comic epic in prose as he called it, and perhaps still the greatest of all English novels.

Tom Jones has imperfections obvious enough to present-day readers. There are progressive developments in the techniques of the arts. A Titian stands on the shoulders of his predecessors, benefits by their experiments and discoveries, and so, from the collective efforts of many striving painters, acquires a sure mastery of color and line and composition which might well seem miraculous to a Giotto, could he come back from the grave after two centuries to survey the work of his successors. Yet we may still prefer the work of Giotto because we find expressed in it, though imperfectly and rudely, something we value which was completely beyond the sympathetic comprehension of Titian. Browning in "Andrea del Sarto" has shown once and for all how technical mastery is in itself nothing. So it is that though Fielding, one of the originators of a new kind of writing, does not display the technical competence of a Trollope or the mastery of a Hardy, he still holds a supreme place because he had something centrally important and sound to communicate and saw it with the great artist's eye—*embodied* to the life in full-blooded characters. Fielding is incomparably vivid; he makes us see with delight what he saw with delight, converts us, and carries us triumphantly with him over the English countryside, through all manner of escapades, into London and out again, until we not only catch the perfect flavor of the eighteenth century but feel the glow of a hearty healthy life which is simply and soundly human, and independent of time or place. Fielding does not see everything; he does not carry us quite to the heights or to the depths of life, as Shakespeare does; he is like his own century in preferring the broad level space between extremes; but this after all is the center, and Fielding is completely at home in it. Probably the secret of Fielding's genius, as nearly as one can put one's finger on it, lies in his directness and his confident sanity. He pierces through all perplexed, sickly, one-sided or conventional thought, and all strained or morbid feeling. He comes straight out with what he sees and feels, and shows us everything without hesitation or fear. Thackeray in his Preface to *Pendennis* said the right thing about Fielding: "Since the author of *Tom Jones* was buried, no writer of fiction among us has been permitted to depict to his utmost power A MAN."

Fielding did it, against the background of the time—the intellectual as well as the social background. And the historical student finds in *Tom Jones* a simple clear-cut picture of the difficulty with which the eighteenth century was wrestling, and to which much attention has been paid in this chapter. The logic of events in the seventeenth century had brought about an unnatural separation, we may say, between head and heart. Thence had issued, on the one side, in the name of "reason," a callous pursuit of selfish advantage, which was really corrupt and brutal, but which justified itself on the ground that it was realistic. By way of reaction, an equally one-sided cult of "noble sentiment" was growing up, which already in Fielding's time was degenerating into what he thought a mawkish hypocrisy. He succeeded no more than Shaftesbury in getting to the bottom of the trouble. He felt such contempt for mean-spirited calculating people and for hypocrites that he made young Blifil, who personifies these types, an unplausible monster; and he was hardly better in portraying the perfect altruist in Squire Allworthy. Nevertheless, he did steer clear of both utilitarianism and sentimentalism. He presented an example of morality based on sentiment without the slightest trace of sentimentalism, and did not blink at any consequence of handing over self-direction to spontaneous impulse. Thus he ranged himself on the side of the rising belief in the natural goodness of earthly human nature. But his greatness as a novelist remains secure whatever may be our estimate of eighteenth-century dilemmas or beliefs, because he did see and portray human nature as it is, without expurgation, honestly and fairly.

The Period as a Whole

The century and a quarter which we have been surveying was dominated, in the field of letters, by three men: Dryden, and then Pope, and finally Dr. Johnson. The middle period has usually been called the neoclassical age of English literature, sometimes the Augustan age, and occasionally the pseudoclassical age. All three terms are seriously misleading, and the last betrays not only misunderstanding but prejudice. Hence in these pages they have been ignored, in an attempt to show and explain the controlling influences really at work in the shaping of eighteenth-century letters. From the beginning of the English Renaissance to the end of the nineteenth century two influences are pervasively present in English literature —that of the classics and that of the Bible —and it is impossible to single out any brief space during which one influence or the other was uniquely important. The kind of influence exerted by the Greek and Latin classics varied greatly from one generation to another, because classically educated men—and nearly all English writers for over three centuries were classically educated—took from the varied wealth of the ancient world what they could understand and use. And this was a varying quantity, controlled by native conditions. Some historians and critics insist on distinguishing what they like as the "really classical" element in the classics—very often it turns out to be "the ancient Greek's joy in life, his delight in the flesh and the senses," and so on—and then assess classical influence by this touchstone. A warning against such folly has been given in an earlier chapter, and it need not be repeated; but it should not be forgotten.

If we try to generalize about the age, we may come nearest the truth if we say it was a time when newly emancipated reason got into the saddle and attempted the control of the whole domain of life. Men hopefully laid the foundations of a "science" of literary creation, of a "science" of morals, as well as of the sciences of physical phenomena. But reason overreached herself, was perplexed by unforeseen consequences of her activity, and then began to dissolve under critical scrutiny. Meanwhile distrusted emotion began to say something on her own account, first by way of satire; but then more rebelliously and alarmingly by claiming to represent what was good in human nature. Reason had made this exclusive claim, had been given her opportunity, and was showing herself grossly incompetent to sustain it. As we have had occasion to observe before, when false oppositions are set up, indefensible extremes are encouraged. Against a one-sided rationalism, there grew up the hardy weed of sentimentalism.

As the century advanced, men tended increasingly to withdraw themselves from problems they did not know how to solve, and found that they could live contentedly without solving them. The day of the professional author was dawning, and men were beginning, not to lead, but to follow the taste of the reading public. The fierce political differences of the early years of the century had died away. There was no serious concern about religion. Methodism might be exciting the lower classes, but their devotion was a spectacle more amusing than disturbing to men of the polite world. The spirit of dilettantism was growing, and along with it, taking the place of concentrated interest in abstract or public questions, a new interest in people. Great ambitions, high hopes, heroic achievement—these were becoming legendary. A bad time for literature, we are tempted to say, and many have said it. Certainly it was a bad time for the more stirring or grander kinds of literature, but it was not an unfruitful time. It was in these placid days that Dr. Johnson talked freely and magnificently with the tireless Boswell at his side, and so sat for a literary portrait that has never been rivaled. And it was in these days that Gray and Horace Walpole and Cowper and others wrote innumerable letters which form a priceless addition to English literature. It was in these days, too, that England's greatest historian, Edward Gibbon, composed the stately paragraphs which trace out *The Decline and Fall of the Roman Empire*. We have much reason for gratitude when we really consider what the last quarter-century of this period has left us. Other literature, before and after this quiet time, we read with astonishment, with awe, with deeply stirred emotion; but of the companionable authors with whom we can live pleasantly, and who can give us day after day, year in year out, a never-failing yet serene delight, some of the best lived in the latter part of the "excellent and indispensable eighteenth century."

SAMUEL PEPYS

1633–1703

Samuel Pepys was born in London on 23 February, 1633. His father, a poor tailor, had migrated thither from the region of the fens, or bogs, north of Cambridge; Samuel, who inherited the strong natural instincts of a fensman, was brought up in an urban world of lower middle-class Puritanism. He received most of his early education at St. Paul's School in London, a foundation which displayed, among others, the sensible motto: *Aut doce, aut disce, aut discede*—"Teach, or learn, or get out." The schoolboy also enjoyed the more questionable advantage of living in the capital during the stormy years of the Civil War; on 30 January, 1649, when he was fifteen, young Pepys saw the beheading of Charles I and remarked that, were he to preach on the event, his text would be: "The memory of the wicked shall rot." A year later he was admitted to Magdalene College, Cambridge, as a sizar, i. e., a scholar whose expenses were paid in return for certain menial duties. Before he received the B. A. degree in 1653 he showed that in spite of his Puritan upbringing he was not averse to drink and boon companionship. In 1655, once more back in London, he married Elizabeth St. Michel, the fifteen-year-old daughter of a penniless Huguenot gentleman. Although the young couple undoubtedly felt a real affection for each other, their life together was frequently made unhappy by jealousy on both sides; in 1668, only a year before Elizabeth's death, they were finally reconciled as a result of their most serious quarrel. In the beginning, moreover, Pepys was a poor man, who had to be contented with a position little better than that of an upper servant in the household of a well-to-do cousin, Edward Montagu. This connection eventually proved to be a fortunate one, for Montagu, a naval official of the Commonwealth, was one of the men most influential in procuring the Restoration of Charles II; in the spring of 1660 he was appointed admiral of the fleet which brought the new king over from the Continent, and he was subsequently made Earl of Sandwich. Pepys, who had been Montagu's secretary on the voyage, was now advanced to the post of Clerk of the Acts for the Navy Office; from this time on he was among the most loyal supporters of the Stuart cause. His new position at first interested him only as a source of profit and prestige; of marine affairs he was almost completely ignorant; but as soon as his curiosity had been aroused, he set out to learn all that was to be known about the Navy. Before long his bourgeois love of order, thoroughness, and discipline came into conflict with a corrupt and inefficient administration; unfortunately, a Clerk of the Acts could effect only minor reforms. The Plague (1665), the Fire of London (1666), and the success of the Dutch in destroying a large part of the English fleet in the dockyards along the Medway (1667) were national disasters which placed the government in a difficult position; Pepys, now recognized to be the most able member of the Navy Office, faced and defeated Parliamentary criticism of that department in 1669. Four years later his worth was rewarded by advancement to the important post of Secretary to the Admiralty; with the backing of his immediate superior, the Duke of York, he was now able to reform the Navy. He not only established military convoys for trading vessels and an efficient system of victualing the fleet; he was also responsible for building thirty new men-of-war; and he made so radical and permanent an improvement in the discipline required of naval officers that he may be called the founder of the British Civil Service. In 1679, after the discovery of the "Popish Plot," he was falsely accused of being a Papist and a traitor, compelled to resign his position, and for a short time even imprisoned in the Tower; his Whig enemies later dropped the case without allowing him to establish his innocence. Another political shift, however, restored him to the Admiralty in 1684, with a salary equivalent to £10,000 in modern money; a year later, when the Duke of York ascended the throne as James II, Pepys reached the brief climax of his career. Although the fleet had been badly neglected during the period when he was out of office, it was quickly rehabilitated through his own energy and the special interest of the king in naval affairs. By 1688 the finances and discipline of the service were so well established that from now on, the Navy was the right hand of national greatness. But in 1688 the Glorious Revolution compelled James to flee the country; and early in the next year, upon the accession of William and Mary, Pepys laid down the secretaryship for ever. The remainder of his life was passed in learned retirement. His *Memoirs of the Royal Navy,* for which he had long been collecting material, appeared in 1690. When he died in 1703, he left a select and valuable library which, in accordance with his instructions, eventually came into the possession of Magdalene College, Cambridge.

The most valuable part of this Bibliotheca Pepysiana, as it is called, is the manuscript journal which Pepys kept for a period of almost ten years, from 1660 to 1669. It consists of about 3000 pages, written in a seventeenth-century form of shorthand which he doubtless used, not only to save time, but also to prevent the contents from being read. The *Diary* was discontinued in 1669 because Pepys was suffering from an acute eye trouble which made it almost impossible for him to write shorthand. In 1660 he may have begun to keep a minute record of his actions with the idea of securing an alibi during the political troubles of the period; soon, however, his chief motive can only have been the satisfaction he took in describing, without restraint, exactly what he had done and seen and thought. The personality which he thus uncovers has been variously interpreted. After the first and very fragmentary publication of the *Diary* in 1825, Coleridge remarked that Pepys was a "pollard," or stunted, man; and Lowell once referred to him as a naïve and humorless Philistine. More recent critics, who are better acquainted with both the *Diary* and the facts of his life, are not so inclined to emphasize his limitations. With a middle-class respect for virtue and piety he combined the instinct to confess the most unpalatable truths; if he frequently displayed a narrow, hard-headed selfishness, he was also a faithful and charming friend; his genius as a practical administrator was mingled with a keen artistic sensibility—witness his love of music and his gift for literary expression. It is precisely because his nature was neither simple nor commonplace that Pepys can tell us so much about himself and about his world.

The best edition of the *Diary* is still that edited by Henry B. Wheatley (London, 1893–1899), but in many passages it omits or modifies what Pepys actually wrote. Arthur Bryant's *Samuel Pepys,* three of whose four volumes have already appeared (Cambridge, 1933–1938), is an outstanding biography, important for its interpretation of Pepys as a public servant as well as a domestic personality. Bryant is also the author of an interesting study of the life of the time, *The England of Charles II* (London, 1934). Thomas Babington Macaulay's *History of England from the Accession of James the Second* (London, 1848–1861) is the standard, although not an unbiased, political account of the period in which Pepys was a public figure.

PASSAGES FROM *THE DIARY*

I

22 May, 1660.[1] Up very early, and now beginning to be settled in my wits again, I went about setting down my last four days' observations this morning. After that, was trimmed by a barber that has not trimmed me yet, my Spaniard being on shore. News brought that the two Dukes[2] are coming on board, which, by and by, they did, in a Dutch boat, the Duke of York in yellow trimmings, the Duke of Gloucester in gray and red. My Lord[3] went in a boat to meet them, the Captain, myself, and others, standing at the entering port. So soon as they were entered we shot the guns off round the fleet. After that they went to view the ship all over, and were most exceedingly pleased with it. They seem to be both very fine gentlemen. After that done, upon the quarter-deck table, under the

[1] At this time Pepys was aboard ship off the coast of Holland, serving as secretary to the commander of the English fleet sent to bring Charles II back to England at the beginning of the Restoration era.

[2] Brothers of the new king. The Duke of York later became James II.

[3] Sir Edward Montagu, commander of the expedition.

awning, the Duke of York, and my Lord, Mr. Coventry, and I, spent an hour at allotting to every ship their service, in their return to England; which having done, they went to dinner, where the table was very full: the two Dukes at the upper end, my Lord Opdam next on one side, and my Lord on the other. Two guns given to every man while he was drinking the King's health, and so likewise to the Dukes' health. I took down Monsieur d'Esquier to the great cabin below, and dined with him in state alone with only one or two friends of his. All dinner the harper belonging to Captain Sparling played to the Dukes. After dinner, the Dukes and my Lord to see the Vice and Rear-Admirals, and I in a boat after them. After that done, they made to the shore in the Dutch boat that brought them, and I got into the boat with them; but the shore was so full of people to expect their coming, as that it was as black (which otherwise is white sand), as every one could stand by another. When we came near the shore, my Lord left them and came into his own boat, and General Penn[4] and I with him; my Lord being very well pleased with this day's work. By the time we came on board again, news is sent us that the King is on shore; so my Lord fired all his guns round twice, and all the fleet after him, which in the end fell into disorder, which seemed very handsome. The gun over against my cabin I fired myself to the King, which was the first time that he had been saluted by his own ships since this change; but holding my head too much over the gun, I had almost spoiled my right eye. Nothing in the world but going of guns almost all this day. In the evening we began to remove cabins; I to the carpenter's cabin, and Dr. Clerke with me, who came on board this afternoon, having been twice ducked in the sea to-day coming from shore, and Mr. North and John Pickering the like. Many of the King's servants came on board to-night; and so many Dutch of all sorts came to see the ship till it was quite dark, that we could not pass by one another, which was a great trouble to us all. This afternoon Mr. Downing[5] (who was knighted yesterday by the King) was here on board, and had a ship for his passage into England, with his lady and servants. By the same token he called me to him when I was going to write the order, to tell me that I must write him Sir G. Downing. My Lord lay in the roundhouse to-night. This evening I was late writing a French letter myself by my Lord's order to Monsieur Krag, Ambassador *de Denmarke à la Haye,*[6] which my Lord signed in bed. After that I to bed, and the Doctor, and sleep well.

23rd. The Doctor and I waked very merry, only my eye was very red and ill in the morning from yesterday's hurt. In the morning came infinity of people on board from the King to go along with him. My Lord, Mr. Crew, and others, go on shore to meet the King as he comes off from shore, where Sir R. Stayner bringing His Majesty into the boat, I hear that His Majesty did with a great deal of affection kiss my Lord upon his first meeting. The King, with the two Dukes and Queen of Bohemia, Princess Royal, and Prince of Orange,[7] came on board, where I in their coming in kissed the King's, Queen's, and Princess's hands, having done the other before. Infinite shooting off of the guns, and that in a disorder on purpose, which was better than if it had been otherwise. All day nothing but Lords and persons of honor on board, that we were exceeding full. Dined in a great deal of state, the Royal company by themselves in the coach,[8] which was a blessed sight to see. I dined with Dr. Clerke, Dr. Quartermaine, and Mr. Darcy in my cabin. This morning Mr. Lucy came on board, to whom and his company of the King's Guard in another ship my Lord did give three dozen of bottles of wine. He made friends between Mr. Pierce and me. After dinner the King and Duke altered the name of some of the ships, *viz.*, the *Naseby* into *Charles;* the *Richard, James;* the *Speaker, Mary;* the *Dunbar* (which was not in company with us), the

[4]Admiral William Penn, father of the founder of Pennsylvania.

[5]One of the principal negotiators for the return of Charles.

[6]Ambassador of Denmark to The Hague.

[7]The aunt, sister, and nephew of the King.

[8]Apartment in the stern of a man of war.

Henry; Winsby, Happy Return; Wakefield, Richmond; Lambert, the *Henrietta; Cheriton,* the *Speedwell; Bradford,* the *Success.*[9] That done, the Queen, Princess Royal, and Prince of Orange, took leave of the King, and the Duke of York went on board the *London,* and the Duke of Gloucester, the *Swiftsure.* Which done, we weighed anchor, and with a fresh gale and most happy weather we set sail for England. All the afternoon the King walked here and there, up and down (quite contrary to what I thought him to have been), very active and stirring. Upon the quarter-deck he fell into discourse of his escape from Worcester,[10] where it made me ready to weep to hear the stories that he told of his difficulties that he had passed through, as his traveling four days and three nights on foot, every step up to his knees in dirt, with nothing but a green coat and a pair of country breeches on, and a pair of country shoes that made him so sore all over his feet, that he could scarce stir. Yet he was forced to run away from a miller and other company, that took them for rogues. His sitting at table at one place, where the master of the house, that had not seen him in eight years, did know him, but kept it private; when at the same table there was one that had been of his own regiment at Worcester, could not know him, but made him drink the King's health, and said that the King was at least four fingers higher than he. At another place he was by some servants of the house made to drink, that they might know him not to be a Roundhead, which they swore he was. In another place at his inn, the master of the house, as the King was standing with his hands upon the back of a chair by the fire-side, kneeled down and kissed his hand, privately, saying, that he would not ask him who he was, but bid God bless him whither he was going. Then the difficulty of getting a boat to get into France, where he was fain to plot with the master thereof to keep his design from the four men and a boy (which was all his ship's company), and so got to Fécamp in France. At Rouen he looked so poorly, that the people went into the rooms before he went away to see whether he had not stole something or other. In the evening I went up to my Lord to write letters for England, which we sent away with word of our coming, by Mr. Edw. Pickering. The King supped alone in the coach; after that I got a dish, and we four supped in my cabin, as at noon. About bed-time my Lord Bartlett[11] (who I had offered my service to before) sent for me to get him a bed, who with much ado I did get to bed to my Lord Middlesex in the great cabin below, but I was cruelly troubled before I could dispose of him, and quit myself of him. So to my cabin again, where the company still was, and were talking more of the King's difficulties; as how he was fain to eat a piece of bread and cheese out of a poor boy's pocket; how, at a Catholic house, he was fain to lie in the priest's hole a good while in the house for his privacy. After that our company broke up, and the Doctor and I to bed. We have all the Lords Commissioners on board us, and many others. Under sail all night, and most glorious weather.

24th. Up, and make myself as fine as I could, with the linen stockings on and wide canons[12] that I bought the other day at Hague. Extraordinary press of noble company, and great mirth all the day. There dined with me in my cabin (that is, the carpenter's) Dr. Earle and Mr. Holles, the King's Chaplains, Dr. Scarborough, Dr. Quartermaine, and Dr. Clerke, Physicians, Mr. Darcy, and Mr. Fox (both very fine gentlemen), the King's servants, where we had brave discourse. Walking upon the decks, where persons of honor all the afternoon, among others, Thomas Killigrew[13] (a merry droll, but a gentleman of great esteem with the King), who told us many merry stories: one, how he wrote a letter three or four days ago to the Princess Royal, about a Queen Dowager of Judaea and Palestine, that was at The Hague *incognita,* that made love to the King, *etc.,* which was Mr. Cary (a

[9]Thus the names of various Roundhead leaders and victories were exchanged for Royalist or for traditional names of ships in the English fleet.

[10]The last stand of the Royalists against Cromwell's army (1651).

[11]Mistake for Lord Berkeley.

[12]Ornaments for the legs.

[13]A well-known wit of the time (1612–1683).

courtier's) wife that had been a nun, who are all married to Jesus. At supper the three Drs. of Physic again at my cabin; where I put Dr. Scarborough in mind of what I heard him say about the use of the eyes, which he owned, that children do, in every day's experience, look several ways with both their eyes, till custom teaches them otherwise. And that we do now see but with one eye, our eyes looking in parallel lines. After this discourse I was called to write a pass for my Lord Mandeville to take up horses to London, which I wrote in the King's name, and carried it to him to sign, which was the first and only one that ever he signed in the ship *Charles*. To bed, coming in sight of land a little before night.

25th. By the morning we were come close to the land, and everybody made ready to get on shore. The King and the two Dukes did eat their breakfast before they went, and there being set some ship's diet before them, only to show them the manner of the ship's diet, they eat of nothing else but pease and pork, and boiled beef. I had Mr. Darcy in my cabin and Dr. Clerke, who eat with me, told me how the King had given £50 to Mr. Shepley for my Lord's servants, and £500 among the officers and common men of the ship. I spoke with the Duke of York about business, who called me Pepys by name, and upon my desire did promise me his future favor. Great expectation of the King's making some Knights, but there was none. About noon (though the brigantine that Beale made was there ready to carry him) yet he would go in my Lord's barge with the two Dukes. Our Captain steered, and my Lord went along bare with him. I went, and Mr. Mansell, and one of the King's footmen, with a dog that the King loved, (which [dirted][14] the boat, which made us laugh, and methink that a King and all that belonged to him are but just as others are), in a boat by ourselves, and so got on shore when the King did, who was received by General Monk[15] with all imaginable love and respect at his entrance upon the land of Dover. Infinite the crowd of people and the horsemen, citizens, and noblemen of all sorts. The Mayor of the town came and gave him his white staff, the badge of his place, which the King did give him again. The Mayor also presented him from the town a very rich Bible, which he took and said it was the thing that he loved above all things in the world. A canopy was provided for him to stand under, which he did, and talked awhile with General Monk and others, and so into a stately coach there set for him, and so away through the town towards Canterbury, without making any stay at Dover. The shouting and joy expressed by all is past imagination. Seeing that my Lord did not stir out of his barge, I got into a boat, and so into his barge, whither Mr. John Crew stepped, and spoke a word or two to my Lord, and so returned, we back to the ship, and going did see a man almost drowned that fell out of his boat into the sea, but with much ado was got out. My Lord almost transported with joy that he had done all this without any the least blur or obstruction in the world, that could give an offense to any, and with the great honor he thought it would be to him. Being overtook by the brigantine, my Lord and we went out of our barge into it, and so went on board with Sir W. Batten and the Vice and Rear-Admirals. At night my Lord supped and Mr. Thomas Crew with Captain Stokes, I supped with the Captain, who told me what the King had given us. My Lord returned late, and at his coming did give me order to cause the mark to be gilded, and a Crown and C. R. to be made at the head of the coach table, where the King to-day with his own hand did mark his height, which accordingly I caused the painter to do, and is now done as is to be seen.

II

13 October, 1660. To my Lord's in the morning, where I met with Captain Cuttance, but my Lord not being up I went out to Charing Cross, to see Major-general Harrison[16]

[14]Here and elsewhere in the selections from the Diary brackets indicate changes by Pepys's editor, Henry B. Wheatley.

[15]General of the Commonwealth instrumental in bringing about the return of the Stuarts; created Duke of Albemarle by Charles II.

[16]General Thomas Harrison, signer of the warrant for the execution of Charles I in 1649.

hanged, drawn, and quartered; which was done there, he looking as cheerful as any man could do in that condition. He was presently cut down, and his head and heart shown to the people, at which there was great shouts of joy. It is said, that he said that he was sure to come shortly at the right hand of Christ to judge them that now had judged him; and that his wife do expect his coming again. Thus it was my chance to see the King beheaded at Whitehall, and to see the first blood shed in revenge for the blood of the King at Charing Cross. From thence to my Lord's, and took Captain Cuttance and Mr. Shepley to the Sun Tavern, and did give them some oysters. After that I went by water home, where I was angry with my wife for her things lying about, and in my passion kicked the little fine basket, which I bought her in Holland, and broke it, which troubled me after I had done it. Within all the afternoon setting up shelves in my study. At night to bed.

14th (Lord's day). Early to my Lord's, in my way meeting with Dr. Fairbrother, who walked with me to my father's[17] back again, and there we drank my morning draft, my father having gone to church and my mother asleep in bed. Here he caused me to put my hand among a great many honorable hands to a paper or certificate in his behalf. To Whitehall chapel, where one Dr. Croft made an indifferent sermon, and after it an anthem, ill sung, which made the King laugh. Here I first did see the Princess Royal since she came into England. Here I also observed, how the Duke of York and Mrs. Palmer[18] did talk to one another very wantonly through the hangings that parts the King's closet and the closet where the ladies sit. To my Lord's, where I found my wife, and she and I did dine with my Lady (my Lord dining with my Lord Chamberlain), who did treat my wife with a good deal of respect. In the evening we went home through the rain by water in a sculler, having borrowed some coats of Mr. Shepley. So home, wet and dirty, and to bed.

15th. Office all the morning. My wife and I by water; I landed her at Whitefriars, she went to my father's to dinner, it being my father's wedding day, there being a very great dinner, and only the Fenners and Joyces there. This morning Mr. Carew[19] was hanged and quartered at Charing Cross; but his quarters, by a great favor, are not to be hanged up. I was forced to go to my Lord's to get him to meet the officers of the Navy this afternoon, and so could not go along with her, but I missed my Lord, who was this day upon the bench at the Sessions house. So I dined there, and went to Whitehall, where I met with Sir W. Batten and Penn, who with the Comptroller, Treasurer, and Mr. Coventry (at his chamber) made up a list of such ships as are fit to be kept out for the winter guard, and the rest to be paid off by the Parliament when they can get money, which I doubt will not be a great while. That done, I took coach, and called my wife at my father's, and so homewards, calling at Thos. Pepys[20] the turner's for some things that we wanted. And so home, where I fell to read *The Fruitless Precaution* (a book formerly recommended by Dr. Clerke at sea to me), which I read in bed till I had made an end of it, and do find it the best writ tale that ever I read in my life. After that done to sleep, which I did not very well do, because that my wife having a stopping in her nose she snored much, which I never did hear her do before.

III

CORONATION DAY

23 April, 1661. About 4 I rose and got to the Abbey, where I followed Sir J. Denham,[21] the Surveyor, with some company that he was leading in. And with much ado, by the favor of Mr. Cooper, his man, did get up into a great scaffold across the North end of the Abbey, where with a great deal of patience I sat from past 4 till 11 before the King came in. And a great pleasure it was to see the Abbey raised in the middle, all covered with red, and a throne

[17] John Pepys, tailor (1601–1680).

[18] Mistress of Charles II, later made Countess of Castlemaine and Duchess of Cleveland.

[19] John Carew, who had signed the death warrant of Charles I.

[20] A cousin.

[21] A well-known poet (1615–1669).

(that is a chair) and footstool on the top of it; and all the officers of all kinds, so much as the very fiddlers, in red vests. At last comes in the dean and prebends of Westminster, with the bishops (many of them in cloth of gold copes), and after them the nobility, all in their Parliament robes, which was a most magnificent sight. Then the Duke, and the King with a scepter (carried by my Lord Sandwich) and sword and mond[22] before him, and the crown too. The King in his robes, bareheaded, which was very fine. And after all had placed themselves, there was a sermon and the service; and then in the choir at the high altar, the King passed through all the ceremonies of the coronation, which to my great grief I and most in the Abbey could not see. The crown being put upon his head, a great shout begun, and he came forth to the throne, and there passed more ceremonies: as taking the oath, and having things read to him by the Bishop; and his lords (who put on their caps as soon as the King put on his crown) and bishops come, and kneeled before him. And three times the King at Arms went to the three open places on the scaffold, and proclaimed, that if any one could show any reason why Charles Stuart should not be King of England, that now he should come and speak. And a General Pardon also was read by the Lord Chancellor, and medals flung up and down by my Lord Cornwallis, of silver, but I could not come by any. But so great a noise that I could make but little of the music; and indeed, it was lost to everybody. But I had so great a lust to . . .[23] that I went out a little while before the King had done all his ceremonies, and went round the Abbey to Westminster Hall, all the way within rails, and 10,000 people, with the ground covered with blue cloth; and scaffolds all the way. Into the Hall I got, where it was very fine with hangings and scaffolds one upon another full of brave ladies; and my wife in one little one, on the right hand. Here I stayed walking up and down, and at last upon one of the side stalls I stood and saw the King come in with all the persons (but the soldiers) that were yesterday in the cavalcade; and a most pleasant sight it was to see them in their several robes. And the King came in with his crown on, and his scepter in his hand, under a canopy borne up by six silver staves, carried by Barons of the Cinque Ports,[24] and little bells at every end. And after a long time, he got up to the farther end, and all set themselves down at their several tables; and that was also a brave sight: and the King's first course carried up by the Knights of the Bath. And many fine ceremonies there was of the Heralds leading up people before him, and bowing; and my Lord Albemarle's going to the kitchen and eat a bit of the first dish that was to go to the King's table. But, above all, was these three Lords, Northumberland, and Suffolk, and the Duke of Ormond,[25] coming before the courses on horseback, and staying so all dinner-time, and at last to bring up [Dymock] the King's Champion, all in armor on horseback, with his spear and target carried before him. And a Herald proclaims "That if any dare deny Charles Stuart to be lawful King of England, here was a Champion that would fight with him"; and with these words, the Champion flings down his gauntlet, and all this he do three times in his going up towards the King's table. At last when he is come, the King drinks to him, and then sends him the cup which is of gold, and he drinks it off, and then rides back again with the cup in his hand. I went from table to table to see the bishops and all others at their dinner, and was infinitely pleased with it. And at the lords' table, I met with William Howe, and he spoke to my Lord for me, and he did give me four rabbits and a pullet, and so I got it and Mr. Creed and I got Mr. Michell to give us some bread, and so we at a stall eat it, as everybody else did what they could get. I took a great deal of pleasure to go up and down, and look upon the ladies, and to hear the music of all sorts, but above all, the 24 violins. About six at night they had

[22]Orb of gold, topped by a cross set with jewels.

[23]Apparently a word or words omitted by Wheatley.

[24]Members of Parliament for five (later seven) ports of the southeastern coast which enjoyed special privileges.

[25]Respectively Lord High Constable, acting Earl Marshal, and acting Lord High Steward of England.

dined, and I went up to my wife, and there met with a pretty lady (Mrs. Franklеyn, a Doctor's wife, a friend of Mr. Bowyer's), and kissed them both, and by and by took them down to Mr. Bowyer's. And strange it is to think, that these two days have held up fair till now that all is done, and the King gone out of the Hall; and then it fell a-raining and thundering and lightening as I have not seen it do for some years: which people did take great notice of; God's blessing of the work of these two days, which is a foolery to take too much notice of such things. I observed little disorder in all this, but only the King's footmen had got hold of the canopy, and would keep it from the Barons of the Cinque Ports, which they endeavored to force from them again, but could not do it till my Lord Duke of Albemarle caused it to be put into Sir R. Pye's hand till to-morrow to be decided. At Mr. Bowyer's; a great deal of company, some I knew, others I did not. Here we stayed upon the leads[26] and below till it was late, expecting to see the fire-works, but they were not performed to-night: only the City[27] had a light like a glory round about it with bonfires. At last I went to King Street, and there sent Crockford to my father's and my house, to tell them I could not come home to-night, because of the dirt, and a coach could not be had. And so after drinking a pot of ale alone at Mrs. Harper's I returned to Mr. Bowyer's, and after a little stay more I took my wife and Mrs. Frankleyn (who I proffered the civility of lying with my wife at Mrs. Hunt's to-night) to Axe Yard, in which at the further end there were three great bonfires, and a great many great gallants, men and women; and they laid hold of us, and would have us drink the King's health upon our knees, kneeling upon a fagot, which we all did, they drinking to us one after another. Which we thought a strange frolic; but these gallants continued thus a great while, and I wondered to see how the ladies did tipple. At last I sent my wife and her bedfellow to bed, and Mr. Hunt and I went in with Mr. Thornbury (who did give the company all their wine, he being yeoman of the wine-cellar to the King) to his house; and there, with his wife and two of his sisters, and some gallant sparks that were there, we drank the King's health, and nothing else, till one of the gentlemen fell down stark drunk, and there lay spewing; and I went to my Lord's pretty well. But no sooner a-bed with Mr. Shepley but my head began to hum, and I to vomit, and if ever I was foxed it was now, which I cannot say yet, because I fell asleep and slept till morning. Only when I waked I found myself wet with my spewing. Thus did the day end with joy everywhere; and blessed be God, I have not heard of any mischance to anybody through it all, but only to Serjt. Glynne, whose horse fell upon him yesterday, and is like to kill him, which people do please themselves to see how just God is to punish the rogue at such a time as this; he being now one of the King's Serjeants, and rode in the cavalcade with Maynard,[28] to whom people wish the same fortune. There was also this night in King Street, [a woman] had her eye put out by a boy's flinging a firebrand into the coach. Now, after all this, I can say that, besides the pleasure of the sight of these glorious things, I may now shut my eyes against any other objects, nor for the future trouble myself to see things of state and show, as being sure never to see the like again in this world.

IV

14 August, 1666. (Thanksgiving[29] day.) Up, and comes Mr. Foley and his man, with a box of a great variety of carpenter's and joiner's tools, which I had bespoke, to me, which please me mightily; but I will have more. Then I abroad down to the Old Swan, and there I called and kissed Betty Michell, and would have got her to go with me to Westminster, but I find her a little colder than she used to be, methought, which did a little molest me. So I away not

[26]On the roof.

[27]The small inner section of London included within the ancient boundaries.

[28]Glynne and Maynard, although eminent under the government of Cromwell, had now contrived to win recognition as King's serjeants, lawyers by royal patent.

[29]Thanksgiving for a late victory over the Dutch.

pleased, and to Whitehall, where I find them at Chapel, and met with Povy, and he and I together, who tells me how mad my letter makes my Lord Peterborough, and what a furious letter he hath writ to me in answer, though it is not come yet. This did trouble me; for though there be no reason, yet to have a nobleman's mouth open against a man may do a man hurt; so I endeavored to have found him out and spoke with him, but could not. So to the chapel, and heard a piece of the Dean of Westminster's sermon, and a special good anthem before the King, after a sermon, and then home by coach with Captain Cocke, who is in pain about his hemp, of which he says he hath bought great quantities, and would gladly be upon good terms with us for it, wherein I promise to assist him. So we 'light at the 'Change, where, after a small turn or two, taking no pleasure nowadays to be there, because of answering questions that would be asked there which I cannot answer; so home and dined, and after dinner, with my wife and Mercer to the Bear-garden[30] where I have not been, I think, of many years, and saw some good sport of the bull's tossing of the dogs: one into the very boxes. But it is a very rude and nasty pleasure. We had a great many hectors in the same box with us (and one very fine went into the pit, and played his dog for a wager, which was a strange sport for a gentleman), where they drank wine, and drank Mercer's health first, which I pledged with my hat off; and who should be in the house but Mr. Pierce the surgeon, who saw us and spoke to us. Thence home, well enough satisfied, however, with the variety of this afternoon's exercise; and so I to my chamber, till in the evening our company come to supper. We had invited to a venison pasty Mr. Batelier and his sister Mary, Mrs. Mercer,[31] her daughter Anne, Mr. Le Brun, and W. Hewer;[32] and so we supped, and very merry. And then about nine o'clock to Mrs. Mercer's gate, where the fire and boys expected us, and her son had provided abundance of serpents[33] and rockets; and there mighty merry (my Lady Penn and Pegg going thither with us, and Nan Wright), till about twelve at night, flinging our fireworks, and burning one another and the people over the way. And at last our businesses being most spent, we into Mrs. Mercer's, and there mighty merry, smutting one another with candle grease and soot, till most of us were like devils. And that being done, then we broke up, and to my house; and there I made them drink, and upstairs we went, and then fell into dancing (W. Batelier dancing well), and dressing, him and I and one Mr. Banister (who with his wife come over also with us) like women; and Mercer put on a suit of Tom's, like a boy, and mighty mirth we had, and Mercer danced a jig; and Nan Wright and my wife and Pegg Penn put on periwigs. Thus we spent till three or four in the morning, mighty merry; and then parted, and to bed.

V

2 SEPTEMBER, 1666 (Lord's day). Some of our maids sitting up late last night to get things ready against our feast to-day, Jane called us up about three in the morning, to tell us of a great fire they saw in the City. So I rose and slipped on my night-gown, and went to her window, and thought it to be on the back-side of Mark Lane at the farthest; but, being unused to such fires as followed, I thought it far enough off; and so went to bed again and to sleep. About seven rose again to dress myself, and there looked out at the window, and saw the fire not so much as it was and further off. So to my closet to set things to rights after yesterday's cleaning. By and by Jane comes and tells me that she hears that above 300 houses have been burned down to-night by the fire we saw, and that it is now burning down all Fish Street, by London Bridge. So I made myself ready presently, and walked to the Tower, and there got up upon one of the high places, Sir J. Robinson's little son going up with me; and there I did see the houses at that end of the bridge all on fire, and an infinite great fire on this and the other side

[30]A theater for animal combats on the south side of the Thames.

[31]Mother of Mary Mercer, Mrs. Pepys's servant.

[32]Pepys's chief clerk.

[33]Firework that burns with a serpentine motion or flame.

the end of the bridge; which, among other people, did trouble me for poor little Michell and our Sarah on the bridge. So down, with my heart full of trouble, to the Lieutenant of the Tower, who tells me that it begun this morning in the King's baker's house in Pudding Lane, and that it hath burned St. Magnus's Church and most part of Fish Street already. So I down to the water-side, and there got a boat and through bridge, and there saw a lamentable fire. Poor Michell's house, as far as the Old Swan, already burned that way, and the fire running further, that in a very little time it got as far as the Steelyard, while I was there. Everybody endeavoring to remove their goods, and flinging into the river or bringing them into lighters that lay off; poor people staying in their houses as long as till the very fire touched them, and then running into boats, or clambering from one pair of stairs by the waterside to another. And among other things, the poor pigeons, I perceive, were loath to leave their houses, but hovered about the windows and balconies till they some of them burned their wings, and fell down. Having stayed, and in an hour's time seen the fire rage every way, and nobody, to my sight, endeavoring to quench it, but to remove their goods, and leave all to the fire, and having seen it get as far as the Steelyard, and the wind mighty high and driving it into the City; and everything, after so long a drought, proving combustible, even the very stones of churches, and among other things the poor steeple by which pretty Mrs. —— lives, and whereof my old schoolfellow Elborough is parson, taken fire in the very top, and there burned till it fell down: I to Whitehall (with a gentleman with me who desired to go off from the Tower, to see the fire, in my boat); to Whitehall, and there up to the King's closet in the Chapel, where people come about me, and I did give them an account dismayed them all, and word was carried in to the King. So I was called for, and did tell the King and Duke of York what I saw, and that unless His Majesty did command houses to be pulled down nothing could stop the fire. They seemed much troubled, and the King commanded me to go to my Lord Mayor from him, and command him to spare no houses, but to pull down before the fire every way. The Duke of York bid me tell him that if he would have any more soldiers he shall; and so did my Lord Arlington[34] afterwards, as a great secret. Here meeting with Captain Cocke, I in his coach, which he lent me, and Creed with me to Paul's, and there walked along Watling Street, as well as I could, every creature coming away loaden with goods to save, and here and there sick people carried away in beds. Extraordinary good goods carried in carts and on backs. At last met my Lord Mayor in Canning Street, like a man spent, with a handkercher about his neck. To the King's message he cried, like a fainting woman, "Lord! what can I do? I am spent: people will not obey me. I have been pulling down houses; but the fire overtakes us faster than we can do it." That he needed no more soldiers; and that, for himself, he must go and refresh himself, having been up all night. So he left me, and I him, and walked home, seeing people all almost distracted, and no manner of means used to quench the fire. The houses, too, so very thick thereabouts, and full of matter for burning, as pitch and tar, in Thames Street; and warehouses of oil, and wines, and brandy, and other things. Here I saw Mr. Isaac Houblon, the handsome man, prettily dressed and dirty, at his door at Dowgate, receiving some of his brothers' things, whose houses were on fire; and, as he says, have been removed twice already; and he doubts (as it soon proved) that they must be in a little time removed from his house also, which was a sad consideration. And to see the churches all filling with goods by people who themselves should have been quietly there at this time. By this time it was about twelve o'clock; and so home, and there find my guests, which was Mr. Wood and his wife Barbary Sheldon, and also Mr. Moone: she mighty fine, and her husband, for aught I see, a likely man. But Mr. Moone's design and mine, which was to look over my closet and please him with the sight thereof, which he hath long desired, was wholly disappointed; for we were in great trouble and disturbance at this fire, not knowing what to

[34]Secretary of State.

think of it. However, we had an extraordinary good dinner, and as merry as at this time we could be. While at dinner Mrs. Batelier come to inquire after Mr. Wolfe and Stanes (who, it seems, are related to them), whose houses in Fish Street are all burned, and they in a sad condition. She would not stay in the fright. Soon as dined, I and Moone away, and walked through the City, the streets full of nothing but people and horses and carts loaden with goods, ready to run over one another, and removing goods from one burned house to another. They now removing out of Canning Street (which received goods in the morning) into Lombard Street, and further; and among others I now saw my little goldsmith, Stokes, receiving some friend's goods, whose house itself was burned the day after. We parted at Paul's; he home, and I to Paul's Wharf, where I had appointed a boat to attend me, and took in Mr. Carcasse and his brother, whom I met in the street, and carried them below and above bridge to and again to see the fire, which was now got further, both below and above, and no likelihood of stopping it. Met with the King and Duke of York in their barge, and with them to Queenhithe, and there called Sir Richard Browne to them. Their order was only to pull down houses apace, and so below bridge at the water-side; but little was or could be done, the fire coming upon them so fast. Good hopes there was of stopping it at the Three Cranes above, and at Buttolph's Wharf below bridge, if care be used; but the wind carries it into the City, so as we know not by the water-side what it do there. River full of lighters and boats taking in goods, and good goods swimming in the water, and only I observed that hardly one lighter or boat in three that had the goods of a house in, but there was a pair of virginals[35] in it. Having seen as much as I could now, I away to Whitehall by appointment, and there walked to St. James's Park, and there met my wife and Creed and Wood and his wife, and walked to my boat; and there upon the water again, and to the fire up and down, it still increasing, and the wind great. So near the fire as we could for smoke; and all over the Thames, with one's face in the wind, you were almost burned with a shower of fire-drops. This is very true; so as houses were burned by these drops and flakes of fire, three or four, nay, five or six houses, one from another. When we could endure no more upon the water, we to a little ale-house on the Bankside, over against the Three Cranes, and there stayed till it was dark almost, and saw the fire grow; and, as it grew darker, appeared more and more, and in corners and upon steeples, and between churches and houses, as far as we could see up the hill of the City, in a most horrid malicious bloody flame, not like the fine flame of an ordinary fire. Barbary and her husband away before us. We stayed till, it being darkish, we saw the fire as only one entire arch of fire from this to the other side the bridge, and in a bow up the hill for an arch of above a mile long: it made me weep to see it. The churches, houses, and all on fire and flaming at once; and a horrid noise the flames made, and the cracking of houses at their ruin. So home with a sad heart, and there find everybody discoursing and lamenting the fire; and poor Tom Hater come with some few of his goods saved out of his house, which is burned upon Fish Street Hill. I invited him to lie at my house, and did receive his goods, but was deceived in his lying there, the news coming every moment of the growth of the fire; so as we were forced to begin to pack up our own goods, and prepare for their removal; and did by moonshine (it being brave dry, and moonshine, and warm weather) carry much of my goods into the garden, and Mr. Hater and I did remove my money and iron chests into my cellar, as thinking that the safest place. And got my bags of gold into my office, ready to carry away, and my chief papers of accounts also there, and my tallies into a box by themselves. So great was our fear, as Sir W. Batten hath carts come out of the country to fetch away his goods this night. We did put Mr. Hater, poor man, to bed a little; but he got but very little rest, so much noise being in my house, taking down of goods.

3rd. About four o'clock in the morning, my Lady Batten sent me a cart to carry away

[35]A spinet-like musical instrument.

all my money, and plate, and best things, to Sir W. Rider's at Bethnal Green. Which I did, riding myself in my night-gown in the cart; and, Lord! to see how the streets and the highways are crowded with people running and riding, and getting of carts at any rate to fetch away things. I find Sir W. Rider tired with being called up all night, and receiving things from several friends. His house full of goods, and much of Sir W. Batten's and Sir W. Penn's. I am eased at my heart to have my treasure so well secured. Then home, with much ado to find a way, nor any sleep all this night to me nor my poor wife. But then and all this day she and I, and all my people laboring to get away the rest of our things, and did get Mr. Tooker to get me a lighter to take them in, and we did carry them (myself some) over Tower Hill, which was by this time full of people's goods, bringing their goods thither; and down to the lighter, which lay at the next quay, above the Tower Dock. And here was my neighbor's wife, Mrs. ——, with her pretty child, and some few of her things, which I did willingly give way to be saved with mine; but there was no passing with anything through the postern, the crowd was so great. The Duke of York come this day by the office, and spoke to us, and did ride with his guard up and down the City to keep all quiet (he being now General, and having the care of all). This day, Mercer being not at home, but against her mistress's order gone to her mother's, and my wife going thither to speak with W. Hewer, met her there, and was angry; and her mother saying that she was not a 'prentice girl, to ask leave every time she goes abroad, my wife with good reason was angry, and, when she came home, bid her be gone again. And so she went away, which troubled me, but yet less than it would, because of the condition we are in, fear of coming into in a little time of being less able to keep one in her quality. At night lay down a little upon a quilt of W. Hewer's in the office, all my own things being packed up or gone; and after me my poor wife did the like, we having fed upon the remains of yesterday's dinner, having no fire nor dishes, nor any opportunity of dressing anything.

4th. Up by break of day to get away the remainder of my things; which I did by a lighter at the Iron gate: and my hands so few, that it was the afternoon before we could get them all away. Sir W. Penn and I to Tower Street, and there met the fire burning three or four doors beyond Mr. Howell's, whose goods, poor man, his trays, and dishes, shovels, &c., were flung all along Tower Street in the kennels, and people working therewith from one end to the other; the fire coming on in that narrow street, on both sides, with infinite fury. Sir W. Batten not knowing how to remove his wine, did dig a pit in the garden, and laid it in there; and I took the opportunity of laying all the papers of my office that I could not otherwise dispose of. And in the evening Sir W. Penn and I did dig another, and put our wine in it; and I my Parmesan cheese, as well as my wine and some other things. The Duke of York was at the office this day, at Sir W. Penn's; but I happened not to be within. This afternoon, sitting melancholy with Sir W. Penn in our garden, and thinking of the certain burning of this office, without extraordinary means, I did propose for the sending up of all our workmen from Woolwich and Deptford yards[36] (none whereof yet appeared), and to write to Sir W. Coventry to have the Duke of York's permission to pull down houses, rather than lose this office, which would much hinder the King's business. So Sir W. Penn he went down this night, in order to the sending them up to-morrow morning; and I wrote to Sir W. Coventry about the business, but received no answer. This night Mrs. Turner (who, poor woman, was removing her goods all this day, good goods into the garden, and knows not how to dispose of them), and her husband supped with my wife and I at night, in the office, upon a shoulder of mutton from the cook's, without any napkin or anything, in a sad manner, but were merry. Only now and then walking into the garden, and saw how horridly the sky looks, all on a fire in the night, was enough to put us out of our wits; and, indeed, it was extremely dreadful, for it looks just as if it was at us, and the whole

[36]Workmen at the naval yards.

heaven on fire. I after supper walked in the dark down to Tower Street, and there saw it all on fire, at the Trinity House on that side, and the Dolphin Tavern on this side, which was very near us; and the fire with extraordinary vehemence. Now begins the practice of blowing up of houses in Tower Street, those next the Tower, which at first did frighten people more than anything; but it stopped the fire where it was done, it bringing down the houses to the ground in the same places they stood, and then it was easy to quench what little fire was in it, though it kindled nothing almost. W. Hewer this day went to see how his mother did, and comes late home, telling us how he hath been forced to remove her to Islington, her house in Pye Corner being burned; so that the fire is got so far that way, and all the Old Bailey, and was running down to Fleet Street; and Paul's is burned, and all Cheapside. I wrote to my father this night, but the post-house being burned, the letter could not go.

5th. I lay down in the office again upon W. Hewer's quilt, being mighty weary, and sore in my feet with going till I was hardly able to stand. About two in the morning my wife calls me up and tells me of new cries of fire, it being come to Barking Church, which is the bottom of our lane. I up, and finding it so, resolved presently to take her away, and did, and took my gold, which was about £2,350, W. Hewer, and Jane, down by Poundy's boat to Woolwich; but, Lord! what a sad sight it was by moon-light to see the whole City almost on fire, that you might see it plain at Woolwich, as if you were by it. There, when I come, I find the gates shut, but no guard kept at all, which troubled me, because of discourse now begun, that there is plot in it, and that the French had done it. I got the gates open, and to Mr. Sheldon's, where I locked up my gold, and charged my wife and W. Hewer never to leave the room without one of them in it, night or day. So back again, by the way seeing my goods well in the lighters at Deptford, and watched well by people. Home, and whereas I expected to have seen our house on fire, it being now about seven o'clock, it was not. But to the fire, and there find greater hopes than I expected; for my confidence of finding our Office on fire was such, that I durst not ask anybody how it was with us, till I come and saw it not burned. But going to the fire, I find by the blowing up of houses, and the great help given by the workmen out of the King's yards, sent up by Sir W. Penn, there is a good stop given to it, as well as at Mark Lane end as ours; it having only burned the dial of Barking Church, and part of the porch, and was there quenched. I up to the top of Barking steeple, and there saw the saddest sight of desolation that I ever saw; everywhere great fires, oil-cellars, and brimstone, and other things burning. I became afeard to stay there long, and therefore down again as fast as I could, the fire being spread as far as I could see it; and to Sir W. Penn's, and there eat a piece of cold meat, having eaten nothing since Sunday, but the remains of Sunday's dinner. Here I met with Mr. Young and Whistler; and having removed all my things, and received good hopes that the fire at our end is stopped, they and I walked into the town, and find Fenchurch Street, Gracious Street, and Lombard Street all in dust. The Exchange a sad sight, nothing standing there, of all the statues or pillars, but Sir Thomas Gresham's picture[37] in the corner. Walked into Moorfields (our feet ready to burn, walking through the town among the hot coals), and find that full of people, and poor wretches carrying their goods there, and everybody keeping his goods together by themselves (and a great blessing it is to them that it is fair weather for them to keep abroad night and day); drank there, and paid twopence for a plain penny loaf. Thence homeward, having passed through Cheapside and Newgate Market, all burned, and seen Anthony Joyce's house in fire. And took up (which I keep by me) a piece of glass of Mercers' Chapel in the street, where much more was, so melted and buckled with the heat of the fire like parchment. I also did see a poor cat taken out of a hole in the chimney, joining to the wall of the Exchange, with the hair all burned off the body, and yet alive. So home at night,

[37]Statue (Gresham was the Elizabethan founder of the Royal Exchange).

and find there good hopes of saving our office; but great endeavors of watching all night, and having men ready; and so we lodged them in the office, and had drink and bread and cheese for them. And lay down and slept a good night about midnight, though when I rose I heard that there had been a great alarm of French and Dutch being risen, which proved nothing. But it is a strange thing to see how long this time did look since Sunday, having been always full of variety of actions, and little sleep, that it looked like a week or more, and I had forgot almost the day of the week.

6th. Up about five o'clock, and there met Mr. Gauden at the gate of the office (I intending to go out, as I used, every now and then to-day, to see how the fire is) to call our men to Bishop's Gate, where no fire had yet been near, and there is now one broke out: which did give great grounds to people, and to me too, to think that there is some kind of plot in this (on which many by this time have been taken, and it hath been dangerous for any stranger to walk in the streets), but I went with the men, and we did put it out in a little time; so that that was well again. It was pretty to see how hard the women did work in the kennels,[38] sweeping of water; but then they would scold for drink, and be as drunk as devils. I saw good butts of sugar broke open in the street, and people go and take handsfull out, and put into beer, and drink it. And now all being pretty well, I took boat, and over to Southwark, and took boat on the other side the bridge, and so to Westminster, thinking to shift myself, being all in dirt from top to bottom; but could not there find any place to buy a shirt or pair of gloves, Westminster Hall being full of people's goods, those in Westminster having removed all their goods, and the Exchequer money put into vessels to carry to Nonsuch;[39] but to the Swan, and there was trimmed; and then to Whitehall, but saw nobody; and so home. A sad sight to see how the river looks: no houses nor church near it, to the Temple, where it stopped. At home, did go with Sir W. Batten, and our neighbor, Knightly (who, with one more, was the only man of any fashion left in all the neighborhood thereabouts, they all removing their goods and leaving their houses to the mercy of the fire), to Sir R. Ford's, and there dined in an earthen platter—a fried breast of mutton; a great many of us, but very merry, and indeed as good a meal, though as ugly a one, as ever I had in my life. Thence down to Deptford, and there with great satisfaction landed all my goods at Sir G. Carteret's safe, and nothing missed I could see, or hurt. This being done to my great content, I home, and to Sir W. Batten's, and there with Sir R. Ford, Mr. Knightly, and one Withers, a professed lying rogue, supped well, and mighty merry, and our fears over. From them to the office, and there slept with the office full of laborers, who talked, and slept, and walked all night long there. But strange it was to see Clothworkers' Hall on fire these three days and nights in one body of flame, it being the cellar full of oil.

VI

5 October, 1667. . . . And I to my tailor's, and there took up my wife and Willet,[40] who stayed there for me, and to the Duke of York's playhouse, but the house so full, it being a new play, *The Coffee House,*[41] that we could not get in, and so to the King's house: and there, going in, met with Knepp,[42] and she took us up into the tiring-rooms: and to the women's shift, where Nell[43] was dressing herself, and was all unready, and is very pretty, prettier than I thought. And so walked all up and down the house above, and then below into the scene-room, and there sat down, and she gave us fruit: and here I read the questions to Knepp, while she answered me, through all her part of *Flora's Vagaries* which was acted to-day. But, Lord! to see how they were both painted would make a man mad, and did make me loath them; and what base company of men

[38]Gutters.

[39]A place more than ten miles southwest of London.

[40]Deborah Willet, Mrs. Pepys's servant.

[41]A comedy by Thomas St. Serfe, printed 1668.

[42]Mrs. Knepp, a well-known actress.

[43]Nell Gwynn, actress and one-time mistress of Charles II.

comes among them, and how lewdly they talk! and how poor the men are in clothes, and yet what a show they make on the stage by candle-light, is very observable. But to see how Nell cursed, for having so few people in the pit, was pretty; the other house carrying away all the people at the new play, and is said, nowadays, to have generally most company, as being better players. By and by into the pit, and there saw the play, which is pretty good, but my belly was full of what I had seen in the house, and so, after the play done, away home, and there to the writing my letters, and so home to supper and to bed.

VII

5 December, 1668. Up, after a little talk with my wife, which troubled me, she being ever since our late difference mighty watchful of sleep and dreams, and will not be persuaded but I do dream of Deb.,[44] and do tell me that I speak in my dreams and that this night I did cry, Huzzy, and it must be she, and now and then I start otherwise than I used to do, she says, which I know not, for I do not know that I dream of her more than usual, though I cannot deny that my thoughts waking do run now and then against my will and judgment upon her, for that only is wanting to undo me, being now in every other thing as to my mind most happy, and may still be so but for my own fault, if I be catched loving anybody but my wife again. So up and to the office, and at noon to dinner, and thence to office, where late, mighty busy, and dispatching much business, settling papers in my own office, and so home to supper, and to bed. No news stirring, but that my Lord of Ormond is likely to go to Ireland again, which do show that the Duke of Buckingham[45] do not rule all so absolutely; and that, however, we shall speedily have more changes in the Navy: and it is certain that the Nonconformists[46] do now preach openly in houses, in many places, and among others the house that was heretofore Sir G. Carteret's, in Leadenhall Street, and have ready access to the King. And now the great dispute is, whether this Parliament or another; and my great design, if I continue in the Navy, is to get myself to be a Parliament man.

6th (Lord's day). Up, and with my wife to church; which pleases me mightily, I being full of fear that she would never go to church again, after she had declared to me that she was a Roman Catholic. But though I do verily think she fears God, and is truly and sincerely righteous, yet I do see she is not so strictly so a Catholic as not to go to church with me, which pleases me mightily. Here Mills made a lazy sermon, upon Moses's meekness, and so home, and my wife and I alone to dinner, and then she to read a little book concerning speech in general,[47] a translation late out of French, a most excellent piece as ever I read, proving a soul in man, and all the ways and secrets by which nature teaches speech in man, which do please me most infinitely to read. By and by my wife to church, and I to my Office to complete my Journal for the last three days, and so home to my chamber to settle some papers, and so to spend the evening with my wife and W. Hewer talking over the business of the Office, and particularly my own Office, how I will make it, and it will become, in a little time, an Office of ease, and not slavery, as it hath for so many years been. So to supper, and to bed.

---

[44] Deborah Willet, her servant.

[45] George Villiers, second Duke of Buckingham, the Zimri of Dryden's *Absalom and Achitophel.*

[46] Protestants outside the Church of England.

[47] William Holder, *Elements of Speech* (1669).

JOHN BUNYAN

1628–1688

The Bunyan family was settled in Bedfordshire from at least the end of the twelfth century. Bunyan's grandfather was a "petty chapman," or small retail trader. Thomas, his father, called himself a "brazier";—he made and mended pots and kettles, but did not belong to the more or less disreputable tribe of wandering tinkers. Bunyan carried on the same trade. His father married three times, and John, the first child of his second wife, was born at the village of Elstow, about a mile south of the town of Bedford, in November, 1628. His baptism was recorded on 30 November. As a child he had some schooling, learning to read and to write, probably at Elstow. In 1644 he became a soldier in the Commonwealth army, fighting against his king until July, 1647. Towards the close of 1648 or the beginning of 1649 he married. No record of his marriage remains, and the name of his wife is not known; but she came of a godly family, and, though she brought little else, she contributed to the new household two books inherited from her father—*The Plain Man's Pathway to Heaven* and *The Practice of Piety.* Her own devout conversation and the former of these books combined to send Bunyan off on that quest of the spirit for religious certitude and for the right pathway to salvation which ended by making him a nonconformist preacher, a writer for edification, and—something that he himself never suspected and would not have desired—one of the great figures in the annals of English literature. Sensitive, highly strung, vividly imaginative, he came to manhood at a time of general religious excitement, and could scarcely in any event have escaped its influence. His long and agonized conflict with himself and final victory he described years later in a book which (though not trustworthy as a record of fact) is a classic of spiritual autobiography: *Grace Abounding to the Chief of Sinners: or, A Brief and Faithful Relation of the Exceeding Mercy of God in Christ to his Poor Servant, John Bunyan; Wherein is particularly showed the manner of his conversion, his sight and trouble for sin, his dreadful temptations, also how he despaired of God's mercy, and how the Lord at length through Christ did deliver him from all the guilt and terror that lay upon him. Whereunto is added a brief relation of his call to the work of the ministry, of his temptations therein, as also what he hath met with in prison. All which was written by his own hand there, and now published for the support of the weak and tempted people of God* (1666).

This was not Bunyan's first book; it was in fact his twelfth publication. In 1653 he had joined a nonconformist body which met in St. John's Church, at Bedford, and he had moved there in 1655. Soon thereafter he lost his wife, who had borne him four children. About the same time he was made a deacon, and in 1656 he published (at Newport Pagnell, where he had been stationed while in the army) his first book, *Some Gospel Truths Opened,* written in confutation of the Quakers. In the following year his calling as a preacher was formally recognized, and his fame began to spread. In 1658 he published his third book, *A Few Sighs from Hell, or the Groans of a Damned Soul.* Probably late in 1659 he married a second time. In the next year, after the accession of Charles II, steps were taken to restore the Church of England to her former position, and Bunyan's preaching at public assemblies became illegal. He determined, however, to persist, and was accordingly arrested on 12 November at the hamlet of Lower Samsell by Harlington (about 13 miles south of Bedford). He was imprisoned for the next 12 years, with the exception, probably, of a brief interval in 1666. While in jail he made long tagged laces to support his family. During part of this period he was allowed much freedom, was often present at church meetings in Bedford, and even went to "see Christians in London." In 1672, following Charles's Declaration of Indulgence, he was pardoned, but was again imprisoned in 1675;—and it was during this period of confinement that he wrote the first part of *The Pilgrim's Progress* (published in 1678). Thereafter, though he continued to be active in preaching, and ran some risks, he escaped molestation. *The Life and Death of Mr. Badman* was published in 1680, *The Holy War* in 1682, and the second part of *The Pilgrim's Progress* in 1684. In 1688 he was caught in a severe storm while riding to London after aiding in the reconciliation of a father and son. He came down with a severe cold followed by a fever, and died on 31 August. He was buried in Bunhill Fields, Finsbury.

In all, Bunyan wrote 60 books and tracts. It is thought that no fewer than 100,000 copies of *The Pilgrim's Progress* were sold before his death; and during the first century of the book's existence 33 editions of Part I were published, and 59 editions of Parts I and II together. There are said to be versions of the book in no less than 108 languages and dialects. No book has had a comparable circulation save the Bible. And on the Bible, almost alone, Bunyan was nourished, and its language and rhythms mingle pleasantly with the homelier speech of the seventeenth-century English countryside in his great allegory of the spiritual life. Bunyan was no poet, but he chose to tell in verse the genesis of his book, and one may best learn from his own words one reason for its enduring vitality:

"When at the first I took my pen in hand
Thus for to write, I did not understand
That I at all should make a little Book
In such a mode. Nay, I had undertook
To make another; which when almost done,
Before I was aware, I this begun;
. . . . . . but yet I did not think
To show to all the world my pen and ink
In such a mode. I only thought to make
I knew not what; nor did I undertake
Thereby to please my neighbor. No, not I,
I did it mine own self to gratify."

When he had been humanized by a full experience of life, knowing the workings of the human heart and mind as few in any age are given to know them, he wrote this book, not of set purpose nor expressly for the improvement of mankind, but almost in his own despite—just because it so "gratified" him to dramatize the spiritual conflict within the soul's dark habitation. And thus was one of the world's few great books born.

The best edition of *The Pilgrim's Progress* is that edited by James B. Wharey (Oxford, 1928). The standard biography is still John Brown's *John Bunyan (1628–1688), His Life, Times, and Work,* rev. Frank M. Harrison (London, 1928); and the most sensible of many critical estimates is W. H. Hutton's *John Bunyan* (London, 1928). That Bunyan was only the best of many similar writers has been demonstrated by William Y. Tindall in his *John Bunyan, Mechanick Preacher* (New York, 1934).

PASSAGES FROM *THE PILGRIM'S PROGRESS*

From This World to That Which Is to Come: Delivered Under the Similitude of a Dream

THE FIRST PART (1678)

I

As I walked through the wilderness of this world, I lighted on a certain place where was 5 a Den, and I laid me down in that place to sleep: and as I slept I dreamed a dream. I dreamed, and behold, I saw a man clothed with rags, standing in a certain place, with his face from his own house, a book in his 10 hand, and a great burden upon his back. I looked, and saw him open the book, and read therein; and, as he read, he wept, and trembled; and, not being able longer to contain, he brake out with a lamentable cry, saying, 15 What shall I do?

In this plight, therefore, he went home and refrained himself as long as he could, that his wife and children should not perceive his distress; but he could not be silent long, because that his trouble increased. Wherefore at length he brake his mind to his wife and children; and thus he began to talk to them: O my dear wife, said he, and you the children of my bowels, I, your dear friend, am in myself undone by reason of a burden that lieth hard upon me; moreover, I am for certain informed that this our city will be burned with fire from heaven; in which fearful overthrow, both myself, with thee my wife, and you my sweet babes, shall miserably come to ruin, except (the which yet I see not) some way of escape can be found, whereby we may be delivered. At this his relations were sore amazed; not for that they believed that what he had said to them was true, but because

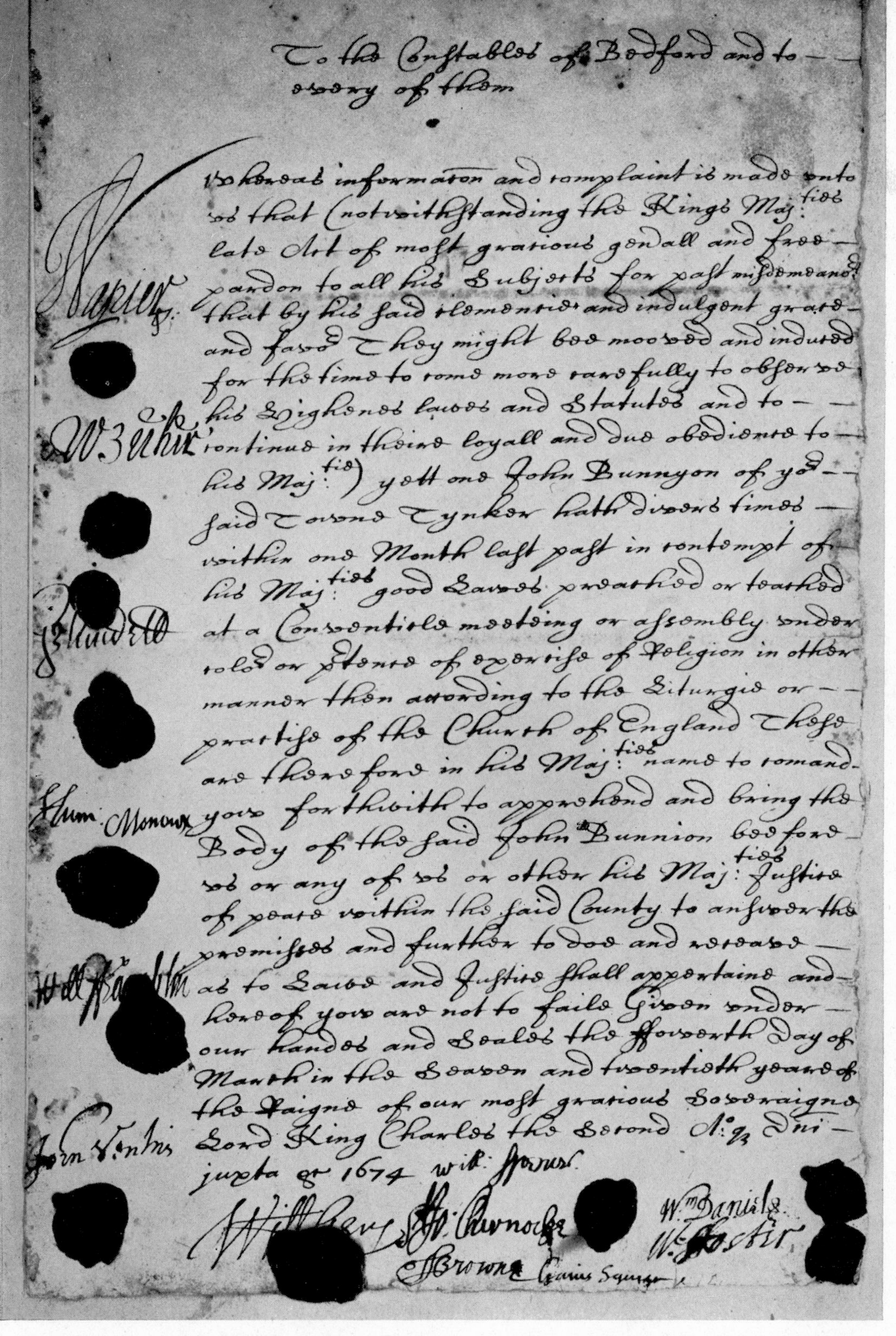

To the Constables of Bedford and to every of them

Whereas information and complaint is made unto us that (notwithstanding the Kings Maj:ties late Act of most gracious generall and free pardon to all his Subjects for past misdemeanors that by his said clemencie and indulgent grace and favor They might bee mooved and induced for the time to come more carefully to observe his Highnes lawes and Statutes and to continue in theire loyall and due obedience to his Maj:tie) yett one John Bunnyon of yor said Towne Tynker hath divers times within one Month last past in contempt of his Maj:ties good Lawes preached or teached at a Conventicle meeting or assembly under colour or pretence of exercise of Religion in other manner then according to the Liturgie or practise of the Church of England These are therefore in his Maj:ties name to comand you forthwith to apprehend and bring the Body of the said John Bunnion before us or any of us or other his Maj:ties Justice of peace within the said County to answer the premisses and further to doe and receave as to Lawe and Justice shall appertaine and hereof you are not to faile Given under our handes and Seales this ffowerth day of March in the Seaven and twentieth yeare of the Raigne of our most gracious Soveraigne Lord King Charles the Second Ao: Dni: juxta &c 1674 wit: ffoster

This is the warrant issued for the apprehension of John Bunyan, tinker, of the town of Bedford. It is dated 4 March, 1674; but according to our style of reckoning it was issued in 1675. (From the thirteenth century until 1752, the new year began officially in England on 25 March.) It was during the months of imprisonment following his arrest that Bunyan wrote the first part of *The Pilgrim's Progress*. (Courtesy of the Pierpont Morgan Library.)

3

Some safer World, in depth of woods embrac'd,
Some happier Island, in the watry waste,
Where Gold nergrows, & never Spaniards come
Where Trees bear maize, & rivers flow wth. Ru
Exil'd or chain'd, he lets you understand
Death but returns him to his native Land;
Or firm as Martyrs, smiling yields the ghost,
Rich of a Life, that is not to be lost.

Where slaves once more their native land behold,
No fiends torment, nor Christians thirst for Gold.

But does He say, the Maker is not good,
Till he's exalted to the State he would;
Himself alone high heav'ns peculiar Care?
Himself alone made happy, when he will, and where; (9)
Go, wiser Thou! and in thy Scale of Sense
Weigh thy Opinion against Providence;
Call Imperfection what you fancy such;
Pronounce He acts too little or too much;
Destroy all Creatures for thy Sport or Gust;
Yet, if unhappy, think tis He's unjust;
Snatch from his hand the Balance & the Rod,
Re-judge his Justice; be the God of God!

In Pride, my Friend, in Pride, our Error lies,
Our Sphere we quit, and rush into the Skies.
Pride still is aiming at the blest Abodes;
Men would be Angels, Angels would be Gods;
Aspiring to be Gods if Angels fell,
Aspiring to be Angels, Men rebell:
And who but wishes to invert the Laws (10
Of Order, sins against th' Eternal Cause.

Ask

Above is a page of the original manuscript of Alexander Pope's *Essay on Man,* Epistle I, lines 105–130 (see page 896 for these lines). (Courtesy of the Pierpont Morgan Library.) To the right is a picture of Gulliver amongst the Lilliputians, engraved from a drawing by Thomas Stothard for an eighteenth-century edition of Swift's *Gulliver's Travels.* The picture shows Gulliver being searched by the Emperor's officers (see page 847). (Courtesy of the New York Public Library.)

they thought that some frenzy distemper had got into his head; therefore, it drawing towards night, and they hoping that sleep might settle his brains, with all haste they got him to bed. But the night was as troublesome to him as the day; wherefore, instead of sleeping, he spent it in sighs and tears. So, when the morning was come, they would know how he did. He told them, Worse and worse: he also set to talking to them again; but they began to be hardened. They also thought to drive away his distemper by harsh and surly carriages to him; sometimes they would deride, sometimes they would chide, and sometimes they would quite neglect him. Wherefore he began to retire himself to his chamber, to pray for and pity them, and also to condole his own misery; he would also walk solitarily in the fields, sometimes reading, and sometimes praying: and thus for some days he spent his time.

Now, I saw, upon a time, when he was walking in the fields, that he was, as he was wont, reading in his book, and greatly distressed in his mind; and, as he read, he burst out, as he had done before, crying, What shall I do to be saved?

I saw also that he looked this way and that way, as if he would run; yet he stood still, because, as I perceived, he could not tell which way to go. I looked then, and saw a man named *Evangelist* coming to him, and asked, Wherefore dost thou cry?

He answered, Sir, I perceive by the book in my hand, that I am condemned to die, and after that to come to judgment; and I find that I am not willing to do the first, nor able to do the second.

Then said *Evangelist,* Why not willing to die, since this life is attended with so many evils? The man answered, Because I fear that this burden that is upon my back will sink me lower than the grave, and I shall fall into Tophet. And, Sir, if I be not fit to go to prison, I am not fit to go to judgment, and from thence to execution; and the thoughts of these things make me cry.

Then said *Evangelist,* If this be thy condition, why standest thou still? He answered, Because I know not whither to go. Then he gave him a parchment roll, and there was written within, Fly from the wrath to come.

The man, therefore, read it, and looking upon *Evangelist* very carefully, said, Whither must I fly? Then said *Evangelist,* pointing with his finger over a very wide field, Do you see yonder wicket-gate? The man said, No. Then said the other, Do you see yonder shining light? He said, I think I do. Then said *Evangelist,* Keep that light in your eye, and go up directly thereto: so shalt thou see the gate; at which, when thou knockest, it shall be told thee what thou shalt do. So I saw in my dream that the man began to run. Now, he had not run far from his own door, but his wife and children, perceiving it, began to cry after him to return; but the man put his fingers in his ears, and ran on, crying, Life! life! eternal life! So he looked not behind him, but fled towards the middle of the plain.

The neighbors also came out to see him run; and, as he ran, some mocked, others threatened, and some cried after him to return; and, among those that did so, there were two that resolved to fetch him back by force. The name of the one was *Obstinate,* and the name of the other *Pliable*. Now, by this time, the man was got a good distance from them; but, however, they were resolved to pursue him, which they did, and in a little time they overtook him. Then said the man, Neighbors, wherefore are you come? They said, To persuade you to go back with us. But he said, That can by no means be; you dwell, said he, in the *City of Destruction,* the place also where I was born: I see it to be so; and, dying there, sooner or later, you will sink lower than the grave, into a place that burns with fire and brimstone: be content, good neighbors, and go along with me.

OBST. What! said *Obstinate,* and leave our friends and our comforts behind us?

CHR. Yes, said *Christian,* for that was his name, because that ALL which you shall forsake is not worthy to be compared with a little of that, that I am seeking to enjoy; and, if you will go along with me, and hold it, you shall fare as I myself; for there, where I go, is enough and to spare. Come away, and prove my words.

OBST. What are the things you seek, since you leave all the world to find them?

CHR. I seek an inheritance incorruptible,

undefiled, and that fadeth not away, and it is laid up in heaven, and safe there, to be bestowed, at the time appointed, on them that diligently seek it. Read it so, if you will, in my book.

OBST. Tush! said *Obstinate,* away with your book; will you go back with us or no?

CHR. No, not I, said the other, because I have laid my hand to the plow.

OBST. Come, then, neighbor *Pliable,* let us turn again, and go home without him; there is a company of these crazed-headed coxcombs, that, when they take a fancy by the end, are wiser in their own eyes than seven men that can render a reason.

PLI. Then said *Pliable,* Don't revile; if what the good *Christian* says is true, the things he looks after are better than ours: my heart inclines to go with my neighbor.

OBST. What! more fools still? Be ruled by me, go back; who knows whither such a brain-sick fellow will lead you? Go back, go back, and be wise.

CHR. Nay, but do thou come with thy neighbor, *Pliable;* there are such things to be had which I spoke of, and many more glories besides. If you believe not me, read here in this book; and for the truth of what is expressed therein, behold, all is confirmed by the blood of Him that made it.

PLI. Well, neighbor *Obstinate,* saith *Pliable,* I begin to come to a point; I intend to go along with this good man, and to cast in my lot with him: but, my good companion, do you know the way to this desired place?

CHR. I am directed by a man, whose name is *Evangelist,* to speed me to a little gate that is before us, where we shall receive instructions about the way.

PL. Come, then, good neighbor, let us be going. Then they went both together.

OBST. And I will go back to my place, said *Obstinate;* I will be no companion of such misled, fantastical fellows.

Now I saw in my dream, that when *Obstinate* was gone back, *Christian* and *Pliable* went talking over the plain; and thus they began their discourse.

CHR. Come, neighbor *Pliable,* how do you do? I am glad you are persuaded to go along with me. Had even *Obstinate* himself but felt what I have felt of the powers and terrors of what is yet unseen, he would not thus lightly have given us the back.

PLI. Come, neighbor *Christian,* since there is none but us two here, tell me now further what the things are, and how to be enjoyed, whither we are going.

CHR. I can better conceive of them with my mind, than speak of them with my tongue: but yet, since you are desirous to know, I will read of them in my book.

PLI. And do you think that the words of your book are certainly true?

CHR. Yes, verily; for it was made by Him that cannot lie.

PLI. Well said; what things are they?

CHR. There is an endless kingdom to be inhabited, and everlasting life to be given us, that we may inhabit that kingdom for ever.

PLI. Well said; and what else?

CHR. There are crowns of glory to be given us, and garments that will make us shine like the sun in the firmament of heaven.

PLI. This is very pleasant; and what else?

CHR. There shall be no more crying, nor sorrow: for He that is owner of the place will wipe all tears from our eyes.

PLI. And what company shall we have there?

CHR. There we shall be with seraphims and cherubims, creatures that will dazzle your eyes to look on them. There also you shall meet with thousands and ten thousands that have gone before us to that place; none of them are hurtful, but loving and holy; every one walking in the sight of God, and standing in his presence with acceptance for ever. In a word, there we shall see the elders with their golden crowns, there we shall see the holy virgins with their golden harps, there we shall see men that by the world were cut in pieces, burnt in flames, eaten of beasts, drowned in the seas, for the love that they bear to the Lord of the place; all well, and clothed with immortality as with a garment.

PLI. The hearing of this is enough to ravish one's heart. But are these things to be enjoyed? How shall we get to be sharers thereof?

CHR. The Lord, the Governor of the country, hath recorded that in this book; the substance of which is, If we be truly willing to have it, he will bestow it upon us freely.

PLI. Well, my good companion, glad am I to hear of these things: come on, let us mend our pace.

CHR. I cannot go so fast as I would, by reason of this burden that is on my back.

Now I saw in my dream, that just as they had ended this talk they drew near to a very miry slough, that was in the midst of the plain; and they, being heedless, did both fall suddenly into the bog. The name of the slough was *Despond*. Here, therefore, they wallowed for a time, being grievously bedaubed with dirt; and *Christian,* because of the burden that was on his back, began to sink in the mire.

PLI. Then said *Pliable,* Ah! neighbor *Christian,* where are you now?

CHR. Truly, said *Christian,* I do not know.

PLI. At that *Pliable* began to be offended, and angrily said to his fellow, Is this the happiness you have told me all this while of? If we have such ill speed at our first setting out, what may we expect betwixt this and our journey's end? May I get out again with my life, you shall possess the brave country alone for me. And, with that, he gave a desperate struggle or two, and got out of the mire on that side of the slough which was next to his own house: so away he went, and *Christian* saw him no more.

Wherefore *Christian* was left to tumble in the *Slough of Despond* alone: but still he endeavored to struggle to that side of the slough that was further from his own house, and next to the wicket-gate; the which he did, but could not get out, because of the burden that was upon his back: but I beheld in my dream, that a man came to him, whose name was *Help,* and asked him, What he did there?

CHR. Sir, said *Christian,* I was bid go this way by a man called *Evangelist,* who directed me also to yonder gate, that I might escape the wrath to come; and as I was going thither I fell in here.

HELP. But why did not you look for the steps?

CHR. Fear followed me so hard, that I fled the next way, and fell in.

HELP. Then said he, Give me thy hand: so he gave him his hand, and he drew him out, and set him upon sound ground, and bid him go on his way.

Then I stepped to him that plucked him out, and said, Sir, wherefore, since over this place is the way from the *City of Destruction* to yonder gate, is it that this plat[1] is not mended, that poor travelers might go thither with more security? And he said unto me, This miry slough is such a place as cannot be mended; it is the descent whither the scum and filth that attends conviction for sin doth continually run, and therefore it was called the *Slough of Despond;* for still, as the sinner is awakened about his lost condition, there ariseth in his soul many fears, and doubts, and discouraging apprehensions, which all of them get together, and settle in this place. And this is the reason of the badness of this ground.

It is not the pleasure of the King that this place should remain so bad. His laborers also have, by the direction of His Majesty's surveyors, been for above these sixteen hundred years employed about this patch of ground, if perhaps it might have been mended: yea, and to my knowledge, said he, here have been swallowed up at least twenty thousand cart-loads, yea, millions of wholesome instructions, that have at all seasons been brought from all places of the King's dominions, and they that can tell, say they are the best materials to make good ground of the place; if so be, it might have been mended, but it is the *Slough of Despond* still, and so will be when they have done what they can.

True, there are, by the direction of the Law-giver, certain good and substantial steps, placed even through the very midst of this slough; but at such time as this place doth much spew out its filth, as it doth against change of weather, these steps are hardly seen; or, if they be, men, through the dizziness of their heads, step beside, and then they are bemired to purpose, notwithstanding the steps be there; but the ground is good when they are once got in at the gate.

Now, I saw in my dream, that by this time *Pliable* was got home to his house, so his

[1] Plot of ground.

neighbors came to visit him; and some of them called him wise man for coming back, and some called him fool for hazarding himself with *Christian:* others again did mock at his cowardliness; saying, Surely, since you began to venture, I would not have been so base to have given out for a few difficulties. So *Pliable* sat sneaking among them. But at last he got more confidence, and then they all turned their tales, and began to deride poor *Christian* behind his back. And thus much concerning *Pliable*.

Now, as *Christian* was walking solitarily by himself, he espied one afar off, come crossing over the field to meet him; and their hap was to meet just as they were crossing the way of each other. The gentleman's name that met him was Mr. *Worldly Wiseman;* he dwelt in the town of *Carnal Policy,* a very great town, and also hard by from whence *Christian* came. This man, then, meeting with *Christian,* and having some inkling of him—for *Christian's* setting forth from the *City of Destruction* was much noised abroad, not only in the town where he dwelt, but also it began to be the town talk in some other places—Master *Worldly Wiseman,* therefore, having some guess of him, by beholding his laborious going, by observing his sighs and groans, and the like, began thus to enter into some talk with *Christian.*

WORLD. How now, good fellow, whither away after this burdened manner?

CHR. A burdened manner, indeed, as ever, I think, poor creature had! And whereas you ask me, Whither away? I tell you, Sir, I am going to yonder wicket-gate before me; for there, as I am informed, I shall be put into a way to be rid of my heavy burden.

WORLD. Hast thou a wife and children?

CHR. Yes; but I am so laden with this burden that I cannot take that pleasure in them as formerly; methinks I am as if I had none.

WORLD. Wilt thou hearken to me if I give thee counsel?

CHR. If it be good, I will; for I stand in need of good counsel.

WORLD. I would advise thee, then, that thou with all speed get thyself rid of thy burden; for thou wilt never be settled in thy mind till then; nor canst thou enjoy the benefits of the blessing which God hath bestowed upon thee till then.

CHR. That is that which I seek for, even to be rid of this heavy burden; but get it off myself, I cannot; nor is there any man in our country that can take it off my shoulders; therefore am I going this way, as I told you, that I may be rid of my burden.

WORLD. Who bid you go this way to be rid of your burden?

CHR. A man that appeared to me to be a very great and honorable person; his name, as I remember, is *Evangelist*.

WORLD. I beshrew him for his counsel! there is not a more dangerous and troublesome way in the world than is that unto which he hath directed thee; and that thou shalt find, if thou will be ruled by his counsel. Thou hast met with something, as I perceive already; for I see the dirt of the *Slough of Despond* is upon thee; but that slough is the beginning of the sorrows that do attend those that go on in that way. Hear me, I am older than thou; thou art like to meet with, in the way which thou goest, wearisomeness, painfulness, hunger, perils, nakedness, sword, lions, dragons, darkness, and, in a word, death, and what not! These things are certainly true, having been confirmed by many testimonies. And should a man so carelessly cast away himself, by giving heed to a stranger?

CHR. Why, Sir, this burden upon my back is more terrible to me than are all these things which you have mentioned; nay, methinks I care not what I meet with in the way, if so be I can also meet with deliverance from my burden.

WORLD. How camest thou by the burden at first?

CHR. By reading this book in my hand.

WORLD. I thought so; and it is happened unto thee as to other weak men, who, meddling with things too high for them, do suddenly fall into thy distractions; which distractions do not only unman men, as thine, I perceive, has done thee, but they run them upon desperate ventures to obtain they know not what.

CHR. I know what I would obtain; it is ease for my heavy burden.

II

Then he went on till he came to the house of the *Interpreter,* where he knocked over and over; at last one came to the door, and asked who was there.

CHR. Sir, here is a traveler, who was bid by an acquaintance of the good-man of this house to call here for my profit; I would therefore speak with the master of the house. So he called for the master of the house, who, after a little time, came to *Christian,* and asked him what he would have.

CHR. Sir, said *Christian,* I am a man that am come from the *City of Destruction,* and am going to the Mount *Zion;* and I was told by the man that stands at the gate, at the head of this way, that if I called here, you would show me excellent things, such as would be an help to me in my journey.

INTER. Then said the *Interpreter,* Come in; I will show that which will be profitable to thee. So he commanded his man to light the candle, and bid *Christian* follow him: so he had him into a private room, and bid his man open a door; the which when he had done, *Christian* saw the picture of a very grave person hang up against the wall; and this was the fashion of it. It had eyes lifted up to heaven, the best of books in his hand, the law of truth was written upon its lips, the world was behind his back. It stood as if it pleaded with men, and a crown of gold did hang over its head.

CHR. Then said *Christian,* What meaneth this?

INTER. The man whose picture this is, is one of a thousand; he can beget children, travail in birth with children, and nurse them himself when they are born. And whereas thou seest him with his eyes lift up to heaven, the best of books in his hand, and the law of truth writ on his lips, it is to show thee that his work is to know and unfold dark things to sinners; even as also thou seest him stand as if he pleaded with men: and whereas thou seest the world as cast behind him, and that a crown hangs over his head, that is to show thee that slighting and despising the things that are present, for the love that he hath to his Master's service, he is sure in the world that comes next to have glory for his reward. Now, said the *Interpreter,* I have showed thee this picture first, because the man whose picture this is, is the only man whom the Lord of the place whither thou art going, hath authorized to be thy guide in all difficult places thou mayest meet with in the way; wherefore, take good heed to what I have showed thee, and bear well in thy mind what thou hast seen, lest in thy journey thou meet with some that pretend to lead thee right, but their way goes down to death.

Then he took him by the hand, and led him into a very large parlor that was full of dust, because never swept; the which after he had reviewed a little while, the *Interpreter* called for a man to sweep. Now, when he began to sweep, the dust began so abundantly to fly about, that *Christian* had almost therewith been choked. Then said the *Interpreter* to a damsel that stood by, Bring hither water, and sprinkle the room; the which, when she had done, it was swept and cleansed with pleasure.

CHR. Then said *Christian,* What means this?

INTER. The *Interpreter* answered, This parlor is the heart of a man that was never sanctified by the sweet grace of the gospel; the dust is his original sin and inward corruptions, that have defiled the whole man. He that began to sweep at first, is the *Law;* but she that brought water, and did sprinkle it, is the *Gospel.* Now, whereas thou sawest, that so soon as the first began to sweep, the dust did so fly about that the room by him could not be cleansed, but that thou wast almost choked therewith; this is to show thee, that the law, instead of cleansing the heart (by its working) from sin, doth revive, put strength into, and increase it in the soul, even as it doth discover and forbid it, for it doth not give power to subdue.

Again, as thou sawest the damsel sprinkle the room with water, upon which it was cleansed with pleasure; this is to show thee, that when the gospel comes in the sweet and precious influences thereof to the heart, then, I say, even as thou sawest the damsel lay the dust by sprinkling the floor with water, so is sin vanquished and subdued, and the soul made clean through the faith of it, and consequently fit for the King of glory to inhabit.

I saw, moreover, in my dream, that the *Interpreter* took him by the hand, and had him into a little room, where sat two little children, each one in his chair. The name of the eldest was *Passion,* and the name of the other *Patience. Passion* seemed to be much discontented; but *Patience* was very quiet. Then *Christian* asked, What is the reason of the discontent of *Passion?* The *Interpreter* answered, The Governor of them would have him stay for his best things till the beginning of the next year; but he will have all now: but *Patience* is willing to wait.

Then I saw that one came to *Passion,* and brought him a bag of treasure, and poured it down at his feet, the which he took up and rejoiced therein, and withal laughed *Patience* to scorn. But I beheld but a while, and he had lavished all away, and had nothing left him but rags.

CHR. Then said *Christian* to the *Interpreter,* Expound this matter more fully to me.

INTER. So he said, These two lads are figures: *Passion,* of the men of this world; and *Patience,* of the men of that which is to come; for as here thou seest, *Passion* will have all now this year, that is to say, in this world; so are the men of this world, they must have all their good things now, they cannot stay till next year, that is until the next world, for their portion of good. That proverb, "A bird in the hand is worth two in the bush," is of more authority with them than are all the Divine testimonies of the good of the world to come. But as thou sawest that he had quickly lavished all away, and had presently left him nothing but rags; so will it be with all such men at the end of this world.

CHR. Then said *Christian,* Now I see that *Patience* has the best wisdom, and that upon many accounts. First, because he stays for the best things. Second, and also because he will have the glory of his, when the other had nothing but rags.

INTER. Nay, you may add another, to wit, the glory of the next world will never wear out; but these are suddenly gone. Therefore *Passion* had not so much reason to laugh at *Patience,* because he had his good things first, as *Patience* will have to laugh at *Passion,* because he had his best things last; for first must give place to last, because last must have his time to come; but last gives place to nothing; for there is not another to succeed. He, therefore, that hath his portion first, must needs have a time to spend it; but he that has his portion last, must have it lastingly; therefore it is said of Dives, In thy lifetime thou receivedst thy good things, and likewise Lazarus evil things; but now he is comforted, and thou art tormented.

CHR. Then I perceive 'tis not best to covet things that are now, but to wait for things to come.

INTER. You say the truth: For the things that are seen are temporal; but the things which are not seen are eternal. But though this be so, yet since things present and our fleshly appetite are such near neighbors one to another; and again, because things to come, and carnal sense, are such strangers one to another; therefore it is that the first of these so suddenly fall into amity, and that distance is so continually between the second.

Then I saw in my dream that the *Interpreter* took *Christian* by the hand, and led him into a place where was a fire burning against a wall, and one standing by it, always casting much water upon it, to quench it; yet did the fire burn higher and hotter.

Then said *Christian,* What means this? The *Interpreter* answered, This fire is the work of grace that is wrought in the heart; he that casts water upon it, to extinguish and put it out, is the Devil; but in that thou seest the fire notwithstanding burn higher and hotter, thou shalt also see the reason of that. So he had him about to the backside of the wall, where he saw a man with a vessel of oil in his hand, of the which he did also continually cast, but secretly, into the fire.

Then said *Christian,* What means this?

The *Interpreter* answered, This is Christ, who continually, with the oil of his grace, maintains the work already begun in the heart: by the means of which, notwithstanding what the devil can do, the souls of his people prove gracious still. And in that thou sawest that the man stood behind the wall to maintain the fire, this is to teach thee that it is hard for the tempted to see how this work of grace is maintained in the soul.

I saw also, that the *Interpreter* took him again by the hand, and led him into a pleasant place, where was builded a stately palace, beautiful to behold; at the sight of which *Christian* was greatly delighted. He saw also, upon the top thereof, certain persons walking, who were clothed all in gold.

Then said *Christian,* May we go in thither?

Then the *Interpreter* took him, and led him up towards the door of the palace; and behold, at the door stood a great company of men, as desirous to go in, but durst not. There also sat a man at a little distance from the door, at a table-side, with a book and his inkhorn before him, to take the name of him that should enter therein; he saw also, that in the doorway stood many men in armor to keep it, being resolved to do to the men that would enter what hurt and mischief they could. Now was *Christian* somewhat in amaze. At last, when every man started back for fear of the armed men, *Christian* saw a man of a very stout countenance come up to the man that sat there to write, saying, Set down my name, Sir: the which when he had done, he saw the man draw his sword, and put an helmet upon his head, and rush toward the door upon the armed men, who laid upon him with deadly force; but the man, not at all discouraged, fell to cutting and hacking most fiercely. So after he had received and given many wounds to those that attempted to keep him out, he cut his way through them all, and pressed forward into the palace, at which there was a pleasant voice heard from those that were within, even of those that walked upon the top of the palace, saying—

> Come in, come in;
> Eternal glory thou shalt win.

So he went in, and was clothed with such garments as they. Then *Christian* smiled and said, I think verily I know the meaning of this.

Now, said *Christian,* let me go hence. Nay, stay, said the *Interpreter,* till I have showed thee a little more, and after that thou shalt go on thy way. So he took him by the hand again, and led him into a very dark room, where there sat a man in an iron cage.

Now the man, to look on, seemed very sad; he sat with his eyes looking down to the ground, his hands folded together, and he sighed as if he would break his heart. Then said *Christian,* What means this? At which the *Interpreter* bid him talk with the man.

Then said *Christian* to the man, What art thou? The man answered, I am what I was not once.

CHR. What wast thou once?

MAN. The man said, I was once a fair and flourishing professor,[2] both in mine own eyes, and also in the eyes of others; I once was, as I thought, fair for the *Celestial City,* and had then even joy at the thoughts that I should get thither.

CHR. Well, but what art thou now?

MAN. I am now a man of despair, and am shut up in it, as in this iron cage. I cannot get out. Oh, now I cannot!

CHR. But how camest thou in this condition?

MAN. I left off to watch and be sober; I laid the reins upon the neck of my lusts; I sinned against the light of the Word and the goodness of God; I have grieved the Spirit, and he is gone; I tempted the devil, and he is come to me; I have provoked God to anger, and he has left me: I have so hardened my heart, that I cannot repent.

Then said *Christian* to the *Interpreter,* But is there no hopes for such a man as this? Ask him, said the *Interpreter.*

CHR. Then said *Christian,* Is there no hope, but you must be kept in the iron cage of despair?

MAN. No, none at all.

CHR. Why, the Son of the Blessed is very pitiful.

MAN. I have crucified him to myself afresh; I have despised his person; I have despised his righteousness; I have counted his blood an unholy thing; I have done despite to the Spirit of grace. Therefore I have shut myself out of all the promises, and there now remains to me nothing but threatenings, dreadful threatenings, faithful threatenings, of certain judgment and fiery

[2]Professing Christian.

indignation, which shall devour me as an adversary.

CHR. For what did you bring yourself into this condition?

MAN. For the lusts, pleasures, and profits of this world; in the enjoyment of which I did then promise myself much delight; but now every one of those things also bite me, and gnaw me like a burning worm.

CHR. But canst thou not now repent and turn?

MAN. God hath denied me repentance. His Word gives me no encouragement to believe; yea, himself hath shut me up in this iron cage; nor can all the men in the world let me out. O eternity, eternity! how shall I grapple with the misery that I must meet with in eternity!

INTER. Then said the *Interpreter* to *Christian,* Let this man's misery be remembered by thee, and be an everlasting caution to thee.

CHR. Well, said *Christian,* this is fearful! God help me to watch and be sober, and to pray that I may shun the cause of this man's misery! Sir, is it not time for me to go on my way now?

INTER. Tarry till I shall show thee one thing more, and then thou shalt go on thy way.

So he took *Christian* by the hand again, and led him into a chamber, where there was one rising out of bed; and as he put on his raiment he shook and trembled. Then said *Christian,* Why doth this man thus tremble? The *Interpreter* then bid him tell to *Christian* the reason of his so doing. So he began and said, This night, as I was in my sleep, I dreamed, and behold the heavens grew exceeding black; also it thundered and lightened in most fearful wise, that it put me into an agony; so I looked up in my dream, and saw the clouds rack at an unusual rate, upon which I heard a great sound of a trumpet, and saw also a man sit upon a cloud, attended with the thousands of heaven; they were all in flaming fire: also the heavens were in a burning flame. I heard then a voice saying, Arise, ye dead, and come to judgment; and with that the rocks rent, the graves opened, and the dead that were therein came forth. Some of them were exceeding glad, and looked upward; and some sought to hide themselves under the mountains. Then I saw the man that sat upon the cloud open the book, and bid the world draw near. Yet there was, by reason of a fierce flame that issued out and came before him, a convenient distance betwixt him and them, as betwixt the judge and the prisoners at the bar. I heard it also proclaimed to them that attended on the man that sat on the cloud, Gather together the tares, the chaff, and stubble, and cast them into the burning lake. And with that, the bottomless pit opened, just whereabout I stood; out of the mouth of which there came, in an abundant manner, smoke and coals of fire, with hideous noises. It was also said to the same persons, Gather my wheat into the garner. And with that I saw many catched up and carried away into the clouds, but I was left behind. I also sought to hide myself, but I could not, for the man that sat upon the cloud still kept his eye upon me; my sins also came into my mind; and my conscience did accuse me on every side. Upon this I awaked from my sleep.

CHR. But what is it that made you so afraid of this sight?

MAN. Why, I thought that the day of judgment was come, and that I was not ready for it: but this frighted me most, that the angels gathered up several, and left me behind; also the pit of hell opened her mouth just where I stood. My conscience, too, afflicted me; and, as I thought, the Judge had always his eye upon me, showing indignation in his countenance.

Then said the *Interpreter* to *Christian,* Hast thou considered all these things?

CHR. Yes, and they put me in hope and fear.

INTER. Well, keep all things so in thy mind that they may be as a goad in thy sides, to prick thee forward in the way thou must go. Then *Christian* began to gird up his loins, and to address himself to his journey. Then said the *Interpreter,* The Comforter be always with thee, good *Christian,* to guide thee in the way that leads to the City.

So *Christian* went on his way, saying—

Here I have seen things rare and profitable;
Things pleasant, dreadful, things to make me stable

In what I have began to take in hand;
Then let me think on them and understand
Wherefore they showed me were, and let me be
Thankful, O good *Interpreter,* to thee.

Now I saw in my dream, that the highway up which *Christian* was to go, was fenced on either side with a wall, and that wall was called *Salvation.* Up this way, therefore, did burdened *Christian* run, but not without great difficulty, because of the load on his back.

He ran thus till he came at a place somewhat ascending, and upon that place stood a cross, and a little below, in the bottom, a sepulcher. So I saw in my dream, that just as *Christian* came up with the cross, his burden loosed from off his shoulders, and fell from off his back, and began to tumble, and so continued to do, till it came to the mouth of the sepulcher, where it fell in, and I saw it no more.

Then was *Christian* glad and lightsome, and said, with a merry heart, He hath given me rest by his sorrow, and life by his death. Then he stood still awhile to look and wonder; for it was very surprising to him, that the sight of the cross should thus ease him of his burden. He looked therefore, and looked again, even till the springs that were in his head sent the waters down his cheeks. Now, as he stood looking and weeping, behold three Shining Ones came to him and saluted him with, Peace be unto thee. So the first said to him, Thy sins be forgiven thee; the second stripped him of his rags, and clothed him with change of raiment; the third also set a mark in his forehead, and gave him a roll with a seal upon it, which he bade him look on as he ran, and that he should give it in at the *Celestial Gate.*

III

So he went on, and *Apollyon* met him. Now the monster was hideous to behold; he was clothed with scales, like a fish (and they are his pride); he had wings like a dragon, feet like a bear, and out of his belly came fire and smoke, and his mouth was as the mouth of a lion. When he was come up to *Christian,* he beheld him with a disdainful countenance, and thus began to question with him.

APOL. Whence come you? and whither are you bound?

CHR. I am come from the *City of Destruction,* which is the place of all evil, and am going to the *City of Zion.*

APOL. By this I perceive thou art one of my subjects, for all that country is mine, and I am the prince and god of it. How is it, then, that thou hast run away from thy king? Were it not that I hope thou mayest do me more service, I would strike thee now, at one blow, to the ground.

CHR. I was born, indeed, in your dominions, but your service was hard, and your wages such as a man could not live on, for the wages of sin is death; therefore, when I was come to years, I did, as other considerate persons do, look out, if, perhaps, I might mend myself.

APOL. There is no prince that will thus lightly lose his subjects, neither will I as yet lose thee; but since thou complainest of thy service and wages, be content to go back: what our country will afford, I do here promise to give thee.

CHR. But I have let myself to another, even to the King of princes; and how can I, with fairness, go back with thee?

APOL. Thou hast done in this, according to the proverb, "Change a bad for a worse"; but it is ordinary for those that have professed themselves his servants, after a while to give him the slip, and return again to me. Do thou so too, and all shall be well.

CHR. I have given him my faith, and sworn my allegiance to him; how, then, can I go back from this, and not be hanged as a traitor?

APOL. Thou didst the same by me, and yet I am willing to pass by all, if now thou wilt yet turn again and go back.

CHR. What I promised thee was in my nonage;[3] and, besides, I count that the Prince under whose banner now I stand is able to absolve me; yea, and to pardon also what I did as to my compliance with thee; and besides, O thou destroying *Apollyon!* to speak truth, I like his service, his wages, his servants, his government, his company, and

[3]Immaturity.

country, better than thine; and, therefore, leave off to persuade me further; I am his servant, and I will follow him.

APOL. Consider, again, when thou art in cool blood, what thou art like to meet with in the way that thou goest. Thou knowest that, for the most part, his servants come to an ill end, because they are transgressors against me and my way. How many of them have been put to shameful death! and, besides, thou countest his service better than mine, whereas he never came yet from the place where he is to deliver any that served him out of their hands; but as for me, how many times, as all the world very well knows, have I delivered, either by power, or fraud, those that have faithfully served me, from him and his, though taken by them; and so I will deliver thee.

CHR. His forbearing at present to deliver them is on purpose to try their love, whether they will cleave to him to the end; and as for the ill end thou sayest they come to, that is most glorious in their account; for, for present deliverance, they do not much expect it, for they stay for their glory, and then they shall have it when their Prince comes in his and the glory of the angels.

APOL. Thou hast already been unfaithful in thy service to him; and how dost thou think to receive wages of him?

CHR. Wherein, O *Apollyon!* have I been unfaithful to him?

APOL. Thou didst faint at first setting out, when thou wast almost choked in the *Gulf of Despond;* thou didst attempt wrong ways to be rid of thy burden, whereas thou shouldst have stayed till thy Prince had taken it off; thou didst sinfully sleep and lose thy choice things; thou wast, also, almost persuaded to go back at the sight of the lions; and when thou talkest of thy journey, and of what thou hast heard and seen, thou art inwardly desirous of vain-glory in all that thou sayest or doest.

CHR. All this is true, and much more which thou hast left out; but the Prince whom I serve and honor is merciful, and ready to forgive; but, besides, these infirmities possessed me in thy country, for there I sucked them in; and I have groaned under them, being sorry for them, and have obtained pardon of my Prince.

APOL. Then *Apollyon* broke out into a grievous rage, saying, I am an enemy to this Prince; I hate his person, his laws, and people; I am come out on purpose to withstand thee.

CHR. *Apollyon,* beware what you do; for I am in the King's highway, the way of holiness; therefore take heed to yourself.

APOL. Then *Apollyon* straddled quite over the whole breadth of the way, and said, I am void of fear in this matter: prepare thyself to die; for I swear by my infernal den, that thou shalt go no further; here will I spill thy soul.

And with that he threw a flaming dart at his breast; but *Christian* had a shield in his hand, with which he caught it, and so prevented the danger of that.

Then did *Christian* draw, for he saw it was time to bestir him; and *Apollyon* as fast made at him, throwing darts as thick as hail; by the which, notwithstanding all that *Christian* could do to avoid it, *Apollyon* wounded him in his head, his hand, and foot. This made *Christian* give a little back; *Apollyon,* therefore, followed his work amain, and *Christian* again took courage, and resisted as manfully as he could. This sore combat lasted for above half a day, even till *Christian* was almost quite spent; for you must know that *Christian,* by reason of his wounds, must needs grow weaker and weaker.

Then *Apollyon,* espying his opportunity, began to gather up close to *Christian,* and wrestling with him, gave him a dreadful fall; and with that *Christian's* sword flew out of his hand. Then said *Apollyon,* I am sure of thee now. And with that he had almost pressed him to death, so that *Christian* began to despair of life; but as God would have it, while *Apollyon* was fetching his last blow, thereby to make a full end of this good man, *Christian* nimbly stretched out his hand for his sword, and caught it, saying, Rejoice not against me, O mine enemy; when I fall I shall arise; and with that gave him a deadly thrust, which made him give back, as one that had received his mortal wound. *Christian* perceiving that, made at him again, saying, Nay, in all these things we are more than conquerors through him that loved us.

And with that *Apollyon* spread forth his dragon's wings, and sped him away, that *Christian* saw him no more.

In this combat no man can imagine, unless he had seen and heard as I did, what yelling 5 and hideous roaring *Apollyon* made all the time of the fight—he spake like a dragon; and, on the other side, what sighs and groans burst from *Christian's* heart. I never saw him all the while give so much as one pleas- 10 ant look, till he perceived he had wounded *Apollyon* with his two-edged sword; then, indeed, he did smile, and look upward; but it was the dreadfulest sight that ever I saw.

So when the battle was over, *Christian* 15 said, I will here give thanks to him that delivered me out of the mouth of the lion, to him that did help me against *Apollyon*. And so he did, saying—

> Great Beelzebub, the captain of this fiend,
> Designed my ruin; therefore to this end
> He sent him harnessed out: and he with rage
> That hellish was, did fiercely me engage.
> But blessed Michael helpéd me, and I,
> By dint of sword, did quickly make him fly.
> Therefore to him let me give lasting praise,
> And thanks, and bless his holy name always.

Then there came to him an hand, with some of the leaves of the tree of life, the 30 which *Christian* took, and applied to the wounds that he had received in the battle, and was healed immediately. He also sat down in that place to eat bread, and to drink of the bottle that was given him a little 35 before; so, being refreshed, he addressed himself to his journey, with his sword drawn in his hand; for he said, I know not but some other enemy may be at hand. But he met with no other affront from *Apollyon* 40 quite through this valley.

Now, at the end of this valley was another, called the *Valley of the Shadow of Death,* and *Christian* must needs go through it, because the way to the *Celestial City* lay 45 through the midst of it. Now, this valley is a very solitary place. The prophet Jeremiah thus describes it:—A wilderness, a land of deserts and of pits, a land of drought, and of the shadow of death, a land 50 that no man (but a Christian) passeth through, and where no man dwelt.

Now here *Christian* was worse put to it than in his fight with *Apollyon,* as by the sequel you shall see.

I saw then in my dream, that when *Christian* was got on the borders of the *Shadow of Death,* there met him two men, children of them that brought up an evil report of the good land, making haste to go back; to whom *Christian* spake as follows:—

CHR. Whither are you going?

MEN. They said, Back! back! and we would have you do so too, if either life or peace is prized by you.

CHR. Why, what's the matter? said *Christian.*

MEN. Matter! said they; we were going that way as you are going, and went as far as we durst; and indeed we were almost past coming back; for had we gone a little further, we had not been here to bring the news to thee.

CHR. But what have you met with? said *Christian.*

MEN. Why, we were almost in the *Valley of the Shadow of Death;* but that, by good hap, we looked before us, and saw the danger before we came to it.

CHR. But what have you seen? said *Christian.*

MEN. Seen! Why, the Valley itself, which is as dark as pitch; we also saw there the hobgoblins, satyrs, and dragons of the pit; we heard also in that Valley a continual howling and yelling, as of a people under unutterable misery, who were sat down in affliction and irons; and over that Valley hangs the discouraging clouds of confusion. Death also doth always spread his wings over it. In a word, it is every whit dreadful, being utterly without order.

CHR. Then, said *Christian,* I perceive not yet, by what you have said, but that this is my way to the desired heaven.

MEN. Be it thy way; we will not choose it for ours. So they parted, and *Christian* went on his way, but still with his sword drawn in his hand, for fear lest he should be assaulted.

I saw then in my dream, so far as this valley reached, there was on the right hand a very deep ditch; that ditch is it into which the blind hath led the blind in all ages, and have both there miserably perished. Again, behold, on the left hand, there was a very dangerous quag, into which, if even a good man falls, he finds no bottom for his foot to stand on. Into this quag King David once did fall, and had no doubt there been smothered, had not He that is able plucked him out.

The pathway was here also exceeding narrow, and therefore good *Christian* was the more put to it; for when he sought, in the dark, to shun the ditch on the one hand, he was ready to tip over into the mire on the other; also when he sought to escape the mire, without great carefulness he would be ready to fall into the ditch. Thus he went on, and I heard him here sigh bitterly; for, besides the danger mentioned above, the pathway was here so dark, that ofttimes, when he lift up his foot to go forward, he knew not where or upon what he should set it next.

About the midst of this valley, I perceived the mouth of hell to be, and it stood also hard by the way-side. Now, thought *Christian,* what shall I do? And ever and anon the flame and smoke would come out in such abundance, with sparks and hideous noises (things that cared not for *Christian's* sword, as did *Apollyon* before), that he was forced to put up his sword, and betake himself to another weapon called *all-prayer.* So he cried, in my hearing, O Lord, I beseech thee, deliver my soul! Thus he went on a great while, yet still the flames would be reaching towards him. Also he heard doleful voices, and rushings to and fro, so that sometimes he thought he should be torn in pieces, or trodden down like mire in the streets. This frightful sight was seen, and these dreadful noises were heard by him for several miles together; and, coming to a place where he thought he heard a company of fiends coming forward to meet him, he stopped, and began to muse what he had best to do. Sometimes he had half a thought to go back; then again he thought he might be half way through the valley; he remembered also how he had already vanquished many a danger, and that the danger of going back might be much more than for to go forward; so he resolved to go on. Yet the fiends seemed to come nearer and nearer; but when they were come even almost at him, he cried out with a most vehement voice, I will walk in the strength of the Lord God!—so they gave back, and came no further.

One thing I would not let slip; I took notice that now poor *Christian* was so confounded, that he did not know his own voice; and thus I perceived it. Just when he was come over against the mouth of the burning pit, one of the wicked ones got behind him, and stepped up softly to him, and whisperingly suggested many grievous blasphemies to him, which he verily thought had proceeded from his own mind. This put *Christian* more to it than anything that he met with before, even to think that he should now blaspheme him that he loved so much before; yet, if he could have helped it, he would not have done it; but he had not the discretion neither to stop his ears, nor to know from whence these blasphemies came.

When *Christian* had traveled in this disconsolate condition some considerable time, he thought he heard the voice of a man, going before him, saying, Though I walk through the valley of the shadow of death, I will fear none ill, for thou art with me.

Then was he glad.

IV

Then I saw in my dream, that when they[4] were got out the wilderness, they presently saw a town before them, and the name of that town is *Vanity;* and at the town there is a fair kept, called *Vanity Fair:* it is kept all the year long; it beareth the name of *Vanity Fair,* because the town where it is kept is lighter than vanity; and also because all that is there sold, or that cometh thither, is vanity. As is the saying of the wise, all that cometh is vanity.

This fair is no new-erected business, but a thing of ancient standing; I will show you the original of it.

Almost five thousand years agone, there were pilgrims walking to the *Celestial City,* as these two honest persons are: and *Beelze-*

[4]Shortly after he had passed through the *Valley of the Shadow of Death, Christian* met *Faithful,* journeying likewise towards the *Celestial City,* and they went on together.

bub, *Apollyon,* and *Legion,* with their companions, perceiving by the path that the pilgrims made, that their way to the city lay through this town of *Vanity,* they contrived here to set up a fair; a fair wherein should be sold all sorts of vanity, and that it should last all the year long: therefore at this fair are all such merchandise sold, as houses, lands, trades, places, honors, preferments, titles, countries, kingdoms, lusts, pleasures, and delights of all sorts, as whores, bawds, wives, husbands, children, masters, servants, lives, blood, bodies, souls, silver, gold, pearls, precious stones, and what not.

And, moreover, at this fair there is at all times to be seen jugglings, cheats, games, plays, fools, apes, knaves, and rogues, and that of every kind.

Here are to be seen, too, and that for nothing, thefts, murders, adulteries, false swearers, and that of a blood-red color.

And, as in other fairs of less moment, there are several rows and streets, under their proper names, where such wares are vended; so here likewise you have the proper places, rows, streets (*viz.,* countries and kingdoms), where the wares of this fair are soonest to be found. Here is the *Britain Row,* the *French Row,* the *Italian Row,* the *Spanish Row,* the *German Row,* where several sorts of vanities are to be sold. But, as in other fairs, some one commodity is as the chief of all the fair, so the ware of *Rome* and her merchandise is greatly promoted in this fair; only our *English* nation, with some others, have taken a dislike thereat.

Now, as I said, the way to the *Celestial City* lies just through this town where this lusty fair is kept; and he that will go to the city, and yet not go through this town, must needs go out of the world. The Prince of princes himself, when here, went through this town to his own country, and that upon a fair day too; yea, and as I think, it was *Beelzebub,* the chief lord of this fair, that invited him to buy of his vanities; yea, would have made him lord of the fair, would he but have done him reverence as he went through the town. Yea, because he was such a person of honor, *Beelzebub* had him from street to street, and showed him all the kingdoms of the world in a little time, that he might, if possible, allure that Blessed One to cheapen and buy some of his vanities; but he had no mind to the merchandise, and therefore left the town, without laying out so much as one farthing upon these vanities. This fair, therefore, is an ancient thing, of long standing, and a very great fair. Now these pilgrims, as I said, must needs go through this fair. Well, so they did: but, behold, even as they entered into the fair, all the people in the fair were moved, and the town itself as it were in a hubbub about them; and that for several reasons: for—

First, the Pilgrims were clothed with such kind of raiment as was diverse from the raiment of any that traded in that fair. The people, therefore, of the fair, made a great gazing upon them: some said they were fools, some they were bedlams, and some they were outlandish men.

Secondly, And as they wondered at their apparel, so they did likewise at their speech; for few could understand what they said; they naturally spoke the language of Canaan, but they that kept the fair were the men of this world; so that, from one end of the fair to the other, they seemed barbarians each to the other.

Thirdly, But that which did not a little amuse the merchandisers was, that these pilgrims set very light by all their wares; they cared not so much as to look upon them; and if they called upon them to buy, they would put their fingers in their ears, and cry, Turn away mine eyes from beholding vanity, and look upwards, signifying that their trade and traffic was in heaven.

One chanced mockingly, beholding the carriages of the men, to say unto them, What will ye buy? But they, looking gravely upon him, said, We buy the truth. At that there was an occasion taken to despise the men the more; some mocking, some taunting, some speaking reproachfully, and some calling upon others to smite them. At last things came to an hubbub and great stir in the fair, insomuch that all order was confounded. Now was word presently brought to the great one of the fair, who quickly came down, and deputed some of his most trusty friends to take these men into examination, about whom the fair was almost overturned. So the men were brought to examination; and they that sat upon them, asked them whence they came, whither they went, and what they did there, in such an unusual garb? The men told them that they were pilgrims and strangers in the world, and that they were going to their own country, which was the heavenly *Jerusalem,* and that they had given no occasion to the men of the town, nor yet to the merchandisers, thus to abuse them, and to let[5] them in their journey, except it was for that, when one asked them what they would buy, they said they would buy the truth. But they that were appointed to examine them did not believe them to be any other than bedlams and mad, or else such as came to put all things into a confusion in the fair. Therefore they took them and beat them, and besmeared them with dirt, and then put them into the cage, that they might be made a spectacle to all the men of the fair.

There, therefore, they lay for some time, and were made the objects of any man's sport, or malice, or revenge, the great one of the fair laughing still at all that befell them. But the men being patient, and not rendering railing for railing, but contrariwise, blessing, and giving good words for bad, and kindness for injuries done, some men in the fair that were more observing, and less prejudiced than the rest, began to check and blame the baser sort for their continual abuses done by them to the men; they, therefore, in angry manner, let fly at them again, counting them as bad as the men in the cage, and telling them that they seemed confederates, and should be made partakers of their misfortunes. The other replied that, for aught they could see, the men were quiet, and sober, and intended nobody any harm; and that there were many that traded in their fair that were more worthy to be put into the cage, yea, and pillory too, than were the men that they had abused. Thus, after divers words had passed on both sides, the men behaving themselves all the while very wisely and soberly before them, they fell to some blows among themselves, and did harm one to another. Then were these two poor men brought before their examiners again, and there charged as being guilty of the late hubbub that had been in the fair. So they beat them pitifully, and hanged irons upon them, and led them in chains up and down the fair, for an example and a terror to others, lest any should speak in their behalf, or join themselves unto them. But *Christian* and *Faithful* behaved themselves yet more wisely, and received the ignominy and shame that was cast upon them with so much meekness and patience, that it won to their side, though but few in comparison of the rest, several of the men in the fair. This put the other party yet into a greater rage, insomuch that they concluded the death of these two men. Wherefore they threatened, that neither the cage nor irons should serve their turn, but that they should die, for the abuse they had done, and for deluding the men of the fair.

Then were they remanded to the cage again, until further order should be taken with them. So they put them in, and made their feet fast in the stocks.

Here, therefore, they called again to mind what they had heard from their faithful friend *Evangelist,* and were the more confirmed in their way and sufferings by what he told them would happen to them. They also now comforted each other, that whose lot it was to suffer, even he should have the best on't; therefore each man secretly wished that he might have that preferment: but committing themselves to the all-wise dispose of Him that ruleth all things, with much content, they abode in the condition in which they were, until they should be otherwise disposed of.

Then a convenient time being appointed, they brought them forth to their trial, in order to their condemnation. When the time was come, they were brought before their enemies and arraigned. The judge's name was Lord *Hate-good.* Their indictment was one and the same in substance, though somewhat varying in form, the contents whereof was this:—

That they were enemies to and disturbers of their trade; that they had made commotions and divisions in the town, and had won a party to their own most dangerous opin-

[5]Hinder.

ions, in contempt of the law of their prince.

Then *Faithful* began to answer, that he had only set himself against that which hath set itself against Him that is higher than the highest. And, said he, as for disturbance, I make none, being myself a man of peace; the parties that were won to us, were won by beholding our truth and innocence, and they are only turned from the worse to the better. And as to the king you talk of, since he is *Beelzebub*, the enemy of our Lord, I defy him and all his angels.

Then proclamation was made, that they that had aught to say for their lord the king against the prisoner at the bar, should forthwith appear and give in their evidence. So there came in three witnesses, to wit, *Envy, Superstition,* and *Pickthank*.[6] They were then asked, if they knew the prisoner at the bar; and what they had to say for their lord the king against him.

Then stood forth *Envy*, and said to this effect: My Lord, I have known this man a long time, and will attest upon my oath before this honorable bench that he is—

JUDGE. Hold! Give him his oath. So they sware him. Then he said—

ENVY. My Lord, this man, notwithstanding his plausible name, is one of the vilest men in our country. He neither regardeth prince nor people, law nor custom; but doth all that he can to possess all men with certain of his disloyal notions, which he in the general calls principles of faith and holiness. And, in particular, I heard him once myself affirm that Christianity and the customs of our town of *Vanity* were diametrically opposite, and could not be reconciled. By which saying, my Lord, he doth at once not only condemn all our laudable doings, but us in the doing of them.

JUDGE. Then did the Judge say unto him, Hast thou any more to say?

ENVY. My Lord, I could say much more, only I would not be tedious to the court. Yet, if need be, when the other gentlemen have given in their evidence, rather than anything shall be wanting that will dispatch him, I will enlarge my testimony against him. So he was bid to stand by.

Then they called *Superstition*, and bid him look upon the prisoner. They also asked, what he could say for their lord the king against him. Then they sware him; so he began.

SUPER. My Lord, I have no great acquaintance with this man, nor do I desire to have farther knowledge of him; however, this I know, that he is a very pestilent fellow, from some discourse that, the other day, I had with him in this town; for then, talking with him, I heard him say, that our religion was nought, and such by which a man could by no means please God. Which saying of his, my Lord, your Lordship very well knows, what necessarily thence will follow, to wit, that we still do worship in vain, are yet in our sins, and finally shall be damned; and this is that which I have to say.

Then was *Pickthank* sworn, and bid say what he knew, in behalf of their lord the king, against the prisoner at the bar.

PICK. My Lord, and you gentlemen all, This fellow I have known of a long time, and have heard him speak things that ought not to be spoke; for he hath railed on our noble prince *Beelzebub*, and hath spoken contemptible of his honorable friends, whose names are the Lord *Old Man*, the Lord *Carnal Delight*, the Lord *Luxurious*, the Lord *Desire of Vain Glory*, my old Lord *Lechery*, Sir *Having Greedy*, with all the rest of our nobility; and he hath said, moreover, That if all men were of his mind, if possible, there is not one of these noblemen should have any longer a being in this town. Besides, he hath not been afraid to rail on you, my Lord, who are now appointed to be his judge, calling you an ungodly villain, with many other such like villifying terms, with which he hath bespattered most of the gentry of our town.

When this *Pickthank* had told his tale, the Judge directed his speech to the prisoner at the bar, saying, Thou runagate, heretic, and traitor, hast thou heard what these honest gentlemen have witnessed against thee?

FAITH. May I speak a few words in my own defense?

JUDGE. Sirrah! sirrah! thou deservest to live no longer, but to be slain immediately upon the place; yet, that all men may see our gentleness towards thee, let us hear what thou, vile runagate, hast to say.

[6] Flatterer.

FAITH. 1. I say, then, in answer to what Mr. *Envy* hath spoken, I never said aught but this, That what rule, or laws, or custom, or people, were flat against the Word of God, are diametrically opposite to Christianity. If I have said amiss in this, convince me of my error, and I am ready here before you to make my recantation.

2. As to the second, to wit, Mr. *Superstition,* and his charge against me, I said only this, That in the worship of God there is required a Divine faith; but there can be no Divine faith without a Divine revelation of the will of God. Therefore, whatever is thrust into the worship of God that is not agreeable to Divine revelation, cannot be done but by a human faith, which faith will not be profitable to eternal life.

3. As to what Mr. *Pickthank* hath said, I say (avoiding terms, as that I am said to rail, and the like) that the prince of this town, with all the rabblement, his attendants, by this gentleman named, are more fit for being in hell, than in this town and country: and so, the Lord have mercy upon me!

Then the Judge called to the jury (who all this while stood by, to hear and observe): Gentlemen of the jury, you see this man about whom so great an uproar hath been made in this town. You have also heard what these worthy gentlemen have witnessed against him. Also you have heard his reply and confession. It lieth now in your breast to hang him or save his life; but yet I think meet to instruct you in our law.

There was an Act made in the days of Pharaoh the Great, servant to our prince, that lest those of a contrary religion should multiply and grow too strong for him, their males should be thrown into the river. There was an Act also made in the days of Nebuchadnezzar the Great, another of his servants, that whoever would not fall down and worship his golden image, should be thrown into a fiery furnace. There was also an Act made in the days of Darius, that whoso, for some time, called upon any god but him, should be cast into the lions' den. Now the substance of these laws this rebel has broken, not only in thought (which is not to be borne), but also in word and deed, which must therefore needs be intolerable.

For that of Pharaoh, his law was made upon supposition, to prevent mischief, no crime yet being apparent; but here is a crime apparent. For the second and third, you see he disputeth against our religion; and for the treason he hath confessed, he deserveth to die the death.

Then went the jury out, whose names were, Mr. *Blind-man,* Mr. *No-good,* Mr. *Malice,* Mr. *Love-lust,* Mr. *Live-loose,* Mr. *Heady,* Mr. *High-mind,*[7] Mr. *Enmity,* Mr. *Liar,* Mr. *Cruelty,* Mr. *Hate-light,* and Mr. *Implacable;* who every one gave in his private verdict against him among themselves, and afterwards unanimously concluded to bring him in guilty before the Judge. And first, among themselves, Mr. *Blind-man,* the foreman, said, I see clearly that this man is a heretic. Then said Mr. *No-good,* Away with such a fellow from the earth. Ay, said Mr. *Malice,* for I hate the very looks of him. Then said Mr. *Love-lust,* I could never endure him. Nor I, said Mr. *Live-loose,* for he would always be condemning my way. Hang him, hang him, said Mr. *Heady.* A sorry scrub, said Mr. *High-mind.* My heart riseth against him, said Mr. *Enmity.* He is a rogue, said Mr. *Liar.* Hanging is too good for him, said Mr. *Cruelty.* Let's dispatch him out of the way, said Mr. *Hate-light.* Then said Mr. *Implacable,* Might I have all the world given me, I could not be reconciled to him; therefore, let us forthwith bring him in guilty of death. And so they did; therefore he was presently condemned to be had from the place where he was, to the place from whence he came, and there to be put to the most cruel death that could be invented.

They, therefore, brought him out, to do with him according to their law; and, first, they scourged him, then they buffeted him, then they lanced his flesh with knives; after that, they stoned him with stones, then pricked him with their swords; and, last of all, they burned him to ashes at the stake. Thus came *Faithful* to his end.

Now I saw that there stood behind the multitude a chariot and a couple of horses, waiting for *Faithful,* who (so soon as his adversaries had dispatched him) was taken

[7]Arrogance.

up into it, and straightway was carried up through the clouds, with sound of trumpet, the nearest way to the *Celestial Gate.*

But as for *Christian,* he had some respite, and was remanded back to prison. So he there remained for a space; but He that overrules all things, having the power of their rage in his own hand, so wrought it about, that *Christian* for that time escaped them, and went his way.

V

Now there was, not far from the place where they[8] lay, a castle called *Doubting Castle,* the owner whereof was *Giant Despair;* and it was in his grounds they were now sleeping: wherefore he, getting up in the morning early, and walking up and down in his fields, caught *Christian* and *Hopeful* asleep in his grounds. Then, with a grim and surly voice, he bid them awake; and asked them whence they were, and what they did in his grounds. They told him they were pilgrims, and that they had lost their way. Then said the Giant, You have this night trespassed on me, by trampling in and lying on my ground, and therefore you must go along with me. So they were forced to go, because he was stronger than they. They also had but little to say, for they knew themselves in a fault. The Giant, therefore, drove them before him, and put them into his castle, into a very dark dungeon, nasty and stinking to the spirits of these two men. Here, then, they lay from Wednesday morning till Saturday night, without one bit of bread, or drop of drink, or light, or any to ask how they did; they were, therefore, here in evil case, and were far from friends and acquaintance. Now in this place *Christian* had double sorrow, because 'twas through his unadvised counsel that they were brought into this distress.

Now, *Giant Despair* had a wife, and her name was *Diffidence.* So when he was gone to bed, he told his wife what he had done; to wit, that he had taken a couple of prisoners and cast them into his dungeon, for trespassing on his grounds. Then he asked her also what he had best to do further to them. So she asked what they were, whence they came, and whither they were bound; and he told her. Then she counseled him that when he arose in the morning he should beat them without mercy. So, when he arose, he getteth him a grievous crab-tree cudgel, and goes down into the dungeon to them, and there first falls to rating of them as if they were dogs, although they gave him never a word of distaste. Then he falls upon them, and beats them fearfully, in such sort that they were not able to help themselves, or to turn them upon the floor. This done, he withdraws and leaves them, there to condole their misery and to mourn under their distress. So all that day they spent the time in nothing but sighs and bitter lamentations. The next night, she, talking with her husband about them further, and understanding that they were yet alive, did advise him to counsel them to make away themselves. So when morning was come, he goes to them in a surly manner as before, and perceiving them to be very sore with the stripes that he had given them the day before, he told them, that since they were never like to come out of that place, their only way would be forthwith to make an end of themselves, either with knife, halter, or poison, for why, said he, should you choose life, seeing it is attended with so much bitterness? But they desired him to let them go. With that he looked ugly upon them, and, rushing to them, had doubtless made an end of them himself, but that he fell into one of his fits (for he sometimes, in sunshiny weather, fell into fits), and lost for a time the use of his hand; wherefore he withdrew, and left them as before, to consider what to do. Then did the prisoners consult between themselves whether 'twas best to take his counsel or no; and thus they began to discourse:—

CHR. Brother, said *Christian,* what shall we do? The life that we now live is miserable. For my part I know not whether is best, to live thus, or to die out of hand. My soul chooseth strangling rather than life, and the grave is more easy for me than this

[8]At his escape from *Vanity Fair,* "*Christian* went not forth alone, for there was one whose name was *Hopeful* (being so made by the beholding of *Christian* and *Faithful* in their words and behavior, in their sufferings at the *Fair*), who joined himself unto him."

dungeon. Shall we be ruled by the Giant?

HOPE. Indeed, our present condition is dreadful, and death would be far more welcome to me than thus for ever to abide; but yet, let us consider, the Lord of the country to which we are going hath said, Thou shalt do no murder: no, not to another man's person; much more, then, are we forbidden to take his counsel to kill ourselves. Besides, he that kills another, can but commit murder upon his body; but for one to kill himself is to kill body and soul at once. And, moreover, my brother, thou talkest of ease in the grave; but hast thou forgotten the hell, whither for certain the murderers go? For no murderer hath eternal life, *etc.* And let us consider, again, that all the law is not in the hand of *Giant Despair*. Others, so far as I can understand, have been taken by him, as well as we; and yet have escaped out of his hand. Who knows, but that God that made the world may cause that *Giant Despair* may die? or that, at some time or other, he may forget to lock us in? or but he may, in a short time, have another of his fits before us, and may lose the use of his limbs? and if ever that should come to pass again, for my part, I am resolved to pluck up the heart of a man, and to try my utmost to get from under his hand. I was a fool that I did not try to do it before; but, however, my brother, let us be patient, and endure a while. The time may come that may give us a happy release; but let us not be our own murderers. With these words *Hopeful* at present did moderate the mind of his brother; so they continued together (in the dark) that day, in their sad and doleful condition.

Well, towards evening, the Giant goes down into the dungeon again, to see if his prisoners had taken his counsel; but when he came there he found them alive; and truly, alive was all; for now, what for want of bread and water, and by reason of the wounds they received when he beat them, they could do little but breathe. But, I say, he found them alive; at which he fell into a grievous rage, and told them that, seeing they had disobeyed his counsel, it should be worse with them than if they had never been born.

At this they trembled greatly, and I think that *Christian* fell into a swoon; but, coming a little to himself again, they renewed their discourse about the Giant's counsel; and whether yet they had best take it or no. Now *Christian* again seemed to be for doing it, but *Hopeful* made his second reply as followeth:—

HOPE. My brother, said he, rememberest thou not how valiant thou hast been heretofore? *Apollyon* could not crush thee, nor could all that thou didst hear, or see, or feel, in the *Valley of the Shadow of Death.* What hardship, terror, and amazement hast thou already gone through! And art thou now nothing but fears? Thou seest that I am in the dungeon with thee, a far weaker man by nature than thou art; also, this Giant has wounded me as well as thee, and hath also cut off the bread and water from my mouth; and with that I mourn without the light. But let's exercise a little more patience; remember how thou playedest the man at *Vanity Fair,* and wast neither afraid of the chain or cage, nor yet of bloody death. Wherefore let us (at least to avoid the shame, that becomes not a Christian to be found in) bear up with patience as well as we can.

Now, night being come again, and the Giant and his wife being in bed, she asked him concerning the prisoners, and if they had taken his counsel. To which he replied, They are sturdy rogues, they choose rather to bear all hardship, than to make away themselves. Then said she, Take them into the castle-yard to-morrow, and show them the bones and skulls of those that thou hast already dispatched, and make them believe, ere a week comes to an end, thou also wilt tear them in pieces, as thou hast done their fellows before them.

So when the morning was come, the Giant goes to them again, and takes them into the castle-yard, and shows them, as his wife had bidden him. These, said he, were pilgrims as you are, once, and they trespassed in my grounds, as you have done; and when I thought fit, I tore them in pieces, and so, within ten days, I will do you. Get you down into your den again; and with that he beat them all the way thither. They lay, therefore, all day on Saturday in a lamentable case, as before. Now, when night was come, and when Mrs. *Diffidence* and her husband, the Giant, were got to bed, they began to renew their discourse of their prisoners; and withal the old Giant wondered, that he could neither by his blows nor his counsel 5 bring them to an end. And with that his wife replied, I fear, said she, that they live in hopes that some will come to relieve them, or that they have picklocks about them, by the means of which they hope to escape. 10 And sayest thou so, my dear? said the Giant; I will, therefore, search them in the morning.

Well, on Saturday, about midnight, they began to pray, and continued in prayer till 15 almost break of day.

Now, a little before it was day, good *Christian,* as one half amazed, brake out in this passionate speech:—What a fool, quoth he, am I, thus to lie in a stinking dungeon, when 20 I may as well walk at liberty! I have a key in my bosom, called *Promise,* that will, I am persuaded, open any lock in *Doubting Castle.* Then said *Hopeful,* That's good news, good brother; pluck it out of thy bosom, and try. 25

Then *Christian* pulled it out of his bosom, and began to try at the dungeon door, whose bolt (as he turned the key) gave back, and the door flew open with ease, and *Christian* and *Hopeful* both came out. Then he went 30 to the outward door that leads into the castle-yard, and, with his key, opened that door also. After, he went to the iron gate, for that must be opened too; but that lock went damnable hard, yet the key did open it. 35 Then they thrust open the gate to make their escape with speed, but that gate, as it opened, made such a cracking, that it waked *Giant Despair,* who, hastily rising to pursue his prisoners, felt his limbs to fail, for his fits took him again, so that he could by no means go after them. Then they went on, and came to the King's highway, and so were safe, because they were out of his jurisdiction.

VI

They went then till they came to the *Delectable Mountains,* which mountains belong to the Lord of that hill of which we have spoken before; so they went up to the mountains, to behold the gardens and orchards, the vineyards and fountains of water; where also they drank and washed themselves, and did freely eat of the vineyards. Now there were on the tops of these mountains Shepherds feeding their flocks, and they stood by the highway side. The Pilgrims therefore went to them, and leaning upon their staves (as is common with weary pilgrims when they stand to talk with any by the way), they asked, Whose *Delectable Mountains* are these? And whose be the sheep that feed upon them?

SHEP. These mountains are *Immanuel's Land,* and they are within sight of His city; and the sheep also are His, and He laid down His life for them.

CHR. Is this the way to the *Celestial City?*

SHEP. You are just in your way.

CHR. How far is it thither?

SHEP. Too far for any but those that shall get thither indeed.

CHR. Is the way safe or dangerous?

SHEP. Safe for those for whom it is to be safe; but transgressors shall fall therein.

JOHN DRYDEN

1631–1700

Dryden was born on 9 August, 1631, at Aldwinkle, a Northamptonshire village. His parents belonged to good families which had been conspicuous for their Puritanism. Dryden was sent to Westminster School, in London, and in 1650 entered Trinity College, Cambridge. Like Milton, Dryden did not escape trouble with his college authorities. He took his B. A. in 1654. His first notable poem was *Heroic Stanzas consecrated to the Memory of his Highness Oliver Cromwell,* written in 1658. It is significant of much in Dryden's life and character that two years later, in *Astraea Redux,* he was among the first to celebrate the return of Charles II. If he changed, Dr. Johnson said, he changed with the nation; but it is also true that Dryden as a working man of letters was dependent for his livelihood upon the favor of the great. This was an influence constantly determining what he should write, and how he should write, and it was undeniably harmful to him as a poet. Moreover, if Dryden's own sense of personal integrity did not suffer from the life of dependence he was condemned to lead, this was only because his warmly felt interests were specifically literary rather than broadly human; in other words, he suffered from essentially the same kind of moral obtuseness as did Bacon. Dryden was dramatist as well as poet, but here too his need of money drove him into close dependence on the taste of his day, with harmful results which are particularly evident in his comedies. The serious plays of the Restoration were of the so-called heroic type. They tended to sensationalism in plot, they were sentimental in conception, and in form they were more or less obedient to classical rule as that was laid down by seventeenth-century criticism. French influences were strong in England after 1660, and played a part in the development of Restoration drama, though the relative strength of the French and native influences entering into the drama of this period is still a debated question. The more notable of Dryden's heroic plays are *The Indian Emperor* (1665), *Tyrannic Love* (1669), *The Conquest of Granada* (in two parts, 1670–1672), and *Aurengzebe* (1675). All of these were written in rimed couplets, a practice which Dryden defended in his *Essay of Dramatic Poesy* (1668). In *All for Love* (1678), however, Dryden returned to blank verse. Some of his comedies are *The Rival Ladies* (1664), *Sir Martin Mar-All* (1667), *Marriage à la Mode* (1672), and *The Spanish Friar* (1681).

In 1670 Dryden attained office, being made historiographer-royal and poet laureate, and some years later he was made collectoı of customs for the port of London, posts which to some extent relieved his financial burdens until the Revolution of 1688, when he lost all his offices and was again reduced to the necessity of earning his living by his pen. The satires for which Dryden is best known as a poet were written in 1681 and 1682—*Absalom and Achitophel, MacFlecknoe,* and *The Medal.* In 1682 he also published his defense of the Church of England, *Religio Laici.* In 1686 he became a Roman Catholic, and in the following year published a defense of his new faith in the form of a beast-fable, *The Hind and the Panther.* The latter part of the seventeenth century was little favorable to lyric poetry, nor did Dryden attempt to write much in that kind, though his ode, *Alexander's Feast,* written in 1697, is a brilliant performance. One can hardly escape astonishment at the range of Dryden's power, successfully exerted despite the handicaps of his circumstances and character. In panegyric and satire, in comedy and heroic play and tragedy, in criticism and translation—in all these he excelled; and as England's greatest and most fully representative man of letters in the latter years of the seventeenth century he amply deserved the dictatorship of literature which he attained in his old age.

A standard, although by no means a new, edition is *The Works of John Dryden, Illustrated with Notes, Historical, Critical, and Explanatory, and a Life of the Author,* ed. Sir Walter Scott and George Saintsbury (Edinburgh and London, 1882–1893). The literary side of Dryden has been well treated by Mark Van Doren in *The Poetry of John Dryden* (New York, 1931) and by T. S. Eliot in *John Dryden, the Poet, the Dramatist, the Critic* (New York, 1932). In his *Intellectual Milieu of John Dryden; Studies in Some Aspects of Seventeenth Century Thought* (Ann Arbor, 1934) Louis I. Bredvold has placed the emphasis on the skeptical and conservative side of Dryden's creed. For a short but provocative study see Bonamy Dobrée, "Milton and Dryden: A Comparison and Contrast in Poetic Ideas and Poetic Method," *Journal of English Literary History,* III (1936), 83–100. The same writer supplies an excellent background for *All for Love* in his *Restoration Tragedy, 1660–1720* (London, 1929). See also Allardyce Nicoll, *A History of Restoration Drama, 1660–1700* (London, 1923), and Montague Summers, *The Restoration Theatre* (London, 1934).

ALL FOR LOVE

or,

The World Well Lost[1]

PREFACE

THE death of Antony and Cleopatra is a subject which has been treated by the greatest wits of our nation, after Shakespeare; and 5 by all so variously, that their example has given me the confidence to try myself in this bow of Ulysses amongst the crowd of suitors; and, withal, to take my own measures in aiming at the mark. I doubt not but the 10 same motive has prevailed with all of us in this attempt; I mean the excellency of the moral; for the chief persons represented were famous patterns of unlawful love, and their end accordingly was unfortunate. All rea- 15 sonable men have long since concluded that the hero of the poem ought not to be a character of perfect virtue, for then he could not without injustice be made unhappy; nor yet altogether wicked, because he could not then 20 be pitied: I have therefore steered the middle course, and have drawn the character of Antony as favorably as Plutarch, Appian, and Dion Cassius would give me leave; the like I have observed in Cleopatra. That 25 which is wanting to work up the pity to a greater height was not afforded me by the story; for the crimes of love which they both committed were not occasioned by any necessity, or fatal ignorance, but were wholly 30 voluntary; since our passions are, or ought to be, within our power. The fabric of the play is regular enough as to the inferior parts of it; and the unities of time, place and action, 5 more exactly observed than, perhaps, the English theater requires. Particularly, the action is so much one that it is the only of the kind without episode or underplot; every scene in the tragedy conducing 10 to the main design, and every act concluding with a turn of it. The greatest error in the contrivance seems to be in the person of Octavia; for, though I might use the privilege of a poet, to introduce her into 15 Alexandria, yet I had not enough considered that the compassion she moved to herself and children was destructive to that which I reserved for Antony and Cleopatra; whose mutual love being founded upon vice, must 20 lessen the favor of the audience to them, when virtue and innocence were oppressed by it. And though I justified Antony in some measure by making Octavia's departure to proceed wholly from herself, yet the 25 force of the first machine[2] still remained; and the dividing of pity, like the cutting of a river into many channels, abated the strength of the natural stream. But this is an objection which none of my critics have urged 30 against me; and therefore I might have let it pass, if I could have resolved to have been partial to myself. The faults my enemies have found are rather cavils concerning little and not essential decencies; which a

[1]First performed in the winter of 1677–1678; first published in the latter year. The source of the play is Shakespeare's *Antony and Cleopatra.* In the Preface Dryden mentions Plutarch, Appian, and Dion Cassius, but the play affords no evidence that he actually used them.

[2]I. e., dramatic motive.

master of the ceremonies may decide betwixt us. The French poets, I confess, are strict observers of these punctilios; they would not, for example, have suffered Cleopatra and Octavia to have met; or if they had met, there must only have passed betwixt them some cold civilities, but no eagerness of repartee, for fear of offending against the greatness of their characters and the modesty of their sex. This objection I foresaw and at the same time contemned; for I judged it both natural and probable that Octavia, proud of her new-gained conquest, would search out Cleopatra to triumph over her; and that Cleopatra, thus attacked, was not of a spirit to shun the encounter; and 'tis not unlikely that two exasperated rivals should use such satire as I have put into their mouths; for after all, though the one were a Roman and the other a queen, they were both women. 'Tis true, some actions, though natural, are not fit to be represented; and broad obscenities in words ought in good manners to be avoided: expressions therefore are a modest clothing of our thoughts, as breeches and petticoats are of our bodies. If I have kept myself within the bounds of modesty, all beyond it is but nicety and affectation; which is no more but modesty depraved into a vice; they betray themselves who are too quick of apprehension in such cases, and leave all reasonable men to imagine worse of them than of the poet.

Honest Montaigne goes yet farther: *Nous ne sommes que ceremonie; la ceremonie nous emporte, et laissons la substance des choses. Nous nous tenons aux branches, et abandonnos le tronc et le corps. Nous avons appris aux dames de rougir, oyans seulement nommer ce qu'elles no craignent aucunement a faire; nous n'osons appeller a droict nos membres, et ne craignons pas de les employer a toute sorte de debauche. La ceremonie nous defend d'exprimer par paroles les choses licites et naturelles, et nous l'en croyons; la raison nous defend de n'en faire d'illictes et mauvaises, et personne ne l'en croid.*[3]

My comfort is that by this opinion my enemies are but sucking critics, who would fain be nibbling ere their teeth are come.

Yet in this nicety of manners does the excellency of French poetry consist; their heroes are the most civil people breathing; but their good breeding seldom extends to a word of sense; all their wit is in their ceremony; they want the genius which animates our state; and therefore 'tis but necessary, when they cannot please, that they should take care not to offend. But as the civilest man in the company is commonly the dullest, so these authors, while they are afraid to make you laugh or cry, out of pure good manners make you sleep. They are so careful not to exasperate a critic that they never leave him any work; so busy with the broom, and make so clean a riddance, that there is little left either for censure or for praise; for no part of a poem is worth our discommending where the whole is insipid; as when we have once tasted of palled[4] wine, we stay not to examine it glass by glass. But while they affect to shine in trifles, they are often careless in essentials. Thus, their Hippolitus[5] is so scrupulous in point of decency that he will rather expose himself to death than accuse his stepmother to his father; and my critics, I am sure, will commend him for it: but we of grosser apprehensions are apt to think that this excess of generosity is not practicable but with fools and madmen. This was good manners with a vengeance; and the audience is like to be much concerned at the misfortunes of this admirable hero; but take Hippolitus out of his poetic fit, and I suppose he would think it a wiser part to set the saddle on the right horse, and choose rather to live with the reputation of a plain-spoken honest man, than to die with the infamy of an incestuous villain. In the mean time we may take notice, that where the poet ought to have preserved the charac-

[3]Florio's translation is: We are nought but ceremony; ceremony doth transport us, and we leave the substance of things; we hold fast by the boughs, and leave the trunk or body. We have taught ladies to blush, only by hearing that named, which they nothing fear to do. We dare not call our members by their proper names, and fear not to employ them in all kind of dissoluteness. Ceremony forbids us by words to express lawful and natural things, and we believe it. Reason willeth us to do no bad or unlawful things, and no man giveth credit unto it (*Essais,* II, xvii).

[4]Grown flat.

[5]In Racine's *Phèdre.*

ter as it was delivered to us by antiquity, when he should have given us the picture of a rough young man of the Amazonian strain, a jolly huntsman, and both by his profession and his early rising a mortal enemy to love, he has chosen to give him the turn of gallantry, sent him to travel from Athens to Paris, taught him to make love, and transformed the Hippolitus of Euripides into Monsieur Hippolite. I should not have troubled myself thus far with French poets, but that I find our *Chedreux* critics[6] wholly form their judgments by them. But for my part, I desire to be tried by the laws of my own country; for it seems unjust to me that the French should prescribe here, till they have conquered. Our little sonneteers who follow them have too narrow souls to judge of poetry. Poets themselves are the most proper, though I conclude not the only critics. But till some genius as universal as Aristotle shall arise, one who can penetrate into all arts and sciences without the practice of them, I shall think it reasonable that the judgment of an artificer in his own art should be preferable to the opinion of another man; at least where he is not bribed by interest or prejudiced by malice; and this, I suppose, is manifest by plain induction: for, first, the crowd cannot be presumed to have more than a gross instinct of what pleases or displeases them: every man will grant me this; but then, by a particular kindness to himself, he draws his own stake first, and will be distinguished from the multitude, of which other men may think him one. But, if I come closer to those who are allowed for witty men, either by the advantage of their quality or by common fame, and affirm that neither are they qualified to decide sovereignly concerning poetry, I shall yet have a strong party of my opinion; for most of them severally will exclude the rest, either from the number of witty men, or at least of able judges. But here again they are all indulgent to themselves; and every one who believes himself a wit, that is, every man, will pretend at the same time to a right of judging. But to press it yet farther, there are many witty men but few poets; neither have all poets a taste of tragedy. And this is the rock on which they are daily splitting. Poetry, which is a picture of nature, must generally please; but 'tis not to be understood that all parts of it must please every man; therefore is not tragedy to be judged by a witty man, whose taste is only confined to comedy. Nor is every man who loves tragedy a sufficient judge of it; he must understand the excellencies of it too, or he will only prove a blind admirer, not a critic. From hence it comes that so many satires on poets and censures of their writings fly abroad. Men of pleasant conversation (at least esteemed so) and indued with a trifling kind of fancy, perhaps helped out with some smattering of Latin, are ambitious to distinguish themselves from the herd of gentlemen by their poetry.

Rarus enim ferme sensus communis in illa Fortuna.[7]

And is not this a wretched affectation, not to be contented with what fortune has done for them, and sit down quietly with their estates, but they must call their wits in question, and needlessly expose their nakedness to public view? Not considering that they are not to expect the same approbation from sober men, which they have found from their flatterers after the third bottle? If a little glittering in discourse has passed them on us for witty men, where was the necessity of undeceiving the world? Would a man who has an ill title to an estate, but yet is in possession of it, would he bring it of his own accord to be tried at Westminster? We who write, if we want the talent, yet have the excuse that we do it for a poor subsistence; but what can be urged in their defence, who, not having the vocation of poverty to scribble,[8] out of mere wantonness take pains to make themselves ridiculous? Horace was certainly in the right, where he said that "no man is satisfied with his condition." A poet is not pleased because he is not rich; and the rich are discontented because the poets will

[6] I. e., our Frenchified critics (*Chedreux* was a kind of wig, so named from the man who first made it).

[7] For common sense is quite scarce among men of that sort (Juvenal, *Satires*, viii, 73-74).

[8] I. e., the call of poverty to summon them to scribble.

not admit them of their number. Thus the case is hard with writers: if they succeed not, they must starve; and if they do, some malicious satire is prepared to level them for daring to please without their leave. But while they are so eager to destroy the fame of others, their ambition is manifest in their concernment: some poem of their own is to be produced, and the slaves are to be laid flat with their faces on the ground, that the monarch may appear in the greater majesty.

Dionysius and Nero had the same longings, but with all their power they could never bring their business well about. 'Tis true, they proclaimed themselves poets by sound of trumpet; and poets they were, upon pain of death to any man who durst call them otherwise. The audience had a fine time on't, you may imagine; they sat in a bodily fear, and looked as demurely as they could, for 'twas a hanging matter to laugh unseasonably; and the tyrants were suspicious, as they had reason, that their subjects had 'em in the wind; so every man in his own defence set as good a face upon the business as he could; 'twas known beforehand that the monarchs were to be crowned laureates; but when the show was over, and an honest man was suffered to depart quietly, he took out his laughter which he had stifled; with a firm resolution never more to see an emperor's play, though he had been ten years a making it. In the mean time the true poets were they who made the best markets; for they had wit enough to yield the prize with a good grace, and not contend with him who had thirty legions: they were sure to be rewarded, if they confessed themselves bad writers, and that was somewhat better than to be martyrs for their reputation. Lucan's example was enough to teach them manners; and after he was put to death, for overcoming Nero, the emperor carried it without dispute for the best poet in his dominions; no man was ambitious of that grinning honor; for if he heard the malicious trumpeter proclaiming his name before his betters, he knew there was but one way with him. Maecenas took another course, and we know he was more than a great man, for he was witty too; but finding himself far gone in poetry, which Seneca assures us was not his talent, he thought it his best way to be well with Virgil and with Horace; that at least he might be a poet at the second hand; and we see how happily it has succeeded with him; for his own bad poetry is forgotten, and their panegyrics of him still remain. But they who should be our patrons are for no such expensive ways to fame; they have much of the poetry of Maecenas, but little of his liberality. They are for persecuting Horace and Virgil, in the persons of their successors (for such is every man who has any part of their soul and fire, though in a less degree). Some of their little zanies[9] yet go farther; for they are persecutors even of Horace himself, as far as they are able, by their ignorant and vile imitations of him; by making an unjust use of his authority, and turning his artillery against his friends. But how would he disdain to be copied by such hands! I dare answer for him, he would be more uneasy in their company than he was with Crispinus, their forefather, in the Holy Way;[10] and would no more have allowed them a place amongst the critics than he would Demetrius the mimic and Tigellius the buffoon:

——*Demetri, teque, Tigelli,*
Discipulorum inter jubeo plorare cathedras.[11]

With what scorn would he look down on such miserable translators, who make doggerel of his Latin, mistake his meaning, misapply his censures, and often contradict their own? He is fixed as a landmark to set out the bounds of poetry:

——*Saxum antiquum ingens,*
Limes agro positus, litem ut discerneret arvis.[12]

But other arms than theirs and other sinews are required to raise the weight of

[9] A zany was an attendant clown who awkwardly mimicked the chief clown in a show.

[10] A wretched poet mentioned by Horace (*Satires,* I, i, 120), whom Dryden identifies with the bore Horace met on the *Via Sacra* (*Satires,* I, ix).

[11] Demetrius and Tigellius, go whine among the benches of your pupils (Horace, *Satires,* I, x, 90–91; Dryden's *discipulorum* should be *discipularum*).

[12] A huge old rock, set down to mark the boundary of the field, and ward off all disputes (*Aeneid,* XII, 897–898; Dryden omits some words in the original).

such an author; and when they would toss him against their enemies,

Genua labant, gelidus concrevit frigore sanguis;
Tum lapis ipse viri vacuum per inane volutus
Nec spatium evasit totum, nec pertulit ictum.[13]

For my part, I would wish no other revenge, either for myself or the rest of the poets, from this rhyming judge of the twelvepenny gallery, this legitimate son of Sternhold,[14] than that he would subscribe his name to his censure, or (not to tax him beyond his learning) set his mark; for should he own himself publicly, and come from behind the lion's skin, they whom he condemns would be thankful to him, they whom he praises would choose to be condemned; and the magistrates whom he has elected, would modestly withdraw from their employment, to avoid the scandal of his nomination. The sharpness of his satire, next to himself, falls most heavily on his friends, and they ought never to forgive him for commending them perpetually the wrong way, and sometimes by contraries. If he have a friend whose hastiness in writing is his greatest fault, Horace would have taught him to have minced the matter, and to have called it readiness of thought and a flowing fancy; for friendship will allow a man to christen an imperfection by the name of some neighbor virtue:

Vellem in amicitia sic erraremus; et isti
Errori, nomen virtus posuisset honestum.[15]

But he would never have allowed him to have called a slow man hasty, or a hasty writer a slow drudge, as Juvenal explains it:

——*Canibus pigris, scabieque vetusta*
Levibus, et siccae lambentibus ora lucernae,
Nomen erit Pardus, Tygris, Leo; si quid adhuc est
Quod fremit in terris violentius.[16]

Yet Lucretius laughs at a foolish lover, even for excusing the imperfections of his mistress:

Nigra μελίχροος *est, immunda et foetida* ἄκοσμος.
Balba loqui non quit, τραυλίζει; *muta pudens est, etc.*[17]

But to drive it *ad Aethiopem cygnum*[18] is not to be endured. I leave him to interpret this by the benefit of his French version on the other side, and without further considering him than I have the rest of my illiterate censors, whom I have disdained to answer because they are not qualified for judges. It remains that I acquaint the reader that I have endeavored in this play to follow the practice of the ancients, who, as Mr. Rymer[19] has judiciously observed, are and ought to be our masters. Horace likewise gives it for a rule in his *Art of Poetry:*

——*Vos exemplaria Graeca*
Nocturna versate manu, versate diurna.[20]

Yet, though their models are regular, they are too little for English tragedy, which requires to be built in a larger compass. I could give an instance in the *Oedipus Tyrannus,* which was the masterpiece of Sophocles; but I reserve it for a more fit occasion, which I hope to have hereafter. In my style I have professed to imitate the divine Shakespeare; which that I might perform more freely, I have disencumbered myself from rhyme. Not that I condemn my former way, but that this is more proper to my present purpose. I hope I need not to explain myself, that I have not copied my author servilely;

[13]Their knees grow weak, their blood runs cold with fear, and the rock itself, hurtling through the empty air, neither traverses the distance nor reaches its mark (*Aeneid,* XII, 905–907; the translation is slightly inexact, to suit Dryden's sense).

[14]The author, with others, of a metrical version of the Psalms once widely popular. Dryden means to say that his "rhyming judge" (who was Lord Rochester) is a wretched poet.

[15]Would that in friendship we might thus name things wrong, and that to our error virtue had given an honorable name (Horace, *Satires,* I, iii, 41–42).

[16]Lazy dogs, grown bald with mange, that lick the edge of a dry lamp, will be named Leopard, Tiger, Lion, or any other beast on earth that roars more furiously (Juvenal, *Satires,* VIII, 83–86).

[17]The dark-skinned maid is a brunette, the sluttish and untidy, unconventional. The stutterer lisps; the dumb is modest (Lucretius, *On the Nature of Things,* IV, 1160, 1164).

[18]To the point of terming an Ethiopian a swan (Juvenal, *Satires,* VIII, 33).

[19]Thomas Rymer (1641–1713), a critic of the drama.

[20]Con night and day the models furnished by the Greeks (ll. 268–269).

words and phrases must of necessity receive a change in succeeding ages; but 'tis almost a miracle that much of his language remains so pure; and that he who began dramatic poetry amongst us, untaught by any, and as Ben Jonson tells us, without learning, should by the force of his own genius perform so much that in a manner he has left no praise for any who come after him. The occasion is fair, and the subject would be pleasant, to handle the difference of styles betwixt him and Fletcher, and wherein and how far they are both to be imitated. But since I must not be over-confident of my own performance after him, it will be prudence in me to be silent. Yet I hope I may affirm, and without vanity, that by imitating him I have excelled myself throughout the play; and particularly, that I prefer the scene betwixt Antony and Ventidius in the first act to anything which I have written in this kind.

PROLOGUE TO *ANTONY AND CLEOPATRA*

What flocks of critics hover here to-day,
As vultures wait on armies for their prey,
All gaping for the carcass of a play!
With croaking notes they bode some dire event,
And follow dying poets by the scent. 5
Ours gives himself for gone; y'have watched your time!
He fights this day unarmed—without his rhyme;
And brings a tale which often has been told,
As sad as Dido's and almost as old.
His hero, whom you wits his bully call, 10
Bates of his mettle and scarce rants at all:
He's somewhat lewd, but a well-meaning mind;
Weeps much; fights little; but is wond'rous kind.
In short, a pattern and companion fit
For all the keeping Tonyes[1] of the pit. 15
I could name more: a wife, and mistress too;
Both (to be plain) too good for most of you:
The wife well-natured, and the mistress true.
Now, poets, if your fame has been his care,
Allow him all the candor you can spare. 20
A brave man scorns to quarrel once a day,
Like Hectors[2] in at every petty fray.
Let those find fault whose wit's so very small,
They've need to show that they can think at all;
Errors like straws upon the surface flow; 25
He who would search for pearls must dive below.
Fops may have leave to level all they can,
As pigmies would be glad to lop a man.
Half-wits are fleas; so little and so light,
We scarce could know they live, but that they bite. 30
But, as the rich, when tired with daily feasts,
For change become their next poor tenants' guests;
Drink hearty draughts of ale from plain brown bowls,
And snatch the homely rasher from the coals,
So you, retiring from much better cheer, 35
For once may venture to do penance here.
And since that plenteous autumn now is past,
Whose grapes and peaches have indulged your taste,
Take in good part, from our poor poet's board,
Such rivelled[3] fruits as winter can afford. 40

[1]Fools.

[2]This name was applied to the ruffians who infested London.

[3]Shrunken.

DRAMATIS PERSONAE

MARC ANTONY
VENTIDIUS, *his General*
DOLLABELLA, *his Friend*
ALEXAS, *the Queen's Eunuch*
SERAPION, *Priest of Isis*
MYRIS, *another Priest*
SERVANTS *to Antony*
CLEOPATRA, *Queen of Egypt*
OCTAVIA, *Antony's Wife*
CHARMION, IRAS, *Cleopatra's Maids*
Antony's two little DAUGHTERS

SCENE—ALEXANDRIA.

ACT I

SCENE, *The Temple of Isis.*

Enter SERAPION, MYRIS, *Priests of Isis.*

SERAPION. Portents and prodigies are grown so frequent
That they have lost their name. Our fruitful Nile

Flowed ere the wonted season, with a torrent
So unexpected and so wondrous fierce,
That the wild deluge overtook the haste 5
E'en of the hinds that watched it: men and beasts
Were born above the tops of trees that grew
On th'utmost margin of the water-mark.
Then with so swift an ebb the flood drove backward,
It slipped from underneath the scaly herd; 10
Here monstrous *phocae*[1]—panted on the shore;
Forsaken dolphins there, with their broad tails,
Lay lashing the departing waves; hard by 'em,
Sea-horses flound'ring in the slimy mud,
Tossed up their heads, and dashed the ooze about 'em. 15

Enter ALEXAS *behind them.*

MYRIS. Avert these omens, Heaven!
SERAP. Last night, between the hours of twelve and one,
In a lone aisle o' th' temple while I walked,
A whirl-wind rose, that with a violent blast
Shook all the dome: the doors around me clapped; 20
The iron wicket that defends the vault
Where the long race of Ptolomies is laid,
Burst open, and disclosed the mighty dead.
From out each monument, in order placed,
An armèd ghost start[2] up: the boy-king last 25
Reared his inglorious head. A peal of groans
Then followed, and a lamentable voice
Cried, "Egypt is no more." My blood ran back;
My shaking knees against each other knocked; 29
On the cold pavement down I fell intranced,
And so unfinished left the horrid scene.
ALEXAS (*showing himself*). And dreamed you this? or did invent the story,
To frighten our Egyptian boys withal,
And train 'em up betimes in fear of priesthood?
SERAP. My lord, I saw you not, 35
Nor meant my words should reach your ears; but what
I uttered was most true.
ALEX. A foolish dream,
Bred from the fumes of indigested feasts
And holy luxury.
SERAP. I know my duty;
This goes no farther.

[1]Seals. [2]I. e., started.

AEX. 'Tis not fit it should. 40
Nor would the times now bear it, were it true.
All southern from yon hills, the Roman camp
Hangs o'er us black and threat'ning, like a storm
Just breaking on our heads.
SERAP. Our faint Egyptians pray for Antony; 45
But in their servile hearts they own Octavius.
MYR. Why then does Antony dream out his hours,
And tempts not fortune for a noble day,
Which might redeem what Actium[3] lost?
ALEX. He thinks 'tis past recovery.
SERAP. Yet the foe
Seems not to press the siege. 51
ALEX. O, there's the wonder.
Mecaenas and Agrippa, who can most[4]
With Caesar,[5] are his foes. His wife Octavia,
Driv'n from his house, solicits her revenge;
And Dollabella, who was once his friend, 55
Upon some private grudge now seeks his ruin;
Yet still war seems on either side to sleep.
SERAP. 'Tis strange that Antony for some days past
Has not beheld the face of Cleopatra;
But here in Isis temple lives retired, 60
And makes his heart a prey to black despair.
ALEX. 'Tis true; and we much fear he hopes by absence
To cure his mind of love.
SERAP. If he be vanquished,
Or make his peace, Egypt is doomed to be
A Roman province; and our plenteous harvests 65
Must then redeem the scarceness of their soil.
While Antony stood firm, our Alexandria
Rivaled proud Rome (dominion's other seat),
And Fortune, striding like a vast Colossus,
Could fix an equal foot of empire here. 70
ALEX. Had I my wish, these tyrants of all nature
Who lord it o'er mankind, should perish—perish
Each by the other's sword; but, since our will
Is lamely followed by our power, we must
Depend on one, with him to rise or fall. 75

[3]The naval battle (B. C. 31) which Marc Antony lost by fleeing after Cleopatra.
[4]Who prevail most.
[5]Octavius, later known as Augustus.

SERAP. How stands the queen affected?
ALEX. O, she dotes,
She dotes, Serapion, on this vanquished man,
And winds herself about his mighty ruins;
Whom would she yet forsake, yet yield him up,
This hunted prey, to his pursuer's hands, 80
She might preserve us all; but 'tis in vain—
This changes my designs, this blasts my counsels,
And makes me use all means to keep him here,
Whom I could wish divided from her arms,
Far as the earth's deep center. Well, you know 85
The state of things; no more of your ill omens
And black prognostics; labor to confirm
The people's hearts.

Enter VENTIDIUS, *talking aside with a* GENTLEMAN *of Antony's.*

SERAP. These Romans will o'erhear us.
But who's that stranger? By his warlike port,
His fierce demeanor, and erected look, 90
He's of no vulgar note.
ALEX. O, 'tis Ventidius,
Our emp'ror's great lieutenant in the East,
Who first showed Rome that Parthia could be conquered.
When Antony returned from Syria last,
He left this man to guard the Roman frontiers. 95
SERAP. You seem to know him well.
ALEX. Too well. I saw him in Cilicia first,
When Cleopatra there met Antony;
A mortal foe he was to us, and Egypt.
But, let me witness to the worth I hate, 100
A braver Roman never drew a sword.
Firm to his prince; but as a friend, not slave.
He ne'er was of his pleasures; but presides
O'er all his cooler hours and morning counsels;
In short, the plainness, fierceness, rugged virtue 105
Of an old true-stamped Roman lives in him.
His coming bodes I know not what of ill
To our affairs. Withdraw, to mark him better;
And I'll acquaint you why I sought you here,
And what's our present work.
(*They withdraw to a corner of the stage; and* VENTIDIUS, *with the other, comes forward to the front*)

VENTIDIUS. Not see him, say you?
I say, I must and will.
GENTLEMAN. He has commanded,
On pain of death none should approach his presence. 112
VEN. I bring him news will raise his drooping spirits,
Give him new life.
GENT. He sees not Cleopatra.
VEN. Would he had never seen her! 115
GENT. He eats not, drinks not, sleeps not, has no use
Of any thing, but thought; or, if he talks,
'Tis to himself, and then 'tis perfect raving;
Then he defies the world, and bids it pass;
Sometimes he gnaws his lip, and curses loud 120
The boy Octavius; then he draws his mouth
Into a scornful smile, and cries, "Take all,
The world's not worth my care."
VEN. Just, just his nature.
Virtue's his path; but sometimes 'tis too narrow
For his vast soul; and then he starts out wide, 125
And bounds into a vice that bears him far
From his first course, and plunges him in ills:
But when his danger makes him find his fault,
Quick to observe and full of sharp remorse,
He censures eagerly his own misdeeds, 130
Judging himself with malice to himself,
And not forgiving what as a man he did,
Because his other parts are more than man.
He must not thus be lost.
(ALEXAS *and the* PRIESTS *come forward*)
ALEX. You have your full instructions, now advance; 135
Proclaim your orders loudly.
SERAP. Romans, Egyptians, hear the queen's command.
Thus Cleopatra bids: "Let labor cease,
To pomp and triumphs give this happy day,
That gave the world a lord: 'tis Antony's."
Live, Antony; and, Cleopatra, live! 141
Be this the general voice sent up to Heaven,
And every public place repeat this echo.
VEN. (*aside*). Fine pageantry!
SERAP. Set out before your doors
The images of all your sleeping fathers, 145
With laurels crowned; with laurels wreath your posts,
And strew with flowers the pavement; let the priests
Do present sacrifice; pour out the wine,
And call the gods to join with you in gladness.

VEN. Curse on the tongue that bids this general joy! 150
Can they be friends of Antony, who revel
When Antony's in danger? Hide, for shame,
You Romans, your great grandsires' images,
For fear their souls should animate their marbles,
To blush at their degenerate progeny. 155

ALEX. A love, which knows no bounds, to Antony,
Would mark the day with honors, when all Heaven
Labored for him, when each propitious star
Stood wakeful in his orb, to watch that hour,
And shed his better influence. Her own birth-day 160
Our queen neglected, like a vulgar fête
That passed obscurely by.

VEN. Would it had slept,
Divided far from his; till some remote
And future age had called it out, to ruin
Some other prince, not him.

ALEX. Your emperor, 165
Though grown unkind, would be more gentle than
T' upbraid my queen for loving him too well.

VEN. Does the mute sacrifice upbraid the priest?
He knows him not his executioner.
O, she has decked his ruin with her love, 170
Led him in golden bands to gaudy slaughter,
And made perdition pleasing; she has left him
The blank of what he was;
I tell thee, eunuch, she has quite unmanned him.
Can any Roman see, and know him now, 175
Thus altered from the lord of half mankind,
Unbent, unsinewed, made a woman's toy,
Shrunk from the vast extent of all his honors,
And cramped within a corner of the world?
O Antony! 180
Thou bravest soldier and thou best of friends!
Bounteous as nature; next to nature's God!
Couldst thou but make new worlds, so wouldst thou give 'em,
As bounty were thy being. Rough in battle
As the first Romans when they went to war; 185
Yet after victory more pitiful
Than all their praying virgins left at home!

ALEX. Would you could add to those more shining virtues,
His truth to her who loves him.

VEN. Would I could not!
But wherefore waste I precious hours with thee? 190
Thou art her darling mischief, her chief engine,
Antony's other fate. Go, tell thy queen,
Ventidius is arrived, to end her charms.
Let your Egyptian timbrels play alone;
Nor mix effeminate sounds with Roman trumpets. 195
You dare not fight for Antony; go pray,
And keep your cowards'-holy-day in temples.

[*Exeunt* ALEXAS, SERAPION.

Re-enter the GENTLEMEN *of M. Antony.*

2 GENTLEMAN. The emperor approaches, and commands,
On pain of death, that none presume to stay.

1 GENT. I dare not disobey him.

[*Going out with the other.*

VEN. Well, I dare. 200
But I'll observe him first unseen, and find
Which way his humor drives, the rest I'll venture. [*Withdraws.*

Enter ANTONY, *walking with a disturbed motion, before he speaks.*

ANTONY. They tell me, 'tis my birth-day, and I'll keep it
With double pomp of sadness.
'Tis what the day deserves which gave me breath. 205
Why was I raised the meteor of the world,
Hung in the skies, and blazing as I traveled,
Till all my fires were spent; and then cast downward
To be trod out by Caesar?

VEN. *(aside).* On my soul;
'Tis mournful, wondrous mournful!

ANT. Count thy gains. 210
Now, Antony, wouldst thou be born for this?
Glutton of fortune, thy devouring youth
Has starved thy wanting age.

VEN. *(aside).* How sorrow shakes him!
So, now the tempest tears him up by th' roots,
And on the ground extends the noble ruin. 215

(ANTONY *having thrown himself down*)

ANT. Lie there, thou shadow of an emperor;
The place thou pressest on thy mother earth
Is all thy empire now: now it contains thee:
Some few days hence, and then 't will be too large,
When thou'rt contracted in thy narrow urn, 220
Shrunk to a few cold ashes; then Octavia

(For Cleopatra will not live to see it),
Octavia then will have thee all her own,
And bear thee in her widowed hand to Caesar;
Caesar will weep, the crocodile will weep, 225
To see his rival of the universe
Lie still and peaceful there. I'll think no more on 't.
Give me some music; look that it be sad;
I'll soothe my melancholy, till I swell
And burst my self with sighing. *(Soft music)* 230
'Tis somewhat to my humor; stay, I fancy
I'm now turned wild, a commoner of nature,
Of all forsaken and forsaking all;
Live in a shady forest's sylvan scene,
Stretched at my length beneath some blasted oak, 235
I lean my head upon the mossy bark,
And look just of a piece as I grew from it;
My uncombed locks, matted like mistletoe,
Hang o'er my hoary face; a murm'ring brook
Runs at my foot.

VEN. *(aside)*. Methinks I fancy 240
Myself there too.

ANT. The herd come jumping by me,
And, fearless, quench their thirst, while I look on,
And take me for their fellow-citizen.
More of this image, more; it lulls my thoughts. *(Soft music again)*

VEN. *(aside)*. I must disturb him; I can hold no longer. *(Stands before him)* 245

ANT. *(starting up)*. Art thou Ventidius?

VEN. Art you Antony?
I'm liker what I was, than you to him
I left you last.

ANT. I'm angry.

VEN. So am I.

ANT. I would be private; leave me.

VEN. Sir, I love you,
And therefore will not leave you.

ANT. Will not leave me! 250
Where have you learned that answer? Who am I?

VEN. My emperor; the man I love next Heaven;
If I said more, I think 'twere scarce a sin;
Y' are all that's good, and god-like.

ANT. All that's wretched.
You will not leave me then?

VEN. 'Twas too presuming 255
To say I would not; but I dare not leave you;
And, 'tis unkind in you to chide me hence
So soon, when I so far have come to see you.

ANT. Now thou hast seen me, art thou satisfied?
For, if a friend, thou hast beheld enough; 260
And, if a foe, too much.

VEN. *(weeping)*. Look, emperor, this is no common dew.
I have not wept this forty year; but now
My mother comes afresh into my eyes;
I cannot help her softness. 265

ANT. By Heav'n, he weeps, poor good old man, he weeps!
The big round drops course[6] one another down
The furrows of his cheeks. Stop 'em. Ventidius,
Or I shall blush to death; they set my shame,
That caused 'em, full before me.

VEN. I'll do my best. 270

ANT. Sure there's contagion in the tears of friends:
See, I have caught it too. Believe me, 'tis not
For my own griefs, but thine—Nay, father.

VEN. Emperor.

ANT. Emperor! Why, that's the style of victory,
The conqu'ring soldier, red with unfelt wounds, 275
Salutes his general so: but never more
Shall that sound reach my ears.

VEN. I warrant you.

ANT. Actium, Actium! Oh——

VEN. It sits too near you

ANT. Here, here it lies; a lump of lead by day,
And, in my short distracted nightly slumbers, 280
The hag that rides my dreams—

VEN. Out with it, give it vent.

ANT. Urge not my shame.
I lost a battle.

VEN. So has Julius done.

ANT. Thou favor'st me, and speak'st not half thou think'st;
For Julius fought it out, and lost it fairly: 285
But Antony—

VEN. Nay, stop not.

ANT. Antony
(Well, thou wilt have it), like a coward, fled,
Fled while his soldiers fought; fled first, Ventidius.
Thou long'st to curse me, and I give thee leave.
I know thou cam'st prepared to rail.

VEN. I did. 290

ANT. I'll help thee.—I have been a man, Ventidius—

VEN. Yes, and a brave one; but—

[6] Pursue.

ANT. I know thy meaning,
But I have lost my reason, have disgraced
The name of soldier with inglorious ease;
In the full vintage of my flowing honors, 295
Sat still, and saw it pressed by other hands.
Fortune came smiling to my youth, and wooed it,
And purple greatness met my ripened years.
When first I came to empire, I was borne
On tides of people, crowding to my triumphs, 300
The wish of nations; and the willing world
Received me as its pledge of future peace;
I was so great, so happy, so belov'd,
Fate could not ruin me; till I took pains,
And worked against my fortune, chid her from me, 305
And turned her loose; yet still she came again.
My careless days, and my luxurious nights,
At length have wearied her, and now she's gone,
Gone, gone, divorced for ever. Help me, soldier,
To curse this madman, this industrious fool, 310
Who labored to be wretched; prithee, curse me.
VEN. No.
ANT. Why?
VEN. You are too sensible already
Of what y' have done, too conscious of your failings;
And, like a scorpion, whipped by others first
To fury, sting yourself in mad revenge. 315
I would bring balm and pour it in your wounds,
Cure your distempered mind, and heal your fortunes.
ANT. I know thou wouldst.
VEN. I will.
ANT. Ha, ha, ha, ha!
VEN. You laugh.
ANT. I do, to see officious love
Give cordials to the dead.
VEN. You would be lost then? 320
ANT. I am.
VEN. I say you are not. Try your fortune.
ANT. I have, to th' utmost. Dost thou think me desperate
Without just cause? No, when I found all lost
Beyond repair, I hid me from the world,
And learned to scorn it here; which now I do 325
So heartily, I think it is not worth
The cost of keeping.
VEN. Caesar thinks not so;
He'll thank you for the gift he could not take.
You would be killed like Tully,[7] would you? Do,
Hold out your throat to Caesar, and die tamely. 330
ANT. No, I can kill myself; and so resolve.
VEN. I can die with you too, when time shall serve;
But fortune calls upon us now to live,
To fight, to conquer.
ANT. Sure thou dream'st, Ventidius.
VEN. No; 'tis you dream; you sleep away your hours 335
In desperate sloth, miscalled philosophy.
Up, up, for honor's sake; twelve legions wait you,
And long to call you chief; by painful journeys
I led 'em, patient both of heat and hunger,
Down from the Parthian marches to the Nile. 340
'Twill do you good to see their sun-burned faces,
Their scarred cheeks, and chopped hands; there's virtue in 'em.
They'll sell those mangled limbs at dearer rates
Than yon trim bands can buy.
ANT. Where left you them?
VEN. I said in Lower Syria.
ANT. Bring 'em hither; 345
There may be life in these.
VEN. They will not come.
ANT. Why didst thou mock my hopes with promised aids,
To double my despair? They're mutinous.
VEN. Most firm and loyal.
ANT. Yet they will not march
To succor me. O trifler!
VEN. They petition 350
You would make hast to head 'em.
ANT. I'm besieged.
VEN. There's but one way shut up; how came I hither?
ANT. I will not stir.
VEN. They would perhaps desire
A better reason.
ANT. I have never used[8]
My soldiers to demand a reason of 355
My actions. Why did they refuse to march?
VEN. They said they would not fight for Cleopatra.

[7]Cicero. [8]I. e., accustomed.

ANT. What was 't they said?
VEN. They said they would not fight for Cleopatra.
Why should they fight, indeed, to make her conquer, 360
And make you more a slave? to gain you kingdoms,
Which, for a kiss, at your next midnight feast
You'll sell to her? Then she new-names her jewels,
And calls this diamond such or such a tax;
Each pendant in her ear shall be a province. 365
ANT. Ventidius, I allow your tongue free licence
On all my other faults; but, on your life,
No word of Cleopatra; she deserves
More worlds than I can lose.
VEN. Behold, you Powers,
To whom you have entrusted humankind; 370
See Europe, Afric', Asia, put in balance,
And all weighed down by one light, worthless woman!
I think the gods are Antonys, and give
Like prodigals this nether world away
To none but wasteful hands.
ANT. You grow presumptuous. 375
VEN. I take the privilege of plain love to speak.
ANT. Plain love! plain arrogance, plain insolence!
Thy men are cowards; thou, an envious traitor;
Who, under seeming honesty, hast vented
The burden of thy rank, o'erflowing gall. 380
O that thou wert my equal, great in arms
As the first Caesar was, that I might kill thee
Without a stain to honor!
VEN. You may kill me;
You have done more already, called me traitor.
ANT. Art thou not one?
VEN. For showing you your self, 385
Which none else durst have done? But had I been
That name which I disdain to speak again,
I needed not have sought your abject fortunes,
Come to partake your fate, to die with you.
What hindred me t' have led my conqu'ring eagles 390
To fill Octavius's bands? I could have been
A traitor then, a glorious, happy traitor,
And not have been so called.
ANT. Forgive me, soldier;
I've been too passionate.
VEN. You thought me false;
Thought my old age betrayed you; kill me, sir; 395
Pray, kill me; yet you need not, your unkindness
Has left your sword no work.
ANT. I did not think so;
I said it in my rage; prithee, forgive me;
Why didst thou tempt my anger, by discovery
Of what I would not hear?
VEN. No prince but you 400
Could merit that sincerity I used,
Nor durst another man have ventured it;
But you, ere love misled your wandering eyes,
Were sure the chief and best of human race,
Framed in the very pride and boast of nature; 405
So perfect, that the gods, who formed you, wondered
At their own skill, and cried, "A lucky hit
Has mended our design." Their envy hindered,
Else you had been immortal, and a pattern,
When Heav'n would work for ostentation's sake, 410
To copy out again.
ANT. But Cleopatra—
Go on; for I can bear it now.
VEN. No more.
ANT. Thou dar'st not trust my passion; but thou may'st;
Thou only lov'st, the rest have flattered me.
VEN. Heav'n's blessing on your heart for that kind word! 415
May I believe you love me? Speak again.
ANT. Indeed I do. Speak this, and this, and this. *(Hugging him)*
Thy praises were unjust; but I'll deserve 'em,
And yet mend all. Do with me what thou wilt;
Lead me to victory, thou know'st the way. 420
VEN. And will you leave this—
ANT. Prithee, do not curse her,
And I will leave her; though, Heav'n knows, I love
Beyond life, conquest, empire, all but honor:
But I will leave her.
VEN. That's my royal master;
And shall we fight?
ANT. I warrant thee, old soldier. 425
Thou shalt behold me once again in iron;
And at the head of our old troops, that beat

The Parthians, cry aloud, "Come, follow me!"

VEN. O, now I hear my emperor! in that word
Octavius fell. Gods, let me see that day, 430
And, if I have ten years behind, take all;
I'll thank you for th'exchange.

ANT. Oh, Cleopatra!

VEN. Again?

ANT. I've done; in that last sigh she went.
Caesar shall know what 'tis to force a lover
From all he holds most dear.

VEN. Methinks you breathe 435
Another soul; your looks are more divine;
You speak a hero, and you move a god.

ANT. O, thou hast fired me; my soul's up in arms,
And mans each part about me; once again,
That noble eagerness of fight has seized me; 440
That eagerness with which I darted upward
To Cassius's camp;[9] in vain the steepy hill
Opposed my way; in vain a war of spears
Sung round my head and planted all my shield;
I won the trenches while my foremost men 445
Lagged on the plain below.

VEN. Ye gods, ye gods,
For such another hour!

ANT. Come on, my soldier!
Our hearts and arms are still the same; I long
Once more to meet our foes; that thou and I,
Like Time and Death, marching before our troops, 450
May taste[10] fate to 'em; mow 'em out a passage,
And ent'ring where the foremost squadrons yield,
Begin the noble harvest of the field.

[*Exeunt.*

ACT II

CLEOPATRA, IRAS, *and* ALEXAS.

CLEOPATRA. What shall I do, or whither shall I turn?
Ventidius has o'ercome, and he will go.

ALEXAS. He goes to fight for you.

CLEOP. Then he would see me, ere he went to fight;
Flatter me not; if once he goes, he's lost, 5
And all my hopes destroyed.

ALEX. Does this weak passion
Become a mighty queen?

CLEOP. I am no queen:
Is this to be a queen, to be besieged
By yon insulting Roman, and to wait
Each hour the victor's chain? These ills are small: 10
For Antony is lost, and I can mourn
For nothing else but him. Now come, Octavius,
I have no more to lose; prepare thy bands;
I'm fit to be a captive; Antony
Has taught my mind the fortune of a slave. 15

IRAS. Call reason to assist you.

CLEOP. I have none.
And none would have; my love's a noble madness,
Which shows the cause deserved it. Moderate sorrow
Fits vulgar love, and for a vulgar man;
But I have loved with such transcendent passion, 20
I soared, at first, quite out of reason's view,
And now am lost above it. No, I'm proud
'Tis thus; would Antony could see me now!
Think you he would not sigh? Though he must leave me,
Sure he would sigh; for he is noble-natured, 25
And bears a tender heart: I know him well.
Ah, no, I know him not; I knew him once,
But now 'tis past.

IRAS. Let it be past with you:
Forget him, madam.

CLEOP. Never, never, Iras.
He once was mine; and once, though now 'tis gone, 30
Leaves a faint image of possession still.

ALEX. Think him unconstant, cruel, and ungrateful.

CLEOP. I cannot; if I could, those thoughts were vain;
Faithless, ungrateful, cruel though he be,
I still must love him.

Enter CHARMION.

Now, what news, my Charmion? 35
Will he be kind? and will he not forsake me?
Am I to live, or die?—nay, do I live?
Or am I dead? for when he gave his answer,
Fate took the word, and then I lived or died.

CHARMION. I found him, madam—

CLEOP. A long speech preparing? 40
If thou bring'st comfort, haste, and give it me,
For never was more need.

[9]A reference to the battle of Philippi (B. C. 42).

[10]I. e., foreshadow.

IRAS. I know he loves you.
CLEOP. Had he been kind, her eyes had told me so,
Before her tongue could speak it; now she studies
To soften what he said; but give me death, 45
Just as he sent it, Charmion, undisguised,
And in the words he spoke.
CHAR. I found him, then,
Encompassed round, I think, with iron statues;
So mute, so motionless his soldiers stood,
While awfully he cast his eyes about, 50
And every leader's hopes or fears surveyed;
Methought he looked resolved, and yet not pleased.
When he beheld me struggling in the crowd,
He blushed, and bade make way.
ALEX. There's comfort yet.
CHAR. Ventidius fixed his eyes upon my passage 55
Severely, as he meant to frown me back.
And sullenly gave place; I told my message,
Just as you gave it, broken and disordered;
I numbered in it all your sighs and tears,
And while I moved your pitiful request, 60
That you but only begged a last farewell,
He fetched an inward groan, and every time
I named you, sighed, as if his heart were breaking,
But shunned my eyes, and guiltily looked down;
He seemed not now that awful Antony, 65
Who shook an armed assembly with his nod;
But, making show as he would rub his eyes,
Disguised and blotted out a falling tear.
CLEOP. Did he then weep? And was I worth a tear?
If what thou hast to say be not as pleasing, 70
Tell me no more, but let me die contented.
CHAR. He bid me say, he knew himself so well,
He could deny you nothing, if he saw you;
And therefore—
CLEOP. Thou wouldst say, he would not see me?
CHAR. And therefore begged you not to use a power, 75
Which he could ill resist; yet he should ever
Respect you as he ought.
CLEOP. Is that a word
For Antony to use to Cleopatra?
Oh, that faint word, respect! how I disdain it!
Disdain myself, for loving after it! 80
He should have kept that word for cold Octavia;
Respect is for a wife; am I that thing,
That dull, insipid lump, without desires,
And without power to give 'em?
ALEX. You misjudge,
You see through love, and that deludes your sight, 85
As what is straight seems crooked through the water;
But I, who bear my reason undisturbed,
Can see this Antony, this dreaded man,
A fearful slave, who fain would run away,
And shuns his master's eyes; if you pursue him, 90
My life on 't, he still drags a chain along,
That needs must clog his flight.
CLEOP. Could I believe thee!—
ALEX. By every circumstance I know he loves.
True, he's hard pressed, by interest and by honor;
Yet he but doubts, and parleys and casts out 95
Many a long look for succor.
CLEOP. He sends word,
He fears to see my face.
ALEX. And would you more?
He shows his weakness who declines the combat,
And you must urge your fortune. Could he speak
More plainly? To my ears, the message sounds— 100
"Come to my rescue, Cleopatra, come;
Come, free me from Ventidius; from my tyrant;
See me, and give me a pretence to leave him!"—
I hear his trumpets. This way he must pass.
Please you, retire a while; I'll work him first, 105
That he may bend more easy.
CLEOP. You shall rule me;
But all, I fear, in vain.
[*Exit with* CHARMION *and* IRAS.
ALEX. I fear so too;
Though I concealed my thoughts, to make her bold;
But 'tis our utmost means, and fate befriend it! [*Withdraws.*

Enter LICTORS *with fasces; one bearing the eagle; then enter* ANTONY *with* VENTIDIUS, *followed by other* COMMANDERS.

ANTONY. Octavius is the minion of blind chance, 110
But holds from virtue nothing.
VENTIDIUS. Has he courage?

ANT. But just enough to season him from
coward.
O, 'tis the coldest youth upon a charge,
The most deliberate fighter! if he ventures
(As in Illyria once they say he did 115
To storm a town), 'tis when he cannot
choose,
When all the world have fixed their eyes
upon him;
And then he lives on that for seven years
after;
But at a close[1] revenge he never fails.
VEN. I heard you challenged him.
ANT. I did, Ventidius. 120
What think'st thou was his answer? 'Twas
so tame!—
He said, he had more ways than one to
die;
I had not.
VEN. Poor!
ANT. He has more ways than one;
But he would choose 'em all before that one.
VEN. He first would choose an ague or a
fever. 125
ANT. No; it must be an ague, not a fever;
He has not warmth enough to die by that.
VEN. Or old age and a bed.
ANT. Ay, there's his choice.
He would live, like a lamp, to the last wink,
And crawl upon the utmost verge of life; 130
O Hercules! Why should a man like this,
Who dares not trust his fate for one great
action,
Be all the care of Heav'n? Why should he
lord it
O'er fourscore thousand men, of whom each
one
Is braver than himself?
VEN. You conquered for him; 135
Philippi knows it; there you shared with him
That empire which your sword made all your
own.
ANT. Fool that I was, upon my eagle's
wings
I bore this wren, till I was tired with soaring,
And now he mounts above me. 140
Good Heav'ns, is this,—is this the man who
braves me?
Who bids my age make way, drives me be-
fore him,
To the world's ridge, and sweeps me off
like rubbish?
VEN. Sir, we lose time; the troops are
mounted all.
ANT. Then give the word to march; 145
I long to leave this prison of a town,

[1] Secret.

To join thy legions, and in open field
Once more to show my face. Lead, my
deliverer.

Enter ALEXAS.

ALEX. Great emperor,
In mighty arms renowned above man-
kind, 150
But, in soft pity to th' oppressed a god:
This message sends the mournful Cleopatra
To her departing lord.
VEN. Smooth sycophant!
ALEX. A thousand wishes, and ten thou-
sand prayers,
Millions of blessings wait you to the wars; 155
Millions of sighs and tears she sends you too,
And would have sent
As many dear embraces to your arms,
As many parting kisses to your lips;
But those, she fears, have wearied you al-
ready. 160
VEN. *(aside)*. False crocodile!
ALEX. And yet she begs not now, you
would not leave her;
That were a wish too mighty for her hopes,
Too presuming
For her low fortune, and your ebbing
love; 165
That were a wish for her more prosp'rous
days,
Her blooming beauty, and your growing
kindness.
ANT. *(aside)*. Well, I must man it out:
—what would the queen?
ALEX. First, to these noble warriors, who
attend
Your daring courage in the chase of fame 170
(Too daring, and too dang'rous for her
quiet),
She humbly recommends all she holds dear,
All her own cares and fears—the care of you.
VEN. Yes, witness Actium.
ANT. Let him speak, Ventidius.
ALEX. You, when his matchless valor
bears him forward, 175
With ardor too heroic, on his foes,
Fall down, as she would do, before his feet;
Lie in his way, and stop the paths of death:
Tell him, this god is not invulnerable;
That absent Cleopatra bleeds in him; 180
And, that you may remember her petition,
She begs you wear these trifles, as a pawn,
Which, at your wished return, she will re-
deem
(Gives jewels to the COMMANDERS)
With all the wealth of Egypt;
This to the great Ventidius she presents, 185

Whom she can never count her enemy,
Because he loves her lord.

VEN. Tell her, I'll none on't;
I'm not ashamed of honest poverty;
Not all the diamonds of the East can bribe
Ventidius from his faith. I hope to see 190
These and the rest of all her sparkling store,
Where they shall more deservingly be placed.

ANT. And who must wear 'em then?

VEN. The wronged Octavia.

ANT. You might have spared that word.

VEN. And he that bribe.

ANT. But have I no remembrance?

ALEX. Yes, a dear one; 195
Your slave the queen—

ANT. My mistress.

ALEX. Then your mistress;
Your mistress would, she says, have sent her soul,
But that you had long since; she humbly begs
This ruby bracelet, set with bleeding hearts
(The emblems of her own), may bind your arm. (*Presenting a bracelet*)

VEN. Now, my best lord, in honor's name, I ask you,
For manhood's sake and for your own dear safety,
Touch not these poisoned gifts,
Infected by the sender; touch 'em not; 204
Myriads of bluest plagues lie underneath 'em,
And more than aconite[2] has dipped the silk.

ANT. Nay, now you grow too cynical, Ventidius.
A lady's favors may be worn with honor.
What, to refuse her bracelet! On my soul,
When I lie pensive in my tent alone, 210
'Twill pass the wakeful hours of winter nights,
To tell[3] these pretty beads upon my arm,
To count for every one a soft embrace,
A melting kiss at such and such a time,
And now and then the fury of her love, 215
When— And what harm's in this?

ALEX. None, none, my lord,
But what's to her, that now 'tis past for ever.

ANT. (*going to tie it*). We soldiers are so awkward—help me tie it.

ALEX. In faith, my lord, we courtiers, too, are awkward
In these affairs; so are all men indeed; 220
E'en I, who am not one. But shall I speak?

ANT. Yes, freely.

ALEX. Then, my lord, fair hands alone
Are fit to tie it; she who sent it can.

[2]A deadly poison. [3]Count.

VEN. Hell, death! this eunuch pander ruins you.
You will not see her?

(ALEXAS *whispers an* ATTENDANT, *who goes out*)

ANT. But to take my leave. 225

VEN. Then I have washed an Ethiop. Y'are undone;
Y'are in the toils; y'are taken; y'are destroyed;
Her eyes do Caesar's work.

ANT. You fear too soon.
I'm constant to myself: I know my strength;
And yet she shall not think me barbarous neither, 230
Born in the depths of Afric'; I'm a Roman,
Bred in the rules of soft humanity.
A guest, and kindly used, should bid farewell.

VEN. You do not know
How weak you are to her, how much an infant; 235
You are not proof against a smile or glance;
A sigh will quite disarm you.

ANT. See, she comes!
Now you shall find your error. Gods, I thank you;
I formed[4] the danger greater than it was,
And now 'tis near, 'tis lessened.

VEN. Mark the end yet. 240

Enter CLEOPATRA, CHARMION, *and* IRAS.

ANT. Well, madam, we are met.

CLEOP. Is this a meeting?
Then we must part?

ANT. We must.

CLEOP. Who says we must?

ANT. Our own hard fates.

CLEOP. We make those fates ourselves.

ANT. Yes, we have made 'em; we have loved each other
Into our mutual ruin. 245

CLEOP. The gods have seen my joys with envious eyes;
I have no friends in Heav'n; and all the world
(As 'twere the bus'ness of mankind to part us)
Is armed against my love; e'en you yourself
Join with the rest; you, you are armed against me. 250

ANT. I will be justified in all I do
To late posterity, and therefore hear me.
If I mix a lie
With any truth, reproach me freely with it;
Else favor me with silence.

[4]Conceived.

CLEOP. You command me, 255
And I am dumb.
VEN. I like this well; he shows authority.
ANT. That I derive my ruin
From you alone—
CLEOP. O Heav'ns! I ruin you!
ANT. You promised me your silence, and you break it 260
Ere I have scarce begun.
CLEOP. Well, I obey you.
ANT. When I beheld you first, it was in Egypt,
Ere Caesar[5] saw your eyes; you gave me love,
And were too young to know it; that I settled 264
Your father in his throne, was for your sake;
I left th'acknowledgment for time to ripen.
Caesar stepped in, and, with a greedy hand,
Plucked the green fruit, ere the first blush of red,
Yet cleaving to the bough. He was my lord,
And was, beside, too great for me to rival;
But I deserved you first, though he enjoyed you. 271
When, after, I beheld you in Cilicia,
An enemy to Rome, I pardoned you.
CLEOP. I cleared myself—
ANT. Again you break your promise. 274
I loved you still, and took your weak excuses,
Took you into my bosom, stained by Caesar,
And not half mine; I went to Egypt with you,
And hid me from the bus'ness of the world,
Shut out enquiring nations from my sight,
To give whole years to you. 280
VEN. (*aside*). Yes, to your shame be't spoken.
ANT. How I loved,
Witness, ye days and nights, and all ye hours,
That danced away with down upon your feet,
As all your bus'ness were to count my passion!
One day passed by, and nothing saw but love; 285
Another came, and still 'twas only love;
The suns were wearied out with looking on,
And I untired with loving.
I saw you every day, and all the day;
And every day was still but as the first, 290
So eager was I still to see you more.
VEN. 'Tis all too true.
ANT. Fulvia, my wife, grew jealous,

[5]Julius Caesar.

As she indeed had reason; raised a war
In Italy, to call me back.
VEN. But yet
You went not.
ANT. While within your arms I lay, 295
The world fell mold'ring from my hands each hour,
And left me scarce a grasp (I thank your love for't).
VEN. Well pushed: that last was home.
CLEOP. Yet may I speak?
ANT. If I have urged a falsehood, yes; else not. 299
Your silence says I have not. Fulvia died
(Pardon, you gods, with my unkindness died);
To set the world at peace, I took Octavia,
This Caesar's[6] sister; in her pride of youth
And flower of beauty did I wed that lady,
Whom blushing I must praise, because I left her. 305
You called; my love obeyed the fatal summons;
This raised the Roman arms; the cause was yours.
I would have fought by land, where I was stronger;
You hindered it; yet, when I fought at sea,
Forsook me fighting; and (O stain to honor!
O lasting shame!) I knew not that I fled;
But fled to follow you. 312
VEN. What haste she made to hoist her purple sails!
And, to appear magnificent in flight,
Drew half our strength away.
ANT. All this you caused. 315
And would you multiply more ruins on me?
This honest man, my best, my only friend,
Has gathered up the shipwreck of my fortunes;
Twelve legions I have left, my last recruits.
And you have watched the news, and bring your eyes 320
To seize them too. If you have aught to answer,
Now speak, you have free leave.
ALEX. (*aside*). She stands confounded;
Despair is in her eyes.
VEN. Now lay a sigh i'th' way to stop his passage:
Prepare a tear, and bid it for his legions; 325
'Tis like they shall be sold.
CLEOP. How shall I plead my cause, when you, my judge,
Already have condemned me? Shall I bring

[6]Octavius's.

The love you bore me for my advocate?
That now is turned against me, that destroys me; 330
For love, once past, is at the best forgotten;
But oft'ner sours to hate; 'twill please my lord
To ruin me, and therefore I'll be guilty.
But could I once have thought it would have pleased you,
That you would pry with narrow searching eyes 335
Into my faults, severe to my destruction,
And watching all advantages with care
That serve to make me wretched? Speak, my lord,
For I end here. Though I deserve this usage,
Was it like you to give it?

ANT. Oh, you wrong me, 340
To think I sought this parting, or desired
To accuse you more than what will clear myself,
And justify this breach.

CLEOP. Thus low I thank you.
And, since my innocence will not offend,
I shall not blush to own it.

VEN. After this, 345
I think she'll blush at nothing.

CLEOP. You seem grieved
(And therein you are kind) that Caesar first
Enjoyed my love, though you deserved it better;
I grieve for that, my lord, much more than you;
For, had I first been yours, it would have saved 350
My second choice: I never had been his,
And ne'er had been but yours. But Caesar first,
You say, possessed my love. Not so, my lord;
He first possessed my person; you, my love:
Caesar loved me; but I loved Antony. 355
If I endured him after, 'twas because
I judged it due to the first name of men;
And, half constrained, I gave, as to a tyrant,
What he would take by force.

VEN. O Siren! Siren!
Yet grant that all the love she boasts were true, 360
Has she not ruined you? I still urge that,
The fatal consequence.

CLEOP. The consequence indeed,
For I dare challenge him, my greatest foe,
To say it was designed; 'tis true, I loved you,
And kept you far from an uneasy wife— 365
Such Fulvia was.
Yes, but he'll say, you left Octavia for me;—
And can you blame me to receive that love,
Which quitted such desert for worthless me?
How often have I wished some other Caesar,
Great as the first, and as the second young,
Would court my love, to be refused for you!

VEN. Words, words; but Actium, sir; remember Actium.

CLEOP. E'en there, I dare his malice. True, I counseled
To fight at sea; but I betrayed you not. 375
I fled, but not to the enemy. 'Twas fear;
Would I had been a man, not to have feared!
For none would then have envied me your friendship,
Who envy me your love.

ANT. We're both unhappy;
If nothing else, yet our ill fortune parts us.
Speak; would you have me perish by my stay? 381

CLEOP. If as a friend you ask my judgment, go;
If, as a lover, stay. If you must perish—
'Tis a hard word—but stay.

VEN. See now th' effects of her so boasted love! 385
She strives to drag you down to ruin with her;
But could she scape without you, oh, how soon
Would she let go her hold, and haste to shore,
And never look behind!

CLEOP. Then judge my love by this. (*Giving* ANTONY *a writing.*) Could I have born 390
A life or death, a happiness or woe,
From yours divided, this had giv'n me means.

ANT. By Hercules, the writing of Octavius!
I know it well: 'tis that proscribing hand,
Young as it was, that led the way to mine,
And left me but the second place in murder.— 396
See, see, Ventidius! here he offers Egypt,
And joins all Syria to it, as a present,
So, in requital, she forsake my fortunes,
And join her arms with his.

CLEOP. And yet you leave me!
You leave me, Antony; and yet I love you,
Indeed I do: I have refused a kingdom; 402
That's a trifle;
For I could part with life, with anything,
But only you. Oh, let me die but with you!
Is that a hard request?

ANT. Next living with you,
'Tis all that Heav'n can give. 407

ALEX. (*aside*). He melts; we conquer.
CLEOP. No; you shall go; your int'rest calls you hence;
Yes; your dear interest pulls too strong for these
Weak arms to hold you here.—(*Takes his hand.*) Go; leave me, soldier 410
(For you're no more a lover); leave me dying;
Push me all pale and panting from your bosom,
And, when your march begins, let one run after,
Breathless almost for joy, and cry, "She's dead":
The soldiers shout; you then, perhaps, may sigh, 415
And muster all your Roman gravity:
Ventidius chides; and straight your brow clears up,
As I had never been.
ANT. Gods, 'tis too much; too much for man to bear!
CLEOP. What is't for me then, 420
A weak, forsaken woman, and a lover?—
Here let me breathe my last: envy me not
This minute in your arms: I'll die apace,
As fast as ere I can, and end your trouble.
ANT. Die! Rather let me perish;—loosened nature 425
Leap from its hinges, sink the props of Heaven,
And fall the skies to crush the nether world!
My eyes, my soul, my all! (*Embraces her*)
VEN. And what's this toy,
In balance with your fortune, honor, fame?
ANT. What is't, Ventidius?—it outweighs 'em all; 430
Why, we have more than conquered Caesar now:
My queen's not only innocent, but loves me.
This, this is she who drags me down to ruin!
"But, could she 'scape without me, with what haste
Would she let slip her hold, and make to shore, 435
And never look behind!"
Down on thy knees, blasphemer as thou art,
And ask forgiveness of wronged innocence.
VEN. I'll rather die than take it. Will you go?
ANT. Go! whither? Go from all that's excellent? 440
Faith, honor, virtue, all good things forbid
That I should go from her, who sets my love
Above the price of kingdoms! Give, you gods,
Give to your boy, your Caesar,
This rattle of a globe to play withal, 445
This gewgaw world, and put him cheaply off:
I'll not be pleased with less than Cleopatra.
CLEOP. She's wholly yours. My heart's so full of joy,
That I shall do some wild extravagance
Of love in public; and the foolish world, 450
Which knows not tenderness, will think me mad.
VEN. O women! women! women! all the gods
Have not such power of doing good to man,
As you of doing harm. [*Exit.*
ANT. Our men are armed.
Unbar the gate that looks to Caesar's camp;
I would revenge the treachery he meant me;
And long security makes conquest easy. 457
I'm eager to return before I go;
For all the pleasures I have known beat thick
On my remembrance; how I long for night!
That both the sweets of mutual love may try, 461
And once triumph o'er Caesar ere we die.
[*Exeunt.*

ACT III

At one door enter CLEOPATRA, CHARMION, IRAS, *and* ALEXAS, *a train of* EGYPTIANS; *at the other,* ANTONY *and* ROMANS. *The entrance on both sides is prepared by music; the trumpets first sounding on Antony's part: then answered by timbrels, etc., on Cleopatra's. Charmion and Iras hold a laurel wreath betwixt them. A dance of Egyptians. After the ceremony, Cleopatra crowns Antony.*

ANTONY. I thought how those white arms would fold me in,
And strain me close, and melt me into love;
So pleased with that sweet image, I sprung forwards,
And added all my strength to every blow.
CLEOPATRA. Come to me, come, my soldier, to my arms! 5
You've been too long away from my embraces;
But when I have you fast and all my own,
With broken murmurs, and with amorous sighs,
I'll say, you were unkind, and punish you,
And mark you red with many an eager kiss.
ANT. My brighter Venus!
CLEOP. O my greater Mars!

ANT. Thou join'st us well, my love! 12
Suppose me come from the Phlegraean plains,[1]
Where gasping giants lay, cleft by my sword,
And mountain tops, pared off each other blow, 15
To bury those I slew; receive me, goddess!
Let Caesar spread his subtle nets like Vulcan;[2]
In thy embraces I would be beheld
By Heav'n and earth at once,
And make their envy what they meant their sport. 20
Let those who took us blush; I would love on
With awful state, regardless of their frowns,
As their superior god.
There's no satiety of love in thee:
Enjoyed, thou still art new; perpetual spring
Is in thy arms; the ripened fruit but falls, 26
And blossoms rise to fill its empty place;
And I grow rich by giving.

Enter VENTIDIUS, *and stands apart.*

ALEXAS. O, now the danger's past, your general comes!
He joins not in your joys, nor minds your triumphs; 30
But with contracted brows looks frowning on,
As envying your success.

ANT. Now, on my soul, he loves me; truly loves me:
He never flattered me in any vice,
But awes me with his virtue: e'en this minute, 35
Methinks, he has a right of chiding me.
Lead to the temple; I'll avoid his presence;
It checks too strong upon me.

(*Exeunt the rest. As* ANTONY *is going,* VENTIDIUS *pulls him by the robe*)

VENTIDIUS. Emperor!

ANT. (*looking back*). 'Tis the old argument; I prithee, spare me.

VEN. But this one hearing, emperor.

ANT. Let go 40
My robe; or, by my father Hercules—

VEN. By Hercules his father, that's yet greater,
I bring you somewhat you would wish to know.

ANT. Thou see'st we are observed, attend me here,
And I'll return. [*Exit.* 45

[1] In Macedonia, where the giants unsuccessfully did battle with the gods.

[2] Who caught his wife, Venus, in the arms of Mars.

VEN. I'm waning in his favor, yet I love him;
I love this man, who runs to meet his ruin;
And sure the gods, like me, are fond of him;
His virtues lie so mingled with his crimes,
As would confound their choice to punish one, 50
And not reward the other.

Enter ANTONY.

ANT. We can conquer,
You see, without your aid.
We have dislodged their troops;
They look on us at distance, and, like curs
Scaped from the lion's paws, they bay far off, 55
And lick their wounds and faintly threaten war.
Five thousand Romans, with their faces upward,
Lie breathless on the plain.

VEN. 'Tis well; and he
Who lost 'em, could have spared ten thousand more.
Yet if by this advantage you could gain 60
An easier peace, while Caesar doubts the chance
Of arms—

ANT. O, think not on't, Ventidius!
The boy pursues my ruin, he'll no peace;
His malice is considerate in advantage.
O, he's the coolest murderer! so staunch, 65
He kills and keeps his temper.

VEN. Have you no friend
In all his army, who has power to move him?
Mecaenas or Agrippa might do much.

ANT. They're both too deep in Caesar's interests. 69
We'll work it out by dint of sword, or perish.

VEN. Fain I would find some other.

ANT. Thank thy love.
Some four or five such victories as this
Will save thy farther pains.

VEN. Expect no more; Caesar is on his guard:
I know, sir, you have conquered against odds;
But still you draw supplies from one poor town, 76
And of Egyptians; he has all the world,
And at his back nations come pouring in,
To fill the gaps you make. Pray, think again.

ANT. Why dost thou drive me from myself, to search 80
For foreign aids?—to hunt my memory,
And range all o'er a waste and barren place,

To find a friend? The wretched have no friends.
Yet I had one, the bravest youth of Rome,
Whom Caesar loves beyond the love of women; 85
He could resolve his mind as fire does wax,
From that hard rugged image melt him down,
And mold him in what softer form he pleased.

VEN. Him would I see; that man of all the world;
Just such a one we want.

ANT. He loved me too;
I was his soul; he lived not but in me: 91
We were so closed within each other's breasts,
The rivets were not found that joined us first.
That does not reach us yet: we were so mixed
As meeting streams, both to ourselves were lost; 95
We were one mass; we could not give or take
But from the same; for he was I, I he.

VEN. (*aside*). He moves as I would wish him.

ANT. After this,
I need not tell his name;—'twas Dollabella.

VEN. He's now in Caesar's camp.

ANT. No matter where, 100
Since he's no longer mine. He took unkindly
That I forbade him Cleopatra's sight
Because I feared he loved her: he confessed
He had a warmth, which for my sake he stifled;
For 'twere impossible that two, so one, 105
Should not have loved the same. When he departed,
He took no leave; and that confirmed my thoughts.

VEN. It argues that he loved you more than her,
Else he had stayed; but he perceived you jealous,
And would not grieve his friend; I know he loves you. 110

ANT. I should have seen him then ere now.

VEN. Perhaps
He has thus long been lab'ring for your peace.

ANT. Would he were here!

VEN. Would you believe he loved you?
I read your answer in your eyes, you would.
Not to conceal it longer, he has sent 115
A messenger from Caesar's camp, with letters.

ANT. Let him appear.

VEN. I'll bring him instantly.
(*Exit* VENTIDIUS; *re-enters immediately with* DOLLABELLA)

ANT. 'Tis he himself! himself, by holy friendship! (*Runs to embrace him*)
Art thou returned at last, my better half?
Come, give me all myself! Let me not live,
If the young bridegroom, longing for his night, 121
Was ever half so fond.

DOLLABELLA. I must be silent, for my soul is busy
About a nobler work: she's new come home,
Like a long-absent man, and wanders o'er 125
Each room, a stranger to her own, to look
If all be safe.

ANT. Thou hast what's left of me;
For I am now so sunk from what I was,
Thou find'st me at my lowest water-mark.
The rivers that ran in and raised my fortunes
Are all dried up, or take another course: 131
What I have left is from my native spring;
I've still a heart that swells in scorn of fate,
And lifts me to my banks.

DOLLA. Still you are lord of all the world to me. 135

ANT. Why, then I yet am so; for thou art all.
If I had any joy when thou wert absent,
I grudged it to myself; methought I robbed
Thee of thy part. But, oh my Dollabella!
Thou hast beheld me other than I am. 140
Hast thou not seen my morning chambers[3] filled
With sceptered slaves who waited to salute me?
With eastern monarchs who forgot the sun
To worship my uprising? Menial kings
Ran coursing up and down my palace-yard,
Stood silent in my presence, watched my eyes, 146
And at my least command all started out,
Like racers to the goal.

DOLLA. Slaves to your fortune.

ANT. Fortune is Caesar's now; and what am I?

VEN. What you have made yourself; I will not flatter. 150

ANT. Is this friendly done?

DOLLA. Yes; when his end is so, I must join with him;
Indeed I must, and yet you must not chide;
Why am I else your friend?

ANT. Take heed, young man,
How thou upbraid'st my love; the queen has eyes, 155

[3] I. e., my chambers in the morning.

And thou, too, hast a soul. Canst thou remember,
When, swelled with hatred, thou beheld'st her first,
As accessory to thy brother's death?

DOLLA. Spare my remembrance; 'twas a guilty day,
And still the blush hangs here.

ANT. To clear herself, 160
For sending him no aid, she came from Egypt.
Her galley down the silver Cydnos rowed;
The tackling silk, the streamers waved with gold;
The gentle winds were lodged in purple sails;
Her nymphs, like Nereids, round her couch were placed, 165
Where she, another sea-born Venus, lay.

DOLLA. No more; I would not hear it.

ANT. Oh, you must!
She lay, and leaned her cheek upon her hand
And cast a look so languishingly sweet,
As if, secure of all beholders' hearts, 170
Neglecting, she could take 'em: boys, like Cupids,
Stood fanning with their painted wings the winds
That played about her face; but if she smiled,
A darting glory seemed to blaze abroad,
That men's desiring eyes were never wearied,
But hung upon the object; to soft flutes 176
The silver oars kept time; and while they played,
The hearing gave new pleasure to the sight;
And both to thought; 'twas Heaven, or somewhat more;
For she so charmed all hearts that gazing crowds 180
Stood panting on the shore, and wanted breath
To give their welcome voice.
Then, Dollabella, where was then thy soul?
Was not thy fury quite disarmed with wonder?
Didst thou not shrink behind me from those eyes, 185
And whisper in my ear, "Oh, tell her not
That I accused her with my brother's death?"

DOLLA. And should my weakness be a plea for yours?
Mine was an age when love might be excused,
When kindly warmth, and when my springing youth 190
Made it a debt to nature. Yours—

VEN. Speak boldly.
Yours, he would say, in your declining age,
When no more heat was left but what you forced,
When all the sap was needful for the trunk,
When it went down, then you constrained the course, 195
And robbed from nature, to supply desire;
In you (I would not use so harsh a word)
But 'tis plain dotage.

ANT. Ha!

DOLLA. 'Twas urged too home.
But yet the loss was private that I made;
'Twas but myself I lost: I lost no legions;
I had no world to lose, no people's love. 201

ANT. This from a friend?

DOLLA. Yes, Antony, a true one;
A friend so tender that each word I speak
Stabs my own heart before it reach your ear.
Oh, judge me not less kind, because I chide!
To Caesar I excuse you.

ANT. O ye gods! 206
Have I then lived to be excused to Caesar?

DOLLA. As to your equal.

ANT. Well, he's but my equal:
While I wear this he never shall be more.

DOLLA. I bring conditions from him.

ANT. Are they noble? 210
Methinks thou shouldst not bring 'em else; yet he
Is full of deep dissembling; knows no honor
Divided from his int'rest. Fate mistook him;
For nature meant him for an usurer:
He's fit indeed to buy, not conquer kingdoms.

VEN. Then, granting this, 216
What power was theirs, who wrought so hard a temper
To honorable terms?

ANT. It was my Dollabella, or some god.

DOLLA. Nor I, nor yet Mecaenas, nor Agrippa: 220
They were your enemies; and I, a friend
Too weak alone; yet 'twas a Roman's deed.

ANT. 'Twas like a Roman done: show me that man,
Who has preserved my life, my love, my honor;
Let me but see his face.

VEN. That task is mine, 225
And, Heav'n, thou know'st how pleasing.

[*Exit* VENTIDIUS.

DOLLA. You'll remember
To whom you stand obliged?

ANT. When I forget it,
Be thou unkind; and that's my greatest curse.
My queen shall thank him too.

DOLLA. I fear she will not.
ANT. But she shall do't. The queen, my Dollabella! 230
Hast thou not still some grudgings of thy fever?
DOLLA. I would not see her lost.
ANT. When I forsake her,
Leave me, my better stars! for she has truth
Beyond her beauty. Caesar tempted her,
At no less price than kingdoms, to betray me; 235
But she resisted all; and yet thou chid'st me
For loving her too well. Could I do so?
DOLLA. Yes; there's my reason.

Re-enter VENTIDIUS, *with* OCTAVIA, *leading Antony's two little* DAUGHTERS.

ANT. Where?—Octavia there! (*Starting back*)
VEN. What, is she poison to you? a disease?
Look on her, view her well, and those she brings: 240
Are they all strangers to your eyes? Has nature
No secret call, no whisper they are yours?
DOLLA. For shame, my lord, if not for love, receive 'em
With kinder eyes. If you confess a man,[4]
Meet 'em, embrace 'em, bid 'em welcome to you. 245
Your arms should open, e'en without your knowledge,
To clasp 'em in; your feet should turn to wings,
To bear you to 'em; and your eyes dart out
And aim a kiss, ere you could reach the lips.
ANT. I stood amazed, to think how they came hither. 250
VEN. I sent for 'em; I brought 'em in, unknown
To Cleopatra's guards.
DOLLA. Yet are you cold?
OCTAVIA. Thus long I have attended for my welcome;
Which, as a stranger, sure I might expect.
Who am I?
ANT. Caesar's sister.
OCTAV. That's unkind. 255
Had I been nothing more than Caesar's sister,
Know, I had still remained in Caesar's camp:
But your Octavia, your much injured wife,
Though banished from your bed, driv'n from your house,
In spite of Caesar's sister, still is yours. 260
'Tis true, I have a heart disdains your coldness,
And prompts me not to seek what you should offer,
But a wife's virtue still surmounts that pride;
I come to claim you as my own: to show
My duty first; to ask, nay beg, your kindness: 265
Your hand, my lord; 'tis mine, and I will have it. (*Taking his hand*)
VEN. Do, take it; thou deserv'st it.
DOLLA. On my soul,
And so she does: she's neither too submissive,
Nor yet too haughty; but so just a mean
Shows, as it ought, a wife and Roman too. 270
ANT. I fear, Octavia, you have begged my life.
OCTAV. Begged it, my lord?
ANT. Yes, begged it, my ambassadress;
Poorly and basely begged it of your brother.
OCTAV. Poorly and basely I could never beg;
Nor could my brother grant. 275
ANT. Shall I, who to my kneeling slave could say,
"Rise up, and be a king," shall I fall down
And cry, "Forgive me, Caesar"? Shall I set
A man, my equal, in the place of Jove,
As he could give me being? No; that word,
"Forgive," would choke me up, 281
And die upon my tongue.
DOLLA. You shall not need it.
ANT. I will not need it. Come, you've all betrayed me,—
My friend too!—to receive some vile conditions.
My wife has bought me with her prayers and tears, 285
And now I must become her branded slave:
In every peevish mood she will upbraid
The life she gave: if I but look awry,
She cries, "I'll tell my brother."
OCTAV. My hard fortune
Subjects me still to your unkind mistakes. 290
But the conditions I have brought are such
You need not blush to take; I love your honor,
Because 'tis mine; it never shall be said,
Octavia's husband was her brother's slave.
Sir, you are free; free, e'en from her you loathe; 295
For, though my brother bargains for your love,
Makes me the price and cement of your peace,
I have a soul like yours; I cannot take
Your love as alms, nor beg what I deserve.

---

[4] I. e., if you confess yourself a man.

I'll tell my brother we are reconciled; 300
He shall draw back his troops, and you shall march
To rule the East; I may be dropped at Athens,
No matter where; I never will complain,
But only keep the barren name of wife,
And rid you of the trouble. 305

VEN. Was ever such a strife of sullen honor!
Both scorn to be obliged.

DOLLA. Oh, she has touched him in the tender'st part;
See how he reddens with despite and shame,
To be outdone in generosity! 310

VEN. See how he winks! how he dries up a tear,
That fain would fall!

ANT. Octavia, I have heard you, and must praise
The greatness of your soul, 314
But cannot yield to what you have proposed:
For I can ne'er be conquered but by love;
And you do all for duty. You would free me,
And would be dropped at Athens; was't not so?

OCTAV. It was, my lord.

ANT. Then I must be obliged
To one who loves me not; who to herself 320
May call me thankless and ungrateful man:—
I'll not endure it; no.

VEN. (*aside*). I am glad it pinches there.

OCTAV. Would you triumph o'er poor Octavia's virtue?
That pride was all I had to bear me up;
That you might think you owed me for your life, 325
And owed it to my duty, not my love.
I have been injured, and my haughty soul
Could brook but ill the man who slights my bed.

ANT. Therefore you love me not.

OCTAV. Therefore, my lord,
I should not love you.

ANT. Therefore you would leave me? 330

OCTAV. And therefore I should leave you —if I could.

DOLLA. Her soul's too great, after such injuries,
To say she loves; and yet she lets you see it.
Her modesty and silence plead her cause.

ANT. O Dollabella, which way shall I turn? 335
I find a secret yielding in my soul;
But Cleopatra, who would die with me,
Must she be left? Pity pleads for Octavia;
But does it not plead more for Cleopatra?

VEN. Justice and pity both plead for Octavia; 340
For Cleopatra, neither.
One would be ruined with you; but she first
Had ruined you; the other, you have ruined,
And yet she would preserve you.
In every thing their merits are unequal. 345

ANT. O my distracted soul!

OCTAV. Sweet Heav'n compose it!—
Come, come, my lord, if I can pardon you,
Methinks you should accept it. Look on these;
Are they not yours? Or stand they thus neglected
As they are mine? Go to him, children, go; 350
Kneel to him, take him by the hand, speak to him;
For you may speak, and he may own you too,
Without a blush; and so he cannot all
His children: go, I say, and pull him to me,
And pull him to yourselves, from that bad woman. 355
You, Agrippina, hang upon his arms;
And you, Antonia, clasp about his waist:
If he will shake you off, if he will dash you
Against the pavement, you must bear it, children; 359
For you are mine, and I was born to suffer.

(*Here the* CHILDREN *go to him, etc.*)

VEN. Was ever sight so moving?—Emperor!

DOLLA. Friend!

OCTAV. Husband!

BOTH CHILDREN. Father!

ANT. I am vanquished; take me,
Octavia; take me, children; share me all.

(*Embracing them*)

I've been a thriftless debtor to your loves, 364
And run out[5] much, in riot, from your stock;
But all shall be amended.

OCTAV. O blest hour!

DOLLA. O happy change!

VEN. My joy stops at my tongue;
But it has found two channels here for one,
And bubbles out above.

ANT. (*to* OCTAVIA). This is thy triumph; lead me where thou wilt; 370
E'en to thy brother's camp.

OCTAV. All there are yours.

Enter ALEXAS *hastily.*

ALEXAS. The queen, my mistress, sir, and yours—

[5]Squandered.

ANT. 'Tis past.—
Octavia, you shall stay this night; to-morrow
Caesar and we are one.

[*Exit leading* OCTAVIA; DOLLABELLA *and the* CHILDREN *follow.*

VEN. There's news for you; run, my officious eunuch, 375
Be sure to be the first; haste forward:
Haste, my dear eunuch, haste. [*Exit*

ALEX. This downright fighting fool, this thick-skulled hero,
This blunt, unthinking instrument of death,
With plain dull virtue has outgone my wit. 380
Pleasure forsook my earli'st infancy;
The luxury of others robbed my cradle,
And ravished thence the promise of a man;
Cast out from nature, disinherited 384
Of what her meanest children claim by kind,[6]
Yet greatness kept me from contempt; that's gone.
Had Cleopatra followed my advice,
Then he had been betrayed who now forsakes.
She dies for love; but she has known its joys:
Gods, is this just, that I, who know no joys,
Must die because she loves? 391

Enter CLEOPATRA, CHARMION, IRAS, *and train.*

O madam, I have seen what blasts my eyes!
Octavia's here!

CLEOP. Peace with that raven's note.
I know it too; and now am in
The pangs of death.

ALEX. You are no more a queen; 395
Egypt is lost.

CLEOP. What tell'st thou me of Egypt?
My life, my soul is lost! Octavia has him!
O fatal name to Cleopatra's love!
My kisses, my embraces, now are hers;
While I— But thou hast seen my rival; speak, 400
Does she deserve this blessing? Is she fair?
Bright as a goddess? And is all perfection
Confined to her? It is. Poor I was made
Of that coarse matter which, when she was finished,
The gods threw by for rubbish. 405

ALEX. She's indeed a very miracle.

CLEOP. Death to my hopes, a miracle!

ALEX. (*bowing*). A miracle;
I mean of goodness; for in beauty, madam,
You make all wonders cease.

CLEOP. I was too rash:
Take this in part of recompense. (*Giving a ring.*) But, oh! 410
I fear thou flatter'st me.

CHARMION. She comes! she's here!

IRAS. Fly, madam, Caesar's sister!

CLEOP. Were she the sister of the thund'rer Jove,
And bore her brother's lightning in her eyes,
Thus would I face my rival. 415

(*Meets* OCTAVIA *with* VENTIDIUS. *Octavia bears up to her. Their trains*[7] *come up on either side*)

OCTAV. I need not ask if you are Cleopatra;
Your haughty carriage—

CLEO. Shows I am a queen;
Nor need I ask you who you are.

OCTAV. A Roman;
A name that makes and can unmake a queen.

CLEOP. Your lord, the man who serves me, is a Roman. 420

OCTAV. He was a Roman till he lost that name
To be a slave in Egypt; but I come
To free him thence.

CLEOP. Peace, peace, my lover's Juno.
When he grew weary of that household-clog,
He chose my easier bonds.

OCTAV. I wonder not 425
Your bonds are easy: you have long been practised
In that lascivious art: he's not the first
For whom you spread your snares: let Caesar[8] witness.

CLEOP. I loved not Caesar; 'twas but gratitude
I paid his love; the worst your malice can 430
Is but to say the greatest of mankind
Has been my slave. The next, but far above him
In my esteem, is he whom law calls yours,
But whom his love made mine.

OCTAV. (*coming up close to her*). I would view nearer
That face which has so long usurped my right, 435
To find th'inevitable charms that catch
Mankind so sure, that ruined my dear lord.

CLEOP. O, you do well to search; for had you known
But half these charms, you had not lost his heart.

OCTAV. Far be their knowledge from a Roman lady, 440
Far from a modest wife! Shame of our sex,

---

[6]By nature.

[7]I. e., attendants. [8]Julius Caesar.

Dost thou not blush to own those black endearments,
That make sin pleasing?

CLEOP. You may blush, who want 'em.
If bounteous nature, if indulgent Heav'n
Have giv'n me charms to please the bravest man, 445
Should I not thank 'em? Should I be ashamed,
And not be proud? I am, that he has loved me;
And, when I love not him, Heav'n change this face
For one like that.

OCTAV. Thou lov'st him not so well.

CLEOP. I love him better, and deserve him more. 450

OCTAV. You do not; cannot; you have been his ruin.
Who made him cheap at Rome, but Cleopatra?
Who made him scorned abroad, but Cleopatra?
At Actium who betrayed him? Cleopatra.
Who made his children orphans, and poor me 455
A wretched widow? Only Cleopatra.

CLEOP. Yet she who loves him best is Cleopatra.
If you have suffered, I have suffered more.
You bear the specious title of a wife,
To gild your cause, and draw the pitying world 460
To favor it; the world contemns poor me.
For I have lost my honor, lost my fame,
And stained the glory of my royal house,
And all to bear the branded name of mistress.
There wants but life, and that too I would lose 465
For him I love.

OCTAV. Be't so, then; take thy wish.
[*Exit cum suis.*[9]

CLEOP. And 'tis my wish,
Now he is lost for whom alone I lived.
My sight grows dim, and every object dances
And swims before me in the maze of death.
My spirits, while they were opposed, kept up; 471
They could not sink beneath a rival's scorn;
But now she's gone, they faint.

ALEX. Mine have had leisure
To recollect their strength, and furnish counsel
To ruin her who else must ruin you.

CLEOP. Vain promiser! 475
Lead me, my Charmion; nay, your hand too, Iras.
My grief has weight enough to sink you both.
Conduct me to some solitary chamber,
And draw the curtains round;
Then leave me to myself, to take alone 480
My fill of grief:
There I till death will his unkindness weep;
As harmless infants moan themselves asleep. [*Exeunt.*

ACT IV

ANTONY, DOLLABELLA.

DOLLABELLA. Why would you shift it from yourself on me?
Can you not tell her you must part?

ANTONY. I cannot.
I could pull out an eye and bid it go,
And t'other should not weep. O Dollabella,
How many deaths are in this word, "Depart"! 5
I dare not trust my tongue to tell her so:
One look of hers would thaw me into tears,
And I should melt till I were lost again.

DOLLA. Then let Ventidius;
He's rough by nature.

ANT. Oh, he'll speak too harshly; 10
He'll kill her with the news; thou, only thou.

DOLLA. Nature has cast me in so soft a mold,
That but to hear a story feigned for pleasure
Of some sad lover's death, moistens my eyes
And robs me of my manhood. I should speak 15
So faintly, with such fear to grieve her heart,
She'd not believe it earnest.

ANT. Therefore—therefore
Thou only, thou art fit; think thyself me;
And when thou speak'st (but let it first be long), 19
Take off the edge from every sharper sound,
And let our parting be as gently made
As other loves begin; wilt thou do this?

DOLLA. What you have said so sinks into my soul,
That, if I must speak, I shall speak just so.

ANT. I leave you then to your sad task; farewell. 25
I sent her word to meet you. (*Goes to the door, and comes back*) I forgot;
Let her be told, I'll make her peace with mine:
Her crown and dignity shall be preserved,

[9] *Exit* with her train.

If I have power with Caesar.—Oh, be sure
To think on that.

DOLLA. Fear not, I will remember. 30

(ANTONY *goes again to the door, and comes back*)

ANT. And tell her, too, how much I was constrained;
I did not this but with extremest force;
Desire her not to hate my memory,
For I still cherish hers;—insist on that.

DOLLA. Trust me, I'll not forget it.

ANT. Then that's all. 35

(*Goes out, and returns again*)

Wilt thou forgive my fondness this once more?
Tell her, though we shall never meet again,
If I should hear she took another love
The news would break my heart.—Now I must go;
For every time I have returned, I feel 40
My soul more tender; and my next command
Would be to bid her stay, and ruin both.

[*Exit.*

DOLLA. Men are but children of a larger growth;
Our appetites as apt to change as theirs,
And full as craving too, and full as vain; 45
And yet the soul, shut up in her dark room,
Viewing so clear abroad, at home sees nothing;
But, like a mole in earth, busy and blind,
Works all her folly up, and casts it outward
To the world's open view; thus I discovered,
And blamed the love of ruined Antony; 51
Yet wish that I were he, to be so ruined.

Enter VENTIDIUS *above.*

VENTIDIUS. Alone? and talking to himself? concerned too?
Perhaps my guess is right; he loved her once,
And may pursue it still.

DOLLA. O friendship! friendship! 55
Ill canst thou answer this; and reason, worse:
Unfaithful in th'attempt; hopeless to win;
And if I win, undone: mere madness all.
And yet th'occasion's fair. What injury
To him, to wear the robe which he throws by! 60

VEN. None, none at all. This happens as I wish,
To ruin her yet more with Antony.

Enter CLEOPATRA, *talking with* ALEXAS; CHARMION *and* IRAS *on the other side.*

DOLLA. She comes! What charms has sorrow on that face!
Sorrow seems pleased to dwell with so much sweetness;
Yet, now and then, a melancholy smile 65
Breaks loose, like lightning in a winter's night,
And shows a moment's day.

VEN. If she should love him too! Her eunuch there?
That porpoise bodes ill weather. Draw, draw nearer,
Sweet devil, that I may hear.

ALEXAS. Believe me; try 70

(DOLLABELLA *goes over to* CHARMION *and* IRAS; *seems to talk with them.*)

To make him jealous; jealousy is like
A polished glass held to the lips when life's in doubt;
If there be breath, 'twill catch the damp, and show it.

CLEOPATRA. I grant you, jealousy's a proof of love,
But 'tis a weak and unavailing med'cine; 75
It puts out the disease,[1] and makes it show,
But has no power to cure.

ALEX. 'Tis your last remedy, and strongest too.
And then this Dollabella, who so fit
To practise on? He's handsome, valiant, young, 80
And looks as he were laid for nature's bait
To catch weak women's eyes.
He stands already more than half suspected
Of loving you; the least kind word or glance
You give this youth will kindle him with love: 85
Then, like a burning vessel set adrift,
You'll send him down amain[2] before the wind,
To fire the heart of jealous Antony.

CLEOP. Can I do this? Ah, no; my love's so true
That I can neither hide it where it is, 90
Nor show it where it is not. Nature meant me
A wife; a silly, harmless, household dove,
Fond without art and kind without deceit;
But fortune, that has made a mistress of me,
Has thrust me out to the wide world, unfurnished 95
Of falsehood to be happy.

ALEX. Force yourself.
Th'event[3] will be, your lover will return
Doubly desirous to possess the good
Which once he feared to lose.

CLEOP. I must attempt it;
But oh, with what regret! 100

[*Exit* ALEXAS.] (*She comes up to* DOLLABELLA.)

---

[1]It brings the disease to the surface.
[2]In all haste. [3]Outcome.

VEN. So, now the scene draws near; they're in my reach.

CLEOP. (*to* DOLLA.). Discoursing with my women! Might not I
Share in your entertainment?

CHARMION. You have been
The subject of it, madam.

CLEOP. How, and how?

IRAS. Such praises of your beauty!

CLEOP. Mere poetry. 105
Your Roman wits, your Gallus and Tibullus,[4]
Have taught you this from Cytheris and Delia.

DOLLA. Those Roman wits have never been in Egypt;
Cytheris and Delia else had been unsung:
I, who have seen—had I been born a poet, 110
Should choose a nobler name.

CLEOP. You flatter me.
But 'tis your nation's vice; all of your country
Are flatterers, and all false. Your friend's like you.
I'm sure, he sent you not to speak these words.

DOLLA. No, madam; yet he sent me—

CLEOP. Well, he sent you— 115

DOLLA. Of a less pleasing errand.

CLEOP. How less pleasing?
Less to yourself, or me?

DOLLA. Madam, to both;
For you must mourn, and I must grieve to cause it.

CLEOP. You, Charmion, and your fellow, stand at distance.—
(*Aside*) Hold up, my spirits.—Well, now your mournful matter; 120
For I'm prepared, perhaps can guess it too.

DOLLA. I wish you would; for 'tis a thankless office
To tell ill news; and I, of all your sex,
Most fear displeasing you.

CLEOP. Of all your sex,
I soonest could forgive you, if you should. 125

VEN. Most delicate advances! Woman! woman!
Dear, damned, inconstant sex!

CLEOP. In the first place,
I am to be forsaken; is't not so?

DOLLA. I wish I could not answer to that question.

CLEOP. Then pass it o'er, because it troubles you: 130
I should have been more grieved another time.
Next, I'm to lose my kingdom—Farewell, Egypt!
Yet is there any more?

DOLLA. Madam, I fear
Your too deep sense of grief has turned your reason.

CLEOP. No, no, I'm not run mad; I can bear fortune: 135
And love may be expelled by other love,
As poisons are by poisons.

DOLLA. You o'erjoy me, madam,
To find your griefs so moderately borne;
You've heard the worst; all are not false like him. 140

CLEOP. No; Heav'n forbid they should.

DOLLA. Some men are constant.

CLEOP. And constancy deserves reward, that's certain.

DOLLA. Deserves it not; but give it leave to hope.

VEN. I'll swear thou hast my leave. I have enough: 144
But how to manage this! Well, I'll consider. [*Exit.*

DOLLA. I came prepared
To tell you heavy news, news which I thought
Would fright the blood from your pale cheeks to hear;
But you have met it with a cheerfulness
That makes my task more easy; and my tongue, 150
Which on another's message was employed,
Would gladly speak its own.

CLEOP. Hold, Dollabella.
First tell me, were you chosen by my lord?
Or sought you this employment?

DOLLA. He picked me out; and, as his bosom-friend, 155
He charged me with his words.

CLEOP. The message then
I know was tender, and each accent smooth,
To mollify that rugged word, "Depart."

DOLLA. Oh, you mistake; he chose the harshest words; 159
With fiery eyes, and with contracted brows,
He coined his face in the severest stamp;
And fury shook his fabric, like an earthquake;
He heaved for vent, and burst like bellowing Etna,
In sounds scarce human—"Hence, away for ever;
Let her begone, the blot of my renown, 165
And bane of all my hopes!

(*All the time of this speech,* CLEOPATRA *seems more and more concerned, till she sinks quite down*)

[4]Two Latin writers of love poetry in the first century B. C.

Let her be driv'n as far as men can think
From man's commerce! she'll poison to the center."

CLEOP. Oh, I can bear no more!

DOLLA. Help, help!—O wretch! O curséd, curséd wretch! 170
What have I done!

CHAR. Help, chafe her temples, Iras.

IRAS. Bend, bend her forward quickly.

CHAR. Heav'n be praised,
She comes again.

CLEOP. Oh, let him not approach me.
Why have you brought me back to this loathed being,
Th'abode of falsehood, violated vows, 175
And injured love? For pity, let me go;
For if there be a place of long repose,
I'm sure I want it. My disdainful lord
Can never break that quiet, nor awake
The sleeping soul with hollowing in my tomb 180
Such words as fright her hence.—Unkind, unkind!

DOLLA. *(kneeling)*. Believe me; 'tis against myself I speak;
That sure desires belief; I injured him:
My friend ne'er spoke those words. Oh, had you seen
How often he came back, and every time 185
With something more obliging and more kind,
To add to what he said; what dear farewells;
How almost vanquished by his love he parted
And leaned to what unwillingly he left!
I, traitor as I was, for love of you 190
(But what can you not do, who made me false?)
I forged that lie; for whose forgiveness kneels
This self-accused, self-punished criminal.

CLEOP. With how much ease believe we what we wish!
Rise, Dollabella; if you have been guilty, 195
I have contributed, and too much love
Has made me guilty too.
Th'advance of kindness, which I made, was feigned,
To call back fleeting love by jealousy;
But 'twould not last. Oh, rather let me lose, 200
Than so ignobly trifle with his heart.

DOLLA. I find your breast fenced round from human reach,
Transparent as a rock of solid crystal;
Seen through, but never pierced. My friend, my friend!
What endless treasure hast thou thrown away; 205
And scattered, like an infant, in the ocean,
Vain sums of wealth, which none can gather thence!

CLEOP. Could you not beg
An hour's admittance to his private ear?
Like one who wanders through long barren wilds 210
And yet foreknows no hospitable inn
Is near to succor hunger, eats his fill
Before his painful march;
So would I feed a while my famished eyes
Before we part; for I have far to go, 215
If death be far, and never must return.

VENTIDIUS *with* OCTAVIA, *behind*.

VEN. From hence you may discover—
Oh, sweet, sweet!
Would you indeed? the pretty hand in earnest?

DOLLA. I will, for this reward.—*(Takes her hand.)* Draw it not back.
'Tis all I e'er will beg.

VEN. They turn upon us. 220

OCTAVIA. What quick eyes has guilt!

VEN. Seem not to have observed 'em, and go on.

They enter.

DOLLA. Saw you the emperor, Ventidius?

VEN. No,
I sought him; but I heard that he was private,
None with him but Hipparchus, his freedman. 225

DOLLA. Know you his bus'ness?

VEN. Giving him instructions,
And letters to his brother Caesar.

DOLLA. Well,
He must be found.

[*Exeunt* DOLLABELLA *and* CLEOPATRA.

OCTAV. Most glorious impudence!

VEN. She looked, methought,
As she would say, "Take your old man, Octavia; 230
Thank you, I'm better here." Well, but what use
Make we of this discovery?

OCTAV. Let it die.

VEN. I pity Dollabella; but she's dangerous:
Her eyes have power beyond Thessalian charms,
To draw the moon from Heav'n; for eloquence, 235
The sea-green Sirens taught her voice their flatt'ry;

And while she speaks, night steals upon the day,
Unmarked of those that hear; then she's so charming,
Age buds at sight of her, and swells to youth:
The holy priests gaze on her when she smiles; 240
And with heaved hands, forgetting gravity,
They bless her wanton eyes; even I, who hate her,
With a malignant joy behold such beauty:
And, while I curse, desire it. Antony
Must needs have some remains of passion still, 245
Which may ferment into a worse relapse,
If now not fully cured. I know, this minute,
With Caesar he's endeavoring her peace.

OCTAV. You have prevailed; but for a further purpose (*Walks off*)
I'll prove[5] how he will relish this discovery. 250
What, make a strumpet's peace! it swells my heart:
It must not, sha' not be.

VEN. His guards appear.
Let me begin, and you shall second me.

Enter ANTONY.

ANT. Octavia, I was looking you, my love;
What, are your letters ready? I have giv'n 255
My last instructions.

OCTAV. Mine, my lord, are written.

ANT. Ventidius. (*Drawing him aside*)

VEN. My lord?

ANT. A word in private.
When saw you Dollabella?

VEN. Now, my lord,
He parted hence, and Cleopatra with him.

ANT. Speak softly.—'Twas by my command he went, 260
To bear my last farewell.

VEN. (*aloud*). It looked indeed
Like your farewell.

ANT. More softly.—My farewell?
What secret meaning have you in those words
Of "My farewell"? He did it by my order.

VEN. (*aloud*). Then he obeyed your order. I suppose 265
You bid him do it with all gentleness,
All kindness, and all—love.

ANT. How she mourned,
The poor forsaken creature!

VEN. She took it as she ought; she bore your parting
As she did Caesar's, as she would another's, 270
Were a new love to come.

ANT. (*aloud*). Thou dost belie her;
Most basely and maliciously belie her.

VEN. I thought not to displease you; I have done.

OCTAV. (*coming up*). You seem disturbed, my lord.

ANT. A very trifle.
Retire, my love.

VEN. It was indeed a trifle. 275
He sent—

ANT. (*angrily*). No more. Look how thou disobey'st me;
Thy life shall answer it.

OCTAV. Then 'tis no trifle.

VEN. (*to* OCTAVIA). 'Tis less; a very nothing; you too saw it,
As well as I, and therefore 'tis no secret.

ANT. She saw it!

VEN. Yes; she saw young Dollabella— 280

ANT. Young Dollabella!

VEN. Young, I think him young,
And handsome too; and so do others think him.
But what of that? He went by your command,
Indeed, 'tis probable, with some kind message;
For she received it graciously; she smiled; 285
And then he grew familiar with her hand,
Squeezed it, and worried it with ravenous kisses;
She blushed, and sighed, and smiled, and blushed again;
At last she took occasion to talk softly,
And brought her cheek up close, and leaned on his; 290
At which he whispered kisses back on hers;
And then she cried aloud that constancy
Should be rewarded.

OCTAV. This I saw and heard.

ANT. What woman was it whom you heard and saw
So playful with my friend? 295
Not Cleopatra?

VEN. Even she, my lord.

ANT. My Cleopatra?

VEN. Your Cleopatra;
Dollabella's Cleopatra; every man's Cleopatra.

ANT. Thou liest.

VEN. I do not lie, my lord.

[5] Test.

Is this so strange? Should mistresses be left, 300
And not provide against a time of change?
You know she's not much used to lonely nights.

ANT. I'll think no more on't.
I know 'tis false, and see the plot betwixt you.
You needed not have gone this way, Octavia. 305
What harms it you that Cleopatra's just?
She's mine no more. I see, and I forgive:
Urge it no farther, love.

OCTAV. Are you concerned,
That she's found false?

ANT. I should be, were it so;
For, though 'tis past, I would not that the world 310
Should tax my former choice, that I loved one
Of so light note; but I forgive you both.

VEN. What has my age deserved that you should think
I would abuse your ears with perjury?
If Heav'n be true, she's false.

ANT. Though Heav'n and earth 315
Should witness it, I'll not believe her tainted.

VEN. I'll bring you, then, a witness
From Hell, to prove her so.—Nay, go not back,
(Seeing ALEXAS *just entering, and starting back)*
For stay you must and shall.

ALEX. What means my lord?

VEN. To make you do what most you hate,—speak truth. 320
You are of Cleopatra's private counsel,
Of her bed-counsel, her lascivious hours;
Are conscious of each nightly change she makes,
And watch her, as Chaldeans do the moon,
Can tell what signs she passes through, what day. 325

ALEX. My noble lord!

VEN. My most illustrious pander,
No fine speech, no cadence, no turned periods,
But a plain homespun truth, is what I ask;
I did, myself, o'erhear your queen make love
To Dollabella. Speak; for I will know 330
By your confession what more passed betwixt 'em;
How near the bus'ness draws to your employment;
And when the happy hour.

ANT. Speak truth, Alexas; whether it offend
Or please Ventidius, care not; justify 335
Thy injured queen from malice; dare his worst.

OCTAV. *(aside)*. See how he gives him courage! how he fears
To find her false! and shuts his eyes to truth,
Willing to be misled!

ALEX. As far as love may plead for woman's frailty, 340
Urged by desert and greatness of the lover,
So far, divine Octavia, may my queen
Stand e'en excused to you for loving him
Who is your lord; so far, from brave Ventidius,
May her past actions hope a fair report. 345

ANT. 'Tis well, and truly spoken: mark, Ventidius.

ALEX. To you, most noble emperor, her strong passion
Stands not excused, but wholly justified.
Her beauty's charms alone, without her crown,
From Ind and Meroe[6] drew the distant vows 350
Of sighing kings; and at her feet were laid
The scepters of the earth, exposed on heaps
To choose where she would reign;
She thought a Roman only could deserve her,
And of all Romans only Antony; 355
And to be less than wife to you, disdained
Their lawful passion.

ANT. 'Tis but truth.

ALEX. And yet, though love, and your unmatched desert,
Have drawn her from the due regard of honor,
At last Heav'n opened her unwilling eyes 360
To see the wrongs she offered fair Octavia,
Whose holy bed she lawlessly usurped;
The sad effects of this improsperous war
Confirmed those pious thoughts.

VEN. *(aside)*. O, wheel you there?
Observe him now; the man begins to mend, 365
And talk substantial reason. Fear not, eunuch;
The emperor has giv'n thee leave to speak.

ALEX. Else had I never dared t'offend his ears
With what the last necessity has urged
On my forsaken mistress; yet I must not 370
Presume to say, her heart is wholly altered.

ANT. No, dare not for thy life; I charge thee dare not
Pronounce that fatal word!

[6]A kingdom of Ethiopia.

OCTAV. *(aside)*. Must I bear this?
Good Heav'n, afford me patience.
VEN. On, sweet eunuch; my dear half man, proceed. 375
ALEX. Yet Dollabella
Has loved her long; he, next my god-like lord,
Deserves her best; and should she meet his passion,
Rejected, as she is, by him she loved—
ANT. Hence from my sight! for I can bear no more; 380
Let Furies drag thee quick to Hell; let all
The longer damned have rest; each torturing hand
Do thou employ, till Cleopatra comes;
Then join thou too, and help to torture her!
[*Exit* ALEXAS, *thrust out by* ANTONY.
OCTAV. 'Tis not well, 385
Indeed, my lord, 'tis much unkind to me,
To show this passion, this extreme concernment,
For an abandoned, faithless prostitute.
ANT. Octavia, leave me; I am much disordered;
Leave me, I say.
OCTAV. My lord?
ANT. I bid you leave me. 390
VEN. Obey him, madam; best withdraw a while,
And see how this will work.
OCTAV. Wherein have I offended you, my lord,
That I am bid to leave you? Am I false,
Or infamous? Am I a Cleopatra? 395
Were I she,
Base as she is, you would not bid me leave you;
But hang upon my neck, take slight excuses,
And fawn upon my falsehood.
ANT. 'Tis too much,
Too much, Octavia; I am pressed with sorrows 400
Too heavy to be borne; and you add more;
I would retire, and recollect what's left
Of man within, to aid me.
OCTAV. You would mourn,
In private, for your love, who has betrayed you.
You did but half return to me; your kindness 405
Lingered behind with her. I hear, my lord,
You make conditions for her,
And would include her treaty. Wondrous proofs
Of love to me!
ANT. Are you my friend, Ventidius?
Or are you turned a Dollabella too, 410
And let this Fury loose?
VEN. Oh, be advised,
Sweet madam, and retire.
OCTAV. Yes, I will go; but never to return.
You shall no more be haunted with this Fury.
My lord, my lord, love will not always last, 415
When urged with long unkindness and disdain:
Take her again whom you prefer to me;
She stays but to be called. Poor cozened man!
Let a feigned parting give her back your heart,
Which a feigned love first got; for injured me, 420
Though my just sense of wrongs forbid my stay,
My duty shall be yours.
To the dear pledges of our former love
My tenderness and care shall be transferred,
And they shall cheer, by turns, my widowed nights; 425
To take my last farewell; for I despair
To have you whole, and scorn to take you half. [*Exit.*
VEN. I combat Heav'n, which blasts my best designs:
My last attempt must be to win her back;
But oh! I fear in vain. [*Exit.*
ANT. Why was I framed with this plain, honest heart, 431
Which knows not to disguise its griefs and weakness,
But bears its workings outward to the world?
I should have kept the mighty anguish in,
And forced a smile at Cleopatra's falsehood; 435
Octavia had believed it, and had stayed.
But I am made a shallow-forded stream,
Seen to the bottom: all my clearness scorned,
And all my faults exposed.—See where he comes,

Enter DOLLABELLA.

Who has profaned the sacred name of friend, 440
And worn it into vileness!
With how secure a brow, and specious form,
He guilds the secret villain! Sure that face
Was meant for honesty; but Heav'n mismatched it,

And furnished treason out with nature's pomp, 445
To make its work more easy.
DOLLA. O my friend!
ANT. Well, Dollabella, you performed my message?
DOLLA. I did, unwillingly.
ANT. Unwillingly?
Was it so hard for you to bear our parting?
You should have wished it.
DOLLA. Why?
ANT. Because you love me. 450
And she received my message with as true,
With as unfeigned a sorrow as you brought it?
DOLLA. She loves you, e'en to madness.
ANT. Oh, I know it.
You, Dollabella, do not better know
How much she loves me. And should I 455
Forsake this beauty, this all-perfect creature?
DOLLA. I could not, were she mine.
ANT. And yet you first
Persuaded me; how come you altered since?
DOLLA. I said at first I was not fit to go;
I could not hear her sighs and see her tears, 460
But pity must prevail; and so, perhaps,
It may again with you; for I have promised,
That she should take her last farewell; and, see,
She comes to claim my word.

Enter CLEOPATRA.

ANT. False Dollabella!
DOLLA. What's false, my lord?
ANT. Why, Dollabella's false, 465
And Cleopatra's false; both false and faithless.
Draw near, you well-joined wickedness, you serpents,
Whom I have in my kindly bosom warmed
Till I am stung to death.
DOLLA. My lord, have I
Deserved to be thus used?
CLEOP. Can Heav'n prepare 470
A newer torment? Can it find a curse
Beyond our separation?
ANT. Yes, if fate
Be just, much greater; Heav'n should be ingenious
In punishing such crimes. The rolling stone
And gnawing vulture[7] were slight pains, invented 475
When Jove was young, and no examples known
Of mighty ills; but you have ripened sin
To such a monstrous growth, 'twill pose[8] the gods
To find an equal torture. Two, two such!—
Oh, there's no farther name,—two such! to me, 480
To me, who locked my soul within your breasts,
Had no desires, no joys, no life, but you;
When half the globe was mine, I gave it you
In dowry with my heart; I had no use,
No fruit of all, but you; a friend and mistress 485
Was what the world could give. O Cleopatra!
O Dollabella! how could you betray
This tender heart, which with an infant-fondness
Lay lulled betwixt your bosoms, and there slept,
Secure of injured faith?
DOLLA. If she has wronged you, 490
Heav'n, Hell, and you revenge it.
ANT. If she wronged me,
Thou wouldst evade thy part of guilt; but swear
Thou lov'st not her.
DOLLA. Not so as I love you.
ANT. Not so! Swear, swear, I say, thou dost not love her.
DOLLA. No more than friendship will allow.
ANT. No more? 495
Friendship allows thee nothing; thou art perjured—
And yet thou didst not swear thou lov'dst her not;
But not so much, no more. O trifling hypocrite,
Who dar'st not own to her, thou dost not love,
Nor own to me, thou dost! Ventidius heard it; 500
Octavia saw it.
CLEOP. They are enemies.
ANT. Alexas is not so: he, he confessed it;
He who next Hell best knew it, he avowed it.
(*To* DOLLA.) Why do I seek a proof beyond yourself?
You, whom I sent to bear my last farewell, 505
Returned to plead her stay.
DOLLA. What shall I answer?
If to have loved be guilt, then I have sinned;

[7]The stone rolled by Sisyphus and the vulture which gnawed Prometheus.

[8]Puzzle.

But if to have repented of that love
Can wash away my crime, I have repented.
Yet, if I have offended past forgiveness, 510
Let not her suffer; she is innocent.
CLEOP. Ah, what will not a woman do, who loves?
What means will she refuse, to keep that heart
Where all her joys are placed? 'Twas I encouraged,
'Twas I blew up the fire that scorched his soul, 515
To make you jealous, and by that regain you.
But all in vain; I could not counterfeit:
In spite of all the dams my love broke o'er,
And drowned my heart again; fate took th'occasion;
And thus one minute's feigning has destroyed 520
My whole life's truth.
ANT. Thin cobweb arts of falsehood;
Seen, and broke through at first.
DOLLA. Forgive your mistress.
CLEOP. Forgive your friend.
ANT. You have convinced yourselves;
You plead each other's cause; what witness have you,
That you but meant to raise my jealousy? 525
CLEOP. Ourselves, and Heaven.
ANT. Guilt witnesses for guilt. Hence, love and friendship!
You have no longer place in human breasts,
These two have driv'n you out. Avoid my sight;
I would not kill the man whom I have loved, 530
And cannot hurt the woman; but avoid me;
I do not know how long I can be tame;
For if I stay one minute more to think
How I am wronged, my justice and revenge
Will cry so loud within me, that my pity 535
Will not be heard for either.
DOLLA. Heav'n has but
Our sorrow for our sins; and then delights
To pardon erring man; sweet mercy seems
Its darling attribute, which limits justice;
As if there were degrees in infinite, 540
And infinite would rather want perfection
Than punish to extent.[9]
ANT. I can forgive
A foe; but not a mistress and a friend.
Treason is there in its most horrid shape
Where trust is greatest, and the soul resigned 545
Is stabbed by its own guards: I'll hear no more;
Hence from my sight for ever!
CLEOP. How? for ever!
I cannot go one moment from your sight,
And must I go for ever?
My joys, my only joys, are centered here: 550
What place have I to go to? my own kingdom?
That I have lost for you; or to the Romans?
They hate me for your sake: or must I wander
The wide world o'er, a helpless, banished woman,
Banished for love of you; banished from you? 555
Ay, there's the banishment! Oh, hear me; hear me,
With strictest justice; for I beg no favor;
And if I have offended you, then kill me,
But do not banish me.
ANT. I must not hear you.
I have a fool within me takes your part; 560
But honor stops my ears.
CLEOP. For pity hear me!
Would you cast off a slave who followed you?
Who crouched beneath your spurn?—He has no pity!
See if he gives one tear to my departure;
One look, one kind farewell; Oh iron heart! 565
Let all the gods look down, and judge betwixt us
If he did ever love!
ANT. No more; Alexas!
DOLLA. A perjured villain!
ANT. (*to* CLEOP.) Your Alexas; yours.
CLEOP. O, 'twas his plot; his ruinous design,
T'engage you in my love by jealousy. 570
Hear him; confront him with me; let him speak.
ANT. I have; I have.
CLEOP. And if he clear me not—
ANT. Your creature! one who hangs upon your smiles!
Watches your eye, to say or to unsay
Whate'er you please! I am not to be moved. 575
CLEOP. Then must we part? Farewell, my cruel lord!
Th'appearance is against me; and I go,
Unjustified, for ever from your sight.
How I have loved, you know; how yet I love,
My only comfort is, I know myself: 580
I love you more, e'en now you are unkind,

[9] I. e., strictly, or to the fullest extent.

Than when you loved me most; so well, so truly,
I'll never strive against it; but die pleased,
To think you once were mine.

ANT. Good Heav'n, they weep at parting! 585
Must I weep too? that calls 'em innocent.
I must not weep; and yet I must, to think
That I must not forgive.—
Live, but live wretched; 'tis but just you should,
Who made me so; live from each other's sight; 590
Let me not hear you meet; set all the earth
And all the seas betwixt your sundered loves;
View nothing common but the sun and skies;
Now, all take several ways;
And each your own sad fate, with mine, deplore; 595
That you were false, and I could trust no more. [*Exeunt severally.*

ACT V

CLEOPATRA, CHARMION, IRAS.

CHARMION. Be juster, Heav'n; such virtue punished thus
Will make us think that Chance rules all above,
And shuffles with a random hand the lots
Which man is forced to draw.

CLEOPATRA. I could tear out these eyes, that gained his heart 5
And had not power to keep it. Oh, the curse
Of doting on, e'en when I find it dotage!
Bear witness, gods, you heard him bid me go;
You, whom he mocked with imprecating vows
Of promised faith!—I'll die; I will not bear it. 10
You may hold me—
(She pulls out her dagger, and they hold her)
But I can keep my breath; I can die inward,
And choke this love.

Enter ALEXAS.

IRAS. Help, O Alexas, help!
The queen grows desperate; her soul struggles in her
With all the agonies of love and rage, 15
And strives to force its passage.

CLEOP. Let me go.
Art thou there, traitor!—Oh,
Oh, for a little breath, to vent my rage,
Give, give me way, and let me loose upon him.

ALEXAS. Yes, I deserve it, for my ill-timed truth. 20
Was it for me to prop
The ruins of a falling majesty?
To place myself beneath the mighty flaw,
Thus to be crushed, and pounded into atoms,
By its o'erwhelming weight? 'Tis too presuming 25
For subjects to preserve that wilful power
Which courts its own destruction.

CLEOP. I would reason
More calmly with you. Did you not o'errule
And force my plain, direct, and open love
Into these crooked paths of jealousy? 30
Now, what's th'event? Octavia is removed;
But Cleopatra's banished. Thou, thou, villain,
Hast pushed my boat to open sea, to prove,[1]
At my sad cost, if thou canst steer it back.
It cannot be; I'm lost too far; I'm ruined; 35
Hence, thou impostor, traitor, monster, devil!—
I can no more; thou, and my griefs, have sunk
Me down so low that I want voice to curse thee.

ALEX. Suppose some shipwrecked seaman near the shore,
Dropping and faint with climbing up the cliff; 40
If from above some charitable hand
Pull him to safety, hazarding himself,
To draw the other's weight; would he look back,
And curse him for his pains? The case is yours;
But one step more, and you have gained the height. 45

CLEOP. Sunk, never more to rise.

ALEX. Octavia's gone, and Dollabella banished.
Believe me, madam, Antony is yours.
His heart was never lost, but started off
To jealousy, love's last retreat and covert; 50
Where it lies hid in shades, watchful in silence,
And list'ning for the sound that calls it back.
Some other, any man ('tis so advanced),
May perfect this unfinished work, which I
(Unhappy only to myself) have left 55
So easy to his hand.

CLEOP. Look well thou do't; else—

[1] I. e., to see.

ALEX. Else, what your silence threatens.—Antony
Is mounted up the Pharos;[2] from whose turret
He stands surveying our Egyptian galleys.
Engaged with Caesar's fleet. Now death or conquest! 60
If the first happen, fate acquits my promise;
If we o'ercome, the conqueror is yours.
(A distant shout within)

CHAR. Have comfort, madam; did you mark that shout? *(Second shout nearer)*

IRAS. Hark! they redouble it.

ALEX. 'Tis from the port.
The loudness shows it near; good news, kind heavens! 65

CLEOP. Osiris make it so!

Enter SERAPION.

SERAPION. Where, where's the queen?

ALEX. How frightfully the holy coward stares
As if not yet recovered of th'assault,
When all his gods, and, what's more dear to him,
His offerings, were at stake.

SERAP. O horror, horror! 70
Egypt has been; our latest hour is come:
The queen of nations, from her ancient seat,
Is sunk for ever in the dark abyss;
Time has unrolled her glories to the last,
And now closed up the volume.

CLEOP. Be more plain: 75
Say, whence thou com'st (though fate is in thy face,
Which from thy haggard eyes looks wildly out,
And threatens ere thou speak'st).

SERAP. I came from Pharos;
From viewing (spare me, and imagine it)
Our land's last hope, your navy—

CLEOP. Vanquished?

SERAP. No; 80
They fought not.

CLEOP. Then they fled.

SERAP. Nor that. I saw,
With Antony, your well-appointed fleet
Row out; and thrice he waved his hand on high,
And thrice with cheerful cries they shouted back;
'Twas then false Fortune, like a fawning strumpet, 85
About to leave the bankrupt prodigal,
With a dissembled smile would kiss at parting,
And flatter to the last; the well-timed oars,
Now dipped from every bank, now smoothly run
To meet the foe; and soon indeed they met, 90
But not as foes. In few,[3] we saw their caps
On either side thrown up; th'Egyptian galleys,
(Received like friends) passed through, and fell behind
The Roman rear; and now, they all come forward,
And ride within the port.

CLEOP. Enough, Serapion; 95
I've heard my doom.—This needed not, you gods:
When I lost Antony, your work was done;
'Tis but superfluous malice.—Where's my lord?
How bears he this last blow?

SERAP. His fury cannot be expressed by words: 100
Thrice he attempted headlong to have fallen
Full on his foes, and aimed at Caesar's galley;
Withheld, he raves on you; cries he's betrayed.
Should he now find you—

ALEX. Shun him; seek your safety,
Till you can clear your innocence.

CLEOP. I'll stay. 105

ALEX. You must not; haste you to your monument,
While I make speed to Caesar.

CLEOP. Caesar! No,
I have no business with him.

ALEX. I can work him
To spare your life, and let this madman perish.

CLEOP. Base fawning wretch! wouldst thou betray him too? 110
Hence from my sight! I will not hear a traitor;
'Twas thy design brought all this ruin on us;
Serapion, thou art honest; counsel me;
But haste, each moment's precious.

SERAP. Retire; you must not yet see Antony. 115
He who began this mischief,
'Tis just he tempt the danger; let him clear you;
And, since he offered you his servile tongue,
To gain a poor precarious life from Caesar,
Let him expose that fawning eloquence, 120
And speak to Antony.

ALEX. O heavens! I dare not;
I meet my certain death.

---

[2]Lighthouse.

[3]In few words.

CLEOP. Slave, thou deserv'st it.—
Not that I fear my lord, will I avoid him;
I know him noble: when he banished me,
And thought me false, he scorned to take my life; 125
But I'll be justified, and then die with him.
ALEX. O pity me, and let me follow you.
CLEOP. To death, if thou stir hence. Speak, if thou canst,
Now for thy life, which basely thou wouldst save;
While mine I prize at—this! Come, good Serapion. 130
[*Exeunt* CLEOPATRA, SERAPION, CHARMION *and* IRAS.
ALEX. O that I less could fear to lose this being,
Which, like a snow-ball in my coward hand,
The more 'tis grasped, the faster melts away.
Poor reason! what a wretched aid art thou!
For still, in spite of thee, 135
These two long lovers, soul and body, dread
Their final separation. Let me think:
What can I say to save myself from death?
No matter what becomes of Cleopatra.
ANT. *(within)*. Which way? where?
VEN. *(within)*. This leads to th'monument. 140
ALEX. Ah me! I hear him; yet I'm unprepared;
My gift of lying's gone;
And this court-devil, which I so oft have raised,
Forsakes me at my need. I dare not stay;
Yet cannot far go hence. [*Exit*. 145

Enter ANTONY *and* VENTIDIUS.

ANTONY. O happy Caesar! thou hast men to lead:
Think not 'tis thou hast conquered Antony;
But Rome has conquered Egypt. I'm betrayed.
VENTIDIUS. Curse on this treach'rous train!
Their soil and Heav'n infect 'em all with baseness, 150
And their young souls come tainted to the world
With the first breath they draw.
ANT. Th'original villain sure no god created;
He was a bastard of the sun, by Nile,
Aped into man; with all his mother's mud 155
Crusted about his soul.
VEN. The nation is
One universal traitor; and their queen
The very spirit and extract of 'em all.
ANT. Is there yet left
A possibility of aid from valor? 160
Is there one god unsworn to my destruction?
The least unmortgaged hope? for, if there be,
Methinks I cannot fall beneath the fate
Of such a boy as Caesar.
The world's one half is yet in Antony; 165
And from each limb of it that's hewed away,
The soul comes back to me.
VEN. There yet remain
Three legions in the town. The last assault
Lopped off the rest; if death be your design
(As I must wish it now), these are sufficient 170
To make a heap about us of dead foes,
An honest pile for burial.
ANT. They're enough.
We'll not divide our stars; but, side by side,
Fight emulous, and with malicious eyes
Survey each other's acts; so every death 175
Thou giv'st, I'll take on me as a just debt,
And pay thee back a soul.
VEN. Now you shall see I love you. Not a word
Of chiding more. By my few hours of life,
I am so pleased with this brave Roman fate,
That I would not be Caesar, to outlive you.
When we put off this flesh, and mount together, 182
I shall be shown to all th'ethereal crowd,—
"Lo, this is he who died with Antony!"
ANT. Who knows but we may pierce through all their troops, 185
And reach my veterans yet? 'Tis worth the tempting,
T'o'erleap this gulf of fate,
And leave our wond'ring destinies behind.

Enter ALEXAS, *trembling*.

VEN. See, see, that villain!
See Cleopatra stamped upon that face, 190
With all her cunning, all her arts of falsehood!
How she looks out through those dissembling eyes!
How he has set his count'nance for deceit,
And promises a lie before he speaks!
Let me dispatch him first. (*Drawing*)
ALEX. O spare me, spare me! 195
ANT. Hold; he's not worth your killing.— On thy life
(Which thou mayst keep, because I scorn to take it),
No syllable to justify thy queen;
Save thy base tongue its office.
ALEX. Sir, she's gone,

Where she shall never be molested more 200
By love, or you.

ANT. Fled to her Dollabella!
Die, traitor! I revoke my promise! die!
(*Going to kill him*)

ALEX. O hold! she is not fled.

ANT. She is: my eyes
Are open to her falsehood; my whole life
Has been a golden dream of love and friendship; 205
But, now I wake, I'm like a merchant, roused
From soft repose to see his vessel sinking,
And all his wealth cast o'er. Ingrateful woman!
Who followed me but as the swallow summer,
Hatching her young ones in my kindly beams, 210
Singing her flatt'ries to my morning wake;
But now my winter comes, she spreads her wings,
And seeks the spring of Caesar.

ALEX. Think not so:
Her fortunes have in all things mixed with yours. 214
Had she betrayed her naval force to Rome,
How easily might she have gone to Caesar,
Secure by such a bribe!

VEN. She sent it first,
To be more welcome after.

ANT. 'Tis too plain,
Else would she have appeared, to clear herself.

ALEX. Too fatally she has: she could not bear 220
To be accused by you; but shut herself
Within her monument; looked down and sighed;
While from her unchanged face the silent tears
Dropped, as they had not leave, but stole their parting.
Some undistinguished words she inly murmured; 225
At last, she raised her eyes; and, with such looks
As dying Lucrece cast—

ANT. My heart forbodes—

VEN. All for the best; go on.

ALEX. She snatched her poniard,
And, ere we could prevent the fatal blow,
Plunged it within her breast; then turned to me; 230
"Go, bear my lord (said she) my last farewell;
And ask him, if he yet suspect my faith."
More she was saying, but death rushed betwixt.
She half pronounced your name with her last breath,
And buried half within her.

VEN. Heav'n be praised! 235

ANT. Then art thou innocent, my poor dear love?
And art thou dead?
O those two words! their sound should be divided;
Hadst thou been false, and died; or hadst thou lived,
And hadst been true—But innocence and death! 240
This shows not well above. Then what am I?
The murderer of this truth, this innocence!
Thoughts cannot form themselves in words so horrid
As can express my guilt!

VEN. Is't come to this? The gods have been too gracious; 245
And thus you thank 'em for't!

ANT. (*to* ALEX.) Why stay'st thou here?
Is it for thee to spy upon my soul,
And see its inward mourning? Get thee hence;
Thou art not worthy to behold what now
Becomes a Roman emperor to perform. 250

ALEX. (*aside*). He loves her still;
His grief betrays it. Good! The joy to find
She's yet alive, completes the reconcilement.
I've saved myself, and her. But, oh! the Romans!
Fate comes too fast upon my wit, 255
Hunts me too hard, and meets me at each double. [*Exit.*

VEN. Would she had died a little sooner, though,
Before Octavia went! you might have treated;
Now 'twill look tame, and would not be received.
Come, rouse yourself, and let's die warm together. 260

ANT. I will not fight; there's no more work for war.
The bus'ness of my angry hours is done.

VEN. Caesar is at your gates.

ANT. Why, let him enter;
He's welcome now.

VEN. What lethargy has crept into your soul? 265

ANT. 'Tis but a scorn of life, and just desire
To free myself from bondage.

VEN. Do it bravely.
ANT. I will; but not by fighting. O Ventidius!
What should I fight for now? My queen is dead.
I was but great for her; my power, my empire, 270
Were but my merchandise to buy her love;
And conquered kings, my factors. Now she's dead,
Let Caesar take the world—
An empty circle, since the jewel's gone
Which made it worth my strife: my being's nauseous; 275
For all the bribes of life are gone away.
VEN. Would you be taken?
ANT. Yes, I would be taken;
But, as a Roman ought—dead, my Ventidius;
For I'll convey my soul from Caesar's reach,
And lay down life myself. 'Tis time the world 280
Should have a lord, and know whom to obey.
We two have kept its homage in suspense,
And bent the globe, on whose each side we trod,
Till it was dinted inwards; let him walk
Alone upon't; I'm weary of my part. 285
My torch is out; and the world stands before me,
Like a black desert at th'approach of night;
I'll lay me down, and stray no farther on.
VEN. I could be grieved,
But that I'll not outlive you: choose your death; 290
For, I have seen him in such various shapes,
I care not which I take; I'm only troubled,
The life I bear is worn to such a rag,
'Tis scarce worth giving. I could wish, indeed,
We threw it from us with a better grace; 295
That, like two lions taken in the toils,
We might at least thrust out our paws, and wound
The hunters that inclose us.
ANT. I have thought on't.
Ventidius, you must live.
VEN. I must not, sir.
ANT. Wilt thou not live, to speak some good of me? 300
To stand by my fair fame, and guard th'approaches
From the ill tongues of men?
VEN. Who shall guard mine,
For living after you?
ANT. Say I command it.
VEN. If we die well, our deaths will speak themselves
And need no living witness.
ANT. Thou hast loved me, 305
And fain I would reward thee; I must die;
Kill me, and take the merit of my death,
To make thee friends with Caesar.
VEN. Thank your kindness.
You said I loved you; and in recompense,
You bid me turn a traitor; did I think 310
You would have used me thus?—that I should die
With a hard thought of you?
ANT. Forgive me, Roman.
Since I have heard of Cleopatra's death,
My reason bears no rule upon my tongue,
But lets my thoughts break all at random out. 315
I've thought better; do not deny me twice.
VEN. By Heav'n I will not.
Let it not be t'outlive you.
ANT. Kill me first,
And then die thou; 'tis but just thou serve
Thy friend before thyself.
VEN. Give me your hand. 320
We soon shall meet again. Now, farewell, emperor!— *(Embrace)*
Methinks that word's too cold to be my last;
Since death sweeps all distinctions, farewell, friend!
That's all.—
I will not make a bus'ness of a trifle; 325
And yet I cannot look on you, and kill you;
Pray turn your face.
ANT. I do: strike home, be sure.
VEN. Home as my sword will reach.
(Kills himself)
ANT. O, thou mistak'st;
That wound was not of thine; give it me back:
Thou robb'st me of my death.
VEN. I do indeed; 330
But think 'tis the first time I e'er deceived you,
If that may plead my pardon.—And you, gods,
Forgive me, if you will; for I die perjured,
Rather than kill my friend. *(Dies)*
ANT. Farewell! Ever my leader, e'en in death! 335
My queen and thou have got the start of me,
And I'm the lag of honor.—Gone so soon?
Is Death no more? He used him carelessly,
With a familiar kindness; ere he knocked,
Ran to the door, and took him in his arms,
As who should say, "Y'are welcome at all hours; 341

A friend need give no warning." Books had[4] spoiled him;
For all the learn'd are cowards by profession.
'Tis not worth
My farther thought; for death, for aught I know, 345
Is but to think no more. Here's to the satisfied. (*Falls on his sword*)
I've missed my heart. O unperforming hand!
Thou never could'st have erred in a worse time.
My fortune jades me to the last; and death,
Like a great man, takes state,[5] and makes me wait 350
For my admittance.—(*Trampling within*)
Some, perhaps, from Caesar:
If he should find me living, and suspect
That I played booty with my life! I'll mend
My work ere they can reach me.
(*Rises upon his knees*)

Enter CLEOPATRA, CHARMION, *and* IRAS.

CLEOP. Where is my lord? where is he?
CHAR. There he lies, 355
And dead Ventidius by him.
CLEOP. My fears were prophets; I am come too late.
O that accursed Alexas! (*Runs to him*)
ANT. Art thou living?
Or am I dead before I knew, and thou
The first kind ghost that meets me?
CLEOP. Help me seat him. 360
Send quickly, send for help!
(*They place him in a chair*)
ANT. I am answered.
We live both. Sit thee down, my Cleopatra;
I'll make the most I can of life, to stay
A moment more with thee.
CLEOP. How is it with you?
ANT. 'Tis as with a man 365
Removing in a hurry; all packed up,
But one dear jewel that his haste forgot;
And he, for that, returns upon the spur;
So I come back for thee.
CLEOP. Too long, you heav'ns, you have been cruel to me: 370
Now show your mended faith, and give me back
His fleeting life!
ANT. It will not be, my love;
I keep my soul by force.
Say but, thou art not false.
CLEOP. 'Tis now too late
To say I'm true: I'll prove it, and die with you. 375

[4] I. e., would have. [5] Assumes dignity.

Unknown to me, Alexas feigned my death;
Which when I knew, I hasted to prevent
This fatal consequence. My fleet betrayed
Both you and me.
ANT. And Dollabella—
CLEOP. Scarce
Esteemed before he loved; but hated now.
ANT. Enough: my life's not long enough for more. 381
Thou say'st thou wilt come after; I believe thee;
For I can now believe whate'er thou say'st,
That we may part more kindly.
CLEOP. I will come:
Doubt not, my life, I'll come, and quickly too: 385
Caesar shall triumph o'er no part of thee.
ANT. But grieve not, while thou stay'st,
My last disastrous times;
Think we have had a clear and glorious day,
And Heav'n did kindly to delay the storm,
Just till our close of ev'ning. Ten years' love, 391
And not a moment lost, but all improved
To th'utmost joys—what ages have we lived!
And now to die each other's; and so dying,
While hand in hand we walk in groves below,
Whole troops of lovers' ghosts shall flock about us, 396
And all the train be ours.
CLEOP. Your words are like the notes of dying swans,
Too sweet to last. Were there so many hours
For your unkindness, and not one for love?
ANT. No, not a minute.—This one kiss—more worth 401
Than all I leave to Caesar. (*Dies*)
CLEOP. O tell me so again,
And take ten thousand kisses for that word.
My lord, my lord! speak, if you yet have being; 405
Sign to me, if you cannot speak; or cast
One look! Do anything that shows you live.
IRAS. He's gone too far to hear you;
And this you see, a lump of senseless clay,
The leavings of a soul.
CHAR. Remember, madam, 410
He charged you not to grieve.
CLEOP. And I'll obey him.
I have not loved a Roman, not to know
What should become his wife; his wife, my Charmion;
For 'tis to that high title I aspire; 414
And now I'll not die less. Let dull Octavia
Survive, to mourn him dead; my nobler fate

Shall knit our 'spousals with a tie too strong
For Roman laws to break.

IRAS. Will you then die?

CLEOP. Why shouldst thou make that question?

IRAS. Caesar is merciful.

CLEOP. Let him be so 420
To those who want his mercy; my poor lord
Made no such cov'nant with him, to spare me
When he was dead. Yield me to Caesar's pride?
What! to be led in triumph through the streets,
A spectacle to base plebeian eyes; 425
While some dejected friend of Antony's,
Close in a corner, shakes his head, and mutters
A secret curse on her who ruined him?
I'll none of that.

CHAR. Whatever you resolve,
I'll follow, e'en to death.

IRAS. I only feared 430
For you; but more should fear to live without you.

CLEOP. Why, now 'tis as it should be. Quick, my friends,
Dispatch; ere this, the town's in Caesar's hands:
My lord looks down concerned, and fears my stay,
Lest I should be surprised; 435
Keep him not waiting for his love too long.
You, Charmion, bring my crown and richest jewels;
With 'em, the wreath of victory I made
(Vain augury!) for him who now lies dead;
You, Iras, bring the cure of all our ills. 440

IRAS. The aspics, madam?

CLEOP. Must I bid you twice?

[*Exeunt* CHARMION *and* IRAS.

'Tis sweet to die, when they would force life on me,
To rush into the dark abode of death,
And seize him first; if he be like my love,
He is not frightful, sure. 445
We're now alone, in secrecy and silence;
And is not this like lovers? I may kiss
These pale, cold lips; Octavia does not see me;
And, oh! 'tis better far to have him thus,
Than see him in her arms.—O, welcome, welcome! 450

Enter CHARMION *and* IRAS.

CHAR. What must be done?

CLEOP. Short ceremony, friends;
But yet it must be decent. First, this laurel
Shall crown my hero's head; he fell not basely,
Nor left his shield behind him.—Only thou
Couldst triumph o'er thyself; and thou alone
Wert worthy so to triumph.

CHAR. To what end 456
These ensigns of your pomp and royalty?

CLEOP. Dull, that thou art! why 'tis to meet my love;
As when I saw him first, on Cydnos' bank,
All sparkling, like a goddess: so adorned, 460
I'll find him once again; my second 'spousals
Shall match my first in glory. Haste, haste, both,
And dress the bride of Antony.

CHAR. 'Tis done.

CLEOP. Now seat me by my lord. I claim this place;
For I must conquer Caesar too, like him, 465
And win my share o'th'world.—Hail, you dear relics
Of my immortal love!
O let no impious hand remove you hence:
But rest for ever here! Let Egypt give
His death that peace, which it denied his life.— 470
Reach me the casket.

IRAS. Underneath the fruit
The aspic lies.

CLEOP. (*putting aside the leaves*). Welcome, thou kind deceiver!
Thou best of thieves; who with an easy key
Dost open life, and, unperceived by us,
E'en steal us from ourselves; discharging so 475
Death's dreadful office better than himself;
Touching our limbs so gently into slumber,
That Death stands by, deceived by his own image,
And thinks himself but Sleep.

SERAP. (*within*). The queen, where is she?
The town is yielded, Caesar's at the gates.

CLEOP. He comes too late t'invade the rights of death. 481
Haste, bare my arm, and rouse the serpent's fury.
(*Holds out her arm, and draws it back*)
Coward flesh,
Wouldst thou conspire with Caesar to betray me,
As thou wert none of mine? I'll force thee to't, 485
And not be sent by him,
But bring, myself, my soul to Antony.
(*Turns aside, and then shows her arm bloody*)

Take hence; the work is done.
SERAP. (*within*). Break ope the door,
And guard the traitor well.
IRAS. Now, Charmion, to be worthy 490
Of our great queen and mistress.
(*They apply the aspics*)
CLEOP. Already, Death, I feel thee in my veins:
I go with such a will to find my lord,
That we shall quickly meet.
A heavy numbness creeps through every limb, 495
And now 'tis at my head; my eye-lids fall,
And my dear love is vanished in a mist.
Where shall I find him, where? O turn me to him,
And lay me on his breast!—Caesar, thy worst;
Now part us, if thou canst. (*Dies*)
(IRAS *sinks down at her feet, and dies;* CHARMION *stands behind her chair, as dressing her head*)

Enter SERAPION, *two* PRIESTS, ALEXAS *bound,* EGYPTIANS.

2 PRIESTS. Behold, Serapion, 500
What havoc death has made!
SERAP. 'Twas what I feared.—
Charmion, is this well done?
CHAR. Yes, 'tis well done, and like a queen, the last
Of her great race; I follow her.
(*Sinks down: dies*)
ALEXAS. 'Tis true,
She has done well: much better thus to die,
Than live to make a holiday in Rome. 506
SERAP. See, see how the lovers sit in state together,
As they were giving laws to half mankind!
Th'impression of a smile, left in her face,
Shows she died pleased with him for whom she lived, 510
And went to charm him in another world.
Caesar's just ent'ring: grief has now no leisure.
Secure that villain, as our pledge of safety,
To grace th'imperial triumph.—Sleep, blest pair,
Secure from human chance, long ages out,
While all the storms of fate fly o'er your tomb; 516
And fame to late posterity shall tell,
No lovers lived so great, or died so well.
[*Exeunt.*

EPILOGUE

Poets, like disputants, when reasons fail,
Have one sure refuge left—and that's to rail.
Fop, coxcomb, fool, are thundered through the pit;
And this is all their equipage of wit.
We wonder how the devil this diff'rence grows, 5
Betwixt our fools in verse, and yours in prose;
For, 'faith, the quarrel rightly understood,
'Tis civil war with their own flesh and blood.
The threadbare author hates the gaudy coat;
And swears at the gilt coach, but swears afoot: 10
For 'tis observed of every scribbling man,
He grows a fop as fast as e'er he can;
Prunes up, and asks his oracle, the glass,
If pink or purple best become his face.
For our poor wretch, he neither rails nor prays; 15
Nor likes your wit just as you like his plays;
He has not yet so much of Mr. Bays.[1]
He does his best; and if he cannot please,
Would quietly sue out his writ of ease.[2]
Yet, if he might his own grand-jury call, 20
By the fair sex he begs to stand or fall.
Let Caesar's power the men's ambition move,
But grace you him who lost the world for love!
Yet if some antiquated lady say,
The last age is not copied in his play; 25
Heav'n help the man who for that face must drudge,
Which only has the wrinkles of a judge.
Let not the young and beauteous join with those;
For should you raise such numerous hosts of foes,
Young wits and sparks he to his aid must call; 30
'Tis more than one man's work to please you all.

[1]Dryden was caricatured under this name in *The Rehearsal* (1671), a farce written by the Duke of Buckingham and others.

[2]A certificate of discharge from employment.

ABSALOM AND ACHITOPHEL

(1681)

Si propius stes
Te capiat magis.[1]

TO THE READER

'Tis not my intention to make an apology for my poem: some will think it needs no excuse, and others will receive none. The design, I am sure, is honest; but he who draws his pen for one party must expect to make enemies of the other. For wit and fool are consequents of Whig and Tory; and every man is a knave or an ass to the contrary side. There's a treasury of merits in the Fanatic Church, as well as in the Papist; and a pennyworth to be had of saintship, honesty, and poetry, for the lewd, the factious, and the blockheads; but the longest chapter in Deuteronomy has not curses enough for an anti-Bromingham.[2] My comfort is, their manifest prejudice to my cause will render their judgment of less authority against me. Yet if a poem have a genius, it will force its own reception in the world; for there's a sweetness in good verse, which tickles even while it hurts, and no man can be heartily angry with him who pleases him against his will. The commendation of adversaries is the greatest triumph of a writer, because it never comes unless extorted. But I can be satisfied on more easy terms: if I happen to please the more moderate sort, I shall be sure of an honest party, and, in all probability, of the best judges; for the least concerned are commonly the least corrupt. And, I confess, I have laid in for those, by rebating[3] the satire (where justice would allow it) from carrying too sharp an edge. They who can criticize so weakly, as to imagine I have done my worst, may be convinced, at their own cost, that I can write severely with more ease than I can gently. I have but laughed at some men's follies, when I could have declaimed against their vices; and other men's virtues I have commended, as freely as I have taxed their crimes. And now, if you are a malicious reader, I expect you should return upon me that I affect to be thought more impartial than I am. But if men are not to be judged by their professions, God forgive you commonwealth's-men for professing so plausibly for the government. You cannot be so unconscionable as to charge me for not subscribing of my name; for that would reflect too grossly upon your own party, who never dare, though they have the advantage of a jury to secure them. If you like not my poem, the fault may, possibly, be in my writing (though 'tis hard for an author to judge against himself); but, more probably, 'tis in your morals, which cannot bear the truth of it. The violent, on both sides, will condemn the character of Absalom, as either too favorably or too hardly drawn. But they are not the violent whom I desire to please. The fault on the right hand is to extenuate, palliate, and indulge; and, to confess freely, I have endeavored to commit it. Besides the respect which I owe his birth I have a greater for his heroic virtues; and David himself could not be more tender of the young man's life than I would be of his reputation. But since the most excellent natures are always the most easy, and, as being such, are the soonest perverted by ill counsels, especially when baited with fame and glory; 't is no more a wonder that he withstood not the temptations of Achitophel, than it was for Adam not to have resisted the two devils, the serpent and the woman. The conclusion of the story I purposely forbore to prosecute, because I could not obtain from myself to show Absalom unfortunate. The frame of it was cut out but for a picture to the waist, and if the draught be so far true, 't is as much as I designed.

Were I the inventor, who am only the historian, I should certainly conclude the piece with the reconcilement of Absalom to David. And who knows but this may come to pass? Things were not brought to an extremity where I left the story; there seems yet to be

[1] The closer you stand, the more it takes your fancy (Horace, *Art of Poetry,* 361).
[2] Anti-Whig. [3] Blunting.

room left for a composure; hereafter there may only be for pity. I have not so much as an uncharitable wish against Achitophel, but am content to be accused of a good-natured error, and to hope with Origen, that the 5 Devil himself may at last be saved. For which reason, in this poem, he is neither brought to set his house in order, nor to dispose of his person afterwards as he in wisdom shall think fit. God is infinitely merci- 10 ful; and his vicegerent is only not so, because he is not infinite.

The true end of satire is the amendment of vice by correction. And he who writes honestly is no more an enemy to the offender, 15 than the physician to the patient, when he prescribes harsh remedies to an inveterate disease; for those are only in order to prevent the chirurgeon's work of an *ense rescindendum,*[4] which I wish not to my very enemies. 20 To conclude all; if the body politic have any analogy to the natural, in my weak judgment an act of oblivion were as necessary in a hot, distempered state, as an opiate would be in a raging fever. 25

ABSALOM AND ACHITOPHEL[1]

In pious times, ere priestcraft did begin,
Before polygamy was made a sin;
When man on many multiplied his kind,
Ere one to one was cursedly confined;
When nature prompted, and no law denied 5
Promiscuous use of concubine and bride;
Then Israel's monarch[2] after Heaven's own heart,
His vigorous warmth did variously impart
To wives and slaves; and, wide as his command,
Scattered his Maker's image through the land. 10

[4]Cutting out with the knife (Ovid, *Metamorphoses,* I, 191).

[1]As Dryden's preface indicates, this is a political poem. The Biblical story of the revolt of Absalom (II Samuel, 13–18) was used as a thin veil for satire in support of the king and the Tories. Charles II's rightful successor to the throne was his brother James, Duke of York, who was, however, opposed by the Whigs because he was a Roman Catholic. The Whig leader, the first Earl of Shaftesbury, wished to make James, Duke of Monmouth, an illegitimate son of Charles, his successor. It was against this project that Dryden directed his satire.

[2]David; Charles II.

Michal[3] of royal blood, the crown did wear;
A soil ungrateful to the tiller's care:
Not so the rest; for several mothers bore
To godlike David several sons before.
But since like slaves his bed they did ascend, 15
No true succession could their seed attend.
Of all this numerous progeny was none
So beautiful, so brave, as Absalon:[4]
Whether, inspired by some diviner lust,
His father got him with a greater gust; 20
Or that his conscious destiny made way,
By manly beauty, to imperial sway.
Early in foreign fields he won renown
With kings and states[5] allied to Israel's crown;
In peace the thoughts of war he could remove, 25
And seemed as he were only born for love.
Whate'er he did, was done with so much ease,
In him alone 't was natural to please:
His motions all accompanied with grace;
And paradise was opened in his face. 30
With secret joy indulgent David viewed
His youthful image in his son renewed:
To all his wishes nothing he denied;
And made the charming Annabel[6] his bride.
What faults he had (for who from faults is free?) 35
His father could not or he would not see.
Some warm excesses which the law forbore,
Were construed youth that purged by boiling o'er,
And Amnon's murder, by a specious name,
Was called a just revenge for injured fame. 40
Thus praised and loved the noble youth remained,
While David, undisturbed, in Sion[7] reigned.
But life can never be sincerely blest;
Heav'n punishes the bad, and proves the best.
The Jews,[8] a headstrong, moody, murm'ring race, 45
As ever tried th' extent and stretch of grace;
God's pampered people, whom, debauched with ease,
No king could govern, nor no God could please
(Gods they had tried of every shape and size,
That god-smiths could produce, or priests devise); 50
These Adam-wits, too fortunately free,
Began to dream they wanted liberty;

[3]Catharine of Portugal, Charles II's queen.

[4]James, Duke of Monmouth. [5]Republics.

[6]Anne Scott, Countess of Buccleuch.

[7]London. [8]The English.

And when no rule, no precedent was found,
Of men by laws less circumscribed and bound;
They led their wild desires to woods and caves, 55
And thought that all but savages were slaves.
They who, when Saul[9] was dead, without a blow,
Made foolish Ishbosheth[10] the crown forgo;
Who banished David did from Hebron[11] bring,
And with a general shout proclaimed him king: 60
Those very Jews, who, at their very best,
Their humor more than loyalty expressed,
Now wondered why so long they had obeyed
An idol monarch, which their hands had made;
Thought they might ruin him they could create, 65
Or melt him to that golden calf, a State.
But these were random bolts; no formed design,
Nor interest made the factious crowd to join:
The sober part of Israel, free from stain,
Well knew the value of a peaceful reign; 70
And, looking backward with a wise affright,
Saw seams of wounds, dishonest to the sight:
In contemplation of whose ugly scars
They cursed the memory of civil wars.
The moderate sort of men, thus qualified, 75
Inclined the balance to the better side;
And David's mildness managed it so well,
The bad found no occasion to rebel.
But when to sin our biased nature leans,
The careful Devil is still at hand with means;
And providently pimps for ill desires: 81
The Good Old Cause, revived, a plot requires.
Plots, true or false, are necessary things,
To raise up commonwealths and ruin kings.
  Th' inhabitants of old Jerusalem 85
Were Jebusites;[12] the town so called from them;
And theirs the native right.
But when the chosen people grew more strong,
The rightful cause at length became the wrong;
And every loss the men of Jebus bore, 90
They still were thought God's enemies the more.
Thus worn and weakened, well or ill content,
Submit they must to David's government:
Impoverished and deprived of all command,
Their taxes doubled as they lost their land; 95
And, what was harder yet to flesh and blood,
Their gods disgraced, and burned like common wood.
This set the heathen priesthood in a flame;
For priests of all religions are the same:
Of whatsoe'er descent their godhead be, 100
Stock, stone, or other homely pedigree,
In his defense his servants are as bold,
As if he had been born of beaten gold.
The Jewish rabbins,[13] though their enemies,
In this conclude them honest men and wise: 105
For 'twas their duty, all the learnéd think,
T' espouse his cause, by whom they eat and drink.
From hence began that Plot,[14] the nation's curse,
Bad in itself, but represented worse, 109
Raised in extremes, and in extremes decried,
With oaths affirmed, with dying vows denied,
Not weighed or winnowed by the multitude;
But swallowed in the mass, unchewed and crude.[15]
Some truth there was, but dashed and brewed with lies,
To please the fools, and puzzle all the wise: 115
Succeeding times did equal folly call,
Believing nothing, or believing all.
Th' Egyptian[16] rites the Jebusites embraced;
Where gods were recommended by their taste.
Such sav'ry deities must needs be good, 120
As served at once for worship and for food.
By force they could not introduce these gods,
For ten to one in former days was odds;
So fraud was used (the sacrificer's trade):
Fools are more hard to conquer than persuade. 125
Their busy teachers mingled with the Jews,
And raked for converts e'en the court and stews:
Which Hebrew priests[17] the more unkindly took,
Because the fleece accompanies the flock.
Some thought they God's anointed meant to slay 130
By guns, invented since full many a day:

---

[9]Oliver Cromwell. [10]Richard Cromwell.

[11]Apparently Scotland, though one would expect it here to mean Brussels.

[12]Roman Catholics.

[13]Doctors of the Anglican Church.

[14]The so-called Popish Plot (1678).

[15]Undigested.

[16]French (the immediate reference is to transubstantiation).

[17]Clergymen of the Anglican Church.

Our author swears it not; but who can know
How far the Devil and Jebusites may go?
This Plot, which failed for want of common sense,
Had yet a deep and dangerous consequence: 135
For, as when raging fevers boil the blood,
The standing lake soon floats into a flood,
And every hostile humor, which before
Slept quiet in its channels, bubbles o'er;
So several factions from this first ferment 140
Work up to foam, and threat the government.
Some by their friends, more by themselves thought wise,
Opposed the power to which they could not rise.
Some had in courts been great, and thrown from thence,
Like fiends were hardened in impenitence. 145
Some, by their monarch's fatal mercy, grown
From pardoned rebels kinsmen to the throne,
Were raised in power and public office high;
Strong bands, if bands ungrateful men could tie.

Of these the false Achitophel[18] was first; 150
A name to all succeeding ages curst:
For close[19] designs and crooked counsels fit;
Sagacious, bold, and turbulent of wit;
Restless, unfixed in principles and place;
In power unpleased, impatient of disgrace: 155
A fiery soul, which, working out its way,
Fretted the pigmy body to decay,
And o'er-informed the tenement of clay.
A daring pilot in extremity;
Pleased with the danger, when the waves went high, 160
He sought the storms; but, for a calm unfit,
Would steer too nigh the sands, to boast his wit.
Great wits are sure to madness near allied,
And thin partitions do their bounds divide;
Else why should he, with wealth and honor blest, 165
Refuse his age the needful hours of rest?
Punish a body which he could not please;
Bankrupt of life, yet prodigal of ease?
And all to leave what with his toil he won,
To that unfeathered two-legg'd thing, a son;
Got, while his soul did huddled notions try
And born a shapeless lump, like anarchy. 172
In friendship false, implacable in hate;
Resolved to ruin or to rule the State.
To compass this the triple bond he broke,
The pillars of the public safety shook;
And fitted Israel for a foreign yoke;[20]
Then seized with fear, yet still affecting fame,
Usurped a patriot's all-atoning name.
So easy still it proves in factious times, 180
With public zeal to cancel private crimes.
How safe is treason, and how sacred ill,
Where none can sin against the people's will!
Where crowds can wink, and no offense be known, 184
Since in another's guilt they find their own!
Yet fame deserved no enemy can grudge;
The statesman we abhor, but praise the judge.
In Israel's courts ne'er sat an Abbethdin[21]
With more discerning eyes, or hands more clean;
Unbribed, unsought, the wretched to redress; 190
Swift of dispatch, and easy of access.
Oh, had he been content to serve the crown,
With virtues only proper to the gown;
Or had the rankness of the soil been freed
From cockle, that oppressed the noble seed; 195
David for him his tuneful harp had strung,
And Heav'n had wanted[22] one immortal song.
But wild Ambition loves to slide, not stand,
And Fortune's ice prefers to Virtue's land.
Achitophel, grown weary to possess 200
A lawful fame, and lazy happiness,
Disdained the golden fruit to gather free,
And lent the crowd his arm to shake the tree.
Now, manifest of crimes contrived long since,
He stood at bold defiance with his prince; 205
Held up the buckler of the people's cause
Against the crown, and skulked behind the laws.
The wished occasion of the Plot he takes;
Some circumstances finds, but more he makes.
By buzzing emissaries fills the ears 210
Of list'ning crowds with jealousies and fears
Of arbitrary counsels brought to light,
And proves the king himself a Jebusite.
Weak arguments! which yet he knew full well
Were strong with people easy to rebel. 215
For, governed by the moon, the giddy Jews

---

[18]Anthony Ashley Cooper, Earl of Shaftesbury (1621–1683).

[19]Secret.

[20]Dryden here refers to England's alliance with France against Holland in 1670. The broken "triple bond" was an alliance made in 1667 between England, Holland, and Sweden, which was directed against France. As a matter of fact Shaftesbury had nothing to do with the alliance of 1670, but Dryden did not know this.

[21]Judge. [22]Lacked.

Tread the same track when she the prime renews;
And once in twenty years, their scribes record,
By natural instinct they change their lord.
Achitophel still wants a chief, and none 220
Was found so fit as warlike Absalon:
Not that he wished his greatness to create,
For politicians neither love nor hate,
But, for he knew his title not allowed,
Would keep him still depending on the crowd, 225
That kingly pow'r, thus ebbing out, might be
Drawn to the dregs of a democracy.
Him he attempts with studied arts to please,
And sheds his venom in such words as these:
"Auspicious prince, at whose nativity 230
Some royal planet ruled the southern sky;
Thy longing country's darling and desire;
Their cloudy pillar and their guardian fire:
Their second Moses, whose extended wand
Divides the seas, and shows the promised land; 235
Whose dawning day in every distant age
Has exercised the sacred prophets' rage;
The people's prayer, the glad diviners' theme,
The young men's vision, and the old men's dream!
Thee, Savior, thee, the nation's vows confess, 240
And, never satisfied with seeing, bless:
Swift unbespoken pomps thy steps proclaim,
And stammering babes are taught to lisp thy name.
How long wilt thou the general joy detain,
Starve and defraud the people of thy reign?
Content ingloriously to pass thy days 246
Like one of Virtue's fools that feeds on praise;
Till thy fresh glories, which now shine so bright,
Grow stale and tarnish with our daily sight.
Believe me, royal youth, thy fruit must be
Or gathered ripe, or rot upon the tree. 251
Heav'n has to all allotted, soon or late,
Some lucky revolution of their fate;
Whose motions if we watch and guide with skill
(For human good depends on human will), 255
Our Fortune rolls as from a smooth descent,
And from the first impression takes the bent;
But, if unseized, she glides away like wind,
And leaves repenting Folly far behind.
Now, now she meets you with a glorious prize, 260
And spreads her locks before her as she flies.
Had thus old David, from whose loins you spring,
Not dared, when Fortune called him, to be king,
At Gath[23] an exile he might still remain, 264
And Heaven's anointing oil had been in vain.
Let his successful youth your hopes engage;
But shun th' example of declining age:
Behold him setting in his western skies,
The shadows lengthening as the vapors rise.
He is not now, as when on Jordan's sand[24] 270
The joyful people thronged to see him land,
Cov'ring the beach, and black'ning all the strand;
But, like the Prince of Angels, from his height
Comes tumbling downward with diminished light;
Betrayed by one poor plot to public scorn, 275
(Our only blessing since his curst return;)
Those heaps of people which one sheaf did bind,
Blown off and scattered by a puff of wind.
What strength can he to your designs oppose,
Naked of friends and round beset with foes? 280
If Pharaoh's[25] doubtful succor he should use,
A foreign aid would more incense the Jews:
Proud Egypt would dissembled friendship bring;
Foment the war, but not support the king:
Nor would the royal party e'er unite 285
With Pharaoh's arms t'assist the Jebusite;
Or if they should, their interest soon would break,
And with such odious aid make David weak.
All sorts of men by my successful arts,
Abhorring kings, estrange their altered hearts 290
From David's rule: and 't is the general cry,
'Religion, commonwealth, and liberty.'
If you, as champion of the public good,
Add to their arms a chief of royal blood,
What may not Israel hope, and what applause 295
Might such a general gain by such a cause?
Not barren praise alone, that gaudy flower
Fair only to the sight, but solid power;
And nobler is a limited command,
Giv'n by the love of all your native land, 300
Than a successive title, long and dark,
Drawn from the moldy rolls of Noah's ark."

---

[23]Brussels.

[24]Jordan represents the sea surrounding England.

[25]Louis XIV of France (Egypt).

What cannot praise effect in mighty minds,
When flattery soothes, and when ambition blinds!
Desire of power, on earth a vicious weed, 305
Yet, sprung from high, is of celestial seed:
In God 't is glory; and when men aspire,
'T is but a spark too much of heavenly fire.
Th' ambitious youth, too covetous of fame,
Too full of angels' metal in his frame, 310
Unwarily was led from virtue's ways,
Made drunk with honor, and debauched with praise.
Half loath, and half consenting to the ill—
For loyal blood within him struggled still—
He thus replied: "And what pretense have I
To take up arms for public liberty? 316
My father governs with unquestioned right;
The faith's defender, and mankind's delight;
Good, gracious, just, observant of the laws:
And Heav'n by wonders has espoused his cause. 320
Whom has he wronged in all his peaceful reign?
Who sues for justice to his throne in vain?
What millions has he pardoned of his foes,
Whom just revenge did to his wrath expose?
Mild, easy, humble, studious of our good; 325
Inclined to mercy, and averse from blood;
If mildness ill with stubborn Israel suit,
His crime is God's belovéd attribute.
What could he gain, his people to betray,
Or change his right for arbitrary sway? 330
Let haughty Pharaoh curse with such a reign
His fruitful Nile, and yoke a servile train.
If David's rule Jerusalem displease,
The Dog-star heats their brains to this disease.
Why then should I, encouraging the bad, 335
Turn rebel and run popularly mad?
Were he a tyrant, who, by lawless might
Oppressed the Jews, and raised the Jebusite,
Well might I mourn; but nature's holy bands
Would curb my spirits and restrain my hands: 340
The people might assert their liberty;
But what was right in them were crime in me.
His favor leaves me nothing to require,
Prevents[26] my wishes, and outruns desire.
What more can I expect while David lives? 345
All but his kingly diadem he gives:
And that"—But there he paused; then sighing, said—
"Is justly destined for a worthier head.
For when my father from his toils shall rest,
And late augment the number of the blest, 350
His lawful issue shall the throne ascend,
Or the collat'ral line, where that shall end.
His brother,[27] though oppressed with vulgar spite,
Yet dauntless, and secure of native right,
Of every royal virtue stands possessed, 355
Still dear to all the bravest and the best.
His courage foes, his friends his truth proclaim;
His loyalty the king, the world his fame.
His mercy e'en th' offending crowd will find;
For sure he comes of a forgiving kind. 360
Why should I then repine at Heav'n's decree,
Which gives me no pretense to royalty?
Yet O that fate, propitiously inclined,
Had raised my birth, or had debased my mind;
To my large soul not all her treasure lent, 365
And then betrayed it to a mean descent!
I find, I find my mounting spirits bold,
And David's part disdains my mother's mold.
Why am I scanted by a niggard birth?
My soul disclaims the kindred of her earth; 370
And, made for empire, whispers me within,
'Desire of greatness is a godlike sin.'"

Him staggering so when hell's dire agent found,
While fainting Virtue scarce maintained her ground,
He pours fresh forces in, and thus replies: 375
"Th' eternal God, supremely good and wise,
Imparts not these prodigious gifts in vain:
What wonders are reserved to bless your reign!
Against your will, your arguments have shown,
Such virtue's only giv'n to guide a throne. 380
Not that your father's mildness I contemn;
But manly force becomes the diadem.
'T is true he grants the people all they crave;
And more, perhaps, than subjects ought to have:
For lavish grants suppose a monarch tame, 385
And more his goodness than his wit proclaim.
But when should people strive their bonds to break,
If not when kings are negligent or weak?
Let him give on till he can give no more,
The thrifty Sanhedrin[28] shall keep him poor;
And every shekel which he can receive, 391
Shall cost a limb of his prerogative.

[26] Anticipates.

[27] The Duke of York, later James II.

[28] Parliament.

To ply him with new plots shall be my care;
Or plunge him deep in some expensive war;
Which when his treasure can no more supply,
He must, with the remains of kingship, buy. 396
His faithful friends, our jealousies and fears
Call Jebusites, and Pharaoh's pensioners;
Whom when our fury from his aid has torn,
He shall be naked left to public scorn. 400
The next successor, whom I fear and hate,
My arts have made obnoxious to the State;
Turned all his virtues to his overthrow,
And gained our elders to pronounce a foe.
His right, for sums of necessary gold, 405
Shall first be pawned, and afterwards be sold;
Till time shall ever-wanting David draw,
To pass your doubtful title into law:
If not, the people have a right supreme
To make their kings; for kings are made for them. 410
All empire is no more than power in trust,
Which, when resumed, can be no longer just.
Succession, for the general good designed,
In its own wrong a nation cannot bind;
If altering that the people can relieve, 415
Better one suffer than a nation grieve.
The Jews well know their power: ere Saul they chose,
God was their king, and God they durst depose.[29]
Urge now your piety, your filial name,
A father's right, and fear of future fame; 420
The public good, that universal call,
To which e'en Heav'n submitted, answers all.
Nor let his love enchant your generous mind;
'T is Nature's trick to propagate her kind.
Our fond begetters, who would never die, 425
Love but themselves in their posterity.
Or let his kindness by th' effects be tried,
Or let him lay his vain pretense aside.
God said he loved your father; could he bring
A better proof, than to anoint him king? 430
It surely showed he loved the shepherd well,
Who gave so fair a flock as Israel.
Would David have you thought his darling son?
What means he then, to alienate the crown?
The name of godly he may blush to bear; 435
'T is after God's own heart to cheat his heir.
He to his brother gives supreme command;
To you a legacy of barren land,
Perhaps th' old harp, on which he thrums his lays,
Or some dull Hebrew ballad in your praise. 440
Then the next heir, a prince sèvere and wise,
Already looks on you with jealous eyes;
Sees through the thin disguises of your arts,
And marks your progress in the people's hearts.
Though now his mighty soul its grief contains, 445
He meditates revenge who least complains;
And, like a lion, slumb'ring in the way,
Or sleep dissembling, while he waits his prey,
His fearless foes within his distance draws,
Constrains his roaring, and contracts his paws; 450
Till at the last, his time for fury found,
He shoots with sudden vengeance from the ground;
The prostrate vulgar passes o'er and spares,
But with a lordly rage his hunters tears.
Your case no tame expedients will afford: 455
Resolve on death, or conquest by the sword,
Which for no less a stake than life you draw;
And self-defense is nature's eldest law.
Leave the warm people no considering time;
For then rebellion may be thought a crime. 460
Prevail[30] yourself of what occasion gives,
But try your title while your father lives;
And that your arms may have a fair pretense,
Proclaim you take them in the king's defense;
Whose sacred life each minute would expose
To plots, from seeming friends, and secret foes. 466
And who can sound the depth of David's soul?
Perhaps his fear his kindness may control.
He fears his brother, though he loves his son,
For plighted vows too late to be undone. 470
If so, by force he wishes to be gained,
Like women's lechery, to seem constrained.
Doubt not: but, when he most affects the frown,
Commit a pleasing rape upon the crown.
Secure his person to secure your cause: 475
They who possess the prince, possess the laws."

He said, and this advice above the rest,
With Absalom's mild nature suited best:
Unblamed of life (ambition set aside),
Not stained with cruelty, nor puffed with pride, 480
How happy had he been, if destiny
Had higher placed his birth, or not so high!

---

[29] The government of the Commonwealth previous to Cromwell's protectorate is represented as a theocracy.

[30] Avail.

His kingly virtues might have claimed a throne,
And blessed all other countries but his own.
But charming greatness since so few refuse, 485
'T is juster to lament him than accuse.
Strong were his hopes a rival to remove,
With blandishments to gain the public love;
To head the faction while their zeal was hot,
And popularly prosecute the Plot. 490
To further this, Achitophel unites
The malcontents of all the Israelites;
Whose differing parties he could wisely join,
For several ends, to serve the same design:
The best (and of the princes some were such), 495
Who thought the pow'r of monarchy too much;
Mistaken men, and patriots in their hearts;
Not wicked, but seduced by impious arts.
By these the springs of property were bent,
And wound so high, they cracked the government. 500
The next for interest sought t' embroil the State,
To sell their duty at a dearer rate;
And make their Jewish markets of the throne,
Pretending public good, to serve their own.
Others thought kings an useless heavy load,
Who cost too much, and did too little good.
These were for laying honest David by, 507
On principles of pure good husbandry.
With them joined all th' haranguers of the throng,
That thought to get preferment by the tongue. 510
Who follow next, a double danger bring,
Not only hating David, but the king:
The Solymaean rout,[31] well-versed of old
In godly faction, and in treason bold;
Cow'ring and quaking at a conqu'ror's sword,
But lofty to a lawful prince restored, 516
Saw with disdain an Ethnic plot[32] begun,
And scorned by Jebusites to be outdone.
Hot Levites[33] headed these; who, pulled before
From th' ark, which in the Judges' days they bore, 520
Resumed their cant, and with a zealous cry
Pursued their old belov'd Theocracy:
Where Sanhedrin and priest enslaved the nation,
And justified their spoils by inspiration:
For who so fit for reign as Aaron's race,[34] 525
If once dominion they could find in grace?
These led the pack; though not of surest scent,
Yet deepest mouthed against the government.
A numerous host of dreaming saints succeed,
Of the true old enthusiastic breed: 530
'Gainst form and order they their power employ,
Nothing to build, and all things to destroy.
But far more numerous was the herd of such,
Who think too little, and who talk too much.
These, out of mere instinct, they knew not why, 535
Adored their fathers' God and property;
And, by the same blind benefit of fate,
The Devil and the Jebusite did hate:
Born to be saved, even in their own despite,
Because they could not help believing right.
Such were the tools; but a whole Hydra more 541
Remains, of sprouting heads too long to score.
Some of their chiefs were princes of the land:
In the first rank of these did Zimri[35] stand;
A man so various, that he seemed to be 545
Not one, but all mankind's epitome:
Stiff in opinions, always in the wrong;
Was everything by starts, and nothing long;
But, in the course of one revolving moon,
Was chemist, fiddler, statesman, and buffoon: 550
Then all for women, painting, riming, drinking,
Besides ten thousand freaks that died in thinking.
Blest madman, who could every hour employ,
With something new to wish, or to enjoy! 554
Railing and praising were his usual themes;
And both (to show his judgment) in extremes:
So over-violent, or over-civil,
That every man, with him, was God or Devil.
In squand'ring wealth was his peculiar art:
Nothing went unrewarded but desert. 560
Beggared by fools, whom still he found too late,
He had his jest, and they had his estate.
He laughed himself from court; then sought relief
By forming parties, but could ne'er be chief;
For, spite of him, the weight of business fell 565

[31] The London rabble. [32] The Popish Plot.

[33] Presbyterian ministers, who had been displaced after the Restoration.

[34] The clergy.

[35] George Villiers, Duke of Buckingham.

On Absalom and wise Achitophel:
Thus, wicked but in will, of means bereft,
He left not faction, but of that was left.
Titles and names 't were tedious to rehearse
Of lords, below the dignity of verse. 570
Wits, warriors, commonwealth's-men, were the best;
Kind husbands, and mere nobles, all the rest.
And therefore, in the name of dullness, be
The well-hung Balaam[36] and cold Caleb[37] free;
And canting Nadab[38] let oblivion damn, 575
Who made new porridge for the paschal lamb.
Let friendship's holy band some names assure;
Some their own worth, and some let scorn secure.
Nor shall the rascal rabble here have place,
Whom kings no titles gave, and God no grace: 580
Not bull-faced Jonas[39] who could statutes draw
To mean rebellion, and make treason law.
But he, though bad, is followed by a worse,
The wretch who Heav'n's anointed dared to curse:
Shimei,[40] whose youth did early promise bring 585
Of zeal to God and hatred to his king,
Did wisely from expensive sins refrain,
And never broke the Sabbath, but for gain;
Nor ever was he known an oath to vent,
Or curse, unless against the government. 590
Thus heaping wealth, by the most ready way
Among the Jews, which was to cheat and pray,
The city, to reward his pious hate
Against his master, chose him magistrate.
His hand a vare[41] of justice did uphold; 595
His neck was loaded with a chain of gold.
During his office, treason was no crime;
The sons of Belial had a glorious time;
For Shimei, though not prodigal of pelf,
Yet loved his wicked neighbor as himself. 600
When two or three were gathered to declaim
Against the monarch of Jerusalem,
Shimei was always in the midst of them;
And if they cursed the king when he was by,
Would rather curse than break good company. 605
If any durst his factious friends accuse,
He packed a jury of dissenting Jews;
Whose fellow-feeling in the godly cause
Would free the suff'ring saint from human laws.
For laws are only made to punish those 610
Who serve the king, and to protect his foes.
If any leisure time he had from power,
(Because 't is sin to misemploy an hour,)
His bus'ness was, by writing, to persuade
That kings were useless, and a clog to trade;
And, that his noble style he might refine, 616
No Rechabite more shunned the fumes of wine.
Chaste were his cellars, and his shrieval board[42]
The grossness of a city feast abhorred:
His cooks, with long disuse, their trade forgot; 620
Cool was his kitchen, though his brains were hot.
Such frugal virtue malice may accuse,
But sure 't was necessary to the Jews;
For towns once burned such magistrates require
As dare not tempt God's providence by fire. 625
With spiritual food he fed his servants well,
But free from flesh that made the Jews rebel;
And Moses' laws he held in more account,
For forty days of fasting in the mount.
To speak the rest, who better are forgot, 630
Would tire a well-breathed witness of the Plot.
Yet, Corah,[43] thou shalt from oblivion pass:
Erect thyself, thou monumental brass,
High as the serpent of thy metal made,
While nations stand secure beneath thy shade. 635
What though his birth were base, yet comets rise
From earthy vapors, ere they shine in skies.
Prodigious actions may as well be done
By weaver's issue, as by prince's son.
This arch-attestor for the public good 640
By that one deed ennobles all his blood.

[36]The Earl of Huntingdon.

[37]Lord Grey of Wark.

[38]Lord Howard of Escrick (the allusion in the following line is to the story that Howard had taken the Sacrament in "lamb's wool"—ale poured on roasted apples and sauce—instead of wine).

[39]Sir William Jones.

[40]Slingsby Bethel, a sheriff of London in 1680.

[41]Wand.

[42]His table when he was a sheriff.

[43]Titus Oates.

Who ever asked the witnesses' high race,
Whose oath with martyrdom did Stephen grace?
Ours was a Levite, and as times went then,
His tribe were God Almighty's gentlemen. 645
Sunk were his eyes, his voice was harsh and loud,
Sure signs he neither choleric was nor proud:
His long chin proved his wit; his saintlike grace
A church vermilion, and a Moses' face.
His memory, miraculously great, 650
Could plots, exceeding man's belief, repeat;
Which therefore cannot be accounted lies,
For human wit could never such devise.
Some future truths are mingled in his book;
But where the witness failed, the prophet spoke: 655
Some things like visionary flights appear;
The spirit caught him up, the Lord knows where;
And gave him his rabbinical degree,
Unknown to foreign university.[44]
His judgment yet his mem'ry did excel; 660
Which pieced his wondrous evidence so well,
And suited to the temper of the times,
Then groaning under Jebusitic crimes.
Let Israel's foes suspect his heav'nly call,
And rashly judge his writ apocryphal; 665
Our laws for such affronts have forfeits made;
He takes his life, who takes away his trade.
Were I myself in witness Corah's place,
The wretch who did me such a dire disgrace,
Should whet my memory, though once forgot, 670
To make him an appendix of my plot.
His zeal to Heav'n made him his prince despise,
And load his person with indignities;
But zeal peculiar privilege affords,
Indulging latitude to deeds and words; 675
And Corah might for Agag's[45] murder call,
In terms as coarse as Samuel used to Saul.
What others in his evidence did join
(The best that could be had for love or coin),
In Corah's own predicament will fall; 680
For *witness* is a common name to all.
Surrounded thus with friends of every sort,
Deluded Absalom forsakes the court;
Impatient of high hopes, urged with renown,
And fired with near possession of a crown. 685
Th' admiring crowd are dazzled with surprise,
And on his goodly person feed their eyes.
His joy concealed, he sets himself to show,
On each side bowing popularly low;
His looks, his gestures, and his words he frames, 690
And with familiar ease repeats their names.
Thus formed by nature, furnished out with arts,
He glides unfelt into their secret hearts.
Then, with a kind compassionating look,
And sighs, bespeaking pity ere he spoke, 695
Few words he said; but easy those and fit,
More slow than Hybla-drops, and far more sweet.
"I mourn, my countrymen, your lost estate;
Though far unable to prevent your fate:
Behold a banished man,[46] for your dear cause 700
Exposed a prey to arbitrary laws!
Yet oh, that I alone could be undone,
Cut off from empire, and no more a son!
Now all your liberties a spoil are made;
Egypt and Tyrus[47] intercept your trade, 705
And Jebusites your sacred rites invade.
My father, whom with reverence yet I name,
Charmed into ease, is careless of his fame;
And, bribed with petty sums of foreign gold,
Is grown in Bathsheba's[48] embraces old; 710
Exalts his enemies, his friends destroys;
And all his power against himself employs.
He gives, and let him give, my right away;
But why should he his own and yours betray?
He, only he, can make the nation bleed, 715
And he alone from my revenge is freed.
Take then my tears (with that he wiped his eyes),
'T is all the aid my present power supplies:
No court-informer can these arms accuse;
These arms may sons against their fathers use: 720
And 't is my wish, the next successor's reign
May make no other Israelite complain."
Youth, beauty, graceful action seldom fail;
But common interest always will prevail;

---

[44] Oates pretended to have the degree of D.D. from Salamanca.

[45] Sir Edmund Bury Godfrey, before whom Oates testified concerning the Popish Plot, and who was soon thereafter murdered.

[46] Monmouth had been sent from England in 1679, but had returned.

[47] France and Holland.

[48] Louise de Querouaille, Duchess of Portsmouth, Charles's mistress.

And pity never ceases to be shown 725
To him who makes the people's wrongs his own.
The crowd, that still believe their kings oppress,
With lifted hands their young Messiah bless:
Who now begins his progress to ordain
With chariots, horsemen, and a num'rous train; 730
From east to west his glories he displays,
And, like the sun, the promised land surveys.
Fame runs before him as the morning star,
And shouts of joy salute him from afar:
Each house receives him as a guardian god,
And consecrates the place of his abode. 736
But hospitable treats did most commend
Wise Issachar,[49] his wealthy western friend,
This moving court, that caught the people's eyes,
And seemed but pomp, did other ends disguise: 740
Achitophel had formed it, with intent
To sound the depths, and fathom, where it went,
The people's hearts; distinguish friends from foes,
And try their strength, before they came to blows.
Yet all was colored with a smooth pretense 745
Of specious love, and duty to their prince.
Religion, and redress of grievances,
Two names that always cheat and always please,
Are often urged; and good King David's life
Endangered by a brother and a wife. 750
Thus in a pageant show a plot is made,
And peace itself is war in masquerade.
O foolish Israel! never warned by ill!
Still the same bait, and circumvented still!
Did ever men forsake their present ease, 755
In midst of health imagine a disease;
Take pains contingent mischiefs to foresee,
Make heirs for monarchs, and for God decree?
What shall we think! Can people give away,
Both for themselves and sons, their native sway? 760
Then they are left defenseless to the sword
Of each unbounded, arbitrary lord:
And laws are vain, by which we right enjoy,
If kings unquestioned can those laws destroy.
Yet if the crowd be judge of fit and just, 765
And kings are only officers in trust,
Then this resuming cov'nant was declared
When kings were made, or is for ever barred.
If those who gave the scepter could not tie
By their own deed their own posterity, 770
How then could Adam bind his future race?
How could his forfeit on mankind take place?
Or how could heavenly justice damn us all,
Who ne'er consented to our father's fall?
Then kings are slaves to those whom they command, 775
And tenants to their people's pleasure stand.
Add, that the power for property allowed
Is mischievously seated in the crowd;
For who can be secure of private right,
If sovereign sway may be dissolved by might? 780
Nor is the people's judgment always true:
The most may err as grossly as the few;
And faultless kings run down, by common cry,
For vice, oppression, and for tyranny.
What standard is there in a fickle rout, 785
Which, flowing to the mark, runs faster out?
Nor only crowds, but Sanhedrins may be
Infected with this public lunacy,
And share the madness of rebellious times,
To murder monarchs for imagined crimes.
If they may give and take whene'er they please, 791
Not kings alone (the Godhead's images),
But government itself at length must fall
To nature's state, where all have right to all.
Yet, grant our lords the people kings can make, 795
What prudent men a settled throne would shake?
For whatsoe'er their sufferings were before,
That change they covet makes them suffer more.
All other errors but disturb a state,
But innovation is the blow of fate. 800
If ancient fabrics nod and threat to fall,
To patch the flaws and buttress up the wall,
Thus far 't is duty: but here fix the mark;
For all beyond it is to touch our ark.[50] 804
To change foundations, cast the frame anew,
Is work for rebels, who base ends pursue,
At once divine and human laws control,
And mend the parts by ruin of the whole.
The tamp'ring world is subject to this curse,
To physic their disease into a worse. 810
Now what relief can righteous David bring?
How fatal 't is to be too good a king!

---

[49] Thomas Thynne of Longleat.

[50] To commit sacrilege.

Friends he has few, so high the madness grows:
Who dare be such, must be the people's foes.
Yet some there were, e'en in the worst of days; 815
Some let me name, and naming is to praise.
In this short file Barzillai[51] first appears;
Barzillai, crowned with honor and with years.
Long since, the rising rebels he withstood
In regions waste, beyond the Jordan's flood:
Unfortunately brave to buoy the State; 821
But sinking underneath his master's fate:
In exile with his godlike prince he mourned;
For him he suffered, and with him returned.
The court he practiced, not the courtier's art: 825
Large was his wealth, but larger was his heart,
Which well the noblest objects knew to choose,
The fighting warrior, and recording Muse.
His bed could once a fruitful issue boast;
Now more than half a father's name is lost. 830
His eldest hope,[52] with every grace adorned,
By me (so Heav'n will have it) always mourned,
And always honored, snatched in manhood's prime
B' unequal fates, and Providence's crime;
Yet not before the goal of honor won, 835
All parts fulfilled of subject and of son:
Swift was the race, but short the time to run.
O narrow circle, but of power divine,
Scanted in space, but perfect in thy line!
By sea, by land, thy matchless worth was known, 840
Arms thy delight, and war was all thy own:
Thy force, infused, the fainting Tyrians propped;
And haughty Pharaoh found his fortune stopped.
O ancient honor! O unconquered hand,
Whom foes unpunished never could withstand! 845
But Israel was unworthy of thy name;
Short is the date of all immoderate fame.
It looks as Heav'n our ruin had designed,
And durst not trust thy fortune and thy mind.
Now, free from earth, thy disencumbered soul 850
Mounts up, and leaves behind the clouds and starry pole:
From thence thy kindred legions may'st thou bring,
To aid the guardian angel of thy king.
Here stop, my Muse, here cease thy painful flight;
No pinions can pursue immortal height: 855
Tell good Barzillai thou canst sing no more,
And tell thy soul she should have fled before:
Or fled she with his life, and left this verse
To hang on her departed patron's hearse?
Now take thy steepy flight from heav'n, and see 860
If thou canst find on earth another he:
Another he would be too hard to find;
See then whom thou canst see not far behind.
Zadoc[53] the priest, whom, shunning power and place,
His lowly mind advanced to David's grace.
With him the Sagan of Jerusalem,[54] 866
Of hospitable soul, and noble stem;
Him of the western dome,[55] whose weighty sense
Flows in fit words and heavenly eloquence.
The prophets' sons, by such example led, 870
To learning and to loyalty were bred:
For colleges on bounteous kings depend,
And never rebel was to arts a friend.
To these succeed the pillars of the laws;
Who best could plead, and best can judge a cause. 875
Next them a train of loyal peers ascend;
Sharp-judging Adriel,[56] the Muses' friend;
Himself a Muse—in Sanhedrin's debate
True to his prince, but not a slave of state:
Whom David's love with honors did adorn,
That from his disobedient son were torn. 881
Jotham[57] of piercing wit, and pregnant thought;
Endued by nature, and by learning taught
To move assemblies, who but only tried
The worse a while, then chose the better side: 885
Nor chose alone, but turned the balance too;
So much the weight of one brave man can do.
Hushai,[58] the friend of David in distress;
In public storms, of manly steadfastness:

---

[51]The Duke of Ormond.

[52]Ormond's oldest son, the Earl of Ossory, who had died in 1680.

[53]William Sancroft, Archbishop of Canterbury.

[54]Henry Compton, Bishop of London.

[55]John Dolben, Bishop of Rochester and Dean of Westminster. The "western dome" is Westminster Abbey.

[56]John Sheffield, Earl of Mulgrave, later Duke of Buckinghamshire.

[57]George Savile, Marquis of Halifax.

[58]Lawrence Hyde, after 1682 Earl of Rochester.

By foreign treaties he informed his youth, 890
And joined experience to his native truth.
His frugal care supplied the wanting throne;
Frugal for that, but bounteous of his own:
'T is easy conduct when exchequers flow,
But hard the task to manage well the low; 895
For sovereign power is too depressed or high,
When kings are forced to sell, or crowds to buy.
Indulge one labor more, my weary Muse,
For Amiel:[59] who can Amiel's praise refuse?
Of ancient race by birth, but nobler yet 900
In his own worth, and without title great:
The Sanhedrin long time as chief he ruled,
Their reason guided, and their passion cooled:
So dext'rous was he in the crown's defense,
So formed to speak a loyal nation's sense, 905
That, as their band was Israel's tribes in small,
So fit was he to represent them all.
Now rasher charioteers the seat ascend,
Whose loose careers his steady skill commend:
They, like th' unequal ruler of the day,[60] 910
Misguide the seasons, and mistake the way;
While he withdrawn at their mad labor smiles,
And safe enjoys the sabbath of his toils.
These were the chief, a small but faithful band
Of worthies, in the breach who dared to stand, 915
And tempt th' united fury of the land.
With grief they viewed such powerful engines bent,
To batter down the lawful government:
A numerous faction, with pretended frights,
In Sanhedrins to plume[61] the regal rights; 920
The true successor from the court removed;
The Plot, by hireling witnesses, improved.
These ills they saw, and, as their duty bound,
They showed the king the danger of the wound;
That no concessions from the throne would please, 925
But lenitives fomented the disease;
That Absalom, ambitious of the crown,
Was made the lure to draw the people down;
That false Achitophel's pernicious hate
Had turned the Plot to ruin Church and State; 930
The council violent, the rabble worse;
That Shimei taught Jerusalem to curse.
With all these loads of injuries oppressed,
And long revolving in his careful breast
Th' event of things, at last, his patience tired,
Thus from his royal throne, by Heav'n inspired, 936
The godlike David spoke: with awful fear
His train their Maker in their master hear.
"Thus long have I, by native mercy swayed,
My wrongs dissembled, my revenge delayed;
So willing to forgive th' offending age; 941
So much the father did the king assuage.
But now so far my clemency they slight,
Th' offenders question my forgiving right.
That one was made for many, they contend;
But 'tis to rule; for that's a monarch's end. 946
They call my tenderness of blood, my fear;
Though manly tempers can the longest bear.
Yet, since they will divert my native course,
'T is time to show I am not good by force. 950
Those heaped affronts that haughty subjects bring,
Are burdens for a camel, not a king.
Kings are the public pillars of the State,
Born to sustain and prop the nation's weight;
If my young Samson will pretend a call 955
To shake the column, let him share the fall:
But O that yet he would repent and live!
How easy 't is for parents to forgive!
With how few tears a pardon might be won
From nature, pleading for a darling son! 960
Poor pitied youth, by my paternal care
Raised up to all the height his frame could bear!
Had God ordained his fate for empire born,
He would have giv'n his soul another turn:
Gulled with a patriot's name, whose modern sense 965
Is one that would by law supplant his prince;
The people's brave, the politician's tool;
Never was patriot yet, but was a fool.
Whence comes it that religion and the laws
Should more be Absalom's than David's cause? 970
His old instructor, ere he lost his place,
Was never thought indued with so much grace.
Good heav'ns, how faction can a patriot paint!
My rebel ever proves my people's saint. 974
Would *they* impose an heir upon the throne?
Let Sanhedrins be taught to give their own.
A king's at least a part of government,
And mine as requisite as their consent;
Without my leave a future king to choose,

---

[59] Edward Seymour, Speaker of the House of Commons from 1673 to 1679.
[60] Phaëton. [61] I. e., to pluck out.

Infers a right the present to depose. 980
True, they petition me t'approve their choice;
But Esau's hands suit ill with Jacob's voice.
My pious subjects for my safety pray;
Which to secure, they take my power away.
From plots and treasons Heav'n preserve my years, 985
But save me most from my petitioners!
Unsatiate as the barren womb or grave;
God cannot grant so much as they can crave.
What then is left, but with a jealous eye
To guard the small remains of royalty? 990
The law shall still direct my peaceful sway,
And the same law teach rebels to obey:
Votes shall no more established power control—
Such votes as make a part exceed the whole:
No groundless clamors shall my friends remove, 995
Nor crowds have power to punish ere they prove;
For gods and godlike kings their care express,
Still to defend their servants in distress.
O that my power to saving were confined!
Why am I forced, like Heav'n, against my mind, 1000
To make examples of another kind?
Must I at length the sword of justice draw?
O curst effects of necessary law!
How ill my fear they by my mercy scan!
Beware the fury of a patient man. 1005
Law they require, let Law then show her face;
They could not be content to look on Grace,
Her hinder parts, but with a daring eye
To tempt the terror of her front and die. 1009
By their own arts, 't is righteously decreed,
Those dire artificers of death shall bleed.
Against themselves their witnesses will swear,
Till viper-like their mother Plot they tear;
And suck for nutriment that bloody gore,
Which was their principle of life before. 1015
Their Belial with their Belzebub will fight;
Thus on my foes, my foes shall do me right.
Nor doubt th' event; for factious crowds engage,
In their first onset, all their brutal rage.
Then let 'em take an unresisted course; 1020
Retire, and traverse, and delude their force;
But, when they stand all breathless, urge the fight,
And rise upon 'em with redoubled might;
For lawful power is still superior found;
When long driv'n back, at length it stands the ground." 1025
He said. Th' Almighty, nodding, gave consent;
And peals of thunder shook the firmament.
Henceforth a series of new time began,
The mighty years in long procession ran: 1029
Once more the godlike David was restored,
And willing nations knew their lawful lord.

MAC FLECKNOE

or,

A Satire upon the True-Blue-Protestant Poet T. S.[1]

(1682)

All human things are subject to decay,
And when fate summons, monarchs must obey.
This Flecknoe[2] found, who, like Augustus, young
Was called to empire, and had governed long;
In prose and verse was owned, without dispute, 5
Through all the realms of Nonsense absolute.
This aged prince, now flourishing in peace,
And bless'd with issue of a large increase;
Worn out with business, did at length debate
To settle the succession of the State; 10
And, pond'ring which of all his sons was fit
To reign, and wage immortal war with wit,
Cried: "'T is resolved; for nature pleads, that he
Should only rule, who most resembles me.
Sh—— alone my perfect image bears, 15
Mature in dullness from his tender years:
Sh—— alone, of all my sons, is he
Who stands confirmed in full stupidity.
The rest to some faint meaning make pretense,
But Sh—— never deviates into sense. 20
Some beams of wit on other souls may fall,
Strike through, and make a lucid interval;

[1] Dryden published *The Medal* in the spring of 1682. One of the answers to it was *The Medal of John Bayes,* by Thomas Shadwell. Dryden and Shadwell had once been friends, but Shadwell was a strong Whig, the two were now enemies, and Shadwell's poem was savagely abusive. *Mac Flecknoe* was Dryden's reply.

[2] Flecknoe died in 1678. He was a Roman Catholic priest before the restoration of Charles II. At one time he was entertained at Lisbon by King John of Portugal.

But Sh——'s genuine night admits no ray,
His rising fogs prevail upon the day.
Besides, his goodly fabric fills the eye, 25
And seems designed for thoughtless majesty;
Thoughtless as monarch oaks that shade the plain,
And, spread in solemn state, supinely reign.
Heywood and Shirley[3] were but types of thee,
Thou last great prophet of tautology. 30
Even I, a dunce of more renown than they,
Was sent before but to prepare thy way;
And, coarsely clad in Norwich drugget, came
To teach the nations in thy greater name.
My warbling lute, the lute I whilom strung, 35
When to King John of Portugal I sung,
Was but the prelude to that glorious day,
When thou on silver Thames didst cut thy way,
With well-timed oars before the royal barge,
Swelled with the pride of thy celestial charge; 40
And big with hymn, commander of a host,
The like was ne'er in Epsom blankets tossed.[4]
Methinks I see the new Arion[5] sail,
The lute still trembling underneath thy nail.
At thy well-sharpened thumb from shore to shore 45
The treble squeaks for fear, the basses roar;
Echoes from Pissing Alley Sh—— call,
And Sh—— they resound from Aston Hall.
About thy boat the little fishes throng,
As at the morning toast that floats along. 50
Sometimes, as prince of thy harmonious band,
Thou wield'st thy papers in thy threshing hand.
St. André's[6] feet ne'er kept more equal time,
Not e'en the feet of thy own *Psyche's*[7] rime;
Though they in number as in sense excel: 55
So just, so like tautology, they fell,
That, pale with envy, Singleton[8] forswore
The lute and sword, which he in triumph bore,
And vowed he ne'er would act Villerius[9] more."
Here stopped the good old sire, and wept for joy 60
In silent raptures of the hopeful boy.
All arguments, but most his plays, persuade,
That for anointed dullness he was made.
Close to the walls which fair Augusta[10] bind
(The fair Augusta much to fears inclined), 65
An ancient fabric raised t' inform the sight,
There stood of yore, and Barbican it hight:
A watchtower once; but now, so fate ordains,
Of all the pile an empty name remains.
From its old ruins brothel-houses rise, 70
Scenes of lewd loves, and of polluted joys,
Where their vast courts the mother-strumpets keep,
And, undisturbed by watch, in silence sleep.
Near these a Nursery[11] erects its head,
Where queens are formed, and future heroes bred; 75
Where unfledged actors learn to laugh and cry,
Where infant punks their tender voices try,
And little Maximins[12] the gods defy.
Great Fletcher never treads in buskins here,
Nor greater Jonson dares in socks appear; 80
But gentle Simkin[13] just reception finds
Amidst this monument of vanished minds:
Pure clinches[14] the suburbian Muse affords,
And Panton waging harmless war with words.
Here Flecknoe, as a place to fame well known, 85
Ambitiously designed his Sh——'s throne;
For ancient Dekker[15] prophesied long since,
That in this pile should reign a mighty prince,
Born for a scourge of wit, and flail of sense;
To whom true dullness should some *Psyches* owe, 90
But worlds of *Misers* from his pen should flow;
Humorists and hypocrites it should produce,

[3]Thomas Heywood and James Shirley, both dramatists of the early seventeenth century.

[4]A play of Shadwell's was entitled *Epsom Wells;* tossing in a blanket is also the punishment given a character in Shadwell's *The Virtuoso.*

[5]A Greek musician of the eighth century B. C. Shadwell was a musician as well as a poet.

[6]A French dancing-master.

[7]An opera in rime by Shadwell.

[8]A singer of the day.

[9]A character in Davenant's *Siege of Rhodes.*

[10]London, at the time fearful of the King and Roman Catholicism.

[11]A theater for the training of young actors.

[12]The name of the chief character in Dryden's *Tyrannic Love.*

[13]A clown.

[14]Puns. Panton is said to have been a celebrated punster.

[15]Thomas Dekker, the dramatist of the early seventeenth century, author of *The Shoemakers' Holiday.*

Whole Raymond families, and tribes of Bruce.[16]
 Now Empress Fame had published the renown
Of Sh——'s coronation through the town. 95
Roused by report of Fame, the nations meet,
From near Bunhill, and distant Watling Street.
No Persian carpets spread th' imperial way,
But scattered limbs of mangled poets lay;
From dusty shops neglected authors come, 100
Martyrs of pies, and relics of the bum.
Much Heywood, Shirley, Ogleby[17] there lay,
But loads of Sh—— almost choked the way.
Bilked stationers for yeomen stood prepared,
And Herringman[18] was captain of the guard.
The hoary prince in majesty appeared, 106
High on a throne of his own labors reared.
At his right hand our young Ascanius sate,
Rome's other hope, and pillar of the State.
His brows thick fogs, instead of glories, grace,
And lambent dullness played around his face.
As Hannibal did to the altars come, 112
Sworn by his sire a mortal foe to Rome;
So Sh—— swore, nor should his vow be vain,
That he till death true dullness would maintain; 115
And, in his father's right, and realm's defense,
Ne'er to have peace with wit, nor truce with sense.
The king himself the sacred unction made,
As king by office, and as priest by trade.
In his sinister hand, instead of ball, 120
He placed a mighty mug of potent ale;
Love's Kingdom[19] to his right he did convey,
At once his scepter, and his rule of sway;
Whose righteous lore the prince had practiced young,
And from whose loins recorded *Psyche* sprung.
His temples, last, with poppies were o'erspread, 126
That nodding seemed to consecrate his head.
Just at that point of time, if fame not lie,
On his left hand twelve reverend owls did fly.
So Romulus, 't is sung, by Tiber's brook, 130
Presage of sway from twice six vultures took.
Th' admiring throng loud acclamations make,
And omens of his future empire take.
The sire then shook the honors of his head,
And from his brows damps of oblivion shed
Full on the filial dullness: long he stood, 136
Repelling from his breast the raging god;
At length burst out in this prophetic mood:
 "Heavens bless my son, from Ireland let him reign
To far Barbadoes on the western main; 140
Of his dominion may no end be known,
And greater than his father's be his throne;
Beyond *Love's Kingdom* let him stretch his pen!"
He paused, and all the people cried, "Amen."
Then thus continued he: "My son, advance
Still in new impudence, new ignorance. 146
Success let others teach, learn thou from me
Pangs without birth, and fruitless industry.
Let *Virtuosos* in five years be writ;
Yet not one thought accuse thy toil of wit. 150
Let gentle George[20] in triumph tread the stage,
Make Dorimant betray, and Loveit rage;
Let Cully, Cockwood, Fopling, charm the pit,
And in their folly show the writer's wit.
Yet still thy fools shall stand in thy defense,
And justify their author's want of sense. 156
Let 'em be all by thy own model made
Of dullness, and desire no foreign aid;
That they to future ages may be known,
Not copies drawn, but issue of thy own. 160
Nay, let thy men of wit too be the same,
All full of thee, and differing but in name.
But let no alien S—dl—y[21] interpose,
To lard with wit thy hungry *Epsom* prose.
And when false flowers of rhetoric thou wouldst cull, 165
Trust nature, do not labor to be dull;
But write thy best, and top; and, in each line,
Sir Formal's[22] oratory will be thine:
Sir Formal, though unsought, attends thy quill,
And does thy northern dedications[23] fill. 170
Nor let false friends seduce thy mind to fame,
By arrogating Jonson's hostile name.[24]

[16] *The Miser* and *The Humorists* are plays by Shadwell. Raymond is a character in the latter, Bruce a character in Shadwell's *The Virtuoso*.

[17] Ogleby had been a dancing-master and had afterwards translated Homer, Virgil, and Aesop, besides writing other poems.

[18] A London publisher.

[19] A play by Flecknoe.

[20] Sir George Etherege. The names in the two following lines are those of characters in Etherege's plays.

[21] Sir Charles Sedley, who had written the prologue for Shadwell's *Epsom Wells,* and who probably, as Dryden suggests, gave Shadwell other assistance.

[22] Sir Formal Trifle is a character in Shadwell's *Virtuoso.*

[23] An allusion to Shadwell's dedication of various books to the Duke of Newcastle and members of his family.

[24] Shadwell frequently eulogized Jonson and professed to imitate him.

Let father Flecknoe fire thy mind with praise,
And uncle Ogleby thy envy raise.
Thou art my blood, where Jonson has no part: 175
What share have we in nature, or in art?
Where did his wit on learning fix a brand,
And rail at arts he did not understand?
Where made he love in Prince Nicander's[25] vein,
Or swept the dust in *Psyche's* humble strain?
Where sold he bargains, 'whip-stitch, kiss my arse,'[26] 181
Promised a play and dwindled to a farce?
When did his Muse from Fletcher scenes purloin,
As thou whole Eth'rege dost transfuse to thine?
But so transfused as oil on water's flow, 185
His always floats above, thine sinks below.
This is thy province, this thy wondrous way,
New humors to invent for each new play:
This is that boasted bias of thy mind,
By which one way, to dullness, 't is inclined;
Which makes thy writings lean on one side still, 191
And, in all changes, that way bends thy will.
Nor let thy mountain-belly make pretense
Of likeness; thine's a tympany of sense.

[25]A character in Shadwell's *Psyche.*

[26]Such phrases are used by Sir Samuel Hearty in Shadwell's *Virtuoso.*

A tun of man in thy large bulk is writ, 195
But sure thou 'rt but a kilderkin[27] of wit.
Like mine, thy gentle numbers freely creep;
Thy tragic Muse gives smiles, thy comic sleep.
With whate'er gall thou sett'st thyself to write,
Thy inoffensive satires never bite. 200
In thy felonious heart though venom lies,
It does but touch thy Irish pen, and dies.
Thy genius calls thee not to purchase fame
In keen iambics, but mild anagram.
Leave writing plays, and choose for thy command 205
Some peaceful province in acrostic land.
There thou may'st wings display the altars raise,
And torture one poor word ten thousand ways.
Or, if thou wouldst thy diff'rent talents suit,
Set thy own songs, and sing them to thy lute."
He said: but his last words were scarcely heard; 211
For Bruce and Longvil had a trap prepared,[28]
And down they sent the yet declaiming bard.
Sinking he left his drugget robe behind,
Borne upwards by a subterranean wind. 215
The mantle fell to the young prophet's part,
With double portion of his father's art.

[27]The fourth part of a tun.

[28]These characters thus make Sir Formal Trifle disappear in Shadwell's *Virtuoso.*

RELIGIO LAICI

or,

A Layman's Faith. A Poem

(1682)

Ornari res ipsa negat, contenta doceri.[1]

THE PREFACE

A POEM with so bold a title, and a name prefixed from which the handling of so serious a subject would not be expected, may reasonably oblige the author to say somewhat in defense both of himself and of his undertaking. In the first place, if it be objected to me that, being a layman, I ought not to have concerned myself with speculations which belong to the profession of divinity, I could answer that perhaps laymen, with equal advantages of parts and knowledge, are not the most incompetent judges of sacred things; but, in the due sense of my own weakness and want of learning, I plead not this; I pretend not to make myself a judge of faith in others, but only to make a confession of my own; I lay no unhallowed hand upon the ark, but wait on it, with the reverence that becomes me, at a distance. In the next place I will ingenuously confess that the helps I have used in this small treatise were many of them taken from the works of our own reverend divines of the Church of England; so that the weapons with which I combat irreligion are already consecrated; though I

[1]Truth desires not to be embellished, but simply to be told (Manilius, *Astronom.,* iii, 39).

suppose they may be taken down as lawfully as the sword of Goliath was by David, when they are to be employed for the common cause, against the enemies of piety. I intend not by this to entitle them to any of my errors, which yet, I hope, are only those of charity to mankind; and such as my *own* charity has caused me to commit, that of *others* may more easily excuse. Being naturally inclined to scepticism in philosophy I have no reason to impose my opinions in a subject which is above it; but whatever they are, I submit them with all reverence to my Mother Church,[2] accounting them no further mine, than as they are authorized, or at least uncondemned by her. And, indeed, to secure myself on this side, I have used the necessary precaution of showing this paper before it was published to a judicious and learned friend, a man indefatigably zealous in the service of the Church and State; and whose writings have highly deserved of both. He was pleased to approve the body of the discourse, and I hope he is more my friend than to do it out of complaisance. 'T is true, he had too good a taste to like it all; and amongst some other faults recommended to my second view what I have written, perhaps too boldly, on St. Athanasius, which he advised me wholly to omit. I am sensible enough that I had done more *prudently* to have followed his opinion; but then I could not have satisfied myself that I had done honestly not to have written what was my own. It has always been my *thought* that heathens who never did, nor without miracle could, hear of the name of Christ, were yet in a possibility of salvation. Neither will it enter easily into my belief that, before the coming of our Savior, the whole world, excepting only the Jewish nation, should lie under the inevitable necessity of everlasting punishment, for want of that revelation which was confined to so small a spot of ground as that of Palestine. Among the sons of Noah we read of one only who was accursed; and if a blessing in the ripeness of time was reserved for Japhet (of whose progeny we are), it seems unaccountable to me why so many generations of the same offspring as preceded our Savior in the flesh should be all involved in one common condemnation, and yet that their posterity should be entitled to the hopes of salvation: as if a bill of exclusion had passed only on the fathers, which debarred not the sons from their succession. Or that so many ages had been *delivered over* to hell, and so many *reserved* for heaven, and that the Devil had the first choice, and God the next. Truly I am apt to think that the revealed religion which was taught by Noah to all his sons might continue for some ages in the whole posterity. That afterwards it was included wholly in the family of Sem is manifest; but when the progenies of Cham and Japhet swarmed into colonies, and those colonies were subdivided into many others, in process of time their descendants lost by little and little the primitive and purer rites of divine worship, retaining only the notion of one deity; to which succeeding generations added others; for men took their degrees in those ages from conquerors to gods. Revelation being thus eclipsed to almost all mankind, the light of nature, as the next in dignity, was substituted; and that is it which St. Paul concludes to be the rule of the heathens, and by which they are hereafter to be judged. If my supposition be true, then the consequence which I have assumed in my poem may be also true; namely, that Deism, or the principles of natural worship, are only the faint remnants or dying flames of revealed religion in the posterity of Noah: and that our modern philosophers, nay, and some of our philosophizing divines, have too much exalted the faculties of our souls, when they have maintained that by their force mankind has been able to find out that there is one supreme agent or intellectual being which we call God; that praise and prayer are his due worship; and the rest of those deducements, which I am confident are the remote effects of revelation, and unattainable by our discourse; I mean as simply considered, and without the benefit of divine illumination. So that we have not lifted up ourselves to God by the weak pinions of our reason, but he has been pleased to descend to us; and what Socrates said of him, what Plato writ, and the rest of the heathen philosophers of several nations, is all no

[2] I. e., the Church of England.

more than the twilight of revelation, after the sun of it was set in the race of Noah. That there is something above us, some principle of *motion,* our reason can apprehend, though it cannot discover what it is, by its own virtue. And indeed 't is very improbable that we, who by the strength of our faculties cannot enter into the knowledge of any *being,* not so much as of our *own,* should be able to find out by them that supreme nature, which we cannot otherwise define than by saying it is infinite; as if infinite were definable, or infinity a subject for our narrow understanding. They who would prove religion by reason do but weaken the cause which they endeavor to support: 't is to take away the pillars from our faith, and to prop it only with a twig; 't is to design a tower like that of Babel, which, if it were possible (as it is not) to reach heaven, would come to nothing by the confusion of the workmen. For every man is building a several way; impotently conceited of his own model and his own materials: reason is always striving, and always at a loss; and of necessity it must so come to pass, while 't is exercised about that which is not its proper object. Let us be content at last to know God by his own methods; at least, so much of him as he is pleased to reveal to us in the sacred Scriptures; to apprehend them to be the word of God is all our reason has to do; for all beyond it is the work of faith, which is the seal of heaven impressed upon our human understanding.

And now for what concerns the holy bishop Athanasius, the preface of whose creed seems inconsistent with my opinion;[3] which is, that heathens may possibly be saved: in the first place I desire it may be considered that it is the preface only, not the creed itself, which (till I am better informed) is of too hard a digestion for my charity. 'T is not that I am ignorant how many several texts of Scripture seemingly support that cause; but neither am I ignorant how all those texts may receive a kinder and more mollified interpretation. Every man who is read in Church history knows *that* belief was drawn up after a long contestation with Arius concerning the divinity of our blessed Savior, and his being one substance with the Father; and that, thus compiled, it was sent abroad among the Christian churches, as a kind of test, which whosoever took was looked on as an orthodox believer. 'T is manifest from hence that the heathen part of the empire was not concerned in it; for its business was not to distinguish betwixt pagans and Christians, but betwixt heretics and true believers. This, well considered, takes off the heavy weight of censure, which I would willingly avoid from so venerable a man; for if this proportion, "whosoever will be saved," be restrained only to those to whom it was intended, and for whom it was composed, I mean the Christians; then the anathema reaches not the heathens, who had never heard of Christ, and were nothing interested in that dispute. After all, I am far from blaming even that prefatory addition to the creed, and as far from caviling at the continuation of it in the liturgy of the Church, where, on the days appointed, 't is publicly read: for I suppose there is the same reason for it now, in opposition to the Socinians,[4] as there was then against the Arians; the one being a heresy which seems to have been refined out of the other; and with how much more plausibility of reason it combats our religion, with so much more caution to be avoided; and therefore the prudence of our Church is to be commended, which has interposed her authority for the recommendation of this creed. Yet, to such as are grounded in the true belief, those explanatory creeds, the Nicene and this of Athanasius, might perhaps be spared; for what is super-natural will always be a mystery in spite of exposition, and, for my own part, the plain Apostles' Creed is most suitable to my weak understanding, as the simplest diet is the most easy of digestion.

I have dwelt longer on this subject than I intended, and longer than, perhaps, I ought; for having laid down, as my foundation, that the Scripture is a rule; that in all things needful to salvation it is clear, sufficient, and ordained by God Almighty for that purpose,

[3]The Preface is as follows: "Whosoever will be saved, before all things it is necessary that he hold the Catholic faith. Which faith except every one do keep whole and undefiled, without doubt he shall perish everlastingly."

[4]A sect which denied the divinity of Christ.

I have left myself no right to interpret obscure places, such as concern the possibility of eternal happiness to heathens; because whatsoever is obscure is concluded not necessary to be known.

But, by asserting the Scripture to be the canon of our faith, I have unavoidably created to myself two sorts of enemies: the Papists indeed, more directly, because they have kept the Scripture from us, what they could;[5] and have reserved to themselves a right of interpreting what they have delivered under the pretense of infallibility: and the Fanatics more collaterally, because they have assumed what amounts to an infallibility in the private spirit; and have detorted[6] those texts of Scripture which are not necessary to salvation, to the damnable uses of sedition, disturbance, and destruction of the civil government. To begin with the Papists, and to speak freely, I think them the less dangerous, at least in appearance, to our present State, for not only the penal laws are in force against them, and their number is contemptible; but also their peerage and commons are excluded from parliaments, and consequently those laws in no probability of being repealed. A general and uninterrupted plot of their clergy, ever since the Reformation, I suppose all Protestants believe. For 't is not reasonable to think but that so many of their orders, as were outed from their fat possessions, would endeavor a reentrance against those whom they account heretics. As for the late design, Mr. Coleman's[7] letters, for aught I know, are the best evidence; and what they discover, without wiredrawing their sense, or malicious glosses, all men of reason conclude credible. If there be anything more than this required of me, I must believe it as well as I am able, in spite of the witnesses, and out of a decent conformity to the votes of parliament; for I suppose the Fanatics will not allow the private spirit in this case. Here the infallibility is at least in one part of the government; and our understandings as well as our wills are represented. But to return to the Roman Catholics, how can we be secure from the practice of Jesuited Papists in that religion? For not two or three of that order, as some of them would impose upon us, but almost the whole body of them, are of opinion that their infallible master has a right over kings, not only in spirituals but temporals. Not to name Mariana, Bellarmine, Emanuel Sa, Molina, Santarel, Simancha,[8] and at least twenty others of foreign countries; we can produce, of our own nation, Campian, and Doleman or Parsons,[9] besides many are named whom I have not read, who all of them attest this doctrine, that the Pope can depose and give away the right of any sovereign prince, *si vel paulum deflexerit,* if he shall never so little warp; but if he once comes to be excommunicated, then the bond of obedience is taken off from subjects; and they may and ought to drive him, like another Nebuchadnezzar, *ex hominum Christianorum dominatu,* from exercising dominion over Christians; and to this they are bound by virtue of divine precept, and by all the ties of conscience under no less penalty than damnation. If they answer me (as a learned priest has lately written) that this doctrine of the Jesuits is not *de fide;*[10] and that consequently they are not obliged by it, they must pardon me if I think they have said nothing to the purpose; for 't is a maxim in their Church, where points of faith are not decided, and that doctors are of contrary opinions, they may follow which part they please; but more safely the most received and most authorized. And their champion Bellarmine has told the world, in his *Apology,* that the king of England is a vassal to the Pope, *ratione directi dominii,*[11] and that he holds in villanage of his Roman landlord. Which is no new claim put in for England. Our chronicles are his authentic witnesses that King John was deposed by the same plea, and Philip Augustus admitted tenant. And which makes the more for Bellarmine,

[5]As far as they could. [6]Twisted.

[7]Coleman had been secretary to the Duke of York and had engaged in correspondence looking to the establishment of Roman Catholicism in England. He was executed in 1678.

[8]All of them Catholic writers of the sixteenth century.

[9]English Jesuits of the sixteenth century. "Doleman" was a pseudonym used by Parsons.

[10]A matter of faith.

[11]By reason of direct control.

the French king was again ejected when our king submitted to the Church, and the crown received under the sordid condition of a vassalage.

'T is not sufficient for the more moderate and well-meaning Papists (of which I doubt not there are many) to produce the evidences of their loyalty to the late king, and to declare their innocency in this Plot:[12] I will grant their behavior in the first to have been as loyal and as brave as they desire; and will be willing to hold them excused as to the second (I mean when it comes to my turn, and after my betters; for 't is a madness to be sober alone, while the nation continues drunk), but that saying of their Father Cres.[13] is still running in my head, that they may be dispensed with in their obedience to an heretic prince, while the necessity of the times shall oblige them to it: for that (as another of them tells us) is only the effect of Christian prudence; but when once they shall get power to shake him off, an heretic is no lawful king, and consequently to rise against him is no rebellion. I should be glad, therefore, that they would follow the advice which was charitably given them by a reverend prelate of our Church; namely, that they would join in a public act of disowning and detesting those Jesuitic principles; and subscribe to all doctrines which deny the Pope's authority of deposing kings, and releasing subjects from their oath of allegiance: to which I should think they might easily be induced, if it be true that this present Pope has condemned the doctrine of king-killing (a thesis of the Jesuits), amongst others, *ex cathedra* (as they call it), or in open consistory.

Leaving them, therefore, in so fair a way (if they please themselves) of satisfying all reasonable men of their sincerity and good meaning to the government, I shall make bold to consider that other extreme of our religion, I mean the Fanatics, or Schismatics, of the English Church. Since the Bible has been translated into our tongue, they have used it so, as if their business was not to be saved but to be damned by its contents. If we consider only them, better had it been for the English nation that it had still remained in the original Greek and Hebrew, or at least in the honest Latin of St. Jerome, than that several texts in it should have been prevaricated to the destruction of that government which put it into so ungrateful hands.

How many heresies the first translation of Tyndal produced in few years, let my Lord Herbert's[14] history of Henry the Eighth inform you; insomuch that for the gross errors in it, and the great mischiefs it occasioned, a sentence passed on the first edition of the Bible, too shameful almost to be repeated. After the short reign of Edward the Sixth (who had continued to carry on the Reformation on other principles than it was begun), everyone knows that not only the chief promoters of that work, but many others whose consciences would not dispense with Popery, were forced, for fear of persecution, to change climates: from whence returning at the beginning of Queen Elizabeth's reign, many of them who had been in France, and at Geneva, brought back the rigid opinions and imperious discipline of Calvin, to graft upon our Reformation. Which, though they cunningly concealed at first (as well knowing how nauseously that drug would go down in a lawful monarchy, which was prescribed for a rebellious commonwealth), yet they always kept it in reserve; and were never wanting to themselves either in court or parliament, when either they had any prospect of a numerous party of Fanatic members in the one, or the encouragement of any favorite in the other, whose covetousness was gaping at the patrimony of the Church. They who will consult the works of our venerable Hooker,[15] or the account of his life,[16] or more particularly the letter written to him on this subject by George Cranmer, may see by what gradations they proceeded: from the dislike of cap and surplice, the very next step was admonitions to the parliament against the whole government ecclesiastical; then came out

[12]The Popish Plot (1678).

[13]Serenus Cressy, chaplain to Queen Catharine, wife of Charles II.

[14]Edward Herbert, brother of the poet George Herbert.

[15]Richard Hooker (*c.* 1554–1600), author of the *Ecclesiastical Polity*.

[16]Dryden refers to the account by Izaak Walton, where, also, Cranmer's letter is printed.

volumes in English and Latin in defense of their tenets; and immediately practices were set on foot to erect their discipline without authority. Those not succeeding, satire and railing was the next; and Martin Marprelate[17] (the Marvell[18] of those times) was the first Presbyterian scribbler who sanctified libels and scurrility to the use of the Good Old Cause. Which was done (says my author) upon this account; that (their serious treatises having been fully answered and refuted) they might compass by railing what they had lost by reasoning; and, when their cause was sunk in court and parliament, they might at least hedge in a stake amongst the rabble: for to their ignorance all things are wit which are abusive. But if Church and State were made the theme, then the doctoral degree of wit was to be taken at Billingsgate: even the most saintlike of the party, though they durst not excuse this contempt and vilifying of the government, yet were pleased, and grinned at it with a pious smile, and called it a judgment of God against the hierarchy. Thus Sectaries, we may see, were born with teeth, foul-mouthed and scurrilous from their infancy; and if spiritual pride, venom, violence, contempt of superiors, and slander, had been the marks of orthodox belief, the Presbytery and the rest of our Schismatics, which are their spawn, were always the most visible Church in the Christian world.

'T is true, the government was too strong at that time for a rebellion; but to show what proficiency they had made in Calvin's school, even then their mouths watered at it; for two of their gifted brotherhood (Hacket and Coppinger), as the story tells us, got up into a pease-cart and harangued the people, to dispose them to an insurrection, and to establish their discipline by force: so that, however it comes about that now they celebrate Queen Elizabeth's birthnight as that of their saint and patroness, yet then they were for doing the work of the Lord by arms against her; and, in all probability, they wanted but a Fanatic lord mayor and two sheriffs of their party, to have compassed it. Our venerable Hooker, after many admonitions which he had given them, toward the end of his preface breaks out into this prophetic speech: "There is in every one of these considerations most just cause to fear, lest our hastiness to embrace a thing of so perilous consequence" (meaning the Presbyterian discipline) "should cause posterity to feel those evils, which as yet are more easy for us to prevent, than they would be for them to remedy."[19]

How fatally this Cassandra has foretold, we know too well by sad experience: the seeds were sown in the time of Queen Elizabeth, the bloody harvest ripened in the reign of King Charles the Martyr; and, because all the sheaves could not be carried off without shedding some of the loose grains, another crop is too like to follow; nay, I fear 't is unavoidable if the conventiclers be permitted still to scatter.

A man may be suffered to quote an adversary to our religion, when he speaks truth; and 't is the observation of Maimbourg, in his *History of Calvinism,*[20] that wherever that discipline was planted and embraced, rebellion, civil war, and misery attended it. And how indeed should it happen otherwise? Reformation of Church and State has always been the ground of our divisions in England. While we were Papists, our Holy Father rid us, by pretending authority out of the Scriptures to depose princes; when we shook off his authority, the Sectaries furnished themselves with the same weapons; and out of the same magazine, the Bible: so that the Scriptures, which are in themselves the greatest security of governors, as commanding express obedience to them, are now turned to their destruction; and never since the Reformation has there wanted a text of their interpreting to authorize a rebel. And 't is to be noted by the way that the doctrines of king-killing and deposing, which have been taken up only by the worst party of the Papists, the most frontless flatterers of the Pope's authority, have been espoused, defended, and are still maintained by the whole body of Noncomformists and Republicans.

[17] The name under which a series of Puritan pamphlets were published in 1588–1590.

[18] Andrew Marvell (1621–1678), the poet and satirist.

[19] *Ecclesiastical Polity,* Preface.

[20] A French work which had appeared in 1682.

'T is but dubbing themselves the people of God, which 't is the interest of their preachers to tell them they are, and their own interest to believe; and after that, they cannot dip into the Bible, but one text or another will turn up for their purpose; if they are under persecution (as they call it), then that is a mark of their election; if they flourish, then God works miracles for their deliverance, and the saints are to possess the earth.

They may think themselves to be too roughly handled in this paper; but I, who know best how far I could have gone on this subject, must be bold to tell them they are spared: though at the same time I am not ignorant that they interpret the mildness of a writer to them, as they do the mercy of the government; in the one they think it fear, and conclude it weakness in the other. The best way for them to confute me is, as I before advised the Papists, to disclaim their principles and renounce their practices. We shall all be glad to think them true Englishmen when they obey the king, and true Protestants when they conform to the Church discipline.

It remains that I acquaint the reader that the verses were written for an ingenious young gentleman,[21] my friend, upon his translation of the *Critical History of the Old Testament,* composed by the learned Father Simon: the verses therefore are addressed to the translator of that work, and the style of them is, what it ought to be, epistolary.

If anyone be so lamentable a critic as to require the smoothness, the numbers, and the turn of heroic poetry in this poem, I must tell him that, if he has not read Horace, I have studied him, and hope the style of his *Epistles* is not ill imitated here. The expressions of a poem designed purely for instruction ought to be plain and natural, and yet majestic; for here the poet is presumed to be a kind of lawgiver, and those three qualities which I have named are proper to the legislative style. The florid, elevated, and figurative way is for the passions; for love and hatred, fear and anger, are begotten in the soul by showing their objects out of their true proportion, either greater than the life, or less; but instruction is to be given by showing them what they naturally are. A man is to be cheated into passion, but to be reasoned into truth.

[21]The young man's name was Henry Dickinson. His translation of Père Richard Simon's French work appeared in 1682.

RELIGIO LAICI

Dim as the borrowed beams of moon and stars
To lonely, weary, wand'ring travelers,
Is Reason to the soul; and, as on high
Those rolling fires discover but the sky,
Not light us here, so Reason's glimmering ray 5
Was lent, not to assure our doubtful way,
But guide us upward to a better day.
And as those nightly tapers disappear,
When day's bright lord ascends our hemisphere;
So pale grows Reason at Religion's sight; 10
So dies, and so dissolves in supernatural light.
Some few, whose lamp shone brighter, have been led
From cause to cause, to nature's secret head;
And found that one first principle must be:
But what, or who, that UNIVERSAL HE; 15
Whether some soul encompassing this ball,
Unmade, unmoved; yet making, moving all;
Or various atoms' interfering dance
Leapt into form (the noble work of chance),
Or this great all was from eternity; 20
Not e'en the Stagirite[1] himself could see,
And Epicurus guessed as well as he:
As blindly groped they for a future state;
As rashly judged of providence and fate:
But least of all could their endeavors find 25
What most concerned the good of humankind;
For happiness was never to be found,
But vanished from 'em like enchanted ground.
One thought content the good to be enjoyed;
This every little accident destroyed: 30
The wiser madmen did for virtue toil,
A thorny, or at best a barren soil;
In pleasure some their glutton souls would steep,
But found their line too short, the well too deep,
And leaky vessels which no bliss could keep. 35
Thus anxious thoughts in endless circles roll,

Opinions of the several sects of philosophers concerning the Summum Bonum.

[1]Aristotle.

Without a center where to fix the soul;
In this wild maze their vain endeavors end:
How can the less the greater comprehend?
Or finite reason reach Infinity? 40
For what could fathom GOD were more than He.

System of Deism.

The Deist thinks he stands on firmer ground;
Cries: "Εὕρηκα, the mighty secret's found:
God is that spring of good; supreme and best; 44
We, made to serve, and in that service blest."
If so, some rules of worship must be given,
Distributed alike to all by Heaven:
Else God were partial, and to some denied
The means his justice should for all provide.
This general worship is to PRAISE and PRAY,
One part to borrow blessings, one to pay; 51
And when frail nature slides into offense,
The sacrifice for crimes is penitence.
Yet, since th' effects of providence, we find,
Are variously dispensed to humankind; 55
That vice triumphs, and virtue suffers here
(A brand that sovereign justice cannot bear),
Our reason prompts us to a future state,
The last appeal from fortune and from fate:
Where God's all-righteous ways will be declared, 60
The bad meet punishment, the good reward.
Thus man by his own strength to heaven would soar,

Of revealed Religion.

And would not be obliged to God for more.
Vain, wretched creature, how art thou misled 64
To think thy wit these godlike notions bred!
These truths are not the product of thy mind,
But dropped from heaven, and of a nobler kind.
Revealed Religion first informed thy sight,
And Reason saw not, till Faith sprung the light.
Hence all thy natural worship takes the source: 70
'T is revelation what thou think'st discourse.[2]
Else, how com'st thou to see these truths so clear,
Which so obscure to heathens did appear?
Not Plato these, nor Aristotle found;
Nor he whose wisdom oracles renowned. 75

Socrates.

Hast thou a wit so deep, or so sublime,
Or canst thou lower dive, or higher climb?
Canst thou, by Reason, more of Godhead know
Than Plutarch, Seneca, or Cicero?

[2] Reason.

Those giant wits, in happier ages born 80
(When arms and arts did Greece and Rome adorn),
Knew no such system; no such piles could raise
Of natural worship, built on prayer and praise,
To One Sole GOD:
Nor did remorse to expiate sin prescribe, 85
But slew their fellow creatures for a bribe:
The guiltless victim groaned for their offense,
And cruelty and blood was penitence.
If sheep and oxen could atone for men,
Ah! at how cheap a rate the rich might sin! 90
And great oppressors might Heaven's wrath beguile,
By offering his own creatures for a spoil!
Dar'st thou, poor worm, offend Infinity?
And must the terms of peace be given by thee?
Then thou art Justice in the last appeal: 95
Thy easy God instructs thee to rebel;
And, like a king remote, and weak, must take
What satisfaction thou art pleased to make.
But if there be a power too just and strong
To wink at crimes, and bear unpunished wrong; 100
Look humbly upward, see his will disclose
The forfeit first, and then the fine impose:
A mulct thy poverty could never pay,
Had not eternal wisdom found the way, 104
And with celestial wealth supplied thy store:
His justice makes the fine, his mercy quits the score.
See God descending in thy human frame;
Th' offended suff'ring in th' offender's name;
All thy misdeeds to him imputed see,
And all his righteousness devolved on thee. 110
For granting we have sinned, and that th' offense
Of man is made against Omnipotence,
Some price that bears proportion must be paid,
And infinite with infinite be weighed.
See then the Deist lost: remorse for vice, 115
Not paid; or paid, inadequate in price:
What farther means can Reason now direct,
Or what relief from human wit expect?
That shows us sick; and sadly are we sure
Still to be sick, till Heav'n reveal the cure: 120
If then Heav'n's will must needs be understood
(Which must, if we want cure, and Heaven be good),
Let all records of will revealed be shown;
With Scripture all in equal balance thrown,
And our one sacred book will be that one.

Proof needs not here, for whether we compare 126
That impious, idle, superstitious ware
Of rites, lustrations, offerings (which before,
In various ages, various countries bore),
With Christian faith and virtues, we shall find 130
None answ'ring the great ends of humankind,
But this one rule of life, that shows us best
How God may be appeased, and mortals blest.
Whether from length of time its worth we draw,
The world is scarce more ancient than the law: 135
Heav'n's early care prescribed for every age;
First, in the soul, and after, in the page.
Or, whether more abstractedly we look,
Or on the writers, or the written book,
Whence, but from heav'n, could men unskilled in arts, 140
In several ages born, in several parts,
Weave such agreeing truths? or how, or why,
Should all conspire to cheat us with a lie?
Unasked their pains, ungrateful their advice,
Starving their gain, and martyrdom their price. 145
If on the book itself we cast our view,
Concurrent heathens prove the story true;
The doctrine, miracles; which must convince,
For Heav'n in them appeals to human sense:
And though they prove not, they confirm the cause, 150
When what is taught agrees with nature's laws.
Then for the style; majestic and divine,
It speaks no less than God in every line:
Commanding words; whose force is still the same
As the first fiat that produced our frame. 155
All faiths beside or did by arms ascend,
Or sense indulged has made mankind their friend:
This only doctrine does our lusts oppose,
Unfed by nature's soil, in which it grows; 159
Cross to our interests, curbing sense and sin;
Oppressed without, and undermined within,
It thrives through pain; its own tormentors tires;
And with a stubborn patience still aspires.
To what can Reason such effects assign,
Transcending nature, but to laws divine? 165
Which in that sacred volume are contained;
Sufficient, clear, and for that use ordained.
But stay: the Deist here will urge anew, *Objection of the Deist.*
No supernatural worship can be true;
Because a general law is that alone 170
Which must to all, and everywhere, be known:
A style so large as not this book can claim,
Nor aught that bears revealed Religion's name.
'T is said the sound of a Messiah's birth
Is gone through all the habitable earth; 175
But still that text must be confined alone
To what was then inhabited, and known:
And what provision could from thence accrue
To Indian souls, and worlds discovered new?
In other parts it helps, that, ages past, 180
The Scriptures there were known, and were embraced,
Till Sin spread once again the shades of night:
What's that to these who never saw the light?
Of all objections this indeed is chief *The objection answered.*
To startle Reason, stagger frail Belief: 185
We grant, 't is true, that Heav'n from human sense
Has hid the secret paths of Providence;
But boundless wisdom, boundless mercy, may
Find e'en for those bewildered souls a way.
If from his nature foes may pity claim, 190
Much more may strangers who ne'er heard his name.
And though no name be for salvation known,
But that of his eternal Son's alone;
Who knows how far transcending goodness can
Extend the merits of that Son to man? 195
Who knows what reasons may his mercy lead,
Or ignorance invincible may plead?
Not only charity bids hope the best,
But more the great apostle has expressed:
That if the Gentiles (whom no law inspired)
By nature did what was by law required, 201
They, who the written rule had never known,
Were to themselves both rule and law alone:
To nature's plain indictment they shall plead,
And by their conscience be condemned or freed. 205
Most righteous doom! because a rule revealed
Is none to those from whom it was concealed.
Then those who followed Reason's dictates right,
Lived up, and lifted high their natural light;
With Socrates may see their Maker's face, 210
While thousand rubric-martyrs want a place.
Nor does it balk my charity, to find
Th' Egyptian bishop[3] of another mind:
For though his creed eternal truth contains,

[3]Athanasius, Bishop of Alexandria.

'T is hard for man to doom to endless pains
All who believed not all his zeal required, 216
Unless he first could prove he was inspired.
Then let us either think he meant to say
This faith, where published, was the only way;
Or else conclude that, Arius to confute, 220
The good old man, too eager in dispute,
Flew high; and, as his Christian fury rose,
Damned all for heretics who durst oppose.

Digression to the translator of Father Simon's Critical History of the Old Testament.

Thus far my charity this path has tried;
(A much unskilful, but well-meaning guide:) 225
Yet what they are, e'en these crude thoughts were bred.
By reading that which better thou hast read:
Thy matchless author's work; which thou, my friend,
By well translating better dost commend:
Those youthful hours which of thy equals most 230
In toys have squandered, or in vice have lost,
Those hours hast thou to nobler use employed;
And the severe delights of truth enjoyed.
Witness this weighty book, in which appears
The crabbed toil of many thoughtful years,
Spent by thy author in the sifting care 236
Of Rabbins' old sophisticated ware
From gold divine; which he who well can sort
May afterwards make algebra a sport:
A treasure, which if country·curates buy, 240
They Junius and Tremellius[4] may defy;
Save pains in various readings and translations,
And without Hebrew make most learn'd quotations:
A work so full with various learning fraught,
So nicely pondered, yet so strongly wrought,
As nature's height and art's last hand required; 246
As much as man could compass, uninspired;
Where we may see what errors have been made
Both in the copier's and translator's trade;
How Jewish, Popish interests have prevailed,
And where infallibility has failed. 251

For some, who have his secret meaning guessed,
Have found our author not too much a priest:
For fashion's sake he seems to have recourse
To Pope, and councils, and tradition's force;
But he that old traditions could subdue, 256
Could not but find the weakness of the new:

[4]Calvinistic divines.

If Scripture, though derived from heav'nly birth,
Has been but carelessly preserved on earth;
If God's own people, who of God before 260
Knew what we know, and had been promised more,
In fuller terms, of Heaven's assisting care,
And who did neither time nor study spare
To keep this book untainted, unperplexed,
Let in gross errors to corrupt the text, 265
Omitted paragraphs, embroiled the sense,
With vain traditions stopped the gaping fence,
Which every common hand pulled up with ease;
What safety from such brushwood-helps as these? 269
If written words from time are not secured,
How can we think have oral sounds endured?
Which thus transmitted, if one mouth has failed,
Immortal lies on ages are entailed;
And that some such have been, is proved too plain;
If we consider interest, Church, and gain. 275

Of the infallibility of tradition in general.

"O, but," says one, "tradition set aside,
Where can we hope for an unerring guide?
For since th' original Scripture has been lost,
All copies disagreeing, maimed the most,
Or Christian faith can have no certain ground, 280
Or truth in Church tradition must be found."

Such an omniscient Church we wish indeed;
'T were worth both Testaments; and cast in the Creed:
But if this mother be a guide so sure,
As can all doubts resolve, all truth secure, 285
Then her infallibility as well
Where copies are corrupt or lame can tell;
Restore lost canon with as little pains,
As truly explicate what still remains; 289
Which yet no council dare pretend to do,
Unless like Esdras they could write it new:
Strange confidence, still to interpret true,
Yet not be sure that all they have explained,
Is in the blest original contained. 294
More safe, and much more modest 't is to say
God would not leave mankind without a way;
And that the Scriptures, though not everywhere
Free from corruption, or entire, or clear,
Are uncorrupt, sufficient, clear, entire,
In all things which our needful faith require.
If others in the same glass better see, 301

'T is for themselves they look, but not for me:
For MY salvation must its doom receive,
Not from what OTHERS but what *I* believe.

Must all tradition then be set aside?
This to affirm were ignorance or pride. 306

Objection in behalf of tradition, urged by Father Simon.

Are there not many points, some needful sure
To saving faith, that Scripture leaves obscure?
Which every sect will wrest a several way 309
(For what one sect interprets, all sects may):
We hold, and say we prove from Scripture plain,
That Christ is GOD; the bold Socinian
From the same Scripture urges he's but MAN.
Now what appeal can end th' important suit; 314
Both parts talk loudly, but the rule is mute?

Shall I speak plain, and in a nation free
Assume an honest layman's liberty?
I think (according to my little skill, 318
To my own Mother Church submitting still)
That many have been saved, and many may,
Who never heard this question brought in play.
Th' unlettered Christian, who believes in gross,
Plods on to heaven, and ne'er is at a loss;
For the strait gate would be made straiter yet,
Were none admitted there but men of wit. 325
The few by nature formed, with learning fraught,
Born to instruct, as others to be taught,
Must study well the sacred page, and see
Which doctrine, this, or that, does best agree
With the whole tenor of the work divine, 330
And plainliest points to Heaven's revealed design;
Which exposition flows from genuine sense,
And which is forced by wit and eloquence.
Not that tradition's parts are useless here, 334
When general, old, disinterested and clear:
That ancient Fathers thus expound the page
Gives truth the reverend majesty of age;
Confirms its force, by biding every test;
For best authority's next rules are best.
And still the nearer to the spring we go, 340
More limpid, more unsoiled the waters flow.
Thus, first traditions were a proof alone,
Could we be certain such they were, so known;
But since some flaws in long descent may be,
They make not truth, but probability. 345
Even Arius and Pelagius[5] durst provoke
To what the centuries preceding spoke.
Such difference is there in an oft-told tale;
But truth by its own sinews will prevail.
Tradition written therefore more commends
Authority, than what from voice descends; 351
And this, as perfect as its kind can be,
Rolls down to us the sacred history,
Which, from the Universal Church received,
Is tried, and after for itself believed. 355

The partial Papists would infer from hence

The second objection.

Their Church, in last resort, should judge the sense;
But first they would assume, with wondrous art,

Answer to the objection.

Themselves to be the whole, who are but part
Of that vast frame, the Church; yet grant they were 360
The handers down, can they from thence infer
A right t' interpret? or would they alone
Who brought the present, claim it for their own?
The book's a common largess to mankind,
Not more for them than every man designed:
The welcome news is in the letter found; 366
The carrier's not commissioned to expound.
It speaks itself, and what it does contain,
In all things needful to be known, is plain.

In times o'ergrown with rust and ignorance, 370
A gainful trade their clergy did advance;
When want of learning kept the laymen low,
And none but priests were authorized to know;
When what small knowledge was, in them did dwell,
And he a god who could but read or spell: 375
Then Mother Church did mightily prevail;
She parceled out the Bible by retail;
But still expounded what she sold or gave,
To keep it in her power to damn and save:
Scripture was scarce, and, as the market went, 380
Poor laymen took salvation on content;
As needy men take money, good or bad:
God's word they had not, but the priest's they had.
Yet, whate'er false conveyances they made,
The lawyer still was certain to be paid. 385
In those dark times they learned their knack so well,
That by long use they grew infallible:
At last, a knowing age began t'enquire
If they the book, or that did them inspire;
And, making narrower search, they found, though late, 390

[5] Heretics of the fourth and fifth centuries respectively.

That what they thought the priest's was their estate,
Taught by the will produced (the written word),
How long they had been cheated on record.
Then every man who saw the title fair
Claimed a child's part, and put in for a share; 395
Consulted soberly his private good,
And saved himself as cheap as e'er he could.
'T is true, my friend (and far be flattery hence),
This good had full as bad a consequence:
The book thus put in every vulgar hand, 400
Which each presumed he best could understand,
The common rule was made the common prey,
And at the mercy of the rabble lay.
The tender page with horny fists was galled,
And he was gifted most that loudest bawled: 405
The spirit gave the doctoral degree;
And every member of a company
Was of his trade and of the Bible free.[6]
Plain truths enough for needful use they found,
But men would still be itching to expound: 410
Each was ambitious of th' obscurest place,
No measure ta'en from knowledge, all from GRACE.
Study and pains were now no more their care;
Texts were explained by fasting and by prayer:
This was the fruit the private spirit brought, 415
Occasioned by great zeal and little thought.
While crowds unlearn'd, with rude devotion warm,
About the sacred viands buzz and swarm,
The fly-blown text creates a crawling brood,
And turns to maggots what was meant for food. 420
A thousand daily sects rise up and die;
A thousand more the perished race supply:
So all we make of Heaven's discovered will
Is, not to have it, or to use it ill.
The danger's much the same; on several shelves 425
If others wreck us, or we wreck ourselves.
What then remains, but, waiving each extreme,
The tides of ignorance and pride to stem?
Neither so rich a treasure to forego;
Nor proudly seek beyond our pow'r to know: 430
Faith is not built on disquisitions vain;
The things we must believe are few and plain:
But since men will believe more than they need,
And every man will make himself a creed,
In doubtful questions 't is the safest way 435
To learn what unsuspected ancients say;
For 't is not likely we should higher soar
In search of heav'n, than all the Church before;
Nor can we be deceived, unless we see
The Scripture and the Fathers disagree. 440
If, after all, they stand suspected still
(For no man's faith depends upon his will),
'T is some relief that points not clearly known
Without much hazard may be let alone:
And after hearing what our Church can say, 445
If still our Reason runs another way,
That private Reason 't is more just to curb,
Than by disputes the public peace disturb.
For points obscure are of small use to learn;
But common quiet is mankind's concern. 450
Thus have I made my own opinions clear;
Yet neither praise expect, nor censure fear:
And this unpolished, rugged verse, I chose,
As fittest for discourse, and nearest prose;
For while from sacred truth I do not swerve, 455
Tom Sternhold's,[7] or Tom Shadwell's rimes will serve.

[6]To be "free" of a trade was to be possessed of the rights of membership in it.

[7]Translator of the Psalms, known for the roughness of his versification.

A SONG FOR ST. CECILIA'S DAY[1]

(1687)

I

From harmony, from heav'nly harmony
This universal frame began:
When Nature underneath a heap
Of jarring atoms lay,
And could not heave her head, 5

[1]St. Cecelia is said to have invented the organ, and was canonized as the patron saint of music. A musical society was organized in London in 1683 for the celebration of St. Cecilia's day, 22 November, and each year an ode, composed for the occasion, was sung. This and the following poem were written by Dryden for this purpose.

The tuneful voice was heard from high:
"Arise, ye more than dead."
Then cold, and hot, and moist, and dry,
In order to their stations leap,
And Music's pow'r obey. 10
From harmony, from heav'nly harmony
This universal frame began:
From harmony to harmony
Through all the compass of the notes it ran,
The diapason closing full in Man. 15

II

What passion cannot Music raise and quell!
When Jubal[2] struck the corded shell,
His list'ning brethren stood around,
And, wond'ring, on their faces fell
To worship that celestial sound. 20
Less than a god they thought there could not dwell
Within the hollow of that shell
That spoke so sweetly and so well.
What passion cannot Music raise and quell!

III

The Trumpet's loud clangor 25
Excites us to arms,
With shrill notes of anger,
And mortal alarms.
The double double double beat
Of the thund'ring Drum 30
Cries: "Hark! the foes come;
Charge, charge, 't is too late to retreat."

IV

The soft complaining Flute
In dying notes discovers
The woes of hopeless lovers, 35
Whose dirge is whispered by the warbling Lute.

V

Sharp Violins proclaim
Their jealous pangs, and desperation,
Fury, frantic indignation,
Depth of pains, and height of passion, 40
For the fair, disdainful dame.

VI

But O! what art can teach,
What human voice can reach,
The sacred Organ's praise?
Notes inspiring holy love, 45
Notes that wing their heav'nly ways
To mend the choirs above.

[2]See Genesis, 4:21.

VII

Orpheus could lead the savage race;
And trees unrooted left their place,
Sequacious of[3] the lyre; 50
But right Cecilia raised the wonder high'r:
When to her Organ vocal breath was giv'n,
An angel heard, and straight appeared,
Mistaking earth for heav'n.

GRAND CHORUS

As from the pow'r of sacred lays 55
The spheres began to move,
And sung the great Creator's praise
To all the blest above;
So, when the last and dreadful hour
This crumbling pageant shall devour, 60
The Trumpet shall be heard on high,
The dead shall live, the living die,
And Music shall untune the sky.

ALEXANDER'S FEAST

or,

The Power of Music

AN ODE IN HONOR OF ST. CECILIA'S DAY

(1697)

I

'T was at the royal feast, for Persia won
By Philip's warlike son:[1]
Aloft in awful state
The godlike hero sate
On his imperial throne: 5
His valiant peers were placed around;
Their brows with roses and with myrtles bound
(So should desert in arms be crowned).
The lovely Thais, by his side,
Sate like a blooming Eastern bride 10
In flow'r of youth and beauty's pride.
Happy, happy, happy pair!
None but the brave,
None but the brave, 14
None but the brave deserves the fair.

CHORUS

Happy, happy, happy pair!
None but the brave,
None but the brave,
None but the brave deserves the fair.

[3]Following.
[1]Alexander the Great.

II

Timotheus,[2] placed on high 20
Amid the tuneful choir,
With flying fingers touched the lyre:
The trembling notes ascend the sky,
And heav'nly joys inspire.
The song began from Jove, 25
Who left his blissful seats above
(Such is the power of mighty love).
A dragon's fiery form belied the god:
Sublime on radiant spires[3] he rode,
When he to fair Olympia pressed; 30
And while he sought her snowy breast:
Then, round her slender waist he curled,
And stamped an image of himself, a sov'reign of the world.
The list'ning crowd admire the lofty sound;
"A present deity," they shout around; 35
"A present deity," the vaulted roofs rebound:
With ravished ears
The monarch hears,
Assumes the god,
Affects to nod, 40
And seems to shake the spheres.

CHORUS

With ravished ears
The monarch hears,
Assumes the god,
Affects to nod, 45
And seems to shake the spheres.

III

The praise of Bacchus then the sweet musician sung,
Of Bacchus ever fair and ever young:
The jolly god in triumph comes;
Sound the trumpets; beat the drums; 50
Flushed with a purple grace
He shows his honest face:
Now give the hautboys breath; he comes, he comes.
Bacchus, ever fair and young,
Drinking joys did first ordain; 55
Bacchus' blessings are a treasure.
Drinking is the soldier's pleasure:
Rich the treasure,
Sweet the pleasure,
Sweet is pleasure after pain. 60

CHORUS

Bacchus' blessings are a treasure,
Drinking is the soldier's pleasure:
Rich the treasure,
Sweet the pleasure,
Sweet is pleasure after pain. 65

IV

Soothed with the sound, the king grew vain;
Fought all his battles o'er again;
And thrice he routed all his foes; and thrice he slew the slain.
The master saw the madness rise;
His glowing cheeks, his ardent eyes; 70
And, while he heav'n and earth defied,
Changed his hand, and checked his pride.
He chose a mournful Muse,
Soft pity to infuse:
He sung Darius[4] great and good, 75
By too severe a fate,
Fallen, fallen, fallen, fallen,
Fallen from his high estate,
And welt'ring in his blood;
Deserted, at his utmost need, 80
By those his former bounty fed;
On the bare earth exposed he lies,
With not a friend to close his eyes.
With downcast looks the joyless victor sate,
Revolving in his altered soul 85
The various turns of chance below;
And, now and then, a sigh he stole;
And tears began to flow.

CHORUS

Revolving in his altered soul
The various turns of chance below; 90
And, now and then, a sigh he stole;
And tears began to flow.

V

The mighty master smiled, to see
That love was in the next degree:
'Twas but a kindred sound to move, 95
For pity melts the mind to love.
Softly sweet, in Lydian measures,
Soon he soothed his soul to pleasures.
"War," he sung, "is toil and trouble;
Honor, but an empty bubble; 100
Never ending, still beginning,
Fighting still, and still destroying;
If the world be worth thy winning,
Think, O think it worth enjoying;
Lovely Thais sits beside thee, 105
Take the good the gods provide thee."
The many rend the skies with loud applause;
So Love was crowned, but Music won the cause.

[2] A Boeotian musician, a favorite of Alexander.
[3] Spirals.
[4] The Persian monarch conquered by Alexander.

The prince, unable to conceal his pain,
Gazed on the fair 110
Who cause his care,
And sighed and looked, sighed and looked,
Sighed and looked, and sighed again:
At length, with love and wine at once oppressed, 114
The vanquished victor sunk upon her breast.

CHORUS

The prince, unable to conceal his pain,
Gazed on the fair
Who caused his care,
And sighed and looked, sighed and looked,
Sighed and looked, and sighed again: 120
At length, with love and wine at once oppressed,
The vanquished victor sunk upon her breast.

VI

Now strike the golden lyre again:
A louder yet, and yet a louder strain.
Break his bands of sleep asunder, 125
And rouse him, like a rattling peal of thunder.
Hark, hark, the horrid sound
Has raised up his head:
As awaked from the dead,
And amazed, he stares around. 130
"Revenge, revenge!" Timotheus cries,
"See the Furies arise!
See the snakes that they rear,
How they hiss in their hair, 134
And the sparkles that flash from their eyes!
Behold a ghastly band,
Each a torch in his hand!
Those are Grecian ghosts, that in battle were slain,
And unburied remain
Inglorious on the plain: 140
Give the vengeance due
To the valiant crew.
Behold how they toss their torches on high,
How they point to the Persian abodes,
And glitt'ring temples of their hostile gods!"
The princes applaud, with a furious joy; 146
And the king seized a flambeau with zeal to destroy;
Thais led the way,
To light him to his prey,
And, like another Helen, fired another Troy.

CHORUS

And the king seized a flambeau with zeal to destroy; 151
Thais led the way,
To light him to his prey,
And, like another Helen, fired another Troy.

VII

Thus, long ago, 155
Ere heaving bellows learned to blow,
While organs yet were mute;
Timotheus, to his breathing flute,
And sounding lyre,
Could swell the soul to rage, or kindle soft desire. 160
At last, divine Cecilia came,
Inventress of the vocal frame;[5]
The sweet enthusiast, from her sacred store,
Enlarged the former narrow bounds,
And added length to solemn sounds, 165
With nature's mother wit, and arts unknown before.
Let old Timotheus yield the prize,
Or both divide the crown;
He raised a mortal to the skies;
She drew an angel down. 170

GRAND CHORUS

At last, divine Cecilia came,
Inventress of the vocal frame;
The sweet enthusiast, from her sacred store,
Enlarged the former narrow bounds,
And added length to solemn sounds, 175
With nature's mother wit, and arts unknown before.
Let old Timotheus yield the prize,
Or both divide the crown;
He raised a mortal to the skies;
She drew an angel down. 180

PREFACE TO THE *FABLES*[1]

(1700)

'TIS with a Poet, as with a man who designs to build, and is very exact, as he sup-

[5] I. e., organ.

[1] Full title: *Fables Ancient and Modern; translated into verse, from Homer, Ovid, Boccace, and Chaucer; with Original Poems. The Preface,* "addressed to the Duke of Ormond, is a piece of work of which it is hard to speak except in some such terms as those which Dryden himself employs in it when he has to write about Chaucer. . . . [It] is more full of life than anything else in Dryden's prose; . . . while nothing, either in prose or verse, brings out more admirably or to better advantage the qualities of Dryden as the great English man of letters. For this is what he was, rather than essentially a poet; his genius is one that commands both vehicles of expression, it is not one that is specially inclined to verse; and the free movement of his mind and speech is scarcely less wonderful in a prose tract like this *Preface* than in the verse of *Absalom and Achitophel*" (W. P. Ker).

poses, in casting up the cost beforehand; but, generally speaking, he is mistaken in his account, and reckons short of the expense he first intended. He alters his mind as the work proceeds, and will have this or that convenience more, of which he had not thought when he began. So has it happened to me; I have built a house, where I intended but a lodge; yet with better success than a certain nobleman,[2] who, beginning with a dog-kennel, never lived to finish the palace he had contrived.

From translating the first of Homer's *Iliads* (which I intended as an essay to the whole work), I proceeded to the translation of the twelfth book of Ovid's *Metamorphoses,* because it contains, among other things, the causes, the beginning, and ending, of the Trojan war. Here I ought in reason to have stopped; but the speeches of Ajax and Ulysses lying next in my way, I could not balk 'em. When I had compassed them, I was so taken with the former part of the fifteenth book (which is the masterpiece of the whole *Metamorphoses*), that I enjoined myself the pleasing task of rendering it into English. And now I found, by the number of my verses, that they began to swell into a little volume; which gave me an occasion of looking backward on some beauties of my author, in his former books: there occurred to me the *Hunting of the Boar, Cinyras and Myrrha,* the good-natured story of *Baucis and Philemon,* with the rest, which I hope I have translated closely enough, and given them the same turn of verse which they had in the original; and this, I may say, without vanity, is not the talent of every poet. He who has arrived the nearest to it, is the ingenious and learned Sandys,[3] the best versifier of the former age; if I may properly call it by that name, which was the former part of this concluding century. For Spenser and Fairfax[4] both flourished in the reign of Queen Elizabeth; great masters in our language, and who saw much further into the beauties of our numbers than those who immediately followed them. Milton was the poetical son of Spenser, and Mr. Waller of Fairfax; for we have our lineal descents and clans as well as other families. Spenser more than once insinuates that the soul of Chaucer was transfused into his body;[5] and that he was begotten by him two hundred years after his decease. Milton has acknowledged to me, that Spenser was his original; and many besides myself have heard our famous Waller own that he derived the harmony of his numbers from *Godfrey of Bulloign,* which was turned into English by Mr. Fairfax.

But to return: having done with Ovid for this time, it came into my mind that our old English poet, Chaucer, in many things resembled him, and that with no disadvantage on the side of the modern author, as I shall endeavor to prove when I compare them; and as I am, and always have been, studious to promote the honor of my native country, so I soon resolved to put their merits to the trial, by turning some of the *Canterbury Tales* into our language, as it is now refined; for by this means, both the poets being set in the same light, and dressed in the same English habit, story to be compared with story, a certain judgment may be made betwixt them by the reader, without obtruding my opinion on him. Or, if I seem partial to my countryman and predecessor in the laurel, the friends of antiquity are not few; and, besides many of the learned, Ovid has almost all the beaux, and the whole fair sex, his declared patrons. Perhaps I have assumed somewhat more to myself than they allow me, because I have adventured to sum up the evidence; but the readers are the jury, and their privilege remains entire, to decide according to the merits of the cause; or, if they please, to bring it to another hearing before some other court. In the mean time, to follow the thread of my discourse (as thoughts, according to Mr. Hobbes,[6] have always some connection), so from Chaucer I was led to think on Boccaccio, who was not only his contemporary, but also pursued the same studies; wrote novels

[2]The Duke of Buckingham (Zimri in *Absalom and Achitophel*).

[3]George Sandys (1578–1644), who translated Ovid's *Metamorphoses.*

[4]Edward Fairfax (died 1635) published his translation of Tasso's *Godfrey of Bulloigne, or the Recovery of Jerusalem* in 1600.

[5]See *Faerie Queene,* Bk. IV, 2, 34.

[6]Thomas Hobbes (1588–1679). The reference is to Pt. I, Chap. 3, of the *Leviathan.*

in prose, and many works in verse; particularly is said to have invented the octave rime, or stanza of eight lines, which ever since has been maintained by the practice of all Italian writers who are, or at least assume the title of, heroic poets. He and Chaucer, among other things, had this in common, that they refined their mother-tongues; but with this difference, that Dante had begun to file their language, at least in verse, before the time of Boccaccio, who likewise received no little help from his master Petrarch; but the reformation of their prose was wholly owing to Boccaccio himself, who is yet the standard of purity in the Italian tongue, though many of his phrases are become obsolete, as in process of time it must needs happen. Chaucer (as you have formerly been told by our learned Mr. Rymer[7]) first adorned and amplified our barren tongue from the Provençal, which was then the most polished of all the modern languages; but this subject has been copiously treated by that great critic, who deserves no little commendation from us his countrymen. For these reasons of time, and resemblance of genius, in Chaucer and Boccaccio, I resolved to join them in my present work; to which I have added some original papers of my own, which whether they are equal or inferior to my other poems, an author is the most improper judge; and therefore I leave them wholly to the mercy of the reader. I will hope the best, that they will not be condemned; but if they should, I have the excuse of an old gentleman, who, mounting on horseback before some ladies, when I was present, got up somewhat heavily, but desired of the fair spectators that they would count fourscore and eight before they judged him. By the mercy of God, I am already come within twenty years of his number; a cripple in my limbs, but what decays are in my mind the reader must determine. I think myself as vigorous as ever in the faculties of my soul, excepting only my memory, which is not impaired to any great degree; and if I lose not more of it, I have no great reason to complain. What judgment I had, increases rather than diminishes; and thoughts, such as they are, come crowding in so fast upon me that my only difficulty is to choose or to reject, to run them into verse, or to give them the other harmony of prose: I have so long studied and practiced both, that they are grown into a habit, and become familiar to me. In short, though I may lawfully plead some part of the old gentleman's excuse, yet I will reserve it till I think I have greater need, and ask no grains of allowance for the faults of this my present work, but those which are given of course to human frailty. I will not trouble my reader with the shortness of time in which I writ it, or the several intervals of sickness. They who think too well of their own performances are apt to boast in their prefaces how little time their works have cost them, and what other business of more importance interfered; but the reader will be as apt to ask the question, why they allowed not a longer time to make their works more perfect? and why they had so despicable an opinion of their judges as to thrust their indigested stuff upon them, as if they deserved no better?

With this account of my present undertaking, I conclude the first part of this discourse: in the second part, as at a second sitting, though I alter not the draft, I must touch the same features over again, and change the dead-coloring[8] of the whole. In general I will only say, that I have written nothing which savors of immorality or profaneness; at least, I am not conscious to myself of any such intention. If there happen to be found an irreverent expression, or a thought too wanton, they are crept into my verses through my inadvertency; if the searchers find any in the cargo, let them be

[7]Thomas Rymer (1641–1713), author of *The Tragedies of the Last Age* (1678) and of *A Short View of Tragedy* (1693). It is in the latter that Rymer puts forward his notion that Chaucer belongs to the "Provençal School": "They who attempted verse in English, down till Chaucer's time, made an heavy pudder, and are always miserably put to 't for a word to clink; which commonly fall so awkward and unexpectedly as dropping from the clouds by some machine or miracle. Chaucer found an Herculean labor on his hands; and did perform to admiration. He seizes all Provençal, French, and Latin that came in his way, gives them a new garb and livery, and mingles them amongst our English: turns out English, gouty or superannuated, to place in their room the foreigners fit for service, trained and accustomed to poetical discipline."

[8]First coat of paint applied to a canvas.

staved[9] or forfeited, like counterbanded goods; at least, let their authors be answerable for them, as being but imported merchandise, and not of my own manufacture. On the other side, I have endeavored to choose such fables, both ancient and modern, as contain in each of them some instructive moral; which I could prove by induction, but the way is tedious, and they leap foremost into sight, without the reader's trouble of looking after them. I wish I could affirm, with a safe conscience, that I had taken the same care in all my former writings; for it must be owned, that supposing verses are never so beautiful or pleasing, yet, if they contain anything which shocks religion or good manners, they are at best what Horace says of good numbers without good sense, *Versus inopes rerum, nugaeque canorae.*[10] Thus far, I hope, I am right in court, without renouncing to my other right of self-defense, where I have been wrongfully accused, and my sense wire-drawn into blasphemy or bawdry, as it has often been by a religious lawyer,[11] in a late pleading against the stage; in which he mixes truth with falsehood, and has not forgotten the old rule of calumniating strongly, that something may remain.

I resume the thread of my discourse with the first of my translations, which was the first *Iliad* of Homer. If it shall please God to give me longer life, and moderate health, my intentions are to translate the whole *Ilias;* provided still that I meet with those encouragements from the public which may enable me to proceed in my undertaking with some cheerfulness. And this I dare assure the world beforehand, that I have found, by trial, Homer a more pleasing task than Virgil, though I say not the translation will be less laborious; for the Grecian is more according to my genius than the Latin poet. In the works of the two authors we may read their manners, and natural inclinations, which are wholly different. Virgil was of a quiet, sedate temper; Homer was violent, impetuous, and full of fire. The chief talent of Virgil was propriety of thoughts, and ornament of words: Homer was rapid in his thoughts, and took all the liberties, both of numbers and of expressions, which his language, and the age in which he lived, allowed him. Homer's invention was more copious, Virgil's more confined; so that if Homer had not led the way, it was not in Virgil to have begun heroic poetry; for nothing can be more evident than that the Roman poem is but the second part of the *Ilias;* a continuation of the same story, and the persons already formed. The manners of Aeneas are those of Hector, superadded to those which Homer gave him. The adventures of Ulysses in the *Odysseis* are imitated in the first six books of Virgil's *Aeneis;* and though the accidents are not the same (which would have argued him of a servile copying, and total barrenness of invention), yet the seas were the same in which both the heroes wandered; and Dido cannot be denied to be the poetical daughter of Calypso. The six latter books of Virgil's poem are the four-and-twenty *Iliads* contracted; a quarrel occasioned by a lady, a single combat, battles fought, and a town besieged. I say not this in derogation to Virgil, neither do I contradict anything which I have formerly said in his just praise; for his episodes are almost wholly of his own invention, and the form which he has given to the telling makes the tale his own, even though the original story had been the same. But this proves, however, that Homer taught Virgil to design; and if invention be the first virtue of an epic poet, then the Latin poem can only be allowed the second place. Mr. Hobbes, in the preface to his own bald translation of the *Ilias* (studying poetry as he did mathematics, when it was too late), Mr. Hobbes, I say, begins the praise of Homer where he should have ended it. He tells us that the first beauty of an epic poem consists in diction; that is, in the choice of words, and harmony of numbers. Now the words are the coloring of the work, which, in the order of nature, is last to be considered. The design, the disposition, the manners, and the thoughts, are all before it: where any of

[9] Destroyed, as contraband hogsheads were, by breaking holes in them.

[10] Verses lacking substance, and melodious trumpery (*De Arte Poetica,* 322).

[11] Jeremy Collier (1650–1726), in his *Short View of the Immorality and Profaneness of the English Stage* (1698).

those are wanting or imperfect, so much wants or is imperfect in the imitation of human life, which is in the very definition of a poem. Words, indeed, like glaring colors, are the first beauties that arise and strike the sight; but, if the draft be false or lame, the figures ill disposed, the manners obscure or inconsistent, or the thoughts unnatural, then the finest colors are but daubing, and the piece is a beautiful monster at the best. Neither Virgil nor Homer were deficient in any of the former beauties; but in this last, which is expression, the Roman poet is at least equal to the Grecian, as I have said elsewhere; supplying the poverty of his language by his musical ear, and by his diligence.

But to return: our two great poets being so different in their tempers, one choleric and sanguine, the other phlegmatic and melancholic; that which makes them excel in their several ways is, that each of them has followed his own natural inclination, as well in forming the design, as in the execution of it. The very heroes show their authors: Achilles is hot, impatient, revengeful—

Impiger, iracundus, inexorabilis, acer, etc.,[12]

Aeneas patient, considerate, careful of his people, and merciful to his enemies; ever submissive to the will of heaven—

quo fata trahunt retrahuntque, sequamur.[13]

I could please myself with enlarging on this subject, but am forced to defer it to a fitter time. From all I have said, I will only draw this inference, that the action of Homer, being more full of vigor than that of Virgil, according to the temper of the writer, is of consequence more pleasing to the reader. One warms you by degrees; the other sets you on fire all at once, and never intermits his heat. 'Tis the same difference which Longinus makes betwixt the effects of eloquence in Demosthenes and Tully;[14] one persuades, the other commands. You never cool while you read Homer, even not in the second book (a graceful flattery to his countrymen); but he hastens from the ships, and concludes not that book till he has made you an amends by the violent playing of a new machine.[15] From thence he hurries on his action with variety of events, and ends it in less compass than two months. This vehemence of his, I confess, is more suitable to my temper; and, therefore, I have translated his first book with greater pleasure than any part of Virgil; but it was not a pleasure without pains. The continual agitations of the spirits must needs be a weakening of any constitution, especially in age; and many pauses are required for refreshment betwixt the heats; the *Iliad* of itself being a third part longer than all Virgil's works together.

This is what I thought needful in this place to say of Homer. I proceed to Ovid and Chaucer, considering the former only in relation to the latter. With Ovid ended the golden age of the Roman tongue; from Chaucer the purity of the English tongue began. The manners of the poets were not unlike. Both of them were well-bred, well-natured, amorous, and libertine, at least in their writings; it may be, also in their lives. Their studies were the same, philosophy and philology.[16] Both of them were knowing in astronomy; of which Ovid's books of the *Roman Feasts,* and Chaucer's *Treatise of the Astrolabe,* are sufficient witnesses. But Chaucer was likewise an astrologer, as were Virgil, Horace, Persius, and Manilius. Both writ with wonderful facility and clearness; neither were great inventors: for Ovid only copied the Grecian fables, and most of Chaucer's stories were taken from his Italian contemporaries, or their predecessors. Boccaccio his *Decameron* was first published, and from thence our Englishman has borrowed many of his *Canterbury Tales*:[17] yet that of *Palamon and Arcite* was written, in all probability, by some Italian wit, in a former age, as I shall prove hereafter. The tale of *Griselda* was the invention of Pe-

[12]Impatient, fiery, ruthless, keen (Horace, *De Arte Poetica,* 121).

[13]Whither the Fates, in their ebb and flow, draw us, let us follow (Virgil, *Aeneid,* V, 709).

[14]M. Tullius Cicero.

[15]This is a slip. The dream of Agamemnon (referred to at the end of the sentence) *precedes* the catalogue of the ships in Bk. II.

[16]The word here denotes all studies connected with literature.

[17]"In all probability, Chaucer was unacquainted with" the *Decameron* (R. K. Root, *The Poetry of Chaucer*).

trarch; by him sent to Boccaccio,[18] from whom it came to Chaucer. *Troilus and Cressida* was also written by a Lombard author,[19] but much amplified by our English translator, as well as beautified; the genius of our countrymen, in general, being rather to improve an invention than to invent themselves, as is evident not only in our poetry, but in many of our manufactures. I find I have anticipated already, and taken up from Boccaccio before I come to him: but there is so much less behind; and I am of the temper of most kings, who love to be in debt, are all for present money, no matter how they pay it afterwards: besides, the nature of a preface is rambling, never wholly out of the way, nor in it. This I have learned from the practice of honest Montaigne, and return at my pleasure to Ovid and Chaucer, of whom I have little more to say.

Both of them built on the inventions of other men; yet since Chaucer had something of his own, as *The Wife of Bath's Tale, The Cock and the Fox,*[20] which I have translated, and some others, I may justly give our countryman the precedence in that part; since I can remember nothing of Ovid which was wholly his. Both of them understood the manners; under which name I comprehend the passions, and, in a larger sense, the descriptions of persons, and their very habits. For an example, I see Baucis and Philemon as perfectly before me, as if some ancient painter had drawn them; and all the Pilgrims in the *Canterbury Tales,* their humors, their features, and the very dress, as distinctly as if I had supped with them at the *Tabard* in Southwark. Yet even there, too, the figures of Chaucer are much more lively, and set in a better light; which though I have not time to prove, yet I appeal to the reader, and am sure he will clear me from partiality. The thoughts and words remain to be considered, 5 in the comparison of the two poets, and I have saved myself one-half of the labor, by owning that Ovid lived when the Roman tongue was in its meridian; Chaucer, in the dawning of our language: therefore that 10 part of the comparison stands not on an equal foot, any more than the diction of Ennius and Ovid, or of Chaucer and our present English. The words are given up, as a post not to be defended in our poet, be- 15 cause he wanted the modern art of fortifying. The thoughts remain to be considered; and they are to be measured only by their propriety; that is, as they flow more or less naturally from the persons described, on 20 such and such occasions. The vulgar judges, which are nine parts in ten of all nations, who call conceits and jingles wit, who see Ovid full of them, and Chaucer altogether without them, will think me little less 25 than mad for preferring the Englishman to the Roman. Yet, with their leave, I must presume to say that the things they admire are only glittering trifles, and so far from being witty, that in a serious poem they are 30 nauseous, because they are unnatural. Would any man, who is ready to die for love, describe his passion like Narcissus? Would he think of *inopem me copia fecit,*[21] and a dozen more of such expressions, poured on 35 the neck of one another, and signifying all the same thing? If this were wit, was this a time to be witty, when the poor wretch was in the agony of death? This is just John Littlewit, in *Bartholomew Fair,*[22] who had a 40 conceit (as he tells you) left him in his misery; a miserable conceit. On these occasions the poet should endeavor to raise pity; but, instead of this, Ovid is tickling you to laugh. Virgil never made use of such 45 machines when he was moving you to commiserate the death of Dido: he would not destroy what he was building. Chaucer

[18]"What Petrarch sent to Boccaccio was a Latin version of Boccaccio's story of Griselda in the *Decameron*" (W. P. Ker). Chaucer took the tale from Petrarch's version.

[19]The *Filostrato,* by Boccaccio, was Chaucer's immediate source. Dryden was misled by Chaucer's reference to one Lollius as his authority. This Lollius seems to be the *Maxime Lolli* of Horace's Second *Epistle* (Bk. I). Chaucer, probably, saw the first verse without its context, and mistakenly inferred that "Lollius was the name of a writer on the Trojan war" (Skeat).

[20]Chaucer invented neither of these tales. Both contain traditional matter—though Chaucer's immediate sources remain still unknown, and are probably lost.

[21]My very riches have made me poor (Ovid, *Metamorphoses,* III, 466).

[22]By Ben Jonson. Dryden's memory betrays him, not as to Jonson's intention, but as to Littlewit's words.

makes Arcite violent in his love, and unjust in the pursuit of it; yet, when he came to die, he made him think more reasonably: he repents not of his love, for that had altered his character; but acknowledges the injustice of his proceedings, and resigns Emilia to Palamon. What would Ovid have done on this occasion? He would certainly have made Arcite witty on his deathbed; he had complained he was further off from possession, by being so near, and a thousand such boyisms, which Chaucer rejected as below the dignity of the subject. They who think otherwise, would, by the same reason, prefer Lucan and Ovid to Homer and Virgil, and Martial to all four of them. As for the turn of words, in which Ovid particularly excels all poets, they are sometimes a fault, and sometimes a beauty, as they are used properly or improperly; but in strong passions always to be shunned, because passions are serious, and will admit no playing. The French have a high value for them; and, I confess, they are often what they call delicate, when they are introduced with judgment; but Chaucer writ with more simplicity, and followed Nature more closely than to use them. I have thus far, to the best of my knowledge, been an upright judge betwixt the parties in competition, not meddling with the design nor the disposition of it; because the design was not their own; and in the disposing of it they were equal. It remains that I say somewhat of Chaucer in particular.

In the first place, as he is the father of English poetry, so I hold him in the same degree of veneration as the Grecians held Homer, or the Romans Virgil. He is a perpetual fountain of good sense; learned in all sciences; and, therefore, speaks properly on all subjects. As he knew what to say, so he knows also when to leave off; a continence which is practiced by few writers, and scarcely by any of the ancients, excepting Virgil and Horace. One of our late great poets[23] is sunk in his reputation, because he could never forgive[24] any conceit which came in his way; but swept like a drag-net, great and small. There was plenty enough, but the dishes were ill sorted; whole pyramids of sweetmeats for boys and women, but little of solid meat for men. All this proceeded not from any want of knowledge, but of judgment. Neither did he want that in discerning the beauties and faults of other poets, but only indulged himself in the luxury of writing; and perhaps knew it was a fault, but hoped the reader would not find it. For this reason, though he must always be thought a great poet, he is no longer esteemed a good writer; and for ten impressions which his works have had in so many successive years, yet at present a hundred books are scarcely purchased once a twelvemonth; for, as my last Lord Rochester said, though somewhat profanely, "Not being of God, he could not stand."

Chaucer followed Nature everywhere, but was never so bold to go beyond her; and there is a great difference of being *poeta* and *nimis poeta,* if we may believe Catullus,[25] as much as betwixt a modest behavior and affectation. The verse of Chaucer, I confess, is not harmonious to us; but 'tis like the eloquence of one whom Tacitus commends, it was *auribus istius temporis accommodata:*[26] they who lived with him, and some time after him, thought it musical; and it continues so, even in our judgment, if compared with the numbers of Lidgate and Gower, his contemporaries: there is the rude sweetness of a Scotch tune in it, which is natural and pleasing, though not perfect. 'Tis true, I cannot go so far as he who published the last edition of him;[27] for he would make us believe the fault is in our ears, and that there were really ten syllables in a verse where we find but nine: but this opinion is not worth confuting; 'tis so gross and obvious an error, that common sense (which is a rule in everything but matters of Faith and Revelation) must convince the reader, that equality of

[23]Abraham Cowley (1618–1667). [24]Give up.

[25]Another slip. The man "too much a poet" is admonished by Martial, *Epigrams,* III, 44.

[26]Well suited to the taste of that time (*De Oratoribus,* 21, where, however, Tacitus has *auribus judicum,* "to the taste of a law-court").

[27]Thomas Speght, 1598. This edition was reprinted with additions in 1602, and again reprinted in 1687. As everybody now knows, Speght was right;—though it should be remembered in Dryden's favor that the text of Chaucer was very imperfectly printed in Speght's edition, and that the principles of Chaucerian pronunciation were unknown in the seventeenth century.

numbers, in every verse which we call *heroic,* was either not known, or not always practiced, in Chaucer's age. It were an easy matter to produce some thousands of his verses, which are lame for want of half a foot, and sometimes a whole one, and which no pronunciation can make otherwise. We can only say, that he lived in the infancy of our poetry, and that nothing is brought to perfection at the first. We must be children before we grow men. There was an Ennius, and in process of time a Lucilius, and a Lucretius, before Virgil and Horace; even after Chaucer there was a Spenser, a Harrington,[28] a Fairfax, before Waller and Denham[29] were in being; and our numbers were in their nonage till these last appeared. I need say little of his parentage, life, and fortunes; they are to be found at large in all the editions of his works. He was employed abroad, and favored, by Edward the Third, Richard the Second, and Henry the Fourth, and was poet, as I suppose, to all three of them. In Richard's time, I doubt, he was a little dipped in the rebellion of the Commons; and being brother-in-law to John of Gaunt, it was no wonder if he followed the fortunes of that family; and was well with Henry the Fourth when he had deposed his predecessor. Neither is it to be admired, that Henry, who was a wise as well as a valiant prince, who claimed by succession, and was sensible that his title was not sound, but was rightfully in Mortimer, who had married the heir of York; it was not to be admired, I say, if that great politician should be pleased to have the greatest Wit of those times in his interest, and to be the trumpet of his praises. Augustus had given him the example, by the advice of Maecenas, who recommended Virgil and Horace to him; whose praises helped to make him popular while he was alive, and after his death have made him precious to posterity. As for the religion of our poet, he seems to have some little bias towards the opinions of Wyclif, after John of Gaunt his patron; somewhat of which appears in the tale of *Piers Plowman:*[30] yet I cannot blame him for inveighing so sharply against the vices of the clergy in his age: their pride, their ambition, their pomp, their avarice, their worldly interest, deserved the lashes which he gave them, both in that, and in most of his *Canterbury Tales.* Neither has his contemporary Boccaccio spared them: yet both those poets lived in much esteem with good and holy men in orders; for the scandal which is given by particular priests reflects not on the sacred function. Chaucer's Monk, his Canon, and his Friar, took not from the character of his Good Parson. A satirical poet is the check of the laymen on bad priests. We are only to take care, that we involve not the innocent with the guilty in the same condemnation. The good cannot be too much honored, nor the bad too coarsely used; for the corruption of the best becomes the worst. When a clergyman is whipped, his gown is first taken off, by which the dignity of his order is secured. If he be wrongfully accused, he has his action of slander; and 'tis at the poet's peril if he transgress the law. But they will tell us that all kind of satire, though never so well deserved by particular priests, yet brings the whole order into contempt. Is then the peerage of England anything dishonored when a peer suffers for his treason? If he be libeled, or any way defamed, he has his *scandalum magnatum*[31] to punish the offender. They who use this kind of argument, seem to be conscious to themselves of somewhat which has deserved the poet's lash, and are less concerned for their public capacity than for their private; at least there is pride at the bottom of their reasoning. If the faults of men in orders are only to be judged among themselves, they are all in some sort parties; for, since they say the honor of their order is concerned in every member of it, how can we be sure that they will be impartial judges? How far I may be allowed to speak my opinion in this case, I know not; but I am sure a dispute of this nature caused mischief in abundance betwixt a King of

[28] Sir John Harington (1561–1612), whose translation of Ariosto's *Orlando Furioso* was published in 1591.

[29] Sir John Denham (1618–1669).

[30] That is, the *Plowman's Tale,* which Dryden found in Speght's edition. It was not, however, written by Chaucer, but by the unknown author of the *Plowman's Creed.*

[31] The offense of defaming magnates of the realm.

England and an Archbishop of Canterbury;[32] one standing up for the laws of his land, and the other for the honor (as he called it) of God's Church; which ended in the murder of the prelate, and in the whipping of His Majesty from post to pillar for his penance. The learned and ingenious Dr. Drake[33] has saved me the labor of inquiring into the esteem and reverence which the priests have had of old; and I would rather extend than diminish any part of it: yet I must needs say that when a priest provokes me without any occasion given him, I have no reason, unless it be the charity of a Christian, to forgive him: *prior laesit*[34] is justification sufficient in the civil law. If I answer him in his own language, self-defense I am sure must be allowed me; and if I carry it further, even to a sharp recrimination, somewhat may be indulged to human frailty. Yet my resentment has not wrought so far but that I have followed Chaucer, in his character of a holy man, and have enlarged on that subject with some pleasure; reserving to myself the right, if I shall think fit hereafter, to describe another sort of priests, such as are more easily to be found than the Good Parson; such as have given the last blow to Christianity in this age, by a practice so contrary to their doctrine. But this will keep cold till another time. In the meanwhile, I take up Chaucer where I left him.

He must have been a man of a most wonderful comprehensive nature, because, as it has been truly observed of him, he has taken into the compass of his *Canterbury Tales* the various manners and humors (as we now call them) of the whole English nation, in his age. Not a single character has escaped him. All his pilgrims are severally distinguished from each other; and not only in their inclinations, but in their very physiognomies and persons. Baptista Porta[35] could not have described their natures better than by the marks which the poet gives them. The matter and manner of their tales, and of their telling, are so suited to their different educations, humors, and callings, that each of them would be improper in any other mouth. Even the grave and serious characters are distinguished by their several sorts of gravity: their discourses are such as belong to their age, their calling, and their breeding; such as are becoming of them, and of them only. Some of his persons are vicious, and some virtuous; some are unlearned, or (as Chaucer calls them) lewd, and some are learned. Even the ribaldry of the low characters is different: the Reeve, the Miller, and the Cook, are several men, and distinguished from each other as much as the mincing Lady-Prioress and the broad-speaking, gap-toothed Wife of Bath. But enough of this; there is such a variety of game springing up before me that I am distracted in my choice, and know not which to follow. 'Tis sufficient to say, according to the proverb, that "Here is God's plenty." We have our forefathers and great-grand-dames all before us, as they were in Chaucer's days: their general characters are still remaining in mankind, and even in England, though they are called by other names than those of Monks, and Friars, and Canons, and Lady Abbesses, and Nuns; for mankind is ever the same, and nothing lost out of Nature, though everything is altered. May I have leave to do myself the justice (since my enemies will do me none, and are so far from granting me to be a good poet, that they will not allow me so much as to be a Christian, or a moral man), may I have leave, I say, to inform my reader, that I have confined my choice to such tales of Chaucer as savor nothing of immodesty. If I had desired more to please than to instruct, the Reeve, the Miller, the Shipman, the Merchant, the Sumner, and, above all, the Wife of Bath, in the *Prologue* to her *Tale*, would have procured me as many friends and readers as there are beaux and ladies of pleasure in the town. But I will no more offend against good manners: I am sensible as I ought to be of the scandal I have given by my loose writings; and make what reparation I am able, by this public acknowledgment. If anything of this nature, or of profaneness, be crept into these

[32] Henry II and Thomas à Becket.

[33] James Drake (1667–1707) wrote an answer to Jeremy Collier, *The Ancient and Modern Stages Reviewed,* 1699.

[34] He gave the provocation (Terence, *Eunuchus,* Prologue 6).

[35] A famous Italian physiognomist (1538–1615).

poems, I am so far from defending it, that I disown it. *Totum hoc indictum volo.*[36] Chaucer makes another manner of apology for his broad speaking, and Boccaccio makes the like; but I will follow neither of them. Our countryman, in the end of his Characters, before the *Canterbury Tales,* thus excuses the ribaldry, which is very gross in many of his novels:—

But firste, I pray you, of your courtesy,
That ye ne arrete it not my villany,
Though that I plainly speak in this mattere,
To tellen you her words, and eke her chere:
Ne though I speak her words properly,
For this ye knowen as well as I,
Who shall tellen a tale after a man,
He mote rehearse as nye as ever he can:
Everich word of it ben in his charge,
All speke he, never so rudely, ne large:
Or else he mote tellen his tale untrue,
Or feine things, or find words new:
He may not spare, altho he were his brother,
He mote as wel say o word as another.
Crist spake himself ful broad in holy Writ,
And well I wote no villany is it,
Eke Plato saith, who so can him rede,
The words mote been cousin to the dede.

Yet if a man should have inquired of Boccaccio or of Chaucer, what need they had of introducing such characters, where obscene words were proper in their mouths, but very indecent to be heard; I know not what answer they could have made; for that reason, such tales shall be left untold by me. You have here a specimen of Chaucer's language, which is so obsolete, that his sense is scarce to be understood; and you have likewise more than one example of his unequal numbers, which were mentioned before. Yet many of his verses consist of ten syllables, and the words not much behind our present English: as for example, these two lines, in the description of the Carpenter's young wife:—

Wincing she was, as is a jolly colt,
Long as a mast, and upright as a bolt.[37]

I have almost done with Chaucer, when I have answered some objections relating to my present work. I find some people are offended that I have turned these tales into modern English; because they think them unworthy of my pains, and look on Chaucer as a dry, old-fashioned wit, not worth reviving. I have often heard the late Earl of Leicester say, that Mr. Cowley himself was of that opinion; who, having read him over at my Lord's request declared he had no taste of him. I dare not advance my opinion against the judgment of so great an author; but I think it fair, however, to leave the decision to the public. Mr. Cowley was too modest to set up for a dictator; and being shocked perhaps with his old style, never examined into the depth of his good sense. Chaucer, I confess, is a rough diamond, and must first be polished, ere he shines. I deny not likewise, that, living in our early days of poetry, he writes not always of a piece; but sometimes mingles trivial things with those of greater moment. Sometimes also, though not often, he runs riot, like Ovid, and knows not when he has said enough. But there are more great wits besides Chaucer, whose fault is their excess of conceits, and those ill sorted. An author is not to write all he can, but only all he ought. Having observed this redundancy in Chaucer (as it is an easy matter for a man of ordinary parts to find a fault in one of greater), I have not tied myself to a literal translation; but have often omitted what I judged unnecessary, or not of dignity enough to appear in the company of better thoughts. I have presumed further, in some places, and added somewhat of my own where I thought my author was deficient, and had not given his thoughts their true luster, for want of words in the beginning of our language. And to this I was the more emboldened, because (if I may be permitted to say it of myself) I found I had a soul congenial to his, and that I had been conversant in the same studies. Another poet, in another age, may take the same liberty with my writings; if at least they live long enough to deserve correction. It was also necessary sometimes to restore the sense of Chaucer, which was lost or mangled in the errors of the press. Let this example suffice at present: in the story of *Palamon and Arcite,* where the temple of Diana is described, you find these verses in all the editions of our author:—

[36] I wish this wholly unsaid.

[37] *The Miller's Tale,* II, 77–78.

There saw I Danè turned unto a tree,
I mean not the goddess Diane,
But Venus daughter, which that hight Danè.[38]

Which, after a little consideration, I knew was to be reformed into this sense, that Daphne, the daughter of Peneus, was turned into a tree. I durst not make thus bold with Ovid, lest some future Milbourne[39] should arise, and say, I varied from my author, because I understood him not.

But there are other judges, who think I ought not to have translated Chaucer into English, out of a quite contrary notion: they suppose there is a certain veneration due to his old language; and that it is little less than profanation and sacrilege to alter it. They are farther of opinion, that somewhat of his good sense will suffer in this transfusion, and much of the beauty of his thoughts will infallibly be lost, which appear with more grace in their old habit. Of this opinion was that excellent person, whom I mentioned, the late Earl of Leicester, who valued Chaucer as much as Mr. Cowley despised him. My Lord dissuaded me from this attempt (for I was thinking of it some years before his death), and his authority prevailed so far with me as to defer my undertaking while he lived, in deference to him; yet my reason was not convinced with what he urged against it. If the first end of a writer be to be understood, then, as his language grows obsolete, his thoughts must grow obscure:—

Multa renascentur, quae nunc cecidere; cadentque
Quae nunc sunt in honore vocabula, si volet usus,
Quem penes arbitrium est et jus et norma loquendi.[40]

When an ancient word, for its sound and significancy, deserves to be revived, I have that reasonable veneration for antiquity to restore it. All beyond this is superstition. Words are not like landmarks, so sacred as never to be removed; customs are changed, and even statutes are silently repealed, when the reason ceases for which they were enacted. As for the other part of the argument, that his thoughts will lose of their original beauty by the innovation of words; in the first place, not only their beauty, but their being is lost, where they are no longer understood, which is the present case. I grant that something must be lost in all transfusion, that is, in all translations; but the sense will remain, which would otherwise be lost, or at least be maimed, when it is scarce intelligible, and that but to a few. How few are there, who can read Chaucer, so as to understand him perfectly? And if imperfectly, then with less profit, and no pleasure. It is not for the use of some old Saxon friends[41] that I have taken these pains with him: let them neglect my version, because they have no need of it. I made it for their sakes who understand sense and poetry as well as they, when that poetry and sense is put into words which they understand. I will go farther, and dare to add, that what beauties I lose in some places, I give to others which had them not originally: but in this I may be partial to myself; let the reader judge, and I submit to his decision. Yet I think I have just occasion to complain of them who, because they understand Chaucer, would deprive the greater part of their countrymen of the same advantage, and hoard him up, as misers do their grandam gold, only to look on it themselves, and hinder others from making use of it. In sum, I seriously protest that no man ever had, or can have, a greater veneration for Chaucer than myself. I have translated some part of his works, only that I might perpetuate his memory, or at least refresh it, amongst my countrymen. If I have altered him anywhere for the better, I must at the same time acknowledge that I could have done nothing without him. *Facile est inventis addere*[42] is no great commendation; and I am not so vain to think I have deserved a greater. I will conclude what I have to say of him singly, with this one remark: A lady of my acquaintance, who keeps a kind of cor-

[38] *The Knight's Tale*, ll. 1204–1206.

[39] Luke Milbourne (1649–1720), author of *Notes on Dryden's Virgil*, 1698.

[40] . . . Words long faded may again revive,
And words may fade now blooming and alive,
If usage wills it so, to whom belongs
The rule, the law, the government of tongues.
(Horace, *De Arte Poetica*, ll. 70–72; Conington's translation. In the first line *nunc* should be *jam.*)

[41] That is, friends acquainted with very early English, the study of which was making progress at this time, through the industry of several antiquaries.

[42] It is easy to make additions to inventions.

respondence with some authors of the fair sex in France, has been informed by them, that Mademoiselle de Scudéry,[43] who is as old as Sibyl, and inspired like her by the same God of Poetry, is at this time translating Chaucer into modern French. From which I gather that he has been formerly translated into the old Provençal;[44] for how she should come to understand old English, I know not. But the matter of fact being true, it makes me think that there is something in it like fatality; that, after certain periods of time, the fame and memory of great wits should be renewed, as Chaucer is both in France and England. If this be wholly chance, 'tis extraordinary; and I dare not call it more, for fear of being taxed with superstition.

Boccaccio comes last to be considered, who, living in the same age with Chaucer, had the same genius, and followed the same studies. Both writ novels, and each of them cultivated his mother-tongue. But the greatest resemblance of our two modern authors being in their familiar style, and pleasing way of relating comical adventures, I may pass it over, because I have translated nothing from Boccaccio of that nature. In the serious part of poetry, the advantage is wholly on Chaucer's side; for though the Englishman has borrowed many tales from the Italian, yet it appears that those of Boccaccio were not generally of his own making, but taken from authors of former ages, and by him only modeled; so that what there was of invention, in either of them, may be judged equal. But Chaucer has refined on Boccaccio, and has mended the stories which he has borrowed, in his way of telling; though prose allows more liberty of thought, and the expression is more easy when unconfined by numbers. Our countryman carries weight, and yet wins the race at disadvantage. I desire not the reader should take my word; and, therefore, I will set two of their discourses, on the same subject, in the same light, for every man to judge betwixt them. I translated Chaucer first, and, amongst the rest, pitched on *The Wife of Bath's Tale;* not daring, as I have said, to adventure on her *Prologue,* because 'tis too licentious. There Chaucer introduces an old woman, of mean parentage, whom a youthful knight, of noble blood, was forced to marry, and consequently loathed her. The crone being in bed with him on the wedding-night, and finding his aversion, endeavors to win his affection by reason, and speaks a good word for herself (as who could blame her?), in hope to mollify the sullen bridegroom. She takes her topics from the benefits of poverty, the advantages of old age and ugliness, the vanity of youth, and the silly pride of ancestry and titles, without inherent virtue, which is the true nobility. When I had closed Chaucer, I returned to Ovid, and translated some more of his fables; and, by this time, had so far forgotten *The Wife of Bath's Tale* that, when I took up Boccaccio, unawares I fell on the same argument, of preferring virtue to nobility of blood and titles, in the story of *Sigismonda;* which I had certainly avoided, for the resemblance of the two discourses, if my memory had not failed me. Let the reader weigh them both; and, if he thinks me partial to Chaucer, 'tis in him to right Boccaccio.

I prefer, in our countryman, far above all his other stories, the noble poem of *Palamon and Arcite,* which is of the epic kind, and perhaps not much inferior to the *Ilias,* or the *Aeneis.* The story is more pleasing than either of them, the manners as perfect, the diction as poetical, the learning as deep and various, and the disposition full as artful: only it includes a greater length of time, as taking up seven years at least; but Aristotle has left undecided the duration of the action; which yet is easily reduced into the compass of a year, by a narration of what preceded the return of Palamon to Athens. I had thought, for the honor of our narration, and more particularly for his, whose laurel, though unworthy, I have worn after him, that this story was of English growth, and Chaucer's own: but I was undeceived by Boccaccio; for, casually looking on the end of his seventh *Giornata,*[45] I found Dioneo (under which name he shadows himself), and Fiammetta (who represents his mistress,

[43]Madeleine de Scudéry (1607–1701), poet and author of huge romances (*Artamenes, Clelia, Cleopatra*) which live now only in the histories.

[44]Here, as earlier in the *Preface,* Dryden supposes Provençal to be identical with early French.

[45]Day (in the *Decameron*).

the natural daughter of Robert, King of Naples), of whom these words are spoken: *Dioneo e Fiametta gran pezza cantarono insieme d'Arcita, e di Palemone;*[46] by which it appears that this story was written before the time of Boccaccio; but the name of its author being wholly lost, Chaucer is now become an original; and I question not but the poem has received many beauties, by passing through his noble hands. Besides this tale, there is another of his own invention, after the manner of the Provençals, called *The Flower and the Leaf,*[47] with which I was so particularly pleased, both for the invention and the moral, that I cannot hinder myself from recommending it to the reader.

As a corollary to this preface, in which I have done justice to others, I owe somewhat to myself; not that I think it worth my time to enter the lists with one M——, and one B——,[48] but barely to take notice that such men there are, who have written scurrilously against me, without any provocation. M——, who is in orders, pretends, amongst the rest, this quarrel to me, that I have fallen foul on priesthood: if I have, I am only to ask pardon of good priests, and am afraid his part of the reparation will come to little. Let him be satisfied, that he shall not be able to force himself upon me for an adversary. I contemn him too much to enter into competition with him. His own translations of Virgil have answered his criticisms on mine. If (as they say, he has declared in print), he prefers the version of Ogilby to mine, the world has made him the same compliment; for 'tis agreed, on all hands, that he writes even below Ogilby. That, you will say, is not easily to be done; but what cannot M—— bring about? I am satisfied, however, that, while he and I live together, I shall not be thought the worst poet of the age. It looks as if I had desired him underhand to write so ill against me; but upon my honest word I have not bribed him to do me this service, and am wholly guiltless of his pamphlet. 'Tis true, I should be glad if I could persuade him to continue his good offices, and write such another critique on anything of mine; for I find, by experience, he has a great stroke with the reader, when he condemns any of my poems, to make the world have a better opinion of them. He has taken some pains with my poetry; but nobody will be persuaded to take the same with his. If I had taken to the Church, as he affirms, but which was never in my thoughts, I should have had more sense, if not more grace, than to have turned myself out of my benefice, by writing libels on my parishioners. But his account of my manners and my principles are of a piece with his cavils and his poetry; and so I have done with him for ever.

As for the City Bard, or Knight Physician, I hear his quarrel to me is, that I was the author of *Absalom and Achitophel,* which, he thinks, is a little hard on his fanatic patrons in London.

But I will deal the more civilly with his two poems, because nothing ill is to be spoken of the dead; and therefore peace be to the *manes* of his *Arthurs*. I will only say that it was not for this noble Knight that I drew the plan of an epic poem on King Arthur, in my preface to the translation of Juvenal. The Guardian Angels of kingdoms were machines too ponderous for him to manage; and therefore he rejected them, as Dares did the whirlbats[49] of Eryx when they were thrown before him by Entellus:[50] yet from that preface, he plainly took his hint; for he began immediately upon the story, though he had the baseness not to acknowledge his benefactor, but instead of it, to traduce me in a libel.

I shall say the less of Mr. Collier, because in many things he has taxed me justly; and I have pleaded guilty to all thoughts and expressions of mine, which can be truly argued of obscenity, profaneness, or immorality, and retract them. If he be my enemy, let him triumph; if he be my friend, as I have given him no personal occasion to be otherwise, he will be glad of my repentance. It becomes me not to draw my pen in the defense of a

[46]Dioneo and Fiammetta sang together a great while of Arcite and Palamon. (Dryden did not know Boccaccio's *Teseide,* the immediate source of *The Knight's Tale.*)

[47]It has now been shown that Chaucer did not write this.

[48]Milbourne; and Sir Richard Blackmore (died 1729), author of *Prince Arthur* (1695), *King Arthur* (1697), and other poetical pieces.

[49]Coverings worn by boxers on their hands.

[50]Cf. *Aeneid,* V, 400.

bad cause, when I have so often drawn it for a good one. Yet it were not difficult to prove that in many places he has perverted my meaning by his glosses, and interpreted my words into blasphemy and bawdry, of which they were not guilty. Besides that, he is too much given to horse-play in his raillery, and comes to battle like a dictator from the plow. I will not say, "The zeal of God's house has eaten him up"; but I am sure it has devoured some part of his good manners and civility. It might also be doubted, whether it were altogether zeal which prompted him to this rough manner of proceeding; perhaps, it became not one of his function to rake into the rubbish of ancient and modern plays: a divine might have employed his pains to better purpose, than in the nastiness of Plautus and Aristophanes, whose examples, as they excuse not me, so it might be possibly supposed that he read them not without some pleasure. They who have written commentaries on those poets, or on Horace, Juvenal, and Martial, have explained some vices, which, without their interpretation, had been unknown to modern times. Neither has he judged impartially betwixt the former age and us. There is more bawdry in one play of Fletcher's, called *The Custom of the Country,* than in all ours together. Yet this has been often acted on the stage, in my remembrance. Are the times so much more reformed now, than they were five-and-twenty years ago? If they are, I congratulate the amendment of our morals. But I am not to prejudice the cause of my fellow poets, though I abandon my own defense: they have some of them answered for themselves; and neither they nor I can think Mr. Collier so formidable an enemy that we should shun him. He has lost ground, at the latter end of the day, by pursuing his point too far, like the Prince of Condé, at the battle of Senneph:[51] from immoral plays to no plays, *ab abusu ad usum, non valet consequentia.*[52] But, being a party, I am not to erect myself into a judge. As for the rest of those who have written against me, they are such scoundrels, that they deserve not the least notice to be taken of them. B—— and M—— are only distinguished from the crowd by being remembered to their infamy:—

> . . . *Demetri, teque, Tigelli,*
> *Discipulorum inter jubeo plorare cathedras.*[53]

[51]At this battle (11 August, 1674) Condé attacked the rearguard of the Prince of Orange, then in retreat between Charleroi and Mons.

[52]The argument from abuse against use is weak.

[53]Demetrius, and you, Tigellius, go weep amidst your pupils' chairs (Horace, *Satires,* I, x, 90–91. Horace has *discipularum*).

LYRIC POETRY OF THE RESTORATION

The Restoration poets may with some justice be said to have inherited the lyric tradition of the earlier seventeenth century. They did not, however, inherit the whole of that tradition, nor did the surviving elements remain unchanged. By 1660 the Spenserian school had virtually disappeared, and that of Donne was on the wane. Devotional poetry of an imaginative and personal character could still be written by a man like Thomas Traherne; but if his lyrics are compared with those of George Herbert, it is apparent that a decisive change has taken place. Traherne was an obscure Welsh clergyman, a childlike and highly gifted mystic, who contributed nothing to the main literary currents of his time. His work remained in manuscript until the beginning of the twentieth century; and even his most appealing poems betray, in their lack of self-assurance and in their failure to express his inspiration fully, how little he relied upon the achievements of his predecessors and contemporaries. Far more typical of the ecclesiastical life of the period was Henry Aldrich, Doctor of Divinity, Dean of Christ Church, Oxford, at one time Vice-Chancellor of the University: a scholar whose wide interests embraced logic, mathematics, and classical literature, as well as architecture and music, and whose sincere piety was no bar to the composition of such verses as "The Five Reasons for Drinking" and a Latin rendering of Congreve's song, "A Soldier and a Sailor."

But the most compact and important group of Restoration lyric poets were in a very real sense the inheritors of an earlier tradition: Sir George Etherege, the Earl of Dorset, Sir Charles Sedley, and the Earl of Rochester brought to the court of Charles II much of the spirit and technique of the poetry written at the court of Charles I. Distinguished men of letters from the Cavalier period—for example, Edmund Waller and Sir William Davenant—were not only alive in 1660 but personally connected with the newer writers; and Dorset supplied a link with a still remoter past, since he was a great-great-grandson of that Thomas Sackville who had been eminent both as a poet and as a courtier in the reign of Queen Elizabeth. The court lyrics of the Restoration are, in fact, the last fruit of an aristocratic tradition which had first appeared in the lyrics of Wyatt and Surrey a century and a half before.

One of the distinguishing marks of this tradition is an indifference to publication. The poems of Etherege and Dorset and Sedley and Rochester were intended, at least originally, for circulation in manuscript; Dorset's indeed have never been adequately collected and printed. The best of their lyrics, on the other hand, are also marked by poetic skill of a high order, even though they may have been written in great haste: how much they owe to Cavalier models is revealed by the delicate phrasing and the exquisite naturalness of their lines. The themes which they set forth may appear to be a new departure since they are occasionally, and in the case of Rochester far more than occasionally, licentious; but it is well to remember that not all the love poetry written at the court of Charles I had been idealistic. The view which the aristocratic tradition took of love, its most important subject, had undergone a steady development from the first. Petrarchian imitation, as well as other influences, had led to the idealizing of woman; but this very interest caused in turn a closer and closer study of her actual qualities. The court poets of the Restoration, while they preserved an attitude of deferential gallantry, were also students of certain, if not all, sides of feminine character: woman as woman assumes a new prominence in their lyrics. At the same time their realistic view of her completed, rather than violated, the courtly ideal. If they are frequently cynical, there has never been a cynicism better-humored or more graceful than theirs.

William Kerr has edited a convenient anthology, *Restoration Verse, 1660–1715* (London, 1930). Traherne's *Poetical Works* were first edited by B. Dobell (1903), since revised and completed by Gladys I. Wade; Helen C. White's *Metaphysical Poets; a Study in Religious Experience* (New York, 1936) contains a recent evaluation of Traherne. *The Dramatic*

Works of Sir George Etherege are edited with an authoritative introduction by H. F. B. Brett-Smith (Oxford, 1927), but Etherege's few poems are accessible only in the earlier *Works,* edited by A. W. Verity (1888); in the first of his *Essays in Biography, 1680–1726* (London, 1925) Bonamy Dobrée gives a spirited study of Etherege's last years. Vivian de Sola Pinto, the editor of *The Poetical and Dramatic Works of Sir Charles Sedley* (London, 1928), has also written the most complete account of the poet, *Sir Charles Sedley, 1639–1701, A Study in the Life and Literature of the Restoration* (London, 1927). The *Collected Works of John Wilmot, Earl of Rochester* have been edited by John Hayward (London, 1926); a shrewd commentary on Rochester and his times appears in the last of three essays in Kenneth B. Murdock's *Sun at Noon* (New York, 1939). The standard edition of *The Complete Works of William Congreve* is that edited by Montague Summers (London, 1923).

SIR GEORGE ETHEREGE

(1635?–1691)

TO CHLORIS

Chloris, 'tis not in our power
To say how long our love will last:
It may be, we within this hour
May lose those joys we now may taste.
The blessèd that immortal be 5
From change in love are only free.

And though you now immortal seem,
Such is th'exactness of your fame:
Those that your beauty so esteem,
Will find it cannot last the same: 10
Love from mine eyes has stol'n my fire,
As apt to waste, and to expire.

Then since we mortal Lovers are,
Let's question not how long 'twill last;
But while we love let us take care, 15
Each minute be with pleasure past:
It were a madness, to deny
To live, because w'are sure to die.

Fear not, though love and beauty fail,
My reason shall my heart direct: 20
Your kindness now will then prevail,
And passion turn into respect:
Chloris, at worst, you'll in the end
But change your Lover for a Friend.

THOMAS TRAHERNE

(1636?–1674)

WONDER

How like an Angel came I down!
How bright are all things here!
When first among his Works I did appear
O how their Glory me did crown!
The World resembled his *Eternity,* 5
In which my Soul did walk;
And ev'ry thing that I did see,
Did with me talk.

The skies in their magnificence,
The lively, lovely air; 10
O how divine, how soft, how sweet, how fair!
The stars did entertain my sense,
And all the Works of God so bright and pure,
So rich and great did seem,
As if they ever must endure, 15
In my esteem.

A native health and innocence
Within my bones did grow,
And while my God did all his Glories show,
I felt a vigor in my sense 20
That was all Spirit. I within did flow
With seas of life, like wine;
I nothing in the World did know,
But 'twas Divine.

Harsh ragged objects were concealed, 25
Oppressions, tears and cries,
Sins, griefs, complaints, dissensions, weeping eyes,
Were hid: and only things revealed,
Which Heavenly Spirits, and the Angels prize.
The state of innocence 30
And bliss, not trades and poverties,
Did fill my sense.

The streets were paved with golden stones,
The boys and girls were mine,
O how did all their lovely faces shine! 35
The sons of men all holy ones,
In joy, and beauty, then appeared to me,
And ev'ry thing which here I found,
While like an Angel I did see,
Adorned the ground. 40

Rich diamond and pearl and gold
In ev'ry place was seen;
Rare splendors, yellow, blue, red, white and green,
Mine eyes did ev'rywhere behold.
Great Wonders clothed with Glory did appear, 45
Amazement was my bliss.
That and my wealth met ev'rywhere:
No joy to this!

Cursed and devised proprieties,
With envy, avarice 50
And fraud, those fiends that spoil even Paradise,
Fled from the splendor of mine eyes.
And so did hedges, ditches, limits, bounds,
I dreamed not aught of those,
But wandered over all men's grounds, 55
And found repose.

Proprieties themselves were mine,
And hedges ornaments;
Walls, boxes, coffers, and their rich contents
Did not divide my joys, but all combine. 60
Clothes, ribbons, jewels, laces, I esteemed
My joys by others worn;
For me they all to wear them seemed
When I was born.

SHADOWS IN THE WATER

In unexperienced infancy
Many a sweet mistake doth lie:
Mistake though false, intending true;
A *Seeming* somewhat more than *View;*
That doth instruct the mind 5
In things that lie behind,
And many secrets to us show
Which afterwards we come to know.

Thus did I by the water's brink
Another world beneath me think; 10
And while the lofty spacious skies
Reverséd there abused mine eyes,
I fancied other feet
Came mine to touch or meet;
As by some puddle I did play 15
Another world within it lay.

Beneath the water people drowned,
Yet with another Heaven crowned,
In spacious regions seemed to go
As freely moving to and fro: 20
In bright and open space
I saw their very face;
Eyes, hands, and feet they had like mine;
Another sun did with them shine.

'Twas strange that people there should walk,
And yet I could not hear them talk: 26
That through a little wat'ry chink,
Which one dry ox or horse might drink,
We other worlds should see,
Yet not admitted be; 30
And other confines there behold
Of light and darkness, heat and cold.

I called them oft, but called in vain;
No speeches we could entertain:
Yet did I there expect to find 35
Some other world, to please my mind.
I plainly saw by these
A new Antipodes,
Whom, though they were so plainly seen,
A film kept off that stood between. 40

By walking men's reverséd feet
I chanced another world to meet;
Though it did not to view exceed
A phantasm, 'tis a world indeed,
Where skies beneath us shine, 45
And earth by art divine
Another face presents below,
Where people's feet against ours go.

Within the regions of the air,
Compassed about with heav'ns fair, 50
Great tracts of land there may be found
Enriched with fields and fertile ground;
Where many num'rous hosts,
In those far distant coasts,
For other great and glorious ends, 55
Inhabit, my yet unknown friends.

O ye that stand upon the brink,
Whom I so near me, through the chink,
With wonder see: What faces there,
Whose feet, whose bodies, do ye wear? 60
I my companions see
In you, another me.
They seeméd others, but are we;
Our second selves those shadows be.

Look how far off those lower skies 65
Extend themselves! scarce with mine eyes
I can them reach. O ye my friends,
What *Secret* borders on those ends?
Are lofty heavens hurled
'Bout your inferior world? 70
Are ye the representatives
Of other people's distant lives?

Of all the playmates which I knew
That here I do the image view
In other selves; what can it mean? 75
But that below the purling stream
Some unknown joys there be
Laid up in store for me;
To which I shall, when that thin skin
Is broken, be admitted in. 80

CHARLES SACKVILLE, EARL OF DORSET

(1638–1706)

SONG, WRITTEN AT SEA,

In the First Dutch War, 1665, the Night before an Engagement[1]

To all you ladies now at land
We men at sea indite;
But first would have you understand
How hard it is to write;
The Muses now, and Neptune too, 5
We must implore to write to you,
With a fa, la, la, la, la.

For though the Muses should prove kind,
And fill our empty brain;
Yet if rough Neptune rouse the wind, 10
To wave the azure main,
Our paper, pen, and ink, and we,
Roll up and down our ships at sea,
With a fa, la, la, la, la.

Then, if we write not by each post, 15
Think not we are unkind;
Nor yet conclude our ships are lost
By Dutchmen, or by wind:
Our tears we'll send a speedier way,
The tide shall bring 'em twice a day, 20
With a fa, la, la, la, la.

The king with wonder, and surprise,
Will swear the seas grow bold;
Because the tides will higher rise,
Than e'er they used of old: 25
But let him know it is our tears
Bring floods of grief to Whitehall stairs.
With a fa, la, la, la, la.

Should foggy Opdam[2] chance to know
Our sad and dismal story; 30
The Dutch would scorn so weak a foe,
And quit their fort at Goree:
For what resistance can they find
From men who've left their hearts behind!
With a fa, la, la, la, la. 35

Let wind and weather do its worst,
Be you to us but kind;
Let Dutchmen vapor, Spaniards curse,
No sorrow we shall find:
'Tis then no matter how things go, 40
Or who's our friend, or who's our foe.
With a fa, la, la, la, la.

To pass our tedious hours away,
We throw a merry main;[3]
Or else at serious ombre[4] play; 45
But, why should we in vain
Each other's ruin thus pursue?
We were undone when we left you.
With a fa, la, la, la, la.

But now our fears tempestuous grow, 50
And cast our hopes away;
Whilst you, regardless of our woe,
Sit careless at a play:
Perhaps permit some happier man
To kiss your hand, or flirt your fan. 55
With a fa, la, la, la, la.

When any mournful tune you hear,
That dies in ev'ry note;
As if it sighed with each man's care,
For being so remote; 60
Think then how often love we've made
To you, when all those tunes were played.
With a fa, la, la, la, la.

In justice you cannot refuse,
To think of our distress; 65
When we for hopes of honor lose
Our certain happiness;
All those designs are but to prove
Ourselves more worthy of your love.
With a fa, la, la, la, la. 70

And now we've told you all our loves,
And likewise all our fears;
In hopes this declaration moves
Some pity from your tears:
Let's hear of no inconstancy, 75
We have too much of that at sea.
With a fa, la, la, la, la.

---

[1]The poem may have been written as early as the end of 1664 and later given this title to suggest that it was written on the eve of the English naval victory of 3 June, 1665.

[2]Jacob van Wassenaer, Baron d'Opdam, admiral of the Dutch fleet.

[3]Number to be thrown for in games of dice.

[4]Game of cards, usually played by three people.

SONG

Dorinda's sparkling wit, and eyes,
United, cast too fierce a light,
Which blazes high, but quickly dies,
Pains not the heart, but hurts the sight.

Love is a calmer, gentler joy, 5
Smooth are his looks, and soft his pace;
Her Cupid is a blackguard boy,
That runs his link[5] full in your face.

SIR CHARLES SEDLEY

(1639?–1701)

SONG

Not *Celia,* that I juster am
Or better than the rest,
For I would change each hour like them,
Were not my heart at rest.

But I am tied to very thee, 5
By every thought I have;
Thy face I only care to see,
Thy heart I only crave.

All that in woman is adored,
In thy dear self I find, 10
For the whole sex can but afford,
The handsome and the kind.

Why then should I seek farther store,
And still make love anew;
When change itself can give no more, 15
'Tis easy to be true.

SONG

Love still has something of the sea,
From whence his Mother rose;[1]
No time his slaves from doubt can free,
Nor give their thoughts repose:

They are becalmed in clearest days, 5
And in rough weather tost;
They wither under cold delays,
Or are in tempests lost.

One while they seem to touch the port,
Then straight into the main, 10
Some angry wind in cruel sport
The vessel drives again.

At first disdain and pride they fear,
Which if they chance to 'scape,
Rivals and falsehood soon appear 15
In a more dreadful shape.

By such degrees to joy they come,
And are so long withstood,
So slowly they receive the sum,
It hardly does them good. 20

'Tis cruel to prolong a pain,
And to defer a joy;
Believe me, gentle *Celemene*
Offends the wingéd boy.

An hundred thousand oaths your fears 25
Perhaps would not remove;
And if I gazed a thousand years
I could no deeper love.

HENRY ALDRICH

(1647–1710)

A CATCH

If all be true that I do think
There are Five Reasons we should drink;
Good wine, a friend, or being dry,
Or lest we should be by and by;
Or any other reason why. 5

JOHN WILMOT, EARL OF ROCHESTER

(1647–1680)

THE MISTRESS

A Song

An age in her embraces past,
Would seem a winter's day;
Where life and light with envious haste,
Are torn and snatched away.

But, oh! how slowly minutes roll, 5
When absent from her eyes,
That fed my love, which is my soul;
It languishes and dies.

For then no more a soul but shade,
It mournfully does move; 10
And haunts my breast, by absence made
The living tomb of love.

---

[5] Torch.

[1] Venus, according to one myth, was born from the sea.

You wiser men despise me not,
  Whose love-sick fancy raves,
On shades of souls, and Heav'n knows what;
  Short ages live in graves. 16

Whene'er those wounding eyes, so full
  Of sweetness, you did see;
Had you not been profoundly dull,
  You had gone mad like me. 20

Nor censure us, you who perceive
  My best belov'd and me,
Sigh and lament, complain and grieve;
  You think we disagree.

Alas! 'tis sacred jealousy, 25
  Love raised to an extreme;
The only proof 'twixt them and me,
  We love, and do not dream.

Fantastic fancies fondly move;
  And in frail joys believe, 30
Taking false pleasure for true love;
  But pain can ne'er deceive.

Kind jealous doubts, tormenting fears,
  And anxious cares, when past,
Prove our hearts' treasure fixed and dear, 35
  And make us blest at last.

LOVE AND LIFE

A Song

All my past life is mine no more,
  The flying hours are gone:
Like transitory dreams giv'n o'er,
Whose images are kept in store,
  By memory alone. 5

The time that is to come is not;
  How can it then be mine?
The present moment's all my lot;
And that, as fast as it is got,
  Phyllis, is only thine. 10

Then talk not of inconstancy,
  False hearts, and broken vows;
If I, by miracle, can be
This live-long minute true to thee,
  'Tis all that Heav'n allows. 15

UPON HIS LEAVING HIS MISTRESS

'Tis not that I am weary grown
Of being yours, and yours alone:
But with what face can I incline,
To damn you to be only mine?

You, whom some kinder Pow'r did fashion, 5
By merit, and by inclination,
The joy at least of a whole nation.

Let meaner spirits of your sex,
With humble aims their thoughts perplex:
And boast, if, by their arts they can 10
Contrive to make *one* happy man.
While, moved by an impartial sense,
Favors, like Nature, you dispense,
With universal influence.

See the kind seed-receiving earth, 15
To every grain affords a birth:
On her no show'rs unwelcome fall,
Her willing womb retains 'em all.
And shall my *Caelia* be confined?
No, live up to thy mighty mind; 20
And be the mistress of mankind.

UPON NOTHING

Nothing! thou elder brother ev'n to shade,
Thou hadst a being ere the world was made,
And (well fixt) art alone, of ending not
  afraid.

Ere time and place were, time and place were
  not,
When primitive *Nothing* something straight
  begot, 5
Then all proceeded from the great united—
  What.

Something the gen'ral attribute of all,
Severed from thee, its sole original,
Into thy boundless self must undistinguished
  fall.

Yet something did thy mighty pow'r command, 10
And from thy fruitful emptiness's hand,
Snatched men, beasts, birds, fire, air, and
  land.

Matter, the wickedst off-spring of thy race,
By Form assisted, flew from thy embrace,
And Rebel Light obscured thy reverend
  dusky face. 15

With Form, and Matter, Time and Place did
  join,
Body, thy foe, with thee did leagues combine,
To spoil thy peaceful realm, and ruin all thy
  line.

But turn-coat Time assists the foe in vain,
And, bribed by thee, assists thy short-lived reign, 20
And to thy hungry womb drives back thy slaves again.

Though mysteries are barred from laic eyes,
And the Divine alone, with warrant, pries
Into thy bosom, where the Truth in private lies.

Yet this of thee the wise may freely say, 25
Thou from the Virtuous nothing tak'st away,
And to be part with thee the Wicked wisely pray.

Great Negative, how vainly would the Wise
Inquire, define, distinguish, teach, devise,
Didst thou not stand to point their dull philosophies? 30

Is, or *is not*, the two great ends of Fate,
And, true or false, the subject of debate,
That perfect, or destroy, the vast designs of Fate.

When they have racked the Politician's breast,
Within thy bosom must securely rest, 35
And, when reduced to thee, are least unsafe and best.

But, *Nothing*, why does *Something* still permit,
That sacred Monarchs should at council sit,
With persons highly thought, at best, for nothing fit.

Whilst weighty *Something* modestly abstains,
From Princes' coffers, and from Statesmen's brains, 41
And nothing there like stately *Nothing* reigns.

Nothing, who dwell'st with fools in grave disguise,
For whom they reverend shapes and forms devise,
Lawn sleeves and furs and gowns, when they like thee look wise. 45

French truth, Dutch prowess, British policy,
Hibernian learning, Scotch civility,
Spaniards' dispatch, Danes' wit, are mainly seen in thee.

The great man's gratitude to his best friend,
King's promises, Whore's vows, towards thee they bend, 50
Flow swiftly into thee, and in thee ever end.

THE KING'S EPITAPH

Here lies a great and mighty King,
Whose promise none relies on;
He never said a foolish thing,
Nor ever did a wise one.

WILLIAM CONGREVE

(1670–1729)

SONG[1]

A Soldier, and a Sailor,
A Tinker, and a Tailor,
Had once a doubtful strife, Sir,
To make a maid a wife, Sir,
Whose name was Buxom *Joan*. 5
For now the time was ended,
When she no more intended,
To lick her lips at men, Sir,
And gnaw the sheets in vain, Sir,
And lie o' nights alone. 10

The Soldier swore like thunder,
He loved her more than plunder;
And showed her many a scar, Sir,
That he had brought from far, Sir,
With fighting for her sake. 15
The Tailor thought to please her,
With off'ring her his measure.
The Tinker too with mettle,
Said he could mend her kettle,
And stop up ev'ry leak. 20

But while these three were prating,
The Sailor slyly waiting,
Thought if it came about, Sir:
That they should all fall out, Sir:
He then might play his part. 25
And just e'en as he meant, Sir,
To loggerheads they went, Sir,
And then he let fly at her,
A shot 'twixt wind and water,
That won this Fair Maid's heart. 30

[1]From the end of Act III of Congreve's *Love for Love* (1695). It is quite possible that the dramatist merely shortened a popular broadside ballad of the time in order to secure a suitable song for his play. (Cf. D.Crane Taylor, *William Congreve*, pp. 77–79.)

JOSEPH ADDISON 1672–1719 *and* RICHARD STEELE 1672–1729

Addison was born at Milston, Wiltshire, on 1 May, 1672. His father was a clergyman, and the boy was brought up in a cultivated environment. He was sent to the Charterhouse School in London and then to Queen's College, Oxford. At Oxford he distinguished himself both as a scholar and as a writer of smooth English and Latin verse, and he won a fellowship at Magdalen College which he held until 1699. His Latin poem on the peace of Ryswick, together with his general ability as a man of letters, won him a pension from the Whigs, who wished to secure his continued support. This enabled him to spend four years in travel and study on the Continent. Immediately on his return in 1704 he was asked to write a poem celebrating Marlborough's victory at Blenheim. He produced *The Campaign,* which was at once successful and which ensured his political position. He was somewhat reserved and cautious in temperament, yet nevertheless became intimate with many of the "wits" of the day. He wrote three plays which would hardly be remembered now were it not that one of them, *Cato,* which was put on the stage in 1713, attained a remarkable factitious success. It had a long run, not because of its dramatic interest or power, but because it was believed to contain good Whig doctrine. When the Whigs returned to power in 1714, Addison was made Chief Secretary for Ireland. Later he became Commissioner for Trade and the Colonies, and finally Secretary of State in 1717. After he had held this post for only a few months he resigned it, chiefly because of ill-health. He died on 17 June, 1719, and was buried in Westminster Abbey.

Richard Steele was born in Dublin in March, 1672. He was sent to Charterhouse, where he became acquainted with Addison; and like Addison he went up to Oxford. He entered Christ Church, at Oxford, in 1690, but left without a degree to become a soldier. His career in the army was not without irregularities, but he rose to a captaincy by 1700. In the following year he began writing for the theater, his first play being *The Funeral, or Grief à la Mode.* In 1703 *The Lying Lover* was produced at Drury Lane, and in 1705 *The Tender Husband.* In these plays Steele attempted to reform the taste of the day; he proved successfully that a comedy could be genuinely amusing without descending to ribaldry and the exhibition of gross immorality, and thus he foreshadowed one of the prominent aims of later work which he and Addison were to do together. In 1707 Steele was appointed Gazetteer, a post which he lost in 1710. In 1713 he sat in Parliament for Stockbridge, but in the following spring was expelled from the House of Commons for uttering seditious sentiments—a charge without real foundation, the vote on which served to show, not Steele's guilt, but simply the solid Tory majority in the House. On the accession of George I in the fall of 1714 Steele was rewarded for his support of the Hanoverian succession by the gift of several offices, and in 1715 he was again elected to Parliament, and was knighted. He also became in that year the Patentee, or manager, of Drury Lane Theater. In spite, however, of these and other turns of fortune in his favor, Steele, owing to his reckless expenditures, was never out of financial difficulties, and his difficulties of this sort grew worse as he grew older. In the fall of 1723 he left London for Bath, then lived for a time at Hereford, and finally retired to Carmarthen in Wales—all this being done in pursuit of an arrangement designed to aid his creditors. At Carmarthen he died on 1 September, 1729, and was buried there in St. Peter's Church.

Both Steele and Addison are remembered today for their two periodicals, the *Tatler* and the *Spectator.* While Steele was editing the *Gazette,* an official government paper, he conceived the idea of a livelier periodical than that organ, and in 1709 began the *Tatler.* Addison soon joined him in writing for it, and the paper ran successfully until they stopped it in January, 1711, in order a few months later to begin the *Spectator* on a somewhat different plan. The

Spectator was issued daily until 6 December, 1712, reaching a total of 555 numbers. The purposes of Steele and Addison are indicated by themselves in numbers of the two papers printed below. Briefly, their most general aim was the reformation of manners, and to this end they freely employed good-humored satire. Their style was marked by simplicity, as the content of their papers was marked by common sense. Of the two writers Addison was easily the superior, his style exhibiting a fine urbanity and quiet distinction which Steele could not attain. Addison, too, extended the *Spectator's* reforming activities to the sphere of taste, and made effective attacks on pedantry which have not yet lost either their force or their applicability. It should be remembered, however, that the whole design was of Steele's invention, and that Steele's reputation has suffered in a sense unfairly from the constant comparison of his essays with those of Addison.

Both the *Tatler* and the *Spectator* have been ably edited by George A. Aitken (London, 1898–1899 and 1898). A standard critical and biographical essay on Addison is Samuel Johnson's, in *The Lives of the English Poets,* ed. George B. Hill (Oxford, 1905), vol. II; a valuable recent study of Addison's life appears in Bonamy Dobrée's *Studies in Biography, 1680–1726* (London, 1925). For the life of Steele see Willard Connely, *Sir Richard Steele* (New York, 1934).

THE TATLER

No. 1. Tuesday, 12 April, 1709.

[Steele.]

Quicquid agunt homines——
nostri est farrago libelli.[1]
—Juv. *Sat.* i. 85, 86.

Though the other papers, which are published for the use of the good people of England, have certainly very wholesome effects, and are laudable in their particular kinds, they do not seem to come up to the main design of such narrations, which, I humbly presume, should be principally intended for the use of politic persons, who are so public-spirited as to neglect their own affairs to look into transactions of state. Now these gentlemen, for the most part, being persons of strong zeal, and weak intellects, it is both a charitable and necessary work to offer something, whereby such worthy and well-affected members of the commonwealth may be instructed, after their reading, what to think; which shall be the end and purpose of this my paper, wherein I shall, from time to time, report and consider all matters of what kind soever that shall occur to me, and publish such my advices and reflections every Tuesday, Thursday, and Saturday in the week, for the convenience of the post. I resolve to have something which may be of entertainment to the fair sex, in honor of whom I have invented the title of this paper. I therefore earnestly desire all persons, without distinction, to take it in for the present *gratis,* and hereafter at the price of one penny, forbidding all hawkers to take more for it at their peril. And I desire all persons to consider, that I am at a very great charge for proper materials for this work, as well as that, before I resolved upon it, I had settled a correspondence in all parts of the known and knowing world. And forasmuch as this globe is not trodden upon by mere drudges of business only, but that men of spirit and genius are justly to be esteemed as considerable agents in it, we shall not, upon a dearth of news, present you with musty foreign edicts, and dull proclamations, but shall divide our relation of the passages which occur in action or discourse throughout this town, as well as elsewhere, under such dates of places as may prepare you for the matter you are to expect in the following manner.

All accounts of gallantry, pleasure, and entertainment, shall be under the article of White's Chocolate-house; poetry under that of Will's Coffee-house; Learning, under the title of Grecian; foreign and domestic news, you will have from St. James's Coffee-house;[2]

[1]Whate'er men do, or say, or think, or dream,
Our motley paper seizes for its theme. (Pope.)

[2]These famous institutions occupied an important place in London life in the late seventeenth and early eighteenth centuries, serving as informal clubs and as centers of social, political, and literary influence. Steele indicates in a general way the kinds of people who frequented the four he mentions.

and what else I have to offer on any other subject shall be dated from my own Apartment.

I once more desire my reader to consider, that as I cannot keep an ingenious man to go daily to Will's under two-pence each day, merely for his charges; to White's under sixpence; nor to the Grecian, without allowing him some plain Spanish,[3] to be as able as others at the learned table; and that a good observer cannot speak with even Kidney[4] at St. James's without clean linen; I say, these considerations will, I hope, make all persons willing to comply with my humble request (when my *gratis* stock is exhausted) of a penny apiece; especially since they are sure of some proper amusement, and that it is impossible for me to want means to entertain them, having, besides the force of my own parts, the power of divination, and that I can, by casting a figure, tell you all that will happen before it comes to pass.

But this last faculty I shall use very sparingly, and speak but of few things until they are passed, for fear of divulging matters which may offend our superiors.

No. 25. Tuesday, 7 June, 1709.

[Steele.]

A letter from a young lady, written in the most passionate terms, wherein she laments the misfortune of a gentleman, her lover, who was lately wounded in a duel, has turned my thoughts to that subject, and inclined me to examine into the causes which precipitate men into so fatal a folly. And as it has been proposed to treat of subjects of gallantry in the article from hence,[5] and no one point in nature is more proper to be considered by the company who frequent this place than that of duels, it is worth our consideration to examine into this chimerical groundless humor, and to lay every other thought aside, until we have stripped it of all its false pretenses to credit and reputation amongst men.

But I must confess, when I consider what I am going about, and run over in my imagination all the endless crowd of men of honor who will be offended at such a discourse; I am undertaking, methinks, a work worthy an invulnerable hero in romance, rather than a private gentleman with a single rapier: but as I am pretty well acquainted by great opportunities with the nature of man, and know of a truth that all men fight against their will, the danger vanishes, and resolution rises upon this subject. For this reason, I shall talk very freely on a custom which all men wish exploded, though no man has courage enough to resist it.

But there is one unintelligible word, which I fear will extremely perplex my dissertation, and I confess to you I find very hard to explain, which is the term "satisfaction." An honest country gentleman had the misfortune to fall into company with two or three modern men of honor, where he happened to be very ill-treated; and one of the company, being conscious of his offense, sends a note to him in the morning, and tells him, he was ready to give him satisfaction. "This is fine doing," says the plain fellow; "last night he sent me away cursedly out of humor, and this morning he fancies it would be a satisfaction to be run through the body."

As the matter at present stands, it is not to do handsome actions denominates a man of honor; it is enough if he dares to defend ill ones. Thus you often see a common sharper in competition with a gentleman of the first rank; though all mankind is convinced, that a fighting gamester is only a pickpocket with the courage of an highwayman. One cannot with any patience reflect on the unaccountable jumble of persons and things in this town and nation, which occasions very frequently, that a brave man falls by a hand below that of a common hangman, and yet his executioner escapes the clutches of the hangman for doing it. I shall therefore hereafter consider, how the bravest men in other ages and nations have behaved themselves upon such incidents as we decide by combat; and show, from their practice, that this resentment neither has its foundation from true reason or solid fame; but is an imposture, made of cowardice, falsehood, and want of understanding. For this work, a good history of quarrels would be very edify-

[3]Wine. [4]One of the waiters at St. James's.

[5]This number of the *Tatler* is dated from White's Chocolate-House.

ing to the public, and I apply myself to the town for particulars and circumstances within their knowledge, which may serve to embellish the dissertation with proper cuts.[6] Most of the quarrels I have ever known, have proceeded from some valiant coxcomb's persisting in the wrong, to defend some prevailing folly, and preserve himself from the ingenuousness of owning a mistake.

By this means it is called "giving a man satisfaction," to urge your offense against him with your sword; which puts me in mind of Peter's order to the keeper, in *The Tale of a Tub*.[7] "If you neglect to do all this, damn you and your generation for ever: and so we bid you heartily farewell." If the contradiction in the very terms of one of our challenges were as well explained and turned into downright English, would it not run after this manner?

"Sir,

"Your extraordinary behavior last night, and the liberty you were pleased to take with me, makes me this morning give you this, to tell you, because you are an ill-bred puppy, I will meet you in Hyde Park, an hour hence; and because you want both breeding and humanity, I desire you would come with a pistol in your hand, on horseback, and endeavor to shoot me through the head, to teach you more manners. If you fail of doing me this pleasure, I shall say, you are a rascal, on every post in town: and so, sir, if you will not injure me more, I shall never forgive what you have done already. Pray, sir, do not fail of getting everything ready; and you will infinitely oblige, sir, your most obedient humble servant, *etc.*"

No. 85. Tuesday, 25 October, 1709.
[Steele.]

My brother Tranquillus, who is a man of business, came to me this morning into my study, and after very many civil expressions in return for what good offices I had done him, told me, "he desired to carry his wife, my sister, that very morning, to his own house." I readily told him, "I would wait upon him," without asking why he was so impatient to rob us of his good company.

[6]Illustrations. [7]By Jonathan Swift.

He went out of my chamber, and I thought seemed to have a little heaviness upon him, which gave me some disquiet. Soon after my sister came to me, with a very matronlike air, and most sedate satisfaction in her looks, which spoke her very much at ease; but the traces of her countenance seemed to discover that she had been lately in a passion, and that air of content to flow from a certain triumph upon some advantage obtained. She no sooner sat down by me, but I perceived she was one of those ladies who begin to be managers within the time of their being brides. Without letting her speak, which I saw she had a mighty inclination to do, I said, "Here has been your husband, who tells me he has a mind to go home this very morning, and I have consented to it." "It is well," said she, "for you must know——" "Nay, Jenny," said I. "I beg your pardon, for it is you must know—— You are to understand, that now is the time to fix or alienate your husband's heart for ever; and I fear you have been a little indiscreet in your expressions or behavior towards him, even here in my house." "There has," says she, "been some words; but I will be judged by you if he was not in the wrong; nay I need not be judged by anybody, for he gave it up himself, and said not a word when he saw me grow passionate, but, 'Madam, you are perfectly in the right of it'; as you shall judge——" "Nay, Madam," said I, "I am judge already, and tell you that you are perfectly in the wrong of it; for if it was a matter of importance, I know he has better sense than you; if a trifle, you know what I told you on your wedding-day, that you were to be above little provocations." She knows very well I can be sour upon occasion, therefore gave me leave to go on.

"Sister," said I, "I will not enter into the dispute between you, which I find his prudence put an end to before it came to extremity; but charge you to have a care of the first quarrel, as you tender your happiness; for then it is that the mind will reflect harshly upon every circumstance that has ever passed between you. If such an accident is ever to happen, which I hope never will, be sure to keep to the circumstance before you; make no allusions to what is passed, or conclusions referring to what is to come: do not show a hoard of matter for dissension in your breast: but, if it is necessary, lay before him the thing as you understand it, candidly, without being ashamed of acknowledging an error, or proud of being in the right. If a young couple be not careful in this point, they will get into a habit of wrangling: and when to displease is thought of no consequence, to please is always of as little moment. There is a play, Jenny, I have formerly been at when I was a student: we got into a dark corner with a porringer of brandy, and threw raisins into it, then set it on fire. My chamber-fellow and I diverted ourselves with the sport of venturing our fingers for the raisins; and the wantonness of the thing was to see each other look like a demon, as we burned ourselves, and snatched out the fruit. This fantastical mirth was called Snap-Dragon. You may go into many a family, where you see the man and wife at this sport; every word at their table alludes to some passage between themselves; and you see by the paleness and emotion in their countenances, that it is for your sake, and not their own, that they forbear playing out the whole game in burning each other's fingers. In this case, the whole purpose of life is inverted, and the ambition turns upon a certain contention who shall contradict best, and not upon an inclination to excel in kindnesses and good offices. Therefore, dear Jenny, remember me, and avoid Snap-Dragon."

"I thank you, brother," said she, "but you do not know how he loves me; I find I can do anything with him." "If you can so, why should you desire to do anything but please him? but I have a word or two more before you go out of the room; for I see you do not like the subject I am upon: let nothing provoke you to fall upon an imperfection he cannot help; for, if he has a resenting spirit, he will think your aversion as immovable as the imperfection with which you upbraid him. But, above all, dear Jenny, be careful of one thing, and you will be something more than woman; that is, a levity you are almost all guilty of, which is, to take a pleasure in your power to give pain. It is even in a mistress an argument of meanness of spirit, but in a wife it is injustice and ingratitude. When a sensible man once observes this in a woman, he must have a very great, or very little spirit, to overlook it. A woman ought, therefore, to consider very often, how few men there are who will regard a meditated offense as a weakness of temper.

I was going on in my confabulation, when Tranquillus entered. She cast all her eyes upon him with much shame and confusion, mixed with great complacency and love, and went up to him. He took her in his arms, and looked so many soft things at one glance, that I could see he was glad I had been talking to her, sorry she had been troubled, and angry at himself that he could not disguise the concern he was in an hour before. After which he says to me, with an air awkward enough, but, methought, not unbecoming, "I have altered my mind, brother; we will live upon you a day or two longer." I replied, "That is what I have been persuading Jenny to ask you, but she is resolved never to contradict your inclination, and refused me."

We were going on in that way which one hardly knows how to express; as when two people mean the same thing in a nice case, but come at it by talking as distantly from it as they can; when very opportunely came in upon us an honest inconsiderable fellow Tim Dapper, a gentleman well known to us both. Tim is one of those who are very necessary, by being very inconsiderable. Tim dropped in at an incident when we knew not how to fall into either a grave or a merry way. My sister took this occasion to make off, and Dapper gave us an account of all the company he has been in to-day, who was and was not at home where he visited. This Tim is the head of a species; he is a little out of his element in this town; but he is a relation of Tranquillus, and his neighbor in the country, which is the true place of residence for this species. The habit of a Dapper, when he is at home, is a light broadcloth, with calamanco[8] or red waistcoat and breeches; and it is remarkable that their wigs seldom hide the collar of their coats. They have always a peculiar spring in their arms, a wriggle in their bodies, and a trip in their gait. All which motions they express at once in their drinking, bowing, or saluting ladies; for a

[8]A woolen material.

distant imitation of a forward fop, and a resolution to overtop him in his way, are the distinguishing marks of a Dapper. These under-characters of men, are parts of the sociable world by no means to be neglected: they are like pegs in a building; they make no figure in it, but hold the structure together, and are as absolutely necessary as the pillars and columns. I am sure we found it so this morning; for Tranquillus and I should, perhaps, have looked cold at each other the whole day, but Dapper fell in with his brisk way, shook us both by the hand, rallied the bride, mistook the acceptance he met with amongst us for extraordinary perfection in himself, and heartily pleased, and was pleased all the while he stayed. His company left us all in good humor, and we were not such fools as to let it sink, before we confirmed it by great cheerfulness and openness in our carriage the whole evening.

No. 132. SATURDAY, 11 FEBRUARY, 1710.
[STEELE.]

Habeo senectuti magnam gratiam, quae mihi sermonis aviditatem auxit, potionis et cibi sustulit.[9]

—TULL. *de Sen.*

AFTER having applied my mind with more than ordinary attention to my studies, it is my usual custom to relax and unbend it in the conversation of such, as are rather easy than shining companions. This I find particularly necessary for me before I retire to rest, in order to draw my slumbers upon me by degrees, and fall asleep insensibly. This is the particular use I make of a set of heavy honest men, with whom I have passed many hours with much indolence, though not with great pleasure. Their conversation is a kind of preparative for sleep; it takes the mind down from its abstractions, leads it into the familiar traces of thought, and lulls it into that state of tranquillity which is the condition of a thinking man, when he is but half awake. After this, my reader will not be surprised to hear the account, which I am about to give of a club of my own contemporaries, among whom I pass two or three hours every evening. This I look upon as taking my first nap before I go to bed. The truth of it is, I should think myself unjust to posterity, as well as to the society at the Trumpet, of which I am a member, did not I in some part of my writings give an account of the persons among whom I have passed almost a sixth part of my time for these last forty years. Our club consisted originally of fifteen; but, partly by the severity of the law in arbitrary times, and partly by the natural effects of old age, we are at present reduced to a third part of that number: in which, however, we hear this consolation, that the best company is said to consist of five persons. I must confess, besides the aforementioned benefit which I meet with in the conversation of this select society, I am not the less pleased with the company, in that I find myself the greatest wit among them, and am heard as their oracle in all points of learning and difficulty.

Sir Jeoffrey Notch, who is the oldest of the club, has been in possession of the right-hand chair time out of mind, and is the only man among us that has the liberty of stirring the fire. This our foreman is a gentleman of an ancient family, that came to a great estate some years before he had discretion, and run it out in hounds, horses, and cock-fighting; for which reason he looks upon himself as an honest, worthy gentleman, who has had misfortunes in the world, and calls every thriving man a pitiful upstart.

Major Matchlock is the next senior, who served in the last civil wars, and has all the battles by heart. He does not think any action in Europe worth talking of since the fight of Marston Moor; and every night tells us of his having been knocked off his horse at the rising of the London apprentices; for which he is in great esteem among us.

Honest old Dick Reptile is the third of our society. He is a good-natured indolent man, who speaks little himself, but laughs at our jokes; and brings his young nephew along with him, a youth of eighteen years old, to show him good company, and give him a taste of the world. This young fellow sits generally silent; but whenever he opens his mouth, or laughs at anything that passes, he

[9]I owe much gratitude to old age, which has sharpened my appetite for conversation and dulled my appetite for food and drink (Cicero, *De Senectute*).

is constantly told by his uncle, after a jocular manner, "Ay, ay, Jack, you young men think us fools; but we old men know you are."

The greatest wit of our company, next to myself, is a Bencher of the neighboring Inn,[10] who in his youth frequented the ordinaries about Charing Cross, and pretends to have been intimate with Jack Ogle. He has about ten distichs of Hudibras without book, and never leaves the club until he has applied them all. If any modern wit be mentioned, or any town-frolic spoken of, he shakes his head at the dullness of the present age, and tells us a story of Jack Ogle.

For my own part, I am esteemed among them, because they see I am something respected by others; though at the same time I understand by their behavior, that I am considered by them as a man of a great deal of learning, but no knowledge of the world; insomuch, that the Major sometimes, in the height of his military pride, calls me the Philosopher: and Sir Jeoffrey, no longer ago than last night, upon a dispute what day of the month it was then in Holland, pulled his pipe out of his mouth, and cried, "What does the scholar say to it?"

Our club meets precisely at *six o'clock in the evening;* but I did not come last night until half an hour after seven, by which means I escaped the battle of Naseby, which the Major usually begins at about three-quarters after six: I found also, that my good friend the Bencher had already spent three of his distichs; and only waited an opportunity to hear a sermon spoken of, that he might introduce the couplet where "a stick" rimes to "ecclesiastic." At my entrance into the room, they were naming a red petticoat and a cloak, by which I found that the Bencher had been diverting them with a story of Jack Ogle.

I had no sooner taken my seat, but Sir Jeoffrey, to show his good-will towards me, gave me a pipe of his own tobacco, and stirred up the fire. I look upon it as a point of morality, to be obliged by those who endeavor to oblige me; and therefore, in requital for his kindness, and to set the conversation a-going, I took the best occasion I could to put him upon telling us the story of old Gantlett, which he always does with very particular concern. He traced up his descent on both sides for several generations, describing his diet and manner of life, with his several battles, and particularly that in which he fell. This Gantlett was a gamecock, upon whose head the knight, in his youth, had won five hundred pounds, and lost two thousand. This naturally set the Major upon the account of Edge Hill fight, and ended in a duel of Jack Ogle's.

Old Reptile was extremely attentive to all that was said, though it was the same he had heard every night for these twenty years, and, upon all occasions, winked upon his nephew to mind what passed.

This may suffice to give the world a taste of our innocent conversation, which we spun out until about ten of the clock, when my maid came with a lantern to light me home. I could not but reflect with myself, as I was going out, upon the talkative humor of old men, and the little figure which that part of life makes in one who cannot employ his natural propensity in discourses which would make him venerable. I must own, it makes me very melancholy in company, when I hear a young man begin a story; and have often observed, that one of a quarter of an hour long in a man of five-and-twenty, gathers circumstances every time he tells it, until it grows into a long Canterbury tale of two hours by that time he is threescore.

The only way of avoiding such a trifling and frivolous old age is, to lay up in our way to it such stores of knowledge and observation, as may make us useful and agreeable in our declining years. The mind of man in a long life will become a magazine of wisdom or folly, and will consequently discharge itself in something impertinent or improving. For which reason, as there is nothing more ridiculous than an old trifling story-teller, so there is nothing more venerable, than one who has turned his experience to the entertainment and advantage of mankind.

In short, we, who are in the last stage of life, and are apt to indulge ourselves in talk, ought to consider, if what we speak be worth being heard, and endeavor to make our discourse like that of Nestor, which Homer compares to the flowing of honey for its sweetness.

[10] A senior member of one of the London legal colleges.

I am afraid I shall be thought guilty of this excess I am speaking of, when I cannot conclude without observing, that. Milton certainly thought of this passage in Homer, when, in his description of an eloquent spirit, he says, "His tongue dropped manna."[11]

No. 158. THURSDAY, 13 APRIL, 1710.

[ADDISON.]

Faciunt nae intelligendo, ut nihil intelligant.[12]

—TER.

TOM FOLIO is a broker in learning, employed to get together good editions, and stock the libraries of great men. There is not a sale of books begins until Tom Folio is seen at the door. There is not an auction where his name is not heard, and that too in the very nick of time, in the critical moment, before the last decisive stroke of the hammer. There is not a subscription goes forward in which Tom is not privy to the first rough draught of the proposals; nor a catalogue printed, that doth not come to him wet from the press. He. is an universal scholar, so far as the title-page of all authors; knows the manuscripts in which they were discovered, the editions through which they have passed, with the praises or censures which they have received from the several members of the learned world. He has a greater esteem for Aldus and Elzevir,[13] than for Virgil and Horace. If you talk of Herodotus, he breaks out into panegyric upon Harry Stephens.[14] He thinks he gives you an account of an author, when he tells you the subject he treats of, the name of the editor, and the year in which it was printed. Or if you draw him into farther particulars, he cries up the goodness of the paper, extols the diligence of the corrector, and is transported with the beauty of the letter. This he looks upon to be sound learning, and substantial criticism. As for those who talk of the fineness of style, and the justness of thought, or describe the brightness of any particular passages; nay, though they themselves write in the genius and spirit of the author they admire; Tom looks upon them as men of superficial learning, and flashy parts.

I had yesterday morning a visit from this learned *idiot,* for *that* is the light in which I consider every pedant, when I discovered in him some little touches of the coxcomb, which I had not before observed. Being very full of the figure which he makes in the republic of letters, and wonderfully satisfied with his great stock of knowledge, he gave me broad intimations, that he did not believe in all points as his forefathers had done. He then communicated to me a thought of a certain author upon a passage of Virgil's account of the dead, which I made the subject of a late paper. This thought hath taken very much among men of Tom's pitch and understanding, though universally exploded by all that know how to construe Virgil, or have any relish of antiquity. Not to trouble my reader with it, I found, upon the whole, that Tom did not believe a future state of rewards and punishments, because Aeneas, at his leaving the empire of the dead, passed through the gate of ivory, and not through that of horn. Knowing that Tom had not sense enough to give up an opinion which he had once received, that I might avoid wrangling, I told him "that Virgil possibly had his oversights as well as another author." "Ah! Mr. Bickerstaff,"[15] says he, "you would have another opinion of him, if you would read him in Daniel Heinsius's edition. I have perused him myself several times in that edition," continued he; "and after the strictest and most malicious examination, could find but two faults in him; one of them is in the Aeneids, where there are two commas instead of a parenthesis; and another in the third Georgic, where you may find a semicolon turned upside down." "Perhaps," said I, "these were not Virgil's faults, but those of the transcriber." "I do not design it," says Tom, "as a reflection on Virgil; on the contrary, I know that all the manuscripts

[11]Said of Belial, *Paradise Lost,* II, 112–113.

[12]While they pretend to know more than others, they really know nothing (Terence, *Andr.,* Prol., 17).

[13]Famous publishers of books.

[14]Henri Estienne, a sixteenth-century editor of and apologist for Herodotus.

[15]The *Tatler* papers, it was pretended, were written by Isaac Bickerstaff, a fictitious astrologer invented several years before by Swift for the purpose of making fun of one Partridge, an astrologer who published predictions much after the manner of the old-fashioned almanac still occasionally to be met with.

declaim against such a punctuation. Oh! Mr. Bickerstaff," says he, "what would a man give to see one simile of Virgil writ in his own hand?" I asked him which was the simile he meant; but was answered, any simile in Virgil. He then told me all the secret history in the commonwealth of learning; of modern pieces that had the names of ancient authors annexed to them; of all the books that were now writing or printing in the several parts of Europe; of many amendments which are made, and not yet published, and a thousand other particulars, which I would not have my memory burdened with for a Vatican.

At length, being fully persuaded that I thoroughly admired him, and looked upon him as a prodigy of learning, he took his leave. I know several of Tom's class, who are professed admirers of Tasso, without understanding a word of Italian: and one in particular, that carries a *Pastor Fido*[16] in his pocket, in which, I am sure, he is acquainted with no other beauty but the clearness of the character.

There is another kind of pedant, who, with all Tom Folio's impertinences, hath greater superstructures and embellishments of Greek and Latin; and is still more insupportable than the other, in the same degree as he is more learned. Of this kind very often are editors, commentators, interpreters, scholiasts, and critics; and, in short, all men of deep learning without common sense. These persons set a greater value on themselves for having found out the meaning of a passage in Greek, than upon the author for having written it; nay, will allow the passage itself not to have any beauty in it, at the same time that they would be considered as the greatest men of the age, for having interpreted it. They will look with contempt on the most beautiful poems that have been composed by any of their contemporaries; but will lock themselves up in their studies for a twelvemonth together, to correct, publish, and expound such trifles of antiquity, as a modern author would be contemned for. Men of the strictest morals, severest lives, and the gravest professions, will write volumes upon an idle sonnet, that is originally in Greek or Latin; give editions of the most immoral authors; and spin out whole pages upon the various readings of a lewd expression. All that can be said in excuse for them is, that their works sufficiently show they have no taste of their authors; and that what they do in this kind, is out of their great learning, and not out of any levity or lasciviousness of temper.

A pedant of this nature is wonderfully well described in six lines of Boileau, with which I shall conclude his character:

Un Pédant enyvré de sa vaine science,
Tout herissé de Grec, tout bouffi d'arrogance;
Et qui de mille auteurs retenus mot pour mot,
Dans sa tête entassés n'a souvent fait qu'un sot,
Croit qu'un livre fait tout, et que sans Aristote
La raison ne voit goute, et le bon sens radote.

Brim-full of learning see that pedant stride,
Bristling with horrid Greek, and puffed with
pride!
A thousand authors he in vain has read,
And with their maxims stuffed his empty head;
And thinks that, without Aristotle's rule,
Reason is blind, and common sense a fool.

[16]Italian pastoral drama of the late sixteenth century by G. B. Guarini.

THE SPECTATOR

No. 1. Thursday, 1 March, 1711.

[Addison.]

Non fumum ex fulgore, sed ex fumo dare lucem
Cogitat, ut speciosa dehinc miracula promat.[1]

—Horace.

I have observed that a reader seldom peruses a book with pleasure till he knows whether the writer of it be a black or a fair man, of a mild or choleric disposition, married or a bachelor, with other particulars of the like nature that conduce very much to the right understanding of an author. To gratify this curiosity, which is so natural to a reader, I design this paper and my next as prefatory discourses to my following writings, and shall give some account in them of the several persons that are engaged in this work. As the chief trouble of compiling,

[1]Not smoke from fire his object is to bring,
But fire from smoke, a very different thing.
(*Art of Poetry*, 143–144; Conington's translation.)

digesting, and correcting will fall to my share, I must do myself the justice to open the work with my own history. I was born to a small hereditary estate, which, according to the tradition of the village where it lies, was bounded by the same hedges and ditches in William the Conqueror's time that it is at present, and has been delivered down from father to son whole and entire, without the loss or acquisition of a single field or meadow, during the space of six hundred years. There runs a story in the family, that my mother dreamed that she was brought to bed of a judge: whether this might proceed from a lawsuit which was then depending in the family, or my father's being a justice of the peace, I cannot determine; for I am not so vain as to think it presaged any dignity that I should arrive at in my future life, though that was the interpretation which the neighborhood put upon it. The gravity of my behavior at my very first appearance in the world seemed to favor my mother's dream: for, as she has often told me, I threw away my rattle before I was two months old, and would not make use of my coral till they had taken away the bells from it.

As for the rest of my infancy, there being nothing in it remarkable, I shall pass it over in silence. I find that, during my nonage, I had the reputation of a very sullen youth, but was always a favorite of my schoolmaster, who used to say *that my parts were solid and would wear well.* I had not been long at the University before I distinguished myself by a most profound silence; for during the space of eight years, excepting in the public exercises of the college, I scarce uttered the quantity of an hundred words; and indeed do not remember that I ever spoke three sentences together in my whole life. Whilst I was in this learned body, I applied myself with so much diligence to my studies that there are very few celebrated books, either in the learned or the modern tongues, which I am not acquainted with.

Upon the death of my father I was resolved to travel into foreign countries, and therefore left the University with the character of an odd, unaccountable fellow, that had a great deal of learning if I would but show it. An insatiable thirst after knowledge carried me into all the countries of Europe in which there was anything new or strange to be seen; nay, to such a degree was my curiosity raised, that having read the controversies of some great men concerning the antiquities of Egypt, I made a voyage to Grand Cairo, on purpose to take the measure of a pyramid; and as soon as I had set myself right in that particular, returned to my native country with great satisfaction.

I have passed my latter years in this city, where I am frequently seen in most public places, though there are not above half a dozen of my select friends that know me; of whom my next paper shall give a more particular account. There is no place of general sort wherein I do not often make my appearance; sometimes I am seen thrusting my head into a round of politicians at Will's, and listening with great attention to the narratives that are made in those little circular audiences. Sometimes I smoke a pipe at Child's, and whilst I seem attentive to nothing but *The Postman,* overhear the conversation of every table in the room. I appear on Sunday nights at St. James's Coffee-house, and sometimes join the little committee of politics in the Inner room, as one who comes there to hear and improve. My face is likewise very well known at the Grecian, the Cocoa-Tree, and in the theaters both of Drury Lane and the Hay-Market. I have been taken for a merchant upon the Exchange for above these ten years, and sometimes pass for a Jew in the assembly of stock-jobbers at Jonathan's. In short, wherever I see a cluster of people, I always mix with them, though I never open my lips but in my own club.

Thus I live in the world rather as a SPECTATOR of mankind than as one of the species; by which means I have made myself a speculative statesman, soldier, merchant, and artisan, without ever meddling with any practical part in life. I am very well versed in the theory of an husband or a father, and can discern the errors in the economy, business, and diversion of others better than those who are engaged in them; as standers-by discover blots which are apt to escape those who are in the game. I never espoused any party with violence, and am resolved to observe an exact neutrality between the Whigs and Tories, unless I shall be forced to declare myself by the hostilities of either side. In short, I have acted in all the parts of my life as a looker-on, which is the character I intend to preserve in this paper.

I have given the reader just so much of my history and character as to let him see I am not altogether unqualified for the business I have undertaken. As for other particulars in my life and adventures, I shall insert them in following papers as I shall see occasion. In the meantime, when I consider how much I have seen, read, and heard, I began to blame my own taciturnity: and since I have neither time nor inclination to communicate the fullness of my heart in speech, I am resolved to do it in writing, and to print myself out, if possible, before I die. I have been often told by my friends that it is a pity so many useful discoveries which I have made, should be in the possession of a silent man. For this reason, therefore, I shall publish a sheetful of thoughts every morning for the benefit of my contemporaries; and if I can in any way contribute to the diversion or improvement of the country in which I live, I shall leave it, when I am summoned out of it, with the secret satisfaction of thinking that I have not lived in vain.

There are three very material points which I have not spoken to in this paper, and which, for several important reasons, I must keep to myself, at least for some time: I mean, an account of my name, my age, and my lodgings. I must confess, I would gratify my reader in anything that is reasonable; but, as for these three particulars, though I am sensible they might tend very much to the embellishment of my paper, I cannot yet come to a resolution of communicating them to the public. They would indeed draw me out of that obscurity which I have enjoyed for many years, and expose me in public places to several salutes and civilities which have been always very disagreeable to me; for the greatest pain I can suffer is the being talked to and being stared at. It is for this reason, likewise, that I keep my complexion and dress as very great secrets, though it is not impossible but I may make discoveries of both in the progress of the work I have undertaken.

After having been thus particular upon myself, I shall in to-morrow's paper give an account of those gentlemen who are concerned with me in this work; for, as I have before intimated, a plan of it is laid and concerted (as all other matters of importance are) in a club. However, as my friends have engaged me to stand in the front, those who have a mind to correspond with me may direct their letters *To The Spectator, at Mr. Buckley's, in Little Britain.* For I must further acquaint the reader that, though our club meets only on Tuesdays and Thursdays, we have appointed a committee to sit every night for the inspection of all such papers as may contribute to the advancement of the public weal.

No. 2. Friday, 2 March, 1711.

[Steele.]

—*Haec alii sex*
Vel plures uno conclamant ore.[2]
—Juvenal.

The first of our society is a gentleman of Worcestershire, of ancient descent, a baronet, his name Sir Roger de Coverley. His great-grandfather was inventor of that famous country-dance which is called after him. All who know that shire are very well acquainted with the parts and merits of Sir Roger. He is a gentleman that is very singular in his behavior, but his singularities proceed from his good sense, and are contradictions to the manners of the world only as he thinks the world is in the wrong. However, this humor creates him no enemies, for he does nothing with sourness of obstinacy; and his being unconfined to modes and forms, makes him but the readier and more capable to please and oblige all who know him. When he is in town, he lives in Soho Square. It is said he keeps himself a bachelor by reason he was crossed in love by a perverse, beautiful widow of the next county to him. Before this disappointment, Sir Roger was what you call a fine gentleman, had often supped with my Lord Rochester and Sir George Ether-

[2]Six others and more cry out with one voice (*Satires,* VII, 167).

ege,[3] fought a duel upon his first coming to town, and kicked Bully Dawson in a public coffee-house for calling him "youngster." But being ill-used by the above-mentioned widow, he was very serious for a year and a half; and though, his temper being naturally jovial, he at last got over it, he grew careless of himself, and never dressed afterward. He continues to wear a coat and doublet of the same cut that were in fashion at the time of his repulse, which, in his merry humors, he tells us, has been in and out twelve times since he first wore it. 'Tis said Sir Roger grew humble in his desires after he had forgot this cruel beauty; but this is looked upon by his friends rather as matter of raillery than truth. He is now in his fifty-sixth year, cheerful, gay, and hearty; keeps a good house in both town and country; a great lover of mankind; but there is such a mirthful cast in his behavior that he is rather beloved than esteemed. His tenants grow rich, his servants look satisfied, all the young women profess love to him, and the young men are glad of his company; when he comes into a house he calls the servants by their names, and talks all the way up stairs to a visit. I must not omit that Sir Roger is a justice of the quorum; that he fills the chair at a quarter-session with great abilities; and, three months ago, gained universal applause by explaining a passage in the Game Act.

The gentleman next in esteem and authority among us is another bachelor, who is a member of the Inner Temple; a man of great probity, wit, and understanding; but he has chosen his place of residence rather to obey the direction of an old humorsome father, than in pursuit of his own inclinations. He was placed there to study the laws of the land, and is the most learned of any of the house in those of the stage. Aristotle and Longinus are much better understood by him than Littleton or Coke.[4] The father sends up, every post, questions relating to marriage-articles, leases, and tenures, in the neighborhood; all which questions he agrees with an attorney to answer and take care of in the lump. He is studying the passions themselves, when he should be inquiring into the debates among men which arise from them. He knows the argument of each of the orations of Demosthenes and Tully,[5] but not one case in the reports of our own courts. No one ever took him for a fool, but none, except his intimate friends, know he has a great deal of wit. This turn makes him at once both disinterested and agreeable; as few of his thoughts are drawn from business, they are most of them fit for conversation. His taste of books is a little too just for the age he lives in; he has read all, but approves of very few. His familiarity with the customs, manners, actions, and writings of the ancients makes him a very delicate observer of what occurs to him in the present world. He is an excellent critic, and the time of the play is his hour of business; exactly at five he passes through New Inn, crosses through Russell Court, and takes a turn at Will's till the play begins; he has his shoes rubbed and his periwig powdered at the barber's as you go into the Rose. It is for the good of the audience when he is at a play, for the actors have an ambition to please him.

The person of next consideration is Sir Andrew Freeport, a merchant of great eminence in the city of London, a person of indefatigable industry, strong reason, and great experience. His notions of trade are noble and generous, and (as every rich man has usually some sly way of jesting which would make no great figure were he not a rich man) he calls the sea the British Common. He is acquainted with commerce in all its parts, and will tell you that it is a stupid and barbarous way to extend dominion by arms; for true power is to be got by arts and industry. He will often argue that if this part of our trade were well cultivated, we should gain from one nation; and if another, from another. I have heard him prove that diligence makes more lasting acquisitions than valor, and that sloth has ruined more nations than the sword. He abounds in several frugal maxims, among which the greatest favorite is, "A penny saved is a penny got." A general trader of good sense is pleasanter company than a general scholar; and Sir Andrew having a natural unaffected eloquence, the

[3]Men of letters during the Restoration period, a generation earlier.

[4]Outstanding English legal authorities.

[5]Cicero.

perspicuity of his discourse gives the same pleasure that wit would in another man. He has made his fortunes himself, and says that England may be richer than other kingdoms by as plain methods as he himself is richer than other men; though at the same time I can say this of him, that there is not a point in the compass but blows home a ship in which he is an owner.

Next to Sir Andrew in the club-room sits Captain Sentry, a gentleman of great courage, good understanding, but invincible modesty. He is one of those that deserve very well, but are very awkward at putting their talents within the observation of such as should take notice of them. He was some years a captain, and behaved himself with great gallantry in several engagements and at several sieges; but having a small estate of his own, and being next heir to Sir Roger, he has quitted a way of life in which no man can rise suitably to his merit who is not something of a courtier as well as a soldier. I have heard him often lament that in a profession where merit is placed in so conspicuous a view, impudence should get the better of modesty. When he has talked to this purpose I never heard him make a sour expression, but frankly confess that he left the world because he was not fit for it. A strict honesty and an even, regular behavior are in themselves obstacles to him that must press through crowds who endeavor at the same end with himself,—the favor of a commander. He will, however, in this way of talk, excuse generals for not disposing according to men's desert, or inquiring into it, "For," says he, "that great man who has a mind to help me, has as many to break through to come at me as I have to come at him"; therefore he will conclude that the man who would make a figure, especially in a military way, must get over all false modesty, and assist his patron against the importunity of other pretenders by a proper assurance in his own vindication. He says it is a civil cowardice to be backward in asserting what you ought to expect, as it is a military fear to be slow in attacking when it is your duty. With this candor does the gentleman speak of himself and others. The same frankness runs through all his conversation. The military part of his life has furnished him with many adventures, in the relation of which he is very agreeable to the company; for he is never overbearing, though accustomed to command men in the utmost degree below him; nor ever too obsequious from an habit of obeying men highly above him.

But that our society may not appear a set of humorists unacquainted with the gallantries and pleasures of the age, we have among us the gallant Will Honeycomb, a gentleman who, according to his years, should be in the decline of his life, but having ever been very careful of his person, and always had a very easy fortune, time has made but very little impression either by wrinkles on his forehead or traces in his brain. His person is well turned and of a good height. He is very ready at that sort of discourse with which men usually entertain women. He has all his life dressed very well, and remembers habits as others do men. He can smile when one speaks to him, and laughs easily. He knows the history of every mode, and can inform you from which of the French king's wenches our wives and daughters had this manner of curling their hair, that way of placing their hoods; whose frailty was covered by such a sort of petticoat, and whose vanity to show her foot made that part of the dress so short in such a year. In a word, all his conversation and knowledge has been in the female world. As other men of his age will take notice to you what such a minister said upon such and such an occasion, he will tell you when the Duke of Monmouth danced at court such a woman was then smitten, another was taken with him at the head of his troop in the Park. In all these important relations, he has ever about the same time received a kind glance or a blow of a fan from some celebrated beauty, mother of the present Lord Such-a-one. If you speak of a young commoner that said a lively thing in the House, he starts up: "He has good blood in his veins; Tom Mirabell, the rogue, cheated me in that affair; that young fellow's mother used me more like a dog than any woman I ever made advances to." This way of talking of his very much enlivens the conversation among us of a more sedate turn; and I find there is not one of the company but myself, who rarely speak at all, but speaks of him as of that sort of man who is usually called a well-bred, fine gentleman. To conclude his character, where women are not concerned, he is an honest, worthy man.

I cannot tell whether I am to account him whom I am next to speak of as one of our company, for he visits us but seldom; but when he does, it adds to every man else a new enjoyment of himself. He is a clergyman, a very philosophic man, of general learning, great sanctity of life, and the most exact good breeding. He has the misfortune to be of a very weak constitution, and consequently cannot accept of such cares and business as preferments in his function would oblige him to; he is therefore among divines what a chamber-counselor is among lawyers. The probity of his mind and the integrity of his life create him followers, as being eloquent or loud advances others. He seldom introduces the subject he speaks upon; but we are so far gone in years that he observes, when he is among us, an earnestness to have him fall on some divine topic, which he always treats with much authority, as one who has no interest in this world, as one who is hastening to the object of all his wishes and conceives hope from his decays and infirmities. These are my ordinary companions.

No. 10. Monday, 12 March, 1711.

[Addison.]

Non aliter quam qui adverso vix flumine lembum
Remigiis subigit, si brachia forte remisit,
Atque illum in praeceps prono rapit alveus amni.[6]

—Virg.

It is with much satisfaction that I hear this great city inquiring day by day after these my papers, and receiving my morning lectures with a becoming seriousness and attention. My publisher tells me that there are already three thousand of them distributed every day. So that if I allow twenty readers to every paper, which I look upon as a modest computation, I may reckon about three-score thousand disciples in London and Westminster, who I hope will take care to distinguish themselves from the thoughtless herd of their ignorant and unattentive brethren. Since I have raised to myself so great an audience, I shall spare no pains to make their instruction agreeable, and their diversion useful. For which reasons I shall endeavor to enliven morality with wit, and to temper wit with morality, that my readers may, if possible, both ways find their account in the speculation of the day. And to the end that their virtue and discretion may not be short, transient, intermitting starts of thought, I have resolved to refresh their memories from day to day, till I have recovered them out of that desperate state of vice and folly into which the age is fallen. The mind that lies fallow but a single day, sprouts up in follies that are only to be killed by a constant and assiduous culture. It was said of Socrates, that he brought philosophy down from heaven, to inhabit among men; and I shall be ambitious to have it said of me, that I have brought philosophy out of closets and libraries, schools and colleges, to dwell in clubs and assemblies, at tea-tables and in coffee-houses.

I would therefore in a very particular manner recommend these my speculations to all well-regulated families, that set apart an hour in every morning for tea and bread and butter; and would earnestly advise them for their good to order this paper to be punctually served up, and to be looked upon as a part of the tea-equipage.

Sir Francis Bacon observes, that a well written book, compared with its rivals and antagonists, is like Moses' serpent, that immediately swallowed up and devoured those of the Egyptians. I shall not be so vain as to think, that where *The Spectator* appears, the other public prints will vanish; but shall leave it to my reader's consideration, whether, is it not much better to be let into the knowledge of one's self, than to hear what passes in Muscovy or Poland; and to amuse ourselves with such writings as tend to the wearing out of ignorance, passion, and prejudice, than such as naturally conduce to inflame hatreds, and make enmities irreconcilable?

[6] Like a man whose oars can barely force the boat upstream, and if he relaxes his arms the current carries it headlong down the river (*Georgics*, I, 201).

In the next place, I would recommend this paper to the daily perusal of those gentlemen whom I cannot but consider as my good brothers and allies, I mean the fraternity of spectators, who live in the world without having anything to do in it; and either by the affluence of their fortunes, or laziness of their dispositions, have no other business with the rest of mankind, but to look upon them. Under this class of men are comprehended all contemplative tradesmen, titular physicians, fellows of the Royal Society, Templars that are not given to be contentious, and statesmen that are out of business; in short, every one that considers the world as a theater, and desires to form a right judgment of those who are the actors on it.

There is another set of men that I must likewise lay a claim to, whom I have lately called the blanks of society, as being altogether unfurnished with ideas, till the business and conversation of the day has supplied them. I have often considered these poor souls with an eye of great commiseration, when I have heard them asking the first man they have met with, whether there was any news stirring? and by that means gathering together materials for thinking. These needy persons do not know what to talk of, till about twelve o'clock in the morning; for by that time they are pretty good judges of the weather, know which way the wind sits, and whether the Dutch mail be come in. As they lie at the mercy of the first man they meet, and are grave or impertinent all the day long, according to the notions which they have imbibed in the morning, I would earnestly entreat them not to stir out of their chambers till they have read this paper, and do promise them that I will daily instil into them such sound and wholesome sentiments, as shall have a good effect on their conversation for the ensuing twelve hours.

But there are none to whom this paper will be more useful, than to the female world. I have often thought there has not been sufficient pains taken in finding out proper employments and diversions for the fair ones. Their amusements seem contrived for them, rather as they are women, than as they are reasonable creatures; and are more adapted to the sex than to the species. The toilet is their great scene of business, and the right adjusting of their hair the principal employment of their lives. The sorting of a suit of ribbons is reckoned a very good morning's work; and if they make an excursion to a mercer's or a toy-shop, so great a fatigue makes them unfit for anything else all the day after. Their more serious occupations are sewing and embroidery, and their greatest drudgery the preparation of jellies and sweetmeats. This, I say, is the state of ordinary women; though I know there are multitudes of those of a more elevated life and conversation, that move in an exalted sphere of knowledge and virtue, that join all the beauties of the mind to the ornaments of dress, and inspire a kind of awe and respect, as well as love, into their male beholder. I hope to increase the number of these by publishing this daily paper, which I shall always endeavor to make an innocent if not an improving entertainment, and by that means at least divert the minds of my female readers from greater trifles. At the same time, as I would fain give some finishing touches to those which are already the most beautiful pieces in human nature, I shall endeavor to point out all those imperfections that are the blemishes, as well as those virtues which are the embellishments of the sex. In the meanwhile I hope these my gentle readers, who have so much time on their hands, will not grudge throwing away a quarter of an hour in a day on this paper, since they may do it without any hindrance to business.

I know several of my friends and well-wishers are in great pain for me, lest I should not be able to keep up the spirit of a paper which I oblige myself to furnish every day: but to make them easy in this particular, I will promise them faithfully to give it over as soon as I grow dull. This I know will be matter of great raillery to the small wits; who will frequently put me in mind of my promise, desire me to keep my word, assure me that it is high time to give over, with many other little pleasantries of the like nature, which men of a little smart genius cannot forbear throwing out against their best friends, when they have such a handle given them of being witty. But let them remember that I do hereby enter my caveat against this piece of raillery.

No. 81. SATURDAY, 2 JUNE, 1711.
[ADDISON.]

Qualis ubi audito venantum murmure tigris
Horruit in maculas—[7]

—STATIUS.

ABOUT the middle of last winter I went to see an opera at the theater in the Haymarket, where I could not but take notice of two parties of very fine women, that had placed themselves in the opposite side-boxes, and seemed drawn up in a kind of battle array one against another. After a short survey of them, I found they were patched differently; the faces on one hand being spotted on the right side of the forehead, and those upon the other on the left. I quickly perceived that they cast hostile glances upon one another; and that their patches were placed in those different situations, as party-signals to distinguish friends from foes. In the middle boxes, between these two opposite bodies, were several ladies who patched indifferently on both sides of their faces, and seemed to sit there with no other intention but to see the opera. Upon inquiry I found, that the body of Amazons on my right hand, were Whigs, and those on my left, Tories; and that those who had placed themselves in the middle boxes were a neutral party, whose faces had not yet declared themselves. These last, however, as I afterwards found, diminished daily, and took their party with one side or the other; insomuch that I observed in several of them, the patches, which were before dispersed equally, are now all gone over to the Whig or Tory side of the face. The censorious say, that the men, whose hearts are aimed at, are very often the occasions that one part of the face is thus dishonored, and lies under a kind of disgrace, while the other is so much set off and adorned by the owner; and that the patches turn to the right or to the left, according to the principles of the man who is most in favor. But whatever may be the motives of a few fantastical coquettes, who do not patch for the public good so much as for their own private advantage, it is certain, that there are several women of honor who patch out of principle, and with an eye to the interest of their country. Nay, I am informed that some of them adhere so steadfastly to their party, and are so far from sacrificing their zeal for the public to their passion for any particular person, that in a late draft of marriage articles a lady has stipulated with her husband, that, whatever his opinions are, she shall be at liberty to patch on which side she pleases.

I must here take notice, that Rosalinda, a famous Whig partisan, has most unfortunately a very beautiful mole on the Tory part of her forehead; which being very conspicuous, has occasioned many mistakes, and given a handle to her enemies to misrepresent her face, as though it had revolted from the Whig interest. But, whatever this natural patch may seem to intimate, it is well-known that her notions of government are still the same. This unlucky mole, however, has misled several coxcombs; and like the hanging out of false colors, made some of them converse with Rosalinda in what they thought the spirit of her party, when on a sudden she has given them an unexpected fire, that has sunk them all at once. If Rosalinda is unfortunate in her mole, Nigranilla is as unhappy in a pimple, which forces her, against her inclinations, to patch on the Whig side.

I am told that many virtuous matrons, who formerly have been taught to believe that this artificial spotting of the face was unlawful, are now reconciled by a zeal for their cause, to what they could not be prompted by a concern for their beauty. This way of declaring war upon one another, puts me in mind of what is reported of the tigress, that several spots rise in her skin when she is angry, or as Mr. Cowley has imitated the verses that stands as the motto on this paper,

——She swells with angry pride,
And calls forth all her spots on ev'ry side.[8]

When I was in the theater the time abovementioned, I had the curiosity to count the

[7] Like the tigress when, at the sound of the hunters, spots appear upon her skin (*Theb.*, II, 128).

[8] *Davideis*, III, 403-404.

patches on both sides, and found the Tory patches to be about twenty stronger than the Whig; but to make amends for this small inequality, I the next morning found the whole puppet-show filled with faces spotted after the Whiggish manner. Whether or no the ladies had retreated hither in order to rally their forces I cannot tell; but the next night they came in so great a body to the opera, that they outnumbered the enemy.

This account of party patches will, I am afraid, appear improbable to those who live at a distance from the fashionable world; but as it is a distinction of a very singular nature, and what perhaps may never meet with a parallel, I think I should not have discharged the office of a faithful Spectator had I not recorded it.

I have, in former papers, endeavored to expose this party-rage in women, as it only serves to aggravate the hatreds and animosities that reign among men, and in a great measure deprive the fair sex of those peculiar charms with which nature has endowed them.

When the Romans and Sabines were at war, and just upon the point of giving battle, the women, who were allied to both of them, interposed with so many tears and entreaties, that they prevented the mutual slaughter which threatened both parties, and united them together in a firm and lasting peace.

I would recommend this noble example to our British ladies, at a time when their country is torn with so many unnatural divisions, that if they continue, it will be a misfortune to be born in it. The Greeks thought it so improper for women to interest themselves in competitions and contentions, that for this reason, among others, they forbade them, under pain of death, to be present at the Olympic games, notwithstanding these were the public diversions of all Greece.

As our English women excel those of all nations in beauty, they should endeavor to outshine them in all other accomplishments proper to the sex, and to distinguish themselves as tender mothers, and faithful wives, rather than as furious partisans. Female virtues are of a domestic turn. The family is the proper province for private women to shine in. If they must be showing their zeal for the public, let it not be against those who are perhaps of the same family, or at least of the same religion or nation, but against those who are the open, professed, undoubted enemies of their faith, liberty, and country. When the Romans were pressed with a foreign enemy, the ladies voluntarily contributed all their rings and jewels to assist the government under a public exigence, which appeared so laudable an action in the eyes of their countrymen, that from thenceforth it was permitted by a law to pronounce public orations at the funeral of a woman in praise of the deceased person, which till that time was peculiar to men. Would our English ladies, instead of sticking on a patch against those of their own country, show themselves so truly public-spirited as to sacrifice every one her necklace against the common enemy, what decrees ought not to be made in favor of them?

Since I am recollecting upon this subject such passages as occur to my memory out of ancient authors, I cannot omit a sentence in the celebrated funeral oration of Pericles, which he made in honor of those brave Athenians that were slain in a fight with the Lacedaemonians. After having addressed himself to the several ranks and orders of his countrymen, and shown them how they should behave themselves in the public cause, he turns to the female part of his audience: "And as for you (says he) I shall advise you in very few words: Aspire only to those virtues that are peculiar to your sex; follow your natural modesty, and think it your greatest commendation not to be talked of one way or other."[9]

No. 112. Monday, 9 July, 1711.

[Addison.]

Ἀθανάτους μὲν πρῶτα θεοὺς, νόμῳ ὡς διάκειται, Τίμα.[10]

—Pythagoras.

I am always very well pleased with a country Sunday, and think, if keeping holy the seventh day were only a human institution, it would be the best method that

---

[9]Thucydides, II, xlv.

[10]First reverence the immortal gods, as custom decrees (*Carmina Aurea*, 1–2).

could have been thought of for the polishing and civilizing of mankind. It is certain the country people would soon degenerate into a kind of savages and barbarians were there not such frequent returns of a stated time, in which the whole village meet together with their best faces, and in their cleanliest habits, to converse with one another upon indifferent subjects, hear their duties explained to them, and join together in adoration of the Supreme Being. Sunday clears away the rust of the whole week, not only as it refreshes in their minds the notions of religion, but as it puts both the sexes upon appearing in their most agreeable forms, and exerting all such qualities as are apt to give them a figure in the eye of the village. A country fellow distinguishes himself as much in the churchyard as a citizen does upon the 'Change, the whole parish politics being generally discussed in that place either after sermon or before the bell rings.

My friend Sir Roger, being a good churchman, has beautified the inside of his church with several texts of his own choosing; he has likewise given a handsome pulpit-cloth, and railed in the communion-table at his own expense. He has often told me that, at his coming to his estate, he found his parishioners very irregular; and that, in order to make them kneel and join in the responses, he gave every one of them a hassock and a common-prayer-book, and at the same time employed an itinerant singing-master, who goes about the country for that purpose, to instruct them rightly in the tunes of the Psalms; upon which they now very much value themselves, and indeed outdo most of the country churches that I have ever heard.

As Sir Roger is landlord to the whole congregation, he keeps them in very good order, and will suffer nobody to sleep in it besides himself; for, if by chance he has been surprised into a short nap at sermon, upon recovering out of it he stands up and looks about him, and, if he sees anybody else nodding, either wakes them himself, or sends his servant to them. Several other of the old knight's particularities break out upon these occasions; sometimes he will be lengthening out a verse in the Singing-Psalms half a minute after the rest of the congregation have done with it; sometimes, when he is pleased with the matter of his devotion, he pronounces "Amen" three or four times to the same prayer; and sometimes stands up when everybody else is upon their knees, to count the congregation, or see if any of his tenants are missing.

I was yesterday very much surprised to hear my old friend, in the midst of the service, calling out to one John Matthews to mind what he was about, and not disturb the congregation. This John Matthews, it seems, is remarkable for being an idle fellow, and at that time was kicking his heels for his diversion. This authority of the knight, though exerted in that odd manner which accompanies him in all circumstances of life, has a very good effect upon the parish, who are not polite enough to see anything ridiculous in his behavior; besides that the general good sense and worthiness of his character makes his friends observe these little singularities as foils that rather set off than blemish his good qualities.

As soon as the sermon is finished, nobody presumes to stir till Sir Roger is gone out of the church. The knight walks down from his seat in the chancel between a double row of his tenants, that stand bowing to him on each side, and every now and then inquires how such an one's wife, or mother, or son, or father do, whom he does not see at church,—which is understood as a secret reprimand to the person that is absent.

The chaplain has often told me that, upon a catechizing day, when Sir Roger had been pleased with a boy that answers well, he has ordered a Bible to be given him next day for his encouragement, and sometimes accompanies it with a flitch of bacon to his mother. Sir Roger has likewise added five pounds a year to the clerk's place; and, that he may encourage the young fellows to make themselves perfect in the church service, has promised, upon the death of the present incumbent, who is very old, to bestow it according to merit.

The fair understanding between Sir Roger and his chaplain, and their mutual concurrence in doing good, is the more remarkable because the very next village is famous for the differences and contentions that rise b-tween the parson and the squire, who live in a perpetual state of war. The parson is always preaching at the squire, and the squire, to be revenged on the parson, never comes to church. The squire has made all his tenants atheists and tithe-stealers; while the parson instructs them every Sunday in the dignity of his order, and insinuates to them in almost every sermon that he is a better man than his patron. In short, matters are come to such an extremity that the squire has not said his prayers either in public or private this half year; and that the parson threatens him, if he does not mend his manners, to pray for him in the face of the whole congregation.

Feuds of this nature, though too frequent in the country, are very fatal to the ordinary people, who are so used to be dazzled with riches that they pay as much deference to the understanding of a man of an estate as of a man of learning; and are very hardly brought to regard any truth, how important soever it may be, that is preached to them, when they know there are several men of five hundred a year who do not believe it.

No. 122. FRIDAY, 20 JULY, 1711.

[ADDISON.]

Comes jucundus in via pro vehiculo est.[11]

—PUBL. SYR.

A MAN'S first care should be to avoid the reproaches of his own heart; his next, to escape the censures of the world. If the last interferes with the former, it ought to be entirely neglected; but otherwise there cannot be a greater satisfaction to an honest mind than to see those approbations which it gives itself seconded by the applauses of the public. A man is more sure of his conduct when the verdict which he passes upon his own behavior is thus warranted and confirmed by the opinion of all that know him.

My worthy friend Sir Roger is one of those who is not only at peace with himself but beloved and esteemed by all about him. He receives a suitable tribute for his universal benevolence to mankind in the returns of affection and good-will which are paid him by every one that lives within his neighborhood. I lately met with two or three odd instances of that general respect which is shown to the good old knight. He would needs carry Will Wimble and myself with him to the county assizes. As we were upon the road, Will Wimble joined a couple of plain men who rid before us, and conversed with them for some time, during which my friend Sir Roger acquainted me with their characters.

"The first of them," says he, "that has a spaniel by his side, is a yeoman of about an hundred pounds a year, an honest man. He is just within the Game Act, and qualified to kill an hare or a pheasant. He knocks down a dinner with his gun twice or thrice a week; and by that means lives much cheaper than those who have not so good an estate as himself. He would be a good neighbor if he did not destroy so many partridges; in short he is a very sensible man, shoots flying, and has been several times foreman of the petty-jury.

"The other that rides along with him is Tom Touchy, a fellow famous for taking the law of everybody. There is not one in the town where he lives that he has not sued for a quarter-sessions. The rogue had once the impudence to go to law with the widow. His head is full of costs, damages, and ejectments; he plagued a couple of honest gentlemen so long for a trespass in breaking one of his hedges, till he was forced to sell the ground it enclosed to defray the charges of the prosecution. His father left him fourscore pounds a year, but he has cast and been cast so often that he is not now worth thirty. I suppose he is going upon the old business of the willow tree."

As Sir Roger was giving me this account of Tom Touchy, Will Wimble and his two companions stopped short till we came up to them. After having paid their respects to Sir Roger, Will told him that Mr. Touchy and he must appeal to him upon a dispute that arose between them. Will, it seems, had been giving his fellow-traveler an account of his angling one day in such a hole; when Tom Touchy, instead of hearing out his story, told him that Mr. Such-an-one, if

[11] A pleasant comrade on a journey is as good as a carriage (Publilius Syrus, *Fragments*).

he pleased, might take the law of him for fishing in that part of the river. My friend Sir Roger heard them both, upon a round trot; and, after having paused some time, told them, with the air of a man who would 5 not give his judgment rashly, *that much might be said on both sides.* They were neither of them dissatisfied with the knight's determination, because neither of them found himself in the wrong by it. Upon which we 10 made the best of our way to the assizes.

The court was sat before Sir Roger came; but notwithstanding all the justices had taken their places upon the bench, they made room for the old knight at the head of 15 them; who, for his reputation in the country, took occasion to whisper in the judge's ear that he was glad his lordship had met with so much good weather in his circuit. I was listening to the proceeding of the court with 20 much attention, and infinitely pleased with that great appearance and solemnity which so properly accompanies such a public administration of our laws, when, after about an hour's sitting, I observed, to my great 25 surprise, in the midst of a trial, that my friend Sir Roger was getting up to speak. I was in some pain for him, till I found he had acquitted himself of two or three sentences, with a look of much business and great in- 30 trepidity.

Upon his first rising the court was hushed, and a general whisper ran among the country people that Sir Roger was up. The speech he made was so little to the purpose that I 35 shall not trouble my readers with an account of it; and I believe was not so much designed by the knight himself to inform the court, as to give him a figure in my eye, and keep up his credit in the country. 40

I was highly delighted, when the court rose, to see the gentlemen of the country gathering about my old friend, and striving who should compliment him most; at the same time that the ordinary people gazed 45 upon him at a distance, not a little admiring his courage that was not afraid to speak to the judge.

In our return home we met with a very odd accident, which I cannot forbear relating, be- 50 cause it shows how desirous all who know Sir Roger are of giving him marks of their esteem. When we were arrived upon the verge of his estate, we stopped at a little inn to rest ourselves and our horses. The man of the house had, it seems, been formerly a 5 servant in the knight's family; and, to do honor to his old master, had some time since, unknown to Sir Roger, put him up in a sign-post before the door; so that the knight's head had hung out upon the road about a 10 week before he himself knew anything of the matter. As soon as Sir Roger was acquainted with it, finding that his servant's indiscretion proceeded wholly from affection and good-will, he only told him that he had made him 15 too high a compliment; and when the fellow seemed to think that could hardly be, added, with a more decisive look, that it was too great an honor for any man under a duke; but told him at the same time that it might be 20 altered with a very few touches, and that he himself would be at the charge of it. Accordingly they got a painter, by the knight's directions, to add a pair of whiskers to the face, and by a little aggravation to the fea- 25 tures to change it into the Saracen's Head. I should not have known this story had not the inn-keeper, upon Sir Roger's alighting, told him in my hearing that his honor's head was brought back last night with the altera- 30 tions that he had ordered to be made in it. Upon this, my friend, with his usual cheerfulness, related the particulars above mentioned, and ordered the head to be brought into the room. I could not forbear discovering 35 greater expressions of mirth than ordinary upon the appearance of this monstrous face, under which, notwithstanding it was made to frown and stare in a most extraordinary manner, I could still discover a distant re- 40 semblance of my old friend. Sir Roger, upon seeing me laugh, desired me to tell him truly if I thought it possible for people to know him in that disguise. I at first kept my usual silence; but upon the knight's conjur- 45 ing me to tell him whether it was not still more like himself than a Saracen, I composed my countenance in the best manner I could, and replied that much might be said on both sides.

50 These several adventures, with the knight's behavior in them, gave me as pleasant a day as ever I met with in any of my travels.

No. 159. SATURDAY, 1 SEPTEMBER, 1711. [ADDISON.]

—Omnem, quae nunc obducta tuenti
Mortales hebetat visus tibi, et humida circum
Caligat, nubem eripiam—[12]

—VIRG.

WHEN I was at Grand Cairo, I picked up several Oriental manuscripts, which I have still by me. Among others I met with one entitled The Visions of Mirza, which I have read over with great pleasure. I intend to give it to the public when I have no other entertainment for them; and shall begin with the first vision, which I have translated word for word as follows:—

"On the fifth day of the moon, which according to the custom of my forefathers I always keep holy, after having washed myself, and offered up my morning devotions, I ascended the high hills of Bagdad, in order to pass the rest of the day in meditation and prayer. As I was here airing myself on the tops of the mountains, I fell into a profound contemplation on the vanity of human life; and passing from one thought to another, 'Surely,' said I, 'man is but a shadow, and life a dream.' Whilst I was thus musing, I cast my eyes towards the summit of a rock that was not far from me, where I discovered one in the habit of a shepherd, with a musical instrument in his hand. As I looked upon him he applied it to his lips, and began to play upon it. The sound of it was exceedingly sweet, and wrought into a variety of tunes that were inexpressibly melodious, and altogether different from anything I had ever heard. They put me in mind of those heavenly airs that are played to the departed souls of good men upon their first arrival in Paradise, to wear out the impressions of their last agonies, and qualify them for the pleasures of that happy place. My heart melted away in secret raptures.

"I had been often told that the rock before me was the haunt of a Genius;[13] and that several had been entertained with music who had passed by it, but never heard that the musician had before made himself visible. When he had raised my thoughts by those transporting airs which he played to taste the pleasures of his conversation, as I looked upon him like one astonished, he beckoned to me, and by the waving of his hand directed me to approach the place where he sat. I drew near with that reverence which is due to a superior nature; and as my heart was entirely subdued by the captivating strains I had heard, I fell down at his feet and wept. The Genius smiled upon me with a look of compassion and affability that familiarized him to my imagination, and at once dispelled all the fears and apprehensions with which I approached him. He lifted me from the ground, and taking me by the hand, 'Mirza,' said he, 'I have heard thee in thy soliloquies; follow me.'

"He then led me to the highest pinnacle of the rock, and placing me on the top of it, 'Cast thy eyes eastward,' said he, 'and tell me what thou seest.' 'I see,' said I, 'a huge valley, and a prodigious tide of water rolling through it.' 'The valley that thou seest,' said he, 'is the Vale of Misery, and the tide of water that thou seest is part of the great Tide of Eternity.' 'What is the reason,' said I, 'that the tide I see rises out of a thick mist at one end, and again loses itself in a thick mist at the other?' 'What thou seest,' said he, 'is that portion of eternity which is called time, measured out by the sun, and reaching from the beginning of the world to its consummation. Examine now,' said he, 'this sea that is bounded with darkness at both ends, and tell me what thou discoverest in it.' 'I see a bridge,' said I, 'standing in the midst of the tide.' 'The bridge thou seest,' said he, 'is Human Life: consider it attentively.' Upon a more leisurely survey of it, I found that it consisted of three-score and ten entire arches, with several broken arches, which added to those that were entire, made up the number about a hundred. As I was counting the arches, the Genius told me that this bridge consisted at first of a thousand arches; but that a great flood swept away the rest, and left the bridge in the ruinous condition I now beheld it. 'But tell me farther,' said he, 'what thou discoverest on it.' 'I see multitudes of people passing over

[12]All the cloud which, drawn across your eyes, now dulls your mortal vision and shrouds you in mist, I shall snatch away (*Aeneid,* II, 604–606).

[13]Spirit.

it,' said I, 'and a black cloud hanging on each end of it.' As I looked more attentively, I saw several of the passengers dropping through the bridge into the great tide that flowed underneath it; and upon farther examination, perceived there were innumerable trap-doors that lay concealed in the bridge, which the passengers no sooner trod upon, but they fell through them into the tide, and immediately disappeared. These hidden pitfalls were set very thick at the entrance of the bridge, so that throngs of people no sooner broke through the cloud, but many of them fell into them. They grew thinner towards the middle, but multiplied and lay closer together towards the end of the arches that were entire.

"There were indeed some persons, but their number was very small, that continued a kind of hobbling march on the broken arches, but fell through one after another, being quite tired and spent with so long a walk.

"I passed some time in the contemplation of this wonderful structure, and the great variety of objects which it presented. My heart was filled with a deep melancholy to see several dropping unexpectedly in the midst of mirth and jollity, and catching at everything that stood by them to save themselves. Some were looking up towards the heavens in a thoughtful posture, and in the midst of a speculation stumbled and fell out of sight. Multitudes were very busy in the pursuit of bubbles that glittered in their eyes and danced before them; but often when they thought themselves within the reach of them, their footing failed and down they sunk. In this confusion of objects, I observed some with scimitars in their hands, and others with urinals, who ran to and fro upon the bridge, thrusting several persons on trap-doors which did not seem to lie in their way, and which they might have escaped had they not been thus forced upon them.

"The Genius seeing me indulge myself on this melancholy prospect, told me I had dwelt long enough upon it. 'Take thine eyes off the bridge,' said he, 'and tell me if thou yet seest anything thou dost not comprehend.' Upon looking up, 'What mean,' said I, 'those great flights of birds that are perpetually hovering about the bridge, and settling upon it from time to time? I see vultures, harpies, ravens, cormorants, and among many other feathered creatures several little winged boys, that perch in great numbers upon the middle arches.' 'These,' said the Genius, 'are Envy, Avarice, Superstition, Despair, Love, with the like cares and passions that infest human life.'

"I here fetched a deep sigh. 'Alas,' said I, 'Man was made in vain! how is he given away to misery and mortality! tortured in life, and swallowed up in death!' The Genius being moved with compassion towards me, bid me quit so uncomfortable a prospect. 'Look no more,' said he, 'on man in the first stage of his existence, in his setting out for eternity; but cast thine eye on that thick mist into which the tide bears the several generations of mortals that fall into it.' I directed my sight as I was ordered, and (whether or no the good Genius strengthened it with any supernatural force, or dissipated part of the mist that was before too thick for the eye to penetrate) I saw the valley opening at the farther end, and spreading forth into an immense ocean, that had a huge rock of adamant running through the midst of it, and dividing it into two equal parts. The clouds still rested on one half of it, insomuch that I could discover nothing in it; but the other appeared to me a vast ocean planted with innumerable islands, that were covered with fruits and flowers, and interwoven with a thousand little shining seas that ran among them. I could see persons dressed in glorious habits with garlands upon their heads, passing among the trees, lying down by the sides of fountains, or resting on beds of flowers; and could hear a confused harmony of singing birds, falling waters, human voices and musical instruments. Gladness grew in me upon the discovery of so delightful a scene. I wished for the wings of an eagle, that I might fly away to those happy seats; but the Genius told me there was no passage to them, except through the gates of death that I saw opening every moment upon the bridge. 'The islands,' said he, 'that lie so fresh and green before thee, and with which the whole face of the ocean appears spotted as far as thou canst see, are more in number than the sands on the seashore: there are myriads of islands behind those which thou here discoverest, reaching farther than thine eye, or even thine imagination can extend itself. These are the mansions of good men after death, who, according to the degree and kinds of virtue in which they excelled, are distributed among these several islands, which abound with pleasures of different kinds and degrees, suitable to the relishes and perfections of those who are settled in them: every island is a paradise accommodated to its respective inhabitants. Are not these, O Mirza, habitations worth contending for? Does life appear miserable that gives thee opportunities of earning such a reward? Is death to be feared that will convey thee to so happy an existence? Think not man was made in vain, who has such an eternity reserved for him.' I gazed with inexpressible pleasure on these happy islands. At length, said I, 'Show me now, I beseech thee, the secrets that lie hid under those dark clouds which cover the ocean on the other side of the rock of adamant.' The Genius making me no answer, I turned me about to address myself to him a second time, but I found that he had left me; I then turned again to the vision which I had been so long contemplating; but instead of the rolling tide, the arched bridge, and the happy islands, I saw nothing but the long hollow valley of Bagdad, with oxen, sheep, and camels grazing upon the sides of it."

No. 323. Tuesday, 11 March, 1712.

[Addison.]

Modo vir, modo femina.[14]

—Ovid.

The Journal with which I presented my readers on Tuesday last,[15] has brought me in several letters with accounts of many private lives cast into that form. I have the Rake's Journal, the Sot's Journal, the Whoremaster's Journal, and among several others a very curious piece, entitled, The Journal of a Mohock.[16] By these instances I find that the intention of my last Tuesday's paper has been mistaken by many of my readers. I did not design so much to expose vice as idleness, and aimed at those persons who pass away their time rather in trifles and impertinence, than in crimes and immoralities. Offenses of this later kind are not to be dallied with, or treated in so ludicrous a manner. In short, my journal only holds up folly to the light, and shows the disagreeableness of such actions as are indifferent in themselves, and blamable only as they proceed from creatures endowed with reason.

My following correspondent, who calls herself Clarinda, is such a journalist as I require: she seems by her letter to be placed in a modish state of indifference between vice and virtue, and to be susceptible of either, were there proper pains taken with her. Had her journal been filled with gallantries, or such occurrences as had shown her wholly divested of her natural innocence, notwithstanding it might have been more pleasing to the generality of readers, I should not have published it; but as it is only the picture of a life filled with a fashionable kind of gayety and laziness, I shall set down five days of it, as I have received it from the hand of my correspondent.

Dear Mr. Spectator,

You having set your readers an exercise in one of your last week's papers, I have performed mine according to your orders, and herewith send it you enclosed. You must know, Mr. Spectator, that I am a maiden lady of good fortune, who have had several matches offered me for these ten years last past, and have at present warm applications made to me by a very pretty fellow. As I am at my own disposal, I come up to town every winter, and pass my time after the manner you will find in the following journal, which I began to write upon the very day after your *Spectator* upon that subject.

Tuesday *night*. Could not go to sleep till one in the morning for thinking of my journal.

Wednesday. *From Eight till Ten.* Drank two dishes of chocolate in bed, and fell asleep after them.

[14] Sometimes a man, sometimes a woman (*Metamorphoses,* IV, 280).

[15] *Spectator* No. 317. The journal was that of a "sober citizen," "of greater consequence in his own thoughts than in the eye of the world."

[16] The name given to the ruffians and thieves who infested London and terrorized many at night. They had formerly been called "Hectors."

From Ten to Eleven. Eat a slice of bread and butter, drank a dish of bohea,[17] read *The Spectator.*

From Eleven to One. At my toilette, tried a new head.[18] Gave orders for Veny to be combed and washed. Mem. I look best in blue.

From One till half an hour after Two. Drove to the Change. Cheapened a couple of fans.

Till Four. At dinner. Mem. Mr. Froth passed by in his new liveries.

From Four to Six. Dressed, paid a visit to old Lady Blithe and her sister, having before heard they were gone out of town that day.

From Six to Eleven. At basset. Mem. Never set again upon the ace of diamonds.

THURSDAY. *From Eleven at night to Eight in the morning.* Dreamed that I punted to Mr. Froth.

From Eight to Ten. Chocolate. Read two acts in *Aurenzebe*[19] a-bed.

From Ten to Eleven. Tea-table. Sent to borrow Lady Faddle's Cupid for Veny. Read the play-bills. Received a letter from Mr. Froth. Mem. Locked it up in my strong box.

Rest of the morning. Fontange,[20] the tire-woman, her account of my Lady Blithe's wash. Broke a tooth in my little tortoise-shell comb. Sent Frank to know how my Lady Hectic rested after her monkey's leaping out at window. Looked pale. Fontange tells me my glass is not true. Dressed by Three.

From Three to Four. Dinner cold before I sat down.

From Four to Eleven. Saw company. Mr. Froth's opinion of Milton. His account of the Mohocks. His fancy for a pin-cushion. Picture in the lid of his snuff-box. Old Lady Faddle promises me her woman to cut my hair. Lost five guineas at crimp.

Twelve a clock at night. Went to bed.

[17]Tea. [18]I. e., head-dress.

[19]Heroic play by Dryden.

[20]Mlle. de Fontange introduced a new type of head-dress which was fashionable among English-women at the end of the seventeenth century.

FRIDAY. *Eight in the morning.* A-bed. Read over all Mr. Froth's letters. Cupid and Veny.

Ten a clock. Stayed within all day, not at home.

From Ten to Twelve. In conference with my mantua-maker. Sorted a suit of ribands. Broke my blue china cup.

From Twelve to One. Shut myself up in my chamber, practiced Lady Betty Modely's skuttle.

One in the afternoon. Called for my flowered handkerchief. Worked half a violet leaf in it. Eyes ached and head out of order. Threw by my work, and read over the remaining part of *Aurenzebe.*

From Three to Four. Dined.

From Four to Twelve. Changed my mind, dressed, went abroad, and played at crimp till midnight. Found Mrs. Spitely at home. Conversation: Mrs. Brilliant's necklace false stones. Old Lady Loveday going to be married to a young fellow that is not worth a groat. Miss Prue gone into the country. Tom Townley has red hair. Mem. Mrs. Spitely whispered in my ear that she had something to tell me about Mr. Froth; I am sure it is not true.

Between Twelve and One. Dreamed that Mr. Froth lay at my feet, and called me Indamora.[21]

SATURDAY. Rose at eight a clock in the morning. Sat down to my toilette.

From Eight to Nine. Shifted a patch for half an hour before I could determine it. Fixed it above my left eyebrow.

From Nine to Twelve. Drank my tea, and dressed.

From Twelve to Two. At Chapel. A great deal of good company. Mem. The third air in the new opera. Lady Blithe dressed frightfully.

From Three to Four. Dined. Mrs. Kitty called upon me to go to the opera before I was risen from table.

From dinner to Six. Drank tea. Turned off a footman for being rude to Veny.

Six a clock. Went to the opera. I did not see Mr. Froth till the beginning of the second act. Mr. Froth talked to a gentleman

[21]The "Captive Queen" in Dryden's *Aureng-Zebe.*

in a black wig. Bowed to a lady in the front box. Mr. Froth and his friend clapped Nicolini[22] in the third act. Mr. Froth cried out *Ancora.*[23] Mr. Froth led me to my chair. I think he squeezed my hand.

Eleven at night. Went to bed. Melancholy dreams. Methought Nicolini said he was Mr. Froth.

SUNDAY. Indisposed.

MONDAY. *Eight a clock.* Waked by Miss Kitty. *Aurenzebe* lay upon the chair by me. Kitty repeated without book the eight best lines in the play. Went in our mobs to the dumb man, according to appointment. Told me that my lover's name began with a G. Mem. The conjurer was within a letter of Mr. Froth's name, *etc.*

Upon looking back into this my journal, I find that I am at a loss to know whether I pass my time well or ill; and indeed never thought of considering how I did it, before I perused your speculation upon that subject. I scarce find a single action in these five days that I can thoroughly approve of, except the working upon the violet leaf, which I am resolved to finish the first day I am at leisure. As for Mr. Froth and Veny, I did not think they took up so much of my time and thoughts, as I find they do upon my journal. The latter of them I will turn off if you insist upon it; and if Mr. Froth does not bring matters to a conclusion very suddenly, I will not let my life run away in a dream.

Your humble servant,
Clarinda.

To resume one of the morals of my first paper, and to confirm Clarinda in her good inclinations, I would have her consider what a pretty figure she would make among posterity, were the history of her whole life published like these five days of it. I shall conclude my paper with an epitaph written by an uncertain author[24] on Sir Philip Sidney's sister, a lady who seems to have been of a temper very much different from that of Clarinda. The last thought of it is so very noble, that I dare say my reader will pardon the quotation.

ON THE COUNTESS DOWAGER OF PEMBROKE

Underneath this marble hearse
Lies the subject of all verse,
Sidney's sister, Pembroke's mother;
Death, ere thou hast killed another,
Fair and learn'd and good as she,
Time shall throw a dart at thee.

No. 377. TUESDAY, 13 MAY, 1712.

[ADDISON.]

Quid quisque vitet, nunquam homini satis
Cautum est in horas.[25]

—HOR.

LOVE was the mother of poetry, and still produces, among the most ignorant and barbarous, a thousand imaginary distresses and poetical complaints. It makes a footman talk like Oroondates,[26] and converts a brutal rustic into a gentle swain. The most ordinary plebeian or mechanic in love bleeds and pines away with a certain elegance and tenderness of sentiments which this passion naturally inspires.

These inward languishings of a mind infected with this softness have given birth to a phrase which is made use of by all the melting tribe, from the highest to the lowest, I mean that of *dying for love.*

Romances, which owe their very being to this passion, are full of these metaphorical deaths. Heroes and heroines, knights, squires, and damsels, are all of them in a dying condition. There is the same kind of mortality in our modern tragedies, where every one gasps, faints, bleeds, and dies. Many of the poets, to describe the execution which is done by this passion, represent the fair sex as Basilisks that destroy with their eyes; but I think Mr. Cowley has with great justness of thought compared a beautiful

[22]Nicolino Grimaldi, a famous Italian singer, who came to England in 1708.

[23]I. e., Encore.

[24]The poem (of which Addison quotes only the first half) has been generally ascribed to Ben Jonson, but in recent years has been claimed for William Browne of Tavistock.

[25]The dangers of the hour! no thought
We give them.
(Horace, *Odes,* II, xiii, 13–14; Conington's translation.)

[26]A character in de Scudéry's romance of *Artamène ou le Grand Cyrus.*

woman to a porcupine, that sends an arrow from every part.

I have often thought, that there is no way so effectual for the cure of this general infirmity, as a man's reflecting upon the motives that produce it. When the passion proceeds from the sense of any virtue or perfection in the person beloved, I would by no means discourage it; but if a man considers that all his heavy complaints of wounds and deaths rise from some little affectations of coquetry, which are improved into charms by his own fond imagination, the very laying before himself the cause of his distemper may be sufficient to effect the cure of it.

It is in this view that I have looked over the several bundles of letters which I have received from dying people, and composed out of them the following bill of mortality, which I shall lay before my reader without any further preface, as hoping that it may be useful to him in discovering those several places where there is most danger, and those fatal arts which are made use of to destroy the heedless and unwary.

Lysander, slain at a puppet-show on the 3rd of September.

Thyrsis, shot from a casement in Pickadilly.

T. S., wounded by Zelinda's scarlet stocking as she was stepping out of a coach.

Will. Simple, smitten at the opera by the glance of an eye that was aimed at one who stood by him.

Tho. Vainlove, lost his life at a ball.

Tim. Tattle, killed by the tap of a fan on his left shoulder by Coquetilla, as he was talking carelessly with her in a bow-window.

Sir Simon Softly, murdered at the play-house in Drury Lane by a frown.

Philander, mortally wounded by Cleora, as she was adjusting her tucker.

Ralph Gapely, Esq., hit by a random shot at the ring.

F. R., caught his death upon the water, April the 31st.

W. W., killed by an unknown hand, that was playing, with the glove off, upon the side of the front box in Drury Lane.

Sir Christopher Crazy, Bar., hurt by the brush of a whalebone petticoat.

Sylvius, shot through the sticks of a fan at St. James's Church.

Damon, struck through the heart by a diamond necklace.

Thomas Trusty, Francis Goosequill, William Meanwell, Edward Callow, Esqrs., standing in a row, fell all four at the same time by an ogle of the Widow Trapland.

Tom Rattle, chancing to tread upon a lady's tail as he came out of the play-house, she turned full upon him, and laid him dead upon the spot.

Dick Tastewell, slain by a blush from the Queen's box in the third act of the *Trip to the Jubilee.*

Samuel Felt, Haberdasher, wounded in his walk to Islington by Mrs. Susannah Cross-stitch, as she was clambering over a stile.

R. F. T., W. S. I., M. P., etc., put to death in the last birthday massacre.

Roger Blinko, cut off in the twenty-first year of his age by a white-wash.

Musidorus, slain by an arrow that flew out of a dimple in Belinda's left cheek.

Ned Courtly, presenting Flavia with her glove (which she had dropped on purpose) she received it, and took away his life with a curtsy.

John Gosselin, having received a slight hurt from a pair of blue eyes, as he was making his escape was dispatched by a smile.

Strephon, killed by Clarinda as she looked down into the pit.

Charles Careless, shot flying by a girl of fifteen who unexpectedly popped her head upon him out of a coach.

Josiah Wither, aged threescore and three, sent to his long home by Elizabeth Jettwell, spinster.

Jack Freelave, murdered by Melissa in her hair.

William Wiseaker, Gent., drowned in a flood of tears by Moll Common.

John Pleadwell, Esq., of the Middle Temple, barrister at law, assassinated in his chambers the sixth instant by Kitty Sly, who pretended to come to him for his advice.

JONATHAN SWIFT

1667–1745

One of the things Swift was heard to say to himself in his dreadful last days was "I am what I am; I am what I am." This has been difficult for many, particularly for comfortable people, to believe, and Swift has often been explained away. Yet he lives on, not merely in the minds and hearts of children who, by a consummate irony, find Lilliput amusing, but as a man speaking to men. For Swift, by virtue of a simplicity of outlook which has its parallel only in the lives and words of a few of the world's great religious figures, attained an insight into human folly which pierces the hearts of men by its profound truth. Uneasily men may squirm, attempting to minimize or to disregard his words, but they do not succeed; for in the end they cannot deny that beneath his coarseness and exaggeration, beneath the contemporary trappings in which he clothed his thought, and beneath his grotesque imaginings, Swift was essentially right. He wrote satirically in accordance with his own bent and the temper of his age, but he does not live simply as the prose counterpart of Pope; not alone for his mastery of satire, nor for its unexampled fierceness, nor yet for the downright plainness and directness and daemonic force of his speech does he live, but because he was what he was, beneath all else a noble personality, deeply sensitive to the confused splendor and misery of humankind.

The first blow of adverse fortune which Swift had to endure came with his birth, for he always considered it an indignity that, though his parents were English, he happened to be born in Ireland, which he hated. He was born on 30 November, 1667, in Dublin. His father had died a short time before his birth, leaving his mother practically destitute. As a consequence he was dependent through his early years on the charity of an uncle—a kind of dependence which was inevitably galling to him, though there is no evidence that his uncle treated him worse than victims of charity are generally treated. In 1673 he was sent to Kilkenny School; in 1681 he proceeded to Trinity College, Dublin, from which he was graduated in 1685, with a poor academic record. In 1689 he was employed as an amanuensis and secretary by Sir William Temple, a kinsman and a man now largely forgotten, though of great note in his day. Temple was a man of the world and had been a diplomat; he was on intimate terms with many of the great and influential people of the time, and he was a smooth and polished writer. There can be no doubt that he did much for Swift, whose association with him lasted, with several interruptions, until Temple's death in 1699. Through his employer's influence Swift was in 1692 admitted an M. A. at Oxford, and in 1694 he took holy orders. He had earlier considered this method of making a living, but had refused to take the step as long as he could not at least say that he had other alternatives and so had not entered the priesthood simply for the sake of income. It was during Swift's stay with Temple that he experimented until he learned how to write and what he could best do. He began apparently with poems, but was told by Dryden that he would never be a poet—a blunt verdict which may have been wrong and which Swift never forgave, although he acted on it and thereafter devoted himself chiefly to prose. It was as a result, too, of a controversy in which Temple had been involved over the relative merits of the ancients and the moderns that Swift wrote one of his most effective satirical pamphlets, *The Battle of the Books,* chiefly composed in 1697. And it was while he was living with Temple that he first met Esther Johnson, the Stella of the famous *Journal,* whose devoted friend he remained, spite of passing attachments to other women, and spite of Hester Vanhomrigh's love for him, until Stella's death in 1728. It has been maintained that Swift was secretly married to Stella, and the truth about this cannot be determined. It is not, however, a matter of very great importance, it being sufficiently plain that only the ceremony is in question, the relations between the two having been simply those of close friends. In 1699

Swift returned to Ireland and in the following year was made Vicar of Laracor. He became attached to the place and did much to improve the living, though he never remained there very long at a time. From 1701, indeed, until 1714 he was much in England. He returned in the first instance to present to the government certain grievances of the Irish clergy; but, particularly after the publication of *A Tale of a Tub* and *The Battle of the Books* in 1704, it was recognized that he would make a powerful political writer and both Whigs and Tories made bids for his support. In the end he threw himself in with the Tories and for several years worked hard and brilliantly for them. His reward, however, was not the bishopric he desired and thought he deserved, nor even a lesser post in England, but the Deanery of St. Patrick's Cathedral, in Dublin. Thus, to his bitter disappointment, was Swift's exile perpetuated, and after 1714—save for two visits to England in 1726 and 1727—he remained in Ireland until his death. He never ceased to hate Ireland, but in the course of time he was moved by the wretched condition of the island and the character of English misrule to write indignantly in support of Irish causes, as, for example, in the *Drapier's Letters*. Gulliver's *Travels into several remote Nations of the World*—unquestionably Swift's greatest and most fully representative book—was also written during these years, and published in 1726. It comprises four voyages, all intended "to vex the world rather than divert it." During the last years of his life Swift became hopelessly mad. He died on 19 October, 1745, and was buried in his own cathedral.

For the text of Swift's more important works see *A Tale of a Tub, to Which Is Added the Battle of the Books and the Mechanical Operation of the Spirit,* ed. A. C. Guthkelch and D. Nichol Smith (Oxford, 1920); *Gulliver's Travels and Selected Writings in Prose and Verse,* ed. John Hayward (New York, 1934); and *The Poems of Jonathan Swift,* ed. Harold H. Williams (Oxford, 1937). Carl Van Doren's *Swift* (New York, 1930) is the most recent of the standard biographies. A literary estimate which has become a classic is William M. Thackeray's "Swift" in *The English Humorists of the Eighteenth Century,* ed. W. L. Phelps (New York, 1900). For one aspect of Swift's thought G. B. Harrison's "Jonathan Swift" may be recommended, in *The Social and Political Ideas of Some English Thinkers of the Augustan Age, A. D. 1650–1750,* ed. F. J. C. Hearnshaw (London, 1928); but the best general commentary is Ricardo B. Quintana's *Mind and Art of Jonathan Swift* (New York, 1936). See also Richard F. Jones, *Ancients and Moderns: A Study of the Background of the Battle of the Books* (St. Louis, 1936).

THE SPIDER AND THE BEE[1]

THINGS were at this crisis, when a material accident fell out. For, upon the highest corner of a large window, there dwelt a certain spider, swollen up to the first magnitude by the destruction of infinite numbers of flies, 5 whose spoils lay scattered before the gates of his palace, like human bones before the cave of some giant. The avenues to his castle were guarded with turnpikes and palisadoes, all after the modern way of fortification.[2] 10 After you had passed several courts, you came to the center, wherein you might behold the constable himself in his own lodgings, which had windows fronting to each avenue, and ports to sally out, upon all occasions of prey or defense. In this mansion he had for some time dwelt in peace and plenty, without danger to his person by swallows from above, or to his palace, by brooms from below; when it was the pleasure of fortune to conduct thither a wandering bee, to whose curiosity

[1]This well-known passage occurs near the beginning of *The Battle of the Books* (published 1704), Swift's contribution to the so-called Quarrel of the Ancients and the Moderns. The party of the ancients, to which he belonged through his connection with Sir William Temple, had used *Aesop's Fables* and the *Epistles of Phalaris* as evidence that modern writing was not superior to the ancient. Unfortunately the leaders of the opposite party, William Wotton and Richard Bentley, keeper of the Royal Library, had been able to prove that both *Fables* and *Epistles* were spurious works of late origin. Swift replies, not with scholarship, but with a mock-epic description of a battle among the books in the Royal Library; and his central theme is cunningly introduced in the guise of a quarrel between a spider and a bee in the same place.

[2]"Fortification was one of the arts, upon the improvement of which the argument in favor of the moderns was founded by their advocates" (Scott).

a broken pane in the glass had discovered itself, and in he went; where, expatiating a while, he at last happened to alight upon one of the outward walls of the spider's citadel; which, yielding to the unequal weight, sunk down to the very foundation. Thrice he endeavored to force his passage, and thrice the center shook. The spider within, feeling the terrible convulsion, supposed at first that nature was approaching to her final dissolution; or else, that Beelzebub,[3] with all his legions, was come to revenge the death of many thousands of his subjects, whom his enemy had slain and devoured. However, he at length valiantly resolved to issue forth, and meet his fate. Meanwhile the bee had acquitted himself of his toils, and, posted securely at some distance, was employed in cleansing his wings, and disengaging them from the ragged remnants of the cobweb. By this time the spider was adventured out, when, beholding the chasms, and ruins, and dilapidations of his fortress, he was very near at his wit's end; he stormed and swore like a madman, and swelled till he was ready to burst. At length, casting his eye upon the bee, and wisely gathering causes from events (for they knew each other by sight): "A plague split you," said he, "for a giddy son of a whore. Is it you, with a vengeance, that have made this litter here? Could not you look before you, and be damned? Do you think I have nothing else to do (in the devil's name) but to mend and repair after your arse?"—"Good words, friend," said the bee (having now pruned himself, and being disposed to droll), "I'll give you my hand and word to come near your kennel no more; I was never in such a confounded pickle since I was born."—"Sirrah," replied the spider, "if it were not for breaking an old custom in our family, never to stir abroad against an enemy, I should come and teach you better manners."—"I pray, have patience," said the bee, "or you will spend your substance, and, for aught I see, you may stand in need of it all, towards the repair of your house."—"Rogue, rogue," replied the spider, "yet, methinks you should have more respect to a person, whom all the world allows to be so much your betters."—"By my troth," said the bee, "the comparison will amount to a very good jest, and you will do me a favor to let me know the reasons that all the world is pleased to use in so hopeful a dispute." At this the spider, having swelled himself into the size and posture of a disputant, began his argument in the true spirit of controversy, with a resolution to be heartily scurrilous and angry, to urge on his own reasons, without the least regard to the answers or objections of his opposite, and fully predetermined in his mind against all conviction.

"Not to disparage myself," said he, "by the comparison with such a rascal, what art thou but a vagabond without house or home, without stock or inheritance? Born to no possession of your own, but a pair of wings and a drone-pipe. Your livelihood is an universal plunder upon nature; a freebooter over fields and gardens; and, for the sake of stealing, will rob a nettle as readily as a violet. Whereas I am a domestic animal, furnished with a native stock within myself. This large castle (to show my improvements in the mathematics) is all built with my own hands, and the materials extracted altogether out of my own person."

"I am glad," answered the bee, "to hear you grant at least that I am come honestly by my wings and my voice; for then, it seems, I am obliged to Heaven alone for my flights and my music; and Providence would never have bestowed on me two such gifts, without designing them for the noblest ends. I visit indeed all the flowers and blossoms of the field and the garden; but whatever I collect from thence, enriches myself, without the least injury to their beauty, their smell, or their taste. Now, for you and your skill in architecture, and other mathematics, I have little to say: in that building of yours there might, for aught I know, have been labor and method enough; but, by woeful experience for us both, 'tis too plain, the materials are naught, and I hope you will henceforth take warning, and consider duration and matter, as well as method and art. You boast, indeed, of being obliged to no other creature, but of drawing and spinning out all from yourself; that is to say, if we may judge of the liquor in the vessel by what issues out,

[3] "Supposed to be the tutelar deity of the flies" (Scott).

you possess a good plentiful store of dirt and poison in your breast; and, though I would by no means lessen or disparage your genuine stock of either, yet, I doubt you are somewhat obliged, for an increase of both, to a little foreign assistance. Your inherent portion of dirt does not fail of acquisitions, by sweepings exhaled from below; and one insect furnishes you with a share of poison to destroy another. So that, in short, the question comes all to this—Whether is the nobler being of the two, that which, by a lazy contemplation of four inches round, by an overweening pride, which feeding and engendering on itself, turns all into excrement and venom, producing nothing at all, but flybane and a cobweb; or that which, by an universal range, with long search, much study, true judgment, and distinction of things, brings home honey and wax."

This dispute was managed with such eagerness, clamor, and warmth, that the two parties of books, in arms below, stood silent a while, waiting in suspense what would be the issue, which was not long undetermined: For the bee, grown impatient at so much loss of time, fled straight away to a bed of roses, without looking for a reply, and left the spider, like an orator, collected in himself, and just prepared to burst out.

It happened upon this emergency, that Aesop broke silence first. He had been of late most barbarously treated by a strange effect of the regent's[4] humanity, who had tore off his title-page, sorely defaced one half of his leaves, and chained him fast among a shelf of Moderns. Where, soon discovering how high the quarrel was like to proceed, he tried all his arts, and turned himself to a thousand forms. At length, in the borrowed shape of an ass, the regent mistook him for a Modern; by which means he had time and opportunity to escape to the Ancients, just when the spider and the bee were entering into their contest, to which he gave his attention with a world of pleasure; and when it was ended, swore in the loudest key, that in all his life he had never known two cases so parallel and adapt to each other, as that in the window, and this upon the shelves. "The disputants," said he, "have admirably managed the dispute between them, have taken in the full strength of all that is to be said on both sides, and exhausted the substance of every argument *pro* and *con*. It is but to adjust the reasonings of both to the present quarrel, then to compare and apply the labors and fruits of each, as the bee has learnedly deduced them, and we shall find the conclusion fall plain and close upon the Moderns and us. For, pray, gentlemen, was ever anything so modern as the spider in his air, his turns, and his paradoxes? He argues in the behalf of you his brethren and himself, with many boastings of his native stock and great genius; that he spins and spits wholly from himself, and scorns to own any obligation or assistance from without. Then he displays to you his great skill in architecture, and improvement in the mathematics. To all this the bee, as an advocate, retained by us the Ancients, thinks fit to answer—that, if one may judge of the great genius or inventions of the Moderns by what they have produced, you will hardly have countenance to bear you out, in boasting of either. Erect your schemes with as much method and skill as you please; yet if the materials be nothing but dirt, spun out of your own entrails (the guts of modern brains) the edifice will conclude at last in a cobweb, the duration of which, like that of other spiders' webs, may be imputed to their being forgotten, or neglected, or hid in a corner. For anything else of genuine that the Moderns may pretend to, I cannot recollect; unless it be a large vein of wrangling and satire, much of a nature and substance with the spider's poison; which, however, they pretend to spit wholly out of themselves, is improved by the same arts, by feeding upon the insects and vermin of the age. As for us the Ancients, we are content, with the bee, to pretend to nothing of our own, beyond our wings and our voice, that is to say, our flights and our language. For the rest, whatever we have got, has been by infinite labor and search, and ranging through every corner of nature; the difference is, that, instead of dirt and poison, we have rather chosen to fill our hives with honey and wax, thus furnishing mankind with the two noblest of things, which are sweetness and light."

[4] The librarian, Richard Bentley.

AN ARGUMENT TO PROVE THAT THE ABOLISHING OF CHRISTIANITY IN ENGLAND

May, As Things Now Stand, Be Attended with Some Inconveniences, and Perhaps Not Produce Those Many Good Effects Proposed Thereby.

WRITTEN IN THE YEAR 1708.

I AM very sensible what a weakness and presumption it is, to reason against the general humor and disposition of the world. I remember it was with great justice, and a due regard to the freedom both of the public and the press, forbidden upon several penalties to write, or discourse, or lay wagers against the Union,[1] even before it was confirmed by parliament, because that was looked upon as a design, to oppose the current of the people, which, besides the folly of it, is a manifest breach of the fundamental law that makes this majority of opinion the voice of God. In like manner, and for the very same reasons, it may perhaps be neither safe nor prudent to argue against the abolishing of Christianity, at a juncture when all parties seem so unanimously determined upon the point, as we cannot but allow from their actions, their discourses, and their writings. However, I know not how, whether from the affection of singularity, or the perverseness of human nature, but so it unhappily falls out, that I cannot be entirely of this opinion. Nay, though I were sure an order were issued out for my immediate prosecution by the Attorney-General, I should still confess that in the present posture of our affairs at home or abroad, I do not yet see the absolute necessity of extirpating the Christian religion from among us.

This perhaps may appear too great a paradox even for our wise and paradoxical age to endure; therefore I shall handle it with all tenderness, and with the utmost deference to that great and profound majority which is of another sentiment.

And yet the curious may please to observe, how much the genius of a nation is liable to alter in half an age. I have heard it affirmed for certain by some very old people, that the contrary opinion was even in their memories as much in vogue as the other is now; and, that a project for the abolishing of Christianity would then have appeared as singular, and been thought as absurd, as it would be at this time to write or discourse in its defense.

Therefore I freely own that all appearances are against me. The system of the Gospel, after the fate of other systems, is generally antiquated and exploded; and the mass or body of the common people, among whom it seems to have had its latest credit, are now grown as much ashamed of it as their betters; opinions, like fashions, always descending from those of quality to the middle sort, and thence to the vulgar, where at length they are dropped and vanish.

But here I would not be mistaken, and must therefore be so bold as to borrow a distinction from the writers on the other side, when they make a difference betwixt nominal and real Trinitarians.[2] I hope no reader imagines me so weak to stand up in the defense of real Christianity, such as used in primitive times (if we may believe the authors of those ages) to have an influence upon men's belief and actions: to offer at the restoring of that would indeed be a wild project; it would be to dig up foundations; to destroy at one blow all the wit, and half the learning of the kingdom; to break the entire frame and constitution of things; to ruin trade, extinguish arts and sciences with the professors of them; in short, to turn our courts, exchanges, and shops into deserts; and would be full as absurd as the proposal of Horace,[3] where he advises the Romans all in a body to leave their city, and seek a new seat in some remote part of the world, by way of a cure for the corruption of their manners.

Therefore I think this caution was in it-

[1]The parliamentary union of England and Scotland (1707).

[2]Between believers in the nominal and in the real nature of the Trinity.

[3]*Epodes*, xvi.

self altogether unnecessary (which I have inserted only to prevent all possibility of caviling), since every candid reader will easily understand my discourse to be intended only in defense of nominal Christianity; the other having been for some time wholly laid aside by general consent, as utterly inconsistent with all our present schemes of wealth and power.

But why we should therefore cast off the name and title of Christians, although the general opinion and resolution be so violent for it, I confess I cannot (with submission) apprehend the consequence necessary. However, since the undertakers propose such wonderful advantages to the nation by this project, and advance many plausible objections against the system of Christianity, I shall briefly consider the strength of both, fairly allow them their greatest weight, and offer such answers as I think most reasonable. After which I will beg leave to show what inconveniences may possibly happen by such an innovation, in the present posture of our affairs.

First, One great advantage proposed by the abolishing of Christianity is, that it would very much enlarge and establish liberty of conscience, that great bulwark of our nation, and of the Protestant Religion, which is still too much limited by priestcraft, notwithstanding all the good intentions of the legislature, as we have lately found by a severe instance. For it is confidently reported, that two young gentlemen of real hopes, bright wit, and profound judgment, who upon a thorough examination of causes and effects, and by the mere force of natural abilities, without the least tincture of learning, having made a discovery, that there was no God, and generously communicating their thoughts for the good of the public, were some time ago, by an unparalleled severity, and upon I know not what obsolete law, broke[4] for blasphemy. And as it hath been wisely observed, if persecution once begins, no man alive knows how far it may reach, or where it will end.

In answer to all which, with deference to wiser judgments, I think this rather shows the necessity of a nominal religion among us. Great wits love to be free with the highest objects; and if they cannot be allowed a God to revile or renounce, they will speak evil of dignities, abuse the government, and reflect upon the ministry; which I am sure few will deny to be of much more pernicious consequence, according to the saying of Tiberius, *Deorum offensa diis curae.*[5] As to the particular fact related, I think it is not fair to argue from one instance, perhaps another cannot be produced; yet (to the comfort of all those who may be apprehensive of persecution) blasphemy we know is freely spoken a million of times in every coffeehouse and tavern, or wherever else good company meet. It must be allowed indeed, that to break an English free-born officer only for blasphemy, was, to speak the gentlest of such an action, a very high strain of absolute power. Little can be said in excuse for the general; perhaps he was afraid it might give offense to the allies, among whom, for aught we know, it may be the custom of the country to believe a God. But if he argued, as some have done, upon a mistaken principle, that an officer who is guilty of speaking blasphemy, may some time or other proceed so far as to raise a mutiny, the consequence is by no means to be admitted; for, surely the commander of an English army is like to be but ill obeyed, whose soldiers fear and reverence him as little as they do a Deity.

It is further objected against the Gospel System, that it obliges men to the belief of things too difficult for freethinkers, and such who have shaken off the prejudices that usually cling to a confined education. To which I answer, that men should be cautious how they raise objections which reflect upon the wisdom of the nation. Is not everybody freely allowed to believe whatever he pleases, and to publish his belief to the world whenever he thinks fit, especially if it serves to strengthen the party which is in the right? Would any indifferent foreigner, who should read the trumpery lately written by Asgil, Tindal, Toland, Coward,[6] and forty more, imagine the Gospel to be our rule of faith,

[4] I. e., tortured.

[5] Let the gods take care of their own offences (Tacitus, *Annals,* I, lxxiii).

[6] These were deists, who believed that religion derived its authority from human reason and not from divine revelation.

and to be confirmed by parliaments? Does any man either believe, or say he believes, or desire to have it thought that he says he believes one syllable of the matter? And is any man worse received upon that score, or does he find his want of nominal faith a disadvantage to him in the pursuit of any civil or military employment? What if there be an old dormant statute or two against him, are they not now obsolete, to a degree, that Empsom and Dudley[7] themselves if they were now alive, would find it impossible to put them in execution?

It is likewise urged, that there are, by computation, in this kingdom, above ten thousand parsons, whose revenues added to those of my lords the bishops, would suffice to maintain at least two hundred young gentlemen of wit and pleasure, and free-thinking, enemies to priestcraft, narrow principles, pedantry, and prejudices; who might be an ornament to the Court and Town: and then, again, so great a number of able [bodied][8] divines might be a recruit to our fleet and armies. This indeed appears to be a consideration of some weight: but then, on the other side, several things deserve to be considered likewise: as, first, whether it may not be thought necessary that in certain tracts of country, like what we call parishes, there should be one man at least of abilities to read and write. Then it seems a wrong computation, that the revenues of the Church throughout this island would be large enough to maintain two hundred young gentlemen, or even half that number, after the present refined way of living; that is, to allow each of them such a rent, as in the modern form of speech, would make them easy. But still there is in this project a greater mischief behind; and we ought to beware of the woman's folly, who killed the hen that every morning laid her a golden egg. For, pray what would become of the race of men in the next age, if we had nothing to trust to besides the scrofulous, consumptive productions, furnished by our men of wit and pleasure, when, having squandered away their vigor, health and estates, they are forced by some disagreeable marriage to piece up their broken fortunes, and entail rottenness and politeness on their posterity? Now, here are ten thousand persons reduced by the wise regulations of Henry VIII,[9] to the necessity of a low diet, and moderate exercise, who are the only great restorers of our breed, without which the nation would in an age or two become one great hospital. Another advantage proposed by the abolishing of Christianity, is the clear gain of one day in seven, which is now entirely lost, and consequently the kingdom one seventh less considerable in trade, business, and pleasure; besides the loss to the public of so many stately structures now in the hands of the Clergy, which might be converted into playhouses, exchanges, market-houses, common dormitories, and other public edifices.

I hope I shall be forgiven a hard word, if I call this a perfect cavil. I readily own there hath been an old custom time out of mind, for people to assemble in the churches every Sunday, and that shops are still frequently shut, in order as it is conceived, to preserve the memory of that ancient practice, but how this can prove a hindrance to business or pleasure, is hard to imagine. What if the men of pleasure are forced one day in the week, to game at home instead of the chocolate-house? Are not the taverns and coffeehouses open? Can there be a more convenient season for taking a dose of physic? Are fewer claps got upon Sunday than other days? Is not that the chief day for traders to sum up the accounts of the week, and for lawyers to prepare their briefs? But I would fain know how it can be pretended that the churches are misapplied? Where are more appointments and rendezvouzes of gallantry? Where more care to appear in the foremost box with greater advantage of dress? Where more meetings for business? Where more bargains driven of all sorts? And where so many conveniences or enticements to sleep?

There is one advantage greater than any of the foregoing, proposed by the abolishing of Christianity: that it will utterly extinguish parties among us, by removing those factious distinctions of High and Low Church, of

[7] Tyrannous officers of the crown in the reign of Henry VII.

[8] Brackets in the original edition.

[9] His seizures of church revenues.

Whig and Tory, Presbyterian and Church of England, which are now so many mutual clogs upon public proceedings, and are apt to prefer the gratifying themselves, or depressing their adversaries, before the most important interest of the state.

I confess, if it were certain that so great an advantage would redound to the nation by this expedient, I would submit and be silent. But will any man say, that if the words *whoring, drinking, cheating, lying, stealing,* were by act of parliament ejected out of the English tongue and dictionaries, we should all awake next morning chaste and temperate, honest and just, and lovers of truth? Is this a fair consequence? Or, if the physicians would forbid us to pronounce the words *pox, gout, rheumatism* and *stone,* would that expedient serve like so many talismans to destroy the diseases themselves? Are party and faction rooted in men's hearts no deeper than phrases borrowed from religion, or founded upon no firmer principles? And is our language so poor that we cannot find other terms to express them? Are *envy, pride, avarice* and *ambition* such ill nomenclators, that they cannot furnish appellations for their owners? Will not *heyducks*[10] and *mamalukes, mandarins* and *pashas,* or any other words formed at pleasure, serve to distinguish those who are in the ministry from others who would be in it if they could? What, for instance, is easier than to vary the form of speech, and instead of the word *church,* make it a question in politics, whether the Monument be in danger? Because religion was nearest at hand to furnish a few convenient phrases, is our invention so barren, we can find no other? Suppose, for argument sake, that the Tories favored Margarita, the Whigs Mrs. Tofts, and the Trimmers Valentini,[11] would not *Margaritians, Toftians* and *Valentinians* be very tolerable marks of distinction? The *Prasini* and *Veniti,*[12] two most virulent factions in Italy, began (if I remember right) by a distinction of colors in ribbons, which we might do with as good a grace about the dignity of the blue and the green, and would serve as properly to divide the Court, the Parliament, and the Kingdom between them, as any terms of art whatsoever, borrowed from religion. And therefore I think there is little force in this objection against Christianity, or prospect of so great an advantage as is proposed in the abolishing of it.

'Tis again objected, as a very absurd ridiculous custom, that a set of men should be suffered, much less employed and hired, to bawl one day in seven against the lawfulness of those methods most in use toward the pursuit of greatness, riches and pleasure, which are the constant practice of all men alive on the other six. But this objection is, I think, a little unworthy so refined an age as ours. Let us argue this matter calmly: I appeal to the breast of any polite freethinker, whether in the pursuit of gratifying a predominant passion, he hath not always felt a wonderful incitement, by reflecting it was a thing forbidden; and therefore we see, in order to cultivate this taste, the wisdom of the nation hath taken special care, that the ladies should be furnished with prohibited silks, and the men with prohibited wine. And indeed it were to be wished, that some other prohibitions were promoted, in order to improve the pleasures of the town; which, for want of such expedients, begin already, as I am told, to flag and grow languid, giving way daily to cruel inroads from the spleen.

'Tis likewise proposed as a great advantage to the public, that if we once discard the system of the Gospel, all religion will of course be banished forever; and consequently, along with it, those grievous prejudices of education, which under the names of *virtue, conscience, honor, justice,* and the like, are so apt to disturb the peace of human minds, and the notions whereof are so hard to be eradicated by right reason or freethinking, sometimes during the whole course of our lives.

Here first, I observe how difficult it is to get rid of a phrase, which the world is once grown fond of, though the occasion that first produced it, be entirely taken away. For

[10] Slavic name for foot-soldiers or members of a noble's retinue.

[11] Margarita, Mrs. Tofts, and Valentini were famous opera singers. The Trimmers were the political party who believed in compromise.

[12] Rival parties in the Roman chariot races.

some years past, if a man had but an ill-favored nose, the deep-thinkers of the age would some way or other contrive to impute the cause to the prejudice of his education. From this fountain are said to be derived all our foolish notions of justice, piety, love of our country, all our opinions of God, or a future state, Heaven, Hell, and the like: and there might formerly perhaps have been some pretense for this charge. But so effectual care hath been taken to remove those prejudices, by an entire change in the methods of education, that (with honor I mention it to our polite innovators) the young gentlemen who are now on the scene, seem to have not the least tincture left of those infusions, or string of those weeds; and, by consequence, the reason for abolishing nominal Christianity upon that pretext, is wholly ceased.

For the rest, it may perhaps admit a controversy, whether the banishing all notions of religion whatsoever, would be convenient for the vulgar. Not that I am in the least of opinion with those who hold religion to have been the invention of politicians, to keep the lower part of the world in awe by the fear of invisible powers; unless mankind were then very different from what it is now: for I look upon the mass or body of our people here in England, to be as freethinkers, that is to say, as stanch unbelievers, as any of the highest rank. But I conceive some scattered notions about a superior power to be of singular use for the common people, as furnishing excellent materials to keep children quiet when they grow peevish, and providing topics of amusement in a tedious winter-night.

Lastly, 'tis proposed as a singular advantage, that the abolishing of Christianity will very much contribute to the uniting of Protestants, by enlarging the terms of communion so as to take in all sorts of dissenters, who are now shut out of the pale upon account of a few ceremonies which all sides confess to be things indifferent: that this alone will effectually answer the great ends of a scheme for comprehension, by opening a large noble gate, at which all bodies may enter; whereas the chaffering with dissenters, and dodging about this or t'other ceremony, is but like opening a few wickets, and leaving them at jar, by which no more than one can get in at a time, and that, not without stooping, and sideling, and squeezing his body.

To all this I answer; that there is one darling inclination of mankind, which usually affects to be a retainer to religion, though she be neither its parent, its godmother, nor its friend; I mean the spirit of opposition, that lived long before Christianity, and can easily subsist without it. Let us, for instance, examine wherein the opposition of sectaries among us consists, we shall find Christianity to have no share in it at all. Does the Gospel anywhere prescribe a starched, squeezed countenance, a stiff, formal gait, a singularity of manners and habit, or any affected forms and modes of speech different from the reasonable part of mankind? Yet, if Christianity did not lend its name to stand in the gap, and to employ or divert these humors, they must of necessity be spent in contraventions to the laws of the land, and disturbance of the public peace. There is a portion of enthusiasm assigned to every nation, which, if it hath not proper objects to work on, will burst out, and set all into a flame. If the quiet of a state can be bought by only flinging men and a few ceremonies to devour, it is a purchase no wise man would refuse. Let the mastiffs amuse themselves about a sheep's skin stuffed with hay, provided it will keep them from worrying the flock. The institution of convents abroad, seems in one point a strain of great wisdom, there being few irregularities in human passions, which may not have recourse to vent themselves in some of those orders, which are so many retreats for the speculative, the melancholy, the proud, the silent, the politic and the morose, to spend themselves, and evaporate the noxious particles; for each of whom we in this island are forced to provide a several sect of religion, to keep them quiet: and whenever Christianity shall be abolished, the legislature must find some other expedient to employ and entertain them. For what imports it how large a gate you open, if there will be always left a number who place a pride and a merit in not coming in?

Having thus considered the most important objections against Christianity, and the chief advantages proposed by the abolishing thereof; I shall now with equal deference and submission to wiser judgments as before, proceed to mention a few inconveniences that may happen, if the Gospel should be repealed; which perhaps the projectors may not have sufficiently considered.

And first, I am very sensible how much the gentlemen of wit and pleasure are apt to murmur, and be choqued[13] at the sight of so many daggled-tail parsons, that happen to fall in their way, and offend their eyes; but at the same time, these wise reformers do not consider what an advantage and felicity it is, for great wits to be always provided with objects of scorn and contempt, in order to exercise and improve their talents, and divert their spleen from falling on each other or on themselves; especially when all this may be done without the least imaginable danger to their persons.

And to urge another argument of a parallel nature: if Christianity were once abolished, how would the freethinkers, the strong reasoners, and the men of profound learning, be able to find another subject so calculated in all points whereon to display their abilities? What wonderful productions of wit should we be deprived of, from those whose genius by continual practice hath been wholly turned upon raillery and invectives against religion, and would therefore never be able to shine or distinguish themselves upon any other subject! We are daily complaining of the great decline of wit among us, and would we take away the greatest, perhaps the only topic we have left? Who would ever have suspected Asgil for a wit, or Toland for a philosopher, if the inexhaustible stock of Christianity had not been at hand to provide them with materials? What other subject, through all art or nature, could have produced Tindal for a profound author, or furnished him with readers? It is the wise choice of the subject that alone adorns and distinguishes the writer. For, had a hundred such pens as these been employed on the side of religion, they would have immediately sunk into silence and oblivion.

[13]Shocked.

Nor do I think it wholly groundless, or my fears altogether imaginary, that the abolishing of Christianity may perhaps bring the Church into danger, or at least put the senate to the trouble of another securing vote. I desire I may not be mistaken; I am far from presuming to affirm or think that the Church is in danger at present, or as things now stand; but we know not how soon it may be so when the Christian religion is repealed. As plausible as this project seems, there may a dangerous design lurk under it: nothing can be more notorious, than that the Atheists, Deists, Socinians,[14] Antitrinitarians, and other subdivisions of freethinkers, are persons of little zeal for the present ecclesiastical establishment: their declared opinion is for repealing the Sacramental Test;[15] they are very indifferent with regard to ceremonies; nor do they hold the *jus divinum*[16] of Episcopacy. Therefore they may be intended as one politic step towards altering the constitution of the Church established, and setting up Presbytery in the stead, which I leave to be further considered by those at the helm.

In the last place, I think nothing can be more plain, than that by this expedient, we shall run into the evil we chiefly pretend to avoid; and that the abolishment of the Christian religion will be the readiest course we can take to introduce popery. And I am the more inclined to this opinion, because we know it has been the constant practice of the Jesuits to send over emissaries, with instructions to personate themselves members of the several prevailing sects among us. So it is recorded, that they have at sundry times appeared in the guise of Presbyterians, Anabaptists, Independents and Quakers, according as any of these were most in credit; so, since the fashion hath been taken up of exploding religion, the popish missionaries have not been wanting to mix with the freethinkers; among whom, Toland, the great oracle of the Antichristians, is an Irish priest, the son of an Irish priest; and the most learned and ingenious author of a book

[14]A sect which denied the divinity of Christ.

[15]The law requiring all holders of office under the crown to take communion in the Anglican Church.

[16]Divine right.

called *The Rights of the Christian Church,*[17] was in a proper juncture reconciled to the Romish faith, whose true son, as appears by a hundred passages in his treatise, he still continues. Perhaps I could add some others to the number; but the fact is beyond dispute, and the reasoning they proceed by is right: for, supposing Christianity to be extinguished, the people will never be at ease till they find out some other method of worship; which will as infallibly produce superstition, as this will end in popery.

And therefore, if notwithstanding all I have said, it still be thought necessary to have a bill brought in for repealing Christianity, I would humbly offer an amendment; that instead of the word, *Christianity,* may be put *religion in general;* which I conceive will much better answer all the good ends proposed by the projectors of it. For, as long as we leave in being a God and his providence, with all the necessary consequences which curious and inquisitive men will be apt to draw from such premises, we do not strike at the root of the evil, though we should ever so effectually annihilate the present scheme of the Gospel; for, of what use is freedom of thought, if it will not produce freedom of action, which is the sole end, how remote soever in appearance, of all objections against Christianity? And therefore, the freethinkers consider it as a sort of edifice, wherein all the parts have such a mutual dependence on each other, that if you happen to pull out one single nail, the whole fabric must fall to the ground. This was happily expressed by him who had heard of a text brought for proof of the Trinity, which in an ancient manuscript was differently read; he thereupon immediately took the hint, and by a sudden deduction of a long *sorites,*[18] most logically concluded; "Why, if it be as you say, I may safely whore and drink on, and defy the parson." From which, and many the like instances easy to be produced, I think nothing can be more manifest, than that the quarrel is not against any particular points of hard digestion in the Christian system, but against religion in general; which, by laying restraints on human nature, is supposed the great enemy to the freedom of thought and action.

Upon the whole, if it shall still be thought for the benefit of Church and State, that Christianity be abolished; I conceive however, it may be more convenient to defer the execution to a time of peace, and not venture in this conjuncture to disoblige our allies, who, as it falls out, are all Christians, and many of them, by the prejudices of their education, so bigoted, as to place a sort of pride in the appellation. If upon being rejected by them, we are to trust to an alliance with the Turk, we shall find ourselves much deceived: for, as he is too remote, and generally engaged in war with the Persian emperor, so his people would be more scandalized at our infidelity, than our Christian neighbors. For they[19] are not only strict observers of religious worship, but what is worse, believe a God; which is more than is required of us even while we preserve the name of Christians.

To conclude: Whatever some may think of the great advantages to trade by this favorite scheme, I do very much apprehend, that in six months' time after the act is passed for the extirpation of the Gospel, the Bank, and East-India Stock, may fall at least one *per cent.* And since that is fifty times more than ever the wisdom of our age thought fit to venture for the preservation of Christianity, there is no reason we should be at so great a loss, merely for the sake of destroying it.

17 Dr. Matthew Tindal.

18 Chain of propositions in logic.

19 The Turks.

GULLIVER'S TRAVELS

(1726)

THE PUBLISHER TO THE READER

THE author of these Travels, Mr. Lemuel Gulliver, is my ancient and intimate friend; there is likewise some relation between us by the mother's side. About three years ago, Mr. Gulliver growing weary of the concourse of curious people coming to him at his house in Redriff, made a small purchase of land, with a convenient house, near Newark, in Nottinghamshire, his native country; where he now lives retired, yet in good esteem among his neighbors.

Although Mr. Gulliver was born in Nottinghamshire, where his father dwelt, yet I have heard him say his family came from Oxfordshire; to confirm which, I have observed in the churchyard at Banbury, in that county, several tombs and monuments of the Gullivers.

Before he quitted Redriff, he left the custody of the following papers in my hands, with the liberty to dispose of them as I should think fit. I have carefully perused them three times: the style is very plain and simple; and the only fault I find is, that the author, after the manner of travelers, is a little too circumstantial. There is an air of truth apparent through the whole; and indeed the author was so distinguished for his veracity, that it became a sort of proverb among his neighbors at Redriff, when any one affirmed a thing, to say it was as true as if Mr. Gulliver had spoke it.

By the advice of several worthy persons, to whom, with the author's permission, I communicated these papers, I now venture to send them into the world, hoping they may be at least, for some time, a better entertainment to our young noblemen, than the common scribbles of politics and party.

This volume would have been at least twice as large, if I had not made bold to strike out innumerable passages relating to the winds and tides, as well as to the variations and bearings in the several voyages; together with the minute descriptions of the management of the ship in storms, in the style of sailors: likewise the account of longitudes and latitudes; wherein I have reason to apprehend that Mr. Gulliver may be a little dissatisfied: but I was resolved to fit the work as much as possible to the general capacity of readers. However, if my own ignorance in sea-affairs shall have led me to commit some mistakes, I alone am answerable for them: and if any traveler hath a curiosity to see the whole work at large, as it came from the hand of the author, I will be ready to gratify him.

As for any further particulars relating to the author, the reader will receive satisfaction from the first pages of the book.

RICHARD SYMPSON.

PART I

A Voyage to Lilliput[1]

CHAPTER I

The Author Gives Some Account of Himself and Family, His First Inducements to Travel. He Is Shipwrecked, and Swims for His Life, Gets Safe on Shore in the Country of Lilliput, *Is Made a Prisoner, and Is Carried up Country.*

MY FATHER had a small estate in Nottinghamshire; I was the third of five sons. He sent me to Emanuel College in Cambridge, at fourteen years old, where I resided three years, and applied myself close to my studies; but the charge of maintaining me (although I had a very scanty allowance) being too great for a narrow fortune, I was bound apprentice to Mr. James Bates, an eminent surgeon in London, with whom I continued four years; and my father now and then sending me small sums of money, I laid them out in learning navigation, and other parts of the mathematics, useful to those who intend to travel, as I always believed it would be some time or other my fortune to do. When

[1] Lilliput means "little fellow."

I left Mr. Bates, I went down to my father; where, by the assistance of him and my uncle John, and some other relations, I got forty pounds, and a promise of thirty pounds a year to maintain me at Leyden: there I studied physic two years and seven months, knowing it would be useful in long voyages.

Soon after my return from Leyden, I was recommended by my good master, Mr. Bates, to be surgeon to the *Swallow,* Captain Abraham Pannell, commander; with whom I continued three years and a half, making a voyage or two into the Levant, and some other parts. When I came back, I resolved to settle in London, to which Mr. Bates, my master, encouraged me, and by him I was recommended to several patients. I took part of a small house in the Old Jury; and being advised to alter my condition, I married Mrs. Mary Burton, second daughter to Mr. Edmund Burton, hosier, in Newgate-Street, with whom I received four hundred pounds for a portion.

But, my good master Bates dying in two years after, and I having few friends, my business began to fail; for my conscience would not suffer me to imitate the bad practice of too many among my brethren. Having therefore consulted with my wife, and some of my acquaintance, I determined to go again to sea. I was surgeon successively in two ships, and made several voyages, for six years, to the East and West Indies, by which I got some addition to my fortune. My hours of leisure I spent in reading the best authors, ancient and modern, being always provided with a good number of books; and when I was ashore, in observing the manners and dispositions of the people, as well as learning their language, wherein I had a great facility by the strength of my memory.

The last of these voyages not proving very fortunate, I grew weary of the sea, and intended to stay at home with my wife and family. I removed from the Old Jury to Fetter-Lane, and from thence to Wapping, hoping to get business among the sailors; but it would not turn to account. After three years' expectation that things would mend, I accepted an advantageous offer from Captain William Prichard, master of the *Antelope,* who was making a voyage to the South Sea. We set sail from Bristol, May 4, 1699, and our voyage at first was very prosperous.

It would not be proper, for some reasons, to trouble the reader with the particulars of our adventures in those seas; let it suffice to inform him, that in our passage from thence to the East Indies, we were driven by a violent storm to the north-west of Van Diemen's Land.[2] By an observation, we found ourselves in the latitude of 30 degrees 2 minutes south. Twelve of our crew were dead by immoderate labor, and ill food, the rest were in a very weak condition. On the fifth of November, which was the beginning of summer in those parts, the weather being very hazy, the seamen spied a rock, within half a cable's length of the ship; but the wind was so strong, that we were driven directly upon it, and immediately split. Six of the crew, of whom I was one, having let down the boat into the sea, made a shift to get clear of the ship, and the rock. We rowed, by my computation, about three leagues, till we were able to work no longer, being already spent with labor while we were in the ship. We therefore trusted ourselves to the mercy of the waves, and in about half an hour the boat was overset by a sudden flurry from the north. What became of my companions in the boat, as well as of those who escaped on the rock, or were left in the vessel, I cannot tell; but conclude they were all lost. For my own part, I swam as fortune directed me, and was pushed forward by wind and tide. I often let my legs drop, and could feel no bottom: but when I was almost gone, and able to struggle no longer, I found myself within my depth; and by this time the storm was much abated. The declivity was so small, that I walked near a mile before I got to the shore, which I conjectured was about eight o'clock in the evening. I then advanced forward near half a mile, but could not discover any sign of houses or inhabitants; at least I was in so weak a condition, that I did not observe them. I was extremely tired, and with that, and the

[2]Perhaps Tasmania is meant, or a part of New Zealand. The latitude mentioned in the next sentence would indicate that Swift meant Australia, were it not for the fact that western Australia was very vaguely known in the early eighteenth century.

heat of the weather, and about half a pint of brandy that I drank as I left the ship, I found myself much inclined to sleep. I lay down on the grass, which was very short and soft, where I slept sounder than ever I remember to have done in my life; and, as I reckoned, above nine hours; for when I awaked, it was just day-light. I attempted to rise, but was not able to stir: for as I happened to lie on my back, I found my arms and legs were strongly fastened on each side to the ground; and my hair, which was long and thick, tied down in the same manner. I likewise felt several slender ligatures across my body, from my arm-pits to my thighs. I could only look upwards, the sun began to grow hot, and the light offended my eyes. I heard a confused noise about me, but in the posture I lay, could see nothing except the sky. In a little time I felt something alive moving on my left leg, which advancing gently forward over my breast, came almost up to my chin; when bending my eyes downwards as much as I could, I perceived it to be a human creature not six inches high, with a bow and arrow in his hands, and a quiver at his back. In the mean time, I felt at least forty more of the same kind (as I conjectured) following the first. I was in the utmost astonishment, and roared so loud, that they all ran back in a fright; and some of them as I was afterwards told, were hurt with the falls they got by leaping from my sides upon the ground. However, they soon returned, and one of them, who ventured so far as to get a full sight of my face, lifting up his hands and eyes by way of admiration, cried out in a shrill, but distinct voice, *Hekinah degul:* the others repeated the same words several times, but then I knew not what they meant. I lay all this while, as the reader may believe, in great uneasiness: at length, struggling to get loose, I had the fortune to break the strings, and wrench out the pegs that fastened my left arm to the ground; for, by lifting it up to my face, I discovered the methods they had taken to bind me, and at the same time with a violent pull, which gave me excessive pain, I a little loosened the strings that tied down my hair on the left side, so that I was just able to turn my head about two inches. But the creatures ran off a second time, before I could seize them; whereupon there was a great shout in a very shrill accent, and after it ceased, I heard one of them cry aloud *Tolgo phonac;* when in an instant I felt above an hundred arrows discharged on my left hand, which pricked me like so many needles; and besides, they shot another flight into the air, as we do bombs in Europe, whereof many, I suppose, fell on my body (though I felt them not), and some on my face, which I immediately covered with my left hand. When this shower of arrows was over, I fell a groaning with grief and pain, and then striving again to get loose, they discharged another volley larger than the first, and some of them attempted with spears to stick me in the sides; but, by good luck, I had on a buff jerkin, which they could not pierce. I thought it the most prudent method to lie still, and my design was to continue so till night, when, my left hand being already loose, I could easily free myself: and as for the inhabitants, I had reason to believe I might be a match for the greatest armies they could bring against me, if they were all of the same size with him that I saw. But fortune disposed otherwise of me. When the people observed I was quiet, they discharged no more arrows; but, by the noise I heard, I knew their numbers increased; and about four yards from me, over-against my right ear, I heard a knocking for above an hour, like that of people at work; when turning my head that way, as well as the pegs and strings would permit me, I saw a stage erected, about a foot and a half from the ground, capable of holding four of the inhabitants, with two or three ladders to mount it: from whence one of them, who seemed to be a person of quality, made me a long speech, whereof I understood not one syllable. But I should have mentioned, that before the principal person began his oration, he cried out three times, *Langro dehul san* (these words and the former were afterwards repeated and explained to me). Whereupon immediately about fifty of the inhabitants came and cut the strings that fastened the left side of my head, which gave me the liberty of turning it to the right, and of observing the person and gesture of him that was to speak. He appeared to be of a middle age, and taller than any of the other three who attended him, whereof one was a page that held up his train, and seemed to be somewhat longer than my middle finger; the other two stood one on each side to support him. He acted every part of an orator, and I could observe many periods of threatenings, and others of promises, pity, and kindness. I answered in a few words, but in the most submissive manner, lifting up my left hand, and both my eyes to the sun, as calling him for a witness; and being almost famished with hunger, having not eaten a morsel for some hours before I left the ship, I found the demands of nature so strong upon me, that I could not forbear showing my impatience (perhaps against the strict rules of decency) by putting my finger frequently on my mouth to signify that I wanted food. The *Hurgo* (for so they call a great lord, as I afterwards learned) understood me very well. He descended from the stage, and commanded that several ladders should be applied to my sides, on which above an hundred of the inhabitants mounted and walked towards my mouth, laden with baskets full of meat, which had been provided and sent thither by the King's orders, upon the first intelligence he received of me. I observed there was the flesh of several animals, but could not distinguish them by the taste. There were shoulders, legs, and loins, shaped like those of mutton, and very well dressed, but smaller than the wings of a lark. I ate them by two or three at a mouthful, and took three loaves at a time, about the bigness of musket bullets. They supplied me as fast as they could, showing a thousand marks of wonder and astonishment at my bulk and appetite. I then made another sign that I wanted drink. They found by my eating, that a small quantity would not suffice me: and being a most ingenious people, they slung up with great dexterity one of their largest hogsheads, then rolled it towards my hand, and beat out the top; I drank it off at a draught, which I might well do, for it did not hold half a pint, and tasted like a small wine of Burgundy, but much more delicious. They brought me a second hogshead, which I drank in the same manner, and made signs for more, but they had none to give me. When I had performed these wonders, they shouted for joy, and danced upon my breast, repeating several times as they did at first, *Hekinah degul.* They made me a sign that I should throw down the two hogsheads, but first warning the people below to stand out of the way, crying aloud, *Borach mivola,* and when they saw the vessels in the air, there was an universal shout of *Hekinah degul.* I confess I was often tempted while they were passing backwards and forwards on my body, to seize forty or fifty of the first that came in my reach, and dash them against the ground. But the remembrance of what I had felt, which probably might not be the worst they could do, and the promise of honor I made them, for so I interpreted my submissive behavior, soon drove out these imaginations. Besides, I now considered myself as bound by the laws of hospitality to a people who had treated me with so much expense and magnificence. However, in my thoughts, I could not sufficiently wonder at the intrepidity of these diminutive mortals, who durst venture to mount and walk upon my body, while one of my hands was at liberty, without trembling at the very sight of so prodigious a creature as I must appear to them. After some time, when they observed that I made no more demands for meat, there appeared before me a person of high rank from his Imperial Majesty. His Excellency, having mounted on the small of my right leg, advanced forwards up to my face, with about a dozen of his retinue. And producing his credentials under the Signet Royal, which he applied close to my eyes, spoke about ten minutes, without any signs of anger, but with a kind of determinate resolution; often pointing forwards, which, as I afterwards found, was towards the capital city, about half a mile distant, whither it was agreed by his Majesty in council that I must be conveyed. I answered in few words, but to no purpose, and made a sign with my hand that was loose, putting it to the other (but over his Excellency's head for fear of hurting him or his train), and then to my own head and body, to signify that I desired my liberty. It appeared that he understood me well enough, for he shook his head by way of disapprobation, and held his hand in a posture to show that I must be carried as a prisoner. However, he made other signs to let me understand that I should have meat and drink enough, and very good treatment. Whereupon I once more thought of attempting to break my bonds; but again, when I felt the smart of their arrows, upon my face and hands, which were all in blisters, and many of the darts still sticking in them, and observing likewise that the number of my enemies increased, I gave tokens to let them know that they might do with me what they pleased. Upon this, the *Hurgo* and his train withdrew, with much civility and cheerful countenances. Soon after I heard a general shout, with frequent repetitions of the words, *Peplom selan,* and I felt great numbers of people on my left side relaxing the cords to such a degree, that I was able to turn upon my right, and to ease myself with making water; which I very plentifully did, to the great astonishment of the people, who conjecturing by my motions what I was going to do, immediately opened to the right and left on that side to avoid the torrent which fell with such noise and violence from me. But before this, they had daubed my face and both my hands with a sort of ointment very pleasant to the smell, which in a few minutes removed all the smart of their arrows. These circumstances, added to the refreshment I had received by their victuals and drink, which were very nourishing, disposed me to sleep. I slept about eight hours, as I was afterwards assured; and it was no wonder, for the physicians, by the Emperor's order, had mingled a sleepy potion in the hogshead of wine.

It seems that upon the first moment I was discovered sleeping on the ground after my landing, the Emperor had early notice of it by an express; and determined in council that I should be tied in the manner I have related (which was done in the night while I slept), that plenty of meat and drink should be sent to me, and a machine prepared to carry me to the capital city.

This resolution perhaps may appear very bold and dangerous, and I am confident would not be imitated by any prince in Europe on the like occasion; however, in my opinion, it was extremely prudent, as well as generous: for supposing these people had endeavored to kill me with their spears and arrows while I was asleep, I should certainly have awaked with the first sense of smart, which might so far have roused my rage and strength, as to have enabled me to break the strings wherewith I was tied; after which, as they were not able to make resistance, so they could expect no mercy.

These people are most excellent mathematicians, and arrived to a great perfection in mechanics, by the countenance and encouragement of the Emperor, who is a renowned patron of learning. This prince hath several machines fixed on wheels, for the carriage of trees and other great weights. He often builds his largest men of war, whereof some are nine foot long, in the woods where the timber grows, and has them carried on these engines three or four hundred yards to the sea. Five hundred carpenters and engineers were immediately set at work to prepare the greatest engine they had. It was a frame of wood raised three inches from the ground, about seven foot long and four wide, moving upon twenty-two wheels. The shout I heard was upon the arrival of this engine, which it seems set out in four hours after my landing. It was brought parallel to me as I lay. But the principal difficulty was to raise and place me in this vehicle. Eighty poles, each of one foot high, were erected for this purpose, and very strong cords of the bigness of packthread were fastened by hooks to many bandages, which the workmen had girt round my neck, my hands, my body, and my legs. Nine hundred of the strongest men were employed to draw up these cords by many pulleys fastened on the poles, and thus, in less than three hours, I was raised and slung into the engine, and there tied fast. All this I was told, for, while the whole operation was performing, I lay in a profound sleep, by the force of that soporiferous medicine infused into my liquor. Fifteen hundred of the Emperor's largest horses, each about four inches and a half high, were employed to draw me towards the metropolis, which, as I said, was half a mile distant.

About four hours after we began our journey, I awaked by a very ridiculous accident; for the carriage being stopped a while to adjust something that was out of order, two or three of the young natives had the curiosity to see how I looked when I was asleep; they climbed up into the engine, and advancing very softly to my face, one of them, an officer in the guards, put the sharp end of his half-pike a good way up into my left nostril, which tickled my nose like a straw, and made me sneeze violently: whereupon they stole off unperceived, and it was three weeks before I knew the cause of my awakening so suddenly. We made a long march the remaining part of that day, and rested at night with five hundred guards on each side of me, half with torches, and half with bows and arrows, ready to shoot me if I should offer to stir. The next morning at sun-rise we continued our march, and arrived within two hundred yards of the city gates about noon. The Emperor, and all his court, came out to meet us; but his great officers would by no means suffer his Majesty to endanger his person by mounting on my body.

At the place where the carriage stopped, there stood an ancient temple, esteemed to be the largest in the whole kingdom; which having been polluted some years before by an unnatural murder, was, according to the zeal of those people, looked upon as profane, and therefore had been applied to common uses, and all the ornaments and furniture carried away. In this edifice it was determined I should lodge. The great gate fronting to the north was about four foot high, and almost two foot wide, through which I could easily creep. On each side of the gate was a small window not above six inches from the ground: into that on the left side, the King's smiths conveyed fourscore and eleven chains, like those that hang to a lady's watch in Europe, and almost as large, which were locked to my left leg with six and thirty padlocks. Over-against this temple, on t'other side of the great highway, at twenty foot distance, there was a turret at least five foot high. Here the Emperor ascended, with many principal lords of his court, to have an opportunity of viewing me, as I was told, for I could not see them. It was reckoned that above an hundred thousand inhabitants came out of the town upon the same errand; and, in spite of my guards, I believe there could not be fewer than ten thousand at several times, who mounted my body by the help of ladders. But a proclamation was soon issued to forbid it upon pain of death. When the workmen found it was impossible for me to break loose, they cut all the strings that bound me; whereupon I rose up, with as melancholy a disposition as ever I had in my life. But the noise and astonishment of the people at seeing me rise and walk, are not to be expressed. The chains that held my left leg were about two yards long, and gave me not only the liberty of walking backwards and forwards in a semicircle; but, being fixed within four inches of the gate, allowed me to creep in, and lie at my full length in the temple.

CHAPTER II

The Emperor of Lilliput, *Attended by Several of the Nobility, Comes to See the Author in His Confinement. The Emperor's Person and Habit Described. Learned Men Appointed to Teach the Author Their Language. He Gains Favor by His Mild Disposition. His Pockets Are Searched, and His Sword and Pistols Taken from Him.*

When I found myself on my feet, I looked about me, and must confess I never beheld a more entertaining prospect. The country round appeared like a continued garden, and the inclosed fields, which were generally forty foot square, resembled so many beds of flowers. These fields were intermingled with woods of half a stang,[3] and the tallest trees, as I could judge, appeared to be seven foot high. I viewed the town on my left hand, which looked like the painted scene of a city in a theater.

I had been for some hours extremely pressed by the necessities of nature; which was no wonder, it being almost two days since I had last disburdened myself. I was under great difficulties between urgency and shame. The best expedient I could think on, was to creep into my house, which I accordingly did; and shutting the gate after me, I went as far as the length of my chain

[3] I. e., half a square rod.

would suffer, and discharged my body of that uneasy load. But this was the only time I was ever guilty of so uncleanly an action; for which I cannot but hope the candid reader will give some allowance, after he hath maturely and impartially considered my case, and the distress I was in. From this time my constant practice was, as soon as I rose, to perform that business in open air, at the full extent of my chain, and due care was taken every morning before company came, that the offensive matter should be carried off in wheel-barrows, by two servants appointed for that purpose. I would not have dwelt so long upon a circumstance, that perhaps at first sight may appear not very momentous, if I had not thought it necessary to justify my character in point of cleanliness to the world; which I am told some of my maligners have been pleased, upon this and other occasions, to call in question.

When this adventure was at an end, I came back out of my house, having occasion for fresh air. The Emperor was already descended from the tower, and advancing on horseback towards me, which had like to have cost him dear; for the beast, though very well trained, yet wholly unused to such a sight, which appeared as if a mountain moved before him, reared up on his hinder feet: but that prince, who is an excellent horseman, kept his seat, till his attendants ran in, and held the bridle, while his Majesty had time to dismount. When he alighted, he surveyed me round with great admiration, but kept beyond the length of my chain. He ordered his cooks and butlers, who were already prepared, to give me victuals and drink, which they pushed forward in a sort of vehicles upon wheels, till I could reach them. I took these vehicles, and soon emptied them all; twenty of them were filled with meat, and ten with liquor; each of the former afforded me two or three good mouthfuls, and I emptied the liquor of ten vessels, which was contained in earthen vials, into one vehicle, drinking it off at a draught; and so I did with the rest. The Empress, and young Princes of the blood of both sexes, attended by many ladies, sat at some distance in their chairs; but upon the accident that happened to the Emperor's horse, they alighted, and came near his person, which I am now going to describe. He is taller by almost the breadth of my nail, than any of his court; which alone is enough to strike an awe into the beholders. His features are strong and masculine, with an Austrian lip and arched nose, his complexion olive, his countenance erect, his body and limbs well proportioned, all his motions graceful, and his deportment majestic. He was then past his prime, being twenty-eight years and three-quarters old, of which he had reigned about seven, in great felicity, and generally victorious. For the better convenience of beholding him, I lay on my side, so that my face was parallel to his, and he stood but three yards off: however, I have had him since many times in my hand, and therefore cannot be deceived in the description. His dress was very plain and simple, and the fashion of it between the Asiatic and the European: but he had on his head a light helmet of gold, adorned with jewels, and a plume on the crest. He held his sword drawn in his hand, to defend himself, if I should happen to break loose; it was almost three inches long, the hilt and scabbard were gold enriched with diamonds. His voice was shrill, but very clear and articulate, and I could distinctly hear it when I stood up. The ladies and courtiers were all most magnificently clad, so that the spot they stood upon seemed to resemble a petticoat spread on the ground, embroidered with figures of gold and silver. His Imperial Majesty spoke often to me, and I returned answers, but neither of us could understand a syllable. There were several of his priests and lawyers present (as I conjectured by their habits) who were commanded to address themselves to me, and I spoke to them in as many languages as I had the least smattering of, which were High and Low Dutch, Latin, French, Spanish, Italian, and Lingua Franca;[4] but all to no purpose. After about two hours the court retired, and I was left with a strong guard, to prevent the impertinence, and probably the malice of the rabble, who were very impatient to crowd about me as near as

[4]The mixed language used in communication between European travelers and the Greeks and others at the eastern end of the Mediterranean.

they durst, and some of them had the impudence to shoot their arrows at me as I sat on the ground by the door of my house, whereof one very narrowly missed my left eye. But the colonel ordered six of the ring-leaders to be seized, and thought no punishment so proper as to deliver them bound into my hands, which some of his soldiers accordingly did, pushing them forwards with the butt-ends of their pikes into my reach; I took them all in my right hand, put five of them into my coat-pocket, and as to the sixth, I made a countenance as if I would eat him alive. The poor man squalled terribly, and the colonel and his officers were in much pain, especially when they saw me take out my pen-knife: but I soon put them out of fear: for, looking mildly, and immediately cutting the strings he was bound with, I set him gently on the ground, and away he ran. I treated the rest in the same manner, taking them one by one out of my pocket, and I observed both the soldiers and people were highly obliged at this mark of my clemency, which was represented very much to my advantage at court.

Towards night I got with some difficulty into my house, where I lay on the ground, and continued to do so about a fortnight; during which time the Emperor gave orders to have a bed prepared for me. Six hundred beds of the common measure were brought in carriages, and worked up in my house; an hundred and fifty of their beds sewn together made up the breadth and length, and these were four double, which however kept me but very indifferently from the hardness of the floor, that was of smooth stone. By the same computation they provided me with sheets, blankets, and coverlets, tolerable enough for one who had been so long inured to hardships as I.

As the news of my arrival spread through the kingdom, it brought prodigious numbers of rich, idle, and curious people to see me; so that the villages were almost emptied, and great neglect of tillage and household affairs must have ensued, if his Imperial Majesty had not provided, by several proclamations and orders of state, against this inconveniency. He directed that those who had already beheld me should return home, and not presume to come within fifty yards of my house without license from court; whereby the secretaries of state got considerable fees.

In the mean time, the Emperor held frequent councils to debate what course should be taken with me; and I was afterwards assured by a particular friend, a person of great quality, who was looked upon to be as much in the secret as any, that the court was under many difficulties concerning me. They apprehended my breaking loose, that my diet would be very expensive, and might cause a famine. Sometimes they determined to starve me, or at least to shoot me in the face and hands with poisoned arrows, which would soon dispatch me; but again they considered, that the stench of so large a carcass might produce a plague in the metropolis, and probably spread through the whole kingdom. In the midst of these consultations, several officers of the army went to the door of the great council-chamber; and two of them being admitted, gave an account of my behavior to the six criminals above-mentioned, which made so favorable an impression in the breast of his Majesty and the whole board, in my behalf, that an Imperial Commission was issued out, obliging all the villages nine hundred yards round the city, to deliver in every morning six beeves, forty sheep, and other victuals for my sustenance; together with a proportionable quantity of bread, and wine, and other liquors; for the due payment of which his Majesty gave assignments upon his treasury. For this prince lives chiefly upon his own demesnes, seldom, except upon great occasions, raising any subsidies upon his subjects, who are bound to attend him in his wars at their own expense. An establishment was also made of six hundred persons to be my domestics, who had board-wages allowed for their maintenance, and tents built for them very conveniently on each side of my door. It was likewise ordered, that three hundred tailors should make me a suit of clothes after the fashion of the country: that six of his Majesty's greatest scholars should be employed to instruct me in their language: and, lastly, that the Emperor's horses, and those of the nobility, and troops of guards, should be frequently exercised in my sight, to accustom themselves to me. All these orders were duly put in execution, and in about three weeks I made a great progress in learning their language; during which time, the Emperor frequently honored me with his visits, and was pleased to assist my masters in teaching me. We began already to converse together in some sort; and the first words I learned were to express my desire that he would please give me my liberty, which I every day repeated on my knees. His answer, as I could comprehend it, was, that this must be a work of time, not to be thought on without the advice of his council, and that first I must *Lumos kelmin pesso desmar lon Emposo;* that is, swear a peace with him and his kingdom. However, that I should be used with all kindness; and he advised me to acquire, by my patience and discreet behavior, the good opinion of himself and his subjects. He desired I would not take it ill, if he gave orders to certain proper officers to search me; for probably I might carry about me several weapons, which must needs be dangerous things, if they answered the bulk of so prodigious a person. I said, his Majesty should be satisfied, for I was ready to strip myself, and turn up my pockets before him. This I delivered part in words, and part in signs. He replied, that by the laws of the kingdom I must be searched by two of his officers; that he knew this could not be done without my consent and assistance; that he had so good an opinion of my generosity and justice, as to trust their persons in my hands: that whatever they took from me should be returned when I left the country, or paid for at the rate which I would set upon them. I took up the two officers in my hands, put them first into my coat-pockets, and then into every other pocket about me, except my two fobs, and another secret pocket which I had no mind should be searched, wherein I had some little necessaries that were of no consequence to any but myself. In one of my fobs there was a silver watch, and in the other a small quantity of gold in a purse. These gentlemen, having pen, ink, and paper about them, made an exact inventory of everything they saw; and when they had done, desired I would set them down, that they might deliver it to the Emperor. This inventory I afterwards translated into English, and is word for word as follows:

Imprimis, In the right coat-pocket of the Great Man-Mountain (for so I interpret the words *Quinbus Flestrin*) after the strictest search, we found only one great piece of coarse cloth, large enough to be a foot-cloth for your Majesty's chief room of state. In the left pocket we saw a huge silver chest, with a cover of the same metal, which we, the searchers, were not able to lift. We desired it should be opened, and one of us stepping into it, found himself up to the mid leg in a sort of dust, some part whereof flying up to our faces, set us both a sneezing for several times together. In his right waistcoat-pocket we found a prodigious bundle of white thin substances, folded one over another, about the bigness of three men, tied with a strong cable, and marked with black figures, which we humbly conceive to be writings, every letter almost half as large as the palm of our hands. In the left there was a sort of engine, from the back of which were extended twenty long poles, resembling the palisadoes before your Majesty's court; wherewith we conjecture the Man-Mountain combs his head; for we did not always trouble him with questions, because we found it a great difficulty to make him understand us. In the large pocket on the right side of his middle cover (so I translate the word *ranfulo,* by which they meant my breeches) we saw a hollow pillar of iron, about the length of a man, fastened to a strong piece of timber, larger than the pillar; and upon one side of the pillar were huge pieces of iron sticking out, cut into strange figures, which we know not what to make of. In the left pocket, another engine of the same kind. In the smaller pocket on the right side, were several round flat pieces of white and red metal, of different bulk; some of the white, which seemed to be silver, were so large and heavy, that my comrade and I could hardly lift them. In the left pocket were two black pillars irregularly shaped: we could not, without difficulty, reach the top of them as we stood at the bottom of his pocket. One of them was covered, and seemed all of a piece: but at the upper end of the other, there appeared a white round substance, about twice the bigness of our heads. Within each of these was enclosed a prodigious plate of steel; which, by our orders, we obliged him to show us, because we apprehended they might be dangerous engines. He took them out of their cases, and told us, that in his own country his practice was to shave his beard with one of these, and cut his meat with the other. There were two pockets which we could not enter: these he called his fobs; they were two large slits cut into the top of his middle cover, but squeezed close by the pressure of his belly. Out of the right fob hung a great silver chain, with a wonderful kind of engine at the bottom. We directed him to draw out whatever was fastened to that chain; which appeared to be a globe, half silver, and half of some transparent metal; for, on the transparent side, we saw certain strange figures circularly drawn, and thought we could touch them, till we found our fingers stopped by that lucid substance. He put this engine to our ears, which made an incessant noise like that of a water-mill. And we conjecture it is either some unknown animal, or the god that he worships; but we are more inclined to the latter opinion, because he assured us (if we understood him right, for he expressed himself very imperfectly), that he seldom did anything without consulting it. He called it his oracle, and said it pointed out the time for every action of his life. From the left fob he took out a net almost large enough for a fisherman, but contrived to open and shut like a purse, and served him for the same use: we found therein several massy pieces of yellow metal, which, if they be real gold, must be of immense value.

Having thus, in obedience to your Majesty's commands, diligently searched all his pockets, we observed a girdle about his waist made of the hide of some prodigious animal; from which, on the left side, hung a sword of the length of five men; and on the right, a bag or pouch divided into two cells, each cell capable of holding three of your Majesty's subjects. In one of these cells were several globes or balls of a most ponderous metal, about the bigness of our heads, and requiring a strong hand to lift them: the other cell contained a heap of certain black grains, but of no great bulk or weight, for we could hold above fifty of them in the palms of our hands.

This is an exact inventory of what we found about the body of the Man-Mountain, who used us with great civility, and due respect to your Majesty's Commission. Signed and sealed on the fourth day of the eighty-ninth moon of your Majesty's auspicious reign.

Clefrin Frelock, Marsi Frelock.

When this inventory was read over to the Emperor, he directed me, although in very gentle terms, to deliver up the several particulars. He first called for my scimitar, which I took out, scabbard and all. In the mean time he ordered three thousand of his choicest troops (who then attended him) to surround me at a distance, with their bows and arrows just ready to discharge: but I did not observe it, for my eyes were wholly fixed upon his Majesty. He then desired me to draw my scimitar, which, although it had got some rust by the sea-water, was in most parts exceeding bright. I did so, and immediately all the troops gave a shout between terror and surprise; for the sun shone clear, and the reflection dazzled their eyes, as I waved the scimitar to and fro in my hand. His Majesty, who is a most magnanimous prince, was less daunted than I could expect; he ordered me to return it into the scabbard, and cast it on the ground as gently as I could, about six foot from the end of my chain. The next thing he demanded, was one of the hollow iron pillars, by which he meant my pocket-pistols. I drew it out, and at his desire, as well as I could, expressed to him the use of it; and charging it only with powder, which, by the closeness of my pouch, happened to escape wetting in the sea (an inconvenience against which all prudent mariners take special care to provide), I first cautioned the Emperor not to be afraid, and then I let it off in the air. The astonishment here was much greater than at the sight of my scimitar. Hundreds fell down, as if they had been struck dead; and even the Emperor, although he stood his ground, could not recover himself in some time. I delivered up both my pistols in the same manner as I had done my scimitar, and then my pouch of powder and bullets; begging him that the former might be kept from fire, for it would kindle with the smallest spark, and blow up his imperial palace into the air. I likewise delivered up my watch, which the Emperor was very curious to see, and commanded two of his tallest yeomen of the guards to bear it on a pole upon their shoulders, as draymen in England do a barrel of ale. He was amazed at the continual noise it made, and the motion of the minute-hand, which he could easily discern; for their sight is much more acute than ours: and asked the opinions of his learned men about him, which were various and remote,[5] as the reader may well imagine without my repeating; although indeed I could not very perfectly understand them. I then gave up my silver and copper money, my purse, with nine large pieces of gold, and some smaller ones; my knife and razor, my comb and silver snuff-box, my handkerchief and journal-book. My scimitar, pistols, and pouch, were conveyed in carriages to his Majesty's stores; but the rest of my goods were returned to me.

I had, as I before observed, one private pocket which escaped their search, wherein there was a pair of spectacles (which I sometimes use for the weakness of my eyes), a pocket perspective,[6] and several other little conveniences; which being of no consequence to the Emperor, I did not think myself bound in honor to discover, and I apprehended they might be lost or spoiled if I ventured them out of my possession.

CHAPTER III

The Author Diverts the Emperor, and His Nobility of Both Sexes, in a Very Uncommon Manner. The Diversions of the Court of Lilliput *Described. The Author Has His Liberty Granted Him upon Certain Conditions.*

MY GENTLENESS and good behavior had gained so far on the Emperor and his court, and indeed upon the army and people in general, that I began to conceive hopes of getting my liberty in a short time. I took all possible methods to cultivate this favorable disposition. The natives came by degrees to be less apprehensive of any danger from me. I would sometimes lie down, and let five or six of them dance on my hand. And at last the boys and girls would venture to come and play at hide and seek in my hair. I had now made a good progress in understanding and speaking their language. The Emperor had a mind one day to entertain me with several of the country shows, wherein they exceed all nations I have known, both for dexterity and magnificence. I was diverted with none so much as that of the rope-dancers, performed upon a slender white thread, extended about two foot, and twelve inches from the ground. Upon which I shall desire liberty, with the reader's patience, to enlarge a little.

This diversion is only practiced by those persons who are candidates for great employments, and high favor, at court.[7] They are trained in this art from their youth, and are not always of noble birth, or liberal education. When a great office is vacant, either by death or disgrace (which often happens), five or six of those candidates petition the Emperor to entertain his Majesty and the court with a dance on the rope, and whoever jumps the highest without falling succeeds in the office. Very often the chief ministers themselves are commanded to show their skill, and to convince the Emperor that they have not lost their faculty. Flimnap,[8] the Treasurer, is allowed to cut a caper on the straight rope, at least an inch higher than any other lord in the whole empire. I have seen him do the summerset several times together upon a trencher fixed on the rope, which is no thicker than a common packthread in England. My friend Reldresal, principal Secretary for Private Affairs, is, in my opinion, if I am not partial, the second after the Treasurer; the rest of the great officers are much upon a par.

[5]Recondite. [6]Telescope.

[7]Swift, of course, has the English court in mind.

[8]Sir Robert Walpole, a Whig. One should remember, however, that the analogies with English affairs cannot be pushed too far.

These diversions are often attended with fatal accidents, whereof great numbers are on record. I myself have seen two or three candidates break a limb. But the danger is much greater when the ministers themselves are commanded to show their dexterity; for, by contending to excel themselves and their fellows, they strain so far, that there is hardly one of them who hath not received a fall, and some of them two or three. I was assured that a year or two before my arrival, Flimnap would have infallibly broke his neck, if one of the King's cushions, that accidentally lay on the ground, had not weakened the force of his fall.

There is likewise another diversion, which is only shown before the Emperor and Empress, and first minister, upon particular occasions. The Emperor lays on the table three fine silken threads of six inches long.[9] One is blue, the other red, and the third green. These threads are proposed as prizes for those persons whom the Emperor hath a mind to distinguish by a peculiar mark of his favor. The ceremony is performed in his Majesty's great chamber of state, where the candidates are to undergo a trial of dexterity very different from the former, and such as I have not observed the least resemblance of in any other country of the old or the new world. The Emperor holds a stick in his hands, both ends parallel to the horizon, while the candidates advancing one by one, sometimes leap over the stick, sometimes creep under it backwards and forwards several times, according as the stick is advanced or depressed. Sometimes the Emperor holds one end of the stick, and his first minister the other; sometimes the minister has it entirely to himself. Whoever performs his part with most agility, and holds out the longest in leaping and creeping, is rewarded with the blue-colored silk; the red is given to the next, and the green to the third, which they all wear girt twice round about the middle; and you see few great persons about this court, who are not adorned with one of these girdles.

The horses of the army, and those of the royal stables, having been daily led before me, were no longer shy, but would come up to my very feet without starting. The riders would leap them over my hand as I held it on the ground, and one of the Emperor's huntsmen, upon a large courser, took my foot, shoe and all; which was indeed a prodigious leap. I had the good fortune to divert the Emperor one day after a very extraordinary manner. I desired he would order several sticks of two foot high, and the thickness of an ordinary cane, to be brought me; whereupon his Majesty commanded the master of his woods to give directions accordingly; and the next morning six woodmen arrived with as many carriages, drawn by eight horses to each. I took nine of these sticks, fixing them firmly in the ground in a quadrangular figure, two foot and a half square. I took four other sticks, and tied them parallel at each corner, about two foot from the ground; then I fastened my handkerchief to the nine sticks that stood erect, and extended it on all sides, till it was tight as the top of a drum; and the four parallel sticks rising about five inches higher than the handkerchief, served as ledges on each side. When I had finished my work, I desired the Emperor to let a troop of his best horse, twenty-four in number, come and exercise upon this plain. His Majesty approved of the proposal, and I took them up, one by one, in my hands, ready mounted and armed, with the proper officers to exercise them. As soon as they got into order, they divided into two parties, performed mock skirmishes, discharged blunt arrows, drew their swords, fled and pursued, attacked and retired, and in short discovered the best military discipline I ever beheld. The parallel sticks secured them and their horses from falling over the stage; and the Emperor was so much delighted that he ordered this entertainment to be repeated several days, and once was pleased to be lifted up and give the word of command; and, with great difficulty, persuaded even the Empress herself to let me hold her in her close chair within two yards of the stage, from whence she was able to take a full view of the whole performance. It was my good fortune that no ill accident happened in these entertainments, only once a fiery

[9] The ribbons of the Garter, the Thistle, and the Bath.

horse, that belonged to one of the captains, pawing with his hoof, struck a hole in my handkerchief, and his foot slipping, he overthrew his rider and himself; but I immediately relieved them both, and covering the hole with one hand, I set down the troop with the other, in the same manner as I took them up. The horse that fell was strained in the left shoulder, but the rider got no hurt, and I repaired my handkerchief as well as I could: however, I would not trust to the strength of it any more in such dangerous enterprises.

About two or three days before I was set at liberty, as I was entertaining the court with these kind of feats, there arrived an express to inform his Majesty, that some of his subjects riding near the place where I was first taken up, had seen a great black substance lying on the ground, very oddly shaped, extending its edges round as wide as his Majesty's bedchamber, and rising up in the middle as high as a man; that it was no living creature, as they at first apprehended, for it lay on the grass without motion, and some of them had walked round it several times: that by mounting upon each other's shoulders, they had got to the top, which was flat and even, and stamping upon it they found it was hollow within; that they humbly conceived it might be something belonging to the Man-Mountain; and if his Majesty pleased, they would undertake to bring it with only five horses. I presently knew what they meant, and was glad at heart to receive this intelligence. It seems upon my first reaching the shore after our ship-wreck, I was in such confusion, that before I came to the place where I went to sleep, my hat, which I had fastened with a string to my head while I was rowing, and had stuck on all the time I was swimming, fell off after I came to land; the string, as I conjecture, breaking by some accident which I never observed, but thought my hat had been lost at sea. I entreated his Imperial Majesty to give orders it might be brought to me as soon as possible, describing to him the use and the nature of it: and the next day the wagoners arrived with it, but not in a very good condition; they had bored two holes in the brim, within an inch and half of the edge, and fastened two hooks in the holes; these hooks were tied by a long cord to the harness, and thus my hat was dragged along for above half an English mile; but the ground in that country being extremely smooth and level, it received less damage than I expected.

Two days after this adventure, the Emperor having ordered that part of his army which quarters in and about his metropolis to be in readiness, took a fancy of diverting himself in a very singular manner. He desired I would stand like a Colossus, with my legs as far asunder as I conveniently could. He then commanded his General (who was an old experienced leader, and a great patron of mine) to draw up the troops in close order, and march them under me; the foot by twenty-four in a breast, and the horse by sixteen, with drums beating, colors flying, and pikes advanced. This body consisted of three thousand foot, and a thousand horse. His Majesty gave orders, upon pain of death, that every soldier in his march should observe the strictest decency with regard to my person; which, however, could not prevent some of the younger officers from turning up their eyes as they passed under me. And, to confess the truth, my breeches were at that time in so ill a condition, that they afforded some opportunities for laughter and admiration.

I had sent so many memorials and petitions for my liberty, that his Majesty at length mentioned the matter, first in the cabinet, and then in a full council; where it was opposed by none, except Skyresh Bolgolam, who was pleased, without any provocation, to be my mortal enemy. But it was carried against him by the whole board, and confirmed by the Emperor. That minister was *Galbet,* or Admiral of the Realm, very much in his master's confidence, and a person well versed in affairs, but of a morose and sour complexion. However, he was at length persuaded to comply; but prevailed that the articles and conditions upon which I should be set free, and to which I must swear, should be drawn up by himself. These articles were brought to me by Skyresh Bolgolam in person, attended by two under-secretaries, and several persons of distinction. After they were read, I was demanded to swear to the performance of them; first in the manner of my own country, and afterwards in the method prescribed by their laws; which was to hold my right foot in my left hand, to place the middle finger of my right hand on the crown of my head, and my thumb on the tip of my right ear. But because the reader may be curious to have some idea of the style and manner of expression peculiar to that people, as well as to know the articles upon which I recovered my liberty, I have made a translation of the whole instrument word for word, as near as I was able, which I here offer to the public.

GOLBASTO MOMAREM EVLAME GURDILO SHEFIN MULLY ULLY GUE, most mighty Emperor of Lilliput, delight and terror of the universe, whose dominions extend five thousand *blustrugs* (about twelve mile in circumference) to the extremities of the globe; monarch of all monarchs, taller than the sons of men; whose feet press down to the center, and whose head strikes against the sun; at whose nod the princes of the earth shake their knees; pleasant as the spring, comfortable as the summer, fruitful as autumn, dreadful as winter. His most sublime Majesty proposeth to the Man-Mountain, lately arrived to our celestial dominions, the following articles, which by a solemn oath he shall be obliged to perform.

First, The Man-Mountain shall not depart from our dominions, without our license under our great seal.

2d, He shall not presume to come into our metropolis, without our express order; at which time, the inhabitants shall have two hours' warning to keep within their doors.

3rd, The said Man-Mountain shall confine his walks to our principal high-roads, and not offer to walk or lie down in a meadow or field of corn.

4th, As he walks the said roads, he shall take the utmost care not to trample upon the bodies of any of our loving subjects, their horses, or carriages, nor take any of our subjects into his hands, without their own consent.

5th, If an express requires extraordinary dispatch, the Man-Mountain shall be obliged to carry in his pocket the messenger and horse a six days' journey once in every moon, and return the said messenger back (if so required) safe to our Imperial Presence.

6th, He shall be our ally against our enemies in the Island of Blefuscu,[10] and do his utmost to destroy their fleet, which is now preparing to invade us.

7th, That the said Man-Mountain shall, at his times of leisure, be aiding and assisting our workmen, in helping to raise certain great stones, towards covering the wall of the principal park, and other our royal buildings.

8th, That the said Man-Mountain shall, in two moons' time, deliver in an exact survey of the circumference of our dominions by a computation of his own paces round the coast.

Lastly, That upon his solemn oath to observe all the above articles, the said Man-Mountain shall have a daily allowance of meat and drink sufficient for the support of 1728 of our subjects, with free access to our Royal Person, and other marks of our favor. Given at our Palace at Belfaborac the twelfth day of the ninety-first moon of our reign.

I swore and subscribed to these articles with great cheerfulness and content, although some of them were not so honorable as I could have wished; which proceeded wholly from the malice of Skyresh Bolgolam, the High-Admiral: whereupon my chains were immediately unlocked, and I was at full liberty; the Emperor himself in person did me the honor to be by at the whole ceremony. I made my acknowledgments by prostrating myself at his Majesty's feet:

[10] This country probably represents France under Louis XIV.

but he commanded me to rise; and after many gracious expressions, which, to avoid the censure of vanity, I shall not repeat, he added, that he hoped I should prove a useful servant, and well deserve all the favors he had already conferred upon me, or might do for the future.

The reader may please to observe, that in the last article for the recovery of my liberty, the Emperor stipulates to allow me a quantity of meat and drink sufficient for the support of 1728 Lilliputians. Some time after, asking a friend at court how they came to fix on that determinate number; he told me that his Majesty's mathematicians, having taken the height of my body by the help of a quadrant, and finding it to exceed theirs in the proportion of twelve to one, they concluded from the similarity of their bodies, that mine must contain at least 1728 of theirs, and consequently would require as much food as was necessary to support that number of Lilliputians. By which, the reader may conceive an idea of the ingenuity of that people, as well as the prudent and exact economy of so great a prince.

CHAPTER IV

Mildendo, *the Metropolis of* Lilliput, *Described, together with the Emperor's Palace. A Conversation between the Author and a Principal Secretary, concerning the Affairs of That Empire. The Author's Offer to Serve the Emperor in His Wars.*

THE first request I made after I had obtained my liberty, was, that I might have license to see Mildendo, the metropolis; which the Emperor easily granted me, but with a special charge to do no hurt either to the inhabitants or their houses. The people had notice by proclamation of my design to visit the town. The wall which encompassed it, is two foot and an half high, and at least eleven inches broad, so that a coach and horses may be driven very safely round it; and it is flanked with strong towers at ten foot distance. I stepped over the great Western Gate, and passed very gently, and sideling through the two principal streets, only in my short waistcoat, for fear of damaging the roofs and eaves of the houses with the skirts of my coat. I walked with the utmost circumspection, to avoid treading on any stragglers, that might remain in the streets, although the orders were very strict, that all people should keep in their houses, at their own peril. The garret windows and tops of houses were so crowded with spectators, that I thought in all my travels I had not seen a more populous place. The city is an exact square, each side of the wall being five hundred foot long. The two great streets, which run cross and divide it into four quarters, are five foot wide. The lanes and alleys, which I could not enter, but only viewed them as I passed, are from twelve to eighteen inches. The town is capable of holding five hundred thousand souls. The houses are from three to five stories. The shops and markets well provided.

The Emperor's palace is in the center of the city, where the two great streets meet. It is enclosed by a wall of two foot high, and twenty foot distant from the buildings. I had his Majesty's permission to step over this wall; and the space being so wide between that and the palace, I could easily view it on every side. The outward court is a square of forty foot, and includes two other courts: in the inmost are the royal apartments, which I was very desirous to see, but found it extremely difficult; for the great gates, from one square into another, were but eighteen inches high, and seven inches wide. Now the buildings of the outer court were at least five foot high, and it was impossible for me to stride over them without infinite damage to the pile, though the walls were strongly built of hewn stone, and four inches thick. At the same time the Emperor had a great desire that I should see the magnificence of his palace; but this I was not able to do till three days after, which I spent in cutting down with my knife some of the largest trees in the royal park, about an hundred yards distant from the city. Of these trees I made two stools, each about three foot high, and strong enough to bear my weight. The people having received notice a second time, I went again through the city to the palace, with my two stools in my hands. When I came to the side of the outer court, I stood upon one stool, and took the other in my hand: this I lifted over the roof, and gently set it down on the space between the first and second court, which was eight 5 foot wide. I then stepped over the buildings very conveniently from one stool to the other, and drew up the first after me with a hooked stick. By this contrivance I got into the inmost court; and lying down upon my side, 10 I applied my face to the windows of the middle stories, which were left open on purpose, and discovered the most splendid apartments that can be imagined. There I saw the Empress and the young Princes, in their 15 several lodgings, with their chief attendants about them. Her Imperial Majesty[11] was pleased to smile very graciously upon me, and gave me out of the window her hand to kiss.

But I shall not anticipate the reader with 20 farther descriptions of this kind, because I reserve them for a greater work, which is now almost ready for the press, containing a general description of this empire, from its first erection, through a long series of 25 Princes, with a particular account of their wars and politics, laws, learning, and religion: their plants and animals, their peculiar manners and customs, with other matters very curious and useful; my chief design at 30 present being only to relate such events and transactions as happened to the public, or to myself, during a residence of about nine months in that empire.

One morning, about a fortnight after I 35 had obtained my liberty, Reldresal, principal Secretary (as they style him) of Private Affairs, came to my house attended only by one servant. He ordered his coach to wait at a distance, and desired I would give him 40 an hour's audience; which I readily consented to, on account of his quality and personal merits, as well as the many good offices he had done me during my solicitations at court. I offered to lie down, that he might the more 45 conveniently reach my ear; but he chose rather to let me hold him in my hand during our conversation. He began with compliments on my liberty; said he might pretend to some merit in it: but, however, added, that 50 if it had not been for the present situation of things at court, perhaps I might not have obtained it so soon. For, said he, as flourishing a condition as we may appear to be in to foreigners, we labor under two mighty 5 evils; a violent faction at home, and the danger of an invasion by a most potent enemy from abroad. As to the first, you are to understand, that for about seventy moons past there have been two struggling 10 parties in this empire, under the names of *Tramecksan* and *Slamecksan,* from the high and low heels on their shoes,[12] by which they distinguish themselves. It is alleged indeed, that the high heels are most agreeable to our 15 ancient constitution; but, however this be, his Majesty hath determined to make use of only low heels in the administration of the government, and all offices in the gift of the Crown, as you cannot but observe; and par- 20 ticularly, that his Majesty's Imperial heels are lower at least by a *drurr* than any of his court *(drurr* is a measure about the fourteenth part of an inch). The animosities between these two parties run so high, that 25 they will neither eat nor drink, nor talk with each other. We compute the *Trameckson,* or High-Heels, to exceed us in number; but the power is wholly on our side. We apprehend his Imperial Highness, the Heir to the 30 Crown, to have some tendency towards the High-Heels;[13] at least we can plainly discover one of his heels higher than the other, which gives him a hobble in his gait. Now, in the midst of these intestine disquiets, we 35 are threatened with an invasion from the Island of Blefuscu, which is the other great empire of the universe, almost as large and powerful as this of his Majesty. For as to what we have heard you affirm, that there 40 are other kingdoms and states in the world inhabited by human creatures as large as yourself, our philosophers are in much doubt, and would rather conjecture that you dropped from the moon, or one of the stars; 45 because it is certain, that an hundred mortals of your bulk would, in a short time, destroy

[11] Probably Queen Anne.

[12] This and what follows is a satire upon party government, but it is a mistake to suppose, from Swift's terms, that it refers specially to the High and Low Church parties in England.

[13] This probably refers to intrigues of the Prince of Wales (later George II) directed against his father's policies.

all the fruits and cattle of his Majesty's dominions. Besides, our histories of six thousand moons make no mention of any other regions, than the two great empires of Lilliput and Blefuscu. Which two mighty powers have, as I was going to tell you, been engaged in a most obstinate war for six and thirty moons past. It began upon the following occasion. It is allowed on all hands, that the primitive way of breaking eggs before we eat them, was upon the larger end: but his present Majesty's grandfather, while he was a boy going to eat an egg, and breaking it according to the ancient practice, happened to cut one of his fingers. Whereupon the Emperor his father published an edict, commanding all his subjects, upon great penalties, to break the smaller end of their eggs.[14] The people so highly resented this law, that our histories tell us there have been six rebellions raised on that account; wherein one Emperor lost his life, and another his crown. These civil commotions were constantly fomented by the monarchs of Blefuscu; and when they were quelled, the exiles always fled for refuge to that empire. It is computed, that eleven thousand persons have, at several times, suffered death, rather than submit to break their eggs at the smaller end. Many hundred large volumes have been published upon this controversy: but the books of the Big-Endians have been long forbidden, and the whole party rendered incapable by law of holding employments. During the course of these troubles, the Emperors of Blefuscu did frequently expostulate by their ambassadors, accusing us of making a schism in religion, by offending against a fundamental doctrine of our great prophet Lustrog, in the fifty-fourth chapter of the Blundecral (which is their Alcoran). This, however, is thought to be a mere strain upon the text: for the words are these; *That all true believers break their eggs at the convenient end:* and which is the convenient end, seems, in my humble opinion, to be left to every man's conscience, or at least in the power of the chief magistrate to determine. Now the Big-Endian exiles have found so much credit in the Emperor of Blefuscu's court, and so much private assistance and encouragement from their party here at home, that a bloody war has been carried on between the two empires for six and thirty moons with various success; during which time we have lost forty capital ships, and a much greater number of smaller vessels, together with thirty thousand of our best seamen and soldiers; and the damage received by the enemy is reckoned to be somewhat greater than ours. However, they have now equipped a numerous fleet, and are just preparing to make a descent upon us; and his Imperial Majesty, placing great confidence in your valor and strength, has commanded me to lay this account of his affairs before you.

I desired the Secretary to present my humble duty to the Emperor, and to let him know, that I thought it would not become me, who was a foreigner, to interfere with parties; but I was ready, with the hazard of my life, to defend his person and state against all invaders.

CHAPTER V

The Author, by an Extraordinary Stratagem, Prevents an Invasion. A High Title of Honor Is Conferred upon Him. Ambassadors Arrive from the Emperor of Blefuscu, *and Sue for Peace. The Emperor's Apartment on Fire by an Accident; the Author Instrumental in Saving the Rest of the Palace.*

THE Empire of Blefuscu is an island situated to the north north-east side of Lilliput, from whence it is parted only by a channel of eight hundred yards wide. I had not yet seen it, and upon this notice of an intended invasion, I avoided appearing on that side of the coast, for fear of being discovered by

[14] This controversy is usually said to refer to the troubles between Catholics and Protestants in England, and no doubt correctly; though the full force of the satire is lost, here and elsewhere in the book, if we tend to think of it as having only, or even chiefly, a particular application. The Little-Endians are explained to be the Protestants, the Big-Endians the Catholics. The Emperor's grandfather is thus Henry VIII and, in the next sentence, the Emperor who lost his life is Charles I, he who lost his crown James II. France (Blefuscu), of course, encouraged the English Catholics.

some of the enemy's ships, who had received no intelligence of me, all intercourse between the two empires having been strictly forbidden during the war, upon pain of death, and an embargo laid by our Emperor upon all vessels whatsoever. I communicated to his Majesty a project I had formed of seizing the enemy's whole fleet: which, as our scouts assured us, lay at anchor in the harbor ready to sail with the first fair wind. I consulted the most experienced seamen, upon the depth of the channel, which they had often plumbed, who told me, that in the middle at high-water it was seventy *glumgluffs* deep, which is about six foot of European measure; and the rest of it fifty *glumgluffs* at most. I walked towards the north-east coast over against Blefuscu; and lying down behind a hillock, took out my small pocket perspective-glass, and viewed the enemy's fleet at anchor, consisting of about fifty men of war, and a great number of transports: I then came back to my house, and gave order (for which I had a warrant) for a great quantity of the strongest cable and bars of iron. The cable was about as thick as packthread, and the bars of the length and size of a knitting-needle. I trebled the cable to make it stronger, and for the same reason I twisted three of the iron bars together, binding the extremities into a hook. Having thus fixed fifty hooks to as many cables, I went back to the north-east coast, and putting off my coat, shoes, and stockings, walked into the sea in my leathern jerkin, about half an hour before high water. I waded with what haste I could, and swam in the middle about thirty yards till I felt ground; I arrived at the fleet in less than half an hour. The enemy was so frighted when they saw me, that they leaped out of their ships, and swam to shore, where there could not be fewer than thirty thousand souls. I then took my tackling, and fastening a hook to the hole at the prow of each, I tied all the cords together at the end. While I was thus employed, the enemy discharged several thousand arrows, many of which stuck in my hands and face; and besides the excessive smart, gave me much disturbance in my work. My greatest apprehension was for my eyes, which I should have infallibly lost, if I had not suddenly thought of an expedient. I kept among other little necessaries a pair of spectacles in a private pocket, which, as I observed before, had scaped the Emperor's searchers. These I took out and fastened as strongly as I could upon my nose, and thus armed went on boldly with my work in spite of the enemy's arrows, many of which struck against the glasses of my spectacles, but without any other effect, further than a little to discompose them. I had now fastened all the hooks, and taking the knot in my hand, began to pull; but not a ship would stir, for they were all too fast held by their anchors, so that the boldest part of my enterprise remained. I therefore let go the cord, and leaving the hooks fixed to the ships, I resolutely cut with my knife the cables that fastened the anchors, receiving about two hundred shots in my face and hands; then I took up the knotted end of the cables, to which my hooks were tied, and with great ease drew fifty of the enemy's largest men of war after me.

The Blefuscudians, who had not the least imagination of what I intended, were at first confounded with astonishment. They had seen me cut the cables, and thought my design was only to let the ships run adrift, or fall foul on each other: but when they perceived the whole fleet moving in order, and saw me pulling at the end, they set up such a scream of grief and despair, that it is almost impossible to describe or conceive. When I had got out of danger, I stopped awhile to pick out the arrows that stuck in my hands and face; and rubbed on some of the same ointment that was given me at my first arrival, as I have formerly mentioned. I then took off my spectacles, and waiting about an hour, till the tide was a little fallen, I waded through the middle with my cargo, and arrived safe at the royal port of Lilliput.

The Emperor and his whole court stood on the shore, expecting the issue of this great adventure. They saw the ships move forward in a large half-moon, but could not discern me, who was up to my breast in water. When I advanced in the middle of the channel, they were yet in more pain, because I was under water to my neck. The Emperor concluded me to be drowned, and that the enemy's fleet was approaching in a hostile manner: but he was soon eased of his fears, for the channel growing shallower every step I made, I came in a short time within hearing, and holding up the end of the cable by which the fleet was fastened, I cried in a loud voice, *Long live the most puissant Emperor of Lilliput!* This great prince received me at my landing with all possible encomiums, and created me a *Nardac* upon the spot, which is the highest title of honor among them.

His Majesty desired I would take some other opportunity of bringing all the rest of his enemy's ships into his ports. And so unmeasurable is the ambition of princes, that he seemed to think of nothing less than reducing the whole empire of Blefuscu into a province, and governing it by a viceroy; of destroying the Big-Endian exiles, and compelling the people to break the smaller end of their eggs, by which he would remain the sole monarch of the whole world. But I endeavored to divert him from this design, by many arguments drawn from the topics[15] of policy as well as justice; and I plainly protested, that I would never be an instrument of bringing a free and brave people into slavery. And when the matter was debated in council, the wisest part of the ministry were of my opinion.

This open bold declaration of mine was so opposite to the schemes and politics of his Imperial Majesty, that he could never forgive it; he mentioned it in a very artful manner at council, where I was told that some of the wisest appeared, at least by their silence, to be of my opinion; but others, who were my secret enemies, could not forbear some expressions, which by a side-wind reflected on me. And from this time began an intrigue between his Majesty and a junto of ministers maliciously bent against me, which broke out in less than two months, and had like to have ended in my utter destruction. Of so little weight are the greatest services to princes, when put into the balance with a refusal to gratify their passions.

About three weeks after this exploit, there arrived a solemn embassy from Blefuscu, with humble offers of a peace; which was soon concluded upon conditions very advantageous to our Emperor, wherewith I shall not trouble the reader. There were six ambassadors, with a train of about five hundred persons, and their entry was very magnificent, suitable to the grandeur of their master, and the importance of their business. When their treaty was finished, wherein I did them several good offices by the credit I now had, or at least appeared to have at court, their Excellencies, who were privately told how much I had been their friend, made me a visit in form. They began with many compliments upon my valor and generosity, invited me to that kingdom in the Emperor their master's name, and desired me to show them some proofs of my prodigious strength, of which they had heard so many wonders; wherein I readily obliged them, but shall not trouble the reader with the particulars.

When I had for some time entertained their Excellencies, to their infinite satisfaction and surprise, I desired they would do me the honor to present my most humble respects to the Emperor their master, the renown of whose virtues had so justly filled the whole world with admiration, and whose royal person I resolved to attend before I returned to my own country: accordingly, the next time I had the honor to see our Emperor, I desired his general license to wait on the Blefuscudian monarch, which he was pleased to grant me, as I could perceive, in a very cold manner; but could not guess the reason, till I had a whisper from a certain person that Flimnap and Bolgolam had represented my intercourse with those ambassadors as a mark of disaffection, from which I am sure my heart was wholly free. And this was the first time I began to conceive some imperfect idea of courts and ministers.

It is to be observed, that these ambassadors spoke to me by an interpreter, the languages of both empires differing as much from each other as any two in Europe, and each nation priding itself upon the antiquity, beauty, and energy of their own tongues, with an avowed contempt for that of their neighbor; yet our Emperor, standing upon the advantage he

[15]Principles.

had got by the seizure of their fleet, obliged them to deliver their credentials, and make their speech in the Lilliputian tongue. And it must be confessed, that from the great intercourse of trade and commerce between both realms, from the continual reception of exiles, which is mutual among them, and from the custom in each empire to send their young nobility and richer gentry to the other, in order to polish themselves by seeing the world, and understanding men and manners; there are few persons of distinction, or merchants, or seamen, who dwell in the maritime parts, but what can hold conversation in both tongues; as I found some weeks after, when I went to pay my respects to the Emperor of Blefuscu, which in the midst of great misfortunes, through the malice of my enemies, proved a very happy adventure to me, as I shall relate in its proper place.

The reader may remember, that when I signed those articles upon which I recovered my liberty, there were some which I disliked upon account of their being too servile, neither could anything but an extreme necessity have forced me to submit. But being now a *Nardac* of the highest rank in that empire, such offices were looked upon as below my dignity, and the Emperor (to do him justice) never once mentioned them to me. However, it was not long before I had an opportunity of doing his Majesty, at least, as I then thought, a most signal service. I was alarmed at midnight with the cries of many hundred people at my door; by which being suddenly awaked, I was in some kind of terror. I heard the word *burglum* repeated incessantly: several of the Emperor's court, making their way through the crowd, entreated me to come immediately to the palace, where her Imperial Majesty's apartment was on fire, by the carelessness of a maid of honor, who fell asleep while she was reading a romance. I got up in an instant; and orders being given to clear the way before me, and it being likewise a moonshine night, I made a shift to get to the Palace without trampling on any of the people. I found they had already applied ladders to the walls of the apartment, and were well provided with buckets, but the water was at some distance. These buckets were about the size of a large thimble, and the poor people supplied me with them as fast as they could; but the flame was so violent that they did little good. I might easily have stifled it with my coat, which I unfortunately left behind me for haste, and came away only in my leathern jerkin. The case seemed wholly desperate and deplorable; and this magnificent palace would have infallibly been burned down to the ground, if, by a presence of mind, unusual to me, I had not suddenly thought of an expedient. I had the evening before drunk plentifully of a most delicious wine, called *glimigrim* (the Blefuscudians call it *flunec,* but ours is esteemed the better sort), which is very diuretic. By the luckiest chance in the world, I had not discharged myself of any part of it. The heat I had contracted by coming very near the flames, and by laboring to quench them, made the wine begin to operate by urine; which I voided in such a quantity, and applied so well to the proper places, that in three minutes the fire was wholly extinguished, and the rest of that noble pile, which had cost so many ages in erecting, preserved from destruction.

It was now day-light, and I returned to my house without waiting to congratulate with the Emperor: because, although I had done a very eminent piece of service, yet I could not tell how his Majesty might resent the manner by which I had performed it: for, by the fundamental laws of the realm, it is capital in any person, of what quality soever, to make water within the precincts of the palace. But I was a little comforted by a message from his Majesty, that he would give orders to the Grand Justiciary for passing my pardon in form; which, however, I could not obtain. And I was privately assured, that the Empress, conceiving the greatest abhorrence of what I had done, removed to the most distant side of the court, firmly resolved that those buildings should never be repaired for her use: and, in the presence of her chief confidents could not forbear vowing revenge.[16]

[16]This episode may have reference to Swift's failure to obtain a bishopric because of his authorship of *A Tale of a Tub.*

CHAPTER VI

Of the Inhabitants of Lilliput; *Their Learning, Laws, and Customs, the Manner of Educating Their Children. The Author's Way of Living in That Country. His Vindication of a Great Lady.*

ALTHOUGH I intend to leave the description of this empire to a particular treatise, yet in the mean time I am content to gratify the curious reader with some general ideas. As the common size of the natives is somewhat under six inches high, so there is an exact proportion in all other animals, as well as plants and trees: for instance, the tallest horses and oxen are between four and five inches in height, the sheep an inch and a half, more or less: their geese about the bigness of a sparrow, and so the several gradations downwards till you come to the smallest, which, to my sight, were almost invisible; but nature hath adapted the eyes of the Lilliputians to all objects proper for their view: they see with great exactness, but at no great distance. And to show the sharpness of their sight towards objects that are near, I have been much pleased with observing a cook pulling a lark, which was not so large as a common fly; and a young girl threading an invisible needle with invisible silk. Their tallest trees are about seven foot high: I mean some of those in the great royal park, the tops whereof I could but just reach with my fist clinched. The other vegetables are in the same proportion; but this I leave to the reader's imagination.

I shall say but little at present of their learning, which for many ages hath flourished in all its branches among them: but their manner of writing is very peculiar, being neither from the left to the right, like the Europeans; nor from the right to the left, like the Arabians; nor from up to down, like the Chinese; nor from down to up, like the Cascagians; but aslant from one corner of the paper to the other, like ladies in England.

They bury their dead with their heads directly downwards, because they hold an opinion, that in eleven thousand moons they are all to rise again, in which period the earth (which they conceive to be flat) will turn upside down, and by this means they shall, at their resurrection, be found ready standing on their feet. The learned among them confess the absurdity of this doctrine, but the practice still continues, in compliance to the vulgar.

There are some laws and customs in this empire very peculiar; and if they were not so directly contrary to those of my own dear country, I should be tempted to say a little in their justification. It is only to be wished, that they were as well executed. The first I shall mention, relates to informers. All crimes against the state are punished here with the utmost severity; but if the person accused maketh his innocence plainly to appear upon his trial, the accuser is immediately put to an ignominious death; and out of his goods or lands, the innocent person is quadruply recompensed for the loss of his time, for the danger he underwent, for the hardship of his imprisonment, and for all the charges he hath been at in making his defense. Or, if that fund be deficient, it is largely supplied by the Crown. The Emperor does also confer on him some public mark of his favor, and proclamation is made of his innocence through the whole city.

They look upon fraud as a greater crime than theft, and therefore seldom fail to punish it with death; for they allege, that care and vigilance, with a very common understanding, may preserve a man's goods from thieves, but honesty has no fence against superior cunning; and since it is necessary that there should be a perpetual intercourse of buying and selling, and dealing upon credit, where fraud is permitted and connived at, or hath no law to punish it, the honest dealer is always undone, and the knave gets the advantage. I remember when I was once interceding with the Emperor for a criminal who had wronged his master of a great sum of money, which he had received by order, and ran away with; and happening to tell his Majesty, by way of extenuation, that it was only a breach of trust; the Emperor thought it monstrous in me to offer, as a defense, the greatest aggravation of the crime: and truly I had little to say in return, farther than the common answer, that different nations had different customs; for, I confess, I was heartily ashamed.

Although we usually call reward and punishment the two hinges upon which all government turns, yet I could never observe this maxim to be put in practice by any nation except that of Lilliput. Whoever can there bring sufficient proof that he hath strictly observed the laws of his country for seventy-three moons, hath a claim to certain privileges, according to his quality and condition of life, with a proportionable sum of money out of a fund appropriated for that use: he likewise acquires the title of *Snilpall,* or Legal, which is added to his name, but does not descend to his posterity. And these people thought it a prodigious defect of policy among us, when I told them that our laws were enforced only by penalties, without any mention of reward. It is upon this account that the image of Justice, in their courts of judicature, is formed with six eyes, two before, as many behind, and on each side one, to signify circumspection; with a bag of gold open in her right hand, and a sword sheathed in her left, to show she is more disposed to reward than to punish.

In choosing persons for all employments, they have more regard to good morals than to great abilities; for, since government is necessary to mankind, they believe that the common size of human understandings is fitted to some station or other, and that Providence never intended to make the management of public affairs a mystery, to be comprehended only by a few persons of sublime genius, of which there seldom are three born in an age: but they suppose truth, justice, temperance, and the like, to be in every man's power; the practice of which virtues, assisted by experience and a good intention, would qualify any man for the service of his country, except where a course of study is required. But they thought the want of moral virtues was so far from being supplied by superior endowments of the mind, that employments could never be put into such dangerous hands as those of persons so qualified; and at least, that the mistakes committed by ignorance in a virtuous disposition, would never be of such fatal consequence to the public weal, as the practices of a man whose inclinations led him to be corrupt, and had great abilities to manage, and multiply, and defend his corruptions.

In like manner, the disbelief of a Divine Providence renders a man uncapable of holding any public station; for, since kings avow themselves to be the deputies of Providence, the Lilliputians think nothing can be more absurd than for a prince to employ such men as disown the authority under which he acts.

In relating these and the following laws, I would only be understood to mean the original institutions, and not the most scandalous corruptions into which these people are fallen by the degenerate nature of man. For as to that infamous practice of acquiring great employments by dancing on the ropes, or badges of favor and distinction by leaping over sticks and creeping under them, the reader is to observe, that they were first introduced by the grandfather of the Emperor now reigning, and grew to the present height, by the gradual increase of party and faction.

Ingratitude is among them a capital crime, as we read it to have been in some other countries: for they reason thus, that whoever makes ill returns to his benefactor, must needs be a common enemy to the rest of mankind, from whom he hath received no obligation, and therefore such a man is not fit to live.

Their notions relating to the duties of parents and children differ extremely from ours. For, since the conjunction of male and female is founded upon the great law of nature, in order to propagate and continue the species, the Lilliputians will needs have it, that men and women are joined together like other animals, by the motives of concupiscence; and that their tenderness towards their young proceeds from the like natural principle: for which reason they will never allow, that a child is under any obligation to his father for begetting him, or to his mother for bringing him into the world, which, considering the miseries of human life, was neither a benefit in itself, nor intended so by his parents, whose thoughts in their love-encounters were otherwise employed. Upon these, and the like reasonings, their opinion is, that parents are the last of all others to be trusted with the education of their own children; and therefore they have in every town public nurseries, where all parents, 5 except cottagers and laborers, are obliged to send their infants of both sexes to be reared and educated when they come to the age of twenty moons, at which time they are supposed to have some rudiments of docility. 10 These schools are of several kinds, suited to different qualities, and to both sexes. They have certain professors well skilled in preparing children for such a condition of life as befits the rank of their parents, and 15 their own capacities as well as inclinations. I shall first say something of the male nurseries, and then of the female.

The nurseries for males of noble or eminent birth, are provided with grave and 20 learned professors, and their several deputies. The clothes and food of the children are plain and simple. They are bred up in the principles of honor, justice, courage, modesty, clemency, religion, and love of 25 their country; they are always employed in some business, except in the times of eating and sleeping, which are very short, and two hours for diversions, consisting of bodily exercises. They are dressed by men till 30 four years of age, and then are obliged to dress themselves, although their quality be ever so great; and the women attendants, who are aged proportionably to ours at fifty, perform only the most menial offices. They 35 are never suffered to converse with servants, but go together in small or greater numbers to take their diversions, and always in the presence of a professor, or one of his deputies; whereby they avoid those early 40 bad impressions of folly and vice to which our children are subject. Their parents are suffered to see them only twice a year; the visit is to last but an hour. They are allowed to kiss the child at meeting and part- 45 ing; but a professor, who always stands by on those occasions, will not suffer them to whisper, or use any fondling expressions, or bring any presents of toys, sweetmeats, and the like. 50

The pension from each family for the education and entertainment of a child, upon failure of due payment, is levied by the Emperor's officers.

The nurseries for children of ordinary gentlemen, merchants, traders, and handicrafts, are managed proportionably after the same manner; only those designed for trades, are put out apprentices at eleven years old, whereas those of persons of quality continue in their exercises till fifteen, which answers to one and twenty with us: but the confinement is gradually lessened for the last three years.

In the female nurseries, the young girls of quality are educated much like the males, only they are dressed by orderly servants of their own sex; but always in the presence of a professor or deputy, till they come to dress themselves, which is at five years old. And if it be found that these nurses ever presume to entertain the girl with frightful or foolish stories, or the common follies practiced by chambermaids among us, they are publicly whipped thrice about the city, imprisoned for a year, and banished for life to the most desolate part of the country. Thus the young ladies there are as much ashamed of being cowards and fools, as the men, and despise all personal ornaments beyond decency and cleanliness: neither did I perceive any difference in their education, made by their difference of sex, only that the exercises of the females were not altogether so robust; and that some rules were given them relating to domestic life, and a smaller compass of learning was enjoined them: for their maxim is, that among people of quality, a wife should be always a reasonable and agreeable companion, because she cannot always be young. When the girls are twelve years old, which among them is the marriageable age, their parents or guardians take them home, with great expressions of gratitude to the professors, and seldom without tears of the young lady and her companions.

In the nurseries of females of the meaner sort, the children are instructed in all kinds of works proper for their sex, and their several degrees: those intended for apprentices, are dismissed at seven years old, the rest are kept to eleven.

The meaner families who have children at

these nurseries, are obliged, besides their annual pension, which is as low as possible, to return to the steward of the nursery a small monthly share of their gettings, to be a portion for the child; and therefore all parents are limited in their expenses by the law. For the Lilliputians think nothing can be more unjust, than for people, in subservience to their own appetites, to bring children into the world, and leave the burden of supporting them on the public. As to persons of quality, they give security to appropriate a certain sum for each child, suitable to their condition; and these funds are always managed with good husbandry, and the most exact justice.

The cottagers and laborers keep their children at home, their business being only to till and cultivate the earth, and therefore their education is of little consequence to the public; but the old and diseased among them are supported by hospitals: for begging is a trade unknown in this empire.

And here it may perhaps divert the curious reader, to give some account of my domestic, and my manner of living in this country, during a residence of nine months and thirteen days. Having a head mechanically turned, and being likewise forced by necessity, I had made for myself a table and chair convenient enough, out of the largest trees in the royal park. Two hundred sempstresses were employed to make me shirts, and linen for my bed and table, all of the strongest and coarsest kind they could get; which, however, they were forced to quilt together in several folds, for the thickest was some degrees finer than lawn. Their linen was usually three inches wide, and three foot make a piece. The sempstresses took my measure as I lay on the ground, one standing at my neck, and another at my mid-leg, with a strong cord extended, that each held by the end, while the third measured the length of the cord with a rule of an inch long. Then they measured my right thumb, and desired no more; for by a mathematical computation, that twice round the thumb is once round the wrist, and so on to the neck and the waist, and by the help of my old shirt, which I displayed on the ground before them for a pattern, they fitted me exactly. Three hundred tailors were employed in the same manner to make me clothes; but they had another contrivance for taking my measure. I kneeled down, and they raised a ladder from the ground to my neck; upon this ladder one of them mounted, and let fall a plumb-line from my collar to the floor, which just answered the length of my coat: but my waist and arms I measured myself. When my clothes were finished, which was done in my house, (for the largest of theirs would not have been able to hold them) they looked like the patchwork made by the ladies in England, only that mine were all of a color.

I had three hundred cooks to dress my victuals, in little convenient huts built about my house, where they and their families lived, and prepared me two dishes apiece. I took up twenty waiters in my hand, and placed them on the table: an hundred more attended below on the ground, some with dishes of meat, and some with barrels of wine, and other liquors, slung on their shoulders; all which the waiters above drew up as I wanted, in a very ingenious manner, by certain cords, as we draw the bucket up a well in Europe. A dish of their meat was a good mouthful, and a barrel of their liquor a reasonable draught. Their mutton yields to ours, but their beef is excellent. I have had a sirloin so large, that I have been forced to make three bites of it; but this is rare. My servants were astonished to see me eat it bones and all, as in our country we do the leg of a lark. Their geese and turkeys I usually ate at a mouthful, and I must confess they far exceed ours. Of their smaller fowl I could take up twenty or thirty at the end of my knife.

One day his Imperial Majesty, being informed of my way of living, desired that himself and his Royal Consort, with the young Princes of the blood of both sexes, might have the happiness (as he was pleased to call it) of dining with me. They came accordingly, and I placed them in chairs of state on my table, just over against me, with their guards about them. Flimnap, the Lord High Treasurer, attended there likewise with his white staff; and I observed he often looked on me with a sour countenance, which I would not seem to regard, but ate more than usual, in honor to my dear country, as well as to fill the court with admiration. I have some private reasons to believe, that this visit from his Majesty gave Flimnap an opportunity of doing me ill offices to his master. That minister had always been my secret enemy, though he outwardly caressed me more than was usual to the moroseness of his nature. He represented to the Emperor the low condition of his treasury; that he was forced to take up money at great discount; that exchequer bills would not circulate under nine *per cent.* below par; that in short I had cost his Majesty above a million and a half of *sprugs* (their greatest gold coin, about the bigness of a spangle); and upon the whole, that it would be advisable in the Emperor to take the first fair occasion of dismissing me.

I am here obliged to vindicate the reputation of an excellent lady, who was an innocent sufferer upon my account. The Treasurer took a fancy to be jealous of his wife, from the malice of some evil tongues, who informed him that her Grace had taken a violent affection for my person; and the court-scandal ran for some time, that she once came privately to my lodging. This I solemnly declare to be a most infamous falsehood, without any grounds, farther than that her Grace was pleased to treat me with all innocent marks of freedom and friendship. I own she came often to my house, but always publicly, nor ever without three more in the coach, who were usually her sister and young daughter, and some particular acquaintance; but this was common to many other ladies of the court. And I still appeal to my servants round, whether they at any time saw a coach at my door without knowing what persons were in it. On those occasions, when a servant had given me notice, my custom was to go immediately to the door; and, after paying my respects, to take up the coach and two horses very carefully in my hands (for, if there were six horses, the postillion always unharnessed four), and place them on a table, where I had fixed a moveable rim quite round, of five inches high, to prevent accidents. And I have often had four coaches and horses at once on my table full of company, while I sat in my chair leaning my face towards them; and when I was engaged with one set, the coachmen would gently drive the others round my table. I have passed many an afternoon very agreeably in these conversations. But I defy the Treasurer, or his two informers (I will name them, and let them make their best of it) Clustril and Drunlo, to prove that any person ever came to me *incognito,* except the secretary Reldresal, who was sent by express command of his Imperial Majesty, as I have before related. I should not have dwelt so long upon this particular, if it had not been a point wherein the reputation of a great lady is so nearly concerned, to say nothing of my own; though I then had the honor to be a *Nardac,* which the Treasurer himself is not; for all the world knows he is only a *Clumglum,* a title inferior by one degree, as that of a Marquis is to a Duke in England, although I allow he preceded me in right of his post. These false informations, which I afterwards came to the knowledge of, by an accident not proper to mention, made Flimnap, the Treasurer, show his lady for some time an ill countenance, and me a worse; and although he were at last undeceived and reconciled to her, yet I lost all credit with him, and found my interest decline very fast with the Emperor himself, who was indeed too much governed by that favorite.

CHAPTER VII

The Author, Being Informed of a Design to Accuse Him of High Treason, Makes His Escape to Blefuscu. *His Reception There.*

Before I proceed to give an account of my leaving this kingdom, it may be proper to inform the reader of a private intrigue which had been for two months forming against me.

I had been hitherto all my life a stranger to courts, for which I was unqualified by the meanness of my condition. I had indeed heard and read enough of the dispositions of great princes and ministers; but never expected to have found such terrible effects of them in so remote a country, governed, as I thought, by very different maxims from those in Europe. 5

When I was just preparing to pay my attendance on the Emperor of Blefuscu, a considerable person at court (to whom I had been very serviceable at a time when he lay under the highest displeasure of his Imperial Majesty) came to my house very privately at night in a close chair, and without sending his name, desired admittance. The chairmen were dismissed; I put the chair, with his Lordship in it, into my coat-pocket: and giving orders to a trusty servant to say I was indisposed and gone to sleep, I fastened the door of my house, placed the chair on the table, according to my usual custom, and sat down by it. After the common salutations were over, observing his Lordship's countenance full of concern, and inquiring into the reason, he desired I would hear him with patience in a matter that highly concerned my honor and my life. His speech was to the following effect, for I took notes of it as soon as he left me.

You are to know, said he, that several Committees of Council have been lately called in the most private manner on your account; and it is but two days since his Majesty came to a full resolution.

You are very sensible that Skyresh Bolgolam (*Galbet,* or High-Admiral) hath been your mortal enemy almost ever since your arrival. His original reasons I know not; but his hatred is much increased since your great success against Blefuscu, by which his glory, as Admiral, is obscured. This Lord, in conjunction with Flimnap the High-Treasurer, whose enmity against you is notorious on account of his lady, Limtoc the General, Lalcon the Chamberlain, and Balmuff the Grand Justiciary, have prepared articles of impeachment against you, for treason, and other capital crimes.

This preface made me so impatient, being conscious of my own merits and innocence, that I was going to interrupt; when he entreated me to be silent, and thus proceeded.

Out of gratitude for the favors you have done me, I procured information of the whole proceedings, and a copy of the articles, wherein I venture my head for your service.

Articles of Impeachment against Quinbus Flestrin (the Man-Mountain)

ARTICLE I

Whereas, by a statute made in the reign of his Imperial Majesty Calin Deffar Plune, it is enacted, that whoever shall make water within the precincts of the royal palace, shall be liable to the pains and penalties of high treason; notwithstanding, the said Quinbus Flestrin, in open breach of the said law, under color of extinguishing the fire kindled in the apartment of his Majesty's most dear Imperial Consort, did maliciously, traitorously, and devilishly, by discharge of his urine, put out the said fire kindled in the said apartment, lying and being within the precincts of the said royal palace, against the statute in that case provided, *etc.*, against the duty, *etc.*

ARTICLE II

That the said Quinbus Flestrin having brought the imperial fleet of Blefuscu into the royal port, and being afterwards commanded by his Imperial Majesty to seize all the other ships of the said empire of Blefuscu, and reduce that empire to a province, to be governed by a viceroy from hence, and to destroy and put to death not only all the Big-Endian exiles, but likewise all the people of that empire, who would not immediately forsake the Big-Endian heresy: He, the said Flestrin, like a false traitor against his most Auspicious, Serene, Imperial Majesty, did petition to be excused from the said service, upon pretense of unwillingness to force the consciences, or destroy the liberties and lives of an innocent people.

ARTICLE III

That, whereas certain ambassadors arrived from the court of Blefuscu, to sue for peace in his Majesty's court: He, the said Flestrin, did, like a false traitor, aid, abet, comfort, and divert the said ambassadors, although he knew them to be servants to a Prince who was lately an open enemy to his Imperial Majesty, and in open war against his said Majesty.

ARTICLE IV

That the said Quinbus Flestrin, contrary to the duty of a faithful subject, is now preparing to make a voyage to the court and empire of Blefuscu, for which he hath received only verbal license from his Imperial Majesty; and under color of the said license, doth falsely and traitorously intend to take the said voyage, and thereby to aid, comfort, and abet the Emperor of Blefuscu, so late an enemy, and in open war with his Imperial Majesty aforesaid.

There are some other articles, but these are the most important, of which I have read you an abstract.

In the several debates upon this impeachment, it must be confessed that his Majesty gave many marks of his great lenity, often urging the services you had done him, and endeavoring to extenuate your crimes. The Treasurer and Admiral insisted that you should be put to the most painful and ignominious death, by setting fire on your house at night, and the General was to attend with twenty thousand men armed with poisoned arrows to shoot you on the face and hands. Some of your servants were to have private orders to strew a poisonous juice on your shirts, which would soon make you tear your own flesh, and die in the utmost torture. The General came into the same opinion; so that for a long time there was a majority against you. But his Majesty resolving, if possible, to spare your life, at last brought off the Chamberlain.

Upon this incident, Reldresal, principal Secretary for Private Affairs, who always approved himself your true friend, was commanded by the Emperor to deliver his opinion, which he accordingly did; and therein justified the good thoughts you have of him. He allowed your crimes to be great, but that still there was room for mercy, the most commendable virtue in a prince, and for which his Majesty was so justly celebrated. He said, the friendship between you and him was so well known to the world, that perhaps the most honorable board might think him partial: however, in obedience to the command he had received, he would freely offer his sentiments. That if his Majesty, in consideration of your services, and pursuant to his own merciful disposition, would please to spare your life, and only give orders to put out both your eyes, he humbly conceived, that by this expedient, justice might in some measure be satisfied, and all the world would applaud the lenity of the Emperor, as well as the fair and generous proceedings of those who have the honor to be his counselors. That the loss of your eyes would be no impediment to your bodily strength, by which you might still be useful to his Majesty. That blindness is an addition to courage, by concealing dangers from us; that the fear you had for your eyes, was the greatest difficulty in bringing over the enemy's fleet, and it would be sufficient for you to see by the eyes of the ministers, since the greatest princes do no more.

This proposal was received with the utmost disapprobation by the whole board. Bolgolam, the Admiral, could not preserve his temper; but rising up in fury, said, he wondered how the Secretary durst presume to give his opinion for preserving the life of a traitor: that the services you had performed, were, by all true reasons of state, the great aggravation of your crimes; that you, who were able to extinguish the fire, by discharge of urine in her Majesty's apartment (which he mentioned with horror), might, at another time, raise an inundation by the same means, to drown the whole palace; and the same strength which enabled you to bring over the enemy's fleet, might serve, upon the first discontent, to carry it back: that he had good reasons to think you were a Big-Endian in your heart; and as treason begins in the heart, before it appears in overt acts, so he accused you as a traitor on that account, and therefore insisted you should be put to death.

The Treasurer was of the same opinion; he showed to what straits his Majesty's revenue was reduced by the charge of maintaining you, which would soon grow insupportable: that the Secretary's expedient of putting out your eyes was so far from being a remedy against this evil, that it would probably increase it, as it is manifest from the common practice of blinding some kind of fowl, after which they fed the faster, and grew sooner fat: that his sacred Majesty and the Council, who are your judges, were in their own consciences fully convinced of your guilt, which was a sufficient argument to condemn you to death, without the formal proofs required by the strict letter of the law.

But his Imperial Majesty, fully determined

against capital punishment, was graciously pleased to say, that since the Council thought the loss of your eyes too easy a censure, some other may be inflicted hereafter. And your friend the Secretary humbly desiring to be heard again, in answer to what the Treasurer had objected concerning the great charge his Majesty was at in maintaining you, said, that his Excellency, who had the sole disposal of the Emperor's revenue, might easily provide against that evil, by gradually lessening your establishment; by which, for want of sufficient food, you would grow weak and faint, and lose your appetite, and consequently decay and consume in a few months; neither would the stench of your carcass be then so dangerous, when it should become more than half diminished; and immediately upon your death, five or six thousand of his Majesty's subjects might, in two or three days, cut your flesh from your bones, take it away by cartloads, and bury it in distant parts to prevent infection, leaving the skeleton as a monument of admiration to posterity.

Thus by the great friendship of the Secretary, the whole affair was compromised. It was strictly enjoined, that the project of starving you by degrees should be kept a secret, but the sentence of putting out your eyes was entered on the books; none dissenting except Bolgolam the Admiral, who, being a creature of the Empress, was perpetually instigated by her Majesty to insist upon your death, she having borne perpetual malice against you, on account of that infamous and illegal method you took to extinguish the fire in her apartment.

In three days your friend the Secretary will be directed to come to your house, and read before you the articles of impeachment; and then to signify the great lenity and favor of his Majesty and Council, whereby you are only condemned to the loss of your eyes, which his Majesty doth not question you will gratefully and humbly submit to; and twenty of his Majesty's surgeons will attend, in order to see the operation well performed, by discharging very sharp-pointed arrows into the balls of your eyes, as you lie on the ground.

I leave to your prudence what measures you will take; and to avoid suspicion, I must immediately return in as private a manner as I came.

His Lordship did so, and I remained alone, under many doubts and perplexities of mind.

It was a custom introduced by this prince and his ministry (very different, as I have been assured, from the practices of former times), that after the court had decreed any cruel execution, either to gratify the monarch's resentment, or the malice of a favorite, the Emperor always made a speech to his whole Council, expressing his great lenity and tenderness, as qualities known and confessed by all the world. This speech was immediately published through the kingdom; nor did anything terrify the people so much as those encomiums on his Majesty's mercy; because it was observed, that the more these praises were enlarged and insisted on, the more inhuman was the punishment, and the sufferer more innocent. And as to myself, I must confess, having never been designed for a courtier either by my birth or education, I was so ill a judge of things, that I could not discover the lenity and favor of his sentence, but conceived it (perhaps erroneously) rather to be rigorous than gentle. I sometimes thought of standing my trial, for although I could not deny the facts alleged in the several articles, yet I hoped they would admit of some extenuations. But having in my life perused many state-trials, which I ever observed to terminate as the judges thought fit to direct, I durst not rely on so dangerous a decision, in so critical a juncture, and against such powerful enemies. Once I was strongly bent upon resistance, for while I had liberty, the whole strength of that empire could hardly subdue me, and I might easily with stones pelt the metropolis to pieces; but I soon rejected that project with horror, by remembering the oath I had made to the Emperor, the favors I received from him, and the high title of *Nardac* he conferred upon me. Neither had I so soon learned the gratitude of courtiers, to persuade myself that his Majesty's present severities acquitted me of all past obligations.

At last I fixed upon a resolution, for which it is probable I may incur some censure, and not unjustly; for I confess I owe the preserving my eyes, and consequently my liberty, to my own great rashness and want of experience: because if I had then known the nature of princes and ministers, which I have since observed in many other courts, and their methods of treating criminals less obnoxious than myself, I should with great alacrity and readiness have submitted to so easy a punishment. But hurried on by the precipitancy of youth, and having his Imperial Majesty's licence to pay my attendance upon the Emperor of Blefuscu, I took this opportunity, before the three days were elapsed, to send a letter to my friend the Secretary, signifying my resolution of setting out that morning for Blefuscu pursuant to the leave I had got; and without waiting for an answer, I went to that side of the island where our fleet lay. I seized a large man of war, tied a cable to the prow, and, lifting up the anchors, I stripped myself, put my clothes (together with my coverlet, which I brought under my arm) into the vessel, and drawing it after me between wading and swimming, arrived at the royal port of Blefuscu, where the people had long expected me: they lent me two guides to direct me to the capital city, which is of the same name. I held them in my hands till I came within two hundred yards of the gate, and desired them to signify my arrival to one of the secretaries, and let him know, I there waited his Majesty's command. I had an answer in about an hour, that his Majesty, attended by the Royal Family, and great officers of the court, was coming out to receive me. I advanced a hundred yards. The Emperor and his train alighted from their horses, the Empress and ladies from their coaches, and I did not perceive they were in any fright or concern. I lay on the ground to kiss his Majesty's and the Empress's hands. I told his Majesty, that I was come according to my promise, and with the license of the Emperor my master, to have the honor of seeing so mighty a monarch, and to offer him any service in my power, consistent with my duty to my own prince; not mentioning a word of my disgrace, because I had hitherto no regular information of it, and might suppose myself wholly ignorant of any such design; neither could I reasonably conceive that the Emperor would discover the secret while I was out of his power: wherein, however, it soon appeared I was deceived.

I shall not trouble the reader with the particular account of my reception at this court, which was suitable to the generosity of so great a prince; nor of the difficulties I was in for want of a house and bed, being forced to lie on the ground, wrapped up in my coverlet.

CHAPTER VIII

The Author, by a Lucky Accident, Finds Means to Leave Blefuscu: *and, after Some Difficulties, Returns Safe to His Native Country.*

THREE days after my arrival, walking out of curiosity to the north-east coast of the island, I observed, about half a league off, in the sea, somewhat that looked like a boat overturned. I pulled off my shoes and stockings, and wading two or three hundred yards, I found the object to approach nearer by force of the tide; and then plainly saw it to be a real boat, which I suppose might, by some tempest, have been driven from a ship; whereupon I returned immediately towards the city, and desired his Imperial Majesty to lend me twenty of the tallest vessels he had left after the loss of his fleet, and three thousand seamen under the command of his Vice-Admiral. This fleet sailed round, while I went back the shortest way to the coast where I first discovered the boat; I found the tide had driven it still nearer. The seamen were all provided with cordage, which I had beforehand twisted to a sufficient strength. When the ships came up, I stripped myself, and waded till I came within an hundred yards of the boat, after which I was forced to swim till I got up to it. The seamen threw me the end of the cord, which I fastened to a hole in the fore-part of the boat, and the other end to a man of war; but I found all my labor to little purpose; for being out of my depth, I was not able to work. In this necessity, I was forced to swim behind, and push the boat forwards as often as I could, with one of my hands; and the tide favoring me, I advanced so far, that I could just hold up my chin and feel the ground. I rested two or three minutes, and then gave the boat another shove, and so on till the sea was no higher than my arm-pits; and now the most laborious part being over, I took out 5 my other cables, which were stowed in one of the ships, and fastening them first to the boat, and then to nine of the vessels which attended me; the wind being favorable, the seamen towed, and I shoved till we arrived 10 within forty yards of the shore; and waiting till the tide was out, I got dry to the boat, and by the assistance of two thousand men, with ropes and engines, I made a shift to turn it on its bottom, and found it was but 15 little damaged.

I shall not trouble the reader with the difficulties I was under by the help of certain paddles, which cost me ten days making, to get my boat to the royal port of Blefuscu, 20 where a mighty concourse of people appeared upon my arrival, full of wonder at the sight of so prodigious a vessel. I told the Emperor that my good fortune had thrown this boat in my way, to carry me to 25 some place from whence I might return into my native country, and begged his Majesty's orders for getting materials to fit it up, together with his license to depart; which, after some kind of expostulations, he was pleased 30 to grant.

I did very much wonder, in all this time, not to have heard of any express relating to me from our Emperor to the court of Blefuscu. But I was afterwards given privately 35 to understand, that his Imperial Majesty, never imagining I had the least notice of his designs, believed I was only gone to Blefuscu in performance of my promise, according to the license he had given me, which 40 was well known at our court, and would return in a few days when that ceremony was ended. But he was at last in pain at my long absence; and after consulting with the Treasurer, and the rest of that cabal, a per- 45 son of quality was dispatched with a copy of the articles against me. This envoy had instructions to represent to the monarch of Blefuscu, the great lenity of his master, who was content to punish me no farther than 50 with the loss of my eyes; that I had fled from justice, and if I did not return in two hours, I should be deprived of my title of *Nardac,* and declared a traitor. The envoy further added, that in order to maintain the peace and amity between both empires, his 5 master expected that his brother of Blefuscu would give orders to have me sent back to Lilliput, bound hand and foot, to be punished as a traitor.

The Emperor of Blefuscu having taken 10 three days to consult, returned an answer consisting of many civilities and excuses. He said, that as for sending me bound, his brother knew it was impossible; that although I had deprived him of his fleet, yet 15 he owed great obligations to me for many good offices I had done him in making the peace. That, however, both their Majesties would soon be made easy; for I had found a prodigious vessel on the shore, able to 20 carry me on the sea, which he had given order to fit up with my own assistance and direction and he hoped in a few weeks both empires would be freed from so insupportable an incumbrance.

25 With this answer the envoy returned to Lilliput, and the monarch of Blefuscu related to me all that had passed; offering me at the same time (but under the strictest confidence) his gracious protection, if I 30 would continue in his service; wherein although I believed him sincere, yet I resolved never more to put any confidence in princes or ministers, where I could possibly avoid it; and therefore, with all due acknowl- 35 edgments for his favorable intentions, I humbly begged to be excused. I told him, that since fortune, whether good or evil, had thrown a vessel in my way, I was resolved to venture myself in the ocean, rather than be 40 an occasion of difference between two such mighty monarchs. Neither did I find the Emperor at all displeased; and I discovered by a certain accident, that he was very glad of my resolution, and so were most of his 45 ministers.

These considerations moved me to hasten my departure somewhat sooner than I intended; to which the court, impatient to have me gone, very readily contributed. Five 50 hundred workmen were employed to make two sails to my boat, according to my directions, by quilting thirteen fold of their strongest linen together. I was at the pains of making ropes and cables, by twisting ten, twenty, or thirty of the thickest and strongest of theirs. A great stone that I happened to find, after a long search, by the sea-shore, served me for an anchor. I had the tallow of three hundred cows for greasing my boat, and other uses. I was at incredible pains in cutting down some of the largest timber-trees for oars and masts, wherein I was, however, much assisted by his Majesty's ship-carpenters, who helped me in smoothing them, after I had done the rough work.

In about a month, when all was prepared, I sent to receive his Majesty's commands, and take my leave. The Emperor and Royal Family came out of the palace; I lay down on my face to kiss his hand, which he very graciously gave me: so did the Empress and young Princes of the blood. His Majesty presented me with fifty purses of two hundred *sprugs* apiece, together with his picture at full length, which I put immediately into one of my gloves, to keep it from being hurt. The ceremonies at my departure were too many to trouble the reader with at this time.

I stored the boat with the carcasses of an hundred oxen, and three hundred sheep, with bread and drink proportionable, and as much meat ready dressed as four hundred cooks could provide. I took with me six cows and two bulls alive, with as many ewes and rams, intending to carry them into my own country, and propagate the breed. And to feed them on board, I had a good bundle of hay, and a bag of corn. I would gladly have taken a dozen of the natives, but this was a thing the Emperor would by no means permit; and besides a diligent search into my pockets, his Majesty engaged my honor not to carry away any of his subjects, although with their own consent and desire.

Having thus prepared all things as well as I was able, I set sail on the twenty-fourth day of September, 1701, at six in the morning; and when I had gone about four leagues to the northward, the wind being at southeast, at six in the evening I descried a small island about half a league to the north-west. I advanced forward, and cast anchor on the lee-side of the island, which seemed to be uninhabited. I then took some refreshment, and went to my rest. I slept well, and as I conjectured at least six hours, for I found the day broke in two hours after I awaked. It was a clear night. I ate my breakfast before the sun was up; and heaving anchor, the wind being favorable, I steered the same course that I had done the day before, wherein I was directed by my pocket-compass. My intention was to reach, if possible, one of those islands, which I had reason to believe lay to the north-east of Van Diemen's Land. I discovered nothing all that day; but upon the next, about three in the afternoon, when I had by my computation made twenty-four leagues from Blefuscu, I descried a sail steering to the south-east; my course was due east. I hailed her, but could get no answer; yet I found I gained upon her, for the wind slackened. I made all the sail I could, and in half an hour she spied me, then hung out her ancient, and discharged a gun. It is not easy to express the joy I was in upon the unexpected hope of once more seeing my beloved country, and the dear pledges I had left in it. The ship slackened her sails, and I came up with her between five and six in the evening, September 26; but my heart leaped within me to see her English colors. I put my cows and sheep into my coat-pockets, and got on board with all my little cargo of provisions. The vessel was an English merchantman returning from Japan by the North and South Seas; the Captain, Mr. John Biddel of Deptford, a very civil man, and an excellent sailor. We were now in the latitude of 30 degrees south; there were about fifty men in the ship; and here I met an old comrade of mine, one Peter Williams, who gave me a good character to the Captain. This gentleman treated me with kindness, and desired I would let him know what place I came from last, and whither I was bound; which I did in a few words, but he thought I was raving, and that the dangers I underwent had disturbed my head; whereupon I took my black cattle and sheep out of my pocket, which, after great astonishment, clearly convinced him of my veracity. I then showed him the gold given me by the Emperor of Blefuscu, together with his Majesty's picture at full length, and some other rarities of that country. I gave him two purses of two hundred *sprugs* each, and promised, when we arrived in England, to make him a present of a cow and a sheep big with young.

I shall not trouble the reader with a particular account of this voyage, which was very prosperous for the most part. We arrived in the Downs on the 13th of April, 1702. I had only one misfortune, that the rats on board carried away one of my sheep; I found her bones in a hole, picked clean from the flesh. The rest of my cattle I got safe on shore, and set them a grazing in a bowling-green at Greenwich, where the fineness of the grass made them feed very heartily, though I had always feared the contrary: neither could I possibly have preserved them in so long a voyage, if the Captain had not allowed me some of his best biscuit, which, rubbed to powder, and mingled with water, was their constant food. The short time I continued in England, I made a considerable profit by showing my cattle to many persons of quality, and others: and before I began my second voyage, I sold them for six hundred pounds. Since my last return, I find the breed is considerably increased, especially the sheep; which I hope will prove much to the advantage of the woolen manufacture, by the fineness of the fleeces.

I stayed but two months with my wife and family; for my insatiable desire of seeing foreign countries would suffer me to continue no longer. I left fifteen hundred pounds with my wife, and fixed her in a good house at Redriff. My remaining stock I carried with me, part in money, and part in goods, in hopes to improve my fortunes. My eldest uncle John had left me an estate in land, near Epping, of about thirty pounds a year; and I had a long lease of the Black Bull in Fetter-Lane, which yielded me as much more; so that I was not in any danger of leaving my family upon the parish. My son Johnny, named so after his uncle, was at the Grammar School, and a towardly child. My daughter Betty (who is now well married, and has children) was then at her needle-work. I took leave of my wife, and boy and girl, with tears on both sides, and went on board the *Adventure*, a merchant-ship of three hundred tons, bound for Surat, Captain John Nicholas, of Liverpool, Commander. But my account of this voyage must be referred to the second part of my Travels.

A DESCRIPTION OF A CITY SHOWER

(OCTOBER, 1710)

Careful observers may foretell the hour,
(By sure prognostics) when to dread a show'r.
While rain depends, the pensive cat gives o'er
Her frolics, and pursues her tail no more. 4
Returning home at night, you'll find the sink
Strike your offended sense with double stink.
If you be wise, then, go not far to dine:
You'll spend in coach-hire more than save in wine.
A coming show'r your shooting corns presage,
Old achés throb, your hollow tooth will rage.
Saunt'ring in coffeehouse is Dulman seen; 11
He damns the climate, and complains of spleen.

Meanwhile the South, rising with dabbled wings,
A sable cloud athwart the welkin flings,
That swill'd more liquor than it could contain, 15
And, like a drunkard, gives it up again.
Brisk Susan whips her linen from the rope,
While the first drizzling show'r is borne aslope;
Such is that sprinkling which some careless quean
Flirts on you from her mop, but not so clean: 20
You fly, invoke the gods; then, turning, stop
To rail; she singing, still whirls on her mop.
Not yet the dust had shunn'd th'unequal strife,
But, aided by the wind, fought still for life,
And wafted with its foe by violent gust, 25
'Twas doubtful which was rain, and which was dust.
Ah! where must needy poet seek for aid,
When dust and rain at once his coat invade?
His only coat, where dust confused with rain,
Roughen the nap, and leave a mingled stain.
Now in contiguous drops the flood comes down, 31
Threat'ning with deluge this *devoted* town.

To shops in crowds the daggled females fly,
Pretend to cheapen goods, but nothing buy.
The Templar[1] spruce, while every spout's abroach, 35
Stays till 'tis fair, yet seems to call a coach.
The tucked-up sempstress walks with hasty strides,
While streams run down her oiled umbrella's sides. 38
Here various kinds, by various fortunes led,
Commence acquaintance underneath a shed.
Triumphant Tories, and desponding Whigs,
Forget their feuds, and join to save their wigs.
Boxed in a chair the beau impatient sits,
While spouts run clattering o'er the roof by fits,
And ever and anon with frightful din 45
The leather sounds; he trembles from within.
So when Troy chairmen bore the wooden steed,
Pregnant with Greeks impatient to be freed,
(Those bully Greeks, who, as the moderns do,
Instead of paying chairmen, run them through) 50
Laoco'n struck the outside with his spear,
And each imprisoned hero quaked for fear.
Now from all parts the swelling kennels[2] flow,
And bear their trophies with them as they go:
Filth of all hues and odors, seem to tell 55
What street they sailed from, by their sight and smell.
They, as each torrent drives with rapid force,
From Smithfield or St. Pulchre's shape their course,
And in huge confluent join at Snowhill ridge,
Fall from the conduit prone to Holborn bridge. 60
Sweepings from butchers' stalls, dung, guts, and blood,
Drowned puppies, stinking sprats, all drenched in mud,
Dead cats, and turnip-tops, come tumbling down the flood.

[1]Legal student, attending one of the London Inns of Court which occupied land once belonging to the Knights Templars.

[2]Gutters.

ON THE DAY OF JUDGMENT

With a whirl of thought oppressed,
I sink from reverie to rest.
An horrid vision seized my head;
I saw the graves give up their dead!
Jove, armed with terrors, burst the skies, 5
And thunder roars and lightning flies!
Amazed, confused, its fate unknown,
The world stands trembling at his throne!
While each pale sinner hangs his head,
Jove, nodding, shook the heav'ns, and said: 10
"Offending race of human kind,
By nature, reason, learning, blind;
You who, through frailty, stepped aside;
And you, who never fell—*through pride:*
You who in different sects were shammed, 15
And come to see each other damned;
(So some folks told you, but they knew
No more of Jove's designs than you;)
The world's mad business now is o'er,
And I resent these pranks no more. 20
I to such blockheads set my wit!
I damn such fools!—Go, go, you're bit."

ALEXANDER POPE

1688–1744

What Dryden was in the latter part of the seventeenth century Pope became in the first half of the eighteenth—the foremost man of letters of the age and the acknowledged arbiter of literary taste. He was born in the year of the Revolution, on 21 May. His father was a London merchant and a Roman Catholic. The latter fact colored Pope's whole life, because for many years after the Revolution Catholics suffered oppressive disabilities, both social and legal, which marked them as a class apart from the rest of the nation and almost forced them to live in an atmosphere of suspicion, intrigue, and evasion of the law. Among other things, they were debarred from the universities, they were burdened with heavy taxes, and they could hold no public offices. Pope, moreover, always refused to change his religion, although the heaviest inducements were held before him from time to time, and although, too, his adherence to Catholicism was merely formal, the result rather of filial piety than of personal conviction. It is doubtful, however, if Pope would have been able to attend one of the universities, even had his parents been Church-of-England people, for from his birth he was deformed and delicate in health. In his *Epistle to Arbuthnot* he called his life one long disease, which was scarcely an exaggeration; there must have been hardly a day when he was free from pain, and his face was lined and contorted from his intense sufferings. His education was largely got through his own eager and wide reading in classical and English poetry, with the result that his scholarship always remained seriously defective and that he had no methodical training save such as was administered by his father in the correction of his youthful verses. He was a precocious boy, and determined at an early age to be a poet. At an early age, too, he succeeded in attracting the interest of several men of taste and cultivation, at least one of whom, William Walsh, deserves to be mentioned in any account of Pope. For "knowing Walsh," whether he exerted a decisive influence or not, marked out precisely the direction in which Pope was to travel. "He used to encourage me much," Pope in later years wrote to a friend, "and used to tell me there was one way left of excelling: for though we had several great poets, we never had any one great poet that was *correct;* and he desired me to make that my study and aim." Pope did so; and in correctness of form, in clarity, pointed wit, polish, studied concision, smoothness, and metrical precision, Pope excelled remarkably, as is witnessed, for example, by the number of familiar sayings he has given to the English-speaking world, and as no one who reads more than a few pages of his poetry needs to be told.

Pope's *Pastorals* were his first published poems, printed in 1709, but written, as he always claimed, when he was only sixteen years old. They were followed by his *Essay on Criticism* in 1711 and by his *Rape of the Lock,* in its earlier form, in 1712. These poems made his reputation immediately, placing him by general consent at the head of living poets. He was not, however, too well off and could not expect, on account of his Catholicism, either public office or a pension, the usual rewards bestowed on successful and useful men of letters by the government in his day. Consequently Pope had to find some new way of securing an income, and he found it. In 1713 he issued proposals for a translation of the *Iliad,* inviting immediate subscriptions in support of the project. Warm friends helped him with enthusiasm to secure subscriptions, a publisher offered him a large sum for the right of publication, and, as the combined result of his reputation and of his persistent hard work with the translation, Pope managed to clear over £5000 on the work, and later made another large sum when, with the help of assistants, he translated the *Odyssey.* Such profits from literary work were unprecedented, and they were sufficient to enable him to buy a country house with a small estate at Twickenham and to live there comfortably through the remainder of his life, independent of private patronage or the favor of public men.

The *Essay on Criticism,* though didactic in character, had shown Pope's gift as a satirist, and his greatest success came in that field, particularly in the *Dunciad* and in the poems collected under the title, *Satires and Epistles.* His satire was never, like Dryden's, political; and though in *The Rape of the Lock* his ridicule was general, he chiefly devoted himself to personal attacks. In this he was biting, even venomous, and he has often been blamed for the number and virulence of his enmities, for his spitefulness, and for his treachery. It cannot be pretended that Pope's character had many edifying qualities; yet no one who has not read widely in the literature of the early eighteenth century can know the extent and kind of provocation he had for his angry retorts. And despite all blemishes and all limitations he remains an arresting figure in his own right, besides embodying more completely than any of his contemporaries the classicism of his age.

The Works of Alexander Pope are edited by John W. Croker, Whitwell Elwin, and William J. Courthope (London, 1871–1879); *The Best of Pope* (New York, 1929) is a convenient volume of selections, carefully edited by George Sherburn. George Sherburn is also the author of a standard work on *The Early Career of Alexander Pope* (Oxford, 1934). Edith Sitwell's *Alexander Pope* (New York, 1930) is one of the most notable of recent attempts to rehabilitate the poet's reputation; but more sober and effectual efforts have been made in this direction by Austin Warren in *Alexander Pope as Critic and Humanist* (Princeton, 1929) and by Geoffrey Tillotson in *On the Poetry of Pope* (Oxford, 1938).

ODE ON SOLITUDE[1]

Happy the man whose wish and care
  A few paternal acres bound,
Content to breathe his native air
    In his own ground.

Whose herds with milk, whose fields with bread, 5
  Whose flocks supply him with attire,
Whose trees in summer yield him shade,
    In winter fire.

Bless'd, who can unconcern'dly find
  Hours, days, and years slide soft away, 10
In health of body, peace of mind,
    Quiet by day,

Sound sleep by night; study and ease
  Together mixed; sweet recreation;
And Innocence, which most does please, 15
    With meditation.

Thus let me live, unseen, unknown,
  Thus unlamented let me die;
Steal from the world, and not a stone
    Tell where I lie. 20

AN ESSAY ON CRITICISM[2]

CONTENTS

PART I

Introduction. That 'tis as great a fault to judge ill, as to write ill, and a more dangerous one to the public, v. 1. That a true Taste is as rare to be found, as a true Genius, v. 9 to 18. That most men are born with some Taste, but spoiled by false Education, v. 19 to 25. The multitude of Critics, and causes of them, v. 26 to 45. That we are to study our own Taste, and know the Limits of it, v. 46 to 67. Nature the best guide of Judgment, v. 68 to 87. Improved by Art and Rules, which are but methodized Nature, 88. Rules derived from the Practice of the Ancient Poets, *v. id.* to 110. That therefore the Ancients are necessary to be studied, by a Critic, particularly Homer and Virgil, v. 120 to 138. Of Licenses, and the use of them by the Ancients, v. 140 to 180. Reverence due to the Ancients, and praise of them, v. 181, *etc.*

PART II. VER. 201, *etc.*

Causes hindering a true Judgment. 1. Pride, v. 208. 2. Imperfect Learning, v. 215. 3. Judging by parts, and not by the whole, v. 233 to 288. Critics in Wit, Language, Versification,

[1]According to Pope himself this poem was written when he was only twelve years old, in 1700. Pope's statements about the dates of his earlier works are unreliable, and it seems unlikely that this one can be true. In any case, however, this is in all probability the earliest poem by Pope which has been preserved.

[2]Pope began to write the *Essay* perhaps as early as 1707. It was finished in 1709, and published in 1711.

only, v. 288, 305, 399, *etc.* 4. Being too hard to please, or too apt to admire, v. 384. 5. Partiality—too much Love to a Sect—to the Ancients or Moderns, v. 394. 6. Prejudice or Prevention, v. 408. 7. Singularity, v. 424. 8. Inconstancy, v. 430. 9. Party Spirit, v. 452, *etc.* 10. Envy, v. 466. Against Envy, and in praise of Good-nature, v. 508, *etc.* When Severity is chiefly to be used by Critics, v. 526, *etc.*

PART III. VER. 560, *etc.*

Rules for the Conduct of Manners in a Critic. 1. Candor, v. 563. Modesty, v. 566. Good-breeding, v. 572. Sincerity, and Freedom of advice, v. 578. 2. When one's Counsel is to be restrained, v. 584. Character of an incorrigible Poet, v. 600. And of an impertinent Critic, v. 610, *etc.* Character of a good Critic, v. 629. The History of Criticism, and Characters of the best Critics, Aristotle, v. 645. Horace, v. 653. Dionysius, v. 665. Petronius, v. 667. Quintilian, v. 670. Longinus, v. 675. Of the Decay of Criticism, and its Revival. Erasmus, v. 693. Vida, v. 705. Boileau, v. 714. Lord Roscommon, *etc.*, v. 725. Conclusion.

PART I

'Tis hard to say, if greater want of skill
Appear in writing or in judging ill;
But, of the two, less dang'rous is th' offense
To tire our patience, than mislead our sense.
Some few in that, but numbers err in this, 5
Ten censure wrong for one who writes amiss;
A fool might once himself alone expose,
Now one in verse makes many more in prose.
'Tis with our judgments as our watches, none
Go just alike, yet each believes his own. 10
In Poets as true genius is but rare,
True Taste as seldom is the Critic's share;
Both must alike from Heav'n derive their light,
These born to judge, as well as those to write.
Let such teach others who themselves excel,
And censure freely who have written well. 16
Authors are partial to their wit, 'tis true,
But are not Critics to their judgment too?
Yet if we look more closely, we shall find
Most have the seeds of judgment in their mind: 20
Nature affords at least a glimm'ring light;
The lines, though touched but faintly, are drawn right.
But as the slightest sketch, if justly traced,
Is by ill-coloring but the more disgraced, 24
So by false learning is good sense defaced:
Some are bewildered in the maze of schools,
And some made coxcombs Nature meant but fools.
In search of wit these lose their common sense,
And then turn Critics in their own defense:
Each burns alike, who can, or cannot write, 30
Or with a Rival's, or an Eunuch's spite.
All fools have still an itching to deride,
And fain would be upon the laughing side.
If Maevius[3] scribble in Apollo's spite,
There are who judge still worse than he can write. 35
Some have at first for Wits, then Poets passed,
Turned Critics next, and proved plain fools at last.
Some neither can for Wits nor Critics pass,
As heavy mules are neither horse nor ass.
Those half-learn'd witlings, num'rous in our isle, 40
As half-formed insects on the banks of Nile;
Unfinished things, one knows not what to call,
Their generation's so equivocal:
To tell 'em, would a hundred tongues require,
Or one vain wit's, that might a hundred tire.
But you who seek to give and merit fame,
And justly bear a Critic's noble name, 47
Be sure yourself and your own reach to know,
How far your genius, taste, and learning go;
Launch not beyond your depth, but be discreet, 50
And mark that point where sense and dullness meet.
Nature to all things fixed the limits fit,
And wisely curbed proud man's pretending wit.
As on the land while here the ocean gains,
In other parts it leaves wide sandy plains; 55
Thus in the soul while memory prevails,
The solid pow'r of understanding fails;
Where beams of warm imagination play,
The memory's soft figures melt away.
One science only will one genius fit; 60
So vast is art, so narrow human wit:
Not only bounded to peculiar arts,
But oft in those confined to single parts.
Like kings we lose the conquests gained before,
By vain ambition still to make them more; 65
Each might his sev'ral province well command,
Would all but stoop to what they understand.

[3]A Roman poet of no ability, whose name has been preserved by Virgil and Horace.

First follow Nature, and your judgment frame
By her just standard, which is still the same:
Unerring Nature, still divinely bright, 70
One clear, unchanged, and universal light,
Life, force, and beauty, must to all impart,
At once the source, and end, and test of Art.
Art from that fund each just supply provides,
Works without show, and without pomp presides: 75
In some fair body thus th' informing soul
With spirits feeds, with vigor fills the whole,
Each motion guides, and ev'ry nerve sustains;
Itself unseen, but in th' effects, remains.
Some, to whom Heav'n in wit has been profuse, 80
Want as much more, to turn it to its use;
For wit and judgment often are at strife,
Though meant each other's aid, like man and wife.
'Tis more to guide, than spur the Muse's steed;
Restrain his fury, than provoke his speed; 85
The wingéd courser, like a gen'rous horse,
Shows most true mettle when you check his course.
Those Rules of old discovered, not devised,
Are Nature still, but Nature methodized;
Nature, like liberty, is but restrained 90
By the same laws which first herself ordained.
Hear how learn'd Greece her useful rules indites,
When to repress, and when indulge our flights:
High on Parnassus' top her sons she showed,
And pointed out those arduous paths they trod; 95
Held from afar, aloft, th' immortal prize,
And urged the rest by equal steps to rise.
Just precepts thus from great examples giv'n,
She drew from them what they derived from Heav'n.
The gen'rous Critic fanned the Poet's fire, 100
And taught the world with reason to admire.
Then Criticism the Muse's handmaid proved,
To dress her charms, and make her more beloved:
But following wits from that intention strayed,
Who could not win the mistress, wooed the maid; 105
Against the Poets their own arms they turned,
Sure to hate most the men from whom they learned.
So modern 'Pothecaries, taught the art
By Doctors' bills to play the Doctor's part,
Bold in the practice of mistaken rules, 110
Prescribe, apply, and call their masters fools.
Some on the leaves of ancient authors prey,
Nor time nor moths e'er spoiled so much as they.
Some dryly plain, without invention's aid, 114
Write dull receipts how poems may be made.
These leave the sense, their learning to display,
And those explain the meaning quite away.
You then whose judgment the right course would steer,
Know well each Ancient's proper character;
His fable,[4] subject, scope in ev'ry page; 120
Religion, Country, genius of his Age:
Without all these at once before your eyes,
Cavil you may, but never criticize.
Be Homer's works your study and delight,
Read them by day, and meditate by night; 125
Thence form your judgment, thence your maxims bring,
And trace the Muses upward to their spring.
Still with itself compared, his text peruse;
And let your comment be the Mantuan Muse.[5]
When first young Maro[5] in his boundless mind 130
A work t' outlast immortal Rome designed,
Perhaps he seemed above the critic's law,
And but from Nature's fountains scorned to draw:
But when t' examine every part he came, 134
Nature and Homer were, he found, the same.
Convinced, amazed, he checks the bold design;
And rules as strict his labored work confine,
As if the Stagirite[6] o'erlooked each line.
Learn hence for ancient rules a just esteem;
To copy nature is to copy them. 140
Some beauties yet no Precepts can declare,
For there's a happiness as well as care.
Music resembles Poetry, in each
Are nameless graces which no methods teach,
And which a master-hand alone can reach.
If, where the rules not far enough extend 146
(Since rules were made but to promote their end),
Some lucky License answer to the full
Th' intent proposed, that License is a rule.
Thus Pegasus, a nearer way to take, 150
May boldly deviate from the common track;
From vulgar bounds with brave disorder part,

[4] Story. [5] Virgil. [6] Aristotle.

And snatch a grace beyond the reach of art,
Which without passing through the judgment, gains
The heart, and all its end at once attains. 155
In prospects thus, some objects please our eyes,
Which out of nature's common order rise,
The shapeless rock, or hanging precipice.
Great wits sometimes may gloriously offend,
And rise to faults true Critics dare not mend.
But though the Ancients thus their rules invade 161
(As Kings dispense with laws themselves have made),
Moderns, beware! or if you must offend
Against the precept, ne'er transgress its End;
Let it be seldom, and compelled by need; 165
And have, at least, their precedent to plead.
The Critic else proceeds without remorse,
Seizes your fame, and puts his laws in force.
I know there are, to whose presumptuous thoughts
Those freer beauties, e'en in them, seem faults. 170
Some figures monstrous and mis-shaped appear,
Considered singly, or beheld too near,
Which, but proportioned to their light, or place,
Due distance reconciles to form and grace.
A prudent chief not always must display 175
His powers in equal ranks, and fair array.
But with th' occasion and the place comply,
Conceal his force, nay seem sometimes to fly.
Those oft are stratagems which error seem,
Nor is it Homer nods, but we that dream. 180
Still green with bays each ancient Altar stands,
Above the reach of sacrilegious hands;
Secure from Flames, from Envy's fiercer rage,
Destructive War, and all-involving Age.
See, from each clime the learn'd their incense bring! 185
Hear, in all tongues consenting paeans ring!
In praise so just let ev'ry voice be joined,
And fill the gen'ral chorus of mankind.
Hail, Bards triumphant! born in happier days;
Immortal heirs of universal praise! 190
Whose honors with increase of ages grow,
As streams roll down, enlarging as they flow;
Nations unborn your mighty names shall sound,
And worlds applaud that must not yet be found!
Oh may some spark of your celestial fire, 195
The last, the meanest of your sons inspire
(That on weak wings, from far, pursues your flights;
Glows while he reads, but trembles as he writes),
To teach vain Wits a science little known,
T' admire superior sense, and doubt their own! 200

PART II

Of all the Causes which conspire to blind
Man's erring judgment, and misguide the mind,
What the weak head with strongest bias rules,
Is Pride, the never-failing voice of fools.
Whatever nature has in worth denied, 205
She gives in large recruits of needful pride;
For as in bodies, thus in souls, we find
What wants in blood and spirits, swelled with wind:
Pride, where wit fails, steps in to our defense,
And fills up all the mighty Void of sense. 210
If once right reason drives that cloud away,
Truth breaks upon us with resistless day.
Trust not yourself; but your defects to know,
Make use of ev'ry friend—and ev'ry foe.
A little learning is a dang'rous thing; 215
Drink deep, or taste not the Pierian spring.[7]
There shallow draughts intoxicate the brain,
And drinking largely sobers us again.
Fired at first sight with what the Muse imparts,
In fearless youth we tempt the heights of Arts, 220
While from the bounded level of our mind
Short views we take, nor see the lengths behind;
But more advanced, behold with strange surprise
New distant scenes of endless science rise!
So pleased at first the tow'ring Alps we try,
Mount o'er the vales, and seem to tread the sky, 226
Th' eternal snows appear already past,
And the first clouds and mountains seem the last;
But, those attained, we tremble to survey
The growing labors of the lengthened way,
Th' increasing prospect tires our wand'ring eyes, 231
Hills peep o'er hills, and Alps on Alps arise!
A perfect Judge will read each work of Wit

[7]Pieria was said to be the birthplace of the muses.

With the same spirit that its author writ:
Survey the Whole, nor seek slight faults to find 235
Where nature moves, and rapture warms the mind;
Nor lose, for that malignant dull delight,
The gen'rous pleasure to be charmed with Wit.
But in such lays as neither ebb, nor flow,
Correctly cold, and regularly low, 240
That, shunning faults, one quiet tenor keep,
We cannot blame indeed—but we may sleep.
In wit, as nature, what affects our hearts
Is not th' exactness of peculiar parts;
'Tis not a lip, or eye, we beauty call, 245
But the joint force and full result of all.
Thus when we view some well-proportioned dome
(The world's just wonder, and e'en thine, O Rome![8]),
No single parts unequally surprise,
All comes united to th' admiring eyes; 250
No monstrous height, or breadth, or length appear;
The Whole at once is bold and regular.
Whoever thinks a faultless piece to see,
Thinks what ne'er was, nor is, nor e'er shall be.
In every work regard the writer's End, 255
Since none can compass more than they intend;
And if the means be just, the conduct true,
Applause, in spite of trivial faults, is due;
As men of breeding, sometimes men of wit,
T' avoid great errors, must the less commit:
Neglect the rules each verbal Critic lays, 261
For not to know some trifles is a praise.
Most Critics, fond of some subservient art,
Still make the Whole depend upon a Part:
They talk of principles, but notions prize, 265
And all to one loved Folly sacrifice.
Once on a time, La Mancha's Knight,[9] they say,
A certain bard encount'ring on the way,
Discoursed in terms as just, with looks as sage,
As e'er could Dennis[10] of the Grecian stage;
Concluding all were desp'rate sots and fools,
Who durst depart from Aristotle's rules. 272
Our Author, happy in a judge so nice,
Produced his Play, and begged the Knight's advice;
Made him observe the subject, and the plot,
The manners, passions, unities; what not? 276

[8]St. Peter's. [9]Don Quixote.

[10]John Dennis, critic and playwright contemporary with Pope.

All which, exact to rule, were brought about,
Were but a Combat in the lists left out.
"What! leave the Combat out?" exclaims the Knight;
Yes, or we must renounce the Stagirite. 280
"Not so, by Heav'n" (he answers in a rage),
"Knights, squires, and steeds, must enter on the stage."
So vast a throng the stage can ne'er contain.
"Then build a new, or act it in a plain."
Thus Critics, of less judgment than caprice, 285
Curious, not knowing, not exact but nice,
Form short Ideas; and offend in arts
(As most in manners) by a love to parts.
Some to Conceit alone their taste confine,
And glitt'ring thoughts struck out at ev'ry line; 290
Pleased with a work where nothing 's just or fit;
One glaring Chaos and wild heap of wit.
Poets like painters, thus, unskilled to trace
The naked nature and the living grace,
With gold and jewels cover ev'ry part, 295
And hide with ornaments their want of art.
True Wit is Nature to advantage dressed,
What oft was thought, but ne'er so well expressed;
Something, whose truth convinced at sight we find,
That gives us back the image of our mind. 300
As shades more sweetly recommend the light,
So modest plainness sets off sprightly wit.
For works may have more wit than does 'em good,
As bodies perish through excess of blood.
Others for Language all their care express, 305
And value books, as women men, for Dress:
Their praise is still—the Style is excellent:
The Sense, they humbly take upon content.
Words are like leaves; and where they most abound, 309
Much fruit of sense beneath is rarely found,
False Eloquence, like the prismatic glass,
Its gaudy colors spreads on ev'ry place;
The face of Nature we no more survey,
All glares alike, without distinction gay:
But true expression, like th' unchanging Sun, 315
Clears and improves whate'er it shines upon,
It gilds all objects, but it alters none.
Expression is the dress of thought, and still
Appears more decent, as more suitable;
A vile conceit in pompous words expressed,

Is like a clown in regal purple dressed: 321
For diff'rent styles with diff'rent subjects sort,
As sev'ral garbs with country, town, and court.
Some by old words to fame have made pretense,
Ancients in phrase, mere moderns in their sense; 325
Such labored nothings, in so strange a style,
Amaze th' unlearn'd, and make the learned smile.
Unlucky, as Fungoso[11] in the play,
These sparks with awkward vanity display
What the fine gentleman wore yesterday;
And but so mimic ancient wits at best, 331
As apes our grandsires, in their doublets dressed.
In words, as fashions, the same rule will hold;
Alike fantastic, if too new, or old:
Be not the first by whom the new are tried, 335
Nor yet the last to lay the old aside.
But most by Numbers judge a Poet's song;
And smooth or rough, with them is right or wrong:
In the bright Muse though thousand charms conspire, 339
Her voice is all these tuneful fools admire;
Who haunt Parnassus but to please their ear,
Not mend their minds; as some to Church repair,
Not for the doctrine, but the music there.
These equal syllables alone require,
Though oft the ear the open vowels tire; 345
While expletives their feeble aid do join;
And ten low words oft creep in one dull line:
While they ring round the same unvaried chimes,
With sure returns of still expected rimes;
Where'er you find "the cooling western breeze," 350
In the next line, it "whispers through the trees";
If crystal streams "with pleasing murmurs creep,"
The reader's threatened (not in vain) with "sleep";
Then, at the last and only couplet fraught
With some unmeaning thing they call a thought, 355
A needless Alexandrine ends the song
That, like a wounded snake, drags its slow length along.

[11]A character in Ben Jonson's *Every Man out of His Humor.*

Leave such to tune their own dull rimes, and know
What's roundly smooth or languishingly slow;
And praise the easy vigor of a line, 360
Where Denham's strength, and Waller's sweetness join.[12]
True ease in writing comes from art, not chance,
As those move easiest who have learned to dance.
'T is not enough no harshness gives offense,
The sound must seem an echo to the sense:
Soft is the strain when Zephyr gently blows,
And the smooth stream in smoother numbers flows; 367
But when loud surges lash the sounding shore,
The hoarse, rough verse should like the torrent roar:
When Ajax strives some rock's vast weight to throw, 370
The line too labors, and the words move slow;
Not so, when swift Camilla scours the plain,
Flies o'er th' unbending corn, and skims along the main.
Hear how Timotheus' varied lays surprise,
And bid alternate passions fall and rise![13] 375
While, at each change, the son of Libyan Jove
Now burns with glory, and then melts with love,
Now his fierce eyes with sparkling fury glow,
Now sighs steal out, and tears begin to flow:
Persians and Greeks like turns of nature found, 380
And the world's victor stood subdued by Sound!
The pow'r of Music all our hearts allow,
And what Timotheus was, is Dryden now.
Avoid Extremes; and shun the fault of such,
Who still are pleased too little or too much.
At ev'ry trifle scorn to take offense, 386
That always shows great pride, or little sense;
Those heads, as stomachs, are not sure the best,
Which nauseate all, and nothing can digest.

[12]Both poets of the mid-seventeenth century, long highly praised as the "fathers" of the plain style and the closed couplet which Dryden developed and Pope perfected.

[13]The reference in these and the following lines is to Dryden's *Alexander's Feast.*

Yet let not each gay Turn thy rapture move;
For fools admire, but men of sense approve:
As things seem large which we through mists descry, 392
Dullness is ever apt to magnify.
Some foreign writers, some our own despise;
The Ancients only, or the Moderns prize. 395
Thus Wit, like Faith, by each man is applied
To one small sect, and all are damned beside.
Meanly they seek the blessing to confine,
And force that sun but on a part to shine, 399
Which not alone the southern wit sublimes,
But ripens spirits in cold northern climes;
Which from the first has shone on ages past,
Enlights the present, and shall warm the last;
Though each may feel increases and decays,
And see now clearer and now darker days. 405
Regard not then if Wit be old or new,
But blame the false, and value still the true.
Some ne'er advance a Judgment of their own,
But catch the spreading notion of the Town;
They reason and conclude by precedent, 410
And own stale nonsense which they ne'er invent.
Some judge of authors' names, not works, and then
Nor praise nor blame the writings, but the men.
Of all this servile herd the worst is he
That in proud dullness joins with Quality, 415
A constant Critic at the great man's board,
To fetch and carry nonsense for my Lord.
What woeful stuff this madrigal would be,
In some starved hackney sonneteer, or me!
But let a Lord once own the happy lines, 420
How the wit brightens! how the style refines!
Before his sacred name flies ev'ry fault,
And each exalted stanza teems with thought!
The Vulgar thus through Imitation err;
As oft the Learn'd by being singular; 425
So much they scorn the crowd, that if the throng
By chance go right, they purposely go wrong;
So Schismatics the plain believers quit,
And are but damned for having too much wit.
Some praise at morning what they blame at night; 430
But always think the last opinion right.
A Muse by these is like a mistress used,
This hour she's idolized, the next abused;
While their weak heads like towns unfortified,
'Twixt sense and nonsense daily change their side. 435
Ask them the cause; they're wiser still, they say;
And still to-morrow's wiser than to-day.
We think our fathers fools, so wise we grow,
Our wiser sons, no doubt, will think us so.
Once School-divines this zealous isle o'erspread; 440
Who knew most Sentences,[14] was deepest read;
Faith, Gospel, all, seemed made to be disputed,
And none had sense enough to be confuted:
Scotists and Thomists,[15] now, in peace remain,
Amidst their kindred cobwebs in Duck-lane.
If Faith itself has different dresses worn, 446
What wonder modes in Wit should take their turn?
Oft', leaving what is natural and fit,
The current folly proves the ready wit;
And authors think their reputation safe, 450
Which lives as long as fools are pleased to laugh.
Some valuing those of their own side or mind,
Still make themselves the measure of mankind:
Fondly we think we honor merit then, 454
When we but praise ourselves in other men.
Parties in Wit attend on those of State,
And public faction doubles private hate.
Pride, Malice, Folly, against Dryden rose,
In various shapes of Parsons, Critics, Beaus;
But sense survived, when merry jests were past; 460
For rising merit will buoy up at last.
Might he return, and bless once more our eyes,
New Blackmores and new Milbourns must arise:[16]
Nay should great Homer lift his awful head,
Zoilus[17] again would start up from the dead.
Envy will merit, as its shade, pursue; 466
But like a shadow, proves the substance true;
For envied Wit, like Sol eclipsed, makes known
Th' opposing body's grossness, not its own,

[14]The reference is to the *Book of Sentences* of Peter Lombard.

[15]Followers of Duns Scotus and St. Thomas Aquinas, scholastic philosophers of the thirteenth century. Duck Lane was a London street where second-hand books were formerly sold.

[16]Blackmore was a physician and a dull poet, Milbourne a clergman; both attacked Dryden.

[17]Greek critic (fourth century, B. C.) who attacked Homer.

When first that sun too powerful beams displays, 470
It draws up vapors which obscure its rays;
But e'en those clouds at last adorn its way,
Reflect new glories, and augment the day.
Be thou the first true merit to befriend; 474
His praise is lost, who stays till all commend.
Short is the date, alas, of modern rimes,
And 't is but just to let them live betimes.
No longer now that golden age appears,
When Patriarch-wits survived a thousand years:
Now length of Fame (our second life) is lost, 480
And bare threescore is all e'en that can boast;
Our sons their fathers' failing language see,
And such as Chaucer is, shall Dryden be.
So when the faithful pencil has designed
Some bright Idea of the master's mind, 485
Where a new world leaps out at his command,
And ready Nature waits upon his hand;
When the ripe colors soften and unite,
And sweetly melt into just shade and light;
When mellowing years their full perfection give, 490
And each bold figure just begins to live,
The treach'rous colors the fair art betray,
And all the bright creation fades away!
Unhappy Wit, like most mistaken things,
Atones not for that envy which it brings. 495
In youth alone its empty praise we boast,
But soon the short-lived vanity is lost:
Like some fair flow'r the early spring supplies,
That gaily blooms, but e'en in blooming dies.
What is this Wit, which must our cares employ? 500
The owner's wife, that other men enjoy;
Then most our trouble still when most admired,
And still the more we give, the more required;
Whose fame with pains we guard, but lose with ease,
Sure some to vex, but never all to please; 505
'Tis what the vicious fear, the virtuous shun,
By fools 'tis hated, and by knaves undone!
If Wit so much from Ign'rance undergo,
Ah, let not Learning too commence its foe!
Of old, those met rewards who could excel,
And such were praised who but endeavored well: 511
Though triumphs were to gen'rals only due,
Crowns were reserved to grace the soldiers too.
Now, they who reach Parnassus' lofty crown,
Employ their pains to spurn some others down; 515
And while self-love each jealous writer rules,
Contending wits become the sport of fools:
But still the worst with most regret commend,
For each ill Author is as bad a Friend.
To what base ends, and by what abject ways,
Are mortals urged through sacred lust of praise! 521
Ah ne'er so dire a thirst of glory boast,
Nor in the Critic let the Man be lost.
Good-nature and good-sense must ever join;
To err is human, to forgive, divine. 525
But if in noble minds some dregs remain
Not yet purged off, of spleen and sour disdain;
Discharge that rage on more provoking crimes,
Nor fear a dearth in these flagitious times.
No pardon vile Obscenity should find, 530
Though wit and art conspire to move your mind;
But Dullness with Obscenity must prove
As shameful sure as Impotence in love.
In the fat age of pleasure, wealth, and ease
Sprung the rank weed, and thrived with large increase: 535
When love was all an easy Monarch's care;[18]
Seldom at council, never in a war:
Jilts ruled the state, and statesmen farces writ;
Nay wits had pensions, and young Lords had wit:
The Fair sate panting at a Courtier's play, 540
And not a Mask[19] went unimproved away:
The modest fan was lifted up no more,
And Virgins smiled at what they blushed before.
The following license of a Foreign reign[20]
Did all the dregs of bold Socinus[21] drain; 545
Then unbelieving priests reformed the nation,
And taught more pleasant methods of salvation;
Where Heav'n's free subjects might their rights dispute,
Lest God himself should seem too absolute:
Pulpits their sacred satire learned to spare, 550
And Vice admired[22] to find a flatt'rer there!
Encouraged thus, Wit's Titans braved the skies,

[18]During the reign of Charles II.

[19]I. e., woman wearing a mask.

[20]The reign of William and Mary.

[21]The name of two Italians of the sixteenth century who revived Arianism and may be regarded as forerunners of modern Unitarianism.

[22]Wondered.

And the press groaned with licensed blasphemies.
These monsters, Critics! with your darts engage,
Here point your thunder, and exhaust your rage! 555
Yet shun their fault, who, scandalously nice,
Will needs mistake an author into vice;
All seems infected that th' infected spy,
As all looks yellow to the jaundiced eye.

PART III

Learn then what Morals Critics ought to show,
For 'tis but half a Judge's task, to know. 560
'Tis not enough, taste, judgment, learning, join;
In all you speak, let truth and candor shine:
That not alone what to your sense is due 564
All may allow; but seek your friendship too.
Be silent always when you doubt your sense;
And speak, though sure, with seeming diffidence:
Some positive, persisting fops we know,
Who, if once wrong, will needs be always so;
But you, with pleasure own your errors past,
And make each day a Critic on the last. 571
'Tis not enough, your counsel still be true;
Blunt truths more mischief than nice falsehoods do;
Men must be taught as if you taught them not,
And things unknown proposed as things forgot. 575
Without Good Breeding, truth is disapproved;
That only makes superior sense beloved.
Be niggards of advice on no pretense;
For the worst avarice is that of sense.
With mean complacence ne'er betray your trust, 580
Nor be so civil as to prove unjust.
Fear not the anger of the wise to raise;
Those best can bear reproof, who merit praise.
'Twere well might critics still this freedom take,
But Appius[23] reddens at each word you speak,
And stares, tremendous, with a threat'ning eye, 586
Like some fierce Tyrant in old tapestry.
Fear most to tax an Honorable fool,
Whose right it is, uncensured, to be dull;
Such, without wit, are Poets when they please, 590
As without learning they can take Degrees.
Leave dang'rous truths to unsuccessful Satires,
And flattery to fulsome Dedicators,
Whom, when they praise, the world believes no more,
Than when they promise to give scribbling o'er. 595
'Tis best sometimes your censure to restrain,
And charitably let the dull be vain:
Your silence there is better than your spite,
For who can rail so long as they can write!
Still humming on, their drowsy course they keep, 600
And lashed so long, like tops, are lashed asleep.
False steps but help them to renew the race,
As, after stumbling, Jades will mend their pace.
What crowds of these, impenitently bold,
In sounds and jingling syllables grown old,
Still run on Poets, in a raging vein, 606
E'en to the dregs and squeezings of the brain,
Strain out the last dull droppings of their sense,
And rime with all the rage of Impotence.
Such shameless Bards we have; and yet 'tis true, 610
There are as mad abandoned Critics too.
The bookful blockhead, ignorantly read,
With loads of learnéd lumber in his head,
With his own tongue still edifies his ears,
And always list'ning to himself appears. 615
All books he reads, and all he reads assails,
From Dryden's Fables down to Durfey's[24] Tales.
With him, most authors steal their works, or buy;
Garth did not write his own Dispensary.[25]
Name a new Play, and he's the Poet's friend,
Nay showed his faults—but when would Poets mend? 621
No place so sacred from such fops is barred,
Nor is Paul's church more safe than Paul's churchyard:
Nay, fly to Altars; there they'll talk you dead:
For Fools rush in where Angels fear to tread. 625

---

[23]I. e., John Dennis. The name was taken from his tragedy, *Appius and Virginia.*

[24]Scurrilous writer (1653–1723).

[25]Samuel Garth's *Dispensary* (1699), a burlesque poem on apothecaries.

Distrustful sense with modest caution speaks,
It still looks home, and short excursions makes;
But rattling nonsense in full volleys breaks,
And never shocked, and never turned aside,
Bursts out, resistless, with a thund'ring tide.
But where's the man, who counsel can bestow, 631
Still pleased to teach, and yet not proud to know?
Unbiassed, or by favor, or by spite;
Not dully prepossessed, nor blindly right;
Though learn'd, well-bred; and though well-bred, sincere, 635
Modestly bold, and humanly severe:
Who to a friend his faults can freely show,
And gladly praise the merit of a foe?
Bless'd with a taste exact, yet unconfined;
A knowledge both of books and human kind:
Gen'rous converse; a soul exempt from pride; 641
And love to praise, with reason on his side?
Such once were Critics; such the happy few,
Athens and Rome in better ages knew.
The mighty Stagirite first left the shore, 645
Spread all his sails, and durst the deeps explore:
He steered securely, and discovered far,
Led by the light of the Maeonian Star.[26]
Poets, a race long unconfined, and free,
Still fond and proud of savage liberty, 650
Received his laws; and stood convinced 'twas fit,
Who conquered Nature, should preside o'er Wit.
Horace still charms with graceful negligence,
And without method talks us into sense,
Will, like a friend, familiarly convey 655
The truest notions in the easiest way.
He, who supreme in judgment, as in wit,
Might boldly censure, as he boldly writ,
Yet judged with coolness, though he sung with fire;
His Precepts teach but what his works inspire. 660
Our Critics take a contrary extreme,
They judge with fury, but they write with fle'me:[27]
Nor suffers Horace more in wrong Translations
By Wits, than Critics in as wrong Quotations. 664

[26]Homer. [27]Phlegm, i. e., dullness.

See Dionysius[28] Homer's thoughts refine,
And call new beauties forth from every line!
Fancy and art in gay Petronius please,
The scholar's learning, with the courtier's ease.
In grave Quintilian's copious work, we find
The justest rules, and clearest method joined:
Thus useful arms in magazines we place, 671
All ranged in order, and disposed with grace,
But less to please the eye, than arm the hand,
Still fit for use, and ready at command.
Thee, bold Longinus! all the Nine[29] inspire, 675
And bless their Critic with a Poet's fire.
An ardent Judge, who zealous in his trust,
With warmth gives sentence, yet is always just;
Whose own example strengthens all his laws;
And is himself that great Sublime he draws. 680
Thus long succeeding Critics justly reigned,
License repressed, and useful laws ordained.
Learning and Rome alike in empire grew;
And Arts still followed where her Eagles flew;
From the same foes, at last, both felt their doom, 685
And the same age saw Learning fall, and Rome.
With Tyranny, then Superstition joined,
As that the body, this enslaved the mind;
Much was believed, but little understood,
And to be dull was construed to be good; 690
A second deluge Learning thus o'er-run,
And the Monks finished what the Goths begun.
At length Erasmus, that great injured name
(The glory of the Priesthood, and the shame!),[30]
Stemmed the wild torrent of a barb'rous age, 695
And drove those holy Vandals off the stage.
But see! each Muse, in Leo's[31] golden days,
Starts from her trance, and trims her withered bays,
Rome's ancient Genius, o'er its ruins spread,
Shakes off the dust, and rears his rev'rend head. 700
Then Sculpture and her sister-arts revive;

[28]Dionysius of Halicarnassus, Greek critic.

[29]The muses.

[30]Though himself a monk, Erasmus attacked the narrowness of monastic life.

[31]Leo X.

Stones leaped to form, and rocks began to live;
With sweeter notes each rising Temple rung;
A Raphael painted, and a Vida[32] sung.
Immortal Vida: on whose honored brow 705
The Poet's bays and Critic's ivy grow:
Cremona now shall ever boast thy name,
As next in place to Mantua, next in fame!
But soon by impious arms from Latium chased,
Their ancient bounds the banished Muses passed; 710
Thence Arts o'er all the northern world advance,
But Critic-learning flourished most in France:
The rules a nation, born to serve, obeys;
And Boileau still in right of Horace sways.
But we, brave Britons, foreign laws despised,
And kept unconquered, and uncivilized; 716
Fierce for the liberties of wit, and bold,
We still defied the Romans, as of old.
Yet some there were, among the sounder few
Of those who less presumed, and better knew, 720
Who durst assert the juster ancient cause,
And here restored Wit's fundamental laws.
Such was the Muse, whose rules and practice tell,
"Nature's chief Master-piece is writing well."

[32]Girolamo Vida (1489–1566), author of a Latin critical poem, *De Arte Poetica.*

Such was Roscommon,[33] not more learn'd than good, 725
With manners gen'rous as his noble blood;
To him the wit of Greece and Rome was known,
And ev'ry author's merit, but his own.
Such late was Walsh[34]—the Muse's judge and friend, 729
Who justly knew to blame or to commend:
To failings mild, but zealous for desert;
The clearest head, and the sincerest heart.
This humble praise, lamented shade! receive,
This praise at least a grateful Muse may give:
The Muse, whose early voice you taught to sing, 735
Prescribed her heights, and pruned her tender wing
(Her guide now lost), no more attempts to rise,
But in low numbers short excursions tries:
Content, if hence th' unlearn'd their wants may view,
The learn'd reflect on what before they knew: 740
Careless of censure, nor too fond of fame;
Still pleased to praise, yet not afraid to blame,
Averse alike to flatter, or offend;
Not free from faults, nor yet too vain to mend.

[33]Wentworth Dillon, Earl of Roscommon.

[34]See the introductory account of Pope above.

THE RAPE OF THE LOCK[1]

An Heroi-Comical Poem

Nolueram, Belinda, tuos violare capillos;
Sed juvat, hoc precibus me tribuisse tuis.[2]
—MART.

TO MRS. ARABELLA FERMOR

Madam,

It will be in vain to deny that I have some regard for this piece, since I dedicate it to You. Yet you may bear me witness, it was intended only to divert a few young Ladies, who have good sense and good humor enough to laugh not only at their sex's little unguarded follies, but at their own. But as it was communicated with the air of a Secret, it soon found its way into the world. An imperfect copy having been offered to a Bookseller, you had the good nature for my sake to consent to the publication of one more correct: This I was forced to, before I had executed half my design, for the Machinery was entirely wanting to complete it.

The Machinery, Madam, is a term invented by the Critics, to signify that part which the Deities, Angels, or Demons are made to act in a Poem: For the ancient Poets are in one respect

[1]First published in 1712, but rewritten and published in its present form in 1714. The occasion of the poem was as follows: Lord Petre had in a moment of fun cut off a lock of Miss Arabella Fermor's hair. Miss Fermor became angry, the families of both took up the quarrel, and serious consequences seemed likely to follow. At this point a common friend, Mr. John Caryll, suggested to Pope that he write a poem to make a jest of the whole affair. The result was the earlier version of the *Rape of the Lock,* which is said to have succeeded in its immediate purpose.

[2]I did not want, Belinda, to do violence to your lock, but I am glad to yield this gift to your entreaties (Martial, *Epigrams,* xii, 84; Pope alters the name).

like many modern Ladies: let an action be never so trivial in itself, they always make it appear of the utmost importance. These Machines I determined to raise on a very new and odd foundation, the Rosicrucian doctrine of Spirits.

I know how disagreeable it is to make use of hard words before a Lady; but 'tis so much the concern of a Poet to have his works understood, and particularly by your Sex, that you must give me leave to explain two or three difficult terms.

The Rosicrucians are a people I must bring you acquainted with. The best account I know of them is in a French book called *Le Comte de Gabalis,* which both in its title and size is so like a Novel, that many of the Fair Sex have read it for one by mistake. According to these Gentlemen, the four Elements are inhabited by Spirits, which they call Sylphs, Gnomes, Nymphs, and Salamanders. The Gnomes or Demons of Earth delight in mischief; but the Sylphs, whose habitation is in the Air, are the best-conditioned creatures imaginable. For, they say, any mortals may enjoy the most intimate familiarities with these gentle Spirits, upon a condition very easy to all true Adepts, an inviolate preservation of Chastity.

As to the following Cantos, all the passages of them are as fabulous as the Vision at the beginning, or the Transformation at the end (except the loss of your Hair, which I always mention with reverence). The Human persons are as fictitious as the airy ones; and the character of Belinda, as it is now managed, resembles you in nothing but in Beauty.

If this Poem had as many Graces as there are in your Person, or in your Mind, yet I could never hope it should pass through the world half so Uncensured as You have done. But let its fortune be what it will, mine is happy enough, to have given me this occasion of assuring you that I am, with the truest esteem, Madam,

Your most obedient, Humble Servant,

A. Pope.

CANTO I

What dire offense from am'rous causes springs,
What mighty contests rise from trivial things,
I sing—This verse to Caryl, Muse! is due:
This, e'en Belinda may vouchsafe to view:
Slight is the subject, but not so the praise, 5
If She inspire, and He approve my lays.
Say what strange motive, Goddess! could compel
A well-bred Lord t' assault a gentle Belle?
O say what stranger cause, yet unexplored,
Could make a gentle Belle reject a Lord? 10
In tasks so bold, can little men engage,
And in soft bosoms dwells such mighty Rage?
Sol through white curtains shot a tim'rous ray,
And oped those eyes that must eclipse the day:
Now lap-dogs give themselves the rousing shake, 15
And sleepless lovers, just at twelve, awake:
Thrice rung the bell, the slipper knocked the ground,[3]
And the pressed watch returned a silver sound.
Belinda still her downy pillow pressed,
Her guardian Sylph prolonged the balmy rest: 20
'Twas He had summoned to her silent bed
The morning-dream that hovered o'er her head;
A youth more glitt'ring than a Birth-night[4] Beau
(That e'en in slumber caused her cheek to glow),
Seemed to her ear his winning lips to lay, 25
And thus in whispers said, or seemed to say:
"Fairest of mortals, thou distinguished care
Of thousand bright Inhabitants of Air!
If e'er one vision touched thy infant thought,
Of all the Nurse and all the Priest have taught; 30
Of airy Elves by moonlight shadows seen,
The silver token, and the circled green,
Or virgins visited by Angel-pow'rs,
With golden crowns and wreaths of heav'nly flow'rs;
Hear and believe! thy own importance know, 35
Nor bound thy narrow views to things below.
Some secret truths, from learnèd pride concealed,
To Maids alone and Children are revealed:
What though no credit doubting Wits may give?
The Fair and Innocent shall still believe. 40
Know, then, unnumbered Spirits round thee fly,
The light Militia of the lower sky:
These, though unseen, are ever on the wing,
Hang o'er the Box, and hover round the Ring.[5]

[3]To call her maid, who had not come when the bell was rung.

[4]Dressed for the king's birthday entertainment.

[5]Drive in Hyde Park.

Think what an equipage thou hast in Air, 45
And view with scorn two Pages and a Chair.
As now your own, our beings were of old,
And once enclosed in Woman's beauteous mold;
Thence, by a soft transition, we repair
From earthly Vehicles to these of air. 50
Think not, when Woman's transient breath is fled,
That all her vanities at once are dead;
Succeeding vanities she still regards,
And though she plays no more, o'erlooks the cards.
Her joy in gilded Chariots, when alive, 55
And love of Ombre, after death survive.
For when the Fair in all their pride expire,
To their first Elements their Souls retire:
The Sprites of fiery Termagants in Flame
Mount up, and take a Salamander's name. 60
Soft yielding minds to Water glide away,
And sip, with Nymphs, their elemental Tea.
The graver Prude sinks downward to a Gnome,
In search of mischief still on Earth to roam.
The light Coquettes in Sylphs aloft repair, 65
And sport and flutter in the fields of Air.
"Know further yet; whoever fair and chaste
Rejects mankind, is by some Sylph embraced:
For Spirits, freed from mortal laws, with ease
Assume what sexes and what shapes they please.[6] 70
What guards the purity of melting Maids,
In courtly balls, and midnight masquerades,
Safe from the treach'rous friend, the daring spark,
The lance by day, the whisper in the dark,
When kind occasion prompts their warm desires, 75
When music softens, and when dancing fires?
'Tis but their Sylph, the wise Celestials know,
Though Honor is the word with Men below.
"Some nymphs there are, too conscious of their face,
For life predestined to the Gnomes' embrace. 80
These swell their prospects and exalt their pride,
When offers are disdained, and love denied:
Then gay Ideas crowd the vacant brain,
While Peers, and Dukes, and all their sweeping train,
And Garters, Stars, and Coronets appear, 85
And in soft sounds, Your Grace salutes their ear.
'Tis these that early taint the female soul,
Instruct the eyes of young Coquettes to roll,
Teach Infant-cheeks a bidden blush to know,
And little hearts to flutter at a Beau. 90
"Oft, when the world imagine women stray,
The Sylphs through mystic mazes guide their way,
Through all the giddy circle they pursue,
And old impertinence expel by new.
What tender maid but must a victim fall 95
To one man's treat, but for another's ball?
When Florio speaks what virgin could withstand,
If gentle Damon did not squeeze her hand?
With varying vanities, from ev'ry part,
They shift the moving Toyshop of their heart; 100
Where wigs with wigs, with sword-knots sword-knots strive,
Beaux banish beaux, and coaches coaches drive.
This erring mortals Levity may call;
Oh blind to truth! the Sylphs contrive it all.
"Of these am I, who thy protection claim,
A watchful sprite, and Ariel is my name. 106
Late, as I ranged the crystal wilds of air,
In the clear Mirror of thy ruling Star
I saw, alas! some dread event impend,
Ere to the main this morning sun descend, 110
But heav'n reveals not what, or how, or where:
Warned by the Sylph, oh pious maid, beware!
This to disclose is all thy guardian can:
Beware of all, but most beware of Man!"
He said; when Shock, who thought she slept too long, 115
Leaped up, and waked his mistress with his tongue.
'Twas then, Belinda, if report say true,
Thy eyes first opened on a Billet-doux;
Wounds, Charms, and Ardors were no sooner read,
But all the Vision vanished from thy head. 120
And now, unveiled, the Toilet stands displayed,
Each silver Vase in mystic order laid.
First, robed in white, the Nymph intent adores,
With head uncovered, the Cosmetic pow'rs.
A heav'nly image in the glass appears, 125
To that she bends, to that her eyes she rears;
Th' inferior Priestess,[7] at her altar's side,

[6] Cf. *Paradise Lost,* I, 423–431.

[7] Betty, the maid.

Trembling begins the sacred rites of Pride.
Unnumbered treasures ope at once, and here
The various off'rings of the world appear; 130
From each she nicely culls with curious toil,
And decks the Goddess with the glitt'ring spoil.
This casket India's glowing gems unlocks,
And all Arabia breathes from yonder box.
The Tortoise here and Elephant unite, 135
Transformed to combs, the speckled, and the white.
Here files of pins extend their shining rows,
Puffs, Powders, Patches, Bibles, Billet-doux.
Now awful Beauty put on all its arms;
The fair each moment rises in her charms, 140
Repairs her smiles, awakens ev'ry grace,
And calls forth all the wonders of her face;
Sees by degrees a purer blush arise,
And keener lightnings quicken in her eyes.
The busy Sylphs surround their darling care,
These set the head, and those divide the hair,
Some fold the sleeve, whilst others plait the gown; 147
And Betty's praised for labors not her own.

CANTO II

Not with more glories, in th' ethereal plain,
The Sun first rises o'er the purple main,
Than, issuing forth, the rival of his beams
Launched on the bosom of the silver Thames.
Fair Nymphs, and well-dressed Youths around her shone, 5
But ev'ry eye was fixed on her alone.
On her white breast a sparkling Cross she wore,
Which Jews might kiss, and Infidels adore.
Her lively looks a sprightly mind disclose,
Quick as her eyes, and as unfixed as those: 10
Favors to none, to all she smiles extends;
Oft she rejects, but never once offends.
Bright as the sun, her eyes the gazers strike,
And, like the sun, they shine on all alike.
Yet graceful ease, and sweetness void of pride, 15
Might hide her faults, if Belles had faults to hide:
If to her share some female errors fall,
Look on her face, and you'll forget 'em all.
This Nymph, to the destruction of mankind,
Nourished two Locks which graceful hung behind 20
In equal curls, and well conspired to deck
With shining ringlets the smooth iv'ry neck.
Love in these labyrinths his slaves detains,
And mighty hearts are held in slender chains.
With hairy springes we the birds betray, 25
Slight lines of hair surprise the finny prey,
Fair tresses man's imperial race ensnare,
And beauty draws us with a single hair.
Th' advent'rous Baron the bright locks admired;
He saw, he wished, and to the prize aspired. 30
Resolved to win, he meditates the way,
By force to ravish, or by fraud betray;
For when success a Lover's toil attends,
Few ask, if fraud or force attained his ends.
For this, ere Phoebus rose, he had implored 35
Propitious heav'n, and every pow'r adored,
But chiefly Love—to Love an Altar built,
Of twelve vast French Romances, neatly gilt.
There lay three garters, half a pair of gloves;
And all the trophies of his former loves; 40
With tender Billet-doux he lights the pyre,
And breathes three am'rous sighs to raise the fire.
Then prostrate falls, and begs with ardent eyes
Soon to obtain, and long possess the prize:
The pow'rs gave ear, and granted half his pray'r, 45
The rest, the winds dispersed in empty air.
But now secure the painted vessel glides,
The sun-beams trembling on the floating tides:
While melting music steals upon the sky,
And softened sounds along the waters die; 50
Smooth flow the waves, the Zephyrs gently play,
Belinda smiled, and all the world was gay.
All but the Sylph—with careful thoughts oppressed,
Th' impending woe sat heavy on his breast.
He summons straight his Denizens of air; 55
The lucid squadrons round the sails repair:
Soft o'er the shrouds aërial whispers breathe,
That seemed but Zephyrs to the train beneath.
Some to the sun their insect-wings unfold,
Waft on the breeze, or sink in clouds of gold; 60
Transparent forms, too fine for mortal sight,
Their fluid bodies half dissolved in light,
Loose to the wind their airy garments flew,
Thin glitt'ring textures of the filmy dew,
Dipped in the richest tincture of the skies, 65
Where light disports in ever-mingling dyes,
While ev'ry beam new transient colors flings,
Colors that change whene'er they wave their wings.
Amid the circle, on the gilded mast,
Superior by the head, was Ariel placed; 70

His purple pinions op'ning to the sun,
He raised his azure wand, and thus begun:
"Ye Sylphs and Sylphids, to your chief give ear!
Fays, Fairies, Genii, Elves, and Demons, hear!
Ye know the spheres and various tasks assigned 75
By laws eternal to th' aërial kind.
Some in the fields of purest ether play,
And bask and whiten in the blaze of day.
Some guide the course of wand'ring orbs on high,
Or roll the planets through the boundless sky. 80
Some less refined, beneath the moon's pale light
Pursue the stars that shoot athwart the night,
Or suck the mists in grosser air below,
Or dip their pinions in the painted bow, 84
Or brew fierce tempests on the wintry main,
Or o'er the glebe distil the kindly rain.
Others on earth o'er human race preside,
Watch all their ways, and all their actions guide:
Of these the chief the care of Nations own,
And guard with Arms divine the British Throne. 90
"Our humbler province is to tend the Fair,
Not a less pleasing, though less glorious care;
To save the powder from too rude a gale,
Nor let th' imprisoned essences exhale;
To draw fresh colors from the vernal flow'rs; 95
To steal from rainbows e'er they drop in show'rs
A brighter wash; to curl their waving hairs,
Assist their blushes, and inspire their airs;
Nay oft, in dreams, invention we bestow,
To change a Flounce, or add a Furbelow. 100
"This day, black Omens threat the brightest Fair,
That e'er deserved a watchful spirit's care;
Some dire disaster, or by force, or slight;
But what, or where, the fates have wrapped in night.
Whether the nymph shall break Diana's law, 105
Or some frail China jar receive a flaw;
Or stain her honor or her new brocade;
Forget her pray'rs, or miss a masquerade;
Or lose her heart, or necklace, at a ball;
Or whether Heav'n has doomed that Shock must fall. 110
Haste, then, ye spirits! to your charge repair:
The flutt'ring fan be Zephyretta's care;
The drops[8] to thee, Brillante, we consign;
And, Momentilla, let the watch be thine;
Do thou, Crispissa, tend her fav'rite Lock; 115
Ariel himself shall be the guard of Shock.
"To fifty chosen Sylphs, of special note,
We trust th' important charge, the Petticoat:
Oft have we known that seven-fold fence to fail,
Though stiff with hoops, and armed with ribs of whale; 120
Form a strong line about the silver bound,
And guard the wide circumference around.
"Whatever spirit, careless of his charge,
His post neglects, or leaves the fair at large,
Shall feel sharp vengeance soon o'ertake his sins, 125
Be stopped in vials, or transfixed with pins;
Or plunged in lakes of bitter washes lie,
Or wedged whole ages in a bodkin's eye:
Gums and Pomatums shall his flight restrain,
While clogged he beats his silken wings in vain; 130
Or Alum styptics with contracting pow'r
Shrink his thin essence like a riveled[9] flow'r:
Or, as Ixion fixed, the wretch shall feel
The giddy motion of the whirling Mill,
In fumes of burning Chocolate shall glow, 135
And tremble at the sea that froths below!"
He spoke; the spirits from the sails descend;
Some, orb in orb, around the nymph extend;
Some thread the mazy ringlets of her hair;
Some hang upon the pendants of her ear: 140
With beating hearts the dire event they wait,
Anxious, and trembling for the birth of Fate.

CANTO III

Close by those meads, for ever crowned with flow'rs,
Where Thames with pride surveys his rising tow'rs,
There stands a structure of majestic frame,[10]
Which from the neighb'ring Hampton takes its name.
Here Britain's statesmen oft the fall foredoom 5
Of foreign Tyrants and of Nymphs at home;
Here thou, great Anna! whom three realms obey,
Dost sometimes counsel take—and sometimes Tea.
Hither the heroes and the nymphs resort,
To taste awhile the pleasures of a Court; 10

[8]Earrings. [9]Shrunken.
[10]Hampton Court, a royal palace.

In various talk th' instructive hours they passed,
Who gave the ball, or paid the visit last;
One speaks the glory of the British Queen,
And one describes a charming Indian screen;
A third interprets motions, looks, and eyes; 15
At ev'ry word a reputation dies.
Snuff, or the fan, supply each pause of chat,
With singing, laughing, ogling, *and all that.*
Meanwhile, declining from the noon of day,
The sun obliquely shoots his burning ray; 20
The hungry Judges soon the sentence sign,
And wretches hang that jurymen may dine;
The merchant from th' Exchange returns in peace,
And the long labors of the Toilet cease.
Belinda now, whom thirst of fame invites, 25
Burns to encounter two advent'rous Knights,
At Ombre[11] singly to decide their doom;
And swells her breast with conquests yet to come.
Straight the three bands prepare in arms to join,
Each band the number of the sacred nine. 30
Soon as she spreads her hand, th' aërial guard
Descend, and sit on each important card:
First Ariel perched upon a Matadore,
Then each, according to the rank they bore;
For Sylphs, yet mindful of their ancient race, 35
Are, as when women, wondrous fond of place.
Behold, four Kings in majesty revered,
With hoary whiskers and a forky beard;
And four fair Queens whose hands sustain a flow'r,
Th' expressive emblem of their softer pow'r; 40
Four Knaves in garbs succinct, a trusty band,
Caps on their heads, and halberts in their hand;
And particolored troops, a shining train,
Draw forth to combat on the velvet plain.
The skillful Nymph reviews her force with care: 45

[11]A game of cards, of Spanish origin, usually played by three people. Each player received nine cards. The one who declared the trump became the "ombre" and played against the other two. If one of these took more tricks than the "ombre" the latter was defeated, which was called "codille." The three highest cards were called "matadores." They were, in the order of their value, "Spadillio" (ace of spades), "Manillio" (when trumps were black, the two of trumps; when red, the seven of trumps). and "Basto" (ace of clubs).

"Let Spades be trumps!" she said, and trumps they were.
Now move to war her sable Matadores,
In show like leaders of the swarthy Moors.
Spadillio first, unconquerable Lord!
Led off two captive trumps, and swept the board. 50
As many more Manillio forced to yield,
And marched a victor from the verdant field.
Him Basto followed, but his fate more hard
Gained but one trump and one plebeian card.
With his broad saber next, a chief in years, 55
The hoary Majesty of Spades appears,
Puts forth one manly leg, to sight revealed,
The rest, his many-colored robe concealed.
The rebel Knave, who dares his prince engage,
Proves the just victim of his royal rage. 60
E'en mighty Pam,[12] that Kings and Queens o'erthrew
And mowed down armies in the fights of Lu,
Sad chance of war! now destitute of aid,
Falls undistinguished by the victor spade!
Thus far both armies to Belinda yield; 65
Now to the Baron fate inclines the field.
His warlike Amazon her host invades,
Th' imperial consort of the crown of Spades.
The Club's black Tyrant first her victim died,
Spite of his haughty mien, and barb'rous pride: 70
What boots the regal circle on his head,
His giant limbs, in state unwieldy spread;
That long behind he trails his pompous robe,
And, of all monarchs, only grasps the globe?
The Baron now his Diamonds pours apace; 75
Th' embroidered King who shows but half his face,
And his refulgent Queen, with pow'rs combined
Of broken troops an easy conquest find.
Clubs, Diamonds, Hearts, in wild disorder seen,
With throngs promiscuous strew the level green. 80
Thus when dispersed a routed army runs,
Of Asia's troops, and Afric's sable sons,
With like confusion different nations fly,
Of various habit, and of various dye,
The pierced battalions dis-united fall, 85
In heaps on heaps; one fate o'erwhelms them all.
The Knave of Diamonds tries his wily arts,
And wins (oh shameful chance!) the Queen of Hearts.

[12]Knave of clubs, highest card in the game of loo.

At this, the blood the virgin's cheek forsook,
A livid paleness spreads o'er all her look; 90
She sees, and trembles at th' approaching ill,
Just in the jaws of ruin, and Codille.
And now (as oft in some distempered State)
On one nice Trick depends the gen'ral fate.
An Ace of Hearts steps forth: The King unseen 95
Lurked in her hand, and mourned his captive Queen:
He springs to Vengeance with an eager pace,
And falls like thunder on the prostrate Ace.
The nymph exulting fills with shouts the sky;
The walls, the woods, and long canals reply. 100

O thoughtless mortals! ever blind to fate,
Too soon dejected, and too soon elate.
Sudden, these honors shall be snatched away,
And cursed for ever this victorious day.

For lo! the board with cups and spoons is crowned, 105
The berries[13] crackle, and the mill turns round;
On shining Altars of Japan they raise
The silver lamp; the fiery spirits blaze:
From silver spouts the grateful liquors glide,
While China's earth receives the smoking tide: 110
At once they gratify their scent and taste,
And frequent cups prolong the rich repast.
Straight hover round the Fair her airy band;
Some, as she sipped, the fuming liquor fanned,
Some o'er her lap their careful plumes displayed, 115
Trembling, and conscious of the rich brocade.
Coffee (which makes the politician wise,
And see through all things with his half-shut eyes),
Sent up in vapors to the Baron's brain
New Stratagems, the radiant Lock to gain. 120
Ah cease, rash youth! desist ere 't is too late,
Fear the just Gods, and think of Scylla's Fate!
Changed to a bird, and sent to flit in air,
She dearly pays for Nisus' injured hair!

But when to mischief mortals bend their will, 125
How soon they find fit instruments of ill!
Just then, Clarissa drew with tempting grace
A two-edged weapon from her shining case:
So Ladies in Romance assist their Knight,
Present the spear, and arm him for the fight.
He takes the gift with rev'rence, and extends
The little engine on his fingers' ends; 132
This just behind Belinda's neck he spread,
As o'er the fragrant steams she bends her head.
Swift to the Lock a thousand Sprites repair,
A thousand wings, by turns, blow back the hair; 136
And thrice they twitched the diamond in her ear;
Thrice she looked back, and thrice the foe drew near.
Just in that instant, anxious Ariel sought
The close recesses of the Virgin's thought; 140
As on the nosegay in her breast reclined,
He watched th' Ideas rising in her mind,
Sudden he viewed, in spite of all her art,
An earthly Lover lurking at her heart.
Amazed, confused, he found his pow'r expired, 145
Resigned to fate, and with a sigh retired.

The Peer now spreads the glitt'ring Forfex wide,
T' enclose the Lock; now joins it, to divide.
E'en then, before the fatal engine closed,
A wretched Sylph too fondly interposed; 150
Fate urged the shears, and cut the Sylph in twain
(But airy substance soon unites again),
The meeting points the sacred hair dissever
From the fair head, for ever, and for ever!

Then flashed the living lightning from her eyes, 155
And screams of horror rend th' affrighted skies.
Not louder shrieks to pitying heav'n are cast,
When husbands, or when lapdogs breathe their last;
Or when rich China vessels fall'n from high,
In glitt'ring dust and painted fragments lie!

Let wreaths of triumph now my temples twine 161
(The victor cried) the glorious Prize is mine!
While fish in streams, or birds delight in air,
Or in a coach and six the British Fair,
As long as Atalantis[14] shall be read, 165
Or the small pillow grace a Lady's bed,
While visits shall be paid on solemn days,
When num'rous wax-lights in bright order blaze,
While nymphs take treats, or assignations give,
So long my honor, name, and praise shall live! 170
What Time would spare, from Steel receives its date,

[13]Coffee beans.

[14]*The New Atalantis* by Mrs. Manley (published in 1709), a voluminous work which chronicled contemporary scandal.

And monuments, like men, submit to fate!
Steel could the labor of the Gods destroy,
And strike to dust th' imperial towers of Troy;
Steel could the works of mortal pride confound, 175
And hew triumphal arches to the ground.
What wonder then, fair nymph! thy hairs should feel,
The conqu'ring force of unresisted steel?

CANTO IV

But anxious cares the pensive nymph oppressed,
And secret passions labored in her breast.
Not youthful kings in battle seized alive,
Not scornful virgins who their charms survive,
Not ardent lovers robbed of all their bliss, 5
Not ancient ladies when refused a kiss,
Not tyrants fierce that unrepenting die,
Not Cynthia when her manteau's pinned awry,
E'er felt such rage, resentment, and despair,
As thou, sad Virgin! for thy ravished Hair. 10
For, that sad moment, when the Sylphs withdrew
And Ariel weeping from Belinda flew,
Umbriel, a dusky, melancholy sprite,
As ever sullied the fair face of light,
Down to the central earth, his proper scene, 15
Repaired to search the gloomy Cave of Spleen.[15]
Swift on his sooty pinions flits the Gnome,
And in a vapor reached the dismal dome.
No cheerful breeze this sullen region knows,
The dreaded East is all the wind that blows. 20
Here in a grotto, sheltered close from air,
And screened in shades from day's detested glare,
She sighs for ever on her pensive bed,
Pain at her side, and Megrim[16] at her head.
Two handmaids wait the throne: alike in place, 25
But diff'ring far in figure and in face.
Here stood Ill-nature like an ancient maid,
Her wrinkled form in black and white arrayed;
With store of pray'rs, for mornings, nights, and noons, 29
Her hand is filled; her bosom with lampoons.
There Affectation, with a sickly mien,
Shows in her cheek the roses of eighteen,
Practiced to lisp, and hang the head aside,
Faints into airs, and languishes with pride,
On the rich quilt sinks with becoming woe, 35
Wrapped in a gown, for sickness, and for show.
The fair ones feel such maladies as these,
When each new night-dress gives a new disease.
A constant Vapor o'er the palace flies;
Strange phantoms rising as the mists arise; 40
Dreadful, as hermit's dreams in haunted shades,
Or bright, as visions of expiring maids.
Now glaring fiends, and snakes on rolling spires,
Pale specters, gaping tombs, and purple fires:
Now lakes of liquid gold, Elysian scenes, 45
And crystal domes, and angels in machines.[17]
Unnumbered throngs on every side are seen,
Of bodies changed to various forms by Spleen.
Here living Tea-pots stand, one arm held out,
One bent; the handle this, and that the spout: 50
A Pipkin[18] there, like Homer's Tripod walks;
Here sighs a Jar, and there a Goose-pie talks;
Men prove with child, as powerful fancy works,
And maids turned bottles, call aloud for corks.
Safe passed the Gnome through this fantastic band, 55
A branch of healing Spleenwort in his hand.
Then thus addressed the pow'r: "Hail, wayward Queen!
Who rule the sex to fifty from fifteen:
Parent of vapors and of female wit,
Who give th' hysteric, or poetic fit, 60
On various tempers act by various ways,
Make some take physic, others scribble plays;
Who cause the proud their visits to delay,
And send the godly in a pet to pray. 64
A nymph there is, that all thy pow'r disdains,
And thousands more in equal mirth maintains.
But oh! if e'er thy Gnome could spoil a grace,
Or raise a pimple on a beauteous face,
Like Citron-waters matrons' cheeks inflame,

[15] Low spirits, or ill temper.

[16] Headache, but the word was used in the early eighteenth century (as was "vapors") for what we should call "the blues."

[17] The "*deus ex machina.*"

[18] A small jar. "Homer's tripod" is one of the self-moving tripods made by Vulcan, described in the *Iliad* (XVIII, 373–377).

Or change complexions at a losing game; 70
If e'er with airy horns I planted heads,
Or rumpled petticoats, or tumbled beds,
Or caused suspicion when no soul was rude,
Or discomposed the head-dress of a Prude,
Or e'er to costive lap-dog gave disease, 75
Which not the tears of brightest eyes could ease:
Hear me, and touch Belinda with chagrin,
That single act gives half the world the spleen."
The Goddess with a discontented air
Seems to reject him, though she grants his pray'r. 80
A wondrous Bag with both her hands she binds,
Like that where once Ulysses held the winds;
There she collects the force of female lungs,
Sighs, sobs, and passions, and the war of tongues.
A Vial next she fills with fainting fears, 85
Soft sorrows, melting griefs, and flowing tears.
The Gnome rejoicing bears her gifts away,
Spreads his black wings, and slowly mounts to day.
Sunk in Thalestris'[19] arms the nymph he found,
Her eyes dejected and her hair unbound. 90
Full o'er their heads the swelling bag he rent,
And all the Furies issued at the vent.
Belinda burns with more than mortal ire,
And fierce Thalestris fans the rising fire.
"O wretched maid!" she spread her hands, and cried 95
(While Hampton's echoes, "Wretched maid!" replied),
"Was it for this you took such constant care
The bodkin, comb, and essence to prepare?
For this your locks in paper durance bound,
For this with tort'ring irons wreathed around? 100
For this with fillets strained your tender head,
And bravely bore the double loads of lead?[20]
Gods! shall the ravisher display your hair,
While the Fops envy, and the Ladies stare!
Honor forbid! at whose unrivaled shrine 105
Ease, pleasure, virtue, all our sex resign.
Methinks already I your tears survey,
Already hear the horrid things they say,
Already see you a degraded toast,[21]
And all your honor in a whisper lost! 110
How shall I, then, your helpless fame defend?
'Twill then be infamy to seem your friend!
And shall this prize, th' inestimable prize,
Exposed through crystal to the gazing eyes,
And heightened by the diamond's circling rays, 115
On that rapacious hand for ever blaze?
Sooner shall grass in Hyde-park Circus grow,
And wits take lodgings in the sound of Bow;[22]
Sooner let earth, air, sea, to Chaos fall, 119
Men, monkeys, lap-dogs, parrots, perish all!"
She said; then raging to Sir Plume[23] repairs,
And bids her Beau demand the precious hairs:
(Sir Plume of amber snuff-box justly vain,
And the nice conduct of a clouded[24] cane)
With earnest eyes, and round unthinking face, 125
He first the snuff-box opened, then the case,
And thus broke out—"My Lord, why, what the devil?
Z—ds! damn the lock! 'fore Gad, you must be civil!
Plague on 't! 'tis past a jest—nay prithee, pox!
Give her the hair"—he spoke, and rapped his box. 130
"It grieves me much" (replied the Peer again)
"Who speaks so well should ever speak in vain.
But by this Lock, this sacred Lock I swear
(Which never more shall join its parted hair;
Which never more its honors shall renew, 135
Clipped from the lovely head where late it grew),
That while my nostrils draw the vital air,
This hand, which won it, shall for ever wear."
He spoke, and speaking, in proud triumph spread
The long-contended honors of her head. 140
But Umbriel, hateful Gnome! forbears not so;
He breaks the Vial whence the sorrows flow.
Then see! the nymph in beauteous grief appears,

[19]A friend of Belinda's, said to be a Mrs. Morley.

[20]Fastenings for curl-papers.

[21]A slang term for a woman whose health was drunk by her admirers.

[22]The bells of the church of St. Mary le Bow, in Cheapside, an unfashionable quarter of the city.

[23]Sir George Brown, brother of Mrs. Morley. He is said to have threatened Pope with violence for the picture of him which follows.

[24]Covered with cloudy markings.

Her eyes half-languishing, half-drowned in tears;
On her heaved bosom hung her drooping head, 145
Which, with a sigh, she raised; and thus she said:
"For ever cursed be this detested day,
Which snatched my best, my fav'rite curl away!
Happy! ah, ten times happy had I been,
If Hampton Court these eyes had never seen! 150
Yet am not I the first mistaken maid,
By love of Courts to num'rous ills betrayed.
O had I rather un-admired remained
In some lone isle, or distant Northern land;
Where the gilt Chariot never marks the way,
Where none learn Ombre, none e'er taste Bohea![25] 156
There kept my charms concealed from mortal eye,
Like roses, that in deserts bloom and die.
What moved my mind with youthful Lords to roam?
O had I stayed, and said my pray'rs at home!
'T was this, the morning omens seemed to tell, 161
Thrice from my trembling hand the patch-box[26] fell;
The tott'ring Chine shook without a wind,
Nay, Poll sat mute, and Shock was most unkind!
A Sylph too warned me of the threats of fate, 165
In mystic visions, now believed too late!
See the poor remnants of these slighted hairs!
My hands shall rend what e'en thy rapine spares:
These in two sable ringlets taught to break,
Once gave new beauties to the snowy neck;
The sister-lock now sits uncouth, alone, 171
And in its fellow's fate foresees its own;
Uncurled it hangs, the fatal shears demands,
And tempts once more thy sacrilegious hands.
O hadst thou, cruel! been content to seize 175
Hairs less in sight, or any hairs but these!"

CANTO V

She said: the pitying audience melt in tears.
But Fate and Jove had stopped the Baron's ears.
In vain Thalestris with reproach assails,
For who can move when fair Belinda fails?
Not half so fixed the Trojan[27] could remain, 5
While Anna begged and Dido raged in vain.
Then grave Clarissa graceful waved her fan;
Silence ensued, and thus the nymph began:
"Say why are Beauties praised and honored most,
The wise man's passion, and the vain man's toast? 10
Why decked with all that land and sea afford,
Why Angels called, and Angel-like adored?
Why round our coaches crowd the white-gloved Beaux,
Why bows the side-box from its inmost rows;
How vain are all these glories, all our pains, 15
Unless good sense preserve what beauty gains;
That men may say, when we the front-box grace:
'Behold the first in virtue as in face!'
Oh! if to dance all night, and dress all day,
Charmed the small-pox, or chased old age away; 20
Who would not scorn what housewife's cares produce,
Or who would learn one earthly thing of use?
To patch, nay ogle, might become a Saint,
Nor could it sure be such a sin to paint.
But since, alas! frail beauty must decay, 25
Curled or uncurled, since Locks will turn to gray;
Since painted, or not painted, all shall fade,
And she who scorns a man, must die a maid;
What then remains but well our pow'r to use,
And keep good-humor still whate'er we lose 30
And trust me, dear! good-humor can prevail,
When airs, and flights, and screams, and scolding fail.
Beauties in vain their pretty eyes may roll;
Charms strike the sight, but merit wins the soul."
So spoke the Dame, but no applause ensued; 35
Belinda frowned, Thalestris called her Prude.
"To arms, to arms!" the fierce Virago cries,
And swift as lightning to the combat flies.
All side in parties, and begin th' attack;
Fans clap, silks rustle, and tough whalebones crack; 40
Heroes' and Heroines' shouts confus'dly rise,

[25] Tea.

[26] Box which held patches of sticking plaster for the face.

[27] Aeneas.

And bass, and treble voices strike the skies.
No common weapons in their hands are found,
Like Gods they fight, nor dread a mortal wound.
So when bold Homer makes the Gods engage, 45
And heav'nly breasts with human passions rage;
'Gainst Pallas, Mars; Latona, Hermes arms;
And all Olympus rings with loud alarms:
Jove's thunder roars, heav'n trembles all around,
Blue Neptune storms, the bellowing deeps resound: 50
Earth shakes her nodding tow'rs, the ground gives way,
And the pale ghosts start at the flash of day!
Triumphant Umbriel on a sconce's height
Clapped his glad wings, and sat to view the fight:
Propped on the bodkin spears, the Sprites survey 55
The growing combat, or assist the fray.
While through the press enraged Thalestris flies,
And scatters death around from both her eyes,
A Beau and Witling perished in the throng,
One died in metaphor, and one in song. 60
"O cruel nymph! a living death I bear,"
Cried Dapperwit, and sunk beside his chair.
A mournful glance Sir Fopling upwards cast,
"Those eyes are made so killing"—was his last.
Thus on Maeander's flowery margin lies 65
Th' expiring Swan, and as he sings he dies.
When bold Sir Plume had drawn Clarissa down,
Chloe stepped in, and killed him with a frown;
She smiled to see the doughty hero slain,
But at her smile, the Beau revived again. 70
Now Jove suspends his golden scales in air,
Weighs the Men's wits against the Lady's hair;
The doubtful beam long nods from side to side;
At length the wits mount up, the hairs subside.
See, fierce Belinda on the Baron flies, 75
With more than usual lightning in her eyes:
Nor feared the Chief th' unequal fight to try,
Who sought no more than on his foe to die.
But this bold Lord with manly strength endued,
She with one finger and a thumb subdued: 80
Just where the breath of life his nostrils drew,
A charge of Snuff the wily virgin threw;
The Gnomes direct, to ev'ry atom just,
The pungent grains of titillating dust.
Sudden, with starting tears each eye o'erflows, 85
And the high dome re-echoes to his nose.
"Now meet thy fate," incensed Belinda cried,
And drew a deadly bodkin from her side.
(The same, his ancient personage to deck,
Her great great grandsire wore about his neck, 90
In three seal-rings; which after, melted down,
Formed a vast buckle for his widow's gown:
Her infant grandame's whistle next it grew,
The bells she jingled, and the whistle blew;
Then in a bodkin graced her mother's hairs, 95
Which long she wore, and now Belinda wears.)
"Boast not my fall" (he cried) "insulting foe!
Thou by some other shalt be laid as low,
Nor think, to die dejects my lofty mind:
All that I dread is leaving you behind! 100
Rather than so, ah, let me still survive,
And burn in Cupid's flames—but burn alive."
"Restore the Lock!" she cries; and all around
"Restore the Lock!" the vaulted roofs rebound.
Not fierce Othello in so loud a strain 105
Roared for the handkerchief that caused his pain.
But see how oft ambitious aims are crossed,
And chiefs contend 'till all the prize is lost!
The Lock, obtained with guilt, and kept with pain, 109
In every place is sought, but sought in vain:
With such a prize no mortal must be bless'd,
So heav'n decrees! with heav'n who can contest?
Some thought it mounted to the Lunar sphere,
Since all things lost on earth are treasured there.
There Heroes' wits are kept in pond'rous vases, 115
And beaux' in snuff-boxes and tweezer-cases.
There broken vows and death-bed alms are found,
And lovers' hearts with ends of riband bound,
The courtier's promises, and sick man's pray'rs, 119

The smiles of harlots, and the tears of heirs,
Cages for gnats, and chains to yoke a flea,
Dried butterflies, and tomes of casuistry.
But trust the Muse—she saw it upward rise,
Though marked by none but quick, poetic eyes
(So Rome's great founder[28] to the heav'ns withdrew, 125
To Proculus alone confessed in view);
A sudden Star, it shot through liquid air,
And drew behind a radiant trail of hair.
Not Berenice's[29] Locks first rose so bright,
The heav'ns bespangling with disheveled light. 130
The Sylphs behold it kindling as it flies,
And pleased pursue its progress through the skies.
This the Beau monde shall from the Mall[30] survey,
And hail with music its propitious ray. 134

[28]Romulus (the legend Pope alludes to is to be found in Livy, I, xvi).

[29]An Egyptian queen who dedicated a lock of hair for her husband's safe return from war. It was said to have become a constellation.

[30]Upper side of St. James's Park, London.

This the bless'd Lover shall for Venus take,
And send up vows from Rosamonda's lake.[31]
This Partridge[32] soon shall view in cloudless skies,
When next he looks through Galileo's eyes;
And hence th' egregious wizard shall foredoom
The fate of Louis, and the fall of Rome.[33] 140
Then cease, bright Nymph! to mourn thy ravished hair,
Which adds new glory to the shining sphere!
Not all the tresses that fair head can boast,
Shall draw such envy as the Lock you lost.
For, after all the murders of your eye, 145
When, after millions slain, yourself shall die:
When those fair suns shall set, as set they must,
And all those tresses shall be laid in dust,
This Lock, the Muse shall consecrate to fame,
And 'midst the stars inscribe Belinda's name.

[31]A pond in St. James's Park.

[32]An astrologer who published predictions. Swift made fun of him in his Bickerstaff papers, foretelling his death, and later pretending that the astrologer had duly died at the appointed time.

[33]Louis XIV and the Papacy.

AN ESSAY ON MAN[1]

To H. St. John Lord Bolingbroke

ARGUMENT OF EPISTLE I

Of the Nature and State of Man, with Respect to the Universe.

Of Man in the abstract. I. That we can judge only with regard to our own system, being ignorant of the relations of systems and things, v. 17, *etc.* II. That Man is not to be deemed imperfect, but a Being suited to his place and rank in the creation, agreeable to the general Order of things, and conformable to Ends and Relations to him unknown, v. 35, *etc.* III. That it is partly upon his ignorance of future events, and partly upon the hope of a future state, that all his happiness in the present depends, v. 77, *etc.* IV. The pride of aiming at more knowledge, and pretending to more Perfection, the cause of Man's error and misery. The impiety of putting himself in the place of God, and judging of the fitness or unfitness, perfection or imperfection, justice or injustice of his dispensations, v. 109, *etc.* V. The absurdity of conceiting himself the final cause of the creation, or expecting that perfection in the moral world, which is not in the natural, v. 131, *etc.* VI. The unreasonableness of his complaints against Providence, while on the one hand he demands the Perfections of the Angels, and on the other the bodily qualifications of the Brutes; though, to possess any of the sensitive faculties in a higher degree, would render him miserable, v. 173, *etc.* VII. That throughout the whole visible world, an universal order and gradation in the sensual and mental faculties is observed, which causes a subordination of creature to creature, and of all creatures to Man. The gradations of sense, instinct, thought, reflection, reason; that Reason alone countervails all the other faculties, v. 207. VIII. How much further this order and subordination of living creatures may extend, above and below us; were any part of which broken, not that part only, but the whole connected creation must be destroyed, v. 233. IX. The extravagance, madness, and

[1]The first epistle, all that is here printed, was written in 1732, though the complete work (four epistles) was not finished and published until 1734. The *Essay* purports to be a philosophical poem, an aim characteristic of the age. Pope, however, had not a philosophic mind, and the interest of the poem lies in its detached sayings. It has even been claimed that Pope merely put into verse material given him by Lord Bolingbroke, his "guide, philosopher, and friend," to whom the poem is addressed. Though this can hardly be true, at least in the literal sense of the words, doubtless the matter of the poem was a subject of frequent discussion between the two.

pride of such a desire, v. 250. X. The consequence of all, the absolute submission due to Providence, both as to our present and future state, v. 281, *etc.* to the end.

EPISTLE I

Awake, my St. John! leave all meaner things
To low ambition, and the pride of Kings.
Let us (since Life can little more supply
Than just to look about us and to die)
Expatiate[2] free o'er all this scene of Man; 5
A mighty maze! but not without a plan;[3]
A Wild, where weeds and flow'rs promiscuous shoot;
Or Garden, tempting with forbidden fruit.
Together let us beat[4] this ample field,
Try what the open, what the covert yield; 10
The latent tracts, the giddy heights, explore
Of all who blindly creep, or sightless soar;
Eye Nature's walks, shoot Folly as it flies,
And catch the Manners living as they rise;
Laugh where we must, be candid where we can; 15
But vindicate the ways of God to Man.

I. Say first, of God above, or Man below,
What can we reason, but from what we know?
Of Man, what see we but his station here,
From which to reason, or to which refer? 20
Through worlds unnumbered though the God be known,
'T is ours to trace him only in our own.
He, who through vast immensity can pierce,
See worlds on worlds compose one universe,
Observe how system into system runs, 25
What other planets circle other suns,
What varied Being peoples ev'ry star,
May tell why Heav'n has made us as we are.
But of this frame the bearings, and the ties,
The strong connections, nice dependencies, 30
Gradations just, has thy pervading soul
Looked through? or can a part contain the whole?
Is the great chain, that draws all to agree,
And drawn supports, upheld by God, or thee?

II. Presumptuous Man! the reason wouldst thou find, 35
Why formed so weak, so little, and so blind?
First, if thou canst, the harder reason guess,
Why formed no weaker, blinder, and no less?
Ask of thy mother earth, why oaks are made
Taller or stronger than the weeds they shade?
Or ask of yonder argent fields above, 41
Why Jove's satellites are less than Jove?
Of Systems possible, if 'tis confessed
That Wisdom infinite must form the best,
Where all must full or not coherent be, 45
And all that rises, rise in due degree;
Then, in the scale of reas'ning life, 'tis plain,
There must be, somewhere, such a rank as Man:
And all the question (wrangle e'er so long)
Is only this, if God has placed him wrong? 50
Respecting Man, whatever wrong we call,
May, must be right, as relative to all.
In human works, though labored on with pain,
A thousand movements scarce one purpose gain;
In God's, one single can its end produce; 55
Yet serves to second too some other use.
So Man, who here seems principal alone,
Perhaps acts second to some sphere unknown,
Touches some wheel, or verges to some goal:
'Tis but a part we see, and not a whole. 60
When the proud steed shall know why Man restrains
His fiery course, or drives him o'er the plains:
When the dull Ox, why now he breaks the clod,
Is now a victim, and now Egypt's God:
Then shall Man's pride and dullness comprehend 65
His actions', passions', being's, use and end;
Why doing, suff'ring, checked, impelled; and why
This hour a slave, the next a deity.
Then say not Man's imperfect, Heav'n in fault;
Say rather, Man's as perfect as he ought: 70
His knowledge measured to his state and place;
His time a moment, and a point his space.
If to be perfect in a certain sphere,
What matter, soon or late, or here or there?
The bless'd to-day is as completely so, 75
As who began a thousand years ago.

III. Heav'n from all creatures hides the book of Fate,
All but the page prescribed, their present state:
From brutes what men, from men what spirits know:
Or who could suffer Being here below? 80
The lamb thy riot dooms to bleed to-day,

---

[2] Wander.

[3] This line in the original editions stood,
"A mighty maze of walks without a plan;"
and it has been remarked (by Lowell) that "perhaps this came nearer Pope's real opinion than the verse he substituted for it."

[4] Scour, as in hunting game.

Had he thy Reason, would he skip and play?
Pleased to the last, he crops the flow'ry food,
And licks the hand just raised to shed his blood.
O blindness to the future! kindly giv'n, 85
That each may fill the circle marked by Heav'n:
Who sees with equal eye, as God of all,
A hero perish, or a sparrow fall,
Atoms or systems into ruin hurled,
And now a bubble burst, and now a world. 90
Hope humbly then; with trembling pinions soar;
Wait the great teacher Death: and God adore.
What future bliss, he gives not thee to know,
But gives that Hope to be thy blessing now.
Hope springs eternal in the human breast: 95
Man never Is, but always To be bless'd:
The soul, uneasy and confined from home,
Rests and expatiates in a life to come.
Lo, the poor Indian! whose untutored mind
Sees God in clouds, or hears him in the wind:
His soul proud Science never taught to stray
Far as the solar walk, or milky way; 102
Yet simple Nature to his hope has giv'n,
Behind the cloud-topped hill, an humbler heav'n;
Some safer world in depth of woods embraced, 105
Some happier island in the wat'ry waste,
Where slaves once more their native land behold,
No fiends torment, no Christians thirst for gold.
To Be, contents his natural desire,
He asks no Angel's wing, no Seraph's fire; 110
But thinks, admitted to that equal[5] sky,
His faithful dog shall bear him company.

IV. Go, wiser thou! and, in thy scale of sense,
Weigh thy Opinion against Providence;
Call imperfection what thou fanci'st such, 115
Say, here he gives too little, there too much:
Destroy all Creatures for thy sport or gust,[6]
Yet cry, If Man's unhappy, God's unjust;
If Man alone engross not Heav'n's high care,
Alone made perfect here, immortal there: 120
Snatch from his hand the balance and the rod,
Re-judge his justice, be the God of God.
In Pride, in reas'ning Pride, our error lies;
All quit their sphere, and rush into the skies.
Pride still is aiming at the bless'd abodes, 125
Men would be Angels, Angels would be Gods
Aspiring to be Gods, if Angels fell,
Aspiring to be Angels, Men rebel:
And who but wishes to invert the laws
Of Order, sins against th' Eternal Cause. 130

V. Ask for what end the heav'nly bodies shine,
Earth for whose use? Pride answers, "'Tis for mine:
For me kind Nature wakes her genial Pow'r,
Suckles each herb, and spreads out ev'ry flow'r;
Annual for me, the grape, the rose renew 135
The juice nectareous, and the balmy dew;
For me, the mine a thousand treasures brings;
For me, health gushes from a thousand springs;
Seas roll to waft me, suns to light me rise;
My foot-stool earth, my canopy the skies." 140
But errs not Nature from his gracious end,
From burning suns when livid deaths descend,
When earthquakes swallow, or when tempests sweep
Towns to one grave, whole nations to the deep?
"No," ('tis replied) "the first Almighty Cause 145
Acts not by partial, but by gen'ral laws;
Th' exceptions few; some change since all began:
And what created perfect?"—Why then Man?
If the great end be human Happiness, 149
Then Nature deviates; and can Man do less?
As much that end a constant course requires
Of show'rs and sun-shine, as of Man's desires;
As much eternal springs and cloudless skies,
As Men for ever temp'rate, calm, and wise.
If plagues or earthquakes break not Heav'n's design, 155
Why then a Borgia, or a Catiline?
Who knows but he, whose hand the lightning forms,
Who heaves old Ocean, and who wings the storms;
Pours fierce Ambition in a Caesar's mind,
Or turns young Ammon,[7] loose to scourge mankind? 160
From pride, from pride, our very reas'ning springs;
Account for moral as for nat'ral things:
Why charge we Heav'n in those, in these acquit?
In both, to reason right is to submit.
Better for Us, perhaps, it might appear, 165
Were there all harmony, all virtue here;

[5]Impartial. [6]Pleasure.

[7]Alexander the Great, who allowed himself to be called the son of Jupiter Ammon.

That never air or ocean felt the wind;
That never passion discomposed the mind.
But all subsists by elemental strife;
And Passions are the elements of Life. 170
The gen'ral Order, since the whole began
Is kept in Nature, and is kept in Man.

VI. What would this Man? Now upward will he soar,
And, little less than Angel, would be more;
Now looking downwards, just as grieved appears 175
To want the strength of bulls, the fur of bears.
Made for his use all creatures if he call,
Say what their use, had he the pow'rs of all?
Nature to these, without profusion, kind, 179
The proper organs, proper pow'rs assign'd;
Each seeming want compensated of course,
Here with degrees of swiftness, there of force;
All in exact proportion to the state;
Nothing to add, and nothing to abate.
Each beast, each insect, happy in its own: 185
Is Heav'n unkind to Man, and Man alone?
Shall he alone, whom rational we call,
Be pleased with nothing, if not bless'd with all?

The bliss of Man (could Pride that blessing find)
Is not to act or think beyond mankind; 190
No pow'rs of body or of soul to share,
But what his nature and his state can bear.
Why has not Man a microscopic eye?
For this plain reason, Man is not a Fly.
Say what the use, were finer optics giv'n, 195
T' inspect a mite, not comprehend the heav'n?
Or touch, if tremblingly alive all o'er,
To smart and agonize at every pore?
Or quick effluvia darting through the brain,
Die of a rose in aromatic pain? 200
If Nature thundered in his op'ning ears,
And stunned him with the music of the spheres,
How would he wish that Heav'n had left him still
The whisp'ring Zephyr, and the purling rill?
Who finds not Providence all good and wise,
Alike in what it gives, and what denies? 206

VII. Far as Creation's ample range extends,
The scale of sensual,[8] mental pow'rs ascends:
Mark how it mounts, to Man's imperial race,
From the green myriads in the peopled grass:
What modes of sight betwixt each wide extreme, 211
The mole's dim curtain, and the lynx's beam:
Of smell, the headlong lioness between,
And hound sagacious on the tainted green:
Of hearing, from the life that fills the Flood,
To that which warbles through the vernal wood: 216
The spider's touch, how exquisitely fine!
Feels at each thread, and lives along the line:
In the nice bee, what sense so subtly true
From pois'nous herbs extracts the healing dew? 220
How Instinct varies in the grov'ling swine,
Compared, half-reas'ning elephant, with thine!
'Twixt that, and Reason, what a nice barrier,
For ever sep'rate, yet for ever near!
Remembrance and Reflection how allied; 225
What thin partitions Sense from Thought divide:
And Middle natures, how they long to join,
Yet never pass th' insuperable line!
Without this just gradation, could they be
Subjected, these to those, or all to thee? 230
The pow'rs of all subdued by thee alone,
Is not thy Reason all these pow'rs in one?

VIII. See, through this air, this ocean, and this earth,
All matter quick, and bursting into birth.
Above, how high progressive life may go! 235
Around, how wide! how deep extend below!
Vast chain of Being! which from God began,
Natures ethereal, human, angel, man,
Beast, bird, fish, insect, what no eye can see,
No glass can reach; from Infinite to thee, 240
From thee to Nothing.—On superior pow'rs
Were we to press, inferior might on ours:
Or in the full creation leave a void,
Where, one step broken, the great scale's destroyed:
From Nature's chain whatever link you strike, 245
Tenth or ten-thousandth, breaks the chain alike.

And, if each system in gradation roll
Alike essential to th' amazing Whole,
The least confusion but in one, not all 249
That system only, but the Whole must fall.
Let Earth unbalanced from her orbit fly,
Planets and Suns run lawless through the sky;
Let ruling Angels from their spheres be hurled,
Being on Being wrecked, and world on world;
Heav'n's whole foundations to their center nod, 255
And Nature tremble to the throne of God.

[8]Sensory.

All this dread Order break—for whom? for thee?
Vile worm!—O Madness! Pride! Impiety!
IX. What if the foot, ordained the dust to tread,
Or hand, to toil, aspired to be the head? 260
What if the head, the eye, or ear repined
To serve mere engines to the ruling Mind?
Just as absurd for any part to claim
To be another, in this gen'ral frame:
Just as absurd, to mourn the tasks or pains,
The great directing Mind of all ordains, 266
All are but parts of one stupendous whole,
Whose body Nature is, and God the soul;
That, changed through all, and yet in all the same;
Great in the earth, as in th' ethereal frame; 270
Warms in the sun, refreshes in the breeze,
Glows in the stars, and blossoms in the trees,
Lives through all life, extends through all extent,
Spreads undivided, operates unspent;
Breathes in our soul, informs our mortal part,
As full, as perfect, in a hair as heart: 276
As full, as perfect, in vile Man that mourns,
As the rapt Seraph that adores and burns:
To him no high, no low, no great, no small;
He fills, he bounds, connects, and equals all.
X. Cease then, nor Order Imperfection name: 281
Our proper bliss depends on what we blame.
Know thy own point: This kind, this due degree
Of blindness, weakness, Heav'n bestows on thee.
Submit.—In this, or any other sphere, 285
Secure to be as bless'd as thou canst bear:
Safe in the hand of one disposing Pow'r,
Or in the natal, or the mortal hour.
All Nature is but Art, unknown to thee;
All Chance, Direction, which thou canst not see; 290
All Discord, Harmony not understood;
All partial Evil, universal Good:
And, spite of Pride, in erring Reason's spite,
One truth is clear, *Whatever is, is right.*

EPISTLE TO DR. ARBUTHNOT[1]

Advertisement to the First Publication of This EPISTLE

This paper is a sort of bill of complaint, begun many years since, and drawn up by snatches, as the several occasions offered. I had no thoughts of publishing it, till it pleased some Persons of Rank and Fortune (the Authors of *Verses to the Imitator of Horace,* and of an *Epistle to a Doctor of Divinity from a Nobleman of Hampton Court*) to attack, in a very extraordinary manner, not only my Writings (of which, being public, the Public is judge), but my Person, Morals, and Family, whereof, to those who know me not, a truer information may be requisite. Being divided between the necessity to say something of myself, and my own laziness to undertake so awkward a task, I thought it the shortest way to put the last hand to this Epistle. If it have anything pleasing, it will be that by which I am most desirous to please, the Truth and the Sentiment; and if anything offensive, it will be only to those I am least sorry to offend, the vicious or the ungenerous.

Many will know their own pictures in it, there being not a circumstance but what is true; but I have, for the most part, spared their Names, and they may escape being laughed at, if they please.

I would have some of them know, it was owing to the request of the learned and candid Friend to whom it is inscribed, that I make not as free use of theirs as they have done of mine. However, I shall have this advantage, and honor, on my side, that whereas, by their proceeding, any abuse may be directed at any man, no injury can possibly be done by mine, since a nameless character can never be found out, but by its truth and likeness. P.

P. Shut, shut the door, good John![2] fatigued, I said,
Tie up the knocker, say I'm sick, I'm dead.
The Dog-star rages! nay 'tis past a doubt,

[1]Pope indicates, in the "Advertisement" here printed, the purpose of this *Epistle,* but his statement concerning the time of its composition cannot be taken literally. A few passages were written earlier than 1734 (the portraits of Addison and Bufo, and the reference to his mother), but the *Epistle* as a whole dates from this year, or from 1735. Its immediate occasion was the abusive attack on Pope contained in the two poems he mentions in the "Advertisement." The first of these is said to have been written by Lady Mary Wortley Montagu and Lord John Hervey together; the second was written by Hervey. Dr. John Arbuthnot was both physician and man of letters, and Pope's close friend until his death in 1735, only a short time after the publication of the *Epistle.* The poem is cast in the form of a dialogue between Pope himself and Arbuthnot.

[2]John Searl, Pope's body-servant.

All Bedlam, or Parnassus, is let out:
Fire in each eye, and papers in each hand, 5
They rave, recite, and madden round the land.
What walls can guard me, or what shade can hide?
They pierce my thickets, through my Grot[3] they glide;
By land, by water, they renew the charge;
They stop the chariot, and they board the barge. 10
No place is sacred, not the Church is free;
E'en Sunday shines no Sabbath-day to me;
Then from the Mint[4] walks forth the Man of rime,
Happy to catch me just at Dinner-time.
Is there a Parson, much bemused in beer, 15
A maudlin Poetess, a riming Peer,
A Clerk,[5] foredoomed his father's soul to cross,
Who pens a Stanza, when he should *engross?*
Is there, who, locked from ink and paper, scrawls
With desp'rate charcoal round his darkened walls? 20
All fly to Twit'nam,[6] and in humble strain
Apply to me, to keep them mad or vain.
Arthur,[7] whose giddy son neglects the Laws,
Imputes to me and my damned works the cause:
Poor Cornus[8] sees his frantic wife elope, 25
And curses Wit, and Poetry, and Pope.
Friend to my Life (which did not you prolong,
The world had wanted many an idle song)
What Drop or Nostrum can this plague remove?
Or which must end me, a Fool's wrath or love? 30
A dire dilemma! either way I'm sped,[9]
If foes, they write, if friends, they read me dead.
Seized and tied down to judge, how wretched I!
Who can't be silent, and who will not lie.
To laugh, were want of goodness and of grace, 35

---

[3]An artificial grotto that formed a passage-way under a road which ran through Pope's grounds at Twickenham. This grotto and its ornamentation gave Pope a particular pleasure.

[4]A district in London where debtors could not be arrested; nor could they be arrested anywhere on Sundays.

[5]Law clerk.

[6]Twickenham, where Pope lived.

[7]Arthur Moore, a politician.

[8]Robert, Lord Walpole. [9]Done for.

And to be grave, exceeds all Pow'r of face.
I sit with sad civility, I read
With honest anguish, and an aching head;
And drop at last, but in unwilling ears,
This saving counsel, "Keep your piece nine years."[10] 40
"Nine years!" cries he, who high in Drury-Lane,
Lulled by soft Zephyrs through the broken pane,
Rimes ere he wakes, and prints before Term ends,[11]
Obliged by hunger, and request of friends:
"The piece, you think, is incorrect? why, take it, 45
I'm all submission, what you'd have it, make it."
Three things another's modest wishes bound,
My Friendship, and a Prologue, and ten pound.
Pitholeon sends to me: "You know his Grace,
I want a Patron; ask him for a Place." 50
Pitholeon libeled me—"but here's a letter
Informs you, Sir, 'twas when he knew no better.
Dare you refuse him? Curll[12] invites to dine,
He'll write a *Journal,* or he'll turn Divine."
Bless me! a packet.—"'Tis a stranger sues, 55
A Virgin Tragedy, an Orphan Muse."
If I dislike it, "Furies, death and rage!"
If I approve, "Commend it to the Stage."
There (thank my stars) my whole Commission ends,
The Play'rs and I are, luckily, no friends. 60
Fired that the house reject him, "'Sdeath I'll print it,
And shame the fools——Your Int'rest, Sir, with Lintot!"[13]
Lintot, dull rogue! will think your price too much:
"Not, Sir, if you revise it, and retouch."
All my demurs but double his Attacks; 65
At last he whispers, "Do; and we go snacks."
Glad of a quarrel, straight I clap the door,
Sir, let me see your works and you no more.
'Tis sung, when Midas' Ears began to spring
(Midas, a sacred person and a king), 70

---

[10]Horace's advice in his *Art of Poetry* (line 388).

[11]I. e., before the season is over.

[12]A piratical publisher and an enemy of Pope.

[13]Another publisher, who published much of Pope's work.

His very Minister who spied them first,
(Some say his Queen) was forced to speak, or burst.
And is not mine, my friend, a sorer case,
When ev'ry coxcomb perks them in my face?
A. Good friend, forbear! you deal in dang'rous things. 75
I'd never name Queens, Ministers, or Kings;[14]
Keep close to Ears, and those let asses prick;
'Tis nothing— P. Nothing? if they bite and kick?
Out with it, *Dunciad!* let the secret pass,
That secret to each fool, that he's an Ass: 80
The truth once told (and wherefore should we lie?)
The Queen of Midas slept, and so may I.
You think this cruel? take it for a rule,
No creature smarts so little as a fool.
Let peals of laughter, Codrus! round thee break, 85
Thou unconcerned canst hear the mighty crack:
Pit, Box, and gall'ry in convulsions hurled,
Thou stand'st unshook amidst a bursting world.
Who shames a Scribbler? break one cobweb through,
He spins the slight, self-pleasing thread anew: 90
Destroy his fib or sophistry, in vain,
The creature's at his dirty work again,
Throned in the center of his thin designs,
Proud of a vast extent of flimsy lines!
Whom have I hurt? has Poet yet, or Peer, 95
Lost the arched eye-brow, or Parnassian sneer?
And has not Colley[15] still his Lord and Whore?
His butchers Henley? his freemasons Moore?
Does not one table Bavius still admit?
Still to one Bishop Philips[16] seem a wit? 100
Still Sappho[17]— A. Hold! for God's sake—you'll offend,
No Names!—be calm!—learn prudence of a friend!
I too could write, and I am twice as tall;
But foes like these— P. One Flatt'rer's worse than all.
Of all mad creatures, if the learn'd are right,
It is the slaver kills, and not the bite. 106
A fool quite angry is quite innocent:
Alas! 'tis ten times worse when they *repent*.

One dedicates in high heroic prose,
And ridicules beyond a hundred foes: 110
One from all Grubstreet will my fame defend,
And, more abusive, calls himself my friend.
This prints my *Letters*, that expects a bribe,
And others roar aloud, "Subscribe, subscribe."
There are, who to my person pay their court: 115
I cough like Horace, and, though lean, am short,
Ammon's great son[18] one shoulder had too high,
Such Ovid's nose, and "Sir! you have an Eye"—
Go on, obliging creatures, make me see
All that disgraced my Betters, met in me. 120
Say for my comfort, languishing in bed,
"Just so immortal Maro[19] held his head:"
And when I die, be sure you let me know
Great Homer died three thousand years ago.
Why did I write? what sin to me unknown 125
Dipped me in ink, my parents', or my own?
As yet a child, nor yet a fool to fame,
I lisped in numbers, for the numbers came.
I left no calling for this idle trade,
No duty broke, no father disobeyed. 130
The Muse but served to ease some friend, not Wife,
To help me through this long disease, my Life,
To second, Arbuthnot! thy Art and Care,
And teach the Being you preserved, to bear.
But why then publish? Granville[20] the polite, 135
And knowing Walsh,[21] would tell me I could write;
Well-natured Garth[22] inflamed with early praise;
And Congreve loved, and Swift endured my lays;
The courtly Talbot, Somers, Sheffield,[23] read;
E'en mitered Rochester[24] would nod the head,
And St. John's self[25] (great Dryden's friends before) 141
With open arms received one Poet more.

---

[14]A glance at Queen Caroline, Walpole, and George II.

[15]Colley Cibber. [16]Ambrose Philips.

[17]Lady Mary Wortley Montagu.

[18]Alexander the Great. [19]Virgil.

[20]George Granville, Lord Lansdowne.

[21]See introductory account of Pope above.

[22]Samuel Garth, physician and man of letters.

[23]All statesmen and patrons of letters.

[24]Francis Atterbury, Bishop of Rochester.

[25]Lord Bolingbroke, to whom Pope's *Essay on Man* is dedicated.

Happy my studies, when by these approved!
Happier their author, when by these beloved!
From these the world will judge of men and books, 145
Not from the Burnets, Oldmixons, and Cookes.[26]
Soft were my numbers; who could take offense,
While pure Description held the place of Sense?
Like gentle Fanny's[27] was my flow'ry theme,
A painted mistress, or a purling stream. 150
Yet then did Gildon draw his venal quill;—
I wished the man a dinner, and sat still.
Yet then did Dennis[28] rave in furious fret;
I never answered,—I was not in debt.
If want provoked, or madness made them print, 155
I waged no war with Bedlam or the Mint.
Did some more sober Critic come abroad;
If wrong, I smiled; if right, I kissed the rod.
Pains, reading, study, are their just pretense,
And all they want is spirit, taste, and sense. 160
Commas and points they set exactly right,
And 'twere a sin to rob them of their mite.
Yet ne'er one sprig of laurel graced these ribalds,
From slashing Bentley down to pidling Tibalds:[29]
Each wight, who reads not, and but scans and spells, 165
Each Word-catcher, that lives on syllables,
E'en such small Critics some regard may claim,
Preserved in Milton's or in Shakespeare's name.
Pretty! in amber to observe the forms
Of hairs, or straws, or dirt, or grubs, or worms! 170
The things, we know, are neither rich nor rare,
But wonder how the devil they got there.
Were others angry: I excused them too;
Well might they rage, I gave them but their due.
A man's true merit 'tis not hard to find; 175
But each man's secret standard in his mind,
That Casting-weight pride adds to emptiness,
This, who can gratify? for who can guess?
The Bard[30] whom pilfered Pastorals renown,
Who turns a Persian tale for half a Crown, 180
Just writes to make his barrenness appear,
And strains, from hard-bound brains, eight lines a year;
He, who still wanting, though he lives on theft,
Steals much, spends little, yet has nothing left:
And He, who now to sense, now nonsense leaning, 185
Means not, but blunders round about a meaning:
And He, whose fustian's so sublimely bad,
It is not Poetry, but prose run mad:
All these, my modest Satire bade translate,
And owned that nine such Poets made a Tate.[31] 190
How did they fume, and stamp, and roar, and chafe!
And swear, not Addison himself was safe.
Peace to all such! but were there One whose fires
True Genius kindles, and fair Fame inspires;
Bless'd with each talent and each art to please, 195
And born to write, converse, and live with ease:
Should such a man, too fond to rule alone,
Bear, like the Turk, no brother near the throne,
View him with scornful, yet with jealous eyes,
And hate for arts that caused himself to rise; 200
Damn with faint praise, assent with civil leer,
And without sneering, teach the rest to sneer;
Willing to wound, and yet afraid to strike,
Just hint a fault, and hesitate dislike;
Alike reserved to blame, or to commend, 205
A tim'rous foe, and a suspicious friend;
Dreading e'en fools, by Flatterers besieged,
And so obliging, that he ne'er obliged;
Like Cato, give his little Senate laws,
And sit attentive to his own applause; 210
While Wits and Templars[32] ev'ry sentence raise,
And wonder with a foolish face of praise:——
Who but must laugh, if such a man there be?
Who would not weep, if Atticus[33] were he?

[26]Authors of secret and scandalous history (Pope's note).

[27]John, Lord Hervey.

[28]Gildon and Dennis were critics of the day.

[29]Bentley was a famous classical scholar who published an edition of *Paradise Lost;* Theobald a scholar and editor of Shakespeare.

[30]Ambrose Philips.

[31]Nahum Tate, at the time poet laureate.

[32]Legal student, attending one of the London Inns of Court which occupied land once belonging to the Knights Templars.

[33]Addison.

What though my Name stood rubric[34] on the walls 215
Or plastered posts, with claps,[35] in capitals?
Or smoking forth, a hundred hawkers' load,
On wings of winds came flying all abroad?
I sought no homage from the Race that write;
I kept, like Asian Monarchs, from their sight: 220
Poems I heeded (now be-rimed so long)
No more than thou, great George! a birthday song.
I ne'er with wits or witlings passed my days,
To spread about the itch of verse and praise;
Nor like a puppy, daggled through the town, 225
To fetch and carry sing-song up and down;
Nor at Rehearsals sweat, and mouthed, and cried,
With handkerchief and orange at my side;
But sick of fops, and poetry, and prate,
To Bufo,[36] left the whole Castalian state. 230
Proud as Apollo on his forkéd hill,[37]
Sat full-blown Bufo, puffed by ev'ry quill;
Fed with soft Dedication all day long,
Horace and he went hand in hand in song.
His Library (where busts of Poets dead 235
And a true Pindar stood without a head),
Received of wits an undistinguished race,
Who first his judgment asked, and then a place:
Much they extolled his pictures, much his seat,
And flattered ev'ry day, and some days eat:
Till grown more frugal in his riper days, 241
He paid some bards with port, and some with praise:
To some a dry rehearsal saw assigned,
And others (harder still) he paid in kind.
Dryden alone (what wonder?) came not nigh,
Dryden alone escaped this judging eye: 246
But still the Great have kindness in reserve,
He helped to bury whom he helped to starve.
May some choice patron bless each gray goose quill!
May ev'ry Bavius have his Bufo still! 250
So, when a Statesman wants a day's defense,
Or Envy holds a whole week's war with Sense,
Or simple pride for flatt'ry makes demands,
May dunce by dunce be whistled off my hands!
Bless'd be the Great! for those they take away, 255
And those they left me; for they left me Gay;[38]
Left me to see neglected Genius bloom,
Neglected die, and tell it on his tomb:
Of all thy blameless life the sole return
My Verse, and Queensb'ry weeping o'er thy urn. 260
Oh, let me live my own, and die so too!
(To live and die is all I have to do)
Maintain a Poet's dignity and ease,
And see what friends, and read what books I please;
Above a Patron, though I condescend 265
Sometimes to call a minister my friend.
I was not born for Courts or great affairs;
I pay my debts, believe, and say my pray'rs;
Can sleep without a Poem in my head;
Nor know, if Dennis be alive or dead. 270
Why am I asked what next shall see the light?
Heav'ns! was I born for nothing but to write?
Has Life no joys for me? or (to be grave)
Have I no friend to serve, no soul to save?
"I found him close with Swift"—"Indeed? no doubt" 275
(Cries prating Balbus), "something will come out."
'Tis all in vain, deny it as I will.
"No, such a Genius never can lie still;"
And then for mine obligingly mistakes
The first Lampoon Sir Will or Bubo[39] makes.
Poor guiltless I! and can I choose but smile,
When ev'ry Coxcomb knows me by my Style?
Cursed be the verse, how well soe'er it flow,
That tends to make one worthy man my foe,
Give Virtue scandal, Innocence a fear, 285
Or from the soft-eyed Virgin steal a tear!
But he who hurts a harmless neighbor's peace,
Insults fall'n worth, or Beauty in distress,
Who loves a Lie, lame slander helps about,
Who writes a Libel, or who copies out: 290
That Fop, whose pride affects a patron's name,
Yet absent, wounds an author's honest fame:
Who can your merit selfishly approve,
And show the sense of it without the love;
Who has the vanity to call you friend, 295
Yet wants the honor, injured, to defend;
Who tells whate'er you think, whate'er you say,

[34]The reference is to Lintot's practice of posting on the walls of his shop the titles of new books in red letters.

[35]Posters.

[36]Probably the Earl of Halifax (the following portrait is said to have been intended, when first written, for Bubb Doddington).

[37]The cleft summit of Parnassus.

[38]John Gay, the poet (1685–1732).

[39]Sir William Yonge and Bubb Doddington.

And, if he lie not, must at least betray:
Who to the Dean, and silver bell can swear,
And sees at Canons[40] what was never there;
Who reads, but with a lust to misapply, 301
Make Satire a Lampoon, and Fiction, Lie.
A lash like mine no honest man shall dread,
But all such babbling blockheads in his stead.
Let Sporus[41] tremble— A. What? that thing of silk, 305
Sporus, that mere white curd of Ass's milk!
Satire or sense, alas! can Sporus feel?
Who breaks a butterfly upon a wheel?
P. Yet let me flap this bug with gilded wings,
This painted child of dirt, that stinks and stings; 310
Whose buzz the witty and the fair annoys,
Yet wit ne'er tastes, and beauty ne'er enjoys:
So well-bred spaniels civilly delight
In mumbling of the game they dare not bite.
Eternal smiles his emptiness betray, 315
As shallow streams run dimpling all the way.
Whether in florid impotence he speaks,
And, as the prompter breathes, the puppet squeaks;
Or at the ear of Eve,[42] familiar Toad,
Half froth, half venom, spits himself abroad,
In puns, or politics, or tales, or lies, 321
Or spite, or smut, or rimes, or blasphemies.
His wit all see-saw, between that and this,
Now high, now low, now master up, now miss,
And he himself one vile Antithesis. 325
Amphibious thing! that acting either part,
The trifling head or the corrupted heart,
Fop at the toilet, flatt'rer at the board,
Now trips a Lady, and now struts a Lord.
Eve's tempter thus the Rabbins have expressed, 330
A Cherub's face, a reptile all the rest;
Beauty that shocks you, parts that none will trust;
Wit that can creep, and pride that licks the dust. 333
Not Fortune's worshiper, nor fashion's fool,
Not Lucre's madman, nor Ambition's tool,
Not proud, nor servile;—be one Poet's praise,
That, if he pleased, he pleased by manly ways:
That Flatt'ry, e'en to Kings, he held a shame,
And thought a Lie in verse or prose the same. 339
That not in Fancy's maze he wandered long,
But stooped to Truth, and moralized his song:
That not for Fame, but Virtue's better end,
He stood the furious foe, the timid friend,
The damning critic, half approving wit,
The coxcomb hit, or fearing to be hit; 345
Laughed at the loss of friends he never had,
The dull, the proud, the wicked, and the mad;
The distant threats of vengeance on his head,
The blow unfelt, the tear he never shed; 349
The tale revived, the lie so oft o'erthrown,
Th' imputed trash, and dullness not his own;
The morals blackened when the writings 'scape,
The libeled person, and the pictured shape;
Abuse, on all he loved, or loved him, spread,
A friend in exile, or a father dead; 355
The whisper, that to greatness still too near,
Perhaps, yet vibrates on his Sov'reign's ear:—
Welcome for thee, fair Virtue! all the past;
For thee, fair Virtue! welcome e'en the last!
A. But why insult the poor, affront the great? 360
P. A knave's a knave, to me, in ev'ry state:
Alike my scorn, if he succeed or fail.
Sporus at court, or Japhet[43] in a jail,
A hireling scribbler, or a hireling peer,
Knight of the post corrupt, or of the shire;
If on a Pillory, or near a Throne, 366
He gain his Prince's ear, or lose his own.
Yet soft by nature, more a dupe than wit,
Sappho can tell you how this man was bit;
This dreaded Sat'rist Dennis will confess 370
Foe to his pride, but friend to his distress:
So humble, he has knocked at Tibbald's door,
Has drunk with Cibber, nay has rimed for Moore.
Full ten years slandered, did he once reply?
Three thousand suns went down on Welsted's[44] lie. 375
To please a Mistress one aspersed his life;
He lashed him not, but let her be his wife.
Let Budgell[45] charge low Grubstreet on his quill,
And write whate'er he pleased, except his Will;

[40] Estate of the Duke of Chandos, which Pope was supposed to have satirized in the fourth of his *Moral Essays*.

[41] Lord Hervey, whom ill health forced to drink ass's milk.

[42] Queen Caroline. Cf. *Paradise Lost*, IV, 799–809.

[43] Japhet Crooke, a forger.

[44] A hack-writer of the day.

[45] Budgell was charged with forging a will, to his own profit.

Let the two Curlls[46] of Town and Court, abuse 380
His father, mother, body, soul and muse.
Yet why? that Father held it for a rule,
It was a sin to call our neighbor fool;
That harmless Mother thought no wife a whore:
Hear this, and spare his family, James Moore! 385
Unspotted names, and memorable long!
If there be force in Virtue, or in Song.
Of gentle blood (part shed in Honor's cause,
While yet in Britain Honor had applause)
Each parent sprung— A. What fortune, pray?— P. Their own, 390
And better got, than Bestia's from the throne.
Born to no Pride, inheriting no Strife,
Nor marrying Discord in a noble wife,[47]
Stranger to civil and religious rage,
The good man walked innoxious through his age. 395
Nor Courts he saw, no suits would ever try,
Nor dared an Oath, nor hazarded a Lie.

[46]The bookseller and Lord Hervey.

[47]Alluding to Addison's marriage with the Countess of Warwick.

Unlearn'd, he knew no schoolman's subtle art,
No language, but the language of the heart.
By Nature honest, by Experience wise, 400
Healthy by temp'rance, and by exercise:
His life, though long, to sickness past unknown,
His death was instant, and without a groan.
O grant me, thus to live, and thus to die!
Who sprung from Kings shall know less joy than I. 405
O Friend! may each domestic bliss be thine!
Be no unpleasing Melancholy mine:
Me, let the tender office long engage,
To rock the cradle of reposing Age,
With lenient arts extend a Mother's breadth,
Make Languor smile, and smooth the bed of Death, 411
Explore the thought, explain the asking eye,
And keep a while one parent from the sky!
On cares like these if length of days attend,
May Heav'n, to bless those days, preserve my friend, 415
Preserve him social, cheerful and serene,
And just as rich as when he served a Queen.[48]
A. Whether that blessing be denied or giv'n,
Thus far was right, the rest belongs to Heav'n.

[48]Arbuthnot had been physician to Queen Anne.

THOMAS GRAY

1716–1771

Gray was born in Cornhill, London, on 26 December, 1716. When he was about eleven years old he was sent to Eton, where he formed close friendships with Horace Walpole, Richard West, whose early death in 1742 caused him deep grief, and Thomas Ashton. In 1734 he entered Peterhouse, Cambridge. He made but few acquaintances there, his life-long habit of reserve already asserting itself, and he left Cambridge in 1738 without taking a degree, because of his hatred of mathematics. In 1739 he went with Horace Walpole to travel on the Continent, and they spent some months together very agreeably, though in Italy there arose a difference between them which caused them to part company, Gray returning home alone in the summer of 1741. He spent about a year living with his mother at Stoke Poges, and then in 1742 returned to Peterhouse. He made some efforts to study the law, and was given the bachelor's degree in law in 1743, but he never took any steps looking to active practice. Instead, he settled down to a life of study at Cambridge, where he remained, save for one interruption, through the rest of his life. In consequence of some disturbance by undergraduates he moved from Peterhouse to Pembroke in 1756, and in a life outwardly so quiet as his this was a great event. When the British Museum was opened in 1759 he took lodgings in London and remained there two years, studying manuscripts and old books in the Museum. He is said to have become one of the most learned men in Europe in his time, his studies including classical literature, history, modern languages and literatures, architecture, botany, and music. He made extensive collections and notes for a history of English poetry, but gave over his design when he learned that Thomas Warton was engaged on the same subject. His few poems he wrote slowly and with difficulty, and he had no ambition for fame. He was occupied with the famous *Elegy* for about eight years before he completed it, and then was induced to publish it in 1751 only when he learned that a mutilated copy was about to be printed without his permission. Nevertheless, the few poems he published in 1753 and 1757 won him immediate recognition, and he was offered the post of poet laureate in the latter year. This he refused without hesitation, regarding it, in view of the character of recent incumbents, as a questionable honor, and as one in any case for which he did not care. In 1768 he was made professor of modern history at Cambridge, a post which in his day did not necessarily carry any duties with it; and, though he planned to deliver some lectures, he never did so. Gray died on 30 July, 1771, and was buried at Stoke Poges, by the side of his mother.

Gray's poems are almost as few in number as those of his contemporary, Collins, and like Collins's they are characterized by an exquisite sense of form. Gray's fastidious classicism of style and form issued from qualities of temperament which were reënforced by his close study of the Greeks and, among English poets, of Milton and Dryden. His antiquarianism, which found expression in the *Bard* and in his Norse and other Welsh poems, together with admiration which he felt for rugged natural scenery, has caused him to be regarded as a forerunner of the romantic poets of the early nineteenth century. This to a certain extent he was, but the point may be unduly insisted on to the obscuration of his more important qualities. His interesting letters are of a piece with his poems in showing that he was "romantic" in only a very partial and external sense.

The Poems of Gray and Collins have most recently been edited by Austin L. Poole (London, 1937), and the *Correspondence of Thomas Gray* by Paget Toynbee and Leonard Whibley (Oxford, 1935). In addition to the biographical material supplied by the *Correspondence* the brief life, by R. W. Ketton Cremer, *Thomas Gray* (London, 1935), may be recommended. A more limited side of Gray is investigated by William P. Jones in *Thomas Gray, Scholar; the True Tragedy of an Eighteenth-Century Gentleman* (Cambridge, U. S. A., 1937). Matthew Arnold's well-known essay on Gray appears in *Essays in Criticism*, Second Series (London, 1888).

ODE ON THE DEATH OF A FAVORITE CAT

Drowned in a Tub of Gold Fishes[1]

'Twas on a lofty vase's side,
Where China's gayest art had dyed
  The azure flowers, that blow;
Demurest of the tabby kind,
The pensive Selima reclined, 5
  Gazed on the lake below.

Her conscious tail her joy declared;
The fair round face, the snowy beard,
  The velvet of her paws,
Her coat, that with the tortoise vies, 10
Her ears of jet, and emerald eyes,
  She saw; and purred applause.

Still had she gazed; but 'midst the tide
Two angel forms were seen to glide,
  The Genii of the stream: 15
Their scaly armor's Tyrian hue
Through richest purple to the view
  Betrayed a golden gleam:

The hapless Nymph with wonder saw:
A whisker first and then a claw, 20
  With many an ardent wish,
She stretched in vain to reach the prize.
What female heart can gold despise?
  What Cat's averse to fish?

Presumptuous Maid! with looks intent 25
Again she stretched, again she bent,
  Nor knew the gulf between.
(Malignant Fate sat by, and smiled)
The slipp'ry verge her feet beguiled,
  She tumbled headlong in. 30

Eight times emerging from the flood
She mewed to ev'ry wat'ry God,
  Some speedy aid to send.
No Dolphin came, no Nereid stirred:
Nor cruel Tom, nor Susan heard. 35
  A Fav'rite has no friend!

From hence, ye Beauties, undeceived,
Know, one false step is ne'er retrieved,
  And be with caution bold.
Not all that tempts your wand'ring eyes 40
And heedless hearts, is lawful prize;
  Nor all, that glisters, gold.

[1]Written early in 1747; first published in 1748. The cat belonged to Gray's friend, Horace Walpole.

ODE ON A DISTANT PROSPECT OF ETON COLLEGE[1]

"Ἄνθρωπος· ἱκανὴ πρόφασις εἰς τὸ δυστυχεῖν.[2]
—MENANDER.

Ye distant spires, ye antique towers,
  That crown the wat'ry glade,
Where grateful Science still adores
  Her Henry's[3] holy Shade;
And ye, that from the stately brow 5
Of Windsor's[4] heights th' expanse below
  Of grove, of lawn, of mead survey,
Whose turf, whose shade, whose flowers among
Wanders the hoary Thames along
  His silver-winding way. 10

Ah happy hills, ah pleasing shade,
  Ah fields beloved in vain,
Where once my careless childhood strayed,
  A stranger yet to pain!
I feel the gales, that from ye blow, 15
A momentary bliss bestow,
  As waving fresh their gladsome wing,
My weary soul they seem to sooth,
And, redolent of joy and youth,
  To breathe a second spring. 20

Say, Father Thames, for thou hast seen
  Full many a sprightly race
Disporting on thy margent green
  The paths of pleasure trace,
Who foremost now delight to cleave 25
With pliant arm thy glassy wave?
  The captive linnet which enthrall?
What idle progeny succeed
To chase the rolling circle's speed,[5]
  Or urge the flying ball? 30

While some on earnest business bent
  Their murm'ring labors ply
'Gainst graver hours, that bring constraint
  To sweeten liberty:
Some bold adventurers disdain 35
The limits of their little reign,
  And unknown regions dare descry:
Still as they run they look behind,
They hear a voice in every wind,
  And snatch a fearful joy. 40

[1]Written in 1742; first published in 1747.
[2]A human being: sufficient cause for misery.
[3]Henry VI, founder of Eton College (1440).
[4]Windsor Castle, a royal palace near Eton.
[5]Roll the hoop.

Gay hope is theirs by fancy fed,
  Less pleasing when possessed;
The tear forgot as soon as shed,
  The sunshine of the breast:
Theirs buxom health of rosy hue, 45
Wild wit, invention ever-new,
  And lively cheer of vigor born;
The thoughtless day, the easy night,
The spirits pure, the slumbers light,
  That fly th' approach of morn. 50

Alas, regardless of their doom,
  The little victims play!
No sense have they of ills to come,
  Nor care beyond to-day:
Yet see how all around 'em wait 55
The Ministers of human fate,
  And black Misfortune's baleful train!
Ah, show them where in ambush stand
To seize their prey the murd'rous band!
  Ah, tell them, they are men! 60

These shall the fury Passions tear,
  The vultures of the mind,
Disdainful Anger, pallid Fear,
  And Shame that skulks behind;
Or pining Love shall waste their youth, 65
Or Jealousy with rankling tooth,
  That inly gnaws the secret heart,
And Envy wan, and faded Care,
Grim-visaged comfortless Despair,
  And Sorrow's piercing dart. 70

Ambition this shall tempt to rise,
  Then whirl the wretch from high,
To bitter Scorn a sacrifice,
  And grinning Infamy.
The stings of Falsehood those shall try, 75
And hard Unkindness' altered eye,
  That mocks the tear it forced to flow;
And keen Remorse with blood defiled,
And moody Madness laughing wild
  Amid severest woe. 80

Lo, in the vale of years beneath
  A grisly troop are seen,
The painful family of Death,
  More hideous than their Queen:
This racks the joints, this fires the veins, 85
That every laboring sinew strains,
  Those in the deeper vitals rage:
Lo, Poverty, to fill the band,
That numbs the soul with icy hand,
  And slow-consuming Age. 90

To each his suff'rings: all are men,
  Condemned alike to groan;
The tender for another's pain,
  Th' unfeeling for his own.
Yet ah! why should they know their fate? 95
Since sorrow never comes too late,
  And happiness too swiftly flies.
Thought would destroy their paradise.
No more; where ignorance is bliss,
  'Tis folly to be wise. 100

HYMN TO ADVERSITY[1]

——Ζῆνα
τὸν φρονεῖν βροτοὺς ὁδώ-
σαντα, τῷ πάθει μαθάν
θέντα κυρίως ἔχειν.[2]
—AESCHYLUS, *Agamemnon.*

Daughter of Jove, relentless Power,
Thou Tamer of the human breast,
Whose iron scourge and tort'ring hour,
The Bad affright, afflict the Best!
Bound in thy adamantine chain 5
The Proud are taught to taste of pain,
And purple Tyrants vainly groan
With pangs unfelt before, unpitied and alone.

When first thy Sire to send on earth
Virtue, his darling Child, designed, 10
To thee he gave the heav'nly Birth,
And bade to form her infant mind.
Stern rugged Nurse! thy rigid lore
With patience many a year she bore:
What sorrow was, thou bad'st her know, 15
And from her own she learned to melt at
  others' woe.

Scared at thy frown terrific, fly
Self-pleasing Folly's idle brood,
Wild Laughter, Noise, and thoughtless Joy,
And leave us leisure to be good. 20
Light they disperse, and with them go
The summer Friend, the flatt'ring Foe;
By vain Prosperity received,
To her they vow their truth, and are again
  believed.

Wisdom is sable garb arrayed 25
Immersed in rapt'rous thought profound,
And Melancholy, silent maid
With leaden eye, that loves the ground,
Still on thy solemn steps attend:
Warm Charity, the gen'ral Friend, 30

[1]Written in 1742; first published in 1753.

[2]Zeus has set men on the way to wisdom and decreed that they shall learn through suffering (lines 167–171).

With Justice to herself severe,
And Pity dropping soft the sadly-pleasing tear.

Oh, gently on thy Suppliant's head,
Dread Goddess, lay thy chast'ning hand!
Not in thy Gorgon terrors clad,[3] 35
Nor circled with the vengeful Band
(As by the Impious thou art seen)
With thund'ring voice, and threat'ning mien,
With screaming Horror's funeral cry,
Despair, and fell Disease, and ghastly Poverty. 40

Thy form benign, O Goddess, wear,
Thy milder influence impart,
Thy philosophic Train be there
To soften, not to wound my heart,
The gen'rous spark extinct revive, 45
Teach me to love and to forgive,
Exact my own defects to scan,
What others are, to feel, and know myself a Man.

THE PROGRESS OF POESY[1]

A Pindaric Ode

Φωνᾶντα συνετοῖσιν· ἐς
Δὲ τὸ πᾶν ἑρμηνέων χατίζει.[2]
—PINDAR, *Olymp. II.*

I. STROPHE

Awake, Aeolian lyre,[3] awake,
And give to rapture all thy trembling strings.
From Helicon's harmonious springs
A thousand rills their mazy progress take:
The laughing flowers, that round them blow,
Drink life and fragrance as they flow. 6
Now the rich stream of music winds along
Deep, majestic, smooth, and strong,
Through verdant vales, and Ceres' golden reign:[4]
Now rolling down the steep amain, 10
Headlong, impetuous, see it pour:
The rocks, and nodding groves rebellow to the roar.

ANTISTROPHE

Oh! Sovereign of the willing soul,
Parent of sweet and solemn-breathing airs,
Enchanting shell![5] the sullen Cares, 15
And frantic Passions hear thy soft control.
On Thracia's hills the Lord of War,[6]
Has curbed the fury of his car,
And dropped his thirsty lance at thy command.
Perching on the sceptered hand 20
Of Jove, thy magic lulls the feathered king[7]
With ruffled plumes, and flagging wing:
Quenched in dark clouds of slumber lie
The terror of his beak, the lightnings of his eye.

EPODE

Thee the voice, the dance, obey, 25
Tempered to thy warbled lay.
O'er Idalia's[8] velvet-green
The rosy-crownéd Loves are seen
On Cytherea's day
With antic Sports, and blue-eyed Pleasures,
Frisking light in frolic measures; 31
Now pursuing, now retreating,
Now in circling troops they meet:
To brisk notes in cadence beating
Glance their many-twinkling feet. 35
Slow melting strains their Queen's approach declare:
Where'er she turns the Graces homage pay.
With arms sublime, that float upon the air,
In gliding state she wins her easy way:
O'er her warm cheek, and rising bosom, move
The bloom of young Desire, the purple light of Love. 41

II. STROPHE

Man's feeble race what Ills await,
Labor and Penury, the racks of Pain,
Disease, and Sorrow's weeping train,
And Death, sad refuge from the storms of Fate! 45
The fond complaint, my Song, disprove,
And justify the laws of Jove.
Say, has he giv'n in vain the heav'nly Muse?
Night, and all her sickly dews,

[3]Gorgon means dreadful; the reference is to the image on the shield of Pallas Athene. In the next line "the vengeful Band" are the Furies.

[1]Written in 1754; first published in 1757.

[2]A voice intelligible to the wise, but one that needs interpreters for the rabble (lines 153–154).

[3]The lyre of Pindar.

[4]Fields over which Ceres reigns.

[5]The lyre was said to have been made first by Hermes from a tortoise shell.

[6]Mars. Thrace was thought to be his favorite abode.

[7]The eagle.

[8]A town in Cyprus containing a temple to Venus, or Cytherea, as she was sometimes called.

Her Specters wan, and Birds of boding cry, 50
He gives to range the dreary sky:
Till down the eastern cliffs afar
Hyperion's march[9] they spy, and glitt'ring shafts of war.

ANTISTROPHE

In climes beyond the solar road,
Where shaggy forms o'er ice-built mountains roam, 55
The Muse has broke the twilight-gloom
To cheer the shiv'ring Native's dull abode.
And oft, beneath the od'rous shade
Of Chili's boundless forests laid,
She deigns to hear the savage Youth repeat 60
In loose numbers wildly sweet
Their feather-cinctured Chiefs, and dusky Loves.
Her track, where'er the Goddess roves,
Glory pursue, and generous Shame,
Th' unconquerable Mind, and Freedom's holy flame. 65

EPODE

Woods, that wave o'er Delphi's steep,
Isles, that crown th' Aegean deep,
Fields, that cool Ilissus[10] laves,
Or where Maeander's[11] amber waves
In lingering Lab'rinths creep, 70
How do your tuneful Echoes languish,
Mute, but to the voice of Anguish?
Where each old poetic Mountain
Inspiration breathed around:
Ev'ry shade and hallowed Fountain 75
Murmured deep a solemn sound:
Till the sad Nine in Greece's evil hour
Left their Parnassus for the Latian plains.
Alike they scorn the pomp of tyrant-Power,
And coward Vice, that revels in her chains.
When Latium had her lofty spirit lost, 81
They sought, O Albion! next thy sea-encircled coast.[12]

[9]The sunrise.

[10]A stream flowing through Athens.

[11]A river in Asia Minor.

[12]Gray's note on this epode is as follows: Progress of poetry from Greece to Italy, and from Italy to England. Chaucer was not unacquainted with the writings of Dante or of Petrarch. The Earl of Surrey and Sir Tho. Wyatt had traveled in Italy [Gray is wrong about Surrey, who was never in Italy, though he spent some time in France], and formed their taste there; Spenser imitated the Italian writers; Milton improved on them: but this school expired soon after the Restoration, and a new one arose on the French model, which has subsisted ever since.

III. STROPHE

Far from the sun and summer-gale,
In thy green lap was Nature's Darling[13] laid,
What time, where lucid Avon strayed, 85
To Him the mighty Mother did unveil
Her awful face: The dauntless Child
Stretched forth his little arms, and smiled.
This pencil take (she said) whose colors clear
Richly paint the vernal year: 90
Thine too these golden keys, immortal Boy!
This can unlock the gates of Joy;
Of Horror that, and thrilling Fears,
Or ope the sacred source of sympathetic Tears.

ANTISTROPHE

Nor second He,[14] that rode sublime 95
Upon the seraph-wings of Ecstasy,
The secrets of th' Abyss to spy.
He passed the flaming bounds of Place and Time:
The living Throne, the sapphire-blaze,
Where Angels tremble, while they gaze, 100
He saw; but blasted with excess of light,
Closed his eyes in endless night.
Behold, where Dryden's less presumptuous car,
Wide o'er the fields of Glory bear
Two Coursers of ethereal race, 105
With necks in thunder clothed, and long-resounding pace.

EPODE

Hark, his hands the lyre explore!
Bright-eyed Fancy hovering o'er
Scatters from her pictured urn 109
Thoughts that breathe, and words that burn.
But ah! 'tis heard no more——
Oh! Lyre divine, what daring Spirit
Wakes thee now? though he inherit
Nor the pride, nor ample pinion,
That the Theban Eagle bear[15] 115
Sailing with supreme dominion
Through the azure deep of air:
Yet oft before his infant eyes would run
Such forms, as glitter in the Muse's ray 119
With orient hues, unborrowed of the Sun:
Yet shall he mount, and keep his distant way
Beyond the limits of a vulgar fate,
Beneath the Good how far—but far above the Great.

[13]Shakespeare. [14]Milton.

[15]Pindar compares himself to that bird, and his enemies to ravens that croak and clamor in vain below, while it pursues its flight, regardless of their noise (Gray's note).

THE BARD[1]

A Pindaric Ode

ADVERTISEMENT

The following Ode is founded on a Tradition current in Wales, that Edward the First, when he completed the conquest of that country, ordered all the Bards that fell into his hands to be put to death.[2]

I. STROPHE

"Ruin seize thee, ruthless King!
Confusion on thy banners wait,
Though fanned by Conquest's crimson wing
They mock the air with idle state.
Helm, nor Hauberk's twisted mail, 5
Nor even thy virtues, Tyrant, shall avail
To save thy secret soul from nightly fears,
From Cambria's[3] curse, from Cambria's tears!"
Such were the sounds, that o'er the crested pride 9
Of the first Edward scattered wild dismay,
As down the steep of Snowdon's[4] shaggy side
He wound with toilsome march his long array.
Stout Glo'ster[5] stood aghast in speechless trance;
To arms! cried Mortimer,[6] and couched his quiv'ring lance.

ANTISTROPHE

On a rock, whose haughty brow 15
Frowns o'er old Conway's foaming flood,
Robed in the sable garb of woe,
With haggard eyes the Poet stood;
(Loose his beard, and hoary hair 19
Streamed, like a meteor, to the troubled air)
And with a Master's hand, and Prophet's fire,
Struck the deep sorrows of his lyre.
"Hark, how each giant-oak, and desert cave,
Sighs to the torrent's awful voice beneath!
O'er thee, O King! their hundred arms they wave, 25
Revenge on thee in hoarser murmurs breathe;
Vocal no more, since Cambria's fatal day,
To high-born Hoel's harp, or soft Llewellyn's lay.

EPODE

"Cold is Cadwallo's tongue,
That hushed the stormy main: 30
Brave Urien sleeps upon his craggy bed:
Mountains, ye mourn in vain
Modred, whose magic song
Made huge Plinlimmon[7] bow his cloud-topped head.
On dreary Arvon's shore they lie,[8] 35
Smeared with gore, and ghastly pale:
Far, far aloof th' affrighted ravens sail;
The famished Eagle screams, and passes by.
Dear lost companions of my tuneful art, 39
Dear, as the light that visits these sad eyes,
Dear, as the ruddy drops that warm my heart,
Ye died amidst your dying country's cries—
No more I weep. They do not sleep.
On yonder cliffs, a grisly band,
I see them sit, they linger yet, 45
Avengers of their native land:
With me in dreadful harmony they join,
And weave with bloody hands the tissue of thy line.

II. STROPHE

" 'Weave the warp, and weave the woof,
The winding-sheet of Edward's race. 50
Give ample room, and verge enough
The characters of hell to trace.
Mark the year, and mark the night,
When Severn shall re-echo with affright
The shrieks of death, through Berkeley's roofs that ring, 55
Shrieks of an agonizing King![9]
She-Wolf[10] of France, with unrelenting fangs,
That tear'st the bowels of thy mangled Mate,

[1]Begun in 1754 and finished in 1757, when it was first published.

[2]This tradition has no foundation in fact. Edward I reigned from 1272 to 1307.

[3]Wales.

[4]A name given by the Saxons to that mountainous tract which the Welsh themselves call *Craigianeryri:* it included all the highlands of Carnarvonshire and Merionethshire, as far east as the river Conway (Gray's note).

[5]Gilbert de Clare, surnamed the Red, Earl of Gloucester and Hertford, son-in-law to King Edward (Gray's note).

[6]Edmond de Mortimer, Lord of Wigmore. They were both Lords-Marchers, whose lands lay on the borders of Wales, and probably accompanied the king in this expedition (Gray's note).

[7]A mountain in Wales.

[8]The shores of Carnarvonshire opposite to the isle of Anglesey (Gray's note).

[9]Edward II, murdered in Berkeley Castle, 1327.

[10]Isabel of France, Edward II's adulterous queen (Gray's note).

From thee be born, who o'er thy country hangs[11]
The scourge of Heav'n. What Terrors round him wait! 60
Amazement in his van, with Flight combined,
And sorrow's faded form, and solitude behind.

ANTISTROPHE

" 'Mighty Victor, mighty Lord,
Low on his funeral couch he lies!
No pitying heart, no eye, afford 65
A tear to grace his obsequies.
Is the sable Warrior[12] fled?
Thy son is gone. He rests among the Dead.
The Swarm, that in thy noon-tide beam were born?
Gone to salute the rising Morn. 70
Fair laughs[13] the Morn, and soft the Zephyr blows,
While proudly riding o'er the azure realm
In gallant trim the gilded Vessel goes;
Youth on the prow, and Pleasure at the helm;
Regardless of the sweeping Whirlwind's sway, 75
That, hushed in grim repose, expects his evening prey.

EPODE

" 'Fill high the sparkling bowl,
The rich repast prepare,
Reft of a crown, he yet may share the feast:
Close by the regal chair 80
Fell Thirst and Famine scowl
A baleful smile upon their baffled Guest.
Heard ye the din of battle bray,
Lance to lance, and horse to horse?
Long Years of havoc[14] urge their destined course, 85
And through the kindred squadrons mow their way.
Ye Towers of Julius,[15] London's lasting shame,
With many a foul and midnight murder fed,
Revere his Consort's[16] faith, his Father's[17] fame,
And spare the meek Usurper's[18] holy head. 90
Above, below, the rose,[19] of snow,
Twined with her blushing foe, we spread:
The bristled Boar[20] in infant gore
Wallows beneath the thorny shade.
Now, Brothers, bending o'er th' accursèd loom 95
Stamp we our vengeance deep, and ratify his doom.

III. STROPHE

" 'Edward, lo! to sudden fate
(Weave we the woof. The thread is spun.)
Half of thy heart we consecrate.
(The web is wove. The work is done.)' 100
Stay, O stay! nor thus forlorn
Leave me unblessed, unpitied, here to mourn:
In yon bright track, that fires the western skies,
They melt, they vanish from my eyes.
But oh! what solemn scenes on Snowdon's height 105
Descending slow their glitt'ring skirts unroll?
Visions of glory, spare my aching sight,
Ye unborn Ages, crowd not on my soul!
No more our long-lost Arthur we bewail.
All-hail, ye genuine Kings,[21] Britannia's Issue, hail! 110

ANTISTROPHE

"Girt with many a Baron bold
Sublime their starry fronts they rear;
And gorgeous Dames, and Statesmen old
In bearded majesty, appear.
In the midst a Form divine![22] 115
Her eye proclaims her of the Briton-Line;
Her lion-port, her awe-commanding face,
Attempered sweet to virgin grace.
What strings symphonious tremble in the air,
What strains of vocal transport round her play! 120
Hear from the grave, great Taliessin, hear:
They breathe a soul to animate thy clay.

[11]Edward III. The reference is to his triumphs in France.

[12]The Black Prince.

[13]These lines describe the reign of Richard II and (in the epode) his death by starvation.

[14]The Wars of the Roses.

[15]The Tower of London. The oldest part of that structure is vulgarly attributed to Julius Caesar (Gray's note).

[16]Margaret of Anjou. [17]Henry V.

[18]Henry VI, who was "very near being canonized" (Gray).

[19]The white and red roses, devices of York and Lancaster (Gray).

[20]The silver boar was the device of Richard III (Gray). The "infant gore" is that of the murdered princes.

[21]Both Merlin and Taliessin [Cymric bard, sixth century] had prophesied that the Welsh should regain their sovereignty over this island, which seemed to be accomplished in the House of Tudor [beginning with Henry VII] (Gray).

[22]Queen Elizabeth.

Bright Rapture calls, and soaring, as she sings,
Waves in the eye of Heav'n her many-colored wings.

EPODE

"The verse adorn again 125
Fierce War, and faithful Love,
And Truth severe, by fairy Fiction dressed.[23]
In buskined measures move
Pale Grief, and pleasing Pain,
With Horror, Tyrant of the throbbing breast.[24]
A Voice, as of the Cherub-Choir, 131
Gales from blooming Eden bear;[25]
And distant warblings lessen on my ear,
That lost in long futurity expire.[26]
Fond impious Man, think'st thou, yon sanguine cloud, 135
Raised by thy breath, has quenched the Orb of day?
To-morrow he repairs the golden flood,
And warms the nations with redoubled ray.
Enough for me: With joy I see
The different doom our Fates assign. 140
Be thine Despair, and sceptered Care,
To triumph, and to die, are mine."
He spoke, and headlong from the mountain's height
Deep in the roaring tide he plunged to endless night.

THE FATAL SISTERS

An Ode[1]

PREFACE

In the Eleventh Century Sigurd, Earl of the Orkney Islands, went with a fleet of ships and a considerable body of troops into Ireland, to the assistance of Sictryg with the silken beard, who was then making war on his father-in-law Brian King of Dublin: the Earl and all his forces were cut to pieces, and Sictryg was in danger of a total defeat; but the enemy had a greater loss by the death of Brian, their King, who fell in action. On Christmas day (the day of the battle), a Native of Caithness in Scotland saw at a distance a number of persons on horseback riding full speed towards a hill, and seeming to enter into it. Curiosity led him to follow them, till looking through an opening in the rocks he saw twelve gigantic figures resembling women: they were all employed about a loom; and as they wove, they sung the following dreadful Song; which when they had finished, they tore the web into twelve pieces, and (each taking her portion) galloped Six to the North and as many to the South.

Now the storm begins to lower
(Haste, the loom of Hell prepare),
Iron-sleet of arrowy shower
Hurtles in the darkened air.

Glitt'ring lances are the loom, 5
Where the dusky warp we strain,
Weaving many a Soldier's doom,
Orkney's woe, and Randver's bane.

See the grisly texture grow
('Tis of human entrails made), 10
And the weights, that play below,
Each a gasping Warrior's head.

Shafts for shuttles, dipped in gore,
Shoot the trembling cords along.
Sword, that once a Monarch bore, 15
Keep the tissue close and strong.

Mista black, terrific Maid,
Sangrida, and Hilda[2] see,
Join the wayward work to aid:
'Tis the woof of victory. 20

Ere the ruddy sun be set,
Pikes must shiver, javelins sing,
Blade with clattering buckler meet,
Hauberk crash, and helmet ring.

(Weave the crimson web of war) 25
Let us go, and let us fly,
Where our Friends the conflict share,
Where they triumph, where they die.

[23]The reference is to Spenser's *Faerie Queene*.
[24]Shakespeare. [25]Milton.
[26]The succession of poets after Milton's time (Gray).

[1]Written in 1761; first published in 1768. Gray made this version from a Latin translation of an Old Norse poem. The original text, with an English prose translation, is to be found in Vigfusson and Powell's *Corpus Poeticum Boreale,* I, 281–283. The prose which precedes and follows the poem Gray embodied in the Preface printed above. The event which it celebrates is the Battle of Clontarf, fought 23 April (not on Christmas day, as Gray says), 1014. Sictryg, it may be noted, was King of Dublin; Brian, King of Ireland. Brian was Sictryg's stepfather, which may be what Gray means when he says "father-in-law." The "gigantic figures resembling women" are the Valkyries, who in the poem are represented as weaving the web of battle.

[2]These are names of Valkyries, as are also the names in the third stanza below.

The pictures on this page illustrate eighteenth-century London. At the top is an aquatint by Pugin and Rowlandson, showing the pillory at Charing Cross, with a crowd gathered to enjoy the spectacle of two culprits undergoing punishment. It was not unusual for such culprits to have to suffer the additional discomfort of being pelted with rotten fruit and vegetables. The lower pictures present three views of London (1738) by William Hogarth, the great English master of pictorial realism and satire. That to the left is entitled "Morning," and shows Covent Garden Market in winter. It was from the figure of the old maid in this print that Fielding drew his conception of Miss Bridget Allworthy in *Tom Jones*. The picture in the middle is entitled "Noon," and shows the congregation leaving what was then the French Church in Hog Lane (now a part of Charing Cross Road). The print to the right is entitled "Night," and shows the narrow portion of Charing Cross and environs of St. Martin's Church on an evening of public rejoicing. (Courtesy of the Metropolitan Museum of Art.)

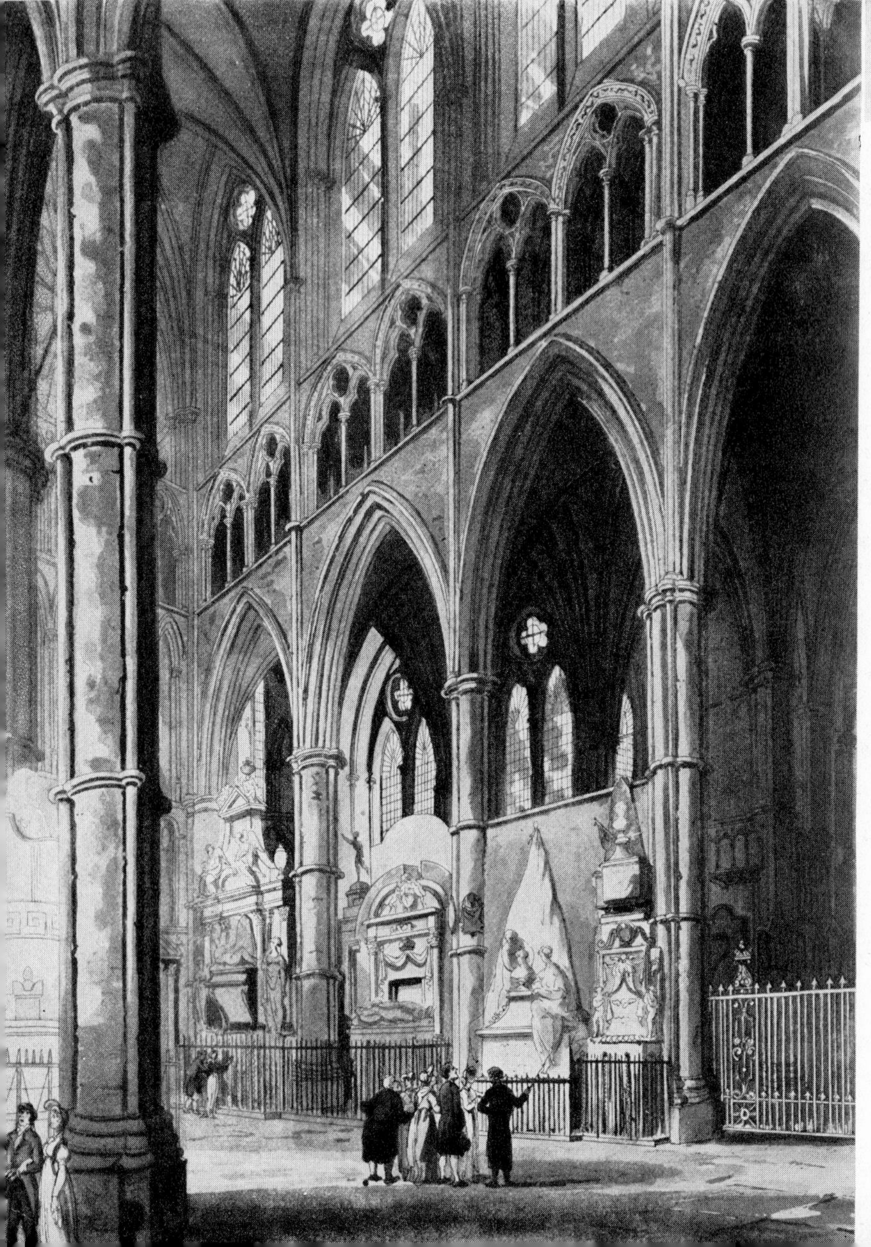

Above is a picture of Eton College from the River Thames, made by W. Westall. Here Thomas Gray was sent to school when he was about eleven; and it was a glimpse of the towers rising above the great hall of the college which later inspired his "Ode on a Distant Prospect of Eton College." (Courtesy of the Metropolitan Museum of Art.)

To the left is an aquatint of the interior of Westminster Abbey by Pugin and Rowlandson. Goldsmith's "Chinese Philosopher," in Letter XIII of *The Citizen of the World* (pages 1007–1010), comments on the monuments which in this print are being pointed out to one group of visitors. (Courtesy of the Metropolitan Museum of Art.)

As the paths of fate we tread,
Wading through th' ensanguined field: 30
Gondula, and Geira, spread
O'er the youthful King[3] your shield.

We the reins to slaughter give,
Ours to kill, and ours to spare:
Spite of danger he shall live. 35
(Weave the crimson web of war.)

They, whom once the desert-beach
Pent within its bleak domain,
Soon their ample sway shall stretch
O'er the plenty of the plain. 40

Low the dauntless Earl is laid,
Gored with many a gaping wound:
Fate demands a nobler head;
Soon a King[4] shall bite the ground.

Long his loss shall Eirin[5] weep, 45
Ne'er again his likeness see;
Long her strains in sorrow steep,
Strains of Immortality!

Horror covers all the heath,
Clouds of carnage blot the sun. 50
Sisters, weave the web of death;
Sisters, cease, the work is done.

Hail the task, and hail the hands!
Songs of joy and triumph sing!
Joy to the victorious bands; 55
Triumph to the younger King.

Mortal, thou that hear'st the tale,
Learn the tenor of our song.
Scotland, through each winding vale
Far and wide the notes prolong. 60

Sisters, hence with spurs of speed:
Each her thundering falchion[6] wield;
Each bestride her sable steed.
Hurry, hurry to the field.

ELEGY

Written in a Country Church-Yard[1]

The Curfew tolls the knell of parting day,
The lowing herd wind slowly o'er the lea,
The plowman homeward plods his weary way,
And leaves the world to darkness and to me.

Now fades the glimmering landscape on the sight, 5
And all the air a solemn stillness holds,
Save where the beetle wheels his droning flight,
And drowsy tinklings lull the distant folds;

Save that from yonder ivy-mantled tower
The moping owl does to the moon complain 10
Of such, as wand'ring near her secret bower,
Molest her ancient solitary reign.

Beneath those rugged elms, that yew-tree's shade,
Where heaves the turf in many a mold'ring heap,
Each in his narrow cell for ever laid, 15
The rude Forefathers of the hamlet sleep.

The breezy call of incense-breathing Morn,
The swallow twitt'ring from the straw-built shed,
The cock's shrill clarion, or the echoing horn,
No more shall rouse them from their lowly bed. 20

For them no more the blazing hearth shall burn,
Or busy housewife ply her evening care:
No children run to lisp their sire's return,
Or climb his knees the envied kiss to share.

Oft did the harvest to their sickle yield, 25
Their furrow oft the stubborn glebe has broke;
How jocund did they drive their team afield!
How bowed the woods beneath their sturdy stroke!

Let not Ambition mock their useful toil,
Their homely joys, and destiny obscure; 30
Nor Grandeur hear with a disdainful smile,
The short and simple annals of the poor.

The boast of heraldry, the pomp of pow'r,
And all that beauty, all that wealth e'er gave,
Awaits alike th' inevitable hour. 35
The paths of glory lead but to the grave.

Nor you, ye Proud, impute to These the fault,
If Mem'ry o'er their Tomb no Trophies raise,
Where through the long-drawn aisle and fretted vault
The pealing anthem swells the note of praise. 40

---

[3]Sictryg. [4]Brian. [5]Ireland. [6]Short sword.
[1]Completed in 1750; first published in 1751.

Can storied[2] urn or animated bust
Back to its mansion call the fleeting breath?
Can Honor's voice provoke the silent dust,
Or Flatt'ry sooth the dull cold ear of Death?

Perhaps in this neglected spot is laid 45
Some heart once pregnant with celestial fire;
Hands, that the rod of empire might have swayed,
Or waked to ecstasy the living lyre.

But Knowledge to their eyes her ample page
Rich with the spoils of time did ne'er unroll; 50
Chill Penury repressed their noble rage,
And froze the genial[3] current of the soul.

Full many a gem of purest ray serene,
The dark unfathomed caves of ocean bear:
Full many a flower is born to blush unseen,
And waste its sweetness on the desert air. 56

Some village-Hampden,[4] that with dauntless breast
The little Tyrant of his fields withstood;
Some mute inglorious Milton here may rest,
Some Cromwell guiltless of his country's blood. 60

Th' applause of list'ning senates to command,
The threats of pain and ruin to despise,
To scatter plenty o'er a smiling land,
And read their hist'ry in a nation's eyes,

Their lot forbade: nor circumscribed alone
Their growing virtues, but their crimes confined; 66
Forbade to wade through slaughter to a throne,
And shut the gates of mercy on mankind,

The struggling pangs of conscious truth to hide,
To quench the blushes of ingenuous shame,
Or heap the shrine of Luxury and Pride 71
With incense kindled at the Muse's flame.

Far from the madding crowd's ignoble strife,
Their sober wishes never learned to stray;
Along the cool sequestered vale of life 75
They kept the noiseless tenor of their way.

Yet e'en these bones from insult to protect
Some frail memorial still erected nigh,
With uncouth rimes and shapeless sculpture decked,
Implores the passing tribute of a sigh. 80

Their name, their years, spelt by th' unlettered muse,
The place of fame and elegy supply:
And many a holy text around she strews,
That teach the rustic moralist to die.

For who to dumb Forgetfulness a prey, 85
This pleasing anxious being e'er resigned,
Left the warm precincts of the cheerful day,
Nor cast one longing ling'ring look behind?

On some fond breast the parting soul relies,
Some pious drops the closing eye requires;
E'en from the tomb the voice of Nature cries, 91
E'en in our Ashes live their wonted Fires.

For thee, who mindful of th' unhonored Dead
Dost in these lines their artless tale relate;
If chance, by lonely contemplation led, 95
Some kindred Spirit shall inquire thy fate,

Haply some hoary-headed Swain may say,
"Oft have we seen him at the peep of dawn
Brushing with hasty steps the dews away
To meet the sun upon the upland lawn. 100

"There at the foot of yonder nodding beech
That wreathes its old fantastic roots so high,
His listless length at noontide would he stretch,
And pore upon the brook that babbles by.

"Hard by yon wood, now smiling as in scorn,
Mutt'ring his wayward fancies he would rove, 106
Now drooping, woeful wan, like one forlorn,
Or crazed with care, or crossed in hopeless love.

"One morn I missed him on the customed hill,
Along the heath and near his fav'rite tree;
Another came; nor yet beside the rill, 111
Nor up the lawn, nor at the wood was he;

[2] Inscribed. [3] Enlivening.

[4] John Hampden, who in 1636 refused to pay the ship-money demanded by Charles I.

"The next with dirges due in sad array
Slow through the church-way path we saw him borne.
Approach and read (for thou can'st read) the lay, 115
Graved on the stone beneath yon agéd thorn."

THE EPITAPH

Here rests his head upon the lap of Earth
A Youth to Fortune and to Fame unknown.
Fair Science[5] *frowned not on his humble birth,*
And Melancholy marked him for her own.

Large was his bounty, and his soul sincere, 121
Heav'n did a recompense as largely send:
He gave to Mis'ry all he had, a tear,
He gained from Heav'n ('twas all he wished) a friend.

No farther seek his merits to disclose, 125
Or draw his frailties from their dread abode
(There they alike in trembling hope repose),
The bosom of his Father and his God.

SONNET

On the Death of Richard West[1]

In vain to me the smiling Mornings shine,
And redd'ning Phoebus lifts his golden Fire:
The Birds in vain their amorous Descant[2] join;
Or cheerful Fields resume their green Attire:
These Ears, alas! for other Notes repine, 5
A different Object do these Eyes require.
My lonely Anguish melts no Heart, but mine;
And in my Breast the imperfect Joys expire.
Yet Morning smiles the busy Race to cheer,
And new-born Pleasure brings to happier Men: 10
The Fields to all their wonted Tribute bear;
To warm their little Loves the Birds complain;
I fruitless mourn to him that cannot hear,
And weep the more, because I weep in vain.

[5]Learning.

[1]Written in 1742; first published in 1775.

[2]Melody.

SKETCH OF HIS OWN CHARACTER[3]

Too poor for a bribe, and too proud to importune;
He had not the method of making a fortune;
Could love, and could hate, so was thought somewhat odd;
No very great wit, he believed in a God.
A Post or a Pension he did not desire, 5
But left Church and State to Charles Townshend and Squire.[4]

[3]Written in 1761; first published in 1775.

[4]Townshend was Chancellor of the Exchequer in 1767; he was a politician, orator, and man of the world. Samuel Squire was a fellow of St. John's College, Cambridge; in 1761 he was Bishop of St. David's.

LETTERS

1. To Horace Walpole[1]

Cambridge, 31 October, 1734

For God's sake, send me your *quaere's,*[2] and I'll do my best to get information upon 5 those points you don't understand. I warrant, you imagine that people in one college know the customs of others; but you mistake, they are quite little societies by themselves. The dresses, language, customs, 10 *etc.*, are different in different colleges. What passes for wit in one would not be understood if it were carried to another. Thus the men of Peterhouse,[3] Pembroke, and Clare Hall, of course, must be Tories; those of Trinity, rakes; of King's, scholars; of Sidney, Whigs; of St. John's, worthy men; and so on. Now what to say about this *terra incognita*[4] I don't know. First, then, it is a great old town, shaped like a spider, with a nasty lump in the middle of it, and half a dozen scrambling long legs. It has fourteen parishes, twelve colleges, and four halls;

[1]Son of the Whig prime-minister, Sir Robert Walpole. Gray, his former school-fellow at Eton, had been at Cambridge only three weeks when this letter was written.

[2]Questions.

[3]Gray's own college. [4]Unknown land.

these halls only entertain students, who after a term of years are elected into the colleges. There are five ranks in the University subordinate to the vice-chancellor: these are masters, fellows, fellow-commoners, pensioners,[5] and sizars.[6] The masters of colleges are twelve grey-haired gentlefolks, who are all mad with pride; the fellows are sleepy, drunken, dull, illiterate things; the fellow-commoners are imitators of the fellows, or else *beaux,* or else nothing; the pensioners, grave, formal sots, who would be thought old, or else drink ale and sing songs against the excise; the sizars are graziers' eldest sons, who come to get good learning that they may all be archbishops of Canterbury. These two last orders are qualified to take scholarships; one of which your humble servant has had given him.[7] First they led me into the hall, and there I swore allegiance to the king; then I went to a room where I took 50,000 Latin oaths, such as: to wear a square cap, to make six verses upon the epistle or gospel[8] every Sunday morning, to chant very loud in chapel, to wear a clean surplice, *etc., etc.* Now as to eating: the fellow-commoners dine at the fellows' table; their commons is worth 6*s.* 4*d.* a week; the pensioners pay but 2*s.* 4*d.* If anybody don't like their commons, they send down into the kitchen to know what's for sizing;[9] the cook sends up a catalogue of what there is, and they choose what they please. They are obliged to pay for the commons whether they eat it or no. There is always plenty enough; the sizars feast upon the leavings of the rest. As to dress: the fellow-commoners usually wear a prunella[10] gown with sleeves, a hat and no band; but their proper habit has its sleeves trimmed with gold lace; this they only wear at public ceremonies. Neither do the noblemen use their proper habit commonly, but wear only a black paduasoy[11] gown. The men of King's are a sort of university by themselves, and differ in customs from all the rest; everybody hates 'em, and when Almanzor[12] comes to me, our peoples stare at him like a lord mayor's show and wonder to see a human creature among them. If I tell you I never stir out, perhaps you won't believe me; especially when you know there's a club of wits kept at the Mitre (all such as come from Eton), where Almanzor would introduce me if I so pleased. Yet you will not think it strange that I don't go abroad when I tell you that I am got into a room, such a hugeous one that little i is quite lost in it; so that when I get up in the morning, I begin to travel towards the middle of it with might and main, and with much ado about noon bait at a great table which stands half-way it; so then by that time (after having pursued my journey full speed) that I arrive at the door, it is so dark and late, and I am so tired that I am obliged to turn back again; so about midnight I get to the bedside. Then, thinks you, I suppose, he goes to sleep; hold you a bit. In this country it is so far from that, that we go to bed to wake and rise to sleep; in short, those that go along the street do nothing but walk in their sleep; they run against every post they meet. But I beg pardon for talking so much of myself, since that's not what you care for.—(To be continued.)

[5]Undergraduates who paid for their own commons.

[6]Undergraduates who received special allowances for doing menial labor.

[7]Gray had received the scholarship two weeks earlier.

[8]Passages from the New Testament read in the communion service.

[9]What can be had as an extra dish.

[10]Strong cloth, silk or worsted.

[11]Strong silk cloth.

[12]The name of a character in Dryden's *Conquest of Granada,* here applied to Gray's Eton friend, Thomas Ashton.

II. To Richard West[1]

Cambridge, December, 1736

You must know that I do not take degrees, and after this term shall have nothing more of college impertinencies to undergo; which I trust will be some pleasure to you, as it is a great one to me. I have endured lectures daily and hourly since I came last, supported by the hopes of being shortly at full liberty to give myself up to my friends and classical companions, who, poor souls! though I see them fallen into great contempt with most people here, yet I cannot help sticking to

[1]One of the closest of Gray's early friends, with whom he had become acquainted at Eton.

them, and out of a spirit of obstinacy (I think) love them the better for it; and indeed what can I do else? Alas, I cannot see in the dark; nature has not furnished me with the optics of a cat. Must I pore upon mathematics? Alas, I cannot see in too much light; I am no eagle. It is very possible that two and two make four, but I would not give four farthings to demonstrate this ever so clearly; and if these be the profits of life, give me the amusements of it. The people I behold all around me, it seems, know all this and more, and yet I do not know one of them who inspires me with any ambition of being like him. Surely it was of this place, now Cambridge but formerly known by the name of Babylon, that the prophet spoke when he said, "The wild beasts of the desert shall dwell there, and their houses shall be full of doleful creatures, and owls shall build there, and satyrs shall dance there; their forts and towers shall be a den forever, a joy of wild asses; there shall the great owl make her nest, and lay and hatch and gather under her shadow; it shall be a court of dragons; the screech owl also shall rest there, and find for herself a place of rest."[2] You see, here is a pretty collection of desolate animals, which is verified in this town to a tittle; and perhaps it may also allude to your habitation,[3] for you know all types may be taken by abundance of handles; however, I defy your owls to match mine.

If the default of your spirits and nerves be nothing but the effect of the hyp,[4] I have no more to say. We all must submit to that wayward queen; I too in no small degree own her sway:

I feel her influence while I speak her power.

But if it be a real distemper, pray take more care of your health, if not for your own at least for our sakes; and do not be so soon weary of this little world. I do not know what refined friendships you may have contracted in the other, but pray do not be in a hurry to see your acquaintance above; among your terrestrial familiars, however, though I say it that should not say it, there positively is not one that has a greater esteem for you than

Yours most sincerely, *etc.*

[2]A fusion of Isaiah, 13:21; 32:14; 34:15, 13, and 14.

[3]Oxford. [4]Hypochondria.

III. To His Mother[1]

Amiens, 1 April, 1739

As WE made but a very short journey today and came to our inn early, I sit down to give you some account of our expedition. On the twenty-ninth (according to the style here)[2] we left Dover at twelve at noon, and with a pretty brisk gale, which pleased everybody mighty well, except myself, who was extremely sick the whole time; we reached Calais by five. The weather changed, and it began to snow hard the minute we came into the harbor, where we took the boat and soon landed. Calais is an exceeding old but very pretty town, and we hardly saw anything there that was not so new and so different from England that it surprised us agreeably. We went the next morning to the great church, and were at high mass (it being Easter Monday). We also saw the convent of the Capuchins and the nuns of St. Dominic; with these last we held much conversation, especially with an English nun, a Mrs. Davis, of whose work I sent you, by the return of the packet, a letter-case to remember her by. In the afternoon we took a post-chaise (it still snowing very hard) for Boulogne, which was only eighteen miles further. This chaise is a strange sort of conveyance, of much greater use than beauty, resembling an ill-shaped chariot,[3] only with the door opening before instead of the side; three horses draw it, one between the shafts and the other two on each side, on one of which the postilion rides and drives too. This vehicle will, upon occasion, go fourscore miles a day; but Mr. Walpole, being in no hurry, chooses to make easy journeys of it; and they are easy ones indeed, for the

[1]In this letter Gray describes the beginning of a trip which he and Horace Walpole made to the Continent in 1739–1741.

[2]The New Style of dating, used in most continental countries from 1582 on, but not adopted in England until 1752.

[3]Light four-wheeled carriage.

motion is much like that of a sedan. We go about six miles an hour, and commonly change horses at the end of it. It is true they are no very graceful steeds; but they go well, and through roads which they say are bad for France, but to me they seem gravel walks and bowling-greens. In short, it would be the finest traveling in the world, were it not for the inns, which are mostly terrible places indeed. But to describe our progress somewhat more regularly: we came into Boulogne when it was almost dark, and went out pretty early on Tuesday morning; so that all I can say about it is that it is a large, old, fortified town with more English in it than French. On Tuesday we were to go to Abbéville, seventeen leagues, or fifty-one short English miles; but by the way we dined at Montreuil, much to our hearts' content, on stinking mutton cutlets, addle eggs, and ditch water. Madame the hostess made her appearance in long lappets[4] of bone lace and a sack[5] of linsey-woolsey. We supped and lodged pretty well at Abbéville, and had time to see a little of it before we came out this morning. There are seventeen convents in it, out of which we saw the chapels of the Minims and the Carmelite nuns. We are now come further thirty miles to Amiens, the chief city of the province of Picardy. We have seen the cathedral, which is just what that of Canterbury must have been before the Reformation. It is about the same size, a huge Gothic building, beset on the outside with thousands of small statues, and within adorned with beautiful painted windows and a vast number of chapels dressed out in all their finery of altar-pieces, embroidery, gilding, and marble. Over the high altar is preserved, in a very large wrought shrine of massy gold, the relics of St. Firmin, their patron saint. We went also to the chapels of the Jesuits and Ursuline nuns, the latter of which is very richly adorned. Tomorrow we shall lie at Clermont, and next day reach Paris. The country we have passed through hitherto has been flat, open, but agreeably diversified with villages, fields well-cultivated, and little rivers. On every hillock is a windmill, a crucifix, or a Virgin Mary dressed in flowers and a sarsenet[6] robe. One sees not many people or carriages on the road; now and then, indeed, you meet a strolling friar, a countryman with his great muff, or a woman riding astride on a little ass, with short petticoats and a great head-dress of blue wool. * * *

[4]Streamers adorning the head.

[5]Loose gown.

[6]Fine, soft silk.

IV. To His Mother

Rheims, 21 June, 1739

We have now been settled almost three weeks in this city, which is more considerable upon account of its size and antiquity than from the number of its inhabitants or any advantages of commerce. There is little in it worth a stranger's curiosity, besides the cathedral church, which is a vast Gothic building of a surprising beauty and lightness, all covered over with a profusion of little statues and other ornaments. It is here the kings of France are crowned by the archbishop of Rheims, who is the first peer and the primate of the kingdom. The holy vessel made use of on that occasion, which contains the oil, is kept in the church of St. Nicasius hard by, and is believed to have been brought by an angel from heaven at the coronation of Clovis, the first Christian king. The streets in general have but a melancholy aspect, the houses all old; the public walks run along the side of a great moat under the ramparts, where one hears a continual croaking of frogs; the country round about is one great plain covered with vines, which at this time of the year afford no very pleasing prospect, as being not above a foot high. What pleasures the place denies to the sight it makes up to the palate, since you have nothing to drink but the best champagne in the world, and all sorts of provisions equally good. As to other pleasures, there is not that freedom of conversation among the people of fashion here that one sees in other parts of France; for, though they are not very numerous in this place, and consequently must live a good deal together, yet they never come to any great familiarity with one another. As my Lord Conway had spent a good part of his time among them, his brother[1] and we with him were soon introduced into all their assemblies. As soon as you enter, the lady of the house presents each of you a card, and offers you a party at quadrille;[2] you sit down and play forty deals without intermission, excepting one quarter of an hour when everybody rises to eat of what they call the *gouter,* which supplies the place of our tea, and is a service of wine, fruits, cream, sweetmeats, crawfish, and cheese. People take what they like and sit down again to play; after that they make little parties to go to the walks together, and then all the company retire to their separate habitations. Very seldom any suppers or dinners are given; and this is the manner they live among one another, not so much out of any aversion they have to pleasure as out of a sort of formality they have contracted by not being much frequented by people who have lived at Paris. It is sure they do not hate gaiety any more than the rest of their country-people, and can enter into diversions that are once proposed, with a good grace enough. For instance, the other evening we happened to be got together in a company of eighteen people, men and women of the best fashion here, at a garden in the town to walk; when one of the ladies bethought herself of asking, "Why should not we sup here?" Immediately the cloth was laid by the side of a fountain under the trees, and a very elegant supper served up; after which another said, "Come, let us sing"; and directly began herself. From singing we insensibly fell to dancing and singing in a round;[3] when somebody mentioned the violins, and immediately a company of them was ordered. Minuets were begun in the open air, and then came country-dances, which held till four o'clock next morning; at which hour the gayest lady there proposed that such as were weary should get into their coaches, and the rest of them should dance before them with the music in the van; and in this manner we paraded through all the principal streets of the city, and waked everybody in it. Mr. Walpole had a mind to make a custom of the thing, and would have given a ball in the same manner next week, but the women did not come into it; so I believe it will drop, and they will return to their dull cards and usual formalities. We are not to stay above a month longer here, and shall then go to Dijon, the chief city of Burgundy, a very splendid and very gay town; at least such is the present design.

[1]Henry Seymour Conway, a first cousin and school-fellow of Walpole's.

[2]Four-handed card game.

[3]Each singing the melody in turn.

V. To Richard West

Turin, 16 November, 1739

AFTER eight days' journey through Greenland,[1] we arrived at Turin. You approach it by a handsome avenue of nine miles long and quite straight. The entrance is guarded by certain vigilant dragons, called *douaniers,*[2] who mumbled us for some time. The city is not large, as being a place of strength and consequently confined within its fortifications. It has many beauties and some faults: among the first are streets all laid out by the line, regular, uniform buildings, fine walks that surround the whole, and in general a good lively, clean appearance. But the houses are of brick plastered, which is apt to want repairing; the windows of oiled paper, which is apt to be torn; and everything very slight, which is apt to tumble down. There is an excellent opera, but it is only in the Carnival; balls every night, but only in the Carnival; masquerades too, but only in the Carnival. This Carnival lasts only from Christmas to Lent; one half of the remaining part of the year is passed in remembering the last, the other in expecting the future Carnival. We cannot well subsist upon such slender diet, no more than upon an execrable Italian comedy and a puppet-show called *Rappresentazione d'un Anima Dannata,*[3] which, I think, are all the present diversions of the place; except the Marquise de Cavaillac's *conversazione,*[4] where one goes to see people play at ombre and taroc, a game of seventy-two cards all painted with suns, and moons, and devils, and monks. Mr. Walpole has been at

[1]I. e., through the arctic climate of the Alps.

[2]Custom-house officials.

[3]*Spectacle of a Lost Soul.* [4]Social assembly.

court;[5] the family are at present at a country palace called La Venerie. The palace here in town is the very quintessence of gilding and looking-glass: inlaid floors, carved panels, and painting wherever they could stick a brush. I own I have not, as yet, anywhere met with those grand and simple works of art that are to amaze one, and whose sight one is to be the better for. But those of Nature have astonished me beyond expression. In our little journey up to the Grande Chartreuse[6] I do not remember to have gone ten paces without an exclamation that there was no restraining. Not a precipice, not a torrent, not a cliff but is pregnant with religion and poetry. There are certain scenes that would awe an atheist into belief, without the help of other argument. One need not have a very fantastic imagination to see spirits there at noonday. You have Death perpetually before your eyes, only so far removed as to compose the mind without frighting it. I am well persuaded St. Bruno was a man of no common genius to choose such a situation for his retirement; and perhaps should have been a disciple of his, had I been born in his time. You may believe Abelard and Heloïse were not forgot upon this occasion. If I do not mistake, I saw you too every now and then at a distance among the trees; *il me semble que j'ai vu ce chien de visage là quelque part.*[7] You seemed to call to me from the other side of the precipice, but the noise of the river below was so great that I really could not distinguish what you said; it seemed to have a cadence like verse. In your next you will be so good to let me know what it was. The week we have since passed among the Alps has not equaled the single day upon that mountain, because the winter was rather too far advanced and the weather a little foggy. However, it did not want its beauties; the savage rudeness of the view is inconceivable without seeing it: I reckoned in one day thirteen cascades, the least of which was, I dare say, one hundred feet in height. I had Livy in the chaise with me, and beheld his *"Nives caelo prope immistae; tecta informia imposita rupibus; pecora iumentaque torrida frigore; homines intonsi et inculti; animalia inanimaque omnia rigentia gelu; omnia confragosa praeruptaque."*[8] The creatures that inhabit them are in all respects below humanity; and most of them, especially women, have the *tumidum guttur,*[9] which they call *goscia.* Mont Cenis, I confess, carries the permission mountains have of being frightful rather too far; and its horrors were accompanied with too much danger to give one time to reflect upon their beauties. There is a family of the Alpine monsters I have mentioned, upon its very top, that in the middle of winter calmly lay in their stock of provisions and firing, and so are buried in their hut for a month or two under the snow. When we were down it, and got a little way into Piedmont, we began to find *"Apricos quosdam colles, rivosque prope silvas, et iam humano cultu digniora loca."*[10] I read Silius Italicus[11] too, for the first time, and wished for you according to custom. We set out for Genoa in two days' time.

VI. To Thomas Wharton[1]

Florence, 12 March, 1740

Proposals for printing by subscription in

THIS LARGE LETTER[2]

The Travels of T. G. Gent., which will consist of the following particulars:

Chap. 1

The author arrives at Dover; his conversation with the mayor of that corporation; sets

[5]The court of the King of Sardinia.

[6]A famous monastery in Savoy.

[7]I seem to have seen that homely face of yours somewhere there.

[8]Snows almost mingled with the sky; shapeless dwellings perched upon the rocks; cattle and beasts of burden pinched with cold; men unshorn and wild; all things, living and lifeless, frozen stiff; all things rough and rugged (Livy, xxi, 32).

[9]Goiter.

[10]Sunny hillsides, and streams running beside groves, and now places worthier of human toil (Livy, xxi, 37).

[11]A Latin poet who in his *Punica,* like Livy in the passages from which Gray has just quoted, describes how the army of Hannibal crossed the Alps.

[1]An intimate friend whose acquaintance Gray had made at Cambridge. In time Wharton became a well-known physician.

[2]Written in large capitals to indicate the type in which the proposed work was to be printed.

out in the packet-boat, grows very sick; the author spews (a very minute account of all the circumstances thereof); his arrival at Calais; how the inhabitants of that country speak French, and are said to be all Papishes; the author's reflections thereupon.

2

How they feed him with soup, and what soup is. How he meets with a *Capucin,*[3] and what a *Capucin* is. How they shut him up in a post-chaise, and send him to Paris; he goes wandering along during six days; and how there are trees and houses just as in England. Arrives at Paris without knowing it.

3

Full account of the river Seine, and of the various animals and plants its borders produce. Description of the little creature called an *abbé,*[4] its parts, and their uses; with the reasons why they will not live in England, and the methods that have been used to propagate them there. A cut of the inside of a nunnery; its structure wonderfully adapted to the use of the animals that inhabit it; a short account of them, how they propagate without the help of a male, and how they eat up their own young ones, like cats and rabbits; supposed to have both sexes in themselves, like a snail. Dissection of a duchess, with copper-plates (very curious).

4

Goes to the opera; grand orchestra of humstrums, bagpipes, salt-boxes, tabors,[5] and pipes. Anatomy of a French ear, showing the formation of it to be entirely different from that of an English one, and that sounds have a directly contrary effect upon one and the other. Farinelli[6] at Paris said to have a fine manner, but no voice. Grand ballet, in which there is no seeing the dance for petticoats. Old women with flowers and jewels stuck in the curls of their grey hair; red-heeled shoes and roll-ups[7] innumerable, hoops and panniers[8] immeasurable, paint unspeakable. Tables wherein is calculated with the utmost exactness the several degrees of red now in use, from the rising blush of an advocate's wife to the flaming crimson of a princess of the blood, done by a limner[9] in great vogue.

5

The author takes unto him a tailor: his character; how he covers him with silk and fringe, and widens his figure with buckram a yard on each side; waistcoat and breeches so straight he can neither breath nor walk. How the barber curls him *en bequille et à la négligée,*[10] and ties a vast solitaire[11] about his neck; how the milliner lengthens his ruffles to his fingers' ends, and sticks his two arms into a muff. How he cannot stir, and how they cut him in proportion to his clothes.

6

He is carried to Versailles; despises it infinitely. A dissertation upon taste. Goes to an installation[12] in the Chapel-Royal: enter the king and fifty fiddlers *solus,*[13] kettle-drums and trumpets, queens and dauphins, princesses and cardinals, incense and the mass; old knights making curtsies; Holy Ghosts and fiery tongues.

7

Goes into the country, to Rheims in Champagne. Stays there three months; what he did there (he must beg the reader's pardon, but) he has really forgot.

8

Proceeds to Lyons. Vastness of that city. Can't see the streets for houses. How rich it is, and how much it stinks. Poem upon

[3]A Capuchin, a member of one branch of the Franciscan order.

[4]Any man entitled to wear ecclesiastical dress.

[5]Drums.

[6]Famous Italian soprano (1705–1782).

[7]Stockings of which the tops could be rolled up or down.

[8]Frames used to distend skirts at the hips.

[9]Painter.

[10]Apparently a fashionable but informal manner of dressing the hair.

[11]Neck-tie of black silk.

[12]Initiation into an order of knighthood.

[13]Alone (a joke already traditional by the time of Addison).

the confluence of the Rhône and the Saône, by a friend of the author's: very pretty!

9

Makes a journey into Savoy, and in his way visits the Grande Chartreuse; he is set astride upon a mule's back, and begins to climb up the mountain; rocks and torrents beneath; pine-trees and snows above; horrors and terrors on all sides. The author dies of the fright.

10

He goes to Geneva. His mortal antipathy to a Presbyterian, and the cure for it. Returns to Lyons. Gets a surfeit with eating ortolans and lampreys;[14] is advised to go into Italy for the benefit of the air.

11

Sets out the latter end of November[15] to cross the Alps. He is devoured by a wolf, and how it is to be devoured by a wolf.[16] The seventh day he comes to the foot of Mont Cenis. How he is wrapped up in bear-skins and bever-skins, boots on his legs, caps on his head, muffs on his hands, and taffeta over his eyes; he is placed on a bier, and is carried to heaven by the savages blindfold. How he lights among a certain fat nation called Clouds; how they are always in a sweat, and never speak but they fart; how they flock about him and think him very odd for not doing so too. He falls flump into Italy.

12

Arrives at Turin; goes to Genoa, and from thence to Placentia;[17] crosses the river Trebbia;[18] the ghost of Hannibal appears to him, and what it and he say upon the occasion. Locked out of Parma in a cold winter's night: the author by an ingenious stratagem gains admittance. Despises that city, and proceeds through Reggio to Modena; how the duke and duchess lie over their own stables, and go every night to a vile Italian comedy. Despises them and it; and proceeds to Bologna.

13

Enters into the Dominions of the Pope o' Rome. Meets the devil, and what he says on that occasion. Very public and scandalous doings between the vines and the elm-trees,[19] and how the olive-trees are shocked thereupon. Author longs for bologna sausages and hams; and how he grows as fat as a hog.

14

Observations on antiquities. The author proves that Bologna was the ancient Tarentum;[20] that the battle of Salamis,[21] contrary to the vulgar opinion, was fought by land, and that not far from Ravenna; that the Romans were a colony of the Jews; and that Aeneas was the same with Ehud.

15

Arrival at Florence. Is of opinion that the Venus of Medicis is a modern performance, and that a very indifferent one, and much inferior to the King Charles at Charing Cross.[22] Account of the city and manners of the inhabitants. A learned dissertation on the true situation of Gomorrah.

And here will end the first part of these instructive and entertaining voyages. The subscribers are to pay twenty guineas, nineteen down and the remainder upon delivery of the book. *N.B.* A few are printed on the softest royal brown paper for the use of the curious.

My dear, dear Wharton:

(Which is a *dear* more than I give anybody else. It is very odd to begin with a parenthesis, but) You may think me a beast for not having sooner wrote to you; and, to be sure, a beast I am. Now when one owns

[14]Respectively small birds of delicate flavor and eel-like fishes.

[15]A mistake for October.

[16]At this point in their journey a little dog belonging to Walpole had actually been carried off by a wolf.

[17]Piacenza.

[18]The scene of Hannibal's victory in 218 B. C.

[19]In Italy grapevines are frequently entwined around elm-trees.

[20]A port in southern Italy.

[21]Fought off the coast of Attica in Greece in 480 B. C.

[22]In the heart of London.

it, I don't see what you have left to say. I take this opportunity to inform you (an opportunity I have had every week this twelvemonth) that I am arrived safe at Calais, and am at present at Florence, a city in Italy in I don't know how many degrees north latitude; under the line[23] I am sure it is not, for I am at this instant expiring with cold. You must know that not being certain what circumstances of my history would particularly suit your curiosity, and knowing that all I had to say to you would overflow the narrow limits of many a good quire of paper, I have taken this method of laying before you the contents, that you may pitch upon what you please, and give me your orders accordingly to expatiate thereupon; for I conclude you will write to me. Won't you? Oh, yes, when you know that in a week I set out for Rome, and that the pope[24] is dead, and that I shall be (I should say, "God willing; and if nothing extraordinary intervene; and if I'm alive and well; and in all human probability") at the coronation of a new one. Now, as you have no other correspondent there, and as, if you do not,[25] I certainly shall not write again (observe my impudence), I take it to be your interest to send me a vast letter, full of all sorts of news, and bawdy, and politics, and such other ingredients as to you shall seem convenient, with all decent expedition. Only do not be too severe upon the Pretender;[26] and, if you like my style, pray say so. This *à la Française;*[27] and if you think it a little too foolish and impertinent, you shall be treated *alla Toscana* with a thousand *Signoria Illustrissima's.*[28] In the mean time I have the honor to remain

Your lofing Frind tell Deth,

T. Gray

P.S. This is *à l'Anglaise.*[29] I don't know where you are; if at Cambridge, pray let me know all how and about it; and if my old friends Thompson or Clark fall in your way, say I am extremely theirs. But if you are in town, I entreat you to make my best compliments to Mrs. Wharton. Adieu, yours sincerely a second time.

[23]The equator. [24]Clement XII.

[25]Do not write.

[26]The Old Pretender, James Edward Stuart, son of James II of England.

[27]In the French manner.

[28]In the Tuscan manner with a thousand *your most illustrious lordship's.*

[29]In the English manner.

VII. To His Mother

Rome, 2 April, 1740

THIS is the eighth day since we came to Rome, but the first hour I have had to write to you in. The journey from Florence cost us four days; one of which was spent at Siena, an agreeable, clean, old city, of no great magnificence or extent, but in a fine situation and good air. What it has most considerable is its cathedral, a huge pile of marble, black and white laid alternately, and labored with a Gothic niceness and delicacy in the old-fashioned way. Within too are some paintings and sculpture of considerable hands. The sight of this and some collections that were showed us in private houses were a sufficient employment for the little time we were to pass there; and the next morning we set forward on our journey through a country very oddly composed. For some miles you have continual scene of little mountains cultivated from top to bottom with rows of olive-trees, or else elms, each of which has its vine twining about it and mixing with the branches, and corn[1] sown between all the ranks. This, diversified with numerous small houses and convents, makes the most agreeable prospect in the world. But, all of a sudden, it alters to black, barren hills, as far as the eye can reach, that seem never to have been capable of culture, and are as ugly as useless. Such is the country for some time before one comes to Mount Radicofani, a terrible black hill, on the top of which we were to lodge that night. It is very high and difficult of ascent; and at the foot of it we were much embarrassed by the fall of one of the poor horses that drew us. This accident obliged another chaise, which was coming down, to stop also; and out of it peeped a figure in a red cloak, with a handkerchief tied round

[1]Wheat.

its head, which, by its voice and mien, seemed a fat old woman; but, upon its getting out, appeared to be Senesino,[2] who was returning from Naples to Siena, the place of his birth and residence. On the highest part of the mountain is an old fortress, and near it a house built by one of the grand dukes for a hunting-seat, but now converted into an inn. It is the shell of a large fabric, but such an inside, such chambers and accommodations that your cellar is a palace in comparison, and your cat sups and lies much better than we did; for, it being a saint's eve, there was nothing but eggs. We devoured our meager fare and, after stopping up the windows with quilts, were obliged to lie upon the straw beds in our clothes: such are the conveniences in a road that is, as it were, the great thoroughfare of all the world. Just on the other side of the mountain, at Ponte Centino, one enters the Patrimony of the Church: a most delicious country, but thinly inhabited. That night brought us to Viterbo, a city of a more lively appearance than any we had lately met with; the houses have glass windows, which is not very usual here, and most of the streets are terminated by a handsome fountain. Here we had the pleasure of breaking our fast on the leg of an old hare and some broiled crows. Next morning, in descending Mount Viterbo, we first discovered (though at near thirty miles' distance) the cupola of St. Peter's, and a little after began to enter on an old Roman pavement, with now and then a ruined tower, or a sepulcher on each hand. We now had a clear view of the city, though not to the best advantage, as coming along a plain quite upon a level with it; however, it appeared very vast, and surrounded with magnificent villas and gardens. We soon after crossed the Tiber, a river that ancient Rome made more considerable than any merit of its own could have done; however, it is not contemptibly small, but a good handsome stream, very deep, yet somewhat of a muddy complection. The first entrance of Rome is prodigiously striking: it is by a noble gate, designed by Michael Angelo and adorned with statues; this brings you into a large square, in the midst of which is a vast obelisk of granite, and in front you have at one view two churches of a handsome architecture and so much alike that they are called the twins, with three streets, the middlemost of which is one of the longest in Rome. As high as my expectation was raised, I confess the magnificence of this city infinitely surpasses it. You cannot pass along a street but you have views of some palace, or church, or square, or fountain, the most picturesque and noble one can imagine. We have not yet set about considering its beauties, ancient and modern, with attention; but have already taken a slight, transient view of some of the most remarkable. St. Peter's I saw the day after we arrived, and was struck dumb with wonder. I there saw the Cardinal d'Auvergne, one of the French ones, who, upon coming off his journey, immediately repaired hither to offer up his vows at the high altar, and went directly into the conclave; the doors of which we saw opened to him, and all the other immured cardinals came thither to receive him; upon his entrance they were closed again directly. It is supposed they will not come to an agreement about a pope till after Easter,[3] though the confinement is very disagreeable. I have hardly philosophy enough to see the infinity of fine things that are here daily in the power of anybody that has money, without regretting the want of it; but custom has the power of making things easy to one. I have not yet seen His Majesty of Great Britain, *etc.*, though I have the two boys[4] in the gardens of the Villa Borghese, where they go a-shooting almost every day; it was at a distance, indeed, for we did not choose to meet them, as you may imagine. This letter (like all those the English send or receive) will pass through the hands of that family before it comes to those it was intended for. They do it more honor than it deserves; and all they will learn from thence will be that I desire you to give my duty to my father, and wherever else it is due, and that I am, *etc.*

[2]Famous Italian soprano.

[3]I. e., until more than two weeks had passed.

[4]The Old Pretender, mentioned in the preceding letter, and his two sons, later known as the Young Pretender and the Cardinal of York.

VIII. To Richard West

London, 8 April, 1742

You are the first who ever made a Muse of a cough; to me it seems a much more easy task to versify in one's sleep (that, indeed, you were of old famous for) than for want of it. Not the wakeful nightingale (when she had a cough) ever sung so sweetly. I give you thanks for your warble, and wish you could sing yourself to rest. These wicked remains of your illness will sure give way to warm weather and gentle exercise, which I hope you will not omit as the season advances. Whatever low spirits and indolence, the effect of them, may advise to the contrary, I pray you add five steps to your walk daily for my sake; by the help of which, in a month's time, I propose to set you on horseback.[1]

I talked of the *Dunciad*[2] as concluding you had seen it; if you have not, do you choose I should get and send it you? I have myself, upon your recommendation, been reading *Joseph Andrews*.[3] The incidents are ill-laid and without invention; but the characters have a great deal of Nature, which always pleases, even in her lowest shapes. Parson Adams is perfectly well; so is Mrs. Slipslop, and the story of Wilson; and throughout he[4] shows himself well-read in stage-coaches, country squires, inns, and Inns of Court. His reflections upon high people and low people, and misses and masters, are very good. However the exaltedness of some minds (or rather, as I shrewdly suspect, their insipidity and want of feeling or observation) may make them insensible to these light things (I mean such as characterize and paint Nature), yet surely they are as weighty and much more useful than your grave discourses upon the mind, the passions, and what not. Now as the paradisaical pleasures of the Mahometans consist in playing upon the flute and lying with houris, be mine to read eternal new romances of Marivaux and Crébillon.[5]

You are very good in giving yourself the trouble to read and find fault with my long harangues.[6] Your freedom (as you call it) has so little need of apologies that I should scarce excuse your treating me any otherwise; which, whatever compliment it might be to my vanity, would be making a very ill one to my understanding. As to matter of style, I have this to say: The language of the age is never the language of poetry, except among the French, whose verse, where the thought or image does not support it, differs in nothing from prose. Our poetry, on the contrary, has a language peculiar to itself, to which almost every one that has written has added something, by enriching it with foreign idioms and derivatives: nay, sometimes words of their own composition or invention. Shakespeare and Milton have been great creators this way, and no one more licentious than Pope or Dryden, who perpetually borrow expressions from the former. Let me give you some instances from Dryden, whom everybody reckons a great master of our poetical tongue:—Full of *museful mopings*—unlike the *trim* of love—a pleasant *beverage*—a *roundelay* of love—stood silent in his *mood*—with knots and *knars*[7] deformed—his *ireful mood*—in proud *array*—his *boon* was granted—and *disarray* and shameful rout—*wayward* but wise—*furbished* for the field—the *foiled, doddard*[8] oaks—*disherited*—*smoldering* flames—*retchless*[9] of laws—*crones* old and ugly—the *beldam* at his side—the *grandam-hag*—*villainize* his father's fame.—But they are infinite; and our language, not being a settled thing (like the French), has an undoubted right to words of an hundred years old, provided antiquity have not rendered them unintelligible. In truth, Shakespeare's language is one of his

[1]West died less than two months later (1 June, 1742). See above Gray's "Sonnet on the Death of Richard West."

[2]Apparently *The New Dunciad,* the fourth book of Pope's *Dunciad* as it is now printed, which had appeared 20 March, 1742.

[3]The novel by Henry Fielding, which had just been published.

[4]Fielding.

[5]Contemporary French novelists.

[6]Here and later in the same letter, where he speaks of his own imitation of Shakespeare's language, Gray is referring to his fragment of a tragedy, called *Agrippina* and founded on Tacitus (*Annals,* xiii and xiv).

[7]Knots. [8]Injured and with tops decayed.

[9]Reckless.

principal beauties; and he has no less advantage over your Addisons and Rowes in this than in those other great excellencies you mention. Every word in him is a picture. Pray put me the following lines into the tongue of your modern dramatics:

> But I, that am not shaped for sportive tricks,
> Nor made to court an amorous looking-glass:
> I, that am rudely stamped, and want love's majesty
> To strut before a wanton, ambling nymph:
> I, that am curtailed of this fair proportion,
> Cheated of feature by dissembling nature,
> Deformed, unfinished, sent before my time
> Into this breathing world, scarce half made up——[10]

and what follows. To me they appear untranslatable; and if this be the case, our language is greatly degenerated. However, the affectation of imitating Shakespeare may doubtless be carried too far, and is no sort of excuse for sentiments ill-suited, or speeches ill-timed, which I believe is a little the case with me. I guess the most faulty expressions may be these:—*silken* son of *dalliance*—*drowsier* pretensions—wrinkled *beldams*—*arched* the hearer's brow and *riveted* his eyes in *fearful ecstasy*. These are easily altered or omitted; and indeed, if the thoughts be wrong or superfluous, there is nothing easier than to leave out the whole. The first ten or twelve lines are, I believe, the best; and as for the rest, I was betrayed into a good deal of it by Tacitus; only, what he has said in five words I imagine I have said in fifty lines. Such is the misfortune of imitating the inimitable. Now, if you are of my opinion, *una litura*[11] may do the business better than a dozen; and you need not fear unraveling my web. I am a sort of spider, and have little else to do but spin it over again, or creep to some other place and spin there. Alas, for one who has nothing to do but amuse himself, I believe my amusements are as little amusing as most folks'. But no matter; it makes the hours pass, and is better than ἐν ἀμαθίᾳ καὶ ἀμουσια καταβιῶναι.[12] Adieu.

[10] *Richard III*, I, i, 14–21. [11] A single erasure.

[12] To pass one's life in grossness and ignorance (probably adopted from Aelian, *Variae Historiae*, vii, 15).

IX. *To Horace Walpole*

Cambridge, 11 February, 1751

My dear sir:

As you have brought me into a little sort of distress, you must assist me, I believe, to get out of it as well as I can. Yesterday I had the misfortune of receiving a letter from certain gentlemen (as their bookseller expresses it) who have taken the *Magazine of Magazines* into their hands. They tell me that an "ingenious" poem, called *Reflections in a Country Church-yard,* has been communicated to them, which they are printing forthwith; that they are informed that the "excellent" author of it is I by name; and that they beg not only his "indulgence," but the "honor of his correspondence," etc. As I am not at all disposed to be either so indulgent or so correspondent as they desire, I have but one bad way left to escape the honor they would inflict upon me; and therefore am obliged to desire you would make Dodsley print it immediately (which may be done in less than a week's time) from your copy, but without my name, in what form is most convenient for him, but in his best paper and character.[1] He must correct the press himself, and print it without any interval between the stanzas, because the sense is in some places continued beyond them; and the title must be *Elegy, Wrote in a Country Church-yard.* If he should add a line or two to say it came into his hands by accident, I should like it better. If you think fit, the 102nd line may be read:

> Awake and faithful to her wonted fires.

But if this be worse than before, it must go as it was. In the 126th, for "*ancient* thorn" read "*aged.*"

If you behold the *Magazine of Magazines* in the light that I do, you will not refuse to give yourself this trouble on my account, which you have taken of your own accord before now. Adieu, sir; I am

Yours ever,
T. G.[2]

[1] Type.

[2] Dodsley succeeded in publishing the first edition of the *Elegy* four days later; and Gray's authorship was announced in the *Magazine of Magazines* on the day following publication.

X. To James Brown[1]

Durham, 24 July, 1753

Dear sir:

We[2] performed our journey, a very agreeable one, within the time appointed, and left out scarce anything worth seeing in or near our way. The Doctor and Mrs. Wharton had expected us about two hours when we arrived at Studley on Friday; we passed that night at Ripon, and the next at Richmond, and on Sunday evening got to Durham. I cannot now enter into the particulars of my travels because I have not yet gathered up my quotations from the classics to intersperse, like Mr. Addison;[3] but I hope to be able soon to entertain you with a dish of very choice erudition. I have another reason too, which is that the post is just setting out. Suffice it to tell you that I have one of the most beautiful vales here in England to walk in, with prospects that change every ten steps and open something new wherever I turn me, all rude and romantic; in short, the sweetest spot to break your neck or drown yourself in that ever was beheld. I have done neither yet, but I have been twice at the races, once at the assembly; have had a visit from Dr. Chapman, and dined with the bishop. I am very shabby, for Stonhewer's box with my coat in it, which went by sea, is not yet arrived. You are desired therefore to send Lee, the bedmaker at Peterhouse, to the master of the Lynn boats to inquire what vessel it was sent by, and why it has not come. I was directed to Dr. Stonhewer of Houghton, to be left with the rector of Sunderland. Another trouble I have to give you, which is to order Barnes to bring any letters Stonhewer or I may have, to you, and direct 'em hither. The Doctor and Mrs. Wharton desire their particular compliments to you, and are sorry you could not be with us. Adieu. I am ever sincerely

Yours,
T. G.

P.S. I have left my watch hanging (I believe) in my bedroom. Will you be so good as to ask after it?

[1]A Cambridge friend, Vice-Master of Pembroke College, which Gray had made his permanent residence.

[2]Gray and his friend, Richard Stonhewer.

[3]In *Remarks on Several Parts of Italy* (1705).

XI. To Richard Hurd[1]

Stoke, 25 August, 1757

Dear sir:

I do not know why you should thank me for what you had a right and title to,[2] but attribute it to the excess of your politeness, and the more so because almost no one else has made me the same compliment. As your acquaintance in the University (you say) do me the honor to admire, it would be ungenerous in me not to give them notice that they are doing a very unfashionable thing, for all people of condition are agreed not to admire, nor even to understand. One very great man, writing to an acquaintance of his and mine, says that he had read them seven or eight times, and that now, when he next sees him, he shall not have above thirty questions to ask. Another, a peer, believes that the last stanza of the second ode relates to King Charles I and Oliver Cromwell. Even my friends tell me they do not succeed, and write me moving topics of consolation on that head. In short, I have heard of nobody but a player[3] and a doctor of divinity that profess their esteem for them. Oh, yes! a lady of quality, a friend of Mason's, who is a great reader: she knew there was a compliment to Dryden, but never suspected there was anything said about Shakespeare or Milton, till it was explained to her, and wishes that there had been titles prefixed to tell what they were about.

From this mention of Mason's name you may think, perhaps, we are great correspondents; no such thing; I have not heard from him these two months. I will be sure to scold in my own name as well as in yours. I rejoice to hear you are so ripe for the

[1]A prominent scholar and ecclesiastic, best known as the author of *Letters on Chivalry and Romance* (1762).

[2]Gray had sent Hurd a copy of the first edition of his *Odes* ("The Progress of Poesy" and "The Bard").

[3]Garrick.

press, and so voluminous,[4]—not for my own sake only, whom you flatter with the hopes of seeing your labors both public and private, but for yours too; for to be employed is to be happy. This principle of mine, and I am convinced of its truth, has, as usual, no influence on my practice. I am alone and *ennuyé*[5] to the last degree, yet do nothing. Indeed I have one excuse: my health, which you so kindly inquire after, is not extraordinary ever since I came hither. It is no great malady, but several little ones that seem brewing no good to me.

It will be a particular pleasure to me to hear whether Content dwells in Leicestershire,[6] and how she entertains herself there; only do not be too happy, nor forget entirely the quiet ugliness of Cambridge. I am, dear sir,

Your friend and obliged humble servant,
T. Gray

If Mr. Brown falls in your way, be so good to show him the beginning of this letter, and it will save me the labor of writing the same thing twice. His first letter, I believe, was in the mail that was robbed, for it was delayed many days; his second I have just received.

XII. To William Mason

Cambridge, 19 December, 1757

Dear Mason:

Though I very well know the bland, emollient, saponaceous qualities both of sack and silver,[1] yet if any great man would say to me, "I make you Rat-Catcher to His Majesty, with a salary of £300 a year and two butts of the best malaga; and though it has been usual to catch a mouse or two (for form's sake) in public once a year, yet to you, sir, we shall not stand upon these things,"—I cannot say I should jump at it. Nay, if they would drop the very name of the office, and call me Sinecure to the King's Majesty, I should still feel a little awkward, and think everybody I saw smelt a rat about me; but I do not pretend to blame any one else that has not the same sensations. For my part, I would rather be Sergeant-Trumpeter, or Pin-Maker to the Palace. Nevertheless I interest myself a little in the history of it, and rather wish somebody may accept it that will retrieve the credit of the thing, if it be retrievable, or ever had any credit. Rowe[2] was, I think, the last man of character that had it. As to Settle, whom you mention, be belonged to my lord mayor, not to the king.[3] Eusden was a person of great hopes in his youth, though at last he turned out a drunken parson.[4] Dryden was as disgraceful to the office from his character as the poorest scribbler could have been from his verses. In short, the office itself has always humbled the possessor hitherto (even in an age when kings were somebody): if he were a poor writer, by making him more conspicuous, and if he were a good one, by setting him at war with the little fry of his own profession; for there are poets little enough to envy even a Poet Laureate.

I am obliged to you for your news; pray send me some more, and better of the sort. I can tell you nothing in return; so your generosity will be the greater. Only Dick[5] is going to give up his rooms and live at Ashwell. Mr. Treasurer sets Sir Matthew Lamb at naught, and says he has sent him reasons half a sheet at a time; and Mr. Brown attests his veracity, as an eye-witness. I have had nine pages of criticism on "The Bard" sent me in an anonymous letter, directed to the "Reverend" Mr. Gray at Strawberry Hill;[6] and if I have a mind to hear as much more on the other ode, I am

---

[4]In this year Hurd published two works of scholarship and finished writing his *Moral and Political Dialogues*.

[5]Mentally weary.

[6]Hurd had recently been presented to a living in Leicestershire.

[1]The office of Poet Laureate carried with it both a salary and an allowance of wine. Gray had recently declined the position.

[2]Nicholas Rowe, Poet Laureate 1715–1718.

[3]Elkanah Settle had been City Poet, not Poet Laureate.

[4]Laurence Eusden, Poet Laureate 1718–1730. He is said to have been Pope's "parson, much bemused in beer" (*Epistle to Dr. Arbuthnot,* l. 15).

[5]Richard Forester, whose rooms subsequently became Gray's.

[6]Walpole's residence, where the *Odes* had been printed.

told where I may direct. He seems a good sensible man, and I dare say a clergyman; he is very frank, and indeed much ruder than he means to be. Adieu, dear Mason, and believe that I am too.

XIII. *To Thomas Wharton*

London, *c.* 20 June, 1760

Dear Doctor:

I heard yesterday from our old friend Mr. Field that Mrs. Wharton had brought you a son; and as I sincerely hope this may be some addition to your happiness, I heartily congratulate you both on this occasion. Another thing I rejoice in is to know that you not only grow reconciled to your scene, but discover beauties round you that once were deformities. I am persuaded the whole matter is to have always something going forward. Happy they that can create a rose-tree, or erect a honeysuckle; that can watch the brood of a hen, or see a fleet of their own ducklings launch into the water! It is with a sentiment of envy I speak it, who never shall have even a thatched roof of my own, nor gather a strawberry but in Covent Garden.[1] I will not believe in the *vocality* of Old Park[2] till next summer, when perhaps I may trust my own ears.

I remain (bating[3] some few little excursions that I have made) still in town, though for these three weeks I have been going into Oxfordshire with Madam Speed; but her affairs, as she says, or her vagaries, as I say, have obliged her to alter her mind ten times within that space; no wonder, for she has got at least £30,000 with a house in town, plate, jewels, china, and old-japan[4] infinite, so that indeed it would be ridiculous for her to know her own mind. I, who know mine, do intend to go to Cambridge; but that owl, Fobus,[5] is going thither to the commencement, so that I am forced to stay till his nonsense is at an end. Chapman, you see, is dead at last; which signifies not much, I take it, for anybody; for his family (they say) are left in good circumstances. I am neither sorry nor glad, for Mason (I doubt) will scarce succeed to his prebend.[6] The old creature is down at Aston, where my lord[7] has paid him a visit lately, as the town says, in a *miff* about the Garter, and other *frumps*[8] he has met with of late. I believe this at least is certain, that he has deserted his old attachments and worships another idol, who receives his incense with a good deal of coldness and negligence.

I can tell you but little of St. Germain. He saw M. d'Affry[9] at The Hague, who in a day or two (on receiving a courier from his own court) asked the States' leave to apprehend him; but he has gone, and arrived safe at St. Mary Axe,[10] where he had lodgings (I fancy) at his old friend La Cour's, the Jew physician. After some days a messenger took charge of him, and he was examined (I believe) before Mr. Pitt. They, however, dismissed him, but with orders to leave England directly; yet I know care was taken that he should be furnished with proper passports to go safe through Holland to Hamburg; which gives some room to believe, what many at first imagined, that he was charged with some proposal from the French court. He is a likely person enough to make them believe at Paris that he could somehow serve them on such an occasion.

We are in great alarms about Quebec. The force in the town was not 3000 men, sufficient to defend the place (naturally strong) against any attack of the French forces, unfurnished as they must be for a formal siege, but by no means to meet[11] them in the field. This, however, is what Murray[12] has chose to do, whether from rashness, or deceived by false intelligence, I cannot tell. The returns of our loss are undoubtedly false, for we have above a hun-

---

[1]The London fruit market.

[2]Wharton's estate near Durham.

[3]Except for. [4]Lacquer work.

[5]The Duke of Newcastle, then Chancellor of the University.

[6]Ecclesiastical living.

[7]Lord Holdernesse, Mason's patron.

[8]In a huff about not having received the Order of the Garter, and other mocks.

[9]French ambassador to Holland.

[10]A London street.

[11]Sufficient to meet.

[12]Commander of the British garrison in Quebec.

dred officers killed or taken. All depends upon the arrival of our garrison from Louisburg, which was daily expected; but even that (unless they bring provisions with them) may increase the distress, for at the time when we were told of the plenty and cheapness of all things at Quebec, I am assured a piece of fresh meat could not be had for twenty guineas.

If you have seen Stonhewer, he has probably told you of my old Scotch (or rather Irish) poetry. I am gone mad about them. They are said to be translations (literal and in prose) from the Erse tongue, done by one Macpherson, a young clergyman in the Highlands.[13] He means to publish a collection he has of these specimens of antiquity, if it be antiquity; but what plagues me is I cannot come at any certainty on that head. I was so struck, so *extasié*[14] with their infinite beauty that I writ into Scotland to make a thousand inquiries. The letters I have in return are ill-wrote, ill-reasoned, unsatisfactory, calculated (one would imagine) to deceive one, and yet not cunning enough to do it cleverly. In short, the whole external evidence would make one believe these fragments (for so he calls them, though nothing can be more entire) counterfeit; but the internal is so strong on the other side that I am resolved to believe them genuine, spite of the devil and the kirk. It is impossible to convince me that they were invented by the same man that writes me these letters. On the other hand, it is almost as hard to suppose, if they are original, that he should be able to translate them so admirably. What can one do? Since Stonhewer went, I have received another of a very different and inferior kind (being merely descriptive), much more modern than the former (he says), yet very old too; this too in its way is extremely fine. In short, this man is the very demon of poetry, or he has lighted on a treasure hid for ages. The Welsh poets are also coming to light: I have seen a discourse in manuscripts[15] about them (by one Mr. Evans, a clergyman) with specimens of their writings; this is in Latin, and, though it don't approach the other, there are fine scraps among it.

You will think I am grown mighty poetical of a sudden; you would think so still more if you knew there was a satire printed against me and Mason jointly. It is called *Two Odes:* the one is inscribed to Obscurity (that is me), the other to Oblivion. It tells me what I never heard before, for (speaking of himself) the author says, though he has

Nor the pride, nor self-opinion
That possess the happy pair,
Each of Taste the fav'rite minion,
Prancing through the desert air:
Yet shall he mount, with classic housings graced,
By help mechanic of equestrian block;
And all unheedful of the critic's mock,
Spur his light courser o'er the bounds of Taste.

The writer is a Mr. Coleman, who published the *Connoisseur,* nephew to the late Lady Bath, and a friend of Garrick's. I believe his *Odes* sell no more than mine did, for I saw a heap of them lie in a bookseller's window, who recommended them to me as a very pretty thing.

If I did not mention *Tristram*[16] to you, it was because I thought I had done so before. There is much good fun in it, and humor sometimes hit and sometimes missed. I agree with your opinion of it, and shall see the two future volumes with pleasure. Have you read his *Sermons*[17] (with his own comic figure at the head of them)? They are in the style I think most proper for the pulpit, and show a very strong imagination and a sensible heart; but you see him often tottering on the verge of laughter, and ready to throw his periwig in the face of his audience. Now for my season:

April 10. I observed the elm putting out.
12. That and the pear looked green. Thermometer at 62.
13. Very fine. White-poplar and willow put out.

[13]James Macpherson (1736–1796), the so-called translator of the Ossianic poems. Gray's doubts that they really were translations of Erse, or Gaelic, originals were by no means so pronounced as those of Samuel Johnson.

[14]Ravished.

[15]*De Bardis Dissertatio,* which Evan Evans published in 1764.

[16]The first installment of Laurence Sterne's *Tristram Shandy* had appeared a few months earlier.

[17]Sterne's *Sermons of Mr. Yorick* (1760).

15. Standard[18] pear (sheltered) in full bloom.
18. Lime and hornbeam[19] green.
19. Swallows flying.
20. Thermometer at 60. Wind southwest. Skylark, chaffinch, thrush, wren, and robin singing. Horse-chestnut, wild briar, bramble, and sallow had spread their leaves. Hawthorn and lilac had formed their blossoms. Black-thorn, double-flowered peach, and pears in full bloom. Double jonquils, hyacinths, anemones, single wallflowers, and auriculas in flower. In the fields, dog-violets, daisies, dandelion, buttercups, red archangel, and shepherd's purse.
21. Almond out of bloom and spreading its leaves.
26. Lilacs flowering.

May 1. Gentianella in flower.
2. Pear goes off. Apple blooms. Thermometer at 63. Wind northeast. Still fair and dry.
3. Evening and all night hard rain.
4. Thermometer at 40. Wind northeast, rain.
11. Very fine. Wind northeast. Horse-chestnut in full bloom. Walnut and vine spread. Lilacs, Persian jasmine, tulips, wallflowers, pheasant-eye, lily-in-the-valley in flower. In the fields, furze, cowslips, harebells, and cow-parsnip.
13. Jasmine and acacia spread. Fine weather.
18. Showery. Wind high.
19. Same. Thermometer at 56.
20. Thunder, rain. 54.
21. Rain. Wind northeast. 52.
31. Green peas 15*d.* a quart.

June 1. At 78.
2. Scarlet strawberries, duke cherries; hay-making here.
3. Wind south southeast. Thermometer at 84 (the highest I ever saw it); it was at noon.

[18]Growing as a tree, not trained to a wall.

[19]Small English tree.

Since which till last week we had hot, dry weather. Now it rains like mad. Cherries and strawberries in bushels.

I believe there is no fear of war with Spain.

XIV. To Horace Walpole

Cambridge, 25 February, 1768

To YOUR friendly accusation I am glad I can plead not guilty with a safe conscience. Dodsley told me in the spring that the plates from Mr. Bentley's designs[1] were worn out, and he wanted to have them copied and reduced to a smaller scale for a new edition. I dissuaded him from so silly an expense, and desired he would put in no ornaments at all. The "Long Story" was to be totally omitted, as its only use (that of explaining the prints) was gone; but to supply the place of it in bulk, lest my works should be mistaken for the works of a flea or a pismire,[2] I promised to send him an equal weight of poetry or prose. So, since my return hither, I put up about two ounces of stuff: *viz.,* "The Fatal Sisters," "The Descent of Odin" (of both which you have copies), a bit of something from the Welsh,[3] and certain little notes, partly from justice (to acknowledge the debt where I had borrowed anything), partly from ill temper, just to tell the gentle reader that Edward I was not Oliver Cromwell, nor Queen Elizabeth the Witch of Endor. This is literally all; and with all this I shall be but a shrimp of an author. I gave leave also to print the same thing at Glasgow; but I doubt my packet has miscarried, for I hear nothing of its arrival as yet. To what you say to me so civilly, that I ought to write more, I reply in your own words (like the pamphleteer[4] who

[1]Richard Bentley, son of the great scholar of the same name, had provided illustrations for previous editions of Gray's poems.

[2]Ant.

[3]"The Triumphs of Owen" and "The Death of Hoel."

[4]F. W. Guidickins in his reply to Walpole's *Historic Doubts on the Reign and Life of King Richard the Third.*

is going to confute you out of your own mouth): What has one to do, when turned of fifty, but really to think of finishing? However, I will be candid (for you seem to be so with me) and avow to you that till fourscore and ten, whenever the humor takes me, I will write because I like it, and because I like myself better when I do so. If I do not write much, it is because I cannot. As you have not this last plea, I see no reason why you should not continue as long as it is agreeable to yourself, and to all such as have any curiosity of judgment in the subjects you choose to treat. By the way, let me tell you (while it is fresh) that Lord Sandwich, who was lately dining at Cambridge, speaking (as I am told) handsomely of your book,[5] said it was pity you did not know that his cousin Manchester[6] had a genealogy of the kings, which came down no lower than to Richard III, and at the end of it were two portraits of Richard and his son, in which that king appeared to be a handsome man. I tell you it as I heard it; perhaps you may think it worth inquiring into.

I have looked into Speed and Leslie.[7] It appears very odd that Speed in the speech he makes for Perkin Warbeck,[8] addressed to James IV of Scotland, should three times cite the manuscript proclamation of Perkin, then in the hands of Sir Robert Cotton;[9] and yet when he gives us the proclamation afterwards (on occasion of the insurrection in Cornwall) he does not cite any such manuscript. In Casley's catalogue of the Cotton Library you may see whether this manuscript proclamation still exists or not; if it does, it may be found in the Museum.[10] Leslie will give you no satisfaction at all; though no subject of England, he could not write freely on this matter as the title of Mary, his mistress, to the crown of England was derived from that of Henry VII. Accordingly, he everywhere treats Perkin as an impostor, yet drops several little expressions inconsistent with that supposition. He has preserved no proclamation; he only puts a short speech into Perkin's mouth, the substance of which is taken by Speed and translated at the end of his, which is a good deal longer; the whole matter is treated by Leslie very concisely and superficially. I can easily transcribe it, if you please; but I do not see that it could answer any purpose.

Mr. Boswell's book[11] I was going to recommend to you, when I received your letter; it has pleased and moved me strangely, all (I mean) that relates to Paoli.[12] He is a man born two thousand years after his time! The pamphlet proves what I have always maintained, that any fool may write a most valuable book by chance, if he will only tell us what he heard and saw with veracity. Of Mr. Boswell's truth I have not the least suspicion, because I am sure he could invent nothing of this kind. The true title of this part of his work is: "A Dialogue between a Green Goose and a Hero."

I have been told of a manuscript in Benet Library;[13] the inscription of it is *Itinerarium Fratris Simonis Simeonis et Hugonis Illuminatoris,* 1322. Would not one think that this should promise something? They were two Franciscan friars that came from Ireland, and passed through Wales to London, to Canterbury, to Dover, and so to France in their way to Jerusalem. All that relates to our own country has been transcribed for me, and (sorry am I to say) signifies not a halfpenny. Only this little bit might be inserted in your next edition of the *Painters:*[14] *"Ad aliud caput civitatis (Londoniae) est monasterium nigrorum*

[5]Walpole's *Historic Doubts.*

[6]George Montagu, fourth Duke of Manchester.

[7]John Speed's *History of Great Britaine* (1611), and John Leslie's *De Origine, Moribus, et Rebus Gestis Scotorum* (1578).

[8]Pretended son of Edward IV, who led an unsuccessful attempt to unthrone Henry VII and was executed in 1499.

[9]Founder of the famous Cottonian Library (1571–1631).

[10]The royal collection, of which the Cottonian Library had become a part and out of which the British Museum has developed.

[11]James Boswell's first important book, *An Account of Corsica* (1768).

[12]General Pascal Paoli, leader of an unsuccessful movement to liberate Corsica from Genoa.

[13]Corpus Christi Library.

[14]Walpole's *Anecdotes of Painting in England* (1762).

monachorum nomine Westmonasterium, in quo constanter et communiter omnes reges Angliae sepeliuntur;—et eidem monasterio quasi immediate conjungitur illud famosissimum palatium regis in quo est illa vulgata camera in cuius parietibus sunt omnes historiae bellicae totius Bibliae ineffabiliter depictae, atque in Gallico completissime et perfectissime conscriptae, in non modica intuentium admiratione et maxima regali magnificentia."[15]

I have had certain observations on your *Royal and Noble Authors* given me to send you perhaps about three years ago; last week I found them in a drawer, and (my conscience being troubled) now enclose them to you. I have even forgot whose they are.

I have been also told of a passage in Philippe de Comines,[16] which (if you know) ought not to have been passed over. The book is not at hand at present, and I must conclude my letter. Adieu!

I am ever yours,
T. Gray

[15]At the other end of the city of London is a monastery of the black monks, called Westminster, in which all the kings of England are uniformly buried together;—and almost immediately adjoining the same monastery is that most famous palace of the king in which is that celebrated chamber on whose walls all the military history of the whole Bible is indescribably portrayed, and also written out, entire and perfect, in the French language, to the no little admiration of spectators and the great display of royal grandeur.

[16]French Historian (c. 1445–1519).

XV. To the Duke of Grafton[1]

Cambridge, 27 or 28 July, 1768

My Lord:

Your Grace has dealt nobly with me; and the same delicacy of mind that induced you to confer this favor on me, unsolicited and unexpected, may perhaps make you averse to receive my sincerest thanks and grateful acknowledgments. Yet your Grace must excuse me; they will have their way; they are indeed but words, yet I know and feel they come from my heart, and therefore are not wholly unworthy of your Grace's acceptance. I even flatter myself (such is my pride) that you have some little satisfaction in your own work. If I did not deceive myself in this, it would complete the happiness of,

My Lord,
Your Grace's
Most obliged and devoted servant.

[1]As Chancellor of Cambridge University the Duke of Grafton had offered Gray the Regius Professorship of Modern History. This letter is an immediate acceptance of the honor.

SAMUEL JOHNSON

1709–1784

Johnson's father was a bookseller doing business in Lichfield, and there Johnson was born on 18 September, 1709. There was little money in the family, and his struggle with poverty began almost with his birth. The one fortunate circumstance of his youth was the fact that he had the freedom of his father's shop; his early education was got largely from wide reading in the books which the people of Lichfield did not buy. In 1728 Johnson entered Pembroke College, Oxford, but was able to remain there only fourteen months. He then did not know where to turn for a living. He took a position in a school, but such were schools in that time that after a few months "he relinquished a situation which all his life long he recollected with the strongest aversion, and even a degree of horror." He next made unsuccessful attempts to obtain appointment to headmasterships, and almost equally unsuccessful attempts to earn money by literary hackwork. When he was twenty-six he married Mrs. Porter, a widow who was many years older than himself, whom he regarded with true and undiminished affection until her death in 1752, and the loss of whom he did not cease to lament until his own death. With a little money which his wife had, Johnson opened a school at Edial, near Lichfield—a school which was never attended by more than three pupils and which he soon abandoned. Other efforts having failed, he now determined to try his fortune in London, whither he went in the company of one of his three former pupils, David Garrick, who was to become the greatest of English actors.

Johnson found employment in the capital, managing to make a bare living, often enough to do little better than escape starvation, by means of hackwriting for the booksellers. In 1738 he published *London,* a satirical poem, imitated from Juvenal after the manner of Pope's imitations of Horace, which won him immediate recognition from the best judges of the day, including Pope himself, but which brought him very little money. Gradually he became known, but could not cease struggling, by means of all kinds of literary work that offered, for a bare subsistence. In 1745 he projected a new edition of Shakespeare, but did not actually publish it until 1765. In 1747 he announced his plan for what was his greatest work, though a work which has now little more than historical interest and one whose value it is not entirely easy for us to grasp. This was his *Dictionary of the English Language,* which it took him and his assistants eight years of hard work to complete. Meanwhile Johnson had published *The Vanity of Human Wishes* in 1749, had seen his classical tragedy, *Irene,* acted with little success, and had published two series of periodical essays, *The Rambler* (1750–1752) and *The Adventurer* (1753). A third series, *The Idler,* was written from 1758 to 1760. Early in 1759 occurred the death of his mother, and it was to meet the expenses of her illness and death that he wrote *Rasselas.* His need was urgent, and he wrote the tale within the space of a single week or, at the most, if we are to accept O. F. Emerson's criticism of Boswell's account, within a period of ten days—a period during which he was distracted by fears and sorrow and was expecting daily to hear the news of his mother's death. Though Johnson all his life had a pronounced tendency to indolence, his mind could on occasion work, as this instance proves, with astonishing rapidity. In 1762, two years after the accession of George III, however, his long struggle with poverty ceased. The Tories at that time returned to power; and Johnson, who was strongly attached to their party, was granted a pension of £300, which was sufficient to make him fairly comfortable through the remainder of his life. From this time until within a few years of the end of his life, he wrote but little. These years after 1762 were the years of his famous talk. It was in 1763 that he met Boswell, who was to record it all in the greatest of English biographies, and it was in 1764 that the Club (later called the Literary Club) was founded, which brought together at once some of Johnson's closest friends and a remarkable group of the men of that age whose names time has not obliterated—Sir Joshua Reynolds, Edmund Burke, Garrick, Boswell, Goldsmith, Charles James Fox, Thomas and Joseph Warton, Edward Gibbon, and others, including R. B. Sheridan and Bishop Percy. These were the happiest years of Johnson's life, and at the close they were crowned by a great achievement. In the late 1770's a group of booksellers planned to issue a collection of the works of the English poets, and Johnson undertook to write biographical and critical notices of those included in the series. The result was his *Lives of the Poets,* which contains some of his best and easiest writing, and which, as a monument of the man and of his type of criticism, is of lasting interest and importance.

Johnson's fame remains secure, as secure as that of any man in the annals of English literature. As a writer, he has had the curious fate to be overshadowed by his own biography, but the day has now happily passed when one can think that one sufficiently knows Johnson from the pages of Boswell. The man, truly enough, was greater than any of his works; yet those works have a vitality which Johnson's enemies have belittled in vain. In them still lives a man "who cared passionately for truth and nothing at all for novelty." And one must go to the writer, as well as to the talker, if one is to understand what Sir Joshua Reynolds gratefully said of his friend: "I acknowledge the highest obligations to him. He may be said to have formed my mind, and to have brushed from it a great deal of rubbish. . . . He qualified my mind to think justly."

The best of the collected editions of Johnson is usually considered to be *The Works of Samuel Johnson, LL.D.* (Oxford, 1825); of *The Lives of the English Poets* there is also an excellent modern edition, ed. George B. Hill (Oxford, 1905); *London* and *The Vanity of Human Wishes* have been published in a volume with an introduction by T. S. Eliot (London, 1930). *The Critical Opinions of Samuel Johnson* have been gathered together in a convenient form by J. E. Brown (Princeton, 1926). The most important biographical account is, naturally, *Boswell's Life of Johnson together with Boswell's Journal of a Tour of the Hebrides and Johnson's Diary of a Journey into North Wales,* ed. George B. Hill, rev. L. F. Powell (Oxford, 1934). Of interest and importance are *Macaulay's and Carlyle's Essays on Samuel Johnson,* ed. William Strunk, Jr. (New York, 1895). The background of the period is thoroughly covered in the collection of essays, *Johnson's England; an Account of the Life and Manners of His Age,* ed. A. S. Turberville (Oxford, 1933).

THE VANITY OF HUMAN WISHES

In Imitation of the Tenth Satire of Juvenal

Let Observation with extensive view
Survey mankind, from China to Peru;
Remark each anxious toil, each eager strife,
And watch the busy scenes of crowded life;
Then say how hope and fear, desire and hate,
O'erspread with snares the clouded maze of fate, 6
Where wav'ring man, betrayed by vent'rous pride
To chase the dreary paths without a guide,
As treach'rous phantoms in the mist delude,
Shuns fancied ills, or chases airy[1] good; 10
How rarely reason guides the stubborn choice,
Rules the bold hand, or prompts the suppliant voice,
How Nations sink, by darling schemes oppressed,
When vengeance listens to the fool's request.
Fate wings with ev'ry wish th'afflictive dart,
Each gift of nature and each grace of art; 16
With fatal heat impetuous courage glows,
With fatal sweetness elocution flows,
Impeachment stops the speaker's pow'rful breath,
And restless fire precipitates on death. 20
But, scarce observed, the knowing and the bold
Fall in the gen'ral massacre of gold;
Wide wasting pest! that rages unconfined,
And crowds with crimes the records of mankind;
For gold his sword the hireling ruffian draws,
For gold the hireling judge distorts the laws;
Wealth heaped on wealth, nor truth nor safety buys, 27
The dangers gather as the treasures rise.
Let Hist'ry tell where rival kings command,
And dubious title shakes the madded land, 30

[1]Unreal.

When statutes glean the refuse of the sword,[2]
How much more safe the vassal than the lord:
Low skulks the hind beneath the rage of power,
And leaves the wealthy traitor in the Tower,
Untouched his cottage, and his slumbers sound, 35
Though Confiscation's vultures hover round.
The needy traveller, serene and gay,
Walks the wild heath, and sings his toil away.
Does envy seize thee? crush th'upbraiding joy,
Increase his riches, and his peace destroy; 40
Now fears in dire vicissitude invade,
The rustling brake alarms, and quiv'ring shade,
Nor light nor darkness bring his pain relief,
One shows the plunder, and one hides the thief.
Yet still one gen'ral cry the skies assails, 45
And gain and grandeur load the tainted gales:
Few know the toiling statesman's fear or care,
Th'insidious rival and the gaping heir.
Once more, Democritus,[3] arise on earth,
With cheerful wisdom and instructive mirth,
See motley life in modern trappings dressed,
And feed with varied fools th'eternal jest: 52
Thou who could'st laugh where want enchained caprice,
Toil crushed conceit,[4] and man was of a piece;
Where wealth unloved without a mourner died; 55
And scarce a sycophant was fed by pride;
Where ne'er was known the form of mock debate,[5]
Or seen a new-made mayor's unwieldy state;
Where change of fav'rites made no change of laws,
And senates heard before they judged a cause; 60
How would'st thou shake at Britain's modish tribe,
Dart the quick taunt, and edge the piercing gibe?
Attentive truth and nature to descry,
And pierce each scene with philosophic eye,
To thee were solemn toys, or empty show, 65
The robes of pleasure and the veils of woe:
All aid the farce, and all thy mirth maintain,
Whose joys are causeless, or whose griefs are vain.
Such was the scorn that filled the sage's mind,
Renewed at ev'ry glance on human kind; 70
How just that scorn ere yet thy voice declare,
Search ev'ry state, and canvass ev'ry pray'r.
Unnumbered suppliants crowd Preferment's gate,
Athirst for wealth, and burning to be great;
Delusive Fortune hears th'incessant call, 75
They mount, they shine, evaporate, and fall.
On ev'ry stage the foes of peace attend,
Hate dogs their flight, and insult mocks their end.
Love ends with hope, the sinking statesman's door
Pours in the morning worshipper no more; 80
For growing names the weekly scribbler lies,
To growing wealth the dedicator flies;
From ev'ry room descends the painted face,
That hung the bright palladium[6] of the place;
And, smoked in kitchens, or in auctions sold,
To better features yields the frame of gold;
For now no more we trace in ev'ry line 87
Heroic worth, benevolence divine:
The form distorted justifies the fall,
And detestation rids th'indignant wall. 90
But will not Britain hear the last appeal,
Sign her foes' doom, or guard her fav'rites' zeal?
Through Freedom's sons no more remonstrance rings,
Degrading nobles and controlling kings; 94
Our supple tribes repress their patriot throats,
And ask no questions but the price of votes;
With weekly libels and septennial ale,[7]
Their wish is full to riot and to rail.
In full-blown dignity see Wolsey[8] stand,
Law in his voice, and fortune in his hand; 100
To him, the church, the realm, their pow'rs consign,
Through him the rays of regal bounty shine,
Turned by his nod the stream of honor flows,
His smile alone security bestows:
Still to new heights his restless wishes tow'r,
Claim leads to claim, and pow'r advances pow'r; 106

---

[2]Statutes execute those spared by war.

[3]The laughing philosopher, a Greek of the fifth century B. C.

[4]Empty opinion.

[5]Parliamentary debate that was unnecessary since the government had already made up its mind.

[6]Protective image.

[7]Ale dispersed during the parliamentary elections which had to be held every seven years.

[8]Cardinal Wolsey (*c.* 1471–1530), chief minister to Henry VIII. After losing the king's favor, he retired and died in a monastery shortly before he was to be executed.

Till conquest unresisted ceased to please,
And rights submitted left him none to seize.
At length his sov'reign frowns—the train of state
Mark the keen glance, and watch the sign to hate. 110
Where'er he turns, he meets a stranger's eye,
His suppliants scorn him, and his followers fly;
Now drops at once the pride of awful state,
The golden canopy, the glitt'ring plate,
The regal palace, the luxurious board, 115
The liv'ried army, and the menial lord.
With age, with cares, with maladies oppressed,
He seeks the refuge of monastic rest.
Grief aids disease, remembered folly stings,
And his last sighs reproach the faith of kings.

Speak thou, whose thoughts at humble peace repine, 121
Shall Wolsey's wealth, with Wolsey's end, be thine?
Or liv'st thou now, with safer pride content,
The wisest justice on the banks of Trent?
For, why did Wolsey, near the steeps of fate,
On weak foundations raise th'enormous weight? 126
Why but to sink beneath misfortune's blow,
With louder ruin to the gulfs below?

What gave great Villiers[9] to th'assassin's knife,
And fixed disease on Harley's[10] closing life?
What murdered Wentworth,[11] and what exiled Hyde,[12] 131
By kings protected, and to kings allied?
What but their wish indulged in courts to shine,
And pow'r too great to keep, or to resign?

When first the college rolls receive his name, 135
The young enthusiast quits his ease for fame;
Through all his veins the fever of renown
Burns from the strong contagion of the gown;
O'er Bodley's dome[13] his future labors spread,
And Bacon's mansion[14] trembles o'er his head. 140
Are these thy views? Proceed, illustrious youth,
And Virtue guard thee to the throne of Truth!
Yet, should thy soul indulge the gen'rous heat
Till captive Science yields her last retreat;
Should reason guide thee with her brightest ray, 145
And pour on misty Doubt resistless day;
Should no false kindness lure to loose delight,
Nor praise relax, nor difficulty fright;
Should tempting Novelty thy cell refrain,
And Sloth effuse her opiate fumes in vain;
Should Beauty blunt on fops her fatal dart,
Nor claim the triumph of a lettered heart; 152
Should no disease thy torpid veins invade,
Nor Melancholy's phantoms haunt thy shade;
Yet hope not life from grief or danger free,
Nor think the doom of man reversed for thee: 156
Deign on the passing world to turn thine eyes,
And pause awhile from Letters to be wise;
There mark what ills the scholar's life assail,
Toil, envy, want, the patron, and the gaol. 160
See nations, slowly wise and meanly just,
To buried merit raise the tardy bust.
If dreams yet flatter, once again attend;
Here Lydiat's life, and Galileo's, end.[15]

Nor deem, when Learning her vast prize bestows, 165
The glitt'ring eminence exempt from foes;
See, when the vulgar 'scape, despised or awed,
Rebellion's vengeful talons seize on Laud.[16]
From meaner minds, though smaller fines content,
The plundered palace, or sequestered rent;
Marked out for dang'rous parts, he meets the shock, 171
And fatal Learning leads him to the block:
Around his tomb let Art and Genius weep,

[9]George Villiers, first Duke of Buckingham, favorite of James I and Charles I, slain by an assassin in 1628.

[10]Robert Harley, first Earl of Oxford, leader of the Tories during the reign of Queen Anne, but impeached in 1717.

[11]Sir Thomas Wentworth, first Earl of Strafford, the adviser of Charles I, executed by a bill of Parliament in 1641.

[12]Edward Hyde, first Earl of Clarendon, the adviser of Charles II and author of the great *History of the Rebellion.* He was exiled in 1667; previously his daughter had married the Duke of York, who later became James II.

[13]The Bodleian Library at Oxford.

[14]A cell in an old tower at Oxford, said to have been built by Roger Bacon in the thirteenth century.

[15]Lydiat (1572–1646) was an English mathematician who died in misery after having been imprisoned by the Roundheads; Galileo (1564–1642) spent the end of his life in blindness and as the prisoner of the Inquisition.

[16]William Laud (1573–1645), Archbishop of Canterbury and one of the strongest opponents of the Puritans. His palace was plundered, his rents sequestered; and in the end he was executed by his enemies.

But hear his death, ye blockheads, hear and sleep.
The festal blazes, the triumphal show, 175
The ravished standard, and the captive foe,
The senate's thanks, the Gazette's pompous tale,
With force resistless o'er the brave prevail.
Such bribes the rapid Greek o'er Asia whirled,
For such the steady Romans shook the world;
For such in distant lands the Britons shine,
And stain with blood the Danube or the Rhine;[17] 182
This pow'r has praise, that virtue scarce can warm
Till Fame supplies the universal charm.
Yet Reason frowns on War's unequal game,
Where wasted nations raise a single name;
And mortgaged states their grandsires' wreaths regret, 187
From age to age in everlasting debt;
Wreaths which at last the dear-bought right convey
To rust on medals, or on stones decay. 190
On what foundation stands the warrior's pride,
How just his hopes, let Swedish Charles[18] decide;
A frame of adamant, a soul of fire,
No dangers fright him, and no labors tire;
O'er love, o'er fear, extends his wide domain,
Unconquered lord of pleasure and of pain;
No joys to him pacific sceptres yield, 197
War sounds the trump, he rushes to the field;
Behold surrounding kings their pow'rs combine,
And one capitulate, and one resign;[19] 200
Peace courts his hand, but spreads her charms in vain;
"Think nothing gained," he cries, "till nought remain,
On Moscow's walls till Gothic standards fly,
And all be mine beneath the polar sky."
The march begins in military state, 205
And nations on his eye suspended wait;
Stern Famine guards the solitary coast,
And Winter barricades the realms of Frost;
He comes, nor want nor cold his course delay;—
Hide, blushing Glory, hide Pultowa's day:[20]
The vanquished hero leaves his broken bands,
And shows his miseries in distant lands; 212
Condemned a needy suppliant to wait,
While ladies interpose, and slaves debate.
But did not Chance at length the error mend?
Did no subverted empire mark his end? 216
Did rival monarchs give the fatal wound?
Or hostile millions press him to the ground?
His fall was destined to a barren strand,
A petty fortress, and a dubious hand;[21] 220
He left the name at which the world grew pale,
To point a moral, or adorn a tale.
All times their scenes of pompous woes afford,
From Persia's tyrant to Bavaria's lord.
In gay hostility and barb'rous pride, 225
With half mankind embattled at his side,
Great Xerxes[22] comes to seize the certain prey,
And starves exhausted regions in his way;
Attendant Flatt'ry counts his myriads o'er,
Till counted myriads soothe his pride no more; 230
Fresh praise is tried till madness fires his mind,
The waves he lashes, and enchains the wind;
New pow'rs are claimed, new pow'rs are still bestowed,
Till ride resistance lops the spreading god;
The daring Greeks deride the martial show,
And heap their valleys with the gaudy foe; 236
Th'insulted sea with humbler thought he gains,
A single skiff to speed his flight remains;
Th'incumbered oar scarce leaves the dreaded coast
Through purple billows and a floating host.
The bold Bavarian,[23] in a luckless hour, 241
Tries the dread summits of a Caesarean pow'r,
With unexpected legions bursts away,
And sees defenseless realms receive his sway;
Short sway! fair Austria spreads her mournful charms, 245
The queen, the beauty, sets the world in arms;

[17] References to the brilliant campaigns of the Duke of Marlborough in 1702–1704.

[18] Charles XII of Sweden (1682–1718).

[19] Respectively Charles IV of Denmark and August II of Poland.

[20] The battle of Pultowa on July 9, 1709, after which the defeated Charles sought refuge in Turkey.

[21] Charles was slain, it is not known by whom, while besieging a small place on the coast of Norway.

[22] King of Persia 485–465 B. C. The naval battle of Salamis, to which Johnson alludes, took place in 480 B. C.

[23] Charles Albert, Elector of Bavaria, whose attempt to gain the crown of the Holy Roman Empire led to the struggle with Queen Maria Theresa which is known as the War of the Austrian Succession (1740–1748). The Elector died in disgrace in 1745.

From hill to hill the beacon's rousing blaze
Spreads wide the hope of plunder and of praise;
The fierce Croatian, and the wild Hussar,[24]
With all the sons of ravage crowd the war;
The baffled prince, in honor's flatt'ring bloom
Of hasty greatness, finds the fatal doom, 252
His foes' derision, and his subjects' blame,
And steals to death from anguish and from shame.

Enlarge my life with multitude of days! 255
In health, in sickness, thus the suppliant prays;
Hides from himself his state, and shuns to know,
That life protracted is protracted woe.
Time hovers o'er, impatient to destroy,
And shuts up all the passages of joy: 260
In vain their gifts the bounteous seasons pour,
The fruit autumnal, and the vernal flow'r;
With listless eyes the dotard views the store,
He views, and wonders that they please no more.
Now pall the tasteless meats, and joyless wines, 265
And Luxury with sighs her slave resigns.
Approach, ye minstrels, try the soothing strain,
Diffuse the tuneful lenitives of pain:
No sounds, alas! would teach th'impervious ear,
Though dancing mountains witnessed Orpheus near; 270
Nor lute nor lyre his feeble pow'rs attend,
Nor sweeter music of a virtuous friend;
But everlasting dictates crowd his tongue,
Perversely grave, or positively wrong.
The still returning tale, and ling'ring jest, 275
Perplex the fawning niece and pampered guest,
While growing hopes scarce awe the gath'ring sneer,
And scarce a legacy can bribe to hear;
The watchful guests still hint the last offense;
The daughter's petulance, the son's expense,
Improve his heady rage with treach'rous skill,
And mould his passions till they make his will. 282

Unnumbered maladies his joints invade,
Lay siege to life, and press the dire blockade;
But unextinguished Av'rice still remains, 285
And dreaded losses aggravate his pains;
He turns, with anxious heart and crippled hands,
His bonds of debt, and mortgages of lands;
Or views his coffers with suspicious eyes,
Unlocks his gold, and counts it till he dies. 290

But grant, the virtues of a temp'rate prime
Bless with an age exempt from scorn and crime;
An age that melts with unperceived decay,
And glides in modest innocence away;
Whose peaceful day Benevolence endears, 295
Whose night congratulating Conscience cheers;
The gen'ral fav'rite as the gen'ral friend:
Such age there is, and who shall wish its end?

Yet ev'n on this her load Misfortune flings,
To press the weary minutes' flagging wings;
New sorrow rises as the day returns, 301
A sister sickens, or a daughter mourns.
Now kindred Merit fills the sable bier,
Now lacerated Friendship claims a tear;
Year chases year, decay pursues decay, 305
Still drops some joy from with'ring life away;
New forms arise, and diff'rent views engage,
Superfluous lags the vet'ran on the stage,
Till pitying Nature signs the last release,
And bids afflicted worth retire to peace. 310

But few there are whom hours like these await,
Who set unclouded in the gulfs of Fate.
From Lydia's monarch[25] should the search descend,
By Solon cautioned to regard his end,
In life's last scene what prodigies surprise,
Fears of the brave, and follies of the wise! 316
From Marlb'rough's eyes the streams of dotage flow,
And Swift expires a driv'ler and a show.[26]

The teeming mother anxious for her race,
Begs for each birth the fortune of a face; 320
Yet Vane[27] could tell what ills from beauty spring;
And Sedley[28] cursed the form that pleased a king.
Ye nymphs of rosy lips and radiant eyes,
Whom Pleasure keeps too busy to be wise;
Whom joys with soft varieties invite, 325
By day the frolic, and the dance by night;
Who frown with vanity, who smile with art,
And ask the latest fashion of the heart;
What care, what rules, your heedless charms shall save,

---

[24]Originally a Hungarian light cavalryman.

[25]Croesus.

[26]Allusions to the paralytic strokes suffered by Marlborough and to Swift's madness.

[27]Anne Vane, mistress of Frederick, Prince of Wales, son of George II and father of George III.

[28]Catherine Sedley, Countess of Dorchester, mistress of James II.

Each nymph your rival, and each youth your slave? 330
Against your fame with fondness hate combines,
The rival batters, and the lover mines.
With distant voice neglected Virtue calls,
Less heard and less, the faint remonstrance falls;
Tired with contempt, she quits the slipp'ry reign, 335
And Pride and Prudence take her seat in vain.
In crowd at once, where none the pass defend,
The harmless freedom and the private friend.
The guardians yield, by force superior plied:
To int'rest, Prudence: and to Flatt'ry, Pride.
Here Beauty falls betrayed, despised, distressed, 341
And hissing infamy proclaims the rest.
Where then shall Hope and Fear their objects find?
Must dull suspense corrupt the stagnant mind?
Must helpless man, in ignorance sedate, 345
Roll darkling down the torrent of his fate?
Must no dislike alarm, no wishes rise,
No cries invoke the mercies of the skies?
Enquirer, cease; petitions yet remain
Which Heav'n may hear, nor deem Religion vain. 350
Still raise for good the supplicating voice,
But leave to Heav'n the measure and the choice.
Safe in his pow'r whose eyes discern afar
The secret ambush of a specious pray'r;
Implore his aid, in his decisions rest, 355
Secure, whate'er he gives, he gives the best.
Yet, when the sense of sacred presence fires,
And strong devotion to the skies aspires,
Pour forth thy fervors for a healthful mind,
Obedient passions, and a will resigned; 360
For love, which scarce collective man can fill;
For patience, sov'reign o'er transmuted ill;
For faith, that, panting for a happier seat,
Counts death kind Nature's signal of retreat.
These goods for man the laws of Heav'n ordain, 365
These goods he grants, who grants the pow'r to gain;
With these celestial Wisdom calms the mind,
And makes the happiness she does not find.

THE RAMBLER

No. 50. Saturday, 8 September, 1750.

Credebant hoc grande nefas, et morte piandum,
Si juvenis vetulo non assurrexerat, atque
Barbato cuicunque puer, licet ipse videret
Plura domi fraga, et majores glandis acervos.
—Juvenal.[1]

And had not men the hoary head revered,
And boys paid rev'rence when a man appeared,
Both must have died, though richer skids they wore,
And saw more heaps of acorns in their store.
—Creech.

I have always thought it the business of those who turn their speculations upon the living world, to commend the virtues, as well as to expose the faults of their contemporaries, and to confute a false as well as to support a just accusation; not only because it is peculiarly the business of a monitor to keep his own reputation untainted, lest those who can once charge him with partiality, should indulge themselves afterwards in disbelieving him at pleasure; but because he may find real crimes sufficient to give full employment to caution or repentance, without distracting the mind by needless scruples and vain solicitudes.

There are certain fixed and stated reproaches that one part of mankind has in all ages thrown upon another, which are regularly transmitted through continued successions, and which he that has once suffered them is certain to use with the same undistinguishing vehemence, when he has changed his station, and gained the prescriptive right of inflicting on others what he had formerly endured himself.

To these hereditary imputations, of which no man sees the justice, till it becomes his interest to see it, very little regard is to be shown; since it does not appear that they are produced by ratiocination or inquiry, but received implicitly, or caught by a kind of instantaneous contagion, and supported rather by willingness to credit, than ability to prove, them.

[1] *Satires*, XIII, 54–57. In the 2nd line *atque* should be *et si*. Often Johnson's quotations are somewhat inexact, but these unimportant slips will not be noted here.

It has been always the practice of those who are desirous to believe themselves made venerable by length of time, to censure the new-comers into life, for want of respect to gray hairs and sage experience, for heady confidence in their own understandings, for hasty conclusions upon partial views, for disregard of counsels, which their fathers and grandsires are ready to afford them, and a rebellious impatience of that subordination to which youth is condemned by nature, as necessary to its security from evils into which it would be otherwise precipitated, by the rashness of passion, and the blindness of ignorance.

Every old man complains of the growing depravity of the world, of the petulance and insolence of the rising generation. He recounts the decency and regularity of former times, and celebrates the discipline and sobriety of the age in which his youth was passed; a happy age, which is now no more to be expected, since confusion has broken in upon the world and thrown down all the boundaries of civility and reverence.

It is not sufficiently considered how much he assumes who dares to claim the privilege of complaining; for as every man has, in his own opinion, a full share of the miseries of life, he is inclined to consider all clamorous uneasiness, as a proof of impatience rather than of affliction, and to ask, What merit has this man to show, by which he has acquired a right to repine at the distributions of nature? Or, why does he imagine that exemptions should be granted him from the general condition of man? We find ourselves excited rather to captiousness than pity, and instead of being in haste to soothe his complaints by sympathy and tenderness, we inquire, whether the pain be proportionate to the lamentation; and whether, supposing the affliction real, it is not the effect of vice and folly, rather than calamity.

The querulousness and indignation which is observed so often to disfigure the last scene of life, naturally leads us to inquiries like these. For surely it will be thought at the first view of things, that if age be thus contemned and ridiculed, insulted and neglected, the crime must at least be equal on either part. They who have had opportunities of establishing their authority over minds ductile and unresisting, they who have been the protectors of helplessness, and the instructors of ignorance, and who yet retain in their own hands the power of wealth, and the dignity of command, must defeat their influence by their own misconduct, and make use of all these advantages with very little skill, if they cannot secure to themselves an appearance of respect, and ward off open mockery, and declared contempt.

The general story of mankind will evince, that lawful and settled authority is very seldom resisted when it is well employed. Gross corruption, or evident imbecility, is necessary to the suppression of that reverence with which the majority of mankind look upon their governors, and on those whom they see surrounded by splendor, and fortified by power. For though men are drawn by their passions into forgetfulness of invisible rewards and punishments, yet they are easily kept obedient to those who have temporal dominion in their hands, till their veneration is dissipated by such wickedness and folly as can neither be defended nor concealed.

It may, therefore, very reasonably be suspected that the old draw upon themselves the greatest part of those insults which they so much lament, and that age is rarely despised but when it is contemptible. If men imagine that excess of debauchery can be made reverend by time, that knowledge is the consequence of long life, however idly or thoughtlessly employed, that priority of birth will supply the want of steadiness or honesty, can it raise much wonder that their hopes are disappointed, and that they see their posterity rather willing to trust their own eyes in their progress into life, than enlist themselves under guides who have lost their way?

There are indeed, many truths which time necessarily and certainly teaches, and which might, by those who have learned them from experience, be communicated to their successors at a cheaper rate; but dictates, though liberally enough bestowed, are generally without effect, the teacher gains few proselytes by instruction which his own behavior contradicts; and young men miss the benefit of counsel, because they are not very ready to believe that those who fall below them in practice, can much excel them in theory. Thus the progress of knowledge is retarded, the world is kept long in the same state, and every new race is to gain the prudence of their predecessors by committing and redressing the same miscarriages.

To secure to the old that influence which they are willing to claim, and which might so much contribute to the improvement of the arts of life, it is absolutely necessary that they give themselves up to the duties of declining years; and contentedly resign to youth its levity, its pleasures, its frolics, and its fopperies. It is a hopeless endeavor to unite the contrarieties of spring and winter; it is unjust to claim the privileges of age, and retain the playthings of childhood. The young always form magnificent ideas of the wisdom and gravity of men, whom they consider as placed at a distance from them in the ranks of existence, and naturally look on those whom they find trifling with long beards, with contempt and indignation, like that which women feel at the effeminacy of men. If dotards will contend with boys in those performances in which boys must always excel them; if they will dress crippled limbs in embroidery, endeavor at gayety with faltering voices, and darken assemblies of pleasure with the ghastliness of disease, they may well expect those who find their diversions obstructed will hoot them away; and that if they descend to competition with youth, they must bear the insolence of successful rivals.

Lusisti satis, edisti satis atque bibisti:
Tempus abire tibi est.[2]

You've had your share of mirth, of meat and drink;
'Tis time to quit the scene—'tis time to think.
—Elphinston.

Another vice of age, by which the rising generation may be alienated from it, is severity and censoriousness, that gives no allowance to the failings of early life, that expects artfulness[3] from childhood, and constancy from youth, that is peremptory in every command, and inexorable to every failure. There are many who live merely to hinder happiness, and whose descendants can only tell of long life, that it produces suspicion, malignity, peevishness, and persecution; and yet even these tyrants can talk of the ingratitude of the age, curse their heirs for impatience, and wonder that young men cannot take pleasure in their father's company.

He that would pass the latter part of life with honor and decency, must, when he is young, consider that he shall one day be old; and remember, when he is old, that he has once been young. In youth, he must lay up knowledge for his support, when his powers of acting shall forsake him; and in age forbear to animadvert with rigor on faults which experience only can correct.

No. 59. Tuesday, 9 October, 1750.

Est aliquid fatale malum per verba levare:
Hoc querulam Prognen Halcyonenque facit.
Hoc erat, in solo quare Paeantius antro
Voce fatigaret Lemnia saxa sua.
Strangulat inclusus dolor, atque exaestuat intus;
Cogitur et vires multiplicare suas.
—Ovid.[4]

Complaining oft gives respite to our grief;
From hence the wretched Progne sought relief,
Hence the Paeantian chief his fate deplores,
And vents his sorrow to the Lemnian shores;
In vain by secrecy we would assuage
Our cares; concealed they gather tenfold rage.
—F. Lewis.

It is common to distinguish men by the names of animals which they are supposed to resemble. Thus a hero is frequently termed a lion, and a statesman a fox, an extortioner gains the appellation of vulture, and a fop the title of monkey. There is also among the various anomalies of character, which a survey of the world exhibits, a species of beings in human form, which may be properly marked out as the screech-owls of mankind.

These screech-owls seem to be settled in an opinion that the great business of life is to complain, and that they were born for no other purpose than to disturb the happiness of others, to lessen the little comforts, and shorten the short pleasures of our condition, by painful remembrances of the past, or melancholy prognostics of the future; their

[2] Horace, *Epistles,* II, ii, 214–215. [3] Skill.

[4] *Tristia,* V, i, 59–64.

only care is to crush the rising hope, to damp the kindling transport, and allay the golden hours of gayety with the hateful dross of grief and suspicion.

To those whose weakness of spirits, or timidity of temper, subjects them to impressions from others, and who are to suffer by fascination, and catch the contagion of misery, it is extremely unhappy to live within the compass of a screech-owl's voice; for it will often fill their ears in the hour of dejection, terrify them with apprehensions, which their own thoughts would never have produced, and sadden, by intruded sorrows, the day which might have been passed in amusements or in business; it will burden the heart with unnecessary discontents, and weaken for a time that love of life which is necessary to the vigorous prosecution of any undertaking.

Though I have, like the rest of mankind, many failings and weaknesses, I have not yet, by either friends or enemies, been charged with superstition; I never count the company which I enter, and I look at the new moon indifferently over either shoulder. I have, like most other philosophers, often heard the cuckoo without money in my pocket, and have been sometimes reproached as foolhardy for not turning down my eyes when a raven flew over my head. I never go home abruptly because a snake crosses my way, nor have any particular dread of a climacterical year;[5] yet I confess that, with all my scorn of old women, and their tales, I consider it as an unhappy day when I happen to be greeted, in the morning, by Suspirius the screech-owl.

I have now known Suspirius fifty-eight years and four months, and have never yet passed an hour with him in which he has not made some attack upon my quiet. When we were first acquainted, his great topic was the misery of youth without riches; and whenever we walked out together, he solaced me with a long enumeration of pleasures, which, as they were beyond the reach of my fortune, were without the verge of my desires, and which I should never have considered as the objects of a wish, had not his unseasonable representations placed them in my sight.

Another of his topics is the neglect of merit, with which he never fails to amuse[6] every man whom he sees not eminently fortunate. If he meets with a young officer, he always informs him of gentlemen whose personal courage is unquestioned, and whose military skill qualifies them to command armies, that have, notwithstanding all their merit, grown old with subaltern commissions. For a genius in the church, he is always provided with a curacy for life. The lawyer he informs of many men of great parts and deep study, who have never had an opportunity to speak in the courts: And meeting Serenus the physician, "Ah, doctor," says he, "what, a-foot still, when so many blockheads are rattling in their chariots? I told you seven years ago that you would never meet with encouragement, and I hope you will now take more notice, when I tell you that your Greek, and your diligence, and your honesty, will never enable you to live like yonder apothecary, who prescribes to his own shop, and laughs at the physician."

Suspirius has, in his time, intercepted fifteen authors in their way to the stage; persuaded nine and thirty merchants to retire from a prosperous trade for fear of bankruptcy, broke off an hundred and thirteen matches by prognostications of unhappiness, and enabled the smallpox to kill nineteen ladies, by perpetual alarm of the loss of beauty.

Whenever my evil stars bring us together, he never fails to represent to me the folly of my pursuits, and informs me that we are much older than when we began our acquaintance, that the infirmities of decrepitude are coming fast upon me, that whatever I now get, I shall enjoy but a little time, that fame is to a man tottering on the edge of the grave of very little importance, and that the time is at hand when I ought to look for no other pleasures than a good dinner and an easy chair.

Thus he goes on in his unharmonious strain,

[5]"Certain observable years are supposed to be attended with some considerable change in the body; as the 7th year; the 21st, made up of three times seven; the 49th, made up of seven times seven; the 63rd, being nine times seven; and the 81st, which is nine times nine; which two last are called the grand climacterics." (Johnson's *Dictionary.*)

[6]To engage the attention of.

displaying present miseries, and foreboding more, νυκτικόραξ ᾄδει θανατηφόρον,[7] every syllable is loaded with misfortune, and death is always brought nearer to the view. Yet, what always raises my resentment and indignation, I do not perceive that his mournful meditations have much effect upon himself. He talks and has long talked of calamities, without discovering otherwise than by the tone of his voice, that he feels any of the evils which he bewails or threatens, but has the same habit of uttering lamentations, as others of telling stories, and falls into expressions of condolence for past, or apprehension of future mischiefs, as all men studious of their ease have recourse to those subjects upon which they can most fluently or copiously discourse.

It is reported of the Sybarites,[8] that they destroyed all their cocks, that they might dream out their morning dreams without disturbance. Though I would not so far promote effeminacy as to propose the Sybarites for an example, yet since there is no man so corrupt or foolish, but something useful may be learned from him, I could wish that, in imitation of a people not often to be copied, some regulations might be made to exclude screech-owls from all company, as the enemies of mankind, and confine them to some proper receptacle, where they may mingle sighs at leisure, and thicken the gloom of one another.

"Thou prophet of evil," says Homer's Agamemnon, "thou never foretellest me good, but the joy of thy heart is to predict misfortunes."[9] Whoever is of the same temper, might there find the means of indulging his thoughts, and improving his vein of denunciation, and the flock of screech-owls might hoot together without injury to the rest of the world.

Yet, though I have so little kindness for this dark generation, I am very far from intending to debar the soft and tender mind from the privilege of complaining, when the sigh arises from the desire not of giving pain, but of gaining ease. To hear complaints with patience, even when complaints are vain, is one of the duties of friendship; and though it must be allowed that he suffers most like a hero that hides his grief in silence,

Spem vultu simulat, premit altum corde dolorem,[10]

His outward smiles concealed his inward smart.
—DRYDEN.

yet it cannot be denied, that he who complains acts like a man, like a social being, who looks for help from his fellow-creatures. Pity is to many of the unhappy a source of comfort in hopeless distresses, as it contributes to recommend them to themselves, by proving that they have not lost the regard of others; and heaven seems to indicate the duty even of barren compassion, by inclining us to weep for evils which we cannot remedy.

NO. 137. TUESDAY, 9 JULY, 1751.

Dum vitant stulti vitia, in contraria currunt.
—HORACE.[11]

——— Whilst fools one vice condemn,
They run into the opposite extreme.
—CREECH.

THAT wonder is the effect of ignorance, has been often observed. The awful stillness of attention, with which the mind is overspread at the first view of an unexpected effect, ceases when we have leisure to disentangle complications and investigate causes. Wonder is a pause of reason, a sudden cessation of the mental progress, which lasts only while the understanding is fixed upon some single idea, and is at an end when it recovers force enough to divide the object into its parts, or mark the intermediate gradations from the first agent to the last consequence.

It may be remarked with equal truth, that ignorance is often the effect of wonder. It is common for those who have never accustomed themselves to the labor of inquiry, nor invigorated their confidence by conquests over difficulty, to sleep in the gloomy quiescence of astonishment, without any effort to animate inquiry or dispel obscurity. What

[7] The night-raven's song bodes death. (*Greek Anthology,* XI, Satirical Epigrams, 186. In one of his sleepless nights Johnson turned this epigram into Latin verse.)

[8] Inhabitants of Sybaris in southern Italy, known for their love of luxury.

[9] *Iliad,* I, 106.

[10] *Aeneid,* I, 209.

[11] *Satires,* I, ii, 24.

Vauxhall Gardens, on the outskirts of London, pictured here by Thomas Rowlandson, was popular throughout the eighteenth century. People came to see and be seen, to gossip, to enjoy varied entertainments, and to eat and drink. In the box at the left, eating supper, are Boswell, Dr. Johnson, and Mrs. Thrale. Goldsmith is standing in front of the box. (Courtesy of the New York Public Library.)

At the top are four unflattering prints made by Rowlandson in 1786 to poke fun at Boswell's *Journal of a Tour to the Hebrides with Samuel Johnson,* published in the previous year. The print at the upper left is entitled "The Procession"; the one directly beneath it, "Tea" (with Mrs. Boswell). At the upper right is "Walking up the High Street" (in Edinburgh), and directly beneath it is "Chatting" ("We talked of Murder," Boswell wrote in the *Journal,* "and of the ancient trial by Duel"). (Courtesy of the Metropolitan Museum of Art.) The two bottom pictures are Sir Godfrey Kneller's portrait of Joseph Addison and Jonathan Richardson's portrait of Sir Richard Steele. (Courtesy of the New York Public Library.)

they cannot immediately conceive, they consider as too high to be reached, or too extensive to be comprehended; they therefore content themselves with the gaze of folly, forbear to attempt what they have no hopes of performing, and resign the pleasure of rational contemplation to more pertinacious study of more active faculties.

Among the productions of mechanic art, many are of a form so different from that of their first materials, and many consist of parts so numerous and so nicely adapted to each other, that it is not possible to view them without amazement. But when we enter the shops of artificers, observe the various tools by which every operation is facilitated, and trace the progress of a manufacture through the different hands, that, in succession to each other, contribute to its perfection, we soon discover that every single man has an easy task, and that the extremes, however remote, of natural rudeness and artificial elegance, are joined by a regular concatenation of effects, of which every one is introduced by that which precedes it, and equally introduces that which is to follow.

The same is the state of intellectual and manual performances. Long calculations or complex diagrams affright the timorous and unexperienced from a second view; but if we have skill sufficient to analyze them into simple principles, it will be discovered that our fear was groundless. *Divide and Conquer,* is a principle equally just in science as in policy. Complication is a species of confederacy which, while it continues united, bids defiance to the most active and vigorous intellect; but of which every member is separately weak, and which may therefore be quickly subdued, if it can once be broken.

The chief art of learning, as Locke has observed, is to attempt but little at a time.[12] The widest excursions of the mind are made by short flights frequently repeated; the most lofty fabrics of science are formed by the continued accumulation of single propositions.

It often happens, whatever be the cause, that impatience of labor, or dread of miscarriage, seizes those who are most distinguished for quickness of apprehension; and that they who might with greatest reason promise themselves victory, are least willing to hazard the encounter. This diffidence, where the attention is not laid asleep by laziness, or dissipated by pleasures, can arise only from confused and general views, such as negligence snatches in haste, or from the disappointment of the first hopes formed by arrogance without reflection. To expect that the intricacies of science will be pierced by a careless glance, or the eminences of fame ascended without labor, is to expect a particular privilege, a power denied to the rest of mankind; but to suppose that the maze is inscrutable to diligence, or the heights inaccessible to perseverance, is to submit tamely to the tyranny of fancy, and enchain the mind in voluntary shackles.

It is the proper ambition of the heroes in literature to enlarge the boundaries of knowledge by discovering and conquering new regions of the intellectual world. To the success of such undertakings perhaps some degree of fortuitous happiness is necessary, which no man can promise or procure to himself; and therefore doubt and irresolution may be forgiven in him that ventures into the unexplored abysses of truth, and attempts to find his way through the fluctuations of uncertainty, and the conflicts of contradiction. But when nothing more is required than to pursue a path already beaten, and to trample obstacles which others have demolished, why should any man so much distrust his own intellect as to imagine himself unequal to the attempt?

It were to be wished that they who devote their lives to study would at once believe nothing too great for their attainment, and consider nothing as too little for their regard; that they would extend their notice alike to science and to life; and unite some knowledge of the present world to their acquaintance with past ages and remote events.

Nothing has so much exposed men of learning to contempt and ridicule, as their ignorance of things which are known to all but themselves. Those who have been taught to consider the institutions of the schools[13] as giving the last perfection to hu-

[12] See *Some Thoughts concerning Education,* Sect. 160, Writing.

[13] I. e., of the university.

man abilities, are surprised to see men wrinkled with study, yet wanting to be instructed in the minute circumstances of propriety, or the necessary forms of daily transaction; and quickly shake off their reverence for modes of education which they find to produce no ability above the rest of mankind.

"Books," says Bacon, "can never teach the use of books."[14] The student must learn by commerce with mankind to reduce his speculations to practice, and accommodate his knowledge to the purposes of life.

It is too common for those who have been bred to scholastic professions, and passed much of their time in academies where nothing but learning confers honors, to disregard every other qualification, and to imagine that they shall find mankind ready to pay homage to their knowledge, and to crowd about them for instruction. They therefore step out from their cells into the open world with all the confidence of authority and dignity of importance; they look round about them at once with ignorance and scorn on a race of beings to whom they are equally unknown and equally contemptible, but whose manners they must imitate, and with whose opinions they must comply, if they desire to pass their time happily among them.

To lessen that disdain with which scholars are inclined to look on the common business of the world, and the unwillingness with which they condescend to learn what is not to be found in any system of philosophy, it may be necessary to consider that though admiration is excited by abstruse researches and remote discoveries, yet pleasure is not given, nor affection conciliated, but by softer accomplishments, and qualities more easily communicable to those about us. He that can only converse upon questions about which only a small part of mankind has knowledge sufficient to make them curious, must lose his days in unsocial silence, and live in the crowd of life without a companion. He that can be only useful on great occasions may die without exerting his abilities, and stand a helpless spectator of a thousand vexations which fret away happiness, and which nothing is required to remove but a little dexterity of conduct and readiness of expedients.

No degree of knowledge attainable by man is able to set him above the want of hourly assistance, or to extinguish the desire of fond endearments, and tender officiousness;[15] and therefore, no one should think it unnecessary to learn those arts by which friendship may be gained. Kindness is preserved by a constant reciprocation of benefits or interchange of pleasures; but such benefits only can be bestowed, as others are capable to receive, and such pleasures only imparted, as others are qualified to enjoy.

By this descent from the pinnacles of art no honor will be lost; for the condescensions of learning are always overpaid by gratitude. An elevated genius employed in little things, appears, to use the simile of Longinus, like the sun in his evening declination, he remits his splendor but retains his magnitude, and pleases more though he dazzles less.

No. 191. Tuesday, 14 January, 1752.

Cereus in vitium flecti, monitoribus asper.
—Horace.[16]

The youth—
Yielding like wax, th' impressive folly bears;
Rough to reproof, and slow to future cares.
—Francis.

TO THE RAMBLER

Dear Mr. Rambler:

I have been four days confined to my chamber by a cold, which has already kept me from three plays, nine sales, five shows, and six card-tables, and put me seventeen visits behindhand; and the doctor tells my mamma, that if I fret and cry, it will settle in my head, and I shall not be fit to be seen these six weeks. But, dear Mr. Rambler, how can I help it? At this very time Melissa is dancing with the prettiest gentleman; she will breakfast with him to-morrow, and then run to two auctions, and hear compliments, and have presents; then she will be dressed, and visit, and get a ticket to the play; then go

[14] See *Essays,* "Of Studies" ("They teach not their own use").

[15] Readiness in doing good offices.

[16] *De Arte Poetica,* 163.

to cards and win, and come home with two flambeaux before her chair. Dear Mr. Rambler, who can bear it?

My aunt has just brought me a bundle of your papers for my amusement. She says, you are a philosopher, and will teach me to moderate my desires, and look upon the world with indifference. But, dear sir, I do not wish, nor intend, to moderate my desires, nor can I think it proper to look upon the world with indifference, till the world looks with indifference on me. I have been forced, however, to sit this morning a whole quarter of an hour with your paper before my face; but just as my aunt came in, Phyllida had brought me a letter from Mr. Trip, which I put within the leaves; and read about "absence" and "inconsolableness," and "ardor," and "irresistible passion," and "eternal constancy," while my aunt imagined that I was puzzling myself with your philosophy, and often cried out, when she saw me look confused, "If there is any word that you do not understand, child, I will explain it."

Dear soul! How old people that think themselves wise may be imposed upon! But it is fit that they should take their turn, for I am sure, while they can keep poor girls close in the nursery, they tyrannize over us in a very shameful manner, and fill our imaginations with tales of terror, only to make us live in quiet subjection, and fancy that we can never be safe but by their protection.

I have a mamma and two aunts, who have all been formerly celebrated for wit and beauty, and are still generally admired by those that value themselves upon their understanding, and love to talk of vice and virtue, nature and simplicity, and beauty and propriety; but if there was not some hope of meeting me, scarcely a creature would come near them that wears a fashionable coat. These ladies, Mr. Rambler, have had me under their government fifteen years and a half, and have all that time been endeavoring to deceive me by such representations of life as I now find not to be true; but I know not whether I ought to impute them to ignorance or malice, as it is possible the world may be much changed since they mingled in general conversation.

Being desirous that I should love books, they told me that nothing but knowledge could make me an agreeable companion to men of sense, or qualify me to distinguish the superficial glitter of vanity from the solid merit of understanding; and that a habit of reading would enable me to fill up the vacuities of life without the help of silly or dangerous amusements, and preserve me from the snares of idleness and the inroads of temptation.

But their principal intention was to make me afraid of men; in which they succeeded so well for a time, that I durst not look in their faces, or be left alone with them in a parlor; for they made me fancy that no man ever spoke but to deceive, or looked but to allure; that the girl who suffered him that had once squeezed her hand, to approach her a second time, was on the brink of ruin; and that she who answered a billet, without consulting her relations, gave love such power over her that she would certainly become either poor or infamous.

From the time that my leading-strings were taken off, I scarce heard any mention of my beauty but from the milliner, the mantua-maker, and my own maid; for my mamma never said more, when she heard me commended, but "The girl is very well," and then endeavored to divert my attention by some inquiry after my needle, or my book.

It is now three months since I have been suffered to pay and receive visits, to dance at public assemblies, to have a place kept for me in the boxes, and to play at Lady Racket's rout;[17] and you may easily imagine what I think of those who have so long cheated me with false expectations, disturbed me with fictitious terrors, and concealed from me all that I have found to make the happiness of woman.

I am so far from perceiving the usefulness or necessity of books, that if I had not dropped all pretensions to learning, I should have lost Mr. Trip, whom I once frighted into another box, by retailing some of Dryden's remarks upon a tragedy; for Mr. Trip declares that he hates nothing like hard words, and, I am sure, there is not a better partner to be found; his very walk is a dance. I have talked once or twice among ladies

[17]Large evening assembly.

about principles and ideas, but they put their fans before their faces, and told me I was too wise for them, who for their part never pretended to read anything but the play-bill, and then asked me the price of my best head.[18]

Those vacancies of time which are to be filled up with books I have never yet obtained; for, consider, Mr. Rambler, I go to bed late, and therefore cannot rise early; as soon as I am up, I dress for the gardens; then walk in the park; then always go to some sale or show, or entertainment at the little theater; then must be dressed for dinner; then must pay my visits; then walk in the park; then hurry to the play; and from thence to the card-table. This is the general course of the day, when there happens nothing extraordinary; but sometimes I ramble into the country, and come back again to a ball; sometimes I am engaged for a whole day and part of the night. If, at any time, I can gain an hour by not being at home, I have so many things to do, so many orders to give to the milliner, so many alterations to make in my clothes, so many visitants' names to read over, so many invitations to accept or refuse, so many cards to write, and so many fashions to consider, that I am lost in confusion, forced at last to let in company or step into my chair, and leave half my affairs to the direction of my maid.

This is the round of my day; and when shall I either stop my course, or so change it as to want a book? I suppose it cannot be imagined, that any of these diversions will soon be at an end. There will always be gardens, and a park, and auctions, and shows, and playhouses, and cards; visits will always be paid, and clothes always be worn; and how can I have time unemployed upon my hands?

But I am most at a loss to guess for what purpose they related such tragic stories of the cruelty, perfidy, and artifices of men, who, if they ever were so malicious and destructive, have certainly now reformed their manners. I have not, since my entrance into the world, found one who does not profess himself devoted to my service, and ready to live or die as I shall command him. They are so far from intending to hurt me, that their only contention is, who shall be allowed most closely to attend, and most frequently to treat me. When different places of entertainment or schemes of pleasure are mentioned, I can see the eye sparkle and the cheeks glow of him whose proposals obtain my approbation; he then leads me off in triumph, adores my condescension, and congratulates himself that he has lived to the hour of felicity. Are these, Mr. Rambler, creatures to be feared? Is it likely that any injury will be done me by those who can enjoy life only while I favor them with my presence?

As little reason can I yet find to suspect them of stratagems and fraud. When I play at cards, they never take advantage of my mistakes, nor exact from me a rigorous observation of the game. Even Mr. Shuffle, a grave gentleman, who has daughters older than myself, plays with me so negligently that I am sometimes inclined to believe he loses his money by design, and yet he is so fond of play, that he says he will one day take me to his house in the country, that we may try by ourselves who can conquer. I have not yet promised him; but when the town grows a little empty, I shall think upon it, for I want some trinkets, like Letitia's, to my watch. I do not doubt my luck, but must study some means of amusing[19] my relations.

For all these distinctions I find myself indebted to that beauty which I was never suffered to hear praised, and of which, therefore, I did not before know the full value. The concealment was certainly an intentional fraud, for my aunts have eyes like other people, and I am every day told that nothing but blindness can escape the influence of my charms. Their whole account of that world which they pretend to know so well has been only one fiction entangled with another; and though the modes of life oblige me to continue some appearances of respect, I cannot think that they, who have been so clearly detected in ignorance or imposture, have any right to the esteem, veneration, or obedience of,

Sir, Yours,
Bellaria.

[18] I. e., head-dress.

[19] Of distracting the attention of.

THE IDLER

No. 16. Saturday, 29 July, 1758.

I paid a visit yesterday to my old friend Ned Drugget, at his country lodgings. Ned began trade with a very small fortune; he took a small house in an obscure street, and for some years dealt only in remnants. Knowing that *light gains make a heavy purse,* he was content with moderate profit; having observed or heard the effects of civility, he bowed down to the counter-edge at the entrance and departure of every customer, listened without impatience to the objections of the ignorant, and refused without resentment the offers of the penurious. His only recreation was to stand at his own door and look into the street. His dinner was sent him from a neighboring alehouse, and he opened and shut the shop at a certain hour with his own hands.

His reputation soon extended from one end of the street to the other; and Mr. Drugget's exemplary conduct was recommended by every master to his apprentice, and by every father to his son. Ned was not only considered as a thriving trader, but as a man of elegance and politeness, for he was remarkably neat in his dress, and would wear his coat threadbare without spotting it; his hat was always brushed, his shoes glossy, his wig nicely curled, and his stockings without a wrinkle. With such qualifications it was not very difficult for him to gain the heart of Miss Comfit, the only daughter of Mr. Comfit the confectioner.

Ned is one of those whose happiness marriage has increased. His wife had the same disposition with himself; and his method of life was very little changed, except that he dismissed the lodgers from the first floor,[1] and took the whole house into his own hands.

He had already, by his parsimony, accumulated a considerable sum, to which the fortune of his wife was now added. From this time he began to grasp at greater acquisitions, and was always ready, with money in his hand, to pick up the refuse of a sale, or to buy the stock of a trader who retired from business. He soon added his parlor to his shop, and was obliged a few months afterwards to hire a warehouse.

He had now a shop splendidly and copiously furnished with everything that time had injured, or fashion had degraded, with fragments of tissues, odd yards of brocade, vast bales of faded silk, and innumerable boxes of antiquated ribbons. His shop was soon celebrated through all quarters of the town, and frequented by every form of ostentatious poverty. Every maid, whose misfortune it was to be taller than her lady, matched[2] her gown at Mr. Drugget's; and many a maiden, who had passed a winter with her aunt in London, dazzled the rustics, at her return, with cheap finery which Drugget had supplied. His shop was often visited in a morning by ladies who left their coaches in the next street, and crept through the alley in linen gowns. Drugget knows the rank of his customers by their bashfulness; and, when he finds them unwilling to be seen, invites them upstairs, or retires with them to the back window.

I rejoiced at the increasing prosperity of my friend, and imagined, that as he grew rich, he was growing happy. His mind has partaken the enlargement of his fortune. When I stepped in for the first five years, I was welcomed only with a shake of the hand; in the next period of his life, he beckoned across the way for a pot of beer; but for six years past, he invites me to dinner; and if he bespeaks me the day before, never fails to regale me with a fillet of veal.

His riches neither made him uncivil nor negligent; he rose at the same hour, attended with the same assiduity, and bowed with the same gentleness. But for some years he has been much inclined to talk of the fatigues of business, and the confinement of a shop, and to wish that he had been so happy as to have renewed his uncle's lease of a farm, that he might have lived without noise and hurry, in a pure air, in the artless society of honest

[1] I. e., the first floor above the ground-floor.

[2] I. e., shopped for; found one there which (in this instance) accorded with her height.

villagers, and the contemplation of the works of nature.

I soon discovered the cause of my friend's philosophy. He thought himself grown rich enough to have a lodging in the country, like the mercers on Ludgate Hill, and was resolved to enjoy himself in the decline of life. This was a revolution not to be made suddenly. He talked three years of the pleasures of the country, but passed every night over his own shop. But at last he resolved to be happy, and hired a lodging in the country, that he may steal some hours in the week from business; for, says he, *when a man advances in life, he loves to entertain himself sometimes with his own thoughts.*

I was invited to this seat of quiet and contemplation among those whom Mr. Drugget considers as his most reputable friends, and desires to make the first witnesses of his elevation to the highest dignities of a shopkeeper. I found him at Islington, in a room which overlooked the high road, amusing himself with looking through the window, which the clouds of dust would not suffer him to open. He embraced me, told me I was welcome into the country, and asked me, if I did not feel myself refreshed. He then desired that dinner might be hastened, for fresh air always sharpened his appetite, and ordered me a toast and a glass of wine after my walk. He told me much of the pleasure he found in retirement, and wondered what had kept him so long out of the country. After dinner, company came in, and Mr. Drugget again repeated the praises of the country, recommended the pleasures of meditation, and told them, that he had been all the morning at the window, counting the carriages as they passed before him.

No. 19. Saturday, 19 August, 1758.

Some of those ancient sages that have exercised their abilities in the inquiry after the *supreme good,* have been of opinion, that the highest degree of earthly happiness is quiet; a calm repose both of mind and body undisturbed by the sight of folly or the noise of business, the tumults of public commotion, or the agitations of private interest; a state in which the mind has no other employment but to observe and regulate her own motions, to trace thought from thought, combine one image with another, raise systems of science and form theories of virtue.

To the scheme of these solitary speculatists, it has been justly objected, that if they are happy, they are happy only by being useless. That mankind is one vast republic, where every individual receives many benefits from the labors of others, which, by laboring in his turn for others, he is obliged to repay; and that where the united efforts of all are not able to exempt all from misery, none have a right to withdraw from their task of vigilance, or to be indulged in idle wisdom, or solitary pleasures.

It is common for controvertists, in the heat of disputation, to add one position to another till they reach the extremities of knowledge, where truth and falsehood lose their distinction. Their admirers follow them to the brink of absurdity, and then start back from each side towards the middle point. So it has happened in this great disquisition. Many perceive alike the force of the contrary arguments, find quiet shameful, and business dangerous, and therefore pass their lives between them, in bustle without business, and negligence without quiet.

Among the principal names of this moderate set is that great philosopher Jack Whirler,[3] whose business keeps him in perpetual motion, and whose motion always eludes his business; who is always to do what he never does, who cannot stand still because he is wanted in another place, and who is wanted in many places because he stays in none.

Jack has more business than he can conveniently transact in one house; he has therefore one habitation near Bow Church, and another about a mile distant. By this ingenious distribution of himself between two houses, Jack has contrived to be found at neither. Jack's trade is extensive, and he has many dealers; his conversation is sprightly, and he has many companions; his disposition is kind, and he has many friends. Jack neither forbears pleasure for business, nor

[3]It is said that John Newbury, a bookseller (and one of the publishers of the collected edition of *The Idler*), was the original of Whirler.

omits business for pleasure, but is equally invisible to his friends and his customers; to him that comes with an invitation to a club, and to him that waits to settle an account.

When you call at his house, his clerk tells you, that Mr. Whirler was just stepped out, but will be at home exactly at two; you wait at a coffee-house till two, and then find that he has been at home, and is gone out again, but left word that he should be at the Half Moon Tavern at seven, where he hopes to meet you. At seven you go to the tavern. At eight in comes Mr. Whirler to tell you that he is glad to see you, and only begs leave to run for a few minutes to a gentleman that lives near the Exchange, from whom he will return before supper can be ready. Away he runs to the Exchange, to tell those who are waiting for him, that he must beg them to defer the business till to-morrow, because his time is come at the Half Moon.

Jack's cheerfulness and civility rank him among those whose presence never gives pain, and whom all receive with fondness and caresses. He calls often on his friends, to tell them, that he will come again to-morrow; on the morrow he comes again, to tell them how an unexpected summons hurries him away. When he enters a house, his first declaration is, that he cannot sit down; and so short are his visits, that he seldom appears to have come for any other reason but to say, He must go.

The dogs of Egypt, when thirst brings them to the Nile, are said to run as they drink for fear of the crocodiles. Jack Whirler always dines at full speed. He enters, finds the family at table, sits familiarly down, and fills his plate; but while the first morsel is in his mouth, hears the clock strike, and rises; then goes to another house, sits down again, recollects another engagement; has only time to taste the soup, makes a short excuse to the company, and continues through another street his desultory dinner.

But, overwhelmed as he is with business, his chief desire is to have still more. Every new proposal takes possession of his thoughts; he soon balances probabilities, engages in the project, brings it almost to completion, and then forsakes it for another, which he catches with some alacrity, urges with the same vehemence, and abandons with the same coldness.

Every man may be observed to have a certain strain of lamentation, some peculiar theme of complaint on which he dwells in his moments of dejection. Jack's topic of sorrow is the want of time. Many an excellent design languishes in empty theory for want of time. For the omission of any civilities, want of time is his plea to others; for the neglect of any affairs, want of time is his excuse to himself. That he wants time, he sincerely believes; for he once pined away many months with a lingering distemper, for want of time to attend his health.

Thus Jack Whirler lives in perpetual fatigue without proportionate advantage, because he does not consider that no man can see all with his own eyes, or do all with his own hands; that whoever is engaged in multiplicity of business, must transact much by substitution, and leave something to hazard: and that he who attempts to do all, will waste his life in doing little.

No. 48. Saturday, 17 March, 1759.

There is no kind of idleness by which we are so easily seduced, as that which dignifies itself by the appearance of business, and, by making the loiterer imagine that he has something to do which must not be neglected, keeps him in perpetual agitation, and hurries him rapidly from place to place.

He that sits still, or reposes himself upon a couch, no more deceives himself than he deceives others; he knows that he is doing nothing, and has no other solace of his insignificance than the resolution, which the lazy hourly make, of changing his mode of life.

To do nothing every man is ashamed: and to do much almost every man is unwilling or afraid. Innumerable expedients have therefore been invented to produce motion without labor, and employment without solicitude. The greater part of those whom the kindness of fortune has left to their own direction, and whom want does not keep chained to the counter or the plow, play throughout life with the shadows of business, and know not at last what they have been doing.

These imitators of action are of all denominations. Some are seen at every auction without intention to purchase; others appear punctually at the Exchange, though they are known there only by their faces. Some are always making parties to visit collections for which they have no taste; and some neglect every pleasure and every duty to hear questions, in which they have no interest, debated in parliament.

These men never appear more ridiculous than in the distress which they imagine themselves to feel, from some accidental interruption of those empty pursuits. A tiger newly imprisoned is indeed more formidable, but not more angry, than Jack Tulip withheld from a florist's feast, or Tom Distich hindered from seeing the first representation of a play.

As political affairs are the highest and most extensive of temporal concerns, the mimic of a politician is more busy and important than any other trifler. Monsieur le Noir, a man who, without property or importance in any corner of the earth, has, in the present confusion of the world, declared himself a steady adherent to the French, is made miserable by a wind that keeps back the packet-boat, and still more miserable by every account of a Malouin privateer[4] caught in his cruise; he knows well that nothing can be done or said by him which can produce any effect but that of laughter, that he can neither hasten nor retard good or evil, that his joys and sorrows have scarcely any partakers; yet such is his zeal, and such his curiosity, that he would run barefooted to Gravesend, for the sake of knowing first that the English had lost a tender, and would ride out to meet every mail from the continent if he might be permitted to open it.

Learning is generally confessed to be desirable, and there are some who fancy themselves always busy in acquiring it. Of these ambulatory students, one of the most busy is my friend Tom Restless.[5]

[4]A privateer of St. Malo.

[5]Johnson said that Restless was meant for Thomas Tyers, son of the founder of Vauxhall Gardens. He was "bred to the law; but, having a handsome fortune, vivacity of temper, and eccentricity of mind, he could not confine himself to the regularity of practice. He therefore ran about the world with a pleasant carelessness, amusing everybody by his desultory conversation" (Boswell, *Life of Johnson*).

Tom has long had a mind to be a man of knowledge, but he does not care to spend much time among authors; for he is of opinion that few books deserve the labor of perusal, that they give the mind an unfashionable cast, and destroy that freedom of thought and easiness of manners indispensably requisite to acceptance in the world. Tom has therefore found another way to wisdom. When he rises he goes into a coffee-house, where he creeps so near to men whom he takes to be reasoners as to hear their discourse, and endeavors to remember something which, when it has been strained through Tom's head, is so near to nothing, that what it once was cannot be discovered. This he carries round from friend to friend through a circle of visits, till, hearing what each says upon the question, he becomes able at dinner to say a little himself; and, as every great genius relaxes himself among his inferiors, meets with some who wonder how so young a man can talk so wisely.

At night he has a new feast prepared for his intellects; he always runs to a disputing society, or a speaking club, where he half hears what, if he had heard the whole, he would but half understand; goes home pleased with the consciousness of a day well spent, lies down full of ideas, and rises in the morning empty as before.

No. 60. Saturday, 9 June, 1759.

Criticism is a study by which men grow important and formidable at a very small expense. The power of invention has been conferred by nature upon few, and the labor of learning those sciences which may by mere labor be obtained is too great to be willingly endured; but every man can exert such judgment as he has upon the works of others; and he whom nature has made weak, and idleness keeps ignorant, may yet support his vanity by the name of a Critic.

I hope it will give comfort to great numbers who are passing through the world in obscurity, when I inform them how easily distinction may be obtained. All the other powers of literature are coy and haughty, they must be long courted, and at last are not always gained; but Criticism is a goddess easy of access and forward of advance, who will meet the slow, and encourage the timorous; the want of meaning she supplies with words, and the want of spirit she recompenses with malignity.

This profession has one recommendation peculiar to itself, that it gives vent to malignity without real mischief. No genius was ever blasted by the breath of critics. The poison, which, if confined, would have burst the heart, fumes away in empty hisses, and malice is set at ease with very little danger to merit. The Critic is the only man whose triumph is without another's pain, and whose greatness does not rise upon another's ruin.

To a study at once so easy and so reputable, so malicious and so harmless, it cannot be necessary to invite my readers by a long or labored exhortation; it is sufficient, since all would be Critics if they could, to show by one eminent example that all can be critics if they will.

Dick Minim, after the common course of puerile studies, in which he was no great proficient, was put an apprentice to a brewer, with whom he had lived two years, when his uncle died in the city, and left him a large fortune in the stocks. Dick had for six months before used the company of the lower players, of whom he had learned to scorn a trade, and, being now at liberty to follow his genius, he resolved to be a man of wit and humor. That he might be properly initiated in his new character, he frequented the coffee-houses near the theaters, where he listened very diligently, day after day, to those who talked of language and sentiments, and unities and catastrophes, till by slow degrees he began to think that he understood something of the stage, and hoped in time to talk himself.

But he did not trust so much to natural sagacity as wholly to neglect the help of books. When the theaters were shut, he retired to Richmond with a few select writers,[6] whose opinions he impressed upon his memory by unwearied diligence; and, when he returned with other wits to the town, was able to tell, in very proper phrases, that the chief business of art is to copy nature; that a perfect writer is not to be expected, because genius decays as judgment increases; that the great art is the art of blotting; and that, according to the rule of Horace, every piece should be kept nine years.

Of the great authors he now began to display the characters, laying down as an universal position, that all had beauties and defects. His opinion was, that Shakespeare, committing himself wholly to the impulse of nature, wanted that correctness which learning would have given him; and that Jonson, trusting to learning, did not sufficiently cast his eye on nature. He blamed the *stanza* of Spenser, and could not bear the *hexameters* of Sidney. Denham and Waller he held the first reformers of English numbers; and thought that if Waller could have obtained the strength of Denham, or Denham the sweetness of Waller, there had been nothing wanting to complete a poet. He often expressed his commiseration of Dryden's poverty, and his indignation at the age which suffered him to write for bread; he repeated with rapture the first lines of *All for Love,* but wondered at the corruption of taste which could bear anything so unnatural as riming tragedies. In Otway he found uncommon powers of moving the passions, but was disgusted by his general negligence, and blamed him for making a conspirator his hero; and never concluded his disquisition, without remarking how happily the sound of the clock is made to alarm the audience. Southern[7] would have been his favorite, but that he mixes comic with tragic scenes, intercepts the natural course of the passions, and fills the mind with a wild confusion of mirth and melancholy. The versification of Rowe he thought too melodious for the stage, and too little varied in different passions. He made it the great fault of Congreve, that all his persons were wits, and that he always wrote with more art than nature. He considered *Cato* rather as a poem than a play, and allowed Addison to be the complete master of allegory and grave humor, but paid no great deference to him as a critic. He thought the

[6]The opinions which follow come from these writers—from Pope chiefly, but also from Collins's *Epistle to Hanmer,* from Dryden, from Addison, and from Joseph Warton.

[7]Thomas Southerne (1660–1746).

chief merit of Prior was in his easy tales and lighter poems, though he allowed that his *Solomon* had many noble sentiments elegantly expressed. In Swift he discovered an inimitable vein of irony, and an easiness which all would hope and few would attain. Pope he was inclined to degrade from a poet to a versifier, and thought his numbers rather luscious than sweet. He often lamented the neglect of *Phaedra and Hippolitus,*[8] and wished to see the stage under better regulations.

These assertions passed commonly uncontradicted; and if now and then an opponent started up, he was quickly repressed by the suffrages of the company, and Minim went away from every dispute with elation of heart and increase of confidence.

He now grew conscious of his abilities, and began to talk of the present state of dramatic poetry; wondered what was become of the comic genius which supplied our ancestors with wit and pleasantry, and why no writer could be found that durst now venture beyond a farce. He saw no reason for thinking that the vein of humor was exhausted, since we live in a country where liberty suffers every character to spread itself to its utmost bulk, and which therefore produces more originals than all the rest of the world together. Of tragedy he concluded business to be the soul, and yet often hinted that love predominates too much upon the modern stage.

He was now an acknowledged critic, and had his own seat in a coffee-house, and headed a party in the pit. Minim has more vanity than ill-nature, and seldom desires to do much mischief; he will perhaps murmur a little in the ear of him that sits next him, but endeavors to influence the audience to favor, by clapping when an actor exclaims "Ye gods!" or laments the misery of his country.

By degrees he was admitted to rehearsals, and many of his friends are of opinion that our present poets are indebted to him for their happiest thoughts; by his contrivance the bell was rung twice in *Barbarossa,*[9] and by his persuasion the author of *Cleone*[10] concluded his play without a couplet; for what can be more absurd, said Minim, than that part of a play should be rimed, and part written in blank verse? and by what acquisition of faculties is the speaker, who never could find rimes before, enabled to rime at the conclusion of an act?

He is the great investigator of hidden beauties, and is particularly delighted when he finds *the sound an echo to the sense.* He has read all our poets with particular attention to this delicacy of versification, and wonders at the supineness with which their works have been hitherto perused, so that no man has found the sound of a drum in this distich:

When pulpit, drum ecclesiastic,
Was beat with fist instead of a stick;[11]

and that the wonderful lines upon honor and a bubble have hitherto passed without notice:

Honor is like the glassy bubble,
Which cost philosophers such trouble;
Where, one part cracked, the whole does fly,
And wits are cracked to find out why.[12]

In these verses, says Minim, we have two striking accommodations of the sound to the sense. It is impossible to utter the two lines emphatically without an act like that which they describe; *bubble* and *trouble* causing a momentary inflation of the cheeks by the retention of the breath, which is afterwards forcibly emitted, as in the practice of *blowing bubbles.* But the greatest excellence is in the third line, which is *cracked* in the middle to express a crack, and then shivers into monosyllables. Yet has this diamond laid neglected with common stones, and among the innumerable admirers of *Hudibras* the observation of this superlative passage has been reserved for the sagacity of Minim.

[8]A tragedy by Edmund Smith (1672–1710), which pleased Addison, but not the public.

[9]A tragedy by Dr. John Brown (1715–1766).

[10]A tragedy by Robert Dodsley (1703–1764). "Mr. Langton, when a very young man," read this play to Johnson. At the end of an act, Johnson said: "Come, let's have some more, let's go into the slaughter-house again, Lanky. But I am afraid there is more blood than brains" (Boswell, *Life of Johnson*).

[11]Samuel Butler's *Hudibras,* I, i, 11–12.

[12]*Ibid.,* II, ii, 385–388. The "bubble" (Prince Rupert's drop) of which Butler speaks is made of glass, and the "philosophers" whom it puzzled were the members of the Royal Society.

No. 61. Saturday, 15 June, 1759.

Mr. Minim had now advanced himself to the zenith of critical reputation; when he was in the pit, every eye in the boxes was fixed upon him; when he entered his coffee-house, he was surrounded by circles of candidates, who passed their novitiate of literature under his tuition; his opinion was asked by all who had no opinion of their own, and yet loved to debate and decide; and no composition was supposed to pass in safety to posterity, till it had been secured by Minim's approbation.

Minim professes great admiration of the wisdom and munificence by which the academies of the continent were raised; and often wishes for some standard of taste, for some tribunal, to which merit may appeal from caprice, prejudice, and malignity. He has formed a plan for an academy of criticism, where every work of imagination may be read before it is printed, and which shall authoritatively direct the theaters what pieces to receive or reject, to exclude or to revive.

Such an institution would, in Dick's opinion, spread the fame of English literature over Europe, and make London the metropolis of elegance and politeness, the place to which the learned and ingenious of all countries would repair for instruction and improvement, where nothing would any longer be applauded or endured that was not conformed to the nicest rules, and finished with the highest elegance.

Till some happy conjunction of the planets shall dispose our princes or ministers to make themselves immortal by such an academy, Minim contents himself to preside four nights in a week in a critical society selected by himself, where he is heard without contradiction, and whence his judgment is disseminated through the great vulgar and the small.[13]

When he is placed in the chair of criticism, he declares loudly for the noble simplicity of our ancestors, in opposition to the petty refinements, and ornamental luxuriance. Sometimes he is sunk in despair, and perceives false delicacy daily gaining ground, and sometimes brightens his countenance with a gleam of hope, and predicts the revival of the true sublime. He then fulminates his loudest censures against the monkish barbarity of rime; wonders how beings that pretend to reason can be pleased with one line always ending like another; tells how unjustly and unnaturally sense is sacrificed to sound; how often the best thoughts are mangled by the necessity of confining or extending them to the dimensions of a couplet; and rejoices that genius has, in our days, shaken off the shackles which had encumbered it so long. Yet he allows that rime may sometimes be borne, if the lines be often broken, and the pauses judiciously diversified.

From blank verse he makes an easy transition to Milton, whom he produces as an example of the slow advance of lasting reputation. Milton is the only writer in whose books Minim can read for ever without weariness. What cause it is that exempts this pleasure from satiety he has long and diligently inquired, and believes it to consist in the perpetual variation of the numbers, by which the ear is gratified and the attention awakened. The lines that are commonly thought rugged and unmusical, he conceives to have been written to temper the melodious luxury of the rest, or to express things by a proper cadence: for he scarcely finds a verse that has not this favorite beauty; he declares that he could shiver in a hot-house when he reads that

> The ground
> Burns frore, and cold performs th' effect of fire;[14]

and that, when Milton bewails his blindness, the verse,

> So thick a drop serene has quenched these orbs,[15]

has, he knows not how, something that strikes him with an obscure sensation like that which he fancies would be felt from the sound of darkness.

Minim is not so confident of his rules of judgment as not very eagerly to catch new light from the name of the author. He is commonly so prudent as to spare those whom he cannot resist, unless, as will sometimes

[13] See Abraham Cowley, *Several Discourses by Way of Essays, in Verse and Prose*, 6. Of Greatness (at end, imitation of Horace, *Odes*, III, i, 2).

[14] *Paradise Lost*, II, 594–595. [15] *Ibid.*, III, 25.

happen, he finds the public combined against them. But a fresh pretender to fame he is strongly inclined to censure, till his own honor requires that he commend him. Till he knows the success of a composition, he intrenches himself in general terms; there are some new thoughts and beautiful passages, but there is likewise much which he would have advised the author to expunge. He has several favorite epithets, of which he has never settled the meaning, but which are very commodiously applied to books which he has not read, or cannot understand. One is *manly,* another is *dry,* another *stiff,* and another *flimsy;* sometimes he discovers delicacy of style, and sometimes meets with *strange expressions.*

He is never so great, or so happy, as when a youth of promising parts is brought to receive his directions for the prosecution of his studies. He then puts on a very serious air; he advises the pupil to read none but the best authors, and, when he finds one congenial to his own mind, to study his beauties, but avoid his faults; and, when he sits down to write, to consider how his favorite author would think at the present time on the present occasion. He exhorts him to catch those moments when he finds his thoughts expanded and his genius exalted, but to take care lest imagination hurry him beyond the bounds of nature. He holds diligence the mother of success; yet enjoins him, with great earnestness, not to read more than he can digest, and not to confuse his mind by pursuing studies of contrary tendencies. He tells him, that every man has his genius, and that Cicero could never be a poet. The boy retires illuminated, resolves to follow his genius, and to think how Milton would have thought: and Minim feasts upon his own beneficence till another day brings another pupil.

LIVES OF THE ENGLISH POETS

PASSAGES FROM *THE LIFE OF MILTON*[1]

He took both the usual degrees, that of bachelor in 1628, and that of master in 1632; but he left the university with no kindness for its institution, alienated either by the injudicious severity of his governors, or his own captious perverseness. The cause cannot now be known, but the effect appears in his writings. His scheme of education, inscribed to Hartlib,[2] supersedes all academical instruction, being intended to comprise the whole time which men usually spend in literature, from their entrance upon grammar "till they proceed, as it is called, masters of arts." And in his discourse *On the likeliest Way to Remove Hirelings out of the Church* he ingeniously proposes that "the profits of the lands forfeited by the act for superstitious uses, should be applied to such academies all over the land, where languages and arts may be taught together; so that youth may be at once brought up to a competency of learning and an honest trade, by which means such of them as had the gift, being enabled to support themselves (without tithes) by the latter, may, by the help of the former, become worthy preachers."

One of his objections to academical education, as it was then conducted, is that men designed for orders in the church were permitted to act plays, "writhing and unboning their clergy limbs to all the antic and dishonest gestures of Trincalos,[3] buffoons, and bawds, prostituting the shame of that ministry which they had, or were near having, to the eyes of courtiers and court-ladies, their grooms and mademoiselles."[4]

This is sufficiently peevish in a man who, when he mentions his exile from the college, relates, with great luxuriance, the compensation which the pleasures of the theater afford him. Plays were therefore only criminal when they were acted by academics.

[1]The first thirteen paragraphs, dealing with Milton's life before he left Cambridge University, are omitted from the present abridgment.

[2]*Of Education,* a letter addressed to Samuel Hartlib (1644).

[3]Trincalo was a character in Thomas Tomkis's *Albumazar,* a play acted before James I at Cambridge in 1615.

[4]From the *Apology for Smectymnuus* (1642).

He went to the university with a design of entering into the church, but in time altered his mind; for he declared that whoever became a clergyman must "subscribe slave, and take an oath withal which, unless he took with a conscience that could retch, he must straight perjure himself. He thought it better to prefer a blameless silence before the office of speaking, bought and begun with servitude and forswearing."[5]

These expressions are, I find, applied to the subscription of the Articles;[6] but it seems more probable that they relate to canonical obedience. I know not any of the Articles which seem to thwart his opinions; but the thoughts of obedience, whether canonical or civil, raised his indignation.

His unwillingness to engage in the ministry, perhaps not yet advanced to a settled resolution of declining it, appears in a letter to one of his friends[7] who had reproved his suspended and dilatory life, which he seems to have imputed to an insatiable curiosity and fantastic luxury of various knowledge. To this he writes a cool and plausible answer, in which he endeavors to persuade him that the delay proceeds not from the delights of desultory study, but from the desire of obtaining more fitness for his task; and that he goes on, "not taking thought of being late, so it give advantage to be more fit."

When he left the university, he returned to his father, then residing at Horton in Buckinghamshire, with whom he lived five years; in which time he is said to have read all the Greek and Latin writers. With what limitations this universality is to be understood, who shall inform us?

It might be supposed that he who read so much should have done nothing else; but Milton found time to write the masque of *Comus,* which was presented at Ludlow, then the residence of the Lord President of Wales,[8] in 1634; and had the honor of being acted by the Earl of Bridgewater's sons and daughter. The fiction is derived from Homer's *Circe;* but we never can refuse to any modern the liberty of borrowing from Homer:

> —*a quo ceu fonte perenni*
> *Vatum Pieriis ora rigantur aquis.*[9]

His next production was *Lycidas,* an elegy written in 1637 on the death of Mr. King,[10] the son of Sir John King, secretary for Ireland in the time of Elizabeth, James, and Charles. King was much a favorite at Cambridge, and many of the wits joined to do honor to his memory. Milton's acquaintance with the Italian writers may be discovered by a mixture of longer and shorter verses, according to the rules of Tuscan poetry, and his malignity to the church by some lines which are interpreted as threatening its extermination.

He is supposed about this time to have written his *Arcades;* for while he lived at Horton he used sometimes to steal from his studies a few days, which he spent at Harefield, the house of the Countess Dowager of Derby,[11] where the *Arcades* made part of a dramatic entertainment.

He began now to grow weary of the country, and had some purpose of taking chambers in the Inns of Court,[12] when the death of his mother set him at liberty to travel, for which he obtained his father's consent and Sir Henry Wotton's directions, with the celebrated precept of prudence, *i pensieri stretti, ed il viso sciolto,* "thoughts close, and looks loose."[13]

In 1638 he left England, and went first to Paris; where, by the favor of Lord Scudamore, he had the opportunity of visiting Grotius,[14] then residing at the French court as ambassador from Christina of Sweden.

---

[5]From *The Reason of Church Government Urged against Prelaty* (1642).

[6]Assent to the Thirty-nine Articles of the Anglican Church.

[7]A letter probably written in 1632. The name of the friend is unknown.

[8]John Egerton, first Earl of Bridgewater.

[9]From whom as from an ever-flowing fountain the mouths of poets are moistened by the muses' waters (Ovid, *Amores,* III, ix, 25).

[10]Edward King, a fellow student of Milton's at Christ's College, Cambridge.

[11]Alice Spenser, who had been celebrated by Edmund Spenser in her youth and was the grandmother of the three children who performed in *Comus.*

[12]The legal colleges in London.

[13]In Wotton's letter (13 April, 1638), prefixed to *Comus* in 1645.

[14]Hugo Grotius (1583–1645), the Dutch poet, scholar, and statesman.

From Paris he hasted into Italy, of which he had with particular diligence studied the language and literature, and, though he seems to have intended a very quick perambulation of the country, stayed two months at Florence; where he found his way into the academies, and produced his compositions with such applause as appears to have exalted him in his own opinion, and confirmed him in the hope that "by labor and intense study, which," says he, "I take to be my portion in this life, joined with a strong propensity of nature," he might "leave something so written to after-times as they should not willingly let it die."[15]

It appears, in all his writings, that he had the usual concomitant of great abilities, a lofty and steady confidence in himself, perhaps not without some contempt of others; for scarcely any man ever wrote so much, and praised so few. Of his praise he was very frugal, as he set its value high, and considered his mention of a name as a security against the waste of time and a certain preservative from oblivion.

At Florence he could not indeed complain that his merit wanted distinction. Carlo Dati presented him with an encomiastic inscription, in the tumid lapidary style;[16] and Francini wrote him an ode, of which the first stanza is only empty noise; the rest are perhaps too diffuse on common topics, but the last is natural and beautiful.

From Florence he went to Siena, and from Siena to Rome, where he was again received with kindness by the learned and the great. Holstenius, the keeper of the Vatican Library, who had resided three years at Oxford, introduced him to Cardinal Barberini; and he, at a musical entertainment, waited for him at the door, and led him by the hand into the assembly. Here Selvaggi praised him in a distich, and Salsilli in a tetrastich:[17] neither of them of much value. The Italians were gainers by this literary commerce; for the encomiums with which Milton repaid Salsilli, though not secure against a stern grammarian, turn the balance indisputably in Milton's favor.

Of these Italian testimonies, poor as they are, he was proud enough to publish them before his poems; though he says he cannot be suspected but to have known that they were said *"non tam de se quam supra se."*[18]

At Rome, as at Florence, he stayed only two months; a time indeed sufficient, if he desired only to ramble with an explainer of its antiquities, or to view palaces and count pictures, but certainly too short for the contemplation of learning, policy, or manners.

From Rome he passed on to Naples, in company of a hermit, a companion from whom little could be expected; yet to him Milton owed his introduction to Manso, Marquis of Villa, who had been before the patron of Tasso. Manso was enough delighted with his accomplishments to honor him with a sorry distich, in which he commends him for everything but his religion; and Milton, in return, addressed him in a Latin poem[19] which must have raised an high opinion of English elegance and literature.

His purpose was now to have visited Sicily and Greece; but, hearing of the differences between the king and parliament, he thought it proper to hasten home rather than pass his life in foreign amusements while his countrymen were contending for their rights. He therefore came back to Rome, though the merchants informed him of plots laid against him by the Jesuits for the liberty of his conversations on religion. He had sense enough to judge that there was no danger, and therefore kept on his way, and acted as before, neither obtruding nor shunning controversy. He had perhaps given some offence by visiting Galileo,[20] then a prisoner in the Inquisition for philosophical heresy; and at Naples he was told by Manso that, by his declarations on religious questions, he had excluded himself from some distinctions which he should otherwise have paid him. But such conduct, though it did not please, was yet

[15]From *The Reason of Church Government Urged against Prelaty* (1642).

[16]The style of monumental inscriptions.

[17]A distich is a couplet; a tetrastich, a stanza of four lines.

[18]Not so much about as above his real character (words before Latin section in Milton's *Poems*, 1645).

[19]The *Mansus,* written in 1639.

[20]Galileo Galilei (1564–1642). Cf. *Paradise Lost,* I, 286–291.

sufficiently safe; and Milton stayed two months more at Rome, and went on to Florence without molestation.

From Florence he visited Lucca. He afterwards went to Venice; and having sent away a collection of music and other books, traveled to Geneva, which he probably considered as the metropolis of orthodoxy.[21]

Here he reposed as in a congenial element, and became acquainted with John Diodati and Frederick Spanheim, two learned professors of divinity. From Geneva he passed through France, and came home, after an absence of a year and three months.

At his return he heard of the death of his friend Charles Diodati,[22] a man whom it is reasonable to suppose of great merit since he was thought by Milton worthy of a poem, entitled *Epitaphium Damonis,* written with the common but childish imitation of pastoral life.

He now hired a lodging at the house of one Russel, a tailor, in St. Bride's Church-yard, and undertook the education of John and Edward Phillips, his sister's sons. Finding his rooms too little, he took a house and garden in Aldersgate Street, which was not then so much out of the world as it is now, and chose his dwelling at the upper end of a passage that he might avoid the noise of the street. Here he received more boys, to be boarded and instructed.

Let not our veneration for Milton forbid us to look with some degree of merriment on great promises and small performance, on the man who hastens home because his countrymen are contending for their liberty, and, when he reaches the scene of action, vapors away his patriotism in a private boarding-school. This is the period of his life from which all his biographers seem inclined to shrink. They are unwilling that Milton should be degraded to a schoolmaster; but, since it cannot be denied that he taught boys, one finds out that he taught for nothing, and another that his motive was only zeal for the propagation of learning and virtue; and all tell what they do not know to be true, only to excuse an act which no wise man will consider as in itself disgraceful. His father was alive; his allowance was not ample; and he supplied its deficiencies by an honest and useful employment.

It is told that in the art of education he performed wonders; and a formidable list is given of the authors, Greek and Latin, that were read in Aldersgate Street by youth between ten and fifteen or sixteen years of age. Those who tell or receive these stories should consider that nobody can be taught faster than he can learn. The speed of the horseman must be limited by the power of his horse. Every man that has ever undertaken to instruct others can tell what slow advances he has been able to make, and how much patience it requires to recall vagrant inattention, to stimulate sluggish indifference, and to rectify absurd misapprehension.

The purpose of Milton, as it seems, was to teach something more solid than the common literature of schools, by reading those authors that treat of physical subjects, such as the Georgic[23] and astronomical treatises of the ancients. This was a scheme of improvement which seems to have busied many literary projectors of that age. Cowley,[24] who had more means than Milton of knowing what was wanting to the embellishments of life, formed the same plan of education in his imaginary college.

But the truth is that the knowledge of external nature, and the sciences which that knowledge requires or includes, are not the great or the frequent business of the human mind. Whether we provide for action or conversation, whether we wish to be useful or pleasing, the first requisite is the religious and moral knowledge of right and wrong; the next is an acquaintance with the history of mankind, and with those examples which may be said to embody truth, and prove by events the reasonableness of opinions. Prudence and justice are virtues and excellences of all times and of all places; we are perpetually moralists, but we are geometricians only by chance. Our intercourse with intellectual nature is necessary; our specula-

[21]Since it was the seat of Calvinism.

[22]Schoolfellow of Milton's and nephew of John Diodati. He had died a year before Milton's return.

[23]Agricultural.

[24]Abraham Cowley (1618–1667), poet. Johnson refers to his tract, *A proposition for the Advancement of Experimental Philosophy* (1661).

tions upon matter are voluntary, and at leisure. Physiological learning[25] is of such rare emergence that one man may know another half his life without being able to estimate his skill in hydrostatics or astronomy; but his moral and prudential character immediately appears.

Those authors, therefore, are to be read at schools that supply most axioms of prudence, most principles of moral truth, and most materials for conversation; and these purposes are best served by poets, orators, and historians.

Let me not be censured for this digression as pedantic or paradoxical; for if I have Milton against me, I have Socrates on my side. It was his labor to turn philosophy from the study of nature to speculations upon life; but the innovators whom I oppose are turning off attention from life to nature. They seem to think that we are placed here to watch the growth of plants, or the motions of the stars. Socrates was rather of opinion that what we had to learn was how to do good and avoid evil.

"Ὅττι τοι ἐν μεγάροισι κακόν τ' ἀγαθόν τε τέτυκται."[26]

Of institutions we may judge by their effects. From this wonder-working academy I do not know that there ever proceeded any man very eminent for knowledge; its only genuine product, I believe, is a small history of poetry, written in Latin by his nephew, Phillips,[27] of which perhaps none of my readers has ever heard.

That in his school, as in everything else which he undertook, he labored with great diligence there is no reason for doubting. One part of his method deserves general imitation. He was careful to instruct his scholars in religion. Every Sunday was spent upon theology, of which he dictated a short system, gathered from the writers that were then fashionable in the Dutch universities.

He set his pupils an example of hard study and spare diet; only now and then he allowed himself to pass a day of festivity and indulgence with some gay gentlemen of Gray's Inn.[28]

He now began to engage in the controversies of the times, and lent his breath to blow the flames of contention. In 1641 he published a treatise *Of Reformation* in two books, against the Established Church, being willing to help the Puritans, who were, he says, "inferior to the prelates in learning."[29]

* * *

His next[30] work was *The Reason of Church Government urged against Prelacy, by Mr. John Milton,* 1642. In this book he discovers, not with ostentatious exultation, but with calm confidence, his high opinion of his own powers; and promises to undertake something, he yet knows not what, that may be of use and honor to his country. "This," says he, "is not to be obtained but by devout prayer to that Eternal Spirit that can enrich with all utterance and knowledge, and sends out his Seraphim with the hallowed fire of his altar, to touch and purify the lips of whom he pleases. To this must be added industrious and select reading, steady observation, and insight into all seemly and generous arts and affairs; till which in some measure be compassed, I refuse not to sustain this expectation." From a promise like this, at once fervid, pious, and rational, might be expected the *Paradise Lost.*

He published the same year two more pamphlets upon the same question. To one of his antagonists, who affirms that he was "vomited out of the university," he answers in general terms: "The fellows of the college wherein I spent some years, at my parting, after I had taken two degrees, as the manner is, signified many times how much better it would content them that I should stay.—As for the common approbation or dislike of that place, as now it is, that I should esteem or disesteem myself the more for that, too simple is the answerer, if he think to obtain

[25]Knowledge of natural science.

[26]
What good, what ill
Hath in thine house befallen.
(*Odyssey*, IV, 392; Cowper's translation.)

[27]Probably Edward Phillips, author of *Tractatulus de Carmine Dramatico* (1670).

[28]One of the London legal colleges.

[29]Milton actually says they were inferior in eloquence (*Defensio Secunda,* 1654).

[30]Next after *Of Prelatical Episcopacy* (1641).

with me. Of small practice were the physician who could not judge, by what she and her sister have of long time vomited, that the worser stuff she strongly keeps in her stomach, but the better she is ever kecking[31] at, and is queasy; she vomits now out of sickness; but before it be well with her, she must vomit by strong physic. The university, in the time of her better health, and my younger judgment, I never greatly admired, but now much less."[32]

This is surely the language of a man who thinks that he has been injured. He proceeds to describe the course of his conduct and the train of his thoughts; and, because he has been suspected of incontinence, gives an account of his own purity: "That if I be justly charged," says he, "with this crime, it may come upon me with tenfold shame."

The style of his piece is rough, and such perhaps was that of his antagonist. This roughness he justifies by great examples in a long digression. Sometimes he tries to be humorous: "Lest I should take him for some chaplain in hand, some squire of the body to his prelate, one who serves not at the altar only but at the court-cupboard,[33] he will bestow on us a pretty model of himself; and sets me out half a dozen phthisical mottoes, wherever he had them, hopping short in the measure of convulsion fits; in which labor the agony of his wit having escaped narrowly, instead of well-sized periods, he greets us with a quantity of thumb-ring posies.[34]—And thus ends this section, or rather dissection, of himself." Such is the controversial merriment of Milton; his gloomy seriousness is yet more offensive. Such is his malignity "that hell grows darker at his frown."[35]

His father, after Reading was taken by Essex,[36] came to reside in his house; and his school increased. At Whitsuntide in his thirty-fifth year he married Mary, the daughter of Mr. Powell, a justice of the peace in Oxfordshire. He brought her to town with him, and expected all the advantages of a conjugal life. The lady, however, seems not much to have delighted in the pleasures of spare diet and hard study; for, as Phillips relates, "having for a month led a philosophical life, after having been used at home to a great house and much company and joviality, her friends, possibly by her own desire, made earnest suit to have her company the remaining part of the summer; which was granted, upon a promise of her return at Michaelmas."

Milton was too busy to much miss his wife; he pursued his studies, and now and then visited the Lady Margaret Leigh, whom he has mentioned in one of his sonnets. At last Michaelmas arrived; but the lady had no inclination to return to the sullen gloom of her husband's habitation, and therefore very willingly forgot her promise. He sent her a letter, but had no answer; he sent more with the same success. It could be alleged that letters miscarry; he therefore despatched a messenger, being by this time too angry to go himself. His messenger was sent back with some contempt. The family of the lady were Cavaliers.

In a man whose opinion of his own merit was like Milton's, less provocation than this might have raised violent resentment. Milton soon determined to repudiate her for disobedience; and, being one of those who could easily find arguments to justify inclination, published (in 1644)[37] *The Doctrine and Discipline of Divorce,* which was followed by *The Judgment of Martin Bucer concerning Divorce,* and the next year his *Tetrachordon, Expositions upon the Four Chief Places of Scripture Which Treat of Marriage.*

This innovation was opposed, as might be expected, by the clergy, who, then holding their famous assembly at Westminster, procured that the author should be called before the Lords; "but that house," says Wood,[38] "whether approving the doctrine or not favoring his accusers, did soon dismiss him."

There seems not to have been much written

[31]Making a noise as if about to vomit.

[32]Both this and the two following quotations are from the *Apology for Smectymnuus* (1642).

[33]Sideboard on which plates were displayed.

[34]Mottoes.

[35]*Paradise Lost,* II, 719–720.

[36]The third Earl of Essex (1591–1646), general of the parliamentary army.

[37]The first of the three tracts was published in 1643, the second in 1644, and third in 1645.

[38]Anthony à Wood in *Athenae Oxonienses* (1691–1692).

against him, nor anything by any writer of eminence. The antagonist that appeared is styled by him "a serving man turned solicitor."[39] Howell[40] in his letters mentions the new doctrine with contempt; and it was, I suppose, thought more worthy of derision than of confutation. He complains of this neglect in two sonnets,[41] of which the first is contemptible, and the second not excellent.

From this time it is observed that he became an enemy to the Presbyterians, whom he had favored before. He that changes his party by his humor is not more virtuous than he that changes it by his interest; he loves himself rather than truth.

His wife and her relations now found that Milton was not an unresisting sufferer of injuries; and perceiving that he had begun to put his doctrine in practice by courting a young woman of great accomplishments, the daughter of one Dr. Davis, who was, however, not ready to comply, they resolved to endeavor a reunion. He went sometimes to the house of one Blackborough, his relation, in the lane of St. Martin's-le-Grand, and at one of his usual visits was surprised to see his wife come from another room and implore forgiveness on her knees. He resisted her intreaties for a while; "but partly," says Phillips,[42] "his own generous nature, more inclinable to reconciliation than to perseverance in anger or revenge, and partly the strong intercession of friends on both sides, soon brought him to an act of oblivion and a firm league of peace." It were injurious to omit that Milton afterwards received her father and her brothers in his own house when they were distressed, with other Royalists.

He published about the same time[43] his *Areopagitica, a Speech of Mr. John Milton for the Liberty of Unlicensed Printing.* The danger of such unbounded liberty and the danger of bounding it have produced a problem in the science of government which human understanding seems hitherto unable to solve. If nothing may be published but what civil authority shall have previously approved, power must always be the standard of truth; if every dreamer of innovations may propagate his projects, there can be no settlement; if every murmurer at government may diffuse discontent, there can be no peace; and if every sceptic in theology may teach his follies, there can be no religion. The remedy against these evils is to punish the authors, for it is yet allowed that every society may punish, though not prevent, the publication of opinions which that society shall think pernicious; but this punishment, though it may crush the author, promotes the book; and it seems not more reasonable to leave the right of printing unrestrained because writers may be afterwards censured than it would be to sleep with doors unbolted because by our laws we can hang a thief.

But whatever were his engagements, civil or domestic, poetry was never long out of his thoughts.

* * *

Being now forty-seven years old,[44] and seeing himself disencumbered from external interruptions, he seems to have recollected his former purposes, and to have resumed three great works which he had planned for his future employment: an epic poem, the history of his country, and a dictionary of the Latin tongue.

To collect a dictionary seems a work of all others least practicable in a state of blindness, because it depends upon perpetual and minute inspection and collation. Nor would Milton probably have begun it after he had lost his eyes; but, having had it always before him, he continued it, says Phillips, "almost to his dying day; but the papers were so discomposed and deficient that they could not be fitted for the press." The compilers of the Latin dictionary printed at Cambridge had the use of those collections in three folios; but what was their fate afterwards is not known.

To compile a history from various authors, when they can only be consulted by other

[39]In *Colasterion* (1645).

[40]James Howell (1596–1666), author of *Epistolae Ho-elianae.*

[41]Sonnets XI and XII in the present collection.

[42]Edward Phillips, in the preface to Milton's *Letters of State* (1694).

[43]In 1644.

[44]In 1656, about four years after Milton had become totally blind.

eyes, is not easy nor possible but with more skilful and attentive help than can be commonly obtained; and it was probably the difficulty of consulting and comparing that stopped Milton's narrative at the Conquest, a period at which affairs were not yet very intricate, nor authors very numerous.

For the subject of his epic poem, after much deliberation, "long choosing, and beginning late,"[45] he fixed upon *Paradise Lost,* a design so comprehensive that it could be justified only by success. He had once designed to celebrate King Arthur, as he hints in his verses to Mansus; but "Arthur was reserved," says Fenton,[46] "to another destiny."

It appears, by some sketches of poetical projects left in manuscript and to be seen in a library[47] at Cambridge, that he had digested his thoughts on this subject into one of those wild dramas which were anciently called mysteries;[48] and Phillips had seen what he terms part of a tragedy, beginning with the first ten lines of Satan's address to the sun. These mysteries consist of allegorical persons, such as Justice, Mercy, Faith. Of the tragedy or mystery of *Paradise Lost* there are two plans:

THE PERSONS

MICHAEL.
CHORUS OF ANGELS.
HEAVENLY LOVE.
LUCIFER.
ADAM, } *with the*
EVE, } *Serpent.*
CONSCIENCE.
DEATH.
LABOR,
SICKNESS,
DISCONTENT, } *Mutes.*
IGNORANCE,
with others;
FAITH.
HOPE.
CHARITY.

THE PERSONS

MOSES.
DIVINE JUSTICE, WISDOM, HEAVENLY LOVE.
THE EVENING STAR, HESPERUS.
CHORUS OF ANGELS.
LUCIFER.
ADAM.
EVE.
CONSCIENCE.
LABOR,
SICKNESS,
DISCONTENT, } *Mutes.*
IGNORANCE,
FEAR,
DEATH;
FAITH.
HOPE.
CHARITY.

PARADISE LOST

THE PERSONS

ACT I

MOSES προλογίζει,[49] recounting how he assumed his true body; that it corrupts not, because it is with God in the mount; declares the like of Enoch and Elijah; besides the purity of the place, that certain pure winds, dews, and clouds preserve it from corruption; whence exhorts to the sight of God; tells they cannot see ADAM in the state of innocence, by reason of their sin.

JUSTICE, }
MERCY, } debating what should become of man, if he fall.
WISDOM, }

CHORUS OF ANGELS singing a hymn of the Creation.

ACT II

HEAVENLY LOVE.
EVENING STAR.
CHORUS sing the marriage-song, and describe Paradise.

ACT III

LUCIFER contriving Adam's ruin.
CHORUS fears for ADAM, and relates Lucifer's rebellion and fall.

ACT IV

ADAM, }
EVE, } fallen.

CONSCIENCE cites them to God's examination.
CHORUS bewails, and tells the good ADAM has lost.

ACT V

ADAM and EVE driven out of Paradise.
——— presented by an angel with
LABOR, GRIEF, HATRED, ENVY, WAR, FAMINE, PESTILENCE, SICKNESS, DISCONTENT, IGNORANCE, FEAR, DEATH, } *Mutes.*
To whom he gives their names. Likewise WINTER, HEAT, TEMPEST, *etc.*
FAITH, }
HOPE, } comfort him and instruct him.
CHARITY, }
CHORUS briefly concludes.

Such was his first design, which could have produced only an allegory, or mystery. The

[45] *Paradise Lost,* IX, 26.

[46] Elijah Fenton (1683–1730). He alludes to the notorious *Prince Arthur* (1695) of Sir Richard Blackmore.

[47] Library of Trinity College.

[48] Miracle-plays.

[49] Delivers a prologue.

following sketch seems to have attained more maturity:

ADAM UNPARADISED

The angel Gabriel, either descending or entering, showing, since this globe was created, his frequency as much on earth as in heaven; describes Paradise. Next, the Chorus, showing the reason of his coming to keep his watch in Paradise, after Lucifer's rebellion, by command from God; and withal expressing his desire to see and know more concerning this excellent new creature, man. The angel Gabriel, as by his name signifying a prince of power, tracing Paradise with a more free office, passes by the station of the Chorus, and, desired by them, relates what he knew of man, as the creation of Eve, with their love and marriage. After this Lucifer appears; after his overthrow, bemoans himself, seeks revenge on man. The Chorus prepare resistance at his first approach. At last, after discourse of enmity on either side, he departs; whereat the Chorus sings of the battle and victory in heaven, against him and his accomplices, as before, after the first act, was sung a hymn of the creation. Here again may appear Lucifer, relating and insulting in what he had done to the destruction of man. Man next, and Eve having by this time been seduced by the Serpent, appears confusedly covered with leaves. Conscience, in a shape,[50] accuses him; Justice cites him to the place whither Jehovah called for him. In the meanwhile the Chorus entertains the stage, and is informed by some angel the manner of the Fall. Here the Chorus bewails Adam's fall; Adam then and Eve return; accuse one another; but especially Adam lays the blame to his wife; is stubborn in his offence. Justice appears, reasons with him, convinces him. The Chorus admonisheth Adam, and bids him beware Lucifer's example of impenitence. The Angel is sent to banish them out of Paradise, but before causes to pass before his eyes, in shapes, a masque of all the evils of this life and world. He is humbled, relents, despairs: at last appears Mercy, comforts him, promises the Messiah; then calls in Faith, Hope, and Charity; instructs him; he repents, gives God the glory, submits to his penalty. The Chorus briefly concludes. Compare this with the former draught.

These are very imperfect rudiments of *Paradise Lost;* but it is pleasant to see great works in their seminal state, pregnant with latent possibilities of excellence; nor could there be any more delightful entertainment than to trace their gradual growth and expansion, and to observe how they are some times suddenly advanced by accidental hint and sometimes slowly improved by stea meditation.

Invention is almost the only literary la which blindness cannot obstruct, and therefore he naturally solaced his solitude by the indulgence of his fancy, and the melody of his numbers. He had done what he knew to be necessarily previous to poetical excellence; he had made himself acquainted with "seemly arts and affairs";[51] his comprehension was extended by various knowledge, and his memory stored with intellectual treasures. He was skillful in many languages, and had by reading and composition attained the full mastery of his own. He would have wanted little help from books, had he retained the power of perusing them.

* * *

He was now busied by *Paradise Lost.* Whence he drew the original design has been variously conjectured by men who cannot bear to think themselves ignorant of that which, at last, neither diligence nor sagacity can discover. Some find the hint in an Italian tragedy. Voltaire[52] tells a wild and unauthorized story of a farce seen by Milton in Italy, which opened thus: "Let the rainbow be the fiddlestick of the fiddle of heaven." It has been already shown that the first conception was a tragedy or mystery, not of a narrative but a dramatic work, which he is supposed to have begun to reduce to its present form about the time (1655) when he finished his dispute with the defenders of the king.

He long before had promised to adorn his native country by some great performance, while he had yet perhaps no settled design, and was stimulated only by such expectations as naturally arose from the survey of his attainments and the consciousness of his powers. What he should undertake it was

[50] Suitable costume and make-up.

[51] From *The Reason of Church Government.*

[52] In his *Essai sur la Poésie Épique.* The "farce" is G. B. Andreini's religious drama, the *Adamo* (1613).

difficult to determine. He was "long choosing, and began late."

While he was obliged to divide his time between his private studies and affairs of state, his poetical labor must have been often interrupted; and perhaps he did little more in that busy time than construct the narrative, adjust the episodes, proportion the parts, accumulate images and sentiments, and treasure in his memory, or preserve in writing, such hints as books or meditation would supply. Nothing particular is known of his intellectual operations while he was a statesman; for, having every help and accommodation at hand, he had no need of uncommon expedients.

Being driven from all public stations, he is yet too great not to be traced by curiosity to his retirement; where he has been found by Mr. Richardson,[53] the fondest of his admirers, sitting "before his door in a grey coat of coarse cloth, in warm sultry weather, to enjoy the fresh air, and so, as well as in his own room, receiving the visits of people of distinguished parts as well as quality." His visitors of high quality must now be imagined to be few; but men of parts might reasonably court the conversation of a man so generally illustrious that foreigners are reported by Wood to have visited the house in Bread Street where he was born.

According to another account, he was seen in a small house, "neatly enough dressed in black clothes, sitting in a room hung with rusty green; pale but not cadaverous, with chalkstones[54] in his hands. He said that if it were not for the gout, his blindness would be tolerable."

In the intervals of his pain, being made unable to use the common exercises, he used to swing in a chair, and sometimes played upon an organ.

He was now confessedly and visibly employed upon his poem, of which the progress might be noted by those with whom he was familiar; for he was obliged, when he had composed as many lines as his memory would conveniently retain, to employ some friend in writing them, having, at least for part of the time, no regular attendant. This gave opportunity to observations and reports.

Mr. Phillips observes that there was a very remarkable circumstance in the composure of *Paradise Lost,* "which I have a particular reason," says he, "to remember; for whereas I had the perusal of it from the very beginning, for some years, as I went from time to time to visit him, in parcels of ten, twenty, or thirty verses at a time (which, being written by whatever hand came next, might possibly want correction as to the orthography and pointing[55]), having as the summer came on not been showed any for a considerable while, and desiring the reason thereof, was answered that his vein never happily flowed but from the autumnal equinox to the vernal; and that whatever he attempted at other times was never to his satisfaction, though he courted his fancy never so much; so that, in all the years he was about this poem, he may be said to have spent half his time therein."

Upon this relation Toland[56] remarks that in his opinion Phillips has mistaken the time of the year; for Milton in his elegies declares that with the advance of the spring he feels the increase of his poetical force, *"redeunt in carmina vires."*[57] To this it is answered that Phillips could hardly mistake time so well marked; and it may be added that Milton might find different times of the year favorable to different parts of life. Mr. Richardson conceives it impossible that "such a work should be suspended for six months, or for one. It may go on faster or slower, but it must go on." By what necessity it must continually go on, or why it might not be laid aside and resumed, it is not easy to discover.

This dependence of the soul upon the seasons, those temporary and periodical ebbs and flows of intellect, may, I suppose, justly be derided as the fumes of vain imagination. *Sapiens dominabitur astris.*[58] The author that thinks himself weatherbound will find, with a little help from hellebore,[59] that he is

[53]Jonathan Richardson, author of *Explanatory Notes and Remarks on Paradise Lost* (1734).

[54]Concretions of hard matter in the joints, an evidence of gout.

[55]Punctuation.

[56]John Toland in his life of Milton (1698).

[57]My powers of song return (Elegy V, 5).

[58]The wise man will rule the stars (an adage attributed to the astronomer Ptolemy).

[59]A plant from which was derived a cure for mental diseases.

only idle or exhausted. But while this notion has possession of the head, it produces the inability which it supposes. Our powers owe much of their energy to our hopes; *possunt quia posse videntur.*[60] When success seems attainable, diligence is enforced; but when it is admitted that the faculties are suppressed by a cross wind or a cloudy sky, the day is given up without resistance; for who can contend with the course of nature?

From such prepossessions Milton seems not to have been free. There prevailed in his time an opinion that the world was in its decay, and that we have had the misfortune to be produced in the decrepitude of nature. It was suspected that the whole creation languished, that neither trees nor animals had the height or bulk of their predecessors, and that everything was daily sinking by gradual diminution. Milton appears to suspect that souls partake of the general degeneracy, and is not without some fear that his book is to be written in "an age too late" for heroic poesy.[61]

Another opinion wanders about the world, and sometimes finds reception among wise men, an opinion that restrains the operations of the mind to particular regions, and supposes that a luckless mortal may be born in a degree of latitude too high or too low for wisdom or for wit. From this fancy, wild as it is, he had not wholly cleared his head when he feared lest the "climate" of his country might be "too cold" for flights of imagination.

Into a mind already occupied by such fancies another not more reasonable might easily find its way. He that could fear lest his genius had fallen upon too old a world, or too chill a climate, might consistently magnify to himself the influence of the seasons, and believe his faculties to be vigorous only half the year.

His submission to the seasons was at least more reasonable than his dread of decaying nature, or a frigid zone, for general causes must operate uniformly in a general abatement of mental power; if less could be performed by the writer, less likewise would content the judges of his work. Among this lagging race of frosty grovelers he might still have risen into eminence by producing something which "they should not willingly let die."[62] However inferior to the heroes who were born in better ages, he might still be great among his contemporaries, with the hope of growing every day greater in the dwindle of posterity. He might still be the giant of the pygmies, the one-eyed monarch of the blind.

Of his artifices of study, or particular hours of composition, we have little account, and there was perhaps little to be told. Richardson, who seems to have been very diligent in his inquiries, but discovers always a wish to find Milton discriminated from other men, relates that "he would sometimes lie awake whole nights, but not a verse could he make; and on a sudden his poetical faculty would rush upon him with an *impetus* or *oestrum,*[63] and his daughter was immediately called to secure what came. At other times he would dictate perhaps forty lines in a breath, and then reduce them to half the number."

These bursts of lights and involutions of darkness, these transient and involuntary excursions and retrocessions of invention, having some appearance of deviation from the common train of nature, are eagerly caught by the lovers of a wonder. Yet something of this inequality happens to every man in every mode of exertion, manual or mental. The mechanic cannot handle his hammer and his file at all times with equal dexterity; there are hours, he knows not why, when his hand is out. By Mr. Richardson's relation, casually conveyed, much regard cannot be claimed. That in his intellectual hour Milton called for his daughter "to secure what came" may be questioned; for unluckily it happens to be known that his daughters were never taught to write; nor would he have been obliged, as is universally confessed, to have employed any casual visiter in disburthening his memory, if his daughter could have performed the office.

The story of reducing his exuberance has

[60] They are able because they seem to be able.

[61] This fear and that discussed in the following paragraph seem to be derived from *The Reason of Church Government.*

[62] From *The Reason of Church Government.*

[63] Impulse or inspiration.

been told of other authors, and, though doubtless true of every fertile and copious mind, seems to have been gratuitously transferred to Milton.

What he has told us, and we cannot now know more, is that he composed much of his poem in the night and morning, I suppose before his mind was disturbed with common business; and that he poured out with great fluency his "unpremeditated verse."[64] Versification, free, like his, from the distresses of rime, must by a work so long be made prompt and habitual; and, when his thoughts were once adjusted, the words would come at his command.

* * *

The slow sale and tardy reputation of this poem[65] have been always mentioned as evidences of neglected merit, and of the uncertainty of literary fame; and inquiries have been made, and conjectures offered, about the causes of its long obscurity and late reception. But has the case been truly stated? Have not lamentation and wonder been lavished on an evil that was never felt?

That in the reigns of Charles and James the *Paradise Lost* received no public acclamations is readily confessed. Wit and literature were on the side of the court; and who that solicited favor or fashion would venture to praise the defender of the regicides? All that he himself could think his due, from "evil tongues" in "evil days,"[66] was that reverential silence which was generously preserved. But it cannot be inferred that his poem was not read, or not, however unwillingly, admired.

The sale, if it be considered, will justify the public. Those who have no power to judge of past times but by their own should always doubt their conclusions. The call for books was not in Milton's age what it is in the present. To read was not then a general amusement; neither traders, nor often gentlemen, thought themselves disgraced by ignorance. The women had not then aspired to literature, nor was every house supplied with a closet of knowledge. Those, indeed, who professed learning, were not less learned than at any other time; but of that middle race of students who read for pleasure or accomplishment, and who buy the numerous products of modern typography, the number was then comparatively small. To prove the paucity of readers it may be sufficient to remark that the nation had been satisfied from 1623 to 1664, that is forty-one years, with only two editions of the works of Shakespeare,[67] which probably did not together make one thousand copies.

The sale of thirteen hundred copies in two years, in opposition to so much recent enmity, and to a style of versification new to all and disgusting to many, was an uncommon example of the prevalence of genius. The demand did not immediately increase; for many more readers than were supplied at first the nation did not afford. Only three thousand were sold in eleven years, for it forced its way without assistance; its admirers did not dare to publish their opinion, and the opportunities now given of attracting notice by advertisements were then very few; the means of proclaiming the publication of new books have been produced by that general literature which now pervades the nation through all its ranks.

But the reputation and price of the copy still advanced till the Revolution[68] put an end to the secrecy of love, and *Paradise Lost* broke into open view with sufficient security of kind reception.

Fancy can hardly forbear to conjecture with what temper Milton surveyed the silent progress of his work, and marked his reputation stealing its way in a kind of subterraneous current through fear and silence. I cannot but conceive him calm and confident, little disappointed, not at all dejected, relying on his own merit with steady consciousness, and waiting without impatience the vicissitudes of opinion, and the impartiality of a future generation.

* * *

Milton has the reputation of having been in his youth eminently beautiful, so as to have been called the lady of his college. His hair, which was of a light brown, parted at the

[64] *Paradise Lost,* IX, 21–24. [65] *Paradise Lost.*
[66] *Paradise Lost,* VII, 26.

[67] There were editions in 1623, 1632, and 1664.
[68] The Glorious Revolution of 1688.

foretop and hung down upon his shoulders, according to the picture which he has given of Adam. He was, however, not of the heroic stature, but rather below the middle size, according to Mr. Richardson, who mentions him as having narrowly escaped from being "short and thick." He was vigorous, and active, and delighted in the exercise of the sword, in which he is related to have been eminently skilful. His weapon was, I believe, not the rapier, but the back-sword,[69] of which he recommends the use in his book on education.

His eyes are said never to have been bright; but, if he was a dexterous fencer, they must have been once quick.

His domestic habits, so far as they are known, were those of a severe student. He drank little strong drink of any kind, and fed without excess in quantity, and in his earlier years without delicacy of choice. In his youth he studied late at night; but afterwards changed his hours, and rested in bed from nine to four in the summer, and five in the winter. The course of his day was best known after he was blind. When he first rose, he heard a chapter in the Hebrew Bible, and then studied till twelve; then took some exercise for an hour; then dined; then played on the organ, and sang or heard another sing; then studied to six; then entertained his visitors till eight; then supped, and, after a pipe of tobacco and a glass of water, went to bed.

So is his life described; but this even tenor appears attainable only in colleges. He that lives in the world will sometimes have the succession of his practice broken and confused. Visitors, of whom Milton is represented to have had great numbers, will come and stay unseasonably; business, of which every man has some, must be done when others will do it.

When he did not care to rise early, he had something read to him by his bedside; perhaps at this time his daughters were employed. He composed much in the morning, and dictated in the day, sitting obliquely in an elbow-chair, with his leg thrown over the arm.

Fortune appears not to have had much of his care. In the civil wars he lent his personal estate to the parliament; but when, after the contest was decided, he solicited repayment, he met not only with neglect but "sharp rebuke," and, having tired both himself and his friends, was given up to poverty and hopeless indignation, till he showed how able he was to do greater service. He was then made Latin secretary, with two hundred pounds a-year, and had a thousand pounds for his *Defence of the People*.[70] His widow, who, after his death, retired to Nantwich in Cheshire, and died about 1729, is said to have reported that he lost two thousand pounds by entrusting it to a scrivener; and that, in the general depredation upon the church, he had grasped an estate of about sixty pounds a year belonging to Westminster Abbey, which, like other sharers of the plunder of rebellion, he was afterwards obliged to return. Two thousand pounds which he had placed in the Excise Office were also lost. There is yet no reason to believe that he was ever reduced to indigence. His wants, being few, were competently supplied. He sold his library before his death, and left his family fifteen hundred pounds, on which his widow laid hold, and only gave one hundred to each of his daughters.

His literature was unquestionably great. He read all the languages which are considered either as learned or polite: Hebrew, with its two dialects, Greek, Latin, Italian, French, and Spanish. In Latin his skill was such as places him in the first rank of writers and critics; and he appears to have cultivated Italian with uncommon diligence. The books in which his daughter, who used to read to him, represented him as most delighting, after Homer, which he could almost repeat, were Ovid's *Metamorphoses* and Euripides. His Euripides is, by Mr. Craddock's kindness, now in my hands; the margin is sometimes noted, but I have found nothing remarkable.

Of the English poets he set most value upon Spenser, Shakespeare, and Cowley. Spenser was apparently his favorite; Shakespeare he may easily be suppose to like, with every other skilful reader; but I should not

[69] Sword with only one cutting edge.

[70] The *Pro Populo Anglicano Defensio* (1651), written to defend the execution of Charles I.

have expected that Cowley, whose ideas of excellence were different from his own, would have had much of his approbation. His character of Dryden, who sometimes visited him, was that he was a good rimist but no poet.

His theological opinions are said to have been first Calvinistical; and afterwards, perhaps when he began to hate the Presbyterians, to have tended towards Arminianism.[71] In the mixed questions of theology and government he never thinks that he can recede far enough from popery, or prelacy; but what Baudius says of Erasmus seems applicable to him: *"magis habuit quod fugeret quam quod sequeretur."*[72] He had determined rather what to condemn than what to approve. He has not associated himself with any denomination of Protestants; we know rather what he was not than what he was. He was not of the Church of Rome; he was not of the Church of England.

To be of no church is dangerous. Religion, of which the rewards are distant, and which is animated only by faith and hope, will glide by degrees out of the mind, unless it be invigorated and reimpressed by external ordinances, by stated calls to worship and the salutary influence of example. Milton, who appears to have had full conviction of the truth of Christianity, and to have regarded the Holy Scriptures with the profoundest veneration, to have been untainted by any heretical peculiarity of opinion, and to have lived in a confirmed belief of the immediate and occasional agency of Providence, yet grew old without any visible worship. In the distribution of his hours there was no hour of prayer, either solitary or with his household; omitting public prayers, he omitted all.

Of this omission the reason has been sought, upon a supposition which ought never to be made, that men live with their own approbation, and justify their conduct to themselves. Prayer certainly was not thought superfluous by him who represents our first parents as praying acceptably in the state of innocence, and efficaciously after their fall. That he lived without prayer can hardly be affirmed; his studies and meditations were an habitual prayer. The neglect of it in his family was probably a fault for which he condemned himself, and which he intended to correct, but that death, as too often happens, intercepted his reformation.

His political notions were those of an acrimonious and surly republican, for which it is not known that he gave any better reason than "a popular government was the most frugal; for the trappings of a monarchy would set up an ordinary commonwealth."[73] It is surely very shallow policy that supposes money to be the chief good; and even this, without considering that the support and expense of a court is, for the most part, only a particular kind of traffic by which money is circulated without any national impoverishment.

Milton's republicanism was, I am afraid, founded in an envious hatred of greatness, and a sullen desire of independence; in petulance impatient of control, and pride disdainful of superiority. He hated monarchs in the state, and prelates in the church; for he hated all whom he was required to obey. It is to be suspected that his predominant desire was to destroy rather than establish, and that he felt not so much the love of liberty as repugnance to authority.

It has been observed that they who most loudly clamor for liberty do not most liberally grant it. What we know of Milton's character in domestic relations is that he was severe and arbitrary. His family consisted of women; and there appears in his books something like a Turkish contempt of females, as subordinate and inferior beings. That his own daughters might not break the ranks, he suffered them to be depressed by a mean and penurious education. He thought woman made only for obedience, and man only for rebellion.

* * *

In the examination of Milton's poetical works I shall pay so much regard to time as to begin with his juvenile productions. For his early pieces he seems to have had a degree of fondness not very laudable; what he has once written he resolves to preserve, and

[71]The anti-Calvinistic doctrines of James Arminius, the Dutch theologian.

[72]He knew what to avoid rather than what to follow.

[73]Remark of Milton's reported in Toland's life.

gives to the public an unfinished poem[74] which he broke off because he was "nothing satisfied with what he had done," supposing his readers less nice than himself. These preludes to his future labors are in Italian, Latin, and English. Of the Italian I cannot pretend to speak as a critic; but I have heard them commended by a man well qualified to decide their merit. The Latin pieces are lusciously elegant; but the delight which they afford is rather by the exquisite imitation of the ancient writers, by the purity of the diction and the harmony of the numbers, than by any power of invention or vigor of sentiment. They are not all of equal value; the elegies excell the odes; and some of the exercises on Gunpowder Treason might have been spared.

The English poems, though they make no promises of *Paradise Lost,* have this evidence of genius, that they have a cast original and unborrowed. But their peculiarity is not excellence; if they differ from the verses of others, they differ for the worse; for they are too often distinguished by repulsive harshness; the combinations of words are new, but they are not pleasing; the rimes and epithets seem to be laboriously sought, and violently applied.

That in the early parts of his life he wrote with much care appears from his manuscripts, happily preserved at Cambridge, in which many of his smaller works are found as they were first written, with the subsequent corrections. Such relics show how excellence is acquired; what we hope ever to do with ease, we must learn first to do with diligence.

Those who admire the beauties of this great poet sometimes force their own judgment into false approbation of his little pieces, and prevail upon themselves to think that admirable which is only singular. All that short compositions can commonly attain is neatness and elegance. Milton never learned the art of doing little things with grace; he overlooked the milder excellence of suavity and softness; he was a lion that had no skill "in dandling the kid."[75]

One of the poems on which much praise has been bestowed is *Lycidas,* of which the diction is harsh, the rimes uncertain, and the numbers unpleasing. What beauty there is we must therefore seek in the sentiments and images. It is not to be considered as the effusion of real passion; for passion runs not after remote allusions and obscure opinions. Passion plucks no berries from the myrtle and ivy, nor calls upon Arethuse and Mincius, nor tells of rough "satyrs" and "fauns with cloven heel." Where there is leisure for fiction there is little grief.

In this poem there is no nature, for there is no truth; there is no art, for there is nothing new. Its form is that of a pastoral, easy, vulgar, and therefore disgusting: whatever images it can supply are long ago exhausted; and its inherent improbability always forces dissatisfaction on the mind. When Cowley tells of Hervey[76] that they studied together, it is easy to suppose how much he must miss the companion of his labors and the partner of his discoveries; but what image of tenderness can be excited by these lines?

> We drove afield, and both together heard
> What time the grey fly winds her sultry horn,
> Battening our flocks with the fresh dews of night.[77]

We know that they never drove afield, and that they had no flocks to batten;[78] and though it be allowed that the representation may be allegorical, the true meaning is so uncertain and remote that it is never sought because it cannot be known when it is found.

Among the flocks, and copses, and flowers appear the heathen deities, Jove and Phoebus, Neptune and Aeolus, with a long train of mythological imagery, such as a college[79] easily supplies. Nothing can less display knowledge, or less exercise invention, than to tell how a shepherd has lost his companion, and must now feed his flocks alone, without any judge of his skill in piping; and how one god asks another god what is become of Lycidas, and how neither god can tell. He who thus grieves will excite no sympathy; he who thus praises will confer no honor.

This poem has yet a grosser fault. With

[74] "The Passion." Johnson quotes from Milton's note at the end of the poem.

[75] *Paradise Lost,* IV, 343.

[76] In his poem "On the Death of Mr. William Hervey."

[77] *Lycidas,* 27–29.

[78] Fatten.

[79] A college education.

these trifling fictions are mingled the most awful and sacred truths, such as ought never to be polluted with such irreverent combinations. The shepherd likewise is now a feeder of sheep, and afterwards an ecclesiastical pastor, a superintendent of a Christian flock. Such equivocations are always unskilful; but here they are indecent, and at least approach to impiety, of which, however, I believe the writer not to have been conscious.

Such is the power of reputation justly acquired that its blaze drives away the eye from nice examination. Surely no man could have fancied that he read *Lycidas* with pleasure, had he not known its author.

Of the two pieces, *L'Allegro* and *Il Penseroso,* I believe opinion is uniform; every man that reads them reads them with pleasure. The author's design is not, what Theobald[80] has remarked, merely to show how objects derive their colors from the mind, by representing the operation of the same things upon the gay and the melancholy temper, or upon the same man as he is differently disposed; but rather how, among the successive variety of appearances, every disposition of mind takes hold on those by which it may be gratified.

The cheerful man hears the lark in the morning; the pensive man hears the nightingale in the evening. The cheerful man sees the cock strut, and hears the horn and hounds echo in the wood; then walks "not unseen" to observe the glory of the rising sun, or listen to the singing milk-maid, and view the labors of the plowman and the mower; then casts his eyes about him over scenes of smiling plenty, and looks up to the distant tower, the residence of some fair inhabitants; thus he pursues rural gaiety through a day of labor or of play, and delights himself at night with the fanciful narratives of superstitious ignorance.

The pensive man at one time walks "unseen" to muse at midnight, and at another hears the sullen curfew. If the weather drives him home, he sits in a room lighted only by "glowing embers"; or by a lonely lamp outwatches the North Star, to discover the habitation of separate souls, and varies the shades of meditation by contemplating the magnificent or pathetic scenes of tragic and epic poetry. When the morning comes, a morning gloomy with rain and wind, he walks into the dark, trackless woods, falls asleep by some murmuring water, and with melancholy enthusiasm expects some dream of prognostication, or some music played by aërial performers.

Both mirth and melancholy are solitary, silent inhabitants of the breast that neither receive nor transmit communication; no mention is therefore made of a philosophical friend, or a pleasant companion. The seriousness does not arise from any participation of calamity, nor the gaiety from the pleasures of the bottle.

The man of cheerfulness, having exhausted the country, tries what "towered cities" will afford, and mingles with scenes of splendor, gay assemblies, and nuptial festivities; but he mingles a mere spectator, as, when the learned comedies of Jonson, or the wild dramas of Shakespeare, are exhibited, he attends the theater.

The pensive man never loses himself in crowds, but walks the cloister, or frequents the cathedral. Milton probably had not yet forsaken the church.

Both his characters delight in music; but he seems to think that cheerful notes would have obtained from Pluto a complete dismission of Eurydice,[81] of whom solemn sounds only procured a conditional release.

For the old age of cheerfulness he makes no provision; but melancholy he conducts with great dignity to the close of life. His cheerfulness is without levity, and his pensiveness without asperity.

Through these two poems the images are properly selected and nicely distinguished; but the colors of the diction seem not sufficiently discriminated. I know not whether the characters are kept sufficiently apart. No mirth can, indeed, be found in his melancholy; but I am afraid that I always meet some melancholy in his mirth. They are two noble efforts of imagination.

The greatest of his juvenile performances is the masque of *Comus,* in which may very

[80] Lewis Theobald (1688–1744), the editor of Shakespeare.

[81] She was almost rescued from the nether world by the music of her husband, Orpheus.

plainly be discovered the dawn or twilight of *Paradise Lost*. Milton appears to have formed very early that system of diction and mode of verse which his maturer judgment approved, and from which he never endeavored nor desired to deviate.

Nor does *Comus* afford only a specimen of his language; it exhibits likewise his power of description and his vigor of sentiment, employed in the praise and defence of virtue. A work more truly poetical is rarely found; allusions, images, and descriptive epithets embellish almost every period with lavish decoration. As a series of lines, therefore, it may be considered as worthy of all the admiration with which the votaries have received it.

As a drama it is deficient. The action is not probable. A masque, in those parts where supernatural intervention is admitted, must indeed be given up to all the freaks of imagination; but, so far as the action is merely human, it ought to be reasonable; which can hardly be said of the conduct of the two brothers, who, when their sister sinks with fatigue in a pathless wilderness, wander both away together in search of berries too far to find their way back, and leave a helpless lady to all the sadness and danger of solitude. This, however, is a defect overbalanced by its convenience.

What deserves more reprehension is that the prologue spoken in the wild wood by the attendant spirit is addressed to the audience, a mode of communication so contrary to the nature of dramatic representation that no precedents can support it.

The discourse of the spirit is too long, an objection that may be made to almost all the following speeches; they have not the sprightliness of a dialogue animated by reciprocal contention, but seem rather declamations deliberately composed, and formally repeated, on a moral question. The auditor therefore listens as to a lecture, without passion, without anxiety.

The song of Comus has airiness and jollity; but, what may recommend Milton's morals as well as his poetry, the invitations to pleasure are so general that they excite no distinct images of corrupt enjoyment, and take no dangerous hold on the fancy.

The following soliloquies of Comus and the lady are elegant but tedious. The song must owe much to the voice, if it ever can delight. At last the brothers enter with too much tranquillity; and when they have feared lest their sister should be in danger, and hoped that she is not in danger, the elder makes a speech in praise of chastity, and the younger finds how fine it is to be a philosopher.

Then descends the spirit in form of a shepherd; and the brother, instead of being in haste to ask his help, praises his singing, and inquires his business in that place. It is remarkable that at this interview the brother is taken with a short fit of riming. The spirit relates that the lady is in the power of Comus; the brother moralises again; and the spirit makes a long narration, of no use because it is false, and therefore unsuitable to a good being.

In all these parts the language is poetical, and the sentiments are generous; but there is something wanting to allure attention.

The dispute between the lady and Comus is the most animated and affecting scene of the drama, and wants nothing but a brisker reciprocation of objections and replies to invite attention, and detain it.

The songs are vigorous, and full of imagery; but they are harsh in their diction, and not very musical in their numbers.

Throughout the whole the figures are too bold, and the language too luxuriant for dialogue. It is a drama in the epic style, inelegantly splendid, and tediously instructive.

The sonnets were written in different parts of Milton's life, upon different occasions. They deserve not any particular criticism; for of the best it can only be said that they are not bad; and perhaps only the eighth and the twenty-first[82] are truly entitled to this slender commendation. The fabric of a sonnet, however adapted to the Italian language, has never succeeded in ours, which, having greater variety of termination, requires the rimes to be often changed.

Those little pieces may be despatched without much anxiety; a greater work calls for greater care. I am now to examine *Para-*

[82] Sonnets VIII and XVIII in the present collection.

dise Lost, a poem which, considered with respect to design, may claim the first place, and with respect to performance the second, among the productions of the human mind.

By the general consent of critics the first praise of genius is due to the writer of an epic poem, as it requires an assemblage of all the powers which are singly sufficient for other compositions. Poetry is the art of uniting pleasure with truth by calling imagination to the help of reason. Epic poetry undertakes to teach the most important truths by the most pleasing precepts, and therefore relates some great event in the most affecting manner. History must supply the writer with the rudiments of narration, which he must improve and exalt by a nobler art, must animate by dramatic energy, and diversify by retrospection and anticipation; morality must teach him the exact bounds, and different shades, of vice and virtue; from policy and the practice of life he has to learn the discriminations of character and the tendency of the passions, either single or combined; and physiology must supply him with illustrations and images. To put these materials to poetical use is required an imagination capable of painting nature, and realizing fiction. Nor is he yet a poet till he has attained the whole extension of his language, distinguished all the delicacies of phrase and all the colors of words, and learned to adjust their different sounds to all the varieties of metrical modulation.

Bossu[83] is of opinion that the poet's first work is to find a moral, which his fable[84] is afterwards to illustrate and establish. This seems to have been the process only of Milton; the moral of other poems is incidental and consequent; in Milton's only it is essential and intrinsic. His purpose was the most useful and the most arduous: "to vindicate the ways of God to man,"[85] to show the reasonableness of religion and the necessity of obedience to the divine law.

To convey this moral there must be a fable, a narration artfully constructed, so as to excite curiosity and surprise expectation. In this part of his work Milton must be confessed to have equaled every other poet. He has involved in his account of the Fall of Man the events which preceded, and those that were to follow it; he has interwoven the whole system of theology with such propriety that every part appears to be necessary; and scarcely any recital is wished shorter for the sake of quickening the progress of the main action.

The subject of an epic poem is naturally an event of great importance. That of Milton is not the destruction of a city, the conduct of a colony, or the foundation of an empire. His subject is the fate of worlds, the revolutions of heaven and of earth; rebellion against the Supreme King, raised by the highest order of created beings; the overthrow of their host, and the punishment of their crimes; the creation of a new race of reasonable creatures; their original happiness and innocence, their forfeiture of immortality, and their restoration to hope and peace.

Great events can be hastened or retarded only by persons of elevated dignity. Before the greatness displayed in Milton's poem all other greatness shrinks away. The weakest of his agents are the highest and noblest of human beings, the original parents of mankind; with whose actions the elements consented;[86] on whose rectitude, or deviation of will, depended the state of terrestrial nature, and the condition of all the future inhabitants of the globe.

Of the other agents in the poem the chief are such as it is irreverence to name on slight occasions. The rest are lower powers,

> ——of which the least could wield
> Those elements, and arm him with the force
> Of all their regions;[87]

powers which only the control of Omnipotence restrains from laying creation waste, and filling the vast expanse of space with ruin and confusion. To display the motives and actions of beings thus superior, so far as human reason can examine them, or human imagination represent them, is the task which this mighty poet has undertaken and performed.

[83]René le Bossu (1631–1689) in his *Traité du Poème Épique.*

[84]Story. [85]*Paradise Lost,* I, 26.

[86]Sympathized. [87]*Paradise Lost,* VI, 221–223.

In the examination of epic poems much speculation is commonly employed upon the characters. The characters in the *Paradise Lost* which admit of examination are those of angels and of man, of angels good and evil, of man in his innocent and sinful state.

Among the angels, the virtue of Raphael is mild and placid, of easy condescension and free communication; that of Michael is regal and lofty and, as may seem, attentive to the dignity of his own nature. Abdiel and Gabriel appear occasionally, and act as every incident requires; the solitary fidelity of Abdiel is very amiably painted.

Of the evil angels the characters are more diversified. To Satan, as Addison observes, such sentiments are given as suit "the most exalted and most depraved being."[88] Milton has been censured by Clarke[89] for the impiety which sometimes breaks from Satan's mouth; for there are thoughts, as he justly remarks, which no observation of character can justify, because no good man would willingly permit them to pass, however transiently, through his own mind. To make Satan speak as a rebel, without any such expressions as might taint the reader's imagination, was indeed one of the great difficulties in Milton's undertaking, and I cannot but think that he has extricated himself with great happiness. There is in Satan's speeches little that can give pain to a pious ear. The language of rebellion cannot be the same with that of obedience. The malignity of Satan foams in haughtiness and obstinacy; but his expressions are commonly general, and no otherwise offensive than as they are wicked.

The other chiefs of the celestial rebellion are very judiciously discriminated in the first and second books; and the ferocious character of Moloch appears, both in the battle and the council, with exact consistency.

To Adam and to Eve are given, during their innocence, such sentiments as innocence can generate and utter. Their love is pure benevolence and mutual veneration; their repasts are without luxury, and their diligence without toil. Their addresses to their Maker have little more than the voice of admiration and gratitude. Fruition left them nothing to ask, and innocence left them nothing to fear.

But with guilt enter distrust and discord, mutual accusation, and stubborn self-defence; they regard each other with alienated minds, and dread their Creator as the avenger of their transgression. At last they seek shelter in his mercy, soften to repentance, and melt in supplication. Both before and after the Fall the superiority of Adam is diligently sustained.

Of the probable and the marvelous, two parts of a vulgar epic poem which immerge the critic in deep consideration, the *Paradise Lost* requires little to be said. It contains the history of a miracle, of creation and redemption; it displays the power and the mercy of the Supreme Being; the probable therefore is marvelous, and the marvelous is probable. The substance of the narrative is truth; and as truth allows no choice, it is, like necessity, superior to rule. To the accidental or adventitious parts, as to everything human, some slight exceptions may be made. But the main fabric is immovably supported.

It is justly remarked by Addison that this poem has, by the nature of its subject, the advantage above all others that it is universally and perpetually interesting.[90] All mankind will, through all ages, bear the same relation to Adam and to Eve, and must partake of that good and evil which extend to themselves.

Of the machinery, so called from Θεὸς ἀπὸ μηχανῆς,[91] by which is meant the occasional interposition of supernatural power, another fertile topic of critical remarks, here is no room to speak, because everything is done under the immediate and visible direction of Heaven; but the rule is so far observed that no part of the action could have been accomplished by any other means.

Of episodes I think there are only two, contained in Raphael's relation of the war in heaven, and Michael's prophetic account of the changes to happen in this world. Both are closely connected with the great action;

[88] *Spectator*, no. 303.

[89] John Clarke in *An Essay upon Study*.

[90] *Spectator*, no. 273.

[91] *Deus ex machina*, an artificial solution of difficulties (Aristotle, *Poetics*, xv, 7).

one was necessary to Adam as a warning, the other as a consolation.

To the completeness or integrity of the design nothing can be objected; it has distinctly and clearly what Aristotle requires, a beginning, a middle, and an end. There is perhaps no poem of the same length from which so little can be taken without apparent mutilation. Here are no funeral games, nor is there any long description of a shield. The short digressions at the beginning of the third, seventh, and ninth books, might doubtless be spared; but superfluities so beautiful who would take away? or who does not wish that the author of the *Iliad* had gratified succeeding ages with a little knowledge of himself? Perhaps no passages are more frequently or more attentively read than those extrinsic paragraphs; and, since the end of poetry is pleasure, that cannot be unpoetical with which all are pleased.

The questions whether the action of the poem be strictly one, whether the poem can be properly termed heroic, and who is the hero, are raised by such readers as draw their principles of judgment rather from books than from reason. Milton, though he entitled *Paradise Lost* only a "poem," yet calls it himself "heroic song." Dryden[92] petulantly and indecently denies the heroism of Adam because he was overcome; but there is no reason why the hero should not be unfortunate, except established practice, since success and virtue do not go necessarily together. Cato is the hero of Lucan; but Lucan's authority will not be suffered by Quintilian to decide. However, if success be necessary, Adam's deceiver was at last crushed; Adam was restored to his Maker's favor, and therefore may securely resume his human rank.

After the scheme and fabric of the poem must be considered its component parts, the sentiments and the diction.

The sentiments, as expressive of manners, or appropriated to characters, are for the greater part unexceptionally just.

Splendid passages, containing lessons of morality or precepts of prudence, occur seldom. Such is the original formation of this poem that as it admits no human manners till the Fall, it can give little assistance to human conduct. Its end is to raise the thoughts above sublunary cares or pleasures. Yet the praise of that fortitude with which Abdiel maintained his singularity of virtue against the scorn of multitudes may be accommodated to all times; and Raphael's reproof of Adam's curiosity after the planetary motions, with the answer returned by Adam, may be confidently opposed to any rule of life which any poet has delivered.

The thoughts which are occasionally called forth in the progress are such as could only be produced by an imagination in the highest degree fervid and active, to which materials were supplied by incessant study and unlimited curiosity. The heat of Milton's mind may be said to sublimate his learning, to throw off into his work the spirit of science, unmingled with its grosser parts.

He had considered creation in its whole extent, and his descriptions are therefore learned. He had accustomed his imagination to unrestrained indulgence, and his conceptions therefore were extensive. The characteristic quality of his poem is sublimity. He sometimes descends to the elegant, but his element is the great. He can occasionally invest himself with grace; but his natural port is gigantic loftiness. He can please when pleasure is required; but it is his peculiar power to astonish.

He seems to have been well acquainted with his own genius, and to know what it was that nature had bestowed upon him more bountifully than upon others, the power of displaying the vast, illuminating the splendid, enforcing the awful, darkening the gloomy, and aggravating the dreadful; he therefore chose a subject on which too much could not be said, on which he might tire his fancy without the censure of extravagance.

The appearances of nature, and the occurrences of life, did not satiate his appetite of greatness. To paint things as they are requires a minute attention, and employs the memory rather than the fancy. Milton's delight was to sport in the wide regions of possibility; reality was a scene too narrow for his mind. He sent his faculties out upon discovery, into worlds where only imagination can travel, and delighted to form new

[92]In his *Essay on Satire* (1692).

modes of existence, and furnish sentiment and action to superior beings, to trace the counsels of hell, or accompany the choirs of heaven.

But he could not be always in other worlds; he must sometimes revisit earth; and tell of things visible and known. When he cannot raise wonder by the sublimity of his mind, he gives delight by its fertility.

Whatever be his subject, he never fails to fill the imagination. But his images and descriptions of the scenes or operations of nature do not seem to be always copied from original form, nor to have the freshness, raciness, and energy of immediate observation. He saw nature, as Dryden expresses it, "through the spectacles of books,"[93] and on most occasions calls learning to his assistance. The garden of Eden brings to his mind the vale of Enna, where Proserpine was gathering flowers. Satan makes his way through fighting elements, like Argo between the Cyanean rocks, or Ulysses between the two Sicilian whirlpools, when he shunned Charybdis on the larboard. The mythological allusions have been justly censured as not being always used with notice of their vanity; but they contribute variety to the narration, and produce an alternate exercise of the memory and the fancy.

His similes are less numerous, and more various, than those of his predecessors. But he does not confine himself within the limits of rigorous comparison; his great excellence is amplitude, and he expands the adventitious image beyond the dimensions which the occasion required. Thus, comparing the shield of Satan to the orb of the moon, he crowds the imagination with the discovery of the telescope, and all the wonders which the telescope discovers.

Of his moral sentiments it is hardly praise to affirm that they excell those of all other poets; for this superiority he was indebted to his acquaintance with the sacred writings. The ancient epic poets, wanting the light of revelation, were very unskilful teachers of virtue; their principal characters may be great, but they are not amiable. The reader may rise from their works with a greater degree of active or passive fortitude, and sometimes of prudence; but he will be able to carry away few precepts of justice, and none of mercy.

From the Italian writers it appears that the advantages of even Christian knowledge may be possessed in vain. Ariosto's pravity[94] is generally known; and though the *Deliverance of Jerusalem*[95] may be considered as a sacred subject, the poet has been very sparing of moral instruction.

In Milton every line breathes sanctity of thought, and purity of manners, except when the train of the narration requires the introduction of the rebellious spirits; and even they are compelled to acknowledge their subjection to God in such a manner as excites reverence, and confirms piety.

Of human beings there are but two; but those two are the parents of mankind, venerable before their fall for dignity and innocence, and amiable after it for repentance and submission. In their first state their affection is tender without weakness, and their piety sublime without presumption. When they have sinned, they show how discord begins in mutual frailty, and how it ought to cease in mutual forbearance; how confidence of the divine favor is forfeited by sin, and how hope of pardon may be obtained by penitence and prayer. A state of innocence we can only conceive, if indeed, in our present misery, it be possible to conceive it; but the sentiments and worship proper to a fallen and offending being we have all to learn, as we have all to practise.

The poet, whatever be done, is always great. Our progenitors in their first state conversed with angels; even when folly and sin had degraded them, they had not in their humiliation "the port of mean suitors";[96] and they rise again to reverential regard when we find that their prayers were heard.

As human passions did not enter the world before the Fall, there is in the *Paradise Lost* little opportunity for the pathetic; but what little there is has not been lost. That passion which is peculiar to rational nature, the

[93]In the *Essay on Dramatic Poesy* (1668). Dryden applies the phrase to Shakespeare.

[94]The immorality of Ariosto (in his *Orlando Furioso*).

[95]The *Gerusalemme Liberata* of Tasso.

[96]*Paradise Lost,* XI, 8–9.

anguish arising from the consciousness of transgression, and the horrors attending the sense of the divine displeasure, are very justly described and forcibly impressed. But the passions are moved only on one occasion; sublimity is the general and prevailing quality in this poem, sublimity variously modified, sometimes descriptive, sometimes argumentative.

The defects and faults of *Paradise Lost,* for faults and defects every work of man must have, it is the business of impartial criticism to discover. As, in displaying the excellence of Milton, I have not made long quotations, because of selecting beauties there had been no end, I shall in the same general manner mention that which seems to deserve censure; for what Englishman can take delight in transcribing passages which, if they lessen the reputation of Milton, diminish in some degree the honor of our country?

The generality of my scheme does not admit the frequent notice of verbal inaccuracies; which Bentley,[97] perhaps better skilled in grammar than in poetry, has often found, though he sometimes made them, and which he imputed to the obtrusions of a reviser whom the author's blindness obliged him to employ,—a supposition rash and groundless, if he thought it true, and vile and pernicious, if, as is said, he in private allowed it to be false.

The plan of *Paradise Lost* has this inconvenience, that it comprises neither human actions nor human manners. The man and woman who act and suffer, are in a state which no other man or woman can ever know. The reader finds no transaction in which he can be engaged, beholds no condition in which he can by any effort of imagination place himself; he has, therefore, little natural curiosity or sympathy.

We all, indeed, feel the effects of Adam's disobedience; we all sin like Adam, and like him must all bewail our offences; we have restless and insidious enemies in the fallen angels, and in the blessed spirits we have guardians and friends; in the redemption of mankind we hope to be included; in the description of heaven and hell we are surely interested, as we are all to reside hereafter either in the regions of horror or of bliss.

But these truths are too important to be new; they have been taught to our infancy; they have mingled with our solitary thoughts and familiar conversation, and are habitually interwoven with the whole texture of life. Being therefore not new, they raise no unaccustomed emotion in the mind; what we knew before we cannot learn; what is not unexpected cannot surprise.

Of the ideas suggested by these awful scenes, from some we recede with reverence, except when stated hours require their association; and from others we shrink with horror, or admit them only as salutary inflictions, as counterpoises to our interests and passions. Such images rather obstruct the career of fancy than incite it.

Pleasure and terror are indeed the genuine sources of poetry; but poetical pleasure must be such as human imagination can at least conceive, and poetical terror such as human strength and fortitude may combat. The good and evil of eternity are too ponderous for the wings of wit; the mind sinks under them in passive helplessness, content with calm belief and humble adoration.

Known truths, however, may take a different appearance, and be conveyed to the mind by a new train of intermediate images. This Milton has undertaken, and performed with pregnancy and vigor of mind peculiar to himself. Whoever considers the few radical positions[98] which the Scriptures afforded him will wonder by what energetic operation he expanded them to such extent, and ramified them to so much variety, restrained as he was by religious reverence from licentiousness of fiction.[99]

Here is a full display of the united force of study and genius, of a great accumulation of materials with judgment to digest, and fancy to combine them: Milton was able to select from nature or from story, from ancient fable or from modern science, whatever could illustrate or adorn his thoughts. An accumulation of knowledge impregnated his mind, fermented by study and exalted by imagination.

[97]Richard Bentley (1682–1742), editor and emendator of *Paradise Lost.*

[98]Original statements.

[99]Freedom in handling the story.

It has been therefore said, without an indecent hyperbole, by one of his encomiasts, that in reading *Paradise Lost* we read a book of universal knowledge.

But original deficience cannot be supplied. The want of human interest is always felt. *Paradise Lost* is one of the books which the reader admires and lays down, and forgets to take up again. None ever wished it longer than it is. Its perusal is a duty rather than a pleasure. We read Milton for instruction, retire harassed and overburdened, and look elsewhere for recreation; we desert our master, and seek for companions.

Another inconvenience of Milton's design is that it requires the description of what cannot be described, the agency of spirits. He saw that immateriality supplied no images, and that he could not show angels acting but by instruments of action; he therefore invested them with form and matter. This, being necessary, was therefore defensible; and he should have secured the consistency of his system by keeping immateriality out of sight, and enticing his reader to drop it from his thoughts. But he has unhappily perplexed his poetry with his philosophy. His infernal and celestial powers are sometimes pure spirit, and sometimes animated body. When Satan walks with his lance upon the "burning marl," he has a body; when, in his passage between hell and the new world, he is in danger of sinking in the vacuity, and is supported by a gust of rising vapors, he has a body; when he animates the toad, he seems to be mere spirit, that can penetrate matter at pleasure; when he "starts up in his own shape," he has at least a determined form; and when he is brought before Gabriel, he has "a spear and a shield," which he had the power of hiding in the toad, though the arms of the contending angels are evidently material.

The vulgar inhabitants of Pandaemonium, being "incorporeal spirits," are "at large, though without number," in a limited space; yet in the battle, when they were overwhelmed by mountains, their armor hurt them, "crushed in upon their substance, now grown gross by sinning." This likewise happened to the uncorrupted angels, who were overthrown the "sooner for their arms, for unarmed they might easily as spirits have evaded by contraction or remove." Even as spirits they are hardly spiritual, for "contraction" and "remove" are images of matter; but if they could have escaped without their armor, they might have escaped from it, and left only the empty cover to be battered. Uriel, when he rides on a sunbeam, is material; Satan is material when he is afraid of the prowess of Adam.

The confusion of spirit and matter which pervades the whole narration of the war of heaven fills it with incongruity; and the book in which it is related[100] is, I believe, the favorite of children, and gradually neglected as knowledge is increased.

After the operation of immaterial agents, which cannot be explained, may be considered that of allegorical persons, which have no real existence. To exalt causes into agents, to invest abstract ideas with form, and animate them with activity, has always been the right of poetry. But such airy beings are, for the most part, suffered only to do their natural office, and retire. Thus Fame tells a tale, and Victory hovers over a general, or perches on a standard; but Fame and Victory can do no more. To give them any real employment, or ascribe to them any material agency, is to make them allegorical no longer, but to shock the mind by ascribing effects to nonentity. In the *Prometheus* of Aeschylus we see Violence and Strength, and in the *Alcestis* of Euripides we see Death, brought upon the stage, all as active persons of the drama; but no precedents can justify absurdity.

Milton's allegory of Sin and Death is undoubtedly faulty. Sin is indeed the mother of Death, and may be allowed to be the portress of hell; but when they stop the journey of Satan, a journey described as real, and when Death offers him battle, the allegory is broken. That Sin and Death should have shown the way to hell might have been allowed; but they cannot facilitate the passage by building a bridge, because the difficulty of Satan's passage is described as real and sensible, and the bridge ought to be only figurative. The hell assigned to the rebellious spirits is described as not less local

[100] Book VI.

than the residence of man. It is placed in some distant part of space, separated from the regions of harmony and order by a chaotic waste and an unoccupied vacuity; but Sin and Death worked up a "mole of aggravated soil," cemented with asphaltus, a work too bulky for ideal architects.

This unskilful allegory appears to me one of the greatest faults of the poem; and to this there was no temptation but the author's opinion of its beauty.

To the conduct of the narrative some objections may be made. Satan is with great expectation brought before Gabriel in Paradise, and is suffered to go away unmolested. The creation of man is represented as the consequence of the vacuity left in heaven by the expulsion of the rebels; yet Satan mentions it as a report "rife in heaven" before his departure.

To find sentiments for the state of innocence was very difficult; and something of anticipation perhaps is now and then discovered. Adam's discourse of dreams seems not to be the speculation of a new-created being. I know not whether his answer to the angel's reproof for curiosity does not want something of propriety; it is the speech of a man acquainted with many other men. Some philosophical notions, especially when the philosophy is false, might have been better omitted. The angel, in a comparison, speaks of "timorous deer" before deer were yet timorous, and before Adam could understand the comparison.

Dryden remarks that Milton has some flats among his elevations.[101] This is only to say that all the parts are not equal. In every work one part must be for the sake of others; a palace must have passages; a poem must have transitions. It is no more to be required that wit should always be blazing than that the sun should always stand at noon. In a great work there is a vicissitude of luminous and opaque parts, as there is in the world a succession of day and night. Milton, when he has expatiated in the sky, may be allowed sometimes to revisit earth; for what other author ever soared so high, or sustained his flight so long?

Milton, being well versed in the Italian poets, appears to have borrowed often from them; and, as every man catches something from his companions, his desire of imitating Ariosto's levity[102] has disgraced his work with the Paradise of Fools, a fiction not in itself ill-imagined, but too ludicrous for its place.

His play on words, in which he delights too often; his equivocations, which Bentley endeavors to defend by the example of the ancients; his unnecessary and ungraceful use of terms of art, it is not necessary to mention, because they are easily remarked, and generally censured, and at last bear so little proportion to the whole that they scarcely deserve the attention of a critic.

Such are the faults of that wonderful performance *Paradise Lost;* which he who can put in balance with its beauties must be considered not as nice but as dull, as less to be censured for want of candor than pitied for want of sensibility.

Of *Paradise Regained* the general judgment seems now to be right, that it is in many parts elegant and everywhere instructive. It was not to be supposed that the writer of *Paradise Lost* could ever write without great effusions of fancy, and exalted precepts of wisdom. The basis of *Paradise Regained* is narrow; a dialogue without action can never please like an union of the narrative and dramatic powers. Had this poem been written not by Milton, but by some imitator, it would have claimed and received universal praise.

If *Paradise Regained* has been too much depreciated, *Samson Agonistes* has in requital been too much admired. It could only be by long prejudice and the bigotry of learning that Milton could prefer the ancient tragedies, with their encumbrance of a chorus, to the exhibitions of the French and English stages; and it is only by a blind confidence in the reputation of Milton that a drama can be praised in which the intermediate parts have neither cause nor consequence, neither hasten nor retard the catastrophe.

In this tragedy are, however, many particular beauties, many just sentiments and striking lines; but it wants that power of attracting the attention which a well-connected plan produces.

[101] In the *Essay on Satire* (1692).

[102] In the *Orlando Furioso,* XXXIV.

Milton would not have excelled in dramatic writing; he knew human nature only in the gross, and had never studied the shades of character, nor the combinations of concurring, or the perplexity of contending passions. He had read much, and knew what books could teach; but had mingled little in the world, and was deficient in the knowledge which experience must confer.

Through all his greater works there prevails an uniform peculiarity of diction, a mode and cast of expression which bears little resemblance to that of any former writer, and which is so far removed from common use that an unlearned reader, when he first opens his book, finds himself surprised by a new language.

This novelty has been, by those who can find nothing wrong in Milton, imputed to his laborious endeavors after words suitable to the grandeur of his ideas. "Our language," says Addison, "sunk under him."[103] But the truth is that, both in prose and verse, he had formed his style by a perverse and pedantic principle. He was desirous to use English words with a foreign idiom. This in all his prose is discovered and condemned, for there judgment operates freely, neither softened by the beauty, nor awed by the dignity of his thoughts; but such is the power of his poetry that his call is obeyed without resistance, the reader feels himself in captivity to a higher and a nobler mind, and criticism sinks in admiration.

Milton's style was not modified by his subject; what is shown with greater extent in *Paradise Lost* may be found in *Comus.* One source of his peculiarity was his familiarity with the Tuscan poets; the disposition of his words is, I think, frequently Italian, perhaps sometimes combined with other tongues. Of him, at last, may be said what Jonson says of Spenser, that "he wrote no language,"[104] but has formed what Butler calls a "Babylonish dialect,"[105] in itself harsh and barbarous, but made by exalted genius and extensive learning the vehicle of so much instruction and so much pleasure that, like other lovers, we find grace in its deformity.

[103]*Spectator,* no. 297. [104]In *Discoveries.*
[105]*Hudibras,* I, i, 89.

Whatever be the faults of his diction, he cannot want the praise of copiousness and variety; he was master of his language in its full extent, and has selected the melodious words with such diligence that from his book alone the art of English poetry might be learned.

After his diction, something must be said of his versification. The measure, he says, "is the English heroic verse without rime."[106] Of this mode he had many examples among the Italians, and some in his own country. The Earl of Surrey is said to have translated one of Virgil's books without rime; and, besides our tragedies, a few short poems had appeared in blank verse, particularly one tending to reconcile the nation to Raleigh's wild attempt upon Guiana, and probably written by Raleigh himself. These petty performances cannot be supposed to have much influenced Milton, who more probably took his hint from Trissino's *Italia Liberata,* and, finding blank verse easier than rime, was desirous of persuading himself that it is better.

"Rime," he says, and says truly, "is no necessary adjunct of true poetry."[106] But, perhaps, of poetry as a mental operation meter or music is no necessary adjunct; it is, however, by the music of meter that poetry has been discriminated in all languages; and in languages melodiously constructed with a due proportion of long and short syllables, meter is sufficient. But one language cannot communicate its rules to another; where meter is scanty and imperfect, some help is necessary. The music of the English heroic[107] line strikes the ear so faintly that it is easily lost, unless all the syllables of every line co-operate together; this co-operation can be only obtained by the preservation of every verse unmingled with another, as a distinct system of sounds; and this distinctness is obtained and preserved by the artifice of rime. The variety of pauses, so much boasted by the lovers of blank verse, changes the measures of an English poet to the periods of a declaimer; and there are only a few skilful and happy readers of Milton who enable their audience

[106]"The Verse," at the beginning of *Paradise Lost.*
[107]Iambic pentameter.

to perceive where the lines end or begin. "Blank verse," said an ingenious critic,[108] "seems to be verse only to the eye."

Poetry may subsist without rime, but English poetry will not often please; nor can rime ever be safely spared but where the subject is able to support itself. Blank verse makes some approach to that which is called the lapidary style, has neither the easiness of prose nor the melody of numbers, and therefore tires by long continuance. Of the Italian writers without rime, whom Milton alleges as precedents, not one is popular; what reason could urge in its defence has been confuted by the ear.

But, whatever be the advantage of rime, I cannot prevail on myself to wish that Milton had been a rimer, for I cannot wish his work to be other than it is; yet, like other heroes, he is to be admired rather than imitated. He that thinks himself capable of astonishing may write blank verse; but those that hope only to please must condescend to rime.

The highest praise of genius is original invention. Milton cannot be said to have contrived the structure of an epic poem, and therefore owes reverence to that vigor and amplitude of mind to which all generations must be indebted for the art of poetical narration, for the texture of the fable, the variation of incidents, the interposition of dialogue, and all the stratagems that surprise and enchain attention. But, of all the borrowers from Homer, Milton is perhaps the least indebted. He was naturally a thinker for himself, confident of his own abilities, and disdainful of help or hindrance; he did not refuse admission to the thoughts or images of his predecessors, but he did not seek them. From his contemporaries he neither courted nor received support; there is in his writings nothing by which the pride of other authors might be gratified, or favor gained, no exchange of praise, nor solicitation of support. His great works were performed under discountenance, and in blindness, but difficulties vanished at his touch; he was born for whatever is arduous; and his work is not the greatest of heroic poems, only because it is not the first.

[108]A Mr. Lock of Norbury Park, Surrey.

ON THE DEATH OF MR. ROBERT LEVET, A PRACTICER IN PHYSIC[1]

Condemned to Hope's delusive mine,
As on we toil from day to day,
By sudden blasts, or slow decline,
Our social comforts drop away.

Well tried through many a varying year,
See Levet to the grave descend,
Officious,[2] innocent, sincere,
Of every friendless name the friend.

Yet still he fills affection's eye,
Obscurely wise and coarsely kind;
Nor lettered arrogance deny
Thy praise to merit unrefined.

When fainting nature called for aid,
And hovering death prepared the blow,
His vigorous remedy displayed
The power of art without the show.

In misery's darkest cavern known,
His useful care was ever nigh,
Where hopeless anguish poured his groan,
And lonely want retired to die.

No summons mocked by chill delay,
No petty gain disdained by pride;
The modest wants of every day
The toil of every day supplied.

His virtues walked their narrow round,
Nor made a pause, nor left a void;
And sure th' Eternal master found
The single talent well employed.[3]

The busy day—the peaceful night,
Unfelt, uncounted, glided by;
His frame was firm—his powers were bright,
Though now his *eightieth* year was nigh.

Then with no fiery throbbing pain,
No cold gradations of decay,
Death broke at once the vital chain,
And freed his soul the nearest way.

[1]Levett died on 17 January, 1782. Johnson wrote this poem in the same year. It was published in the *Gentleman's Magazine,* August, 1783. Boswell says: "[He was] an obscure practicer in physic amongst the lower people. . .". It appears from Johnson's diary that their acquaintance commenced about the year 1746." For many years Levett "had an apartment in his house, or his chambers, and waited upon him every morning, through the whole course of his late and tedious breakfast. He was of a strange, grotesque appearance, stiff and formal in his manner, and seldom said a word while any company was present."

[2]Ready in doing good offices.

[3]An allusion to the parable of the servant to whom one talent (sum of money) was entrusted (St. Matthew, 25: 24–28).

JAMES BOSWELL

1740–1795

Boswell's parents were both members of distinguished and ancient Scottish families. His father, Alexander Boswell, was an able lawyer and judge and, moreover, the master of Auchinleck, in Ayrshire—an estate conferred by James IV upon his ancestor, Thomas Boswell, in 1504. James was born at Edinburgh on 29 October, 1740. He was educated privately and at the Edinburgh High School, proceeding thence to Edinburgh University. His father designed him for the law, and to pursue that study he went to Glasgow in November, 1759, "where he also attended the lectures of Dr. Adam Smith on moral philosophy and rhetoric." James's own inclination was not for the law, however, but for the army, and for a characteristic reason. He discovered in soldiers "an animation and relish of existence" unequaled except, perhaps, amongst actors; and he also "had acquired, from reading and conversation, an almost enthusiastic notion of the felicity of London"—a notion which experience did not disappoint. Hence he "was now earnest to have a commission as an officer of the Guards," in order at once to gratify his love of London and of the most animated society. Early in 1760 his father took him to the metropolis, apparently yielding to martial ardor, but continuing to press the claims of the law. After a year, a commission not being obtained, Boswell returned to Edinburgh and legal studies. But he was again in London in the autumn of 1762, still trying to obtain a commission. In the following spring, on 16 May, he was introduced to Dr. Johnson. During the summer he finally agreed to follow the law and in August, 1763, left for Utrecht to continue his studies. In the summer of 1764 he was in Berlin, and thereafter in Switzerland, where he contrived to meet both Rousseau and Voltaire. Thence he journeyed to Italy, where he managed to renew his acquaintance with John Wilkes, then a political exile, and whence he traveled to Corsica, armed with an introduction from Rousseau to General Paoli. He returned to England in February, 1766, and became an advocate at the Scottish bar in the same year. On 25 November, 1769, he married his cousin Margaret Montgomery. He was already the father of two natural children. His wife bore him four sons (two of whom died in infancy) and three daughters.

In 1772 Boswell was again in London, and saw much of Johnson. From this time, indeed, he was with him as much as possible, spending long periods in London in 1773, 1775, 1776, 1778, 1779, 1781, 1783, and 1784. He was kept in Scotland by lack of money—of which he never had enough to free him from embarrassments—in 1774, 1780, and 1782. In April, 1773, he was elected a member of the Literary Club, despite some opposition. In August of the same year Johnson went to Scotland and journeyed with Boswell to the Hebrides. In 1776 they also visited Lichfield and other places together. It has been calculated that, in all, Boswell saw Johnson on 276 days. Meanwhile he had begun in 1775 to keep terms at the Inner Temple, and in 1786 (two years after Johnson's death) he was called to the English bar. In 1788 he was in London, and in the following year took a house there. And in London he died, on 19 May, 1795.

Boswell began writing very early, publishing in 1760 a pamphlet which "is a rather strained imitation of the style of Sterne," with whom he had been intimate in London during his first visit. Other minor publications followed rapidly, including in 1761 *An Ode to Tragedy* which Boswell gaily dedicated to himself, and in 1763 a series of letters "which is the first considerable example of his life-long willingness to be indiscreet provided thereby he could be interesting." (F. A. Pottle, *Literary Career of Boswell.*) Through many years he contributed steadily and voluminously to periodicals; and one series of his essays, numbering 70—originally published in the *London Magazine*, 1777–1783—has recently been reprinted (*The Hypochondriack*, edited by Margery Bailey, 2 vols., 1928). The mass of his publications is in fact very large, though only three of his books give him any claim to remembrance: *An Account of Corsica* (1768); *The Journal of a Tour to the Hebrides with Samuel Johnson, LL. D.* (1785); and *The Life of Samuel Johnson, LL.D.* (1791). It is for the last, of course, that he *is* remembered; because, as Macaulay has splendidly and truly said: "Homer is not more decidedly the first of heroic poets, Shakespeare is not more decidedly the first of dramatists, Demosthenes is not more decidedly the first of orators, than Boswell is the first of biographers. He has no second. He has distanced all his competitors so decidedly that it is not worth while to place them. Eclipse is first, and the rest nowhere."

Yet Boswell, despite his literary genius, and despite the amiable qualities which endeared him to Johnson and which enabled him all his life to gratify his passion for association with the great, has never attained a place amongst English writers commensurate with his magnificent achievement. A contemporary, echoing a very general feeling, asked: "Who would purchase fame as an author, or in any other way, on such terms as this creature, Boswell?" His close friend and devoted correspondent, William Johnston Temple, considered him the most thinking man he ever knew, but, nevertheless, confided to his Diary (25 May, 1783): "Boswell irregular in his conduct and manners, selfish, indelicate, thoughtless, no sensibility or feeling for others who have not his coarse and rustic strength and spirits. Sorry I came to town to meet him. Detaining me here to no purpose. Seems often absurd and almost mad I think. No composure or rational view of things. Years do not improve him." Macaulay, paying every tribute to his great *book,* thought the *man* "one of the smallest that ever lived," and "of the meanest and feeblest intellect": "servile and impertinent, shallow and pedantic, a bigot and a sot; bloated with family pride, and eternally blustering about the dignity of a born gentleman, yet stooping to be a talebearer, an eavesdropper, a common butt in the taverns of London; so curious to know everybody who was talked about that, Tory and high Churchman as he was, he maneuvered, we have been told, for an introduction to Tom Paine; so vain of the most childish distinctions that, when he had been to court, he drove to the office where his book was printing without changing his clothes, and summoned all the printer's devils to admire his new ruffles and sword; such was this man, and such he was content and proud to be." And Macaulay's accusations cannot be disputed, though his strong language has been of late years universally deplored, as taking into account only one side of a complex nature. The other side has been presented by the accomplished editor of Boswell's *Letters* (2 vols., 1924), Professor C. B. Tinker, in a volume of frank special-pleading (*Young Boswell,* 1922). Probably the case for Boswell has best been stated by Raleigh: "He had simplicity, candor, fervor, a warmly affectionate nature, a quick intelligence, and a passion for telling all that he knew. These are qualities which make for good literature. They enabled Boswell to portray Johnson with an intimacy and truth that has no parallel in any language" (*Six Essays on Johnson*).

The great biography has recently been reissued in *Boswell's Life of Johnson together with Boswell's Journal of a Tour to the Hebrides and Johnson's Diary of a Journey into North Wales,* ed. George B. Hill, rev. L. F. Powell (Oxford, 1934). No less valuable for the student of Boswell are the *Private Papers of James Boswell from Malahide Castle,* ed. Geoffrey Scott and Frederick A. Pottle (New York, 1928–1936); only one volume of these invaluable papers has as yet been republished in a popular edition, i. e., *Boswell's Journal of a Tour to the Hebrides with Samuel Johnson,* edited from the original manuscript by Frederick A. Pottle and Charles H. Bennett (New York, 1936). For further primary material see Claude C. Abbott, *A Catalogue of Papers Relating to Boswell, Johnson, and Sir William Forbes, Found at Fettercairn House, 1930–1931* (Oxford, 1936).

PASSAGES FROM *THE LIFE OF SAMUEL JOHNSON, LL.D.*

(1791)

The Dictionary (1747–1756)

The year 1747 is distinguished as the epoch when Johnson's arduous and important work, his Dictionary of the English Language was announced to the world, by the publication of its Plan or *Prospectus.*

How long this immense undertaking had been the object of his contemplation, I do not know. I once asked him by what means he had attained to that astonishing knowledge of our language, by which he was enabled to realize a design of such extent, and accumulated difficulty. He told me, that "it was not the effect of particular study; but that it had grown up in his mind insensibly." I have been informed by Mr. James Dodsley, that several years before this period, when Johnson was one day sitting in his brother Robert's shop, he heard his brother suggest to him, that a Dictionary of the English Language would be a work that would be well received by the public; that Johnson seemed at first to catch at the proposition, but, after a pause, said, in his abrupt decisive manner, "I believe I shall not undertake it." That he, however, had bestowed much thought upon the subject, before he published his *Plan,* is evident from the enlarged, clear, and accurate views which it exhibits; and we find him mentioning in that tract, that many of the writers whose testimonies were to be produced as authorities, were selected by Pope; which proves that he had been furnished, probably by Mr. Robert Dodsley, with whatever hints that eminent poet had contributed towards a great literary project, that had been the subject of important consideration in a former reign.

The booksellers who contracted with Johnson, single and unaided, for the execution of a work, which in other countries has not been effected but by the co-operating exertions of many, were Mr. Robert Dodsley, Mr. Charles Hitch, Mr. Andrew Millar, the two Messieurs Longman, and the two Messieurs Knapton. The price stipulated was fifteen hundred and seventy-five pounds.

The *Plan* was addressed to Philip Dormer, Earl of Chesterfield, then one of his Majesty's Principal Secretaries of State; a nobleman who was very ambitious of literary distinction, and who, upon being informed of the design, had expressed himself in terms very favorable to its success. There is, perhaps in everything of any consequence, a secret history which it would be amusing to know, could we have it authentically communicated. Johnson told me, "Sir, the way in which the *Plan* of my *Dictionary* came to be inscribed to Lord Chesterfield, was this: I had neglected to write it by the time appointed. Dodsley suggested a desire to have it addressed to Lord Chesterfield. I laid hold of this as a pretext for delay, that it might be better done, and let Dodsley have his desire. I said to my friend, Dr. Bathurst, 'Now if any good comes of my addressing to Lord Chesterfield, it will be ascribed to deep policy, when, in fact, it was only a casual excuse for laziness.' " * * *

Dr. Adams found him one day busy at his *Dictionary,* when the following dialogue ensued. "Adams. This is a great work, Sir. How are you to get all the etymologies? Johnson. Why, Sir, here is a shelf with Junius, and Skinner,[1] and others; and there is a Welsh gentleman who has published a collection of Welsh proverbs, who will help me with the Welsh. Adams. But, Sir, how can you do this in three years? Johnson. Sir, I have no doubt that I can do it in three years. Adams. But the French Academy, which consists of forty members, took forty years to compile their Dictionary. Johnson. Sir, thus it is. This is the proportion. Let me see; forty times forty is sixteen hundred. As three to sixteen hundred, so is the proportion of an Englishman to a Frenchman." With so much ease and pleasantry

[1]Previous lexicographers.

could he talk of that prodigious labor which he had undertaken to execute. * * *

For the mechanical part he employed, as he told me, six amanuenses; and let it be remembered by the natives of North-Britain,[2] to whom he is supposed to have been so hostile, that five of them were of that country. * * *

1754: AETAT. 45.] * * * The *Dictionary,* we may believe, afforded Johnson full occupation this year. As it approached to its conclusion, he probably worked with redoubled vigor, as seamen increase their exertion and alacrity when they have a near prospect of their haven.

Lord Chesterfield, to whom Johnson had paid the high compliment of addressing to his Lordship the *Plan* of his *Dictionary,* had behaved to him in such a manner as to excite his contempt and indignation. The world has been for many years amused with a story confidently told, and as confidently repeated with additional circumstances, that a sudden disgust was taken by Johnson upon occasion of his having been one day kept long in waiting in his Lordship's antechamber, for which the reason assigned was, that he had company with him; and that at last, when the door opened, out walked Colley Cibber;[3] and that Johnson was so violently provoked when he found for whom he had been so long excluded, that he went away in a passion, and never would return. I remember having mentioned this story to George Lord Lyttelton, who told me, he was very intimate with Lord Chesterfield; and holding it as a well-known truth, defended Lord Chesterfield, by saying, that "Cibber, who had been introduced familiarly by the back-stairs, had probably not been there above ten minutes." It may seem strange even to entertain a doubt concerning a story so long and so widely current, and thus implicitly adopted, if not sanctioned, by the authority which I have mentioned; but Johnson himself assured me that there was not the least foundation for it. He told me that there never was any particular incident which produced a quarrel between Lord Chesterfield and him; but that his Lordship's continued neglect was the reason why he resolved to have no connection with him. When the *Dictionary* was upon the eve of publication, Lord Chesterfield, who, it is said, had flattered himself with expectations that Johnson would dedicate the work to him, attempted, in a courtly manner, to soothe, and insinuate himself with the Sage, conscious, as it should seem, of the cold indifference with which he had treated its learned author; and further attempted to conciliate him, by writing two papers in *The World,* in recommendation of the work; and it must be confessed, that they contain some studied compliments, so finely turned, that if there had been no previous offense, it is probable that Johnson would have been highly delighted. Praise, in general, was pleasing to him; but by praise from a man of rank and elegant accomplishments, he was peculiarly gratified. * * *

This courtly device failed of its effect. Johnson, who thought that "all was false and hollow," despised the honeyed words, and was even indignant that Lord Chesterfield should, for a moment, imagine that he could be the dupe of such an artifice. His expression to me concerning Lord Chesterfield, upon this occasion, was, "Sir, after making great professions, he had, for many years, taken no notice of me; but when my *Dictionary* was coming out, he fell a scribbling in *The World* about it. Upon which, I wrote him a letter expressed in civil terms, but such as might show him that I did not mind what he said or wrote, and that I had done with him."

This is that celebrated letter of which so much has been said, and about which curiosity has been so long excited, without being gratified. I for many years solicited Johnson to favor me with a copy of it, that so excellent a composition might not be lost to posterity. He delayed from time to time to give it me; till at last in 1781, when we were on a visit at Mr. Dilly's, at Southill in Bedfordshire, he was pleased to dictate it to me from memory. He afterwards found among his papers a copy of it, which he had dictated to Mr. Baretti, with its title and corrections, in his own handwriting. This he gave to Mr. Langton; adding that if it were to come into

[2]Scotland.

[3]Dramatist and Poet Laureate. Cibber was held in general contempt.

print, he wished it to be from that copy. By Mr. Langton's kindness, I am enabled to enrich my work with a perfect transcript of what the world has so eagerly desired to see.

To the Right Honorable the Earl of Chesterfield.

February 7, 1755.

My Lord, I have been lately informed, by the proprietor of *The World,* that two papers, in which my Dictionary is recommended to the public, were written by your Lordship. To be so distinguished, is an honor, which, being very little accustomed to favors from the great, I know not well how to receive, or in what terms to acknowledge.

When, upon some slight encouragement, I first visited your Lordship, I was overpowered, like the rest of mankind, by the enchantment of your address; and could not forbear to wish that I might boast myself *Le vainqueur du vainqueur de la terre;*[4]—that I might obtain that regard for which I saw the world contending; but I found my attendance so little encouraged, that neither pride nor modesty would suffer me to continue it. When I had once addressed your Lordship in public, I had exhausted all the art of pleasing which a retired and uncourtly scholar can possess. I had done all that I could; and no man is well pleased to have his all neglected, be it ever so little.

Seven years, my Lord, have now passed, since I waited in your outward rooms, or was repulsed from your door; during which time I have been pushing on my work through difficulties, of which it is useless to complain, and have brought it, at last, to the verge of publication, without one act of assistance, one word of encouragement, or one smile of favor. Such treatment I did not expect, for I never had a Patron before.

The shepherd in Virgil grew at last acquainted with Love, and found him a native of the rocks.[5]

Is not a Patron, my Lord, one who looks with unconcern on a man struggling for life in the water, and, when he has reached ground, encumbers him with help? The notice which you have been pleased to take of my labors, had it been early, had been kind; but it has been delayed till I am indifferent, and cannot enjoy it; till I am solitary,[6] and cannot impart it; till I am known, and do not want it. I hope it is no very cynical asperity not to confess obligations where no benefit has been received, or to be unwilling that the Public should consider me as owing that to a Patron, which Providence has enabled me to do for myself.

Having carried on my work thus far with so little obligation to any favorer of learning, I shall not be disappointed though I should conclude it, if less be possible, with less; for I have been long wakened from that dream of hope, in which I once boasted myself with so much exultation, my Lord, your Lordship's most humble, most obedient servant,

Sam. Johnson.

* * *

The *Dictionary,* with a *Grammar and History of the English Language,* being now at length published, in two volumes folio, the world contemplated with wonder so stupendous a work achieved by one man, while other countries had thought such undertakings fit only for whole academies. Vast as his powers were, I cannot but think that his imagination deceived him, when he supposed that by constant application he might have performed the task in three years. * * *

The extensive reading which was absolutely necessary for the accumulation of authorities, and which alone may account for Johnson's retentive mind being enriched with a very large and various store of knowledge and imagery, must have occupied several years. The Preface furnishes an eminent instance of a double talent, of which Johnson was fully conscious. Sir Joshua Reynolds heard him say, "There are two things which I am confident I can do very well: one is an introduction to any literary work, stating what it is to contain, and how it should be executed in the most perfect manner; the other is a conclusion, showing from various causes why the execution has not been equal to what the author promised to himself and to the public." * * *

A few of his definitions must be admitted to be erroneous. Thus, *Windward* and *Leeward,* though directly of opposite meaning, are defined identically the same way; as to which inconsiderable specks it is enough to observe, that his Preface announces that he

[4]The conqueror of the conqueror of the earth (Boileau, *L'Art Poétique,* III, 272).

[5]*Eclogues,* VIII, 43.

[6]Johnson's wife had died on 17 March, 1752.

was aware there might be many such in so immense a work; nor was he at all disconcerted when an instance was pointed out to him. A lady once asked him how he came to define *Pastern* the *knee* of a horse: instead of making an elaborate defense, as she expected, he at once answered, "Ignorance, Madam, pure ignorance." His definition of *Network*[7] has been often quoted with sportive malignity, as obscuring a thing in itself very plain. But to these frivolous censures no other answer is necessary than that with which we are furnished by his own Preface. * * *

His introducing his own opinions, and even prejudices, under general definitions of words, while at the same time the original meaning of the words is not explained, as his *Tory, Whig, Pension, Oats, Excise,*[8] and a few more, cannot be fully defended, and must be placed to the account of capricious and humorous indulgence. Talking to me upon this subject when we were at Ashbourne in 1777, he mentioned a still stronger instance of the predominance of his private feelings in the composition of this work, than any now to be found in it. "You know, Sir, Lord Gower forsook the old Jacobite interest. When I came to the word *Renegado,* after telling that it meant 'one who deserts to the enemy, a revolter,' I added, *Sometimes we say a* GOWER. Thus it went to the press; but the printer had more wit than I, and struck it out."

Let it, however, be remembered, that this indulgence does not display itself only in sarcasm towards others, but sometimes in playful allusion to the notions commonly entertained of his own laborious task. Thus: "*Grubstreet,* the name of a street in London, much inhabited by writers of small histories, *dictionaries,* and temporary poems; whence any mean production is called *Grubstreet.*"—"*Lexicographer,* a writer of dictionaries, a *harmless drudge.*" * * *

He had spent, during the progress of the work, the money for which he had contracted to write his *Dictionary.* We have seen that the reward of his labor was only fifteen hundred and seventy-five pounds; and when the expense of amanuenses and paper, and other articles are deducted, his clear profit was very inconsiderable. I once said to him, "I am sorry, Sir, you did not get more for your *Dictionary.*" His answer was, "I am sorry, too. But it was very well. The booksellers are generous, liberal-minded men." He, upon all occasions, did ample justice to their character in this respect. He considered them as the patrons of literature; and, indeed, although they have eventually been considerable gainers by his *Dictionary,* it is to them that we owe its having been undertaken and carried through at the risk of great expense, for they were not absolutely sure of being indemnified.

Christopher Smart (1763)

CONCERNING this unfortunate poet, Christopher Smart, who was confined in a madhouse, he had, at another time, the following conversation with Dr. Burney:—BURNEY. "How does poor Smart do, Sir; is he likely to recover?" JOHNSON. "It seems as if his mind had ceased to struggle with the disease; for he grows fat upon it." BURNEY. "Perhaps, Sir, that may be from want of exercise." JOHNSON. "No, Sir; he has partly as much exercise as he used to have, for he digs in the garden. Indeed, before his confinement, he used for exercise to walk to the ale-house; but he was *carried* back again. I did not think he ought to be shut up. His infirmities were not noxious to society. He insisted on people praying with him; and I'd as lief pray with Kit Smart as any one else. Another charge was, that he did not love clean linen; and I have no passion for it."—Johnson continued. "Mankind have a great aversion to intellectual labor; but even supposing knowledge to be easily attainable, more people would be content to be ignorant

[7] "Anything reticulated or decussated, at equal distances, with interstices between the intersections."

[8] *Tory*: "One who adheres to the ancient constitution of the state, and the apostolical hierarchy of the Church of England; opposed to a whig." *Whig:* "The name of a faction." *Pension:* "An allowance made to any one without an equivalent. In England it is generally understood to mean pay given to a state hireling for treason to his country." *Oats:* "A grain which in England is generally given to horses, but in Scotland supports the people." *Excise:* "A hateful tax levied upon commodities, and adjudged not by the common judges of property, but wretches hired by those to whom Excise is paid."

than would take even a little trouble to acquire it."

The Social Order (1763)

I DESCRIBED to him an impudent fellow from Scotland, who affected to be a savage, and railed at all establishing systems. JOHNSON. "There is nothing surprising in this, Sir. He wants to make himself conspicuous. He would tumble in a hog-sty, as long as you looked at him and called to him to come out. But let him alone, never mind him, and he'll soon give it over."

I added, that the same person maintained that there was no distinction between virtue and vice. JOHNSON. "Why, Sir, if the fellow does not think as he speaks, he is lying; and I see not what honor he can propose to himself from having the character of a liar. But if he does really think that there is no distinction between virtue and vice, why, Sir, when he leaves our houses let us count our spoons." * * *

He recommended to me to keep a journal of my life, full and unreserved. He said it would be a very good exercise, and would yield me great satisfaction when the particulars were faded from my remembrance. I was uncommonly fortunate in having had a previous coincidence of opinion with him upon this subject, for I had kept such a journal for some time; and it was no small pleasure to me to have this to tell him, and to receive his approbation. He counseled me to keep it private, and said I might surely have a friend who would burn it in case of my death. From this habit I have been enabled to give the world so many anecdotes, which would otherwise have been lost to posterity. I mentioned that I was afraid I put into my journal too many little incidents. JOHNSON. "There is nothing, Sir, too little for so little a creature as man. It is by studying little things that we attain the great art of having as little misery and as much happiness as possible."

Next morning Mr. Dempster happened to call on me, and was so much struck even with the imperfect account which I gave him of Dr. Johnson's conversation, that to his honor be it recorded, when I complained that drinking port and sitting up late with him affected my nerves for some time after, he said, "One had better be palsied at eighteen than not to keep company with such a man."

On Tuesday, July 18, I found tall Sir Thomas Robinson sitting with Johnson. Sir Thomas said, that the King of Prussia valued himself upon three things;—upon being a hero, a musician, and an author. JOHNSON. "Pretty well, Sir, for one man. As to his being an author, I have not looked at his poetry; but his prose is poor stuff. He writes just as you might suppose Voltaire's footboy to do, who has been his amanuensis. He has such parts as the valet might have, and about as much of the coloring of the style as might be got by transcribing his works." When I was at Ferney, I repeated this to Voltaire, in order to reconcile him somewhat to Johnson, whom he, in affecting the English mode of expression, had previously characterized as "a superstitious dog"; but after hearing such a criticism on Frederick the Great, with whom he was then on bad terms, he exclaimed, "An honest fellow!" * * *

Mr. Levet[9] this day showed me Dr. Johnson's library, which was contained in two garrets over his Chambers, where Lintot, son of the celebrated bookseller of that name, had formerly his warehouse. I found a number of good books, but very dusty and in great confusion. The floor was strewed with manuscript leaves, in Johnson's own handwriting, which I beheld with a degree of veneration, supposing they perhaps might contain portions of *The Rambler* or of *Rasselas*. I observed an apparatus for chemical experiments, of which Johnson was all his life very fond. The place seemed to be very favorable for retirement and meditation. Johnson told me that he went up thither without mentioning it to his servant, when he wanted to study, secure from interruption; for he would not allow his servant to say he was not at home when he really was. "A servant's strict regard for truth (said he), must be weakened by such a practice. A philosopher may know that it is

[9]See Johnson's poem on his death and the note concerning him, printed at the end of the selections from Johnson in this volume.

merely a form of denial; but few servants are such nice distinguishers. If I accustom a servant to tell a lie for *me,* have I not reason to apprehend that he will tell many lies for *himself?*" * * *

Mr. Temple,[10] now vicar of St. Gluvias, Cornwall, who had been my intimate friend for many years, had at this time chambers in Farrar's Buildings, at the bottom of Inner Temple Lane, which he kindly lent me upon my quitting my lodgings, he being to return to Trinity Hall, Cambridge. I found them particularly convenient for me, as they were so near Dr. Johnson's.

On Wednesday, July 20, Dr. Johnson, Mr. Dempster, and my uncle Dr. Boswell, who happened to be now in London, supped with me at these Chambers. JOHNSON. "Pity is not natural to man. Children are always cruel. Savages are always cruel. Pity is acquired and improved by the cultivation of reason. We may have uneasy sensations from seeing a creature in distress, without pity; for we have not pity unless we wish to relieve them. When I am on my way to dine with a friend, and finding it late, have bid the coachman make haste, if I happen to attend when he whips his horses, I may feel unpleasantly that the animals are put to pain, but I do not wish him to desist. No, Sir, I wish him to drive on." * * *

Rousseau's treatise on the inequality of mankind was at this time a fashionable topic. It gave rise to an observation by Mr. Dempster, that the advantages of fortune and rank were nothing to a wise man, who ought to value only merit. JOHNSON. "If man were a savage, living in the woods by himself, this might be true; but in civilized society we all depend upon each other, and our happiness is very much owing to the good opinion of mankind. Now, Sir, in civilized society, external advantages make us more respected. A man with a good coat upon his back meets with a better reception than he who has a bad one. Sir, you may analyze this, and say what is there in it? But that will avail you nothing, for it is a part of a general system. Pound St. Paul's Church into atoms, and consider any single atom; it is, to be sure, good for nothing: but, put all these atoms together, and you have St. Paul's Church. So it is with human felicity, which is made up of many ingredients, each of which may be shown to be very insignificant. In civilized society, personal merit will not serve you so much as money will. Sir, you may make the experiment. Go into the street, and give one man a lecture on morality, and another a shilling, and see which will respect you most. If you wish only to support nature, Sir William Petty[11] fixes your allowance at three pounds a year; but as times are much altered, let us call it six pounds. This sum will fill your belly, shelter you from the weather, and even get you a strong lasting coat, supposing it to be made of good bull's hide. Now, Sir, all beyond this is artificial, and is desired in order to obtain a greater degree of respect from our fellow-creatures. And, Sir, if six hundred pounds a year procure a man more consequence, and, of course, more happiness than six pounds a year, the same proportion will hold as to six thousand, and so on as far as opulence can be carried. Perhaps he who has a large fortune may not be so happy as he who has a small one; but that must proceed from other causes than from his having the large fortune: for, *caeteris paribus,*[12] he who is rich in a civilized society, must be happier than he who is poor; as riches, if properly used (and it is a man's own fault if they are not), must be productive of the highest advantages. Money, to be sure, of itself is of no use, for its only use is to part with it. Rousseau, and all those who deal in paradoxes, are led away by a childish desire of novelty. When I was a boy, I used always to choose the wrong side of a debate, because most ingenious things, that is to say, most new things, could be said upon it. Sir, there is nothing for which you may not muster up more plausible arguments, than those which are urged against wealth and other external advantages. Why, now, there is stealing; why should it be thought a crime? When we consider by what unjust methods property has been often acquired, and that what was

[10] William Johnston Temple (1739–1796).

[11] Author of a *Treatise on Taxes* (1662), and *The Multiplication of Mankind* (1682).

[12] Other things being equal.

unjustly got it must be unjust to keep, where is the harm in one man's taking the property of another from him? Besides, Sir, when we consider the bad use that many people make of their property, and how much better use the thief may make of it, it may be defended as a very allowable practice. Yet, Sir, the experience of mankind has discovered stealing to be so very bad a thing, that they make no scruple to hang a man for it. When I was running about this town a very poor fellow, I was a great arguer for the advantages of poverty; but I was, at the same time, very sorry to be poor. Sir, all the arguments which are brought to represent poverty as no evil, show it to be evidently a great evil. You never find people laboring to convince you that you may live very happily upon a plentiful fortune.—So you hear people talking how miserable a King must be; and yet they all wish to be in his place."

It was suggested that Kings must be unhappy, because they are deprived of the greatest of all satisfactions, easy and unreserved society. JOHNSON. "That is an ill-founded notion. Being a King does not exclude a man from such society. Great Kings have always been social. The King of Prussia, the only great King at present, is very social. Charles the Second, the last King of England who was a man of parts, was social; and our Henrys and Edwards were all social."

Mr. Dempster having endeavored to maintain that intrinsic merit *ought* to make the only distinction amongst mankind. JOHNSON. "Why, Sir, mankind have found that this cannot be. How shall we determine the proportion of intrinsic merit? Were that to be the only distinction amongst mankind, we should soon quarrel about the degrees of it. Were all distinctions abolished, the strongest would not long acquiesce, but would endeavor to obtain a superiority by their bodily strength. But, Sir, as subordination is very necessary for society, and contentions for superiority very dangerous, mankind, that is to say, all civilized nations, have settled it upon a plain invariable principle. A man is born to hereditary rank; or his being appointed to certain offices, gives him a certain rank. Subordination tends greatly to human happiness. Were we all upon an equality, we should have no other enjoyment than mere animal pleasure." * * *

He took care to guard himself against any possible suspicion that his settled principles of reverence for rank and respect for wealth were at all owing to mean or interested motives; for he asserted his own independence as a literary man. "No man (said he) who ever lived by literature, has lived more independently than I have done."

Young People (*1763*)

"SIR, I love the acquaintance of young people; because, in the first place, I don't like to think myself growing old. In the next place, young acquaintances must last longest, if they do last; and then, Sir, young men have more virtue than old men: they have more generous sentiments in every respect. I love the young dogs of this age: they have more wit and humor and knowledge of life than we had; but then the dogs are not so good scholars. Sir, in my early years I read very hard. It is a sad reflection, but a true one, that I knew almost as much at eighteen as I do now. My judgment, to be sure, was not so good; but I had all the facts. I remember very well, when I was at Oxford, an old gentleman said to me, 'Young man, ply your book diligently now, and acquire a stock of knowledge; for when years come upon you, you will find that poring upon books will be but an irksome task.' "

A Woman's Preaching (*1763*)

NEXT day, Sunday, July 31, I told him I had been that morning at a meeting of the people called Quakers, where I had heard a woman preach. JOHNSON. "Sir, a woman's preaching is like a dog's walking on his hinder legs. It is not done well; but you are surprised to find it done at all."

George III (*1767*)

IN FEBRUARY, 1767, there happened one of the most remarkable incidents of Johnson's life, which gratified his monarchical enthusiasm, and which he loved to relate with all its circumstances, when requested by his friends. This was his being honored by a private conversation with his Majesty, in the library at the Queen's house. He had frequently visited those splendid rooms and noble collection of books, which he used to say was more numerous and curious than he supposed any person could have made in the time which the King had employed. Mr. Barnard, the librarian, took care that he should have every accommodation that could contribute to his ease and convenience, while indulging his literary taste in that place; so that he had here a very agreeable resource at leisure hours.

His Majesty having been informed of his occasional visits, was pleased to signify a desire that he should be told when Dr. Johnson came next to the library. Accordingly, the next time that Johnson did come, as soon as he was fairly engaged with a book, on which, while he sat by the fire, he seemed quite intent, Mr. Barnard stole round to the apartment where the King was, and, in obedience to his Majesty's commands, mentioned that Dr. Johnson was then in the library. His Majesty said he was at leisure, and would go to him; upon which Mr. Barnard took one of the candles that stood on the King's table, and lighted his Majesty through a suite of rooms, till they came to a private door into the library, of which his Majesty had the key. Being entered, Mr. Barnard stepped forward hastily to Dr. Johnson, who was still in a profound study, and whispered him, "Sir, here is the King." Johnson started up, and stood still. His Majesty approached him, and at once was courteously easy.

His Majesty began by observing, that he understood he came sometimes to the library; and then mentioning his having heard that the Doctor had been lately at Oxford, asked him if he was not fond of going thither. To which Johnson answered, that he was indeed fond of going to Oxford sometimes, but was likewise glad to come back again. The King then asked him what they were doing at Oxford. Johnson answered, he could not much commend their diligence, but that in some respects they were mended, for they had put their press under better regulations, and were at that time printing Polybius. He was then asked whether there were better libraries at Oxford or Cambridge. He answered, he believed the Bodleian was larger than any they had at Cambridge; at the same time adding, "I hope, whether we have more books or not than they have at Cambridge, we shall make as good use of them as they do." Being asked whether All-Souls or Christ-Church library was the largest, he answered, "All-Souls library is the largest we have, except the Bodleian." "Aye (said the King), that is the public library."

His Majesty inquired if he was then writing anything. He answered, he was not, for he had pretty well told the world what he knew, and must now read to acquire more knowledge. The King, as it should seem with a view to urge him to rely on his own stores as an original writer, and to continue his labors, then said "I do not think you borrow much from anybody." Johnson said, he thought he had already done his part as a writer. "I should have thought so too (said the King), if you had not written so well."—Johnson observed to me, upon this, that "No man could have paid a handsomer compliment; and it was fit for a King to pay. It was decisive." When asked by another friend, at Sir Joshua Reynolds's, whether he made any reply to this high compliment, he answered, "No, Sir. When the King had said it, it was to be so. It was not for me to bandy civilities with my Sovereign." Perhaps no man who had spent his whole life in courts could have shown a more nice and dignified sense of true politeness, than Johnson did in this instance.

His Majesty having observed to him that he supposed he must have read a great deal; Johnson answered, that he thought more than he read; that he had read a great deal in the early part of his life, but having fallen into ill health, he had not been able to read much, compared with others: for instance, he said he had not read much, compared with Dr. Warburton. Upon which the King said, that he heard Dr. Warburton[13] was a man of such

[13] William Warburton (1698–1779), Bishop of Gloucester, author of *The Divine Legation of Moses*, and editor of Pope's works.

general knowledge that you could scarce talk with him on any subject on which he was not qualified to speak; and that his learning resembled Garrick's acting, in its universality. His Majesty then talked of the controversy between Warburton and Lowth, which he seemed to have read, and asked Johnson what he thought of it. Johnson answered, "Warburton has most general, most scholastic learning; Lowth is the more correct scholar. I do not know which of them calls names best." The King was pleased to say he was of the same opinion; adding, "You do not think, then, Dr. Johnson, that there was much argument in the case." Johnson said, he did not think there was. "Why truly (said the King), when once it comes to calling names, argument is pretty well at an end."

Criticism (*1769*)

MRS. MONTAGU, a lady distinguished for having written an Essay on Shakespeare, being mentioned; REYNOLDS. "I think that essay does her honor." JOHNSON. "Yes, Sir; it does *her* honor, but it would do nobody else honor. I have, indeed, not read it all. But when I take up the end of a web, and find it packthread, I do not expect, by looking further, to find embroidery. Sir, I will venture to say, there is not one sentence of true criticism in her book." GARRICK. "But, Sir, surely it shows how much Voltaire has mistaken Shakespeare, which nobody else has done." JOHNSON. "Sir, nobody else has thought it worth while. And what merit is there in that? You may as well praise a schoolmaster for whipping a boy who has construed ill. No, Sir, there is no real criticism in it: none showing the beauty of thought, as formed on the workings of the human heart."

The admirers of this Essay may be offended at the slighting manner in which Johnson spoke of it; but let it be remembered, that he gave his honest opinion unbiased by any prejudice, or any proud jealousy of a woman intruding herself into the chair of criticism; for Sir Joshua Reynolds has told me, that when the Essay first came out, and it was not known who had written it, Johnson wondered how Sir Joshua could like it. At this time Sir Joshua himself had received no information concerning the author, except being assured by one of our most eminent literati, that it was clear its author did not know the Greek tragedies in the original. One day at Sir Joshua's table, when it was related that Mrs. Montagu, in an excess of compliment to the author of a modern tragedy, had exclaimed, "I tremble for Shakespeare"; Johnson said "When Shakespeare has got —— for his rival, and Mrs. Montagu for his defender, he is in a poor state indeed."

Johnson proceeded: "The Scotchman[14] has taken the right method in his *Elements of Criticism*. I do not mean that he has taught us anything; but he has told us old things in a new way." MURPHY. "He seems to have read a great deal of French criticism, and wants to make it his own; as if he had been for years anatomizing the heart of man, and peeping into every cranny of it." GOLDSMITH. "It is easier to write that book, than to read it." JOHNSON. "We have an example of true criticism in Burke's *Essay on the Sublime and Beautiful;* and, if I recollect, there is also Du Bos; and Bouhours, who shows all beauty to depend on truth. There is no great merit in telling how many plays have ghosts in them, and how this Ghost is better than that. You must show how terror is impressed on the human heart. In the description of night in *Macbeth,* the beetle and the bat detract from the general idea of darkness,—inspissated gloom."

Sympathy (*1769*)

TALKING of our feeling for the distresses of others;—JOHNSON. "Why, Sir, there is much noise made about it, but it is greatly exaggerated. No, Sir, we have a certain degree of feeling to prompt us to do good: more than that, Providence does not intend. It would be misery to no purpose." BOSWELL. "But suppose now, Sir, that one of your intimate friends were apprehended for an offense for which he might be hanged." JOHNSON. "I should do what I could to bail him, and give him any other assistance;

[14] Henry Home, Lord Kames (1696–1782).

but if he were once fairly hanged, I should not suffer." BOSWELL. "Would you eat your dinner that day, Sir?" JOHNSON. "Yes, Sir; and eat it as if he were eating it with me. Why, there's Baretti, who is to be tried for his life to-morrow; friends have risen up for him on every side; yet if he should be hanged, none of them will eat a slice of plum-pudding the less. Sir, that sympathetic feeling goes a very little way in depressing the mind."

I told him that I had dined lately at Foote's, who showed me a letter which he had received from Tom Davies, telling him that he had not been able to sleep from the concern which he felt on account of "This sad affair of Baretti," begging of him to try if he could suggest anything that might be of service; and, at the same time, recommending to him an industrious young man who kept a pickle-shop. JOHNSON. "Ay, Sir, here you have a specimen of human sympathy; a friend hanged, and a cucumber pickled. We know not whether Baretti or the pickle-man has kept Davies from sleep; nor does he know himself. And as to his not sleeping, Sir; Tom Davies is a very great man; Tom has been upon the stage, and knows how to do those things. I have not been upon the stage, and cannot do those things." BOSWELL. "I have often blamed myself, Sir, for not feeling for others as sensibly as many say they do." JOHNSON. "Sir, don't be duped by them any more. You will find these very feeling people are not very ready to do you good. They *pay* you by *feeling*."

Good Beings (*1772*)

I TALKED of the recent expulsion of six students from the University of Oxford, who were methodists and would not desist from publicly praying and exhorting. JOHNSON. "Sir, that expulsion was extremely just and proper. What have they to do at an University who are not willing to be taught, but will presume to teach? Where is religion to be learned but at an University? Sir, they were examined, and found to be mighty ignorant fellows." BOSWELL. "But, was it not hard, Sir, to expell them, for I am told they were good beings?" JOHNSON. "I believe they might be good beings; but they were not fit to be in the University of Oxford. A cow is a very good animal in the field; but we turn her out of a garden." Lord Elibank used to repeat this as an illustration uncommonly happy.

Reading (*1773*)

ON MONDAY, April 19, he called on me with Mrs. Williams, in Mr. Strahan's coach, and carried me out to dine with Mr. Elphinston, at his academy at Kensington. A printer having acquired a fortune sufficient to keep his coach, was a good topic for the credit of literature. Mrs. Williams said, that another printer, Mr. Hamilton, had not waited so long as Mr. Strahan, but had kept his coach several years sooner. JOHNSON. "He was in the right. Life is short. The sooner that a man begins to enjoy his wealth the better."

Mr. Elphinston talked of a new book that was much admired, and asked Dr. Johnson if he had read it. JOHNSON. "I have looked into it." "What (said Elphinston), have you not read it through?" Johnson, offended at being thus pressed, and so obliged to own his cursory mode of reading, answered tartly, "No, Sir, do *you* read books *through?*"

Ossian (*1775*)

MR. BOSWELL TO DR. JOHNSON.

Edinburgh, Feb. 2, 1775.

. . . As TO Macpherson,[15] I am anxious to have from yourself a full and pointed account of what has passed between you and him. It is confidently told here, that before your book came out he sent to you, to let you know that he understood you meant to deny the authenticity of Ossian's poems; that the originals were in his possession; that you might have inspection of them, and might take the evidence of people skilled in the Erse language; and that he hoped,

[15] James Macpherson (1736–1796) had in 1760 begun publishing what he claimed were translations of ancient poetry composed in the Gaelic (or Erse) tongue by Ossian. These "translations" (it is now agreed they were forgeries) were eagerly accepted in Scotland, were popular on the Continent, and occupy an important place in the rise of Romanticism. Macpherson's prose translation of the *Iliad* of Homer was published in 1773.

after this fair offer, you would not be so uncandid as to assert that he had refused reasonable proof. That you paid no regard to his message, but published your strong attack upon him; and then he wrote a letter to you, in such terms as he thought suited to one who had not acted as a man of veracity. * * *

TO JAMES BOSWELL, ESQ.

My dear Boswell,—I am surprised that, knowing as you do the disposition of your countrymen to tell lies in favor of each other,[16] you can be at all affected by any reports that circulate among them. Macpherson never in his life offered me a sight of any original or of any evidence of any kind; but thought only of intimidating me by noise and threats, till my last answer—that I would not be deterred from detecting what I thought a cheat, by the menaces of a ruffian—put an end to our correspondence.

The state of the question is this. He, and Dr. Blair, whom I consider as deceived, say, that he copied the poem from old manuscripts. His copies, if he had them, and I believe him to have none, are nothing. Where are the manuscripts? They can be shown if they exist, but they were never shown. *De non existentibus et non apparentibus,* says our law, *eadem est ratio.*[17] No man has a claim to credit upon his own word, when better evidence, if he had it, may be easily produced. But, so far as we can find, the Erse language was never written till very lately for the purposes of religion. A nation that cannot write, or a language that was never written, has no manuscripts.

But whatever he has he never offered to show. If old manuscripts should now be mentioned, I should, unless there were more evidence than can be easily had, suppose them another proof of Scotch conspiracy in national falsehood.

Do not censure the expression; you know it to be true. * * *

My compliments to Madam and Veronica.[18]

I am, Sir, Your most humble servant,

Sam. Johnson.

February 7, 1775.

What words were used by Mr. Macpherson in his letter to the venerable Sage, I have never heard; but they are generally said to have been of a nature very different from the language of literary contest. Dr. Johnson's answer appeared in the newspapers of the day, and has since been frequently republished; but not with perfect accuracy. I give it as dictated to me by himself, written down in his presence, and authenticated by a note in his own handwriting, "This, I think, is a true copy."

Mr. James Macpherson,—I received your foolish and impudent letter. Any violence offered me I shall do my best to repel; and what I cannot do for myself, the law shall do for me. I hope I shall never be deterred from detecting what I think a cheat, by the menaces of a ruffian. What would you have me retract? I thought your book an imposture; I think it an imposture still. For this opinion I have given my reasons to the public, which I here dare you to refute. Your rage I defy. Your abilities, since your Homer, are not so formidable; and what I hear of your morals, inclines me to pay regard not to what you shall say, but to what you shall prove. You may print this if you will.

Sam. Johnson.

Mr. Macpherson little knew the character of Dr. Johnson, if he supposed that he could be easily intimidated; for no man was ever more remarkable for personal courage. He had, indeed, an awful dread of death, or rather, "of something after death"; and what rational man, who seriously thinks of quitting all that he has ever known, and going into a new and unknown state of being, can be without that dread? But his fear was from reflection; his courage natural. His fear, in that one instance, was the result of philosophical and religious consideration. He feared death, but he feared nothing else, not even what might occasion death. Many instances of his resolution may be mentioned. One day, at Mr. Beauclerk's house in the country, when two large dogs were fighting, he went up to them, and beat them till they separated; and at another time, when told of the danger there was that a gun might burst if charged with many balls, he put in six or seven, and fired it off against a wall. Mr. Langton told me, that when they were swimming together near Oxford, he cautioned Dr. Johnson against a pool, which was reckoned particularly dangerous; upon which Johnson directly swam into it. He told me

[16] My friend has, in this letter, relied upon my testimony, with a confidence, of which the ground has escaped my recollection (Boswell's note).

[17] Reasoning is identical, says our law, concerning the nonexistent and concerning the invisible.

[18] Boswell's wife and daughter.

himself that one night he was attacked in the street by four men, to whom he would not yield, but kept them all at bay, till the watch came up, and carried both him and them to the round-house. In the playhouse at Lichfield, as Mr. Garrick informed me, Johnson having for a moment quitted a chair which was placed for him between the side-scenes, a gentleman took possession of it, and when Johnson on his return civilly demanded his seat, rudely refused to give it up; upon which Johnson laid hold of it, and tossed him and the chair into the pit. Foote, who so successfully revived the old comedy, by exhibiting living characters, had resolved to imitate Johnson on the stage, expecting great profits from his ridicule of so celebrated a man. Johnson being informed of his intention, and being at dinner at Mr. Thomas Davies's the bookseller, from whom I had the story, he asked Mr. Davies "what was the common price of an oak stick"; and being answered six-pence, "Why then, Sir (said he), give me leave to send your servant to purchase me a shilling one. I'll have a double quantity; for I am told Foote means to *take me off,* as he calls it, and I am determined the fellow shall not do it with impunity." Davies took care to acquaint Foote of this, which effectually checked the wantonness of the mimic. Mr. Macpherson's menaces made Johnson provide himself with the same implement of defense; and had he been attacked, I have no doubt that, old as he was, he would have made his corporal prowess be felt as much as his intellectual.

The Irish (*1775*)

MY MUCH-VALUED friend Dr. Barnard, now Bishop of Killaloe, having once expressed to him an apprehension, that if he should visit Ireland he might treat the people of that country more unfavorably than he had done the Scotch, he answered, with strong pointed double-edged wit, "Sir, you have no reason to be afraid of me. The Irish are not in a conspiracy to cheat the world by false representations of the merits of their countrymen. No, Sir; the Irish are a FAIR PEOPLE;—they never speak well of one another."

The Indistinct Relater (*1775*)

I VISITED him by appointment in the evening, and we drank tea with Mrs. Williams.[19] He told me that he had been in the company of a gentleman whose extraordinary travels had been much the subject of conversation. But I found that he had not listened to him with that full confidence, without which there is little satisfaction in the society of travelers. I was curious to hear what opinion so able a judge as Johnson had formed of his abilities, and I asked if he was not a man of sense. JOHNSON. "Why, Sir, he is not a distinct relater; and I should say, he is neither abounding nor deficient in sense. I did not perceive any superiority of understanding." BOSWELL. "But will you not allow him a nobleness of resolution, in penetrating into distant regions?" JOHNSON. "That, Sir, is not to the present purpose. We are talking of his sense. A fighting cock has a nobleness of resolution."

A Good Thing (*1775*)

NO MORE of his conversation for some days appears in my journal, except that when a gentleman told him he had bought a suit of lace for his lady, he said, "Well, Sir, you have done a good thing and a wise thing." "I have done a good thing (said the gentleman), but I do not know that I have done a wise thing." JOHNSON. "Yes, Sir; no money is better spent than what is laid out for domestic satisfaction. A man is pleased that his wife is dressed as well as other people; and a wife is pleased that she is dressed."

The Felicity of England in Its Taverns (*1776*)

WE DINED at an excellent inn at Chapel House, where he expatiated on the felicity of England in its taverns and inns, and triumphed over the French for not having, in any perfection, the tavern life. "There is no private house (said he), in which people can enjoy themselves so well, as at a capital tav-

[19] A blind and aged woman of letters whom Johnson supported as a member of his household.

ern. Let there be ever so great plenty of good things, ever so much grandeur, ever so much elegance, ever so much desire that everybody should be easy; in the nature of things it cannot be: there must always be some degree of care and anxiety. The master of the house is anxious to entertain his guests; the guests are anxious to be agreeable to him: and no man, but a very impudent dog indeed, can as freely command what is in another man's house, as if it were his own. Whereas, at a tavern, there is a general freedom from anxiety. You are sure you are welcome: and the more noise you make, the more trouble you give, the more good things you call for, the welcomer you are. No servants will attend you with the alacrity which waiters do, who are incited by the prospect of an immediate reward in proportion as they please. No, Sir; there is nothing which has yet been contrived by man, by which so much happiness is produced as by a good tavern or inn."[20] He then repeated, with great emotion, Shenstone's lines:—

> Whoe'er has traveled life's dull round,
> Where'er his stages may have been,
> May sigh to think he still has found
> The warmest welcome at an inn.

Marriage (1776)

WHEN he again talked of Mrs. Careless tonight, he seemed to have had his affection revived; for he said, "If I had married her, it might have been as happy for me." BOSWELL. "Pray, Sir, do you not suppose that there are fifty women in the world, with any one of whom a man may be as happy, as with any one woman in particular?" JOHNSON. "Ay, Sir, fifty thousand." BOSWELL. "Then, Sir, you are not of opinion with some who imagine that certain men and certain women are made for each other; and that they cannot be happy if they miss their counterparts?" JOHNSON. "To be sure not, Sir. I believe marriages would in general be as happy, and often more so, if they were all made by the Lord Chancellor, upon a due consideration of characters and circumstances, without the parties having any choice in the matter."

The Reviews (1776)

"THE Monthly Reviewers (said he) are not Deists;[21] but they are Christians with as little Christianity as may be; and are for pulling down all establishments. The Critical Reviewers are for supporting the constitution both in church and state. The Critical Reviewers, I believe, often review without reading the books through; but lay hold of a topic, and write chiefly from their own minds. The Monthly Reviewers are duller men, and are glad to read the books through."

John Wilkes (1776)

MY DESIRE of being acquainted with celebrated men of every description had made me, much about the same time, obtain an introduction to Dr. Samuel Johnson and to John Wilkes, Esq.[22] Two men more different could perhaps not be selected out of all mankind. They had even attacked one another with some asperity in their writings; yet I lived in habits of friendship with both. I could fully relish the excellence of each;

---

[20] Sir John Hawkins has preserved very few *Memorabilia* of Johnson. There is, however, to be found, in his bulky tome, a very excellent one upon this subject:—"In contradiction to those, who, having a wife and children, prefer domestic enjoyments to those which a tavern affords, I have heard him assert, *that a tavern chair was the throne of human felicity.*—'As soon,' said he, 'as I enter the door of a tavern, I experience an oblivion of care, and a freedom from solicitude: when I am seated, I find the master courteous, and the servants obsequious to my call; anxious to know and ready to supply my wants: wine there exhilarates my spirits, and prompts me to free conversation and an interchange of discourse with those whom I most love. I dogmatize and am contradicted, and in this conflict of opinions and sentiments I find delight' " (Boswell's note).

[21] One who believes in God on the testimony of reason, not of revelation.

[22] Demagogue and man of loose life (1727–1797); editor of the political periodical *The North Briton,* for one number of which he suffered a brief imprisonment, which helped to make him popular. Later he was outlawed, but in 1768 returned to England and was elected to Parliament for Middlesex. He was then imprisoned and in 1769 expelled from Parliament. He was several times reëlected, but each time declared ineligible. In 1774 he became lord mayor of London, and, again elected to Parliament, he was now allowed to sit, and remained a member until 1790.

for I have ever delighted in that intellectual chemistry, which can separate good qualities from evil in the same person.

Sir John Pringle, "mine own friend and my Father's friend," between whom and Dr. Johnson I in vain wished to establish an acquaintance, as I respected and lived in intimacy with both of them, observed to me once, very ingeniously, "It is not in friendship as in mathematics, where two things, each equal to a third, are equal between themselves. You agree with Johnson as a middle quality, and you agree with me as a middle quality; but Johnson and I should not agree." Sir John was not sufficiently flexible; so I desisted; knowing, indeed, that the repulsion was equally strong on the part of Johnson; who, I know not from what cause, unless his being a Scotchman, had formed a very erroneous opinion of Sir John. But I conceived an irresistible wish, if possible, to bring Dr. Johnson and Mr. Wilkes together. How to manage it, was a nice and difficult matter.

My worthy booksellers and friends, Messieurs Dilly in the Poultry, at whose hospitable and well-covered table I have seen a greater number of literary men, than at any other, except that of Sir Joshua Reynolds, had invited me to meet Mr. Wilkes and some more gentlemen on Wednesday, May 15. "Pray (said I), let us have Dr. Johnson."—"What, with Mr. Wilkes? not for the world (said Mr. Edward Dilly): Dr. Johnson would never forgive me."—"Come (said I), if you'll let me negotiate for you, I will be answerable that all shall go well." DILLY. "Nay, if you will take it upon you, I am sure I shall be very happy to see them both here."

Notwithstanding the high veneration which I entertained for Dr. Johnson, I was sensible that he was sometimes a little actuated by the spirit of contradiction, and by means of that I hoped I should gain my point. I was persuaded that if I had come upon him with a direct proposal, "Sir, will you dine in company with Jack Wilkes?" he would have flown into a passion, and would probably have answered, "Dine with Jack Wilkes, Sir! I'd as soon dine with Jack Ketch."[23] I therefore, while we were sitting quietly by ourselves at his house in an evening, took occasion to open my plan thus:—"Mr. Dilly, Sir, sends his respectful compliments to you, and would be happy if you would do him the honor to dine with him on Wednesday next along with me, as I must soon go to Scotland." JOHNSON. "Sir, I am obliged to Mr. Dilly. I will wait upon him—" BOSWELL. "Provided, Sir, I suppose, that the company which he is to have, is agreeable to you." JOHNSON. "What do you mean, Sir? What do you take me for? Do you think I am so ignorant of the world as to imagine that I am to prescribe to a gentleman what company he is to have at his table?" BOSWELL. "I beg your pardon, Sir, for wishing to prevent you from meeting people whom you might not like. Perhaps he may have some of what he calls his patriotic friends with him." JOHNSON. "Well, Sir, and what then? What care *I* for his *patriotic friends?* Poh!" BOSWELL. "I should not be surprised to find Jack Wilkes there." JOHNSON. "And if Jack Wilkes *should* be there, what is that to *me,* Sir? My dear friend, let us have no more of this. I am sorry to be angry with you; but really it is treating me strangely to talk to me as if I could not meet any company whatever, occasionally." BOSWELL. "Pray forgive me, Sir: I meant well. But you shall meet whoever comes, for me." Thus I secured him, and told Dilly that he would find him very well pleased to be one of his guests on the day appointed.

Upon the much-expected Wednesday, I called on him about half an hour before dinner, as I often did when we were to dine out together, to see that he was ready in time, and to accompany him. I found him buffeting his books, as upon a former occasion, covered with dust, and making no preparation for going abroad. "How is this, Sir? (said I). Don't you recollect that you are to dine at Mr. Dilly's?" JOHNSON. "Sir, I did not think of going to Dilly's: it went out of my head. I have ordered dinner at home with Mrs. Williams." BOSWELL. "But, my dear Sir, you know you were engaged to Mr. Dilly, and I told him so. He will expect you, and will be much disap-

[23] An executioner of the seventeenth century, notorious for his barbarity.

pointed if you don't come." JOHNSON. "You must talk to Mrs. Williams about this."

Here was a sad dilemma. I feared that what I was so confident I had secured would yet be frustrated. He had accustomed himself to show Mrs. Williams such a degree of humane attention, as frequently imposed some restraint upon him; and I knew that if she should be obstinate, he would not stir. I hastened down stairs to the blind lady's room, and told her I was in great uneasiness, for Dr. Johnson had engaged to me to dine this day at Mr. Dilly's, but that he had told me he had forgotten his engagement, and had ordered dinner at home. "Yes, Sir (said she, pretty peevishly), Dr. Johnson is to dine at home."—"Madam (said I), his respect for you is such, that I know he will not leave you unless you absolutely desire it. But as you have so much of his company, I hope you will be good enough to forgo it for a day; as Mr. Dilly is a very worthy man, has frequently had agreeable parties at his house for Dr. Johnson, and will be vexed if the Doctor neglects him to-day. And then, Madam, be pleased to consider my situation; I carried the message, and I assured Mr. Dilly that Dr. Johnson was to come, and no doubt he has made a dinner, and invited a company, and boasted of the honor he expected to have. I shall be quite disgraced if the Doctor is not there." She gradually softened to my solicitations, which were certainly as earnest as most entreaties to ladies upon any occasion, and was graciously pleased to empower me to tell Dr. Johnson, "That all things considered, she thought he should certainly go." I flew back to him, still in dust, and careless of what should be the event, "indifferent in his choice to go or stay"; but as soon as I had announced to him Mrs. Williams's consent, he roared, "Frank,[24] a clean shirt," and was very soon dressed. When I had him fairly seated in a hackney-coach with me, I exulted as much as a fortune-hunter who has got an heiress into a post-chaise with him to set out for Gretna Green.[25]

When we entered Mr. Dilly's drawing room, he found himself in the midst of a company he did not know. I kept myself snug and silent, watching how he would conduct himself. I observed him whispering to Mr. Dilly, "Who is that gentleman, Sir?" —"Mr. Arthur Lee."—JOHNSON. "Too, too, too" (under his breath), which was one of his habitual mutterings. Mr. Arthur Lee could not but be very obnoxious to Johnson, for he was not only a *patriot* but an *American*. He was afterwards minister from the United States at the court of Madrid. "And who is the gentleman in lace?"—"Mr. Wilkes, Sir." This information confounded him still more; he had some difficulty to restrain himself, and taking up a book, sat down upon a window-seat and read, or at least kept his eye upon it intently for some time, till he composed himself. His feelings, I dare say, were awkward enough. But he no doubt recollected his having rated me for supposing that he could be at all disconcerted by any company, and he, therefore, resolutely set himself to behave quite as an easy man of the world, who could adapt himself at once to the disposition and manners of those whom he might chance to meet.

The cheering sound of "Dinner is upon the table," dissolved his reverie, and we *all* sat down without any symptom of ill humor. There were present, beside Mr. Wilkes, and Mr. Arthur Lee, who was an old companion of mine when he studied physic at Edinburgh, Mr. (now Sir John) Miller, Dr. Lettsom, and Mr. Slater the druggist. Mr. Wilkes placed himself next to Dr. Johnson, and behaved to him with so much attention and politeness, that he gained upon him insensibly. No man ate more heartily than Johnson, or loved better what was nice and delicate. Mr. Wilkes was very assiduous in helping him to some fine veal. "Pray give me leave, Sir:—It is better here—A little of the brown—Some fat, Sir—A little of the stuffing—Some gravy—Let me have the pleasure of giving you some butter—Allow me to recommend a squeeze of this orange;—or the lemon, perhaps, may have more zest."—"Sir, Sir, I am obliged to you, Sir," cried Johnson, bowing, and turning his head to him with a look for some time of "surly virtue," but, in a short while, of complacency.

Foote being mentioned, Johnson said, "He

[24] Francis Barber, Johnson's negro servant.

[25] The Scotch town, just over the border from England, where run-away marriages were made.

is not a good mimic." One of the company added, "A merry Andrew, a buffoon." JOHNSON. "But he has wit too, and is not deficient in ideas, or in fertility and variety of imagery, and not empty of reading; he has knowledge enough to fill up his part. One species of wit he has in an eminent degree, that of escape. You drive him into a corner with both hands; but he's gone, Sir, when you think you have got him—like an animal that jumps over your head. Then he has a great range for wit; he never lets truth stand between him and a jest, and he is sometimes mighty coarse. Garrick is under many restraints from which Foote is free." WILKES. "Garrick's wit is more like Lord Chesterfield's." JOHNSON. "The first time I was in company with Foote was at Fitzherbert's. Having no good opinion of the fellow, I was resolved not to be pleased; and it is very difficult to please a man against his will. I went on eating my dinner pretty sullenly, affecting not to mind him. But the dog was so very comical, that I was obliged to lay down my knife and fork, throw myself back upon my chair, and fairly laugh it out. No, Sir, he was irresistible. He upon one occasion experienced, in an extraordinary degree, the efficacy of his powers of entertaining. Amongst the many and various modes which he tried of getting money, he became a partner with a small-beer brewer, and he was to have a share of the profits for procuring customers amongst his numerous acquaintance. Fitzherbert was one who took his small-beer; but it was so bad that the servants resolved not to drink it. They were at some loss how to notify their resolution, being afraid of offending their master, who they knew liked Foote much as a companion. At last they fixed upon a little black boy, who was rather a favorite, to be their deputy, and deliver their remonstrance; and having invested him with the whole authority of the kitchen, he was to inform Mr. Fitzherbert, in all their names, upon a certain day, that they would drink Foote's small-beer no longer. On that day Foote happened to dine at Fitzherbert's, and this boy served at table; he was so delighted with Foote's stories, and merriment, and grimace, that when he went down stairs, he told them, 'This is the finest man I have ever seen. I will not deliver your message. I will drink his small-beer.'"

Somebody observed that Garrick could not have done this. WILKES. "Garrick would have made the small-beer still smaller. He is now leaving the stage; but he will play *Scrub*[26] all his life." I knew that Johnson would let nobody attack Garrick but himself, as Garrick once said to me, and I had heard him praise his liberality; so to bring out his commendation of his celebrated pupil, I said, loudly, "I have heard Garrick is liberal." JOHNSON. "Yes, Sir, I know that Garrick has given away more money than any man in England that I am acquainted with, and that not from ostentatious views. Garrick was very poor when he began life; so when he came to have money, he probably was very unskillful in giving away, and saved when he should not. But Garrick began to be liberal as soon as he could; and I am of opinion, the reputation of avarice which he has had, has been very lucky for him, and prevented his having many enemies. You despise a man for avarice, but do not hate him. Garrick might have been much better attacked for living with more splendor than is suitable to a player: if they had had the wit to have assaulted him in that quarter, they might have galled him more. But they have kept clamoring about his avarice, which has rescued him from much obloquy and envy."

Talking of the great difficulty of obtaining authentic information for biography, Johnson told us, "When I was a young fellow I wanted to write the *Life of Dryden*, and in order to get materials, I applied to the only two persons then alive who had seen him; these were old Swinney, and old Cibber. Swinney's information was no more than this, 'That at Will's coffee-house Dryden had a particular chair for himself, which was set by the fire in winter, and was then called his winter-chair; and that it was carried out for him to the balcony in summer, and was then called his summer-chair.' Cibber could tell no more but 'That he remembered him a decent old man, arbiter of critical disputes at Will's.' You are to con-

[26]A servant in George Farquhar's *Beaux' Stratagem.*

sider that Cibber was then at a great distance from Dryden, had perhaps one leg only in the room, and durst not draw in the other." BOSWELL. "Yet Cibber was a man of observation?" JOHNSON. "I think not." BOSWELL. "You will allow his *Apology* to be well done." JOHNSON. "Very well done, to be sure, Sir. That book is a striking proof of the justice of Pope's remark:

> Each might his several province well command,
> Would all but stoop to what they understand."[27]

BOSWELL. "And his plays are good." JOHNSON. "Yes; but that was his trade; *l'esprit du corps:* he had been all his life among players and play-writers. I wondered that he had so little to say in conversation, for he had kept the best company, and learned all that can be got by the ear. He abused Pindar to me, and then showed me an Ode of his own, with an absurd couplet, making a linnet soar on an eagle's wing. I told him that when the ancients made a simile, they always made it like something real."

Mr. Wilkes remarked, that "among all the bold flights of Shakespeare's imagination, the boldest was making Birnam Wood march to Dunsinane; creating a wood where there never was a shrub; a wood in Scotland! ha! ha! ha!" And he also observed, that "the clannish slavery of the Highlands of Scotland was the single exception to Milton's remark of 'The Mountain Nymph, sweet Liberty,'[28] being worshiped in all hilly countries."—"When I was at Inverary (said he) on a visit to my old friend, Archibald, Duke of Argyle, his dependents congratulated me on being such a favorite of his Grace. I said, 'It is then, gentlemen, truly lucky for me; for if I had displeased the Duke, and he had wished it, there is not a Campbell among you but would have been ready to bring John Wilkes's head to him in a charger. It would have been only

> Off with his head! So much for Aylesbury.'

I was then member for Aylesbury." * * *

Mr. Arthur Lee mentioned some Scotch who had taken possession of a barren part of America, and wondered why they should choose it. JOHNSON. "Why, Sir, all barrenness is comparative. The *Scotch* would not know it to be barren." BOSWELL. "Come, come, he is flattering the English. You have now been in Scotland, Sir, and say if you did not see meat and drink enough there." JOHNSON. "Why yes, Sir; meat and drink enough to give the inhabitants sufficient strength to run away from home." All these quick and lively sallies were said sportively, quite in jest, and with a smile, which showed that he meant only wit. Upon this topic he and Mr. Wilkes could perfectly assimilate; here was a bond of union between them, and I was conscious that as both of them had visited Caledonia, both were fully satisfied of the strange narrow ignorance of those who imagine that it is a land of famine. But they amused themselves with persevering in the old jokes. When I claimed a superiority for Scotland over England in one respect, that no man can be arrested there for a debt merely because another swears it against him; but there must first be the judgment of a court of law ascertaining its justice; and that a seizure of the person, before judgment is obtained, can take place only if his creditor should swear that he is about to fly from the country, or, as it is technically expressed, is *in meditatione fugae:* WILKES. "That, I should think, may be safely sworn of all the Scotch nation." JOHNSON. (to Mr. Wilkes) "You must know, Sir, I lately took my friend Boswell and showed him genuine civilized life in an English provincial town. I turned him loose at Lichfield, my native city, that he might see for once real civility: for you know he lives among savages in Scotland, and among rakes in London." WILKES. "Except when he is with grave, sober, decent people like you and me." JOHNSON. (smiling) "And we ashamed of him."

A Bad Style of Poetry (1777)

HE OBSERVED, that a gentleman of eminence in literature had got into a bad style of poetry of late. "He puts (said he) a very common thing in a strange dress till he does not know it himself, and thinks other people do not know it." BOSWELL. "That is owing to his being so much versant in old

[27] *Essay on Criticism,* I, 66–67. [28] *L'Allegro,* 36.

English poetry." JOHNSON. "What is that to the purpose, Sir? If I say a man is drunk, and you tell me it is owing to his taking much drink, the matter is not mended. No, Sir, ——[29] has taken to an odd mode. For example, he'd write thus:

Hermit hoar, in solemn cell,
Wearing out life's evening gray.

Gray evening is common enough; but *evening gray* he'd think fine.—Stay;—we'll make out the stanza:

Hermit hoar, in solemn cell,
Wearing out life's evening gray;
Smite thy bosom, sage, and tell,
What is bliss? and which the way?"

BOSWELL. "But why smite his bosom, Sir?" JOHNSON. "Why, to show he was in earnest" (smiling).—He at an after period added the following stanza:

Thus I spoke; and speaking sighed;
—Scarce repressed the starting tears;—
When the smiling sage replied—
—Come, my lad, and drink some beer.

Happiness (*1777*)

IN OUR way, Johnson strongly expressed his love of driving fast in a post-chaise. "If (said he) I had no duties, and no reference to futurity, I would spend my life in driving briskly in a post-chaise with a pretty woman; but she should be one who could understand me, and would add something to the conversation."

London (*1777*)

WE ENTERED seriously upon a question of much importance to me, which Johnson was pleased to consider with friendly attention. I had long complained to him that I felt myself discontented in Scotland, as too narrow a sphere, and that I wished to make my chief residence in London, the great scene of ambition, instruction, and amusement: a scene, which was to me, comparatively speaking, a heaven upon earth. JOHNSON. "Why, Sir, I never knew any one who had such a *gust* for London as you have: and I cannot blame you for your wish to live there: yet, Sir, were I in your father's place, I should not consent to your settling there; for I have the old feudal notions, and I should be afraid that Auchinleck would be deserted, as you would soon find it more desirable to have a country-seat in a better climate." * * *

I suggested a doubt, that if I were to reside in London, the exquisite zest with which I relished it in occasional visits might go off, and I might grow tired of it. JOHNSON. "Why, Sir, you find no man, at all intellectual, who is willing to leave London. No, Sir, when a man is tired of London, he is tired of life; for there is in London all that life can afford."

Oliver Edwards (*1778*)

AND now I am to give a pretty full account of one of the most curious incidents in Johnson's life, of which he himself has made the following minute on this day: "In my return from church, I was accosted by Edwards, an old fellow-collegian, who had not seen me since 1729. He knew me, and asked if I remembered one Edwards; I did not at first recollect the name, but gradually as we walked along, recovered it, and told him a conversation that had passed at an ale-house between us. My purpose is to continue our acquaintance."

It was in Butcher Row that this meeting happened. Mr. Edwards, who was a decent-looking elderly man in gray clothes, and a wig of many curls, accosted Johnson with familiar confidence, knowing who he was, while Johnson returned his salutation with a courteous formality, as to a stranger. But as soon as Edwards had brought to his recollection their having been at Pembroke College together nine-and-forty years ago, he seemed much pleased, asked where he lived, and said he should be glad to see him in Bolt Court. EDWARDS. "Ah, Sir! we are old men now." JOHNSON. (who never liked to think of being old), "Don't let us discourage one another." EDWARDS. "Why, Doctor, you look stout and hearty, I am happy to see you so; for the newspapers told us you were very ill." JOHNSON. "Ay, Sir, they are always telling lies of *us old fellows.*"

Wishing to be present at more of so singu-

[29]Thomas Warton (1728–1790).

lar a conversation as that between two fellow-collegians, who had lived forty years in London without ever having chanced to meet, I whispered to Mr. Edwards that Dr. Johnson was going home, and that he had better accompany him now. So Edwards walked along with us, I eagerly assisting to keep up the conversation. Mr. Edwards informed Dr. Johnson that he had practiced long as a solicitor in Chancery, but that he now lived in the country upon a little farm, about sixty acres, just by Stevenage in Hertfordshire, and that he came to London (to Barnard's Inn, No. 6), generally twice a week. Johnson appearing to me in a reverie, Mr. Edwards addressed himself to me, and expatiated on the pleasure of living in the country. BOSWELL. "I have no notion of this, Sir. What you have to entertain you, is, I think, exhausted in half an hour." EDWARDS. "What? don't you love to have hope realized? I see my grass, and my corn, and my trees growing. Now, for instance, I am curious to see if this frost has not nipped my fruit-trees." JOHNSON. (who we did not imagine was attending) "You find, Sir, you have fears as well as hopes."—So well did he see the whole, when another saw but the half of a subject.

When we got to Dr. Johnson's house, and were seated in his library, the dialogue went on admirably. EDWARDS. "Sir, I remember you would not let us say *prodigious* at College. For even then, Sir (turning to me), he was delicate in language, and we all feared him."[30] JOHNSON. (to Edwards) "From your having practiced the law long, Sir, I presume you must be rich." EDWARDS. "No, Sir; I got a good deal of money; but I had a number of poor relations to whom I gave a great part of it." JOHNSON. "Sir, you have been rich in the most valuable sense of the word." EDWARDS. "But I shall not die rich." JOHNSON. "Nay, sure, Sir, it is better to *live* rich than to *die* rich." EDWARDS. "I wish I had continued at College." JOHNSON. "Why do you wish that, Sir?" EDWARDS. "Because I think I should have had a much easier life than mine has been. I should have been a parson, and had a good living, like Bloxam and several others, and lived comfortably." JOHNSON. "Sir, the life of a parson, of a conscientious clergyman, is not easy. I have always considered a clergyman as the father of a larger family than he is able to maintain. I would rather have Chancery suits upon my hands than the cure of souls. No, Sir, I do not envy a clergyman's life as an easy life, nor do I envy the clergyman who makes it an easy life." Here taking himself up all of a sudden, he exclaimed, "O! Mr. Edwards! I'll convince you that I recollect you. Do you remember our drinking together at an alehouse near Pembroke gate? At that time, you told me of the Eton boy, who, when verses on our SAVIOR's turning water into wine were prescribed as an exercise, brought up a single line, which was highly admired,—

Vidit et erubuit lympha pudica DEUM,[31]

and I told you of another fine line in Camden's *Remains,* an eulogy upon one of our Kings, who was succeeded by his son, a prince of equal merit:—

Mira cano, Sol occubuit, nox nulla secuta est."[32]

EDWARDS. "You are a philosopher, Dr. Johnson. I have tried too in my time to be a philosopher; but, I don't know how, cheerfulness was always breaking in."—Mr. Burke, Sir Joshua Reynolds, Mr. Courtenay, Mr. Malone, and, indeed, all the eminent men to whom I have mentioned this, have thought it an exquisite trait of character. The truth is, that philosophy, like religion, is too generally supposed to be hard and severe, at least so grave as to exclude all gayety.

EDWARDS. "I have been twice married, Doctor. You, I suppose, have never known

[30]Johnson said to me afterwards, "Sir, they respected me for my literature; and yet it was not great but by comparison. Sir, it is amazing how little literature there is in the world" (Boswell's note).

[31]The line is really lifted (as the "Mr. Malone" of the next paragraph later discovered) from an epigram, on the miracle of the water turned into wine, by Richard Crashaw: "The modest spring has seen her God and blushed."

[32]Camden says that some ascribe this line, written to "honor King Henry II, then departed, and King Richard succeeding," to Giraldus Cambrensis: "I sing of wonders, the Sun has set, yet no night has followed."

what it was to have a wife." JOHNSON. "Sir, I have known what it was to have a wife, and (in a solemn, tender, faltering tone) I have known what it was to *lose a wife.*—It had almost broke my heart." 5

EDWARDS. "How do you live, Sir? For my part, I must have my regular meals, and a glass of good wine. I find I require it." JOHNSON. "I now drink no wine, Sir. Early in life I drank wine: for many years 10 I drank none. I then for some years drank a great deal." EDWARDS. "Some hogsheads, I warrant you." JOHNSON. "I then had a severe illness, and left it off, and I have never begun it again. I never felt any 15 difference upon myself from eating one thing rather than another, nor from one kind of weather rather than another. There are people, I believe, who feel a difference; but I am not one of them. And as to 20 regular meals, I have fasted from the Sunday's dinner to the Tuesday's dinner, without any inconvenience. I believe it is best to eat just as one is hungry: but a man who is in business, or a man who has a family, 25 must have stated meals. I am a straggler. I may leave this town and go to Grand Cairo, without being missed here or observed there." EDWARDS. "Don't you eat supper, Sir?" JOHNSON. "No, Sir." EDWARDS. 30 "For my part, now, I consider supper as a turnpike through which one must pass, in order to get to bed."

JOHNSON. "You are a lawyer, Mr. Edwards. Lawyers know life practically. A 35 bookish man should always have them to converse with. They have what he wants." EDWARDS. "I am grown old: I am sixty-five." JOHNSON. "I shall be sixty-eight next birthday. Come, Sir, drink water, and 40 put in for a hundred." * * *

This interview confirmed my opinion of Johnson's most humane and benevolent heart. His cordial and placid behavior to an old fellow-collegian, a man so different 45 from himself; and his telling him that he would go down to his farm and visit him, showed a kindness of disposition very rare at an advanced age. He observed, "how wonderful it was that they had both been 50 in London forty years, without having ever once met, and both walkers in the street too!"

Mr. Edwards, when going away, again recurred to his consciousness of senility, and looking full in Johnson's face, said to him, "You'll find in Dr. Young,

O my coevals! remnants of yourselves."[33]

Johnson did not relish this at all; but shook his head with impatience. Edwards walked off, seemingly highly pleased with the honor of having been thus noticed by Dr. Johnson. When he was gone, I said to Johnson, I thought him but a weak man. JOHNSON. "Why, yes, Sir. Here is a man who has passed through life without experience: yet I would rather have him with me than a more sensible man who will not talk readily. This man is always willing to say what he has to say." Yet Dr. Johnson had himself by no means that willingness which he praised so much, and I think so justly; for who has not felt the painful effect of the dreary void, when there is a total silence in a company, for any length of time; or, which is as bad, or perhaps worse, when the conversation is with difficulty kept up by a perpetual effort?

Johnson once observed to me, "Tom Tyers described me the best: 'Sir (said he), you are like a ghost: you never speak till you are spoken to.'"

Bad Management (*1778*)

ON MONDAY, April 20, I found him at home in the morning. We talked of a gentleman who we apprehended was gradually involving his circumstances by bad management. JOHNSON. "Wasting a fortune is evaporation by a thousand imperceptible means. If it were a stream, they'd stop it. You must speak to him. It is really miserable. Were he a gamester, it could be said he had hopes of winning. Were he a bankrupt in trade, he might have grown rich; but he has neither spirit to spend nor resolution to spare. He does not spend fast enough to have pleasure from it. He has the crime of prodigality, and the wretchedness of parsimony. If a man is killed in a duel, he is killed as many a one has been killed; but it is a sad thing for a man to lie down and die; to bleed to death, because he

[33] *Night Thoughts,* IV, 109.

has not fortitude enough to sear the wound, or even to stitch it up." I cannot but pause a moment to admire the fecundity of fancy, and choice of language, which in this instance, and, indeed, on almost all occasions, he displayed. It was well observed by Dr. Percy, now Bishop of Dromore, "The conversation of Johnson is strong and clear, and may be compared to an antique statue, where every vein and muscle is distinct and bold. Ordinary conversation resembles an inferior cast."

The First Whig (1778)

BOSWELL. "I drank chocolate, Sir, this morning with Mr. Eld; and, to my no small surprise, found him to be a *Staffordshire Whig,* a being which I did not believe had existed." JOHNSON. "Sir, there are rascals in all countries." BOSWELL. "Eld said, a Tory was a creature generated between a non-juring parson and one's grandmother." JOHNSON. "And I have always said, the first whig was the Devil." BOSWELL. "He certainly was, Sir. The Devil was impatient of subordination; he was the first who resisted power:—

Better to reign in Hell, than serve in Heaven."[34]

Kindness (1783)

JOHNSON's love of little children, which he discovered upon all occasions, calling them "pretty dears," and giving them sweetmeats, was an undoubted proof of the real humanity and gentleness of his disposition.

His uncommon kindness to his servants, and serious concern, not only for their comfort in this world, but their happiness in the next, was another unquestionable evidence of what all, who were intimately acquainted with him, knew to be true.

Nor would it be just, under this head, to omit the fondness which he showed for animals which he had taken under his protection. I never shall forget the indulgence with which he treated Hodge, his cat: for whom he himself used to go out and buy oysters, lest the servants having that trouble should take a dislike to the poor creature. I am, unluckily, one of those who have an antipathy to a cat, so that I am uneasy when in the room with one; and I own, I frequently suffered a good deal from the presence of this same Hodge. I recollect him one day scrambling up Dr. Johnson's breast, apparently with much satisfaction, while my friend smiling and half-whistling, rubbed down his back, and pulled him by the tail; and when I observed he was a fine cat, saying, "Why yes, Sir, but I have had cats whom I liked better than this"; and then as if perceiving Hodge to be out of countenance, adding, "but he is a very fine cat, a very fine cat indeed."

This reminds me of the ludicrous account which he gave Mr. Langton, of the despicable state of a young Gentleman of good family. "Sir, when I heard of him last, he was running about town shooting cats." And then in a sort of kindly reverie, he bethought himself of his own favorite cat, and said, "But Hodge shan't be shot; no, no, Hodge shall not be shot."

Cant (1783)

BOSWELL. "I wish much to be in Parliament, Sir." JOHNSON. "Why, Sir, unless you come resolved to support any administration, you would be the worse for being in Parliament, because you would be obliged to live more expensively." BOSWELL. "Perhaps, Sir, I should be the less happy for being in Parliament. I never would sell my vote, and I should be vexed if things went wrong." JOHNSON. "That's cant, Sir. It would not vex you more in the House, than in the gallery: public affairs vex no man." BOSWELL. "Have not they vexed yourself a little, Sir? Have not you been vexed by all the turbulence of this reign, and by that absurd vote of the House of Commons, 'That the influence of the Crown has increased, is increasing, and ought to be diminished?'" JOHNSON. "Sir, I have never slept an hour less, nor eat an ounce less meat. I would have knocked the factious dogs on the head, to be sure; but I was not *vexed.*" BOSWELL. "I declare, Sir, upon my honor, I did imagine I was vexed, and took a pride in it; but it *was,* perhaps, cant; for I own I neither ate

[34]*Paradise Lost,* I, 263.

less, nor slept less." JOHNSON. "My dear friend, clear your *mind* of cant. You may *talk* as other people do: you may say to a man, 'Sir, I am your most humble servant.' You are *not* his most humble servant. You may say, 'These are bad times; it is a melancholy thing to be reserved to such times.' You don't mind the times. You tell a man, 'I am sorry you had such bad weather the last day of your journey, and were so much wet.' You don't care six-pence whether he is wet or dry. You may *talk* in this manner; it is a mode of talking in Society: but don't *think* foolishly."

OLIVER GOLDSMITH

1728–1774

Goldsmith's family was of English origin, but had long been settled in Ireland when he was born there on 10 November, 1728. His father was a clergyman and farmer, with a small income and a large family. Oliver has sketched the elder Goldsmith's character in the narrative of the Man in Black in *The Citizen of the World,* and it is said that all members of the family were "equally generous, credulous, simple," and improvident. The greater part of Oliver's boyhood was passed in the village of Lissoy, where he was given some rather irregular instruction, and whence he proceeded in 1744 to Trinity College, Dublin. There he was entered as a poor scholar, or "sizar," a position humiliating to one of his sensitiveness of temper. He was also unfortunate in having a tutor who delighted in two subjects which Goldsmith detested—logic and mathematics—and who was apparently rather brutal besides. In addition, Goldsmith's awkwardness, ungainly appearance, and mental unreadiness—not to speak of his infractions of collegiate rules—all made against his academic success. He did, however, manage to obtain the degree of B. A. in 1749. His relatives wanted him to become a clergyman, and he unwillingly undertook to prepare himself for ordination; but when he presented himself to Bishop Synge of Elphin he was rejected because, according to tradition, he was wearing a pair of flaming scarlet breeches. A period of uncertain groping for a career followed, in which money was spent or lost which Goldsmith's relatives and now widowed mother could ill afford. Finally, early in 1753, Goldsmith reached Edinburgh to study medicine. There he attended some lectures, probably not working overmuch, and then went to Leyden to continue his studies. From Leyden he presently set out, "with one shirt in his pocket and a devout reliance on Providence," as Sir Walter Scott says, to travel through Europe on foot. By one means or another he succeeded in procuring subsistence as he walked through Flanders, France, Germany, Switzerland, and Italy, learning much which he afterwards put to literary use, and obtaining, it is said, a medical degree at either Louvain or Padua. Early in 1756 he was back again in England, living miserably in London, and trying with little or no success to earn a bare living by various occupations. By 1760 he had drifted into hackwriting for the booksellers, and this he continued until his death on 4 April, 1774.

Goldsmith was the master of an easy, finished style—he touched no branch of literature that he did not adorn, wrote Dr. Johnson in the Latin epitaph inscribed on his monument in Westminster Abbey—and, despite his irregular habits, the booksellers found him a profitable servant. He compiled histories of Rome, Greece, and England, *A History of the Earth and Animated Nature,* and many another work which cannot even be mentioned here. Of the *Animated Nature* Dr. Johnson said: "He is now writing a Natural History, and will make it as interesting as a Persian tale." According to Lee Lewes, an actor, Goldsmith used to say that of all his compilations "his *Selections of English Poetry* showed more 'the art of profession.' Here he did nothing but mark the particular passages with a red lead pencil, and for this he got *two hundred pounds*—but then he used to add, 'a man shows his judgment in these selections, and he may be often twenty years of his life cultivating that judgment.'" It has been estimated that in the later years of his life Goldsmith's income from literary work may have been as high as £800 a year. He never learned, however, how to control his expenditures; as his income rose so did his debts, with the result that he was never free from financial difficulties, and at the time of his death owed not less than £2000. "Was ever poet," asked Dr. Johnson, "so trusted before?"

Much of Goldsmith's writing was ephemeral and perished with his age, yet he contrived to give lasting interest to a surprising variety of work, and is still remembered as essayist (*The Citizen of the World,* 1760–1761), as poet (*The Traveler,* 1764; *The Deserted Village,* 1770; *Retaliation,* 1774), as novelist (*The Vicar of*

Wakefield, 1766), and as playwright (*The Good-Natured Man,* 1768; *She Stoops to Conquer,* 1773). Probably he took greater care with his poems than with anything else, as we know that he wrote them very slowly and spent much time in revising them. *The Vicar of Wakefield,* on the other hand, he never revised, although it was not published until several years after it was written. It was, he explained, already paid for, so that there was no need to take further trouble with it. Yet, as Scott says, "we read *The Vicar of Wakefield* in youth and in age. We return to it again and again, and bless the memory of an author who contrives so well to reconcile us to human nature." Keen observation lay always behind Goldsmith's quiet satire, to give substance to this happy reconciliation; but it is his exquisite good humor which his readers remember best and longest. "Who," asked Thackeray, "of the millions whom he has amused, does not love him? To be the most beloved of English writers, what a title that is for a man!"

Goldsmith's *Citizen of the World* has been edited by Austin Dobson (London, 1891); his poems are available in *The Miscellaneous Works of Oliver Goldsmith,* ed. David Masson (London, 1868). Of the older biographies the best known is John Forster's *Life and Adventures of Oliver Goldsmith* (London, 1848); Stephen Gwynn's *Oliver Goldsmith* (London, 1935) is a more up-to-date and sympathetic account. William M. Thackeray has written one of his most typical essays on "Sterne and Goldsmith" in *The English Humorists of the Eighteenth Century,* ed. W. L. Phelps (New York, 1900).

THE CITIZEN OF THE WORLD[1]

or,

Letters from a Chinese Philosopher, Residing in London, to His Friends in the East

LETTER XIII

From Lien Chi Altangi to Fum Hoam, First President of the Ceremonial Academy at Pekin, in China

AN ACCOUNT OF WESTMINSTER ABBEY

I AM just returned from Westminster Abbey, the place of sepulture for the philosophers, heroes, and kings of England. What a gloom do monumental inscriptions, and all the venerable remains of deceased merit inspire! Imagine a temple marked with the hand of antiquity, solemn as religious awe, adorned with all the magnificence of barbarous profusion, dim windows, fretted pillars, long colonnades, and dark ceilings. Think, then, what were my sensations at being introduced to such a scene. I stood in the midst of the temple, and threw my eyes round on the walls, filled with the statues, the inscriptions, and the monuments of the dead.

Alas! I said to myself, how does pride attend the puny child of dust even to the grave! Even humble as I am, I possess more consequence in the present scene than the greatest hero of them all: they have toiled for an hour to gain a transient immortality, and are at length retired to the grave, where they have no attendant but the worm, none to flatter but the epitaph.

As I was indulging such reflections, a gentleman dressed in black, perceiving me to be a stranger, came up, entered into conversation, and politely offered to be my instructor and guide through the temple. "If any monument," said he, "should particularly excite your curiosity, I shall endeavor to satisfy your demands." I accepted, with thanks, the gentleman's offer, adding, that "I was come to observe the policy, the wisdom, and the justice of the English, in conferring rewards upon deceased merit. If adulation like this," continued I, "be properly conducted, as it can

[1]These essays first appeared in a newspaper, *The Public Ledger,* in 1760–1761, and were then collected and published (with some changes and additions) in 1762. Goldsmith's device of writing over the name of an imaginary Asiatic was not of his own invention. He had before him the example of Montesquieu, of Voltaire, and of other French writers, and also, closer at hand, of Horace Walpole's very popular *Letter from Xo Ho, a Chinese Philosopher at London, to his Friend Lien-Chi, at Peking* (1757).

no ways injure those who are flattered, so it may be a glorious incentive to those who are now capable of enjoying it. It is the duty of every good government to turn this monumental pride to its own advantage; to become strong in the aggregate from the weakness of the individual. If none but the truly great have a place in this awful repository, a temple like this will give the finest lessons of morality, and be a strong incentive to true ambition. I am told that none have a place here but characters of the most distinguished merit." The man in black seemed impatient at my observations, so I discontinued my remarks, and we walked on together to take a view of every particular monument in order as it lay.

As the eye is naturally caught by the finest objects, I could not avoid being particularly curious about one monument, which appeared more beautiful than the rest: "That," said I to my guide, "I take to be the tomb of some very great man. By the peculiar excellence of the workmanship, and the magnificence of the design, this must be a trophy raised to the memory of some king who has saved his country from ruin, or lawgiver who has reduced his fellow-citizens from anarchy into just subjection."—"It is not requisite," replied my companion, smiling, "to have such qualifications in order to have a very fine monument here: more humble abilities will suffice."—"What, I suppose, then, the gaining two or three battles, or the taking half a score towns, is thought a sufficient qualification?"—"Gaining battles, or taking towns," replied the man in black, "may be of service; but a gentleman may have a very fine monument here without ever seeing a battle or a siege."—"This, then, is the monument of some poet, I presume—of one whose wit has gained him immortality?"—"No, Sir," replied my guide, "the gentleman who lies here never made verses; and as for wit, he despised it in others, because he had none himself."—"Pray tell me, then, in a word," said I, peevishly, "what is the great man who lies here particularly remarkable for?" —"Remarkable, Sir?" said my companion; "why, Sir, the gentleman that lies here is remarkable, very remarkable—for a tomb in Westminster Abbey."—"But, head of my Ancestors! how has he got here? I fancy he could never bribe the guardians of the temple to give him a place: should he not be ashamed to be seen among company where even moderate merit would look like infamy?"—"I suppose," replied the man in black, "the gentleman was rich, and his friends, as is usual in such a case, told him he was great. He readily believed them; the guardians of the temple, as they got by the self-delusion, were ready to believe him too; so he paid his money for a fine monument; and the workman, as you see, has made him one of the most beautiful. Think not, however, that this gentleman is singular in his desire of being buried among the great; there are several others in the temple, who, hated and shunned by the great while alive, have come here, fully resolved to keep them company now they are dead."

As we walked along to a particular part of the temple, "There," says the gentleman, pointing with his finger, "that is the Poet's Corner; there you see the monuments of Shakespeare, and Milton, and Prior, and Drayton."—"Drayton!" I replied; "I never heard of him before; but I have been told of one Pope—is he there?"—"It is time enough," replied my guide, "these hundred years; he is not long dead; people have not done hating him yet."—"Strange," cried I; "can any be found to hate a man whose life was wholly spent in entertaining and instructing his fellow-creatures?"—"Yes," says my guide, "they hate him for that very reason. There are a set of men called answerers of books, who take upon them to watch the republic of letters, and distribute reputation by the sheet; they somewhat resemble the eunuchs in a seraglio, who are incapable of giving pleasure themselves, and hinder those that would. These answerers have no other employment but to cry out Dunce and Scribbler; to praise the dead, and revile the living; to grant a man of confessed abilities some small share of merit; to applaud twenty blockheads in order to gain the reputation of candor; and to revile the moral character of the man whose writings they cannot injure. Such wretches are kept in pay by some mercenary bookseller, or, more frequently, the bookseller himself takes this dirty work off their hands, as all that is required is to be very abusive and very dull. Every poet of any genius is sure to find such enemies; he feels, though he seems to despise their malice; they make him miserable here, and in the pursuit of empty fame, at last he gains solid anxiety."

"Has this been the case with every poet I see here?" cried I. "Yes, with every mother's son of them," replied he, "except he happened to be born a mandarin. If he has much money, he may buy reputation from your book-answerers, as well as a monument from the guardians of the temple."

"But are there not some men of distinguished taste, as in China, who are willing to patronize men of merit, and soften the rancor of malevolent dullness?"

"I own there are many," replied the man in black; "but, alas! Sir, the book-answerers crowd about them, and call themselves the writers of books; and the patron is too indolent to distinguish: thus poets are kept at a distance, while their enemies eat up all their rewards at the mandarin's table."

Leaving this part of the temple, we made up to an iron gate, through which my companion told me we were to pass, in order to see the monuments of the kings. Accordingly, I marched up without further ceremony, and was going to enter, when a person, who held the gate in his hand, told me I must pay first. I was surprised at such a demand; and asked the man, whether the people of England kept a *show*—whether the paltry sum he demanded was not a national reproach?—whether it was not more to the honor of the country to let their magnificence, or their antiquities, be openly seen, than thus meanly to tax a curiosity which tended to their own honor? "As for your questions," replied the gate-keeper, "to be sure they may be very right, because I don't understand them; but, as for that there threepence, I farm it from one—who rents it from another—who hires it from a third—who leases it from the guardians of the temple, —and we all must live." I expected, upon paying here, to see something extraordinary, since what I had seen for nothing filled me with so much surprise: but in this I was disappointed; there was little more within than black coffins, rusty armor, tattered standards, and some few slovenly figures in wax. I was sorry I had paid, but I comforted myself by considering it would be my last payment. A person attended us, who, without once blushing, told a hundred lies: he talked of a lady who died by pricking her finger;[2] of a king with a golden head,[3] and twenty such pieces of absurdity. "Look ye there, gentleman," says he, pointing to an old oak chair, "there's a curiosity for ye; in that chair the kings of England were crowned: you see also a stone underneath, and that stone is Jacob's pillow." I could see no curiosity either in the oak chair or the stone: could I, indeed, behold one of the old kings of England seated in this, or Jacob's head laid upon the other, there might be something curious in the sight; but in the present case, there was no more reason for my surprise, than if I should pick a stone from their streets, and call it a curiosity, merely because one of the kings happened to tread upon it as he passed in the procession.

From hence our conductor led us through several dark walks and winding ways, uttering lies, talking to himself, and flourishing a wand which he held in his hand. He reminded me of the black magicians of Kobi.[4] After we had been almost fatigued with a variety of objects, he at last desired me to consider attentively a certain suit of armor, which seemed to show nothing remarkable, "This armor," said he, "belonged to General Monk."[5]—"Very surprising that a general should wear armor!"—"And pray," added he, "observe this cap; this is General Monk's cap."—"Very strange, indeed, very strange, that a general should have a cap also! Pray, friend, what might this cap have cost originally?"—"That, Sir," says he, "I don't know; but this cap is all the wages I have for my trouble."—"A very small recompense, truly," said I. "Not so very small," replied he, "for every gentleman puts some money into

[2]Lady Elizabeth Russell. Her tomb is in the chapel of St. Edmund.

[3]The head (of the figure of Henry V, chapel of St. Edward) was of silver, but it had disappeared before the close of the sixteenth century.

[4]Or Gobi, the desert of central Asia.

[5]George Monk (1608–1670), parliamentary general in the Civil Wars.

it, and I spend the money." "What—more money! still more money!"—"Every gentleman gives something, Sir."—"I'll give thee nothing," returned I; "the guardians of the temple should pay you your wages, friend, and not permit you to squeeze thus from every spectator. When we pay our money at the door to see a show, we never give more as we are going out. Sure, the guardians of the temple can never think they get enough. Show me the gate; if I stay longer I may probably meet with more of those ecclesiastical beggars."

Thus leaving the temple precipitately, I returned to my lodgings, in order to ruminate over what was great, and to despise what was mean, in the occurrences of the day.

LETTER XXI

To the Same

THE CHINESE GOES TO SEE A PLAY

THE English are as fond of seeing plays acted as the Chinese; but there is a vast difference in the manner of conducting them. We play our pieces in the open air, the English theirs under cover; we act by daylight, they by the blaze of torches. One of our plays continues eight or ten days successively; an English piece seldom takes up above four hours of the representation.

My companion in black, with whom I am now beginning to contract an intimacy, introduced me a few nights ago to the playhouse, where we placed ourselves conveniently at the foot of the stage. As the curtain was not drawn before my arrival, I had an opportunity of observing the behavior of the spectators, and indulging those reflections which novelty generally inspires.

The rich in general were placed in the lowest seats, and the poor rose above them in degrees proportioned to their poverty. The order of precedence seemed here inverted; those who were undermost all the day, now enjoyed a temporary eminence, and became masters of the ceremonies. It was they who called for the music, indulging every noisy freedom, and testifying all the insolence of beggary in exaltation.

They who held the middle region seemed not so riotous as those above them, nor yet so tame as those below: to judge by their looks, many of them seemed strangers there as well as myself. They were chiefly employed, during this period of expectation, in eating oranges, reading the story of the play, or making assignations.

Those who sat in the lowest rows, which are called the pit, seemed to consider themselves as judges of the merit of the poet and the performers; they were assembled partly to be amused, and partly to show their taste; appearing to labor under that restraint which an affectation of superior discernment generally produces. My companion, however, informed me, that not one in a hundred of them knew even the first principles of criticism; that they assumed the right of being censors because there was none to contradict their pretensions; and that every man who now called himself a connoisseur, became such to all intents and purposes.

Those who sat in the boxes appeared in the most unhappy situation of all. The rest of the audience came merely for their own amusement; these, rather to furnish out a part of the entertainment themselves. I could not avoid considering them as acting parts in dumb show—not a courtesy or nod, that was not all the result of art; not a look nor a smile that was not designed for murder. Gentlemen and ladies ogled each other through spectacles; for, my companion observed, that blindness was of late become fashionable; all affected indifference and ease, while their hearts at the same time burned for conquest. Upon the whole, the lights, the music, the ladies in their gayest dresses, the men with cheerfulness and expectation in their looks, all conspired to make a most agreeable picture, and to fill a heart that sympathizes at human happiness with inexpressible serenity.

The expected time for the play to begin at last arrived; the curtain was drawn, and the actors came on. A woman, who personated a queen, came in curtseying to the audience, who clapped their hands upon her appearance. Clapping of hands is, it seems, the manner of applauding in England; the manner is absurd, but every country, you know, has its peculiar absurdities. I was equally surprised, however, at the submission of the actress, who should have considered herself as a queen, as at the little discernment of the audience who gave her such marks of applause before she attempted to deserve them. Preliminaries between her and the audience being thus adjusted, the dialogue was supported between her and a most hopeful youth, who acted the part of her confidant. They both appeared in extreme distress, for it seems the queen had lost a child some fifteen years before, and still kept its dear resemblance next her heart, while her kind companion bore a part in her sorrows.

Her lamentations grew loud; comfort is offered, but she detests the very sound: she bids them preach comfort to the winds. Upon this her husband comes in, who, seeing the queen so much afflicted, can himself hardly refrain from tears, or avoid partaking in the soft distress. After thus grieving through three scenes, the curtain dropped for the first act.

"Truly," said I to my companion, "these kings and queens are very much disturbed at no very great misfortune: certain I am, were people of humbler stations to act in this manner, they would be thought divested of common sense." I had scarcely finished this observation, when the curtain rose, and the king came on in a violent passion. His wife had, it seems, refused his proffered tenderness, had spurned his royal embrace, and he seemed resolved not to survive her fierce disdain. After he had thus fretted, and the queen had fretted through the second act, the curtain was let down once more.

"Now," says my companion, "you perceive the king to be a man of spirit; he feels at every pore: one of your phlegmatic sons of clay would have given the queen her own way, and let her come to herself by degrees; but the king is for immediate tenderness, or instant death: death and tenderness are leading passions of every modern buskined[6] hero, this moment they embrace, and the next stab, mixing daggers and kisses in every period."

I was going to second his remarks, when my attention was engrossed by a new object; a man came in balancing a straw upon his nose, and the audience were clapping their hands in all the raptures of applause. "To what purpose," cried I, "does this unmeaning figure make his appearance? is he a part of the plot?"—"Unmeaning do you call him?" replied my friend in black; "this is one of the most important characters of the whole play; nothing pleases the people more than seeing a straw balanced: there is a good deal of meaning in the straw: there is something suited to every apprehension in the sight; and a fellow possessed of talents like these is sure of making his fortune."

The third act now began with an actor who came to inform us that he was the villain of the play, and intended to show strange things before all was over. He was joined by another who seemed as much disposed for mischief as he: their intrigues continued through this whole division. "If that be a villain," said I, "he must be a very stupid one to tell his secrets without being asked; such soliloquies of late are never admitted in China."

The noise of clapping interrupted me once more; a child of six years old was learning to dance on the stage, which gave the ladies and mandarins infinite satisfaction. "I am sorry," said I, "to see the pretty creature so early learning so very bad a trade; dancing being, I presume, as contemptible here as in China."—"Quite the reverse," interrupted my companion; "dancing is a very reputable and genteel employment here; men have a greater chance for encouragement from the merit of their heels than their heads. One who jumps up and flourishes his toes three times before he comes to the ground, may have three hundred a year; he who flourishes them four times, gets four hundred; but he who arrives at five is inestimable, and may demand what salary he thinks proper. The female dancers, too, are valued for this sort of jumping and crossing; and it is a cant word amongst them, that she deserves most who shows highest. But the fourth act is begun; let us be attentive."

In the fourth act the queen finds her long lost child, now grown up into a youth of smart parts and great qualifications; wherefore she wisely considers that the crown will fit his head better than that of her husband, whom she knows to be a driveler. The king discovers her design, and here comes on the

[6]Tragic.

deep distress: he loves the queen, and he loves the kingdom; he resolves, therefore, in order to possess both, that her son must die. The queen exclaims at his barbarity, is frantic with rage, and at length, overcome with sorrow, falls into a fit; upon which the curtain drops, and the act is concluded.

"Observe the art of the poet," cries my companion. "When the queen can say no more, she falls into a fit. While thus her eyes are shut, while she is supported in the arms of Abigail, what horrors do we not fancy! We feel it in every nerve: take my word for it, that fits are the true *aposiopesis*[7] of modern tragedy."

The fifth act began, and a busy piece it was. Scenes shifting, trumpets sounding, mobs hallooing, carpets spreading, guards bustling from one door to another; gods, demons, daggers, racks, and ratsbane. But whether the king was killed, or the queen was drowned, or the son was poisoned, I have absolutely forgotten.

When the play was over, I could not avoid observing that the persons of the drama appeared in as much distress in the first act as the last. "How is it possible," said I, "to sympathize with them through five long acts? Pity is but a short-lived passion. I hate to hear an actor mouthing trifles. Neither startings, strainings, nor attitudes, affect me, unless there be cause: after I have been once or twice deceived by those unmeaning alarms, my heart sleeps in peace, probably unaffected by the principal distress. There should be one great passion aimed at by the actor as well as the poet; all the rest should be subordinate, and only contribute to make that the greater; if the actor, therefore, exclaims upon every occasion, in the tones of despair, he attempts to move us too soon; he anticipates the blow, he ceases to affect, though he gains our applause."

I scarce perceived that the audience were almost all departed; wherefore, mixing with the crowd, my companion and I got into the street, where, essaying a hundred obstacles from coach-wheels and palanquin poles, like birds in their flight through the branches of a forest, after various turnings, we both at length got home in safety. Adieu.

[7]Sudden breaking-off in the middle of a speech.

LETTER XXXIII

To the Same

THE MANNER OF WRITING AMONG THE CHINESE—THE EASTERN TALES OF MAGAZINES, *ETC.*, RIDICULED

I AM disgusted, O Fum Hoam, even to sickness disgusted. Is it possible to bear the presumption of those islanders, when they pretend to instruct me in the ceremonies of China! They lay it down as a maxim, that every person who comes from thence must express himself in metaphor, swear by Alla, rail against wine, and behave, and talk, and write, like a Turk or Persian. They make no distinction between our elegant manners, and the voluptuous barbarities of our Eastern neighbors. Wherever I come, I raise either diffidence or astonishment: some fancy me no Chinese, because I am formed more like a man than a monster; and others wonder to find one born five thousand miles from England, endued with common sense. "Strange," say they, "that a man who has received his education at such a distance from London, should have common sense; to be born out of England, and yet have common sense! Impossible! He must be some Englishman in disguise; his very visage has nothing of the true exotic barbarity."

I yesterday received an invitation from a lady of distinction, who, it seems, had collected all her knowledge of Eastern manners from fictions every day propagated here, under the titles of Eastern Tales and Oriental Histories. She received me very politely, but seemed to wonder that I neglected bringing opium and a tobacco-box: when chairs were drawn for the rest of the company, I was assigned my place on a cushion on the floor. It was in vain that I protested the Chinese used chairs as in Europe; she understood decorums too well to entertain me with the ordinary civilities.

I had scarce been seated according to her directions, when the footman was ordered to pin a napkin under my chin: this I protested against, as being no way Chinese; however, the whole company, who, it seems, were a club of connoisseurs, gave it unanimously against me, and the napkin was pinned accordingly.

It was impossible to be angry with people, who seemed to err only from an excess of politeness, and I sat contented, expecting their importunities were now at an end; but as soon as ever dinner was served, the lady demanded, whether I was for a plate of bear's claws, or a slice of birds' nests. As these were dishes with which I was utterly unacquainted, I was desirous of eating only what I knew, and therefore begged to be helped from a piece of beef that lay on the side-table: my request at once disconcerted the whole company. A Chinese eat beef! that could never be: there was no local propriety in Chinese beef, whatever there might be in Chinese pheasant. "Sir," said my entertainer, "I think I have some reason to fancy myself a judge of these matters; in short, the Chinese never eat beef; so that I must be permitted to recommend the pilaw.[8] There was never better dressed at Pekin; the saffron and rice were well boiled, and the spices in perfection.

I had no sooner begun to eat what was laid before me, than I found the whole company as much astonished as before: it seems I made no use of my chop-sticks. A grave gentleman, whom I take to be an author, harangued very learnedly (as the company seemed to think) upon the use which was made of them in China. He entered into a long argument with himself about their first introduction, without once appealing to me, who might be supposed best capable of silencing the inquiry. As the gentleman therefore took my silence for a mark of his own superior sagacity, he was resolved to pursue the triumph: he talked of our cities, mountains, and animals, as familiarly as if he had been born in Quamsi, but as erroneously as if a native of the moon. He attempted to prove that I had nothing of the true Chinese cut in my visage; showed that my cheek-bones should have been higher, and my forehead broader. In short, he almost reasoned me out of my country, and effectually persuaded the rest of the company to be of his opinion.

I was going to expose his mistakes, when it was insisted, that I had nothing of the true Eastern manner in my delivery. "This gentleman's conversation," says one of the ladies, who was a great reader, "is like our own,—mere chit-chat and common sense: there is nothing like sense in the true Eastern style, where nothing more is required but sublimity. Oh! for a history of Aboulfaouris, the grand voyager, of genii, magicians, rocks, bags of bullets, giants, and enchanters, where all is great, obscure, magnificent, and unintelligible!"—"I have written many a sheet of Eastern tale myself," interrupts the author, "and I defy the severest critic to say but that I have stuck close to the true manner. I have compared a lady's chin to the snow upon the mountains of Bomek; a soldier's sword to the clouds that obscure the face of heaven. If riches are mentioned, I compare them to the flocks that graze the verdant Tefflis; if poverty, to the mists that veil the brow of Mount Baku. I have used *thee* and *thou* upon all occasions; I have described fallen stars, and splitting mountains, not forgetting the little houries, who make a pretty figure in every description. But you shall hear how I generally begin—'Eben-ben-bolo, who was the son of Ban, was born on the foggy summits of Benderabassi. His beard was whiter than the feathers which veil the breast of the penguin; his eyes were like the eyes of doves when washed by the dews of the morning; his hair, which hung like the willow weeping over the glassy stream, was so beautiful that it seemed to reflect its own brightness; and his feet were as the feet of a wild deer which fleeth to the tops of the mountains.' There, there is the true Eastern taste for you; every advance made towards sense, is only a deviation from sound. Eastern tales should always be sonorous, lofty, musical, and unmeaning."

I could not avoid smiling, to hear a native of England attempt to instruct me in the true Eastern idiom; and after he looked round some time for applause, I presumed to ask him, whether he had ever traveled into the East? to which he replied in the negative. I demanded whether he understood Chinese, or Arabic? to which also he answered as before. "Then how, Sir," said I, "can you pretend to determine upon the Eastern style, who are entirely unacquainted with the Eastern writ-

[8]An oriental dish of rice with meat, spices, etc.

ings? Take, Sir, the word of one who is professedly a Chinese, and who is actually acquainted with the Arabian writers, that what is palmed upon you daily for an imitation of Eastern writing, no way resembles their manner, either in sentiment or diction. In the East, similes are seldom used, and metaphors almost wholly unknown; but in China particularly, the very reverse of what you allude to takes place: a cool phlegmatic method of writing prevails there. The writers of that country, ever more assiduous to instruct than to please, address rather the judgment than the fancy. Unlike many authors of Europe who have no consideration of the reader's time, they generally leave more to be understood than they express.

"Besides, Sir, you must not expect from an inhabitant of China the same ignorance, the same unlettered simplicity, that you find in a Turk, Persian, or native of Peru. The Chinese are versed in the sciences as well as you, and are masters of several arts unknown to the people of Europe. Many of them are instructed not only in their own national learning, but are perfectly well acquainted with the languages and learning of the West. If my word in such a case is not to be taken, consult your own travelers on this head, who affirm, that the scholars of Pekin and Siam sustain theological theses in Latin. 'The college of Masprend, which is but a league from Siam,' says one of your travelers, 'came in a body to salute our ambassador. Nothing gave me more sincere pleasure, than to behold a number of priests, venerable both from age and modesty, followed by a number of youths of all nations, Chinese, Japanese, Tonquinese, of Cochin China, Pegu, and Siam, all willing to pay their respects in the most polite manner imaginable. A Cochin Chinese made an excellent Latin oration upon this occasion; he was succeeded and even outdone by a student of Tonquin, who was as well skilled in the Western learning as any scholar of Paris.' Now, Sir, if youths who never stirred from home are so perfectly skilled in your laws and learning, surely more must be expected from one like me, who have traveled so many thousand miles, who have conversed familiarly for several years with the English factors established at Canton, and the missionaries sent us from every part of Europe. The unaffected of every country nearly resemble each other, and a page of our Confucius and of your Tillotson[9] have scarce any material difference. Paltry affectation, strained allusions, and disgusting finery, are easily attained by those who choose to wear them: and they are but too frequently the badges of ignorance or of stupidity, whenever it would endeavor to please."

I was proceeding in my discourse, when, looking round, I perceived the company no way attentive to what I attempted, with so much earnestness, to enforce. One lady was whispering her that sat next, another was studying the merits of a fan, a third began to yawn, and the author himself fell fast asleep. I thought it, therefore, high time to make a retreat, nor did the company seem to show any regret at my preparations for departure: even the lady who had invited me, with the most mortifying insensibility, saw me seize my hat, and rise from my cushion; nor was I invited to repeat my visit, because it was found that I aimed at appearing rather a reasonable creature, than an outlandish idiot. Adieu.

LETTER LI

To the Same

A BOOKSELLER'S VISIT TO THE CHINESE

As I was yesterday seated at breakfast over a pensive dish of tea, my meditations were interrupted by my old friend and companion, who introduced a stranger, dressed pretty much like himself. The gentleman made several apologies for his visit, begged of me to impute his intrusion to the sincerity of his respect, and the warmth of his curiosity.

As I am very suspicious of my company when I find them very civil without any apparent reason, I answered the stranger's caresses at first with reserve; which my friend perceiving, instantly let me into my visitant's trade and character, asking Mr. Fudge, whether he had lately published any-

[9] John Tillotson (1630–1694), Archbishop of Canterbury, whose sermons were used as models of a lucid prose style.

thing new. I now conjectured that my guest was no other than a bookseller, and his answer confirmed my suspicions.

"Excuse me, Sir," says he, "it is not the season; books have their time as well as cucumbers. I would no more bring out a new work in summer than I would sell pork in the dog days. Nothing in my way goes off in summer, except very light good indeed. A review, a magazine, or a Sessions paper,[10] may amuse a summer reader; but all our stock of value we reserve for a spring and winter trade." "I must confess, Sir," says I, "a curiosity to know what you call a valuable stock, which can only bear a winter perusal."—"Sir," replied the bookseller, "it is not my way to cry up my own goods; but, without exaggeration, I will venture to show with any of the trade: my books at least have the peculiar advantage of being always new; and it is my way to clear off my old to the trunk-makers every season. I have ten new title-pages now about me, which only want books to be added to make them the finest things in nature. Others may pretend to direct the vulgar; but that is not my way; I always let the vulgar direct me; wherever popular clamor arises, I always echo the million. For instance, should the people in general say that such a man is a rogue, I instantly give orders to set him down in print a villain; thus every man buys the book, not to learn new sentiments, but to have the pleasure of seeing his own reflected."—"But, Sir," interrupted I, "you speak as if you yourself wrote the books you publish; may I be so bold as to ask a sight of some of those intended publications which are shortly to surprise the world?"—"As to that, Sir," replied the talkative book-seller, "I only draw out the plans myself; and though I am very cautious of communicating them to any, yet, as in the end I have a favor to ask, you shall see a few of them. Here, Sir, here they are; diamonds of the first water, I assure you. *Imprimis,* a Translation of several Medical precepts for the use of such physicians as do not understand Latin. *Item,* the Young Clergyman's art of placing patches regularly, with a Dissertation on the different manners of smiling without distorting the face. *Item,* the whole Art of Love made perfectly easy, by a broker of 'Change Alley. *Item,* the proper manner of Cutting blacklead pencils, and making crayons, by the Right Hon. the Earl of ——. *Item,* the Muster-master-general, or the review of reviews."—"Sir," cried I, interrupting him, "my curiosity, with regard to title-pages, is satisfied; I should be glad to see some longer manuscript, a history, or an epic poem."—"Bless me!" cries the man of industry, "now you speak of an epic poem, you shall see an excellent farce. Here it is; dip into it where you will, it will be found replete with true modern humor. Strokes, Sir; it is filled with strokes of wit and satire in every line."—"Do you call these dashes of the pen strokes," replied I, "for I must confess I can see no other?"—"And pray, Sir," returned he, "what do you call them? Do you see anything good now-a-days, that is not filled with strokes—and dashes?—Sir, a well placed dash makes half the wit of our writers of modern humor. I bought a piece last season that had no other merit upon earth than nine hundred and ninety-five breaks, seventy-two ha-ha's, three good things, and a garter. And yet it played off, and bounced, and cracked, and made more sport than a firework."[11]—"I fancy, then, Sir, you were a considerable gainer?"—"It must be owned the piece did pay; but, upon the whole, I cannot much boast of last winter's success; I gained by two murders; but then I lost by an ill-timed charity sermon. I was a considerable sufferer by my Direct Road to an Estate, but the Infernal Guide brought me up again. Ah, Sir, that was a piece touched off by the hand of a master; filled with good things from one end to the other. The author had nothing but the jest in view; no dull moral lurking beneath, nor ill-natured satire to sour the reader's good-humor; he wisely considered that moral and humor at the same time were quite overdoing the business."—"To what purpose was the book then published?" cried I.—"Sir, the book was published in order to be sold; and no book sold better, except the criticisms upon it, which

[10] List of cases put down for trial.

[11] Here Goldsmith is probably satirizing Laurence Sterne's *Tristram Shandy,* which had begun to appear shortly before this.

came out soon after: of all kinds of writing, that goes off best at present; and I generally fasten a criticism upon every selling book that is published.

"I once had an author who never left the least opening for the critics: close was the word; always very right and very dull; ever on the safe side of an argument; yet, with all his qualifications, incapable of coming into favor. I soon perceived that his bent was for criticism; and, as he was good for nothing else, supplied him with pens and paper, and planted him, at the beginning of every month, as a censor on the works of others. In short, I found him a treasure; no merit could escape him; but what is most remarkable of all, he ever wrote best and bitterest when drunk." "But are there not some works," interrupted I, "that, from the very manner of their composition, must be exempt from criticism; particularly such as profess to disregard its laws?"—"There is no work whatsoever but he can criticize," replied the bookseller; "even though you wrote in Chinese, he would have a pluck at you. Suppose you should take it into your head to publish a book, let it be a volume of Chinese letters, for instance; write how you will, he shall show the world you could have written better. Should you, with the most local exactness, stick to the manners and customs of the country from whence you come; should you confine yourself to the narrow limits of Eastern knowledge, and be perfectly simple, and perfectly natural, he has then the strongest reason to exclaim. He may, with a sneer, send you back to China for readers. He may observe that after the first or second letter, the iteration of the same simplicity is insupportably tedious. But the worst of all is, the public, in such a case, will anticipate his censures, and leave you, with all your uninstructive simplicity, to be mauled at discretion."

"Yes," cried I, "but in order to avoid his indignation, and, what I should fear more, that of the public, I would, in such a case, write with all the knowledge I was master of. As I am not possessed of much learning, at least I would not suppress what little I had; nor would I appear more stupid than nature made me."—"Here, then," cries the bookseller, "we should have you entirely in our power; unnatural, un-Eastern, quite out of character, erroneously sensible, would be the whole cry. Sir, we should then hunt you down like a rat."—"Head of my father!" said I, "sure there are but two ways; the door must either be shut or it must be open. I must either be natural or unnatural."—"Be what you will, we shall criticize you," returned the bookseller, "and prove you a dunce in spite of your teeth. But, Sir, it is time that I should come to business. I have just now in the press a history of China; and if you will but put your name to it as the author, I shall repay the obligation with gratitude."—"What, Sir!" replied I, "put my name to a work which I have not written? Never, while I retain a proper respect for the public and myself." The bluntness of my reply quite abated the ardor of the bookseller's conversation; and, after about half an hour's disagreeable reserve, he, with some ceremony, took his leave, and withdrew. Adieu.

LETTER LXVII

To Hingpo, a Slave in Persia

THE FOLLY OF ATTEMPTING TO LEARN WISDOM BY BEING RECLUSE

Books, my son, while they teach us to respect the interests of others, often make us unmindful of our own; while they instruct the youthful reader to grasp at social happiness, he grows miserable in detail, and, attentive to universal harmony, often forgets that he himself has a part to sustain in the concert. I dislike, therefore, the philosopher, who describes the inconveniences of life in such pleasing colors that the pupil grows enamored of distress, longs to try the charms of poverty, meets it without dread, nor fears its inconveniences till he severely feels them.

A youth who has thus spent his life among books, new to the world, and unacquainted with man but by philosophic information, may be considered as a being whose mind is filled with the vulgar errors of the wise; utterly unqualified for a journey through life, yet confident of his own skill in the direction, he sets out with confidence, blunders on with vanity, and finds himself at last undone.

He first has learned from books, and then lays it down as a maxim, that all mankind are virtuous or vicious in excess; and he has been long taught to detest vice, and love virtue: warm, therefore in attachments, and steadfast in enmity, he treats every creature as a friend or foe; expects from those he loves unerring integrity, and consigns his enemies to the reproach of wanting every virtue. On this principle he proceeds; and here begin his disappointments. Upon a closer inspection of human nature he perceives that he should have moderated his friendship, and softened his severity; for he often finds the excellencies of one part of mankind clouded with vice, and the faults of the other brightened with virtue; he finds no character so sanctified that has not its failings, none so infamous but has somewhat to attract our esteem; he beholds impiety in lawn,[12] and fidelity in fetters.

He now, therefore, but too late, perceives that his regards should have been more cool, and his hatred less violent; that the truly wise seldom court romantic friendships with the good, and avoid, if possible, the resentment even of the wicked: every moment gives him fresh instances that the bonds of friendship are broken if drawn too closely, and that those whom he has treated with disrespect more than retaliate the injury; at length, therefore, he is obliged to confess that he has declared war upon the vicious half of mankind, without being able to form an alliance among the virtuous to espouse his quarrel.

Our book-taught philosopher, however, is now too far advanced to recede; and though poverty be the just consequence of the many enemies his conduct has created, yet he is resolved to meet it without shrinking. Philosophers have described poverty in most charming colors, and even his vanity is touched in thinking that he shall show the world, in himself, one more example of patience, fortitude, and resignation. "Come, then, O Poverty! for what is there in thee dreadful to the WISE? Temperance, Health, and Frugality walk in thy train; Cheerfulness and Liberty are ever thy companions. Shall any be ashamed of thee, of whom Cincinnatus was not ashamed? The running brook, the herbs of the field, can amply satisfy nature; man wants but little, nor that little long.[13] Come, then, O Poverty, while kings stand by, and gaze with admiration at the true philosopher's resignation!"

The goddess appears; for Poverty ever comes at the call; but, alas! he finds her by no means the charming figure books and his warm imagination had painted. As when an Eas[illegible]de, whom her friends and rela[illegible] long described as a model of perfection, pays her first visit, the longing bridegroom lifts the veil to see a face he had never seen before; but instead of a countenance blazing with beauty like the sun, he beholds deformity shooting icicles to his heart: such appears Poverty to her new entertainer; all the fabric of enthusiasm is at once demolished, and a thousand miseries rise up on its ruins, while Contempt, with pointing finger, is foremost in the hideous procession.

The poor man now finds that he can get no kings to look at him while he is eating; he finds that in proportion as he grows poor, the world turns its back upon him, and gives him leave to act the philosopher in all the majesty of solitude. It might be agreeable enough to play the philosopher while we are conscious that mankind are spectators: but what signifies wearing the mask of sturdy contentment, and mounting the stage of restraint, when not one creature will assist at the exhibition! Thus is he forsaken of men, while his fortitude wants the satisfaction even of self-applause: for either he does not feel his present calamities, and that is natural insensibility; or he disguises his feelings, and that is dissimulation.

Spleen now begins to take up the man: not distinguishing in his resentments, he regards all mankind with detestation, and commencing man-hater, seeks solitude to be at liberty to rail.

It has been said, that he who retires to solitude is either a beast or an angel.[14] The censure is too severe, and the praise unmerited; the discontented being, who retires from society, is generally some good-natured man, who has begun life without experience, and

[12] The sleeves of a bishop are made of lawn.

[13] Lifted from Young's *Night Thoughts,* IV, 9.

[14] See Aristotle, *Politics,* I, ii (1253a, 2–4).

knew not how to gain it in his intercourse with mankind. Adieu.

LETTER LXXXVI

To Fum Hoam

THE RACES OF NEWMARKET RIDICULED. DESCRIPTION OF A CART RACE

OF ALL the places of amusement where gentlemen and ladies are entertained, I have not been yet to visit Newmarket. This, I am told, is a large field, where, upon certain occasions, three or four horses are brought together, then set a-running, and that horse which runs fastest wins the wager.

This is reckoned a very polite and fashionable amusement here, much more followed by the nobility than partridge fighting at Java, or paper kites in Madagascar. Several of the great here, I am told, understand as much of farriery as their grooms; and a horse, with any share of merit, can never want a patron among the nobility.

We have a description of this entertainment almost every day in some of the gazettes, as for instanc[illegible] "On such a day the Give and Take Plate [illegible] run for between his Grace's Crab, his Lor[illegible]p's Periwinkle, and 'Squire Smacken's [illegible]nerkin. All rode their own horses. Th[illegible] was the greatest concourse of nobility [illegible] has been known here for several season[illegible] The odds were in favor of Crab in the beginning; but Slamerkin, after the first heat, seemed to have the match hollow: however, it was soon seen that Periwinkle improved in wind, which at last turned out accordingly; Crab was run to a standstill, Slamerkin was knocked up, and Periwinkle was brought in with universal applause." Thus, you see, Periwinkle received universal applause, and, no doubt, his lordship came in for some share of that praise which was so liberally bestowed upon Periwinkle. Sun of China! how glorious must the senator appear in his cap and leather breeches, his whip crossed in his mouth, and thus coming to the goal, amongst the shouts of grooms, jockeys, pimps, stable-bred dukes, and degraded generals!

From the description of this princely amusement, now transcribed, and from the great veneration I have for the characters of its principal promoters, I make no doubt but I shall look upon a horse-race with becoming reverence, predisposed as I am by a similar amusement, of which I have lately been a spectator; for just now I happened to have an opportunity of being present at a cart race.

Whether this contention between three carts of different parishes was promoted by a subscription among the nobility, or whether the grand jury, in council assembled, had gloriously combined to encourage plaustral[15] merit, I cannot take upon me to determine; but certain it is, the whole was conducted with the utmost regularity and decorum, and the company, which made a brilliant appearance, were universally of opinion, that the sport was high, the running fine, and the riders influenced by no bribe.

It was run on the road from London, to a village called Brentford, between a turnip-cart, a dust-cart, and a dung-cart; each of the owners condescending to mount, and be his own driver. The odds, at starting, were Dust against Dung, five to four; but, after half a mile's going, the knowing ones found themselves all on the wrong side, and it was Turnip against the field, brass to silver.

Soon, however, the contest became more doubtful; Turnip indeed kept the way, but it was perceived that Dung had better bottom. The road re-echoed with the shouts of the spectators—"Dung against Turnip! Turnip against Dung!" was now the universal cry; neck and neck; one rode lighter, but the other had more judgment. I could not but particularly observe the ardor with which the fair sex espoused the cause of the different riders on this occasion; one was charmed with the unwashed beauties of Dung; another was captivated with the patibulary[16] aspect of Turnip; while, in the meantime, unfortunate gloomy Dust, who came whipping behind, was cheered by the encouragement of some, and pity of all.

The contention now continued for some time, without a possibility of determining to whom victory designed the prize. The win-

[15] Pertaining to a cart or wagon. (The word was apparently introduced into English by Goldsmith.)

[16] Gallows-like.

ning post appeared in view, and he who drove the turnip-cart assured himself of success; and successful he might have been, had his horse been as ambitious as he; but, upon approaching a turn from the road, which led homewards, the horse fairly stood still, and refused to move a foot farther. The dung-cart had scarce time to enjoy this temporary triumph, when it was pitched headlong into a ditch by the way-side, and the rider left to wallow in congenial mud. Dust, in the meantime, soon came up, and not being far from the post, came in, amidst the shouts and acclamations of all the spectators, and greatly caressed by all the quality of Brentford. Fortune was kind only to one, who ought to have been favorable to all; each had peculiar merit, each labored hard to earn the prize, and each richly deserved the cart he drove.

I do not know whether this description may not have anticipated that which I intended giving of Newmarket. I am told, there is little else to be seen even there. There may be some minute differences in the dress of the spectators, but none at all in their understandings: the quality of Brentford are as remarkable for politeness and delicacy as the breeders of Newmarket. The quality of Brentford drive their own carts, and the honorable fraternity of Newmarket ride their own horses. In short, the matches in one place are as rational as those in the other; and it is more than probable that turnips, dust, and dung, are all that can be found to furnish out description in either.

Forgive me, my friend; but a person like me, bred up in a philosophic seclusion, is apt to regard perhaps with too much asperity, those occurrences which sink man below his station in nature, and diminish the intrinsic value of humanity. Adieu.

LETTER CVI

To the Same

FUNERAL ELEGIES WRITTEN UPON THE GREAT RIDICULED. A SPECIMEN OF ONE

It was formerly the custom here, when men of distinction died, for their surviving acquaintance to throw each a slight present into the grave. Several things of little value were made use of for that purpose,—perfumes, relics, spices, bitter herbs, camomile, wormwood, and verses. This custom, however, is almost discontinued, and nothing but verses alone are now lavished on such occasions; an oblation which they suppose may be interred with the dead, without any injury to the living.

Upon the death of the great, therefore, the poets and undertakers are sure of employment. While one provides the long cloak, black staff, and mourning coach, the other produces the pastoral or elegy, the monody or apotheosis. The nobility need be under no apprehensions, but die as fast as they think proper; the poet and undertaker are ready to supply them; these can find metaphorical tears and family escutcheons at an hour's warning; and when the one has soberly laid the body in the grave, the other is ready to fix it figuratively among the stars.

There are several ways of being poetically sorrowful on such occasions. The bard is now some pensive youth of science, who sits deploring among the tombs; again, he is Thyrsis, complaining in a circle of harmless sheep. Now Britannia sits upon her own shore, and gives a loose to maternal tenderness; at another time, Parnassus, even the mountain Parnassus, gives way to sorrow, and is bathed in tears of distress.

But the most usual manner is this: Damon meets Menalcas, who has got a most gloomy countenance. The shepherd asks his friend, whence that look of distress? To which the other replies, that Pollio is no more. "If that be the case, then," cries Damon, "let us retire to yonder bower at some distance off, where the cypress and the jessamine add fragrance to the breeze; and let us weep alternately for Pollio, the friend of shepherds, and the patron of every muse."—"Ah!" returns his fellow shepherd, "what think you rather of that grotto by the fountain side? the murmuring stream will help to assist our complaints, and a nightingale on a neighboring tree will join her voice to the concert!" When the place is thus settled, they begin: the brook stands still to hear their lamentations; the cows forget to graze; and the very tigers start from the forest with sympathetic concern. By the tombs of our ancestors, my dear Fum, I am quite unaffected in all this distress: the whole is liquid laudanum to my spirits; and a tiger of common sensibility has twenty times more tenderness than I.

But though I could never weep with the complaining shepherd, yet I am sometimes induced to pity the poet, whose trade is thus to make demigods and heroes for a dinner. There is not in nature a more dismal figure than a man who sits down to premeditated flattery: every stanza he writes tacitly reproaches the meanness of his occupation, till, at last, his stupidity becomes more stupid, and his dullness more diminutive.

I am amazed, therefore, that none have yet found out the secret of flattering the worthless, and yet of preserving a safe conscience. I have often wished for some method, by which a man might do himself and his deceased patron justice, without being under the hateful reproach of self-conviction. After long lucubration, I have hit upon such an expedient; and send you the specimen of a poem upon the decease of a great man, in which the flattery is perfectly fine, and yet the poet perfectly innocent.

ON THE DEATH OF THE RIGHT HONORABLE ——

Ye Muses, pour the pitying tear
For Pollio snatched away;
Oh, had he lived another year!
—*He had not died to-day.*

Oh, were he born to bless mankind,
In virtuous times of yore,
Heroes themselves had fall'n behind!
—*Whene'er he went before.*

How sad the groves and plains appear,
And sympathetic sheep;
E'en pitying hills would drop a tear!
—*If hills could learn to weep.*

His bounty in exalted strain
Each bard may well display;
Since none implored relief in vain!
—*That went relieved away.*

And hark! I hear the tuneful throng
His obsequies forbid;
He still shall live, shall live as long
—*As ever dead man did.*

STANZAS ON WOMAN[1]

When lovely woman stoops to folly,
And finds, too late, that men betray,
What charm can soothe her melancholy,
What art can wash her guilt away?

The only art her guilt to cover,
To hide her shame from every eye,
To give repentance to her lover,
And wring his bosom, is—to die.

[1]From *The Vicar of Wakefield* (1766), chap. 24.

THE DESERTED VILLAGE

(1770)

To Sir Joshua Reynolds

Dear Sir,—I can have no expectations, in an address of this kind, either to add to your reputation, or to establish my own. You can gain nothing from my admiration, as I am ignorant of that art in which you are said to excel; and I may lose much by the severity of your judgment, as few have a juster taste in poetry than you. Setting interest, therefore, aside, to which I never paid much attention, I must be indulged at present in following my affections. The only dedication I ever made was to my brother, because I loved him better than most other men. He is since dead. Permit me to inscribe this Poem to you.

How far you may be pleased with the versification and mere mechanical parts of this attempt, I don't pretend to inquire; but I know you will object (and indeed several of our best and wisest friends concur in the opinion), that the depopulation it deplores is nowhere to be seen, and the disorders it laments are only to be found in the poet's own imagination. To this I can scarce make any other answer, than that I sincerely believe what I have written; that I have taken all possible pains, in my country excursions, for these four or five years past, to be certain of what I allege; and that all my views and inquiries have led me to believe those miseries real, which I here attempt to display. But this is not the place to enter into an inquiry whether the country be depopulating or not: 5 the discussion would take up much room, and I should prove myself, at best, an indifferent politician, to tire the reader with a long preface, when I want his unfatigued attention to a long poem. 10

In regretting the depopulation of the country, I inveigh against the increase of our luxuries; and here also I expect the shout of modern politicians against me. For twenty or thirty years past, it has been the fashion to 15 consider luxury as one of the greatest national advantages; and all the wisdom of antiquity in that particular as erroneous. Still, however, I must remain a professed ancient on that head, and continue to think 20 those luxuries prejudicial to states by which so many vices are introduced, and so many kingdoms have been undone. Indeed, so much has been poured out of late on the other side of the question, that, merely for 25 the sake of novelty and variety, one would sometimes wish to be in the right.

I am, dear sir, your sincere friend, and ardent admirer,

Oliver Goldsmith. 30

Sweet Auburn![1] loveliest village of the plain,
Where health and plenty cheered the laboring swain,
Where smiling Spring its earliest visit paid,
And parting Summer's lingering blooms delayed:
Dear lovely bowers of innocence and ease, 5
Seats of my youth, when every sport could please:
How often have I loitered o'er thy green,
Where humble happiness endeared each scene!
How often have I paused on every charm,
The sheltered cot, the cultivated farm, 10
The never-failing brook, the busy mill,
The decent church that topped the neighboring hill;
The hawthorn bush, with seats beneath the shade,
For talking age and whispering lovers made!
How often have I blessed the coming day, 15
When toil, remitting, lent its turn to play,
And all the village train, from labor free,
Led up their sports beneath the spreading tree!
While many a pastime circled in the shade,
The young contending as the old surveyed; 20
And many a gambol frolicked o'er the ground,
And sleights of art and feats of strength went round;
And still, as each repeated pleasure tired,
Succeeding sports the mirthful band inspired—
The dancing pair that simply[2] sought renown, 25
By holding out to tire each other down;
The swain mistrustless of his smutted face,
While secret laughter tittered round the place;
The bashful virgin's side-long looks of love;
The matron's glance, that would those looks reprove. 30
These were thy charms, sweet village! sports like these,
With sweet succession, taught e'en toil to please;
These round thy bowers their cheerful influence shed;
These were thy charms—but all these charms are fled. 34
Sweet smiling village, loveliest of the lawn,
Thy sports are fled, and all thy charms withdrawn;
Amidst thy bowers the tyrant's hand is seen,
And Desolation saddens all thy green:
One only master grasps the whole domain,[3]
And half a tillage stints thy smiling plain. 40
No more thy glassy brook reflects the day,
But, choked with sedges, works its weedy way;
Along thy glades, a solitary guest,
The hollow-sounding bittern guards its nest:
Amidst thy desert walks the lapwing flies, 45
And tires their echoes with unvaried cries:
Sunk are thy bowers in shapeless ruin all,
And the long grass o'ertops the moldering wall;
And, trembling, shrinking from the spoiler's hand,
Far, far away thy children leave the land. 50

[1]It is practically certain that Goldsmith had Lissoy in mind (which has changed its name to Auburn), though this has been disputed.

[2]In a simple way.

[3]Landlords were empowered by the Enclosure Acts (of which there were 700 between 1760 and 1774) to enclose common land, for the improvement of their estates. This often involved ejectments.

Ill fares the land, to hastening ills a prey,
Where wealth accumulates, and men decay.
Princes and lords may flourish, or may fade;
A breath can make them, as a breath has made:
But a bold peasantry, their country's pride, 55
When once destroyed, can never be supplied.
A time there was, ere England's griefs began,
When every rood of ground maintained its man;
For him light Labor spread her wholesome store,
Just gave what life required, but gave no more: 60
His best companions, Innocence and Health;
And his best riches, ignorance of wealth.
But times are altered: Trade's unfeeling train
Usurp the land, and dispossess the swain;
Along the lawn, where scattered hamlets rose, 65
Unwieldy wealth and cumbrous pomp repose;
And every want to opulence allied,
And every pang that folly pays to pride.
Those gentle hours that plenty bade to bloom,
Those calm desires that asked but little room,
Those healthful sports that graced the peaceful scene, 71
Lived in each look, and brightened all the green—
These, far departing, seek a kinder shore,
And rural mirth and manners are no more.
Sweet Auburn! parent of the blissful hour, 75
Thy glades forlorn confess the tyrant's power.
Here, as I take my solitary rounds,
Amidst thy tangling walks and ruined grounds,
And, many a year elapsed, return to view
Where once the cottage stood, the hawthorn grew— 80
Remembrance wakes with all her busy train,
Swells at my breast, and turns the past to pain.
In all my wanderings round this world of care,
In all my griefs—and God has given my share—
I still had hopes, my latest hours to crown, 85
Amidst these humble bowers to lay me down;
To husband out life's taper at the close,
And keep the flame from wasting by repose:
I still had hopes, for pride attends us still,
Amidst the swains to show my book-learn'd skill, 90
Around my fire an evening group to draw,
And tell of all I felt, and all I saw;
And, as a hare, whom hounds and horns pursue,
Pants to the place from whence at first she flew,
I still had hopes, my long vexations past, 95
Here to return—and die at home at last.
O blest retirement, friend to life's decline,
Retreats from care, that never must be mine,
How happy he who crowns, in shades like these,
A youth of labor with an age of ease; 100
Who quits a world where strong temptations try,
And, since 'tis hard to combat, learns to fly!
For him no wretches, born to work and weep,
Explore the mine, or tempt the dangerous deep;
No surly porter stands, in guilty state, 105
To spurn imploring famine from the gate;
But on he moves to meet his latter end,
Angels around befriending virtue's friend;
Bends to the grave with unperceived decay,
While resignation gently slopes the way; 110
And, all his prospects brightening to the last,
His heaven commences ere the world be past!
Sweet was the sound, when oft, at evening's close,
Up yonder hill the village murmur rose.
There, as I passed with careless[4] steps and slow, 115
The mingled notes came softened from below;
The swain responsive as the mikmaid sung,
The sober herd that lowed to meet their young;
The noisy geese that gabbled o'er the pool,
The playful children just let loose from school; 120
The watch-dog's voice that bayed the whispering wind,
And the loud laugh that spoke the vacant[5] mind;—
These all in sweet confusion sought the shade,
And filled each pause the nightingale had made.
But now the sounds of population fail, 125
No cheerful murmurs fluctuate in the gale,
No busy steps the grass-grown footway tread,
For all the bloomy flush of life is fled—

[4]Care-free.
[5]Untroubled, perhaps, rather than stupid.

All but yon widowed, solitary thing,
That feebly bends beside the plashy spring;
She, wretched matron—forced, in age, for bread, 131
To strip the brook with mantling cresses spread,
To pick her wintry faggot from the thorn,
To seek her nightly shed, and weep till morn,—
She only left of all the harmless train, 135
The sad historian of the pensive plain.

Near yonder copse, where once the garden smiled,
And still where many a garden-flower grows wild,
There, where a few torn shrubs the place disclose,
The village preacher's[6] modest mansion rose.
A man he was to all the country dear, 141
And passing rich with forty pounds a year.
Remote from towns he ran his godly race,
Nor e'er had changed, nor wished to change, his place; 144
Unpracticed he to fawn, or seek for power
By doctrines fashioned to the varying hour;
Far other aims his heart had learned to prize,
More skilled to raise the wretched than to rise.
His house was known to all the vagrant train;
He chid their wanderings, but relieved their pain; 150
The long-remembered beggar was his guest,
Whose beard descending swept his aged breast;
The ruined spendthrift, now no longer proud,
Claimed kindred there, and had his claims allowed;
The broken soldier, kindly bade to stay, 155
Sat by his fire, and talked the night away;—
Wept o'er his wounds, or, tales of sorrow done,
Shouldered his crutch, and showed how fields were won.
Pleased with his guests, the good man learned to glow,
And quite forgot their vices in their woe; 160
Careless their merits or their faults to scan,
His pity gave ere charity began.

Thus to relieve the wretched was his pride,
And e'en his failings leaned to virtue's side;
But in his duty prompt at every call, 165
He watched and wept, he prayed and felt for all;
And, as a bird each fond endearment tries,
To tempt its new-fledged offspring to the skies,
He tried each art, reproved each dull delay,
Allured to brighter worlds, and led the way.

Beside the bed where parting life was laid,
And sorrow, guilt, and pain, by turns dismayed, 172
The reverend champion stood. At his control,
Despair and anguish fled the struggling soul;
Comfort came down the trembling wretch to raise, 175
And his last faltering accents whispered praise.

At church, with meek and unaffected grace,
His looks adorned the venerable place;
Truth from his lips prevailed with double sway,
And fools, who came to scoff, remained to pray. 180
The service past, around the pious man
With steady zeal, each honest rustic ran;
E'en children followed, with endearing wile,
And plucked his gown, to share the good man's smile;
His ready smile a parent's warmth expressed; 185
Their welfare pleased him, and their cares distressed:
To them his heart, his love, his griefs were given,
But all his serious thoughts had rest in heaven.
As some tall cliff that lifts its awful form,
Swells from the vale, and midway leaves the storm, 190
Though round its breast the rolling clouds are spread,
Eternal sunshine settles on its head.

Beside yon straggling fence that skirts the way,
With blossomed furze unprofitably gay, 194
There, in his noisy mansion, skilled to rule,
The village master taught his little school.
A man severe he was, and stern to view;
I knew him well, and every truant knew:
Well had the boding tremblers learned to trace
The day's disasters in his morning face; 200
Full well they laughed with counterfeited glee
At all his jokes, for many a joke had he;
Full well the busy whisper, circling round,
Conveyed the dismal tidings when he frowned.
Yet he was kind, or if severe in aught, 205

[6]Probably Goldsmith had both his father and his brother, Henry, in mind in describing the preacher.

The love he bore to learning was in fault.
The village all declared how much he knew;
'Twas certain he could write, and cipher too;
Lands he could measure, terms and tides presage, 209
And e'en the story ran that he could gauge.
In arguing, too, the parson owned his skill,
For e'en though vanquished, he could argue still;
While words of learned length and thundering sound
Amazed the gazing rustics ranged around;
And still they gazed, and still the wonder grew, 215
That one small head could carry all he knew.
But past is all his fame;—the very spot
Where many a time he triumphed, is forgot.
Near yonder thorn, that lifts its head on high,
Where once the sign-post caught the passing eye, 220
Low lies that house where nut-brown drafts inspired,
Where gray-beard mirth and smiling toil retired,
Where village statesmen talked with looks profound,
And news much older than their ale went round.
Imagination fondly stoops to trace 225
The parlor splendors of that festive place;
The whitewashed wall, the nicely-sanded floor,
The varnished clock that clicked behind the door,
The chest, contrived a double debt to pay,
A bed by night, a chest of drawers by day, 230
The pictures placed for ornament and use,
The twelve good rules,[7] the royal game of goose,[8]
The hearth, except when winter chilled the day,
With aspen boughs, and flowers, and fennel, gay;— 234
While broken tea-cups, wisely kept for show,
Ranged o'er the chimney, glistened in a row.
Vain transitory splendors! could not all
Reprieve the tottering mansion from its fall?
Obscure it sinks, nor shall it more impart
An hour's importance to the poor man's heart. 240
Thither no more the peasant shall repair,
To sweet oblivion of his daily care;
No more the farmer's news, the barber's tale,
No more the woodman's ballad shall prevail;
No more the smith his dusky brow shall clear,
Relax his ponderous strength, and lean to hear; 246
The host himself no longer shall be found
Careful to see the mantling bliss go round;
Nor the coy maid, half willing to be pressed,
Shall kiss the cup to pass it to the rest. 250
Yes! let the rich deride, the proud disdain,
These simple blessings of the lowly train;
To me more dear, congenial to my heart,
One native charm, than all the gloss of art.
Spontaneous joys, where nature has its play,
The soul adopts, and owns their first-born sway; 256
Lightly they frolic o'er the vacant mind,
Unenvied, unmolested, unconfined:
But the long pomp, the midnight masquerade,
With all the freaks of wanton wealth arrayed,
In these, ere triflers half their wish obtain,
The toiling pleasure sickens into pain; 262
And, e'en while Fashion's brightest arts decoy,
The heart distrusting asks, if this be joy.
Ye friends to truth, ye statesmen, who survey 265
The rich man's joys increase, the poor's decay,
'Tis yours to judge how wide the limits stand
Between a splendid and a happy land.
Proud swells the tide with loads of freighted ore,
And shouting Folly hails them from her shore; 270
Hoards, e'en beyond the miser's wish, abound,
And rich men flock from all the world around.
Yet count our gains. This wealth is but a name
That leaves our useful products still the same.
Not so the loss. The man of wealth and pride 275
Takes up a space that many poor supplied;
Space for his lake, his park's extended bounds,
Space for his horses, equipage, and hounds;
The robe that wraps his limbs in silken sloth,
Has robbed the neighboring fields of half their growth; 280
His seat, where solitary sports are seen,
Indignant spurns the cottage from the green;
Around the world each needful product flies,
For all the luxuries the world supplies;

[7]These rules were said to have been found in the study of Charles I after his death. Printed on a card, they were hung on the wall.

[8]Played with dice on a board divided into compartments.

While thus the land, adorned for pleasure all, 285
In barren splendor feebly waits the fall.
As some fair female, unadorned and plain,
Secure to please while youth confirms her reign,
Slights every borrowed charm that dress supplies,
Nor shares with art the triumph of her eyes; 290
But when those charms are past, for charms are frail,
When time advances, and when lovers fail,
She then shines forth, solicitous to bless,
In all the glaring impotence of dress:
Thus fares the land by luxury betrayed; 295
In nature's simplest charms at first arrayed;—
But verging to decline, its splendors rise,
Its vistas strike, its palaces surprise;
While, scourged by famine, from the smiling land 299
The mournful peasant leads his humble band;
And while he sinks, without one arm to save,
The country blooms—a garden and a grave!
Where, then, ah! where shall poverty reside,
To 'scape the pressure of contiguous pride?
If to some common's fenceless limits strayed, 305
He drives his flock to pick the scanty blade,
Those fenceless fields the sons of wealth divide,
And e'en the bare-worn common is denied.
If to the city sped—what waits him there?
To see profusion that he must not share; 310
To see ten thousand baneful arts combined
To pamper luxury and thin mankind;
To see those joys the sons of pleasure know
Extorted from his fellow-creature's woe:
Here while the courtier glitters in brocade,
There the pale artist[9] plies the sickly trade; 316
Here while the proud their long-drawn pomps display,
There the black gibbet glooms beside the way:
The dome where Pleasure holds her midnight reign,
Here, richly decked, admits the gorgeous train; 320
Tumultuous grandeur crowds the blazing square,
The rattling chariots clash, the torches glare.
Sure scenes like these no troubles e'er annoy!
Sure these denote one universal joy!—
Are these thy serious thoughts?—ah, turn thine eyes 325
Where the poor houseless shivering female lies:
She once, perhaps, in village plenty blessed,
Has wept at tales of innocence distressed;
Her modest looks the cottage might adorn,
Sweet as the primrose peeps beneath the thorn: 330
Now lost to all, her friends, her virtue, fled,
Near her betrayer's door she lays her head,
And, pinched with cold, and shrinking from the shower,
With heavy heart deplores that luckless hour,
When idly first, ambitious of the town, 335
She left her wheel, and robes of country brown.
Do thine, sweet Auburn, thine, the loveliest train,
Do thy fair tribes participate her pain?
E'en now, perhaps, by cold and hunger led,
At proud men's doors they ask a little bread! 340
Ah, no. To distant climes, a dreary scene,
Where half the convex world intrudes between,
Through torrid tracts with fainting steps they go,
Where wild Altama[10] murmurs to their woe.
Far different there from all that charmed before, 345
The various terrors of that horrid shore;
Those blazing suns that dart a downward ray,
And fiercely shed intolerable day;
Those matted woods where birds forget to sing,
But silent bats in drowsy clusters cling; 350
Those poisonous fields, with rank luxuriance crowned,
Where the dark scorpion gathers death around;
Where at each step the stranger fears to wake
The rattling terrors of the vengeful snake;
Where crouching tigers[11] wait their hapless prey, 355
And savage men more murderous still than they:
While oft in whirls the mad tornado flies,
Mingling the ravaged landscape with the skies.

[9]Craftsman.

[10]Altamaha, a river in Georgia.

[11]Goldsmith had not yet became the historian of Animated Nature; but Noah Webster later called the jaguar "the American tiger."

Far different these from every former scene,
The cooling brook, the grassy-vested green,
The breezy covert of the warbling grove, 361
That only sheltered thefts of harmless love.
Good Heaven! what sorrows gloomed that parting day,
That called them from their native walks away;
When the poor exiles, every pleasure past, 365
Hung round their bowers, and fondly looked their last,
And took a long farewell, and wished in vain,
For seats like these beyond the western main;
And shuddering still to face the distant deep,
Returned and wept, and still returned to weep! 370
The good old sire the first prepared to go
To new-found worlds, and wept for others' woe;
But for himself, in conscious virtue brave,
He only wished for worlds beyond the grave.
His lovely daughter, lovelier in her tears, 375
The fond companion of his helpless years,
Silent went next, neglectful of her charms,
And left a lover's for a father's arms.
With louder plaints the mother spoke her woes,
And blessed the cot where every pleasure rose, 380
And kissed her thoughtless babes with many a tear,
And clasped them close, in sorrow doubly dear;
Whilst her fond husband strove to lend relief
In all the silent manliness of grief.
O Luxury, thou cursed by Heaven's decree, 385
How ill exchanged are things like these for thee!
How do thy potions, with insidious joy,
Diffuse their pleasures only to destroy!
Kingdoms by thee to sickly greatness grown,
Boast of a florid vigor not their own; 390
At every draft more large and large they grow,
A bloated mass of rank unwieldy woe;
Till sapped their strength, and every part unsound,
Down, down they sink, and spread a ruin round.
E'en now the devastation is begun, 395
And half the business of destruction done;
E'en now, methinks, as pondering here I stand,
I see the rural Virtues leave the land.
Down where yon anchoring vessel spreads the sail
That idly waiting flaps with every gale, 400
Downward they move, a melancholy band,
Pass from the shore, and darken all the strand;
Contented Toil, and hospitable Care,
And kind connubial Tenderness are there;
And Piety with wishes placed above, 405
And steady Loyalty, and faithful Love.
And thou, sweet Poetry, thou loveliest maid,
Still first to fly where sensual joys invade!
Unfit, in these degenerate times of shame, 409
To catch the heart, or strike for honest fame;
Dear charming nymph, neglected and decried,
My shame in crowds, my solitary pride;
Thou source of all my bliss and all my woe,
That found'st me poor at first, and keep'st me so;
Thou guide by which the nobler arts excel, 415
Thou nurse of every virtue, fare thee well!
Farewell! and oh! where'er thy voice be tried,
On Torno's[12] cliffs, or Pambamarca's[13] side,
Whether where equinoctial[14] fervors glow,
Or winter wraps the polar world in snow, 420
Still let thy voice, prevailing over time,
Redress the rigors of th'inclement clime;
Aid slighted Truth with thy persuasive strain;
Teach erring man to spurn the rage of gain;
Teach him that states, of native strength possessed, 425
Though very poor, may still be very blest;
That Trade's proud empire hastes to swift decay,
As ocean sweeps the labored mole away;
While self-dependent power can time defy,
As rocks resist the billows and the sky.[15] 430

---

[12]Tornea, Gulf of Bothnia, Sweden.

[13]Mountain in Ecuador. [14]Equatorial.

[15]According to Boswell, Dr. Johnson wrote the last four lines.

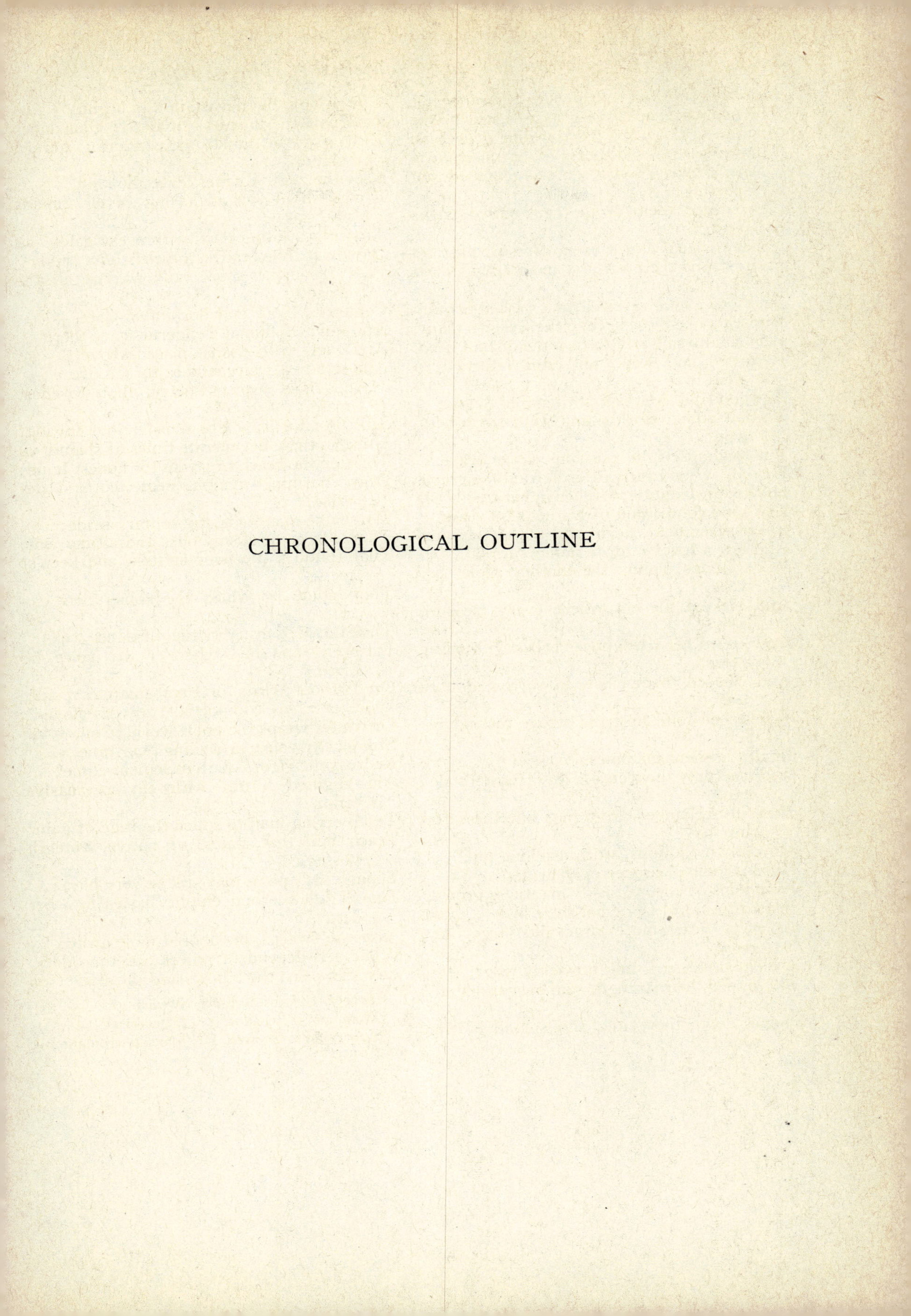

CHRONOLOGICAL OUTLINE

CHRONOLOGICAL OUTLINE

Abbreviations: c. (for *circa*) prefixed to a date means "about"; *fl.* (for *floruit*) following a person's name means that he was in middle age at about the year given.

Political, Social, Religious		Literary, Philosophical
St. Patrick.	373–463	
St. Patrick consecrated Bishop of Ireland.	405	
Traditional date for the departure of the Roman legions from Britain.	410	
Traditional date for the Anglo-Saxon invasion of Britain.	449	
	*c.*510	Date at which the action of the first part of *Beowulf* is conjectured to have been laid.
	516?–570?	Gildas, author of *De Excidio Britanniae.*
Battle of Mount Badon, victory of the Britons over invading Saxons.	516?	
Battle of Camlan, in which Arthur was later said to have fallen.	537?	
St. Columba at Iona.	563	
Papacy of St. Gregory the Great.	590–604	
Reign of Ethelbert of Kent.	*c.*560–616	
St. Augustine's mission to Kent.	597	
Reign of Edwin of Northumbria.	617–633	
St. Aidan sets forth for Lindisfarne.	635	
	639–709	Aldhelm.
Synod of Whitby.	664	
	670	Caedmon, author of *Hymns, fl.*
	672?–735	Bede.
	679–800	*Historia Britonum,* first account of Arthur.
Death of Abbess Hilda of Whitby.	680	
	*c.*690	Adamnan's *Life of St. Columba.*
	*c.*700	*Genesis, Daniel,* and *Exodus,* the so-called Caedmon group.
	*c.*725	*Deor's Lament.* *The Seafarer.* *Widsith.* *The Wanderer.*
	731	Bede's *Ecclesiastical History.*
	735–804	Alcuin.
	*c.*740	*Beowulf.*
Charlemagne.	742–814	

Political, Social, Religious		Literary, Philosophical
Beginning of the Danish raids.	c.790	
	796	Nennius, reviser of the *Historia Britonum, fl.*
	c.800	Cynewulf's *Juliana, Elene,* and *Fates of the Apostles.*
		Cynewulfian *Crist, Phoenix, Andreas, Dream of the Rood.*
	c.825	*Heliand,* translation of the four Gospels.
	856 or 915?	*Judith.*
Reign of Alfred.	871–899	Alfred's translations of Bede's *Ecclesiastical History,* Gregory's *Pastoral Care,* and Boethius's *Consolation of Philosophy.*
	c.875	First *Quem Quaeritis?* trope (beginning of medieval drama).
Beginning of the Norman raids on northern France.	886	
	c.887	Asser's *Life of Alfred the Great.*
	c.890–1154	*Anglo-Saxon Chronicle.*
Rollo becomes Duke of Normandy.	911	
Reign of Aethelstan.	924–939	
	c.937	*Battle of Brunanburh.*
	971	*Blickling Homilies.*
	c.991	*Battle of Maldon.*
	c.1000	British Museum Manuscript *Vitellius A.xv,* containing *Beowulf, Judith.*
		The Exeter Book, manuscript containing *Deor's Lament, The Seafarer, The Wanderer, Widsith.*
		The Vercelli Book, manuscript containing *Andreas, Elene, Dream of the Rood.*
	1000–1100	*Chanson de Roland.*
	1006	Aelfric, translator of *Genesis,* author of *Homilies* and *Lives of the Saints, fl.*
Reign of Canute.	1017–1035	
Reign of Edward the Confessor.	1042–1066	
Battle of Hastings.	1066	
Reign of William I (the Conqueror, first of the Norman kings).	1066–1087	
	1079–1142	Abelard.
	1084?–1155	Henry of Huntingdon, chronicler.
Doomesday Book.	1086	
Reign of William II (Rufus).	1087–1100	
Anselm appointed Archbishop of Canterbury.	1093	
	c.1095–1143	William of Malmesbury, chronicler.
First Crusade.	1096–1099	
	c.1100	Earliest Norse sagas.
		Earliest tales in the Welsh *Mabinogion.*
Reign of Henry I.	1100–1135	
	1100?–1154	Geoffrey of Monmouth, author of the *Historia Regum Britanniae* (first appearance of King Arthur as a romantic hero).

Political, Social, Religious		Literary, Philosophical
Reign of Stephen.	1135–1154	
	1136–1198?	William of Newburgh, author of the *Historia Rerum Anglicarum.*
Civil wars of Stephen and Matilda.	1139–1153	
	c.1140	Eadmer's *Life of Anselm.*
	1146?–1220?	Giraldus Cambrensis, author of the *Expugnatio Hibernica* and the *Itinerarium Cambriae.*
Second Crusade.	1147	
Reign of Henry II (first of the Plantagenet kings).	1154–1189	
	c.1154	Wace of Jersey's *Geste des Bretons* (based on Geoffrey of Monmouth).
	c.1160	Benoît de Sainte Maure's *Roman de Troie* (based on Dares Phrygius and Dictys Cretensis; first romantic treatment of Troilus and Cressida).
First English invasion of Ireland. Murder of St. Thomas à Becket	1170	
	1175–1253	Robert Grosseteste.
	1180	Death of John of Salisbury, author of the *Policraticus.*
Third Crusade.	1189–1192	
Reign of Richard I (the Lion-Hearted).	1189–1199	
Reign of John.	1199–1216	
	1200	Walter Map or Mapes, *fl.*
	c.1200	Orm's *Ormulum* (paraphrases of the Gospels in English). Layamon's *Brut* (first important poem in Middle English; fairy element added to Arthurian legends).
	1201?	Death of Roger of Hoveden, chronicler.
King John acknowledges the overlordship of the Pope.	1213	
Battle of Bouvines (defeat of the English pretensions in France).	1214	
	c.1214–1292	Roger Bacon
Magna Charta.	1215	
Reign of Henry III.	1216–1272	
	c.1225	"Sumer is Icumen In" (earliest secular lyric extant in English).
	c.1225–1274	St. Thomas Aquinas.
Death of Stephen Langton, Archbishop of Canterbury.	1228	
	c.1230	First part of the *Roman de la Rose,* by Guillaume de Lorris.
Foundation of University College (first college at Oxford).	1249	
	c.1250	*The Owl and the Nightingale.* *Gesta Romanorum.* *King Horn* (earliest verse romance extant in English).
Murder of Hugh of Lincoln.	1255	
Henry III begins to use English as well as French in proclamations.	1258	
	1259	Death of Matthew Paris, chronicler.

Political, Social, Religious		Literary, Philosophical
Simon de Montfort's Parliament (first representation of towns).	1265	
	1265–1308	John Duns Scotus.
	1265–1321	Dante.
	c.1270	Second part of the *Roman de la Rose*, by Jean de Meung.
Reign of Edward I.	1272–1307	
	1280–c.1347	William of Ockham.
	1281–1345	Richard de Bury, author of the *Philobiblion*.
Conquest of Wales completed.	1284	
	1287	Guido della Colonna's *Historia Troiana* (based on Benoît de Sainte Maure).
Model Parliament.	1295	
Confirmation of the Charters (restriction of the royal power of taxation by Parliament).	1297	
	c.1300	Manuscript of "Judas" (earliest ballad extant in English).
		Amis and Amiloun, Bevis of Hampton, Guy of Warwick, Havelok the Dane (verse romances).
		Cursor Mundi (religious history in didactic verse).
	c.1300–1320	Dante's *Divina Commedia*.
	c.1300–1349	Richard Rolle of Hampole.
	1304–1374	Petrarch.
Babylonian Captivity of the Papacy.	1305–1376	
Edward le Bruce crowned in Scotland.	1306	
Reign of Edward II.	1307–1327	
Feast of Corpus Christi established.	1311	Beginning of the guild cycle plays, of which the earliest extant are probably those performed at York.
	1313–1375	Boccaccio.
Battle of Bannockburn.	1314	
John Wiclif.	c.1320–1384	
	c.1325–1408	John Gower.
Reign of Edward III.	1327–1377	
	c.1328	Chester cycle of guild plays composed.
Hundred Years' War.	1338–1453	
	c.1338	Boccaccio's *Filostrato* (founded on Benoît de Sainte Maure and Guido della Colonna).
Battle of Sluys (first important English victory in the Hundred Years' War).	1340	
	c.1340–1400	Geoffrey Chaucer.
Battle of Crécy.	1346	
Capture of Calais.	1347	
First epidemic of the Black Death.	1348–1350	
	1348–1358	Boccaccio's *Decamerone*.
Statute of Laborers.	1349	
Order of the Garter established.		
English replaces French in the schools.	c.1350	
Battle of Poitiers.	1356	
English used in opening Parliament.	1362	
	c.1362	*Piers Plowman*, A-text.

Political, Social, Religious		Literary, Philosophical
	1364	Death of Ranulf Higden, author of the *Polychronicon.*
	1367	John de Trevisa's English translation of Higden's *Polychronicon.*
	*c.*1370	Chaucer's *Book of the Duchess.* *Sir Gawain and the Green Knight.* *The Pearl.*
	1372–1373	Chaucer's first trip to Italy.
	*c.*1375	John Barbour's *Bruce.*
Reign of Richard II.	1377–1399	
	*c.*1377	*Piers Plowman,* B-text (first allusion to Robin Hood).
Great Schism.	1378–1417	
	1378	Chaucer's second trip to Italy.
	*c.*1378	Gower's *Speculum Meditantis* (in French).
	*c.*1380	Chaucer's *Hous of Fame.* Wiclif's translation of the Bible.
Peasants' Revolt.	1381	
	*c.*1382	Chaucer's *Parlement of Foules.* Gower's *Vox Clamantis.*
	*c.*1385	Chaucer's *Troilus and Criseyde* (founded on Boccaccio's *Filostrato*), *Legend of Good Women* (early version), and the "Knightes Tale" in the *Canterbury Tales.*
	1387	Departure of Canterbury pilgrims from the Tabard Inn, Southwark, on 17 April.
	*c.*1387	In Chaucer's *Canterbury Tales* the "Prologue" and the "Prioresses Tale." Thomas Usk's *Testament of Love.*
Battle of Otterburn, described in the ballad *The Hunting of the Cheviot.*	1388	
	1390	Gower's *Confessio Amantis* (in English).
	*c.*1390	*Piers Plowman,* C-text.
	1390–1447	Humphrey, Duke of Gloucestor, patron of letters.
	*c.*1393	The "Pardoners Tale" in Chaucer's *Canterbury Tales.*
	1393–1464	John Capgrave, chronicler.
	*c.*1395	The "Nonne Preestes Tale" in Chaucer's *Canterbury Tales.* Chaucer's *Legend of Good Women* (revised version).
	1396	Death of Walter Hilton, author of the *Scala Perfectionis.*
Reign of Henry IV (first of the Lancastrian kings).	1399–1413	
	*c.*1400	Froissart's *Chroniques.*
	1400–1425	Two English translations of *The Voiage and Travaile of Sir John Maundeville* (another, quite imperfect, may be earlier).

Political, Social, Religious		Literary, Philosophical
	1400–1500	Composition of the best of the English and Scottish popular ballads.
	c.1412	Thomas Occleve's *De Regimine Principum* (in English).
Reign of Henry V.	1413–1422	
Battle of Agincourt.	1415	
Reign of Henry VI.	1422–1461	
	1422–1509	*Paston Letters.*
	c.1423	*The Kingis Quair* of James I of Scotland.
	c.1425	*Castle of Perseverance* (first complete morality play extant).
		The Pride of Life (early fragment of a morality play).
		Wakefield (Towneley) cycle of guild plays.
Capture and execution of Joan of Arc.	1430–1431	
	1430?–1506	Robert Henryson, Scottish Chaucerian.
	1438	John Lydgate's *Falls of Princes* (founded on Boccaccio's *De Casibus Virorum Illustrium*).
	1446?–1519	William Grocyn.
Jack Cade's rebellion.	1450	
	1455	Reginald Pecock's *Repressor of Over-Much Blaming of the Clergy.*
Wars of the Roses.	1455–1485	
	1456	The Gutenberg Bible.
	1460?–1524	Thomas Linacre.
	c.1460–1529	John Skelton.
	c.1460–c.1530	William Dunbar, Scottish Chaucerian.
Reign of Edward IV (first of the Yorkist kings).	1461–1483	
	1466–1536	Erasmus.
	c.1467–1519	John Colet.
	1469 or 1470	Sir Thomas Malory's *Morte d'Arthur* completed.
	1469–1527	Machiavelli.
	1471	Death of Sir Thomas Malory.
Thomas Wolsey.	1471–1530	
	c.1474	Caxton prints at Bruges the *Recuyell of the Histories of Troy* (first book printed in English).
	1474–1533	Ariosto.
	1477	*Dictes and Seyings of the Philosophers* printed by Caxton at Westminster (the first dated book printed in England).
	1478–1535	St. Thomas More.
Reign of Edward V.	1483	
Reign of Richard III.	1483–1485	
	1483–1540	Guicciardini.
	1483–1546	Luther.
Battle of Bosworth Field.	1485	Caxton publishes Malory's *Morte d'Arthur.*
Reign of Henry VII (first of the Tudor kings).	1485–1509	

Political, Social, Religious		Literary, Philosophical
Thomas Cranmer.	1489–1556	
	*c.*1490	Henry Medwall's *Fulgens and Lucrece* (first extant interlude).
	*c.*1490–1536	William Tyndale.
	1491	Greek taught at Oxford.
First voyage of Columbus.	1492	
	1493–1537	Earliest editions of *Everyman.*
	1495?–1553	Rabelais.
Vasco da Gama reaches India by the Cape of Good Hope.	1497–1498	
John Cabot in America.	1497–1499	
	1499–1500	First visit of Erasmus to England.
	1503?–1542	Sir Thomas Wyatt.
	*c.*1505	Skelton's *Bowge of Court* written.
	1505–1506	Second visit of Erasmus to England.
	1509	Alexander Barclay's *Ship of Fools.* Erasmus's *Praise of Folly.* Stephen Hawes's *Pastime of Pleasure.*
	1509–1514	Third visit of Erasmus to England.
Reign of Henry VIII.	1509–1547	
Calvin.	1509–1564	
Battle of Flodden Field.	1513	
Wolsey chief minister of State.	1515–1529	
	1515–1568	Roger Ascham.
	1516	More's *Utopia* (in Latin).
	1516–1532	Ariosto's *Orlando Furioso.*
Luther posts his theses in Wittenberg.	1517	
	1517?–1547	Henry Howard, Earl of Surrey.
Circumnavigation of the earth by Magellan's fleet.	1519–1522	
William Cecil, Lord Burghley.	1520–1598	
Diet of Worms.	1521	
	1523	Skelton's *Garland of Laurel* published.
	1523–1525	Lord Berners's English translation of Froissart's *Chronicles.*
	1524–1585	Ronsard.
	1525–1526	Tyndale's New Testament (published in Germany).
	1525?–1577	George Gascoigne.
	1528	Castiglione's *Book of the Courtier.*
	1529	Simon Fish's *Supplication of Beggars.*
	1530	Tyndale's Pentateuch.
	1531	Sir Thomas Elyot's *Governour.*
	1532	Chaucer's *Works,* ed. William Thynne. Machiavelli's *Prince* published.
	1532–1548	Rabelais's *Pantagruel* and *Gargantua.*
Henry VIII marries Anne Boleyn. Separation of the English Church from Rome.	1533	
Thomas Cromwell in power.	1533–1540	
	1533–1592	Montaigne.
Act of Supremacy (Henry VIII head of the Church of England).	1534	
	1535	Miles Coverdale's first complete English Bible.

Political, Social, Religious		Literary, Philosophical
	1536	Calvin's *Institutes of the Christian Religion.*
	1536–1608	Thomas Sackville, Lord Buckhurst.
	1539	The Great Bible (prepared under Cranmer).
	1540	Sir David Lindsay's *Satyr of Three Estates.*
	*c.*1540	Nicholas Udall's *Ralph Roister Doister* written.
	1542–1550	Edward Hall's *Chronicle.*
	1543–1607	Sir Edward Dyer.
	1545	Ascham's *Toxophilus.*
	*c.*1545	John Heywood's *Four P.P.* published.
Council of Trent.	1546–1563	
Reign of Edward VI.	1547–1553	
	1547–1562	English version of the Psalms by Thomas Sternhold and John Hopkins.
	1547–1616	Cervantes.
First Book of Common Prayer and Act of Uniformity.	1549	Joachim Du Bellay's *Défense et Illustration de la Langue Française.*
	1551	Translation of More's *Utopia* into English by Ralph Robinson.
Second Book of Common Prayer and Second Act of Uniformity.	1552	
	1552?–1599	Edmund Spenser.
	1552?–1618	Sir Walter Ralegh.
	1553	Thomas Wilson's *Arte of Rhetorique.*
Reign of Mary I (Mary Tudor).	1553–1558	
Marriage of Mary and Philip of Spain. Execution of Lady Jane Grey.	1554	
	1554–1586	Sir Philip Sidney.
	1554?–1606	John Lyly.
	*c.*1555	George Cavendish's *Life of Cardinal Wolsey* written. William Roper's *Life of Sir Thomas More* written.
Mary's religious executions.	1555–1558	
	1557	St. Thomas More's English *Works* (ed. William Rastell). *Songs and Sonnets* (*Tottel's Miscellany*). Surrey's blank verse translation of the *Aeneid,* Books II and IV, published.
Loss of Calais.	1558	John Knox's *First Blast of the Trumpet against the Monstrous Regiment of Women.*
	1558–1562	Thomas Phaer's English translation of the *Aeneid.*
Reign of Elizabeth.	1558–1603	
	1558?–1597?	George Peele.
Elizabethan Prayer Book. Elizabethan Acts of Supremacy and Uniformity.	1559	
	1559–1610	*Mirror for Magistrates.*
	1559?–1634	George Chapman.

Political, Social, Religious		Literary, Philosophical
	c.1560	*Gammer Gurton's Needle.*
		Geneva Bible.
	1560?–1592	Robert Greene.
	1561	Sir Thomas Hoby's English translation of Castiglione's *Cortegiano* (*The Courtier*).
		Thomas Norton's English translation of Calvin's *Institutes.*
		Sackville and Norton's *Gorboduc* acted.
		Joseph Scaliger's *Poetics.*
	1561–1626	Francis Bacon.
	1562	Richard Grafton's *Abridgement of the Chronicles of England.*
Wars of Religion in France.	1562–1598	
	1562–1619	Samuel Daniel.
	1563	John Foxe's *Actes and Monuments* (*The Book of Martyrs*).
		Sackville's *Induction* to the *Mirror for Magistrates.*
	1563–1631	Michael Drayton.
	1564–1593	Christopher Marlowe.
	1564–1616	William Shakespeare.
	1565	John Stow's *Summarie of English Chronicles.*
	1565–1567	Arthur Golding's English translation of Ovid's *Metamorphoses.*
	1566	Gascoigne's *Supposes* and *Jocasta.*
	1566–1567	William Painter's *Palace of Pleasure.*
	1567–1619	Thomas Campion.
Battle of Langside (Mary of Scotland surrenders to Elizabeth).	1568	
Northern Rising.	1569	
Pius V excommunicates Elizabeth.	1570	Ascham's *Scholemaster.*
	1570?–1632?	Thomas Dekker.
Thirty-nine Articles issued.	1571	
Massacre of St. Bartholomew.	1572	Gascoigne's *Hundred Sundry Flowers.*
	1572–1637	Ben Jonson.
	1572?–1631	John Donne.
William Laud.	1573–1645	
First executions of Catholic missionaries.	1575	
	1576	Gascoigne's *Steel Glass.*
		A Paradise of Dainty Devices (ed. Richard Edwards).
		George Pettie's *Petite Palace of Pettie his Pleasure.*
		The Theater built (first London playhouse).
Sir Francis Drake circumnavigates the earth in the *Golden Hind.*	1577–1580	
	1578	*A Gorgeous Gallery of Gallant Inventions.*
		Raphael Holinshed's *Chronicles* (revised edition 1586–1587).
		Lyly's *Euphues, the Anatomy of Wit.*

Political, Social, Religious		Literary, Philosophical
	1579	Stephen Gosson's *School of Abuse.*
		Sir Thomas North's English translation of Plutarch's *Lives.*
		Spenser's *Shepherd's Calendar.*
	1579–1625	John Fletcher.
	1580	Lyly's *Euphues and his England.*
	1580	John Stowe's *Chronicles of England.*
	*c.*1580	Sidney's *Arcadia* and *Astrophel and Stella* written; his *Defense of Poesy* begun.
	1580–1597	Montaigne's *Essays.*
	1581	Tasso's *Jerusalem Delivered.*
		English translation of Seneca's *Tragedies,* by Thomas Newton and others.
	*c.*1581	Peele's *Arraignment of Paris* written.
	1582	Richard Stanyhurst's translation of Virgil's *Aeneid,* Books I–IV.
	1583	Philip Stubbes's *Anatomie of Abuses.*
	1584	Lyly's *Alexander and Campaspe.*
		A Handful of Pleasant Delights (ed. Clement Robinson).
		Reginald Scot's *Discovery of Witchcraft.*
	1584–1616	Francis Beaumont.
	1586	William Webbe's *Discourse of English Poetrie.*
		William Warner's *Albion's England.*
		William Camden's *Britannia.*
Execution of Mary Queen of Scots.	1587	
	*c.*1587	Marlowe's *Tamburlaine,* Part I, written.
		Thomas Kyd's *Spanish Tragedy* written.
Defeat of the Spanish Armada.	1588	
	*c.*1588	Marlowe's *Doctor Faustus* written.
	1588–1589	Martin Marprelate tracts.
	1588–1679	Thomas Hobbes.
	1589	Greene's *Menaphon.*
		George Puttenham's *Art of English Poesie.*
		Richard Hakluyt's *Principall Navigations, Voyages, and Discoveries of the English Nation* (enlarged 1598–1600).
	1590	Thomas Lodge's *Rosalynde.*
		Spenser's *Faerie Queene,* Books I–III.
	*c.*1590	Greene's *James IV* performed.
		Peele's *Old Wives' Tale* written.
	1590–1593	Sidney's *Arcadia* published (earlier, shorter version first printed, from manuscript, 1926).
	1591	John Harington's English translation of Ariosto's *Orlando Furioso.*
		Sidney's *Astrophel and Stella* published.
		Spenser's *Complaints.*
	1591–1592	Greene's Conny-Catching pamphlets.
	1591–1674	Robert Herrick.
	1592	Daniel's *Delia.*

Political, Social, Religious		Literary, Philosophical
	1593	*The Phoenix' Nest.*
		Shakespeare's *Venus and Adonis.*
	1593–1633	George Herbert.
	1593–1683	Izaak Walton.
	1594	Drayton's *Idea.*
		Thomas Nashe's *Unfortunate Traveler.*
		Shakespeare's *Rape of Lucrece.*
	1594–1595	Shakespeare's *Romeo and Juliet* probably written.
	1594–1597	Richard Hooker's *Of Ecclesiastical Polity,* Books I–V.
	1595	Daniel's *Civil Wars.*
		Sidney's *Defense of Poesy* published.
		Spenser's *Amoretti* and *Epithalamion.*
Cadiz Expedition (under Essex and Ralegh)	1596	Ralegh's *Discovery of Guiana.*
		Spenser's *Faerie Queene,* Books IV–VI.
	*c.*1596	Thomas Deloney's *Thomas of Reading.*
	1597	Bacon's *Essays* (first edition, ten essays).
		Drayton's *Heroical Epistles.*
	1597–1598	Shakespeare's *Henry IV* probably written.
Edict of Nantes.	1598	Jonson's *Every Man in His Humor.*
		Francis Meres's *Palladis Tamia.*
		John Stow's *Survey of London.*
	1598–1600	Shakespeare's *As You Like It, Twelfth Night, Julius Caesar,* and *Hamlet* probably written.
The rebellion of Hugh O'Neill, Earl of Tyrone.	1598–1603	
	1598–1611	Chapman's English translation of the *Iliad.*
	1599	Sir John Davies's *Nosce Teipsum.*
		The Globe Theater built.
Oliver Cromwell.	1599–1658	
	1600	*England's Helicon* (ed. John Bodenham).
		England's Parnassus (ed. Robert Allot).
		Dekker's *Shoemakers' Holiday* and *Old Fortunatus* published.
Elizabethan Poor Law.	1601	
Execution of the Earl of Essex.		
	1602.	Founding of the Bodleian Library.
		Campion's *Observations in the Art of English Poesie.*
		Poetical Rhapsody (ed. Francis and Walter Davison).
	*c.*1602	Daniel's *Defense of Ryme.*
	1603	John Florio's English translation of Montaigne's *Essays.*
		Thomas Heywood's *Woman Killed with Kindness* acted.
Reign of James I (first of the Stuart kings).	1603–1625	

Political, Social, Religious		Literary, Philosophical
Hampton Court Conference.	1604	
	1604–1605	Shakespeare's *Othello* probably written.
	1604	Dekker's *Honest Whore,* Part I.
Gunpowder Plot.	1605	Bacon's *Advancement of Learning.*
	1605–1615	Cervantes's *Don Quixote.*
	1605–1682	Sir Thomas Browne.
	1606	Jonson's *Volpone* written.
	1606–1607	Shakespeare's *Macbeth, King Lear,* and *Antony and Cleopatra* probably written.
	1606–1668	Sir William Davenant.
	1606–1684	Corneille.
	1606–1687	Edmund Waller.
First settlement in Virginia	1607	Chapman's *Bussy D'Ambois.*
	c.1608	John Webster's *White Devil* acted.
	1608–1661	Thomas Fuller.
	1608–1674	John Milton.
	1609	Shakespeare's *Sonnets* published. Dekker's *Gull's Hornbook* and *Four Birds of Noah's Ark.*
	c.1609	Beaumont and Fletcher's *Knight of the Burning Pestle* and *Philaster* acted.
	1609–1642	Sir John Suckling.
	1609–1674	Edward Hyde, Earl of Clarendon (*History of the Rebellion* published 1702–1704).
	1610	Giles Fletcher's *Christ's Victory and Triumph.* Jonson's *Alchemist* written.
	1611	King James Bible, often referred to as the Authorized Version.
	1611–1612	Shakespeare's *Tempest* probably written.
	1612	Bacon's *Essays* (second edition, thirty-eight essays). Donne's *Second Anniversary.* Thomas Shelton's English translation of Cervantes's *Don Quixote.*
	1612–1622	Drayton's *Polyolbion.*
	1612–1680	Samuel Butler.
	1612?–1649	Richard Crashaw.
	1613–1616	William Browne of Tavistock's *Britannia's Pastorals.*
	1614	Sir Thomas Overbury's *Characters.* Ralegh's *History of the World.*
	c.1614	John Webster's *Duchess of Malfi* acted.
	1614–1615	Chapman's English translation of the *Odyssey.*
Bacon made Lord Chancellor. Synod of Dort.	1618	
Thirty Years' War.	1618–1648	
	1618–1658	Richard Lovelace.
	1618–1667	Abraham Cowley.
Pilgrim Fathers establish Plymouth.	1620	Bacon's *Novum Organum.*
	1620–1706	John Evelyn (*Diary* first published 1818).

Political, Social, Religious		Literary, Philosophical
	1621	Robert Burton's *Anatomy of Melancholy.*
	1621–1678	Andrew Marvell.
	1622–1673	Molière.
	1622–1695	Henry Vaughan.
	1623	First folio of Shakespeare's *Plays.*
		Thomas Middleton's *Changeling* acted.
	1625	Bacon's *Essays* (third edition, fifty-eight essays).
Reign of Charles I.	1625–1649	
	1626	Bacon's *New Atlantis.*
Duke of Buckingham murdered.	1628	Sir Edward Coke's *Institutes of the Laws of England.*
	1628–1688	John Bunyan.
	1629	Milton's *On the Morning of Christ's Nativity* written.
Personal government of Charles I.	1629–1640	
Puritan settlement of Massachusetts Bay.	1630	Dekker's *Honest Whore,* Part II.
	c.1631	Milton's *L'Allegro* and *Il Penseroso* written.
	1631–1700	John Dryden.
	1632	Second folio of Shakespeare's *Plays.*
	1632–1704	John Locke.
Laud made Archbishop of Canterbury.	1633	William Prynne's *Histriomastix.*
		Donne's *Poems.*
		Phineas Fletcher's *Purple Island.*
		John Ford's *'Tis Pity She's a Whore.*
		Philip Massinger's *New Way to Pay Old Debts.*
		Herbert's *Temple.*
	1633–1703	Samuel Pepys.
First levy of ship-money in England.	1634	Milton's *Comus* written.
	1635–1691	George Etherege.
	1636?–1674	Thomas Traherne (*Poetical Works* first published 1903; *Centuries of Meditations,* 1908).
Hampden's Case.	1637	Descartes's *Discours sur la Méthode.*
		Milton's *Lycidas* written.
		James Shirley's *Lady of Pleasure.*
	1638–1639	Milton's trip to Italy.
	1638–1706	Charles Sackville, Earl of Dorset.
	1639–1699	Racine.
	1639?–1701	Sir Charles Sedley.
Short Parliament.	1640	Walton's *Life of Donne* (with Donne's *LXXX Sermons*).
Long Parliament.	1640–1660	
	1640?–1716	William Wycherley.
Triennial Act.	1641	
Execution of the Earl of Strafford.		
	1642	Browne's *Religio Medici* (first, unauthorized edition).
		Sir John Denham's *Cooper's Hill.*
		Fuller's *Holy State.*
		Theaters closed by the Puritans.

Political, Social, Religious		Literary, Philosophical
	*c.*1642	Milton's drafts for a play on the subject of *Paradise Lost.*
Civil War.	1642–1651	
	1642–1727	Sir Isaac Newton.
	1643	Sir Richard Baker's *Chronicle of the Kings of England.* Browne's *Religio Medici* (authorized edition).
Battle of Marston Moor.	1644	Milton's *Areopagitica* and *On Education.*
Cromwell's Model Army (following the Self-Denying Ordinance). Battle of Naseby.	1645	James Howell's *Epistolae Ho-elianae.* First collection of Milton's minor poems published.
	1646	Browne's *Pseudodoxia Epidemica.*
	1647	Cowley's *Mistress.*
	1647–1680	John Wilmot, Earl of Rochester.
	1647–1710	Henry Aldrich.
	1648	Herrick's *Hesperides* and *Noble Numbers* (second edition, 1823).
Execution of Charles I.	1649	Milton's *Tenure of Kings and Magistrates.*
Commonwealth.	1649–1660	
	1650	Marvell's *Horatian Ode upon Cromwell's Return from Ireland.*
	1650–1651	Jeremy Taylor's *Holy Living* and *Holy Dying.*
	1650–1655	Vaughan's *Silex Scintillans.*
John Churchill, Duke of Marlborough.	1650–1722	
Battle of Worcester. Navigation Act.	1651	Davenant's *Gondibert.* Hobbes's *Leviathan.* Milton's *Pro Populo Anglicano Defensio.*
First Dutch Naval War.	1652–1654	Dorothy Osborne's *Letters* written (first published 1888).
Rump Parliament ejected. Barebone's Parliament. Cromwell Lord Protector.	1653	Walton's *Compleat Angler,* Part I.
	1656	Cowley's *Davideis* and *Pindaric Odes.* Davenant's *Siege of Rhodes.*
	1658	Browne's *Hydriotaphia.* Dryden's *Stanzas on the Death of Cromwell.*
Restoration.	1660	
	1660–1669	Pepys's *Diary* written (first published 1825).
Reign of Charles II.	1660–1685	
	1660–1672	Bunyan's first imprisonment.
	1660?–1731	Daniel Defoe.
	1661	Joseph Glanvill's *Vanity of Dogmatizing.*
Final version of the Prayer Book.	1662	Fuller's *Worthies of England.* Royal Society chartered.
	1662–1678	Samuel Butler's *Hudibras.*
	1663	Third Folio of Shakespeare's *Plays.* Drury Lane Theater built.

Political, Social, Religious		Literary, Philosophical
Great Plague.	1665	Dryden and Sir Robert Howard's *Indian Queen.*
Second Dutch War.	1665–1667	
Great Fire of London.	1666	Bunyan's *Grace Abounding.*
		Molière's *Misanthrope.*
	1667	Dryden's *Annus Mirabilis.*
		Milton's *Paradise Lost* (first edition, in ten books).
		Molière's *Tartuffe.*
		Thomas Sprat's *History of the Royal Society.*
	1667–1745	Jonathan Swift.
	1668	Dryden's *Essay of Dramatic Poesy.*
		Sir Charles Sedley's *Mulberry Garden.*
	1668–1688	Dryden poet laureate.
	1668–1694	La Fontaine's *Fables.*
Secret Treaty of Dover.	1670	Pascal's *Pensées.*
	1670–1672	Dryden's *Conquest of Granada.*
	1670–1729	William Congreve.
	1671	Milton's *Paradise Regained* and *Samson Agonistes.*
		The Rehearsal acted (the work of George Villiers, Duke of Buckingham, and others).
	1672–1719	Joseph Addison.
	1672–1729	Sir Richard Steele.
	1674	Boileau's *Art Poétique.*
		Milton's *Paradise Lost* (second edition, in twelve books).
	*c.*1674	Wycherley's *Plain-Dealer* acted.
	1676	Charles Cotton's *Compleat Angler,* Part II.
		Etherege's *Man of Mode.*
	1677	Mme. de Lafayette's *Princesse de Clèves.*
		Nathaniel Lee's *Rival Queens.*
		Racine's *Phèdre.*
		Wycherley's *Plain-Dealer* published.
Popish Plot.	1678	Dryden's *All for Love.*
		Thomas Rymer's *Tragedies of the Last Age Considered.*
		Bunyan's *Pilgrim's Progress,* Part I.
	*c.*1678	Mrs. Aphra Behn's *Oroonoko.*
	1679–1714	Gilbert Burnet's *History of the Reformation.*
	1680	Bunyan's *Life and Death of Mr. Badman.*
	1681–1682	Dryden's *Absalom and Achitophel.*
	1682	Dryden's *MacFlecknoe* and *Religio Laici.*
		Thomas Otway's *Venice Preserved.*
	1684	Bunyan's *Pilgrim's Progress,* Part II.
Monmouth's Rebellion.	1685	
Revocation of the Edict of Nantes.		
Reign of James II.	1685–1688	
	1685–1753	George Berkeley.

Political, Social, Religious		Literary, Philosophical
	1687	Newton's *Principia.*
		Dryden's *Hind and the Panther.*
Glorious or Bloodless Revolution.	1688	George Savile, Marquis of Halifax's *Character of a Trimmer.*
	1688–1692	Thomas Shadwell poet laureate.
Reign of William III and Mary II.	1688–1694	
	1688–1744	Alexander Pope.
Bill of Rights.	1689	
Toleration Act.		
	1689–1761	Samuel Richardson.
	1690	Locke's *Essay Concerning the Human Understanding.*
	1691–1692	Anthony à Wood's *Athenae Oxonienses.*
A society for the reformation of manners founded.	1692	Thomas Rymer's *Short View of Tragedy.*
		Sir William Temple's *Essays.*
	1692–1699	English Quarrel of the Ancients and the Moderns.
	1692–1715	Nahum Tate poet laureate.
	1693	Locke's *Thoughts concerning Education.*
	1694	William Wotton's *Reflections on Ancient and Modern Learning.*
Reign of William III.	1694–1702	
	1694–1773	Philip Stanhope, Earl of Chesterfield.
	1694–1778	Voltaire.
	1695	Congreve's *Love for Love.*
	1696	John Toland's *Christianity not Mysterious.*
Treaty of Ryswick.	1697	Dryden's *Alexander's Feast.*
		Sir John Vanbrugh's *Relapse.*
	1697–1698	Swift's *Tale of a Tub* and *Battle of the Books* written.
	1698	Jeremy Collier's *Short View of the Immorality and Profaneness of the English Stage.*
	1698–1703	Edward Ward's *London Spy.*
	1699	Samuel Garth's *Dispensary.*
	1700	Congreve's *Way of the World.*
		Dryden's *Fables.*
		John Pomfret's *Choice.*
		Tom Brown's *Amusements Serious and Comical.*
Act of Settlement.	1701	Defoe's *True-Born Englishman.*
		Steele's *Christian Hero.*
War of the Spanish Succession.	1701–1714	
	1702	Defoe's *Shortest Way with the Dissenters.*
	1702–1704	Clarendon's *History of the Rebellion and Civil Wars in England* first published.
Reign of Queen Anne.	1702–1714	
	1703	Nicholas Rowe's *Fair Penitent.*
		Steele's *Lying Lover.*
John Wesley.	1703–1791	

Political, Social, Religious		Literary, Philosophical
Capture of Gibraltar. Battles of Blenheim and Malaga.	1704	Swift's *Tale of a Tub* and *Battle of the Books* published.
	1705	Addison's *Campaign*. Steele's *Tender Husband*.
Parliamentary Union of England and Scotland.	1707	George Farquhar's *Beaux' Stratagem*.
	1707–1754	Henry Fielding.
William Pitt, Earl of Chatham.	1708–1778	
	1709	Pope's *Pastorals*.
	1709–1711	The *Tatler*.
	1709–1784	Samuel Johnson.
	1710–1713	Swift's *Journal to Stella* written.
	1711	Pope's *Essay on Criticism*. Anthony Ashley Cooper, Earl of Shaftesbury's *Characteristics of Men and Manners*.
	1711–1712	The *Spectator*.
	1711–1776	David Hume.
	1712–1714	Pope's *Rape of the Lock*.
	1712–1778	Rousseau.
Treaty of Utrecht.	1713	Pope's *Windsor Forest*. Scriblerus Club formed. Addison's *Cato*. Berkeley's *Dialogues between Hylas and Philonous*. Steele's *Guardian*. Anne Finch, Countess of Winchilsea's *Miscellany Poems*.
	1713–1768	Laurence Sterne.
	1714–1723	Bernard Mandeville's *Fable of the Bees*.
Reign of George I (first of the Hanoverian kings).	1714–1727	
George Whitefield.	1714–1770	
First Jacobite Rebellion.	1715	Isaac Watts's *Divine Songs for Children*.
	1715–1718	Nicholas Rowe poet laureate.
	1715–1720	Pope's translation of the *Iliad*.
	1716	John Gay's *Trivia*.
	1716–1771	Thomas Gray.
	1717–1779	David Garrick.
	1717–1797	Horace Walpole.
	1718–1730	Laurence Eusden poet laureate.
	1719	Defoe's *Robinson Crusoe*. Isaac Watts's *Psalms of David*.
South Sea Bubble.	1720	
Sir Robert Walpole head of the cabinet.	1721–1742	
	1721–1771	Tobias Smollett.
	1722	Defoe's *Journal of the Plague Year* and *Moll Flanders*. Steele's *Conscious Lovers* acted.
	1723–1734	Gilbert Burnet's *History of My Own Time*.
	1723–1792	Sir Joshua Reynolds.

Political, Social, Religious		Literary, Philosophical
	1724	*The Evergreen* (collection of old Scotch poetry, ed. Allan Ramsay).
		Swift's *Drapier's Letters.*
	1724–1804	Kant.
	1725	Allan Ramsay's *Gentle Shepherd.*
		Pope's edition of Shakespeare.
	1725–1726	Pope's translation of the *Odyssey.*
Robert Clive, Lord Clive.	1725–1774	
	1726	Swift's *Gulliver's Travels.*
	1726–1727	John Dyer's *Grongar Hill.*
	1726–1729	Voltaire's visit to England.
	1726–1730	James Thomson's *Seasons.*
	1727–1737	The period covered in the *Memoirs of the Reign of George II* by Lord Hervey (first published 1848).
	1727–1750	John Gay's *Fables.*
Reign of George II.	1727–1760	
	1728	John Gay's *Beggar's Opera.*
		William Law's *Serious Call to a Devout and Holy Life.*
	1728–1743	Pope's *Dunciad.*
	1728–1774	Oliver Goldsmith.
	1729	Swift's *Modest Proposal.*
	1729–1797	Edmund Burke.
	1730–1731	Fielding's *Tom Thumb.*
	1730–1757	Colley Cibber poet laureate.
	1731	George Lillo's *London Merchant, or George Barnwell.*
	1731–1800	William Cowper.
	1731–1914	The *Gentleman's Magazine.*
	1732	Covent Garden Theater built.
Warren Hastings.	1732–1818	
	1733	Pope's *Essay on Man.*
	1734	Lewis Theobald's edition of Shakespeare.
	1735	Pope's *Epistle to Dr. Arbuthnot.*
	1736	Joseph Butler's *Analogy of Religion.*
	1737	William Shenstone's *Schoolmistress.*
		Act for licensing the theaters.
		Wesley's *Psalms and Hymns.*
	1737–1741	William Warburton's *Divine Legation of Moses.*
	1737–1768	Chesterfield's *Letters to His Natural Son* written.
	1737–1794	Edward Gibbon.
	1738	Johnson's *London.*
	1739–1740	Hume's *Treatise of Human Nature.*
	1739–1741	Gray's trip to the Continent with Horace Walpole.
	1740	Colley Cibber's *Apology for the Life of Colley Cibber.*
		Richardson's *Pamela, or Virtue Rewarded.*
War of the Austrian Succession.	1740–1748	
	1740–1795	James Boswell.

Political, Social, Religious		Literary, Philosophical
	1742	Fielding's *Joseph Andrews.*
		Edward Young's *Complaint, or Night Thoughts.*
	1743	Robert Blair's *Grave.*
		Fielding's *Jonathan Wild the Great.*
	1744	Mark Akenside's *Pleasures of Imagination.*
Second Jacobite Rebellion.	1745–1746	
Battle of Culloden.	1746	William Collins's *Odes.*
		Joseph Warton's *Odes.*
	1747	Thomas Warton's *Pleasures of Melancholy.*
	1748	James Thomson's *Castle of Indolence.*
		Richardson's *Clarissa Harlowe.*
		Smollett's *Roderick Random.*
		Hume's *Inquiry concerning Human Understanding.*
		Montesquieu's *Esprit des Lois.*
	1748–1832	Jeremy Bentham.
	1749	Fielding's *Tom Jones.*
		Henry St. John, Lord Bolingbroke's *Idea of a Patriot King.*
		Johnson's *Vanity of Human Wishes.*
Charles James Fox	1749–1806	
	1749–1832	Goethe.
	1750–1752	Johnson's *Rambler.*
	1751	Gray's *Elegy Written in a Country Churchyard.*
		Fielding's *Amelia.*
		Smollett's *Peregrine Pickle.*
	1751–1816	Richard Brinsley Sheridan.
Gregorian Calendar adopted by act of Parliament.	1752	
	1752–1770	Thomas Chatterton.
	1753	British Museum chartered.
	1753–1754	Richardson's *Sir Charles Grandison.*
	1754	Thomas Warton's *Observations on the Fairie Queene of Spenser.*
	1754–1762	Hume's *History of England.*
	1754–1832	George Crabbe.
	1755	Johnson's *English Dictionary.*
Black Hole of Calcutta.	1756	John Home's *Douglas* acted.
William Pitt the elder, head of the cabinet.	1756–1761	
Seven Years' War.	1756–1763	
	1756–1782	Joseph Warton's *Genius and Writings of Pope.*
Clive's victory at Plassey.	1757	Gray's *Odes* (*The Bard* and *The Progress of Poesy*).
	1757–1785	William Whitehead poet laureate.
	1757–1827	William Blake.
Capture of Louisburg.	1758	
	1758–1760	Johnson's *Idler.*

Political, Social, Religious		Literary, Philosophical
Wolfe takes Quebec.	1759	Goldsmith's *Bee.* Johnson's *Rasselas.* Voltaire's *Candide.* British Museum opened.
	1759–1796	Robert Burns.
	1759–1805	Schiller.
	1760	James Macpherson's *Fragments of Ancient Poetry* (*Ossian*). Rousseau's *Nouvelle Héloise.*
	1760–1761	Goldsmith's *Citizen of the World* (*Chinese Letters*).
	1760–1767	Sterne's *Tristram Shandy.*
Reign of George III.	1760–1820	
	1761	Charles Churchill's *Rosciad.*
	1762	Richard Hurd's *Letters on Chivalry and Romance.* Rousseau's *Contrat Social.*
	1762–1763	Smollett's *Briton.* John Wilkes's *North Briton.*
	1763	Boswell meets Johnson, 16 May.
	1763–1766	Boswell's visit to the Continent.
Spinning jenny invented by James Hargreaves.	1764	Goldsmith's *Traveler.* The Literary Club established. Walpole's *Castle of Otranto.*
Invention of the steam engine by James Watt.	1765	Johnson's edition of Shakespeare. Thomas Percy's *Reliques of Ancient English Poetry.*
	1765–1769	Sir William Blackstone's *Commentaries on the Laws of England.*
	1766	Goldsmith's *Vicar of Wakefield.* Lessing's *Laokoön.*
	1766–1767	Rousseau's visit to England.
	1768	Boswell's *Account of Corsica.* Goldsmith's *Good-Natured Man.* Hugh Kelly's *False Delicacy.* Sterne's *Sentimental Journey.*
	1768–1772	*Letters of Junius* (perhaps by Sir Philip Francis).
	1768–1840	Francis Burney's *Letters and Diaries* written (first published 1842–1889).
	1768–1848	Chateaubriand.
	1769	William Robertson's *History of Charles V.*
Controversy over the election of John Wilkes for Middlesex.	1769–1774	
	1769–1790	Reynold's *Discourses to the Royal Academy.*
	1770	Burke's *Thoughts on the Present Discontent.* Goldsmith's *Deserted Village.*
Lord North head of the cabinet.	1770–1782	
	1770–1850	William Wordsworth.
	1771	Henry Mackenzie's *Man of Feeling.* Smollett's *Humphry Clinker.*
	1771–1774	James Beattie's *Minstrel.*

Political, Social, Religious		Literary, Philosophical
	1771–1832	Sir Walter Scott.
	1772	Richard Graves's *Spiritual Quixote.*
	1772–1834	Samuel Taylor Coleridge.
	1773	Goldsmith's *She Stoops to Conquer.*
	1773–1779	Robert Fergusson's *Poems.*
	1774	Chesterfield's *Letters to His Natural Son* published.
		Goethe's *Sorrows of Werther.*
	1774–1781	Thomas Warton's *History of English Poetry.*
	1774–1843	Robert Southey.
	1775	Burke's *Speech on Conciliation.*
		Sheridan's *Rivals* performed.
War with the American Colonies.	1775–1783	
	1775–1817	Jane Austen.
	1775–1834	Charles Lamb.
	1775–1864	Walter Savage Landor.
Declaration of American Independence.	1776	Thomas Paine's *Common Sense.*
		Adam Smith's *Wealth of Nations.*
	1776–1788	Gibbon's *Decline and Fall of the Roman Empire.*
	1777	Chatterton's *Rowley Poems* published.
		Maurice Morgann's *Essay on the Character of Falstaff.*
		Clara Reeve's *Champion of Virtue (The Old English Baron).*
		Sheridan's *School for Scandal* performed.
	1778	Frances Burney's *Evelina.*
	1778–1830	William Hazlitt.
	1779	Hume's *Natural History of Religion.*
		Cowper and John Newton's *Olney Hymns.*
	1779–1781	Johnson's *Lives of the Poets.*
Gordon Riots.	1780	
	1781	Charles Macklin's *Man of the World* acted.
		Sheridan's *Critic.*
		Kant's *Critique of Pure Reason.*
	1781–1788	Rousseau's *Confessions.*
	1782	Cowper's *Poems* and *Diverting History of John Gilpin.*
	1783	William Blake's *Poetical Sketches.*
		George Crabbe's *Village.*
		Joseph Ritson's *Collection of English Songs.*
William Pitt the younger, head of the cabinet.	1783–1801	

Glossary

(Words are included which occur in the poems by Chaucer, in the *Popular Ballads*, and in Book I of Spencer's *Faerie Queene*. Words unfamiliar only by reason of their spelling, whose meaning can be determined by pronunciation, are not included. Unfamiliar words not contained in any good modern dictionary which occur in texts other than those mentioned above are explained in footnotes.)

a, one; of.
a', all.
abon, above.
about, out of.
abrayde, awoke.
abused, deceived.
abye, pay for.
accident, outward appearance.
accordaunt, according.
achat, buying.
achatours, buyers.
acord, agree; agreement.
acquite, release.
addrest, prepared; ready; directed.
admired, wondered at.
adrad, afraid.
advauncing, praising.
afferm, establish as true.
afflicted, downcast.
affray, alarm; panic; terror.
affyle his tonge, polish his speech.
after, along; according to.
agayn, toward; in.
agayns, when you meet.
ageyn, against.
aghast, frightened.
ago, gone.
agraste, favored.
agrief, amiss.
al, although; awl.
albe, although.
alday, at any time.
alderbest, best of all.
ale-stake, a stake projecting horizontally from a house to indicate that ale could be bought there.
algate, in every case; nevertheless.
Algezir, Algeciras in north Africa.
Alisaundre, Alexandria.
alkin, of every kind.
alle and somme, one and all.
aller, of all.
almner, giver of alms.
als, also.
al-so, as.
amate, dismay; dishearten.
amazed, bewildered.
amazement, perplexity.
amblere, pacer.
amende, improve.
amis, hood; cape; wrongly.
a-morwe, on the morrow.
amoved, stirred.
an(d), if.
and, an.
ane, one.
anlas, dagger.
annoy, distress.
anon, instantly.
antiphoner, anthem-book.
ape, fool; dupe.
applyde, accommodated.
approving, proving.
apyked, sharpened; trimmed.
archery, archers.
aread, point out; tell; make known.
areeds, counsels.
areste, stop.
arette, impute; consider.
aright, wholly; well.
arise, depart.
armory, armor.
arras, tapestry.
array, dress.
arrayed, ordered; dressed.
aryve, disembarcation of troops.
ascendent, part of the zodiac rising above the horizon.
aslake, appease.
aspire, grow up.
aspye, spy.
assay, try; touch; assail; attack; value.
assent, conspiracy.
assoile, pardon.
assoilling, absolution.
assured, secure.
assynd, pointed out.
asterte, escape.
as that, as one who.
aston(ie)d, stunned.
attaint, dim.
attained, broached.
atte beste, in the best fashion.
attempree, temperate.
Austin, St. Augustine.
avale, fall.
avaunce, profit.
avaunt, boast.
avauntour, boaster.
Ave-Mary, prayer to the Virgin.
avenge, take vengeance on.
aventure, chance.
avision, vision.
avize, perceive; consider.
avouchen, prove.
avys, opinion.
avysed, well advised.
awkwarde, backhanded.
axe, ask.
ay, always.

ba, ball.
bachelere, young aspirant to knighthood.
bains, banns.
bairn, child.
baite, feed.
baith, both.
bake mete, meat pie.
bale, injury; evil influence; sorrow; fire.
ballade, poem consisting of one or more triplets of seven or eight-line stanzas, each ending with the same refrain, and an envoy.
bands, bonds.
banes, banns.
bar, bore.
barne, man.
barres, stripes; ornaments.
baser, too humble.
basnites, light helmets.
bastard, ignoble.
batailed, battlemented.
battailous, warlike.
bawdrik, belt worn over one shoulder.
be, by.
beadmen, men of prayer.
beare up, put the helm up.
become, gone.
bed, command.
beggestere, beggar-woman.
beguiled of, disappointed in.
beguyld, foiled.
behight, call; name; entrusted.
behot, held out hope for; promised.
bekke, nod.
bel amy, fair friend.
belive, quickly.
Belmarye, Benmarin, a district in north Africa.
bemes, trumpets.
ben, are.
bene, bean; jot.
Beneit, St. Benedict.
bent, coarse grass; field; purpose; levelled.
bequeathed, entrusted.
beseene, well, good looking.
bestedd, sorely pressed; situated.
bet, beaten; better.
bet, go, go as quickly as possible.
betake, deliver.

bete, relieve.
beth, be.
bethinkes, determines.
bethrall, enslave.
betide, happen.
bever, visor.
bewray, disclose.
beye, buy.
bicched bones, cursed dice.
bidding bedes, saying prayers.
biknowe, acknowledge.
bile, bill; beak.
bilive, quickly; immediately.
birk, birch.
bisette, set to work.
bismotered, stained.
bisy, anxious.
bisyde, of, from near.
bisydes, him, near him.
bit, commands.
bits, food.
biwraye, reveal.
blakeberied, a-, blackberrying.
blame, injury.
blane, stopped.
blankmanger, creamed fowl.
blaze, proclaim.
blent, blinds; blinded; deceived; stained.
bless, preserve; brandish.
blubbred, tear-stained.
Boece, Boethius.
boght, redeemed.
boist, box.
bokeler, small shield.
boles, bulls.
boot, help; remedy; avail.
bootelesse, unavailing.
bord bigonne, sat at the head of the table.
borne, brook.
borrow, ransom.
bosses, knobs.
bote, boot; remedy; salvation.
boughtes, coils.
bounty, virtue.
bour, bedroom.
bourde, jest.
bouzing can, drinking cup.
bowne, make ready; ready.
bowr, bedroom; house; muscle.
boÿs, bows.
bracer, guard for the arm in archery.
brae, hillside.
braid, broad; long; written on a long sheet.
brand, sword.
bras, money.
brast, broke; burst.
braun, muscle.
braw, fine.
bray, cry out.
breach, breaking.
bred, were born.
breem, fresh-water fish.
brend, burned.
brenninge, burning.
bret-ful, brimful.
brimstoon, sulphur.
brode, plainly.
brook, enjoy.
brotch, brooch.
brouke, enjoy the use of.
bryttlynge, cutting up.
buckle, make ready.
buffe, blow.
bugle, wild ox.
bulte it to the bren, sift it to the bran.
burdoun, bass.
burn, brook.
buske, bush; make ready.
buskin, high boot.
but, unless.
but-if, unless.
buxom, yielding.
buxumnesse, submission.
by, along; pay for.
by and by, immediately.
byckarte, attacked.
byddys, abides.
byde, endure.
byears, biers.
bylive, quickly; immediately.
bylle, sword.
byre, cow-house.
bystode, hard pressed.

caas, legal cases.
caityf, captive; wretch.
cake, round loaf of bread.
call, netted head-dress.
can, did; know; began.
cancred, venomous; corrupt.
canon bitt, smooth, round bit.
capull-hyde, horse-hide.
car'd, cared for.
car'd for, shrank from.
cardiacle, pain in the heart.
carefull, full of care.
carelesse, uncared for.
carke, anxiety.
carl(e), fellow.
carline, old; low-born.
carpe, talk; joke.
carpyng, discussion.
carver, used for carving.
cas, accident.
cast, intend; devise; plan.
casuelly, by chance.
catapuce, spurge.
catel, property.
caytive, captive; wretch.
ceint, girdle.
celle, subordinate convent.
centaure, centaury.
centonell, sentinel.
certes, certainly.
ceruce, lead ointment.
chaffare, merchandise.
channerin, fretting.
chapman, merchant.
charge, memory; care.
chauffed, heated; rubbed.
chaunce, term in the game of hazard.
chaunterie, endowment to pay for masses.
chaw, jaw; chew.
cheare, countenance; behavior.
chearen, cheer himself.
cheffe, chief.
chere, countenance; behavior; appearance.
cherl, fellow.
chevisaunce, dealing for profit.
chide, champ.
chiknes, chickens.
chivachye, military expedition.
chivalrye, knighthood.
cink, five.
clappeth, chatters.
clause, in a, briefly.
clepen, call.
clere, bright; pure.
clergeon, choir-boy.
clerk, scholar.
clinke, tinkle.
clos(s), enclosure.
cloutes, rags; clothes.
clowe, claw; clutch.
coast, region.
cod, bag; stomach.
coillons, testicles.
cokewold, cuckold.
cold, baneful; could.
colera, bile.
colerik, of a bilious temperament.
col-fox, fox with black in its fur.
colpons, shreds.
combred, impeded.
combrous, harassing.
comfortlesse, helpless.
commonly, sociably.
commune, as in, alike.
compeer, comrade.
compeld, summoned.
complecciouns, collections of humors; temperaments.
composicioun, arrangement.
comyn-bell, town-bell.
condicioun, rank.
confiture, mixture.
conne, learn; know how.
conning, skill; knowledge.
conscience, tenderness.
conseil, secret.
consort, accord.
constraint, distress.
construe, translate.
contek, strife.
contenaunce, outward show.
contrairie, foe.
cop, top; tip.
cope, priest's cloak.
coppe, cup.
corages, hearts.
cordial, heart stimulant.
corn, grain.
corny, strong in corn or malt.
corpus bones, bones of the Lord's body.
corrosives, remedies.
cors(e), body.
cote, small house.
couch, set; place.
coude, knew how to.
counterfesaunce, imposture.
counterfete, imitate.
countour, king's legal representative in a county.
courtepy, short upper coat.
courting, courtier-like.

couthe, known; knew; best knew how.
coveityse, covetousness.
covenaunt, contract.
coverchiefs, coverings for the head.
covyne, trickery.
coy, quiet.
craftes, handicrafts.
crew, company.
crime, reproach.
cristofre, figure of St. Christopher.
crokke, earthenware pot.
crop, reward.
crope, crept.
croppes, shoots.
croslet, small cross.
crounyng, tonsure.
crowned, capital.
crownes with cups, salutes with full cups.
croys, cross.
cruddy, curdled.
crudled, curdled.
crulle, curled.
cryke, creek.
curat, parish-priest.
cure, cure of souls; care.
curious, careful.
cursednesse, malice.
curst turne, spiteful feat.
cut, lot.

daint, choice.
dainty dear, exceedingly precious.
dalliance, amorous talk; trifling; social entertainment.
dam(e), mother.
darrayne, prepare for battle; prove by battle.
date, term of life.
daun, master.
daunce, dance; game.
daunger, control; risk.
daungerous, overbearing.
daunte, tame; subdue.
dayesye, daisy.
deadly, deathlike.
deadly made, mortal.
deare, injury.
debate, quarrel; fight.
debonaire, gracious.
deceivable, deceitful.
deceived, cheated.
dee, do.
deel, bit.
dees, dice.
deeth, the, the pestilence.
deface, disgrace.
defame, dishonor.
defaute, fault.
defeasaunce, defeat.
defenden, forbid.
defye, renounce.
degree, rank; order.
delices, pleasures.
deliver, active; set free.
deliverly, quickly.
delyces, pleasures.
demen, judge.
departed, divided.
depeint, painted.
dere, injury.
derive, divert.
descryde, declared.
despight, anger; ill treatment.
despit(e) ous, cruel; malicious; scornful.
desport, amusement.
devys, decision.
devyse, relate; describe.
dewties, dues.
deye, dairy-woman.
deyntee, good.
deys, dais.
diamond, adamant.
dight, adorn; put on.
dighted, wiped.
digne, worthy; haughty.
dint, stroke.
disaventrous, unfortunate.
dischevele, disheveled.
discolourd, many-colored.
disdaine, that which would excite disdain.
disdainfull, indignant.
disese, grief.
dishonesty, unchastity.
dismaid, overcame.
dispart, divide.
dispence, make amends; expenditure.
dispence, esy of, spending little.
dispiteous, cruel.
disple, subject to penance.
disport, amusement; pleasantry.
dispredden, spread out.
disputisoun, disputation.
disseized, deprived.
dissolute, enfeebled.
distayned, stained.
distraine, afflict.
dites, lifts.
ditty, theme.
diverse, distracting; perverse.
divide, play an elaborate passage in music.
doctryne, teaching.
documents, lessons.
doen to, betake.
doghtren, daughters.
dois, does.
dokked, cut short.
dolour, grief; pain.
dome, judgment.
doune, ended.
doome, decree.
doon us honge, have us hanged.
dormant, table, a side-table kept permanently filled with food.
dorste, dared.
doted, imbecile.
doubtfull, fearful.
dre, endured.
dreadfull, full of dread.
drecched, troubled.
drede, doubt; fear.
dree, can do.
dreed, object of reverence.
drenched, drowned.
drere, sadness.
dreriment, gloom; sorrow.
drery, bloody; ghastly.
dresse, set in order.
dreynt, drowned.
drie, feel; endure.
drift, impetus; plot.
dronkelewe, addicted to drink.
drouped, were draggled.
drumlie, gloomy.
dryve, pass.
dugs, breasts.
dule, grief.
dye, hazard.
dynte, stroke.

each where, everywhere.
earne, yearn.
earst, formerly.
edifyde, built.
ee, eye.
eek, also.
eeke, increase.
eft, then.
eftsoones, forthwith.
eke, also.
eld, old age.
ellebor, hellabore.
elles, otherwise.
else, already.
elyng, miserable.
embalme, anoint.
embard, imprisoned.
embay, enclose; bathe.
embosse, plunge.
embost, driven to extremity; encased.
embowd, arched over.
emboyled, agitated; heated.
embrouded, embroidered.
emmove, move.
empeach, hinder.
emperst, penetrated.
emprize, enterprise.
emys, uncle's.
enchace, serve as setting for.
encombred, involved.
encounter, go to meet.
endyte, write.
enfouldred, thunderous.
engorged, devoured.
engrave, bury.
engyned, put on the rack for torture.
enhaunst, raised; exalted.
enraged, frantic.
ensample, example.
ensewen, follow; befall.
entente, mind.
entire, with full vigor.
entraile, twisted coil.
entune, intone.
envious, envied.
envoy, postscript of a poem.
envyned, well provided of wine.
equall, impartial.
erbe yve, ground ivy.
erme, grief.
erst, first.
ese, doon, provide entertainment.
esloyne, withdraw.
espye, perceive.
essoyne, excuse; exemption.
estatlich, stately.

eugh, yew.
even(e), smooth; medium.
ever-dying dread, constant fear of death.
everich, every.
everichon, everyone.
everilkon, everyone.
ever-mo, continually.
every-deel, in every respect.
ewghen, of yew.
excheat, gain.
expire, come to a term; breathe out.
extirpe, extirpate.
ey, egg.
eyas, young hawk, newly fledged.
eyne, eyes.

fa', fall.
fact, deed.
facultee, as by his, considering his authority or disposition.
fade, decay.
fader, father's.
faine, glad.
fairlies, wonders.
fairnesse, honesty of life.
faitor, villain; impostor.
falding, coarse cloth.
fanglenesse, showy modernity.
faren, gone.
farsed, stuffed.
fashes, troubles.
faste, close; soundly; intently.
fatal, prophetic.
faynd, disguised.
faytor, impostor.
feare, object of fear; make afraid.
fearefull, full of fear.
fee, wealth.
fell, befell; fierce.
felly, fiercely; cruelly.
fen, chapter of a book by Avicenna.
ferd, fear.
fere, mate; comrade.
fere, on, together.
fered, frightened.
ferly, wonder.
ferme, rent.
ferne, distant.
ferre, further.
ferreste, furthest.
ferthing, small portion.
fest, fist.
fet, feeds; fetched.
fetis, neat; graceful.
fetisly, gracefully.
fey, faith.
feyne, invent.
ffaine, glad.
ffare, go.
ffarley, strange.
ffetteled, made ready.
fil, befell.
file, smoothe.
fille, fell.
finch, pulle a, pluck a dupe (?).
find, provide for; choose.
fit, division of a song; strain of music; emotion; condition.
fithele, fiddle.
flaggy, drooping.
flake, flash.
flatour, flatterer.
flee, fly.
fleigh, flew.
fleshly, carnally.
flit, give way; move.
florin, English coin, first coined at Florence.
flowen, flew.
floytinge, fluting.
foile, thin sheet of metal.
fond, foolish; provided for.
fone, foes.
food, feud.
foole-happie, blindly lucky.
foot-mantel, outer skirt.
for, against; why.
for that, because.
for-by, past.
fordonne, ruined; overcome.
for-dronke, very drunk.
foreby, near.
forecast, pause to reflect.
forelifting, lifting up in front.
forespent, utterly wasted.
forlete, give up; abandon.
forlorne, utterly lost; abandoned.
forn-cast, premeditated.
forneys, furnace.
for-pyned, wasted away by torment.
fors, matter.
fors, do no, take no account.
forsake, avoid.
for-sleuthen, waste in idleness.
forster, forester.
forth right, straight.
for-thi, therefore.
fortunen, forecast; give a good or bad fortune to.
forwandred, tired out with wandering.
forward, agreement.
for-wearied, utterly wearied.
for-why, because.
forwiting, foreknowledge.
forworne, worn out.
forwoot, knows beforehand.
forwrapped, wrapped up; concealed.
fother, load.
fou, dry measure varying from two to six Winchester, or slightly less than standard, bushels.
foulys, birds.
frame, steady.
francklin, freeman; freeholder; substantial farmer.
fraternitee, guild.
fray, frighten.
frayneth, beseeches.
freck, bold man.
fredom, liberality.
free, generous; noble.
frend, friend; help.
frend, to, as friend.
fret, gnaw.
freyke, bold man.
frie, good.
frounce, gather in folds.
fruytesteres, female fruit-sellers.
fry, swarm.
ful, very.
fume, harmful vapor rising from stomach to brain.
fumetere, fumitory.
fumositee, fumes caused by drunkenness.
funerall, death.
furlong, eighth of a mile.
fustian, coarse cloth.
fynde, end; finish (?).

gabbe, jest; prate.
gae, go.
gage, pledge.
gain, serve.
galingale, spice made from the root of sweet cyperus.
gall, gall-bladder.
game, in, jokingly.
gamed, it pleased.
gamen, play.
gan, began; did.
gang, go.
gar, make.
gare, ready.
garget, throat.
garlande, wreath hung on a wand for a target in archery.
gate, way; path.
gat-tothed, with teeth widely spaced; goat-toothed and so lascivious (?).
gaude, trick.
gauded, fitted with gauds or beads that in a rosary marked the five joys of the Virgin.
gaytres beryies, berries of the buckthorn.
gede, went.
gent, gentle.
gentils, gentlefolk.
gere, utensils; apparel.
german, brother.
Gernade, Granada.
gerner, garner.
gest, exploit.
ghost, soul; spirit.
gied, gave.
gin, instrument of torture; begin; if.
gipoun, short coat worn under the armor.
gipser, wallet.
girles, young people of both sexes.
giternes, guitars.
glade, rejoice.
glede, glowing coal; fire.
glee, cheer; entertainment.
glent, glanced; darted.
glister, shine.
glosed, commented on; explained.
gnarre, growl; snarl.
go, walk.
gobbet, piece; fragment.
golett, throat; part covering the throat.
goliardeys, buffoon.
good, income; property.
good, knew his, knew how to act.

gorge, throat; what has been swallowed.
gory blood, clotted blood.
gossib, friend; relative.
gost, soul; spirit.
governaunce, control; manner.
government, control; self-control.
gowe, go we.
graile, gravel.
graine, died in, dyed thoroughly.
grate, chafe.
gree, favor.
green, grass plot.
greetin, weeping.
Grete See, Mediterranean.
grette, greeted.
greved, grew angry.
grevis, groves.
greyn, grain; corn.
griesie, gray; grizzled.
griple, grasp; tenacious.
grisly, horrible.
grith, peace; charter of peace.
grope, test.
grosse, heavy.
grotes, four-penny pieces.
ground, land; earth; texture.
grucche, murmur.
gruf, on his face.
gryfon, fabulous animal; vulture (?).
gryping, grasp.
grys, gray fur.
gryte, great.
guerdon, reward.
guise, behavior.
gypon, short coat.
gyse, way.

ha', hall.
habergeoun, coat of mail.
hable, powerful; able.
hagard hauke, untamed hawk.
hals, neck.
halse, beseech.
halwes, saints; shrines of saints.
halyde, hauled.
han, have.
handeling, usage.
harbour, shelter.
hardily, certainly.
hardiment, courage.
hardly, with difficulty.
harlot, rogue.
harlotryes, ribald actions or tales.
harneised, equipped.
harre, hinge.
harrow, help.
hasard, game of hazard.
hasardrye, gambling.
haughtie, lofty; high-pitched.
haunt, limit; usual resort; skill.
haunteden, practiced.
hauteyn, loud.
hawe, yard.
he(e), high.
heben, ebony.
heep, crowd.
heft, raised.
heig, high.
heigh ymaginacioun, Heaven's foreknowledge.
heled, hidden.
helpless, unavoidable.
hem, them.
hende, noble; gracious.
hente, obtain; seize.
her(e), their.
herbergage, lodging.
herberwe, harbor; inn.
herde, shepherd.
herien, praise.
heryinge, praising.
heste, command.
hethenesse, heathen lands.
hevinesse, sorrow.
hew, shape; condition; pretense; expression.
hight, commanded; called; promise.
hight, on, aloud.
hind, deer.
hinde, courteous.
hindreste, hindmost.
hir, their; her.
hit, it.
hold, possession.
holde, wager.
holland, a kind of linen.
holme, evergreen oak; holly (?).
holpen, helped.
holt, wood.
hond, out of, at once.
honest, honorable.
hoomly, simply.
hoor, gray.
hord, treasure.
hore, frosty; hoary.
horned, horny.
horrid, bristling; rough.
horro, roughness.
hors, horses.
hot, was called.
houped, whooped.
houres, astrological hours.
housbondrye, economy.
housling, sacramental.
hove, rise.
humour, one of the four chief fluids of the body (blood, phlegm, bile, and black bile) in Gelenical medicine.
hurtlen, rush jostling.
hussyfskap, housewifery.
hyne, farm servant.
hyre, reward.

ilk(e), each; every; same.
ilkone, each one.
imbrew, shed blood.
impe, scion; offspring.
implyes, enfolds.
improvided, unforeseen.
in, dwelling.
incontinent, at once.
infect, invalidated.
infected, ingrained.
infest, attack; make hostile.
inspire, breathe in.
intended, stretched forth.
intendiment, careful consideration; knowledge.
intent, purpose; gaze; pleasure.
intreat, persuade.
invent, find.
inwith, within.
irkesome, troubled; weary.
Ise, I shall.
ith, in the.

Jacob's staff, pilgrim's staff.
janglere, babbler.
jangleth, chatters.
jape, trick; deception.
japers, jesters.
jaw, wave.
jet, fashion.
jolif, merry.
jolitee, comfort; smartness.
jolly, brave; gallant; handsome.
jordanes, pots.
jott, least bit.
journall, daily.
juste, joust.
justyse, judge; administration of justice.

keep(e), heed; watch.
keeping, be at your, be on your guard.
ken, know.
kepe, protect; care.
kest, cast.
kind(e), nature.
kind, beastly, in the nature of a beast.
kindly, natural.
kirk, church.
kirtle, tunic; cloak.
kithe, of the same country or people.
kitte, cut.
knarre, stump of a fellow.
knave, servant-boy.
knees, jagged projections of the rock.
knobbes, swellings.
knowes, knees.
kyn, cows.

laas, cord.
Lacidomie, Lacedaemonia.
lady, lady's.
lafte, leave; leave off.
laike, play.
laith, loath.
lake, pit; cavity.
lap, leaped.
large, coarsely.
last, loads.
lat be, do away with.
later, late.
latoun, alloy similar in appearance to brass.
laude, praise.
laugte, caught.
launcht, pierced.
lauriol, spurge-laurel.
lay, lodged.
layn, lying.
lay-stall, refuse-heap.
lazar, leper.
lea, grassy field.
leach, physician.
leaned, lay.
learne, teach.

leasing, lie.
leche, physician.
leed, stationary cauldron above a furnace.
leet, caused; left; let.
leman, lover.
lemes, flames.
lene, lend.
lere, teach; learn.
lesinges, lies.
lessoun, reading from Scripture.
lest, delight.
leste, pleased.
let, prevent; hinder; hindrance; obstacle.
leten, allowed; considered.
lette, stop; wait; hindered.
letterure, learning.
Lettow, Lithuania.
letuaries, prescriptions.
leute, loyalty.
leve, cease; grant; permission; dear.
leved, believed.
leven, lawn.
lever, rather.
lewed, ignorant; rude; common.
lewte, loyalty.
leye, wager.
libbard, leopard.
libbying, living.
licentiat, provided with a papal license to hear confession.
licour, sap.
lief(e), loved one; dear.
liggen, lie.
light, quickly; easily; befall.
likerous, dainty; gluttonous.
lilled, lolled; put out.
lillie, lovely.
limitour, one licensed to beg within certain limits.
lin, cease.
line, in a, by a cord.
lipsed, lisped.
list, pleased.
litarge, ointment made from protoxide of lead.
lith, limb.
lively, living.
loathed, disgusted.
lodemenage, pilotage.
loe, love.
loft, roof.
logge, resting-place.
loken, locked.
lond, in, away.
lond, up-on, in the country.
long a, many a.
long of, owing to.
longs, belongs.
lordinges, gentlemen.
lore, doctrine; learning.
lorn(e), lost; deserted.
losengeour, flatterer.
loset, loosed.
lough, laughed; lake.
lout, bow.
love-dayes, days appointed for the settlement of disputes.
lovely, affectionate; amorously.
lowe, hill.
lowed, stooped.
lowly, modest; humble.
Loy, St. Eligius.
luce, carp.
lucre of vilanye, vile gain.
lumpish, dull.
lust, delight; desire.
lustlesse, feeble.
lusty, gay.
Lyde, Lydia.
Lyes, Ayas in Asiatic Turkey.
lyking, pleasure; desire.
lynde, linden-tree.
lyne, linden; lineage.
lyng, furze; bent grass.
lyte, small.
lyvinge, manner of life.

magger of, in spite of.
maile, link armor.
maine, force.
maistrye, for the, to take the prize; as regards authority.
make, mate.
making, composition; poetry.
male, wallet.
mall, club.
maner, kind of.
manly, human.
many, multitude.
March-parti, borders.
mark, money worth two thirds of a pound.
marshal, master of ceremonies.
Mart, Mars.
mart, trade.
Martinmass, 11 November.
mary, marrow.
mase, state of confusion; confused fancy.
masteryes, feats of skill.
mated, stupefied; overcome.
maugree your heed, in spite of all you can do.
maun, must.
maunciple, officer who purchased victuals for an inn or college.
Maure, St. Maur, a disciple of St. Benedict.
may, maid.
mayne, strength; force.
maynly, violently.
mealt'h, melteth.
meany, troop.
mede, field; reward.
mell, mingle.
menage, control.
ment, mingled; joined.
mercenarie, hireling.
Mercenrike, Mercia.
merciable, merciful.
mery, pleasant.
meschief, mishap.
mesurable, moderate.
mete, measure.
meten, dream.
mew(e), coop; den.
meynee, followers.
minisht, diminished.
ministres, officers of justice.
mirk, murky.
mirkesome, dark.
mirthe, amusement.
mischieves, misfortunes.
misdeeming, misleading.
misdeem'd, misjudged.
misfeigning, feigning with evil purpose.
misseeming, unseemly; false show.
mistake, mislead.
misweening, misjudgment.
mister, kind of; trade.
miteyn, glove.
mo, more.
mochel, much; many.
moder, mother's.
molde, earth.
momme, mumbling.
moniments, relics; traces.
moot, men, one should.
mormal, running sore.
morne milk, morning milk.
mort, note on a horn to announce the death of a deer.
mortall, deadly.
mortreux, stew.
morwe, morning.
moss, bog.
moste, might.
mote, may; must.
mottelee, parti-colored costume.
mould, form; shape.
mountance, amount.
mowe(n), way.
moyste, new.
muche, great.
muchell, much.
muckle, much.
myd, with.
mykel, much.
myllan, Milan steel.
mylner, miller.
myneyeple, gauntlet (?).

name, by; especially.
name, great, great value.
namely, especially.
namo, no more.
narette, do not impute.
nas, was not.
natheles, nevertheless.
neare, close.
nedely, of necessity.
needments, things needed.
neet, cattle.
nere, were not.
never-a-del, not a bit.
newe, afresh.
nextin, next.
nicer, too nice.
nicetie, reserve.
nightertale, night-time.
ni'll, will not.
nis, is not.
niste, did not know.
nobles, coins worth a third of a pound.
noblesse, nobleness.
noder, none other.
nolde, would not.
nominate, call.
nones, for the, for the occasion.
nonne pre(e)st, nun's priest.

noot, know not.
nose-thirles, nostrils.
nosethrill, nostril.
notabilitee, notable fact.
note, know not.
not-heed, cropped head.
nould, would not.
noursled, trained; reared.
nouthe, as, just now.
nouther, neither.
noyd, vexed; grieved.
noyous, harmful.
ny, close.
nyce, scrupulous; foolish.

o, one.
observe, favor.
of, by.
offring, the offering by the congregation of the bread and wine to be consecrated in the mass; voluntary gifts to a parish-priest from his congregation.
ofspring, family.
oght, at all.
on, one.
onely, mere; especial.
ones, united in design.
onis, once.
oon, alwey after, uniform in quality.
oon, ever in, ever alike.
oppyned, opened.
or, ere.
origane, wild marjoram (?).
original, source; cause.
orlogge, clock.
ought, owned; aught.
ounces, bunches.
oures, hours of the breviary.
out of, without.
outrage, clamor; violence.
outragious, violent.
outrely, utterly.
out-rydere, inspector of the farms of a monastery.
over, besides.
over-al, everywhere.
overcraw, exult over.
overest, uppermost.
overlepe, outrun; catch.
oversight, escape.
owches, gems.
oweth, owns.
o-wher, somewhere.

paas, a, at a footpace.
pace, proceed; surpass; steps.
paire, impair.
Palatye, Palathia in Anatolia.
paled, fenced with pales.
palfrey, saddle-horse, especially for ladies.
pall, cloak.
palmer, pilgrim.
par, by.
paramours, lovers.
parbreake, vomit.
pardale, panther.
pardee, par dieux, a common oath.
pardoner, one who sold indulgences.
parfourned, performed.
parisshens, parishioners.
parti, upon a, aside.
parvys, church porch, especially that of St. Paul's in London.
pas, foot-pace; pace.
passion, suffering.
passionate, express with feeling.
pastes, pasties.
patente, letter of privilege.
Pater-Noster, Our Father (the Lord's Prayer).
patrone, preserver.
paynim, pagan.
peece, structure; fabric; fortified place.
peire, series; set.
pennes, feathers.
perceable, penetrable.
peren, appear.
pers, dark shade of blue or crimson.
persant, piercing.
persoun, parson.
peyne, take trouble.
pight, placed; struck.
piled, thin.
pilwe-beer, pillowcase.
pin, whit.
pinche at, find fault with.
pinched, pleated.
pine, suffering; sorrow.
pined, exhausted by suffering.
pitaunce, charitable gift.
pitous, compassionate.
pitty, fill with pity.
place, rank.
place, in, present; to the spot.
plat, flat; plainly; interfolded; entwined.
platane, oriental plane-tree.
plate, plate armor.
pledges, children.
plentevous, plenteous.
pleyen, play; joke.
pleyn, full; unlimited.
plight, plait; fold; pledge.
point, whit.
point, in good, in good condition.
point, to, completely; exactly.
pokkes, pustules.
pollicie, Machiavellian tactics.
pomely, dappled.
poraille, poor people.
portesse, portable breviary.
post, pillar.
potage, broth.
poudre-marchant, flavoring powder.
pouldred, powdered; pulverized.
pounces, talons.
pouped, puffed.
pourtraiture, image.
povert, poverty.
povre, poor.
poyse, force.
practicke, artful.
prancke, adjust.
praunce, stalk.
pray, preying; ravage.
prease, strive; press; crowd.
predicacioun, preaching.
prees, crowd.
presage, point out beforehand.
presence, chamber in which a sovereign receives guests.
presently, immediately.
presse, device for pressing; mould.
pretence, importance.
prevaile, avail.
pricasour, hard rider.
price, pay the price of.
pricke-wande, rod used as a mark in archery.
prickes, rods used as marks in archery.
pricking, riding; spurring.
priefe, experience; power.
priketh, incites.
prime, nine o'clock in the morning; spring-time.
privily, secretly.
properly, exactly.
propre, own; well-made.
propretee, peculiar quality.
prouder, too proud.
prove, test; try.
provost, chief magistrate.
prow, brave; profit.
Pruce, Prussia.
prys, renown.
puddings, sausages.
puissance, might.
pulled, plucked.
purchas(e), proceeds from begging; acquisition.
purchasing, conveyancing.
purchasour, conveyancer.
purf(i)led, fringed; decorated with an ornamental border.
purposes, discourses.
purtreye, draw.
purveyaunce, provision.
pyned, tortured.

quad, bad.
quaile, become dismayed.
quayd, subdued.
quell, frighten; kill.
quick, alive.
quight, release.
quit, release.
quited, requited.
quyrry, slaughtered game.
quyte, requite.

rablement, mob.
radly, quickly.
raft, struck off.
rage, romp.
raile, flow.
ramp, tear; attack.
rank, bold.
rape, haste.
rapt, carried off.
rare, thin; faint.
raskall, base; worthless.
rather, earlier; sooner.
ratones, small rats.
raug(h)te, reached; obtained.
ravin, plunder; booty.
ravisedest, didst draw.
raw, unstrung.
rawbone, excessively lean.

rawstye by the roote, rusted at the end with blood (?).
reacheles on, heedless about.
read, counsel; advice; advise.
reas, rouse.
reave, take away.
rebownded, reverberated.
rebutte, recoil; drive back.
recche, direct.
recchelees, heedless.
recorde, call to mind.
recoyle, retreat; retire.
recure, restore.
red, named; known.
rede, read; advise.
redily, quickly.
redound, overflow.
redresse, heal.
reed, counsel; adviser.
reele, roll.
refrain, restrain.
rekeninges, bills.
rekke, care.
remes, realms.
renne, run.
rente, income; burst.
renverst, upside down.
repast, refreshment.
repining, indignant.
repleccioun, over-eating.
reprevable, reprehensible.
repreve, shame.
repriefe, reproach.
requere, request.
resons, opinions.
respire, take breath.
restore, reward.
rethor, rhetorician.
retyrd, withdrawn.
reve, steward.
revenging will, desire for revenge.
reverence, respectful manner.
revers(e), contrary; bring back.
rew, pity; be sorry.
reysed, gone on a military expedition.
ribaudye, ribaldry.
richesse, wealth.
riddes, dispatches.
rife, strong; strongly.
rift, split; fissure; rent asunder.
right, straight ahead.
rightwisnesse, righteousness.
rigorous, violent.
rigour, violence.
ring, hammer of a door-knocker.
riotise, riotous living.
ritt, runs about; rides.
rive, split; tear.
rode, harbor; rood.
roghte, cared.
roome, station.
roste, roast meat.
rote, root; stringed instrument.
rouncy, farm horse.
round lists, enclosed ground for set combats as distinguished from open fields.
route, band.
rouze, shake up.
rove, shoot an arrow from an elevation.
rowels, polling parts of a bit.
rowd, rolled.
Ruce, Russia.
rue, pity.
ruefulnesse, pathos.
rueth, cause to pity.
ruffin, disorderly; ruffian.
ruine, fall.
rule, taking on.
ruth, pity; grief.
ryden out, go on expeditions.
ryotour, roisterer.
ryve, pierce.

sacred, accursed.
sad, serious; sober; firm.
saffron with, color.
sair, sore.
sallow, variety of willow.
salue, salute.
salvage, savage.
sam, together.
sanguin, red.
sangwyn, of a complexion, according to Galenical medicine, which implied jollity and generosity.
sapience, wisdom.
Satalye, Adalia in Asiatic Turkey.
sautrye, psaltery.
savour, have a relish for.
sawcefleem, covered with pimples caused by an excess of the salty humor.
sawten, assault.
say, fine woolen cloth; saw.
sayling, used for masts.
scad, scald.
scald, scab.
scalle, scab.
scalled, scabby.
scalpe, skull.
Scariot, Judas Iscariot.
scarlot, rich cloth.
scarsly, economically.
scath(e), harm; injury; pity.
schrewe, sinner.
science, knowledge; learned writing.
scole, manner.
scoleye, attend the university.
scored, inscribed.
scowre, run; pursue.
scrip, bag.
scriveyn, scribe.
scryne, chest for keeping books and papers.
se, protect; saw.
seare, burning.
seasd, penetrated.
second tenor, melody of lower pitch.
secree, able to keep secrets.
securly, surely.
see, save.
seeled, closed.
seely, innocent.
seeming meet, seemly.
seeming wise, appearance.
seigh, saw.
seintuarie, consecrated object.
seised, reached.
seke, sick.
selde, seldom.
selle, barter.
sely, innocent; good; simple.
sembled, met.
semi-cope, short cloak worn by priests.
seminge, to my, as it seems to me.
sen, since.
sendal, thin silk.
sene, visible.
sent, sense.
sentence, meaning; subject; judgment.
sermone, preach.
servisable, willing to serve.
sete, inflicted.
sethe, boil.
sette, care.
sette hir aller cappe, made fools of them all.
settyng, planting.
sew, follow; pursue.
seye, was to, meant.
seynd, broiled.
shapen, plan.
shaply, fit.
share, slice.
shaume, musical instrument similar to an oboe.
shawes, woods.
shear, several.
sheeldes, French crowns.
sheene, bright; beautiful.
shend, reproach.
shent(e), scolded; injured.
shepe, shepherd.
shete a peny, shoot for a penny.
sheugh, trench; furrow.
shewes, appearances; marks.
shiten, defiled.
shone, shoes.
shoop, planned.
shopen, arrayed.
shorte with, shorten.
shradds, coppices.
shrewe, curse; rascal.
shrighte, shrieked.
shroggs, wands serving for marks.
shroudes, garments.
shrowd, take shelter.
sic, such.
sight, of in appearance.
signe, watch-word.
sike, sick.
siker, sure.
sikerer, surer.
sikerly, surely.
silly, simple; harmless; innocent.
sin, since.
sinfull hire, service to sin.
sinke, deposit.
sits, fits.
sith, afterward; since.
sithens, since.
slade, valley.
slake, moderate; abate.
slawe, slain.
sleighte, craft; trick.
sleuthe, sloth.

slight, trick; device.
slon, slay.
smale fowles, little birds; nightingales (?).
smart, agony.
smerte, sharply; hurt.
snibben, rebuke.
snubbes, snags; knobs.
softly, gently.
solas, amusement; pleasure.
solempne, important; cheerful.
solempnely, importantly.
som-del, somewhat.
somnour, officer who cited culprits before an ecclesiastical court.
somtyme, once.
soothly, truly.
sop in wyn, bread or cake broken in wine.
sort, chance; manner.
sorwe, with, bad luck to him; to his harm.
sote, sweet.
soth, truth.
sothfastnesse, truth.
souce, strike; swoop upon.
souded, confirmed.
soukinge, sucking.
soun, sound.
souninge in, tending to.
soust, dipped; steeped.
sovereygne, excellent.
sovereynly, chiefly.
sownd, clash; wield.
sowne, sound.
space, length of time; course.
spanne, about nine inches.
sparred, shut.
spendyd, got ready.
spent, worn out.
spersed, dispersed.
spies, glances; thrusts.
spill, destroy.
sporne, kick.
spousd, betrothed.
sprente, sprang; spurted.
spreyned, sprinkled.
spright, spirit.
spring, flood.
spurn, kick (?); encounter (?).
spyced, over-fastidious.
spyrred, asked.
stadle, prop.
stage, at a, from a floor.
stal, stole away.
stape in age, advanced in years.
starke, stiff.
stayd, caused to stay.
sted, place.
stelths, thefts.
stemed, shone.
stepe, prominent; bulging.
stere, steersman; rudder.
sterlinges, silver coins.
sterne, stern; men.
sterte, move quickly; leap.
sterve, die.
steven, voice.
steven, unsett, unexpected time.
stew(e), hot place; fish-pond; brothel.
stiked, stuck.
still, ever.
stinte, stop.
stockes, posts; stumps.
stole, mantle.
stoor, farm-stock.
stop, obstacle.
storie, series of readings from Scripture.
storven, died.
stot, hack; cob.
stound, stunned; moment; time; peril; trouble.
stour, brawl; fight.
stowre, conflict; danger; distress.
straunge, foreign.
streightes, closes.
streit, strict; stinted; cramped.
streite, tightly; drawn.
stremes, currents.
streyneth, constrains.
strete and stalle, on the road and housed (?).
streyte, strictly.
strike, hank.
stroke, moved rapidly forward.
strowd, scattered.
stryving, strife.
stub, stock of a tree.
studieth, meditate; delay.
sturre, disturbance; tumult.
stye, alley; mount.
subject, underlying.
subtilly, secretly.
suffisaunce, contentment.
suffised, satisfied.
suffyce unto, be content with.
suppress, overcome.
surcote, upper coat.
sure, genuine.
suspect, fear.
sustened, maintained.
swaid, swung.
swaine, youth.
swal, swelled.
swapte, smote with swords.
swat, were sweating.
sway, swing.
swelt, swelled; raged; fainted.
swevene, dream.
sweyved, sounded.
swich, such.
swinged, singed.
swink, toil.
swinken, work.
swonken, worked.
swote, sweet.
swouwn(d) e, swoon.
swythe, quickly.
syen, see.
syke, ditch; trench.
syne, afterwards.
sythes, times.

tabard, rough coat worn by laborers.
table, picture.
tackles, equipment of a ship; rigging.
taffetie, fine silk.
taille, by, on account.
take in hand, maintain.
takel, archery-gear; arrows.
talants, claws.
tale, tell, give heed.
talen, tell stories.
talent, desire.
tapicer, upholsterer.
tappestere, barmaid.
targe, small shield.
Tartary, Tartarus; hell.
taught, told.
teade, torch.
tear, there (?).
teene, affliction; grief.
telle no store, set no store.
tellen, count over.
tempest thee, distress thyself severely.
temple, college of law.
tempred, accommodated.
termes, in, in set phrases; verbatim.
tett, lock of hair.
than, then.
that, so that; when; what.
the, they.
the(e), so mot I, so may I thrive.
thee'ch, so, so may I thrive.
thegither, together.
then, than.
ther-as, where.
there, where.
ther-to, in addition.
thewes, manners; habits.
thilke, that.
thing, make a, draw up a writ.
tho, the; those; then.
thombe of gold, thumb of a good miller.
thral, slave.
thraldome, slavery.
thrast, pressed.
three square, with three equal sides.
thriftily, carefully.
thrill, pierce; penetrate.
thrillant, piercing.
throly, strenuously.
tide, time.
tikelnesse, instability.
timely, measured.
tipet, hood.
tire, dress; head-dress; train; crew.
toft, exposed elevation.
told, counted.
tollen, take toll.
tombesteres, female tumblers.
ton, one.
tool, weapon.
toon, toes.
to-rente, tore asunder; torn asunder.
tort, wrong.
to-swinke, work much.
to-tere, tear asunder.
touch, touchstone.
toun, farm.
toy, sport.
trace, walk.
tract, trace; track.
traine, tail; trickery.

Tramissene, Tremeyen, a district in north Africa.
transmew, transmute.
trayne, artifice; snare.
treachour, traitor.
treatie, diplomacy.
treen mould, form of a tree.
trenchand, sharp; piercing.
trespas, sin; wrong.
tretys, well-proportioned.
treye, three.
triacle, sovereign remedy.
trielich, choicely.
trinall, threefold.
tristil-tre, tree used as a meeting-place.
trowe, believe.
truncked, beheaded.
trusse, seize and carry away.
twinn, in, in twain; in two's; apart.
twinne, depart from; separate; deprive.
twyne, band.
tyde, time.
tyne, pain; sorrow.
type of thine, symbol of thee.
tyre, head-dress.

unacquainted, unaccustomed.
unbid, unprayed for.
unbrent, unburned.
uncoupled, loose.
uncouth, strange.
undern, noon; from nine to twelve.
undertake, conduct an enterprise.
undight, unfastened; removed.
uneasie, uncomfortable; disturbed.
uneath, difficult; with difficulty; almost.
unhardy, timid.
unkinde, unnatural.
unkindly, against nature; unnatural.
unlese, unloose.
unnethe(s), scarcely.
unprovided, unforeseen.
unthrifty, wicked; destructive.
untill, towards; unto.
unty, loosen.
unused, from disuse.
unwary, unexpected.
unweeting, unconscious; unknowing.
upright, flat on the back.
up so doun, upside down.
upstaring, bristling; upstarting.

vavasour, sub-vassal; landholder.
veiwe, yew.
venerye, hunting.
verament, truly.
vere, turn.
vernicle, copy of the Veronica picture of Christ.
verraily, truly.
verray, true; very.
vers, verses.
vertu, quickening power; valor.
vertuous, virtuous; efficacious; manly.
vew, appearance.
viage, journey.
viewe, yew.
vigilyës, ceremonies held the evening before a festival.
vilde, vile.
vile, lowly.
vileinye, rudeness; unfit speech.
visour, mask; disguise.
vitaille, victuals.
voyage, journey.

wade, go.
wafereres, confectioners.
wage, pledge.
wake, watch; wake.
wallowd, rolled.
wan, pale; gloomy.
wane, number (?); vehicle for a missile (?).
wanto(w) n, wild; playful.
war, aware; cautious.
war him, let him beware.
ward, guard.
wardles make, earthly mate.
wardrobe, privy.
ware, guard; wary; sharp.
warely, carefully.
warente, protect.
warison, reward.
warrayd, made war upon.
warsle, wrestle.
waryce, cure.
wast, useless.
wastel-breed, fine white bread.
wastfull, barren.
watering, brook or watering-place for horses.
Watte, Walter.
wayne, chariot.
wayted, observed.
wayted after, demanded; expected.
wayting, watching.
weaker, too weak.
weal, clench hard.
weare, spend.
webbe, weaver.
weeds, clothes.
weene, think.
weet, know; wet.
wel, fully; very.
welawey, alas.
weld, wield.
wele, happiness.
welke, fade; wane.
welked, withered.
welkin, sky.
well to donne, well-doing.
wende, would have supposed.
wenden, go.
wenen, think.
wered, wore.
werken, act.
werre, war.
wex, grow; wax.
whally, streaked.
what, why.
whelkes, pustules.
whelp, puppy.
wher, whether.
whereas, where.
whether, which.
whiche, what sort.
whilom, formerly; ever.
whot, hot.
whyleare, erewhile; lately.
whylom, formerly; ever.
wi, with.
wide, away.
wif, woman.
wight, man; person; strong.
wighty, strong.
wike, week.
wikke, wicked.
wilfull, ignorant.
wilfully, by choice.
will or nill, willy-nilly.
wimpel, covering for the head.
wimpled, pleated.
win, go.
winne, gain.
winning, profit.
wis, surely.
wise, manner.
wisly, surely.
wist, knew.
wit, bit of wisdom; genius; intelligence; judgment.
with, by.
with-alle, withal; however.
withouten, besides.
withseye, oppose.
witing, knowledge.
wize, manner.
wlatsom, loathsome.
wolden, wished.
wombe, belly.
won, overcome.
wone, custom; number; plenty; one.
won(n)e, dwell; live; abide.
woning, dwelling.
wood, mad.
woodnesse, madness.
woodweele, woodlark (?).
woot, know.
worm, snake; dragon.
worship, honor.
wortes, herbs.
worth, be.
worthy, noble; distinguished.
wot, know.
wouche, evil.
woxen, grown; become.
wrattheth, becomes angry.
wreke, avenge.
wrighte, workman.
wring, distress.
wrizled, wrinkled; shriveled.
wrocken, avenged.
wroghte, contrived.
wyde, aside; away.
wyde, a little, a short distance away.
wyf, woman.
wyld, deer.
wynning, profit.
wys, to make it, to make it a subject for deliberation.
wysly, surely.

y-, a prefix used especially with the past participles of verbs.
yaf, gave.
yblent, blinded.
y-chaped, with the metal point of a scabbard; mounted.
y-corven, cut.
ydel, in vain.
ydrad, dreaded.
yë, eyes.
yeddinges, songs.
yede, go.
yeldéd, yelled.
yeldhalle, guildhall.
yemen, yeomen.
yerde, switch.
yerle, earl.
yerly, early.
yerne, briskly.
yersel, yourself.
yes, you shall.
yeve, give.
yfere, together.
yiftes, gifts.
yive, give.
y-lad, carried.
ymages, wax images of the patient (?); signs of the zodiac (?).
ympe, scion; offspring.
yod, went.
ypight, placed.
yplaste, placed.
Ypocras, Hippocrates.
y-preved, proved.
y-sene, visible.
y-wimpled, covered with a wimple.
y-wis, certainly.

Index of Historical and Critical Introductions

Index of Authors, Titles, and First Line of Poems